INDEX

to

BROWN, DRIVER & BRIGGS

HEBREW LEXICON

INDEX

to
BROWN, DRIVER & BRIGGS

HEBREW LEXICON

•

Compiled by
Bruce Einspahr

See Addenda (p. 453) for additional listings.

MOODY PRESS

CHICAGO

© 1976 by
THE MOODY BIBLE INSTITUTE
OF CHICAGO

All rights reserved.
Second printing, Revised edition, 1977

ISBN: 0-8024-4082-7

Library of Congress Cataloging in Publication Data
Einspahr, Bruce.
    Index to the Brown, Driver and Briggs Hebrew and
English lexicon of the Old Testament.

    1. Brown, Francis, 1849-1916. A Hebrew and English
lexicon of the Old Testament—Indexes.   I. Brown,
Francis, 1849-1916. A Hebrew and English lexicon of the
Old Testament.   II. Title.
PJ4833.B683E35   221.2   76-25479
ISBN 0-8024-4082-7

Printed in the United States of America

FOREWORD

The importance of this work is directly related to the importance of *A Hebrew and English Lexicon of the Old Testament,* by Francis Brown, S. R. Driver and C. A. Briggs (hereafter referred to as the *Lexicon* or *BDB*). To appreciate *BDB,* one must first understand the nature of a lexicon in contrast to the ordinary dictionary. Dictionaries generally list only the meanings of words, whereas a thorough lexicon relates the various meanings to specific passages in literature—the Old Testament in the case of *BDB.* Obviously, then, a lexicon's value is judged by the author's skills both as philologist and as interpreter.

In spite of some weaknesses noted below, *BDB* remains unsurpassed in its philological depth and scope—reflected, for example, in its etymological studies and its sensitivity to the nuances of words within various contexts. Driver's Notes on the Hebrew Text of the Books of Samuel is but one evidence of the thoroughness of research that underlies his own contribution.

Another strength of *BDB,* and so of this *Index,* is that it lists cognates of a given Hebrew root as they exist in other Semitic languages. As pointed out in the preface to the *Lexicon,* this can sometimes be a risky business, but nevertheless a necessary and helpful one.

BDB does have weaknesses. It espouses the documentary hypothesis, which has been called into question by discoveries in archaeology and form-critical work. Moreover, since it antedates the important finds at Ugarit (Ras Shamra), no Ugaritic cognates are listed. In addition, *BDB* seems to be overly influenced by word meanings found in the English Revised Version of 1885. Another limitation, in the opinion of some users (such as first year Hebrew students!), is that words are listed according to Hebrew root instead of alphabetically. In some ways, of course, this feature is a strength, in that all derivatives of a given root are found together.

BDB shares the limitations of most scholarly work done in its era (the early 20th century). Since it preceded the discovery of the Dead Sea Scrolls, it exercised undue freedom in emending the text. Consequently, scholars who have a high regard for the Masoretic Text (the traditional Hebrew text) find it difficult to give *BDB* unqualified endorsement.

On the other hand, the authors of *BDB* had at their disposal a surprisingly large number of sources, which were meticulously consulted. One need only read the list of abbreviations at the front of the *Lexicon* to be impressed with the wealth of material of which the authors took advantage. Consequently, *BDB* has not successfully been replaced as the standard Hebrew lexicon.

Still, the greatest difficulty in using *BDB* (because of its listing by root) is simply that of finding the lexical treatment of a given word of the Hebrew text. This *Index* will enable the user to find readily both the root and the appropriate contextual nuances of the word he is studying.

It perhaps should be stressed that this new tool is in no way intended to replace *BDB*. Rather, its aim is to simplify the *Lexicon's* use. The writers of this Foreword hope that the *Index to BDB,* by facilitating the study of biblical Hebrew, will contribute to deeper and more effective teaching and preaching of the Word of God.

BRUCE K. WALTKE   KENNETH L. BARKER
Th.D., Ph.D.   Th.M., Ph.D.

Editors' note: Great care has been exercised to ensure accuracy, but in a work of this size and complexity some errors are bound to occur. Users of this *Index,* therefore, are encouraged to notify the publisher of errors, discrepancies, inconsistencies, etc., that are discovered. Please write to

MOODY PRESS
820 N. LaSalle
Chicago, IL 60610

INTRODUCTION

ORIGIN AND PURPOSE OF THE INDEX

This project was inspired by the Index to the *Bauer/ Arndt and Gingrich Greek Lexicon* by John R. Alsop, published by Zondervan Publishing House. It was felt that a similar tool for the Hebrew student would be extremely valuable. For many Bible students, translation is difficult and frustrating, largely because often few results are evident after many hours of work. Though a student may have been well-trained in Hebrew, he can easily become disenchanted with his new ability and within a few years forget most of what he had learned. Unfortunately, this pattern is typical of Hebrew students. An index to a popular and reliable Hebrew lexicon would encourage the Hebrew student by directing him quickly to the appropriate entries in the lexicon. He would therefore enjoy greater results in a shorter period of time, regardless of his skill in the language.

For reasons explained in the Foreword, *A Hebrew and English Lexicon of the Old Testament* (hereafter referred to as *BDB* or the *Lexicon*) by Francis Brown, S. R. Driver and Charles A. Briggs (Oxford University Press), was chosen for this project. This *Index* is not meant in any way to replace the *Lexicon*, but rather to enable the translator to get into the *Lexicon* faster and more easily in order to take advantage of the wealth of material it contains. Nor is it intended to weaken or eliminate the use of good Hebrew translating principles. There is no substitute for fundamental language skills. This tool is designed to make more efficient use of whatever skill the user may have.

PRODUCTION OF THE INDEX

The basic compilation took ten months and the resources of seven men to complete. Each man was assigned a section of the *Lexicon,* from which he recorded each individual entry. These records were then keypunched onto cards, loaded into the computer and programmed for a printout in exact lexical order. Corrections were made by comparing the computer printout with the *Lexicon.* Four series of corrections were made in order to reduce errors to the minimum.

The original information was recorded on 7,947 sheets of paper and was then transferred to 832 pounds of computer cards. The computer took 45 minutes to sort the information and four hours to print it. The final computer printout contained 139,924 references on 2,596 pages of computer paper weighing 46 pounds! Finally, the data was recorded on computer tape in biblical sequence and readied for typesetting by additional programming.

EXPLANATION OF FORMAT

Hebrew words

The unpointed Hebrew words are listed under each verse in the form and in the order in which the words appear in *BDB*—making the order alphabetical in most cases. In a few instances the Hebrew word was longer than what we were able to record in the initial data entry. In these cases, as much of the word as possible was included to make it sufficiently distinct from other Hebrew words.

The basic, singular form of the Hebrew is listed in the *Index,* even when the text form is plural.

Since the *Index* lists only the words that are discussed in the *Lexicon,* occasional omissions in the *Index* will be noticed. For example, though ארץ (earth) is found both in Genesis 1:1 and 2, it is listed in the *Index* only under verse 2, since the *BDB* discussion does not include verse 1.

Frequently the same word is listed more than once under a given verse, though used only once in the verse. In such cases, the word is discussed in more than one place in the *Lexicon* for that contextual use.

English words

A general English equivalent is listed immediately to the right of its corresponding Hebrew word. These are given solely to help properly identify the word being studied. Precise meanings for a given context are located in *BDB*. It is the purpose of the *Index* to furnish these locations. The *Index* should not be used as a simplified, substitute lexicon. Otherwise one would be much wiser simply to rely on standard English versions.

Since the *Lexicon* does not usually define or give a transliteration of proper names, the *Index* uses the forms of the *New American Standard Bible.*

Lexicon page and quadrant

The next to last column indicates the page number and quadrant where the contextual meaning of the Hebrew word is found in the *Lexicon*. To expedite location, each page is divided into four imaginary quadrants. The left column is divided into A and B and the right column into C and D.

Article sections

The last column indicates the specific section, or sections, within the quadrant where the word is discussed for the given context. Short articles are not divided into sections and in such cases, of course, there is no entry in the section column in the *Index*. Up to six sections and subsections may be listed. For technical reasons concerning data entry and typesetting, where a Roman numeral is used in the *Lexicon* to designate a section, an Arabic number is substituted in the *Index*. Where Greek letters are used in the *Lexicon,* the customary English equivalents are substituted in the *Index,* except that *theta* (θ) is represented by **t** instead of **th.**

Parenthetical discussions

In front of the page number there will occasionally be an asterisk, indicating a parenthetical discussion in the *Lexicon.* Such discussions may or may not actually contain the Hebrew word under consideration, but the closely related information to be so gleaned was felt to be helpful enough to warrant the listings.

Special editorial considerations

The *Lexicon* normally has a section where the different *forms* of a word are illustrated, with Scripture references to where these forms occur. Since almost all of these references are repeated in the section which discusses the *definition* of the word, only the references in the definition section are listed.

The *BDB* appendix entitled "Addenda et Corrigenda" (pp. 1119-1126) lists lexical corrections, which are also noted in the *Index.* Where such correction is involved, the phrase "ADDENDA ET CORRIGENDA" is entered in the English column. The page and quadrant indicated refer to this supplement in the *Lexicon.*

HOW TO USE THE *INDEX*

Though the *Index* is relatively simple to use, it is helpful, of course, to know fundamental principles of Hebrew in order more quickly to identify a root word in the *Index* from the Hebrew text. Some users will need to rely on the process of elimination and a letter by letter comparison of the Hebrew words listed in the *Index* under the verse in which the word is located.

After determining the word that needs to be defined, turn to the *Lexicon* page number, quadrant, and section (if any) that are indicated. By this simple process, the valuable information in the *Lexicon* is quickly made available.

ACKNOWLEDGMENTS

In a project of this size many people are inevitably involved, and it would be impossible to name them all. The men who worked most closely with me and helped initially record the vast amount of data need to be mentioned first. Through long, laborious hours of work, they have become part of this *Index*. These men, all graduates of the class of 1976 from Dallas Theological Seminary, are: Tom Diffenderfer, Grover Gunn, Grant McCallister, Dick Olsen, Mike Powell, and Dave Sanford.

One of the most critical needs was for a computer and a qualified programmer that would involve the least possible expense. God provided the answer through John Thompson, a 1978 graduate candidate at the seminary. Because of his programming skills and access to a computer, this project was able to be completed.

I want to give special thanks to the two professors at Dallas Theological Seminary who were deeply involved in the project. Dr. Bruce K. Waltke, Chairman of the Department of Semitic Languages and Old Testament Exegesis, authorized the *Index* as fulfillment of the master's thesis requirement for the seven seminary students involved in the compilation. Without his important and continuing support, this book would never have been published. My advisor was Dr. Kenneth L. Barker, Professor of Semitics and Old Testament, who listened patiently to all the problems and gave me the guidance that was much needed for this complex undertaking.

Another group of individuals, too numerous to list, gave financial support, many of them sacrificially. Especially because there were times of doubt, due to lack of funds, that this project would ever be completed, I cannot give them enough thanks.

Finally, I would like to thank Moody Press and Textbook Editor, David Douglass. The project would be relatively worthless if it were never made available to translators and students of Hebrew throughout the world. If, because of this work, more students will study the Old Testament from the original Hebrew text, God will receive the glory and those involved in the project will be satisfied.

BRUCE EINSPAHR
Dallas, Texas
February, 1976

GENESIS

Ch v.	Heb	Eng	Page	Sec
1 1	אלה	GOD	42a	3 b
	אל	GOD	43a	7
	את	MARK OF THE AC-CUSATIVE	84d	1 a
	ב	IN	88d	15
	ברא	CREATE	135b	1
	ה	THE	207a	1 a
	ראשית	BEGINNING	912a	1 a
	שמי	HEAVENS	1030a	1 a
1 2	ארץ	EARTH	76a	1 b
	בהו	EMPTINESS	96a	
	היה	BE	227a	3 4b
	חשך	DARKNESS	365a	1
	מי	WATER	565c	1 i
	פנה	FACE	816b	15
	פנה	FACE	819a	2 7b
	רוח	BREATH	926a	9 e
	רחף	HOVER	934b	
	תהו	FORMLESSNESS	1062c	1
	תהום	DEEP	1063a	3
1 3	אור	LIGHT	21c	1
	אמר	SAY	55d	1
	היה	BECOME	225c	2 1a
1 4	אור	LIGHT	21c	1
	בדל	BE DIVIDED	95b	1
	חשך	DARKNESS	365a	1
	טוב	PLEASANT	374a	3 a
	ראה	TO SEE	907a	2 1
1 5	אור	LIGHT	21c	1
	בקר	MORNING	134a	1 e
	היה	BECOME	225c	2 1a
	ו	AND	*252a	1
	חשך	DARKNESS	365a	1
	יום	DAY	398b	1
	יום	DAY	398c	2 d
	לילה	NIGHT	538c	1
	קרא	CALL	896a	6 e2
1 6	בדל	BE DIVIDED	95b	1
	בין	INTERVAL	107c	1 b
	היה	BE	227c	3 5a
	מי	WATER	565c	1 i
	רקיע	EXTENDED SUR-FACE	956b	2
	תוך	MIDST	1063c	
1 7	בדל	BE DIVIDED	95b	1
	היה	COME TO PASS	224b	1 1b
	מן	FROM	578d	1 c
	על	UPON	759b	4 2e a
	עשה	DO	794d	2 1b
	רקיע	EXTENDED SUR-FACE	956b	2
	שמי	HEAVENS	*1029d	1 a
	תחת	UNDERNEATH	1066b	3 2a
	תחת	UNDERNEATH	1066b	3 2a
1 8	בקר	MORNING	134a	1 e
	ה	THE	208b	1 i
	היה	BECOME	225c	2 1a
	יום	DAY	398c	2 d
	קרא	CALL	896a	6 e2
	רקיע	EXTENDED SUR-FACE	956b	2
	שמי	HEAVENS	1029d	1 a
1 9	היה	COME TO PASS	224b	1 1b
	ו	AND	252b	1 b
	יבשה	DRY LAND	387a	
	קוה	COLLECT	876b	
	מקוה	COLLECTION	876c	
	מקום	STANDING PLACE	880b	4
	ראה	TO SEE	908c	1 c
	שמי	HEAVENS	1029d	1 a
1 10	טוב	PLEASANT	374a	3 a
	יבשה	DRY LAND	387a	
	ים	SEA	*411a	5
	כי	THAT	471c	1 a
	מקוה	COLLECTION	876c	
	ראה	TO SEE	907b	5 a
1 11	ארץ	EARTH	76b	3 b
	אשר	PARTICLE OF RE-LATION	81d	2
	דשא	SPROUT	206a	
	דשא	GRASS	206a	
	היה	COME TO PASS	224b	1 1b
	זרע	SOW	282a	1
	זרע	SOWING	282b	2 c
	זרע	SOWING	282c	2 e
	ל	TO	516a	5 ja
	מין	KIND	568b	
	על	UPON	752c	2 1
	עץ	TREE	781c	1 b
	עשב	HERB	793c	
	עשה	DO	794d	2 2
	פרי	FRUIT	826b	1
1 12	ארץ	EARTH	76b	3 b
	דשא	GRASS	206a	
	זרע	SOW	282a	1
	זרע	SOWING	282b	2 c
	טוב	PLEASANT	374a	3 a
	יצא	BRING OUT	425b	4 j
	מין	KIND	568b	
	עשב	HERB	793c	
	עשה	DO	794d	2 2

Ch v.	Heb	Eng	Page	Sec
1 13	ראה	TO SEE	907b	5 a
	בקר	MORNING	134a	1 e
	היה	BECOME	225c	2 1a
	יום	DAY	398c	2 d -
	שלישי	THIRD	1026a	
1 14	אות	SIGN	17a	8
	מאור	LUMINARY	22c	
	בדל	BE DIVIDED	95b	1
	בין	INTERVAL	107c	1 d
	היה	BECOME	226c	2 2e
	יום	DAY	398b	1
	מועד	APPOINTED TIME	417d	1 b
	רקיע	EXTENDED SUR-FACE	956b	2
	שמי	HEAVENS	1029d	1 a
1 15	אור	BECOME LIGHT	21b	1
	מאור	LUMINARY	22c	
	היה	COME TO PASS	224b	1 1b
	היה	BECOME	226c	2 2e
	רקיע	EXTENDED SUR-FACE	956b	2
	שמי	HEAVENS	1029d	1 a
1 16	מאור	LUMINARY	22c	
	את	MARK OF THE AC-CUSATIVE	84d	1 a
	ה	THE	207a	1 b
	ו	AND	253a	1 g
	יום	DAY	398b	1
	כוכב	STAR	456d	
	ל	TO	515a	5 ha
	ממשלה	RULE	606a	2
	עשה	DO	794d	2 1b
	קטן	SMALL	882b	1 b
1 17	אור	BECOME LIGHT	21b	1
	ל	TO	517b	7 a
	נתן	PUT	680b	2 a
	רקיע	EXTENDED SUR-FACE	956b	2
	שמי	HEAVENS	1029d	1 a
1 18	תחת	UNDERNEATH	1066b	3 2b
	בדל	BE DIVIDED	95b	1
	חשך	DARKNESS	365a	1
	טוב	PLEASANT	374a	3 a
	יום	DAY	398b	1
	משל	RULE	605d	2
1 19	בקר	MORNING	134a	1 e
	היה	BECOME	225c	2 1a
	יום	DAY	398c	2 d
	רביעי	FOURTH	917d	1
	שמי	HEAVENS	1029d	1 a
1 20	חי	ALIVE	312b	1 d
	נפש	SOUL	659c	2
	עוף	FLY	733c	1
	עוף	FLYING CREATURES	733d	1
	על	UPON	755d	2 5
	פנה	FACE	816b	15
	פנה	FACE	819a	2 7a e
	רקיע	EXTENDED SUR-FACE	956b	2
	שמי	HEAVENS	1029d	1 a
	שרץ	SWARM	1056c	1
	שרץ	SWARMING THINGS	1056d	
1 21	ברא	CREATE	135b	1
	גדול	GREAT	153a	1
	ה	THE	209a	2 b
	חי	ALIVE	312b	1 d
	טוב	PLEASANT	374a	3 a
	כל	ALL	481b	1 b
	כנף	WING	489c	1 a
	מין	KIND	568b	
	נפש	SOUL	659c	
	עוף	FLY	733d	1
	רמש	CREEP	943a	2 b
	שרץ	SWARM	1056c	1
	תנין	SEA-MONSTER	1072c	3
1 22	אמר	SAY	56b	1
	ברך	BLESS	139a	2 a
	ל	TO	517c	7 ba
	מלא	FILL	570b	2
	עוף	FLY	733d	1
	פרה	BEAR FRUIT	826a	1
	רבה	BECOME MANY	915a	1 b
1 23	בקר	MORNING	134a	1 e
	היה	BECOME	225c	2 1a
	חמישי	FIFTH	332c	1
	יום	DAY	398c	2 d
1 24	בהמה	BEAST	97a	2
	היה	COME TO PASS	224b	1 1b
	חי	ALIVE	312b	1 d
	חיה	LIVING THING	312c	1 b
	יצא	BRING OUT	425b	4 j
	מין	KIND	568b	
	נפש	SOUL	659c	2
	רמש	CREEPING THINGS	943a	1
1 25	אדמה	GROUND	9d	4
	בהמה	BEAST	97a	2
	היה	LIVING THING	312c	1 b
	טוב	PLEASANT	374a	3 a
	מין	KIND	568b	
	עשה	DO	794b	2 1b
	רמש	CREEPING THINGS	943a	1
1 26	אדם	MAN	9b	2
	אדם	MAN	9b	2

Ch v.	Heb	Eng	Page	Sec
	ארץ	EARTH	76b	3 a
	ב	IN	90d	3 8
	בהמה	BEAST	97a	2
	דגה	FISH	185d	
	דמות	LIKENESS	198b	1
	ו	AND	252b	1 b
	ים	SEA	411a	5
	ך	LIKE	454a	1 c1
	עוף	FLY	733d	1
	על	UPON	752c	2 1
	צלם	IMAGE	854a	2
	רדה	HAVE DOMINION	922a	
	רמש	CREEP	943a	2 a
	רמש	CREEPING THINGS	943a	1
	תאר	FORM	1061b	
1 27	אדם	MAN	9b	2
	אדם	MAN	9b	2
	אלהים	GOD	43b	1 b
	ברא	CREATE	135b	1
	זכר	MALE	271c	1 1b
	נקבה	FEMALE	666c	1
	צלם	IMAGE	854a	2
1 28	ברך	BLESS	139a	2 a
	דגה	FISH	185d	
	ה	THE	209a	2 b
	חי	ALIVE	312b	1 c
	ים	SEA	411a	5
	כבש	SUBDUE	461b	3
	מלא	FILL	570b	2
	עוף	FLY	733d	1
	פרה	BEAR FRUIT	826a	1
	רדה	HAVE DOMINION	922a	
	רמש	CREEP	943a	2 c
1 29	אכלה	FOOD	38a	1
	את	MARK OF THE AC-CUSATIVE	84d	1 a
	הנה	BEHOLD	244a	B a
	זרע	SOW	281c	2
	זרע	SOWING	282b	2 c
	כל	ALL	481c	1 b
	ל	TO	512c	4 b
	נתן	GIVE	678b	1 b
	עץ	TREE	781c	1 b
	עשב	HERB	793c	
	פנה	FACE	816b	15
	פנה	FACE	819a	2 7b
	אכלה	FOOD	38a	1
1 30	ארץ	EARTH	76b	3 a
	את	MARK OF THE AC-CUSATIVE	84d	1 a
	היה	COME TO PASS	224b	1 1b
	חי	ALIVE	312b	1 d
	חיה	LIVING THING	312c	1 b
	ירק	GREEN	438d	
	נפש	SOUL	659c	2
	עוף	FLY	733d	1
	עשב	HERB	793c	
	רמש	CREEP	943a	2 a
1 31	בקר	MORNING	134a	1 e
	ה	THE	209a	2 b
	היה	BECOME	225c	2 1a
	הנה	BEHOLD	244b	C
	טוב	PLEASANT	374a	3 a
	יום	DAY	398c	2 d
	כל	ALL	481c	1 c
	מאד	EXCEEDINGLY	547b	2 a
	ששי	SIXTH	995d	
2 1	צבא	HOST	839b	1 d
2 2	אשר	PARTICLE OF RE-LATION	82b	4 a
	ב	IN	88d	15
	יום	DAY	398c	2 d
	יום	DAY	400c	7 g
	כלה	FINISH	478a	1 a
	כל	ALL	481a	1 a
	מלאכה	WORK	522a	3 a
	מן	FROM	578a	1 a
	עשה	DO	793d	1 1a l
	שבת	CEASE	991d	2 a
2 3	ברא	CREATE	135b	1
	ברך	BLESS	139a	2 b
	ה	THE	209a	2 b
	יום	DAY	398c	2 d
	כי	BECAUSE	473c	3 b
	ל	TO	517b	7 ba
	מלאכה	WORK	522a	3 a
	קדש	BE SET APART	873a	1 d
	שביעי	SEVENTH	988d	1
	שבת	CEASE	991d	2 a
2 4	אלה	THESE	41c	A
	ב	IN	91a	5 l
	ברא	CREATE	135c	1
	ה	THE	208d	1 i
	יהוה	YAHWEH	218c	1
	יהוה	YAHWEH	219a	2 1h
	יום	DAY	400a	7 d1 g
	תולדות	GENERATIONS	410a	B
2 5	אדם	MAN	9a	2
	אדמה	GROUND	9c	1
	אין	NOT	34c	2 c
	יהוה	YAHWEH	219a	2 1h
	היה	BE	226d	3 1
	טרם	NOT YET	382c	1
	כי	BECAUSE	473d	2
	כל	ALL	482b	1 ec
	לא	NOT	*518c	1 aa

GENESIS

Ch v.	Heb	Eng	Page	Sec
	מטר	RAIN	565a	
	עבד	WORK	713a	1
	על	UPON	756b	27 a a
	עשׂב	HERB	793b	
	צמח	SPROUT	855b	1
	שׂדה	FIELD	961c	1 d
	שׂדה	FIELD	961c	1 d
	שׂיח	BUSH	967b	
2 6	אדמה	GROUND	9d	4
	אד	MIST	15d	
	עלה	GO UP	748d	5
	פנה	FACE	816b	1 5
	שׁקה	GIVE TO DRINK	1052c	1
	אד	ADDENDA ET COR-RIGENDA	1119d	
2 7	אדם	MAN	9a	1
	אדמה	EARTH	9d	3
	אף	NOSE	60a	1
	יהוה	YAHWEH	219a	2 1h
	היה	BECOME	226b	2 2e
	חי	ALIVE	312b	1 d
	חיים	LIFE	313b	1
	יצר	FORM	427d	2 a
	ל	TO	512b	4 a
	מן	OUT OF	579c	2 cc
	נפח	BREATHE	656a	
	נפשׁ	SOUL	659c	2
	נשׁמה	BREATH	675a	2
	עפר	DRY EARTH	779d	1 b
2 8	אדם	MAN	9a	1
	גן	GARDEN	171a	
	יהוה	YAHWEH	219a	2 1h
	יצר	FORM	427d	2 a
	מן	FROM	578c	1 c
	נטע	PLANT	642c	1
	עדן		726d	
	עדן	EDEN	727a	
	קדם	FRONT	869b	1 b 1
	שׂום	TO PLACE	962c	1 a
	שׁם	THERE	1027a	1 a
2 9	אדמה	GROUND	9c	1
	מאכל	FOOD	38b	
	גן	GARDEN	171a	
	ה	THE	208b	1 ha
	יהוה	YAHWEH	219a	2 1h
	ו	AND	253a	1 g
	חיים	LIFE	313b	2
	חמד	DESIRE	326c	
	טוב	PLEASANT	373d	1 b
	טוב	A GOOD THING	375b	4
	דעת	KNOWLEDGE	395d	1 d
	כל	ALL	481b	1 b
	עץ	TREE	781c	1
	צמח	SPROUT	855c	1
	מראה	VISION	909c	1 b
	רע	EVIL	949a	3
	תוך	MIDST	1063c	
2 10	גן	GARDEN	171a	
	היה	BECOME	226b	2 2e
	יצא	GO OUT	423a	1
	נהר	STREAM	625d	1
	עדן	EDEN	727a	
	פרד	DIVIDE	825b	1
	ראשׁ	HEAD	911b	4 c
	ארבע	FOUR	917a	1 b1
	שׁם	THERE	1027c	4 a
	שׁקה	GIVE TO DRINK	1052c	1
2 11	אשׁר	PARTICLE OF RELATION	81d	2
	את	MARK OF THE ACCUSATIVE	84d	1 a
	ה	THE	209b	2 c
	הוא	HE, SHE, IT	215b	1 a
	זהב	GOLD	262c	1
	זהב	GOLD	263b	7
	חוילה	HAVILAH	296c	
	חוילה	HAVILAH	296c	
	חוילה	HAVILAH	296c	
	סבב	GO AROUND	685d	2 b
	פישׁון	PISHON	810b	
	שׁם	THERE	1027b	1 b
	שׁם	NAME	1027d	1
2 12	אבן	STONE	6d	3
	בדלח	BDELLIUM	95d	
	ה	THE	208d	2 a
	הוא	HE, SHE, IT	216d	7
	זהב	GOLD	262c	1
	זהב	GOLD	263b	7
	טוב	PLEASANT	374b	3 e
	שׁהם	CARNELIAN	995d	
	שׁם	THERE	1027a	1 a
2 13	הוא	HE, SHE, IT	215b	1 a
	כושׁ	CUSH	469a	3
	כל	ALL	481a	1 a
	נהר	STREAM	625d	1
	סבב	GO AROUND	685d	2 b
	שׁם	NAME	1027d	1
2 14	אשׁור	ASSYRIA	78d	3
	הוא	HE, SHE, IT	215b	1 a
	הוא	HE, SHE, IT	215d	2 b
	חדקל	TIGRIS	293c	
	חוילה	HAVILAH	*296d	
	נהר	STREAM	625d	1
	נהר	STREAM	*625d	1 f
	פרת	EUPHRATES	832b	
	קדמה	EAST	870b	1

Ch v.	Heb	Eng	Page	Sec
	רביעי	FOURTH	917d	1
	שׁם	NAME	1027d	1
2 15	אדם	MAN	9a	1
	גן	GARDEN	171a	
	יהוה	YAHWEH	219a	2 1h
	ל	TO	517b	7 a
	נוח	REST	628d	B 1
	עבד	WORK	713a	1
	עדן	EDEN	727a	
	שׁמר	KEEP	1036b	1 a
2 16	אדם	MAN	9a	1
	אמר	SAY	56b	1
	גן	GARDEN	171a	
	יהוה	YAHWEH	219a	2 1h
	על	UPON	753b	2 1c
	עץ	TREE	781c	1
	עץ	TREE	781c	1 b
	צוה	LAY CHARGE UPON	845c	1 a
2 17	ו	AND	252d	1 e
	טוב	A GOOD THING	375b	4
	דעת	KNOWLEDGE	395d	1 d
	יום	DAY	400a	7 d1 g
	לא	NOT	518c	1 aa
	מות	DIE	560a	2 b
	רע	EVIL	949a	3
2 18	אדם	MAN	9a	1
	בד	SEPARATION	94c	1 b
	יהוה	YAHWEH	219a	2 1h
	היה	BE	227b	3 4c
	טוב	PLEASANT	374c	5
	כי	THAT	*471d	1 a
	ל	TO	515a	5 hb a
	לא	NOT	519a	1 ba
	נגד	IN FRONT	617c	2 a
	עזר	HELP	740d	2
2 19	אדמה	EARTH	9d	3
	אל	TO	39c	1
	בוא	COME	99b	2
	הוא	HE, SHE, IT	215d	2 b
	יהוה	YAHWEH	219a	2 1h
	חי	ALIVE	312b	1 d
	חיה	LIVING THING	312c	1 b
	יצר	FORM	427d	2 a
	ל	TO	517b	7 a
	מה	WHAT	552d	1 b
	מן	OUT OF	579b	2 ba
	נפשׁ	SOUL	659c	2
	עוף	FLY	733d	1
	קרא	CALL	896a	6 e2
	ראה	TO SEE	907b	1
	שׂדה	FIELD	961b	1 c
	שׁם	NAME	1027d	1
	שׁמי	HEAVENS	1029d	1 a
2 20	אדם	ADAM	9c	3
	בהמה	BEAST	97a	2
	חיה	LIVING THING	312c	1 b
	ל	TO	515a	5 hb a
	מצא	FIND	592c	1 a
	נגד	IN FRONT	617c	2 a
	עוף	FLY	733d	1
	עזר	HELP	740d	2
	קרא	CALL	896a	6 f
	שׂדה	FIELD	961b	1 c
	שׁם	NAME	1027d	1
2 21	בשׂר	FLESH	142c	1 b
	יהוה	YAHWEH	219a	2 1h
	ישׁן	SLEEP	445c	
	נפל	FALL	658b	5
	סגר	CLOSE	689d	2 a
	על	UPON	756b	27 a b
	צלע	RIB	854b	1
	תרדמה	DEEP SLEEP	922b	
	רוח	BREATH	*925b	3 h
	תחת	INSTEAD	1065d	2 2b a
2 22	אדם	MAN	9b	1
	אל	TO	39c	1
	אשׁה	WOMAN	61a	1
	בוא	COME	99b	2
	בנה	BUILD	124c	1 c
	יהוה	YAHWEH	219a	2 1h
	ל	TO	512b	4 a
	לקח	TAKE	542d	3 a
	צלע	RIB	854b	1
2 23	אדם	MAN	9b	1
	אישׁ	MAN	35d	
	אשׁה	WOMAN	61a	1
	בשׂר	FLESH	142d	4
	זה	THIS	260c	1 a
	כי	BECAUSE	473d	3 b
	לקח	TAKE	544a	1
	מן	OUT OF	579b	2 ba
	עצם	BONE	782d	1 a
	פעם	OCCURRENCE	822b	3 d2
	קרא	CALL	896b	2 d1
2 24	אב	FATHER	3b	1
	אישׁ	MAN	35d	
	אם	MOTHER	51d	1
	אשׁה	WOMAN	61b	2
	בשׂר	FLESH	142d	4
	דבק	CLING	179d	2 a
	כן	SO	487b	3 f
	עזב	LEAVE	737b	2 b1
2 25	אדם	MAN	9b	1
	אשׁה	WOMAN	61b	2
	בושׁ	BE ASHAMED	102a	

Ch v.	Heb	Eng	Page	Sec
	היה	BE	227a	3 4a
	ערום	NAKED	736a	
3 1	שׁנים	TWO	1041a	1 a
	אל	TO	40a	3 b
	אלהים	GOD	44a	4 a
	אמר	SAY	55d	1
	אמר	SAY	55d	1
	אמר	SAY	56a	1
	אשׁה	WOMAN	61a	1
	אף	ALSO	65b	2
	גן	GARDEN	171a	
	יהוה	YAHWEH	219a	2 1h
	היה	BE	227a	3 4a
	חיה	LIVING THING	312d	1 b
	כל	ALL	482a	1 ea
	לא	NOT	518c	1 aa
	מן	THAN	582c	6 b
	נחשׁ	SERPENT	638b	1 d
	עץ	TREE	781c	1 b
	ערום	CRAFTY	791a	1
	עשׂה	DO	794b	2 1b
	שׂדה	FIELD	961b	1 c
3 2	אשׁה	WOMAN	61a	1
	גן	GARDEN	171a	
	נחשׁ	SERPENT	638b	1 d
	עץ	TREE	781c	1 b
	פרי	FRUIT	826b	1
3 3	אלהים	GOD	44a	4 a
	אשׁר	PARTICLE OF RELATION	82c	4 a
	גן	GARDEN	171a	
	לא	NOT	518c	1 aa
	מות	DIE	559d	2 b
	נגע	TOUCH	619a	1
	פן	LEST	814c	1
	פרי	FRUIT	826b	1
3 4	לא	NOT	*518c	1 aa
	מות	DIE	560a	2 b
	נחשׁ	SERPENT	638b	1 d
3 5	אלהים	GOD	44a	4 a
	היה	BECOME	226a	2 2c
	ו	AND	254d	5 a
	טוב	A GOOD THING	375b	4
	יום	DAY	400a	7 d1 g
	ך	LIKE	453d	1 b
	עין	EYE	744b	1 j
	עין	EYE	744c	3 a
	פקח	OPEN	824d	
	רע	EVIL	949a	3
3 6	תאוה	DESIRE	16c	2
	אישׁ	MAN	35d	
	מאכל	FOOD	38b	
	חמד	DESIRE	326c	
	טוב	PLEASANT	373d	1 b
	כי	THAT	471c	1 a
	כי	THAT	471d	1 a
	עין	EYE	744a	1 a
	פרי	FRUIT	826b	1
	שׂכל	BE PRUDENT	968b	1
3 7	הם	THEY	241c	3 a
	חגורה	GIRDLE	292b	
	ל	TO	515d	5 ia
	ערום	NAKED	736a	1
	עין	EYE	744b	1 j
	עין	EYE	744c	3 a
	עלה	LEAF	750a	
	פקח	OPEN	824d	
	תאה	FIG-TREE	1061a	1
	תפר	SEW TOGETHER	1074c	
	אנן	THEY	*1081c	
3 8	אדם	MAN	9b	1
	אשׁה	WOMAN	61b	2
	גן	GARDEN	171a	
	יהוה	YAHWEH	219a	2 1h
	הלך	WALK	236a	1 b
	חבא	WITHDRAW	285b	1
	יום	DAY	398b	3
	ל	TO	516d	6 a
	עץ	TREE	781c	1 b
	פנה	FACE	818b	26 a
	קול	VOICE	877a	1 b
	קול	VOICE	877b	2 c
	רוח	BREATH	924d	2 a
3 9	אי	WHERE	32b	1 a
	יהוה	YAHWEH	219a	2 1h
	היך	HOW	*228a	
	קרא	CALL	895b	2 a
3 10	אנכי	I	59a	
	גן	GARDEN	171a	
	חבא	WITHDRAW	285b	
	ירא	FEAR	431a	1 a
	ערום	NAKED	736a	1
	קול	VOICE	877a	1 b
	שׁמע	HEAR	1033c	1 a
3 11	אכל	EAT	37b	1
	אתה	THOU	61c	
	בלת	NOT	116d	4 a
	כי	THAT	471c	1 a
	מי	WHO	566a	
	נגד	BE CONSPICUOUS	616d	2
	ערום	NAKED	736a	1
3 12	אדם	MAN	9b	1
	הוא	HE, SHE, IT	215d	2 a
	חכם	WISE	314d	2
3 13	אמר	SAY	56a	1
	יהוה	YAHWEH	219a	2 1h

2

Ch	v.	Heb	Eng	Page	Sec
		זה	THIS	261c	4 d
		מה	WHAT	552c	1 ab
		נחש	SERPENT	638b	1 d
		נשא	DECEIVE	674a	
3	14	ארר	CURSE	76d	
		בהמה	BEAST	97a	2
		יהוה	YAHWEH	219a	2 1h
		הלך	WALK	232a	1 2
		זה	THIS	260c	1 a
		חיה	LIVING THING	312c	1 b
		חיים	LIFE	313b	1
		יום	DAY	399a	4 a
		כי	BECAUSE	473c	3 a
		מן	THAN	582c	6 b
		נחש	SERPENT	*638b	1 c
		נחש	SERPENT	638d	1 d
		על	UPON	752c	2 1
		עפר	DRY EARTH	779d	1 a
		עשה	DO	793d	1 1a 1
		שדה	FIELD	961b	1 c
3	15	איבה	ENMITY	33c	
		בין	INTERVAL	107c	1 d
		הוא	HE, SHE, IT	215b	1 a
		זרע	SOWING	282c	4 b
		זרע	SOWING	282c	4 a
		עקב	HEEL	784a	A
		ראש	HEAD	910d	1 b
		שוף	BRUISE	1003a	
		שות	PUT	1011b	2 a
3	16	איש	MAN	35d	
		אל	TO	40a	3 c
		בן	SON	121b	2
		הריון	CONCEPTION	248a	
		ו	AND	252b	1 a
		ילד	BEAR	408a	1 a
		משל	RULE	605d	1
		נתן	PUT	680b	2 a
		על	UPON	757c	2 7 c c
		עצב	PAIN	780d	1
		עצבון	PAIN	781a	
		רבה	BECOME MANY	915b	
		רבה	BECOME MANY	915c	1 c
		רבה	BECOME MANY	915d	1 e1
		תשוקה	LONGING	1003c	
		תשוקה	LONGING	1003c	
3	17	אדם	MAN	9b	1
		אדם	ADAM	9c	3
		אדמה	GROUND	9c	1
		אמר	SAY	56a	1
		אמר	SAY	56b	1
		אשה	WOMAN	61b	2
		ארר	CURSE	76d	
		אשר	PARTICLE OF RE-LATION	82d	4 d
		חיים	LIFE	313b	1
		יום	DAY	399a	4 a
		כי	BECAUSE	473c	3 a
		עבור	FOR THE SAKE OF	721a	1 a
		עצבון	PAIN	781a	
		קול	VOICE	877b	3 a1
		שמע	HEAR	1034a	11
3	18	אכל	EAT	37b	1
		דרדר	THISTLES	205a	
		עשב	HERB	793c	
		צמח	SPROUT	855c	1
		קוץ	THORN-BUSH	881a	1
		שדה	FIELD	961c	1 d
3	19	אדמה	EARTH	9d	3
		אכל	EAT	37b	1
		אל	TO	39c	1
		אף	NOSE	60b	2
		אתה	THOU	61c	
		זעה	SWEAT	402c	
		כי	BECAUSE	474b	3 d
		לקח	TAKE	544a	1
		עד	AS FAR AS	724b	12a b
		על	UPON	757c	2 7 c ab
		עפר	DRY EARTH	779d	1 b
		עפר	DRY EARTH	779d	1 b
		שוב	TURN BACK	997c	4 a
3	20	אדם	MAN	9b	1
		אם	MOTHER	51c	1
		הוא	HE, SHE, IT	215b	1 a
		יהוה	YAHWEH	218a	2
		היה	BECOME	226a	2 2a
		חוה	EVE	295d	
		חי	ALIVE	312b	1 d
		כי	BECAUSE	473d	3 b
		קרא	CALL	896a	6 a
3	21	אדם	MAN	9b	1
		אדם	ADAM	9c	3
		יהוה	YAHWEH	219a	2 1h
		כתנת	TUNIC	509a	
		ל	TO	515a	5 hb a
		לבש	CLOTHE	528c	3
		עור	SKIN	736b	2
3	22	יהוה	YAHWEH	219a	2 1h
		היה	BECOME	226a	2 2c
		הן	BEHOLD	243c	A
		חיים	LIFE	313b	2
		טוב	A GOOD THING	375b	4
		יד	HAND	388d	1
		ידע	KNOW	393c	1
		ל	TO	514a	5 fb
		לקח	TAKE	542a	3 a
		עולם	LONG DURATION	762d	2 i

Ch	v.	Heb	Eng	Page	Sec
		עתה	NOW	774b	2 b
		עץ	TREE	781c	1 a
		פן	LEST	814d	1 a
		רע	EVIL	949a	3
		שלח	SEND	1018c	3 a
3	23	אדמה	GROUND	9c	1
		אדמה	EARTH	9d	3
		אשר	PARTICLE OF RE-LATION	81d	2
		גן	GARDEN	171a	
		יהוה	YAHWEH	219a	2 1h
		לקח	TAKE	544a	1
		מן	OUT OF	579a	2 aa
		עבד	WORK	713a	1
		עדן	EDEN	727a	
		פן	LEST	814d	1 a
		שם	THERE	1027c	4 c
3	24	אדם	ADAM	9c	3
		גן	GARDEN	171a	
		גרש	DRIVE OUT	176a	1
		דרך	WAY	202d	1
		הפך	TURN	246a	1
		חיים	LIFE	313b	2
		חרב	SWORD	352d	1 j
		כרוב	CHERUB	500c	2
		ל	TO	513d	5 d
		להט	FLAME	529d	1
		מן	FROM	578d	1 c
		עדן	EDEN	727a	
		עץ	TREE	781c	1 a
		קדם	FRONT	869c	1 b 2
		שכן	SETTLE DOWN	1015c	1 b
		שמר	KEEP	1036c	1 b
4	1	איש	MAN	35d	
		אשה	WOMAN	61b	2
		את	MARK OF THE AC-CUSATIVE	84d	1 a
		את	WITH	86a	1 a
		הרה	CONCEIVE	247d	1
		חוה	EVE	295d	
		ידע	KNOW	394b	3
		ילד	BEAR	408a	1 a
		קין	CAIN	884b	
		קין	CAIN	884a	
		קנה	ACQUIRE	889a	1 c
4	2	אדמה	GROUND	9c	1
		אח	BROTHER	26b	1
		את	MARK OF THE AC-CUSATIVE	84d	1 a
		הבל	ABEL	211b	
		היה	BECOME	226a	2 2a
		ו	AND	252d	1 e
		יסף	DO AGAIN	415c	2 a
		ל	TO	517d	7 bc
		עבד	WORK	713a	1
		קין	CAIN	884a	
		רעה	TEND	945a	1 d1
4	3	אדמה	GROUND	9c	1
		בוא	COME	99b	2
		היה	COME TO PASS	224c	2 a1 az
		יום	DAY	399c	5 a
		מן	FROM	580d	3 ba
		מן	FROM	581c	4 b
		מנחה	OFFERING	585a	1
		מנחה	OFFERING	585c	6
		פרי	FRUIT	826b	1
		קין	CAIN	884a	
		קין	END	893d	1
4	4	בוא	COME	99b	2
		בכור	FIRST-BORN	114b	2 c
		הבל	ABEL	211b	
		הוא	HE, SHE, IT	215c	1 b
		ו	AND	252c	1 b
		חלב	FAT	317a	2 b
		מנחה	OFFERING	585a	1
		צאן	SMALL CATTLE	838b	1 a4
		שעה	GAZE	1043a	
4	5	ו	AND	252d	1 e
		חרה	BURN	354a	1 b
		לא	NOT	*518c	1 aa
		מאד	EXCEEDINGLY	547b	2 a
		מנחה	OFFERING	585a	1
		נפל	FALL	657c	5
		פנה	FACE	815d	1 1a
		קין	CAIN	884a	
		שעה	GAZE	1043a	
4	6	אמר	SAY	55d	1
		חרה	BURN	354a	1 b
		ל	TO	511a	1
		מה	HOW	554a	4 d
		מה	HOW	554a	4 d
		נפל	FALL	657c	5
		פנה	FACE	815d	1 1a
		פנה	FACE	817d	2 5a a
		קין	CAIN	884a	
4	7	אל	TO	40a	3 c
		חטאת	SIN	308c	1 b
		יטב	DO RIGHT	406a	5 a
		ל	TO	511d	2
		לא	NOT	520b	4 b
		משל	RULE	605d	1
		שאת	UPRISING	673b	4
		על	UPON	757c	2 7 c c
		פתח	OPENING	835d	
		רבץ	LIE DOWN	918c	
		תשוקה	LONGING	1003c	

Ch	v.	Heb	Eng	Page	Sec
4	8	אח	BROTHER	26b	1
		אל	TO	40a	4
		אמר	SAY	56a	1
		ב	IN	91a	5 1
		הבל	ABEL	211b	
		היה	COME TO PASS	224c	2 a1 ab
		היה	BE	227a	3 3
		הרג	KILL	247a	1 a
		עמד	STAND	764c	6 c
		קום	STAND	878a	2
		קין	CAIN	884a	
		שדה	FIELD	961b	1 b
4	9	אח	BROTHER	26b	1
		אי	WHERE	32b	1 a
		ה	INTERROG PART	209d	1 b
		הבל	ABEL	211b	
		ידע	KNOW	393c	1 a
		קין	CAIN	884a	
		שמר	KEEP	1036c	1 a
4	10	אדמה	GROUND	9d	4
		אח	BROTHER	26b	1
		דם	BLOOD	196d	2 f
		מה	WHAT	552b	1 a
		מן	OUT OF	579a	2 ab
		צעק	CRY	858c	1 b
		קול	VOICE	877a	1 f
4	11	אדמה	GROUND	9d	4
		אח	BROTHER	26b	1
		ארר	CURSE	76d	
		דם	BLOOD	196d	2 f
		יד	HAND	388d	1
		לקח	TAKE	543b	4 f
		מן	FROM	578c	1 b
		פה	MOUTH	804d	1 a
		פצה	PART	822c	1 a
4	12	אדמה	GROUND	9c	1
		יסף	DO AGAIN	415c	2 a
		כח	STRENGTH	471a	5
		כי	WHEN	473a	2 a
		ל	TO	517d	7 bc
		מן	FROM	578c	1 b
		נוד	WANDER	626d	1 a
		נוד	NOD	*627a	
		נוע	TOTTER	631b	2
		נצה	FLY	*663b	
		נתן	GIVE	679c	1 t
		עבד	WORK	713a	1
4	13	גדל	GREAT	153a	3
		מן	THAN	582d	6 d
		נשא	LIFT	671a	2 b
		עון	INIQUITY	731c	3
		קין	CAIN	884a	
4	14	אדמה	GROUND	9d	4
		גרש	DRIVE OUT	176d	
		ה	THE	207b	1 ca
		היה	COME TO PASS	225a	2 1b ag
		הן	BEHOLD	243c	A
		הרג	KILL	247a	1 a
		יום	DAY	399d	7 a1
		כל	ALL	482a	1 eb
		מן	FROM	578c	1 b
		מצא	FIND	593b	3 a
		נוד	WANDER	626d	1 a
		נוד	NOD	*627a	
		נוע	TOTTER	631b	2
		נצה	FLY	*663b	
		סתר	HIDE	711c	2
		על	UPON	758c	4 2a
		פנה	FACE	816b	15
		פנה	FACE	818b	26a
		פנה	FACE	819b	28b
4	15	אות	SIGN	16d	1
		אמר	SAY	56a	1
		בלת	NOT	116d	4 a
		הרג	KILL	247a	1 a
		כל	ALL	482a	1 eb
		כל	ALL	482b	1 ec
		כן	SO	487a	3 da
		מצא	FIND	593b	3 a
		נכה	SMITE	646a	2 c
		נקם	AVENGE	668b	
		קין	CAIN	884a	
		שבעתים	SEVEN FOLD	988d	1
4	16	יצא	GO OUT	422d	1 b
		ישב	DWELL	443a	3
		נוד	NOD	627a	
		עדן	EDEN	727a	
		קדמה	EAST	870b	1
		קין	CAIN	884a	
4	17	אשה	WOMAN	61b	2
		בנה	BUILD	124b	1 aa
		הרה	CONCEIVE	247d	1
		חנוך	ENOCH	335c	1
		ידע	KNOW	394b	3
		עיר	CITY	746b	1
		קין	CAIN	884a	
		קרא	CALL	896a	6 a
		שם	NAME	1027d	2 a
4	18	את	MARK OF THE AC-CUSATIVE	85a	1 b
		חנוך	ENOCH	335c	1
		ילד	BEGET	408c	2 a
		ילד	BE BORN	408d	
		למך	LAMECH	541a	1
		מחויאל	MEHUJAEL	562c	
		מתושאל	METHUSHAEL	607b	

GENESIS

Ch v.	Heb	Eng	Page	Sec
4 19	עירד	IRAD	747a	
	למך	LAMECH	541a	1
	לקח	TAKE	543b	4 e2
	עדה	ADAH	725d	1
	צלה	ZILLAH	853c	
	שם	NAME	1027d	2 a
	שנים	TWO	1041a	1 a
4 20	אב	FATHER	3c	5
	אהל	TENT	13d	1
	הוא	HE, SHE, IT	215b	1 a
	ו	AND	253a	1 g
	יבל	JABAL	385b	
	ישב	DWELL	443a	3
	עדה	ADAH	725d	1
	מקנה	CATTLE	889b	1
4 21	אב	FATHER	3c	5
	הוא	HE, SHE, IT	215b	1 a
	יובל	JUBAL	385b	
	כנור	LYRE	490a	
	כנור	LYRE	490b	
	עוגב	PIPE	721d	
	תפש	LAY HOLD OF	1074d	2
4 22	אחות	SISTER	27d	1
	ברזל	IRON	137c	1 b
	חרש	CUT IN	360c	1
	לטש	HAMMER	538b	1
	נחשת	COPPER	638d	1
	נעמה	NAAMAH	653d	1
	צלה	ZILLAH	853c	
	תובלקין	TUBAL-CAIN	1063b	
4 23	אזן	HEAR	24c	1
	אמרה	UTTERANCE	57b	
	הרג	KILL	247a	1 a
	חבורה	STRIPE	289a	
	חלף	EXCHANGE	*322b	
	ילד	CHILD	409c	D
	ל	TO	514d	5 g
	למך	LAMECH	541a	1
	עדה	ADAH	725d	1
	פצע	BRUISE	822d	
	צלה	ZILLAH	853c	
	קול	VOICE	877b	3 a1
4 24	כי	BECAUSE	474a	3 c
	למך	LAMECH	541a	1
	נקם	AVENGE	668a	
	קין	CAIN	884a	
	שבע	SEVEN	988b	5 c
	שבעים	SEVENTY	988c	3 a
	שבעתים	SEVEN FOLD	988d	1
4 25	אחר	ANOTHER	29c	
	בן	SON	120a	1
	הבל	ABEL	211b	
	הרג	KILL	247a	1 a
	זרע	SOWING	282d	4 d
	ידע	KNOW	394b	3
	כי	THAT	*472a	1 a
	כי	BECAUSE	473a	3 b
	עוד	STILL	729b	1 b
	קין	CAIN	884a	
	קרא	CALL	896a	6 a
	שת	PUT	1011b	1
	שת	SETH	1011d	
	תחת	INSTEAD	1065d	2 2b a
4 26	אז	THEN	23a	1 a
	אנוש	ENOSH	60d	
	ב	IN	90b	3 4
	הוא	HE, SHE, IT	215c	1 b
	חלל	POLLUTE	320d	
	ילד	BE BORN	408d	
	קרא	CALL	845b	2 c
	קרא	CALL	896a	6 a
	שת	SETH	1011d	
	שם	NAME	1028b	3
5 1	אדם	MAN	9b	2
	אדם	ADAM	9c	3
	ב	IN	90d	3 8
	ברא	CREATE	135b	1
	דמות	LIKENESS	198b	1
	זה	THIS	261a	1
	תולדות	GENERATIONS	410a	A
	ספר	MISSIVE	707b	3 b
5 2	אדם	MAN	9b	2
	ברא	CREATE	135b	1
	ברא	CREATE	135c	1
	ברך	BLESS	139a	2 a
	זכר	MALE	271c	11 b
	נקבה	FEMALE	666c	1
	קרא	CALL	896a	6 a
5 3	אדם	ADAM	9c	3
	ב	IN	90d	3 8
	דמות	LIKENESS	198b	1
	חיה	LIVE	311a	1 a
	ילד	BEGET	409a	1
	צלם	IMAGE	854a	2
	קרא	CALL	896a	6 a
	שת	SETH	1011d	
	שלשים	THIRTY	1026c	1
	שנה	YEAR	1040b	
5 4	אדם	ADAM	9c	3
	אחר	AFTER	30a	2 b
	בן	SON	120a	1
	בן	SON	120a	1
	בת	DAUGHTER	123a	1
	בת	DAUGHTER	123a	1
	חיה	BE	227b	3 4b
	יום	DAY	399a	4 a
	ילד	BEGET	409a	1
	שת	SETH	1011d	
5 5	אדם	ADAM	9c	3
	חיה	BE	*226d	3 1
	חיה	BE	227b	3 4b
	כל	ALL	481a	1 a
	כל	ALL	482c	
	שלשים	THIRTY	1026c	1
	שנה	YEAR	1040c	
5 6	אנוש	ENOSH	60d	
	חמש	FIVE	332a	5 a1
	שת	SETH	1011d	
5 7	אנוש	ENOSH	60d	
	בן	SON	120a	1
	בת	DAUGHTER	123a	1
	בת	DAUGHTER	123a	1
	שבע	SEVEN	988b	5 b2
	שת	SETH	1011d	
5 8	חיה	BE	227b	3 4b
	יום	DAY	399a	4 a
	שת	SETH	1011d	
5 9	אנוש	ENOSH	60d	
	קינן	KENAN	884b	
	שנה	YEAR	1040b	
	תשעים	NINETY	1077d	
5 10	אנוש	ENOSH	60d	
	בן	SON	120a	1
	בת	DAUGHTER	123a	1
	חמש	FIVE	332a	2 a
	קינן	KENAN	884b	
5 11	אנוש	ENOSH	60d	
	חיה	BE	227b	3 4b
	יום	DAY	399a	4 a
5 12	מהללאל	MAHALALEL	239d	1
	קינן	KENAN	884b	
5 13	מהללאל	MAHALALEL	239d	1
	קנן	KENAN	884b	
	ארבעים	FORTY	917c	2 c
5 14	חיה	BE	227b	3 4b
	עשר	TEN	797a	3 b
	קינן	KENAN	884b	
5 15	מהללאל	MAHALALEL	239d	1
	ירד	JARED	434b	1
	ששים	SIXTY	995d	
5 16	מהללאל	MAHALALEL	239d	1
	ירד	JARED	434b	1
5 17	מהללאל	MAHALALEL	239d	1
	חמש	FIVE	332a	5 a2
	תשעים	NINETY	1077d	
5 18	חנוך	ENOCH	335c	2
	ירד	JARED	434b	1
5 19	ששים	SIXTY	995d	
	חנוך	ENOCH	335c	2
	ירד	JARED	434b	1
5 20	ירד	JARED	434b	1
5 21	חנוך	ENOCH	335c	2
	מתושלח	METHUSELAH	607b	
5 22	אלהים	GOD	43d	3
	את	WITH	85d	1
	בוא	COME	*98d	3
	הלך	WALK	236b	2
	חנוך	ENOCH	335c	2
	מתושלח	METHUSELAH	607b	
	שלש	THREE	1025d	3
5 23	חנוך	ENOCH	335c	2
	מאה	HUNDRED	548c	2 b
5 24	אין	NOT	34b	2 b
	אלהים	GOD	43d	3
	את	WITH	85d	1
	בוא	COME	*98d	3
	הלך	WALK	236b	2
	חנוך	ENOCH	335c	2
	כי	BECAUSE	473d	3 b
	לקח	TAKE	543a	3 a
5 25	למך	LAMECH	541a	2
	מתושלח	METHUSELAH	607b	
	שבע	SEVEN	988b	5 b2
	שמנים	EIGHTY	1033b	
	מתושלח	METHUSELAH	607b	
5 26	למך	LAMECH	541a	2
	מתושלח	METHUSELAH	607b	
	שמנים	EIGHTY	1033b	
5 27	מתושלח	METHUSELAH	607b	
5 28	בן	SON	120a	1
	למך	LAMECH	541a	2
5 29	אדמה	GROUND	9c	1
	ארר	CURSE	76d	
	זה	THIS	260c	1 a
	יד	HAND	389a	1 a
	מן	FROM	578a	1 a
	נח	NOAH	629b	
	נחם	CONSOLE ONESELF	637b	
	עצבון	PAIN	781a	1
	מעשה	DEED	795d	1 a3
	קרא	CALL	896a	6 a
5 30	חיה	LIVE	311a	1 a
	חמש	FIVE	332a	3
	למך	LAMECH	541a	2
	תשעים	NINETY	1077d	
5 31	למך	LAMECH	541a	2
	שבע	SEVEN	988b	5 b2
	שבעים	SEVENTY	988c	3 b
5 32	בן	SON	121d	9 a
	ו	AND	252a	1
	חם	HAM	325d	1
	חמש	FIVE	332a	3
	יפת	JAPHETH	834d	
	שם	SHEM	1028d	
6 1	אדם	MAN	9b	2
	אדמה	GROUND	9d	4
	היה	COME TO PASS	224c	2 a1 at
	חלל	POLLUTE	320d	2
	ילד	BE BORN	408d	
	כי	WHEN	473a	2 a
	ל	TO	517d	7 bc
	למד	LEARN	540d	
	על	UPON	752d	2 1
	פנה	FACE	819a	2 7b
	רבב	BECOME MANY	912d	1
6 2	אלהים	GOD	43b	1 c
	בחר	CHOOSE	104a	2 b
	בן	SON	120b	1 d
	בת	DAUGHTER	123a	1
	טוב	PLEASANT	373c	1 a
	כי	THAT	471c	1 a
	לקח	TAKE	543b	4 e2
	מן	FROM	581b	3 be
	ראה	TO SEE	907a	2 1
	אנון	THEY	*1081c	
	בר	SON	*1085b	1
6 3	בשר	FLESH	142d	5
	דור	DWELL	189c	
	דין	JUDGE	192c	1
	יום	DAY	399a	4 a
	עשרים	TWENTY	797d	1 2d
	רוח	BREATH	925b	4 c
	ש	WHO	980a	4 a
	ש	WHO	980b	4 c
	שגג	GO ASTRAY	993a	2
	ידן	ADDENDA ET COR-RIGENDA	1122b	
6 4	אחר	AFTER	30a	2 b
	אלהים	GOD	43b	1 c
	אשר	PARTICLE OF RE-LATION	82c	4 ba
	בוא	COME	98a	1 e
	בן	SON	120b	1 d
	בת	DAUGHTER	123a	1
	גבור	STRONG	150b	2
	הם	THEY	241b	1 a
	הם	THEY	241d	7
	יום	DAY	400d	7 g
	ילד	BEAR	408b	1 a
	מן	FROM	581d	4 c
	נפל	LIE	*657d	7
	נפלים	GIANTS	558c	
	עולם	LONG DURATION	762a	1 a
	שם	NAME	1028a	2 b1
6 5	אדם	MAN	9b	2
	מחשבה	THOUGHT	364b	1 a
	יום	DAY	400c	7 f
	יצר	PURPOSE	428a	4
	כי	THAT	471c	1 a
	לב	HEART	524d	2 3c
	רב	GREAT	913c	2 a
	רע	EVIL	948c	0 c
	רק	ONLY	956c	2 c
6 6	אדם	MAN	9b	2
	אל	TO	39d	2
	כי	THAT	471c	1 a
	נחם	BE SORRY	637a	2
	עצב	HURT	780d	
6 7	אדם	MAN	9b	2
	אדם	MAN	9b	2
	אדמה	GROUND	9d	4
	בהמה	BEAST	96d	1
	ברא	CREATE	135b	1
	כי	THAT	471c	1 a
	כי	BECAUSE	473d	3 b
	מחה	WIPE OUT	562b	3
	מן	FROM	582a	5 b
	נחם	BE SORRY	637a	2
	על	UPON	758c	4 2a
	פנה	FACE	819b	2 8b
	רמש	CREEPING THINGS	943a	1
6 8	ו	AND	252b	1 e
	חן	FAVOR	336b	2 b2
	מצא	FIND	592d	1 a
6 9	אלהים	GOD	43d	3
	את	WITH	85d	1
	בוא	COME	*98d	3
	דור	GENERATION	190a	2 b
	הלך	WALK	236b	2
	תולדות	GENERATIONS	410a	A
	תמים	SOUND	1071a	4
6 10	חם	HAM	325d	1
	יפת	JAPHETH	834d	
	שלש	THREE	1025d	
	שם	SHEM	1028d	
6 11	אלהים	GOD	43d	3
	ארץ	EARTH	76a	1 c
	חמס	VIOLENCE	329c	
	ים	SEA	*411a	5
	מלא	BE FULL	570c	1
	שחת	GO TO RUIN	1007d	
6 12	בשר	FLESH	142d	6 c
	דרך	WAY	203c	6 a
	הנה	BEHOLD	244b	C
	כי	BECAUSE	473d	3 b
	כל	ALL	481c	1 b
	שחת	GO TO RUIN	1007d	
	שחת	GO TO RUIN	1008b	2

Ch	v.	Heb	Eng	Page	Sec
6	13	את	WITH	85d	1
		בוא	COME	98c	2 d
		בשר	FLESH	142d	6 c
		הנה	BEHOLD	243d	
		חמס	VIOLENCE	329c	
		כי	BECAUSE	473d	3 b
		מלא	BE FULL	570a	1 b
		פנה	FACE	817a	24a c
		פנה	FACE	818c	26c a
		קץ	END	893d	1
6	14	בית	HOUSE	110c	8 a
		בקר	CATTLE	133b	1 a
		גפר	GOPHER	172d	
		חוץ	THE OUTSIDE	299d	1 bd
		כפר	PITCH	498d	
		כפר	SMEAR	498d	
		ל	TO	515c	5 ia
		מן	FROM	578d	1 c
		עץ	TREE	781d	2 a
		קן	NEST	890a	2
		תבה	ARK	1061c	
6	15	אמה	CUBIT	52b	1
		ארך	LENGTH	73d	A
		זה	THIS	261b	3
		חמשים	FIFTY	332c	2 a
		קומה	HEIGHT	879b	3
		רחב	WIDTH	931d	
		שלשים	THIRTY	1026c	1
		תבה	ARK	1061c	
6	16	אל	TO	39c	1
		אמה	CUBIT	52b	1
		כלה	FINISH	478a	1 a
		מעל	ABOVE	752a	2 d
		פתח	OPENING	835d	
		צד	SIDE	841a	
		צהר	ROOF	844a	
		שני	SECOND	1041c	
		תבה	ARK	1061c	
		תחתי	LOWER	1066c	
6	17	אני	I	59a	
		אנכי	I	59c	
		בשר	FLESH	142d	6 a
		גוע	EXPIRE	157c	
		הנה	BEHOLD	244b	B b
		חיים	LIFE	313b	1
		מבול	FLOOD	550a	2
		מי	WATER	565c	1 d
		רוח	BREATH	924d	1 e
		שחת	GO TO RUIN	1008a	1
		שמי	HEAVENS	1029d	1 a
		תחת	UNDERNEATH	1066a	3 2a
6	18	אל	TO	39d	2
		את	WITH	85d	1
		בוא	COME	97d	1
		קום	STAND	879a	6 d
		תבה	ARK	1061c	
6	19	בוא	COME	99a	1
		בשר	FLESH	142d	6 a
		זכר	MALE	271c	12
		חיה	LIVE	311c	1
		חי	ALIVE	312b	1 d
		כל	ALL	482c	2 a
		מן	FROM	580c	3 a
		נקבה	FEMALE	666c	2
		תבה	ARK	1061c	
6	20	אדמה	GROUND	9d	4
		ה	THE	207d	1 e
		חיה	LIVE	311c	1
		כל	ALL	482c	2 a
		מין	KIND	568b	
		רמש	CREEPING THINGS	943a	1
6	21	אכל	EAT	37d	1
		אכלה	FOOD	38a	1
		מאכל	FOOD	38b	
		אסף	GATHER	62b	1 c
		ל	TO	515d	5 ia
		לקח	TAKE	543a	4 b
6	22	כ	LIKE	454d	2 d
		כן	SO	486c	2 cc
		עשה	DO	794a	1 1a 7
7	1	אל	TO	39d	
		את	MARK OF THE AC-CUSATIVE	85a	1 a
		בית	HOUSE	109d	5 a
		דור	GENERATION	190a	2 a
		זה	THIS	261a	2 bb
		פנה	FACE	817a	24a g
		צדיק	JUST	843a	3 a
		ראה	TO SEE	907a	2 3
		תבה	ARK	1061c	
7	2	איש	MAN	35d	
		אשה	WOMAN	61b	3
		אשר	PARTICLE OF RE-LATION	82b	2 b
		הוא	HE, SHE, IT	216b	3 c
		טהור	CLEAN	373a	1
		שבע	SEVEN	988a	1 b
		שנים	TWO	1041a	1 b1
7	3	זכר	MALE	271c	12
		זרע	SOWING	282c	4 a
		זרע	SOWING	283a	4 e
		חיה	LIVE	311c	1
		נקבה	FEMALE	666c	2
		פנה	FACE	816b	15
		פנה	FACE	819a	27b
		שבע	SEVEN	988a	1 b
7	4	אדמה	GROUND	9d	4
		אנכי	I	59a	
		יום	DAY	398b	1
		יום	DAY	398c	2 c
		ל	TO	517a	6 b
		לילה	NIGHT	538d	1
		מחה	WIPE OUT	562b	3
		מטר	RAIN	565a	
		עוד	STILL	729a	1 ab
		על	UPON	758c	4 2a
		פנה	FACE	816b	15
		פנה	FACE	819b	28b
		צבא	ARMY	839a	1 a
		יקום	SUBSTANCE	879c	
		שבע	SEVEN	988a	1 b
7	5	צוה	CHARGE	846a	3
7	6	בן	SON	121d	9 a
		מבול	FLOOD	550a	2
		מי	WATER	565c	1 d
		על	UPON	752c	2 1
		שש	SIX	995c	3
7	7	את	WITH	85d	1
		מבול	FLOOD	550a	1
		מי	WATER	565c	1 d
		תבה	ARK	1061c	
7	8	אדמה	GROUND	9d	4
		ה	THE	207d	1 e
		טהור	CLEAN	373a	1
		מן	FROM	580c	3 a
		עוף	FLY	733d	1
		רמש	CREEP	943a	2 a
7	9	בוא	COME	97d	1
		זכר	MALE	271c	12
		כאשר	AS	455b	1 a
		נקבה	FEMALE	666c	2
		צוה	CHARGE	846a	3
		שנים	TWO	1041a	1 b1
		תבה	ARK	1061c	
7	10	חיה	BECOME	225d	2 1b
		יום	DAY	398c	2 c
		ל	TO	517a	6 b
		מבול	FLOOD	550a	2
		מי	WATER	565c	1 d
7	11	ארבה	LATTICE	70d	
		ארץ	EARTH	76a	1 b
		בקע	BREAK OPEN OR THROUGH	132a	1
		דלת	DOOR	*195b	4
		חדש	NEW MOON	294d	2 b2
		חיים	LIFE	313b	1
		יום	DAY	398c	2 e
		יום	DAY	400d	7 g
		ל	TO	513d	5 cb g
		מען	SPRING	746a	
		עשר	TEN	797b	7 a
		פתח	OPEN	835c	
		רב	GREAT	913c	2 a
		שבע	SEVEN	*988b	2 b
		שמי	HEAVENS	1030a	1 b
		תהום	DEEP	1062d	1
7	12	גשם	RAIN	177c	
		יום	DAY	398b	1
		לילה	NIGHT	538d	1
		ארבעים	FORTY	917b	1 a
7	13	את	WITH	85d	1
		בוא	COME	97d	1
		זה	THIS	261a	2 bb
		חם	HAM	325d	1
		יום	DAY	400d	7 g
		עצם	BONE	783a	3
		יפת	JAPHETH	834d	
		שם	SHEM	1028d	
		תבה	ARK	1061c	
7	14	בהמה	BEAST	97a	2
		חיה	LIVING THING	312c	1
		כל	ALL	481c	1 b
		כנף	WING	489c	1 a
		מין	KIND	568b	
		צפור	BIRD	862a	2
		רמש	CREEP	943a	2 a
		רמש	CREEPING THINGS	943a	1
7	15	בשר	FLESH	142d	6 b
		חיים	LIFE	313b	1
		רוח	BREATH	924d	1 e
		תבה	ARK	1061c	
7	16	בוא	COME	97d	1
		בעד	BEHIND	126b	1 b
		בשר	FLESH	142d	6 b
		זכר	MALE	271c	12
		כאשר	AS	455b	1 a
		נקבה	FEMALE	666c	2
		סגר	SHUT	689a	1
7	17	יום	DAY	398c	2 c
		מבול	FLOOD	550a	2
		מי	WATER	565c	1 d
		נשא	LIFT	670a	1 a
		על	UPON	758c	4 2a
		רבה	BECOME MANY	915b	1 c
		ארבעים	FORTY	917b	1 a
		ארבעים	FORTY	917b	1 a
		רום	BE HIGH	927a	3
		תבה	ARK	1061c	
7	18	גבר	BE STRONG	149d	2 a
		הלך	WALK	232b	13
		מאד	EXCEEDINGLY	547b	2 a
		מי	WATER	565c	
		פנה	FACE	816b	15
		רבה	BECOME MANY	915b	1 c
		תבה	ARK	1061c	
7	19	גבה	HIGH	147a	1
		גבר	BE STRONG	149d	2 a
		הר	MOUNTAIN	250a	1 c
		הר	MOUNTAIN	250b	1 d
		כסה	BE COVERED	492b	
		מאד	EXCEEDINGLY	547c	2 d
		מי	WATER	565c	1 d
		שמי	HEAVENS	1029d	1 a
		תחת	UNDERNEATH	1065b	2 1
7	20	גבר	BE STRONG	149d	2 a
		הר	MOUNTAIN	250a	1 c
		חמש	FIVE	332a	1
		כסה	BE COVERED	492b	1
		מעל	ABOVE	752a	2 d
7	21	ב	IN	88c	12c
		בהמה	BEAST	97a	2
		בשר	FLESH	142d	6 a
		גוע	EXPIRE	157c	
		ה	THE	209a	2 b
		ו	AND	252a	1
		חיה	LIVING THING	312c	1 b
		כל	ALL	481c	1 b
		רמש	CREEP	943a	2 c
		שרץ	SWARM	1056c	2
		שרץ	SWARMING THINGS	1056d	
7	22	אף	NOSE	60a	1
		חיים	LIFE	313b	1
		חרבה	DRY GROUND	351c	
		כל	ALL	481c	1 c
		מן	FROM	581b	3 be
		נשמה	BREATH	675d	2
		רוח	BREATH	924d	1 e
7	23	אדם	MAN	9b	2
		אדמה	GROUND	9d	4
		אך	ONLY	36c	2 ba
		בהמה	BEAST	96d	1
		מחה	WIPE OUT	562b	3
		מחה	WIPE OUT	562b	3
		מן	FROM	582a	5 b
		פנה	FACE	819a	27b
		יקום	SUBSTANCE	879c	
		רמש	CREEPING THINGS	943a	1
		שאר	REMAIN	984a	1
		תבה	ARK	1061c	
7	24	גבר	BE STRONG	149d	2 a
		חמשים	FIFTY	332c	3 a
		יום	DAY	398c	2 c
8	1	בהמה	BEAST	96d	1
		זכר	REMEMBER	270b	2 1 a
		חיה	LIVING THING	312c	1
		עבר	PASS OVER	718d	1 b
		רוח	BREATH	924d	2 a
		שבך	DECREASE	1013c	
		תבה	ARK	1061c	
8	2	ארבה	LATTICE	70d	
		גשם	RAIN	177c	
		כלא	BE RESTRAINED	476b	
		סכר	SHUT UP	698c	
		מען	SPRING	746a	
		שמי	HEAVENS	1029d	1 a
		שמי	HEAVENS	1030a	1 b
		תהום	DEEP	1062d	1
8	3	הלך	WALK	232c	13
		הלך	WALK	233c	14c 4
		חסר	LACK	341b	3
		יום	DAY	398c	2 c
		מי	WATER	565c	1 d
		מן	FROM	581c	4 b
		על	UPON	758c	4 2a
		שוב	TURN BACK	997a	2
		שוב	TURN BACK	998a	7 a
8	4	אררט	ARARAT	76d	
		חדש	NEW MOON	294d	2 b2
		יום	DAY	398c	2 e
		נוח	REST	628a	1
		על	UPON	752d	2 1
		שביעי	SEVENTH	988d	1
		תבה	ARK	1061c	
8	5	חיה	BE	227a	3 4b
		הלך	WALK	232c	13
		הלך	WALK	233c	14c 5
		הר	MOUNTAIN	250a	1 c
		הר	MOUNTAIN	250d	1 m
		חדש	NEW MOON	294d	2 b2
		חדש	NEW MOON	294d	2 b2
		חסר	LACK	341b	3
		יום	DAY	*398c	2 e
		ל	TO	513d	5 cb g
		מי	WATER	565c	1 d
		עד	AS FAR AS	724b	12 a a
		עשירי	TENTH	798a	1
		עשירי	TENTH	798a	1
		ראה	TO SEE	908c	1 c
		ראש	HEAD	910d	2 a
8	6	חיה	COME TO PASS	224c	2 a1 az
		חלון	WINDOW	319d	
		יום	DAY	398c	2 c
		עשה	DO	794b	2 1a
		פתח	OPEN	835a	
		קץ	END	893d	1
		תבה	ARK	1061c	
8	7	יבש	BE DRY	386c	2

Ch v.	Heb	Eng	Page	Sec
	יצא	GO OUT	424a	3
	מי	WATER	565c	1 d
	עד	AS FAR AS	724b	1 2a b
	על	UPON	758c	4 2a
	ערב	RAVEN	788b	
	שוב	TURN BACK	997a	2
	שלח	SEND	1019b	3
8 8	אדמה	GROUND	9d	4
	את	WITH	86c	4 a
	ה	INTERROG PART	210b	2
	יונה	DOVE	401d	
	מי	WATER	565c	1 d
	פנה	FACE	819b	2 8b
	קלל	BE SLIGHT	886c	1
	ראה	TO SEE	907b	5 a
8 9	אל	TO	39c	1
	יד	HAND	388d	1
	יונה	DOVE	401d	
	כף	SOLE OF FOOT	496d	3
	ל	TO	515a	5 hb a
	לקח	TAKE	542d	1
	מי	WATER	565c	1 d
	מצא	FIND	592c	1 a
	מנוח	RESTING PLACE	629d	1
	פנה	FACE	816b	1 5
	רגל	FOOT	919d	1 d
	שוב	TURN BACK	997b	3 b
	תבה	ARK	1061c	
8 10	אחר	ANOTHER	*29c	
	חול	WHIRL	*297b	2 d
	יום	DAY	398c	2 c
	יונה	DOVE	401d	
	יסף	DO AGAIN	415c	2 a
	עוד	STILL	729a	1 ab
	שבע	SEVEN	988b	1 c
	תבה	ARK	1061c	
8 11	זית	OLIVE TREE	268c	1
	טרף	FRESH-PLUCKED	383a	
	טרף	PREY	*383c	3
	יונה	DOVE	401d	
	ל	TO	516d	6 a
	מי	WATER	565c	1 d
	עלה	LEAF	750a	
	על	UPON	758c	4 2a
	עת	TIME	773c	1 b
	ערב	SUNSET	787d	1 a
	פה	MOUTH	805b	3
	קלל	BE SLIGHT	886b	1
8 12	יום	DAY	398c	2 c
	יונה	DOVE	401d	
	יחל	WAIT	403d	
	יסף	ADD	414d	
	עוד	STILL	729a	1 ab
8 13	אדמה	GROUND	9d	4
	היה	COME TO PASS	224d	1 2a 1b
	הנה	BEHOLD	244b	C
	חדש	NEW MOON	294d	2 b2
	חרב	BE DRY	351a	1
	חרב	BE DRY	351a	1
	יום	DAY	*398c	2 c
	מכסה	COVERING	492c	1
	סור	TURN ASIDE	694b	1
	על	UPON	758c	4 2a
	ראה	TO SEE	907c	6 c
	ראשון	FIRST	911d	2
	תבה	ARK	1061c	
8 14	חדש	NEW MOON	294d	2 b2
	יבש	BE DRY	386b	1 c
	יום	DAY	398c	2 e
	ל	TO	513d	5 cb g
	שבע	SEVEN	988b	5 b1
8 15	אל	TO	40a	3 b
	אמר	SAY	56b	1
	דבר	SPEAK	181a	3 b
8 16	יצא	GO OUT	422d	1 a
	תבה	ARK	1061c	
8 17	ב	IN	88c	1 2c
	בהמה	BEAST	96d	1
	בשר	FLESH	142d	6 b
	היה	LIVING THING	312c	1 a
	יצא	BRING OUT	425a	3
	פרה	BEAR FRUIT	826a	1
	רבה	BECOME MANY	915a	1 b
	רמש	CREEPING THINGS	943a	1
	רמש	CREEP	943a	2 a
	שרץ	SWARM	1056c	2
8 18	את	WITH	85d	1
8 19	היה	LIVING THING	312c	1 b
	יצא	GO OUT	422d	1 a
	ל	TO	516a	5 ja
	רמש	CREEPING THINGS	943a	1
	רמש	CREEP	943a	2 c
	תבה	ARK	1061c	
8 20	ב	IN	89a	2 2
	בנה	BUILD	124c	1 at
	מזבח	ALTAR	258b	1
	מזבח	ALTAR	258d	8
	מזבח	ALTAR	259a	1
	טהור	CLEAN	373a	1
	עוף	FLY	733d	1
	עלה	GO UP	749d	8
	עלה	WHOLE BURNT OF-FERING	750d	
8 21	אדמה	GROUND	9c	1
	אמר	SAY	56b	2
	חי	ALIVE	312b	1 d
	יסף	DO AGAIN	415c	2 a
	יצר	PURPOSE	428a	4
	כאשר	AS	455b	1 a
	לא	NOT	*518c	1 aa
	לב	HEART	524d	2 3c
	לב	HEART	525c	2 7
	נוחח	SOOTHING	629c	
	נכה	SMITE	646a	2 c
	נעורים	YOUTH	655b	
	עבור	FOR THE SAKE OF	721a	1 a
	קלל	BE SLIGHT	886d	3
	ריח	SMELL	926b	
	ריח	SCENT	926b	2
	רע	EVIL	948c	0 c
8 22	זרע	SOWING	282a	1 b
	חם	HEAT	328d	
	חרף	HARVEST-TIME	358b	
	יום	DAY	398b	1
	לא	NOT	*518c	1 aa
	לילה	NIGHT	538c	1
	עוד	STILL	729a	1 ab
	קין	SUMMER	884d	1
	קציר	HARVESTING	894c	2
	קר	COLD	903b	
	שבת	CEASE	991d	1
9 1	ברך	BLESS	139a	2 a
	מלא	FILL	570b	2
	פרה	BEAR FRUIT	826a	1
9 2	אדמה	GROUND	9d	4
	דג	FISH	185c	
	דג	FISH	*185d	
	היה	BECOME	225d	2 1b
	חיה	LIVING THING	312c	1 b
	חת	TERROR	369c	
	ים	SEA	411a	5
	מורא	FEAR	432b	1
	נתן	GIVE	681c	1 e
	על	UPON	756b	2 7a b
	רמש	CREEP	943a	1
9 3	אך	ONLY	36d	2 c
	אכלה	FOOD		
	אשר	PARTICLE OF RE-LATION	82a	2 a
	את	MARK OF THE AC-CUSATIVE	84d	1 a
	הוא	HE, SHE, IT	215d	2 c
	חי	ALIVE	312b	1 c
	ירק	GREEN	438d	
	כ	LIKE	454a	1 c1
	כל	ALL	482c	2 a
	עשב	HERB	793c	
	רמש	CREEPING THINGS	943a	3
9 4	אך	HOWBEIT	36c	2 a
	בשר	FLESH	142c	1 a
	דם	BLOOD	196b	1
	נפש	A LIVING BEING	659d	3 a
9 5	אדם	MAN	9b	2
	אדם	MAN	9b	2
	את	BROTHER	26b	4
	איש	MAN	36a	
	אך	ONLY	36d	2 c
	דם	BLOOD	196b	1
	דם	BLOOD	197b	2 k
	דרש	SEEK	205c	5
	חיה	LIVING THING	312c	1 b
	יד	HAND	391b	5 g3
	יד	HAND	391b	5 g3
	נפש	A LIVING BEING	659d	3 a
9 6	אדם	MAN	9b	2
	אדם	MAN	9b	2
	ב	IN	89d	3 2c
	דם	BLOOD	196c	2 b
	דם	BLOOD	196c	2 b
	צלם	IMAGE	854a	2
	שפך	POUR OUT	1049c	1 b
	שפך	POUR OUT	1049d	
9 7	אתם	YOU	61d	
	פרה	BEAR FRUIT	826a	1
	שרץ	SWARM	1056d	2
9 8	את	WITH	85d	1
9 9	אחר	AFTER	30a	2 b
	אני	I	59a	
	אנכי	I	59c	
	את	WITH	86a	1 da
	ברית	COVENANT	136c	2 2a
	ברית	COVENANT	137a	3 1
	הנה	BEHOLD	244b	B b
	זרע	SOWING	282d	4 c
	קום	STAND	879a	6 d
9 10	ב	IN	88c	1 2c
	בהמה	BEAST	97a	1
	ברית	COVENANT	136c	2 2a
	ה	THE	209a	2 b
	חי	ALIVE	312b	1 d
	חיה	LIVING THING	312c	1 d
	יצא	GO OUT	422d	1 a
	ל	TO	514c	5 fd
	מן	FROM	581b	3 be
	נפש	SOUL	659c	2
	תבה	ARK	1061c	
9 11	ברית	COVENANT	136c	2 2a
	ברית	COVENANT	137a	3 1
	בשר	FLESH	142d	6 a
	כרת	BE CUT OFF	504a	1 b
	מבול	FLOOD	550a	2
	מי	WATER	565c	1 d
	מן	OUT OF	580a	2 eb
	עוד	STILL	729b	1 b
	קום	STAND	879a	6 d
	שחת	GO TO RUIN	1008a	1
9 12	אות	SIGN	17a	6
	אני	I	59a	
	בין	INTERVAL	107c	1 d
	ברית	COVENANT	136c	2 2a
	ברית	COVENANT	*137a	3 1
	דור	GENERATION	190a	2 c
	זה	THIS	261a	3
	חי	ALIVE	312b	1 d
	נפש	SOUL	659c	2
	עולם	LONG DURATION	762c	2 d
9 13	אות	SIGN	17a	6
	ברית	COVENANT	136c	2 2a
	היה	BECOME	226c	2 2e
	נתן	PUT	680b	2 a
	ענן	CLOUD	778a	1 b
	קשת	BOW	906c	2
9 14	ברית	COVENANT	136c	2 2a
	היה	COME TO PASS	225b	1 2b ae
	ענן	BRING 0A CLOUD0	778a	
	ענן	CLOUD	778a	1 b
	קשת	BOW	906c	2
	ראה	TO SEE	908c	1 c
9 15	בין	INTERVAL	107c	1 d
	ברית	COVENANT	136c	2 2a
	ברית	COVENANT	137a	3 2
	בשר	FLESH	142d	6 a
	זכר	REMEMBER	270b	2 3 a
	חי	ALIVE	312b	1 d
	מבול	FLOOD	550a	
	מי	WATER	565c	1 d
	נפש	SOUL	659c	2
	שחת	GO TO RUIN	1008a	1
9 16	ב	IN	88c	1 2c
	ברית	COVENANT	136c	2 2a
	ברית	COVENANT	137a	3 2
	ברית	COVENANT	137a	3 2
	בשר	FLESH	142d	6 a
	היה	BECOME	225c	2 1a
	זכר	REMEMBER	270b	2 3 a
	חי	ALIVE	312b	1 d
	נפש	SOUL	659c	2
	עולם	LONG DURATION	762c	2 d
	ענן	CLOUD	778a	1 b
	קשת	BOW	906c	2
	ראה	TO SEE	907c	6 b
9 17	אות	SIGN	17a	6
	ברית	COVENANT	136c	2 2a
	ברית	COVENANT	137a	3 1
	בשר	FLESH	142d	6 a
9 18	קום	STAND	879a	6 d
	הוא	HE, SHE, IT	215d	2 b
	היה	BE	227a	3 4b
	חם	HAM	325d	1
	יצא	GO OUT	422d	1 a
	כנען	CANAAN	488d	1
	יפת	JAPHETH	834d	
	שם	SHEM	1028d	
	תבה	ARK	1061c	
9 19	אלה	THESE	41c	A
	אלה	THESE	41c	D
	נפץ	DISPERSE	659a	
9 20	אדמה	GROUND	9c	1
	איש	MAN	36a	
	חלל	POLLUTE	320d	2
	כרם	VINEYARD	501d	
	כרם	VINEYARD	501d	
	נטע	PLANT	642c	1
9 21	חוץ	THE OUTSIDE	*299d	1 bb
	יין	WINE	406c	C
	מן	OUT OF	579b	2 bb
	שכר	BE DRUNK	1016b	
	שתה	DRINK	1059b	1 a
	תוך	MIDST	1063c	
9 22	חוץ	THE OUTSIDE	299d	1 bb
	חם	HAM	326a	1
	כנען	CANAAN	488d	1
	נגד	BE CONSPICUOUS	616d	1
	ערוה	NAKEDNESS	788d	1
	ראה	TO SEE	907c	6 a
9 23	אחרנית	BACKWARDS	30d	
	כסה	COVER	491c	1
	ערוה	NAKEDNESS	788d	1
	ערוה	NAKEDNESS	789a	1
	יפת	JAPHETH	834d	
	ראה	TO SEE	907c	6 a
	שמלה	WRAPPER	971a	
	שכם	SHOULDER	1014b	1 a
	שם	SHEM	1028d	
9 24	יין	WINE	406c	C
	יקץ	AWAKE	429c	
	קטן	SMALL	882a	1 a
9 25	ארר	CURSE	76d	
	כנען	CANAAN	488d	1
	עבד	SLAVE	713d	1
9 26	אלהים	GOD	44c	4 ba
	ברך	BLESS	138c	2 a
	עבד	SLAVE	714c	7
	שם	SHEM	1028d	
9 27	אלהים	GOD	44a	4 a
	ו	AND	252b	1 b
	כנען	CANAAN	488d	1

Ch	v.	Heb	Eng	Page	Sec
		ל	TO	511d	3 a
		עבד	SLAVE	714c	7
		פתה	BE SPACIOUS	834b	
		יפת	JAPHETH	834d	
		שכן	SETTLE DOWN	1015b	2 c
		שם	SHEM	1028d	
9	28	אחר	AFTER	29d	2 b
		חיה	LIVE	311a	1 a
		חמשים	FIFTY	332c	4 b
		מבול	FLOOD	550a	2
9	29	חמשים	FIFTY	332c	4 b
		יום	DAY	399a	4 a
10	1	ו	AND	252a	1
		חם	HAM	326a	1
		ילד	BE BORN	408d	
		תולדות	GENERATIONS	410a	A
		מבול	FLOOD	550a	
		יפת	JAPHETH	834d	
		שם	SHEM	1028d	
10	2	מגוג	MAGOG	156a	
		מגוג	MAGOG	156a	
		גמר	GOMER	170a	1
		ו	AND	252a	1
		יון	JAVAN	402a	
		מדי	MEDES	552a	1
		יפת	JAPHETH	834d	
		תובל	TUBAL	1063a	
		תירס	TIRAS	1066d	
10	3	אשכנז	ASHKENAZ	79b	2
		אשכנז	ASHKENAZ	79b	
		גמר	GOMER	170a	1
		ריפת	DIPHATH	193d	
		ריפת	RIPHATH	937d	
		תגרמה	TOGARMAH	1062b	
10	4	אלישה	ELISHAH	47a	
		דדנים	DODANIM	187a	1
		יון	JAVAN	402a	
		כתי	KITTIM	508c	
		רודנים	RHODIANS	922c	
		תרשיש	TARSHISH	1077a	1
10	5	אי	COAST	16a	
		איש	MAN	36a	
		ארץ	EARTH	76c	5
		גוי	NATION	156c	1
		ל	TO	516a	5 ja
		לשון	TONGUE	546c	2
10	6	חם	HAM	326a	1
		כוש	CUSH	469a	3
		כוש	CUSH	469a	1
		כנען	CANAAN	488d	1
		מצרים	EGYPT	595d	2 a
		פוט	LIBYANS	806c	
10	7	דדן	DEDAN	187a	1
		דדן	DEDAN	187a	1
		חוילה	HAVILAH	296c	
		חוילה	HAVILAH	296c	
		כוש	CUSH	469a	1
		סבא	SEBA	685b	
		סבתה	SABTAH	688b	
		סבתכא	SABTECA	688b	
		רעמה	RAAMAH	947c	
		שבא	SHEBA	985b	
10	8	גבור	STRONG	150b	2
		הוא	HE, SHE, IT	215b	1 a
		חלל	POLLUTE	320d	1
		ילד	BEGET	408c	2 a
		כוש	CUSH	469a	3
		נמרד	NIMROD	650a	2
10	9	אמר	SAY	56c	
		גבור	STRONG	150b	2
		כן	SO	487b	3 f
		ל	TO	*513a	5 ad
		נמרד	NIMROD	650a	2
		פנה	FACE	817a	2 4a g
		ציד	HUNTING	844d	1
10	10	אכד	AKKAD	37a	
		ארך	ERECH	74b	
		ארץ	EARTH	76a	2 a
		בבל	BABEL	93c	
		כלנה	CALNEH	484c	
		ממלכה	KINGDOM	575a	1
		נמרד	NIMROD	*650a	2
		ראשית	BEGINNING	912a	1 a
		שנער	SHINAR	1042c	
10	11	ארץ	EARTH	76a	2 a
		אשור	ASSYRIA	78d	3
		בנה	BUILD	124b	1 aa
		יצא	GO OUT	422d	1 a
		כלח	CALAH	480d	
		נינוה	NINEVEH	644b	
		רחבת	REHOBOTH	932c	1
10	12	גדול	GREAT	153a	1
		הוא	HE, SHE, IT	215b	1 a
		כלח	CALAH	480d	
		נינוה	NINEVEH	644b	
		עיר	CITY	746b	1
		רסן	RESEN	944a	
10	13	ילד	BEGET	408c	2 a
		להבים	LEHABIM	529c	
		לובים	LUBIM	530c	
		לוד	LUD	530d	2
		מצרים	EGYPT	595d	2 a
		נפתחים	NAPHTUHIM	661d	
		ענמים	ANAMIM	777d	
10	14	יצא	GO OUT	422d	1 a
		כסלחים	CASLUHIM	493b	

Ch	v.	Heb	Eng	Page	Sec
		כפתרי	CAPHTORIM	499c	
		פלשת	PHILISTIA	814b	
		פלשתי	PHILISTINE	814c	
		פתרסים	PATHRUSIM	837d	
		שם	THERE	1027c	4 c
10	15	אתבעל	ETHBAAL	87a	
		חת	HETH	366c	
		ילד	BEGET	408c	2 a
		כנען	CANAAN	488d	1
		צידון	SIDON	*850d	
		צידון	SIDON	851a	
10	16	אמרי	AMORITES	57c	1
		יבוסי	JEBUSITE	101a	1
		גרגשי	GIRGASHITE	173a	
		גרגשי	GIRGASHITE	173b	
10	17	חוי	HIVITE	295d	2
		סיני	SINITE	696b	
		ערקי	ARKITE	792b	
10	18	אחר	AFTERWARDS	29d	1 b
		אלחנן	ELHANAN	45a	
		ארוד	ARVAD	71c	
		ארודי	ARVADITE	71c	
		חמתי	HAMATHITE	333b	
		כנעני	CANAANITE	489a	2 b
		פוץ	BE DISPERSED	807a	2
		צמרי	ZAMARITE	856b	
10	19	אדמה	ADMAH	10a	
		בוא	COME	98c	2 e
		גבול	BORDER	147d	1 a
		גרר	GERAR	176b	
		כנעני	CANAANITE	489a	2 b
		לשע	LASHA	546d	
		מן	FROM	581d	5 a
		סדם	SODOM	690a	
		עד	AS FAR AS	724a	1 b
		עזה	GAZA	738b	
		עמרה	GOMORRAH	771d	
		צביים	ZEBOIIM	840b	
		צידון	SIDON	851a	
10	20	אלה	THESE	41c	A
		ארץ	EARTH	76c	5
		גוי	NATION	156c	1
		חם	HAM	326a	1
		לשון	TONGUE	546c	2
10	21	אב	FATHER	3c	4 b
		בן	SON	120d	1 ja
		גדול	GREAT	153a	5
		הוא	HE, SHE, IT	215c	1 b
		ילד	BE BORN	408c	
		עבר	EBER	720a	1
		יפת	JAPHETH	834d	
		שם	SHEM	1028d	
10	22	ארם	ARAM	74b	1
		ארם	ARAM	74c	A
		ארפכשד	ARPACHSHAD	75d	
		ארפכשד	ARPACHSHAD	75d	
		אשור	ASSHUR	78d	1
		לוד	LUD	530d	1
		עילם	ELAM	743d	1
		שם	SHEM	1028d	
10	23	ארם	ARAM	74b	1
		גתר	GETHER	178c	
		חול	HUL	299a	
		מש	MASH	602a	
		עוץ	UZ	734b	1 a
10	24	ילד	BEGET	408c	2 a
		עבר	EBER	720a	1
		שלח	SHELAH	1019d	
10	25	יום	DAY	399a	4 b
		ילד	BE BORN	408c	
		יקטן	JOKTAN	429b	
		עבר	EBER	720a	1
		פלג	SPLIT	811a	
		פלג	PELEG	811b	
10	26	אלמודד	ALMODAD	38d	
		חצרמות	HAZARMAVETH	348a	
		ילד	BEGET	408c	2 a
		יקטן	JOKTAN	429b	
		ירח	JERAH	437b	
		שלף	SHELEPH	1025c	
10	27	אוזל	UZAL	23d	
		דקלה	DIKLAH	200c	
		דקלה	DIKLAH	200d	
		הדורם	HADORAM	*213b	1
		הדורם	HADORAM	213b	1
10	28	אבימאל	ABIMAEL	4b	
		עובל	OBAL	716c	
		שבא	SHEBA	985b	
10	29	אופיר	OPHIR	20c	1
		אופיר	OPHIR	20d	4
		חוילה	HAVILAH	296c	
		חוילה	HAVILAH	296d	
		יובב	JOBAB	384d	1
		יקטן	JOKTAN	429b	
10	30	אופיר	OPHIR	20c	1
		בוא	COME	98c	2 e
		מושב	DWELLING	444b	2 a
		מן	FROM	582b	5 d3
		משא	MESHA	602a	
		ספר	SEPHAR	708c	
		קדם	FRONT	869c	1 b
10	31	אלה	THESE	41c	A
		ארץ	EARTH	76c	5
		גוי	NATION	156c	1
		ל	TO	516a	5 ja
		לשון	TONGUE	546c	2

Ch	v.	Heb	Eng	Page	Sec
		שם	SHEM	1028d	
10	32	אלה	THESE	41c	A
		גוי	NATION	156c	1
		תולדות	GENERATIONS	410a	A
		ל	TO	516a	5 ja
		מבול	FLOOD	550a	
11	1	ארץ	EARTH	76a	1 c
		דבר	WORD	183b	3 1
		שפה	SPEECH	974a	1 h
11	2	בקעה	PLAIN	132c	2
		היה	COME TO PASS	224c	2 a1 ab
		מן	FROM	578d	1 c
		מצא	FIND	593b	3 a
		נסע	JOURNEY	652b	3
		קדם	FRONT	869d	1 b 3
		שם	THERE	1027c	1 a
		שנער	SHINAR	1042c	
11	3	אבן	STONE	6c	2
		איש	MAN	36b	
		היה	BECOME	226c	2 2f
		חמר	CEMENT	330c	1
		חמר	BITUMEN	330c	
		יהב	GIVE	396d	5
		לבנה	BRICK	527c	1
		לבן	MAKE BRICK	527c	
		רע	FRIEND	946a	3
		שרפה	BURNING	977b	
11	4	בנה	BUILD	124b	1 aa
		בל	BEL	128c	
		מגדל	TOWER	153d	1
		ו	AND	253a	1 k
		יהב	GIVE	396d	5
		ל	TO	515d	5 ia
		פוץ	BE DISPERSED	807a	
		פן	LEST	814d	1
		פנה	FACE	816b	15
		פנה	FACE	819a	27 b
		ראש	HEAD	910d	2 a
		שם	NAME	1028a	2 b1
		שמי	HEAVENS	1029d	1 a
11	5	בנה	BUILD	124b	1 aa
		מגדל	TOWER	153d	1
		ירד	GO DOWN	433b	2
		ראה	TO SEE	907c	6 b
11	6	בצר	MAKE INACCESSIBLE	131a	
		הן	BEHOLD	243c	A
		הנה	BEHOLD	*244a	B a
		זמם	CONSIDER	273b	2 b
		חלל	POLLUTE	320d	2
		כל	ALL	481b	1 a
		עם	PEOPLE	766c	1
		עתה	NOW	774b	2 b
		שפה	SPEECH	974a	2
11	7	איש	MAN	36b	
		אשר	THAT	83c	8 b
		בלל	MINGLE	117c	1
		בלע	SWALLOW UP	*118b	2 a
		יהב	GIVE	396d	5
		ירד	GO DOWN	433b	2
		רע	FRIEND	946a	3
		שם	THERE	1027a	1 a
		שמע	HEAR	1033d	1 g
11	8	ברד	BE SEPARATE	*94b	1
		בנה	BUILD	124b	1 aa
		חדל	CEASE	293a	2
		ל	TO	517d	7 bc
		פוץ	BE DISPERSED	807a	1 a
		פנה	FACE	816b	15
		שם	THERE	1027c	4 a
11	9	בבל	BABEL	*93c	
		בבל	BABEL	93c	
		בלל	MINGLE	117c	1
		בלע	SWALLOW UP	*118b	2 a
		כן	SO	487b	3 f
		פוץ	BE DISPERSED	807a	1 a
		פנה	FACE	816b	15
		קרא	CALL	896a	6 a
		שפה	SPEECH	974a	2
		שם	THERE	1027a	1 a
		שם	THERE	1027c	4 a
11	10	ארפכשד	ARPACHSHAD	75d	
		תולדות	GENERATIONS	410a	A
		מאה	HUNDRED	548b	1 d6
		מבול	FLOOD	550a	
		שם	SHEM	1028d	
11	11	בן	SON	120a	1
		בן	SON	120a	1
		בת	DAUGHTER	123a	1
		חיה	LIVE	311a	1 a
		שם	SHEM	1028d	
11	12	ארפכשד	ARPACHSHAD	75d	
		שלח	SHELAH	1019d	
		שלשים	THIRTY	1026c	1
11	13	בן	SON	120a	1
		בת	DAUGHTER	123a	1
		ארבע	FOUR	916d	1 a1
		שלח	SHELAH	1019d	
11	14	עבר	EBER	720a	1
		שלח	SHELAH	1019d	
11	15	בן	SON	120a	1
		בת	DAUGHTER	123a	1
		עבר	EBER	720a	1
		שלח	SHELAH	1019d	
11	16	עבר	EBER	720a	1
		פלג	PELEG	811b	

Ch	v.	Heb	Eng	Page	Sec
11	17	ארבע	FOUR	917b	2 c
		עבר	EBER	720a	1
11	18	פלג	PELEG	811b	
		פלג	PELEG	811b	
11	19	רעו	REU	946c	
		פלג	PELEG	811b	
		תשע	NINE	1077c	1 a
11	20	רעו	REU	946c	
		שרוג	SERUG	974d	
11	21	רעו	REU	946c	
		שרוג	SERUG	974d	
		שבע	SEVEN	988b	5 b2
11	22	נחור	NAHOR	637d	1
		שרוג	SERUG	974d	
11	23	מאה	HUNDRED	548a	1 b1
		נחור	NAHOR	637d	1
		שרוג	SERUG	974d	
11	24	נחור	NAHOR	637d	1
		עשרים	TWENTY	797d	1 2a
		תרח	TERAH	1076b	1
		תשע	NINE	1077c	4
11	25	נחור	NAHOR	637d	1
		עשר	TEN	797b	9
		תרח	TERAH	1076b	1
		תשע	NINE	1077c	2
11	26	אברם	ABRAM	4d	
		חיה	LIVE	311a	1 a
		נחור	NAHOR	637d	2
		תרח	TERAH	1076b	1
11	27	אברם	ABRAM	4d	
		הרן	HARAN	248c	1
		תולדות	GENERATIONS	410a	A
		לום	LOT	532b	
		נחור	NAHOR	637d	1
		תרח	TERAH	1076b	1
11	28	אב	FATHER	3b	1
		אור	UR	22d	
		ארץ	EARTH	76a	2a
		הרן	HARAN	248c	1
		מולדת	KINDRED	409d	1
		כשדים	CHALDEANS	505a	1 a
		פנה	FACE	818d	2 7a a
		תרח	TERAH	1076b	1
		אור	ADDENDA ET COR-RIGENDA	1119d	
11	29	אב	FATHER	3b	1
		בת	DAUGHTER	123a	1
		הרן	HARAN	248c	1
		יסכה	ISCAH	414d	
		לקח	TAKE	543b	4 e2
		מלכה	MILCAH	574c	1
		נחור	NAHOR	637d	2
11	30	אין	NOT	34d	3
		עקר	BARREN	785d	
		שרי	SARAI	979c	
11	31	אור	UR	22d	
		ארץ	EARTH	76a	2 a
		ארץ	EARTH	76b	2e
		את	WITH	85d	1
		הלך	WALK	230d	1 1d 3b
		חרן	HARAN	248c	1
		חרן	HARAN	357a	
		חרן	HARAN	357a	
		כלה	DAUGHTER-IN-LAW	483c	1
		כנען	CANAAN	488d	2 a
		כשדים	CHALDEANS	505a	1 a
		לום	LOT	532b	
		עד	AS FAR AS	724a	1 1a
		שרי	SARAI	979c	
		שם	THERE	1027a	1 a
		תרח	TERAH	1076b	1
		אור	ADDENDA ET COR-RIGENDA	1119d	
11	32	חיה	BE	227b	3 4b
		חרן	HARAN	357a	
		יום	DAY	399a	4 a
		תרח	TERAH	1076b	1
12	1	ארץ	EARTH	76b	2e
		בית	HOUSE	109d	5 a
		הלך	WALK	231d	1 1d 5h
		מולדת	KINDRED	409d	1
		ל	TO	515d	5 ib
		ראה	TO SEE	908d	
		ראה	TO SEE	908d	1 a2
12	2	ברך	BLESS	139a	2 a
		ברכה	BLESSING	139d	2
		גדל	BECOME GREAT	152b	2
		גדול	GREAT	153a	2
		גוי	NATION	156c	1 a
		ו	AND	254b	3
		ל	TO	512b	4 a
		שם	NAME	1028a	2 b1
12	3	אדמה	EARTH	10a	6
		ארץ	EARTH	76a	1 a
		ארר	CURSE	76c	
		ברך	BLESS	138d	
		ברך	BLESS	139a	2 a
		ברך	BLESS	139b	4 f
		קלל	BE SLIGHT	886c	1
12	4	את	WITH	85d	1
		חרן	HARAN	357a	
		יצא	GO OUT	422d	1 a
		כאשר	AS	455b	1 a
		לום	LOT	532b	

Ch	v.	Heb	Eng	Page	Sec
12	5	שבעים	SEVENTY	988c	3 a
		ארץ	EARTH	76b	2 e
		הלך	WALK	230d	1 1d 3b
		חרן	HARAN	357a	
		כנען	CANAAN	488d	2 a
		לום	LOT	532b	
		נפש	SOUL	660c	4 c3
		עשה	DO	795a	2 7
		רכוש	PROPERTY	940d	1
		רכש	COLLECT	940d	
		שרי	SARAI	979c	
12	6	אלון	TEREBINTH	18d	
		אז	THEN	23a	1 a
		ארץ	EARTH	76b	2 e
		ב	IN	88b	1 1
		מורה	TEACHER	435c	
		כנעני	CANAANITE	489a	2 b
		עד	AS FAR AS	724a	1 1a
		מקום	STANDING PLACE	880b	4
		שכם	SHECHEM	1014b	1
12	7	ארץ	EARTH	76b	2 e
		בנה	BUILD	124c	1 at
		ה	THE	209c	3
		מזבח	ALTAR	258b	1
		זה	THIS	261a	2 bb
		ראה	TO SEE	908b	1 a
12	8	ב	IN	90b	3 4
		ביתאל	BETHEL	110d	
		בנה	BUILD	124c	1 at
		מזבח	ALTAR	258b	1
		ים	SEA	411b	9
		מן	FROM	578c	1 c
		נטה	SPREAD OUT	640a	2
		עי	AI	743b	1
		עתק	MOVE	801b	1
		קרא	CALL	845b	2 c
		קדם	FRONT	869c	1 b 2
		קדם	FRONT	869d	1 b 2
		שם	THERE	1027c	4 a
		שם	NAME	1028b	3
12	9	הלך	WALK	233c	1 4c 4
		נגב	SOUTH-COUNTRY	616b	2
		נסע	JOURNEY	652b	3
		נסע	JOURNEY	652b	3
12	10	גור	SOJOURN	157d	2 1
		חיה	BECOME	225c	2 1a
		ירד	GO DOWN	432d	1 d
		כבד	HEAVY	458a	1 a
		רעב	FAMINE	944b	1
		רעב	FAMINE	944b	1
12	11	אדן	LORD	11b	3 1g
		אשה	WOMAN	61a	1
		את	THOU	61d	
		בוא	COME	97d	1
		חיה	COME TO PASS	224c	2 a1 ah
		הנה	BEHOLD	244a	B a
		ידע	KNOW	393c	1 a
		יפה	BEAUTIFUL	421c	
		כאשר	WHEN	455c	3
		ל	TO	517c	7 bb
		נא	PART OF EN-TREATY	609c	4 d
		קרב	COME NEAR	897d	2
		קרב	COME NEAR	898a	2
		מראה	VISION	909c	1 b
		שרי	SARAI	979c	
12	12	חיה	COME TO PASS	225b	1 2b ba
		הרג	KILL	247a	1 a
		זה	THIS	260c	1 a
		חיה	LIVE	311c	1
		כי	WHEN	473b	2 a
		מצרי	EGYPTIAN	596a	2
		ראה	TO SEE	906d	1 a
12	13	אחות	SISTER	27d	1
		את	THOU	61d	
		חיה	LIVE	311a	1 b
		יטב	BE WELL	405c	3
		נא	PART OF EN-TREATY	609a	1
		נפש	SOUL	659c	2
		עבור	FOR THE SAKE OF	721a	1 a
		מען	PURPOSE	775c	2 b
		ש	WHO	*980b	4 d
12	14	חיה	COME TO PASS	224c	2 a1 aa
		יפה	BEAUTIFUL	421c	
		כי	THAT	471c	1 a
		מאד	EXCEEDINGLY	547b	2 a
		מצרי	EGYPTIAN	596a	2
		ראה	TO SEE	907a	2 1
		אל	TO	40a	3 b
12	15	הלל	PRAISE	238a	1
		לקח	TAKE	544a	1
		פרעה	PHARAOH	829a	
		ראה	TO SEE	906d	1 a
		שר	CHIEFTAIN	978a	2 a
12	16	אתון	SHE-ASS	87d	
		בקר	CATTLE	133b	1 a
		חיה	BECOME	226c	2 2h
		חמור	HE-ASS	331b	1
		יטב	DO GOOD TO	405d	2
		עבד	SLAVE	713d	1
		שפחה	MAID	1046c	1
12	17	בית	HOUSE	109d	5 a
		דבר	WORD	184a	4 8
		ו	AND	253a	1 g

Ch	v.	Heb	Eng	Page	Sec
		זרע	SOWING	282c	4 b
		נגע	STRIKE	619b	
		נגע	STROKE	619c	2
		פרעה	PHARAOH	829a	
		צבא	ARMY	839a	1 a
		שרי	SARAI	979c	
12	18	הוא	HE, SHE, IT	216a	3 a
		זה	THIS	261c	4 d
		כי	THAT	471c	1 a
		מה	WHAT	552c	1 ab
		מה	HOW	554a	4 da
		נגד	BE CONSPICUOUS	616d	2
		קרא	CALL	895c	5 a
12	19	אחות	SISTER	27d	1
		אשה	WOMAN	61b	2
		הנה	BEHOLD	243d	A
		לקח	TAKE	543a	4 b
		לקח	TAKE	543b	4 e2
		מה	HOW	554a	4 da
		עתה	NOW	774a	1 a
12	20	צוה	COMMAND	845d	1 e
13	1	הוא	HE, SHE, IT	215c	1 d
		כל	ALL	481c	1 c
		לום	LOT	532b	
		מצרים	EGYPT	595d	1 b2
		נגב	SOUTH-COUNTRY	616b	2
		מצרים	EGYPT	695c	1
13	2	עם	WITH	767b	1 e
		ה	THE	207c	1 e
		זהב	GOLD	262d	2
		זהב	GOLD	263c	1
		כבד	MASSIVE	458b	2 c
		כסף	SILVER	494a	3
		מאד	EXCEEDINGLY	547b	2 a
		מקנה	CATTLE	889b	2
13	3	בין	INTERVAL	107c	1 a
		חיה	BE	227a	3 3
		הלך	WALK	231b	1 d3 gd
		תחלה	BEGINNING	321b	
		ל	TO	516a	5 ja
		נגב	SOUTH-COUNTRY	616b	1 a
		מסע	JOURNEY	652c	2
		עד	AS FAR AS	724a	1 1a
		עי	AI	743b	1
		מקום	STANDING PLACE	880b	4
		שם	THERE	1027b	1 b
13	4	מזבח	ALTAR	259a	8
		עשה	DO	794b	2 1a
		מקום	STANDING PLACE	880b	4
		ראשון	FIRST	911d	3 a1
		שם	NAME	1028b	3
13	5	בקר	CATTLE	133b	1 a
		ה	THE	208d	2
		לום	LOT	532b	
13	6	יחדו	TOGETHER	403b	A
		יכל	BE ABLE	407c	1
		ישב	DWELL	443a	3
		ל	TO	517d	7 bc
		נשא	LIFT	671b	2 c
		רכוש	PROPERTY	940d	2
13	7	אז	THEN	23a	1 a
		בין	INTERVAL	107c	1 a
		חיה	BECOME	225c	2 1a
		ישב	DWELL	443a	3
		כנעני	CANAANITE	489a	2 b
		לום	LOT	532b	
		פרזי	PERIZZITE	827a	
		מקנה	CATTLE	889b	2
		ריב	STRIFE	936d	1
		רעה	TEND	945a	1 d1
13	8	אח	BROTHER	26b	2
		אל	NOT	39a	A a
		אנחנו	WE	59d	
		חיה	BECOME	225c	2 1a
		לום	LOT	532b	
		נא	PART OF EN-TREATY	609b	3 c
		ריב	STRIFE	*936d	1
		מריבה	STRIFE	937b	
		רעה	TEND	945a	1 d1
13	9	ו	AND	254d	5 ca
		ימין	RIGHT HAND	412a	2 b
		ימן	GO TO THE RIGHT	412b	
		לא	NOT	520b	4 ba
		נא	PART OF EN-TREATY	609a	1
		פנה	FACE	817a	2 4a f
		פרד	DIVIDE	825b	1
		שמאל	LEFT	969d	1
		שמאל	TAKE THE LEFT	970a	1
13	10	ארץ	EARTH	76a	2 a
		בוא	COME	98c	2 e
		גן	GARDEN	171a	
		ירדן	JORDAN	434c	
		ירדן	JORDAN	434d	
		ד	LIKE	454a	1 c2
		כל	ALL	481b	1 a
		כבר	ROUND	503b	1
		לום	LOT	532b	
		נשא	LIFT	670c	1 b 4
		סדם	SODOM	690a	
		מצרים	EGYPT	695c	1
		עין	EYE	744b	1 f
		פנה	FACE	817d	2 4e
		צער	ZOAR	858d	
		צער	ZOAR	858d	

Ch v.	Heb	Eng	Page	Sec
	שחת	GO TO RUIN	1008a	1
	משקה	IRRIGATION	1052d	1
13 11	אח	BROTHER	26b	4
	בחר	CHOOSE	104a	3 b
	ירדן	JORDAN	434d	1
	כבר	ROUND	503b	1
	ל	TO	515b	5 ia
	לוט	LOT	532b	1
	מן	FROM	578d	1 c
	נסע	JOURNEY	652b	3
	על	UPON	759a	4 2b
	פרד	DIVIDE	825b	1
	קדם	FRONT	869d	1 b 3
13 12	אהל	MOVE TENT	14b	
	ישב	DWELL	443a	3
	כנען	CANAAN	488d	2 a
	כבר	ROUND	503b	1
	לוט	LOT	532b	1
	סדם	SODOM	690a	
	עד	AS FAR AS	724a	1 1a
13 13	חטא	SINFUL	308b	2
	ל	TO	511a	1 d
	מאד	EXCEEDINGLY	547b	2 a
	סדם	SODOM	690a	
	רע	EVIL	948c	0 b
13 14	אחר	AFTER	30a	2 b
	ים	SEA	411b	9
	לוט	LOT	532b	1
	נא	PART OF EN-TREATY	609a	1
	נגב	SOUTH-COUNTRY	616b	2
	נשא	LIFT	670c	1 b 4
	עין	EYE	744d	1 f
	מעם	FROM WITH	768d	A
	פרד	DIVIDE	825b	1
	צפון	NORTH	861a	
	קדם	EASTWARD	870a	
	מקום	STANDING PLACE	879d	2 b1
	ראה	TO SEE	907c	6 c
	שם	THERE	1027b	1 b
13 15	זרע	SOWING	282c	4 b
	עד	AS FAR AS	724a	1 2a a
	עולם	LONG DURATION	762d	2 f
	ראה	TO SEE	906d	1 b
	ראה	TO SEE	906d	1 b
13 16	אם	IF	49d	1 al c
	אשר	THAT	83c	8 b
	גם	ALSO	169d	4
	זרע	SOWING	282c	4 b
	מנה	COUNT	284a	1
	יכל	BE ABLE	407c	1
	יכל	BE ABLE	407c	1 a
	כ	LIKE	453d	1 b
	מנה	COUNT	584a	1
	עפר	DRY EARTH	780a	2 a
	שום	TO PLACE	964a	3 e
13 17	ארך	LENGTH	73d	A
	ב	IN	88b	1 1
	הלך	WALK	235d	1 a
	קום	STAND	878b	6 c
	ל	TO	516b	5 ja
	רחב	WIDTH	931d	
13 18	אהל	MOVE TENT	14b	
	אלון	TEREBINTH	18d	
	בנה	BUILD	124c	1 at
	מזבח	ALTAR	258b	1
	חברון	HEBRON	289b	1
	ממרא	MAMRE	577b	1
14 1	אלסר	ELLASAR	48c	
	אמרפל	AMRAPHEL	57d	
	אריוך	ARIOCH	73c	
	גוים	NATION	156d	3
	גוים	GOIM	157a	
	גוים	GOIM	157a	
	היה	COME TO PASS	224d	1 2a 1b
	יום	DAY	399b	4 b
	כדרלעמר	CHEDORLAOMER	462a	
	מלך	KING	573a	1
	עולם	ELAM	743d	
	שנאב	SHINAB	*1039c	
	שנער	SHINAR	1042d	
	תדעל	TIDAL	1062b	
14 2	אדמה	ADMAH	10a	
	את	WITH	86b	1 dd
	בלע	BELA	118d	
	ברע	BERA	140b	
	ברשע	BIRSHA	141d	
	הוא	HE, SHE, IT	*214d	
	מלחמה	WAR	536a	
	מלחמה	WAR	536c	
	מלך	KING	573a	1
	עשה	DO	794c	2 1e
	צביים	ZEBOIIM	840b	
	צער	ZOAR	858d	
	שמאבר	SHEMEMBER	1028d	
	שנאב	SHINAB	1039c	
14 3	אל	TO	39c	1
	אלה	THESE	41c	A
	הוא	HE, SHE, IT	215c	1 a
	חבר	UNITE	288a	1 a
	ים	SEA	411a	3
	מלח	SALT	571d	
	שדים	SIDDIM	961a	
14 4	כדרלעמר	CHEDORLAOMER	462a	
	מרד	REBEL	597c	1
	עשר	TEN	797b	3 b
	עשר	TEN	797b	8 a
	שלש	THREE	1025d	2
	שנה	YEAR	1040b	
14 5	שנים	TWO	1041b	2
	אימם	EMIM	34a	
	חם	HAM	241a	
	זוזים	ZUZIM	265c	
	זמזמים	ZAMZUMMIN	273d	
	כדרלעמר	CHEDORLAOMER	462a	
	נכה	SMITE	646b	3
	עשתרות	ASHTAROTH	800b	
	קריתים	KIRIATHAIM	900b	1
	קרנים	KARNAIM	902b	
	ארבע	FOUR	917a	2 al a
	רפאים	REPHAIM	952b	
	רפאים	REPHAIM	952b	
	שוה	LEVEL PLAIN	1001a	
14 6	אילפאראן	ELPARAN	18c	
	אילים	ELIM	18c	
	אילת	ELATH	19a	
	חרי	HORITE	360a	1
	על	UPON	755d	2 6a
	שעיר	SEIR	973a	1 b
	שעיר	SEIR	973a	1 b
14 7	אמרי	AMORITES	57c	2 c
	בא	COME	98b	2
	חצצנתמר	HAZAZON-TAMAR	346c	
	נכה	SMITE	646b	3
	עינמשפט	EN-MISHPAT	745c	1
	עמלקי	AMALEKITES	766a	
	קדש	KADESH	874a	1
	שדה	FIELD	961d	2 d
	שוב	TURN BACK	996d	1
14 8	אדמה	ADMAH	10a	
	את	WITH	86b	1 dd
	בלע	BELA	118d	
	הוא	HE, SHE, IT	215c	1 a
	מלחמה	WAR	536a	
	מלחמה	WAR	536c	
	ערך	ARRANGE	789c	1 d
	צביים	ZEBOIIM	840b	
	צער	ZOAR	858d	
	שדים	SIDDIM	961a	
14 9	אלסר	ELLASAR	48c	
	אמרפל	AMRAPHEL	57d	
	אריוך	ARIOCH	73c	
	את	WITH	86b	1 dd
	גוי	NATION	156d	3
	גוים	GOIM	157a	
	חמש	FIVE	331d	1 b
	כדרלעמר	CHEDORLAOMER	462a	
	עילם	ELAM	743d	
	ארבע	FOUR	917a	1 b1
	שנער	SHINAR	1042c	
	תדעל	TIDAL	1062b	
14 10	באר	WELL	91d	2
	הר	MOUNTAIN	250c	1 e
	חמר	BITUMEN	330c	
	נוס	FLEE	630d	1
	נפל	FALL	656d	1
	שדים	SIDDIM	961a	
	שאר	REMAIN	984a	1
14 11	אכל	FOOD	38a	
	לקח	TAKE	543d	9 a
	רכוש	PROPERTY	940d	3
14 12	לוט	LOT	532b	
	לקח	TAKE	543d	9 b
	רכוש	PROPERTY	940d	3
14 13	אלון	TEREBINTH	18d	
	אמרי	AMORITES	57c	3
	אשכל	ESHCOL	79b	1
	בעל	LORD	127c	1 5b
	ברית	COVENANT	136b	1 1
	ה	THE	208a	1 g
	ממרא	MAMRE	577b	2
	עברי	HEBREW	720b	2 b
	ענר	ANER	778d	1
	פליט	ESCAPED ONE	812c	
14 14	אח	BROTHER	26b	2
	בית	HOUSE	109c	4
	דן	DAN	193a	3
	חניך	TRAINED	335c	
	יליד	BORN	409d	
	כי	THAT	471c	1 a
	רדף	PURSUE	922d	1 c
	ריק	MAKE EMPTY	938a	3
	שבה	TAKE CAPTIVE	985c	
	שמנה	EIGHT	1033a	2 b
14 15	דמשק	DAMASCUS	199d	
	הוא	HE, SHE, IT	215c	1 d
	חובה	HOBAH	295b	
	חלק	DIVIDE	323c	
	חלק	DIVIDE	323d	1
	לילה	NIGHT	539a	1
	נכה	SMITE	646b	3
	רדף	PURSUE	922d	1 b
	שמאל	LEFT	969d	3
14 16	אח	BROTHER	26b	2
	לוט	LOT	532b	
	עם	PEOPLE	766c	2 c
	רכוש	PROPERTY	940d	3
	שוב	TURN BACK	998d	1 a
	שוב	TURN BACK	999a	1 a
14 17	אחר	AFTER	30a	2 b
	כדרלעמר	CHEDORLAOMER	462a	
	ל	TO	514a	5 e
	נכה	SMITE	646b	3
	עמק	VALE	771a	
	שוב	TURN BACK	997a	2
	שוה	SHAVEH	1001a	
14 18	יין	WINE	406c	A
	יצא	BRING OUT	425a	4 e
	כהן	PRIEST-KING	463a	1
	מלך	KING	573a	1
	מלכיצדק	MELCHIZEDEK	575d	
	עליון	HIGHEST	751b	1
	שלם	SALEM	1024a	
14 19	ברך	BLESS	138d	2 b
	ברך	BLESS	139a	3
	עליון	HIGHEST	751b	1
	קנה	ACQUIRE	888d	1 a
14 20	ברך	BLESS	138d	2 a
	מגן	DELIVER UP	171c	
	כל	ALL	482c	2 a
	עליון	HIGHEST	751b	1
	מעשר	TENTH PART	798b	2
14 21	צר	ADVERSARY	865b	
	רכוש	PROPERTY	940d	3
14 22	אל	TO	39c	1
	יד	HAND	389d	1 d
	עליון	HIGHEST	751b	1
	קנה	ACQUIRE	888d	1 a
	רום	BE HIGH	927b	1 1
14 23	אם	IF	50b	1 b2
	אשר	PARTICLE OF RE-LATION	83a	7 a
	חוט	THREAD	296c	1
	מן	FROM	582a	5 b
	נעל	SANDAL	653b	1
	עשר	BE RICH	799b	1
	שרוך	THONG	976c	
14 24	אשכל	ESHCOL	79b	1
	בלעדי	APART FROM	116b	A
	הלך	WALK	231c	1 1d 5a
	הם	THEY	241b	2
	חלק	PORTION	324a	1 a
	ממרא	MAMRE	577b	2
	נער	RETAINER	655a	2 b
	ענר	ANER	778d	1
	רק	ONLY	956b	2 a
15 1	אחר	AFTER	29d	2 b
	אל	NOT	39a	A a
	אלה	THESE	41c	C
	אנכי	I	59a	
	מגן	SHIELD	171c	
	דבר	WORD	182c	1 2a
	דבר	WORD	183c	4 4
	היה	BECOME	225d	2 1b
	מחזה	VISION	303d	
	ירא	FEAR	431a	1 a
	ל	TO	513a	5 ad
	מאד	EXCEEDINGLY	547b	2 a
	רבה	BECOME MANY	915b	1
	רבה	BECOME MANY	915d	1 e4
	שכר	HIRE	969a	2
15 2	אדון	LORD	11c	4 a
	אליעזר	ELIEZER	45c	A
	אנכי	I	59a	
	בן	SON	*120a	1
	בן	SON	121d	8 l
	דמשק	DAMASCUS	199d	
	הוא	HE, SHE, IT	215d	2 b
	הלך	WALK	234b	2 1
	הלך	WALK	234c	2 2
	ו	AND	253c	1 k
	משק	ACQUISITION	606c	
	עירירי	STRIPPED	792d	
	זי	WHO	*1087d	1 a
15 3	בית	HOUSE	109d	4
	בן	SON	120c	1 h
	הן	BEHOLD	243c	A
	זרע	SOWING	282c	4 b
	זרע	SOWING	283a	4 e
	ירש	INHERIT	439c	2
15 4	דבר	WORD	182c	1 2a
	הוא	HE, SHE, IT	215d	2 a
	ירש	INHERIT	439c	2
	כיאם	BUT	*475a	2
	כיאם	BUT	475a	2 b
	מן	OUT OF	579c	2 ca
	מעה	BELLY	589a	2
15 5	היה	BECOME	226a	2 2c
	זרע	SOWING	282c	4 b
	חול	SAND	*297d	A
	חוץ	THE OUTSIDE	299d	1
	יכל	BE ABLE	407c	1 a
	יצא	BRING OUT	424d	1 g
	כוכב	STAR	457a	
	כה	THUS	462a	1
	נא	PART OF EN-TREATY	609a	1
	נבט	LOOK	613c	1
	ספר	COUNT	707d	1
	שמי	HEAVENS	1029d	1 a
15 6	אמן	CONFIRM	53b	2
	ו	AND	*252b	1 b
	חשב	THINK	363b	2 3
	צדקה	RIGHTEOUSNESS	842b	5
15 7	אור	UR	22d	
	אמר	SAY	56a	1
	אנכי	I	59c	
	יהוה	YAHWEH	219a	2 2a

Ch v.	Heb	Eng	Page	Sec
	זה	THIS	261a	2 bb
	ירש	TAKE POSSESSION	439b	1 a
	כשדים	CHALDEANS	505a	1 a
	אור	ADDENDA ET COR-RIGENDA	1119d	
15 8	אדון	LORD	11c	4 a
	ב	IN	90a	3 2e
	ידע	KNOW	*393d	1 a
	ירש	TAKE POSSESSION	439b	1 a
	מה	HOW	553d	4 a
15 9	איל	RAM	18a	2
	גוזל	YOUNG OF BIRDS	160a	
	עגלה	HEIFER	722b	
	עז	SHE-GOAT	777c	3 b
	שלש	DO A THIRD TIME	1026a	
	שלש	DO A THIRD TIME	1026a	
	תר	TURTLE-DOVE	1076a	
	תר	TURTLE-DOVE	*1076a	
15 10	איש	MAN	36b	
	בתר	CUT IN TWO	144a	
	בתר	PART	144a	1
	בתר	CUT IN TWO	144a	
	כרת	CUT	503d	4
	ל	TO	515d	5 ia
	נתן	PUT	680b	2 a
	צפור	BIRD	862a	2
	רע	FRIEND	946b	3
	תוך	MIDST	1063c	
	קבל	BEFORE	*1110a	
15 11	ירד	COME DOWN	432d	1 a
	נשב	BLOW	674b	
	עיט	BIRD OF PREY	743c	
	על	UPON	756b	27 a a
	פגר	CORPSE	803d	2
15 12	אימה	TERROR	34a	
	בוא	COME	98a	1 i
	היה	BE	227a	3 5b
	הנה	BEHOLD	244b	C
	חשכה	DARKNESS	365b	
	ל	TO	518a	7 bg
	נפל	FALL	657c	5
	נפל	FALL	657c	5
	על	UPON	756b	27 a b
	תרדמה	DEEP SLEEP	922b	
	רוח	BREATH	*925b	3 h
	שמש	SUN	1039b	1
15 13	גר	SOJOURNER	158b	1
	זרע	SOWING	282c	4 b
	ל	TO	513d	5 cb d
	לא	NOT	519c	2 c
	מאה	HUNDRED	548a	1 c2
	ענה	BE BOWED DOWN	776b	1
15 14	אחר	AFTER	30a	2 b
	גדול	GREAT	153a	1
	גוי	NATION	156d	1 c
	דין	JUDGE	192b	4
	רכוש	PROPERTY	940d	1
15 15	אב	FATHER	3c	4 a
	ב	IN	88d	16
	בוא	COME	98a	1 h
	טוב	PLEASANT	374a	4 a
	קבר	BURY	868c	
	קבר	BURY	868c	
	שיבה	OLD AGE	966d	2
	שלום	PEACE	1023a	4
15 16	אמרי	AMORITES	57c	2 d
	דור	GENERATION	190a	2 c
	הנה	HITHER	244c	A a
	הנה	HITHERTO	244d	B
	עון	INIQUITY	731b	2 b
	רביעי	FOURTH	917d	1
	שוב	TURN BACK	997b	3 b
	שלם	COMPLETE	1024a	1 a
15 17	אש	FIRE	77d	6
	בוא	COME	98a	1 i
	בין	INTERVAL	107b	1
	גזר	PART	160c	
	היה	BECOME	225c	2 1a
	לפיד	TORCH	542a	
	עבר	PASS OVER	717d	3 d
	עלטה	THICK DARKNESS	759c	
	עשן	SMOKE	798c	2 a
	שמש	SUN	1039b	1
	תנור	FIRE-POT	1072b	
15 18	את	WITH	86a	1 da
	ברית	COVENANT	136c	2 2b
	ברית	COVENANT	137a	3 1
	גדול	GREAT	153a	1
	זרע	SOWING	282c	4 b
	יום	DAY	400c	7 g
	כרת	CUT	503d	4
	מן	FROM	581d	5 a
	נהר	STREAM	625d	1
	נהר	STREAM	625d	1
	נתן	GIVE	678c	1 b
	מצרים	EGYPT	695c	1 a
	עז	SHE-GOAT	777c	3 b
	פרת	EUPHRATES	832b	
15 19	קדמני	KADMONITES	870d	
	קיני	KENITE	884a	1
	קניזי	KENIZZITE	889d	
15 20	חתי	HITTITE	366d	2 a
	פריזי	PERIZZITE	827a	
	רפאים	REPHAIM	952b	
15 21	יבוסי	JEBUSITE	101a	1
	גרגשי	GIRGASHITE	173a	

Ch v.	Heb	Eng	Page	Sec
16 1	כנעני	CANAANITE	489a	2 b
	אמה	MAID	51a	1
	הגר	HAGAR	212b	
	ילד	BEAR	408b	1 a
	מצרי	EGYPTIAN	596a	1
	שרי	SARAI	979c	
	שפחה	MAID	1046a	1
16 2	אולי	PERADVENTURE	19c	1
	בוא	COME	98a	1 e
	בן	SON	*120a	1
	בנה	BUILD	125a	2 c
	הנה	BEHOLD	244a	B a
	מן	OUT OF	579c	2 ca
	מן	FROM	583a	7 b
	נא	PART OF EN-TREATY	609c	4 d
	עצר	RESTRAIN	783c	1
	שרי	SARAI	979c	
	שפחה	MAID	1046c	1
16 3	איש	MAN	35d	
	אשה	WOMAN	61b	2
	הגר	HAGAR	212b	
	כנען	CANAAN	488d	2 a
	ל	TO	513d	5 cb g
	מצרי	EGYPTIAN	596a	
	קץ	END	893d	1
	שרי	SARAI	979c	
	שפחה	MAID	1046c	1
16 4	גברת	MISTRESS	150c	2
	הגר	HAGAR	212b	
	הרה	CONCEIVE	247d	1
	עין	EYE	744d	3 c
	קלל	BE SLIGHT	886c	3
16 5	אנכי	I	59a	
	בין	INTERVAL	107c	1 d
	הרה	CONCEIVE	247d	1
	חיק	BOSOM	300d	3 a
	חמס	VIOLENCE	329c	
	נתן	PUT	680b	2 a
	עין	EYE	744d	3 c
	על	UPON	756c	27 a b
	קלל	BE SLIGHT	886c	3
	שפחה	MAID	1046c	1
	שפט	JUDGE	1047c	2 a
16 6	ברח	FLEE	138a	2
	טוב	PLEASANT	374a	2 f
	יד	HAND	391a	5 c3
	עין	EYE	744d	3 c
	ענה	BE BOWED DOWN	776b	1
	שפחה	MAID	1046c	1
16 7	באר	WELL	*91c	1
	דרך	WAY	202d	1
	מלאך	MESSENGER	521a	3
	מי	WATER	565b	1 a
	מצא	FIND	593b	3 a
	עין	SPRING	745a	
	עין	SPRING	745b	
	על	UPON	755d	26 a
	שור	SHUR	1004b	
16 8	אי	WHERE	32b	2 b
	אין	WHENCE	32d	
	אן	WHERE	33a	A
	בוא	COME	98b	2
	ברח	FLEE	138a	2
	גברת	MISTRESS	150c	2
	הגר	HAGAR	212b	
	הלך	WALK	230d	1 1d 3b
	שפחה	MAID	1046c	1
16 9	אל	TO	39c	1
	גברת	MISTRESS	150c	2
	יד	HAND	*391a	5 c3
	יד	HAND	391c	5 i
	מלאך	MESSENGER	521d	3
	ענה	BE BOWED DOWN	776b	1
16 10	זרע	SOWING	282c	4 b
	מלאך	MESSENGER	521d	3
	מן	ON ACCOUNT OF	580b	2 f
	ספר	COUNT	708a	
	רב	MULTITUDE	914a	1
	רבה	BECOME MANY	915b	
	רבה	BECOME MANY	915c	1 a
	רבה	BECOME MANY	915d	1 e1
16 11	אל	TO	40a	3 b
	בן	SON	120a	1
	הנה	BEHOLD	243d	
	הרה	PREGNANT	248a	
	מלאך	MESSENGER	521d	3
	עני	AFFLICTION	777a	1
	שמע	HEAR	1034b	2 f
	ישמעאל	ISHMAEL	1035d	1
16 12	אדם	MAN	9a	1
	אח	BROTHER	26b	2
	ב	IN	89b	2 4a
	כל	ALL	482c	2 a
	כל	ALL	482d	2 ba
	פנה	FACE	818d	27 a d
	פרא	WILD ASS	825b	
	שכן	SETTLE DOWN	1015b	2 a
16 13	אל	GOD	42c	6 c
	גם	ALSO	169b	2
	דבר	SPEAK	180c	
	ה	THE	208d	2 a
	ה	INTERROG PART	210a	1 c
	הלם	HITHER	241a	
	ראה	TO SEE	906d	1 a
	ראה	TO SEE	907c	6 a

Ch v.	Heb	Eng	Page	Sec
	ראי	LOOKING	909b	1
	ראי	LOOKING	909b	3
16 14	באר	WELL	91c	1
	בארלחירואי	BEER-LAHAI-ROI	91d	
	בארלחירואי	BEER-LAHAI-ROI	91d	
	בין	INTERVAL	107c	1 a
	ברד	BERED	136a	1
	הנה	BEHOLD	244a	A
	כן	SO	487b	3 f
	קדש	KADESH	873d	1
	ראה	TO SEE	906d	1 a
16 15	בן	SON	120a	1
	הגר	HAGAR	212b	
	ישמעאל	ISHMAEL	1035d	1
16 16	הגר	HAGAR	212b	
	שמנים	EIGHTY	1033b	
	ישמעאל	ISHMAEL	1035d	1
17 1	היה	BE	227a	3 4b
	הלך	WALK	236b	2
	פנה	FACE	817a	24 ad
	שדי	ALMIGHTY	995a	2
	תמים	SOUND	1071a	4
17 2	ברית	COVENANT	136c	2 2b
	ברית	COVENANT	137a	3 1
	ו	AND	252b	1 b
	מאד	MUCHNESS	547c	2 e
	נתן	PUT	680d	2 b
17 3	את	WITH	86a	1 db
	ברית	COVENANT	136c	2 2b
	דבר	SPEAK	181b	3 d
	נפל	FALL	657c	3 b
	על	UPON	756b	27 a a
17 4	אב	FATHER	3c	4 b
	את	WITH	85c	
	את	WITH	86a	1 da
	ברית	COVENANT	136c	2 2b
	גוי	NATION	156c	1 a
	גוי	NATION	*156d	1 b
	המון	CROWD	242d	3 c
17 5	אב	FATHER	3c	4 b
	אברם	ABRAM	4d	
	את	MARK OF THE AC-CUSATIVE	85a	1 b
	ברית	COVENANT	136c	2 2b
	גוי	NATION	156c	1 a
	גוי	NATION	*156d	1 b
	המון	CROWD	242d	3 c
	נתן	GIVE	681a	3 a
	עוד	STILL	729a	1 ab
	שם	NAME	1027d	2 a
	את	ADDENDA ET COR-RIGENDA	1121b	
17 6	ברית	COVENANT	136c	2 2b
	גוי	NATION	156c	1 a
	גוי	NATION	*156d	1 b
	מאד	MUCHNESS	547c	2 e
	נתן	GIVE	681a	3 b
	פרה	BEAR FRUIT	826a	2
17 7	אחר	AFTER	30a	2 b
	אלהים	GOD	44b	4 a
	בין	INTERVAL	107c	1 a
	ברית	COVENANT	136c	2 2b
	ברית	COVENANT	137a	3 1
	ברית	COVENANT	137a	3 1
	דור	GENERATION	190a	2 c
	זרע	SOWING	282c	4 b
	עולם	LONG DURATION	762c	2 d
	קום	STAND	879a	6 d
17 8	אחזה	POSSESSION	28d	
	אלהים	GOD	44b	4 a
	ברית	COVENANT	136c	2 2b
	מגור	SOJOURNING PLACE	158c	
	זרע	SOWING	282c	4 b
	כנען	CANAAN	488d	2 a
	נתן	GIVE	678c	1 b
	עולם	LONG DURATION	762d	2 f
17 9	אברם	ABRAM	4d	
	ברית	COVENANT	136c	2 2b
	דור	GENERATION	190a	2 c
	זרע	SOWING	282c	4 b
17 10	אחר	AFTER	30a	2 b
	ברית	COVENANT	136c	2 2b
	זה	THIS	261a	3
	זכר	MALE	271c	1 1 b
	זרע	SOWING	282c	4 b
	ל	TO	512c	5 aa
	מול	CIRCUMCIZE	557d	
17 11	את	SIGN	17a	6
	את	MARK OF THE AC-CUSATIVE	85b	2 c
	ברית	COVENANT	136c	2 2b
	בשר	FLESH	142d	3
	היה	BECOME	226c	2 2e
	מול	CIRCUMCIZE	557d	
	מלל	CIRCUMCIZE	576d	
	עולה	FORESKIN	790b	
17 12	אשר	PARTICLE OF RE-LATION	82b	2 b
	בית	HOUSE	109c	4
	בן	SON	121c	7 a
	ברית	COVENANT	136c	2 2b
	דור	GENERATION	190a	2 c
	הוא	HE, SHE, IT	216b	3 c
	זכר	MALE	271c	1 1 b
	זרע	SOWING	282d	4 e

Ch	v.	Heb	Eng	Page	Sec
		ילד	BORN	409d	
		כסף	SILVER	494c	8 e
		מול	CIRCUMCIZE	557d	
		נכר	FOREIGNNESS	648d	2
		מקנה	PURCHASE	889c	
		שמנה	EIGHT	1033a	1 c
17	13	בית	HOUSE	109c	4
		ברית	COVENANT	136c	2 2b
		ברית	COVENANT	137a	3 2
		ילד	BORN	409d	
		כסף	SILVER	494c	8 e
		מול	CIRCUMCIZE	557d	
		עולם	LONG DURATION	762c	2 d
		מקנה	PURCHASE	889c	1
17	14	את	MARK OF THE AC-CUSATIVE	85b	2 c
		ברית	COVENANT	136c	2 2b
		ברית	COVENANT	137b	3 3
		בשר	FLESH	142d	3
		בשר	FLESH	142d	3
		זכר	MALE	271c	11 b
		כרת	BE CUT OFF	504b	1 c
		מול	CIRCUMCIZE	557d	
		נפש	SOUL	660b	4 c2
		עם	KINSMAN	769b	
		ערל	HAVING FORESKIN	790c	
		פרר	BREAK	830b	1 b
17	15	אברם	ABRAM	4d	
		ברית	COVENANT	136c	2 2b
		כי	BUT	474b	3 e
		כי אם	BUT	*475a	2 b
		שרה	SARAH	979a	
		שם	NAME	1027d	2 a
17	16	בן	SON	120a	1
		ברית	COVENANT	136c	2 2b
		ברך	BLESS	139a	2 a
		גוי	NATION	156c	1 a
		גוי	NATION	*156d	1 b
		היה	BECOME	226a	2 1b
		מן	OUT OF	579c	2 ca
		נתן	GIVE	678c	1 b
17	17	אם	IF	50d	2 ab b
		בן	SON	*120a	1
		בת	DAUGHTER	123d	9
		ברית	COVENANT	136c	2 2b
		ילד	BE BORN	408d	
		לב	HEART	525c	2 7
		מאה	HUNDRED	547d	1 a1
		נפל	FALL	657c	3
		על	UPON	756b	2 7aa
		צחק	LAUGH	850a	
		יצחק	ISAAC	850c	
		שרה	SARAH	979a	
		תשעים	NINETY	1077d	
17	18	אלהים	GOD	43d	3
		ברית	COVENANT	136c	2 2b
		ברית	COVENANT	137a	3 2
		חיה	LIVE	311a	1 b
		לו	IF	530b	2 a
		פנה	FACE	817a	2 4a b
17	19	אבל	VERILY	6a	1
		אחר	AFTER	30a	2 b
		בן	SON	120a	1
		ברית	COVENANT	136c	2 2b
		ברית	COVENANT	137a	3 1
		ברית	COVENANT	137a	3 2
		זרע	SOWING	282c	4 b
		עולם	LONG DURATION	762c	2 d
		יצחק	ISAAC	850c	
		יצחק	ISAAC	850c	
		קום	STAND	879a	6 d
		שרה	SARAH	979a	
17	20	ברית	COVENANT	136c	2 2b
		ברך	BLESS	139a	2 a
		גוי	NATION	156c	1 a
		הנה	BEHOLD	244a	B a
		ל	TO	514b	5 fa
		מאד	MUCHNESS	547c	1 a
		נשיא	PRINCE	672b	3
		נתן	GIVE	681a	3 b
		פרה	BEAR FRUIT	826a	2
		רבה	BECOME MANY	915c	1 a
		שמע	HEAR	1034b	2 h
		שנים	TWO	1041b	2
17	21	אחר	ANOTHER	29d	
		ברית	COVENANT	136c	2 2b
		ברית	COVENANT	137a	3 1
		ו	AND	252d	1 e
		זה	THIS	261a	2 bb
		מועד	APPOINTED TIME	417c	1 a
		ל	TO	517a	6 a
		יצחק	ISAAC	850c	
		קום	STAND	879a	6 d
		שרה	SARAH	979a	
17	22	דבר	SPEAK	181b	3 d
		כלה	FINISH	478b	1 c
		עלה	GO UP	748c	2 e
		על	UPON	759a	4 2c
17	23	ב	IN	88c	2 2c
		בשר	FLESH	142d	3
		דבר	SPEAK	181b	3 d
		זה	THIS	261a	2 bb
		זכר	MALE	271c	11 b
		כאשר	AS	455b	1 a
		כסף	SILVER	494c	8 e
		מול	CIRCUMCIZE	557d	

Ch	v.	Heb	Eng	Page	Sec
		עצם	BONE	783a	3
		מקנה	PURCHASE	889c	1
17	24	בשר	FLESH	142d	3
		מול	CIRCUMCIZE	557d	
		שנה	YEAR	1040b	
17	25	בשר	FLESH	142d	3
		מול	CIRCUMCIZE	557d	
		שלש	THREE	1025d	2
17	26	מול	CIRCUMCIZE	557d	
		עצם	BONE	783a	3
17	27	את	WITH	86c	4 a
		בית	HOUSE	109d	4
		בן	SON	121c	7 a
		ילד	BORN	409d	
		כסף	SILVER	494c	8 e
		מול	CIRCUMCIZE	557d	
		נכר	FOREIGNNESS	648d	2
		מקנה	PURCHASE	889c	1
18	1	אלון	TEREBINTH	18d	
		חם	HEAT	328d	1
		יום	DAY	398b	1
		ממרא	MAMRE	577b	1
		פתח	OPENING	835d	
18	2	ארץ	EARTH	76b	3 a
		הנה	BEHOLD	244b	C
		נשא	LIFT	670c	1 b 4
		על	UPON	756a	2 6c
		פתח	OPENING	835d	
		ראה	TO SEE	906d	1 a
		ראה	TO SEE	907d	6 c
		רוץ	RUN	930b	1
		שחה	BOW DOWN	1005c	2 d
		שלש	THREE	1025d	1 a
18	3	אדון	LORD	11b	3 2a
		אל	NOT	39a	A a
		אם	IF	49d	1 a3 a
		חן	FAVOR	336b	2 b2
		מצא	FIND	592d	1 a
		נא	PART OF EN-TREATY	609b	3 b
		נא	PART OF EN-TREATY	609c	4 c
		עבד	SLAVE	714c	6
		עבר	PASS OVER	718a	5 a
		על	UPON	759a	4 2c
18	4	לקח	TAKE	544a	1
		מי	WATER	565b	1 a
		מעט	A FEW	590a	1 b
		נא	PART OF EN-TREATY	609b	3 c
		עץ	TREE	781c	1 a
		רגל	FOOT	919d	1 a
		רחץ	WASH OFF	934c	1
		שען	LEAN	1043d	
		תחת	UNDERNEATH	1065b	2 1
		אחר	AFTERWARDS	29d	1 b
18	5	כאשר	AS	455b	1 b
		כי על כן	FOR THEREFORE	475c	
		כן	SO	486c	2 db
		לב	HEART	525c	2 8
		לחם	FOOD	537a	1 a
		סעד	SUPPORT	703c	1
		עבר	PASS OVER	717d	4 a
		עבר	PASS OVER	718a	5 a
		על	UPON	756a	2 6a
		על	UPON	759a	4 2c
		פת	FRAGMENT	837d	
18	6	לוש	KNEAD	534c	
		מהר	HASTEN	554d	1
		מהר	HASTEN	555a	3
		סלת	FINE FLOUR	701c	
		עגה	BREAD-CAKE	728b	
		קמח	FLOUR	887d	
		שרה	SARAH	979a	
		שלש	THREE	1025d	
18	7	בן	SON	121c	7 b
		בקר	HERD	133b	1 b
		בקר	CATTLE	133b	1 a
		טוב	PLEASANT	374b	3 d
		ל	TO	517a	7 bc
		מהר	HASTEN	555a	2
		עשה	DO	794d	2 3
		רוץ	RUN	930b	1
		רך	TENDER	940a	1
18	8	בן	SON	121c	7 b
		בקר	CATTLE	133b	1 a
		חלב	MILK	316b	A
		חמאה	CURD	326a	
		על	UPON	756b	2 6c
		עמד	STAND	763d	1 a
		עץ	TREE	781c	1 a
		עשה	DO	794d	2 3
		פנה	FACE	817c	2 4b f
18	9	איה	WHERE	32c	
		הנה	BEHOLD	243d	A
18	10	אחר	BEHIND	30a	2 a
		בן	SON	120a	1
		בן	SON	*120a	1
		חי	ALIVE	312b	3
		פתח	OPENING	835d	
		שוב	TURN BACK	998a	6 g
18	11	אשה	WOMAN	61a	1
		ארח	WAY	73a	2 1
		היה	BE	227b	3 4c
		זקן	OLD	278c	1
		חדל	CEASE	293a	1

Ch	v.	Heb	Eng	Page	Sec
18	12	יום	DAY	399b	4 a
		אדון	LORD	11b	3 1b
		אחר	AFTER	30a	2 b
		בלה	BECOME OLD AND WORN OUT	115a	
		בלה	WORN OUT	*115b	
		ו	AND	253c	1 k
		זקן	BE OLD	278b	
		עדנה	DELIGHT	726d	
		צחק	LAUGH	850b	
		יצחק	ISAAC	850c	
		קרב	INWARD PART	899a	1 a
18	13	אמנם	VERILY	53d	
		אף	ALSO	65a	1
		ו	AND	253c	1 k
		זה	THIS	261c	4 e
		זקן	BE OLD	278b	
		מה	HOW	554a	4 d
		צחק	LAUGH	850b	
18	14	בן	SON	120a	1
		דבר	WORD	183d	4 6
		חי	ALIVE	312b	3
		מועד	APPOINTED TIME	417c	1 a
		מן	THAN	582d	6 d
		פלא	BE SURPASSING	810c	1
		שוב	TURN BACK	998a	6 g
18	15	ירא	FEAR	431a	1
		כחש	DECEIVE	471b	1
		כי	BUT	474b	3 e
		לא	NOT	519a	1 ad b
		צחק	LAUGH	850b	
18	16	עם	WITH	767b	1 a
		פנה	FACE	819a	2 7ae
		שלח	SEND	1019a	1 d
		שם	THERE	1027c	4 a
		שקף	LOOK DOWN	1054c	
18	17	אני	I	59a	1
		ה	INTERROG PART	209d	1 b
18	18	כסה	COVER	491d	2
		ארץ	EARTH	76a	1 a
		ברך	BLESS	138d	
		גוי	NATION	156c	1 a
		גוי	NATION	156c	1
		עצום	MIGHTY	783a	1
		שום	TO PLACE	964b	4 c
18	19	אב	FATHER	3b	1
		אחר	AFTER	30a	2 b
		בית	HOUSE	109d	5 b
		דבר	SPEAK	181c	5
		דרך	WAY	204a	6 ec
		ידע	KNOW	393d	1 a
		ידע	KNOW	394b	2
		מען	PURPOSE	775b	1 c
		מען	PURPOSE	775c	2 a
		צדקה	RIGHTEOUSNESS	842b	5
		צוה	CHARGE	845d	2 b
		שמר	KEEP	1037a	3 c
18	20	זעקה	CRY	277d	1
		חטאת	SIN	309a	2
		כבד	BE HEAVY	457b	1
		כי	BECAUSE	473c	3 a
		מאד	EXCEEDINGLY	547d	1 a
		רבב	BECOME MUCH	912d	2
18	21	בוא	COME	98b	2
		ה	THE	209c	3
		ה	INTERROG PART	210b	1
		ירד	GO DOWN	433b	2
		כלה	COMPLETE	478d	1
		לא	NOT	519a	1 ad a
		נא	PART OF EN-TREATY	609b	3 a
		עשה	DO	794a	1 1a 7
		פנה	FACE	817a	2 4a c
		צעקה	CRY	858d	1
		ראה	TO SEE	907b	5 a
18	22	הלך	WALK	230d	1 1d 3b
		סדם	SODOM	690a	
		עוד	STILL	728d	1 aa
		עמד	STAND	763d	1 a
		פנה	TURN	815b	1 b
		פנה	FACE	816d	2 4
		כען	NOW	*1107b	
18	23	אף	ALSO	65a	1
		נגש	DRAW NEAR	620d	1
		ספה	SWEEP AWAY	705a	2
		עם	WITH	767d	1 e
		צדיק	JUST	843a	3 a
		רשע	WICKED	957b	1
18	24	אולי	PERADVENTURE	19d	2
		אף	ALSO	65a	1
		יש	THERE IS	441c	2 b
		נשא	LIFT	671c	3 c
		ספה	SWEEP AWAY	705a	2
		מען	PURPOSE	775a	1 a
		צדיק	JUST	843a	3 a
		מקום	STANDING PLACE	880a	3 a
		קרב	INWARD PART	899a	1 c
		תוך	MIDST	1063c	
18	25	ארץ	EARTH	76a	1 a
		דבר	WORD	183d	4 7
		היה	BECOME	226b	2 2c
		חלילה	FAR BE IT	321a	
		כ	LIKE	454a	1 b
		כ	LIKE	454a	2 a
		מות	DIE	560b	1
		עם	WITH	767d	1 e

GENESIS

Ch	v.	Heb	Eng	Page	Sec
		צדיק	JUST	843a	3 a
		רשע	WICKED	957b	1
		שפט	JUDGE	1047b	1
		משפט	JUDGMENT	1048d	2 a
18	26	אם	IF	49c	1 a1 a
		מצא	FIND	593a	1 a
		נשא	LIFT	671c	3 c
		עבור	FOR THE SAKE OF	721a	1 a
		צדיק	JUST	843a	3 a
		מקום	STANDING PLACE	880a	3 a
18	27	אדון	LORD	11b	3 2a
		אפר	ASHES	68a	
		הנה	BEHOLD	244a	^ B a
		יאל	SHOW-WILLING-NESS	384a	2
		ל	TO	517d	7 bc
		נא	PART OF EN-TREATY	609c	4 d
		ענה	ANSWER	772d	1
		עפר	DRY EARTH	780a	2 d
18	28	אולי	PERADVENTURE	19d	2
		ב	IN	90c	3 5
		חמש	FIVE	332b	5 g
		חסר	LACK	341d	1 a
		מצא	FIND	593a	1 a
		צדיק	JUST	843a	3 a
		ארבעים	FORTY	917c	2 a
		שחת	GO TO RUIN	1008b	1
18	29	אולי	PERADVENTURE	19d	2
		יסף	DO AGAIN	415c	2 a
		מצא	FIND	594a	1 f
		עבור	FOR THE SAKE OF	721a	1 a
		עוד	STILL	729b	1 b
		ארבעים	FORTY	917c	1 c
18	30	אדון	LORD	11b	3 2a
		חרה	BURN	354b	2 b
		מצא	FIND	593a	1 a
		מצא	FIND	594a	1 f
		נא	PART OF EN-TREATY	609b	3 c
18	31	אדון	LORD	11b	3 2a
		יאל	SHOW-WILLING-NESS	384a	2
		ל	TO	517d	7 bc
		מצא	FIND	594a	1 f
		נא	PART OF EN-TREATY	609c	4 d
		עשרים	TWENTY	797d	1 1e
18	32	אדון	LORD	11b	3 2a
		אולי	PERADVENTURE	19d	2
		אך	ONLY	36c	2 ba
		ה	THE	207b	1 ca
		חרה	BURN	354b	2 b
		מצא	FIND	594a	1 f
		עשר	TEN	796c	2 b
		עשר	TEN	797a	2 b
		פעם	OCCURRENCE	822b	3 d1
18	33	רק	ONLY	956c	2 a
		הלך	WALK	230b	1 1b
		כאשר	WHEN	455c	3
		כלה	FINISH	478b	1 c
		ל	TO	511b	1 ga
		שוב	TURN BACK	997a	3 a
19	1	אף	NOSE	60b	2
		מלאאך	MESSENGER	521d	2
		סדם	SODOM	690a	
		ערב	SUNSET	787d	1 a
		קום	STAND	877d	1 a
		קרא	ENCOUNTER	896d	1
		ראה	TO SEE	906d	1 a
		שחה	BOW DOWN	1005c	2 d
		שער	GATE	1045a	2 a
19	2	אדון	LORD	11b	3 2a
		בית	HOUSE	108c	1 a
		דרך	JOURNEY	203a	2
		הלך	WALK	231b	1 d3 gd
		כי	BUT	474c	3 e
		לא	NOT	519a	1 ad b
		לון	LODGE	533c	1 a
		נא	PART OF EN-TREATY	609c	4 d
		סור	TURN ASIDE	693c	1
		רגל	FOOT	919d	1 a
		רחוב	PLAZA	932b	
		רחץ	WASH OFF	934c	1
		שכם	START EARLY	1014c	
		שער	GATE	1045a	2 a
19	3	אל	TO	39d	2
		אפה	BAKE	66a	
		בית	HOUSE	108c	1 a
		מאד	EXCEEDINGLY	547d	2 a
		סור	TURN ASIDE	693c	1
		מצה	UNLEAVENED BREAD	695b	
		פצר	PUSH	823a	
		משתה	FEAST	1059d	1
19	4	בית	HOUSE	108c	1 a
		זקן	OLD	278a	2 a
		חזק	BE FIRM	305a	6 a
		טרם	NOT YET	382c	1
		מן	FROM	581d	5 b
		נער	YOUTH	655a	1 d
		סבב	TURN AROUND	686a	1 a
		עד	AS FAR AS	724a	1 1b
		עם	PEOPLE	766c	2 a
		קצה	END	892b	3

Ch	v.	Heb	Eng	Page	Sec
		שכב	LIE DOWN	1012a	1 b
19	5	איה	WHERE	32c	
		אל	TO	40a	3 b
		ה	THE	207b	1 ca
		ידע	KNOW	394b	3
		יצא	BRING OUT	424d	1 h
		לילה	NIGHT	538d	1
		קרא	CALL	895b	2 a
19	6	בעד	BEHIND	*126c	1 b
		דלת	DOOR	*195a	1
		סגר	SHUT	689a	1
		פתח	OPENING	835d	
19	7	נא	PART OF EN-TREATY	609b	3 b
		רעע	BE EVIL	949d	1
19	8	איש	MAN	35d	
		אל	THESE	41b	
		ב	IN	88c	1 4
		בוא	COME	97d	1
		בת	DAUGHTER	123a	1
		טוב	PLEASANT	374a	2 f
		סלל	COVER OVER	*378d	
		ידע	KNOW	394b	3
		יצא	BRING OUT	424d	1 h
		בעל-כן	FOR THEREFORE	475c	
		ל	TO	510d	1 d
		נא	PART OF EN-TREATY	609b	3 a
		נא	PART OF EN-TREATY	609c	4 d
		צל	SHADOW	853b	2
		קורה	RAFTER	900a	
		רק	ONLY	956c	2 b
19	9	גור	SOJOURN	157d	1
		דלת	DOOR	195a	1
		הלאה	OUT THERE	229b	A
		מאד	EXCEEDINGLY	547b	2 a
		מן	THAN	582b	6 a
		נגש	DRAW NEAR	620d	1
		נגש	DRAW NEAR	620d	1
		עתה	NOW	774a	1 b
		פער	PUSH	823a	
		רעע	BE EVIL	949c	1
		שבר	BREAK	990c	
		שפט	JUDGE	1047b	1 b
19	10	בוא	COME	99a	1
		דלת	DOOR	195a	1
		סגר	SHUT	688d	1
19	11	בית	HOUSE	108c	1 a
		גדול	GREAT	153b	7
		ה	THE	208c	1 hb
		לאה	BE WEARY	521a	1
		מן	FROM	581d	5 b
		מצא	FIND	593a	1 b
		נכה	SMITE	646b	4 a
		סנורים	SUDDEN BLIND-NESS	703a	
		פתח	OPENING	835d	
		קטן	SMALL	882b	1 a
19	12	חתן	DAUGHTER:S HUS-BAND	368c	1
		יצא	CAUSE TO GO	424b	1 a
		מי	WHO	567b	G
		עד	STILL	729b	1 c
		פה	HERE	805d	1 a
19	13	אנחנו	WE	59d	
		גדל	BECOME GREAT	152b	2 d
		פנה	FACE	816c	2 2a
		צעקה	CRY	858d	1
		שחת	GO TO RUIN	1008a	1
		שחת	GO TO RUIN	1008b	1
19	14	קום	STAND	278b	6 c
		חתן	DAUGHTER:S HUS-BAND	368c	1
		יצא	GO OUT	422d	1 a
		עין	EYE	744d	3 c
		צחק	LAUGH	850b	1
		שחת	GO TO RUIN	1008b	1
19	15	ו	AND	254d	5 b
		קום	STAND	278b	6 c
		כמו	LIKE	455d	1
		כמו	LIKE	456a	1 a
		מלאך	MESSENGER	521d	2
		מצא	FIND	594b	2 e
		ספה	SWEEP AWAY	705a	1
		עון	INIQUITY	731c	3
		עלה	GO UP	748d	5
		פן	LEST	814d	1
		שחר	DAWN	1007b	1
19	16	ב	IN	91a	5 2
		חוץ	THE OUTSIDE	300a	1 bd
		חמלה	COMPASSION	328b	
		יד	HAND	389a	1 a
		יצא	BRING OUT	424d	1 g
		מהה	LINGER	554c	
		נוח	REST	628d	B 1
19	17	אחר	BEHIND	30a	2 a
		אל	TO	40c	6
		חיה	COME TO PASS	224c	2 al aa
		הר	MOUNTAIN	250b	1 e
		חוץ	THE OUTSIDE	299d	1 a
		יצא	BRING OUT	424d	1 g
		כ	LIKE	454d	3 b
		כבר	ROUND	503b	1
		מלט	SLIP AWAY	572c	2
		מלט	SLIP AWAY	572c	2

Ch	v.	Heb	Eng	Page	Sec
		נבט	LOOK	613c	1 a
		ספה	SWEEP AWAY	705a	1
		על	UPON	754b	2 lf c
		פן	LEST	814d	1
19	18	אדון	LORD	11b	3 2a
		אל	NOT	39b	A bb
		בי	I PRAY	*106c	
		נא	PART OF EN-TREATY	609b	3 b
		עלה	GO UP	748d	5
19	19	גדל	BECOME GREAT	152c	2
		דבק	CLING	180a	2 c
		חיה	LIVE	311c	1
		חן	FAVOR	336b	2 b2
		חסד	GOODNESS	339a	2 1a
		יכל	BE ABLE	407c	1 a
		מות	DIE	559d	2 b
		מלט	SLIP AWAY	572c	2
		מצא	FIND	592d	1 a
		נא	PART OF EN-TREATY	609c	4 d
		נפש	SOUL	659c	2
		עם	WITH	767d	1 d
		עשה	DO	794b	1 3
		פן	LEST	814d	1
19	20	חיה	LIVE	311a	1 b
		ל	TO	517b	7 a
		לא	NOT	520b	4 ba
		מלט	SLIP AWAY	572c	2
		נא	PART OF EN-TREATY	609b	3 a
		נא	PART OF EN-TREATY	609c	4 d
		נפש	SOUL	659c	2
		עיר	CITY	*746b	1
		צער	ZOAR	858d	
		צער	ZOAR	*858d	
		מצער	SMALL THING	859b	1
		קרב	NEAR	898b	1
		שם	THERE	1027b	1
19	21	בלת	NOT	116d	4 a
		הפך	TURN	245c	1 b
		ל	TO	514b	5 fa
19	22	נשא	LIFT	670c	1 b 3
		יכל	BE ABLE	407c	1 a
		כן	SO	487b	3 f
		מהר	HASTEN	555a	2
		מלט	SLIP AWAY	572c	2
		עד	AS FAR AS	724b	1 2a b
		צער	ZOAR	858d	
		שם	THERE	1027b	3 a
19	23	בוא	COME	*98a	1 i
		יצא	GO OUT	423b	1 f
		יצא	GO OUT	*423b	1 f
		על	UPON	755d	2 5
		שמש	SUN	1039a	1
19	24	את	WITH	86d	4 c
		גפרית	BRIMSTONE	172d	
		מטר	RAIN	565a	
		על	UPON	756b	2 7a a
		שמי	HEAVENS	1030a	2 a
19	25	אדמה	GROUND	9c	1
		אל	THESE	41b	
		הפך	TURN	245c	1 b
		ישב	DWELL	443b	3
		ככר	ROUND	503b	1
		צמח	SPROUT	855c	1
19	26	אחר	BEHIND	30b	4 aa
		מלח	SALT	571d	
		נבט	LOOK	613c	1 a
		נציב	PILLAR	662d	1
19	27	אל	TO	39c	1
		בקר	MORNING	134a	1 f
		בקר	MORNING	134b	1 h
		עמד	STAND	763d	1 a
		פנה	FACE	816c	2 2a
		מקום	STANDING PLACE	879d	1 a
		שכם	START EARLY	1014d	
19	28	שם	THERE	1027b	1 b
		ארץ	EARTH	76a	2 b
		ה	THE	207d	1 f
		כבשן	KILN	461c	
		ככר	ROUND	503b	1
		עלה	GO UP	748d	5
		פנה	FACE	816b	15
		פנה	FACE	819a	2 7a e
		קיטור	SMOKE	882c	
		שקף	LOOK DOWN	1054c	
19	29	חיה	COME TO PASS	224c	2 al ab
		הם	THEY	241d	8 d
		הפך	TURN	245c	1 b
		הפכה	OVERTHROW	246b	
		זכר	REMEMBER	270b	2 1 a
		ישב	DWELL	443a	3
		ככר	ROUND	503b	1
		שחת	GO TO RUIN	1008a	1
		שלח	SEND	1019a	2 a
		תוך	MIDST	1063d	
19	30	הוא	HE, SHE, IT	215c	1 d
		ירא	FEAR	431b	1 d
		עם	WITH	767b	1 a
		מערה	CAVE	792c	
		צער	ZOAR	858d	
19	31	אב	FATHER	3b	1
		אין	NOT	34c	2 c
		בוא	COME	98a	1 e

Ch v.	Heb	Eng	Page	Sec
	בכורה	FIRST-BORN	114c	
	דרך	WAY	*203a	1
	דרך	WAY	203b	4 a
	זקן	BE OLD	278b	
	על	UPON	757a	27c a
	צעיר	YOUNG	859a	2
19 32	אב	FATHER	3b	1
	הלך	WALK	234a	15f 2
	זרע	SOWING	282d	4 c
	זרע	SOWING	283a	4 e
	חיה	LIVE	311c	1
	יין	WINE	406c	C
	שכב	LIE DOWN	1012b	3
	שקה	GIVE TO DRINK	1052c	2
19 33	אב	FATHER	3b	1
	בכורה	FIRST-BORN	114c	
	הוא	HE, SHE, IT	216d	7
	ידע	KNOW	393d	1 b
	יין	WINE	406c	C
	לילה	NIGHT	538d	1
	קום	STAND	877c	1 a
	שכב	LIE DOWN	1012b	1e
	שכב	LIE DOWN	1012b	3
	שקה	GIVE TO DRINK	1052c	2
19 34	אמש	YESTERDAY	57d	
	בוא	COME	98a	1e
	בכורה	FIRST-BORN	114c	
	היה	COME TO PASS	224c	2 a1 az
	הן	BEHOLD	243c	A
	זרע	SOWING	282d	4 c
	זרע	SOWING	283a	4 e
	חיה	LIVE	311c	1
	יין	WINE	406c	C
	לילה	NIGHT	538d	1
	מחרת	THE MORROW	564a	
	מן	FROM	581c	4 b
	צעיר	YOUNG	859a	2
	שכב	LIE DOWN	1012b	3
	שכב	LIE DOWN	1012b	3
	שקה	GIVE TO DRINK	1052c	2
19 35	הוא	HE, SHE, IT	216d	7
	ידע	KNOW	393d	1 b
	יין	WINE	406c	C
	לילה	NIGHT	538d	1
	קום	STAND	877c	1 a
	שכב	LIE DOWN	1012b	1e
	שכב	LIE DOWN	1012b	3
	שקה	GIVE TO DRINK	1052c	2
19 36	הרה	CONCEIVE	247d	1
	מן	OUT OF	580a	2 ea
19 37	אב	FATHER	3c	4 b
	בכורה	FIRST-BORN	114c	
	בן	SON	120a	1
	יום	DAY	401b	71
	מואב	MOAB	555d	2 a
	מואב	MOAB	555d	1
	עד	AS FAR AS	724b	12a a
19 38	אב	FATHER	3c	4 b
	בן	SON	120a	1
	בן	SON	120d	1 jb
	בנעמי	BEN-AMMI	122c	
	יום	DAY	401b	71
	עד	AS FAR AS	724b	12a a
	עמון	AMMON	769d	
	צעיר	YOUNG	859a	2
20 1	גור	SOJOURN	157d	1
	גרר	GERAR	176b	
	ה	THE	208a	2 a
	ישב	DWELL	443a	3
	נגב	SOUTH-COUNTRY	616a	1 a
	נסע	JOURNEY	652b	3
	קדש	KADESH	873d	1
	שור	SHUR	1004b	
20 2	אבמלך	ABIMELECH	4b	1
	אחות	SISTER	27d	1
	אל	TO	40c	6
	גרר	GERAR	176b	
	לקח	TAKE	543b	4 e2
	מלך	KING	573a	1
	שרה	SARAH	979a	
20 3	אבמלך	ABIMELECH	4b	1
	בעט	MARRY	127a	1
	בעל	OWNER	127b	12
	הנה	BEHOLD	243d	
	הנה	BEHOLD	244b	B b
	ו	AND	253c	1 k
	חלום	DREAM	321c	1
	לילה	NIGHT	538d	1
	לקח	TAKE	543b	4 e2
	מות	DIE	559d	2 b
	על	UPON	754b	21f b
20 4	אבמלך	ABIMELECH	4b	1
	אדון	LORD	11b	3 2a
	גם	ALSO	169b	2
	הרג	KILL	247b	2
	צדיק	JUST	843a	3 a
	קרב	COME NEAR	897b	1 a
20 5	אח	BROTHER	26b	1
	אחות	SISTER	27d	1
	הוא	HE, SHE, IT	*214d	
	הוא	HE, SHE, IT	215b	1 a
	הוא	HE, SHE, IT	215c	1 b
	זה	THIS	260c	1a
	כף	HOLLOW OF THE HAND	496c	1 d7
	לא	NOT	520b	4 ba

Ch v.	Heb	Eng	Page	Sec
	לבב	HEART	523d	2 6a
	נקיון	INNOCENCY	667d	1
	תם	INTEGRITY	1070d	3
20 6	גם	ALSO	169c	4
	זה	THIS	260c	1 a
	חטא	MISS A GOAL OR WAY	307a	2 b
	חלום	DREAM	321c	2 a
	חשך	WITHHOLD	362b	1 b
	כן	SO	487a	3 f
	ל	TO	517d	7 bc
	לבב	HEART	523d	2 6a
	מן	FROM	583a	7 b
	נגע	TOUCH	619a	3
	נתן	GIVE	679a	1 g
	תם	INTEGRITY	1070d	3
20 7	אין	NOT	34b	2 c
	בעד	ON BEHALF OF	126c	2
	חיה	LIVE	311a	1 b
	מות	DIE	560a	2 b
	נביא	PROPHET	611c	1
	עתה	NOW	774b	2 b
	פלל	INTERVENE	813b	1
	שוב	TURN BACK	999a	1 d
	שוב	TURN BACK	999b	1 d
20 8	אזן	EAR	24a	2 a
	בקר	MORNING	134b	1 h
	דבר	SPEAK	181c	1 a
	דבר	WORD	183b	3 2
	ירא	FEAR	431a	1 a
	מאד	EXCEEDINGLY	*547b	2 a
	קרא	CALL	895c	5 a
20 9	בוא	COME	99c	2 a
	גדול	GREAT	153a	3
	חטא	MISS A GOAL OR WAY	306d	2 a
	חטאה	SIN	308b	1
	כי	THAT	472c	1 f
	ל	TO	*510d	1 d
	מה	WHAT	552d	1 ac
	מה	WHAT	553a	1 db
	ממלכה	KINGDOM	575a	1
	על	UPON	756c	27a b
	עשה	DO	793d	1 1a 2
	עשה	DO	795b	1 b
	קרא	CALL	895c	5 a
20 10	מה	WHAT	552c	1 a
	עשה	DO	793d	1 1a 1
	ראה	TO SEE	907b	3
20 11	אמר	SAY	56b	2
	דבר	WORD	184a	4 8
	הרג	KILL	247a	1 a
	יראה	FEAR	432a	3
	מקום	STANDING PLACE	880a	3 a
	רק	ONLY	956c	2 e
20 12	אח	BROTHER	26b	1
	אחות	SISTER	27d	1
	אחות	SISTER	*27d	2
	אך	HOWBEIT	36c	2 a
	אם	MOTHER	51c	1
	אם	MOTHER	51d	1
	אמנה	VERILY	53d	
	אשה	WOMAN	61b	2
	בת	DAUGHTER	123a	1
	בת	DAUGHTER	123a	1
	בת	DAUGHTER	123b	1 d
	היה	BECOME	226c	2 2f
20 13	אח	BROTHER	26b	1
	אל	TO	40d	1
	אמר	SAY	56b	1
	אשר	PARTICLE OF RELATION	81d	2
	הוא	HE, SHE, IT	216a	3 a
	היה	COME TO PASS	224c	2 a1 ah
	זה	THIS	261a	3
	חסד	GOODNESS	338c	1 1
	כאשר	WHEN	455c	3
	ל	TO	514b	5 fa
	עם	WITH	767d	1 d
	מקום	STANDING PLACE	879d	2 b1
	שם	THERE	1027b	3 a
	שם	THERE	1027c	3 b
	תעה	ERR	1073c	1
20 14	בקר	CATTLE	133b	1 a
	צאן	SMALL CATTLE	838b	1 a4
	שרה	SARAH	979a	
	שוב	TURN BACK	999a	1 d
	שפחה	MAID	1046c	1
20 15	טוב	PLEASANT	373d	2 b
	פנה	FACE	817a	24a f
20 16	אח	BROTHER	26b	1
	אלף	THOUSAND	49a	1 a
	את	WITH	86a	1 c
	הנה	BEHOLD	243d	
	יכח	REASON	407a	
	כל	ALL	482c	2
	כסות	COVERING	492b	2
	כסף	SILVER	494b	8 b
	נתן	GIVE	678b	1 b
	עין	EYE	744d	3 d
	שרה	SARAH	979a	
	אל	TO	40a	3 b
20 17	אמה	MAID	51a	1
	פלל	INTERVENE	813b	1
	רפא	HEAL	950c	1
20 18	עד	BEHIND	*126c	1 b

Ch v.	Heb	Eng	Page	Sec
	דבר	WORD	184a	4 8
	ל	TO	512d	5 ac
	עצר	RESTRAIN	783c	1
	רחם	WOMB	933b	1
	שרה	SARAH	979a	
21 1	כאשר	AS	455b	1 a
	פקד	ATTEND TO	823b	A 2
	שרה	SARAH	979a	
	שרה	SARAH	979a	
21 2	דבר	SPEAK	181b	3 d
	הרה	CONCEIVE	247d	1
	זקנים	OLD AGE	279a	
	מועד	APPOINTED TIME	417c	1 a
	שרה	SARAH	979a	
21 3	ה	THE	209c	3
	ילד	BE BORN	408d	
	יצחק	ISAAC	850c	
	שרה	SARAH	979a	
21 4	מול	CIRCUMCIZE	557d	
	יצחק	ISAAC	850c	
	שמנה	EIGHT	1033a	1
21 5	את	MARK OF THE ACCUSATIVE	85a	1 b
	ילד	BE BORN	408d	
	מאה	HUNDRED	548b	1 d6
	יצחק	ISAAC	850c	
	את	ADDENDA ET CORRIGENDA	1121b	
21 6	צחק	LAUGHTER	850b	
	צחק	LAUGH	850b	
	יצחק	ISAAC	850c	
	שרה	SARAH	979a	
21 7	בן	SON	121b	2
	זקנים	OLD AGE	279a	
	ינק	NURSE	413c	
	מלל	SPEAK	576b	
	שרה	SARAH	979a	
21 8	גדל	GROW UP	152b	1 a
	ילד	CHILD	409b	A
	משתה	FEAST	1059d	1
21 9	הגר	HAGAR	212b	
	מצרי	EGYPTIAN	596a	
	צחק	LAUGH	850b	
	צחק	LAUGH	850b	2
21 10	אמה	MAID	51a	1
	גרש	DRIVE OUT	176d	
	עם	WITH	767c	1 b
21 11	אודה	CAUSE	15c	
	מאד	EXCEEDINGLY	547b	2 a
	עין	EYE	744d	3 c
	רעע	BE EVIL	949c	1
	אמה	MAID	51a	1
21 12	זרע	SOWING	282c	4 b
	נער	YOUTH	655a	1 c
	עין	EYE	744d	3 c
	על	UPON	754b	21f b
	קרא	CALL	896c	6 d7
	קשת	BOW	906c	1 d
	רעע	BE EVIL	949c	1
	שרה	SARAH	979a	
21 13	אמה	MAID	51a	1
	גוי	NATION	156c	1 a
	הוא	HE, SHE, IT	216a	3 a
	זרע	SOWING	282d	4 c
	שם	TO PLACE	964b	5 a
21 14	אל	TO	39c	1
	בארשבע	BEERSHEBA	92a	
	בקר	MORNING	134b	1 h
	מדבר	WILDERNESS	185a	3 b
	הגר	HAGAR	212b	
	חמת	WATERSKIN	333a	
	ילד	CHILD	409b	A
	נתן	GIVE	678b	1 a
	על	UPON	756b	27a a
	שכם	SHOULDER	1014b	1 a
	שלח	SEND	1019a	1 b
	תעה	ERR	1073c	1
21 15	חמת	WATERSKIN	333a	
	ילד	CHILD	409b	A
	כלה	BE FINISHED	477c	2 a
	שיח	BUSH	967b	
	שלך	THROW	1021a	1 b
	תחת	UNDERNEATH	1065b	2 l
21 16	אל	NOT	39a	A a
	בכה	WEEP	113c	1
	מטה	HURL	377b	
	ילד	CHILD	409b	A
	ישב	SIT	442c	1 a
	מן	FROM	578d	1 c
	נגד	IN FRONT	617d	2 ca
	נשא	LIFT	670c	1 b 5
	קול	VOICE	876d	1 a
	קול	VOICE	877a	1 a
	קשת	BOW	906c	1 d
	ראה	TO SEE	908a	8 a3
	רחק	BE DISTANT	935a	1
21 17	אשר	PARTICLE OF RELATION	82c	4 bg
	הגר	HAGAR	212b	
	ירא	FEAR	431a	1 a
	מלאך	MESSENGER	521d	3
	מה	WHAT	552d	1 ac
	שם	THERE	1027b	1 b
	שמי	HEAVENS	1030a	2 a
	שמע	HEAR	1034a	2 a
	שמע	HEAR	1034b	2 f

GENESIS

Ch	v.	Heb	Eng	Page	Sec
21	18	גוי	NATION	156c	1 a
		חזק	BE FIRM	305a	6 a
		נשא	LIFT	670a	1 a
		קום	STAND	878b	6 b
		שום	TO PLACE	964b	5 a
21	19	באר	WELL	91c	1
		חמת	WATERSKIN	333a	
		מי	WATER	565b	1 a
		מלא	FILL	570c	1
		עין	EYE	744b	1 j
		פקח	OPEN	824d	1 b
		שקה	GIVE TO DRINK	1052c	2
21	20	גדל	GROW UP	152b	1 a
		היה	BE	227b	3 4d b
		קשת	BOWMAN	906c	
		רבה	SHOOT	916c	
		רמה	SHOOT	941a	1
21	21	אם	MOTHER	51d	1
		ארץ	EARTH	76a	2a
		לקח	TAKE	543b	4 e1
		פארן	PARAN	803a	
21	22	אבימלך	ABIMELECH	4b	1
		הוא	HE, SHE, IT	216d	7
		היה	COME TO PASS	224c	2 a1 ag
		עם	WITH	767b	1 a
		עת	TIME	773b	1 a
		פיכל	PHICOL	810a	
		צבא	ARMY	839a	1 a
		שר	CHIEFTAIN	978b	3 a
21	23	אם	IF	50b	1 b2
		גור	SOJOURN	157a	1
		הנה	HITHER	244d	A b
		חסד	GOODNESS	338c	1 1
		נין	OFFSPRING	630c	
		נכד	STIRPS	*644d	
		נכד	PROGENY	645a	
		עתה	NOW	774b	2 b
		שבע	SWEAR	989b	1 a
		שקר	DEAL FALSELY	1055c	
21	24	שבע	SWEAR	989a	1 a
21	25	אבימלך	ABIMELECH	4b	1
		אודה	CAUSE	15c	
		באר	WELL	*91c	1
		באר	WELL	91c	1
		גזל	TEAR AWAY	159d	
		ו	AND	*252b	1 b
		יכח	REPROVE	407a	5 b
		מי	WATER	565b	1 a
		עבד	SLAVE	713d	2
21	26	בלת	EXCEPT	116c	2
		ה	THE	207b	1 ca
		מי	WHO	566c	C
21	27	בקר	CATTLE	133b	1 a
		ברית	COVENANT	136b	1 1
		כרת	CUT	503d	4
		צאן	SMALL CATTLE	838b	1 a4
21	28	בד	SEPARATION	94c	1 b
		כבשה	EWE-LAMBS	461a	
		נצב	STAND	662c	1
		שבע	SEVEN	988a	1 a
		שבע	SEVEN	988b	5 c
21	29	אלה	THESE	41c	C
		הוא	HE, SHE, IT	*216c	4 bb
		הם	THEY	241c	4 bb
		כבשה	EWE-LAMBS	461a	
		נצב	STAND	662c	1
21	30	את	MARK OF THE AC-CUSATIVE	85a	1 a
		באר	WELL	91c	1
		באר-שבע	BEERSHEBA	92a	
		חפר	DIG	343c	1 a
		כבשה	EWE-LAMBS	461a	
		כי	THAT	471d	1 b
		עבור	FOR THE SAKE OF	721a	2
		עדה	TESTIMONY	729d	
21	31	באר-שבע	BEERSHEBA	92a	
		כן	SO	487b	3 f
		שבע	SWEAR	989a	1 a
		שם	THERE	1027a	1 a
21	32	באר-שבע	BEERSHEBA	92a	
		ברית	COVENANT	136b	1 1
		כרת	CUT	503d	4
		פיכל	PHICOL	810a	
		פלשתי	PHILISTINE	814c	
		צבא	ARMY	839a	1 a
		שר	CHIEFTAIN	978b	3 a
		שוב	TURN BACK	997a	3 a
21	33	אל	GOD	42c	6 c
		אשל	TAMARISK TREE	79b	
		באר-שבע	BEERSHEBA	92a	
		יהוה	YAHWEH	218c	1
		יהוה	YAHWEH	218c	1
		נטע	PLANT	642b	1
		עולם	LONG DURATION	762b	2 c
		שם	NAME	1028b	3
21	34	גור	SOJOURN	157d	1
		יום	DAY	399c	5 b
		פלשתי	PHILISTINE	814c	
		רב	MUCH	913a	1 b
22	1	אחר	AFTER	29d	2 b
		דבר	WORD	183c	4 4
		היה	COME TO PASS	224d	1 2a 1b
		הנה	BEHOLD	243d	
		הנה	BEHOLD	244a	A
		נסה	TEST	650b	3 a
22	2	אב	FATHER	3b	1

Ch	v.	Heb	Eng	Page	Sec
		אהב	LOVE	12d	1
		אמר	SAY	56a	1
		ארץ	EARTH	76a	2 b
		הלך	WALK	231a	1 d3 ga
		הלך	WALK	231d	1 1d 5h
		הר	MOUNTAIN	249c	1 a
		יחיד	ONLY ONE	402d	1
		ל	TO	515d	5 ib
		מריה	MORIAH	599a	
		נא	PART OF EN-TREATY	609a	1
		עלה	GO UP	749d	8
		עלה	WHOLE BURNT OF-FERING	750c	
22	3	אמר	SAY	56a	1
		בקע	CLEAVE	132a	
		בקר	MORNING	134b	1 h
		הלך	WALK	230d	1 d3 ga
		חבש	BIND	289d	1 c
		חמור	HE-ASS	331b	3
		עץ	TREE	782a	2 d
22	4	מקום	STANDING PLACE	880b	4
		ו	AND	254d	5 b
		מקום	STANDING PLACE	880b	4
		רחק	DISTANT	935c	2 a1
22	5	הלך	WALK	231a	1 d3 gc
		חמור	HE-ASS	331b	3
		ישב	REMAIN	442d	2 a
		כה	THUS	462b	2
		נער	YOUTH	655a	1 c
		פה	HERE	805d	1 a
		שחה	BOW DOWN	1005c	2 c
22	6	מאכלת	KNIFE	38c	
		אש	FIRE	77c	3
		הלך	WALK	230a	1 1a
		חמור	HE-ASS	*331b	3
		יד	HAND	391a	5 c4
		יחדו	TOGETHER	403b	A
		על	UPON	756b	27 a a
		עץ	TREE	782a	2 d
22	7	איה	WHERE	32c	1
		אמר	SAY	56a	1
		אמר	SAY	56b	1
		אש	FIRE	77c	3
		הנה	BEHOLD	243d	
		הנה	BEHOLD	244a	A
		ל	TO	515a	5 ha
		עץ	TREE	782a	2 d
		שה	A SHEEP	962a	1
22	8	הלך	WALK	230a	1 1a
		יחדו	TOGETHER	403b	A
		ראה	TO SEE	907d	6 g
		שה	A SHEEP	962a	1
22	9	בנה	BUILD	124c	1 at
		מזבח	ALTAR	258b	1
		מזבח	ALTAR	259a	1
		מן	FROM	578d	1 c
		מעל	ABOVE	751c	1 b
		על	UPON	756b	27 a a
		עץ	TREE	782a	2 d
		עקד	BIND	785b	
		ערך	ARRANGE	789c	1 b
		מקום	STANDING PLACE	880b	4
22	10	מאכלת	KNIFE	38c	
		שחט	SLAUGHTER	1006b	3
22	11	הנה	BEHOLD	243d	
		הנה	BEHOLD	244a	A
		מלאך	MESSENGER	521d	3
		שמי	HEAVENS	1030a	2 a
22	12	אל	NOT	39a	A a
		אל	TO	40a	A
		חשך	WITHHOLD	362b	1 a
		ידע	KNOW	393c	1 a
		יחיד	ONLY ONE	402d	1
		כי	THAT	471c	1 a
		מאומה	ANYTHING	548d	
		נער	YOUTH	655a	1 c
		עתה	NOW	774a	1 a
		שלח	SEND	1018c	3 a
22	13	איל	RAM	18a	2
		אחז	GRASP	28c	1
		אחר	BEHIND	29d	1 a
		הלך	WALK	233d	1 5b
		סבך	THICKET	687c	
		עלה	GO UP	749d	8
		עלה	WHOLE BURNT OF-FERING	750c	
		קרן	HORN	901d	1 a
		תחת	INSTEAD	1065d	2 2b a
22	14	אמר	SAY	56c	1
		אשר	THAT	83c	8 b
		יהוה	YAHWEH	219b	2 3
		מקום	STANDING PLACE	880b	4
		ראה	TO SEE	907d	6 g
		ראה	TO SEE	908b	1 a
22	15	מלאך	MESSENGER	521d	3
		שמי	HEAVENS	1030a	2 a
		שני	SECOND	1041c	
22	16	דבר	WORD	183c	4 6
		חשך	WITHHOLD	362b	1 a
		יחיד	ONLY ONE	402d	1
		כי	THAT	471d	1 a
		כי	THAT	472a	1 c
		נאם	UTTERANCE	610b	1
		יען	ON ACCOUNT OF	774d	2 a1
		שבע	SWEAR	989b	2

Ch	v.	Heb	Eng	Page	Sec
22	17	ברך	BLESS	139a	2 a
		ו	AND	252b	1 b
		זרע	SOWING	282c	4 b
		חול	SAND	297d	A
		חול	SAND	297d	C
		ים	SEA	411a	8 a
		ירש	TAKE POSSESSION	439c	1 a
		ד	LIKE	453d	1 b
		כוכב	STAR	457a	
		כי	THAT	472d	1 e
		רבה	BECOME MANY	915b	
		רבה	BECOME MANY	915d	1 e1
		שפה	SPEECH	974a	3
		שמי	HEAVENS	1029d	1 a
		שער	GATE	1044c	1 a
22	18	ארץ	EARTH	76a	1 a
		ברך	BLESS	139c	
		גוי	NATION	156c	1
		זרע	SOWING	282c	4 b
		עקב	CONSEQUENCE	784d	1
		קול	VOICE	877b	3 b
22	19	באר-שבע	BEERSHEBA	92a	
		הלך	WALK	231a	1 d3 ga
		הלך	WALK	234a	1 5c
22	20	דבר	WORD	183c	4 4
		היה	COME TO PASS	224c	2 a1 ai
		מלכה	MILCAH	574c	1
		נגד	BE CONSPICUOUS	617a	1
		נחור	NAHOR	637d	2
22	21	ארם	ARAM	74b	2
		בוז	BUZ	100c	1
		חזו	HAZO	*304a	
		עוץ	UZ	734b	1 b
		קמואל	KEMUEL	887d	1
22	22	בתואל	BETHUEL	143d	
		חזו	HAZO	303d	
		ידלף	JIDLAPH	393b	
		כשד	CHESED	505a	
		מעכה	MAACAH	590d	1 a
		פלדש	PILDASH	811c	
22	23	ילד	BEGET	408c	2 a
		מלכה	MILCAH	574c	1
		נחור	NAHOR	637d	2
		רבקה	REBEKAH	918d	
		שמנה	EIGHT	1033a	1 b
22	24	טבה	TEBAH	370d	
		מעכה	MAACAH	*591a	3
		פלגש	CONCUBINE	811c	1
		ראומה	REUMAH	910b	
		תחש	TAHASH	1065a	
23	1	היה	BE	227b	3 4b
		חיים	LIFE	313a	1
		חיים	LIFE	313a	1
		מאה	HUNDRED	548b	2 a2
		שרה	SARAH	979a	
		שבע	SEVEN	988b	5 a4
		שנה	YEAR	1040b	
23	2	בכה	WEEP	113c	4
		חברון	HEBRON	289b	
		ספד	WAIL	704c	
		קרית-ארבע	FOURFOLD CITY	900a	
		שרה	SARAH	979a	
23	3	בן	SON	120d	1 ja
		חת	HETH	366c	A
		פנה	FACE	819a	2 8a
		קום	STAND	877d	1 a
23	4	אחזה	POSSESSION	28d	
		אנכי	I	59c	
		גר	SOJOURNER	158a	1
		גר	SOJOURNER	*158c	2
		תושב	SOJOURNER	444c	
		עם	WITH	768b	3
		פנה	FACE	818a	2 5a b
		קבר	BURY	868c	
23	5	קצבער	GRAVE	868d	
		בן	SON	120d	1 ja
		חת	HETH	366c	A
		לו	IF	*530b	2
23	6	ענה	ANSWER	773a	1 d
		אדון	LORD	11b	3 1d
		כלא	RESTRAIN	476b	3
		מן	FROM	583a	7 ba
		נשיא	PRINCE	672b	3
		עפרון	EPHRON	780b	1
		קבר	BURY	868c	
		קבר	BURY	868c	
		שמע	HEAR	1034a	1 i
		תוך	MIDST	1063d	
23	7	ארץ	EARTH	76b	4 a
		בן	SON	120d	1 ja
		עם	PEOPLE	766d	5 c
		קום	STAND	877d	1 a
		שחה	BOW DOWN	1005b	1 c
23	8	את	WITH	86c	3 b
		דבר	SPEAK	181b	3 d
		נפש	SOUL	661b	8
		עפרון	EPHRON	780b	1
		פגע	MEET	803c	4
		פנה	FACE	818a	2 5a b
		צחר	ZOHAR	850c	1
		קבר	BURY	868c	
		שמע	HEAR	1034a	1 i
23	9	אחזה	POSSESSION	28d	
		אשר	PARTICLE OF RE-LATION	83a	7 b

Ch v.	Heb	Eng	Page	Sec
	ב	IN	90b	3 3b
	כסף	SILVER	494c	8 e
	כסף	SILVER	494d	9
	מכפלה	MACHPELAH	495d	
	מלא	FULL	571a	
	קצבר	GRAVE	868d	
	קצה	END	892a	1
23 10	שדה	FIELD	961d	2 b
	אזן	EAR	24a	2 a
	בוא	COME	97d	1
	בן	SON	120d	1 ja
	חתי	HITTITE	366c	1
	חת	HETH	366c	A
	ישב	DWELL	443a	3
	ל	TO	514c	5 fd
	ענה	ANSWER	773a	1 d
	עפרון	EPHRON	780b	1
	שער	GATE	1045a	2 a
23 11	אדון	LORD	11b	3 1d
	בן	SON	120d	1 ja
	לא	NOT	519a	1 ad b
	עין	EYE	745a	5
	עם	PEOPLE	766d	5 a
	שדה	FIELD	961d	2 b
	שמע	HEAR	1034a	1 i
23 12	ארץ	EARTH	76b	4 a
	עם	PEOPLE	766d	5 c
	פנה	FACE	817c	24b b
	שחה	BOW DOWN	1005b	1 c
23 13	אזן	EAR	24a	2 a
	אך	HOWBEIT	36c	2 a
	אם	IF	50b	1 b3
	ארץ	EARTH	76b	4 a
	כסף	SILVER	494c	8 e
	כסף	SILVER	494d	9
	לו	IF	530b	2
	נתן	GIVE	679b	1 n
	עם	PEOPLE	766d	5 c
	עפרון	EPHRON	780b	1
	קבר	BURY	868c	
	שדה	FIELD	961d	2 b
	שם	THERE	1027b	3
	שמע	HEAR	1034a	1 i
23 14	ענה	ANSWER	773a	1 d
23 15	אדון	LORD	11b	3 1d
	ארץ	EARTH	76b	2 d
	הוא	HE, SHE, IT	216a	3 b
	כסף	SILVER	494b	8 a
	לו	IF	*530b	2
	מה	WHAT	553a	1 da
	שמע	HEAR	1034a	1 i
23 16	אזן	EAR	24a	2 a
	בן	SON	120d	1 ja
	דבר	SPEAK	181c	4 b
	חת	HETH	366c	A
	כסף	SILVER	494b	8 a
	כסף	SILVER	494c	9
	ל	TO	512b	5 aa
	סחר	GO AROUND	695c	1
	עבר	PASS OVER	717d	4 e
	עפרון	EPHRON	780b	1
	שקל	WEIGH	1053c	2
23 17	גבול	BOUNDARY	148a	1 c
	קום	STAND	278b	7 b
	מכפלה	MACHPELAH	495d	
	ממרא	MAMRE	577b	3
	סביב	ROUND ABOUT	686d	1 b
	עפרון	EPHRON	780b	1
	פנה	FACE	817c	24 d
23 18	בוא	COME	97d	1
	בן	SON	120d	1 ja
	חת	HETH	366c	A
	עין	EYE	745a	5
	מקנה	PURCHASE	889c	3
	שער	GATE	1045a	2 a
23 19	אחר	AFTER	30a	2 b
	אל	TO	39d	2
	חברון	HEBRON	289b	
	מכפלה	MACHPELAH	495d	
	פנה	FACE	818d	27a d
	קבר	BURY	868c	
	קבר	BURY	868c	
	שרה	SARAH	979a	
23 20	אחוזה	POSSESSION	28d	
	את	WITH	86d	4 b
	בן	SON	120d	1 ja
	חת	HETH	366c	A
	קצבר	GRAVE	868d	
	קום	STAND	878b	7 b
24 1	בוא	COME	98b	1 k
	ברך	BLESS	139a	2 a
	זקן	BE OLD	278b	
	יום	DAY	399b	4 a
	כל	ALL	482d	2 ba
24 2	בית	HOUSE	109b	5 a
	זקן	OLD	278c	2 a
	יד	HAND	389c	1 d
	ירך	THIGH	438a	1 b
	משל	RULE	605d	1
	נא	PART OF EN-TREATY	609a	1
	שום	TO PLACE	963c	1 d
	תחת	UNDERNEATH	1065b	2 1
24 3	אלהים	GOD	44c	4 bb
	בת	DAUGHTER	123b	1 i
	ישב	DWELL	443a	3

Ch v.	Heb	Eng	Page	Sec
	כי	BUT	474b	3 e
	כנעני	CANAANITE	489a	2 b
	ל	TO	515b	5 hb a
	קרב	INWARD PART	899a	1 fl
	שבע	SWEAR	989c	1
	שמי	HEAVENS	*1030b	1 a
24 4	הלך	WALK	231a	1 d3 ga
	מולדת	KINDRED	409d	1
	ל	TO	515b	5 hb a
	לקח	TAKE	543b	4 e1
	משפחה	CLAN	*1046d	1 a
24 5	אבה	BE WILLING		2c
	אולי	PERADVENTURE	19c	1
	ה	INTERROG PART	209d	1 b
	הלך	WALK	231c	1 1d 5z
	יצא	GO OUT	422d	1 a
	ל	TO	517d	7 bc
	שוב	TURN BACK	998d	1 a
	שם	THERE	1027c	4 b
24 6	ל	TO	516a	5 ic
	פן	LEST	814d	1
	שם	THERE	1027b	3 a
	שמר	KEEP	1037b	1
24 7	אלהים	GOD	44c	4 bb
	אמר	SAY	56b	1
	דבר	SPEAK	181b	3 c
	הוא	HE, SHE, IT	215d	2 a
	זרע	SOWING	282c	4 b
	מולדת	KINDRED	409d	1
	ל	TO	510d	1 b
	מלאך	MESSENGER	521d	3
	לקח	TAKE	543b	4 e1
	שבע	SWEAR	989c	2
	שלח	SEND	1018c	2
	שם	THERE	1027c	4 a
	שמי	HEAVENS	*1030b	2 a
24 8	אבה	BE WILLING		2c
	אם	IF	49c	1 al a
	הלך	WALK	231c	1 1d 5z
	זה	THIS	260d	2 ba
	לא	NOT	518c	1 aa
	נקה	BE CLEAN	667b	4
	רק	ONLY	956c	2 b
	שבועה	OATH	990a	1 a
24 9	אדון	LORD	11a	2 1b
	ירך	THIGH	438a	1 b
	על	UPON	753d	2 1f
	שום	TO PLACE	963c	1 d
	שבע	SWEAR	989b	1 a
24 10	ארם	ARAM	74c	B
	הלך	WALK	231a	1 d3 ga
	הלך	WALK	234a	1 5c
	טוב	GOOD THINGS	375c	2
	נחור	NAHOR	637d	2
24 11	אל	TO	39c	1
	אל	TO	40c	8
	באר	WELL	91c	1
	באר	WELL	91c	1
	ברך	BLESS	139b	
	חוץ	THE OUTSIDE	300a	1 bd
	מי	WATER	565b	1 a
	עת	TIME	773c	1 b
	ערב	SUNSET	787d	1 a
	שאב	DRAW	980c	
24 12	אדון	LORD	11b	3 1a
	אלהים	GOD	44b	4 ba
	חסד	GOODNESS	338c	1 1
	עם	WITH	767d	1 d
	עשה	DO	794b	13
	פנה	FACE	817a	24
	קרה	ENCOUNTER	899d	1
24 13	אנכי	I	59c	
	באר	WELL	*91c	1
	בת	DAUGHTER	123b	1 i
	הנה	BEHOLD	243d	
	מי	WATER	565b	1 a
	נצב	STAND	662a	1 a
	עין	SPRING	745b	
	על	UPON	755d	2 6a
	שאב	DRAW	980c	
	את	MARK OF THE AC-CUSATIVE	85a	1 a
	היה	COME TO PASS	225b	1 2b bd
	חסד	GOODNESS	338c	1 1
	יכח	APPOINT	407a	2
	כד	JAR	461c	
	כי	THAT	471c	1 a
	נטה	INCLINE	640d	3 a
	נערה	GIRL	655b	1
	עבד	SLAVE	714a	3
	עשה	DO	794b	13
	שקה	GIVE TO DRINK	1052c	2
	שתה	DRINK	1059b	1a
24 15	בתואל	BETHUEL	143d	
	היה	COME TO PASS	224d	1 2a 1c
	טרם	NOT YET	382c	1
	ילד	BE BORN	408d	
	כד	JAR	461c	
	כלה	FINISH	478b	1 c
	מלכה	MILCAH	574c	1
	נחור	NAHOR	637d	2
	עד	UNTIL	725b	2 2d
	רבקה	REBEKAH	918d	
	שכם	SHOULDER	1014b	1 a
24 16	איש	MAN	35d	
	באר	WELL	*91c	1

Ch v.	Heb	Eng	Page	Sec
	בתולה	VIRGIN	143d	
	טוב	PLEASANT	373c	1 a
	ידע	KNOW	394b	3
	ירד	GO DOWN	433a	1 g
	כד	JAR	461c	
	מאד	EXCEEDINGLY	547b	2 a
	מלא	FILL	570c	1
	נערה	GIRL	655b	1
	עין	SPRING	745a	
	מראה	VISION	909d	1 b
24 17	כד	JAR	461c	
	מעט	A FEW	590a	1 b
	קרא	ENCOUNTER	896d	1
	רוץ	RUN	930b	1
	שום	TO PLACE	963b	1 b
24 18	אדון	LORD	11b	3 1k
	ו	AND	254a	2 a
	ירד	LET DOWN	434b	3
	כד	JAR	461c	
	מהר	HASTEN	555a	2
	שקה	GIVE TO DRINK	1052c	2
24 19	אם	IF	50c	1 cd
	כלה	FINISH	478b	1 c
	עד	UNTIL	725a	2 1b a
	שאב	DRAW	980c	
	שקה	GIVE TO DRINK	1052c	2
	שתה	DRINK	1059c	1 d
24 20	באר	WELL	91c	1
	כד	JAR	461c	
	מהר	HASTEN	555a	2
	עוד	STILL	729b	1 b
	ערה	BE NAKED	788d	2
	רוץ	RUN	930b	1
	שאב	DRAW	980c	
	שקת	WATER-TROUGH	1052d	
24 21	דרך	JOURNEY	203a	2
	ה	INTERROG PART	210b	2 b
	חרש	BE SILENT	361b	1 a
	ל	TO	510c	1 a
	לא	NOT	519a	1 ad b
	צלח	ADVANCE	852c	1
	שאה	GAZE	981b	
24 22	בקע	HALF	132c	
	זהב	GOLD	263a	6
	זהב	GOLD	263b	9 a
	יד	HAND	389a	1 b
	כאשר	WHEN	455c	3
	כלה	FINISH	478b	1 c
	נזם	RING	633d	1
	על	UPON	756b	27a a
	עשר	TEN	796d	2 b
	צמיד	BRACELET	855b	
	שנים	TWO	1041a	1 a
	משקל	WEIGHT	1054a	
	שרה	BRACELET	1057b	
	שתה	DRINK	1059c	1 d
24 23	את	THOU	61d	
	בית	HOUSE	108d	1 a
	בת	DAUGHTER	123b	1 h
	יש	THERE IS	441c	2 b
	יש	BE	*442a	2 ch
	מי	WHO	566b	8
	נגד	BE CONSPICUOUS	616d	1
	מקום	STANDING PLACE	880b	5 a
24 24	בת	DAUGHTER	123b	1 h
	בתואל	BETHUEL	143d	
	מלכה	MILCAH	574c	1
	נחור	NAHOR	637d	2
24 25	מספוא	FODDER	704c	
	עם	WITH	768b	3 b
	מקום	STANDING PLACE	880b	5 a
	רב	MUCH	913b	1 f
	תבן	STRAW	1062a	
24 26	קדד	BOW DOWN	869a	
	שחה	BOW DOWN	1005c	2 a
24 27	אלהים	GOD	44b	4 ba
	אמת	FIRMNESS	54b	3 b
	ברך	BLESS	138c	2 a
	חסד	GOODNESS	339a	2 2
	נחה	LEAD	634d	
	עזב	LEAVE	737a	1 g
	על	UPON	756b	27a a
	מעם	FROM WITH	769a	B
24 28	אם	MOTHER	51d	1
	ך	LIKE	454a	1 b
	נערה	GIRL	655b	1
	רוץ	RUN	930b	1
24 29	חוץ	THE OUTSIDE	299d	1 a
	לבן	LABAN	526c	
	עין	SPRING	745a	
	רוץ	RUN	930b	1
24 30	אחות	SISTER	27d	1
	הנה	BEHOLD	244b	C
	יד	HAND	389a	1 b
	ך	LIKE	454a	3 b
	נזם	RING	633d	1
	עין	SPRING	745a	
	על	UPON	753a	2 la a
	על	UPON	755d	2 6a
	על	UPON	756b	2 6c
	צמיד	BRACELET	855b	
24 31	בוא	COME	97d	1
	ברך	BLESS	138d	2 b
	חוץ	THE OUTSIDE	299d	1 b
	מה	HOW	554a	4 d
	פנה	TURN	815c	

GENESIS

Ch v.	Heb	Eng	Page	Sec
24 32	מקום	STANDING PLACE	880b	5 a
	מי	WATER	565b	1 a
	מספוא	FODDER	704c	
	פתח	OPEN	835c	1
	רחץ	WASH OFF	934c	1
	תבן	STRAW	1062a	
24 33	אם	IF	50c	1 cd
	דבר	SPEAK	181a	2
	עד	UNTIL	725a	2 lb a
	פנה	FACE	817c	24b f
	שום	TO PLACE	964d	
24 34	זהב	GOLD	262d	2
24 35	בקר	CATTLE	133b	1 a
	ברך	BLESS	139a	2 e
	גדל	BECOME GREAT	152b	2 e
	ו	AND	252a	
	זהב	GOLD	263c	1
	חמור	HE-ASS	331b	1
	מאד	EXCEEDINGLY	547b	2 a
	שפחה	MAID	1046c	1
24 36	זקנה	OLD AGE	279a	
	שרה	SARAH	979a	
24 37	בת	DAUGHTER	123b	1 i
	ישב	DWELL	443a	3
	כנעני	CANAANITE	489a	2 b
	שבע	SWEAR	989c	1
24 38	אם	IF	50b	1 b2
	אם	IF	50b	1 b
	אם	IF	50c	1 ce
	הלך	WALK	231a	1 d3 ga
	לקח	TAKE	543b	4 e1
	משפחה	CLAN	1046a	1 a
	לחן	EXCEPT	*1099a	
24 39	אולי	PERADVENTURE	19c	1
	הלך	WALK	231c	1 1d 5z
24 40	אב	FATHER	3c	3
	דרך	JOURNEY	203a	2
	הלך	WALK	236b	2
	מלאך	MESSENGER	521d	3
	לקח	TAKE	543b	4 e1
	צלח	ADVANCE	852c	1
	שלח	SEND	1018c	2 a
	משפחה	CLAN	1046d	1 a
24 41	אז	THEN	23a	1 b
	אלה	OATH	46d	1
	כי	WHEN	473a	2 a
	נקה	BE CLEAN	667b	4
	נקי	FREE FROM	667d	3
	משפחה	CLAN	1046d	1 a
24 42	אלהים	GOD	44b	4 ba
	אם	IF	49d	1 a2
	דרך	JOURNEY	203a	2
	יש	THERE IS	441d	2 ca
	נא	PART OF ENTREATY	609c	4 c
	עין	SPRING	745a	
	צלח	ADVANCE	852c	1
24 43	אנכי	I	59c	
	באר	WELL	*91c	
	היה	COME TO PASS	225b	1 2b f
	הנה	BEHOLD	243d	
	כד	JAR	461c	
	מי	WATER	565b	1 a
	מעט	A FEW	590a	1 b
	נצב	STAND	662a	1 a v
	עין	SPRING	745b	
	עלמה	YOUNG WOMAN	761c	1
	שאב	DRAW	980c	
	שקה	GIVE TO DRINK	1052c	2
24 44	גם	ALSO	169b	1
	יכח	APPOINT	407a	2
	שאב	DRAW	980c	
24 45	באר	WELL	*91c	1
	דבר	SPEAK	181a	3 b
	טרם	NOT YET	382c	1
	ירד	GO DOWN	433a	1 g
	כד	JAR	461c	
	לב	HEART	525c	2 7
	עין	SPRING	745a	
	על	UPON	757c	27c b
	שאב	DRAW	980c	
	שכם	SHOULDER	1014b	1 a
	שקה	GIVE TO DRINK	1052c	2
24 46	ירד	LET DOWN	434b	3
	כד	JAR	461c	
	מהר	HASTEN	555a	2
	שקה	GIVE TO DRINK	1052c	2
24 47	אף	NOSE	60a	1 b
	בת	DAUGHTER	123b	1 h
	בתואל	BETHUEL	143d	
	יד	HAND	389a	1 b
	מי	WHO	566b	B
	מלכה	MILCAH	574c	1
	נום	RING	633d	1
	נחור	NAHOR	637d	2
	צמיד	BRACELET	855d	
	שאל	ASK	981d	2 a
24 48	אלהים	GOD	44b	4 ba
	אמת	FIRMNESS	54a	1
	ברך	BLESS	139a	2
	לקח	TAKE	543b	4 e1
	נחה	LEAD	635a	
	קדד	BOW DOWN	869a	
	שחה	BOW DOWN	1005c	2 a
24 49	או	OR	14d	1
	אם	IF	49d	1 a2
	אמת	FIRMNESS	54a	3 a
	את	WITH	86a	1 db
	חסד	GOODNESS	338d	1 2
	ימן	RIGHT HAND	412a	2 b
	יש	THERE IS	441d	2 ca
	לא	NOT	519a	1 ad a
	על	UPON	757b	27c ab
	עשה	DO	794b	1 3
	פנה	TURN	815a	1 a
	שמאל	LEFT	969d	1
	חסד	ADDENDA ET CORRIGENDA	1123c	
24 50	בתואל	BETHUEL	143d	
	טוב	PLEASANT	374a	2 f
	יכל	BE ABLE	407c	1 b
	יצא	GO OUT	423b	1 g
	לבן	LABAN	526c	
	מן	OUT OF	579d	2 d
	רע	EVIL	948b	2
24 51	היה	BECOME	226b	2 2d
	פנה	FACE	817a	24a f
24 52	כאשר	WHEN	455c	3
	שחה	BOW DOWN	1005c	2 b
24 53	בגד	GARMENT	94a	1
	זהב	GOLD	263a	6
	זהב	GOLD	263c	1
	יצא	BRING OUT	425a	4 b
	כלי	ARTICLE	479c	1
	כסף	SILVER	494b	7
	מגדנה	EXCELLENT THING	550c	
	נתן	GIVE	678b	1 b
24 54	בקר	MORNING	134b	1 h
	עם	WITH	767b	1 a
24 55	או	OR	14d	1
	אחר	AFTERWARDS	29d	1 b
	יום	DAY	399c	5 a
	ישב	REMAIN	442a	2 a
	נערה	GIRL	655b	1
	עשור	A TEN	797c	1 a
24 56	אחר	DELAY	29b	2
	דרך	JOURNEY	203a	2
	הלך	WALK	231b	1 d3 gd
	צלח	ADVANCE	852c	1
	שלח	SEND	1019b	3
24 57	נערה	GIRL	655b	1
	שאל	ASK	982a	2 a
24 59	אחות	SISTER	27d	1
	ינק	NURSE	413c	
	שלח	SEND	1019a	1 d
24 60	אחות	SISTER	27d	1
	אלף	THOUSAND	48d	1 a
	ברך	BLESS	139a	4 b
	זרע	SOWING	282d	4 c
	ירש	TAKE POSSESSION	439c	1 a
	רבבה	MULTITUDE	914b	
	שנא	HATE	971c	3
	שער	GATE	1044c	1 a
	הלך	WALK	231c	1 1d 5z
24 61	נערה	GIRL	655b	2
	רכב	RIDE	938c	1
24 62	באר-לחי-ראי	BEER-LAHAI-ROI	91d	
	בוא	COME	98d	2 e
	ו	AND	253a	1 k
	ישב	DWELL	443a	3
	נגב	SOUTH-COUNTRY	616b	1 a
	יצחק	ISAAC	850c	
24 63	ל	TO	517a	6 a
	ערב	SUNSET	787d	1 a
	פנה	TURN	815a	1 e
	יצחק	ISAAC	850c	
	שדה	FIELD	961b	1 b
	שוח	STROLL	962b	
	שוט	GO ABOUT	1002a	
24 64	נפל	FALL	657d	6
	על	UPON	758c	4 2a
	ה	THE	208d	2 a
24 65	הוא	HE, SHE, IT	*216a	3 a
	הלזה	THIS	229d	
	הלך	WALK	230b	1 1a
	כסה	COVER	492b	1
	מי	WHO	566a	
	צעיף	VEIL	858b	
	שדה	FIELD	961b	1 b
24 66	ספר	COUNT	708a	1
24 67	אהב	LOVE	12d	1
	אם	MOTHER	51d	1
	בוא	COME	99a	1
	היה	BECOME	226c	2 2f
	נחם	CONSOLE ONESELF	637a	3
	יצחק	ISAAC	850c	
	שרה	SARAH	979a	
25 1	ו	AND	254a	2 a
	יסף	DO AGAIN	415c	2 b
	קטורה	KETURAH	882c	
25 2	מדן	MEDAN	193c	
	מדין	MIDIAN	193c	1
	יקשן	ISHBAK	430d	
	ישבק	ISHBAK	990b	
	שוח	SHUAH	1001d	
25 3	אשורם	ASSHURIM	79a	
	דדן	DEDAN	187a	2
	דדן	DEDAN	187a	2
	היה	BE	227a	3 4b
	ילד	BEGET	408c	2 a
	יקשן	JOKSHAN	430d	
	לאמים	LEUMMIM	522c	
	לטושם	LETUSHIM	538c	
	שבא	SHEBA	985b	
25 4	אבידע	ABIDA	4a	
	אלה	THESE	41c	A
	אלדעה	ELDAAH	44d	
	מדין	MIDIAN	193c	1
	חנוך	ENOCH	335c	3
	עיפה	EPHAH	734a	1
	עפר	EPHER	780b	1
	קטורה	KETURAH	882c	
25 6	חי	ALIVE	312a	1 b
	מתנה	GIFT	682b	
	על	UPON	759a	4 2b
	פלגש	CONCUBINE	811c	1
	קדם	FRONT	869c	1 b
	קדם	EASTWARD	870a	
	שלח	SEND	1019a	1 b
25 7	חיים	LIFE	313a	1
	חמש	FIVE	332a	5 b1
	יום	DAY	399a	4 a
	מאה	HUNDRED	548b	1 d6
	שבעים	SEVENTY	988c	3 c
	שנה	YEAR	1040b	
	שנה	YEAR	1040c	
25 8	אסף	GATHER	62d	2 a
	גוע	EXPIRE	157c	
	זקן	OLD	278c	1
	טוב	PLEASANT	374a	4 a
	מות	DIE	*559c	1 a1
	מות	DIE	559c	1 a1
	עם	KINSMAN	769b	
	שבע	SATISFIED	960b	1 b
	שיבה	OLD AGE	966d	2
25 9	אל	TO	39d	2
	חתי	HITTITE	366c	1
	מכפלה	MACHPELAH	495d	
	ממרא	MAMRE	577b	3
	עפרון	EPHRON	780b	1
	פנה	FACE	818d	27a d
	צחר	ZOHAR	850c	1
	קבר	BURY	868c	
25 10	את	WITH	86c	4 a
	בן	SON	120d	1 ja
	חת	HETH	366c	A
	קבר	BURY	868d	
	קנה	ACQUIRE	888d	
	שרה	SARAH	979a	
	שם	THERE	1027b	1
25 11	אחר	AFTER	30a	2 b
	באר-לחי-ראי	BEER-LAHAI-ROI	91d	
	ברך	BLESS	139a	2 a
	מות	DEATH	560d	1
	עם	WITH	768a	2
25 12	הגר	HAGAR	212b	
	תולדות	GENERATIONS	410a	A
	מצרי	EGYPTIAN	596a	
	שרה	SARAH	979a	
	שפחה	MAID	1046c	1
25 13	אדבאל	ADBEEL	9a	
	בכור	FIRST-BORN	114a	1
	מבשם	MIBSAM	142a	1
	תולדות	GENERATIONS	410a	A
	נביות	NEBAIOTH	614a	
	קדר	KEDAR	871b	2
25 14	משא	BABYLON	601c	1
	משמע	MISHMA	1036a	1
25 15	דומה	DUMAH	189a	1
	חדד	HADAD	292c	
	יטור	JETUR	377b	
	נודב	NODAB	*622a	
	נפיש	NAPHISH	661c	
	קדמה	KEDEMAH	870b	
	תימא	TEMA	1066d	
25 16	אמה	TRIBE	52c	
	הם	THEY	241c	4 bg
	חצר	SETTLED ABODE	347b	A
	טירה	ENCAMPMENT	377b	1
	יטור	JETUR	*377b	
	נשיא	PRINCE	672b	3
25 17	אסף	GATHER	62d	2 a
	גוע	EXPIRE	157c	
	חיים	LIFE	313a	1
	מות	DIE	559c	1 a1
	עם	KINSMAN	769b	
	שבע	SEVEN	988b	5 a4
25 18	אח	BROTHER	26b	2
	אשור	ASSYRIA	78d	3
	בוא	COME	98c	2 e
	חוילה	HAVILAH	296d	
	מן	FROM	581d	5 a
	נפל	FALL	657d	6
	פנה	FACE	818d	27a d
	פנה	FACE	818d	27a d
	שור	SHUR	1004b	
	שכן	SETTLE DOWN	1015b	1 a
25 19	תולדות	GENERATIONS	410a	A
25 20	ארמי	ARAMEAN	74c	
	ארם	ARAM	74c	B
	בת	DAUGHTER	123b	1 h
	בתואל	BETHUEL	143d	
	לבן	LABAN	526c	
	פדן	PADDAN	804c	
25 21	הרה	CONCEIVE	247d	1
	ל	TO	514a	5 e
	נכח	FRONT	647b	2 bb
	עקר	BARREN	785d	

Ch	v.	Heb	Eng	Page	Sec
25	22	עתר	PRAY	801c	
		דרש	SEEK	205a	2 a
		הלך	WALK	233d	15a
		זה	THIS	261c	4 e
		מה	HOW	554a	4 d
		קרב	INWARD PART	899a	1 a
		רצץ	CRUSH	954d	
25	23	אמץ	BE STRONG	55a	1
		בטן	WOMB	106a	3
		גוי	NATION	156c	1 a
		לאם	PEOPLE	522c	
		מן	THAN	582c	6 a
		מעה	BELLY	589a	3
		פרד	DIVIDE	825b	1
		צעיר	YOUNG	859a	2
		רב	GREAT	913c	2 c
25	24	בטן	WOMB	106a	3
		יום	TIME	399d	6 a
		מלא	BE FULL	570b	1 b
		תואם	TWIN	1060d	
25	25	אדמוני	RED	10c	
		אדרת	MANTLE	12b	2
		יצא	GO OUT	423c	1 h
		כל	ALL	481b	1 a
		עשו	ESAU	796c	
		ראשון	FIRST	911c	1 a
		שער	HAIR	972b	1
25	26	אחז	GRASP	28b	
		אחר	AFTER	30a	2 b
		יצא	GO OUT	423c	1 h
		עקב	HEEL	784a	A
		עקב	FOLLOW AT THE HEEL	*784b	
		יעקב	JACOB	785a	1
		עשו	ESAU	796c	
		ארבע	FOUR	916d	1 a2
25	27	אהל	TENT	13d	1
		איש	MAN	36a	
		גדל	GROW UP	152b	1 a
		ידע	KNOW	394b	4 b
		ישב	DWELL	443a	3
		ציד	HUNTING	844d	1
		שדה	FIELD	961b	1 d
		שדה	FIELD	961b	1 c
		תם	COMPLETE	1071a	2
25	28	אב	FATHER	3b	1
		אהב	LOVE	12d	1
		פה	MOUTH	804d	1 a
		ציד	GAME	844d	2
25	29	זיד	BOIL UP	267c	1
		נזיד	THING BOILED	268a	
		עיף	FAINT	746a	
		שדה	FIELD	961b	1 c
25	30	אדם	RED	10b	
		אדם	A CONDIMENT	10b	
		אדום	EDOM	10b	1
		כן	SO	487b	3 f
		לעט	SWALLOW	542a	
		עיף	FAINT	746a	
25	31	בכרה	RIGHT OF FIRST-BORN	114c	
		יום	DAY	400d	7 h
		מכר	SELL	569b	
25	32	אנכי	I	59c	
		בכרה	RIGHT OF FIRST-BORN	114c	
		הלך	WALK	234c	2 1
		הנה	BEHOLD	243d	
25	33	בכרה	RIGHT OF FIRST-BORN	114c	
		יום	DAY	400d	7 h
		מכר	SELL	569b	
25	34	בזה	DESPISE	102b	
		בכרה	RIGHT OF FIRST-BORN	114c	
		נזיד	THING BOILED	268a	
		עדשה	LENTILE	727d	
		קום	STAND	877d	1 a
26	1	אבימלך	ABIMELECH	4b	1
		בד	SEPARATION	94d	1 e
		גרר	GERAR	176b	
		היה	BECOME	225c	2 1a
		הלך	WALK	231a	1 d3 ga
		מלך	KING	573a	1
		פלשתי	PHILISTINE	814c	
		רעב	FAMINE	944b	1
26	2	ירד	GO DOWN	432d	1 d
26	3	אל	THESE	41b	
		ארץ	EARTH	76c	5
		ארץ	EARTH	76c	5
		ברך	BLESS	139a	2 a
		גור	SOJOURN	157d	1
		היה	BE	227b	3 4d a
		זרע	SOWING	282c	4 b
		עם	WITH	767c	1 a
		קום	STAND	879a	6 f
		שבועה	OATH	990a	1 a
26	4	אל	THESE	41b	
		ארץ	EARTH	76c	5
		ארץ	EARTH	76c	5
		ברך	BLESS	139c	
		גוי	NATION	156c	1
		זרע	SOWING	282c	4 b
		כוכב	STAR	457a	
		נתן	GIVE	678c	1 b
		נתן	GIVE	679c	1 t
		הא	DEMONSTRATIVE PARTICLE	*1089c	A
26	5	חקה	SOMETHING PRESCRIBED	350b	2 d
		חקה	SOMETHING PRESCRIBED	350b	2 e
		תורה	LAW	436a	2 a
		עקב	CONSEQUENCE	784d	1
		מצוה	COMMANDMENT	846c	2 b2
		קול	VOICE	877b	3 b
		משמרת	GUARD	1038c	3
26	6	גרר	GERAR	176b	
26	7	הרג	KILL	247a	1a
		טוב	PLEASANT	373c	1a
		ירא	FEAR	431b	1 d
		כי	BECAUSE	474b	3 d
		ל	TO	514b	5 fa
		על	UPON	754b	2 1f b
		פן	LEST	814d	1 a
		מראה	VISION	909d	1 b
		שאל	ASK	981d	2 a
26	8	אבימלך	ABIMELECH	4b	1
		ארך	BE LONG	73c	
		בעד	AWAY FROM	126b	1 a
		חלון	WINDOW	319d	
		יום	DAY	399d	5 b
		כי	WHEN	473a	2 a
		מלך	KING	573a	1
		עשתי	ONE	799d	
		פלשתי	PHILISTINE	814c	
		צחק	LAUGH	850b	2
		יצחק	ISAAC	850c	
		שקף	LOOK DOWN	1054c	
26	9	איך	HOW	32c	1
		אך	SURELY	36c	1
		אמר	SAY	56b	2
		על	UPON	754b	2 1f b
		פן	LEST	814d	1 a
26	10	אשם	OFFENCE	79d	2
		בוא	COME	99c	2 a
		זה	THIS	261c	4 d
		מה	WHAT	552c	1 ab
		שכב	LIE DOWN	1012b	3
26	11	מות	DIE	559d	2 a
		נגע	TOUCH	619a	3
		צוה	CHARGE	845d	2 c
26	12	ברך	BLESS	139a	1
		זרע	SOW	281c	1 a
		מצא	FIND	*394a	1 h
		מאה	HUNDRED	547d	1 a2
		מצא	FIND	592d	1 a
		שער	MEASURE	1045c	
26	13	גדל	BECOME GREAT	152b	2 a
		גדל	BECOMING GREAT	152d	
		הלך	WALK	233b	14c 3
		עד	UNTIL	724d	2 1a a
26	14	היה	BECOME	226c	2 2h
		עבדה	SERVICE	715c	
		פלשתי	PHILISTINE	814c	
		קנא	BE ZEALOUS	888c	2
		מקנה	CATTLE	889b	2
		רב	MUCH	913a	1 a2
26	15	באר	WELL	91c	1
		חפר	DIG	343c	1 a
		מלא	FILL	570c	1
		סתם	STOP UP	711b	
		עבד	SLAVE	713d	2
		עפר	DRY EARTH	779d	1 a
		פלשתי	PHILISTINE	814c	
26	16	מן	THAN	582c	6 a
		מן	THAN	582c	6 d
		מעם	FROM WITH	768d	2
		עצם	BE VAST	782c	1
26	17	גרר	GERAR	176b	
		חנה	DECLINE	333c	2 a
		נחל	WADY	636c	2
26	18	באר	WELL	91c	1
		באר	WELL	*91c	1
		ו	AND	254a	2 a
		חפר	DIG	343c	1 a
		מות	DEATH	560d	1
		סתם	STOP UP	711b	
		פלשתי	PHILISTINE	814c	
		קרא	CALL	896a	6 f
		שוב	TURN BACK	998b	8
		הא	DEMONSTRATIVE PARTICLE	*1089c	A
26	19	באר	WELL	91c	1
		באר	WELL	*91c	1
		בן	SON	*121a	1 jd
		חי	ALIVE	312b	1 f
		חפר	DIG	343c	1 a
		מצא	FIND	592d	1 a
		נחל	WADY	636c	2
		עבד	SLAVE	713d	2
26	20	גרר	GERAR	176b	
		עם	WITH	767c	1 c
		עשק	ESEK	796c	
		עשק	CONTEND	796c	
		ריב	STRIVE	936c	2
26	21	באר	WELL	91c	1
		חפר	DIG	343c	1 a
		על	UPON	754d	2 1f g
		ריב	STRIVE	936c	2
		שטנה	SITNAH	966c	
26	22	באר	WELL	91c	1
		חפר	DIG	343c	1 a
		כי	THAT	*472a	1 b
		עתה	NOW	774a	1 a
		עתק	MOVE	801b	1
		פרה	BEAR FRUIT	826a	1
		רחב	BE LARGE	931c	2
		רחבות	REHOBOTH	932c	2
		ריב	STRIVE	936c	2
		הא	DEMONSTRATIVE PARTICLE	*1089c	A
26	23	בארשבע	BEERSHEBA	92a	
		עלה	GO UP	748b	1 c
26	24	אלהים	GOD	44b	4 ba
		ברך	BLESS	139a	2 a
		זרע	SOWING	282c	4 b
		ירא	FEAR	431a	1 a
		עבד	SLAVE	714c	3
		עבור	FOR THE SAKE OF	721a	1 a
26	25	באר	WELL	91c	1
		בנה	BUILD	124c	1 at
		מזבח	ALTAR	258b	1
		כרה	DIG	500a	
		נטה	SPREAD OUT	640a	2
		עבד	SLAVE	713d	2
26	26	אחזת	AHUZZATH	28d	
		גרר	GERAR	176b	
		הלך	WALK	231a	1 d3 ga
		פיכל	PHICOL	810a	
		צבא	ARMY	839a	1 a
		מרע	FRIEND	946d	
		מרע	FRIEND	946d	
		שר	CHIEFTAIN	978b	3 a
26	27	אתם	YOU	61d	
		את	WITH	86c	4 a
		ו	AND	253a	1 k
		מדוע	WHEREFORE	396c	
		שנא	HATE	971c	1 a
26	28	אלה	OATH	46d	2
		בין	INTERVAL	107c	1 d
		ברית	COVENANT	136b	1 1
		ברית	COVENANT	136c	1 5
		היה	COME TO PASS	224b	1 1b
		כרת	CUT	503d	4
		נא	PART OF ENTREATY	609b	3 c
26	29	עם	WITH	767c	1 b
		אם	IF	50b	1 b2
		ברך	BLESS	138d	2 b
		טוב	A GOOD THING	375b	3
		כאשר	SINCE	455c	2
		נגע	TOUCH	619b	3
		עתה	NOW	774a	1 a
		עשה	DO	794b	1 3
		רעה	MISERY	949b	2
		רק	ONLY	956c	2 c
		שלום	PEACE	1023a	5 a
26	30	משתה	FEAST	1059d	1
26	31	את	WITH	86c	4 a
		בקר	MORNING	134b	1
		הלך	WALK	231c	1 d 4
		הלך	WALK	231d	1 d5 ta
		שלום	PEACE	1023a	5 a
26	32	אודה	CAUSE	15c	1
		באר	WELL	91c	1
		היה	COME TO PASS	224c	2 a1 ag
		חפר	DIG	343c	1 a
		מצא	FIND	592c	1 a
		עבד	SLAVE	713d	2
26	33	בארשבע	BEERSHEBA	92a	
		יום	DAY	401b	7 1
		כן	SO	487b	3 f
		עד	AS FAR AS	724b	1 2a a
		עם	WITH	767c	1
		שם	NAME	1027d	1
26	34	אלון	ELON	19a	2
		בארי	BEERI	92b	1
		בת	DAUGHTER	123b	1 h
		בשמת	BASEMATH	142a	1
		חתי	HITTITE	366c	1
		יהודית	JUDITH	397c	
		ל	TO	*512a	3 b
		עשו	ESAU	796c	
26	35	מרה	BITTERNESS	601a	
		רוח	BREATH	925b	3 e
		שם	NAME	1028b	3
27	1	ברך	BLESS	139a	3
		בן	SON	120a	1
		גדול	GREAT	153a	5
		ה	THE	207b	1 b
		הנה	BEHOLD	244a	A
		זקן	BE OLD	278b	
		כהה	GROW DIM	462c	
		כי	WHEN	473a	2 a
		מן	FROM	583a	7 ba
		עשו	ESAU	796c	
		ראה	TO SEE	907b	4
27	2	זקן	BE OLD	278b	
		ידע	KNOW	393c	1 a
		מות	DEATH	560c	1
		נא	PART OF ENTREATY	609c	4 d
27	3	יצא	GO OUT	423d	2 a
		כלי	IMPLEMENT	479d	2 a
		עתה	NOW	774b	2 b
		צוד	HUNT	844c	
		ציד	GAME	844d	2

GENESIS

Ch v.	Heb	Eng	Page	Sec
	צידה	PROVISION	845b	
	קשת	BOW	906a	1 a
	שדה	FIELD	961b	1 c
	תלי	QUIVER	1068a	
27 4	אב	FATHER	3b	1
	אהב	LOVE	13a	2
	ברך	BLESS	139a	3
	מטעם	TASTY	381b	
	טרם	NOT YET	382c	2
	עבור	FOR THE SAKE OF	721a	2
27 5	הלך	WALK	230d	1 1d 3a
	צוד	HUNT	844c	
	ציד	GAME	844d	2
	שדה	FIELD	961b	1 c
27 6	אח	BROTHER	26b	1
	הנה	BEHOLD	244a	B a
	שמע	HEAR	1033c	1 b
27 7	מטעם	TASTY	381b	
	מות	DEATH	560d	1
	פנה	FACE	817b	24a h
	פנה	FACE	817d	24e
	ציד	GAME	844d	2
27 8	אשר	PARTICLE OF RE-LATION	82a	1
	ו	AND	254c	4
	ל	TO	514b	5 fa
	עתה	NOW	774b	2 b
27 9	גדי	KID	152a	
	טוב	PLEASANT	374b	3 d
	מטעם	TASTY	381b	
	לקח	TAKE	543c	6
	עז	SHE-GOAT	777c	2
	עשה	DO	794c	2 1g
	צאן	SMALL CATTLE	838b	1 a
	שם	THERE	1027a	4 d
27 10	בוא	COME	99b	1
	מות	DEATH	560d	1
	עבור	FOR THE SAKE OF	721a	2
27 11	אח	BROTHER	26b	1
	אם	MOTHER	51d	1
	הן	BEHOLD	243c	A
	חלק	SMOOTH	325b	1
	שער	HAIRY	972c	
27 12	אולי	PERADVENTURE	19c	1
	בוא	COME	99c	2 a
	ברכה	BLESSING	139c	1 a
	על	UPON	756c	27a b
	קללה	CURSE	887a	
	תעע	MOCK	1073d	
27 13	אך	HOWBEIT	36c	2 a
	אם	MOTHER	51d	1
	ברכה	BLESSING	139c	1 a
	הלך	WALK	234a	1 5f 1
	לקח	TAKE	543c	6
	על	UPON	756c	27a b
	קללה	CURSE	887a	
27 14	אם	MOTHER	51d	1
	ברכה	BLESSING	139c	1 a
	הלך	WALK	233d	1 5b
	מטעם	TASTY	381b	
	עשה	DO	794d	2 3
27 15	את	WITH	86b	3 a
	בגד	GARMENT	94a	
	בית	HOUSE	108c	1 a
	בית	HOUSE	108d	1 aa
	בן	SON	120a	1
	בן	SON	120a	1
	ברכה	BLESSING	139c	1 a
	חמדה	DESIRABLENESS	326d	
	לבש	CLOTHE	528b	3
	קטן	SMALL	882a	1 a
27 16	ברכה	BLESSING	139c	1 a
	גדי	KID	152a	
	חלקה	SMOOTH PART	325c	1
	לבש	CLOTHE	528b	2
	עור	SKIN	736b	2
	עז	SHE-GOAT	777c	2
	צואר	NECK	848c	1
27 17	ב	IN	88c	1 4
	ברכה	BLESSING	139c	1 a
	מטעם	TASTY	381b	
	יד	HAND	390d	5 b1
	לחם	FOOD	537a	1 a
	עשה	DO	794d	2 3
27 18	ברכה	BLESSING	139c	1 a
	הנה	BEHOLD	243d	
	הנה	BEHOLD	244a	A
	מי	WHO	566b	
27 19	ברכה	BLESSING	139c	1 a
	עבור	FOR THE SAKE OF	721a	2
	עשה	DO	794a	1 1a 7
	ציד	GAME	844d	2
27 20	ברכה	BLESSING	139c	1 a
	יהוה	YAHWEH	218d	2 1a
	זה	THIS	261c	4 c
	כי	BECAUSE	473c	3 a
	ל	TO	517c	7 bb
	מה	HOW	553c	2 aa
	מהר	HASTEN	555a	2
	מצא	FIND	592d	1 a
	פנה	FACE	816d	24
	קרה	ENCOUNTER	899d	1
27 21	אם	IF	50d	2 bb
	ברכה	BLESSING	139c	1 a
	ה	INTERROG PART	210b	2 b
	זה	THIS	261c	4 f

Ch v.	Heb	Eng	Page	Sec
	לא	NOT	519a	1 ad b
	מוש	FEEL	559b	
	נגש	DRAW NEAR	620d	1
27 22	ברכה	BLESSING	139c	1 a
	יד	HAND	389a	1 a
	נגש	DRAW NEAR	620d	1
	קול	VOICE	876d	1 a
27 23	ברכה	BLESSING	139c	1 a
	היה	BECOME	226b	2 2c
	נכר	RECOGNIZE	648a	2
27 24	שער	HAIRY	972c	
	אני	I	59a	
	אנכי	I	59a	
	ברכה	BLESSING	139c	1 a
	זה	THIS	261c	4 f
27 25	ברכה	BLESSING	139c	1 a
	יין	WINE	406c	A
	נגש	APPROACH	621b	
	מען	PURPOSE	775c	2 b
	ציד	GAME	844d	2
	שתה	DRINK	1059b	1 a
27 26	ברכה	BLESSING	139c	1 a
	נגש	DRAW NEAR	620d	1
	נשק	KISS	676b	
27 27	ברך	BLESS	139a	2 b
	ברכה	BLESSING	139c	1 a
	נגש	DRAW NEAR	620d	1
	נשק	KISS	676b	
	ראה	TO SEE	907d	7 a
	ריח	SCENT	926b	1
	ריח	SCENT	926b	1
	ריח	SMELL	926b	1
27 28	ברכה	BLESSING	139c	1 a
	דגן	CORN	186c	
	טל	NIGHT-MIST	378c	
	תירוש	NEW WINE	440d	
	רב	MULTITUDE	914a	1
	שמי	HEAVENS	1029d	1 a
	שמן	FAT	1032a	
27 29	אם	MOTHER	51d	1
	ארר	CURSE	76c	
	ארר	CURSE	76d	
	בן	SON	120b	1 a
	ברך	BLESS	138d	2
	ברך	BLESS	139b	4 f
	ברכה	BLESSING	139c	1 a
	גביר	LORD	150c	
	הוה	BECOME	217c	
	ו	AND	252b	1 b
	לאם	PEOPLE	522c	
	עם	PEOPLE	766c	1
	שחה	BOW DOWN	1005b	1 c
27 30	אך	ONLY	36d	2 c
	את	WITH	86d	4 a
	ברכה	BLESSING	139c	1 a
	כאשר	WHEN	455c	3
27 31	ציד	HUNTING	844d	1
	ברכה	BLESSING	139c	1 a
	מטעם	TASTY	381b	
	עבור	FOR THE SAKE OF	721a	2
	עשה	DO	794d	2 3
	ציד	GAME	844d	2
27 32	בן	SON	120a	1
	ברכה	BLESSING	139c	1 a
	אפו	THEN	66b	1
27 33	ברך	BLESS	138d	2 b
	ברכה	BLESSING	139c	1 a
	גם	YEA	169c	3
	גם	ALSO	169c	4
	הוא	HE, SHE, IT	216c	4 bb
	חרד	TREMBLE	353b	2
	טרם	NOT YET	382c	2
	כל	ALL	482c	2 a
	מאד	EXCEEDINGLY	547c	2 b
	צוד	HUNT	844c	
	ציד	GAME	844d	2
27 34	אנכי	I	59b	
	ברכה	BLESSING	139c	1 a
	ו	AND	254d	5 b
	מר	BITTER	600c	2 a
	צעק	CRY	858c	2
	צעקה	CRY	858d	2
27 35	ברכה	BLESSING	139c	1 a
	מרמה	DECEIT	941b	
27 36	אצל	LAY ASIDE	69b	
	בכרה	RIGHT OF FIRST-BORN	114c	
	ברכה	BLESSING	139c	1 a
	ה	INTERROG PART	210a	1 c
	זה	THIS	261c	4 i
	כי	THAT	472b	1 da
	לא	NOT	520b	4 ba
	לקח	TAKE	543a	3 a
	עתה	NOW	774a	1 a
	עקב	FOLLOW AT THE HEEL	784b	
27 37	אפו	THEN	66b	1
	ברכה	BLESSING	139c	1 a
	גביר	LORD	150c	
	דגן	CORN	186c	
	תירוש	NEW WINE	440d	
	מה	WHAT	553a	1 da
	נתן	GIVE	678c	1 b
	סמך	LEAN	702a	2
	עבד	SLAVE	713d	2
	ענה	ANSWER	772d	1 d

Ch v.	Heb	Eng	Page	Sec
27 38	שום	TO PLACE	964a	3 d
	בכה	WEEP	113c	1
	ברכה	BLESSING	139c	1 a
27 39	נשא	LIFT	670c	1 b 5
	ברכה	BLESSING	139c	1 a
	טל	NIGHT-MIST	378c	
	מושב	DWELLING	444b	2 a
	מן	FROM	578c	1 b
	על	HEIGHT	752c	1
	ענה	ANSWER	772d	1 d
	שמי	HEAVENS	1029d	1 a
	שמן	FAT	1032a	
27 40	ברכה	BLESSING	139c	1 a
	חיה	COME TO PASS	225b	1 2b be
	חיה	LIVE	311b	1 c
	חרב	SWORD	353a	1 k
	כאשר	WHEN	455c	3
	על	UPON	753d	2 1e
	על	UPON	758c	4 2a
	על	YOKE	760d	
	פרק	TEAR APART	830a	
	צואר	NECK	848c	1
	רוד	ROAM	923d	1
27 41	אב	FATHER	3b	1
	אבל	MOURNING	5c	
	ברכה	BLESSING	139c	1 a
	הרג	KILL	247a	1 a
	לב	HEART	525c	2 7
	על	UPON	754b	2 1f b
	קרב	COME NEAR	897c	2
	שטם	BEAR A GRUDGE	966b	
27 42	את	MARK OF THE AC-CUSATIVE	85a	1 b
	בן	SON	120a	1
	בן	SON	120a	1
	הרג	KILL	247a	1 a
	ל	TO	510d	1 d
	נגד	BE CONSPICUOUS	617a	
	נחם	CONSOLE ONESELF	637b	4
	קטן	SMALL	882a	1 a
27 43	ברח	FLEE	138a	2
	חרן	HARAN	357a	
	חרן	HARAN	357a	
	ל	TO	515b	5 ib
	לבן	LABAN	526c	
27 44	יום	DAY	399b	5 a
	חמה	RAGE	404c	2
	חמה	RAGE	*404d	2 c
	ישב	REMAIN	442d	2 a
	עד	UNTIL	725a	2 1a b
	עם	WITH	768b	3
	שוב	TURN BACK	997d	6 f
27 45	אם	MOTHER	51d	1
	אף	NOSE	60b	3
	גם	ALSO	169c	4
	יום	DAY	400a	7 a6
	מה	HOW	554b	4 d
	עד	AS FAR AS	724b	12a b
	שוב	TURN BACK	997d	6 f
	שכח	FORGET	1013a	1 a
	שכל	BE BEREAVED	1013c	
	שלח	SEND	1018b	1 c
	שנים	TWO	1041a	1 a
27 46	אלה	THESE	41d	D
	בת	DAUGHTER	123b	1 i
	בת	DAUGHTER	123b	1 i
	חיים	LIFE	313a	1
	חיים	LIFE	313b	1
	חת	HETH	366c	B
	ל	TO	513a	5 ad
	מה	HOW	554a	4 d
	פנה	FACE	818c	2 6c a
	קוץ	FEEL A LOATHING	881a	1
28 1	אב	FATHER	3b	1
	אב	FATHER	3b	1
	בת	DAUGHTER	123b	1 i
	ברך	BLESS	139a	3
	חת	HETH	*366c	B
	כנען	CANAAN	488d	2 a
	צוה	CHARGE	845d	2 c
28 2	אח	BROTHER	26b	1
	ארם	ARAM	74c	B
	בגד	GARMENT	94a	
	בת	DAUGHTER	123a	1
	בתואל	BETHUEL	143d	
	הלך	WALK	230d	1 1d 3b
	לבן	LABAN	526c	
	לבן	LABAN	526c	
	פדן	PADDAN	804c	
28 3	ברך	BLESS	139a	2 a
	עם	PEOPLE	766c	1
	פרה	BEAR FRUIT	826b	2
	קהל	ASSEMBLY	874d	2 d
	רבה	BECOME MANY	915c	1 a
	שדי	ALMIGHTY	995a	2
28 4	ברכה	BLESSING	139d	1 b
	מגור	SOJOURNING PLACE	158c	
	זרע	SOWING	282c	4 b
	ירש	TAKE POSSESSION	439c	1 a
28 5	ארם	ARAM	74c	B
	ארמי	ARAMEAN	74c	
	בתואל	BETHUEL	143d	
	הלך	WALK	230d	1 1d 3b
	לבן	LABAN	526c	
	לבן	LABAN	526c	

Ch	v.	Heb	Eng	Page	Sec
		רבקה	REBEKAH	918d	
28	6	שלח	SEND	1018d	4
		אמר	SAY	56b	1
		ארם	ARAM	74c	B
		בת	DAUGHTER	123b	1 i
		ברך	BLESS	139a	1
		ו	AND	252b	1 b
		כנען	CANAAN	488d	2 a
		צוה	LAY CHARGE UPON	845c	1 a
28	7	שלח	SEND	1019a	1 a
		אב	FATHER	3b	1
		אם	MOTHER	51d	1
		ארם	ARAM	74c	B
		הלך	WALK	230d	1 1d 3b
28	8	בת	DAUGHTER	123b	1 i
		כנען	CANAAN	488d	2 a
		רע	EVIL	948a	1
28	9	בשמת	BASEMATH	*142a	1
		מחלת	MAHALATH	563b	1
		נביות	NEBAIOTH	614a	
		על	UPON	755b	2 4b
		ישמעאל	ISHMAEL	1035a	1
28	10	בארשבע	BEERSHEBA	92a	1
		הלך	WALK	230d	1 1d 3b
		חרן	HARAN	357a	
28	11	אבן	STONE	6b	1
		בוא	COME	98a	1 i
		לון	LODGE	533c	1 a
		מן	FROM	580d	3 bb
		פגע	MEET	803b	1
		מקום	STANDING PLACE	880b	4
		מראשות	HEAD-PLACE	912b	
		שום	TO PLACE	962d	1 a
		שכב	LIE DOWN	1012a	1 b
28	12	חלם	DREAM	321c	B
		ירד	GO DOWN	433c	2
		מלאך	MESSENGER	521d	2
		נגע	REACH	619c	2
		נצב	STAND	662c	2
		סלם	LADDER	700c	
		עלה	GO UP	748c	1 f
		ראש	HEAD	910d	2 a
28	13	אב	FATHER	3c	4 a
		אלהים	GOD	44b	4 ba
		אנכי	I	59c	
		יהוה	YAHWEH	219a	2 2a
		זרע	SOWING	282c	4 b
		נצב	STAND	662a	1 a
		על	UPON	756b	2 6c
		שכב	LIE DOWN	1012a	1 b
28	14	אדמה	EARTH	10a	6
		ברך	BLESS	138d	1
		זרע	SOWING	282c	4 b
		ים	SEA	411b	9
		נגב	SOUTH-COUNTRY	616b	
		עפר	DRY EARTH	780a	2 a
		פרץ	BREAK THROUGH	829c	8
		צפון	NORTH	861a	
		קדם	EASTWARD	870a	
28	15	אדמה	LAND	10a	5
		אם	IF	50c	1 cd
		דבר	SPEAK	181b	1 a
		הלך	WALK	230d	1 1d 3a
		עד	UNTIL	725a	2 1a a
		שוב	TURN BACK	998d	1 a
		שמר	KEEP	1037a	4 a
28	16	אכן	SURELY	38c	A
		ידע	KNOW	393c	1 a
		יקץ	AWAKE	429c	
		יש	BE	441c	2 a
		שנה	SLEEP	446a	
		מקום	STANDING PLACE	880a	4
28	17	בית	HOUSE	109b	1 ae 0
		בלת	EXCEPT	*116c	2
		ירא	FEAR	431a	1 a
		ירא	BE REVERED	431b	3 c
		כיאם	EXCEPT	474d	2 a
		מה	HOW	553c	2 b
		מקום	STANDING PLACE	880a	4
		שמי	HEAVENS	1030b	2 a
		שער	GATE	1045b	4
		קבל	BEFORE	*1110b	2 b
28	18	אבן	STONE	6b	1
		אבן	STONE	6b	1
		ביתאל	BETHEL	110d	1
		בקר	MORNING	134b	1 h
		יצק	POUR	427a	1
		מצבה	PILLAR	663a	1 b
		על	UPON	756b	2 7a a
		ראש	HEAD	910d	2 a
		מראשות	HEAD-PLACE	912b	
		שמן	OIL	1032b	2 f
28	19	אלם	BUT	19d	
		בית	HOUSE	*109b	1 ae 0
		ביתאל	BETHEL	110d	1
		ביתאל	BETHEL	110d	1
		לוז	LUZ	531c	1
		לוז	LUZ	531c	1
		מקום	STANDING PLACE	880b	4
		ראשון	FIRST	911d	3 a1
		קדמה	FORMER TIME	1110c	
28	20	אמר	SAY	56b	1
		בגד	GARMENT	94a	1
		היה	BE	227b	3 4d a
		לבש	PUT ON	528a	C
		נדר	VOW	623d	
		נדר	VOW	624a	1 b
		נתן	GIVE	678c	1
28	21	שמר	KEEP	1037a	4 a
		אלהים	GOD	44b	4 a
		היה	BECOME	226c	2 2f
		שוב	TURN BACK	997a	3 a
		שלם	COMPLETE	1024a	2
28	22	אבן	STONE	6b	1
		בית	HOUSE	109b	1 ae 0
		מצבה	PILLAR	663b	1 b
		עשר	TAKE THE TENTH OF	797c	
29	1	שום	TO PLACE	964b	4 c
		בן	SON	121b	1 jl
		הלך	WALK	230b	1 1c
		הלך	WALK	230d	1 1d 3b
		נשא	LIFT	670a	1 a
		קדם	FRONT	869c	1
		רגל	FOOT	920a	1 f
29	2	אבן	STONE	6b	1
		באר	WELL	91c	1
		באר	WELL	91c	1
		באר	WELL	91d	1
		עדר	FLOCK	727c	1 a
		על	UPON	755d	2 6a
		פה	MOUTH	805b	4
		רבץ	LIE DOWN	918b	
		שדה	FIELD	961b	1 a
		שם	THERE	1027a	1 a
		שקה	GIVE TO DRINK	1052c	2
29	3	אבן	STONE	6b	1
		אסף	GATHER	62d	1 b
		באר	WELL	91c	1
		באר	WELL	91d	1
		עדר	FLOCK	727c	1 a
		על	UPON	758c	4 2a
		פה	MOUTH	805b	4
		מקום	STANDING PLACE	879d	2 a
		שוב	TURN BACK	999a	1 b
		שם	THERE	1027b	3 a
		שקה	GIVE TO DRINK	1052c	2
29	4	אין	WHENCE	32d	
		אנחנו	WE	59d	
		אתם	YOU	61d	
		חרן	HARAN	357a	
29	5	בן	SON	120b	1 f
		ידע	KNOW	394a	2
		נחור	NAHOR	637d	2
29	6	רחל	RACHEL	932d	1
		שלום	PEACE	1022d	3
		שלום	PEACE	1022d	3
29	7	אסף	GATHER	62d	1 b
		גדול	GREAT	153b	7
		הלך	WALK	234a	1 5f 1
		הן	BEHOLD	243c	A
		יום	DAY	398b	1
		לא	NOT	519b	1 bb
		עוד	STILL	728d	1 aa
		מקנה	CATTLE	889b	2
		רעה	TEND	944d	1 a
		שקה	GIVE TO DRINK	1052c	2
29	8	אבן	STONE	6b	1
		אסף	GATHER	62d	1 b
		באר	WELL	91c	1
		באר	WELL	91d	1
		יכל	BE ABLE	407d	1 c
		עד	UNTIL	725a	2 1a b
		עדר	FLOCK	727c	1 a
		פה	MOUTH	805b	4
		שקה	GIVE TO DRINK	1052c	2
29	9	אשר	PARTICLE OF RELATION	83a	7 b
		דבר	SPEAK	181b	3 e
		עוד	STILL	729a	1 aa
		רחל	RACHEL	932d	
		רעה	TEND	945a	1 d1
29	10	אבן	STONE	6b	1
		אח	BROTHER	26b	1
		באר	WELL	91c	1
		באר	WELL	91d	1
		בת	DAUGHTER	123b	1 h
		נגש	DRAW NEAR	620d	1
		פה	MOUTH	805b	4
		רחל	RACHEL	932d	
		שקה	GIVE TO DRINK	1052c	2
29	11	בכה	WEEP	113c	1
		נשא	LIFT	670c	1 b 5
		נשק	KISS	676b	
29	12	רחל	RACHEL	932d	
		אח	BROTHER	26b	2
		כי	THAT	471d	1 a
		רבקה	REBEKAH	918d	
		רוץ	RUN	930b	1
29	13	חבק	CLASP	287d	
		כ	LIKE	454d	3 b
		נשק	KISS	676c	
		נשק	KISS	676c	
		רוץ	RUN	930b	1
		שמע	REPORT	1034d	1
29	14	אך	SURELY	36c	1
		בשר	FLESH	142d	4
		חדש	NEW MOON	294c	2 a
		יום	TIME	399d	6 b
		עם	WITH	768b	3 a
		עצם	BONE	782d	1
29	15	אח	BROTHER	26b	2
		ו	AND	254d	5 a
		חנם	OUT OF FAVOR	336c	A
		כי	THAT	472b	1 da
		לבן	LABAN	526c	
		עבד	WORK	713a	2
		משכרת	WAGES	969b	
29	16	גדל	GREAT	153a	5
		לאה	LEAH	521b	
		לבן	LABAN	526c	
		קטן	SMALL	882a	1 a
29	17	יפה	BEAUTIFUL	421c	
		לאה	LEAH	521b	
		עין	EYE	744d	1 p
		מראה	VISION	909c	1
		רך	TENDER	940a	1
		תאר	FORM	1061b	1
29	18	אהב	LOVE	12d	1
		ב	IN	90a	3 3b
		בת	DAUGHTER	123a	1
		עבד	WORK	713a	2
		קטן	SMALL	882a	1 a
		שבע	SEVEN	988a	1 a
		שבע	SEVEN	988b	5 c
29	19	אחר	ANOTHER	29c	
		טוב	PLEASANT	374c	6
		ישב	REMAIN	442d	2 a
		לבן	LABAN	526c	
		מן	THAN	582b	6 a
		נתן	GIVE	678c	1 c
29	20	אהב	LOVE	12d	1
		ב	IN	90a	3 3b
		יום	DAY	399b	5 a
		עבד	WORK	713a	2
29	21	יהב	GIVE	396c	1
		לבן	LABAN	526c	
		מלא	BE FULL	570b	1 b
29	22	אסף	GATHER	62b	1 a
		לבן	LABAN	526c	
		עשה	DO	794c	2 1c
		משתה	FEAST	*1059d	1
29	23	לאה	LEAH	521b	
		ערב	SUNSET	787d	1 a
29	24	אמה	MAID	51a	1
		זלפה	ZILPAH	273a	
		לאה	LEAH	521b	
		לבן	LABAN	526c	
		שפחה	MAID	1046c	1
		שפחה	MAID	1046c	1
29	25	בקר	MORNING	133d	1 b
		היה	COME TO PASS	225a	1 2a 1c
		ו	AND	254c	4
		זה	THIS	261c	4 d
		לא	NOT	520b	4 ba
		לאה	LEAH	521b	
		מה	WHAT	552c	1 ab
		מה	HOW	554a	4 da
		מן	FROM	583a	7 b
		עבד	WORK	713a	2
		עבד	WORK	713a	2
		עם	WITH	768b	3 a
		רמה	BEGUILE	941a	1
29	26	בת	DAUGHTER	*123a	1
		כן	SO	486a	1 ca
		לבן	LABAN	526c	
		נתן	GIVE	678c	1 c
		עשה	DO	795b	1 b
		פנה	FACE	817d	2 4e
		צעיר	YOUNG	859a	1
29	27	את	MARK OF THE ACCUSATIVE	84d	1 a
		זה	THIS	260c	1 a
		זה	THIS	260d	1 a
		מלא	FILL	570d	3
		עבד	WORK	713a	2
		עבדה	LABOR	715b	2
		עוד	STILL	729a	1 ab
		שבוע	PERIOD OF SEVEN	988d	1
29	28	זה	THIS	260c	1 a
		מלא	FILL	570d	3
		נתן	GIVE	678c	1 c
		רחל	RACHEL	932d	
		שבוע	PERIOD OF SEVEN	988d	1
29	29	אמה	MAID	51a	1
		בלהה	BILHAH	117b	
		לבן	LABAN	526c	
		רחל	RACHEL	932d	
		שפחה	MAID	1046c	1
		שפחה	MAID	1046c	1
29	30	אהב	LOVE	12d	1
		לאה	LEAH	521b	
		מן	THAN	582c	6 a
		עבד	WORK	713a	2
		עוד	STILL	729a	1 ab
		עם	WITH	768b	3 a
		רחל	RACHEL	933a	1
29	31	לאה	LEAH	521b	
		עקר	BARREN	785d	
		פתח	OPEN	835b	
		רחם	WOMB	933b	1
		שנא	HATE	971c	1 1
29	32	אהב	LOVE	12d	1
		איש	MAN	35d	
		הרה	CONCEIVE	247d	1
		כי	THAT	*472a	1 b
		כי	THAT	*472c	1 db

GENESIS

Ch	v.	Heb	Eng	Page	Sec
		לאה	LEAH	521b	
		עתה	NOW	774a	1 b
		עני	AFFLICTION	777a	
		ראה	TO SEE	908a	8 a2
29	33	ראובן	REUBEN	910a	1
		את	MARK OF THE AC-CUSATIVE	84d	1 a
		הרה	CONCEIVE	247d	1
		כי	THAT	471c	1 a
		כי	THAT	471d	1 b
		לאה	LEAH	*521b	
		עוד	STILL	729b	1 b
		שמע	HEAR	1034b	2 b
29	34	שמעון	SIMEON	1035c	1
		איש	MAN	35d	
		הרה	CONCEIVE	247d	1
		כן	SO	487b	3 f
		לאה	LEAH	*521b	
		לוה	BE JOINED	531a	
		לוי	LEVI	532c	1 a
		עתה	NOW	774a	1 b
29	35	פעם	OCCURRENCE	822b	3 d2
		הרה	CONCEIVE	247d	1
		ידה	PRAISE	392b	1 a2
		יהודה	JUDAH	397a	1 1
		כן	SO	487b	3 f
		לאה	LEAH	*521b	
		עמד	STAND	764a	2 d
		פעם	OCCURRENCE	822b	3 d2
30	1	אין	NOT	34c	2 dd
		יהב	GIVE	396d	1
		קנא	BE ZEALOUS	888c	2
30	2	אף	NOSE	60b	3
		בטן	WOMB	106a	3
		בן	SON	120a	1
		ה	INTERROG PART	209d	1 b
		חרה	BURN	354a	1 a
		מנע	WITHHOLD	586a	
		פרי	FRUIT	826b	2
		תחת	INSTEAD	1065d	2 2b a
30	3	אמה	MAID	51a	1
		בוא	COME	98a	1 e
		בלהה	BILHAH	117b	
		בנה	BUILD	125a	2 c
		ברך	KNEE	139c	
		הנה	BEHOLD	244a	A
		ילד	BEAR	408c	1 b
		מן	OUT OF	579c	2 ca
30	4	אמה	MAID	51a	1
		בלהה	BILHAH	117b	
		שפחה	MAID	1046c	1
30	5	בלהה	BILHAH	117b	
		הרה	CONCEIVE	247d	1
30	6	בן	SON	120a	1
		דין	JUDGE	192b	2 b
		דן	DAN	192d	1
		כן	SO	487b	3 f
		שמע	HEAR	1034b	2 e
30	7	בלהה	BILHAH	117b	
		הרה	CONCEIVE	247d	1
		שפחה	MAID	1046c	
30	8	גם	ALSO	169d	4
		יכל	PREVAIL	408a	2 a
		עם	WITH	767c	1 c
		פתל	TWIST	836c	
		נפתולים	WRESTLINGS	836d	
		נפתלי	NAPHTALI	836d	1
30	9	זלפה	ZILPAH	273a	
		לאה	LEAH	521b	
		מן	FROM	583a	7 b
		עמד	STAND	764a	2 d
		שפחה	MAID	1046c	
30	10	זלפה	ZILPAH	273a	
		שפחה	MAID	1046c	1
30	11	גדוד	BAND	*151b	1
		גד	GAD	151c	1 a
		גד	FORTUNE	151c	1
30	12	זלפה	ZILPAH	273a	
		שפחה	MAID	1046c	1
30	13	אשר	GO STRAIGHT	80d	4
		אשר	HAPPINESS	81a	
		אשר	ASHER	81b	1
		ב	IN	89c	3 1c
		בת	DAUGHTER	123c	2
30	14	דודי	MANDRAKE	*188b	
		חטה	WHEAT	334d	
		יום	TIME	399d	6 a
		מן	FROM	580d	3 ba
		קציר	HARVESTING	894d	3
		ראובן	REUBEN	910a	1
		שדה	FIELD	961b	1 d
30	15	ה	THE	207b	1 ca
		כן	SO	487a	3 da
		ל	TO	518a	7 bg
		לילה	NIGHT	538d	1
		לקח	TAKE	543a	3 a
		מעט	A FEW	590a	1 ea
		שכב	LIE DOWN	1012b	3
		תחת	INSTEAD	1065d	2 2b b
30	16	ב	IN	90a	3 3a
		הוא	HE, SHE, IT	216d	7
		לילה	NIGHT	538d	1
		שדה	FIELD	961b	1 a
		שכר	HIRE	969a	
		שכב	LIE DOWN	1012b	3
30	17	הרה	CONCEIVE	247d	1
30	18	חמישי	FIFTH	332c	1
		אשר	THAT	83c	8 c
		יששכר	ISSACHAR	441a	1
		נתן	GIVE	679b	1 n
		שכר	HIRE	969a	1
		שפחה	MAID	1046c	1
30	19	הרה	CONCEIVE	247d	1
30	20	זבד	ENDOWMENT	256b	
		זבד	BESTOW UPON	256b	
		זבל	EXALT	259c	
		זבולן	ZEBULUN	259d	1
30	21	טוב	PLEASANT	374b	4 a
		פעם	OCCURRENCE	822b	3 d2
		שש	SIX	995c	1 a
		אחר	AFTERWARDS	29d	1 b
		בת	DAUGHTER	123a	1
		דינה	DINAH	192d	
30	22	זכר	REMEMBER	270b	2 1 a
		עז	SHE-GOAT	777c	1
		פתח	OPEN	835b	
		רחם	WOMB	933b	1
30	23	אסף	GATHER	62c	4
		הרה	CONCEIVE	247d	1
		חרפה	REPROACH	358a	2 b
		יוסף	JOSEPH	*415c	1 a
30	24	יסף	ADD	415a	1
		יוסף	JOSEPH	415c	1 a
30	25	הלך	WALK	230d	1 d3 ga
		ל	TO	511b	1 ga
30	26	הם	THEY	241d	8 d
		ילד	CHILD	409b	A
		עבד	WORK	713a	2
		עבדה	LABOR	715b	2
30	27	ברך	BLESS	139a	2 a
		ו	AND	254a	2 a
		חן	FAVOR	336b	2 b1
		מצא	FIND	592d	1 a
		נא	PART OF EN-TREATY	609c	4 c
		נחש	OBSERVE SIGNS	638c	2
		ש	WHO	*980b	4 d
30	28	ו	AND	254a	3
		נקב	PIERCE	666b	2
		על	UPON	753b	2 lc
		שכר	HIRE	969a	1
30	29	את	WITH	86b	3 a
		עבד	WORK	713a	2
30	30	ברך	BLESS	139a	2 a
		היה	BE	227c	3 4d c
		ו	AND	254d	5 b
		מעט	A FEW	589d	1 a
		מתי	WHEN	607d	A
		עתה	NOW	774b	2 b
		עשה	DO	794a	1 1b
		פנה	FACE	817d	2 4e
		פרץ	BREAK THROUGH	829c	8
		רב	MULTITUDE	914a	1
		רגל	FOOT	919d	1 f
30	31	מאומה	ANYTHING	548d	
		עשה	DO	793d	1 1a 3
		צאן	SMALL CATTLE	838b	1 a
		רעה	TEND	944d	1 a
		שוב	TURN BACK	998b	8
		שמר	KEEP	1036c	1 a
30	32	חום	DARKENED	299b	
		מלא	PATCH	378a	
		כשב	LAMB	461b	
		נקד	SPECKLED	666d	
		צאן	SMALL CATTLE	838a	2
		שה	A SHEEP	961d	1
		שכר	HIRE	969a	1
		שם	THERE	1027c	4 d
30	33	את	WITH	86b	3 a
		גנב	STEAL	170b	
		חום	DARKENED	299b	
		מלא	PATCH	378a	
		יום	DAY	400a	7 a2
		כשב	LAMB	461b	
		כי	WHEN	473a	2 a
		מחר	TO-MORROW	564a	1 a
		מחר	TO-MORROW	564a	2
		על	UPON	757a	2 7c a
		ענה	ANSWER	773a	3 a
		עז	SHE-GOAT	777c	1
		צדקה	RIGHTEOUSNESS	842b	5
		שכר	HIRE	969a	1
30	34	היה	COME TO PASS	224b	1 1b
		הן	BEHOLD	243c	A
		לו	IF	530b	2
30	35	חום	DARKENED	299b	
		מלא	PATCH	378a	
		יד	HAND	390d	5 b4
		כשב	LAMB	461b	
		לבן	WHITE	526b	
		נקד	SPECKLED	666d	
		נתן	GIVE	679c	1 r
		עז	SHE-GOAT	777c	1
		עקד	STRIPED	785b	
		תיש	HE-GOAT	1067a	
30	36	דרך	JOURNEY	203a	2
		יום	DAY	398b	2 b
		יתר	BE LEFT OVER	451c	
		רעה	TEND	944d	1 a
		שום	TO PLACE	963c	1 d
30	37	חם	THEY	241d	8 d
		מחשף	A LAYING BARE	362d	
		לבן	WHITE	526b	
		לבנה	POPLAR	527b	
		לוז	ALMOND-TREE	531c	1
		לח	FRESH	535a	1
		מקל	ROD	596c	1
		ערמון	PLANE-TREE	790d	
		פצל	PEEL	822d	
		פצלה	PEELED SPOT	822d	
30	38	חמם	BE OR BECOME WARM	328d	3
		יצג	SET	426c	
		מקל	ROD	596c	1
		נכח	FRONT	647b	2 bb
		פצל	PEEL	822d	
		רהט	TROUGH	923d	
		שום	TO PLACE	964b	4 c
		שקת	WATER-TROUGH	1052d	
		שתה	DRINK	1059c	1 d
30	39	חמם	BE OR BECOME WARM	328d	3
		מלא	PATCH	378a	
		ילד	BEAR	408b	1 a
		מקל	ROD	596c	1
		נקד	SPECKLED	666d	
		עקד	STRIPED	785b	
30	40	אל	TO	39d	3 a
		חום	DARKENED	299b	
		כשב	LAMB	461b	
		נתן	PUT	680b	2 a
		עדר	FLOCK	727c	1 a
		על	UPON	755b	2 4a
		עקד	STRIPED	785b	
		פנה	FACE	816a	14
		פרד	DIVIDE	825c	1
		שית	PUT	1011b	2 a
30	41	היה	COME TO PASS	225b	1 2b bg
		יחם	CONCEIVE	404b	
		כל	ALL	481b	1
		מקל	ROD	596c	1
		עין	EYE	744a	1 d
		קשר	BIND	905c	
		רהט	TROUGH	923d	
		שום	TO PLACE	963c	1 c
		שום	TO PLACE	964b	4 c
30	42	עטף	BE FEEBLE	742c	
		קשר	BIND	905b	1 c
		שום	TO PLACE	964b	4 c
30	43	היה	BECOME	226c	2 2h
		חמור	HE-ASS	331b	1
		מאד	EXCEEDINGLY	547c	2 d
		פרץ	BREAK THROUGH	829c	8
		רב	MUCH	913a	1 b
		שפחה	MAID	1046c	1
31	1	אמר	SAY	56b	1
		אשר	PARTICLE OF RE-LATION	83a	7 a
		מאשר	FROM THAT WHICH	84a	A
		כבוד	RICHES	458c	1
		לקח	TAKE	543c	3 a
		עשה	DO	795a	2 7
31	2	עם	WITH	768b	3 e
		ראה	TO SEE	906d	1 a
		שלשם	THREE DAYS AGO	1026b	
		תמול	YESTERDAY	1070a	2 b
31	3	ארץ	EARTH	76b	2a
		היה	BE	227b	3 4d a
		מולדת	KINDRED	409d	1
		עם	WITH	767c	1 a
31	5	אל	TO	40a	3 a
		אלהים	GOD	44b	4 ba
		היה	BE	227b	3 4d a
		עם	WITH	767c	1 a
		עם	WITH	768b	3 e
		ראה	TO SEE	907a	2 1
		שלשם	THREE DAYS AGO	1026b	
		תמול	YESTERDAY	1070a	2 b
31	6	אתן	YOU	61d	
		כח	STRENGTH	470d	1 b
		עבד	WORK	713a	2
31	7	חלף	PASS ON OR AWAY	322b	1
		מנה	TIME	584c	
		נתן	GIVE	679a	1 g
		עם	WITH	767d	1 d
		רעע	BE EVIL	949d	1
		משכרת	WAGES	969b	
		תלל	MOCK	1068d	
31	8	אם	IF	49c	1 a1 a
		ילד	BEAR	408b	1 a
		כה	THUS	462b	1 a
		נקד	SPECKLED	666d	
		עקד	STRIPED	785b	
		שכר	HIRE	969a	1
31	9	נצל	SNATCH AWAY	664d	1
		מקנה	CATTLE	889b	2
31	10	ברד	SPOTTED	136a	
		ו	AND	252d	1 e
		חלום	DREAM	321c	2 a
		יחם	CONCEIVE	404b	
		עלה	GO UP	748d	3
		עת	TIME	773c	2 a
		עקד	STRIPED	785b	
		עתד	HE-GOAT	800d	
31	11	אלהים	GOD	44a	3 b
		הנה	BEHOLD	244a	A
		חלום	DREAM	321c	2 a

20

Ch	v.	Heb	Eng	Page	Sec
31	12	מלאך	MESSENGER	521d	3
		ברד	SPOTTED	136a	
		עלה	GO UP	748d	3
		עקד	STRIPED	785b	
		עתוד	HE-GOAT	800d	
		ראה	TO SEE	906d	1 b
31	13	אל	GOD	42c	6 a
		מולדת	KINDRED	409b	
		משח	ANOINT	603b	3 b
		נדר	VOW	623d	
		נדר	VOW	624a	1
		מצבה	PILLAR	663a	1 b
		עתה	NOW	774a	1 a
		עתה	NOW	774b	1 e
31	14	חלק	PORTION	324a	1 c
		נחלה	INHERITANCE	635c	3
		עוד	STILL	728d	1 aa
31	15	אכל	EAT	37c	1
		גם	ALSO	169b	2
		חשב	THINK	363c	1
		כסף	SILVER	494c	8 e
		ל	TO	514a	5 e
		מכר	SELL	569b	
		נכרי	FOREIGN	648d	1 b
31	16	הוא	HE, SHE, IT	*216a	3 b
		הוא	HE, SHE, IT	216a	3 b
		ל	TO	513b	5 ba
		נצל	SNATCH AWAY	664d	1
		עתה	NOW	774b	2 b
		עשר	RICHES	799b	
31	17	נשא	LIFT	670a	1 a
		קום	STAND	877c	1 a
31	18	ארם	ARAM	74c	B
		נהג	DRIVE	624b	1
		קנין	ACQUISITION	889a	1
		מקנה	CATTLE	889b	2
		רכוש	PROPERTY	940a	2
		רכש	COLLECT	940d	
31	19	גזז	SHEAR	159c	
		גנב	STEAL	170b	
		הלך	WALK	233d	1 5a
		צאן	SMALL CATTLE	838b	1 a2
		תרפים	IDOL	1076c	
31	20	ארמי	ARAMEAN	74c	
		בלי	WEARING OUT	115a	2 a
		ברח	FLEE	137d	2
		גנב	STEAL	170c	
		הוא	HE, SHE, IT	216a	3 a
		לבב	HEART	*523c	2 3a
		לב	HEART	524d	2 3a
		על	UPON	758b	3 ca
31	21	ברח	FLEE	137d	2
		נהר	STREAM	625d	1
		עבר	PASS OVER	717a	1 a1
		שום	TO PLACE	963b	2 c
31	22	ברח	FLEE	137d	2
		נגד	BE CONSPICUOUS	617a	
31	23	דבק	KEEP CLOSE	180a	3
		דרך	JOURNEY	203a	2
		יום	DAY	398c	2 b
		רדף	PURSUE	922c	1 a
		שבע	SEVEN	988b	5 c
31	24	ארמי	ARAMEAN	74c	
		דבר	SPEAK	181b	3 e
		חלום	DREAM	321c	2 a
		טוב	PLEASANT	374a	2 f
		לבן	LABAN	*526c	
		לילה	NIGHT	538d	1
		מן	FROM	582a	5 b
		מן	FROM	*583b	7 ba
		פן	LEST	814d	1
		רע	EVIL	948b	2
31	25	נשג	OVERTAKE	673c	1 a
		תקע	THRUST	1075c	1
		תקע	THRUST	1075c	1
31	26	גנב	STEAL	170c	
		חרב	SWORD	352d	1 i
		לבב	HEART	523c	2 3a
		נהג	DRIVE	624b	1
		שבה	TAKE CAPTIVE	985c	1 c
31	27	ברח	FLEE	138d	2
		גנב	STEAL	*170c	
		גנב	STEAL	170c	
		ובא	WITHDRAW	285b	
		כנור	LYRE	490a	
		ל	TO	517c	7 bb
		לבב	HEART	*523c	2 3a
		מה	HOW	554a	4 da
		שמחה	JOY	970d	1
		שיר	SONG	1010b	1
		שלח	SEND	1019a	1 d
		תף	TIMBREL	1074b	
31	28	בן	SON	120c	1 f
		נטש	PERMIT	644a	3
		נשק	KISS	676c	
		סכל	BE FOOLISH	698a	
		עתה	NOW	774a	1 a
31	29	אלה	GOD	42a	3 b
		אל	GOD	43a	7
		אלהים	GOD	44b	4 ba
		אמש	YESTERDAY	57d	
		דבר	SPEAK	181b	3 e
		טוב	PLEASANT	374a	2 f
		יד	HAND	390b	2
		יש	BE	442a	2 ce
		מן	FROM	582a	5 b
		מן	FROM	583b	7 ba
		רע	EVIL	948b	2
		רע	EVIL	948d	2
		שמר	KEEP	1037b	1
31	30	גנב	STEAL	170b	
		הלך	WALK	233a	14b 1
		כסף	LONG	493d	
		עתה	NOW	774b	2 b
		תרפים	IDOL	*1076c	
31	31	גזל	TEAR AWAY	159d	
		ירא	FEAR	431b	1 e
		מעם	FROM WITH	769a	C
		פן	LEST	814d	1
31	32	אשר	PARTICLE OF RELATION	82a	2
		גנב	STEAL	170b	
		חיה	LIVE	311a	1 a
		מה	WHAT	552d	1 b
		נגד	IN FRONT	617b	1 aa
		נכר	REGARD	648a	1
		עם	WITH	768b	3 b
		קבל	BEFORE	*1110b	2 b
31	33	אמה	MAID	51a	1
		יצא	GO OUT	422c	1 a
		מצא	FIND	593a	1 b
31	34	ישב	SIT	442b	1 a
		כר	SADDLE	468b	
		לקח	TAKE	543b	4 g
		מצא	FIND	593a	1 b
		מוש	FEEL	607a	1
		שום	TO PLACE	963a	1 a
		תרפים	IDOL	1076c	
31	35	אדון	LORD	11b	3 1f
		אשה	WOMAN	61a	1
		חפש	SEARCH	344c	2 b
		חרה	BURN	354a	1 b
		יכל	BE ABLE	407c	1 a
		כי	BECAUSE	473d	3 b
		מצא	FIND	593a	1 b
		פנה	FACE	818c	2 6b
		קום	STAND	877d	1 a
		תרפים	IDOL	1076c	
31	36	דלק	HOTLY PURSUE	196b	2
		חטאת	SIN	308c	1 a
		חרה	BURN	354a	1 b
		מה	WHAT	552c	1 a
		פשע	TRANSGRESSION	833c	1
		ריב	STRIVE	936c	2
31	37	יכח	DECIDE	407a	1
		כה	THUS	462b	2
		כלי	ARTICLE	479c	1
		כלי	ARTICLE	479c	1
		מצא	FIND	593a	1 b
		מוש	FEEL	607a	1
		נגד	IN FRONT	617b	1 aa
		שום	TO PLACE	963c	1 c
		שנים	TWO	1041a	1 a
31	38	איל	RAM	17d	1
		זה	THIS	261d	4 i
		עם	WITH	768b	3 a
		עז	SHE-GOAT	777c	1
		עשרים	TWENTY	797d	1 1a
		צאן	SMALL CATTLE	838b	1 a
		רחל	EWE	932d	
		שכל	BE BEREAVED	1013d	2 b1
31	39	בוא	COME	99b	2
		בקש	SEEK	135a	5 b
		גנב	STEAL	170b	
		חטא	MISS A GOAL OR WAY	307b	1
		טרפה	ANIMAL TORN	383c	1
		טרפה	ANIMAL TORN	*383c	1
		יום	DAY	398b	1
31	40	אכל	EAT	37c	5
		חרב	DRYNESS	351b	3
		יום	DAY	398b	1
		שנה	SLEEP	446a	
		נדד	FLEE	622b	2
		קרח	FROST	901c	1
31	41	זה	THIS	261d	4 i
		חלף	PASS ON OR AWAY	322b	1
		מנה	TIME	584c	2
		עבד	WORK	713a	2
		עשר	TEN	797b	4 b
		ארבע	FOUR	917a	2 a1 a
		משכרת	WAGES	969b	
31	42	אלה	GOD	41d	1 b
		אלהים	GOD	44b	4 ba
		אלהים	GOD	44b	4 ba
		אמש	YESTERDAY	57d	
		יגיע	TOIL	388c	1
		יכח	DECIDE	406d	1
		כי	THAT	472c	1 db
		כף	HOLLOW OF THE HAND	496d	1 d7
		ל	TO	515c	5 hc
		לולא	IF NOT	530c	A
		עתה	NOW	774c	2 gb
		עני	AFFLICTION	777a	1
		פחד	DREAD	808c	3
		ריקם	EMPTILY	938b	1
		שלח	SEND	1019a	1 c
31	43	או	OR	14d	1
		בן	SON	120c	1 f
		הוא	HE, SHE, IT	216a	3 b
		יום	DAY	399d	7 a1
31	44	ל	TO	513b	5 ba
		ברית	COVENANT	136b	1 1
		הלך	WALK	234a	1 5f 2
		כרת	CUT	503d	4
		עד	WITNESS	729c	1
		עתה	NOW	774b	2 b
31	45	אבן	STONE	6b	1
		מצבה	PILLAR	663a	1 b
		רום	BE HIGH	927c	1
		שום	TO PLACE	964b	4 c
31	46	אבן	STONE	6c	1
		לקט	GATHER UP	544d	1
31	47	שהד	WITNESS	962a	
		יגר	HEAP	1094d	1
		שהדו	TESTIMONY	1113d	
31	48	יום	DAY	399d	7 a1
		עד	WITNESS	729c	1
31	49	אשר	THAT	83c	8 c
		בין	INTERVAL	107c	1 d
		כי	WHEN	473a	2 a
		סתר	HIDE	711c	2
		צפה	KEEP WATCH	859c	
		מצפה	MIZPAH	860a	1
		רע	FRIEND	946b	3
31	50	אם	IF	50b	1 b2
		בין	INTERVAL	107c	1 a
		עד	WITNESS	729d	2 a
		על	UPON	755b	24 b
		ענה	BE BOWED DOWN	776b	1
		צפה	KEEP WATCH	859c	
		ראה	TO SEE	907d	7 a
		בין	INTERVAL	107c	1 a
31	51	הנה	BEHOLD	244a	A
		ירה	CAST	435a	2
		מצבה	PILLAR	663a	1 b
31	52	אם	IF	50a	1 b1
		מצבה	PILLAR	663a	1 b
		עבר	PASS OVER	717c	2
		עד	WITNESS	729c	1
		עדה	TESTIMONY	729d	
		רעה	MISERY	949b	2
31	53	אלהים	GOD	44b	4 ba
		אלהים	GOD	44c	4 ba
		נחור	NAHOR	637d	2
		פחד	DREAD	808c	3
		שבע	SWEAR	989b	1 a
		שפט	JUDGE	1047c	2 a
31	54	אכל	EAT	37b	1
		זבח	SLAUGHTER FOR SACRIFICE	256d	1 1 a
		זבח	SLAUGHTER FOR SACRIFICE	257a	14
		זבח	SACRIFICE	257c	2 1
		לחם	FOOD	537a	1 a
32	1	בן	SON	120c	1 f
		בקר	MORNING	134b	1 h
		ברך	BLESS	139a	3
		נשק	KISS	676c	
32	2	דרך	JOURNEY	203a	2
		הלך	WALK	231b	1 d3 gd
		מחנים	MAHANAIM	334b	
		ל	TO	511b	1 ga
		פגע	MEET	803b	1
32	3	כאשר	WHEN	455c	3
32	4	אדום	EDOM	10c	3
		מלאך	MESSENGER	521c	1 a
		עשו	ESAU	796c	
		שדה	FIELD	961d	2 d
		שעיר	SEIR	973a	1 a
32	5	אדון	LORD	11b	3 1k
		אמר	SAY	55d	1
		אמר	SAY	56a	1
		חמור	HE-ASS	331b	1
		עתה	NOW	774c	2 f
32	6	חן	FAVOR	336b	2 b1
		מצא	FIND	592d	1 a
		נגד	BE CONSPICUOUS	616d	1
		עבד	SLAVE	713d	1
		שור	A HEAD OF CATTLE	1004b	
		שלח	SEND	1018b	1 c
		שפחה	MAID	1046c	1
32	7	אמר	SAY	56b	1
		מחנה	ENCAMPMENT	334b	3 b
32	8	חצה	DIVIDE	345b	1
		ירא	FEAR	431a	1 a
		ל	TO	512b	4
		עם	PEOPLE	766c	2 c
		צרר	BIND	864d	B
32	9	אם	IF	49c	1 a1 a
		בוא	COME	98c	2 b
		מחנה	ENCAMPMENT	334b	3 b
		נכה	SMITE	646b	3
		פליטה	ESCAPE	812c	2 b
32	10	אב	FATHER	3c	4 a
		אלהים	GOD	44b	4 ba
		יטב	DO GOOD TO	405d	2
		מולדת	KINDRED	409d	1
		עם	WITH	767d	1 d
32	11	אמת	FIRMNESS	54a	3 b
		ב	IN	89c	3 1b
		ה	THE	208b	1 ha
		זה	THIS	261a	2 bb
		מחנה	ENCAMPMENT	334b	3 b
		חסד	GOODNESS	339b	4
		ירדן	JORDAN	434c	
		מן	THAN	582d	6 d

GENESIS

Ch v.	Heb	Eng	Page	Sec
	מקל	STAFF	596c	2
	עבר	PASS OVER	717a	1 a1
	עתה	NOW	774a	1 a
	עשה	DO	794b	1 3
	קטן	BE SMALL	881d	1
32 12	אם	MOTHER	51c	1
	יד	HAND	391b	5 g1
	ירא	FEAR	431b	1 e
	נכה	SMITE	646b	3
	נצל	DELIVER	665a	3 a
	על	UPON	755c	2 4c
	פן	LEST	814a	1
32 13	זרע	SOWING	282c	4 b
	חול	SAND	297a	A
	חול	SAND	297a	C
	יטב	DO GOOD TO	405d	2
	ים	SEA	411b	8 b
	ספר	COUNT	708a	1
	עם	WITH	767d	1 d
	רב	MULTITUDE	914a	1
	שום	TO PLACE	964a	3 e
32 14	לון	LODGE	533c	1 a
	מנחה	GIFT	585a	1
	עדר	FLOCK	727d	2 a
32 15	איל	RAM	17d	1
	מאה	HUNDRED	548a	1 b3
	עשרים	TWENTY	797d	1 1d
	רחל	EWE	932d	1
	תיש	HE-GOAT	1067a	1
32 16	אתון	SHE-ASS	87d	
	ינק	NURSE	413c	
	עיר	MALE ASS	747a	
	עשר	TEN	796d	2 b
	עשרים	TWENTY	797d	1 1d
	פר	YOUNG BULL	830d	1
	פרה	HEIFER	831a	
	ארבעים	FORTY	917c	1 b
	שלשים	THIRTY	1026c	1
32 17	בד	SEPARATION	94c	1
	יד	HAND	390d	5 b4
	עבד	SLAVE	713d	2
	עבר	PASS OVER	718a	5 c
	עדר	FLOCK	727d	2 a
	רוח	SPACE	926c	1
	שום	TO PLACE	963a	1 d
32 18	אן	WHERE	33a	A
	הלך	WALK	230d	1 1d 3b
	כי	WHEN	473a	2 a
	מי	WHO	566b	B
	פגש	MEET	803c	
	פנה	FACE	817c	2 4c a
	צוה	CHARGE	845c	2 c
	שאל	ASK	981c	2 a
32 19	מנחה	GIFT	585a	1
	שלח	SEND	1018b	a
32 20	דבר	WORD	183d	4 7
	מצא	FIND	593a	1 c
	עדר	FLOCK	727d	2 a
	צוה	CHARGE	845c	2 c
32 21	אחר	AFTER	30a	2 b
	ה	THE	208c	2 a
	כפר	COVER OVER	497b	1
	מנחה	GIFT	585a	1
	נשא	LIFT	670c	1 b 3
	פנה	FACE	816a	1 b
	פנה	FACE	817c	2 4c a
32 22	מחנה	ENCAMPMENT	334a	1 a
	לון	LODGE	533c	1 a
	מנחה	GIFT	585a	1
	עבר	PASS OVER	718a	5 c
	פנה	FACE	818d	2 7a a
32 23	יבק	JABBOK	132d	2
	הוא	HE, SHE, IT	216d	7
	ילד	CHILD	409b	A
	עבר	PASS OVER	717a	1 a1
	מעבר	FORD	721b	1
	עשר	TEN	797a	1 a
	שפחה	MAID	1046c	1
32 24	אשר	PARTICLE OF RE-LATION	83a	7 a
	נחל	WADY	636c	2
	עבר	PASS OVER	718d	1 a
32 25	אבק	WRESTLE	7c	
	אדון	LORD	11b	3 1g
	יתר	BE LEFT OVER	451b	
	עד	AS FAR AS	724b	1 2a b
	שחר	DAWN	1007b	
32 26	אבק	WRESTLE	7c	
	יכל	PREVAIL	408a	2 b
	יקע	DISLOCATED	429b	
	ירך	THIGH	437d	1 a
	כף	HOLLOW	497a	4 a
	נגע	TOUCH	619a	1 a
32 27	ברך	BLESS	139a	2 a
	כיאם	EXCEPT	474d	2 b
	שחר	DAWN	1007b	
32 28	מי	WHO	*566a	A
	שם	NAME	1028a	2 a
	להן	EXCEPT	*1099a	
	מן	WHO	*1100d	1
32 29	איש	MAN	35d	
	אמר	SAY	56d	
	יכל	PREVAIL	408a	2 a
	כיאם	BUT	475a	2 b
	לא	NOT	518d	1 ac
	עוד	STILL	729a	1 ab
	עם	WITH	767c	1 c
	שרה	PERSIST	975b	
	ישראל	ISRAEL	975c	1
	שם	NAME	1027d	2 a
32 30	ברך	BLESS	139a	2 a
	זה	THIS	261c	4 e
	מה	HOW	554a	4 d
	שאל	ASK	981d	2 a
	שאל	ASK	981d	2 a
32 31	אל	TO	40a	3 a
	ו	AND	254a	2 b
	נצל	BE DELIVERED	664c	2
	פנה	FACE	815d	1 1c
	פנל	PENVEL	819c	1
	ראה	TO SEE	906d	1 a
32 32	זרח	RISE	280b	1 a
	ירך	THIGH	438a	1 a
	כאשר	WHEN	455c	3
	ל	TO	*512d	5 aa
	עבר	PASS OVER	717d	4 a
	על	UPON	752d	2 1
	פנל	PENVEL	819c	1
	צלע	LIMP	854b	
32 33	יום	DAY	401b	7 l
	ירך	THIGH	437d	1 a
	כן	SO	487b	3 f
	כף	HOLLOW	497a	4 a
	נגע	TOUCH	619a	1 a
	נשה	A NERVE IN THE THIGH	675a	
	עד	AS FAR AS	724b	1 2a a
	ישראל	ISRAEL	975d	2 b1
33 1	חצה	DIVIDE	345b	1 a
	ילד	CHILD	409b	A
	לאה	LEAH	521b	
	שפחה	MAID	1046c	1
33 2	אחרון	BEHIND	30d	A
	ילד	CHILD	409b	A
	לאה	LEAH	521b	
	ראשון	FIRST	912a	3 b2
	שום	TO PLACE	964a	4 a
	שפחה	MAID	1046c	1
33 3	ארץ	EARTH	76b	3 a
	נגש	DRAW NEAR	620d	1
	עבר	PASS OVER	718a	5 c
	עד	AS FAR AS	724b	1 2a b
	שבע	SEVEN	988a	1 a
	שבע	SEVEN	988b	5 c
	שחה	BOW DOWN	1005b	1 b
33 4	בכה	WEEP	113c	3
	חבק	CLASP	287d	
	נפל	FALL	657c	3 c
	נשק	KISS	676b	
	על	UPON	756b	27a a
	צואר	NECK	848c	1
33 5	רוץ	RUN	930b	1
	חנן	SHOW FAVOR	336a	2 a
	ילד	CHILD	409b	A
	ל	TO	513a	5 ad
	מי	WHO	566b	
33 6	הם	THEY	241b	1 d
	ילד	CHILD	409b	A
	נגש	DRAW NEAR	620d	1
	שחה	BOW DOWN	1005b	1 c
	שפחה	MAID	1046c	1
33 7	ילד	CHILD	409b	A
	לאה	LEAH	521b	
	נגש	DRAW NEAR	620d	1
	נגש	DRAW NEAR	621a	
	שחה	BOW DOWN	1005b	1 c
33 8	אדון	LORD	11b	3 1k
	מחנה	ENCAMPMENT	334b	3 b
	חן	FAVOR	336b	2 b1
	ל	TO	513a	5 ad
	מי	WHO	566b	A
	פגש	MEET	803d	
33 9	יש	HAVE	441d	2 cb
	רב	MUCH	913b	1 f
	חן	FAVOR	336b	2 b1
33 10	כיעלכן	FOR THEREFORE	475c	
	מנחה	GIFT	585a	1
	נא	PART OF EN-TREATY	609b	3 b
	נא	PART OF EN-TREATY	609c	4 c
	פנה	FACE	816a	1 2b
	רצה	BE PLEASED WITH	953a	1 b
33 11	בוא	COME	99c	B
	ברכה	BLESSING	139d	5
	חנן	SHOW FAVOR	336a	2 a
	יש	HAVE	441d	2 cb
	כי	BECAUSE	474b	3 d
	כל	ALL	482c	2 a
	פצר	PUSH	823a	
33 12	הלך	WALK	231c	1 1d 5e
	הלך	WALK	234a	1 5c
	נגד	IN FRONT	617c	2 b
33 13	בקר	CATTLE	*133a	
	דפק	BEAT	200c	
	ו	AND	254b	2 db
	יום	DAY	400a	7 a6
	ילד	CHILD	409b	A
	מות	DIE	559d	1 b
	עול	GIVE SUCK	732b	
	על	UPON	753b	2 1b
	רך	TENDER	940a	1
33 14	אט	GENTLENESS	31d	B
	ילד	CHILD	409b	A
	ל	TO	516c	5 jb
	מלאכה	WORK	522a	2
	נא	PART OF EN-TREATY	609b	3 c
	נחל	JOURNEY BY STAGES	625d	
	עבר	PASS OVER	718a	5 c
	פנה	FACE	817c	2 4c a
	רגל	FOOT	919d	1 f
	שעיר	SEIR	973a	1 a
33 15	חן	FAVOR	336b	2 b1
	יצג	SET	426c	
	מה	HOW	554a	4 d
	מן	FROM	580d	3 ba
	עם	PEOPLE	766c	2 c
33 16	דרך	JOURNEY	203a	2
	יום	DAY	400c	7 g
	שעיר	SEIR	973a	1 a
	שוב	TURN BACK	997a	3 a
33 17	בית	HOUSE	108c	1 a
	בית	HOUSE	108d	1 aa
	בנה	BUILD	124b	1 ab
	נסע	JOURNEY	652b	3
	סכה	THICKET	697c	2
	סכות	SUCCOTH	697d	1
	עשה	DO	794c	2 1c
33 18	ארם	ARAM	74c	B
	ב	IN	91a	5 1
	חנה	DECLINE	333c	2 a
	פנה	FACE	816d	2 2b
	שכם	SHECHEM	1014b	1
	שכם	SHECHEM	*1014c	1
	שלם	COMPLETE	1024a	2
33 19	בן	SON	120d	1 ja
	חלקה	PORTION OF GROUND	324c	1 a
	חמור	HAMOR	331c	
	מאה	HUNDRED	547d	1 a1
	נטה	SPREAD OUT	640a	2
	קשיטה	WEIGHT	903d	
	שכם	SHECHEM	1014c	2
33 20	אל	GOD	42d	6 f
	אלהים	GOD	44b	4 ba
	מזבח	ALTAR	258b	1
	מזבח	ALTAR	258d	8
	נצב	STAND	662c	1
	מצבה	PILLAR	663a	1 b
34 1	בת	DAUGHTER	123a	1
	בת	DAUGHTER	123b	1 i
	דינה	DINAH	192d	
	לאה	LEAH	521b	
	ראה	TO SEE	908a	8 a1
34 2	את	WITH	85c	
	חוי	HIVITE	295d	1
	חמור	HAMOR	331c	
	נשיא	PRINCE	672b	3
	נשיא	PRINCE	672c	8
	ענה	BE BOWED DOWN	776b	2
	שכב	LIE DOWN	1012b	3
	שכם	SHECHEM	1014c	2
34 3	אהב	LOVE	12d	1
	דבק	CLING	179d	2 a
	דבר	SPEAK	181d	5
	דינה	DINAH	192d	
	לב	HEART	525c	2 9a
	נערה	GIRL	655b	1
	נפש	SOUL	660d	6 e
34 4	חמור	HAMOR	331c	
	ילדה	GIRL	409c	
34 5	דינה	DINAH	192d	
	חיה	BE	227b	3 4d b
	ו	AND	*252b	1 b
	חרש	BE SILENT	361b	1 a
	טמא	BE UNCLEAN	379c	1
	עד	AS FAR AS	724b	1 2a b
34 6	דבר	SPEAK	181b	3 d
	חמור	HAMOR	331c	
34 7	בן	SON	*120d	1 jb
	חרה	BURN	354a	1 b
	כן	SO	486a	1 ca
	ל	TO	517c	7 bb
	נבלה	SENSELESSNESS	615a	1
	עצב	HURT	780d	
	עשה	DO	795b	1 b
	ישראל	ISRAEL	975c	2 a1
	שכב	LIE DOWN	1012b	3
34 8	בת	DAUGHTER	123a	1 a
	דבר	SPEAK	181b	3 d
	חמור	HAMOR	331c	
	חשק	BE ATTACHED TO	366a	
	נפש	SOUL	660d	6 e
34 9	נתן	GIVE	678c	1 c
	חתן	MAKE ONESELF A SON IN LAW	368d	2
34 10	נתן	GIVE	678c	1 c
	אחז	GRASP	28c	
	חיה	BE	227a	3 3
	סחר	GO AROUND	695b	1
	פנה	FACE	817a	2 4a f
34 11	חן	FAVOR	336b	2 b1
34 12	ו	AND	254c	3
	כאשר	AS	455b	1 a
	מהר	PURCHASE-PRICE	555c	
	נערה	GIRL	655b	1

Ch	v.	Heb	Eng	Page	Sec
		נתן	GIVE	678c	1 c
		מתן	GIFTS	682b	
		על	UPON	753b	2 1c
		רבה	BECOME MANY	915b	
		רבה	BECOME MANY	915c	1 c
34	13	אשר	THAT	83c	8 c
		בן	SON	*120d	1 jb
		דינה	DINAH	192d	
		חמור	HAMOR	331c	
		טמא	BE UNCLEAN	379c	1
		ענה	ANSWER	773a	1 e
		מרמה	DECEIT	941b	
34	14	הוא	HE, SHE, IT	*216d	6 a
		חרפה	REPROACH	358a	2 d
		יכל	BE ABLE	407c	1 a
		נתן	GIVE	678c	1 c
		ערלה	FORESKIN	790b	
34	15	אות	CONSENT	22d	
		אך	ONLY	36c	2 ba
		ב	IN	90a	3 2e
		זה	THIS	261d	6 ba
		זכר	MALE	271c	1 1b
		ל	TO	512d	5 aa
		ל	TO	514b	5 fb
		מול	CIRCUMCIZE	557d	
34	16	ישב	DWELL	443a	3
		נתן	GIVE	678c	1 c
34	17	בת	DAUGHTER	123a	1 a
		הלך	WALK	230b	1 1b
		מול	CIRCUMCIZE	557d	
34	18	חמור	HAMOR	331c	
		יטב	BE PLEASING	405c	4
		עין	EYE	744d	3 c
34	19	אחר	DELAY	29b	1
		חפץ	DELIGHT IN	342d	1 a
		כבד	BE HONORED	457c	1 b
		נער	YOUTH	655a	1 e
34	20	חמור	HAMOR	331c	
		שער	GATE	1045a	2 a
34	21	אשה	WOMAN	61b	2
		הם	THEY	241c	3 b
		ו	AND	254c	4
		יד	HAND	390c	3 d
		סחר	GO AROUND	695b	1
		רחב	WIDE	932a	
		רחב	WIDE	932a	
		שלם	COMPLETE	1024a	3
34	22	אות	CONSENT	22d	
		ב	IN	90a	3 2e
		זה	THIS	261d	6 ba
		זכר	MALE	271c	1 1b
		ישב	DWELL	443a	3
		כאשר	AS	455b	1 a
		ל	TO	512d	5 aa
		מול	CIRCUMCIZE	557d	
34	23	אות	CONSENT	23a	
		הם	THEY	241c	3 b
		קנין	ACQUISITION	889a	1
		מקנה	CATTLE	889b	2
34	24	זכר	MALE	271c	1 1b
		חמור	HAMOR	331c	
		יצא	GO OUT	422d	1 a
		מול	CIRCUMCIZE	557d	
		שער	GATE	1045a	2 a
34	25	בטח	SECURITY	105b	
		בן	SON	*120d	1 jb
		דינה	DINAH	192d	
		היה	COME TO PASS	224d	2 a1 a1
		היה	BE	227a	3 4a
		הרג	KILL	247a	1 a
		זכר	MALE	271c	1 1b
		כאב	BE IN PAIN	456a	1
		לוי	LEVI	532c	1 a
		על	UPON	757c	2 7d
		שמעון	SIMEON	*1035c	1
34	26	דינה	DINAH	192d	
		הרג	KILL	247a	1 a
		חמור	HAMOR	331c	
		חרב	SWORD	352d	1 f
		מן	OUT OF	579a	2 aa
		פה	MOUTH	805c	6 c2
34	27	אשר	THAT	83c	8 c
		בוא	COME	98c	2 b
		בזז	SPOIL	102d	
		בן	SON	*120d	1 jb
		חלל	PIERCED	319c	2
		טמא	BE UNCLEAN	379c	1
		על	UPON	757d	2 7d
34	28	ו	AND	253a	1 h
		חמור	HE-ASS	331b	1
34	29	בזז	SPOIL	102d	
		חיל	STRENGTH	299a	3
		טף	CHILDREN	382a	
		שבה	TAKE CAPTIVE	985c	1 a
34	30	אסף	GATHER	62c	1 a
		באש	STINK	93a	2
		ישב	DWELL	443b	3
		כנעני	CANAANITE	489a	2 b
		לוי	LEVI	532c	1 a
		מת	MALE	607b	2 a
		נכה	SMITE	646b	3
		מספר	NUMBER	709a	1 a
		עכר	STIR UP	747d	
		על	UPON	757d	2 7d
		פרזי	PERIZZITE	827a	
		שמד	BE EXTERMINATED	1029b	1
		שמעון	SIMEON	*1035c	1
34	31	זנה	COMMIT FORNICATION	275d	1
35	1	אל	GOD	42c	6 a
		ברח	FLEE	138a	2
		ה	THE	209c	3
		מזבח	ALTAR	259a	8
		עלה	GO UP	748b	1 c
		ראה	TO SEE	908b	1 a
35	2	אלהים	GOD	43c	1 d
		בית	HOUSE	109d	5 a
		חלף	PASS ON OR AWAY	322b	1
		טהר	BE CLEAN	372c	1
		נכר	FOREIGNNESS	648c	1
		סור	TURN ASIDE	694b	1
		שמלה	WRAPPER	971a	
35	3	אל	GOD	42c	6 a
		דרך	WAY	202c	3
		היה	BE	227b	3 4d a
		הלך	WALK	230c	1 1d 1a
		מזבח	ALTAR	259a	8
		יום	DAY	*398c	2 f
		עלה	GO UP	748b	1 c
		צרה	DISTRESS	865b	
35	4	אלה	TEREBINTH	18c	
		אלון	TEREBINTH	18d	1
		אזן	EAR	23d	1
		אל	TO	39c	1
		אלהים	GOD	43c	1 d
		טמן	HIDE	380b	1
		נזם	RING	634a	2
		נכר	FOREIGNNESS	648c	1
		עם	WITH	768a	2
35	5	בן	SON	*120d	1 jb
		היה	BECOME	225d	2 1b
		חתת	TERROR	369d	
		נסע	SET OUT	652a	2 a
		סביב	ROUND ABOUT	687b	2 bb
		רדף	PURSUE	922c	1
35	6	ביתאל	BETHEL	110d	1
		כנען	CANAAN	488d	2 a
		לוז	LUZ	531c	1
		עם	PEOPLE	766c	2 c
35	7	אל	GOD	42c	6 c
		ביתאל	BETHEL	110d	1
		בנה	BUILD	124c	1 at
		ברח	FLEE	138a	2
		מזבח	ALTAR	258b	1
		מזבח	ALTAR	258d	8
		שם	THERE	1027a	1 a
35	8	אלון	TEREBINTH	18d	1
		אלון	OAK	47c	
		בכות	WEEPING	113d	
		בכים	BOCHIM	114a	1
		דבורה	DEBORAH	184b	1
		ינק	NURSE	413c	
		קבר	BURY	868d	
		רבקה	REBEKAH	918d	
		תחת	UNDERNEATH	1066b	3 2b
35	9	ארם	ARAM	74c	B
		ברך	BLESS	139a	2 a
		עוד	STILL	729b	1 b
		ראה	TO SEE	908b	1 a
35	10	קרא	CALL	896b	2 d2
		שם	NAME	1027d	1
35	11	גוי	NATION	156c	1 a
		גוי	NATION	*156d	1 b
		היה	BECOME	226a	2 1b
		חלץ	LOINS	323b	1
		יצא	GO OUT	423c	1 h
		מן	OUT OF	579c	2 ca
		פרה	BEAR FRUIT	826a	1
		קהל	ASSEMBLY	874d	2 1
		שדי	ALMIGHTY	995a	2
35	12	אחר	AFTER	30a	2 b
		זרע	SOWING	282c	4 b
35	13	אשר	PARTICLE OF RELATION	82c	4 bb
		דבר	SPEAK	181b	3 d
		עלה	GO UP	748c	2 e
		על	UPON	759a	4 2c
35	14	אבן	STONE	6b	1
		אשר	PARTICLE OF RELATION	82c	4 bb
		ביתאל	BETHEL	110d	1
		דבר	SPEAK	181b	3 d
		יצק	POUR	427a	1
		נסך	POUR OUT	650d	
		נסך	DRINK-OFFERING	651a	1
		נצב	STAND	662c	2
		מצבה	PILLAR	663a	1 b
		שמן	OIL	1032b	2 f
35	15	ביתאל	BETHEL	110d	1
		דבר	SPEAK	181b	3 d
35	16	אפרתה	EPHRATH	68d	1
		ארץ	EARTH	76b	4 b
		בוא	COME	*98d	2 e
		ילד	BEAR	408b	1 a
		כברה	DISTANCE	460c	
		נסע	SET OUT	652b	2 a
		עוד	STILL	729c	2 ab
		קשה	BE SEVERE	904b	
35	17	ילד	BEAR	408b	1 a
		ילד	MIDWIFE	408d	
		ירא	FEAR	431a	1 a
		קשה	BE SEVERE	904b	1
35	18	און	TROUBLE	19d	1
		בנאוני	BEN-ONI	122b	
		בנימן	BENJAMIN	122c	1
		יצא	GO OUT	423a	1 e
		נפש	SOUL	659c	1 c
		קרא	CALL	896a	6 e1
35	19	אפרתה	EPHRATH	68d	1
		ביתלחם	BETHLEHEM	111d	1
		ביתלחם	BETHLEHEM	112a	1
		דרך	WAY	202d	1 c
		קבר	BURY	868c	
35	20	יום	DAY	401b	7 l
		נצב	STAND	662c	2
		מצבה	PILLAR	663a	1 b
		צברה	GRAVE	869a	1
		רחל	RACHEL	933a	
35	21	מגדלעדר	MIGDAL-EDER	154a	1
		הלאה	OUT THERE	229b	A
		נטה	SPREAD OUT	640a	2
35	22	בלהה	BILHAH	117b	
		בן	SON	*120d	1 jb
		עשר	TEN	797b	2 a
		פלגש	CONCUBINE	811c	1
		שכב	LIE DOWN	1012b	3
35	23	זבולן	ZEBULUN	259d	1
		יהודה	JUDAH	397b	1 1
		ישכר	ISSACHAR	441a	1
		לאה	LEAH	521b	
		לוי	LEVI	532c	1 a
35	24	שמעון	SIMEON	1035c	1
		בנימן	BENJAMIN	122d	1
		יוסף	JOSEPH	415d	1 a
35	25	בלהה	BILHAH	117b	
		דן	DAN	192d	1
		נפתלי	NAPHTALI	836d	1
		שפחה	MAID	1046c	1
35	26	ארם	ARAM	74c	B
		אשר	ASHER	81b	1
		בן	SON	*120d	1 jb
		גד	GAD	151c	1
		זלפה	ZILPAH	273a	
		ילד	BE BORN	408d	1
		לאה	LEAH	521b	
		שפחה	MAID	1046c	1
35	27	גור	SOJOURN	157d	1
		חברון	HEBRON	*289b	
		חברון	HEBRON	289b	
		קריתארבע	FOURFOLD CITY	900c	
35	29	אסף	GATHER	62d	2 a
		זקן	OLD	278c	1
		מות	DIE	559c	1 a1
		עם	KINSMAN	769b	
		שבע	SATISFIED	960a	1 b
36		בשמת	BASEMATH	*142a	1
36	1	אדום	EDOM	10b	1
		הוא	HE, SHE, IT	215c	1 a
		חרי	HORITE	*360a	2
		יהודית	JUDITH	*397c	
		תולדות	GENERATIONS	410a	A
		עשו	ESAU	796c	
36	2	אהליבמה	OHOLIBAMA	14c	1
		אלון	ELON	19a	1
		חוי	HIVITE	295d	1
		חרי	HORITE	360a	1
		חתי	HITTITE	366c	1
		כנען	CANAAN	488d	2 a
		עדה	ADAH	725d	2
		ענה	ANAH	777b	1
		צבעון	ZIBEON	840d	
36	3	בשמת	BASEMATH	142a	1
		נביות	NEBAIOTH	614a	
		ישמעאל	ISHMAEL	1035d	1
36	4	אליפז	ELIPHAZ	45c	A
		בשמת	BASEMATH	142a	1
		עדה	ADAH	725d	2
		רעואל	REUEL	946c	1
36	5	אהליבמה	OHOLIBAMA	14c	1
		בן	SON	120d	1 ja
		ילד	BE BORN	408d	1
		יעוש	JEUSH	736c	1
		יעלם	JALAM	761c	
		קרח	KORAH	901b	1 a
36	6	בית	HOUSE	109d	4
		בית	HOUSE	109d	5 a
		הלך	WALK	231a	1 d3 ga
		נפש	SOUL	660c	4 c4
		קנין	ACQUISITION	889a	1
		מקנה	CATTLE	889b	2
		רכש	COLLECT	940d	
36	7	מגור	SOJOURNING PLACE	158c	
		יכל	BE ABLE	407c	1
		יכל	BE ABLE	407c	1 a
		ישב	DWELL	443a	3
		מן	THAN	582d	6 d
		נשא	LIFT	671b	2 c
		פנה	FACE	818c	2 6c a
		מקנה	CATTLE	889b	2
		רב	MUCH	913b	1 e
		רכש	PROPERTY	940d	2
36	8	אדום	EDOM	10b	1
		עשו	ESAU	796c	
		עשו	ESAU	796c	
		שעיר	SEIR	973a	1 b
36	9	אב	FATHER	3c	4 b
		אדום	EDOM	10c	2

23

GENESIS

Ch v.	Heb	Eng	Page	Sec
	תולדות	GENERATIONS	410a	A
	עשו	ESAU	796c	
36 10	שעיר	SEIR	973a	1 b
	אליפז	ELIPHAZ	45c	A
36 10	בשמת	BASEMATH	142a	1
	עדה	ADAH	725d	2
	רעואל	REUEL	946c	2
36 11	אליפז	ELIPHAZ	45c	A
	אומר	OMAR	57b	
	געתם	GATTAM	172b	
	תימן	TEMAN	412d	
	צפו	ZEPHO	859d	
	קנז	KENAZ	889d	
36 12	אליפז	ELIPHAZ	45c	A
	תמנע	TIMNA	286b	2
	עדה	ADAH	725d	2
	עמלק	AMALEK	766a	
	פלגש	CONCUBINE	811c	1
36 13	בשמת	BASEMATH	142a	1
	זרח	ZERAH	280c	2 a
	מזה	MIZZAH	561a	
	נחת	NAHATH	639c	1
	רעואל	REUEL	946c	2
	שמה	SHAMMAH	1031c	1
36 14	אהליבמה	OHOLIBAMA	14c	1
	היה	BE	227a	3 4b
	יעיש	JEUSH	736c	1
	יעלם	JALAM	761c	
	ענה	ANAH	777b	1
	צבעון	ZIBEON	840d	
	קרח	KORAH	901b	1 a
36 15	אליפז	ELIPHAZ	45c	A
	אלוף	CHIEF	49b	
	אומר	OMAR	57b	
	בן	SON	120d	1 ja
	תמנע	TIMNA	*286b	1 b
	תימן	TEMAN	412d	
	צפו	ZEPHO	859d	
	קנז	KENAZ	889d	
36 16	אדום	EDOM	10c	3
	אליפז	ELIPHAZ	45c	A
	געתם	GATTAM	172b	
	תמנע	TIMNA	*286b	1 b
	עדה	ADAH	725d	
	עמלק	AMALEK	766a	
	קרח	KORAH	901b	1 b
36 17	אדום	EDOM	10c	3
	בשמת	BASEMATH	142a	1
	זרח	ZERAH	280c	2 a
	מזה	MIZZAH	561a	
	נחת	NAHATH	639c	1
	רעואל	REUEL	946c	2
	שמה	SHAMMAH	1031c	1
36 18	אהליבמה	OHOLIBAMA	14c	1
	יעיש	JEUSH	736c	1
	יעלם	JALAM	761c	
	ענה	ANAH	777b	1
	קרח	KORAH	901b	1 a
36 19	אדום	EDOM	10b	1
	בן	SON	120d	1 ja
	עשו	ESAU	796c	
36 20	בן	SON	120d	1 ja
	חרי	HORITE	*360a	2
	חרי	HORITE	360a	1
	לוטן	LOTAN	532b	
	ענה	ANAH	777b	1
	צבעון	ZIBEON	840d	
	שעיר	SEIR	973a	1 d
	שובל	SHOBAL	987c	1
36 21	אדום	EDOM	10c	3
	אצר	EZER	69d	
	בן	SON	120d	1 ja
	דישן	DISHAN	190d	1
	דישן	DISHAN	190d	
	חרי	HORITE	360a	2
	שעיר	SEIR	973a	1 d
36 22	חומם	HOMAM	243a	
	תמנע	TIMNA	286b	2
	חרי	HORITE	360a	3 a
	לוטן	LOTAN	532b	
36 23	אונם	ONAM	20c	1
	מנחת	MANAHATH	630a	
	עיבל	EBAL	716c	
	עלון	ALVAN	759b	
	שובל	SHOBAL	987c	1
	שפו	SHEPHO	1046a	
36 24	איה	AIAH	17b	1
	חמור	HE-ASS	331b	1
	ימם	HOT SPRINGS	411b	
	מצא	FIND	593a	1 b
	ענה	ANAH	777b	2
	צבעון	ZIBEON	840d	
	רעה	TEND	944d	1 a
36 25	אהליבמה	OHOLIBAMA	14c	1
	דישן	DISHON	190d	2
	מואב	MOAB	555d	2 b
	ענה	ANAH	777b	1
36 26	אשבן	ESHBAN	78b	
	דישן	DISHAN	190d	
	דישן	DISHON	190d	2
	חמדן	HEMDAN	326d	
	חמרן	HAMRAN	331c	
	יתרן	ITHRAN	452d	1
	כרן	CHERAN	502b	
36 27	אצר	EZER	69d	
	בלהן	BILHAN	117b	1

Ch v.	Heb	Eng	Page	Sec
	בניעקן	BENE-JAAKAN	122c	
	יעון	AZZVAN	266b	
	זעון	ZAAVAN	276c	
	עקן	AKAN	785c	
36 28	ארן	ARAN	75a	
	דישן	DISHAN	*190d	
	דישן	DISHAN	190d	
	עוץ	UZ	734b	1 c
36 29	חרי	HORITE	*360a	2
	חרי	HORITE	360a	2
	לוטן	LOTAN	532b	
	ענה	ANAH	777b	1
	צבעון	ZIBEON	840d	
36 30	אצר	EZER	69d	
	דישן	DISHAN	*190d	
	דישן	DISHAN	190d	
	דישן	DISHON	190d	2
	חרי	HORITE	360a	2
	חרי	HORITE	*360a	2
	שעיר	SEIR	973a	1 a
36 31	אדום	EDOM	10c	3
	מלך	KING	573a	1
	מלך	KING	573a	1
	מלך	BE KING	574a	
	מלך	BE KING	574a	
36 32	אדום	EDOM	10c	3
	בלע	BELA	*118c	1
	בלע	BELA	118c	1
	בעור	BEOR	129d	2
	דנהבה	DINHABAH	200b	
36 33	בלע	BELA	118c	1
	בצרה	BOZRAH	131b	1
	זרח	ZERAH	280c	2 b
	יובב	JOBAB	384d	2
	מות	DIE	559c	1 a1
	מלך	BE KING	574a	
	תחת	INSTEAD	1065d	2 2b a
36 34	חשם	HUSHAM	302a	
	יובב	JOBAB	384d	2
	תימני	TEMANITE	412d	
	מות	DIE	559c	1 a1
36 35	בדד	BEDAD	95a	
	מדין	MIDIAN	193c	2
	הדד	HADAD	212d	1 a
	חשם	HUSHAM	302a	
	מות	DIE	559c	1 a1
	עוית	AVITH	732a	
36 36	הדד	HADAD	212d	1 a
	מות	DIE	559c	1 a1
	שמלה	SAMLAH	971a	
	משקה	MASREKAH	977d	
36 37	מות	DIE	559c	1 a1
	נחר	STREAM	625d	1
	רחבות	REHOBOTH	932c	3
	שמלה	SAMLAH	971a	
	שאול	SAUL	982c	2
36 38	מות	DIE	559c	1 a1
	בעלחנן	BAAL-HANAN	128a	1
	עכבור	ACHBOR	747b	1
	שאול	SAUL	982c	2
36 39	בעלחנן	BAAL-HANAN	128a	1
	הדד	HADAD	*212d	1 b
	הדר	HADAR	214c	
	מטרד	MATRED	382b	
	מהיטבאל	MEHETABEL	406b	1
	מות	DIE	559c	1 a1
	מיזהב	ME-ZAHAB	566a	
	עכבור	ACHBOR	747b	1
	פעו	PAU	821b	
	תחת	INSTEAD	1065d	2 2b a
36 40	תמנע	TIMNA	286b	1 a
	יתת	JETHETH	453c	
	עלוה	ALVAH	759b	
36 41	אהליבמה	OHOLIBAMA	14c	2
	אילפאן	ELPARAN	18c	
	אלה	ELAH	18d	1
	אילת	ELATH	19a	
36 42	מבצר	MIBZAR	550b	
	קנז	KENAZ	889d	
36 43	אב	FATHER	3c	4 b
	אדום	EDOM	10c	2
	אדום	EDOM	10c	3
	אחזה	POSSESSION	28c	
	מושב	DWELLING	444b	2 a
	מגדיאל	MAGDIEL	550c	
	עירם	IRAM	747a	
	עשו	ESAU	796c	
	צפו	ZEPHO	859d	
37 1	מגור	SOJOURNING PLACE	158c	
37 2	אח	BROTHER	26b	1
	בלהה	BILHAH	117b	
	דבה	EVIL REPORT	179b	3
	זלפה	ZILPAH	273a	
	תולדות	GENERATIONS	410a	A
	יוסף	JOSEPH	415d	1 a
	נער	YOUTH	655a	1 c
	עשר	TEN	797b	7 b
	רעה	TEND	945a	1 d1
	רע	EVIL	948b	2
	שבע	SEVEN	988a	2 a
37 3	אב	FATHER	3b	1
	אהב	LOVE	12d	1
	בן	SON	120c	1 h

Ch v.	Heb	Eng	Page	Sec
	הוא	HE, SHE, IT	216a	3 a
	ו	AND	252b	1 b
	זקנים	OLD AGE	279a	
	כתנת	TUNIC	509a	
	מן	THAN	582c	6 b
	פס	FLAT OF HAND	821a	
37 4	אב	FATHER	3b	1
	אח	BROTHER	26b	1
	את	MARK OF THE AC-CUSATIVE	85a	1 a
	דבר	SPEAK	181a	3 a
	יכל	BE ABLE	407c	1 b
	שלום	PEACE	1022d	3
37 5	אח	BROTHER	26b	1
	חלום	DREAM	321c	2 a
	חלם	DREAM	321c	B
	יסף	DO AGAIN	415c	2 a
	שנא	HATE	971c	1 a
37 6	חלום	DREAM	321c	2 a
	חלם	DREAM	321c	B
37 7	אלמה	SHEAF	48a	
	אלם	BIND	48a	2
	אנחנו	WE	59d	
	הנה	BEHOLD	244b	C
	נצב	STAND	662b	1 c
	סבב	SURROUND	685d	2 d
	קום	STAND	877d	1 d
	שדה	FIELD	961d	2 a
	תוך	MIDST	1063d	
37 8	אם	IF	50d	2 ab a
	חלום	DREAM	321c	2 a
	יסף	DO AGAIN	415c	2 a
	משל	RULE	605d	1
	שנא	HATE	971c	1 a
37 9	הנה	BEHOLD	244b	C
	חלום	DREAM	321c	B
	חלם	DREAM	321c	2 a
	ירח	MOON	437a	
	כוכב	STAR	456d	
	עד	STILL	729b	1 b
	שחה	BOW DOWN	1005b	1 c
	שמש	SUN	1039a	
37 10	אב	FATHER	3b	1
	אם	MOTHER	51d	1
	גער	REBUKE	172a	1
	חלום	DREAM	321c	2 a
	חלם	DREAM	321c	B
	ל	TO	*510b	1
	מה	WHAT	552d	1 c
	ספר	COUNT	708a	1
37 11	קנא	BE ZEALOUS	888c	2
	שמר	KEEP	1036d	2 a
37 12	רעה	TEND	944d	1 a
37 13	הנה	BEHOLD	244a	A
	רעה	TEND	944d	1 a
	שלח	SEND	1018b	1 a
37 14	דבר	WORD	182b	1 1c
	הלך	WALK	234a	1 5f 1
	חברון	HEBRON	289b	
	עמק	VALE	771a	
	ראה	TO SEE	907d	6 d
	שוב	TURN BACK	999c	3
	שכם	SHECHEM	1014b	1
	שלח	SEND	1018b	1 a
37 15	בקש	SEEK	134c	1 b
	הנה	BEHOLD	244b	C
	מצא	FIND	593b	3 a
	תעה	ERR	1073c	1
37 16	איפה	WHERE	33a	1
	בקש	SEEK	134c	1 b
	רעה	TEND	944d	1 a
37 17	אחר	BEHIND	29d	2
	דתן	DOTHAN	206d	
	דתן	DOTHAN	206d	
	הלך	WALK	231c	1 1d 5z
	זה	THIS	262a	6 e
	מצא	FIND	593b	3 a
	נסע	SET OUT	652b	2 b
	שמע	HEAR	1033c	1 b
37 18	ו	AND	254d	5 b
	טרם	NOT YET	382c	2
	נכל	KNAVISH	647d	
	קרב	COME NEAR	897b	1 a
	רחק	DISTANT	935c	2 a1
37 19	בעל	LORD	127c	1 5a
	הזה	THIS	229d	
	חלום	DREAM	321c	2 a
37 20	אכל	EAT	37c	2
	אמר	SAY	55d	1
	בור	PIT	92c	3
	היה	BECOME	226a	2 2b
	הרג	KILL	247a	1 a
	חיה	LIVING THING	312c	1 b
	חלום	DREAM	321c	2 a
	מה	WHAT	552d	1 b
	עתה	NOW	774b	2 b
	ראה	TO SEE	907b	5 a
	רע	EVIL	948a	1
	שלך	THROW	1021a	1 b
37 21	נכה	SMITE	645d	2 a
	נפש	SOUL	659d	3 c
37 22	אל	TO	39d	2
	בור	PIT	92c	3
	דם	BLOOD	196c	2 b
	מען	PURPOSE	775b	1 c
	שוב	TURN BACK	999a	1 d

Ch	v.	Heb	Eng	Page	Sec
		שלח	SEND	1018c	3 a
		שלך	THROW	1021a	1 b
		שפך	POUR OUT	1049c	1 b
37	23	בוא	COME	98b	2
		כתנת	TUNIC	509a	
		על	UPON	753c	2 la a
		פס	FLAT OF HAND	821a	
		פשט	STRIP OFF	833a	1
37	24	אין	NOT	34c	2 c
		בור	PIT	*92c	4
		בור	PIT	92c	3
		רב	MUCH	913a	1 b
		ריק	EMPTY	938a	1
		שלך	THROW	1021a	1 b
37	25	ארחה	TRAVELLING COM-PANY	73c	
		הלך	WALK	233d	1 5a
		ירד	BRING DOWN	433d	1 a
		ישב	SIT	442d	1 a
		לחם	FOOD	537a	1 a
		לט	MYRRH	538b	
		נכאת	A SPICE	644d	
		נשא	LIFT	671a	2 a
		צרי	BALM	863b	
		ישמעאלי	ISHMAELITE	1035d	
37	26	בצע	PROFIT	130c	
		דם	BLOOD	196d	2 f
		הרג	KILL	247a	1 a
		יהודה	JUDAH	397a	1 l
		כי	THAT	471d	1
		כסה	COVER	491d	2
		מה	WHAT	552c	1 aa
		מה	WHAT	553a	1 db
37	27	אל	NOT	39a	A a
		בשר	FLESH	142d	4
		היה	BECOME	225c	2 1b
		מכר	SELL	569b	
		נא	PART OF EN-TREATY	609b	3 c
		שמע	HEAR	1034a	1 j
		ישמעאלי	ISHMAELITE	1035d	
37	28	איש	MAN	36a	
		בור	PIT	92c	3
		מדיני	MIDIANITE	193c	
		כסף	SILVER	494b	8 b
		כסף	SILVER	494d	9
		מכר	SELL	569b	
		משך	DRAW	604b	1
		סחר	GO AROUND	695c	2
		עלה	GO UP	749b	1 b1
		ישמעאלי	ISHMAELITE	1035d	
37	29	אין	NOT	34b	2 c
		בור	PIT	92c	3
		הנה	BEHOLD	244b	C
		קרע	TEAR	902c	1 a1
37	30	אין	NOT	34b	2 b
		ילד	CHILD	409b	A
37	31	דם	BLOOD	196c	2 a
		טבל	DIP	371b	1
		כתנת	TUNIC	509a	
		עז	SHE-GOAT	777c	2
		שעיר	HE-GOAT	972c	
		שחט	SLAUGHTER	1006a	1
37	32	ה	INTERROG PART	210b	2 b
		כתנת	TUNIC	509a	
		לא	NOT	519a	1 ad b
		נכר	REGARD	648a	1
		פס	FLAT OF HAND	821a	
37	33	אכל	EAT	37c	2
		חיה	LIVING THING	312c	1 b
		טרף	TEAR	382d	
		טרף	TEAR	383a	
		כתנת	TUNIC	509a	
		נכר	RECOGNIZE	648a	2
		רע	EVIL	948a	1
37	34	אבל	MOURN	5c	
		יום	DAY	399c	5 b
		מתנים	LOINS	608b	1 e
		קרע	TEAR	902c	1 a1
		קרע	TEAR	902c	1 a1
		שום	TO PLACE	963a	1 a
		שמלה	WRAPPER	971a	
		שמלה	WRAPPER	971a	
		שק	SACK	974c	2 a
37	35	אב	FATHER	3b	1
		אבל	MOURNING	5d	
		בכה	WEEP	113c	4
		בת	DAUGHTER	123b	1 g
		ירד	GO DOWN	433a	1 i
		כל	ALL	481b	1 a
		מאן	REFUSE	549a	
		נחם	CONSOLE ONESELF	637a	
		נחם	CONSOLE ONESELF	637b	3
		שאול	SHEOL	982d	1
		אל	TO	39c	1
37	36	מדיני	MIDIANITE	193c	
		טבח	COOK	371a	2
		מכר	SELL	569b	
		סריס	EUNUCH	710c	
		פוטיפר	POTIPHAR	806c	
		שר	CHIEFTAIN	978c	4 a
38	1	איש	MAN	36a	
		את	WITH	86d	4 a
		חירה	HIRAH	301b	
		יהודה	JUDAH	397a	1 l
		נטה	BEND	640b	3 a

Ch	v.	Heb	Eng	Page	Sec
		עדלמי	ADULLAMITE	726c	
		עת	TIME	773b	1 a
38	2	איש	MAN	36a	
		בת	DAUGHTER	123b	1 h
		בתשוע	BATH-SHUA	124a	2
		שוע	SHUA	447d	
		כנעני	CANAANITE	489a	1
38	3	הרה	CONCEIVE	247d	1
		ער	ER	735c	1
38	4	הרה	CONCEIVE	247d	1
38	5	ו	AND	252b	1 b
		יסף	DO AGAIN	415c	2 b
		כזיב	CHEZIB	469d	
		שלה	SHELAH	1017c	
38	6	ער	ER	735c	1
		תמר	TAMAR	1071c	1 a
38	7	היה	BECOME	226a	2 2b
		מות	DIE	560b	2
		ער	ER	735c	1
		רע	EVIL	948c	0 b
38	8	בוא	COME	98a	1 e
		זרע	SOWING	282d	4 c
		זרע	SOWING	283a	4 e
		יבם	DO DUTY OF HUS-BAND:S BROTH	386a	
		יבמת	SISTER-IN-LAW	*386a	
		יבם	HUSBAND:S BROTHER	*386a	
		קום	STAND	878a	3
38	9	אם	IF	50b	1 b4 a
		ארץ	EARTH	76b	3 a
		בוא	COME	98a	1 e
		בלת	NOT	116d	4 a
		היה	COME TO PASS	225b	1 2b bb
		היה	BECOME	226c	2 2h
		זרע	SOWING	282d	4 c
		זרע	SOWING	283a	4 e
		לא	NOT	518d	1 ac
		שחת	GO TO RUIN	1008a	1
38	10	מות	DIE	560b	2
		רעע	BE EVIL	949c	4
38	11	אב	FATHER	3c	1
		אלמנה	WIDOW	48b	
		גדל	GROW UP	152b	1
		כלה	DAUGHTER-IN-LAW	483c	1
		מות	DIE	559d	2 b
		פן	LEST	814d	1 a
		שלה	SHELAH	1017c	
		תמר	TAMAR	1071c	1 a
38	12	בת	DAUGHTER	123b	1 h
		בתשוע	BATH-SHUA	124a	2
		גזז	SHEAR	159c	
		חירה	HIRAH	301b	
		יום	DAY	399c	5 b
		שוע	SHUA	447d	
		נחם	CONSOLE ONESELF	637a	3
		עדלמי	ADULLAMITE	726c	
		עלה	GO UP	748c	2 a
		על	UPON	757b	27c aa
		רבה	BECOME MANY	915b	1 c
38	13	אמר	SAY	56b	1
		גזז	SHEAR	159c	
		חם	HUSBAND'S FA-THER	327b	
		תמנה	TIMNAH	584d	1
		גדל	BE CONSPICUOUS	617a	
		תמר	TAMAR	1071c	1 a
38	14	אלמנות	WIDOWHOOD	48c	
		גדל	GROW UP	152b	1
		דרך	WAY	202d	1
		ישב	SIT	442c	1 a
		כסה	COVER	491c	1
		תמנה	TIMNAH	584d	1
		נתן	GIVE	681b	1 b
		סור	TURN ASIDE	694b	1
		עינים	ENAIM	734d	
		עטה	WRAP ONESELF	*742a	
		על	UPON	758c	4 2a
		עלף	COVER	763b	
		פתח	OPENING	836a	
		ציעיף	VEIL	858b	
		שלה	SHELAH	1017c	
38	15	זנה	COMMIT FORNICA-TION	275d	1
		חשב	THINK	363a	1 l
		כסה	COVER	491c	1
		ל	TO	512b	4 a
		ל	TO	514a	5 e
38	16	דרך	WAY	202c	1
		יהב	GIVE	396d	5
		כי	IF	473b	2 b
		כלה	DAUGHTER-IN-LAW	483c	1
		נטה	BEND	640b	3 a
38	17	אם	IF	50c	2 aa
		גדי	KID	152a	
		ערבון	PLEDGE	786d	
		צאן	SMALL CATTLE	838b	1 a4
		שלח	SEND	1018b	1 b
38	18	הרה	CONCEIVE	247d	1
		חתם	SEAL	368b	
		חתמת	SIGNET-RING	*368b	
		יד	HAND	390d	5 c1
		ל	TO	514a	5 e

Ch	v.	Heb	Eng	Page	Sec
		מטה	STAFF	641c	1
		ערבון	PLEDGE	786d	
		פתיל	CORD	836d	
38	19	אלמנות	WIDOWHOOD	48c	
		לבש	PUT ON	527d	A
		סור	TURN ASIDE	694b	1
		עדה	PASS ON	*723c	
		על	UPON	758c	4 2a
		ציעיף	VEIL	858b	
38	20	גדי	KID	152a	
		יד	HAND	391a	5 d
		מצא	FIND	593a	1 b
		עדלמי	ADULLAMITE	726c	
38	21	דרך	WAY	202c	1
		זה	THIS	261d	6 a
		עינים	ENAIM	734d	
		על	UPON	756a	2 6a
		קדש	TEMPLE-PROSTI-TUTE	873d	
38	22	זה	THIS	261d	6 a
		מצא	FIND	593a	1 b
		קדש	TEMPLE-PROSTI-TUTE	873d	
38	23	בוז	CONTEMPT	*100b	
		בוז	CONTEMPT	100b	1
		גדי	KID	152a	
		מצא	FIND	593a	1 b
		פן	LEST	814d	1
		שלח	SEND	1018b	1 b
		פן	ADDENDA ET COR-RIGENDA	1126b	
38	24	אמר	SAY	56b	1
		היה	COME TO PASS	224d	2 al a1
		זנה	COMMIT FORNICA-TION	275d	1
		זנונים	FORNICATION	276a	A
		חדש	NEW MOON	*294c	2 a
		חדש	NEW MOON	294c	2 a
		יצא	CAUSE TO GO	424c	1 b
		כ	LIKE	455a	2
		כלה	DAUGHTER-IN-LAW	483c	1
		ל	TO	516a	5 jb
		מן	FROM	581c	4 b
		נגד	BE CONSPICUOUS	617a	
		שרף	BURN	977a	
		שלש	THREE	*1025d	1 a
		תמר	TAMAR	1071c	1 a
38	25	איש	MAN	35d	
		הוא	HE, SHE, IT	*214d	
		חם	HUSBAND'S FA-THER	327b	
		חתמת	SIGNET-RING	368d	
		חתם	SEAL	*368b	
		יצא	BE BROUGHT FORTH	425c	
		מי	WHO	566b	B
		מטה	STAFF	641c	1
		נכר	REGARD	648a	1
		פתיל	CORD	836d	
		שלח	SEND	1018b	1 c
38	26	ידע	KNOW	394b	3
		יסף	ADD	414d	
		כעלכן	FOR THEREFORE	475c	
		מן	THAN	582c	6 a
		נכר	RECOGNIZE	648a	2
		נתן	GIVE	678c	1 c
		צדק	BE JUST	842c	1
		שלה	SHELAH	1017c	
38	27	בטן	WOMB	106a	3
		היה	COME TO PASS	225a	1 2a 1c
		ילד	BEAR	408b	1 a
		תואם	TWIN	1060d	
38	28	זה	THIS	260c	1 a
		יד	HAND	389a	1 b
		ילד	BEAR	408b	1 a
		ילד	MIDWIFE	408d	
		יצא	GO OUT	423c	1 h
		נתן	GIVE	679d	1 y
		קשר	BIND	905b	1 a
		ראשון	FIRST	912a	3 b1
		שני	SCARLET	1040c	
38	29	היה	COME TO PASS	225a	1 2a 1c
		יד	HAND	389a	1 b
		יצא	GO OUT	423c	1 h
		כ	LIKE	454d	3 b
		מה	HOW	553c	2 b
		על	UPON	756c	2 7a b
		פרץ	BREAK THROUGH	829a	1
		פרץ	PEREZ	829d	1
		פרץ	BURSTING FORTH	829d	1
		שוב	TURN BACK	999a	1 c
38	30	זרח	ZERAH	280b	1
		יד	HAND	389a	1 b
		יצא	GO OUT	423c	1 h
		על	UPON	753c	2 la a
		שני	SCARLET	1040c	
39	1	איש	MAN	36a	
		טבח	COOK	371a	2
		ירד	BRING DOWN	433d	1 a
		ירד	BE BROUGHT DOWN	434b	1
		מצרי	EGYPTIAN	596a	1
		סריס	EUNUCH	710c	
		פוטיפר	POTIPHAR	806c	
		ישמעאלי	ISHMAELITE	1035d	

Ch	v.	Heb	Eng	Page	Sec
39	2	היה	BE	227b	3 4 d b
		מצרי	EGYPTIAN	596a	2
		עם	WITH	767c	1 a
		צלח	ADVANCE	852c	2
39	3	עם	WITH	767c	1 a
		צלח	ADVANCE	852c	1
39	4	בית	HOUSE	110b	6
		חן	FAVOR	336b	2 b1
		יש	HAVE	442a	2 cb
		כל	ALL	481d	1 c
		נתן	GIVE	679c	1 r
		פקד	ATTEND TO	823d	1
		שרת	SERVE	1058a	1 a
39	5	מאז	FROM THAT TIME	23b	2
		בית	HOUSE	110b	6
		ברך	BLESS	139a	2 a
		ברכה	BLESSING	139d	1 b
		היה	COME TO PASS	224c	2 a1 az
		היה	BECOME	225d	2 1b
		יש	HAVE	441d	2 cb
		כל	ALL	*481d	1 c
		מצרי	EGYPTIAN	596a	2
		פקד	ATTEND TO	824a	1
		ש	WHO	*980b	4 d
39	6	את	WITH	86a	1 b
		היה	BE	227a	3 4a
		ידע	KNOW	393c	1 a
		ידע	KNOW	394b	2
		יפה	BEAUTIFUL	421c	
		מאומה	ANYTHING	548d	
		עזב	LEAVE	737b	1 h
		מראה	VISION	909c	1 b
		תאר	FORM	1061b	
39	7	אחר	AFTER	29d	2 b
		אל	TO	39d	3 a
		דבר	WORD	183a	4 4
		היה	COME TO PASS	224c	2 a1 ai
		נשא	LIFT	670c	1 b 4
		שכב	LIE DOWN	1012a	3
39	8	את	WITH	86a	1 b
		ידע	KNOW	393c	1 a
		יש	HAVE	441d	2 cb
		כל	ALL	*481d	1 c
		מאן	REFUSE	549a	
		מה	WHAT	552d	1 b
		נתן	GIVE	679c	1 r
39	9	איך	HOW	32c	1
		אלהים	GOD	44a	4 a
		באשר	IN THAT	84a	C
		גדול	GREAT	153a	3
		חטא	MISS A GOAL OR WAY	307a	2 b
		חשך	WITHHOLD	362b	1 a
		כיאם	EXCEPT	474d	2 a
		מאומה	ANYTHING	548d	
		רעה	MISERY	949b	3
		ש	WHO	980b	4 c
39	10	אצל	BESIDE	69b	A
		היה	COME TO PASS	224d	1 2a 1b
		היה	BE	227b	3 4d a
		היה	BE	227b	3 4d a
		יום	DAY	400b	7 e1
		ך	LIKE	454d	1 b
		שכב	LIE DOWN	1012b	3
39	11	היה	COME TO PASS	224c	2 a1 ae
		יום	DAY	*400c	7 g
		יום	DAY	400d	7 h
		מלאכה	WORK	522a	1
		מן	FROM	580c	3 a
39	12	יצא	GO OUT	423a	1
		נוס	FLEE	630d	1
		עזב	LEAVE	737a	1 b
		שכב	LIE DOWN	1012b	3
		תפש	LAY HOLD OF	1074d	1
39	13	ך	LIKE	454d	3 b
		עזב	LEAVE	737a	1 b
39	14	איש	MAN	36a	4
		בוא	COME	98a	1 e
		בוא	COME	99b	2
		גדול	GREAT	153a	4
		עברי	HEBREW	720b	1 a
		צחק	LAUGH	850b	2
		קול	VOICE	*877a	1 a
		קרא	CALL	895a	1
		ראה	TO SEE	907d	7 a
		שכב	LIE DOWN	1012b	3
39	15	אצל	BESIDE	69b	A
		יצא	GO OUT	423a	1 d
		נוס	FLEE	630d	1
		עזב	LEAVE	737a	1 b
		קול	VOICE	876d	1 a
		קול	VOICE	877a	1 a
		קרא	CALL	895a	1 a
		רום	BE HIGH	927c	1 b
39	16	נוח	REST	628d	B 1
39	17	בוא	COME	99b	2
		עבד	SLAVE	713d	1
		עברי	HEBREW	720b	1 a
		צחק	LAUGH	850b	2
39	18	עזב	LEAVE	737a	1 b
		קול	VOICE	876d	1 a
		קרא	CALL	895a	1 a
		רום	BE HIGH	927c	1 b
39	19	אף	NOSE	60b	3
		דבר	WORD	183d	4 7
		חרה	BURN	354a	1 a

Ch	v.	Heb	Eng	Page	Sec
39	20	עבד	SLAVE	713d	1
		אל	TO	39d	2
		אסר	TIE	63d	3
		אסר	TIE	63d	3
		אסיר	PRISONER	64a	
		אשר	PARTICLE OF RELATION	82c	4 bb
		בית	HOUSE	109a	1 ae 2
		מלך	KING	573a	1
		סהר	ROUNDNESS	690c	
		מקום	STANDING PLACE	880b	4
		ש	WHO	*979d	2
39	21	בית	HOUSE	109a	1 ae 2
		היה	BE	227b	3 4d b
		חן	FAVOR	336c	2 b1
		חסד	GOODNESS	339a	2 1a
		נטה	BEND	640c	3 b
		נתן	PUT	680d	2 b
		סהר	ROUNDNESS	690c	
		על	UPON	758a	2 8
		עם	WITH	767c	1 a
		שר	CHIEFTAIN	978c	4 b
39	22	אסיר	PRISONER	64a	
		בית	HOUSE	109a	1 ae 2
		היה	BE	227c	3 5a
		נתן	GIVE	679c	1 r
		סהר	ROUNDNESS	690c	
39	23	אין	NOT	34b	2 c
		באשר	IN THAT	84a	C
		בית	HOUSE	109a	1 ae 2
		יד	HAND	391a	5 c3
		מאומה	ANYTHING	548d	
		סהר	ROUNDNESS	690c	
		עם	WITH	767c	1 a
		צלח	ADVANCE	852c	1
		ראה	TO SEE	907d	6 h
		שר	CHIEFTAIN	978c	4 b
40	1	אחר	AFTER	29d	2 b
		אפה	BAKE	66a	
		דבר	WORD	183c	4 4
		חטא	MISS A GOAL OR WAY	306d	2 a
		משקה	CUP-BEARER	1052d	
40	2	אפה	BAKE	66a	
		סרים	EUNUCH	710c	
		על	UPON	757d	2 7d
		קצף	BE WROTH	893b	2
		שר	CHIEFTAIN	978c	4 a
		משקה	CUP-BEARER	1052d	
40	3	אסר	TIE	63d	3
		בית	HOUSE	109a	1 ae 2
		טבח	COOK	371a	2
		סהר	ROUNDNESS	690c	
		מקום	STANDING PLACE	880b	4
		משמר	PRISON	1038b	1
		טבח	COOK	371a	2
40	4	יום	DAY	399b	5 a
		פקד	ATTEND TO	823c	B 1
		משמר	PRISON	1038b	1
		שרת	SERVE	1058a	1 a
40	5	איש	MAN	36a	
		אסר	TIE	63d	3
		אפה	BAKE	66a	
		אשר	PARTICLE OF RELATION	83a	7 b
		אשר	PARTICLE OF RELATION	83a	7 b
		בית	HOUSE	109a	1 ae 2
		חלום	DREAM	321c	2 a
		חלום	DREAM	321c	B
		סהר	ROUNDNESS	690c	
		פתרון	INTERPRETATION	837c	
		משקה	CUP-BEARER	1052d	
40	6	בקר	MORNING	133d	1 a
		הנה	BEHOLD	243d	
		זעף	BE VEXED	277a	1
40	7	אדון	LORD	11a	2 1b
		מדוע	WHEREFORE	396c	
		סרים	EUNUCH	710c	
		פנה	FACE	815d	1 1a
		רע	EVIL	948b	7
		משמר	PRISON	1038b	1
40	8	אין	NOT	34c	2 c
		חלם	DREAM	321c	B
		חלום	DREAM	321c	2 a
		ספר	COUNT	708a	1
		פתר	INTERPRET	837c	
		פתרון	INTERPRETATION	837c	
40	9	גפן	VINE	172c	
		הנה	BEHOLD	244b	C
		ו	AND	255a	5 cg
		חלום	DREAM	321c	2 a
		משקה	CUP-BEARER	1052d	
40	10	אשכל	CLUSTER	79a	1
		בשל	GROW RIPE	143b	
		גפן	VINE	172c	
		ך	LIKE	454d	3 b
		ניץ	BLOSSOM	665b	
		נצה	BLOSSOM	665b	
		עלה	GO UP	748d	4
		ענב	GRAPE	772a	
		פרח	BUD	827a	
		שריג	TENDRIL	974d	
40	11	אל	TO	39d	2
		כוס	CUP	468a	

Ch	v.	Heb	Eng	Page	Sec
		כף	HOLLOW OF THE HAND	496b	1 a
		לקח	TAKE	542d	1
		על	UPON	756b	2 7a a
		ענב	GRAPE	772a	
		שחט	SQUEEZE OUT	965c	
40	12	פתרון	INTERPRETATION	837c	
		שריג	TENDRIL	974d	
40	13	אשר	PARTICLE OF RELATION	82c	4 ba
		היה	BE	227d	3 4b
		ך	LIKE	454a	1 c1
		כוס	CUP	468a	
		כן	PLACE	487d	2
		נשא	LIFT	670b	1 b 2
		נתן	PUT	680b	2 a
		עוד	STILL	729c	2 ab
		על	UPON	757a	2 7c a
		מקום	STANDING PLACE	879d	1 a
		שוב	TURN BACK	999b	1 d
		משפט	JUDGMENT	1049a	6 b
		משקה	CUP-BEARER	1052d	
40	14	אל	TO	40a	3 b
		את	WITH	86c	3 b
		זכר	REMEMBER	269d	1 2 a
		זכר	REMEMBER	270d	3 a
		חסד	GOODNESS	338c	1 1
		יטב	BE WELL	405c	3
		יצא	CAUSE TO GO	424b	1 a
		כאשר	WHEN	455c	3
		כיאם	BUT	475b	2 b
		נא	PART OF ENTREATY	609b	2
40	15	עם	WITH	767d	1 d
		בור	PIT	92c	4
		גגב	STEAL	170c	
		כי	THAT	472d	1 f
		מאומה	ANYTHING	548d	
		מן	OUT OF	579a	2 aa
		עברי	HEBREW	720b	2 b
		פה	HERE	806a	1 a
		שום	TO PLACE	962d	1 a
40	16	אף	ALSO	64d	1
		אפה	BAKE	66a	
		הנה	BEHOLD	244b	C
		ו	AND	255a	5 cg
		חרי	WHITE BREAD	301a	
		חלום	DREAM	321c	2 a
		טוב	PLEASANT	374b	5
		סל	BASKET	700d	
		פתר	INTERPRET	837c	
		ראש	HEAD	910d	1 a
		נקה	ADDENDA ET CORRIGENDA	1125b	
40	17	אכל	EAT	37c	2
		מאכל	FOOD	38b	
		אפה	BAKE	66a	
		סל	BASKET	700d	
		עוף	FLYING CREATURES	733d	1
		עליון	HIGH	751b	2
		מעשה	DEED	796a	2 a1
		ראש	HEAD	910d	1 a
40	18	סל	BASKET	700d	
		פתרון	INTERPRETATION	837c	
40	19	אכל	EAT	37c	2
		בשר	FLESH	142c	1
		נשא	LIFT	670b	1 b 2
		נשא	LIFT	671b	3 b
		עוד	STILL	729c	2 ab
		עוף	FLYING CREATURES	733d	1
		על	UPON	758a	4 2a
		עין	TREE	781d	2 b
		תלה	HANG	1068a	2
		אפה	BAKE	66a	
40	20	יום	DAY	398c	2 f
		ילד	BE BORN	409b	
		נשא	LIFT	670b	1 b 2
		עבד	SLAVE	713d	1
		עשה	DO	794c	2 1c
		משקה	CUP-BEARER	1052d	
		משתה	FEAST	1059d	1
		תוך	MIDST	1063d	
40	21	כוס	CUP	468a	
		כף	HOLLOW OF THE HAND	496b	1 a
		על	UPON	756b	2 7a a
		שוב	TURN BACK	999b	1 d
		משקה	DRINK	1052d	3
		משקה	CUP-BEARER	1052d	
40	22	אפה	BAKE	66a	
		פתר	INTERPRET	837c	
		תלה	HANG	1068a	2
40	23	זכר	REMEMBER	269d	1 2 a
		שכח	FORGET	1013a	1 b
		משקה	CUP-BEARER	1052d	
41	1	היה	COME TO PASS	224d	1 2a 1b
		הנה	BEHOLD	244b	C
		חלם	DREAM	321c	B
		יאר	STREAM	384b	1
		יום	TIME	399d	6 b
		על	UPON	755d	2 6a
		עמד	STAND	763d	1 a
		קץ	END	893d	1
		שנה	YEAR	1040b	

Ch	v.	Heb	Eng	Page	Sec
41	2	אחו	REEDS	28a	
		ברא	FAT	135d	
		בשר	FLESH	142c	1 a
		הנה	BEHOLD	244b	C
		יאר	STREAM	384b	1
		יפה	BEAUTIFUL	421c	
		עלה	GO UP	748d	1
		פרה	HEIFER	831a	
		מראה	VISION	909a	1 b
		רעה	TEND	945b	2 a
		שבע	SEVEN	988d	5 c
41	3	אצל	BESIDE	69b	A
		בשר	FLESH	142c	1 a
		דק	THIN	201a	1
		היה	COME TO PASS	224b	1 1b
		הנה	BEHOLD	244b	C
		יאר	STREAM	384b	1
		עלה	GO UP	748d	3
		עמד	STAND	763d	1 a
		פרה	HEIFER	831a	
		מראה	VISION	909a	1 b
		רע	EVIL	948b	4
		רק	THIN	*956b	
		שפה	SPEECH	974a	3
41	4	ברא	FAT	135d	
		בשר	FLESH	142c	1 a
		דק	THIN	201a	1
		יפה	BEAUTIFUL	421c	
		יקץ	AWAKE	429c	
		מראה	VISION	909a	1 b
		רע	EVIL	948b	4
		רק	THIN	*956b	
41	5	ברא	FAT	135d	
		בשר	FLESH	142c	1 a
		חלם	DREAM	321c	B
		טוב	PLEASANT	373d	1 b
		ישן	SLEEP	445c	
		עלה	GO UP	748d	4
		קנה	STALK	889c	1
		שבלת	EAR OF GRAIN	987c	
		שבלת	EAR OF GRAIN	987c	
41	6	בשר	FLESH	142c	1 a
		דק	THIN	201a	1
		צמח	SPROUT	855b	1
		קדים	EAST WIND	870b	1
		ריק	EMPTY	*938a	1
		שבלת	EAR OF GRAIN	987c	
		שדף	SCORCH	995b	
41	7	בלע	SWALLOW DOWN	118a	1
		ברא	FAT	135d	
		בשר	FLESH	142c	1 a
		דק	THIN	201a	1
		חלום	DREAM	321c	2 a
		יקץ	AWAKE	429c	
		מלא	FULL	571a	
		ריק	EMPTY	*938a	1
		שבלת	EAR OF GRAIN	987c	
41	8	בקר	MORNING	133d	1 a
		בשר	FLESH	142c	1 a
		חכם	WISE	314d	4
		חלום	DREAM	321c	1
		חרטם	ENGRAVER	355a	1
		פעם	THRUST	821d	
		פתר	INTERPRET	837c	
		קרא	CALL	895d	5 c
		רוח	BREATH	925b	3 e
41	9	בשר	FLESH	142c	1 a
		דבר	SPEAK	181b	3
		זכר	REMEMBER	271a	3 b
		חטא	SIN	308a	1 a
		משקה	CUP-BEARER	1052d	
41	10	אפה	BAKE	66a	
		בשר	FLESH	142c	1 a
		טבח	COOK	371a	2
		עבד	SLAVE	713d	2
		קצף	BE WROTH	893b	2
		משמר	PRISON	1038b	1
41	11	בשר	FLESH	142c	1 a
		חלום	DREAM	321c	2 a
		חלם	DREAM	321c	B
		פתרון	INTERPRETATION	837c	
41	12	בשר	FLESH	142c	1 a
		חלום	DREAM	321c	2 a
		טבח	COOK	371a	2
		ל	TO	513c	5 cb a
		עבד	SLAVE	713d	1
		עברי	HEBREW	720b	1 a
		פתר	INTERPRET	837c	
		שם	THERE	1027a	1
41	13	את	MARK OF THE AC-CUSATIVE	85a	1 a
		בשר	FLESH	142c	1 a
		כן	SO	486c	2 ca
		כן	PLACE	487d	2
		על	UPON	757a	2 7c a
		פתר	INTERPRET	837c	
		מקום	STANDING PLACE	879d	1 c
		תלה	HANG	1068a	2
41	14	בור	PIT	92c	4
		בשר	FLESH	142c	1 a
		חלף	PASS ON OR AWAY	322b	
		קרא	CALL	895d	5 c
		רוץ	RUN	930c	1
		שמלה	WRAPPER	971a	
41	15	אין	NOT	34c	2 c
		בשר	FLESH	142c	1 a
		חלם	DREAM	321c	B
		חלום	DREAM	321c	2 a
		על	UPON	754d	2 lf g
		פתר	INTERPRET	837c	
		שמע	HEAR	1033c	1 c
41	16	אמר	SAY	56b	1
		בלעדי	APART FROM	116b	A
		בשר	FLESH	142c	1 a
		ענה	ANSWER	772d	1 c
		ענה	ANSWER	773a	1 d
41	17	בשר	FLESH	142c	1 a
		חלום	DREAM	321c	2 a
		יאר	STREAM	384b	1
		עמד	STAND	763d	1 a
		שפה	SPEECH	974a	3
41	18	אחו	REEDS	28a	
		ברא	FAT	135d	
		בשר	FLESH	142c	1 a
		יאר	STREAM	384b	1
		יפה	BEAUTIFUL	421c	
		עלה	GO UP	748d	3
		רעה	TEND	945b	2 a
		תאר	FORM	1061c	
41	19	בשר	FLESH	142c	1 a
		דל	WEAK	195d	
		הם	THEY	241d	8 c
		ל	TO	514b	5 fb
		עלה	GO UP	748d	3
		ראה	TO SEE	907a	1 b
		רע	EVIL	947d	1
		רע	EVIL	948b	4
		רק	THIN	956b	1
		תאר	FORM	1061c	
41	20	ברא	FAT	135d	
		ראשון	FIRST	911c	1
		רע	EVIL	948b	4
		רק	THIN	956b	1
41	21	אל	TO	39d	2
		בוא	COME	97d	1
		ידע	BE PERCEIVED	394d	3
		יקץ	AWAKE	429c	
		כאשר	AS	455b	1 a
		קרב	INWARD PART	899a	1 b
		מראה	VISION	909a	1 b
		רע	EVIL	948b	4
41	22	חלום	DREAM	321c	2 a
		טוב	PLEASANT	373d	1 b
		מלא	FULL	571a	
		עלה	GO UP	748d	4
		קנה	STALK	889c	1
		שבלת	EAR OF GRAIN	987c	
41	23	דק	THIN	201a	1
		צמם	DRY UP	856d	
		קדים	EAST WIND	870b	1
		ריק	EMPTY	*938a	1
		שבלת	EAR OF GRAIN	987c	
		שדף	SCORCH	995b	
41	24	בלע	SWALLOW DOWN	118a	1
		דק	THIN	201a	1
		חרטם	ENGRAVER	355a	1
		טוב	PLEASANT	373d	1 b
		ריק	EMPTY	*938a	1
		שבלת	EAR OF GRAIN	987c	
41	25	הוא	HE, SHE, IT	216a	3
		חלום	DREAM	321c	2 a
		נגד	BE CONSPICUOUS	616d	2
41	26	הם	THEY	241d	3 b
		חלום	DREAM	321c	2 a
		טוב	PLEASANT	373d	1 b
		טוב	PLEASANT	374b	3 d
		שבלת	EAR OF GRAIN	987c	
41	27	כחש	LEANNESS	*471c	
		קדים	EAST WIND	870b	1
		ריק	EMPTY	938a	1
		רעב	FAMINE	944b	1
		רע	EVIL	948b	4
		רק	THIN	956b	1
		שבלת	EAR OF GRAIN	987c	
		שדף	SCORCH	995b	
41	28	ראה	TO SEE	908a	
41	29	ראה	TO SEE	908d	1 a2
		שבעה	PLENTY	960a	1
41	30	קום	STAND	878a	4
		רעב	FAMINE	944b	1
		רעב	FAMINE	944b	1
		שבעה	PLENTY	960a	1
		שכח	FORGET	1013b	
41	31	אחר	AFTER	30a	2 b
		ידע	BE MADE KNOWN	394c	1
		כבד	HEAVY	458a	1 a
		פנה	FACE	818c	2 6c a
		רעב	FAMINE	944b	1
		שבעה	PLENTY	960a	1
41	32	חלום	DREAM	321c	2 a
		כון	BE FIRM	465d	1 d
		מהר	HASTEN	555a	1
		על	UPON	754d	2 lf h
		מעם	FROM WITH	769a	D
		פעם	OCCURRENCE	822a	3 a
		שנה	DO AGAIN	1040d	1
41	33	בין	DISCERN	106d	
		חכם	WISE	314d	2
		על	UPON	755a	2 3
		ראה	TO SEE	907a	6 g
		שית	PUT	1011b	2 a
41	34	חמש	TAKE A FIFTH PART	332b	
		על	UPON	755a	2 3
		פקד	COMMISSIONER	824b	
		שבע	PLENTY	960a	1
41	35	אכל	FOOD	38a	
		בר	GRAIN	141b	
		טוב	PLEASANT	373d	2 a
		צבר	HEAP UP	840d	
		קבץ	GATHER	867c	1
		שמר	KEEP	1036d	2 a
		תחת	UNDERNEATH	1065c	2 1d
41	36	כרת	BE CUT OFF	504a	1 b
		פקדון	DEPOSIT	824c	
		רעב	FAMINE	944b	1
41	37	יטב	BE PLEASING	405c	4
41	38	זה	THIS	262a	6 ca
		מצא	FIND	593a	1 a
41	39	אין	NOT	34b	2 c
		בין	DISCERN	106d	
		זה	THIS	260c	1 a
		חכם	WISE	314d	2
		ידע	KNOW	395a	
		צבר	HEAP UP	840d	
41	40	גדל	BECOME GREAT	152b	2 a
		כסא	SEAT OF HONOR	490d	1 a
		נשק	KISS	676c	
		על	UPON	755a	2 3
		עם	PEOPLE	766c	1
		פה	MOUTH	805d	6 d1 a
		רק	ONLY	956b	1
		נתן	PUT	680d	2 c
41	41	ראה	TO SEE	907d	7 a
41	42	זהב	GOLD	263a	6
		טבעת	SIGNET	371d	1
		יד	HAND	389a	1 b
		לבש	CLOTHE	528b	1 a
		נתן	PUT	680a	2 a
		סור	TURN ASIDE	694b	1
		על	UPON	758c	4 2a
		צואר	NECK	848c	1
		ירבעם	CHAIN	914d	
		שום	TO PLACE	963b	1 b
		שש	BYSSUS	1058c	
41	43	אשר	PARTICLE OF RE-LATION	83a	7 b
		על	UPON	755a	2 3
		קרא	CALL	845b	3 a
		רכב	RIDE	938d	1
		מרכבה	CHARIOT	939d	
		משנה	SECOND	1041c	3 a
41	44	בלעדי	APART FROM	116b	A
		בלעדי	APART FROM	*116b	B a
		רגל	FOOT	920a	1 f
		רום	BE HIGH	927b	1 a1
41	45	און	ON	58a	
		אסנת	ASENATH	62a	
		כהן	PRIEST	463a	2
		על	UPON	752d	2 1
		פוטיפרע	POTIPHERA	806c	
		צפנתפענח	ZEPHENATH-PA-NEAH	861c	
41	46	יוסף	JOSEPH	415d	1 a
		יצא	GO OUT	422d	1 b
		פנה	FACE	817d	2 5a a
		פרעה	PHARAOH	829a	
41	47	ל	TO	516b	5 ja
		עשה	DO	794d	2 2
		קמץ	FIST	888a	
		שבע	PLENTY	960a	1
41	48	נתן	PUT	680b	2 a
		סביב	ROUND ABOUT	687b	2 bb
		קבץ	GATHER	867c	1
		שדה	FIELD	961d	2 c
41	49	בר	GRAIN	141b	
		חדל	CEASE	293a	2
		חול	SAND	297d	A
		חול	SAND	297d	C
		ים	SEA	411b	8 b
		מאד	EXCEEDINGLY	547b	2 a
		ספר	COUNT	707d	1
		מספר	NUMBER	708d	1 a
		עד	UNTIL	724d	2 1a a
		רבה	BECOME MANY	915d	1 e3
41	50	און	ON	58a	
		אסנת	ASENATH	62a	
		טרם	NOT YET	382c	2
		ילד	BE BORN	408d	
		כהן	PRIEST	463a	2
		פוטיפרע	POTIPHERA	806c	
		רעב	FAMINE	944b	1
41	51	אב	FATHER	3c	3
		מנשה	MANASSEH	286c	1 a
		כי	THAT	*472a	1 b
		נשה	FORGET	674d	
		עמל	TROUBLE	765d	1
		אפרים	EPHRAIM	68b	1
41	52	כי	THAT	*472a	1 b
		עני	AFFLICTION	777a	1
		פרה	BEAR FRUIT	826a	1
41	53	כלה	BE FINISHED	477c	1 a
		שבע	PLENTY	960a	1
41	54	ארץ	EARTH	76c	5
		היה	BECOME	225c	2 1a
		חלל	POLLUTE	320d	2
		כלה	BE FINISHED	*477c	1 a

GENESIS

Ch	v.	Heb	Eng	Page	Sec
41	55	לחם	FOOD	537b	1 b
		הלך	WALK	231a	1 d3 ga
		ל	TO	515a	5 ha
		לחם	FOOD	537b	1 b
		מצרים	EGYPTIANS	595d	2 b
		צעק	CRY	858c	1 a
		רעב	BE HUNGRY	945b	
41	56	חזק	BE FIRM	304c	1 4b
		מצרים	EGYPTIANS	595d	2 b
		פתח	OPEN	835a	
		רעב	FAMINE	944b	1
		שבר	BUY GRAIN	991b	
		שבר	BUY GRAIN	991d	
41	57	בוא	COME	97d	1
		חזק	BE FIRM	304c	1 4b
		רעב	FAMINE	944b	1
		שבר	BUY GRAIN	991c	
42	1	יש	THERE IS	441d	2 b
		מה	HOW	554a	4 da
		ראה	TO SEE	908c	
		שבר	GRAIN	991c	
42	2	ירד	GO DOWN	433a	1 d
		שבר	GRAIN	991c	
		שבר	BUY GRAIN	991c	
		שם	THERE	1027a	4 a
42	3	בר	GRAIN	141b	
		ירד	GO DOWN	432d	1 d
		שבר	GRAIN	991c	
		שבר	BUY GRAIN	991c	
42	4	אסון	MISCHIEF	62a	
		בנימין	BENJAMIN	122d	1
		פן	LEST	814d	1 a
		קרא	ENCOUNTER	897a	2
		שלח	SEND	1018b	1 a
42	5	בן	SON	*120d	1 jg
		כנען	CANAAN	488d	1
		ישראל	ISRAEL	975c	1
		שבר	BUY GRAIN	991c	
42	6	אף	NOSE	60b	2
		הוא	HE, SHE, IT	215d	2 b
		שבר	BUY GRAIN	991c	
		שחה	BOW DOWN	1005b	1 b
		שליט	HAVING MASTERY	1020c	1
42	7	אין	WHENCE	32d	
		דבר	SPEAK	181a	2
		דבר	SPEAK	181b	3 d
		כנען	CANAAN	488d	2
		נכר	RECOGNIZE	648a	2
		נכר	TREAT AS FOREIGN	649b	
		קשה	SEVERE	904d	2 a
		שבר	BUY GRAIN	991c	
42	8	נכר	RECOGNIZE	648a	2
42	9	זכר	REMEMBER	269c	1 l a
		חלם	DREAM	321c	B
		חלום	DREAM	321c	2 a
		ל	TO	514b	5 fa
		ערוה	NAKEDNESS	789a	3
		ראה	TO SEE	907c	6 a
		רגל	GO ABOUT	920b	2
42	10	אדון	LORD	11b	3 ld
		אדון	LORD	11b	2 lf
		ו	AND	252d	1 d
		לא	NOT	519a	1 ad b
		שבר	BUY GRAIN	991c	
42	11	אנחנו	WE	59d	
		נחנו	WE	59d	
		כן	HONEST	467b	3
		כל	ALL	481b	1 a
		עבד	SLAVE	714c	6
		רגל	GO ABOUT	920b	2
42	12	כי	BUT	474c	3 e
		ערוה	NAKEDNESS	789a	3
		ראה	TO SEE	907c	6 a
42	13	אין	NOT	34b	2 b
		אנחנו	WE	59d	
		ה	THE	207b	1 b
		כנען	CANAAN	488d	2 a
		קטן	SMALL	882b	1 a
		שנים	TWO	1041b	2
42	14	הוא	HE, SHE, IT	216c	6 a
		רגל	GO ABOUT	920b	2
42	15	אם	IF	50b	1 b2
		ב	IN	90a	3 2e
		בחן	TRY	103c	
		הנה	HITHER	244c	A a
		זה	THIS	261d	6 bb
		זה	THIS	262a	6 e
		חי	ALIVE	312a	1 b
		כיאם	EXCEPT	474d	2 a
42	16	אמת	FIRMNESS	54b	4 a
		אסר	TIE	64a	
		את	WITH	86b	3 a
		בחן	TRY	103c	
		חי	ALIVE	312a	1 b
		כי	THAT	472a	1 c
		לא	NOT	519a	1 ad a
		מן	FROM	580a	3 a
		רגל	GO ABOUT	920b	2
42	17	אל	TO	39d	2
		אסף	GATHER	62b	1 a
		משמר	PRISON	1038b	1
42	18	ו	AND	254c	3
		זה	THIS	260d	1 a
42	19	אסר	TIE	64a	
		בית	HOUSE	109a	1 ae 2
		הלך	WALK	234a	1 5f 1
		כן	HONEST	467b	3
		רעבון	HUNGER	944c	
		שבר	GRAIN	991c	
		משמר	PRISON	1038b	1
42	20	אמן	CONFIRM	53a	4
		מות	DIE	559d	2 a
42	21	אבל	VERILY	6a	1
		אל	TO	40b	4
		אשם	GUILTY	79d	
		אשר	THAT	83c	8 c
		חנן	SHOW FAVOR	336b	1
		כן	SO	487a	3 f
		נפש	SOUL	660d	6 a
		על	UPON	754b	2 lf b
		צרה	DISTRESS	865b	
		צרה	DISTRESS	865b	
		ראה	TO SEE	907b	5 b
		שמע	HEAR	1034a	1 j
42	22	דם	BLOOD	197b	2 k
		דרש	SEEK	205d	3
		חטא	MISS A GOAL OR WAY	306d	2 a
		ילד	CHILD	409b	A
42	23	ענה	ANSWER	773a	1 d
		ליץ	SCORN	539c	2
		שמע	HEAR	1033d	1 g
42	24	אסר	TIE	63d	3
		את	WITH	86c	4 a
		בכה	WEEP	113b	1
		סבב	TURNABOUT	685c	1
		עין	EYE	745a	5
		על	UPON	759a	4 2c
42	25	בר	GRAIN	141b	
		מזון	FOOD	*266a	
		כלי	VESSEL	480a	3
		כסף	SILVER	494c	8 e
		ל	TO	515a	5 ha
		מלא	FILL	570c	1
		צידה	PROVISION	845b	
		צוה	CHARGE	845d	2 d
		שק	SACK	974b	1
		שוב	TURN BACK	999a	1 d
		עיה	ADDENDA ET CORRIGENDA	1124a	
42	26	הלך	WALK	231b	1 ld 4
		חמור	HE-ASS	331b	3
		נשא	LIFT	670a	1 a
		שבר	GRAIN	991c	
42	27	הנה	BEHOLD	243d	
		חמור	HE-ASS	331b	3
		כלי	VESSEL	*480a	3
		כסף	SILVER	494c	8 e
		מלון	INN	533d	1
		אמתחת	SACK	607d	
		מספוא	FODDER	704c	
		פה	MOUTH	805b	4
		פתח	OPEN	835a	
		שק	SACK	974b	1
42	28	אל	TO	40a	3 a
		זה	THIS	261c	4 d
		חרד	TREMBLE	353c	4
		יצא	GO OUT	423a	1 e
		מה	WHAT	552c	1 ab
		אמתחת	SACK	607d	
		עשה	DO	793d	1 la 2
		שוב	TURN BACK	1000a	
42	29	כנען	CANAAN	488d	2 a
		קרה	ENCOUNTER	899c	2
42	30	אדון	LORD	11b	2 lf
		איש	MAN	36a	
		את	WITH	86a	1 db
		דבר	SPEAK	181a	2
		כ	LIKE	453d	1 b
		נתן	GIVE	681b	3 c
		קשה	SEVERE	904d	2 a
		רגל	GO ABOUT	920b	2
		משמר	PRISON	1038b	1
42	31	כן	HONEST	467b	3
		רגל	GO ABOUT	920b	2
42	32	כנען	CANAAN	488d	2 a
42	33	אדון	LORD	11b	2 lf
		איש	MAN	36a	
		ב	IN	90a	3 2e
		בית	HOUSE	109d	5 a
		זה	THIS	261d	6 bb
		כן	HONEST	467b	3
		נוח	REST	629a	B 2
		רעבון	HUNGER	944c	
42	34	כן	HONEST	467b	3
		סחר	GO AROUND	695b	1
		רגל	GO ABOUT	920b	2
42	35	ירא	FEAR	431a	1 a
		צרור	BUNDLE	865c	
		ריק	MAKE EMPTY	937d	1
		שק	SACK	974b	1
42	36	אין	NOT	34b	2 b
		בנימין	BENJAMIN	122d	1
		היה	BECOME	225d	2 lb
		לקח	TAKE	543a	3 a
		על	UPON	756c	27a b
		שכל	BE BEREAVED	1013d	1
42	37	אם	IF	49c	1 al a
		יד	HAND	391b	5 h1
		על	UPON	753b	2 lc
		על	UPON	757b	27c ab
42	38	שוב	TURN BACK	998d	1 a
		אסון	MISCHIEF	62a	
		בד	SEPARATION	94c	1 b
		ו	AND	254b	2 db
		יגון	GRIEF	387b	
		ירד	GO DOWN	432d	1 d
		ירד	BRING DOWN	434a	1 d
		קרא	ENCOUNTER	897a	2
		שיבה	OLD AGE	966d	1
		שאול	SHEOL	982d	1
		שאר	REMAIN	984a	2
43	1	כבד	HEAVY	458a	1 a
43	2	אכל	EAT	37b	1
		מעט	A FEW	590a	1 b
		שבר	BUY GRAIN	991c	
		שבר	GRAIN	991c	
43	3	שוב	TURN BACK	997b	3 a
		בלת	EXCEPT	116c	3
		יהודה	JUDAH	397b	1 l
		עוד	BEAR WITNESS	730a	3
		עשר	TEN	796d	2 b
		פנה	FACE	816a	1 2b
		ראה	TO SEE	906d	1 a
		לתן	EXCEPT	*1099a	
43	4	יש	THERE IS	441d	2 ca
		שבר	BUY GRAIN	991c	
43	5	אין	NOT	34b	2 c
		בלת	EXCEPT	116c	3
		פנה	FACE	816a	1 2b
		ראה	TO SEE	906d	1 a
43	6	ה	INTERROG PART	210b	2 a
		מה	HOW	554a	4 da
		עוד	STILL	729b	1 c
		רעע	BE EVIL	949c	1
43	7	חי	ALIVE	312a	1 b
		מולדת	KINDRED	409d	
		ירד	BRING DOWN	433d	1 a
		יש	HAVE	441d	2 cb
		יש	BE	*442a	2 ch
		עוד	STILL	728d	1 aa
		פה	MOUTH	805d	6 d2
		שאל	ASK	981d	2 a
43	8	גם	ALSO	169a	1
		הלך	WALK	234a	1 5c
		יהודה	JUDAH	397b	1 l
		נער	YOUTH	655a	1 c
		שלח	SEND	1018b	1 a
43	9	אם	IF	49d	1 a3 a
		בוא	COME	99b	2
		בקש	SEEK	135a	5 b
		חטא	MISS A GOAL OR WAY	307b	3
		יום	DAY	400c	7 f
		יצג	SET	426d	
		כל	ALL	481b	1 a
		ערב	TAKE ON PLEDGE	786c	1
43	10	זה	THIS	*261d	4 i
		כי	THAT	472c	1 db
		לולא	IF NOT	530c	A
		מהה	LINGER	554c	
		שוב	TURN BACK	997b	3 b
43	11	אפו	THEN	66b	3
		בטנים	PISTACHIO	106c	
		דבש	HONEY	*185b	
		דבש	HONEY	185b	
		זה	THIS	260d	1 a
		זמרה	MELODY	274b	3
		זמרה	BEST PRODUCT	275a	
		ירד	BRING DOWN	433d	1 a
		כלי	VESSEL	480a	3
		לט	MYRRH	538b	
		מנחה	GIFT	585a	1
		נכאת	A SPICE	644d	
		צרי	BALM	863b	
		שקד	ALMOND	1052b	1
43	12	כסף	SILVER	494c	8 e
		לקח	TAKE	542d	2
		אמתחת	SACK	607d	
		פה	MOUTH	805b	4
		משנה	MISTAKE	993b	
		שוב	TURN BACK	999a	1 a
		שוב	TURN BACK	1000a	
		שלו	EASE	1017b	
		משנה	DOUBLE	1041c	1
43	14	כאשר	WHEN	455c	3
		נתן	GIVE	678c	1 b
		רחמים	COMPASSION	933c	2
		שדי	ALMIGHTY	995a	2
		שכל	BE BEREAVED	1013c	
43	15	ירד	GO DOWN	433a	1 d
		כסף	SILVER	494c	8 e
		לקח	TAKE	542d	2
		מנחה	GIFT	585a	1
		מצרים	EGYPT	595d	1 b1
		עמד	STAND	763d	1 d
		משנה	DOUBLE	1041c	1
43	16	אכל	EAT	37b	1
		אשר	PARTICLE OF RELATION	82a	1
		טבח	SLAUGHTER	370c	1
		טבח	SLAUGHTERING	370d	1
		כן	ESTABLISH	466b	2 a
		על	UPON	755b	2 3
		צהר	MIDDAY	843d	1
43	18	בוא	COME	99c	A
		בוא	COME	99c	A

Ch	v.	Heb	Eng	Page	Sec
		דבר	WORD	184a	4 8
		חמור	HE-ASS	331b	3
		ירא	FEAR	431a	1 a
		כי	BECAUSE	473d	3 b
		כסף	SILVER	494c	8 e
		אמתחת	SACK	607d	
		נפל	FALL	658b	1
		עבד	SLAVE	714c	7
		שוב	TURN BACK	998a	7 b
43	19	נגש	DRAW NEAR	620d	1
		על	UPON	755b	2 3
43	20	אדון	LORD	11b	3 1d
		בי	I PRAY	106c	
		שבר	BUY GRAIN	991c	
43	21	כסף	SILVER	494c	8 e
		מלון	INN	533d	
		אמתחת	SACK	607d	
		אמתחת	SACK	607d	
		פה	MOUTH	805b	4
		פתח	OPEN	835a	
		שוב	TURN BACK	999a	1 a
		משקל	WEIGHT	1054a	
43	22	ירד	BRING DOWN	433d	1 a
		מי	WHO	566c	C
		אמתחת	SACK	607d	
		שבר	BUY GRAIN	991c	
43	23	אלהים	GOD	44b	4 ba
		בוא	COME	98b	2
		ממון	HIDDEN TREASURE	380c	
		יצא	BRING OUT	424d	1 h
		ירא	FEAR	431a	1 a
		אמתחת	SACK	607d	
		שלום	PEACE	1022d	3
43	24	חמור	HE-ASS	331b	3
		מי	WATER	565b	1 a
		מספוא	FODDER	704c	
		רחץ	WASH OFF	934c	1
43	25	אכל	EAT	37b	1
		כון	ESTABLISH	466b	2 a
		לחם	FOOD	537a	1 a
		מנחה	GIFT	585a	1
		עד	AS FAR AS	724c	12 a b
		צהר	MIDDAY	843a	1
43	26	בוא	COME	99b	2
		מנחה	GIFT	585a	1
43	27	אמר	SAY	56a	1
		זקן	OLD	278c	2 a
		חי	ALIVE	312a	1 b
		עוד	STILL	728d	1 aa
		שאל	ASK	981d	2 a
		שלום	PEACE	1022d	3
		שלום	PEACE	1022d	3
43	28	חי	ALIVE	312a	1 b
		קדד	BOW DOWN	869a	
		שחה	BOW DOWN	1005b	1 a
		שלום	PEACE	1022d	3
43	29	אם	MOTHER	51d	1
		אמר	SAY	56a	1
		בן	SON	120b	1 a
		בנימין	BENJAMIN	122d	1
		חנן	SHOW FAVOR	336a	2 a
43	30	אל	TO	40a	3 c
		בכה	WEEP	113b	1
		בקש	SEEK	134d	2 d
		חדר	CHAMBER	293c	
		כמר	GROW WARM	485b	1
		מהר	HASTEN	555a	2
		על	UPON	756d	27 a c
		רחמים	COMPASSION	933c	2 a
		שם	THERE	1027c	3 c
43	31	אפק	HOLD	67d	2
		פנה	FACE	815d	1 1a
		רחץ	WASH OFF	934c	1
		שום	TO PLACE	963b	1 c
43	32	בד	SEPARATION	94c	1 b
		יכל	BE ABLE	407c	1 a
		יכל	BE ABLE	407d	1 d
		כי	BECAUSE	474b	3 d
		ל	TO	513a	5 ad
		לחם	FOOD	537a	1 a
		מצרי	EGYPTIAN	596a	2
		עברי	HEBREW	720b	2 b
		שום	TO PLACE	963b	1 c
		תועבה	ABOMINATION	1072d	1 a
43	33	אל	TO	40a	3 a
		בכור	FIRST-BORN	114a	1 a
		בכרה	RIGHT OF FIRST-BORN	114c	
		ישב	SIT	442c	1 a
		צעירה	YOUTH	859a	
		צעיר	YOUNG	859a	2
		רע	FRIEND	946b	3
		תמה	BE ASTOUNDED	1069b	
43	34	את	WITH	86d	4 a
		חמש	FIVE	331d	1 a
		יד	TIME	390c	4 c
		כל	ALL	481b	1 a
		נשא	LIFT	671b	2 e
		משאת	PORTION	673a	4 a
		רבה	BECOME MANY	915b	2 a1
		שכר	BE DRUNK	1016b	
		שתה	DRINK	1059a	1
44	1	בית	HOUSE	110b	6
		יכל	BE ABLE	407c	1 b
		כאשר	AS	455b	1 a
		מלא	FILL	570c	1
		אמתחת	SACK	607d	
		אמתחת	SACK	607d	
44	2	נשא	LIFT	671a	2 a
		על	UPON	755b	2 3
		פה	MOUTH	805b	4
		גביע	CUP	149b	
		דבר	WORD	182b	1 1b
		ו	AND	253a	1 g
		כ	LIKE	454a	1 c1
		כסף	SILVER	494b	7
		אמתחת	SACK	607d	
		פה	MOUTH	805b	4
		שבר	GRAIN	991c	
44	3	אור	BECOME LIGHT	21b	
		בעיר	BEASTS	*129c	
		בקר	MORNING	133d	1 b
		בקר	MORNING	133d	1 b
		חם	THEY	241b	1 d
		חמור	HE-ASS	331b	3
		שלח	SEND	1019b	
44	4	בית	HOUSE	110b	6
		טובה	WELFARE	375d	3
		יצא	GO OUT	422d	1 a
		לא	NOT	518c	1 aa
		נשג	OVERTAKE	673c	1 a
		על	UPON	755b	2 3
		רדף	PURSUE	922c	1 a
		רחק	BE DISTANT	935a	1
		רעה	MISERY	949b	2
		שלם	BE COMPLETE	1022c	5
		תחת	INSTEAD	1066a	2 2b b
44	5	אדון	LORD	11b	3 1a
		ב	IN	89d	3 2a
		נחש	PRACTISE DIVINATION	638c	1
		רעע	BE EVIL	949c	1
		שתה	DRINK	1059b	1
44	6	נשג	OVERTAKE	673c	1 a
44	7	אדון	LORD	11b	3 1k
		דבר	WORD	183d	4 7
		חלילה	FAR BE IT	321a	
44	8	אדון	LORD	11b	1 f
		איך	HOW	32c	1
		גנב	STEAL	170b	
		זהב	GOLD	263c	1
		כנען	CANAAN	488d	2 a
		כסף	SILVER	494b	7
		מצא	FIND	593b	3 a
		אמתחת	SACK	607d	
		פה	MOUTH	805b	4
		שוב	TURN BACK	998d	1 a
44	9	אשר	PARTICLE OF RELATION	82a	2
		מות	DIE	559d	2 a
		מצא	FIND	593d	1 a
		עבד	SLAVE	714c	7
44	10	כ	LIKE	454c	2 d
		כן	SO	485d	
		כן	SO	486b	2 aa
		מצא	FIND	593d	1 a
		נקי	FREE FROM	667c	3
		עבד	SLAVE	714c	7
		עתה	NOW	774d	2 d
44	11	ירד	LET DOWN	434b	3
		מהר	HASTEN	555a	2
		אמתחת	SACK	607d	
		פתח	OPEN	835a	
44	12	גביע	CUP	149b	
		חלל	POLLUTE	320d	2
		חפש	SEARCH	344c	2 b
		כלה	FINISH	478b	1 d
		מצא	FIND	593d	1 a
		אמתחת	SACK	607d	
44	13	בעיר	BEASTS	*129c	
		חמור	HE-ASS	331b	3
		עמס	LOAD	770c	1
		קרע	TEAR	902c	1 a1
		קרע	TEAR	902c	1 a1
		שמלה	WRAPPER	971a	
		שוב	TURN BACK	997b	3 a
44	14	יהודה	JUDAH	397b	11
		נפל	FALL	657b	3 b
		עוד	STILL	*728d	1 aa
44	15	מה	WHAT	553a	1
		נחש	PRACTISE DIVINATION	638c	1
		מעשה	DEED	795c	1 a2
		אלהים	GOD	43d	3
44	16	אמר	SAY	55d	1
		גביע	CUP	149b	
		הנה	BEHOLD	243d	2
		הנה	BEHOLD	*244a	A
		יהודה	JUDAH	397b	11
		מה	HOW	553c	2 aa
		מצא	FIND	593b	2 b
		מצא	FIND	593d	1 a
		עבד	SLAVE	714c	7
		עון	INIQUITY	731b	2
		צדק	MAKE RIGHTEOUS	843a	2 b
44	17	גביע	CUP	149b	
		הוא	HE, SHE, IT	215d	2 a
		חלילה	FAR BE IT	321a	
		ל	TO	516d	5 k
		מן	FROM	583b	7 ba
		מצא	FIND	593d	1 a
		עבד	SLAVE	714c	7
		עלה	GO UP	748c	2 a
		שלום	PEACE	1022d	3
44	18	אדון	LORD	11b	3 1d
		אזן	EAR	24a	2 a
		בי	I PRAY	106c	
		חרה	BURN	354a	1 a
		יהודה	JUDAH	397b	11
		כ	LIKE	454b	2 a
		נא	PART OF ENTREATY	609b	3 c
		נגש	DRAW NEAR	620d	1
44	19	יש	BE	*442a	2 ch
		שאל	ASK	981d	1
44	20	אב	FATHER	3b	1
		אהב	LOVE	12d	1
		אח	BROTHER	26b	1
		אם	MOTHER	51c	1
		זקן	OLD	278c	1
		זקנים	OLD AGE	279a	
		ילד	CHILD	409b	A
		יש	HAVE	441d	2 cb
		יש	BE	*442a	2 ch
		יתר	BE LEFT OVER	451b	
		קטן	SMALL	882a	1 a
44	21	ירד	BRING DOWN	433d	1 a
		שום	TO PLACE	963d	2 c
		עין	ADDENDA ET CORRIGENDA	1125d	
44	22	ו	AND	254b	2 db
		יכל	BE ABLE	407c	1 a
		נער	YOUTH	655a	1 c
		עזב	LEAVE	737a	1
44	23	יסף	DO AGAIN	415c	2
		פנה	FACE	816a	1 2b
		עלה	GO UP	748c	2 a
44	24	עלה	GO UP	748c	2 a
44	25	מעט	A FEW	590a	1 b
		שבר	BUY GRAIN	991c	
44	26	אם	IF	49d	1 a2
		יכל	BE ABLE	407c	1 a
		יש	BE	441c	2 a
		פנה	FACE	816a	1 2b
44	27	שנים	TWO	1041a	1 b1
44	28	אך	SURELY	36c	1
		הנה	HITHERTO	244d	B
		טרף	TEAR	382d	
		טרף	TEAR	383a	
		יצא	GO OUT	422d	1 b
44	29	אסון	MISCHIEF	62a	1
		את	MARK OF THE ACCUSATIVE	84d	1 a
		ירד	BRING DOWN	434a	1 d
		לקח	TAKE	543a	3 a
		מעם	FROM WITH	769a	A
		קרה	ENCOUNTER	899c	2
		רעה	MISERY	949b	1
		שיבה	OLD AGE	966d	1
		שאול	SHEOL	982d	1
44	30	כ	LIKE	454d	3 b
		נפש	SOUL	659d	3 c
		קשר	BIND	905b	1
		היה	COME TO PASS	225b	1 2b be
44	31	יגון	GRIEF	387b	1
		ירד	BRING DOWN	434a	1 d
		כ	LIKE	454d	3 b
		שיבה	OLD AGE	966d	1
		שאול	SHEOL	982d	1
44	32	חטא	MISS A GOAL OR WAY	307b	3
		יום	DAY	400c	7 f
		מעם	FROM WITH	769a	C
		ערב	TAKE ON PLEDGE	786c	1
44	33	נא	PART OF ENTREATY	609b	3 c
		עבד	SLAVE	714c	7
		תחת	INSTEAD	1065d	2 2b a
44	34	איך	HOW	32c	1
		מצא	FIND	593c	3 e
		עלה	GO UP	748c	2 a
		פן	LEST	814d	1
		ראה	TO SEE	908a	8 a3
		רע	EVIL	948d	1
		פן	ADDENDA ET CORRIGENDA	1126b	
45	1	אפק	HOLD	67d	2
		ידע	MAKE ONESELF KNOWN	395b	
		יכל	BE ABLE	407c	1 a
		יצא	BRING OUT	424d	1 e
		נצב	STAND	662a	1 b
		על	UPON	756b	2 6c
		על	UPON	759a	4 2c
		עמד	STAND	764c	7 a
		קרא	CALL	895b	1 b
45	2	בכי	WEEPING	113b	
		נתן	GIVE	679d	1 x
45	3	בהל	BE DISTURBED	96b	1
		חי	ALIVE	312a	1 b
		יכל	BE ABLE	407c	1 a
		עוד	STILL	728d	1 aa
		ענה	ANSWER	772d	1 a
		פנה	FACE	818b	2 6b
45	4	מכר	SELL	569b	
		נגש	DRAW NEAR	620d	1
		נגש	DRAW NEAR	620d	1
45	5	הנה	HITHER	244c	A a

Ch	v.	Heb	Eng	Page	Sec
		מחיה	PRESERVATION OF LIFE	313c	1
		חרה	BURN	354a	1 b
		כי	BECAUSE	473d	3 b
		מכר	SELL	569b	
		עצב	HURT	780c	
		שלח	SEND	1018c	2 a
45	6	אשר	PARTICLE OF RELATION	82c	4 ba
		זה	THIS	261d	4 i
		חריש	PLOUGHING	361a	
		עוד	STILL	729a	1 ab
		קרב	INWARD PART	899a	1 e
45	7	חיה	LIVE	311c	1
		ל	TO	511c	3 a
		פליטה	ESCAPE	812c	1
		שום	TO PLACE	964d	5 b
		שארית	REST	984d	2
45	8	אב	FATHER	3d	8
		אדון	LORD	11a	1 1a
		הנה	HITHER	244c	A a
		כי	BUT	474b	3 e
		ל	TO	512c	4 b
		לא	NOT	518d	1 ac
		משל	RULE	605d	1
		עתה	NOW	774b	2 b
		שום	TO PLACE	964a	3 d
45	9	אדון	LORD	11a	1 1a
		ירד	GO DOWN	432d	1 d
		מהר	HASTEN	555a	2
		עלה	GO UP	748c	2 a
		עמד	STAND	764a	3 a
		שום	TO PLACE	964a	3 d
45	10	גשן	GOSHEN	*177d	1
		גשן	GOSHEN	177d	1
		גשן	GOSHEN	*177d	1
		קרב	NEAR	898c	2 a
45	11	ירש	BE IMPOVERISHED	439d	
		כול	SUSTAIN	465a	1
		פן	LEST	814d	1
45	12	בנימין	BENJAMIN	122d	1
		ה	THE	209c	2 c
		עין	EYE	744b	1 f
		פה	MOUTH	805a	2 a
45	13	הנה	HITHER	244c	A a
		ירד	BRING DOWN	433d	1 a
		כבוד	HONOR	458c	2 a
		מהר	HASTEN	555a	2
45	14	בכה	WEEP	113c	3
		בכה	WEEP	113c	3
		בנימין	BENJAMIN	122d	1
		נפל	FALL	657c	3 c
		על	UPON	756d	27 a c
		צואר	NECK	848c	1
		צואר	NECK	848c	1
45	15	אחר	AFTER	30a	2 b
		בכה	WEEP	113c	3
		בנימין	BENJAMIN	122d	1
		דבר	SPEAK	181b	3 d
		נשק	KISS	676c	
		על	UPON	756d	27 a c
45	16	בוא	COME	98b	2
		יטב	BE PLEASING	405c	4
		קול	VOICE	877b	3 a2
		שמע	HEAR	1034b	1
45	17	בוא	GO	98d	4
		בעיר	BEASTS	129c	
		מען	LOAD	381b	
		כנען	CANAAN	488d	2 a
		צען	WANDER	858a	
45	18	חלב	FAT	317a	3
		טוב	GOOD THINGS	375c	1
45	19	זה	THIS	260c	1 a
		לקח	TAKE	543a	4 b
		עגלה	CART	722c	
		צוה	CHARGE	846b	3
45	20	חום	PITY	299b	A
		טוב	GOOD THINGS	375c	1
		כלי	ARTICLE	479c	1
		מצרים	EGYPT	695c	1 a
		עין	EYE	744c	2 a
45	21	בן	SON	*120d	1 jg
		מזון	FOOD	*266a	
		עגלה	CART	722c	
		על	UPON	754a	2 1f
		פה	MOUTH	805d	6 d1 a
		צידה	PROVISION	845b	
45	22	חלפה	A CHANGE	322c	1
		כסף	SILVER	494b	8 b
		מאה	HUNDRED	548b	1 c6
		שמלה	WRAPPER	971a	
45	23	אתון	SHE-ASS	87d	
		בר	GRAIN	141b	
		זה	THIS	262a	6 d
		מזון	FOOD	266a	
		חמור	HE-ASS	331b	3
		טוב	GOOD THINGS	375c	1
		נשא	LIFT	671a	2 a
		עשר	TEN	796d	2 a
		עשר	TEN	796d	2 a
45	24	הלך	WALK	234a	1 5d
		רגז	BE AGITATED	919b	
		רגז	BE AGITATED	919b	
45	25	כנען	CANAAN	488d	2 a
		עלה	GO UP	748b	1 a
45	26	אמן	CONFIRM	53a	2 b
		חי	ALIVE	312a	1 b
		כי	THAT	471d	1 a
		משל	RULE	605d	1
		פוג	GROW NUMB	806a	
45	27	חיה	LIVE	311b	2 b
		עגלה	CART	722c	
		רוח	BREATH	925a	3 a
45	28	חי	ALIVE	312a	1 b
		טרם	NOT YET	*382c	2
		רב	MUCH	913b	1 f
46	1	אכל	EAT	37b	1
		בארשבע	BEERSHEBA	92a	
		זבח	SLAUGHTER FOR SACRIFICE	257a	13
		זבח	SACRIFICE	257b	11
		נסע	SET OUT	652b	2 a
46	2	הנה	BEHOLD	244a	A
		לילה	NIGHT	538d	1
		מראה	VISION	909b	
46	3	אל	GOD	42c	6 a
		אלהים	GOD	44b	4 ba
		גוי	NATION	156c	1 a
		ירא	FEAR	431b	1 d
		ירד	GO DOWN	432d	1 d
		ל	TO	512b	4 a
46	4	גם	ALSO	169b	2
		ירד	GO DOWN	432d	1 d
		עלה	GO UP	749d	7
		שות	PUT	1011a	1
46	5	בארשבע	BEERSHEBA	92a	
		בן	SON	*120d	1 jg
		עגלה	CART	722c	
46	6	זרע	SOWING	282d	4 d
		מקנה	CATTLE	889b	2
		רכוב	PROPERTY	940d	3
		רכש	COLLECT	940d	
46	7	בוא	COME	99a	1
		בת	DAUGHTER	123b	1 g
		זרע	SOWING	282d	4 d
46	9	חנוך	ENOCH	335c	4
		חצרון	HEZRON	348a	2 a
		כרמי	CARMI	501d	1
		פלוא	PALLU	811a	
46	10	אהד	OHAD	13c	
		זרח	ZERAH	*280c	4
		ימואל	JEMUEL	410c	
		ימין	JAMIN	412c	1
		יכין	JACHIN	467c	1
		כנעני	CANAANITE	489a	2 a
		נמואל	NEMUEL	*649c	1
		צחר	ZOHAR	850c	2
		שאול	SAUL	982c	3
46	11	בן	SON	*121a	1 je
		גרשון	GERSHON	177a	
		לוי	LEVI	532c	1 a
		מררי	MERARI	601b	
		קהת	KOHATH	875b	
46	12	בן	SON	*121a	1 jd
		זרח	ZERAH	280b	1
		חמול	HAMUL	328b	
		חצרון	HEZRON	348a	2 b
		יהודה	JUDAH	397b	11
		ער	ER	735c	1
		פרץ	PEREZ	829d	1
		שלה	SHELAH	1017c	1
46	13	יוב	IOB	398a	
		יששכר	ISSACHAR	441a	1
		פואה	PUAH	806a	
		שמרון	SHIMRON	1038a	
		תולע	TOLA	1069a	
46	14	אלון	ELON	19a	1
		זבולן	ZEBULUN	259d	1
		יחלאל	JAHLEEL	404b	
		סרד	SERED	710a	
46	15	ארם	ARAM	74c	B
		דינה	DINAH	192d	1
		ו	AND	253a	1 g
		לאה	LEAH	521b	
		נפש	SOUL	660c	4 c3
46	16	אזני	OZNI	24c	
		אצבון	EZBON	69a	1
		ארוד	AROD	71b	
		ארודי	ARODI	71b	
		אראלי	ARELITES	72a	
		גד	GAD	151c	1 a
		חגי	HAGGI	291b	1
		עירי	ERI	735c	
		צפיון	ZIPHION	859d	
		שוני	SHUNI	1002c	1
46	17	אשר	ASHER	81b	1
		בריעה	BERIAH	140b	1
		חבר	HEBER	288c	2
		ימנה	IMNAH	412c	1
		מלכיאל	MALCHIEL	575c	
		שרח	SERAH	976b	
		ישוה	ISHVAH	1001a	
		ישוי	ISHVI	1001a	1
46	18	את	MARK OF THE ACCUSATIVE	84d	1 a
		זלפה	ZILPAH	273a	
		לאה	LEAH	521b	
		לבן	LABAN	526c	
		נפש	SOUL	660c	4 c3
		נתן	GIVE	678c	1 b
		עשר	TEN	797b	6 b
		שש	SIX	995c	2
46	19	יוסף	JOSEPH	415d	1 a
46	20	און	ON	58a	
		אסנת	ASENATH	62a	
		אפרים	EPHRAIM	68b	1
		מנשה	MANASSEH	286c	1 a
		ילד	BE BORN	408d	
		יוסף	JOSEPH	415d	1 a
		כהן	PRIEST	463a	2
		פוטיפרע	POTIPHERA	806c	
46	21	אדר	ADDAR	12b	1
		אחוד	EHUD	26a	
		אחירם	AHIRAM	27c	
		אחי	EHI	29a	
		ארד	ARD	71b	
		אשבל	ASHBEL	78a	
		בכר	BECHER	114b	2
		בלע	BELA	118c	2
		בנימין	BENJAMIN	*122d	1
		גרא	GERA	173a	
		חופם	HUPHAM	*299c	
		חפים	HUPPIM	342c	
		מפים	MUPPIM	592b	
		נעמן	NAAMAN	654a	1
		ראש	ROSH	912c	
		שפופם	SHEPHUPHAM	*1051b	
46	22	ילד	BE BORN	408d	
		נפש	SOUL	660c	4 c3
		עשר	TEN	797b	4 a
		ארבע	FOUR	917b	2 a2 e
46	23	אחר	AHER	31b	
		דן	DAN	192d	2
46	24	חושים	HUSHIM	302a	
		שוחם	SHUHAM	1001d	
		גוני	GUNI	157b	1
		יחצאל	JAHZEEL	345d	
		יצר	JEZER	428a	
		נפתלי	NAPHTALI	836d	1
		שלם	SHILLEM	1024a	
46	25	בלהה	BILHAH	117b	
		לבן	LABAN	526c	
		נפש	SOUL	660c	4 c3
		נתן	GIVE	678c	1 b
		שבע	SEVEN	988a	1 b
46	26	בד	SEPARATION	94d	1 e
		ה	THE	209c	3
		יצא	GO OUT	423c	1 h
		ירך	THIGH	438a	1 b
		ל	TO	512c	5 ac
		נפש	SOUL	660c	4 c3
		שש	SIX	995d	4
46	27	בית	HOUSE	109d	1
		בית	HOUSE	110a	5 dg
		בן	SON	*120d	1 ja
		ה	THE	*209c	3
		ילד	BE BORN	408d	
		יוסף	JOSEPH	415d	1 a
		ל	TO	512c	5 ac
		נפש	SOUL	660c	4 c3
		שבעים	SEVENTY	988c	1 d
		שנים	TWO	1041a	1 b1
46	28	גשן	GOSHEN	177d	1
		גשן	GOSHEN	177d	1
		יהודה	JUDAH	397b	11
		ירה	POINT OUT	435b	4
46	29	אסר	TIE	63d	2
		בכה	WEEP	113c	3
		גשן	GOSHEN	177d	1
		נפל	FALL	657c	3 c
		עוד	STILL	729a	1 ab
		עלה	GO UP	748c	2 a
		צואר	NECK	848c	1
		צואר	NECK	848c	1
		ראה	TO SEE	908b	1 b
		מרכבה	CHARIOT	939d	
		מרכבה	CHARIOT	939d	
46	30	חי	ALIVE	312a	1 b
		פעם	OCCURRENCE	822b	3 d2
		ראה	TO SEE	906d	1 a
46	31	אב	FATHER	3c	3
		כנען	CANAAN	488d	2 a
46	32	בוא	COME	99b	2
		מקנה	CATTLE	889b	2
		רעה	TEND	945a	1 d1
46	33	חיה	COME TO PASS	225b	1 2b ba
		כי	WHEN	473b	2 a
		מעשה	DEED	795d	1 b2
46	34	אב	FATHER	3c	4 a
		גשן	GOSHEN	177d	1
		מן	FROM	582a	5 c
		נעורים	YOUTH	655c	
		עבור	FOR THE SAKE OF	721b	2
		עתה	NOW	774c	2 f
		מקנה	CATTLE	889b	2
		רעה	TEND	945a	1 d1
		תועבה	ABOMINATION	1072d	1 a
47	1	גשן	GOSHEN	177d	1
		כנען	CANAAN	488d	2 a
47	2	חמש	FIVE	331d	1 b
		יצג	SET	426d	
		פנה	FACE	816d	2 4
		קצה	END	892b	3
		קצה	END	*1111c	
47	3	מעשה	DEED	795d	1 b2
		רעה	TEND	945a	1 d1
47	4	אשר	PARTICLE OF RELATION	83a	7 b

Ch	v.	Heb	Eng	Page	Sec
		גור	SOJOURN	157d	1
		גשן	GOSHEN	177d	1
		כבד	HEAVY	458a	1
		כנען	CANAAN	488d	2 a
		רעב	FAMINE	944b	1
		מרעה	PASTURAGE	945c	
		מרעה	PASTURAGE	945c	
47	5	יוסף	JOSEPH	415d	1 a
47	6	אם	IF	49d	1 a3 a
		ארץ	EARTH	76a	2
		גשן	GOSHEN	177d	1
		ו	AND	254a	2
		חיל	STRENGTH	298d	2
		מיטב	THE BEST	406b	
		ישב	CAUSE TO SIT	443b	3 a
		מצרים	EGYPT	695c	1 a
		פנה	FACE	817a	2 4a f
		מקנה	CATTLE	889b	2
		שום	TO PLACE	964a	1
		שר	CHIEFTAIN	978c	4 b
47	7	ברך	BLESS	139d	4 a
		יוסף	JOSEPH	415d	1 a
		עמד	STAND	764d	4
47	8	חיים	LIFE	313a	1
		יום	DAY	399d	4 a
		מה	HOW	553d	4 ca
47	9	מגור	SOJOURNING PLACE	158c	
		מגור	SOJOURNING PLACE	158c	
		חיים	LIFE	313a	1
		יום	DAY	399a	4 a
		מעט	A FEW	589d	1 a
		נשג	REACH	673a	2 a
		רע	EVIL	948a	2
47	10	ברך	BLESS	139b	4 b
		יצא	GO OUT	422d	1 b
		פנה	FACE	817d	2 5a a
47	11	אחזה	POSSESSION	28c	
		גשן	GOSHEN	*177d	1
		מיטב	THE BEST	406b	
		יוסף	JOSEPH	415d	1 a
		ישב	CAUSE TO SIT	443d	3 a
		רעמסס	RAMSES	947c	
		רעמסס	RAMSES	947d	
47	12	כל	SUSTAIN	465a	1
		ל	TO	516c	5 jb
		פה	MOUTH	805c	6 c1
		טף	ADDENDA ET CORRIGENDA	1123d	
47	13	כבד	HEAVY	458a	1 a
		כנען	CANAAN	488d	2 a
		להה	FAINT	529c	
		לחם	FOOD	537b	1 b
		מצרים	EGYPT	695c	1 a
		פנה	FACE	818c	2 6c a
		רעב	FAMINE	944b	1
47	14	זרע	SOWING	*282b	2 a
		כנען	CANAAN	488d	2 a
		לקט	GATHER UP	544d	2
		מצא	FIND	594a	2 c
		שבר	BUY GRAIN	991c	
		שבר	GRAIN	991c	
47	15	אפס	CEASE	67a	
		יתן	GIVE	396d	1
		כנען	CANAAN	488d	2 a
		לחם	FOOD	537b	1 b
		נגד	IN FRONT	617b	1 aa
		תמם	BE FINISHED	1070c	4
47	16	אפס	CEASE	67a	
		ב	IN	90b	3 3b
		יתן	GIVE	396c	1
		מקנה	CATTLE	889b	1
47	17	בקר	CATTLE	133b	1 a
		הלך	WALK	234b	1 5f 3
		חמור	HE-ASS	331b	1
		חמור	HE-ASS	331b	1
		לחם	FOOD	537b	1 b
		נהל	REFRESH	625a	5
		סוס	HORSE	692c	1
		מקנה	CATTLE	889b	1
		מקנה	CATTLE	889b	2
47	18	אדמה	GROUND	9d	2
		אדון	LORD	11b	3 1d
		אל	TO	39c	1
		אם	IF	50c	1 ca
		בהמה	BEAST	97a	2
		בלת	EXCEPT	116c	2
		גויה	BODY	156b	1
		כחד	HIDE	470b	
		כיאם	BUT	475a	2 b
		מקנה	CATTLE	889b	1
		שאר	REMAIN	984a	1
		שני	SECOND	1041c	
		תמם	BE FINISHED	1070b	2
		תמם	BE FINISHED	1070c	4
47	19	אדמה	LAND	9d	5
		אדמה	GROUND	9d	2
		זרע	SOWING	282b	2 a
		ישם	BE DESOLATE	445b	
		לחם	FOOD	537b	1 b
		מה	HOW	554d	4 d
		עבד	SLAVE	713d	1
		עבד	SLAVE	714c	7
		עין	EYE	745a	1
47	20	אדמה	LAND	9d	5

Ch	v.	Heb	Eng	Page	Sec
		אדמה	GROUND	9d	2
		חזק	BE FIRM	304c	1 4b
		כי	BECAUSE	474b	3 d
		מכר	SELL	569b	
		מצרים	EGYPT	695c	1 a
		קנה	ACQUIRE	889a	2
		רעב	FAMINE	944c	1
		שדה	FIELD	961d	2 b
47	21	גבול	BOUNDARY	148a	2 a
		מן	FROM	581d	5 a
		עבד	WORK	713c	1
		עבר	PASS OVER	719a	4
		קצה	END	892a	1
47	22	אדמה	GROUND	9d	2
		את	WITH	86d	4 b
		חק	SOMETHING PRESCRIBED	349b	2
		כהן	PRIEST	463a	2
		כן	SO	487b	3 f
		מכר	SELL	569b	
		קנה	ACQUIRE	889a	2
		רק	ONLY	956b	2 a
47	23	אדמה	GROUND	9c	1
		אדמה	GROUND	9d	2
		הא	LO	210c	
		זרע	SOW	281c	1 b
		זרע	SOWING	282b	2 a
47	24	אכל	FOOD	38a	
		אשר	PARTICLE OF RELATION	82a	1
		תבואה	PRODUCT	100a	1
		היה	COME TO PASS	225b	1 2b bg
		זרע	SOWING	282a	1 a
		זרע	SOWING	*282b	2 d
		חמישי	FIFTH	332d	3
		יד	PART	390c	4 b
		נתן	GIVE	679b	1 n
		שדה	FIELD	961d	2 b
47	25	חיה	LIVE	311c	1
		חן	FAVOR	336b	2 b1
		עבד	SLAVE	714c	7
47	26	אדמה	LAND	9d	5
		אדמה	GROUND	9d	2
		חמש	FIFTH PART	332b	
		חק	SOMETHING PRESCRIBED	349c	6 a
		יום	DAY	401a	7 j
		יום	DAY	401b	7 l
		כהן	PRIEST	463a	2
		ל	TO	512c	4 b
		ל	TO	514c	5 fc
		מצרים	EGYPT	695c	1 a
		על	UPON	753b	2 1c
		שום	TO PLACE	963d	3 b
47	27	אחז	GRASP	28c	
		ארץ	EARTH	76a	2 a
		גשן	GOSHEN	177d	1
		פרה	BEAR FRUIT	826a	1
		רבה	BECOME MANY	915a	1 a
		ישראל	ISRAEL	975c	2 a1
47	28	חיה	LIVE	311a	1 a
		חיים	LIFE	313a	1
		ארבעים	FORTY	917c	2 c
		שבע	SEVEN	988b	5 b2
47	29	אמת	FIRMNESS	54a	3 a
		חן	FAVOR	336b	2 b1
		חסד	GOODNESS	338d	1 2
		יום	DAY	399b	4 a
		ירך	THIGH	438a	1
		נא	PART OF ENTREATY	609b	3 b
		נא	PART OF ENTREATY	609c	4 c
		עשה	DO	794b	1 3
		קרב	COME NEAR	897c	2
		שום	TO PLACE	963c	1 d
		דבר	WORD	182b	1 1b
47	30	קבר	BURY	868c	
		צברה	GRAVE	869a	1
		שכב	LIE DOWN	1012c	4 b
47	31	מטה	COUCH	641d	
		ראש	HEAD	910d	2 a
		שחה	BOW DOWN	1005c	2 c
48	1	אפרים	EPHRAIM	68b	1
		דבר	WORD	183c	4 4
		מנשה	MANASSEH	286c	1 a
		חלה	BE WEAK	317d	2
		לקח	TAKE	543c	7
48	2	חזק	BE FIRM	305b	2
		ישב	SIT	442b	1 a
		מטה	COUCH	641d	
48	3	ברך	BLESS	139a	2 a
		יוסף	JOSEPH	415d	1 a
		לוז	LUZ	531c	1
		ראה	TO SEE	908b	1 a
		שדי	ALMIGHTY	995a	2
48	4	אחזה	POSSESSION	28d	
		אחר	AFTER	30a	2 b
		זרע	SOWING	282c	4 b
		נתן	GIVE	681a	3 b
		עולם	LONG DURATION	762d	2 f
		עם	PEOPLE	766c	1
		פרה	BEAR FRUIT	826b	2
		קהל	ASSEMBLY	874d	2 d
		רבה	BECOME MANY	915c	1 a
48	5	אפרים	EPHRAIM	68b	1

Ch	v.	Heb	Eng	Page	Sec
		ה	THE	*209c	3
		הוא	HE, SHE, IT	216a	3 b
		הם	THEY	241c	3 b
		מנשה	MANASSEH	286c	1 a
		ילד	BE BORN	408d	
		ל	TO	513b	5 ba
48	6	מולדת	BORN	409d	3
		על	UPON	754a	2 1f
48	7	קרא	CALL	896c	6 d5
		אפרתה	EPHRATH	68d	1
		ארץ	EARTH	76b	4 b
		בוא	COME	*98d	2 e
		ביתלחם	BETHLEHEM	111d	1
		ביתלחם	BETHLEHEM	112a	1
		דרך	WAY	202c	1
		דרך	WAY	202d	1
		כברה	DISTANCE	460c	
		עוד	STILL	729c	2 ab
		על	UPON	753b	2 1b
		פדן	PADDAN	804c	
48	8	בן	SON	*120d	1 ja
		מי	WHO	566b	
48	9	ברך	BLESS	139a	3
48	10	זקן	OLD AGE	279a	
		חבק	CLASP	287d	
		יכל	BE ABLE	407c	1 a
		כבד	BE HEAVY	457b	2
		נגש	APPROACH	*621b	
		נשק	KISS	676b	
		עין	EYE	744b	1 i
		ראה	TO SEE	907b	4
48	11	זרע	SOWING	282d	4 c
		פלל	INTERVENE	813a	
		ראה	TO SEE	906d	1 a
		ראה	TO SEE	908d	1 a2
48	12	אף	NOSE	60b	2
		ברך	KNEE	139c	
		יצא	CAUSE TO GO	424c	1 a
		ל	TO	511c	1 gb
		מעם	FROM WITH	769a	A
		שחה	BOW DOWN	1005b	1 b
48	13	אפרים	EPHRAIM	68b	1
		מנשה	MANASSEH	286c	1 a
		ימין	RIGHT HAND	411c	1
		נגש	APPROACH	*621b	
		שמאל	LEFT	969d	2
48	14	אפרים	EPHRAIM	68b	1
		ה	THE	207b	1 b
		מנשה	MANASSEH	286c	1 a
		ימין	RIGHT HAND	411c	1
		צעיר	YOUNG	859a	2
		ראש	HEAD	910d	1 a
		שכל	LAY CROSSWISE	968d	
		שמאל	LEFT	969d	2
		שית	PUT	1011a	1
48	15	ברך	BLESS	139a	3
		הלך	WALK	236b	2
		יום	DAY	401b	7 l
		עוד	STILL	729c	2 b
		רעה	TEND	944d	1 b
48	16	ברך	BLESS	139a	2 a
		גאל	REDEEM	145c	3 a
		דגה	MULTIPLY	185c	
		מלאך	MESSENGER	521d	3
		קרא	CALL	896c	6 d7
		קרב	INWARD PART	899a	1 e
		רב	MULTITUDE	914a	1
		רע	EVIL	948d	1
48	17	אפרים	EPHRAIM	68b	1
		מנשה	MANASSEH	286c	1 a
		יד	HAND	389a	1
		ימין	RIGHT HAND	411d	1 a
		רעע	BE EVIL	949c	1
		שית	PUT	1011a	1
		תמך	GRASP	1069c	1
48	18	בכור	FIRST-BORN	114a	1
		ימין	RIGHT HAND	*411c	1 a
		כן	SO	486b	1 cd
		שום	TO PLACE	963b	1 b
48	19	אולם	BUT	19d	
		אפרים	EPHRAIM	68b	1
		גדל	BECOME GREAT	152b	2 e
		גוי	NATION	156c	1 a
		היה	BECOME	226b	2 e
		זרע	SOWING	282d	4 c
		מאן	REFUSE	549a	
		מן	THAN	582c	6 a
		קטן	SMALL	882b	1 a
48	20	אפרים	EPHRAIM	68b	1
		ב	IN	90a	3 2d
		ברך	BLESS	139a	3
		ברך	BLESS	139b	4
		מנשה	MANASSEH	286c	1 a
		פנה	FACE	817c	2 4c c
		שום	TO PLACE	963b	1 b
		שום	TO PLACE	964a	3 e
		שוה	SET	1001b	
48	21	היה	BE	227b	3 4d a
		הנה	BEHOLD	243d	
		שוב	TURN BACK	998d	1 a
48	22	אמרי	AMORITES	57c	2 d
		חרב	SWORD	352c	1 a
		לקח	TAKE	543d	8
		על	UPON	755a	2 2
		קשת	BOW	906a	1 b
		שכם	SHOULDER	1014b	1 b

Ch	v.	Heb	Eng	Page	Sec
49	1	אחרית	END	31b	B
		אסף	GATHER	62c	1 a
		קרא	ENCOUNTER	897a	2
49	2	אסף	GATHER	62c	1 a
		בן	SON	*120d	1 jb
		קבץ	GATHER	867d	
		שמע	HEAR	1034a	1 k
49	3	און	VIGOUR	20b	1
		יתר	SUPERIORITY	452a	3
		כח	STRENGTH	470c	1 a
		שאת	DIGNITY	673b	1
		ראשית	BEGINNING	912b	1 a
49	4	אב	FATHER	3b	1
		אז	THEN	23a	1 c
		אל	NOT	39a	A a
		חלל	POLLUTE	320b	1 a
		יצוע	BED	427a	
		יתר	EXCEL	451c	2
		מי	WATER	565d	4 d
		עלה	GO UP	748b	1 c
		פחז	WANTONNESS	808d	
		משכב	COUCH	1012d	1
		הא	DEMONSTRATIVE PARTICLE	*1089c	A
49	5	אח	BROTHER	26b	1
		חמס	VIOLENCE	329c	
		מכרה	SWORD	468d	2 a
		כלי	IMPLEMENT	479d	2 a
		לוי	LEVI	532c	1 a
		שמעון	SIMEON	*1035c	1
49	6	אף	NOSE	60b	3
		בוא	COME	98a	1 f
		הרג	KILL	247a	1 a
		יחד	BE UNITED	402d	
		כבד	HONOR	459b	5
		נפש	SOUL	660a	4 a1
		סוד	ASSEMBLY	691c	1 b
		עקר	HAMSTRING	785d	
		קהל	ASSEMBLY	874c	1 a
		רצון	GOODWILL	953c	3 b
		שור	A HEAD OF CATTLE	1004a	
49	7	אף	NOSE	60b	3
		ארר	CURSE	76d	
		חלק	DIVIDE	323d	3
		עברה	OVERFLOW	720c	3 a
		עז	STRONG	738d	
		פוץ	BE DISPERSED	807a	1 a
		קשה	BE SEVERE	904b	2
		ישראל	ISRAEL	975c	2 a1
49	8	בן	SON	120b	1
		ידה	PRAISE	392b	1 a1
		יהודה	JUDAH	397a	1 1
		ערף	BACK OF NECK	791b	1
		שחה	BOW DOWN	1005b	1 c
49	9	אריה	LION	71d	
		אריה	LION	71d	
		גור	WHELP	158d	1
		טרף	PREY	383c	1
		יהודה	JUDAH	397a	1 1
		כרע	BOW DOWN	502c	2
		לביא	LION	522d	
		מי	WHO	566d	F c
		עלה	GO UP	748d	3
		קום	STAND	879a	4 a
		קשה	SEVERE	904d	2 b
		רבץ	LIE DOWN	918c	
49	10	בין	INTERVAL	107d	D
		חקק	CUT IN	349b	
		יהודה	JUDAH	397a	1 1
		יקהה	OBEDIENCE	429b	
		סור	TURN ASIDE	693d	2
		עד	UNTIL	725a	2 1a b
		עד	UNTIL	725a	2 1b b
		שבט	ROD	987a	1 d
		שילה	SHILOH	1010a	
49	11	אסר	TIE	63c	1 1
		אתון	SHE-ASS	87d	
		בן	SON	121c	7 b
		גפן	VINE	172c	
		דם	BLOOD	197d	4
		כבס	WASH	460a	1
		לבוש	CLOTHING	528c	
		סות	VESTURE	691d	
		עיר	MALE ASS	747a	
		ענב	GRAPE	772a	
		שרקה	VINE	977d	
49	12	חכלילי	DARK	314b	
		חלב	MILK	316c	B
		לבן	WHITE	526b	
		מן	ON ACCOUNT OF	580b	2 f
		עין	EYE	744c	1 s
		שן	TOOTH	1042a	1
49	13	אניה	A SHIP	58b	
		זבולן	ZEBULUN	259d	1
		חוף	SHORE	342b	
		ים	SEA	411b	8 a
		ירכה	SIDE	438a	1
		ל	TO	511d	2
		על	UPON	757c	2 7c ab
		צידון	SIDON	850d	
		שכן	SETTLE DOWN	1015b	2 a
49	14	גרם	STRENGTH	175a	2
		חמור	HE-ASS	331c	2
		יששכר	ISSACHAR	441a	1
		רבץ	LIE DOWN	918b	
		משפתים	FIRE-PLACES	1046b	
49	15	היה	BECOME	226b	2 2e
		טוב	PLEASANT	374a	2 e
		מס	LABOUR-GANG	*587a	1
		מס	LABOUR-GANG	*587a	2 b
		מס	LABOUR-GANG	587a	3
		מנוח	RESTING PLACE	629d	1
		מנוחה	RESTING PLACE	629d	1
		נטה	BEND	640b	3 b
		נעם	BE DELIGHTFUL	653c	
		סבל	BEAR	687d	
		עבד	WORK	713a	3
		ראה	TO SEE	907a	2 1
		שכם	SHOULDER	1014a	1 a
49	16	דין	JUDGE	192b	3
		דן	DAN	192d	2
		שבט	TRIBE	987a	2 a
49	17	אחור	HINDER SIDE	30c	A
		ארח	WAY	73a	1
		דן	DAN	192d	2
		דרך	WAY	202c	1
		נחש	SERPENT	638b	1 a
		נפל	FALL	656d	1
		נשך	BITE	675a	
		עקב	HEEL	784b	A
		רכב	RIDE	938d	3
		שפיפן	HORNED SNAKE	1051b	
49	18	ישועה	DELIVERANCE	447b	3
		קוה	WAIT FOR	875d	1
49	19	גדוד	BAND	151b	1
		גד	GAD	151c	1 a
		גוד	ATTACK	156a	
		עקב	HEEL	784d	C
49	20	אשר	ASHER	81b	2
		לחם	FOOD	537b	1 b
		מלך	KING	573c	5 d
		מעדן	DAINTY	726d	
		שמן	FAT	1032a	1
49	21	אלה	TEREBINTH	18d	
		אילה	HIND	19b	
		אמר	WORD	57a	2
		ה	TOP	57b	
		ה	THE	209a	2 a
		נפתלי	NAPHTALI	836b	1
		שלח	SEND	1018d	3 d
		שפר	BEAUTY	1051c	
49	22	בן	SON	121b	5
		בת	DAUGHTER	123d	8
		יוסף	JOSEPH	415c	1 a
		עין	SPRING	745b	
		פרה	BEAR FRUIT	826a	2
		צעד	STEP	857c	
		צעד	STEP	857c	
		שור	WALL	1004b	
49	23	בעל	LORD	127c	1 5b
		חץ	ARROW	346c	1
		מרר	BE BITTER	600b	1
		מצרים	EGYPT	695c	1 a
		ירבעם	SHOOT	914d	
		שטם	BEAR A GRUDGE	966b	
49	24	אבן	STONE	6b	1
		אביר	STRONG	7d	
		זרוע	ARM	283d	1 a
		יד	HAND	389a	1 c
		יד	HAND	390a	1 e2
		ישב	REMAIN	443a	2 b
		איתן	ENDURING	450d	2
		מן	OUT OF	580d	2 eb
		פזז	BE SUPPLE	808a	
		קשת	BOW	906a	1 e
		רעה	TEND	945a	1 d3
		שם	THERE	1027c	4 a
49	25	אל	GOD	42c	6 c
		את	WITH	86a	1 a
		ברך	BLESS	139a	2 a
		ברכה	BLESSING	139d	3
		טל	NIGHT-MIST	*378c	
		מן	OUT OF	580a	2 ea
		עזר	HELP	740b	
		על	HEIGHT	752c	1
		רבץ	LIE DOWN	918c	
		רחם	WOMB	933b	1
		שד	BREAST	994d	3
		שדי	ALMIGHTY	995a	1
		שמי	HEAVENS	1029d	1 a
		תהום	DEEP	1062d	1
		תחת	UNDERNEATH	1065b	1
49	26	ברכה	BLESSING	139d	3
		גבעה	HILL	149a	3
		גבר	BE STRONG	149d	2 b
		הור	MOUNTAIN	223c	
		היה	BECOME	225d	2 1b
		הרה	CONCEIVE	248a	
		הר	MOUNTAIN	250b	1 c
		יוסף	JOSEPH	415c	1 a
		נזיר	CONSECRATED	634c	1
		עולם	LONG DURATION	762a	1 d
		קדקד	HEAD	869a	
		תאוה	BOUNDARY	1063b	
		עד	ADDENDA ET CORRIGENDA	1125d	
49	27	בקר	MORNING	134a	1 e
		זאב	WOLF	255d	
		חלק	DIVIDE	323d	1
		טרף	TEAR	382d	
		ל	TO	517d	6 a
		עד	BOOTY	723d	
		שלל	SPOIL	1022a	1
49	28	ברך	BLESS	139a	3
		ברכה	BLESSING	139d	1 a
		דבר	SPEAK	181b	3 c
		ל	TO	510d	1 b
		שבט	TRIBE	987a	2 a
49	29	אל	TO	39d	1
		אסף	GATHER	62d	2 a
		חתי	HITTITE	366c	1
		עם	KINSMAN	769b	
		עפרון	EPHRON	780b	1
		צוה	CHARGE	845d	2 c
		קבר	BURY	868c	
49	30	אחזה	POSSESSION	28d	
		אשר	PARTICLE OF RELATION	82d	6 c
		חתי	HITTITE	366c	1
		מכפלה	MACHPELAH	495d	
		ממרא	MAMRE	577b	3
		עפרון	EPHRON	780b	1
		פנה	FACE	818d	2 7a d
		קצצר	GRAVE	868d	
49	31	לאה	LEAH	521b	
		קבר	BURY	868c	
		רבקה	REBEKAH	918d	
		שרה	SARAH	979a	
		שם	THERE	1027b	3
49	32	בן	SON	120d	1 ja
		חת	HETH	366c	A
		מקנה	CATTLE	889b	
49	33	אסף	GATHER	62c	2 d
		אסף	GATHER	62d	2 a
		גוע	EXPIRE	157c	
		ממה	COUCH	641d	
		עם	KINSMAN	769b	
		צוה	CHARGE	845d	2 c
50	1	אב	FATHER	3b	1
		בכה	WEEP	113c	3
		נפל	FALL	657c	3 c
		נשק	KISS	676b	
50	2	חנט	SPICE	334d	2
		ל	TO	517d	7 bc
		עבד	SLAVE	713d	1
		צוה	CHARGE	845d	2 b
		רפא	HEAL	950d	1 b
50	3	בכה	WEEP	113c	4
		חנטים	EMBALMING	334d	
		מלא	BE FULL	570b	1 b
50	4	אזן	EAR	24a	2 a
		בכית	WEEPING	114a	
		חן	FAVOR	336b	2 b1
		נא	PART OF ENTREATY	609c	4 c
		עבר	PASS OVER	*717d	4 d
50	5	אב	FATHER	3b	1
		כנען	CANAAN	488a	2 a
		כרה	DIG	500a	
		קבר	BURY	868c	
		שבע	SWEAR	989c	1
		שם	THERE	1027b	3
50	6	שבע	SWEAR	989c	1
50	7	בית	HOUSE	109d	5 a
50	8	ארץ	EARTH	76a	2
		בית	HOUSE	110a	5 dz
		גשן	GOSHEN	177d	1
		עזב	LEAVE	737a	1 b
		רק	ONLY	956b	1
50	9	מחנה	ENCAMPMENT	334b	3 b
		כבד	MASSIVE	458b	1
		פרש	HORSEMAN	832a	
		רכב	CHARIOT	939a	1
50	10	אבל	MOURNING	5c	
		אטד	BRAMBLE	31d	
		גרן	THRESHING-FLOOR	175b	
		גרן	THRESHING-FLOOR	175b	
		ירדן	JORDAN	434c	
		כבד	HEAVY	458b	2 a
		מספד	WAILING	704d	1
		ספד	WAIL	704d	
		עבר	REGION ACROSS	719c	1 a
50	11	אבל	MOURNING	5c	
		אבל	MOURNING	5d	
		אבל	ABEL	6a	6
		אטד	BRAMBLE	31d	
		גרן	THRESHING-FLOOR	175b	
		גרן	THRESHING-FLOOR	175b	
		ירדן	JORDAN	434c	
		ישב	DWELL	443b	3
		כבד	HEAVY	458a	1
		כנעני	CANAANITE	489a	2 b
		עבר	REGION ACROSS	719c	1 a
50	12	כאשר	AS	455b	1 b
		כן	SO	486c	2 da
50	13	אחזה	POSSESSION	28d	
		אשר	PARTICLE OF RELATION	82d	6 c
		חתי	HITTITE	366c	1
		כנען	CANAAN	488d	2 a
		מכפלה	MACHPELAH	495d	
		עפרון	EPHRON	780b	1
		פנה	FACE	818d	2 7a d
		קצצר	GRAVE	868d	
		קנה	ACQUIRE	889a	2
50	14	שוב	TURN BACK	997b	3 b
50	15	לו	IF	530b	1 d
		רעה	MISERY	949b	2

Ch	v.	Heb	Eng	Page	Sec
		שטם	BEAR A GRUDGE	966b	
		שוב	TURN BACK	999c	4 a
50	16	אב	FATHER	3b	1
		מות	DEATH	560d	1
		צוה	CHARGE	846a	2 e
		צוה	CHARGE	846a	4 a
50	17	אלהים	GOD	44b	4 ba
		אנא	AH, NOW	58a	
		בכה	WEEP	113c	3
		חטאת	SIN	308c	1 a
		נשא	LIFT	671b	3 c
		נשא	LIFT	671c	3 c
		עבד	SLAVE	714a	3
		פשע	TRANSGRESSION	833c	1
		רעה	MISERY	949b	2
50	18	הנה	BEHOLD	243d	
		הנה	BEHOLD	*244a	A
		נפל	FALL	657b	3 b
		עבד	SLAVE	714c	7
50	19	ה	INTERROG PART	209d	1 b
		ירא	FEAR	431a	1 a
		תחת	INSTEAD	*1065d	2 2b a
50	20	חיה	LIVE	311c	1
		חשב	THINK	363a	1 2
		חשב	THINK	363b	2 2
		טובה	WELFARE	375d	1
		יום	DAY	400d	7 h
		על	UPON	757d	2 7d
		עם	PEOPLE	766d	4
		מען	PURPOSE	775d	1 c
		רעה	MISERY	949b	2
50	21	דבר	SPEAK	181d	5
		ירא	FEAR	431a	1 a
		כול	SUSTAIN	465a	1
		לב	HEART	525c	2 9a
		נחם	CONSOLE ONESELF	637a	
50	22	בית	HOUSE	109d	5 a
		חיה	LIVE	311a	1 a
		עשר	TEN	797a	3 a
50	23	אפרים	EPHRAIM	68b	1
		ברך	KNEE	139c	
		מנשה	MANASSEH	286c	1 a
		ילד	BEAR	408c	1
		ילד	BE BORN	409a	
		ל	TO	512d	5 aa
		מנשה	MANASSEH	*586c	1 b2 d
		שלש	PERTAINING TO THE THIRD	1026d	
50	24	פקד	ATTEND TO	823d	A 2
		שבע	SWEAR	989c	2
50	25	זה	THIS	262a	6 e
		עלה	GO UP	749c	4
		עצם	BONE	782d	1 f
		פקד	ATTEND TO	823b	A 2
		שבע	SWEAR	989d	1
50	26	ארון	CHEST	75b	2
		בן	SON	121d	9 a
		חנט	SPICE	334d	2
		עשר	TEN	797a	3 a
		שום	TO PLACE	964d	

EXODUS

Ch	v.	Heb	Eng	Page	Sec
1	1	בית	HOUSE	109d	5 a
		בן	SON	*120d	1 jg
		בנה	BUILD	124b	1 aa
1	2	לוי	LEVI	532c	1 a
		ראובן	REUBEN	910a	1
		שמעון	SIMEON	1035c	1
1	3	זבולן	ZEBULUN	259d	1
		יששכר	ISSACHAR	441a	1
1	4	אשר	ASHER	81b	1
		גד	GAD	151c	1 a
		דן	DAN	192d	1
		שדה	FIELD	961c	1 f
1	5	יוסף	JOSEPH	415d	1 a
		יצא	GO OUT	423a	1 h
		ירך	THIGH	438a	1 b
		נפש	SOUL	660c	4 c3
1	6	דור	GENERATION	190a	2 a
		יוסף	JOSEPH	415d	1
1	7	את	MARK OF THE AC-CUSATIVE	85a	1 b
		בן	SON	120d	1 jg
		מאד	MUCHNESS	547c	2 e
		מלא	FILL	570b	1
		עצם	BE VAST	782c	2
		פרה	BEAR FRUIT	826a	1
		רבה	BECOME MANY	915a	1 a
		ישראל	ISRAEL	975c	1
		שרץ	SWARM	1056d	2
1	8	חדש	NEW	294a	A
		ידע	KNOW	394a	2
		יוסף	JOSEPH	415d	1 a
		מלך	KING	573a	1
		קום	STAND	878a	4
1	9	בן	SON	120d	1 jg
		הנה	BEHOLD	244a	B a
		עם	PEOPLE	766c	1
		עצום	MIGHTY	783a	1
		רב	MUCH	913b	1 e
1	10	הוא	HE, SHE, IT	215c	1 b
		חיה	COME TO PASS	225b	1 2b ba
		חכם	BE WISE	314c	
		יהב	GIVE	396d	5

Ch	v.	Heb	Eng	Page	Sec
		יסף	JOIN	415a	1
		לחם	ENGAGE IN BAT-TLE	535c	
		מלחמה	WAR	536a	
		פן	LEST	814d	1
		קרא	ENCOUNTER	897a	2
		רבה	BECOME MANY	915a	1 a
		שנא	HATE	971c	3
1	11	מס	LABOUR-GANG	587a	2 a
		סבלה	BURDEN	688a	
		מסכנות	SUPPLY	698b	
		עיר	CITY	746c	1 e
		על	UPON	755a	2 3
		מען	PURPOSE	775b	1 c
		ענה	BE BOWED DOWN	776b	1
		פתם	PITHOM	837a	
		שום	TO PLACE	963d	1
		שר	CHIEFTAIN	978d	4 b
1	12	כאשר	AS	455b	1
		כן	SO	486c	2 cb
		ענה	BE BOWED DOWN	776b	1
		פרץ	BREAK THROUGH	829c	8
		קוץ	FEEL A LOATHING	881a	2
		רבה	BECOME MANY	915a	1 a
		ישראל	ISRAEL	975d	2 b1
1	13	עבד	WORK	713c	1
		פרך	HARSHNESS	827d	
1	14	את	MARK OF THE AC-CUSATIVE	85b	3 a
		ב	IN	89d	3 2b
		חיים	LIFE	313a	1
		חמר	CEMENT	330c	1
		לבנה	BRICK	527c	1
		מרר	BE BITTER	600b	2
		עבד	WORK	713a	2
		עבדה	LABOR	715a	1
		עבדה	LABOR	715b	3
		פרך	HARSHNESS	827d	2
		קשה	SEVERE	904c	2 a
1	15	ילד	MIDWIFE	408d	1
		עברי	HEBREW	720b	2 b
		פועה	PUAH	806d	
		שפרה	SHIPHRAH	1051c	
1	16	אבן	WHEEL	7a	2
		בת	DAUGHTER	123a	1
		ילד	HELP TO BRING FORTH	408d	
		ילד	CHILD	*409b	A
		מות	DIE	560b	1 b
		עברי	HEBREW	720b	2 a
		ראה	TO SEE	908a	8 b
1	17	חיה	LIVE	311c	1
		ילד	MIDWIFE	408d	1
		ילד	CHILD	409b	A
		ירא	FEAR	431c	3 b
		עשה	DO	794a	1 1a 7
1	18	חיה	LIVE	311c	1
		מדוע	WHEREFORE	396c	1
		ילד	MIDWIFE	408d	
		ילד	CHILD	409b	A
1	19	חיה	HAVING THE VIGOR OF LIFE	313a	
		טרם	NOT YET	382c	2
		ילד	MIDWIFE	408d	
		כי	BECAUSE	473c	2
		כי	BUT	474b	3 e
		מצרי	EGYPTIAN	596a	1
		עברי	HEBREW	720b	2 a
1	20	יטב	DO GOOD TO	405d	2
		ילד	MIDWIFE	408d	
		עם	PEOPLE	*766b	1
		עם	PEOPLE	766c	1
		עצם	BE VAST	782c	2
		רבה	BECOME MANY	915a	1 a
1	21	בית	HOUSE	109d	5 b
		בית	HOUSE	109d	5 a
		ילד	MIDWIFE	408d	
		ירא	FEAR	431c	3 b
		בת	DAUGHTER	123a	1
1	22	ה	THE	208a	1 g
		חיה	LIVE	311c	1
		יאר	STREAM	384b	1
		ילוד	BORN	409c	
		כל	ALL	481c	1
		עם	PEOPLE	766c	1
		צוה	GIVE CHARGE TO	845c	1 b
		שלך	THROW	1021a	1 b
2	1	בית	HOUSE	110b	5 dk
		בת	DAUGHTER	123c	1 i
		לוי	LEVI	532a	1
		לוי	LEVI	532c	1 b
		משה	MOSES	602c	
2	2	אשה	WOMAN	61a	1
		הרה	CONCEIVE	247d	1
		טוב	PLEASANT	373c	1 a
		ירח	MONTH	437b	1
		צפן	HIDE	860c	1
		ראה	TO SEE	907a	2 1
2	3	זפת	PITCH	278a	
		חמר	BITUMEN	330c	
		חמר	COVER WITH AS-PHALT	330d	
		יאר	STREAM	384b	1
		יכל	BE ABLE	407c	1 b
		ילד	CHILD	409b	A
		סוף	REEDS	693a	1

Ch	v.	Heb	Eng	Page	Sec
		עוד	STILL	729a	1 ab
		צפן	HIDE	860d	
		שום	TO PLACE	963a	1 a
		תבה	ARK	1061c	
2	4	אחות	SISTER	27d	1
		יצב	STATION ONESELF	426b	A
		מה	WHAT	552d	1 b
		מן	FROM	578d	1 c
		עשה	DO	795b	1 c
		רחק	DISTANT	935c	2 a2
2	5	אמה	MAID	51a	1
		בת	DAUGHTER	123b	1 h
		הלך	WALK	230d	1 1d 2b
		יאר	STREAM	384b	1
		יד	HAND	391c	5 h3
		ירד	GO DOWN	433a	1 g
		נערה	GIRL	655b	2
		סוף	REEDS	693a	1
		רחץ	WASH OFF	934c	2
		שלח	SEND	1018b	1 a
		תבה	ARK	1061c	
2	6	בכה	WEEP	113b	1
		הנה	BEHOLD	244b	C
		חמל	SPARE	328b	
		ילד	CHILD	409b	A
		מן	FROM	580d	3 bb
		נער	YOUTH	654d	1 a
		עברי	HEBREW	720b	2 a
		פתח	OPEN	835a	
2	7	אחות	SISTER	27d	1
		אשה	WOMAN	61a	1
		בת	DAUGHTER	123b	1 h
		ה	INTERROG PART	209d	1 a
		ילד	CHILD	409b	A
		ינק	NURSE	413c	
		ינק	NURSE	413c	
		עברי	HEBREW	720b	2 a
		קרא	CALL	895c	5 c
2	8	אם	MOTHER	51c	1
		אם	MOTHER	51d	1
		בת	DAUGHTER	123b	1 h
		הלך	WALK	233d	1 5b
		ילד	CHILD	409b	A
		עלמה	YOUNG WOMAN	761c	
2	9	אם	MOTHER	51d	1
		בת	DAUGHTER	123b	1 h
		הלך	WALK	237a	3 b
		ילד	CHILD	409b	A
		ינק	NURSE	413c	
		נוק	SUCKLE	632d	1
		נתן	GIVE	679b	1 n
		שכר	HIRE	969a	1
2	10	בת	DAUGHTER	123b	1 h
		גדל	GROW UP	152b	1 a
		חיה	BECOME	226c	2 2f
		ילד	CHILD	409b	A
		כי	THAT	*472a	1 b
		מי	WATER	565c	1 b
		מן	OUT OF	579a	2 aa
		משה	MOSES	602c	1
		משה	DRAW	602c	
		קרא	CALL	896a	6 a
		שלה	DRAW OUT	*1017d	
2	11	אח	BROTHER	26b	2
		איש	MAN	36a	
		גדל	GROW UP	152b	1 a
		הם	THEY	241d	7
		מצרי	EGYPTIAN	596a	1
		סבלה	BURDEN	688a	
		עברי	HEBREW	720b	1 b
		ראה	TO SEE	908a	8 a3
2	12	אין	NOT	34b	2 b
		הנה	HITHER	*244b	A a
		חול	SAND	297c	
		טמן	HIDE	380b	1
		כה	THUS	462b	1
		מצרי	EGYPTIAN	596a	2
		נכה	SMITE	646c	2 c
		פנה	TURN	815b	2 a
2	13	נצה	STRUGGLE	663c	1
		עברי	HEBREW	720b	1 b
		רע	FRIEND	946a	2
		רשע	WICKED	957b	1
		שני	SECOND	1041b	
2	14	איש	MAN	36a	
		אכן	SURELY	38c	A
		אמר	SAY	56b	2
		הרג	KILL	247a	1 a
		ידע	BE MADE KNOWN	394c	1
		ירא	FEAR	431a	1 a
		ל	TO	517d	7 bc
		מצרי	EGYPTIAN	596a	2
		נכה	SMITE	645b	1 a
		שום	TO PLACE	964a	3 d
		שר	CHIEFTAIN	978d	1
		שפט	JUDGE	1047c	1 b
2	15	באר	WELL	91c	1
		בקש	SEEK	134d	2
		ברח	FLEE	138a	2
		מדין	MIDIAN	193c	3
		ה	THE	207b	1 cb
		הרג	KILL	247a	1 a
		ישב	SIT	442c	1 a
		ל	TO	517d	7 bc
		משה	MOSES	602c	
		על	UPON	756b	2 6c

Ch v.	Heb	Eng	Page	Sec
2 16	באר	WELL	*91c	1
	מדין	MIDIAN	193c	2
	דלה	DRAW	194d	
	כהן	PRIEST-KING	463a	1
	מלא	FILL	570c	1
	רהט	TROUGH	923d	
	שקה	GIVE TO DRINK	1052c	2
2 17	גרש	DRIVE OUT	176d	
	ישע	DELIVER	446c	1
	רעה	TEND	945a	1 d1
	שקה	GIVE TO DRINK	1052c	2
2 18	מדוע	WHEREFORE	396c	
	מהר	HASTEN	555b	2
	רעואל	REUEL	946c	1
2 19	איש	MAN	36a	
	דלה	DRAW	194d	
	יד	HAND	391b	5 g1
	ל	TO	515c	5 hc
	מצרי	EGYPTIAN	596a	1
	נצל	DELIVER	665a	3 a
	רעה	TEND	945a	1 d1
	שקה	GIVE TO DRINK	1052c	2
2 20	אורי	URI	22b	1
	אי	WHERE	32b	1 a
	אכל	EAT	37b	1
	ו	AND	254c	4
	מה	HOW	554a	4 d
	עזב	LEAVE	737a	1 b
2 21	יאל	SHOW WILLING-NESS	384a	1
	ישב	DWELL	443a	3
	נתן	GIVE	678c	1 c
	צפרה	ZIPPORAH	862a	
2 22	גר	SOJOURNER	158a	1
	גרשם	GERSHOM	177a	1
	נכרי	FOREIGN	648d	1 a
	קרא	CALL	896a	6 a
2 23	אנח	SIGN	58d	2
	זעק	CRY	277b	2 d
	מן	ON ACCOUNT OF	580b	2 f
	עבדה	LABOR	715b	3
	עלה	GO UP	749a	8
	פנה	FACE	817a	2 4a c
	שועה	CRY FOR HELP	1003a	
2 24	ברית	COVENANT	136c	2 2b
	ברית	COVENANT	137b	3 2
	זכר	REMEMBER	270b	2 3 a
	נאקה	GROANING	611a	
2 25	ראה	TO SEE	907c	6 a
3 1	אחר	BEHIND	29d	
	אלהים	GOD	44a	3 b
	מדין	MIDIAN	193c	
	היה	BE	227c	3 5a
	הר	MOUNTAIN	249b	1 a
	חרב	HOREB	352a	
	חתן	WIFE'S FATHER	368c	1
	יתרו	JETHRO	452b	
	כהן	PRIEST-KING	463a	1
	נהג	DRIVE	624b	1
	רעה	TEND	944d	1 a
3 2	אין	NOT	34c	2 f
	אכל	EAT	37d	
	אש	FIRE	77b	1
	אש	FIRE	77c	2
	אש	FIRE	77d	6
	בער	BURN	129a	
	מלאך	MESSENGER	521d	3
	לחבה	FLAME	529b	1
	סנה	BLACKBERRY BUSH	702d	
	ראה	TO SEE	907c	6 c
	ראה	TO SEE	908b	1 a
	תוך	MIDST	1063d	
3 3	בער	BURN	129a	2
	מדוע	WHEREFORE	396c	
	נא	PART OF EN-TREATY	609b	3 a
	סור	TURN ASIDE	693c	1
	סנה	BLACKBERRY BUSH	702d	
	ראה	TO SEE	906d	1 b
	מראה	VISION	909c	1 a
3 4	הנה	BEHOLD	244a	A
	סור	TURN ASIDE	693c	1
	סנה	BLACKBERRY BUSH	702d	
	קרא	CALL	895b	2 a
	ראה	TO SEE	907b	5 a
3 5	אדמה	GROUND	9d	4
	הוא	HE, SHE, IT	216a	3 b
	הלם	HITHER	240d	
	נעל	SANDAL	653b	
	נשל	DRAW OFF	675c	2
	על	UPON	758c	4 2a
	עמד	STAND	763d	1 a
	קדש	APARTNESS	871c	2 b
	מקום	STANDING PLACE	879d	1 a
	קרב	COME NEAR	897c	1 f
	רגל	FOOT	919d	1 a
3 6	אלהים	GOD	44b	4 ba
	אלהים	GOD	44b	4 ba
	ירא	FEAR	431b	1 d
	מן	FROM	583c	7 b
	נבט	LOOK	613c	1 a
	סתר	HIDE	711d	2 a
3 7	מכאוב	PAIN	456b	1
	נגש	DRIVE	620c	3
	עם	PEOPLE	766c	1
	עני	AFFLICTION	777a	1
	פנה	FACE	818a	2 5b
	פנה	FACE	818c	2 6c a
	צעקה	CRY	858d	2
3 8	אמרי	AMORITES	57c	2 e
	יבוסי	JEBUSITE	101a	1
	דבש	HONEY	185b	
	זוב	FLOW	264d	2
	חוי	HIVITE	295d	2
	חלב	MILK	316c	A 4
	חתי	HITTITE	366d	2 a
	טוב	PLEASANT	374a	3 b
	ירד	GO DOWN	433b	1
	כנעני	CANAANITE	489a	2 b
	פרזי	PERIZZITE	827a	1
	רחב	WIDE	932a	
	רחב	WIDE	932a	
3 9	בוא	COME	98b	2
	לחץ	OPPRESSION	537d	
	לחץ	OPPRESS	537d	2
	עתה	NOW	774b	2 c
	צעקה	CRY	858d	2
	ישראל	ISRAEL	975d	2 b1
3 10	בן	SON	120d	1 jg
	יצא	CAUSE TO GO	424c	1 a
3 11	יצא	CAUSE TO GO	424c	1 a
	כי	THAT	472d	1 f
	מי	WHO	566d	F b
3 12	אות	SIGN	16d	2
	ב	IN	91a	5 1
	יהוה	YAHWEH	218b	1
	יהוה	YAHWEH	218b	1
	יהוה	YAHWEH	218b	1
	יהוה	YAHWEH	*218b	1
	יהוה	YAHWEH	218b	1
	זה	THIS	261b	3
	יצא	CAUSE TO GO	424c	1 a
	כי	THAT	471d	1 b
	עבד	WORK	713b	4 a
	עם	WITH	767c	1 a
	שלח	SEND	1018c	2 a
3 13	אב	FATHER	3c	4 b
	אלהים	GOD	44b	4 ba
	אכי	I	59c	
	יהוה	YAHWEH	218b	1
	מה	WHAT	552b	
	מי	WHO	*566b	A
	שלח	SEND	1018c	2 a
	שם	NAME	1028a	2 a
	מן	WHO	*1100d	1
3 14	יהוה	YAHWEH	218b	1
	יהוה	YAHWEH	218b	1
	יהוה	YAHWEH	218b	1
	היה	BE	226d	3 1
	כה	THUS	462a	1 a
3 15	אב	FATHER	3c	4 b
	אלהים	GOD	44b	4 ba
	דור	PERIOD	189d	1 b
	יהוה	YAHWEH	218b	1
	יהוה	YAHWEH	218b	1
	זכר	REMEMBRANCE	271b	2 a
	כה	THUS	462a	1 a
	עוד	STILL	729b	1 b
	עולם	LONG DURATION	762b	2 c
	שם	NAME	1028c	3
3 16	אב	FATHER	3c	4 b
	אלהים	GOD	44b	4 ba
	אסף	GATHER	62b	1 a
	זקן	OLD	278d	2 b
	פקד	ATTEND TO	823b	A 1a
3 17	אמרי	AMORITES	57c	2 e
	יבוסי	JEBUSITE	101a	1
	דבש	HONEY	185b	
	זוב	FLOW	264d	2
	חוי	HIVITE	295d	2
	חלב	MILK	316c	A 4
	חתי	HITTITE	366d	2 a
	כנעני	CANAANITE	489a	2 b
	עני	AFFLICTION	777a	1
3 18	אלהים	GOD	44c	4 ba
	דרך	JOURNEY	203a	2
	יהוה	YAHWEH	218d	2 1c
	הלך	WALK	230c	1 1d 1b
	זבח	SLAUGHTER FOR SACRIFICE	257a	1 3
	זקן	OLD	278d	2 b
	יום	DAY	398d	2 b
	נא	PART OF EN-TREATY	609b	3 a
	עברי	HEBREW	720b	2 b
	קול	VOICE	877b	3 a1
	קרה	ENCOUNTER	899d	1
3 19	הלך	WALK	230b	1 b
	חזק	STRONG	305c	1 b
	נתן	GIVE	679a	1 g
	נכה	SMITE	646c	4 a
	פלא	BE SURPASSING	810d	4
	שלח	SEND	1018d	3
3 20	היה	COME TO PASS	224c	2 a1 at
	היה	COME TO PASS	225b	1 2b c
	הלך	WALK	232a	1 1d 5k
	חן	FAVOR	336c	2 b1
	נתן	PUT	680d	2 b
3 21	ריקם	EMPTILY	938b	1
3 22	גור	SOJOURN	157d	1
	זהב	GOLD	263a	6
	זהב	GOLD	263c	1
	כלי	ARTICLE	479c	1
	נצל	STRIP	664d	1
	שמלה	WRAPPER	971a	
	שאל	ASK	981d	1 b
	שכן	NEIGHBOR	1015c	2
4 1	אמן	CONFIRM	53a	2 b
	הן	IF	243c	B
	ענה	ANSWER	772d	1 d
	קול	VOICE	877b	3 a1
4 2	הם	THEY	241d	7
	זה	THIS	261c	4 c
	מה	WHAT	552b	1 ab
	מטה	STAFF	641c	1
4 3	ארץ	EARTH	76b	3 a
	היה	BECOME	226b	2 2e
	נוס	FLEE	630d	1
	נחש	SERPENT	638b	1 b
	פנה	FACE	818c	2 6a
	שלך	THROW	1021a	1 a
4 4	אחז	GRASP	28b	
	היה	BECOME	226b	2 2e
	זנב	TAIL	275c	1 a
	חזק	BE FIRM	305a	6 a
	כף	HOLLOW OF THE HAND	496b	1 a
	מטה	STAFF	641c	1
4 5	אלהים	GOD	44b	4 ba
	אמן	CONFIRM	53b	2 d
	כי	THAT	471d	1 a
	מען	PURPOSE	775c	2 b
4 6	בוא	COME	99b	1 f
	חזק	BOSOM	300d	1
	יצא	BRING OUT	425a	4 b
	עוד	STILL	729b	1 b
	צרע	BE STRUCK WITH LEPROSY	864a	
	שלג	SNOW	1017a	
4 7	בשר	FLESH	142c	1 b
	חזק	BOSOM	300d	1
	יצא	BRING OUT	425a	4 b
	שוב	TURN BACK	998b	7 i
	שוב	TURN BACK	999a	1 a
4 8	אות	SIGN	16d	4
	אחרון	BEHIND	30d	B
	אמן	CONFIRM	53a	2 b
	אמן	CONFIRM	53a	2 b
	היה	COME TO PASS	225b	1 2b bb
	קול	VOICE	877b	3 a1
4 9	אות	SIGN	16d	4
	אמן	CONFIRM	53a	2 b
	גם	ALSO	169b	2
	דם	BLOOD	197c	2 o
	היה	COME TO PASS	225b	1 2b bb
	יאר	STREAM	384b	1
	יבשת	DRY LAND	387a	
	יבשה	DRY LAND	387a	
	מי	WATER	565c	1 b
	קול	VOICE	877b	3 a1
	שפך	POUR OUT	1049c	1 a
4 10	אדון	LORD	11b	3 2a
	מאז	FROM THAT TIME	23b	B
	בי	I PRAY	106c	
	גם	ALSO	169a	1
	דבר	WORD	183b	3 1
	כבד	HEAVY	458b	1 c
	לשון	TONGUE	546b	1 b
	עבד	SLAVE	714c	6
	פה	MOUTH	805a	2 a
	שלשם	THREE DAYS AGO	1026b	
	תמול	YESTERDAY	1070a	2 c
4 11	או	OR	14d	1
	אלם	DUMB	48a	
	יהוה	YAHWEH	219b	2 2d
	חרש	DEAF	361b	
	לא	NOT	520b	4 ba
	מי	WHO	567b	F e
	עור	BLIND	734c	1 a
	פקח	SEEING	824d	
	רכב	RIDE	938d	1
	שום	TO PLACE	964c	5 b
	שום	TO PLACE	964c	5 b
4 12	אשר	PARTICLE OF RE-LATION	82a	1
	ירה	DIRECT	435c	5 c
	פה	MOUTH	805a	2 a
4 13	אדון	LORD	11b	3 2a
	בי	I PRAY	106c	
4 14	אהרן	AARON	14d	
	אח	BROTHER	26b	1
	אף	NOSE	60b	3
	הוא	HE, SHE, IT	215c	1 c
	ו	AND	254b	2 db
	חרה	BURN	354a	2
	לב	HEART	525c	2 9a
	לוי	LEVITE	532d	1
	משה	MOSES	602c	
	שמח	REJOICE	970b	2 a
	שמח	REJOICE	970b	1 a
4 15	ירה	DIRECT	435c	5 c
	פה	MOUTH	805a	2 a
	פה	MOUTH	805a	2 a
	שום	TO PLACE	963a	1 a
4 16	אלהים	GOD	43d	2 b

Ch v.	Heb	Eng	Page	Sec	Ch v.	Heb	Eng	Page	Sec	Ch v.	Heb	Eng	Page	Sec
	הוא	HE, SHE, IT	215c	1 c		שלח	SEND	1019a	3	5 19	ב	IN	88d	1 6
	ל	TO	515c	5 hc	5 3	אלהים	GOD	44c	4 ba		גרע	DIMINISH	175c	1
	לא	NOT	519a	1 bb		ב	IN	89c	3 2a		דבר	WORD	183b	4 1
	פה	MOUTH	805a	2 a		דבר	PESTILENCE	184a	1		יום	DAY	400c	7 e3
4 17	אות	SIGN	16d	4		דרך	JOURNEY	203a	2		לבנה	BRICK	527c	1
	יד	HAND	391a	5 c4		יהוה	YAHWEH	218d	2 1c		ראה	TO SEE	907a	2 5
	לקח	TAKE	542d	1		הלך	WALK	230c	1 1d 1b		רע	EVIL	948d	1
	מטה	STAFF	641c	1		יום	DAY	398b	2		שטר	OFFICIAL	1009c	
	עשה	DO	793d	1 1a 1		עברי	HEBREW	720b	2 b	5 20	את	WITH	86d	4 a
4 18	אח	BROTHER	26b	2		פגע	MEET	803b	3		יצא	GO OUT	422d	1 b
	ה	INTERROG PART	210b	2 a		קרא	ENCOUNTER	897a			נצב	STAND	662a	1
	הלך	WALK	231d	1 d5 tc	5 4	הלך	WALK	231b	1 d3 gd		פגע	MEET	803b	1
	הלך	WALK	233d	1 5b		סבלה	BURDEN	688a			קרא	ENCOUNTER	897a	1
	חי	ALIVE	312a	1 b		פרע	LET GO	829a	1	5 21	באש	STINK	93a	2
	חתן	WIFE'S FATHER	368c	1	5 5	הן	BEHOLD	243c	A		הרג	KILL	247a	1 a
	יתרו	JETHRO	452b	1		ו	AND	252d	1 f		על	UPON	757d	2 7c d
	יתר	JETHER	452b	1		סבלה	BURDEN	688a			ראה	TO SEE	908a	8 b
	נא	PART OF ENTREATY	609b	3 a		עתה	NOW	774a	1 a		ריח	SCENT	926b	1
	עוד	STILL	728d	1 aa		מעשה	DEED	795d	1 b1		שפט	JUDGE	1047c	2 a
	ראה	TO SEE	907a	5 a		רב	MUCH	913a	1 b	5 22	אדון	LORD	11b	3 2a
	שלום	PEACE	1022d	3		שבת	CEASE	992a	1		זה	THIS	261c	4 e
4 19	בקש	SEEK	134d	2 a	5 6	נגש	DRIVE	620c	3		מה	HOW	554a	4 d
	מדין	MIDIAN	193c	3		שטר	OFFICIAL	1009c			רעע	BE EVIL	949c	1
	הלך	WALK	234a	1 5f 1	5 7	הם	THEY	241b	1 a		שוב	TURN BACK	997a	3 a
	נפש	SOUL	659d	3 c		יסף	DO AGAIN	415c	2 a	5 23	מאז	FROM THAT TIME	23b	B
4 20	אלהים	GOD	44a	3 b		לבנה	BRICK	527c	1		דבר	SPEAK	181c	4 a
	חמור	HE-ASS	331b	2 a		לבן	MAKE BRICK	527c			נצל	DELIVER	664d	3 a
	יד	HAND	391a	5 c4		קשש	GATHER STUBBLE	905d			רעע	BE EVIL	949c	1
	מטה	STAFF	641c	1		קשש	GATHER STUBBLE	905d			שם	NAME	1028b	3
	רכב	RIDE	938d	1		שלשם	THREE DAYS AGO	1026b		6 1	גרש	DRIVE OUT	177a	
	שוב	TURN BACK	997b	3 a		תבן	STRAW	1062a			חזק	STRONG	305c	1 b
4 21	מופת	WONDER	68d	1		תמול	YESTERDAY	1070a	2 b		יד	HAND	390a	1 e2
	מופת	SIGN	69a	2		אסף	ADDENDA ET CORRIGENDA	1120c			עתה	NOW	774a	1 b
	מופת	SIGN	69a	2	5 8	גרע	DIMINISH	175c	1	6 2	אנכי	I	59b	
	הלך	WALK	233d	1 5a		הם	THEY	241c	3 a		יהוה	YAHWEH	219a	2 2a
	חזק	BE FIRM	304d	5		כן	SO	487a	3 f	6 3	ב	IN	89a	1 7b
	יד	HAND	391a	5 c4		לבנה	BRICK	527c	1		יהוה	YAHWEH	218c	1
	לב	HEART	525b	2 6d		על	UPON	753b	2 1c		ידע	MAKE ONESELF KNOWN	394c	2
	עשה	DO	793d	1 1a 1		צעק	CRY	858c	1 a		ראה	TO SEE	908b	1 a
	פנה	FACE	816d	2 4		רפה	SINK	951d			שדי	ALMIGHTY	995a	2
	ראה	TO SEE	907a	7 a		שלשם	THREE DAYS AGO	1026b			שם	NAME	1028c	3
	שום	TO PLACE	963a	1 a		מתכנת	MEASUREMENT	1067c	1	6 4	ברית	COVENANT	136c	2 2b
	שוב	TURN BACK	997b	3 a		תמול	YESTERDAY	1070a	2 ab		ברית	COVENANT	137a	3 1
4 22	אב	FATHER	3b	2	5 9	ב	IN	88c	2 1b		גור	SOJOURN	157d	1
	בכור	FIRST-BORN	114b	3		דבר	WORD	183b	3 1		מגור	SOJOURNING PLACE	158c	
	בן	SON	120b	1 c		כבד	BE HEAVY	457b	1	6 5	קום	STAND	879a	6 d
	כה	THUS	462a	1 a		עבדה	LABOR	715b	3		ברית	COVENANT	136c	2 2b
4 23	בן	SON	120b	1 c		על	UPON	753a	2 1b		ברית	COVENANT	137a	3 2
	הנה	BEHOLD	243d			עשה	DO	794a	1 1b		נאקה	GROANING	611a	
	הנה	BEHOLD	244b	B b		שעה	GAZE	1043a			עבד	WORK	713c	1
	הרג	KILL	247b	2	5 10	אין	NOT	34b	2 c		שמש	SUN	1039b	4 b
	מאן	REFUSE	549b			נגש	DRIVE	620c	3	6 6	אנכי	I	59b	
	עבד	WORK	713b	4 a		שטר	OFFICIAL	1009c			גאל	REDEEM	145c	3 b
	שלח	SEND	1019a	3		תבן	STRAW	1062a			יהוה	YAHWEH	219a	2 2a
4 24	בקש	SEEK	134d	2 c	5 11	אשר	PARTICLE OF RELATION	82c	4 bg		זרוע	ARM	284a	1 c
	מלון	INN	533d			גרע	WITHDRAW	175d	1		יצא	CAUSE TO GO	424c	1 a
	מות	DIE	560b	2		דבר	WORD	183d	4 6		כן	SO	486d	3 d
	פגש	MEET	803d			לקח	TAKE	543a	4 b		סבלה	BURDEN	688a	
4 25	דם	BLOOD	*196c	2 a		מצא	FIND	592c	1 a		עבדה	LABOR	715b	3
	דם	BLOOD	197a	2 h		עבדה	LABOR	715b	3		קצר	SHORTNESS	894b	
	חתן	DAUGHTER:S HUSBAND	368d	2		תבן	STRAW	1062a			שפט	JUDGEMENT	1048a	
	כרת	CUT OFF	503d	1 a	5 12	פוץ	BE DISPERSED	807b	2		תחת	UNDERNEATH	1066b	3 2a
	ל	TO	511a	1 f		קשש	GATHER STUBBLE	905d		6 7	אלהים	GOD	44b	4 a
	נגע	TOUCH	619b	1		תבן	STRAW	1062a			יהוה	YAHWEH	219a	2 2b b
	ערלה	FORESKIN	790b		5 13	אוץ	PRESS	21a	1		ידע	KNOW	393d	1 a
	צפרה	ZIPPORAH	862a			אמר	SAY	56b	1		יצא	CAUSE TO GO	424c	1 a
	רגל	FOOT	919d	1 a		בלה	BECOME OLD AND WORN OUT	*115b	B		סבלה	BURDEN	688a	
4 26	אז	THEN	23a	1 a		דבר	WORD	183b	4 1		תחת	UNDERNEATH	1066b	3 2a
	דם	BLOOD	*196c	2 a		יום	DAY	400c	7 e3	6 8	אנכי	I	59b	
	דם	BLOOD	197a	2 h		כאשר	AS	455b	1 a		בוא	COME	99b	2
	חתן	DAUGHTER:S HUSBAND	368d	2		כלה	FINISH	478a	1 a		יהוה	YAHWEH	219b	2 2d
	ל	TO	514d	5 g		נגש	DRIVE	620c	3		יד	HAND	389c	1 d
	מולה	CIRCUMCISION	558a			מעשה	DEED	795d	1 b1		מורשה	POSSESSION	440c	
	רפה	SINK	951d	4		תבן	STRAW	1062a			נשא	LIFT	670b	1 b 1
	רפה	SINK	952a	1	5 14	חק	SOMETHING PRESCRIBED	349b	1		נתן	GIVE	678c	1 b
4 27	אלהים	GOD	44a	3 b		מדוע	WHEREFORE	396c		6 9	דבר	SPEAK	181a	3 b
	הלך	WALK	233d	1 5b		יום	DAY	399d	7 a1		כן	SO	486a	1 ca
	הר	MOUNTAIN	249b	1 a		כלה	FINISH	478a	1 a		מן	ON ACCOUNT OF	580b	2 f
	הר	MOUNTAIN	249d	1 a		לבן	MAKE BRICK	527c			עבדה	LABOR	715b	3
	נשק	KISS	676b			נגש	DRIVE	620c	3		קשה	SEVERE	904c	2 a
	פגש	MEET	803d			נכה	SMITE	646c	3		רוח	BREATH	925a	3 d
4 28	אות	SIGN	16d	4		שטר	OFFICIAL	1009c			דבר	SPEAK	181a	3 b
	דבר	WORD	183b	3 2		שלשם	THREE DAYS AGO	1026b		6 10	דבר	SPEAK	181a	3 b
4 29	אסף	GATHER	62b	1 a		תמול	YESTERDAY	1070a	2 b	6 11	פרעה	PHARAOH	829a	
	הלך	WALK	233d	1 5b		תמול	YESTERDAY	1070a	2 aa	6 12	דבר	SPEAK	181c	3 f
4 30	אות	SIGN	16d	4		זמן	AGREE TOGETHER	*1091c			הן	BEHOLD	243c	A
	דבר	WORD	183b	3 2	5 15	כה	THUS	462b	1 a		ערל	HAVING FORESKIN	790d	
	עין	EYE	745a	5		צעק	CRY	858c	1 a		שפה	SPEECH	973d	1 a1
4 31	אמן	CONFIRM	53a	1 a		שטר	OFFICIAL	1009c			שמע	HEAR	1034a	1 n
	כי	THAT	471d	1 a	5 16	אין	NOT	34c	2 c	6 13	יצא	CAUSE TO GO	424c	1 a
	עני	AFFLICTION	777a	1		חטא	MISS A GOAL OR WAY	306d	2 a		פרעה	PHARAOH	829a	
	פקד	ATTEND TO	823b	A 1a		לבנה	BRICK	527c	1		צוה	CHARGE	846a	4 a
	קדד	BOW DOWN	869a			נכה	SMITE	646c	3	6 14	אב	FATHER	3c	4
	שמע	HEAR	1033c	1 a		נתן	GIVE	681c	1 c		בית	HOUSE	110b	5 e
5 1	אלהים	GOD	44b	4 ba		כן	SO	487a	3 f		חנוך	ENOCH	335c	4
	אמר	SAY	56a	1	5 17	רפה	SINK	951d			חצרון	HEZRON	348a	2 a
	חגג	MAKE PILGRIMAGE	290c	1	5 18	לבנה	BRICK	527c	1		כרמי	CARMI	501d	1
	כה	THUS	462a	1 a		נתן	GIVE	681c	1 c		פלוא	PALLU	811a	
	עם	PEOPLE	766c	1		עבד	WORK	713a	1		ראובן	REUBEN	910a	1
	שלח	SEND	1019b	3		תבן	STRAW	1062a			ראש	HEAD	911a	3 f
5 2	ידע	KNOW	394a	2		תכן	MEASUREMENT	1067c			ישראל	ISRAEL	975c	1
	מי	WHO	566c	F b							משפחה	CLAN	1047a	1 d
	קול	VOICE	877b	3 b						6 15	אהד	OHAD	13c	
											זרח	ZERAH	*280c	4
											ימואל	JEMUEL	410c	

Ch	v.	Heb	Eng	Page	Sec
		ימין	JAMIN	412c	1
		יכין	JACHIN	467c	1
		כנעני	CANAANITE	489a	2a
		נמואל	NEMUEL	*649c	1
		צחר	ZOHAR	850c	2
		שאול	SAUL	982c	3
		משפחה	CLAN	1047a	1 d
6	16	בן	SON	*121a	1 je
		גרשון	GERSHON	177a	
		חיים	LIFE	313a	1
		תולדות	GENERATIONS	410a	A
		לוי	LEVI	532c	1a
		מאה	HUNDRED	548b	2 b
		מררי	MERARI	601b	
		קהת	KOHATH	875b	
		שבע	SEVEN	988b	5 b1
6	17	גרשון	GERSHON	177a	
		לבני	LIBNI	526d	
		שמעי	SHIMEI	1035c	3 a
6	18	חברון	HEBRON	289b	1
		חיים	LIFE	313a	1
		עזיאל	UZZIEL	739c	1a
		עמרם	AMRAM	771d	1
		יצהר	IZHAR	844b	
		קהת	KOHATH	875b	
		קהת	KOHATH	875b	
6	19	תולדות	GENERATIONS	410a	A
		לוי	LEVITE	532d	2
		מושי	MUSHI	559b	
		מחלי	MAHLI	563a	1
		מררי	MERARI	601b	
		משפחה	CLAN	1047a	1 d
6	20	דדה	AUNT	187d	1
		יוכבד	JOCHEBED	222c	
		חיים	LIFE	313a	1
		משה	MOSES	602c	
		עמרם	AMRAM	771d	1
		שבע	SEVEN	988b	5 b1
6	21	זכרי	ZICHRI	271d	3 a
		נפג	NEPHEG	655d	1
		יצהר	IZHAR	844b	
		קרח	KORAH	901b	2
6	22	אליצפן	ELIZAPHAN	45d	A
		מישאל	MISHAEL	567d	1
		סתרי	SITHRI	712c	
		עזיאל	UZZIEL	739c	1a
6	23	איתמר	ITHAMAR	16a	
		אלישבע	ELISHEBA	45d	
		אלעזר	ELEAZAR	46b	A
		נדב	NADAB	621c	1
		נחשון	NAHSHON	638c	
		עמינדב	AMMINADAB	770b	1
6	24	אביאסף	ABIASAPH	4a	
		אלקנה	ELKANAH	46c	B
		אסיר	ASSIR	64b	
		קרח	KORAH	901b	2
		קרחי	KORAHITES	901c	1
6	25	אב	FATHER	3c	3
		זכר	REMEMBER	270b	2 3 a
		לוי	LEVITE	533a	3 1c
		מן	FROM	580d	3 bb
		פוטיאל	PUTIEL	806c	
		פינחס	PHINEHAS	810a	1
		ראש	HEAD	911a	3 f
		משפחה	CLAN	1047a	1 d
6	26	יצא	CAUSE TO GO	424c	1 a
		על	UPON	754a	2 1f
		צבא	ARMY	839a	1a
6	27	הוא	HE, SHE, IT	215c	1 e
		יצא	CAUSE TO GO	424c	1 a
		פרעה	PHARAOH	829a	
6	28	דבר	SPEAK	*180d	
		היה	COME TO PASS	224c	2 a1 ag
		יום	DAY	400b	7 d3 a
6	29	דבר	SPEAK	180c	
		יהוה	YAHWEH	219a	2 2a
		פרעה	PHARAOH	829a	
6	30	הן	BEHOLD	243c	A
		ערל	HAVING FORESKIN	790d	
		שפה	SPEECH	973d	1 a1
7	1	אלהים	GOD	43d	2 b
		משה	MOSES	602c	
		נביא	PROPHET	611c	1
		נתן	GIVE	681a	3 a
7	2	משה	MOSES	602c	
7	3	אות	SIGN	16d	4
		מופת	WONDER	68d	1
		לב	HEART	525b	2 6d
		קשה	BE SEVERE	904c	3 a
7	4	בן	SON	120d	1 jg
		יצא	CAUSE TO GO	424c	1 a
		נתן	PUT	680d	2 b
		שפט	JUDGEMENT	1048a	
7	5	יהוה	YAHWEH	219a	2 2b a
		יצא	CAUSE TO GO	424c	1 a
		נטה	EXTEND	640d	1 a
		תוך	MIDST	1063d	
7	6	כאשר	AS	455b	1 b
		כן	SO	486b	2 ca
7	7	אהרן	AARON	14d	
		משה	MOSES	602c	
7	9	מופת	WONDER	68d	1
		מופת	SIGN	69a	2
		כי	WHEN	473a	2 a
		ל	TO	515d	5 ia
		מטה	STAFF	641c	1
		נתן	GIVE	679b	1 m
		תנין	SERPENT	1072c	1
7	10	היה	BECOME	226b	2
		כאשר	AS	455b	1 b
		כן	SO	486c	2 da
		מטה	STAFF	641c	1
		צוה	CHARGE	846a	3
		תנין	SERPENT	1072c	1
7	11	חכם	WISE	314d	4
		חרטם	ENGRAVER	355a	1
		כשף	PRACTICE SORCERY	506c	
		לט	SECRECY	532b	2
		שמש	SUN	1039b	4 b
7	12	בלע	SWALLOW DOWN	118a	1
		מטה	STAFF	641c	1
		תנין	SERPENT	1072c	1
7	13	חזק	BE FIRM	304c	1 4a
		לב	HEART	525b	2 6d
7	14	כבד	HEAVY	458b	1 c
		ל	TO	517d	7 bc
		לב	HEART	525b	2 6d
		מאן	REFUSE	549b	
7	15	בקר	MORNING	134b	2
		הפך	TURN	246a	1 b
		יאר	STREAM	384b	1
		ל	TO	512b	4 a
		לקח	TAKE	542d	1
		נחש	SERPENT	638b	1 b
		מטה	STAFF	641c	1
		נצב	STAND	662a	1 a
		קרא	ENCOUNTER	897a	1
7	16	אלהים	GOD	44c	4 ba
		כה	THUS	462b	3
		עבד	WORK	713b	4 a
		עברי	HEBREW	720b	2 b
7	17	אמר	SAY	56a	1
		ב	IN	90a	3 2e
		דם	BLOOD	197c	2 o
		יהוה	YAHWEH	219a	2 2b a
		הנה	BEHOLD	243d	
		הנה	BEHOLD	244b	B b
		הפך	TURN	246a	2 c
		זה	THIS	261d	6 bb
		יאר	STREAM	384b	1
7	18	יד	HAND	390d	5 c1
		כה	THUS	462a	1 a
		מטה	STAFF	641c	1
		באש	STINK	92d	1
		דגה	FISH	185d	
		יאר	STREAM	384b	1
		לאה	BE WEARY	521a	1
		מות	DIE	559d	1 b
		שתה	DRINK	1059b	1 a
7	19	אבן	STONE	6c	2
		אגם	POOL	8c	2
		דם	BLOOD	197c	2 o
		יאר	STREAM	384c	2 a
		מי	WATER	565c	2
		נהר	STREAM	625d	1
		נטה	EXTEND	639d	1 a
		מטה	STAFF	641c	1
		מצרים	EGYPT	695c	1 a
		עץ	TREE	781d	2 b
		מקוה	COLLECTION	876c	
7	20	ב	IN	90b	3 4
		דם	BLOOD	197c	2 o
		הפך	TURN	246a	2 c
		יאר	STREAM	384b	1
		כאשר	AS	455b	1 b
		כן	SO	486c	2 da
		מטה	STAFF	641c	1
		נכה	SMITE	645b	1 a
		רום	BE HIGH	927c	1 a1
7	21	באש	STINK	92d	1
		דגה	FISH	185d	
		דם	BLOOD	197c	2 o
		יאר	STREAM	384b	1
		יכל	BE ABLE	407c	1 a
		שתה	DRINK	1059b	1 a
7	22	חזק	BE FIRM	304c	1 4a
		חרטם	ENGRAVER	355a	1
		לב	HEART	525b	2 6d
		לט	SECRECY	532b	2
7	23	לב	HEART	524d	2 3c
		פנה	TURN	815b	1 c
		שית	PUT	1011b	2 b
7	24	חפר	DIG	343c	1 a
		יאר	STREAM	384b	1
		יכל	BE ABLE	407c	1 a
		סביב	ROUND ABOUT	687b	2 bb
		שתה	DRINK	1059b	1 a
		שתה	DRINK	1059b	1 a
7	25	מלא	BE FULL	570c	2
		נכה	SMITE	646c	4 a
7	26	אמר	SAY	56a	1
		כה	THUS	462a	1 a
		עבד	WORK	713b	4 a
7	27	גבול	BOUNDARY	148a	2 a
		מאן	REFUSING	549b	
		נגף	STRIKE	619d	
		צפרדע	FROGS	862c	
7	28	ב	IN	*88a	
		חדר	CHAMBER	293d	
		יאר	STREAM	384b	1
		משארת	A HOUSEHOLD VESSEL	602b	
		מטה	COUCH	641d	
		עבד	SLAVE	713d	2
		עלה	GO UP	748d	3
		צפרדע	FROGS	862c	
		שרץ	SWARM	1056c	1
		תנור	FIRE-POT	1072b	
7	29	עבד	SLAVE	713d	2
		עלה	GO UP	748d	3
		צפרדע	FROGS	862c	
8	1	אגם	POOL	8c	2
		ב	IN	89c	3 1a
		יאר	STREAM	384c	2 a
		נהר	STREAM	625d	1
		נטה	EXTEND	639d	1 a
		מטה	STAFF	641c	1
		עלה	GO UP	749c	3
		צפרדע	FROGS	862c	
8	2	כסה	COVER	492a	5
		מי	WATER	565c	2
		מצרים	EGYPT	695c	1 a
		עלה	GO UP	748d	3
		צפרדע	FROGS	862c	
8	3	חרטם	ENGRAVER	355a	1
		לט	SECRECY	532b	2
		עלה	GO UP	749c	3
		צפרדע	FROGS	862c	
8	4	סור	TURN ASIDE	694b	1
		סור	TURN ASIDE	694b	1
		עתר	PRAY	801c	
		צפרדע	FROGS	862c	
8	5	יאר	STREAM	384b	1
		כרת	CUT OFF	504c	2 a
		ל	TO	*517a	6 a
		מן	OUT OF	579a	2 aa
		מתי	WHEN	607d	B
		עתר	PRAY	801c	
		פאר	BEAUTIFY	802b	1
		צפרדע	FROGS	862c	
		רק	ONLY	956b	2 a
		שאר	REMAIN	984a	1
8	6	יהוה	YAHWEH	218d	2 1c
		ל	TO	517a	6 a
		מחר	TO-MORROW	564a	1 a
		מען	PURPOSE	775c	2 b
8	7	יאר	STREAM	384b	1
		סור	TURN ASIDE	693d	2
		צפרדע	FROGS	862c	
		שאר	REMAIN	984a	1
8	8	דבר	WORD	184a	4 8
		מעם	FROM WITH	769a	A
		צעק	CRY	858c	1 b
		צפרדע	FROGS	862c	
		שום	TO PLACE	964a	3 f
		לות	BESIDE	1099a	
8	9	דבר	WORD	182b	1 1b
		חצר	ENCLOSURE	346d	1
		מות	DIE	559d	1 b
		צפרדע	FROGS	862c	
		שדה	FIELD	961c	1 f
8	10	באש	STINK	92d	1
		חמר	HEAP	330d	
		צבר	HEAP UP	840d	
8	11	היה	BECOME	225c	2 1a
		כבד	MAKE HEAVY	458a	2
		לב	HEART	525b	2 6d
		ראה	TO SEE	907b	5 a
		רוחה	RESPITE	926c	
8	12	כן	GNAT	487d	
		נטה	EXTEND	639d	1 a
		מטה	STAFF	641c	1
		נכה	SMITE	645b	1 a
		עפר	DRY EARTH	779d	1 c
8	13	אדם	MAN	9b	2
		ב	IN	89c	3 1a
		בהמה	BEAST	96d	1
		כן	GNAT	487d	
		כן	GNAT	487d	
		נטה	EXTEND	639d	1 a
		מטה	STAFF	641c	1
		נכה	SMITE	645b	1 a
		עפר	DRY EARTH	779d	1 c
8	14	אדם	MAN	9b	2
		בהמה	BEAST	96d	1
		חרטם	ENGRAVER	355a	1
		יכל	BE ABLE	407d	1 a
		יצא	BRING OUT	425a	4 j
		כן	GNAT	487d	
		כן	GNAT	487d	
		לט	SECRECY	532b	2
8	15	הוא	HE, SHE, IT	*216d	6 a
		חזק	BE FIRM	304c	1 4a
		חרטם	ENGRAVER	355a	1
		לב	HEART	525b	2 6d
8	16	אמר	SAY	56a	1
		בקר	MORNING	134b	1 h
		יצב	STATION ONESELF	426c	C
		כה	THUS	462a	1 a
8	17	אין	NOT	34b	2 c
		הנה	BEHOLD	244b	B b
		כיאם	FOR IF	474d	1
		מלא	BE FULL	570a	1 a
		ערב	SWARM	786c	
		שלח	SEND	1019c	
8	18	בלת	NOT	116d	4 a

Ch	v.	Heb	Eng	Page	Sec
		גשן	GOSHEN	177d	1
		יהוה	YAHWEH	219a	2 2b a
		עמד	STAND	764b	3 c
		מען	PURPOSE	775c	2 b
8	19	פלה	BE SEPARATED	811d	2
		אות	SIGN	16d	4
		ל	TO	517a	6 a
		מחר	TO-MORROW	564a	1 a
		פדות	RANSOM	804b	
8	20	שום	TO PLACE	963c	1 d
		כבד	MASSIVE	458a	1 a
		ערב	SWARM	786c	
		פנה	FACE	818c	2 6c a
		שחת	GO TO RUIN	1007d	
8	21	אלהים	GOD	44d	4 c
		קרא	CALL	895c	5 b
8	22	יהוה	YAHWEH	218d	2 1c
		הן	IF	243d	B
		ו	AND	254d	5 cb
		זבח	SLAUGHTER FOR SACRIFICE	257d	1 1 c
		כן	BE FIRM	465d	2
		ל	TO	517d	7 bd
		לא	NOT	519a	1 ae
		סקל	STONE	709c	
		תועבה	ABOMINATION	1072d	1 a
8	23	דרך	JOURNEY	203a	2
		יהוה	YAHWEH	218d	2 1c
		הלך	WALK	230c	1 1d 1b
		יום	DAY	398b	2 b
		כאשר	AS	455b	1 a
8	24	בעד	ON BEHALF OF	126c	2
		יהוה	YAHWEH	218d	2 1b
		ל	TO	517c	7 bb
		עתר	PRAY	801c	
		רחק	BE DISTANT	935a	1
		רק	ONLY	956c	2 b
8	25	בלת	NOT	116d	4 a
		יסף	DO AGAIN	415c	2
		מחר	TO-MORROW	564a	1 b
		סור	TURN ASIDE	693d	2
		מעם	FROM WITH	769a	A
		עתר	PRAY	801c	
		רק	ONLY	956c	2 b
		תלל	MOCK	1068b	
8	26	יצא	GO OUT	422d	1 b
		מעם	FROM WITH	769a	A
		עתר	PRAY	801c	
8	27	דבר	WORD	182b	1 1b
		סור	TURN ASIDE	694b	1
		שאר	REMAIN	984a	1
8	28	כבד	MAKE HEAVY	458a	2
		לב	HEART	525b	2 6d
		פעם	OCCURRENCE	822b	3 c
9	1	אלהים	GOD	44c	4 ba
		עברי	HEBREW	720b	2 b
9	2	חזק	BE FIRM	305b	6 d
		כיאם	FOR IF	474d	1 b
		מאן	REFUSING	549b	
		עוד	STILL	728d	1 aa
9	3	דבר	PESTILENCE	184a	2
		הנה	BEHOLD	244b	B b
		חמור	HE-ASS	331b	1
		כבד	HEAVY	458a	2 a
		סוס	HORSE	692c	1
		מקנה	CATTLE	889b	1
		שדה	FIELD	961b	1 a
9	4	דבר	WORD	183d	4 6
		כל	ALL	481d	1 c
		פלה	BE SEPARATED	811d	2
9	5	אמר	SAY	83b	7 c
		אשר	PARTICLE OF RELATION		
		מועד	APPOINTED TIME	417c	1 a
		מחר	TO-MORROW	564a	1 b
		שום	TO PLACE	963d	3 b
9	6	מחרת	THE MORROW	564a	
9	7	כבד	BE HEAVY	457b	2
		לב	HEART	525b	2 6d
		עד	AS FAR AS	724d	1 3
9	8	זרק	TO TOSS	284c	1 a
		חפן	HOLLOW OF HAND	342b	
		כבשן	KILN	461c	
		מלא	FULNESS	571b	1
		פיח	SOOT	806b	
		שמי	HEAVENS	1030a	1 b
9	9	אבק	DUST	7c	
		אדם	MAN	9b	2
		בהמה	BEAST	96d	1
		אבעבעת	BLISTERS	101b	
		פרח	BREAK OUT	827c	
		שחין	BOIL	1006c	
9	10	אדם	MAN	9b	2
		בהמה	BEAST	96d	1
		אבעבעת	BLISTERS	101b	
		זרק	TO TOSS	284c	1 a
		כבשן	KILN	461c	
		עמד	STAND	763d	1 d
		פיח	SOOT	806b	
		פרח	BREAK OUT	827c	
		שחין	BOIL	1006c	
		שמי	HEAVENS	1030a	1 b
9	11	חרשם	ENGRAVER	355a	1
		יכל	BE ABLE	407c	1 a
		פנה	FACE	817b	2 4b d
		פנה	FACE	818c	2 6c a
		שחין	BOIL	1006c	
9	12	חזק	BE FIRM	304d	5
		לב	HEART	525b	2 6d
9	13	אלהים	GOD	44c	4 ba
		בקר	MORNING	134b	1 h
		יצב	STATION ONESELF	426c	C
		עברי	HEBREW	720b	2 b
9	14	אלה	THESE	41c	A
		מגפה	BLOW	620a	1
		עבור	FOR THE SAKE OF	721b	2
		עתה	NOW	774c	2 ga
		פעם	OCCURRENCE	822b	3 c
		שלח	SEND	1018c	2 b
9	15	דבר	PESTILENCE	184a	1
		יד	HAND	390a	1 e2
		כחד	BE HIDDEN	470b	1
		כי	THAT	*472c	1 db
		נכה	SMITE	646c	4 a
		עתה	NOW	774c	2 ga
		שלח	SEND	1018d	3 b
9	16	אולם	BUT	19d	
		זה	THIS	260d	1 a
		כח	STRENGTH	470d	3
		ספר	COUNT	708a	1
		עבור	FOR THE SAKE OF	721a	1 a
		עבור	FOR THE SAKE OF	721a	1 b
		עמד	STAND	764d	2
		מען	PURPOSE	775b	1 c
		קול	VOICE	877a	2 a
		ראה	TO SEE	908a	1 a2
9	17	בלת	ONLY	*1085c	
		זה	NOT	116d	4 a
		סלל	LIFT UP	699d	
		עוד	STILL	729a	1 aa
9	18	ברד	HAIL	135d	
		היה	BECOME	225c	2 1a
		הנה	BEHOLD	244b	B b
		יום	DAY	401b	7 k
		יסד	BE FOUNDED	414a	2
		כ	LIKE	453c	1 a
		כבד	HEAVY	458b	2 a
		מחר	TO-MORROW	564a	1 a
		מטר	RAIN	*565a	
		מטר	RAIN	565a	
		מן	FROM	583d	9 b2
		עת	TIME	773c	1 a
		עתה	NOW	774c	2 f
9	19	אדם	MAN	9b	2
		אסף	GATHER	62d	2 b
		בית	HOUSE	108d	1 a
		בית	HOUSE	109b	1 b
		ברד	HAIL	135d	
		ירד	GO DOWN	433c	3 a
		מצא	FIND	593d	1 c
		עוז	TAKE REFUGE	731d	
9	20	ירא	FEAR	431c	3 b
		נום	FLEE	631a	2
9	21	אל	TO	40a	3 c
		ו	AND	254d	5 b
		לב	HEART	524d	2 3c
		עזב	LEAVE	737a	1 b
		שום	TO PLACE	963c	2 b
9	22	אדם	MAN	9b	2
		בהמה	BEAST	96d	1
		ברד	HAIL	135d	
		נטה	EXTEND	639d	1 a
		על	UPON	757a	2 7b
		עשב	HERB	793b	
		שמי	HEAVENS	1030a	1 b
9	23	אש	FIRE	77c	2
		ברד	HAIL	135d	
		הלך	WALK	232c	1 3
		הלך	WALK	*232c	1 3
		מטר	RAIN	565a	
		נטה	EXTEND	639d	1 a
		מטה	STAFF	641c	1
		נתן	GIVE	678d	1 d
		קול	VOICE	877a	2 b
		שמי	HEAVENS	1030a	1 b
9	24	מאז	FROM THAT TIME	23b	B
		אש	FIRE	77c	2
		ברד	HAIL	135d	
		גוי	NATION	156d	1 c
		היה	BECOME	225c	2 1a
		כבד	HEAVY	458b	2 a
		להבה	FLAME	529b	1
		לקח	TAKE	544a	
9	25	אדם	MAN	9b	2
		בהמה	BEAST	96d	1
		ברד	HAIL	135d	
		מן	FROM	582a	5 b
		נכה	SMITE	645c	1 b
		עץ	TREE	781d	1 b
		עשב	HERB	793b	
		שדה	FIELD	961c	1 d
		שבר	BREAK	991a	
9	26	ברד	HAIL	135d	
		גשן	GOSHEN	177d	1
		היה	BECOME	225c	2 1a
9	27	חטא	MISS A GOAL OR WAY	307a	2 b
		פעם	OCCURRENCE	822b	3 d2
		צדיק	JUST	843a	1 d
		רשע	WICKED	957b	1
9	28	יסף	DO AGAIN	415c	2 a
		מן	THAN	583a	6 d
		עתר	PRAY	801c	
		קול	VOICE	877a	2 b
		רב	MUCH	913b	1 f
9	29	חדל	CEASE	293a	1
		יצא	GO OUT	422d	1 a
		כף	HOLLOW OF THE HAND	496c	1 d4
		מען	PURPOSE	775c	2 b
		פרש	SPREAD OUT	831b	2
		קול	VOICE	877a	2 b
9	30	יהוה	YAHWEH	219a	2 1h
		טרם	NOT YET	382c	1
		ירא	FEAR	431c	2
		פנה	FACE	818b	2 6b
9	31	אביב	YOUNG EARS	1b	1
		גבעל	BUD	149c	
		נכה	SMITE	645a	
		פשתה	FLAX	834a	1
		שערה	BARLEY	972d	1
9	32	אפיל	LATE	66d	
		חטה	WHEAT	334d	
		כסמת	SPELT	493c	2
		נכה	SMITE	645a	
9	33	חדל	CEASE	293a	1
		יצא	GO OUT	422d	1 b
		כף	HOLLOW OF THE HAND	496c	1 d4
		מטר	RAIN	564d	
		נתך	POUR FORTH	677d	
		מעם	FROM WITH	769a	A
		פרש	SPREAD OUT	831b	2
		קול	VOICE	877a	2 b
		לות	BESIDE	*1099a	
9	34	חדל	CEASE	293a	1
		חטא	MISS A GOAL OR WAY	306d	2 b
		יסף	DO AGAIN	415c	2 a
		כבד	MAKE HEAVY	458a	2
		לב	HEART	525b	2 6d
		מטר	RAIN	564d	
		קול	VOICE	877a	2 b
9	35	חזק	BE FIRM	304c	1 4a
		יד	HAND	391a	5 d
		לב	HEART	525b	2 6d
10	1	אות	SIGN	16d	4
		אלה	THESE	41c	A
		ה	THE	209a	2
		כבד	MAKE HEAVY	458a	2
		לב	HEART	525b	2 6d
10	2	שית	PUT	1011c	1
		אות	SIGN	16d	4
		בן	SON	120b	1 f
		יהוה	YAHWEH	219a	2 2b a
		ידע	KNOW	393d	1 a
		נתן	GIVE	*681b	3 d
		ספר	COUNT	708a	1
		עלל	ACT ARBITRARILY	759d	1
		מען	PURPOSE	775c	2 b
		שום	TO PLACE	964d	5 c
10	3	מאן	REFUSE	549b	
		מתי	WHEN	607d	C
		עברי	HEBREW	720b	2 b
		ענה	BE BOWED DOWN	776a	1
		פנה	FACE	818b	2 6b
10	4	גבול	BOUNDARY	148a	2 a
		הנה	BEHOLD	244b	B b
		כיאם	FOR IF	474d	1 b
		מכתב	WRITING	508b	2
		מאן	REFUSING	549b	
		מחר	TO-MORROW	564a	1 b
		ארבה	LOCUST	916a	
10	5	ברד	HAIL	135d	
		יכל	BE ABLE	407c	1 a
		יתר	REMAINDER	451d	1 a
		כסה	COVER	492a	5
		ל	TO	512d	5 aa
		עין	EYE	744d	4 a
		פליטה	ESCAPE	812c	1
		צמח	SPROUT	855b	1
		שדה	FIELD	961b	1 d
		שאר	REMAIN	984a	1
		שאר	REMAIN	984a	1
10	6	אב	FATHER	3c	4 a
		אדמה	GROUND	9d	2
		יום	DAY	401a	7 j
		יום	DAY	401b	7 l
		יצא	GO OUT	422d	1 b
		מלא	BE FULL	570a	1 a
		מן	FROM	582a	5 c
10	7	אבד	PERISH	1c	1
		יהוה	YAHWEH	218d	2 1d
		זה	THIS	260c	1
		טרם	NOT YET	382c	1
		מוקש	BAIT	430d	
		מצרים	EGYPTIANS	595d	2 b
		מתי	WHEN	607d	C
10	8	יהוה	YAHWEH	218d	2 1b
		מי	WHO	566b	
		שוב	TURN BACK	1000a	
10	9	הלך	WALK	231c	1 1d 5g
		זקן	OLD	278c	2 a
		חג	FESTIVAL-GATHERING	291a	1 a
		נער	YOUTH	655a	1 d
10	10	כאשר	AS	455b	1 b
		כן	SO	486c	2 da

Ch	v	Heb	Eng	Page	Sec
		נגד	IN FRONT	617b	1 b
		ראה	TO SEE	907d	7 c
		סוף	ADDENDA ET CORRIGENDA	1123d	
10	11	את	WITH	86d	4 a
		בקש	SEEK	135c	4 a
		גבר	MAN	150a	
		גרש	DRIVE OUT	176d	
		כן	SO	486b	1 cd
10	12	ברד	HAIL	135d	
		נטה	EXTEND	639d	1 a
		עלה	GO UP	748d	3
		על	UPON	756d	2 7b
		עשב	HERB	793b	
		ארבה	LOCUST	916a	
		שאר	REMAIN	984b	1
10	13	בקר	MORNING	133d	1 a
		היה	BECOME	225d	2 1a
		נהג	DRIVE	624c	2
		נטה	EXTEND	639d	1 a
		מטה	STAFF	641c	1
		נשא	LIFT	671a	2 a
		קדם	EAST WIND	870b	1
		ארבה	LOCUST	916a	
		רוח	BREATH	924d	2 a
10	14	אחר	AFTER	30a	2 b
		גבול	BOUNDARY	148a	2 a
		כבד	MASSIVE	458b	2 b
		כן	SO	485d	1 a
		נוח	REST	628a	1
		עלה	GO UP	748d	3
		פנה	FACE	817d	2 4e
		ארבה	LOCUST	916a	
10	15	ברד	HAIL	135d	
		חשך	GROW DARK	364d	2
		ירק	GREEN	438d	
		יתר	BE LEFT OVER	451b	
		יתר	LEAVE OVER	451c	1 a
		כל	ALL	482b	1 ec
		כסה	COVER	492a	5
		עין	EYE	744d	4 a
		עץ	TREE	781c	1 b
		עשב	HERB	793b	
10	16	יהוה	YAHWEH	218d	2 1b
		חטא	MISS A GOAL OR WAY	307a	2 b
		מהר	HASTEN	555a	2
10	17	אך	ONLY	36c	2 ba
		יהוה	YAHWEH	218d	2 1b
		ו	AND	254d	3
		חטאת	SIN	308d	1 d2
		נשא	LIFT	671a	3 c
		סור	TURN ASIDE	694b	1
		על	UPON	758d	4 2b
		עתר	PRAY	801c	
		פעם	OCCURRENCE	822b	3 d1
		רק	ONLY	956c	2 a
		רק	ONLY	956c	2 a
10	18	עתר	PRAY	801c	
10	19	גבול	BOUNDARY	148a	2 a
		הפך	TURN	245c	1 a
		חזק	STRONG	305c	1 c
		ים	SEA	*410d	2
		ים	SEA	411b	9
		סוף	REEDS	693a	2 a
		ארבה	LOCUST	916a	
		ארבה	LOCUST	916a	
		רוח	BREATH	924d	2 a
		שאר	REMAIN	984b	1
		תקע	THRUST	1075c	1
10	20	חזק	BE FIRM	304d	5
		לב	HEART	525b	2 6d
10	21	חשך	DARKNESS	365a	1
		משש	GROPE	607a	
		נטה	EXTEND	639d	1 a
		על	UPON	757a	2 7b
		שמי	HEAVENS	1030a	1 b
10	22	אפלה	DARKNESS	66c	1
		חשך	DARKNESS	365a	1
		נטה	EXTEND	639d	1 a
		שמי	HEAVENS	1030a	1 b
10	23	מושב	DWELLING	444b	2 a
		קום	STAND	877c	
		תחת	UNDERNEATH	1066b	3 2a
10	24	יצג	BE STOPPED	426d	
		קרא	CALL	895d	5 b
		סוף	ADDENDA ET CORRIGENDA	1123d	
10	25	גם	ALSO	169b	1
		יהוה	YAHWEH	218d	2 1c
		זבח	SACRIFICE	257b	1 1
		יד	HAND	390d	5 b2
		עשה	DO	794d	2 4
10	26	יהוה	YAHWEH	218d	2 1c
		הלך	WALK	232a	1 2
		מה	HOW	553c	2 aa
		עבד	WORK	713b	4 a
		פרסה	HOOF	828b	1
		מקנה	CATTLE	889b	1
		שאר	REMAIN	984a	2
10	27	אבה	BE WILLING	2c	
		אבה	BE WILLING	2c	
		חזק	BE FIRM	304d	5
		לב	HEART	525b	2 6d
10	28	יסף	DO AGAIN	415c	2 a
		מות	DIE	559d	2 a
		על	UPON	759a	4 2b
		פנה	FACE	816a	1 2b
		שמר	KEEP	1037b	1
10	29	יסף	DO AGAIN	415c	2 a
		כן	RIGHT	467a	1
		פנה	FACE	816a	1 2b
11	1	בוא	COME	99c	2 a
		גרש	DRIVE OUT	177a	
		זה	THIS	262a	6 e
		כלה	COMPLETE	478d	1
		נגע	STROKE	619c	2
		עוד	STILL	729a	1 ab
11	2	אשה	WOMAN	61b	4
		דבר	SPEAK	181c	8 a
		זהב	GOLD	263a	6
		זהב	GOLD	263c	1
		כלי	ARTICLE	479c	1
		רע	FRIEND	946b	3
		שאל	ASK	981d	1 b
11	3	גדול	GREAT	153a	6 b
		חן	FAVOR	336c	2 b1
		נתן	PUT	680d	2 b
11	4	חצות	DIVISION	345c	
		תוך	MIDST	1063c	
11	5	אחר	BEHIND	29d	2 a
		בכור	FIRST-BORN	114b	2 b
		בכור	FIRST-BORN	114b	1 d
		ישב	SIT	442b	1 a
		כסא	SEAT OF HONOR	490d	1 a
		מות	DIE	560a	2 b
		מן	FROM	582a	5 b
		על	UPON	752d	2 1
		שפחה	MAID	*1046c	1
		שפחה	MAID	1046c	1
11	6	גדול	GREAT	153a	4
		היה	COME TO PASS	227d	2
		יסף	DO AGAIN	415c	2
		צעקה	CRY	858d	2
11	7	איש	MAN	35d	
		אשר	THAT	83b	8 ab
		חרץ	CUT	358c	2
		כלב	DOG	476d	A
		ל	TO	510d	1 d
		לשון	TONGUE	546d	3
		מן	FROM	583d	9 b1
		פלה	BE SEPARATED	811d	2
		שמש	SUN	1039b	4 b
11	8	אלה	THESE	41c	A
		חרי	BURNING	354c	
		רגל	FOOT	920a	1 f
		שחה	BOW DOWN	1005b	1 c
11	9	מופת	WONDER	68d	1
		רבה	BECOME MANY	915b	1 c
11	10	מופת	WONDER	68d	1
		מופת	SIGN	69c	2
		חזק	BE FIRM	304d	5
		לב	HEART	525b	2 6d
		פנה	FACE	816d	2 4
12	2	אביב	ABIB	1b	2
		חדש	NEW MOON	*294d	2 b1
		חדש	NEW MOON	294d	2 b2
		ל	TO	512d	5 ab
		ל	TO	512d	5 aa
		עבר	PASS OVER	717c	3 a
		ראש	HEAD	911b	4 b
		ראשון	FIRST	911d	2
		שמש	SUN	1039b	4 b
12	3	אב	FATHER	3c	3
		איש	MAN	36a	
		בית	HOUSE	110b	5 e
		בית	HOUSE	110b	5 e
		דבר	SPEAK	181a	8 a
		ו	AND	254d	5 ca
		עדה	CONGREGATION	417b	3
		ל	TO	513d	5 cb g
		עשור	A TEN	797c	1 b
		פסח	PASSOVER	820b	2
		שה	A SHEEP	962a	1
12	4	אכל	EAT	37b	1
		ב	IN	90c	3 8
		בית	HOUSE	109d	5 a
		כסס	COMPUTE	493c	
		מכסה	COMPUTATION	493d	A
		מן	THAN	582d	6 d
		מסת	SUFFICIENCY	*588b	
		מעט	BE SMALL	589c	
		נפש	SOUL	660c	4 c4
		על	UPON	754c	2 1f d
		פה	MOUTH	805c	6 c1
		פסח	PASSOVER	820b	2
		קרב	NEAR	898c	2 a
		שה	A SHEEP	962a	1
		שכן	NEIGHBOUR	1015c	2
12	5	בן	SON	122a	9 b
		זכר	MALE	271c	1 2
		ל	TO	512d	5 aa
		עז	SHE-GOAT	777c	3 c
		פסח	PASSOVER	820b	2
		שה	A SHEEP	962a	1
		תמים	SOUND	1071a	2
12	6	יום	DAY	398c	2 e
		עדה	CONGREGATION	417b	3
		ל	TO	513d	5 cb g
		עד	AS FAR AS	724b	1 2a a
		ערב	SUNSET	788a	1 b
		עשר	TEN	797b	4 a
		פסח	PASSOVER	*820b	3
		קהל	ASSEMBLY	874d	2 a
		ארבע	FOUR	917a	2 a2 a
		שחט	SLAUGHTER	1006b	2
		משמרת	GUARD	1038c	2
12	7	בית	HOUSE	108c	1 a
		בית	HOUSE	108d	1 ab
		דם	BLOOD	197c	3 a
		מזוזה	DOOR-POST	265b	1
		מן	FROM	580d	3 ba
		נתן	PUT	680d	2 a
		משקוף	LINTEL	1054d	1
12	8	אש	FIRE	77c	3
		בשל	BOIL	*143b	2
		לילה	NIGHT	538d	1
		מרר	BITTER HERB	601a	
		מצה	UNLEAVENED BREAD	695b	
		על	UPON	755c	2 4c
		עשרים	TWENTY	798a	2 2b
		צלי	ROASTED	852a	
12	9	אש	FIRE	77c	3
		בשל	BOIL	143b	
		בשל	BOIL	*143b	2
		בשל	COOKED	143b	
		כי אם	BUT	475a	2 b
		כרע	LEG	502d	
		מי	WATER	565b	1 a
		נא	RAW	644b	
		על	UPON	755c	2 4c
		צלי	ROASTED	852a	
		קרב	INWARD PART	899b	3
		ראש	HEAD	910d	1 b
12	10	בקר	MORNING	134b	
		יום	DAY	*398d	2 e
		יתר	LEAVE OVER	451c	1 a
		עד	AS FAR AS	724b	1 2a a
12	11	חגר	GIRD	291d	1
		חפזון	TREPIDATION	342a	1
		ככה	THUS	462c	
		ל	TO	515b	5 hb b
		מקל	STAFF	596c	2
		מתנים	LOINS	608a	1 c
		נעל	SANDAL	653a	
		פסח	PASSOVER	820b	
12	12	אדם	MAN	9b	2
		אלהים	GOD	43c	1 d
		בהמה	BEAST	96d	1
		בכור	FIRST-BORN	114b	1 d
		יהוה	YAHWEH	219b	2 2d
		לילה	NIGHT	538d	1
		נכה	SMITE	646a	2 c
		שפט	JUDGEMENT	1048a	1
12	13	אות	SIGN	16d	1
		דם	BLOOD	197c	3 a
		היה	BECOME	225d	2 1b
		ו	AND	254d	2 db
		נגף	BLOW	620a	1
		נכה	SMITE	646c	4 a
		פסח	PASS OVER	820a	
		משחית	DESTRUCTION	1008c	
12	14	דור	GENERATION	190a	2 c
		זכרון	MEMORIAL	272a	1 a
		חגג	MAKE PILGRIMAGE	290d	1
		חגג	MAKE PILGRIMAGE	290d	1
		חג	FESTIVAL-GATHERING	291a	1 b2
		חג	FESTIVAL-GATHERING	291b	1 b
		חקה	SOMETHING PRESCRIBED	350a	1
12	15	עולם	LONG DURATION	762c	2 e
		אך	SURELY	36c	1
		ה	THE	209a	2 b
		ו	AND	254d	5 a
		חמץ	THAT WHICH IS LEAVENED	329d	
		יום	DAY	401a	7 j
		כרת	BE CUT OFF	504b	1 c
		נפש	SOUL	660b	4 c2
		מצה	UNLEAVENED BREAD	695b	
		עד	AS FAR AS	724b	1 2a a
		ראשון	FIRST	911d	2 a
		שאר	LEAVEN	959a	
		ישראל	ISRAEL	975c	2 a1
		שבת	CEASE	992a	4
12	16	אך	ONLY	36c	2 ba
		אכל	EAT	37d	1
		כל	ALL	482b	1 ec
		ל	TO	514a	5 e
		מלאכה	WORK	522a	3 b
		נפש	SOUL	660c	4 c3
		עשה	DO	795a	1 a
		עשה	DO	795b	2 c
		קדש	APARTNESS	872b	5
		מקרא	CONVOCATION	896d	1
		ראשון	FIRST	911d	2 a
12	17	דור	GENERATION	190a	2 c
		חקה	SOMETHING PRESCRIBED	350a	1
		יצא	CASUE TO GO	424c	1 a
		מצה	UNLEAVENED BREAD	695b	
		עולם	LONG DURATION	762c	2 e
		עצם	BONE	783a	3

Ch	v.	Heb	Eng	Page	Sec
12	18	שמר	KEEP	1036d	3 a
		ה	THE	209a	2 b
		יום	DAY	398c	2 e
		יום	DAY	401b	71
		מצה	UNLEAVENED BREAD	695b	
		עד	AS FAR AS	724b	12a a
		ערב	SUNSET	787a	1 a
		ראשון	FIRST	911d	2 a
		ארבע	FOUR	917a	2a2 a
12	19	ב	IN	88c	1 2c
		גר	SOJOURNER	158a	1
		גר	SOJOURNER	158b	2
		אזרח	A NATIVE	280c	1
		מחמצת	ANYTHING LEAVENED	330a	
		עדה	CONGREGATION	417b	3
		מושב	DWELLING	444b	2 c
		כרת	BE CUT OFF	504b	1
		מצא	FIND	594a	2 c
		נפש	SOUL	660b	4 c2
		שאר	LEAVEN	959a	
12	20	מחמצת	ANYTHING LEAVENED	330a	
		מושב	DWELLING	444b	2 c
		מצה	UNLEAVENED BREAD	695b	
12	21	זקן	OLD	278d	2 b
		משך	DRAW	604b	1
		פסח	PASSOVER	820b	2
		פסח	PASSOVER	820b	2
		שחט	SLAUGHTER	1006b	2
		משפחה	CLAN	1046d	1 a
12	22	אגדה	BUNCH	8a	2
		אזוב	HYSSOP	23c	
		בקר	MORNING	133d	1 a
		דם	BLOOD	197c	3 a
		זבח	SACRIFICE	258a	2 5
		מזוזה	DOOR-POST	265b	1
		טבל	DIP	371b	1
		יצא	GO OUT	422c	1 a
		לקח	TAKE	542d	1
		נגע	TOUCH	619b	1
		סף	BASIN	706b	
		משקוף	LINTEL	1054d	
12	23	דם	BLOOD	197c	3 a
		מזוזה	DOOR-POST	265b	1
		נגף	STRIKE	619d	
		עבר	PASS OVER	717c	3 a
		פסח	PASS OVER	820a	
		שחת	GO TO RUIN	1008b	1
		משקוף	LINTEL	1054d	
12	24	חק	SOMETHING PRESCRIBED	349c	6 a
		עולם	LONG DURATION	762c	2 e
12	25	דבר	SPEAK	*180d	
		עבדה	LABOR	715b	4
12	26	ל	TO	513a	5 ad
		מה	WHAT	552b	1 a
		עבדה	LABOR	715b	4
12	27	אמר	SAY	56a	1
		זבח	SACRIFICE	257c	2 2
		מאה	HUNDRED	548a	1 c2
		נגף	STRIKE	619d	
		נצל	DELIVER	664d	3 a
		פסח	PASS OVER	820a	
		פסח	PASSOVER	820b	1
		קדד	BOW DOWN	869a	
12	28	הלך	WALK	230b	1 1b
		כאשר	AS	455b	1 b
		כן	SO	486b	2 ca
		צוה	CHARGE	846a	3
12	29	בור	PIT	92c	4
		בכור	FIRST-BORN	114b	1 d
		בכור	FIRST-BORN	114b	2 b
		חצי	HALF	345d	2
		ישב	SIT	442b	1 a
		כסא	SEAT OF HONOR	490d	1 a
		לילה	NIGHT	538d	1
		נכה	SMITE	646a	2 c
		שבי	CAPTIVITY	985d	3
12	30	אין	NOT	34c	2
		היה	BECOME	225d	2 1a
		צעקה	CRY	858d	2
12	31	עצב	PAIN	*1107d	
12	32	ברך	BLESS	139d	3
		לקח	TAKE	543c	7
12	33	חזק	BE FIRM	304b	13
		מהר	HASTEN	555a	2
		מות	DIE	560a	2 b
		מצרים	EGYPTIANS	595d	2 b
12	34	בצק	DOUGH	130d	
		חמץ	BE SOUR	329d	
		טרם	NOT YET	382c	1
		משארת	A HOUSEHOLD VESSEL	602b	
		משארת	A HOUSEHOLD VESSEL	*602b	
		צרר	BIND	864c	A
		שמלה	WRAPPER	971a	
		שכם	SHOULDER	1014b	1 a
12	35	דבר	WORD	182b	1 1b
		זהב	GOLD	263a	6
		זהב	GOLD	263c	1
		כלי	ARTICLE	479c	1
		שמלה	WRAPPER	971a	

Ch	v.	Heb	Eng	Page	Sec
		שאל	ASK	981d	1 b
12	36	חן	FAVOR	336c	2 b1
		נצל	STRIP	664d	1
		נתן	PUT	680d	2 b
12	37	אלף	THOUSAND	49a	1 c
		אלף	THOUSAND	49a	1 c
		בד	SEPARATION	94c	1 d
		גבר	MAN	150a	
		ך	LIKE	453b	1 a
		נסע	JOURNEY	652b	3
		סכת	SUCCOTH	697d	2
		רגלי	ON FOOT	920b	2
		רעמסס	RAMSES	947c	
		סוף	ADDENDA ET CORRIGENDA	1123d	
12	38	כבד	MASSIVE	458b	2 b
		ערב	MIXTURE	786b	
12	39	אפה	BAKE	66a	
		אפה	BAKE	66a	
		בצק	DOUGH	130d	
		גרש	DRIVE OUT	177a	
		חמץ	BE SOUR	329d	
		יכל	BE ABLE	407c	1 a
		יצא	BRING OUT	425a	4 a
		מהה	LINGER	554c	
		מצרים	EGYPT	595d	1 b2
		מצה	UNLEAVENED BREAD	695b	
		מצה	UNLEAVENED BREAD	695b	
		עגה	BREAD-CAKE	728b	
		עשה	DO	794d	2 3
		צידה	PROVISION	845b	
12	40	מושב	TIME OF DWELLING	444b	4
12	41	יצא	GO OUT	422d	1 a
		עצם	BONE	783a	3
		צבא	ARMY	839a	1 a
12	42	דור	GENERATION	190a	2 c
		הוא	HE, SHE, IT	215c	1 e
		יצא	CASUE TO GO	424c	1
		לילה	NIGHT	538d	1
		שמר	WATCHING	1037d	
12	43	אכל	EAT	37b	1
		בן	SON	121c	7 a
		חקה	SOMETHING PRESCRIBED	350a	1
		נכר	FOREIGNNESS	648d	2
		פסח	PASSOVER	820b	3
12	44	אז	THEN	23a	1 b
		ו	AND	254c	5 a
		כסף	SILVER	494c	8 e
		מול	CIRCUMCIZE	557d	
		עבד	SLAVE	713d	1
		מקנה	PURCHASE	889c	1
12	45	תושב	SOJOURNER	444c	
		שכיר	HIRED	969b	2
12	46	אכל	EAT	37d	1
		חוץ	THE OUTSIDE	299d	1
		עצם	BONE	782d	2
		שבר	BREAK	990c	
12	47	עדה	CONGREGATION	417b	3
		עשה	DO	795a	2 6
12	48	אז	THEN	23a	1 b
		גור	SOJOURN	157d	1
		גר	SOJOURNER	158b	2
		גר	SOJOURNER	*158c	2
		זכר	MALE	271c	1 1b
		אזרח	A NATIVE	280c	1
		ל	TO	512d	5 aa
		מול	CIRCUMCIZE	557d	
		ערל	HAVING FORESKIN	790c	
		עשה	DO	795a	2 6
		עשה	DO	795a	2 6
		פסח	PASSOVER	820b	3
		קרב	COME NEAR	897c	1 g
12	49	גור	SOJOURN	157d	1
		גר	SOJOURNER	158b	2
		גר	SOJOURNER	*158c	2
		אזרח	A NATIVE	280c	1
		תורה	LAW	436a	2 a
12	50	כאשר	AS	455b	1 b
		כן	SO	486b	2 ca
		צוה	CHARGE	846a	3
12	51	יצא	CASUE TO GO	424c	1 a
		על	UPON	754a	2 lf
		עצם	BONE	783a	3
		צבא	ARMY	839a	1 a
13	1	ראה	TO SEE	907a	1 b
13	2	אדם	MAN	9b	2
		בכור	FIRST-BORN	114b	1 d
		פטר	THAT WHICH SEPARATES	809d	
		קדש	BE SET APART	873a	1 c
		רחם	WOMB	933b	1
13	3	אכל	EAT	37d	1
		בית	HOUSE	109a	1 ae 9
		זה	THIS	262a	6 e
		זכר	REMEMBER	270a	1 g
		חזק	STRENGTH	305d	1
		חמץ	THAT WHICH IS LEAVENED	329d	
		יד	HAND	390a	1 e2
		יצא	GO OUT	422d	1 a
		יצא	CAUSE TO GO	424c	1 a
		עבד	SLAVE	713d	1

Ch	v.	Heb	Eng	Page	Sec
13	4	אביב	ABIB	1b	2
		חדש	NEW MOON	294d	2 b1
		יום	DAY	399d	7 a1
13	5	אמרי	AMORITES	57c	2 e
		יבוסי	JEBUSITE	101a	1
		דבש	HONEY	185b	
		זוב	FLOW	264d	2
		חוי	HIVITE	295d	2
		חלב	MILK	316c	A 4
		חתי	HITTITE	366d	2
		כנעני	CANAANITE	489a	2 b
		עבד	WORK	713b	4 a
		עבדה	LABOR	715b	4
		שבע	SWEAR	989c	2
13	6	חג	FESTIVAL-GATHERING	291a	1 b2
		ל	TO	515b	5 hb b
		מצה	UNLEAVENED BREAD	695b	
13	7	אכל	EAT	37d	1
		את	MARK OF THE ACCUSATIVE	85b	2 b
		גבול	BOUNDARY	148a	2 a
		חמץ	THAT WHICH IS LEAVENED	329d	
		ל	TO	514a	5 e
		מצה	UNLEAVENED BREAD	695b	
		ראה	TO SEE	908c	2 c
		שאר	LEAVEN	959a	
13	8	אמר	SAY	56b	1
		זה	THIS	260d	1 a
		זה	THIS	*261d	1
		יצא	GO OUT	422d	1 a
		עבור	FOR THE SAKE OF	721a	1 a
13	9	אות	SIGN	17a	5
		בין	INTERVAL	107b	1
		זכרון	MEMORIAL	272a	1 b
		חזק	STRONG	305c	1 b
		טוטפת	BANDS	*377d	
		יד	HAND	390a	1 e2
		יצא	CAUSE TO GO	424c	1 a
		תורה	LAW	436a	2 a
		עין	EYE	745a	5
13	10	חקה	SOMETHING PRESCRIBED	350a	1
		יום	YEAR	399d	6 c
		מועד	APPOINTED TIME	*417c	1 b
		מועד	APPOINTED TIME	417c	1 a
		מן	FROM	582b	5 d3
13	11	כנעני	CANAANITE	489a	2 b
		שבע	SWEAR	989c	2
13	12	זכר	MALE	271c	1
		עבר	PASS OVER	718d	1 c
		פטר	THAT WHICH SEPARATES	809d	
		פטר	THAT WHICH SEPARATES	809d	
		רחם	WOMB	933b	1
		שגר	OFFSPRING	993d	1
13	13	אדם	MAN	9b	2
		בכור	FIRST-BORN	114b	1 d
		חמור	HE-ASS	331b	1
		ערף	BREAK THE NECK	791c	
		פדה	RANSOM	804a	1
		פטר	THAT WHICH SEPARATES	809d	
		שה	A SHEEP	962a	1
		בית	HOUSE	109a	1 ae 9
13	14	חזק	STRENGTH	305d	1
		יד	HAND	390a	1 e2
		יצא	CAUSE TO GO	424c	1 a
		מה	WHAT	552b	1 a
		מחר	TO-MORROW	564a	2
		עבד	SLAVE	713d	1
13	15	אדם	MAN	9b	2
		בכור	FIRST-BORN	114b	2 b
		בכור	FIRST-BORN	114b	1 d
		הרג	KILL	247b	2
		זבח	SLAUGHTER FOR SACRIFICE	256d	1 1 ba
		זכר	MALE	271c	1
		כן	SO	487b	3 f
		מן	FROM	582b	5 b
		פדה	RANSOM	804a	1
		פטר	THAT WHICH SEPARATES	809d	
		קשה	BE SEVERE	904b	1
		רחם	WOMB	933b	1
13	16	אות	SIGN	17a	5
		חזק	STRENGTH	305d	1
		טוטפת	BANDS	*378d	
		טוטפת	BANDS	378a	
		יד	HAND	390a	1 e2
		יצא	CAUSE TO GO	424c	1 a
		עין	EYE	745a	5
13	17	ב	IN	91a	5 l
		דרך	WAY	202d	1
		היה	COME TO PASS	224d	2a 1b
		נחה	LEAD	634d	
		נחם	BE SORRY	637a	2
		פן	LEST	814d	1 a
		קרב	NEAR	898b	1
		ראה	TO SEE	907a	1 b
		שוב	TURN BACK	997b	3 a
13	18	דרך	WAY	202d	1
		חרש	HASTE	*301d	

EXODUS

Ch v.	Heb	Eng	Page	Sec
	כנען	CANAAN	488d	2a
	מוג	MELT	556a	
	רעד	TREMBLING	944d	
15 16	אבן	STONE	7a	8
	אבן	STONE	7a	8
	אימה	TERROR	34a	
	גדול	GREAT	153c	0
	דמם	BE DUMB	199a	3
	זו	THIS	262b	2
	זרוע	ARM	284a	1 c
	נפל	FALL	657c	5
	עבר	PASS OVER	717c	3 a
	עד	UNTIL	725a	2 1b b
	פחד	DREAD	808c	1
	קנה	ACQUIRE	889a	1 b
	גדל	ADDENDA ET COR-RIGENDA	1121d	
15 17	אדון	LORD	11b	3 2a
	ישב	DWELL	443a	3
	מכון	FIXED PLACE	467c	1 e
	נחלה	PROPERTY	635b	1 e
	נטע	PLANT	642c	2
	מקדש	SACRED PLACE	874a	1
15 18	מלך	BE KING	574a	1
	עד	PERPETUITY	723c	2 e
	עולם	LONG DURATION	762c	2 c
15 19	הלך	WALK	230c	1 1d 2a
	יבשה	DRY LAND	387a	1
	מי	WATER	565c	1 c
	סוס	HORSE	692a	1
	פרש	HORSEMAN	832a	1
15 20	אהרן	AARON	14d	
	מחלה	DANCING	298b	
	מחלה	DANCING	298b	
	מחלה	DANCING	298b	
	מרים	MIRIAM	599b	1
	משה	MOSES	*602a	
	נביאה	PROPHETESS	612c	1 a
	תף	TIMBREL	1074c	
15 21	גאה	RISE UP	144b	3
	מרים	MIRIAM	599b	1
	סוס	HORSE	692c	1
	ענה	SING	777b	
	רכב	RIDE	938d	3
	רמה	SHOOT	941a	
	שיר	SING	1010d	
15 22	מדבר	WILDERNESS	185a	3 a
	הלך	WALK	230c	1 1d 1b
	יום	DAY	398c	2 b
	מצא	FIND	592a	1 a
	נסע	SET OUT	652c	1
	סוף	REEDS	693b	2 a
	שור	SHUR	1004b	
15 23	הם	THEY	241c	3 a
	יכל	BE ABLE	407c	1 a
	כן	SO	487b	3 f
	מי	WATER	565d	3
	מן	ON ACCOUNT OF	580b	2 f
	מר	BITTER	600c	1
	מרה	MARAH	600d	
	מרה	MARAH	600d	
	שתה	DRINK	1059b	1 a
15 24	לון	MURMUR	534a	
	על	UPON	757d	2 7d
	שתה	DRINK	1059b	1 a
15 25	חק	SOMETHING PRE-SCRIBED	349c	6 a
	ירה	POINT OUT	435b	4
	מי	WATER	565d	3
	מתק	BE SWEET	608c	1
	נסה	TEST	650b	3 a
	עץ	TREE	781c	1 a
	צעק	CRY	858c	1 b
	שום	TO PLACE	963b	3 b
	שלך	THROW	1021a	1 a
	שם	THERE	1027a	1 a
	משפט	JUDGMENT	1048d	3
15 26	אזן	HEAR	24c	1
	אם	IF	50a	1 a5
	יהוה	YAHWEH	218d	2 1a
	יהוה	YAHWEH	219b	2 2c
	מחלה	SICKNESS	318b	
	חק	SOMETHING PRE-SCRIBED	349d	7 g
	ישר	STRAIGHT	449a	2 a
	על	UPON	757a	2 7b
	מצוה	COMMANDMENT	846c	2 b1
	קול	VOICE	877b	3 b
	רפא	HEAL	950d	2 a
	שום	TO PLACE	963b	1 b
	שמע	HEAR	1034a	11
15 27	אילים	ELIM	18c	
	חנה	DECLINE	333c	2 c2
	מי	WATER	565b	1 a
	עין	SPRING	745b	
	שבעים	SEVENTY	988c	1 b
	שם	THERE	1027a	1 a
	שנים	TWO	1041b	2
	תמר	PALM-TREE	1071c	
16 1	אילים	ELIM	18c	
	בן	SON	120d	1 jg
	מדבר	WILDERNESS	185a	3 a
	חמש	FIVE	332a	2 b2
	עדה	CONGREGATION	417b	3
	נסע	SET OUT	652b	2 a
	סין	SIN	695d	

Ch v.	Heb	Eng	Page	Sec
	סיני	SINAI	696a	
	עשר	TEN	797b	5 a
16 2	בן	SON	120d	1 jg
	עדה	CONGREGATION	417b	3
	לון	MURMUR	534a	
	לון	MURMUR	534a	
16 3	ב	IN	89d	3 2a
	יד	HAND	391a	5 d
	יצא	BRING OUT	424d	1 g
	ל	TO	516c	5 jb
	לחם	FOOD	537a	1 a
	לחם	FOOD	537a	1 a
	מות	DIE	560a	2 b
	נתן	GIVE	678d	1 f
	סיר	POT	696c	1
	על	UPON	756a	2 6b
	קהל	ASSEMBLY	874d	1
	רעב	FAMINE	944b	1
	שבע	ABUNDANCE	960a	1
16 4	דבר	WORD	183b	4 1
	ה	INTERROG PART	210b	2 b
	הלך	WALK	234c	2 3a 1d
	יום	DAY	400c	7 e3
	תורה	LAW	436a	2 3
	לא	NOT	519a	1 ad b
	לקט	GATHER UP	544d	1
	מטר	RAIN	*565a	
	נסה	TEST	650b	3 a
	שמי	HEAVENS	1030a	2 a
16 5	היה	COME TO PASS	225b	12b bg
	יום	DAY	400b	7 e1
	לקט	GATHER UP	544d	1
	על	UPON	755a	2 2
	משנה	DOUBLE	1041c	1
	חד	A	*1079c	2
16 6	ו	AND	254a	5 a
	יצא	CAUSE TO GO	424c	1 a
	ערב	SUNSET	787d	1 a
16 7	נחנו	WE	59d	
	ב	IN	91a	5 2
	בקר	MORNING	134a	1 e
	בקר	MORNING	134c	2
	ו	AND	254d	5 a
	כבוד	GLORY	458d	2 c1
	כי	THAT	472d	1 f
	לון	MURMUR	534a	
	לון	MURMUR	534a	
	תלנה	MURMURING	534b	
	מה	WHAT	552c	1 a
	מה	WHAT	553a	1 db
	נחנו	WE	59d	
16 8	בקר	MORNING	134a	1 e
	כי	BUT	474b	3 e
	לא	NOT	518d	1 ac
	לון	MURMUR	534a	
	תלנה	MURMURING	534b	
	לחם	FOOD	537a	1 a
	שבע	SATISFIED	959b	1 a
	שבע	SATESFIED	959b	1 a
	בן	SON	120d	1 jg
16 9	עדה	CONGREGATION	417b	3
	תלנה	MURMURING	534b	
	פנה	FACE	817b	2 4a h
	קרב	COME NEAR	897c	1 c
	בן	SON	120d	1 jg
16 10	היה	COME TO PASS	224c	2 a1 aa
	עדה	CONGREGATION	417b	3
	כבוד	GLORY	458d	2 c1
	ענן	CLOUD	778a	1 a
	פנה	TURN	815b	2 a
	ראה	TO SEE	908b	1 a
16 12	בקר	MORNING	134a	1 e
	יהוה	YAHWEH	219a	2 2b b
	ידע	KNOW	393d	1 a
	תלנה	MURMURING	534b	
	לחם	FOOD	537a	1 a
	ערב	SUNSET	788a	1 b
	שבע	SATISFIED	959b	1 b
	בקר	MORNING	134a	1 e
16 13	היה	COME TO PASS	224c	2 a1 ag
	מחנה	ENCAMPMENT	334a	1 a
	טל	NIGHT-MIST	378c	
	כסה	COVER	492a	5
	סביב	ROUND ABOUT	687a	1 cb
	עלה	GO UP	748d	3
	שלו	QUAIL	969c	
	שכבה	LYING	1012c	2
16 14	ארץ	EARTH	76b	3 a
	דק	SMALL	201a	2
	הלך	WALK	234c	2 3a 1d
	חספס	SCALE-LIKE	341a	
	טל	NIGHT-MIST	378c	
	ך	LIKE	454a	1 c2
	כפור	HOARFROST	499b	
	מן	MANNA	577b	
	עלה	GO UP	748d	5
	פנה	FACE	818d	2 7a d
	פנה	FACE	819a	2 7b
	שדה	FIELD	961c	1 f
	שכבה	LYING	1012c	2
16 15	אלה	FOOD	38a	1 a
	מה	WHAT	552d	1 b
	מן	WHAT IS IT	577c	
	נתן	GIVE	678c	1 b
	אכל	EAT	37b	1
16 16	דבר	WORD	182d	1 2a

Ch v.	Heb	Eng	Page	Sec
	זה	THIS	261a	3
	נפש	SOUL	660c	4 c4
	מספר	NUMBER	709a	1 b
	עמר	OMER	771c	
	פה	MOUTH	805c	6 bb
	פה	MOUTH	805c	6 cl
	צוה	CHARGE	845d	2 d
16 17	לקט	GATHER UP	544d	1
	מעט	BE SMALL	589d	B
	רבה	BECOME MANY	915c	1 c
	רבה	BECOME MANY	915c	
16 18	אכל	EAT	37b	1
	חסר	LACK	341c	
	לקט	GATHER UP	544d	1
	מדד	MEASURE	551a	1
	מעט	BE SMALL	589d	B
	עדף	REMAIN OVER	727b	
	עמר	OMER	771c	
	פה	MOUTH	805c	6 bb
	פה	MOUTH	805c	6 cl
	רבה	BECOME MANY	915c	1 c
16 19	בקר	MORNING	134b	1
	יתר	LEAVE OVER	451c	1 a
16 20	באש	STINK	92d	
	באש	STINK	*93a	1
	בקר	MORNING	134b	1
	יתר	LEAVE OVER	451c	1 a
	קצף	BE WROTH	893b	2
	רמם	BE WORMY	933d	
	תולע	WORM	1068d	1
16 21	אכל	EAT	37b	1
	בקר	MORNING	134b	1 f
	ו	AND	254a	2 da
	חמם	BE OR BECOME WARM	328c	1
	מסס	MELT	587d	1
	פה	MOUTH	805c	6 bb
	שמש	SUN	1039b	1
16 22	עדה	CONGREGATION	417b	3
	נשיא	PRINCE	672b	4
	עמר	OMER	771c	
	שנים	TWO	1041a	1 a
	משנה	DOUBLE	1041c	1
16 23	אפה	BAKE	66a	
	בקר	MORNING	134b	2
	הוא	HE, SHE, IT	216d	6 a
	מחר	TO-MORROW	563d	1 a
	נוח	REST	628d	B 1
	עד	AS FAR AS	724b	1 2a a
	עדף	REMAIN OVER	727b	
	קדש	APARTNESS	872b	5
	שבת	SABBATH	992b	1 d
	שבתון	SABBOTH OBSERV-ANCE	992d	1
	משמרת	GUARD	1038c	2
16 24	באש	STINK	93a	2
	בקר	MORNING	134b	2
	היה	BECOME	225c	2 1a
	כאשר	AS	455b	1 a
	נוח	REST	628d	B 1
	רחום	WORM	933d	
16 25	ל	TO	515b	5 hb b
	שדה	FIELD	961c	1 f
	שבת	SABBATH	992b	1 a
16 26	יום	DAY	398c	2 a
	לקט	GATHER UP	544d	1
	שבת	SABBATH	992b	1 a
16 27	מן	FROM	580c	3 ba
	אן	WHERE	33a	D
	תורה	LAW	436a	2 a
16 28	מאן	REFUSE	549b	
	מצוה	COMMANDMENT	846c	2 b3
16 29	כן	SO	487a	3 f
	נתן	GIVE	678c	1 b
	שבת	SABBATH	992b	1 a
	תחת	UNDERNEATH	1065d	2 a
16 30	יום	DAY	398b	2 a
	שבת	CEASE	991d	2 b
16 31	בית	HOUSE	110a	5 dd
	גד	CORIANDER	151c	
	דבש	HONEY	185b	
	זרע	SOWING	282b	2 c
	טעם	TASTE	381a	1
	לבן	WHITE	526b	
	מן	MANNA	577b	
	צפיחת	FLAT CAKE	860c	
	ישראל	ISRAEL	975d	2 c
16 32	אכל	EAT	37d	1
	דבר	WORD	182d	1 2a
	דור	GENERATION	190a	2 c
	יצא	CAUSE TO GO	424c	1 a
	מלא	FULNESS	571b	2
	עמר	OMER	771c	
	צוה	CHARGE	845d	2 d
	משמרת	GUARD	1038c	2
16 33	דור	GENERATION	190a	2 c
	מלא	FULLNESS	571b	2
	מן	MANNA	577b	
	נוח	REST	628d	B 1
	עמר	OMER	771c	
	פנה	FACE	817b	2 4a h
	צנצנת	JAR	857a	
	שם	THERE	1027b	3 a
	משמרת	GUARD	1038c	2
16 34	ו	AND	254d	5 b
	כאשר	AS	455c	1 c

Ch v.	Heb	Eng	Page	Sec
	נוח	REST	628d	B 1
	עדות	TESTIMONY	730b	1
	פנה	FACE	817b	2 4a h
	פנה	FACE	817d	2 4d
	צוה	GIVE CHARGE UNTO	845d	1 c
	משמרת	GUARD	1038c	2
16 35	אכל	EAT	37b	1
	ישב	BE INHABITED	443c	
	מן	MANNA	577b	
	קצה	END	892d	2
16 36	איפה	EPHAH	35b	1
	עמר	OMER	771c	
	עשירי	TENTH	798a	2
17 1	בן	SON	120d	1 jg
	עדה	CONGREGATION	417b	3
	ל	TO	516b	5 ja
	נסע	JOURNEY	652b	2
	מסע	JOURNEY	652d	2
	סין	SIN	695d	
	פה	MOUTH	805d	6 d1 a
	רפידים	REPHIDIM	951c	
17 2	מה	WHAT	553c	2 ab
	נסה	TEST	650d	3 b
	ריב	STRIVE	936c	2
	ריב	STRIVE	936c	2
17 3	ל	TO	*510b	1 a
	לון	MURMUR	534a	
	מה	HOW	554a	4 d
	עלה	GO UP	749b	1 a
	צמא	THIRST	854d	
	צמא	BE THIRSTY	854d	
17 4	אמר	SAY	56b	1
	מעט	A FEW	590b	1 eb
	סקל	STONE	709c	
	עוד	STILL	729a	1 ab
	צעק	CRY	858c	1 b
17 5	הלך	WALK	230a	1 1a
	זקן	OLD	278d	2 b
	יאר	STREAM	384b	1
	לקח	TAKE	542d	1
	מן	FROM	580d	3 ba
	מטה	STAFF	641c	1
	נכה	SMITE	645b	1 a
	עבר	PASS OVER	718a	5 c
	פנה	FACE	817c	2 4c a
17 6	זקן	OLD	278d	2 b
	חרב	HOREB	352a	
	יצא	GO OUT	423a	1 f
	מי	WATER	565b	1 a
	נכה	SMITE	645b	1 a
	נכה	SMITE	645b	1 a
	צור	ROCK	849c	1 a
	שתה	DRINK	1059b	1 a
17 7	אין	NOT	34c	2 db
	יש	BE	441c	2 a
	נסה	TEST	650d	3 b
	מסה	MASSAH	650c	
	על	UPON	754d	2 1f b
	ריב	STRIFE	936d	1
	מריבה	MERIBAH	937b	1
17 8	עמלק	AMALEK	766a	
	רפידים	REPHIDIM	951c	
17 9	אלהים	GOD	44a	3 b
	בחר	CHOOSE	104a	3 b
	גבעה	HILL	149a	1
	יהושע	JOSHUA	221c	1
	יד	HAND	390d	5 c1
	לחם	ENGAGE IN BATTLE	535c	
	מחר	TO-MORROW	564a	1 b
	מטה	STAFF	641c	1
	נצב	STAND	662a	1 a
	ראש	HEAD	910d	2 a
17 10	אהרן	AARON	14d	
	גבעה	HILL	149a	1
	יהושע	JOSHUA	221c	1
	חור	HUR	301b	1
	לחם	ENGAGE IN BATTLE	535c	
	ראש	HEAD	910d	2 a
17 11	גבר	BE STRONG	149d	2 a
	כאשר	AS	455b	1 b
	נוח	REST	628d	A 1a
	רום	BE HIGH	927b	1 a1
17 12	אבן	STONE	6b	1
	אמונה	FIRMNESS	53c	1
	בוא	COME	98a	1 i
	זה	THIS	262a	6 e
	חור	HUR	301b	1
	ישב	SIT	442b	1 a
	כבד	HEAVY	458a	1 a
	תמך	SUPPORT	1069d	2
17 13	יהושע	JOSHUA	221c	1
	חלש	BE WEAK	325d	2
	חרב	SWORD	352d	1 f
	פה	MOUTH	805d	6 c2
17 14	ה	THE	*207d	1 d
	יהושע	JOSHUA	221c	1
	זה	THIS	260c	1 a
	זכר	MEMORIAL	271a	
	זכר	REMEMBRANCE	271b	1 a
	זכרון	MEMORIAL	272a	1 d
	מחה	WIPE OUT	562a	2
	ספר	MISSIVE	707a	3
	ספר	MISSIVE	*707c	4

Ch v.	Heb	Eng	Page	Sec
	שום	TO PLACE	963b	1 b
	שמי	HEAVENS	1029d	1 a
	תחת	UNDERNEATH	1066a	1 b
17 15	בנה	BUILD	124c	1 at
	יהוה	YAHWEH	219b	2 3
	מזבח	ALTAR	258b	1
	נס	STANDARD	651d	1 a
17 16	דור	PERIOD	189d	1 b
	יה	YAH	219c	
	יד	HAND	389c	1 d
	כסא	SEAT OF HONOR	490d	1 b
	על	UPON	757a	2 b
18 1	מדין	MIDIAN	193c	1
	חתן	WIFE'S FATHER	368c	1
	יצא	CAUSE TO GO	424c	1 a
	יתרו	JETHRO	452b	
	כהן	PRIEST-KING	463a	1
	שמע	HEAR	1033d	1 d1
18 2	חתן	WIFE'S FATHER	368c	1
	יתרו	JETHRO	452b	
	יתרו	JETHRO	452b	
	צפרה	ZIPPORAH	862a	
	שלוחים	SENDING AWAY	1019d	1
18 3	גר	SOJOURNER	158a	1
	גרשם	GERSHOM	177a	1
	נכרי	FOREIGN	648d	1 a
18 4	אלהים	GOD	44b	4 ba
	אליעזר	ELIEZER	45c	B
	ב	IN	88d	1 7a
	עזר	HELP	740d	2
18 5	אלהים	GOD	44a	3 b
	הר	MOUNTAIN	249d	1 a
	הר	MOUNTAIN	249d	1 a
	חנה	DECLINE	333c	2 c2
	חתן	WIFE'S FATHER	368c	1
	יתרו	JETHRO	452b	
18 6	חתן	WIFE'S FATHER	368c	1
	יתרו	JETHRO	452b	
18 7	חתן	WIFE'S FATHER	368c	1
	נשק	KISS	676b	
	רע	FRIEND	946b	3
	שאל	ASK	981d	2 a
	שחה	BOW DOWN	1005c	1 c
	שלום	PEACE	1022d	3
18 8	אודה	CAUSE	15c	
	חתן	WIFE'S FATHER	368c	1
	תלאה	WEARINESS	521b	
	מצא	FIND	593c	3 e
	נצל	DELIVER	664d	3 a
18 9	חדה	REJOICE	292d	
	טובה	WELFARE	375d	3
	יד	HAND	391b	5 g1
	יתרו	JETHRO	452b	
	על	UPON	754b	2 1f b
	על	UPON	756d	27 a c
	עשה	DO	793d	1 1a 2
18 10	ברך	BLESS	138c	2 a
	יד	HAND	391b	5 g1
	יד	HAND	391b	5 g1
	יתרו	JETHRO	452b	
	נצל	DELIVER	665a	3 a
	תחת	UNDERNEATH	1066a	3 2a
18 11	אלהים	GOD	43c	1 d
	גדול	GREAT	153b	6 c
	זיד	BOIL UP	267c	
	זיד	BOIL UP	*267d	2
	כי	THAT	472d	1 e
	עתה	NOW	774a	1 a
18 12	אכל	EAT	37b	1
	זבח	SACRIFICE	257c	1 1
	זקן	OLD	278d	2 b
	חתן	WIFE'S FATHER	368c	1
	יתרו	JETHRO	452b	
	פנה	FACE	817c	2 4a h
18 13	בקר	MORNING	134a	1 e
	היה	COME TO PASS	224c	2 a1 az
	ישב	SIT	442c	1 a
	מחרת	THE MORROW	564a	
	מן	FROM	582a	5 c
	עד	AS FAR AS	724b	12a a
	על	UPON	756b	2 6c
	שפט	JUDGE	1047b	1 b
18 14	בד	SEPARATION	94c	1 b
	בקר	MORNING	134a	1 e
	חתן	WIFE'S FATHER	368c	1
	מדוע	WHEREFORE	396c	
	ישב	SIT	442c	1 a
	נצב	STAND	662a	1 a
	עד	AS FAR AS	724b	12a a
	על	UPON	756b	2 6c
18 15	דרש	SEEK	205b	2 a
	חתן	WIFE'S FATHER	368c	1
	כי	BECAUSE	473c	3 a
18 16	אלהים	GOD	44a	3 b
	דבר	WORD	183d	4 5
	חק	SOMETHING PRESCRIBED	349d	7 f
	ידע	KNOW	395a	
	תורה	LAW	436a	2 a
	כי	WHEN	473a	2 a
	רע	FRIEND	946b	3
	שפט	JUDGE	1047b	1 b
	שפט	JUDGE	1047c	2 b
18 17	חתן	WIFE'S FATHER	368c	1
	טוב	PLEASANT	374b	5
	לא	NOT	519a	1 ba

Ch v.	Heb	Eng	Page	Sec
18 18	יכל	BE ABLE	407c	1 b
	כבד	HEAVY	458b	1 d
	מן	THAN	582d	6 d
	נבל	SINK	615b	1
18 19	אתה	THOU	61c	
	יעץ	ADVISE	419d	
	מול	IN FRONT OF	557c	2
	עתה	NOW	774b	1 e
18 20	דרך	WAY	203c	6 b
	זהר	ADMONISH	264b	
	חק	SOMETHING PRESCRIBED	349d	7 f
	ידע	MAKE KNOWN	395a	
	תורה	LAW	436a	2 a
	עשה	DO	793d	1 a
	מעשה	DEED	795d	1 a3
18 21	אלף	THOUSAND	49a	2
	אמת	FIRMNESS	54a	3 a
	בצע	UNJUST GAIN	130c	
	חיל	STRENGTH	298d	2
	חיל	STRENGTH	298d	2
	חזה	SEE	302c	3 c
	חמשים	FIFTY	332b	1 a
	ירא	FEAR	431c	3 b
	מאה	HUNDRED	548a	1 c1
	על	UPON	755a	2 3
	עשר	TEN	796d	1
	שום	TO PLACE	963d	3 d
	שנא	HATE	971c	1 b
	שנא	HATE	971d	3
	חיתין	CHIEFTAIN	978b	2 b
18 22	את	WITH	86a	1
	גדול	GREAT	153a	6 a
	דבר	WORD	183d	4 5
	הם	THEY	241b	1 c
	נשא	LIFT	671a	2
	על	UPON	758d	4 2b
	עת	TIME	773b	1 a
	קטן	SMALL	882b	2
	קלל	BE SLIGHT	886d	1
	שפט	JUDGE	1047b	1 b
18 23	בוא	COME	98b	2
	יכל	BE ABLE	407c	1 b
	על	UPON	757a	27 c a
	עמד	STAND	764b	3 d
	צוה	CHARGE	845d	1 c
	שלום	PEACE	1023a	4
18 24	חתן	WIFE'S FATHER	368c	1
18 25	אלף	THOUSAND	49a	2
	חיל	STRENGTH	298d	2
	חמשים	FIFTY	332b	1 a
	מאה	HUNDRED	548a	1 c1
	מן	OUT OF	579b	2 ac
	עשר	TEN	796d	1
	ראש	HEAD	911a	3 a
18 26	הם	THEY	241b	1 c
	עת	TIME	773b	1 a
	קטן	SMALL	882b	2
	קשה	SEVERE	904c	1
	שפט	JUDGE	1047b	1 b
18 27	הלך	WALK	231d	1 1d 5h
	חתן	WIFE'S FATHER	368c	1
18 28	בחר	CHOOSE	104b	5 b
19 1	מדבר	WILDERNESS	185a	3 a
	ל	TO	513d	5 cb g
	סיני	SINAI	696a	
19 2	הר	MOUNTAIN	249b	1 a
	נגד	IN FRONT	617b	1 aa
	נסע	SET OUT	652b	2 a
	סיני	SINAI	696a	
	רפידים	REPHIDIM	951c	
19 3	בית	HOUSE	110a	5 dg
	כה	THUS	462a	1 a
	עלה	GO UP	748c	2 b
19 4	אב	FATHER	3b	2
	כנף	WING	489c	1 a
	נשא	LIFT	671b	2 c
	נשר	EAGLE	677a	
19 5	אם	IF	50a	1 a5
	ברית	COVENANT	136c	2 2c
	ל	AND	254c	
	ל	TO	513a	5 ad
	ל	TO	513b	5 ba
	מן	OUT OF	579b	2 ac
	סגלה	PROPERTY	688c	1
	עם	PEOPLE	766c	1
	קול	VOICE	877b	3 b
19 6	גוי	NATION	156c	1
	דבר	SPEAK	181a	3 b
	דבר	WORD	183b	3 2
	כהן	PRIEST-KING	463a	1
	ממלכה	KINGDOM	575b	1
	קדוש	HOLY	872d	2 b
19 7	דבר	WORD	182d	12a
	זקן	OLD	278d	2 b
	פנה	FACE	817c	2 4b g
	שום	TO PLACE	963b	1 b
19 8	דבר	WORD	182b	1 1c
	יחדו	TOGETHER	403c	B
	ענה	ANSWER	772d	1 d
	שוב	TURN BACK	999b	3
19 9	אמן	CONFIRM	53b	2 c
	אנכי	I	59c	
	דבר	SPEAK	181b	3 e
	עבי	THICKNESS	716a	
	עבור	FOR THE SAKE OF	721b	2

Ch	v.	Heb	Eng	Page	Sec
		עם	WITH	767d	1 d
19	10	ענן	CLOUD	778a	1 a
		הלך	WALK	231a	1 d3 ga
		יום	DAY	400a	7 a l
		כבס	WASH	460a	1
		מחר	TO-MORROW	564a	1 b
		קדש	BE SET APART	873b	4 b
		שמלה	WRAPPER	971a	
19	11	הר	MOUNTAIN	249b	1 a
		יום	DAY	401a	7 i
		ירד	GO DOWN	433b	2
		כון	BE READY	466a	3
		ל	TO	*517a	6 a
		סיני	SINAI	696a	
19	12	גבל	BOUND	148b	
		מות	DIE	559d	2 a
		נגע	TOUCH	619a	1 a
		סביב	ROUND ABOUT	687a	1 b
		קצה	END	892b	2
		שמר	KEEP	1037b	1
19	13	אם	IF	50a	1 b1
		יובל	RAM	385c	1
		ירה	SHOOT	435b	3
		ירה	SHOT THROUGH	435a	
		משך	DRAW	604c	4
		נגע	TOUCH	619a	1 a
		סקל	STONE	709c	
19	14	ירד	COME DOWN	432d	1 a
		כבס	WASH	460a	1
		מן	FROM	578d	1 a
		קדש	BE SET APART	873b	4 b
		שמלה	WRAPPER	971a	
19	15	כון	BE READY	466a	3
		ל	TO	517a	6 b
		נגש	DRAW NEAR	620d	1
		שלש	THREE	1025d	1 b
19	16	בקר	MORNING	134a	1 f
		ברק	LIGHTNING	140c	1
		היה	COME TO PASS	224d	2 al al
		היה	BECOME	225c	2 la
		היה	BECOME	225c	2 la
		חזק	BE FIRM	304b	1 l
		חזק	STRONG	305c	1 c
		מחנה	ENCAMPMENT	334a	1 a
		חרד	TREMBLE	353c	2
		כבד	HEAVY	458a	1 a
		ענן	CLOUD	778a	1 a
		קול	VOICE	877a	2 b
		שפר	HORN	1051d	
19	17	מחנה	ENCAMPMENT	334a	1 a
		יצא	CAUSE TO GO	424c	1 b
		יצב	STATION ONESELF	426b	A
		תחתי	LOWER	1066c	
19	18	אש	FIRE	77c	2
		הר	MOUNTAIN	249b	1 a
		הר	MOUNTAIN	*249b	1 a
		חרד	TREMBLE	353b	1
		ירד	GO DOWN	433b	2
		כבשן	KILN	461c	
		כל	ALL	481b	1 a
		סיני	SINAI	696a	
		עשן	SMOKE	798c	2 a
		עשן	SMOKE	798c	1 a
		פנה	FACE	818c	26 c c
19	19	הלך	WALK	232c	13
		הלך	WALK	233d	14d
		חזק	BE FIRM	304b	1 1f
		קול	VOICE	877a	1 b
		שפר	HORN	1051d	
19	20	הר	MOUNTAIN	249b	1 a
		ירד	GO DOWN	433b	2
		סיני	SINAI	696a	
		קרא	CALL	895d	5 a
		ראש	HEAD	910d	2 a
19	21	הרס	THROW DOWN	248d	3
		ירד	COME DOWN	432d	1 a
		עוד	BEAR WITNESS	730a	3
		רב	MUCH	913a	1 c
19	22	כהן	PRIEST-KING	463a	1
		נגש	DRAW NEAR	621a	
		פרץ	BREAK THROUGH	829c	6
		קדש	BE SET APART	873c	4
19	23	גבל	BOUND	148b	
		הר	MOUNTAIN	249b	1 a
		הר	MOUNTAIN	249d	1 a
		יכל	BE ABLE	407c	1 a
		סיני	SINAI	696a	
		עוד	BEAR WITNESS	730a	3
		עלה	GO UP	748b	1 c
		קדש	BE SET APART	873b	4
19	24	הלך	WALK	234b	1 5f 3
		הרס	THROW DOWN	248d	3
		ירד	COME DOWN	432d	1 a
		כהן	PRIEST-KING	463a	1
		עלה	GO UP	748c	2 b
		פרץ	BREAK THROUGH	829c	6
19	25	אמר	SAY	56a	1
		ירד	COME DOWN	432d	1 a
20	1	דבר	SPEAK	180d	2
20	2	אנכי	I	59c	
		בית	HOUSE	109a	1 ae 9
		יהוה	YAHWEH	218d	2 la
		יהוה	YAHWEH	219b	2 2d
		יצא	CAUSE TO GO	424c	1 b
		עבד	SLAVE	713d	1
20	3	אחר	ANOTHER	29d	
		אלהים	GOD	43c	1 d
		היה	BE	227c	3 4d c
		חוץ	THE OUTSIDE	*300a	1 b
		לא	NOT	518c	1 aa
		פנה	FACE	818d	27 a b
20	4	ארץ	EARTH	76a	1 b
		ארץ	EARTH	76a	1 b
		מי	WATER	565c	1 e
		תמונה	LIKENESS	568b	
		מן	FROM	578d	1 c
		מעל	ABOVE	751c	1 a
		על	HEIGHT	752c	1
		עשה	DO	794c	2 1c
		פסל	IDOL	820d	
		שמי	HEAVENS	1030a	1 a
		תחת	UNDERNEATH	1065b	1
		תחת	UNDERNEATH	1066b	3 2b
20	5	אל	GOD	42d	6 d
		יהוה	YAHWEH	218d	2 1a
		יהוה	YAHWEH	219b	2 2d
		ים	SEA	*411a	5
		ל	TO	513d	5 cb g
		עון	INIQUITY	731a	1 c1
		פקד	ATTEND TO	823c	A 3
		קנא	JEALOUS	888d	
		רבע	PERTAINING TO THE FOURTH	918a	
		שנא	HATE	971d	3
		שחה	BOW DOWN	1005c	3
		שלש	PERTAINING TO THE THIRD	1026d	
		שם	NAME	*1028c	3
20	6	אהב	LOVE	13a	3
		אלף	THOUSAND	49a	1 a
		חסד	GOODNESS	339b	2 3b
		ל	TO	513d	5 cb g
		עשה	DO	794b	13
		שמר	KEEP	1037a	3 c
20	7	יהוה	YAHWEH	218a	1
		יהוה	YAHWEH	218d	2 1a
		ל	TO	515a	5 ha
		נקה	BE CLEAN	667c	2
		נשא	LIFT	670d	1 b 7
		שוא	EMPTINESS	996a	1
		שם	NAME	1028b	3
20	8	זכר	REMEMBER	270a	1 g
		יום	DAY	398d	2 i
		קדש	BE SET APART	873a	2
		שבת	SABBATH	992b	1 b
		שבת	SABBATH	992b	1 a
20	9	יום	DAY	398b	2 a
		מלאכה	WORK	522a	3 b
		עבד	WORK	713a	1
		עשה	DO	793d	1 1a l
		שבת	SABBATH	992b	1 a
20	10	אמה	MAID	51a	1
		ב	IN	88c	13
		בהמה	BEAST	97a	2
		בן	SON	120a	1
		גר	SOJOURNER	158b	2
		ה	THE	209a	2 b
		יהוה	YAHWEH	218d	2 1a
		ו	AND	252d	1 d
		יום	DAY	398b	2 a
		מלאכה	WORK	522a	3 b
		עבד	SLAVE	713d	1
		עשה	DO	793d	1 1a l
		שבת	SABBATH	992b	1 a
		שבת	SABBATH	992b	1 a
		שער	GATE	1045a	2 c
20	11	ברך	BLESS	139a	2 b
		יהוה	YAHWEH	218d	2 1a
		יום	DAY	398c	2 d
		יום	DAY	398d	2 i
		ים	SEA	411a	5
		כן	SO	487a	3 f
		נוח	REST	628b	2
		קדש	BE SET APART	873a	1 d
		שבת	SABBATH	992c	1 d
		שבת	SABBOTH	992c	1 d
		שמי	HEAVENS	1030a	1 a
20	12	אב	FATHER	3b	1
		אדמה	LAND	10a	5
		אם	MOTHER	51d	1
		ארך	BE LONG	73d	2
		יהוה	YAHWEH	218d	2 1a
		יום	DAY	399b	4 a
		כבד	MAKE HONORABLE	457d	2 a
		על	UPON	752d	2 1
20	13	לא	NOT	518c	1 aa
		ענה	ANSWER	773a	3 a
		רצח	MURDER	953d	
		רצח	MURDER	953d	
20	14	נאף	COMMIT ADUL-TERY	610c	1
		שור	A HEAD OF CATTLE	1004a	
20	15	גנב	STEAL	170b	
		עם	PEOPLE	*766b	1
		עשן	SMOKING	*798c	
		קול	VOICE	*877a	2 a
		קול	VOICE	877b	2 b
		ראה	TO SEE	*907a	1 b
		שפר	HORN	*1051d	
20	16	עד	WITNESS	729d	2 c
		עד	WITNESS	729d	2 c
		ענה	ANSWER	773a	3 a
		רע	FRIEND	946a	2
		שוא	EMPTINESS	996b	2
		שקר	DECEPTION	1055c	2
20	17	אמה	MAID	51a	1
		ו	AND	252d	1 d
		חמד	DESIRE	326b	A
		חמור	HE-ASS	331b	1
		רע	FRIEND	946a	2
		שור	A HEAD OF CATTLE	1004a	
20	18	אש	FIRE	77d	6
		דת	LAW	206d	1
		הר	MOUNTAIN	249b	1 a
		לפיד	TORCH	542b	1
		נוע	WAVE	631b	1
		עמד	STAND	764a	1 f
		ערפל	CLOUD	791d	
		עשן	SMOKING	798c	
		קול	VOICE	877a	2 a
		קול	VOICE	877a	2 b
		ראה	TO SEE	907a	1 b
		רחק	DISTANT	935c	2 a2
		שפר	HORN	1051d	
20	19	דבר	SPEAK	181b	3 e
		משה	MOSES	602c	
		שמי	HEAVENS	*1030a	2 a
20	20	בלת	NOT	117a	4 a
		חטא	MISS A GOAL OR WAY	306d	2 b
		ירא	FEAR	431a	1 a
		יראה	FEAR	432a	3
		משה	MOSES	602c	
		נסה	TEST	650b	3 a
		עבור	FOR THE SAKE OF	721a	1 b
		עבור	FOR THE SAKE OF	721b	2
20	21	משה	MOSES	602c	
		נגש	DRAW NEAR	621a	
		עמד	STAND	764a	1 f
		ערפל	CLOUD	*791d	
		רחק	DISTANT	935c	2 a2
		שם	THERE	1027b	1 b
		שם	NAME	*1028b	3
20	22	דבר	SPEAK	181b	3 e
		כה	THUS	462a	1 a
		משה	MOSES	602c	
		שמי	HEAVENS	1030a	2 a
20	23	אלהים	GOD	43c	1 d
		את	WITH	86a	1 b
		זהב	GOLD	263a	6
		כסף	SILVER	494b	7
		עלה	GO UP	748c	1 f
		עירה	NAKEDNESS	788d	1
20	24	אדמה	EARTH	9d	3
		ברך	BLESS	139a	2 a
		זבח	SLAUGHTER FOR SACRIFICE	256d	1 1 a
		זבח	SLAUGHTER FOR SACRIFICE	257a	14
		מזבח	ALTAR	258b	1
		מזבח	ALTAR	259a	8
		זכר	REMEMBER	270d	2
		כל	ALL	481c	1 b
		עלה	WHOLE BURNT OF-FERING	750d	
		מקום	STANDING PLACE	880a	4
		שלם	PEACE-OFFERING	1023c	
		שלם	PEACE-OFFERING	1023c	
		שם	NAME	1028b	3
20	25	אבן	STONE	6c	1
		בנה	BUILD	124c	1 at
		בנה	BUILD	124c	1 b
		גזית	HEWING	159b	
		מזבח	ALTAR	258b	1
		חלל	POLLUTE	320b	1 b
		חרב	SWORD	353a	3
		כי	THAT	474c	
		גוף	MOVE TO AND FRO	631d	1
		שלם	COMPLETE	*1024a	1
20	26	אשר	THAT	83c	8 b
		מזבח	ALTAR	258b	1
		מזבח	ALTAR	259a	1
		מעלה	STEP	752b	1
		על	UPON	756d	2 7b
		עירה	NAKEDNESS	*788d	1
21	1	פנה	FACE	817c	24 b g
		שום	TO PLACE	963b	1 c
		משה	JUDGMENT	1049a	4
21	2	חנם	OUT OF FAVOR	336c	A
		חפשי	FREE	344d	1
		יצא	GO OUT	422d	1 c
		כי	IF	473b	2 b
		ל	TO	512c	4 a
		עבד	WORK	713a	1
		עבד	SLAVE	713d	1
		עברי	HEBREW	720b	1 b
		קנה	ACQUIRE	889a	2
		שביעי	SEVENTH	988d	2
		שש	SIX	995c	1 a
		שנה	YEAR	1040b	
21	3	אשה	WOMAN	61b	2
		בעל	OWNER	127b	1 2
		גף	BODY	172d	1
		יצא	GO OUT	422d	1 c
		כי	IF	473b	2 b
21	4	אדון	LORD	11a	2 1b
		בת	DAUGHTER	123a	1
		גף	BODY	172d	1

EXODUS

Ch v.	Heb	Eng	Page	Sec
	ו	AND	253a	1 g
	ילד	CHILD	409b	A
	יצא	GO OUT	422d	1 c
	כי	IF	473b	2 b
21 5	אדון	LORD	11b	3 1a
	אהב	LOVE	12d	1
	אם	IF	50a	1 a5
	בן	SON	120a	1
	בן	SON	121b	2
	חפשי	FREE	344d	1
	ילד	CHILD	*409b	A
	יצא	GO OUT	422d	1 c
	כי	IF	473b	2 b
	כי	IF	473b	2 b
21 6	אדון	LORD	11a	2 1b
	אזן	EAR	23d	1
	אלהים	GOD	43b	1 a
	דלת	DOOR	195a	1
	מזוזה	DOOR-POST	265b	1
	נגש	APPROACH	*621b	
	עבד	WORK	713a	2
	עין	EYE	744a	1 a
	עולם	LONG DURATION	762a	2 a
	רצע	BORE	954a	
	מרצע	AWL	954b	
21 7	אמה	MAID	51a	1
	יצא	GO OUT	422d	1 c
	כי	IF	473b	2 b
	ל	TO	512b	4 a
	מכר	SELL	569b	
21 8	אדון	LORD	11a	2 1b
	בגד	ACT TREACHEROUSLY	93d	B
	יעד	APPOINT	416d	
	כי	IF	473b	2 b
	לא	NOT	520c	
	מכר	SELL	569b	
	משל	RULE	605d	1
	נכרי	FOREIGN	648d	1 a
	עם	PEOPLE	*766b	1
	עם	PEOPLE	767a	5 h
	פדה	RANSOM	804b	
	רע	EVIL	948a	1
21 9	יעד	APPOINT	416d	
	כי	IF	473b	2 b
	משפט	JUDGMENT	1049a	6 b
21 10	גרע	DIMINISH	175c	2
	כי	IF	473b	2 b
	כסות	COVERING	492b	1
	ענה	COHABITATION	773b	
	שאר	FLESH	985a	1 a
21 11	אין	NOT	34d	4 a
	חנם	OUT OF FAVOR	336c	A
	יצא	GO OUT	422d	1 c
	כי	IF	473b	2 b
	שלש	THREE	1025d	
	די	WHO	*1087d	1
21 12	מות	DIE	559d	2 a
	נכה	SMITE	645d	2 a
21 13	אנה	BE OPPORTUNE	58c	
	צדה	LIE IN WAIT	841b	
	שום	TO PLACE	963d	3 b
21 14	הרג	KILL	247a	1 a
	מזבח	ALTAR	258c	1
	זיד	BOIL UP	267d	2
	כי	IF	473b	2 b
	לחם	FOOD	537a	1 a
	מות	DIE	559d	2 a
	מעם	FROM WITH	769a	A
	ערמה	CRAFTINESS	791a	1
	רע	FRIEND	946a	2
21 15	אב	FATHER	3b	1
	אם	MOTHER	51d	1
	מות	DIE	559d	2 a
	נכה	SMITE	645b	1 a
21 16	גנב	STEAL	170b	
	ו	AND	252d	1 d
	יד	HAND	390d	5 c2
	מות	DIE	559d	2 a
	מכר	SELL	569b	
	מצא	FIND	593d	1 a
21 17	אב	FATHER	3b	1
	אם	MOTHER	51d	1
	ו	AND	252d	1 d
	מות	DIE	559d	2 a
	קלל	BE SLIGHT	886c	1
21 18	אבן	STONE	6b	1
	אגרף	FIST	175d	
	ו	AND	252d	1 e
	כי	IF	473b	2 b
	מות	DIE	559c	1 a1
	נכה	SMITE	645b	1 a
	נפל	FALL	657d	6
	ריב	STRIVE	936c	1
	רע	FRIEND	946a	2
	משכב	COUCH	1012d	1
21 19	הלך	WALK	235d	1 b
	חוץ	THE OUTSIDE	299d	1 bb
	כי	IF	473b	2 b
	נכה	SMITE	645b	1 a
	נקה	BE CLEAN	667b	3
	נתן	GIVE	679b	1 n
	קום	STAND	877c	1 a
	רפא	HEAL	951a	1
	שבת	CESSATION	992a	
	משענת	STAFF	1044a	
21 20	אמה	MAID	51a	1
	כי	IF	473b	2 b
	מות	DIE	559c	1 a1
	נכה	SMITE	645d	2 a
	נקם	AVENGE	668a	1 d
	נקם	AVENGE	668b	2
	שבט	ROD	987a	1 a
21 21	אך	HOWBEIT	36c	2
	יום	DAY	399d	5 a
	כי	IF	473b	2 b
	כסף	SILVER	494b	3
	נקם	AVENGE	668b	
	ברם	ONLY	*1085c	
21 22	אשה	WOMAN	61b	2
	אסון	MISCHIEF	62a	
	ב	IN	89b	3 la
	בעל	OWNER	127b	1 2
	ילד	CHILD	409b	A
	יצא	GO OUT	423c	1 h
	כי	IF	473b	2 b
	מות	DIE	559c	1 a1
	נגף	STRIKE	619d	
	נצה	STRUGGLE	663c	
	נתן	GIVE	679b	1 n
	על	UPON	753b	2 1c
	ענש	FINE	779a	
	פליל	JUDGE	813d	
	ארבע	FOUR	917a	1 c3
	שית	PUT	1011b	1
21 23	אסון	MISCHIEF	62a	
	נפש	SOUL	659d	3 c
	נתן	GIVE	679b	1 p
	תחת	INSTEAD	1065d	2 2b b
21 24	עין	EYE	745a	5
	שן	TOOTH	1042a	1
	תחת	INSTEAD	1065d	2 2b b
21 25	חבורה	STRIPE	289d	1
	פצע	BRUISE	822d	
	פצע	BRUISE	822d	
	תחת	INSTEAD	1065d	2 2b b
21 26	אמה	MAID	51a	1
	חפשי	FREE	344d	1
	ל	TO	*512c	4 a
	נכה	SMITE	645b	1 a
	שחת	GO TO RUIN	1008a	1
	תחת	INSTEAD	1065d	2 2b b
21 27	אמה	MAID	51a	1
	חפשי	FREE	344d	1
	ל	TO	*512c	4 a
	נפל	FALL	658a	1 c
	שן	TOOTH	1042a	1
	תחת	INSTEAD	1065d	2 2b b
21 28	אכל	EAT	37d	1
	את	MARK OF THE ACCUSATIVE	85a	1 a
	בעל	OWNER	127b	1 1
	בשר	FLESH	142c	1 a
	כי	IF	473b	2 b
	נגח	PUSH	618c	
	נקי	FREE FROM	667c	2
	סקל	STONE	709c	
	שור	A HEAD OF CATTLE	1004a	
21 29	בעל	OWNER	127b	1 1
	כי	IF	473b	2 b
	מות	DIE	560c	2
	מות	DIE	560c	3
	נגח	ADDICTED TO GORING	618c	
	עוד	BEAR WITNESS	730a	
	שלשם	THREE DAYS AGO	1026b	
	שמר	KEEP	1036d	2 b
	תמול	YESTERDAY	1070a	2 c
21 30	כי	IF	473b	2 b
	כפר	RANSOM	497b	1
	נתן	GIVE	679b	1 n
	על	UPON	753b	2 1c
	פדיום	RANSOM	804b	
	שית	PUT	1011c	
21 31	או	OR	15a	2
	כי	IF	473b	2 b
	נגח	PUSH	618c	
	עשה	DO	795b	1 c
	משפט	JUDGMENT	1048d	4
21 32	אדון	LORD	11a	2 1b
	אמה	MAID	51a	1
	כי	IF	473b	2 b
	כסף	SILVER	494b	8 a
	נגח	PUSH	618c	
	נתן	GIVE	679b	1 n
	שקל	SHEKEL	1053d	
21 33	בור	PIT	92c	3
	חמור	HE-ASS	331b	1
	כי	IF	473b	2 b
	כסה	COVER	491d	3
	כרה	DIG	500a	
	נפל	FALL	656d	1
	פתח	OPEN	835a	
	שור	A HEAD OF CATTLE	1004a	
	שם	THERE	1027b	3 a
21 34	בור	PIT	92c	3
	בעל	OWNER	127b	1 1
	שוב	TURN BACK	999c	4 b
21 35	חי	ALIVE	312b	1 c
	חצה	DIVIDE	345b	1
	כי	IF	473b	2 b
	מכר	SELL	569b	
	נגף	STRIKE	619d	
	רע	FRIEND	946a	2
21 36	או	OR	15a	2
	בעל	OWNER	127b	1 1
	ידע	BE MADE KNOWN	394c	1
	נגח	ADDICTED TO GORING	618c	
	שלשם	THREE DAYS AGO	1026b	
	שמר	KEEP	1036d	2 b
	תחת	INSTEAD	1065d	2 2b b
	תמול	YESTERDAY	1070a	2 c
21 37	בקר	CATTLE	133c	2
	גנב	STEAL	170b	
	טבח	SLAUGHTER	370c	1
	כי	IF	473b	2 b
	מכר	SELL	569b	
	צאן	SMALL CATTLE	838b	1 b
	ארבע	FOUR	916d	1 a3
	שה	A SHEEP	962a	1
	שור	A HEAD OF CATTLE	1004a	
	שור	A HEAD OF CATTLE	1004a	
	שלם	BE COMPLETE	1022c	3
	תחת	INSTEAD	1065d	2 2b b
22 1	אין	NOT	34c	2 c
	גנב	THIEF	170c	
	דם	BLOOD	197a	2 g
	דם	BLOOD	197b	2 i
	מחתרת	BREAKING IN	369a	
	מצא	FIND	394a	1 g2
	נכה	SMITE	646c	4
22 2	אין	NOT	34d	3
	אם	IF	49d	1 a2
	גנבה	THING STOLEN	170c	
	דם	BLOOD	197b	2 i
	זרח	RISE	280b	1 a
	מכר	SELL	569c	
	על	UPON	755d	2 5
	שמש	SUN	1039a	1
22 3	אם	IF	50a	1 a5
	גנבה	THING STOLEN	170c	
	חי	ALIVE	312b	1 c
	חמור	HE-ASS	331b	1
	מצא	FIND	394a	1 g1
	מן	FROM	582a	5 b
	שה	A SHEEP	962a	1
	שור	A HEAD OF CATTLE	1004a	
	שנים	TWO	1041a	1 b1
22 4	אחר	ANOTHER	29c	
	בער	BE BRUTISH	129c	
	בעיר	BEASTS	129c	
	בער	BE BRUTISH	129c	
	מיטב	THE BEST	406b	
	כי	IF	473b	2 b
	כרם	VINEYARD	501d	
	שדה	FIELD	961d	2 a
	שלח	SEND	1019b	3
22 5	אש	FIRE	77b	1
	אש	FIRE	77c	1
	בער	BURN	129b	
	בערה	BURNING	129c	
	גדיש	HEAP	155c	
	יצא	GO OUT	424a	2 c
	כי	IF	473b	2 b
	כרם	VINEYARD	501d	
	מצא	FIND	593b	3 d
	קמה	STANDING GRAIN	879b	
	קוץ	THORN-BUSH	881a	1
	שדה	FIELD	961d	2 a
22 6	גנב	STEAL	170c	
	גנב	THIEF	170c	
	מצא	FIND	394a	1 g2
	כלי	ARTICLE	479c	1
	מה	HOW	553d	4 a
	נתן	GIVE	679c	1 r
	רע	FRIEND	946a	2
	שמר	KEEP	1036c	1 a
	שנים	TWO	1041a	1 b1
22 7	אלהים	GOD	43b	1 a
	בעל	OWNER	127b	1 1
	גנב	THIEF	170c	
	יד	HAND	389b	1 c
	מצא	FIND	394a	1 g2
	מלאכה	WORK	522a	2
	רע	FRIEND	946a	2
	שלח	SEND	1018c	3 a
22 8	אבדה	LOST THING	2b	
	אלהים	GOD	43b	1 a
	אשר	PARTICLE OF RELATION	82d	4 d
	דבר	WORD	183d	4 5
	חמור	HE-ASS	331b	1
	עד	AS FAR AS	724a	1 a
	על	UPON	754d	2 1f h
	פשע	TRANSGRESSION	833d	1
	רע	FRIEND	946a	2
	רשע	BE WICKED	957d	1
	שה	A SHEEP	962a	1
	שלמה	GARMENT	971b	
	שור	A HEAD OF CATTLE	1004a	
	שנים	TWO	1041a	1 b1
22 9	אין	NOT	34d	4 a
	חמור	HE-ASS	331b	1
	נתן	GIVE	679c	1 r
	ראה	TO SEE	907a	1 b
	רע	FRIEND	946a	2
	שבה	TAKE CAPTIVE	985c	

Ch v.	Heb	Eng	Page	Sec
	שבר	BREAK	990d	
	שור	A HEAD OF CATTLE	1004a	
	שמר	KEEP	1036c	1 a
22 10	בעל	OWNER	127b	1 1
	מלאכה	WORK	522a	2
	לקח	TAKE	543b	4 f
	רע	FRIEND	946a	2
	שבועה	OATH	989d	1 a
	שלח	SEND	1018c	3 a
22 11	בעל	OWNER	127b	1 1
	גנב	STEAL	170c	
	גנב	STEAL	170c	
	מעם	FROM WITH	769c	C
22 12	אם	IF	50a	1 a5
	טרף	TEAR	382d	
	טרף	TEAR	383a	1
	טרפה	ANIMAL TORN	383c	1
22 13	עד	WITNESS	729c	1 1
	בעל	OWNER	127b	1 1
	מעם	FROM WITH	768d	A
	רע	FRIEND	946a	2
	שאל	ASK	981c	1 b
22 14	שבר	BREAK	990d	
	בעל	OWNER	127b	1 1
	שכר	HIRE	969a	1
	שכור	HIRED	969b	1
22 15	איש	MAN	35d	
	ארש	BETROTH	77a	
	בתולה	VIRGIN	143d	
	מהר	ACQUIRE BY PAYING PURCHASE	555c	
	פתה	BE SIMPLE	834c	1
	שכב	LIE DOWN	1012b	3
22 16	אם	IF	50a	1 a5
	בתולה	VIRGIN	144a	
	כסף	SILVER	494c	9
	מאן	REFUSE	549a	
	מהר	PURCHASE-PRICE	555c	
	שקל	WEIGH	1053c	2
22 17	חיה	LIVE	311c	1
	כשף	PRACTICE SORCERY	506c	
22 18	מות	DIE	559d	2 a
	שכב	LIE DOWN	1012b	3
22 19	אלהים	GOD	43c	1 d
	בד	SEPARATION	94c	1 b
	בלת	EXCEPT	116c	2
	חרם	BAN	*355d	
	חרם	BAN	356a	1
22 20	גר	SOJOURNER	158b	1
	גר	SOJOURNER	158b	1
	ינה	OPPRESS	413b	
	לחץ	OPPRESS	537d	2
22 21	אלמנה	WIDOW	48b	
	יתום	ORPHAN	450c	
	ענה	BE BOWED DOWN	776b	1
22 22	אם	IF	50a	1 a5
	כי	THAT	472c	1 db
	כיאם	THAT IF	474c	1 a
	ענה	BE BOWED DOWN	776b	1
	צעק	CRY	858c	1 b
	צעק	CRY	858d	2
22 23	אלמנה	WIDOW	48b	
	אף	NOSE	60b	3
	בן	SON	121b	2
	הרג	KILL	247b	2
	חרה	BURN	354a	2 a
	יתום	ORPHAN	450c	
22 24	כסף	SILVER	494d	9
	ל	TO	513a	5 ad
	לוה	BORROW	531a	
	נשה	LEND	674c	
	נשך	INTEREST	675b	
	על	UPON	753b	2 1c
	עם	WITH	768a	2
	עני	POOR	776d	1
22 25	בוא	COME	98a	1 i
	חבל	BIND	286b	2
	עד	AS FAR AS	724c	1 2a b
	רע	FRIEND	946a	2
	שלמה	GARMENT	971b	
	שוב	TURN BACK	999a	1 d
22 26	חנן	GRACIOUS	337a	
	כסות	COVERING	492b	1
	עור	SKIN	736a	1
	צעק	CRY	858c	1 b
	שמלה	WRAPPER	971a	
22 27	אלהים	GOD	43b	1 a
	ארר	CURSE	76c	
	נשיא	PRINCE	672b	1
	קלל	BE SLIGHT	886c	2
22 28	אחר	DELAY	29b	2
	בכור	FIRST-BORN	114b	1 d
	דמע	JUICE	199c	
	מלאה	FULL PRODUCE	571b	
22 29	אם	MOTHER	52a	3
	נתן	GIVE	679b	11
	שור	A HEAD OF CATTLE	1004a	
	שמיני	EIGHTH	1033b	
22 30	בשר	FLESH	142c	1 a
	טרפה	ANIMAL TORN	383c	1
	כלב	DOG	476d	A
	ל	TO	513a	5 ad
	קדש	APARTNESS	872b	4 b
	שדה	FIELD	961b	1 b
	שלך	THROW	1021a	1 a

Ch v.	Heb	Eng	Page	Sec
23 1	חמס	VIOLENCE	329c	
	נשא	LIFT	670d	1 b 7
	עד	WITNESS	729d	2 c
	עם	WITH	767c	1 a
	רשע	WICKED	957b	1
	שוא	EMPTINESS	996b	2
	שית	PUT	1011a	1
	שמע	REPORT	1034d	
23 2	היה	BECOME	225d	2 1b
	נטה	BEND	640b	3 a
	נטה	BEND	641a	3 g
	על	UPON	754c	2 1f e
	ענה	ANSWER	773a	3 a
	רב	MUCH	913b	1 c
	ריב	STRIFE	937a	3
	רעה	MISERY	949b	2
23 3	דל	POOR	195d	
	הדר	HONOUR	214a	2
	ריב	STRIFE	937a	3
23 4	איב	BE HOSTILE TO	33c	
	חמור	HE-ASS	331b	1
	פגע	MEET	803b	1
	שוב	TURN BACK	999a	1 d
	תעה	ERR	1073b	1
23 5	איב	BE HOSTILE TO	33c	
	חדל	CEASE	293a	2
	חמור	HE-ASS	331b	1
	מן	FROM	583a	7 b
	משא	LOAD	672c	1
	עזב	LEAVE	737b	1 i
	עזב	LEAVE	737c	3
	עם	WITH	767b	1 a
	ראה	TO SEE	907a	2 3
	רבץ	LIE DOWN	918b	
	שנא	HATE	971c	3
23 6	אביון	NEEDY	2d	
	נטה	BEND	641a	3 g
	ריב	STRIFE	937a	3
	משפט	JUDGEMNT	1049a	5
	משפט	JUDGMENT	1049a	5
23 7	דבר	WORD	183b	3 1
	הרג	KILL	247a	1 a
	מן	FROM	578a	1 a
	נקי	CLEAN	667c	1
	צדק	DECLARE RIGHTEOUS	842d	2
	צדיק	JUST	843a	2
	רחק	BE DISTANT	935a	
	רשע	WICKED	957b	1
23 8	ו	AND	252b	1 b
	סלף	TWIST	701b	1
	עור	MAKE BLIND	734c	
	פקח	SEEING	824d	
	צדיק	JUST	843a	2
	צדיק	JUST	843a	1 a
	שחד	BRIBE	1005a	
	שחד	BRIBE	1005a	
23 9	גר	SOJOURNER	158b	2
	גר	SOJOURNER	158b	1
	לחץ	OPPRESS	537d	2
	נפש	SOUL	661a	6 g
23 10	אסף	GATHER	62b	1 c
	תבואה	PRODUCT	100a	1
	זרע	SOW	281c	1 b
23 11	אביון	NEEDY	2d	
	זית	OLIVE TREE	268c	1
	חיה	LIVING THING	312c	1 b
	יתר	REMAINDER	451d	1 a
	כרם	VINEYARD	501d	
	נטש	LEAVE	643d	1
	שדה	FIELD	961b	1 c
	שביעי	SEVENTH	988d	2
	שמט	LET DROP	1030c	
23 12	אמה	MAID	51a	1
	גר	SOJOURNER	158b	2
	חמור	HE-ASS	331b	1
	יום	DAY	398b	2 a
	נוח	REST	628b	2
	נפש	REFRESH ONESELF	661c	1 a 1
	עשה	DO	793d	1 a 1
	מעשה	DEED	795d	1 b1
	שבת	CEASE	991d	2 b
	שבת	SABBATH	992b	1
	שש	SIX	995c	1 a
	שור	A HEAD OF CATTLE	1004a	
23 13	אלהים	GOD	43c	1 d
	זכר	REMEMBER	270d	3 a
	על	UPON	752d	2 1
	פה	MOUTH	805a	2 a
	שם	NAME	1028d	4
	שמר	KEEP	1037b	1
23 14	חגג	MAKE PILGRIMAGE	290d	1
	חג	FESTIVAL-GATHERING	290d	1
	רגל	FOOT	920a	2
	שנה	YEAR	1040b	
23 15	אביב	ABIB	1b	2
	חג	FESTIVAL-GATHERING	291a	1 b2
	חג	FESTIVAL-GATHERING	291b	1 b
	חדש	NEW MOON	294d	2 b1
	מועד	APPOINTED TIME	417c	1 a
	מועד	APPOINTED TIME	*417c	1 b
	יצא	GO OUT	422d	1 a
	ל	TO	517a	6 a

Ch v.	Heb	Eng	Page	Sec
	מצה	UNLEAVENED BREAD	695b	
	מצה	UNLEAVENED BREAD	695b	
	פנה	FACE	816c	2 2a
	פנה	FACE	816d	2 2a
	צוה	CHARGE	846a	3
	ריקם	EMPTILY	938b	1
	שמר	KEEP	1036c	3 a
23 16	אסף	GATHER	62b	1 c
	אסיף	INGATHERING	63b	
	בכורים	FIRST-FRUITS	114c	
	זרע	SOW	281c	1 c
	חג	FESTIVAL-GATHERING	291a	1 b2
	חג	FESTIVAL-GATHERING	291a	1 b2
	יצא	GO OUT	423a	1 e
	מעשה	DEED	795d	1 b
	מעשה	DEED	795d	1 b1
	קציר	HARVESTING	894a	3
	שנה	YEAR	1040b	
23 17	אדון	LORD	11a	1 2
	זכור	MALE	271d	
	חג	FESTIVAL-GATHERING	290d	1
	פנה	FACE	816c	2 1a
	פנה	FACE	816d	2 2a
	ראה	TO SEE	908b	1 b
	שנה	YEAR	1040b	
23 18	בקר	MORNING	133d	1 a
	דם	BLOOD	197d	3 b
	זבח	SLAUGHTER FOR SACRIFICE	256d	1 1 a
	זבח	SACRIFICE	257c	2 2
	חג	FESTIVAL-GATHERING	291a	1 b2
	חלב	FAT	316d	2 b
	חמץ	THAT WHICH IS LEAVENED	329d	
	ל	TO	517a	6 c
	לון	LODGE	533d	1 c
	על	UPON	755c	2 4c
23 19	אדמה	GROUND	9c	1
	אם	MOTHER	52a	3
	בכורים	FIRST-FRUITS	114c	
	בשל	BOIL	143a	1
	גדי	KID	152a	
	יהוה	YAHWEH	218d	2 1a
	חלב	MILK	316c	A 2
	ראשית	BEGINNING	912b	1 b
23 20	כן	ESTABLISH	466b	2 a
	מלאך	MESSENGER	521d	3
	פנה	FACE	817c	2 4c a
	מקום	STANDING PLACE	880a	3 b
	שמר	KEEP	1037a	4 a
23 21	ישב	DWELL	443b	3
	כי	BECAUSE	474b	3 d
	מרה	BE REBELLIOUS	598b	
	נשא	LIFT	671c	3 c
	פשע	TRANSGRESSION	833c	3 c
	קול	VOICE	877b	3 b
	שם	NAME	1028c	3
	שמר	KEEP	1037b	1
23 22	איב	BE HOSTILE TO	33c	
	איב	BE HOSTILE TO	33c	
	ו	AND	254c	5 a
	כי	BECAUSE	474b	3 d
	צור	SHOW HOSTILITY TO	849a	
	צרר	SHEW HOSTILITY TOWARD	865d	
	קול	VOICE	877b	3 b
23 23	אמרי	AMORITES	57c	2 e
	בוא	COME	99b	2
	יבוסי	JEBUSITE	101a	1
	הלך	WALK	231c	1 1d 5e
	חוי	HIVITE	295d	2
	חתי	HITTITE	366d	2 a
	כחד	HIDE	470c	2
	כנעני	CANAANITE	489a	2 b
	מלאך	MESSENGER	521d	3
23 24	הרם	THROW DOWN	248d	
	מצבה	PILLAR	663b	1 c
	מעשה	DEED	795d	1 a2
	שבר	BREAK	991a	
	שחה	BOW DOWN	1005c	3
23 25	ברך	BLESS	139a	2 b
	יהוה	YAHWEH	218d	2 1b
	מחלה	SICKNESS	318b	
	סור	TURN ASIDE	694b	1
	קרב	INWARD PART	899a	1 f1
23 26	מלא	FILL	570d	3
	מספר	NUMBER	709a	1 a
	עקר	BARREN	785d	
	שכל	BE BEREAVED	1013d	2 b1
23 27	אימה	TERROR	34a	
	המם	CONFUSE	243a	2
	נתן	GIVE	681a	3 a
	ערף	BACK OF NECK	791b	1
23 28	גרש	DRIVE OUT	177a	
	חוי	HIVITE	295d	2
	חתי	HITTITE	366d	2 a
	כנעני	CANAANITE	489a	2 b
	פנה	FACE	818a	2 5a e
	צרעה	HORNETS	864a	

EXODUS

Ch	v.	Heb	Eng	Page	Sec
23	29	גרש	DRIVE OUT	177a	
		חיה	LIVING THING	312c	1 b
		פן	LEST	814d	1
		רבב	BECOME MANY	912d	1
		שדה	FIELD	961b	1 c
		שממה	WASTE	1031b	
23	30	גרש	DRIVE OUT	177a	
		מעט	A FEW	590a	1 d
		נחל	TAKE AS A POSSESSION	635c	1 a
		עד	UNTIL	725a	2 la b
		פנה	FACE	818b	26a
		פרה	BEAR FRUIT	826a	1
23	31	גבול	BORDER	147d	1 a
		גרש	DRIVE OUT	177a	
		ים	SEA	410d	1
		מן	FROM	581d	5 a
		נהר	STREAM	625d	1
		סוף	REEDS	693b	2 a
		פלשתי	PHILISTINE	814c	
		שית	PUT	1011b	2 c
23	32	ברית	COVENANT	136b	11
		ברית	COVENANT	136c	15
		כרת	CUT	503d	4
		צחק	LAUGHTER	850c	
23	33	חטא	MISS A GOAL OR WAY	307c	2
		מוקש	BAIT	430d	
		כי	BECAUSE	474b	3 d
		פן	LEST	814d	1
24	1	אהרן	AARON	14d	
		זקן	OLD	278d	2 b
		זקן	OLD	*278d	2 b
		נדב	NADAB	621c	
		עלה	GO UP	748b	2 b
		רחק	DISTANT	935c	2 a1
		שבעים	SEVENTY	988c	1 e
		שחה	BOW DOWN	1005c	2 c
24	2	נגש	DRAW NEAR	620d	1
		נגש	DRAW NEAR	620d	1
		עם	PEOPLE	*766b	1
24	3	דבר	WORD	183a	22
		קול	VOICE	877a	1 a
		משפט	JUDGMENT	1049a	4
24	4	בנה	BUILD	124c	1 at
		בקר	MORNING	134b	1 h
		דבר	WORD	183a	22
		הר	MOUNTAIN	249d	1 a
		מזבח	ALTAR	258b	1
		מצבה	PILLAR	663b	1 c
		עשר	TEN	797b	1
		שבט	TRIBE	987a	2 a
		שנים	TWO	1041b	2
		תחת	UNDERNEATH	1065c	2 1a
24	5	זבח	SACRIFICE	*257c	2 1
		זבח	SACRIFICE	257d	2 5
		עלה	GO UP	749d	8
		עלה	WHOLE BURNT OFFERING	750d	
		פר	YOUNG BULL	830d	2 a
		שלח	SEND	1018b	1 a
		שלם	PEACE-OFFERING	1023c	
		שלם	PEACE-OFFERING	1023c	
		שלם	PEACE-OFFERING	1023c	
24	6	אגן	BASIN	8c	1
		דם	BLOOD	197c	3 b
		דם	BLOOD	197d	3 b
		זרק	TO TOSS	284c	1 b
		חצי	HALF	345c	1
24	7	ברית	COVENANT	136c	2 2c
		ברית	COVENANT	136d	2 2c
		ו	AND	252b	1 b
		ספר	MISSIVE	707b	3 c
		קרא	CALL	895c	1
24	8	ברית	COVENANT	136c	2 2c
		דבר	WORD	183a	22
		דם	BLOOD	197c	3 b
		דם	BLOOD	197d	3 a
		הנה	BEHOLD	244a	A
		זבח	SACRIFICE	258a	2 5
		זרק	TO TOSS	284c	1 b
		כרת	CUT	503d	4
		על	UPON	754a	2 1f
24	9	זקן	OLD	278d	2 b
		זקן	OLD	*278d	2 b
		נדב	NADAB	621c	1 e
		שבעים	SEVENTY	988c	1 e
24	10	אלהים	GOD	44b	4 ba
		מהר	PURITY	372d	1
		כ	LIKE	453d	1 b
		ל	TO	514b	5 fb
		לבנה	BRICK	527c	3
		ספיר	SAPPHIRE	705d	
		עצם	BONE	782d	3
		מעשה	DEED	796a	2 a1
		רגל	FOOT	919d	1 b
24	11	אכל	EAT	37b	1
		אציל	NOBLES	69c	2
		חזה	SEE	302b	1 a
		שלח	SEND	1018d	3 b
24	12	אבן	STONE	6c	2
		ירה	DIRECT	435c	5 b
		תורה	LAW	436a	2 b1
		כתב	WRITE	507b	1 a
		לוח	TABLET	531d	1
		עלה	GO UP	748c	2 b
		מצוה	COMMANDMENT	846b	2 a
24	13	אלהים	GOD	44a	3 b
		יהושוע	JOSHUA	221c	1
		הר	MOUNTAIN	249d	1 a
		הר	MOUNTAIN	249d	1 a
		הר	MOUNTAIN	249d	1 a
		עלה	GO UP	748b	1 d
		שרת	SERVE	1058a	1 c
24	14	בעל	LORD	127c	1 5a
		דבר	WORD	183d	4 5
		זה	THIS	261d	6 a
		זקן	OLD	278d	2 b
		חור	HUR	301b	1
		ל	TO	515a	5 ha
		מי	WHO	567b	G
		עד	UNTIL	725a	2 la b
		שוב	TURN BACK	997b	3 b
24	15	כסה	COVER	491d	4
		עלה	GO UP	748b	1 c
		ענן	CLOUD	778a	1 a
24	16	הר	MOUNTAIN	249b	1 a
		כבוד	GLORY	458d	2 c1
		כסה	COVER	491d	4
		סיני	SINAI	696a	
		שכן	SETTLE DOWN	1015a	1 c
24	17	אש	FIRE	77c	1
		ב	IN	88b	1 1
		כבוד	GLORY	458d	2 c1
		מראה	VISION	909c	1 b
		ראש	HEAD	910d	2 a
24	18	ב	IN	88b	1 1
		היה	BE	226d	3 2
		יום	DAY	398b	1
		לילה	NIGHT	538d	1
		עלה	GO UP	748b	1 c
		ארבעים	FORTY	917b	1 a
25	2	את	WITH	86c	4 a
		לב	HEART	525a	24
		נדב	INCITE	621c	
		תרומה	OFFERING	929b	5
		תרומה	OFFERING	929b	7
25	3	זהב	GOLD	263a	6
		זהב	GOLD	263c	1
		תרומה	OFFERING	929b	5
25	4	ארגמן	PURPLE THREAD	71b	1 a
		עז	SHE-GOAT	777c	4
		שני	SCARLET	1040d	
		שש	BYSSUS	1058c	
		תכלת	VIOLET THREAD	1067b	1 a
		תולעה	WORM	1069a	2
25	5	אדם	BE RED	10a	
		איל	RAM	18a	3
		עור	SKIN	736b	2
		עץ	TREE	781d	2 a
		שטה	ACACIA	1008d	
		תחש	SEALSKIN	1065a	
25	6	מאור	LUMINARY	22d	
		בשם	SPICE	142a	1
		משחה	OINTMENT	603c	1
		סם	SPICE	702c	
		קטרת	SMOKE	882d	2
		שמן	OIL	1032c	2 g
		שמן	OIL	1032c	2 g
25	7	אבן	STONE	6d	3
		אבן	STONE	6d	3
		אבן	STONE	6d	3
		אפוד	EPHOD	65c	1 b
		חשן	BREAST-PIECE	365d	
		מלוא	SETTING	571b	1
		שהם	CARNELIAN	996a	
25	8	שכן	SETTLE DOWN	1015b	2 c
		תוך	MIDST	1063d	
25	9	אשר	PARTICLE OF RELATION	82d	6 b
		תבנית	PATTERN	125d	2
		תבנית	PATTERN	125d	2
		כלי	UTENSIL	480a	2 f
		כן	SO	486c	2 cc
		ראה	TO SEE	908d	1 a2
		משכן	DWELLING-PLACE	1015c	2 c
		משכן	DWELLING-PLACE	1015d	2 c
25	10	אמה	CUBIT	52b	1
		אמה	CUBIT	52b	1
		אמה	CUBIT	52c	1
		ארך	LENGTH	73d	A
		ארון	CHEST	75b	3 a
		זרת	SPAN	*285a	
		עץ	TREE	781d	2 a
		קומה	HEIGHT	879b	3
		רחב	WIDTH	931b	1
		שטה	ACACIA	1008d	
25	11	בית	HOUSE	110c	8 a
		זהב	GOLD	263a	6
		זהב	GOLD	263b	8
		זהב	GOLD	263c	2 a
		זהב	GOLD	263d	2 c
		זר	CIRCLET	267a	
		חוץ	THE OUTSIDE	299d	1 bd
		מהור	CLEAN	373a	2
		סביב	ROUND ABOUT	687a	1 b
		צפה	LAY OUT	860a	
		צפה	LAY OUT	860a	
25	12	זהב	GOLD	263d	2 b
		טבעת	SIGNET	371d	3
		יצק	CAST	427b	2
		נתן	PUT	680b	2 a
		פעם	FOOT	822a	1 c
		צלע	RIB	854b	6
		ארבע	FOUR	916d	1 a1
25	13	בד	PART	94d	3 c
		זהב	GOLD	263d	2 c
		צפה	LAY OUT	860a	
		שטה	ACACIA	1008d	
25	14	ארון	CHEST	75b	3 b
		בד	PART	94d	3 c
		בוא	COME	99b	1 f
		צלע	RIB	854b	6
25	15	בד	PART	94d	3 c
		סור	TURN ASIDE	694a	3
25	16	ארון	CHEST	75c	3 g
		נתן	PUT	680b	2 a
		עדות	TESTIMONY	730b	1
25	17	אמה	CUBIT	52b	1
		אמה	CUBIT	52c	1
		ארך	LENGTH	73d	A
		זהב	GOLD	263b	8
		זהב	GOLD	263c	
		מהור	CLEAN	373a	2
		כפרת	PROPITIATORY	498c	
25	18	זהב	GOLD	263c	2 a
		כפרת	PROPITIATORY	498c	
		כרוב	CHERUB	500d	4 a
		עשה	DO	794c	2 1g
		קצה	END	892c	1
25	19	זה	THIS	262a	6 e
		כפרת	PROPITIATORY	498c	
		כרוב	CHERUB	500d	4 a
		מן	OUT OF	579b	2 ba
		קצה	END	892c	1
		קצה	END	892c	1
25	20	אח	BROTHER	26c	4
		אל	TO	39d	3 a
		כנף	WING	489c	1 c
		כפרת	PROPITIATORY	498c	
		כרוב	CHERUB	500d	4 a
		סכך	OVERSHADOW	697a	1
		מעל	ABOVE	751d	2 ca
		פנה	FACE	816a	13
		פרש	SPREAD OUT	831a	1
25	21	כפרת	PROPITIATORY	498c	
		כרוב	CHERUB	500d	4 a
		נתן	PUT	680b	2 a
		עדות	TESTIMONY	730b	1
		מעל	ABOVE	752a	2 d
25	22	ארון	CHEST	75c	3 g
		בין	INTERVAL	107d	D
		דבר	SPEAK	181b	3 d
		יעד	MEET AT AN APPOINTED PLACE	416d	1
		כפרת	PROPITIATORY	498c	
		כרוב	CHERUB	500d	4 a
		עדות	TESTIMONY	730b	1
		על	UPON	758c	4 2a
		צוה	CHARGE	846a	1
25	23	אמה	CUBIT	52b	1
		אמה	CUBIT	52b	1
		קומה	HEIGHT	879b	3
		שלחן	TABLE	1020b	3
25	24	זהב	GOLD	263a	6
		זהב	GOLD	263b	8
		זהב	GOLD	263d	2 c
		זר	CIRCLET	267a	
		מהור	CLEAN	373a	2
		סביב	ROUND ABOUT	687a	1 b
25	25	זר	CIRCLET	267a	
		מפח	SPAN	381c	
		סביב	ROUND ABOUT	687a	1 b
		מסגרת	BORDER	689d	1
25	26	נתן	PUT	680b	2 a
		פאה	CORNER	802a	1
		רגל	FOOT	919d	1 e
25	27	בד	PART	94d	3 c
		בית	HOUSE	109c	3
		מסגרת	BORDER	689d	1
25	28	עמה	CLOSE BY	769c	A
		בד	PART	94d	3 c
		זהב	GOLD	263d	2 c
		נשא	LIFT	671d	3
		מקדש	SACRED PLACE	874a	3
25	29	הם	THEY	241d	8 d
		מהור	CLEAN	373a	2
		כף	PAN	497a	4 b
		נסך	POUR OUT	650d	
		מנקיה	SACRIFICIAL BOWL	667d	
		קערה	DISH	891a	
		קשוה	JAR	903b	
25	30	לחם	FOOD	537b	1 a
		תמיד	CONTINUITY	556c	1 a
		נתן	PUT	680b	2 a
25	31	גביע	CUP	149b	
		מהור	CLEAN	373a	2
		ירך	BASE	438a	2
		כפתור	KNOB	499c	2
		מן	OUT OF	579b	2 ba
		מנורה	LAMPSTAND	633b	3
		עשה	DO	795b	2 a
		פרח	BUD	827b	
		קנה	STALK	889d	4 d
		מקשה	HAMMERED WORK	904d	
25	32	יצא	GO OUT	423d	1 h
		מנורה	LAMPSTAND	633b	3
		צד	SIDE	841a	

Ch	v.	Heb	Eng	Page	Sec
25	33	קנה	STALK	889d	4 e
		גביע	CUP	149b	
		יצא	GO OUT	423d	1 h
		כן	SO	485d	1 a
		כפתור	KNOB	499c	2
		פרח	BUD	827b	
		שקד	CUPS SHAPED LIKE ALMOND	1052b	
25	34	גביע	CUP	149b	
		כפתור	KNOB	499c	2
		פרח	BUD	827b	
		ארבע	FOUR	917a	1 b1
		שקד	CUPS SHAPED LIKE ALMOND	1052b	
25	35	יצא	GO OUT	423d	1 h
		כפתור	KNOB	499c	2
		מן	OUT OF	579b	2 ba
25	36	טהור	CLEAN	373a	2
		כל	ALL	481b	1 a
		כפתור	KNOB	499c	2
		מן	OUT OF	579b	2 ba
		מקשה	HAMMERED WORK	904d	
25	37	אור	BECOME LIGHT	21b	1
		נר	LAMP	632d	
		עבר	REGION ACROSS	719d	2
		עלה	GO UP	749d	4
		על	UPON	758a	2 9
		שבע	SEVEN	988a	1 b
25	38	מחתה	FIRE-HOLDER	367b	1
		טהור	CLEAN	373a	2
		מלקחים	TONGS	544c	2
25	39	טהור	CLEAN	373a	2
		כלי	UTENSIL	480a	2 f
25	40	ב	IN	90d	3 8
		תבנית	PATTERN	125d	2
		הר	MOUNTAIN	249b	1 a
		הר	MOUNTAIN	250a	1 a
		ראה	TO SEE	907d	7 c
		ראה	TO SEE	909a	1
26	1	ארגמן	PURPLE THREAD	71b	1 a
		חשב	THINK	363b	1 5
		יריעה	CURTAIN	438c	
		כרוב	CHERUB	500d	4 b
		מעשה	DEED	796a	2 a1
		שזר	BE TWISTED	1005a	
		שני	SCARLET	1040d	
		שש	BYSSUS	1058c	
		תכלת	VIOLET THREAD	1067b	1 a
		תולעה	WORM	1069a	2
26	2	אמה	CUBIT	52c	1
		ארך	LENGTH	73d	A
		יריעה	CURTAIN	438c	
		מדה	SIZE	551c	2
		עשרים	TWENTY	797d	1 2a
		ארבע	FOUR	*916a	1 a1
		רחב	WIDTH	931d	
		שמנה	EIGHT	1033a	3 c
26	3	אחות	ANOTHER	28a	5
		אשה	WOMAN	61c	4
		חבר	UNITE	288b	1 b
		חמש	FIVE	331d	1 c
26	4	חברת	A THING THAT JOINS	289a	
		מחברת	THING JOINED	289c	1
		ללי	LOOP	533b	
		קצה	END	892c	1
		קיצון	OUTERMOST	894a	
		שפה	SPEECH	974a	3
		תכלת	VIOLET THREAD	1067b	1 a
26	5	אחות	ANOTHER	28a	5
		אשה	WOMAN	61c	4
		מחברת	THING JOINED	289c	1
		ללי	LOOP	533b	
		קבל	RECEIVE	867b	
		קצה	END	892a	1
26	6	אחות	ANOTHER	28a	5
		אשה	WOMAN	61c	4
		חבר	UNITE	288b	2
		קרס	HOOK	902b	
		קרס	HOOK	902b	
26	7	ל	TO	512b	4 a
		עשר	TEN	797a	1 d
		עשתי	ONE	799d	
		משכן	DWELLING-PLACE	1015d	2 c
26	8	אמה	CUBIT	52c	1
		ארך	LENGTH	73d	A
		יריעה	CURTAIN	438c	
		מדה	SIZE	551c	2
		ארבע	FOUR	*916d	1 a1
		רחב	WIDTH	931d	
		שלשים	THIRTY	1026c	1
26	9	בד	SEPARATION	94c	1 a
		חבר	UNITE	288b	2
		חמש	FIVE	331d	1 c
		כפל	DOUBLE OVER	495c	
		מול	IN FRONT OF	557c	2 a
26	10	חברת	A THING THAT JOINS	289a	
		חברת	A THING THAT JOINS	289a	
		ללי	LOOP	533b	
		קיצון	OUTERMOST	894a	
26	11	בוא	COME	99b	1 f
		חבר	UNITE	288b	2
		חמשים	FIFTY	332c	2 b
		ללי	LOOP	533b	
26	12	קרם	HOOK	902b	
		אחור	HINDER PART	30d	
		חצי	HALF	345c	1
		סרח	EXCESS	710b	
		סרח	GO FREE	710b	2
		עדף	REMAIN OVER	727a	
		משכן	DWELLING-PLACE	1015d	2 c
26	13	זה	THIS	262a	6 e
		כסה	COVER	491d	
		סרח	GO FREE	710b	2
		עדף	REMAIN OVER	727b	
		צד	SIDE	841a	
		צד	SIDE	841a	
		משכן	DWELLING-PLACE	1015d	2 c
26	14	אדם	BE RED	10a	
		איל	RAM	18a	3
		מכסה	COVERING	492c	2
		מעל	ABOVE	752a	2 d
		תחש	SEALSKIN	1065a	
26	15	עמד	STAND	764b	5 d
		קרש	BOARD	903c	2
26	16	אמה	CUBIT	52b	1
		אמה	CUBIT	52c	1
		חצי	HALF	345c	1
		קרש	BOARD	903c	2
26	17	אחות	ANOTHER	28a	5
		אשה	WOMAN	61c	4
		יד	TENONS	390c	4 f
		שלב	BE BOUND	1016d	
26	18	תימן	SOUTH	412d	1 b
		ל	TO	511c	1 h
		נגב	SOUTH-COUNTRY	616b	2
		צלע	RIB	*854b	2
26	19	אדן	BASE	10d	3
		יד	TENONS	390c	4 f
		ארבעים	FORTY	917b	1 a
		פאה	CORNER	802b	2 a
		צלע	RIB	854b	6
		צפן	NORTH	861a	
26	20	—	—	—	
26	21	ארבעים	FORTY	917b	1 a
26	22	ים	SEA	411b	9
		ירכה	EXTREME PARTS	438b	2
26	23	ירכה	EXTREME PARTS	438b	2
		מקצע	CORNER-BUTRESS	893a	
		מקצע	CORNER-BUTRESS	893a	
		מקצע	SET IN CORNERS	893b	
26	24	כן	SO	*485d	1 a
		ממה	DOWNWARDS	641b	3
		מקצע	CORNER-BUTRESS	893a	
		מקצע	CORNER-BUTRESS	893a	
		ראש	HEAD	910d	2 a
		תאם	BE DOUBLE	1061a	
		תם	COMPLETE	1071a	3
26	25	עשר	TEN	797b	6 a
		שש	SIX	995c	2
26	26	בריח	BAR	138b	1 a
		צלע	RIB	854b	6
26	27	בריח	BAR	138b	1 a
		ים	SEA	411b	9
		ירכה	EXTREME PARTS	438b	2
		צלע	RIB	854b	6
26	28	אל	TO	39d	1
		ברח	GO THROUGH	138a	1
		בריח	BAR	138b	1 a
		מן	FROM	582a	5 d1
		קצה	END	892a	1
		תיכן	MIDDLE	1064a	
26	29	בית	HOUSE	109c	3
		בריח	BAR	138b	1 a
26	30	הר	MOUNTAIN	249b	1 a
		הר	MOUNTAIN	250a	1 a
		קום	STAND	878d	2 b
		ראה	TO SEE	909a	1
		משכן	DWELLING-PLACE	1015d	2 c
		משפט	JUDGMENT	1049b	6 d
26	31	ארגמן	PURPLE THREAD	71b	1 a
		חשב	THINK	363b	1 5
		כרוב	CHERUB	500d	4 b
		פרכת	CURTAIN	827d	
		שזר	BE TWISTED	1005a	
		שש	BYSSUS	1058c	
26	32	וו	HOOK	255b	
		נתן	PUT	*680c	2 a
		עמוד	PILLAR	765a	1
		צפה	LAY OUT	860b	
		שטה	ACACIA	1008d	
26	33	בדל	BE DIVIDED	95b	1
		בוא	COME	99b	1
		בוא	COME	99b	2
		בית	HOUSE	110c	8 b
		ל	TO	512b	5 aa
		עדות	TESTIMONY	730b	1
		קדש	APARTNESS	871d	2 c
		קדש	APARTNESS	871d	2 c
		קרם	HOOK	902b	
26	34	נתן	PUT	680b	2 a
		עדות	TESTIMONY	730b	1
		כפרת	PROPITIATORY	498c	
		קדש	APARTNESS	871d	2 c
26	35	חוץ	THE OUTSIDE	300a	1 bd
		תימן	SOUTH	412d	1 b
		נכח	FRONT	647b	1
		צלע	RIB	854b	6
		צפון	NORTH	861a	
26	36	ארגמן	PURPLE THREAD	71b	1 a
		מסך	COVERING	697b	2 b
		מעשה	DEED	796a	2 a1
		פתח	OPENING	835d	
		רקם	VARIEGATE	955c	
		שזר	BE TWISTED	1005a	
		שש	BYSSUS	1058c	
26	37	וו	HOOK	255b	
		יצק	CAST	427b	2
		מסך	COVERING	697b	2 b
		עמוד	PILLAR	765a	1
		שטה	ACACIA	1008d	
27	1	אמה	CUBIT	52b	1
		ארך	LENGTH	73d	A
		מזבח	ALTAR	258c	3
		מזבח	ALTAR	259a	8
		רבע	SQUARED	917c	
		רחב	WIDTH	931d	
		שלש	THREE	1025d	1 a
27	2	מן	OUT OF	579b	2 ba
		פנה	CORNER	819c	1 a
		קרן	HORN	902a	3
27	3	דשן	BE FAT	206b	
		מזלגה	THREE PRONGED FORK	272c	
		מזרק	BOWL	284d	2 a
		מחתה	FIRE-HOLDER	367b	1
		יע	SHOVEL	418b	
		כלי	UTENSIL	480a	2 f
		ל	TO	514c	5 fd
		סור	POT	696c	2
		עשה	DO	794c	2 1g
		רשת	NET	440c	2
27	4	מכבר	GRATING	460d	
		מעשה	DEED	796a	2 a1
		קצה	END	892c	1
		קצה	END	892c	1
27	5	היה	BE	227a	3 2
		חצי	HALF	345d	
		רשת	NET	440c	2
		מכבר	GRATING	*460d	
		כרכב	RIM	501b	
		ממה	DOWNWARDS	641b	3
27	6	בד	PART	94d	3 c
27	7	בד	PART	94d	3 c
		בוא	COME	99d	C
		צלע	RIB	854b	6
27	8	הר	MOUNTAIN	249b	1 a
		הר	MOUNTAIN	250a	1 a
		מזבה	ALTAR	258c	3 a
		כן	SO	*486c	2 ca
		כן	SO	486c	2 cd
		לוח	BOARD	531d	2
		נבב	HOLLOW OUT	612c	
		ראה	TO SEE	908d	1 a2
27	9	אמה	CUBIT	52c	1
		ארך	LENGTH	73d	A
		חצר	ENCLOSURE	347a	3 a
		תימן	SOUTH	412d	1 b
		נגב	SOUTH-COUNTRY	616b	2
		פאה	CORNER	802b	2 a
		קלע	CURTAIN	887c	
		שש	BYSSUS	1058c	
27	10	וו	HOOK	255b	
		חשוק	FILLET	366a	
		חשוק	FILLET	366a	
		חשוק	FILLET	366a	
		עמוד	PILLAR	765a	1
		עשרים	TWENTY	797d	1 1e
27	11	וו	HOOK	255b	
		חשוק	FILLET	366a	
		כן	SO	485d	1 a
		עמוד	PILLAR	765a	1
		עשרים	TWENTY	797d	1 1e
		צפן	NORTH	861a	
27	12	אמה	CUBIT	52b	1
		חצר	ENCLOSURE	347a	3 a
		ים	SEA	411b	9
		עשר	TEN	797a	2 b
		פאה	CORNER	802b	2 a
		רחב	WIDTH	931d	
27	13	אמה	CUBIT	52b	1
		מזרח	PLACE OF SUNRISE	281a	2 cI
		חצר	ENCLOSURE	347a	3 a
		פאה	CORNER	802b	2 a
		קדם	EASTWARD	870a	
		רחב	WIDTH	931d	
27	14	חמש	FIVE	332a	2 a
		כתף	SIDE	509c	2 b
27	15	חמש	FIVE	332a	2 a
		כתף	SIDE	509c	2 b
27	16	ארגמן	PURPLE THREAD	71b	1 a
		מסך	COVERING	697b	2 a
		ארבע	FOUR	917a	1 b3
		רקם	VARIEGATE	955c	
		שער	GATE	1045b	3 d
		שש	BYSSUS	1058c	
27	17	וו	HOOK	255b	
		חשק	FURNISH WITH FILLETS	366b	
		עמוד	PILLAR	765a	1
27	18	אמה	CUBIT	52c	1
		רחב	WIDTH	931d	
		שש	BYSSUS	1058c	
27	19	יתד	PEG	450b	A
		כלי	UTENSIL	480a	2 f
		ל	TO	514c	5 fd
		עבדה	LABOR	715c	4

Ch v.	Heb	Eng	Page	Sec
	מעיל	ROBE	591c	3
29 6	שום	TO PLACE	963b	1 b
	נזר	CROWN	634b	1 b
	מצנפת	TURBAN	857b	
29 7	קדש	APARTNESS	872a	4 a
	יצק	POUR	427a	1
	משח	ANOINT	603b	3 a
	משחה	OINTMENT	603c	1
29 8	כתנת	TUNIC	509a	
	לבש	CLOTHE	528b	1 a
	קרב	COME NEAR	898a	2 a1
29 9	אבנט	GIRDLE	126a	
	מגבעות	HEAD-GEAR	149c	
	היה	BECOME	226c	2 2f
	חבש	BIND	289d	1 a
	חגר	GIRD	291d	1
	חקה	SOMETHING PRE-SCRIBED	350a	1
	יד	HAND	389a	1
	יד	HAND	389b	1 c
	כהנה	PRIESTHOOD	464d	
	מלא	FILL	570d	2
	עולם	LONG DURATION	762c	2 e
29 10	יד	HAND	389a	1
	סמך	LEAN	701d	1 a
	פנה	FACE	817a	24
	פר	YOUNG BULL	830d	2 c
	קרב	COME NEAR	898a	2 b1
29 11	פר	YOUNG BULL	830d	2 c
	שחט	SLAUGHTER	1006a	2
29 12	אל	TO	40c	8
	דם	BLOOD	197d	3 b
	דם	BLOOD	197d	3 b
	מזבח	ALTAR	259b	3
	מזבח	ALTAR	259b	2
	יסוד	FOUNDATION	414b	2
	פר	YOUNG BULL	830d	2 c
	אצבע	FINGER	840c	1 a
	שפך	POUR OUT	1049c	1 a
29 13	מזבח	ALTAR	259a	1
	חלב	FAT	316d	2 b
	יתרת	APPENDAGE	452c	
	כבד	LIVER	458b	
	כליה	KIDNEYS	480c	1 b
	כסה	COVER	491d	4
	קטר	MAKE SACRAFICES SMOKE	883a	1 a
	קרב	INWARD PART	899b	3
29 14	חטאת	SIN	309c	4 b
	מחנה	ENCAMPMENT	334a	1 a
	עור	SKIN	736b	2
	פר	YOUNG BULL	830d	2 c
	פרש	OFFAL	831d	
	שרף	BURN	977a	2 a
29 15	יד	HAND	389a	1 a
	סמך	LEAN	701d	1 a
	ראש	HEAD	910d	1 b
29 16	דם	BLOOD	197c	3 b
	מזבח	ALTAR	259a	1
	זרק	TO TOSS	284c	1 b
29 17	כרע	LEG	502d	2
	נתח	CUT IN PIECES	677c	
	נתח	PIECE OF A DI-VIDED CARCASS	677c	
	קרב	INWARD PART	899b	3
	רחץ	WASH OFF	934c	1
29 18	אשה	OFFERING MADE BY FIRE	78a	
	אשה	OFFERING MADE BY FIRE	78a	
	ניחח	SOOTHING	629c	
	עלה	WHOLE BURNT OF-FERING	750c	
	קטר	MAKE SACRAFICES SMOKE	883a	1 a
	ריח	SCENT	926b	2
29 19	יד	HAND	389a	1 a
	סמך	LEAN	701d	1 a
	ראש	HEAD	910d	1 b
29 20	בהן	THUMB	97b	
	דם	BLOOD	197c	3 b
	דם	BLOOD	197d	3 b
	מזבח	ALTAR	259a	1
	זרק	TO TOSS	284c	1 b
	יד	HAND	389a	1 a
	יד	HAND	389a	1 b
	ימני	RIGHT	412c	
	רגל	FOOT	919d	1 a
	תנוך	TIP	1072a	
29 21	דם	BLOOD	197c	3 b
	משחה	OINTMENT	603c	1
	נזה	SPURT	633c	
	קדש	BE SET APART	872d	1
29 22	איל	RAM	18a	2 a
	אליה	FAT TAIL	47a	2 b
	חלב	FAT	316d	2 b
	ימין	RIGHT	412a	3
	יתרת	APPENDAGE	452c	
	כבד	LIVER	458b	
	כליה	KIDNEYS	480c	1 b
	כסה	COVER	491d	4
	מלא	INSTALLATION	571c	2
	קרב	INWARD PART	899b	3
29 23	חלה	A KIND OF CAKE	319c	2 c
	ככר	ROUND	503b	2
	לחם	FOOD	537a	1 a

Ch v.	Heb	Eng	Page	Sec
	מצה	UNLEAVENED BREAD	695b	
	סל	BASKET	700d	
	רקיק	A THIN CAKE	956d	
	שמן	OIL	1032c	2 g
29 24	כל	ALL	482d	2 ba
	נוף	WAVE	632b	4
	תנופה	WAVING	632c	2 a
29 25	אשה	OFFERING MADE BY FIRE	78a	
	ניחח	SOOTHING	629c	
	נוף	WAVE	*632b	4
	קטר	MAKE SACRAFICES SMOKE	883a	1 a
29 26	ריח	SCENT	926b	2
	איל	RAM	18a	2 a
	חזה	BREAST	303d	
	מלוא	INSTALLATION	571c	2
	מנה	PORTION	584b	
	נוף	WAVE	632a	4
	תנופה	WAVING	632c	2 a
29 27	איל	RAM	18a	2 a
	מאשר	FROM THAT WHICH	84a	A
	חזה	BREAST	303d	
	מלוא	INSTALLATION	571c	2
	נוף	WAVE	632b	
	תנופה	WAVING	632c	2 a
	קדש	BE SET APART	873a	1 a
	רום	BE HIGH	927d	
	תרומה	OFFERING	929b	4 b
29 28	היה	BECOME	226c	2 2f
	חק	SOMETHING PRE-SCRIBED	349c	4
	עולם	LONG DURATION	762c	2
	תרומה	OFFERING	929b	4 b
	שלם	PEACE-OFFERING	1023c	
29 29	אחר	AFTER	30a	2 b
	יד	HAND	389b	1 c
	ל	TO	513c	5 ca
	מלא	FILL	570d	2
	משח	ANOINT	603b	3 a
29 30	לבש	PUT ON	527d	A
29 31	איל	RAM	18a	2 a
	בשל	BOIL	143a	2
	מלוא	INSTALLATION	571c	2
	קדוש	HOLY	872d	2 a
	מקום	STANDING PLACE	880b	4
29 32	איל	RAM	17d	1
	אכל	EAT	37b	1
	לחם	FOOD	537a	1 a
	סל	BASKET	700d	
29 33	שוק	LEG	1003b	2
	המה	THEY	241c	3 a
	זור	BE A STRANGER	266c	2 a
	יד	HAND	389b	1 c
	כפר	BE COVERED OVER	498b	2
	מלא	FILL	570d	2
	קדש	BE SET APART	873a	1 c
29 34	אכל	EAT	37d	1
	בקר	MORNING	134b	2
	יתר	BE LEFT OVER	451b	
	יתר	BE LEFT OVER	451c	
	לחם	FOOD	537a	1 a
	מלוא	INSTALLATION	571c	2
	מן	FROM	581a	3 bc
	שרף	BURN	977a	2 a
29 35	יד	HAND	389b	1 c
	ככה	THUS	462c	
	מלא	FILL	570d	3
	צוה	CHARGE	846a	3
29 36	חטא	MISS A GOAL OR WAY	307c	2
	חטאת	SIN	309c	4 b
	יום	DAY	401a	7 i
	כפר	COVER OVER	497d	3 b1
	כפרים	ATONEMENT	498c	
	ל	TO	515a	5 ha
	משח	ANOINT	603b	3 b
	על	UPON	754c	2 1f d
	פר	YOUNG BULL	830d	2 c
	קדש	BE SET APART	873a	1 a
29 37	מזבח	ALTAR	259a	1
	מזבח	ALTAR	259b	4
	כפר	COVER OVER	497d	3 b1
	נגע	TOUCH	619a	1 a
	קדש	APARTNESS	872a	3 a
	קדש	BE SET APART	873a	1 a
	קדש	BE SET APART	873a	2
29 38	בן	SON	122a	9 b
	זה	THIS	261b	3
	יום	DAY	401a	7 i
	כבש	LAMB	461a	1
	תמיד	CONTINUITY	556c	1 b
29 39	בקר	MORNING	134a	1 e
	כבש	LAMB	461a	1
	ערב	SUNSET	788a	1 b
29 40	בלל	MIX	117c	2
	הין	HIN	228d	1 a
	הין	HIN	229a	1 c
	הין	HIN	229a	2
	הין	HIN	229a	2
	יין	WINE	406c	B
	כבש	LAMB	461a	1
	כתית	BEATEN	510c	
	נסך	DRINK-OFFERING	651a	1

Ch v.	Heb	Eng	Page	Sec
	סלת	FINE FLOUR	701c	
	עשרון	TENTH PART	798a	
	רבע	FOURTH PART	917d	1
	רביעי	FOURTH	918a	4
29 41	בקר	MORNING	134a	1 e
	כבש	LAMB	461a	1
	מנחה	OFFERING	585c	5 e
	ניחח	SOOTHING	629c	
	נסך	DRINK-OFFERING	651a	1
	ערב	SUNSET	788a	1 b
	ריח	SCENT	926b	2
29 42	דור	GENERATION	190a	2 c
	יעד	MEET AT AN AP-POINTED PLACE	416d	1
	תמיד	CONTINUITY	556c	2 b
	עלה	WHOLE BURNT OF-FERING	750b	
	שם	THERE	1027b	1 b
	שם	THERE	1027b	3
29 43	יעד	MEET AT AN AP-POINTED PLACE	416d	1
	כבוד	GLORY	458d	2 c1
	קדש	BE SET APART	873a	3
	שם	THERE	1027b	3
29 44	מזבח	ALTAR	259b	4
	כהן	ACT AS PRIEST	464c	1
	קדש	BE SET APART	873a	1 c
	קדש	BE SET APART	873a	1 a
29 45	אלהים	GOD	44b	4 a
	שכן	SETTLE DOWN	1015b	2 c
	תוך	MIDST	1063d	
29 46	יהוה	YAHWEH	218d	2 1d
	יהוה	YAHWEH	219a	2 2b g
	יהוה	YAHWEH	219b	2 2d
	ידע	KNOW	393d	1 a
	יצא	CASUE TO GO	424c	1 a
	שכן	SETTLE DOWN	1015b	2 c
	תוך	MIDST	1063d	
30 1	מזבח	ALTAR	258c	3 b
	מזבח	ALTAR	259a	8
	קטרת	SMOKE	882d	2
	מקטר	PLACE OF SACRIFE-CIAL SMOKE	883b	
30 2	אמה	CUBIT	52b	1
	מן	OUT OF	579b	2 ba
	רבע	SQUARED	917c	
30 3	גג	TOP	151a	2
	זר	CIRCLET	267a	
	מהור	CLEAN	373a	2
	קיר	WALL	885b	4
30 4	ב	IN	*88a	
	בד	PART	94d	3 c
	הם	THEY	241d	8 a
	זר	CIRCLET	267a	
	צד	SIDE	841a	
	צלע	RIB	854b	6
30 5	בד	PART	94d	3 c
30 6	מזבח	ALTAR	258c	3 b
	יעד	MEET AT AN AP-POINTED PLACE	416d	1
	כפרת	PROPITIATORY	498c	
	נתן	PUT	680d	2 a
	עדות	TESTIMONY	730b	1
	עדות	TESTIMONY	730b	1
	פנה	FACE	817d	24 d
	שם	THERE	1027b	3
30 7	בקר	MORNING	134b	1 f
	טוב	MAKE GOOD	406a	4
	קטרת	SMOKE	882d	2
	קטר	MAKE SACRAFICES SMOKE	883b	2
30 8	דור	GENERATION	190a	2 c
	תמיד	CONTINUITY	556c	2 b
	ערב	SUNSET	788a	1 b
	קטרת	SMOKE	882d	2
	קטר	MAKE SACRAFICES SMOKE	883b	2
30 9	זור	BE A STRANGER	266c	2 d
	מנחה	OFFERING	585b	5
	נסך	POUR OUT	650d	2
	עלה	GO UP	749d	8
	עלה	WHOLE BURNT OF-FERING	750d	
	קטרת	SMOKE	882d	2
30 10	דור	GENERATION	190a	2 c
	דם	BLOOD	197d	3 b
	חטאת	SIN	309d	4 c
	כפר	COVER OVER	497d	3 b1
	כפר	COVER OVER	497d	3 b1
	כפרים	ATONEMENT	498c	
	על	UPON	756d	2 7a c
	קדש	APARTNESS	872a	3 a
30 12	כפר	RANSOM	497b	2
	ל	TO	516a	5 ja
	נגף	BLOW	620a	1
	נשא	LIFT	671c	3 e
	נתן	GIVE	679b	1 n
	פקד	ATTEND TO	823c	A 4
	ראש	HEAD	911b	7
30 13	ב	IN	90c	3 8
	גרה	GERAH	176a	
	מחצית	HALF	346a	1
	עבר	PASS OVER	718b	5 g
	על	UPON	755b	2 4c
	פקד	ATTEND TO	823c	A 4
	קדש	APARTNESS	871d	2 c

Ch v.	Heb	Eng	Page	Sec
	תרומה	OFFERING	929b	6
	שקל	SHEKEL	1053d	
	שקל	SHEKEL	1053d	
	שקל	SHEKEL	1053d	
30 14	בן	SON	122a	9 a
	עבר	PASS OVER	718b	5 g
	מעל	ABOVE	751d	2 bb a
	על	UPON	755b	2 4a
	פקד	ATTEND TO	823c	A 4
	תרומה	OFFERING	929b	6
30 15	דל	POOR	195d	
	מחצית	HALF	346a	1
	כפר	COVER OVER	497d	3 b2
	מעט	BE SMALL	589d	B
	נפש	SOUL	660b	4 c1
	נתן	GIVE	679a	1 k
	עשיר	RICH	799b	
	רבה	BECOME MANY	915c	1 c
	תרומה	OFFERING	929b	6
	שקל	SHEKEL	1053d	
30 16	זכרון	MEMORIAL	272a	1 d
	כסף	SILVER	494c	8 e
	כפר	COVER OVER	497d	3 b2
	כפרים	ATONEMENT	498c	
	נפש	SOUL	660b	4 c1
	נתן	GIVE	679a	1 j
	עבדה	LABOR	715b	4
	על	UPON	754c	2 lf d
30 18	כיור	POT	468c	3 a
	כן	BASE	487c	1
	נתן	PUT	680b	2 a
	נתן	PUT	680c	2 a
	שם	THERE	1027b	3 a
30 19	רחץ	WASH OFF	934c	1
30 20	אשה	OFFERING MADE BY FIRE	78a	
	את	WITH	86b	2
	מות	DIE	560a	2 b
	מי	WATER	565b	1 a
	נגש	DRAW NEAR	620d	1
	קטר	MAKE SACRIFICES SMOKE	883a	1 a
30 21	דור	GENERATION	190a	2 c
	היה	BECOME	226b	2 2d
	זרע	SOWING	282d	4 c
	חק	SOMETHING PRESCRIBED	349c	6 a
	עולם	LONG DURATION	762c	2
	רחץ	WASH OFF	934c	1
30 23	בשם	SPICE	141d	1
	דרור	A FLOWING	204d	1
	חמשים	FIFTY	332b	1 b2
	מחצית	HALF	346a	1
	מר	MYRRH	600d	1
	קנה	STALK	889c	3
	קנמון	CINNAMON	890a	
	ראש	HEAD	911b	5
	שמן	OIL	*1032b	2 a
30 24	הין	HIN	229a	2
	הין	HIN	229a	1 b
	זית	OLIVE TREE	268d	2
	מאה	HUNDRED	548b	1 c5
	קדה	CASSIA	869b	
	שמן	OIL	1032c	2 g
	שקל	SHEKEL	1053d	
30 25	משחה	OINTMENT	603c	1
	מעשה	DEED	796a	2 a1
	קדש	APARTNESS	872a	3 d
	רקח	PERFUME	955b	
	רקח	MIX OIL	955b	
	מרקחת	OINTMENT-MIX-TURE	955c	1
	שמן	OIL	1032c	2 g
30 26	משח	ANOINT	603b	3 b
	עדות	TESTIMONY	730b	1
30 27	מזבח	ALTAR	258c	3 b
	קטרת	SMOKE	882d	2
30 28	מזבח	ALTAR	258c	3 a
	כיור	POT	468c	3 a
	כן	BASE	487c	1
	עלה	WHOLE BURNT OF-FERING	750d	
30 29	נגע	TOUCH	619a	1 a
	קדש	APARTNESS	872a	3 a
	קדש	BE SET APART	873a	1 a
	קדש	BE SET APART	873a	2
30 30	כהן	ACT AS PRIEST	464c	1
	משח	ANOINT	603b	3 a
	קדש	BE SET APART	873a	1 c
30 31	דור	GENERATION	190a	2 c
	זה	THIS	260d	1 a
	משחה	OINTMENT	603c	1
30 32	בשר	FLESH	142c	2
	סך	BE POURED	692a	3
	מתכנת	MEASUREMENT	1067c	2
30 33	זור	BE A STRANGER	266c	2 a
	כרת	BE CUT OFF	504b	1 c
	עם	KINSMAN	769c	
	רקח	MIX OIL	955b	
	רקח	MIX OIL	955b	
30 34	בד	PART	94d	2
	זך	PURE	269b	1
	חלבנה	GALBANUM	317b	
	לבנה	FRANKINCENSE	526d	
	נטף	MYRRH	643b	
	סם	SPICE	702c	
30 35	שחלת	ONYCHA	1006c	
	טהור	CLEAN	373a	2
	מלח	SALT	572a	
	קדש	APARTNESS	872a	3 d
	קטרת	SMOKE	882d	2
30 36	רקח	MIX OIL	955b	
	רקח	PERFUME	955b	
	דקק	PULVERISE	200d	
	יעד	MEET AT AN AP-POINTED PLACE	416d	1
	עדות	TESTIMONY	730b	1
	קדש	APARTNESS	872a	3 d
	שחק	RUB AWAY	1007a	
30 37	קדש	APARTNESS	872a	3 d
	קטרת	SMOKE	882d	2
	מתכנת	MEASUREMENT	1067c	2
30 38	כרת	BE CUT OFF	504b	1 c
	עם	KINSMAN	769c	
	ריח	SMELL	926b	
31 2	אורי	URI	22b	1
	בצלאל	BEZALEL	130b	1
	חור	HUR	301b	2
	יהודה	JUDAH	397b	12
	ל	TO	512b	5 ac
	מטה	TRIBE	641d	3
	קרא	CALL	896a	5 e
31 3	תבונה	UNDERSTANDING	108b	2
	חכמה	WISDOM	315b	1
	דעת	SKILL	395c	1 b
	מלאכה	WORK	522b	4
	מלא	FILL	570c	1
	רוח	BREATH	926a	9 d
31 4	ב	IN	90c	3 6
	ה	THE	207c	1 e
	זהב	GOLD	263c	1
	זהב	GOLD	263c	2 a
	חשב	THINK	363a	1 5
	מחשבה	THOUGHT	364c	3
	עשה	DO	794a	1 1b
31 5	אבן	STONE	6d	3
	חרשת	CARVING	360d	
	מלאכה	WORK	522b	4
	מלא	FILL	570d	2
	עשה	DO	794a	1 1b
31 6	אהליאב	OHOLIAB	14c	
	אחיסמך	AHISAMACH	27b	
	אנכי	I	59c	3
	דן	DAN	192d	2
	חכם	WISE	314d	1
	חכמה	WISDOM	315b	1
	לב	HEART	524d	2 3b
	נתן	PUT	680b	2 a
	נתן	PUT	680c	2 b
31 7	כפרת	PROPITIATORY	498c	
	ל	TO	513d	5 cb b
	עדות	TESTIMONY	730b	1
31 8	מזבח	ALTAR	258c	3 b
	טהור	CLEAN	373a	2
31 9	מזבח	ALTAR	258c	3 a
	כיור	POT	468c	3 a
	כן	BASE	487c	1
	עלה	WHOLE BURNT OF-FERING	750d	
31 10	אהרן	AARON	14d	
	אהרן	AARON	14d	
	כהן	ACT AS PRIEST	464c	1
	שרד	BRAIDED WORK	975b	
	שרד	BRAIDED WORK	975b	
31 11	משחה	OINTMENT	603c	1
	קטרת	SMOKE	882d	2
31 13	אות	SIGN	17a	6
	אך	SURELY	36c	1
	בין	INTERVAL	107c	1 d
	דור	GENERATION	190a	2 c
	יהוה	YAHWEH	219b	2 2b e
	קדש	BE SET APART	873a	4 d
	שבת	SABBOTH	992c	1 c
	שמר	KEEP	1036d	3 b
31 14	ו	AND	254d	5 a
	חלל	POLLUTE	320b	1 b
	כרת	BE CUT OFF	504b	1 c
	מות	DIE	559d	2 a
	נפש	SOUL	660b	4 c2
	עם	KINSMAN	769c	
	קדש	APARTNESS	872b	5
	קרב	INWARD PART	899b	1 f4
	שבת	SABBOTH	992c	1 c
	שמר	KEEP	1036d	3 b
31 15	יום	DAY	398b	2 a
	יום	DAY	398d	2 i
	מות	DIE	559d	2 a
	קדש	APARTNESS	872b	5
	שבת	SABBATH	992b	1 a
	שבת	SABBATH	992c	1 c
	שבתון	SABBOTH OBSERV-ANCE	992d	1
31 16	ברית	COVENANT	136c	2 2c
	ברית	COVENANT	137a	3 2
	דור	GENERATION	190a	2 c
	עולם	LONG DURATION	762c	2 d
	עשה	DO	795a	2 c
	שבת	SABBOTH	992c	1 c
	שבת	SABBATH	992c	1 c
	שמר	KEEP	1036d	3 b
31 17	אות	SIGN	17a	6
	נפש	REFRESH ONESELF	661c	
	עולם	LONG DURATION	762c	2 d
	שבת	CEASE	991d	2 b
	שבת	SABBATH	992c	1 d
31 18	אבן	STONE	6c	2
	דבר	SPEAK	181b	3 d
	הר	MOUNTAIN	249b	1 a
	הר	MOUNTAIN	250a	1 a
	כלה	FINISH	478b	1 c
	כתב	WRITE	507b	1 c
	כתב	WRITE	507d	1 c
	לוח	TABLET	*531d	1
	לוח	TABLET	531d	1
	לוח	TABLET	531d	1
	סיני	SINAI	696a	
	עדות	TESTIMONY	730b	1
	אצבע	FINGER	840c	1 c
32 1	אלהים	GOD	43c	1 d
	בוש	BE ASHAMED	101d	
	היה	FALL OUT	224b	1 1a
	הלך	WALK	231c	1 d 5e
	הר	MOUNTAIN	249b	1 a
	הר	MOUNTAIN	250a	1 a
	זה	THIS	260d	2 a
	ירד	COME DOWN	432d	1 a
	מה	WHAT	552d	1 b
	עלה	GO UP	749b	1 a
	על	UPON	757b	2 7c aa
	קהל	ASSEMBLE AS	874d	1
	קום	STAND	878b	6 b
32 2	אזן	EAR	23d	1
	זהב	GOLD	263a	6
	נזם	RING	634a	2
	פרק	TEAR APART	830a	
32 3	אזן	EAR	23d	1
	זהב	GOLD	263a	6
	נזם	RING	634a	2
	פרק	TEAR APART	830a	
32 4	חרט	GRAVING-TOOL	355a	1
	מסכה	MOLTEN IMAGE	651b	2
	עגל	CALF	722b	
	צור	FASHION	849b	
32 5	בנה	BUILD	124c	1 at
	מזבח	ALTAR	258d	8
	חג	FESTIVAL-GATHER-ING	290d	1 a
	מחר	TO-MORROW	564a	1 b
	ישב	SIT	442d	1 b
32 6	מחרת	THE MORROW	564a	
	נגש	APPROACH	621b	
	עלה	GO UP	749d	8
	עלה	WHOLE BURNT OF-FERING	750d	
	צחק	LAUGH	850b	2
	שכם	START EARLY	1014d	
	שלם	PEACE-OFFERING	1023c	
32 7	דבר	SPEAK	181a	3 b
	הלך	WALK	234b	1 5f 3
	שחת	GO TO RUIN	1008a	1
32 8	דרך	WAY	203c	6 b
	מהר	QUICKLY	555b	
	מסכה	MOLTEN IMAGE	651b	2
	סור	TURN ASIDE	693c	1
	עגל	CALF	722b	
	ערף	BACK OF NECK	791c	2
	צוה	CHARGE	845d	2 a
32 9	קשה	SEVERE	904d	3
32 10	אף	NOSE	60b	3
	גוי	NATION	156c	1 a
	חרה	BURN	354a	2
	כלה	FINISH	478c	2 c2
	ל	TO	512b	4 a
	נוח	REST	629a	B 5
32 11	אף	NOSE	60b	3
	גדול	GREAT	153a	3
	יהוה	YAHWEH	218d	2 1e
	חזק	STRONG	305c	1 b
	חלה	MOLLIFY	318c	1 a
	חרה	BURN	354a	2
	יד	HAND	390a	1 e2
	יצא	CAUSE TO GO	424c	1 a
	כח	STRENGTH	470d	3
	כח	STRENGTH	470d	3
32 12	אדמה	GROUND	9d	3
	אף	NOSE	60b	3
	אף	NOSE	60b	3
	ב	IN	89c	3 1c
	חרון	BURNING OF AN-GER	354c	
	ל	TO	511a	1 d
	מה	HOW	554b	4 d
	נחם	BE SORRY	637a	2
	על	UPON	758c	4 2a
	פנה	FACE	819b	2 8b
	רעה	MISERY	949b	2
	רעה	MISERY	949b	1
	שוב	TURN BACK	997d	6 f
32 13	אמר	SAY	56a	1
	זכר	REMEMBER	270b	2 1 c
	זרע	SOWING	282c	4 b
	כוכב	STAR	457a	
	נחל	TAKE AS A POSSES-SION	635c	1 a
	עבד	SLAVE	714a	3
	עולם	LONG DURATION	762d	2 f
	ישראל	ISRAEL	·975c	1
32 14	דבר	SPEAK	181d	6

Ch v.	Heb	Eng	Page	Sec
	נחם	BE SORRY	637a	2
	על	UPON	754b	2 lf b
	רעה	MISERY	949b	1
32 15	הר	MOUNTAIN	249b	1 a
	הר	MOUNTAIN	250a	1 a
	זה	THIS	262a	6 e
	יד	HAND	390d	5 c1
	ירד	COME DOWN	432d	1 a
	כתב	WRITE	507b	1 a
	לוח	TABLET	*531d	1
	לוח	TABLET	531d	1
	עבר	REGION ACROSS	719d	2
	עדות	TESTIMONY	730b	1
	פנה	TURN	815b	1 c
32 16	הם	THEY	241c	3 b
	חרת	GRAVE	362a	1
	יצא	CAUSE TO GO	424c	1 b
	מכתב	WRITING	508b	1
	לוח	TABLET	*531d	1
	לוח	TABLET	531d	1
	מעשה	DEED	796b	2 b
32 17	יהושע	JOSHUA	221c	1
	יום	DAY	398c	2 d
	קול	VOICE	876a	1 a
	קול	VOICE	877b	2 j
	רע	ROAR	929d	1
32 18	גבורה	MIGHT	150c	2
	חלושה	WEAKNESS	325d	1
	ענה	SING	777b	
	ענה	SING	777b	
	קול	VOICE	876a	1 a
32 19	הר	MOUNTAIN	249b	1 a
	חג	FESTIVAL-GATHER-ING	*291a	1 a
	מחולה	DANCING	298b	
	חרה	BURN	354a	1 a
	כאשר	WHEN	455c	3
	לוח	TABLET	531d	1
	עגל	CALF	722b	
	קרב	COME NEAR	897c	1 b
	שבר	BREAK	991a	
	שלך	THROW	1021a	1 a
32 20	אש	FIRE	77b	1
	דקק	BE FINE	200d	2
	זרה	SCATTER	279d	1
	טחן	GRIND	377c	
	נחל	TORRENT	*636a	1
	עגל	CALF	722b	
	עד	UNTIL	724d	2 la a
	עפר	DRY EARTH	779d	1 d
	פנה	FACE	819a	2 7b
	שרף	BURN	976d	2 a
	שוף	BRUISE	1003a	
	שקה	GIVE TO DRINK	1052c	2
32 21	בוא	COME	99c	2 a
	חטאה	SIN	308b	1
	מה	WHAT	552c	1 a
32 22	אדון	LORD	11b	3 lg
	חרה	BURN	354a	1 a
	רע	EVIL	949c	3
32 23	אלהים	GOD	43c	1 d
	היה	FALL OUT	224b	1 la
	הלך	WALK	231c	1 ld 5e
	זה	THIS	260d	2 a
32 24	אש	FIRE	77c	3
	יצא	GO OUT	423a	1 f
	מי	WHO	567b	G
	עגל	CALF	722b	
	פרק	TEAR APART	830a	
	שלך	THROW	1021a	1 a
32 25	פרע	LET GO	828a	1
	קום	STAND	878a	2
	שמצה	WHISPER	1036b	
32 26	בן	SON	121a	1 je
	מחנה	ENCAMPMENT	334a	1 a
	ל	TO	515c	5 hc
	לוי	LEVI	532c	1 c
	מי	WHO	567b	G
	עמד	STAND	763d	1 a
	שער	GATE	1044a	1 a
32 27	אח	BROTHER	26b	4
	איש	MAN	36a	
	אלהים	GOD	44b	4 ba
	הרג	KILL	247b	1
	חרב	SWORD	352c	1 b
	ירך	THIGH	437d	1 a
	מן	FROM	582b	5 d2
	עבר	PASS OVER	717c	3 a
	קרב	NEAR	898c	2 a
	רע	FRIEND	946b	3
	שום	TO PLACE	964b	4 b
	שוב	TURN BACK	997a	1 a
	שער	GATE	1044d	1 a
32 28	אלף	THOUSAND	49a	1 a
	בן	SON	121a	1 je
	דבר	WORD	182b	1 lb
	ך	LIKE	453b	1 a
	לוי	LEVI	532c	1 c
32 29	ברכה	BLESSING	139d	1 b
	יד	HAND	*389b	1 c
	יד	HAND	389b	1 c
	ל	TO	518b	7 bh
	מלא	FILL	570b	2
	מלא	FILL	570d	2
	על	UPON	756c	27 a b
32 30	בעד	ON BEHALF OF	126c	2

Ch v.	Heb	Eng	Page	Sec
	חטא	MISS A GOAL OR WAY	307b	2 b
	חטאה	SIN	308b	1
	חטאת	SIN	309a	1 e
	כפר	COVER OVER	497c	2 a
	מחרת	THE MORROW	564a	
32 31	עלה	GO UP	748c	2 b
	אלהים	GOD	43c	1 d
	אנא	AH, NOW	58a	
	זהב	GOLD	263a	6
	חטא	MISS A GOAL OR WAY	307b	2 b
	חטאה	SIN	308b	1
	ל	TO	515d	5 ia
32 32	שוב	TURN BACK	997a	3 a
	אין	NOT	34c	2 dd
	אם	IF	50b	1 b3
	חטאת	SIN	308d	1 d2
	כתב	WRITE	507b	1 a
	מחה	WIPE	562a	1
	נשא	LIFT	671b	3 c
	ספר	MISSIVE	*707c	4
	ספר	MISSIVE	*707c	3 g
32 33	חטא	MISS A GOAL OR WAY	307b	2 b
	מחה	WIPE	562a	1
	מי	WHO	567b	G
	ספר	MISSIVE	*707c	3 g
	ספר	MISSIVE	*707c	4
32 34	אשר	PARTICLE OF RELATION	82c	4 bg
	דבר	SPEAK	181b	3 c
	הלך	WALK	231c	1 ld 5e
	הנה	BEHOLD	244a	B b
	ו	AND	254d	5 a
	חטאת	SIN	308d	1 d1
	מלאך	MESSENGER	521d	3
	נחה	LEAD	634d	
	פקד	ATTEND TO	823c	A 2
32 35	נגף	STRIKE	619d	
	עגל	CALF	722b	
	על	UPON	758d	3 a
33 1	דבר	SPEAK	181a	3 b
	הלך	WALK	234b	1 5f 3
	זרע	SOWING	282c	4 b
	שבע	SWEAR	989c	2
33 2	אמרי	AMORITES	57c	2 e
	יבוסי	JEBUSITE	101a	1
	גרש	DRIVE OUT	177a	
	חוי	HIVITE	295d	2
	חתי	HITTITE	366d	2 a
	כנעני	CANAANITE	489a	2 b
	מלאך	MESSENGER	521d	3
	שלח	SEND	1018c	2 a
33 3	דבש	HONEY	185b	
	זוב	FLOW	264d	2
	חלב	MILK	316c	A 4
	כלה	FINISH	478c	2 c2
	ערף	BACK OF NECK	791c	2
	קשה	SEVERE	904d	3
33 4	אבל	MOURN	5c	
	דבר	WORD	182b	1 1c
	עדי	ORNAMENTS	726a	2
	רע	EVIL	948a	2
	שית	PUT	1011a	1
33 5	ירד	BRING DOWN	434b	2
	כלה	FINISH	478c	2 c2
	עדי	ORNAMENTS	726a	2
	על	UPON	758c	4 2a
	ערף	BACK OF NECK	791c	2
	קשה	SEVERE	904d	3
	רגע	A MOMENT	921a	BA A
	הר	MOUNTAIN	249b	1 a
33 6	חרב	HOREB	352a	
	מן	FROM	581c	4 a
	נצל	DELIVER	665a	
	עדי	ORNAMENTS	726a	2
33 7	אהל	TENT	14a	3
	בקש	SEEK	134c	3 c
	מחנה	ENCAMPMENT	334a	1 a
	מועד	TENT OF MEETING	418a	5
	נטה	SPREAD OUT	640a	2
	קרא	CALL	896a	6 e2
	רחק	BE DISTANT	935a	1
33 8	היה	COME TO PASS	225a	1 2b ae
	נבט	LOOK	613c	1 a
	נצב	STAND	662b	1 c
	פתח	OPENING	835d	
	קום	STAND	877d	1 a
33 9	דבר	SPEAK	181b	3 e
	היה	COME TO PASS	225a	1 2b ae
	ירד	GO DOWN	433b	2
	פתח	OPENING	835d	
33 10	ו	AND	254a	2 da
	פתח	OPENING	835d	
	פתח	OPENING	835d	
	קום	STAND	877d	1 a
	ראה	TO SEE	907a	2 3
	שחה	BOW DOWN	1005d	2 c
33 11	אהל	TENT	14a	1a
	יהושע	JOSHUA	221c	1
	כאשר	AS	455c	1 d
	מוש	REMOVE	559a	
	נון	NUN	630c	
	פנה	FACE	815d	1 1c
	רע	FRIEND	946a	2

Ch v.	Heb	Eng	Page	Sec
	שרת	SERVE	1058a	1 c
	תוך	MIDST	1063d	
33 12	חן	FAVOR	336b	2 b2
	ידע	KNOW	394b	2
	ידע	MAKE KNOWN	395a	
	מצא	FIND	592d	1 a
	שם	NAME	1028d	2 a
33 13	גוי	NATION	156c	1 b
	דרך	WAY	204a	6 eb
	חן	FAVOR	336b	2 b2
	ידע	KNOW	395a	
	מצא	FIND	592d	1 a
	נא	PART OF EN-TREATY	609c	4 c
33 14	הלך	WALK	231b	1 ld 5e
	נוח	REST	628c	A lb l
	פנה	FACE	816a	1 2a
33 15	אין	NOT	34b	2 c
	הלך	WALK	231c	1 ld 5e
	פנה	FACE	816a	1 2a
33 16	אדמה	GROUND	9d	4
	אפו	THEN	66b	1
	ב	IN	91a	5 2
	חן	FAVOR	336b	2 b2
	ידע	BE MADE KNOWN	394c	1
	לא	NOT	520b	4 ba
	מה	HOW	553d	4 a
	מצא	FIND	592d	1 a
	עם	PEOPLE	766d	4
	פלה	BE SEPARATED	811d	1
33 17	חן	FAVOR	336b	2 b2
	מצא	FIND	592d	1 a
	שם	NAME	1028a	2 a
33 18	כבוד	GLORY	458d	2 c1
	ראה	TO SEE	908d	1 a2
	ראה	TO SEE	908d	
33 19	ב	IN	90b	3 4
	חנן	SHOW FAVOR	336a	2 b
	טוב	GOOD THINGS	375c	3 a
	עבר	PASS OVER	719a	3 a
	פנה	FACE	818d	2 7a a
	קרא	CALL	895c	3 b
	רחם	LOVE	933c	1
33 20	אדם	MAN	9b	2
	חיה	LIVE	311a	1 a
	פנה	FACE	815d	1 a
	ראה	TO SEE	906d	1 1b
33 21	את	WITH	86b	2
	נצב	STAND	662a	1 a
	צור	ROCK	849c	1 a
	מקום	STANDING PLACE	879d	1 a
33 22	היה	COME TO PASS	225b	1 2b be
	כבוד	GLORY	458d	2 c1
	כף	HOLLOW OF THE HAND	496c	1 b
	נקרה	HOLE	669b	
	עבר	PASS OVER	717d	4 a
	עד	AS FAR AS	724c	1 2b
	צור	ROCK	849c	1 a
	שכך	COVER	967d	
33 23	אחור	HINDER PART	30d	
	כף	HOLLOW OF THE HAND	496c	1 b
	סור	TURN ASIDE	694b	1
	פנה	FACE	815d	1 1b
	ראה	TO SEE	906d	1 a
	ראה	TO SEE	908c	3
34 1	אבן	STONE	6c	2
	דבר	WORD	183a	2 2
	כתב	WRITE	507c	1 b1
	לוח	TABLET	531d	1
	לוח	TABLET	*531d	1
	פסל	HEW	820d	
	שבר	BREAK	991a	
34 2	בכור	FIRST-BORN	114b	1 d
	בקר	MORNING	133d	1 a
	בקר	MORNING	134a	1 f
	הר	MOUNTAIN	249b	1 a
	הר	MOUNTAIN	249b	1 3
	כון	BE READY	466a	3
	ל	TO	*517a	6 a
	נצב	STAND	662a	1 a
	סיני	SINAI	696a	
	עלה	GO UP	748b	1 c
	ראש	HEAD	910d	2 a
34 3	איש	MAN	36a	
	הר	MOUNTAIN	249b	1 a
	הר	MOUNTAIN	250a	1 a
	מול	IN FRONT OF	557c	2 a
	ראה	TO SEE	908c	2 c
	רעה	TEND	945b	2 a
	אבן	STONE	6c	2
34 4	בקר	MORNING	134b	1 h
	הר	MOUNTAIN	249b	1 a
	הר	MOUNTAIN	249d	1 a
	לוח	TABLET	531d	1
	סיני	SINAI	696a	
	עלה	GO UP	748b	1 c
	פסל	HEW	820d	
34 5	ב	IN	90b	3 4
	יצב	STATION ONESELF	426b	A
	ירד	GO DOWN	433b	1
	ענן	CLOUD	778a	1 a
	קרא	CALL	895c	3
34 6	אל	GOD	42d	6 d
	אלה	GOD	43a	2

51

EXODUS

Ch v.	Heb	Eng	Page	Sec
	אמת	FIRMNESS	54a	3 b
	אף	NOSE	60b	3
	ארך	LONG	74a	
	חנון	GRACIOUS	337a	
	חסד	GOODNESS	339b	2 2
	חסד	GOODNESS	*339b	2 3a
	עבר	PASS OVER	717d	4 a
	קרא	CALL	895b	3 a
	רחום	COMPASSIONATE	933d	
34 7	אלף	THOUSAND	49a	1 a
	בן	SON	120b	1 f
	חטאה	SINFUL THING	308b	
	חסד	GOODNESS	339b	2 3b
	לא	NOT	*519b	1 bc
	נצר	KEEP	665d	3
	נקה	BE CLEAN	667c	2
	נשא	LIFT	671b	3 c
	עון	INIQUITY	731a	1 c2
	עון	INIQUITY	731a	1 c1
	פקד	ATTEND TO	823c	A 3
	פשע	TRANSGRESSION	833c	3 d
	רבע	PERTAINING TO THE FOURTH	918a	
	שלש	PERTAINING TO THE THIRD	1026d	
34 8	מהר	HASTEN	555a	2
	קדד	BOW DOWN	869a	2
	שחה	BOW DOWN	1005c	2 a
34 9	אדון	LORD	11b	3 2a
	הלך	WALK	231c	1 1d 5d
	חטאת	SIN	309a	1 d2
	חן	FAVOR	336b	2 b2
	מצא	FIND	592d	1 a
	נא	PART OF ENTREATY	609c	4 c
	נחל	TAKE AS A POSSESSION	635c	1 d
	סלח	FORGIVE	699b	
	עון	INIQUITY	731a	1 c2
	ערף	BACK OF NECK	791c	2
	קשה	SEVERE	904d	3
34 10	ברא	CREATE	135c	3
	ברית	COVENANT	136c	2 2c
	ברית	COVENANT	137a	3 1
	גוי	NATION	156d	1 c
	ירא	CAUSE FEAR	431d	2
	כרת	CUT	504a	4
	עשה	DO	794a	1 1a 4
	פלא	BE SURPASSING	810d	4
34 11	אמרי	AMORITES	57c	2 e
	יבוסי	JEBUSITE	101a	1
	גרש	CAST OUT	176c	2
	הנה	BEHOLD	244b	B b
	חוי	HIVITE	295d	2
	חתי	HITTITE	366d	2 a
	כנעני	CANAANITE	489a	2 b
	פנה	FACE	818b	26a
	צוה	CHARGE	845d	2 a
34 12	ברית	COVENANT	136c	1 1
	מוקש	BAIT	430d	
	ישב	DWELL	443b	3
	כרת	CUT	503d	4
	על	UPON	757a	2 7c a
34 13	אשרה	ASHERA	81c	B
	מזבח	ALTAR	259a	1
	כרת	CUT OFF	503d	2
	מצבה	PILLAR	663b	1 c
	נתץ	PULL DOWN	683b	1
	שבר	BREAK	991a	
34 14	אחר	ANOTHER	29d	
	אל	GOD	42c	3
	אל	GOD	42d	6 d
	קנא	JEALOUS	888d	
	קנא	JEALOUS	888d	
	שם	NAME	1028c	3
34 15	אכל	EAT	37b	2
	אכל	EAT	37b	1
	ברית	COVENANT	136b	1 1
	זבח	SLAUGHTER FOR SACRIFICE	257a	1 3
	זבח	SACRIFICE	257c	1 2
	זנה	COMMIT FORNICATION	275d	3
	ישב	DWELL	443b	3
	כרת	CUT	503d	4
	פן	LEST	814d	1 b
	קרא	CALL	895d	5 a
34 16	זנה	COMMIT FORNICATION	275d	3
	זנה	COMMIT FORNICATION	276a	1 b
34 17	אלהים	GOD	43c	1 d
	מסכה	MOLTEN IMAGE	651b	2
34 18	אביב	ABIB	1b	2
	חג	FESTIVAL-GATHERING	291a	1 b2
	חג	FESTIVAL-GATHERING	291b	1 b
	חדש	NEW MOON	294d	2 b1
	מועד	APPOINTED TIME	*417c	1 a
	מועד	APPOINTED TIME	417c	1 a
	יצא	GO OUT	422d	1 a
	מצה	UNLEAVENED BREAD	695d	
	מצה	UNLEAVENED BREAD	695b	
	שמר	KEEP	1036d	3 a

Ch v.	Heb	Eng	Page	Sec
34 19	זכר	MALE	271c	1 2
	פטר	THAT WHICH SEPARATES	809d	
	רחם	WOMB	933b	1
	שה	A SHEEP	962a	1
	שור	A HEAD OF CATTLE	1004b	1
34 20	ב	IN	90a	3 3a
	חמור	HE-ASS	331b	1
	ערף	BREAK THE NECK	791c	2
	פדה	RANSOM	804a	1
	פטר	THAT WHICH SEPARATES	809d	
	פנה	FACE	816b	2 2a
	ריקם	EMPTILY	938b	1
	שה	A SHEEP	962a	1
34 21	חריש	PLOUGHING	361a	1
	עבד	WORK	713a	1
	קציר	HARVESTING	894d	3
	שבת	CEASE	991d	2 b
	שבת	CEASE	991d	2 b
	שבת	SABBATH	992b	1 a
34 22	אסיף	INGATHERING	63b	
	בכורים	FIRST-FRUITS	114c	
	חג	FESTIVAL-GATHERING	291a	1 b2
	חג	FESTIVAL-GATHERING	291a	1 b2
	חג	FESTIVAL-GATHERING	291b	1 b
	חטה	WHEAT	334d	
	ל	TO	*517a	6 a
	תקופה	COMING ROUND	880d	
	קציר	HARVESTING	894c	2
	שבוע	PERIOD OF SEVEN	989a	1
	שנה	YEAR	1040b	
34 23	אדון	LORD	11a	1 2
	אלהים	GOD	44b	4 ba
	זכור	MALE	271d	
	פנה	FACE	816c	2 1a
	פנה	FACE	816d	2 2a
34 24	איש	MAN	36a	
	גבול	BORDER	147d	1 a
	יהוה	YAHWEH	218d	2 1a
	חמד	DESIRE	326b	A
	ירש	CAUSE TO POSSESS	440a	2 a
	עלה	GO UP	748b	1 d
	פנה	FACE	816d	2 2a
	פנה	FACE	818b	26a
	ראה	TO SEE	908b	1 b
	רחב	BE LARGE	931c	2
34 25	בקר	MORNING	133d	1 a
	בקר	MORNING	134a	1 f
	בקר	MORNING	134b	2
	דם	BLOOD	197d	3 b
	זבח	SACRIFICE	257c	2 2
	זבח	SACRIFICE	257c	2 2
	חג	FESTIVAL-GATHERING	291a	1 b2
	חמץ	THAT WHICH IS LEAVENED	329d	
	ל	TO	517a	6 c
	לון	LODGE	533d	1 c
	על	UPON	755c	2 4c
	פסח	PASSOVER	820b	3
	ראה	TO SEE	907a	2 1
	שחט	SLAUGHTER	1006a	2
34 26	אדמה	GROUND	9c	1
	אם	MOTHER	52a	3
	בכורים	FIRST-FRUITS	114c	
	בשל	BOIL	143a	1
	גדי	KID	152a	
	יהוה	YAHWEH	218d	2 1a
	חלב	MILK	316c	A 2
	ראשית	BEGINNING	912b	1 b
34 27	ברית	COVENANT	136c	2 2c
	ברית	COVENANT	136d	2 2c
	ברית	COVENANT	137a	3 1
	דבר	WORD	183a	2 2
	כרת	CUT	503d	4
	כתב	WRITE	507b	1 a
	על	UPON	754a	2 1fa
	פה	MOUTH	805d	6 d2
34 28	ברית	COVENANT	136c	2 2c
	ברית	COVENANT	136d	2 2c
	דבר	WORD	183a	2 2
	היה	BE	226d	3 2
	יום	DAY	398b	1
	לוח	TABLET	*531d	1
	לוח	TABLET	531d	1
	לילה	NIGHT	538d	1
	עשר	TEN	797a	2 c
	שתה	DRINK	1059b	1 a
34 29	ב	IN	91a	5 2
	דבר	SPEAK	181b	3 d
	היה	COME TO PASS	224c	2 a1 ab
	הר	MOUNTAIN	249b	1 a
	הר	MOUNTAIN	249b	1 a
	הר	MOUNTAIN	250a	1 a
	ירד	COME DOWN	432d	1 a
	לוח	TABLET	531d	1
	סיני	SINAI	696a	
	עדות	TESTIMONY	730b	1
	עור	SKIN	736a	1
	פנה	FACE	815d	1 1a
	קרן	SEND OUT RAYS	902a	
34 30	ירא	FEAR	431b	2

Ch v.	Heb	Eng	Page	Sec
	נגש	DRAW NEAR	620d	1
	עור	SKIN	736a	1
	פנה	FACE	815d	1 1a
	קרן	SEND OUT RAYS	902a	1
34 31	עדה	CONGREGATION	417b	3
	נשיא	PRINCE	672b	4
34 32	הר	MOUNTAIN	249b	1 a
	הר	MOUNTAIN	250a	1 a
	נגש	DRAW NEAR	621a	1
	סיני	SINAI	696a	
34 33	דבר	SPEAK	181b	3 d
	כלה	FINISH	478b	1 c
	מן	FROM	583a	7 b
	מסוה	VEIL	691d	
34 34	דבר	SPEAK	181b	3 d
	יצא	GO OUT	422d	1 a
	מסוה	VEIL	691d	
	סור	TURN ASIDE	694b	1
	צוה	CHARGE	846b	4 c
34 35	דבר	SPEAK	181b	3 d
	מסוה	VEIL	691d	
	פנה	FACE	815d	1 1a
	קרן	SEND OUT RAYS	902a	
	שוב	TURN BACK	999a	1 b
35 1	דבר	WORD	182a	1 2a
	עדה	CONGREGATION	417b	3
35 2	מות	DIE	560c	2
	קדש	APARTNESS	872b	5
	שעיר	SEIR	973a	1 b
	שבת	SABBATH	992c	1 d
	שבתון	SABBOTH OBSERVANCE	992d	1
35 3	בער	BURN	129b	1
	מושב	DWELLING	444b	2 c
	שעיר	SEIR	973a	1 b
35 4	דבר	WORD	182a	1 2a
	זה	THIS	261a	3
	עדה	CONGREGATION	417b	3
35 5	זהב	GOLD	263c	1
	לב	HEART	525a	2 4
	נדיב	INCLINED	622a	1
	רוח	BREATH	925c	7
	תרומה	OFFERING	929b	5
35 6	ארגמן	PURPLE THREAD	71b	1 a
	שש	BYSSUS	1058c	
35 7	אדם	BE RED	10a	1
	איל	RAM	18a	3
	שעיר	SEIR	973a	1 b
	תחש	SEALSKIN	1065a	
	תחש	SEALSKIN	1065a	
35 8	מאור	LUMINARY	22d	1
	בשם	SPICE	142a	1
	משחה	OINTMENT	603c	1
35 9	אבן	STONE	6d	3
	אבן	STONE	6d	3
	אבן	STONE	6d	3
	אפוד	EPHOD	65c	1 b
	חשן	BREAST-PIECE	365d	
	מלוא	SETTING	571b	1
	שהם	CARNELIAN	996a	
35 10	חכם	WISE	314d	1
	לב	HEART	524d	2 3b
35 11	אהל	TENT	14a	3
	בריח	BAR	138b	1 a
	מכסה	COVERING	492c	2
	קרס	HOOK	902b	
	רצח	MURDER	953d	
35 12	בד	PART	94d	3 c
	כפרת	PROPITIATORY	498c	
	מסך	COVERING	697b	2 c
	פרכת	CURTAIN	827d	
35 13	בד	PART	94d	3 c
	לחם	FOOD	537b	1 a
35 14	מאור	LUMINARY	22c	
35 15	בד	PART	94d	3 c
	מזבח	ALTAR	258c	3 b
	משחה	OINTMENT	603c	1
	מסך	COVERING	697b	2 b
	פתח	OPENING	835d	
	שעיר	SEIR	973a	1 b
35 16	בד	PART	94d	3 c
	מזבח	ALTAR	258c	3 a
	מכבר	GRATING	460d	
	כיור	POT	468c	3 a
	כן	BASE	487c	1
	עלה	WHOLE BURNT OFFERING	750d	
35 17	חצר	ENCLOSURE	*347a	3 a
	מסך	COVERING	697b	2 a
	קלע	CURTAIN	887c	
	שער	GATE	1045b	3
35 18	יתד	PEG	450b	A
	מיתר	CORD	452d	
35 19	אהרן	AARON	14d	
	כהן	ACT AS PRIEST	464c	1
	שרד	BRAIDED WORK	975b	
35 20	עדה	CONGREGATION	417b	3
	בוא	COME	99b	2
35 21	מלאכה	WORK	522b	6 b
	לב	HEART	525a	2 4
	נדב	INCITE	621c	
	נשא	LIFT	670d	1 b1
	עבדה	LABOR	715b	4
	רוח	BREATH	925c	7
	תרומה	OFFERING	929b	5
35 22	בוא	COME	99b	2

Ch v.	Heb	Eng	Page	Sec	Ch v.	Heb	Eng	Page	Sec	Ch v.	Heb	Eng	Page	Sec
	ו	AND	253a	1 g		חכם	WISE	314d	1		צלע	RIB	854b	6
	זהב	GOLD	263a	6		חכמה	WISDOM	315b	1	36 26	ארבעים	FORTY	917b	1 a
	חח	HOOK	296b	2		ל	TO	514c	5 fd	36 27	ירכה	EXTREME PARTS	438b	2
	מבעת	SIGNET	371d	2		מלאכה	WORK	522a	3 b	36 28	ירכה	EXTREME PARTS	438b	2
	כלי	ARTICLE	479c	1		לב	HEART	524d	2 3b		מקצע	CORNER-BUTRESS	893a	
	כומז	A GOLD ORNAMENT	484d			נתן	PUT	680c	2 b		מקצע	CORNER-BUTRESS	893a	
	לב	HEART	525a	2 4		עבדה	LABOR	715b	1	36 29	ו	AND	252b	1 b
	נדיב	INCLINED	622a	1		עשה	DO	794b	1 1b		מטה	DOWNWARDS	641b	3
	נוף	WAVE	632b	4		צוה	CHARGE	846a	3		מקצע	CORNER-BUTRESS	893a	
	תנופה	OFFERING	632c	2 b	36 2	אהליאב	OHOLIAB	14c			מקצע	CORNER-BUTRESS	893a	
	נזם	RING	634a	2		בצלאל	BEZALEL	130b	1		ראש	HEAD	910d	2 a
	על	UPON	755c	2 4c		חכם	WISE	314d	1		תאם	BE DOUBLE	1061a	
	רוח	BREATH	925c	7		חכמה	WISDOM	315b	1		תם	COMPLETE	1071a	3
35 23	אדם	BE RED	10a	1		מלאכה	WORK	522a	3 b	36 30	שש	SIX	995c	
	איל	RAM	18a	3		לב	HEART	524d	2 3b	36 31	בריח	BAR	138b	1 a
	בוא	COME	99b	2		לב	HEART	524d	2 3b		צלע	RIB	854b	6
	מצא	FIND	594a	2 b		לב	HEART	525a	2 4	36 32	בריח	BAR	138b	1 a
	שש	BYSSUS	1058c			נשא	LIFT	670d	1 b 1		ירכה	EXTREME PARTS	438b	2
	תחש	SEALSKIN	1065a			נתן	PUT	680d	2 b		צלע	RIB	854b	6
35 24	בוא	COME	99b	2		קרב	COME NEAR	897c	1 b	36 33	ברח	GO THROUGH	137d	1
	מלאכה	WORK	522a	3 b	36 3	בוא	COME	99b	2		בריח	BAR	138b	1 a
	מצא	FIND	594a	2 b		בקר	MORNING	134b	1 f		מן	FROM	582a	5 d1
	עבדה	LABOR	715b	1		מלאכה	WORK	522a	3 b		קצה	END	892a	1
	רום	BE HIGH	927d	3 a		נדבה	FREEWILL-OFFERING	621d	2 a	36 34	תיכן	MIDDLE	1064a	
	תרומה	OFFERING	929a	5		נדבה	FREEWILL-OFFERING	621d	2 c		בית	HOUSE	109c	3
35 25	ארגמן	PURPLE THREAD	71a	1		עבדה	LABOR	715b	1		בריח	BAR	138b	1 a
	ארגמן	PURPLE THREAD	71b	1 a		פנה	FACE	818a	2 5a b	36 35	ארגמן	PURPLE THREAD	71b	1 a
	חכם	WISE	314d	1		תרומה	OFFERING	929b	5		חשב	THINK	363b	1 5
	מוה	SPIN	376a		36 4	איש	MAN	36a			כרוב	CHERUB	500d	4 b
	מטוה	THAT WHICH IS SPUN	376a			חכם	WISE	314d	1		שש	BYSSUS	1058c	
	לב	HEART	524d	2 3b		מלאכה	WORK	522b	6 b	36 36	וו	HOOK	255b	
	שש	BYSSUS	*1058c		36 5	די	SUFFICIENCY	191c	1		יצק	CAST	427b	2
	שש	BYSSUS	1058c			מלאכה	WORK	522a	3 b		עמוד	PILLAR	765b	1
	תכלת	VIOLET THREAD	1067b	1 a		עבדה	LABOR	715b	1		שטה	ACACIA	1008d	
	תכלת	VIOLET THREAD	*1067b	1		רבה	BECOME MANY	915c	1 d1	36 37	ארגמן	PURPLE THREAD	71b	1 a
35 26	חכמה	WISDOM	315b	1	36 6	אשה	WOMAN	61a	1		מסך	COVERING	697b	2 b
	מוה	SPIN	376a			כלא	BE RESTRAINED	476c			פתח	OPENING	835d	
	לב	HEART	525a	2 4		מן	FROM	583a	7 b		רקם	VARIEGATE	955d	
	נשא	LIFT	670d	1 b 1		עבר	PASS OVER	718d	2 a		שש	BYSSUS	1058c	
	עז	SHE-GOAT	*777c	4		קול	VOICE	877b	3 a3	36 38	וו	HOOK	255b	
35 27	אבן	STONE	6d	3		תרומה	OFFERING	929b	5		חמש	FIVE	331d	1 b
	אבן	STONE	6d	3	36 7	די	SUFFICIENCY	191c	1		חשוק	FILLET	366a	
	אפוד	EPHOD	65c	1 b		יתר	SHOW EXCESS	451c	3		עמוד	PILLAR	765a	1
	בוא	COME	99b	2		מסת	SUFFICIENCY	*588b		37 1	אמה	CUBIT	52b	1
	חשן	BREAST-PIECE	365d		36 8	ארגמן	PURPLE THREAD	71b	1 a		בצלאל	BEZALEL	130b	1
	מלוא	SETTING	571b	1		חכם	WISE	314d	1		רחב	WIDTH	931d	
	נשיא	PRINCE	672b	4		חשב	THINK	363b	1 5	37 2	בית	HOUSE	110c	8 a
	שהם	CARNELIAN	996a			כרוב	CHERUB	500d	4 b		זר	CIRCLET	267a	
35 28	מאור	LUMINARY	22c	1		לב	HEART	524d	2 3b		חוץ	THE OUTSIDE	299d	1 bd
	בשם	SPICE	142a	1		שש	BYSSUS	1058c			טהור	CLEAN	373a	2
	משחה	OINTMENT	603c	1	36 9	אמה	CUBIT	52c	1	37 3	זהב	GOLD	263d	2 b
35 29	אשה	WOMAN	61a	1		מדה	SIZE	551c	2		יצק	CAST	427b	2
	בוא	COME	99b	2		עשרים	TWENTY	797d	1 2a		פעם	FOOT	822a	1 c
	מלאכה	WORK	522b	4		ארבע	FOUR	*916a	1 a1		צלע	RIB	854b	6
	לב	HEART	525a	2 4		שמנה	EIGHT	1033a	3 c	37 4	בד	PART	94d	3 c
	נדב	INCITE	621c		36 10	חבר	UNITE	288b	2	37 5	בד	PART	94d	3 c
	נדבה	FREEWILL-OFFERING	621d	2 c		חמש	FIVE	331d	1 c		בוא	COME	99b	1 f
	נדבה	FREEWILL-OFFERING	621d	2 a	36 11	מחברת	THING JOINED	289c	1		צלע	RIB	854b	6
35 30	אורי	URI	22b	1		לולי	LOOP	533b		37 6	אמה	CUBIT	52b	1
	בצלאל	BEZALEL	130b	1		קצה	END	892a	1		טהור	CLEAN	373a	2
	חור	HUR	301b	2		קיצון	OUTERMOST	894a			כפרת	PROPITIATORY	498c	
	יהודה	JUDAH	397b	1 2		תכלת	VIOLET THREAD	1067b	1 a	37 7	חוץ	THE OUTSIDE	300a	1 bd
	קרא	CALL	896a	5 e	36 12	מחברת	THING JOINED	289c	1		כפרת	PROPITIATORY	498c	
35 31	תבונה	UNDERSTANDING	108b	2		לולי	LOOP	533b			כרוב	CHERUB	500d	4 a
	חכמה	WISDOM	315b	1		קבל	RECEIVE	867b			קצה	END	892c	1
	דעת	SKILL	395c	1 b		קצה	END	892a	1		מקשה	HAMMERED WORK	904d	
	מלאכה	WORK	522b	4	36 13	היה	BECOME	226a	2 b	37 8	כפרת	PROPITIATORY	498c	
	מלא	FILL	570c	1		חבר	UNITE	288b	2		כרוב	CHERUB	500d	4 a
	רוח	BREATH	926a	9 d		קרס	HOOK	902b			קצה	END	892c	1
35 32	זהב	GOLD	263c	1		קרס	HOOK	902b			קצה	END	892c	1
	זהב	GOLD	263c	2 a	36 14	עשתי	ONE	799d		37 9	אח	BROTHER	26c	4
	חשב	THINK	363a	1 5		משכן	DWELLING-PLACE	1015d	2 c		כפרת	PROPITIATORY	498c	
	מחשבה	THOUGHT	364c	3	36 15	אמה	CUBIT	52c	1		כרוב	CHERUB	500d	4 a
	עשה	DO	794a	1 1b		מדה	SIZE	551c	2		סכך	OVERSHADOW	697a	1
35 33	אבן	STONE	6d	3		עשתי	ONE	799d			מעל	ABOVE	751d	2 ca
	חרשת	CARVING	360d		36 16	בד	SEPARATION	*94c	1 a		פנה	FACE	816a	1 3
	מחשבה	THOUGHT	364c	3		חבר	UNITE	288b	2		פרש	SPREAD OUT	831a	1
	מלאכה	WORK	522b	4		חמש	FIVE	331d	1 c	37 11	זר	CIRCLET	267a	
	מלא	FILL	570c	2	36 17	חברת	A THING THAT JOINS	289a			טהור	CLEAN	373a	2
35 34	אהליאב	OHOLIAB	14c			מחברת	THING JOINED	289c	2 a	37 12	זר	CIRCLET	267a	
	אחיסמך	AHISAMACH	27b			לולי	LOOP	533b			שפה	SPAN	381c	
	דן	DAN	192d	2		קיצון	OUTERMOST	894a			מסגרת	BORDER	689d	1
	ירה	DIRECT	435b	5 a	36 18	חבר	UNITE	288b	2	37 13	זהב	GOLD	263d	2 b
	לב	HEART	525a	2 4		קרס	HOOK	902b			יצק	CAST	427b	2
	נתן	PUT	680d	2 b	36 19	מכסה	COVERING	492c	2		פאה	CORNER	802a	1
35 35	ארג	WEAVE	71a			מעל	ABOVE	752a	2 d		רגל	FOOT	919d	1 e
	ארגמן	PURPLE THREAD	71b	1 a		שפה	SPEECH	974a	3	37 14	בד	PART	94d	3 c
	חכמה	WISDOM	315b	1		תחש	SEALSKIN	1065a			בית	HOUSE	109c	1
	חרש	GRAVER	360d	1 d	36 20	עמד	STAND	764b	5 d		מסגרת	BORDER	689d	1
	חשב	THINK	363a	1 5	36 21	אמה	CUBIT	52c	1		עמה	CLOSE BY	*769c	A
	חשב	THINK	363b	1 5		חצי	HALF	345c	1	37 15	בד	PART	94d	3 c
	מחשבה	THOUGHT	364c	3	36 22	יד	TENONS	390c	4 f	37 16	חם	THEY	241d	8 d
	מלאכה	WORK	522b	4		שלב	BE BOUND	1016d			טהור	CLEAN	373a	2
	לב	HEART	524d	2 3b	36 23	תימן	SOUTH	412d	1 b		כף	PAN	497a	4 b
	מלא	FILL	570c	1		נגב	SOUTH-COUNTRY	616b	2		מקטרה	SACRIFICIAL BOWL	667d	
	רקם	VARIEGATE	955c			עשרים	TWENTY	797d	1 1b		קערה	DISH	891a	
	שש	BYSSUS	1058c			צלע	RIB	*854b	6		קשוה	JAR	903d	
36 1	אהליאב	OHOLIAB	14c		36 24	יד	TENONS	390c	4 f		ישראל	ISRAEL	975d	2 c
	ב	IN	*88a			עשרים	TWENTY	797d	1 1b	37 17	גביע	CUP	149b	
	תבונה	UNDERSTANDING	108b	2		ארבעים	FORTY	917b	1 a		טהור	CLEAN	373a	2
	בצלאל	BEZALEL	130b	1	36 25	עשרים	TWENTY	797d	1 1b		ירך	BASE	438a	3
	חם	THEY	241d	8 a							כפתור	KNOB	499c	2
											עשה	DO	794c	2 1g
											פרח	BUD	827b	
											קנה	STALK	889d	4 d

Ch	v.	Heb	Eng	Page	Sec
37	18	יצא	GO OUT	423d	1 h
		צד	SIDE	841a	
37	19	גביע	CUP	149b	
		יצא	GO OUT	423d	1 h
		כפתור	KNOB	499c	2
		פרח	BUD	827b	
		שקד	CUPS SHAPED LIKE ALMOND	1052b	
37	20	גביע	CUP	149b	
		כפתור	KNOB	499c	2
		פרח	BUD	827b	
		שקד	CUPS SHAPED LIKE ALMOND	1052b	
37	21	יצא	GO OUT	423d	1 h
		כפתור	KNOB	499c	
		כפתור	KNOB	499c	2
37	22	מהור	CLEAN	373a	2
		כפתור	KNOB	499c	
37	23	מחתה	FIRE-HOLDER	367b	1
		מהור	CLEAN	373a	2
		מלקחים	TONGS	544c	2
		שבע	SEVEN	988b	5 c
37	24	מהור	CLEAN	373a	2
		עשה	DO	794c	2 1g
37	25	מזבח	ALTAR	258c	3 b
		מזבח	ALTAR	259c	8
		רבע	SQUARED	917c	
37	26	גג	TOP	151a	2
		זר	CIRCLET	267a	
		מהור	CLEAN	373a	2
		קיר	WALL	885b	4
37	27	בד	PART	94d	3 c
		בית	HOUSE	109c	3
		זר	CIRCLET	267a	
		צד	SIDE	841a	
		צלע	RIB	854b	6
37	28	בד	PART	94d	3 c
37	29	מהור	CLEAN	373a	2
		משחה	OINTMENT	603c	1
		רקח	MIX OIL	955b	
38	1	מזבח	ALTAR	258c	3 a
		מזבח	ALTAR	258c	3 a
		מזבח	ALTAR	259a	8
		עלה	WHOLE BURNT OFFERING	750d	
		רבע	SQUARED	917c	
		רחב	WIDTH	931d	
38	2	פנה	CORNER	819c	1 a
38	3	מזלגה	THREE PRONGED FORK	272c	
		מזרק	BOWL	284d	2 a
		מחתה	FIRE-HOLDER	367b	2
		יע	SHOVEL	418b	
		כלי	UTENSIL	480a	2 f
		סור	POT	696c	2
38	4	רשת	NET	440c	
		מכבר	GRATING	460d	
		כרכב	RIM	501b	
38	5	בד	PART	94d	3 c
		בית	HOUSE	109c	3
		יצק	CAST	427b	2
		מכבר	GRATING	460d	
		קצת	END	892c	1
38	6	בד	PART	94d	3 c
38	7	בד	PART	94d	3 c
		בוא	COME	99b	1 f
		מזבח	ALTAR	258c	3 a
		לוח	BOARD	531d	2
		נבב	HOLLOW OUT	612c	
		עשה	DO	794c	2 1g
		צלע	RIB	854b	6
38	8	ב	IN	90c	3 6
		כיור	POT	468c	3 a
		כן	BASE	487c	1
		צבא	SERVE	838d	2
		מראה	MIRROR	909c	
38	9	תימן	SOUTH	412d	1 b
		נגב	SOUTH-COUNTRY	616b	2
		שש	BYSSUS	1058c	
38	10	וו	HOOK	255b	
		חשוק	FILLET	366a	
38	11	וו	HOOK	255b	
		חשוק	FILLET	366a	
38	12	וו	HOOK	255b	
		חמשים	FIFTY	332c	2 a
		חשוק	FILLET	366a	
		חשוק	FILLET	366a	
		ים	SEA	411b	9
		עשר	TEN	797a	2 b
38	13	אמה	CUBIT	52b	1
		מזרח	PLACE OF SUNRISE	281a	2 c1
		קדם	EASTWARD	870a	
38	14	אמה	CUBIT	52b	1
		חמש	FIVE	332a	2 a
		כתף	SIDE	509c	2 b
38	15	אמה	CUBIT	52b	1
		זה	THIS	262a	6 e
		חמש	FIVE	332a	2 a
		חצר	ENCLOSURE	*347a	3 a
		כתף	SIDE	509c	2 b
		ל	TO	514a	5 d
38	16	שש	BYSSUS	1058c	
38	17	וו	HOOK	255b	
		חשוק	FILLET	366a	
		חשוק	FILLET	366a	
		חשק	FURNISH WITH FILLETS	366b	
38	18	צפוי	METAL PLATING	860b	
		ארגמן	PURPLE THREAD	71b	1 a
		חצר	ENCLOSURE	*347a	3 a
		מסך	COVERING	697b	2 a
		עמה	CLOSE BY	769d	B
		עשרים	TWENTY	797c	1 1a
		רקם	VARIEGATE	955c	
		שש	BYSSUS	1058c	
38	19	וו	HOOK	255b	
		חשוק	FILLET	366a	
		צפוי	METAL PLATING	860b	
		ארבע	FOUR	917a	1 b3
38	20	יתד	PEG	450b	A
38	21	אהרן	AARON	14d	
		איתמר	ITHAMAR	16a	
		לוי	LEVITE	533a	3 1d
		עבדה	LABOR	715b	4
		עדות	TESTIMONY	730b	1
		פה	MOUTH	805d	6 d1 a
		פקד	ATTEND TO	823d	
		פרדים	MUSTERINGS	824b	
		משכן	DWELLING-PLACE	1015d	2 c
38	22	אורי	URI	22b	1
		בצלאל	BEZALEL	130b	1
		חור	HUR	301b	2
		יהודה	JUDAH	397b	1 2
38	23	אהליאב	OHOLIAB	14c	
		אחיסמך	AHISAMACH	27b	
		ארגמן	PURPLE THREAD	71b	1 a
		דן	DAN	192d	2
		חרש	GRAVER	360d	1
		חשב	THINK	363b	1 5
		רקם	VARIEGATE	955c	
		שש	BYSSUS	1058c	
38	24	היה	BE	227b	3 4b
		זהב	GOLD	263a	6
		מלאכה	WORK	522b	6 b
		תנופה	OFFERING	632c	2 b
		עשה	DO	795b	2 0
		עשה	DO	795b	2 f
		עשרים	TWENTY	797d	1 2a
		קדש	APARTNESS	871d	2 c
38	25	אלף	THOUSAND	49a	1 b
		אלף	THOUSAND	49a	1 b
		פקד	ATTEND TO	823c	A 4
		שבעים	SEVENTY	988c	3 b
38	26	אלף	THOUSAND	49a	1 c
		בן	SON	122a	9 a
		בקע	HALF	132c	
		חמשים	FIFTY	332c	1 b3
		מחצית	HALF	346a	1
		עבר	PASS OVER	718b	5 g
		פקד	ATTEND TO	823c	A 4
		שקל	SHEKEL	1053d	
38	27	יצק	CAST	427b	2
		כסף	SILVER	494b	8 c
		מטה	DOWNWARDS	641b	3
		אלף	THOUSAND	49a	1 b
38	28	וו	HOOK	255b	
		חמש	FIVE	332b	5 h
		חשק	FURNISH WITH FILLETS	366b	
		צפה	LAY OUT	860a	
		שבעים	SEVENTY	988c	3 b
38	29	כבר	ROUND	503b	3 b
		תנופה	OFFERING	632c	2 b
38	30	אשר	PARTICLE OF RELATION	83a	7 b
		מזבח	ALTAR	258c	3 a
		מזבח	ALTAR	259a	8
		מכבר	GRATING	460d	
		נחשת	COPPER	638d	1
38	31	חצר	ENCLOSURE	*347a	3 a
		יתד	PEG	450b	A
39	1	ארגמן	PURPLE THREAD	71b	1 a
		כאשר	AS	455b	1 a
		מן	OUT OF	579b	2 ba
		משה	MOSES	602c	
		צוה	CHARGE	846a	3
		שרד	BRAIDED WORK	975b	
		שרד	BRAIDED WORK	975b	
39	2	אפוד	EPHOD	65c	1 b
		ארגמן	PURPLE THREAD	71b	1 a
		שש	BYSSUS	1058c	
39	3	ארגמן	PURPLE THREAD	71a	1
		ארגמן	PURPLE THREAD	71b	1 a
		חשב	THINK	363b	1 5
		פח	PLATE OF METAL	809a	
		פתיל	CORD	836d	
		קצין	CUT OFF	893d	
		קצין	CUT OFF	893d	
		רקע	BEAT	956a	
		שש	BYSSUS	1058c	
		תוך	MIDST	1063c	
		תכלת	VIOLET THREAD	*1067b	1
39	4	חבר	UNITE	288a	1 b
		חבר	UNITE	288b	2
		כתף	SHOULDER	509c	1 c
		ל	TO	513c	5 ca
		קצה	END	892c	1
		קצת	END	892c	1
39	5	אפדה	EPHOD	66a	1
		ארגמן	PURPLE THREAD	71b	1 a
		חשב	INGENIOUS WORK	363d	1 5
		כאשר	AS	455b	1 a
		משה	MOSES	602c	
		צוה	CHARGE	846a	3
		שש	BYSSUS	1058c	
39	6	אבן	STONE	6d	3
		חתם	SEAL	368b	
		סבב	TURN ABOUT	686d	2
		פתח	ENGRAVE	836c	
		פתוח	ENGRAVING	836c	
		משבצות	CHEQUERED WORK	990b	
39	7	שהם	CARNELIAN	996a	
		אפוד	EPHOD	65c	1 b
		זכרון	MEMORIAL	272a	1 d
		כאשר	AS	455b	1 a
		כתף	SHOULDER	509c	1 c
		משה	MOSES	602c	
39	8	ארגמן	PURPLE THREAD	71b	1 a
		חשב	THINK	363b	1 5
		חשן	BREAST-PIECE	365d	
		שש	BYSSUS	1058c	
39	9	זרת	SPAN	285a	
		חשן	BREAST-PIECE	365d	
		כנף	WING	489c	1 c
		כפל	DOUBLE OVER	495c	
		עשה	DO	794c	2 1g
39	10	אדם	CARNELIAN	10b	
		ברקת	EMERALD	140c	
		טור	ROW	377a	2
		מלא	FILL	570d	2
		פטדה	TOPAZ	809c	
39	11	יהלם	ROW	240d	
		טור	ROW	377a	2
		נפך	EMERALD	656c	
		ספיר	SAPRHIRE	705d	
		שרד	BRAIDED WORK	975b	
39	12	אחלמה	AMETHYST	29b	
		טור	ROW	377a	2
		לשם	JACINTH	545d	
		שבו	AGAGTE	986b	
39	13	טור	ROW	377a	2
		ישפה	JASPER	448a	
		מלאה	SETTING OF JEWEL	571b	
		סבב	TURN ABOUT	686d	2
		רביעי	FOURTH	917d	1
		משבצות	CHEQUERED WORK	990b	
		שהם	CARNELIAN	996a	
		תרשיש	YELLOW JASPAR	1076d	
39	14	חתם	SEAL	368b	
		פתוח	ENGRAVING	836c	
39	15	גבלת	TWISTING	148b	
		חשן	BREAST-PIECE	365d	
		מהור	CLEAN	373a	2
		עבת	CORD	721c	1 c
		שרשרה	CHAIN	1057c	
39	16	חשן	BREAST-PIECE	365d	
		קצה	END	892c	1
		משבצות	CHEQUERED WORK	990b	
39	17	חשן	BREAST-PIECE	365d	
		עבת	CORD	721c	1 c
		קצה	END	892c	1
39	18	כתף	SHOULDER	509c	1 c
		מול	IN FRONT OF	*557c	2 a
		עבת	CORD	721c	1 c
		משבצות	CHEQUERED WORK	990b	
39	19	בית	HOUSE	110b	7
		חשן	BREAST-PIECE	365d	
		קצה	END	892c	1
39	20	אפוד	EPHOD	65c	1 b
		מחברת	THING JOINED	289c	2 b
		חשב	INGENIOUS WORK	363d	
		כתף	SHOULDER	509c	1 c
		מול	IN FRONT OF	557c	2 bb
		מטה	DOWNWARDS	641b	3
		מעל	ABOVE	751c	1 b
		עמה	CLOSE BY	*769c	A
39	21	אפוד	EPHOD	65c	1 b
		זחה	REMOVE	267b	
		חשב	INGENIOUS WORK	363d	
		חשן	BREAST-PIECE	365d	
		משה	MOSES	602c	
		פתיל	CORD	836d	
		רכס	BIND	940c	
		תכלת	VIOLET THREAD	1067b	1 a
		אפוד	EPHOD	65c	1 b
39	22	ארג	WEAVE	71a	
		כליל	WHOLE	483a	2 a
		מעיל	ROBE	591c	3
		תכלת	VIOLET THREAD	1067b	1 a
39	23	קרע	TEAR	902d	
		שהה	SPEECH	974a	3
		תחרא	CORSELET	1065a	
39	24	ארגמן	PURPLE THREAD	71b	1 a
		מעיל	ROBE	591c	3
		רמון	POMEGRANATE	942a	3
		שול	SKIRT	1002c	
		שזר	BE TWISTED	1005a	
		שש	BYSSUS	1058c	
39	25	מהור	CLEAN	373a	2
		מעיל	ROBE	591c	3
		פעמן	BELL	822b	
		פעמן	BELL	822b	
		רמון	POMEGRANATE	942a	3
		שול	SKIRT	1002c	
		תוך	MIDST	1063c	

Ch	v.	Heb	Eng	Page	Sec
39	26	מעיל	ROBE	591c	3
		משה	MOSES	602c	
		פעמן	BELL	822b	
		רמן	POMEGRANATE	942a	3
		שול	SKIRT	1002c	
39	27	ארג	WEAVE	71a	
		כתנת	TUNIC	509a	
		שש	BYSSUS	1058c	
39	28	בד	WHITE LINEN	94b	
		מגבעות	HEAD-GEAR	149c	
		מכנס	BREECH	488b	
		מעיל	ROBE	591c	3
		פאר	HEAD-DRESS	802c	
		מצנפת	TURBAN	857b	
		שש	BYSSUS	1058c	
		שש	BYSSUS	1058c	
39	29	ארגמן	PURPLE THREAD	71b	1 a
		אבנט	GIRDLE	126a	
		משה	MOSES	602c	
		רקם	VARIEGATE	955d	
		שש	BYSSUS	1058c	
39	30	חתם	SEAL	368b	
		מהור	CLEAN	373a	2
		כתב	WRITE	507b	1 a
		כתב	WRITE	507c	1 b1
		מכתב	WRITING	508b	2
		נזר	CROWN	634b	1 b
		פתח	ENGRAVING	836c	
		ציץ	BLOSSOM	847d	2
		קדש	APARTNESS	872b	4 a
		קדש	APARTNESS	872a	4 a
39	31	משה	MOSES	602c	
		מעל	ABOVE	752a	2 d
		פתיל	CORD	836d	
		מצנפת	TURBAN	857b	
		תכלת	VIOLET THREAD	1067b	1 a
39	32	אהל	TENT	14a	3
		כלה	BE FINISHED	477c	1 b
		כן	SO	486c	2 cc
		עבדה	LABOR	715b	4
		צוה	CHARGE	846a	3
		משכן	DWELLING-PLACE	1015d	2 c
39	33	קרס	HOOK	902b	
39	34	אדם	BE RED	10a	
		איל	RAM	18a	3
		מכסה	COVERING	492c	2
		מסך	COVERING	697b	2 c
		פרכת	CURTAIN	827d	
		תחש	SEALSKIN	1065a	
39	35	בד	PART	94d	3 c
		כפרת	PROPITIATORY	498c	
		עדות	TESTIMONY	730b	1
39	36	לחם	FOOD	537b	1 a
39	37	מאור	LUMINARY	22d	
		מהור	CLEAN	373a	2
		מערכה	ROW	790b	2
39	38	מזבח	ALTAR	258c	3 b
		משחה	OINTMENT	603c	1
		מסך	COVERING	697b	2 b
		פתח	OPENING	835d	
39	39	בד	PART	94d	3 c
		מזבח	ALTAR	258c	3 a
		מכבר	GRATING	460d	
		כיור	POT	468c	3 a
		כן	BASE	487c	1
		ל	TO	513c	5 ca
		נחשת	COPPER	638d	1
39	40	חצר	ENCLOSURE	*347a	3 a
		יתד	PEG	450b	A
		מיתר	CORD	452d	
		מסך	COVERING	697b	2 a
		עבדה	LABOR	715b	4
39	41	אהרן	AARON	14d	
		כהן	ACT AS PRIEST	464c	1
		שרד	BRAIDED WORK	975b	
39	42	כן	SO	486c	2 cc
		עבדה	LABOR	715b	1
		צוה	CHARGE	846a	3
39	43	ברך	BLESS	139a	3
		כאשר	AS	455b	1 b
		כן	SO	486c	2 ca
40	2	אהל	TENT	14a	3
		קום	STAND	878d	2 b
		ראשון	FIRST	911d	2 a
		משכן	DWELLING-PLACE	1015d	2 c
40	3	עדות	TESTIMONY	730b	1
40	4	ערך	ARRANGE	789c	1 b
		ערך	ORDER	789d	1
40	5	מזבח	ALTAR	258c	3 b
		נתן	PUT	680b	2 a
		מסך	COVERING	697b	2 b
		עדות	TESTIMONY	730b	1
		פנה	FACE	817d	2 4d
		פתח	OPENING	835d	
		קטרת	SMOKE	882d	2
40	6	אהל	TENT	14a	3
		מזבח	ALTAR	258c	3 a
		נתן	PUT	680b	2 a
		עלה	WHOLE BURNT OF-FERING	750d	
		פנה	FACE	817d	2 4d
		פתח	OPENING	835d	
		משכן	DWELLING-PLACE	1015d	2 c
40	7	כיור	POT	468c	3 a
40	8	חצר	ENCLOSURE	*347a	3 a
		נתן	PUT	680c	2 a

Ch	v.	Heb	Eng	Page	Sec
40	9	מסך	COVERING	697b	2 a
		משחה	OINTMENT	603c	1
		קדש	APARTNESS	871d	2 c
		קדש	BE SET APART	873a	1 a
40	10	מזבח	ALTAR	258c	3 a
		מזבח	ALTAR	259a	9
		מזבח	ALTAR	259b	4
		מזבח	ALTAR	259b	4
		משח	ANOINT	603b	3
		עלה	WHOLE BURNT OF-FERING	750d	
		קדש	APARTNESS	872a	3 a
		קדש	BE SET APART	873a	1 a
40	11	כיור	POT	468c	3 a
		כן	BASE	487c	1
		משח	ANOINT	603b	3
		קדש	BE SET APART	873a	1 a
40	12	קרב	COME NEAR	898a	2 a1
		רחץ	WASH OFF	934c	1
40	13	כהן	ACT AS PRIEST	464c	1
		לבש	CLOTHE	528b	1 a
		משח	ANOINT	603b	3
		קדש	BE SET APART	873a	1 c
40	14	כתנת	TUNIC	509a	
		לבש	CLOTHE	528b	1 a
		קרב	COME NEAR	898a	2 a1
40	15	דור	GENERATION	190a	2 c
		היה	BECOME	226c	2 2f
		כהן	ACT AS PRIEST	464c	1
		כתנה	PRIESTHOOD	464d	
		משח	ANOINT	603b	3 a
40	16	כן	SO	486c	2 cc
40	17	נתן	PUT	680b	2 a
		ראשון	FIRST	911d	2 a
40	18	בריח	BAR	138b	1 a
		קום	STAND	878a	2 a
		קום	STAND	878d	2 b
40	19	מכסה	COVERING	492c	2
		משה	MOSES	602c	
		מעל	ABOVE	752a	2 d
		פרש	SPREAD OUT	831b	2
		משכן	DWELLING-PLACE	1015d	2 c
40	20	בד	PART	94d	3 c
		כפרת	PROPITIATORY	498c	
		עדות	TESTIMONY	730b	1
		מעל	ABOVE	752a	2 d
		שום	TO PLACE	964b	4 b
40	21	משה	MOSES	602c	
		סכך	OVERSHADOW	697a	2
		מסך	COVERING	697b	2 c
		עדות	TESTIMONY	730b	1
		פרכת	CURTAIN	827d	
40	22	ירך	SIDE	438a	2
40	23	לחם	FOOD	537b	1 a
		ערך	ARRANGE	789c	1 b
		ערך	ORDER	789d	1
40	24	ירך	SIDE	438a	2
		נגב	SOUTH-COUNTRY	616b	2
40	25	גבח	FRONT	647b	1
		משה	MOSES	602c	
40	26	מזבח	ALTAR	258c	3 b
40	27	משה	MOSES	602c	
		קטרת	SMOKE	882d	2
		קמר	MAKE SACRAFICES SMOKE	883b	2
40	28	מסך	COVERING	697b	2 b
		פתח	OPENING	835d	
40	29	אהל	TENT	14a	3
		מזבח	ALTAR	258c	3 a
		מנחה	OFFERING	585b	5
		משה	MOSES	602c	
		עלה	GO UP	750a	8
		עלה	WHOLE BURNT OF-FERING	750d	
		פתח	OPENING	835d	
		משכן	DWELLING-PLACE	1015d	2 c
40	30	כיור	POT	468c	3 a
40	31	רחץ	WASH OFF	934c	1
40	32	משה	MOSES	602c	
40	33	חצר	ENCLOSURE	*347a	3 a
		כלה	FINISH	478a	1 a
		סביב	ROUND ABOUT	687a	1 cb
		מסך	COVERING	697b	2 a
		קום	STAND	878d	2 b
40	34	כבוד	GLORY	458d	2 c1
		כסה	COVER	491d	4
		מלא	FILL	570b	2
		משכן	DWELLING-PLACE	1015d	2 c
40	35	יכל	BE ABLE	407c	1 a
		כבוד	GLORY	458d	2 c1
		מלא	FILL	570b	2
		שכן	SETTLE DOWN	1015a	1 c
		משכן	DWELLING-PLACE	1015d	2 c
40	36	נסע	JOURNEY	652b	3
		עלה	GO UP	749a	1 c1
40	37	אם	IF	49c	1 a1 b
		נסע	SET OUT	652a	2 a
		עד	AS FAR AS	724b	12a a
		עלה	GO UP	749a	1 c1
40	38	בית	HOUSE	110a	5 dd
		ישראל	ISRAEL	975d	2 c

Ch	v.	Heb	Eng	Page	Sec
1	1	מועד	TENT OF MEETING	418a	5
1	2	אדם	MAN	9b	1
		בקר	CATTLE	133b	1 a
		כי	IF	473b	2 b
		כי	IF	473c	2 b
		מן	FROM	580c	3 a
		צאן	SMALL CATTLE	838b	1 a4
		קרב	COME NEAR	898a	2 b6
		קרבן	OFFERING	898d	
1	3	אם	IF	49d	1 a2
		זכר	MALE	271c	1 2
		מועד	TENT OF MEETING	418a	5
		כי	IF	473b	2 b
		ל	TO	515a	5 ha
		עלה	WHOLE BURNT OF-FERING	750b	
		פנה	FACE	817a	2 4a g
		פתח	OPENING	835d	
		קרבן	OFFERING	898d	
		רצון	GOODWILL	953c	2
1	4	כפר	COVER OVER	497d	3 b2
		ל	TO	511a	1 e
		סמך	LEAN	701d	1 a
		עלה	WHOLE BURNT OF-FERING	750d	
		ראש	HEAD	910d	1 b
		רצה	BE PLEASED WITH	953b	1
1	5	אהרן	AARON	14d	
		בן	SON	121a	1 jz
		בקר	CATTLE	133b	1 a
		דם	BLOOD	197c	3 b
		דם	BLOOD	197c	3 b
		זוית	CORNER	265a	
		זרק	TO TOSS	284c	1 b
		כהן	PRIEST	464a	7
		סביב	ROUND ABOUT	687a	1 b
		עלה	WHOLE BURNT OF-FERING	750d	
		על	UPON	752d	2 1
		פנה	FACE	817b	2 4a h
		קרב	COME NEAR	898a	2 b3
		שחט	SLAUGHTER	1006a	2
1	6	נתח	PIECE OF A DI-VIDED CARCASS	677c	
		נתח	CUT IN PIECES	677c	
		עלה	WHOLE BURNT OF-FERING	750d	
1	7	פשמ	STRIP OFF	833a	3
		אש	FIRE	77c	4
		בן	SON	121a	1 jz
		עץ	TREE	782a	2 d
		ערך	ARRANGE	789c	1 b
1	8	בן	SON	121a	1 jz
		כהן	PRIEST	464a	7
		נתח	PIECE OF A DI-VIDED CARCASS	677c	
		ערך	ARRANGE	789c	1 b
		פדר	SUET	804d	
		ראש	HEAD	910d	1 b
1	9	אשה	OFFERING MADE BY FIRE	78a	
		אשה	OFFERING MADE BY FIRE	78a	
		כל	ALL	482d	2 ba
		כרע	LEG	502d	
		ל	TO	515b	5 hb b
		מי	WATER	565b	1 a
		ניחח	SOOTHING	629c	
		עלה	WHOLE BURNT OF-FERING	750d	
		קרב	INWARD PART	899b	3
		ריח	SCENT	926b	2
		רחץ	WASH OFF	934c	1
1	10	זכר	MALE	271c	1 2
		כשב	LAMB	461b	
		כי	IF	473b	2 b
		עלה	WHOLE BURNT OF-FERING	750b	
		עז	SHE-GOAT	777c	3 d
		צאן	SMALL CATTLE	838b	1 a4
		קרבן	OFFERING	898d	
1	11	בן	SON	121a	1 jz
		דם	BLOOD	197c	3 b
		זוית	CORNER	265a	
		זרק	TO TOSS	284c	1 b
		ירך	SIDE	438a	2
		כהן	PRIEST	464a	7
		סביב	ROUND ABOUT	687a	1 b
		פנה	FACE	817b	2 4a h
		שחט	SLAUGHTER	1006a	2
1	12	נתח	PIECE OF A DI-VIDED CARCASS	677c	
		נתח	CUT IN PIECES	677c	
		ערך	ARRANGE	789c	1 b
		פדר	SUET	804d	
		ראש	HEAD	910d	1 b
1	13	כל	ALL	482d	2 ba
		כרע	LEG	502d	
		מי	WATER	565b	1 a
		ניחח	SOOTHING	629c	
		עלה	WHOLE BURNT OF-FERING	750d	
		קרב	INWARD PART	899b	3
		רחץ	WASH OFF	934c	1
1	14	אם	IF	49d	1 a2

Ch v.	Heb	Eng	Page	Sec
	בן	SON	121c	7 b
	יונה	DOVE	401d	
	עוף	FLY	733d	1
	עלה	WHOLE BURNT OF-FERING	750b	
	קרב	COME NEAR	898a	2 b6
1 15	תר	TURTLE-DOVE	1076a	
	דם	BLOOD	197d	3 b
	מלק	NIP	577a	
	מצה	DRAIN	594c	
	קיר	WALL	885b	4
	קרב	COME NEAR	898a	2 b1
	ראש	HEAD	910d	1 b
1 16	אצל	BESIDE	69b	A
	דשן	FAT ASHES	206c	2
	מראה	CROP	597b	
	נוצה	PLUMAGE	663c	
	קדם	EASTWARD	870a	
1 17	בדל	BE DIVIDED	95c	4
	כנף	WING	489c	1 a
	ניחח	SOOTHING	629c	
	עלה	WHOLE BURNT OF-FERING	750d	
2 1	שסע	DIVIDE	1042d	
	יצק	POUR	427b	1
	כי	IF	473c	2 b
	לבנה	FRANKINCENSE	526d	
	מנחה	OFFERING	585c	5 e
	מנחה	OFFERING	585c	5 b
	מנחה	OFFERING	585c	6
	נפש	SOUL	660b	4 c2
	סלת	FINE FLOUR	701c	
	קרב	COME NEAR	898a	2 b6
	קרבן	OFFERING	898d	
	שמן	OIL	1032c	2 g
2 2	בוא	COME	99b	2
	בן	SON	121a	1 jz
	אזכרה	MEMORIAL-OFFER-ING	272c	
	כהן	PRIEST	464a	7
	כף	HOLLOW OF THE HAND	*496b	1 a
	לבנה	FRANKINCENSE	526d	
	מלא	FULNESS	571b	1
	מנחה	OFFERING	585c	6
	על	UPON	755c	2 4c
	קמץ	GRASP	888a	
	קמץ	FIST	888a	
	שם	THERE	1027a	4 d
2 3	אהרן	AARON	14d	
	אשה	OFFERING MADE BY FIRE	78a	
2 4	מאפה	THING BAKED	66b	
	בלל	MIX	117c	2
	בלל	MIX	117c	2
	חלה	A KIND OF CAKE	319d	2 d
	מנחה	OFFERING	585c	5 e
	מנחה	OFFERING	585c	5 c
	משח	ANOINT	603a	1
	מצה	UNLEAVENED BREAD	695b	
	קרב	COME NEAR	898a	2 b6
	קרבן	OFFERING	898d	
	רקיק	A THIN CAKE	956d	
	שמן	OIL	1032c	2 g
	שמן	OIL	1032c	2
	תנור	FIRE-POT	1072b	
2 5	בלל	MIX	117c	2
	מחבת	FLAT PLATE	290b	1
	מנחה	OFFERING	585c	5 c
	מצה	UNLEAVENED BREAD	695b	
	קרבן	OFFERING	898d	
	שמן	OIL	1032c	2 g
2 6	יצק	POUR	427b	1
	פתת	BREAK UP	837d	
	פת	FRAGMENT	837d	
2 7	מנחה	OFFERING	585c	5 c
	עשה	DO	795b	2 a
	מרחשת	STEW PAN	935d	
	שמן	OIL	1032c	2 g
2 8	מנחה	OFFERING	585c	6
	מנחה	OFFERING	585c	6
	נגש	APPROACH	621b	
	עשה	DO	795b	2 d
	קדש	APARTNESS	872a	3 b
	קרב	COME NEAR	898a	2 b4
2 9	אזכרה	MEMORIAL-OFFER-ING	272c	
	רום	BE HIGH	927c	2
2 10	אהרן	AARON	14d	
	קדש	APARTNESS	872a	3 b
2 11	אשה	OFFERING MADE BY FIRE	78a	
	דבש	HONEY	185b	
	חמץ	THAT WHICH IS LEAVENED	329d	
	מנחה	OFFERING	585c	6
	מנחה	OFFERING	585c	5 c
	עשה	DO	795b	2 d
	קטר	MAKE SACRAFICES SMOKE	883a	1 a
	שאר	LEAVEN	959a	
2 12	קרבן	OFFERING	898d	
	ראשית	BEGINNING	912b	1 b
2 13	ברית	COVENANT	136c	2 2c
	ברית	COVENANT	137b	3 2

Ch v.	Heb	Eng	Page	Sec
	מלח	SALT	571d	
	מלח	SALT	*571d	
	מלח	SALT	572a	
	מנחה	OFFERING	585c	5 e
	קרבן	OFFERING	898d	
	שבת	CEASE	992a	5
2 14	אביב	YOUNG EARS	1b	1
	אש	FIRE	77c	3
	בכורים	FIRST-FRUITS	114c	
	בכורים	FIRST-FRUITS	114c	
	גרש	A CRUSHING	176c	
	כרמל	GARDEN	502a	2
	מנחה	OFFERING	585c	5 a
	מנחה	OFFERING	585c	5 e
	קלה	ROAST	885d	
2 15	לבנה	FRANKINCENSE	526d	
	מנחה	OFFERING	585c	5 a
2 16	אשה	OFFERING MADE BY FIRE	78a	
	גרש	A CRUSHING	176c	
	אזכרה	MEMORIAL-OFFER-ING	272c	
	לבנה	FRANKINCENSE	526d	
	על	UPON	755c	2 4c
	קטר	MAKE SACRAFICES SMOKE	883a	1 a
3 1	זבח	SACRIFICE	257d	2 5
	זכר	MALE	271c	1 2
	נקבה	FEMALE	666c	2
	פנה	FACE	817b	2 4a h
	שלם	PEACE-OFFERING	1023c	
3 2	בן	SON	121a	1 jz
	דם	BLOOD	197c	3 b
	זרק	TO TOSS	284c	1 b
	זרק	TO TOSS	284c	1 b
	כהן	PRIEST	464a	7
3 3	חלב	FAT	317a	2 b
	כסה	COVER	491d	4
	קרב	COME NEAR	898a	2 b2
	קרב	INWARD PART	899b	3
3 4	חלב	FAT	317a	2 b
	יתרת	APPENDAGE	452c	
	כבד	LIVER	458b	
	כליה	KIDNEYS	480b	1 b
	כסל	LOINS	492d	1
	על	UPON	755c	2 4c
3 5	בן	SON	121a	1 jz
3 6	זכר	MALE	271c	1 2
	נקבה	FEMALE	666c	2
	קרב	COME NEAR	898a	2 a1
3 7	כשב	LAMB	461b	
	פנה	FACE	817b	2 4a h
	קרב	COME NEAR	898a	2 b1
3 8	בן	SON	121a	1 jz
	דם	BLOOD	197c	3 b
	זרק	TO TOSS	284c	1 b
3 9	אליה	FAT TAIL	47a	
	חלב	FAT	317a	2 b
	כסה	COVER	491d	4
	עמה	CLOSE BY	769c	A
	עצה	SPINE	782b	
	קרב	INWARD PART	899b	3
3 10	חלב	FAT	317a	2 b
	יתרת	APPENDAGE	452c	
	כבד	LIVER	458b	
	כליה	KIDNEYS	480b	1 b
	כסל	LOINS	492d	1
	על	UPON	755c	2 4c
3 11	לחם	FOOD	537b	2 c
3 12	עז	SHE-GOAT	777c	3 e
	קרב	COME NEAR	898a	2 b1
3 13	בן	SON	121a	1 jz
	דם	BLOOD	197c	3 b
	זרק	TO TOSS	284c	1 b
3 14	חלב	FAT	317a	2 b
	כסה	COVER	491d	4
	קרב	COME NEAR	898a	2 b2
	קרבן	OFFERING	898d	
	קרב	INWARD PART	899b	3
3 15	חלב	FAT	317a	2 b
	יתרת	APPENDAGE	452c	
	כבד	LIVER	458b	
	כליה	KIDNEYS	480b	1 b
	כסל	LOINS	492d	1
	על	UPON	755c	2 4c
3 16	אשה	OFFERING MADE BY FIRE	78a	
	לחם	FOOD	537b	2 c
3 17	דור	GENERATION	190a	2 c
	דם	BLOOD	196c	1
	חלב	FAT	317a	2 b
	חקה	SOMETHING PRE-SCRIBED	350a	1
	מושב	DWELLING	444b	2 c
	עולם	LONG DURATION	762c	2 e
4 2	הם	THEY	241d	8 c
	חטא	MISS A GOAL OR WAY	307b	2 b
	חטאת	SIN	*309d	4 c
	כי	IF	473c	2 b
	כי	IF	473c	2 b
	כל	ALL	482a	1 eb
	מן	FROM	581a	3 bd
	נפש	SOUL	660b	4 c2
	עשה	DO	793d	1 1a 1
	עשה	DO	795b	1 b

Ch v.	Heb	Eng	Page	Sec
	שגגה	SIN OF ERROR	993a	
4 3	אשמה	WRONG-DOING	80b	2
	אשר	THAT	83d	8 d
	בן	SON	121c	7 b
	חטא	MISS A GOAL OR WAY	306d	2 b
	חטא	MISS A GOAL OR WAY	307b	2 b
	חטאת	SIN	308d	1 b
	חטאת	SIN	309c	4 b
	חטאת	SIN	309d	4 b
	כהן	PRIEST	464b	8
	כי	IF	473b	
	משיח	ANOINTED	603c	2
	על	UPON	754b	2 1f b
	פר	YOUNG BULL	830d	2 c
	קרב	COME NEAR	898a	2 b
4 4	פר	YOUNG BULL	830d	2 c
4 5	דם	BLOOD	197c	3 b
	כהן	PRIEST	464b	8
	משיח	ANOINTED	603c	2
4 6	דם	BLOOD	197c	3 b
	טבל	DIP	371b	1
	נזה	SPURT	633c	
	פנה	FACE	816d	2 2b
	פרכת	CURTAIN	827d	
	אצבע	FINGER	840c	1 a
	קדש	APARTNESS	871d	2
	שבע	SEVEN	988a	1 a
	שבע	SEVEN	988b	5 c
4 7	אל	TO	40c	8
	דם	BLOOD	197d	3 b
	דם	BLOOD	197d	3 b
	מזבח	ALTAR	258c	3
	מזבח	ALTAR	258c	3 a
	מזבח	ALTAR	259b	3
	מזבח	ALTAR	259b	2
	יסוד	FOUNDATION	414b	2
	סם	SPICE	702c	
	עלה	WHOLE BURNT OF-FERING	750d	
	קטרת	SMOKE	882d	2
	קרן	HORN	902a	3
	שפך	POUR OUT	1049c	1 a
4 8	חטאת	SIN	309c	4 b
	כסה	COVER	491d	4
	קרב	INWARD PART	899b	3
	רום	BE HIGH	927c	2
4 9	יתרת	APPENDAGE	452c	
	כבד	LIVER	458b	
	כליה	KIDNEYS	480b	1 b
	כסל	LOINS	492d	1
	על	UPON	755c	2 4c
4 10	מזבח	ALTAR	258c	3 a
	מזבח	ALTAR	259a	1
	עלה	WHOLE BURNT OF-FERING	750d	
	קטר	MAKE SACRAFICES SMOKE	883a	1 a
	רום	BE HIGH	927d	
	שור	A HEAD OF CATTLE	1004b	
4 11	כרע	LEG	502d	
	עור	SKIN	736b	2
	על	UPON	755c	2 4c
	פרש	OFFAL	831d	
	קרב	INWARD PART	899b	3
4 12	אל	TO	40d	9
	דשן	FAT ASHES	206c	2
	חוץ	THE OUTSIDE	300a	1 bd
	מחנה	ENCAMPMENT	334a	1
	טהור	CLEAN	373a	1
	יצא	BRING OUT	425a	4 d
	שרף	BURN	977a	
	שרף	BURN	977a	2 a
	שפך	POURING	1050a	
4 13	אשם	OFFEND	79c	2
	אשר	THAT	83d	8 d
	עדה	CONGREGATION	417b	3
	כי	IF	473b	2 b
	עין	EYE	744d	3 d
	עלם	CONCEAL	761a	
	עשה	DO	793d	1 1a 1
	עשה	DO	795b	1 b
	קהל	ASSEMBLY	874d	2 a
	שגה	GO ASTRAY	993b	4
4 14	בן	SON	121c	7 b
	חטא	MISS A GOAL OR WAY	307b	2 b
	חטאת	SIN	308c	1 b
	חטאת	SIN	309c	4 b
	ידע	BE MADE KNOWN	394c	1
	על	UPON	754d	2 1f b
	קהל	ASSEMBLY	874d	2 a
	קרב	COME NEAR	898a	2 b1
4 15	זקן	OLD	278d	2 b
	עדה	CONGREGATION	417b	3
4 16	דם	BLOOD	197c	3 b
	כהן	PRIEST	464b	8
	משיח	ANOINTED	603c	2
4 17	דם	BLOOD	197c	3 b
	טבל	DIP	371b	1
	נזה	SPURT	633c	
	פנה	FACE	816d	2 2b
	אצבע	FINGER	840c	1 a
	שבע	SEVEN	988b	5 c
4 18	דם	BLOOD	197d	3 b

Ch	v.	Heb	Eng	Page	Sec
		דם	BLOOD	197d	3 b
		מזבח	ALTAR	259b	3
		מזבח	ALTAR	259b	2
		יסוד	FOUNDATION	414b	2
		עלה	WHOLE BURNT OF-FERING	750d	
		קרן	HORN	902a	3
		שפך	POUR OUT	1049c	1 a
4	19	רום	BE HIGH	927c	2
4	20	חטאת	SIN	309c	4 b
		כפר	EXPIATION	*497a	
		כפר	COVER OVER	497d	3 b2
		סלח	FORGIVE	669c	
4	21	אל	TO	40d	9
		חוץ	THE OUTSIDE	300a	1 bd
		חטאת	SIN	309c	4 b
		חטאת	SIN	309d	4 b
		יצא	BRING OUT	425a	4 d
		קהל	ASSEMBLY	874d	2 a
		ראשון	FIRST	911c	1 a
		שרף	BURN	977a	2 a
4	22	אשם	OFFEND	79c	2
		אשר	THAT	83d	8 d
		יהוה	YAHWEH	218d	2 1e
		חטא	MISS A GOAL OR WAY	307b	2 b
		חטאת	SIN	*309c	4 a
		חטאת	SIN	*309d	4 c
		מן	FROM	581a	3 bc
		נשיא	PRINCE	672b	4
		עם	PEOPLE	766d	3
		עשה	DO	793d	1 1a 1
		עשה	DO	795b	1 b
4	23	או	OR	15a	2
		זכר	MALE	271c	1 2
		חטא	MISS A GOAL OR WAY	307a	2 b
		חטאת	SIN	308c	1 b
		ידע	BE MAKE KNOWN	395b	
		על	UPON	754d	2 1f h
		עז	SHE-GOAT	777c	3 f
		שעיר	HE-GOAT	972c	
4	24	חטאת	SIN	309c	4 a
		עלה	WHOLE BURNT OF-FERING	750d	
		מקום	STANDING PLACE	880b	4
		שעיר	HE-GOAT	972c	
		שחט	SLAUGHTER	1006a	2
		שחט	SLAUGHTER	1006b	2
4	25	דם	BLOOD	197d	3 b
		דם	BLOOD	197d	3 b
		מזבח	ALTAR	258c	3 a
		מזבח	ALTAR	259b	2
		מזבח	ALTAR	259b	3
		חטאת	SIN	309c	4 a
		יסוד	FOUNDATION	414b	2
		עלה	WHOLE BURNT OF-FERING	750d	
4	26	מאשר	FROM THAT WHICH	84a	A
		חטאת	SIN	308d	1 b
		חטאת	SIN	309a	1 f
		כפר	COVER OVER	498a	3 c
		ל	TO	511a	1 e
		סלח	FORGIVE	699c	
4	27	ארץ	EARTH	76b	4 a
		אשם	OFFEND	79c	2
		אשר	THAT	83d	8 d
		חטא	MISS A GOAL OR WAY	307b	2 b
		חטאת	SIN	*309d	4 c
		כי	IF	473b	2 b
		מן	FROM	581a	3 bc
		נפש	SOUL	660b	4 c2
		עם	PEOPLE	766d	3
		עשה	DO	795b	1 b
		שגגה	SIN OF ERROR	993a	
4	28	או	OR	15a	2
		חטא	MISS A GOAL OR WAY	307b	2 b
		חטאת	SIN	308c	1 b
		חטאת	SIN	308d	1 b
		חטאת	SIN	*309c	4 a
		ידע	BE MAKE KNOWN	395b	
		נקבה	FEMALE	666c	2
		על	UPON	754d	2 1f b
		על	UPON	754d	2 1f h
		עז	SHE-GOAT	777c	3 f
		שעירה	SHE-GOAT	972d	
4	29	חטאת	SIN	309c	4 a
4	30	דם	BLOOD	197d	3 b
		דם	BLOOD	197d	3 b
		מזבח	ALTAR	258c	3 a
		מזבח	ALTAR	259b	3
		מזבח	ALTAR	259b	2
		יסוד	FOUNDATION	414b	2
		עלה	WHOLE BURNT OF-FERING	750d	
		שפך	POUR OUT	1049c	1 a
4	31	כפר	COVER OVER	497d	3 b2
		סור	TURN ASIDE	694c	
		סלח	FORGIVE	699c	
4	32	בוא	COME	99b	2
		חטאת	SIN	309c	4 a
		כבש	LAMB	461a	1
		כי	IF	473b	2 b
		נקבה	FEMALE	666c	2
4	33	חטאת	SIN	309c	4 a
		עלה	WHOLE BURNT OF-FERING	750d	
		מקום	STANDING PLACE	880b	4
4	34	דם	BLOOD	197d	3 b
		דם	BLOOD	197d	3 b
		מזבח	ALTAR	258c	3 a
		מזבח	ALTAR	259b	2
		מזבח	ALTAR	259b	3
		חטאת	SIN	309c	4 a
		יסוד	FOUNDATION	414b	2
		עלה	WHOLE BURNT OF-FERING	750d	
		שפך	POUR OUT	1049c	1 a
4	35	אשה	OFFERING MADE BY FIRE	78a	
		חטא	MISS A GOAL OR WAY	307b	2 b
		חטאת	SIN	308d	1 b
		חטאת	SIN	309a	1 f
		חטאת	SIN	*309c	4 a
		כבש	LAMB	461b	
		כפר	COVER OVER	498a	3 c
		סלח	FORGIVE	669c	
		סור	TURN ASIDE	694c	
5	1	או	OR	15a	1
		אלה	OATH	46d	1
		חטא	MISS A GOAL OR WAY	306d	2 b
		חטאת	SIN	*309d	4 c
		כי	IF	473c	2 b
		נגד	BE CONSPICUOUS	617a	3
		נפש	SOUL	660b	4 c2
		נשא	LIFT	671a	2 b
		עון	INIQUITY	731c	3
		קול	VOICE	877b	3 a4
5	2	אשם	OFFEND	79c	2
		חיה	LIVING THING	312c	1 b
		טמא	UNCLEAN	379d	2 b
		טמא	UNCLEAN	379d	2 a
		נבלה	CARCASS	615d	2
		נגע	TOUCH	619a	1 a
		נפש	SOUL	660b	4 c2
		עלם	CONCEAL	761a	
		שרץ	SWARMING THINGS	1056d	
5	3	אשם	OFFEND	79c	2
		טמא	BE UNCLEAN	379a	3
		טמאה	UNCLEANNESS	380a	4
		ל	TO	514c	5 fd
		נגע	TOUCH	619a	1 a
		עלם	CONCEAL	761a	
5	4	אדם	MAN	9b	1
		אשם	OFFEND	79c	2
		בטה	SPEAK RASHLY	104d	
		בטה	SPEAK RASHLY	104d	
		יטב	DO RIGHT	406a	5 a
		כי	IF	473c	2 b
		ל	TO	514c	5 fc
		ל	TO	514c	5 fd
		נפש	SOUL	660b	4 c2
		עלם	CONCEAL	761a	
		רעע	BE EVIL	949d	1
		שפה	SPEECH	973c	1 a1
		שבע	SWEAR	989b	1 a
		שבועה	OATH	989d	1 a
5	5	אשם	OFFEND	79c	2
		אשר	THAT	83c	8 ab
		חטא	MISS A GOAL OR WAY	307b	2 b
		ידה	CONFESS	392d	1
		ל	TO	514c	5 fc
		על	UPON	754d	2 1f h
5	6	חטא	MISS A GOAL OR WAY	307b	2 b
		חטאת	SIN	308d	1 b
		חטאת	SIN	308d	1 b
		חטאת	SIN	309a	1 f
		חטאת	SIN	309c	4 a
		חטאת	SIN	*309d	4 c
		כשבה	EWE-LAMB	461b	
		כפר	COVER OVER	498a	3 c
		נקבה	FEMALE	666c	2
		עז	SHE-GOAT	777c	3 f
		שעירה	SHE-GOAT	972d	
5	7	די	SUFFICIENCY	191c	1
		חטא	MISS A GOAL OR WAY	307b	3
		חטאת	SIN	309c	4 a
		יד	HAND	390b	2
		יונה	DOVE	401d	
		מסת	SUFFICIENCY	*588b	
		נגע	REACH	619c	2
		עלה	WHOLE BURNT OF-FERING	750b	
		תר	TURTLE-DOVE	1076a	
5	8	בדל	BE DIVIDED	95c	4
		חטאת	SIN	309c	4 a
		מול	IN FRONT OF	557c	2 bb
		מלק	NIP	577a	
		ערף	BACK OF NECK	791c	3
5	9	ראשון	FIRST	912a	3 b1
		דם	BLOOD	197c	3 b
		דם	BLOOD	197d	3 b
		מזבח	ALTAR	259b	3
		חטאת	SIN	309c	4 a
		יסוד	FOUNDATION	414b	2
		מצה	DRAIN	594c	
		נזה	SPURT	633c	
		קיר	WALL	885b	4
		שאר	REMAIN	984a	1
5	10	חטא	MISS A GOAL OR WAY	307b	2 b
		חטאת	SIN	308d	1 b
		חטאת	SIN	309a	1 f
		כפר	COVER OVER	498a	3 c
		סלח	FORGIVE	669c	
		עלה	WHOLE BURNT OF-FERING	750d	
		משפט	JUDGMENT	1048d	3
		חזה	SEE	*1092c	4
5	11	איפה	EPHAH	35b	1
		חטא	MISS A GOAL OR WAY	306d	2 b
		חטא	MISS A GOAL OR WAY	307b	3
		חטאת	SIN	309c	4 a
		יד	HAND	390b	2
		יונה	DOVE	401d	
		לבנה	FRANKINCENSE	526d	
		מנחה	OFFERING	585c	5 b
		נשג	REACH	673c	3
		עשירי	TENTH	798a	2
		שמן	OIL	1032c	2 g
		תר	TURTLE-DOVE	1076a	
5	12	אזכרה	MEMORIAL-OFFERING	272c	
		חטאת	SIN	*309c	4 a
		חטאת	SIN	309c	4 a
		כף	HOLLOW OF THE HAND	*496b	1 a
		מלא	FULNESS	571b	1
		קמץ	FIST	888a	
		קמץ	GRASP	888a	
		שה	A SHEEP	962a	1
5	13	חטא	MISS A GOAL OR WAY	307b	2 b
		חטאת	SIN	308d	1 b
		חטאת	SIN	309a	1 f
		חטאת	SIN	309c	4 a
		כפר	COVER OVER	498a	3 c
		מן	FROM	581a	3 bd
		סלח	FORGIVE	669c	
5	14	אשם	OFFENCE	80a	4
5	15	איל	RAM	18a	2 b
		חטא	MISS A GOAL OR WAY	307b	2 b
		כי	IF	473c	2 b
		כסף	SILVER	494b	8 a
		מעל	ACT TREACHEROUSLY	591b	1 a
		נפש	SOUL	660b	4 c2
		ערך	ORDER	790a	2
		שגגה	SIN OF ERROR	993a	
		שקל	SHEKEL	1053d	
		שקל	SHEKEL	1053d	
5	16	איל	RAM	18a	2 b
		חטא	MISS A GOAL OR WAY	307b	3
		חמישי	FIFTH	332d	3
		יסף	ADD	415a	1
		כפר	COVER OVER	497d	3 b2
		כפר	COVER OVER	498a	3 c
		סלח	FORGIVE	669c	
		נתן	GIVE	678b	1 a
		שלם	BE COMPLETE	1022c	3
5	17	אשם	OFFEND	79c	2
		חטא	MISS A GOAL OR WAY	306d	2 b
		נפש	SOUL	660b	4 c2
		נשא	LIFT	671a	2 b
		עון	INIQUITY	731c	3
		עשה	DO	793d	1 1a 1
		עשה	DO	795b	1 b
5	18	איל	RAM	18a	2 b
		כפר	COVER OVER	497d	3 b2
		כפר	COVER OVER	498a	3 c
		סלח	FORGIVE	669c	
		על	UPON	754b	2 1f b
		ערך	ORDER	790a	2
		שגג	GO ASTRAY	993a	2
		שגגה	SIN OF ERROR	993a	
5	19	אשם	OFFEND	79c	1
		ל	TO	*510d	1 d
5	21	או	OR	15a	2
		גזל	ROBBERY	160a	
		חטא	MISS A GOAL OR WAY	306d	2 b
		כחש	DECEIVE	471b	1
		מעל	ACT TREACHEROUSLY	591b	1 a
		נפש	SOUL	660b	4 c2
		עמית	ASSOCIATE	765c	
		עשק	OPPRESS	798d	1
		פקרון	DEPOSIT	824c	
		תשומת	SECURETY	964d	
5	22	אבדה	LOST THING	2b	
		או	OR	15a	2

Ch	v.	Heb	Eng	Page	Sec
		אשמה	WRONG-DOING	80a	1
		ב	IN	88a	
		הם	THEY	241d	6 a
		הם	THEY	241d	8 c
		חטא	MISS A GOAL OR WAY	307a	2 b
		כחש	DECEIVE	471b	
		מצא	FIND	593a	1 b
		על	UPON	754c	2 If e
		על	UPON	754d	2 If h
		שבע	SWEAR	989b	1 a
		שקר	DECEPTION	1055c	3
5	23	אבדה	LOST THING	2b	
		אשם	OFFEND	79c	2
		את	WITH	86b	3 a
		גזל	TEAR AWAY	159d	
		גזלה	PLUNDER	160a	
		חטא	MISS A GOAL OR WAY	306d	2 b
		מצא	FIND	593a	1 b
		עשק	OPPRESS	798d	1
		עשק	OPPRESSION	799a	3
		פקד	ATTEND TO	824a	2
		פקדון	DEPOSIT	824c	
		שוב	TURN BACK	999a	1 d
5	24	אשמה	WRONG-DOING	80b	3
		חמישי	FIFTH	332d	3
		יסף	ADD	415a	1
		מן	FROM	581a	3 bc
		ראש	HEAD	911b	7
		שבע	SWEAR	989b	1 a
5	25	איל	RAM	18a	2 b
		ב	IN	90c	3 8
		ערך	ORDER	790a	2
5	26	אשמה	WRONG-DOING	80a	1
		כפר	COVER OVER	497d	3 b2
		סלח	FORGIVE	669c	
		על	UPON	754d	2 If h
6	2	אהרן	AARON	14d	
		אש	FIRE	77c	4
		בקר	MORNING	133d	1 a
		זה	THIS	261a	3
		יקד	BE BURNING	428d	
		מוקדה	HEARTH	429a	
		תורה	LAW	436a	2 a
		צוה	CHARGE	845d	2 c
6	3	אכל	EAT	37c	3
		אצל	BESIDE	69b	A
		אש	FIRE	77c	4
		בד	WHITE LINEN	94b	
		בשר	FLESH	142c	2
		דשן	FAT ASHES	206c	2
		מזבח	ALTAR	259a	1
		מכנס	BREECH	488b	
		לבש	PUT ON	527d	A
		מד	GARMENT	551c	3
		רום	BE HIGH	927c	1 c
		שום	TO PLACE	963c	1 d
6	4	אחר	ANOTHER	29c	
		בגד	GARMENT	94a	
		דשן	FAT ASHES	206c	2
		חוץ	THE OUTSIDE	300a	1 bd
		מהור	CLEAN	373a	1
		יצא	BRING OUT	425a	4 d
		לבש	PUT ON	527d	A
		פשט	STRIP OFF	833a	1
6	5	אש	FIRE	77c	4
		בער	BURN	129b	2
		בקר	MORNING	134b	1 f
		חלב	FAT	317a	2 b
		יקד	BE BURNING	428d	
		כבה	BE QUENCHED	459c	
		עלה	WHOLE BURNT OF-FERING	750d	
		ערך	ARRANGE	789c	1 b
		קטר	MAKE SACRIFICES SMOKE	883a	1 a
		שלם	PEACE-OFFERING	1023c	
6	6	יקד	BE BURNING	428d	
		כבה	BE QUENCHED	459c	
		תמיד	CONTINUITY	556b	1 a
6	7	בן	SON	121a	1 jz
		תורה	LAW	436a	2 a
		מנחה	OFFERING	585c	5 b
		מנחה	OFFERING	585c	6
		פנה	FACE	816c	2 1b
		קרב	COME NEAR	898a	2 b4
6	8	אזכרה	MEMORIAL-OFFERING	272c	
		אזכרה	MEMORIAL-OFFERING	272c	
		כף	HOLLOW OF THE HAND	*496b	1 a
		לבנה	FRANKINCENSE	526d	
		מנחה	OFFERING	585c	5 b
		עלה	WHOLE BURNT OF-FERING	750d	
		קטר	MAKE SACRIFICES SMOKE	883a	1 a
		קמץ	FIST	888a	
		רום	BE HIGH	927c	2
6	9	אכל	EAT	37d	1
		חצר	ENCLOSURE	347a	3 a
		מצה	UNLEAVENED BREAD	695b	
		קדש	HOLY	872d	2 a
6	10	מקום	STANDING PLACE	880b	4
		אפה	BAKE	66b	
		אפה	BAKE	66b	
		אשה	OFFERING MADE BY FIRE	78a	
		אשה	OFFERING MADE BY FIRE	78a	
		אשם	OFFENCE	79d	4
		חטאת	SIN	309c	4 a
		חלק	PORTION	324a	1 b
		חמץ	THAT WHICH IS LEAVENED	329d	
		קדש	APARTNESS	872a	3 b
6	11	בן	SON	121a	1 jz
		דור	GENERATION	190a	2 c
		זכר	MALE	271c	1 1 b
		חטאת	SIN	*309c	4 a
		חק	SOMETHING PRESCRIBED	349c	4
		עולם	LONG DURATION	762c	2
		קדש	BE SET APART	873a	2
6	13	איפה	EPHAH	35b	1
		בקר	MORNING	134a	1 e
		זה	THIS	261a	3
		מחצית	HALF	346a	1
		תמיד	CONTINUITY	556c	2 b
		מנחה	OFFERING	585c	4
		עשירי	TENTH	798a	2
6	14	מחבת	FLAT PLATE	290b	1
		מנחה	OFFERING	585c	5 e
		מנחה	OFFERING	585c	5 c
		עשה	DO	795b	2 c
		פת	FRAGMENT	837d	
		רבך	MIX	916c	
6	15	חק	SOMETHING PRESCRIBED	349c	4
		כהן	PRIEST	464b	8
		כליל	WHOLE	483b	2 b
		משיח	ANOINTED	603c	2
		עולם	LONG DURATION	762c	2
		קטר	MAKE SACRIFICES SMOKE	883b	
6	16	אכל	EAT	37d	1
		אש	FIRE	77c	4
		כהן	PRIEST	464a	7
		כליל	WHOLE	483b	2 b
6	18	דבר	SPEAK	181a	3 b
		זה	THIS	261a	3
		חטאת	SIN	309c	4 a
		תורה	LAW	436a	2 a
		קדש	APARTNESS	872a	3 b
		מקום	STANDING PLACE	880b	4
		שחט	SLAUGHTER	1006a	1
6	19	אכל	EAT	37d	1
		חטא	MISS A GOAL OR WAY	307c	2
		חטאת	SIN	309c	4 a
		חצר	ENCLOSURE	347a	3 a
		קדוש	HOLY	872d	2 a
		מקום	STANDING PLACE	880b	4
6	20	בגד	GARMENT	*93d	
		דם	BLOOD	197c	3 b
		כבס	WASH	460a	1
		נזה	SPURT	633b	
		קדוש	HOLY	872d	2 a
		קדש	BE SET APART	873a	2
		מקום	STANDING PLACE	880b	4
6	21	בשל	BOIL	143b	
		חרש	EARTHENWARE	360a	1
		כלי	VESSEL	480b	3
		מי	WATER	565b	1 a
		מרק	POLISH	599d	
		נחשת	COPPER	638d	1
		נחשת	COPPER	*638d	1
		שבר	BREAK	990d	
		שטף	OVERFLOW	1009b	
6	22	זכר	MALE	271c	1 1 b
		כהן	PRIEST	464a	7
		קדש	APARTNESS	872a	3 b
6	23	אכל	EAT	37d	1
		בוא	COME	99c	B
		דם	BLOOD	197c	3 b
		חטאת	SIN	309c	4 a
		חטאת	SIN	309d	4 b
		כפר	COVER OVER	498d	3 d
		שרף	BURN	977a	
7	1	זה	THIS	261a	3
		תורה	LAW	436a	2 a
7	2	דם	BLOOD	197c	3 b
		זרק	TO TOSS	284c	1 b
		עלה	WHOLE BURNT OF-FERING	750d	
		מקום	STANDING PLACE	880b	4
		שחט	SLAUGHTER	1006b	2
7	3	אליה	FAT TAIL	47a	
		כסה	COVER	491d	4
		קרב	INWARD PART	899b	3
7	4	יתרת	APPENDAGE	452c	
		כבד	LIVER	458b	
		כליה	KIDNEYS	480b	1 b
		כסל	LOINS	492d	1
		על	UPON	755c	2 4c
7	5	ארם	ARAM	74b	A
7	6	אכל	EAT	37d	1
		זכר	MALE	271c	1 1 b
		כהן	PRIEST	464a	7
7	7	קדוש	HOLY	872d	2 a
		חטאת	SIN	309c	4 a
		תורה	LAW	436a	2 a
		ד	LIKE	454c	2 a
		כפר	COVER OVER	497d	3 b2
		כפר	COVER OVER	498a	3 d
7	8	עלה	WHOLE BURNT OF-FERING	750d	
7	9	אפה	BAKE	66b	
		מחבת	FLAT PLATE	290b	1
		מנחה	OFFERING	585c	5 c
		מנחה	OFFERING	585c	5 c
		מנחה	OFFERING	585c	5 c
		עשה	DO	795b	2 c
		מרחשת	STEW PAN	935d	
		תנור	FIRE-POT	1072b	
7	10	בלל	MIX	117c	2
		בן	SON	121a	1 jz
		חרב	DRY	351b	
7	11	זבח	SACRIFICE	258a	2 7
		זה	THIS	261a	3
		תורה	LAW	436a	2 a
7	12	בלל	MIX	117c	2
		זבח	SACRIFICE	257c	2 4
		זבח	SACRIFICE	257d	2 5
		חלה	A KIND OF CAKE	319d	2 d
		תודה	THANK-OFFERING	392d	4
		תודה	THANK-OFFERING	393a	4
		משח	ANOINT	603a	1
		מצה	UNLEAVENED BREAD	695b	
		על	UPON	753d	2 1f
		על	UPON	755c	2 4b
		קרב	COME NEAR	898a	2 b4
		רבך	MIX	916c	
		רקיק	A THIN CAKE	956d	
		שלם	PEACE-OFFERING	1023c	
7	13	זבח	SACRIFICE	257c	2 4
		חלה	A KIND OF CAKE	319d	2 e
		חמץ	THAT WHICH IS LEAVENED	329d	
		תודה	THANK-OFFERING	392d	4
		לחם	FOOD	537a	1 a
		על	UPON	755c	2 4b
		שלם	PEACE-OFFERING	1023c	
		שלם	PEACE-OFFERING	1023c	
7	14	דם	BLOOD	197c	3 b
		דם	BLOOD	*197d	3 b
		זרק	TO TOSS	284c	1 b
		תרומה	OFFERING	929b	7
		תרומה	OFFERING	929b	4 a
		שלם	PEACE-OFFERING	1023c	
7	15	אכל	EAT	37d	1
		בקר	MORNING	134b	2
		זבח	SACRIFICE	257c	2 4
		תודה	THANK-OFFERING	392d	4
		נוח	REST	629a	B 2
		שלם	PEACE-OFFERING	1023c	
7	16	אכל	EAT	37d	1
		ו	AND	254d	5 cb
		זבח	SACRIFICE	257c	2 4
		זבח	SACRIFICE	257d	2 5
		זבח	SACRIFICE	258a	2 4
		מחרת	THE MORROW	564b	
		נדבה	FREEWILL-OFFERING	621d	2 c
		נדר	VOW	624a	5
		קרב	COME NEAR	898a	2 b2
		שלם	PEACE-OFFERING	1023c	
7	17	זבח	SACRIFICE	257c	2 4
		שרף	BURN	977a	
7	18	אכל	EAT	37d	1
		חשב	THINK	363c	4
		נפש	SOUL	660b	4 c2
		נשא	LIFT	671a	2 b
		עון	INIQUITY	731c	3
		פגול	FOUL THING	803b	
		רצה	BE PLEASED WITH	953b	1
7	19	אכל	EAT	37d	1
		מהור	CLEAN	373a	1
		ממא	UNCLEAN	379d	2 d
		שרף	BURN	977a	
7	20	ממא	UNCLEANNESS	380a	4
		כרת	BE CUT OFF	504b	1 c
		ל	TO	513c	5 ca
		נפש	SOUL	660b	4 c2
		נפש	SOUL	660b	4 c2
		על	UPON	753d	2 1b
		עם	KINSMAN	769c	
		ממא	UNCLEAN	379d	2 d
7	21	ממא	UNCLEAN	379d	2 d
		ממאה	UNCLEANNESS	380a	4
		כרת	BE CUT OFF	504b	1 c
		ל	TO	513c	5 ca
		נפש	SOUL	660b	4 c2
		נפש	SOUL	660b	4 c2
		עם	KINSMAN	769c	
		שקץ	DETESTATION	1054d	
7	23	חלב	FAT	317a	2 b
		כשב	LAMB	461b	
		עז	SHE-GOAT	777c	2
		שור	A HEAD OF CATTLE	1004b	
7	24	חלב	FAT	317a	2 b
		טרפה	ANIMAL TORN	383c	1
		מלאכה	WORK	522b	5
		נבלה	CARCASS	615d	2

Ch v.	Heb	Eng	Page	Sec
7 25	עשה	DO	795b	2 f
	חלב	FAT	317a	2 b
	כרת	BE CUT OFF	504b	1 c
	נפש	SOUL	660b	4 c2
	עם	KINSMAN	769c	
7 26	דם	BLOOD	196c	1
	מושב	DWELLING	444b	2 c
	ל	TO	514c	5 fc
	עוף	FLY	733d	1
7 27	דם	BLOOD	196c	1
	כרת	BE CUT OFF	504b	1 c
	נפש	SOUL	660b	4 c2
	נפש	SOUL	660b	4 c2
	עם	KINSMAN	769c	
7 30	חזה	BREAST	303d	
	נוף	WAVE	632a	4
7 31	חזה	BREAST	303d	
7 32	ימין	RIGHT	412a	3
7 33	בן	SON	121a	1 jz
	דם	BLOOD	197d	3 b
	ימין	RIGHT	412a	3
	מנה	PORTION	584b	
	קרב	COME NEAR	898a	2 b3
	שלם	PEACE-OFFERING	1023c	
7 34	אהרן	AARON	14d	
	את	WITH	86d	4 b
	בן	SON	121a	1 jz
	חזה	BREAST	303d	
	חק	SOMETHING PRESCRIBED	349c	4
	תנופה	WAVING	632c	2 a
	עולם	LONG DURATION	762c	2
	תרומה	OFFERING	929b	4 b
	שוק	LEG	1003b	2
7 35	יום	DAY	400b	7 d3 a
	כהן	ACT AS PRIEST	464c	1
	משחה	CONSECRATED PORTION	603c	2
	קרב	COME NEAR	898a	2 a1
	דור	GENERATION	190a	2 c
7 36	חקה	SOMETHING PRESCRIBED	350a	1
	משח	ANOINT	603b	3 a
	עולם	LONG DURATION	762c	2 e
7 37	זה	THIS	261b	3
	חטאת	SIN	309b	4
	תורה	LAW	436a	2 a
	ל	TO	514c	5 fa
	מלוא	INSTALLATION	571b	2
	מנחה	OFFERING	585b	5
7 38	הר	MOUNTAIN	249b	1 a
	הר	MOUNTAIN	250a	1 a
	משה	MOSES	602c	
	סיני	SINAI	*696a	
8 2	איל	RAM	18a	2 a
	חטאת	SIN	309c	4 b
	משחה	OINTMENT	603c	1
	מצה	UNLEAVENED BREAD	695b	
	סל	BASKET	700d	
	שמן	OIL	1032c	2 g
8 3	עדה	CONGREGATION	417b	3
	קהל	ASSEMBLE AS	875a	2
8 4	עדה	CONGREGATION	417b	3
	קהל	ASSEMBLE AS	875a	2
8 5	דבר	WORD	182d	12a
	צוה	CHARGE	845d	2 d
8 6	קרב	COME NEAR	898a	2 a1
	רחץ	WASH OFF	934c	1
8 7	אפוד	EPHOD	65c	1 b
	אפוד	EPHOD	65c	1 b
	אפוד	EPHOD	65c	1 b
	אפד	GIRD ON EPHOD	65d	
	אבנט	GIRDLE	126a	
	חגר	GIRD	291d	1
	חשב	INGENIOUS WORK	363d	
	כתנת	TUNIC	509a	
	לבש	CLOTHE	528b	1 a
	מעיל	ROBE	591c	3
8 8	אורים	URIM	22a	
	אל	TO	39d	2
	חשן	BREAST-PIECE	365d	
	שום	TO PLACE	963b	1 b
	תם	INTEGRITY	1070d	4
8 9	זהב	GOLD	263a	6
	מול	IN FRONT OF	557c	2 a
	משה	MOSES	602c	
	נזר	CROWN	634b	1 b
	ציץ	BLOSSOM	847d	2
	מצנפת	TURBAN	857b	
	קדש	APARTNESS	872b	4 a
	שום	TO PLACE	963b	1 b
8 10	משה	ANOINT	603b	3 b
	משחה	OINTMENT	603c	1
	קדש	BE SET APART	873a	1 a
	שמן	OIL	1032c	2 g
8 11	מזבח	ALTAR	259a	9
	כיור	POT	468c	3 a
	כן	BASE	487c	1
	משה	ANOINT	603b	3 b
	נזה	SPURT	633c	
	קדש	BE SET APART	873a	1 a
	שבע	SEVEN	988b	5 c
8 12	אהרן	AARON	14d	
	יצק	POUR	427a	1
	משח	ANOINT	603b	3 a
8 13	משחה	OINTMENT	603c	1
	קדש	BE SET APART	873a	1 c
	אבנט	GIRDLE	126a	
	מגבעות	HEAD-GEAR	149c	
	חבש	BIND	289d	1 a
	חגר	GIRD	291d	1
	כתנת	TUNIC	509a	
	לבש	CLOTHE	528b	1 a
	משה	MOSES	602c	
	קרב	COME NEAR	898a	2 a1
8 14	חטאת	SIN	309c	4 b
	נגש	APPROACH	621b	
8 15	דם	BLOOD	197d	3 b
	דם	BLOOD	197d	3 b
	מזבח	ALTAR	259b	4
	מזבח	ALTAR	259b	4
	מזבח	ALTAR	259b	3
	חטא	MISS A GOAL OR WAY	307c	3
	יסוד	FOUNDATION	414b	2
	יצק	POUR	427b	1
	כפר	COVER OVER	497d	3 b1
	קדש	BE SET APART	873a	1 a
8 16	חטאת	SIN	309d	4 b
	יתרת	APPENDAGE	452c	
	כבד	LIVER	458b	
	כליה	KIDNEYS	480c	1 b
	קרב	INWARD PART	899b	3
8 17	חוץ	THE OUTSIDE	300a	1 bd
	חטאת	SIN	309d	4 b
	משה	MOSES	602c	
	פרש	OFFAL	831d	
8 18	איל	RAM	18a	2 a
	עלה	WHOLE BURNT OFFERING	750c	
	קרב	COME NEAR	898a	2 b1
8 19	דם	BLOOD	197c	3 b
	זרק	TO TOSS	284c	1 b
8 20	נתח	PIECE OF A DIVIDED CARCASS	677c	
	נתח	CUT IN PIECES	677c	
	פדר	SUET	804d	
	קטר	MAKE SACRAFICES SMOKE	883a	1 a
8 21	כרע	LEG	502d	
	מי	WATER	565b	1 a
	עלה	WHOLE BURNT OFFERING	750d	
	קרב	INWARD PART	899b	3
	רחץ	WASH OFF	934c	1
8 22	איל	RAM	18a	2 a
	מלוא	INSTALLATION	571c	2
	קרב	COME NEAR	898a	2 b1
8 23	אהרן	AARON	14d	
	אזן	EAR	23d	1
	אשם	OFFENCE	80a	4
	בהן	THUMB	97b	
	דם	BLOOD	197d	3 b
	זבח	SACRIFICE	258a	2 5
	יד	HAND	389a	1 a
	ימין	RIGHT	412c	
	תנוך	TIP	1072a	
8 24	אזן	EAR	23d	1
	בהן	THUMB	97b	
	גוי	NATION	156a	1 c
	דם	BLOOD	197c	3 b
	דם	BLOOD	197d	3 b
	זרק	TO TOSS	284c	1 b
	יד	HAND	389a	1 a
	יד	HAND	389a	1 a
	ימין	RIGHT	412c	
	קרב	COME NEAR	898a	2 a1
	תנוך	TIP	1072a	
8 25	אליה	FAT TAIL	47a	
	יד	HAND	*389b	1 c
	ימין	RIGHT	412a	3
	יתרת	APPENDAGE	452c	
	כבד	LIVER	458b	
	כליה	KIDNEYS	480c	1 b
	קרב	INWARD PART	899b	3
8 26	חלה	A KIND OF CAKE	319c	2 c
	חלה	A KIND OF CAKE	319d	2 d
	ימין	RIGHT	412a	3
	מצה	UNLEAVENED BREAD	695b	
	סל	BASKET	700d	
	רקיק	A THIN CAKE	956d	
	שמן	OIL	1032c	2 g
8 27	כל	ALL	482d	2 ba
	כף	HOLLOW OF THE HAND	496b	1 a
	משה	MOSES	602c	
	נוף	WAVE	632b	4
	תנופה	WAVING	632c	2 a
8 28	גוי	NATION	156d	1 c
	מלוא	INSTALLATION	571c	2
	נוף	WAVE	*632b	4
	על	UPON	758c	4 2a
8 29	איל	RAM	18a	2 d
	חזה	BREAST	303d	
	מלוא	INSTALLATION	571c	2
	מנה	PORTION	584b	
	משה	MOSES	602c	
	נוף	WAVE	632a	4
8 30	דם	BLOOD	197c	3 b
	משחה	OINTMENT	603c	1
	נזה	SPURT	633c	
8 31	קדש	BE SET APART	873a	1 c
	איל	RAM	17d	1
	בשל	BOIL	143a	2
	לחם	FOOD	537a	1 a
	מלוא	INSTALLATION	571c	2
	סל	BASKET	700d	
8 32	יתר	BE LEFT OVER	451b	
8 33	יד	HAND	389b	1 c
	יום	DAY	398d	2 f
	יצא	GO OUT	422c	1 a
	מלא	BE FULL	570b	1 b
	מלא	FILL	570d	2
	מלוא	INSTALLATION	571b	2
8 34	כפר	COVER OVER	497d	3 b2
8 35	מות	DIE	560a	2 b
	צוה	CHARGE	846b	4 c
	שמר	KEEP	1037a	3 c
	משמרת	GUARD	1038c	4 a
8 36	דבר	WORD	182d	1 2a
	יד	HAND	391a	5 d
	צוה	CHARGE	846a	4 b
9 1	זקן	OLD	278d	2 b
9 2	איל	RAM	18a	2 c
	בן	SON	121c	7 b
	בקר	CATTLE	133b	1 a
	חטאת	SIN	309c	4 b
	עגל	CALF	722b	
	עלה	WHOLE BURNT OFFERING	750c	
9 3	בן	SON	122a	9 b
	חטאת	SIN	309d	4 b
	עגל	CALF	722b	
	שעיר	HE-GOAT	972c	
9 4	איל	RAM	18a	2 d
	בלל	MIX	117c	2
	זבח	SLAUGHTER FOR SACRIFICE	257a	1 4
	ראה	TO SEE	908b	1 a
	שור	A HEAD OF CATTLE	1004b	
	שלם	PEACE-OFFERING	1023c	
9 5	עמד	STAND	764a	1 d
	פנה	FACE	816c	2 1b
9 6	דבר	WORD	182d	1 2a
	כבוד	GLORY	458d	2 c1
	צוה	CHARGE	845d	2 d
	ראה	TO SEE	908b	1 a
9 7	בעד	ON BEHALF OF	126c	2
	חטאת	SIN	309c	4 b
	חטאת	SIN	309d	4 b
	כפר	COVER OVER	498a	3 e
	עלה	WHOLE BURNT OFFERING	750d	
9 8	אשר	PARTICLE OF RELATION	83a	7 b
	חטאת	SIN	309c	4 b
	עגל	CALF	722b	
	שחט	SLAUGHTER	1006a	2
9 9	דם	BLOOD	197d	3 b
	מזבח	ALTAR	259b	3
	מזבח	ALTAR	259b	2
	חטאת	SIN	*309d	4 b
	טבל	DIP	371b	1
	יסוד	FOUNDATION	414b	2
	יצק	POUR	427b	1
	קרב	COME NEAR	898a	2 b3
9 10	חטאת	SIN	309c	4 b
	חטאת	SIN	309d	4 b
	יתרת	APPENDAGE	452c	
	כבד	LIVER	458b	
	כליה	KIDNEYS	480c	1 b
9 11	חטאת	SIN	309d	4 b
9 12	דם	BLOOD	197c	3 b
	זרק	TO TOSS	284c	1 b
	מצא	FIND	594b	4
	עלה	WHOLE BURNT OFFERING	750d	
9 13	מצא	FIND	594b	4
	נתח	PIECE OF A DIVIDED CARCASS	677c	
9 14	כרע	LEG	502d	
	קרב	INWARD PART	899b	3
	רחץ	WASH OFF	934c	1
9 15	חטא	MISS A GOAL OR WAY	307c	3
	חטאת	SIN	309d	4 b
	ראשון	FIRST	911c	1 a
	שעיר	HE-GOAT	972c	
9 16	עלה	WHOLE BURNT OFFERING	750d	
9 17	משפט	JUDGMENT	1048b	3
	בד	SEPARATION	94d	1 e
	כף	HOLLOW OF THE HAND	496b	1 a
	מלא	FILL	570d	2
	עלה	WHOLE BURNT OFFERING	750b	
9 18	איל	RAM	18a	2 d
	דם	BLOOD	197c	3 b
	זרק	TO TOSS	284c	1 b
	מצא	FIND	594b	4
	שור	A HEAD OF CATTLE	1004b	
9 19	איל	RAM	18a	2 d
	אליה	FAT TAIL	47a	

Ch	v.	Heb	Eng	Page	Sec
		יתרת	APPENDAGE	452c	
		כבד	LIVER	458b	
		כליה	KIDNEYS	480b	1 b
		מכסה	COVERING	492c	
		שור	A HEAD OF CATTLE	1004b	
9	20	חזה	BREAST	303d	
9	21	חזה	BREAST	303d	
		ימין	RIGHT	412a	3
		נוף	WAVE	632a	4
9	22	ברך	BLESS	139a	3
		מזבח	ALTAR	*259a	1
		חטאת	SIN	309d	4 b
		חטאת	SIN	309d	4 c
		ירד	GO DOWN	433a	1 f
		נשא	LIFT	670b	1 b 1
		עלה	WHOLE BURNT OF-FERING	750d	
		על	UPON	756d	2 7b
		עשה	DO	794d	2 4
		שלם	PEACE-OFFERING	1023c	
9	23	ברך	BLESS	139a	3
		כבוד	GLORY	458d	2 c1
		ראה	TO SEE	908b	1 a
9	24	אש	FIRE	77c	4
		יצא	GO OUT	423b	1 g
		עלה	WHOLE BURNT OF-FERING	750d	
		פנה	FACE	817d	2 5a a
		רנן	GIVE A RINGING CRY	943b	1
10	1	אש	FIRE	77c	4
		אש	FIRE	77c	4
		הם	THEY	241d	8 d
		זור	BE A STRANGER	266d	2 d
		מחתה	FIRE-HOLDER	367b	3
		נדב	NADAB	621c	1
		קטרת	SMOKE	882d	2
		קרב	COME NEAR	898a	2 b5
10	2	אכל	EAT	37c	3
		אש	FIRE	77c	4
		יצא	GO OUT	423b	1 g
		מות	DIE	560a	2 b
		פנה	FACE	817d	2 5a a
10	3	דמם	BE SILENT	198d	1
		הוא	HE, SHE, IT	216d	6 a
		כבד	BE HONORED	457c	2
		פנה	FACE	818d	2 7a a
		קדש	BE SET APART	873a	2
		קרב	NEAR	898c	2 e
10	4	אליצפן	ELIZAPHAN	45d	A
		את	WITH	86d	4 a
		דוד	UNCLE	187c	2
		חוץ	THE OUTSIDE	300a	1 bd
		מישאל	MISHAEL	567d	1
		עזיאל	UZZIEL	739d	1 a
		קדש	APARTNESS	871d	2 c
		קרב	COME NEAR	897c	1 g
10	5	כתנת	TUNIC	509a	
		קרב	COME NEAR	897c	1 g
10	6	איתמר	ITHAMAR	16a	
		בית	HOUSE	110a	5 dd
		בכה	WEEP	113c	4
		מות	DIE	560a	2 b
		פרם	TEAR GARMENT	828a	
		פרע	LET GO	828d	1
		קצף	BE WROTH	893b	1
		שרף	BURN	977a	2 b1
		שרפה	BURNING	977c	
10	7	דבר	WORD	182b	1 1b
		יצא	GO OUT	422c	1 a
		מות	DIE	560a	2 b
		משחה	OINTMENT	603c	1
		שמן	OIL	1032c	2 g
10	9	דור	GENERATION	190a	2 c
		חקה	SOMETHING PRE-SCRIBED	350a	1
		יין	WINE	406c	C
		מות	DIE	560a	2 b
		עולם	LONG DURATION	762c	2 e
		שכר	INTOXICATING DRINK	1016b	
10	10	בדל	BE DIVIDED	95c	3
		בין	INTERVAL	107c	1 d
		חל	PROFANENESS	320d	
		טהור	CLEAN	373a	1
		טמא	UNCLEAN	379d	2 d
		ל	TO	518b	7 bh
		קדש	APARTNESS	872b	6
10	11	חק	SOMETHING PRE-SCRIBED	349d	7 g
		יד	HAND	391a	5 d
		ירה	DIRECT	435c	5 b
10	12	איתמר	ITHAMAR	16a	
		יתר	BE LEFT OVER	451c	
		מצה	UNLEAVENED BREAD	695b	
		קדש	APARTNESS	872a	3 b
10	13	אכל	EAT	37b	1
		חק	SOMETHING PRE-SCRIBED	349c	4
		צוה	CHARGE	846b	4 c
		קדוש	HOLY	872d	2 a
10	14	חזה	BREAST	303d	
		חק	SOMETHING PRE-SCRIBED	349c	4
		טהור	CLEAN	373a	1
		תנופה	WAVING	632c	2 a
		נתן	GIVE	681b	1 a
		תרומה	OFFERING	929b	4 b
		שלם	PEACE-OFFERING	1023c	
10	15	אשה	OFFERING MADE BY FIRE	78a	
		היה	BECOME	226c	2 2f
		חזה	BREAST	303d	
		חק	SOMETHING PRE-SCRIBED	349c	4
		נוף	WAVE	632a	4
		תנופה	WAVING	632c	2 a
		עולם	LONG DURATION	762c	2
		תרומה	OFFERING	929b	4 b
10	16	איתמר	ITHAMAR	16a	
		דרש	SEEK	205c	4 a
		חטאת	SIN	309c	4 a
		יתר	BE LEFT OVER	451c	
		קצף	BE WROTH	893b	2
		שרף	BURN	977a	
10	17	את	MARK OF THE AC-CUSATIVE	85a	1 a
		חטאת	SIN	309c	4 a
		מדוע	WHEREFORE	396c	
		כפר	COVER OVER	497d	3 b2
		נשא	LIFT	671a	2 b
		נתן	PUT	681a	2 d
		עון	INIQUITY	731b	3
		קדש	APARTNESS	871d	2 c
		קדש	APARTNESS	872a	3 b
		מקום	STANDING PLACE	880b	4
10	18	בוא	COME	99c	B
		דם	BLOOD	197c	3 b
		הן	IF	243c	B
		הן	BEHOLD	243c	A
		פנימה	TOWARDS THE SIDE	819b	1
		קדש	APARTNESS	871d	2 c
10	19	אלה	THESE	41d	D
		הן	BEHOLD	243c	A
		חטאת	SIN	309c	4 a
		חטאת	SIN	310a	4 c
		יטב	BE PLEASING	405c	4
		כ	LIKE	453d	1 b
		עלה	WHOLE BURNT OF-FERING	750d	
10	20	קרא	ENCOUNTER	897a	2
		יטב	BE PLEASING	405c	4
11	2	דישן	PYGARG	190d	
11	3	חיה	LIVING THING	312c	1 a
		גרה	CUD	176a	
		עלה	GO UP	749c	3
		פרם	BREAK IN TWO	828b	1
		פרסה	HOOF	828b	1
		פרסה	HOOF	828b	1
		שסע	DIVIDE	1042d	
		שסע	CLEFT	1043a	
11	4	גרה	CUD	176a	
		זה	THIS	260c	1 a
		טמא	UNCLEAN	379d	2 b
		ל	TO	*512d	5 aa
		עלה	GO UP	749c	3
		פרם	BREAK IN TWO	828b	1
		פרם	BREAK IN TWO	828b	1
11	5	גרה	CUD	176a	
		טמא	UNCLEAN	379d	2 b
		ל	TO	*512d	5 aa
		עלה	GO UP	749c	3
		פרם	BREAK IN TWO	828b	1
		שפן	ROCK-BADGER	1051a	
11	6	ארנבת	HARE	58a	
		בעד	ON BEHALF OF	126c	2
		גרה	CUD	176a	
		טמא	UNCLEAN	379d	2 b
		ל	TO	*512d	5 aa
		עלה	GO UP	749c	3
		פרם	BREAK IN TWO	828b	1
11	7	גרה	CUD	176a	
		גרר	DRAG	176a	
		גרה	CUD	176a	
		חזיר	SWINE	306b	1
		טמא	UNCLEAN	379d	2 b
		ל	TO	*512d	5 aa
		פרסה	HOOF	828b	1
		פרם	BREAK IN TWO	828b	1
		שסע	DIVIDE	1042d	
		שסע	CLEFT	1043a	
11	8	טמא	UNCLEAN	379d	2 b
		ל	TO	*512d	5 aa
		נבלה	CARCASS	615d	2
11	9	זה	THIS	260c	1 a
		נחל	TORRENT	636b	1
		סנפיר	FIN	703b	
		קשקשת	SCALE OF FISH	903d	
11	10	ה	THE	209a	2 b
		חי	ALIVE	312b	1 d
		נחל	TORRENT	636b	1
		נפש	SOUL	659c	2
		סנפיר	FIN	703b	
		קשקשת	SCALE OF FISH	903d	
		שקץ	DETESTATION	1055a	
		שרץ	SWARMING THINGS	1056d	
11	11	בעד	ON BEHALF OF	126c	2
		נבלה	CARCASS	615d	2
		שקץ	DETEST	1055a	1
11	12	שקץ	DETESTATION	1055a	
		סנפיר	FIN	703b	
		קשקשת	SCALE OF FISH	903d	
		שקץ	DETESTATION	1055a	
11	13	אכל	EAT	37d	1
		נשר	EAGLE	676c	
		נשר	EAGLE	*677a	1
		עוף	FLY	733d	1
		עזניה	BIRD OF PREY	740a	
		פרם	BEARDED VUL-TURE	828b	
		שקץ	DETEST	1055a	1
		שקץ	DETESTATION	1055a	
11	14	איה	HAWK	17b	
		דאה	KITE	178d	
		מין	KIND	568b	
11	15	מין	KIND	568b	
		ערב	RAVEN	788b	
11	16	בת	DAUGHTER	123d	6
		תחמס	MALE OSTRICH	329d	
		יענה	OSTRICH	419a	
		מין	KIND	568b	
		נץ	HAWK	665c	
		שחף	SEA-MEW	1006d	
11	17	ברבריס	FATTENED FOWL	*141b	
		כוס	OWL	468b	
		ינשוף	OWL	676b	
		שלח	DRAW OUT	*1017d	
		שלך	CORMORANT	1021c	
11	18	תנשמת	PELICAN	675d	1
		קאת	PELICAN	866b	
		רחם	CARRION-VUL-TURE	934b	
11	19	אנפה	HERON	60b	
		דוכיפת	HOOPOE	189a	
		חסידה	STORK	339d	
		מין	KIND	568b	
		עטלף	BAT	742b	
11	20	הלך	WALK	232a	1 2
		עוף	FLY	733d	2
		ארבע	FOUR	917a	1 a5
		שקץ	DETESTATION	1055a	
		שרץ	SWARMING THINGS	1056d	
11	21	הלך	WALK	232a	1 2
		הם	THEY	241d	8 d
		זה	THIS	260c	1 a
		כרע	LEG	502d	
		לא	NOT	520c	
		נתר	SPRING	684a	
		עוף	FLY	733d	2
		מעל	ABOVE	751c	1 b
		ארבע	FOUR	917a	1 a5
		רגל	FOOT	919d	1 d
		שרץ	SWARMING THINGS	1056d	
11	22	את	MARK OF THE AC-CUSATIVE	84d	1 a
		חגב	LOCUST	290b	
		חרגל	LOCUST	353d	
		מין	KIND	568b	
		סלעם	LOCUST	701b	
		ארבה	LOCUST	916a	
		ארבה	LOCUST	*916a	
11	23	עוף	FLY	733d	2
		ארבע	FOUR	916d	1 a2
		רגל	FOOT	919d	1 d
		שקץ	DETESTATION	1055a	
		שרץ	SWARMING THINGS	1056d	
11	24	אלה	THESE	41c	D
		טמא	BE UNCLEAN	379a	3
		טמא	BE UNCLEAN	379b	3
		טמא	BE UNCLEAN	379d	
		ל	TO	514d	5 g
		נבלה	CARCASS	615d	2
		ערב	SUNSET	787d	1 a
11	25	טמא	BE UNCLEAN	379b	3
		כבס	WASH	460a	1
		נבלה	CARCASS	615d	2
11	26	אשר	PARTICLE OF RE-LATION	82a	2 a
		גרה	CUD	176a	
		טמא	BE UNCLEAN	379b	3
		טמא	UNCLEAN	379d	2 b
		ל	TO	514d	5 fe
		עלה	GO UP	749c	3
		פרם	BREAK IN TWO	828b	1
		שסע	DIVIDE	1042d	
		שסע	CLEFT	1043a	
11	27	הלך	WALK	232a	1 2
		הלך	WALK	232a	1 2
		חיה	LIVING THING	312c	1 a
		טמא	BE UNCLEAN	379a	3
		טמא	BE UNCLEAN	379b	3
		טמא	BE UNCLEAN	379b	3
		טמא	UNCLEAN	379d	2 b
		כף	HOLLOW OF THE HAND	496c	1 c
11	28	ארבע	FOUR	917a	1 a5
		טמא	BE UNCLEAN	379a	3
		טמא	BE UNCLEAN	379b	3
		טמא	UNCLEAN	379d	2 b
		כבס	WASH	460a	1
		נבלה	CARCASS	615d	2
11	29	זה	THIS	260c	1 a

Ch	v	Heb	Eng	Page	Sec
		חלד	WEASEL	317c	
		טמא	UNCLEAN	379d	2 b
		ל	TO	512d	5 aa
		מין	KIND	568b	
		עכבר	MOUSE	747b	
		צב	LIZARD	839d	
		שרץ	SWARM	1056c	2
		שרץ	SWARMING THINGS	1056d	
11	30	אנקה	FERRET	60c	
		חמט	SAND REPTILE	328a	
		כח	REPTILE	470a	
		לטאה	LIZARD	538b	
		תנשמת	LIZARD	675d	2
11	31	טמא	BE UNCLEAN	379a	3
		טמא	BE UNCLEAN	379b	3
		טמא	UNCLEAN	379d	2 b
		מות	DEATH	560d	1
		שרץ	SWARMING THINGS	1056d	
11	32	בוא	COME	99d	C
		טהר	BE CLEAN	372b	2
		טמא	BE UNCLEAN	379a	3
		טמא	BE UNCLEAN	379b	3
		מלאכה	WORK	522b	5
		מות	DEATH	560d	1
		מי	WATER	565b	1 a
		מן	FROM	581a	3 bc
		מן	FROM	581b	3 be
		נפל	FALL	656d	1
		עור	SKIN	736b	2
		עץ	TREE	781d	2 a
		שק	SACK	974b	1
11	33	את	MARK OF THE ACCUSATIVE	85a	1 a
		חרש	EARTHENWARE	360a	1
		טמא	BE UNCLEAN	379a	3
		מן	FROM	581a	3 bc
		נפל	FALL	656d	1
		שבר	BREAK	990c	
		תוך	MIDST	1063d	
11	34	אכל	EAT	37d	1
		אכל	FOOD	38a	
		טמא	BE UNCLEAN	379a	3
		מי	WATER	565b	1 a
		מן	FROM	581a	3 bc
		משקה	DRINK	1052d	2
		שתה	DRINK	1059c	2
11	35	טמא	BE UNCLEAN	379a	3
		טמא	UNCLEAN	379d	2 c
		כור	OVEN	468c	
		מן	FROM	581a	3 bc
		נבלה	CARCASS	615d	2
		נפל	FALL	656d	1
		תנור	FIRE-POT	1072b	
11	36	בור	WELL	92b	1
		טהר	CLEAN	373a	1
		טמא	BE UNCLEAN	379a	3
		נבלה	CARCASS	615d	2
		מעין	SPRING	746a	
11	37	זרע	SOW	281d	1 b
		זרע	SOWING	282b	2 b
		זרע	SOWING	283b	
		טהור	CLEAN	373a	1
		מן	FROM	581a	3 bc
		נבלה	CARCASS	615d	2
		נפל	FALL	656d	1
11	38	זרע	SOWING	282b	2 b
		טמא	UNCLEAN	379d	2 c
		נבלה	CARCASS	615d	2
		נפל	FALL	656d	1
		נתן	PUT	681d	2
11	39	אכלה	FOOD	38a	1
		הוא	HE, SHE, IT	*214d	
		הוא	HE, SHE, IT	215d	2 c
		טמא	BE UNCLEAN	379b	3
		מות	DIE	559d	1 b
		מן	FROM	581a	3 bc
		נבלה	CARCASS	615d	2
		מקוה	COLLECTION	876c	
11	40	טמא	BE UNCLEAN	379a	3
		טמא	BE UNCLEAN	379b	3
		נבלה	CARCASS	615d	2
11	41	אכל	EAT	37d	1
		שקץ	DETESTATION	1055a	
		שרץ	SWARM	1056c	2
		שרץ	SWARMING THINGS	1056d	
11	42	הלך	WALK	232a	1 2
		הלך	WALK	232a	1 2
		ל	TO	514c	5 fd
		מן	FROM	582a	5 b
		עד	AS FAR AS	724b	1 1b
		רבה	BECOME MANY	915c	1 c
		רבה	BECOME MANY	915c	
		ארבע	FOUR	917a	1 a5
		רגל	FOOT	919d	1 d
		שקץ	DETESTATION	1055a	
		שרץ	SWARM	1056c	2
		שרץ	SWARMING THINGS	1056d	
11	43	טמא	BE UNCLEAN	379b	3
		טמא	BE UNCLEAN	379d	
		שקץ	MAKE DETESTABLE	1055a	2
		שרץ	SWARM	1056c	2
		שרץ	SWARMING THINGS	1056d	
11	44	יהוה	YAHWEH	219b	2 2c
		טמא	BE UNCLEAN	379c	3
		קדוש	HOLY	872c	1 b
		קדוש	HOLY	872d	2 b
		קדש	BE SET APART	873c	1
		רמש	CREEP	943a	2 a
		שרץ	SWARMING THINGS	1056d	
11	45	אלהים	GOD	44b	4 a
		יהוה	YAHWEH	219b	2 2c
		עלה	GO UP	749b	1 a
		קדוש	HOLY	872c	1 b
		קדוש	HOLY	872d	2 b
11	46	ח	THE	209a	2 b
		זה	THIS	261b	3
		חי	ALIVE	312b	1 c
		תורה	LAW	436a	2 d
		ל	TO	514c	5 fc
		נפש	SOUL	659c	2
		עוף	FLY	733d	1
		רמש	CREEP	943a	2 b
		שרץ	SWARM	1056c	2
11	47	אכל	EAT	37d	1
		בדל	BE DIVIDED	95c	3
		חיה	LIVING THING	312c	1 a
		טהור	CLEAN	373a	1
		טמא	UNCLEAN	380a	2 d
12	2	אשה	WOMAN	61a	1
		דוה	BE ILL	188c	2
		זכר	MALE	271c	1 1 b
		זרע	SOW	282a	2
		טמא	BE UNCLEAN	379b	3
		נדה	IMPURITY	622c	1
12	3	בשר	FLESH	142c	1 b
		מול	CIRCUMCIZE	557d	
12	4	דם	BLOOD	196c	2
		טהר	PURITY	372d	2
		טהרה	PURIFYING	372d	1
		ישב	REMAIN	443a	2 b
		מלא	BE FULL	570b	1 b
12	5	דם	BLOOD	196c	2 a
		טהרה	PURIFYING	372d	1
		טמא	BE UNCLEAN	379b	3
		ישב	REMAIN	443a	2 b
		נדה	IMPURITY	622c	1
		נקבה	FEMALE	666c	1
		שבוע	PERIOD OF SEVEN	988d	1
		ששים	SIXTY	995d	
12	6	בן	SON	121c	7 b
		בן	SON	121d	7 b
		בן	SON	122a	9 b
		בת	DAUGHTER	123a	1
		חטאת	SIN	309c	4 a
		חטאת	SIN	*309d	4 c
		טהר	PURITY	372d	1
		יונה	DOVE	401d	
		כבש	LAMB	461a	1
		מלא	BE FULL	570b	1 b
		עלה	WHOLE BURNT OFFERING	750b	1
		תר	TURTLE-DOVE	1076a	
12	7	דם	BLOOD	196c	2 a
		זכר	MALE	271c	1 1 b
		טהר	BE CLEAN	372b	2
		תורה	LAW	436a	2 a
		כפר	COVER OVER	497d	3 b2
		נקבה	FEMALE	666c	1
		מקור	SPRING	881b	4
12	8	די	SUFFICIENCY	191c	1
		חטאת	SIN	309c	4 a
		חטאת	SIN	*309d	4 c
		טהר	BE CLEAN	372b	2
		יונה	DOVE	401d	
		כפר	COVER OVER	497d	3 b2
		לקח	TAKE	543c	6
		מסת	SUFFICIENCY	*588b	
		מצא	FIND	593c	4
		עלה	WHOLE BURNT OFFERING	750b	1
		שה	A SHEEP	962a	1
		תר	TURTLE-DOVE	1076a	
13	2	אדם	MAN	9b	1
		בהרת	BRIGHTNESS	97c	
		בוא	COME	99c	B
		בשר	FLESH	142c	1 b
		כהן	PRIEST	464a	7
		כי	IF	473b	2 b
		כי	IF	473c	2 b
		נגע	MARK	619d	3
		שאת	SWELLING	673b	2
		עור	SKIN	736b	1
		צרעת	LEPROSY	863d	A
13	3	הפך	TURN	245d	2 b
		טמא	BE UNCLEAN	379c	3
		לבן	WHITE	526b	
		עור	SKIN	*736b	1
		עמק	DEEP	771b	1
		ראה	TO SEE	907c	6 a
		ראה	TO SEE	907c	6 a
		מראה	VISION	909c	1 b
		שער	HAIR	972b	1
13	4	בהרת	BRIGHTNESS	97c	
		הפך	TURN	245d	2 b
		לבן	WHITE	526b	
		לבן	WHITE	526b	
		לבן	WHITE	*526b	
		נגע	MARK	619d	3
		עור	SKIN	*736b	1
13	5	הנה	IF	244c	D
		נגע	MARK	619d	3
		סגר	SHUT UP	689c	2 a
		עין	EYE	744b	4 b
		עמד	STAND	764b	3 c
		פשה	SPREAD	832c	
		ראה	TO SEE	907c	6 a
		שני	SECOND	1041c	
13	6	בהרת	BRIGHTNESS	97c	
		הנה	IF	244c	D
		טהר	BE CLEAN	372b	2
		טהר	BE CLEAN	372c	2
		כבס	WASH	460a	1
		כהה	DIM	462d	
		נגע	MARK	619d	3
		מספחת	ERUPTION	705c	
13	7	טהרה	PURIFYING	372d	2
		מספחת	ERUPTION	705c	
		פשה	SPREAD	832c	
		ראה	TO SEE	908b	1 b
13	8	הנה	IF	244c	D
		טמא	BE UNCLEAN	379c	4
		מספחת	ERUPTION	705c	
		ראה	TO SEE	907c	6 c
13	9	אדם	MAN	9b	B
		בוא	COME	99c	B
13	10	הוא	HE, SHE, IT	*214d	
		הנה	IF	244c	D
		הפך	TURN	245c	1 c4
		חי	ALIVE	312b	1 c
		מחיה	PRESERVATION OF LIFE	313c	4
		לבן	WHITE	526b	
		לבן	WHITE	526b	
		שאת	SWELLING	673b	2
13	11	טמא	BE UNCLEAN	379c	4
		טמא	UNCLEAN	379d	2 a
		ישן	BECOME INACTIVE	445d	
		סגר	SHUT UP	689c	2 a
		עור	SKIN	*736b	1
13	12	כסה	COVER	491d	4
		ל	TO	*516d	5 jb
		מן	FROM	581d	5 a
		נגע	MARK	619d	3
		עין	EYE	744b	1 f
		פרח	BREAK OUT	827c	
		מראה	VISION	909d	2
		רגל	FOOT	919d	1 a
13	13	הפך	TURN	245d	2 b
		טהר	BE CLEAN	372c	2
		טהור	CLEAN	373a	1
		כל	ALL	481b	1 a
		כסה	COVER	491d	4
		לבן	WHITE	526b	
		נגע	MARK	619d	3
13	14	חי	ALIVE	312b	1 c
		טמא	BE UNCLEAN	379a	3
		ראה	TO SEE	908c	1 c
13	15	חי	ALIVE	312b	1 c
		טמא	BE UNCLEAN	379c	4
		טמא	UNCLEAN	379d	2 c
		ראה	TO SEE	907c	6 a
13	16	הפך	TURN	245d	1 b
		חי	ALIVE	312b	1 c
		לבן	WHITE	526b	
		שוב	TURN BACK	998b	7 i
13	17	הפך	TURN	245d	1 b
		טהר	BE CLEAN	372c	2
		טהור	CLEAN	373a	1
		לבן	WHITE	526b	
		נגע	MARK	619d	3
		נגע	MARK	619d	3
13	18	רפא	HEAL	950d	1
		שחין	BOIL	1006c	
13	19	אדמדם	REDDISH	10c	
		בהרת	BRIGHTNESS	97c	
		בהרת	BRIGHTNESS	97c	
		לבן	WHITE	526b	
		לבן	WHITE	*526b	
		לבן	WHITE	526b	
		שאת	SWELLING	673b	2
		מקום	STANDING PLACE	880b	4
		ראה	TO SEE	908b	1 b
		שחין	BOIL	1006c	
13	20	הפך	TURN	245d	2 b
		טמא	BE UNCLEAN	379c	4
		לבן	WHITE	526b	
		פרח	BREAK OUT	827c	
		שחין	BOIL	1006c	
		שפל	LOW	1050c	1
13	21	הוא	HE, SHE, IT	*214d	
		כהה	DIM	462d	
		לבן	WHITE	526b	
		סגר	SHUT UP	689c	2 a
		שפל	LOW	1050c	1
13	22	טמא	BE UNCLEAN	379c	4
		פשה	SPREAD	832c	
13	23	בהרת	BRIGHTNESS	97c	
		בהרת	BRIGHTNESS	97c	
		טהר	BE CLEAN	372c	2
		עמד	STAND	764a	2 a
		פשה	SPREAD	832c	

Ch v.	Heb	Eng	Page	Sec
	צרבת	SCAB	863a	
	שחין	BOIL	1006c	
	תחת	UNDERNEATH	1065d	2 2a
13 24	אדמדם	REDDISH	10c	
	או	OR	14d	1
	בהרת	BRIGHTNESS	97b	
	מחיה	PRESERVATION OF LIFE	313c	4
	מכוה	BURN	465a	
	לבן	WHITE	526b	
	לבן	WHITE	*526b	
	לבן	WHITE	526b	
13 25	בהרת	BRIGHTNESS	97b	1 b
	הפך	TURN	245d	1
	טמא	BE UNCLEAN	379d	4
	מכוה	BURN	465a	
	לבן	WHITE	*526b	
	לבן	WHITE	526b	
	ספחת	ERUPTION	705c	
	פרח	BREAK OUT	827c	
13 26	בהרת	BRIGHTNESS	97b	
	כהה	DIM	462d	
	לבן	WHITE	*526b	
	לבן	WHITE	526b	
	סגר	SHUT UP	689d	2 a
	שפל	LOW	1050c	1
13 27	טמא	BE UNCLEAN	379d	4
	פשה	SPREAD	832c	
13 28	בהרת	BRIGHTNESS	97b	
	טהר	BE CLEAN	372d	2
	כהה	DIM	462d	
	מכוה	BURN	465a	
	שאת	SWELLING	673d	2
	עמד	STAND	764d	2 a
	צרבת	SCAB	863a	
	תחת	UNDERNEATH	1065d	2 2a
13 29	זקן	BEARD	278d	1
	נגע	MARK	619d	3
13 30	דק	SMALL	201a	2
	זקן	BEARD	278b	1
	טמא	BE UNCLEAN	379c	4
	נגע	MARK	619d	3
	נתק	SCAB	683d	
	צהב	YELLOW	843c	
13 31	נגע	MARK	619d	3
	נתק	SCAB	684a	
	צהב	YELLOW	*843c	
	צהב	LOVE	843c	
	שחר	BLACK	1007b	
13 32	נגע	MARK	619d	3
	נתק	SCAB	683d	
	פשה	SPREAD	832c	
	צהב	YELLOW	843c	
13 33	נתק	SCAB	683d	
	שני	SECOND	1041c	
13 34	טהר	BE CLEAN	372b	2
	טהר	BE CLEAN	372c	2
	כבס	WASH	460a	1
	נתק	SCAB	683d	
13 35	מהרה	PURIFYING	372d	2
	נתק	SCAB	683d	
	פשה	SPREAD	832c	
13 36	בקר	SEEK	133a	4
	טמא	UNCLEAN	379d	2 a
	נתק	SCAB	683d	
	צהב	YELLOW	843c	
13 37	טהר	BE CLEAN	372c	2
	טהור	CLEAN	373a	1
	נתק	SCAB	683d	
	עין	EYE	744d	4 b
	עמד	STAND	764a	2 a
	צהב	DISTANT	843c	2 a2
	צמח	SPROUT	855c	2
	רפא	HEAL	950d	1
	שחר	BLACK	1007b	
13 38	בהרת	BRIGHTNESS	97c	
	לבן	WHITE	*526b	
	לבן	WHITE	526b	
	עור	SKIN	*736b	1
13 39	בהק	ERUPTION	97b	
	בהרת	BRIGHTNESS	97c	
	טהור	CLEAN	373a	1
	כהה	DIM	462d	
	לבן	WHITE	526b	
	עור	SKIN	*736b	1
	פרח	BREAK OUT	827b	
13 40	גבח	HAVING A BALD FOREHEAD	147c	
	טהור	CLEAN	373a	1
	מרט	MAKE BALD	599a	
	קרח	BALD	901b	
13 41	גבח	HAVING A BALD FOREHEAD	147c	
	טהור	CLEAN	373a	1
	מרט	MAKE BALD	599a	
	פאה	CORNER	802b	2 b
	פנה	FACE	815d	1 1a
	קרח	BALD	901b	
13 42	אדמדם	REDDISH	10c	
	גבחת	BALD FOREHEAD	147c	
	גבחת	BALD FOREHEAD	147c	
	לבן	WHITE	526b	
	נגע	MARK	619d	3
	פרח	BREAK OUT	827c	
	קרחת	BALDNESS OF HEAD	901b	

Ch v.	Heb	Eng	Page	Sec
13 43	אדמדם	REDDISH	10c	
	גבחת	BALD FOREHEAD	147c	
	לבן	WHITE	526b	
	נגע	MARK	619d	3
	שאת	SWELLING	673b	
	עור	SKIN	*736b	1
	קרחת	BALDNESS OF HEAD	901b	
13 44	טמא	BE UNCLEAN	379c	4
	טמא	UNCLEAN	379d	2 a
	נגע	MARK	619d	3
	צרע	BE STRUCK WITH LEPROSY	863d	
13 45	טמא	UNCLEAN	379d	2 a
	עטה	WRAP ONESELF	741d	
	פרם	TEAR GARMENT	828a	
	פרע	LET GO	829a	1
	צרע	BE STRUCK WITH LEPROSY	863d	
	קרא	CALL	895a	1 b
	שפם	MOUSTACHE	974a	
13 46	בדד	ISOLATION	94d	
	טמא	BE UNCLEAN	379a	3
	טמא	UNCLEAN	379d	2 a
	מושב	DWELLING	444b	2 c
13 47	נגע	MARK	619d	3
	פשת	FLAX	833d	
	צמר	WOOL	856a	
13 48	או	OR	15a	1
	כלי	ARTICLE	*479c	1
	ל	TO	513d	5 cb g
	מלאכה	WORK	522a	3 b
	עור	SKIN	736b	2
	ערב	WOOF	786c	
	פשת	FLAX	833d	
	צמר	WOOL	856a	
	שתי	WARP	1060a	
13 49	אדמדם	REDDISH	10c	
	ירקרק	GREENISH	439a	
	כלי	ARTICLE	479c	1
	ראה	TO SEE	909a	2
13 50	זה	THIS	261b	3
	נגע	MARK	619d	3
13 51	או	OR	15a	1
	טמא	UNCLEAN	379d	2 c
	ל	TO	*514c	5 fd
	מלאכה	WORK	522a	3 b
	מלאכה	WORK	522b	5
	מאר	PAIN	549d	2
	נגע	MARK	619d	3
	עשה	DO	795b	2 f
13 52	ב	IN	90c	3 6
	כלי	ARTICLE	479c	1
	מאר	PAIN	549d	2
	פשת	FLAX	833d	
	צמר	WOOL	856a	
	שרף	BURN	977a	
13 53	כלי	ARTICLE	479c	1
13 54	סגר	SHUT UP	689d	2 a
	צוה	CHARGE	845d	2 d
	שני	SECOND	1041c	
13 55	גבחת	BALD FOREHEAD	147c	
	הפך	TURN	245c	1 2
	טמא	UNCLEAN	379d	2 c
	כבס	BE WASHED	460b	
	עין	EYE	745a	4 b
	פחתת	A BORING OUT	809b	
	פשה	SPREAD	832c	
	קרחת	BALDNESS OF HEAD	901b	
13 56	כבס	BE WASHED	460b	
	כהה	DIM	462d	
	קרע	TEAR	902c	1 b
	כלי	ARTICLE	479c	1
13 57	פרח	BREAK OUT	827c	
	ראה	TO SEE	908c	1 c
13 58	טהר	BE CLEAN	372b	2
	כבס	BE WASHED	460b	
	כלי	ARTICLE	479c	1
13 59	טהר	BE CLEAN	372c	2
	טמא	BE UNCLEAN	379c	4
	תורה	LAW	436a	2 a
	כלי	ARTICLE	479c	1
	נגע	MARK	619d	3
	פשת	FLAX	833d	
	צמר	WOOL	856a	
14 2	בוא	COME	99c	B
	מהרה	PURIFYING	372d	2
	תורה	LAW	436a	2 a
	צרע	BE STRUCK WITH LEPROSY	864a	
14 3	נגע	MARK	619d	3
	צרע	BE STRUCK WITH LEPROSY	863d	
	רפא	HEAL	950d	1
14 4	אזוב	HYSSOP	23c	
	ארז	CEDAR	72d	3
	חי	ALIVE	312b	1 c
	טהר	BE CLEAN	372d	2
	טהור	CLEAN	373a	1
	עץ	TREE	782a	2 e
	צפור	BIRD	862a	1
	שני	SCARLET	1040d	
	תולעה	WORM	1069a	2
14 5	חי	ALIVE	312b	1 f
	חרש	EARTHENWARE	360a	1

Ch v.	Heb	Eng	Page	Sec
	מי	WATER	565d	3
	צפור	BIRD	862a	1
	שחט	SLAUGHTER	1006a	2
14 6	אזוב	HYSSOP	23c	
	ארז	CEDAR	72d	3
	דם	BLOOD	196c	2 a
	חי	ALIVE	312b	1 c
	חי	ALIVE	312b	1 f
	טבל	DIP	371b	1
	מי	WATER	565d	3
	עץ	TREE	782a	2 e
	שחט	SLAUGHTER	1006a	2
	שני	SCARLET	1040d	
	תולעה	WORM	1069a	2
14 7	חי	ALIVE	312b	1 c
	טהר	BE CLEAN	372c	2
	טהר	BE CLEAN	372d	2
	נזה	SPURT	633c	
	פנה	FACE	819a	2 7b
	שדה	FIELD	961c	1 f
	שלח	SEND	1019b	3
14 8	אחר	AFTERWARDS	29d	1 b
	חוץ	THE OUTSIDE	300a	1 bd
	טהר	BE CLEAN	372b	2
	טהר	BE CLEAN	372d	2
	ישב	REMAIN	442d	2 a
	כבס	WASH	460a	1
	רחץ	WASH OFF	934c	2
14 9	שער	HAIR	972b	2
	בשר	FLESH	142c	2
	גב	BACK	146c	5
	זקן	BEARD	278b	1
	טהר	BE CLEAN	372b	2
	כבס	WASH	460a	1
	עין	EYE	744c	1 r
	רחץ	WASH OFF	934c	2
	שער	HAIR	972b	2
14 10	בלל	MIX	117c	2
	בת	DAUGHTER	123d	9
	כבש	LAMB	461a	1
	כבשה	EWE-LAMBS	461a	
	לג	LOG	528d	2
	מנחה	OFFERING	585c	5 b
	עשרון	TENTH PART	798a	
	שער	HAIR	972b	2
	שמן	OIL	1032c	2 g
14 11	טהר	BE CLEAN	372c	3
	טהר	BE CLEAN	372d	2
	עמד	STAND	764d	4
14 12	לג	LOG	528d	2
	נוף	WAVE	632a	4
	תנופה	WAVING	632c	2 a
14 13	חטא	SIN	309c	4 a
	חטאת	SIN	*309d	4 c
	חטאת	SIN	310a	4 c
	עלה	WHOLE BURNT OF-FERING	750d	
	קדש	APARTNESS	872a	3 b
	מקום	STANDING PLACE	880b	4
	שחט	SLAUGHTER	1006b	2
14 14	אזן	EAR	23d	1
	בהן	THUMB	97b	
	דם	BLOOD	197d	3 b
	דם	BLOOD	*197d	3 b
	טהר	BE CLEAN	372d	2
	יד	HAND	389a	1 a
	ימני	RIGHT	412c	
	תנוך	TIP	1072a	
14 15	יצק	POUR	427b	1
	כף	HOLLOW OF THE HAND	496b	1 a
	לג	LOG	528d	2
	שמאלי	LEFT	970a	
	שמאלי	LEFT	970a	
14 16	טבל	DIP	371b	1
	ימני	RIGHT	412c	
	כף	HOLLOW OF THE HAND	496b	1 a
	נזה	SPURT	633c	
	אצבע	FINGER	840c	1 a
	שמאלי	LEFT	970a	
14 17	אזן	EAR	23d	1
	בהן	THUMB	97b	
	דם	BLOOD	197d	3 b
	טהר	BE CLEAN	372d	2
	יד	HAND	389a	1 a
	ימני	RIGHT	412c	
	יתר	REMAINDER	451d	1 b
	כף	HOLLOW OF THE HAND	496b	1 a
	תנוך	TIP	1072a	
14 18	טהר	BE CLEAN	372d	2
	יתר	BE LEFT OVER	451b	
	כף	HOLLOW OF THE HAND	496b	1 a
	כפר	COVER OVER	498a	3 b2
14 19	אחר	AFTERWARDS	29d	1 b
	חטאת	SIN	309c	4 a
	חטאת	SIN	310a	4 c
	טהר	BE CLEAN	372d	2
	טמאה	UNCLEANNESS	380a	4
	כפר	COVER OVER	497d	3 b2
	כפר	COVER OVER	498a	3 c
	עלה	WHOLE BURNT OF-FERING	750d	
	עשה	DO	794d	2 4

Ch v.	Heb	Eng	Page	Sec
14 20	מזבח	ALTAR	259a	1
	מהר	BE CLEAN	372b	2
	כפר	COVER OVER	497d	3 b2
	עלה	GO UP	749d	8
	עלה	WHOLE BURNT OF-FERING	750d	
14 21	בלל	MIX	117c	2
	דל	POOR	195d	
	יד	HAND	390b	2
	כפר	COVER OVER	497d	3 b2
	לג	LOG	528d	
	מנחה	OFFERING	585c	5 b
	תנופה	WAVING	632c	2 a
	נשג	REACH	673c	3
	עשרון	TENTH PART	798a	
14 22	אשר	PARTICLE OF RE-LATION	82c	4 c
	חמאת	SIN	309c	4 a
	יד	HAND	390b	2
	יונה	DOVE	401d	
	נשג	REACH	673c	3
	עלה	WHOLE BURNT OF-FERING	750b	
	תר	TURTLE-DOVE	1076a	
14 23	מהרה	PURIFYING	372d	2
14 24	לג	LOG	528d	
	גוף	WAVE	632a	4
	תנופה	WAVING	632c	2 a
14 25	אזן	EAR	23d	1
	בהן	THUMB	97b	
	דם	BLOOD	197d	3 b
	דם	BLOOD	*197d	3 b
	מהר	BE CLEAN	372d	2
	יד	HAND	389a	1 a
	ימני	RIGHT	412c	
	תנוך	TIP	1072a	
14 26	יצק	POUR	427b	1
	כף	HOLLOW OF THE HAND	496b	1 a
	שמאלי	LEFT	970a	
14 27	ימני	RIGHT	412c	
	כף	HOLLOW OF THE HAND	496b	1 a
	נזה	SPURT	633c	
	אצבע	FINGER	840c	1 a
	שמאלי	LEFT	970a	
	שבע	SEVEN	988b	5 c
14 28	אזן	EAR	23d	1
	בהן	THUMB	97b	
	דם	BLOOD	197d	3 b
	מהר	BE CLEAN	372d	2
	יד	HAND	389a	1 a
	ימני	RIGHT	412c	
	כף	HOLLOW OF THE HAND	496b	1 a
	על	UPON	752d	2 1
	תנוך	TIP	1072a	
14 29	מהר	BE CLEAN	372d	2
	כפר	COVER OVER	498a	3 b2
14 30	אשר	PARTICLE OF RE-LATION	82c	4 c
	יד	HAND	390b	2
	יונה	DOVE	401d	
	נשג	REACH	673c	3
	עשה	DO	794d	2 4
	מקום	STANDING PLACE	880b	4
	תר	TURTLE-DOVE	1076a	
14 31	אשר	PARTICLE OF RE-LATION	82c	4 c
	חמאת	SIN	309c	4 a
	מהר	BE CLEAN	372d	2
	יד	HAND	390b	2
	כפר	COVER OVER	497d	3 b2
	נשג	REACH	673c	3
	עלה	WHOLE BURNT OF-FERING	750d	
14 32	מהרה	PURIFYING	372d	2
	יד	HAND	390b	2
	תורה	LAW	436a	2 a
	נגע	MARK	619d	3
	נשג	REACH	673c	3
14 34	אחזה	POSSESSION	28c	
	אחזה	POSSESSION	28c	
	ארץ	EARTH	76b	2 e
	נגע	MARK	619d	3
	צרעת	LEPROSY	863d	C
14 35	כ	LIKE	453d	1 b
	נגד	BE CONSPICUOUS	616d	1
	נגע	MARK	619d	3
	ראה	TO SEE	908c	1 c
14 36	אחר	AFTER	29d	2
	טרם	NOT YET	302c	2
	טמא	BE UNCLEAN	379a	3
	נגע	MARK	619d	3
	פנה	TURN	815c	
	ראה	TO SEE	907c	6 a
14 37	אדמדם	REDDISH	10c	
	בית	HOUSE	108d	1 ab
	ירקרק	GREENISH	439a	
	נגע	MARK	619d	3
	שקערורה	DEPRESSION	891a	
	שפל	LOW	1050c	1
14 38	סגר	SHUT UP	689d	2 b
14 39	בית	HOUSE	108d	1 ab
	נגע	MARK	619d	3
	פשה	SPREAD	832c	

Ch v.	Heb	Eng	Page	Sec
14 40	אבן	STONE	6c	2
	בית	HOUSE	*108d	1 ab
	הם	THEY	241d	8 d
	חוץ	THE OUTSIDE	300a	1 bd
	חלץ	DRAW OFF OR OUT	322d	1
	טמא	UNCLEAN	380a	3
	נגע	MARK	619d	3
14 41	בית	HOUSE	110c	8 a
	חוץ	THE OUTSIDE	300a	1 bd
	טמא	UNCLEAN	380a	3
	עפר	DRY EARTH	779d	1 g
	קצה	CUT OFF	892a	
	קצע	SCRAPE	892d	
	שפך	POUR OUT	1049c	1 a
14 42	אבן	STONE	6c	2
	אחר	ANOTHER	29c	
	בוא	COME	99b	1 f
	בית	HOUSE	*108d	1 ab
	טוח	OVER-SPREAD	376b	
	עפר	DRY EARTH	779d	1 g
	תחת	UNDERNEATH	1066a	3 1b
14 43	אבן	STONE	6c	2
	אחר	BESIDES	30a	3
	בית	HOUSE	*108d	1 ab
	חלץ	DRAW OFF OR OUT	322d	1
	טוח	OVER-SPREAD	376b	
	נגע	MARK	619d	3
	פרח	BREAK OUT	827b	
	קצה	CUT OFF	892a	
	שוב	TURN BACK	998a	7 a
14 44	טמא	UNCLEAN	379d	2 c
	מאר	PAIN	549d	2
	נגע	MARK	619d	3
	פשה	SPREAD	832c	
	צרעת	LEPROSY	863d	C
14 45	אבן	STONE	6c	2
	בית	HOUSE	108d	1 ab
	טמא	UNCLEAN	380a	3
	יצא	BRING OUT	425a	4 d
	נתץ	PULL DOWN	683b	1
	עפר	DRY EARTH	779d	2 a
	עץ	TREE	781d	2 b
14 46	טמא	BE UNCLEAN	379a	3
	טמא	BE UNCLEAN	379b	3
	יום	DAY	400b	7 d5
	סגר	SHUT UP	689c	2 b
14 47	שכב	LIE DOWN	1012b	2
14 48	מהר	BE CLEAN	372c	2
	טוח	OVER-SPREAD	376b	
	נגע	MARK	619d	3
	פשה	SPREAD	832c	
	רפא	HEAL	950d	1
14 49	אזוב	HYSSOP	23c	
	ארז	CEDAR	72d	3
	חמא	MISS A GOAL OR WAY	307c	4
	עץ	TREE	782a	2 e
	צפור	BIRD	862a	1
	שני	SCARLET	1040d	
	תולעה	WORM	1069a	2
14 50	חי	ALIVE	312b	1 f
	חרש	EARTHENWARE	360a	1
	מי	WATER	565d	3
	שחט	SLAUGHTER	1006a	2
14 51	אזוב	HYSSOP	23c	
	ארז	CEDAR	72d	3
	דם	BLOOD	196c	2 a
	חי	ALIVE	312b	1 c
	חי	ALIVE	312b	1 f
	טבל	DIP	371b	1
	מי	WATER	565d	3
	נזה	SPURT	633c	
	עץ	TREE	782a	2 e
	שחט	SLAUGHTER	1006a	2
	שני	SCARLET	1040d	
	תולעה	WORM	1069a	2
14 52	אזוב	HYSSOP	23c	
	ארז	CEDAR	72d	3
	דם	BLOOD	196c	2 a
	חמא	MISS A GOAL OR WAY	307c	4
	חי	ALIVE	312b	1 f
	מי	WATER	565d	3
	עץ	TREE	782a	2 e
	שני	SCARLET	1040d	
	תולעה	WORM	1069a	2
14 53	חי	ALIVE	312b	1 c
	מהר	BE CLEAN	372b	2
	כפר	COVER OVER	497d	3 b1
	פנה	FACE	816c	2 1d
	פנה	FACE	819a	2 7b
	שדה	FIELD	961c	1 f
	שלח	SEND	1019b	3
14 54	תורה	LAW	436a	2 a
	ל	TO	514b	5 fa
	נגע	MARK	619d	3
14 55	צרעת	LEPROSY	863d	C
14 56	בהרת	BRIGHTNESS	97b	
	שאת	SWELLING	673b	2
	ספחת	ERUPTION	705c	
14 57	מהור	CLEAN	373a	1
	טמא	UNCLEAN	379d	2 c
	ירה	DIRECT	435c	5 b
	תורה	LAW	436a	2 a
	צרעת	LEPROSY	863d	

Ch v.	Heb	Eng	Page	Sec
15 2	איש	MAN	36a	
	בשר	FLESH	142d	3
	זוב	ISSUE	264d	
	טמא	UNCLEAN	379d	2 a
	כי	IF	473c	2 b
15 3	בשר	FLESH	142d	3
	זוב	ISSUE	264d	
	חתם	SEAL	368a	
	טמאה	UNCLEANNESS	380a	4
	רור	FLOW	938b	
15 4	בשר	FLESH	142d	3
	זוב	FLOW	264d	4
	טמא	BE UNCLEAN	379a	3
	טמא	BE UNCLEAN	379a	3
	כלי	ARTICLE	479c	1
	שכב	LIE DOWN	1012b	1 b
15 5	בשר	FLESH	142d	3
	טמא	BE UNCLEAN	379b	3
	כבס	WASH	460a	1
15 6	מי	WATER	565b	1 a
	בשר	FLESH	142d	3
	זוב	FLOW	264d	4
	טמא	BE UNCLEAN	379b	3
	כבס	WASH	460a	1
	כלי	ARTICLE	479c	1
	מי	WATER	565b	1 a
15 7	בשר	FLESH	142d	3
	זוב	FLOW	264d	4
	טמא	BE UNCLEAN	379b	3
	כבס	WASH	460a	1
15 8	בשר	FLESH	142d	3
	זוב	FLOW	264d	4
	טמא	BE UNCLEAN	379b	3
	כבס	WASH	460a	1
	רקק	SPIT	956d	
15 9	בשר	FLESH	142d	3
	זוב	FLOW	264d	4
	טמא	BE UNCLEAN	379a	3
	כל	ALL	481c	1 b
	רכב	RIDE	938d	
	מרכב	CHARIOT	939c	2
15 10	בשר	FLESH	142d	3
	חמשים	FIFTY	332c	5
	טמא	BE UNCLEAN	379b	3
	כבס	WASH	460a	1
	תחת	UNDER	*1117d	
15 11	בשר	FLESH	142d	3
	זב	FLOW	264d	4
	חמשים	FIFTY	332c	5
	טמא	BE UNCLEAN	379b	3
	כבס	WASH	460a	1
	כבס	WASH	460a	1
	שטף	OVERFLOW	1009b	3
15 12	בשר	FLESH	142d	3
	זב	FLOW	264d	4
	חרש	EARTHENWARE	360a	1
	עץ	TREE	781d	2 a
	שבר	BREAK	990d	
	שטף	OVERFLOW	1009b	
15 13	בשר	FLESH	142c	2
	בשר	FLESH	142d	3
	זוב	ISSUE	264d	
	זב	FLOW	264d	4
	חי	ALIVE	312b	1 f
	מהר	BE CLEAN	372b	2
	מהר	BE CLEAN	372b	2
	מהרה	PURIFYING	372d	2
	ספר	COUNT	707d	1
	רחץ	WASH OFF	934c	1
15 14	בשר	FLESH	142d	3
	יונה	DOVE	401d	
	נתן	GIVE	678b	1
	עלה	WHOLE BURNT OF-FERING	750b	
	תר	TURTLE-DOVE	1076a	
15 15	בשר	FLESH	142d	3
	זוב	ISSUE	264d	
	חמאת	SIN	309c	4 a
	חמאת	SIN	*309d	4 c
	כפר	COVER OVER	498a	3 c
	עלה	WHOLE BURNT OF-FERING	750b	
	עלה	WHOLE BURNT OF-FERING	750d	
15 16	עשה	DO	794d	2 4
	איש	MAN	35d	
	בשר	FLESH	142c	2
	בשר	FLESH	142d	3
	זרע	SOWING	282c	3
	טמא	BE UNCLEAN	379b	3
	יצא	GO OUT	423a	1 f
	כי	IF	473c	2 b
	קרה	CHANCE	*899d	
15 17	שכבה	LYING	1012c	1
	בשר	FLESH	142d	3
	זרע	SOWING	282c	3
	טמא	BE UNCLEAN	379b	3
	כבס	BE WASHED	460b	
	מי	WATER	565b	1 a
	שכבה	LYING	1012c	1
15 18	איש	MAN	35d	
	בשר	FLESH	142d	3
	זרע	SOWING	282c	3
	טמא	BE UNCLEAN	379b	3
	שכב	LIE DOWN	1012b	1
	שכבה	LYING	1012c	1

LEVITICUS

Ch	v.	Heb	Eng	Page	Sec
15	19	בשר	FLESH	142d	3
		דם	BLOOD	196c	2 a
		זוב	FLOW	264d	4
		זוב	ISSUE	264d	
		טמא	BE UNCLEAN	379b	3
		כי	IF	473c	2 b
		נדה	IMPURITY	622c	1
15	20	טמא	BE UNCLEAN	379a	3
		נדה	IMPURITY	622c	1
		שכב	LIE DOWN	1012b	1 b
15	21	טמא	BE UNCLEAN	379b	3
		מות	DIE	560a	2 b
15	22	טמא	BE UNCLEAN	379b	3
		כלי	ARTICLE	479c	1
15	23	טמא	BE UNCLEAN	379b	3
		כלי	ARTICLE	479c	1
15	24	טמא	BE UNCLEAN	379a	3
		טמא	BE UNCLEAN	379b	3
		נדה	IMPURITY	622c	1
		שכב	LIE DOWN	1012b	1 b
		שכב	LIE DOWN	1012b	1 b
15	25	דם	BLOOD	196c	2 a
		זוב	ISSUE	264d	
		זוב	FLOW	264d	4
		טמא	UNCLEAN	379d	2 a
		טמאה	UNCLEANNESS	380a	4
		כי	IF	473c	2 b
		לא	NOT	520a	4 ab
		נדה	IMPURITY	622c	1
		על	UPON	755a	2 2
15	26	זוב	ISSUE	264d	
		טמא	UNCLEAN	379d	2 c
		טמאה	UNCLEANNESS	380a	4
		כלי	ARTICLE	479c	1
		כל	ALL	481c	1 b
		נדה	IMPURITY	622c	1
		שכב	LIE DOWN	1012b	1 b
		משכב	COUCH	1012d	1
15	27	טמא	BE UNCLEAN	379a	3
		טמא	BE UNCLEAN	379b	3
15	28	אחר	AFTERWARDS	29d	1 b
		זוב	ISSUE	264d	
		טהר	BE CLEAN	372b	2
		ספר	COUNT	707d	1
15	29	יונה	DOVE	401d	2
		עלה	WHOLE BURNT OF-FERING	750b	
		תר	TURTLE-DOVE	1076a	
15	30	זוב	ISSUE	264d	
		חטאת	SIN	309c	4 a
		טמאה	UNCLEANNESS	380a	4
		כפר	COVER OVER	498a	3 c
		עלה	WHOLE BURNT OF-FERING	750b	
		עלה	WHOLE BURNT OF-FERING	750d	
15	31	עשה	DO	794d	2 4
		טמא	BE UNCLEAN	379c	3
		טמאה	UNCLEANNESS	380a	4
		נזר	SEPARATE	634a	
		תוך	MIDST	1063d	
15	32	זוב	FLOW	264d	4
		זרע	SOWING	282c	3
		טמא	BE UNCLEAN	379a	3
		יצא	GO OUT	423a	1 f
		תורה	LAW	436a	2 a
		שכבה	LYING	1012c	1
15	33	דוה	UNWELL	188c	2
		זוב	ISSUE	264d	
		זוב	FLOW	264d	4
		זכר	MALE	271c	1 1 b
		טמא	UNCLEAN	379d	2 a
		נדה	IMPURITY	622c	1
		נקבה	FEMALE	666c	1
		שכב	LIE DOWN	1012b	3
16	1	מות	DIE	560a	2 b
		מות	DEATH	560d	1
		קרב	COME NEAR	897c	1 c
16	2	בית	HOUSE	110c	8 b
		כפרת	PROPITIATORY	498c	
		מות	DIE	560a	2 b
		מן	FROM	578d	1 c
		עת	TIME	773d	1 a
		פנה	FACE	816c	2 1 b
		קדש	APARTNESS	871d	2 c
		ראה	TO SEE	908b	1 a
16	3	איל	RAM	18a	2 c
		ב	IN	89c	3 1b
		בוא	COME	98c	2 a
		בן	SON	121c	7 b
		זה	THIS	261d	6 ba
		חטאת	SIN	309d	4 c
		לבש	PUT ON	527d	A
		עלה	WHOLE BURNT OF-FERING	750c	
16	4	בד	WHITE LINEN	94b	
		אבנט	GIRDLE	126a	
		בשר	FLESH	142c	2
		חגר	GIRD	292a	3
		מכנס	BREECH	488b	
		כתנת	TUNIC	509a	
		לבש	PUT ON	527d	A
		על	UPON	753a	2 1a a
		מצנפת	TURBAN	857b	
		צנוע	WRAP	857b	
		קדש	APARTNESS	872b	4 a
16	5	איל	RAM	18a	2 c
		בן	SON	120d	1 jg
		חטאת	SIN	309d	4 c
		עדה	CONGREGATION	417b	3
		עלה	WHOLE BURNT OF-FERING	750c	
		סעיר	HE-GOAT	972c	
		שעיר	HE-GOAT	972c	
16	6	בית	HOUSE	109d	5 a
		חטאת	SIN	309d	4 c
		כפר	COVER OVER	498a	3 e
		ל	TO	513c	5 ca
16	7	עמד	STAND	764d	4
		שעיר	HE-GOAT	972c	
16	8	גורל	LOT	174c	2 a
		חטאת	SIN	*309d	4 c
		חטאת	SIN	*309d	4 c
		נתן	PUT	680b	2 a
		עזאזל	ENTIRE REMOVAL	736d	
		שעיר	HE-GOAT	972c	
16	9	גורל	LOT	174c	2 a
		חטאת	SIN	309d	4 c
		עלה	GO UP	749a	6
		על	UPON	756c	2 7b
		עשה	DO	794d	2 4
16	10	גורל	LOT	174c	2 a
		חטאת	SIN	*309d	4 c
		חי	ALIVE	312b	1 c
		כפר	COVER OVER	497d	3 b1
		עזאזל	ENTIRE REMOVAL	736d	
		עלה	GO UP	749a	6
		עמד	STAND	765a	
		שלח	SEND	1019a	1 a
16	11	בית	HOUSE	109d	5 a
		חטאת	SIN	309d	4 c
		כפר	COVER OVER	498a	3 e
16	12	בית	HOUSE	110c	8 b
		גחלת	COAL	160d	
		דק	SMALL	201a	2
		חטאת	SIN	*309d	4 c
		חפן	HOLLOW OF HAND	342b	
		מחתה	FIRE-HOLDER	367b	3
		מלא	FULNESS	571b	1
		סם	SPICE	702c	
		על	UPON	758c	4 2a
		פנה	FACE	817d	2 5a a
		כסה	COVER	491d	3
16	13	כפרת	PROPITIATORY	498c	
		מות	DIE	560a	2 b
		עדות	TESTIMONY	730b	1
		ענן	CLOUD	778a	2
		קטרת	SMOKE	882d	2
		קטרת	SMOKE	882d	2
16	14	דם	BLOOD	197c	3 b
		דם	BLOOD	*197c	3 b
		חטאת	SIN	*309d	4 c
		כפרת	PROPITIATORY	498c	
		נזה	SPURT	633c	
		נזה	SPURT	633c	
		פנה	FACE	819d	2 7a e
		קדם	EASTWARD	870a	
		תפינים	BREAK	1074a	
16	15	אל	TO	40d	9
		בית	HOUSE	110c	8 b
		דם	BLOOD	197c	3 b
		חטאת	SIN	309d	4 c
		כפרת	PROPITIATORY	498c	
		ל	TO	513c	5 ca
		נזה	SPURT	633b	
16	16	חטאת	SIN	308d	1 b
		חטאת	SIN	*309d	4 c
		חטאת	SIN	*309d	4 c
		טמאה	UNCLEANNESS	380a	3
		טמאה	UNCLEANNESS	380a	3
		כפר	COVER OVER	497d	3 b1
		כפר	COVER OVER	498a	3 c
		ל	TO	514c	5 fd
		פשע	TRANSGRESSION	833d	3 d
		שכן	SETTLE DOWN	1015b	2 d
		תוך	MIDST	1063d	
16	17	בוא	COME	98a	1 b
		בית	HOUSE	109d	5 a
		חטאת	SIN	*309d	4 c
		כפר	COVER OVER	498a	3 e
		כפר	COVER OVER	498a	3 d
		קהל	ASSEMBLY	874d	2 a
16	18	דם	BLOOD	197d	3 b
		מזבח	ALTAR	259b	2
		כפר	COVER OVER	497d	3 b1
16	19	דם	BLOOD	197c	3 b
		חטאת	SIN	*309d	4 c
		טהר	BE CLEAN	372c	1 b
		טמאה	UNCLEANNESS	380a	3
		נזה	SPURT	633c	
		קדש	BE SET APART	873b	4 a
16	20	מזבח	ALTAR	259b	4
		חטאת	SIN	*309d	4 c
		חי	ALIVE	312b	1 c
		כלה	FINISH	478b	1 c
		כפר	COVER OVER	497d	3 a
16	21	חטאת	SIN	308d	1 b
		חי	ALIVE	312b	1 c
		יד	HAND	389a	1 a
		ידה	CONFESS	392d	1
		ל	TO	514c	5 fd
		עון	INIQUITY	731a	1 b
		על	UPON	756d	2 7a c
		עתי	TIMELY	774c	
		פשע	TRANSGRESSION	833d	3 d
		שנים	TWO	1041a	1 a
16	22	ב	IN	88c	1 4
		גזרה	SEPARATION	160c	
		חטאת	SIN	*309d	4 c
		נשא	LIFT	671a	2 b
		עון	INIQUITY	731c	3
		שלח	SEND	1019b	3
16	23	בד	WHITE LINEN	94b	
		בוא	COME	97d	1 b
		לבש	PUT ON	527d	A
		נוח	REST	628d	B 1
		פשט	STRIP OFF	833a	1
16	24	בשר	FLESH	142c	2
		כפר	COVER OVER	497d	3 b2
		כפר	COVER OVER	498a	3 e
		לבש	PUT ON	527d	A
		עלה	WHOLE BURNT OF-FERING	750d	
		עשה	DO	794d	2 4
		קדש	HOLY	872d	2 a
16	25	חטאת	SIN	309d	4 c
16	26	בשר	FLESH	142c	2
		עזאזל	ENTIRE REMOVAL	736d	
		שלח	SEND	1019a	1 a
16	27	בוא	COME	99d	B
		דם	BLOOD	197c	3 b
		חטאת	SIN	309d	4 c
		יצא	BRING OUT	425a	4 a
		כפר	COVER OVER	498a	3 d
		פרש	OFFAL	831d	
16	28	בשר	FLESH	142c	2
16	29	גור	SOJOURN	157d	1
		גר	SOJOURNER	158b	2
		גר	SOJOURNER	*158c	2
		אזרח	A NATIVE	280c	1
		חדש	NEW MOON	294d	2 b2
		חקה	SOMETHING PRE-SCRIBED	350a	1
		מלאכה	WORK	522a	3 b
		נפש	SOUL	660b	4 b6
		עולם	LONG DURATION	762c	2 e
		ענה	BE BOWED DOWN	776b	4
		עשור	A TEN	797c	1 b
16	30	חטאת	SIN	309a	1 f
		טהר	BE CLEAN	372b	3
		טהר	BE CLEAN	372c	1 c
		כפר	COVER OVER	497d	3 a
		כפר	COVER OVER	498a	3 b2
16	31	הוא	HE, SHE, IT	*214d	
		חקה	SOMETHING PRE-SCRIBED	350a	1
		נפש	SOUL	660b	4 b6
		עולם	LONG DURATION	762c	2 e
		ענה	BE BOWED DOWN	776b	4
		שבת	SABBATH	992c	2
		שבתון	SABBOTH OBSERV-ANCE	992d	2
16	32	בד	WHITE LINEN	94b	
		יד	HAND	389b	1 c
		כהן	PRIEST	464b	1
		כהן	ACT AS PRIEST	464c	1
		כפר	COVER OVER	497d	3
		לבש	PUT ON	527d	A
		מלא	FILL	570d	2
		משח	ANOINT	603b	3 a
		קדש	APARTNESS	872b	4 a
		תחת	INSTEAD	1065d	2 2b a
16	33	מזבח	ALTAR	259b	3
		כהן	PRIEST	464a	7
		כפר	COVER OVER	497d	3 a
		כפר	COVER OVER	497d	3 b1
		עם	PEOPLE	766c	1
		מקדש	SACRED PLACE	874b	3
		קהל	ASSEMBLY	874d	2 a
16	34	חטאת	SIN	308d	1 b
		חטאת	SIN	309a	1 f
		חקה	SOMETHING PRE-SCRIBED	350a	1
		כפר	COVER OVER	498a	3 c
		עולם	LONG DURATION	762c	2 e
17	2	דבר	WORD	182d	1 2a
		צוה	CHARGE	845d	2 d
17	3	בית	HOUSE	110a	5 dd
		כשב	LAMB	461b	
		עז	SHE-GOAT	777c	3 e
		שור	A HEAD OF CATTLE	1004b	
		שחט	SLAUGHTER	1006a	1
17	4	דם	BLOOD	196c	2 b
		דם	BLOOD	197b	2 i
		חשב	THINK	363c	3
		כרת	BE CUT OFF	504b	1 c
		ל	TO	510d	1 c
		עם	KINSMAN	*769c	
		משכן	DWELLING-PLACE	1015d	2 c
17	5	זבח	SLAUGHTER FOR SACRIFICE	257a	13
		זבח	SLAUGHTER FOR SACRIFICE	257a	14
		זבח	SACRIFICE	257d	2 5
		טהר	BE CLEAN	372b	2
		כהן	PRIEST	464a	7
		עז	SHE-GOAT	777c	3 e
		פנה	FACE	819a	2 7b

Ch	v.	Heb	Eng	Page	Sec
17		שדה	FIELD	961c	1 f
		שלם	PEACE-OFFERING	1023c	
17	6	דם	BLOOD	197c	3 b
		זרק	TO TOSS	284c	1 b
		חלב	FAT	317a	2 b
		כהן	PRIEST	464a	7
		קטר	MAKE SACRAFICES SMOKE	883a	1 a
17	7	דור	GENERATION	190a	2 c
		זבח	SLAUGHTER FOR SACRIFICE	257a	13
		זבח	SACRIFICE	257d	2 5
		זנה	COMMIT FORNICATION	275d	3
		חקה	SOMETHING PRESCRIBED	350a	1
		עולם	LONG DURATION	762c	2 e
		שעיר	SATYR	972d	
17	8	בית	HOUSE	110a	5 dd
		גור	SOJOURN	157d	1
		גר	SOJOURNER	158b	2
		גר	SOJOURNER	*158c	2
		ה	THE	208a	1 g
		זבח	SACRIFICE	257d	2 5
		זבח	SACRIFICE	258a	2 7
		עלה	GO UP	749d	8
		עלה	WHOLE BURNT OFFERING	750d	
		תוך	MIDST	1063d	
17	9	כרת	BE CUT OFF	504b	1 c
		עם	KINSMAN	769c	
		עשה	DO	794d	2 4
17	10	בית	HOUSE	110a	5 dd
		גור	SOJOURN	157d	1
		גר	SOJOURNER	158b	2
		גר	SOJOURNER	*158c	2
		דם	BLOOD	196c	1
		ה	THE	208a	1 g
		כרת	CUT OFF	504c	2 c
		נפש	A LIVING BEING	659d	3 a
		נפש	SOUL	660b	4 c2
		נתן	PUT	680d	2 b
		עם	KINSMAN	*769c	
		תוך	MIDST	1063d	
17	11	דם	BLOOD	196b	1
		דם	BLOOD	197c	3 b
		כפר	COVER OVER	497d	3 b2
		כפר	COVER OVER	498a	3 d
		נפש	A LIVING BEING	659d	3 a
		נפש	SOUL	660b	4 c1
		נתן	PUT	681a	2 d
17	12	גור	SOJOURN	157d	1
		גר	SOJOURNER	158b	2
		גר	SOJOURNER	*158c	2
		דם	BLOOD	196c	1
		מן	FROM	580c	3 a
		נפש	A LIVING BEING	659d	3 a
		נפש	SOUL	660b	4 c2
17	13	אכל	EAT	37d	1
		גור	SOJOURN	157d	1
		גר	SOJOURNER	158b	2
		גר	SOJOURNER	*158c	2
		דם	BLOOD	196c	1
		חיה	LIVING THING	312c	1 b
		כסה	COVER	491d	2
		עוף	FLY	733d	1
		עפר	DRY EARTH	779d	1 a
		צוד	HUNT	844c	
		ציד	GAME	844d	
		שפך	POUR OUT	1049c	1 a
		תוך	MIDST	1063d	
17	14	בשר	FLESH	142d	6 a
		דם	BLOOD	196b	1
		דם	BLOOD	196c	1
		כרת	BE CUT OFF	504b	1 c
		נפש	A LIVING BEING	659d	3 a
17	15	גר	SOJOURNER	158b	2
		טמא	BE UNCLEAN	379a	3
		טמא	BE UNCLEAN	379b	3
		טרפה	ANIMAL TORN	383c	1
		נבלה	CARCASS	615d	2
		נפש	SOUL	660b	4 c2
17	16	בשר	FLESH	142c	2
		נשא	LIFT	671a	2 b
		עון	INIQUITY	731c	3
18	2	אנכי	I	59b	
		יהוה	YAHWEH	219b	2 2d
18	3	הלך	WALK	234d	2 3a 2d
		חקה	SOMETHING PRESCRIBED	350b	2 e
		מעשה	DEED	795c	1 a2
18	4	אנכי	I	59b	
		יהוה	YAHWEH	219b	2 2d
		חקה	SOMETHING PRESCRIBED	350a	2 d
		חקה	SOMETHING PRESCRIBED	350b	2 e
		משפט	JUDGMENT	1049a	4
18	5	יהוה	YAHWEH	219b	2 2d
		חיה	LIVE	311b	1 c
		חקה	SOMETHING PRESCRIBED	350a	2 d
		חקה	SOMETHING PRESCRIBED	350b	2 e
		משפט	JUDGMENT	1049a	4
18	6	אנכי	I	59b	

Ch	v.	Heb	Eng	Page	Sec
		בשר	FLESH	142d	4
		יהוה	YAHWEH	219b	2 2d
		ערוה	NAKEDNESS	789a	1
		קרב	COME NEAR	897b	1 a
		שאר	FLESH	985a	2
18	7	אב	FATHER	3b	1
18	8	אב	FATHER	3b	1
		אשה	WOMAN	61b	2
		ערוה	NAKEDNESS	789a	1
18	9	אחות	SISTER	27d	1
		אם	MOTHER	51d	1
		בת	DAUGHTER	123a	1
		בת	DAUGHTER	123b	1 d
		חוץ	THE OUTSIDE	299d	1 a
		מולדת	BORN	409d	3
18	10	בת	DAUGHTER	123b	1 g
		ערוה	NAKEDNESS	789a	1
18	11	אב	FATHER	3b	1
		אחות	SISTER	27d	1
		אשה	WOMAN	61b	2
		בת	DAUGHTER	123b	1 d
		מולדת	BORN	409d	3
18	12	שאר	FLESH	985a	2
18	13	שאר	FLESH	985a	2
18	14	דדה	AUNT	187d	
		קרב	COME NEAR	897b	1 a
18	15	תבל	CONFUSION	117d	
		כלה	DAUGHTER-IN-LAW	483c	1
18	16	ערוה	NAKEDNESS	789a	1
18	17	בת	DAUGHTER	123b	1 g
		זמה	PLAN	273c	2 c
		שאר	FLESH	985a	2
18	18	אל	TO	40b	5
		חיים	LIFE	313b	1
		על	UPON	753d	2 1d
		על	UPON	755b	2 4b
		צרר	SHEW HOSTILITY TOWARD	865d	
		צרר	MAKE A RIVAL-WIFE	865d	
18	19	בית	HOUSE	109d	4
		טמאה	UNCLEANNESS	380a	4
		נדה	IMPURITY	622c	1
18	20	קרב	COME NEAR	897b	1 a
		זרע	SOWING	282c	3
		טמא	BE UNCLEAN	379a	1
		נתן	GIVE	680a	1 z
		עמית	ASSOCIATE	765c	
		שכבת	COPULATION	1012d	
18	21	יהוה	YAHWEH	219b	2 2d
		זרע	SOWING	282d	4 d
		חלל	POLLUTE	320b	1 c
		מלך	MOLECH	574c	
		נתן	GIVE	679b	1 k
		עבר	PASS OVER	718d	1 d
		שם	NAME	1028b	3
18	22	זכר	MALE	271c	1 1 b
		שכב	LIE DOWN	1012b	3
		משכב	ACT OF LYING	1012d	2 b
		תועבה	ABOMINATION	1073a	2 b
18	23	בהמה	BEAST	96d	1
		תבל	CONFUSION	117d	
		טמא	BE UNCLEAN	379a	1
		נתן	GIVE	680a	1 z
		עמד	STAND	764c	7 f
		רבע	LIE DOWN	918b	
		שכבת	COPULATION	1012d	
18	24	טמא	BE UNCLEAN	379b	1
		טמא	BE UNCLEAN	379d	
		פנה	FACE	818b	2 6a
		שלח	SEND	1019a	2 c
18	25	טמא	BE UNCLEAN	379a	1
		ישב	DWELL	443b	3
		עון	INIQUITY	731a	1 c1
		קיא	SPUE OUT	883c	
18	26	גור	SOJOURN	157d	1
		גר	SOJOURNER	158b	2
		גר	SOJOURNER	*158c	2
		חקה	SOMETHING PRESCRIBED	350a	2 d
		חקה	SOMETHING PRESCRIBED	350b	2 e
		משפט	JUDGMENT	1049a	4
		תועבה	ABOMINATION	1073a	2 b
18	27	אל	THESE	41b	
		טמא	BE UNCLEAN	379a	1
		תועבה	ABOMINATION	1073a	2 b
18	28	טמא	BE UNCLEAN	379c	1
		קיא	SPUE OUT	883c	
18	29	כרת	BE CUT OFF	504b	1 c
		מן	FROM	581a	3 bc
		נפש	SOUL	660b	4 c4
		עם	KINSMAN	*769c	
		תועבה	ABOMINATION	1073a	2 b
18	30	בלת	NOT	116d	4 a
		יהוה	YAHWEH	219b	2 2d
		חקה	SOMETHING PRESCRIBED	350a	2 b
		טמא	BE UNCLEAN	379d	
		מן	FROM	580d	3 ba
		משמרת	GUARD	1038c	3
		תועבה	ABOMINATION	*1073a	2 b
19	2	בן	SON	120d	1 jg
		דבר	SPEAK	181a	3 b
		יהוה	YAHWEH	219b	2 2d

Ch	v.	Heb	Eng	Page	Sec
		עדה	CONGREGATION	417b	3
		קדוש	HOLY	872c	1 b
		קדוש	HOLY	872d	2 b
19	3	אם	MOTHER	51d	1
		יהוה	YAHWEH	219b	2 2d
		ירא	FEAR	431c	3
		שבת	SABBOTH	992c	1 c
		שבת	SABBOTH	992c	1 c
		שמר	KEEP	1036d	3 b
19	4	אלהים	GOD	43c	1 d
		אליל	WORTHLESSNESS	47c	B
		יהוה	YAHWEH	219b	2 2d
		מסכה	MOLTEN IMAGE	651b	2
		פנה	TURN	815b	1 a
19	5	זבח	SLAUGHTER FOR SACRIFICE	257a	13
		רצון	GOODWILL	953c	2
		שלם	PEACE-OFFERING	1023c	
19	6	אכל	EAT	37d	1
		ה	THE	209a	2 b
		זבח	SACRIFICE	257d	2 5
		יום	DAY	401b	7 l
		יתר	BE LEFT OVER	451c	
		מחרת	THE MORROW	564b	
		שרף	BURN	977a	
19	7	אכל	EAT	37d	1
		פגול	FOUL THING	803b	
		רצה	BE PLEASED WITH	953b	1
19	8	חלל	POLLUTE	320b	1 b
		כרת	BE CUT OFF	504b	1 c
		נפש	SOUL	660b	4 c2
		נשא	LIFT	671a	2 b
		עון	INIQUITY	731c	3
		עם	KINSMAN	769c	
19	9	ארץ	EARTH	76b	3 b
		בית	HOUSE	*108d	1 a
		בת	DAUGHTER	123a	1
		כלה	FINISH	*478b	1 c
		כלה	FINISH	478b	1 c
		לקט	GLEAN	544d	3
		לקט	GLEANING	545a	
		פאה	CORNER	802a	1
		קצר	HARVEST	894b	
		קצר	HARVEST	894b	
		קציר	HARVESTING	894c	2
		קצר	HARVEST	894c	
		קציר	HARVESTING	894c	2
19	10	גר	SOJOURNER	158b	2
		יהוה	YAHWEH	219b	2 2d
		כרם	VINEYARD	501d	
		לקט	GATHER UP	544d	1
		עזב	LEAVE	737b	1 j
		עלל	GLEAN	760a	
		עני	POOR	776d	1
		פרט	THE BROKEN OFF	827d	
19	11	גנב	STEAL	170c	
		כחש	DECEIVE	471b	1
		עמית	ASSOCIATE	765c	
		שקר	DEAL FALSELY	1055d	
19	12	יהוה	YAHWEH	219b	2 2d
		חלל	POLLUTE	320b	1 c
		לא	NOT	518c	1 aa
		שבע	SWEAR	989b	1 1
		שם	NAME	1028b	3
19	13	את	WITH	86b	3 a
		בקר	MORNING	133d	1 a
		גזל	TEAR AWAY	159d	
		לון	LODGE	533d	1 c
		עשק	OPPRESS	798d	1
		פעלה	WORK	821d	2
		רע	FRIEND	946a	2
		שכיר	HIRED	969b	2
19	14	אלהים	GOD	44d	4 c
		יהוה	YAHWEH	219b	2 2d
		חרש	DEAF	361c	
		ירא	FEAR	431b	2
		מכשול	STUMBLING	506b	2 a
		עור	BLIND	734c	1 a
		קלל	BE SLIGHT	886c	1
19	15	גדול	GREAT	153b	6 b
		הדר	HONOUR	214a	2
		הדר	HONOUR	*214a	2
		נשא	LIFT	670c	1 b 3
		עול	INJUSTICE	732c	
		עמית	ASSOCIATE	765c	
		צדק	RIGHTEOUSNESS	841c	2 a
		שפט	JUDGE	1047c	2
		משפט	JUDGMENT	1048b	1 a
19	16	דם	BLOOD	197b	2
		יהוה	YAHWEH	219b	2 2d
		הלך	WALK	231d	1 1d 5k
		על	UPON	757d	2 7d
		עמד	STAND	763d	1 c
		רכיל	SLANDER	940c	
		רע	FRIEND	946a	2
19	17	אח	BROTHER	26b	2
		חמא	SIN	308a	3
		יכח	REPROVE	407a	5 b
		לבב	HEART	524b	2 9b
		נשא	LIFT	670d	1 b 0
		על	UPON	754b	2 1f b
		עמית	ASSOCIATE	765c	
19	18	אהב	LOVE	12d	1
		בן	SON	121b	1 ji
		יהוה	YAHWEH	219b	2 2d
		ל	TO	512a	3 b

LEVITICUS

Ch	v.	Heb	Eng	Page	Sec
		נצר	KEEP	643c	1
		נקם	AVENGE	668a	2
		עם	PEOPLE	766a	5 a
		רע	FRIEND	946a	1
19	19	בהמה	BEAST	97a	2
		זרע	SOW	281c	1 d
		חקה	SOMETHING PRE-SCRIBED	350b	2 e
		כלאים	TWO KINDS	476d	6
		עלה	GO UP	748d	6
		על	UPON	753a	2 l a a
		על	UPON	756d	2 7b
		רבע	LIE DOWN	918b	
		שעטנז	MIXED STUFF	1043b	
19	20	בקרת	PUNISHMENT	134c	
		זרע	SOWING	282c	3
		חפשה	FREEDOM	344d	
		חפש	BE FREE	344d	
		חרב	ATTACK	352b	
		חרף	ACQUIRE	358c	
		מות	DIE	560c	2
		נתן	GIVE	681b	1 a
		פדה	RANSOM	804b	
		שכב	LIE DOWN	1012b	3
		שכבה	LYING	1012c	1
		שפחה	MAID	1046c	1
19	21	איל	RAM	18a	2 b
		אשם	OFFENCE	79d	4
19	22	איל	RAM	18a	2 b
		אשם	OFFENCE	79d	4
		חטא	MISS A GOAL OR WAY	307b	2 b
		חטאת	SIN	308d	1 b
		חטאת	SIN	308d	1 b
		חטאת	SIN	309a	1 f
		כפר	COVER OVER	497d	3 b2
		כפר	COVER OVER	498a	3 d
		כפר	COVER OVER	498a	3 c
		סלח	FORGIVE	669c	
19	23	אכל	EAT	37d	1
		מאכל	FOOD	38b	
		חלל	POLLUTE	*320c	4
		כל	ALL	482a	1 eb
		ל	TO	512d	5 aa
		נטע	PLANT	642b	1 1
		עץ	TREE	781c	1 b
		ערל	HAVING FORESKIN	790c	
		ערל	COUNT AS FORE-SKIN	790c	
		ערלה	FORESKIN	790c	
19	24	הלל	REJOICING	239b	2
		קדש	APARTNESS	872a	3 b
		רביעי	FOURTH	918a	1
		שנה	YEAR	1040c	
19	25	תבואה	PRODUCT	100a	1
		יהוה	YAHWEH	219b	2 2d
		חלל	POLLUTE	*320c	4
		חמישי	FIFTH	332c	2
		יסף	ADD	415b	1
19	26	דם	BLOOD	196c	1
		נחש	PRACTISE DIVINA-TION	638c	1
		על	UPON	755c	2 4c
		ענן	PRACTISE SOOTH-SAYING	778b	1
19	27	זקן	BEARD	278b	2
		נקף	GO AROUND	669a	3
		פאה	CORNER	802a	1
		שחת	GO TO RUIN	1008b	1
19	28	בשר	FLESH	142c	2
		יהוה	YAHWEH	219b	2 2d
		כתבת	WRITING	508b	
		ל	TO	514d	5 g
		נפש	SOUL	660c	4 c5
		נתן	PUT	680b	2 a
		שרט	INCISION	976b	
19	29	ארץ	EARTH	76b	2 f
		זמה	PLAN	273c	2 c
		זנה	COMMIT FORNICA-TION	275d	1
		זנה	COMMIT FORNICA-TION	276a	1 a
		חלל	POLLUTE	320b	1 a
		לא	NOT	518c	1 aa
		מלא	BE FULL	570a	1 b
19	30	יהוה	YAHWEH	219b	2 2d
		ירא	FEAR	431c	3
		שבת	SABBOTH	992c	1 c
		שבת	SABBOTH	992c	1 c
		שמר	KEEP	1036d	3 b
19	31	אוב	NECROMANCER	15b	2
		בקש	SEEK	135a	3 d
		יהוה	YAHWEH	219b	2 2d
		ממא	BE UNCLEAN	379a	2
		ידעני	FAMILIAR SPIRIT	396b	
		פנה	TURN	815b	1 a
19	32	אלהים	GOD	44d	4 c
		הדר	HONOUR	213d	2
		יהוה	YAHWEH	219b	2 2d
		זקן	OLD	278c	2 a
		ירא	FEAR	431c	2
		פנה	FACE	818c	2 6b
		קום	STAND	877d	1 a
		שיבה	OLD AGE	966d	1
19	33	גור	SOJOURN	157d	1
		גר	SOJOURNER	158b	2
		גר	SOJOURNER	*158c	2
		ינה	OPPRESS	413b	1
19	34	אהב	LOVE	13a	1
		גור	SOJOURN	157d	1
		גר	SOJOURNER	158b	2
		גר	SOJOURNER	158b	1
		יהוה	YAHWEH	219b	2 2d
		אזרח	A NATIVE	280c	1
		ל	TO	512a	3 b
		מן	FROM	580c	3 a
19	35	מדה	MEASURE	551c	1
		משורה	MEASURE	601c	
		עול	INJUSTICE	732c	
		משפט	JUDGMENT	1048b	1 a
		משקל	WEIGHT	1054a	
19	36	אבן	STONE	6d	5
		מאזן	BALANCES	24d	
		איפה	EPHAH	35b	2
		יהוה	YAHWEH	219b	2 2d
		הין	HIN	*228d	
		הין	HIN	229a	1
		יצא	CAUSE TO GO	424c	1 a
		צדק	RIGHTNESS	841c	1
19	37	יהוה	YAHWEH	219b	2 2d
		חקה	SOMETHING PRE-SCRIBED	350a	2 d
		חקה	SOMETHING PRE-SCRIBED	350b	2 e
20	2	משפט	JUDGMENT	1049a	4
		אבן	STONE	6b	1
		ב	IN	89d	3 2a
		גור	SOJOURN	157d	1
		גר	SOJOURNER	158b	2
		גר	SOJOURNER	*158c	2
		זרע	SOWING	282d	4 d
		מות	DIE	559d	2 a
		מלך	MOLECH	574c	
		מן	FROM	580d	3 ba
		נתן	GIVE	679b	1 k
		עם	PEOPLE	766d	5 c
		רגם	TO STONE	920c	1
20	3	זרע	SOWING	282d	4 d
		חלל	POLLUTE	320b	1 c
		ממא	BE UNCLEAN	379c	2
		כרת	CUT OFF	504c	2 c
		מלך	MOLECH	574c	
		קדש	APARTNESS	871c	1 c
20	4	ארץ	EARTH	76b	4 a
		ב	NOT	116d	4 a
		זרע	SOWING	282d	4 d
		מות	DIE	560b	1 b
		מלך	MOLECH	574c	
		נתן	GIVE	679b	1 k
		עין	EYE	744d	3 d
20	5	עלם	CONCEAL	761a	
		אנכי	I	59b	
		זנה	COMMIT FORNICA-TION	275d	3
		כרת	CUT OFF	504c	2 c
		מלך	MOLECH	574c	
		שום	TO PLACE	963d	2 c
		משפחה	CLAN	1046a	1
20	6	אוב	NECROMANCER	15b	2
		זנה	COMMIT FORNICA-TION	275d	3
		ידעני	FAMILIAR SPIRIT	396b	
		כרת	CUT OFF	504c	2 c
		נפש	SOUL	660b	4 c2
		נתן	PUT	680d	2 b
		פנה	TURN	815b	1 a
20	7	יהוה	YAHWEH	219b	2 2c
		קדוש	HOLY	872d	2 b
		קדש	BE SET APART	873c	1
20	8	יהוה	YAHWEH	219b	2 2d
		חקה	SOMETHING PRE-SCRIBED	350b	2 e
20	9	קדש	BE SET APART	873b	4 d
		אם	MOTHER	51d	1
		ב	IN	89b	2 4b
		דם	BLOOD	197a	2 i
		מות	DIE	559d	2 a
20	10	איש	MAN	35d	
		מות	DIE	559d	2 a
		נאף	COMMIT ADUL-TERY	610c	1 b
		נאף	COMMIT ADUL-TERY	610c	1 a
		רע	FRIEND	946a	1
20	11	אשה	WOMAN	61b	2
		דם	BLOOD	197a	2 i
		מות	DIE	559d	2 a
20	12	תבל	CONFUSION	117d	
		דם	BLOOD	197a	2 i
		כלה	DAUGHTER-IN-LAW	483c	1
		מות	DIE	559d	2 a
20	13	דם	BLOOD	197a	2 i
		זכר	MALE	271c	1 1b
		מות	DIE	559d	2 a
		עשה	DO	793d	1 1a 1
		שכב	LIE DOWN	1012b	3
		משכב	ACT OF LYING	1012d	2 b
		תועבה	ABOMINATION	1073a	2
20	14	את	MARK OF THE AC-CUSATIVE	85a	1 a
		זמה	PLAN	273c	2 c
20	15	שרף	BURN	977a	2 b1
		איש	MAN	35d	
		הרג	KILL	247b	4
		הרג	KILL	247b	3
		מות	DIE	559d	2 a
		נתן	GIVE	680a	1 z
		שכבת	COPULATION	1012d	
20	16	בהמה	BEAST	*96d	1
		דם	BLOOD	197a	2 i
		הרג	KILL	247b	3
		מות	DIE	559d	2 a
		קרב	COME NEAR	897b	1 a
		רבע	LIE DOWN	918a	
20	17	אם	MOTHER	51d	1
		בן	SON	121b	1 ji
		בת	DAUGHTER	123b	1 d
		הוא	HE, SHE, IT	*214d	
		חסד	GOODNESS	339c	4
		חסד	SHAME	340a	
		כרת	BE CUT OFF	504b	1 c
		נשא	LIFT	671a	2 b
		עון	INIQUITY	731c	3
		ערוה	NAKEDNESS	789a	1
20	18	דוה	UNWELL	188c	2
		דם	BLOOD	196c	2 a
		כרת	BE CUT OFF	504b	1 c
		ערה	BE NAKED	788d	1
		מקור	SPRING	881b	3
20	19	נשא	LIFT	671a	2 b
		עון	INIQUITY	731c	3
		ערה	BE NAKED	788d	1
		שאר	FLESH	985a	2
20	20	דוד	UNCLE	187c	3
		דדה	AUNT	187d	
		חטא	SIN	308a	3
		מות	DIE	559d	2 a
		נשא	LIFT	671a	2 b
		ערירי	STRIPPED	792d	
20	21	נדה	IMPURITY	622c	1
		ערירי	STRIPPED	792d	
20	22	חקה	SOMETHING PRE-SCRIBED	350a	2 d
		חקה	SOMETHING PRE-SCRIBED	350b	2 e
		קיא	SPUE OUT	883c	
20	23	גוי	NATION	156d	1 c
		הלך	WALK	234d	2 3a 2d
		חקה	SOMETHING PRE-SCRIBED	350a	2 b
		חקה	SOMETHING PRE-SCRIBED	350b	2 e
		קוץ	FEEL A LOATHING	881a	1
		שלח	SEND	1019a	2 c
20	24	אדמה	LAND	9d	5
		בדל	BE DIVIDED	95b	2
		דבש	HONEY	185b	
		יהוה	YAHWEH	219b	2 2d
		זוב	FLOW	264d	2
		חלב	MILK	316c	A 4
		ירש	TAKE POSSESSION	439c	1 a
20	25	אדמה	GROUND	9d	4
		בדל	BE DIVIDED	95b	2
		בדל	BE DIVIDED	95c	3
		בין	INTERVAL	107c	1 b
		מהור	CLEAN	373a	1
		ממא	BE UNCLEAN	379c	4
		ממא	UNCLEAN	379d	2 b
		נפש	SOUL	660c	4 c4
		עוף	FLY	733d	1
		רמש	CREEP	943a	1
		שקץ	MAKE DETESTABLE	1055a	2
		בדל	BE DIVIDED	95b	2
20	26	יהוה	YAHWEH	219b	2 2c
		קדוש	HOLY	872c	2 b
		קדש	HOLY	872d	2 b
20	27	אבן	STONE	6b	1
		אוב	NECROMANCER	15b	2
		איש	MAN	35d	
		דם	BLOOD	197a	2 i
		ידעני	FAMILIAR SPIRIT	396b	
		מות	DIE	559d	2 a
		רגם	TO STONE	920c	1
21	1	אמר	SAY	56a	1
		אמר	SAY	56b	1
		ממא	BE UNCLEAN	379d	
		כהן	PRIEST	464a	7
		ל	TO	514d	5 g
		נפש	SOUL	660c	4 c5
		עם	KINSMAN	769c	
21	2	אם	MOTHER	51d	1
		כיאם	EXCEPT	474d	2 a
		ל	TO	514d	5 g
		קרב	NEAR	898c	2 c
		שאר	FLESH	985a	2
21	3	בתולה	VIRGIN	143d	
		היה	BECOME	226d	2 2h
		ממא	BE UNCLEAN	379d	
		ל	TO	514d	5 g
		קרב	NEAR	898c	2 c
21	4	בעל	LORD	*127c	1 5b
		חלל	POLLUTE	320a	1 a
		ממא	BE UNCLEAN	379d	
		עם	KINSMAN	769c	
21	5	בשר	FLESH	142c	2
		זקן	BEARD	278b	2
		פאה	CORNER	802b	1

Ch	v.	Heb	Eng	Page	Sec
		קרח	MAKE BALD	901a	
		קרחה	BALD SPOT	901b	
		שרטת	MAKE CUTS	976b	
		שרט	INCISE	976b	
21	6	חלל	POLLUTE	320a	1 c
		לחם	FOOD	537b	2 c
		קדש	APARTNESS	872b	4 a
		קדוש	HOLY	872d	2 b
		קרב	COME NEAR	898a	2 b4
		קדש	APARTNESS	872ba	4 a
21	7	איש	MAN	35d	
		גרש	CAST OUT	176c	
		זנה	COMMIT FORNICATION	275d	1
		חלל	PROFANED	321a	
21	8	קדוש	HOLY	872d	2 b
		יהוה	YAHWEH	219b	2 2c
		לחם	FOOD	537b	2 c
		קדוש	HOLY	872c	1 b
		קדוש	HOLY	872d	2 b
		קדש	BE SET APART	873b	3 b
		קדש	BE SET APART	873b	4 d
		קרב	COME NEAR	898a	2 b4
21	9	איש	MAN	36a	
		הוא	HE, SHE, IT	*214d	
		זנה	COMMIT FORNICATION	275d	1
		חלל	POLLUTE	320a	1 b
		חלל	POLLUTE	320b	1 a
		כהן	PRIEST	464a	7
		שרף	BURN	977a	
21	10	גדול	GREAT	153a	6 b
		ה	THE	207b	1 b
		יד	HAND	389b	1 c
		יצק	BE POURED	427b	1
		כהן	PRIEST	464b	8
		לבש	PUT ON	527d	A
		מלא	FILL	570d	2
		מן	THAN	582b	6 a
		משחה	OINTMENT	603c	1
		פרם	TEAR GARMENT	828a	
		פרע	LET GO	828d	1
21	11	אם	MOTHER	51d	1
		בוא	COME	98b	2
		טמא	BE UNCLEAN	379d	
		נפש	SOUL	660c	4 c5
		על	UPON	757a	2 7c a
21	12	יהוה	YAHWEH	219b	2 2d
		חלל	POLLUTE	320b	1 b
		יצא	GO OUT	422c	1 a
		משחה	OINTMENT	603c	1
		נזר	CONSECRATION	634b	3 a
		שמן	OIL	1032c	2 g
21	13	בתולים	VIRGINITY	144a	
21	14	אלה	THESE	41c	A
		אלמנה	WIDOW	48b	
		בתולה	VIRGIN	143d	1
		גרש	CAST OUT	176c	
		ו	AND	252d	1 d
		זנה	COMMIT FORNICATION	275d	1
		חלל	PROFANED	321a	
		כיאם	BUT	475a	2 b
		עם	KINSMAN	769c	
21	15	יהוה	YAHWEH	219b	2 2c
		זרע	SOWING	282d	4 c
		חלל	POLLUTE	320b	1 a
		עם	KINSMAN	769c	
		קדש	BE SET APART	873b	4 d
21	17	דור	GENERATION	190a	2 c
		זרע	SOWING	282d	4 c
		לחם	FOOD	537b	2 c
		מום	BLEMISH	548c	1 a
		קרב	COME NEAR	897c	1 g
		קרב	COME NEAR	898a	2 b4
21	18	חרם	SLIT	357a	
		מום	BLEMISH	548c	1 a
		עור	BLIND	734c	1 a
		פסח	LAME	820c	
		קרב	COME NEAR	897c	1 g
		שרע	EXTEND	976d	
21	19	יד	HAND	389d	1 d
		שבר	BREAKING	991a	1
21	20	אשך	TESTICLE	79a	
		תבלל	CONFUSION	117d	
		גבן	CROOK-BACKED	148c	
		גרב	ITCH	173a	
		דק	THIN	201a	1
		ילפת	SCAB	410c	
		מרוח	RUB	598c	
		עין	EYE	744a	1 a
		שכה	HAVING STRONG TESTICLES	1013a	
21	21	זרע	SOWING	282d	4 c
		כהן	PRIEST	464a	7
		לחם	FOOD	537b	2 c
		מום	BLEMISH	548c	1 a
		נגש	DRAW NEAR	620d	1
		נגש	DRAW NEAR	620d	1
		קרב	COME NEAR	898a	2 b4
21	22	לחם	FOOD	537b	2 c
		קדש	APARTNESS	872a	3 b
21	23	אך	HOWBEIT	36c	2 a
		יהוה	YAHWEH	219b	2 2c
		חלל	POLLUTE	320b	1 b
		מום	BLEMISH	548c	1 a

Ch	v.	Heb	Eng	Page	Sec
		נגש	DRAW NEAR	620d	1
		קדש	BE SET APART	873b	4 d
		מקדש	SACRED PLACE	874b	3
22	2	יהוה	YAHWEH	219b	2 2d
		חלל	POLLUTE	320b	1 c
		נזר	DEDICATE	634a	
		קדש	APARTNESS	871c	1 c
		קדש	BE SET APART	873b	1 b
22	3	דור	GENERATION	190a	2 c
		יהוה	YAHWEH	219b	2 2d
		זרע	SOWING	282d	4 c
		טמאה	UNCLEANNESS	380a	4
		כרת	BE CUT OFF	504b	1 c
		נפש	SOUL	660b	4 c2
		על	UPON	753b	2 1b
		פנה	FACE	818a	2 5a d
		קדש	BE SET APART	873b	1 b
		קרב	COME NEAR	897c	1 b
22	4	איש	MAN	36a	
		זב	FLOW	264d	4
		זרע	SOWING	282c	3
		זרע	SOWING	282d	4 c
		טהר	BE CLEAN	372b	2
		טמא	UNCLEAN	379d	2 a
		יצא	GO OUT	423b	1 f
		נפש	SOUL	660c	4 c5
		עד	UNTIL	725a	2 1a b
		צרע	BE STRUCK WITH LEPROSY	863d	
22	5	שכבה	LYING	1012c	1
		טמא	BE UNCLEAN	379a	3
		טמא	BE UNCLEAN	379b	3
		טמאה	UNCLEANNESS	380a	4
		ל	TO	514c	5 fc
		שרץ	SWARMING THINGS	1056d	
22	6	בשר	FLESH	142c	2
		טמא	BE UNCLEAN	379a	3
		טמא	BE UNCLEAN	379b	3
		כיאם	EXCEPT	474d	2 a
		נפש	SOUL	660b	4 c2
		ערב	SUNSET	787d	1 a
22	7	אחר	AFTERWARDS	29d	1 b
		בוא	COME	98a	1 i
		טהר	BE CLEAN	372b	2
22	8	יהוה	YAHWEH	219b	2 2d
		טמא	BE UNCLEAN	379a	3
		טרפה	ANIMAL TORN	383c	1
		נבלה	CARCASS	615d	2
22	9	יהוה	YAHWEH	219b	2 2d
		חטא	SIN	308a	3
		חלל	POLLUTE	320b	1 b
		כי	BECAUSE	473c	3 a
		מות	DIE	560a	2 b
		נשא	LIFT	670d	1 b0
		משמרת	GUARD	1038c	4 a
22	10	זור	BE A STRANGER	266c	2 a
		תושב	SOJOURNER	444c	
		כהן	PRIEST	464a	7
		שכיר	HIRED	969b	2
22	11	יליד	BORN	409d	
		כהן	PRIEST	464a	7
		כסף	SILVER	494d	9
		נפש	SOUL	660b	4 c2
		קנין	ACQUIRE	889a	1
22	12	זור	BE A STRANGER	266c	2 a
		כהן	PRIEST	464a	7
		כי	IF	473c	2 b
22	13	תרומה	OFFERING	929a	4
		אב	FATHER	3c	3
		אלמנה	WIDOW	48b	
		גרש	CAST OUT	176c	
		זור	BE A STRANGER	266c	2 a
		זרע	SOWING	282d	4 d
		חק	SOMETHING PRESCRIBED	349d	7 g
		כהן	PRIEST	464a	7
		כי	IF	473c	2 b
		לחם	FOOD	537b	2 c
		נעורים	YOUTH	655c	
22	14	חמישי	FIFTH	332d	3
		יסף	ADD	414d	
		כהן	PRIEST	464a	7
		כי	IF	473c	2 b
		נתן	GIVE	678b	1 a
		שגגה	SIN OF ERROR	993a	
22	15	חלל	POLLUTE	320b	1 b
		רום	BE HIGH	927d	3 b
22	16	אשמה	WRONG-DOING	80b	3
		יהוה	YAHWEH	219b	2 2c
		נשא	LIFT	*671a	2 b
		נשא	LIFT	672a	1
		עון	INIQUITY	731c	3
22	18	איש	MAN	36a	
		בית	HOUSE	110a	5 dd
		גר	SOJOURNER	158b	2
		ל	TO	514c	5 fd
		נדבה	FREEWILL-OFFERING	621d	2 c
		נדבה	FREEWILL-OFFERING	621d	2 c
		נדר	VOW	624a	5
		עלה	WHOLE BURNT OFFERING	750b	
		עלה	WHOLE BURNT OFFERING	751a	

Ch	v.	Heb	Eng	Page	Sec
22	19	קרב	COME NEAR	898a	2 b6
		זכר	MALE	271c	1 2
		כשב	LAMB	461b	
		עלה	WHOLE BURNT OFFERING	750b	
		עז	SHE-GOAT	777c	3 d
		רצון	GOODWILL	953c	2
22	20	מום	BLEMISH	548d	1 b
		רצון	GOODWILL	953c	2
22	21	זבח	SACRIFICE	258a	2 7
		מום	BLEMISH	548d	1 b
		נדבה	FREEWILL-OFFERING	621d	2 c
		נדר	VOW	624a	5
		נדר	VOW	624a	6
		רצון	GOODWILL	953c	2
		שלם	PEACE-OFFERING	1023c	
22	22	אלה	THESE	41c	A
		אשה	OFFERING MADE BY FIRE	78a	
		גרב	ITCH	173a	
		חרץ	CUT	358c	1
		יבל	RUNNING	385c	
		עורת	BLINDNESS	734d	
		שבר	BREAK	990c	
22	23	ו	AND	252d	1 d
		נדבה	FREEWILL-OFFERING	621d	2 c
		נדר	VOW	624a	5
		קלט	BE STUNTED	886b	
		רצה	BE PLEASED WITH	953b	1
		שה	A SHEEP	962a	1
		שרע	EXTEND	976d	
		שור	A HEAD OF CATTLE	1004b	
22	24	ו	AND	252d	1 d
		כרת	CUT OFF	503d	1 a
		כתת	BEAT	510a	1
		מעד	PRESS	590c	
		נתק	TEAR AWAY	683c	3
22	25	בן	SON	121c	7 a
		יד	HAND	391b	5 g3
		לחם	FOOD	537b	2 c
		מום	BLEMISH	548d	1 b
		נכר	FOREIGNNESS	648d	2
		רצה	BE PLEASED WITH	953b	1
		משחת	CORRUPTION	1008c	
22	27	אם	MOTHER	52a	3
		אשה	OFFERING MADE BY FIRE	78a	
		ה	THE	209a	2 b
		היה	BE	226d	3 2
		הלאה	ONWARDS	229c	B
		ילד	BE BORN	408d	
		כשב	LAMB	461b	
		מן	FROM	581b	4 a
		עז	SHE-GOAT	777c	3 a
		קרבן	OFFERING	898d	
		רצה	BE PLEASED WITH	953b	1
		שור	A HEAD OF CATTLE	1004b	
22	28	בן	SON	121b	4
		שה	A SHEEP	962a	1
		שור	A HEAD OF CATTLE	1004b	
22	29	זבח	SLAUGHTER FOR SACRIFICE	257a	1 3
		זבח	SACRIFICE	257c	2 4
		תודה	THANK-OFFERING	393a	4
		רצון	GOODWILL	953c	2
22	30	אכל	EAT	37d	1
		בקר	MORNING	134b	2
		יהוה	YAHWEH	219b	2 2d
		יתר	LEAVE OVER	451c	1 a
22	31	יהוה	YAHWEH	219b	2 2d
22	32	יהוה	YAHWEH	219b	2 2d
		חלל	POLLUTE	320b	1 c
		קדש	APARTNESS	871c	1 c
		קדש	BE SET APART	873a	2
22	33	אלהים	GOD	44b	4 a
		יהוה	YAHWEH	219b	2 2d
		יצא	CAUSE TO GO	424c	1 a
23	2	הם	THEY	241c	4 bg
		מועד	APPOINTED TIME	417c	1 b
		מועד	APPOINTED TIME	417c	1 b
		קרא	CALL	895b	3 a
		מקרא	CONVOCATION	896d	1
23	3	יום	DAY	398b	2 a
		מושב	DWELLING	444b	2 c
		מלאכה	WORK	522a	3 b
		שבת	SABBATH	992b	1 a
		שבת	SABBATH	992c	1 d
		שבתון	SABBOTH OBSERVANCE	992d	1
23	4	מועד	APPOINTED TIME	417c	1 b
		מועד	APPOINTED TIME	417c	1 b
		קרא	CALL	895b	3 a
		מקרא	CONVOCATION	896d	1
23	5	ערב	SUNSET	788a	1 b
		פסח	PASSOVER	820b	3
		פסח	PASSOVER	820b	3
		ראשון	FIRST	911d	2 a
23	6	חג	FESTIVAL-GATHERING	291a	1 b2
		חמש	FIVE	*332a	2 b2
		מצה	UNLEAVENED BREAD	695b	

67

Ch	v.	Heb	Eng	Page	Sec
		מצה	UNLEAVENED BREAD	695b	
23	7	מלאכה	WORK	522a	3 b
		עבדה	LABOR	715b	1
23	8	מלאכה	WORK	522a	3 b
		עבדה	LABOR	715b	1
23	10	קרב	COME NEAR	898a	2 b2
		כהן	PRIEST	464a	7
		עמר	SHEAF	771c	
		קציר	HARVEST	894b	
		קציר	HARVESTING	894c	2
23	11	ראשית	BEGINNING	912b	1 b
		כהן	PRIEST	464a	7
		מחרת	THE MORROW	564a	
		נוף	WAVE	632a	4
		עמר	SHEAF	771c	
		רצון	GOODWILL	953c	2
		שבת	SABBATH	992c	1 c
23	12	בן	SON	122a	9 b
		נוף	WAVE	632a	4
		עלה	WHOLE BURNT OF-FERING	750b	
		עלה	WHOLE BURNT OF-FERING	750d	
23	13	עמר	SHEAF	771c	
		אשה	OFFERING MADE BY FIRE	78a	
		בלל	MIX	117c	2
		הין	HIN	229a	1 c
		יין	WINE	406c	B
		מנחה	OFFERING	585c	5 b
		נסך	DRINK-OFFERING	651a	1
		רביעי	FOURTH	918a	4
23	14	בוא	COME	99b	2
		דור	GENERATION	190a	2 c
		חקה	SOMETHING PRE-SCRIBED	350a	1
		יום	DAY	*401b	7 l
		מושב	DWELLING	444b	2 c
		כרמל	GARDEN	502a	2
		עולם	LONG DURATION	762c	2 e
		עצם	BONE	783a	3
		קלי	PARCHED GRAIN	885d	
23	15	בוא	COME	99b	2
		יום	DAY	400a	7 d l e
		יום	DAY	401a	7 j
		מחרת	THE MORROW	564a	
		תנופה	WAVING	632c	2 a
		ספר	COUNT	707d	1
		עמר	SHEAF	771c	
		ארבע	FOUR	917b	2 a2 z
		שבת	SABBATH	992c	4
		שבת	SABBATH	992c	1 c
		תמים	COMPLETE	1071a	3
23	16	חדש	NEW	294a	A
		מחרת	THE MORROW	564a	
		מנחה	OFFERING	585c	5 d
		עד	AS FAR AS	724b	12 a a
		קרב	COME NEAR	898a	2 b4
		שביעי	SEVENTH	988d	1
		שבת	SABBATH	992c	1 c
23	17	אפה	BAKE	66b	
		בכורים	FIRST-FRUITS	114c	
		חמץ	THAT WHICH IS LEAVENED	329d	
		מושב	DWELLING	444b	2 c
		לחם	FOOD	537b	1 a
		מנחה	OFFERING	585c	5 d
		תנופה	WAVING	632c	2 a
		עשרון	TENTH PART	798b	
23	18	איל	RAM	18a	2 c
		בן	SON	121c	7 b
		בן	SON	122a	9 b
		לחם	FOOD	537a	1 a
		נסך	DRINK-OFFERING	651a	1
		עלה	WHOLE BURNT OF-FERING	750c	
		פר	YOUNG BULL	830d	2 b
23	19	בן	SON	122a	9 b
		חטאת	SIN	309b	4
		שעיר	HE-GOAT	972c	
		שלם	PEACE-OFFERING	1023c	
23	20	בכורים	FIRST-FRUITS	114c	
		בכורים	FIRST-FRUITS	114c	
		כהן	PRIEST	464a	7
		לחם	FOOD	537b	1 a
		נוף	WAVE	632a	4
		תנופה	WAVING	632c	2 a
		קדש	APARTNESS	872a	3 b
23	21	דור	GENERATION	190a	2 c
		חקה	SOMETHING PRE-SCRIBED	350a	1
		מושב	DWELLING	444b	2 c
		מלאכה	WORK	522a	3 b
		עבדה	LABOR	715b	1
		עולם	LONG DURATION	762c	2 e
		עצם	BONE	783a	3
23	22	גר	SOJOURNER	158b	1
		יהוה	YAHWEH	219b	2 2d
		כלה	FINISH	478b	1 a
		כלה	FINISH	*478b	1 c
		לקט	GLEAN	544d	3
			GLEANING	545a	
		עזב	LEAVE	737b	1 j
		עני	POOR	776d	1
		פאה	CORNER	802a	1

Ch	v.	Heb	Eng	Page	Sec
		קצר	HARVEST	894b	
		קצר	HARVEST	894b	
		קצר	HARVEST	894b	
		קציר	HARVESTING	894c	2
		קציר	HARVESTING	894c	2
23	24	זכרון	MEMORIAL	272a	1 d
		תרועה	SHOUT OF WAR	929d	2
		שבתון	SABBOTH OBSERV-ANCE	992d	4
23	25	מלאכה	WORK	522a	3 b
		עבדה	LABOR	715b	1
23	27	קרב	COME NEAR	898a	2 b2
		אך	SURELY	36c	1
		יום	DAY	398d	2 i
		כפרים	ATONEMENT	498c	
		נפש	SOUL	660b	4 b6
		ענה	BE BOWED DOWN	776b	4
		עשור	A TEN	797c	1 b
23	28	יום	DAY	398d	2 i
		כפר	COVER OVER	497d	3 b2
		כפרים	ATONEMENT	498c	
		מלאכה	WORK	522a	3 b
		עצם	BONE	783a	3
23	29	אבד	DESTROY	2b	1
		כרת	BE CUT OFF	504b	1 c
		נפש	SOUL	660b	4 c2
		עם	KINSMAN	769c	
		ענה	BE BOWED DOWN	776b	2
		עצם	BONE	783a	3
23	30	אבד	DESTROY	2b	1
		מלאכה	WORK	522a	3 b
		נפש	SOUL	660b	4 c2
		עצם	BONE	783a	3
23	31	דור	GENERATION	190a	2 c
		חקה	SOMETHING PRE-SCRIBED	350a	1
		מושב	DWELLING	444b	2 c
		מלאכה	WORK	522a	3 b
		עולם	LONG DURATION	762c	2 e
23	32	נפש	SOUL	660b	4 b6
		ענה	BE BOWED DOWN	776b	4
		ערב	SUNSET	787d	1 a
		שבת	CEASE	991d	2 c
		שבת	SABBATH	992c	2
		שבתון	SABBOTH OBSERV-ANCE	992d	2
		שבת	KEEP	992d	
23	34	חג	FESTIVAL-GATHER-ING	291a	1 b2
		סכה	THICKET	697d	3
23	35	מלאכה	WORK	522a	3 b
		עבדה	LABOR	715b	1
23	36	מלאכה	WORK	522a	3 b
		עבדה	LABOR	715b	1
		עצרה	ASSEMBLY	783d	1
23	37	דבר	WORD	183b	4 l
		זבח	SACRIFICE	257d	2 5
		יום	DAY	400c	7 e3
		מועד	APPOINTED TIME	417c	1 b
		מנחה	OFFERING	585c	1
		נסך	DRINK-OFFERING	651a	1
		עלה	WHOLE BURNT OF-FERING	750d	
		מקרא	CONVOCATION	896d	1
23	38	בד	SEPARATION	94d	1 e
		נדבה	FREEWILL-OFFER-ING	621d	2 c
		נדבה	FREEWILL-OFFER-ING	621d	2 c
		נדר	VOW	624a	5
		מתנה	GIFT	682b	
		שבת	SABBATH	992c	1 d
23	39	אך	SURELY	36c	1
		אסף	GATHER	62b	1 c
		תבואה	PRODUCT	100a	1
		חגג	MAKE PILGRIMAGE	290d	1
		חג	FESTIVAL-GATHER-ING	291a	1 b2
		חג	FESTIVAL-GATHER-ING	291b	1 b
		שבתון	SABBOTH OBSERV-ANCE	992d	4
23	40	הדר	ORNAMENT	214b	1
		כף	HOLLOW	497a	4 d
		נחל	WADY	636c	2
		עבות	LEAFY	721c	
		ענף	BRANCH	778c	
		עץ	TREE	781c	1 b
		ערבה	POPLAR	788b	
		שמח	REJOICE	970b	2 a
		תמר	PALM-TREE	1071c	
23	41	דור	GENERATION	190a	2 c
		חגג	MAKE PILGRIMAGE	290d	1
		חג	FESTIVAL-GATHER-ING	291a	1 b1
		חג	FESTIVAL-GATHER-ING	291b	1 b
		חקה	SOMETHING PRE-SCRIBED	350a	1
		עולם	LONG DURATION	762c	2 e
23	42	אזרח	A NATIVE	280c	1
		סכה	THICKET	697d	3
23	43	דור	GENERATION	190a	2 c
		יהוה	YAHWEH	219b	2 2d
		יצא	CAUSE TO GO	424c	1 a
		ישב	CAUSE TO SIT	443d	3 a
		סכה	THICKET	697d	3

Ch	v.	Heb	Eng	Page	Sec
23	44	מועד	APPOINTED TIME	417c	1 b
24	2	מאור	LUMINARY	22d	
		זית	OLIVE TREE	268d	2
		זך	PURE	269b	1
		כתית	BEATEN	510c	
		תמיד	CONTINUITY	556c	1 a
		שמן	OIL	1032c	2 g
24	3	בקר	MORNING	134a	1 e
		דור	GENERATION	190a	2 c
		חקה	SOMETHING PRE-SCRIBED	350a	1
		תמיד	CONTINUITY	556c	1 a
		עדות	TESTIMONY	*730b	1
		עולם	LONG DURATION	762c	2 e
		ערך	ARRANGE	789c	1 b
		פרכת	CURTAIN	827d	
24	4	מהור	CLEAN	373a	2
		תמיד	CONTINUITY	556c	1 a
		מנגרה	LAMPSTAND	633b	3
		ערך	ARRANGE	789c	1 b
24	5	אפה	BAKE	66a	
		אפה	BAKE	66a	
		חלה	A KIND OF CAKE	319c	2 a
24	6	מהור	CLEAN	373a	2
		מערכת	ROW	790b	
		שום	TO PLACE	962d	1 a
		שש	SIX	995c	1 a
		שלחן	TABLE	1020b	3
24	7	אשה	OFFERING MADE BY FIRE	78a	
		זך	PURE	269b	1
		אזכרה	MEMORIAL-OFFER-ING	272c	
		לבנה	FRANKINCENSE	526d	
		מערכת	ROW	790b	
24	8	את	WITH	86d	4 b
		ברית	COVENANT	136c	2 2c
		ברית	COVENANT	137a	3 2
		יום	DAY	398d	2 i
		תמיד	CONTINUITY	556c	1 a
		עולם	LONG DURATION	762c	2 d
		עולם	LONG DURATION	762c	2 e
		ערך	ARRANGE	789c	1 b
		שבת	SABBATH	992c	1 d
24	9	אשה	OFFERING MADE BY FIRE	78a	
		חק	SOMETHING PRE-SCRIBED	349c	4
		עולם	LONG DURATION	762c	2
		קדש	APARTNESS	872a	3 d
		קדוש	HOLY	872d	2 a
24	10	ה	THE	209a	2 b
		מצרי	EGYPTIAN	596a	1
		נצה	STRUGGLE	663c	
		ישראלי	ISARELITE	976a	
24	11	בוא	COME	99b	2
		דברי	DIBRI	184c	
		דן	DAN	192d	2
		יהוה	YAHWEH	218a	1
		ל	TO	512d	5 ac
		מטה	TRIBE	641d	3
		קבב	CURSE	866d	
		קלל	BE SLIGHT	886d	2
		ישראלי	ISARELITE	976a	
		שלמות	SHELOMITH	1025a	1
		שם	NAME	1028c	3
24	12	נוח	REST	628d	B 1
		פרש	MAKE DISTINCT	831c	
		משמר	PRISON	1038b	1
24	14	יצא	BRING OUT	424d	1 g
		סמך	LEAN	702a	1 a
		קלל	BE SLIGHT	886d	2
		רגם	TO STONE	920c	
24	15	חטא	SIN	308a	3
		נשא	LIFT	671a	2 b
		קלל	BE SLIGHT	886d	2
24	16	גר	SOJOURNER	158a	1
		גר	SOJOURNER	158b	2
		כ	LIKE	454c	2 ba
		מות	DIE	559d	2 a
		מות	DIE	560c	2
		נקב	CURSE	666d	
		רגם	TO STONE	920c	
		שם	NAME	1028c	3
24	17	מות	DIE	559d	2 a
		נכה	SMITE	*645d	2 a
		נכה	SMITE	646a	2 a
		נפש	SOUL	660b	4 c1
24	18	נכה	SMITE	*645d	2 a
		נכה	SMITE	646a	2 a
		נפש	SOUL	659d	3 c
		נפש	SOUL	660b	4 c1
		שלם	BE COMPLETE	1022c	1
24	19	כן	SO	486c	2 cd
		מום	BLEMISH	548c	1
		נתן	PUT	680b	2 a
		עמיתה	ASSOCIATE	765c	
		עשה	DO	795b	1 c
24	20	כן	SO	486c	2 cd
		מום	BLEMISH	548c	1
		נתן	PUT	680b	2 a
		נתן	PUT	681d	2 d
		עין	EYE	744a	1 a
		עין	EYE	745a	5
		שבר	BREAKING	991a	1 a
		שן	TOOTH	1042a	1 a

Ch	v.	Heb	Eng	Page	Sec
24	21	מות	DIE	560c	2
		נכה	SMITE	646a	2 c
		שלם	BE COMPLETE	1022c	3
24	22	גר	SOJOURNER	158b	2
		יהוה	YAHWEH	219b	2 2c
		כ	LIKE	454b	2 c
24	23	אבן	STONE	6b	1
		יצא	BRING OUT	424d	1 g
		קלל	BE SLIGHT	886d	2
		רגם	TO STONE	920c	
25	1	הר	MOUNTAIN	249b	1 a
		הר	MOUNTAIN	250a	1 a
		סיני	SINAI	696a	
25	2	שבת	CEASE	991d	2 c
		שבת	SABBATH	992c	3
		שבת	KEEP	992d	
25	3	אסף	GATHER	62b	1 c
		תבואה	PRODUCT	100a	1
		זמר	TRIM	274d	
		זרע	SOW	281c	1 b
		כרם	VINEYARD	501d	
25	4	זמר	TRIM	274d	
		זרע	SOW	281c	1 b
		כרם	VINEYARD	501d	
		שבת	SABBATH	992c	3
		שבתון	SABBOTH OBSERVANCE	992d	3
25	5	בצר	CUT OFF	130d	
		כרם	VINEYARD	*501d	
		נזיר	NAZIRITESHIP	634c	3
		ספיח	GROWTH	705c	
		ענב	GRAPE	772a	
		קצר	HARVEST	894c	
		קציר	HARVESTING	894c	2
		שבתון	SABBOTH OBSERVANCE	992d	3
25	6	אכלה	FOOD	38a	1
		אמה	MAID	51a	1
		גור	SOJOURN	157d	1
		תושב	SOJOURNER	444d	
		עבד	SLAVE	713d	1
		שכיר	HIRED	969b	2
		שבת	SABBATH	992c	5
25	7	תבואה	PRODUCT	100a	1
		חיה	LIVING THING	312c	1 b
25	8	ספר	COUNT	707d	1
		ארבעים	FORTY	917c	2 b
		שבת	SABBATH	992c	4
25	9	יום	DAY	398d	2 i
		כפרים	ATONEMENT	498c	
		עבר	PASS OVER	718c	2 a
		עשור	A TEN	797c	1 b
		ראה	TO SEE	908a	2
		תרועה	SHOUT OF WAR	930a	2
		שפר	HORN	1051d	
		שפר	HORN	1051d	
		שפר	HORN	1051d	
25	10	אחזה	POSSESSION	28c	
		דרור	LIBERTY	204d	2
		דרור	LIBERTY	*204d	2
		חמשים	FIFTY	332c	6
		יובל	RAM	385c	2
		ישב	DWELL	443b	3
		קדש	BE SET APART	873b	2
		קרא	CALL	895b	3 a
		משפחה	CLAN	1046d	1 a
25	11	בצר	CUT OFF	130d	
		הוא	HE, SHE, IT	216b	4 a
		זרע	SOW	281c	1 a
		חמשים	FIFTY	332c	6
		יובל	RAM	385c	2
		כרם	VINEYARD	*501d	
		נזיר	NAZIRITESHIP	634c	3
		ספיח	GROWTH	705c	
		קצר	HARVEST	894c	
25	12	תבואה	PRODUCT	100b	1
		יובל	RAM	385c	2
		קדש	APARTNESS	872b	5
25	13	אחזה	POSSESSION	28c	
		יובל	RAM	385c	2
		שנה	YEAR	1040b	
25	14	ינה	OPPRESS	413b	
		מכר	SELL	569b	
		ממכר	WARE	569d	
		עמית	ASSOCIATE	765c	
25	15	אחר	AFTER	29d	2 b
		ב	IN	90c	3 8
		תבואה	PRODUCT	100a	1
		יובל	RAM	385c	2
		מכר	SELL	569b	
		מספר	NUMBER	709a	1 b
		עמית	ASSOCIATE	765c	
25	16	תבואה	PRODUCT	100a	1
		מכר	SELL	569b	
		מעט	BE SMALL	589c	
		מעט	BE SMALL	589c	A
		פה	MOUTH	805c	6 c1
		פה	MOUTH	805c	6 bb
		פה	MOUTH	805c	6 d2
		מקנה	PURCHASE	889c	1
		רבב	BECOME MUCH	912d	1
		רב	MULTITUDE	914a	2
25	17	אלהים	GOD	44d	4 c
		יהוה	YAHWEH	219b	2 2c
		ינה	OPPRESS	413b	
		ירא	FEAR	431b	2
		עמית	ASSOCIATE	765c	
25	18	בטח	SECURITY	105b	
		חקה	SOMETHING PRESCRIBED	350a	2 d
		חקה	SOMETHING PRESCRIBED	350b	2 e
		ישב	DWELL	443a	3
		ל	TO	516d	5 k
25	19	ארץ	EARTH	76b	3 b
		בטח	SECURITY	105b	
		ישב	DWELL	443a	3
		נתן	GIVE	679c	1 t
		שבע	ABUNDANCE	960a	1
25	20	אסף	GATHER	62b	1 c
		תבואה	PRODUCT	100a	1
		הן	IF	243c	B
		זרע	SOW	281c	1 a
		כי	WHEN	473b	2 a
25	21	תבואה	PRODUCT	100b	1
		ברכה	BLESSING	139d	1 b
		עשה	DO	794d	2 2
		צוה	CHARGE	846a	4 d
		ששי	SIXTH	995d	
		שנה	YEAR	1040b	
25	22	את	MARK OF THE ACCUSATIVE	85b	2 b
		בוא	COME	98a	1 j
		תבואה	PRODUCT	*100a	1
		תבואה	PRODUCT	100b	1
		זרע	SOW	281c	1 a
		ישן	OLD	446a	
		שמיני	EIGHTH	1033b	
		תשיעי	NINTH	1077d	
25	23	גר	SOJOURNER	158b	1
		גר	SOJOURNER	*158c	2
		תושב	SOJOURNER	444c	
		מכר	SELL	569c	
		עם	WITH	768d	3 a
		צמיתת	COMPLETION	856c	
25	24	אחזה	POSSESSION	28c	
		גאלה	REDEMPTION	145d	2
25	25	אחזה	POSSESSION	28c	
		גאל	ACT AS KINSMAN	145b	1
		מוך	BE LOW	557b	
		מכר	SELL	569b	
		ממכר	WARE	569d	
		מן	FROM	581a	3 bc
		קרב	NEAR	898c	2
25	26	גאל	ACT AS KINSMAN	145c	1 c
		גאלה	REDEMPTION	145d	4
		די	SUFFICIENCY	191d	2 b
		יד	HAND	390b	2
		מצא	FIND	593c	4
		נשג	REACH	673c	3
25	27	אחזה	POSSESSION	28c	
		חשב	THINK	363c	3
		מכר	SELL	569b	
		ממכר	SALE	569d	
		עדף	REMAIN OVER	727b	
		שוב	TURN BACK	999b	1 d
		אחזה	POSSESSION	28c	
25	28	די	SUFFICIENCY	191c	1
		היה	BE	226d	3 2
		יובל	RAM	385c	2
		יובל	RAM	385c	2
		יצא	GO OUT	422d	1 c
		ממכר	WARE	569d	
25	29	בית	HOUSE	108c	1 a
		גאלה	REDEMPTION	145d	3
		חומה	WALL	327c	1
		יום	YEAR	399d	6 c
		מושב	DWELLING	444b	2 b
		מכר	SELL	569b	
		ממכר	SALE	569d	
		עד	AS FAR AS	724b	1 2a
		עיר	CITY	746b	1 a
		תמם	BE FINISHED	1070b	2
25	30	גאל	REDEEM	145d	2 a
		דור	GENERATION	190a	2 c
		קום	STAND	288b	7 b
		חומה	WALL	327c	1
		יובל	RAM	385c	2
		יצא	GO OUT	422d	1 c
		ל	TO	512d	5 aa
		לא	NOT	520c	
		מלא	BE FULL	570b	1 b
		עיר	CITY	746b	1 a
		צמיתת	COMPLETION	856c	
		קנה	ACQUIRE	889a	2
		תמים	COMPLETE	1071a	3
25	31	גאלה	REDEMPTION	145d	3
		חומה	WALL	327c	1
		חצר	SETTLED ABODE	347b	A
		חשב	THINK	363c	2
		יובל	RAM	385c	2
		יצא	GO OUT	422d	1 c
		ל	TO	513b	5 ba
		על	UPON	755b	2 4a
		שדה	FIELD	961c	1 f
25	32	אחזה	POSSESSION	28c	
		גאלה	REDEMPTION	145d	3
		לוי	LEVITE	533a	3 1c
		עולם	LONG DURATION	762a	2 a
25	33	אחזה	POSSESSION	28c	
		אחזה	POSSESSION	28c	
		אשר	THAT	83d	8 d
		גאל	ACT AS KINSMAN	145c	1 c
		יובל	RAM	385c	2
		יצא	GO OUT	422d	1 c
		לוי	LEVITE	533a	3 1c
		ממכר	WARE	569d	
		מן	FROM	580d	3 bb
25	34	אחזה	POSSESSION	28d	
		מגרש	COMMON-LAND	177b	
		מכר	SELL	569c	
		עולם	LONG DURATION	762d	2 f
		שדה	FIELD	961d	2 c
25	35	ב	IN	*88b	1 2
		גר	SOJOURNER	158c	2
		גר	SOJOURNER	*158c	2
		חזק	BE FIRM	305b	6 c
		מוט	SLIP	556d	
		מוך	BE LOW	557b	
		עם	WITH	768a	2
25	36	אלהים	GOD	44d	4 c
		את	WITH	86c	2
		חיה	LIVE	311a	1 b
		ירא	FEAR	431b	2
		נשך	INTEREST	675b	
		עם	WITH	768a	2
		תרבית	INTEREST	916b	1
25	37	אכל	FOOD	38a	2
		ב	IN	90b	3 3b
		כסף	SILVER	494d	9
		נשך	INTEREST	675b	
		נתן	GIVE	679c	1 q
		תרבית	INCREASE	916b	1 b
25	38	אלהים	GOD	44b	4 a
		יהוה	YAHWEH	219b	2 2d
		יצא	CAUSE TO GO	424c	1 a
25	39	מוך	BE LOW	557b	
		מכר	SELL	569c	
		עבד	WORK	713a	2
		עבדה	LABOR	715b	2
		עם	WITH	768a	2
25	40	יובל	RAM	385c	2
		תושב	SOJOURNER	444c	
		עבד	WORK	713a	2
		שכיר	HIRED	969b	2
25	41	אחזה	POSSESSION	28c	
		מעם	FROM WITH	769a	C
		משפחה	CLAN	1046d	1 a
25	42	יצא	CAUSE TO GO	424c	1 a
		מכר	SELL	569c	
		ממכרת	SALE	569d	
		עבד	SLAVE	714a	3
25	43	אלהים	GOD	44d	4 c
		ירא	FEAR	431b	2
		פרך	HARSHNESS	827d	
		רדה	HAVE DOMINION	922a	
25	44	אמה	MAID	51a	1
		גוי	NATION	156d	1 c
		סביב	ROUND ABOUT	687b	2 bb
25	45	אחזה	POSSESSION	28c	
		בן	SON	121c	7 a
		גור	SOJOURN	157d	1
		ילד	BEGET	409a	1
		תושב	SOJOURNER	444c	
		משפחה	CLAN	1046d	1 a
25	46	אחזה	POSSESSION	28c	
		אחר	AFTER	30a	2 b
		ירש	INHERIT	439d	2
		נחל	TAKE AS A POSSESSION	635d	
		עבד	WORK	713a	2
		עולם	LONG DURATION	762a	2 a
		פרך	HARSHNESS	827d	
		רדה	HAVE DOMINION	922a	
25	47	גר	SOJOURNER	158b	2
		גר	SOJOURNER	*158c	2
		יד	HAND	390b	2
		תושב	SOJOURNER	444c	
		מוך	BE LOW	557b	
		מכר	SELL	569c	
		נשג	REACH	673d	3
		עם	WITH	768a	2
		עקר	OFFSHOOT	785c	
		משפחה	CLAN	1046d	1 a
25	48	אחר	AFTER THAT	30b	3
		גאל	ACT AS KINSMAN	145c	1 b
		גאלה	REDEMPTION	145d	3
		ל	TO	513b	5 ba
		מכר	SELL	569c	
25	49	או	OR	15a	2
		בשר	FLESH	142d	4
		בשר	FLESH	*142d	4
		גאל	ACT AS KINSMAN	145c	1 b
		גאל	REDEEM	145d	1
		דוד	UNCLE	187c	2
		יד	HAND	390b	2
		מן	FROM	580d	3 ba
		נשג	REACH	673c	3
		שאר	FLESH	985a	2
		משפחה	CLAN	1046d	1 a
25	50	ב	IN	90c	3 8
		חשב	THINK	363c	3
		יובל	RAM	385c	2
		יום	DAY	398d	2 f
		כסף	SILVER	494d	8 e
		מכר	SELL	569c	
		ממכר	SALE	569d	
		שכיר	HIRED	969b	2

LEVITICUS

Ch v.	Heb	Eng	Page	Sec
25 51	גאלה	REDEMPTION	145d	4
	כסף	SILVER	494c	8 e
	פה	MOUTH	805c	6 c1
	פה	MOUTH	805d	6 d2
	מקנה	PURCHASE	889c	2
	רב	MUCH	913a	1 b
	שוב	TURN BACK	999b	1 d
25 52	גאלה	REDEMPTION	145d	4
	חשב	THINK	363c	3
	יובל	RAM	385c	2
	מעט	A FEW	589d	1 a
	פה	MOUTH	805c	6 bb
	שאר	REMAIN	984a	1
	שוב	TURN BACK	999b	1 d
25 53	פרך	HARSHNESS	827d	
	רדה	HAVE DOMINION	922a	
	שכיר	HIRED	969b	2
25 54	אלה	THESE	41c	D
	גאל	REDEEM	145d	2 a
	יובל	RAM	385c	2
	יצא	GO OUT	422d	1 c
25 55	יהוה	YAHWEH	219b	2 2d
	יצא	CAUSE TO GO	424c	1 a
	עבד	SLAVE	714a	3
26 1	אבן	STONE	6c	1
	אליל	WORTHLESSNESS	47c	B
	יהוה	YAHWEH	219b	2 2c
	מצבה	PILLAR	663b	1 c
	נתן	PUT	680c	2 a
	על	UPON	757c	2 7c ab
	קום	STAND	878d	2 a
	משכית	SHOW-PIECE	967d	1
	שחה	BOW DOWN	1005c	3
	משכית	ADDENDA ET CORRIGENDA	1126d	
26 2	יהוה	YAHWEH	219b	2 2d
	ירא	FEAR	431c	3
	שבת	SABBOTH	992c	1 c
	שבת	SABBOTH	992c	1 c
	שמר	KEEP	1036d	3 b
26 3	הלך	WALK	234c	2 3a 1e
	חקה	SOMETHING PRESCRIBED	350b	2 e
	חקה	SOMETHING PRESCRIBED	350b	2 d
26 4	מצוה	COMMANDMENT	846c	2 b2
	ארץ	EARTH	76b	3 b
	גשם	RAIN	177c	
	יובל	PRODUCE	385b	
	נתן	GIVE	678d	1 d
	נתן	GIVE	679c	1 t
	עת	TIME	773c	2 b
	שדה	FIELD	961c	1 d
26 5	את	MARK OF THE ACCUSATIVE	85a	1 a
	בטח	SECURITY	105b	
	בציר	VINTAGE	131b	
	דיש	THRESHING	190c	
	זרע	SOWING	282a	1 b
	ל	TO	512d	5 aa
	נשג	REACH	673c	2 a
	שבע	ABUNDANCE	960a	1
26 6	אין	NOT	34d	4 c
	חיה	LIVING THING	312c	1 b
	חרד	TREMBLE	353c	
	נתן	PUT	680c	2 b
	רע	EVIL	948a	1
	שבת	CEASE	992a	2
	שכב	LIE DOWN	1012a	1 b
	שלום	PEACE	1023b	6
26 7	איב	BE HOSTILE TO	33c	
26 8	מאה	HUNDRED	548a	1 a5
	מן	FROM	580c	3 a
	רבבה	MULTITUDE	914b	
	רדף	PURSUE	922d	1 b
26 9	ברית	COVENANT	136c	2 2c
	ברית	COVENANT	137a	3 1
	פנה	TURN	815c	2 c1
	פרה	BEAR FRUIT	826b	2
	קום	STAND	879a	6 f
26 10	חדש	NEW	294b	A
	יצא	BRING OUT	425a	4 a
	ישן	BECOME INACTIVE	445d	
	ישן	OLD	446a	
26 11	געל	ABHOR	171d	
	נפש	SOUL	660d	6 b
26 12	אלהים	GOD	44b	4 a
	הלך	WALK	236c	2
26 13	יהוה	YAHWEH	219b	2 2d
	הלך	WALK	237a	5 a
	יצא	CAUSE TO GO	424c	1 a
	מוטה	BAR OF YOKE	557b	2
	מן	FROM	583b	7 ba
	עבד	SLAVE	714a	3
	על	YOKE	760d	
	קוממיות	UPRIGHTNESS	879c	
26 14	שמע	HEAR	1034a	1 j
26 15	בלת	NOT	116d	4 a
	ברית	COVENANT	136c	2 2c
	ברית	COVENANT	137b	3 3
	געל	ABHOR	171d	
	חקה	SOMETHING PRESCRIBED	350a	2 d
	חקה	SOMETHING PRESCRIBED	350b	2 e
	מאס	REJECT	549c	1 b

Ch v.	Heb	Eng	Page	Sec
	נפש	SOUL	660d	6 b
	פרר	BREAK	830b	1 b
	מצוה	COMMANDMENT	846c	2 b2
26 16	אף	ALSO	64d	1
	בהלה	DISMAY	96d	
	דאבן	FAINTNESS	178b	
	דוב	PINE AWAY	187b	
	זרע	SOW	281c	1 c
	זרע	SOWING	282b	2 a
	זרע	SOWING	282c	2 e
	כלה	FINISH	478c	2 b
	עין	EYE	744a	1 u
	פקד	ATTEND TO	824a	1
	קדחת	FEVER	869b	
	רבה	BECOME MANY	915c	1 c
	ריק	EMPTINESS	938d	
	שחפת	CONSUMPTION	1006d	
26 17	נגף	STRIKE	620a	
	נוס	FLEE	630d	1
	רדה	HAVE DOMINION	922a	
	שנא	HATE	971c	3
26 18	אלה	THESE	41d	D
	חטאת	SIN	308d	1 b
	יסף	ADD	414d	
	יסר	DISCIPLINE	416b	2 a
	עד	AS FAR AS	724c	1 2a d
	על	UPON	754b	2 1f b
	שבע	SEVEN	988a	1 a
	שמע	HEAR	1034a	1 j
26 19	ברזל	IRON	137d	3
	גאון	EXALTATION	145a	1 a
	נחושה	COPPER	639a	2
	נתן	GIVE	681b	3 c
	עז	STRENGTH	739a	2 a
	שבר	BREAK	990c	
	שמי	HEAVENS	1029d	1 a
	שמי	HEAVENS	1030b	2 a
26 20	יבול	PRODUCE	385b	
	כח	STRENGTH	470c	1 a
	נתן	GIVE	679c	1 t
	נתן	GIVE	679c	1 t
	ריק	EMPTINESS	938b	
	תמם	BE FINISHED	1070c	4
26 21	אבה	BE WILLING	2c	
	חטאת	SIN	308d	1 b
	יסף	ADD	414d	
	מכה	SLAUGHTER	647a	4
	עם	WITH	767d	1 d
	קרי	OPPOSITION	899d	
	שבע	SEVEN	988a	1 a
	שמע	HEAR	1034a	1 j
26 22	בהמה	BEAST	97a	2
	דרך	WAY	202c	1
	חיה	LIVING THING	312c	1 b
	כרת	CUT OFF	504c	2 a
	מעט	BE SMALL	589c	A
	שדה	FIELD	961b	1 c
	שכל	BE BEREAVED	1013d	1
	שלח	SEND	1019c	
	שמם	BE DESOLATED	1031a	1
26 23	אלה	THESE	41c	D
	הלך	WALK	232a	1 1d 5k
	הלך	WALK	234d	2 3b
	יסר	BE CORRECTED	416a	
	ל	TO	514a	5 e
	קרי	OPPOSITION	899d	
26 24	אכי	I	59b	
	אף	ALSO	64d	1
	הלך	WALK	234d	2 3b
	חטאת	SIN	308d	1 b
	נכה	SMITE	646c	4 b
	על	UPON	754b	2 1f b
	קרי	OPPOSITION	899d	
	שבע	SEVEN	988a	1 a
26 25	בוא	COME	99c	2 a
	ברית	COVENANT	136c	2 2c
	דבר	PESTILENCE	184a	1
	נקם	AVENGE	668a	1 a
	נקם	VENGEANCE	668b	1
26 26	אפה	BAKE	66a	
	ל	TO	512d	5 aa
	לחם	FOOD	537a	1 a
	לחם	FOOD	537a	1 a
	מטה	STAFF	641c	1
	שוב	TURN BACK	999a	1 a
	משקל	WEIGHT	1054a	
	תנור	FIRE-POT	1072b	
26 27	ב	IN	90c	3 7
	הלך	WALK	234d	2 3b
	זה	THIS	261d	6 bg
	קרי	OPPOSITION	899d	
	שמע	HEAR	1034a	1 j
26 28	אף	ALSO	64d	1
	הלך	WALK	234d	2 3b
	חטאת	SIN	308d	1 b
	חמה	RAGE	404d	2 c
	יסר	DISCIPLINE	416b	2 a
	על	UPON	754b	2 1f b
	קרי	OPPOSITION	899d	
	שבע	SEVEN	988a	1 a
26 29	בשר	FLESH	142c	1 b
26 30	במה	HIGH PLACE	119c	3
	געל	ABHOR	171d	
	חמן	SUN-PILLAR	329a	
	כרת	CUT OFF	504c	3
	נפש	SOUL	660d	6 b

Ch v.	Heb	Eng	Page	Sec
	פגר	CORPSE	803d	1
	פגר	CORPSE	803d	1
	שמד	BE EXTERMINATED	1029c	2
26 31	חרבה	WASTE	352a	1
	ניחת	SOOTHING	629c	
	מקדש	SACRED PLACE	874a	1
	ריח	SMELL	926b	
	שמם	BE DESOLATED	1031b	1
26 32	אבי	I	59b	
	שמם	BE DESOLATED	1031a	2
	שמם	BE DESOLATED	1031b	1
26 33	גוי	NATION	156d	1 c
	זרה	SCATTER	280a	1
	חרבה	WASTE	352a	1
	חרב	SWORD	352c	1 c
	ריק	MAKE EMPTY	938a	3
	שממה	WASTE	1031b	
26 34	יום	DAY	400b	7 d2 a
	רצה	BE PLEASED WITH	953a	4
	רצה	BE PLEASED WITH	953b	
	שבת	CEASE	991d	2 c
	שבת	SABBATH	992c	3
	שמם	BE DESOLATED	1031b	
26 35	יום	DAY	400b	7 d2 a
	ישב	DWELL	443a	3
	שבת	CEASE	991d	2 c
	שבת	SABBOTH	992c	1 c
	שמם	BE DESOLATED	1031b	
26 36	ארץ	EARTH	76c	5
	ב	IN	88b	1 2
	בוא	COME	99a	1
	לב	HEART	524b	2 9b
	נדף	DRIVE	623d	
	נוס	FLEE	630d	1
	מנוסה	FLIGHT	631a	
	עלה	LEAF	750a	
	קול	VOICE	877b	21
	רדף	PURSUE	922d	1 c
	רדף	PURSUE	922d	1 b
	מרך	WEAKNESS	940b	
	שאר	REMAIN	984a	1
26 37	אין	NOT	34c	2 c
	כ	LIKE	455a	
	כשל	STUMBLE	505c	1
	תקומה	STANDING	879d	
	רדף	PURSUE	922d	1 c
26 38	אבד	PERISH	1c	1
	אכל	EAT	37c	5
	גוי	NATION	156d	1 c
26 39	אף	ALSO	65a	1
	ארץ	EARTH	76c	5
	את	WITH	85d	1
	ב	IN	90c	3 5
	מקק	PINE AWAY	596d	4
	עון	INIQUITY	731c	3
	שאר	REMAIN	984a	1
26 40	אף	ALSO	65a	1
	אשר	THAT	83c	8 ab
	הלך	WALK	234d	2 3b
	ידה	CONFESS	392d	1
	מעל	ACT TREACHEROUSLY	591b	1 c
	עון	INIQUITY	731c	1 b
	קרי	OPPOSITION	899d	
26 41	או	OR	15a	3
	אז	THEN	23a	1 b
	אף	ALSO	64d	1
	בוא	COME	99a	1
	כנע	BE HUMBLE	488c	1
	לב	HEART	524a	2 6d
	עון	INIQUITY	731c	1
	ערל	HAVING FORESKIN	790d	
	קרי	OPPOSITION	899d	
	רצה	BE PLEASED WITH	953b	4
26 42	אף	ALSO	65a	1
	ברית	COVENANT	136c	2 2b
	ברית	COVENANT	137a	3 2
	זכר	REMEMBER	270b	2 3 a
	זכר	REMEMBER	270b	2 1 d
	יצחק	ISAAC	850c	
26 43	געל	ABHOR	171d	
	חקה	SOMETHING PRESCRIBED	350a	2 d
	חקה	SOMETHING PRESCRIBED	350b	2 e
	מן	FROM	583b	7 bb
	נפש	SOUL	660d	6 b
	עון	INIQUITY	731c	3
	עזב	LEAVE	737d	2
	יען	ON ACCOUNT OF	775a	3
	רצה	BE PLEASED WITH	953b	4
	שמם	BE DESOLATED	1031b	
26 44	אף	ALSO	65a	1
	ברית	COVENANT	136c	2 2c
	ברית	COVENANT	137b	3 3
	געל	ABHOR	171d	
	יהוה	YAHWEH	218d	2 1d
	יהוה	YAHWEH	219b	2 2c
	כלה	FINISH	478c	2 c2
	מאס	REJECT	549c	1 a
	פרר	BREAK	830b	1 a
26 45	אלהים	GOD	44b	4 a
	ברית	COVENANT	136c	2 2c
	ברית	COVENANT	137a	3 2
	גוי	NATION	156d	1 c
	יהוה	YAHWEH	219b	2 2d

NUMBERS

Ch	v.	Heb	Eng	Page	Sec
1	47	לוי	LEVITE	533a	3 1c
		פקד	ATTEND TO	823a	
1	49	לוי	LEVI	532c	2
		נשא	LIFT	671c	3 e
		פקד	ATTEND TO	823c	A 4
		ראש	HEAD	911b	7
1	50	חנה	DECLINE	333c	2 c2
		לוי	LEVITE	533a	3 1d
		סביב	ROUND ABOUT	687b	1 cb
		עדות	TESTIMONY	730b	1
		פקד	ATTEND TO	823d	1
		משכן	DWELLING-PLACE	1015d	2 c
		שרת	SERVE	1057b	2 b
1	51	זור	BE A STRANGER	266c	2 a
		ירד	BRING DOWN	434a	2
		לוי	LEVITE	533a	3 1d
		מות	DIE	560c	1
		נסע	SET OUT	652a	2 a
1	52	דגל	STANDARD	186b	
		חנה	DECLINE	333c	2 c2
		מחנה	ENCAMPMENT	334a	1 a
		על	UPON	754a	2 1f
		צבא	ARMY	838d	
1	53	בן	SON	120d	1 jg
		חנה	DECLINE	333c	2 c2
		עדה	CONGREGATION	417b	1
		לוי	LEVITE	533a	3 1d
		סביב	ROUND ABOUT	687a	1 cb
		עדות	TESTIMONY	730b	1
		קצף	WRATH	893c	1
		משכן	DWELLING-PLACE	1015d	2 c
		שמר	KEEP	1037a	3 c
		משמרת	GUARD	1038c	4 a
1	54	כן	SO	486c	2 cc
2	2	אות	SIGN	17a	7
		דגל	STANDARD	186b	
		דגל	STANDARD	*186b	
		חנה	DECLINE	333c	2 c2
		נגד	IN FRONT	617d	2 ca
		סביב	ROUND ABOUT	687a	1 cb
		על	UPON	754a	2 1f
		צבא	ARMY	838d	1 a
2	3	דגל	STANDARD	186b	
		מזרח	PLACE OF SUNRISE	281a	2 c1
		מחנה	ENCAMPMENT	334a	1 a
		נחשון	NAHSHON	638c	
		נשיא	PRINCE	672b	5
		עמינדב	AMMINADAB	770b	1
		צבא	ARMY	838d	1 a
		קדם	EASTWARD	870a	
2	4	צבא	ARMY	838d	1 a
		ארבע	FOUR	917b	2 c
		שבעים	SEVENTY	988c	3 b
2	5	חנה	DECLINE	333c	2 c2
		יששכר	ISSACHAR	441a	1
		יששכר	ISSACHAR	441a	1
		נתנאל	NETHANEL	682a	1
		על	UPON	756a	2 6a
		צוער	ZUAR	859b	
2	6	צבא	ARMY	838d	1 a
		ארבע	FOUR	917b	2 c
2	7	אליאב	ELIAB	45a	A
		זבולן	ZEBULUN	259d	2
		זבולן	ZEBULUN	259d	2
		חלן	HELON	298b	
2	8	נסע	SET OUT	652a	2 a
		שבע	SEVEN	988b	4
2	9	ל	TO	513c	5 cb b
		נסע	JOURNEY	*652b	3
		צבא	ARMY	838d	1 a
		ראשון	FIRST	912a	3 b1
		שנים	EIGHTY	1033b	
2	10	אליצור	ELIZUR	45d	
		דגל	STANDARD	186b	
		תימן	SOUTH	412d	1 b
		צבא	ARMY	838d	1 a
		ראובן	REUBEN	910a	2
		ראובן	REUBEN	910a	2
		שדיאור	SHEDEUR	994d	
2	11	צבא	ARMY	838d	1 a
2	12	חנה	DECLINE	333c	2 c2
		מעט	A FEW	590a	1
		על	UPON	756a	2 6a
		צורישדי	ZURISHADDAI	849d	
		שלמיאל	SHELUMIEL	1025a	
		שמעון	SIMEON	1035c	2
2	14	אליסף	ELIASAPH	45c	A
		גד	GAD	151c	1 b
		דעואל	DEUEL	396a	
		רעואל	REUEL	946c	3
2	16	ל	TO	513c	5 cb b
		ראובן	REUBEN	910a	2
		שני	SECOND	1041c	
2	17	דגל	STANDARD	186b	
		מחנה	ENCAMPMENT	334a	1 a
		מחנה	ENCAMPMENT	334b	1 b
		יד	HAND	390c	3 e
		כאשר	AS	455b	1
		כן	SO	486c	2 cb
		לוי	LEVITE	533a	3 1d
		נסע	SET OUT	*652b	2 a
2	18	אפרים	EPHRAIM	68b	2
		דגל	STANDARD	186b	
		ים	SEA	411b	9
		עמיהוד	AMMIHUD	770b	2
2	19	ארבעים	FORTY	917b	1 a
2	20	מנשה	MANASSEH	586d	1 b3 g
		מנשה	MANASSEH	586d	1 b3 a
		על	UPON	756a	2 6a
		פדהצור	PEDAHZUR	804c	
2	22	אבידן	ABIDAN	4a	
		בנימן	BENJAMIN	122d	1
		בנימן	BENJAMIN	122d	1
		גדעני	GIDEONI	154c	
2	24	אפרים	EPHRAIM	68b	2
		שמנה	EIGHT	1033a	3 b
2	25	אחיזר	AHIEZER	27b	1
		דגל	STANDARD	186b	
		דן	DAN	192d	2
		דן	DAN	192d	2
		עמישדי	AMMISHADDAI	770b	
2	27	אשר	ASHER	81b	2
		אשר	ASHER	81b	2
		חנה	DECLINE	333c	2 c2
		עכרן	OCHRAN	747d	
		על	UPON	756a	2 6a
		פגעיאל	PAGIEL	803c	
2	28	ארבעים	FORTY	917c	2 b
2	29	אחירע	AHIRA	27c	
		עינן	ENAN	734d	
		נפתלי	NAPHTALI	836d	2 a
2	31	אחרן	BEHIND	31a	B g
		דגל	STANDARD	186b	
		דן	DAN	192d	2
		שבע	SEVEN	988b	4
		לוי	LEVITE	533a	3 1c
2	33	פקד	ATTEND TO	823d	1
2	34	דגל	STANDARD	186b	
		חנה	DECLINE	333c	2 c2
		כן	SO	486c	2 cc
		על	UPON	754a	2 1f
		משפחה	CLAN	1046d	1 c
3	1	דבר	SPEAK	*180d	
		דבר	SPEAK	181b	3 d
		הר	MOUNTAIN	249b	1 a
		הר	MOUNTAIN	250a	1 a
		יום	DAY	400b	7 d3 a
		תולדות	GENERATIONS	410a	A
		סיני	SINAI	696a	
3	2	איתמר	ITHAMAR	16a	
		נדב	NADAB	621c	1
3	3	אהרן	AARON	14d	
		בן	SON	121a	1 jz
		יד	HAND	389b	1 c
		כהן	PRIEST	464a	7
		כהן	ACT AS PRIEST	464c	1
		מלא	FILL	570d	2
		משח	ANOINT	603b	3 a
3	4	איתמר	ITHAMAR	16a	
		אש	FIRE	77c	4
		זור	BE A STRANGER	266d	2 d
		כהן	ACT AS PRIEST	464c	1
		מות	DIE	560a	2 b
		נדב	NADAB	621c	1
		סיני	SINAI	696a	
		פנה	FACE	818d	27 a a
		קרב	COME NEAR	898a	2 b5
3	6	לוי	LEVI	532c	2
		שרת	SERVE	1058b	2 b
3	7	עבד	WORK	713b	5
		עבדה	LABOR	715c	4
		משמרת	GUARD	1038c	4 a
		משמרת	GUARD	1038c	4 a
3	8	עבד	WORK	713b	5
		עבדה	LABOR	715c	4
		שמר	KEEP	1036c	1 a
		משמרת	GUARD	1038c	4 a
3	9	את	WITH	86d	4 b
		לוי	LEVITE	533a	3 1d
		נתן	GIVE	678c	1 b
		נתנינים	NETHINIM	*682a	
3	10	זור	BE A STRANGER	266c	2 a
		כהנה	PRIESTHOOD	464d	
		מות	DIE	560c	2
		פקד	ATTEND TO	823c	B 1
		קרב	APPROACHING	898b	2
		שמר	KEEP	1037a	3 c
3	12	אנכי	I	59c	
		בכור	FIRST-BORN	114b	1 d
		לוי	LEVITE	533a	3 1d
		מן	OUT OF	579c	2 cb
		פטר	THAT WHICH SEPARATES	809d	
		רחם	WOMB	933b	1
		תוך	MIDST	1063d	
3	13	בכור	FIRST-BORN	114b	1 d
		יהוה	YAHWEH	219b	2 2d
		נכה	SMITE	646d	2 c
		קדש	BE SET APART	873c	1 c
3	14	סיני	SINAI	696a	
3	15	בן	SON	121a	1 je
		חדש	NEW MOON	294c	2 a
		לוי	LEVI	532c	1 c
		מעל	ABOVE	751d	2 bb a
		משפחה	CLAN	1047a	1 d
		כאשר	AS	455b	1
3	16	פה	MOUTH	805d	6 d1 a
		צוה	CHARGE	846b	4 c
3	17	בן	SON	*121a	1 je
		גרשון	GERSHON	177b	
		לוי	LEVI	532c	1 c
		מררי	MERARI	601b	
		קהת	KOHATH	875b	
3	18	גרשון	GERSHON	177b	
		לבני	LIBNI	526d	
		שמעי	SHIMEI	1035c	3 a
		חברון	HEBRON	289b	1
3	19	עזיאל	UZZIEL	739c	1 a
		יצהר	IZHAR	844b	
		קהת	KOHATH	875b	
		קהת	KOHATH	875b	
3	20	בית	HOUSE	110b	5 e
		ה	THE	208b	1 g
		הם	THEY	241c	4 bg
		לוי	LEVITE	532d	2
		מושי	MUSHI	559b	
		מחלי	MAHLI	563a	1
		מררי	MERARI	601b	
3	21	גרשון	GERSHON	177b	
		גרשני	GERSHONITES	177b	
		הם	THEY	241c	4 bg
		ל	TO	512d	5 ac
		לבני	LIBNITE	526d	
		שמעי	SHEMEITES	1035c	
3	22	חדש	NEW MOON	294c	2 a
		מעל	ABOVE	751d	2 bb a
3	23	גרשני	GERSHONITES	177b	
		ים	SEA	411b	9
3	24	אליסף	ELIASAPH	45c	B
		בית	HOUSE	110b	5 e
		גרשני	GERSHONITES	177b	
		לאל	LAEL	522b	
3	25	אהל	TENT	14a	3
		גרשון	GERSHON	177b	
		גרשון	GERSHON	*177b	
		מכסה	COVERING	492c	2
		מסך	COVERING	697b	2 b
		פתח	OPENING	835d	
		משמרת	GUARD	1038c	4 a
3	26	את	MARK OF THE ACCUSATIVE	85b	3 a
		חצר	ENCLOSURE	347a	3 a
		מיתר	CORD	452d	
		ל	TO	514c	5 fd
		מסך	COVERING	697b	2 a
		עבדה	LABOR	715c	4
		על	UPON	755d	2 6a
		על	UPON	756a	2 6a
		פתח	OPENING	835d	
		קלע	CURTAIN	887c	
3	27	הם	THEY	241c	4 bg
		חברוני	HEBRONITE	289c	
		ל	TO	512d	5 ac
		עזיאלי	UZZIELITES	739c	
		עמרמי	AMRAMITES	771d	
		יצהרי	IZHARITES	844b	
		קהתי	KOHATHITES	875c	
3	28	זכר	MALE	271c	1 1 b
		חדש	NEW MOON	294c	2 a
		קדם	EASTWARD	870a	
		קדש	APARTNESS	871d	2 c
		משמרת	GUARD	1038c	4 c2
3	29	חנה	DECLINE	333c	2 c2
		תימן	SOUTH	412d	1 b
		ירך	SIDE	438a	2
		קהת	KOHATH	875b	
3	30	אב	FATHER	3c	3
		אליצפן	ELIZAPHAN	45d	A
		עזיאל	UZZIEL	739c	1 a
3	31	מזבח	ALTAR	259a	1
		ל	TO	*514c	5 fd
		מנורה	LAMPSTAND	633b	3
		מסך	COVERING	697b	2 b
		עבדה	LABOR	715c	4
		שלחן	TABLE	1020b	1
		משמרת	GUARD	1038c	4 a
		שרת	SERVE	1057b	2 b
3	32	אהרן	AARON	14d	
		לוי	LEVITE	532d	2
		נשיא	PRINCE	*672b	5
		פקדה	OVERSIGHT	824b	2 b
		משמרת	GUARD	1038c	4 a
3	33	הם	THEY	241c	4 bg
		מושי	MUSHITES	559b	
		מחלי	MAHLITES	563a	2
		מררי	MERARI	601b	
3	34	זכר	MALE	271c	1 1 b
		חדש	NEW MOON	294c	2 a
		שש	SIX	995c	3
3	35	אב	FATHER	3c	3
		אביחיל	ABIHAIL	4b	3
		חנה	DECLINE	333c	2 c2
		ירך	SIDE	438a	2
		מררי	MERARI	601b	
		צוריאל	ZURIEL	849d	
3	36	בריח	BAR	138b	1 a
		ל	TO	*514c	5 fd
		מררי	MERARI	601b	
		עבדה	LABOR	715c	4
		פקדה	OVERSIGHT	824a	2
		קרש	BOARD	903c	2
		משמרת	GUARD	1038c	4 a
3	37	חצר	ENCLOSURE	347a	3 a
		יתד	PEG	450b	A
		מיתר	CORD	452d	
		עמוד	PILLAR	765a	1
3	38	זור	BE A STRANGER	266c	2 a
		מזרח	PLACE OF SUNRISE	281a	2 c1

Ch	v.	Heb	Eng	Page	Sec
		מות	DIE	560c	2
		פנה	FACE	817d	2 4d
		קרב	APPROACHING	898b	2
		משמרת	GUARD	1038c	4 a
		משמרת	GUARD	1038c	4 a
3	39	זכר	MALE	271c	1 1 b
		חדש	NEW MOON	294c	2 a
		לוי	LEVITE	533a	3 1c
		פה	MOUTH	805d	6 d1 a
3	40	בכור	FIRST-BORN	114b	1 d
		זכר	MALE	271c	1 d
		חדש	NEW MOON	294c	2 a
		נשא	LIFT	671c	3 e
3	41	בהמה	BEAST	97a	2
		בכור	FIRST-BORN	114b	2 b
		יהוה	YAHWEH	219b	2 2d
3	42	בכור	FIRST-BORN	114b	1 d
		כאשר	AS	455b	1 a
		פקד	ATTEND TO	823c	A 4
3	43	בכור	FIRST-BORN	114b	1 d
		זכר	MALE	271c	2
		חדש	NEW MOON	294c	2 a
		שבעים	SEVENTY	988c	3 b
3	45	בהמה	BEAST	97a	2
		בכור	FIRST-BORN	114b	1 d
		יהוה	YAHWEH	219b	2 2d
3	46	את	MARK OF THE ACCUSATIVE	85b	3 a
		בכור	FIRST-BORN	114a	1 b
		עדף	REMAIN OVER	727b	
		על	UPON	755a	2 2
		פדה	RANSOM	804a	1
		שבעים	SEVENTY	988c	3 b
3	47	גרה	GERAH	176a	
		חמש	FIVE	331d	1 d
		שקל	SHEKEL	1053d	
		שקל	SHEKEL	1053d	
3	48	כסף	SILVER	494c	8 e
		עדף	REMAIN OVER	727b	
		פדה	RANSOM	804a	1
		פדיום	RANSOM	804b	
3	49	כסף	SILVER	494c	8 e
		עדף	REMAIN OVER	727b	
		פדה	RANSOM	804a	1
		פדיום	RANSOM	804b	
		פדיום	RANSOM	804b	
3	50	אלף	THOUSAND	49a	1 b
		בכור	FIRST-BORN	114a	1 b
		שקל	SHEKEL	1053d	
3	51	פדה	RANSOM	804a	1
		פדיום	RANSOM	804b	
4	2	לוי	LEVI	532c	1 c
		נשא	LIFT	671c	3 e
		ראש	HEAD	911b	7
		תוך	MIDST	1063d	
4	3	בן	SON	122a	9 a
		מעל	ABOVE	751d	2 bb a
		צבא	SERVICE	839b	3 a
4	4	עבדה	LABOR	715b	4
		קדש	APARTNESS	872a	3 a
4	5	ארון	CHEST	75c	3 g
		ירד	BRING DOWN	434a	2
		כסה	COVER	491d	3
		נסע	SET OUT	652a	2 a
		מסך	COVERING	697b	2 c
		עדות	TESTIMONY	730b	1
		פרכת	CURTAIN	827d	
4	6	בגד	COVERING	94a	2
		בד	PART	94d	3 c
		כליל	WHOLE	483a	2 a
		כסוי	COVERING	492b	
		עור	SKIN	736b	2
		מעל	ABOVE	752a	2 d
		פרש	SPREAD OUT	831b	2
		שום	TO PLACE	964b	4 b
		תחש	SEALSKIN	1065a	
		תכלת	VIOLET THREAD	1067b	2
4	7	בגד	COVERING	94a	2
		כף	PAN	497a	4 b
		לחם	FOOD	537b	1 a
		תמיד	CONTINUITY	556c	2 a
		נסך	DRINK-OFFERING	651a	1
		מנקיה	SACRIFICIAL BOWL	667d	1
		פרש	SPREAD OUT	831b	2
		קשוה	JAR	903d	
		שלחן	TABLE	1020b	3
		תכלת	VIOLET THREAD	1067b	2
4	8	בגד	COVERING	94a	2
		בד	PART	94d	3 c
		כסה	COVER	491d	3
		מכסה	COVERING	492c	2
		פרש	SPREAD OUT	831b	2
		שום	TO PLACE	964b	4 b
		שני	SCARLET	1040d	
		תחש	SEALSKIN	1065a	
		תולעה	WORM	1069a	2
4	9	מאור	LUMINARY	22d	
		בגד	COVERING	94a	2
		מחתה	FIRE-HOLDER	367b	1
		כלי	VESSEL	480b	3
		כסה	COVER	491d	3
		מלקחים	TONGS	544c	2
		מנורה	LAMPSTAND	633b	3
		שרת	SERVE	1057b	2 b
		תכלת	VIOLET THREAD	1067b	2
4	10	בגד	COVERING	94a	2
4	11	כלי	VESSEL	480b	3
		מכסה	COVERING	492c	2
		מוט	POLE	557a	2
		תחש	SEALSKIN	1065a	
4	11	בגד	COVERING	94a	2
		בד	PART	94d	3 c
		מזבח	ALTAR	258c	3 b
		זהב	GOLD	263a	6
		כסה	COVER	491d	3
		מכסה	COVERING	492c	2
		פרש	SPREAD OUT	831b	2
		שום	TO PLACE	964b	4 b
		תחש	SEALSKIN	1065a	
		תכלת	VIOLET THREAD	1067b	2
4	12	בגד	COVERING	94a	2
		כלי	UTENSIL	480a	2 f
		כסה	COVER	491d	3
		מכסה	COVERING	492c	2
		מוט	POLE	557a	2
		שרת	SERVE	1057b	2 b
		שרת	MINISTRY	1058b	
		תחש	SEALSKIN	1065a	
		תכלת	VIOLET THREAD	1067b	2
4	13	ארגמן	PURPLE THREAD	71b	2
		בגד	COVERING	94a	2
		דשן	BE FAT	206b	
		פרש	SPREAD OUT	831b	2
		בד	PART	94d	3 c
4	14	מזלגה	THREE PRONGED FORK	272c	
		מזרק	BOWL	284d	2 a
		מחתה	FIRE-HOLDER	367b	2
		יע	SHOVEL	418b	
		כסוי	COVERING	492b	
		פרש	SPREAD OUT	831b	2
		שום	TO PLACE	964b	4 b
		שרת	SERVE	1057b	2 b
		תחש	SEALSKIN	1065a	
4	15	כלה	FINISH	478b	1 c
		כסה	COVER	491d	3
		מות	DIE	560a	2 b
		נגע	TOUCH	619a	1 a
		נסע	SET OUT	652a	2 a
		משא	BEARING	672d	3
4	16	מאור	LUMINARY	22d	
		תמיד	CONTINUITY	556c	2 b
		מנחה	OFFERING	585b	4
		משחה	OINTMENT	603c	1
		סם	SPICE	702c	
		פקדה	OVERSIGHT	824a	2 a
		פקדה	OVERSIGHT	824b	2 d
4	18	כרת	CUT OFF	504c	2 b
		לוי	LEVITE	533a	3 1c
		שבט	TRIBE	987b	2 c
		תוך	MIDST	1063d	
4	19	איש	MAN	36a	
		חיה	LIVE	311a	1 a
		מות	DIE	560a	2 b
		נגש	DRAW NEAR	620d	1
		משא	BEARING	672d	3
		עבדה	LABOR	715b	4
		קדש	APARTNESS	872a	3 a
		שום	TO PLACE	964a	3 d
4	20	בלע	SWALLOW UP	118b	1
		בעל	LORD	*127c	1 5b
		מות	DIE	560a	2 b
4	22	גרשון	GERSHON	*177b	
		גרשון	GERSHON	177b	
		נשא	LIFT	671c	3 e
		ראש	HEAD	911b	7
4	23	עבד	WORK	713b	5
		עבדה	LABOR	715b	4
		צבא	SERVE	838d	2
		צבא	SERVICE	839b	3 a
4	24	גרשני	GERSHONITES	177b	
		עבד	WORK	713b	5
		עבדה	LABOR	715b	4
4	25	יריעה	CURTAIN	438c	
		מכסה	COVERING	492c	2
		מסך	COVERING	697b	2 b
		מעל	ABOVE	752a	2 d
		תחש	SEALSKIN	1065a	
4	26	חצר	ENCLOSURE	347a	3 a
		מיתר	CORD	452d	
		כלי	UTENSIL	480a	2 f
		מסך	COVERING	697b	2 b
		עבד	WORK	713b	5
		עבדה	LABOR	715b	2
		עשה	DO	795b	2 a
		פתח	OPENING	835d	
		קלע	CURTAIN	887c	
4	27	גרשני	GERSHONITES	177b	
		ל	TO	514c	5 fd
		משא	BEARING	672d	3
		עבדה	LABOR	715b	4
		פקד	ATTEND TO	823c	B 2
		שם	NAME	1028a	2 a
		משמרת	GUARD	*1038c	4 a
		משמרת	GUARD	1038c	4 a
4	28	איתמר	ITHAMAR	16a	
		גרשני	GERSHONITES	177b	
		עבדה	LABOR	715b	4
		משמרת	GUARD	1038c	4 a
4	29	מררי	MERARI	601b	
4	30	עבד	WORK	713b	5
		עבדה	LABOR	715b	4
4	31	צבא	SERVICE	839b	3 a
		בריח	BAR	138b	1 a
		ל	TO	514c	5 fd
		משא	BEARING	672d	3
		עבדה	LABOR	715b	4
		קרש	BOARD	903d	2
		משמרת	GUARD	1038c	4 a
		משמרת	GUARD	1038c	4 a
4	32	חצר	ENCLOSURE	347a	3 a
		יתד	PEG	450b	A
		מיתר	CORD	452d	
		כלי	UTENSIL	480a	2 f
		ל	TO	514c	5 fd
		משא	BEARING	672d	3
		עבדה	LABOR	715b	2
		פקד	ATTEND TO	823c	B 2
		שם	NAME	1028a	2 a
		משמרת	GUARD	1038c	4 a
		משמרת	GUARD	1038c	4 a
4	33	איתמר	ITHAMAR	16a	
		מררי	MERARI	601b	
		עבדה	LABOR	715b	4
		עבדה	LABOR	715b	4
4	34	עדה	CONGREGATION	417b	3
		קהתי	KOHATHITES	875c	
4	35	עבדה	LABOR	715b	4
		צבא	SERVICE	839b	3 a
4	36	שער	GATE	1045b	3 d
4	37	יד	HAND	391a	5 d
		עבד	WORK	713b	5
4	38	גרשון	GERSHON	*177b	
		גרשון	GERSHON	177b	
4	39	עבדה	LABOR	715b	4
		צבא	SERVICE	839b	3 a
4	41	גרשון	GERSHON	177b	
		גרשון	GERSHON	*177b	
		עבד	WORK	713b	5
4	42	מררי	MERARI	601b	
4	43	עבדה	LABOR	715b	4
		צבא	SERVICE	839b	3 a
4	45	יד	HAND	391a	5 d
		מררי	MERARI	601b	
4	46	לוי	LEVITE	533a	3 1c
4	47	משא	BEARING	672d	3
		עבד	WORK	713b	5
		עבדה	LABOR	715b	4
		עבדה	LABOR	715c	4
4	49	איש	MAN	36a	
		משא	BEARING	672d	3
		עבדה	LABOR	715b	4
5	2	זב	FLOW	264d	4
		טמא	UNCLEAN	379d	2 a
		ל	TO	514d	5 g
		נפש	SOUL	660c	4 c5
		צרע	BE STRUCK WITH LEPROSY	863d	
5	3	זכר	MALE	271c	1 1 b
		טמא	BE UNCLEAN	379c	3
		נקבה	FEMALE	666c	1
		שכן	SETTLE DOWN	1015b	2 c
5	4	כאשר	AS	455b	1 b
		כן	SO	*486c	2 ca
5	4	שדה	FIELD	961d	2 d
5	6	אדם	MAN	9b	2
		אדם	MAN	9b	2
		איש	MAN	35d	
		אשם	OFFEND	79c	2
		חטאת	SIN	308c	1 a
		מן	FROM	581a	3 bc
		מעל	ACT TREACHEROUSLY	591b	1 c
5	7	נפש	SOUL	660b	4 c2
		אשם	OFFEND	79c	1
		אשם	OFFENCE	79d	3
		אשר	PARTICLE OF RELATION	82a	1
		חטאת	SIN	308d	1 c
		חמשי	FIFTH	332d	3
		ידה	CONFESS	392d	1
		יסף	ADD	415a	1
		ראש	HEAD	911b	7
		שוב	TURN BACK	999b	1 d
5	8	איל	RAM	18a	2 b
		אשם	OFFENCE	79d	3
		בד	SEPARATION	94d	1 e
		גאל	ACT AS KINSMAN	145b	1
		כפר	COVER OVER	497d	3 b2
		כפר	COVER OVER	498a	3 d
		כפרים	ATONEMENT	498c	
		שוב	TURN BACK	1000a	1
5	9	ל	TO	514c	5 fd
		קדש	APARTNESS	872a	3 b
		תרומה	OFFERING	929a	4
		תרומה	OFFERING	929b	7
5	10	את	MARK OF THE ACCUSATIVE	85b	3 a
5	12	מעל	UNFAITHFUL	*591b	1
		מעל	ACT TREACHEROUSLY	591b	1 b
5	13	שטה	TURN ASIDE	966b	
		איש	MAN	35d	
		הוא	HE, SHE, IT	*214d	
		זרע	SOWING	282c	3
		טמא	BE UNCLEAN	379b	1
		סתר	HIDE	711c	2
		עד	WITNESS	729d	2 c

NUMBERS

Ch	v.	Heb	Eng	Page	Sec
		צב	LITTER	839d	
		שׁור	A HEAD OF CATTLE	1004a	
		שׁור	A HEAD OF CATTLE	1004b	
7	5	לוי	LEVITE	533a	3 1d
		עבד	WORK	713b	5
		עבדה	LABOR	715b	4
		עבדה	LABOR	715b	4
		פה	MOUTH	805c	6 bb
7	6	בקר	CATTLE	133c	2
		לוי	LEVITE	533a	3 1d
		עגלה	CART	722c	
		קדשׁ	HOLY	872d	2 b
7	7	בקר	CATTLE	133c	2
		גרשׁון	GERSHON	177b	
		גרשׁון	GERSHON	*177b	
		עבדה	LABOR	715b	4
		עגלה	CART	722c	
		פה	MOUTH	805c	6 bb
		ארבע	FOUR	917a	1 c2
7	8	איתמר	ITHAMAR	16a	
		בקר	CATTLE	133c	2
		מררי	MERARI	601b	
		עבדה	LABOR	715b	4
		עגלה	CART	722c	
		עשׂרים	TWENTY	797d	1 2b
		פה	MOUTH	805c	6 bb
		שׁמנה	EIGHT	1033a	1 c
7	9	כתף	SHOULDER	509b	1 a
		עבדה	LABOR	715c	4
		על	UPON	753c	2 1c
7	10	מזבח	ALTAR	259a	9
		מזבח	ALTAR	259a	9
		חנכה	DEDICATION	335c	
		נער	RETAINER	655a	2 a
		פנה	FACE	817d	2 4d
		קרב	COME NEAR	898a	2 b6
7	11	מזבח	ALTAR	259a	9
		חנכה	DEDICATION	335c	
		יום	DAY	401a	7 i
		יום	DAY	401a	7 i
		ל	TO	512d	5 ab
		נער	RETAINER	655a	2 a
		קרב	COME NEAR	898a	2 b6
7	12	יהודה	JUDAH	397b	1 2
		עמינדב	AMMINADAB	770b	1
7	13	בלל	MIX	117c	2
		מזרק	BOWL	284d	2 b
		מלא	FULL	571a	
		מנחה	OFFERING	585c	5 b
		נחשׁון	NAHSHON	638c	
		עצר	RESTRAIN	783d	
		קערה	DISH	891a	
		קרבן	OFFERING	898d	
		שׁבעים	SEVENTY	988c	1 a
		שׁקל	SHEKEL	1053d	
		משׁקל	WEIGHT	1054a	
7	14	זהב	GOLD	263b	9 a
		כף	PAN	497a	4 b
		מלא	FULL	571a	
		עשׂר	TEN	796d	2 b
		קטרת	SMOKE	882d	2
7	15	איל	RAM	18a	2 f
		בן	SON	121c	7 b
		כבשׂ	LAMB	461a	1
		עלה	WHOLE BURNT OF-FERING	750c	
7	16	פר	YOUNG BULL	830d	2 b
		חטאת	SIN	309c	4 a
		עז	SHE-GOAT	777c	3 f
		שׂעיר	HE-GOAT	972c	
7	17	בן	SON	122a	9 b
		בקר	CATTLE	133c	2
		זה	THIS	261b	3
		נחשׁון	NAHSHON	638c	
		עמינדב	AMMINADAB	770b	1
		שׁנים	TWO	1041a	1 b1
7	18	ישׁשכר	ISSACHAR	441a	1
		נתנאל	NETHANEL	682a	1
		צוער	ZUAR	859b	
		קרב	COME NEAR	898a	2 c7
7	19	בלל	MIX	117c	2
		מזרק	BOWL	284d	2 b
		מלא	FULL	571a	
7	20	חנכה	DEDICATION	*335c	
		מלא	FULL	571a	
		ראובן	REUBEN	910a	2
7	21	עלה	WHOLE BURNT OF-FERING	750c	
		פר	YOUNG BULL	830d	2 b
7	22	חטאת	SIN	309c	4 a
7	23	זה	THIS	261b	3
		נתנאל	NETHANEL	682a	1
		צוער	ZUAR	859b	
7	24	אליאב	ELIAB	45a	A
		זבולן	ZEBULUN	259d	2
		חלן	HELON	298b	
		ל	TO	513c	5 cb a
		ל	TO	513c	5 cb b
7	25	בלל	MIX	117c	2
		מזרק	BOWL	284d	2 b
		מלא	FULL	571a	
7	26	מלא	FULL	571a	
7	27	עלה	WHOLE BURNT OF-FERING	750c	
7	28	חטאת	SIN	309c	4 a
7	29	אליאב	ELIAB	45a	A
7	30	חלן	HELON	298b	
		אליצור	ELIZUR	45d	
		ל	TO	513c	5 cb b
		רביעי	FOURTH	917d	1
		שׁדיאור	SHEDEUR	994d	
7	31	בלל	MIX	117c	2
		מזרק	BOWL	284d	2 b
7	32	מלא	FULL	571a	
7	33	עלה	WHOLE BURNT OF-FERING	750c	
7	34	חטאת	SIN	309c	4 a
7	35	אליצור	ELIZUR	45d	
		שׁדיאור	SHEDEUR	994d	
7	36	חמישׁי	FIFTH	332c	1
		ל	TO	513c	5 cb b
		מאה	HUNDRED	548b	2 b
		צורישׁדי	ZURISHADDAI	849d	
		שׁלמיאל	SHELUMIEL	1025a	
7	37	בלל	MIX	117c	2
		מזרק	BOWL	284d	2 b
		מלא	FULL	571a	
7	38	מלא	FULL	571a	
7	39	עלה	WHOLE BURNT OF-FERING	750c	
7	40	חטאת	SIN	309c	4 a
7	41	צורישׁדי	ZURISHADDAI	849d	
		שׁלמיאל	SHELUMIEL	1025a	
7	42	אליסף	ELIASAPH	45c	A
		דעואל	DEUEL	396a	
7	43	בלל	MIX	117c	2
		מזרק	BOWL	284d	2 b
		מלא	FULL	571a	
7	44	מלא	FULL	571a	
7	45	עלה	WHOLE BURNT OF-FERING	750c	
7	46	חטאת	SIN	309c	4 a
7	47	אליסף	ELIASAPH	45c	A
		דעואל	DEUEL	396a	
7	48	אפרים	EPHRAIM	68b	2
		עמיהוד	AMMIHUD	770b	2
7	49	בלל	MIX	117c	2
		מזרק	BOWL	284d	2 b
		מלא	FULL	571a	
7	50	מלא	FULL	571a	
7	51	עלה	WHOLE BURNT OF-FERING	750c	
7	52	חטאת	SIN	309c	4 a
7	53	עמיהוד	AMMIHUD	770b	2
7	54	מנשׁה	MANASSEH	586a	1 b3 a
		פדהצור	PEDAHZUR	804c	
7	55	בלל	MIX	117c	2
		מזרק	BOWL	284d	2 b
		מלא	FULL	571a	
7	56	מלא	FULL	571a	
7	57	עלה	WHOLE BURNT OF-FERING	750c	
7	58	חטאת	SIN	309c	4 a
7	59	פדהצור	PEDAHZUR	804c	
		אבידן	ABIDAN	4a	1
7	60	בנימין	BENJAMIN	122d	1
		גדעני	GIDEONI	154c	
		תשׁיעי	NINTH	1077d	
7	61	בלל	MIX	117c	2
		מזרק	BOWL	284d	2 b
		מלא	FULL	571a	
		ישׂראל	ISRAEL	975d	2 a3
7	62	מלא	FULL	571a	
7	63	עלה	WHOLE BURNT OF-FERING	750c	
7	64	חטאת	SIN	309c	4 a
7	65	אבידן	ABIDAN	4a	
		גדעני	GIDEONI	154c	
7	66	אחיזר	AHIEZER	27b	1
		דן	DAN	192d	2
		עמישׁדי	AMMISHADDAI	770b	
		עשׂירי	TENTH	798a	1
7	67	בלל	MIX	117c	2
		מזרק	BOWL	284d	2 b
		מלא	FULL	571a	
7	68	מלא	FULL	571a	
7	69	עלה	WHOLE BURNT OF-FERING	750c	
7	70	חטאת	SIN	309c	4 a
7	71	אחיזר	AHIEZER	27b	1
		עמישׁדי	AMMISHADDAI	770b	
7	72	אשׁר	ASHER	81b	2
		עכרן	OCHRAN	747d	
		עשׂר	TEN	797c	
		עשׁתי	ONE	799d	
		פגעיאל	PAGIEL	803c	
7	73	בלל	MIX	117c	2
		מזרק	BOWL	284d	2 b
		מלא	FULL	571a	
7	74	מלא	FULL	571a	
7	75	עלה	WHOLE BURNT OF-FERING	750c	
7	76	חטאת	SIN	309c	4 a
7	77	עכרן	OCHRAN	747d	
		פגעיאל	PAGIEL	803c	
7	78	אחירע	AHIRA	27c	
		עינן	ENAN	745d	
		עשׂר	TEN	797c	
		שׁנים	TWO	1041b	2
7	79	בלל	MIX	117c	2
		מזרק	BOWL	284d	2 b
7	80	מלא	FULL	571a	
7	81	מלא	FULL	571a	
		עלה	WHOLE BURNT OF-FERING	750c	
7	82	חטאת	SIN	309c	4 a
7	83	אחירע	AHIRA	27c	
		עינן	ENAN	745d	
7	84	את	WITH	86d	4 b
		מזבח	ALTAR	259a	9
		מזרק	BOWL	284d	2 b
		חנכה	DEDICATION	335c	
		קערה	DISH	891a	
		שׁנים	TWO	1041b	2
7	85	מזרק	BOWL	284d	2 b
		קערה	DISH	891a	
		שׁבעים	SEVENTY	988c	1 e
7	86	מלא	FULL	571a	
		עשׂרים	TWENTY	798a	1 2d
		קטרת	SMOKE	882d	2
7	87	בקר	CATTLE	133b	1 a
		חטאת	SIN	309c	4 a
		עלה	WHOLE BURNT OF-FERING	750c	
		שׂעיר	HE-GOAT	972c	
		שׂעיר	HE-GOAT	972c	
7	88	בקר	CATTLE	133b	1 a
		מזבח	ALTAR	259a	9
		חנכה	DEDICATION	335c	
		פר	YOUNG BULL	830d	2 a
		ארבע	FOUR	917b	2 b
		שׁשׁים	SIXTY	995d	
		ארון	CHEST	75c	3 g
7	89	בין	INTERVAL	*107d	D
		דבר	SPEAK	181b	3 d
		דבר	SPEAK	182a	
		דבר	SPEAK	*182a	
		כפרת	PROPITIATORY	498c	
		כרוב	CHERUB	500d	4 a
		עדות	TESTIMONY	730b	1
		על	UPON	758c	4 2a
8	2	אור	BECOME LIGHT	21b	1
		מול	IN FRONT OF	557c	2 a
		מנורה	LAMPSTAND	633b	3
		שׁבע	SEVEN	988a	1 c
8	3	כן	SO	486c	2 da
		מול	IN FRONT OF	557c	2 a
		מנורה	LAMPSTAND	633b	3
8	4	זהב	GOLD	263a	6
		ירך	BASE	438a	3
		כן	SO	486b	2 ab
		מן	FROM	582a	5 b
		מנורה	LAMPSTAND	633b	3
		עד	AS FAR AS	724b	1 1b
		פרח	BUD	827b	
		מקשׁה	HAMMERED WORK	904d	
		ראה	TO SEE	908d	1 a2
		מראה	VISION	909d	1 c
8	6	מהר	BE CLEAN	372c	1 b
		לוי	LEVITE	533a	3 1d
8	7	בשׂר	FLESH	142c	2
		חטאת	SIN	310a	5
		מהר	BE CLEAN	372c	1 b
		מהר	BE CLEAN	372c	1 b
		מי	WATER	565c	1 a
		נזה	SPURT	633b	
		עבר	PASS OVER	718d	1 b
		תער	RAZOR	789b	1 a
8	8	בלל	MIX	117c	2
		חטאת	SIN	309c	4 b
		מנחה	OFFERING	585c	5 b
		פר	YOUNG BULL	830d	2 c
8	9	בן	SON	120d	1 jg
		עדה	CONGREGATION	417b	3
		כבס	WASH	460a	1
		קהל	ASSEMBLE AS	875a	2
		קרב	COME NEAR	898a	2 a1
8	10	סמך	LEAN	702a	1 a
		קרב	COME NEAR	898a	2 a1
8	11	נוף	WAVE	632a	4
		עבדה	LABOR	715b	4
8	12	חטאת	SIN	309c	4 b
		כפר	COVER OVER	497d	3 b2
		סמך	LEAN	701d	1 a
		עלה	WHOLE BURNT OF-FERING	750c	
		עלה	WHOLE BURNT OF-FERING	750d	
		פר	YOUNG BULL	830d	2 c
8	13	נוף	WAVE	632a	4
		תנופה	WAVING	632c	2
8	14	בדל	BE DIVIDED	95b	2
8	15	מהר	BE CLEAN	372c	1 b
		נוף	WAVE	632a	4
		תנופה	WAVING	632c	2 a
		עבד	WORK	713b	5
8	16	בכור	FIRST-BORN	114b	1 b
		כל	ALL	482c	2 a
		לקח	TAKE	543a	4 a
		נתן	GIVE	678c	1 b
		נתינם	NETHINIM	*682a	
		פטרה	THAT WHICH SEPA-RATES	809d	
		רחם	WOMB	933b	1
8	17	בכור	FIRST-BORN	114b	1 d
		נכה	SMITE	646a	2 c
		קדשׁ	BE SET APART	873c	1 c

Ch v.	Heb	Eng	Page	Sec
8 18	בכור	FIRST-BORN	114b	1 d
8 19	כפר	COVER OVER	498a	3 b2
	לוי	LEVITE	533a	3 1d
	נגף	BLOW	620a	1
	נגש	DRAW NEAR	620d	1
	נתן	GIVE	678c	1 b
	נתינים	NETHINIM	*682a	
	עבד	WORK	713b	5
	עבדה	LABOR	715b	4
8 20	בן	SON	120d	1 jg
	עדה	CONGREGATION	417b	3 *
	כן	SO	486c	2 cc
	ל	TO	514b	5 fa
	תנופה	WAVING	632c	2 a
8 21	חטא	MISS A GOAL OR WAY	307d	2 a
	מהר	BE CLEAN	372c	1 b
	כפר	COVER OVER	497d	3 b2
	כפר	COVER OVER	498a	3 b2
	נוף	WAVE	632a	4
8 22	כן	SO	486c	2 ca
	עבד	WORK	713b	5
	עבדה	LABOR	715b	4
	צוה	COMMAND	845d	1 e
8 24	בן	SON	122a	9 a
	זה	THIS	260d	1 a
	עבדה	LABOR	715b	4
	מעל	ABOVE	751d	2 bb a
	עשרים	TWENTY	797d	1 2a
	צבא	SERVE	838d	2
	צבא	SERVICE	839b	3 a
8 25	בן	SON	122a	9 a
	עבד	WORK	713b	5
	עבדה	LABOR	715c	4
	צבא	SERVICE	839b	3 a
8 26	שוב	TURN BACK	997d	1
	ככה	THUS	462c	
	עבד	WORK	713b	5
	עבדה	LABOR	715b	4
	שרת	SERVE	1058b	2 b
9 1	סיני	SINAI	696a	
9 2	מועד	APPOINTED TIME	417c	1 a
	פסח	PASSOVER	820b	3
9 3	חקה	SOMETHING PRESCRIBED	350a	2 d
	מועד	APPOINTED TIME	417c	1 a
	ערב	SUNSET	788a	1 b
9 4	עשה	DO	795a	2 6
	פסח	PASSOVER	820b	3
9 5	כן	SO	486c	2 cc
	סיני	SINAI	696a	
	ערב	SUNSET	788a	1 b
	פסח	PASSOVER	820b	3
	פסח	PASSOVER	820b	3
	ראשון	FIRST	911d	2 a
9 6	אדם	MAN	9b	1
	היה	BE	226d	3 1
	טמא	UNCLEAN	379d	2 a
	יכל	BE ABLE	407c	1 a
	ל	TO	514d	5 g
	נפש	SOUL	660c	4 c5
	עשה	DO	795a	2 6
	פסח	PASSOVER	820b	3
	קרב	COME NEAR	897c	1 c
9 7	אדם	MAN	9b	1
	אנחנו	WE	59d	
	גרע	RESTRAIN	175d	2
	טמא	UNCLEAN	379d	2 a
	מועד	APPOINTED TIME	417c	1 a
	ל	TO	514d	5 g
	נפש	SOUL	660c	4 c5
	קרבן	OFFERING	898d	
9 8	מה	WHAT	552d	1 b
	צוה	COMMAND	845d	1 e
9 10	דור	GENERATION	190a	2 c
	דרך	JOURNEY	203a	2
	טמא	UNCLEAN	379d	2 a
	ל	TO	512d	5 aa
	ל	TO	514d	5 g
	נפש	SOUL	660c	4 c5
	עשה	DO	795a	2 6
	פסח	PASSOVER	820b	3
	רחק	DISTANT	935b	1 a
9 11	מרר	BITTER HERB	601a	
	מצה	UNLEAVENED BREAD	695b	
	על	UPON	755c	2 4c
	ערב	SUNSET	788a	1 b
9 12	בקר	MORNING	134b	2
	חקה	SOMETHING PRESCRIBED	350a	1
	עצם	BONE	782d	2
	פסח	PASSOVER	820b	3
	שאר	REMAIN	984b	2
	שבר	BREAK	990c	
9 13	אשר	PARTICLE OF RELATION	82a	2 a
	דרך	JOURNEY	203a	2
	הוא	HE, SHE, IT	215d	2 c
	חדל	CEASE	293a	2
	חטא	SIN	308a	3
	מועד	APPOINTED TIME	417c	1 a
	כרת	BE CUT OFF	504b	1 c
	נפש	SOUL	660b	4 c2
	נשא	LIFT	671a	2 b
	עם	KINSMAN	769c	

Ch v.	Heb	Eng	Page	Sec
	עשה	DO	795a	2 6
	פסח	PASSOVER	820b	3
	קרבן	OFFERING	898d	
9 14	גור	SOJOURN	157d	1
	גר	SOJOURNER	158b	2
	גר	SOJOURNER	*158c	2
	ו	AND	253a	1 h
	אזרח	A NATIVE	280c	1
	חקה	SOMETHING PRESCRIBED	350a	1
	חקה	SOMETHING PRESCRIBED	350a	1
	כן	SO	486b	2 ab
	עשה	DO	795a	2 6
	פסח	PASSOVER	820b	3
	פסח	PASSOVER	820b	3
9 15	אהל	TENT	14a	3
	אש	FIRE	77c	1
	בקר	MORNING	134a	1 e
	כ	LIKE	453d	1 b
	כסה	COVER	491d	4
	עדות	TESTIMONY	730b	1
	מראה	VISION	909c	1 b
9 16	אש	FIRE	77c	2
	כן	SO	485d	1 a
	כסה	COVER	491d	4
	לילה	NIGHT	539a	1
	תמיד	CONTINUITY	556c	1 b
	מראה	VISION	909c	1 b
9 17	נסע	SET OUT	652a	2 a
	עלה	GO UP	749a	1 c1
	על	UPON	758c	4 2a
	פה	MOUTH	805d	6 c1
	מקום	STANDING PLACE	880b	4
	שכן	SETTLE DOWN	1015a	1 c
9 18	חנה	DECLINE	333c	2 b
	חנה	DECLINE	333d	2 c2
	יום	DAY	400b	7 d8
	שכן	SETTLE DOWN	1015a	1 c
	משכן	DWELLING-PLACE	1015d	2 c
9 19	ארך	BE LONG	73d	2
	יום	DAY	399c	5 b
	משמרת	GUARD	1038c	3
9 20	חנה	DECLINE	333c	2 b
	חנה	DECLINE	333d	2 c2
	יש	BE	442a	2 cd
	מספר	NUMBER	709a	1 a
9 21	בקר	MORNING	134a	1 e
	בקר	MORNING	134a	1 e
	יומם	DAYTIME	401c	1
	יש	BE	442a	2 cd
	עלה	GO UP	749a	1 c1
9 22	ארך	BE LONG	73d	2
	חדש	NEW MOON	294c	2 a
	חנה	DECLINE	333c	2 b
	חנה	DECLINE	333d	2 c2
	יום	DAY	399c	5 b
	יום	YEAR	399d	6 c
	עלה	GO UP	749a	1 c1
	שכן	SETTLE DOWN	1015a	1 c
	משכן	DWELLING-PLACE	1015d	2 c
9 23	חנה	DECLINE	333c	2 b
	חנה	DECLINE	333d	2 c2
	יד	HAND	391a	5 d
	משמרת	GUARD	1038c	3
10 2	את	MARK OF THE ACCUSATIVE	85b	1 d
	מחנה	ENCAMPMENT	334a	1 a
	כסף	SILVER	494b	7
	מסע	PULLING UP	652c	1 a
	מקרא	CONVOCATION	896d	2
	מקשה	HAMMERED WORK	904d	
10 3	הם	THEY	241d	8 d
	חצצרה	CLARION	348c	2 b
	יעד	GATHER BY APPOINTMENT	417a	3
	תקע	GIVE A BLOW	1075c	2
10 4	אלף	THOUSAND	49b	2
	חצצרה	CLARION	348c	2 a
	יעד	GATHER BY APPOINTMENT	417a	3
	תקע	GIVE A BLOW	1075c	2
	אחד	ADDENDA ET CORRIGENDA	1120a	
10 5	מחנה	ENCAMPMENT	*334a	1 a
	מחנה	ENCAMPMENT	334a	1 a
	מחנה	ENCAMPMENT	334b	3 a
	מחנה	ENCAMPMENT	334b	3 a
	חצצרה	CLARION	348c	2 b
	נסע	SET OUT	652a	2 a
	קדם	EASTWARD	870a	
	תרועה	SHOUT OF WAR	930a	2
	תקע	GIVE A BLOW	1075c	2
10 6	מחנה	ENCAMPMENT	334a	1 a
	מחנה	ENCAMPMENT	*334a	1 a
	מחנה	ENCAMPMENT	334b	3 a
	מחנה	ENCAMPMENT	334b	3 b
	חצצרה	CLARION	348c	2 b
	תימן	SOUTH	412d	1 b
	נסע	SET OUT	652a	2 a
	תרועה	SHOUT OF WAR	930a	2
10 7	חצצרה	CLARION	348c	2 a
	קהל	ASSEMBLE AS	875a	2
	רוע	RAISE A SHOUT	929c	2
	תקע	GIVE A BLOW	1075c	2

Ch v.	Heb	Eng	Page	Sec
10 8	אהרן	AARON	14d	
	בן	SON	121a	1 jz
	דור	GENERATION	190a	2 c
	חצצרה	CLARION	348c	2 a
	חקה	SOMETHING PRESCRIBED	350a	1
	כהן	PRIEST	464a	7
	עולם	LONG DURATION	762c	2 e
	תקע	GIVE A BLOW	1075c	2
10 9	איב	BE HOSTILE TO	33c	
	זכר	REMEMBER	270c	1 b 1
	חצצרה	CLARION	348c	2 b
	ישע	BE DELIVERED	446b	1
	צרר	SHEW HOSTILITY TOWARD	865c	
	צר	ADVERSARY	865d	
	רוע	RAISE A SHOUT	929c	2
10 10	יהוה	YAHWEH	219b	2 2d
	זכרון	MEMORIAL	272a	1 d
	חדש	NEW MOON	*294c	2
	חצצרה	CLARION	348c	2 a
	מועד	APPOINTED TIME	417b	1 b
	על	UPON	755d	2 5
	ראש	HEAD	911b	4 b
	שמחה	JOY	970d	2
	תקע	GIVE A BLOW	1075c	2
10 11	עדות	TESTIMONY	730b	1
	עלה	GO UP	749a	1 c1
	עשרים	TWENTY	798a	2 1
	משכן	DWELLING-PLACE	1015d	2 c
10 12	נסע	JOURNEY	652b	3
	מסע	JOURNEY	652d	2
	סיני	SINAI	696a	
	פארן	PARAN	803a	
	שכן	SETTLE DOWN	1015a	1 c
10 13	יד	HAND	391a	5 d
	נסע	JOURNEY	652b	3
	ראשון	FIRST	912a	3 a1
10 14	דגל	STANDARD	186b	
	נחשון	NAHSHON	638c	
	נסע	JOURNEY	652b	3
	על	UPON	755a	2 3
	עמינדב	AMMINADAB	770b	1
	צבא	ARMY	839a	1 a
	ראשון	FIRST	912a	3 a2
10 15	יששכר	ISSACHAR	441a	1
	נתנאל	NETHANEL	682a	1
	צבא	ARMY	839a	1 a
10 16	צוער	ZUAR	859b	
	אליאב	ELIAB	45a	A
	זבולן	ZEBULUN	259d	2
	חלן	HELON	298b	
10 17	גרשון	GERSHON	177b	
	גרשון	GERSHON	*177b	
	ו	AND	252b	1 b
	ירד	BE BROUGHT DOWN	434b	2
	מררי	MERARI	601b	
	נסע	SET OUT	652a	2 a
10 18	אליצור	ELIZUR	45d	
	דגל	STANDARD	186b	
	נסע	SET OUT	652a	2 a
	נסע	SET OUT	*652b	2 a
	ראובן	REUBEN	910a	2
10 19	שדיאור	SHEDEUR	994d	
	צורישדי	ZURISHADDAI	849d	
	שלמיאל	SHELUMIEL	1025a	
	שמעון	SIMEON	1035c	2
	אליסף	ELIASAPH	45c	A
10 20	גד	GAD	151c	1 b
	דעואל	DEUEL	396a	
10 21	נסע	SET OUT	652a	2 a
	עד	AS FAR AS	724c	12a b
	קהתי	KOHATHITES	875c	
	קהתי	KOHATHITES	875c	
10 22	אפרים	EPHRAIM	68b	2
	דגל	STANDARD	186b	
	נסע	SET OUT	652a	2 a
	נסע	SET OUT	*652b	2 a
	עמיהוד	AMMIHUD	770b	2
10 23	מנשה	MANASSEH	586d	1 b3 g
	פדהצור	PEDAHZUR	804c	
10 24	אבידן	ABIDAN	4a	
	בנימן	BENJAMIN	122d	1
	גדעני	GIDEONI	154c	
10 25	אחיזר	AHIEZER	27b	1
	אסף	GATHER	63a	3
	דגל	STANDARD	186b	
	דן	DAN	192d	2
	מחנה	ENCAMPMENT	334a	1 a
	ל	TO	513a	5 ad
	נסע	SET OUT	652a	2 a
10 26	עמישדי	AMMISHADDAI	770b	
	אשר	ASHER	81b	2
	עכרן	OCHRAN	747d	
	פגעיאל	PAGIEL	803c	
10 27	אחירע	AHIRA	27c	
	עינן	ENAN	745d	
	נפתלי	NAPHTALI	836d	2
10 28	נסע	JOURNEY	652b	3
10 29	אמר	SAY	56a	1
	אנחנו	WE	59d	
	דבר	SPEAK	181c	5
	מדיני	MIDIANITE	193c	2
	חבב	HOBAB	285d	
	חתן	WIFE'S FATHER	368c	1

Ch	v.	Heb	Eng	Page	Sec
		טוב	PLEASANT	374a	2 f
		יטב	DO GOOD TO	405d	2
		נסע	JOURNEY	652b	3
		קין	KENITE	883d	1
10	30	רעואל	REUEL	946c	1
		מולדת	KINDRED	409d	1
		כי אם	BUT	475a	2 b
10	31	חנה	DECLINE	333c	2 c2
		כי על כן	FOR THEREFORE	475c	
		נא	PART OF EN-TREATY	609b	3 b
		עזב		737a	1 a
10	32	היה	COME TO PASS	225b	1 2b bd
		טוב	A GOOD THING	375b	3
		יטב	DO GOOD TO	405d	2
		יטב	DO GOOD TO	405d	2
		כי	IF	473b	2 b
10	33	ארון	CHEST	75c	3 f
		ברית	COVENANT	136d	2 2c
		דרך	JOURNEY	203a	2
		הר	MOUNTAIN	249b	1 a
		הר	MOUNTAIN	*249b	1 a
		יום	DAY	398b	2 b
		מנוחה	RESTING PLACE	629d	1
		נסע	JOURNEY	652b	3
		נסע	JOURNEY	652b	3
		פנה	FACE	817c	2 4c a
		תור	SEEK OUT	1064b	1
10	34	יומם	BY DAY	401c	2
		נסע	SET OUT	652b	2 a
		על	UPON	755d	2 5
		ענן	CLOUD	778a	1 a
10	35	איב	BE HOSTILE TO	33c	
		נוס	FLEE	630d	1
		נסע	SET OUT	652a	2 a
		פוץ	BE DISPERSED	807a	
		קום	STAND	878b	6 a
		שנא	HATE	971d	2
10	36	אלף	THOUSAND	49b	2
		נוח	REST	628b	1
		רבבה	MULTITUDE	914b	
		שוב	TURN BACK	997b	3 a
11	1	אזן	EAR	24b	2 b
		אנן	COMPLAIN	59d	
		אש	FIRE	77c	2
		בער	BURN	129a	3
		היה	BECOME	226a	2 2c
		חרה	BURN	354a	2 a
		כ	LIKE	*454b	1 d
		עם	PEOPLE	766c	1
		קצה	END	892b	2
		רע	EVIL	948d	1
11	2	אש	FIRE	77c	2
		פלל	INTERVENE	813b	1
		שקע	SINK	1054b	
11	3	אש	FIRE	77c	2
		בער	BURN	129a	3
		תבערה	TEBERAH	*129c	
		תבערה	TEBERAH	129c	
		צעק	CRY	858c	1 a
11	4	אוה	DESIRE	16b	
		תאוה	DESIRE	16c	1
		אכל	EAT	37d	1
		אספסף	COLLECTION	63c	
		בכה	WEEP	113b	1
		בשר	FLESH	142c	1 a
		מי	WHO	566c	F a
		שוב	TURN BACK	998b	8
11	5	אבטחים	WATER-MELONS	*105c	
		אבטחים	WATER-MELONS	105d	
		בצל	ONION	130b	
		בשר	FLESH	142c	1 a
		דגה	FISH	185d	
		זכר	REMEMBER	269d	1 1 a
		חנם	OUT OF FAVOR	336c	A
		חציר	GREEN GRASS	348b	1
		קשאה	CUCUMBERS	903d	
		קשא	CUCUMBERS	903d	
		שום	GARLIC	1002c	
11	6	אין	NOT	34d	4 a
		בלת	EXCEPT	116c	3
		בשר	FLESH	142c	1 a
		יבש	DRY	386d	1
		כל	ALL	482c	2 a
		מן	MANNA	577b	
11	7	בדלח	BDELLIUM	95d	
		בשר	FLESH	142c	1 a
		גד	CORIANDER	151c	
		זרע	SOWING	282b	2 c
		מן	MANNA	577b	
11	8	עין	EYE	745a	4 b
		בשר	FLESH	142c	1 a
		בשל	BOIL	143a	1
		דוך	POUND	189a	
		מדכה	MORTAR	189a	
		ה	THE	207d	1 f
		טחן	GRIND	377c	
		טעם	TASTE	381a	1
		לקט	GATHER UP	544d	1
		לשד	DAINTY	545c	
		עגה	BREAD-CAKE	728b	
		עשה	DO	794c	2 1g
		פרור	POT	807d	
		שוט	GO ABOUT	1002a	
		שמן	OIL	1032b	2 b
11	9	בשר	FLESH	142c	1 a

Ch	v.	Heb	Eng	Page	Sec
		טל	NIGHT-MIST	378c	
11	10	ירד	GO DOWN	433c	3 a
		ירד	GO DOWN	433c	3 a
		מן	MANNA	577b	
		בכה	WEEP	113b	1
		בשר	FLESH	142c	1
		חרה	BURN	354a	2 a
		ל	TO	511d	2
		מאד	EXCEEDINGLY	*547b	2 a
		פתח	OPENING	835d	
		רעע	BE EVIL	949c	1
		שמע	HEAR	1033c	1 b
11	11	משפחה	CLAN	1046d	1 c
		בשר	FLESH	142c	1 a
		חן	FAVOR	336b	2 b2
		מצא	FIND	592d	1
		משא	LOAD	672c	1
		עבד	SLAVE	714c	6
		רעע	BE EVIL	949c	1
11	12	אדמה	LAND	10a	5
		אם	IF	50d	2 ab a
		אמן	CONFIRM	52d	2
		אנכי	I	59a	
		בשר	FLESH	142c	1 a
		ה	THE	207d	1 f
		הרה	CONCEIVE	247d	1
		חיק	BOSOM	300d	2
		ילד	BEAR	*408b	2 a
		ילד	BEGET	*408c	2 a
		ינק	SUCK	413b	
		כאשר	AS	455c	1 d
		על	UPON	757a	2 7c a
		עם	PEOPLE	766c	1
		שבע	SWEAR	989c	2
11	13	אין	WHENCE	32d	
		בכה	WEEP	113c	5
		בשר	FLESH	142c	1
		על	UPON	753b	2 1b
		עם	PEOPLE	766c	1
11	14	בד	SEPARATION	94c	1 b
		בשר	FLESH	142c	1 a
		יכל	BE ABLE	407c	1 a
		כבד	HEAVY	458b	1 d
11	15	את	THOU	61d	
		בשר	FLESH	142c	1 a
		גם	ALSO	169b	2
		הרג	KILL	247b	2
		חן	FAVOR	336b	2 b2
		ככה	THUS	462c	
		מצא	FIND	592d	1 a
		ראה	TO SEE	908a	8 a3
		רעה	MISERY	949a	1
11	16	אסף	GATHER	62b	1 a
		בשר	FLESH	142c	1 a
		הם	THEY	*241c	1 a
		זקן	OLD	278d	2 b
		מועד	TENT OF MEETING	418a	5
		יצב	STATION ONESELF	426b	A
		ל	TO	515b	5 hb a
		שטר	OFFICIAL	1009c	
11	17	אצל	LAY ASIDE	69b	
		אצל	LAY ASIDE	69b	
		את	WITH	86a	1 a
		ב	IN	88c	1 2b
		בשר	FLESH	142c	1 a
		דבר	SPEAK	181b	3 e
		ירד	GO DOWN	433b	2
		מן	FROM	580d	3 ba
		נשא	LIFT	671a	2 a
		משא	LOAD	672c	1
		רוח	BREATH	925d	9 a
		שום	TO PLACE	963b	1 b
11	18	אזן	EAR	24b	2 b
		אכל	EAT	37d	1
		בכה	WEEP	113c	1
		בשר	FLESH	142c	1 a
		טוב	PLEASING	373b	4
		ל	TO	*517a	6 a
		מחר	TO-MORROW	564a	1
		מי	WHO	566c	F a
11	19	קדש	BE SET APART	873c	4
		בשר	FLESH	142c	1 a
		יום	DAY	400a	7 a6
11	20	אמר	SAY	56b	1
		אף	NOSE	60a	1
		בכה	WEEP	113c	5
		בשר	FLESH	142c	1 a
		זה	THIS	261c	4 e
		זרא	LOATHSOME THING	266d	
		חדש	NEW MOON	294c	2 a
		חדש	NEW MOON	294c	2 a
		יום	TIME	399d	6 b
		יצא	GO OUT	422d	1 a
		מאס	REJECT	549c	1 a
		עד	UNTIL	725a	2 1a b
		יען	ON ACCOUNT OF	774d	2 b
11	21	אלף	THOUSAND	49a	1 c
		בשר	FLESH	142c	1 a
		חדש	NEW MOON	294c	2 a
		יום	TIME	399d	6 b
		רגלי	ON FOOT	920b	1
11	22	אם	IF	50d	2 ab a
		אסף	GATHER	62d	1 b
		בשר	FLESH	142c	1 a
		דג	FISH	185d	

Ch	v.	Heb	Eng	Page	Sec
		מצא	FIND	593c	4
		מצא	FIND	*594b	3
11	23	שחט	SLAUGHTER	1006b	
		בשר	FLESH	142c	1 a
		ה	INTERROG PART	209d	1 b
		ה	INTERROG PART	210b	2 b
		יד	HAND	390a	1 e2
		לא	NOT	519a	1 ad b
		עתה	NOW	774a	1 b
		קצר	BE SHORT	894a	
		קרה	ENCOUNTER	899c	2
11	24	ראה	TO SEE	907b	5 a
		אהל	TENT	14a	3
		אסף	GATHER	62b	1
		בשר	FLESH	142c	1 a
		דבר	WORD	183b	3 2
		זקן	OLD	278d	2 b
		נביא	PROPHET	611c	1
		סביב	ROUND ABOUT	687b	2 bb
		עמד	STAND	764c	1
11	25	אצל	LAY ASIDE	69b	
		בשר	FLESH	142c	1 a
		זקן	OLD	278d	2 b
		יסף	ADD	414d	
		ירד	GO DOWN	433b	2
		נבא	PROPHESY	612b	1 a
		נוח	REST	628a	1
		ענן	CLOUD	778a	1 a
		רוח	BREATH	925d	9 a
		שבעים	SEVENTY	988c	1 a
11	26	אהל	TENT	14a	3
		אלדד	ELDAD	44d	
		בשר	FLESH	142c	1 a
		חדש	NEW MOON	294c	2 a
		מידד	MEDAD	392a	
		כתב	WRITE	507d	3
		נבא	PROPHESY	612b	1 a
		נוח	REST	628a	1
		רוח	BREATH	925d	9 a
		שאר	REMAIN	984a	2
11	27	אלדד	ELDAD	44d	
		בשר	FLESH	142c	1 a
		ה	THE	207d	1 d
		מידד	MEDAD	392a	
		נבא	PROPHESY	612b	1 a
		רוץ	RUN	930b	1
11	28	אדון	LORD	11b	3 1g
		בחורים	YOUTH	104c	
		בן	SON	120c	1 g
		בשר	FLESH	142c	1 a
		יהושע	JOSHUA	221c	1
		כלא	RESTRAIN	476b	2
		נון	NUN	630c	
		ענה	ANSWER	773a	2 a
		שרת	SERVE	1058a	1 c
11	29	בשר	FLESH	142c	1 a
		ל	TO	515c	5 hc
		מי	WHO	566c	F a
		נתן	GIVE	678d	1 f
		עם	PEOPLE	766c	1
		קנא	BE ZEALOUS	888c	3 a
		רוח	BREATH	925d	9 a
11	30	אסף	GATHER	62d	2 b
		בשר	FLESH	142c	1 a
		זקן	OLD	278d	2 b
11	31	אמה	CUBIT	52b	1
		את	WITH	86d	4 c
		בשר	FLESH	142c	1 a
		דרך	JOURNEY	203a	2
		יום	DAY	398b	2 b
		כ	LIKE	453c	1 a
		כה	THUS	462b	2
		נטש	LEAVE	643d	1
		נסע	JOURNEY	652c	2 a
		סביב	ROUND ABOUT	687b	2 bb
		רוח	BREATH	924d	2 a
		שלו	QUAIL	969c	
11	32	אסף	GATHER	62b	1 c
		בשר	FLESH	142c	1 a
		יום	DAY	398b	1
		לילה	NIGHT	539a	1
		מחרת	THE MORROW	564a	
		מעט	BE SMALL	589d	B
		סביב	ROUND ABOUT	687b	2 bb
		קום	STAND	877d	1 e
		שלו	QUAIL	969c	
11	33	בשר	FLESH	142c	1 a
		חרה	BURN	354a	2 a
		טרם	NOT YET	382c	1
		כרת	BE CUT OFF	504b	3
		נכה	SMITE	646c	4 a
		מכה	SLAUGHTER	647a	4
		עוד	STILL	728d	1 aa
		רב	GREAT	913c	2 a
		שן	TOOTH	1042a	1 a
11	34	אוה	DESIRE	16b	
		תאוה	DESIRE	16c	1
		עם	PEOPLE	766d	4
		קבר	BURY	868c	
		ה קברותהתאו	KIBROTH-HATTA-AVAH	*869a	
11	35	תאוה	DESIRE	16c	1
		חצרות	HAZEROTH	348a	
		נסע	JOURNEY	652b	3
		ה קברותהתאו	KIBROTH-HATTA-AVAH	869a	

Ch	v.	Heb	Eng	Page	Sec
12	1	אודה	CAUSE	15c	
		דבר	SPEAK	181c	4 d
		כושי	CUSHITE	469a	A
		מרים	MIRIAM	599b	1
12	2	ב	IN	89d	3 2b
		דבר	SPEAK	181c	4a
		רק	ONLY	956b	2 a
12	3	אדמה	GROUND	9d	4
		כל	ALL	*481c	1 b
		על	UPON	752d	2 1
		ענו	POOR	776c	4
12	4	מועד	TENT OF MEETING	418a	5
		מרים	MIRIAM	599b	1
		פתאם	SUDDENNESS	837b	
		שלש	THREE	1025d	
12	5	אהל	TENT	14a	3
		ירד	GO DOWN	433b	1
		מרים	MIRIAM	599b	1
		פתח	OPENING	835d	
12	6	דבר	SPEAK	181c	4 a
		דבר	WORD	183b	3 2
		חלום	DREAM	321d	2 a
		ידע	MAKE ONESELF KNOWN	395b	
		נביא	PROPHET	611c	1
		מראה	VISION	909b	
		שמע	HEAR	1033d	1 f
12	7	אמן	CONFIRM	53a	5
		משה	MOSES	602d	
		עבד	SLAVE	714a	3
12	8	אל	TO	40a	3 a
		ב	IN	89b	2 4a
		ב	IN	89d	3 2b
		דבר	SPEAK	181c	4 a
		דבר	SPEAK	181c	4 d
		ו	AND	254c	4
		חידה	RIDDLE	295b	1
		ירא	FEAR	431b	1 d
		תמונה	LIKENESS	568c	
		נבט	LOOK	613c	1 a
		עבד	SLAVE	714a	3
		פה	MOUTH	805a	2 a
		פה	MOUTH	805b	2 c
		מראה	VISION	909c	1 b
12	9	חרה	BURN	354a	2 a
12	10	אהל	TENT	14a	3
		מרים	MIRIAM	599b	1
		סור	TURN ASIDE	693d	2
		על	UPON	758c	4 2a
		פנה	TURN	815b	2 a
		צרע	BE STRUCK WITH LEPROSY	864a	
		שלג	SNOW	1017a	
12	11	בי	I PRAY	106c	
		חטא	MISS A GOAL OR WAY	307b	2 b
		חטאת	SIN	308c	1 a
		יאל	BE FOOLISH	383d	1
		על	UPON	756c	27 a b
		שית	PUT	1011b	1
12	12	אכל	EAT	37d	3
		אם	MOTHER	51c	1
		אם	MOTHER	51c	1
		בשר	FLESH	142c	1 a
		יצא	GO OUT	423c	1 h
		נא	PART OF EN-TREATY	609b	3 c
		רחם	WOMB	933b	1
12	13	אל	GOD	42d	6 e
		בי	I PRAY	*106c	
		נא	PART OF EN-TREATY	609b	3 b
		נא	PART OF EN-TREATY	609b	3
		צעק	CRY	858c	1 b
		רפא	HEAL	950c	1 a
12	14	אסף	GATHER	62d	2 b
		ירק	SPIT	439a	
		כלם	BE HUMILIATED	483d	1
		סגר	BE SHUT UP	689b	1
		פנה	FACE	816d	2 3a
12	15	אסף	GATHER	62d	2 b
		מרים	MIRIAM	599b	1
		נסע	SET OUT	652a	2 a
		סגר	BE SHUT UP	689b	1
12	16	חצרות	HAZEROTH	348a	
		פארן	PARAN	803a	
13	2	כל	ALL	482c	2 a
		פארן	PARAN	803a	
		תור	SPY OUT	1064c	2
13	3	שלח	SEND	1018b	1 a
13	4	זכור	ZACCUR	271d	1
		ראובן	REUBEN	910a	2
13	5	שמוע	SHAMMUA	1035d	
		חרי	HORITE	360a	3 b
		שמעון	SIMEON	1035c	2
		שפט	SHAPHAT	1048b	2
13	6	יהודה	JUDAH	397b	1 2
		כלב	CALEB	477a	
		יפנה	JEPHUNNEH	819c	1
13	7	יגאל	IGAL	145d	1
		יוסף	JOSEPH	415d	2
		יששכר	ISSACHAR	441a	1
13	8	אפרים	EPHRAIM	68b	2
		יהושע	JOSHUA	221c	1
		הושע	HOSHEA	448a	1
		נון	NUN	630c	
13	9	בנימין	BENJAMIN	122d	1
		עיר	CITY	746d	3
		פלטי	PALTI	812d	1
13	10	רפוא	RAPHU	951b	
		גדיאל	GADDIEL	151d	
		זבולן	ZEBULUN	259d	2
		סודי	SODI	691d	
13	11	גדי	GADDI	151d	
		יוסף	JOSEPH	415d	1 b
		מנשה	MANASSEH	586d	1 b3 g
		סוסי	SUSI	692d	
13	12	דן	DAN	192d	2
		עמיאל	AMMIEL	770a	2
13	13	אשר	ASHER	81b	2
		מיכאל	MICHAEL	567c	1
		סתור	SETHUR	712c	
13	14	ופסי	VOPHSI	255c	
		נחבי	NAHBI	286a	
13	15	גאואל	GEUEL	145b	
		גד	GAD	151c	1 b
		מכי	MACHI	568d	
13	16	יהושע	JOSHUA	221c	1
		יהושע	JOSHUA	221c	1
		הושע	HOSHEA	448a	1
		נון	NUN	630c	
		תור	SPY OUT	1064c	2
13	17	את	MARK OF THE ACCUSATIVE	85b	2 a
		הר	MOUNTAIN	251a	2 a
		זה	THIS	261c	4 g
		נגב	SOUTH-COUNTRY	616b	1 a
		עלה	GO UP	748b	1 c
		תור	SPY OUT	1064c	2
13	18	אם	IF	50d	2 bb
		ה	INTERROG PART	210b	2 b
		ה	INTERROG PART	210b	2 b
		חזק	STRONG	305c	1 a
		מה	WHAT	552d	1 b
		מעט	A FEW	590a	1 a
		ראה	TO SEE	907a	2 4
		רב	MUCH	913a	1 c
		רפה	SLACK	952a	
13	19	ב	IN	88a	
		מבצר	FORTIFICATION	131c	
		ה	INTERROG PART	210b	2 b
		ה	INTERROG PART	210b	2 b
		הם	THEY	241d	8 c
		מחנה	ENCAMPMENT	334b	1 b
		טוב	PLEASANT	374a	3 b
		מה	WHAT	552d	1 b
		רע	EVIL	948b	4
13	20	אין	NOT	34c	2 db
		אם	IF	50d	2 bb
		בכורים	FIRST-FRUITS	114c	
		ה	INTERROG PART	210b	2 b
		חזק	BE FIRM	305b	2
		יום	TIME	399d	6 a
		ענב	GRAPE	772a	
		פרי	FRUIT	826b	1
		רזה	LEAN	931a	
		שמן	FAT	1032a	1
13	21	בוא	COME	98d	2 e
		ביתרחוב	BETH-REHOB	112d	
		חמת	HAMATH	333a	
		צן	ZIN	856c	
		רחוב	REHOB	932b	1 a
13	22	אחימן	AHIMAN	27a	1
		אשכל	ESHCOL	79b	2
		בוא	COME	98b	2
		בנה	BUILD	125a	1 a
		חברון	HEBRON	289b	
		חברון	HEBRON	289b	
		יליד	CHILDREN	409d	
		נגב	SOUTH-COUNTRY	616b	1 a
		ענק	NECK	778c	
		פנה	FACE	817d	2 4e
		צען	ZOAN	858a	
		שם	THERE	1027a	1 a
		ששי	SHESHAI	1058d	
		תלמי	TALMAI	1068d	2
13	23	אשכול	CLUSTER	79a	1
		אשכל	ESHCOL	79b	2
		ה	THE	207c	1 d
		זמורה	BRANCH	274d	
		כרת	CUT OFF	503d	1 a
		מוט	POLE	557a	2
		מן	FROM	580d	3 ba
		נחל	WADY	636c	2
		ענב	GRAPE	772a	
		רמון	POMEGRANATE	941d	2
		שם	THERE	1027c	4 a
		תאנה	FIG	1061a	2
13	24	אודה	CAUSE	15c	
		אשכול	CLUSTER	79a	1
		אשכל	ESHCOL	79b	2
		אשכל	ESHCOL	79b	2
		כרת	CUT OFF	503d	1 a
		נחל	WADY	636c	2
13	25	תור	SPY OUT	1064c	2
13	26	בן	SON	120d	1 jg
		דבר	WORD	182b	1 1c
		מדבר	WILDERNESS	185a	3 a
		הלך	WALK	233d	1 5b
		עדה	CONGREGATION	417b	3
		פארן	PARAN	803a	
		פרי	FRUIT	826b	1
		קדש	KADESH	873d	1
		ראה	TO SEE	908d	1 a1
		שוב	TURN BACK	999c	3
13	27	אשר	PARTICLE OF RELATION	82c	4 bb
		דבש	HONEY	185b	
		זוב	FLOW	264d	2
		חלב	MILK	316c	A 4
		פרי	FRUIT	826b	1
13	28	אפס	NON-EXISTENCE	67b	2 cb
		בצר	MAKE INACCESSIBLE	131a	
		יליד	CHILDREN	409d	
		כי	THAT	472b	1 da
		עז	STRONG	738d	2
		ענק	NECK	778c	
13	29	אמרי	AMORITES	57c	2 e
		יבוסי	JEBUSITE	101a	1
		הר	MOUNTAIN	251a	2 a
		חתי	HITTITE	366d	2 a
		יד	HAND	391c	5 h3
		ים	SEA	410d	1
		ירדן	JORDAN	434d	
		כנעני	CANAANITE	489a	2 b
		נגב	SOUTH-COUNTRY	616b	1 a
		על	UPON	755d	2 6a
		עמלק	AMALEK	766a	
13	30	חס	HUSH	245b	
		יכל	PREVAIL	408a	2 b
		ירש	TAKE POSSESSION	439b	1 a
13	31	חזק	STRONG	305c	1 a
		עלה	GO UP	748c	2 c
13	32	דבה	EVIL REPORT	179b	3
		הוא	HE, SHE, IT	216a	3 b
		יצא	BRING OUT	425b	4 k
		ישב	DWELL	443b	1
		מדה	SIZE	551c	2
		תוך	MIDST	1063d	
		תור	SPY OUT	1064c	2
13	33	חגב	LOCUST	290b	
		כן	SO	485d	1 a
		נפלים	GIANTS	658c	
		ענק	NECK	778c	
		שם	THERE	1027a	1 a
14	1	בכה	WEEP	113b	1
		כל	ALL	482c	
		לילה	NIGHT	538d	1
		נשא	LIFT	670c	1 b 5
		נתן	GIVE	679d	1 x
14	2	לו	IF	530b	2
		לון	MURMUR	534a	
		קדש	HOLY	872d	2 b
14	3	בז	SPOIL	103a	2
		טוב	PLEASANT	374c	6
		נפל	FALL	657b	2 a
14	4	נתן	PUT	680d	2 c
		על	UPON	755d	2 5
14	5	עדה	CONGREGATION	417b	3
		קדש	HOLY	872d	2 d
		קהל	ASSEMBLY	874d	2 a
14	6	יהושע	JOSHUA	221c	1
		כלב	CALEB	477a	
		יפנה	JEPHUNNEH	819c	1
		תור	SPY OUT	1064c	2
14	7	ארץ	EARTH	76b	3 b
		טוב	PLEASANT	374a	3 b
		עדה	CONGREGATION	417b	3
		מאד	EXCEEDINGLY	547c	2 d
		תור	SPY OUT	1064c	2
14	8	ארץ	EARTH	76b	3 b
		אשר	PARTICLE OF RELATION	82a	2 a
		דבש	HONEY	185b	
		הוא	HE, SHE, IT	215d	2 c
		זוב	FLOW	264d	2
		חלב	MILK	316c	A 4
		חפץ	DELIGHT IN	342d	2 a
14	9	אכל	EAT	37c	1
		ארץ	EARTH	76b	4 a
		את	WITH	85d	1 a
		ירא	FEAR	431b	1 b
		לחם	FOOD	537c	3 b
		מרד	REBEL	597c	2
		על	UPON	758d	4 2a
		עם	PEOPLE	766d	5 c
		צל	SHADOW	853b	2
14	10	אבן	STONE	6b	1
		ב	IN	89d	3 2a
		כבוד	GLORY	458d	2 c1
		ראה	TO SEE	908b	1 a
		רגם	TO STONE	920c	
14	11	אות	SIGN	16d	4
		אן	WHERE	33a	2
		אמן	CONFIRM	53b	2 c
		ב	IN	90c	3 7
		נאץ	CONTEMN	611a	
14	12	עשה	DO	793d	1 la l
		גוי	NATION	156c	1
		דבר	PESTILENCE	184a	1
		ו	AND	252b	1 b
		ירש	TAKE POSSESSION	440a	4
		מן	THAN	582b	6 a
		נכה	SMITE	646c	4 a
		עצום	MIGHTY	783a	1
14	13	כח	STRENGTH	470d	3

Ch	v.	Heb	Eng	Page	Sec
14	14	ב	IN	88d	1 4
		הלך	WALK	231c	1 1d 5e
		עין	EYE	745a	5
		עמוד	PILLAR	765b	4
		ענן	CLOUD	778a	1a
		ראה	TO SEE	*908a	8 a5
		ראה	TO SEE	908b	1 a
14	15	גוי	NATION	156d	1 c
		מות	DIE	560b	2
		שמע	REPORT	1034d	
14	16	בלי	WEARING OUT	*115d	C a
		בלת	NOT	117a	4 b
		מדבר	WILDERNESS	185a	3
		יכל	BE ABLE	407c	1
		שבע	SWEAR	989c	2
		שחט	SLAUGHTER	1006b	3
14	17	אדן	LORD	11b	3 2a
		גדל	BECOME GREAT	152b	2 f
		כח	STRENGTH	470d	3
14	18	אף	NOSE	60b	3
		ארך	LONG	74a	
		חסד	GOODNESS	339b	2 3a
		נקה	BE CLEAN	667c	2
		נשא	LIFT	671b	3c
		עון	INIQUITY	731a	1 c1
		עון	INIQUITY	731a	1 c2
		פשע	TRANSGRESSION	833c	3 d
		רבע	PERTAINING TO THE FOURTH	918a	
		שלש	PERTAINING TO THE THIRD	1026d	
14	19	גדל	GREATNESS	152d	1
		חנה	HITHER	244c	A a
		חסד	GOODNESS	339b	2 3b
		מן	FROM	582a	5 c
		נשא	LIFT	671c	3 c
		סלח	FORGIVE	699b	
		עון	INIQUITY	731a	1 c2
14	20	סלח	FORGIVE	699b	
14	21	אולם	BUT	19d	
		אנכי	I	59b	
		חי	ALIVE	311d	1 a
		כבוד	GLORY	459a	2 c3
		מלא	BE FULL	570c	1
		קדוש	HOLY	872d	2 b
14	22	אות	SIGN	16d	4
		זה	THIS	261d	4 i
		כבוד	GLORY	458d	2 c1
		כי	THAT	472a	1 c
		נסה	TEST	650b	3 b
		עשה	DO	793d	1 1a 1
		פעם	OCCURRENCE	822a	3 a
14	23	אם	IF	50b	1 b2
		נאץ	CONTEMN	611a	
		שבע	SWEAR	989c	2
14	24	אחר	ANOTHER	29c	
		בוא	COME	97d	1
		זרע	SOWING	282d	4 c
		ירש	TAKE POSSESSION	440a	5
		כלב	CALEB	477a	
		מלא	FILL	570d	2
		עבד	SLAVE	714a	3
		עם	WITH	768c	4 b
		עקב	CONSEQUENCE	784d	1
		רוח	BREATH	925b	3 g
14	25	דרך	WAY	202d	1
		ים	SEA	410d	2
		כנעני	CANAANITE	489a	2 b
		מחר	TO-MORROW	564a	1 b
		נסע	JOURNEY	652b	3
		סוף	REEDS	693b	2 b
		עמלקי	AMALEKITES	766a	
		עמק	VALE	771a	
		פנה	TURN	815b	1 c
14	27	אשר	PARTICLE OF RE-LATION	82a	2 a
		הם	THEY	241c	2 c
		לון	MURMUR	534a	
		תלנה	MURMURING	534b	
		רע	EVIL	948c	0 b
14	28	אזן	EAR	24b	2 b
		אם	IF	50b	1
		דבר	SPEAK	181c	4 b
		חי	ALIVE	311d	1 a
		כאשר	AS	455b	1 b
		כן	SO	486c	2 cd
		נאם	UTTERANCE	610b	2
14	29	מדבר	WILDERNESS	185a	3
		לון	MURMUR	534a	
		נפל	FALL	657b	2 a
		מספר	NUMBER	709a	1 b
		פגר	CORPSE	803d	1
14	30	בן	SON	120c	1 g
		בן	SON	120c	1 g
		יהרשוע	JOSHUA	221c	1
		יד	HAND	389c	1 d
		כיאם	EXCEPT	474d	2 a
		כלב	CALEB	477a	
		נשא	LIFT	670b	1 b1
		שכן	SETTLE DOWN	1015c	2
14	31	אמר	SAY	56a	1
		בז	SPOIL	103a	2
		ו	AND	254c	5 a
		מאם	REJECT	549c	1 b
14	32	מדבר	WILDERNESS	185a	3
		נפל	FALL	657b	2 a
14	33	פגר	CORPSE	803d	1
		מדבר	WILDERNESS	185a	3
		זנות	FORNICATION	276b	C
		נשא	LIFT	671b	2 b
		פגר	CORPSE	803d	1
		תמם	BE FINISHED	1070c	5
14	34	יום	DAY	399d	6 c
		תנואה	OPPOSITION	626b	
		נשא	LIFT	671a	2 b
		עון	INIQUITY	731c	3
		תור	SPY OUT	1064c	2
14	35	יהוה	YAHWEH	219b	2 2d
		זה	THIS	260d	1 a
		יעד	GATHER BY AP-POINTMENT	417a	3
		מות	DIE	560a	2 b
		רע	EVIL	948c	0 b
		תמם	BE FINISHED	1070c	5
14	36	דבה	EVIL REPORT	179b	3
		יצא	BRING OUT	425b	4 k
		לון	MURMUR	534b	
		תור	SPY OUT	1064c	2
		דבה	EVIL REPORT	*179b	3
14	37	דבה	EVIL REPORT	179b	3
		יצא	BRING OUT	425b	4 k
		מות	DIE	559c	1 a1
		מגפה	PLAGUE	620a	1
		רע	EVIL	948b	2
14	38	יהרשוע	JOSHUA	221c	1
		הלך	WALK	233d	1 5a
		הם	THEY	241d	7
		כלב	CALEB	477a	
		תור	SPY OUT	1064c	2
14	39	אבל	MOURN	5c	
14	40	אמר	SAY	56a	1
		בקר	MORNING	134b	1 h
		הנה	BEHOLD	243d	
		הנה	BEHOLD	244a	A
		הר	MOUNTAIN	250d	1 m
		חטא	MISS A GOAL OR WAY	307a	2 b
14	41	הוא	HE, SHE, IT	216b	6 a
		עבר	PASS OVER	717b	1 i
		פה	MOUTH	805b	2 c
14	42	נגף	STRIKE	620a	
14	43	אחר	BEHIND	30b	4 aa
		כיעלכן	FOR THEREFORE	475c	
		כנעני	CANAANITE	489a	2 b
		נפל	FALL	657b	2 a
		עמלקי	AMALEKITES	766a	
		שוב	TURN BACK	997d	6 a
		ארון	CHEST	75c	3 f
14	44	הון	BE EASY	223b	
		הר	MOUNTAIN	250d	1 m
		ל	TO	517c	7 bb
		מוש	DEPART	559a	
		עפל	BE HEEDLESS	779c	
		קרב	INWARD PART	899b	1 f2
		חרמה	HORMAH	356c	
14	45	כנעני	CANAANITE	489a	2 b
		כתת	BEAT	510c	
		נכה	SMITE	646b	3
		עמלקי	AMALEKITES	766a	
15	2	מושב	DWELLING	444b	2 b
15	3	זבח	SACRIFICE	257d	2 5
		זבח	SACRIFICE	258a	2 7
		מועד	APPOINTED TIME	417c	1 b
		נדבה	FREEWILL-OFFER-ING	621d	2 c
		נדבה	FREEWILL-OFFER-ING	621d	2 c
		נדר	VOW	624a	5
		נדר	VOW	624a	6
		עלה	WHOLE BURNT OF-FERING	750d	
		עשה	DO	794d	2 4
		צאן	SMALL CATTLE	838b	1 a4
		ריח	SCENT	926b	2
15	4	בלל	MIX	117c	2
		הין	HIN	228d	1 a
		הין	HIN	229a	1
		מנחה	OFFERING	585c	5 b
		עשרון	TENTH PART	798a	
		רביעי	FOURTH	918a	4
15	5	הין	HIN	229a	1 c
		זבח	SACRIFICE	257d	2 5
		זבח	SACRIFICE	258a	2 7
		יין	WINE	406c	B
		נסך	DRINK-OFFERING	651a	1
		רביעי	FOURTH	918a	4
15	6	אל	RAM	18a	2 c
		בלל	MIX	117c	2
		הין	HIN	228d	1 a
		הין	HIN	229a	1
		הין	HIN	229a	2
		מנחה	OFFERING	585c	5 b
		שלישי	THIRD	1026b	
15	7	הין	HIN	229a	1 c
		יין	WINE	406c	B
		נסך	DRINK-OFFERING	651a	1
15	8	בן	SON	121c	7 b
		בקר	CATTLE	133b	1 a
		זבח	SACRIFICE	257d	2 5
		זבח	SACRIFICE	257d	2 5
		זבח	SACRIFICE	258a	2 7
		נדר	VOW	624a	5
		נדר	VOW	624a	6
		עלה	WHOLE BURNT OF-FERING	750c	
		עלה	WHOLE BURNT OF-FERING	750d	
		שלם	PEACE-OFFERING	1023c	
		שלם	PEACE-OFFERING	1023d	
15	9	בלל	MIX	117c	2
		בן	SON	121c	7 b
		בקר	CATTLE	133b	1 a
		הין	HIN	228d	1 a
		הין	HIN	229a	1
		הין	HIN	229a	1 a
		חצי	HALF	345c	1
		מנחה	OFFERING	585c	5 b
		על	UPON	755c	2 4b
		קרב	COME NEAR	898a	2 b4
15	10	הין	HIN	229a	1 a
		חצי	HALF	345c	1
		יין	WINE	406c	B
		נסך	DRINK-OFFERING	651a	1
		נסך	DRINK-OFFERING	651a	1
15	11	איל	RAM	18a	2 c
		כבה	THUS	462c	
		עז	SHE-GOAT	777c	3 a
		עשה	DO	795b	1
		שה	A SHEEP	962a	1
		שור	A HEAD OF CATTLE	1004b	
15	12	כבה	THUS	462c	
		מספר	NUMBER	709a	1 b
15	13	אלה	THESE	41c	A
		אזרח	A NATIVE	280c	1
		כבה	THUS	462c	
15	14	גור	SOJOURN	157d	1
		גר	SOJOURNER	158b	2
		גר	SOJOURNER	*158c	2
		דור	GENERATION	190a	2 ce
		כן	SO	486c	2 ce
		עשה	DO	794d	24
15	15	גור	SOJOURN	157d	1
		גר	SOJOURNER	158b	2
		גר	SOJOURNER	*158c	2
		דור	GENERATION	190a	2 c
		חקה	SOMETHING PRE-SCRIBED	350a	1
		חקה	SOMETHING PRE-SCRIBED	350a	1
		כ	LIKE	454c	2 a
		נסך	DRINK-OFFERING	651a	1
		על	UPON	758b	4 1b
		עולם	LONG DURATION	762c	2 e
15	16	גור	SOJOURN	157d	1
		גר	SOJOURNER	158b	2
		גר	SOJOURNER	*158c	2
		תורה	LAW	436a	2 a
15	19	לחם	FOOD	537b	1 b
		רום	BE HIGH	927d	3 a
		תרומה	OFFERING	929a	1
15	20	גרן	THRESHING-FLOOR	175b	
		חלה	A KIND OF CAKE	319c	2 b
		כן	SO	486b	2 ab
		מואב	MOAB	555d	2 b
		עריסה	COARSE MEAL	791b	
		ראשית	BEGINNING	912b	1 b
		רום	BE HIGH	927d	3 a
		תרומה	OFFERING	929a	1
15	21	דור	GENERATION	190a	2 c
		עריסה	COARSE MEAL	791b	
		ראשית	BEGINNING	912b	1 b
		תרומה	OFFERING	929a	1
15	22	שגה	GO ASTRAY	993b	4
15	23	דור	GENERATION	190a	2 c
		הלאה	ONWARDS	229c	B
		מן	FROM	581b	4 b
		צוה	CHARGE	846a	4 b
15	24	אם	IF	50a	1 a4 b
		היה	COME TO PASS	225b	1 2b bb
		חטאת	SIN	309d	4 b
		חטאת	SIN	*309d	4 b
		ל	TO	516c	5 jb
		מן	FROM	578b	1 b
		נסך	DRINK-OFFERING	651a	1
		עין	EYE	744d	3 d
		עלה	WHOLE BURNT OF-FERING	750c	
		עלה	WHOLE BURNT OF-FERING	750d	
		עשה	DO	795b	1 a
15	25	אשה	OFFERING MADE BY FIRE	78a	
		בוא	COME	99b	2
		בן	SON	120d	1 jg
		הוא	HE, SHE, IT	*216d	6 a
		חטאת	SIN	309d	4 b
		עדה	CONGREGATION	417b	3
		כפר	COVER OVER	497d	3 b2
		סלח	FORGIVE	669c	
		שגגה	SIN OF ERROR	993a	
		שגגה	SIN OF ERROR	993a	
15	26	בן	SON	120d	1 jg
		גור	SOJOURN	157d	1
		גר	SOJOURNER	158b	2
		גר	SOJOURNER	*158c	2
		עדה	CONGREGATION	417b	3
		סלח	FORGIVE	669c	

Ch	v.	Heb	Eng	Page	Sec
15	27	שׁגגה	SIN OF ERROR	993a	
		בת	DAUGHTER	123d	9
		חטא	MISS A GOAL OR WAY	307b	2 b
		חטאת	SIN	309c	4 a
		חטאת	SIN	*309d	4 c
		נפשׁ	SOUL	660b	4 c2
15	28	שׁגגה	SIN OF ERROR	993a	
		חטא	MISS A GOAL OR WAY	307b	2 b
		כפר	COVER OVER	497d	3 b2
		נפשׁ	SOUL	660b	4 c1
		סלח	FORGIVE	669c	
		שׁגג	GO ASTRAY	993a	2
		שׁגגה	SIN OF ERROR	993a	
15	29	גור	SOJOURN	157d	1
		גר	SOJOURNER	158b	2
		גר	SOJOURNER	*158c	2
		אזרח	A NATIVE	280c	1
		תורה	LAW	436a	2 a
		שׁגגה	SIN OF ERROR	993a	
15	30	גדף	BLASPHEME	154c	2
		גר	SOJOURNER	158b	1
		גר	SOJOURNER	158b	2
		אזרח	A NATIVE	280c	1
		יד	HAND	389d	1 e1
		כרת	BE CUT OFF	504b	1 c
		נפשׁ	SOUL	660b	4 c2
		נפשׁ	SOUL	660b	4 c2
		רום	BE HIGH	926d	2 b
15	31	בזה	DESPISE	102b	
		כרת	BE CUT OFF	504b	1 c
		נפשׁ	SOUL	660b	4 c2
		נשׂא	LIFT	671a	2 b
		עון	INIQUITY	731b	2 a
		פרר	BREAK	830b	1 e
		מצוה	COMMANDMENT	846b	2 a
15	32	קשׁשׁ	GATHER STUBBLE	905d	
		שׁבת	SABBATH	992c	1 d
15	33	מצא	FIND	593b	3 a
		קרב	COME NEAR	897d	1 a
		קשׁשׁ	GATHER STUBBLE	905d	
15	34	מה	WHAT	552d	1 b
		נוח	REST	628d	B 1
		עשׂה	DO	795b	1 c
		פרשׁ	MAKE DISTINCT	831c	
		משׁמר	PRISON	1038b	1
15	35	אבן	STONE	6b	1
		מות	DIE	559d	2 a
		רגם	TO STONE	920c	
15	36	אבן	STONE	6b	1
		יצא	BRING OUT	424d	1 g
		מות	DIE	559d	2 a
		רגם	TO STONE	920c	
15	38	אמר	SAY	56c	4
		גדלים	TWISTED THREADS	*152d	1
		דור	GENERATION	190a	2 c
		כנף	EXTREMITY	489d	2 a
		פתיל	CORD	836d	
		ציצת	TASSEL	851d	
		תכלת	VIOLET THREAD	1067b	1 a
15	39	גדלים	TWISTED THREADS	*152d	1
		זכר	REMEMBER	270a	14 b
		זנה	COMMIT FORNICATION	275d	3
		לבב	HEART	523b	2 1
		עין	EYE	744d	3 c
		עשׂה	DO	793d	1 1a 1
		ציצת	TASSEL	851d	
		תור	EXPLORE	1064c	1
15	40	זכר	REMEMBER	270a	14 b
		קדושׁ	HOLY	872d	2 b
15	41	אלהים	GOD	44b	4 a
		יהוה	YAHWEH	219b	22 d
		יצא	CASUE TO GO	424c	1 a
16	1	אבירם	ABIRAM	4d	1
		און	ON	20b	
		אליאב	ELIAB	45a	B
		דתן	DATHAN	206d	
		לוי	LEVI	532c	1 a
		פלת	PELETH	814c	1
		יצהר	IZHAR	844b	
		קהת	KOHATH	875b	
		קרח	KORAH	901b	2
		ראובן	REUBEN	910a	2
16	2	ו	AND	253a	1 g
		עדה	CONGREGATION	417b	3
		מועד	APPOINTED MEETING	417d	2
		מן	FROM	580c	3 a
		קום	STAND	878a	2
		קריא	CALLED	896c	
		שׁם	NAME	1028a	2 b1
16	3	ו	AND	254c	4
		כל	ALL	481d	1 da
		נשׂא	LIFT	672a	
		קדושׁ	HOLY	872d	2 b
		קהל	ASSEMBLY	874d	2 a
		קהל	ASSEMBLE AS	874d	1 b
		רב	MUCH	913b	1 f
16	5	בחר	CHOOSE	104a	1 a
		בקר	MORNING	134b	2
		בקר	MORNING	134c	2
		ו	AND	254d	5 ca
		ידע	MAKE KNOWN	395a	
		עדה	CONGREGATION	417a	1
		קדושׁ	HOLY	872d	2 b
		קרב	COME NEAR	898a	2 a1
16	6	מחתה	FIRE-HOLDER	367b	3
		עדה	CONGREGATION	417a	1
16	7	בחר	CHOOSE	104a	2 a
		בן	SON	120c	1 g
		בן	SON	121a	1 je
		בקר	MORNING	*134b	2
		הם	THEY	241d	8 d
		לוי	LEVI	532c	1 c
		קדושׁ	HOLY	872d	2 b
		קטרת	SMOKE	882d	2
		רב	MUCH	913b	1 f
16	8	בן	SON	120c	1 g
		בן	SON	121a	1 je
		לוי	LEVI	532c	1 c
16	9	אלהים	GOD	44b	4 ba
		בדל	BE DIVIDED	95b	2
		עדה	CONGREGATION	417b	3
		מן	THAN	582d	6 d
		מעט	A FEW	590b	1 ea
		עבד	WORK	713b	5
		עבדה	LABOR	715c	4
		עמד	STAND	764a	1 e
		קרב	COME NEAR	898a	2 a1
		משׁכן	DWELLING-PLACE	1015d	2 c
		שׁרת	SERVE	1057b	2 b
16	10	אח	BROTHER	26b	2
		בן	SON	121a	1 je
		בקשׁ	SEEK	134d	2
		ו	AND	252d	1 f
		כהנה	PRIESTHOOD	464d	
		לוי	LEVI	532c	1 c
		מעט	A FEW	590b	1 ea
		קרב	COME NEAR	898a	2 a1
16	11	יעד	GATHER BY APPOINTMENT	417a	3
		עדה	CONGREGATION	417a	1
		כן	SO	486a	3 d
		לון	MURMUR	534a	
		לון	MURMUR	534a	
		מה	WHAT	553a	1 db
16	12	אבירם	ABIRAM	4d	1
		אליאב	ELIAB	45a	B
		דתן	DATHAN	206d	
16	13	גם	ALSO	169b	2
		דבשׁ	HONEY	185b	
		זוב	FLOW	264d	2
		חלב	MILK	316c	A 4
		מעט	A FEW	590b	1 ea
		שׂרר	ACT AS PRINCE	979a	
16	14	אף	ALSO	64d	1
		דבשׁ	HONEY	185b	
		זוב	FLOW	264d	2
		חלב	MILK	316c	A 4
		נחלה	PROPERTY	635b	1 b
		נקר	DIG	669b	
16	15	את	MARK OF THE ACCUSATIVE	85a	1 a
		חמור	HE-ASS	331b	1
		חרה	BURN	354a	1 b
		מנחה	OFFERING	585a	3
		נשׂא	LIFT	671b	3 a
		פנה	TURN	815c	2 c1
		רעע	BE EVIL	949c	1
16	16	בקר	MORNING	*134b	2
		עדה	CONGREGATION	417a	1
16	17	מחתה	FIRE-HOLDER	367b	3
		קטרת	SMOKE	882d	2
		קרב	COME NEAR	898a	2 b5
16	18	ו	AND	253a	1 g
		מחתה	FIRE-HOLDER	367b	3
		קטרת	SMOKE	882d	2
		אשׁ	ADDENDA ET CORRIGENDA	1120d	
16	19	כבוד	GLORY	458d	2 c1
		קהל	ASSEMBLE AS	875a	2
		ראה	TO SEE	908b	1 a
16	21	בדל	BE DIVIDED	95c	1 b
		כלה	FINISH	478c	2 c2
		רגע	A MOMENT	921a	BC
		תוך	MIDST	1063d	
16	22	אל	GOD	42d	6 f
		אלהים	GOD	44c	4 bb
		בשׂר	FLESH	142d	6 c
		חטא	MISS A GOAL OR WAY	306d	2 b
		ל	TO	513d	5 cb g
		קצף	BE WROTH	893b	1
		רוח	BREATH	925b	4 b
16	24	אבירם	ABIRAM	4d	1
		דבר	SPEAK	181a	3 b
		דתן	DATHAN	206d	
		סביב	ROUND ABOUT	687a	1 d
		עלה	GO UP	749b	1 c2
		משׁכן	DWELLING-PLACE	1015d	1
16	25	אבירם	ABIRAM	4d	1
		דתן	DATHAN	206d	
		הלך	WALK	231c	1 1d 5z
		הלך	WALK	234a	1 5c
		זקן	OLD	278d	2 b
16	26	ב	IN	90c	3 5
		דבר	SPEAK	181a	3 b
		חטא	SIN	309a	2
		נגע	TOUCH	619a	1 a
		ספה	SWEEP AWAY	705a	1
		על	UPON	759a	4 2c
		רשׁע	WICKED	957c	3
16	27	אבירם	ABIRAM	4d	1
		דתן	DATHAN	206d	
		ו	AND	253a	1 g
		נצב	STAND	662a	1 a
		סביב	ROUND ABOUT	687a	1 d
		עלה	GO UP	749b	1 c2
		על	UPON	759a	4 2c
		פתח	OPENING	835d	
		משׁכן	DWELLING-PLACE	1015d	1
16	28	ב	IN	90a	3 2e
		זה	THIS	261d	6 bb
		לב	HEART	524c	2 3a
		מן	OUT OF	579c	2 cd
		מעשׂה	DEED	795c	1 a1
16	29	אדם	MAN	9b	2
		כל	ALL	*481c	1 b
		לא	NOT	518d	1 ac
		מות	DEATH	560c	1
		פקד	ATTEND TO	823d	3
		פקדה	OVERSIGHT	824a	1 a
16	30	אדמה	GROUND	9d	4
		בלע	SWALLOW UP	118a	2
		ברא	CREATE	135b	3
		בריאה	A CREATION	135c	
		חי	ALIVE	312a	1 b
		ירד	GO DOWN	433a	1 i
		נאץ	CONTEMN	611a	
		פה	MOUTH	804d	1 a
		פצה	PART	822c	1 a
		שׁאול	SHEOL	983d	1
16	31	אדמה	GROUND	9d	4
		בקע	BREAK OPEN OR THROUGH	132a	1
16	32	אדמה	GROUND	9d	4
		בית	HOUSE	109d	5 a
		בית	HOUSE	109d	5 a
		בלע	SWALLOW UP	118a	2
		פה	MOUTH	804d	1 a
		פתח	OPEN	835b	
		רכושׁ	PROPERTY	940d	1
16	33	אבד	PERISH	1d	1
		חי	ALIVE	312a	1 b
		ירד	GO DOWN	433a	1 i
		כסה	COVER	492a	6
		שׁאול	SHEOL	983a	1
		תוך	MIDST	1063d	
16	34	בלע	SWALLOW UP	118a	2
		ל	TO	515a	5 g
		נוס	FLEE	630d	1
		סביב	ROUND ABOUT	687b	2 bb
		פן	LEST	814d	1 a
16	35	אכל	EAT	37c	3.
		את	WITH	86d	4 c
		יצא	GO OUT	423b	1 g
		להבה	FLAME	*529b	1
		קטרת	SMOKE	882d	2
		קרב	COME NEAR	898a	2 b5
16	104	בת	DAUGHTER	123d	9
17	2	בין	INTERVAL	107d	D
		הלאה	OUT THERE	229b	A
		זרה	SCATTER	279d	1
		מחתה	FIRE-HOLDER	367b	3
		קדשׁ	BE SET APART	873a	2
		רום	BE HIGH	927c	1 c
		שׂרפה	BURNING	977c	
17	3	אות	SIGN	16d	5
		חטא	SINFUL	308b	2
		מחתה	FIRE-HOLDER	367b	3 c
		נפשׁ	SOUL	659d	2
		עשׂה	DO	794c	2 1g
		פח	PLATE OF METAL	809a	
		צפוי	METAL PLATING	860b	
		קדשׁ	BE SET APART	873a	2
		קרב	COME NEAR	898a	2 b5
		רקוע	EXPANSION	956b	
17	4	מחתה	FIRE-HOLDER	367b	3
		נחשׁת	COPPER	638d	1
		צפוי	METAL PLATING	860b	
		קרב	COME NEAR	898a	2 b5
		רקע	BEAT	956a	
		שׂרף	BURN	977a	2 b1
17	5	אשׁר	PARTICLE OF RELATION	82b	2 b
		דבר	SPEAK	181c	4 a
		הוא	HE, SHE, IT	216b	3
		זור	BE A STRANGER	266c	2 a
		זכרון	MEMORIAL	272a	1 c
		זרע	SOWING	282d	4 c
		יד	HAND	391a	5 d
		עדה	CONGREGATION	417a	1
		מען	PURPOSE	775c	2 ca
		קטר	MAKE SACRAFICES SMOKE	883b	2
17	6	קרב	COME NEAR	897c	1 a
		בן	SON	121a	1 jg
		עדה	CONGREGATION	417b	3
		לון	MURMUR	534a	
		מחרת	THE MORROW	564c	
17	7	היה	COME TO PASS	224c	2 a1 ab
		כבוד	GLORY	458d	2 c1
		כסה	COVER	491d	4
		פנה	TURN	815b	1
		קהל	ASSEMBLE AS	874d	1 b
		ראה	TO SEE	908b	1 a

Ch	v.	Heb	Eng	Page	Sec
17	8	פנה	FACE	816c	2 1b
17	10	כלה	FINISH	478c	2 c2
		רגע	A MOMENT	921a	BC
		רחום	BE EXALTED	933d	
		תוך	MIDST	1063d	
17	11	את	WITH	86d	4 c
		הלך	WALK	236d	1 d
		חלל	POLLUTE	320d	2
		מחתה	FIRE-HOLDER	367b	3
		יצא	GO OUT	423c	1 g
		כפר	COVER OVER	497c	2 a
		מהרה	HASTE	555b	
		נגף	BLOW	620a	1
		על	UPON	758c	4 2a
		פנה	FACE	817d	2 5 a a
17	12	קצף	WRATH	893c	1
		חלל	POLLUTE	320d	2
		כפר	COVER OVER	497c	2 a
		נגף	BLOW	620a	1
		קטרת	SMOKE	882d	2
		רוץ	RUN	930b	1
		תוך	MIDST	1063d	
17	13	חי	ALIVE	312c	1 b
		מגפה	PLAGUE	620a	3
17	14	בד	SEPARATION	94d	1 e
		דבר	WORD	184a	4 8
		מות	DIE	559c	1 a1
		מות	DIE	560a	2 b
		מגפה	PLAGUE	620a	3
		ארבע	FOUR	917a	2 a2 a
17	15	מגפה	PLAGUE	620a	3
		עצר	RESTRAIN	783d	
		שוב	TURN BACK	997a	3 a
17	17	את	WITH	86c	4 a
		בית	HOUSE	110b	5 e
		כתב	WRITE	507c	1 b1
		מטה	STAFF	641d	1
		עתוד	HE/GOAT	800d	
17	18	בית	HOUSE	110b	5 e
		כתב	WRITE	507c	1 b1
		לוי	LEVI	532c	2
		מטה	STAFF	641c	1
		ראש	HEAD	911a	3 f
17	19	יעד	MEET AT AN AP-POINTED PLACE	416d	1
		נוח	REST	628d	B 1
		עדות	TESTIMONY	730b	1
		שם	THERE	1027b	3
17	20	בחר	CHOOSE	104a	1 a
		היה	COME TO PASS	225a	1 2b ag
		לון	MURMUR	534a	
		תלנה	MURMURING	534b	
		פרח	BUD	827a	
		שכך	DECREASE	1013c	
17	21	בית	HOUSE	110b	5 e
		מטה	STAFF	641c	1
		על	UPON	758c	4 2b
17	22	אהל	TENT	14a	3
		נוח	REST	628d	B 1
		עדות	TESTIMONY	730b	1
17	23	אהל	TENT	14a	3
		בית	HOUSE	110b	5 dk
		יצא	BRING OUT	425b	4 j
		ל	TO	512d	5 ac
		לוי	LEVI	532c	1 b
		מחרת	THE MORROW	564a	
		מטה	STAFF	641c	1
		עדות	TESTIMONY	730b	1
		פרח	BUD	827a	
		פרח	BUD	827b	
		ציץ	BLOSSOM	847d	1
		ציץ	BLOSSOM	847f	1
		שקד	ALMOND	1052b	1
17	24	יצא	BRING OUT	425a	4 f
		פנה	FACE	817d	2 5 a a
17	25	אות	SIGN	16d	5
		בן	SON	121d	8 g
		כלה	FINISH	478c	2 a
		תלנה	MURMURING	534b	
		מות	DIE	560a	2 b
		מרי	REBELLION	598c	
		מטה	STAFF	641c	1
		עדות	TESTIMONY	730b	1
		על	UPON	758c	4 2b
		שוב	TURN BACK	999a	1 b
		משמרת	GUARD	1038c	2
17	26	כאשר	AS	455b	1 b
		כן	SO	486c	2 ca
17	27	אבד	PERISH	1b	1
		גוע	EXPIRE	157c	
		הן	BEHOLD	243c	A
17	28	אם	IF	50d	2 c
		גוע	EXPIRE	157c	
		מות	DIE	560a	2 b
		קרב	APPROACHING	898b	1
		משכן	DWELLING-PLACE	1015d	2 c
		תמם	BE FINISHED	1070b	1
		תמם	BE FINISHED	1070c	5
18	1	אב	FATHER	3c	3
		כהנה	PRIESTHOOD	464d	
		נשא	LIFT	671a	2 b
		עון	INIQUITY	731c	3
18	2	אב	FATHER	3c	3
		אהל	TENT	14a	3
		אח	BROTHER	26b	1
		לוה	BE JOINED	530d	
		לוי	LEVI	532c	2
		עדות	TESTIMONY	730b	1
		על	UPON	755b	2 4a
		קרב	COME NEAR	898a	1 a
		שרת	SERVE	1058b	2 b
18	3	מות	DIE	560a	2 b
		משמרת	GUARD	1038c	4 a
		משמרת	GUARD	1038c	4 a
18	4	זור	BE A STRANGER	266c	2 a
		ל	TO	514c	5 fd
		לוה	BE JOINED	530d	
		עבדה	LABOR	715b	4
		על	UPON	755b	2 4a
		קרב	COME NEAR	897b	1 a
		משמרת	GUARD	1038c	4 a
18	5	מזבח	ALTAR	259a	1
		על	UPON	756c	2 7a b
		קצף	WRATH	893c	1
		משמרת	GUARD	1038c	4 a
		משמרת	GUARD	1038c	4 a
18	6	אח	BROTHER	26b	1
		לוי	LEVITE	533a	3 1d
		נתן	GIVE	678c	1 b
		מתנה	GIFT	682c	
		עבד	WORK	713b	5
		עבדה	LABOR	715b	4
18	7	בית	HOUSE	110c	8 b
		דבר	WORD	183b	4 1
		זור	BE A STRANGER	266c	2 a
		כהנה	PRIESTHOOD	464d	
		ל	TO	514c	5 fc
		מות	DIE	560c	2
		מן	FROM	583d	9 b1
		מתנה	GIFT	682c	
		עבד	WORK	713b	5
		עבדה	LABOR	715b	4
		קטר	MAKE SACRAFICES SMOKE	883a	1 a
		קרב	APPROACHING	898b	2
		שמר	KEEP	1037a	3 c
18	8	חק	SOMETHING PRE-SCRIBED	349c	4
		ל	TO	514c	5 fd
		משחה	CONSECRATED PORTION	603c	
		נתן	PUT	681a	2 d
		עולם	LONG DURATION	762c	2 e
		תרומה	OFFERING	929a	4
		משמרת	GUARD	1038c	4 a
18	9	אשם	OFFENCE	79d	4
		חטאת	SIN	309c	4 a
		ל	TO	514c	5 fd
		מנחה	OFFERING	585b	5
		קדש	APARTNESS	872a	3 b
		שוב	TURN BACK	999c	4 b
18	10	זכר	MALE	271c	1 1 b
		קדש	APARTNESS	*871d	2 c
18	11	חק	SOMETHING PRE-SCRIBED	349c	4
		ל	TO	514c	5 fd
		תנופה	WAVING	632c	2 a
		מתן	GIFTS	682b	
		מתנה	GIFT	*682c	
		עולם	LONG DURATION	762c	2 e
		תרומה	OFFERING	929a	4
18	12	דגן	CORN	186c	
		דגן	CORN	186c	
		חלב	FAT	317a	3
		תירוש	NEW WINE	440d	
		נתן	GIVE	679a	1 k
		יצהר	FRESH OIL	844a	
		ראשית	BEGINNING	912b	1 b
18	13	בכורים	FIRST-FRUITS	114c	
18	14	חרם	DEVOTED THING	356d	2
18	15	אך	HOWBEIT	36c	2 a
		בכור	FIRST-BORN	114b	2 b
		בכור	FIRST-BORN	114b	2 b
		בשר	FLESH	142d	6 a
		טמא	UNCLEAN	379d	2 b
		ל	TO	513d	5 cb g
		פדה	RANSOM	804a	1
		פטר	THAT WHICH SEPA-RATES	809d	
		רחם	WOMB	933b	1
18	16	בן	SON	122a	9 a
		גרה	GERAH	176a	
		חדש	NEW MOON	294c	2 a
		חמש	FIVE	331d	1 d
		כסף	SILVER	494b	8 a
		כסף	SILVER	494d	9
		ערך	ORDER	790a	2
		פדה	RANSOM	804a	1
18	17	אך	HOWBEIT	36c	2 a
		אשה	OFFERING MADE BY FIRE	78a	
		בכור	FIRST-BORN	114b	2 a
		דם	BLOOD	197c	3 b
		זרק	TO TOSS	284c	1 b
		חלב	FAT	317a	2 b
		כשב	LAMB	461b	
		עז	SHE-GOAT	777c	3 e
		פדה	RANSOM	804a	1
		קדש	APARTNESS	872a	3
		קטר	MAKE SACRAFICES SMOKE	883a	1 a
		שור	A HEAD OF CATTLE	1004b	
18	18	חזה	BREAST	303d	
		ימין	RIGHT	412a	3
		תנופה	WAVING	632c	2 a
18	19	ברית	COVENANT	137a	3 2
		זרע	SOWING	*282c	4 b
		זרע	SOWING	283a	4 g
		חק	SOMETHING PRE-SCRIBED	349c	4
		מלח	SALT	571d	
		עולם	LONG DURATION	762c	2 e
		עולם	LONG DURATION	762c	2 d
		רום	BE HIGH	927d	3 a
		תרומה	OFFERING	929a	4
18	20	חלק	PORTION	324a	2 a
		חלק	PORTION	324b	3 b
		נחלה	PROPERTY	635b	1 d
		נחל	TAKE AS A POSSES-SION	635c	1 b
18	21	את	MARK OF THE AC-CUSATIVE	85b	3 a
		בן	SON	121a	1 je
		חלף	EXCHANGE	322b	
		לוי	LEVI	532c	1 c
		נחלה	PROPERTY	635b	1 d
		עבד	WORK	713b	5
		עבדה	LABOR	715b	4
		מעשר	TENTH PART	798b	2
18	22	חטא	SIN	308a	3
		מות	DIE	560a	2 b
		נשא	LIFT	670d	1 b 0
18	23	דור	GENERATION	190a	2 c
		ה	THE	208b	1 g
		הוא	HE, SHE, IT	215c	1 c
		חקה	SOMETHING PRE-SCRIBED	350a	1
		לוי	LEVITE	532d	2
		נחלה	PROPERTY	635b	1 d
		נחל	TAKE AS A POSSES-SION	635c	1 b
		נשא	LIFT	671a	2 b
		עבד	WORK	713b	5
		עבדה	LABOR	715b	4
		עון	INIQUITY	731c	3
		עולם	LONG DURATION	762c	2 e
		תרומה	OFFERING	929b	4 e
18	24	כן	SO	487b	3 f
		לוי	LEVITE	533a	3 1d
		נחלה	PROPERTY	635b	1 d
		נחלה	PROPERTY	635b	1 d
		נחל	TAKE AS A POSSES-SION	635c	1 b
		מעשר	TENTH PART	798b	
		רום	BE HIGH	927d	3 a
18	26	ב	IN	89a	1 7c
		לוי	LEVITE	533a	3 1d
		נחלה	PROPERTY	635b	1 d
		מעשר	TENTH PART	798b	2
		מעשר	TENTH PART	798b	2
		רום	BE HIGH	927d	3 a
		תרומה	OFFERING	929b	4 c
18	27	גרן	THRESHING-FLOOR	175b	
		דגן	CORN	*186c	
		דגן	CORN	186c	
		חשב	THINK	363c	3
		יקב	WINE-VAT	428c	
		מלאה	FULL PRODUCE	571b	
18	28	מעשר	TENTH PART	798b	
		רום	BE HIGH	927d	3 a
		תרומה	OFFERING	929b	4 c
18	29	חלב	FAT	317a	3
		מתנה	GIFT	682c	
		מקדש	SACRED PLACE	874b	6
		רום	BE HIGH	927d	3 a
		תרומה	OFFERING	929b	4 c
18	30	תבואה	PRODUCT	100a	1
		גרן	THRESHING-FLOOR	175b	
		חלב	FAT	317a	3
		חשב	THINK	363c	3
		יקב	WINE-VAT	428c	
		לוי	LEVITE	533a	3 1d
		רום	BE HIGH	927c	2
18	31	בית	HOUSE	109d	5 a
		חלף	EXCHANGE	322b	
		מקום	STANDING PLACE	880a	4
		שכר	HIRE	969a	2
18	32	חטא	SIN	308a	3
		חלב	FAT	317a	3
		חלל	POLLUTE	320b	1 b
		מות	DIE	560a	2 b
		נשא	LIFT	670d	1 b 0
		רום	BE HIGH	927c	2
19	2	אדם	RED	10b	
		חקה	SOMETHING PRE-SCRIBED	350a	1
		תורה	LAW	436a	2 a
		מום	BLEMISH	548d	1 b
		עלה	GO UP	749a	6
		על	YOKE	760d	
		פרה	HEIFER	831a	
19	3	יצא	BRING OUT	425a	3
		נער	RETAINER	655a	2 a
		שחט	SLAUGHTER	1006a	2
19	4	אל	TO	40d	9
		דם	BLOOD	197c	3 b
		נזה	SPURT	633c	

Ch	v.	Heb	Eng	Page	Sec
19	5	נכח	FRONT	647b	2 a
		דם	BLOOD	197d	3 b
		עין	EYE	745a	5
		פרה	HEIFER	831a	
		פרש	OFFAL	831d	
		שרף	BURN	977a	2 a
19	6	אזוב	HYSSOP	23c	
		ארז	CEDAR	72d	3
		עץ	TREE	782a	2 e
		פרה	HEIFER	831a	
		סרפה	BURNING	977b	
		שרפה	BURNING	977c	
		שלך	THROW	1021a	1 a
		שני	SCARLET	1040d	
		תוך	MIDST	1063d	
		תולעה	WORM	1069a	2
19	7	בשר	FLESH	142c	1
		טמא	BE UNCLEAN	379b	3
19	8	בשר	FLESH	142c	1
		טמא	BE UNCLEAN	379b	3
		מי	WATER	565b	1 a
		שרף	BURN	977a	2 a
19	9	אסף	GATHER	62b	1 c
		אפר	ASHES	68a	
		בן	SON	121a	1 jg
		חטאת	SIN	310a	5
		מהור	CLEAN	373a	1
		עדה	CONGREGATION	417b	3
		מי	WATER	565c	1 a
		נדה	IMPURITY	622c	1
		נוח	REST	628d	B 1
		פרה	HEIFER	831a	
		משמרת	GUARD	1038c	2
19	10	אסף	GATHER	62b	1 c
		אפר	ASHES	68a	
		גור	SOJOURN	157d	1
		גר	SOJOURNER	158b	2
		גר	SOJOURNER	*158c	2
		חקה	SOMETHING PRE-SCRIBED	350a	1
		טמא	BE UNCLEAN	379b	3
		עולם	LONG DURATION	762c	2 e
		פרה	HEIFER	831a	
19	11	אדם	MAN	9b	1
		טמא	BE UNCLEAN	379b	3
		ל	TO	514c	5 fc
		נפש	SOUL	660c	4 c5
19	12	חטא	MISS A GOAL OR WAY	307d	2 b
		חטא	MISS A GOAL OR WAY	307d	2 b
		טהר	BE CLEAN	372b	2
19	13	אדם	MAN	9b	1
		זרק	TO TOSS	284c	
		חטא	MISS A GOAL OR WAY	307d	2 b
		טמא	BE UNCLEAN	379c	3
		טמא	UNCLEAN	379d	2 a
		טמאה	UNCLEANNESS	380a	4
		כרת	BE CUT OFF	504b	1 c
		מי	WATER	565c	1 a
		נדה	IMPURITY	622c	1
		נפש	SOUL	660c	4 c2
		נפש	SOUL	660c	4 c5
		עוד	STILL	728d	1 aa
19	14	טמא	BE UNCLEAN	379b	3
		תורה	LAW	436a	2 a
19	15	טמא	UNCLEAN	379d	2 c
		כלי	VESSEL	480b	3
		פתח	OPEN	835a	
		פתיל	CORD	836d	
		צמיד	COVER OF VESSEL	855b	
19	16	חרב	SWORD	352d	1 h
		טמא	BE UNCLEAN	379b	3
		עצם	BONE	782d	1 f
		פנה	FACE	819a	2 7b
		שדה	FIELD	961c	1 f
19	17	חטאת	SIN	310a	5
		חי	ALIVE	312b	1 f
		טמא	UNCLEAN	379d	2 a
		מי	WATER	565d	3
		נתן	PUT	680b	2 a
		עפר	DRY EARTH	779d	1 d
		שרפה	BURNING	977c	
19	18	אזוב	HYSSOP	23c	
		חלל	PIERCED	319c	2
		טבל	DIP	371b	1
		מי	WATER	565c	1 a
		נזה	SPURT	633c	
		נפש	SOUL	660c	4 c4
		עצם	BONE	782d	1 f
19	19	חטא	MISS A GOAL OR WAY	307c	4
		טהר	BE CLEAN	372b	2
		טמא	UNCLEAN	379d	2 a
		נזה	SPURT	633c	
19	20	זרק	TO TOSS	284c	
		חטא	MISS A GOAL OR WAY	307d	2 b
		טמא	BE UNCLEAN	379a	3
		טמא	BE UNCLEAN	379c	3
		טמא	UNCLEAN	379d	2 a
		כרת	BE CUT OFF	504b	1 c
		מי	WATER	565c	1 a
		נדה	IMPURITY	622c	1
		נפש	SOUL	660b	4 c2

Ch	v.	Heb	Eng	Page	Sec
		תוך	MIDST	1063d	
19	21	חקה	SOMETHING PRE-SCRIBED	350a	1
		טמא	BE UNCLEAN	379b	3
		מי	WATER	565c	1 a
		נדה	IMPURITY	622c	1
		נזה	SPURT	633c	
		עולם	LONG DURATION	762c	2 e
19	22	טמא	BE UNCLEAN	379b	3
		טמא	BE UNCLEAN	379b	3
		טמא	UNCLEAN	379d	2 a
		נגע	TOUCH	619a	1 a
		נפש	SOUL	660b	4 c2
20	1	מדבר	WILDERNESS	185a	3 a
		מרים	MIRIAM	599b	1
		צן	ZIN	856c	1
		קבר	BURY	868a	
		קדש	KADESH	873d	1
20	2	קהל	ASSEMBLE AS	874d	1 b
20	3	גוע	EXPIRE	157c	
		לו	IF	530b	2
		ריב	STRIVE	936c	2
20	4	בעיר	BEASTS	129c	
		קהל	ASSEMBLY	874d	2 a
20	5	אין	NOT	34c	2 c
		גפן	VINE	172c	
		זרע	SOWING	282a	1 a
		לא	NOT	519b	1 bb
		מקום	STANDING PLACE	880a	3 d
		רמון	POMEGRANATE	941d	1
		רע	EVIL	948b	4
		שתה	DRINK	1059a	1 a
		תאנה	FIG-TREE	1061a	1
20	6	כבוד	GLORY	458d	2 c1
		ראה	TO SEE	908b	1 a
20	8	בעיר	BEASTS	129c	
		יצא	BRING OUT	425a	4 i
		מי	WATER	565b	1 a
		מטה	STAFF	641c	1
		נתן	GIVE	679c	1 t
		סלע	CRAG	701a	1
		קהל	ASSEMBLE AS	875a	2
		שקה	GIVE TO DRINK	1052c	2
20	9	מטה	STAFF	641c	1
		פנה	FACE	817d	2 5a a
20	10	יצא	BRING OUT	425a	4 i
		מי	WATER	565b	1 a
		מרה	BE REBELLIOUS	598a	2
		נא	PART OF EN-TREATY	609a	1
		סלע	CRAG	701a	1
		פנה	FACE	816c	2 1b
		קהל	ASSEMBLE AS	875a	2
20	11	בעיר	BEASTS	129c	
		עדה	CONGREGATION	417b	3
		יצא	GO OUT	423a	1 f
		מי	WATER	565b	1 a
		מטה	STAFF	641c	1
		נכה	SMITE	645b	1 a
		סלע	CRAG	701a	1
		רב	MUCH	913a	1 b
		רום	BE HIGH	927b	1 a1
		שתה	DRINK	1059b	1 a
20	12	אמן	CONFIRM	53b	2 c
		כן	SO	487a	3 d
		יען	ON ACCOUNT OF	774d	2 c
		קדש	BE SET APART	873c	1
20	13	אשר	THAT	83c	8 c
		את	WITH	86b	1 dd
		מי	WATER	565b	1 a
		קדש	BE SET APART	873a	1
		ריב	STRIVE	936c	2
		מריבה	MERIBAH	937b	2
20	14	אדום	EDOM	10c	3
		אח	BROTHER	26b	2
		אמר	SAY	56a	1
		תלאה	WEARINESS	521b	
		מלך	KING	573a	1
		מצא	FIND	593c	3 e
		קדש	KADESH	873d	1
20	15	ירד	GO DOWN	433a	1 d
		רעע	BE EVIL	949c	1
20	16	גבול	BOUNDARY	148a	2 a
		יצא	CAUSE TO GO	424c	1 a
		מלאך	MESSENGER	521d	3
		קדש	KADESH	873d	1
		קצה	END	892a	1
		שמע	HEAR	1034a	2 a
20	17	באר	WELL	91c	1
		גבול	BOUNDARY	148a	2 a
		דרך	WAY	202d	1
		הלך	WALK	230c	1 1d 1a
		ימין	RIGHT HAND	411d	2 b
		מי	WATER	565b	1 a
		נא	PART OF EN-TREATY	609b	3 a
		נטה	BEND	640b	3 a
		עבר	PASS OVER	717a	
		עד	UNTIL	725a	2 1a b
20	18	אדום	EDOM	10c	2
20	19	דבר	WORD	183d	4 6
		דרך	WAY	*202d	1
		נתן	GIVE	679b	1 n
		מסלה	HIGHWAY	700c	
		עבר	PASS OVER	717c	3 a
		רגל	FOOT	920a	1 f

Ch	v.	Heb	Eng	Page	Sec
		רק	THIN	956b	
		שתה	DRINK	1059b	1 d
20	20	אדום	EDOM	10c	2
		ב	IN	89b	3 1a
		חזק	STRONG	305c	1 b
		יד	HAND	389d	1 e1
		כבד	MASSIVE	458a	1 b
		עבר	PASS OVER	717c	3 a
		עם	PEOPLE	766c	2 d
20	21	אדום	EDOM	10c	2
		גבול	BOUNDARY	148a	2 a
		מאן	REFUSE	549a	
		נטה	BEND	640b	3 a
		נתן	GIVE	679a	1 g
		עבר	PASS OVER	717c	3 a
		על	UPON	759a	4 2b
20	22	מוסרה	MOSERAH	64c	
		הר	HOR	246d	1
		הר	MOUNTAIN	249b	1 a
		נסע	SET OUT	652b	2 a
		קדש	KADESH	873d	1
20	23	אדום	EDOM	10c	3
		גבול	BORDER	147d	1 a
		הר	HOR	246d	1
20	24	אהרן	AARON	14d	
		אסף	GATHER	62d	2 a
		ל	TO	511d	2
		מי	WATER	565b	1 a
		מרה	BE REBELLIOUS	598b	2
		על	UPON	758b	3 a
		עם	KINSMAN	769b	
		פה	MOUTH	805b	2 c
		מריבה	MERIBAH	937b	2
20	25	הר	HOR	246d	1
		הר	MOUNTAIN	249b	1 a
		עלה	GO UP	749c	1 c
20	26	אסף	GATHER	62d	2 a
		לבש	CLOTHE	528b	1 a
		פשט	STRIP OFF	833a	1
20	27	הר	HOR	246d	1
20	28	הר	MOUNTAIN	249b	1 a
		ירד	COME DOWN	432d	1 a
		לבש	CLOTHE	528b	1 a
		פשט	STRIP OFF	833a	1
20	29	בית	HOUSE	110a	5 dd
		בכה	WEEP	113c	4
		גוע	EXPIRE	157c	
21	1	אתרים	ATHARIM	87d	
		כנעני	CANAANITE	489a	2 a
		מלך	KING	573a	1
		מן	FROM	578d	1 c
		נגב	SOUTH-COUNTRY	616b	1 a
		ערד	ARAD	788c	
		שבה	TAKE CAPTIVE	985c	2
		שבי	CAPTIVITY	985d	3
21	2	חרם	BAN	355d	1 a
		נדר	VOW	623d	
		נדר	VOW	624a	4
21	3	חרם	BAN	355d	1 a
		חרמה	HORMAH	356c	
		חרמה	HORMAH	356c	
		כנעני	CANAANITE	489a	2 b
		נתן	GIVE	679c	1 s
21	4	אדום	EDOM	10c	3
		דרך	WAY	202d	1
		הר	HOR	246d	1
		נסע	JOURNEY	652b	3
		נפש	SOUL	661a	6 g
		סוף	REEDS	693b	2
		קצר	BE SHORT	894a	
21	5	אין	NOT	34b	2 b
		דבר	SPEAK	181c	4 d
		לחם	FOOD	537a	1 a
		קוץ	FEEL A LOATHING	881a	1
		קלקל	WORTHLESS	887b	
21	6	נחש	SERPENT	638a	1 a
		נחש	SERPENT	638b	3
		נשך	BITE	675b	
		שרף	FIERY SERPENT	977b	
		שלח	SEND	1019a	2
21	7	בעד	ON BEHALF OF	126c	2
		דבר	SPEAK	181c	4 d
		ה	THE	208a	1 g
		חטא	MISS A GOAL OR WAY	307a	2 b
		נחש	SERPENT	638a	1 a
		סור	TURN ASIDE	694b	1
		על	UPON	758d	4 2b
		פלל	INTERVENE	813b	1
		פלל	INTERVENE	813b	1
21	8	חיה	LIVE	311b	2 a
		כל	ALL	482a	1 eb
		ל	TO	515c	5 ia
		נשך	BITE	675a	
21	9	שום	TO PLACE	963b	1 b
		אם	IF	50b	1 b4 a
		את	MARK OF THE AC-CUSATIVE	85a	1 a
		חיה	COME TO PASS	225b	1 2b bb
		חיה	LIVE	311b	2 a
		נבט	LOOK	613c	1
		נחש	SERPENT	638a	1 a
		נחש	SERPENT	638b	3
		נחשת	COPPER	638d	1
		נחשתן	NEHUSHTAN	639b	
		נשך	BITE	675a	

Ch v.	Heb	Eng	Page	Sec
21 10	שום	TO PLACE	963b	1 b
	אבת	OBOTH	15c	
21 11	אבת	OBOTH	15c	
	מזרח	PLACE OF SUNRISE	280d	1
	מואב	MOAB	555d	2 b
	נסע	JOURNEY	652b	3
	עיים	IYIM	743d	1
	פנה	FACE	818d	27a d
	שמש	SUN	1039b	2
21 12	זרד	ZERED	279d	
	נחל	WADY	636c	2
	נסע	JOURNEY	652b	3
	שם	THERE	1027c	4 a
21 13	אמרי	AMORITES	57c	2a
	ארנון	ARNON	75a	
	ארנון	ARNON	75b	
	גבול	BORDER	147d	1 a
	גבול	BORDER	147d	1 a
	חנה	DECLINE	333d	2 c2
	מואב	MOAB	555d	2 b
	נסע	JOURNEY	652b	3
	עבר	REGION ACROSS	719b	1
21 14	אמר	SAY	56c	
	ארנון	ARNON	75a	
	והב	WAHEB	255a	
	כן	SO	487b	3 f
	מלחמה	WAR	536b	
	נחל	WADY	636c	2
	סופה	SUPHAH	693b	
	ספר	MISSIVE	707b	3 d
21 15	אשד	FOUNDATION	78b	
	גבול	BORDER	147d	1 a
	ו	AND	252b	1 b
	שבת	SEAT	443d	
	מואב	MOAB	555d	2 b
	נחל	WADY	636c	2
	נמה	BEND	640b	3 a
	ער	AR	786b	
	שען	LEAN	1043d	
21 16	אמר	SAY	56a	1
	אסף	GATHER	62b	1 a
	באר	WELL	91c	1
	באר	BEER	91d	3 a
	מי	WATER	565b	1a
21 17	אז	THEN	23a	1 a
	באר	WELL	91c	1
	עלה	GO UP	748d	5
	ענה	SING	777b	
	שור	SING	1010c	
	שירה	SONG	1010c	
21 18	באר	WELL	91c	1
	היה	COME TO PASS	225b	1 2b bd
	חפר	DIG	343c	1 a
	חקק	CUT IN	349b	B
	כרה	DIG	500a	
	מי	WATER	565d	3
	נדיב	NOBLE	622a	2
	מתנה	MATTANAH	682c	
	שר	CHIEFTAIN	978a	1 a
	משענת	STAFF	1044a	
21 19	במות	BAMOTH	119d	
	נחליאל	NAHALIEL	636d	
	מתנה	MATTANAH	682c	
21 20	במות	BAMOTH	119d	
	גיא	VALLEY	161b	2
	ו	AND	252b	1 b
	ישימון	WASTE	445b	a
	פנה	FACE	819a	27a e
	פסגה	PISGAH	820a	
	שדה	FIELD	961d	2 d
	שקף	LOOK DOWN	1054c	
21 21	אמרי	AMORITES	57c	2a
	סיחון	SIHON	695d	
21 22	באר	WELL	91c	1
	גבול	BOUNDARY	148a	2 a
	דרך	WAY	202d	1
	הלך	WALK	230c	1 1d 2a
	נמה	BEND	640b	3 a
	עבר	PASS OVER	717a	1 b
21 23	אסף	GATHER	62b	1 a
	גבול	BOUNDARY	148a	2 a
	יחץ	JAHAZ	397d	
	ל	TO	515a	5 ha
	לחם	ENGAGE IN BATTLE	535c	
	נתן	GIVE	679d	1 g
	עבר	PASS OVER	717c	3 a
21 24	ארנון	ARNON	75b	
	יבק	JABBOK	132d	
	יבק	JABBOK	*133a	
	גבול	BORDER	147d	1 a
	חרב	SWORD	352d	1 f
	ירש	TAKE POSSESSION	439b	1 a
	נכה	SMITE	646b	3
	עז	STRONG	738c	
	יעזר	JAZER	741c	
	עמון	AMMON	770a	
	פה	MOUTH	805d	6 c2
	יבק	ADDENDA ET CORRIGENDA	1121c	
21 25	אמרי	AMORITES	57c	2a
	בת	DAUGHTER	123d	4
	חשבון	HESHBON	363d	
	לקח	TAKE	543d	8
21 26	ארנון	ARNON	75b	
	הוא	HE, SHE, IT	216a	3 b
	חשבון	HESHBON	363d	
	יד	HAND	391b	5 g1
	לחם	ENGAGE IN BATTLE	535c	
	מואב	MOAB	555d	2 a
21 27	ראשון	FIRST	911c	1 a
	בנה	BUILD	125a	1 b
	חשבון	HESHBON	363d	
	כון	BE ESTABLISHED	467a	
	כן	SO	487b	3 f
	משל	USE A PROVERB	605c	
	סיחון	SIHON	695d	
21 28	ארנון	ARNON	75b	
	בין	INTERVAL	*107d	D
	במה	HIGH PLACE	119a	
	בעל	OWNER	127b	1 3
	חשבון	HESHBON	363d	
	יצא	GO OUT	423b	1 g
	להבה	FLAME	529b	1
	ער	AR	786b	
	קריה	TOWN	900a	2
	אש	ADDENDA ET CORRIGENDA	*1120d	
21 29	אבד	PERISH	1c	1
	אוי	WOE	17a	1
	בת	DAUGHTER	123b	1 i
	כמוש	CHEMOSH	484d	1
	מואב	MOAB	555d	2 a
	נתן	GIVE	679c	1 s
	עם	PEOPLE	766c	1
	פליט	ESCAPED ONE	812c	
	שבית	CAPTIVITY	986b	1
21 30	אבד	PERISH	1c	1
	דיבן	DIBON	192a	1
	חשבון	HESHBON	363d	
	ירה	SHOOT	435a	3
	מידבא	MEDEBA	567d	
	נפח	NOPHAH	656a	
	נפח	BLOW	656a	
	שמם	BE DESOLATED	1031b	1
21 32	בת	DAUGHTER	123d	4
	ירש	TAKE POSSESSION	439c	1 b
	ירש	CAUSE TO POSSESS	440a	2 a
	יעזר	JAZER	741c	
	רגל	GO ABOUT	920b	2
	שלח	SEND	1018b	1 c
21 33	בשן	BASHAN	143c	
	דרך	WAY	202d	1
	אדרעי	EDREI	204c	
	עוג	OG	728b	
	עלה	GO UP	748d	1 e
	פנה	TURN	815b	1 c
21 34	חשבון	HESHBON	363d	
	ירא	FEAR	431b	1 b
	נתן	GIVE	679c	1 s
21 35	בלת	NOT	117a	4 c
	ירש	TAKE POSSESSION	439b	1 a
	נכה	SMITE	646a	2 c
	שריד	SURVIVOR	975a	1
	שאר	REMAIN	984b	1
22 1	ירדן	JORDAN	434d	
	מואב	MOAB	555d	2 b
	עבר	REGION ACROSS	719c	1 a
	ערבה	DESERT-PLAIN	787c	3
22 2	בלק	BALAK	119a	
	צפור	ZIPPOR	862a	
22 3	גור	DREAD	159a	1
	מואב	MOAB	555d	2 a
	פנה	FACE	818b	2 6b
	קוץ	FEEL A LOATHING	881a	2
22 4	בלק	BALAK	119a	
	מדין	MIDIAN	193c	2
	זקן	OLD	279a	2 b
	ירק	GREEN	438d	
	ל	TO	513a	5 ad
	לחך	LICK	535a	
	לחך	LICK UP	535b	
	מואב	MOAB	555d	2 a
	מלך	KING	573a	1
	סביב	ROUND ABOUT	687b	2 ba b
	עת	TIME	773b	1 a
	עתה	NOW	774a	1 b
	צפור	ZIPPOR	862a	
	קהל	ASSEMBLY	874c	1 b
	קהל	ASSEMBLY	874d	2 d
	שור	A HEAD OF CATTLE	1004a	
	כען	NOW	*1107b	
22 5	בלעם	BALAAM	118d	
	בן	SON	121b	1 ji
	בעור	BEOR	129d	1
	יצא	GO OUT	422b	1 a
	כסה	COVER	492a	5
	מול	IN FRONT OF	557c	2 bb
	נהר	STREAM	625d	1
	עין	EYE	744d	4 a
	על	UPON	755d	2 6a
	עם	PEOPLE	766d	5 a
	פתור	PETHOR	834d	
	קרא	CALL	895c	5 a
22 6	אולי	PERADVENTURE	19c	1
	ארר	CURSE	76c	
	ארר	CURSE	76d	
	אשר	PARTICLE OF RELATION	82a	1
	ברך	BLESS	139a	3
	ברך	BLESS	139b	3
	גרש	DRIVE OUT	177a	
	הלך	WALK	230c	1 1c
	יבל	BE ABLE	407d	1 e
	ל	TO	515b	5 hb a
	עצום	MIGHTY	783a	1
22 7	בלעם	BALAAM	118d	
	בלק	BALAK	119a	
	מדין	MIDIAN	193c	2
	זקן	OLD	279a	2 b
	קסם	DIVINATION	890c	1
22 8	בלעם	BALAAM	118d	
	דבר	WORD	182b	1 1c
	כאשר	AS	455b	1 a
	לון	LODGE	533c	1 a
	לילה	NIGHT	538d	1
	פה	HERE	806a	1 a
	שר	CHIEFTAIN	978a	2 a
	שוב	TURN BACK	999c	3
22 9	בלעם	BALAAM	118d	
	מי	WHO	566b	
22 10	מואב	MOAB	555d	2 a
	מלך	KING	573a	1
	צפור	ZIPPOR	862a	
22 11	אולי	PERADVENTURE	19c	1
	גרש	DRIVE OUT	177a	
	הלך	WALK	230c	1 1c
	כסה	COVER	492a	5
	לחם	ENGAGE IN BATTLE	535c	
	לחם	ENGAGE IN BATTLE	535c	
22 12	עין	EYE	744d	4 a
	עתה	NOW	774b	1 e
	קבב	CURSE	866d	
	ארר	CURSE	76c	
22 13	ברך	BLESS	138d	2 b
	בקר	MORNING	134b	1 h
	הלך	WALK	231c	1 1d 5b
	מאן	REFUSE	549b	
22 14	הלך	WALK	231c	1 1d 5b
	מאן	REFUSE	549a	
22 15	כבד	BE HONORED	457c	1 b
	רב	MUCH	913b	1 e
	שלח	SEND	1018b	1 a
22 16	הלך	WALK	231a	1 d3 ga
	שלח	SEND	1018b	1 c
	מנע	WITHHOLD	586b	
	צפור	ZIPPOR	862a	
22 17	הלך	WALK	230c	1 1c
	כבד	MAKE HONORABLE	457c	2 a
	קבב	CURSE	866d	
22 18	אם	IF	49d	1 a1 c
	יהוה	YAHWEH	218d	2 1f
	זהב	GOLD	262d	5
	זהב	GOLD	263c	1
	כסף	SILVER	494a	3
	מלא	FULNESS	571b	
	עבד	SLAVE	714a	2
	עבר	PASS OVER	717c	2
	פה	MOUTH	805b	2 c
	מן	SMALL	882a	1 b
22 19	דבר	SPEAK	181b	3 e
	לילה	NIGHT	538d	1
22 20	אך	ONLY	36d	2 c
	אפס	NON-EXISTENCE	67b	2 ca
	לילה	NIGHT	539a	1
	סכן	BE OF USE	698b	
	קרא	CALL	895c	5 a
22 21	אתון	SHE-ASS	87d	
	אתון	SHE-ASS	87d	
	בקר	MORNING	134b	1 h
22 22	חבש	BIND	289d	1 c
	אתון	SHE-ASS	87d	
	אתון	SHE-ASS	87d	
	דרך	WAY	202c	1
	חיה	BURN	354a	2 a
	יצב	STATION ONESELF	426b	A
	ל	TO	512b	4 a
	מלאך	MESSENGER	521d	3
	נער	RETAINER	655a	2 a
	רכב	RIDE	938c	2
	שטן	ADVERSARY	966b	1
22 23	אתון	SHE-ASS	87d	
	דרך	WAY	202c	1
	הלך	WALK	231b	1 d3 ge
	חרב	SWORD	352c	1 c
	יד	HAND	390d	5 c1
	מלאך	MESSENGER	521d	3
	נמה	BEND	640b	3 a
	נמה	INCLINE	640d	3 a
	נכה	SMITE	645b	1 a
	נצב	STAND	662a	1 a
	שדה	FIELD	961c	1 f
	שלף	DRAW OUT	1025b	1
22 24	גדר	WALL	155a	
	זה	THIS	262a	6 e
	מלאך	MESSENGER	521d	3
	עמד	STAND	763d	1 a
	משעול	HOLLOW WAY	1043c	
22 25	אתון	SHE-ASS	87d	
	מלאך	MESSENGER	521d	3
	לחץ	PRESS	537b	1
	לחץ	SQUEEZE ONESELF	537d	
	נכה	SMITE	645b	1 a
	קיר	WALL	885a	2
22 26	אשר	PARTICLE OF RELATION	82c	4 bb

NUMBERS

Ch v.	Heb	Eng	Page	Sec
	ימין	RIGHT HAND	411d	2 b
	יסף	DO AGAIN	415c	2 a
	מלאך	MESSENGER	521d	3
	נטה	BEND	640b	3 a
	עבר	PASS OVER	718a	5 a
	עמד	STAND	763d	1 a
	צר	NARROW	865a	
	מקום	STANDING PLACE	880a	4
22 27	אתון	SHE-ASS	87d	
	חרה	BURN	354a	1 a
	מלאך	MESSENGER	521d	3
	מקל	STAFF	596c	2
	נכה	SMITE	645b	1 a
	רבץ	LIE DOWN	918b	
22 28	אמר	SAY	55d	1
	אתון	SHE-ASS	87d	
	זה	THIS	261d	4 i
	מה	WHAT	552c	1 a
	נכה	SMITE	645b	1 a
	פה	MOUTH	805b	3
	פתח	OPEN	835b	
	רגל	FOOT	920a	2
22 29	אתון	SHE-ASS	87d	
	הרג	KILL	247b	4
	יש	BE	441c	2 a
	כי	THAT	*472c	1 db
	לו	IF	530b	2
	עלל	ACT ARBITRARILY	759d	1
	עתה	NOW	774c	2 ga
22 30	אתון	SHE-ASS	87d	
	יום	DAY	401b	7 l
	כה	THUS	462b	1 b
	סכן	BE OF US	698b	
	עוד	STILL	729c	2 b
	רכב	RIDE	938d	2
22 31	אף	NOSE	60b	2
	דרך	WAY	202c	1
	חרב	SWORD	352c	1 c
	יד	HAND	390d	5 c1
	מלאך	MESSENGER	521d	3
	נצב	STAND	662a	1 a
	עין	EYE	744b	1 j
	קדד	BOW DOWN	869a	
	שחה	BOW DOWN	1005c	2 d
	שלף	DRAW OUT	1025b	1
22 32	אתון	SHE-ASS	87d	
	זה	THIS	261d	4 i
	יצא	GO OUT	423d	2 c
	ירט	BE PRECIPITATE	437c	
	ל	TO	512b	4 a
	מלאך	MESSENGER	521d	3
	מה	HOW	554b	4 f
	נגד	IN FRONT	617c	2 b
	נכה	SMITE	645b	1 a
	רגל	FOOT	920a	2
	שטן	ADVERSARY	966b	1
22 33	אולי	PERADVENTURE	19d	3
	את	MARK OF THE ACCUSATIVE	85a	1 a
	אתון	SHE-ASS	87d	
	גם	ALSO	169b	2
	הרג	KILL	247b	2
	חיה	LIVE	311c	1
	כי	THAT	472c	1 db
	לולא	IF NOT	530c	D
	נטה	BEND	640b	3 a
	רגל	FOOT	920a	2
22 34	דרך	WAY	202c	1
	חטא	MISS A GOAL OR WAY	307a	2 b
	ל	TO	515d	5 ib
	מלאך	MESSENGER	521d	3
	נצב	STAND	662a	1 a
	קרא	ENCOUNTER	897a	1
	רעע	BE EVIL	946c	1
22 35	אפס	NON-EXISTENCE	67b	2 ca
	מלאך	MESSENGER	521d	3
22 36	ארנן	ARNON	75a	
	גבול	BORDER	147d	1 a
	גבול	BORDER	148a	1 d
	קצה	END	892a	1
22 37	אמנם	VERILY	53d	
	הלך	WALK	231a	1 d3 ga
	יכל	BE ABLE	407c	1 b
	כבד	MAKE HONORABLE	457d	2 a
	קרא	CALL	895c	5 a
22 38	ה	INTERROG PART	209d	1 b
	יכל	BE ABLE	407c	1 b
	עתה	NOW	774a	1 a
	פה	MOUTH	805a	2 a
	שום	TO PLACE	963a	1 a
22 39	קריתחצות	KIRIATH-HUZOTH	900c	
22 40	בקר	CATTLE	133b	1 a
	זבח	SLAUGHTER FOR SACRIFICE	256d	1 l ba
22 41	במה	HIGH PLACE	119b	3
	במות	BAMOTH	119d	
	בעל	BAAL	127c	2 l
	בקר	MORNING	134b	2
	עלה	GO UP	749c	1 c
	קצה	END	892b	2
	שם	THERE	1027c	4 a
23	בלק	BALAK	119a	
23 1	איל	RAM	18a	2
	בנה	BUILD	124c	1 at
	מזבח	ALTAR	258b	1
	זה	THIS	261d	6 a
	כון	ESTABLISH	466c	2 b
	ל	TO	515b	5 hb a
	שבע	SEVEN	988a	1 b
23 2	ב	IN	89a	2 2
	מזבח	ALTAR	259a	1
	עלה	GO UP	749d	8
	עלה	GO UP	749d	8
23 3	אולי	PERADVENTURE	19c	1
	דבר	WORD	183d	4 6
	יצב	STATION ONESELF	426b	A
	מה	WHAT	552d	1 ae
	מה	AUGHT	553d	3
	עלה	WHOLE BURNT OFFERING	750c	
	על	UPON	756b	2 6c
	קרא	ENCOUNTER	897a	1
	קרה	ENCOUNTER	899d	1
	ראה	TO SEE	908d	1 a2
	ראה	TO SEE	908d	1
	שפי	BARE HEIGHT	1046a	2
23 4	מזבח	ALTAR	258d	8
	מזבח	ALTAR	259a	1
	עלה	GO UP	749d	8
	עלה	GO UP	749d	8
	ערך	ARRANGE	789c	1 a
	קרה	ENCOUNTER	899d	1
	שבע	SEVEN	988a	1 c
	מערכה	ADDENDA ET CORRIGENDA	1126a	
23 5	שוב	TURN BACK	997a	3 a
23 6	נצב	STAND	662a	1 a
23 6	עלה	WHOLE BURNT OFFERING	750c	
	על	UPON	756b	2 6c
23 7	ארם	ARAM	74c	B
	ארר	CURSE	76c	
	הלך	WALK	230c	1 lc
	זעם	BE INDIGNANT	276d	2
	משל	PARABLE	605b	3
	נחה	LEAD	635a	
	נשא	LIFT	670d	1 b 6
	יעקב	JACOB	785a	2
	קדם	FRONT	869c	1 b
23 8	אל	GOD	42d	6 f
	זעם	BE INDIGNANT	276d	2
	מה	HOW	553c	2 aa
	קבב	CURSE	866d	
	קבב	CURSE	866d	
23 9	בדד	ISOLATION	95a	1
	גוי	NATION	156d	1 c
	הן	BEHOLD	243c	A
	חשב	THINK	363c	
	צור	ROCK	849c	1 a
	ראש	HEAD	910d	2 a
	שור	BEHOLD	1003d	1
	שכן	SETTLE DOWN	1015a	1 a
23 10	אחרית	END	31a	B
	ישר	STRAIGHT	449b	3 c2
	מי	WHO	566d	F c
	מנה	COUNT	584a	1
	נפש	SOUL	660a	4 a1
	מספר	NUMBER	709a	1 b
	עפר	DRY EARTH	780a	2 a
	רבע	FOURTH PART	917d	
23 11	ברך	BLESS	139a	3
	קבב	CURSE	866d	
23 12	פה	MOUTH	805a	2 a
23 13	אפס	NON-EXISTENCE	67b	2 ca
	כל	ALL	*482b	1 ec
	קבב	CURSE	866d	
	מקום	STANDING PLACE	879d	1 a
	קצה	END	892b	2
	שם	THERE	1027c	4 b
23 14	בנה	BUILD	124c	1 at
	מזבח	ALTAR	258b	1
	מזבח	ALTAR	259a	1
	לקח	TAKE	543d	7
	עלה	GO UP	749d	8
	עלה	GO UP	749d	8
	עלה	WHOLE BURNT OFFERING	750c	
	פסגה	PISGAH	820a	
	צפה	KEEP WATCH	859c	
	יצב	STATION ONESELF	426b	A
23 15	כה	THUS	462b	2
	עלה	WHOLE BURNT OFFERING	750c	
	קרה	ENCOUNTER	899d	1
	פה	MOUTH	805a	2 a
23 16	קרה	ENCOUNTER	899d	1
	שוב	TURN BACK	997a	3 a
23 17	הנה	BEHOLD	243d	
	נצב	STAND	662a	1 a
23 18	אזן	HEAR	24c	1
	משל	PARABLE	605b	3
	נשא	LIFT	670d	1 b 6
	עד	AS FAR AS	724a	1 la
	צפור	ZIPPOR	862a	
	קום	STAND	878a	1 g
23 19	אדם	MAN	9b	2
	אנש	MAN	35d	
	אל	GOD	42d	6 f
	ו	AND	252b	1
	ו	AND	254b	3
	כזב	LIE	469c	1
	לא	NOT	519b	1 bb
	נחם	BE SORRY	637b	2
23 20	ברך	BLESS	139a	3
	ברך	BLESS	139a	2 a
	לקח	TAKE	543b	4 f
23 21	שוב	TURN BACK	999d	1
	און	TROUBLE	19d	1
	יהוה	YAHWEH	218d	2 le
	מלך	KING	573a	1
	נבט	LOOK	613d	1
	עמל	TROUBLE	765d	1
	תרועה	SHOUT OF WAR	930a	1
23 22	אל	GOD	42d	6 f
	תועפה	EMINENCE	419c	
	יצא	CAUSE TO GO	424c	1 a
	כ	LIKE	453d	1 b
	ראם	WILD OX	910b	
23 23	אל	GOD	42d	6 f
	אמר	SAY	56c	
	כ	LIKE	453d	1 b
	כי	THAT	472d	1 e
	נחש	DIVINATION	638d	
	עת	TIME	773c	1 a
	פעל	DO	821b	1 a
	קסם	DIVINATION	890c	1
23 24	ארי	LION	71d	
	דם	BLOOD	196c	2 c
	הן	BEHOLD	243c	A
	טרף	PREY	383c	1
	לביא	LION	522d	
	נשא	LIFT	672a	
	עד	UNTIL	725a	2 l b b
	שתה	DRINK	1059c	1 f
23 25	ברך	BLESS	139a	3
	קבב	CURSE	866d	
23 27	אלהים	GOD	44a	3 b
	ישר	BE STRAIGHT	448c	2
	לקח	TAKE	543d	7
	קבב	CURSE	866d	
	מקום	STANDING PLACE	879d	1 a
23 28	ביתפעור	BETH-PEOR	112c	
	ישימון	WASTE	445b	A
	לקח	TAKE	543d	7
	פנה	FACE	819a	2 7a e
	פעור	PEOR	822b	1
23 29	בנה	BUILD	124c	1 at
	מזבח	ALTAR	258b	1
	כון	ESTABLISH	466c	2 b
23 30	מזבח	ALTAR	259a	1
	עלה	GO UP	749d	8
	עלה	GO UP	749d	8
24 1	אל	TO	39d	3 a
	ברך	BLESS	139a	2 a
	הלך	WALK	233d	1 5 a
	טוב	PLEASING	373b	1
	נחש	DIVINATION	638d	
	פעם	OCCURRENCE	822a	3 b
	קרא	ENCOUNTER	897a	1
24 2	היה	BECOME	225d	2 1b
	ל	TO	516b	5 ja
	רוח	BREATH	925d	9 b
	שכן	SETTLE DOWN	1015a	1 a
24 3	בער	BEOR	129d	1
	גבר	MAN	150a	
	משל	PARABLE	605b	3
	נאם	UTTERANCE	610b	1
	נשא	LIFT	670d	1 b 6
	עין	EYE	744c	1 s
	שתם	OPEN	1060c	
24 4	אל	GOD	42d	6 f
	אמר	WORD	57a	1
	חזה	SEE	302c	2
	מחזה	VISION	303d	1
	נאם	UTTERANCE	610b	1
	נפל	FALL	657b	3 a
	עין	EYE	744c	3 a
	שדי	ALMIGHTY	995a	1
24 5	טוב	PLEASING	373b	1
	מה	HOW	553c	2 b
	יעקב	JACOB	785a	2
	משכן	DWELLING-PLACE	1015a	3 a
24 6	אהל	ALOE	14d	1
	ארז	CEDAR	72c	1 a
	גנה	GARDEN	171b	
	נהר	STREAM	625d	1
	נחל	WADY	636c	2
	נחל	PALM TREE	636d	
	נטה	STRETCH OUT	640c	
	נטע	PLANT	642b	1
	על	UPON	755d	2 6a
24 7	אגג	AGAG	8a	
	דלי	BUCKET	194d	
	זרע	SOWING	282b	2 a
	מלך	KING	573a	1
	מלכות	ROYAL POWER	574d	1
	נזל	FLOW	633d	1
	נשא	LIFT	672a	
	רב	MUCH	913a	1 b
	רום	BE HIGH	927a	2 c
24 8	אל	GOD	42d	6 f
	גרם	BREAK BONES	175a	2
	חץ	ARROW	346c	2
	תועפה	EMINENCE	419c	
	יצא	CAUSE TO GO	424c	1 a

Ch v.	Heb	Eng	Page	Sec
	מחץ	SHATTER	563c	
	צר	ADVERSARY	865d	
	ראם	WILD OX	910b	
24 9	ארי	LION	71d	
	ארר	CURSE	76c	
	ארר	CURSE	76d	
	ברך	BLESS	138d	2 b
	ברך	BLESS	139b	4 f
	ה	THE	*207d	1 f
	כרע	BOW DOWN	502c	2
	לביא	LION	522d	
	מי	WHO	566d	F c
	קום	STAND	879a	4 a
24 10	ברך	BLESS	139a	3
	חרה	BURN	354a	1 a
	כף	HOLLOW OF THE HAND	496c	1 d1
	ספק	SLAP	706c	1
	קבב	CURSE	866c	1
	קרא	CALL	895d	5 c
24 11	ברח	FLEE	138a	2
	כבד	MAKE HONORABLE	457d	2 a
	כבוד	HONOR	459a	3
	מנע	WITHHOLD	586a	
24 13	זהב	GOLD	262d	5
	זהב	GOLD	263c	1
	טובה	WELFARE	375d	3
	כסף	SILVER	494a	3
	לב	HEART	524c	2 3a
	מלא	FULNESS	571b	1
	מן	OUT OF	579c	2 cd
	עבר	PASS OVER	717c	2
	פה	MOUTH	805b	2 c
24 14	אחרית	END	31b	B
	יעץ	ADVISE	419d	
	ל	TO	511c	1 gb
24 15	בעור	BEOR	129d	1
	גבר	MAN	150a	
	משל	PARABLE	605b	3
	נאם	UTTERANCE	610b	1
	נשא	LIFT	670d	1 s
	עין	EYE	744c	1 s
	שתם	OPEN	1060c	
24 16	אל	GOD	42d	6 f
	אמר	WORD	57a	1
	חזה	SEE	302c	2
	מחזה	VISION	303d	
	דעת	KNOWLEDGE	395d	1 c
	נאם	UTTERANCE	610b	1
	נפל	FALL	657b	3 a
	עין	EYE	744c	3 a
	עליון	HIGHEST	751b	1
	שדי	ALMIGHTY	995a	1
24 17	בן	SON	*120d	1 ja
	בן	SON	121d	8 i
	דרך	TREAD	202a	1
	כוכב	STAR	456d	
	מחץ	SHATTER	563c	
	עתה	NOW	774a	1 a
	קדקד	HEAD	869b	
	קום	STAND	878a	4
	שאת	DIN OF BATTLE	981b	1
	שבט	ROD	987a	1 d
	שור	BEHOLD	1003d	1
	שת	SETH	1011d	1
24 18	אדום	EDOM	10c	3
	חיל	STRENGTH	298d	1 b
	ירשה	POSSESSION	440b	
	שעיר	SEIR	973a	1 a
24 19	אבד	DESTROY	2b	1
	מן	OUT OF	579a	2 ab
	יעקב	JACOB	785a	2
	רדה	HAVE DOMINION	922a	1
	שריד	SURVIVOR	975a	1
24 20	אבד	DESTRUCTION	2b	
	אחרית	END	31a	B
	אחרית	END	31b	C
	משל	PARABLE	605b	3
	נשא	LIFT	670d	1 b6
	עד	AS FAR AS	724a	1 la
	עמלק	AMALEK	766a	
	ראה	TO SEE	907c	6 a
	ראשית	BEGINNING	912b	1 a
24 21	מושב	DWELLING	444b	2 a
	איתן	ENDURING	450d	2
	משל	PARABLE	605b	3
	נשא	LIFT	670d	1 b6
	סלע	CRAG	701a	1
	קיני	KENITE	884a	
	קן	NEST	890a	1
	ראה	TO SEE	907c	6 a
24 22	אשור	ASSHUR	78d	2
	בער	CONSUME	129b	3
	כי אם	BUT	475b	2 b
	ל	TO	517d	7 bf
	מה	HOW	554b	4 e
	קין	KENITE	883d	1
	שבה	FLAME	985c	1 a
24 23	אוי	WOE	17a	
	אל	GOD	42d	6 f
	מי	WHO	566d	F c
	מן	SINCE	583c	7 c
	משל	PARABLE	605b	3
	נשא	LIFT	670d	1 b6
	שום	TO PLACE	963d	3 a
24 24	אבד	DESTRUCTION	2b	
	אשור	ASSHUR	78d	2
	ו	AND	254c	5 a
	יד	HAND	390c	3 d
	כתי	KITTIM	508c	
	עבר	REGION ACROSS	719d	1 b
	עבר	EBER	720a	1
	עד	AS FAR AS	724a	1 la
	ענה	BE BOWED DOWN	776b	1
	צי	SHIP	850d	
24 25	דרך	JOURNEY	203a	2
	הלך	WALK	231b	1 d3 gd
	הלך	WALK	234a	1 5e
25 1	אבל	ABEL	6a	3
	אל	TO	39c	1
	בת	DAUGHTER	123b	1 i
	זנה	COMMIT FORNICATION	275d	1
	חלל	POLLUTE	320d	2
	שטים	SHITTIM	1008d	1
25 2	זבח	SACRIFICE	257c	1 2
	שחה	BOW DOWN	1005c	3
25 3	בעל	BAAL	127c	2 1
	בעלפעור	BAAL-PEOR	128b	
	בעלפעור	BAAL-PEOR	128b	
	חרה	BURN	354a	2 a
	פעור	PEOR	822c	2
	צמד	BIND	855a	
25 4	אף	NOSE	60b	3
	חרון	BURNING OF ANGER	354c	
	יקע	HANG	429c	
	נגד	IN FRONT	617b	1 aa
	שוב	TURN BACK	997d	6 f
	שמש	SUN	1039b	4 a
25 5	בעל	BAAL	127c	2 1
	בעלפעור	BAAL-PEOR	128b	
	הרג	KILL	247b	3
	ל	TO	511a	1 f
	פעור	PEOR	822c	2
	צמד	BIND	855a	
	שפט	JUDGE	1047b	1 b
25 6	איש	MAN	36a	
	בכה	WEEP	113c	6
	בן	SON	121a	1 jg
	מדיני	MIDIANITE	193c	
	עדה	CONGREGATION	417b	3
	מן	FROM	580c	3 a
	קרב	COME NEAR	897d	1 a
25 7	לקח	TAKE	542d	1
	פינחס	PHINEHAS	810a	1
	רמח	SPEAR	942b	
25 8	דקר	PIERCE	201a	1
	מגפה	PLAGUE	620a	3
	על	UPON	758d	4 2b
	עצר	RESTRAIN	783d	
	קבה	LARGE VAULTED TENT	866d	
	קבה	BELLY	867a	2
25 9	מות	DIE	559c	1 a1
	מגפה	PLAGUE	620a	3
	ארבע	FOUR	917b	2 b
25 11	חמה	RAGE	404d	2 c
	חמה	RAGE	*404d	2 c
	כלה	FINISH	478c	2 c2
	על	UPON	758d	4 2b
	קנאה	ZEAL	888b	2 a
	קנא	BE ZEALOUS	888c	3 a
	שוב	TURN BACK	999d	6 a
25 12	ברית	COVENANT	136d	2 2d
	ברית	COVENANT	137a	3 1
	ברית	COVENANT	137b	3 2
	כן	SO	487a	3 d
	שלום	PEACE	1023a	5 b
25 13	אחר	AFTER	30a	2 b
	ברית	COVENANT	136d	2 2d
	ברית	COVENANT	137a	3 2
	זרע	SOWING	282d	4 c
	כהנה	PRIESTHOOD	464d	
	כפר	COVER OVER	497c	2 a
	קנא	BE ZEALOUS	888c	3 a
	תחת	INSTEAD	1066a	2 3a b
25 14	מדיני	MIDIANITE	193c	
	זמרי	ZIMRI	275b	1
	נכה	SMITE	646c	4
	סלוא	SALU	699a	
	שמעוני	SIMEONITES	1035c	
25 15	אמה	TRIBE	52c	
	מדין	MIDIAN	193c	3
	מדיני	MIDIANITE	193c	
	יסף	DO AGAIN	415c	2 a
	כזבי	COZBI	469d	
	נכה	SMITE	646c	4
	צור	ZUR	849d	1
	ראש	HEAD	911a	3 f
25 17	מדיני	MIDIANITE	193c	
	צרר	SHEW HOSTILITY TOWARD	865c	
25 18	אחות	SISTER	27d	1
	מדין	MIDIAN	193c	2
	כזבי	COZBI	469d	
	ל	TO	513a	5 ad
	מגפה	PLAGUE	620a	3
	נכה	SMITE	646c	4
	נכל	CRAFT	647d	
	נכל	KNAVISH	647d	
	נשיא	PRINCE	672c	8
	על	UPON	754d	2 lf h
	פעור	PEOR	*822c	2
	צרר	SHEW HOSTILITY TOWARD	865d	
	עלדבר	ADDENDA ET CORRIGENDA	1122a	
25 19	יסף	DO AGAIN	415c	2 a
	מגפה	PLAGUE	620a	3
25 25	יסף	DO AGAIN	415c	2 a
26 1	חמול	HAMUL	328b	
26 2	בן	SON	121a	1 jg
	בן	SON	122a	9 a
	עדה	CONGREGATION	417b	3
	נשא	LIFT	671c	3 e
	צבא	WAR	839b	2
	ראש	HEAD	911b	7
26 3	דבר	SPEAK	181a	3 a
	ירדן	JORDAN	434c	
	ירדן	JORDAN	434c	
	מואב	MOAB	555d	2 b
	פואה	PUAH	806a	
26 4	בן	SON	122a	9 a
26 5	חנכי	HANOCHITES	335c	
	חנוך	ENOCH	335c	4
	פלאי	PALLUITES	811a	
	פלוא	PALLU	811a	
	ראובן	REUBEN	910a	1
	ראובן	REUBEN	910a	1
	ישראל	ISRAEL	975c	1
26 6	חצרוני	HEZRONITES	348a	1
	חצרון	HEZRON	348a	2 a
	כרמי	CARMI	501d	1
26 7	ראובני	REUBENITE	910a	1
26 8	אליאב	ELIAB	45a	B
	פלוא	PALLU	811a	
26 9	אבירם	ABIRAM	4d	1
	אליאב	ELIAB	45a	B
	דתן	DATHAN	206d	1
	עדה	CONGREGATION	417a	1
	נמואל	NEMUEL	649c	2
	נצה	STRUGGLE	663c	
	קרא	CALL	896a	5 d
	קריא	CALLED	896d	
	קרח	KORAH	901b	2
26 10	אש	FIRE	77c	2
	בלע	SWALLOW UP	118a	2
	עדה	CONGREGATION	417a	1
	נס	SIGN	652a	4
	פה	MOUTH	804d	1 a
	פתח	OPEN	835b	
	קרח	KORAH	901b	2
26 11	מות	DIE	560a	2 b
	קרח	KORAH	901b	2
26 12	ימואל	JEMUEL	410c	
	ימין	JAMIN	412c	1
	יכין	JACHIN	467c	1
	נמואל	NEMUEL	649c	1
	נמואלי	NEMUELITE	649c	
26 13	זרח	ZERAH	*280c	4
	זרחי	ZERAHITES	280c	2
	זרח	ZERAH	280c	4
	שאול	SAUL	982c	3
	שאולי	SHAULITES	982c	
26 14	שמעוני	SIMEONITES	1035c	
26 15	חגי	HAGGI	291b	2
	חגי	HAGGI	291b	1
	צפיון	ZIPHION	859d	
	צפלוני	ZEPLONITES	859d	
	שוני	SHUNI	1002c	1
	שוני	SHUNITES	1002d	2
26 16	אזני	OZNI	24c	
	אצבון	EZBON	69a	1
	ערי	ERITES	735c	
	ערי	ERI	735c	
26 17	ארוד	AROD	71b	
	ארודי	ARODI	71b	
	אראלי	ARELITES	72a	
	אראלי	ARELITES	72a	
26 18	ארבעים	FORTY	917b	1 a
26 19	יהודה	JUDAH	397b	1 1
	ער	ER	735c	1
	קדוש	HOLY	872d	2 b
26 20	זרח	ZERAH	280b	1
	זרחי	ZERAHITES	280c	1
	פרץ	PEREZ	829d	1
	פרצי	PEREZITES	829d	
	שלני	SHELANITES	1017c	
	שלה	SHELAH	1017c	
26 21	חמולי	HAMULITES	328b	
	חצרוני	HEZRONITES	348a	1
	חצרון	HEZRON	348a	2 b
	פרץ	PEREZ	829d	1
26 23	יששכר	ISSACHAR	441a	1
	פוני	PUNITES	806a	
	תולע	TOLA	1069a	
	תולעי	TOLAITES	1069a	
26 24	יוב	IOB	398a	
	ישוב	JASHUB	1000b	1
	ישבי	JASHUBITES	1000b	
	שמרני	SHIMRONITES	1038a	
26 25	יששכר	ISSACHAR	441a	1
	ארבע	FOUR	917b	2 c
26 26	אלון	ELON	19a	1
	אלני	ELON	19a	
	זבולן	ZEBULUN	259d	2
	יחלאלי	JAHLEELITES	404b	

NUMBERS

Ch	v.	Heb	Eng	Page	Sec
		יחלאל	JAHLEEL	404b	
		סרד	SERED	710a	
		סרי	SERED	710a	
26	27	זבולני	ZEBULUNITE	259d	
26	28	אפרים	EPHRAIM	68b	2
		בן	SON	120d	1 ja
		יוסף	JOSEPH	415d	1 b
		מנשה	MANASSEH	586d	1 b3 b
26	29	ילד	BEGET	409a	1
		מנשה	MANASSEH	586d	1 b3 a
26	30	אביעזר	ABIEZER	4c	1
		אביעזרי	ABIEZRITE	4c	
		חלק	HELEK	324c	
		חלקי	HELEKITES	324c	
26	31	אשריאל	ASRIEL	77b	
		אשראלי	ASRIELITE	77b	
		שכם	SHECHEM	1014c	
		שכמי	SHECHEMITES	1014c	
26	32	חפרי	HEPHERITES	343d	
		חפר	HEPHER	343d	1
		שבעים	SEVENTY	988c	3 b
		שמידעי	SHEMIDAITES	1029a	
		שמידע	SHEMIDA	1029a	
26	33	צלפחד	ZELOPHEHAD	854c	
		חגלה	HOGLAH	291c	
		חפר	HEPHER	343d	1
		מחלה	MAHLAH	563a	1
		מלכה	MILCAH	574c	2
		נעה	NOAH	631c	
		תרצה	TIRZAH	953c	1
26	34	מנשה	MANASSEH	586d	1 b3 b
26	35	אפרים	EPHRAIM	68b	2
		בכר	BECHER	114b	1
		בכרי	BECHERITES	114b	
		תחן	TAHAN	334c	
		תחני	TAHANITES	334c	
		שתלחי	SHUTHELAITES	1004d	
		שותלח	SHUTHELAH	1004d	
26	36	ערני	ERANITES	735d	
		ערן	ERAN	735d	1
		שותלח	SHUTHELAH	1004d	
26	37	אפרים	EPHRAIM	68b	2
		בן	SON	120d	1 ja
		יוסף	JOSEPH	415d	1 b
26	38	אחירמי	AHIRAMITES	27c	
		אחירם	AHIRAM	27c	
		אחי	EHI	29a	
		אחרח	AHARAH	31b	
		אשבלי	ASHBELITE	78a	
		אשבל	ASHBEL	78a	
		בלע	BELA	118c	2
		בלעי	BELAITES	118c	
		בנימין	BENJAMIN	122d	1
		גרא	GERA	*173a	
26	39	גרא	GERA	*173a	
		חופם	HUPHAM	299c	
		חופמי	HUPHAMITES	299c	
		שפופם	SHEPHUPHAM	1051b	
		שופמי	SHEPHUPHAM	1051b	
26	40	אדר	ADDAR	12b	1
		ארד	ARD	71b	
		ארדי	ARDITE	71b	
		בלע	BELA	118c	2
		גרא	GERA	*173a	
26	41	נעמי	NAAMITES	564b	1
		נעמן	NAAMAN	654a	1
		בנימין	BENJAMIN	122d	1
26	42	אחר	AHER	31b	
		דן	DAN	192d	2
		דן	DAN	192d	2
		חשים	HUSHIM	302a	
		שוחמי	SHUHAMITES	1001d	
		שוחם	SHUHAM	1001d	
26	43	חשים	HUSHIM	302a	
		ארבע	FOUR	917b	2 c
		משפחה	CLAN	*1047a	1 d
26	44	אשר	ASHER	81b	2
		בריעה	BERIAH	140b	1
		בריעי	BERIITES	140b	
		ימנה	IMNAH	412c	1
		ישוי	ISHVI	1001a	1
		ישוי	ISHVITES	1001a	
26	45	בריעה	BERIAH	140b	1
		חבר	HEBER	288c	2
		חברי	HEBERITE	288d	
		מלכיאל	MALCHIEL	575c	
		מלכיאלי	MALCHIELITES	575c	
26	46	אשר	ASHER	81b	2
		שרח	SERAH	976b	
26	47	אשר	ASHER	81b	2
26	48	גוני	GUNI	157b	1
		גוני	GUNITES	157b	
		יחצאל	JAHZEEL	345d	
		יחצאלי	JAHZEELITES	345d	
26	49	יצר	JEZER	428a	
		יצרי	JEZERITE	428b	B
		שלם	SHILLEM	1024a	
		שלמי	SHILLEMITES	1024b	
26	51	אלף	THOUSAND	49a	1 c
		ב	IN	89a	1 7b
26	53	חלק	DIVIDE	323c	
		חלק	DIVIDE	323d	2 a
		נחלה	PROPERTY	635b	1 b
26	54	מעט	BE SMALL	589c	A
		מעט	A FEW	589d	1 a
		נתן	GIVE	681d	1 a
		פה	MOUTH	805c	6 c1
		רב	MUCH	913a	1 c
		רבה	BECOME MANY	915c	1 c
26	55	גורל	LOT	174b	1
		חלק	DIVIDE	323c	
		חלק	DIVIDE	323d	2 a
		נחל	TAKE AS A POSSES-SION	635c	1 b
26	56	גורל	LOT	174b	1
		חלק	DIVIDE	323c	
		חלק	DIVIDE	323d	2 a
		מעט	A FEW	589d	1 a
		נחלה	PROPERTY	635b	1 b
		רב	MUCH	913a	1 c
26	57	גרשן	GERSHON	177b	
		גרשני	GERSHONITES	177b	
		לוי	LEVITE	532d	2
		מררי	MERARI	601b	
		מררי	MERARITES	601b	
		קהתי	KOHATHITES	875c	
		חברוני	HEBRONITE	289c	
26	58	ילד	BEGET	409a	1
		לבני	LIBNITE	526d	
		לוי	LEVI	532c	2
		מושי	MUSHITES	559b	
		קהת	KOHATH	875b	
		קרחי	KORAHITES	901c	
26	59	דדה	AUNT	*187d	
		יוכבד	JOCHEBED	222a	
		לוי	LEVI	532c	1 a
		מרים	MIRIAM	599b	1
		משה	MOSES	602c	
26	60	איתמר	ITHAMAR	16a	
		ילד	BE BORN	408d	
		נדב	NADAB	621c	1
26	61	אש	FIRE	77c	4
		זור	BE A STRANGER	266d	2 d
		מות	DIE	560a	2 b
		נדב	NADAB	621c	1
		קרב	COME NEAR	898a	2 b5
26	62	בן	SON	122a	9 a
		זכר	MALE	271c	1 1 b
		חדש	NEW MOON	294c	2 a
		נתן	GIVE	681b	1 a
		פקד	ATTEND TO	823d	
26	63	ירדן	JORDAN	434c	
26	64	מואב	MOAB	555d	2 b
		היה	BE	226d	3 1
		סיני	SINAI	696a	
26	65	יהושע	JOSHUA	221c	1
		יתר	BE LEFT OVER	451b	
		כיאם	EXCEPT	474d	2 a
		כלב	CALEB	477a	
		מות	DIE	560a	2 b
27	1	חגלה	HOGLAH	291c	
		חפר	HEPHER	343d	1
		מחלה	MAHLAH	563a	1
		מלכה	MILCAH	574c	2
		מנשה	MANASSEH	586d	1 b2 d
		מנשה	MANASSEH	586d	1 b3 b
		נעה	NOAH	631c	
		צלפחד	ZELOPHEHAD	854c	
		תרצה	TIRZAH	953c	1
27	2	עמד	STAND	763d	1 d
27	3	חטא	SIN	308a	2
		יעד	GATHER BY AP-POINTMENT	417a	3
		עדה	CONGREGATION	417a	1
		עדה	CONGREGATION	417a	1
		מות	DIE	560a	2 b
		קרח	KORAH	901b	2
27	4	אחזה	POSSESSION	28c	
		גרע	WITHDRAW	175d	1
		שם	NAME	1028b	2 c
		משפחה	CLAN	1046d	1 a
27	5	קרב	COME NEAR	897d	1 a
		משפט	JUDGMENT	1048c	1 d
27	7	אחזה	POSSESSION	28d	
		אחזה	POSSESSION	*28d	
		דבר	SPEAK	180c	
		כן	RIGHT	467a	1
		נחלה	INHERITANCE	635c	3
		עבר	PASS OVER	718d	1 c
		צלפחד	ZELOPHEHAD	854c	
27	8	נחלה	INHERITANCE	635c	3
		עבר	PASS OVER	718d	1 c
27	9	אין	NOT	34d	3
		נחלה	INHERITANCE	635c	3
27	10	נחלה	INHERITANCE	635c	3
27	11	חקה	SOMETHING PRE-SCRIBED	350a	1
		ירש	TAKE POSSESSION	439c	1 a
		נחלה	INHERITANCE	635c	3
		קרב	NEAR	898c	2 c
		שאר	FLESH	985a	2
		משפחה	CLAN	1046d	1 a
		משפט	JUDGMENT	1048d	3
27	12	הר	MOUNTAIN	249d	1 a
		זה	THIS	261a	2 bb
		עברים	ABARIM	720d	
27	13	אסף	GATHER	62d	2 a
		אסף	GATHER	62d	2 a
		עם	KINSMAN	769b	
27	14	כאשר	SINCE	455c	2
		מי	WATER	565a	1
		מרה	BE REBELLIOUS	598b	2
		צן	ZIN	856c	2
		קדש	BE SET APART	873c	2
		קדש	KADESH	873d	1
		מריבה	MERIBAH	937b	2
		מריבה	STRIFE	937b	
27	16	אל	GOD	42d	6 f
		אלהים	GOD	44c	4 bb
		בשר	FLESH	142d	6 c
		ל	TO	*513d	5 cb g
		פקד	ATTEND TO	823c	B 1
27	17	רוח	BREATH	925b	4 b
		בוא	COME	97d	1 a
		בוא	COME	99a	1 a
		עדה	CONGREGATION	417b	3
		יצא	GO OUT	424a	3
		יצא	BRING OUT	424d	1 c
		פנה	FACE	817c	2 4c b
		צאן	SMALL CATTLE	838b	2
27	18	יהושע	JOSHUA	221c	1
		סמך	LEAN	702a	1 a
		רוח	BREATH	925b	3 h
27	19	צוה	GIVE CHARGE OVER	845d	1 d
27	20	הוד	MAJESTY	217b	3 b
		עדה	CONGREGATION	417b	3
		נתן	PUT	680c	2 b
27	21	אורים	URIM	22a	
		עמד	STAND	763d	1 d
		שאל	ASK	982a	2 b
		משפט	JUDGMENT	1048b	1 a
27	22	יהושע	JOSHUA	221c	1
27	23	דבר	SPEAK	181c	4 a
		סמך	LEAN	702a	1 a
		צוה	GIVE CHARGE OVER	845d	1 d
28	2	אשה	OFFERING MADE BY FIRE	78a	
		אשה	OFFERING MADE BY FIRE	78a	
		מועד	APPOINTED TIME	417c	1 a
		לחם	FOOD	537b	2 c
		ניחח	SOOTHING	629c	
28	3	אשה	OFFERING MADE BY FIRE	78a	
		יום	DAY	401a	7 i
		כבש	LAMB	461a	1
		תמיד	CONTINUITY	*556c	2 b
		תמיד	CONTINUITY	556c	2 b
		עלה	WHOLE BURNT OF-FERING	750b	
		עלה	WHOLE BURNT OF-FERING	750d	
28	4	בקר	MORNING	134a	1 e
		כבש	LAMB	461a	1
		ערב	SUNSET	788a	1 b
28	5	איפה	EPHAH	35b	1
		בלל	MIX	117c	2
		הין	HIN	228d	1 a
		הין	HIN	229a	1
		כתית	BEATEN	510c	
		מנחה	OFFERING	585c	5 b
		עשרון	TENTH PART	798a	
		עשירי	TENTH	798a	2
		רביעי	FOURTH	918a	4
28	6	הר	MOUNTAIN	249b	1 a
		הר	MOUNTAIN	250a	1 a
		תמיד	CONTINUITY	556c	2 b
		סיני	SINAI	696a	
		עלה	WHOLE BURNT OF-FERING	750b	
28	7	הין	HIN	229a	1 d
		הין	HIN	229a	1
		נסך	POUR OUT	650d	
		נסך	DRINK-OFFERING	651a	1
		רביעי	FOURTH	918a	4
		שכר	INTOXICATING DRINK	1016c	
28	8	בקר	MORNING	134a	1 e
		מנחה	OFFERING	585c	5 e
		נסך	DRINK-OFFERING	651a	1
		ערב	SUNSET	788a	1 b
28	9	בלל	MIX	117c	2
		נסך	DRINK-OFFERING	651a	1
		עשרון	TENTH PART	798a	
		קדש	HOLY	872d	2 b
28	10	תמיד	CONTINUITY	556c	2 b
		נסך	DRINK-OFFERING	651a	1
		עלה	WHOLE BURNT OF-FERING	750b	
		עלה	WHOLE BURNT OF-FERING	750d	
		על	UPON	755c	2 4b
		שבת	SABBATH	992c	1 d
28	11	איל	RAM	18a	2 d
		בן	SON	121c	7 b
		בקר	CATTLE	133b	1 a
		חדש	NEW MOON	*294c	1
		עלה	WHOLE BURNT OF-FERING	750c	
		עלה	WHOLE BURNT OF-FERING	750d	
		ראש	HEAD	911b	4 b
28	12	איל	RAM	18a	2 d
		בלל	MIX	117c	2
28	13	בלל	MIX	117c	2

Ch	v.	Heb	Eng	Page	Sec
		עלה	WHOLE BURNT OF-FERING	750d	
28	14	עשרון	TENTH PART	798a	
		איל	RAM	18a	2 d
		הין	HIN	229a	1 c
		הין	HIN	229a	1 c
		הין	HIN	229a	2
		הין	HIN	229a	1 c
		הין	HIN	229a	2
		חדש	NEW MOON	295a	2 b3
		חצי	HALF	345c	1
		יין	WINE	406c	B
		נסך	DRINK-OFFERING	651a	1
		עלה	WHOLE BURNT OF-FERING	750c	
		רביעי	FOURTH	918a	4
		שכר	INTOXICATING DRINK	1016c	
28	15	חטאת	SIN	309d	4 b
		תמיד	CONTINUITY	556c	2 b
		נסך	DRINK-OFFERING	651a	1
		עלה	WHOLE BURNT OF-FERING	750b	
		על	UPON	755c	2 4b
		עשה	DO	795b	2 d
28	16	פסח	PASSOVER	820b	3
28	17	אכל	EAT	37d	1
		חג	FESTIVAL-GATHER-ING	291a	1 b2
		מצה	UNLEAVENED BREAD	695b	
28	18	מלאכה	WORK	522a	3 b
		עבדה	LABOR	715b	1
28	19	איל	RAM	18a	2 d
		אשה	OFFERING MADE BY FIRE	78a	
		בן	SON	121c	7 b
		בקר	CATTLE	133b	1 a
		ל	TO	512d	5 aa
		עלה	WHOLE BURNT OF-FERING	750c	
		עלה	WHOLE BURNT OF-FERING	750d	
28	20	איל	RAM	18a	2 d
		בלל	MIX	117c	2
28	22	חטאת	SIN	309d	4 b
		כפר	COVER OVER	497d	3 b2
28	23	תמיד	CONTINUITY	556c	2 b
		עלה	WHOLE BURNT OF-FERING	750b	
		עלה	WHOLE BURNT OF-FERING	750b	
28	24	אלה	THESE	41d	D
		יום	DAY	401a	7 i
		לחם	FOOD	537b	2 c
		תמיד	CONTINUITY	556c	2 b
		נסך	DRINK-OFFERING	651a	1
		עלה	WHOLE BURNT OF-FERING	750b	
		על	UPON	755c	2 4b
		עשה	DO	795b	2 d
28	25	מלאכה	WORK	522a	3 b
		עבדה	LABOR	715b	1
28	26	בכורים	FIRST-FRUITS	114c	
		בכורים	FIRST-FRUITS	114c	
		חדש	NEW	294a	A
		יום	DAY	398d	2 i
		מלאכה	WORK	522a	3 b
		מנחה	OFFERING	585c	5 d
		עבדה	LABOR	715b	1
		שבוע	PERIOD OF SEVEN	989a	1
28	27	בן	SON	121c	7 b
		בקר	CATTLE	133b	1 a
		עלה	WHOLE BURNT OF-FERING	750c	
		עלה	WHOLE BURNT OF-FERING	750d	
28	28	בלל	MIX	117c	2
28	30	חטאת	SIN	309d	4 b
		כפר	COVER OVER	497d	3 b2
		עז	SHE-GOAT	777c	3 d
28	31	תמיד	CONTINUITY	556c	2 b
		מנחה	OFFERING	585c	6
		נסך	DRINK-OFFERING	651a	1
		עלה	WHOLE BURNT OF-FERING	750b	
		על	UPON	755c	2 4b
29	1	מלאכה	WORK	522a	3 b
		עבדה	LABOR	715b	1
		תרועה	SHOUT OF WAR	930a	2
29	2	איל	RAM	18a	2 d
		כבש	LAMB	461a	1
		עלה	WHOLE BURNT OF-FERING	750c	
		עלה	WHOLE BURNT OF-FERING	750d	
29	3	איל	RAM	18a	2 d
		בלל	MIX	117c	2
		מנחה	OFFERING	585c	5 b
29	5	חטאת	SIN	309d	4 b
		כפר	COVER OVER	497d	3 b2
29	6	תמיד	CONTINUITY	556c	2 b
		נסך	DRINK-OFFERING	651a	1
		עלה	WHOLE BURNT OF-FERING	750b	
		עלה	WHOLE BURNT OF-FERING	750c	

Ch	v.	Heb	Eng	Page	Sec
		על	UPON	755c	2 4b
29	7	כון	ESTABLISH	466c	2 b
		מלאכה	WORK	522a	3 b
		נפש	SOUL	660b	4 b6
		ענה	BE BOWED DOWN	776b	4
		עשור	A TEN	797c	1 b
29	8	עלה	WHOLE BURNT OF-FERING	750c	
		עלה	WHOLE BURNT OF-FERING	750d	
29	9	בלל	MIX	117c	2
		מנחה	OFFERING	585c	5 b
29	11	חטאת	SIN	309d	4 b
		כפרים	ATONEMENT	498c	
		תמיד	CONTINUITY	556c	2 b
		נסך	DRINK-OFFERING	651a	1
		עלה	WHOLE BURNT OF-FERING	750b	
29	12	חגג	MAKE PILGRIMAGE	290d	1
		חג	FESTIVAL-GATHER-ING	291a	1 b2
		חג	FESTIVAL-GATHER-ING	291b	1 b
		מלאכה	WORK	522a	3 b
		עבדה	LABOR	715b	1
29	13	בקר	CATTLE	133b	1 a
		עלה	WHOLE BURNT OF-FERING	750c	
		עלה	WHOLE BURNT OF-FERING	750c	
		קרב	COME NEAR	898a	2 b2
		ארבע	FOUR	917b	2 a2 g
		שלש	THREE	1025d	2
29	14	בלל	MIX	117c	2
		מנחה	OFFERING	585c	5 b
		עשר	TEN	797b	3 a
		שלש	THREE	1025d	2
29	15	ארבע	FOUR	917a	2 a2 g
29	16	חטאת	SIN	309d	4 b
		תמיד	CONTINUITY	556c	2 b
		נסך	DRINK-OFFERING	651a	1
		עלה	WHOLE BURNT OF-FERING	750b	
29	17	בן	SON	121c	7 b
		בקר	CATTLE	133b	1 a
		ארבע	FOUR	917b	2 a2 g
29	18	ל	TO	512a	3 b
		נסך	DRINK-OFFERING	651a	1
		מספר	NUMBER	709a	1 b
29	19	חטאת	SIN	309d	4 b
		תמיד	CONTINUITY	556c	2 b
		נסך	DRINK-OFFERING	651a	1
		עלה	WHOLE BURNT OF-FERING	750b	
29	20	עשר	TEN	797a	1 c
		עשתי	ONE	799d	
29	21	ל	TO	512a	3 b
		נסך	DRINK-OFFERING	651a	1
29	22	חטאת	SIN	309d	4 b
		תמיד	CONTINUITY	556c	2 b
		נסך	DRINK-OFFERING	651a	1
		עלה	WHOLE BURNT OF-FERING	750b	
29	23	עשר	TEN	796d	2 b
		רביעי	FOURTH	917d	1
29	24	ל	TO	512a	3 b
		נסך	DRINK-OFFERING	651a	1
29	25	חטאת	SIN	309d	4 b
		תמיד	CONTINUITY	556c	2 b
		נסך	DRINK-OFFERING	651a	1
		עלה	WHOLE BURNT OF-FERING	750b	
29	26	חמישי	FIFTH	332c	1
29	27	תשע	NINE	1077c	1 a
		נסך	DRINK-OFFERING	651a	1
29	28	חטאת	SIN	309d	4 b
		תמיד	CONTINUITY	556c	2 b
		נסך	DRINK-OFFERING	651a	1
		עלה	WHOLE BURNT OF-FERING	750b	
29	29	שמנה	EIGHT	1033a	1 b
29	30	נסך	DRINK-OFFERING	651a	1
		עשר	TEN	797b	
29	31	חטאת	SIN	309d	4 b
		תמיד	CONTINUITY	556c	2 b
		נסך	DRINK-OFFERING	651a	1
		עלה	WHOLE BURNT OF-FERING	750b	
29	33	נסך	DRINK-OFFERING	651a	1
29	34	חטאת	SIN	309d	4 b
		תמיד	CONTINUITY	556c	2 b
		נסך	DRINK-OFFERING	651a	1
		עלה	WHOLE BURNT OF-FERING	750b	
29	35	מלאכה	WORK	522a	3 b
		עבדה	LABOR	715b	1
		עצרה	ASSEMBLY	783d	1
29	36	עלה	WHOLE BURNT OF-FERING	750c	
		עלה	WHOLE BURNT OF-FERING	750d	
		קרב	COME NEAR	898a	2 b2
29	37	נסך	DRINK-OFFERING	651a	1
29	38	חטאת	SIN	309d	4 b
		תמיד	CONTINUITY	556c	2 b
		נסך	DRINK-OFFERING	651a	

Ch	v.	Heb	Eng	Page	Sec
		עלה	WHOLE BURNT OF-FERING	750b	
29	39	בד	SEPARATION	94c	1 d
		מועד	APPOINTED TIME	417c	1 b
		ל	TO	514c	5 fc
		מנחה	OFFERING	585b	5
		נדבה	FREEWILL-OFFER-ING	621d	2 c
		נדר	VOW	624a	5
		נסך	DRINK-OFFERING	651a	1
		עלה	WHOLE BURNT OF-FERING	750d	
		שלם	PEACE-OFFERING	1023c	
		שלם	PEACE-OFFERING	1023d	
30	2	דבר	WORD	182d	1 2a
		צוה	CHARGE	845d	2 d
30	3	אסר	TIE	64a	6
		אסר	BOND	64b	
		דבר	WORD	182d	1 1f
		חלל	POLLUTE	320c	1 b
		יצא	GO OUT	423c	1 g
		כי	IF	473b	2 b
		נדר	VOW	623d	
		נדר	VOW	624a	2
		פה	MOUTH	805a	2 a
		שבע	SWEAR	989a	1 a
		שבועה	OATH	989a	1 a
30	4	אסר	TIE	64a	6
		אסר	BOND	64b	
		נדר	VOW	623d	
		נדר	VOW	624a	2
		נעורים	YOUTH	655c	
30	5	אסר	TIE	64a	6
		אסר	BOND	64b	
		חרש	BE SILENT	361b	1 a
		ל	TO	510c	1 a
		נדר	VOW	624a	6
		נדר	VOW	624a	2
		נפש	SOUL	660a	4 b
		קום	STAND	878b	7 e
30	6	אסר	TIE	64a	6
		אסר	BOND	64b	
		נדר	VOW	624a	2
		נוא	RESTRAIN	626b	1
		נפש	SOUL	660a	4 b
		סלח	FORGIVE	699c	
30	7	איש	MAN	35d	
		אסר	TIE	64a	6
		מבטא	RASH UTTERANCE	105a	
		נדר	VOW	624a	2
		נפש	SOUL	660a	4 b
		על	UPON	753b	2 1c
30	8	אסר	TIE	64a	6
		אסר	BOND	64b	
		חרש	BE SILENT	361b	1 a
		ל	TO	510c	1 a
		נדר	VOW	624a	2
		נדר	VOW	624a	2
		נפש	SOUL	660a	4 b
30	9	אסר	TIE	64a	6
		מבטא	RASH UTTERANCE	105a	
		נדר	VOW	624a	6
		נדר	VOW	624a	2
		נוא	RESTRAIN	626b	1
		נפש	SOUL	660a	4 b
		סלח	FORGIVE	699c	
		על	UPON	753b	2 1c
		פרר	BREAK	830c	2 b
30	10	אלמנה	WIDOW	48b	
		אסר	TIE	64a	6
		גרש	CAST OUT	176c	
		נדר	VOW	624a	2
		נפש	SOUL	660a	4 b
		קום	STAND	878b	7 e
30	11	אסר	TIE	64a	6
		אסר	BOND	64b	
		בית	HOUSE	108d	1 a
		נדר	VOW	623d	
		שבועה	OATH	989d	1 a
30	12	אסר	TIE	64a	6
		אסר	BOND	64b	
		חרש	BE SILENT	361b	1 a
		נדר	VOW	624a	2
		נוא	RESTRAIN	626b	1
		אסר	BOND	64b	
30	13	מוצא	GOING FORTH	425d	2 a
		ל	TO	514c	5 fc
		נדר	VOW	624a	2
		סלח	FORGIVE	699c	
		פרר	BREAK	830c	2 b
		שפה	SPEECH	973d	1 a1
30	14	אסר	BOND	64b	
		נדר	VOW	624a	2
		נדר	VOW	624a	2
		נפש	SOUL	660a	4 b
		ענה	BE BOWED DOWN	776b	4
		פרר	BREAK	830c	2 b
		קום	STAND	879a	6 e
		שבועה	OATH	989d	1 a
30	15	אל	TO	39d	1
		אסר	BOND	64b	
		חרש	BE SILENT	361b	1 a
		מן	FROM	582b	5 d1
		נדר	VOW	624a	6
		נדר	VOW	624a	2

Ch	v.	Heb	Eng	Page	Sec
		על	UPON	753b	2 1c
		קום	STAND	879a	6 e
30	16	נשא	LIFT	671a	2 b
		עון	INIQUITY	731c	3
		פרר	BREAK	830c	2 b
30	17	חק	SOMETHING PRE-SCRIBED	349d	7 g
		חק	SOMETHING PRE-SCRIBED	349d	7 g
		נעורים	YOUTH	655c	
31	2	אסף	GATHER	62d	2 a
		מדיני	MIDIANITE	193c	
		נקם	AVENGE	668a	1 b
		נקמה	VENGEANCE	668c	2
		עם	KINSMAN	769b	
31	3	מדין	MIDIAN	193c	2
		חלץ	EQUIP FOR WAR	323b	
		נקמה	VENGEANCE	668c	2
		נתן	PUT	680d	2 b
		על	UPON	757d	2 7d
31	4	אלף	THOUSAND	49a	1 a
		ל	TO	512b	5 ab
		צבא	WAR	839b	2
31	5	אלף	THOUSAND	49a	1 a
		אלף	THOUSAND	49b	2
		חלץ	EQUIP FOR WAR	323a	2
		מסר	DELIVER UP	588b	
31	6	אלף	THOUSAND	49a	1 a
		חצצרה	CLARION	348c	2 b
		כלי	INSTRUMENT	480a	2 b
		צבא	WAR	839b	2
		תרועה	SHOUT OF WAR	930a	2
31	7	מדין	MIDIAN	193c	2
		הרג	KILL	247b	1 b
		זכר	MALE	271c	1 1 b
		צבא	WAGE WAR	838b	1
31	8	אוי	EVI	16c	
		אל	TO	40b	5
		בלעם	BALAAM	118d	
		בעור	BEOR	129d	1
		מדין	MIDIAN	193c	2
		מדין	MIDIAN	193c	2
		הרג	KILL	247b	1 b
		חור	HUR	301b	3
		חלל	PIERCED	319c	2
		על	UPON	755b	2 4b
		צור	ZUR	849d	1
		רבע	REBA	918b	
		רקם	REKEM	955d	1 a
31	9	בזז	SPOIL	102d	
		מדין	MIDIAN	193c	2
		חיל	STRENGTH	299a	3
		טף	CHILDREN	382a	
		מקנה	CATTLE	889b	2
31	10	טירה	ENCAMPMENT	377b	1
		מושב	DWELLING	444b	2 a
31	11	ב	IN	88c	1 2c
		מלקוח	BOOTY	544b	
31	12	בן	SON	121d	1 jg
		עדה	CONGREGATION	417b	3
		ירדן	JORDAN	434c	
		מלקוח	BOOTY	544b	
		מואב	MOAB	555d	2 b
		שבי	CAPTIVITY	985d	3
31	13	עדה	CONGREGATION	417b	3
31	14	אלף	THOUSAND	49a	2
		חיל	STRENGTH	299a	4
		מלחמה	WAR	536b	
		פקד	ATTEND TO	823d	B 1
		צבא	WAR	839b	2
		קצף	BE WROTH	893b	2
31	15	חיה	LIVE	311c	1
		נקבה	FEMALE	666c	1
31	16	בלעם	BALAAM	118d	
		דבר	WORD	182b	1 1d
		הם	THEY	241b	1 a
		עדה	CONGREGATION	417b	3
		מסר	DELIVER UP	588b	
		מגפה	PLAGUE	620a	3
		על	UPON	754d	2 1f h
		פעור	PEOR	822c	2
		עלדבר	ADDENDA ET COR-RIGENDA	1122a	
31	17	הרג	KILL	247b	1 b
		זכר	MALE	271c	1 1 a
		זכר	MALE	271c	1 1 b
		טף	CHILDREN	382a	
		ידע	KNOW	394b	3
		משכב	ACT OF LYING	1012d	2 b
31	18	אשה	WOMAN	61a	1
		זכר	MALE	271c	1 1 a
		חיה	LIVE	311c	1
		טף	CHILDREN	382a	
		ידע	KNOW	394b	3
		משכב	ACT OF LYING	1012d	2 b
31	19	הרג	KILL	247a	1 a
		חטא	MISS A GOAL OR WAY	307d	2 b
		חלל	PIERCED	319c	2
		חנה	DECLINE	333d	2 c2
		נפש	SOUL	660b	4 c2
		שבי	CAPTIVITY	985d	3
31	20	חטא	MISS A GOAL OR WAY	307d	2 b
		כלי	ARTICLE	479c	1
		עור	SKIN	736b	2

Ch	v.	Heb	Eng	Page	Sec
		עץ	TREE	781d	2 a
		מעשה	DEED	796a	2 a1
31	21	חקה	SOMETHING PRE-SCRIBED	350a	1
		תורה	LAW	436a	2 a
31	22	צבא	WAR	839b	2
		בדיל	TIN	95d	2
		ברזל	IRON	137c	2
		עפרת	LEAD	780c	
31	23	דבר	WORD	183d	4 6
		חטא	MISS A GOAL OR WAY	307d	2 b
		מהר	BE CLEAN	372b	2
		מי	WATER	565c	1 a
		נדה	IMPURITY	622c	1
		עבר	PASS OVER	718d	2 a
31	24	מהר	BE CLEAN	372b	2
31	26	ב	IN	88c	1 2c
		עדה	CONGREGATION	417b	3
		מלקוח	BOOTY	544b	
		נשא	LIFT	671c	3 e
		ראש	HEAD	911a	3 f
		ראש	HEAD	911b	7
		שבי	CAPTIVITY	985d	3
31	27	חצה	DIVIDE	345b	1
		מלקוח	BOOTY	544b	
		צבא	WAR	839b	2
		תפש	LAY HOLD OF	1074d	2
31	28	אדם	MAN	9b	2
		חמור	HE-ASS	331b	1
		מכס	TAX	493d	
		מלחמה	WAR	536b	
		נפש	SOUL	660b	4 c2
		צבא	WAR	839b	2
		רום	BE HIGH	927d	2
31	29	מחצית	HALF	346a	1
		תרומה	OFFERING	929b	4 d
31	30	אדם	MAN	9b	2
		אחז	GRASP	28b	
		חמור	HE-ASS	331b	1
		חמשים	FIFTY	332b	1 b1
		מחצית	HALF	346a	1
		משמרת	GUARD	1038c	4 a
31	32	אלף	THOUSAND	49a	1 c
		בזז	SPOIL	102d	
		בז	SPOIL	103a	2
		זהב	GOLD	263c	1
		חמש	FIVE	332a	4
		יתר	REMAINDER	451d	1 b
		מלקוח	BOOTY	544b	
		עם	PEOPLE	766c	2 d
		צאן	SMALL CATTLE	838b	1 b
		צבא	WAR	839b	2
31	33	אלף	THOUSAND	49a	1 c
		אלף	THOUSAND	49a	1 c
		בקר	CATTLE	133c	2
31	34	שבעים	SEVENTY	988c	3 b
31	35	חמור	HE-ASS	331b	1
		אדם	MAN	9c	2
		זכר	MALE	271c	1 1 a
		ידע	KNOW	394b	3
		נפש	SOUL	660b	4 c1
		משכב	ACT OF LYING	1012d	2 b
31	36	חלק	PORTION	324a	1 a
		מחצה	HALF	345d	
		צאן	SMALL CATTLE	838b	1 b
		צבא	WAR	839b	2
31	37	חמש	FIVE	332a	5 c
		מכס	TAX	493d	
31	38	בקר	CATTLE	133c	2
		מכס	TAX	493d	
31	39	שבעים	SEVENTY	988c	3 a
		חמור	HE-ASS	331b	1
		מכס	TAX	493d	
31	40	אדם	MAN	9c	2
		מכס	TAX	493d	
		נפש	SOUL	660b	4 c1
		נפש	SOUL	660c	4 c3
		שש	SIX	995c	2
		מכס	TAX	493d	
31	41	תרומה	OFFERING	929b	4 d
31	42	מחצית	HALF	346a	1
		צבא	WAGE WAR	838d	1
31	43	מחצה	HALF	345d	
31	44	בקר	CATTLE	133c	2
31	45	שש	SIX	995d	4
		חמור	HE-ASS	331b	1
31	46	אדם	MAN	9c	2
31	47	נפש	SOUL	660b	4 c1
		חמשים	FIFTY	332b	1 b1
		מחצית	HALF	346a	1
		משכן	DWELLING-PLACE	1015d	2 c
		משמרת	GUARD	1038c	4 a
31	48	פקד	ATTEND TO	823c	B 1
		צבא	ARMY	838d	1 a
31	49	איש	MAN	35d	
		יד	HAND	391a	5 c3
		מלחמה	WAR	536b	
		נשא	LIFT	671c	3 e
		פקד	ATTEND TO	823d	1
		ראש	HEAD	911b	7
31	50	מבעת	SIGNET	371d	2
		כלי	ARTICLE	479c	1
		כומז	A GOLD ORNA-MENT	484d	

Ch	v.	Heb	Eng	Page	Sec
		כפר	COVER OVER	497d	3 b2
		מצא	FIND	593c	4
		נפש	SOUL	660b	4 c1
		עגיל	HOOP	722d	
		צמיד	BRACELET	855b	
		צמיד	BRACELET	855b	
		אצעדה	ARMLET	858a	
		קרב	COME NEAR	898a	2 b6
		קרבן	OFFERING	898d	
		קרבן	OFFERING	898d	
31	51	כלי	ARTICLE	479c	1
		מעשה	DEED	796a	2 a1
31	52	אלף	THOUSAND	49a	1 c
		זהב	GOLD	263a	6
		רום	BE HIGH	927d	3 a
		תרומה	OFFERING	929b	4 d
31	53	בזז	SPOIL	102d	
		צבא	WAR	839b	2
31	54	בוא	COME	99a	1
		זכרון	MEMORIAL	272a	1 d
32	1	יעזר	JAZER	741c	
		מקום	STANDING PLACE	880a	3 d
		מקנה	CATTLE	889b	2
		ראובן	REUBEN	910a	2
32	2	עדה	CONGREGATION	417b	3
		ראובן	REUBEN	910a	2
32	3	אלעלא	ELEALEH	46c	
		ביתבעלמעון	BETH-BAAL-MEON	111a	
		ביתבעלמעון	BETH-BAAL-MEON	111a	
		דיבן	DIBON	192a	1
		חשבון	HESHBON	363d	
		נבו	NEBO	612d	1 a
		נמרה	NIMRAH	649d	
		יעזר	JAZER	741c	
		עטרות	ATAROTH	743a	1 a
		סבם	SEBAM	959b	
32	4	עדה	CONGREGATION	417b	3
		נכה	SMITE	646b	3
32	5	אחזה	POSSESSION	28c	
		חן	FAVOR	336b	2 b1
		מצא	FIND	592d	1 a
		נתן	GIVE	681d	1 a
		עבר	PASS OVER	718d	1 a
32	6	בוא	GO	98d	4
		ראובן	REUBEN	910a	2
32	7	מן	FROM	583b	7 ba
		נוא	RESTRAIN	626b	2
		נוא	RESTRAIN	626b	2
		עבר	PASS OVER	717a	1 a2
32	8	קדש	KADESH	874a	1
32	9	אשכל	ESHCOL	79b	2
		נוא	RESTRAIN	626b	2
		נחל	WADY	636c	2
		עלה	GO UP	748b	1 'c
32	10	חרה	BURN	354a	2 a
		שבע	SWEAR	989c	2
32	11	אדמה	LAND	10a	5
		בן	SON	121d	9 a
		בן	SON	122a	9 a
		מלא	FILL	570d	2
		יצחק	ISAAC	850c	
		שבע	SWEAR	989c	2
32	12	בלת	EXCEPT	116c	2 1
		בן	SON	120c	1 g
		בן	SON	120c	1 g
		יהושע	JOSHUA	221c	1
		זולה	EXCEPT	*265d	1
		כיאם	EXCEPT	*474d	2 a
		כלב	CALEB	477a	
		מלא	FILL	570d	2
		קנזי	KENIZZITE	889d	
32	13	דור	GENERATION	190a	2 a
		חרה	BURN	354a	2 a
		נוע	WAVER	631c	4
		רע	EVIL	948c	0 b
		תמם	BE FINISHED	1070c	5
32	14	אל	TO	40b	4
		אף	NOSE	60b	3
		חטא	SINFUL	308b	1 a
		חרון	BURNING OF AN-GER	354c	
		יסף	ADD	414d	
		ספה	SWEEP AWAY	705a	1
		קום	STAND	878a	4
		תרבות	INCREASE	916b	
		תחת	INSTEAD	1065d	2 2b a
32	15	אחר	BEHIND	30b	4 aa
		יסף	ADD	414d	
		ל	TO	512a	3 b
		נח	REST	628d	B 2
		שוב	TURN BACK	997d	6 a
		שחת	GO TO RUIN	1008a	1
32	16	בנה	BUILD	124c	1 a1
		גדרה	WALL	155a	
		נגש	DRAW NEAR	620d	1
		פה	HERE	806a	1 a
		מקנה	CATTLE	889b	2
		טף	ADDENDA ET COR-RIGENDA	1123d	
32	17	אם	IF	50c	1 cd
		מצר	FORTIFICATION	131c	
		חוש	HASTE	301d	
		חלץ	EQUIP FOR WAR	323b	
		חמשים	IN BATTLE ARRAY	332d	2
		עד	UNTIL	725a	2 1 aa

Ch	v.	Heb	Eng	Page	Sec
		סף	ADDENDA ET COR-RIGENDA	1123d	
32	18	נחל	TAKE AS A POSSES-SION	635d	1 a
32	19	בוא	COME	98b	2
		הלאה	OUT THERE	229c	A
		מזרח	PLACE OF SUNRISE	281a	2 c1
		ירדן	JORDAN	434c	
		מן	FROM	579a	1 c
		נחל	TAKE AS A POSSES-SION	635c	1 b
		עבר	REGION ACROSS	719c	1 b
		עבר	REGION ACROSS	719c	1 a
32	20	חלץ	EQUIP FOR WAR	*323a	2
32	21	חלץ	EQUIP FOR WAR	323a	2
		חלץ	EQUIP FOR WAR	*323b	
		ירש	CAUSE TO POSSESS	440a	2 a
		ל	TO	512c	5 aa
32	22	אחזה	POSSESSION	28c	
		כבש	BE SUBDUED	461b	
		מן	OUT OF	579d	2 d
		נקי	FREE FROM	667c	3
32	23	אשר	THAT	83b	8 ab
		חטאת	SIN	309a	2
		מצא	FIND	593a	3 c
32	24	בנה	BUILD	124b	1 aa
		גדרה	WALL	155a	
		יצא	GO OUT	423c	1 g
		פה	MOUTH	805a	2 a
		צנה	FLOCKS	856c	
32	25	צוה	CHARGE	846a	3
		ראובן	REUBEN	910a	2
32	26	מקנה	CATTLE	889b	2
		סף	ADDENDA ET COR-RIGENDA	*1123d	
32	27	אדון	LORD	11b	3 1g
		דבר	SPEAK	180c	1
		חלץ	EQUIP FOR WAR	323a	2
32	28	בן	SON	120c	1 g
		יהושע	JOSHUA	221c	1
		צוה	COMMAND	845d	1 e
		ראש	HEAD	911a	3 f
32	29	אחזה	POSSESSION	28c	
		חלץ	EQUIP FOR WAR	323a	2
		כבש	BE SUBDUED	461b	
		עבר	PASS OVER	717a	1 a1
		ראובן	REUBEN	910a	2
32	30	אחז	GRASP	28c	
		חלץ	EQUIP FOR WAR	323a	1
32	31	ענה	ANSWER	772a	1 d
		ראובן	REUBEN	910a	2
32	32	נחנו	WE	59d	
		חלץ	EQUIP FOR WAR	323a	1
		ירדן	JORDAN	434c	
		עבר	PASS OVER	717a	1 a2
		עבר	REGION ACROSS	719c	1 a
32	33	בשן	BASHAN	143c	
		גבולה	BORDER	148b	
		חטא	MISS 0A GOAL OR WAY0	307a	2 b
		חצי	HALF	345c	1
		יוסף	JOSEPH	415d	1 b
		ל	TO	516b	5 ja
		ממלכה	KINGDOM	575a	1
		מנשה	MANASSEH	586d	1 b2 d
		סיחון	SIHON	695d	
		עוג	OG	728b	
		ראובן	REUBEN	910a	2
32	34	בנה	BUILD	124d	1 i
		דיבן	DIBON	*192a	1
		דיבן	DIBON	192a	1
		עטרות	ATAROTH	743a	1 a
		ערער	AROER	792d	1
32	35	יגבהה	JOGBEHAH	147c	
		יעזר	JAZER	741c	
		עטרות	ATAROTH	743a	1 b
32	36	ביתהרם	BETH-HARAM	111c	
		ביתנמרה	BETH-NIMRAH	112b	
		מבצר	FORTIFICATION	131c	
		גדרה	WALL	155a	
32	37	אלעלא	ELEALEH	46c	
		בנה	BUILD	124d	1 i
		חשבון	HESHBON	363d	1
		קריתים	KIRIATHIAM	900b	1
		ראובן	REUBEN	910a	2
32	38	ביתבעלמעון	BETH-BAAL-MEON	111a	
		ביתבעלמעון	BETH-BAAL-MEON	111a	
		בנה	BUILD	124d	1 i
		מעון	BAAL-MEON	128a	
		נבו	NEBO	612d	1 a
		סבב	TURN ABOUT	686d	1
		קרא	CALL	896a	6 h
		שם	SEBAM	959b	1
32	39	הלך	WALK	230d	1 1d 3b
		ירש	CAUSE TO POSSESS	440a	2 a
		מנשה	MANASSEH	586d	1 b2 d
32	40	מנשה	MANASSEH	586d	1 b2 d
32	41	יאיר	JAIR	22c	1
		חות	TENT-VILLAGE	295d	
		ארגב	ARGOB	419a	1
		מנשה	MANASSEH	586d	1 b2 d
		קרא	CALL	896a	6 c
32	42	בת	DAUGHTER	123d	4
		נבח	NOBAH	613b	1

Ch	v.	Heb	Eng	Page	Sec
		נבח	NOBAH	613b	2
		קנת	KENATH	890b	
33	1	קרא	CALL	896a	6 h
		יצא	GO OUT	422d	1 a
		צבא	ARMY	838d	1 a
33	2	מוצא	GOING FORTH	425d	3 b
		קדש	APARTNESS	872b	6
33	3	יד	HAND	389d	1 e1
		יצא	GO OUT	422d	1 a
		מחרת	THE MORROW	564a	1
		נסע	SET OUT	652b	2 a
		נסע	SET OUT	652b	2 a
		פסח	PASSOVER	820b	3
		רום	BE HIGH	926d	2 b
		רעמסס	RAMSES	947c	
33	4	אשר	PARTICLE OF RE-LATION	82d	6 b
		בכור	FIRST-BORN	114b	1 d
		נכה	SMITE	646a	2 c
		עשה	DO	794a	1 1a 5
		קבר	BURY	868d	
		שפט	JUDGEMENT	1048a	
33	5	נסע	JOURNEY	652b	3
		סכות	SUCCOTH	697d	3
		רעמסס	RAMSES	947c	
33	6	אתם	ETHAM	87c	
		סכות	SUCCOTH	697d	2
		קצה	END	892b	2
33	7	אתם	ETHAM	87c	
		בעלצפון	BAAL-ZEPHON	128b	
		מגדל	MIGDOL	154a	
		נסע	SET OUT	652b	2 a
		על	UPON	757b	2 7c ab
		פיחהירת	PI-BESETH	809d	
		פנה	FACE	817c	2 4d
		פנה	FACE	818d	27a d
		שוב	TURN BACK	996d	1
33	8	אתם	ETHAM	87c	
		מדבר	WILDERNESS	185a	3 a
		דרך	JOURNEY	203a	2
		הלך	WALK	230c	1 1d 1b
		יום	DAY	398c	2 b
		מרה	MARAH	600d	
		נסע	SET OUT	652b	2 a
		עבר	PASS OVER	717c	3 b
		פיחהירת	PI-BESETH	809d	
		תוך	MIDST	1063d	
33	9	אילים	ELIM	18c	
		מרה	MARAH	600d	
		נסע	SET OUT	652b	2 a
		עין	SPRING	745b	
		שבעים	SEVENTY	988c	1 b
		תמר	PALM-TREE	1071c	
		אילים	ELIM	18c	
33	10	חנה	DECLINE	333c	2 c2
		סוף	REEDS	693b	2 a
33	11	לקח	TAKE	543c	6
		סוף	REEDS	693b	2 a
		סין	SIN	695d	
33	12	דפקה	DOPHKAH	200c	
		סין	SIN	695d	
33	13	אלוש	ALUSH	47a	
		דפקה	DOPHKAH	200c	
33	14	אלוש	ALUSH	47a	
		רפידים	REPHIDIM	951c	
		שתה	DRINK	1059b	1 a
		סיני	SINAI	696a	
		רפידים	REPHIDIM	951c	
33	15	סיני	SINAI	696a	
33	16	תאוה	DESIRE	16c	1
		סיני	SINAI	696a	
		קברותהתאוה	KIBROTH-HATTA-AVAH	869a	
33	17	תאוה	DESIRE	16c	1
		חצרות	HAZEROTH	348a	
		קברותהתאוה	KIBROTH-HATTA-AVAH	869a	
33	18	חצרות	HAZEROTH	348a	
		רתמה	RITHMAH	958c	
33	19	רמנפרץ	RIMMON-PEREZ	942b	
		רתמה	RITHMAH	958c	
33	20	לבנה	LIBNAH	526c	2
		רמנפרץ	RIMMON-PEREZ	942b	
33	21	לבנה	LIBNAH	526c	2
		רסה	RISSAH	943d	
33	22	קהלתה	KEHELATHAH	875b	
		רסה	RISSAH	943d	
33	23	קהלתה	KEHELATHAH	875b	
		שפר	SHEPHER	1051c	
33	24	חרדה	HARADAH	354a	
		שפר	SHEPHER	1051c	
33	25	חרדה	HARADAH	354a	
		מקהלת	MAKHELOTH	875b	
33	26	מקהלת	MAKHELOTH	875b	
		תחת	TAHATH	1066c	2
33	27	תחת	TAHATH	1066c	2
		תרח	TERAH	1076c	2
33	28	מתקה	MITHKAH	609a	
		תרח	TERAH	1076c	2
33	29	חשמנה	HASHMONAH	365c	
		מתקה	MITHKAH	609a	
33	30	מסרות	MOSERAH	64c	
		חשמנה	HASHMONAH	365c	
33	31	מסרות	MOSERAH	64c	
		בארתבנייעק	BEEROTH BENE-JA-AKAN	*92b	
		בנייעקן	BENE-JAAKAN	122c	

Ch	v.	Heb	Eng	Page	Sec
		בנייעקן	BENE-JAAKAN	122c	
33	32	בארתבנייעק	BEEROTH BENE-JA-AKAN	*92b	
		בנייעקן	BENE-JAAKAN	122c	
		גדגדה	GUDGODAH	*151d	
		חר	HOLLOW	301b	
33	33	יטבתה	JOTBATHAH	406a	
33	34	יטבתה	JOTBATHAH	406a	
		עברנה	ABRONAH	720d	
33	35	עברנה	ABRONAH	721a	
		עציונגבר	EZION-GEBER	782b	
33	36	עציונגבר	EZION-GEBER	782b	
		צן	ZIN	856c	
		קדש	KADESH	873d	1
33	37	אדום	EDOM	10c	3
		מוסרה	MOSERAH	64c	
		חר	HOR	246d	1
		חר	MOUNTAIN	250a	1 a
		קדש	KADESH	873d	1
		קצה	END	892b	2
33	38	חר	HOR	246d	1
		חמישי	FIFTH	332c	1
		ארבעים	FORTY	917c	3
33	39	אהרן	AARON	14d	1
		חר	HOR	246d	1
33	40	כנעני	CANAANITE	489a	2 a
		נגב	SOUTH-COUNTRY	616b	1 a
		ערד	ARAD	788c	
33	41	חר	HOR	246d	1
		צלמנה	ZALMONAH	854a	2 c
33	42	פונן	PUNON	806d	
		צלמנה	ZALMONAH	854a	1 d
33	43	אבת	OBOTH	15c	
		פונן	PUNON	806d	
33	44	אבת	OBOTH	15c	
		גבול	BORDER	147d	1 a
		עיים	IYIM	743d	1
33	45	דיבן	DIBON	192a	1
		עיים	IYIM	743d	1
33	46	ביתדבלתים	BETH-DIBLATHAIM	111b	
		דבלתים	DIBLATHAIM	179c	
		דיבן	DIBON	192a	1
		עלמנדבלתי	ALMON-DIBLATHA-IM	761b	
33	47	ביתדבלתים	BETH-DIBLATHAIM	111b	
		דבלתים	DIBLATHAIM	179c	
		חר	MOUNTAIN	249b	1 a
		נבו	NEBO	612d	2
		עלמנדבלתי	ALMON-DIBLATHA-IM	761b	
33	48	חר	MOUNTAIN	249b	1 a
		ירדן	JORDAN	434c	
		מואב	MOAB	555d	2 b
33	49	אבל	ABEL	6a	3
		ביתהישימות	BETH-JESHIMOTH	111d	
		ישימון	WASTE	*445c	A
		מואב	MOAB	555d	2 b
		שטים	SHITTIM	1008d	1
33	50	ירדן	JORDAN	434c	
		מואב	MOAB	555d	2 b
33	51	כי	WHEN	473b	2 a
33	52	אבד	CAUSE TO PERISH	2a	1
		במה	HIGH PLACE	119b	3
		ירש	CAUSE TO POSSESS	440a	2 a
		ירש	CAUSE TO POSSESS	440a	2 a
		מסכה	MOLTEN IMAGE	651b	2
		צלם	IMAGE	853d	1
		משכית	SHOW-PIECE	967c	1
33	53	שמד	BE EXTERMINATED	1029c	2
		ירש	TAKE POSSESSION	439c	1 a
		ירש	CAUSE TO POSSESS	440a	2 a
33	54	אל	TO	40d	
		גורל	LOT	174b	1
		גורל	LOT	174b	1
		יצא	GO OUT	423b	1 f
		מעט	BE SMALL	589c	A
		מעט	A FEW	589d	1 a
		נחל	TAKE AS A POSSES-SION	635d	
		רב	MUCH	913a	1 c
		רבה	BECOME MANY	915c	1 c
		שם	THERE	1027c	3 b
		משפחה	CLAN	1046d	1 c
33	55	ירש	CAUSE TO POSSESS	440a	2 a
		ירש	CAUSE TO POSSESS	440a	2 a
		יתר	LEAVE OVER	451c	1 a
		צד	SIDE	841a	
		צד	SIDE	841a	
		צנין	THORN	856d	
		צרר	SHEW HOSTILITY TOWARD	865c	
		שך	THORN	968a	
33	56	דמה	BE LIKE	198a	2
		היה	COME TO PASS	225a	1 2b ad
		ל	TO	517d	7 bc
34	2	ב	IN	89a	1 7b
		גבולה	BORDER	148b	
		כי	WHEN	473b	2 a
		כנען	CANAAN	488d	2 a
		נחלה	PROPERTY	635b	1 b
		נפל	FALL	*657a	1
34	3	גבול	BORDER	147d	1 a
		יד	HAND	391c	5 h3
		ים	SEA	411a	3
		מלח	SALT	571d	
		נגב	SOUTH-COUNTRY	616b	1 a

Ch v.	Heb	Eng	Page	Sec
	נגב	SOUTH-COUNTRY	616b	2
	צן	ZIN	856c	
	קדם	EASTWARD	870a	
	קצה	END	892a	1
34 4	אדר	ADDAR	12b	2
	חצראדר	HAZARADDAR	347b	
	חצרן	HEZRON	348a	1 a
	יצא	GO OUT	423d	1 h
	תוצאה	OUT GOING	426a	1
	ל	TO	512d	5 aa
	נגב	SOUTH-COUNTRY	616b	2
	סבב	TURN AROUND	686a	1 c
	עבר	PASS OVER	718a	5 b
	מעלה	ASCENT	751c	1
	עצמון	AZMON	783b	
	צן	ZIN	856c	
	קדש	KADESH	874a	1
34 5	ים	SEA	410d	1
	תוצאה	OUT GOING	426a	1
	נחל	WADY	636c	2
	סבב	TURN AROUND	686b	1 c
	עצמון	AZMON	783b	
34 6	גדול	GREAT	153a	1
	ו	AND	252c	1 c
	ו	AND	*252d	1 c
	ים	SEA	410d	1
	ים	SEA	411b	9
34 7	אוה	DESIRE	16b	
	הר	HOR	246d	2
	ים	SEA	410d	1
	צפון	NORTH	861a	
	תאה	MARK OUT	1060d	
	תאר	DRAW IN OUTLINE	1061c	
34 8	אוה	DESIRE	16b	
	בוא	COME	98d	2 e
	הר	HOR	246d	2
	חמת	HAMATH	333a	
	תוצאה	OUT GOING	426a	1
	צדד	ZEDAD	841b	
	תאה	MARK OUT	1060d	
	תאר	DRAW IN OUTLINE	1061c	
34 9	זפרן	ZIPHRON	277d	
	חצרעינן	HAZAR-ENAN	347c	
	יצא	GO OUT	423d	1 h
	תוצאה	OUT GOING	426a	1
	צפון	NORTH	861a	
34 10	אוה	DESIRE	16b	
	חצרעינן	HAZAR-ENAN	347c	
	מן	FROM	582b	5 d3
	קדם	EASTWARD	870a	
	שפם	SHEPHAM	1050d	
	תאה	MARK OUT	*1060d	
	תאר	DRAW IN OUTLINE	*1061c	
34 11	ים	SEA	411a	4
	ירד	GO DOWN	433c	3 f
	כנרת	CHINNERETH	490b	2
	כתף	SIDE	509c	2 a
	מחה	STRIKE	562c	3
	עין	AIN	745b	1
	קדם	FRONT	869a	1 b 2
	קדם	EASTWARD	870a	
	רבלה	RIBLAH	916c	2
	שפם	SHEPHAM	1050a	
34 12	גבולה	BORDER	148b	1
	ים	SEA	411a	3
	תוצאה	OUT GOING	426a	1
	ירד	GO DOWN	433c	3 f
	מלח	SALT	571d	
34 13	גורל	LOT	174b	1
	חצי	HALF	345c	1
	נחל	TAKE AS A POSSESSION	635d	
	תשע	NINE	1077c	1 a
34 14	בית	HOUSE	110b	5 e
	חצי	HALF	345c	1
	לקח	TAKE	543b	4 f
	מנשה	MANASSEH	586c	1 b 2 g
	ראובני	REUBENITE	910a	
34 15	מזרח	PLACE OF SUNRISE	281a	2 c 1
	חצי	HALF	345c	1
	ירדן	JORDAN	434d	
	לקח	TAKE	543b	4 f
	עבר	REGION ACROSS	719c	1 a
	קדם	EASTWARD	870a	
34 17	בן	SON	120c	1 g
	יהושע	JOSHUA	221c	1
	נחל	TAKE AS A POSSESSION	635d	3
	נחל	TAKE AS A POSSESSION	635d	
34 18	נחל	TAKE AS A POSSESSION	635d	
	נחל	TAKE AS A POSSESSION	635d	3
34 19	בן	SON	120c	1 g
	יהודה	JUDAH	397b	1 2
	כלב	CALEB	477a	
34 20	עמיהוד	AMMIHUD	770b	1
	שמואל	SAMUEL	1028d	2
	שמעון	SIMEON	1035c	2
34 21	אלדד	ELDAD	44d	
	בנימין	BENJAMIN	122d	1
	כסלון	CHISLON	493b	
34 22	בקי	BUKKI	131c	1
	דן	DAN	192d	2
34 23	אפד	EPHOD	65d	

Ch v.	Heb	Eng	Page	Sec
	בן	SON	120d	1 ja
	חניאל	HANNIEL	337a	1
	יוסף	JOSEPH	415d	1 b
	מנשה	MANASSEH	586d	1 b3 g
34 24	אפרים	EPHRAIM	68b	2
	קמואל	KEMUEL	887d	2
	שפטן	SHIPHTAN	1049b	
34 25	אליצפן	ELIZAPHAN	45d	B
	זבולן	ZEBULUN	259d	2
	פרנך	PARNACH	828a	
34 26	יששכר	ISSACHAR	441a	1
	עזן	AZZAN	740a	
	פלטיאל	PALTIEL	812d	1
34 27	אחיהוד	AHIHUD	26d	
	אשר	ASHER	81b	1
	שלמי	SHELOMI	1025a	
34 28	עמיהוד	AMMIHUD	770b	4
	נפתלי	NAPHTALI	836d	2 a
34 29	נחל	TAKE AS A POSSESSION	635d	
35 1	ירדן	JORDAN	434c	
35 2	מואב	MOAB	555d	2 b
	אחזה	POSSESSION	28d	
	מגרש	COMMON-LAND	177b	
	סביב	ROUND ABOUT	687b	2 bb
	צוה	CHARGE	845d	2 b
35 3	מגרש	COMMON-LAND	177b	
	חיה	LIVING THING	312c	1 a
	רכוש	PROPERTY	940d	2
35 4	אלף	THOUSAND	48d	1
	אלף	THOUSAND	48d	1 a
	אמה	CUBIT	52b	1
	מגרש	COMMON-LAND	177b	
	חוץ	THE OUTSIDE	299d	1 a
	קיר	WALL	885a	2
35 5	אלף	THOUSAND	48d	1 a
	אמה	CUBIT	52c	1
	מגרש	COMMON-LAND	177b	
	חוץ	THE OUTSIDE	300a	1 bd
	ים	SEA	411b	9
	ים	SEA	411b	9
	מדד	MEASURE	551a	1
	מדד	MEASURE	551a	1
	נגב	SOUTH-COUNTRY	616b	2
	קדם	EASTWARD	870b	
	תוך	MIDST	1063c	
35 6	נוס	FLEE	630d	1
	נתן	PUT	681a	2 d
	על	UPON	755c	2 4b
	מקלט	REFUGE	886a	
	ארבעים	FORTY	917c	2 a
	רצח	MURDER	953d	
35 7	מגרש	COMMON-LAND	177b	
35 8	אחזה	POSSESSION	28c	
	מעט	A FEW	589d	1 a
	מעט	BE SMALL	589d	B
	נחל	TAKE AS A POSSESSION	635c	1 b
	פה	MOUTH	805c	6 bb
	רב	MUCH	913a	1 c
	רבה	BECOME MANY	915c	1 c
	דעת	KNOWLEDGE	*395c	1 a
	נכה	SMITE	*645d	2 a
	נכה	SMITE	646a	2 c
	נפש	SOUL	660b	4 c2
	עיר	CITY	746c	1 f
	מקלט	REFUGE	886a	
	קרה	ENCOUNTER	899d	2
	שגגה	SIN OF ERROR	993a	
35 12	גאל	ACT AS KINSMAN	145b	1
	מות	DIE	559d	2 a
	עיר	CITY	746c	1 f
	מקלט	REFUGE	886a	
	רצח	MURDER	953d	
	משפט	JUDGMENT	1048b	1 a
35 13	עיר	CITY	746c	1 f
	מקלט	REFUGE	886a	
	ירדן	JORDAN	434c	
35 14	עבר	REGION ACROSS	719c	1 a
	עיר	CITY	746c	1 f
	מקלט	REFUGE	886a	
35 15	גר	SOJOURNER	158b	2
	דעת	KNOWLEDGE	*395c	1 a
	תושב	SOJOURNER	444c	
	נכה	SMITE	*645d	2 a
	נכה	SMITE	646a	2 c
	נפש	SOUL	660b	4 c2
	מקלט	REFUGE	886a	
	שגגה	SIN OF ERROR	993a	
35 16	ברזל	IRON	137c	2
	כלי	IMPLEMENT	479d	2 a
	מות	DIE	559d	2 a
	נכה	SMITE	645d	2 a
	רצח	MURDER	953d	
35 17	אבן	STONE	6b	1
	יד	HAND	389b	1 c
	מות	DIE	559c	1 a1
	מות	DIE	559d	2 a
	נכה	SMITE	645d	2 a
	רצח	MURDER	953d	
35 18	יד	HAND	389b	1 c
	כלי	IMPLEMENT	479d	2 a
	מות	DIE	559d	2 a
	נכה	SMITE	645d	2 a
	עץ	TREE	781d	2 a

Ch v.	Heb	Eng	Page	Sec
35 19	רצח	MURDER	953d	
	גאל	ACT AS KINSMAN	145c	1 e
	דם	BLOOD	196d	2 e
	מות	DIE	560b	1 b
	פגע	MEET	803b	1
	רצח	MURDER	953d	
35 20	הדף	THRUST	213d	1
	צדיה	LYING IN WAIT	841b	
	שנאה	HATING	971d	1
	שלך	THROW	1021b	2 a
35 21	איבה	ENMITY	33c	
	גאל	ACT AS KINSMAN	145c	1 e
	דם	BLOOD	196d	2 e
	מות	DIE	559d	2 a
	מות	DIE	560b	1 b
	נכה	SMITE	645d	2 a
	נכה	SMITE	646a	2 c
	פגע	MEET	803b	1
	רצח	MURDER	953d	
35 22	איבה	ENMITY	33c	
	אם	IF	50a	1 a4 b
	הדף	THRUST	213d	1
	כלי	IMPLEMENT	479d	2 a
	כל	ALL	482a	1 eb
	לא	NOT	520a	4 aa
	פתע	SUDDENNESS	837b	
	צדיה	LYING IN WAIT	841b	
35 23	אבן	STONE	6b	1
	איב	BE HOSTILE TO	33c	
	בקש	SEEK	134d	2 b
	ל	TO	513a	5 ad
	לא	NOT	*519b	1 bc
	לא	NOT	520a	4 aa
	מות	DIE	559c	1 a1
	נפל	FALL	658a	1 g
	רעה	MISERY	949b	2
35 24	אם	IF	50a	1 a4 b
	גאל	ACT AS KINSMAN	145c	1 e
	דם	BLOOD	196d	2 e
	נכה	SMITE	646a	2 c
	על	UPON	754a	2 1f
	שפט	JUDGE	1047c	2 b
35 25	גאל	ACT AS KINSMAN	145c	1 e
	דם	BLOOD	196d	2 e
	ה	THE	207b	1 b
	ישב	REMAIN	442d	2 a
	כהן	PRIEST	464b	8
	מות	DEATH	560d	1
	משח	ANOINT	603b	3 a
	עיר	CITY	746c	1 f
	מקלט	REFUGE	886a	
	רצח	MURDER	953d	
	שמן	OIL	1032c	2 g
35 26	גבול	BOUNDARY	148a	2 b
	עיר	CITY	746c	1 f
	מקלט	REFUGE	886a	
	רצח	MURDER	953d	
35 27	גאל	ACT AS KINSMAN	145c	1 e
	גבול	BOUNDARY	148a	2 b
	דם	BLOOD	196d	2 e
	דם	BLOOD	197b	2 i
	מצא	FIND	593a	1 c
	עיר	CITY	746c	1 f
	מקלט	REFUGE	886a	
	רצח	MURDER	953d	
35 28	אחזה	POSSESSION	28c	
	כהן	PRIEST	464b	8
	מות	DEATH	560d	1
	מות	DEATH	560d	1
	עיר	CITY	746c	1 f
	מקלט	REFUGE	886a	
	רצח	MURDER	953d	
35 29	דור	GENERATION	190a	2 c
	חקה	SOMETHING PRESCRIBED	350a	1
	מושב	DWELLING	444b	2 c
	משפט	JUDGMENT	1048d	3
35 30	מות	DIE	559d	2 a
	נכה	SMITE	*645d	2 a
	נכה	SMITE	646a	2 c
	נפש	SOUL	660b	4 c2
	עד	WITNESS	729d	2 c
	ענה	ANSWER	773a	3 a
	רצח	MURDER	953d	
	רצח	MURDER	953d	
35 31	אשר	PARTICLE OF RELATION	82a	2 a
	הוא	HE, SHE, IT	215d	2 c
	כפר	RANSOM	497b	1
	ל	TO	515c	5 hc
	מות	DIE	559d	2 a
	רצח	MURDER	953d	
	רשע	WICKED	957b	1
35 32	כפר	RANSOM	497b	1
	מות	DEATH	560d	1
	נוס	FLEE	630d	1
	עיר	CITY	746c	1 f
	מקלט	REFUGE	886a	
	שוב	TURN BACK	997c	3 b
35 33	דם	BLOOD	196c	2 b
	דם	BLOOD	196c	2 b
	דם	BLOOD	197b	2 l
	חנף	BE POLLUTED	338a	1
	כיאם	EXCEPT	474a	2 a
	כפר	BE COVERED OVER	498b	2
	ל	TO	514d	5 g

Ch	v.	Heb	Eng	Page	Sec
35	34	שׁפך	POUR OUT	1049d	
		יהוה	YAHWEH	219b	2 2c
		טמא	BE UNCLEAN	379c	2
36	1	דבר	SPEAK	181c	3 f
		יוסף	JOSEPH	415d	1 b
		ל	TO	513b	5 cb g
		מנשה	MANASSEH	586d	1 b2 d
		ראש	HEAD	911a	3 f
36	2	אדון	LORD	11b	3 1g
		ב	IN	89a	17c
		ב	IN	89d	3 2c
		גורל	LOT	174b	1
		נחלה	PROPERTY	635b	1 b
		צוה	CHARGE	846b	2
		צלפחד	ZELOPHEHAD	854c	
36	3	אשה	WOMAN	61b	2
		גורל	LOT	174d	3
		גרע	WITHDRAW	175d	1
		יסף	BE JOINED	415a	2
		נחלה	INHERITANCE	635c	3
36	4	אם	IF	50c	1 b4 b
		גרע	WITHDRAW	175d	1
		יובל	RAM	385c	2
		יסף	BE JOINED	415a	2
36	5	בן	SON	120d	1 ja
		דבר	SPEAK	180c	
		יוסף	JOSEPH	415d	1 b
		כן	RIGHT	467a	1
36	6	אשה	WOMAN	61b	2
		דבר	WORD	182d	1 2a
		טוב	PLEASANT	374a	2 f
		עין	EYE	744d	3 c
		צוה	CHARGE	845d	2 d
		צלפחד	ZELOPHEHAD	854c	
36	7	דבק	CLING	179d	1 b
		סבב	TURNABOUT	685c	1 a
36	8	ירש	TAKE POSSESSION	439c	1 a
		נחלה	INHERITANCE	635c	3
36	9	דבק	CLING	179d	1 b
		סבב	TURNABOUT	685d	1 a
36	10	כאשר	AS	455b	1 b
		כן	SO	486c	2 ca
		צלפחד	ZELOPHEHAD	854c	
36	11	אשה	WOMAN	61b	2
		בן	SON	120b	1 b
		דוד	UNCLE	187c	2
		היה	BECOME	226c	2 2f
		חגלה	HOGLAH	291c	
		מחלה	MAHLAH	563a	1
		מלכה	MILCAH	574c	2
		נעה	NOAH	631c	
		צלפחד	ZELOPHEHAD	854c	
		תרצה	TIRZAH	953c	1
36	12	אשה	WOMAN	61b	2
		יוסף	JOSEPH	415d	1 b
		מנשה	MANASSEH	586d	1 b3 a
		על	UPON	755b	2 4a
36	13	ירדן	JORDAN	434c	2
		מואב	MOAB	555d	2 b
		צוה	CHARGE	846a	4 b
		מצוה	COMMANDMENT	846c	2 b3
		משפט	JUDGMENT	1049a	4

DEUTERONOMY

Ch	v.	Heb	Eng	Page	Sec
1	1	דיזהב	DIZAHAB	191d	
		חצרות	HAZEROTH	348a	
		לבנה	LIBNAH	*526c	2
		לבן	LABAN	526c	2
		מול	IN FRONT OF	557c	2
		סוף	REEDS	693b	2 b
		סוף	SUPH	693b	
		עבר	REGION ACROSS	719c	1 a
		ערבה	DESERT-PLAIN	787c	2 a
		פארן	PARAN	803a	
		ישראל	ISRAEL	975c	2 a1
		תפל	TOPHEL	1074b	
1	2	דרך	WAY	202d	1
		חרב	HOREB	352a	
		קדש	KADESH	874a	1
		שעיר	SEIR	973a	1 b
1	3	דבר	SPEAK	181a	3 b
		חדש	NEW MOON	294d	2 b2
		עשר	TEN	797a	1 c
		עשתי	ONE	799d	
		צוה	CHARGE	846a	4 a
		ארבעים	FORTY	917c?	3
1	4	אמרי	AMORITES	57c	2 a
		בשן	BASHAN	143c	
		אדרעי	EDREI	204c	
		חשבון	HESHBON	363d	
		ישב	DWELL	443a	3
		מלך	KING	573a	1
		נכה	SMITE	646b	3
		סיחון	SIHON	695d	
		עוג	OG	728b	
		עשתרות	ASHTAROTH	800b	
1	5	באר	MAKE DISTINCT	91c	
		יאל	SHOW-WILLING-NESS	384a	2
		תורה	LAW	436b	2 b2
		מואב	MOAB	555d	2 b
		עבר	REGION ACROSS	719c	1 a
1	6	ב	IN	88b	1 1
		חרב	HOREB	352a	
1	7	רב	MUCH	913b	1 f
		אמרי	AMORITES	57c	2 c
		הר	MOUNTAIN	250b	1 e
		הר	MOUNTAIN	251a	2 b
		הר	MOUNTAIN	251a	2 a
		חוף	SHORE	342b	
		ים	SEA	410d	1
		כנעני	CANAANITE	489a	2 b
		ל	TO	515d	5 ib
		לבנון	LEBANON	527a	
		נגב	SOUTH-COUNTRY	616b	1 a
		נהר	STREAM	625d	1
		נסע	SET OUT	652b	2 a
		ערבה	DESERT-PLAIN	787c	2 a
		פנה	TURN	815b	1 c
		פרת	EUPHRATES	832b	
		שׁבן	NEIGHBOUR	1015c	2
		שׁפלה	LOWLAND	1050c	1
1	8	אב	FATHER	3c	4 b
		אחר	AFTER	*30a	2 b
		זרע	SOWING	282c	4 b
		ירש	TAKE POSSESSION	439b	2
		נתן	PUT	680d	2 b
		פנה	FACE	817b	2 4b c
		ראה	TO SEE	907d	7 a
		שבע	SWEAR	989c	2
1	9	יכל	BE ABLE	407c	1 b
		נשא	LIFT	671a	2 a
1	10	עת	TIME	773b	1 a
		הנה	BEHOLD	243d	
		תורה	LAW	436c	3 b3
		כוכב	STAR	457a	
1	11	אלף	THOUSAND	49a	1 a
		ברך	BLESS	139a	2 a
		דבר	SPEAK	181b	3 c
		יסף	ADD	415b	1
		כ	LIKE	453b	1
		ל	TO	510d	1 b
		פעם	OCCURRENCE	822a	3 a
1	12	איכה	IN WHAT MANNER	32d	1
		טרח	BURDEN	382c	
		נשא	LIFT	671a	2 a
		משא	LOAD	672c	1
		ריב	STRIFE	936d	1
1	13	ב	IN	89a	17c
		בין	DISCERN	107a	
		חכם	WISE	314d	2
		ידע	KNOW	394a	2
		יהב	PROVIDE	396d	1
		ל	TO	515d	5 ia
		שׁום	TO PLACE	964a	3 d
		דבר	SPEAK	181d	6
1	14	טוב	PLEASANT	374b	5
1	15	חכם	WISE	314d	2
		חמשים	FIFTY	332b	1 a
		ידע	KNOW	394a	2
		לקח	TAKE	543b	4 d
		עשר	TEN	796d	1
		ראש	HEAD	911a	3 a
		שר	CHIEFTAIN	978b	2 b
		שטר	OFFICIAL	1009c	
		שטר	OFFICIAL	1009c	
1	16	איש	MAN	36b	1
		גר	SOJOURNER	158b	2
		צדק	RIGHTEOUSNESS	841c	2 a
		שפט	JUDGE	1047b	1 b
		שפט	JUDGE	1047c	2 b
		שמע	HEAR	1033d	1 h
1	17	גדל	GREAT	153b	7
		גור	DREAD	159a	1
		הוא	HE, SHE, IT	216a	3 b
		כ	LIKE	454c	2 bb
		ל	TO	513b	5 ba
		מן	THAN	582d	1
		נכר	REGARD	648a	1
		פנה	FACE	818b	2 6b
		קטן	SMALL	882b	1
		קרב	COME NEAR	897d	1 a
		קשה	BE SEVERE	904b	1
		משפט	JUDGMENT	1048b	1 a
		משפט	JUDGMENT	1048b	1 a
		שמע	HEAR	1033d	1 h
1	19	אמרי	AMORITES	57c	2 c
		את	MARK OF THE AC-CUSATIVE	85b	2
		גדול	GREAT	153a	1
		דרך	WAY	202d	1
		הוא	HE, SHE, IT	216d	7
		הלך	WALK	230c	1 1d 1a
		הר	MOUNTAIN	251a	2 b
		חרב	HOREB	352a	
		ירא	BE FEARFUL	431d	1
		נסע	SET OUT	652b	2 a
		קדש	KADESH	874a	1
		ראה	TO SEE	907b	3
1	20	אמרי	AMORITES	57c	2 c
1	21	ארץ	EARTH	76b	2 e
		דבר	SPEAK	181b	3 c
		חתת	BE SHATTERED	369b	2 a
		ירא	FEAR	431b	1 a
		ירש	TAKE POSSESSION	439b	1 a
		כאשר	AS	455b	1 a
		ל	TO	510d	1 b
		נתן	PUT	680d	2 b
		פנה	FACE	817b	2 4b c
1	22	דבר	WORD	182b	1 1c
		חפר	DIG	343d	2
		כל	ALL	481b	1 a
1	23	שׁוב	TURN BACK	999c	3
		יטב	BE PLEASING	405c	4
		ל	TO	512b	5 ab
		לקח	TAKE	543b	4 d
1	24	אשכל	ESHCOL	79b	2
		הר	MOUNTAIN	*251a	2 b
		נחל	WADY	636c	2
		עלה	GO UP	748b	1 c
		פנה	TURN	815b	1 c
1	25	דבר	WORD	182b	1 1c
		טוב	PLEASANT	374a	3 b
		יד	HAND	389a	1 a
		ירד	BRING DOWN	433d	1 a
		שׁוב	TURN BACK	999c	3
1	26	אבה	BE WILLING	2c	
		מרה	BE REBELLIOUS	598b	
1	27	אמרי	AMORITES	57c	2 c
		ב	IN	91a	5 2
		יד	HAND	390d	5 b3
		יצא	CAUSE TO GO	424c	1 a
		מן	ON ACCOUNT OF	583a	7 a
		רגן	MURMUR	920a	1
		שנא	HATING	972a	2
1	28	שמד	BE EXTERMINATED	1029b	1
		אמר	SAY	56b	1
		אנחנו	WE	59d	
		בצר	MAKE INACCESSI-BLE	131a	
		לבב	HEART	524b	2 9b
		רום	BE HIGH	926d	1 a
1	29	ירא	FEAR	431b	1 c
		ערץ	CAUSE TO TREM-BLE	791d	2
1	30	את	WITH	86b	1 db
		לחם	ENGAGE IN BAT-TLE	535d	
		עם	WITH	767d	1 d
		עשה	DO	794a	1 1a 4
1	31	אשר	PARTICLE OF RE-LATION	82c	4 bb
		אשר	THAT	83b	8 ab
		בן	SON	120a	1
		הלך	WALK	230c	1 1d 1a
		ראה	TO SEE	907b	3
1	32	אמן	CONFIRM	53b	2 c
		ב	IN	90c	3 7
1	33	אש	FIRE	77c	2
		הלך	WALK	230c	1 1d 2a
		יומם	DAYTIME	*401c	1
		לילה	NIGHT	538c	1
		ענן	CLOUD	778a	1 a
		ראה	TO SEE	908d	
		ראה	TO SEE	909a	2 c
		תור	SEEK OUT	1064b	1
1	34	קצף	BE WROTH	893b	1
		שבע	SWEAR	989c	2
1	35	דור	GENERATION	190a	2 a
		טוב	PLEASANT	374a	3 b
		רע	EVIL	948c	0 b
		שבע	SWEAR	989c	2
1	36	דרך	TREAD	202a	1
		זולה	EXCEPT	*265c	1
		זולה	EXCEPT	265d	1
		כלב	CALEB	477a	
		מלא	FILL	570d	2
		יען	ON ACCOUNT OF	774d	2 a
1	37	אנף	BE ANGRY	60a	
		שם	THERE	1027b	2
1	38	יהושוע	JOSHUA	221c	1
		חזק	BE FIRM	304d	3
		נחל	TAKE AS A POSSES-SION	635d	1 a
		פנה	FACE	817b	2 4b a
		שם	THERE	1027b	3 a
1	39	בז	SPOIL	103a	2
		הם	THEY	241b	2 a
		טוב	A GOOD THING	375b	4
		טף	CHILDREN	382a	
		ידע	KNOW	393d	1 d
		ירש	TAKE POSSESSION	439b	1 a
		רע	EVIL	949a	3
1	40	דרך	WAY	202d	1
		ים	SEA	410d	2
		ל	TO	515d	5 ib
		נסע	JOURNEY	652b	3
		סוף	REEDS	693b	2 b
1	41	אנחנו	WE	59d	
		הון	BE EASY	223b	1
		חגר	GIRD	291d	2
		חטא	MISS A GOAL OR WAY	307a	2 b
		כלי	IMPLEMENT	479d	2 a
		ל	TO	517c	7 bb
		לחם	ENGAGE IN BAT-TLE	535d	
		מלחמה	WAR	536c	
1	42	אב	BE HOSTILE TO	33c	2
		נגף	STRIKE	620a	
		הון	BE EASY	*223b	1
1	43	זוד	BOIL UP	267d	2
		מרה	BE REBELLIOUS	598b	
1	44	אמרי	AMORITES	57c	2 c
		דבורה	BEE	184b	

Ch v.	Heb	Eng	Page	Sec
	חרמה	HORMAH	356c	
	כאשר	AS	455c	1 d
	כתת	BEAT	510c	
	רדף	PURSUE	922d	1 b
	שעיר	SEIR	973a	1 a
1 45	אזן	LISTENING	24c	2
	בכה	WEEP	113c	6
	פנה	FACE	817b	24a h
	קול	VOICE	877b	3 a1
	שוב	TURN BACK	997c	3 b
1 46	קדש	KADESH	873d	1
2 1	דרך	WAY	202d	1
	כאשר	AS	455b	1 a
	נסע	JOURNEY	652b	3
	סבב	GO AROUND	685d	2 b
	סוף	REEDS	693b	2 b
	שעיר	SEIR	973a	1 b
2 3	סבב	GO AROUND	685d	2 b
	פנה	TURN	815b	1 a
	רב	MUCH	913b	1 f
2 4	ב	IN	89a	2 1
	בן	SON	120d	1 ja
	גבול	BOUNDARY	148a	2 a
	ו	AND	254c	4
	ירא	FEAR	431b	1 c
	עבר	PASS OVER	*717d	4 b
	עשו	ESAU	796c	
	שעיר	SEIR	973a	1 a
	שמר	KEEP	1037b	1
2 5	גרה	ENGAGE IN STRIFE	173b	1
	מדרך	TREADING-PLACE	204a	
	ירשה	POSSESSION	440b	
	כף	SOLE OF FOOT	496d	3
	עד	AS FAR AS	724d	1 3
	עשו	ESAU	796c	
	רגל	FOOT	919d	1 a
	שעיר	SEIR	973a	1 b
2 6	אכל	EAT	37b	1
	אכל	FOOD	38a	
	כסף	SILVER	494d	9
	כרה	TRADE	500b	
	שבר	BUY GRAIN	991c	
2 7	את	MARK OF THE AC-CUSATIVE	85b	2 a
	ברך	BLESS	139a	2 a
	חסר	LACK	341b	1 a
	מעשה	DEED	795d	1 b3
2 8	אילפארן	ELPARAN	18c	
	אילת	ELATH	19a	
	את	WITH	86d	4 a
	בן	SON	120d	1 ja
	מדבר	WILDERNESS	185a	3 c
	דרך	WAY	202d	1
	דרך	WAY	202d	1
	מואב	MOAB	555d	2 b
	עבר	PASS OVER	718b	5 f
	עציונגבר	EZION-GEBER	782b	
	ערבה	DESERT-PLAIN	787c	2 a
	עשו	ESAU	796c	
	שעיר	SEIR	973a	1 a
2 9	בן	SON	120d	1 ja
	גרה	ENGAGE IN STRIFE	173b	1
	ירשה	POSSESSION	440b	
	לוט	LOT	532b	
	ער	AR	786b	
	צור	SHOW HOSTILITY TO	849b	
2 10	אימים	EMIM	34a	
	ענק	NECK	778c	
	רום	BE HIGH	926d	1 a
	רפאים	REPHAIM	*952b	
2 11	אימים	EMIM	34a	
	אף	ALSO	64d	1
	הם	THEY	241b	1 b
	חשב	THINK	363b	1
	מואבי	MOABITISH	556a	
	ענק	NECK	778c	
	רפאים	REPHAIM	952b	
2 12	בן	SON	120d	1 ja
	חרי	HORITE	360a	2
	ירש	TAKE POSSESSION	439c	1 b
	ירשה	POSSESSION	440b	
	ישב	DWELL	443a	3
	עשו	ESAU	796c	
	פנה	FACE	816b	16
	שעיר	SEIR	973a	1 a
	תחת	INSTEAD	1065d	22b a
2 13	זרד	ZERED	279d	
	זרד	ZERED	279d	
	ל	TO	515d	5 ib
	נחל	WADY	636c	2
	עתה	NOW	774b	1 e
2 14	איש	MAN	35d	
	דור	GENERATION	190a	2 a
	הלך	WALK	230c	1 1d 1b
	זרד	ZERED	279d	
	מלחמה	WAR	536b	
	נחל	WADY	636c	2
	עבר	PASS OVER	717a	1 a1
	עד	UNTIL	724d	2 1a a
	קדש	KADESH	874a	1
	שבע	SWEAR	989c	2
	תמם	BE FINISHED	1070c	5
2 15	תמם	CONFUSE	243a	2 1
	עד	AS FAR AS	724d	1 2a b
	תמם	BE FINISHED	1070c	5
2 16	איש	MAN	35d	
	היה	COME TO PASS	*224c	2 a1 ah
	ל	TO	517d	7 bc
	מלחמה	WAR	536b	
	תמם	BE FINISHED	1070c	5
2 18	גבול	BORDER	147d	1 a
	עבר	PASS OVER	717c	3 a
	ער	AR	786b	
2 19	בן	SON	120d	1 ja
	גרה	ENGAGE IN STRIFE	173b	1
	ירשה	POSSESSION	440b	
	לוט	LOT	532b	
	מול	IN FRONT OF	557c	2
	עמון	AMMON	770a	
	צור	SHOW HOSTILITY TO	849b	
	קרב	COME NEAR	897c	1 d
2 20	אף	ALSO	64d	1
	זמזמים	ZAMZUMMIN	273d	
	חשב	THINK	363b	1
	עמוני	AMMONITE	770a	
	פנה	FACE	816b	16
	רפאים	REPHAIM	952b	
	רפאים	REPHAIM	952b	
2 21	ירש	TAKE POSSESSION	439c	1 b
	ישב	DWELL	443a	3
	ענק	NECK	778c	
	רום	BE HIGH	926d	1 a
	תחת	INSTEAD	1065d	22b a
2 22	בן	SON	120d	1 ja
	חרי	HORITE	360a	2
	יום	DAY	401b	7 1
	ירש	TAKE POSSESSION	439c	1 b
	ישב	DWELL	443a	3
	עשו	ESAU	796c	
	שעיר	SEIR	973a	1 a
	שמד	BE EXTERMINATED	1029b	1
2 23	חצר	SETTLED ABODE	347b	A
	ישב	DWELL	443a	3
	כפתור	CAPHTOR	499c	
	כפתרי	CAPHTORIM	499c	
	עוים	AVVIM	732a	1
	עזה	GAZA	738b	
	אמרי	AMORITES	57c	3
2 24	ארנן	ARNON	75a	
	גרה	ENGAGE IN STRIFE	173b	1
	חלל	POLLUTE	320d	2
	חשבון	HESHBON	363d	
	ירש	TAKE POSSESSION	439b	1 a
	נחל	WADY	636c	2
	נסע	SET OUT	652b	2 a
	נתן	GIVE	679c	1 s
2 25	חול	WHIRL	297a	2 b
	חלל	POLLUTE	320d	2
	יראה	FEAR	432a	1
	עם	PEOPLE	766c	1
	פחד	DREAD	808c	1
	רגז	BE AGITATED	919b	
	שלל	SPOIL	1022a	2
	שמי	HEAVENS	1029d	1 a
	שמע	REPORT	1034d	
	תחת	UNDERNEATH	*1065b	2 1
2 26	מדבר	WILDERNESS	185a	3 c
	חשבון	HESHBON	363d	
	מלאך	MESSENGER	521c	1 a
	קדמת	KEDEMOTH	870d	
2 27	דרך	WAY	202d	1
	הלך	WALK	230c	1 1d 2a
	ימין	RIGHT HAND	412a	2 b
	סור	TURN ASIDE	693c	1
2 28	אכל	FOOD	38a	
	כסף	SILVER	494d	9
	נתן	GIVE	679b	1 o
	עבר	PASS OVER	717c	3 a
	רגל	FOOT	920a	1 f
	רק	ONLY	956c	2 b
	שבר	BUY GRAIN	991d	
2 29	בן	SON	120d	1 ja
	מואבי	MOABITISH	556a	
	ער	AR	786b	
	עשו	ESAU	796c	
	שעיר	SEIR	973a	1 a
2 30	אבה	BE WILLING	2c	
	אבה	BE WILLING	2c	
	אמץ	BE STRONG	55b	3
	ו	AND	252b	1 a
	חשבון	HESHBON	363d	
	יום	DAY	400d	7 h
	לבב	HEART	524d	2 6d
	עבר	PASS OVER	718d	2 b
	מען	PURPOSE	775b	1 c
	קשה	BE SEVERE	904c	3 a
	רוח	BREATH	925b	3 g
2 31	חלל	POLLUTE	320d	2
	חלל	POLLUTE	320d	2
	ירש	TAKE POSSESSION	439b	1 a
2 32	יהץ	JAHAZ	397d	
2 33	נכה	SMITE	646b	3
2 34	חרם	BAN	355d	1 a
	חרם	BAN	*355d	
	טף	CHILDREN	382a	
	מת	MALE	607a	1
	שריד	SURVIVOR	975a	1
	שאר	REMAIN	984b	1
	מתם	SOUNDNESS	*1071b	
2 35	בהמה	BEAST	97a	2
	בז	SPOIL	102d	
	ל	TO	515d	5 ia
	לכד	CAPTURE	540a	1
	רק	ONLY	956b	2 a
2 36	ארנן	ARNON	75a	
	כל	ALL	482d	2 ba
	מן	FROM	581d	5 a
	נחל	WADY	636c	2
	נתן	PUT	680d	2 b
	ערער	AROER	792d	1
	קריה	TOWN	900a	1
	שגב	BE HIGH	960c	1
	שפה	SPEECH	974a	3
2 37	יבק	JABBOK	132d	
	יבק	JABBOK	*133a	
	הר	MOUNTAIN	251a	2b
	יד	HAND	390b	3 c
	נחל	WADY	636c	2
	עמון	AMMON	770a	
	קרב	COME NEAR	897c	1 b
	יבק	ADDENDA ET COR-RIGENDA	*1212d	
3 1	דרך	WAY	202d	1
	אדרעי	EDREI	204c	
	מלך	KING	573a	1
	עוג	OG	728b	
	עלה	GO UP	748b	1 e
3 2	אמרי	AMORITES	57c	2 a
	חשבון	HESHBON	363d	
	ירא	FEAR	431b	1 b
	ישב	DWELL	443a	3
3 3	בלת	NOT	117a	4 c
	נכה	SMITE	646b	3
	עוג	OG	728b	
	שריד	SURVIVOR	975a	1
	שאר	REMAIN	984b	1
3 4	חבל	CORD	286d	3
	ממלכה	KINGDOM	575a	1
	עוג	OG	728b	
	קריה	TOWN	900a	1
	ארגב	ARGOB	918d	1
	ששים	SIXTY	995d	
3 5	בד	SEPARATION	94c	1 d
	בצר	MAKE INACCESSI-BLE	131a	
	בריח	BAR	138b	1 b
	בריח	BAR	138b	1
	גבה	HIGH	147b	1
	דלת	DOOR	195b	3
	חומה	WALL	327c	1
	מאד	EXCEEDINGLY	547b	2 a
	עיר	CITY	746b	1 b
	פרזי	HAMLET-DWELLER	826d	
	רבה	BECOME MANY	915d	1 e4
3 6	חרם	BAN	355d	1 a
	חרם	BAN	*355d	
	חשבון	HESHBON	363d	
	טף	CHILDREN	382a	
	מת	MALE	607a	1
	מתם	SOUNDNESS	*1071b	
3 7	בז	SPOIL	102d	
	חרם	BAN	*355d	
	שלל	SPOIL	1022a	2
3 8	אמרי	AMORITES	57c	2 a
	ארנן	ARNON	75a	
	הר	MOUNTAIN	249b	1 a
	חרמון	HERMON	356d	
	נחל	WADY	636c	2
	עבר	REGION ACROSS	719c	1 a
3 9	אמרי	AMORITES	57c	2 a
	חרמון	HERMON	356d	
	צידני	SIDONIANS	851a	
	שניר	SENIR	972a	1
	שרין	SIRION	976b	1
3 10	אדרעי	EDREI	204c	
	אדרעי	EDREI	204c	
	מישור	LEVEL PLACE	449d	1
	שרון	SHARON	*450a	2
	ממלכה	KINGDOM	575a	1
	סלכה	SALECAH	669c	
	עוג	OG	728b	
3 11	איש	MAN	35d	
	אמה	CUBIT	52b	1
	אנשו	MAN	60d	2
	ב	IN	90c	3 8
	ברזל	IRON	137c	1 d
	יתר	REMAINDER	451d	1 a
	לא	NOT	520b	4 bb
	עוג	OG	728b	
	עמון	AMMON	770a	
	ערש	COUCH	793b	
	רבה	RABBA	913d	1
	ארבע	FOUR	916d	1 a1
	רחב	WIDTH	931d	
	רחב	WIDTH	931d	
	רפאים	REPHAIM	952b	
	רק	ONLY	956b	2 a
	שאר	REMAIN	984a	1
	תשע	NINE	1077c	1 a
3 12	ארנן	ARNON	75a	
	גדי	GADITE	151d	
	נחל	WADY	636c	2
	על	UPON	756a	2 6a
	ערער	AROER	792d	1
	ראובני	REUBENITE	910a	
3 13	חבל	CORD	286d	3

Ch	v	Heb	Eng	Page	Sec
		ארגב	ARGOB	*419a	1
		יתר	REMAINDER	451d	1 b
		ממלכה	KINGDOM	575a	1
		מנשה	MANASSEH	586c	1 b2 d
		עוג	OG	728b	
		קרא	CALL	896b	2 d3
		ארגב	ARGOB	918d	1
		רפאים	REPHAIM	952b	
3	14	יאיר	JAIR	22c	1
		גבול	BOUNDARY	147d	1 b
		גשורי	GESHURITES	178c	1
		חבל	CORD	286d	3
		חוה	TENT-VILLAGE	295d	
		יום	DAY	401b	7 1
		לקח	TAKE	543d	8
		לקח	TAKE	543d	8
		מנשה	MANASSEH	586d	1 b2 d
		מעכתי	MAACATHITE	591a	
		קרא	CALL	896a	6 c
		ארגב	ARGOB	918d	1
		ארגב	ARGOB	918d	1
3	16	ארנון	ARNON	75a	
		יבק	JABBOK	132d	
		יבק	JABBOK	*132d	
		יבק	JABBOK	133a	
		גבול	BORDER	147d	1 a
		גבול	BOUNDARY	147d	1 b
		גדי	GADITE	151d	
		ו	AND	252d	1 c
		נחל	WADY	636c	2
		נחל	WADY	636c	2
		עמן	AMMON	770a	
		ראובני	REUBENITE	910a	
		יבק	ADDENDA ET CORRIGENDA	1212d	
3	17	אשדה	FOUNDATION	78b	1
		גבול	BOUNDARY	147d	1 b
		ו	AND	252d	1 c
		מזרח	PLACE OF SUNRISE	281a	2 c1
		ים	SEA	411a	3
		ים	SEA	411a	3
		כנרת	CHINNERETH	490b	1
		מלח	SALT	571d	
		ערבה	DESERT-PLAIN	787c	1 a
		ערבה	DESERT-PLAIN	787c	2 a
		פסגה	PISGAH	820a	
		תחת	UNDERNEATH	1065c	2 1a
3	18	חיל	STRENGTH	298d	1 c
		חלץ	EQUIP FOR WAR	323a	1
		נתן	GIVE	678c	1 b
		עבר	PASS OVER	718a	5 c
		ישראל	ISRAEL	975d	2 b1
3	19	מקנה	CATTLE	889b	1
		רב	MUCH	913a	1 a2
3	20	ארץ	EARTH	76b	2 e
		הם	THEY	241b	1 b
		ירשה	POSSESSION	440b	
		ל	TO	511b	1 ga
		נוח	REST	628c	A 1b 1
		עבר	REGION ACROSS	719c	1 b
3	21	ה	THE	209b	2 c
		יהושוע	JOSHUA	221c	1
		ממלכה	KINGDOM	575a	1
		עבר	PASS OVER	717a	1 a2
		ראה	TO SEE	906d	1 b
3	22	הוא	HE, SHE, IT	215d	2 b
		ירא	FEAR	431b	1 b
		ל	TO	515c	5 hc
		לחם	ENGAGE IN BATTLE	535d	
3	23	חנן	SHOW FAVOR	336b	2
3	24	אדון	LORD	11c	4 a
		אל	GOD	42b	3
		אשר	THAT	83c	8 c
		גבורה	MIGHT	150c	3
		גדל	GREATNESS	152d	2 b
		חזק	STRONG	305c	1 b
		חלל	POLLUTE	320d	2
		ראה	TO SEE	908d	1 a2
		ראה	TO SEE	908d	
		שמי	HEAVENS	1030a	1 a
3	25	טוב	PLEASANT	374a	3 b
		טוב	PLEASANT	374b	3 b
		לבנון	LEBANON	*526d	
		לבנון	LEBANON	527a	
		עבר	REGION ACROSS	719c	1 b
3	26	יסף	DO AGAIN	415c	2 a
		עבר	BE ARROGANT	720d	2 a
		עוד	STILL	729b	1 b
		מען	PURPOSE	775b	1 b
		רב	MUCH	913b	1 f
		שמע	HEAR	1034b	2 f
3	27	זה	THIS	261a	2 bb
		מזרח	PLACE OF SUNRISE	281a	2 c1
		ים	SEA	411b	9
		תימן	SOUTH	412d	1 b
		ירדן	JORDAN	434c	
		נשא	LIFT	670c	1 b 4
		עין	EYE	744b	1 f
		פסגה	PISGAH	820a	
		ראה	TO SEE	907c	6 c
3	28	אמץ	BE STRONG	55a	1
		יהושוע	JOSHUA	221c	1
		חזק	BE FIRM	304d	3
		עבר	PASS OVER	718a	5 c
3	29	ביתפעור	BETH-PEOR	112c	
		גיא	VALLEY	161b	
		מול	IN FRONT OF	557c	2
		פעור	PEOR	822b	1
4	1	חק	SOMETHING PRESCRIBED	349d	7 g
		חק	SOMETHING PRESCRIBED	349d	7 g
		למד	LEARN	540d	
		משפ	JUDGMENT	1049a	4
4	2	גרע	DIMINISH	175c	1
		דבר	WORD	182d	1 2a
		יסף	ADD	415b	1
4	3	צוה	CHARGE	845d	2 a
		בעל	BAAL	127c	2 1
		בעלפעור	BAAL-PEOR	128b	
		ה	THE	209b	2 c
		הלך	WALK	235a	2 3d 2
		כל	ALL	481c	1 b
4	4	דבק	CLINGING	180a	
		חי	ALIVE	312a	1 b
		כל	ALL	481b	1 a
4	5	יהוה	YAHWEH	218d	2 1f
		חק	SOMETHING PRESCRIBED	349d	7 g
		ירש	TAKE POSSESSION	439c	1 a
		למד	LEARN	540d	
		שם	THERE	1027c	3 b
		משפ	JUDGMENT	1049a	4
4	6	בן	DISCERN	107a	
		בינה	UNDERSTANDING	108a	3
		גוי	NATION	156c	1 b
		הוא	HE, SHE, IT	*216a	3 a
		הוא	HE, SHE, IT	*216d	6 a
		זה	THIS	261a	2 bb
		חכם	WISE	314d	5
		חכמה	WISDOM	315c	4
		חק	SOMETHING PRESCRIBED	349d	7 g
		עם	PEOPLE	766c	1
		רק	ONLY	956c	2
		שמר	KEEP	1037a	3 c
4	7	גוי	NATION	*156c	1 b
		כל	ALL	481b	1 a
		מי	WHO	566b	A
		קרב	NEAR	898c	2 f
4	8	גוי	NATION	*156c	1 b
		חק	SOMETHING PRESCRIBED	349d	7 g
		תורה	LAW	436b	2 b2
		פנה	FACE	817c	2 4b g
		צדיק	JUST	843a	1 a
		משפ	JUDGMENT	1049a	4
4	9	בן	SON	120b	1 f
		חיים	LIFE	313b	1
		ידע	MAKE KNOWN	395a	
		לבב	HEART	523d	2 3d
		נפש	SOUL	660a	4 b2
		פן	LEST	814d	1
		רק	ONLY	956c	2 b
		שכח	FORGET	1013a	1 a
4	10	אדמה	GROUND	9d	4
		אשר	PARTICLE OF RELATION	82c	4 ba
		אשר	THAT	83c	8 b
		דבר	WORD	183a	2 2
		חי	ALIVE	312a	1 b
		חרב	HOREB	352a	
		ירא	FEAR	431c	3 b
		למד	LEARN	540d	
		למד	LEARN	540d	
		עמד	STAND	763d	1 a
		קהל	ASSEMBLE AS	875a	2
		שמע	HEAR	1034c	2 a
4	11	אש	FIRE	77c	2
		בער	BURN	129a	2
		הר	MOUNTAIN	249b	1 a
		חשך	DARKNESS	365a	1
		לבב	HEART	523b	1
		ענן	CLOUD	778a	1 a
		ערפל	CLOUD	791d	
		שמי	HEAVENS	1029d	1 a
		תחת	UNDERNEATH	1065c	2 1a
4	12	אש	FIRE	77c	2
		זולה	EXCEPT	266a	1
		תמונה	LIKENESS	568c	
		תוך	MIDST	1063d	
4	13	אבן	STONE	6c	2
		ברית	COVENANT	136c	2 2c
		דבר	WORD	183a	2 2
		לוח	TABLET	531d	1
		לוח	TABLET	*531d	1
4	14	את	MARK OF THE ACCUSATIVE	85a	1 a
		חק	SOMETHING PRESCRIBED	349d	7 g
		ירש	TAKE POSSESSION	439c	1 a
		למד	LEARN	540d	
		עבר	PASS OVER	717a	1 a2
		שם	THERE	1027c	3 b
		משפ	JUDGMENT	1049a	4
4	15	אש	FIRE	77c	2
		דבר	SPEAK	*180d	
		ו	AND	254c	4
		חרב	HOREB	352a	
		יום	DAY	400b	7 d3 a
		תמונה	LIKENESS	568c	
		נפש	SOUL	660b	4 b6
		שמר	KEEP	1037b	1
4	16	תבנית	FIGURE	125d	3
		זכר	MALE	271c	1
		ל	TO	515d	5 ia
		תמונה	LIKENESS	568b	
		נקבה	FEMALE	666c	2
			IMAGE	702b	
		פסל	IDOL	820d	
4	17	שחת	GO TO RUIN	1008c	2
		תבנית	FIGURE	125d	3
		כנף	WING	489c	1 a
		עוף	FLY	733c	1 a
		צפור	BIRD	862a	1
		שמי	HEAVENS	1029d	1 a
4	18	אדמה	GROUND	9d	4
		תבנית	FIGURE	125d	3
		דגה	FISH	185d	
		מי	WATER	565c	1 e
		רמש	CREEP	943a	2 a
		תחת	UNDERNEATH	*1066d	3 2b
4	19	חלק	DIVIDE	323c	1
		ירח	MOON	437a	
		כוכב	STAR	456d	
		נדח	THRUST	623a	4
		נשא	LIFT	670c	1 b 4
		עבד	WORK	713b	4 b
		צבא	HOST	839a	1 c
		ראה	TO SEE	907c	6 a
		שמי	HEAVENS	1029d	1 a
		שמי	HEAVENS	1029d	1 a
		שמש	SUN	1039b	3
		תחת	UNDERNEATH	*1065b	2 1
4	20	ברזל	IRON	137c	3
		יום	DAY	400d	7 h
		יצא	CAUSE TO GO	424c	1 a
		כור	FURNACE	468b	
		לקח	TAKE	543d	4 d
		נחלה	PROPERTY	635b	1 e
4	21	אנף	BE ANGRY	60a	
		בלת	NOT	116d	4 a
		ברית	COVENANT	137b	3 3
		דבר	WORD	184a	4 8
		טוב	PLEASANT	374a	3 b
		נחלה	PROPERTY	635b	1 e
		שבע	SWEAR	989c	2
4	22	טוב	PLEASANT	374a	3 b
		ל	TO	513a	5 ad
4	23	ברית	COVENANT	137b	3 3
		כרת	CUT	503d	1
		ל	TO	515d	5 ia
		תמונה	LIKENESS	568b	
		פן	LEST	814d	1
		פסל	IDOL	820d	
		שכח	FORGET	1013b	1 c
4	24	אכל	EAT	37c	3
		אל	GOD	42d	6 d
		אש	FIRE	77c	2
		קנא	JEALOUS	888d	
4	25	בן	SON	120b	1 f
		ילד	BEGET	409a	1
		ישן	BECOME INACTIVE	445d	
		כי	WHEN	473b	2 a
		כל	ALL	482c	2 a
		כעם	VEX	495a	2
		תמונה	LIKENESS	568b	
		עין	EYE	744d	3 c
		פסל	IDOL	820d	
		רע	EVIL	948c	0 b
		שחת	GO TO RUIN	1008c	2
4	26	אבד	PERISH	1d	1
		ארך	BE LONG	73d	1 a
		ירש	TAKE POSSESSION	439c	1 a
		מהר	QUICKLY	555b	
		עבר	PASS OVER	717a	1 a1
		עוד	BEAR WITNESS	730a	2
		שמד	BE EXTERMINATED	1029b	1 m
4	27	גוי	NATION	156d	1 c
		מת	MALE	607b	2 a
		נהג	DRIVE	624b	1
		מספר	NUMBER	709a	1 a
		פוץ	BE DISPERSED	807a	1 a
		שאר	REMAIN	984a	1
4	28	אבן	STONE	6c	2
		אלהים	GOD	43c	1 d
		עץ	TREE	782a	2 c
		מעשה	DEED	796a	2 a3
		ראה	TO SEE	907b	4
		ריח	SMELL	926b	
		שמע	HEAR	1033d	1 e.
4	29	בקש	SEEK	134d	3 c
		דרש	SEEK	205b	3
		כי	BECAUSE	473c	3 a
		כל	ALL	481a	1 a
		לבב	HEART	523b	2 2
		מצא	FIND	593a	1 a
		נפש	SOUL	661b	0
		עבר	REGION ACROSS	719c	1 a
		שם	THERE	1027c	4 a
4	30	אחרית	END	31b	B
		מצא	FIND	593c	3 e
		צר	STRAITS	865b	
		שמע	HEAR	1034a	1 m
4	31	אל	GOD	42d	6 d
		רחום	COMPASSIONATE	933d	
		רפה	SINK	952a	1

Ch v.	Heb	Eng	Page	Sec
	שבע	SWEAR	989c	2
	שחת	GO TO RUIN	1008b	1
	שכח	FORGET	1013b	1 c
4 32	אדם	MAN	9b	2
	ברא	CREATE	135b	1
	גדול	GREAT	153a	6 a
	דבר	WORD	*183d	47
	היה	COME TO PASS	227d	2
	יום	DAY	401a	7 k
	כ	LIKE	453d	1 b
	מן	FROM	583d	9 b2
	מן	FROM	583d	9 b1
	קצה	END	892b	1
	שאל	ASK	981d	2 a
	שמי	HEAVENS	1030a	1 a
	שמע	HEAR	1034b	2
4 33	ארץ	EARTH	76b	4 c
	אש	FIRE	77c	2
	ה	INTERROG PART	209a	1 1
	ו	AND	254a	2 b
	שמע	HEAR	1033c	1 a
4 34	אות	SIGN	16d	4
	מופת	WONDER	69a	1
	גדול	GREAT	153a	3
	גוי	NATION	156c	1 b
	זרוע	ARM	284a	1 c
	חזק	STRONG	305c	1 b
	יד	HAND	390a	1 e2
	מורא	FEAR	432b	2
	לקח	TAKE	543b	4 d
	נטה	EXTEND	640d	1 a
	מסה	TEST	650b	
	נסה	TRY	650b	2
	קרב	INWARD PART	899b	1 f1
4 35	אלהים	GOD	43d	3
	אלהים	GOD	43d	3
	בד	SEPARATION	94d	1 e
	הוא	HE, SHE, IT	215d	1 c
	עוד	STILL	729b	1 c
	ראה	TO SEE	909a	1
4 36	אש	FIRE	77c	2
	דבר	WORD	183a	2 2
	יסר	DISCIPLINE	416a	1 a
	מן	OUT OF	579a	2 ab
	ראה	TO SEE	908d	1 a2
	ראה	TO SEE	908d	
	שמע	HEAR	1034c	2 a
	תחת	INSTEAD	1066a	2 3b
4 37	אהב	LOVE	13a	5 a
	אחר	AFTER	*30a	2 b
	בחר	CHOOSE	103d	1 a
	ה	THE	*208d	2 a
	זרע	SOWING	282c	4 b
	יצא	CAUSE TO GO	424c	1 a
	כח	STRENGTH	470d	3
	פנה	FACE	816a	12a
	תחת	INSTEAD	1066a	2 3b
4 38	בוא	COME	99b	2
	יום	DAY	400d	7 h
	ירש	CAUSE TO POSSESS	440a	2 a
	עצום	MIGHTY	783a	1
4 39	אין	NOT	34b	2 a
	אל	TO	39d	2
	אלהים	GOD	43d	3
	אלהים	GOD	43d	3
	ידע	KNOW	394a	1 g
	לבב	HEART	523d	2 3d
	עוד	STILL	729b	1 c
	מעל	ABOVE	751c	1 a
	שוב	TURN BACK	999d	8
	תחת	UNDENEATH	*1065b	1
4 40	אדמה	GROUND	9d	4
	אחר	AFTER	30a	2 b
	ארך	BE LONG	73d	1 a
	אשר	THAT	83c	8 b
	חק	SOMETHING PRESCRIBED	349d	7 g
	יום	DAY	400c	7 f
	יטב	BE WELL	405c	3
	צוה	CHARGE	845d	2 a
	מצוה	COMMANDMENT	846c	2 b1
4 41	בדל	BE DIVIDED	95c	2
	מזרח	PLACE OF SUNRISE	280d	1
	עבר	REGION ACROSS	719c	1 a
	שמש	SUN	1039b	2
4 42	אל	THESE	41b	2
	בלי	WEARING OUT	115d	A
	דעת	KNOWLEDGE	395c	1 a
	לא	NOT	519b	1 bc
	נוס	FLEE	630d	1
	נוס	FLEE	630d	1
	רצח	MURDER	953d	
	שנא	HATE	971d	3
	שלשם	THREE DAYS AGO	1026b	2
	תמול	YESTERDAY	1070a	2 c
4 43	בצר	BEZER	131a	1
	גרי	GADITE	151d	
	גולן	GOLAN	157b	2
	מישור	LEVEL PLACE	449d	1
	מנשי	MANASSITES	586d	
	ראובני	REUBENITE	910a	
	רמות	RAMOTH	928b	1 a
4 44	תורה	LAW	436b	2 b2
	שום	TO PLACE	963b	1 c
4 45	ב	IN	91a	5 1
	דבר	SPEAK	181d	3 b
	חק	SOMETHING PRESCRIBED	349d	7 g
	יצא	GO OUT	422d	1 a
	עדה	TESTIMONIES	730a	
	משפט	JUDGMENT	1049a	4
4 46	ביתפעור	BETH-PEOR	112c	
	גיא	VALLEY	161b	
	חשבון	HESHBON	363d	
	יצא	GO OUT	422d	1 a
	מול	IN FRONT OF	*557c	2
	נכה	SMITE	646b	3
	עבר	REGION ACROSS	719c	1 a
4 47	מזרח	PLACE OF SUNRISE	280d	1
	עבר	REGION ACROSS	719c	1 a
	עוג	OG	728b	2
	שמש	SUN	1039b	2
4 48	ארנן	ARNON	75a	
	הר	MOUNTAIN	249b	1 a
	חרמון	HERMON	356d	
	נחל	WADY	636c	2
	שיאן	SION	673b	
	ערער	AROER	792d	1
4 49	אשדה	FOUNDATION	78b	
	מזרח	PLACE OF SUNRISE	281a	2 c1
	ים	SEA	411a	3
	ירדן	JORDAN	434d	
	עבר	REGION ACROSS	719c	1 a
	ערבה	DESERT-PLAIN	787c	1 a
	ערבה	DESERT-PLAIN	787c	2 a
	פסגה	PISGAH	820a	
5 1	אזן	EAR	24a	2 a
	דבר	SPEAK	180c	
	חק	SOMETHING PRESCRIBED	349d	7 g
	למד	LEARN	540d	
	שמר	KEEP	1037a	3 c
5 2	ברית	COVENANT	137a	3 1
	חרב	HOREB	352a	
5 3	כרת	CUT	503d	4
	ברית	COVENANT	137a	3 1
	חי	ALIVE	312a	1 b
	ים	SEA	*411a	3
	כל	ALL	481b	1 a
	כרת	CUT	503d	4
5 4	ב	IN	88d	1 4
	דבר	SPEAK	181b	3 e
	הר	MOUNTAIN	249b	1 a
	פנה	FACE	815a	1 1c
5 5	הר	MOUNTAIN	249b	1 a
	ירא	FEAR	431b	1 c
	נגד	BE CONSPICUOUS	616d	2
	עלה	GO UP	748b	1 c
	פנה	FACE	818b	2 6b
5 6	בית	HOUSE	109a	1ae 9
	יהוה	YAHWEH	218d	2 1a
	יהוה	YAHWEH	219b	2 2d
	יצא	CAUSE TO GO	424c	1 a
	עבד	SLAVE	713d	1
5 7	אחר	ANOTHER	*29d	
	אלהים	GOD	43c	1 d
	היה	BE	227c	3 4d c
	פנה	FACE	818d	2 7a b
5 8	ארץ	EARTH	76a	1 b
	ארץ	EARTH	76a	1 b
	מי	WATER	565c	1 e
	תמונה	LIKENESS	568b	
	מעל	ABOVE	751c	1 a
	פסל	IDOL	820d	
	שמי	HEAVENS	1030a	1 a
	תחת	UNDENEATH	*1065b	1
	תחת	UNDERNEATH	*1066a	3 2b
5 9	אל	GOD	42d	6 d
	יהוה	YAHWEH	218d	2 1a
	יהוה	YAHWEH	219b	2 2d
	עון	INIQUITY	731a	1 c1
	פקד	ATTEND TO	823c	A 3
	קנא	JEALOUS	888d	2
	רבע	PERTAINING TO THE FOURTH	918a	
	שנא	HATE	971d	3
	שחה	BOW DOWN	1005c	3
	שלש	PERTAINING TO THE THIRD	1026d	
5 10	אהב	LOVE	13a	3
	אלף	THOUSAND	49a	1 a
	חסד	GOODNESS	339b	2 3b
	עשה	DO	794b	1 3
	שמר	KEEP	1037a	3 c
5 11	יהוה	YAHWEH	218d	2 1a
	נקה	BE CLEAN	667c	2
	נשא	LIFT	670d	1 b 7
	שוא	EMPTINESS	996a	1
	שם	NAME	1028b	3
5 12	יהוה	YAHWEH	218d	2 1a
	זכר	REMEMBER	270a	1 g
	יום	DAY	398d	2 i
	קדש	BE SET APART	873a	2
	שבת	SABBATH	992b	1 a
	שבת	SABBATH	992b	1 a
	שמר	KEEP	1036d	3 b
5 13	יום	DAY	398d	2 a
	מלאכה	WORK	522a	3 b
	עבד	WORK	713a	1
5 14	אמה	MAID	51a	1
	בהמה	BEAST	97a	2
	בן	SON	120a	1
	גר	SOJOURNER	158b	2
	ה	THE	*209d	2 b
	יהוה	YAHWEH	218d	2 1a
	חמור	HE-ASS	331b	1
	מלאכה	WORK	522a	3 b
	נוח	REST	628b	2
	עבד	SLAVE	713d	1
	שבת	SABBATH	992b	1 a
	שבת	SABBATH	992b	1 a
	שור	A HEAD OF CATTLE	1004a	
	שער	GATE	1045a	2 c
5 15	יהוה	YAHWEH	218d	2 1a
	זכר	REMEMBER	269d	11 d
	זרוע	ARM	284a	1 c
	חזק	STRONG	305c	1 b
	יום	DAY	398d	2 i
	יצא	CAUSE TO GO	424c	1 a
	עבד	SLAVE	713d	1
	עשה	DO	795a	2 6
	שבת	SABBATH	992b	1 a
	שבת	SABBATH	992b	1 b
5 16	אדמה	LAND	10a	5
	אם	MOTHER	51d	1
	ארך	BE LONG	73d	1
	יהוה	YAHWEH	218d	2 1a
	יום	DAY	399b	4 a
	יטב	BE WELL	405c	3
	כבד	MAKE HONORABLE	457d	2 a
5 17	גנב	STEAL	170c	
	נאף	COMMIT ADULTERY	610c	1 a
	עד	WITNESS	729d	2 c
	ענה	ANSWER	773a	3 a
	רע	FRIEND	946a	2
	רצח	MURDER	953d	
	שוא	EMPTINESS	996b	2
5 18	אוה	DESIRE	16b	
	אמה	MAID	51a	1
	חמד	DESIRE	326b	A
	חמור	HE-ASS	331b	1
	רע	FRIEND	946a	2
	שור	A HEAD OF CATTLE	1004a	
5 19	אבן	STONE	6c	2
	דבר	SPEAK	180d	2
	דבר	WORD	183a	2 2
	הר	MOUNTAIN	249b	1 a
	יסף	ADD	414d	
	לוח	TABLET	*531d	1
	לוח	TABLET	531d	1
	ענן	CLOUD	778a	1 a
	ערפל	CLOUD	791d	
	קהל	ASSEMBLY	874c	1 d
	קול	VOICE	877a	1 b
5 20	בער	BURN	129a	2
	היה	COME TO PASS	224c	2 a1 aa
	הר	MOUNTAIN	249b	1 a
	זקן	OLD	278d	2 b
	חשך	DARKNESS	365a	1
5 21	אדם	MAN	9b	2
	גדל	GREATNESS	152d	2 b
	דבר	SPEAK	181b	3 d
	הן	BEHOLD	243c	A
	כבוד	GLORY	458d	2 c1
	ראה	TO SEE	908d	
	ראה	TO SEE	908d	1 a2
5 22	אכל	EAT	37c	3
	יסף	ADD	414d	
	מות	DIE	560a	2 b
5 23	אלהים	GOD	44b	4 a
	בשר	FLESH	142d	6 c
	חי	ALIVE	311d	1 a
	מי	WHO	566d	F c
5 24	את	THOU	61d	
	קרב	COME NEAR	897c	1 g
	שמע	HEAR	1034a	1 j
5 25	יטב	DO WELL	405d	3
	קול	VOICE	877b	3 a1
5 26	זה	THIS	260d	2 ba
	יום	DAY	400c	7 f
	יטב	BE WELL	405c	3
	ירא	FEAR	431c	3 b
	לבב	HEART	523c	2 2
	נתן	GIVE	679a	1 f
	עולם	LONG DURATION	762d	2 f
5 27	ל	TO	515d	5 ib
5 28	חק	SOMETHING PRESCRIBED	349d	7 g
	למד	LEARN	540d	
	עמד	STAND	764b	3 b
	עם	WITH	768a	2
	פה	HERE	806a	1 a
	מצוה	COMMANDMENT	846b	2 a
5 29	זה	THIS	260d	2 ba
	ימין	RIGHT HAND	412a	2 b
	סור	TURN ASIDE	693c	1
	שמר	KEEP	1037a	3 c
5 30	ארך	BE LONG	73d	1 a
	דרך	WAY	204a	6 ec
	טוב	PLEASING	373b	4
	ל	TO	511a	1 e
	צוה	CHARGE	845d	2 a
6 1	זה	THIS	261a	3
	חק	SOMETHING PRESCRIBED	349d	7 g
	עבר	PASS OVER	717a	1 a2

Ch	v.	Heb	Eng	Page	Sec
6	2	מצוה	COMMANDMENT	846b	2 a
		ארך	BE LONG	73d	2
		בן	SON	120b	1 f
		חיים	LIFE	313b	1
		חקה	SOMETHING PRE-SCRIBED	350b	2 e
		חקה	SOMETHING PRE-SCRIBED	350b	2 d
		ירא	FEAR	431c	3 b
		צוה	CHARGE	845d	2 a
		מצוה	COMMANDMENT	846c	2 b2
6	3	אשר	THAT	83c	8 b
		דבר	SPEAK	181b	3 c
		דבש	HONEY	185b	
		זוב	FLOW	264d	2
		חלב	MILK	316c	A 4
		יטב	BE WELL	405c	3
		כאשר	AS	455b	1 a
		רבה	BECOME MANY	915a	1 a
		נקה	ADDENDA ET COR-RIGENDA	1125b	
6	5	אהב	LOVE	13a	3
		לבב	HEART	523b	2 2
		מאד	FORCE	547b	1
		נפש	SOUL	661b	0
6	6	דבר	WORD	182d	1 2a
		לבב	HEART	523d	2 3d
		צוה	CHARGE	845d	2 a
6	7	ב	IN	90d	4 e
		דבר	SPEAK	181c	4 c
		דרך	WAY	202c	1
		הלך	WALK	230b	1 1a
		הלך	WALK	230d	1 1d 2a
		שנן	SHARPEN	1042a	
6	8	אות	SIGN	17a	5
		טוטפות	BANDS	378a	
		ל	TO	512b	4 a
		עין	EYE	745a	5
		קשר	BIND	905b	1 b
6	9	בית	HOUSE	108d	1 ab
		מזוזה	DOOR-POST	265b	1
		כתב	WRITE	507c	1 b1
		שער	GATE	1044d	1 a
6	10	בנה	BUILD	124b	1 ab
		היה	COME TO PASS	225b	1 2b d
		טוב	PLEASANT	373c	1 a
		כי	WHEN	473b	2 a
6	11	בור	WELL	92b	1
		זית	OLIVE TREE	268d	1
		חצב	HEW	345a	1
		טוב	GOOD THINGS	375c	2
		מלא	FILL	570c	1
		מלא	FULL	571a	
		נטע	PLANT	642c	1
		שבע	SATISFIED	959b	1 a
6	12	בית	HOUSE	109a	1 ae 9
		יצא	CAUSE TO GO	424c	1
		עבד	SLAVE	713d	1
		פן	LEST	814d	1
6	13	את	MARK OF THE AC-CUSATIVE	85a	1 a
		ב	IN	90a	3 2d
		ירא	FEAR	431c	3 b
		שבע	SWEAR	989b	1 a
		שם	NAME	1028b	3
6	14	אחר	ANOTHER	*29d	
		אלהים	GOD	43c	1 d
		הלך	WALK	235a	2 3d 2
		סביב	ROUND ABOUT	687b	2 bb
6	15	אדמה	GROUND	9d	4
		אל	GOD	42d	6 d
		חרה	BURN	354a	1
		על	UPON	758c	4 2a
		פנה	FACE	819b	2 8b
		קנא	JEALOUS	888d	
		קנא	JEALOUS	888d	
		שמד	BE EXTERMINATED	1029b	1
6	16	נסה	TEST	650b	3 b
		מסה	MASSAH	650c	
6	17	חק	SOMETHING PRE-SCRIBED	349d	7 g
		עדה	TESTIMONIES	730a	
		מצוה	COMMANDMENT	846c	2 b1
6	18	טוב	PLEASANT	374a	2 f
		טוב	PLEASANT	374a	3 b
		יטב	BE WELL	405c	3
		ישר	STRAIGHT	449a	2 a
		שבע	SWEAR	989c	2
6	19	איב	BE HOSTILE TO	33c	
		הדף	THRUST	213d	2
		כאשר	AS	455b	1 a
6	20	חק	SOMETHING PRE-SCRIBED	349d	7 g
		כי	WHEN	473b	2 a
		מחר	TO-MORROW	564a	2
		עדה	TESTIMONIES	730a	
6	21	חזק	STRONG	305c	1 b
		יד	HAND	390a	1 e2
		יצא	CAUSE TO GO	424c	1 a
		עבד	SLAVE	714c	7
6	22	אות	SIGN	16d	4
		מופת	WONDER	69a	1
		בית	HOUSE	109d	5 a
		רע	EVIL	948a	1
6	23	את	MARK OF THE AC-CUSATIVE	85a	1 a

Ch	v.	Heb	Eng	Page	Sec
		בוא	COME	99b	2
		יצא	CAUSE TO GO	424c	1 a
		מען	PURPOSE	775b	1 c
6	24	חיה	LIVE	311c	1
		חק	SOMETHING PRE-SCRIBED	349d	7 g
		חק	SOMETHING PRE-SCRIBED	349d	7 g
		טוב	A GOOD THING	375a	1
		יום	DAY	400c	7 f
		יום	DAY	400d	7 h
		ירא	FEAR	431c	3 b
6	25	כי	IF	473b	2 b
		פנה	FACE	817b	24a h
		צדקה	RIGHTEOUSNESS	842b	5
		מצוה	COMMANDMENT	846b	2 a
7	1	אמרי	AMORITES	57c	2 e
		יבוסי	JEBUSITE	101a	1
		גרגשי	GIRGASHITE	173a	
		חוי	HIVITE	295d	2
		חוי	HIVITE	295d	2
		חתי	HITTITE	366d	2 a
		נשל	CLEAR AWAY	675c	2
		רב	GREAT	913c	2 d
7	2	ברית	COVENANT	136b	1 1
		חנן	SHOW FAVOR	336a	1 c
		חרם	BAN	355d	1 a
		כרת	CUT	503d	4
		נכה	SMITE	646b	3
		נתן	GIVE	679c	1 s
		פנה	FACE	817b	24b c
7	3	חתן	MAKE ONESELF A SON IN LAW	368d	2
7	4	אחר	BEHIND	30b	4 aa
		חרה	BURN	354a	2
		חרם	BAN	*355d	1 a
		מהר	QUICKLY	555b	
		סור	TURN ASIDE	694c	2
		עבד	WORK	713b	4 b
7	5	אש	FIRE	77c	1
		אשרה	ASHERA	81c	B
		גדע	HEW	154b	
		מזבח	ALTAR	259a	0
		חרם	BAN	*355d	1 a
		כה	THUS	462b	1 b
		כיאם	BUT	475a	2 b
		מצבה	PILLAR	663b	1
		נתץ	PULL DOWN	683b	1
		פסיל	IDOL	821a	
7	6	אדמה	GROUND	9d	4
		בחר	CHOOSE	103d	1 a
		חרם	BAN	355d	1 a
		מן	OUT OF	579b	2 ac
		סגלה	PROPERTY	688c	1
		עם	PEOPLE	767a	5 g
		בחר	CHOOSE	103d	1 a
7	7	חשק	BE ATTACHED TO	366a	1
		כל	ALL	482a	1 ea
		מן	ON ACCOUNT OF	580b	2 f
		מן	THAN	582c	6 b
		מן	ON ACCOUNT OF	583a	7 a
		מעט	A FEW	589d	1 a
		רבב	BECOME MUCH	912d	1
		רב	MULTITUDE	914a	1
		רבה	MULTITUDE	914b	2
7	8	שכב	LIE DOWN	1012a	1 b
		שמר	KEEP	1037b	4 b
		אהב	LOVE	13a	5 b
		בית	HOUSE	109a	1 ae 9
		חזק	STRONG	305c	1 b
		יד	HAND	390a	1 e2
		יצא	CAUSE TO GO	424c	1 a
		מן	ON ACCOUNT OF	583a	7 a
		עבד	SLAVE	713d	1
		פדה	RANSOM	804a	3 a
		פרעה	PHARAOH	829a	
		שבע	SWEAR	989c	2
		שבועה	OATH	990a	2
		שמר	KEEP	1037b	4 b
7	9	אהב	LOVE	13a	3
		אל	GOD	42c	6 a
		אלהים	GOD	43d	3
		אלהים	GOD	43d	3
		אלף	THOUSAND	48d	1 a
		אמן	CONFIRM	53a	5
		ברית	COVENANT	137b	3 2
		דור	GENERATION	190a	2 c
		ה	THE	208b	1 ha
		הוא	HE, SHE, IT	215d	2 b
		ו	AND	254c	4
		חסד	GOODNESS	339a	2 1e
		חסד	GOODNESS	339b	2 3b
7	10	אבד	DESTROY	2b	1
		אחר	DELAY	29b	1
		שן	HATE	971d	2
		שלם	BE COMPLETE	1022c	5
7	11	חק	SOMETHING PRE-SCRIBED	349d	7 g
7	12	ברית	COVENANT	137b	3 2
		היה	COME TO PASS	225b	1 2b be
		חסד	GOODNESS	339a	2 1e
		ל	TO	515c	5 hc
		עקב	CONSEQUENCE	784d	1
		שמר	KEEP	1037a	3 c
		שמר	KEEP	1037b	4 b
		משפט	JUDGMENT	1049a	4

Ch	v.	Heb	Eng	Page	Sec
7	13	אדמה	GROUND	9c	1
		אהב	LOVE	13a	5 b
		אלף	CATTLE	48c	
		בטן	WOMB	106a	3
		ברך	BLESS	139a	2 a
		דגן	CORN	186c	
		תירוש	NEW WINE	440d	
		עשתרות	EWES	800b	
		פרי	FRUIT	826b	1
		פרי	FRUIT	826b	2
		יצהר	FRESH OIL	844a	
		שגר	OFFSPRING	993d	
7	14	ב	IN	88b	1 2
		ברך	BLESS	138d	2 b
		עקר	BARREN	785d	
7	15	מדוה	SICKNESS	*188c	
		מדוה	SICKNESS	188c	
		חלי	SICKNESS	318b	
		נתן	PUT	680b	2 a
		סור	TURN ASIDE	694b	1
		רע	EVIL	948a	1
7	16	אכל	EAT	37c	1
		חום	PITY	299b	A
		מוקש	BAIT	430d	
		לחם	FOOD	*537c	3 b
		עבד	WORK	713b	4 b
		עין	EYE	744c	2 a
		שום	TO PLACE	963b	1 b
7	17	איכה	IN WHAT MANNER	32d	1
		יכל	BE ABLE	407c	1 a
		ירש	CAUSE TO POSSESS	440a	2 a
		כי	IF	473b	2 b
		לבב	HEART	524a	2 7
		רב	GREAT	913c	2 d
7	18	זכר	REMEMBER	269d	1 1 d
		ירא	FEAR	431b	1 c
7	19	אות	SIGN	16d	4
		מופת	WONDER	69a	1
		אשר	PARTICLE OF RE-LATION	82c	4 c
		זרוע	ARM	284a	1 c
		חזק	STRONG	305c	1 b
		יצא	CAUSE TO GO	424c	1 a
		ירא	FEAR	431b	1 c
		מסה	TEST	650b	
7	20	אבד	PERISH	1c	1
		סתר	HIDE	711b	1
		עד	AS FAR AS	724b	1 2a b
		פנה	FACE	818b	2 6b
		צרעה	HORNETS	864a	
		שלח	SEND	1019a	2 d
7	21	אל	GOD	42d	6 d
		גדול	GREAT	153b	6 c
		ירא	BE REVERED	431d	3 a
		ערץ	CAUSE TO TREM-BLE	792a	2
7	22	אל	THESE	41b	
		חיה	LIVING THING	312c	1 b
		יכל	BE ABLE	407c	1 b
		יכל	BE ABLE	407d	1 d
		כלה	FINISH	478c	2 c1
		מהר	QUICKLY	555b	
		מעט	A FEW	590a	1 d
		נשל	CLEAR AWAY	675c	3
		רבה	BECOME MANY	915a	1 b
		שדה	FIELD	961b	1 c
7	23	מהומה	DISCOMFITURE	223a	2
		הום	DISCOMFIT	223a	
		המם	CONFUSE	243a	2
		נתן	GIVE	679c	1 s
		עד	AS FAR AS	724b	1 2a b
		פנה	FACE	817b	24b c
		שמד	BE EXTERMINATED	1029b	1
7	24	אבד	DESTROY	2b	2
		יצב	STATION ONESELF	426c	D
		עד	AS FAR AS	724b	1 2a b
		פנה	FACE	816d	2 3a
		שם	NAME	1028b	2 c
		שמי	HEAVENS	1029d	1 a
		תחת	UNDERNEATH	1066a	3 2a
7	25	אש	FIRE	77c	1
		זהב	GOLD	263a	6
		זהב	GOLD	263c	1
		חמד	DESIRE	326b	A
		יקש	BE ENSNARED	430c	
		כסף	SILVER	494b	7
		לא	NOT	518c	1 aa
		לקח	TAKE	543a	4 a
		פסיל	IDOL	821a	
		תועבה	ABOMINATION	1072d	1 b
		פן	ADDENDA ET COR-RIGENDA	1126b	
7	26	חרם	DEVOTED THING	356b	1 b
		לא	NOT	518c	1 aa
		שקץ	DETEST	1055a	1
		תועבה	ABOMINATION	*1072a	1 b
		תעב	BE ABHORRED	1073b	1 a2
8	1	מצוה	COMMANDMENT	846b	2 a
		רבה	BECOME MANY	915a	1 a
8	2	ה	INTERROG PART	210b	2 b
		הלך	WALK	236d	1 c
		זה	THIS	261d	4 i
		זכר	REMEMBER	269d	1 1 d
		לא	NOT	519a	1 ad b
		לבב	HEART	523c	2 2
		נסה	TEST	650b	3 a

Ch	v.	Heb	Eng	Page	Sec
		ענה	BE BOWED DOWN	776b	3
8	3	מצוה	COMMANDMENT	846b	2 a
		אכל	EAT	37d	1
		בד	SEPARATION	94c	1 b
		ה	THE	207d	1 e
		חיה	LIVE	311b	1 c
		ידע	MAKE KNOWN	395a	
		מוצא	GOING FORTH	425d	2 a
		לחם	FOOD	537a	1 a
		מן	MANNA	577c	
		על	UPON	753d	2 1e
		ענה	BE BOWED DOWN	776b	3
		פה	MOUTH	805b	2 c
		רעב	BE HUNGRY	944b	
8	4	בלה	BECOME OLD AND WORN OUT	115a	
		בצק	SWELL	130d	
		זה	THIS	261d	4 i
		על	UPON	758d	4 2a
		שמלה	WRAPPER	971a	
8	5	בן	SON	120a	1
		ידע	KNOW	394a	1 g
		יסר	DISCIPLINE	416a	1 b
		יסר	DISCIPLINE	416a	1 a
		לבב	HEART	523c	2 3b
		לבב	HEART	523c	2 2
		עם	WITH	768c	4 a
8	6	דרך	WAY	204a	6 ec
		הלך	WALK	234c	2 3a 1b
		ירא	FEAR	431c	3 b
		ל	TO	517b	7 ba
8	7	בקעה	VALLEY	132c	1
		הר	MOUNTAIN	250b	1 e
		טוב	PLEASANT	374a	3 b
		מי	WATER	565c	1 b
		נחל	WADY	636b	2
		עין	SPRING	745b	
		תהום	DEEP	1063a	4
8	8	גפן	VINE	172c	
		דבש	HONEY	185b	
		זית	OLIVE TREE	268d	1
		חטה	WHEAT	334d	
		רמון	POMEGRANATE	941d	1
		שערה	BARLEY	972d	1
		שמן	OIL	1032a	2 a
		תאנה	FIG-TREE	1061a	1
8	9	אבן	STONE	6d	4
		ברזל	IRON	137c	1 a
		הר	MOUNTAIN	250c	1 f
		חסר	LACK	341b	1
		חצב	HEW	345a	1
		כל	ALL	482c	2 a
		לא	NOT	518d	1 ac
		מסכנת	SCARCITY	587d	
		נחשת	COPPER	638d	1
8	10	ברך	BLESS	139a	1
		טוב	PLEASANT	374a	3 b
		שבע	SATISFIED	959b	1 a
8	11	בלת	NOT	116d	4 a
		חקה	SOMETHING PRESCRIBED	350a	2 d
		חקה	SOMETHING PRESCRIBED	350b	2 e
		פן	LEST	814d	1
		מצוה	COMMANDMENT	846c	2 b2
8	12	בית	HOUSE	108d	1 ab
		בנה	BUILD	124b	1 ab
		טוב	PLEASANT	373c	1 a
		שבע	SATISFIED	959b	1 a
8	13	בקר	CATTLE	133b	1 a
		זהב	GOLD	262d	2
		רבה	BECOME MANY	915a	1 c
		רבה	BECOME MANY	915a	1 c
8	14	בית	HOUSE	109a	1 ae 9
		יצא	CAUSE TO GO	424c	1 a
		לבב	HEART	524a	2 6c
		עבד	SLAVE	713d	1
		רום	BE HIGH	926d	2 b
8	15	אשר	PARTICLE OF RELATION	82c	4 bb
		הלך	WALK	236c	1 a
		חלמיש	FLINT	321d	
		יצא	BRING OUT	425a	4 i
		ירא	BE FEARFUL	431d	1 a
		מי	WATER	565b	1 a
		נחש	SERPENT	638a	1 a
		עקרב	SCORPION	785d	
		אבע	FINGER	840c	1 c
		צור	ROCK	849c	1 a
		צמאון	THIRSTY GROUND	855a	
		שרף	FIERY SERPENT	977b	
8	16	אכל	EAT	37d	1
		יטב	DO GOOD TO	405d	2
		מן	MANNA	577c	
		נסה	TEST	650b	3 a
		ענה	BE BOWED DOWN	776b	3
8	17	אמר	SAY	56b	2
		חיל	STRENGTH	299a	3
		יד	HAND	389d	1 e1
		כח	STRENGTH	470d	1 d
		לבב	HEART	524a	2 7
		עצם	MIGHT	782c	1
		עשה	DO	795a	2 7
8	18	ברית	COVENANT	137a	3 1
		ה	THE	209b	2 c
		זכר	REMEMBER	270a	13 b
		חיל	STRENGTH	299a	3
		יום	DAY	400d	7 h
		כח	STRENGTH	470c	1 b
		נתן	GIVE	678c	1 b
		עשה	DO	795a	2
		קום	STAND	879a	6 f
		שבע	SWEAR	989c	2
8	19	אבד	PERISH	1c	1
		אחר	ANOTHER	*29d	
		היה	COME TO PASS	225b	1 2b e
		הלך	WALK	235a	2 3d 2
		עבד	WORK	713b	4 b
		עוד	BEAR WITNESS	730a	1
		שחה	BOW DOWN	1005c	3
		שכח	FORGET	1013b	1 c
8	20	אבד	PERISH	1c	1
		אבד	DESTROY	2b	1
		כן	SO	486b	2 ab
		עקב	CONSEQUENCE	784d	1
		פנה	FACE	818b	2 6a
		קול	VOICE	877b	3 b
9	1	בצר	MAKE INACCESSIBLE	131a	
		ירש	TAKE POSSESSION	439c	1 b
		אשר	PARTICLE OF RELATION	82d	4 d
9	2	יצב	STATION ONESELF	426c	D
		מי	WHO	566d	F c
		ענק	NECK	778c	
		פנה	FACE	817b	2 4b d
		רום	BE HIGH	926d	1 a
		שמע	HEAR	1033d	1 d2
9	3	אבד	DESTROY	2b	1
		אכל	EAT	37c	3
		אש	FIRE	77c	2
		דבר	SPEAK	181b	3 c
		ירש	CAUSE TO POSSESS	440a	2 a
		כנע	HUMBLE	488c	2
		מהר	QUICKLY	555b	
		עבר	PASS OVER	718a	5 c
9	4	ב	IN	90c	3 5
		גוי	NATION	156c	1 c
		הדף	THRUST	213d	2
		ירש	CAUSE TO POSSESS	440a	2 a
		לבב	HEART	524a	2 7
		פנה	FACE	818a	2 5a e
		רשעה	WICKEDNESS	958a	2
9	5	ב	IN	90c	3 5
		גוי	NATION	156c	1 c
		דבר	WORD	182d	1 2b
		ירש	CAUSE TO POSSESS	440a	2 a
		ישר	STRAIGHTNESS	449c	2
		לבב	HEART	523d	2 6a
		רשעה	WICKEDNESS	958a	2
		שבע	SWEAR	989c	2
9	6	טוב	PLEASANT	374a	3 b
		ערף	BACK OF NECK	791c	2
		קשה	SEVERE	904d	3
9	7	אשר	THAT	83b	8 aa
		זכר	REMEMBER	269d	1 1 c1
		יום	DAY	401a	7 k
		יצא	GO OUT	422d	1 a
		מן	FROM	583d	9 b2
		מרה	BE REBELLIOUS	598b	
		עם	WITH	767d	1 d
		קצף	BE WROTH	893b	
		קצף	BE WROTH	893b	
		שכח	FORGET	1013b	1 a
9	8	אנף	BE ANGRY	60a	
		חרב	HOREB	352a	
		קצף	BE WROTH	893b	
		קצף	BE WROTH	893b	
9	9	אבן	STONE	6c	2
		אשר	PARTICLE OF RELATION	82c	4 bb
		ברית	COVENANT	136d	2 2c
		הר	MOUNTAIN	249d	1
		יום	DAY	398b	1
		כרת	CUT	503d	4
		לוח	TABLET	*531d	1
		לוח	TABLET	531d	1
		לוח	TABLET	531d	1
		לילה	NIGHT	538d	1
		אבן	STONE	6c	2
9	10	דבר	SPEAK	181b	3 e
		דבר	WORD	183a	2 2
		כ	LIKE	453d	1 b
		כתב	WRITE	507b	1 a
		כתב	WRITE	507d	1 a
		לוח	TABLET	531d	1
		לוח	TABLET	*531d	1
		אבע	FINGER	840c	1 c
		קהל	ASSEMBLY	874c	1 d
9	11	אבן	STONE	6c	2
		ברית	COVENANT	136d	2 2c
		יום	DAY	398b	1
		לוח	TABLET	531d	1
		לוח	TABLET	531d	1
		לילה	NIGHT	538d	1
		שנא	HATE	971d	3
9	12	דרך	WAY	203c	6 b
		זה	THIS	262a	6 e
		יצא	CAUSE TO GO	424c	1 a
		מהר	QUICKLY	555b	
		מסכה	MOLTEN IMAGE	651b	2
		סור	TURN ASIDE	693c	1
		עשה	DO	794c	2 1c
		צוה	CHARGE	845d	2 a
		שחת	GO TO RUIN	1008a	2
9	13	הנה	BEHOLD	244b	C
		ערף	BACK OF NECK	791c	2
		עשה	DO	793d	1 1a 1
		קשה	SEVERE	904d	3
9	14	גוי	NATION	156c	1 a
		מחה	WIPE OUT	562a	2
		מן	FROM	578a	1 a
		עשה	DO	794c	2 1g
		רב	GREAT	913c	2 d
		רפה	SINK	952a	3
		שם	NAME	1028b	2 c
		שמי	HEAVENS	1029d	1 a
		תחת	UNDERNEATH	1066a	3 2a
9	15	בער	BURN	129a	2
		ברית	COVENANT	136d	2 2c
		יד	HAND	389a	1 a
		ירד	COME DOWN	432d	1 a
		לוח	TABLET	531d	1
9	16	ראשון	FIRST	911d	3 a1
		חטא	MISS A GOAL OR WAY	307a	2 b
		ל	TO	515d	5 ia
		מהר	QUICKLY	555b	
		מסכה	MOLTEN IMAGE	651b	2
		עגל	CALF	722b	
		צוה	CHARGE	845d	2 a
9	17	יד	HAND	389a	1 a
		לוח	TABLET	531d	1
		על	UPON	758c	4 2a
		שבר	BREAK	991a	2
		שלך	THROW	1021a	1 a
		תפש	LAY HOLD OF	1074d	1
9	18	חטא	MISS A GOAL OR WAY	307b	2 b
		חמאת	SIN	308d	1 b
		יום	DAY	398b	1
		כעם	VEX	495a	2
		לילה	NIGHT	538d	1
		נפל	FALL	658b	2
		על	UPON	754b	2 1f b
		רע	EVIL	948c	0 b
9	19	אף	NOSE	60b	3
		יגר	BE AFRAID	388c	
		חמה	RAGE	404d	2 c
		פנה	FACE	818b	2 6b
		פעם	OCCURRENCE	822b	3 c
		קצף	BE WROTH	893b	
9	20	אנף	BE ANGRY	60a	
		פלל	INTERVENE	813b	1
		שמד	BE EXTERMINATED	1029b	1
9	21	דקק	BE FINE	200d	2
		חמאת	SIN	308d	1 b
		מחן	GRIND	377c	
		יטב	DO WELL	406a	3
		ירד	GO DOWN	433c	3 b
		כתת	BEAT	510a	1
		ל	TO	512b	4 a
		נחל	TORRENT	636a	1
		עגל	CALF	722b	
9	22	עד	UNTIL	724d	2 a
		עפר	DRY EARTH	779d	1 d
		שרף	BURN	976d	2 a
		תאוה	DESIRE	16c	1
		תבערה	TEBERAH	129c	
		מסה	MASSAH	650c	
		קברותהתאוה	KIBROTH-HATTA-AVAH	869a	
		קצף	BE WROTH	893b	
		קצף	BE WROTH	893b	
9	23	אמן	CONFIRM	53a	2 b
		מרה	BE REBELLIOUS	598b	
		קדש	KADESH	874a	1
		קול	VOICE	877b	3 b
		יום	DAY	400a	7 d1 e
9	24	יום	DAY	401a	7 j
		מן	FROM	581b	4 a
		מרה	BE REBELLIOUS	598b	
		עם	WITH	767d	1 d
9	25	אמר	SAY	56c	4
		את	MARK OF THE ACCUSATIVE	85b	2 b
		יום	DAY	398b	1
		לילה	NIGHT	538d	1
		נפל	FALL	658b	2
9	26	אדן	LORD	11c	4 a
		גדל	GREATNESS	152d	2 b
		חזק	STRONG	305c	1 b
		יצא	CAUSE TO GO	424c	1 a
		נחלה	PROPERTY	635b	1 e
		פדה	RANSOM	804a	3 a
		פלל	INTERVENE	813b	1
		שחת	GO TO RUIN	1008b	1
9	27	זכר	REMEMBER	270b	2 1 c
		חמאת	SIN	309a	1 d5
		עבד	SLAVE	714a	3
		פנה	TURN	815c	2 c2
		קשי	STUBBORNNESS	904d	
		רשע	WICKEDNESS	957d	3
9	28	ב	IN	*91a	5 2
		בוא	COME	99a	1 a
		בלי	WEARING OUT	115d	C a
		דבר	SPEAK	181b	3 c
		יכל	BE ABLE	407c	1

Ch	v.	Heb	Eng	Page	Sec
		יצא	CAUSE TO GO	424c	1 b
		יצא	CAUSE TO GO	424c	1 a
		מות	DIE	560b	2
		מן	ON ACCOUNT OF	583a	7 a
		שנאה	HATING	972a	2
9	29	זרוע	ARM	284a	1 c
		יצא	CAUSE TO GO	424c	1 b
		כח	STRENGTH	470d	3
		נחלה	PROPERTY	635b	1 e
10	1	אבן	STONE	6c	2
		ארון	CHEST	75b	3 a
		ל	TO	515c	5 ia
		לוח	TABLET	531d	1
		עלה	GO UP	748c	2 b
		עשה	DO	794c	2 1c
		פסל	HEW	820d	
		ראשון	FIRST	911c	1 a
10	2	דבר	WORD	183a	22
		לוח	TABLET	531d	1
		לוח	TABLET	*531d	1
		ראשון	FIRST	911c	1 a
		שבר	BREAK	991a	
10	3	אבן	STONE	6c	2
		ארון	CHEST	75b	3 a
		לוח	TABLET	531d	1
		עץ	TREE	781d	2 a
		עשה	DO	794c	2 1g
		פסל	HEW	820d	
		ראשון	FIRST	911c	1 a
		שטה	ACACIA	1008d	
10	4	דבר	WORD	183a	22
		כתב	WRITE	507b	1 a
		לוח	TABLET	531d	1
		לוח	TABLET	*531d	1
		קהל	ASSEMBLY	874c	1 d
		ראשון	FIRST	911c	1 a
10	5	ירד	COME DOWN	432d	1 a
		לוח	TABLET	531d	1
10	6	מוסרה	MOSERAH	64c	
		בארתבניעיק	BEEROTH BENE-JA-AKAN	92b	
		בניעקן	BENE-JAAKAN	122c	
		כהן	ACT AS PRIEST	464c	2
		נסע	JOURNEY	652b	3
		קלל	BURNISHED	887a	
		ישראל	ISRAEL	975d	2 b1
10	7	גדגדה	GUDGODAH	151d	
		יטבתה	JOTBATHAH	406a	
		מי	WATER	565c	1 b
		נחל	WADY	636b	2
		נסע	JOURNEY	652b	3
10	8	ארון	CHEST	75c	3 f
		בדל	BE DIVIDED	95b	1 a
		ברך	BLESS	139a	3
		יום	DAY	401b	71
		לוי	LEVITE	532d	2
		עמד	STAND	764a	1 e
		קלל	BURNISHED	887a	
		שם	NAME	1028b	3
		שרת	SERVE	1058a	2 a
10	9	דבר	SPEAK	181b	3 c
		הוא	HE, SHE, IT	215d	2 b
		היה	BECOME	226c	2 2h
		חלק	PORTION	324a	2 a
		כן	SO	487b	3 f
		לוי	LEVI	532c	2
		נחלה	PROPERTY	635b	1 d
		עם	WITH	767c	1 b
10	10	אבה	BE WILLING	2c	
		יום	DAY	398b	1
		לילה	NIGHT	538d	1
		עמד	STAND	764b	3 b
		פעם	OCCURRENCE	822b	3 c
		ראשון	FIRST	911c	1 a
		שחת	GO TO RUIN	1008b	1
10	11	מסע	JOURNEY	652d	2
		פנה	FACE	817c	2 4c b
10	12	דרך	WAY	204a	6 ec
		הלך	WALK	234c	2 3a 1b
		ירא	FEAR	431c	3 b
		כיאם	EXCEPT	475a	2 a
		ל	TO	517d	7 bc
		לבב	HEART	523b	1
		נפש	SOUL	661b	0
		מעם	FROM WITH	768d	A
10	13	חקה	SOMETHING PRE-SCRIBED	350b	2 d
		חקה	SOMETHING PRE-SCRIBED	350b	2 e
		טוב	A GOOD THING	375a	1
		מצוה	COMMANDMENT	846c	2 b2
10	14	שמי	HEAVENS	1030b	2 a
10	15	אחר	AFTER	*30a	2 b
		בחר	CHOOSE	103d	1 a
		זרע	SOWING	282c	4 b
		חשק	BE ATTACHED TO	366a	
		יום	DAY	400d	7 h
		ל	TO	517b	7 ba
		רק	ONLY	956c	2 b
10	16	לבב	HEART	524a	2 6d
		מול	CIRCUMCIZE	557d	
		עלה	FORESKIN	790c	
		ערף	BACK OF NECK	791c	2
		קשה	BE SEVERE	904c	3 a
10	17	אדון	LORD	11a	2
		אדון	LORD	11b	22

Ch	v.	Heb	Eng	Page	Sec
		אל	GOD	42c	6 a
		אלהים	GOD	43c	1 d
		גבור	STRONG	150a	1
		גדול	GREAT	153b	6 c
		ירא	BE REVERED	431d	3 a
		נשא	LIFT	670c	1 b 3
		שחד	BRIBE	1005a	
10	18	אהב	LOVE	13a	1
		אלמנה	WIDOW	48b	
		גר	SOJOURNER	158b	2
		יתום	ORPHAN	450c	
		שמלה	WRAPPER	971a	
		משפט	JUDGMENT	1049a	5
10	19	אהב	LOVE	13a	1
		גר	SOJOURNER	158b	2
		גר	SOJOURNER	158b	1
10	20	דבק	CLING	179d	2 a
		ירא	FEAR	431c	3 b
		שבע	SWEAR	989b	1 a
		שם	NAME	1028b	3
10	21	אלהים	GOD	44d	4 c
		את	WITH	86b	1 db
		גדול	GREAT	153c	9
		תהלה	PRAISE	240c	5 ce
		ירא	CAUSE FEAR	431d	2 a
		עם	WITH	767d	1 f
		עשה	DO	794a	1 1a 4
		ב	IN	89a	17b
10	22	כוכב	STAR	457a	2
		נפש	SOUL	660b	4 c3
		שום	TO PLACE	964a	3 e
11	1	חקה	SOMETHING PRE-SCRIBED	350a	2 d
		חקה	SOMETHING PRE-SCRIBED	350b	2 e
		יום	DAY	400c	7 f
		משמרת	GUARD	1038d	3
11	2	את	MARK OF THE AC-CUSATIVE	85b	3 a
		גדל	GREATNESS	152d	2 b
		זרוע	ARM	284a	1 c
		חזק	STRONG	305c	1 b
		מוסר	DISCIPLINE	416b	1 a
		ראה	TO SEE	907b	3
11	3	אות	SIGN	16d	4
		מלך	KING	573a	1
		עשה	DO	793d	1 1a 1
		פרעה	PHARAOH	829a	
11	4	אבד	CAUSE TO PERISH	2a	1
		יום	DAY	401b	7 1
		סוס	HORSE	692c	1
		סוף	REEDS	693b	2 a
		צוף	FLOW	847b	1
		רדף	PURSUE	922c	1 a
11	6	אבירם	ABIRAM	4d	1
		אליאב	ELIAB	45a	B
		בית	HOUSE	109d	5 a
		בית	HOUSE	109d	5 a
		בלע	SWALLOW UP	118a	2
		דתן	DATHAN	206d	
		פה	MOUTH	804d	1 a
		פצה	PART	822c	1 a
		יקום	SUBSTANCE	879c	
		ראובן	REUBEN	910a	1
		רגל	FOOT	920a	1 f
11	7	גדול	GREAT	153b	6 c
		עשה	DO	793d	1 1a 1
11	8	חזק	BE FIRM	304b	1 1b
		עבר	PASS OVER	717a	1 a2
11	9	ארך	BE LONG	73d	1 a
		דבש	HONEY	185b	1
		זוב	FLOW	264d	2
		זרע	SOWING	282c	4 b
		חלב	MILK	316c	A 4
11	10	גן	GARDEN	171a	
		זרע	SOW	281c	1 c
		זרע	SOWING	282b	2 b
		יצא	GO OUT	422d	1 a
		ירק	HERBS	438d	
		ל	TO	*516c	5 jb
		שקה	GIVE TO DRINK	1052c	1
		בקעה	VALLEY	132c	1
11	11	הר	MOUNTAIN	250b	1 e
		ו	AND	252d	1 e
		ל	TO	516c	5 jb
		מטר	RAIN	564d	
		מי	WATER	565c	1 g
		עבר	PASS OVER	717a	1 a2
		שמי	HEAVENS	1029d	1 a
11	12	אחרית	END	31a	B
		ב	IN	*88d	1 4
		דרש	SEEK	205c	7
		תמיד	CONTINUITY	556b	1 a
		ראשית	BEGINNING	912a	1 a
		שנה	YEAR	1040b	
11	13	היה	COME TO PASS	225b	1 2b bb
		לבב	HEART	523b	22
		נפש	SOUL	661b	0
11	14	אסף	GATHER	62b	1 c
		דגן	CORN	186c	
		יורה	EARLY RAIN	435c	
		תירש	NEW WINE	440d	
		מלקוש	SPRING-RAIN	545b	
		נתן	GIVE	678d	1 d
		עת	TIME	773c	2 b
		יצהר	FRESH OIL	844a	

Ch	v.	Heb	Eng	Page	Sec
11	15	בהמה	BEAST	97a	2
		נתן	GIVE	678d	1 d
		עשב	HERB	793b	
		שדה	FIELD	961b	1 a
11	16	לבב	HEART	523c	2 2
		סור	TURN ASIDE	693c	1
		עבד	WORK	713b	4 b
		פתה	BE SIMPLE	834c	2
		שחה	BOW DOWN	1005c	3
11	17	אבד	PERISH	1d	1
		אדמה	GROUND	9c	1
		חרה	BURN	354a	2a
		טוב	PLEASANT	374a	3 b
		יבול	PRODUCE	385b	
		מהרה	HASTE	555b	
		מטר	RAIN	564d	
11	18	נתן	GIVE	679c	1 t
		עצר	RESTRAIN	783c	1
		אות	SIGN	17a	5
		אלה	THESE	41c	A
		טוטפות	BANDS	378a	
		לבב	HEART	523c	2 2
		נפש	SOUL	661b	0
		עין	EYE	745a	5
11	19	דבר	SPEAK	181c	4 c
		הלך	WALK	230b	1 1a
		הלך	WALK	230d	1 1d 2a
		למד	LEARN	540d	
11	20	בית	HOUSE	108d	1 ab
		מזוזה	DOOR-POST	265b	1
		כיאם	FOR IF	474d	1 b
		כתב	WRITE	507c	1 b1
		שער	GATE	1044d	1 a
11	21	רבה	BECOME MANY	915b	1 c
		שמי	HEAVENS	1030a	1 a
11	22	דבק	CLING	179d	2 a
		דרך	WAY	204a	6 ec
		הלך	WALK	234c	2 3a 1b
		ל	TO	517b	7 ba
11	23	ירש	TAKE POSSESSION	439c	1 b
		ירש	CAUSE TO POSSESS	440a	2 a
		פנה	FACE	818a	2 5a e
11	24	אחרון	BEHIND	30d	1
		גבול	BORDER	147d	1 a
		דרך	TREAD	202a	2
		מדרך	TREADING-PLACE	*204a	
		ים	SEA	410d	1
		כל	ALL	481c	1 b
		כף	SOLE OF FOOT	496d	3
		לבנן	LEBANON	527a	
		פרת	EUPHRATES	832b	
		רגל	FOOT	919d	1 a
11	25	דבר	SPEAK	181b	3 c
		דרך	TREAD	202a	2
		יצב	STATION ONESELF	426c	D
		מורא	FEAR	432b	1
		פחד	DREAD	808c	1
		פנה	FACE	816d	2 3a
11	26	ברכה	BLESSING	139d	1 b
		פנה	FACE	817c	2 4b g
11	27	אשר	THAT	83d	8 d
		אשר	THAT	84a	
		ברכה	BLESSING	139d	1 b
11	28	אשר	THAT	83d	8 d
		דרך	WAY	204a	6 ec
		ידע	KNOW	394a	2
		צוה	CHARGE	845d	2 a
		קללה	CURSE	887a	
11	29	אל	TO	41a	A
		ברכה	BLESSING	139d	1 b
		גרזים	GERIZIM	173d	
		היה	COME TO PASS	225b	1 2b ba
		הר	MOUNTAIN	249b	1 a
		הר	MOUNTAIN	249b	1 a
		נתן	PUT	680c	2 b
		עיבל	EBAL	716d	
11	30	אלון	TEREBINTH	18d	
		אחר	BEHIND	30a	2 a
		אצל	BESIDE	69b	A
		מבוא	ENTERING	99d	2
		מורה	TEACHER	435c	
		כנעני	CANAANITE	489a	2 b
		לא	NOT	520b	4 bb
		מול	IN FRONT OF	557c	2
		עבר	REGION ACROSS	719c	1 b
		ערבה	DESERT-PLAIN	787c	1 b
		שמש	SUN	1039b	2
11	31	ירש	TAKE POSSESSION	439b	1 a
		כי	WHEN	473b	2 a
11	32	חק	SOMETHING PRE-SCRIBED	349a	7 g
		חק	SOMETHING PRE-SCRIBED	349d	7 g
		פנה	FACE	817c	2 4b g
*12	1	אדמה	GROUND	9d	4 a
		חי	ALIVE	312a	1 b
		חק	SOMETHING PRE-SCRIBED	349d	7 g
12	2	אבד	CAUSE TO PERISH	2a	1
		גבעה	HILL	149a	3
		גבעה	HILL	149a	2
		הר	MOUNTAIN	250d	1 1
		ירש	TAKE POSSESSION	439c	1 b
		עבד	WORK	713b	4 b
		עץ	TREE	781c	1 a

97

DEUTERONOMY

Ch v.	Heb	Eng	Page	Sec
	מקום	STANDING PLACE	880b	4
	רום	BE HIGH	926d	1 a
	רענן	LUXURIANT	947d	
12 3	אבד	CAUSE TO VANISH	2a	2
	אש	FIRE	77c	1
	אשרה	ASHERA	81c	B
	גדע	HEW	154b	
	מזבח	ALTAR	259a	0
	מצבה	PILLAR	663b	1 c
	פסיל	IDOL	821a	
	מקום	STANDING PLACE	880b	4
	שם	NAME	1028b	2 c
12 5	בחר	CHOOSE	104a	2 a
	דרש	RESORT TO	205a	1
	מזבח	ALTAR	258c	2
	כי אם	BUT	475a	2 b
	מקום	STANDING PLACE	880b	4
	שום	TO PLACE	962d	1 a
	שכן	SETTLE DOWN	1015c	1
	שכן	DWELLING	1015c	
	שם	NAME	1028b	3
12 6	בכור	FIRST-BORN	114b	2 c
	זבח	SACRIFICE	257d	2 5
	זבח	SACRIFICE	257d	2 5
	זבח	SACRIFICE	258a	2 7
	יד	HAND	389c	1 d
	נדבה	FREEWILL-OFFERING	621d	2 c
	נדר	VOW	624a	5
	עלה	WHOLE BURNT OFFERING	751a	
	מעשר	TENTH PART	798b	2
	תרומה	OFFERING	929a	1
	תרוה	OFFERING	929b	7
12 7	אכל	EAT	37b	1
	ברך	BLESS	139a	2 a
	יד	HAND	389b	1 c
	פנה	FACE	817b	24 a h
	שמח	REJOICE	970b	
	משלוח	OUTSTRETCHING	1020a	1
12 8	ישר	STRAIGHT	449a	2 b
	עין	EYE	744d	3 c
	פה	HERE	806a	1 a
12 9	מנוחה	RESTING PLACE	629d	1
	עתה	NOW	774c	2 f
12 10	בטח	SECURITY	105b	
	מן	FROM	578a	1 a
	מן	FROM	578d	1 c
	נוח	REST	628c	A 1b 2
	סביב	ROUND ABOUT	687a	1 d
12 11	בחר	CHOOSE	104a	1 a
	בחר	CHOOSE	104a	1 a
	היה	COME TO PASS	225a	1 2b ag
	זבח	SACRIFICE	257d	2 5
	זבח	SACRIFICE	258a	2 7
	יד	HAND	389c	1 d
	נדר	VOW	623d	
	נדר	VOW	624a	2
	עלה	WHOLE BURNT OFFERING	751a	
	מעשר	TENTH PART	798b	2
	תרומה	OFFERING	929a	1
	שכן	SETTLE DOWN	1015b	
	שם	NAME	1028b	3
12 12	אמה	MAID	51a	1
	חלק	PORTION	324a	2 a
	לוי	LEVITE	532d	2
	נחלה	PROPERTY	635b	1 d
	פנה	FACE	817b	24 a h
	שמח	REJOICE	970b	2 a
	שער	GATE	1045a	2 c
12 13	עלה	GO UP	749d	8
	עלה	WHOLE BURNT OFFERING	750d	
12 14	מקום	STANDING PLACE	880a	4
	בחר	CHOOSE	104a	2 a
	עלה	GO UP	749d	8
	עלה	WHOLE BURNT OFFERING	750d	
	מקום	STANDING PLACE	880b	4
	שם	THERE	1027a	1 a
12 15	אוה	DESIRE	16b	
	איל	HART	19b	
	ברכה	BLESSING	139d	1 b
	בשר	FLESH	142c	1 a
	זבח	SLAUGHTER FOR SACRIFICE	257a	2
	טמא	UNCLEAN	379d	2 a
	ל	TO	*516c	5 jb
	נפש	SOUL	660d	6 a
	נתן	GIVE	678b	1 b
	צבי	GAZELLE	840b	
	רק	ONLY	956c	2 b
	שער	GATE	1045a	2 c
12 16	דם	BLOOD	196c	1
	רק	ONLY	956c	2 b
	שפך	POUR OUT	1049c	1 a
12 17	בכור	FIRST-BORN	114b	2 c
	דגן	CORN	186c	
	דגן	CORN	186c	
	יד	HAND	389c	1 d
	יכל	BE ABLE	407d	1 d
	תירוש	NEW WINE	440d	
	נדבה	FREEWILL-OFFERING	621d	2 c
	נדר	VOW	623d	

Ch v.	Heb	Eng	Page	Sec
	נדר	VOW	624a	5
	נדר	VOW	624a	2
	מעשר	TENTH PART	798b	2
	יצהר	FRESH OIL	844a	
	תרומה	OFFERING	929a	1
	שער	GATE	1045a	2 c
12 18	אכל	EAT	37b	1
	אמה	MAID	51a	1
	בחר	CHOOSE	104a	1 a
	יד	HAND	389c	1 c
	לוי	LEVITE	532d	2
	פנה	FACE	817b	24 a h
	שמח	REJOICE	970b	2 a
	משלח	OUTSTRETCHING	1020a	1
12 19	אדמה	LAND	10a	5
	לוי	LEVITE	532d	2
	עזב	LEAVE	737c	2 c
12 20	אוה	DESIRE	16a	
	אוה	DESIRE	16b	
	גבול	BORDER	147d	1 a
	דבר	SPEAK	181b	3 c
	כי	BECAUSE	473c	3 a
	נפש	SOUL	660d	6 a
	נפש	SOUL	660d	6 a
	רחב	BE LARGE	931c	1
12 21	אוה	DESIRE	16b	
	בחר	CHOOSE	104a	2 a
	זבח	SLAUGHTER FOR SACRIFICE	257a	2
	נפש	SOUL	660d	6 a
	רחק	BE DISTANT	934d	
	שער	GATE	1045a	2 c
12 22	איל	HART	19b	
	אכל	EAT	37d	1
	טמא	UNCLEAN	379d	2 a
	יחדו	TOGETHER	403c	C
	כן	SO	486c	2 cf
	צבי	GAZELLE	840b	
12 23	דם	BLOOD	196b	1
	דם	BLOOD	196c	1
	חזק	BE FIRM	304b	1 2e
	נפש	SOUL	659b	1 a
	נפש	A LIVING BEING	659d	3 a
	עם	WITH	767b	1 a
	רק	ONLY	956c	2 b
12 24	נפש	A LIVING BEING	659d	3 a
	שפך	POUR OUT	1049c	1 a
12 25	אחר	AFTER	30a	2 b
	יטב	BE WELL	405c	3
	ישר	STRAIGHT	449a	2 a
	כי	BECAUSE	473c	3 a
	עין	EYE	744d	3 c
12 26	בחר	CHOOSE	104a	2 a
	נדר	VOW	624a	6
	נדר	VOW	624a	2
12 27	קדש	APARTNESS	872a	3 c
	דם	BLOOD	197d	3 b
	דם	BLOOD	*197d	3 b
	זבח	SACRIFICE	257c	1 1
	מזבח	ALTAR	258c	2
	מזבח	ALTAR	259a	1
	עלה	WHOLE BURNT OFFERING	750d	
	שפך	POUR OUT	1049d	
12 28	אחר	AFTER	30a	2 b
	טוב	PLEASANT	374a	2 f
	יטב	BE WELL	405c	3
	ישר	STRAIGHT	449a	2 a
	כי	BECAUSE	473c	3 a
	עין	EYE	744d	3 c
12 29	עולם	LONG DURATION	762d	2 f
	ירש	TAKE POSSESSION	439c	1 b
	כרת	CUT OFF	504c	2 c
12 30	איכה	IN WHAT MANNER	32d	I
	אנכי	I	59b	
	אנכי	I	59b	
	דרש	SEEK	205b	3 b
	ל	TO	514b	5 fa
	נקש	STRIKE	669c	
	עבד	WORK	713b	4 b
	שמד	BE EXTERMINATED	1029b	1
12 31	גם	ALSO	169b	2
	שרף	BURN	977a	2 b2
	תועבה	ABOMINATION	1072d	1 b
13 1	גרע	DIMINISH	175c	1
	דבר	WORD	182d	1 2a
	יסף	ADD	415b	1
13 2	אות	SIGN	16d	4
	אל	TO	39c	1
	מופת	WONDER	69a	1
	חלם	DREAM	321c	C
	חלום	DREAM	321d	2 b
	נביא	PROPHET	612a	2
	קום	STAND	878a	4
13 3	אות	SIGN	16d	4
	מופת	WONDER	69a	1
	בוא	COME	98c	2 c
	הלך	WALK	235a	23d 2
	ידע	KNOW	394a	2
13 4	ה	INTERROG PART	210b	2 a
	חלם	DREAM	321c	C
	חלום	DREAM	321d	2 b
	יש	BE	441c	2 a
	לב	HEART	523b	2 2
	נביא	PROPHET	612a	2
	נסה	TEST	650b	3 a

Ch v.	Heb	Eng	Page	Sec
13 5	נפש	SOUL	661b	0
	את	MARK OF THE ACCUSATIVE	85a	1 a
	דבק	CLING	179d	2 a
	הלך	WALK	235a	23d 1
	ירא	FEAR	431c	3 b
	קול	VOICE	877b	3 b
13 6	בית	HOUSE	109a	1 ae 9
	בער	CONSUME	129b	1
	דבר	SPEAK	181a	2
	דרך	WAY	203c	6 b
	חלם	DREAM	321c	C
	חלום	DREAM	321d	2 b
	יצא	CAUSE TO GO	424c	1 a
	מות	DIE	560c	2
	נביא	PROPHET	612a	2
	נדח	THRUST	623b	3
	סרה	A TURNING ASIDE	694c	2
	עבד	SLAVE	713d	1
	על	UPON	757d	2 7d
	פדה	RANSOM	804a	3 a
	צוה	CHARGE	845d	2 a
	רע	EVIL	948d	3
13 7	אם	MOTHER	51d	1
	אמר	SAY	56b	1
	אשה	WOMAN	61b	2
	הלך	WALK	233d	1 5b
	הלך	WALK	235a	23d 2
	חיק	BOSOM	300d	3 a
	ידע	KNOW	394a	2
	סות	INCITE	694d	2
	סתר	COVERING	712a	3
	עבד	WORK	713b	4 b
	רע	FRIEND	946a	1
13 8	אלהים	GOD	43c	1 d
	מן	FROM	581d	5 a
	סביב	ROUND ABOUT	687b	2 bb
	קצה	END	892a	1
	קרב	NEAR	898c	2 a
13 9	אבה	BE WILLING		2 c
	חוס	PITY	299b	A
	חמל	SPARE	328b	
	כסה	COVER	492a	6
13 10	אחרון	BEHIND	31a	B b
	ב	IN	89b	24 a
	הרג	KILL	247b	3
	מות	DIE	560b	1 b
	ראשון	FIRST	911d	3 a1
13 11	אבן	STONE	6b	1
	בית	HOUSE	109a	1 ae 9
	בקש	SEEK	134d	2 d
	יצא	CAUSE TO GO	424c	1 a
	מות	DIE	559d	2 a
	נדח	THRUST	623b	3
	סקל	STONE	709c	
	עבד	SLAVE	713d	1
	על	UPON	759a	2 c
13 12	דבר	WORD	*183d	4 7
	יסף	DO AGAIN	415c	2
	ירא	FEAR	431b	1 a
	רע	EVIL	948c	1 d
13 13	חרם	DEVOTED THING	*356b	1 a
	כי	IF	473b	2 b
	שמע	HEAR	1033c	1 c
13 14	בליעל	WORTHLESSNESS	116a	1
	הלך	WALK	233d	1 5b
	הלך	WALK	235a	23d 2
	ידע	KNOW	394a	2
	ישב	DWELL	443b	3
	נדח	THRUST	623b	3
	עבד	WORK	713b	4 b
13 15	אמת	FIRMNESS	54b	4 a
	דבר	WORD	182c	1 1g
	דרש	SEEK	205c	4 b
	הלך	WALK	234c	23a 1b
	הנה	IF	244c	D
	חקר	SEARCH	350c	1
	חרם	DEVOTED THING	*356b	1 a
	יטב	DO WELL	406a	3
	כון	BE FIRM	465d	1 d
	עשה	DO	795b	1 a
	שאל	ASK	982a	2 a
	תועבה	ABOMINATION	1072d	1 b
13 16	חרב	SWORD	352d	1 f
	חרב	SWORD	352d	1 f
	חרם	BAN	356a	1 d
	חרם	DEVOTED THING	*356b	1 a
	נכה	SMITE	646a	2 c
13 17	בנה	BUILD	125a	1 b
	חרם	DEVOTED THING	356b	1 a
	כליל	WHOLE	483b	2 b
	עוד	STILL	729b	1 b
	קבץ	GATHER	867c	1
	רחוב	PLAZA	932b	
	שלל	SPOIL	1022a	2
	תל	MOUND	1068b	1
13 18	דבק	CLING	179d	1 a
	חרון	BURNING OF ANGER	354c	
	נתן	GIVE	678c	1 b
	רחם	LOVE	933c	1
	רחמים	COMPASSION	933c	
	שוב	TURN BACK	997d	6 f
13 19	ישר	STRAIGHT	449a	2 a
	כי	BECAUSE	473c	3 a
	קול	VOICE	877b	3 b

Ch v.	Heb	Eng	Page	Sec
14 1	בן	SON	120b	1 c
	גדד	CUT	151a	1
	ל	TO	514d	5 g
	עין	EYE	745a	5
	קרח	MAKE BALD	*901a	
	קרחה	BALD SPOT	901b	
14 2	אדמה	EARTH	10a	6
	בחר	CHOOSE	103d	1 a
	מן	OUT OF	579b	2 ac
	סגלה	PROPERTY	688c	1
	עם	PEOPLE	767a	5 g
14 3	את	MARK OF THE AC-CUSATIVE	85b	3 a
	תועבה	ABOMINATION	1072d	1 b
14 4	כשב	LAMB	461b	
	עז	SHE-GOAT	777c	2
	שה	A SHEEP	962a	1
	שור	A HEAD OF CATTLE	1004b	
14 5	איל	HART	19b	
	אקו	WILD GOAT	70a	
	דישן	PYGARG	190d	
	זמר	MOUNTAIN SHEEP	275a	
	יחמור	ROEBUCK	331c	
	צבי	GAZELLE	840b	
	תאו	ANTELOPE	1060d	
14 6	גרה	CUD	176a	
	עלה	GO UP	749c	3
	פרסה	HOOF	828b	1
	פרס	BREAK IN TWO	828b	1
	שסע	DIVIDE	1042d	
	שסע	CLEFT	1043a	
14 7	ארנבת	HARE	58a	
	גרה	CUD	176a	
	זה	THIS	*260c	1 a
	טמא	UNCLEAN	379d	2 b
	עלה	GO UP	749c	3
	פרס	BREAK IN TWO	828b	1
	שסע	DIVIDE	1042d	
	שפן	ROCK-BADGER	1050d	
14 8	גרה	STIR UP STRIFE	173b	
	גרה	CUD	176a	
	גרר	DRAG	176a	
	חזיר	SWINE	306b	1
	טמא	UNCLEAN	379d	2 b
	נבלה	CARCASS	615d	2
	נגע	TOUCH	619a	1 a
	פרס	BREAK IN TWO	828b	1
14 9	זה	THIS	*260c	1 a
	סנפיר	FIN	703b	
	קשקשת	SCALE OF FISH	903d	
14 10	טמא	UNCLEAN	379d	2 b
	סנפיר	FIN	703b	
	קשקשת	SCALE OF FISH	903d	
14 11	טהור	CLEAN	373a	1
	צפור	BIRD	862a	1
14 12	נשר	EAGLE	676d	
	עזניה	BIRD OF PREY	740a	
	פרס	BEARDED VUL-TURE	828b	
14 13	איה	HAWK	17b	
	דאה	KITE	178d	
	דיה	KITE	178d	
	מין	SPLIT	*568b	
	מין	KIND	568b	
14 14	מין	KIND	568b	
	ערב	RAVEN	788b	
14 15	בת	DAUGHTER	123d	6
	תחמס	MALE OSTRICH	329d	
	יענה	OSTRICH	419a	
	מין	KIND	568b	
	נץ	HAWK	665c	
	שחף	SEA-MEW	1006d	
14 16	כוס	OWL	468a	
	תנשמת	PELICAN	675d	1
	ינשוף	OWL	676b	
14 17	קאת	PELICAN	866b	
	רחמה	CARRION-VUL-TURE	934b	
	רחם	CARRION-VUL-TURE	934b	
	שלך	CORMORANT	1021c	
14 18	אנפה	HERON	60b	
	דוכיפת	HOOPOE	189a	
	חסידה	STORK	339d	
	מין	KIND	568b	
	עטלף	BAT	742b	
14 19	טמא	UNCLEAN	379d	2 b
	עוף	FLY	733d	2
	שרץ	SWARMING THINGS	1056d	
14 20	טהור	CLEAN	373a	1
	עוף	FLY	733d	2
14 21	אם	MOTHER	52a	3
	בשל	BOIL	143a	1
	גדי	KID	152a	
	גר	SOJOURNER	158b	2
	חלב	MILK	316c	A 2
	מכר	SELL	569b	
	נבלה	CARCASS	615d	2
	נכרי	FOREIGN	648d	1 b
14 22	תבואה	PRODUCT	100a	1
	זרע	SOWING	282b	2 b
	יצא	GO OUT	423a	1 h
	עשר	TAKE THE TENTH OF	797c	
	שנה	YEAR	1040b	

Ch v.	Heb	Eng	Page	Sec
14 23	אכל	EAT	37b	1
	בחר	CHOOSE	104a	2 a
	בכור	FIRST-BORN	114b	2 c
	דגן	CORN	186c	
	דגן	CORN	186c	
	יום	DAY	400c	7 f
	ירא	FEAR	431c	3 b
	תירוש	NEW WINE	440d	
	ל	TO	517d	7 bc
	למד	LEARN	540d	
	מעשר	TENTH PART	798b	2
	פנה	FACE	817b	24 a h
	יצהר	FRESH OIL	844a	
	מקום	STANDING PLACE	880b	4
	שכן	SETTLE DOWN	1015b	1
14 24	בחר	CHOOSE	104a	2 a
	ברך	BLESS	139a	2 a
	יכל	BE ABLE	407c	1 b
	יכל	BE ABLE	407d	1 d
	כי	IF	473b	2 b
	כי	BECAUSE	473c	3 a
	מן	THAN	582d	6 d
	רבה	BECOME MANY	915b	1 a1
	רחק	BE DISTANT	934d	
14 25	בחר	CHOOSE	104a	1 a
	נתן	GIVE	679b	1 o
	צור	CONFINE	848d	1
	מקום	STANDING PLACE	880b	4
14 26	אוה	DESIRE	16a	
	אכל	EAT	37b	1 e
	ה	THE	207c	1
	יין	WINE	406c	B
	נפש	SOUL	660d	6 a
	נתן	GIVE	679b	1 n
	פנה	FACE	817b	24 a h
	שמח	REJOICE	970b	2 a
	שכר	INTOXICATING DRINK	1016c	
14 27	חלק	PORTION	324a	2 a
	לוי	LEVITE	532d	2
	עזב	LEAVE	737c	2 c
14 28	תבואה	PRODUCT	100a	1
	יצא	BRING OUT	425a	4 d
	מן	FROM	581c	4 b
	נוח	REST	628d	B 1
	מעשר	TENTH PART	798b	2
14 29	אלמנה	WIDOW	48b	
	ברך	BLESS	139a	2 a
	גר	SOJOURNER	158b	2
	חלק	PORTION	324a	2 a
	יתום	ORPHAN	450c	
	לוי	LEVITE	532d	2
15 1	מן	FROM	581c	4 b
	שמטה	A LETTING DROP	1030d	
15 2	אח	BROTHER	26b	4
	בעל	OWNER	127b	1 1
	דבר	WORD	183d	4 7
	יד	HAND	389c	1 d
	נגש	EXACT	620c	2
	נשה	LEND	674c	
	משה	LOAN	674c	
	קרא	CALL	845b	3 a
	שמט	LET DROP	1030c	
	שמטה	A LETTING DROP	1030d	
15 3	את	WITH	86b	3 a
	נגש	EXACT	620c	2
	נכרי	FOREIGN	648d	1 b
	שמט	LET DROP	1030c	
15 4	אביון	NEEDY	2d	
	אפס	NON-EXISTENCE	67b	2 cb
	ב	IN	88b	1 2
	ברך	BLESS	139a	2 a
	נחלה	PROPERTY	635b	1 a
15 5	מצוה	COMMANDMENT	846b	2 a
	רק	ONLY	956d	2 f
15 6	ברך	BLESS	139a	2 a
	גוי	NATION	156d	1 c
	דבר	SPEAK	181b	3 c
	משל	RULE	605d	1
	עבט	TAKE A PLEDGE	716b	
	עבט	TAKE A PLEDGE	716c	
15 7	אביון	NEEDY	2d	
	אביון	NEEDY	2d	
	אמץ	BE STRONG	55b	3
	ב	IN	88b	1 2
	כי	IF	473b	2 b
	לבב	HEART	524a	2 6d
	מן	FROM	581a	3 bd
	די	SUFFICIENCY	191c	1
15 8	חסר	LACK	*341b	1 a
	חסר	LACK	341d	2
	מחסור	NEED	341d	1
	פתח	OPEN	835b	
15 9	אביון	NEEDY	2d	
	אביון	NEEDY	2d	
	בליעל	WORTHLESSNESS	116b	1
	חטא	SIN	308a	2
	לבב	HEART	523d	2 2
	עין	EYE	744c	2 a
	עם	WITH	768c	4 a
	קרא	CALL	895b	2
	קרב	COME NEAR	897c	2
	רעע	BE EVIL	949c	3
	שבע	SEVEN	988a	1 d
	שמטה	A LETTING DROP	1030d	
	שנה	YEAR	1040b	

Ch v.	Heb	Eng	Page	Sec
15 10	ברך	BLESS	139a	2 a
	יד	HAND	389b	1 c
	לבב	HEART	524b	29 b
	מעשה	DEED	795d	1 b3
	רעע	BE EVIL	949c	2
	משלח	OUTSTRETCHING	1020a	1
15 11	אביון	NEEDY	2d	
	אביון	NEEDY	2d	
	חדל	CEASE	293a	1
	כן	SO	*487b	3 f
	עני	POOR	776d	1
	פתח	OPEN	835b	
15 12	אח	BROTHER	26b	2
	אמה	MAID	51a	1
	חפשי	FREE	344d	1
	כי	IF	473b	2 b
	מכר	SELL	569c	
	עבד	WORK	713a	2
	עברי	HEBREW	720b	1 b
	מעם	FROM WITH	*769a	C
15 13	חפשי	FREE	344d	1
	מעם	FROM WITH	*769a	C
	ריקם	EMPTILY	938b	1
	שלח	SEND	1019a	1 c
15 14	ברך	BLESS	139a	2 a
	גרן	THRESHING-FLOOR	175b	
	יקב	WINE-VAT	428c	
	ענק	SERVE AS NECK-LACE	778d	
	צאן	SMALL CATTLE	838b	1 a4
	אשר	ADDENDA ET COR-RIGENDA	1121a	
15 15	דבר	WORD	182d	1 2a
	זכר	REMEMBER	269d	1 1 d
	כן	SO	*487b	3 f
	עבד	SLAVE	713d	1
	פדה	RANSOM	804a	3 a
	צוה	CHARGE	845d	2 a
15 16	אהב	LOVE	12d	1
	טוב	PLEASING	373b	4
	כי	IF	473b	2 b
	כי	WHEN	473d	2 a
	עם	WITH	768b	3 a
	מעם	FROM WITH	769a	C
15 17	אזן	EAR	23d	1
	אמה	MAID	51a	1
	אף	ALSO	65a	1
	דלת	DOOR	195a	1
	לקח	TAKE	542d	1
	נתן	PUT	680b	2 a
	עבד	SLAVE	714c	7
	עולם	LONG DURATION	762a	2 a
	מרצע	AWL	954b	
15 18	ברך	BLESS	139a	2 a
	חפשי	FREE	344d	1
	עבד	WORK	713a	2
	מעם	FROM WITH	*769a	C
	קשה	BE SEVERE	904b	2
	שכר	HIRE	969a	1
	שכיר	HIRED	969b	1
	משנה	DOUBLE	1041c	1
15 19	בכור	FIRST-BORN	114b	2 a
	בכור	FIRST-BORN	114b	2 b
	גזז	SHEAR	159c	
	ילד	BE BORN	408d	
	כל	ALL	481c	1 b
	עבד	WORK	713a	1
	קדש	BE SET APART	873b	1 b
	שור	A HEAD OF CATTLE	1004b	
15 20	ב	IN	90b	3 3b
	בחר	CHOOSE	104a	2 a
	פנה	FACE	817b	24 a h
	מקום	STANDING PLACE	880b	4
15 21	זבח	SLAUGHTER FOR SACRIFICE	257a	13
	מום	BLEMISH	548d	1 b
	עור	BLIND	734c	1 b
	פסח	LAME	820c	
	רע	EVIL	948b	4
15 22	איל	HART	19b	
	טמא	UNCLEAN	379d	2 a
	יחדו	TOGETHER	*403c	C
	צבי	GAZELLE	840b	
15 23	דם	BLOOD	196c	1
	שפך	POUR OUT	1049c	1 a
16 1	אביב	ABIB	1b	2
	יצא	CAUSE TO GO	424c	1 a
	לוי	LEVITE	532d	1
	לילה	NIGHT	539a	1
	עשה	DO	795a	2 6
	פסח	PASSOVER	820b	3
	שמר	KEEP	1036d	3
16 2	בחר	CHOOSE	104a	2 a
	זבח	SLAUGHTER FOR SACRIFICE	256d	1 1 a
	זבח	SLAUGHTER FOR SACRIFICE	257a	13
	פסח	PASSOVER	820b	1
	פסח	PASSOVER	820b	1
	מקום	STANDING PLACE	880b	4
	שכן	SETTLE DOWN	1015b	1
16 3	זכר	REMEMBER	270a	1 g
	חיים	LIFE	313b	1
	חמץ	THAT WHICH IS LEAVENED	329d	
	חפזון	TREPIDATION	342a	

DEUTERONOMY

Ch v.	Heb	Eng	Page	Sec
	יום	DAY	400a	7 d1 a
	יצא	GO OUT	422d	1 a
	מצה	UNLEAVENED BREAD	695b	
	על	UPON	755c	2 4c
	על	UPON	755c	2 4c
	עני	AFFLICTION	777a	
16 4	בקר	MORNING	133d	1 a
	בקר	MORNING	134a	1 f
	גבול	BORDER	147d	1 a
	ל	TO	*514a	5 e
	ל	TO	517a	6 c
	לון	LODGE	533d	1
	מן	FROM	580d	3 bc
	ראה	TO SEE	908c	2 a
	ראשון	FIRST	911d	2 a
	שאר	LEAVEN	959a	
16 5	זבח	SLAUGHTER FOR SACRIFICE	256d	11 a
	יכל	BE ABLE	407d	1 d
	פסח	PASSOVER	820b	1
16 6	אל	TO	40d	
	בוא	COME	98a	1 i
	בחר	CHOOSE	104a	2 a
	זבח	SLAUGHTER FOR SACRIFICE	256d	11 a
	מועד	APPOINTED TIME	417c	1 a
	יצא	GO OUT	422d	1 a
	כיאם	BUT	475a	2 b
	ערב	SUNSET	787d	1 a
	פסח	PASSOVER	820b	3
	פסח	PASSOVER	820b	1
	מקום	STANDING PLACE	880b	4
	שכן	SETTLE DOWN	1015b	1
16 7	בחר	CHOOSE	104a	1 a
	בשל	BOIL	143b	2
	הלך	WALK	231b	1 d3 gd
16 8	מצה	UNLEAVENED BREAD	695b	
16 9	עצרה	ASSEMBLY	783d	1
	חלל	POLLUTE	320b	2
	חלל	POLLUTE	320b	2
	חרמש	SICKLE	357a	
	ל	TO	515d	5 ia
	ספר	COUNT	707d	1
	קמה	STANDING GRAIN	879b	
	שבוע	PERIOD OF SEVEN	988d	1
16 10	ברך	BLESS	139a	2 a
	חג	FESTIVAL-GATHERING	291a	1 b2
	חג	FESTIVAL-GATHERING	291b	1 b
	מסת	SUFFICIENCY	588b	
	נדבה	FREEWILL-OFFERING	621d	2 c
	נדבה	FREEWILL-OFFERING	621d	2 c
	עשה	DO	795d	2 6
	שבוע	PERIOD OF SEVEN	989a	1
16 11	אלמנה	WIDOW	48b	
	אמה	MAID	51a	1
	בחר	CHOOSE	104a	2 a
	בן	SON	120a	1
	גר	SOJOURNER	158b	2
	חדש	NEW MOON	294d	2 b1
	יתום	ORPHAN	450c	
	שמח	REJOICE	970b	2 a
	שכן	SETTLE DOWN	1015b	1
16 12	זכר	REMEMBER	269d	11 d
	חק	SOMETHING PRESCRIBED	349d	7 g
	עבד	SLAVE	713d	1
	עין	EYE	744c	1 p
	עשה	DO	793d	1 la 1
16 13	אסף	GATHER	62b	1c
	גרן	THRESHING-FLOOR	175b	
	חג	FESTIVAL-GATHERING	291a	1 b2
	חג	FESTIVAL-GATHERING	291b	1 b
	יקב	WINE-VAT	428c	
	ל	TO	515d	5 ia
	סכה	THICKET	697d	3
	עשה	DO	795a	2 6
16 14	אלמנה	WIDOW	48b	
	אמה	MAID	51a	1
	בן	SON	120a	1
	גר	SOJOURNER	158b	2
	חג	FESTIVAL-GATHERING	291a	1 b2
	יתום	ORPHAN	450c	
	לוי	LEVITE	532d	2
16 15	אך	ONLY	36d	2 bb
	תבואה	PRODUCT	100a	1
	בחר	CHOOSE	104a	1 a
	ברך	BLESS	139a	2 a
	כי	BECAUSE	473c	3 a
	שמח	JOYFUL	970c	1 a
16 16	זכור	MALE	271d	
	חג	FESTIVAL-GATHERING	291a	1 b2
	חג	FESTIVAL-GATHERING	291a	1 b2
	מצה	UNLEAVENED BREAD	695b	
	סכה	THICKET	697d	3
	פנה	FACE	816a	2 2a
	ראה	TO SEE	908b	1 b
	ריקם	EMPTILY	938b	1
16 17	שבוע	PERIOD OF SEVEN	989a	1
	ברכה	BLESSING	139d	1 b
	יד	HAND	390b	2
	מתנה	GIFT	682c	
16 18	ל	TO	515d	5 ia
	צדק	RIGHTEOUSNESS	841c	2 a
	שטר	OFFICIAL	1009c	
	שפט	JUDGE	1047c	2 b
	שפט	JUDGE	1047d	2 b
	משפט	JUDGMENT	1048b	1 a
16 19	חכם	WISE	314d	2
	נטה	BEND	641a	3 g
	נכר	REGARD	648a	1
	סלף	TWIST	701b	1
	עור	MAKE BLIND	734c	
	עין	EYE	744d	3 d
	צדיק	JUST	843a	2
	שחד	BRIBE	1005a	
	שחד	BRIBE	1005a	
	משפט	JUDGMENT	1049a	5
16 20	רדף	PURSUE	923a	2
16 21	אצל	BESIDE	69b	A
	אשרה	ASHERA	81c	B
	נטע	PLANT	642c	1
	על	UPON	756b	2 6c
	עץ	TREE	782a	2 c
16 22	מצבה	PILLAR	663b	1 c
	קום	STAND	878d	2 a
17 1	זבח	SLAUGHTER FOR SACRIFICE	256d	11 ba
	זבח	SLAUGHTER FOR SACRIFICE	257a	13
	מום	BLEMISH	548d	1 b
	רע	EVIL	948b	4
	שה	A SHEEP	962a	1
	שור	A HEAD OF CATTLE	1004b	
	תועבה	ABOMINATION	1072d	1 b
17 2	איש	MAN	35d	
	אשה	WOMAN	61a	1
	ברית	COVENANT	137b	3 3
	כי	IF	473b	2 b
	מצא	FIND	594a	2 c
	עבר	PASS OVER	717b	1 i
	רע	EVIL	948c	0 b
17 3	הלך	WALK	233d	15 b
	הלך	WALK	235a	23 d 2
	ירח	MOON	437a	
	עבד	WORK	713b	4 b
	צבא	HOST	839a	1 c
17 4	אמת	FIRMNESS	54b	4
	דבר	WORD	182c	1 lg
	דרש	SEEK	205c	4 b
	הנה	IF	244c	D
	יטב	DO WELL	406a	3
	כון	BE FIRM	465d	1 d
	נגד	BE CONSPICUOUS	617a	
	תועבה	ABOMINATION	1072d	1 b
17 5	אבן	STONE	6b	1
	אשה	WOMAN	61a	1
	יצא	BRING OUT	424d	1 g
	מות	DIE	559d	2 a
	מות	DIE	559d	2 a
	סקל	STONE	709c	
	רע	EVIL	948c	0 d
17 6	מות	DIE	559d	2 a
	מות	DIE	560c	2
	סוס	HORSE	692c	2
	עד	WITNESS	729d	2 c
	על	UPON	754a	2 lf
	פה	MOUTH	805d	6 d1 b
17 7	אחרון	BEHIND	31a	B b
	בער	CONSUME	129b	3
	יד	HAND	389a	1 a
	מות	DIE	560b	1 b
17 8	ראשון	FIRST	911d	3 a1
	בחר	CHOOSE	104a	1 a
	בין	INTERVAL	107c	1 b
	דין	JUDGMENT	192c	2
	דם	BLOOD	197b	2 j
	מן	THAN	582d	6 d
	נגע	STROKE	619c	1
	עלה	GO UP	748b	1 c
	פלא	BE SURPASSING	810c	2
	מקום	STANDING PLACE	880b	4
	ריב	STRIFE	937a	3
	משפט	JUDGMENT	1048b	1 a
17 9	דבר	WORD	182c	1 lh
	דרש	SEEK	205c	4 b
	יום	DAY	400d	7 g
	כהן	PRIEST	463d	5
	לוי	LEVITE	532d	3 lb
	שפט	JUDGE	1047d	2 b
	משפט	JUDGMENT	1048b	1 a
17 10	בחר	CHOOSE	104a	2 a
	דבר	WORD	182c	1 lh
	ירה	DIRECT	435b	5 b
	פה	MOUTH	805d	6 d2
17 11	דבר	WORD	182c	1 lh
	ימין	RIGHT HAND	412a	2
	ירה	DIRECT	435b	5 b
	תורה	LAW	436a	2 a
	סור	TURN ASIDE	693c	1
	על	UPON	754a	2 lf
	פה	MOUTH	805d	6 d2
	משפט	JUDGMENT	1048c	1 e
17 12	בלת	NOT	116d	4 a
	בער	CONSUME	129b	3
	ו	AND	254d	5 a
	זדון	INSOLENCE	268a	2
	כהן	PRIEST	463d	5
	שפט	JUDGE	1047d	2 b
	שרת	SERVE	1058a	2 a
17 13	ו	AND	252b	1 b
	זיד	BOIL UP	267d	2
	ירא	FEAR	431b	1 a
17 14	ארץ	EARTH	76b	2 e
	ירש	TAKE POSSESSION	439b	1 a
	מלך	KING	573a	1
	מלך	KING	573c	5 c
	סביב	ROUND ABOUT	687b	2 bb
	שום	TO PLACE	963d	3 d
17 15	אשר	PARTICLE OF RELATION	82b	2 b
	בחר	CHOOSE	103d	1 a
	הוא	HE, SHE, IT	216b	3 c
	יכל	BE ABLE	407d	1 d
	לא	NOT	519b	1 bb
	מלך	KING	573c	5 c
	נכרי	FOREIGN	648d	1 a
	קרב	INWARD PART	899b	1 f3
	שום	TO PLACE	963d	3 d
17 16	יסף	DO AGAIN	415c	2
	סוס	HORSE	692c	2
	רבה	BECOME MANY	915c	1 b
17 17	זהב	GOLD	262d	2
	זהב	GOLD	263c	1
	לב	HEART	523c	2 2
	סור	TURN ASIDE	693c	1
17 18	תורה	LAW	436b	2 b2
	ישב	SIT	442b	1 a
	כהן	PRIEST	463d	5
	כסא	THRONE	491b	3 a
	כתב	WRITE	507c	1 b1
	כתב	WRITE	507d	1 c
	לוי	LEVITE	532d	3 lb
	ממלכה	DOMINION	575b	2
	פנה	FACE	818a	2 5a b
	משנה	COPY	1041c	2
17 19	דבר	WORD	183a	2 2
	יהוה	YAHWEH	218d	2 le
	חיים	LIFE	313b	1
	חק	SOMETHING PRESCRIBED	349d	7 g
	ירא	FEAR	431b	2 b2
	תורה	LAW	436b	2 b2
	למד	LEARN	540d	
	עם	WITH	768b	3 b
	קרא	CALL	895c	4 b
17 20	ארך	BE LONG	73d	1 a
	בלת	NOT	116d	4 a
	ימין	RIGHT HAND	412a	2
	לב	HEART	524a	2 6c
	ממלכה	KINGDOM	575b	1
	על	UPON	752d	2 1
	מצוה	COMMANDMENT	846b	2 a
	קרב	INWARD PART	899b	1 f3
	רום	BE HIGH	926d	2 b
18 1	אשה	OFFERING MADE BY FIRE	78a	
	חלק	PORTION	324a	2 a
	כהן	PRIEST	463d	5
	לוי	LEVI	532c	1
	לוי	LEVITE	532d	3 lb
	עם	WITH	767c	1 b
18 2	דבר	SPEAK	181b	3 c
	נחלה	PROPERTY	635b	1 d
	קרב	INWARD PART	899b	1 f3
18 3	אם	IF	50a	1 b1
	את	WITH	86a	1 da
	את	WITH	86d	4 b
	זבח	SACRIFICE	257c	11
	זרוע	ARM	284b	4
	כהן	PRIEST	463d	5
	כהן	PRIEST	463d	5
	לחי	JAW	534d	1
	קבה	BELLY	867a	1
	שה	A SHEEP	962a	1
	שור	A HEAD OF CATTLE	1004b	
	משפט	JUDGMENT	1049a	5
18 4	גז	SHEARING	159c	
	דגן	CORN	186c	
	דגן	CORN	186c	
	תירש	NEW WINE	440d	
	יצהר	FRESH OIL	844a	
	ראשית	BEGINNING	912b	1 b
	ראשית	BEGINNING	912b	1 b
18 5	בחר	CHOOSE	103d	1 a
	יום	DAY	400c	7 f
	שרת	SERVE	1058b	2 a
18 6	אוה	DESIRE	16b	
	גור	SOJOURN	157d	1
	כי	IF	473b	2 b
	לוי	LEVITE	532d	1
	נפש	SOUL	660d	6 a
	מקום	STANDING PLACE	880b	4
	ישראל	ISRAEL	975c	2 a1
	שער	GATE	*1045a	2 c
18 7	יהוה	YAHWEH	218d	2 le

Ch	v.	Heb	Eng	Page	Sec
		לוי	LEVITE	533a	3 1b
18	8	שרת	SERVE	1058b	2 a
		בד	SEPARATION	94c	1 d
		חלק	PORTION	324a	1 b
		ממכר	WARE	569d	
		על	UPON	754a	2 1f
18	9	ארץ	EARTH	76b	2 e
		גוי	NATION	156d	1 c
		כי	WHEN	473b	2 a
		למד	LEARN	540d	
		תועבה	ABOMINATION	1072d	1 b
18	10	ב	IN	88b	1 2
		ו	AND	252a	1
		כשף	PRACTICE SORCERY	506c	
		מצא	FIND	594a	2 c
		נחש	PRACTISE DIVINATION	638c	1
		עבר	PASS OVER	718d	1 d
		ענן	PRACTISE SOOTHSAYING	778b	
		קסם	DIVINATION	890c	2
		קסם	PRACTICE OF DIVINATION	890d	3
18	11	אוב	NECROMANCER	15b	2
		אל	TO	39c	1
		דרש	SEEK	205b	2 b
		חבר	UNITE	288a	2
		חבר	COMPANY	288c	3 a
		ידעני	FAMILIAR SPIRIT	396b	
		עשה	DO	795a	2 8
		שאל	ASK	982a	2 b
18	12	אלה	THESE	41c	A
		אלה	THESE	41c	A
		ירש	CAUSE TO POSSESS	440a	2 a
		תועבה	ABOMINATION	1072d	1 b
		תועבה	ABOMINATION	1072d	1 b
18	13	עם	WITH	767d	1
		תמים	SOUND	1071a	4
18	14	ירש	TAKE POSSESSION	439c	1 b
		כי	BECAUSE	474a	3 c
		כן	SO	486b	1 cd
		נתן	GIVE	679a	1 g
		ענן	PRACTISE SOOTHSAYING	778b	
		קסם	PRACTICE OF DIVINATION	890d	1
18	15	משה	MOSES	602c	
		נביא	PROPHET	611c	1
		קום	STAND	879a	3
18	16	יהוה	YAHWEH	218d	2 1f
		חרב	HOREB	352a	
		יסף	DO AGAIN	415c	2 a
		מות	DIE	560a	2 b
		קהל	ASSEMBLY	874b	1 d
		שאל	ASK	982b	2 b
18	17	דבר	SPEAK	180d	1
		יטב	DO WELL	405d	3
18	18	משה	MOSES	602c	
		נביא	PROPHET	611c	1
		נתן	PUT	680c	2 b
		קום	STAND	879a	3
		קרב	INWARD PART	899b	1 f3
18	19	דבר	SPEAK	181c	4 a
		דבר	WORD	183b	3 2
		דרש	SEEK	205c	5
		היה	COME TO PASS	225a	1 2b ag
		יד	HAND	391b	5 g3
		מעם	FROM WITH	769a	A
		שמע	HEAR	1034a	1 k
18	20	דבר	SPEAK	181c	4 a
		זיד	BOIL UP	267d	2
		מות	DIE	559d	2 a
		נביא	PROPHET	612a	2
		שם	NAME	1028d	4
18	21	איכה	IN WHAT MANNER	32d	1
		כי	IF	473b	2 a
		כי	WHEN	473b	2 a
		לבב	HEART	524a	2 7
18	22	אשר	THAT	83d	8 d
		גור	DREAD	159a	1
		דבר	SPEAK	181c	4 a
		זדון	INSOLENCE	268a	2
		מן	OUT OF	580a	2 ec
		נביא	PROPHET	612a	2
19	1	ירש	TAKE POSSESSION	439c	1 b
		כרת	CUT OFF	504c	2 c
19	2	בדל	BE DIVIDED	95c	2
		ל	TO	515d	5 ia
19	3	גבול	BOUNDARY	148a	2 a
		כון	ESTABLISH	466b	2 a
		ל	TO	515d	5 ia
		נום	FLEE	630d	1
		רצח	MURDER	953d	
		שלש	DO A THIRD TIME	1026a	
19	4	בלי	WEARING OUT	115d	A
		דבר	WORD	183c	4 3
		דעת	KNOWLEDGE	395c	1 a
		ל	TO	513a	5 ad
		לא	NOT	519b	1 bc
		נום	FLEE	630d	1
		נכה	SMITE	646a	2 c
		רצח	MURDER	953d	
		שנא	HATE	971d	3
		שלשם	THREE DAYS AGO	1026b	
		תמול	YESTERDAY	1070a	2 c
19	5	ברזל	IRON	137c	2
		גרזן	AXE	173d	
		חטב	CUT OR GATHER WOOD	310a	
		יער	WOOD	420c	A
		כרת	CUT OFF	503b	2
		מצא	FIND	593b	3 b
		נדח	IMPEL	623a	1
		נום	FLEE	630d	1
		נשל	SLIP	675c	1
		עד	WITNESS	729d	2 c
		עץ	TREE	781c	1 a
		עץ	TREE	781d	2 b
		עץ	TREE	782a	2 d
19	6	גאל	ACT AS KINSMAN	145c	1 e
		דם	BLOOD	196d	2 e
		חמם	BE OR BECOME WARM	328d	2
		כי	BECAUSE	473c	3 a
		ל	TO	513a	5 ad
		לא	NOT	519b	1 bc
		לבב	HEART	524b	2 9b
		מות	DEATH	560d	1
		נכה	SMITE	645d	2 a
		נכה	SMITE	646a	2 c
		נפש	SOUL	659d	3 c
		נשג	OVERTAKE	673c	1 a
		רבה	BECOME MANY	915b	1 a1
		רדף	PURSUE	922c	1 a
		רצח	MURDER	953d	
		שנא	HATE	971d	3
		שלשם	THREE DAYS AGO	1026b	
		משפט	JUDGMENT	1048c	1 e
		תמול	YESTERDAY	1070a	
19	7	בדל	BE DIVIDED	95c	2
		כן	SO	*487b	3 f
19	8	אם	IF	49c	1 a1 a
		גבול	BOUNDARY	148a	2 a
		דבר	SPEAK	181d	6
		רחב	BE LARGE	931c	2
19	9	דרך	WAY	204a	6 ec
		יום	DAY	400c	7 f
		יסף	ADD	414d	
		כי	BECAUSE	473c	3 a
		ל	TO	515d	5 ia
		ל	TO	517b	7 ba
19	10	דם	BLOOD	196c	2 b
		דם	BLOOD	196d	2 d
		דם	BLOOD	197a	2 i
		היה	BE	227a	3 3
		לא	NOT	518c	1 aa
		נחלה	PROPERTY	635b	1 a
		נקי	CLEAN	667c	1
		על	UPON	756c	2 7ab
		שפך	POUR OUT	1049d	
19	11	אל	THESE	41b	
		ארב	LIE IN WAIT	70b	
		נום	FLEE	630d	1
		נכה	SMITE	645d	2 a
		נפש	SOUL	659d	3 c
		על	UPON	757d	2 7d
		קום	STAND	878a	2 a
19	12	גאל	ACT AS KINSMAN	145c	1 e
		דם	BLOOD	196d	2 e
		זקן	OLD	279a	2 b
		לקח	TAKE	542d	3 a
		מות	DIE	559d	2 a
19	13	בער	CONSUME	129b	2
		דם	BLOOD	196d	2 d
		חום	PITY	299b	A
		טוב	PLEASING	373b	4
		ל	TO	511a	1 e
		נקי	CLEAN	667c	1
		פה	MOUTH	805d	6 d1 b
19	14	גבול	BOUNDARY	148a	1 c
		גבל	BOUND	148b	
		נחל	TAKE AS A POSSESSION	635c	1 b
		סוג	DISPLACE	691a	1
		ראשון	FIRST	911c	1 a
		חטא	MISS A GOAL OR WAY	307b	2 b
		חטא	SIN	308a	1 b
		חטאת	SIN	308d	1 b
		ל	TO	514c	5 fc
		עון	INIQUITY	731a	1 a
		על	UPON	754a	2 1fa
		קום	STAND	877d	1 f
		קום	STAND	878b	7 f
19	16	חמס	VIOLENCE	329c	
		סרה	A TURNING ASIDE	694c	1
		עד	WITNESS	729d	2 c
		ענה	ANSWER	773a	3 a
		קום	STAND	877d	1 f
19	17	יום	DAY	400d	7 g
		כהן	PRIEST	463d	5
		עמד	STAND	763d	1
		ריב	STRIFE	937a	3
		שפט	JUDGE	1047d	2 b
19	18	דרש	SEEK	205c	4 b
		הנה	IF	244c	D
		יטב	DO WELL	406a	3
		עד	WITNESS	729d	2 c
		ענה	ANSWER	773a	3 a
		שפט	JUDGE	1047d	2 b
		שקר	DECEPTION	1055c	3
		שקר	DECEPTION	1055c	3
19	19	בער	CONSUME	129b	3
		זמם	CONSIDER	273b	2 b
19	20	דבר	WORD	*183d	4 7
		יסף	DO AGAIN	415c	2
		ירא	FEAR	431b	1 a
		רע	EVIL	948c	0 d
19	21	ב	IN	90b	3 3b
		חום	PITY	299b	A
		נפש	SOUL	659d	3 c
		עין	EYE	745a	1 a
		שן	TOOTH	1042a	1 a
20	1	ירא	FEAR	431b	1 c
		עלה	GO UP	749b	1 a
		רב	GREAT	913c	2 d
20	2	כ	LIKE	454a	3 b
		כהן	PRIEST	463c	5
		נגש	DRAW NEAR	621a	
		קרב	COME NEAR	897c	1 b
20	3	חפז	BE IN TREPIDATION	342a	2
		ירא	FEAR	431a	1 a
		לבב	HEART	524b	2 9b
		ערץ	CAUSE TO TREMBLE	792a	2
		קרב	APPROACHING	898b	1
		רכך	BE TENDER	940a	1 a
20	4	ישע	DELIVER	446c	1 b
		לחם	ENGAGE IN BATTLE	535c	
20	5	לחם	ENGAGE IN BATTLE	535d	
		אחר	ANOTHER	29c	
		בית	HOUSE	108d	1 a1
		בנה	BUILD	124b	1 ab
		הלך	WALK	233d	1 5b
		חדש	NEW	294a	A
		חנך	TRAIN UP	335b	2
		מות	DIE	559c	1 a1
		מי	WHO	567b	G
		שטר	OFFICIAL	1009c	
20	6	אחר	ANOTHER	29c	
		הלך	WALK	233d	1 5b
		חלל	POLLUTE	320c	4
		כרם	VINEYARD	501d	
		מות	DIE	559c	1 a1
		מי	WHO	567b	G
		נטע	PLANT	642c	1
20	7	אחר	ANOTHER	29c	
		אשה	WOMAN	61b	2
		ארש	BETROTH	77a	
		הלך	WALK	233d	1 5b
		מות	DIE	559c	1 a1
		מי	WHO	567b	G
20	8	יסף	ADD	414d	
		ירא	FEAR	431a	1 a
		לבב	HEART	524b	2 9b
		לבב	HEART	524b	2 9b
		רך	TENDER	940a	2
		שטר	OFFICIAL	1009c	
20	9	כ	LIKE	454a	3 b
		פקד	ATTEND TO	823c	B 1
		צבא	ARMY	839a	1 a
		ראש	HEAD	911a	3 d
		שר	CHIEFTAIN	978b	3 a
		שטר	OFFICIAL	1009c	
20	10	לחם	ENGAGE IN BATTLE	535c	
		על	UPON	757d	2 7d
		קרא	CALL	895c	3 a
		קרב	COME NEAR	897c	1 b
		שלום	PEACE	1023b	6
20	11	היה	COME TO PASS	225b	1 2b ae
		היה	COME TO PASS	*225b	1 2b ae
		מס	LABOUR-GANG	587a	2 b
		מצא	FIND	593d	1 c
		פתח	OPEN	835a	
20	12	מלחמה	WAR	536a	
		מלחמה	WAR	536c	
		על	UPON	757d	2 7d
		עשה	DO	794c	2 1e
		צור	CONFINE	848d	2
		שלם	BE IN COVENANT OF PEACE	1023d	1
20	13	זכור	MALE	271d	
		חרב	SWORD	352d	1 f
		נכה	SMITE	646a	2 c
20	14	בזז	SPOIL	102d	
		זכור	MALE	*271d	
		ל	TO	515d	5 ia
		נתן	GIVE	679a	1 k
		רק	ONLY	956b	2 a
		שלל	SPOIL	1022a	2
		שלל	SPOIL	1022a	2
20	15	אשר	PARTICLE OF RELATION	82b	2 b
		חם	THEY	241c	3 c
		רחק	DISTANT	935b	1 a
20	16	חיה	LIVE	311c	1
		נחלה	PROPERTY	635b	1 a
		נשמה	BREATH	675d	3
		רק	ONLY	956c	2 b
20	17	אמרי	AMORITES	57c	2 e
		יבוסי	JEBUSITE	101a	1

101

Ch	v.	Heb	Eng	Page	Sec
		חוי	HIVITE	295d	2
		חרם	BAN	355d	1 a
		חתי	HITTITE	366d	2 a
20	18	כנעני	CANAANITE	489a	2 b
		חטא	MISS A GOAL OR WAY	307a	2 b
		למד	LEARN	540d	
		מען	PURPOSE	775c	2 ca
		עשה	DO	793d	1 1a 1
		תועבה	ABOMINATION	1072d	1 b
20	19	אדם	MAN	9b	2
		גרזן	AXE	173d	
		ה	INTERROG PART	209d	1 b
		כרת	CUT OFF	503d	2
		לחם	ENGAGE IN BATTLE	535c	
		נדח	IMPEL	623a	1
		פנה	FACE	818c	2 6b
		צור	CONFINE	848d	2
		מצור	SIEGE	849a	1
		שדה	FIELD	961c	1 d
		שחת	GO TO RUIN	1008b	1
		תפש	LAY HOLD OF	1074d	1
20	20	מאכל	FOOD	38b	
		אשר	PARTICLE OF RELATION	82a	2 a
		בנה	BUILD	124c	1 ah
		הוא	HE, SHE, IT	215d	2 c
		ירד	GO DOWN	433b	1 k
		כרת	CUT OFF	503d	2
		לא	NOT	519b	1 bb
		מלחמה	WAR	536c	
		עד	AS FAR AS	724b	1 2a b
		עץ	TREE	781c	1 b
		עשה	DO	794c	2 1e
		מצור	SIEGE	849a	
		שחת	GO TO RUIN	1008b	1
20	22	חדש	NEW	294a	A
21	1	חדש	NEW MOON	*294c	2 a
		ידע	BE MADE KNOWN	394c	1
		מי	WHO	566c	C
		נכה	SMITE	646a	2 c
		נפל	LIE	657d	7
		שדה	FIELD	961b	1 b
21	2	זקן	OLD	279a	2 b
		מדד	MEASURE	551a	
		מדד	MEASURE	551a	1
		מדד	MEASURE	551a	
		סביב	ROUND ABOUT	687b	2 bb
		שפט	JUDGE	1047d	2 b
21	3	בקר	CATTLE	133b	1 a
		היה	COME TO PASS	225b	1 2b bd
		זקן	OLD	279a	2 b
		משך	DRAW	604b	1
		עבד	WORK	713c	
		עגלה	HEIFER	722b	
		על	YOKE	760d	
		קרב	NEAR	898b	1
21	4	זקן	OLD	279a	2 b
		זרע	SOW	281d	1 a
		ירד	BRING DOWN	433d	1 a
		איתן	EVER-FLOWING	450d	1
		נחל	WADY	636b	2
		עבד	WORK	713c	1
		עגלה	HEIFER	722b	
		ערף	BREAK THE NECK	791c	
21	5	בחר	CHOOSE	103d	1 a
		בן	SON	121a	1 je
		ברך	BLESS	139a	3
		כהן	PRIEST	463d	5
		לוי	LEVI	532c	1 c
		נגע	STROKE	619c	1
		נגש	DRAW NEAR	621a	
		על	UPON	754a	2 1f
		פה	MOUTH	805d	6 d1 b
		שרת	SERVE	1058a	2 a
21	6	זקן	OLD	279a	2 b
		נחל	WADY	636b	2
		עגלה	HEIFER	722b	
		על	UPON	754a	2 7a c
		ערף	BREAK THE NECK	791c	
		קרב	NEAR	898b	1
		רחץ	WASH OFF	934c	1
21	7	אמר	SAY	56b	1
		דם	BLOOD	196c	2 b
		ראה	TO SEE	906d	1 b
21	8	דם	BLOOD	196d	2 d
		דם	BLOOD	197b	2 m
		כפר	COVER OVER	497c	2 b
		נתן	PUT	680d	1
		פדה	RANSOM	804a	3 a
		סום	TO PLACE	*963a	1 a
21	9	בער	CONSUME	129b	3
		דם	BLOOD	196d	2 d
		ישר	STRAIGHT	449a	2 a
		נקי	CLEAN	667c	1
21	10	שבה	TAKE CAPTIVE	985c	2
		שביה	CAPTIVITY	986a	3
21	11	חשק	BE ATTACHED TO	366a	
		יפה	BEAUTIFUL	421c	
		שביה	CAPTIVITY	986a	2
		תאר	FORM	1061b	
21	12	עשה	DO	794d	2 5
		צפרן	STYLUS POINT	862b	1
		ראש	HEAD	910d	1 a
		תוך	MIDST	1063d	
21	13	אחר	AFTER	29d	2 b
		אם	MOTHER	51d	1
		בכה	WEEP	113c	4
		בעל	MARRY	127a	1
		יום	TIME	399d	6 b
		ירח	MONTH	437b	1
		סור	TURN ASIDE	694b	1
		שמלה	WRAPPER	971a	
		שבי	CAPTIVITY	985d	2
21	14	ב	IN	90a	3 3b
		חפץ	DELIGHT IN	342d	1 a
		כסף	SILVER	494d	9
		מכר	SELL	569b	
		נפש	SOUL	660d	6 a
		עמר	DEAL TYRANNICALLY	771c	
		ענה	BE BOWED DOWN	776b	2
		תחת	INSTEAD	1066a	2 3a b
21	15	אהב	LOVE	12d	1
		בן	SON	120a	1
		שנא	HATE	971c	1 a
		שנא	HATED	971d	
21	16	אהב	LOVE	12d	1
		בכר	MAKE FIRST-BORN	114a	2
		היה	COME TO PASS	225a	1 2b aa
		נחל	GET AS A POSSESSION	635d	2
		פנה	FACE	818d	2 7a b
		שנא	HATE	971c	1 a
21	17	און	VIGOUR	20b	1
		בכרה	RIGHT OF FIRST-BORN	114c	
		כי	BUT	474b	3 e
		ל	TO	513b	5 ba
		מצא	FIND	594a	2
		נכר	RECOGNIZE	648b	3
		פה	MOUTH	805c	5 b
		ראשית	BEGINNING	912b	1
		שנא	HATE	971c	1 a
		שנים	TWO	1041a	1 b1
		משפט	JUDGMENT	1049a	5
21	18	אב	FATHER	3b	1
		אין	NOT	34b	2 c
		אם	MOTHER	51d	1
		יסר	DISCIPLINE	416b	2 b
		מרה	BE REBELLIOUS	598a	1
		סרר	BE STUBBORN	710d	
		קול	VOICE	877b	3 a1
21	19	אב	FATHER	3b	1
		אם	MOTHER	51d	1
		זקן	OLD	279a	2 b
		יצא	BRING OUT	424d	1 i
		מקום	STANDING PLACE	880a	2
		שער	GATE	*1045a	2 a
		שער	GATE	1045a	2 a
		תפש	LAY HOLD OF	1074d	1
21	20	זה	THIS	261a	2 ba
		זלל	BE LIGHT	272d	2
		זקן	OLD	279a	2 b
		מרה	BE REBELLIOUS	598a	1
		סבא	DRINK LARGELY	685a	
		סרר	BE STUBBORN	710d	
		קול	VOICE	877b	3 a1
21	21	אבן	STONE	6b	1
		בער	CONSUME	129b	3
		ירא	FEAR	431b	1 a
		מות	DIE	559d	2 a
		רגם	TO STONE	920c	
21	22	חטא	SIN	308a	1 b
		מות	DIE	560c	2
		מות	DEATH	560d	2
		עץ	TREE	782a	2 b
		משפט	JUDGMENT	1048c	1 e
		תלה	HANG	1068a	3
21	23	אדמה	LAND	10a	5
		טמא	BE UNCLEAN	379c	2
		לון	LODGE	533d	1 c
		נבלה	CARCASS	615c	1 a
		נחלה	PROPERTY	635b	1 a
		עץ	TREE	782a	2 b
		קבר	BURY	868c	1
		קללה	CURSE	887a	
		תלה	HANG	1068a	3
22	1	ל	TO	510d	1 c
		לא	NOT	518c	1 aa
		נדח	BANISH	623a	3
		עלם	CONCEAL	761b	
		שה	A SHEEP	962a	1
		שוב	TURN BACK	999a	1 d
		שור	A HEAD OF CATTLE	1004a	
22	2	אם	IF	49d	1 a2
		אסף	GATHER	62b	2 b
		דרש	SEEK	205b	4 a
		היה	BE	226d	3 2
		עד	AS FAR AS	724b	1 2a b
		עם	WITH	768b	3 a
		קרב	NEAR	898c	2 a
		שוב	TURN BACK	999a	1 d
		תוך	MIDST	1063d	
22	3	אבד	BE LOST	1d	3
		אבדה	LOST THING	2b	
		חמור	HE-ASS	331b	
		יכל	BE ABLE	407d	1 d
		מצא	FIND	593a	1 b
		עלם	CONCEAL	761b	
		שמלה	WRAPPER	971a	
22	4	דרך	WAY	202c	1
		חמור	HE-ASS	331b	1
		נפל	FALL	656d	1
		עזב	LEAVE	737d	3
		עלם	CONCEAL	761b	
		עם	WITH	767b	1 a
		קום	STAND	878d	1 a
		ראה	TO SEE	907a	2 3
22	5	אלה	THESE	41c	A
		גבר	MAN	150a	
		כלי	ARTICLE	479c	1
		לבש	PUT ON	527d	A
		על	UPON	753a	2 1a a
		שמלה	WRAPPER	971a	
		תועבה	ABOMINATION	1072d	1 b
22	6	אם	MOTHER	52a	3
		ביצה	EGG	101b	
		בן	SON	121b	4
		דרך	WAY	202c	1
		על	UPON	755c	2 4c
		אפרח	YOUNG ONE	827b	
		קן	NEST	890a	1
		קרא	ENCOUNTER	897a	
		רבץ	LIE DOWN	918c	1
22	7	אם	MOTHER	52a	3
		ארך	BE LONG	73d	1 a
		בן	SON	121b	4
		יטב	BE WELL	405c	3
		לקח	TAKE	543a	4 a
22	8	בית	HOUSE	108d	1 ab
		בנה	BUILD	124b	1 ab
		גג	ROOF	150d	1
		דם	BLOOD	197a	2 i
		מן	FROM	577d	1 a
		נפל	FALL	656d	1
		מעקה	PARAPET	785b	
		עשה	DO	794c	2 1c
		שום	TO PLACE	963a	1 a
22	9	תבואה	PRODUCT	100a	1
		זרע	SOW	281c	1 c
		זרע	SOW	281c	1 d
		זרע	SOWING	282b	2 d
		כלאים	TWO KINDS	476d	
		כרם	VINEYARD	501d	
		מלאה	FULL PRODUCE	571b	
		קדש	BE SET APART	873a	3
22	10	חמור	HE-ASS	331c	4
		חרש	CUT IN	360c	2
		יחדו	TOGETHER	403c	A
		שור	A HEAD OF CATTLE	1004b	
22	11	יחדו	TOGETHER	403c	A
		לבש	PUT ON	528a	A
		פשת	FLAX	833d	
		צמר	WOOL	856a	
		שעטנז	MIXED STUFF	1043b	
22	12	גדלים	TWISTED THREADS	152d	1
		כנף	EXTREMITY	489d	2 a
		כסה	COVER	491c	1
		כסות	COVERING	492b	1
22	13	בוא	COME	98a	1 e
		שנא	HATE	971c	1 a
22	14	בתולים	VIRGINITY	144a	
		דבר	WORD	182c	1 1g
		יצא	BRING OUT	425b	4 k
		ל	TO	512b	5 aa
		מצא	FIND	593a	1 d
		עלילה	WANTONNESS	760a	1
		קרב	COME NEAR	897b	1 a
		רע	EVIL	948b	2
		שום	TO PLACE	963a	1
		שם	NAME	1028a	2 b2
		ל	IN REGARD TO	*1098c	4 b
22	15	אם	MOTHER	51d	1
		בתולים	VIRGINITY	144a	
		זקן	OLD	279a	2 b
		נערה	GIRL	655b	1
		שער	GATE	1045a	2 a
		שער	GATE	*1045a	2 a
22	16	זקן	OLD	279a	2 b
		נערה	GIRL	655b	1
		שנא	HATE	971c	1 a
22	17	בתולים	VIRGINITY	144a	
		בתולים	VIRGINITY	144a	
		דבר	WORD	182c	1 1g
		זקן	OLD	279a	2 b
		מצא	FIND	593a	1 d
		עלילה	WANTONNESS	760a	1
		פרש	SPREAD OUT	831a	1
		שום	TO PLACE	963a	1 a
		שמלה	WRAPPER	971a	
22	18	זקן	OLD	279a	2 b
		יסר	DISCIPLINE	416b	2 b
22	19	אשה	WOMAN	61b	2
		בתולה	VIRGIN	143d	1
		יום	DAY	399a	4 a
		יצא	BRING OUT	425b	4 k
		מאה	HUNDRED	547d	1 a4
		נערה	GIRL	655b	1
		נתן	GIVE	679b	1 n
		עניש	FINE	778d	
		רע	EVIL	948b	2
		שלח	SEND	1019a	1 b
		שם	NAME	1028a	2 b2
22	20	אמת	FIRMNESS	54b	4 a
		בתולים	VIRGINITY	144a	

Ch	v.	Heb	Eng	Page	Sec
		דבר	WORD	182c	1 1g
		מצא	FIND	593d	1 c
		נערה	GIRL	655b	1
22	21	אבן	STONE	6b	1
		בער	CONSUME	129b	3
		זנה	COMMIT FORNICATION	275d	1
		יצא	BRING OUT	424d	1 g
		מות	DIE	559d	2 a
		נבלה	SENSELESSNESS	615a	1
		נערה	GIRL	655b	1
		סקל	STONE	709c	
22	22	איש	MAN	35d	
		אשה	WOMAN	61a	1
		בעל	MARRY	127a	1
		בעל	OWNER	127b	1 2
		בער	CONSUME	129b	3
		גם	ALSO	169c	2
		מצא	FIND	394a	1 g2
		מות	DIE	559d	2 a
		שכב	LIE DOWN	1012b	3
22	23	ארש	BETROTH	77a	1
		בתולה	VIRGIN	143d	
		מצא	FIND	593b	3 a
		נערה	GIRL	655b	1
22	24	אבן	STONE	6b	1
		בער	CONSUME	129b	3
		דבר	WORD	184a	4 8
		יצא	BRING OUT	424d	1 g
		מות	DIE	559d	2 a
		נערה	GIRL	655b	1
		סקל	STONE	709c	
		ענה	BE BOWED DOWN	776b	2
		צעק	CRY	858c	2
		שער	GATE	*1045a	2 a
22	25	ארש	BETROTH	77a	1
		חזק	BE FIRM	305a	6 a
		מות	DIE	559d	2 a
		מצא	FIND	593b	3 a
		נערה	GIRL	655b	1
		שדה	FIELD	961b	1 b
22	26	חטא	SIN	308a	1 b
		כאשר	AS	455c	1 d
		כן	SO	486c	2 cf
		מות	DEATH	560d	2
		נערה	GIRL	655b	1
		קום	STAND	878a	2
		רע	FRIEND	946a	2
		רצח	MURDER	953d	1
22	27	אין	NOT	34d	3
		ארש	BETROTH	77a	1
		ישע	DELIVER	446c	1
		מצא	FIND	593b	3 a
		נערה	GIRL	655b	1
		צעק	CRY	858c	2
		שדה	FIELD	961b	1 b
22	28	ארש	BETROTH	77a	1
		בתולה	VIRGIN	143d	
		מצא	FIND	394a	1 g2
		מצא	FIND	593b	3 a
		נערה	GIRL	655b	1
		תפש	LAY HOLD OF	1074d	1
22	29	אשה	WOMAN	61b	2
		יום	DAY	399a	4 a
		יכל	BE ABLE	407c	1 b
		נערה	GIRL	655b	1
		נתן	GIVE	679b	1 n
		ענה	BE BOWED DOWN	776b	2
		שלח	SEND	1019a	1 b
		תחת	INSTEAD	1066a	2 3a b
23	1	כנף	EXTREMITY	489d	2 a
23	2	בוא	COME	97d	1 b
		דכה	CRUSHING	194c	
		כרת	CUT OFF	503d	1 a
		פצע	BRUISE	822d	
		קהל	ASSEMBLY	874d	2 a
		שפכה	MALE ORGAN	1050a	
23	3	בוא	COME	97d	1 b
		גם	YEA	169c	3
		דור	GENERATION	190a	2 c
		ל	TO	512c	5 aa
		ממזר	BASTARD	561c	1
		עשירי	TENTH	798a	1
		קהל	ASSEMBLY	874d	2 a
23	4	בוא	COME	97d	1 b
		גם	YEA	169c	3
		דור	GENERATION	190a	2 c
		ל	TO	512c	5 aa
		מואבי	MOABITISH	556a	
		עמוני	AMMONITE	770a	
		עשירי	TENTH	798a	1
		קהל	ASSEMBLY	874d	2 a
23	5	ארם	ARAM	74c	B
		ב	IN	91a	5 1
		בלעם	BALAAM	118d	
		בעור	BEOR	129d	1
		דבר	WORD	184a	4 8
		דרך	WAY	202c	1
		יצא	GO OUT	422d	1 a
		לחם	FOOD	537a	1 a
		פתור	PETHOR	834d	
		קדם	COME IN FRONT	870a	1 b
		שכר	HIRE	969a	
23	6	אבה	BE WILLING	2c	
		אהב	LOVE	13a	5 b
		בלעם	BALAAM	118d	

Ch	v.	Heb	Eng	Page	Sec
		ברכה	BLESSING	139d	1 b
		הפך	TURN	245c	1 c4
		ל	TO	512b	4 a
		ל	TO	515c	5 hc
		קללה	CURSE	887a	
		משפט	JUDGMENT	1049a	5
23	7	בחר	CHOOSE	104a	2 b
		דרש	SEEK	205c	6
		טובה	WELFARE	375d	1
		יום	DAY	399a	4 a
		שלום	PEACE	1023a	3
23	8	אדמי	EDOMITE	10c	
		גר	SOJOURNER	158b	1
		מצרי	EGYPTIAN	596a	2
		תעב	BE ABHORRED	1073b	1 a2
23	9	דור	GENERATION	190a	2 c
		ילד	BE BORN	408d	
		ל	TO	512c	5 aa
		קהל	ASSEMBLY	874d	2 a
23	10	רע	EVIL	948a	1
		שמר	KEEP	1037b	1
23	11	ב	IN	88b	1 2
		חוץ	THE OUTSIDE	300a	1 bd
		קרה	CHANCE	899d	
		תוך	MIDST	1063d	
23	12	בוא	COME	98a	1 i
		היה	COME TO PASS	225b	1 2b ae
		ערב	SUNSET	787d	1 a
		פנה	TURN	815b	1 e
23	13	אחר	ANOTHER	29d	
		חוץ	THE OUTSIDE	299c	1 a
		יד	HAND	390c	3 e
23	14	אזן	IMPLEMENTS	24c	
		חוץ	THE OUTSIDE	299c	1 a
		חפר	DIG	343c	1 a
		ישב	SIT	442d	1 c
		יתד	PEG	450b	C
		כסה	COVER	491d	2
		על	UPON	755b	2 4b
		צאה	FILTH	844b	
		שוב	TURN BACK	998c	8
23	15	דבר	WORD	183d	4 6
		היה	BE	227d	3 4a
		הלך	WALK	236c	2
		נצל	DELIVER	664d	3 a
		ערוה	NAKEDNESS	789a	2
		קדוש	HOLY	872c	2 a
		שוב	TURN BACK	997d	6 b
		אדון	LORD	11a	2 1b
23	16	נצל	DELIVER ONESELF	664c	1
		סגר	DELIVER UP	689c	1
		עבד	SLAVE	713d	1
		מעם	FROM WITH	*769a	C
23	17	טוב	PLEASANT	373d	2 b
		ינה	OPPRESS	413b	
		ישב	DWELL	443a	1
		עם	WITH	768b	3 a
		שער	GATE	*1045a	2 c
23	18	קדש	TEMPLE-PROSTITUTE	873d	
		קדש	TEMPLE-PROSTITUTE	873d	
23	19	גם	ALSO	169c	2
		זנה	COMMIT FORNICATION	275d	1
		כלב	DOG	477a	B
		ל	TO	514c	5 fc
		מחיר	HIRE	564b	2
		נדר	VOW	624a	2
		אתנן	HIRE	1072c	
		תועבה	ABOMINATION	1072d	1 b
23	20	אכל	FOOD	38a	
		דבר	WORD	183d	4 6
		כסף	SILVER	494d	9
		נשך	PAY INTEREST	675b	
		נשך	INTEREST	675b	
		נשך	INTEREST	675b	
23	21	ברך	BLESS	139a	2 a
		יד	HAND	389d	1 c
		נכרי	FOREIGN	648d	1 b
		נשך	PAY INTEREST	675b	
		משלח	OUTSTRETCHING	1020a	1
23	22	אחר	DELAY	29b	2
		דרש	SEEK	205c	5
		חטא	SIN	308a	1
		נדר	VOW	623d	
		נדר	VOW	624a	2
		מעם	FROM WITH	769a	A
		שלם	BE COMPLETE	1022c	4
23	23	חדל	CEASE	293a	2
		חטא	SIN	308a	2
		נדר	VOW	623d	
23	24	מוצא	GOING FORTH	425d	2 a
		נדבה	VOLUNTARINESS	621d	1
		נדר	VOW	623d	
		שפה	SPEECH	973d	1 a1
		שמר	KEEP	1037a	3 c
		ל	TO	39d	2
23	25	כלי	VESSEL	480a	3
		נפש	SOUL	660d	6 a
		ענב	GRAPE	772a	
		שבע	ABUNDANCE	960a	1
23	26	חרמש	SICKLE	357a	2
		מלילה	EAR	576c	
		נוף	MOVE TO AND FRO	631d	1
		קמה	STANDING GRAIN	879b	

Ch	v.	Heb	Eng	Page	Sec
		קטף	PLUCK OFF	882c	
24	1	בעל	MARRY	127a	1
		דבר	WORD	183d	4 6
		חן	FAVOR	336b	2 b1
		כריתות	DIVORCEMENT	504d	
		כתב	WRITE	507b	1 a
		כתב	WRITE	507b	1 b
		כתב	WRITE	507d	1 c
		מצא	FIND	592d	1 a
		מצא	FIND	593a	1 d
		נתן	GIVE	678b	1 a
		ספר	MISSIVE	707a	2
		ערוה	NAKEDNESS	789a	2
		שלח	SEND	1019a	1 b
24	2	אחר	ANOTHER	29c	
		היה	BECOME	226d	2 2h
		הלך	WALK	233d	1 5b
		יצא	GO OUT	422d	1 c
		יצא	BRING OUT	*424d	1 f
24	3	אחרון	BEHIND	30d	B
		כריתות	DIVORCEMENT	504d	
		נתן	GIVE	678b	1 a
		ספר	MISSIVE	707a	2
		שנא	HATE	971c	1
		שלח	SEND	1019a	1 b
24	4	אחר	AFTER THAT	30b	3
		ארץ	EARTH	76b	2 f
		בעל	OWNER	127b	1 2
		חטא	MISS A GOAL OR WAY	307d	3
		טמא	BE UNCLEAN	379d	
		נחלה	PROPERTY	635b	1 a
		פנה	FACE	817a	2 4a g
		ראשון	FIRST	911c	1 a
		שוב	TURN BACK	998b	1
		תועבה	ABOMINATION	1072d	1 b
24	5	חדש	NEW	294a	A
		ל	TO	514d	5 fe
		נקי	FREE FROM	667c	3
		עבר	PASS OVER	717b	1 h
		על	UPON	753b	2 1c
		צבא	WAR	839b	2
		שמח	REJOICE	970c	
		שמח	REJOICE	970c	
24	6	חבל	BIND	286b	2
		רכב	CHARIOT	939b	3
24	7	בער	CONSUME	129b	3
		גנב	STEAL	170b	
		גנב	THIEF	170c	
		מצא	FIND	394a	1 g2
		מות	DIE	559d	2 a
		מכר	SELL	569b	
		נפש	SOUL	660b	4 c2
		עמר	DEAL TYRANNICALLY	771c	
24	8	ירה	DIRECT	435b	5 b
		תורה	LAW	436c	3 b3
		כהן	PRIEST	463d	5
		לוי	LEVITE	532d	3 1b
		נגע	MARK	619d	3
		עבד	SLAVE	713d	1
24	9	דרך	WAY	202c	1
		זכר	REMEMBER	269d	1 1 d
		יצא	GO OUT	422d	1 a
		מרים	MIRIAM	599b	1
24	10	מאומה	ANYTHING	548d	
		משאה	LOAN	673d	
		נשה	LEND	674c	
		עבט	TAKE A PLEDGE	716b	
		עבוט	PLEDGE	716b	
24	11	חוץ	THE OUTSIDE	299d	1 bb
		נשה	LEND	674d	
		עבוט	PLEDGE	716b	
24	12	עבוט	PLEDGE	716b	
		עני	POOR	776d	1
24	13	בוא	COME	98a	1 i
		ברך	BLESS	139a	2 a
		עבוט	PLEDGE	716b	
		פנה	FACE	817a	2 4a g
		שלמה	GARMENT	971b	
		שוב	TURN BACK	999a	1 d
24	14	אביון	NEEDY	2d	
		אביון	NEEDY	2d	
		גר	SOJOURNER	158b	2
		עני	POOR	776d	1
		עשק	OPPRESS	798d	1
		שכיר	HIRED	969b	2
24	15	אל	TO	40a	3 c
		בוא	COME	98a	1 i
		חטא	SIN	308a	1
		יום	TIME	399d	6 a
		נפש	SOUL	660d	6 a
		נשא	LIFT	670d	1 b 9
		נתן	GIVE	679b	1 n
		על	UPON	755d	2 5
		עני	POOR	776d	1
		קרא	CALL	895b	2 a
		שכר	HIRE	969a	1
24	16	ב	IN	90c	3 5
		חטא	SIN	308a	2
		מות	DIE	560c	2
		על	UPON	754b	2 1f b
24	17	אלמנה	WIDOW	48b	1
		בגד	GARMENT	94a	1
		גר	SOJOURNER	158b	2
		חבל	BIND	286b	1

103

DEUTERONOMY

Ch	v	Heb	Eng	Page	Sec
27	14	איש	MAN	36a	3 1b
		לוי	LEVITE	533a	3 1b
		קול	VOICE	877a	1 a
		רום	BE HIGH	926d	2 a
27	15	אמן	VERILY	53b	
		אמר	SAY	56b	1
		ארר	CURSE	76d	
		חרש	GRAVER	360d	1 a
		מסכה	MOLTEN IMAGE	651b	2
		סתר	COVERING	712a	3
		מעשה	DEED	796a	2 a3
		פסל	IDOL	820d	
		שום	TO PLACE	964b	4 c
		תועבה	ABOMINATION	1072d	1 b
		תועבה	ABOMINATION	*1073a	1 b
27	16	אם	MOTHER	51d	1
		אמר	SAY	55d	1
		קלה	DISHONOURED	885d	
27	17	גבול	BOUNDARY	148a	1 c
		סוג	DISPLACE	691a	1
27	18	עור	BLIND	734c	1
		שגה	GO ASTRAY	993b	1
27	19	אלמנה	WIDOW	48b	
		גר	SOJOURNER	158b	2
		יתום	ORPHAN	450c	
		נטה	BEND	641a	3 g
		משפט	JUDGEMNT	1049a	5
27	20	כנף	EXTREMITY	489d	2 a
27	21	בהמה	BEAST	96d	1
		שכב	LIE DOWN	1012b	3
27	22	אחות	SISTER	27d	1
		אם	MOTHER	51d	1
		בת	DAUGHTER	123a	1
		בת	DAUGHTER	123a	1
27	23	חתן	WIFE:S FATHER	368c	2
27	24	נכה	SMITE	646a	2 c
		סתר	COVERING	712a	3
27	25	דם	BLOOD	196d	2 d
		נכה	SMITE	*645d	2 a
		נכה	SMITE	646a	2 c
		נפש	SOUL	660b	4 c2
		נקי	CLEAN	667c	1
		שחד	BRIBE	1005a	
27	26	אמן	VERILY	53b	
		ארר	CURSE	76d	
		תורה	LAW	436b	2 b2
28	1	גוי	NATION	156c	1
		נתן	PUT	680c	2 b
		עליון	HIGH	751b	1
28	2	ברכה	BLESSING	139d	1 b
		כי	IF	473b	2 b
		נשג	OVERTAKE	673c	1 b
		על	UPON	756c	27 a b
28	3	ברך	BLESS	138d	2 b
28	4	אדמה	GROUND	9c	1
		אלף	CATTLE	48c	
		בטן	WOMB	106a	3
		ברך	BLESS	138d	2 c
		עשתרות	EWES	800b	
		פרי	FRUIT	826b	2
		שגר	OFFSPRING	993d	
28	5	ברך	BLESS	138d	2 c
		טנא	BASKET	380d	
		משארת	A HOUSEHOLD VESSEL	602b	
28	6	בוא	COME	97d	1 a
		ברך	BLESS	138d	2 b
		יצא	GO OUT	424a	3
28	7	נגף	STRIKE	620a	
		נוס	FLEE	630d	1
28	8	אסם	STOREHOUSE	62a	
		את	WITH	86b	1 dg
		ברך	BLESS	139a	2 a
		ברכה	BLESSING	139d	1 c
		יד	HAND	389b	1 c
		צוה	CHARGE	846a	4 d
		משלח	OUTSTRETCHING	1020a	1
28	9	דרך	WAY	204a	6 ec
		הלך	WALK	234c	2 3a 1b
		ל	TO	512c	4 b
		קום	STAND	879a	5
28	10	ירא	FEAR	431b	1 c
		קרא	CALL	896b	2 d4
28	11	אדמה	GROUND	9c	1
		בטן	WOMB	106a	3
		טובה	WELFARE	375d	1
		יתר	SHOW EXCESS	451c	3
		פרי	FRUIT	826b	2
28	12	אוצר	TREASURE	70a	3 d
		ברך	BLESS	139a	2 b
		טוב	PLEASANT	374b	4 a
		לוה	BORROW	531a	
		לוה	BORROW	531a	
		מטר	RAIN	564d	
		פתח	OPEN	835a	
28	13	זנב	TAIL	275c	1 b
		כי	IF	473b	2 b
		מטה	DOWNWARDS	641b	2 b
		נתן	GIVE	681a	3 b
		מעל	ABOVE	752a	2 ca
		ראש	HEAD	910d	1 b
		רק	ONLY	956c	1
28	14	הלך	WALK	235a	2 3d 2
		הלך	WALK	*235a	2 3d 2
		ימין	RIGHT HAND	412a	2 b
		כל	ALL	482b	1 ec
28	15	עבד	WORK	713b	4 b
		חקה	SOMETHING PRE-SCRIBED	350b	2 d
		חקה	SOMETHING PRE-SCRIBED	350b	2 e
		נשג	OVERTAKE	673c	1 b
		על	UPON	756c	27 a b
28	17	טנא	BASKET	380d	
		משארת	A HOUSEHOLD VESSEL	602b	
28	18	אדמה	GROUND	9c	1
		אלף	CATTLE	48c	
		בטן	WOMB	106a	3
		עשתרות	EWES	800b	
		שגר	OFFSPRING	993d	
28	19	בוא	COME	97d	1 a
		יצא	GO OUT	424a	3
28	20	אבד	PERISH	1c	1
		מארה	CURSE	76d	
		אשר	PARTICLE OF RELATION	82d	4 c
		מגערת	REBUKE	172a	
		מהומה	DISCOMFITURE	223a	2
		יד	HAND	389b	1 c
		מהר	QUICKLY	555b	
		עד	AS FAR AS	724b	1 2a b
		עזב	LEAVE	737c	2 d1
		רע	EVIL	948a	1
		שלח	SEND	1019a	2 d
		משלח	OUTSTRETCHING	1020a	1
		שמד	BE EXTERMINATED	1029b	1
28	21	דבק	CLING	180a	1
		דבר	PESTILENCE	184a	1
		כלה	FINISH	478c	2 c2
		על	UPON	758c	4 2a
28	22	אבד	PERISH	1c	1
		דלקת	INFLAMMATION	196b	
		ה	THE	208c	1 hb
		חרב	DRYNESS	351b	2
		חרב	SWORD	352d	1 j
		חרחר	VIOLENT HEAT	359c	
		ירקון	RUST	439a	1
		נכה	SMITE	646c	4 a
		עד	AS FAR AS	724b	1 2a b
		קדחת	FEVER	869b	
		רדף	PURSUE	922d	1 b
		שדפון	SMUT	995b	
		שחפת	CONSUMPTION	1006a	
28	23	ברזל	IRON	137c	3
		נחשת	COPPER	639a	4
		על	UPON	755d	2 5
		שמי	HEAVENS	1029a	1 a
28	24	אבק	DUST	7c	
		ירד	GO DOWN	433c	3 a
		מטר	RAIN	564d	
		עפר	DRY EARTH	779d	1 a
		שמד	BE EXTERMINATED	1029b	1
28	25	זועה	A TREMBLING	266b	
		ל	TO	512c	4 b
		ממלכה	KINGDOM	575a	1
		נגף	STRIKE	620a	
		נוס	FLEE	630d	1
28	26	מאכל	FOOD	38b	
		בהמה	BEAST	97a	3
		חרד	TREMBLE	353c	
		נבלה	CARCASS	615c	1 a
28	27	אשר	THAT	83c	8 b
		גרב	ITCH	173a	
		חרס	AN ERUPTIVE DISEASE	360b	
		שחור	TUMORS	377d	
		יכל	BE ABLE	407d	1 d
		נכה	SMITE	646c	4 a
		עפל	HEMORRHOID	779b	
		רפא	HEAL	950d	1
		שחין	BOIL	1006c	
28	28	ה	THE	*208c	1 hb
		לבב	HEART	524b	2 9b
		נכה	SMITE	646c	4 a
		עורון	BLINDNESS	734d	
		שגעון	MADNESS	993d	
		תמהון	BEWILDERMENT	1069b	
28	29	אך	ONLY	36d	2 bb
		אלה	DARKNESS	66c	1
		גזל	TEAR AWAY	159d	
		ה	THE	207d	1 f
		היה	BE	227c	3 5a
		יום	DAY	400c	7 f
		ישע	DELIVER	446c	1 a
		מששש	GROPE	607a	2
		עור	BLIND	734c	1 a
		עשק	OPPRESS	798d	2
		צהר	MIDDAY	844a	2
		צלח	ADVANCE	852c	1
28	30	אחר	ANOTHER	29c	
		אשה	WOMAN	61b	2
		ארש	BETROTH	77a	
		בית	HOUSE	108d	1 ab
		בנה	BUILD	124b	1 ab
		חלל	POLLUTE	320c	4
		כרם	VINEYARD	501b	
		נטע	PLANT	642c	1
		שגל	VIOLATE	993c	
		שכב	LIE DOWN	1012b	3
28	31	גזל	TEAR AWAY	159d	
		חמור	HE-ASS	331b	1
		מבח	SLAUGHTER	370c	1 a
		ישע	DELIVER	446c	1 a
		ל	TO	510d	1 c
		ל	TO	*512a	3 b
		פנה	FACE	818a	25a b
		שוב	TURN BACK	998a	7 b
		שור	A HEAD OF CATTLE	1004a	
28	32	אחר	ANOTHER	29c	
		אל	TO	40a	3 c
		אל	GOD	43a	7
		יום	DAY	400c	7 f
		כלה	LONGING	479a	
		עם	PEOPLE	767a	5 h
28	33	אדמה	GROUND	9c	1
		אך	ONLY	36d	2 bb
		יגיע	TOIL	388c	2
		יגיע	TOIL	388c	2
		יום	DAY	400c	7 f
		עשק	OPPRESS	798d	2
		רצץ	CRUSH	954c	2
		רק	ONLY	956c	2 c
28	34	מן	ON ACCOUNT OF	580b	2 f
		עין	EYE	744b	1
		מראה	VISION	909d	2
		שגע	BE MAD	993d	
28	35	ברך	KNEE	139c	
		יכל	BE ABLE	407d	1 d
		מן	FROM	581d	5 a
		נכה	SMITE	646c	4 a
		קדקד	HEAD	869b	
		רגל	FOOT	919d	1 a
		רע	EVIL	948a	1
		רפא	HEAL	950d	1
		שוק	LEG	1003b	1
		שחין	BOIL	1006c	
28	36	אבן	STONE	6c	2
		הלך	WALK	236d	1 d
		מלך	KING	573c	5 c
		עבד	WORK	713b	4 b
		עץ	TREE	782a	2 c
		קום	STAND	878d	2 a
28	37	כל	ALL	482c	2
		משל	PROVERB	605b	2
		נהג	DRIVE	624b	1
		שמה	APPALMENT	1031c	1
		שנינה	SHARP WORD	1042b	1
28	38	אסף	GATHER	62b	1 c
		זרע	SOWING	282b	2
		חסל	FINISH OFF	340c	
		יצא	BRING OUT	425a	4 d
		כרסם	TEAR OFF	*493c	
		רב	MUCH	913a	1 a1
		ארבה	LOCUST	916a	
28	39	אגר	GATHER	8d	
		אכל	EAT	37c	2
		נטע	PLANT	642c	1
		עבד	WORK	713a	1
		תולעה	WORM	1069a	1
28	40	גבול	BOUNDARY	148a	2 a
		זית	OLIVE TREE	268d	1
		זית	OLIVE TREE	268d	2
		נשל	SLIP	675c	1
		סוך	ANOINT	692a	1
		שמן	OIL	1032b	2 c
28	41	הלך	WALK	231b	1 d3 ge
		ילד	BEGET	409a	1
		שבי	CAPTIVITY	985d	1
28	42	אדמה	GROUND	9c	1
		ירש	TAKE POSSESSION	439d	1
		צלצל	WHIRRING LOCUST	852d	
28	43	גר	SOJOURNER	158b	2
		ירד	GO DOWN	433b	1 k
		מטה	DOWNWARDS	641b	1
		עלה	GO UP	749a	0
		מעל	ABOVE	751d	2 a
		על	UPON	755a	2 3
		עלא	ABOVE	*1106c	
28	44	זנב	TAIL	275c	1 b
		לוה	BORROW	531a	1
		ראש	HEAD	910d	1 b
28	45	חקה	SOMETHING PRE-SCRIBED	350b	2 d
		חקה	SOMETHING PRE-SCRIBED	350b	2 e
		נשג	OVERTAKE	673c	1 b
		רדף	PURSUE	922d	1 b
		שמד	BE EXTERMINATED	1029b	1
28	46	אות	SIGN	16d	4
		מופת	WONDER	69a	1
		זרע	SOWING	283a	4 g
		עולם	LONG DURATION	762c	1
28	47	טוב	GOOD THINGS	375c	3 b
		כל	ALL	482c	2
		לבב	HEART	524a	2 9a
		רב	MULTITUDE	914a	1
28	48	תחת	INSTEAD	1066a	2 3a b
		ברזל	IRON	137c	3
		חסר	WANT	341c	
		כל	ALL	482c	2
		עד	AS FAR AS	*724b	1 2a b
		עירם	NAKEDNESS	736a	1
		על	YOKE	760d	
		צואר	NECK	848c	1
		צמא	THIRST	854d	
		רעב	FAMINE	944b	2
28	49	דאה	FLY SWIFTLY	178d	

Ch v.	Heb	Eng	Page	Sec
	לשון	TONGUE	546c	2
	נשר	EAGLE	676d	
	קצה	END	892a	1
	רחק	DISTANT	935c	2 a 1
	שמע	HEAR	1033d	1 g
28 50	זקן	OLD	278c	2 a
	חנן	SHOW FAVOR	336a	1 c
	נער	YOUTH	655a	1 d
	נשא	LIFT	670c	1 b 3
	עז	STRONG	738d	
28 51	אבד	DESTROY	2b	1
	אדמה	GROUND	9c	1
	אלף	CATTLE	48c	
	אשר	THAT	83c	8 b
	דגן	CORN	186a	
	תירוש	NEW WINE	440d	
	עשתרות	EWES	800b	
	פרי	FRUIT	826b	2
	יצהר	FRESH OIL	844a	
	שאר	REMAIN	984b	1
	שגר	OFFSPRING	993d	
	שמד	BE EXTERMINATED	1029b	1
28 52	בטח	TRUST	105a	1 3c
	בצר	MAKE INACCESSIBLE	131a	
	גבה	HIGH	147b	1
	הם	THEY	242a	8 d
	חומה	WALL	327b	1
	ירד	GO DOWN	433b	1 k
	צרר	BIND	864d	B
28 53	בטן	WOMB	106a	3
	בשר	FLESH	142c	1 b
	צוק	CONSTRAIN	848a	
	מצוק	STRAITNESS	848a	
	מצור	SIEGE	849a	1
28 54	אשה	WOMAN	61b	2
	חק	IN	88b	1 2
	חיק	BOSOM	300d	3 a
	יתר	LEAVE OVER	451c	1 a
	יתר	REMAINDER	451d	1 a
	עין	EYE	744c	2 a
	ענג	DAINTY	772b	
	רך	TENDER	940a	1
	רעע	BE EVIL	949c	3
28 55	בלי	WEARING OUT	115d	C a
	בשר	FLESH	142c	1 b
	כל	ALL	482c	2 a
	מן	FROM	583a	7 ba
	צוק	CONSTRAIN	848a	
	מצוק	STRAITNESS	848a	
	מצור	SIEGE	849a	1
	שאר	REMAIN	984b	1
28 56	איש	MAN	35d	
	חיק	BOSOM	300d	3 a
	יצג	SET	426c	
	כף	SOLE OF FOOT	496d	3
	עין	EYE	744c	2 a
	ענג	DAINTY	772b	
	ענג	BE SOFT	772b	1
	רגל	FOOT	919d	1 a
	רך	TENDERNESS	940a	
	רך	TENDER	940a	1
	רעע	BE EVIL	949c	3
28 57	בין	INTERVAL	107d	D
	חסר	WANT	341c	
	יצא	GO OUT	423c	1 h
	סתר	COVERING	712a	3
	צוק	CONSTRAIN	848a	
	מצוק	STRAITNESS	848a	
	מצור	SIEGE	849a	1
	רגל	FOOT	920a	1 f
	שליה	AFTER-BIRTH	1017d	
28 58	ירא	FEAR	431c	3 b
	ירא	BE REVERED	431d	3 b2
	תורה	LAW	436b	2 b2
	כבד	BE HONORED	457c	1 b
	שם	NAME	1028c	3
28 59	אמן	CONFIRM	52d	1
	גדול	GREAT	153a	2
	זרע	SOWING	283a	4 g
	חלה	BE WEAK	317d	2
	חלי	SICKNESS	318b	
	מכה	SLAUGHTER	647a	4
	פלא	BE SURPASSING	810d	2
	רע	EVIL	948a	1
28 60	דבק	CLING	179d	2 c
	מדוה	SICKNESS	188c	
	יגר	BE AFRAID	388c	
28 61	גם	ALSO	169b	2
	חלה	BE WEAK	317d	2
	חלי	SICKNESS	318b	
	תורה	LAW	436b	2 b2
	לא	NOT	519b	1 bc
	מכה	SLAUGHTER	647a	4
	ספר	MISSIVE	707b	3 c
	עלה	GO UP	749c	4
	על	UPON	757a	2 7b
	שמד	BE EXTERMINATED	1029b	1
28 62	ב	IN	89a	1 7b
	כוכב	STAR	457a	
	מעט	A FEW	590a	1 b
	מת	MALE	607b	2 b
	שאר	REMAIN	984a	1
	תחת	INSTEAD	1066a	2 3a a
28 63	אבד	DESTROY	2b	1
	היה	COME TO PASS	225a	1 2b ad

Ch v.	Heb	Eng	Page	Sec
	יטב	DO GOOD TO	405d	2
	כאשר	AS	455b	1 b
	כן	SO	486c	2 cd
	נסח	TEAR AWAY	650c	
	על	UPON	758c	4 2a
	רבה	BECOME MANY	915b	
	שוש	REJOICE	965b	
28 64	אבן	STONE	6c	2
	ידע	KNOW	394a	2
	מן	FROM	581d	5 a
	עבד	WORK	713b	4 b
	עץ	TREE	782a	2 c
	פוץ	BE DISPERSED	807a	1 a
	קצה	END	892b	1
28 65	דאבון	FAINTNESS	178b	
	כליון	FAILING	479a	1
	כף	SOLE OF FOOT	496d	3
	לב	HEART	525c	2 9b
	מנוח	RESTING PLACE	629d	1
	רגז	QUIVERING	919c	
	רגל	FOOT	919d	1 a
	רגע	BE AT REST	921b	B
28 66	אמן	CONFIRM	53b	2 c
	חיים	LIFE	313a	1
	יומם	BY DAY	401c	2
	ל	TO	512d	5 aa
	נגד	IN FRONT	617d	2 ca
	פחד	DREAD	808b	1
	תלא	HANG	1067d	
28 67	בקר	MORNING	134a	1 e
	לב	HEART	524b	2 9b
	מי	WHO	566c	F a
	מן	ON ACCOUNT OF	580b	2 f
	נתן	GIVE	678d	1 f
	עין	EYE	744b	1 f
	פחד	DREAD	808b	1
	פחד	DREAD	808c	1
	מראה	VISION	909d	2
28 68	אמר	SAY	56a	1
	אניה	A SHIP	58b	
	אשר	PARTICLE OF RELATION	82d	4 d
	יסף	DO AGAIN	415c	2 a
	קנה	ACQUIRE	889a	2
	שוב	TURN BACK	998d	1 a
	שפחה	MAID	1046c	1
	בד	SEPARATION	94d	1 e
	ברית	COVENANT	136c	2 2c
	ברית	COVENANT	136d	2 2c
	ברית	COVENANT	137a	3 1
	חרב	HOREB	352a	
	כרת	CUT	503d	4
29 1	מואב	MOAB	555d	2 b
29 2	עבד	SLAVE	713d	2
	אות	SIGN	16d	4
	מופת	WONDER	69a	1
	מסה	TEST	650b	
29 3	אזן	EAR	23d	2 a
	יום	DAY	401b	7 1
	לב	HEART	524d	2 3b
	נתן	GIVE	678c	1 b
	ראה	TO SEE	907b	4
	שמע	HEAR	1033d	1 e
29 4	בלה	BECOME OLD AND WORN OUT	115a	
	הלך	WALK	236d	1 b
	נעל	SANDAL	653a	
	על	UPON	758d	4 2a
	שלמה	GARMENT	971b	
29 5	אנכי	I	59b	
	אנכי	I	59c	
	יהוה	YAHWEH	219a	2 2b b
	שכר	INTOXICATING DRINK	1016c	
29 6	חשבון	HESHBON	363d	
	נגח	SMITE	646b	3
	עוג	OG	728b	
29 7	גדי	GADITE	151d	
	לקח	TAKE	543a	4 c
	מנשי	MANASSITES	586d	
	נחלה	PROPERTY	635d	1 b
	ראובני	REUBENITE	910a	
29 8	ברית	COVENANT	136d	2 2c
	שכל	BE PRUDENT	968c	7
	שמר	KEEP	1037a	3 c
29 9	זקן	OLD	278d	2 b
	נצב	STAND	662a	1 a
	שטר	OFFICIAL	1009c	
29 10	גר	SOJOURNER	158b	2
	חטב	CUT OR GATHER WOOD	310a	
	מן	FROM	582a	5 b
	שאב	DRAW	980c	
29 11	אלה	OATH	46d	2
	ברית	COVENANT	137a	3 1
	כרת	CUT	503d	4
	עבר	PASS OVER	718a	5 e
29 12	דבר	SPEAK	181b	3 c
	קום	STAND	879a	5
29 13	אלהים	GOD	44b	4 a
	אלה	OATH	46d	2
	בד	SEPARATION	94c	1 b
	ברית	COVENANT	137a	3 1
	כרת	CUT	503d	4
29 15	אשר	THAT	83b	8 aa
	עבר	PASS OVER	717c	3 a

Ch v.	Heb	Eng	Page	Sec
	קרב	INWARD PART	899b	1 f8
29 16	אבן	STONE	6c	2
	זהב	GOLD	263a	6
	זהב	GOLD	263c	1
	כסף	SILVER	494b	7
	עם	WITH	768b	3 b
	עץ	TREE	782a	2 c
	שקוץ	DETESTED THING	1055a	
29 17	אלהים	GOD	43c	1 d
	הלך	WALK	235a	2 3d 2
	יש	BE	441c	3 a
	לבב	HEART	523d	2 4
	לענה	WORMWOOD	542a	
	עבד	WORK	713b	4 b
	מעם	FROM WITH	768d	A
	פן	LEST	814a	1 b
	פנה	TURN	815b	1 b
	פרה	BEAR FRUIT	826a	2
	ראש	VENOM	912c	1
	משפחה	CLAN	1046d	1 a
	שרש	ROOT	1057d	1
29 18	אלה	OATH	46d	3 a
	ברך	BLESS	139c	
	יש	BE	441c	2
	לבב	HEART	524a	2 7
	לב	HEART	525b	2 6d
	ספה	SWEEP AWAY	705a	2
	מען	PURPOSE	775c	2 1
	צמא	THIRSTY	854d	
	רוה	WATERED	924b	
	שרירות	STUBBORNNESS	1057b	
29 19	אבה	BE WILLING	2c	
	אז	THEN	23a	1 b
	אלה	OATH	46d	3 a
	ישן	SLEEPING	445d	
	מחה	WIPE OUT	562a	2
	סלח	FORGIVE	699b	
	עשן	SMOKE	798c	1 b
	קנאה	ZEAL	888c	3 b
	רבץ	LIE DOWN	918c	
	תחת	UNDERNEATH	1066a	3 2a
29 20	אלה	OATH	46d	3 a
	בדל	BE DIVIDED	95b	2
	ברית	COVENANT	136c	2 2c
	ה	THE	*209a	2 a
	תורה	LAW	436b	2 b2
	מן	OUT OF	579b	2 ac
	ספר	MISSIVE	707b	3 c
	רעה	MISERY	949b	2
29 21	אחר	BEHIND	30b	4 ag
	אחרון	BEHIND	30d	B
	דור	GENERATION	190a	2 c
	תחלאים	DISEASES	316a	
	מן	FROM	581d	4 c
	מכה	SLAUGHTER	647a	4
	נכרי	FOREIGN	648d	1 b
	קום	STAND	878a	4
	רחק	DISTANT	935b	1 a
29 22	אדמה	ADMAH	10a	
	גפרית	BRIMSTONE	172d	
	הפך	TURN	245c	1 b
	מהפכה	OVERTHROW	246b	
	זרע	SOW	281d	1 a
	חמה	RAGE	404d	2 c
	מלח	SALT	571d	
	סדם	SODOM	690a	
	עלה	GO UP	748d	4
	עמרה	GOMORRAH	771d	
	עשב	HERB	793b	
	צביים	ZEBOIIM	840b	
	צמח	SPROUT	855c	1
	שרפה	BURNING	977b	
29 23	גדול	GREAT	153a	3
	חרי	BURNING	354c	
	כה	THUS	462c	
	מה	HOW	554b	4 f
	תחת	INSTEAD	*1066a	2 2b b
29 24	ברית	COVENANT	137a	3 1
	ברית	COVENANT	137b	3 3
	כרת	CUT	503d	4
	עזב	LEAVE	737c	2 d2
	על	UPON	758b	3 a
29 25	חלק	DIVIDE	323c	1
	ידע	KNOW	394a	2
	עבד	WORK	713b	4 b
29 26	בוא	COME	99c	2 a
	חרה	BURN	354a	2
29 27	אדמה	LAND	10a	5
	אחר	ANOTHER	29c	
	יום	DAY	400d	7 h
	חמה	RAGE	404d	2 c
	נתש	PLUCK UP	684c	
	קצף	WRATH	893c	1
	שלך	THROW	1021b	2 b
29 28	תורה	LAW	436b	2 b2
	סתר	HIDE	711c	2
30 1	ברכה	BLESSING	139d	1 b
	לבב	HEART	523d	2 3d
	נדה	THRUST	623b	2
	נתן	PUT	680d	2 b
	פנה	FACE	817c	2 4b g
30 2	שוב	TURN BACK	999d	8
	לבב	HEART	523b	2 2
	נפש	SOUL	661b	0
30 3	מן	OUT OF	579a	2 aa
	פוץ	BE DISPERSED	807b	1 a

Ch v.	Heb	Eng	Page	Sec
	קבץ	GATHER	868a	1
	רחם	LOVE	933c	1
	שבית	CAPTIVITY	986b	1
	שבית	CAPTIVITY	986b	2
	שוב	TURN BACK	998c	8
30 4	לקח	TAKE	543c	6
	נדח	BANISH	623a	2
	קבץ	GATHER	868a	1
	קצה	END	892b	1
	שם	THERE	1027c	4a
	שמי	HEAVENS	1030a	1a
30 5	יטב	DO GOOD TO	405d	2
	רבה	BECOME MANY	915b	
	רבה	BECOME MANY	915c	1a
30 6	זרע	SOWING	283a	4g
	חיים	LIFE	313b	2
	לבב	HEART	523b	22
	לבב	HEART	524a	26d
	מול	CIRCUMCIZE	557d	
	נפש	SOUL	661b	0
	מען	PURPOSE	775a	1a
30 7	אלה	OATH	46d	3a
	נתן	PUT	680c	2b
	על	UPON	756c	27a b
	רדף	PURSUE	922d	1f
30 8	עשה	DO	793d	1 1a 1
	שוב	TURN BACK	997c	3b
30 9	אדמה	GROUND	9c	1
	בטן	WOMB	106a	3
	טוב	A GOOD THING	375a	1
	טובה	WELFARE	375d	1
	יתר	SHOW EXCESS	451c	3
	פרי	FRUIT	826b	2
	שוש	REJOICE	965b	1
	שוב	TURN BACK	998b	8
30 10	חקה	SOMETHING PRE-SCRIBED	350b	2d
	חקה	SOMETHING PRE-SCRIBED	350b	2e
	תורה	LAW	436b	2b2
	לבב	HEART	523b	22
	נפש	SOUL	661b	0
	ספר	MISSIVE	707b	3c
30 11	פלא	BE SURPASSING	810c	1
	מצוה	COMMANDMENT	846b	2a
	רחק	DISTANT	935c	1a
30 12	ו	AND	252b	1b
	ל	TO	515c	5hc
	לא	NOT	519b	1b
	מי	WHO	566d	Fc
	עלה	GO UP	748b	1c
	שמע	HEAR	1034a	1a
30 13	ו	AND	252b	1b
	ל	TO	515c	5hc
	לא	NOT	519b	1bb
	מי	WHO	566d	Fc
	עבר	PASS OVER	717a	1a2
	עבר	REGION ACROSS	719b	1
	שמע	HEAR	1034a	1a
30 14	דבר	WORD	182d	1 2b
	לבב	HEART	523b	21
	מאד	EXCEEDINGLY	547b	2a
	פה	MOUTH	805a	2a
	קרב	NEAR	898c	2f
	קרב	NEAR	898c	2g
30 15	ה	THE	208b	1 ha
	חיים	LIFE	313b	2
	טוב	A GOOD THING	375a	4
	מות	DEATH	560c	1
	נתן	PUT	680d	2b
	פנה	FACE	817c	24b g
	רע	EVIL	948d	3
30 16	ברך	BLESS	139a	2a
	דרך	WAY	204a	6ec
	חיה	LIVE	311a	1a
	חקה	SOMETHING PRE-SCRIBED	350a	2d
	חקה	SOMETHING PRE-SCRIBED	350b	2e
	מצוה	COMMANDMENT	846d	2b2
	רבה	BECOME MANY	915a	1a
	משפט	JUDGMENT	1049a	4
30 17	לבב	HEART	523b	24
	נדח	THRUST	623a	4
	עבד	WORK	713b	4b
	פנה	TURN	815b	1a
30 18	אבד	PERISH	1c	1
	ארך	BE LONG	73d	1a
	ירש	TAKE POSSESSION	439c	1a
30 19	ארץ	EARTH	76a	1b
	בחר	CHOOSE	104a	1b
	ברכה	BLESSING	139d	1b
	ה	THE	208b	1 ha
	ו	AND	254c	4
	זרע	SOWING	283a	4g
	חיים	LIFE	313b	2
	מות	DEATH	560c	1
	נתן	PUT	680d	2b
	עוד	BEAR WITNESS	730a	24b g
	פנה	FACE	817c	24b g
30 20	ארך	LENGTH	73d	B
	דבק	CLING	179d	2a
	הוא	HE, SHE, IT	*216a	3a
	חיים	LIFE	313b	2
31 2	בוא	COME	97d	1a
	בן	SON	121d	9a
	זה	THIS	261a	2bb
	יצא	GO OUT	424a	3
	ירדן	JORDAN	434c	
	עוד	STILL	729a	1 ab
31 3	עשרים	TWENTY	797d	1 2d
	יהושע	JOSHUA	221c	1
	ירש	TAKE POSSESSION	439c	1b
	עבר	PASS OVER	718a	5c
	פנה	FACE	818a	2 5a e
31 4	עוג	OG	728b	
31 5	נתן	GIVE	679c	1s
	מצוה	COMMANDMENT	846b	2a
31 6	אמץ	BE STRONG	55a	2
	חזק	BE FIRM	304b	1 2c
	ירא	FEAR	431a	1a
	ערץ	CAUSE TO TREM-BLE	792a	2
	רפה	SINK	952a	1
31 7	אמץ	BE STRONG	55a	2
	אמר	SAY	56a	1
	יהושע	JOSHUA	221c	1
	חזק	BE FIRM	304b	1 2c
31 8	חתת	BE SHATTERED	369d	2a
	ירא	FEAR	431a	1a
	רפה	SINK	952a	1
31 9	ארון	CHEST	75c	3f
	בן	SON	121a	1je
	זקן	OLD	278d	2b
	תורה	LAW	436b	2b2
	כהן	PRIEST	463d	5
	לוי	LEVI	532c	1c
31 10	חג	FESTIVAL-GATHER-ING	291a	1b2
	מועד	APPOINTED TIME	417c	1b
	סכה	THICKET	697d	3
	שמטה	A LETTING DROP	1030d	
	שנה	YEAR	1040b	
31 11	אזן	EAR	24a	2a
	בחר	CHOOSE	104a	2
	תורה	LAW	436b	2b2
	נגד	IN FRONT	617b	1aa
	פנה	FACE	816d	2a
	קרא	CALL	895c	4a
	ראה	TO SEE	908b	1b
31 12	גר	SOJOURNER	158b	2
	טף	CHILDREN	382a	
	ירא	FEAR	431c	3b
	תורה	LAW	436b	2b2
	למד	LEARN	540d	
	קהל	ASSEMBLE AS	875a	2
31 13	חי	ALIVE	312a	1b
	ירא	FEAR	431c	3b
	למד	LEARN	540d	
	עבר	PASS OVER	717a	1a1
31 14	אהל	TENT	14a	3
	יהושע	JOSHUA	221c	1
	יום	DAY	399b	4a
	מועד	TENT OF MEETING	418a	5
	יצב	STATION ONESELF	426b	A
	קרב	COME NEAR	897c	2
	אהל	TENT	14a	3
31 15	פתח	OPENING	835d	
31 16	אלהים	GOD	43c	1d
	ברית	COVENANT	137b	33
	הנה	BEHOLD	244b	Bb
	זנה	COMMIT FORNICA-TION	275d	2
	כרת	CUT	503d	4
	נכר	FOREIGNNESS	648c	1
	עזב	LEAVE	737c	2d1
	פרר	BREAK	830b	1b
	שבב	LEAVE DOWN	1012c	4b
31 17	אלהים	GOD	44d	4c
	חרה	BURN	354a	2
	יום	DAY	400d	7g
	ל	TO	518a	7bf
	מצא	FIND	593c	3e
	סתר	HIDE	711d	2c
	עזב	LEAVE	737c	2
	על	UPON	758b	3b
	צרה	DISTRESS	865b	
	קרב	INWARD PART	899a	1f1
	רב	MUCH	913a	1b
	רעה	MISERY	949a	1
31 18	אלהים	GOD	43c	1d
	יום	DAY	400d	7g
	סתר	HIDE	711d	2a
	על	UPON	754b	2 1f b
	פנה	TURN	815b	1a
	רעה	MISERY	949b	3
31 19	למד	LEARN	540d	
	עד	WITNESS	729c	1
	שום	TO PLACE	963a	1a
	שירה	SONG	1010c	
31 20	אלהים	GOD	43c	1d
	ברית	COVENANT	137b	33
	דבש	HONEY	185b	
	דשן	BE FAT	206a	
	זוב	FLOW	264d	2
	חלב	MILK	316c	A 4
	נאץ	CONTEMN	611a	
	עבד	WORK	713b	4b
	פנה	TURN	815b	1a
	פרר	BREAK	830b	1b
	שבע	SATISFIED	959b	1a
31 21	זרע	SOWING	283a	4g
	טרם	NOT YET	302c	2
	יצר	PURPOSE	428a	4
	מן	OUT OF	579a	2aa
	מצא	FIND	593c	3e
	עד	WITNESS	729c	1
	ענה	ANSWER	773a	3a
	צרה	DISTRESS	865b	
	רעה	MISERY	949a	1
	שבע	SWEAR	989c	2
	שירה	SONG	1010c	
	שכח	FORGET	1013b	
31 22	למד	LEARN	540d	
	שירה	SONG	1010c	
31 23	אמץ	BE STRONG	55a	2
	יהושע	JOSHUA	221c	1
31 24	היה	COME TO PASS	224c	2 a1 aa
	תורה	LAW	436b	2b2
31 25	ארון	CHEST	75c	3f
	לוי	LEVITE	532d	3 1a
31 26	ארון	CHEST	75c	3f
	תורה	LAW	436b	2b2
	ספר	MISSIVE	707b	3c
	עד	WITNESS	729c	1
	צד	SIDE	841a	
31 27	שום	TO PLACE	963c	1d
	אף	ALSO	65b	3
	חי	ALIVE	312a	1b
	מות	DEATH	560d	1
	מרה	BE REBELLIOUS	598b	
	מרי	REBELLION	598b	
	עוד	STILL	729b	2aa
	עם	WITH	767d	1d
	ערף	BACK OF NECK	791c	1
	קשה	SEVERE	904d	3
31 28	אזן	EAR	24a	2a
	דבר	SPEAK	181c	4b
	זקן	OLD	278d	2b
	עוד	BEAR WITNESS	730a	
	קהל	ASSEMBLE AS	875a	2
	שטר	OFFICIAL	1009c	
31 29	אחרית	END	31b	B
	דרך	WAY	203c	6b
	יד	HAND	389a	1a
	כעס	VEX	495a	2
	כעס	VEX	495a	2
	מות	DEATH	560d	1
	מעשה	DEED	795d	1a2
	צוה	CHARGE	845d	2a
	קרא	ENCOUNTER	897a	2
	רע	EVIL	948c	0b
	שחת	GO TO RUIN	1008c	2
31 30	אזן	EAR	24a	2a
	דבר	SPEAK	181c	4b
	דבר	WORD	182d	2 1a
	קהל	ASSEMBLY	874d	2a
	שירה	SONG	1010c	
	תמן	BE FINISHED	1070b	1
32 1	אזן	HEAR	24b	1
	אמר	WORD	57a	1
	ארץ	EARTH	76a	1
	פה	MOUTH	805a	2a
32 2	אמרה	UTTERANCE	57b	
	דשא	GRASS	206a	
	ה	THE	208a	1f
	ה	THE	208a	1f
	טל	NIGHT-MIST	378c	
	לקח	TEACHING	544b	2
	מטר	RAIN	564d	
	נזל	DISTIL	633d	2
	ערף	DRIP	791d	
	עשב	HERB	793b	
	שעירים	RAIN	973c	
32 3	גדל	GREATNESS	152d	2b
	יהב	ASCRIBE	396d	4
	קרא	CALL	895c	3b
32 4	אין	NOT	34d	4b
	אל	GOD	42d	6c
	אליצור	ELIZUR	45d	
	אמונה	FIRMNESS	53c	3b
	דרך	WAY	204a	6eb
	ישר	STRAIGHT	449a	3a
	עול	INJUSTICE	732c	
	פעל	DOING	821c	1a
	צדיק	JUST	843a	1d
	צור	ROCK	849d	2a
	משפט	JUDGMENT	1048d	2
	תמים	SOUND	1071a	
32 5	בן	SON	120b	1c
	דור	GENERATION	190a	2c
	לא	NOT	519c	2d
	מום	BLEMISH	548d	2b
	עקש	TWISTED	786a	
	פתלתל	TORTUOUS	836d	
	שחת	GO TO RUIN	1008a	2
32 6	אב	FATHER	3b	2
	הל	INTERROG PART	210b	
	זה	THIS	260c	1a
	חכם	WISE	314d	5
	כון	ESTABLISH	466d	1b
	נבל	FOOLISH	614d	
	עשה	DO	794b	2 1b
	קנה	ACQUIRE	888d	1a
32 7	בין	DISCERN	106d	3a
	דור	PERIOD	189d	1a
	ו	AND	*253b	1 ib
	זכר	REMEMBER	269d	1 1d

DEUTERONOMY

Ch v.	Heb	Eng	Page	Sec
	זקן	OLD	278c	2 a
	יום	DAY	399c	5 c
	עולם	LONG DURATION	762d	1 a
	שאל	ASK	981d	2 a
	שנה	YEAR	1040b	
32 8	גבולה	BORDER	148b	
	ל	TO	516b	5 jb
	נחל	TAKE AS A POSSESSION	635d	1 b
	נצב	STAND	662c	4
	עזר	HELP	740b	
	עליון	HIGHEST	751b	1
	פרד	DIVIDE	825c	1
32 9	חבל	CORD	286d	3
	חלק	PORTION	324b	3 a
	נחלה	PROPERTY	635b	1 e
	יעקב	JACOB	785a	2
32 10	אישון	PUPIL	36b	
	בין	DISCERN	107a	
	מדבר	WILDERNESS	184d	2
	ילל	HOWLING	410b	
	ישימון	WASTE	445c	B
	כון	ESTABLISH	467a	4
	מצא	FIND	593b	3 a
	נצר	GUARD	665d	2
	סבב	SURROUND	686b	1
	תהו	FORMLESSNESS	1062c	1
32 11	אב	FATHER	3b	2
	אברה	PINION	7c	
	גוזל	YOUNG OF BIRDS	160a	
	כ	LIKE	454a	1 c2
	כנף	WING	489c	1 a
	לקח	TAKE	543c	5
	נשא	LIFT	671b	2 c
	נשר	EAGLE	677a	
	עוף	FLY	733c	1 b
	עור	ROUSE ONESELF	735b	
	פרש	SPREAD OUT	831a	1
	קן	NEST	890a	1
	רחף	HOVER	934b	1
32 12	אל	GOD	42c	3
	בדד	ISOLATION	94d	
	נחה	LEAD	635a	
	נכר	FOREIGNNESS	648c	1
32 13	במה	HIGH PLACE	119a	2 a
	דבש	HONEY	185b	
	חלמיש	FLINT	321d	
	ינק	NURSE	413c	
	תנובה	FRUIT	626c	
	סלע	CRAG	701a	1
	צור	ROCK	849c	1 a
	צור	ROCK	849c	1 a
	רכב	RIDE	938d	1
	שדה	HIGH PLACES	961a	
	שדי	FIELD	961b	1
	שמן	OIL	1032b	2 b
32 14	איל	RAM	17d	1
	בן	SON	121b	1 jn
	בקר	CATTLE	*133a	
	בקר	CATTLE	133c	2
	בשן	BASHAN	143c	
	דם	BLOOD	197d	4
	חלב	MILK	316b	A
	חלב	FAT	316d	2 a
	חלב	FAT	317a	3
	חמאה	CURD	326a	
	חמר	WINE	330c	
	חמה	WHEAT	334d	
	כליה	KIDNEYS	480c	1 b
	כר	LAMB	503a	
	עם	WITH	767b	1 a
	ענב	GRAPE	772a	
	עתוד	HE-GOAT	800d	
	צאן	SMALL CATTLE	838b	1 a3
32 15	אלה	GOD	43a	2
	בעט	KICK	127a	
	ישועה	DELIVERANCE	447b	3
	ישרון	JESHURUN	449c	
	כשה	BE GORGED	505b	
	נבל	BE SENSELESS	614c	
	נטש	FORSAKE	643d	2
	נשה	FORGET	*674d	
	עבה	BE THICK	716a	
	עשה	DO	794b	2 1b
	צור	ROCK	849d	2 a
	שמן	GROW FAT	1031d	
32 16	זור	BE A STRANGER	266c	2 c
	כעס	VEX	495a	
	קנא	BE ZEALOUS	888c	4
	קנא	BE ZEALOUS	888d	
	קנא	BE ZEALOUS	888d	
	תועבה	ABOMINATION	1073a	1 b
32 17	אלה	GOD	43a	1
	אלהים	GOD	44a	4 a
	זבח	SLAUGHTER FOR SACRIFICE	257c	1 3
	חדש	NEW	294b	A
	ידע	KNOW	394a	2
	לא	NOT	519c	2 d
	מן	FROM	581d	4 c
	קרב	NEAR	898d	3
	שער	BRISTLE	972c	
	שער	BE AQUAINTED WITH	973b	
	שד	DEMON	994a	
	שדי	ALMIGHTY	995a	
32 18	אל	GOD	42d	6 f
	חול	WHIRL	297b	2
	ילד	BEAR	408c	1 c
	ילד	BEGET	*408c	2 a
	צור	ROCK	849d	2 a
	שיח	FORGET	1009d	
32 19	כעס	ANGER	495b	2
	מן	ON ACCOUNT OF	580b	2 f
32 20	אחרית	END	31a	B
	אמן	TRUSTING	53c	1
	בן	SON	120b	1 c
	דור	GENERATION	190a	3
	תהפכה	PERVERSITY	246c	
	סתר	HIDE	711d	2 c
	ראה	TO SEE	907b	5 a
32 21	אל	GOD	42d	6 d
	הבל	VAPOUR	211a	2
	כעס	VEX	495a	2
	כעס	BE ANGRY	495a	
	לא	NOT	519b	1 bb
	לא	NOT	519c	2 d
	לא	NOT	520b	4 ac
	נבל	FOOLISH	614d	
	קנא	BE ZEALOUS	888c	4
	קנא	BE ZEALOUS	888d	
	הר	MOUNTAIN	250d	1 m
32 22	יבל	PRODUCE	385b	
	מוסד	FOUNDATION	414c	
	יקד	BE BURNING	428d	
	יקד	BE KINDLED	428d	
	להט	SET ABLAZE	529d	
	קדח	KINDLE	869b	1
	שאול	SHEOL	982d	1
	תחתי	LOWER	1066c	
32 23	חץ	ARROW	346c	2
	יסף	ADD	415a	1
	כלה	FINISH	478c	2 b
	ספה	SWEEP AWAY	705a	
	רעה	MISERY	949a	1
32 24	בהמה	BEAST	97a	3
	זחל	SHRINK BACK	267d	
	חמה	POISON	404c	1 b
	לחם	EAT	536d	
	מזה	SUCK OUT	*561a	
	מזה	EMPTY	561a	
	מרירי	BITTER	601b	
	מת	MALE	*607b	3 b
	עם	WITH	767b	1 a
	עפר	DRY EARTH	779d	1 a
	קבב	DESTRUCTION	881c	
	רעב	FAMINE	944b	1
	רשף	FLAME	958b	2
	שלח	SEND	1019a	2 d
	שן	TOOTH	1042a	1 b
32 25	אימה	TERROR	34a	
	איש	MAN	36a	
	בחור	YOUNG MAN	104c	2
	בתולה	VIRGIN	143d	
	חדר	CHAMBER	293d	
	חוץ	THE OUTSIDE	299d	1 bd
	חרג	QUAKE	*353a	
	ינק	SUCK	413b	
	עם	WITH	767b	1 a
	שיבה	OLD AGE	966d	1
	שכל	BE BEREAVED	1013d	1
32 26	אנוש	MAN	60d	3
	זכר	REMEMBRANCE	271b	1 a
	פאה	CLEAVE IN PIECES	802a	
	פוץ	BE DISPERSED	807b	1 a
	שבת	CEASE	992a	2
32 27	גור	DREAD	159a	1
	יד	HAND	*389d	1 e1
	כעס	ANGER	495b	2
	לא	NOT	518d	1 ac
	לולא	IF NOT	530c	B
	נכר	TREAT AS FOREIGN	649a	
	פעל	DO	821b	1 a
	צר	ADVERSARY	865d	
	רום	BE HIGH	926d	2 b
	פ	ADDENDA ET CORRIGENDA	1126b	
32 28	אבד	PERISH	1d	2
	תבונה	UNDERSTANDING	108b	2
	גוי	NATION	156d	1 b
	עצה	ADVICE	420a	
32 29	אחרית	END	31a	B
	בין	DISCERN	106d	3 b
	חכם	BE WISE	314c	
	לו	IF	530a	1 a
	שכל	BE PRUDENT	968b	2
32 30	איכה	IN WHAT MANNER	32d	1
	אלף	THOUSAND	49a	1 a
	אם	IF	50a	1 a4 c
	כי	THAT	472b	1 da
	מכר	SELL	569b	
	נוס	FLEE	631a	1
	סגר	DELIVER UP	689c	1
	צור	ROCK	849d	2 a
	רבבה	MULTITUDE	914b	
	רדף	PURSUE	922c	1 b
32 31	פליל	JUDGE	813c	
	צור	ROCK	849d	2 a
	צור	ROCK	849d	2 b
32 32	אשכול	CLUSTER	79a	1
	גפן	VINE	172c	
	מרורה	BITTERNESS	601a	4
	סדם	SODOM	690a	
	עמרה	GOMORRAH	771d	
	ענב	GRAPE	772a	
	ראש	VENOM	912c	1
	שדמה	FIELD	995b	
32 33	חמה	POISON	404c	1 b
	יין	WINE	406c	B
	אכזר	CRUEL	470a	
	פתן	COBRA	837a	
	ראש	VENOM	912c	2
	תנין	SERPENT	1072c	1
32 34	חתם	SEAL	367d	2
	כמס	STORE UP	485a	
	עם	WITH	768b	3 b
32 35	איד	DISTRESS	15d	3
	חוש	HASTE	301d	
	ל	TO	511c	1 gb
	מוט	SLIP	556d	
	נקם	VENGEANCE	668b	1
	עת	TIME	773c	1 d
	עתיד	READY	800c	3
	קרב	NEAR	898b	3
	רגל	FOOT	919d	1 a
	שלם	RECOMPENCE	1024a	
32 36	אזל	GO	23c	
	אפס	NON-EXISTENCE	67b	2 b
	דין	JUDGE	192b	1
	נחם	BE SORRY	637b	i
	עבד	SLAVE	714a	3
	עזב	LEAVE	737d	3
32 37	אי	WHERE	32b	1 a
	איה	WHERE	32c	
	אלהים	GOD	44d	4 c
	חסה	SEEK REFUGE	340a	
	צור	ROCK	849d	2 b
	צור	ROCK	849d	2 a
32 38	אכל	EAT	37c	1
	זבח	SACRIFICE	257c	1 2
	חלב	FAT	317a	2 b
	נסיך	LIBATION	651a	1
	סתרה	SHELTER	712c	
	על	UPON	755d	2 5
32 39	אלהים	GOD	44a	4 a
	הוא	HE, SHE, IT	216c	5
	חיה	LIVE	311c	3
	מות	DIE	560b	2
	מחץ	SHATTER	563c	
	עם	WITH	768b	3 d
	רפא	HEAL	950d	2 a
32 40	אנכי	I	59b	
	חי	ALIVE	311d	1 a
	יד	HAND	389c	1 d
	נשא	LIFT	670b	1 b 1
	עולם	LONG DURATION	762b	1 c
	שמי	HEAVENS	1030a	1 b
32 41	אחז	GRASP	28b	
	ברק	LIGHTNING	140c	2
	חרב	SWORD	352c	1 d
	חרב	SWORD	352d	1 j
	נקם	VENGEANCE	668b	1
	צר	ADVERSARY	865d	
	שן	HATE	971d	2
	שוב	TURN BACK	999c	4 b
	שנן	SHARPEN	1041d	
	משפט	JUDGMENT	1048c	1 f
32 42	אכל	EAT	37c	4
	בשר	FLESH	142c	1 b
	דם	BLOOD	196c	2 c
	דם	BLOOD	197b	2 n
	חץ	ARROW	346c	2
	חרב	SWORD	352d	1 g
	מן	OUT OF	579b	2 bb
	פרע	LEADER	828c	
	שביה	CAPTIVITY	986a	2
	שכר	BE DRUNK	1016b	
32 43	אדמה	LAND	10a	5
	דם	BLOOD	196d	2 f
	כפר	COVER OVER	497c	2 b
	נקם	AVENGE	668a	1 a
	נקם	VENGEANCE	668b	1
	עבד	SLAVE	714a	3
	צר	ADVERSARY	865d	
	רנן	GIVE A RINGING CRY	943c	
32 44	שוב	TURN BACK	999c	4 b
	דבר	SPEAK	181c	4 b
	דבר	WORD	182d	2 1a
	יהושוע	JOSHUA	221c	1
	הושע	HOSHEA	448a	1
	שירה	SONG	1010c	
32 46	תורה	LAW	436b	2 b2
	לב	HEART	523d	2 3c
	עד	BEAR WITNESS	730a	3
	שום	TO PLACE	963c	2 b
32 47	ארך	BE LONG	73d	1
	חיים	LIFE	313b	2
	לא	NOT	519b	1 bb
	מן	THAN	582d	6 d
	עבר	PASS OVER	717a	1 a1
	עברים	ABARIM	720d	
32 48	ריק	EMPTY	938a	2
	עברים	ABARIM	720d	
	עצם	BONE	783a	3
32 49	אחזה	POSSESSION	28c	
	אנכי	I	59b	

Ch v.	Heb	Eng	Page	Sec
	הר	MOUNTAIN	249b	1 a
	הר	MOUNTAIN	249b	1 a
	זה	THIS	261a	2 bb
	יריחו	JERICHO	437d	
	מואב	MOAB	555d	2 b
	נבו	NEBO	612d	2
	עברים	ABARIM	720d	
	פנה	FACE	818d	27a d
32 50	אסף	GATHER	62d	2 a
	הר	HOR	246d	1
	הר	HOR	246d	1
	הר	MOUNTAIN	249b	1 a
	הר	MOUNTAIN	249b	1 a
	עם	KINSMAN	769b	
	עם	KINSMAN	769b	
32 51	מי	WATER	565b	1 a
	מעל	ACT TREACHEROUSLY	591b	2 b
	על	UPON	758b	3 a
	צן	ZIN	856c	
	קדש	BE SET APART	873b	3 a
	קדש	KADESH	873d	1
	מריבה	MERIBAH	937b	2
32 52	אנכי	I	59b	
	נגד	IN FRONT	617d	2 ca
33 1	איש	MAN	36a	
	אלהים	GOD	43d	3 b
	ברך	BLESS	139a	3
	ברכה	BLESSING	139d	1 a
	זה	THIS	261a	3
33 2	אש	FIRE	77d	6
	אתה	COME	87b	
	דת	LAW	206d	
	זרח	RISE	280b	1 b
	חרב	HOREB	*352a	
	יפע	SHINE OUT	422a	1
	סיני	SINAI	696a	
	פארן	PARAN	803a	
	קדש	KADESH	873d	1
	רבבה	MULTITUDE	914b	
	מריבה	MERIBAH	937b	2
	שעיר	SEIR	973a	1 a
33 3	אף	ALSO	64d	1
	דברת	WORD	184c	
	חבב	LOVE	285c	
	נשא	LIFT	671c	3 f
	עם	PEOPLE	766c	2 b
	קדוש	HOLY	872d	2 b
	רגל	FOOT	919d	1 f
	תכה	ASSEMBLE	1067a	
33 4	תורה	LAW	436a	2 b1
	מורשה	POSSESSION	440c	
	משה	MOSES	602c	
	צוה	GIVE CHARGE TO	845c	1 b
	קהלה	ASSEMBLY	875a	
33 5	אסף	GATHER	63a	
	יחד	ALTOGETHER	403b	2 b
	יחדו	TOGETHER	*403c	B
	ישרון	JESHURUN	449c	
	מלך	KING	573b	3
	שבט	TRIBE	987a	2 a
33 6	מת	MALE	607b	2 a
	מספר	NUMBER	709a	1 a
	ראובן	REUBEN	910a	2
33 7	יהודה	JUDAH	397b	12
	ל	TO	514b	5 fa
	מן	FROM	578b	1
	עזר	HELP	740d	2
	צר	ADVERSARY	865d	
	ריב	STRIVE	936c	1
	שמע	HEAR	1034a	2 a
33 8	אורים	URIM	22a	
	איש	MAN	36a	
	חסיד	KIND	339d	2 b
	לוי	LEVI	532c	2
	מי	WATER	565b	1 a
	נסה	TEST	650b	3 a
	מסה	MASSAH	650c	
	ריב	STRIVE	936c	3
	מריבה	MERIBAH	937b	2
	תם	INTEGRITY	1070d	4
33 9	אם	MOTHER	51d	1
	אמר	SAY	56a	1
	אמרה	UTTERANCE	57b	
	ברית	COVENANT	137d	3 2
	ידע	KNOW	394b	2
	נכר	RECOGNIZE	648b	3
	נצר	KEEP	665d	3
	ראה	TO SEE	907b	3
33 10	אף	NOSE	60a	1 a
	ירה	DIRECT	435b	5 b
	תורה	LAW	436a	2 b1
	תורה	LAW	436c	3 b3
	כליל	WHOLE	483a	2 b
	יעקב	JACOB	785a	2
	קטורה	SMOKE OF SACRIFICE	882c	
	שום	TO PLACE	963a	1 a
	ישראל	ISRAEL	975c	2 a1
	משפט	JUDGMENT	1048d	3
33 11	בלת	NOT	*117a	4 a
	ברך	BLESS	139a	1 b
	חיל	STRENGTH	299a	3
	מחץ	SHATTER	563c	
	מתנים	LOINS	608b	2 a
	פעל	DOING	821c	1 c
	קום	STAND	878a	2
	רצה	BE PLEASED WITH	953b	2
	שן	HATE	971d	1
33 12	בטח	SECURITY	105b	
	בנימין	BENJAMIN	122d	1
	חפף	ENCLOSE	342b	
	ידיד	BELOVED	391d	1
	יום	DAY	400c	7 f
	כתף	SHOULDER	509b	1 a
	ל	TO	514b	5 fa
	נסע	SET OUT	652b	2 a
	שכן	SETTLE DOWN	1015a	1 a
33 13	ברך	BLESS	139b	2 b
	טל	NIGHT-MIST	378c	
	יוסף	JOSEPH	415d	1
	ל	TO	514b	5 fa
	מגד	EXCELLENCE	550c	
	רבץ	LIE DOWN	918c	
	שמי	HEAVENS	1029d	1 a
	תהום	DEEP	1062d	1
	תחת	UNDENEATH	*1065b	1
	נגד	STREAM	*1102a	
33 14	תבואה	PRODUCT	100b	1
	גרש	YIELD	177a	
	ירח	MONTH	437b	2
	מגד	EXCELLENCE	550c	
	שמש	SUN	1039b	1
33 15	גבעה	HILL	149a	3
	גבעה	HILL	149a	3
	הר	MOUNTAIN	250b	1 c
	מגד	EXCELLENCE	550c	
	עולם	LONG DURATION	762a	1 d
	קדם	FRONT	869d	2 a
33 16	יוסף	JOSEPH	415d	1 c
	ל	TO	511c	1 gb
	מגד	EXCELLENCE	550c	
	מלא	THAT WHICH FILLS	571b	3
	נזיר	CONSECRATED	634c	1
	סנה	BLACKBERRY BUSH	702d	
	קדקד	HEAD	869b	
	רצון	GOODWILL	953c	1 a
	שכן	SETTLE DOWN	1015b	2 c
33 17	אפס	END	67a	1
	אפרים	EPHRAIM	68b	2
	בכור	FIRST-BORN	114b	2 a
	הדר	SPLENDOUR	214b	2
	יחדו	TOGETHER	403c	B
	מנשה	MANASSEH	586c	1 b1 b
	נגח	PUSH	618c	
	קרן	HORN	901d	2
	קרן	HORN	901d	1 a
	ראם	WILD OX	910b	
	רבבה	MULTITUDE	914b	
	שור	A HEAD OF CATTLE	1004b	
33 18	זבולן	ZEBULUN	259b	2
	יששכר	ISSACHAR	441a	1
	שמח	REJOICE	970b	1 a
33 19	זבח	SACRIFICE	257c	11
	חול	SAND	297c	
	טמן	HIDE	380c	1
	ספן	COVER	706a	
	צדק	RIGHTNESS	841c	1
	קרא	CALL	895d	5 c
	שפע	ABUNDANCE	1051a	
33 20	אף	ALSO	64d	1
	ברך	BLESS	138d	2 b
	גד	GAD	151c	1 b
	זרוע	ARM	283d	1 a
	טרף	TEAR	382d	
	לבא	LION	522d	
	קדקד	HEAD	869b	
	רחב	BE LARGE	931c	2
	שכן	SETTLE DOWN	1015a	1 b
33 21	אתה	COME	87b	
	חלקה	PORTION OF GROUND	324c	2
	חקק	CUT IN	349b	A
	ספן	COVER	706a	
	צדקה	RIGHTEOUSNESS	842a	1 b
	ראה	TO SEE	907d	6 g
	ראשית	BEGINNING	912b	2
	משפט	JUDGMENT	1048d	3
33 22	אריה	LION	71d	
	גור	WHELP	158d	1
	דן	DAN	192d	2
	זנק	LEAP	276c	
	נגד	STREAM	*1102a	
33 23	ברכה	BLESSING	139d	1 b
	דרום	SOUTH	205a	
	ים	SEA	411a	4
	מלא	FULL	571a	
	נפתלי	NAPHTALI	836d	2 a
	רצון	GOODWILL	953c	1 a
	שבע	SATISFIED	960a	1 a
33 24	אשר	ASHER	81b	2
	ברך	BLESS	138d	2 b
	טבל	DIP	371b	1
	מן	THAN	582c	6 b
	רצה	BE PLEASED WITH	953b	1 b
	שמן	OIL	1032b	2 b
33 25	ברזל	IRON	137c	3
	דבא	REST	179a	
	יום	DAY	399b	4 a
	מנעל	BOLT	653b	
33 26	אל	GOD	42d	6 f
	ב	IN	89a	17b
	גאוה	MAJESTY	144d	2
	ישרון	JESHURUN	449c	
	עזר	HELP	740d	2
	רכב	RIDE	938d	2
	רכב	RIDE	938d	2
	שחק	DUST	1007a	2
	שמי	HEAVENS	1030a	2 a
33 27	איב	BE HOSTILE TO	33c	
	אלהים	GOD	44c	4 bb
	גרש	DRIVE OUT	177d	
	זרוע	ARM	284a	1 c
	מענה	DEN	733b	2
	עולם	LONG DURATION	762c	2 c
	קדם	FRONT	869d	2 a
	תחת	UNDENEATH	1065b	1
33 28	אל	TO	40c	8
	אף	ALSO	64d	
	בדד	ISOLATION	94d	
	בדד	ISOLATION	*95a	
	בטח	SECURITY	105b	
	דגן	CORN	186c	
	טל	NIGHT-MIST	378c	
	תירוש	NEW WINE	440d	
	עין	SPRING	745b	
	ערף	DRIP	791d	
	שכן	SETTLE DOWN	1015a	1 a
	שמי	HEAVENS	1029d	1 a
	שמי	HEAVENS	1030b	2 a
33 29	אשר	HAPPINESS	81a	
	ב	IN	89d	3 2c
	במה	HIGH PLACE	119b	2
	גאוה	MAJESTY	144d	2
	דרך	TREAD	202a	2
	ישע	BE DELIVERED	446b	2
	כחש	BE DECEIVED	471a	
	עזר	HELP	740c	1
34 1	דן	DAN	193a	3
	הר	MOUNTAIN	249b	1 a
	יריחו	JERICHO	437d	
	מואב	MOAB	555d	2 b
	נבו	NEBO	612d	2
	פנה	FACE	818d	27a d
	פסגה	PISGAH	820a	
	ראה	TO SEE	908d	1 a2
34 2	אחרון	BEHIND	30d	A
	ארץ	EARTH	76a	2
	ים	SEA	410d	1
	מנשה	MANASSEH	586c	1 b1 b
	נפתלי	NAPHTALI	837a	2 b
34 3	בקעה	PLAIN	132c	2
	יריחו	JERICHO	437d	
	יריחו	JERICHO	*437d	
	כבר	ROUND	503b	1
	נגב	SOUTH-COUNTRY	616b	1 a
	צער	ZOAR	858d	
	תמר	PALM-TREE	1071c	
34 4	זרע	SOWING	282c	4 b
	עבר	PASS OVER	717a	1 a2
	עין	EYE	744a	1 a
	ראה	TO SEE	908d	
	ראה	TO SEE	908d	1 a2
34 5	מואב	MOAB	555d	2 b
	משה	MOSES	602d	
	עבד	SLAVE	714a	3
34 6	ביתפעור	BETH-PEOR	112c	
	גיא	VALLEY	161b	
	יום	DAY	401b	7 l
	מואב	MOAB	555d	2 b
	מול	IN FRONT OF	*557c	2
	קבר	BURY	868c	
	צברה	GRAVE	869a	1
34 7	כהה	GROW DIM	462c	
	לח	FRESHNESS	535a	
	לחום	BOWELS	*536a	
	נום	ESCAPE	630d	3
	עין	EYE	744a	1 a
34 8	אבל	MOURNING	5c	
	בכה	WEEP	113c	4
	בכי	WEEPING	113d	
	מואב	MOAB	555d	2 b
	תמם	BE FINISHED	1070b	2
34 9	יהושע	JOSHUA	221c	1
	חכמה	WISDOM	315b	2
	מלא	FULL	571a	
	סמך	LEAN	702a	1 a
	רוח	BREATH	925c	6
34 10	משה	MOSES	602c	
	נביא	PROPHET	611c	1
	עוד	STILL	729b	1 b
	פנה	FACE	815d	11c
	קום	STAND	878a	4
34 11	אות	SIGN	16d	4
	מופת	WONDER	69a	1
	ל	TO	514b	5 fb
34 12	חזק	STRONG	305c	1 b
	יד	HAND	390b	2
	מורא	FEAR	432b	4
	ל	TO	514b	5 fb
40 9	משה	ANOINT	603b	3

JOSHUA

Ch v.	Heb	Eng	Page	Sec
1 1	יהושע	JOSHUA	221c	1
	משה	MOSES	602d	

109

Ch v.	Heb	Eng	Page	Sec
	עבד	SLAVE	714a	3
	שרת	SERVE	1058a	1 c
1 2	זה	THIS	261a	2 bb
	ירדן	JORDAN	434c	
	עבד	SLAVE	714a	3
1 3	דרך	TREAD	202a	2
	מדרך	TREADING-PLACE	*204a	
	היה	BE	227b	3 4d a
	כף	SOLE OF FOOT	496d	3
1 4	מבוא	ENTERING	99d	2
	גבול	BORDER	147d	1 a
	זה	THIS	261a	2 bb
	חתי	HITTITE	366d	2 b
	ים	SEA	410d	1
	לבנון	LEBANON	527a	
	נהר	STREAM	625d	1
	פרת	EUPHRATES	832b	
1 5	חיים	LIFE	313b	1
	יצב	STATION ONESELF	426c	D
	עם	WITH	767c	1 a
	פנה	FACE	817b	2 4b d
	רפה	SINK	952a	1
1 6	אב	FATHER	3c	4 b
	אמץ	BE STRONG	55a	1
	חזק	BE FIRM	304b	1 2c
	נחל	TAKE AS A POSSESSION	635d	1 a
1 7	שבע	SWEAR	989c	2
	אמץ	BE STRONG	55a	1
	אשר	PARTICLE OF RELATION	82c	4 bg
	הלך	WALK	230d	1 1d 3a
	חזק	BE FIRM	304b	1 2c
	ימין	RIGHT HAND	412a	2b
	תורה	LAW	436b	2 b2
	כל	ALL	481c	1 c
	משה	MOSES	602c	
	עבד	SLAVE	714a	3
	רק	ONLY	956c	2 b
	שכל	BE PRUDENT	968c	6
1 8	או	THEN	23a	1 b
	הגה	MUSE	211d	3 a
	יומם	BY DAY	401c	2
	תורה	LAW	436b	2 b2
	מוש	DEPART	559a	
	ספר	MISSIVE	707b	3 c
	פה	MOUTH	805a	2 a
	צלח	ADVANCE	852c	1
	שכל	BE PRUDENT	968c	6
1 9	אמץ	BE STRONG	55a	2
	אשר	PARTICLE OF RELATION	82c	4 bg
	יהוה	YAHWEH	218d	2 1a
	הלך	WALK	230d	1 1d 3a
	חזק	BE FIRM	304b	1 2c
	חתת	BE SHATTERED	369b	2 c
	לא	NOT	520b	4 b
	לא	NOT	520b	4 ba
	ערץ	CAUSE TO TREMBLE	791d	2
	צוה	CHARGE	845d	2 b
1 10	שטר	OFFICIAL	1009c	
1 11	זה	THIS	261a	2 bb
	ירדן	JORDAN	434c	
	ירש	TAKE POSSESSION	439d	1 a
	כון	ESTABLISH	466b	2 a
	עבר	PASS OVER	717c	3 a
	עוד	STILL	729c	2 ab
	צידה	PROVISION	845b	
	קרב	INWARD PART	899b	1 f2
1 12	גדי	GADITE	151d	2
	מנשה	MANASSEH	586c	1 b2 d
	ראובני	REUBENITE	910a	
1 13	דבר	WORD	182d	1 2a
	זכר	REMEMBER	270a	14 a
	משה	MOSES	602c	
	נוח	REST	628c	A 1b 1
	עבד	SLAVE	714a	3
1 14	גבור	STRONG	150b	2
	חיל	STRENGTH	298d	1 c
	חמשים	IN BATTLE ARRAY	332d	
	טף	CHILDREN	*382a	
	עבר	PASS OVER	718a	5 c
	עבר	REGION ACROSS	719c	1 a
	עזר	HELP	740b	
1 15	מזרח	PLACE OF SUNRISE	280d	1
	ירש	TAKE POSSESSION	439d	1 a
	ירשה	POSSESSION	440b	
	ל	TO	511b	1 ga
	נוח	REST	628c	A 1b 1
	עבד	SLAVE	714a	3
	עבר	REGION ACROSS	719c	1 a
	עבר	REGION ACROSS	719c	1 a
	שוב	TURN BACK	997b	3 b
1 16	אשר	PARTICLE OF RELATION	82c	4 bg
	הלך	WALK	234a	1 5d
	כל	ALL	481d	1 c
	ענה	ANSWER	773a	1 d
1 17	יהוה	YAHWEH	218d	2 1a
	כן	SO	486c	2 cc
1 18	אמץ	BE STRONG	55a	2
	חזק	BE FIRM	304b	1 2c
	ל	TO	514b	5 fa
	מות	DIE	560c	2
	מרה	BE REBELLIOUS	598b	
	צוה	CHARGE	846a	3
	רק	ONLY	956c	2 b
	שמע	HEAR	1034a	1 n
2 1	אשה	WOMAN	61a	1
	זנה	COMMIT FORNICATION	275d	1
	חרש	SILENTLY	361c	
	ראה	TO SEE	907c	6 a
	רחב	RAHAB	932a	
	שטים	SHITTIM	1008d	1
	שכב	LIE DOWN	1012b	2
	שם	THERE	1027c	3 c
2 2	אמר	SAY	56c	
	הנה	HITHER	244c	A a
	חפר	DIG	343d	2
	יריחו	JERICHO	437c	
	לילה	NIGHT	538d	1
	מלך	KING	573a	1
2 3	מן	FROM	580c	3 a
	ה	THE	208d	2 a
	חפר	DIG	343d	
	יצא	CAUSE TO GO	424c	1 b
	יריחו	JERICHO	437c	
	רחב	RAHAB	932a	
2 4	אין	WHENCE	32d	
	כן	TRUE	467b	2
	לקח	TAKE	543c	4 g
	צפן	HIDE	860c	1
2 5	אן	WHERE	33a	A
	היה	BE	227c	3 5b
	הלך	WALK	230d	1 1d 3b
	חשך	DARKNESS	365a	1
	יצא	GO OUT	422d	1 a
	ל	TO	518a	7 bg
	מהר	QUICKLY	555b	
	נשג	OVERTAKE	673c	1 a
	סגר	SHUT	689a	1
	רדף	PURSUE	922c	1 a
	שער	GATE	1044c	1 a
2 6	גג	ROOF	150d	1
	טמן	HIDE	380b	1
	ל	TO	512d	5 aa
	עלה	GO UP	749c	1
	עץ	TREE	782a	2 f
	ערך	ARRANGE	789c	1 a
	פשת	FLAX	833d	1
2 7	אחר	AFTER THAT	30b	3
	דרך	WAY	202d	1 j
	כאשר	WHEN	455c	3
	סגר	SHUT	688d	1
	מעברה	FORD	721b	1
	על	UPON	757c	27c ab
	רדף	PURSUE	922c	1 a
	שער	GATE	1044c	1 a
2 8	גג	ROOF	150d	1
	טרם	NOT YET	382c	1
	עלה	GO UP	748c	1 f
	על	UPON	757b	27c aa
2 9	אימה	TERROR	34a	1
	כי	THAT	471d	1 a
	מוג	MELT	556a	
	נפל	FALL	657c	5
2 10	פנה	FACE	818b	26b
	אשר	THAT	83b	8 aa
	חרם	BAN	355d	1 a
	יבש	BE DRY	386c	1
	ים	SEA	410d	2
	יצא	GO OUT	422d	1 a
	מי	WATER	565c	1 c
	סוף	REEDS	693a	2 a
	סיחון	SIHON	695d	
	עבר	REGION ACROSS	719c	1 a
	עוג	OG	728b	
	פנה	FACE	818b	26a
	שמע	HEAR	1033c	1
2 11	קום	STAND	278b	7 a
	לבב	HEART	524b	2 9b
	מסס	MELT	587d	2
	מעל	ABOVE	751c	1 a
	עמד	STAND	764b	3 c
	פנה	FACE	818b	26c a
	רוח	BREATH	925a	3 b
	תחת	UNDERNEATH	*1065b	1
2 12	אב	FATHER	3c	3
	אות	SIGN	16d	1
	אמת	FIRMNESS	54a	1
	ב	IN	90a	3 2d
	חסד	GOODNESS	338c	1 1
	נתן	GIVE	679b	1 m
	שבע	SWEAR	989b	1 a
2 13	אם	MOTHER	51d	1
	חיה	LIVE	311c	1
	נפש	SOUL	660a	3 c
	נצל	DELIVER	665a	3 b
2 14	אמת	FIRMNESS	54a	3 a
	ה	THE	209a	2 a
	זה	THIS	261a	2 ba
	חסד	GOODNESS	338d	1 2
	מות	DIE	559d	1
	נגד	BE CONSPICUOUS	617a	3
	נפש	SOUL	659b	3 c
	עשה	DO	794b	1 3
	תחת	INSTEAD	1065d	2 2b b
2 15	בית	HOUSE	108d	1 ab
	בעד	AWAY FROM	126b	1 a
	ה	THE	207c	1 d
	חבל	CORD	286c	1
	חלון	WINDOW	319d	
	חומה	WALL	327b	1
	חרכים	LATTICE	*355b	
	ירד	LET DOWN	434b	3
	קיר	WALL	885a	2
2 16	דרך	JOURNEY	203a	2
	הלך	WALK	230d	1 1d 3b
	הלך	WALK	231b	1 d3 gd
	חבה	WITHDRAW	285c	
	פגע	MEET	803b	3
	רדף	PURSUE	922d	1 c
	שם	THERE	1027b	3
2 17	זה	THIS	*261a	2 bb
	נקי	FREE FROM	667d	3
	שבע	SWEAR	989c	1
	שבועה	OATH	990a	1 a
2 18	אב	FATHER	3c	3
	אם	MOTHER	51d	1
	אסף	GATHER	62b	1 a
	חוט	THREAD	296c	1
	חלון	WINDOW	319d	
	ירד	LET DOWN	434b	3
	תקוה	CORD	876b	
	שני	SCARLET	1040c	
2 19	ב	IN	89b	2 4b
	דלת	DOOR	195a	1
	דם	BLOOD	197a	2 i
	היה	COME TO PASS	225b	1 2b f
	חוץ	THE OUTSIDE	299d	1 a
	יצא	GO OUT	422c	1 a
	נקי	FREE FROM	667d	3
2 20	זה	THIS	261a	2 ba
	נגד	BE CONSPICUOUS	617a	3
	נקי	FREE FROM	667d	3
	שבע	SWEAR	989c	1
	שבועה	OATH	990a	1 a
2 21	הוא	HE, SHE, IT	216c	6 a
	חלון	WINDOW	319d	
	כ	LIKE	454c	2 d
	כן	SO	486b	2 aa
	תקוה	CORD	876b	
	שני	SCARLET	1040c	
2 22	בקש	SEEK	134c	1 b
	מצא	FIND	593a	1 a
	נתן	GIVE	679c	1 t
	עד	UNTIL	725a	2 1b a
	רדף	PURSUE	922d	1 c
2 23	מצא	FIND	593c	3 e
	שוב	TURN BACK	998b	8
2 24	כי	THAT	472a	1 b
	מוג	MELT	556a	
	נתן	GIVE	679c	1 s
3 1	בקר	MORNING	134b	1 h
	טרם	NOT YET	382c	1
	נסע	SET OUT	652b	2 a
	שטים	SHITTIM	1008d	1
3 2	היה	COME TO PASS	224c	2 a1 az
	מן	FROM	581c	4 b
	עבר	PASS OVER	717c	3 a
	שטר	OFFICIAL	1009c	
3 3	ארון	CHEST	75c	3 f
	הלך	WALK	231c	1 1d 5z
	ו	AND	254d	5 cb
	כהן	PRIEST	463d	5
	לוי	LEVITE	533a	3 1b
	מקום	STANDING PLACE	879d	1 a
	קרב	COME NEAR	897c	1 b
3 4	אמה	CUBIT	52b	1
	אמה	CUBIT	52c	1
	דרך	WAY	202c	1
	כ	LIKE	453c	1 a
	מדה	MEASURE	551c	1
	עבר	PASS OVER	718b	5 h
	מען	PURPOSE	775c	2
	רחק	DISTANT	935c	2 a
	שלשם	THREE DAYS AGO	1026b	
	תמול	YESTERDAY	1070a	2 c
3 5	פלא	BE SURPASSING	810d	4
	קדש	BE SET APART	873c	4
3 6	ארון	CHEST	75c	3 f
	כהן	PRIEST	463d	5
3 7	גדל	BECOME GREAT	152b	2
	חלל	POLLUTE	320d	2
	עין	EYE	745a	5
3 8	ארון	CHEST	75c	3 f
	ירדן	JORDAN	434d	
	כהן	PRIEST	463d	5
	מי	WATER	565c	1 b
	קצה	END	892b	2
3 9	דבר	WORD	183b	3 2
	הנה	HITHER	244c	A a
	נגש	DRAW NEAR	620d	1
3 10	אל	GOD	42d	6 d
	אמרי	AMORITES	57c	2
	יבוסי	JEBUSITE	101a	1
	גרגשי	GIRGASHITE	173a	
	זה	THIS	261d	6 bb
	חוי	HIVITE	295d	2
	חי	ALIVE	311d	1 a
	חתי	HITTITE	366d	2 a
	ירש	CAUSE TO POSSESS	440a	2 a
	כנעני	CANAANITE	489a	2 b
3 11	אדון	LORD	11a	1 2
	ארון	CHEST	75c	3 e

Ch	v.	Heb	Eng	Page	Sec
3	12	עבר	PASS OVER	718a	5 e
		ל	TO	512d	5 ab
		לקח	TAKE	543b	4 d
3	13	אדון	LORD	11a	1 2
		ארון	CHEST	75c	3 e
		היה	COME TO PASS	225b	1 2b ae
		ו	AND	252b	1 b
		ירד	GO DOWN	433c	3 b
		ירדן	JORDAN	434d	
		כהן	PRIEST	463b	4
		כף	SOLE OF FOOT	496c	3
		כרת	BE CUT OFF	504b	4
		נד	HEAP	622d	
		נוח	REST	628a	1
		מעל	ABOVE	752a	2 d
		עמד	STAND	764b	5 c
3	14	היה	COME TO PASS	224d	2 a1 al
		כהן	PRIEST	463b	4
		נסע	SET OUT	652b	2 a
		עבר	PASS OVER	717a	1 a1
3	15	גדה	BANK OF RIVER	152a	
		יום	TIME	399d	6 a
		כהן	PRIEST	463b	4
		מי	WATER	565c	1 b
		מלא	FILL	570b	1
		מלא	FILL	570d	2
		על	UPON	755a	2 2
		קצה	END	892b	2
		קציר	HARVESTING	894d	3
		טבל	ADDENDA ET COR-RIGENDA	1123d	
3	16	אדם	ADAM	9c	4
		ים	SEA	411a	3
		ים	SEA	411a	3
		ירד	GO DOWN	433c	3 b
		כרת	BE CUT OFF	504b	4
		מי	WATER	565c	1 b
		מלח	SALT	572a	
		נגד	IN FRONT	617b	1 aa
		נד	HEAP	622d	
		מעל	ABOVE	752a	2 d
		על	UPON	757a	2 7c a
		עמד	STAND	764b	5 c
		ערבה	DESERT-PLAIN	787c	1 a
		צד	SIDE	841a	
		צרתן	ZERETHAN	866c	
		קום	STAND	877d	1 d
		רחק	BE DISTANT	935a	1
		תמם	BE FINISHED	1070b	1
3	17	גוי	NATION	156c	1 b
		חרבה	DRY GROUND	351c	
		כהן	PRIEST	463b	4
		כון	ESTABLISH	466b	1 d
		עבר	PASS OVER	717a	1 a1
		עד	UNTIL	724d	2 1a a
		תמם	BE FINISHED	1070b	1
4	1	גוי	NATION	156c	1 b
		עבר	PASS OVER	717a	1 a1
		תמם	BE FINISHED	1070b	1
4	2	לקח	TAKE	543b	4 d
4	3	אבן	STONE	6b	1
		כהן	PRIEST	463b	4
		כון	ESTABLISH	466b	1 d
		לון	LODGE	533c	1 a
		מלון	INN	533d	
		לילה	NIGHT	538d	1
		נוח	REST	628d	B 1
		מצב	STANDING PLACE	662d	1
		עבר	PASS OVER	718d	1 a
4	4	כון	ESTABLISH	466c	2 b
		צידון	SIDON	851a	
		קרא	CALL	895d	5 b
4	5	אבן	STONE	6b	1
		ארון	CHEST	75c	3 e
		מספר	NUMBER	709a	1 b
		רום	BE HIGH	927c	1 c
		שכם	SHOULDER	1014b	1 a
4	6	אבן	STONE	6b	1
		אות	SIGN	16d	5
		אשר	THAT	83d	8 d
		ל	TO	513a	5 ad
		מחר	TO-MORROW	564a	2
		שאל	ASK	981d	2 a
4	7	אבן	STONE	6b	1
		אמר	SAY	56a	1
		ארון	CHEST	75c	3 f
		אשר	THAT	83c	8 c
		זכרון	MEMORIAL	272a	1 c
		ירדן	JORDAN	434d	
		כרת	BE CUT OFF	504b	4
		עבר	PASS OVER	718a	5 e
4	8	אבן	STONE	6b	1
		כן	SO	486c	2 da
		מלון	INN	533d	
		נוח	REST	628d	B 1
		מספר	NUMBER	709a	1 b
		עבר	PASS OVER	718d	1 a
4	9	אבן	STONE	6b	1
		ארון	CHEST	75c	3 f
		יום	DAY	401b	7 1
		כהן	PRIEST	463b	4
		מצב	STANDING PLACE	662d	1
		קום	STAND	878d	2 a
4	10	דבר	WORD	182d	1 2a
		כהן	PRIEST	463b	4
		מהר	HASTEN	555a	2

Ch	v.	Heb	Eng	Page	Sec
4	11	תמם	BE FINISHED	1070b	1
		ארון	CHEST	75c	3 c
		כהן	PRIEST	463d	5
		תמם	BE FINISHED	1070b	1
4	12	גד	GAD	151c	1 b
		חמשים	IN BATTLE ARRAY	332d	
		מנשה	MANASSEH	586c	1 b2 d
		ראובן	REUBEN	910a	2
4	13	אלף	THOUSAND	49a	1 c
		חלץ	EQUIP FOR WAR	323a	2
		יריחו	JERICHO	437d	
		כ	LIKE	453b	1 a
		עבר	PASS OVER	717a	1 a2
		ערבה	DESERT-PLAIN	787c	3
		ארבעים	FORTY	917b	1
4	14	גדל	BECOME GREAT	152b	2
		חיים	LIFE	313b	1
		ירא	FEAR	431c	3
		עין	EYE	745a	5
4	16	ארון	CHEST	75c	3 e
		כהן	PRIEST	464a	7
		עדות	TESTIMONY	730b	1
		עלה	GO UP	748b	1 a
		צוה	CHARGE	845d	2 b
4	17	כהן	PRIEST	463b	4
		עלה	GO UP	748b	1 a
4	18	ארון	CHEST	75c	3 f
		גדה	BANK OF RIVER	152a	
		הלך	WALK	232b	1 3
		חרבה	DRY GROUND	351c	
		ירדן	JORDAN	434d	
		כהן	PRIEST	463b	4
		כף	SOLE OF FOOT	496d	2
		נחל	WADY	636c	2
		נתק	DRAW	683c	1
		על	UPON	755a	2
		מקום	STANDING PLACE	879d	2 a
		שוב	TURN BACK	998a	7 a
		שלשם	THREE DAYS AGO	1026b	
		תמול	YESTERDAY	1070a	2 b
4	19	מזרח	PLACE OF SUNRISE	281a	2
		חנה	DECLINE	333c	2 c1
		חנה	DECLINE	333c	2 c2
		עלה	GO UP	748b	1 a
		עשור	A TEN	797c	1 b
		קצה	END	892b	2
4	20	אבן	STONE	6b	1
		קום	STAND	878d	2 a
4	21	אבן	STONE	6b	1
		אשר	THAT	83d	8 d
		אשר	THAT	84a	1
		זה	THIS	261a	2 bb
4	22	יבשה	DRY LAND	387a	
		ידע	TEACH	395a	
		ירדן	JORDAN	434c	
		יבש	BE DRY	386c	1
		ירדן	JORDAN	434d	
		סוף	REEDS	693b	2 a
		עד	UNTIL	725a	2 1b a
		פנה	FACE	818b	2 6a
4	23	אשר	THAT	83c	8 c
4	24	חזק	STRONG	305c	1 a
		יד	HAND	390a	1 e2
		יום	DAY	400c	7 f
		ירא	FEAR	431c	3 b
		עם	PEOPLE	766a	5 d
		מען	PURPOSE	775d	2 2
5	1	אמרי	AMORITES	57c	1 b
		היה	COME TO PASS	224c	2 a1 aa
		יבש	BE DRY	386c	1
		ים	SEA	410d	1
		ים	SEA	411b	9
		ירדן	JORDAN	434d	
		כנעני	CANAANITE	489a	2 b
		לבב	HEART	524b	2 9b
		עבר	REGION ACROSS	719c	1 b
		עוד	STILL	729a	1 ab
		רוח	BREATH	925a	3 b
		שמע	HEAR	1033c	1 a
5	2	חרב	SWORD	353a	2
		מול	CIRCUMCIZE	557d	
		מלל	CIRCUMCIZE	576d	
		עת	TIME	773b	1 a
		צר	HARD PEBBLE	866a	
		שוב	TURN BACK	998b	8
5	3	אל	TO	40c	8
		גבעה	HILL	149a	4
		חרב	SWORD	353a	2
		מול	CIRCUMCIZE	557d	
		ערלה	FORESKIN	790b	
		צר	HARD PEBBLE	866a	
5	4	איש	MAN	35d	
		אשר	PARTICLE OF RELATION	82c	4 bd
		ב	IN	91a	5 1
		דבר	WORD	184a	4 8
		זה	THIS	261a	3
		זכר	MALE	271c	1 1 b
		יצא	GO OUT	422d	1 a
		מלחמה	WAR	536b	
		מול	CIRCUMCIZE	557d	
5	5	ילוד	BORN	409c	4
		יצא	GO OUT	422d	1 a
		מול	CIRCUMCIZE	557d	
		מול	CIRCUMCIZE	557d	
		עם	PEOPLE	766a	4

Ch	v.	Heb	Eng	Page	Sec
5	6	איש	MAN	35d	
		בלת	NOT	116d	4 a
		גוי	NATION	156c	1 b
		דבש	HONEY	185b	
		הלך	WALK	230c	1 1d 2a
		הלך	WALK	230c	1 1d 1b
		זוב	FLOW	264d	2
		חלב	MILK	316c	A 4
		יצא	GO OUT	422d	1 a
		מלחמה	WAR	536b	
		ראה	TO SEE	908d	1 a2
		שבע	SWEAR	989c	2
		תמם	BE FINISHED	1070c	5
5	7	מול	CIRCUMCIZE	557d	
		ערל	HAVING FORESKIN	790c	
		קום	STAND	878d	3
5	8	גוי	NATION	156c	1 b
		חיה	LIVE	311b	2 a
		מול	CIRCUMCIZE	557d	
		ראה	TO SEE	908c	2 c
		תחת	UNDERNEATH	1065d	2 2a
		תמם	BE FINISHED	1070b	1
5	9	חרפה	REPROACH	358a	2 d
		יום	DAY	401b	7 1
		על	UPON	758d	4.2b
5	10	חנה	DECLINE	333c	2 c1
		יריחו	JERICHO	437d	
		ערבה	DESERT-PLAIN	787c	3
		עשה	DO	795a	2 6
		פסח	PASSOVER	820b	3
5	11	מחרת	THE MORROW	564a	
		מצה	UNLEAVENED BREAD	695b	
		עבור	PRODUCE	721a	
		עצם	BONE	783a	3
		פסח	PASSOVER	820b	3
		קלה	ROAST	885d	
5	12	תבואה	PRODUCT	100a	1
		מחרת	THE MORROW	564a	
		מן	MANNA	577c	
		עבור	PRODUCE	721a	
		עוד	STILL	729a	1 ab
		שבת	CEASE	991d	1
5	13	אם	IF	50c	2 ab a
		ה	INTERROG PART	*210a	1 d
		חרב	SWORD	352c	1 c
		יד	HAND	390d	5 c1
		ל	TO	515c	5 hc
		נגד	IN FRONT	617c	2 b
		שלף	DRAW OUT	1025b	1
5	14	אדון	LORD	11b	3 li
		אל	TO	41a	A
		כי	BUT	474c	3 e
		לא	NOT	519a	1 ad b
		נפל	FALL	657b	3 b
		צבא	HOST	839a	1
		שר	CHIEFTAIN	978b	3 a
		שחה	BOW DOWN	1005c	2 d
		הוא	HE, SHE, IT	216a	3 b
5	15	נעל	SANDAL	653b	
		נשל	DRAW OFF	675c	1
		על	UPON	758c	4 2a
		צבא	HOST	839a	1
		קדש	APARTNESS	871c	2 b
		מקום	STANDING PLACE	879d	1 a
		שר	CHIEFTAIN	978b	3 a
6	1	בוא	COME	97d	1
		יצא	GO OUT	424a	3
		יריחו	JERICHO	437c	
		סגר	SHUT	689a	1
		סגר	BE SHUT UP	689b	1
6	2	גבור	STRONG	150b	2
		חיל	STRENGTH	298d	1 c
		יד	HAND	390d	5 b3
		מלחמה	WAR	536b	
6	3	נקף	GO AROUND	669a	1 a
		סבב	GO AROUND	685d	2 a
		פעם	OCCURRENCE	822a	3 a
6	4	יובל	RAM	385c	1
		כהן	PRIEST	463b	4
		סבב	GO AROUND	685d	2 a
		שפר	HORN	1051d	
		שפר	HORN	1051d	
		שפר	HORN	1051d	
		תקע	GIVE A BLOW	1075c	2
6	5	גדול	GREAT	153a	4
		חומה	WALL	327b	1
		חומה	WALL	327c	1
		יובל	RAM	385c	1
		משך	DRAW	604c	4
		נגד	IN FRONT	617b	1 ab
		נפל	FALL	656d	1
		קרן	HORN	901d	1 c
		רוע	RAISE A SHOUT	929c	1
		תרועה	SHOUT OF WAR	930a	1
		שפר	HORN	1051d	
		תחת	UNDERNEATH	1065d	2 2a
6	6	ארון	CHEST	75c	3 f
		יובל	RAM	385c	1
		כהן	PRIEST	463b	4
		שפר	HORN	1051d	
6	7	ה	THE	208b	1 g
		חלץ	EQUIP FOR WAR	323a	1
		סבב	GO AROUND	685d	2 a
6	8	ארון	CHEST	75c	3 f
		יובל	RAM	385c	1

Ch	v.	Heb	Eng	Page	Sec
		כהן	PRIEST	463b	4
		שפר	HORN	1051d	
		תקע	GIVE A BLOW	1075c	2
6	9	אסף	GATHER	63a	3
		ה	THE	208b	1 g
		הלך	WALK	233a	14c 1g
		חלץ	EQUIP FOR WAR	323a	2
		כהן	PRIEST	463b	4
		שפר	HORN	1051d	
		תקע	GIVE A BLOW	1075c	2
		תקע	GIVE A BLOW	1075c	2
6	10	יום	DAY	400a	7 d1 b
		יצא	GO OUT	423c	1 g
		עד	AS FAR AS	724b	12 a a
		פה	MOUTH	805a	2 a
		קול	VOICE	876d	1 a
		רוע	RAISE A SHOUT	929c	1
		שמע	HEAR	1034c	1 a
6	11	מחנה	ENCAMPMENT	334b	2 b
		נקף	GO AROUND	669a	1 a
		סבב	GO AROUND	686c	1 a
		פעם	OCCURRENCE	822a	3 a
6	12	בקר	MORNING	134b	1 h
6	13	כהן	PRIEST	463b	4
		אסף	GATHER	63a	3
		ה	THE	208b	1 g
		הלך	WALK	233a	14c 1g
		הלך	WALK	233b	14c 2
		חלץ	EQUIP FOR WAR	323a	2
		יובל	RAM	385c	1
		כהן	PRIEST	463b	4
		שפר	HORN	1051d	
		תקע	GIVE A BLOW	1075c	2
6	14	מחנה	ENCAMPMENT	334b	2 b
		כה	THUS	462b	1 b
		סבב	GO AROUND	685d	2 a
		עשה	DO	794a	1 1a 7
		פעם	OCCURRENCE	822a	3 a
6	15	כ	LIKE	454a	1 c1
		סבב	GO AROUND	685d	2 a
		שחר	DAWN	1007b	
		שכם	START EARLY	1014d	
6	16	כהן	PRIEST	463b	4
		רוע	RAISE A SHOUT	929c	1
		שביעי	SEVENTH	988d	2
		תקע	GIVE A BLOW	1075c	2
6	17	זנה	COMMIT FORNICATION	275d	1
		חבא	WITHDRAW	285b	
		חרם	BAN	*355d	1 a
		חרם	BAN	*355d	
		חרם	DEVOTED THING	356a	1 a
		חרם	DEVOTED THING	*356b	2
		רחב	RAHAB	932a	
6	18	חרם	BAN	355d	1 a
		חרם	DEVOTED THING	356a	1 a
		חרם	DEVOTED THING	356b	1 a
		מן	FROM	583a	7 b
		עכר	STIR UP	747d	
		עכר	STIR UP	*747d	
		רק	ONLY	956c	2 b
		שמר	KEEP	1036d	2 b
6	19	אוצר	TREASURE	70a	1
		ברזל	IRON	137c	1
		הוא	HE, SHE, IT	216a	3 b
		זהב	GOLD	262d	3
		זהב	GOLD	263c	1
		חרם	DEVOTED THING	*356a	1
		חרם	DEVOTED THING	*356b	2
		כלי	ARTICLE	479c	1
6	20	חומה	WALL	327b	1
		חומה	WALL	327c	1
		נגד	IN FRONT	617b	1 ab
		נפל	FALL	656d	1
		רוע	RAISE A SHOUT	929c	1
		רוע	RAISE A SHOUT	929c	1
		תרועה	SHOUT OF WAR	930a	1
		שפר	HORN	1051d	
		תחת	UNDERNEATH	1065d	2 2a
		תקע	GIVE A BLOW	1075c	2
6	21	איש	MAN	35d	
		זקן	OLD	278c	2 a
		חמור	HE-ASS	331b	1
		חרב	SWORD	352d	1 f
		חרם	BAN	*355d	
		חרם	BAN	355d	1 a
		ל	TO	516c	5 jb
		מן	FROM	582a	5 b
		נער	YOUTH	655a	1 d
		שה	A SHEEP	962a	1
		שור	A HEAD OF CATTLE	1004b	
6	22	אשה	WOMAN	61a	1
		זנה	COMMIT FORNICATION	275d	1
		יצא	CAUSE TO GO	424b	1 a
		רגל	GO ABOUT	920b	2
		שבע	SWEAR	989b	1 a
6	23	אם	MOTHER	51d	1
		חוץ	THE OUTSIDE	300a	1 bd
		יצא	CAUSE TO GO	424c	1 b
		נוח	REST	628d	B 1
		רחב	RAHAB	932a	
		משפחה	CLAN	1046d	
6	24	אוצר	TREASURE	70a	1
		אש	FIRE	77c	1
		ברזל	IRON	137c	1 d
		ה	THE	*207d	1 e
6	25	זהב	GOLD	262d	3
		זהב	GOLD	263c	1
		חרם	DEVOTED THING	*356a	1
		כלי	ARTICLE	479c	1
		שרף	BURN	976d	2 a
		אב	FATHER	3c	3
		זנה	COMMIT FORNICATION	275d	1
		חבא	WITHDRAW	285b	
		חיה	LIVE	311c	1
		יום	DAY	401b	7 1
		רגל	GO ABOUT	920b	2
		רחב	RAHAB	932a	
		משפחה	CLAN	1046d	1 a
6	26	ב	IN	90a	3 3a
		בנה	BUILD	124d	1 i
		דלת	DOOR	195b	4
		יסד	FOUND	414a	1
		נצב	STAND	662c	2
		פנה	FACE	817a	24 a g
		ציער	YOUNG	859a	2
		ראש	HEAD	910d	2 a
		שבע	SWEAR	989c	1
6	27	היה	BE	227b	3 4d a
		שמע	REPORT	1035a	
7	1	זבדי	ZABDI	256c	1
		זמרי	ZIMRI	*275b	
		זרח	ZERAH	280b	1
		חרה	BURN	354a	2 a
		חרם	DEVOTED THING	356a	1 a
		חרם	DEVOTED THING	356b	1 a
		חרם	DEVOTED THING	356b	1 a
		חרם	DEVOTED THING	*356b	1 a
		יהודה	JUDAH	397b	1 2
		כרמי	CARMI	501d	1
		מעל	ACT TREACHEROUSLY	591b	1 a
		מטה	TRIBE	641d	3
		עכן	ACHAN	747c	
7	2	ביתאל	BETHEL	110d	
		ביתאון	BETH-AVEN	110d	
		עי	AI	743b	1
		עם	WITH	*768a	2
		קדם	FRONT	869d	1 b 2
		רגל	GO ABOUT	920b	2
7	3	אלף	THOUSAND	48d	1 a
		אלף	THOUSAND	48d	1 a
		ו	AND	252b	1 b
		יגע	TOIL	388b	
		כ	LIKE	453b	1 a
		מעט	A FEW	590a	1 a
		נכה	SMITE	646d	3
		עי	AI	743b	1
		שם	THERE	1027b	3
7	4	איש	MAN	36a	
		נוס	FLEE	630d	1
		עי	AI	743b	1
7	5	איש	MAN	36a	
		היה	BECOME	226b	2 2e
		מורד	DESCENT	434c	1
		לבב	HEART	524b	2 9b
		מי	WATER	565d	4 e
		נכה	SMITE	646a	2 c
		עי	AI	743b	1
		רדף	PURSUE	922a	1 b
		שבר	BREAKING	991b	4
7	6	זקן	OLD	278d	2
		נפל	FALL	657b	3 b
		עלה	GO UP	749c	4
		עפר	DRY EARTH	779d	1 a
		קרע	TEAR	*902c	1 a1
		שמלה	WRAPPER	971a	
7	7	אבד	DESTROY	2b	1
		אדון	LORD	11c	4 a
		אהה	ALAS	13c	
		אמרי	AMORITES	57c	2 b
		ו	AND	254a	2 a
		יאל	SHOW WILLINGNESS	384a	1
		יד	HAND	390d	5 b3
		ירדן	JORDAN	434c	
		לו	IF	530b	2
		עבר	PASS OVER	718d	1 a
		עבר	REGION ACROSS	719c	1 a
7	8	אדון	LORD	11b	3 2a
		אחר	AFTER THAT	30b	3
		בי	I PRAY	106c	
		הפך	TURN	245b	1 a
		ערף	BACK OF NECK	791b	1
		פנה	TURN	*815c	1
7	9	גדל	GREAT	153b	6 c
		כנעני	CANAANITE	489a	2 b
		כרת	CUT OFF	504c	2 b
		סבב	TURN AROUND	686a	1
		שם	NAME	1028b	3
7	10	נפל	LIE	657d	2
7	11	ברית	COVENANT	137b	3 3
		גנב	STEAL	170c	
		חטא	MISS 0A GOAL OR WAY0	306d	2 b
		חרם	DEVOTED THING	356a	1 a
		חרם	DEVOTED THING	356b	1 a
		כחש	DECEIVE	471b	1
		כלי	ARTICLE	479c	1
7	12	עבר	PASS OVER	717b	1 i
		קום	STAND	278b	7 a
		חרם	DEVOTED THING	356b	1 a
		חרם	DEVOTED THING	356b	1 a
		יסף	DO AGAIN	415c	2 a
		ערף	BACK OF NECK	791b	1
		פנה	TURN	815b	1 b
		פנה	FACE	817b	24b d
		קרב	INWARD PART	899b	1 f1
		שמד	BE EXTERMINATED	1029b	1
7	13	אלהים	GOD	44b	4 ba
		אלהים	GOD	44c	4 ba
		קום	STAND	278b	7 a
		חרם	DEVOTED THING	356b	1 a
		ל	TO	*517c	6 a
		מחר	TO-MORROW	564a	1
		סור	TURN ASIDE	694b	1
		פנה	FACE	817b	24b d
		קדש	BE SET APART	873b	4 b
		קדש	BE SET APART	873c	4
7	14	אורים	URIM	22b	
		בקר	MORNING	134b	2
		גבר	MAN	150a	
		גורל	LOT	*174c	2 f
		היה	COME TO PASS	225a	1 2b ag
		לכד	TAKING	540a	1
		קרב	COME NEAR	897c	1 h
		משפחה	CLAN	1046d	1 a
7	15	ברית	COVENANT	137b	3 3
		היה	COME TO PASS	225a	1 2b ag
		חרם	DEVOTED THING	356a	1 a
		חרם	DEVOTED THING	*356b	1 a
		כי	BECAUSE	474b	3 d
		לכד	TAKE	540b	3
		נבלה	SENSELESSNESS	615b	1
		עבר	PASS OVER	717b	1 i
		שרף	BURN	977a	
		שרף	BURN	977a	
7	16	אורים	URIM	22b	
		בקר	MORNING	134b	1 h
		יהודה	JUDAH	397b	1 2
		לכד	TAKE	540b	3
		קרב	COME NEAR	898b	2 a2
		ראש	HEAD	911b	6
7	17	גבר	MAN	150a	
		זבדי	ZABDI	256c	1
		זרחי	ZERAHITES	280c	1
		לכד	TAKING	540a	1
		לכד	TAKE	540b	3
		קרב	COME NEAR	898a	2 a2
		משפחה	CLAN	1046d	1 a
		משפחה	CLAN	*1046d	1 a
7	18	גבר	MAN	150a	
		זבדי	ZABDI	256c	1.
		זרח	ZERAH	280b	1
		יהודה	JUDAH	397b	1 2
		כרמי	CARMI	501d	2
		לכד	TAKE	540b	3
		עכן	ACHAN	747c	
		קרב	COME NEAR	898a	2 a2
7	19	אלהים	GOD	44b	4 ba
		תודה	THANKSGIVING	392d	1
		כבוד	HONOR	459b	6 b
		כחד	HIDE	470b	
		נתן	GIVE	679d	1 x
		עכן	ACHAN	747c	
		שום	TO PLACE	963b	1 c
7	20	אלהים	GOD	44b	4 ba
		אמנה	VERILY	53d	
		זה	THIS	262a	6 d
		חטא	MISS A GOAL OR WAY	307a	2 b
		עכן	ACHAN	747c	
		ראש	HEAD	911b	6
7	21	אדרת	MANTLE	12b	2
		זהב	GOLD	262d	3
		זהב	GOLD	263b	9 a
		חמד	DESIRE	326b	A
		טוב	PLEASANT	373c	1
		ממן	HIDE	380b	1
		כסף	SILVER	494b	8 a
		לשון	TONGUE	546d	5
		מאה	HUNDRED	548a	1 b2
		שלל	SPOIL	1022a	2
		שנער	SHINAR	1042c	
		שקל	SHEKEL	1053d	
		שקל	SHEKEL	1053d	
		משקל	WEIGHT	1054a	
7	22	טמן	HIDE	380b	1
		רוץ	RUN	930b	1
		שלח	SEND	1018b	1 a
7	23	יצק	POUR	427b	
7	24	אדרת	MANTLE	12b	2
		ו	AND	252a	1
		זהב	GOLD	262d	3
		זרח	ZERAH	280b	1
		חמור	HE-ASS	331b	1
		חרם	DEVOTED THING	*356b	1 a
		לשון	TONGUE	546d	5
		עכן	ACHAN	747c	
		עכור	DISTURBANCE	747d	
		עלה	GO UP	749c	1 c
		עם	WITH	767b	1 a
		שור	A HEAD OF CATTLE	1004b	
7	25	אבן	STONE	6b	1
		אבן	STONE	6b	1

Ch v.	Heb	Eng	Page	Sec
	חרם	DEVOTED THING	*356b	1 a
	סקל	STONE	709c	
	עבר	STIR UP	747d	
	רגם	TO STONE	920c	
	שרף	BURN	977a	2 b1
7 26	אבן	STONE	6b	1
	חרון	BURNING OF AN-GER	354c	
	יום	DAY	401b	71
	כן	SO	487b	3 f
	עכן	ACHAN	*747c	
	עבור	DISTURBANCE	747d	
	קום	STAND	878d	2 b
	שוב	TURN BACK	997d	6 f
8 1	חתת	BE SHATTERED	369b	1 a
	ירא	FEAR	431a	1 a
	מלחמה	WAR	536b	
	לקח	TAKE	543d	7
	עי	AI	743b	1
8 2	עם	PEOPLE	766c	2 d
	אחר	BEHIND	30b	4 ab
	ארב	LIE IN WAIT	70b	
	ארב	LIE IN WAIT	70b	
	בזז	SPOIL	102d	
	יריחו	JERICHO	437c	
	עי	AI	743b	1
	רק	ONLY	956b	2 a
	שום	TO PLACE	964a	4 a
	שלל	SPOIL	1022a	2
8 3	בחר	CHOOSE	104b	5 b
	גבור	STRONG	150b	1
	חיל	STRENGTH	298d	1 c
	מלחמה	WAR	536b	
	לילה	NIGHT	539a	1
	עי	AI	743b	1
8 4	עם	PEOPLE	766c	2 d
	אחר	BEHIND	30b	4 ab
	ארב	LIE IN WAIT	70b	
	כון	BE READY	466a	3
	רחק	BE DISTANT	935a	1
8 5	כאשר	AS	455b	1 a
	נוס	FLEE	630d	1
	קרב	COME NEAR	897c	1 b
	ראשון	FIRST	911d	3 a1
8 6	כאשר	AS	455b	1 a
	נוס	FLEE	630d	1
	נתק	PULL	683d	1
	ראשון	FIRST	911d	3 a1
8 7	ארב	LIE IN WAIT	70b	
	ירש	CAUSE TO POSSESS	440a	2 a
	קום	STAND	878a	2
8 8	אש	FIRE	77c	1
	היה	COME TO PASS	225b	1 2b ae
	יצת	KINDLE	428c	1
	תפש	LAY HOLD OF	1074d	1
8 9	מארב	AMBUSH	70d	1 a
	הלך	WALK	231a	1 d3 ga
	ים	SEA	411b	9
	לון	LODGE	533c	1 a
	תוך	MIDST	1063c	
8 10	בקר	MORNING	134b	1 h
	זקן	OLD	278d	2 b
8 11	גיא	VALLEY	161b	1
	ה	THE	207b	1 cb
	מלחמה	WAR	536b	
	מן	FROM	578d	1 c
	נגש	DRAW NEAR	620d	1
	עם	PEOPLE	766c	2 d
8 12	ארב	LIE IN WAIT	70b	
	חמש	FIVE	332a	4
	ים	SEA	411b	9
	נכה	SMITE	646b	3
	עי	AI	*743b	1
	שום	TO PLACE	964a	4 a
8 13	הלך	WALK	230c	1 1d 2a
	מחנה	ENCAMPMENT	334b	3 c
	ים	SEA	411b	9
	מן	FROM	578d	1 c
	מן	FROM	578d	1 c
	עמק	VALE	771a	
	עקב	HEEL	784b	C
	שום	TO PLACE	964a	4 a
8 14	אחר	BEHIND	30b	4 ab
	ארב	LIE IN WAIT	70b	
	ארב	LIE IN WAIT	70b	
	מועד	APPOINTED TIME	417c	1 a
	ל	TO	511b	1 ga
	מהר	HASTEN	555a	2
	ערבה	DESERT-PLAIN	787c	1 b
	שכם	START EARLY	1014d	
8 15	דרך	WAY	202d	1
	נגע	STRIKE	619b	
	נוס	FLEE	630d	1
8 16	נתק	DRAW	683c	1
	עי	AI	*743b	1
	רדף	PURSUE	922c	1 a
8 17	עזב	LEAVE	737a	1 e
	פתח	OPEN	835a	
	רדף	PURSUE	922c	1 a
8 18	אל	TO	39d	3 a
	יד	HAND	390d	5 c1
	כידון	JAVELIN	475d	
	נטה	EXTEND	639d	1 a
8 19	ארב	LIE IN WAIT	70b	
	אש	FIRE	77c	1
	ה	THE	208b	1 g

Ch v.	Heb	Eng	Page	Sec
	יצת	KINDLE	428c	
	מהר	HASTEN	555a	2
	מהרה	HASTE	555b	
	נטה	EXTEND	639d	1 a
	קום	STAND	878a	2
	מקום	STANDING PLACE	879d	1 b
	רוץ	RUN	930b	1
8 20	הלם	HITHER	*240d	
	הנה	HITHER	244c	A a
	הפך	TURN	245d	1 a
	יד	HAND	390b	2
	נוס	FLEE	630d	1
	עשן	SMOKE	798c	1 a
	פנה	TURN	815b	2 a
	רדף	PURSUE	922d	1 c
	שמי	HEAVENS	1030a	1 b
8 21	ארב	LIE IN WAIT	70b	
	כי	THAT	471d	1 a
	לכד	CAPTURE	540a	1
	נכה	SMITE	646b	3
	עשן	SMOKE	798c	1 a
	שוב	TURN BACK	996d	1
8 22	אלה	THESE	41c	B
	בלת	NOT	117a	4 c
	פליט	ESCAPED ONE	812c	
	שריד	SURVIVOR	975a	1
	שאר	REMAIN	984b	1
	תוך	MIDST	1063c	
8 23	חי	ALIVE	312a	1 b
	קרב	COME NEAR	897d	1 a
	תפש	LAY HOLD OF	1074d	1
8 24	הרג	KILL	247b	1 b
	חרב	SWORD	352d	1 f
	חרב	SWORD	352d	1 f
	כל	ALL	481b	1 a
	נכה	SMITE	646b	3
	נפל	FALL	657b	2 a
	רדף	PURSUE	922d	1 b
	שדה	FIELD	961c	1 f
	תמם	BE FINISHED	1070c	5
8 25	איש	MAN	35d	
	מן	FROM	582a	5 b
8 26	חרם	BAN	355d	1 a
	כידון	JAVELIN	475d	
	נטה	EXTEND	639d	1 a
	עד	UNTIL	724d	2 1a aa
	שוב	TURN BACK	999a	1 c
8 27	בזז	SPOIL	102d	
	רק	ONLY	956b	2 a
	שלל	SPOIL	1022a	2
8 28	יום	DAY	401b	71
	שום	TO PLACE	964c	1
	תל	MOUND	1068b	1
8 29	אבן	STONE	6b	1
	בוא	COME	98a	1 i
	יום	DAY	401b	71
	ירד	BRING DOWN	434a	2
	גבלה	CARCASS	615c	1 a
	עת	TIME	773c	1 b
	עץ	TREE	781d	2 b
	ערב	SUNSET	787d	1 a
	פתח	OPENING	836a	
	קום	STAND	878d	2 b
	שלך	THROW	1021a	1 a
	תלה	HANG	1068d	2
8 30	אז	THEN	23a	1 a
	אלהים	GOD	44b	4 ba
	בנה	BUILD	124c	1 at
	הר	MOUNTAIN	249b	1 a
	מזבח	ALTAR	258b	1
	עיבל	EBAL	716d	
8 31	אבן	STONE	6c	1
	ברזל	IRON	137c	2
	זבח	SLAUGHTER FOR SACRIFICE	256d	1 1 a
	מזבח	ALTAR	258c	1
	תורה	LAW	436b	2 b2
	כת	LIKE	454a	1 c1
	משה	MOSES	602d	
	נוף	MOVE TO AND FRO	631d	1
	ספר	MISSIVE	707b	3 c
	עבד	SLAVE	714a	3
	עלה	GO UP	750a	8
	עלה	WHOLE BURNT OF-FERING	750d	
	שלם	PEACE-OFFERING	1023c	
	שלם	COMPLETE	1024a	1 a
8 32	אבן	STONE	6b	1
	תורה	LAW	436b	2 b2
	משה	MOSES	602d	
	משנה	COPY	1041c	1
8 33	עיבל	EBAL	716d	
	ארון	CHEST	75c	3 f
	ברך	BLESS	139a	3
	גר	SOJOURNER	158a	1
	גר	SOJOURNER	158b	2
	גריזים	GERIZIM	173d	
	הר	MOUNTAIN	249b	1 a
	הר	MOUNTAIN	249b	1 a
	זה	THIS	262a	6 e
	זקן	OLD	278d	2 b
	אזרח	A NATIVE	280c	1
	כ	LIKE	454c	2 ba
	כהן	PRIEST	463d	5
	לוי	LEVITE	533a	3 1b
	מול	IN FRONT OF	557c	2 a

Ch v.	Heb	Eng	Page	Sec
	עבד	SLAVE	714a	3
	ראשון	FIRST	912a	3 a1
	שטר	OFFICIAL	1009c	
8 34	שפט	JUDGE	1047d	2 b
	ברכה	BLESSING	139d	1 b
	תורה	LAW	436b	2 b2
	תורה	LAW	436b	2 b2
	כ	LIKE	454a	1 c1
	ספר	MISSIVE	707b	3 c
	קללה	CURSE	887a	
	קרא	CALL	895c	4 a
8 35	גר	SOJOURNER	158b	2
	דבר	WORD	183d	46
	טף	CHILDREN	*382a	
	נגד	IN FRONT	617b	1 aa
	קהל	ASSEMBLY	874d	2 a
	קרא	CALL	895c	4 a
9 1	אמרי	AMORITES	57c	2 e
	יבוסי	JEBUSITE	101a	1
	היה	COME TO PASS	224c	2 a1 aa
	הר	MOUNTAIN	251a	2 a
	חוי	HIVITE	295d	2
	חוף	SHORE	342b	
	חתי	HITTITE	366d	2 a
	ים	SEA	410d	1
	ים	SEA	411b	2 b
	כנעני	CANAANITE	489a	2 b
	לבנון	LEBANON	527a	
	מול	IN FRONT OF	557c	2 a
	עבר	REGION ACROSS	719c	1 b
	שפלה	LOWLAND	1050c	1
9 2	יחדו	TOGETHER	403b	A
	לחם	ENGAGE IN BAT-TLE	535c	
	קבץ	GATHER	868b	
9 3	גבעון	GIBEON	149c	
	עי	AI	743b	1
9 4	בלה	WORN OUT	115b	
	בקע	BREAK OPEN OR THROUGH	132b	
	חם	THEY	241b	1 b
	חמור	HE-ASS	331b	3
	יין	WINE	406c	D
	לקח	TAKE	542d	2
	נאד	SKIN	609d	
	ציד	SUPPLY ONES PRO-VISIONS	845b	
	צרר	BIND	864d	
	שק	SACK	974b	1
9 5	בלה	WORN OUT	115b	
	מלא	PATCH	378a	
	יבש	BE DRY	386b	1 a
	לחם	FOOD	537a	1 a
	נעל	SANDAL	653a	
	נקוד	CRUMB	666d	1
	על	UPON	753a	2 1a aa
	ציד	PROVISION	845b	
	שלמה	GARMENT	971b	
9 6	איש	MAN	36a	
	ברית	COVENANT	136b	1 1
	כרת	CUT	503d	4
	רחק	DISTANT	935b	1 a
9 7	איך	HOW	32c	1
	איש	MAN	36a	
	ברית	COVENANT	136b	1 1
	גבעון	GIBEON	*149c	
	חוי	HIVITE	295d	2
	חוי	HIVITE	*295d	2
	כרת	CUT	503d	4
9 9	יהוה	YAHWEH	218d	2 1a
	ל	TO	514d	5 g
	רחק	DISTANT	935b	1 a
	שם	NAME	1028b	3
	שמע	REPORT	1035a	
9 10	אמרי	AMORITES	57c	2 a
	חשבון	HESHBON	363d	
	עבר	REGION ACROSS	719c	1 a
	עוג	OG	728b	
	עשתרות	ASHTAROTH	800b	
9 11	ברית	COVENANT	136b	1 1
	דרך	JOURNEY	203a	1
	הלך	WALK	233d	1 5a
	זקן	OLD	278d	2 b
	יד	HAND	391a	5 c4
	כרת	CUT	503d	4
	לקח	TAKE	542d	2
	ציידה	PROVISION	845b	
9 12	זה	THIS	260d	2 a
	חם	HOT	328d	
	חם	HEAT	*328d	
	יבש	BE DRY	386b	1 a
	לחם	FOOD	537a	1 a
	נקוד	CRUMB	666d	1
	ציד	SUPPLY ONES PRO-VISIONS	845b	
9 13	בלה	BECOME OLD AND WORN OUT	115a	
	בקע	BREAK OPEN OR THROUGH	132b	
	דרך	JOURNEY	203a	2
	חדש	NEW	294a	A
	יין	WINE	406c	D
	מאד	EXCEEDINGLY	547b	2 a
	מלא	FILL	570c	1
	מן	ON ACCOUNT OF	580c	2 f
	נאד	SKIN	609d	

Ch v.	Heb	Eng	Page	Sec
	רבב	BECOME MUCH	912d	2
	רב	MULTITUDE	914a	2
	שלמה	GARMENT	971b	
9 14	ציד	PROVISION	845b	
	שאל	ASK	982a	2b
9 15	ברית	COVENANT	136b	1 1
	חיה	LIVE	311c	1
	עדה	CONGREGATION	417b	3
	כרת	CUT	503d	4
	נשיא	PRINCE	672b	4
	עשה	DO	794c	2 1e
	שלון	PEACE	1023b	6
9 16	אחר	AFTER THAT	30b	3
	ברית	COVENANT	136b	1 1
	חיה	COME TO PASS	224d	2 a1 a1
	כרת	CUT	503d	4
	קצה	END	892b	4
	קרב	NEAR	898c	2a
9 17	בארות	BEEROTH	92a	
	בעלה	BAALAH	128c	
	גבעון	GIBEON	149c	
	כפירה	CHEPHIRAH	499a	
	נסע	SET OUT	652b	2a
	קריתיערים	KIRIATH-JEARIM	900c	
9 18	אלהים	GOD	44b	4 ba
	עדה	CONGREGATION	417b	3
	לון	MURMUR	534a	
	נכה	SMITE	646a	2c
	נשיא	PRINCE	672b	4
	נשיא	PRINCE	672b	4
	שבע	SWEAR	989b	1a
9 19	אלהים	GOD	44b	4 ba
	יכל	BE ABLE	407c	1a
	נגע	TOUCH	619a	3
	נשיא	PRINCE	672b	4
	שבע	SWEAR	989b	1a
9 20	חיה	LIVE	311c	1
	על	UPON	754b	2 1f b
	קצף	WRATH	893c	1
	שבע	SWEAR	989b	1a
	שבועה	OATH	989d	1a
9 21	דבר	SPEAK	181b	3c
	חטב	CUT OR GATHER WOOD	310a	
	נשיא	PRINCE	672b	4
	עץ	TREE	782a	2d
	שאב	DRAW	980c	
9 22	רחק	DISTANT	935b	1a
9 23	אלהים	GOD	44d	4c
	ו	AND	253a	1h
	חטב	CUT OR GATHER WOOD	310a	
	כרת	BE CUT OFF	504b	4
	מעון	REFUGE	*733a	1
	עץ	TREE	782a	2d
	שאב	DRAW	980c	
9 24	יהוה	YAHWEH	218d	2 1a
	ירא	FEAR	431b	1c
	ל	TO	515c	5 hc
	נגד	BE CONSPICUOUS	617a	
	עבד	SLAVE	714a	3
	שמד	BE EXTERMINATED	1029b	1
9 25	הנה	BEHOLD	243d	2
	הנה	BEHOLD	*244a	A
	טוב	PLEASANT	374a	2f
	ישר	STRAIGHT	449a	2b
	עין	EYE	744d	3c
9 27	בחר	CHOOSE	104a	2a
	חטב	CUT OR GATHER WOOD	310a	
	יום	DAY	401b	71
	עץ	TREE	782a	2d
	מקום	STANDING PLACE	880b	4
10 1	אדניצדק	ADONI-ZEDEK	11d	
	גבעון	GIBEON	149c	
	חרם	BAN	355d	1a
	ירושלים	JERUSALEM	436d	
	יריחו	JERICHO	437c	
	כי	THAT	471d	1a
	כן	SO	486c	2 ca
	לכד	CAPTURE	540a	1
	עי	AI	743b	1
	שלם	BE IN COVENANT OF PEACE	1023d	1
10 2	גבעון	GIBEON	149c	
	גבור	STRONG	150b	2
	הוא	HE, SHE, IT	*216a	3a
	ירא	FEAR	431a	1a
	ממלכה	DOMINION	575b	2
	עי	AI	743b	1
	עיר	CITY	746b	1d
10 3	אדניצדק	ADONI-ZEDEK	11d	
	דביר	DEBIR	184c	1
	הוהם	HOHAM	222d	
	חברון	HEBRON	289b	
	יפיע	JAPHIA	422b	1a
	ירושלים	JERUSALEM	436d	
	ירמות	JARMUTH	438b	1
	לכיש	LACHISH	540c	
	עגלון	EGLON	722d	2
	פראם	PIRAM	825b	
10 4	את	WITH	86a	1 da
	גבעון	GIBEON	149c	
	נכה	SMITE	646c	3
	עזר	HELP	740b	
	עלה	GO UP	748c	2a
	שלם	BE IN COVENANT OF PEACE	1023d	1
10 5	אמרי	AMORITES	57c	2b
	אסף	GATHER	62d	1a
	גבעון	GIBEON	149c	
	חברון	HEBRON	289b	
	חמש	FIVE	331d	1d
	חנה	DECLINE	333c	2c2
	מחנה	ENCAMPMENT	334b	3c
	ירושלים	JERUSALEM	436d	
	ירמות	JARMUTH	438b	1
	לחם	ENGAGE IN BATTLE	535c	
	לחם	ENGAGE IN BATTLE	*535c	
	לכיש	LACHISH	540c	
	עגלון	EGLON	722d	2
10 6	אל	TO	40b	4
	אמרי	AMORITES	57c	2b
	גבעון	GIBEON	149c	
	הר	MOUNTAIN	251a	2b
	ישע	DELIVER	446c	1
	מהרה	HASTE	555b	
	עזר	HELP	740b	
	עלה	GO UP	748c	2a
	קבץ	GATHER	867d	1
	רפה	SINK	951d	1
10 7	גבור	STRONG	150b	2
	חיל	STRENGTH	298d	1c
	מלחמה	WAR	536b	
	מן	FROM	578a	1a
	עם	PEOPLE	766c	2d
10 8	ירא	FEAR	431b	1c
	עמד	STAND	764b	2a
	פנה	FACE	816d	2 3a
10 9	לילה	NIGHT	539a	1
10 10	ביתחורון	BETH-HORON	111c	
	ביתחורון	BETH-HORON	*111c	
	ביתחורון	BETH-HORON	111c	B
	גבעון	GIBEON	149c	
	המם	CONFUSE	243a	2
	מקדה	MAKKEDAH	596b	
	נכה	SMITE	646b	3
	מכה	SLAUGHTER	647a	3
	עקה	DIG ABOUT	740a	
	רדף	PURSUE	922d	1b
10 11	אבן	STONE	6d	1
	אבן	STONE	7a	7
	מאשר	FROM THAT WHICH	84a	A
	ביתחורון	BETH-HORON	111c	
	ביתחורון	BETH-HORON	*111c	
	ביתחורון	BETH-HORON	111c	B
	הרג	KILL	247b	1b
	חרב	SWORD	352d	1f
	מורד	DESCENT	434c	1
	מות	DIE	559d	2b
	נוס	FLEE	630d	1
	עקה	DIG ABOUT	740a	
	רב	MUCH	913b	1e
	שלך	THROW	1021b	2a
	שמי	HEAVENS	1030a	2a
10 12	אז	THEN	23a	1a
	אמר	SAY	56a	1
	אמרי	AMORITES	57c	2b
	גבעון	GIBEON	149c	
	דבר	SPEAK	181b	3c
	דמם	BE STILL	198d	1
	ירח	MOON	437a	
	פנה	FACE	817b	2 4b c
	שמש	SUN	1039b	1
10 13	אין	HASTEN	21a	3
	בוא	COME	98a	1i
	גוי	NATION	156c	1b
	דמם	BE STILL	198d	1
	הוא	HE, SHE, IT	216d	6a
	יום	DAY	398b	1
	יום	DAY	400d	7h
	ירח	MOON	437a	
	ישר	STRAIGHT	449b	3c2
	ך	LIKE	453c	1a
	לא	NOT	520c	4 bb
	נקם	AVENGE	668a	1b
	ספר	MISSIVE	707b	3d
	עד	UNTIL	725a	2 1b b
	על	UPON	752d	2 1
	עמד	STAND	764a	2a
	שמש	SUN	1039b	1
	תמים	COMPLETE	1071a	3
10 14	היה	BE	226d	3 1
	יום	DAY	400d	7h
	ך	LIKE	453d	1b
	ל	TO	514b	5 fb
	לחם	ENGAGE IN BATTLE	535d	
10 16	חבא	WITHDRAW	285b	
	מקדה	MAKKEDAH	596b	
	נוס	FLEE	630d	1
	מערה	CAVE	792c	
10 17	חבא	WITHDRAW	285b	
	מצא	FIND	394a	1f
	מקדה	MAKKEDAH	596b	
	נגד	BE CONSPICUOUS	617a	
10 18	אבן	STONE	6b	1
	פה	MOUTH	805b	4
10 19	שמר	KEEP	1036c	1b
	זנב	CUT OFF THE TAIL	275c	
	עמד	STAND	764a	3a
	רדף	PURSUE	922c	1a
10 20	מבצר	FORTIFICATION	131c	
	נכה	SMITE	646a	2c
	שרד	SLAUGHTER	647a	2
	שריד	ESCAPE	974d	
	שריד	SURVIVOR	975a	1
	תמם	BE FINISHED	1070c	5
10 21	חרץ	CUT	358c	1
	ל	TO	*511a	1d
	לשון	TONGUE	546b	1b
	מקדה	MAKKEDAH	596b	
	שלון	PEACE	1023b	6
10 22	יצא	BRING OUT	424d	1i
	יצא	BRING OUT	424d	1g
	פה	MOUTH	805b	4
	פתח	OPEN	835a	
10 23	חברון	HEBRON	289b	
	יצא	BRING OUT	424d	1i
	יצא	BRING OUT	424d	1g
	ירושלים	JERUSALEM	436d	
	ירמות	JARMUTH	438b	1
	לכיש	LACHISH	540c	
	עגלון	EGLON	722d	2
10 24	ה	THE	209b	3
	הלך	WALK	231c	1d 5a
	יצא	BRING OUT	424d	1h
	מלחמה	WAR	536b	
	צואר	NECK	848c	1
	קצין	CHIEF	892d	1
	קרא	CALL	895d	5b
	קרב	COME NEAR	897c	1g
	קרב	COME NEAR	897c	1g
10 25	אמץ	BE STRONG	55a	2
	את	WITH	85c	
	חזק	BE FIRM	304b	1 2c
	חתת	BE SHATTERED	369b	4
	ירא	FEAR	431a	1a
	לחם	ENGAGE IN BATTLE	535c	
10 26	היה	BE	227c	3 5a
	מות	DIE	560b	1a
	נכה	SMITE	645d	2a
	עץ	TREE	781d	2b
	תלה	HANG	1068a	2
10 27	אבן	STONE	6b	1
	בוא	COME	98a	1i
	חבא	WITHDRAW	285b	
	יום	DAY	401b	71
	ירד	BRING DOWN	434a	2
	על	UPON	752d	2 1
	עת	TIME	773c	1c
	עץ	TREE	781d	2b
	עצם	BONE	783a	3
	פה	MOUTH	805b	4
	שלך	THROW	1021a	1a
	חרב	SWORD	352d	1f
10 28	חרם	BAN	355d	1a
	יריחו	JERICHO	437c	
	מקדה	MAKKEDAH	596b	
	נכה	SMITE	646b	3
	נפש	SOUL	660b	4c3
	שריד	SURVIVOR	975a	1
	שאר	REMAIN	984b	1
10 29	לבנה	LIBNAH	526c	1
	לחם	ENGAGE IN BATTLE	535c	
	מקדה	MAKKEDAH	596b	
	עבר	PASS OVER	718a	5a
10 30	חרב	SWORD	352d	1f
	יריחו	JERICHO	437c	
	נכה	SMITE	646b	3
	נפש	SOUL	660b	4c3
	שריד	SURVIVOR	975a	1
	שאר	REMAIN	984b	1
10 31	חנה	DECLINE	333c	2c2
	לבנה	LIBNAH	526c	1
	לחם	ENGAGE IN BATTLE	535c	
	לכיש	LACHISH	540c	
	לכיש	LACHISH	540c	
	עבר	PASS OVER	718a	5a
	שוב	TURN BACK	997a	2
10 32	חרב	SWORD	352d	1f
	לבנה	LIBNAH	526c	1
	לכיש	LACHISH	540c	
	נכה	SMITE	646b	3
	נפש	SOUL	660b	4c3
10 33	אז	THEN	23a	1a
	בלת	NOT	117a	4c
	גב	GOB	*146c	
	גזר	GEZER	160c	
	הרם	HORAM	248b	
	לכיש	LACHISH	540c	
	נכה	SMITE	646b	3
	עזר	HELP	740b	
	שריד	SURVIVOR	975a	1
	שאר	REMAIN	984b	1
10 34	חנה	DECLINE	333c	2c2
	לחם	ENGAGE IN BATTLE	535c	
	לכיש	LACHISH	540c	
	עבר	PASS OVER	718a	5a
	עגלון	EGLON	722d	2

Ch v.	Heb	Eng	Page	Sec
10 35	חרב	SWORD	352d	1 f
	חרם	BAN	355d	1 a
	לכיש	LACHISH	540c	
	נכה	SMITE	646b	3
	נפש	SOUL	660b	4 c3
10 36	חברון	HEBRON	289b	
	לחם	ENGAGE IN BATTLE	535c	
10 37	עגלון	EGLON	722d	2
	חרב	SWORD	352d	1 f
	חרם	BAN	355d	1 a
	נכה	SMITE	646b	3
	נפש	SOUL	660b	4 c3
	עגלון	EGLON	722d	2
	שריד	SURVIVOR	975a	1
	שאר	REMAIN	984b	1
10 38	דביר	DEBIR	184c	2 c
	לחם	ENGAGE IN BATTLE	535c	
10 39	דביר	DEBIR	184c	2 c
	חברון	HEBRON	289b	
	חרב	SWORD	352d	1 f
	חרם	BAN	355d	1 a
	כן	SO	486c	2 ca
	לבנה	LIBNAH	526c	1
	נכה	SMITE	646b	3
	נפש	SOUL	660b	4 c3
	שריד	SURVIVOR	975a	1
	שאר	REMAIN	984b	1
10 40	אלהים	GOD	44b	4 ba
	אשדה	FOUNDATION	78b	
	הר	MOUNTAIN	251a	2 a
	חרם	BAN	355d	1 a
	נגב	SOUTH-COUNTRY	616b	1 a
	נכה	SMITE	646b	3
	נכה	SMITE	646b	3
	נשמה	BREATH	675d	3
	שריד	SURVIVOR	975a	1
	שאר	REMAIN	984b	1
	שפלה	LOWLAND	1050c	1
10 41	גבעון	GIBEON	149c	
	גשן	GOSHEN	177d	2
	עזה	GAZA	738b	
	קדש	KADESH	874a	1
10 42	אלהים	GOD	44b	4 ba
	לחם	ENGAGE IN BATTLE	535d	
	לכד	CAPTURE	540a	1
	פעם	OCCURRENCE	822a	3 a
11 1	יבין	JABIN	108a	1
	מדון	MADON	193c	
	חצור	HAZOR	347d	1
	יובב	JOBAB	384d	3
	אכשף	ACHSHAPH	506d	
	שמרון	SHIMRON	1038a	
11 2	דאר	DOR	190b	
	הר	MOUNTAIN	251a	2 a
	ים	SEA	411b	9
	כנרת	CHINNERETH	490b	1
	נגב	SOUTH-COUNTRY	616c	2
	נפה	HEIGHT	632c	
	ערבה	DESERT-PLAIN	787c	2 a
	שפלל	LOWLAND	1050d	2
11 3	אמרי	AMORITES	57c	2 e
	ארץ	EARTH	76a	2 b
	יבוסי	JEBUSITE	101a	1
	הר	MOUNTAIN	251a	2 b
	מזרח	PLACE OF SUNRISE	281a	2 d
	חוי	HIVITE	295d	2
	חרמון	HERMON	356d	
	חתי	HITTITE	*366d	2 b
	חתי	HITTITE	366d	2 a
	כנעני	CANAANITE	*489a	2 b
	כנעני	CANAANITE	489a	2 b
	מן	FROM	578c	1 c
	מצפה	MIZPAH	860a	3
	תחת	UNDERNEATH	1065c	2 1a
11 4	חול	SAND	297d	A
	חול	SAND	297d	C
	מחנה	ENCAMPMENT	334b	3 c
	ים	SEA	411a	8 a
	סוס	HORSE	692c	1
	רב	MUCH	913a	1 a2
	רב	MULTITUDE	914a	1
	רכב	CHARIOT	939a	1
11 5	אל	TO	40c	8
	חנה	DECLINE	333c	2 c2
	יעד	GATHER BY APPOINTMENT	416d	3
	לחם	ENGAGE IN BATTLE	535c	
	מי	WATER	565c	2
	מרום	MEROM	598c	
11 6	אש	FIRE	77c	1
	ירא	FEAR	431b	1 c
	ך	LIKE	453c	1
	מחר	TO-MORROW	564a	1 b
	סוס	HORSE	692c	1
	עת	TIME	773c	1 a
	עקר	HAMSTRING	785d	
	פנה	FACE	817b	24b c
	מרכבה	CHARIOT	939d	
	שרף	BURN	976d	2 a
11 7	מלחמה	WAR	536b	
	מי	WATER	565c	2
	מרום	MEROM	598c	

Ch v.	Heb	Eng	Page	Sec
	נפל	FALL	657c	4 a
	עם	PEOPLE	766c	2 d
	פתאם	SUDDENNESS	837c	
11 8	בלת	NOT	117a	4 c
	בקעה	PLAIN	132c	2
	מזרח	PLACE OF SUNRISE	281a	2 c1
	מי	WATER	565c	2
	נכה	SMITE	646b	3
	צידון	SIDON	851a	
	מצפה	MIZPEH	859d	2
	מצפה	MIZPAH	860a	3
	רדף	PURSUE	922d	1 b
	שריד	SURVIVOR	975a	1
	משרפותמים	MISREPHOTH-MAIM	977c	
11 9	שאר	REMAIN	984b	1
	אמר	SAY	56c	4
	אש	FIRE	77c	1
	סוס	HORSE	692c	1
	עקר	HAMSTRING	785d	
	מרכבה	CHARIOT	939d	
	שרף	BURN	976d	2 a
11 10	חצור	HAZOR	347d	1
	חרב	SWORD	352d	1 f
	ממלכה	KINGDOM	575a	1
	נכה	SMITE	646a	2 c
	פנה	FACE	816b	16
	ראש	HEAD	911a	3 b
	שוב	TURN BACK	996d	1
11 11	חצור	HAZOR	347d	1
	חרב	SWORD	352d	1 f
	חרם	BAN	355d	1 a
	יתר	BE LEFT OVER	451b	
	נכה	SMITE	646a	2 c
	נפש	SOUL	660b	4 c3
	נשמה	BREATH	675d	3
11 12	חרב	SWORD	352d	1 f
	חרם	BAN	355d	1 a
	חרם	BAN	*355d	1 a
	לכד	CAPTURE	540a	1
	נכה	SMITE	646a	2 c
	עבד	SLAVE	714a	3
11 13	זולה	EXCEPT	266a	2
	חצור	HAZOR	347d	1
	תל	MOUND	1068b	2
11 14	בז	SPOIL	102d	
	חרב	SWORD	352d	1 f
	נכה	SMITE	646a	2 c
	נשמה	BREATH	675d	3
	עד	AS FAR AS	*724b	12a b
	שאר	REMAIN	984b	1
	שלל	SPOIL	1022a	2
11 15	דבר	WORD	183d	4 6
	כן	SO	486c	2 ca
	סור	TURN ASIDE	694b	2
	עבד	SLAVE	714a	3
11 16	גשן	GOSHEN	177d	2
	הר	MOUNTAIN	251a	2 b
	לקח	TAKE	543a	4 c
	נגב	SOUTH-COUNTRY	616b	1 a
	ערבה	DESERT-PLAIN	787c	2 a
	קדש	KADESH	873d	1
	שפלה	LOWLAND	1050a	2
11 17	בעלגד	BAAL-GAD	128a	
	בקעה	PLAIN	132c	2
	הר	MOUNTAIN	249b	1 a
	חלק	SMOOTH	325b	1
	חרמון	HERMON	356d	
	לבנון	LEBANON	527a	
	לכד	CAPTURE	540a	1
	מות	DIE	560b	1 a
	נכה	SMITE	645d	2 a
	קדש	KADESH	873d	1
	שעיר	SEIR	973a	1 a
	תחת	UNDERNEATH	1065c	2 1a
11 18	מלחמה	WAR	536c	
	עשה	DO	794c	2 1e
11 19	בלת	EXCEPT	116c	2
	גבעון	GIBEON	149c	
	גבעון	GIBEON	149c	
	חוי	HIVITE	295d	2
	כל	ALL	482d	2 ba
	לקח	TAKE	543d	8
	שלם	BE IN COVENANT OF PEACE	1023d	1
11 20	את	WITH	86d	4 c
	חזק	BE FIRM	304d	5
	תחנה	FAVOR	337c	1
	חרם	BAN	355d	1 a
	חרם	BAN	*355d	1 a
	לב	HEART	525b	26d
	קרא	ENCOUNTER	897a	1
11 21	דביר	DEBIR	184c	2 c
	הר	MOUNTAIN	251a	2 b
	הר	MOUNTAIN	251a	2 b
	חברון	HEBRON	289b	
	חרם	BAN	355d	1 a
	יהודה	JUDAH	397c	2
	כרת	CUT OFF	504c	2 b
	עם	WITH	767b	1 a
	ענב	ANAB	772b	
	ענק	NECK	778c	
11 22	אשדוד	ASHDOD	78b	
	בצלאל	BEZALEL	*130b	
	גת	GATH	387d	
	יתר	BE LEFT OVER	451b	

Ch v.	Heb	Eng	Page	Sec
	עזה	GAZA	738b	
	ענק	NECK	778c	
	שאר	REMAIN	984a	1
11 23	מחלקת	DIVISION	325a	1
	מלחמה	WAR	536a	
	לקח	TAKE	543a	4 c
	נחלה	PROPERTY	635b	1 b
	שקט	BE QUIET	1053a	1
12 1	ארנון	ARNON	75a	
	הר	MOUNTAIN	249b	1 a
	מזרח	PLACE OF SUNRISE	281a	2 c1
	חרמון	HERMON	356d	
	ירש	TAKE POSSESSION	439c	1 a
	נחל	WADY	636c	2
	נכה	SMITE	646b	3
	עבר	REGION ACROSS	719c	1 b
	עבר	REGION ACROSS	719c	1 b
	ערבה	DESERT-PLAIN	787c	2 a
12 2	ארנון	ARNON	75a	
	יבק	JABBOK	132d	
	יבק	JABBOK	*132d	
	יבק	JABBOK	133a	
	גבול	BORDER	147d	1 a
	חשבון	HESHBON	363d	
	משל	RULE	605d	1
	נחל	WADY	636c	2
	נחל	WADY	636c	2
	עמון	AMMON	770a	
	ערער	AROER	792d	1
	יבק	ADDENDA ET CORRIGENDA	1121d	
12 3	אשדה	FOUNDATION	78b	
	ביתהישימות	BETH-JESHIMOTH	111d	
	דרך	WAY	202d	1
	מזרח	PLACE OF SUNRISE	281a	2 c1
	ים	SEA	411a	3
	ים	SEA	411a	3
	ים	SEA	411a	4
	תימן	TEMAN	412d	
	כנרת	CHINNERETH	490b	2
	מלח	SALT	572a	
	ערבה	DESERT-PLAIN	787c	1 a
	ערבה	DESERT-PLAIN	787c	2 a
	פסגה	PISGAH	820a	
12 4	גבול	BORDER	147d	1 a
	אדרעי	EDREI	204c	
	יתר	REMAINDER	451d	1 a
	מן	OUT OF	579c	2 cb
	עוג	OG	728b	
	עשתרות	ASHTAROTH	800b	
	רפאים	REPHAIM	952b	
12 5	גבול	BOUNDARY	147d	1 b
	גבול	BORDER	147d	1 a
	גשורי	GESHURITES	178c	1
	הר	MOUNTAIN	249b	1 a
	חרמון	HERMON	356d	
	חשבון	HESHBON	363d	
	מעכתי	MAACATHITE	591a	
	משל	RULE	605d	1
	סלכה	SALECAH	669d	
12 6	גדי	GADITE	151d	
	ירשה	POSSESSION	440b	
	מנשה	MANASSEH	586c	1 b2 d
	נכה	SMITE	646b	3
	עבד	SLAVE	714a	3
	ראובני	REUBENITE	910a	
12 7	בעלגד	BAAL-GAD	128a	
	בקעה	PLAIN	132c	2
	מחלקת	DIVISION	325a	1
	חלק	SMOOTH	325b	1
	ירשה	POSSESSION	440b	
	לבנון	LEBANON	527a	
	עבר	REGION ACROSS	719c	1 b
	שעיר	SEIR	973a	1 a
12 8	אמרי	AMORITES	57c	2 e
	אשדה	FOUNDATION	78b	
	יבוסי	JEBUSITE	101a	1
	הר	MOUNTAIN	*250b	1 e
	הר	MOUNTAIN	250b	1
	הר	MOUNTAIN	251a	2 a
	חוי	HIVITE	295d	2
	חתי	HITTITE	366d	2 a
	כנעני	CANAANITE	489a	2 b
	נגב	SOUTH-COUNTRY	616b	1 a
	ערבה	DESERT-PLAIN	787c	2 a
	שפלה	LOWLAND	1050c	1
12 9	ירוחו	JERICHO	437c	
	מן	FROM	578d	1 c
	עי	AI	743b	1
	צד	SIDE	841a	
12 10	חברון	HEBRON	289b	
	ירושלים	JERUSALEM	436d	
12 11	ירמות	JARMUTH	438b	1
	לכיש	LACHISH	540c	
	גזר	GEZER	160c	
12 12	נכה	SMITE	646b	3
	עגלון	EGLON	722d	2
12 13	ביתגדר	BETH-GADER	111b	
	גדר	GEDER	155a	
12 14	חרמה	HORMAH	356c	
	ערד	ARAD	788c	
12 15	לבנה	LIBNAH	526c	1
	עדלם	ADULLAM	726b	
12 16	מקדה	MAKKEDAH	596c	
	חפר	HEPHER	343d	1
12 17	תפח	TAPPUAH	656b	2

Ch	v	Heb	Eng	Page	Sec
12	18	אפק	APHEK	67d	1
		שרון	SHARON	450a	
		ל	TO	513d	5 cb e
		אפק	ADDENDA ET COR-RIGENDA	1120c	
12	19	מדון	MADON	193c	
		חצור	HAZOR	347d	1
12	20	אכשף	ACHSHAPH	506d	
		שמרון	SHIMRON	1038a	
12	21	מגדו	MEGIDDO	152a	
		תענך	TAANACH	1073d	
12	22	יקנעם	JOKNEAM	429b	
		כרמל	CARMEL	502a	1
		קדש	KEDESH	873d	1
12	23	גוי	NATION	156d	1 c
		דאר	DOR	190b	
		דאר	DOR	190b	
		נפת	HEIGHT	632c	
		נפת	HEIGHT	632c	
12	24	תרצה	TIRZAH	953c	2
13	1	בוא	COME	98b	1 k
		זקן	BE OLD	278b	
		יום	DAY	399b	4 a
		ירש	TAKE POSSESSION	439c	1 a
		רבה	BECOME MANY	915d	1 e3
		שאר	REMAIN	984a	1
13	2	גשורי	GESHURITES	178c	1
		זה	THIS	261a	3
		גשורי	ADDENDA ET COR-RIGENDA	1122a	
13	3	אשדודי	ASHDODITE	78c	
		אשקלוני	ASHKELONITES	80d	1 d
		חמש	FIVE	331d	
		חשב	THINK	363c	2
		גתי	GITTITE	388a	
		כנעני	CANAANITE	489a	2 b
		סרן	TYRANT	710d	
		עוים	AVVIM	732a	1
		עזתי	GAZITE	738b	
		עקרון	EKRON	785d	
		עקרוני	EKRONITE	785d	
		פלשתי	PHILISTINE	814c	
		פנה	FACE	818d	2 7a d
		פנה	FACE	818d	2 7a d
		צפון	NORTH	861a	
		שיחור	SHIHOR	1009d	
13	4	אמרי	AMORITES	57c	2 b
		אפק	APHEK	68a	3
		גבול	BORDER	147d	1 a
		תימן	TEMAN	412d	
		כנעני	CANAANITE	*489a	2 b
		כנעני	CANAANITE	489a	2 b
		צידני	SIDONIANS	851a	
13	5	בוא	COME	98d	2 e
		בעלגד	BAAL-GAD	128a	
		גבל	GEBAL	*148c	
		גבלי	GEBALITE	148c	
		הר	MOUNTAIN	249b	1 a
		חמת	HAMATH	333a	
		חרמון	HERMON	356d	
		לבנון	LEBANON	527a	
		עד	UNTIL	725b	3 1
13	6	ב	IN	89a	1 7c
		ירש	CAUSE TO POSSESS	440a	2 a
		ל	TO	*510d	1 c
		לבנון	LEBANON	527a	
		מי	WATER	565c	2
		נחלה	PROPERTY	635b	1 b
		נפל	FALL	658b	3
		צידני	SIDONIANS	851a	
		רק	ONLY	956c	2 b
		משרפותמים	MISREPHOTH-MAIM	977c	
13	7	ב	IN	89a	1 7c
		חלק	DIVIDE	323c	1
		מנשה	MANASSEH	586c	1 b1 d
		תשע	NINE	1077c	1 a
13	8	גוי	GADITE	151d	
		מזרח	PLACE OF SUNRISE	281a	2 c1
		לקח	TAKE	543b	4 f
		עבד	SLAVE	714a	3
		עבר	REGION ACROSS	719c	1 a
		ראובני	REUBENITE	910a	
13	9	ארנן	ARNON	75a	
		דיבן	DIBON	192a	1
		מישור	LEVEL PLACE	449d	1
		מידבא	MEDEBA	567d	
		נחל	WADY	636c	2
		ערער	AROER	792d	1
13	10	גבול	BORDER	147d	1 a
		חרונים	HORONAIM	357b	
		חשבון	HESHBON	363d	
		מלך	BE KING	574a	
		עמון	AMMON	770a	
13	11	גבול	BOUNDARY	147d	1 b
		גשורי	GESHURITES	178c	
		הר	MOUNTAIN	249b	1 a
		חרמון	HERMON	356d	
		חרונים	HORONAIM	357b	
		מעכתי	MAACATHITE	591a	
		סלכה	SALECAH	669c	
13	12	אדרעי	EDREI	204c	
		ירש	CAUSE TO POSSESS	440a	2 a
		יתר	REMAINDER	451d	1 a
		מלך	BE KING	574a	
		ממלכות	KINGDOM	575c	1
		נכה	SMITE	646b	3
		עוג	OG	728b	
		עשתרות	ASHTAROTH	800b	
		רפאים	REPHAIM	952b	
		שאר	REMAIN	984a	1
13	13	גשור	GESHUR	178a	1
		גשורי	GESHURITES	178c	1
		יום	DAY	401b	7 1
		ירש	CAUSE TO POSSESS	440a	2 a
		ישב	DWELL	443a	3
		מעכתי	MAACATHITE	591a	
		מעכה	MAACAH	591a	3
13	14	אלהים	GOD	44c	4 ba
		אשה	OFFERING MADE BY FIRE	78a	
		דבר	SPEAK	181b	3 c
		הוא	HE, SHE, IT	215d	2 b
		לוי	LEVITE	532d	2
		נחלה	PROPERTY	635b	1 d
13	15	ראובן	REUBEN	910a	2
13	16	ארנון	ARNON	75a	
		גבול	BOUNDARY	147d	1 b
		היה	BE	227c	3 4d d
		מישור	LEVEL PLACE	449d	1
		מידבא	MEDEBA	567d	
		נחל	WADY	636c	2
		ערער	AROER	792d	1
13	17	בעלבלמעון	BETH-BAAL-MEON	111a	
		במות	BAMOTH	119d	
		מען	BAAL-MEON	128b	
		דיבן	DIBON	192a	1
		חשבון	HESHBON	363d	
		מישור	LEVEL PLACE	449d	1
		עיר	CITY	746b	1 c
13	18	יחץ	JAHAZ	397d	
		מיפעת	MEPHAATH	422b	
		קדמת	KEDEMOTH	870d	
13	19	הר	MOUNTAIN	250b	1 e
		עמק	VALE	771a	
		צרתהשחר	ZERETH-SHAHAR	866c	
		קריתים	KIRIATHAIM	900b	1
		שבם	SEBAM	959b	
13	20	אשדה	FOUNDATION	78b	
		ביתהישמות	BETH-JESHIMOTH	111d	
		ביתפעור	BETH-PEOR	112c	
		פסגה	PISGAH	820a	
13	21	אוי	EVI	16c	
		מדין	MIDIAN	193c	2
		חור	HUR	301b	3
		חשבון	HESHBON	363d	
		מישור	LEVEL PLACE	449d	1
		ממלכות	KINGDOM	575c	1
		נסיך	PRINCE	651c	
		נשיא	PRINCE	672c	8
		סיחון	SIHON	695d	
		צור	ZUR	849d	1
		רבע	REBA	918b	
		רקם	REKEM	955d	1 a
13	22	אל	TO	40b	5
		בלעם	BALAAM	*118d	
		בעור	BEOR	129d	1
		הרג	KILL	247b	1 b
		חרב	SWORD	352d	1 f
		על	UPON	755b	2 4b
		קסם	PRACTICE OF DIVI-NATION	890c	1
13	23	ו	AND	252d	1 c
		חצר	SETTLED ABODE	347b	B
		עיר	CITY	746b	1 b
		ראובן	REUBEN	910a	2
13	24	גד	GAD	151c	1 b
13	25	יעזר	JAZER	741c	
		עמון	AMMON	770a	
		ערער	AROER	793a	2
		פנה	FACE	818d	2 7a d
		רבה	RABBA	913d	1
13	26	גבול	BOUNDARY	148a	2 b
		דביר	DEBIR	184c	2 b
		מחנים	MAHANAIM	334b	
		חשבון	HESHBON	363d	
		לאדבר	LO-DEBAR	520d	
		לידבר	LIDEBIR	529a	
		מצפה	MIZPEH	859d	3
		רמת	RAMATH-LEHI	928b	2
13	27	ביתהרם	BETH-HARAM	111b	
		ביתנמרה	BETH-NIMRAH	112b	
		ו	AND	252d	1 c
		מזרח	PLACE OF SUNRISE	281a	2 c1
		חשבון	HESHBON	363d	
		ים	SEA	411a	4
		ירדן	JORDAN	434d	
		יתר	REMAINDER	451d	1 b
		כנרת	CHINNERETH	*490b	1
		כנרת	CHINNERETH	490b	1
		ממלכות	KINGDOM	575c	1
		סיחון	SIHON	695d	
		סכת	SUCCOTH	697d	1
		עבר	REGION ACROSS	719c	1 a
		עמק	VALE	771a	
		צפן	ZAPHON	861b	
		קצה	END	892b	2
13	28	חצר	SETTLED ABODE	347b	B
13	29	היה	BECOME	226c	2 2h
		מנשה	MANASSEH	586c	1 b2 g
		מנשה	MANASSEH	586c	1 b2 d
13	30	מנשה	MANASSEH	586c	1 b1 a
		יאיר	JAIR	22c	1
		גבול	BOUNDARY	147d	1
		היה	BE	227c	3 4d d
		חוה	TENT-VILLAGE	295d	
		מחנים	MAHANAIM	334b	
		ארגב	ARGOB	419a	1
		ממלכות	KINGDOM	575c	1
		עוג	OG	728b	
13	31	אדרעי	EDREI	204c	1
		ממלכות	KINGDOM	575c	1
		מנשה	MANASSEH	586c	1 b2 d
		עוג	OG	728b	
		פך	ASHTAROTH	800b	
13	32	מזרח	PLACE OF SUNRISE	281a	2 c1
		ירדן	JORDAN	434d	
		מואב	MOAB	555d	2 b
		נחל	TAKE AS A POSSES-SION	635d	
		עבר	REGION ACROSS	*719b	1
		עבר	REGION ACROSS	719c	1 a
13	33	אלהים	GOD	44c	4 ba
		דבר	SPEAK	181b	3 c
		הוא	HE, SHE, IT	215d	2 b
		לוי	LEVITE	532d	2
		נחלה	PROPERTY	635b	1 d
14	1	אב	FATHER	3c	
		נחל	TAKE AS A POSSES-SION	635c	1 b
		נחל	TAKE AS A POSSES-SION	635d	
14	2	ראש	HEAD	911a	3 f
		גורל	LOT	174d	3
		יד	HAND	391a	5 d
		תשע	NINE	1077c	1 a
14	3	ירדן	JORDAN	434c	
		לוי	LEVITE	533a	3 1c
		נחלה	PROPERTY	635b	1 d
		עבר	REGION ACROSS	719c	1 a
14	4	אפרים	EPHRAIM	68b	2
		מגרש	COMMON-LAND	177b	
		חלק	PORTION	324a	2 a
		יוסף	JOSEPH	415d	1 b
		כיא	EXCEPT	474d	2 a
		לוי	LEVITE	533a	3 1c
		קנין	ACQUISITION	889a	1
		מקנה	CATTLE	889b	2
14	5	חלק	DIVIDE	323c	1
		כן	SO	486c	2 ca
		שקט	BE QUIET	1053a	1
14	6	אדה	CAUSE	15c	
		איש	MAN	36a	
		אלהים	GOD	43d	3 b
		יהודה	JUDAH	397b	1 2
		כלב	CALEB	477a	
		נגש	DRAW NEAR	620d	1
		יפנה	JEPHUNNEH	819c	1
		קדש	KADESH	874a	1
		קנזי	KENIZZITE	889d	
14	7	בן	SON	121d	9 a
		דבר	WORD	182b	1 1c
		לבב	HEART	523c	2
		עבד	SLAVE	714a	3
		עם	WITH	768c	4 a
		קדש	KADESH	874a	1
		רגל	GO ABOUT	920b	2
		שוב	TURN BACK	999c	3
14	8	יהוה	YAHWEH	218d	2 1f
		לבב	HEART	*524b	2 9b
		מלא	FILL	570d	2
		מסה	DISSOLVE	587b	
14	9	אם	IF	50b	1 b2
		דרך	TREAD	202a	2
		יהוה	YAHWEH	218d	2 1f
		מלא	FILL	570d	2
		שבע	SWEAR	989a	1 a
14	10	מאז	FROM THAT TIME	23b	B
		אשר	PARTICLE OF RE-LATION	82c	4 ba
		בן	SON	121d	9 a
		הלך	WALK	230c	1 1d 1b
		הלך	WALK	230c	1 1d 2a
		חיה	LIVE	311c	1
		עתה	NOW	774b	2 c
		ארבעים	FORTY	917c	2 a
14	11	אז	THEN	23a	1 a
		בוא	COME	97d	1 a
		חזק	STRONG	305c	1 a
		יצא	GO OUT	424a	3
		כ	LIKE	454c	2 c
		כח	STRENGTH	470c	1 a
		עתה	NOW	774a	1 a
		את	WITH	85c	2
14	12	את	WITH	85d	1 a
		בצר	MAKE INACCESSI-BLE	131a	
		ירש	CAUSE TO POSSESS	440a	2 a
		ענק	NECK	778c	2
14	13	ברך	BLESS	139a	3
		חברון	HEBRON	289b	
		כלב	CALEB	477a	
		נחלה	PROPERTY	635b	1 b
		יפנה	JEPHUNNEH	819c	1
14	14	אלהים	GOD	44b	4 ba
		חברון	HEBRON	289b	
		יום	DAY	401b	7 1

Ch	v.	Heb	Eng	Page	Sec
		כלב	CALEB	477a	
		בן	SO	487b	3 f
		מלא	FILL	570d	2
		יען	ON ACCOUNT OF	774d	2 a
		קנזי	KENIZZITE	889d	
14	15	אדם	MAN	9b	1
		ב	IN	88b	12a
		ה	THE	207b	1 b
		חברון	HEBRON	289b	
		מלחמה	WAR	536a	
		ענק	NECK	778c	
		קריתארבע	FOURFOLD CITY	*900b	
		קריתארבע	FOURFOLD CITY	900c	
		ארבע	ARBA	*917b	
		שקט	BE QUIET	1053a	1
15	1	בן	SON	121a	1 jd
		גבול	BORDER	147d	1 a
		גורל	LOT	174d	3
		יהודה	JUDAH	397b	12
		תימן	SOUTH	412d	1 a
		נגב	SOUTH-COUNTRY	616c	2
		צן	ZIN	856c	
		קצה	END	892a	1
15	2	ים	SEA	411a	3
		לשון	TONGUE	546d	6
		מלח	SALT	572a	
		נגב	SOUTH-COUNTRY	616b	2
		נגב	SOUTH-COUNTRY	616c	2
		פנה	TURN	815c	2 b
		קצה	END	892a	1
15	3	אדר	ADDAR	12b	2
		אל	TO	40d	9
		חצראדר	HAZARADDAR	347c	
		חצרון	HEZRON	348a	1 a
		יצא	GO OUT	423d	1 h
		נגב	SOUTH-COUNTRY	616b	2
		סבב	TURN AROUND	686a	1 c
		עבר	PASS OVER	718a	5 b
		עבר	PASS OVER	718a	5 b
		עלה	GO UP	749a	9
		צן	ZIN	856c	
		מעלה	ASCENT	751c	1
		קדש	KADESH	874a	1
		קרקע	KARKA	903a	1
15	4	יצא	GO OUT	423d	1 h
		תוצאה	OUT GOING	426a	1
		נגב	SOUTH-COUNTRY	616b	2
		נחל	WADY	636c	2
		מצרים	EGYPT	695c	1 a
		עבר	PASS OVER	718a	5 b
		עצמון	AZMON	783b	
15	5	ים	SEA	411a	3
		ים	SEA	411b	8 c
		יערים	JEARIM	421b	
		לשון	TONGUE	546d	6
		מלח	SALT	572a	
		צפון	NORTH	861a	
		קדם	EASTWARD	870b	
		קצה	END	892a	1
15	6	אבן	STONE	7a	9
		בהן	BOHAN	97b	
		ביתחגלה	BETH-HOGLAH	111c	
		ביתערבה	BETH-ARABAH	112c	
		עבר	PASS OVER	718a	5 b
		עלה	GO UP	749a	9
		ראובן	REUBEN	910a	2
15	7	דביר	DEBIR	184c	2 a
		תוצאה	OUT GOING	426a	1
		מי	WATER	565c	2
		נגב	SOUTH-COUNTRY	616b	2
		נחל	WADY	636c	2
		נכח	FRONT	*647b	1
		עבר	PASS OVER	718a	5 b
		עינשמש	EN-SHEMESH	734d	1
		עין	SPRING	745b	C
		עגור	DISTURBANCE	747d	1
		מעלה	ASCENT	751c	1
		פנה	TURN	815c	2 b
15	8	יבוסי	JEBUSITE	101a	2
		בן	SON	120d	1 ja
		הנם	HINNOM	244d	
		הנם	HINNOM	245a	
		הר	MOUNTAIN	250d	1 m
		ים	SEA	411b	9
		ירושלים	JERUSALEM	436d	
		כתף	SIDE	509c	2 a
		מן	FROM	578d	1 c
		נגב	SOUTH-COUNTRY	616c	2
		עלה	GO UP	749a	9
		פנה	FACE	818d	27a d
		קצה	END	892a	1
		רפאים	REPHAIM	952b	
15	9	בעלה	BAALAH	128b	
		בעלה	BAALAH	128c	
		הר	MOUNTAIN	250d	1 m
		יצא	GO OUT	423d	1 h
		מי	WATER	565c	2
		מעין	SPRING	745d	
		עפרון	EPHRON	780b	3
		נפתוח	NEPHTOAH	836b	
		קריתיערים	KIRIATH-JEARIM	900c	
		קריתיערים	KIRIATH-JEARIM	900c	
		תאר	INCLINE	1061b	
		תאר	INCLINE	1061b	
15	10	ביתשמש	BETH-SHEMESH	112d	1
		בעלה	BAALAH	128b	
		ים	SEA	411b	9
		ירד	GO DOWN	433c	3 f
		כסלון	CHESALON	493b	
		כתף	SIDE	509c	2 a
		מנה	TIMNAH	584d	2
		סבב	TURN AROUND	686a	1 c
		עבר	PASS OVER	718a	5 b
		קריתיערים	KIRIATH-JEARIM	900c	
		קריתיערים	KIRIATH-JEARIM	900c	
		שעיר	SEIR	973a	2
15	11	יבנאל	JABNEEL	125c	1
		בעלה	BAALAH	128b	
		יצא	GO OUT	423d	1 h
		תוצאה	OUT GOING	426a	1
		כתף	SIDE	509c	2 a
		עבר	PASS OVER	718a	5 b
		קריתיערים	KIRIATH-JEARIM	900c	
		שכרון	SHIKKERON	1016c	
		תאר	INCLINE	1061b	
15	12	הגבול	GREAT	147c	
		ו	AND	252d	1 c
		ים	SEA	410d	1
		ים	SEA	411b	9
15	13	אל	TO	40c	7
		חברון	HEBRON	289b	
		חלק	PORTION	324a	2 a
		כלב	CALEB	477a	
		פה	MOUTH	805d	6 d2
		קריתארבע	FOURFOLD CITY	*900b	
		קריתארבע	FOURFOLD CITY	900c	
		ארבע	ARBA	*917b	
15	14	אחימן	AHIMAN	27a	1
		ילד	CHILDREN	409d	
		ירש	CAUSE TO POSSESS	440a	2 a
		כלב	CALEB	477a	
		ענק	NECK	778c	
		ענק	NECK	778c	
		ששי	SHESHAI	1058d	
		תלמי	TALMAI	1068d	2
15	15	דביר	DEBIR	184c	2 c
		דביר	DEBIR	184c	2 c
		קריתספר	KIRIATH-SEPHER	900d	
15	16	כלב	CALEB	477a	
		נכה	SMITE	646b	3
		נתן	GIVE	678c	1 c
		עכסה	ACHSAH	747c	
		קריתספר	KIRIATH-SEPHER	900d	
15	17	כלב	CALEB	477a	
		נתן	GIVE	678c	1 c
		עכסה	ACHSAH	747c	
		עתניאל	OTHNIEL	801a	
		קנז	KENAZ	889d	
15	18	בא	COME	98a	1 d
		חמור	HE-ASS	331b	2 a
		כלב	CALEB	477a	
		מה	WHAT	552c	1 ac
		סות	INCITE	694d	1 a
		על	UPON	758c	4 2a
		צנח	DESCEND	856c	
15	19	ברכה	BLESSING	139d	5
		ו	AND	254c	4
		נגב	SOUTH-COUNTRY	616b	1 a
		עלי	UPPER	751a	
		תחתי	LOWER	1066c	
15	20	בן	SON	121a	1 jd
		חצר	SETTLED ABODE	*347b	D
		יהודה	JUDAH	397b	12
15	21	בן	SON	121a	1 jd
		גבול	BORDER	147d	1 a
		יגור	JAGUR	158c	
		מן	FROM	582a	5 d1
		נגב	SOUTH-COUNTRY	616a	1 a
		נגב	SOUTH-COUNTRY	616b	1 a
		עדר	EDER	727d	
		קבצאל	KABZEEL	868b	
		קצה	END	892a	1
15	22	דיבן	DIBON	192a	2
		ערער	AROER	793a	3
		קינה	KINAH	884a	2
		קין	KENITE	884a	2
15	23	חצור	HAZOR	347d	2 a
		יתנן	ITHNAN	451a	
		קדש	KEDESH	873a	3
15	24	בעלות	BEALOTH	128c	
		זיף	ZIPH	268b	1 b
		טלם	TELEM	379a	1
		יתנן	ITHNAN	*451a	
15	25	חצורחדתה	HAZOR-HADATTAH	347d	
		חצור	HAZOR	347d	2 b
		חצרון	HEZRON	348a	1 b
		קריות	KERIOTH-HEZRON	901a	1
15	26	אמם	AMAM	52c	
		מולדה	MOLADAH	409d	
		שמע	SHEMA	1035a	
15	27	ביתפלט	BETH-PELET	112c	
		חצרגדה	HAZAR-GADDAH	347c	
		חשמון	HESHMON	365c	
15	28	בארשבע	BEERSHEBA	92a	
		ביותיה	BIZIOTHIAH	103a	
		בת	DAUGHTER	123d	4
		חצרשועל	HAZAR-SHUAL	347c	1
15	29	בלהה	BILHAH	117b	
		בעלה	BAALAH	128b	
		עיים	IYIM	743d	2
		עצם	EZEM	783a	
		קריתיערים	KIRIATH-JEARIM	900c	
15	30	אלתולד	ELTOLAD	39a	
		ביתאל	BETHEL	111a	2
		בתואל	BETHUEL	143d	
		חרמה	HORMAH	356c	
15	31	כסיל	CHESIL	493b	
		מדמנה	MADMANNAH	199b	1
		סנסנה	SANSANNAH	703b	
		צקלג	ZIKLAG	862c	
15	32	ביתלבאות	BETH-LEBAOTH	111d	
		חצר	SETTLED ABODE	347b	B
		חצר	SETTLED ABODE	*347b	D
		לבאות	LEBAOTH	522d	
		עין	AIN	745b	2
		עשרים	TWENTY	797d	12a
		רמון	RIMMON	942a	2
		שלחים	SHILHIM	1019d	
		שערים	SHAARAIM	1045c	2
15	33	אשנה	ASHNAH	80b	1
		אשתאול	ESHTAOL	84b	
		צרעה	ZORAH	864a	
		שפלה	LOWLAND	1050c	1
15	34	זנוח	ZANOAH	276c	1
		תפח	TAPPUAH	656b	1
		עגלון	EGLON	722d	2
		עינם	ENAM	734d	
		עינגנים	EN-GANNIM	745c	1
15	35	ירמות	JARMUTH	438b	1
		עדלם	ADULLAM	726b	
		עוקה	DIG ABOUT	740a	
		שוכה	SOCOH	962c	1
15	36	גדרה	GEDERAH	155b	
		גדרתים	GEDEROTHAIM	155b	
		עדיתים	ADITHAIM	726b	
		ארבע	FOUR	917a	2 a1 b
		שערים	SHAARAIM	1045c	1
15	37	מגדלגד	MIGDAL-GAD	154a	
		חדשה	HADASHAH	295a	
		צאנן	ZENAN	838c	
		דלען	DILEAN	196a	
15	38	יקתאל	JOKTHEEL	430d	1
		מצפה	MIZPEH	859d	1
15	39	בצקת	BOZKATH	130d	
		לכיש	LACHISH	540c	
		עגלון	EGLON	722d	2
15	40	כבון	CABBON	460a	
		כתליש	CHITLISH	508c	
		לחמס	LAHMAS	537c	
15	41	ביתדגון	BETH-DAGON	*111b	1
		ביתדגון	BETH-DAGON	111b	1
		גדרות	GEDEROTH	155b	
		מקדה	MAKKEDAH	596b	
		נעמה	NAAMAH	654a	
		שש	SIX	995c	2
15	42	לבנה	LIBNAH	526c	1
		עשן	ASHAN	798c	
		עתר	ETHER	801d	
15	43	אשנה	ASHNAH	80b	2
		נציב	NEZIB	662d	
15	44	אכזיב	ACHZIB	469d	1
		מרשה	MARESHAH	601c	
		קעילה	KEILAH	890d	
		תשע	NINE	1077c	1 a
15	45	בת	DAUGHTER	123d	4
		חצר	SETTLED ABODE	347b	B
15	46	אשדוד	ASHDOD	78b	
		יבנה	JABNEH	125c	
		חצר	SETTLED ABODE	347b	B
		יד	HAND	391c	5 h3
		מן	FROM	581d	5 a
15	47	אשדוד	ASHDOD	78b	
		בת	DAUGHTER	123d	4
		הגבול	GREAT	147c	
		גבול	BOUNDARY	147d	1 b
		ו	AND	252d	1 c
		חצר	SETTLED ABODE	347b	B
		ים	SEA	410d	1
		נחל	WADY	636c	2
		עזה	GAZA	738b	
15	48	הר	MOUNTAIN	251a	2 b
		יתיר	JATTIR	452d	
		שוכה	SOCOH	962c	2
		שמיר	SHAMIR	1039a	2
		שפיר	SHAPHIR	*1051c	2
15	49	דביר	DEBIR	184c	2 c
		דביר	DEBIR	184c	2 c
		דנה	DANNAH	200b	
		קריתספר	KIRIATH-SEPHER	900d	
15	50	אשתמוע	ESHTEMOA	84c	
		ענים	ANIM	745d	
		ענב	ANAB	772b	
15	51	גשן	GOSHEN	177d	2
		חלן	HOLON	298b	2
		עשר	TEN	797b	
		תשע	NINE	1077c	1 a
15	52	ארב	ARAB	70c	
		רומה	DUMAH	189a	2
		אשן	ESHAN	1043d	
15	53	אפקה	APHEKAH	68a	
		ביתתפוח	BETH-TAPPUAH	113a	
		בן	SON	*121a	1 jd
		ינום	JANUM	630b	
15	54	חברון	HEBRON	289b	
		חמטה	HUMTAH	328a	
		ציער	ZIOR	859b	
		קריתארבע	FOURFOLD CITY	900c	

Ch	v	Heb	Eng	Page	Sec
15	55	זיף	ZIPH	268b	1 a
		כרמל	CARMEL	502b	2
		יטה	JUTTAH	641a	
		מעון	MAON	733a	
15	56	יזרעאל	JEZREEL	283a	1 a
		יקדעם	JOKDEAM	429a	
15	57	גבעה	GIBEAH	149b	1
		תמנה	TIMNAH	584d	1
		עשר	TEN	796d	2 a
		קין	HOBAB	883d	2
15	58	ביתצור	BETH-ZUR	112d	
		גדור	GEDOR	155b	1
		חלחול	HALHUL	319a	
15	59	אלתקן	ELTEKON	49c	
		ביתענות	BETH-ANOTH	112b	
		מערת	MAARATH	789b	
		שש	SIX	995c	1 a
15	60	בעלה	BAALAH	128b	
		קריתיערים	KIRIATH-JEARIM	900c	
		קריתיערים	KIRIATH-JEARIM	900c	
		רבה	RABBA	913d	2
15	61	ביתהערבה	BETH-ARABAH	112c	
		מדבר	WILDERNESS	184d	3
		מדבר	WILDERNESS	185a	3 b
		מדין	MIDDIN	551d	
		מדין	MIDDIN	552a	
		סככה	SECACAH	698a	
15	62	נבשן	NIBSHAN	143c	
		מדבר	WILDERNESS	184d	3
		עינגדי	ENGEDI	745b	
		עירהמלח	CITY OF SALT	746d	
		שש	SIX	995c	1 a
15	63	יבוסי	JEBUSITE	101a	1
		בנימן	BENJAMIN	*122d	1
		יום	DAY	401b	71
		ירושלים	JERUSALEM	436d	
		ירש	CAUSE TO POSSESS	440a	2 a
		ישב	DWELL	443a	3
16	1	אפרים	EPHRAIM	68c	3
		גורל	LOT	174b	1
		מזרח	PLACE OF SUNRISE	281a	2 c1
		יוסף	JOSEPH	415d	1 b
		יצא	GO OUT	423b	1 f
		ירדן	JORDAN	434d	
		ל	TO	511b	1 f
		מי	WATER	565c	2
16	2	ארכי	ARCHITE	74b	
		ביתאל	BETHEL	110d	1
		גבול	BOUNDARY	147d	1 b
		יצא	GO OUT	423d	1 h
		לוז	LUZ	531c	1
		עבר	PASS OVER	718a	5 b
		עטרות	ATAROTH	743a	2 a
16	3	ביתחורון	BETH-HORON	111c	B
		גבול	BOUNDARY	147d	1 b
		גזר	GEZER	160c	
		תוצאה	OUT GOING	426a	1
		ירד	GO DOWN	433c	3 f
		יפלטי	JAPHLETITES	812d	
		תחתון	LOWER	1066b	
16	4	יוסף	JOSEPH	415d	1 b
		נחל	TAKE AS A POSSESSION	635c	1 b
16	5	אפרים	EPHRAIM	68b	2
		ביתחורון	BETH-HORON	111c	A
		מזרח	PLACE OF SUNRISE	281a	2 c1
		עטרות	ATAROTH	743a	2 a
		עליון	HIGH	751b	2
16	6	מזרח	PLACE OF SUNRISE	281a	2 c1
		מזרח	PLACE OF SUNRISE	281a	2 d
		ים	SEA	411b	9
		יצא	GO OUT	423d	1 h
		מכמתת	MICHMETHATH	485c	
		ינוח	JANOAH	629c	
		סבב	TURN AROUND	686b	1 c
		עבר	PASS OVER	718a	5 b
		תאנתשלה	TAANATH-SHILOH	1061b	
16	7	יצא	GO OUT	423d	1 h
		ירד	GO DOWN	433c	3 f
		ינוח	JANOAH	629c	
		נערה	NAARAH	655c	
		עטרות	ATAROTH	743a	2 b
		פגע	MEET	803c	5
16	8	אפרים	EPHRAIM	68b	2
		הלך	WALK	232d	13
		תוצאה	OUT GOING	426a	1
		נחל	WADY	636c	2
		תפח	TAPPUAH	656b	2
		קנה	KANAH	889d	1
16	9	אפרים	EPHRAIM	68b	2
		מבדלה	SEPARATE PLACE	95d	
		מנשה	MANASSEH	286c	1 b1 a
16	10	אפרים	EPHRAIM	68b	2
		גזר	GEZER	160c	
		היה	BECOME	226b	2 2e
		יום	DAY	401b	71
		ירש	CAUSE TO POSSESS	440a	2 a
		ישב	DWELL	443a	3
		כנעני	CANAANITE	489a	2 b
		מס	LABOUR-GANG	*587a	1
		מס	LABOUR-GANG	*587a	3
		מס	LABOUR-GANG	587a	2 b
		עבד	WORK	713a	3
17	1	גורל	LOT	174d	3
		ימין	RIGHT HAND	412a	2 b
		יוסף	JOSEPH	415d	1 b
		מלחמה	WAR	536b	
		מנשה	MANASSEH	586c	1 b2 g
		מנשה	MANASSEH	586d	1 b2 d
17	2	אביעזר	ABIEZER	4c	1
		אשריאל	ASRIEL	77b	
		בן	SON	121b	2
		זכר	MALE	271c	1 1b
		מנשה	MANASSEH	286c	1 b1 a
		חלק	HELEK	324c	
		חפר	HEPHER	343d	1
		יוסף	JOSEPH	415d	1 b
		יתר	BE LEFT OVER	451c	
		שכם	SHECHEM	1014c	
		שמידע	SHEMIDA	1029a	
17	3	חגלה	HOGLAH	291c	
		חפר	HEPHER	343d	1
		מחלה	MAHLAH	563a	1
		מלכה	MILCAH	574c	2
		מנשה	MANASSEH	586d	1 b2 d
		נעה	NOAH	631c	
		נתן	GIVE	681a	3 b
		צלפחד	ZELOPHEHAD	854c	
		תרצה	TIRZAH	953c	1
17	4	אל	TO	40c	7
		נחלה	PROPERTY	635b	1 b
		נשיא	PRINCE	672b	4
		פה	MOUTH	805d	6 d2
17	5	קרב	COME NEAR	897c	1 c
		חבל	CORD	286d	3
		ירדן	JORDAN	434c	
		מנשה	MANASSEH	586c	1 b1 b
		נפל	FALL	657a	1
		עבר	REGION ACROSS	719c	1 a
		עשר	TEN	796d	2 b
17	6	בת	DAUGHTER	123b	1 i
		מנשה	MANASSEH	286c	1 b1 a
		יתר	BE LEFT OVER	451c	
		נחלה	PROPERTY	635b	1 b
		נחל	TAKE AS A POSSESSION	635c	1 b
17	7	אשר	ASHER	81b	3
		הלך	WALK	232d	13
		מכמתת	MICHMETHATH	485c	
		מנשה	MANASSEH	586c	1 b1 b
		תפוח	TAPPUAH	656b	2
		פנה	FACE	818d	27 ad
17	8	אפרים	EPHRAIM	68b	2
		גבול	BOUNDARY	147d	1 b
		מנשה	MANASSEH	586c	1 b1 b
		תפוח	TAPPUAH	656b	2
17	9	אלה	THESE	41c	C
		תוצאה	OUT GOING	426a	1
		ירד	GO DOWN	433c	3 f
		מנשה	MANASSEH	586c	1 b1 b
		מנשה	MANASSEH	586c	1 b1 b
		נגב	SOUTH-COUNTRY	616c	2
		נחל	WADY	636c	2
		קנה	KANAH	889d	1
		אלה	ADDENDA ET CORRIGENDA	1120a	
17	10	אשר	ASHER	81b	3
		מזרח	PLACE OF SUNRISE	281a	2 d
		יששכר	ISSACHAR	441a	1
		מנשה	MANASSEH	586c	1 b1 b
		נגב	SOUTH-COUNTRY	616b	2
		פגע	MEET	803c	5
17	11	אשר	ASHER	81b	3
		את	MARK OF THE ACCUSATIVE	85b	3 a
		ביתשאן	BETH-SHEAN	112d	
		בלעם	BILEAM	118d	
		בת	DAUGHTER	123d	4
		מגדו	MEGIDDO	152a	
		דאר	DOR	190b	
		יבלעם	IBLEAM	385d	
		יששכר	ISSACHAR	441a	1
		מנשה	MANASSEH	586c	1 b1 b
		נפת	HEIGHT	632c	
		עינדר	EN-DOR	745c	
		תענך	TAANACH	1073d	
		תענך	TAANACH	*1073d	
17	12	מנשה	MANASSEH	286c	1 b1 a
		יאל	SHOW-WILLINGNESS	384a	3
		ירש	CAUSE TO POSSESS	440a	2 a
		כנעני	CANAANITE	489a	2 b
		אלה	ADDENDA ET CORRIGENDA	1120a	
17	13	חזק	BE FIRM	304b	1 1b
		ירש	CAUSE TO POSSESS	440a	2 a
		כנעני	CANAANITE	489a	2 b
		מס	LABOUR-GANG	587a	2 b
17	14	ברך	BLESS	139a	2 a
		גורל	LOT	174d	3
		דבר	SPEAK	181b	3 d
		חבל	CORD	286d	3
		מדוע	WHEREFORE	396c	
		יוסף	JOSEPH	*415d	1 b
		יוסף	JOSEPH	415d	1 b
		כה	THUS	462b	3
		נחלה	PROPERTY	635b	1 b
		עד	UNTIL	725b	23
		עם	PEOPLE	*766b	1
17	15	אוץ	BE PRESSED	21a	1
		אפרים	EPHRAIM	68c	3
		ברא	CREATE	135c	1
		הר	MOUNTAIN	251a	2 b
		יער	WOOD	420c	A
		יער	WOOD	*420d	G
		עם	PEOPLE	*766b	1
17	16	ביתשאן	BETH-SHEAN	112d	
		בת	DAUGHTER	123d	4
		ברזל	IRON	137c	1 d
		הר	MOUNTAIN	*251a	2 b
		יזראל	JEZREEL	283c	1 b
		יזרעאל	JEZREEL	*283c	1 b
		יוסף	JOSEPH	415d	1 b
		כנעני	CANAANITE	489a	2 b
		מצא	FIND	*593c	4
		מצא	FIND	594b	3
		עמק	VALE	771a	
		עמק	VALE	771a	
		רכב	CHARIOT	939a	1
17	17	אפרים	EPHRAIM	68b	2
		בית	HOUSE	110a	5 dz
		גורל	LOT	174d	3
		יוסף	JOSEPH	415d	1 b
		כח	STRENGTH	470d	1 c
		מנשה	MANASSEH	586c	1 b1 b
		עם	PEOPLE	*766b	1
17	18	ברא	CREATE	135c	1
		ברזל	IRON	137c	1 d
		הר	MOUNTAIN	*251a	2 b
		חזק	STRONG	305c	1 a
		יער	WOOD	420c	A
		יער	WOOD	*420d	G
		תוצאה	OUT GOING	426a	1
		ירש	CAUSE TO POSSESS	440a	2 a
		כנעני	CANAANITE	489a	2 b
		רכב	CHARIOT	939a	1
18	1	עדה	CONGREGATION	417b	3
		מועד	TENT OF MEETING	418a	5
		כבש	BE SUBDUED	461b	
		קהל	ASSEMBLE AS	875a	2
		שכן	SETTLE DOWN	1015c	1 a
		שלו	SHILOH	1017d	
18	2	חלק	DIVIDE	323c	1
		יתר	BE LEFT OVER	451b	
18	3	עלה	GO UP	749a	9
		אן	WHERE	33a	D
		אלהים	GOD	44b	4 ba
		ירש	TAKE POSSESSION	439b	1 a
		רפה	SINK	952a	
18	4	הלך	WALK	235d	1 a
		יתב	PROVIDE	396d	3
		כתב	WRITE	507d	3
		ל	TO	512d	5 ab
18	5	פה	MOUTH	805c	6 c1
		בית	HOUSE	110a	5 dz
		גבול	BOUNDARY	148a	1 b
		חלק	PORTION	324a	2 a
		חלק	DIVIDE	324a	
		יוסף	JOSEPH	415d	1 b
		מן	FROM	578c	1 c
		נגב	SOUTH-COUNTRY	616b	2
18	6	גורל	LOT	174b	1
		הנה	HITHER	244c	A a
		חלק	PORTION	324a	2 a
		ירה	THROW	435a	1
		כתב	WRITE	507d	3
		ל	TO	515c	5 hc
		פנה	FACE	817b	24 ah
18	7	גד	GAD	151c	1 h
		מזרח	PLACE OF SUNRISE	281a	2 c1
		חלק	PORTION	324a	2 a
		חלק	PORTION	324a	2 a
		ירדן	JORDAN	434c	
		כהנה	PRIESTHOOD	464d	
		לוי	LEVITE	533a	3 1c
		לקח	TAKE	543b	4 f
		מנשה	MANASSEH	586c	1 b2 d
		עבד	SLAVE	714a	3
		עבר	REGION ACROSS	719c	1 a
		ראובן	REUBEN	910a	2
		ראובן	REUBEN	910a	2
18	8	גורל	LOT	174b	3
		הלך	WALK	234b	1 5f 3
		הלך	WALK	235d	1
		כתב	WRITE	507d	2
		שלו	SHILOH	1017d	
		שלך	THROW	1021b	3
18	9	חלק	PORTION	324a	2 a
		כתב	WRITE	507d	3
		ל	TO	516b	5 ja
		ספר	MISSIVE	707a	3
		עבר	PASS OVER	717c	3 a
		שלו	SHILOH	1017d	
18	10	גורל	LOT	174b	1
		חלק	DIVIDE	323c	1
		מחלקת	DIVISION	325a	1
		שלו	SHILOH	1017d	
		שלך	THROW	1021b	3
18	11	בנימן	BENJAMIN	122d	1
		גבול	BOUNDARY	147d	1 b
		גורל	LOT	174b	1
		גורל	LOT	174d	3
		יוסף	JOSEPH	415d	1 b
		יצא	GO OUT	423b	1 f
18	12	ביתאון	BETH-AVEN	110d	
		היה	BE	227b	3 4d d
		הר	MOUNTAIN	251a	2 b

Ch	v.	Heb	Eng	Page	Sec
		תוצאה	OUT GOING	426a	1
18	13	כתף	SIDE	509c	2 a
		ביתאל	BETHEL	110d	1
		ביתחורן	BETH-HORON	111c	B
		ירד	GO DOWN	433c	3 f
		כתף	SIDE	509c	2 a
		לוז	LUZ	531c	1
		נגב	SOUTH-COUNTRY	616b	2
		נגב	SOUTH-COUNTRY	616c	2
		עבר	PASS OVER	718a	5 b
		עטרות	ATAROTH	743a	2 a
		על	UPON	757c	27c ab
		תחתון	LOWER	1066b	
18	14	ביתחורן	BETH-HORON	111c	B
		בעלה	BAALAH	128b	
		ים	SEA	411a	9
		תוצאה	OUT GOING	426a	1
		נגב	SOUTH-COUNTRY	616a	2
		סבב	TURN AROUND	686a	1 c
		פנה	FACE	818d	27a d
		קריתיערים	KIRIATH-JEARIM	900a	
		קריתיערים	KIRIATH-JEARIM	900c	
		תאר	INCLINE	1061b	
18	15	יצא	GO OUT	423d	1 h
		מי	WATER	565c	2
		נגב	SOUTH-COUNTRY	616b	2
		מעין	SPRING	745d	
		נפתוח	NEPHTOAH	836b	
		קצה	END	892b	2
		קריתיערים	KIRIATH-JEARIM	900c	
18	16	יבוסי	JEBUSITE	101a	2
		הנם	HINNOM	244d	
		הנם	HINNOM	245a	
		ירד	GO DOWN	433c	3 f
		כתף	SIDE	509c	2 a
		נגב	SOUTH-COUNTRY	616c	C
		עין	SPRING	745b	2
		פנה	FACE	818d	27a d
		קצה	END	892b	2
		רפאים	REPHAIM	952b	
18	17	אבן	STONE	7a	9
		בהן	BOHAN	97b	
		יצא	GO OUT	423d	1 h
		נכח	FRONT	647b	1
		עינשמש	EN-SHEMESH	734d	
		מעלה	ASCENT	751c	1
		תאר	INCLINE	1061b	
18	18	ביתהערבה	BETH-ARABAH	112c	
		כתף	SIDE	509c	2 a
		מול	IN FRONT OF	557c	2
		עבר	PASS OVER	718a	5 b
18	19	ביתהגלה	BETH-HOGLAH	111c	
		ים	SEA	411a	3
		ים	SEA	411b	8 c
		תוצאה	OUT GOING	426a	1
		כתף	SIDE	509c	2 a
		לשון	TONGUE	546d	6
		מלח	SALT	572a	
		נגב	SOUTH-COUNTRY	616b	2
		נגב	SOUTH-COUNTRY	616c	2
		עבר	PASS OVER	718a	5 b
		קצה	END	892a	1
18	20	בנימין	BENJAMIN	122d	1
		גבל	BOUND	148b	
		גבולה	BORDER	148b	
		קדם	EASTWARD	870b	
18	21	ביתהגלה	BETH-HOGLAH	111c	
		בנימין	BENJAMIN	122d	1
		קציץ	EMEK-KEZIZ	894a	
18	22	ביתהערבה	BETH-ARABAH	112c	
		צמרים	ZEMARAIM	856b	1
18	23	עוים	AVVIM	732a	2
		עפרה	OPHRAH	780b	1 a
		פרה	PARAH	831a	
18	24	גבע	GEBA	148d	
		כפר	VILLAGE	499a	
		עפני	OPHNI	779c	
18	25	בארות	BEEROTH	92a	
		גבעון	GIBEON	149c	
		רמה	RAMA	928a	1
18	26	כפירה	CHEPHIRAH	499a	
		מצה	MOZAH	594c	
		מצפה	MIZPEH	859d	2
		מצפה	MIZPAH	860a	5
18	27	ירפאל	IRPEEL	951b	
		רקם	REKEM	955d	2
		תראלה	TARALAH	1076a	
18	28	אלף	HAELEPH	49b	
		יבוסי	JEBUSITE	101a	2
		בנימין	BENJAMIN	122d	1
		גבעה	GIBEAH	149c	2
		ירושלים	JERUSALEM	436d	
		צלע	ZELAH	854b	
		קריתיערים	KIRIATH-JEARIM	900c	
19	1	גורל	LOT	174b	1
		היה	BE	227a	3 3
		יצא	GO OUT	423b	1 f
		שמעון	SIMEON	1035c	2
19	2	בארשבע	BEERSHEBA	92a	
		מולדה	MOLADAH	409d	
		שבע	SHEBA	989d	
19	3	בלה	BALAH	115a	
		בלהה	BILHAH	117b	
		חצרשועל	HAZAR-SHUAL	347c	2
		עצם	EZEM	783a	
19	4	אלתולד	ELTOLAD	39a	
		ביתאל	BETHEL	111a	2
		בתואל	BETHUEL	143d	
		חרמה	HORMAH	356c	
		כסיל	CHESIL	*493b	
19	5	ביתמרכבות	BETH-MARCABOTH	112b	
		חצרסוסה	HAZAR-SUSAH	347c	
		צקלג	ZIKLAG	862c	
19	6	ביתלבאות	BETH-LEBAOTH	111d	
		לבאות	LEBAOTH	522d	
		שלש	THREE	1025d	2
		שערים	SHAARAIM	1045c	2
		שרוחן	SHARUHEN	1056b	
19	7	עין	AIN	745b	2 b
		עשן	ASHAN	798c	
		עתר	ETHER	801d	
		ארבע	FOUR	917a	1 a4
		רמון	RIMMON	942a	2
19	8	בעלתבאר	BAALATH-BEER	128c	
		זה	THIS	261b	3
		חצר	SETTLED ABODE	347b	B
		נגב	SOUTH-COUNTRY	616b	1 a
		רמת	RAMATH-LEHI	928b	3
		שמעון	SIMEON	1035c	2
		אלה	ADDENDA ET COR-RIGENDA	1120a	
19	9	היה	BE	227a	3 4a
		חבל	CORD	286d	3
		חלק	PORTION	324a	2 a
		חלק	PORTION	324a	2 a
		נחל	TAKE AS A POSSES-SION	635c	1 b
		רב	GREAT	913c	2 d
19	10	גורל	LOT	174b	1
		היה	BE	227a	3 2
		זבולן	ZEBULUN	259d	2
		שריד	SARID	975a	
19	11	דבשת	DABBESHETH	185c	2
		יקנעם	JOKNEAM	429b	
		מרעלה	MAREALAH	599c	
		נחל	WADY	636c	2
		פגע	MEET	803c	5
		פגע	MEET	803c	5
		פנה	FACE	818d	27a d
19	12	גבול	BOUNDARY	147d	1 b
		דברת	DABERATH	184b	
		יפיע	JAPHIA	422b	
		יצא	GO OUT	423d	1 h
		כסלת	CHESULLOTH	493b	
		על	UPON	757c	27c ab
		קדם	EASTWARD	870a	
		שריד	SARID	975a	
		שוב	TURN BACK	998b	7 h
		תבור	TABOR	1061d	3
19	13	דמנה	DIMNAH	199b	
		מזרח	PLACE OF SUNRISE	281a	2 c1
		חפר	HEPHER	343d	2
		גתהחפר	GATH-HEPHER	387d	
		יצא	GO OUT	423d	1 h
		נעה	NEAH	631c	
		עבר	PASS OVER	718a	5 b
		עתקצין	ETH-KAZIN	773d	
		קדם	EASTWARD	870a	
		רמון	RIMMON	942a	2
		תאר	INCLINE	1061b	
19	14	גיא	VALLEY	161b	A
		חנתן	HANNOTHON	337b	
		תוצאה	OUT GOING	426a	1
		סבב	TURN AROUND	686a	1 c
		יפתחאל	IPHTAHEL	836b	
19	15	ביתלחם	BETHLEHEM	112a	2
		ידאלה	IDALAH	391d	
		נהלל	NAHALOL	625b	
		קטת	KATTAH	883a	
		קטרון	KATRON	883c	
		שמרון	SHIMRON	1038a	
19	16	זבולן	ZEBULUN	259d	2
		זה	THIS	261b	3
		אלה	ADDENDA ET COR-RIGENDA	1120a	
19	17	גורל	LOT	174b	1
		יצא	GO OUT	423b	1 f
		יששכר	ISSACHAR	441a	1
		יששכר	ISSACHAR	441a	1
		רביעי	FOURTH	917d	1
19	18	יזרעאל	JEZREEL	283b	1 b
		כסלת	CHESULLOTH	493b	
		שונם	SHUNEM	1002d	
		תענך	TAANACH	*1073d	
19	19	אחרת	ANAHARATH	58d	
		חפרים	HAPHARAIM	343d	
		שיאון	SHION	1009d	
19	20	אבץ	EBEZ	7b	
		קישון	KISHION	904d	
		רבית	RABBITH	914c	
19	21	ביתפצץ	BETH-PAZZEZ	112d	
		עינגנים	EN-GANNIM	745c	2
		עינחדה	EN-HADDAH	745c	
		רמות	RAMOTH	928c	1 c
19	22	ביתשמש	BETH-SHEMESH	113a	3
		תוצאה	OUT GOING	426a	1
		כסלת	CHESULLOTH	493b	
		פגע	MEET	803c	5
		שש	SIX	995c	2
		שחצומה	SHAHAZUMAH	1006d	
		תבור	TABOR	1061d	3
		תבור	TABOR	1061d	1
19	23	זה	THIS	261b	3
19	24	יששכר	ISSACHAR	441a	1
		אשר	ASHER	81b	2
		גורל	LOT	174b	1
		חמישי	FIFTH	332c	1
		יצא	GO OUT	423b	1 f
19	25	בטן	BETEN	106b	
		חוקק	HUKOK	301a	
		חלי	HALI	318d	
		חלקת	HELKATH	324d	
		חוקק	HUKOK	350c	
		אכשף	ACHSHAPH	506d	
19	26	אלמלך	ALLAMMELECH	47d	
		כרמל	CARMEL	502a	1
		מישאל	MISHAL	602b	
		עמעד	AMAD	770c	
		פגע	MEET	803c	5
		שיחורלבנת	SHIHOR-LIBNATH	1009d	
19	27	ביתדגון	BETH-DAGON	111b	2
		ביתהעמק	BETH-EMEK	112b	
		גיא	VALLEY	161b	A
		זבולן	ZEBULUN	259d	3
		יצא	GO OUT	423d	1 h
		כבול	CABUL	459d	1
		נעיאל	NEIEL	653a	
		פגע	MEET	803c	5
		יפתחאל	IPHTAHEL	836b	
		שמאל	LEFT	969d	3
		שוב	TURN BACK	998b	7 h
19	28	חמון	HAMMON	329a	1
		צידון	SIDON	851a	
		צידון	SIDON	*851a	2
		קנה	KANAH	889d	2
		רחוב	REHOB	932b	1 b1
19	29	מבצר	FORTIFICATION	131c	
		מבצר	FORTIFICATION	*131c	
		חבל	CORD	286d	3
		אחלב	HELBAH	317b	
		חסה	HOSAH	340b	2
		תוצאה	OUT GOING	426a	1
		אכזיב	ACHZIB	470a	2
		עיר	CITY	746b	1 a
		צידון	SIDON	*851a	
		צר	TYER	862d	
		רמה	RAMA	928b	3
		שוב	TURN BACK	998b	7 h
19	30	אפק	APHEK	67d	2
		עכו	ACCO	747c	
		עמה	UMMAH	769d	
		עשרים	TWENTY	797d	1 2c
		רחוב	REHOB	932b	1 b2
		אפק	ADDENDA ET COR-RIGENDA	1120c	
19	31	אשר	ASHER	81b	2
		אלה	ADDENDA ET COR-RIGENDA	1120a	
19	32	גורל	LOT	174b	1
		יצא	GO OUT	423b	1 f
19	33	אדמיהנקב	ADAMI-NEKEB	10a	
		אלון	TEREBINTH	18d	
		אלון	ALLON	47d	
		יבנאל	JABNEEL	125c	2
		בצעננים	IN ZAANANNIM	130c	
		חלף	HELEPH	322b	
		תוצאה	OUT GOING	426a	1
		לקום	LAKKUM	542c	
		נקב	NEKEB	666c	
		צעננים	ZAANANNIM	858b	1 d
19	34	אזנתתבור	AZNOTH-TABOR	24d	
		אשר	ASHER	81b	2
		זבולן	ZEBULUN	259d	3
		חוקק	HUKOK	301a	
		חקק	HUKKOK	350c	
		יהודה	JUDAH	397b	2
		יצא	GO OUT	423d	1 h
		נגב	SOUTH-COUNTRY	616b	2
		פגע	MEET	803c	5
		שוב	TURN BACK	998b	7 h
		תבור	TABOR	1061d	1
19	35	מבצר	FORTIFICATION	131c	
		חמת	HAMMATH	329a	
		חמון	HAMMON	*329a	2
		כנרת	CHINNERETH	490b	1
		צדים	ZIDDIM	841b	
		צר	ZER	862d	
		רקת	RAKKATH	957a	
19	36	אדמה	ADAMAH	10a	7
		חצור	HAZOR	347d	1
		רמה	RAMA	928b	4
19	37	אדרעי	EDREI	204c	
		חצור	HAZOR	347d	4
		עינחצור	EN-HAZOR	745c	
		קדש	KEDESH	873d	1
19	38	ביתענת	BETH-ANATH	112c	
		ביתשמש	BETH-SHEMESH	113a	2
		מגדלאל	MIGDAL-EL	154a	
		חרם	HOREM	356c	
		יראון	YIRON	432a	
		עברן	EBRON	720d	
		עשר	TEN	797b	9 b
		תשע	NINE	1077c	2
19	39	נפתלי	NAPHTALI	836d	2 a
19	40	גורל	LOT	174b	1
		דן	DAN	192d	2
		יצא	GO OUT	423b	1 f
		שביעי	SEVENTH	988d	1

120

Ch v.	Heb	Eng	Page	Sec
22 2	ראובני	REUBENITE	910a	
	ל	TO	514b	5 fa
	עבד	SLAVE	714a	3
	צוה	CHARGE	846a	3
22 3	זה	THIS	261d	4 i
	יום	DAY	401b	7 l
	עזב	LEAVE	737b	2 b1
	משמרת	GUARD	1038c	3
22 4	אחזה	POSSESSION	28c	
	דבר	SPEAK	181b	3 c
	הלך	WALK	231d	1 d 5h
	נוח	REST	628c	A 1b 1
	עבד	SLAVE	714a	3
	עבר	REGION ACROSS	719c	1 a
22 5	אהב	LOVE	13a	3
	דבק	CLING	179d	2 a
	דרך	WAY	204a	6 ec
	תורה	LAW	436b	2 b2
	לבב	HEART	523b	2 2
	נפש	SOUL	661b	0
	עבד	SLAVE	714a	3
	מצוה	COMMANDMENT	846b	2 a
	רק	ONLY	956c	2 b
22 6	ברך	BLESS	139a	3
22 7	ברך	BLESS	139a	3
	כי	WHEN	473a	2 a
	מנשה	MANASSEH	586c	1 b2 d
	עבר	REGION ACROSS	719c	1 b
22 8	ב	IN	89b	3 1a
	ברזל	IRON	137c	2
	זהב	GOLD	262c	3
	חלק	DIVIDE	323c	1
	נכס	RICHES	647d	
	עם	WITH	767c	1 b
	שלמה	GARMENT	791b	
	רבה	BECOME MANY	915d	1 e4
22 9	אחזה	POSSESSION	28c	
	אחז	GRASP	28c	
	הלך	WALK	231a	1 d3 ga
	הלך	WALK	231c	1 1d 4
	כנען	CANAAN	488d	2 a
	מנשה	MANASSEH	586c	1 b2 d
	ראובן	REUBEN	910a	2
	שלו	SHILOH	1017d	
22 10	גדול	GREAT	153a	1
	מזבח	ALTAR	258c	3
	ירדן	JORDAN	434d	
	כנען	CANAAN	488d	2 a
	מנשה	MANASSEH	586c	1 b2 d
	מראה	VISION	909c	1 b
22 11	אל	TO	40c	8
	בנה	BUILD	124c	1 at
	ירדן	JORDAN	434d	
	כנען	CANAAN	488d	2 a
	מול	IN FRONT OF	557c	2 a
	מנשה	MANASSEH	586c	1 b2 d
	עבר	REGION ACROSS	719c	1 a
	שמע	HEAR	1033c	1 c
22 12	עדה	CONGREGATION	417b	3
	עלה	GO UP	748c	2 c
	צבא	WAR	839b	2
	קהל	ASSEMBLE AS	874d	1 a
	שלו	SHILOH	1017d	
22 13	מנשה	MANASSEH	586c	1 b2 d
22 14	אב	FATHER	3c	3
	אלף	THOUSAND	49b	2
	בית	HOUSE	110b	5 e
	נשיא	PRINCE	672b	4
	ראש	HEAD	911a	3 f
22 15	בית	HOUSE	109d	5 a
	דבר	SPEAK	181b	3 d
	מנשה	MANASSEH	586c	1 b2 d
22 16	אחר	BEHIND	30b	4 aa
	אלהים	GOD	44b	4 ba
	עדה	CONGREGATION	417b	3
	מה	WHAT	553a	1 c
	מעל	ACT TREACHEROUSLY	591b	1 c
	מרד	REBEL	597c	2
	שוב	TURN BACK	997d	6 a
22 17	את	MARK OF THE ACCUSATIVE	85a	1 c
	היה	COME TO PASS	224d	1 1b
	טהר	BE CLEAN	372c	1 b
	יום	DAY	401b	7 l
	עדה	CONGREGATION	417b	3
	מעט	A FEW	590b	1 ea
	נגף	BLOW	620a	1
	עון	INIQUITY	731b	2
	פעור	PEOR	822c	2
22 18	אחר	BEHIND	30b	4 aa
	היה	COME TO PASS	225b	1 2b ae
	עדה	CONGREGATION	417b	3
	מחר	TO-MORROW	564a	1 b
	מרד	REBEL	597c	2
	קצף	BE WROTH	893b	1
	שוב	TURN BACK	997d	6 a
22 19	אחזה	POSSESSION	28c	
	אחז	GRASP	28c	
	אך	ONLY	36d	2 c
	בלעדי	APART FROM	116b	B b
	טמא	UNCLEAN	380a	3
	מרד	REBEL	597c	2
	עבר	PASS OVER	717a	1 a2
	שכן	SETTLE DOWN	1015b	2 d
	משכן	DWELLING-PLACE	1015d	2 c
22 20	גוע	EXPIRE	157c	
	היה	BECOME	225d	2 1b
	זרח	ZERAH	280b	1
	חרם	DEVOTED THING	356b	1
	עדה	CONGREGATION	417b	3
	מעל	ACT TREACHEROUSLY	591b	1 a
	עון	INIQUITY	731b	2 c
	עכן	ACHAN	747c	
	קצף	WRATH	893c	1
22 21	אלף	THOUSAND	49b	2
	דבר	SPEAK	181b	3 d
	מנשה	MANASSEH	586c	1 b2 d
	ענה	ANSWER	773a	1 e
22 22	אל	GOD	42d	6 f
	ישע	DELIVER	446c	1 b
	מעל	UNFAITHFUL	591b	2
	מרד	REBELLION	597d	
22 23	אחר	BEHIND	30b	4 aa
	בקש	SEEK	135a	5 b
	זבח	SACRIFICE	258a	2 7
	ל	TO	515d	5 ia
	מנחה	OFFERING	585b	5
	עלה	GO UP	750a	8
	עלה	WHOLE BURNT OFFERING	750d	
	שוב	TURN BACK	997d	6 a
22 24	אלהים	GOD	44b	4 ba
	בן	SON	120c	1 f
	דאגה	ANXIETY	178d	
	זה	THIS	260c	1 a
	מה	WHAT	553b	1 dc
	מן	ON ACCOUNT OF	580b	2 f
	בן	SON	120c	1 f
22 25	גבול	BOUNDARY	147d	1 b
	חלק	PORTION	324a	1 c
	ירא	FEAR	431c	3 b
	נתן	GIVE	681a	3 a
	שבת	CEASE	992a	3
22 26	זבח	SACRIFICE	257d	2 5
22 27	אחר	AFTER	30a	2 b
	בין	INTERVAL	107c	1 f
	בן	SON	120c	1 f
	דור	GENERATION	190a	2 c
	זבח	SACRIFICE	257d	2 5
	חלק	PORTION	324a	1 c
	עבד	WORK	713b	5
	עבדה	LABOR	715b	4
	עד	WITNESS	729c	1
	שלם	PEACE-OFFERING	1023c	
22 28	תבנית	CONSTRUCTION	125d	1
	דור	GENERATION	190a	2 c
	מזבח	ALTAR	259a	8
	מחר	TO-MORROW	564a	1 b
	עד	WITNESS	729c	1
22 29	אחר	BEHIND	30b	4 aa
	בד	SEPARATION	94d	1 e
	זבח	SACRIFICE	257d	2 5
	חלילה	FAR BE IT	321a	
	מנחה	OFFERING	585b	5
	מרד	REBEL	597c	
	עלה	WHOLE BURNT OFFERING	750d	
	שוב	TURN BACK	997d	6 a
22 30	אלף	THOUSAND	49b	2
	יטב	BE PLEASING	405c	4
	עדה	CONGREGATION	417b	3
	כהן	PRIEST	464a	7
	מנשה	MANASSEH	586c	1 b2 a
	נשיא	PRINCE	672b	4
22 31	אז	THEN	23b	2
	אשר	THAT	83c	8 c
	מנשה	MANASSEH	586c	1 b2 a
	מעל	ACT TREACHEROUSLY	591b	1 c
22 32	דבר	WORD	182b	1 1c
	נשיא	PRINCE	672b	4
	שוב	TURN BACK	997b	3 b
	שוב	TURN BACK	999c	3
22 33	אמר	SAY	56b	2
	ברך	BLESS	139a	1
	יטב	BE PLEASING	405c	4
	עלה	GO UP	748c	2 c
	צבא	WAR	839b	2
	שחת	GO TO RUIN	1008a	1
22 34	אלהים	GOD	43d	3
	אלהים	GOD	43d	3
	מזבח	ALTAR	258c	3
	עד	WITNESS	729c	1
	קרא	CALL	896a	6 e2
23 1	אחר	AFTER THAT	30b	3
	בוא	COME	98b	1 k
	היה	COME TO PASS	224d	2 a1 a1
	יום	DAY	399b	4 a
	יום	DAY	401a	7 j
	מן	FROM	581c	4 b
	נוח	REST	628c	A 1b 2
	סביב	ROUND ABOUT	687a	1 d
23 2	זקן	OLD	278d	2 b
	יום	DAY	399b	4 a
	שטר	OFFICIAL	1009c	
	שפט	JUDGE	1047d	2 b
23 3	לחם	ENGAGE IN BATTLE	535d	
	פנה	FACE	818c	26 c a
23 4	ב	IN	89a	1 7c
	מבוא	ENTERING	99d	2
	ים	SEA	410d	1
	כרת	CUT OFF	504c	2 c
	נחלה	PROPERTY	635b	1 b
	נפל	FALL	658b	3
23 5	דבר	SPEAK	181b	3 c
	הדף	THRUST	213d	2
	ירש	TAKE POSSESSION	439c	1 a
	ירש	CAUSE TO POSSESS	440a	2 a
23 6	חזק	BE FIRM	304b	1 2c
	ימין	RIGHT HAND	412a	2 b
	משה	MOSES	602d	
	ספר	MISSIVE	707b	3 c
23 7	ב	IN	88c	1 4
	בוא	COME	98a	1 f
	זכר	REMEMBER	271a	3 a
	שאר	REMAIN	984a	1
	שבע	SWEAR	989b	1 a
	שבע	SWEAR	989c	1
	שחה	BOW DOWN	1005c	3
	שם	NAME	1028d	4
23 8	דבק	CLING	179d	2 a
	יום	DAY	401b	7 l
23 9	כיאם	BUT	475a	2 b
	יום	DAY	401b	7 l
	ירש	CAUSE TO POSSESS	440a	2 a
	עמד	STAND	764b	4
	פנה	FACE	816d	2 3a
23 10	דבר	SPEAK	181b	3 c
	לחם	ENGAGE IN BATTLE	535d	
23 11	רדף	PURSUE	922d	1 b
	אהב	LOVE	13a	3
	נפש	SOUL	660b	4 b6
	שמר	KEEP	1037b	1
23 12	ב	IN	88c	1 4
	בוא	COME	98a	1 f
	דבק	CLING	179d	2 a
	חתן	MAKE ONESELF A SON IN LAW	368d	2
	יתר	REMAINDER	451d	1 a
	שאר	REMAIN	984a	1
	שוב	TURN BACK	997d	6 a
23 13	אבד	PERISH	1d	1
	טוב	PLEASANT	374b	3 b
	יסף	DO AGAIN	415c	2 a
	מוקש	BAIT	430d	
	ירש	CAUSE TO POSSESS	440a	2 a
	פח	BIRD-TRAP	809a	2 b
	צד	SIDE	841a	
	צנין	THORN	856d	
	שטט	SCOURGE	1002b	
23 14	בוא	COME	98c	2 c
	דבר	SPEAK	181c	5
	דבר	WORD	183b	3 2
	דבר	WORD	183d	4 6
	דרך	WAY	203a	1
	דרך	WAY	*203b	4 a
	הלך	WALK	234b	2 1
	טוב	PLEASANT	374d	9 b
	ידע	KNOW	393d	1 e
	כל	ALL	*482d	2 ba
	לבב	HEART	523b	2 2
	לבב	HEART	523c	2 3b
	מן	FROM	581a	3 bc
	נפל	FALL	657d	5
	נפש	SOUL	661b	0
23 15	בוא	COME	98c	2 b
	היה	COME TO PASS	225a	1 2b ad
	טוב	PLEASANT	374b	3 b
	טוב	PLEASANT	374d	9 b
	כן	SO	486c	2 cd
	רע	EVIL	948b	1
23 16	אבד	PERISH	1d	1
	אחר	ANOTHER	29d	
	ברית	COVENANT	137b	3 3
	הלך	WALK	235a	2 3d 2
	חרה	BURN	354a	2 a
	טוב	PLEASANT	374b	3 b
	מהרה	HASTE	555b	
	עבד	WORK	713b	4 b
	עבר	PASS OVER	717b	1 i
24 1	אסף	GATHER	62b	1 a
	זקן	OLD	278d	2 b
	יצב	STATION ONESELF	426c	C
	כנעני	CANAANITE	489a	2 b
	פנה	FACE	817b	24a h
	שטר	OFFICIAL	1009c	
	שכם	SHECHEM	1014b	1
	שפט	JUDGE	1047b	2 b
24 2	אחר	ANOTHER	29d	
	אלהים	GOD	43c	1 d
	אלהים	GOD	44b	4 ba
	מן	FROM	581d	4 c
	נהר	STREAM	625d	1
	נחור	NAHOR	637d	2
	עבד	WORK	713b	4 b
	עבר	REGION ACROSS	719c	1 b
	עולם	LONG DURATION	761d	1 a
	תרח	TERAH	1076b	1
24 3	הלך	WALK	236c	1 a
	זרע	SOWING	282c	4 b
	כנען	CANAAN	488d	2 a
	לקח	TAKE	543d	7
	נהר	STREAM	625d	1
	עבר	REGION ACROSS	719c	1 b

JUDGES

Ch	v.	Heb	Eng	Page	Sec
24	4	יצחק	ISAAC	850c	
		ירד	GO DOWN	433a	1 d
		ירש	TAKE POSSESSION	439b	1 a
		מצרים	EGYPT	595d	1 b1
		עשו	ESAU	796c	
		עשו	ESAU	796c	
		יצחק	ISAAC	850c	
24	5	שעיר	SEIR	973a	1 b
		יצא	CAUSE TO GO	424c	1 a
		נגף	STRIKE	619d	
24	6	יצא	CAUSE TO GO	424c	1 a
		סוף	REEDS	693b	2 a
		פרש	HORSEMAN	832a	
		רדף	PURSUE	922c	1 a
		רכב	CHARIOT	939a	1
24	7	מאאל	DARKNESS	66d	
		כסה	COVER	491d	5
		מצרי	EGYPTIAN	596a	
		צעק	CRY	858c	1 b
		ראה	TO SEE	906d	1 b
		שום	TO PLACE	963c	1
24	8	אמרי	AMORITES	57c	2 a
		ירדן	JORDAN	434c	
		ירש	TAKE POSSESSION	439b	1 a
		לחם	ENGAGE IN BATTLE	535c	
		עבר	REGION ACROSS	719c	1 a
24	9	בלעם	BALAAM	118d	
		בלק	BALAK	119a	
		בעור	BEOR	129d	1
		צפור	ZIPPOR	862a	
		קרא	CALL	895d	5 a
24	10	אבה	BE WILLING	2c	
		בלעם	BALAAM	118d	
		ברך	BLESS	139a	2 a
		שמע	HEAR	1034b	2 g
24	11	אמרי	AMORITES	57c	2 e
		יבוסי	JEBUSITE	101a	1
		בעל	OWNER	127b	1 3
		גרגשי	GIRGASHITE	173a	
		חוי	HIVITE	295d	2
		חתי	HITTITE	366d	2 a
24	12	אמרי	AMORITES	57c	2 b
		גרש	DRIVE OUT	177a	
		לא	NOT	518d	1 ac
		צרעה	HORNETS	864a	
		קשת	BOW	906a	1 b
24	13	בנה	BUILD	124b	1 aa
		זית	OLIVE TREE	268d	1
		יגע	TOIL	388b	1
		כרם	VINEYARD	501d	
		נטע	PLANT	642c	1
24	14	אמת	FIRMNESS	54a	3 a
		ירא	FEAR	431c	3 b
		נהר	STREAM	625d	1
		סור	TURN ASIDE	694b	1
		עבר	REGION ACROSS	719c	1 b
		תמים	COMPLETE	1071b	5
24	15	אלהים	GOD	43c	1 d
		אם	IF	50d	2 bb
		אמרי	AMORITES	57c	2 b
		את	MARK OF THE ACCUSATIVE	84d	1 a
		בחר	CHOOSE	104a	3 b
		מי	WHO	566c	C
		נהר	STREAM	625d	1
		עבר	REGION ACROSS	719c	1 b
		רעע	BE EVIL	949c	1
24	16	אחר	ANOTHER	29d	
		אלהים	GOD	43c	1 d
		חלילה	FAR BE IT	321a	
		עבד	WORK	713b	4 b
24	17	אות	SIGN	16d	4
		בית	HOUSE	109a	1 ae 9
		הלך	WALK	230c	1 1d 2a
		עבד	SLAVE	713d	1
		עבר	PASS OVER	717c	3 a
		עלה	GO UP	749b	1 a
		עשה	DO	793d	1 1a 1
		קרב	INWARD PART	899a	1 f8
		שמר	KEEP	1037a	4 a
24	18	אמרי	AMORITES	57c	2 b
		גם	ALSO	169c	4
		גרש	DRIVE OUT	177a	
24	19	אל	GOD	42d	6 d
		אלהים	GOD	44b	4 a
		חטאת	SIN	309a	1 d2
		יכל	BE ABLE	407c	1 a
		נשא	LIFT	671c	3 c
		פשע	TRANSGRESSION	833c	1 c
		קדוש	HOLY	872c	1 b
		קנוא	JEALOUS	888d	
24	20	אחר	AFTER THAT	30b	3
		אלהים	GOD	43c	1 d
		יטב	DO GOOD TO	405d	2
		כלה	FINISH	478c	2 c2
		נכר	FOREIGNNESS	648c	1
		עבד	WORK	713b	4 b
		רעע	BE EVIL	949c	1
		שוב	TURN BACK	998a	6 g
24	21	לא	NOT	519a	1 ad b
24	22	בחר	CHOOSE	104a	3 b
		עד	WITNESS	729d	2 c
24	23	אלהים	GOD	43c	1 d
		אלהים	GOD	44b	4 ba
		לבב	HEART	523d	24
		נטה	INCLINE	640d	3 d
		נכר	FOREIGNNESS	648c	1
		סור	TURN ASIDE	694b	1
24	25	ברית	COVENANT	136d	2 c
		ברית	COVENANT	137a	3 1
		חק	SOMETHING PRESCRIBED	349c	6 a
		כרת	CUT	503d	4
		משפט	JUDGMENT	1048d	3
24	26	אבן	STONE	6b	1
		אלה	TEREBINTH	18c	
		אלה	OAK	47c	
		דבר	WORD	183a	2 2
		תורה	LAW	436a	2 b1
		כתב	WRITE	507c	1 b3
		ספר	MISSIVE	707b	3 c
		מקדש	SACRED PLACE	874a	1
		קום	STAND	878d	2 a
24	27	אבן	STONE	6b	1
		אלהים	GOD	44d	4 c
		אמר	WORD	57a	1
		דבר	SPEAK	181b	3 e
		כחש	DECEIVE	471b	2
		עדה	TESTIMONY	729d	
24	28	ל	TO	511b	1 ga
		שלח	SEND	1019a	1 a
24	29	בן	SON	121d	9 a
		דבר	WORD	183c	4 4
		עבד	SLAVE	714a	3
		עשר	TEN	797a	3 a
24	30	גבול	BOUNDARY	147d	1 c
		גבול	BOUNDARY	148a	1 c
		געש	GAASH	172b	
		הר	MOUNTAIN	251a	2 b
		מן	FROM	578d	1 c
		תמנתסרה	TIMNATH-SERAH	584d	
		קבר	BURY	868c	
24	31	ארך	BE LONG	73d	1 a
		זקן	OLD	278d	2 b
		יום	DAY	399a	4 a
		יום	DAY	399b	4 a
		מעשה	DEED	795d	1 c
24	32	בן	SON	120d	1 ja
		חלקה	PORTION OF GROUND	324c	1 a
		חמור	HAMOR	331c	
		יוסף	JOSEPH	415d	1 b
		יוסף	JOSEPH	415d	1 a
		מאה	HUNDRED	547d	1 a1
		עצם	BONE	782d	1 f
		קבר	BURY	868c	
		קשיטה	WEIGHT	903d	
		שכם	SHECHEM	1014c	2
24	33	גבעה	GIBEAH	149b	3
		הר	MOUNTAIN	251a	2 b
		נתן	GIVE	681b	1 a
29	27	שאב	DRAW	980c	

JUDGES

Ch	v.	Heb	Eng	Page	Sec
1	1	יהושע	JOSHUA	221c	1
		תחלה	BEGINNING	321b	
		כנעני	CANAANITE	489a	2 b
		ל	TO	515c	5 hc
		מי	WHO	566b	
		עלה	GO UP	748c	2
		ישראל	ISRAEL	975d	2 b1
		שאל	ASK	982a	2 b
1	3	אנכי	I	59b	
		את	WITH	85d	1
		גורל	LOT	174d	3
		הלך	WALK	231c	1 1d 5a
		כנעני	CANAANITE	489a	2 b
		עלה	GO UP	748b	1 c
		שמעון	SIMEON	1035c	2
1	4	אלף	THOUSAND	49a	1 c
		בזק	BEZEK	103b	
		בזק	BEZEK	103b	
		כנעני	CANAANITE	489a	2 b
		עשר	TEN	797a	2 c
		פרזי	PERIZZITE	827a	
		בזק	ADDENDA ET CORRIGENDA	1121b	
1	5	אדניבזק	ADONI-BEZEK	11d	
		בזק	BEZEK	103b	
		כנעני	CANAANITE	489a	2 b
		נכה	SMITE	646b	3
		פרזי	PERIZZITE	827a	
		בזק	ADDENDA ET CORRIGENDA	1121b	
1	6	אדניבזק	ADONI-BEZEK	11d	
		אחז	GRASP	28b	
		בהן	THUMB	97b	
		יד	HAND	389a	1 b
		קצץ	CUT OFF	*893d	
		קצץ	CUT OFF	893d	
		רגל	FOOT	919b	1 a
		רדף	PURSUE	922c	1 a
1	7	אדניבזק	ADONI-BEZEK	11d	
		בהן	THUMB	97b	
		יד	HAND	389a	1 b
		ירושלים	JERUSALEM	436d	
		כאשר	AS	455b	1 b
		כן	SO	486c	2 ca
		לקט	GATHER UP	544d	1
		מלך	KING	573a	1
		קצץ	CUT OFF	893d	
		רגל	FOOT	919d	1 a
		שבעים	SEVENTY	988c	1
		שלחן	TABLE	1020b	1
1	8	אש	FIRE	77c	1
		בן	SON	121a	1 jd
		חרב	SWORD	352d	1 f
		יהודה	JUDAH	397b	1 2
		ירושלים	JERUSALEM	436d	
		לכד	CAPTURE	540a	1
		נכה	SMITE	646b	3
		שלח	SEND	1019b	7
1	9	בן	SON	121a	1 jd
		הר	MOUNTAIN	251a	2 a
		ירד	GO DOWN	433a	1 e
		כנעני	CANAANITE	489a	2 b
		נגב	SOUTH-COUNTRY	616b	1 a
		שפלה	LOWLAND	1050c	1
1	10	אחימן	AHIMAN	27a	1
		אל	TO	40b	4
		הלך	WALK	231a	1 d3 ga
		חברון	HEBRON	289b	
		חברון	HEBRON	289b	
		כנעני	CANAANITE	489a	2 b
		ענק	NECK	778c	
		פנה	FACE	816b	16
		קריתארבע	FOURFOLD CITY	900c	
		ששי	SHESHAI	1058d	
		תלמי	TALMAI	1068d	2
1	11	דביר	DEBIR	184c	2 c
		דביר	DEBIR	184c	2 c
		פנה	FACE	816b	16
		קריתספר	KIRIATH-SEPHER	900d	
1	12	כלב	CALEB	477a	
		לכד	CAPTURE	540a	1
		נכה	SMITE	646b	3
		נתן	GIVE	678c	1 c
		עכסה	ACHSAH	747c	
		קריתספר	KIRIATH-SEPHER	900d	
1	13	כלב	CALEB	477a	
		נתן	GIVE	678c	1 c
		עכסה	ACHSAH	747c	
		עתניאל	OTHNIEL	801a	
		קטן	SMALL	882b	1 a
		קנז	KENAZ	889d	
1	14	את	WITH	86d	4 a
		בוא	COME	98a	1 d
		חמור	HE-ASS	331b	2 a
		כלב	CALEB	477a	
		סות	INCITE	694d	1 a
		צנח	DESCEND	856c	
1	15	ברכה	BLESSING	139d	5
		יהב	GIVE	396d	1
		כלב	CALEB	477a	
		נגב	SOUTH-COUNTRY	616b	1 a
		עלי	UPPER	751a	
		תחתי	LOWER	1066c	
1	16	בן	SON	121a	1 jd
		מדבר	WILDERNESS	185a	3 b
		חבב	HOBAB	285d	
		חתן	WIFE:S FATHER	368c	1
		יהודה	JUDAH	397c	2
		יריחו	JERICHO	*437d	
		ישב	DWELL	443a	3
		נגב	SOUTH-COUNTRY	616b	1 a
		עמלקי	AMALEKITES	766b	
		עם	PEOPLE	766c	1
		ערד	ARAD	788c	
		קין	KENITE	883d	1
		קיני	KENITE	884a	
		תמר	PALM-TREE	1071c	
1	17	חרמה	HORMAH	356c	
		כנעני	CANAANITE	489a	2 b
		נכה	SMITE	646b	3
		צפת	ZEPHATH	862c	
		קרא	CALL	896a	6 a
		שמעון	SIMEON	1035c	2
1	18	אשקלון	ASHKELON	80c	
		גבול	BOUNDARY	148a	2 b
		לכד	CAPTURE	*540a	1
		עזה	GAZA	738b	
		עקרון	EKRON	785d	
1	19	את	WITH	85d	1 a
		ברזל	IRON	137c	1 c
		היה	BE	227b	3 4d a
		יכל	BE ABLE	*407c	1 a
		ירש	CAUSE TO POSSESS	440a	2 a
		לא	NOT	518d	1 ab
		עמק	VALE	771a	
		רכב	CHARIOT	939a	1
1	20	חברון	HEBRON	289b	
		ירש	CAUSE TO POSSESS	440a	2 a
		כלב	CALEB	477a	
		ענק	NECK	778c	
1	21	יבוסי	JEBUSITE	101a	1
		בן	SON	*121a	1 jd
		בנימין	BENJAMIN	122d	1
		יום	DAY	401b	7 l
		ירושלים	JERUSALEM	436d	
		ירש	CAUSE TO POSSESS	440a	2 a
		ישב	DWELL	443a	3
1	22	בית	HOUSE	110a	5 dz
		הם	THEY	241b	1
		יוסף	JOSEPH	415d	1 b
1	23	בית	HOUSE	110a	5 dz

Ch v.	Heb	Eng	Page	Sec
	ביתאל	BETHEL	110d	1
	יוסף	JOSEPH	415d	1 b
	לוז	LUZ	531c	1
	פנה	FACE	816b	16
	תור	SPY OUT	1064c	
1 24	מבוא	ENTRANCE	99d	1
	חסד	GOODNESS	338c	11
	עשה	DO	794b	13
	ראה	TO SEE	908d	1 a1
	שמר	KEEP	1036d	1 c
1 25	מבוא	ENTRANCE	99d	1
	חרב	SWORD	352d	1 f
	נכה	SMITE	646b	3
	ראה	TO SEE	908d	1 a1
	משפחה	CLAN	1046d	1 a
1 26	בנה	BUILD	124d	1 aa
	הלך	WALK	230d	1 1d 3a
	חתי	HITTITE	366d	2 b
	יום	DAY	401b	7 1
	לוז	LUZ	531c	2
	קרא	CALL	896a	6 a
1 27	בית שאן	BETH-SHEAN	112d	1
	בת	DAUGHTER	123d	4
	מגדו	MEGIDDO	152a	
	דאר	DOR	190b	
	יאל	SHOW-WILLING-NESS	384a	3
	יבלעם	IBLEAM	385d	
	ירש	CAUSE TO POSSESS	440a	2 a
	כנעני	CANAANITE	489a	2 b
	מנשה	MANASSEH	586c	1 b1 b
	תענך	TAANACH	1073d	
1 28	ירש	CAUSE TO POSSESS	440a	2 a
	כנעני	CANAANITE	489a	2 b
	מס	LABOUR-GANG	587a	2 b
	שום	TO PLACE	964c	5 a
1 29	גזר	GEZER	160c	
	ירש	CAUSE TO POSSESS	440a	2 a
	כנעני	CANAANITE	489a	2 b
1 30	זבולן	ZEBULUN	259d	2
	ירש	CAUSE TO POSSESS	440a	2 a
	ישב	DWELL	443a	3
	כנעני	CANAANITE	489a	2 b
	נהלל	NAHALOL	625b	
	קטרון	KATRON	883c	
1 31	אפק	APHEK	67d	2
	אשר	ASHER	81b	2
	חלבה	HELBAH	317a	
	אחלב	HELBAH	*317b	
	אחלב	HELBAH	317b	
	ירש	CAUSE TO POSSESS	440a	2 a
	אכזיב	ACHZIB	469d	2
	עכו	ACCO	747c	
	צידון	SIDON	851a	
	רחוב	REHOB	932b	1 b2
	אפק	ADDENDA ET CORRIGENDA	1120c	
1 32	אשורי	ASHURITE	79a	
	אשרי	ASHERITE	81b	
	ירש	CAUSE TO POSSESS	440a	2 a
	ישב	DWELL	443a	3
	כנעני	CANAANITE	489a	2 b
	קרב	INWARD PART	899b	1 f1
1 33	בית ענת	BETH-ANATH	112c	
	בית שמש	BETH-SHEMESH	113a	1
	ירש	CAUSE TO POSSESS	440a	2 a
	ישב	DWELL	443a	3
	כנעני	CANAANITE	489a	2 b
	ל	TO	512c	4 b
	מס	LABOUR-GANG	587a	2 b
	נפתלי	NAPHTALI	836d	2 a
	קרב	INWARD PART	899b	1 f1
1 34	אמרי	AMORITES	57c	2 b
	דן	DAN	192d	1
	ירד	GO DOWN	432d	1 b
	ל	TO	511b	1 ga
	לחץ	PRESS	537d	1
	עמק	VALE	771a	
1 35	אילון	AIJALON	19c	1
	אמרי	AMORITES	57c	2 b
	בית	HOUSE	110a	5 dz
	הר	MOUNTAIN	249c	1 a
	חרס	HERES	357c	1
	יאל	SHOW-WILLING-NESS	384b	3
	יוסף	JOSEPH	415d	1 b
	כבד	BE HEAVY	457b	1
	מס	LABOUR-GANG	587a	2 b
	שעלבים	SHAALBIM	1043c	
1 36	אמרי	AMORITES	57c	2 b
	גבול	BORDER	147d	1 a
	מעלה	ASCENT	751c	1
	מעל	ABOVE	751d	2 ba
	סלע	SELA	701aa	
2 1	אב	FATHER	3c	4 b
	בכה	WEEP	113c	6
	בכים	BOCHIM	114a	
	בכים	BOCHIM	114a	
	ברית	COVENANT	137b	3 3
	מלאך	MESSENGER	521d	3
	עולם	LONG DURATION	762c	2 d
	פרר	BREAK	830b	1 a
	רגל	GO ABOUT	920b	2
	שבע	SWEAR	989c	2
2 2	ברית	COVENANT	136b	11
	מזבח	ALTAR	259a	0
	זה	THIS	261c	4 d
	כרת	CUT	503d	4
	נתץ	PULL DOWN	683b	1
	קול	VOICE	877b	3 b
2 3	גם	ALSO	169d	4
	גרש	DRIVE OUT	177a	
	מוקש	BAIT	430d	
	צד	SIDE	841a	
2 4	בכה	WEEP	113c	1
	בכים	BOCHIM	*114a	
	מלאך	MESSENGER	521d	3
	נשא	LIFT	670c	1 b 5
	קול	VOICE	876d	1 a
2 5	בכה	WEEP	113c	6
	בכים	BOCHIM	114a	
	בכים	BOCHIM	114a	
	מקום	STANDING PLACE	880a	4
	קרא	CALL	896a	6 a
	רקד	SKIP ABOUT	955a	
2 6	יהושע	JOSHUA	221c	1
	ירש	TAKE POSSESSION	439b	1 a
2 7	ארך	BE LONG	73d	1 a
	גדול	GREAT	153b	6 c
	יהושע	JOSHUA	221c	1
	יהושע	JOSHUA	221c	1
	זקן	OLD	278d	2 b
	יום	DAY	399d	4 a
	יום	DAY	399b	4 a
	מעשה	DEED	795d	1 c
2 8	בן	SON	121d	9 a
	יהושע	JOSHUA	221c	1
	מאה	HUNDRED	548b	2 a1
2 9	נון	NUN	630c	
	עבד	SLAVE	714a	3
	עשר	TEN	797a	3 a
	אפרים	EPHRAIM	68c	3
	גבול	BOUNDARY	148a	1 c
	געש	GAASH	172b	
	חרם	HERES	357c	
	תמנת סרח	TIMNATH-SERAH	584d	
	תמנת חרם	TIMNATH-HERES	584d	
	קבר	BURY	868c	
2 10	אחר	ANOTHER	*29d	
	אסף	GATHER	62d	2 a
	דור	GENERATION	190a	2
	ידע	KNOW	394a	2
	מעשה	DEED	795d	1 c
	קום	STAND	878a	4
2 11	בעל	BAAL	127d	2 3
	בל	BEL	128c	
	עבד	WORK	713b	4 b
	עין	EYE	744d	3 c
	רע	EVIL	948c	0 b
2 12	אחר	ANOTHER	29d	
	אלהים	GOD	43c	1 d
	אלהים	GOD	43c	1 d
	אלהים	GOD	44b	4 ba
	הלך	WALK	235a	2 3d 2
	יצא	CASUE TO GO	424c	1 a
	כעס	VEX	495a	2
2 13	בעל	BAAL	127d	2 2
	עבד	WORK	713b	4 b
	עשתרת	ASTORETH	800a	
2 14	חרה	BURN	354a	2 a
	יד	HAND	390d	5 b3
	יד	HAND	390d	5 b3
	מכר	SELL	569b	
	סביב	ROUND ABOUT	687a	1 d
	עמד	STAND	764b	4
	פנה	FACE	817b	2 4b d
	שסה	PLUNDER	1042c	
	שסס	PLUNDER	1042d	
2 15	אשר	PARTICLE OF RELATION	82c	4 bg
	יצא	GO OUT	424a	2 c
	צרר	BIND	864d	B
	רעה	MISERY	949d	2 1
2 16	ישע	DELIVER	446c	1 a
	קום	STAND	878d	3
	שסה	PLUNDER	1042c	
	שפט	JUDGE	1047b	1 b
2 17	אחר	ANOTHER	29d	
	אלהים	GOD	43c	1 d
	דרך	WAY	203c	6 b
	הלך	WALK	234c	2 3a 1b
	זנה	COMMIT FORNICATION	275d	3
	מהר	QUICKLY	555b	
	סור	TURN ASIDE	693c	1
	שמע	HEAR	1034a	1 k
	שפט	JUDGE	1047b	1 b
2 18	דחק	OPPRESS	191b	
	היה	BE	227b	3 4d a
	יום	DAY	399a	4 a
	ישע	DELIVER	446d	1 b
	כי	WHEN	473a	2 a
	לחץ	OPPRESS	537d	2
	מן	ON ACCOUNT OF	580b	2 f
	נאקה	GROANING	611a	
	נחם	BE SORRY	637a	1
	פנה	FACE	818c	2 6c a
	קום	STAND	878d	3
	קשר	BIND	905b	1 a
	שפט	JUDGE	1047b	1 b
	שפט	JUDGE	1047b	1 b
2 19	אחר	ANOTHER	29d	
	אלהים	GOD	43c	1 d
	דרך	WAY	203d	6 d
	מן	THAN	582c	6 a
	נפל	FALL	658b	4
	עבד	WORK	713b	4 b
	מעלל	DEED	760b	1
	קשה	SEVERE	904d	3
	שוב	TURN BACK	997d	6 a
	שחת	GO TO RUIN	1008c	2
	שפט	JUDGE	1047b	1 b
2 20	ברית	COVENANT	137b	3 3
	גוי	NATION	156d	1 b
	חרה	BURN	354a	2 a
	עבר	PASS OVER	717c	1 i
	יען	ON ACCOUNT OF	774d	2
	קול	VOICE	877b	3 b
	שמע	HEAR	1034a	1 1
2 21	גם	ALSO	169c	4
	יהושע	JOSHUA	221c	1
	יסף	DO AGAIN	415c	2 a
	ירש	CAUSE TO POSSESS	440a	2 a
2 22	דרך	WAY	204a	6 ec
	ה	INTERROG PART	210b	2 b
	לא	NOT	519a	1 ad b
	נסה	TEST	650b	3 a
	שמר	KEEP	1037a	3 c
2 23	בלת	NOT	116d	4 a
	יהושע	JOSHUA	221c	1
	ירש	CAUSE TO POSSESS	440a	2 a
	מהר	QUICKLY	555b	
	נוח	REST	628d	B 2
3 1	כנען	CANAAN	488d	2 a
	מלחמה	WAR	536b	
	נוח	REST	628d	B 2
	נסה	TEST	650b	3 a
3 2	בן	SON	121a	1 jg
	דור	GENERATION	190a	2 b
	מלחמה	WAR	536b	
	למד	LEARN	540d	
3 3	בוא	COME	98d	2 e
	בעל חרמון	BAAL-HERMON	128a	
	הר	MOUNTAIN	249c	1 a
	חוי	HIVITE	295d	2
	חמש	FIVE	331d	1 d
	חמת	HAMATH	333a	
	חרמון	HERMON	356d	
	חתי	HITTITE	366d	2 a
	חתי	HITTITE	*366d	2 b
	כנעני	CANAANITE	489a	2 b
	לבנון	LEBANON	527a	
	סרן	TYRANT	710d	
	עד	UNTIL	725b	3 1
	פלשתי	PHILISTINE	814c	
	צידני	SIDONIANS	851a	
	צידני	SIDONIANS	851a	
3 4	ה	INTERROG PART	210b	2 a
	נסה	TEST	650b	3 a
	מצוה	COMMANDMENT	*846c	2 b
3 5	אמרי	AMORITES	57c	2 e
	יבוסי	JEBUSITE	101a	1
	חוי	HIVITE	295d	2
	ישב	DWELL	443a	3
	כנעני	CANAANITE	489a	2 b
	קרב	INWARD PART	899b	1 f1
3 7	אשרה	ASHERA	81c	A
	בעל	BAAL	127d	2 3
	יהוה	YAHWEH	218d	2 1d
	עבד	WORK	713b	4 b
	עין	EYE	744d	3 c
	שכח	FORGET	1013b	1 c
3 8	ארם	ARAM	74c	B
	חרה	BURN	354a	2 a
	יד	HAND	390d	5 b3
	כושנרשעתי	CUSHAN-RISHATHAIM	469b	
	מכר	SELL	569b	
	מלך	KING	573a	1
	שמנה	EIGHT	1032d	1 a
3 9	זעק	CRY	277b	2 a
	ישע	DELIVER	446c	1 a
	ישע	DELIVER	446c	1 b
	כלב	CALEB	477a	
	עתניאל	OTHNIEL	801a	
	קום	STAND	879a	3
	קטן	SMALL	882b	1 a
	קנז	KENAZ	889d	
3 10	אגגי	AGAGITE	8a	
	היה	BECOME	225d	2 1b
	כושנרשעתי	CUSHAN-RISHATHAIM	469b	
	מלך	KING	573a	1
	עזז	BE STRONG	738c	
	רוח	BREATH	926a	9 c1
	שפט	JUDGE	1047b	1 b
3 11	עתניאל	OTHNIEL	801a	
	קנז	KENAZ	889d	
	ארבעים	FORTY	917b	1 a
	ארבעים	FORTY	917c	1 a
	שקט	BE QUIET	1053a	1
3 12	חזק	BE FIRM	304c	1 a
	יסף	DO AGAIN	415c	2 a
	מואב	MOAB	555d	2 a
	עגלון	EGLON	722d	1
	על	UPON	758b	3 b

123

Ch	v.	Heb	Eng	Page	Sec
3	13	ירחו	JERICHO	*437d	
		ירש	TAKE POSSESSION	439c	1 a
		עמלק	AMALEK	766a	
		עמון	AMMON	770a	
		תמר	PALM-TREE	1071c	
3	14	עגלון	EGLON	722d	1
		עשר	TEN	797b	8 b
		שמנה	EIGHT	1033a	2
3	15	אהוד	EHUD	13c	1
		אטר	SHUT UP	32a	
		בנימיני	BENJAMITE	122d	
		גרא	GERA	173a	
		זעק	CRY	277b	2 a
		יד	HAND	389a	1 a
		ימין	RIGHT HAND	411d	1 a
		ישע	DELIVER	446c	1 a
		ל	TO	*512a	3 b
		מנחה	TRIBUTE	585a	2
		עגלון	EGLON	722d	1
		קום	STAND	879a	3
		שלח	SEND	1018b	1 b
		ל	MARK OF ACCUSATIVE	*1098b	2
3	16	אהוד	EHUD	13c	1
		חגר	GIRD	291d	2
		חרב	SWORD	352c	1 a
		ימין	RIGHT	412a	3
		ירך	THIGH	437d	1 a
		ל	TO	513b	5 ba
		ל	TO	515d	5 ia
		מד	GARMENT	551c	3
		עלה	WHOLE BURNT OFFERING	750d	
		פה	MOUTH	805b	3
		תחת	UNDERNEATH	1066b	3 2b
3	17	ברא	FAT	135d	
		מנחה	TRIBUTE	585a	2
		עגלון	EGLON	722d	1
		קרב	COME NEAR	897d	1 a
3	18	מנחה	TRIBUTE	585a	2
		עם	PEOPLE	766c	2 c
		קרב	COME NEAR	897d	1 a
3	19	את	WITH	86b	2
		הס	HUSH	245a	
		יצא	GO OUT	422d	1 b
		סתר	COVERING	712a	3
		על	UPON	756b	2 6c
		על	UPON	759a	4 2c
		פסיל	IDOL	821a	
		שוב	TURN BACK	996d	1
3	20	אהוד	EHUD	13c	
		אשר	PARTICLE OF RELATION	83a	7 b
		בד	SEPARATION	94c	1 b
		ה	THE	207b	1 cb
		כסא	SEAT OF HONOR	490d	1 a
		עליה	ROOF-CHAMBER	751a	
		על	UPON	758c	4 2a
		קום	STAND	877d	1 a
		מקרה	COOLNESS	903b	
3	21	אהוד	EHUD	13c	
		בטן	BELLY	105d	1 a
		יד	HAND	389a	1 a
		ירך	THIGH	437d	1 a
		לקח	TAKE	542d	3 a
		עם	WITH	768a	1 g
		שמאל	LEFT	969d	1
		תקע	THRUST	1075b	1
3	22	בטן	BELLY	105d	1 a
		בעד	BEHIND	126c	1 b
		חלב	FAT	316d	1
		חרב	SWORD	352c	1 c
		יצא	GO OUT	423b	2 a
		להב	BLADE	529b	2
		נצב	HAFT	662c	1
		סגר	CLOSE	689a	2 a
		פרשדנה	FECES	832b	
		שלף	DRAW OUT	1025b	1
3	23	אהוד	EHUD	13c	1
		בעד	BEHIND	126c	1 b
		דלת	DOOR	195a	2
		ו	AND	252b	1 b
		נעל	LOCK	653a	
		סגר	SHUT	689a	1
		מסדרון	PORCH	690c	
		עליה	ROOF-CHAMBER	751a	
3	24	אך	SURELY	36c	1
		דלת	DOOR	195a	2
		חדר	CHAMBER	293d	
		ימין	RIGHT	412a	3
		יצא	GO OUT	422d	1 a
		נעל	LOCK	653a	
		סכך	OVERSHADOW	697a	1
		עליה	ROOF-CHAMBER	751a	
		מקרה	COOLNESS	903b	
		רגל	FOOT	920a	1 f
3	25	בוש	BE ASHAMED	101d	3
		דלת	DOOR	195a	2
		חול	WHIRL	297b	2
		לקח	TAKE	543c	4 g
		נפל	LIE	657d	7
		עד	AS FAR AS	724d	12a b
		עליה	ROOF-CHAMBER	751a	
		פתח	OPEN	835a	
		מפתח	KEY	836b	
		בוש	ADDENDA ET CORRIGENDA	1121b	
3	26	אהוד	EHUD	13c	1
		מהה	LINGER	554c	
		מלט	SLIP AWAY	572c	2
		עבר	PASS OVER	717d	4 a
		עד	AS FAR AS	724c	1 2b
		פסיל	IDOL	821a	
		שעירה	SEIRIAH	972d	
3	27	אפרים	EPHRAIM	68c	3
		הר	MOUNTAIN	*251a	2 b
		הר	MOUNTAIN	251a	2 b
		שפר	HORN	1051d	
		תקע	GIVE A BLOW	1075c	2
3	28	ירדן	JORDAN	434d	
		ל	TO	515b	5 hb g
		לכד	CAPTURE	540a	1
		עבר	PASS OVER	717a	1 a2
		מעברה	FORD	721b	1
		רדף	PURSUE	922c	1 a
3	29	אלף	THOUSAND	49a	1 c
		חיל	STRENGTH	298d	1 c
		מלט	SLIP AWAY	572b	2
		שמן	ROBUST	1032a	2
3	30	כנע	BE HUMBLED	488c	2
		שקט	BE QUIET	1053a	1
		תחת	UNDERNEATH	1065a	2 1d
3	31	בקר	CATTLE	133c	2
		היה	BECOME	225c	2 1a
		ישע	DELIVER	446c	1 a
		מלמד	OX-GOAD	541a	
		ענת	ANATH	779a	
		פלשתי	PHILISTINE	814c	
		שמגר	SHAMGAR	1029a	
4	1	אהוד	EHUD	13c	1
		יסף	DO AGAIN	415c	2 a
4	2	יבין	JABIN	108a	2
		יבין	JABIN	*108a	2
		גוי	NATION	156d	1 c
		חצור	HAZOR	347d	1
		חרשת	HAROSHETH	361d	
		יד	HAND	390d	5 b3
		כנען	CANAAN	488d	2 a
		מכר	SELL	569b	
		מלך	BE KING	574a	
		מלך	BE KING	574a	
		סיסרא	SISERA	696b	1
		צבא	ARMY	839a	1 a
		ברזל	IRON	137c	1 d
4	3	חזקה	STRENGTH	306a	1
		לחץ	OPPRESS	537d	2
		מאה	HUNDRED	548a	1 c2
		סוס	HORSE	*692c	1
		צעק	CRY	858c	1 b
		רכב	CHARIOT	939a	1
		תשע	NINE	1077c	3
4	4	אשה	WOMAN	61b	2
		דבורה	DEBORAH	184b	2
		לפידות	LAPPIDOTH	542b	
		נביאה	PROPHETESS	612c	1 a
		שפט	JUDGE	1047b	1 b
4	5	אלון	TEREBINTH	18d	
		אלון	TEREBINTH	18d	
		אפרים	EPHRAIM	68c	3
		דבורה	DEBORAH	184b	2
		הר	MOUNTAIN	251a	2 b
		עלה	GO UP	748c	2 b
		רמה	RAMA	928a	1
		משפט	JUDGMENT	1048b	1 a
		תמר	PALM-TREE	1071c	
4	6	אבינעם	ABINOAM	4c	
		אלהים	GOD	44c	4 ba
		בדן	BEDAN	*96a	1
		ברק	BARAK	140c	
		הר	MOUNTAIN	249c	1 a
		זבולן	ZEBULUN	259d	2
		לא	NOT	520b	4 a
		לקח	TAKE	543d	7
		משך	DRAW	604b	3
		נפתלי	NAPHTALI	836d	2 a
		נפתלי	NAPHTALI	837a	2 a
		צוה	CHARGE	846a	2 d
		קדש	KEDESH	873d	1
		קרא	CALL	895d	5 a
		תבור	TABOR	1061d	1
4	7	יבין	JABIN	108a	2
		המון	CROWD	242c	3 a
		משך	DRAW	604b	1
		נחל	TORRENT	636a	1
		צבא	ARMY	839a	1 a
		קישון	KISHON	885c	
		רכב	CHARIOT	939a	1
4	8	ברק	BARAK	140c	
		הלך	WALK	230b	1 1b
		הלך	WALK	231c	1 1d 5b
		אם	NON-EXISTENCE	67b	2 cb
4	9	ברק	BARAK	140c	
		דבורה	DEBORAH	184b	2
		הלך	WALK	231c	1 1d 5b
		הלך	WALK	233a	14b 1
		הלך	WALK	234a	1 5c
		יד	HAND	390d	5 b3
		מכר	SELL	569b	
		נכר	TREAT AS FOREIGN	*649a	
		תפארה	BEAUTY	802d	3 b
4	10	קדש	KEDESH	873d	1
		אלף	THOUSAND	49a	1 c
		אלף	THOUSAND	49a	1 c
		ברק	BARAK	140c	
		דבורה	DEBORAH	184b	2
		זבולן	ZEBULUN	259d	2
		זעק	CRY	277c	1
		נפתלי	NAPHTALI	836d	2 a
		קדש	KEDESH	873d	1
		רגל	FOOT	920a	1 f
4	11	אלון	TEREBINTH	18d	
		את	WITH	86b	2
		בצעננים	IN ZAANANNIM	130c	
		חבב	HOBAB	285d	
		חבר	HEBER	288c	1
		חתן	WIFE:S FATHER	368c	1
		נטה	SPREAD OUT	640a	2
		פרד	DIVIDE	825b	2
		צעננים	ZAANANNIM	858b	
		קדש	KEDESH	873d	1
		קין	KENITE	883d	1
		קיני	KENITE	884a	
		קיני	KENITE	884a	
4	12	אבינעם	ABINOAM	4c	
		ברק	BARAK	140c	1 a
		הר	MOUNTAIN	249c	1 a
		תבור	TABOR	1061d	1
4	13	את	WITH	85d	1
		ברזל	IRON	137c	1 d
		גוי	NATION	156d	1 c
		זעק	CRY	277c	1
		חרשת	HAROSHETH	361d	
		מאה	HUNDRED	548a	1 c2
		נחל	TORRENT	636a	1
		סוס	HORSE	*692c	1
		קישון	KISHON	885c	
		רכב	CHARIOT	939a	1
		רכב	CHARIOT	939a	1
4	14	אשר	PARTICLE OF RELATION	82c	4 ba
		ברק	BARAK	140c	
		דבורה	DEBORAH	184b	2
		הר	MOUNTAIN	249c	1 a
		יצא	GO OUT	424a	2 c
		לא	NOT	520b	4 ba
		קום	STAND	878b	6 a
		תבור	TABOR	1061d	1
4	15	ברק	BARAK	140c	
		ה	THE	207b	1 cb
		חמם	CONFUSE	243a	2
		מחנה	ENCAMPMENT	334b	3 c
		חרב	SWORD	352d	1 f
		ירד	GO DOWN	433a	1 f
		נוס	FLEE	630d	1
		על	UPON	758c	4 2a
		פנה	FACE	817b	24b c
		רגל	FOOT	920a	1 f
		מרכבה	CHARIOT	939d	
4	16	ברק	BARAK	140c	
		גוי	NATION	156d	1 c
		מחנה	ENCAMPMENT	334b	3 c
		חרב	SWORD	352d	1 f
		חרשת	HAROSHETH	361d	
		נפל	FALL	657b	2 a
		עד	AS FAR AS	724d	1 3
		רדף	PURSUE	922c	1 a
4	17	יבין	JABIN	108a	2
		חבר	HEBER	288c	1
		חצור	HAZOR	347d	1
		יעל	JAEL	418d	
		נוס	FLEE	630d	1
		קיני	KENITE	884a	
		רגל	FOOT	920a	1 f
		שלום	PEACE	1023b	6
4	18	אדון	LORD	11b	3 1d
		ה	THE	207c	1 d
		יעל	JAEL	418d	
		ירא	FEAR	431a	1 a
		כסה	COVER	491d	1
		סור	TURN ASIDE	693c	1
		קרא	ENCOUNTER	896d	1
		שמיכה	RUG	970d	
4	19	ה	THE	207c	1 d
		חלב	MILK	*316b	A
		חלב	MILK	316b	A
		כסה	COVER	491c	1
		נאד	SKIN	609d	
		פתח	OPEN	835a	
		צמא	BE THIRSTY	854d	
		שקה	GIVE TO DRINK	1052c	2
		שקה	GIVE TO DRINK	1052c	2
4	20	אין	NOT	34c	2 dg
		אם	NON-EXISTENCE	67b	2 b
		יש	THERE IS	441d	2 b
		פה	HERE	806a	1 a
		פתח	OPENING	835d	
		שאל	ASK	981d	2 a
4	21	חבר	HEBER	288c	1
		יעל	JAEL	418d	
		יתד	PEG	450b	A
		לט	SECRECY	532a	1
		מקבת	HAMMER	666c	
		עיף	BE FAINT	746a	
		צנח	DESCEND	856c	
		רדם	BE IN HEAVY SLEEP	922b	

Ch	v.	Heb	Eng	Page	Sec
		רקח	THE TEMPLE	956d	
		סום	TO PLACE	963a	1 a
		תקע	THRUST	1075b	1
		תקע	THRUST	*1075c	1
4	22	בקש	SEEK	134c	1 b
		ברק	BARAK	140c	
		יעל	JAEL	418d	
		יתד	PEG	450b	A
		נפל	LIE	657d	7
		קרא	ENCOUNTER	896d	1
		ראה	TO SEE	908d	1 a1
		רדף	PURSUE	922d	1 b
		רקח	THE TEMPLE	956d	
4	23	יבין	JABIN	108a	2
		כנע	HUMBLE	488c	2
		כנען	CANAAN	488d	2 a
4	24	יבין	JABIN	108a	2
		הלך	WALK	233b	1 4c 3
		כנען	CANAAN	488d	2 a
		כרת	CUT OFF	504c	2 b
		עד	UNTIL	724d	2 1a a
		קשה	SEVERE	904c	2 a
5	1	אבינעם	ABINOAM	4c	
		ברק	BARAK	140c	
		דבורה	DEBORAH	184b	2
		שיר	SING	1010d	
5	2	ברך	BLESS	139a	1
		ה	THE	208d	1 i
		נדב	INCITE	621c	1
		פרע	ACT AS LEADER	828c	
		פרע	LEADER	828c	
		ישראל	ISRAEL	975c	2 a1
5	3	אזן	HEAR	24c	1
		אלהים	GOD	44c	4 ba
		זמר	MAKE MUSIC	274a	1
		רזן	BE WEIGHTY	931b	
		שיר	SING	1010d	
		שמע	HEAR	1033d	1 f
5	4	ארץ	EARTH	76a	1 b
		גם	YEA	169c	3
		מי	WATER	565c	1 g
		נטף	DROP	643a	
		עב	DARK CLOUD	728a	1 a
		רעש	SHAKE	950b	
		שעיר	SEIR	973a	1 a
		שמי	HEAVENS	1029d	1 a
5	5	אלהים	GOD	44c	4 ba
		הר	MOUNTAIN	250a	1 c
		זה	THIS	260d	2 a
		זלל	SHAKE	272d	
		נזל	FLOW	633d	1
		סיני	SINAI	696a	
		פנה	FACE	818c	2 6b
5	6	ארח	WAY	73a	1
		הלך	WALK	230c	1 1d 1a
		הלך	WALK	230c	1 1d 1a
		חדל	CEASE	293a	1
		יום	DAY	399b	4 b
		יעל	JAEL	418d	
		נתיבה	PATH	677b	1
		ענת	ANATH	779a	
		עקלקל	CROOKED	785c	
		שמגר	SHAMGAR	1029a	
5	7	אם	MOTHER	52a	2
		דבורה	DEBORAH	184b	2
		חדל	CEASE	293a	1
		עד	UNTIL	724d	2 1a a
		פרזה	OPEN REGION	826d	
		פרזון	RURAL POPULA-TION	826d	
		קום	STAND	878a	4
		ישראל	ISRAEL	975c	2 a1
5	8	אז	THEN	23a	1 c
		אלהים	GOD	43b	1 a
		אם	IF	50c	2 aa
		בחר	CHOOSE	104b	5 b
		מגן	SHIELD	171c	
		חדש	NEW	294b	A
		לחם	WAR	535d	
		עם	PEOPLE	766c	2 b
		עם	PEOPLE	766d	2 d
		ארבעים	FORTY	917b	1 a
		רמח	SPEAR	942b	
		שער	GATE	1044c	1 a
5	9	ברך	BLESS	139a	1
		חקק	CUT IN	349b	4
		ל	TO	510d	1 a
		נדב	INCITE	621c	1
5	10	אתון	SHE-ASS	87d	
		הלך	WALK	230b	1 1a
		הלך	WALK	230d	1 1d 2b
		ירד	GO DOWN	432d	1 b
		מד	CLOTH	551b	2
		צחר	TAWNY	850c	
		רכב	RIDE	938d	3
		שיח	MUSE	967b	3 a
5	11	אז	THEN	23a	1 c
		בין	INTERVAL	107b	1
		חצץ	THOSE DIVIDING	346d	
		ירד	GO DOWN	432d	1 b
		ל	TO	511b	1 ga
		מן	FROM	578b	1 b
		פרזון	RURAL POPULA-TION	826d	
		צדקה	RIGHTEOUSNESS	842c	7 a
		משאב	DRAWING-PLACE	980c	
		שער	GATE	1044c	1 a
		תנה	RECOUNT	1072a	
5	12	אבינעם	ABINOAM	4c	
		ברק	BARAK	140c	
		דבר	SPEAK	181a	2
		דבורה	DEBORAH	184b	2
		עור	ROUSE ONESELF	734d	1
		קום	STAND	878b	6 b
		שבה	TAKE CAPTIVE	985c	2
		שבי	CAPTIVITY	985d	3
		שיר	SONG	1010b	1
5	13	אדיר	MAJESTIC	12b	2
		אז	THEN	23a	1 c
		גבור	STRONG	150b	2
		ל	TO	515c	5 hc
		צר	ADVERSARY	865d	
		רדה	HAVE DOMINION	922a	
		שריד	SURVIVOR	975a	1
5	14	אחר	BEHIND	30a	2 a
		בנימן	BENJAMIN	122d	1
		זבולן	ZEBULUN	259d	2
		חקק	CUT IN	349b	A
		חקק	CUT IN	*349b	4
		יצא	GO OUT	424a	2 c
		ירד	GO DOWN	432d	1 b
		משך	DRAW	604b	3
		ספר	ENUMERATOR	708b	1 a
		ספר	ENUMERATOR	708c	1 b
		עמלק	AMALEK	766a	
		עם	PEOPLE	766c	2 b
		עם	PEOPLE	766d	2 d
		עם	KINSMAN	769c	
		עמק	VALE	*771a	
		שבט	ROD	987b	1 d
		שרש	ROOT	1057c	1
5	15	ברק	BARAK	140c	
		דבורה	DEBORAH	184b	2
		חק	SOMETHING PRE-SCRIBED	349b	3
		יששכר	ISSACHAR	441a	1
		כן	SO	486d	2 db
		ל	TO	*511d	2
		לב	HEART	525a	2 4
		עמק	VALE	771a	
		פלגה	DIVISION	811b	2
		ראובן	REUBEN	910a	1
		רגל	FOOT	920a	1 f
		שר	CHIEFTAIN	978a	1
		שלח	SEND	1019c	
5	16	חק	SOMETHING PRE-SCRIBED	349c	3
		ישב	REMAIN	442d	2 a
		ל	TO	511d	2
		עדר	FLOCK	727d	1 c
		פלגה	DIVISION	811b	2
		ראובן	REUBEN	910a	2
		משפתים	FIRE-PLACES	1046b	
		שפתים	PACK-SADDLES	1046b	
		שריקה	HISSING	1057a	
5	17	אניה	A SHIP	58b	
		אשר	ASHER	81b	2
		גור	SOJOURN	158a	2
		דן	DAN	192d	2
		חוף	SHORE	342b	
		ים	SEA	411b	8 a
		ירדן	JORDAN	434c	
		ל	TO	511d	2
		עבר	REGION ACROSS	719c	1 a
		מפרץ	LANDING-PLACE	830a	
		שכן	SETTLE DOWN	1015a	1 a
		שכן	SETTLE DOWN	1015b	1 a
5	18	זבולן	ZEBULUN	259d	2
		חרף	REPROACH	357d	
		ל	TO	517b	7 ba
		נפש	SOUL	659d	3 c
		נפתלי	NAPHTALI	836d	2 a
		מרום	HEIGHT	928d	1
		שדה	HIGH PLACES	961a	
		שדה	FIELD	961c	1 g
5	19	אז	THEN	23a	1 c
		בצע	GAIN MADE BY VIOLENCE	130c	
		מגדו	MEGIDDO	152a	
		כסף	SILVER	494b	3
		לחם	ENGAGE IN BAT-TLE	535d	
		לקח	TAKE	543d	8
		מלך	KING	573a	1
		על	UPON	756a	2 6a
		תענך	TAANACH	1073d	
5	20	כוכב	STAR	457a	
		לחם	ENGAGE IN BAT-TLE	535c	
		לחם	ENGAGE IN BAT-TLE	535d	
		סיסרא	SISERA	696b	1
		מסלה	HIGHWAY	700c	
		שמי	HEAVENS	1029d	1 a
5	21	גרף	SWEEP AWAY	175d	
		דרך	TREAD	202a	1
		נחל	TORRENT	636a	1
		עז	STRENGTH	739a	1
		קדומים	KISHON	870c	
		קישון	KISHON	885c	
5	22	אביר	MIGHTY	7d	3
		אז	THEN	23a	1 c
		דהרה	RUSHING	187b	
		הלם	SMITE	240c	1
		סום	HORSE	692c	1
		עקב	HEEL	784b	A
		אבביר	ADDENDA ET COR-RIGENDA	1119b	
5	23	מרוז	MEROZ	72d	
		ארר	CURSE	76c	
		גבור	STRONG	150b	2
		מלאך	MESSENGER	521d	3
		עזרה	HELP	740d	1
5	24	ברך	BLESS	139b	4
		חבר	HEBER	288c	1
		יעל	JAEL	418d	
		מן	THAN	582c	6 b
		קיני	KENITE	884a	
5	25	אדיר	MAJESTIC	12b	2
		חלב	MILK	316b	A
		חמאה	CURD	326a	
		נתן	GIVE	678b	1 a
		ספל	BOWL	706a	
		קרב	COME NEAR	897d	1 a
		שאל	ASK	981c	1 a
5	26	הלם	SMITE	240c	1
		הלמות	HAMMER	240d	
		ו	AND	252b	1 a
		חלף	PASS ON OR AWAY	322a	3 a
		יד	HAND	389b	1 c
		ימין	RIGHT HAND	411c	1 a
		יתד	PEG	450b	A
		מחץ	SMITE THROUGH	563c	
		מחק	ANNIHILATE	563d	
		סיסרא	SISERA	696b	1
		עמל	LABOURER	766a	1
		רקח	THE TEMPLE	956d	
5	27	אשר	PARTICLE OF RE-LATION	82c	4 bg
		כרע	BOW DOWN	502c	4
		נפל	FALL	657a	2 a
		שדד	DEAL VIOLENTLY WITH	994a	
		שכב	LIE DOWN	1012a	1 a
		שם	THERE	1027a	1 a
5	28	אחר	DELAY	29b	1
		בוש	BE ASHAMED	101d	
		בעד	AWAY FROM	126b	1
		חלון	WINDOW	319d	
		יבב	CRY SHRILLY	384d	1
		מדוע	WHEREFORE	396c	
		ל	TO	517c	7 bb
		סום	HORSE	*692c	1
		סיסרא	SISERA	696b	1
		פעם	BEAT	822a	1 a
		רכב	CHARIOT	939a	1
		מרכבה	CHARIOT	939d	
		שקף	LOOK DOWN	1054c	
5	29	אמר	WORD	57a	1
		אף	ALSO	65a	1
		חכם	WISE	314d	3
		ענה	ANSWER	772d	1 a
		שרה	PRINCESS	979a	
		שוב	TURN BACK	999c	3
5	30	גבר	MAN	150a	
		חלק	DIVIDE	323d	1
		לא	NOT	520b	4 ba
		מצא	FIND	592d	1 a
		סיסרא	SISERA	696b	1
		צבע	DYE	840c	
		צואר	NECK	848c	1
		ראש	HEAD	910d	1 a
		רחם	WOMB	933b	2
		רקמה	VARIEGATED STUFF	955d	
		שגל	CONSORT	993c	
		שלל	SPOIL	1022a	2
		שלל	SPOIL	1022a	4
5	31	אבד	PERISH	1d	1
		אהב	LOVE	13a	3
		איב	BE HOSTILE TO	33c	
		גבורה	STRENGTH	150b	2
		יצא	GO OUT	423b	1 f
		כן	SO	485d	1 a
		ארבעים	FORTY	917c	1 a
		שמש	SUN	1039a	1
		שקט	BE QUIET	1053a	1
		סיני	SINAI	696a	
6	1				
6	2	הר	MOUNTAIN	250c	1 f
		מנהרה	LIGHT OPENING	626a	
		עזז	BE STRONG	738c	
		מערה	CAVE	792c	
		מצד	FASTNESS	844d	1
6	3	אם	IF	50b	1 b4 a
		זרע	SOW	281c	1 a
		עלה	GO UP	748d	2 c
		עמלק	AMALEK	766a	
		קדם	FRONT	869c	1 b
6	4	בוא	COME	98c	2 e
		מחיה	PRESERVATION OF LIFE	313c	2
		חמור	HE-ASS	331b	1
		חנה	DECLINE	333c	2 c2
		יבול	PRODUCE	385b	
		עזה	GAZA	738b	
		שה	A SHEEP	962a	1
		שאר	REMAIN	984b	1
		שור	A HEAD OF CATTLE	1004a	

JUDGES

Ch v.	Heb	Eng	Page	Sec
6 5	שחת	GO TO RUIN	1008b	1
	די	SUFFICIENCY	191d	2 b
	הם	THEY	241b	1
	ו	AND	253a	1 g
	מספר	NUMBER	708d	1 a
	ארבה	LOCUST	916a	
	שחת	GO TO RUIN	1008a	1
6 6	דלל	BE LOW	195c	
	זעק	CRY	277b	2 a
	פנה	FACE	818c	2 6c a
6 7	אורה	CAUSE	15c	
	זעק	CRY	277b	2 a
6 8	אלהים	GOD	44c	4 ba
	בית	HOUSE	109a	1 ae 9
	יצא	CASUE TO GO	424c	1 a
	נביא	PROPHET	611c	1
	עבד	SLAVE	713d	1
6 9	גרש	DRIVE OUT	177a	
	לחץ	OPPRESS	537d	2
6 10	אלהים	GOD	43c	1 d
	אמרי	AMORITES	57c	2 b
	אנכי	I	59c	
	יהוה	YAHWEH	218d	2 1b
	יהוה	YAHWEH	219a	2 2a
	ירא	FEAR	431c	3
	קול	VOICE	877b	3 b
6 11	אביהעזרי	ABIEZRITE	4c	
	אלה	TEREBINTH	18c	
	אשר	PARTICLE OF RE-LATION	83a	7 b
	גדעון	GIDEON	154c	
	יהואש	JEHOASH	220a	3
	חבט	BEAT OFF	286a	2
	חטה	WHEAT	334d	
	גת	WINE-PRESS	387c	
	ישב	SIT	442c	1 a
	מלאך	MESSENGER	521d	3
	נוס	ESCAPE	631a	3
	עפרה	OPHRAH	780b	1 b
6 12	גבור	STRONG	150b	2
	חיל	STRENGTH	298d	1 c
	מלאך	MESSENGER	521d	3
	ראה	TO SEE	908b	1 a
6 13	אדון	LORD	11b	3 1i
	איה	WHERE	32c	
	בי	I PRAY	106c	
	גדעון	GIDEON	154c	
	יש	BE	442a	2 cf
	כף	POWER	496d	2
	מצא	FIND	593c	3 e
	נטש	FORSAKE	643d	1
	ספר	COUNT	708a	1
	פלא	BE SURPASSING	810d	4
6 14	זה	THIS	261a	2 ba
	ישע	DELIVER	446c	1 a
	כח	STRENGTH	470c	1 a
	כף	POWER	496d	2
	לא	NOT	520b	4 ba
	לא	NOT	520b	4 bb
	פנה	TURN	815a	1
	שלח	SEND	1018c	1
6 15	אדון	LORD	11b	3 2a
	אלף	THOUSAND	49b	2
	ב	IN	90a	3 2e
	בי	I PRAY	106c	
	דל	WEAK	195d	
	ה	THE	207b	1 b
	ישע	DELIVER	446c	1 a
	מנשה	MANASSEH	586c	1 b1 b
	צעיר	YOUNG	859a	1 a
6 16	כי	THAT	471d	1
6 17	אות	SIGN	16d	4
	דבר	SPEAK	181b	1 a
	חן	FAVOR	336b	2 b2
	מצא	FIND	592d	1 a
	נא	PART OF EN-TREATY	609c	4 c
	עשה	DO	794a	1 1a 3
	ש	WHO	980a	3 a
6 18	יצא	BRING OUT	425a	4 e
	מוש	DEPART	559a	
	מנחה	GIFT	585a	1
	נוח	REST	628d	B 1
	שום	TO PLACE	964b	5 a
6 19	אלה	TEREBINTH	18c	
	איפה	EPHAH	35b	1
	אל	TO	40d	9
	בשר	FLESH	142c	1 a
	גדי	KID	152a	
	גדעון	GIDEON	154c	
	יצא	BRING OUT	425a	4 e
	מרק	BROTH	600a	
	נגש	APPROACH	621b	
	מצה	UNLEAVENED BREAD	695b	
	סל	BASKET	700d	
	עשה	DO	794d	2 3
	פרור	POT	807d	
	קמח	FLOUR	887d	
	שום	TO PLACE	963a	1 a
	תחת	UNDERNEATH	1066a	3 1a
6 20	אלהים	GOD	44a	3 b
	בשר	FLESH	142c	1 a
	הלז	THIS	229c	
	מלאך	MESSENGER	521d	3
	מרק	BROTH	600a	
	נוח	REST	628d	B 1
	סלע	CRAG	701a	1
	שפך	POUR OUT	1049c	1 a
6 21	בשר	FLESH	142c	1 a
	הלך	WALK	231c	1 1d 4
	מלאך	MESSENGER	521d	3
	נגע	TOUCH	619a	1 a
	מצה	UNLEAVENED BREAD	695b	
	עלה	GO UP	748d	5
	צור	ROCK	849c	1 c
	קצה	END	892a	1
	שלח	SEND	1018d	3 c
	משענת	STAFF	1044a	
6 22	אדון	LORD	11c	4 a
	אהה	ALAS	13c	
	כיעללכן	FOR THEREFORE	475c	
	מלאך	MESSENGER	521d	3
	פנה	FACE	815d	1 1c
6 23	ירא	FEAR	431a	1 a
	מות	DIE	560a	2 b
	רגל	GO ABOUT	920b	2
	שלום	PEACE	1022d	3
6 24	אביעזרי	ABIEZRITE	4c	
	בנה	BUILD	124c	1 at
	יהוה	YAHWEH	219b	2 3
	מזבח	ALTAR	258b	0
	יום	DAY	401b	7 1
	עוד	STILL	728d	1 aa
	עפרה	OPHRAH	780b	1 b
	שלום	PEACE	1023a	5 b
6 25	אשרה	ASHERA	81c	B
	אשר	PARTICLE OF RE-LATION	83a	7 b
	בעל	BAAL	127d	2 2
	חרם	THROW DOWN	248c	1
	מזבח	ALTAR	259a	0
	כרת	CUT OFF	503d	2
	על	UPON	756b	2 6c
	פר	YOUNG BULL	830d	
	שור	A HEAD OF CATTLE	1004b	
6 26	אשרה	ASHERA	81c	B
	בנה	BUILD	124c	1 at
	יהוה	YAHWEH	218d	2 1a
	כרת	CUT OFF	503d	2
	מעוז	PLACE OF SAFETY	732a	1
	עלה	WHOLE BURNT OF-FERING	750d	
	עץ	TREE	781d	2 b
	מערכה	ROW	790b	2
	פר	YOUNG BULL	830d	2 b
	מערכה	ADDENDA ET COR-RIGENDA	1126a	
6 27	ירא	FEAR	431b	1 b
	כאשר	SINCE	455c	2
	לילה	NIGHT	539a	1
	מן	FROM	583b	7 ba
6 28	אשרה	ASHERA	81c	B
	בנה	BUILD	124c	1 at
	בעל	BAAL	127d	2 2
	בקר	MORNING	134b	1 h
	ה	THE	208d	2 a
	מזבח	ALTAR	259a	0
	כרת	BE CUT OFF	504b	2
	עלה	GO UP	750a	3
	על	UPON	756b	2 6c
	פר	YOUNG BULL	830d	
	שכם	START EARLY	1014d	
6 29	בקש	SEEK	134c	1 a
	דרש	SEEK	205c	4 b
	יהואש	JEHOASH	220a	3
	מי	WHO	566b	
	רע	FRIEND	946b	3
6 30	אשרה	ASHERA	81c	B
	בעל	BAAL	127d	2 2
	יהואש	JEHOASH	220a	3
	מזבח	ALTAR	259a	0
	יצא	CAUSE TO GO	424c	1 b
	כי	BECAUSE	474c	3 d
	כרת	CUT OFF	503d	2
	מות	DIE	559d	2 a
	נתץ	PULL DOWN	683b	1
6 31	אתם	YOU	61d	
	בעל	BAAL	127d	2 2
	בקר	MORNING	134b	2
	יהואש	JEHOASH	220a	3
	מזבח	ALTAR	259a	0
	ישע	DELIVER	446c	1
	ל	TO	515c	5 hc
	מות	DIE	560c	1
	נתץ	PULL DOWN	683b	1
	עד	AS FAR AS	724b	1 2a a
	עמד	STAND	763d	1 c
	ריב	STRIVE	936a	3
6 32	בשת	SHAME	102b	1
	בעל	BAAL	127d	2 2
	גדעון	GIDEON	154c	
	מזבח	ALTAR	259a	0
	נתץ	PULL DOWN	683b	1
	ריב	STRIVE	936c	2
	ירבעל	JERUBBAAL	937c	
6 33	אסף	GATHER	62d	1 a
	יזרעאל	JEZREEL	283c	1 b
	יחדו	TOGETHER	403c	A
	עמלק	AMALEK	766a	
	עמק	VALE	771a	
	קדם	FRONT	869c	1 b
6 34	אביעזור	ABIEZER	4c	1
	זעק	CRY	277c	
	לבש	PUT ON	528b	F
	רוח	BREATH	926a	9 c1
	שפר	HORN	1051d	
	תקע	GIVE A BLOW	1075c	2
6 35	אשר	ASHER	81b	2
	זעק	CRY	277c	
	מלאך	MESSENGER	521c	1 a
	מנשה	MANASSEH	586c	1 b1 b
	עלה	GO UP	748c	2 a
	נפתלי	NAPHTALI	837a	2 b
6 36	אלהים	GOD	43d	3
	אם	IF	49d	1 a2
	יד	HAND	391a	5 d
	יש	THERE IS	441d	2 ca
	ישע	DELIVER	446c	1 b
6 37	אל	TO	41a	B
	גזה	FLEECE	159c	
	גרן	THRESHING-FLOOR	175b	
	חרב	DRYNESS	351b	1
	טל	NIGHT-MIST	378c	
	יצג	SET	426c	
	ישע	DELIVER	446c	1 b
	צמר	WOOL	856a	
6 38	גזה	FLEECE	159c	
	היה	COME TO PASS	224b	1 1b
	זור	PRESS DOWN AND OUT	267a	
	טל	NIGHT-MIST	378c	
	מחרת	THE MORROW	564a	
	מי	WATER	565c	1 h
	מלא	FULNESS	571b	1
	מצה	DRAIN	594c	
	ספל	BOWL	706a	
6 39	אל	TO	41a	B
	אלהים	GOD	43d	3
	גזה	FLEECE	159c	
	חרב	DRYNESS	351b	1
	חרה	BURN	354a	2 a
	טל	NIGHT-MIST	378c	
	נסה	TEST	650b	1
	פעם	OCCURRENCE	822b	3 d1
	רק	ONLY	956b	2 a
6 40	גזה	FLEECE	159c	
	חרב	DRYNESS	351b	1
	טל	NIGHT-MIST	378c	
7 1	את	WITH	85d	1
	גבעה	HILL	149a	4
	גדעון	GIDEON	154c	
	היה	BE	227a	3 3
	חנה	DECLINE	333c	2 c2
	מחנה	ENCAMPMENT	334b	3 c
	חרד	HAROD	353d	
	חרדי	HARODITE	*353d	
	מורה	TEACHER	435d	
	ל	TO	514a	5 d
	עין	SPRING	745b	A
	על	UPON	756a	2 6a
	עמק	VALE	771a	
	ירבעל	JERUBBAAL	937c	
	שכם	START EARLY	1014c	
7 2	ישע	GIVE VICTORY	447a	3 a
	מן	THAN	582d	6 d
	פאר	BEAUTIFY	802b	1
	רב	MUCH	913b	1 e
7 3	אבך	TURN	5b	2
	ו	AND	252b	1 b
	חרד	TREMBLING	353d	
	ירא	FEAR	431a	1 a
	מי	WHO	567b	G
	צפר	RETURN	861d	
	צרף	SMELT	864b	2
	קרא	CALL	895c	2
	שאר	REMAIN	984a	1
	שוב	TURN BACK	996d	1
7 4	אמר	SAY	56a	1
	אשר	PARTICLE OF RE-LATION	82d	4 d
	הוא	HE, SHE, IT	215d	2 a
	היה	COME TO PASS	225a	1 2b ag
	הלך	WALK	231c	1 1d 5a
	הלך	WALK	231c	1 1d 5b
	ירד	BRING DOWN	433d	1 a
	ל	TO	515c	5 hc
	צרף	SMELT	864b	1
	רב	MUCH	*913b	1 e
7 5	בד	SEPARATION	94c	1 a
	ברך	KNEE	139c	
	ירד	BRING DOWN	433d	1 a
	כלב	DOG	476d	A
	כרע	BOW DOWN	502c	1
	לוע	SWALLOW	*534b	
	לקק	LICK	545a	
	לשון	TONGUE	546a	1 a
7 6	ברך	KNEE	139c	
	יתר	REMAINDER	451d	1 b
	כרע	BOW DOWN	502c	1
	לוע	SWALLOW	*534b	
	לקק	LICK	545a	
	מאה	HUNDRED	548a	1 c2
	מספר	NUMBER	708d	1 a
	פה	MOUTH	804d	1 a
7 7	ב	IN	89d	3 2a
	ישע	DELIVER	446d	1 b

Ch	v.	Heb	Eng	Page	Sec
		לוע	SWALLOW	*534b	
		לקק	LICK	545a	
		מאה	HUNDRED	548a	1 c2
		מקום	STANDING PLACE	879d	2 b1
7	8	היה	BE	227a	3 3
		חזק	BE FIRM	305b	6 d
		מחנה	ENCAMPMENT	334b	3 c
		ל	TO	514a	5 d
		מאה	HUNDRED	548a	1 c2
		עמק	VALE	771a	
		צידה	PROVISION	845b	
		שלח	SEND	1019a	1 a
		שפר	HORN	1051d	
		תחת	UNDENEATH	1065d	1
7	9	ירד	GO DOWN	432d	1 b
7	10	ירא	FEAR	431b	1 d
		פרה	PURAH	826c	
7	11	חזק	BE FIRM	304a	1 1a
		חמשים	IN BATTLE ARRAY	332d	
		פרה	PURAH	826c	
		קצה	END	892b	2
		שמע	HEAR	1033c	1 a
7	12	בן	SON	121b	1 jl
		די	SUFFICIENCY	*191d	2 b
		חול	SAND	297d	A
		חול	SAND	297d	C
		ים	SEA	411b	8 a
		ל	TO	514c	5 fb
		נפל	LIE	657d	7
		מספר	NUMBER	708d	1 a
		עמלק	AMALEK	766a	
		עמק	VALE	771a	
		קדם	FRONT	869c	1 b
		ארבה	LOCUST	916a	
		ש	WHO	979d	1
7	13	ה	THE	207c	1 d
		הפך	TURN	245c	1 b
		הפך	TURN	246a	1
		ו	AND	252b	1 b
		חלום	DREAM	321c	1
		חלום	DREAM	321d	2 a
		לחם	FOOD	537a	1 a
		נכה	SMITE	645c	1 a
		נפל	FALL	656d	1
		ספר	COUNT	708a	1
		מעל	ABOVE	751d	2 ca
		צליל	CAKE	853d	3
		רע	FRIEND	946a	2
		שערה	BARLEY	972d	2
7	14	אלהים	GOD	43d	3
		אם	IF	50c	1 ca
		בלת	EXCEPT	116c	2
		יהואש	JEHOASH	220a	3
		זה	THIS	260c	1 a
		חרב	SWORD	352c	1 a
		רע	FRIEND	946a	2
7	15	חלום	DREAM	321d	2 a
		מספר	NUMBER	709a	2
		שבר	BREAKING	991b	3
		שחה	BOW DOWN	1005c	2 c
7	16	חצה	DIVIDE	345b	1
		כד	JAR	461c	
		לפיד	TORCH	542a	
		מאה	HUNDRED	548a	1 c2
		נתן	PUT	680b	2 a
		ריק	EMPTY	938a	1
		שפר	HORN	1051d	
		תוך	MIDST	1063c	
7	17	היה	COME TO PASS	225a	1 2b ad
		כן	SO	486c	2 ce
		מן	FROM	578a	1 a
		קצה	END	892b	2
		ראה	TO SEE	907c	6 c
7	18	סביב	ROUND ABOUT	687b	2 bb
		תקע	GIVE A BLOW	1075c	2
7	19	אך	ONLY	36d	2 c
		כד	JAR	461c	
		מאה	HUNDRED	547d	1 a1
		נפץ	SHATTER	658d	
		קום	STAND	879a	6 a
		קצה	END	892b	2
		ראש	HEAD	911b	4 b
		שמר	KEEP	1036d	1 b
		אשמורה	WATCH	1038a	
		תיכון	MIDDLE	1064a	
		תקע	GIVE A BLOW	1075c	2
7	20	חזק	BE FIRM	305a	6 a
		חרב	SWORD	352c	1 a
		חרב	SWORD	352d	1 j
		יד	HAND	389a	1 a
		יד	HAND	389a	1 a
		יד	HAND	389a	1 a
		ימין	RIGHT HAND	411d	1 a
		כד	JAR	461c	
		ל	TO	515c	5 hc
		לפיד	TORCH	542a	
		קרא	CALL	895a	1 b
		שמאל	LEFT	969d	2
		שבר	BREAK	990c	
		שפר	HORN	1051d	
		תקע	GIVE A BLOW	1075c	2
		תקע	GIVE A BLOW	1075c	2
7	21	סביב	ROUND ABOUT	687a	1 cb
		עמד	STAND	764a	2 a
		רוע	RAISE A SHOUT	929c	1
		רוץ	RUN	930b	1
		תחת	UNDERNEATH	1065d	2 2a
7	22	אבל	ABEL	6a	5
		ביתהשטה	BETH-SHITTAH	112d	
		ו	AND	252c	1 b
		צבת	TABBATH	372a	
		נום	FLEE	630d	
		צררה	ZERERAH	866c	
		צרתן	ZERETHAN	866c	
		רע	FRIEND	946b	3
		שום	TO PLACE	963c	2 a
		שפה	SPEECH	974a	3
		תקע	GIVE A BLOW	1075c	2
7	23	אשר	ASHER	81b	2
		מנשה	MANASSEH	586c	1 b1 b
		נפתלי	NAPHTALI	837a	2 b
7	24	ביתברה	BETH-BARAH	111b	
		הר	MOUNTAIN	251a	2 b
		ירד	GO DOWN	432d	1 b
		ל	TO	515b	5 hb g
		לכד	CAPTURE	540a	1
		קרא	ENCOUNTER	897a	1
7	25	מדין	MIDIAN	193c	2
		הרג	KILL	247b	1 b
		זאב	ZEEB	256a	
		זאב	ZEEB	256a	
		יקב	WINE-PRESS	428c	
		ירדן	JORDAN	434c	
		לכד	CAPTURE	540a	1
		עבר	REGION ACROSS	719c	1 a
		צור	ROCK	849c	1 d
		רדף	PURSUE	922d	1 b
		שר	CHIEFTAIN	978a	1 a
		ערב	ADDENDA ET COR-RIGENDA	1126a	
8	1	הלך	WALK	233d	15a
		חזקה	STRENGTH	306a	2
		מה	WHAT	553a	1 c
		קרא	CALL	895c	5 a
		ריב	STRIVE	936c	1
		ש	WHO	*980b	4 d
8	2	אביעזר	ABIEZER	4c	1
		בציר	VINTAGE	131b	
		טוב	PLEASANT	374c	6
		לא	NOT	520b	4 ba
		עוללות	GLEANING	760a	
		עתה	NOW	774a	1 a
8	3	אז	THEN	23a	1 a
		מדין	MIDIAN	193c	2
		זאב	ZEEB	256a	
		יכל	BE ABLE	407c	1 b
		מה	WHAT	553a	1 da
		על	UPON	758d	4 2b
		רוח	BREATH	925a	3 c
		רפה	SINK	951d	3
		שר	CHIEFTAIN	978a	1 a
		ערב	ADDENDA ET COR-RIGENDA	1126a	
8	4	ירדן	JORDAN	434c	
		מאה	HUNDRED	548a	1 c2
		עבר	PASS OVER	717a	1 a2
		עיף	FAINT	746a	
		רדף	PURSUE	922d	1 c
8	5	מדין	MIDIAN	193c	2
		זבח	ZEBAH	258a	
		כבר	ROUND	503b	2
		מלך	KING	573a	1
		סכות	SUCCOTH	697d	1
		עיף	FAINT	746a	
		עם	PEOPLE	766c	2 c
		צלמנע	ZALMUNNA	854a	
		רגל	FOOT	920a	1 f
8	6	זבח	ZEBAH	258a	
		כי	THAT	472d	1 f
		עתה	NOW	774a	1 a
		צבא	ARMY	838d	1 a
		שר	CHIEFTAIN	978b	2 d
8	7	ברקנים	BRIERS	140d	
		בשר	FLESH	142c	1 b
		דוש	THRESH	190c	
		זבח	ZEBAH	258a	
		כן	SO	487a	3 da
		קוץ	THORN-BUSH	881a	1
8	8	זה	THIS	262a	6 d
		ענה	ANSWER	772d	1
		פנל	PENVEL	819c	1
		מגדל	TOWER	153d	1
8	9	נתן	PULL DOWN	683b	1
		פנל	PENVEL	819c	1
		שוב	TURN BACK	997b	3 b
		שלון	PEACE	1023b	6
8	10	אחז	GRASP	28c	2
		בן	SON	121b	1 jl
		זבח	ZEBAH	258a	
		מחנה	ENCAMPMENT	334b	3 c
		חרב	SWORD	352c	1 c
		יתר	BE LEFT OVER	451b	
		עשר	TEN	797b	5 b
		קדם	FRONT	869c	1 b
		קרקר	KARKOR	903a	
		שלף	DRAW OUT	1025c	1
8	11	בטח	SECURITY	105b	
		יגבהה	JOGBEHAH	147c	
		מחנה	ENCAMPMENT	334b	3 c
		נבח	NOBAH	613b	1
		נכה	SMITE	646b	3
		עלה	GO UP	748d	1 e
8	12	קדם	FRONT	869d	1 b 2
		מדין	MIDIAN	193c	2
		זבח	ZEBAH	258a	
		מחנה	ENCAMPMENT	334b	3 c
		חרד	TREMBLE	353c	
		לכד	CAPTURE	540a	1
		מלך	KING	573a	1
8	13	יהואש	JEHOASH	220a	3
		חרס	HERES	357c	2
		מן	FROM	583d	9 a
		מעלה	ASCENT	751b	2
		שוב	TURN BACK	996d	1
8	14	זן	OLD	279a	2 b
		כתב	WRITE	507d	1 c
		לכד	CAPTURE	540a	1
		מן	FROM	580c	3 a
		שר	CHIEFTAIN	978b	2 d
		שאל	ASK	981d	2 a
		שבע	SEVEN	988b	5 a1
		שבעים	SEVENTY	988c	3 a
8	15	אמר	SAY	56b	1
		אשר	PARTICLE OF RE-LATION	82d	4 d
		אשר	PARTICLE OF RE-LATION	82d	4 c
		זבח	ZEBAH	258a	
		חרף	REPROACH	357d	
		יעף	WEARY	419b	
8	16	ברקנים	BRIERS	140d	
		דוש	THRESH	190c	
		זן	OLD	279a	2 b
		ידע	MAKE KNOWN	395a	
		קוץ	THORN-BUSH	881a	1
8	17	מגדל	TOWER	154a	1
		הרג	KILL	247b	1 b
		נתץ	PULL DOWN	683b	1
		פנל	PENVEL	819c	1
8	18	איפה	OF WHAT KIND	33a	2
		בן	SON	120d	1 ib
		ה	THE	207d	1 f
		הרג	KILL	247a	1 a
		זבח	ZEBAH	258a	
		ד	LIKE	454c	2 a
		תאר	FORM	1061b	
		תבור	TABOR	1061d	2
		תבז	THEBEZ	*1062a	
8	19	אם	MOTHER	51d	1
		בן	SON	120b	1 a
		הרג	KILL	247a	1 a
		חיה	LIVE	311c	1
		חי	ALIVE	311d	1 a
		לו	IF	530a	1 a
		יקום	JAKIM	879c	1
8	20	הרג	KILL	247a	1 a
		חרב	SWORD	352c	1 c
		ירא	FEAR	431a	1 a
		יתר	JETHER	452b	2
		נער	YOUTH	655a	1 d
		עוד	STILL	728d	1 aa
		קום	STAND	878b	6 b
		שלף	DRAW OUT	1025b	1
8	21	ב	IN	89a	2 2
		גבורה	MIGHT	150b	2
		הרג	KILL	247a	1 a
		זבח	ZEBAH	258a	
		ד	LIKE	453d	1 b
		פגע	MEET	803b	3
		צואר	NECK	848c	2
		קום	STAND	878b	6 b
		שהרון	MOON	962a	
8	22	בן	SON	120b	1 f
		ישע	DELIVER	446c	1 a
		משל	RULE	605d	1
8	23	אני	I	59a	
		אנכי	I	59b	
		משל	RULE	605d	3
		משל	RULE	605d	1
8	24	זהב	GOLD	263a	6
		נזם	RING	634a	2
		שאל	ASK	981c	1 a
		שאלה	REQUEST	982c	1
		שלל	SPOIL	1022a	2
		ישמעאלי	ISHMAELITE	1035d	
8	25	ה	THE	207c	1 d
		נזם	RING	634a	2
		פרש	SPREAD OUT	831a	1
		שמלה	WRAPPER	971a	
		שלך	THROW	1021a	1 a
		שלל	SPOIL	1022a	2
		שם	THERE	1027b	3 a
8	26	ארגמן	PURPLE THREAD	71b	2
		בגד	GARMENT	94a	1
		בד	SEPARATION	94c	1 d
		מדין	MIDIAN	193c	2
		זהב	GOLD	263a	6
		זהב	GOLD	263b	9 a
		נזם	RING	634a	2
		נטפה	DROP	643b	
		ענק	NECKLACE	778d	
		צואר	NECK	848c	2
		שהרון	MOON	962a	
		שאל	ASK	981c	1 a
		משקל	WEIGHT	1054a	
8	27	אפוד	EPHOD	65d	2
		היה	BECOME	226c	2 2f

JUDGES

Ch v.	Heb	Eng	Page	Sec
	זנה	COMMIT FORNICA-TION	275d	3
	יצג	SET	426c	
	מוקש	BAIT	430d	
	עפרה	OPHRAH	780b	1 b
	עשה	DO	794c	2 1g
8 28	יום	DAY	399b	4 b
	יסף	ADD	414d	
	כנע	BE HUMBLED	488c	2
	נשא	LIFT	670b	1 b 2
	ארבעים	FORTY	917c	1 a
	שקט	BE QUIET	1053a	1
8 29	יהואש	JEHOASH	220a	3
	ירבעל	JERUBBAAL	937c	
8 30	יצא	GO OUT	423c	1 h
	ירך	THIGH	438a	1 b
	רב	MUCH	913a	1 b
	שבעים	SEVENTY	988c	1 b
8 31	אבימלך	ABIMELECH	4c	3
	פלגש	CONCUBINE	811c	1
	שום	TO PLACE	964c	5 b
	שכם	SHECHEM	1014b	1
	שם	NAME	1027d	2 a
8 32	אביעזרי	ABIEZRITE	4c	
	יהואש	JEHOASH	220a	3
	טוב	PLEASANT	374b	4 a
	מות	DIE	559c	1 a1
	עפרה	OPHRAH	780b	1 b
	קבר	BURY	868a	
	קצבר	GRAVE	868d	
	שיבה	OLD AGE	966d	2
8 33	אל	GOD	42c	4
	בעל	BAAL	127d	2 4
	בעל	BAAL	127d	2 3
	ברית	COVENANT	136c	1 3
	זנה	COMMIT FORNICA-TION	275d	3
	שום	TO PLACE	964a	3 d
	שוב	TURN BACK	997d	6 a
8 34	יהוה	YAHWEH	218d	2 1d
	זכר	REMEMBER	270a	13 b
	סביב	ROUND ABOUT	687a	1 d
8 35	חסד	GOODNESS	338c	1 1
	טובה	WELFARE	375d	3
	עשה	DO	794b	1 3
	ירבעל	JERUBBAAL	937c	
9 1	אבימלך	ABIMELECH	4c	3
	הלך	WALK	230d	1 1d 3b
	הלך	WALK	231a	1 d3 ga
	ירבעל	JERUBBAAL	937c	
	משפחה	CLAN	1046d	1 a
9 2	אם	IF	50d	2 ab a
	בעל	OWNER	127b	1 3
	בשר	FLESH	142d	4
	דבר	SPEAK	181c	4 b
	זכר	REMEMBER	269c	1 1 a
	טוב	PLEASANT	374b	6
	משל	RULE	605d	1
	עצם	BONE	782d	1
	שבעים	SEVENTY	988c	1 a
	שכם	SHECHEM	*1014c	1
9 3	אבימלך	ABIMELECH	4c	3
	דבר	SPEAK	181c	5
	דבר	SPEAK	181c	4 b
	לב	HEART	525a	2 4
	נטה	BEND	640b	3 a
	על	UPON	754d	2 1f g
9 4	אבימלך	ABIMELECH	4c	3
	אל	GOD	42c	4
	בית	HOUSE	109b	1 ae 0
	בעל	BAAL	127d	2 4
	ברית	COVENANT	136c	1 3
	פחז	BE WANTON	808d	1
	ריק	EMPTY	938a	2
	שכר	HIRE	969a	
	שבעים	SEVENTY	988c	1 e
9 5	יותם	JOTHAM	222d	2
	הרג	KILL	247a	1 a
	חבא	WITHDRAW	285b	
	יתר	BE LEFT OVER	451b	
	מלך	KING	573b	1
	עפרה	OPHRAH	780b	1 b
	קטן	SMALL	882b	1 a
9 6	אלון	TEREBINTH	18d	
	אסף	GATHER	62d	1 a
	מלוא	MILLO	571c	1
	מלך	KING	573d	5 c
	מלך	BE KING	574d	
	נצב	STAND	662c	
	עם	WITH	*768a	2
9 7	גרזים	GERIZIM	173d	
	יותם	JOTHAM	222d	2
	הר	MOUNTAIN	249b	1 a
	נסא	LIFT	670c	1 b 5
	קול	VOICE	876d	1 a
	קרא	CALL	895a	1 a
9 8	אמר	SAY	55d	1
	הלך	WALK	233a	1 4b 1
	הלך	WALK	233d	1 5a
	זית	OLIVE TREE	268c	1
	מלך	KING	573b	4
	מלך	KING	573c	5 c
	מלך	BE KING	574b	
	משח	ANOINT	603a	2
	עץ	TREE	781c	1
9 9	דשן	FATNESS	206b	1
	דשן	FAT	*206c	
	הלך	WALK	233d	1 5a
	זית	OLIVE TREE	268c	1
	חדל	CEASE	293b	
	כבד	MAKE HONORABLE	457d	2 d
9 10	נוע	WAVE	631b	1
	מלך	BE KING	574a	
9 11	תאנה	FIG-TREE	1061a	1
	הלך	WALK	233d	1 5a
	חדל	CEASE	293b	
	טוב	PLEASANT	373d	1 b
	מתק	SWEETNESS	608d	
	תנובה	FRUIT	626c	
	נוע	WAVE	631b	1
	תאנה	FIG-TREE	1061a	1
9 12	גפן	VINE	172c	
	מלך	BE KING	574a	
9 13	אלהים	GOD	43c	1 d
	גפן	VINE	172c	
	גפן	VINE	172c	
	הלך	WALK	233d	1 5a
	חדל	CEASE	293b	
	תירוש	NEW WINE	440d	
	נוע	WAVE	631b	1
	נעל	SANDAL	653a	
	שמח	REJOICE	970c	
	שמח	REJOICE	970c	
9 14	אטד	BRAMBLE	31d	
	מלך	BE KING	574a	
9 15	אטד	BRAMBLE	31d	
	אין	NOT	34c	2 dd
	אכל	EAT	37c	3
	אם	IF	49d	1 a2
	אמת	FIRMNESS	54c	5
	ארז	CEDAR	72c	1 a
	חסה	SEEK REFUGE	340a	
	יצא	GO OUT	423b	1 g
	לבנון	LEBANON	527a	
	מלך	KING	573b	4
	מלך	KING	573c	5 c
	משח	ANOINT	603b	2
	צל	SHADOW	853b	2
9 16	אמת	FIRMNESS	54a	3 a
	דרך	WAY	203c	6 b
	טובה	WELFARE	375d	3
	מלך	BE KING	574b	
	עשה	DO	794a	1 1a 7
	עשה	DO	794b	1 3
	תמים	COMPLETE	1071b	5
9 17	אשר	THAT	83c	8 c
	לחם	ENGAGE IN BAT-TLE	535d	
	נגד	IN FRONT	617d	2 ca
	על	UPON	754c	2 1f c
	שלך	THROW	1021b	3
9 18	אמה	MAID	51a	1
	הרג	KILL	247a	1 a
	מלך	BE KING	574b	
	קום	STAND	878a	2
9 19	אמת	FIRMNESS	54a	3 a
	עשה	DO	794b	1 3
	שמח	REJOICE	970a	1 a
	תמים	COMPLETE	1071b	5
9 20	אין	NOT	34c	2 dd
	יצא	GO OUT	423b	1 g
9 21	באר	BEER	91d	3 b
	ברח	FLEE	137d	2
	יותם	JOTHAM	222d	2
	פנה	FACE	818b	2 6a
	פנה	FACE	818b	2 6a
9 22	שור	SAW	965a	
	שרר	ACT AS PRINCE	979a	
9 23	בגד	ACT TREACHER-OUSLY	93d	B
	רוח	BREATH	925a	3 c
	רע	EVIL	948b	9
9 24	דם	BLOOD	197a	2 i
	הרג	KILL	247a	1 a
	חזק	BE FIRM	304d	2
	חמס	VIOLENCE	329c	
	יד	HAND	389d	1 e1
	על	UPON	756c	2 7a b
	ירבעל	JERUBBAAL	937c	
	שום	TO PLACE	963a	1 a
	שבעים	SEVENTY	988c	1 b
9 25	ארב	LIE IN WAIT	70c	
	גזל	TEAR AWAY	159d	
	הר	MOUNTAIN	250d	1 m
	ל	TO	515b	5 hb g
	נגד	BE CONSPICUOUS	617a	
	שום	TO PLACE	964a	1 a
9 26	בטח	TRUST	105a	1 3b
	געל	GAAL	172a	
	הרג	KILL	247b	1 b
	עבד	EBED	714c	1
	עבר	PASS OVER	718a	5 e
9 27	אכל	EAT	37b	1
	אלהים	GOD	43c	2 a
	בצר	CUT OFF	130d	
	הלל	REJOICING	239b	1
	כרם	VINEYARD	501d	1
	קלל	BE SLIGHT	886c	1
9 28	אנחנו	WE	59d	
	געל	GAAL	172a	
	זבל	ZEBUL	259d	
	חמור	HAMOR	331c	
	כי	THAT	472d	1 f
	לא	NOT	520b	4 ba
	מי	WHO	566b	A
	מי	WHO	566d	F b
	עבד	WORK	713a	3
	עבד	EBED	714c	1
	פקיד	COMMISSIONER	824b	
	שכם	SHECHEM	1014c	2
9 29	מי	WHO	566c	F a
	נתן	GIVE	678d	1 f
	סור	TURN ASIDE	694b	1
	צבא	ARMY	838d	1 a
	רבה	BECOME MANY	915b	
9 30	געל	GAAL	172a	
	זבל	ZEBUL	259d	
	חרה	BURN	354a	1 a
	עבד	EBED	714c	1
	שר	CHIEFTAIN	978b	2 d
9 31	געל	GAAL	172a	
	עבד	EBED	714c	1
	על	UPON	757d	2 7d
	צור	CONFINE	848d	2
	רומה	RUMAH	928a	
	תרמה	TREACHEROUSLY	941b	
9 32	ארב	LIE IN WAIT	70b	
	שדה	FIELD	961c	1 f
9 33	את	WITH	85d	1
	בקר	MORNING	133d	1 c
	זרח	RISE	280b	1
	מצא	FIND	593c	4
	עם	WITH	768a	1 g
	פשט	STRIP OFF	833a	2
9 34	ארב	LIE IN WAIT	70b	
	ראש	HEAD	911b	6
9 35	מארב	AMBUSH	70d	1 a
	געל	GAAL	172a	
	עבד	EBED	714c	1
	פתח	OPENING	836a	
	קום	STAND	878a	2
9 36	געל	GAAL	172a	
	הר	MOUNTAIN	250a	1 a
	הר	MOUNTAIN	250d	1 m
	הר	MOUNTAIN	250d	1 m
	זבל	ZEBUL	259d	
	עם	PEOPLE	766d	4
	צל	SHADOW	853b	1
	ראה	TO SEE	907a	2 5
9 37	אלון	TEREBINTH	18d	
	געל	GAAL	172a	
	טבור	HIGHEST PART	371d	
	יסף	DO AGAIN	415c	2 a
	עם	PEOPLE	766d	4
	מעם	FROM WITH	769a	A
	ענן	PRACTISE SOOTH-SAYING	778b	
9 38	ראש	HEAD	911b	6
	תבור	TABOR	*1061d	2
	אפו	THEN	66b	1
	זבל	ZEBUL	259d	
	לא	NOT	520b	4 ba
	מאס	REJECT	549c	2
	מי	WHO	566d	F b
	עבד	WORK	713a	3
9 39	געל	GAAL	172a	
	פנה	FACE	817c	2 4c b
9 40	נפל	FALL	657a	2 a
	פתח	OPENING	836a	
	רב	MUCH	913a	1 b
	שער	GATE	1044c	1 a
9 41	ארומה	ARUMAH	72b	
	געל	GAAL	172a	
	גרש	DRIVE OUT	176d	
	זבל	ZEBUL	259d	
	רומה	RUMAH	928a	
9 42	תרמה	TREACHEROUSLY	941c	
	מחרת	THE MORROW	564a	
	שדה	FIELD	961c	1 f
9 43	ארב	LIE IN WAIT	70b	
	הנה	BEHOLD	244b	C
	חצה	DIVIDE	345b	1
	נכה	SMITE	646b	3
	קום	STAND	878a	2
	ראש	HEAD	911b	6
	שדה	FIELD	961c	1 f
9 44	פשט	STRIP OFF	833a	2
	פתח	OPENING	836a	
	ראש	HEAD	911b	6
	שדה	FIELD	961c	1 f
9 45	הרג	KILL	247b	1 b
	זרע	SOW	281c	1 d
	לחם	ENGAGE IN BAT-TLE	535c	
	מלח	SALT	571d	
	נתץ	PULL DOWN	683b	1
9 46	אל	GOD	42c	4
	בעל	OWNER	127b	1 3
	בעל	BAAL	*127d	2 4
	ברית	COVENANT	136c	1 3
	מגדל	TOWER	154a	
	שכם	SHECHEM	*1014c	1
	שמע	HEAR	1033d	1 d1
9 47	בעל	OWNER	127b	1 3
	מגדל	TOWER	154a	1
	נגד	BE CONSPICUOUS	617a	
	קבץ	GATHER	868b	
	שכם	SHECHEM	*1014c	1

Ch	v.	Heb	Eng	Page	Sec
9	48	את	WITH	85d	1
		ה	THE	207c	1 d
		הר	MOUNTAIN	251a	2 b
		כרת	CUT OFF	503d	1 a
		מה	WHAT	553b	1 ea
		מהר	HASTEN	555a	2
		נשא	LIFT	670a	1 a
		צלמון	ZALMON	854a	1
		קדם	AXE	899c	
		ראה	TO SEE	907b	5 a
		שוכה	BRANCH	962c	
		שכם	SHOULDER	1014b	1 a
9	49	אלף	THOUSAND	48d	1 a
		אש	FIRE	77c	1
		מגדל	TOWER	154a	1
		גם	ALSO	169b	2
		יצת	KINDLE	428c	
		כרת	CUT OFF	503d	1 a
		שוכה	BRANCH	962c	
		שוך	BRANCH	962c	
9	50	תבור	TABOR	*1061d	2
		תבץ	THEBEZ	1062a	
9	51	בעד	BEHIND	126b	1 b
		בעל	OWNER	127b	13
		גג	ROOF	151a	1
		מגדל	TOWER	153d	1
		סגר	SHUT	689a	1
		עז	STRENGTH	738d	1
		עלה	GO UP	748c	1 f
		על	UPON	756d	2 7b
		ירבעל	JERUBBAAL	937c	
9	52	אש	FIRE	77c	1
		מגדל	TOWER	153d	1
		לחם	ENGAGE IN BATTLE	535c	
		נגש	DRAW NEAR	620d	1
		פתח	OPENING	835d	
		שרף	BURN	976d	2 a
9	53	פלח	CLEAVAGE	812a	1
		רכב	CHARIOT	939b	3
		רצץ	CRUSH	954d	
		שלך	THROW	1021a	1 a
9	54	אמר	SAY	56a	1
		דקר	PIERCE	201b	
		הרג	KILL	247a	1 a
		חרב	SWORD	352c	1 c
		כלי	IMPLEMENT	479d	2 a
		ל	TO	514b	5 fa
		מהרה	HASTE	555b	
		מות	DIE	560a	
		נשא	LIFT	671a	2 a
		שלף	DRAW OUT	1025b	1
9	56	הרג	KILL	247a	1 a
		עשה	DO	793d	1 1a 2
		רעה	MISERY	949b	2
		שבעים	SEVENTY	988c	1 b
		שוב	TURN BACK	999c	4 a
9	57	אל	TO	40b	4
		ב	IN	89b	2 4b
		יותם	JOTHAM	222d	1
		קללה	CURSE	887a	
		ראש	HEAD	911b	8
		רעה	MISERY	949b	2
		שוב	TURN BACK	999c	4 a
10	1	אבימלך	ABIMELECH	4c	3
		איש	MAN	36a	
		דודו	DODO	187d	1
		היה	BECOME	*225c	2 1a
		יששכר	ISSACHAR	441a	1
		ישע	DELIVER	446c	1 a
		פואה	PUAH	806a	
		קום	STAND	878a	4
		שמיר	SHAMIR	1039a	1
		תולע	TOLA	1069a	
10	2	מות	DIE	559c	1 a1
		עשרים	TWENTY	797d	1 2a
		שמיר	SHAMIR	1039a	1
		שפט	JUDGE	1047b	1 b
10	3	יאיר	JAIR	22c	2
		אחר	AFTER	30a	2 b
		עשרים	TWENTY	797d	1 2a
		קום	STAND	878a	4
		שנים	TWO	1041b	3
		שפט	JUDGE	1047b	1 b
10	4	יאיר	JAIR	22c	2
		חוה	TENT-VILLAGE	295d	
		יום	DAY	401b	7 l
		ארגב	ARGOB	419a	1
		עיר	MALE ASS	747a	
		רכב	RIDE	938d	2
		שלשים	THIRTY	1026c	1
10	5	יאיר	JAIR	22c	2
		מות	DIE	559c	1 a1
		קמון	KAMON	879c	
10	6	אלהים	GOD	43c	1 d
		ארם	ARAM	74c	C
		בעל	BAAL	127d	
		יסף	DO AGAIN	415c	2 a
		עבד	WORK	713b	4 b
		עמון	AMMON	770a	
		עשתרת	ASTORETH	800a	
		פלשתי	PHILISTINE	814c	
		צידון	SIDON	851a	
10	7	חרה	BURN	354a	2 a
		יד	HAND	390d	5 b3
		מכר	SELL	569b	
10	8	אמרי	AMORITES	57c	2 a
		ב	IN	88d	1 5
		ירדן	JORDAN	434c	
		עבר	REGION ACROSS	719c	1 a
		רעץ	SHATTER	950a	
		רצץ	CRUSH	954d	
10	9	אפרים	EPHRAIM	68b	2
		בית	HOUSE	110b	5 dh
		צרר	BIND	864d	B
10	10	אלהים	GOD	44d	4 c
		בעל	BAAL	127d	2 3
		זעק	CRY	277b	2 a
		חטא	MISS A GOAL OR WAY	307a	2 b
		כי	THAT	471d	1
		עבד	WORK	713b	4 b
		עזב	LEAVE	737c	2 d1
10	11	אמרי	AMORITES	57c	2 a
10	12	ישע	DELIVER	446d	1 b
		לחץ	OPPRESS	537d	2
		מעון	MAON	733a	3
		עמלק	AMALEK	766a	
		ציוני	SIDONIANS	851a	
		צעק	CRY	858c	1 b
10	13	אלהים	GOD	43c	1 d
		יסף	DO AGAIN	415c	2 a
		ישע	DELIVER	446d	1 b
		כן	SO	486d	3 d
		עבד	WORK	713b	4 b
10	14	אלהים	GOD	43d	3
		בחר	CHOOSE	104a	1 b
		זעק	CRY	277b	2 b
		ישע	DELIVER	446c	1
		צרה	DISTRESS	865b	
10	15	אך	HOWBEIT	36c	2 a
		חטא	MISS A GOAL OR WAY	307a	2 b
		טוב	PLEASANT	374a	2 f
10	16	אלהים	GOD	43c	1 d
		נכר	FOREIGNNESS	648c	1
		נפש	SOUL	661a	6 g
		סור	TURN ASIDE	694b	1
		עמל	TROUBLE	765d	1
		קצר	BE SHORT	894b	
		קרב	INWARD PART	899b	1 fl
10	17	אסף	GATHER	62d	1 a
		מצפה	MIZPAH	860a	2
10	18	חלל	POLLUTE	320d	2
		מי	WHO	567b	G
		ראש	HEAD	911a	3 a
		רע	FRIEND	946b	3
		שר	CHIEFTAIN	978a	1 a
11	1	אשה	WOMAN	61a	1
		בן	SON	*120c	1 ia
		גבור	STRONG	150b	2
		היה	BE	227a	3 4a
		זנה	COMMIT FORNICATION	275d	1
		חיל	STRENGTH	298d	1 c
		ילד	BEGET	409a	1
		יפתח	JEPHTHAH	836b	1
11	2	אחר	ANOTHER	29c	
		בן	SON	120c	1 ia
		גדל	GROW UP	152b	1 a
		גרש	DRIVE OUT	176d	1
		נחל	TAKE AS A POSSESSION	635c	1 b
11	3	ברח	FLEE	138a	2
		טוב	TOB	376a	
		מלקח	GATHER UP	545a	
		ריק	EMPTY	938a	2
11	4	היה	COME TO PASS	224c	2 a1 az
		יום	DAY	399c	5 a
		יום	DAY	401a	7 j
		לחם	ENGAGE IN BATTLE	535c	
11	5	מן	FROM	581c	4 b
		זקן	OLD	278d	2 b
		טוב	TOB	376a	
		לחם	ENGAGE IN BATTLE	*535c	
		לחם	ENGAGE IN BATTLE	535c	
		לקח	TAKE	543c	6
		שר	CHIEFTAIN	978a	1 a
11	6	כל	ALL	481b	1 a
		קצין	CHIEF	892d	1
11	7	גרש	DRIVE OUT	176d	1
		זקן	OLD	278d	2 b
		מן	OUT OF	579a	2 aa
		שנא	HATE	971c	1 a
		צרר	ADDENDA ET CORRIGENDA	1126c	
11	8	הלך	WALK	231a	1 1d 5b
		זקן	OLD	278d	2 b
		כן	SO	487a	3 da
		לחם	ENGAGE IN BATTLE	535c	
		עתה	NOW	774a	1 a
		ראש	HEAD	911a	3 a
		שוב	TURN BACK	997c	5 a
11	9	אם	IF	49d	1 a2
		זקן	OLD	278d	2 b
		ראש	HEAD	911a	3 a
11	10	בין	INTERVAL	107c	1 d
		דבר	WORD	182b	1 1b
		זקן	OLD	278d	2 b
		כן	SO	486b	2 ab
		שמע	HEAR	1033d	1 h
11	11	דבר	SPEAK	181c	3 f
		זקן	OLD	278d	2 b
		פנה	FACE	817b	24a h
		מצפה	MIZPAH	860a	1
		קצין	CHIEF	892d	1
		ראש	HEAD	911a	3 a
		שום	TO PLACE	964a	3 d
		שר	CHIEFTAIN	978a	1 a
11	12	לחם	ENGAGE IN BATTLE	535c	
		מה	WHAT	553b	1 dc
		מלך	KING	573a	1
11	13	ארנון	ARNON	75b	
		יבק	JABBOK	132d	
		לקח	TAKE	543a	3 a
		שוב	TURN BACK	999b	1 d
		שלון	PEACE	*1023b	6
11	14	יסף	DO AGAIN	415c	2 a
11	15	לקח	TAKE	543a	3 a
		מואב	MOAB	555d	2 b
11	16	בוא	COME	98b	2
		הלך	WALK	230c	1 1d 2a
		ים	SEA	411a	2
		סוף	REEDS	693b	2 b
11	17	אבה	BE WILLING	2c	
		שמע	HEAR	1034a	1 j
11	18	ארנון	ARNON	75a	
		ארנון	ARNON	75b	
		גבול	BORDER	147d	1 a
		הלך	WALK	230c	1 1d 2a
		מורח	PLACE OF SUNRISE	280d	1
		מואב	MOAB	555d	2 b
		סבב	GO AROUND	685d	2 b
		עבר	REGION ACROSS	719b	1
11	19	אמרי	AMORITES	57c	2 a
		חשבון	HESHBON	363d	
		סיחון	SIHON	695d	
		מקום	STANDING PLACE	879d	2 a
11	20	אמן	CONFIRM	53b	2 e
		אסף	GATHER	62b	1 a
		גבול	BOUNDARY	148a	2 a
		יהץ	JAHAZ	397d	
		לחם	ENGAGE IN BATTLE	535c	
		סיחון	SIHON	695d	
11	21	אלהים	GOD	44c	4 ba
		אמרי	AMORITES	57c	2 a
		ירש	TAKE POSSESSION	439b	1 a
		סיחון	SIHON	695d	
11	22	אמרי	AMORITES	57c	2 a
		ארנון	ARNON	75a	
		יבק	JABBOK	132d	
		גבול	BOUNDARY	148a	2 a
		מדבר	WILDERNESS	185a	3
		ירש	TAKE POSSESSION	439b	1 a
		יבק	ADDENDA ET CORRIGENDA	1121c	
11	23	אלהים	GOD	44c	4 ba
		אמרי	AMORITES	57c	2 a
		ירש	TAKE POSSESSION	439b	1 a
		ירש	CAUSE TO POSSESS	440a	2 a
11	24	אלהים	GOD	43c	2 a
		יהוה	YAHWEH	218d	2 1c
		ירש	TAKE POSSESSION	439b	1 a
		ירש	CAUSE TO POSSESS	439d	1
		ירש	CAUSE TO POSSESS	440a	2 a
11	25	אם	IF	50d	2 ab a
		בלק	BALAK	119a	
		טוב	PLEASING	373b	3
		כמוש	CHEMOSH	484d	
		לחם	ENGAGE IN BATTLE	535c	
		צפור	ZIPPOR	862a	
		ריב	STRIVE	936c	1
11	26	ארנון	ARNON	75b	
		בת	DAUGHTER	123d	4
		חשבון	HESHBON	363d	
		יד	HAND	391c	5 h3
		נצל	DELIVER	664d	2
		ערער	AROER	792d	1
11	27	את	WITH	86b	1 db
		חטא	MISS A GOAL OR WAY	306d	2 a
		רעה	MISERY	949b	2
		שפט	JUDGE	1047c	2 a
11	29	היה	BECOME	225d	2 h
		מנשה	MANASSEH	586c	1 b2 b
		עבר	PASS OVER	717c	3 a
		עבר	PASS OVER	718a	3 a
		מצפה	MIZPEH	859d	3
		רוח	BREATH	926a	9 c1
11	30	אם	IF	50a	1 a5
		נדר	VOW	623d	
		נדר	VOW	624a	3
11	31	דלת	DOOR	195a	1
		היה	COME TO PASS	225b	1 2b bd
		היה	BECOME	226c	2 2h
		יצא	GO OUT	422c	1 a
		עלה	WHOLE BURNT OFFERING	750c	
		שלון	PEACE	1023b	6
11	32	עבר	PASS OVER	717a	1 b
11	33	אבל	ABEL	6a	4

JUDGES

Ch	v	Heb	Eng	Page	Sec
		בוא	COME	98c	2 e
		כנע	BE HUMBLED	488c	2
		מכה	SLAUGHTER	647a	3
		ערער	AROER	793a	2
11	34	פנה	FACE	818b	2 6b
		ב	IN	89b	3 1a
		ב	IN	89c	3 1b
		הנה	BEHOLD	244b	C
		מחולה	DANCING	298b	
		מחולה	DANCING	298b	
		יחיד	ONLY ONE	402d	1
		מצפה	MIZPAH	860a	2
		רק	ONLY	956b	2 a
		תף	TIMBREL	1074c	
11	35	אהה	ALAS	13c	
		ב	IN	89a	1 7a
		כרע	CAUSE TO BOW DOWN	502d	1
		עכר	STIR UP	747d	
		פה	MOUTH	805a	2 a
		פצה	PART	822c	1 b
		שוב	TURN BACK	997a	1
11	36	יצא	GO OUT	423c	1 g
		נקמה	VENGEANCE	668c	1
		עשה	DO	794a	1 1a 3
		פה	MOUTH	805a	2 a
		פה	MOUTH	805a	2 a
		פצה	PART	822c	1 b
11	37	בכה	WEEP	113c	3
		בתולים	VIRGINITY	144a	
		הר	MOUNTAIN	249d	1 a
		חדש	NEW MOON	294c	2 a
		ירד	GO DOWN	433a	1 g
		על	UPON	756d	2 7a c
		עשה	DO	795b	1 c
		רוד	ROAM	923d	
		רעה	COMPANION	946b	
		רעיה	COMPANION	946b	
		רפה	SINK	952a	3
		שנים	TWO	1041a	1 b1
11	38	בכה	WEEP	113c	3
		בתולים	VIRGINITY	144a	
		הר	MOUNTAIN	249d	1 a
		חדש	NEW MOON	294c	2 a
		רעה	COMPANION	946b	
		שלח	SEND	1018d	4
11	39	חדש	NEW MOON	294c	2 a
		חק	SOMETHING PRE-SCRIBED	349c	6 a
		ידע	KNOW	394b	3
		נדר	VOW	623d	
		נדר	VOW	624a	6
		נדר	VOW	624a	3
11	40	בת	DAUGHTER	123b	1 i
		יום	YEAR	399d	6 c
		ארבע	FOUR	917a	1 c1
		תנה	RECOUNT	1072a	
12	1	אש	FIRE	77c	1
		עבר	PASS OVER	718a	5 a
		צפון	ZAPHON	861b	
		קרא	CALL	895d	5 a
		שרף	BURN	976d	2 a
12	2	איש	MAN	36a	
		זעק	CRY	277b	1
		ישע	DELIVER	446c	1 a
		מאד	EXCEEDINGLY	547b	2 a
		ריב	STRIFE	937a	2
12	3	אין	NOT	34b	2 c
		ישע	DELIVER	446c	1 a
		כף	HOLLOW OF THE HAND	496d	1 d6
		נפש	SOUL	659d	3 c
		עבר	PASS OVER	717a	1 b
		עלה	GO UP	748c	2 c
		שום	TO PLACE	963a	1 a
12	4	לחם	ENGAGE IN BAT-TLE	535c	
		מנשה	MANASSEH	586c	1 b2 b
		פליט	ESCAPED ONE	*812c	
		קבץ	GATHER	867d	2
12	5	אפרתי	EPHRATHITE	68d	1
		ירדן	JORDAN	434d	
		כי	WHEN	473a	2 a
		ל	TO	515b	5 hb g
		לא	NOT	519a	1 ad b
		לכד	CAPTURE	540d	1
		מעברה	FORD	721b	1
		פליט	ESCAPED ONE	812c	
12	6	אחז	GRASP	28b	
		אל	TO	40c	8
		אמר	SAY	55d	1
		ירדן	JORDAN	434d	
		כון	ESTABLISH	466c	3
		כן	RIGHT	467a	1
		סבלת	FLOWING STREAM	688a	
		מעברה	FORD	721b	1
		ארבעים	FORTY	917c	2 a
		שבלת	FLOWING STREAM	987c	
		שחט	SLAUGHTER	1006b	3
12	7	מות	DIE	559d	1 a1
12	8	אבצן	IBZAN	7b	
		ביתלחם	BETHLEHEM	111d	1
		ביתלחם	BETHLEHEM	112a	2
		מן	OUT OF	579d	2 cb
12	9	בוא	COME	99a	1 b
		חוץ	THE OUTSIDE	299c	1 a
		חוץ	THE OUTSIDE	299d	1 a
		שלח	SEND	1019a	1 a
		שלשים	THIRTY	1026c	1
12	10	אבצן	IBZAN	7b	
		ביתלחם	BETHLEHEM	112a	2
		מות	DIE	559c	1 a1
12	11	אלון	ELON	19b	3
		זבולוני	ZEBULUNITE	259d	
12	12	אלון	ELON	19a	3
		אילון	AIJALON	19c	2
		זבולוני	ZEBULUNITE	259d	
		זבולון	ZEBULUN	259d	3
		מות	DIE	559c	1 a1
12	13	הלל	HILLEL	239b	
		עבדון	ABDON	715c	1 1
		פרעתוני	PIRATHONITE	828d	
12	14	בן	SON	120b	1 f
		עיר	MALE ASS	747a	
		ארבעים	FORTY	917b	1 a
		רכב	RIDE	938d	2
		שבעים	SEVENTY	988c	1 b
12	15	אפרים	EPHRAIM	68b	2
		הלל	HILLEL	239b	
		הר	MOUNTAIN	251a	2 b
		מות	DIE	559c	1 a1
		עבדון	ABDON	715c	1 1
		עמלקי	AMALEKITES	766a	
		עמלק	AMALEK	766a	
		פרעתון	PIRATHON	828c	
13	1	יד	HAND	390d	5 b3
		יסף	DO AGAIN	415c	2 a
13	2	דני	DANITES	193a	
		היה	BE	226d	3 1
		מן	OUT OF	579c	2 cb
		מנוח	MANOAH	629d	
		עקר	BARREN	785d	
		צרעה	ZORAH	864a	
		משפחה	CLAN	1046d	1 b
13	3	הרה	CONCEIVE	247d	1
		מלאך	MESSENGER	521d	3
		נא	PART OF EN-TREATY	609c	4 d
		עקר	BARREN	785d	
		ראה	TO SEE	908b	1 a
13	4	טמא	UNCLEAN	379d	2 c
		יין	WINE	406c	C
		כל	ALL	482b	1 ec
		נא	PART OF EN-TREATY	609a	1
		שכר	INTOXICATING DRINK	1016c	
		שמר	KEEP	1037b	1
		שתה	DRINK	1059b	1 a
13	5	בטן	WOMB	106a	3
		הוא	HE, SHE, IT	215b	1 a
		חלל	POLLUTE	320d	2
		ישע	DELIVER	446c	1 a
		מורה	RAZOR	559a	
		מן	FROM	581c	4 a
		נזיר	CONSECRATED	634c	2
		נער	YOUTH	654d	1 a
		עלה	GO UP	748d	6
13	6	אי	WHERE	32b	2 b
		איש	MAN	35d	
		אלהים	GOD	43d	3 a
		אלהים	GOD	44a	3 b
		ירא	BE REVERED	431d	3 c
		מלאך	MESSENGER	521d	3
		נגד	BE CONSPICUOUS	616d	1
		מראה	VISION	909c	1 b
		שאל	ASK	981d	2 a
13	7	בטן	WOMB	106a	3
		טמאה	UNCLEANNESS	380a	4
		יום	DAY	398c	2 f
		יום	DAY	401b	7 1
		יין	WINE	406c	C
		מות	DEATH	560c	1
		מן	FROM	581c	4 a
		נזיר	CONSECRATED	634c	2
		נער	YOUTH	654d	1 a
		שכר	INTOXICATING DRINK	1016c	
		שתה	DRINK	1059b	1 a
13	8	אדון	LORD	11b	3 2a
		אלהים	GOD	43d	3 a
		בי	I PRAY	106c	
		י	AND	252b	1 b
		ילד	BE BORN	409a	
		ירה	DIRECT	435c	5 c
		מנוח	MANOAH	629d	
		נער	YOUTH	654d	1 a
		עתר	PRAY	801c	
13	9	אין	NOT	34c	2 c
		אלהים	GOD	44a	3 b
		י	AND	253c	1 k
		מלאך	MESSENGER	521d	3
		שדה	FIELD	961c	1 f
13	10	יום	DAY	400a	7 a5
		מהר	HASTEN	555a	2
		ראה	TO SEE	908b	1 b
		רוץ	RUN	930b	1
13	11	אני	I	59a	
		אנכי	I	59c	
		הוא	HE, SHE, IT	*216b	4 ba
13	12	נער	YOUTH	654d	1 a
		מעשה	DEED	795d	1 b2
13	13	משפט	JUDGMENT	1049b	6 c
		מלאך	MESSENGER	521d	3
		שמר	KEEP	1037b	1
13	14	גפן	VINE	172c	
		טמאה	UNCLEANNESS	380a	4
		יין	WINE	406c	C
		יצא	GO OUT	423c	1 h
		שכר	INTOXICATING DRINK	1016c	
13	15	שתה	DRINK	1059b	1 a
		גדי	KID	152a	
		מלאך	MESSENGER	521d	3
		לחם	FOOD	*537b	2 a
		עצר	RESTRAIN	783c	1
		עשה	DO	794d	2 4
13	16	אם	IF	49c	1 al a
		ב	IN	88c	1 2b
		מלאך	MESSENGER	521d	3
		לחם	FOOD	537b	2 a
		עצר	RESTRAIN	783c	1
		עשה	DO	794d	2 4
13	17	כבד	MAKE HONORABLE	457d	2 c
		מלאך	MESSENGER	521d	3
		מי	WHO	566b	A
		שם	NAME	1028a	2 a
13	18	מלאך	MESSENGER	521d	3
		מה	HOW	*554a	4 d
		פלאי	WONDERFUL	811a	
		שאל	ASK	981d	2 a
13	19	גדי	KID	152a	
		ל	TO	517c	7 bb
		מנחה	OFFERING	585b	4
		עלה	GO UP	749d	8
		פלא	BE SURPASSING	810d	3
		צור	ROCK	849c	1 c
13	20	מלאך	MESSENGER	521d	3
		להב	FLAME	529a	1
		נפל	FALL	657c	3 b
		עלה	GO UP	748d	5
		שמי	HEAVENS	1030a	1 b
13	21	אז	THEN	23a	1 a
		יסף	ADD	414d	
		מלאך	MESSENGER	521d	3
		מות	DIE	560a	2 b
		ראה	TO SEE	908b	1 a
13	22	מות	DIE	560a	2 b
13	23	אלה	THESE	41c	A
		זה	THIS	262a	6 d
		חפץ	DELIGHT IN	343a	2 b
		חפץ	DELIGHT	343b	3
		כ	LIKE	453d	1 a
		כת	LIKE	453d	1 b
		לו	IF	530a	1 a
		מות	DIE	560b	2
		מנחה	OFFERING	585b	4
		עת	TIME	773c	1 a
		ראה	TO SEE	908d	1
		ראה	TO SEE	908d	1 a2
		שמע	HEAR	1034d	2 b
13	24	אשה	WOMAN	61a	1
		ברך	BLESS	139a	2 a
		גדל	GROW UP	152b	1 a
		שמשון	SAMSON	1039c	
13	25	אשתאול	ESHTAOL	84b	
		דן	DAN	192d	2
		חלל	POLLUTE	320d	2
		מחנהדן	MAHANEH-DAN	334b	
		פעם	THRUST	821d	
		צרעה	ZORAH	864a	9 c1
		רוח	BREATH	926a	9 c1
14	1	בת	DAUGHTER	123b	1 i
		תמנה	TIMNAH	584d	2
		שמשון	SAMSON	1039c	
14	2	אם	MOTHER	51d	1
		בת	DAUGHTER	123b	1 i
		תמנה	TIMNAH	584d	2
14	3	אח	BROTHER	26b	2
		את	MARK OF THE AC-CUSATIVE	85a	1 a
		בת	DAUGHTER	123c	1 i
		הוא	HE, SHE, IT	*215b	1 a
		ישר	BE STRAIGHT	448c	2
		כי	THAT	472d	1 f
		עם	KINSMAN	769c	
		ערל	HAVING FORESKIN	790c	
		שמשון	SAMSON	1039c	
14	4	תאנה	OPPORTUNITY	58c	
		בקש	SEEK	134c	1 b
		הוא	HE, SHE, IT	216d	6 a
		מן	OUT OF	579d	2 d
		משל	RULE	605d	1
14	5	ארי	LION	71d	
		כפיר	LION	498d	2
		תמנה	TIMNAH	584d	2
		קרא	ENCOUNTER	897a	1
		שאג	ROAR	980c	1
14	6	אין	NOT	34c	2 c
		גדי	KID	152a	
		ה	THE	207d	1 f
		היה	BECOME	*225d	2 1b
		כ	LIKE	454d	3 a
		מאומה	ANYTHING	548d	
		צלח	RUSH	852b	
		רוח	BREATH	926a	9 c1
		שסע	DIVIDE	1042d	

Ch	v	Heb	Eng	Page	Sec
14	7	דבר	SPEAK	181b	3 c
		ישר	BE STRAIGHT	448c	2
		ל	TO	510d	1 b
14	8	אריה	LION	71d	
		גויה	CORPSE	156c	2 b
		דבורה	BEE	184b	
		דבש	HONEY	185a	
		יום	DAY	401a	7 j
		עדה	CONGREGATION	417b	2
		מן	FROM	581c	4 b
		מפלת	CARCASS	658c	1
		סור	TURN ASIDE	693c	1
		שוב	TURN BACK	997b	3 a
14	9	אריה	LION	71d	
		גויה	CORPSE	156c	2 b
		דבש	HONEY	185a	
		הלך	WALK	233b	1 4c 1g
		רדה	SCRAPE OUT	922b	
14	10	בחור	YOUNG MAN	104c	
		חמש	FIVE	332a	5 b2
		עשה	DO	794c	2 1c
		משתה	FEAST	1059d	1
14	11	את	WITH	85d	1
		מרע	FRIEND	946d	
		מרע	FRIEND	946d	
14	12	אם	IF	50a	1 a5
		חוד	PROPOUND A RIDDLE	295c	
		חידה	RIDDLE	295c	2 a
		חליפה	A CHANGE	322c	1
		מצא	FIND	593b	2 c
		נגד	BE CONSPICUOUS	616d	1
		נתן	GIVE	679b	1 n
		סדין	LINEN WRAPPER	690b	
		שבוע	PERIOD OF SEVEN	988d	1
		משתה	FEAST	1059d	1
14	13	חוד	PROPOUND A RIDDLE	295c	
		חידה	RIDDLE	295c	2 a
		חליפה	A CHANGE	322c	1
		נתן	GIVE	679b	1 n
		סדין	LINEN WRAPPER	690b	
14	14	מאכל	FOOD	38b	
		חידה	RIDDLE	295c	2 b
		מתוק	SWEET	608d	1
		עז	STRONG	738d	
		אחוה	A DECLARING	*1092b	
14	15	אש	FIRE	77c	1
		ה	INTERROG PART	210a	1 d
		הלם	HITHER	241a	
		חידה	RIDDLE	295c	2 b
		ירש	IMPOVERISH	439d	3
		לא	NOT	520c	4 bb
		נגד	BE CONSPICUOUS	616d	2
		פתה	BE SIMPLE	*834d	1
		קרא	CALL	895d	5 a
		קרא	CALL	895d	5 a
		שרף	BURN	977a	2 b1
14	16	אהב	LOVE	12d	1
		בכה	WEEP	113c	5
		בן	SON	121b	1 ji
		ו	AND	252d	1 f
		חידה	RIDDLE	295c	2 a
		חוד	PROPOUND A RIDDLE	295c	
		נגד	BE CONSPICUOUS	616d	2
		על	UPON	753b	2 1b
		עם	PEOPLE	766d	5 a
		רק	ONLY	956c	2 c
		שנא	HATE	971c	1 a
14	17	בכה	WEEP	113c	5
		בן	SON	121b	1 ji
		חידה	RIDDLE	295c	2 b
		על	UPON	753b	2 1b
		עם	PEOPLE	766d	5 a
		צוק	CONSTRAIN	847d	
		משתה	FEAST	1059d	1
14	18	ארי	LION	71d	
		דבש	HONEY	185a	
		חדר	CHAMBER	293c	
		חידה	RIDDLE	295c	2 c
		חרס	SUN	357b	
		חרש	CUT IN	360c	2
		טרם	NOT YET	382c	2
		לולא	IF NOT	530b	A
		מה	WHAT	553a	1 da
		מצא	FIND	593b	2 c
		מתוק	SWEET	608d	1
		עגלה	HEIFER	722b	
		עז	STRONG	738d	
14	19	אשקלון	ASHKELON	80c	
		חידה	RIDDLE	295c	2 b
		חליפה	A CHANGE	322c	1
		חלוצה	WHAT IS STRIPPED OFF	322d	
		חרה	BURN	354a	1 a
		ירד	GO DOWN	433a	1 d
		מן	FROM	580c	3 a
		נגד	BE CONSPICUOUS	616d	1
		נכה	SMITE	646a	2 c
		צלח	RUSH	852b	
		רוח	BREATH	926a	9 c1
		שלשים	THIRTY	1026c	1
14	20	היה	BECOME	226d	2 2h
		רעה	GE A SPECIAL FRIEND	946b	
15	1	מרע	FRIEND	946d	
		ב	IN	89c	3 1b
		בוא	COME	98a	1 e
		גדי	KID	152a	
		היה	COME TO PASS	224c	2 a1 az
		חדר	CHAMBER	293c	
		חמה	WHEAT	334d	
		יום	DAY	399c	5 a
		יום	TIME	399c	6 a
		יום	DAY	401a	7 j
		מן	FROM	581c	4 b
		פקד	ATTEND TO	823b	A 2
		קציר	HARVESTING	894d	3
15	2	אמר	SAY	56b	2
		היה	BECOME	226c	2 2h
		טוב	PLEASANT	374c	6
		נתן	GIVE	678c	1 c
		קטן	SMALL	882a	1 a
		מרע	FRIEND	946d	
		שנא	HATE	971c	1 a
15	3	אני	I	59a	
		מן	OUT OF	579d	2 d
		נקה	BE CLEAN	667b	2
		פעם	OCCURRENCE	822b	3 d2
		רעה	MISERY	949b	2
15	4	זנב	TAIL	275c	1 a
		לכד	CAPTURE	540a	1
		לפיד	TORCH	542a	
		מאה	HUNDRED	548b	1 c3
		פנה	TURN	815c	1
		שועל	FOX	1043c	
		תוך	MIDST	1063b	
15	5	בער	BURN	129b	1
		בער	BURN	129c	2
		גדיש	HEAP	155c	
		זית	OLIVE TREE	268c	1
		כרם	VINEYARD	501d	
		לפיד	TORCH	542a	
15	6	מן	FROM	582a	5 b
		חתן	DAUGHTER:S HUSBAND	368c	1
		לקח	TAKE	543a	3 a
		מי	WHO	566b	
		תמני	TIMNITE	584d	
		נתן	GIVE	678c	1 c
		מרע	FRIEND	946d	
		שרף	BURN	977a	2 b1
15	7	זה	THIS	262a	6 d
		חדל	CEASE	293a	2
		כ	LIKE	453a	1 b
		כיאם	SURELY	475c	2 c
		נקם	AVENGE	668b	1
15	8	ירך	THIGH	438a	1 a
		מכה	SLAUGHTER	647a	3
		נפל	FALL	657c	4 c
		סלע	CRAG	701a	1
		עיטם	ETAM	743c	1
		על	UPON	752d	2 1
		שוק	LEG	1003b	1
15	9	חיה	COMMUNITY	*312d	
		יהודה	JUDAH	397c	2
		לחי	LEHI	534d	
		נטש	FORSAKE	644a	3
		נטש	PERMIT	*644a	3
15	10	אסר	TIE	63d	3
		יהודה	JUDAH	397b	12
		עלה	GO UP	748c	2 c
15	11	זה	THIS	261c	4 d
		כן	SO	486c	2 ca
		מה	WHAT	553a	1 c
		משל	RULE	605d	1
		סלע	CRAG	701a	1
		עיטם	ETAM	743c	1
15	12	אתם	YOU	61d	
		אסר	TIE	63d	3
		יד	HAND	390d	5 b3
		פגע	MEET	803b	3
		פן	LEST	814d	1
15	13	שבע	SWEAR	989b	1 a
		אסר	TIE	63d	3
		חדש	NEW	294a	A
		מות	DIE	560b	1 b
		סלע	CRAG	701a	1
		עבת	CORD	721c	1 a
		עלה	GO UP	749b	1 a
15	14	אסור	BAND	64a	
		בוא	COME	98b	2
		בער	BURN	129a	2
		זרוע	ARM	283d	1 a
		יד	HAND	389a	1 b
		לחי	LEHI	534d	
		מסס	MELT	587d	1
		עבת	CORD	721c	1 a
		פשת	FLAX	833a	1
		צלח	RUSH	852b	
		קרא	ENCOUNTER	897a	1
		רוח	BREATH	926a	9 c1
		רוע	RAISE A SHOUT	929c	1 a
15	15	אלף	THOUSAND	48b	1 a
		חמור	HE-ASS	331c	5
		טרי	FRESH	382b	
		לחי	JAW	534d	1
		מצא	FIND	593b	2
		שלח	SEND	1018d	3 a
15	16	אלף	THOUSAND	48d	1 a
		חמור	HEAP	331a	
		חמור	HE-ASS	331c	5
		לחי	JAW	534d	1
		נכה	SMITE	646a	2 c
15	17	לחי	LEHI	534d	
		לחי	JAW	534d	1
		מן	OUT OF	579a	2 aa
		רמת	RAMATH-LEHI	928b	1
		שלך	THROW	1021a	1 c
15	18	ה	THE	208c	1 hb
		יד	HAND	390d	5 b3
		תשועה	DELIVERANCE	448b	1
		נתן	GIVE	678d	1 d
		עבד	SLAVE	714c	6
		ערל	HAVING FORESKIN	790c	
		צמא	THIRST	854d	
		צמא	BE THIRSTY	854d	
		קרא	CALL	895b	2 a
15	19	בקע	CLEAVE	131d	1
		חיה	LIVE	311b	2
		חיה	LIVE	*311b	2 d
		יום	DAY	401b	71
		יצא	GO OUT	423a	1 f
		כן	SO	487b	3 f
		מכתש	MORTAR	509d	
		לחי	LEHI	534d	
		לחי	JAW	534d	
		מי	WATER	565c	2
		עין	SPRING	745b	B
		קרא	CALL	896a	1
		קרא	PARTRIDGE	896c	
		רוח	BREATH	925a	3 a
		שוב	TURN BACK	998a	7 a
		שתה	DRINK	1059b	1 a
16	1	אשה	WOMAN	61a	1
		בוא	COME	98a	1 e
		זנה	COMMIT FORNICATION	275d	1
		עזה	GAZA	738b	
16	2	אור	LIGHT	21c	2
		ארב	LIE IN WAIT	70b	
		בקר	MORNING	133d	1 b
		הרג	KILL	247a	1 a
		ל	TO	515b	5 hb g
		לילה	NIGHT	539a	1
		סבב	SURROUND	685d	2 d
		עד	AS FAR AS	724b	12a b
		עד	AS FAR AS	724c	12a b
		עד	UNTIL	725a	2 1b b
		עזז	BE STRONG	738c	
		חרש	ADDENDA ET CORRIGENDA	1123d	
16	3	אחז	GRASP	28b	
		בריח	BAR	138b	1 b
		בריח	BAR	138b	2
		דלת	DOOR	195b	3
		הר	MOUNTAIN	250d	1 m
		מזוזה	DOOR-POST	265b	3
		חברון	HEBRON	289b	
		חצי	HALF	345d	2
		כתף	SHOULDER	509b	1 a
		נסע	PULL OUT	652a	1
		עלה	GO UP	749c	4
		עם	WITH	767b	1 a
		פנה	FACE	818d	27a d
		שכב	LIE DOWN	1012a	1 b
16	4	אהב	LOVE	12d	1
		אחר	AFTER	30a	2 b
		דלילה	DELILA	196a	
		היה	COME TO PASS	224c	2 a1 ai
		מנשה	MANASSEH	586c	1 b1 b
		נחל	WADY	636c	2
		שרק	SOREK	977d	
16	5	אסר	TIE	63d	3
		ב	IN	90a	3 2e
		יכל	PREVAIL	408a	2 b
		כח	STRENGTH	470c	1 a
		מה	HOW	553d	4 a
		מה	HOW	553d	4 a
		סרן	TYRANT	710d	
		ענה	BE BOWED DOWN	776b	1
		פתה	BE SIMPLE	834d	1
		ראה	TO SEE	907b	5 a
16	6	אסר	TIE	64a	1
		ב	IN	90a	3 2e
		דלילה	DELILA	196a	
		כח	STRENGTH	470c	1 a
		נא	PART OF ENTREATY	609a	1
		ענה	BE BOWED DOWN	776b	1
16	7	אדם	MAN	9c	2
		אסר	TIE	63d	3
		חלה	BE WEAK	317d	1
		חרב	BE DRY	351b	
		יתר	CORD	452a	
		לח	NEW	535a	2
16	8	אסר	TIE	63d	3
		חרב	BE DRY	351b	
		יתר	CORD	452a	
		לח	NEW	535a	2
		עלה	GO UP	749c	4
16	9	ארב	LIE IN WAIT	70b	
		ה	THE	208a	1 f
		חדר	CHAMBER	293c	
		ידע	BE MADE KNOWN	394c	1
		יתר	CORD	452a	
		כח	STRENGTH	470c	1 a

JUDGES

Ch	v.	Heb	Eng	Page	Sec
18	10	עצל	BE SLUGGISH	782b	
		בטח	TRUST	105b	2
		מחסור	NEED	341d	2
		יד	HAND	390c	3 d
18	11	אשתאול	ESHTAOL	84b	
		דני	DANITES	193a	
		חגר	GIRD	292a	2
		כלי	IMPLEMENT	479b	2a
		מלחמה	WAR	536c	
		נסע	SET OUT	652b	2
		צרעה	ZORAH	864a	
		משפחה	CLAN	1046d	1 b
18	12	דן	DAN	192d	2
		מחנהדן	MAHANEH-DAN	334b	
		יום	DAY	401b	71
		כן	SO	487b	3 f
		קרא	CALL	896a	6 e2
18	13	עבר	PASS OVER	718a	5 a
18	14	אפוד	EPHOD	65d	3 b
		חמש	FIVE	331d	1 d
		ידע	KNOW	394a	1 g
		ליש	LAISH	539d	
		מסכה	MOLTEN IMAGE	651b	2
		ענה	ANSWER	773a	2 a
		רגל	GO ABOUT	920b	2
		תרפים	IDOL	1076c	
18	15	לוי	LEVITE	532d	1
		סור	TURN ASIDE	693c	1
		שאל	ASK	982a	2 a
		שלום	PEACE	1022d	3
18	16	דן	DAN	192d	2
		חגר	GIRD	292a	2
		כלי	IMPLEMENT	479b	2a
		מלחמה	WAR	536c	
		נצב	STAND	662a	1 a
		פתח	OPENING	836a	
		שער	GATE	1044d	1 a
		שער	GATE	*1045a	2 c
18	17	אפוד	EPHOD	65d	3 b
		חגר	GIRD	292a	2
		חמש	FIVE	331d	1 d
		כהן	PRIEST	463b	3 a
		כלי	IMPLEMENT	479b	2a
		מלחמה	WAR	536c	
		מסכה	MOLTEN IMAGE	651b	2
		נצב	STAND	662a	1 a
		פתח	OPENING	836a	
		רגל	GO ABOUT	920b	2
		שער	GATE	1044d	1 a
		תרפים	IDOL	1076c	
18	18	אפוד	EPHOD	65d	3 b
		בוא	COME	97d	1
		כהן	PRIEST	463b	3 a
		מסכה	MOLTEN IMAGE	651b	2
		תרפים	IDOL	1076c	
18	19	אב	FATHER	3d	8
		או	OR	14d	1
		ה	INTERROG PART	210b	1 d
		חרש	BE SILENT	361b	1 a
		טוב	PLEASANT	374c	6
		כהן	PRIEST	463b	3 a
		פה	MOUTH	804d	1 b
		שום	TO PLACE	963b	1 b
		משפחה	CLAN	1046d	1 b
18	20	אפוד	EPHOD	65d	3 b
		יטב	BE GLAD	405c	1
		כהן	PRIEST	463b	3 a
		לב	HEART	525c	2 9a
		תרפים	IDOL	1076c	
18	21	טף	CHILDREN	382a	
		כבודה	RICHES	459c	
		פנה	TURN	815b	1 c
		שום	TO PLACE	963b	1 c
18	22	דבק	KEEP CLOSE	180a	3
		דן	DAN	192d	2
		זעק	CRY	277c	
		עם	WITH	*768a	2
18	23	דן	DAN	192d	2
		זעק	CRY	277c	
		מה	WHAT	552d	1 ac
		סבב	TURN ABOUT	686c	1 a
18	24	זה	THIS	261c	4 c
		כהן	PRIEST	463b	3 a
		לקח	TAKE	543a	3 a
		מה	HOW	553c	2 aa
		עשה	DO	794b	2 1a
18	25	אסף	GATHER	62c	4
		דן	DAN	192d	2
		מר	BITTER	600c	2 b
		נפש	SOUL	660b	6 c
		פגע	MEET	803b	3
		שמע	HEAR	1034c	1 x
18	26	דן	DAN	192d	2
		דרך	JOURNEY	203a	2
		הלך	WALK	231b	1 d3 gd
		חזק	STRONG	305c	1a
18	27	אש	FIRE	77c	1
		בטח	TRUST	105b	2
		היה	BE	227c	3 4d c
		חרב	SWORD	352d	1 f
		כהן	PRIEST	463b	3 a
		ליש	LAISH	539d	
		נכה	SMITE	646a	2 c
		שקט	BE QUIET	1053a	1

Ch	v.	Heb	Eng	Page	Sec
18	28	אדם	MAN	9c	2
		אשר	PARTICLE OF RE-LATION	83a	7 c
		ביתרחוב	BETH-REHOB	112d	
		בנה	BUILD	124b	1 aa
		דבר	WORD	183b	4 1
		נצל	DELIVER	664d	3 a
		עם	WITH	767d	1 d
		עמק	VALE	771a	
		צידון	SIDON	851a	
		רחק	DISTANT	935b	1 a
18	29	אולם	BUT	19d	
		דן	DAN	192d	1
		דן	DAN	193a	3
		ילד	BE BORN	409a	
		ליש	LAISH	539d	
		קרא	CALL	896a	6 a
		ראשון	FIRST	911d	3 a1
		ישראל	ISRAEL	975c	1
18	30	גרשם	GERSHOM	177a	1
		דן	DAN	192d	2
		דן	DAN	*193a	3
		דני	DANITES	193a	
		יהונתן	JOHATHAN	221a	0
		יום	DAY	400a	7 d1 b
		כהן	PRIEST	*463b	3 a
		משה	MOSES	602c	
		עד	AS FAR AS	724a	1 2aa
		קום	STAND	878d	2 a
18	31	אלהים	GOD	44a	3 b
		בית	HOUSE	109a	1 ae 0
		יום	DAY	400a	7 d2 a
		עשה	DO	794b	2 1a
		שום	TO PLACE	964b	4 c
		שלו	SHILOH	1017d	
19	1	אין	NOT	34c	2 c
		אשה	WOMAN	61b	1
		בילחם	BETHLEHEM	111d	1
		גור	SOJOURN	157d	1
		יום	DAY	400d	7 g
		ירכה	EXTREME PARTS	438a	2
		לוי	LEVITE	532d	1
		מלך	KING	573a	1
		פלגש	CONCUBINE	811c	1
19	2	את	WITH	86d	4 a
		בילחם	BETHLEHEM	111d	1
		חדש	NEW MOON	294c	2 a
		יום	TIME	399d	6 b
		יום	YEAR	*399d	6 c
		על	UPON	753d	2 1b
		ארבע	FOUR	917a	1 b1
19	3	דבר	SPEAK	181d	5
		חמור	HE-ASS	331b	2 c
		לב	HEART	525c	2 9a
		נערה	GIRL	655b	1
		צמד	COUPLE	855a	1
		קרא	ENCOUNTER	897a	1
		רמה	RAMA	928a	1
		שוב	TURN BACK	998d	1 a
19	4	את	WITH	85d	1
		חזק	BE FIRM	305b	6 d
		חתן	WIFE'S FATHER	368c	1
		ישב	REMAIN	442d	2 a
		נערה	GIRL	655b	1
19	5	אחר	AFTERWARDS	29d	1 b
		בקר	MORNING	134b	1 h
		חתן	DAUGHTER:S HUS-BAND	368c	1
		לב	HEART	525c	2 8
		לחם	FOOD	537a	1 a
		נערה	GIRL	655b	1
		סעד	SUPPORT	703c	1
		פת	FRAGMENT	837d	
19	6	רביעי	FOURTH	917a	1
		הלך	WALK	231b	1 d3 gd
		יאל	SHOW-WILLING-NESS	384a	1
		יחדו	TOGETHER	403b	A
		יטב	BE GLAD	405c	1
		ישב	SIT	442d	1 b
		לב	HEART	525c	2 9a
		נערה	GIRL	655b	1
19	7	חתן	WIFE'S FATHER	368c	1
		פצר	PUSH	823a	
		שוב	TURN BACK	998b	8
19	8	בקר	MORNING	134b	1 h
		חמישי	FIFTH	332c	1
		חנה	DECLINE	*333c	1
		יום	DAY	398b	1
		יום	DAY	398b	1
		לבב	HEART	524a	2 8
		מהה	LINGER	554c	
		נטה	BEND	640b	3 a
		נערה	GIRL	655b	1
		סעד	SUPPORT	703c	1
		אהל	TENT	13d	2
19	9	חנה	DECLINE	333c	1
		חתן	WIFE'S FATHER	368c	1
		יום	DAY	398b	1
		יום	DAY	398b	1
		יטב	BE GLAD	405c	1
		לבב	HEART	524a	2 8
		נא	PART OF EN-TREATY	609c	4 d
		נטה	BEND	640b	3 a
		נערה	GIRL	655b	1

Ch	v.	Heb	Eng	Page	Sec
		ערב	BECOME EVENING	788a	
		רפה	SINK	951d	1
19	10	אבה	BE WILLING	2c	
		יבום	JEBUS	101a	1
		הלך	WALK	234a	1 5e
		חבש	BIND	290a	1 c
		חמור	HE-ASS	331b	2 c
		ירושלים	JERUSALEM	436d	
		נכח	FRONT	647c	2 bc
		עד	AS FAR AS	724a	1 1a
		צמד	COUPLE	855a	1
19	11	אדון	LORD	11a	2 1b
		יבום	JEBUS	101a	
		יבוסי	JEBUSITE	101a	1
		הלך	WALK	234b	1 5f 2
		חנה	DECLINE	*333c	1
		יום	DAY	398b	1
		יום	DAY	398b	1
		סור	TURN ASIDE	693c	1
		עם	WITH	*768d	2
		רדד	BEAT OUT	921d	1
19	12	אדון	LORD	11a	2 1b
		אשר	PARTICLE OF RE-LATION	82b	2 b
		גבעה	GIBEAH	149b	2
		הם	THEY	241c	3 c
		ו	AND	252d	1 e
		נכרי	FOREIGN	648d	1 b
		סור	TURN ASIDE	693c	1
		עבר	PASS OVER	718a	5 d
19	13	הלך	WALK	234b	1 5f 2
		לון	LODGE	533c	1 a
		קרב	COME NEAR	897c	1 e
19	14	אשר	PARTICLE OF RE-LATION	83a	7 c
		בוא	COME	98a	1 i
		גבעה	GIBEAH	149b	2
		ל	TO	512d	5 aa
19	15	אסף	GATHER	63a	2
		ישב	SIT	442c	1 a
		לון	LODGE	533c	1 a
		סור	TURN ASIDE	693c	1
		רחוב	PLAZA	932b	
		שם	THERE	1027b	2
19	16	בנימיני	BENJAMITE	122d	1
		גבעה	GIBEAH	149b	2
		גור	SOJOURN	157d	1
		זקן	OLD	278c	1
		מעשה	DEED	795d	1 b1
		שדה	FIELD	961c	1 f
19	17	אין	WHENCE	32d	2
		ארה	WANDER	72d	2
		הלך	WALK	230d	1 1d 3b
		זקן	OLD	278c	1
		רחוב	PLAZA	932b	
19	18	אנחנו	WE	59d	1
		אסף	GATHER	63a	2
		את	MARK OF THE AC-CUSATIVE	85b	2 a
		בית	HOUSE	108d	1 a
		בית	HOUSE	109b	1 ae 0
		בילחם	BETHLEHEM	111d	1
		יום	DAY	400c	7 g
		ירכה	EXTREME PARTS	438a	2
		עבר	PASS OVER	718a	5 d
		שם	THERE	1027c	4 c
19	19	אמה	MAID	51a	1
		חמור	HE-ASS	331b	2 c
		מחסור	NEED	341d	2
		יין	WINE	406c	A
		יש	BE	442a	2 c
		כל	ALL	482b	1 ec
		ל	TO	516b	5 ja
		מספוא	FODDER	704c	
		תבן	STRAW	1062a	
19	20	זקן	OLD	278c	1
		מחסור	NEED	341d	1
		על	UPON	753d	2 1c
		רחוב	PLAZA	932b	
		שלום	PEACE	1022d	3
19	21	בוא	COME	99a	1
		בלל	TO GIVE PROVEN-DER	117d	
		חמור	HE-ASS	331b	2 c
		רחץ	WASH OFF	934c	1
19	22	בליעל	WORTHLESSNESS	116a	1
		בעל	OWNER	127b	1 1
		דלת	DOOR	195a	1
		דפק	BEAT	200c	
		זקן	OLD	278c	1
		ידע	KNOW	394b	3
		יום	DAY	*398d	2 g
		יטב	MAKE GLAD	405c	1
		יצא	BRING OUT	424d	1 h
		לב	HEART	525c	2 9a
		סבב	TURN AROUND	686a	1 a
19	23	אל	NOT	39b	A bb
		בעל	OWNER	127b	1 1
		נבלה	SENSELESSNESS	615a	1
19	24	תתולה	VIRGIN	143d	
		טוב	PLEASANT	374a	2 f
		יצא	BRING OUT	424d	1 h
		נבלה	SENSELESSNESS	615a	1
		ענה	BE BOWED DOWN	776b	2
19	25	אבה	BE WILLING	2c	

Ch	v	Heb	Eng	Page	Sec
		בקר	MORNING	*133d	1 b
		בקר	MORNING	133d	1 a
		חוץ	THE OUTSIDE	299c	1 a
		חזק	BE FIRM	305a	6 a
		ידע	KNOW	394b	3
		יצא	BRING OUT	424d	1 i
		לילה	NIGHT	539a	1
		עלה	GO UP	748d	5
		עלל	ACT ARBITRARILY	759d	1
		שחר	DAWN	1007b	
		שלח	SEND	1019b	3
		שמע	HEAR	1034a	1 j
19	26	אדון	LORD	11a	21c
		אור	LIGHT	21c	2
		בקר	MORNING	*133d	1 b
		בקר	MORNING	133d	1 b
		נפל	FALL	657b	3 a
		פנה	TURN	815b	1 e
19	27	אדון	LORD	11a	21c
		אשה	WOMAN	61b	2
		בקר	MORNING	134b	1 h
		דלת	DOOR	195a	1
		דרך	JOURNEY	203a	2
		נפל	FALL	657b	3 a
		סף	THRESHOLD	706b	
		פתח	OPEN	835a	
19	28	חמור	HE-ASS	331b	2 c
		לקח	TAKE	543c	5
19	29	אחז	GRASP	*28b	
		מאכלת	KNIFE	38c	
		גבול	BOUNDARY	148a	2 a
		חזק	BE FIRM	305a	6 a
		ל	TO	512b	4 a
		נתח	PIECE OF A DIVIDED CARCASS	677c	
		נתח	CUT IN PIECES	677c	
		עצם	BONE	782d	1 b
		שלח	SEND	1019a	1 a
19	30	היה	COME TO PASS	225b	12b bd
		היה	COME TO PASS	227d	2
		זה	THIS	262a	6 d
		יום	DAY	400a	7 d1 z
		יום	DAY	401b	71
		כ	LIKE	453d	1 b
		ל	TO	515d	5 ia
		מן	FROM	583d	9 b2
		עוץ	COUNSEL	734a	
		ראה	TO SEE	908c	2 a
		שום	TO PLACE	963c	2 b
20	1	באר־שבע	BEERSHEBA	92a	
		באר־שבע	BEERSHEBA	92a	
		דן	DAN	193a	3
		עדה	CONGREGATION	*417b	3
		מן	FROM	583d	9 b1
		מצפה	MIZPAH	860a	4
		מצפה	MIZPAH	860a	4
		קהל	ASSEMBLE AS	874d	1 a
20	2	אלהים	GOD	44a	3 b
		חרב	SWORD	352c	1 c
		יצב	STATION ONESELF	426b	A
		עם	PEOPLE	766c	1
		פנה	CORNER	819d	2
		קהל	ASSEMBLY	874c	1 b
		רגלי	ON FOOT	920b	
		שלף	DRAW OUT	1025c	1
20	3	איכה	IN WHAT MANNER	32d	1
		בנימין	BENJAMIN	122d	1
		היה	COME TO PASS	227d	2
		מצפה	MIZPAH	860a	4
20	4	אשה	WOMAN	61b	2
		אשר	PARTICLE OF RELATION	83a	7 c
		לוי	LEVITE	532d	1
		רצח	MURDER	954a	
20	5	בעל	OWNER	127b	13
		דמה	BE LIKE	198a	2
		ה	THE	207a	1 a
		הרג	KILL	247a	1 a
		סבב	SURROUND	685d	2 d
		על	UPON	757d	27d
		ענה	BE BOWED DOWN	776b	2
		קום	STAND	878a	2
		רע	FRIEND	946a	2
20	6	אחז	GRASP	28b	
		זמה	PLAN	273c	2 c
		נבלה	SENSELESSNESS	615a	1
		נחלה	PROPERTY	635a	1 a
		נתח	CUT IN PIECES	677c	
		שדה	FIELD	961d	2
		שלח	SEND	1019a	1 a
20	7	דבר	WORD	182b	11d
		הלם	HITHER	240d	
		יהב	PROVIDE	396b	3
		עצה	ADVICE	420a	1
20	8	הלך	WALK	231b	1 d3 gd
		סור	TURN ASIDE	693c	1
		קום	STAND	877d	1 f
20	9	גורל	LOT	174c	2 e
		זה	THIS	261a	3
		על	UPON	758a	27d
20	10	גבע	GEBA	148d	
		גבעה	GIBEAH	149b	2
		גורל	LOT	174c	2 e
		כ	LIKE	454a	1 c1
		ל	TO	511b	1 ga
		ל	TO	512d	5 ab
		ל	TO	513d	5 cb g
		מאה	HUNDRED	548a	1 a5
		נבלה	SENSELESSNESS	615a	1
		צידה	PROVISION	845b	
		רבבה	MULTITUDE	914b	
20	11	איש	MAN	36a	
		אסף	GATHER	62d	1 a
		חבר	UNITED	288d	1
20	12	בנימין	BENJAMIN	122d	1
		היה	COME TO PASS	227d	2
		מה	WHAT	553a	1 c
		שבט	TRIBE	987b	2 a
20	13	אבה	BE WILLING	2c	
		בליעל	WORTHLESSNESS	116a	1
		בער	CONSUME	129b	3
		מות	DIE	560b	1 b
		נתן	GIVE	679c	1 s
		רעה	MISERY	949b	3
20	14	אסף	GATHER	62d	1 a
		בנימין	BENJAMIN	122d	1
		מלחמה	WAR	536c	
20	15	בד	SEPARATION	94c	1 d
		בחר	CHOOSE	104b	7
		בנימין	BENJAMIN	122d	1
		חרב	SWORD	352c	1 c
		מאה	HUNDRED	548a	1 c2
		פקד	ATTEND TO	823d	
		פקד	ATTEND TO	823d	
		שש	SIX	995c	3
		שלף	DRAW OUT	1025c	1
20	16	אבן	STONE	6b	1
		אטר	SHUT UP	32a	
		בחר	CHOOSE	104b	7
		ה	THE	207c	1 d
		זה	THIS	260c	1 a
		חטא	MISS A GOAL OR WAY	307c	1
		יד	HAND	389a	1 a
		ימין	RIGHT HAND	411d	1 a
		מאה	HUNDRED	548a	1 c2
		קלע	SLING	887c	
		שערה	A HAIR	972b	
20	17	זה	THIS	260c	1 a
		חרב	SWORD	352c	1 c
		מלחמה	WAR	536c	
		פקד	ATTEND TO	823d	
		שלף	DRAW OUT	1025c	1
20	18	בנימין	BENJAMIN	122d	1
		תחלה	BEGINNING	321b	
		ל	TO	515d	5 hc
		מי	WHO	566b	
		עלה	GO UP	748c	2 c
		שאל	ASK	982a	2 b
20	19	בקר	MORNING	134b	1 h
		חנה	DECLINE	333c	2 c2
20	20	מלחמה	WAR	536c	
		מלחמה	WAR	536c	
		ערך	ARRANGE	789a	1 d
20	21	בנימין	BENJAMIN	122d	1
		שחת	GO TO RUIN	1008b	1
20	22	חזק	BE FIRM	305b	2
		יסף	DO AGAIN	415c	2 a
		מלחמה	WAR	536c	
		ערך	ARRANGE	789a	1 d
		ערך	ARRANGE	789a	1 d
20	23	בכה	WEEP	113c	6
		בנימין	BENJAMIN	122d	1
		יסף	DO AGAIN	415c	2 a
		מלחמה	WAR	536c	
		נגש	DRAW NEAR	620d	1
		פנה	FACE	817b	2 4a h
		שאל	ASK	982a	2 b
20	24	בנימין	BENJAMIN	122d	1
		קרב	COME NEAR	897b	1 a
20	25	את	MARK OF THE ACCUSATIVE	85b	3 a
		חרב	SWORD	352c	1 c
		קרא	ENCOUNTER	897a	1
		שחת	GO TO RUIN	1008b	1
		שלף	DRAW OUT	1025c	1
		שמנה	EIGHT	1033a	2 b
20	26	בכה	WEEP	113c	6
		בן	SON	121a	1 jg
		ישב	SIT	442c	1 a
		עלה	WHOLE BURNT OFFERING	750d	
		פנה	FACE	817b	2 4a h
		צום	FAST	847a	
		שלם	PEACE-OFFERING	1023c	
20	27	אלהים	GOD	44a	3 b
		ארון	CHEST	75b	3
		ארון	CHEST	75c	3 f
		שאל	ASK	982a	2 b
20	28	אלעזר	ELEAZAR	46b	A
		בנימין	BENJAMIN	122d	1
		חדל	CEASE	293a	2
		יסף	DO AGAIN	415c	2 a
		מלחמה	WAR	536c	
		עמד	STAND	764a	1 e
20	29	ארב	LIE IN WAIT	70b	
		סבב	ROUND ABOUT	687a	1 b
		שום	TO PLACE	964b	4 a
20	30	אל	TO	40b	4
		בנימין	BENJAMIN	122d	1
		ערך	ARRANGE	789d	1 d
		פעם	OCCURRENCE	822a	3 b
20	31	בנימין	BENJAMIN	122d	1
		חלל	POLLUTE	320d	2
		נכה	SMITE	646a	2 a
		נתק	PULL	683d	
		מסלה	HIGHWAY	700c	
		פעם	OCCURRENCE	822a	3 b
		קרא	ENCOUNTER	897a	1
		שדה	FIELD	961c	1 f
20	32	בנימין	BENJAMIN	122d	1
		ך	LIKE	455a	
		נגף	STRIKE	620a	
		נתק	DRAW AWAY	683c	1
		מסלה	HIGHWAY	700c	
		ראשון	FIRST	911d	3 a1
20	33	ארב	LIE IN WAIT	70b	
		בעל־תמר	BAAL-TAMAR	128b	
		גבע	GEBA	148d	
		גבעה	GIBEAH	149b	2
		מערב	WEST	788b	
		מערה	BARE PLACE	789a	1
		ערך	ARRANGE	789c	1 d
		קום	STAND	878a	2
		מקום	STANDING PLACE	879d	1 b
		גיח	ADDENDA ET CORRIGENDA	1121d	
20	34	אלף	THOUSAND	49a	1 c
		בחר	CHOOSE	104b	7
		כבד	BE HEAVY	457b	1
		מלחמה	WAR	536c	
		נגד	IN FRONT	617d	2 cb g
		נגע	TOUCH	619b	3
		על	UPON	757b	27c aa
20	35	אלף	THOUSAND	49a	1 c
		את	MARK OF THE ACCUSATIVE	85b	3 a
		חמש	FIVE	332b	5 e1
		חרב	SWORD	352c	1 c
		נגף	STRIKE	619d	
		שחת	GO TO RUIN	1008b	1
		שלף	DRAW OUT	1025c	1
20	36	ארב	LIE IN WAIT	70b	
		בטח	TRUST	105b	15b
		בנימין	BENJAMIN	122d	1
		נגף	STRIKE	620a	
		נתן	GIVE	680a	1 z
		מקום	STANDING PLACE	880c	7 a
		שום	TO PLACE	964b	4 a
20	37	ארב	LIE IN WAIT	70b	
		חוש	HASTE	301d	1
		חרב	SWORD	352d	1 f
		משך	DRAW	604b	3
		נכה	SMITE	646b	3
		פשט	STRIP OFF	833a	2
20	38	ארב	LIE IN WAIT	70b	
		מועד	SIGNAL	418a	4
		משאת	UPRISING	673a	1 a
		עלה	GO UP	749c	4
		עשן	SMOKE	798c	1 a
		רבה	BECOME MANY	915b	
		רבה	BECOME MANY	915c	1 d1
20	39	אך	SURELY	36c	1
		הפך	TURN	245d	2 a
		חלל	POLLUTE	320d	2
		ך	LIKE	455a	B
		נגף	STRIKE	620a	
		נכה	SMITE	646a	2 a
		ראשון	FIRST	911c	1 a
20	40	חלל	POLLUTE	320d	2
		כליל	WHOLE	483a	2 a
		משאת	UPRISING	673a	1 a
		עלה	GO UP	748d	5
		עמוד	PILLAR	765b	4
		עשן	SMOKE	798c	1 a
		פנה	TURN	815b	2 a
		שמי	HEAVENS	1030a	1 b
		תימרה	COLUMN	*1071d	2
20	41	בהל	BE DISTURBED	96b	1
		בנימין	BENJAMIN	122d	1
		הפך	TURN	245d	2 a
		נגע	TOUCH	619b	3
		על	UPON	757b	27c aa
20	42	דבק	KEEP CLOSE	180a	3
		דרך	WAY	202d	2
		מלחמה	WAR	536c	
		פנה	TURN	815b	1
		שחת	GO TO RUIN	1008b	1
20	43	דרך	TREAD	202b	1
		מזרח	PLACE OF SUNRISE	280d	1
		כתר	SURROUND	509c	
		מנוחה	REST	630a	2
		נכח	FRONT	647c	2 bc
		רדף	PURSUE	923a	
20	44	את	MARK OF THE ACCUSATIVE	85b	3 a
		חיל	STRENGTH	298d	1 c
		שמנה	EIGHT	1033a	2 b
20	45	גדעם	GIDOM	154c	
		דבק	KEEP CLOSE	180a	2
		חמש	FIVE	332a	4
		נכה	SMITE	646a	2 c
		מסלה	HIGHWAY	700c	
		סלע	CRAG	701a	1
		עלל	GLEAN	760a	
		רמון	RIMMON	942a	1
20	46	את	MARK OF THE ACCUSATIVE	85b	3 a

Ch	v.	Heb	Eng	Page	Sec
		חיל	STRENGTH	298d	1 c
		חרב	SWORD	352c	1 c
		שלף	DRAW OUT	1025c	1
20	47	חדש	NEW MOON	294c	2 a
		סלע	CRAG	701a	1
		רמון	RIMMON	942a	1
20	48	אש	FIRE	77c	1
		בנימין	BENJAMIN	122d	1
		מן	FROM	582a	5 b
		מצא	FIND	593d	1 c
		מצא	FIND	593d	1 c
		מת	MALE	607a	1
		נכה	SMITE	646b	3
		שוב	TURN BACK	997b	3 b
		שלח	SEND	1019b	7
		מתם	SOUNDNESS	1071b	
21	1	מצפה	MIZPAH	860a	4
		שבע	SWEAR	989a	1 a
21	2	אלהים	GOD	43d	3
		בכה	WEEP	113c	6
		בכה	WEEP	113c	1
		בכה	WEEP	113c	2
		בכי	WEEPING	113d	
		ישב	SIT	442a	1 a
		פנה	FACE	817b	2 4 a h
21	3	אלהים	GOD	44c	4 ba
		זה	THIS	260c	1 a
		פקד	ATTEND TO	823d	1
21	4	בנה	BUILD	124c	1 at
		מזבח	ALTAR	258b	1
		מחרת	THE MORROW	564a	
		עלה	WHOLE BURNT OF-FERING	750d	
		שלם	PEACE-OFFERING	1023c	
21	5	היה	COME TO PASS	224b	1 1b
		ל	TO	514b	5 fa
		מות	DIE	559d	2 a
		עלה	GO UP	748c	2 b
		מצפה	MIZPAH	860a	4
		קהל	ASSEMBLY	874c	1 b
		שבועה	OATH	990a	1 a
21	6	גדע	HEW OFF	154b	
		נחם	BE SORRY	637a	1
		בלת	NOT	116d	4 a
21	7	יתר	BE LEFT OVER	451c	
		ל	TO	514b	5 fa
		עשה	DO	793d	1 1a 3
		שבע	SWEAR	989a	1 a
21	8	יבש	JABESH	386d	1
		מי	WHO	566c	E b
		מי	WHO	566c	D
		עלה	GO UP	748c	2 b
		מצפה	MIZPAH	860a	4
		קהל	ASSEMBLY	874c	1 b
21	9	יבש	JABESH	386d	1
		פקד	ATTEND TO	823d	
21	10	בן	SON	121d	8 a
		חרב	SWORD	352d	1 f
		טף	CHILDREN	382a	
		יבש	JABESH	386d	1
		עדה	CONGREGATION	*417b	3
		נכה	SMITE	646a	2 c
		שם	THERE	1027b	2
21	11	זה	THIS	261a	3
		זכר	MALE	271c	11 a
		זכר	MALE	271c	11 b
		חרם	BAN	356a	1 d
		ידע	KNOW	394b	3
		משכב	ACT OF LYING	1012d	2 b
21	12	בתולה	VIRGIN	143d	
		זכר	MALE	271c	11 a
		יבש	JABESH	386d	1
		ידע	KNOW	394b	3
		כנען	CANAAN	488d	2 a
		ל	TO	516b	5 jb
		מצא	FIND	592d	1 a
		נערה	GIRL	655b	1
		משכב	ACT OF LYING	1012d	2 b
		שלו	SHILOH	1017d	
21	13	בנימין	BENJAMIN	122d	1
		עדה	CONGREGATION	*417b	3
		סלע	CRAG	701a	1
		קרא	CALL	895c	3 a
		רמון	RIMMON	942a	1
		שלום	PEACE	1023b	6
21	14	חיה	LIVE	311c	1
		יבש	JABESH	386d	1
		כן	SO	485d	1 a
		מצא	FIND	593c	4
		מצא	FIND	*594d	1
21	15	נחם	BE SORRY	637a	1
		עשה	DO	794c	2 1f
		פרץ	BURSTING FORTH	829d	4
21	16	זקן	OLD	278d	2 b
		עדה	CONGREGATION	*417b	3
		יתר	BE LEFT OVER	451c	
		עשה	DO	793d	1 1a 3
		שמד	BE EXTERMINATED	1029b	1
21	17	ירשה	POSSESSION	440b	
		מחה	WIPE OUT	562b	2
		פליטה	ESCAPE	812c	2 b
21	18	ארר	CURSE	76d	
		יכל	BE ABLE	407d	1 d
		שבע	SWEAR	989a	1 a
21	19	ה	THE	209b	2 b
		מזרח	PLACE OF SUNRISE	280d	1

Ch	v.	Heb	Eng	Page	Sec
		חג	FESTIVAL-GATHER-ING	291a	1 a
		יום	YEAR	399d	6 c
		לבונה	LEBONAH	526d	
		נגב	SOUTH-COUNTRY	616b	2
		מסלה	HIGHWAY	700c	
		שלו	SHILOH	1017d	
21	20	ארב	LIE IN WAIT	70b	
		בנימין	BENJAMIN	122d	1
21	21	ארץ	EARTH	76a	2 c
		בנימין	BENJAMIN	122d	1 i
		בת	DAUGHTER	123b	1 c
		הלך	WALK	230d	1 1d 3a
		חול	WHIRL	297a	1
		מחלה	DANCING	298b	
		חטף	CATCH	310c	
		יצא	GO OUT	422d	1 a
		שלו	SHILOH	1017d	
21	22	אשם	OFFEND	79c	2
		חנן	SHOW FAVOR	336a	1 a
		לא	NOT	520d	
		לו	IF	530b	2
		עת	TIME	773c	1 a
		ריב	STRIVE	936d	4
21	23	בנימין	BENJAMIN	122d	1
		בנה	BUILD	124d	1 i
		גזל	TEAR AWAY	159d	
		הלך	WALK	233d	1 5b
		חול	WHIRL	297b	1
		ל	TO	516b	5 jb
		נשא	LIFT	671b	3 b
		מספר	NUMBER	709a	1 b
		ירבעל	JERUBBAAL	937c	
21	24	הלך	WALK	235d	1
		משפחה	CLAN	1046d	1 a
21	25	יום	DAY	400d	7 g
		ישר	STRAIGHT	449a	1
		מלך	KING	573a	1

RUTH

Ch	v.	Heb	Eng	Page	Sec
1	1	ביתלחם	BETHLEHEM	111d	1
		גור	SOJOURN	157d	1
		היה	BECOME	225c	2 a
		יום	DAY	400b	7 d2 b
		מואב	MOAB	555d	2 b
		שדה	FIELD	961d	2 d
		שפט	JUDGE	1047b	1 b
1	2	אלימלך	ELIMELECH	45b	
		אפרתי	EPHRATHITE	68d	2
		ביתלחם	BETHLEHEM	111d	1
		כליון	CHILION	479a	
		מואב	MOAB	555d	2 b
		מחלון	MAHLON	563a	
		נעמי	NAOMI	654a	
		שדה	FIELD	961d	2 d
1	3	אלימלך	ELIMELECH	45b	
		נעמי	NAOMI	654a	
		שאר	REMAIN	984b	2
1	4	כ	LIKE	453c	1 a
		מואבי	MOABITISH	556a	
		נשא	LIFT	671c	3 d
		ערפה	ORPAH	791c	
		רות	RUTH	946c	
1	5	גם	ALSO	169c	2
		ילד	CHILD	409b	A
		כליון	CHILION	479a	
		מחלון	MAHLON	563a	
		שאר	REMAIN	984b	2
1	6	כלה	DAUGHTER-IN-LAW	483c	1
		מואב	MOAB	555d	2 b
		פקד	ATTEND TO	823c	A 2
		שוב	TURN BACK	997a	2
1	7	דרך	WAY	202c	1
		כלה	DAUGHTER-IN-LAW	483c	1
1	8	אשה	WOMAN	61b	4
		הלך	WALK	234b	1 5f 3
		חסד	GOODNESS	339a	2 1a
		כלה	DAUGHTER-IN-LAW	483c	1
		נעמי	NAOMI	654a	
1	9	אשה	WOMAN	61b	4
		בכה	WEEP	113c	1
		מצא	FIND	592c	1 a
		מנוחה	REST	630a	2
		נשק	KISS	676b	
		נתן	GIVE	678d	1 e
		קול	VOICE	876d	1 a
1	10	כי	THAT	472a	1 b
		ל	TO	511c	1 gb
		עם	PEOPLE	766c	1
		שוב	TURN BACK	997b	3 a
1	11	בת	DAUGHTER	123a	1 c
		מעה	BELLY	589a	1
1	12	בת	DAUGHTER	123a	1 c
		הלך	WALK	234b	1 5f 3
		זקן	BE OLD	278c	
		יש	HAVE	441d	2 cb
		כי	THAT	473a	1 f
		לילה	NIGHT	539a	1
		מן	THAN	583a	6 d
		תקוה	HOPE	876b	1
1	13	אל	NOT	39b	A bb

Ch	v.	Heb	Eng	Page	Sec
		בת	DAUGHTER	123a	1 c
		גדל	GROW UP	152b	1 a
		היה	BECOME	226d	2 2h
		הם	THEY	242a	8 d
		יצא	GO OUT	424a	2 c
		ל	TO	511a	1
		לחן	THEREFORE	530a	
		מן	ON ACCOUNT OF	580b	2 f
		מרר	BE BITTER	600a	1
		עצב	SHUT ONESELF IN	723a	
		שבר	HOPE	960b	1
		לחן	THEREFORE	*1099a	
1	14	בכה	WEEP	113c	1
		דבק	CLING	179d	2 a
		חמות	HUSBAND:S MOTHER	327b	1
		נשק	KISS	676b	
		עד	STILL	729a	1 ab
		ערפה	ORPAH	791c	
		קול	VOICE	876d	1 a
		רות	RUTH	946c	
1	15	אלהים	GOD	44d	4 c
		יבמת	SISTER-IN-LAW	386a	
		עם	PEOPLE	766c	1
		שוב	TURN BACK	997b	3 a
1	16	אלהים	GOD	44d	4 c
		אשר	PARTICLE OF RE-LATION	82c	4 bg
		אשר	PARTICLE OF RE-LATION	82c	4 bg
		לון	LODGE	533c	1 a
		עזב	LEAVE	737a	1 a
		עם	PEOPLE	766c	1
		פגע	MEET	803c	4
		רות	RUTH	946d	1
		שוב	TURN BACK	996d	1
1	17	אשר	PARTICLE OF RE-LATION	82c	4 bg
		ה	THE	208b	1 ha
		יסף	ADD	415b	1
		כי	THAT	472a	1 c
		פרד	DIVIDE	825c	2
1	18	אמץ	BE STRONG	55b	1
		חדל	CEASE	293a	1
1	19	ביתלחם	BETHLEHEM	111d	1
		הום	MURMUR	223a	
		עיר	CITY	746c	1 h
		שנים	TWO	1041a	1 a
1	20	מרר	BE BITTER	600b	1
		מרא	MARA	600d	
		מר	BITTER	600d	2 b
		שדי	ALMIGHTY	995a	1
1	21	הלך	WALK	230b	1 1b
		מלא	FULL	571a	
		ענה	ANSWER	773a	3 a
		ריקם	EMPTILY	938b	1
		שדי	ALMIGHTY	995a	1
1	22	ה	THE	209c	3
		תחלה	BEGINNING	321b	
		כלה	DAUGHTER-IN-LAW	483c	1
		מואב	MOAB	555d	2 b
		מואבי	MOABITISH	556a	
		קציר	HARVESTING	894d	3
		רות	RUTH	946c	
		שערה	BARLEY	972d	1
		שוב	TURN BACK	997a	1
2	1	אלימלך	ELIMELECH	45b	
		בעז	BOAZ	126d	1
		גבור	STRONG	150b	2
		ידע	ACQUAINTANCE	394d	
		מודע	KINSMAN	396b	
		ל	TO	513c	5 cb a
		משפחה	CLAN	1046d	1 a
2	2	חן	FAVOR	336b	2 b1
		לקט	GLEAN	544d	3
		מואבי	MOABITISH	556a	
		מצא	FIND	592d	1 a
		רות	RUTH	946c	
		שדה	FIELD	961d	2 a
		שבלת	EAR OF GRAIN	987c	1
2	3	אלימלך	ELIMELECH	45b	
		בעז	BOAZ	126d	1
		הלך	WALK	233d	1 5b
		חלקה	PORTION OF GROUND	324c	1
		ל	TO	513d	5 cb g
		לקט	GLEAN	544d	3
		קצר	HARVEST	894c	
		קרה	ENCOUNTER	899c	1
		מקרה	ACCIDENT	900a	1
		משפחה	CLAN	1046d	1 a
2	4	בעז	BOAZ	126d	1
		ברך	BLESS	139a	2 a
		קצר	HARVEST	894c	
2	5	בעז	BOAZ	126d	1
		נערה	GIRL	655b	2
		נצב	STAND	662b	2
		קצר	HARVEST	894c	
2	6	ה	THE	209c	3
		מואב	MOAB	555d	2 b
		מואבי	MOABITISH	556a	
		נערה	GIRL	655b	2
		נצב	STAND	662b	2
		קצר	HARVEST	894c	
		שוב	TURN BACK	997a	1

RUTH

Ch	v.	Heb	Eng	Page	Sec
2	7	מאז	FROM THAT TIME	23b	B
		אסף	GATHER	62b	1c
		בקר	MORNING	133d	1d
		זה	THIS	261d	4i
		ישב	REMAIN	442d	2a
		לקט	GLEAN	544d	3
		מעט	A FEW	590a	1a
		עמד	STAND	764b	3e
		עמר	SHEAF	771c	
		עתה	NOW	774c	2f
		קצר	HARVEST	894c	
2	8	בעז	BOAZ	126d	1
		דבק	CLING	179d	1c
		כה	THUS	462b	2
		לקט	GLEAN	544d	2
		נערה	GIRL	655b	2
		עבר	PASS OVER	718a	5a
		רות	RUTH	946c	
2	9	אשר	PARTICLE OF RELATION	82c	4bg
		בלת	NOT	116d	4a
		הלך	WALK	231a	1d3 ga
		לא	NOT	520b	4ba
		לא	NOT	520b	4bb
		נגע	TOUCH	619b	3
		צמא	BE THIRSTY	854d	
		קצר	HARVEST	894b	
		קצר	HARVEST	894c	
		שאב	DRAW	980c	
		שתה	DRINK	1059b	1a
2	10	ארץ	EARTH	76b	3a
		חן	FAVOR	336b	2b1
		מצא	FIND	592d	1a
		נכר	REGARD	648a	1a
		נכרי	FOREIGN	648d	1b
		נפל	FALL	657c	3b
		שחה	BOW DOWN	1005b	1a
2	11	אם	MOTHER	51d	1
		בעז	BOAZ	126d	1
		הלך	WALK	230b	1 1c
		חמות	HUSBAND:S MOTHER	327b	
		מולדת		409d	1
		נגד	BE CONSPICUOUS	617a	
		עשה	DO	794a	1 1a 4
		שלשם	THREE DAYS AGO	1026b	
		תמול	YESTERDAY	1070a	2ab
2	12	אלהים	GOD	44c	4ba
		חסה	SEEK REFUGE	340b	
		כנף	WING	489d	1h
		מעם	FROM WITH	769a	D
		פעל	DOING	821c	1c
		משכרת	WAGES	969b	
		שלם	BE COMPLETE	1022c	5
		שלם	COMPLETE	1024a	1a
2	13	אדון	LORD	11b	3 1k
		אמה	MAID	51a	2
		דבר	SPEAK	181d	5
		חן	FAVOR	336b	2b1
		לב	HEART	525c	2 9a
		מצא	FIND	592d	1a
		נחם	CONSOLE ONESELF	637a	
		שפחה	MAID	1046c	2
		שפחה	MAID	1046c	1
2	14	אכל	EAT	37b	1
		אכל	FOOD	38a	
		בעז	BOAZ	127a	1
		בקר	MORNING	*133d	1d
		הלם	HITHER	240d	
		חמץ	VINEGAR	330a	
		טבל	DIP	371b	1
		ישב	SIT	442c	1a
		יתר	LEAVE OVER	451c	1a
		נגש	DRAW NEAR	620d	1
		פת	FRAGMENT	837d	
		צבט	REACH	840b	
		צד	SIDE	841a	
		קלי	PARCHED GRAIN	885d	
		קצר	HARVEST	894c	
2	15	בעז	BOAZ	127a	1
		גם	ALSO	169b	2
		כלם	HUMILIATE	484a	1
		לקט	GLEAN	544d	3
		עמר	SHEAF	771c	
2	16	גער	REBUKE	172a	1
		לקט	GLEAN	544d	3
		עזב	LEAVE	737a	1f
		צבתים	BUNDLES OF GRAIN	841a	
		שלל	DRAW OUT	1021c	
2	17	איפה	EPHAH	35b	1
		חבט	BEAT OFF	286a	2
		ך	LIKE	453c	1a
		לקט	GLEAN	544d	3
		לקט	GLEAN	544d	3
		שערה	BARLEY	972d	2
2	18	חמות	HUSBAND:S MOTHER	327b	
		יצא	BRING OUT	425a	4b
		יתר	LEAVE OVER	451c	1a
		לקט	GLEAN	544d	3
		מן	SINCE	583c	7c
		שבע	ABUNDANCE	960a	1
2	19	איפה	WHERE	33a	1
		אן	WHERE	33a	B
		בעז	BOAZ	127a	1
		ברך	BLESS	138d	2b
		חמות	HUSBAND:S MOTHER	327b	
		לקט	GLEAN	544d	3
		נכר	REGARD	648a	1
		עשה	DO	794b	1 1b
2	20	את	WITH	86a	1db
		ברך	BLESS	138d	2b
		גאל	ACT AS KINSMAN	145b	1
		חי	ALIVE	312a	1b
		חסד	GOODNESS	339a	1a
		כלה	DAUGHTER-IN-LAW	483c	1
		ל	TO	511a	1f
		מן	FROM	580d	8b
		עזב	LEAVE	737b	1g
		קרב	NEAR	898c	2c
2	21	אם	IF	50c	1cd
		אשר	PARTICLE OF RELATION	83a	7b
		גם	YEA	169d	6
		דבק	CLING	179d	1c
		כי	THAT	472a	1b
		כי	THAT	472b	1da
		כלה	FINISH	478a	1a
		מואבי	MOABITISH	556a	
		עד	UNTIL	725a	2 1ba
		עזב	LEAVE	737b	1j
		קציר	HARVESTING	894c	1
		רות	RUTH	946c	
2	22	אשר	THAT	83c	8ab
		טוב	PLEASANT	374c	5
		יצא	GO OUT	423a	2a
		כלה	DAUGHTER-IN-LAW	483c	1
		נערה	GIRL	655b	2
		פגע	MEET	803b	3
		רות	RUTH	946c	
2	23	בעז	BOAZ	127a	1
		דבק	CLING	179d	1c
		חמות	HUSBAND:S MOTHER	327b	
		חטה	WHEAT	334d	
		כלה	BE FINISHED	477c	1a
		לקט	GLEAN	544d	3
		נערה	GIRL	655b	2
		קציר	HARVESTING	894d	3
		קציר	HARVESTING	894d	3
		שערה	BARLEY	972d	1
3	1	בקש	SEEK	134d	1d
		חמות	HUSBAND:S MOTHER	327b	
		יטב	BE WELL	405c	3
		מנוח	CONDITION OF REST	629d	2
		מנוחה	REST	*630a	2
3	2	בעז	BOAZ	127a	1
		גרן	THRESHING-FLOOR	175b	
		הנה	BEHOLD	243d	
		זרה	SCATTER	279d	2
		מדעת	KINDRED	396b	
		לילה	NIGHT	539a	1
		נערה	GIRL	655b	2
		שערה	BARLEY	972d	1
3	3	גרן	THRESHING-FLOOR	175b	
		ידע	MAKE ONESELF KNOWN	394c	1c
		ירד	GO DOWN	432d	1c
		כלה	FINISH	478b	1c
		סוך	ANOINT	692a	1
		רחץ	WASH OFF	934c	2
		שום	TO PLACE	963b	1b
		שמלה	WRAPPER	971a	
3	4	ידע	KNOW	393d	1b
		מרגלות	PLACE OF FEET	920b	
3	5	ירד	GO DOWN	432d	1c
3	6	גרן	THRESHING-FLOOR	175b	
		חמות	HUSBAND:S MOTHER	327b	
3	7	בעז	BOAZ	127a	1
		יטב	BE GLAD	405c	1
		לב	HEART	525c	2 9a
		לט	SECRECY	532a	1
		ערמה	HEAP	790d	
		קצה	END	892b	2
		מרגלות	PLACE OF FEET	920b	
3	8	חצי	HALF	345d	2
		חרד	TREMBLE	353b	2
		לפת	TWIST	542b	
		מרגלות	PLACE OF FEET	920b	
3	9	אמה	MAID	51a	1
		גאל	ACT AS KINSMAN	145c	1
		ו	AND	254c	4
		כנף	EXTREMITY	489d	2a
		מי	WHO	566b	
		פרש	SPREAD OUT	831b	2
		רות	RUTH	946c	
		שפחה	MAID	*1046c	2
3	10	בחור	YOUNG MAN	104c	
		בת	DAUGHTER	123b	1f
		ברך	BLESS	138d	2b
		דל	POOR	195d	
		חסד	GOODNESS	338c	11
		יטב	MAKE GOOD	406a	4
		עשיר	RICH	799c	
3	11	אשה	WOMAN	61b	1
		בת	DAUGHTER	123b	1f
		חיל	STRENGTH	298d	2
		ירא	FEAR	431b	1a
		שער	GATE	1045a	2a
3	12	אמנם	VERILY	54a	
		גאל	ACT AS KINSMAN	145c	1
		יש	THERE IS	441d	2b
		כי	THAT	472d	1e
		כיאם	SURELY	475b	2c
		קרב	NEAR	898c	2c
3	13	בקר	MORNING	133d	1a
		גאל	ACT AS KINSMAN	145c	1a
		חי	ALIVE	311d	1a
		חפץ	DELIGHT IN	342d	1b
		טוב	PLEASANT	374c	5
		לין	LODGE	533c	1a
		לילה	NIGHT	539a	1
		שכב	LIE DOWN	1012a	1b
3	14	בקר	MORNING	133d	1b
		גרן	THRESHING-FLOOR	175b	
		טרם	NOT YET	382d	2
		ידע	BE MADE KNOWN	394c	1
		נכר	RECOGNIZE	648b	2
		קום	STAND	877c	1a
		מרגלות	PLACE OF FEET	920b	
		רע	FRIEND	946a	2
3	15	אחז	GRASP	28b	
		מטפחת	CLOAK	381c	
		יהב	GIVE	396c	1
		מדד	MEASURE	551a	2
		מדד	MEASURE	551a	
		על	UPON	753a	2 1aa
		שערה	BARLEY	972d	1
		שית	PUT	1011a	1
3	16	חמות	HUSBAND:S MOTHER	327b	
		מי	WHO	566b	
3	17	חמות	HUSBAND:S MOTHER	327b	
		ריקם	EMPTILY	938b	1
		שערה	BARLEY	972d	2
3	18	איך	HOW	32c	1
		דבר	WORD	183c	43
		כיאם	EXCEPT	474d	2a
		כלה	FINISH	478b	1e
		נפל	FALL	657d	5
		שקט	BE QUIET	1053a	2
4	1	אלמני	SOME ONE	48c	
		בעז	BOAZ	127a	1
		גאל	ACT AS KINSMAN	145c	1
		זן	OLD	*279a	2b
		ישב	SIT	442d	1b
		סור	TURN ASIDE	693c	1
		עלה	GO UP	748b	1c
		פלני	A CERTAIN ONE	811d	
		שער	GATE	1045a	2a
4	2	זקן	OLD	279a	2b
		ישב	SIT	442d	1b
4	3	אלימלך	ELIMELECH	45b	
		אשר	PARTICLE OF RELATION	83a	7b
		גאל	ACT AS KINSMAN	145c	1
		ה	THE	209c	3
		חלקה	PORTION OF GROUND	324c	1a
		מואב	MOAB	555d	2b
		מכר	SELL	569b	
		שוב	TURN BACK	997a	2
4	4	אזן	EAR	24b	3
		אמר	SAY	56b	1
		אמר	SAY	56b	2
		אנכי	I	59c	
		גאל	ACT AS KINSMAN	145c	1c
		זולה	EXCEPT	265d	1
		זקן	OLD	279a	2b
		ארץ	EARTH	*1083a	1
4	5	בעז	BOAZ	127a	1
		יד	HAND	391b	5g3
		מואבי	MOABITISH	556a	
		קום	STAND	879b	6g
		רות	RUTH	946c	
		שם	NAME	1028b	2c
4	6	גאל	ACT AS KINSMAN	145c	1
		גאל	ACT AS KINSMAN	145c	1c
		גאלה	REDEMPTION	145d	3
		שחת	GO TO RUIN	1008b	1
4	7	גאלה	REDEMPTION	145d	2
		תמורה	RECOMPENSE	558d	2
		נעל	SANDAL	653b	
		נתן	GIVE	678b	1a
		תעודה	TESTIMONY	730c	2
		על	UPON	754d	2 1fh
		קום	STAND	878c	2
		רע	FRIEND	946a	2
		שלף	DRAW OUT	1025c	1
4	8	בעז	BOAZ	127a	1
		גאל	ACT AS KINSMAN	145c	1
		נעל	SANDAL	653b	
		שלף	DRAW OUT	1025c	2
4	9	אלימלך	ELIMELECH	45b	
		בעז	BOAZ	127a	1
		זקן	OLD	279a	2b
		יד	HAND	391b	5g3
		כליון	CHILION	479a	
		מחלון	MAHLON	563a	
		עד	WITNESS	729d	2c

Ch	v.	Heb	Eng	Page	Sec
4	10	כרת	BE CUT OFF	504b	4
		מואבי	MOABITISH	556a	
		מחלון	MAHLON	563a	
		עד	WITNESS	729d	2 c
		מעם	FROM WITH	769a	
		קום	STAND	879b	6 g
		מקום	STANDING PLACE	880a	4
		רות	RUTH	946c	
		שם	NAME	1028b	2 c
		שם	NAME	1028b	2 c
4	11	אפרתה	EPHRATH	68d	2
		בית	HOUSE	109d	5 b
		בנה	BUILD	124d	2 a
		ה	THE	209c	3
		זן	OLD	*279a	2 b
		זקן	OLD	279a	2 b
		חיל	STRENGTH	298d	2
		ישב	SIT	*442c	1 a
		לאה	LEAH	521b	
		נתן	GIVE	681b	3 c
		עד	WITNESS	729d	2 c
		קרא	CALL	895c	3 c
		רחל	RACHEL	933a	
		ישראל	ISRAEL	975c	1
		שנים	TWO	1041a	1 a
		שער	GATE	1045a	2 c
4	12	זרע	SOWING	282d	4 c
		זרע	SOWING	283a	4 e
		יהודה	JUDAH	397b	1 1
		נערה	GIRL	655b	2
		פרץ	PEREZ	829d	1
		תמר	TAMAR	1071c	1 a
4	13	בעז	BOAZ	127a	1
		הריון	CONCEPTION	248a	
		נתן	GIVE	678d	1 d
		רות	RUTH	946c	
4	14	ברך	BLESS	138c	2 a
		גאל	ACT AS KINSMAN	145c	1
		ישב	SIT	442a	1 a
		קרא	CALL	896b	2 a
		שבת	CEASE	992a	5
4	15	אהב	LOVE	12d	1
		אשר	PARTICLE OF RELATION	82b	2 a
		הוא	HE, SHE, IT	215d	2 c
		טוב	PLEASANT	374c	6
		כול	SUSTAIN	465a	1
		סלה	DAUGHTER-IN-LAW	483c	1
		נפש	SOUL	661a	6 g
		שיבה	OLD AGE	966d	2
		שוב	TURN BACK	999b	2 b
4	16	אמן	CONFIRM	52d	3
		חיק	BOSOM	300d	2
		ילד	CHILD	409b	A
		שית	PUT	1011a	1
4	17	בן	SON	120c	1 f
		דוד	DAVID	188a	
		ילד	BE BORN	409a	
		ישי	JESSE	445a	
		עובד	OBED	714d	1
		קרא	CALL	896a	6 f
		שכן	NEIGHBOR	1015c	2
4	18	חצרון	HEZRON	348a	2 b
		ילד	BEGET	409a	1
		תולדות	GENERATIONS	410a	A
		פרץ	PEREZ	829d	1
4	19	חצרון	HEZRON	348a	2 b
		עמינדב	AMMINADAB	770b	
		רם	RAM	928a	1 a
4	20	נחשון	NAHSHON	638c	
		עמינדב	AMMINADAB	770b	1
		שלמון	SALMON	969c	
4	21	בעז	BOAZ	127a	1
		עובד	OBED	714d	1
		שלמון	SALMON	969c	
4	22	דוד	DAVID	188a	
		ישי	JESSE	445a	
		עובד	OBED	*714d	1
		שחת	CORRUPT	*1115a	

1 SAMUEL

Ch	v.	Heb	Eng	Page	Sec
1	1	אליאל	ELIEL	45a	E
		אליאב	ELIAB	45a	D
		אליהו	ELIHU	45b	B
		אפרתי	EPHRATHITE	68d	1
		היה	BE	226d	3 1
		הר	MOUNTAIN	251a	2 b
		מן	OUT OF	579c	2 cb
		נחת	NAHATH	639c	2
		צוף	ZUPH	847c	
		צופי	SUPHITE	847c	
		צפה	KEEP WATCH	859c	
		רמה	RAMA	928a	2
		רמתים	RAMATHAIM	928c	
		ירחם	JEROHAM	934a	1
		שם	NAME	1027d	2 a
		תוח	TOAH	1063c	
1	2	חנה	HANNAH	336d	
		ילד	CHILD	409b	B
		ל	TO	513b	5 ba
		פננה	PENINNAH	819d	
1	3	זבח	SLAUGHTER FOR SACRIFICE	257a	1 3
		זבח	SLAUGHTER FOR SACRIFICE	257a	1 2
		חפני	HOPHNI	342b	
		יום	YEAR	399d	6 c
		כהן	PRIEST	463b	4
		ל	TO	515b	5 hb b
		עלי	ELI	750a	
		פינחס	PHINEHAS	810a	2
		צבא	GOD OF WAR	839c	4 c
		שלו	SHILOH	1017d	
1	4	ה	THE	*207c	1 d
		היה	BECOME	225c	2 1a
		יום	DAY	400a	7 b
		יום	DAY	*400d	7 g
		מנה	PORTION	584b	
		פננה	PENINNAH	819d	
1	5	אהב	LOVE	12d	1
		אף	NOSE	60b	2
		אפס	NON-EXISTENCE	67b	2 cb
		בן	SON	*120a	1
		חנה	HANNAH	336d	
		מנה	PORTION	584b	
		סגר	SHUT	689a	1
		רחם	WOMB	933b	1
1	6	בן	SON	*120a	1
		בעד	BEHIND	126c	1 b
		גם	ALSO	169c	2
		כעס	BE ANGRY	495a	
		כעס	ANGER	495b	1
		סגר	SHUT	689a	1
		עבור	FOR THE SAKE OF	721a	1 b
		צרה	VEXER	865d	
		רחם	WOMB	933b	1
		רעם	THUNDER	947b	
1	7	ב	IN	90b	3 b
		בית	HOUSE	109b	1 ae 0
		בכה	WEEP	113b	1
		בן	SON	*120a	1
		די	SUFFICIENCY	191d	2 ca
		היכל	TEMPLE	*228b	2 a
		כעס	VEX	495a	
		עלה	GO UP	748b	1 d
		שנה	YEAR	1040b	
1	8	בכה	WEEP	113b	1
		בן	SON	*120a	1
		חנה	HANNAH	336d	
		טוב	PLEASANT	374c	6
		ל	TO	511a	1 e
		לבב	HEART	524b	2 9b
		מה	HOW	554a	4 b
		רעע	BE EVIL	949c	2
1	9	בן	SON	*120a	1
		ה	THE	207b	1 cb
		היכל	TEMPLE	*228b	2 a
		היכל	TEMPLE	228b	2 a
		מזוזה	DOOR-POST	265b	2 a
		חנה	HANNAH	336d	
		ישב	SIT	442b	1 a
		כהן	PRIEST	463b	4
		כסא	SEAT OF HONOR	490d	2
		עלי	ELI	750b	
		על	UPON	756a	2 6a
		קום	STAND	877d	1 a
		שלו	SHILOH	1017d	
1	10	אל	TO	41b	
		בכה	WEEP	113b	1
		בכה	WEEP	113c	2
		בן	SON	*120a	1
		מר	BITTER	600c	2 b
		על	UPON	757c	2 7c b
		פלל	INTERVENE	813b	3
1	11	איש	MAN	35d	
		אמה	MAID	51a	2
		בן	SON	*120a	1
		זכר	REMEMBER	270b	2 1 a
		זרע	SOWING	282d	4 d
		חיים	LIFE	313b	1
		מורה	RAZOR	559a	
		נדר	VOW	623d	
		נדר	VOW	624a	1
		נתן	GIVE	678d	1 d
		נתן	GIVE	679b	1 1
		עלה	GO UP	748d	6
		על	UPON	756a	2 7b
		על	UPON	758d	4 2a
		עני	AFFLICTION	777a	1
		צבא	GOD OF WAR	839c	4 c
		ראה	TO SEE	908a	8 a2
		שכח	FORGET	1013b	2 a
1	12	היה	COME TO PASS	225a	1 2a 2
		ו	AND	252b	1 b
		כי	WHEN	473a	2 a
		ל	TO	517c	7 bb
		עלי	ELI	750b	
		פלל	INTERVENE	813b	3
		פנה	FACE	817b	2 4b b
		רבה	BECOME MANY	915c	1 d1
		שמר	KEEP	1036d	1 d
1	13	אל	TO	41b	
		דבר	SPEAK	181a	3 b
		דבר	SPEAK	181d	5
		הוא	HE, SHE, IT	215d	2 a
		חנה	HANNAH	336d	
		חשב	THINK	363a	1 1
		לב	HEART	525c	2 7
		על	UPON	757c	2 7c b
		קול	VOICE	876d	1 a
		רק	ONLY	956b	2 a
		שפה	SPEECH	973d	1 a2
		שכר	DRUNKEN	1016c	
		שמע	HEAR	1034b	1
1	14	יין	WINE	406c	C
		מתי	WHEN	607d	C
		סור	TURN ASIDE	694b	1
		שכר	BE DRUNK	1016b	
1	15	אדון	LORD	11b	3 1h
		חנה	HANNAH	336d	
		יין	WINE	406c	C
		לא	NOT	519a	1 ad b
		קשה	SEVERE	904c	2 a
		רוח	BREATH	925c	5 b
		שכר	INTOXICATING DRINK	1016b	
1	16	שפך	POUR OUT	1049d	2 b
		אמה	MAID	51a	2
		בליעל	WORTHLESSNESS	116a	1
		בת	DAUGHTER	123d	5
		כעס	ANGER	495b	1
		מן	ON ACCOUNT OF	580c	2 f
		נתן	GIVE	681b	3 c
		פנה	FACE	817d	2 4f
		רב	MULTITUDE	914a	2
		שיח	COMPLAINT	967a	3
		שפחה	MAID	*1046c	2
1	17	אלהים	GOD	44c	4 ba
		הלך	WALK	231d	1 d5 tc
		נתן	GIVE	678d	1 e
		מעם	FROM WITH	769a	A
		שאלה	REQUEST	982c	2
1	18	אמה	MAID	51a	2
		דרך	JOURNEY	203a	2
		הלך	WALK	231b	1 d3 gd
		חן	FAVOR	336b	2 b1
		לשכה	ROOM	545d	1 a
		מצא	FIND	592d	1 a
		פנה	FACE	815d	1 1a
		שפחה	MAID	1046c	2
1	19	בקר	MORNING	134b	1 h
		זכר	REMEMBER	270b	2 1 a
		חנה	HANNAH	336d	
		ידע	KNOW	394b	3
		רמה	RAMA	928a	2
		שוב	TURN BACK	997b	3 a
1	20	היה	COME TO PASS	224c	2 a1 ad
		הרה	CONCEIVE	247d	1
		חנה	HANNAH	336d	
		גת	GATH	387d	
		ל	TO	517a	6 a
		תקופה	COMING ROUND	880d	
		שמואל	SAMUEL	1028d	1
1	21	זבח	SACRIFICE	257c	2 3
		יום	YEAR	399d	6 c
		מטר	RAIN	564d	
		נדר	VOW	624a	1
		שמואל	SAMUEL	1028d	1
1	22	חנה	HANNAH	336d	
		ישב	REMAIN	442d	2 a
		נער	YOUTH	654d	1 a
		עד	UNTIL	725a	2 1b b
		עולם	LONG DURATION	762a	2 a
		פנה	FACE	816d	2 2a
		קשת	BOW	905d	
		ראה	TO SEE	908b	1 b
1	23	דבר	WORD	182d	1 2b
		טוב	PLEASANT	374a	2 f
		ינק	NURSE	413c	
		ישב	REMAIN	442d	2 a
		קום	STAND	879a	6 f
1	24	איפה	EPHAH	35b	2
		ב	IN	89c	3 1b
		בית	HOUSE	109b	1 ae 0
		בת	DAUGHTER	123b	1 i
		יין	WINE	406c	D
		נבל	SKIN-BOTTLE	614b	1
		נער	YOUTH	654d	1
		פר	YOUNG BULL	830d	2 a
		קמח	FLOUR	887d	
		שלו	SHILOH	1017d	
		שלש	THREE	*1025d	1 a
		שלש	DO A THIRD TIME	1026a	
1	25	נער	YOUTH	654d	1 b
		פר	YOUNG BULL	830d	2 a
		שחט	SLAUGHTER	1006a	2
1	26	אדון	LORD	11b	3 1h
		אל	TO	41b	
		בי	I PRAY	106c	
		זה	THIS	261d	6 a
		חי	ALIVE	312a	1 b
		נפש	SOUL	659c	2
		נצב	STAND	662a	1 a
		עם	WITH	768a	2
		פלל	INTERVENE	813b	3
		שמואל	SAMUEL	1028d	1
1	27	אל	TO	40b	6
		נער	YOUTH	654d	1 b
		נתן	GIVE	678d	1 e
		פלל	INTERVENE	813b	3
		שאלה	REQUEST	982c	2
1	28	גם	ALSO	169c	2
		היה	BE	226d	3 1
		שאל	ASK	981d	1 b
		שחה	BOW DOWN	1005c	1 a

Ch	v.	Heb	Eng	Page	Sec
2	1	חנה	HANNAH	336d	
		ישועה	DELIVERANCE	447b	3
		לב	HEART	525c	2 9a
		עלץ	REJOICE	763b	
		פה	MOUTH	804d	1 b
		פלל	INTERVENE	813b	4
		קרן	HORN	902a	2
		רום	BE HIGH	927a	2 b
		רחב	BE LARGE	931c	
		שמח	REJOICE	970b	2 a
2	2	בלת	EXCEPT	116c	2
		קדוש	HOLY	872c	1 a
2	3	אל	GOD	42c	6 c
		גבה	HIGH	147b	3
		דבר	SPEAK	181a	2
		דעה	KNOWLEDGE	395c	
		יצא	GO OUT	423c	1 g
		ל	TO	514a	5 e
		לא	NOT	520c	
		עלילה	WANTONNESS	760a	2 a
		עתק	FORWARD	801b	
		רבה	BECOME MANY	915d	1 d2
		תכן	ESTIMATE	1067b	1
2	4	אזר	GIRD	25a	
		גבור	STRONG	150b	2
		חיל	STRENGTH	298c	1 a
		חת	SHATTERED	369c	1
		כשל	BE FEEBLE	505d	2
		קשת	BOW	906c	1 e
2	5	אמל	BE WEAK	51b	
		חדל	CEASE	293a	1
		עד	AS FAR AS	724d	1 3
		עקר	BARREN	785d	
		רב	MUCH	913b	1 d
		רעב	HUNGRY	944c	
		רעב	HUNGRY	944c	
		שבע	SATISFIED	960a	1 a
		שכר	HIRE	969a	
		שבע	SEVEN	988a	1 b
2	6	חיה	LIVE	311c	3 a
		חתי	HITTITE	*367a	2 b
		ירד	BRING DOWN	434a	1 d
		מות	DIE	560b	2
		שאול	SHEOL	982d	1
2	7	אף	ALSO	64d	1
		ירש	IMPOVERISH	440a	3
		עשר	BE RICH	799b	1
		רום	BE HIGH	927b	2 c
		שפל	BECOME LOW	1050b	1
2	8	אביון	NEEDY	2d	
		אפוד	EPHOD	65c	1 a
		ארץ	EARTH	76a	1 b
		דל	POOR	195d	
		תבל	WORLD	385d	1
		ישב	CAUSE TO SIT	443d	3 a
		כבוד	HONOR	458c	2 b
		מן	FROM	578a	1 a
		נדיב	NOBLE	622a	2
		נחל	TAKE AS A POSSES-SION	635d	1 b
		מצוק	PILLAR	748b	
		עפר	DRY EARTH	780a	2 e
		קום	STAND	878d	1 a
		רום	BE HIGH	927c	1 a2
		שית	PUT	1011a	1
		אשפת	REFUSE-HEAP	1046b	
2	9	גבר	BE STRONG	149d	2 a
		דמם	BE SILENT	199a	
		חשך	DARKNESS	365a	1
		כח	STRENGTH	470d	1 d
		רגל	FOOT	919d	1 a
		רשע	WICKED	957c	3
		שמר	KEEP	1037a	4 a
2	10	אפס	END	67a	1
		דין	JUDGE	192b	4
		חתת	BE SHATTERED	369b	4
		מלך	KING	573a	1
		מלך	KING	573b	2
		משיח	ANOINTED	603c	1
		עז	STRENGTH	739a	2 b
		קרן	HORN	902a	2
		רום	BE HIGH	927c	1 f
		ריב	STRIVE	936d	
		רעם	THUNDER	947b	
		שמים	HEAVENS	1030a	2 a
2	11	היה	BE	227c	3 5a
		כהן	PRIEST	463b	1
		על	UPON	757b	2 7c ab
		פנה	FACE	816c	2 2a
		רמה	RAMA	928a	2
		שרת	SERVE	1058b	2 a
		שרת	SERVE	*1058b	2 a
2	12	בליעל	WORTHLESSNESS	116a	1
		ידע	KNOW	394a	1
2	13	את	WITH	86a	1 da
		את	WITH	86d	4 b
		בשר	FLESH	142c	1 a
		בשל	BOIL	143a	1
		ה	THE	207c	1 d
		זבח	SACRIFICE	257c	1 1
		מזלג	THREE PRONGED FORK	272c	
		כהן	PRIEST	463b	4
		כל	ALL	482b	1 eb
		שן	TOOTH	1042a	1 c
		משפט	JUDGEMNT	1049a	6 b
2	14	דוד	POT	188b	A
		מזלג	THREE PRONGED FORK	272c	
		כהן	PRIEST	463b	4
		כיור	POT	468c	1
		נכה	SMITE	645d	1 d
		פרור	POT	807d	
		קלחת	CALDRON	886a	
		שלו	SHILOH	1017d	
		שם	THERE	1027b	2
2	15	בשר	FLESH	142c	1
		בשל	BOIL	143b	
		חי	ALIVE	312b	1 c
		חלב	FAT	316d	2 b
		טרם	NOT YET	382c	2
		כהן	PRIEST	463b	4
		כיאם	BUT	475a	2 b
		צלה	ROAST FLESH	852a	
		קטר	MAKE SACRIFICES SMOKE	*882d	
		קטר	MAKE SACRIFICES SMOKE	883a	1 a
2	16	אוה	DESIRE	16a	
		חזקה	STRENGTH	306a	1
		יום	DAY	400d	7 h
		כאשר	AS	455b	2
		כי	THAT	472a	1
		כי	BUT	474c	3 e
		לא	NOT	519a	1 ad b
		לקח	TAKE	543d	8
		נפש	SOUL	660d	6 a
		עתה	NOW	774a	1 a
		קטר	MAKE SACRIFICES SMOKE	882d	
		קטר	MAKE SACRIFICES SMOKE	883a	1 a
2	17	חטאת	SIN	308c	1 b
		מנחה	OFFERING	585a	3
		נאץ	CONTEMN	611a	
		נער	YOUTH	655a	1 c
		פנה	FACE	816c	2 2a
2	18	בד	WHITE LINEN	94b	
		חגר	GIRD	291d	1
		פנה	FACE	816c	2 2a
		שרת	SERVE	1058b	2 a
2	19	אם	MOTHER	51d	1
		זבח	SACRIFICE	257c	2 3
		יום	YEAR	399d	6 c
		יום	YEAR	399d	6 c
		מעיל	ROBE	591c	1
		עלה	GO UP	749c	4
		עשה	DO	794c	2 1c
		קטן	SMALL	882b	1 b
2	20	ברך	BLESS	139a	3
		הלך	WALK	231b	1 d3 gd
		זרע	SOWING	282d	4 d
		זרע	SOWING	283a	4 e
		מן	OUT OF	579c	2 ca
		מקום	STANDING PLACE	879d	2 b1
		שום	TO PLACE	964d	5 b
		שאל	ASK	981c	1 a
		שאלה	REQUEST	982c	2
		תחת	INSTEAD	1066a	2 2b b
2	21	גדל	GROW UP	152b	1 a
		הרה	CONCEIVE	247d	1
		זרע	SOWING	*282d	4 d
		חנה	HANNAH	336d	
		עם	WITH	768b	3 a
2	22	אהל	TENT	14b	3
		היכל	TEMPLE	*228b	2 a
		ו	AND	252b	1 b
		זקן	BE OLD	278b	
		מועד	TENT OF MEETING	418a	5
		פתח	OPENING	835d	
		צבא	SERVE	838d	2
		שכב	LIE DOWN	1012b	3
2	23	אשר	THAT	83c	8 c
		את	WITH	86d	4 a
		דבר	WORD	184a	4 7
		רע	EVIL	948c	0 d
2	24	טוב	PLEASANT	373d	2 d
		עבר	PASS OVER	719a	4
		עם	PEOPLE	766c	1
		שמענה	REPORT	1035b	1
2	25	אלהים	GOD	43b	1 a
		חטא	MISS A GOAL OR WAY	306d	2 a
		חטא	MISS A GOAL OR WAY	307a	2 b
		חפץ	DELIGHT IN	343a	2 b
		ל	TO	515c	5 hc
		מות	DIE	560b	2
		מי	WHO	566d	F c
		פלל	INTERVENE	813a	
		פלל	INTERVENE	813b	1
		קול	VOICE	877b	3 a1
2	26	גדל	BECOMING GREAT	152d	
		גם	ALSO	169b	1
		הלך	WALK	233c	1 4d
		טוב	PLEASANT	373d	2 c
		נצח	EVERLASTINGNESS	664b	4
		עם	WITH	768a	4 b
2	27	אלהים	GOD	44a	3 b
		ה	INTERROG PART	210a	1 c
		פרעה	PHARAOH	829a	
2	28	אפוד	EPHOD	65c	1 b
		אפוד	EPHOD	65c	2 a
		אשה	OFFERING MADE BY FIRE	78a	
		בחר	CHOOSE	104a	3 a
		מזבח	ALTAR	259a	1
		כהן	PRIEST	463c	4
		ל	TO	512c	4 b
		נשא	LIFT	671a	2 a
		עלה	GO UP	750a	8
		על	UPON	756d	2 7b
		פנה	FACE	817a	2 4ab b
		קטרת	SMOKE	882d	
		קטר	MAKE SACRIFICES SMOKE	883a	1 a
2	29	בעט	KICK	127a	
		ברא	BE FAT	135d	
		זבח	SACRIFICE	257c	1 1
		כבד	MAKE HONORABLE	457d	2
		מן	THAN	582c	6 a
		מנחה	OFFERING	585a	3
		מנחה	OFFERING	585b	3
		מעון	REFUGE	733a	3
		ראשית	BEGINNING	912b	2
2	30	בזה	DESPISE	102c	
		הלך	WALK	236b	2
		חלילה	FAR BE IT	321a	
		כבד	MAKE HONORABLE	457d	2 a
		כבד	MAKE HONORABLE	457d	2 c
		כן	SO	486d	3 d
		עולם	LONG DURATION	762b	2 b3
		קלל	BE SLIGHT	886c	3
2	31	גדע	HEW OFF	154b	
		הנה	BEHOLD	244b	B b
		זקן	OLD	278c	2 a
		זרוע	ARM	284a	2 a
		יום	DAY	400a	7 f
		מן	FROM	583b	7 ba
2	32	אשר	PARTICLE OF RE-LATION	82d	4 c
		זקן	OLD	278c	2 a
		יום	DAY	400c	7 f
		יטב	DO GOOD TO	405d	2 a
		נבט	LOOK	613d	2
		מעון	REFUGE	733a	3
		צר	STRAITS	865b	
2	33	אדב	GRIEVE	9a	
		דוב	PINE AWAY	187b	
		חרב	SWORD	352d	1 f
		כלה	FINISH	478c	2 b
		כרת	CUT OFF	504c	2 c
		ל	TO	512c	5 aa
		מעם	FROM WITH	*769a	A
		תרבית	INCREASE	916b	
		מרבית	INCREASE	916b	1 a
2	34	אות	SIGN	16d	2
		אל	TO	40b	4
		זה	THIS	261b	3
		חפני	HOPHNI	342b	
		פינחם	PHINEHAS	810a	2
2	35	אמן	CONFIRM	52d	3
		אמן	CONFIRM	53a	5
		בית	HOUSE	109d	5 b
		בנה	BUILD	124d	2 a
		הלך	WALK	236b	2
		יום	DAY	400c	7 f
		כהן	PRIEST	463c	4
		לבב	HEART	523c	2 2
		משיח	ANOINTED	603c	1
		נפש	SOUL	661b	
		פנה	FACE	817a	2 4ad d
		קום	STAND	879a	3
2	36	אגורה	PAYMENT	8d	
		היה	COME TO PASS	225a	1 2b ag
		כהנה	PRIESTHOOD	464d	
		כבר	ROUND	503b	2
		ל	TO	515a	5 ha
		לחם	FOOD	537a	1
		לחם	FOOD	537a	1 a
		ספח	JOIN	705b	
		פת	FRAGMENT	837d	
3	1	חזון	VISION	303a	3
		יום	DAY	400d	7 g
		יקר	RARE	430a	2
		פנה	FACE	817a	2 4aa a
		פרץ	BREAK THROUGH	829c	
		שרת	SERVE	1058b	2 a
3	2	חלל	POLLUTE	320d	2
		יום	DAY	400c	7 g
		יכל	BE ABLE	407c	1 a
		כהה	DIM	462d	
		מקום	STANDING PLACE	880a	4
		ראה	TO SEE	907b	4
		שכב	LIE DOWN	1012a	1 b
3	3	ארון	CHEST	75c	3 d
		דלת	DOOR	*195a	1
		היכל	TEMPLE	228b	2 a
		טרם	NOT YET	382c	1
		כבה	BE QUENCHED	459c	
		נר	LAMP	632d	
		שכב	LIE DOWN	1012a	1 b
3	4	הנה	BEHOLD	244a	A
		קרא	CALL	895a	1 b
3	5	הנה	BEHOLD	244a	A
		קרא	CALL	895c	5 a
		קרא	CALL	895d	5 d
		רוץ	RUN	930b	1

Ch	v.	Heb	Eng	Page	Sec
		שוב	TURN BACK	998b	8
		שכב	LIE DOWN	1012a	1 b
3	6	בן	SON	120b	1 c
		הנה	BEHOLD	244a	A
		יסף	DO AGAIN	415c	2 a
		קום	STAND	877c	1 a
		קרא	CALL	895a	1 b
		קרא	CALL	895c	5 a
		קרא	CALL	896a	5 d
		שוב	TURN BACK	998b	8
3	7	דבר	WORD	182d	1 2a
		טרם	NOT YET	382c	1
		ידע	KNOW	394a	2
3	8	בין	DISCERN	106d	2 c
		הנה	BEHOLD	244a	A
		יסף	DO AGAIN	415c	2 c
		קום	STAND	877c	1 a
		קרא	CALL	895a	1 b
		קרא	CALL	895c	5 a
		שלישי	THIRD	1026b	
3	9	היה	COME TO PASS	225b	1 2b d
		עבד	SLAVE	714c	6
		מקום	STANDING PLACE	880a	4
3	10	יצב	STATION ONESELF	426b	B
		עבד	SLAVE	714c	6
		פעם	OCCURRENCE	822a	3 b
3	11	קרא	CALL	895a	1 b
		אזן	EAR	24a	2 a
		הנה	BEHOLD	244b	B b
		צלל	TINGLE	852d	
		צלל	TINGLE	852d	
		שמע	HEAR	1033d	1 d1
3	12	דבר	SPEAK	181a	3 b
		חלל	POLLUTE	320d	2
		יום	DAY	400d	7 g
		כלה	FINISH	478b	1 d
3	13	אני	I	59a	
		ו	AND	252b	1 b
		כהה	REBUKE	462d	
		עון	INIQUITY	731a	1 b
		קלל	BE SLIGHT	886d	1
		שפט	JUDGE	1047d	3 c1
3	14	אם	IF	50b	1 b2
		זבח	SACRIFICE	257c	1 1
		כן	SO	*487a	3 da
		מנחה	OFFERING	585b	3
		עון	INIQUITY	731a	1 c3
3	15	בקר	MORNING	133d	1 a
		דלת	DOOR	195a	1
		היכל	TEMPLE	*228b	2 a
		היכל	TEMPLE	*228b	2 a
		ירא	FEAR	431b	1 d
		פתח	OPEN	835a	
		מראה	VISION	909b	
		שכב	LIE DOWN	1012a	1 b
3	16	בן	SON	120b	1 c
		הנה	BEHOLD	244a	A
		קרא	CALL	895d	5 c
3	17	אם	IF	50b	1 b2
		יסף	ADD	415b	1
		כה	THUS	462b	1 b
		כחד	HIDE	470b	
3	18	עשה	DO	793d	1 1a 2
		דבר	WORD	183b	3 2
		טוב	PLEASANT	374a	2 f
		כחד	HIDE	470b	
3	19	נגד	BE CONSPICUOUS	616d	1
		גדל	GROW UP	152b	1 a
		היה	BE	227b	3 4d a
		מן	FROM	581a	3 bc
		נפל	FALL	658b	4
3	20	אמן	CONFIRM	52d	3
		בארשבע	BEERSHEBA	92a	
		בארשבע	BEERSHEBA	92a	
		דן	DAN	193a	3
		מן	FROM	581d	5 a
		נביא	PROPHET	611c	1
3	21	יסף	DO AGAIN	415c	2 a
		ראה	TO SEE	908b	1 a
		שלו	SHILOH	1017d	
		שלו	SHILOH	1017d	
4	1	אבן	STONE	7a	9
		אפק	APHEK	68a	4
		היה	BECOME	225d	2 1b
		חנה	DECLINE	333c	2 c2
		חנה	DECLINE	333c	2 c2
		חנה	DECLINE	333c	2 c2
		על	UPON	756a	2 6a
		פלשתי	PHILISTINE	814c	
		קרא	ENCOUNTER	897a	1
		אפק	ADDENDA ET COR-RIGENDA	1120c	
4	2	מלחמה	WAR	536c	
		נגף	STRIKE	620a	
		נטש	PERMIT	644a	3
		נכה	SMITE	646c	4
		ערך	ARRANGE	789c	1 d
		מערכה	ROW	790a	1 a
		ארבע	FOUR	917a	1 c1
		שדה	FIELD	961c	1 f
4	3	ברית	COVENANT	136d	2 2c
		זקן	OLD	278d	2 b
		מחנה	ENCAMPMENT	334b	2 b
		ישע	DELIVER	446c	1 a
		כף	POWER	496d	2
		נגף	STRIKE	619d	

Ch	v.	Heb	Eng	Page	Sec
		קרב	INWARD PART	8990	1 f1
		שלו	SHILOH	1017d	
4	4	ארון	CHEST	75c	3 f
		ארון	CHEST	75c	3 f
		ברית	COVENANT	136d	2 2c
		חפני	HOPHNI	342b	
		ישב	SIT	442c	1 a
		כרוב	CHERUB	500d	3
		פינחס	PHINEHAS	810a	2
		צבא	GOD OF WAR	839c	4 c
		שלו	SHILOH	1017d	
4	5	ברית	COVENANT	136d	2 2c
		הום	MURMUR	223a	
		מחנה	ENCAMPMENT	334b	2 b
		רוע	RAISE A SHOUT	929d	5
		תרועה	SHOUT OF WAR	930a	3
		שכב	LIE DOWN	1012a	1 b
4	6	בוא	COME	98b	2
		מחנה	ENCAMPMENT	334b	2 b
		עברי	HEBREW	720b	2 a
		קול	VOICE	876d	1
		תרועה	SHOUT OF WAR	930a	3
4	7	אוי	WOE	17a	
		זה	THIS	262a	6 d
		מחנה	ENCAMPMENT	334b	2 b
		ירא	FEAR	431a	1 a
		פלשתי	PHILISTINE	814c	
		שלשם	THREE DAYS AGO	1026b	
		תמול	YESTERDAY	1070a	2 ab
4	8	אדיר	MAJESTIC	12b	1
		אוי	WOE	17a	
		אלהים	GOD	43c	1 d
		אלהים	GOD	44a	3 b
		דבר	PESTILENCE	184a	1
		הם	THEY	241c	4 bg
		מי	WHO	566d	F c
		נכה	SMITE	646c	4 a
		מכה	SLAUGHTER	647c	4
4	9	איש	MAN	35d	4
		היה	BECOME	226b	2 2e
		היה	BECOME	*226c	2 2f
		חזק	BE FIRM	305b	2
		עבד	WORK	713a	3
		עברי	HEBREW	720b	2 a
4	10	ל	TO	511b	1 ga
		נגף	STRIKE	620a	
		נום	FLEE	630d	1
		מכה	SLAUGHTER	647a	2
		נפל	FALL	657a	2 a
		רגלי	ON FOOT	920b	
4	11	ארון	CHEST	75c	3 d
		חפני	HOPHNI	342b	
		לקח	TAKE	544a	1
		פינחס	PHINEHAS	810a	2
4	12	אדמה	EARTH	9d	3
		בוא	COME	98b	2
		בנימין	BENJAMIN	122d	1
		מד	GARMENT	551c	3
		מערכה	ROW	790a	1 a
		קרע	TEAR	902c	1 a1
		רוץ	RUN	930b	1
		שלו	SHILOH	1017d	
4	13	ארון	CHEST	75c	3 d
		דרך	WAY	202c	1
		זעק	CRY	277b	2 d
		חרד	TREMBLING	353d	
		יד	HAND	390b	3 a
		ישב	SIT	442b	1 a
		כסא	SEAT OF HONOR	490d	2
		עיר	CITY	746c	1 h
		על	UPON	754b	2 1f b
		צפה	KEEP WATCH	859c	
4	14	שער	GATE	1044d	1 a
		המון	SOUND	242c	1
		מהר	HASTEN	555a	2
		צעקה	CRY	858d	2
		קול	VOICE	876d	1 a
		קול	VOICE	877b	2 i
		בן	SON	121d	9 a
4	15	עין	EYE	744b	1 i
		קום	STAND	878c	7 j
		ראה	TO SEE	907b	1 a
		שמנה	EIGHT	1033a	3 c
		תשעים	NINETY	1077d	
4	16	בן	SON	120b	1 c
		דבר	WORD	183c	4 3
		היה	FALL OUT	224b	1 1a
		נום	FLEE	630d	1
		מערכה	ROW	790a	1 a
4	17	בשר	BEAR TIDINGS	142b	2
		גדול	GREAT	153a	2
		היה	COME TO PASS	224b	1 1b
		חפני	HOPHNI	342b	
		לקח	TAKE	544a	1
		מגפה	SLAUGHTER	620a	2
		נום	FLEE	630d	1
		פינחם	PHINEHAS	810a	2
4	18	אחרית	BACKWARDS	30d	
		בעד	ABOUT	126c	1 b
		זכר	REMEMBER	271a	3 b
		זקן	BE OLD	278b	
		יד	HAND	390b	3 b
		כבד	HEAVY	458a	1 a
		כסא	SEAT OF HONOR	490d	2
		נפל	FALL	656d	1
		מפרקת	NECK	830b	

Ch	v.	Heb	Eng	Page	Sec
		ארבעים	FORTY	917b	1 a
		ארבעים	FORTY	917c	1 a
		שבר	BREAK	990d	
		שער	GATE	1044d	1 a
		שפט	JUDGE	1047b	1 b
4	19	אל	TO	40c	6
		הפך	TURN	245d	1 a
		ו	AND	252b	1 b
		חם	HUSBAND'S FA-THER	327b	
		כלה	DAUGHTER-IN-LAW	483c	1
		כרע	BOW DOWN	502c	4
		לקח	TAKE	544a	1
		פינחם	PHINEHAS	810a	2
		ציר	PANG	852a	
		שמועה	REPORT	1035b	
4	20	ירא	FEAR	431a	1 a
		לב	HEART	524d	2 3c
		נצב	STAND	662a	1 b
		על	UPON	756b	2 6c
		ענה	ANSWER	772d	1
		שית	PUT	1011b	2 b
4	21	איכבוד	ICHABOD	33b	
		חם	HUSBAND'S FA-THER	327b	
		כבד	GLORY	458d	2 c1
		לקח	TAKE	544a	1
		נער	YOUTH	654d	1 a
		קרא	CALL	896a	6 e1
4	22	כבד	GLORY	458d	2 c1
		לקח	TAKE	544a	1
5	1	אבן	STONE	7a	9
		אשדוד	AHSDOD	78c	
		לקח	TAKE	543d	8
5	2	אצל	BESIDE	69b	A
		דגון	DAGON	186a	
		דגון	DAGON	186a	
		יצג	SET	426c	
5	3	אשדודי	ASHDODITE	78c	
		דגון	DAGON	186a	
		יד	HAND	390d	1 e2
		מחרת	THE MORROW	564a	1
		נפל	LIE	657d	7
		מקום	STANDING PLACE	879d	2 a
		שוב	TURN BACK	999a	8
5	4	אל	TO	40c	8
		ארץ	EARTH	76b	3 a
		בקר	MORNING	134b	1 h
		בקר	MORNING	134c	2
		דגון	DAGON	186a	
		יד	HAND	389a	1 b
		כף	HOLLOW OF THE HAND	496b	1 a
		כרת	CUT OFF	503d	1 a
		מחרת	THE MORROW	564a	1
		נפל	LIE	657d	7
		מפתן	THRESHOLD	837b	
		ראש	HEAD	910d	1 a
		שאר	REMAIN	984a	1
5	5	אשדוד	AHSDOD	78b	
		בית	HOUSE	109b	1 ae 0
		דגון	DAGON	186a	
		דגון	DAGON	186a	
		דלג	LEAP	194c	
		דרך	TREAD	202a	2
		יום	DAY	401b	7 1
		כהן	PRIEST	463a	1
		כן	SO	487b	3 f
		מפתן	THRESHOLD	837b	
5	6	אשדוד	AHSDOD	78b	
		אשדודי	ASHDODITE	78c	
		גבול	BOUNDARY	148a	2 d
		מחור	TUMORS	377d	
		יד	HAND	390a	1 e2
		כבד	BE HEAVY	457b	1
		נכה	SMITE	646c	4 a
		נכה	SMITE	646c	4 a
		עפל	HEMORRHOID	779b	
		שמם	BE DESOLATED	1031b	1
5	7	אלהים	GOD	43c	2 a
		ארון	CHEST	75c	3 e
		אשדוד	AHSDOD	78c	
		דגון	DAGON	186a	
		ו	AND	252b	1 b
		יד	HAND	390a	1 e2
		קשה	BE SEVERE	904b	2
5	8	אסף	GATHER	62b	1 a
		גת	GATH	387d	
		סבב	TURNABOUT	685d	1 a
		סבב	TURN ABOUT	686c	1 d
		סרן	TYRANT	710d	
5	9	אחר	AFTER THAT	30b	3
		ב	IN	89b	2 4a
		גדול	GREAT	153b	7
		מהומה	TUMULT	223a	
		היה	BECOME	225c	2 1b
		מחור	TUMORS	377d	
		יד	HAND	390a	1 e2
		ל	TO	512d	5 a
		מן	FROM	581d	5 b
		נכה	SMITE	646c	4 a
		סבב	TURN ABOUT	686c	1 d
		עפל	HEMORRHOID	779b	
		קמן	SMALL	882b	1 a
		שתר	BURST	979c	

Ch	v.	Heb	Eng	Page	Sec
5	10	זעק	CRY	277b	2 d
		מות	DIE	560b	2
		סבב	TURN ABOUT	686c	1 d
		עקרון	EKRON	785d	
		עקרוני	EKRONITE	785d	
		שלח	SEND	1019a	1 e
5	11	אלהים	GOD	44a	3 b
		אסף	GATHER	62b	1 a
		מהומה	TUMULT	223a	
		יד	HAND	390a	1 e2
		כבד	BE HEAVY	457b	1
		מות	DIE	560b	2
		מקום	STANDING PLACE	879d	2 a
		שוב	TURN BACK	998b	7 b
		שלח	SEND	1019a	3
5	12	טחור	TUMORS	377d	
		מות	DIE	560a	2 b
		נכה	SMITE	646c	6
		עיר	CITY	746c	1 h
		עלה	GO UP	749a	8
		עפל	HEMORRHOID	779b	
		שועה	CRY FOR HELP	1003a	
6	1	היה	BE	226d	3 2
		חדש	NEW MOON	294c	2 a
		פלשתי	PHILISTINE	814c	
6	2	ידע	MAKE KNOWN	395a	
		כהן	PRIEST	463a	2
		מה	HOW	553d	4 a
		קסם	PRACTICE OF DIVI-NATION	890c	1
6	3	אז	THEN	23a	1 b
		אשם	OFFENCE	80a	4
		יד	HAND	390a	1 e2
		ידע	BE MADE KNOWN	394c	1
		כי	BUT	474b	3 e
		ל	TO	514a	5 e
		מה	HOW	554a	4 d
		סור	TURN ASIDE	693d	2
		ריקם	EMPTILY	938b	1
		רפא	HEAL	950d	1
		שוב	TURN BACK	999c	4 a
		שלח	SEND	1019a	1 e
6	4	אשם	OFFENCE	80a	4
		זהב	GOLD	263a	6
		זהב	GOLD	263a	6
		טחור	TUMORS	377d	
		מגפה	PLAGUE	620a	3
		סרן	TYRANT	710d	
		עכבר	MOUSE	747b	
		עפל	HEMORRHOID	779b	
		שוב	TURN BACK	999c	4 a
6	5	אולי	PERADVENTURE	19c	1
		ו	AND	254c	4
		טחור	TUMORS	377d	
		יד	HAND	390a	1 e2
		כבוד	HONOR	459b	6 b
		נתן	GIVE	679a	1 h
		עכבר	MOUSE	747b	
		עפל	HEMORRHOID	779c	
		צלם	IMAGE	853d	1
		קלל	BE SLIGHT	886d	1
		שחת	GO TO RUIN	1008b	1
6	6	ו	AND	254c	5 b
		כאשר	WHEN	455c	3
		כבד	MAKE HEAVY	457d	1
		לבב	HEART	524a	2 6d
		לב	HEART	525b	2 6d
		עלל	ACT ARBITRARILY	759d	1
		פרעה	PHARAOH	829a	
6	7	אסר	TIE	63d	2
		בית	HOUSE	108d	1 a
		בית	HOUSE	109d	1 b
		בן	SON	121b	4
		בקר	CATTLE	*133c	2
		חדש	NEW	294a	A
		לקח	TAKE	543c	4 g
		עגלה	CART	722c	
		עול	GIVE SUCK	732b	
		עלה	GO UP	749a	6
		על	UPON	756d	2 7b
		על	YOKE	760d	
		פרה	HEIFER	831a	
		שוב	TURN BACK	999a	1 a
6	8	אשם	OFFENCE	80a	4
		ה	THE	207c	1 d
		הלך	WALK	232c	13
		הלך	WALK	234a	1 5d
		זהב	GOLD	263a	6
		כלי	ARTICLE	479b	1
		מן	FROM	578d	1 c
		נתן	PUT	680d	2 a
		עגלה	CART	722c	
		צד	SIDE	841a	
		ארגז	BOX	919c	
		שוב	TURN BACK	999b	1 f
		שלח	SEND	1019a	1 e
6	9	ביתשמש	BETH-SHEMESH	112d	1
		דרך	WAY	202d	1
		היה	FALL OUT	224b	1 1a
		יד	HAND	390a	1 e2
		נגע	TOUCH	619a	2
		עלה	GO UP	748b	1 e
		מקרה	ACCIDENT	900a	1
		ראה	TO SEE	907d	6 e
		רעה	MISERY	949b	2
6	10	אסר	TIE	63d	2
		בית	HOUSE	*108d	1 a
		בית	HOUSE	109b	1 b
		בן	SON	121b	4
		כלא	SHUT UP	476b	1
		עגלה	CART	722c	
		עול	GIVE SUCK	732b	
6	11	פרה	HEIFER	831a	
		זהב	GOLD	263a	6
		טחור	TUMORS	377d	
		עגלה	CART	722c	
		עכבר	MOUSE	747b	
		צלם	IMAGE	853d	1
		ארגז	BOX	919c	
		ביתשמש	BETH-SHEMESH	112d	1
6	12	געה	LOW	171d	
		דרך	WAY	202d	1
		הלך	WALK	232a	1 2
		הלך	WALK	233a	1 4c 1g
		ימין	RIGHT HAND	412a	2 b
		ישר	BE STRAIGHT	448c	1
		סור	TURN ASIDE	693c	1
		מסלה	HIGHWAY	700c	
		פרה	HEIFER	831a	
		שמאל	LEFT	969d	1
6	13	ביתשמש	BETH-SHEMESH	112d	1
		חטה	WHEAT	334d	
		עמק	VALE	771a	
		קציר	HARVEST	894b	
		קציר	HARVESTING	894c	2
		קרא	ENCOUNTER	897a	1
		ראה	TO SEE	*906d	1 b
6	14	אבל	MEADOW	5d	1
		אבן	STONE	6c	1
		ביתשמשי	BETH-SHEMITE	113a	
		בקע	CLEAVE	132a	2
		יהושע	JOSHUA	221c	2
		עגלה	CART	722c	
		עלה	WHOLE BURNT OF-FERING	750d	
		עץ	TREE	781d	2 b
		פרה	HEIFER	831a	
6	15	אבל	MEADOW	5d	1
		אבן	STONE	6c	1
		ביתשמש	BETH-SHEMESH	112d	1
		זבח	SACRIFICE	257c	1 1
		ירד	BRING DOWN	434a	2
		כלי	ARTICLE	479b	1
		לוי	LEVITE	532d	3 1a
		עלה	WHOLE BURNT OF-FERING	750d	
		ארגז	BOX	919c	
		שום	TO PLACE	963c	1 d
		סרן	TYRANT	710d	
6	16	ראה	TO SEE	907d	6 e
6	17	אשדוד	AHSDOD	78b	
		אשם	OFFENCE	80a	4
		אשקלון	ASHKELON	80c	
		זהב	GOLD	263a	6
		טחור	TUMORS	377d	
		גת	GATH	387d	
		עזה	GAZA	738b	
		שוב	TURN BACK	999b	1 f
6	18	אבל	MEADOW	5d	1
		אבן	STONE	6c	1
		ביתשמשי	BETH-SHEMITE	113a	
		מבצר	FORTIFICATION	131c	
		יהושע	JOSHUA	221c	2
		זהב	GOLD	263a	6
		חמש	FIVE	331d	1 d
		יום	DAY	401b	7 1
		כפר	VILLAGE	499a	
		נוח	REST	628d	B 1
		סרן	TYRANT	710d	
		עיר	CITY	746b	1 b
		עכבר	MOUSE	747b	
		פרזי	HAMLET-DWELLER	826d	
6	19	אבל	MOURN	5c	
		ביתשמש	BETH-SHEMESH	112d	1
		הוא	HE, SHE, IT	216b	4 a
		חדה	REJOICE	292d	
		נכה	SMITE	646a	2 c
		נכה	SMITE	646a	2 c
		מכה	SLAUGHTER	647a	2
		ראה	TO SEE	908a	8 a1
		שבעים	SEVENTY	988c	3 b
6	20	אלהים	GOD	43d	1
		ביתשמש	BETH-SHEMESH	112d	1
		יכל	BE ABLE	407c	1 a
		מי	WHO	566b	B
		מי	WHO	566d	F c
		עלה	GO UP	748c	2 e
		על	UPON	758d	4 2b
		קדוש	HOLY	872c	1 b
6	21	מלאך	MESSENGER	521c	1 a
		קריתיערים	KIRIATH-JEARIM	900c	
		שוב	TURN BACK	999a	4
7	1	אבינדב	ABINADAB	4c	1
		אלעזר	ELEAZAR	46c	B
		גבעה	HILL	149a	1
		גבעה	GIBEAH	149b	2
		קדש	BE SET APART	873a	1 c
		קריתיערים	KIRIATH-JEARIM	900c	
		שמר	KEEP	1036c	1 a
7	2	בית	HOUSE	110d	5 dd
		היה	COME TO PASS	224c	2 a1 az
		יום	DAY	399c	5 b
		יום	DAY	400a	7 d1 e
		יום	DAY	401a	7 j
		ישב	REMAIN	442d	2 a
		מן	FROM	581b	4 a
		נהה	LAMENT	624c	
		קריתיערים	KIRIATH-JEARIM	900c	
		רבה	BECOME MANY	915b	1 c
7	3	אלהים	GOD	43c	1 d
		כון	ESTABLISH	466c	3
		לבב	HEART	523b	2 2
		לבב	HEART	523d	2 4
		נכר	FOREIGNNESS	648c	1
		סור	TURN ASIDE	694b	1
		עשתרת	ASTORETH	800a	
7	4	בעל	BAAL	127d	2 3
		סור	TURN ASIDE	694b	1
		עשתרת	ASTORETH	800a	
7	5	בעד	ON BEHALF OF	126c	2
		פלל	INTERVENE	813b	1
		מצפה	MIZPAH	860a	4
		מצפה	MIZPAH	860a	4
		קבץ	GATHER	867c	2
7	6	חטא	MISS A GOAL OR WAY	307a	2 b
		פנה	FACE	817b	2 4a h
		צום	FAST	847a	
		קבץ	GATHER	867d	1
		שאב	DRAW	980c	
		שפט	JUDGE	1047b	1 b
		שפך	POUR OUT	1049c	1 a
7	7	ירא	FEAR	431b	1 c
		עלה	GO UP	748c	2 c
		קבץ	GATHER	868b	
7	8	יהוה	YAHWEH	218d	2 1c
		זעק	CRY	277b	2
		חרש	BE SILENT	361b	3
		ישע	DELIVER	446d	1 b
		מן	FROM	583b	7 ba
7	9	בעד	ON BEHALF OF	126c	2
		זעק	CRY	277b	2 a
		חלב	MILK	316c	A 2
		טלה	LAMB	378b	
		כליל	WHOLE	483b	1
		עלה	WHOLE BURNT OF-FERING	750d	
		ענה	ANSWER	772d	1 b
7	10	היה	BE	227c	3 5a
		המם	CONFUSE	243a	2
		מלחמה	WAR	536c	
		נגף	STRIKE	620a	
		נגש	DRAW NEAR	621a	
		עלה	WHOLE BURNT OF-FERING	750d	
		קול	VOICE	877a	2 b
		קול	VOICE	877b	2 b
		רעם	THUNDER	947b	
7	11	איש	MAN	36a	
		ביתכר	BETHCAR	111d	
		עד	AS FAR AS	724a	1 1a
		תחת	UNDERNEATH	1066b	3 2b
7	12	אבן	STONE	6b	1
		אבן	STONE	7a	9
		אפק	APHEK	68a	A a
		הנה	HITHER	244c	A a
		ישנה	JESHANAH	446a	
		עזר	HELP	740b	
		שום	TO PLACE	964b	4 c
		שן	SHEN	1042b	
7	13	היה	BECOME	225c	2 1b
		יסף	ADD	414d	
		כנע	BE HUMBLED	488c	2
		פלשתי	PHILISTINE	814c	
7	14	אמרי	AMORITES	57c	2b
		גת	GATH	387d	
		לקח	TAKE	543d	8
		שוב	TURN BACK	998a	7 b
		שלום	PEACE	1023b	6
7	15	חיים	LIFE	313b	1
		שפט	JUDGE	1047b	1 b
7	16	את	WITH	86b	2
		די	SUFFICIENCY	191d	2 cb
		הלך	WALK	230b	1 1b
		סבב	GO AROUND	685d	2
		מקום	STANDING PLACE	880a	3 a
		שפט	JUDGE	1047b	1 b
7	17	מזבח	ALTAR	258b	1
		נכה	SMITE	645b	1 a
		רמה	RAMA	928a	2
		שפט	JUDGE	1047b	1 b
8	1	זקן	BE OLD	278b	1
		שום	TO PLACE	964c	5 b
		שפט	JUDGE	1047b	1 b
8	2	ביתו	ABIJAM	4a	2
		בארשבע	BEERSHEBA	92a	
		בן	SON	120a	1
		יואל	JOEL	*222b	1
		יואל	JOEL	222b	1
		שני	SECOND	255c	
		משנה	SECOND	1041d	3 b
		שפט	JUDGE	1047b	1 b
8	3	בצע	UNJUST GAIN	130c	
		דרך	WAY	203c	6 c
		הלך	WALK	234d	2 3a 1t
		לקח	TAKE	543b	4 f

Ch	v	Heb	Eng	Page	Sec
		נטה	BEND	640b	3 a
		נטה	BEND	641a	3 g
		שחד	BRIBE	1005a	
		משפט	JUDGEMNT	1049a	5
8	4	זקן	OLD	278d	2 b
		קבץ	GATHER	868b	
		רמה	RAMA	928a	2
8	5	דרך	WAY	203c	6 c
		הלך	WALK	234d	23a 1t
		זקן	BE OLD	278b	
		מלך	KING	573a	1
		מלך	KING	573c	5 c
		עתה	NOW	774b	1 d
		שום	TO PLACE	964a	3 d
		שפט	JUDGE	1047c	1 b
8	6	כאשר	WHEN	455c	3
		מלך	KING	573c	5 c
		פלל	INTERVENE	813b	3
		רעע	BE EVIL	949c	1
		שפט	JUDGE	1047c	1 b
8	7	לא	NOT	518d	1 ac
		מאס	REJECT	549c	1 a
		מאס	REJECT	549c	1 a
		מלך	BE KING	574a	
		מן	FROM	583b	7 ba
		קול	VOICE	877b	3 a1
		שמע	HEAR	1034a	1 m
8	8	אלהים	GOD	43c	3
		יום	DAY	400a	7 d1 e
		יום	DAY	401b	7 1
		כ	LIKE	454d	2 d
		כן	SO	486b	2 ac
		מן	FROM	581b	4 a
		עבד	WORK	713b	4 b
8	9	אך	HOWBEIT	36c	2 a
		כי	THAT	472b	1 da
		מלך	BE KING	574a	
		עוד	BEAR WITNESS	730a	3
		קול	VOICE	877b	3 a1
		משפט	JUDGMENT	1048d	3
8	10	דבר	WORD	182a	1 1a
		דבר	WORD	183b	3 2
		שאל	ASK	981c	1 a
8	11	מלך	BE KING	574a	
		פרש	HORSE	832a	
		רוץ	RUN	930b	1
		מרכבה	CHARIOT	939d	
		מרכבה	CHARIOT	939d	
		שום	TO PLACE	964a	3 d
		משפט	JUDGMENT	1048d	3
8	12	חמשים	FIFTY	332b	1 a
		חרש	CUT IN	360c	2
		חריש	PLOUGHING	361a	
		כלי	IMPLEMENT	479d	2 a
		כלי	EQUIPMENT	480a	2 e
		ל	TO	518b	7 bh
		מלחמה	WAR	536c	
		קצר	HARVEST	894b	
		קצר	HARVEST	894b	
		קציר	HARVESTING	894c	2
		שום	TO PLACE	964a	3 d
		שר	CHIEFTAIN	978c	3 b
8	13	אפה	BAKE	66a	
		אפה	BAKE	66a	
		טבחה	FEMALE COOK	371a	
		רקחה	OINTMENT-MAKER	955c	
8	14	ה	THE	*208d	2 a
		זית	OLIVE TREE	268d	1
		טוב	PLEASANT	374b	3 c
8	15	זרע	SOWING	282b	2 d
		סריס	EUNUCH	710c	
		עשר	TAKE THE TENTH OF	797c	
8	16	בחור	YOUNG MAN	104c	
		חמור	HE-ASS	331b	1
		טוב	PLEASANT	373b	1 a
		ל	TO	515a	5 ha
		עשה	DO	795c	2 0
		עשה	DO	795b	2 f
		שפחה	MAID	1046c	1
8	17	עבד	SLAVE	714c	7
		עשר	TAKE THE TENTH OF	797c	
8	18	בחר	CHOOSE	104a	3 b
		זעק	CRY	277b	2 a
		פנה	FACE	818a	25b
8	19	כיאם	BUT	475a	2 b
		מאן	REFUSE	549a	
		מלך	KING	573c	5 c
8	20	יצא	GO OUT	424a	2 c
		לחם	ENGAGE IN BATTLE	535d	
		מלחמה	WAR	536b	1
		פנה	FACE	817a	24 c b
		שפט	JUDGE	1047c	1 b
8	21	אזן	EAR	24b	2 b
		דבר	SPEAK	181c	4 b
8	22	ל	TO	511b	1 ga
		מלך	KING	573c	5 c
		מלך	BE KING	574a	
9	1	אפיח	APHIAH	66c	
		בכורת	BECORATH	114c	
		בנימין	BENJAMIN	122d	1
		גבור	STRONG	150b	2
		היה	BE	226d	3 1
		חיל	STRENGTH	298d	1 c
		ימיני	BENJAMITE	412b	
		מן	OUT OF	579c	2 cb
		צרור	ZEROR	866c	
		קיש	KISH	885c	1
		שם	NAME	1027d	2 a
9	2	בחור	YOUNG MAN	104c	
		גבה	HIGH	147b	1
		היה	BE	227c	34d c
		טוב	PLEASANT	373c	1 a
		טוב	PLEASANT	374c	6
		כל	ALL	482a	1 ea
		מן	FROM	581d	5 a
		מן	THAN	582c	6 b
		מעל	ABOVE	751d	2 ba
		שאול	SAUL	982b	1
		שכם	SHOULDER	1014b	1 b
		שם	NAME	1027d	2 a
9	3	אבד	BE LOST	1d	3
		את	MARK OF THE ACCUSATIVE	85a	1 a
		אתון	SHE-ASS	87d	
		בקש	SEEK	134c	1 b
		קום	STAND	278b	6 c
		ל	TO	512d	5 aa
		נער	RETAINER	655a	2 a
		קיש	KISH	885c	1
		שאול	SAUL	982b	1
9	4	אין	NOT	34c	2 da
		ארץ	EARTH	76a	2 c
		ארץ	EARTH	76a	2 c
		בנימיני	BENJAMITE	122d	
		הר	MOUNTAIN	251a	2 b
		ימיני	BENJAMITE	412b	
		מצא	FIND	593a	1 b
		עבר	PASS OVER	717c	3 a
		ערמה	CRAFTINESS	791a	1
		שלשה	SHALISHAH	1027a	
		שעלים	SHAALIM	1043d	
9	5	ארץ	EARTH	76a	2 c
		אתון	SHE-ASS	87d	
		דאג	BE ANXIOUS	178b	1
		הלך	WALK	234b	1 5f 2
		חדל	CEASE	293a	2
		צוף	ZUPH	847c	
		שאול	SAUL	982b	1
9	6	איש	MAN	36a	
		אלהים	GOD	43d	3 b
		אלהים	GOD	44a	3 b
		בוא	COME	98c	2 c
		הלך	WALK	230d	1 1d 2b
		הלך	WALK	230d	1 1d 3b
		כבד	BE HONORED	457c	1 b
		נא	PART OF ENTREATY	609c	4 d
		עתה	NOW	774b	1 d
		שם	THERE	1027b	2
9	7	אזל	GO	23c	4
		את	WITH	86c	3 a
		בוא	COME	99b	2
		הנה	IF	244c	D
		כלי	VESSEL	480a	3
		תשורה	GIFT	1003d	
9	8	יד	HAND	390d	5 c2
		יסף	DO AGAIN	415c	2 a
		כסף	SILVER	494b	8 a
		מצא	FIND	594a	2
		ענה	ANSWER	772d	1 d
		רבע	FOURTH PART	917d	1
		שקל	SHEKEL	1053d	
		שקל	SHEKEL	1053d	
9	9	דרש	SEEK	205b	2 a
		הלך	WALK	231b	1 d3 gc
		הלך	WALK	234a	1 5f 2
		נביא	PROPHET	611c	1
		נביא	PROPHET	611d	1
		עד	AS FAR AS	724a	1 1a
		קרא	CALL	896b	2 d1
		ראה	SEER	909a	
9	10	אלהים	GOD	43d	3 b
		אלהים	GOD	44a	3 b
		דבר	WORD	182a	1 1a
		הלך	WALK	231a	1 d3 ga
		הלך	WALK	234a	1 5f 2
		טוב	PLEASANT	374b	5
		שם	THERE	1027b	1 b
9	11	זה	THIS	261d	6 a
		יש	BE	441c	2 a
		מצא	FIND	593b	3 a
		נערה	GIRL	655b	1
		מעלה	ASCENT	751b	2
		ראה	SEER	909a	
		שאב	DRAW	980c	
9	12	בוא	COME	98b	2 c
		במה	HIGH PLACE	119b	3
		זבח	SACRIFICE	257c	1 1
		יום	DAY	400d	7 h
		יש	BE	441c	2 a
		ל	TO	511b	1 ga
		מהר	HASTEN	554d	1
		עם	PEOPLE	766c	2 a
9	13	במה	HIGH PLACE	119b	3
		ברך	BLESS	139b	3
		זבח	SACRIFICE	257c	1 1
		טרם	NOT YET	302c	1
		יום	DAY	400d	7 h
		כן	SO	486b	2 ad d
9	14	מצא	FIND	593a	1 a
		עלה	GO UP	748b	1 d
		עם	PEOPLE	766c	2 a
		קרא	CALL	895d	5 c
		במה	HIGH PLACE	119b	3
		עיר	CITY	746b	1
		עלה	GO UP	748b	1 d
		תוך	MIDST	1063d	
9	15	אזן	EAR	24b	3
		במה	HIGH PLACE	119b	3
		יום	DAY	400a	7 a6
		פנה	FACE	817d	24e
9	16	ארץ	EARTH	76a	2 c
		בוא	COME	98b	2
		במה	HIGH PLACE	119b	3
		בנימין	BENJAMIN	122d	1
		ישע	DELIVER	446c	1 a
		ל	TO	512b	4 a
		מחר	TO-MORROW	564a	1 a
		משח	ANOINT	603b	2
		נגיד	LEADER	618a	1
		עת	TIME	773c	1 a
		עני	AFFLICTION	777a	1
		צעקה	CRY	858d	2
		ראה	TO SEE	907c	6 a
9	17	אמר	SAY	56a	1
		אשר	PARTICLE OF RELATION	82d	4 d
		במה	HIGH PLACE	119b	3
		ענה	ANSWER	773a	2 a
		עצר	RESTRAIN	783c	1
9	18	אי	WHERE	32b	1 b
		במה	HIGH PLACE	119b	3
		נגש	DRAW NEAR	620d	1
		ראה	SEER	909a	
		שער	GATE	1044d	1 a
9	19	במה	HIGH PLACE	119b	3
		בקר	MORNING	134b	2
		לב	HEART	523c	2 2
		עלה	GO UP	748b	1 d
		ראה	SEER	909a	
9	20	אבד	BE LOST	1d	3
		אתון	SHE-ASS	87d	
		במה	HIGH PLACE	119b	3
		חמדה	DESIRE	326c	
		יום	DAY	400a	7 a4
		ל	TO	512d	5 aa
		לא	NOT	520b	4 ba
		לב	HEART	524d	2 3c
		מצא	FIND	593d	1 a
		שום	TO PLACE	963c	2 b
		שלש	THREE	1025d	1 b
9	21	במה	HIGH PLACE	119b	3
		בנימיני	BENJAMITE	122d	
		בנימין	BENJAMIN	122d	1
		דבר	WORD	183d	4 7
		ה	THE	207b	1 b
		לא	NOT	520b	4 ba
		צעיר	YOUNG	859a	1 a
		מן	SMALL	882a	2 b1
		שבט	TRIBE	987b	2 a
		משפחה	CLAN	1046d	1 a
9	22	בוא	COME	99a	1
		במה	HIGH PLACE	119b	3
		כ	LIKE	453b	1 a
		לשכה	ROOM	545d	1 a
		מקום	STANDING PLACE	880a	4
		קרא	CALL	895d	5 c
		ראש	HEAD	911a	3 d
9	23	אמר	SAY	56a	1
		אשר	PARTICLE OF RELATION	82d	4 d
		במה	HIGH PLACE	119b	3
		טבח	COOK	371a	1
		מנה	PORTION	584b	5
		עם	WITH	768b	3 c
		שום	TO PLACE	963c	1 d
9	24	אליה	FAT TAIL	47a	
		במה	HIGH PLACE	119b	3
		ה	THE	209c	3
		טבח	COOK	371a	1
		מועד	APPOINTED TIME	417c	1 a
		קרא	CALL	895d	5 c
		רום	BE HIGH	927c	1 c
		שום	TO PLACE	963b	1 c
		שאר	REMAIN	984a	1
		שאר	FLESH	985a	1 a
		שוק	LEG	1003b	2
		שמר	KEEP	1037a	3 d
9	25	במה	HIGH PLACE	119b	3
		גג	ROOF	150d	1
		דבר	SPEAK	181b	3 e
9	26	רבע	BE-SPREAD	914d	1
		גג	ROOF	150d	1
		עלה	GO UP	748d	5
		שחר	DAWN	1007b	
		שכב	LIE DOWN	1012a	1 b
		שכם	START EARLY	1014d	
		שכם	START EARLY	1014d	
		שלח	SEND	1019a	1 e
9	27	יום	DAY	400d	7 h
		עמד	STAND	764a	2 a
		קצה	END	892b	2
10	1	אות	SIGN	16d	2
		ה	THE	207c	1 d
		יצק	POUR	427a	1

1 SAMUEL

Ch v.	Heb	Eng	Page	Sec
	כי	THAT	472b	1 da
	משח	ANOINT	603b	2
	נגיד	LEADER	618a	1
	נחלה	PROPERTY	635b	1 e
	נשק	KISS	676b	
	עצר	RESTRAIN	783c	1
	פך	PHIAL	810b	
	שמן	OIL	1032b	2 d
10 2	אפרתה	EPHRATH	68d	1
	אתון	SHE-ASS	87d	
	בנימין	BENJAMIN	122d	1
	בקש	SEEK	134c	1 b
	דאג	BE ANXIOUS	178b	1
	דבר	WORD	183c	4 3
	מצא	FIND	593d	1 a
	נטש	FORSAKE	643d	2
	עם	WITH	768a	2
	מעם	FROM WITH	768d	A
	צלצח	ZELZEH	854c	
	צברה	GRAVE	869a	1
	רחל	RACHEL	933a	
10 3	אלון	TEREBINTH	18d	
	אלון	TEREBINTH	18d	
	אלהים	GOD	43d	3
	ביאל	BETHEL	110d	1
	גדי	KID	152a	
	הלאה	OUT THERE	229d	A
	חלף	PASS ON OR AWAY	322a	1 a
	יין	WINE	406c	D
	ככר	ROUND	503b	2
	נבל	SKIN-BOTTLE	614b	1
	נשא	LIFT	671a	2 a
	עלה	GO UP	748c	2 b
	תבור	TABOR	1061d	4
10 4	לחם	FOOD	537a	1 a
	נתן	GIVE	678b	1 a
	שאל	ASK	982a	2 a
	שנים	TWO	1041a	1 a
10 5	אחר	AFTER	29d	2 b
	אלהים	GOD	44a	3 b
	במה	HIGH PLACE	119b	3
	גבעה	HILL	149a	4
	חבל	CORD	286d	4
	חליל	FLUTE	319d	
	כנור	LYRE	490a	
	נביא	PROPHET	611c	1
	נבא	PROPHESY	612b	1 a
	נבל	HARP	614c	
	נציב	PREFECT	662d	2
	פגע	MEET	803b	1
	רוח	BREATH	*925d	9 a
	תף	TIMBREL	1074c	
10 6	אחר	ANOTHER	29c	
	אל	TO	41a	B
	הפך	TURN	246a	2 c
	נבא	PROPHESY	612b	1 a
	צלח	RUSH	852b	
	רוח	BREATH	925d	9 a
	נבא	PROPHESY	*1101d	1
10 7	אות	SIGN	16d	2
	אלהים	GOD	43d	3
	היה	COME TO PASS	225b	1 2b d
	כי	WHEN	473b	2 a
	מצא	FIND	593c	4
	עשה	DO	794a	1 1a 3
10 8	זבח	SACRIFICE	257d	2 5
	ידע	MAKE KNOWN	395a	
	יחל	WAIT	404a	1
	עלה	WHOLE BURNT OF-FERING	750d	
	שלם	PEACE-OFFERING	1023c	
10 9	אות	SIGN	16d	2
	אחר	ANOTHER	29c	
	היה	COME TO PASS	225a	1 2a 2
	הפך	TURN	245c	1 a
	ו	AND	252b	1 b
	ל	TO	*512d	5 aa
	מעם	FROM WITH	768d	A
	פנה	TURN	815c	1
	שכם	SHOULDER	1014b	2
10 10	גבעה	HILL	149a	1
	גבעה	GIBEAH	149b	2
	חבל	CORD	286d	4
	נביא	PROPHET	611c	1
	נבא	PROPHESY	612b	1 a
	צלח	RUSH	852b	
	קרא	ENCOUNTER	897a	1
	רוח	BREATH	925d	9 a
	תוד	MIDST	1063d	1
	נבא	PROPHESY	*1101d	
10 11	בן	SON	120c	1 g
	גם	ALSO	169b	2
	היה	COME TO PASS	224d	2 ... a1 am
	זה	THIS	261c	4 c
	מה	WHAT	552c	1 ab
	נבא	PROPHESY	612a	1 a
	קיש	KISH	885c	1
	שלשם	THREE DAYS AGO	1026b	
	תמול	YESTERDAY	1070a	2 c
10 12	גם	ALSO	169b	2
	היה	FALL OUT	224b	1 1a
	כן	SO	487b	3 f
	משל	PROVERB	605a	1
	שם	THERE	1027c	4 c
10 13	במה	HIGH PLACE	119b	3
	כלה	FINISH	478b	1 c
	נבא	PROPHESY	612b	1 a
10 14	אן	WHERE	33a	
	אין	NOT	34c	2 dg
	אל	NOT	39b	C
	אתון	SHE-ASS	87d	
	בקש	SEEK	134c	1 b
	דוד	UNCLE	187c	2
	הלך	WALK	*230d	1 1d 3b
10 15	דוד	UNCLE	187c	2
10 16	אמר	SAY	56a	1
	אתון	SHE-ASS	87d	
	דוד	UNCLE	187c	2
	מלוכה	KINGSHIP	574c	
	מצא	FIND	593d	1 a
10 18	לחץ	OPPRESS	537d	2
	ממלכה	KINGDOM	575a	1
10 19	אלהים	GOD	44d	4 c
	אלף	THOUSAND	49b	2
	אשר	PARTICLE OF RE-LATION	82a	2 a
	הוא	HE, SHE, IT	215d	2 c
	יצב	STATION ONESELF	426c	C
	ישע	DELIVER	446d	1 b
	כי	THAT	472a	1 b
	כי אם	BUT	*475a	2 b
	לא	NOT	519a	1 ad b
	מאס	REJECT	549c	1 a
	מלך	KING	573c	5 c
	פנה	FACE	817b	2 4a h
	צרה	DISTRESS	865b	
10 20	אורים	URIM	22b	
	בנימין	BENJAMIN	122d	1
	לכד	TAKE	540b	3
	קרב	COME NEAR	898a	2 a2
10 21	אלף	THOUSAND	49b	2
	בנימין	BENJAMIN	122d	1
	בקש	SEEK	134c	1 b
	גבר	MAN	150a	
	מצא	FIND	394a	1 f
	לכד	TAKE	540b	3
	מטרי	MATRITE	565a	
	קיש	KISH	885c	1
	קרב	COME NEAR	898a	2 a2
	משפחה	CLAN	1046d	1 a
10 22	אל	TO	39d	2
	הלם	HITHER	240d	
	הנה	BEHOLD	243d	
	חבא	WITHDRAW	285b	
	כלי	ARTICLE	479c	1
	עוד	STILL	729b	1 c
	עוד	STILL	729b	1 b
	שאל	ASK	982a	2 b
10 23	גבה	BE HIGH	147a	1
	יצב	STATION ONESELF	426c	A
	מעל	ABOVE	751d	2 ba
	רוץ	RUN	930b	1
	שכם	SHOULDER	1014b	1 b
10 24	בחר	CHOOSE	103d	1 a
	ה	INTERROG PART	210a	1 c
	חיה	LIVE	311b	1 d
	כ	LIKE	453d	1 b
	מלך	KING	573b	5 b
	רוע	RAISE A SHOUT	929d	4
10 25	ה	THE	207c	1 d
	מלוכה	KINGSHIP	574c	
	נוח	REST	628d	B 1
	ספר	MISSIVE	707a	3
	שלח	SEND	1019a	1 a
	משפט	JUDGMENT	1048d	3
10 26	גבעה	GIBEAH	149b	2
	הלך	WALK	231b	1 d3 gd
	חיל	STRENGTH	298d	2
	חיל	STRENGTH	299d	4
	נגע	TOUCH	619a	1 b
10 27	בוא	COME	99b	2
	בזה	DESPISE	102c	
	בליעל	WORTHLESSNESS	116a	1
	זה	THIS	260c	1 a
	חדש	NEW MOON	294c	2 a
	חיל	STRENGTH	*299a	1
	חרש	BE SILENT	361b	1 a
	ישע	DELIVER	446c	1 a
	כ	LIKE	455a	
	מנחה	GIFT	585a	1
	נגה	THIS	*1088d	
11 1	ברית	COVENANT	136b	1 1
	היה	COME TO PASS	224d	2
	חדש	NEW MOON	294c	2 a
	יבש	JABESH	386d	1
	יבש	JABESH	386d	1
	כרת	CUT	503d	4
	נחש	NAHASH	638b	1
	עבד	WORK	713a	3
	על	UPON	757d	2 7d
	עמוני	AMMONITE	770a	
11 2	ב	IN	90a	3 2e
	זה	THIS	261d	6 ba
	חרפה	REPROACH	358a	3
	ימין	RIGHT	412a	3
	כרת	CUT	504a	4
	ל	TO	512d	5 aa
	נחש	NAHASH	638b	1
	נקר	DIG	669b	
	עמוני	AMMONITE	770a	
	שום	TO PLACE	963b	1 b
11 3	זן	OLD	279a	2 b
	יבש	JABESH	386d	1
	יצא	GO OUT	423d	2 a
	ישע	DELIVER	446c	1 a
	רפה	SINK	952a	3
	שלח	SEND	1018b	1 a
11 4	בכה	WEEP	113c	1
	גבעה	GIBEAH	149b	2
	דבר	SPEAK	181c	4 b
	פנה	FACE	819a	2 7b
	קול	VOICE	876d	1 a
	שאל	SAUL	*982c	1
11 5	בכה	WEEP	113b	1
	בקר	CATTLE	133b	1 a
	יבש	JABESH	386d	1
	ספר	COUNT	708a	1
	שדה	FIELD	961b	1 a
11 6	חרה	BURN	354a	1 a
	צלח	RUSH	852b	
	רוח	BREATH	926a	9 c1
11 7	בקר	CATTLE	133c	2
	יד	HAND	391a	5 d
	נפל	FALL	657c	5
	נתח	CUT IN PIECES	677c	
	על	UPON	756b	2 7a b
	עשה	DO	795b	1 c
	פחד	DREAD	808c	1
	צמד	COUPLE	855a	1
11 8	איש	MAN	36a	
	בזק	BEZEK	103b	
	פנה	FACE	819a	2 7b
	פקד	ATTEND TO	823c	A 4
11 9	חמם	BE OR BECOME WARM	328c	1
	יבש	JABESH	386d	1
	יבש	JABESH	386d	1
	תשועה	DELIVERANCE	448b	1
	מחר	TO-MORROW	564a	1 b
	פנה	FACE	819a	2 7b
	שמח	REJOICE	970b	1 a
	שמש	SUN	1039b	1
11 10	טוב	PLEASANT	374a	2 f
	יבש	JABESH	386d	1
	בקר	MORNING	134b	1 h
11 11	חם	HEAT	328d	
	יום	DAY	398b	1
	יחד	UNION	403a	2 a2
	מחרת	THE MORROW	564a	
	נכה	SMITE	646b	3
	עם	PEOPLE	766c	2 d
	עמון	AMMON	*769d	
	עמון	AMMON	770a	
	פוץ	BE DISPERSED	807a	
	ראש	HEAD	911b	6
	שום	TO PLACE	964c	5 b
	שאר	REMAIN	984a	1
	שאר	REMAIN	984a	1
	אשמורה	WATCH	1038a	
11 12	בוא	COME	98c	2 b
	מות	DIE	560b	1 b
	מי	WHO	567b	G
	נתן	GIVE	679c	1 s
11 13	תשועה	DELIVERANCE	448b	1
	מות	DIE	560c	2
	נוע	WAVE	631b	1
	עשה	DO	795a	29
11 14	הלך	WALK	230d	1 1d 3a
	הלך	WALK	234a	1 5f 2
	חדש	RENEW	294a	1
	מלוכה	KINGSHIP	574c	
11 15	הלך	WALK	230d	1 1d 3a
	זבח	SACRIFICE	*257c	2 1
	זבח	SACRIFICE	257d	2 5
	מאד	EXCEEDINGLY	547c	2 b
	מלך	BE KING	574b	
	פנה	FACE	817b	2 4a h
	שמח	REJOICE	970b	2 a
	שלם	PEACE-OFFERING	1023c	
	שלם	PEACE-OFFERING	1023c	
12 1	מלך	KING	573c	5 c
12 2	הלך	WALK	236b	2
	הלך	WALK	236b	2
	ו	AND	252b	1 a
	זקן	BE OLD	278b	1
	יום	DAY	401b	7 1
	מן	FROM	582a	5 c
	נעורים	YOUTH	655c	
	עתה	NOW	774b	2 c
	פנה	FACE	817a	2 4a d
	שיב	BE HOARY	966c	
12 3	את	MARK OF THE AC-CUSATIVE	84d	1 a
	הנה	BEHOLD	244a	A
	חמור	HE-ASS	331b	1
	כפר	RANSOM	497b	1
	לקח	TAKE	543a	3 a
	לקח	TAKE	543b	4 f
	מי	WHO	566b	B
	מי	WHO	566b	B
	נגד	IN FRONT	617b	1 a
	עין	EYE	744d	3 d
	עלם	CONCEAL	761a	
	ענה	ANSWER	773a	3 a
	עשק	OPPRESS	798d	1
	רצץ	CRUSH	954c	1

Ch	v.	Heb	Eng	Page	Sec
		שוב	TURN BACK	999a	1 d
		שוב	TURN BACK	999c	3
		שור	A HEAD OF CATTLE	1004a	
12	4	לקח	TAKE	543b	4 f
		מאומה	ANYTHING	548d	
		עשק	OPPRESS	798d	1
		רצץ	CRUSH	954c	2
12	5	מאומה	ANYTHING	548d	
		מצא	FIND	593b	2 b
		עד	WITNESS	729d	2 c
		עד	WITNESS	729d	2 a
12	6	אב	FATHER	3c	4 b
		משה	MOSES	602c	
		עד	WITNESS	729d	2 a
		עשה	DO	794a	1 b
12	7	את	WITH	86b	1 db
		יצב	STATION ONESELF	426b	1
		פנה	FACE	817b	24 a h
		צדקה	RIGHTEOUSNESS	842d	7 a
		שפט	JUDGE	1048a	1
12	8	ו	AND	254d	5 b
		זעק	CRY	277b	2 a
		יצא	CAUSE TO GO	424c	1 a
		ישב	CAUSE TO SIT	443c	3 a
		כאשר	WHEN	455c	3
		מצרים	EGYPT	595d	1 b1
		משה	MOSES	602c	
		ענה	BE BOWED DOWN	776b	1
		מקום	STANDING PLACE	880a	3 b
12	9	יהוה	YAHWEH	218d	2 1d
		חצור	HAZOR	347d	1
		מואב	MOAB	555d	2 a
		מכר	SELL	569b	
		סיסרא	SISERA	696b	1
		צבא	ARMY	839a	1 a
		שר	CHIEFTAIN	978b	3 a
		שכח	FORGET	1013b	1 c
12	10	בעל	BAAL	127d	2 3
		זעק	CRY	277b	2 a
		חטא	MISS A GOAL OR WAY	307a	2 b
		עבד	WORK	713b	4 b
		עשתרת	ASTORETH	800a	
12	11	בדן	BEDAN	96a	1
		במה	SECURITY	105b	
		סביב	ROUND ABOUT	687a	1 d
		עבדון	ABDON	715c	1 1
		יפתח	JEPHTHAH	836b	1
		ירבעל	JERUBBAAL	937c	
12	12	יהוה	YAHWEH	218d	2 1b
		כי	BUT	474c	3 e
		כיאם	BUT	*475a	2 b
		מלך	KING	573b	3
		נחש	NAHASH	638b	1
		עמון	AMMON	770a	
12	13	בחר	CHOOSE	104a	2 b
		מלך	KING	573c	5 c
		נתן	PUT	680d	2 c
12	14	אחר	BEHIND	29d	2 a
		גם	ALSO	169b	1
		יהוה	YAHWEH	218d	2 1b
		היה	BECOME	225d	2 b
		ירא	FEAR	431c	3 b
		מלך	BE KING	574a	
		מרה	BE REBELLIOUS	598b	
		פה	MOUTH	805b	2 c
		קול	VOICE	877b	3 b
12	15	אב	FATHER	3c	4 b
		היה	BECOME	225c	2 1b
		ו	AND	253b	1 j
		מרה	BE REBELLIOUS	598b	2
		פה	MOUTH	805b	2 c
		קול	VOICE	877b	3 b
12	16	גדול	GREAT	153a	6 a
		יצב	STATION ONESELF	426b	B
		עתה	NOW	774b	2 d
12	17	חטה	WHEAT	334d	
		ידע	KNOW	393d	1 c
		ל	TO	517c	7 bb
		מטר	RAIN	564d	
		קול	VOICE	877a	2 b
		קול	VOICE	877b	2 b
		קציר	HARVESTING	894d	3
		קרא	CALL	895b	2 a
		ראה	TO SEE	907c	5 b
		רעה	MISERY	949b	3
		שאל	ASK	981c	1 a
12	18	ירא	FEAR	431b	1 b
		מטר	RAIN	564d	
		קול	VOICE	877b	2 b
		קרא	CALL	895b	2 a
12	19	חטא	SIN	308d	1 b
		יסף	ADD	414d	
		ל	TO	517c	7 bb
		מות	DIE	560a	2 b
		רעה	MISERY	949b	3
		שאל	ASK	981c	1 a
12	20	ירא	FEAR	431a	1 a
		לבב	HEART	523b	2 2
		סור	TURN ASIDE	693c	1
12	21	יעל	PROFIT	418d	
		נצל	DELIVER	664d	3 a
		תהו	FORMLESSNESS	1062c	2
		תהו	FORMLESSNESS	1062c	2
12	22	גדול	GREAT	153b	6 c

Ch	v.	Heb	Eng	Page	Sec
		יאל	SHOW-WILLING-NESS	384b	3
		נטש	FORSAKE	643d	2
12	23	עבור	FOR THE SAKE OF	721a	1 a
		דרך	WAY	203c	6 c
		ה	THE	209a	3
		חדל	CEASE	293a	2
		חטא	MISS A GOAL OR WAY	307a	2 b
		חלילה	FAR BE IT	321a	
		טוב	PLEASANT	374b	0 a
		ירה	DIRECT	435b	5 a
		ישר	STRAIGHT	449b	3 b
		פלל	INTERVENE	813b	1
12	24	אמת	FIRMNESS	54a	3 a
		גדל	BECOME GREAT	152c	3 a
		ירא	FEAR	431c	3 b
		לבב	HEART	523b	2 2
		עם	WITH	767d	1 d
12	25	ספה	SWEEP AWAY	705a	1
		רעע	BE EVIL	949d	2
13	1	מלך	BE KING	574a	
		מלך	BE KING	574a	
		שנה	YEAR	1040b	
13	2	בחר	CHOOSE	104a	3 b
		בית־אל	BETHEL	110d	1
		גבעה	GIBEAH	149b	2
		יהונתן	JONATHAN	220d	1
		יתר	REMAINDER	451d	1 b
		מכמס	MICHMASH	485a	
13	3	גבע	GEBA	148d	
		יהונתן	JONATHAN	220d	1
		נציב	PREFECT	662d	2
		עברי	HEBREW	720b	2 b
		שפר	HORN	1051d	
13	4	באש	STINK	93a	
		נציב	PREFECT	662d	2
		שמע	HEAR	1033c	1 c
13	5	אלף	THOUSAND	49a	1 c
		בית־און	BETH-AVEN	110d	
		חול	SAND	297d	A
		חול	SAND	297d	C
		חנה	DECLINE	333c	2 c2
		ים	SEA	411b	8 a
		מכמס	MICHMASH	485a	
		לחם	ENGAGE IN BAT-TLE	535c	
		פרש	HORSEMAN	832a	
		קדמה	EAST	870b	2
		רב	MULTITUDE	914a	1
		רכב	CHARIOT	939a	1
		שלשים	THIRTY	1026c	2
13	6	בור	PIT	92c	3
		חבא	WITHDRAW	285b	1
		חוח	BRIER	296b	1 a
		חר	HOLE	359d	
		ל	TO	511a	1 e
		מערה	CAVE	792c	
		צר	ADDENDA ET COR-RIGENDA	1126c	
13	7	אחר	BEHIND	30b	4 aa
		ארץ	EARTH	76a	2 c
		גד	GAD	151c	1 b
		חרד	TREMBLE	353c	4
		עבר	PASS OVER	717a	1 a1
		עברי	HEBREW	720b	2 b
		מעברה	FORD	721b	1
		עוד	STILL	*728d	1 aa
13	8	אשר	PARTICLE OF RE-LATION	83b	7 c
		יחל	WAIT	403d	
		יחל	WAIT	404a	
		מועד	APPOINTED TIME	417c	1 a
		ל	TO	517a	6 c
		על	UPON	759a	4 2c
		פוץ	BE DISPERSED	807b	2
		שום	TO PLACE	963d	3 b
13	9	נגש	APPROACH	621b	
		עלה	WHOLE BURNT OF-FERING	750d	
		שלם	PEACE-OFFERING	1023c	
13	10	ברך	BLESS	139b	4 a
		היה	COME TO PASS	225a	12a 1c
		עלה	WHOLE BURNT OF-FERING	750d	
13	11	אסף	GATHER	62d	1 a
		מועד	APPOINTED TIME	417c	1 a
		מכמס	MICHMASH	485a	
		נפץ	DISPERSE	659a	
		על	UPON	759a	4 2c
13	12	אפק	HOLD	67d	1
		חלה	MOLLIFY	318c	1 b
		עלה	WHOLE BURNT OF-FERING	750d	
		עתה	NOW	774b	1 d
13	13	אל	TO	41a	A
		כון	ESTABLISH	466a	1 a
		כי	THAT	472c	1 db
		לא	NOT	520d	
		לו	IF	530b	2
		ממלכה	DOMINION	575b	2
		סכל	BE FOOLISH	698a	
		עולם	LONG DURATION	762b	2 b3
		עתה	NOW	774c	2 ga
		מצוה	COMMANDMENT	846c	2 c
13	14	בקש	SEEK	134d	1 d

Ch	v.	Heb	Eng	Page	Sec
		כ	LIKE	454a	1 c1
		ל	TO	512b	4 a
		לבב	HEART	523c	2 2
		ממלכה	DOMINION	575b	2
		נגיד	LEADER	618a	1
		צוה	GIVE CHARGE OVER	845d	1 d
13	15	קום	STAND	878b	7 c
		גבעה	GIBEAH	149b	2
		מצא	FIND	594b	2 e
		פקד	ATTEND TO	823a	A 4
13	16	גבע	GEBA	148d	
		גבעה	GIBEAH	149b	2
		חנה	DECLINE	333c	2 c2
		חנה	DECLINE	333c	2 c2
		ישב	REMAIN	442d	2 a
		מכמס	MICHMASH	485a	
		מלחמה	WAR	536b	
		מצא	FIND	594b	2 e
13	17	דרך	WAY	202d	1
		ה	THE	208b	1 g
		יצא	GO OUT	422c	1 a
		עפרה	OPHRAH	780b	1 a
		פנה	TURN	815b	1 a
		ראש	HEAD	911b	6
		שחת	GO TO RUIN	1008b	1
		שועל	SHUAL	1043b	
13	18	בית־חורון	BETH-HORON	111c	B
		גבול	BOUNDARY	148a	1 b
		גבע	GEBA	148d	
		גיא	VALLEY	161b	B
		דרך	WAY	202d	1
		על	UPON	755d	2 5
		פנה	TURN	815b	1 a
		צבעים	ZEBOIM	840d	
		ראש	HEAD	911b	6
		שקף	LOOK DOWN	1054c	
13	19	חנית	SPEAR	333d	1
		חרש	GRAVER	360d	1 a
		מצא	FIND	594b	2 d
		עברי	HEBREW	720b	1 a
		פן	LEST	814d	1 a
13	20	את	PLOUGHSHARE	88c	
		מחרשה	PLOUGHSHARE	361a	
		ירד	GO DOWN	433a	1 d
		לטש	SHARPEN	538c	2
		קרדם	AXE	899c	
13	21	את	PLOUGHSHARE	88c	
		דרבן	GOAD	201c	
		מחרשה	PLOUGHSHARE	*361a	
		נצב	STAND	662c	4
		פצירה	FILE	823a	
		קלשון	GOAD POINTS	887d	
		קרדם	AXE	899c	
13	22	היה	COME TO PASS	225a	1 2a 2
		חנית	SPEAR	333d	1
		יד	HAND	390d	5 c1
		ל	TO	512d	5 aa
		מצא	FIND	594a	2 a
13	23	מכמס	MICHMASH	485a	
		מצב	GARRISON	662d	3
		מעבר	FORD	721b	1
14	1	היה	BECOME	225c	2 1a
		חלו	THIS	229c	
		כלי	IMPLEMENT	479d	2 a
		מצב	GARRISON	662d	3
		נשא	LIFT	671a	2 a
		עבר	PASS OVER	717a	1 b
		עבר	REGION ACROSS	719d	1
		על	UPON	757b	27c aa
14	2	גבעה	GIBEAH	149b	2
		ישב	REMAIN	442d	2 a
		מגרון	MIGRON	550d	1
		קצה	END	892b	2
		רמון	POMEGRANATE	941d	1
14	3	אחיהו	AHIJAH	26d	1
		אחיטוב	AHITUB	26d	1
		איכבוד	ICHABOD	33b	
		אפוד	EPHOD	65c	1 b
		אפוד	EPHOD	65c	2 a
		הלך	WALK	230b	1 1b
		כהן	PRIEST	463b	4
		נשא	LIFT	671a	2 a
		עלי	ELI	750b	
		פינחם	PHINEHAS	810a	2
		שלו	SHILOH	1017d	
14	4	בוצץ	BOZEZ	130d	
		בקש	SEEK	134d	2 d
		זה	THIS	262a	6 e
		מצב	GARRISON	662d	3
		סלע	CRAG	701a	1
		סנה	SENEH	702d	
		עבר	PASS OVER	717b	1 c
		עבר	REGION ACROSS	719d	2
		מעברה	FORD	721b	1
		על	UPON	757b	27c aa
		שן	TOOTH	1042a	1 c
14	5	ארץ	EARTH	76a	1 b
		גבע	GEBA	148d	
		מכמס	MICHMASH	485a	
		מול	IN FRONT OF	557c	2
		מן	FROM	578c	1 c
		נגב	SOUTH-COUNTRY	616b	2
		מצוק	PILLAR	748b	
		שן	TOOTH	1042a	1 c
14	6	ב	IN	89d	3 2a

Ch v.	Heb	Eng	Page	Sec
	יהונתן	JONATHAN	220d	1
	ישע	GIVE VICTORY	447a	3 b
	כלי	IMPLEMENT	479d	2 a
	ל	TO	515a	5 hb a
	מעט	A FEW	589d	1 a
	מצב	GARRISON	662d	3
	עבר	PASS OVER	717a	1 b
	מעצור	RESTRAINT	784a	
	ערל	HAVING FORESKIN	790c	
	עשה	DO	794a	1 1b
	רב	MUCH	913a	1 c
	שמע	HEAR	1033c	1 a
14 7	כלי	IMPLEMENT	479d	2 a
	לבב	HEART	523c	2 2
	לבב	HEART	523c	2 2
	נטה	BEND	640b	3 a
14 8	יהונתן	JONATHAN	220d	1
	הלך	WALK	231b	1 d3 gd
	עבר	PASS OVER	717a	1 b
14 9	דמם	BE STILL	198d	2
	כה	THUS	462b	1 a
	נגע	REACH	619c	2
	על	UPON	757b	2 7c aa
	עמד	STAND	764a	2 a
	תחת	UNDERNEATH	1065d	2 2a
14 10	אות	SIGN	16d	2
	אל	TO	41a	B
	כה	THUS	462b	1 a
	עלה	GO UP	748c	2 c
	על	UPON	757b	2 7c aa
14 11	חבא	WITHDRAW	285b	1
	חוח	BRIER	*296b	1 a
	חר	HOLE	359d	
	מצב	GARRISON	662d	3
	עברי	HEBREW	720b	2 a
14 12	אל	TO	41a	B
	יד	HAND	390d	5 c1
	ידע	KNOW	395a	
	כלי	IMPLEMENT	479d	2 a
	מצב	GARRISON	662d	3
	על	UPON	757b	2 7c aa
14 13	כלי	IMPLEMENT	479d	2 a
	מות	DIE	560a	
	נפל	FALL	657a	2 a
	עלה	GO UP	748c	1 f
	על	UPON	752d	2 1
	פנה	FACE	817b	2 4b c
14 14	חצי	HALF	345c	1
	כ	LIKE	455a	
	כלי	IMPLEMENT	479d	2 a
	נכה	SMITE	646a	2 c
	מכה	SLAUGHTER	647a	2
	מענה	PLACE FOR TASK	776a	
	עשרים	TWENTY	797d	1 la
	צמד	COUPLE	855b	2
	ראשון	FIRST	911d	2 a
14 15	מהומה	DISCOMFITURE	*223a	2
	חרד	TREMBLE	353b	1
	חרדה	TREMBLING	353d	1
	מצב	GARRISON	662d	3
	רגז	BE AGITATED	919a	
	שדה	FIELD	961c	1 f
	שחת	GO TO RUIN	1008b	1
14 16	גבעה	GIBEAH	149b	2
	הלם	SMITE	240c	
	הלם	HITHER	240d	
	המון	CROWD	242c	3 a
	ל	TO	513c	5 cb b
	מוג	MELT	556a	
	צפה	KEEP WATCH	859c	
14 17	הלך	WALK	231c	1 1d 4
	כלי	IMPLEMENT	479d	2 a
	מי	WHO	566c	C
	מעם	FROM WITH	768d	A
	פקד	ATTEND TO	823c	A 4
	ראה	TO SEE	907b	5 a
14 18	אחיהו	AHIJAH	26d	1
	אפוד	EPHOD	65c	2
	אפוד	EPHOD	65c	2
	ארון	CHEST	75c	3 d
	נגש	APPROACH	621b	
	נשא	LIFT	671a	2 a
14 19	אסף	GATHER	62c	4
	היה	COME TO PASS	224c	2 a1 ak
	הלך	WALK	233b	1 4c 3
	המון	TUMULT	242c	1
	ילד	BEAR	408b	1 a
	כהן	PRIEST	463c	4
	עד	UNTIL	725b	2 2a
14 20	את	WITH	85a	1
	מהומה	DISCOMFITURE	223a	2
	זעק	CRY	277c	
	מלחמה	WAR	536b	1
14 21	ל	TO	518a	7 bg
	סבב	TURN ABOUT	685c	1 a
	סביב	ROUND ABOUT	687a	1 d
	עברי	HEBREW	720b	2 b
	שלשם	THREE DAYS AGO	1026b	
	תמול	YESTERDAY	1070a	2 b
14 22	דבק	KEEP CLOSE	180a	2 b
	מהומה	DISCOMFITURE	*223a	2
	הר	MOUNTAIN	251a	2 b
	חבא	WITHDRAW	285b	1
14 23	ביתאון	BETH-AVEN	110d	
	ישע	DELIVER	446d	1 b
	עבר	PASS OVER	717c	2
14 24	אלה	SWEAR	46d	
	ארר	CURSE	76d	
	מעם	TASTE	381a	1
	מלחמה	WAR	536c	
	לחם	FOOD	537b	2 a
	נקם	AVENGE	668d	1 b
	שגה	GO ASTRAY	993a	3
	שגגה	SIN OF ERROR	993a	
14 25	דבש	HONEY	185b	
	יער	WOOD	421a	G
	יער	HONEYCOMB	421a	
	פנה	FACE	819d	2 7b
	שדה	FIELD	961c	1 f
14 26	דבורה	BEE	184b	
	דבש	HONEY	185b	
	הלך	WALK	232a	1 2
	הלך	TRAVELLER	237b	
	יער	WOOD	421a	G
	יער	HONEYCOMB	421a	
	ירא	FEAR	431c	3
	נשג	REACH	673c	2 b
	פה	MOUTH	804d	1 a
	שבועה	OATH	990a	1 a
14 27	אור	BECOME LIGHT	21b	
	דבש	HONEY	185b	
	טבל	DIP	371b	1
	יד	HAND	390d	5 c1
	יערה	HONEYCOMB	421a	
	מטה	STAFF	641c	1
	פה	MOUTH	804d	1 a
	קצה	END	892a	1
	ראה	TO SEE	907b	4
	שבע	SWEAR	989c	1
	שוב	TURN BACK	998d	1 a
	שלח	SEND	1018d	3 a
	שמע	HEAR	1033c	1 a
14 28	ארר	CURSE	76d	
	לחם	FOOD	537b	2 a
	עיף	BE FAINT	746a	
	שבע	SWEAR	989c	1
14 29	אור	BECOME LIGHT	21b	
	דבש	HONEY	185b	
	ה	THE	*209a	2 a
	טעם	TASTE	381a	1
	עכר	STIR UP	747d	
14 30	אף	ALSO	65b	3
	כי	THAT	472c	1 db
	לו	IF	*530a	
	לו	IF	530a	1 a
	מצא	FIND	592d	1 a
	מכה	SLAUGHTER	647a	2
	עתה	NOW	774b	1 d
	רבה	BECOME MANY	915b	1 a1
14 31	אילון	AIJALON	19c	1
	אחר	BEHIND	30a	2 a
	מכמש	MICHMASH	485a	
	נכה	SMITE	646b	3
	עיף	BE FAINT	746a	
14 32	אל	TO	40b	5
	בן	SON	121c	7 b
	בקר	CATTLE	133b	1 a
	בקר	CATTLE	*133b	1 a
	דם	BLOOD	196c	1
	עיט	DART GREEDILY	743c	
	על	UPON	755c	2 4c
	צרחן	SMALL CATTLE	838b	1 a1
	שחט	SLAUGHTER	1006a	1
14 33	בגד	ACT TREACHEROUSLY	93d	A
	דם	BLOOD	196c	1
	הנה	BEHOLD	244a	B a
	חטא	MISS A GOAL OR WAY	307a	2 b
	ל	TO	517c	7 bb
	על	UPON	755c	2 4c
	אל	TO	40b	5
14 34	אל	TO	41a	A
	דם	BLOOD	196c	1
	חטא	MISS A GOAL OR WAY	307a	2 b
	יד	HAND	391a	5 c4
	לילה	NIGHT	538d	1
	נגש	APPROACH	621b	
	נגש	APPROACH	621b	
	על	UPON	755c	2 4c
	פוץ	BE DISPERSED	807a	
	שה	A SHEEP	962a	1
	שור	A HEAD OF CATTLE	1004b	1
	שחט	SLAUGHTER	1006a	1
14 35	את	MARK OF THE ACCUSATIVE	85a	1 a
	מזבח	ALTAR	258b	1
	חלל	POLLUTE	320d	2
14 36	אור	LIGHT	21c	2
	אלהים	GOD	43d	3
	בזז	SPOIL	102d	
	בקר	MORNING	133d	1 b
	הלם	HITHER	240d	
	טוב	PLEASANT	374a	2 f
	ירד	GO DOWN	432d	1 b
	כהן	PRIEST	463c	4
	לא	NOT	518c	1 aa
	קרב	COME NEAR	897b	1 a
	שאר	REMAIN	984b	1
14 37	ענה	ANSWER	772d	1 b
	שאל	ASK	982a	2 b
14 38	הלם	HITHER	240d	
	חטאת	SIN	308c	1 b
	ידע	KNOW	393d	1 c
	מה	HOW	553d	4 a
	נגש	DRAW NEAR	620d	1
	פנה	CORNER	819d	2
	ראה	TO SEE	907b	5 a
	ראה	TO SEE	907c	5 b
14 39	חי	ALIVE	311d	1 a
	ישע	DELIVER	446d	1 b
	כי	THAT	472a	1 c
	כיאם	THAT IF	474c	1 a
	מות	DIE	559d	2 a
	מן	FROM	580c	3 a
	טוב	PLEASANT	374a	2 f
	ל	TO	511d	1 h
14 40	עבר	REGION ACROSS	719d	2
14 41	אורים	URIM	22a	
	אורים	URIM	22b	
	גורל	LOT	*174c	2 f
	יהב	GIVE	396d	1
	יצא	GO OUT	423a	1 d
	לכד	TAKE	540b	3
	תם	INTEGRITY	1070d	4
	תמים	COMPLETE	1071b	5
14 42	אורים	URIM	22b	
	לכד	TAKE	540b	3
	נפל	FALL	658a	3
14 43	דבש	HONEY	185b	
	הנה	BEHOLD	244a	A
	טעם	TASTE	381a	1
	מות	DIE	559d	2 a
	מעט	A FEW	590a	1 b
	מטה	STAFF	641c	1
	קצה	END	892a	1
14 44	יסף	ADD	415b	1
	כי	THAT	472a	1 c
	מות	DIE	559d	2 a
14 45	את	WITH	86a	1 a
	חי	ALIVE	311d	1 a
	חלילה	FAR BE IT	321a	
	ישועה	VICTORY	447c	4
	מות	DIE	559d	2 a
	מן	FROM	581a	3 bd
	נפל	FALL	657a	1
	עם	WITH	767c	1
	עשה	DO	794a	1 1b
	פדה	RANSOM	804a	2
	שערה	A HAIR	972b	
14 46	אחר	BEHIND	30b	4 aa
	הלך	WALK	231b	1 d3 gd
	מקום	STANDING PLACE	880a	3 b
14 47	אדום	EDOM	10c	2
	אשר	PARTICLE OF RELATION	82c	4 bg
	ישע	BE DELIVERED	446b	2
	לכד	CAPTURE	540a	1
	מלוכה	KINGSHIP	574d	
	עמון	AMMON	770a	
	פנה	TURN	815b	1 a
	צובא	ZOBAH	844c	
	רחוב	REHOB	932b	1 a
	רשע	BE WICKED	957d	3
14 48	חיל	STRENGTH	298d	1 b
	עמלק	AMALEK	766a	
	עשה	DO	793d	1 1a 1
	שסה	PLUNDER	1042c	
14 49	בכירה	FIRST-BORN	114c	
	מיכל	MICHAL	568a	
	מלכישוע	MALCHI-SHUA	575d	
	מרב	MERAB	597b	
	קטן	SMALL	882a	1 a
	ישוי	ISHVI	1001a	2
14 50	אבינר	ABNER	4c	
	אחימעץ	AHIMAAZ	27b	2
	אחינעם	AHINOAM	27b	1
	דוד	UNCLE	187c	2
	נר	NER	633a	1
14 51	אבינר	ABNER	4c	
	נר	NER	633a	1
	קיש	KISH	885c	1
14 52	אסף	GATHER	62b	2 b
	בן	SON	121d	8 a
	גבור	STRONG	150a	1
	חזק	STRONG	305c	1 d
	כל	ALL	481c	1 b
	מלחמה	WAR	536d	2
15 1	את	MARK OF THE ACCUSATIVE	85a	1 a
	דבר	WORD	183b	3 2
	ל	TO	512b	4 a
	מלך	KING	573c	5 c
	משח	ANOINT	603b	2
	קול	VOICE	877b	3 b
	שלח	SEND	1018c	2 a
	שמע	HEAR	1034a	1 j
15 2	דרך	WAY	202c	1
	עמלק	AMALEK	766a	
	פקד	ATTEND TO	823c	A 1a
	צבא	GOD OF WAR	839c	4 c
	שום	TO PLACE	964b	4 a
15 3	חמל	SPARE	328b	
	חמור	HE-ASS	331b	1
	חרם	BAN	*355d	
	חרם	BAN	355d	1 a
	חרם	BAN	*355d	1 a

Ch v.	Heb	Eng	Page	Sec
	חרם	DEVOTED THING	*356b	1 a
	ינק	SUCK	413b	
	מן	FROM	582a	5 b
	עולל	CHILD	760c	
	שה	A SHEEP	962a	
15 4	שור	A HEAD OF CATTLE	1004b	
	חוילה	HAVILAH	*296d	
	טלאים	TELAIM	378b	
	טלם	TELEM	379a	1
	מאה	HUNDRED	548a	1 b1
	רגלי	ON FOOT	920b	
	שמע	HEAR	1034c	
15 5	ארב	LIE IN WAIT	70c	
	עיר	CITY	746d	3
	ריב	STRIVE	936d	4
15 6	אסף	GATHER	62c	1 5f 3
	הלך	WALK	234b	
	חסד	GOODNESS	338c	1 1
	סור	TURN ASIDE	693d	2
	עמלקי	AMALEKITES	766a	
	עשה	DO	794b	1 3
	קיני	KENITE	884a	
	תוך	MIDST	1063d	
15 7	בוא	COME	98d	2 e
	חוילה	HAVILAH	296d	
	חכילה	HACHILAH	*314d	
	טלם	TELEM	379a	1
	פנה	FACE	818d	27a d
	שור	SHUR	1004b	
15 8	אגג	AGAG	8a	
	חי	ALIVE	312a	1 b
	חרב	SWORD	352d	1 f
	חרם	BAN	355d	1 a
	חרם	DEVOTED THING	*356b	1 a
	תפש	LAY HOLD OF	1074d	1
15 9	אבה	BE WILLING	2c	
	אגג	AGAG	8a	
	בזה	DESPISE	102c	2
	חמל	SPARE	328b	
	חרם	BAN	355d	1 a
	טוב	A GOOD THING	375b	2
	מוטב	THE BEST	406b	
	כר	LAMB	503a	
	מלאכה	WORK	522a	2
	מסס	MELT	588a	2
	צאן	SMALL CATTLE	838b	1 a4
	שמן	FAT	1032a	1
	משמן	FATNESS	1032d	
	משנה	SECOND	1041d	3 a
15 10	דבר	WORD	182c	1 2a
	היה	BECOME	225b	2 1b
15 11	אחר	BEHIND	30b	4 aa
	דבר	WORD	183a	2 2
	זעק	CRY	277b	2 a
	חרה	BURN	354a	1 b
	חרם	BAN	*355d	1 a
	חרם	DEVOTED THING	*356b	1 a
	לילה	NIGHT	539a	1
	מלך	KING	573c	5 c
	מלך	BE KING	574b	
	נחם	BE SORRY	637a	2
	קום	STAND	879a	6 f
	שוב	TURN BACK	997d	6 a
15 12	בקר	MORNING	134b	1 h
	יד	MONUMENT	390c	4 a
	כרמל	CARMEL	502b	2
	נגד	BE CONSPICUOUS	617a	
	נצב	STAND	662c	2
	סבב	TURN ABOUT	685c	1 a
	שכם	START EARLY	1014c	
15 13	ברך	BLESS	138d	2 b
	קום	STAND	879a	6 f
15 14	אזן	EAR	24a	1
	בקר	CATTLE	133b	1 a
	ה	THE	*209a	2 a
	ו	AND	254c	4
	קול	VOICE	877a	1 e
15 15	אשר	THAT	83c	8 c
	חמל	SPARE	328b	
	חרם	BAN	355d	1 a
	מוטב	THE BEST	406b	
	יתר	LEFT OVER	451b	
	עמלקי	AMALEKITES	766a	
	צאן	SMALL CATTLE	838b	1 a4
15 16	ה	THE	207b	1 ca
	לילה	NIGHT	539a	1
	נגד	BE CONSPICUOUS	616d	2
	רפה	SINK	952a	1
15 17	לא	NOT	520b	4 ba
	מלך	KING	573c	5 c
	משח	ANOINT	603b	2
	קטן	SMALL	882b	2
15 18	חטא	SINFUL	308b	2
	חרם	BAN	355d	1 a
	חרם	BAN	*355d	1 a
	גתי	GITTITE	388a	1
	כלה	FINISH	478c	2 c1
	לחם	ENGAGE IN BAT-TLE	535c	
	עד	AS FAR AS	724b	1 2a b
	שלח	SEND	1018c	2 a
15 19	עיט	DART GREEDILY	743c	
	קול	VOICE	877b	3 b
15 20	אגג	AGAG	8a	
	אשר	THAT	83c	8 ag
	חרם	BAN	355d	1 a

Ch v.	Heb	Eng	Page	Sec
	חרם	BAN	*355d	1 a
	קול	VOICE	877b	3 b
15 21	בקר	CATTLE	133b	1 a
	חרם	DEVOTED THING	356b	1 a
	ראשית	BEGINNING	912b	2
15 22	איל	RAM	18a	2 g
	זבח	SACRIFICE	257c	1 1
	חלב	FAT	317a	2 b
	חסד	GOODNESS	*338d	1 3
	חפץ	DELIGHT	343b	1
	חרם	BAN	*355d	1 a
	טוב	PLEASANT	374c	6
	ל	TO	517d	7 bd
	מן	THAN	582b	6 a
	עלה	WHOLE BURNT OF-FERING	750d	
	קול	VOICE	877b	3 b
	קשב	ATTEND	904a	
15 23	און	TROUBLE	20a	2
	ו	AND	254d	5 b
	חטאת	SIN	308c	1
	חרם	BAN	*355d	1 a
	מאס	REJECT	549c	1 a
	מאס	REJECT	549c	1 a
	מן	FROM	583b	7 bb
	מרי	REBELLION	598b	
	יען	ON ACCOUNT OF	774d	2 c
	פצר	PUSH	823a	
	קסם	DIVINATION	890c	2
	תרפים	IDOL	1076d	
15 24	חטא	MISS A GOAL OR WAY	307a	2 b
	ירא	FEAR	431b	1 b
	עבר	PASS OVER	717c	1 i
	פה	MOUTH	805b	2 c
15 25	חטאת	SIN	308d	1 d2
	נשא	LIFT	671b	3 c
	שחה	BOW DOWN	1005c	2 c
15 26	חרם	DEVOTED THING	*356b	1 a
	מאס	REJECT	549c	1 a
	מאס	REJECT	549c	1 a
	מלך	KING	573b	5 b
	מן	FROM	*583b	7 bb
	הלך	WALK	230b	1 1b
15 27	חזק	BE FIRM	305a	6 a
	כנף	EXTREMITY	489d	2 a
	מעיל	ROBE	*591c	1
	מעיל	ROBE	591c	1
	סבב	TURN ABOUT	685c	1 a
	קרע	TEAR	902d	2
15 28	טוב	PLEASANT	374c	6
	ממלכות	DOMINION	575c	2
	קרע	TEAR	902c	2
	רע	FRIEND	946a	2
	רעות	FELLOW	*946c	
15 29	אדם	MAN	9b	2
	לא	NOT	519b	1 bb
	נחם	BE SORRY	637a	2
	נצח	EMINENCE	664b	1
	שקר	DEAL FALSELY	1055d	
15 30	זקן	OLD	278d	2 b
	חטא	MISS A GOAL OR WAY	307a	2 b
	כבד	MAKE HONORABLE	457d	2 a
	נגד	IN FRONT	617b	1 aa
15 31	שוב	TURN BACK	996d	6 a
15 32	אגג	AGAG	8a	
	אכן	SURELY	38c	A
	הלך	WALK	232a	1 1d 5k
	מעדנות	BONDS	588d	
	מר	BITTER	600d	2 b
	נגש	APPROACH	621b	
	נגש	APPROACH	*621b	
	סור	TURN ASIDE	*694a	4
	מעדנות	BONDS	772c	
15 33	אגג	AGAG	8a	
	חרם	BAN	356a	2
	כן	SO	486c	2 cd
	מן	THAN	582c	6 b
	פנה	FACE	817b	24a h
	פשח	TEAR IN PIECES	832d	
	שכל	BE BEREAVED	1013d	
	שכל	BE BEREAVED	1013d	1
	שסף	HEW IN PIECES	1043a	
15 34	גבעה	GIBEAH	149b	2
	הלך	WALK	230d	1 1d 3b
	רמה	RAMA	928a	2
	שאול	SAUL	*982c	1
15 35	אבל	MOURN	5c	
	אל	TO	40b	6
	יום	DAY	401b	7 1
	יסף	ADD	414d	
	מות	DEATH	560c	1
	מלך	BE KING	574b	
	נחם	BE SORRY	637a	2
	ראה	TO SEE	907d	6 d
16 1	אבל	MOURN	5c	
	בית הלחמי	THE BETHLEHEM-ITE	112a	
	ישי	JESSE	445a	
	מאס	REJECT	549c	1 a
	מן	FROM	583b	7 ba
	מתי	WHEN	607d	C
	קרן	HORN	901d	1 b
	ראה	TO SEE	907d	6 g
	שמן	OIL	1032b	2 d

Ch v.	Heb	Eng	Page	Sec
16 2	בקר	CATTLE	133b	1 a
	הרג	KILL	247a	2 db
	ו	AND	254b	2 db
	יד	HAND	391a	5 c4
	עגלה	HEIFER	722b	
16 3	אמר	SAY	56a	1
	ב	IN	88d	1 4
	זבח	SACRIFICE	257c	1 1
	ידע	MAKE KNOWN	395a	
	ישי	JESSE	445a	
	משח	ANOINT	603b	2
	קרא	CALL	895d	5 a
16 4	זן	OLD	279a	2 b
	חרד	TREMBLE	353c	4
	קרא	ENCOUNTER	897a	1
	שלום	PEACE	1022d	3
16 5	ב	IN	*88d	1 4
	זבח	SACRIFICE	257c	1 1
	קדש	BE SET APART	873b	4 b
	קדש	BE SET APART	873c	4
	קרא	CALL	895d	5 a
16 6	אך	SURELY	36c	1
	אליאב	ELIAB	45a	C
	אליהו	ELIHU	45b	2
	נגד	IN FRONT	617b	1 aa
16 7	אדם	MAN	9b	2
	אשר	THAT	83d	8 e
	גבה	HIGH	147b	4 4
	לבב	HEART	523b	2 1
	מאס	REJECT	549c	1 a
	נבט	LOOK	613d	2
	עין	EYE	745a	4 b
	קומה	HEIGHT	879b	1
	ראה	TO SEE	908a	8 c
	מראה	VISION	909c	1 b
	מראה	VISION	*909d	
16 8	אבינדב	ABINADAB	4c	2
	בחר	CHOOSE	103d	1 a
	זה	THIS	260c	1 a
	עבר	PASS OVER	719a	3 a
16 9	בחר	CHOOSE	103d	1 a
	זה	THIS	260c	1 a
	עבר	PASS OVER	719a	3 a
	שמה	SHAMMAH	1031c	2
	שמעא	SHIMEA	1035a	1
16 10	אלה	THESE	41c	D
	בחר	CHOOSE	103d	1 a
	עבר	PASS OVER	719a	3 a
16 11	לקח	TAKE	543c	6
	נער	YOUTH	655a	1 c
	סבב	GO AROUND	685d	2 a
	עוד	STILL	729b	1 c
	פה	HERE	806a	2
	קטן	SMALL	882a	1 a
	רעה	TEND	945a	1 d1
	שאר	REMAIN	983d	
16 12	אדמוני	RED	10c	
	טוב	PLEASANT	373c	1 a
	יפה	BEAUTIFUL	421c	
	משח	ANOINT	603b	2
	עלם	YOUNG MAN	761c	
	עם	WITH	768d	5
	ראי	LOOKING	909b	2
	תמם	BE COMPLETE	1070c	3
16 13	אל	TO	41a	B
	דוד	DAVID	188a	
	הלך	WALK	230d	1 1d 3b
	יום	DAY	401a	7 j
	מן	FROM	581b	4 a
	משח	ANOINT	603b	2
	מעל	ABOVE	751d	2 bb b
	צלח	RUSH	852b	
	קרב	INWARD PART	899b	1 f3
	קרן	HORN	901d	1 b
	רוח	BREATH	926a	9 c1
	רמה	RAMA	928a	2
	שמן	OIL	1032b	2 d
16 14	את	WITH	86d	4 c
	בעת	FALL UPON	130a	1
	ו	AND	252b	1
	סור	TURN ASIDE	693d	2
	מעם	FROM WITH	768d	A
	רוח	BREATH	925d	9 a
	רוח	BREATH	926a	9 c1
	רע	EVIL	948b	2
16 15	בעת	FALL UPON	*130a	1
	נא	PART OF EN-TREATY	609c	4
	רוח	BREATH	925d	9 a
	רע	EVIL	948b	2
16 16	אל	TO	41a	B
	אמר	SAY	56c	1
	בקש	SEEK	134c	1 b
	היה	BECOME	225d	2 1b
	טוב	PLEASING	373b	4
	ידע	KNOW	394b	4 b
	כנור	LYRE	490a	
	כנור	LYRE	490b	
	נגן	PLAY	618d	
	נגן	PLAY	618d	
	על	UPON	758d	4 2a
	רוח	BREATH	925d	9 a
	רע	EVIL	948b	2
16 17	יטב	DO WELL	405d	3
	ל	TO	*517c	7 bb
	נגן	PLAY	618d	

145

Ch	v.	Heb	Eng	Page	Sec
		עבד	SLAVE	713d	2
16	18	ראה	TO SEE	907d	6 g
		בין	DISCERN	106d	1
		ביתהלחמי	THE BETHLEHEM-ITE	112a	
		גבור	STRONG	150b	2
		דבר	WORD	182a	1 1a
		חיל	STRENGTH	298d	1 c
		ידע	KNOW	394b	4 b
		ישי	JESSE	445a	
		ל	TO	513c	5 cb a
		מלחמה	WAR	536b	
		מן	FROM	580c	3 a
		נגן	PLAY	618d	
		תאר	FORM	1061b	
16	20	גדי	KID	152a	
		חמור	HE-ASS	331c	3
		יד	HAND	391a	5 d
		יין	WINE	406c	D
		לחם	FOOD	537a	1 a
		נאד	SKIN	609d	
		שלח	SEND	1018b	1 b
16	21	אהב	LOVE	13a	1
		היה	BECOME	226b	2 2d
		כלי	IMPLEMENT	479d	2 a
		עמד	STAND	763d	1 d
16	22	חן	FAVOR	336b	2 b1
		עמד	STAND	764a	1 e
16	23	אל	TO	41a	B
		ה	THE	209a	2 b
		היה	BECOME	225d	2 1b
		טוב	PLEASING	373b	4
		כנור	LYRE	490a	
		ל	TO	511a	1 e
		נגן	PLAY	618d	
		סור	TURN ASIDE	693d	2
		על	UPON	758d	4 2a
		רוח	BREATH	925d	9 a
		רוח	BE WIDE	926c	
		רע	EVIL	948b	2
17	1	אסף	GATHER	62b	1 a
		אפסדמים	EPHES-DAMMIM	67c	
		אשר	PARTICLE OF RELATION	83a	7 c
		חנה	DECLINE	333d	2 c2
		מחנה	ENCAMPMENT	334b	3 c
		מלחמה	WAR	536a	
		עזקה	DIG ABOUT	740a	
		שוכה	SOCOH	962c	1
17	2	אלה	TEREBINTH	18d	
		מלחמה	WAR	536a	
		עמק	VALE	771a	
		ערך	ARRANGE	789c	1 d
17	3	אל	TO	41a	A
		גיא	VALLEY	161b	
		ה	THE	207b	1 cb
		הר	MOUNTAIN	250c	1 k
17	4	איש	MAN	36a	
		אמה	CUBIT	52c	1
		בין	SPACE BETWEEN	108a	2
		גבה	HEIGHT	147b	1
		זרת	SPAN	285a	
		גת	GATH	387d	
		שש	SIX	995c	1 a
		שם	NAME	1027d	2 a
17	5	חמש	FIVE	332a	4
		כובע	HELMET	464d	
		כלי	IMPLEMENT	*479d	2 a
		לבש	PUT ON	528a	E
		נחשת	COPPER	638d	1
		קשקשת	SCALE OF FISH	903d	
		שקל	SHEKEL	1053c	
		משקל	WEIGHT	1054a	
		שריון	BODY-ARMOUR	1056b	
		שריון	BODY-ARMOUR	1056b	
17	6	חושי	HUSHAI	302a	1
		כידון	JAVELIN	475d	
		כתף	SHOULDER	509b	1 a
		מצחה	GREAVE	595a	
		נחשת	COPPER	638d	1
		רגל	FOOT	919d	1 a
17	7	ארג	WEAVE	71a	
		ברזל	IRON	137c	1 d
		חושי	HUSHAI	302a	1
		חנית	SPEAR	334a	2 b
		חנית	SPEAR	334a	2 a
		חץ	ARROW	346c	2
		כידון	JAVELIN	*475d	
		להבה	FLAME	529b	2
		מנור	BEAM	644d	
		עץ	TREE	781d	2 b
		צנה	LARGE SHIELD	857a	
		שקל	SHEKEL	1053c	
17	8	ברה	EAT	*136a	
		חושי	HUSHAI	302a	1
		ירד	GO DOWN	432d	1 b
		מלחמה	WAR	536a	
		עבד	SLAVE	714a	2
		עמד	STAND	763d	1 a
		ערך	ARRANGE	789c	1 a
		מערכה	ROW	790b	1 b
		פלשתי	PHILISTINE	814b	
17	9	יכל	PREVAIL	408a	2 b
		לחם	ENGAGE IN BATTLE	535c	
		לחם	ENGAGE IN BATTLE	535d	
		נכה	SMITE	646a	2 c
		עבד	SLAVE	714c	7
17	10	חרף	REPROACH	357d	
		יחד	UNION	403a	2 a1
		לחם	ENGAGE IN BATTLE	535d	
		נתן	GIVE	678c	1 b
		מערכה	ROW	790b	1 b
17	11	ב	IN	89a	1 7b
		חתת	BE SHATTERED	369d	2 a
		ירא	FEAR	431a	1 a
17	12	איש	MAN	36a	
		אפרתי	EPHRATHITE	68d	2
		ב	IN	88b	1 2a
		בוא	COME	98b	1 k
		ביתהלחם	BETHLEHEM	111d	1
		ה	THE	*209b	2 b
		זקן	BE OLD	278b	1
		שמנה	EIGHT	1033a	1 b
17	13	אבינדב	ABINADAB	4c	2
		אליאב	ELIAB	45a	C
		הלך	WALK	231b	1 d3 ge
		שמה	SHAMMAH	1031c	2
		שמעא	SHIMEA	1035a	1
		משנה	SECOND	1041a	3 b
17	14	מן	SMALL	882a	1 a
		שלש	THREE	1025d	1 a
17	15	ביתהלחם	BETHLEHEM	111d	1
		חושי	HUSHAI	302a	1
		על	UPON	759a	4 2c
		רעה	TEND	944d	1 a
		שוב	TURN BACK	997a	2
17	16	יצב	STATION ONESELF	426b	B
		ערב	BECOME EVENING	788a	
		שכם	START EARLY	1014d	
17	17	איפה	EPHAH	35b	1
		ה	THE	*209b	2 b
		לחם	FOOD	537a	1 a
		עשר	TEN	796d	2 b
		קלי	PARCHED GRAIN	885d	
		רוץ	RUN	930c	1
17	18	בוא	COME	99b	2
		חלב	MILK	316b	A
		חריץ	A CUT	358d	1
		ערבה	THING EXCHANGED	786d	
		פקד	ATTEND TO	823b	A 1a
		שר	CHIEFTAIN	978c	3 b
		שלום	PEACE	1022d	3
17	19	אלה	TEREBINTH	18d	
		כל	ALL	481c	1 b
		לחם	ENGAGE IN BATTLE	535c	
17	20	עמק	VALE	771a	
		אב	FATHER	3b	1
		בקר	MORNING	134b	1 h
		חיל	STRENGTH	299a	4
		יצא	GO OUT	424a	2 c
		נטש	LEAVE	643d	1
		מעגל	ENTRENCHMENT	722d	1
		על	UPON	753b	2 1c
		מערכה	ROW	790a	1 a
		רוע	RAISE A SHOUT	929c	1
		שמר	KEEP	1036c	1 a
17	21	ישב	DWELL	*443b	3
		ערך	ARRANGE	789c	1 d
		מערכה	ROW	790a	1 a
		ישראל	ISRAEL	975c	2
17	22	כלי	ARTICLE	479c	1
		נטש	LEAVE	643d	1
		על	UPON	753b	2 1c
		מערכה	ROW	790a	1 a
		רוץ	RUN	930b	1
		שאל	ASK	982a	2 a
		שמר	KEEP	1036c	1 a
		שמר	KEEP	1036c	1 b
17	23	איש	MAN	36a	
		בין	SPACE BETWEEN	108a	2
		דבר	SPEAK	181c	3 e
		גת	GATH	387d	
		מערכה	ROW	790b	1 b
17	24	ירא	FEAR	431a	1 a
		כל	ALL	481c	1 b
		נום	FLEE	630d	1
		פנה	FACE	818b	2 6a
17	25	היה	COME TO PASS	225a	1 2b ag
		חפשי	FREE	344d	2
		חרף	REPROACH	357d	
		כי	THAT	472d	1 e
		עשר	RICHES	799b	
		עשר	BE RICH	799b	1
17	26	אלהים	GOD	44b	4 a
		הלו	THIS	229c	
		חי	ALIVE	311d	1 a
		חרפה	REPROACH	357d	1
		חרפה	REPROACH	357d	1
		חרף	REPROACH	357d	
		כי	THAT	472d	1 f
		מי	WHO	566d	F b
		סור	TURN ASIDE	694d	1
		מערכה	ROW	790b	1 b
		ערל	HAVING FORESKIN	790c	
17	27	דבר	WORD	183d	4 7
17	28	אליאב	ELIAB	45a	C
		הם	THEY	241d	7
		זדון	INSOLENCE	268a	1
		חרה	BURN	354a	1 a
		לבב	HEART	524a	2 6b
		מעט	A FEW	590a	1 b
		נטש	LEAVE	643d	1
		מערכה	ROW	790a	1 a
		ראה	TO SEE	907d	6 e
17	29	רע	EVIL	947d	2
		דבר	WORD	184a	4 8
17	30	אצל	BESIDE	69b	B
		דבר	WORD	182b	1 1c
		דבר	WORD	183d	4 7
		דבר	WORD	183d	4 7
		מול	IN FRONT OF	557c	2
		סבב	TURNABOUT	685c	1 a
		שוב	TURN BACK	999c	3
17	32	לחם	ENGAGE IN BATTLE	535c	
		נפל	FALL	657c	5
		על	UPON	753c	2 1d
17	33	לחם	ENGAGE IN BATTLE	535c	
		מלחמה	WAR	536b	
		נער	YOUTH	655a	1 d
		נערים	YOUTH	655b	
17	34	ארי	LION	71d	
		את	MARK OF THE ACCUSATIVE	85b	3 a
		דב	BEAR	*179a	
		דב	BEAR	179a	
		היה	BE	227a	3 4b
		ו	AND	252b	1 b
		זה	THIS	262b	
		נשא	LIFT	671b	3 a
		עדר	FLOCK	727c	1 a
		רעה	TEND	945a	1 d1
		שה	A SHEEP	962a	1
17	35	זקן	BEARD	278b	1
		חזק	BE FIRM	305a	6 a
		יצא	GO OUT	423d	2 c
		נכה	SMITE	645d	1
		נכה	SMITE	645d	2 a
		נצל	SNATCH AWAY	664d	1
		פה	MOUTH	805b	3
		קום	STAND	877d	1 c
17	36	אלהים	GOD	44b	4 a
		ארי	LION	71d	
		דב	BEAR	179a	
		היה	BECOME	226a	2 2c
		חי	ALIVE	311d	1 a
		חרף	REPROACH	357d	
		נכה	SMITE	646a	2 c
		מערכה	ROW	790b	1 b
		ערל	HAVING FORESKIN	790c	
17	37	ארי	LION	71d	
		דב	BEAR	179a	
		יד	HAND	391b	5 g1
		יד	HAND	391b	5 g1
17	38	ו	AND	252b	1 b
		לבש	CLOTHE	528b	1 a
		מד	GARMENT	551c	3
		נתן	PUT	680a	2 a
		קובע	HELMET	875c	
		קין	SPEAR	*883d	
		שריון	BODY-ARMOUR	1056b	
17	39	אלה	THESE	41c	D
		הלך	WALK	231d	1 d5 ta
		חגר	GIRD	291d	1
		חרב	SWORD	352c	1 b
		יאל	SHOW-WILLINGNESS	384a	1
		מד	GARMENT	551c	3
		נסה	TEST	650b	1
		סור	TURN ASIDE	694b	1
		על	UPON	759b	4 2e a
17	40	אבן	STONE	6b	1
		אשר	PARTICLE OF RELATION	83a	7 b
		בחר	CHOOSE	104a	3 b
		ו	AND	252c	1 b
		חלק	SMOOTH	325c	
		יד	HAND	391a	5 c4
		כלי	INSTRUMENT	*480a	2 c
		כלי	VESSEL	480a	3
		ילקוט	RECEPTACLE	545a	
		מקל	STAFF	596c	2
		נחל	WADY	636b	2
		קלע	SLING	887c	
		רעה	TEND	945a	1 d1
		שבט	ROD	*987a	1 a
17	41	הלך	WALK	233c	1 4d
		צנה	LARGE SHIELD	857a	
		קרב	APPROACHING	898b	1
17	42	אדמוני	RED	10c	
		בוז	DESPISE	102c	
		היה	BE	227a	3 4b
		יפה	BEAUTIFUL	421c	
		נבט	LOOK	613c	1 a
		נער	YOUTH	655a	1 d
		עלם	YOUNG MAN	761c	
		עם	WITH	*768d	5
		מראה	VISION	909c	1 a
17	43	כלב	DOG	477a	B
		מקל	STAFF	596c	2
		קלל	BE SLIGHT	886c	

Ch	v.	Heb	Eng	Page	Sec
17	44	שבט	ROD	*987a	1 a
		במה	BEAST	97a	3
		בשר	FLESH	142c	1 b
		הלך	WALK	230b	1 1c
		עוף	FLY	733d	1
		שדה	FIELD	961b	1 c
17	45	אלהים	GOD	44c	4 ba
		ב	IN	90a	3 2d
		חנית	SPEAR	333d	1
		חרף	REPROACH	357d	1
		כידון	JAVELIN	475d	1
		מערכה	ROW	790b	1 b
		צבא	GOD OF WAR	839b	4
		צבא	GOD OF WAR	839b	4 c
		שם	NAME	1028b	3
17	46	היה	LIVING THING	312c	1 b
		מחנה	ENCAMPMENT	334b	3 c
		יש	HAVE	441d	2 cb
		סגר	DELIVER UP	689b	1
		סור	TURN ASIDE	694b	1
		עוף	FLY	733d	1
		פגר	CORPSE	803d	1
17	47	חנית	SPEAR	333d	1
		חרב	SWORD	*352d	1 j
		ישע	GIVE VICTORY	447a	3 b
		ל	TO	513b	5 ba
		קהל	ASSEMBLY	874c	1 b
17	48	היה	COME TO PASS	225a	1 2a 2
		ו	AND	252b	1 b
		כי	WHEN	473a	2 a
		מהר	HASTEN	555a	2
		קרב	COME NEAR	897c	1 g
		רוץ	RUN	930b	1
17	49	אבן	STONE	6b	1
		טבע	SINK	371c	1
		כלי	VESSEL	480a	3
		לקח	TAKE	542d	3 a
		מצח	FOREHEAD	594d	
		נכה	SMITE	645c	1 a
		נפל	FALL	656d	1
		קלע	SLING	887c	
17	50	אבן	STONE	6b	1
		חזק	BE FIRM	304a	1 1a
		יד	HAND	390d	5 c1
		מות	DIE	560b	1 a
		נכה	SMITE	645d	2 a
		קלע	SLING	887c	
17	51	חרב	SWORD	352c	1 c
		חרב	SWORD	*352d	1 e
		כרת	CUT OFF	503d	1
		מות	DIE	560a	
		עמד	STAND	763d	1 a
		תער	RAZOR	789b	2
		רוץ	RUN	930b	1
		שלף	DRAW OUT	1025b	1
17	52	בוא	COME	98c	2 e
		גיא	VALLEY	161b	1
		דרך	WAY	202d	1
		חלל	PIERCED	319c	2
		גת	GATH	387d	
		נפל	FALL	657a	2 a
		רוע	RAISE A SHOUT	929c	1
		שער	GATE	1044c	1 a
		שערים	SHAARAIM	1045c	1
17	53	דלק	HOTLY PURSUE	196b	2
		מחנה	ENCAMPMENT	334b	
		שוב	TURN BACK	996d	1
		שסס	PLUNDER	1042d	
17 \	54	אהל	TENT	13d	1
		אהל	TENT	13d	1
		ירושלים	JERUSALEM	436d	
		כלי	IMPLEMENT	479d	2 a
17	55	אבינר	ABNER	4c	
		אם	IF	50b	1 b2
		ה	THE	208d	1 i
		זה	THIS	261b	4 b
		חי	ALIVE	312a	1 b
		מי	WHO	566b	B
		נפש	SOUL	659c	2
		אתה	THOU	61c	
17	56	זה	THIS	261b	4 b
		מי	WHO	566c	C
		עלם	YOUNG MAN	761c	
		עם	WITH	*768d	5
		שאל	ASK	982a	2 a
17	57	שוב	TURN BACK	997a	2
17	58	ביתהלחמי	THE BETHLEHEM-ITE	112a	
		ה	THE	208d	1 i
		ישי	JESSE	445a	
18	1	אהב	LOVE	13a	1
		יהונתן	JONATHAN	220d	1
		נפש	SOUL	660a	4 b3
		קשר	BIND	905b	
18	2	שוב	TURN BACK	997b	3 a
18	3	אהב	LOVE	13a	1
		ברית	COVENANT	136c	1 4
		כרת	CUT	503d	4
		נפש	SOUL	660a	4 b3
18	4	חגור	BELT	292a	
		מד	GARMENT	551c	3
		עד	AS FAR AS	724b	1 1b
		פשט	STRIP OFF	833b	
		קשת	BOW	906a	1 b
18	5	אשר	PARTICLE OF RELATION	82c	4 bg

Ch	v.	Heb	Eng	Page	Sec
		יטב	BE PLEASING	405c	4
		על	UPON	755a	2 3
		שכל	BE PRUDENT	968c	6
18	6	חול	WHIRL	297b	1
		מחולה	DANCING	298b	
		מחולה	DANCING	298b	
		פלשתי	PHILISTINE	814b	
		שמחה	JOY	970d	1
		שוב	TURN BACK	997a	2
		שיר	SING	1010d	
		שליש	THREE STRINGED	1026d	
		תף	TIMBREL	1074c	
18	7	נכה	SMITE	646d	2 c
		ענה	SING	777b	
		רבבה	MULTITUDE	914b	
		שחק	LAUGH	965d	3
18	8	אך	ONLY	36c	2 ba
		חרה	BURN	354a	1 b
		מלוכה	KINGSHIP	574c	
		נתן	GIVE	679a	1 h
		עוד	STILL	729b	1 c
		רבבה	MULTITUDE	914b	
18	9	רעע	BE EVIL	949c	1
		היה	BE	227c	3 5a
		הלאה	ONWARDS	229c	B
		יום	DAY	401a	7 j
		מן	FROM	581b	4 a
		עין	EYE	745a	
		שקר	OGLE	974c	
18	10	אל	TO	41a	B
		ב	IN	90b	3 3b
		ה	THE	207b	1 cb
		חנית	SPEAR	333d	1
		יד	HAND	390d	5 c1
		יום	DAY	400b	7 e1
		מחרת	THE MORROW	564a	
		נבא	PROPHESY	612b	1 a
		נגן	PLAY	618d	
		צלח	RUSH	852b	
		רוח	BREATH	925d	9 a
		רע	EVIL	948b	2
18	11	חנית	SPEAR	333d	1
		מול	HURL	376d	
		נכה	SMITE	645c	1 a
		סבב	TURNABOUT	685c	1 a
		פנה	FACE	818b	26a
		קיר	WALL	885a	1 a
18	12	היה	BE	227b	3 4d a
		ירא	FEAR	431b	1 c
		סור	TURN ASIDE	693d	2
		מעם	FROM WITH	768a	A
		פנה	FACE	818a	2 5b
18	13	בוא	COME	97d	1 a
		סור	TURN ASIDE	694b	1
		מעם	FROM WITH	769a	A
		פנה	FACE	817c	2 4c b
		שום	TO PLACE	964c	5 b
18	14	היה	BE	227c	3 5a
		שכל	BE PRUDENT	968c	6
18	15	אשר	THAT	83b	8 ab
		גור	DREAD	159a	1
		ראה	TO SEE	907b	5 a
		שכל	BE PRUDENT	968c	6
18	16	אהב	LOVE	12d	1
		בוא	COME	97d	1 a
		יצא	GO OUT	424a	3
		פנה	FACE	817c	2 4c b
18	17	אך	HOWBEIT	36c	2 a
		את	MARK OF THE ACCUSATIVE	85a	1 a
		ב	IN	89b	2 4a
		בן	SON	121d	8 a
		בת	DAUGHTER	123a	1
		היה	BECOME	226c	2 2f
		לחם	ENGAGE IN BATTLE	535d	
		מלחמה	WAR	536b	
		מרב	MERAB	597c	
18	18	חי	KINSFOLK	312c	
		חתן	DAUGHTER:S HUSBAND	368c	1
		ל	TO	513a	5 ad
		מי	WHO	566b	A
		מי	WHO	566d	F b
		משפחה	CLAN	1046d	1 a
18	19	היה	COME TO PASS	224d	1 2a 1b
		מחולתי	MEHOLATHITE	563b	
		מרב	MERAB	597b	
		נתן	GIVE	681b	1 b
		עדריאל	ADRIEL	727b	
		עת	TIME	773d	2 c
18	20	אהב	LOVE	12d	1
		ישר	BE STRAIGHT	448c	2
		מיכל	MICHAL	568a	
18	21	חתן	MAKE ONESELF A SON IN LAW	368d	1
		מוקש	BAIT	430d	
18	22	אהב	LOVE	12d	1
		חפץ	DELIGHT IN	342d	1 a
		חתן	MAKE ONESELF A SON IN LAW	368d	1
		לט	SECRECY	532a	1
		עבד	SLAVE	713d	2
		צוה	CHARGE	845d	2 b
18	23	ו	AND	253c	1 k

Ch	v.	Heb	Eng	Page	Sec
		חתן	MAKE ONESELF A SON IN LAW	368d	1
		קלה	DISHONOURED	885d	
		קלל	BE SLIGHT	886c	2
		רוש	BE IN WANT	930d	
18	25	חפץ	DELIGHT	343b	1
		חשב	THINK	363a	1 2
		ל	TO	517d	7 bc
		מהר	PURCHASE-PRICE	555c	
		נפל	FALL	658a	2
		נקם	AVENGE	668b	1 b
		ערלה	FORESKIN	790b	
18	26	חתן	MAKE ONESELF A SON IN LAW	368d	1
		ישר	BE STRAIGHT	448c	2
		מלא	BE FULL	570b	1 b
		איש	MAN	36a	
18	27	חתן	MAKE ONESELF A SON IN LAW	368d	1
		מאה	HUNDRED	548a	1 b1
		מיכל	MICHAL	568a	
		מלא	FILL	570d	2
		ערלה	FORESKIN	790b	
18	28	אהב	LOVE	12d	1
		מיכל	MICHAL	568a	
18	29	איב	BE HOSTILE TO	33c	
		איב	BE HOSTILE TO	33c	
		היה	BE	227c	3 5a
		יום	DAY	400c	7 f
		יסף	DO AGAIN	415c	2 a
		ירא	FEAR	431b	1 c
18	30	די	SUFFICIENCY	191d	2 ca
		היה	COME TO PASS	224d	1 2a 1b
		יקר	BE PRECIOUS	429d	1 a
		מן	THAN	582c	6 b
		פלשתי	PHILISTINE	814c	
		שכל	BE PRUDENT	968b	
		שר	CHIEFTAIN	978a	1 a
19	1	חפץ	DELIGHT IN	342d	1 a
		עבד	SLAVE	713d	2
19	2	בקש	SEEK	134d	2 d
		חבא	WITHDRAW	285b	
		סתר	COVERING	712a	2 a
		שמר	KEEP	1037b	
19	3	דבר	SPEAK	181c	4 c
		ו	AND	254b	2 db
		יד	HAND	391b	5 f
		יום	DAY	*400d	7 g
		מה	AUGHT	553d	3
		שדה	FIELD	961c	1 f
19	4	דבר	SPEAK	181a	
		דבר	SPEAK	181c	4 c
		חטא	MISS A GOAL OR WAY	306d	2 a
		חטא	MISS A GOAL OR WAY	306d	2 a
		טוב	PLEASANT	374a	2 f
		טוב	PLEASANT	374d	0 a
		כי	BECAUSE	474b	3 d
		מעשה	DEED	795d	1 a3
19	5	גדול	GREAT	153a	1
		דם	BLOOD	196d	2 d
		חטא	MISS A GOAL OR WAY	306d	2 a
		חנם	OUT OF FAVOR	336d	C
		תשועה	DELIVERANCE	448b	1
		כף	HOLLOW OF THE HAND	496d	1 d6
		ל	TO	517c	7 bb
		מה	HOW	554b	4 db
		נפש	SOUL	659b	3 c
		נקי	CLEAN	667c	1
		פלשתי	PHILISTINE	814b	
		שום	TO PLACE	963a	1 a
19	6	אם	IF	50b	1 b2
		חי	ALIVE	311d	1 a
		מות	DIE	560c	2
		שבע	SWEAR	989b	1 a
19	7	פנה	FACE	817b	2 4b a
		שלשם	THREE DAYS AGO	1026d	
		תמול	YESTERDAY	1070a	2 b
19	8	יסף	DO AGAIN	415c	2 a
		נכה	SLAUGHTER	647a	2
19	9	היה	BECOME	225d	2 1b
		חנית	SPEAR	333d	1
		נגן	PLAY	618d	
		רוח	BREATH	925d	9 a
		רע	EVIL	948b	2
19	10	בקש	SEEK	134d	2 d
		ה	THE	207b	1 cb
		הוא	HE, SHE, IT	216d	7
		חנית	SPEAR	333d	1
		מלט	SLIP AWAY	572b	4
		נכה	SMITE	645c	1 a
		פטר	SEPARATE	809c	1
		פנה	FACE	818b	26a
19	11	בקר	MORNING	133d	1 a
		לילה	NIGHT	539a	1
		מות	DIE	560c	2
		מיכל	MICHAL	568a	
		מלט	SLIP AWAY	572c	3
		נפש	SOUL	660a	3 c
		שמר	KEEP	1036d	1 c
19	12	בעד	AWAY FROM	126b	1 a
		ברח	FLEE	137d	2
		הלך	WALK	234a	1 5e

Ch	v.	Heb	Eng	Page	Sec
		חלון	WINDOW	319d	
		ירד	LET DOWN	434b	3
		מיכל	MICHAL	568a	
		מלט	SLIP AWAY	572b	2
19	13	בגד	GARMENT	94a	1
		בגד	COVERING	94a	1
		ה	THE	207b	1 cb
		ה	THE	*207c	1 d
		כביר	QUILT	460d	
		כסה	COVER	491d	2
		מיכל	MICHAL	568a	
		מטה	COUCH	641d	
		עז	SHE-GOAT	777c	4
		מראשות	HEAD-PLACE	912b	
		שום	TO PLACE	963c	1 d
		תרפים	IDOL	1076c	
19	14	חלה	BE WEAK	317d	2
19	15	מטה	COUCH	641d	
		עלה	GO UP	749c	2 a
		ראה	TO SEE	907c	6 a
19	16	אל	TO	41a	A
		כביר	QUILT	460d	
		מטה	COUCH	641d	
		עז	SHE-GOAT	777c	4
		מראשות	HEAD-PLACE	912b	
		תרפים	IDOL	1076c	
19	17	איב	BE HOSTILE TO	33c	
		ככה	THUS	462c	
		מה	HOW	554b	4 d
		מה	HOW	*554b	4 d
		מיכל	MICHAL	568a	
		מלט	SLIP AWAY	572b	2
		רמה	BEGUILE	941a	
19	18	ברח	FLEE	137d	2
		מלט	SLIP AWAY	572b	2
		נוית	NAIOTH	627d	
		נוית	NAIOTH	*628a	
		רמה	RAMA	928a	2
19	19	נגד	BE CONSPICUOUS	617a	
		נוית	NAIOTH	627d	
		רמה	RAMA	928a	2
19	20	להקה	COMPANY	530a	
		נביא	PROPHET	611c	1
		נבא	PROPHESY	612a	1 a
		נבא	PROPHESY	612b	1 a
		נצב	STAND	662b	2
		רוח	BREATH	925d	9 a
		נבא	PROPHESY	*1101d	
19	21	יסף	DO AGAIN	415c	2 b
		נבא	PROPHESY	612b	1 a
		שלישי	THIRD	1026a	
19	22	איפה	WHERE	33a	1
		בור	WELL	92b	1
		גדול	GREAT	153a	1
		הלך	WALK	230d	1 1d 3b
		נוית	NAIOTH	627d	
		רמה	RAMA	928a	2
		שכו	SECU	967d	
		שאל	ASK	981d	2 a
19	23	הלך	WALK	233b	14c 2
		נבא	PROPHESY	612b	1 a
		נוית	NAIOTH	627d	
		רוח	BREATH	925d	9 a
		רמה	RAMA	928a	2
19	24	גם	ALSO	169b	2
		לילה	NIGHT	539a	1
		נבא	PROPHESY	612b	1 a
		נפל	LIE	657d	7
		ערום	NAKED	736a	
		פשט	STRIP OFF	833a	1
		נבא	PROPHESY	*1101d	
20	1	בקש	SEEK	134d	2 a
		ברח	FLEE	138a	2
		חמאת	SIN	308c	1 a
		כי	THAT	472d	1 f
		נוית	NAIOTH	627d	
		נפש	SOUL	659d	3 c
		עון	INIQUITY	730d	1
		פנה	FACE	817a	24 a g
		רמה	RAMA	928a	2
20	2	אזן	EAR	24b	3
		אמר	SAY	56a	1
		הנה	BEHOLD	244a	B a
		זה	THIS	260c	1 a
		חלילה	FAR BE IT	321a	
		סתר	HIDE	711d	1
		קטן	SMALL	882b	2
20	3	אולם	BUT	19d	
		חי	ALIVE	311d	1a
		חי	ALIVE	312a	1 b
		חן	FAVOR	336b	2 b1
		כי	THAT	472a	1 c
		נפש	SOUL	659c	2
		עצב	HURT	780c	
		פשע	STEP	832c	
		שבע	SWEAR	989a	1a
20	4	אמר	SAY	56b	2
		מה	WHAT	553b	1 ea
		נפש	SOUL	661a	5
		עשה	DO	793d	1 1a 3
20	5	אכל	EAT	37b	1
		הנה	BEHOLD	244a	B a
		חדש	NEW MOON	294c	1
		ישב	SIT	442c	1 a
		מחר	TO-MORROW	564a	1 a
		סתר	HIDE	711b	1
		שדה	FIELD	961c	1 f
		שלישי	THIRD	1026b	
20	6	ביתלחם	BETHLEHEM	111d	1
		זבח	SACRIFICE	257c	2 3
		יום	YEAR	399d	6 c
		פקד	ATTEND TO	823b	A 1d
		רוץ	RUN	930b	1
		שאל	ASK	982b	
		משפחה	CLAN	1046d	1 a
20	7	חרה	BURN	354a	1 b
		טוב	PLEASANT	374c	5
		כה	THUS	462b	1 a
		כלה	BE FINISHED	477c	1 d
		עבד	SLAVE	714c	6
		מעם	FROM WITH	769a	D
		שלום	PEACE	1022d	3
20	8	אם	IF	49d	1 a2
		אתה	THOU	61c	1
		ברית	COVENANT	136c	14
		חסד	GOODNESS	338c	1 1
		יש	BE	441c	2 a
		יש	BE	*442a	2 ch
		מה	HOW	554b	4 d
		עבד	SLAVE	714c	6
		עון	INIQUITY	731b	2 a
		על	UPON	758a	28
20	9	עשה	DO	794b	1 3
		חלילה	FAR BE IT	321a	
		כלה	BE FINISHED	477c	1 d
		מעם	FROM WITH	769a	D
20	10	או	OR	15a	3
		יד	HAND	390d	5 c1
		מה	WHAT	552c	1 aa
		מה	AUGHT	553d	3
		קשה	SEVERE	904d	2 a
20	11	שדה	FIELD	961c	1 f
20	12	אז	THEN	23a	1 b
		און	EAR	24b	3
		הנה	IF	244c	D
		חקר	SEARCH	350d	2 b
		טוב	PLEASING	373b	4
		מחר	TO-MORROW	564a	1 a
		עד	WITNESS	729d	2 a
		עת	TIME	773c	1 a
		שלישי	THIRD	1026b	
20	13	אזן	EAR	24b	3
		את	MARK OF THE AC-CUSATIVE	85b	1 c
		היה	BE	227b	3 4d a
		הלך	WALK	231d	1 d5 tc
		יטב	DO RIGHT	406a	5 b
		יסף	ADD	415b	1
		כי	IF	473b	2 b
20	14	חי	ALIVE	312a	1 b
		חסד	GOODNESS	338c	1 1
		חסד	GOODNESS	338c	1 1
		לא	NOT	519a	1 a
		לא	NOT	520d	
		לו	IF	530b	2
		עם	WITH	767d	1 d
20	15	אדמה	GROUND	9d	4
		חסד	GOODNESS	338c	1 1
		כרת	CUT OFF	504c	2 c
		כרת	CUT OFF	504d	4
		מעם	FROM WITH	*769a	B
		פנה	FACE	819b	2 8b
20	16	בקש	SEEK	135a	5 b
		כרת	CUT	503d	4
20	17	אהב	LOVE	13a	1
		אהבה	LOVE	13b	1
		יסף	DO AGAIN	415c	2 a
		נפש	SOUL	660a	4 b3
		שבע	SWEAR	989b	1 a
		שבע	SWEAR	989d	1 a
20	18	חדש	NEW MOON	294c	1
		מושב	SEAT	444b	1 a
		מחר	TO-MORROW	564a	1 a
		פקד	ATTEND TO	823d	1
		פקד	ATTEND TO	823d	1
20	19	אבן	STONE	7a	9
		אצל	BESIDE	69b	A
		הלז	THIS	*229c	
		ישב	REMAIN	442b	2 a
		סתר	HIDE	711b	1
		מעשה	DEED	795c	1 a1
		פקד	ATTEND TO	823d	1
		ארגב	HEAP	918d	
		שלש	DO A THIRD TIME	1026a	
20	20	חץ	ARROW	346b	1
		ירה	SHOOT	435b	2
		ל	TO	515c	5 ia
		ל	TO	517b	7 ba
		מטרה	TARGET	643c	1
		צד	SIDE	841a	1
		שלח	SEND	1019b	6
		שלש	DO A THIRD TIME	1026a	
20	21	בוא	COME	98b	2
		דבר	WORD	183d	4 6
		ה	THE	207b	1 cb
		הלאה	OUT THERE	*229c	A
		הנה	HITHER	244c	A a
		חי	ALIVE	311d	1 a
		חצי	ARROW	345d	
		חץ	ARROW	*346b	1
		חץ	ARROW	346b	1
		מן	FROM	578d	1 c
		מצא	FIND	592d	1 a
		שלום	PEACE	1022d	3
		בוא	COME	*98b	2
20	22	הלאה	OUT THERE	229b	A
		חצי	ARROW	345d	
		חץ	ARROW	346b	1
		חץ	ARROW	*346b	1
		מן	FROM	579a	1 c
		עלם	YOUNG MAN	761c	
		עם	WITH	*768d	5
20	24	אכל	EAT	37b	1
		חדש	NEW MOON	294c	1
		סתר	HIDE	711b	1
		על	UPON	756a	2 6b
		שדה	FIELD	961c	1 f
20	25	ישב	SIT	442b	1 a
		ישב	SIT	442c	1 a
		מושב	SEAT	444b	1 a
		ל	TO	511b	1 ga
		פעם	OCCURRENCE	822a	3 b
		פקד	ATTEND TO	823d	1
		צד	SIDE	841a	1
		קדם	COME IN FRONT	870a	2 b
		קום	STAND	877d	1 a
		מקום	STANDING PLACE	880a	4
20	26	אמר	SAY	56b	2
		בלת	NOT	116c	1
		טהר	BE CLEAN	372c	
		כי	THAT	472d	1 e
		מאומה	ANYTHING	548d	
		מקרה	ACCIDENT	900a	1
20	27	בן	SON	120c	1 g
		חדש	NEW MOON	294c	1
		יום	DAY	399d	7 a1
		ישי	JESSE	445b	
		לחם	FOOD	537a	1 a
		מחרת	THE MORROW	564b	
		פקד	ATTEND TO	823d	1
		מקום	STANDING PLACE	880a	4
		תמול	YESTERDAY	1070a	2 aa
20	28	ענה	ANSWER	772d	1 c
20	29	שאל	ASK	982b	
		הוא	HE, SHE, IT	215c	1 e
		זבח	SACRIFICE	257c	2 3
		חן	FAVOR	336b	2 b1
		כן	SO	487a	3 f
		מלט	SLIP AWAY	572b	1
		צוה	GIVE CHARGE TO	845c	1 b
		שלחן	TABLE	1020b	1
		משפחה	CLAN	1046d	1 a
20	30	בשת	SHAME	102a	1
		בשת	SHAME	102b	1
		בחר	CHOOSE	104b	7
		בן	SON	120c	1 ia
		בן	SON	120c	1 a
		חרה	BURN	354a	1 a
		ישי	JESSE	445b	
		לא	NOT	520b	4 ba
		מרדות	REBELLIOUSNESS	597d	
		ערוה	NAKEDNESS	789a	1
20	31	אדמה	GROUND	9d	4
		בן	SON	120c	1 g
		ישי	JESSE	445b	
		כון	BE FIRM	465d	1 b
		לקח	TAKE	543c	6
		מות	DEATH	560d	2
		מלכות	ROYAL POWER	574d	1
20	32	מה	HOW	554b	4 d
		מות	DIE	560c	2
20	33	ה	THE	207b	1 cb
		הוא	HE, SHE, IT	216d	6 b
		חנית	SPEAR	333d	1
		טול	HURL	376d	
		כלה	BE FINISHED	477c	1 d
		מעם	FROM WITH	769a	D
20	34	אל	TO	40b	6
		אף	NOSE	60b	3
		ה	THE	207b	1 cb
		חדש	NEW MOON	294c	1
		חרי	BURNING	354c	
		כלם	HUMILIATE	484a	1
		מעם	FROM WITH	769a	A
		עצב	HURT	780c	
		קום	STAND	877d	1 a
		שלחן	TABLE	1020b	1
20	35	בקר	MORNING	134b	2
		מועד	APPOINTED TIME	417c	1 a
		נער	YOUTH	655a	1 c
		קטן	SMALL	882b	1 a
		שדה	FIELD	961c	1 f
20	36	חצי	ARROW	345d	
		חץ	ARROW	346b	1
		ירה	SHOOT	435a	3
		ירה	SHOOT	435b	2
		ל	TO	517b	7 ba
		מצא	FIND	592d	1 a
		עבר	PASS OVER	719a	3 c
		רוץ	RUN	930b	1
20	37	הלאה	OUT THERE	229c	A
		חצי	ARROW	345d	
		ירה	SHOOT	435a	3
		מקום	STANDING PLACE	880a	4
		קרא	CALL	895a	1 a
20	38	חוש	HASTE	301d	
		חצי	ARROW	345d	
		חץ	ARROW	346b	1

Ch	v.	Heb	Eng	Page	Sec
		לקט	GATHER UP	544d	1
		מהרה	HASTE	555b	
		עמד	STAND	764b	3 a
		קרא	CALL	895a	1 b
20	39	ידע	KNOW	393c	1 a
		מאומה	ANYTHING	548d	
20	40	כלי	IMPLEMENT	479d	2 a
20	41	אבן	STONE	7a	9
		אף	NOSE	60b	2
		אצל	BESIDE	69b	B
		בכה	WEEP	113c	3
		גדל	BECOME GREAT	152c	3 c
		נגב	SOUTH-COUNTRY	616b	1 a
		נפל	FALL	657c	3 b
		נשק	KISS	676b	2
		עד	UNTIL	725a	2 lb a
		קום	STAND	877d	1 a
		ארגב	HEAP	918d	
20	42	אשר	THAT	83c	8 c
		הלך	WALK	231d	1 d5 tc
		זרע	SOWING	282d	4 c
		שבע	SWEAR	989b	1 a
		שם	NAME	1028b	3
21	2	אחימלך	AHIMELECH	27a	1
		חרד	TREMBLE	353c	4
		כהן	PRIEST	463c	4
		נב	NOB	611b	1
21	3	קרא	ENCOUNTER	897a	1
		אחימלך	AHIMELECH	27a	1
		אלמני	SOME ONE	48c	
		ידע	CAUSE TO KNOW	394d	
		יעד	APPOINT	417a	
		כהן	PRIEST	463c	4
		מאומה	ANYTHING	549a	
		פלני	A CERTAIN ONE	811d	
		מקום	STANDING PLACE	880a	4
21	4	לחם	FOOD	537a	1 a
		מצא	FIND	594a	2 a
		מצא	FIND	594b	2 e
		תחת	UNDERNEATH	1065c	2 1d
21	5	אך	ONLY	36d	2 ba
		אשה	WOMAN	61a	1
		חל	PROFANENESS	320d	
		יש	BE	442a	2 c
		כהן	PRIEST	463c	4
		כיאם	BUT	475a	2 b
		לחם	FOOD	537b	1 a
		לחם	FOOD	537b	1 a
		קדש	APARTNESS	872a	3 d
		שמר	KEEP	1037b	2
		תחת	UNDERNEATH	1065c	2 1d
		תחת	UNDERNEATH	*1066a	3 1a
21	6	אף	ALSO	65b	3
		דרך	JOURNEY	203a	2
		חל	PROFANENESS	320d	
		כהן	PRIEST	463c	4
		כיאם	SURELY	475c	2 c
		כלי	IMPLEMENT	479d	2 a
		ל	TO	515b	5 hb g
		עצר	RESTRAIN	783c	1
		קדש	APARTNESS	872b	6
		קדש	BE SET APART	872a	1
		שלשם	THREE DAYS AGO	1026b	
		תמול	YESTERDAY	1070a	2 b
21	7	חם	HEAT	328d	
		כהן	PRIEST	463c	4
		לחם	FOOD	537b	1 a
		לקח	TAKE	544a	2
		סור	TURN ASIDE	694c	
		פנה	FACE	817d	2 5a a
		שום	TO PLACE	964b	4 b
21	8	אביר	MIGHTY	7d	1
		אדמי	EDOMITE	10c	
		אשר	PARTICLE OF RELATION	83a	7 b
		דאג	DOEG	178c	
		עבד	SLAVE	713d	2
		עצר	RESTRAIN	783d	
		רעה	TEND	945a	1 d1
		שר	CHIEFTAIN	978d	4 b
21	9	אחימלך	AHIMELECH	27a	1
		אין	NOT	35b	
		גם	ALSO	169b	1
		דבר	WORD	183c	4 l
		חנית	SPEAR	333d	1
		חרב	SWORD	352c	1 a
		יד	HAND	391c	5 i
		כלי	IMPLEMENT	479d	2 a
		כלי	IMPLEMENT	479d	2 a
		לקח	TAKE	543c	6
		נחץ	URGE	637d	
		תחת	UNDERNEATH	1065c	2 1d
21	10	אלה	TEREBINTH	18d	
		אחר	BEHIND	30a	2 a
		אפוד	EPHOD	65c	1 a
		את	MARK OF THE ACCUSATIVE	85a	1 a
		ה	THE	207c	1 d
		זה	THIS	261d	6 a
		זולה	EXCEPT	265d	1
		כהן	PRIEST	463c	4
		לוט	WRAP	532a	
		עמק	VALE	771a	
		פלשתי	PHILISTINE	814b	
		שמלה	WRAPPER	971a	
21	11	אבימלך	ABIMELECH	4b	2
		אכיש	ACHISH	37a	
		גת	GATH	387d	
21	12	פנה	FACE	818b	2 6a
		אכיש	ACHISH	37a	
		מחולה	DANCING	298b	
		מחולה	DANCING	298c	
		לא	NOT	520b	4 bb
		נכה	SMITE	646a	2 c
		ענה	SING	777b	
		רבבה	MULTITUDE	914b	
21	13	אכיש	ACHISH	37a	
		גת	GATH	387d	
		לבב	HEART	523d	2 3d
		שום	TO PLACE	963b	1 b
21	14	דלת	DOOR	195a	1
		הלל	PRAISE	239b	
		זקן	BEARD	278b	1
		טעם	TASTE	381b	2
		ירד	BRING DOWN	434a	1 b
		עין	EYE	745a	5
		ריר	SPITTLE	938c	
		שרט	INCISE	976b	
		שנה	CHANGE	1040a	
		שנה	CHANGE	*1040a	
		שער	GATE	1044c	1 a
		תוה	MAKE A MARK	1063b	
		תפף	SOUND THE TIMBREL	1074c	
21	15	אכיש	ACHISH	37a	
		מה	HOW	554a	4 da
		שגע	BE MAD	993d	
21	16	את	MARK OF THE ACCUSATIVE	84d	1 a
		זה	THIS	260c	1 a
		חסר	NEEDY	341c	
		על	UPON	753b	2 1b
		שגע	BE MAD	993d	
		שגע	BE MAD	993d	
22	1	מלט	SLIP AWAY	572c	2
		עדלם	ADULLAM	726b	
		מערה	CAVE	792c	
		מצודה	FASTNESS	845a	
22	2	היה	BECOME	226c	2 2g
		כל	ALL	481c	1 b
		מר	BITTER	600c	2 b
		נפש	SOUL	660d	6 c
		נשא	BE A CREDITOR	673d	
		מצוק	STRAITNESS	848a	
		קבץ	GATHER	868b	
		שר	CHIEFTAIN	978a	1 b
22	3	אם	MOTHER	52a	1
		יצא	GO OUT	424a	2 c
		עד	UNTIL	725a	2 1a b
		עשה	DO	794a	1 a3
22	4	יום	DAY	400b	7 d2 a
		נוח	REST	629a	B 2
		נחה	LEAD	635a	
		פנה	FACE	816c	2 2a
		מצודה	FASTNESS	845a	
		מצודה	FASTNESS	845a	
22	5	בוא	GO	98d	4
		גד	GAD	151c	2
		הלך	WALK	233d	1 5b
		הלך	WALK	234b	1 5f 3
		חרת	HERETH	362a	
		יהודה	JUDAH	397b	2
		יער	WOOD	420d	B
		יער	WOOD	420d	G
		ל	TO	515d	5 ib
		מצודה	FASTNESS	845a	
22	6	אשל	TAMARISK TREE	79b	
		גבעה	GIBEAH	149b	2
		חנית	SPEAR	333d	1
		ידע	BE MADE KNOWN	394c	1
		נצב	STAND	662a	1 b
		על	UPON	756b	2 6c
		רמה	HEIGH-PLACE	928a	
22	7	בן	SON	120c	1 g
		בנימיני	BENJAMITE	122d	
		גם	ALSO	169b	2
		ישי	JESSE	445b	
		כל	ALL	481b	1 a
		ל	TO	512a	3 b
		נצב	STAND	662a	1 b
		על	UPON	756b	2 6c
		שום	TO PLACE	964c	1 b
		שר	CHIEFTAIN	978c	3 b
22	8	אזן	EAR	24b	3
		ארב	LIE IN WAIT	70b	
		בן	SON	120c	1 g
		חלה	BE WEAK	317d	2
		יום	DAY	400d	7 h
		ישי	JESSE	445b	
		כי	THAT	472d	1 f
		כרת	CUT	503d	4
		ל	TO	512b	4 a
		מן	FROM	580c	3
		מצפה	MIZPEH	859d	2
		קום	STAND	879a	4 b
		קשר	BIND	905b	1
22	9	אדמי	EDOMITE	10c	
		אחימלך	AHIMELECH	27a	1
		אחיטוב	AHITUB	27a	1
		בן	SON	120c	1 g
		דאג	DOEG	178c	
		ישי	JESSE	445b	
22	10	נב	NOB	611b	1
		נכה	SMITE	646a	2 c
		נצב	STAND	662b	2
		נתן	GIVE	678b	1 a
		פלשתי	PHILISTINE	814b	
		צידה	PROVISION	845b	
		שאל	ASK	982a	2 b
22	11	אחימלך	AHIMELECH	27a	1
		אחיטוב	AHITUB	27a	1
		כהן	PRIEST	463c	4
		כהן	PRIEST	463c	4
		קרא	CALL	895d	5 c
		שלח	SEND	1018b	1 c
22	12	אדון	LORD	11b	3 le
		אחימלך	AHIMELECH	27a	1
		אחיטוב	AHITUB	27a	1
		הנה	BEHOLD	244a	A
22	13	ארב	LIE IN WAIT	70b	
		בן	SON	120c	1 g
		יום	DAY	400d	7 h
		ישי	JESSE	445b	
		ל	TO	512b	4 a
		ל	TO	515c	5 hc
		מה	HOW	554a	4 da
		קום	STAND	878a	2
		קשר	BIND	905b	2
		שאל	ASK	982a	2 b
22	14	אחימלך	AHIMELECH	27a	1
		אמן	CONFIRM	53a	5
		חתן	DAUGHTER:S HUSBAND	368c	1
		כבד	BE HONORED	457c	1 b
		מי	WHO	566c	D
		מי	WHO	566c	F c
		סור	TURN ASIDE	694a	4
		סור	TURN ASIDE	694a	4
		משמעת	OBEDIENT BAND	1036a	1
22	15	דבר	WORD	182c	1 1g
		חלל	POLLUTE	320d	2
		חלילה	FAR BE IT	321a	
		ידע	KNOW	393c	1 a
		קטן	SMALL	882b	1 b
		שום	TO PLACE	963a	1 a
		שאל	ASK	982a	2 b
22	16	אחימלך	AHIMELECH	27a	1
		חלב	FAT	316d	2 b
		מות	DIE	559d	2 a
22	17	אבה	BE WILLING	2c	
		אביר	MIGHTY	7d	1
		אזן	EAR	24b	3
		ברח	FLEE	137d	2
		גם	ALSO	169b	2
		כהן	PRIEST	463c	4
		כי	BECAUSE	474b	3 d
		נצב	STAND	662a	1 b
		סבב	TURN ABOUT	685c	1 a
		על	UPON	756b	2 6c
		עם	WITH	767c	1 a
		פגע	MEET	803b	3
		רוץ	RUN	930c	2 a
		שלח	SEND	1018c	3 a
22	18	אדמי	EDOMITE	10c	
		אתה	THOU	61c	
		אפוד	EPHOD	65c	1 a
		אפוד	EPHOD	65c	2 a
		בד	WHITE LINEN	94b	
		דאג	DOEG	178c	
		דאג	DOEG	*178c	
		הוא	HE, SHE, IT	215c	1 c
		כהן	PRIEST	463c	4
		נשא	LIFT	671a	2 a
		סבב	TURN ABOUT	685c	1 a
		פגע	MEET	803b	3
22	19	חמור	HE-ASS	331b	1
		חרב	SWORD	352d	1 f
		ינק	SUCK	413b	
		כהן	PRIEST	463c	4
		מן	FROM	582a	5 b
		נב	NOB	611b	1
		עולל	CHILD	760c	
		שה	A SHEEP	962a	1
		שור	A HEAD OF CATTLE	1004b	
22	20	אביתר	ABIATHAR	5a	
		אחימלך	AHIMELECH	27a	1
		אחיטוב	AHITUB	27a	1
		ברח	FLEE	138a	2
		ל	TO	513c	5 cb a
		מלט	SLIP AWAY	572b	2
22	21	אביתר	ABIATHAR	5a	
		הרג	KILL	247a	1 a
		כהן	PRIEST	463c	4
22	22	אביתר	ABIATHAR	5a	
		אדמי	EDOMITE	10c	
		דאג	DOEG	*178c	
		דאג	DOEG	178c	
		חוב	BE GUILTY	295a	
		סבב	SURROUND	686a	2 d
22	23	בקש	SEEK	134d	2 a
		ירא	FEAR	431a	1 a
		נפש	SOUL	659d	3 c
		עם	WITH	768b	3 c
		משמעת	GUARD	1038b	1
23	1	גרן	THRESHING-FLOOR	175b	
		לחם	ENGAGE IN BATTLE	535c	
		קעילה	KEILAH	890d	

Ch v.	Heb	Eng	Page	Sec
23 2	שסה	PLUNDER	1042c	
	אמר	SAY	56b	1
	ישע	DELIVER	446c	1
	נכה	SMITE	646b	3
	שאל	ASK	982a	2 b
23 3	איש	MAN	36a	
	אף	ALSO	65a	2
	אף	ALSO	65b	3
	ירא	FEAR	431a	1 a
	מערכה	ROW	790b	1 b
	קעילה	KEILAH	890d	
23 4	יסף	DO AGAIN	415c	2 a
	שאל	ASK	982a	2 b
23 5	הלך	WALK	230d	1 ld 3a
	ישע	DELIVER	446c	1
	נהג	DRIVE	624b	1
	נכה	SMITE	646a	2 c
	מכה	SLAUGHTER	647a	1
23 6	אביתר	ABIATHAR	5a	
	אחימלך	AHIMELECH	27a	1
	אפוד	EPHOD	65c	2
	אפוד	EPHOD	65c	2 a
	ברח	FLEE	138a	2
23 7	בריח	BAR	138b	2
	בריח	BAR	138b	1 b
	דלת	DOOR	195b	3
	נגד	BE CONSPICUOUS	617a	
	נכר	TREAT AS FOREIGN	649a	
	סגר	BE SHUT UP	689b	1
	עיר	CITY	746b	1 a
23 8	צור	CONFINE	848d	1
	שמע	HEAR	1034c	
23 9	אביתר	ABIATHAR	5a	
	אפוד	EPHOD	65c	2
	חרש	CUT IN	360c	
	כהן	PRIEST	463b	4
	נגש	APPROACH	621b	
	רעה	MISERY	949b	2
23 10	בקש	SEEK	134d	2 d
	ל	TO	512a	3 b
	שחת	GO TO RUIN	1008a	1
23 11	בעל	OWNER	127c	1 3
	ה	INTERROG PART	209d	1 a
	סגר	DELIVER UP	689c	1
	שמע	HEAR	1033d	1 d1
23 12	בעל	OWNER	127c	1 3
	סגר	DELIVER UP	689c	1
	סגר	DELIVER UP	689c	1
23 13	אשר	PARTICLE OF RELATION	82c	4 bg
	הלך	WALK	236a	1 b
	חדל	CEASE	293a	2
	מלט	SLIP AWAY	572b	2
	נגד	BE CONSPICUOUS	617a	
	קעילה	KEILAH	890d	
23 14	בקש	SEEK	134c	1 b
	זיף	ZIPH	268b	1 a
	חרש	WOOD	*361c	
	יום	DAY	400c	7 f
	מצד	FASTNESS	844d	1
23 15	בקש	SEEK	134c	2 a
	מדבר	WILDERNESS	185a	3 b
	זיף	ZIPH	268b	1 a
	חרש	WOOD	361c	
	יצא	GO OUT	423d	2 c
	נפש	SOUL	659d	3 c
	ראה	TO SEE	907b	5 a
23 16	הלך	WALK	230d	1 ld 3b
	חזק	BE FIRM	304d	2
	חרש	WOOD	361c	
23 17	ירא	FEAR	431a	1 a
	מצא	FIND	593b	3 c
	משנה	SECOND	1041c	3 a
23 18	ברית	COVENANT	136c	14
	הלך	WALK	231b	1 d3 gd
	חרש	WOOD	361c	
	כרת	CUT	504a	4
	פנה	FACE	817b	2 4a h
23 19	גבעה	HILL	149a	4
	זיפי	ZIPHITES	268b	
	חוילה	HAVILAH	*296d	
	חכילה	HACHILAH	314b	
	חרש	WOOD	361c	
	ימין	RIGHT	412a	4
	ישימון	WASTE	445b	A
	לא	NOT	520b	4 bb
	סתר	HIDE	711c	
	מצד	FASTNESS	844d	1
23 20	אוה	DESIRE	16b	
	ל	TO	513b	5 ba
	ל	TO	516c	5 jb
	נפש	SOUL	660d	6 a
	סגר	DELIVER UP	689c	1
23 21	ברך	BLESS	138d	2 b
	חמל	SPARE	328b	
23 22	הוא	HE, SHE, IT	215c	1 c
	ידע	KNOW	393d	1 c
	כון	ESTABLISH	466c	2 a
	מהר	SWIFT	555a	
	ערם	BE SHREWD	791a	
	מקום	STANDING PLACE	880a	4
	ראה	TO SEE	906d	1 a
	ראה	TO SEE	907a	5 b
23 23	אל	TO	40c	7
	אלף	THOUSAND	49b	2
	אם	IF	49d	1 a2
	הלך	WALK	231c	1 ld 5a
	חבא	WITHDRAW	285b	1
	חפש	SEARCH	344c	2 a
	ידע	KNOW	393d	1 a
	ידע	KNOW	393d	1 c
	יש	BE	441c	2 a
	כון	BE FIRM	465d	1 d
	מן	FROM	581a	3 bc
	ראה	TO SEE	907c	5 b
	שוב	TURN BACK	997b	3 b
23 24	מדבר	WILDERNESS	185a	3 b
	זיף	ZIPH	268b	
	ימין	RIGHT	412a	4
	ישימון	WASTE	445b	A
	מעון	MAON	733a	
	ערבה	DESERT-PLAIN	787b	1 a
23 25	בקש	SEEK	134c	1 b
	מדבר	WILDERNESS	185a	3 b
	חרדי	HARODITE	353d	
	ירד	GO DOWN	433a	1 g
	ישב	REMAIN	*442d	2 a
	סלע	CRAG	701a	1
	מעון	MAON	733a	1
23 26	הר	MOUNTAIN	250d	1 m
	חפז	BE IN TREPIDATION	342a	
	עטר	SURROUND	742d	
	פנה	FACE	818b	2 6a
	פנה	FACE	818b	2 6a
	צד	SIDE	841a	
	תפש	LAY HOLD OF	1074d	1
23 27	מהר	HASTEN	555a	2
	מהרה	HASTE	*555b	
	פשט	STRIP OFF	833a	2
23 28	הלך	WALK	233d	1 5a
	מחלקת	DIVISION	325a	
	מחלקות	SMOOTHNESS	325d	
	כן	SO	487b	3 f
	סלע	CRAG	701a	1
	שוב	TURN BACK	996d	1
23 29	עינגדי	ENGEDI	745b	
	מצד	FASTNESS	844d	1
24 1	עינגדי	ENGEDI	745b	
	שוב	TURN BACK	997a	2
24 2	אחר	BEHIND	30b	4 aa
	מדבר	WILDERNESS	185a	3 b
	צור	ROCK	*849c	1 a
	שוב	TURN BACK	997a	2
24 3	איש	MAN	36a	
	בחר	CHOOSE	104b	7
	בקש	SEEK	134c	1 b
	יעל	MOUNTAIN-GOAT	418d	
	על	UPON	757b	2 7c ab
	מערה	CAVE	792c	
	פנה	FACE	818d	2 7a d
	צור	ROCK	849c	1 a
	רגל	FOOT	920a	1 f
24 4	גדרה	WALL	155a	
	דרך	WAY	202c	1
	ירכה	EXTREME PARTS	438a	2
	ישב	REMAIN	442d	2 a
	סכך	OVERSHADOW	697a	1
	על	UPON	756a	2 6a
	מערה	CAVE	*792c	
	קום	STAND	877d	1 a
	רגל	FOOT	920a	1 f
24 5	איב	BE HOSTILE TO	33c	
	אשר	PARTICLE OF RELATION	82c	4 ba
	אשר	PARTICLE OF RELATION	83a	7 b
	יטב	BE PLEASING	405c	4
	כנף	EXTREMITY	489d	2 a
	כרת	CUT OFF	503d	1 a
	לט	SECRECY	532a	1
	מעיל	ROBE	*591c	1
24 6	אחר	AFTER	30a	2 b
	את	MARK OF THE ACCUSATIVE	85a	1 a
	כנף	EXTREMITY	489d	2 a
	כרת	CUT OFF	503d	1 a
	לב	HEART	525a	2 5
	נכה	SMITE	645c	1 a
	על	UPON	758b	3 a
24 7	חלילה	FAR BE IT	321a	
	יד	HAND	389d	1 c
	משיח	ANOINTED	603c	
	מערה	CAVE	792c	
	קום	STAND	*878a	2
24 8	אל	TO	40a	4
	מערה	CAVE	792c	
	מערה	CAVE	*792c	
	קדד	BOW DOWN	869a	
	קום	STAND	878a	2
	קרא	CALL	895a	1 a
	שסע	DIVIDE	1042d	
24 9	אחר	BEHIND	30a	2 a
	אף	NOSE	60b	2
	יצא	GO OUT	422d	1 a
	נבט	LOOK	613c	1 a
	סגר	DELIVER UP	689b	1
	מערה	CAVE	*792c	
	קדד	BOW DOWN	869a	
	קרא	CALL	895a	1 a
	רעה	MISERY	*949b	2
	שחה	BOW DOWN	1005b	1 a
	שמע	HEAR	*1034a	1 k
24 10	בקש	SEEK	134d	2 b
	מה	HOW	554a	4 da
	מערה	CAVE	792c	
	ראה	TO SEE	*906d	1 b
	רעה	MISERY	949b	2
	שמע	HEAR	1034a	1 k
24 11	אמר	SAY	56c	4
	אשר	THAT	83b	8 aa
	הרג	KILL	247a	1 a
	חוס	PITY	299b	A
	יד	HAND	389d	
	יום	DAY	400c	7 g
	משיח	ANOINTED	603c	1
	מערה	CAVE	*792c	
	צדה	LIE IN WAIT	841b	
	ראה	TO SEE	906d	1 b
	שלח	SEND	1018c	3 a
24 12	אב	FATHER	3d	8
	גם	ALSO	169b	2
	הרג	KILL	247a	1 a
	חטא	MISS A GOAL OR WAY	306d	2 a
	ידע	KNOW	393d	1 c
	כנף	EXTREMITY	489d	2 a
	כרת	CUT OFF	503d	1
	מעיל	ROBE	*591c	1
	פשע	TRANSGRESSION	833c	1
	ראה	TO SEE	907c	5 b
	רעה	MISERY	949b	2
24 13	נקם	AVENGE	668a	1 a
	שפט	JUDGE	1047c	2 a
24 14	ה	THE	208b	1
	יצא	GO OUT	423b	1 g
	מן	OUT OF	579d	2 d
	משל	PROVERB	605a	1
	קדמני	FORMER	870d	1
	רשע	WICKED	957b	1
	רשע	WICKEDNESS	957c	1
24 15	יצא	GO OUT	423d	2 c
	מות	DIE	559d	1 b
	מי	WHO	566b	B
	פרעש	FLEA	829a	
	ראה	TO SEE	*907d	7 b
	ריב	STRIVE	936c	3
24 16	דין	JUDGE	193a	
	יד	HAND	391b	5 gl
	מן	FROM	578a	1 a
	ראה	TO SEE	907d	7 b
	ריב	STRIVE	*936c	3
	שפט	JUDGE	1047c	2 a
	שפט	JUDGE	1047d	3 b1
24 17	בכה	WEEP	113c	1
	בן	SON	120b	1 c
	זה	THIS	261a	3
	קול	VOICE	876d	1 a
	רעה	MISERY	*949b	2
	אתה	THOU	61c	
24 18	הרג	KILL	247a	1 a
	טובה	WELFARE	375d	3
	צדיק	JUST	843a	2
	רעה	MISERY	949b	2
24 19	אשר	THAT	83b	8 aa
	טובה	WELFARE	375d	3
	עשה	DO	794b	1 3
24 20	איב	BE HOSTILE TO	33c	
	קום	STAND	*278b	7 b
	טוב	PLEASANT	373d	2 e
	טובה	WELFARE	375d	3
	כי	WHEN	473a	2 a
24 21	שלם	BE COMPLETE	1022c	5
	קום	STAND	278b	7 b
	ממלכה	DOMINION	575b	2
	עתה	NOW	774b	2 c
	שם	NAME	*1028b	2 c
	שמד	BE EXTERMINATED	*1029c	1
24 22	אחר	AFTER	*30a	2 b
	אם	IF	50b	1 b2
	זרע	SOWING	282d	4 c
	כרת	CUT OFF	504c	1
	מצודה	FASTNESS	845a	
	שם	NAME	1028b	2 c
	שמד	BE EXTERMINATED	1029c	1
25 1	ספד	WAIL	704c	1
	מעון	MAON	733a	1
	פארן	PARAN	803a	
	קבץ	GATHER	867d	1
	קבר	BURY	868c	
	רמה	RAMA	928a	2
25 2	אלף	THOUSAND	48d	1 a
	אלף	THOUSAND	49a	1 c
	גדול	GREAT	153a	6 b
	גזז	SHEAR	159c	
	כרמל	CARMEL	502b	2
	מעון	MAON	733a	
	עז	SHE-GOAT	777c	1
	מעשה	DEED	795d	1 b2
	צאן	SMALL CATTLE	838b	1 a
	צאן	SMALL CATTLE	838b	1 b
25 3	אביגיל	ABIGAIL	4a	1
	טוב	PLEASANT	374d	8
	יפה	BEAUTIFUL	421c	
	כלבי	CALEBITE	477a	
	נבל	NABAL	615a	
	מעלל	DEED	760b	1

Ch	v	Heb	Eng	Page	Sec
		קשה	SEVERE	904c	2 a
		רע	EVIL	948a	3
		רע	EVIL	949a	3
		רעע	BE EVIL	949d	2
		שכל	PRUDENCE	968c	1
		תאר	FORM	1061b	
25	4	גזז	SHEAR	159c	
		נבל	NABAL	615a	
25	5	ב	IN	90a	3 2d
		כרמל	CARMEL	502b	2
		נבל	NABAL	615a	
		נער	RETAINER	655a	2 b
		צאן	SMALL CATTLE	838b	2 a
		שאל	ASK	982a	2 a
		שם	NAME	1028a	2 a
25	6	חי	ALIVE	312a	1 b
		שלום	PEACE	1022d	3
25	7	אשר	PARTICLE OF RE-LATION	83a	7 b
		גזז	SHEAR	159c	
		יום	DAY	400b	7 d2 a
		כלם	HUMILIATE	484a	1
		כרמל	CARMEL	502b	2
		ל	TO	513b	5 ba
		ל	TO	514a	5 e
		מאומה	ANYTHING	548d	
		עתה	NOW	774b	1
		פקד	ATTEND TO	823d	1
25	8	חן	FAVOR	336b	2 b1
		טוב	PLEASANT	373d	2 a
		יום	DAY	401b	7 m
		מצא	FIND	593c	4
		על	UPON	754c	2 lf e
		שאל	ASK	981d	2 a
25	9	נבל	NABAL	615a	
		נוח	REST	628b	1
		שם	NAME	1028a	2 a
25	10	בן	SON	120c	1 g
		ה	THE	209b	2 b
		ישי	JESSE	445b	F b
		מי	WHO	566c	F b
		נבל	NABAL	615a	
		עבד	SLAVE	714a	2
		פרץ	BREAK THROUGH	829c	
		רבב	BECOME MANY	912d	1
25	11	אי	WHERE	32b	2 b
		אין	WHENCE	32d	
		גזז	SHEAR	159c	
		ו	AND	252d	1 f
		טבח	SLAUGHTER	370c	1
		טבחה	THING SLAUGH-TERED	370d	1
		לחם	FOOD	537a	1 a
25	12	דרך	JOURNEY	203b	2
		הפך	TURN	245d	2 a
25	13	איש	MAN	36a	
		חגר	GIRD	291d	2
		חרב	SWORD	352c	1 b
		ישב	REMAIN	442b	2 a
		כלי	ARTICLE	479c	1
		עלה	GO UP	748c	2 d
		על	UPON	756a	2 6b
25	14	אביגיל	ABIGAIL	4a	1
		ברך	BLESS	139b	4 c
		נבל	NABAL	615a	
		עיט	SCREAM	743b	
		שלח	SEND	1018b	1 a
25	15	את	WITH	85d	1
		הלך	WALK	236b	2
		טוב	PLEASANT	374d	9 a
		יום	DAY	400b	7 d5
		כלם	BE HUMILIATED	484a	1
		כלם	HUMILIATE	*484a	1
		מאומה	ANYTHING	548d	
		פקד	ATTEND TO	823b	A 1d
		שדה	FIELD	961c	1 f
25	16	חומה	WALL	327d	3
		יום	DAY	400b	7 d2 a
		יומם	DAYTIME	*401c	1
		על	UPON	753a	2 la b
		רעה	TEND	944d	1 a
25	17	אל	TO	41a	B
		בליעל	WORTHLESSNESS	116a	1
		כלה	BE FINISHED	477c	1 d
		מות	DIE	560a	2 b
		מן	THAN	582d	6 d
		ראה	TO SEE	907c	5 b
25	18	אביגיל	ABIGAIL	4a	1
		דבלה	PRESSED FIG-CAKE	179b	
		חמור	HE-ASS	331b	1 a
		חמש	FIVE	331d	1 a
		יין	WINE	406c	D
		לחם	FOOD	537a	1 a
		מאה	HUNDRED	548a	1 b1
		מאה	HUNDRED	548a	1 b2
		נבל	SKIN-BOTTLE	614b	1
		סאה	SEAH	684b	
		עשה	DO	794d	2 3
		צאן	SMALL CATTLE	838b	1 b
		צמק	BUNCH OF RAISINS	856a	
		קלי	PARCHED GRAIN	885d	
25	19	איש	MAN	35d	
		נבל	NABAL	615a	
25	20	ו	AND	252b	1 b
		חמור	HE-ASS	331b	2 a
		סתר	COVERING	712a	1

Ch	v	Heb	Eng	Page	Sec
		פגש	MEET	803d	
		רכב	RIDE	938c	1
25	21	אך	SURELY	36c	1
		זה	THIS	260c	1 a
		טובה	WELFARE	375d	3
		מאומה	ANYTHING	548d	
		פקד	ATTEND TO	823d	1
		שוב	TURN BACK	999c	4 a
		שקר	DECEPTION	1055c	1
		תחת	INSTEAD	1066a	2 2b b
25	22	ב	IN	89b	2 4a
		בקר	MORNING	133d	1 b
		יסף	ADD	415b	1
		קיר	WALL	885a	3
		שאר	REMAIN	984b	1
		שתן	URINATE	1010b	
25	23	אביגיל	ABIGAIL	4a	1
		אף	NOSE	60b	2
		חמור	HE-ASS	331b	2 a
		ירד	GO DOWN	433a	1 f
		מהר	HASTEN	555a	2
		נפל	FALL	657c	3 b
		על	UPON	758c	4 2a
25	24	אדון	LORD	11b	3 lk
		אמה	MAID	51a	2
		אנכי	I	59b	
		דבר	SPEAK	181c	4 b
		נפל	FALL	657c	3 b
		עון	INIQUITY	731c	3
		שפחה	MAID	*1046c	2
25	25	אדם	MAN	9b	1
		אל	TO	41a	B
		אל	TO	41b	
		אמה	MAID	51a	2
		בליעל	WORTHLESSNESS	116a	1
		כ	LIKE	454c	2 d
		כן	SO	486b	2 aa
		לב	HEART	524d	2 3c
		נבל	NABAL	615a	
		נבלה	SENSELESSNESS	615b	1
		על	UPON	757d	27c c
		עם	WITH	768b	3 b
		שום	TO PLACE	963c	2 b
		שם	NAME	1027d	2 a
25	26	אשר	THAT	83c	8 c
		בוא	COME	98a	1 g
		בקש	SEEK	134d	2 b
		דם	BLOOD	197a	2 g
		חי	ALIVE	312a	1 b
		יד	HAND	389c	1 d
		ישע	GIVE VICTORY	447a	3 a
		מן	FROM	583c	7 b
		מנע	WITHHOLD	586a	
		נבל	NABAL	615a	
		נפש	SOUL	659c	2
		רעה	MISERY	949b	2
25	27	אמה	MAID	51a	2
		ברכה	BLESSING	139d	5
		הלך	WALK	236a	1 b
		ו	AND	254c	5 a
		נתן	GIVE	681c	1 c
		רגל	FOOT	920a	1 f
		שפחה	MAID	1046c	2
25	28	אמה	MAID	51a	2
		אמן	CONFIRM	52d	3
		בית	HOUSE	109d	5 b
		מצא	FIND	394a	1 g1
		יום	DAY	399a	4 a
		יום	DAY	399a	4 a
		לחם	ENGAGE IN BAT-TLE	535d	
		מלחמה	WAR	536b	
		מן	FROM	581c	4 a
		נשא	LIFT	671c	3 c
		פשע	TRANSGRESSION	833c	1
25	29	את	WITH	86c	3 a
		בקש	SEEK	134c	2 a
		חי	ALIVE	312a	1 b
		כף	HOLLOW	497a	4 c
		נפש	SOUL	659c	2
		צרר	BIND	864c	A
		צרור	BUNDLE	865c	
		קלע	SLING	887c	
		קלע	SLING	887c	
25	30	אשר	PARTICLE OF RE-LATION	82d	6 b
		דבר	SPEAK	181c	5
		טובה	WELFARE	375d	2 a
		כי	WHEN	473b	2 a
		ל	TO	512b	4 a
		צוה	GIVE CHARGE OVER	845d	1 d
25	31	אמה	MAID	51a	2
		דם	BLOOD	196c	2 b
		זה	THIS	260d	1 a
		זכר	REMEMBER	269d	1 2 a
		חנם	OUT OF FAVOR	336c	C
		חנם	OUT OF FAVOR	*336c	C
		יד	HAND	389c	1 d
		יטב	DO GOOD TO	405d	2
		ישע	GIVE VICTORY	447a	3 a
		מכשול	STUMBLING	506b	2 d
		לב	HEART	525a	2 5
		פוקה	TOTTERING	807c	
		שמר	KEEP	1036c	1 a
		שפך	POUR OUT	1049c	1 b

Ch	v	Heb	Eng	Page	Sec
25	32	אביגיל	ABIGAIL	4a	1
		ברך	BLESS	138c	2 a
25	33	ברך	BLESS	138d	2 b
		ברך	BLESS	138d	2 c
		דם	BLOOD	197a	2 g
		טעם	TASTE	381a	2
		ישע	GIVE VICTORY	447a	3 a
		כלא	RESTRAIN	476b	2
25	34	אולם	BUT	19d	
		אור	LIGHT	21c	2
		אם	IF	50b	1 b2
		בקר	MORNING	133d	1 b
		חי	ALIVE	311d	1 a
		יתר	BE LEFT OVER	451b	
		כי	THAT	472a	1 c
		כיאם	THAT IF	474c	1 a
		ל	TO	512c	5 aa
		לולא	IF NOT	530c	A
		מהר	HASTEN	555a	2
		מנע	WITHHOLD	586a	
		קיר	WALL	885a	3
		שתן	URINATE	1010b	
25	35	נשא	LIFT	670c	1 b 3
		עלה	GO UP	748b	1 c
		שלום	PEACE	1022d	3
25	36	אביגיל	ABIGAIL	4a	1
		אור	LIGHT	21c	2
		בקר	MORNING	133d	1 b
		טוב	PLEASING	373b	2
		ל	TO	513b	5 ba
		לב	HEART	525c	29a
		מאד	EXCEEDINGLY	547c	2 b
		מלך	KING	573c	5 d
		על	UPON	753c	2 ld
		קטן	SMALL	882b	1 b
		שכר	DRUNKEN	1016c	
		משתה	FEAST	1059c	1
25	37	אבן	STONE	7a	3 b
		היה	COME TO PASS	224d	2 al al
		היה	BECOME	226b	2 2e
		יין	WINE	406c	C
		יצא	GO OUT	423a	1 e
		לב	HEART	525c	29b
		מות	DIE	559d	1 a2
25	38	קרב	INWARD PART	899a	1 a
		היה	COME TO PASS	224d	2 al ae
		יום	DAY	398c	2 c
		ד	LIKE	453b	1 a
		מות	DIE	560a	2 b
		נגף	STRIKE	619d	
		עשר	TEN	797a	2 c
25	39	אביגיל	ABIGAIL	4a	1
		אשר	PARTICLE OF RE-LATION	82d	6 c
		ברך	BLESS	138c	2 a
		דבר	SPEAK	181c	4 c
		חרפה	REPROACH	357d	1
		חשך	WITHHOLD	362b	1 b
		יד	HAND	391b	5 g1
		מות	DIE	560a	2 b
		עבד	SLAVE	714c	6
		ראש	HEAD	911b	8
		ריב	STRIVE	936c	3
		ריב	STRIFE	937a	3
		שוב	TURN BACK	999c	4 a
25	40	אביגיל	ABIGAIL	4a	1
		כרמל	CARMEL	502b	2
25	41	אמה	MAID	51a	2
		אף	NOSE	60b	2
		קום	STAND	877d	1 a
		רחץ	WASH OFF	934c	1
		שפחה	MAID	1046c	1
25	42	אביגיל	ABIGAIL	4a	1
		הלך	WALK	231d	1 d5 tc
		ו	AND	253a	1 g
		חמור	HE-ASS	331b	2 a
		נערה	GIRL	655b	2
		רגל	FOOT	919d	1 f
		רכב	RIDE	938c	1
		אחינעם	AHINOAM	27b	2
25	43	גם	ALSO	169c	2
		ו	AND	252c	1 c
		יזרעאל	JEZREEL	283b	1 a
		שנים	TWO	1041a	1 a
25	44	ליש	LAISH	539d	
		מיכל	MICHAL	568a	
		נתן	GIVE	678c	1 c
		פלטי	PALTI	812d	2
		פלטיאל	PALTIEL	*812d	2
26	1	גבעה	HILL	149a	4
		גבעה	GIBEAH	149b	2
		חוילה	HAVILAH	*296d	
		חכילה	HACHILAH	314b	
		חכילה	HACHILAH	*314b	
		ישימון	WASTE	445b	A
		לא	NOT	520b	4 bb
		סתר	HIDE	711c	
		פנה	FACE	818d	2 7a d
		בחר	CHOOSE	104b	7
26	2	בקש	SEEK	134c	1 b
		מדבר	WILDERNESS	185a	3 b
		זיף	ZIPH	268b	1 a
		נצל	SNATCH AWAY	664d	1
26	3	גבעה	HILL	149a	4
		חוילה	HAVILAH	*296d	
		חכילה	HACHILAH	314b	

Ch v.	Heb	Eng	Page	Sec
	רישימון	WASTE	445b	A
	פנה	FACE	818d	27a d
26 4	אל	TO	40c	7
	כון	BE FIRM	465d	1 d
	רגל	GO ABOUT	920b	2
26 5	חנה	DECLINE	333c	2 c2
	נר	NER	633a	1
	סביב	ROUND ABOUT	687b	2 bb
	מעגל	ENTRENCHMENT	722d	1
	שכב	LIE DOWN	1012a	1 b
26 6	אבישי	ABISHAI	5a	
	אחימלך	AHIMELECH	27a	2
	יואב	JOAB	222a	1
	חתי	HITTITE	366c	1
	צרויה	ZERUIAH	863b	
26 7	אבישי	ABISHAI	5a	
	חנית	SPEAR	333d	1
	ישן	SLEEPING	445d	
	מעך	PRESS	590d	
	סביב	ROUND ABOUT	687b	2 bb
	מעגל	ENTRENCHMENT	722d	1
	מראשות	HEAD-PLACE	912b	
	שכב	LIE DOWN	1012a	1 b
	שכב	LIE DOWN	1012a	1 b
26 8	אבישי	ABISHAI	5a	
	חנית	SPEAR	333d	1
	נכה	SMITE	645c	1 a
	סגר	DELIVER UP	689b	1
	שנה	DO AGAIN	1040d	
26 9	אבישי	ABISHAI	5a	
	מי	WHO	566d	F c
	משיח	ANOINTED	603c	1
	נקה	BE CLEAN	667d	3
	שחת	GO TO RUIN	1008b	1
26 10	בוא	COME	98c	2
	ה	THE	207b	1 ca
	חי	ALIVE	311d	1 a
	יום	DAY	398d	2 h1
	ירד	GO DOWN	432d	1 b
	כי אם	BUT	475a	2 b
	נגף	STRIKE	619d	
	ספה	SWEEP AWAY	705a	1
26 11	הלך	WALK	231d	1 1d 5h
	חלילה	FAR BE IT	321a	
	חנית	SPEAR	333d	1
	יד	HAND	389b	1 c
	ל	TO	515d	5 ib
	משיח	ANOINTED	603c	1
	צפחת	JAR	860b	
	מראשות	HEAD-PLACE	912b	
26 12	הלך	WALK	231d	1 1d 5h
	חנית	SPEAR	333d	1
	ישן	SLEEPING	445d	
	ל	TO	515d	5 ib
	נפל	FALL	657c	5
	צפחת	JAR	860b	
	קיץ	AWAKE	884c	1 a
	מראשות	HEAD-PLACE	912c	
	תרדמה	DEEP SLEEP	922b	
26 13	הר	MOUNTAIN	250d	1 m
	עבר	PASS OVER	717a	1 a2
	עבר	REGION ACROSS	719b	1
	עמד	STAND	763d	1 a
	מקום	STANDING PLACE	880b	5 b
	רב	GREAT	913c	2
	רחק	DISTANT	935c	2 a2
26 14	נר	NER	633a	1
26 15	איש	MAN	35d	
	מי	WHO	566d	F c
	שחת	GO TO RUIN	1008b	1
	שמר	KEEP	1036c	1 b
26 16	אי	WHERE	32b	1 a
	את	MARK OF THE AC-CUSATIVE	85b	3 a
	בן	SON	121d	8 e
	חי	ALIVE	311d	1 a
	חנית	SPEAR	333d	1
	טוב	PLEASANT	374b	5
	כי	THAT	472a	1 c
	מות	DEATH	560d	2
	משיח	ANOINTED	603c	1
	צפחת	JAR	860b	
	ראה	TO SEE	907b	5 a
	מראשות	HEAD-PLACE	912b	
	שמר	KEEP	1036c	1 b
26 17	בן	SON	120b	1 c
	נכר	RECOGNIZE	648b	2
	קול	VOICE	876d	1 a
26 18	יד	HAND	390d	5 c1
	מה	WHAT	552c	1 aa
	עבד	SLAVE	714c	6
	רעה	MISERY	949b	3
26 19	אדם	MAN	9b	2
	אחר	ANOTHER	29d	
	אלהים	GOD	43c	1 d
	אם	IF	50a	1 a4 a
	ארר	CURSE	76d	
	גרש	DRIVE OUT	176d	
	מנחה	OFFERING	585a	3
	נחלה	PROPERTY	635b	1 e
	סות	INCITE	694d	2
	ספה	JOIN	705b	
	עבד	WORK	713b	4 b
	עבד	SLAVE	714c	6
	פנה	FACE	817a	2 4a g
	ריח	SMELL	926b	
26 20	בקש	SEEK	134c	1 b
	דם	BLOOD	197b	2 k
	הר	MOUNTAIN	250c	1 g
	יצא	GO OUT	423d	2 c
	נגד	IN FRONT	617d	2 cb a
	נפל	FALL	657d	1
	פרעש	FLEA	829a	
	קרא	PARTRIDGE	896c	
26 21	בן	SON	120b	1 c
	חטא	MISS A GOAL OR WAY	306d	2 a
	יקר	BE PRECIOUS	429d	1 b
	סכל	BE FOOLISH	698a	
	רבה	BECOME MANY	915d	1 e3
	שגה	GO ASTRAY	993a	3
	תחת	INSTEAD	1066a	2 3a b
26 22	ו	AND	254c	4
	חנית	SPEAR	333d	1
26 23	אבה	BE WILLING	2c	
	אמונה	FIRMNESS	53c	3 a
	משיח	ANOINTED	603c	1
	צדקה	RIGHTEOUSNESS	842b	3
	שוב	TURN BACK	999c	4 a
26 24	גדל	BECOME GREAT	152b	2 b
	כן	SO	486c	2 cd
	צרה	DISTRESS	865b	
26 25	בן	SON	120b	1 c
	ברך	BLESS	138d	2 b
	גם	ALSO	169b	1
	דרך	JOURNEY	203a	2
	הלך	WALK	231b	1 d3 gd
	יכל	PREVAIL	408a	2
	שוב	TURN BACK	997a	3 a
27 1	אמר	SAY	56b	2
	בקש	SEEK	134c	1 b
	טוב	PLEASANT	374c	6
	יאש	DESPAIR	384c	
	יום	DAY	400a	7 a6
	כי	BUT	474b	3 e
	לב	HEART	525c	2 7
	מלט	SLIP AWAY	572c	1
	מלט	SLIP AWAY	572c	2
	ספה	SWEEP AWAY	705a	1
	עתה	NOW	774b	1 d
27 2	גת	GATH	387d	
	מעוך	MAOCH	590d	
	עבר	PASS OVER	717a	1 b
27 3	אביגיל	ABIGAIL	4a	1
	אחינעם	AHINOAM	27b	2
	יזרעאלי	JEZREELITE	283c	2
	גת	GATH	387d	
	כרמלי	CARMELITE	502b	
27 4	בקש	SEEK	134c	1 b
	ברח	FLEE	138a	2
	גת	GATH	387d	
	יסף	ADD	414d	
	יסף	DO AGAIN	415c	2 a
	נגד	BE CONSPICUOUS	617a	
27 5	חן	FAVOR	336b	2 b1
	ממלכה	DOMINION	575b	2
	נא	PART OF EN-TREATY	609c	4 c
	עיר	CITY	746c	1 d
	שדה	FIELD	961c	1 f
27 6	יום	DAY	401b	7 l
	כן	SO	486d	3 d
	כן	SO	*487b	3 f
	צקלג	ZIKLAG	862c	
27 7	חדש	NEW MOON	294c	2 a
	יום	TIME	*399d	6 b
	יום	YEAR	399d	6 c
	יום	YEAR	399d	6 c
	פלשתי	PHILISTINE	814c	
27 8	ארבע	FOUR	917a	1 b1
	בוא	COME	98c	2 e
	גורי	GIRZITES	160c	
	גרזי	GIRZITES	173d	
	גשורי	GESHURITES	178c	2
	ישב	DWELL	443b	3
	עולם	LONG DURATION	762a	1 a
	עמלקי	AMALEKITES	766a	
	פשט	STRIP OFF	833a	2
	שור	SHUR	1004b	
	גשורי	ADDENDA ET COR-RIGENDA	*1122a	
27 9	ו	AND	*252b	1 b
	חיה	LIVE	311c	1
	חמור	HE-ASS	331b	1
	לקח	TAKE	543d	9 a
	נכה	SMITE	646b	3
27 10	אן	WHERE	33a	
	אל	NOT	39b	C
	אל	TO	41a	B
	יהודה	JUDAH	397c	2
	נגב	SOUTH-COUNTRY	616b	1 a
	פשט	STRIP OFF	833a	2
	קיני	KENITE	884a	
	ירחמאלי	JERAHMEELITES	934a	
27 11	חיה	LIVE	311c	1
	גת	GATH	387d	
	כה	THUS	462a	1
	כה	THUS	462b	1 b
	על	UPON	754d	2 1f g
	פלשתי	PHILISTINE	814c	
	פן	LEST	814d	1 a
27 12	משפט	JUDGEMNT	1049a	6 b
	אמן	CONFIRM	53b	2 c
	באש	STINK	93a	1
	עבד	SLAVE	714c	7
	עולם	LONG DURATION	762a	2 a
28 1	צבא	WAR	839b	2
	קבץ	GATHER	867d	2
	קבץ	GATHER	867d	2
28 2	יום	DAY	400c	7 f
	כן	SO	487a	3 da
28 3	אוב	NECROMANCER	15b	2
	ו	AND	252c	1 b
	ידעני	FAMILIAR SPIRIT	396b	
	סור	TURN ASIDE	694b	1
	ספד	WAIL	704c	
	רמה	RAMA	928a	2
28 4	קבץ	GATHER	867d	1
	שונם	SHUNEM	1002b	
28 5	חול	WHIRL	*297a	2 b
	חרד	TREMBLE	353c	1
	ירא	FEAR	431a	1 a
	לב	HEART	525c	2 9b
28 6	אורים	URIM	22a	
	גם	ALSO	169a	1
	חלום	DREAM	321d	2 a
	ענה	ANSWER	772d	1 b
	שאל	ASK	982a	2 b
28 7	אוב	NECROMANCER	15b	4
	בעלה	MISTRESS	128b	2
	בקש	SEEK	134d	1 d
	דרש	SEEK	205b	2 b
	עבד	SLAVE	713d	2
	עינדר	EN-DOR	745c	
28 8	אוב	NECROMANCER	15b	4
	אחר	ANOTHER	29c	
	חפש	SEARCH	344c	
	לבש	PUT ON	527d	A
	עלה	GO UP	749c	2 a
	קסם	PRACTICE OF DIVI-NATION	890d	1
28 9	אוב	NECROMANCER	15b	2
	ידע	KNOW	393c	1 a
	ידעני	FAMILIAR SPIRIT	396b	
	כרת	CUT OFF	504c	2 b
	מות	DIE	560b	1 b
	נקש	STRIKE	669c	
28 10	חי	ALIVE	311d	1 a
	עון	INIQUITY	731b	3
	קרה	ENCOUNTER	899c	2
	שבע	SWEAR	989b	1 a
28 11	את	MARK OF THE AC-CUSATIVE	84d	1 a
	מי	WHO	566b	B
	עלה	GO UP	749c	
28 12	זעק	CRY	277b	2 d
	קול	VOICE	*877a	1 a
	רמה	BEGUILE	941a	
28 13	אלהים	GOD	43d	2 b
	ירא	FEAR	431a	1 a
	עלה	GO UP	748b	1 b
28 14	אף	NOSE	60b	2
	זקן	OLD	278c	2 a
	מעיל	ROBE	591c	1
	עטה	WRAP ONESELF	741d	
	קדד	BOW DOWN	869a	
	תאר	FORM	1061c	
28 15	חלום	DREAM	321d	2 a
	יד	HAND	391a	5 d
	ידע	MAKE KNOWN	395a	
	מה	HOW	554a	4 d
	סור	TURN ASIDE	693d	2
	על	UPON	759a	4 2c
	ענה	ANSWER	772d	1 b
	קרא	CALL	895d	5 a
28 16	סור	TURN ASIDE	693d	2
	על	UPON	759a	4 2c
	ער	ADVERSARY	786b	
	שאל	ASK	982a	2 b
28 17	דבר	SPEAK	181c	4 a
	יד	HAND	391a	5 d
	ממלכה	DOMINION	575b	2
	קרע	TEAR	902c	2
	רע	FRIEND	946a	1
28 18	חרון	BURNING OF AN-GER	354c	
	כאשר	SINCE	455c	2
	כן	SO	487a	3 f
	עמלק	AMALEK	766a	
	עשה	DO	794a	1 1a 5
28 20	אכל	EAT	37b	1
	ירא	FEAR	431b	1 c
	כח	STRENGTH	470c	1 a
	לחם	FOOD	537b	2 a
	לילה	NIGHT	539a	1
	מהר	HASTEN	555a	2
	מלא	FULNESS	571b	4
	נפל	FALL	657b	3 a
	קומה	HEIGHT	879b	1
28 21	בהל	BE DISTURBED	96b	1
	גם	ALSO	*169c	
	כף	HOLLOW OF THE HAND	496d	1 d6
	נפש	SOUL	659d	3 c
	שום	TO PLACE	963a	1 a

Ch	v.	Heb	Eng	Page	Sec
28	22	שפחה	MAID	1046c	2
		גם	ALSO	169c	4
		הלך	WALK	230c	1 1d 2a
		כח	STRENGTH	470c	1 a
		לחם	FOOD	537a	1 a
		פת	FRAGMENT	837d	
		שום	TO PLACE	963b	1 c
28	23	שפחה	MAID	1046c	2
		ישב	SIT	442c	1 a
		ישב	SIT	*442d	1 b
		מאן	REFUSE	549b	
		מטה	COUCH	641d	
		פצר	PUSH	823a	
28	24	אפה	BAKE	66a	
		אפה	BAKE	66a	
		זבח	SLAUGHTER FOR SACRIFICE	257a	2
		לוש	KNEAD	534c	
		מהר	HASTEN	555a	2
		מצה	UNLEAVENED BREAD	695b	
		עגל	CALF	722a	
		קמח	FLOUR	887d	
		מרבק	STALL	918d	
28	25	נגש	APPROACH	621b	
29	1	אפק	APHEK	67d	1
		ב	IN	89a	2 1
		יזרעאל	JEZREEL	283b	1 b
		עין	SPRING	745b	
		קבץ	GATHER	*867d	2
		קבץ	GATHER	867d	2
		אפק	ADDENDA ET CORRIGENDA	1120c	
29	2	אחרון	BEHIND	31a	B b
		אלף	THOUSAND	49b	2
		ל	TO	516b	5 ja
		מאה	HUNDRED	548a	1 c1
		שר	CHIEFTAIN	978a	1 a
29	3	או	OR	14d	1
		היה	BE	227b	3 4d b
		יום	DAY	399c	5 b
		יום	DAY	401b	7 l
		לא	NOT	*520b	4 ba
		מאומה	ANYTHING	548d	
		מה	WHAT	553a	1 c
		מצא	FIND	593b	2 b
		נפל	FALL	657c	4 b
		עבד	SLAVE	714a	2
		עברי	HEBREW	720b	2 a
		שר	CHIEFTAIN	978a	1 a
		שנה	YEAR	1040b	
29	4	ירד	GO DOWN	432d	1 b
		פקד	ATTEND TO	824a	1
		קצף	BE WROTH	893b	2
		רצה	BE PLEASED WITH	953a	
		שטן	ADVERSARY	966b	1
		שר	CHIEFTAIN	978a	1 a
		שוב	TURN BACK	997a	3 a
29	5	מחולה	DANCING	298b	
		מחולה	DANCING	298c	
		לא	NOT	520b	4 bb
		נכה	SMITE	646a	2 c
		ענה	SING	777b	
		רבבה	MULTITUDE	914b	
29	6	בוא	COME	97d	1 a
		חי	ALIVE	311d	1 a
		טוב	PLEASANT	373d	2 c
		יום	DAY	400a	7 d1 e
		יום	DAY	401b	7 l
		יצא	GO OUT	424a	3
		ישר	STRAIGHT	449b	3 b
		כי	THAT	472a	1 c
		מצא	FIND	593b	2 b
		שר	CHIEFTAIN	978a	1 a
29	7	הלך	WALK	231d	1 d5 ta
		רע	EVIL	948b	3
		שר	CHIEFTAIN	978a	1 a
		שוב	TURN BACK	997b	3 a
		שלום	PEACE	1023a	5 a
29	8	יום	DAY	400b	7 d7
		יום	DAY	401b	7 l
		כי	THAT	*472a	1 b
		מצא	FIND	593b	2 b
		פנה	FACE	817c	2 4b a
29	9	טוב	PLEASANT	373d	2 c
		מלאך	MESSENGER	521d	2
		עלה	GO UP	748c	2 c
		שר	CHIEFTAIN	978a	1 a
29	10	אדון	LORD	11b	2 1f
		אור	BECOME LIGHT	21b	
		בליעל	WORTHLESSNESS	*116a	1
		בקר	MORNING	133d	1 b
		בקר	MORNING	134b	1 h
		היה	COME TO PASS	225b	1 2b d
		ו	AND	253a	1 g
		טוב	PLEASANT	373d	2 c
		פקד	ATTEND TO	824a	1
		שום	TO PLACE	963a	1 a
		שכם	START EARLY	1014d	
29	11	בקר	MORNING	134b	1 h
		יזרעאל	JEZREEL	283c	1 b
		שכם	START EARLY	1014c	
30	1	היה	COME TO PASS	224d	1 2a 1b
		נגב	SOUTH-COUNTRY	616b	1 a
		נכה	SMITE	646b	3
		עמלקי	AMALEKITES	766a	
		פשט	STRIP OFF	833a	2
		צקלג	ZIKLAG	862c	
		שרף	BURN	976d	2 a
30	2	גדול	GREAT	153b	7
		דרך	JOURNEY	203a	2
		נהג	DRIVE	624b	1
		קטן	SMALL	882b	1 a
		שבה	TAKE CAPTIVE	985c	1 a
30	3	בן	SON	120a	1
		שרף	BURN	976d	2 a
		שבה	TAKE CAPTIVE	985c	
30	4	את	WITH	85d	1
		בכה	WEEP	113b	1
		כח	STRENGTH	470c	1 b
		עד	UNTIL	724d	2 1a a
30	5	אביגיל	ABIGAIL	4a	1
		אחינעם	AHINOAM	27b	2
		יזרעאלי	JEZREELITE	283c	2
		כרמלי	CARMELITE	502b	
		שבה	TAKE CAPTIVE	985c	2
30	6	אמר	SAY	56b	2
		בן	SON	120a	1
		יהוה	YAHWEH	218d	2 1e
		חזק	BE FIRM	305b	1
		מרר	BE BITTER	600a	2
		סקל	STONE	709c	
		על	UPON	754b	2 1f b
		צרר	BIND	864d	B
30	7	אביתר	ABIATHAR	5a	
		אחימלך	AHIMELECH	27a	1
		אפוד	EPHOD	65c	2
		כהן	PRIEST	463c	4
		נגש	APPROACH	621b	
		נגש	APPROACH	621b	
30	8	גדוד	BAND	151b	1
		נצל	DELIVER	664d	2
		נשג	OVERTAKE	673c	1 a
		רדף	PURSUE	922d	1 c
		שאל	ASK	982a	2 b
30	9	בשור	BESOR	143a	
		יתר	BE LEFT OVER	451c	
		נחל	WADY	636c	2
30	10	בשור	BESOR	143a	
		מאה	HUNDRED	548a	1 b1
		נחל	WADY	636c	2
		פגר	BE EXHAUSTED	803c	
		רדף	PURSUE	922d	1 c
30	11	איש	MAN	36a	
		איש	MAN	36a	
		מצא	FIND	593b	3 a
		מצרי	EGYPTIAN	596a	1
		שדה	FIELD	961c	1 f
		שקה	GIVE TO DRINK	1052c	2
30	12	אכל	EAT	37b	1
		דבלה	PRESSED FIG-CAKE	179b	
		יום	DAY	398b	1
		לחם	FOOD	537b	2 a
		לילה	NIGHT	538d	1
		על	UPON	757c	2 7c ab
		פלח	CLEAVAGE	812a	2
		צמוק	BUNCH OF RAISINS	856a	
		רוח	BREATH	925a	3 a
		שוב	TURN BACK	998a	7 a
		שתה	DRINK	1059b	1 a
30	13	אדון	LORD	11b	3 1a
		אי	WHERE	32b	2 b
		אין	WHENCE	32d	
		איש	MAN	36a	
		אנכי	I	59c	
		חלה	BE WEAK	317d	2
		יום	DAY	400a	7 a4
		מצרי	EGYPTIAN	596a	1
		עזב	LEAVE	737b	2 b1
		עמלקי	AMALEKITES	766a	
		שלש	THREE	1025d	1 b
30	14	כלב	CALEB	477a	
		כרתי	CHERETHITE	504d	1
		פשט	STRIP OFF	833a	2
		צקלג	ZIKLAG	862c	4
		שרף	BURN	976d	2 a
30	15	אדון	LORD	11b	3 1a
		גדוד	BAND	151b	
		ירד	BRING DOWN	433d	1 a
		סגר	DELIVER UP	689c	1
		שבע	SWEAR	989b	1 a
30	16	חגג	MAKE PILGRIMAGE	290d	2
		ירד	BRING DOWN	433d	1 a
		לקח	TAKE	543d	9 a
		נטש	LEAVE	643d	1
		כיאם	EXCEPT	474d	2 a
30	17	מחרת	THE MORROW	564b	
		מלט	SLIP AWAY	572b	1
		מן	FROM	582a	5 c
		נשף	TWILIGHT	676a	1
		רכב	RIDE	938c	1
30	18	לקח	TAKE	543d	9 a
		נצל	DELIVER	664d	2
		עמלק	AMALEK	766a	
30	19	גדול	GREAT	153b	7
		כל	ALL	482d	2 ba
		לקח	TAKE	543d	9 a
		מן	FROM	582a	5 b
		עדר	BE LACKING	727c	
		קטן	SMALL	882b	1 a
		שוב	TURN BACK	999a	1 a
30	20	דוד	DAVID	188b	J
		לקח	TAKE	543d	9 a
		נהג	DRIVE	624b	1
		פנה	FACE	817c	2 4c a
		מקנה	CATTLE	889b	2
		שלל	SPOIL	1022a	2
30	21	בשור	BESOR	143a	
		בשור	BESOR	*143a	
		ישב	CAUSE TO SIT	443c	2
		מאה	HUNDRED	548a	1 b2
		נגש	DRAW NEAR	620d	1
		נחל	WADY	636c	2
		פגר	BE EXHAUSTED	803c	
30	22	שאל	ASK	982a	2 a
		בליעל	WORTHLESSNESS	116b	2
		הלך	WALK	231c	1 1d 5b
		כיאם	EXCEPT	474d	2 a
		נהג	DRIVE	624b	1
		נצל	DELIVER	664d	2
		יען	ON ACCOUNT OF	774d	2 a
		רע	EVIL	948c	0 b
30	23	את	MARK OF THE ACCUSATIVE	85c	3 a
		גדוד	BAND	151b	1
		שמר	KEEP	1037a	4 a
30	24	ה	THE	207b	1 ca
		חלק	DIVIDE	323c	4
		חלק	PORTION	324a	1 a
		יחדו	TOGETHER	403c	C
		ירד	GO DOWN	432d	1 b
		ירד	BE BROUGHT DOWN	434b	1
		ישב	REMAIN	442d	2 a
		כ	LIKE	454c	2 c
		כלי	ARTICLE	479c	1
		ל	TO	514b	5 fa
		על	UPON	756a	2 6b
		שמע	HEAR	1034a	1 j
30	25	היה	COME TO PASS	224c	2 a1 az
		חק	SOMETHING PRESCRIBED	349c	6 a
		יום	DAY	401a	7 j
		יום	DAY	401b	7 l
		מן	FROM	581b	4 a
		מעל	ABOVE	751d	2 bb b
		שום	TO PLACE	963d	3 b
		משפט	JUDGMENT	1048d	3
30	26	איב	BE HOSTILE TO	33c	
		ברכה	BLESSING	139d	5
		זקן	OLD	278d	2 b
		צקלג	ZIKLAG	862c	
		רע	FRIEND	946a	1
30	27	ביתאל	BETHEL	111a	2
		בתואל	BETHUEL	143d	
		יתיר	JATTIR	453a	
		נגב	SOUTH-COUNTRY	616b	1 a
		רמת	RAMATH-LEHI	928b	3
		רמות	RAMOTH	928c	1 b
30	28	אשתמוע	ESHTEMOA	84c	
		ערער	AROER	793a	3
		ערער	AROER	793a	3
		שפמות	SIPHMOTH	974a	
		שפמות	SHIPMOTH	1050d	
30	29	קיני	KENITE	884a	
		ירחמאלי	JERAHMEELITES	934a	
		רכל	RACAL	940b	
30	30	בורעשן	BOR-ASHAN	92d	
		חרמה	HORMAH	356c	
		עתך	ATHACH	800d	
30	31	הלך	WALK	236a	1 b
		חברון	HEBRON	289b	
31	1	הר	MOUNTAIN	249c	1 a
		יזרעאל	JEZREEL	*283b	1 b
		נפל	FALL	657a	2 a
31	2	אבינדב	ABINADAB	4c	3
		דבק	KEEP CLOSE	180a	2
		מלכישוע	MALCHI-SHUA	575d	
31	3	חול	WHIRL	297a	2 b
		ירה	SHOOT	435b	2
		כבד	BE HEAVY	457b	1
		מלחמה	WAR	536a	
		מלחמה	WAR	536d	
		מן	OUT OF	580a	2 ea
		מצא	FIND	593b	3 b
		מצודה	FASTNESS	845a	
		קשת	BOW	906b	1 d
31	4	אבה	BE WILLING	2c	
		דקר	PIERCE	201b	
		דקר	PIERCE	201b	
		דקר	PIERCE	*201b	
		חרב	SWORD	352c	1 c
		ירא	FEAR	431a	1 a
		כלי	IMPLEMENT	479d	2 a
		נפל	FALL	656d	1
		עלל	ACT ARBITRARILY	759d	1
		ערל	HAVING FORESKIN	790c	
		שלף	DRAW OUT	1025b	1
31	5	כלי	IMPLEMENT	479d	2 a
		נפל	FALL	656d	1
31	6	יחדו	TOGETHER	403c	B
		כלי	IMPLEMENT	479d	2 a
31	7	איש	MAN	36a	
		ב	IN	88a	
		ירדן	JORDAN	434c	
		כי	THAT	471d	1 a
		עבר	REGION ACROSS	719b	1 a
		עבר	REGION ACROSS	719c	1 a

Ch	v.	Heb	Eng	Page	Sec
		עזב	LEAVE	737b	2 a1
		עמק	VALE	771a	
31	8	הר	MOUNTAIN	249c	1 a
		יזרעאל	JEZREEL	*283b	1 b
		מחרת	THE MORROW	564a	
		נפל	LIE	657d	7
		פשט	STRIP OFF	833a	
31	9	בית	HOUSE	109b	1 ae 0
		בשר	BEAR TIDINGS	142b	1
		כלי	IMPLEMENT	479d	2 a
		כרת	CUT OFF	503d	1 a
		עצב	IDOL	781b	
		פשט	STRIP OFF	833a	2
		שלח	SEND	1018b	1 c
31	10	בית	HOUSE	109b	1 ae 0
		ביתשאן	BETH-SHEAN	112d	
		גויה	CORPSE	156b	2 a
		דגון	DAGON	*186a	
		יזרעאל	JEZREEL	*283b	1 b
		חומה	WALL	327b	1
		כלי	IMPLEMENT	479d	2 a
		עשתרת	ASTORETH	800a	
		תקע	THRUST	1075c	1
31	11	יבש	JABESH	386d	1
31	12	איש	MAN	35d	
		ביתשאן	BETH-SHEAN	112d	
		גויה	CORPSE	156c	2 a
		גופה	BODY	*157c	1
		יזרעאל	JEZREEL	*283b	1 b
		חיל	STRENGTH	298d	1 c
		חומה	WALL	327b	1
		יבש	JABESH	386d	1
		לילה	NIGHT	539a	1
		שרף	BURN	977a	2 a
31	13	אשל	TAMARISK TREE	79c	
		יבש	JABESH	386d	1
		צום	FAST	847a	
		קבר	BURY	868c	

2 SAMUEL

Ch	v.	Heb	Eng	Page	Sec
1	1	עמלק	AMALEK	766a	
		עמלקי	AMALEKITES	766a	
		צקלג	ZIKLAG	862c	
		שוב	TURN BACK	997a	2
		שנים	TWO	1041a	1 b1
1	2	אדמה	EARTH	9d	3
		היה	COME TO PASS	225a	1 2a 1c
		נפל	FALL	657c	3 b
		מעם	FROM WITH	768d	A
		קרע	TEAR	902c	1 a1
1	3	אי	WHERE	32b	2
		מלט	SLIP AWAY	572b	2
1	4	אשר	THAT	83c	8 ag
		דבר	WORD	183c	4 3
		יהונתן	JONATHAN	220d	1
		היה	FALL OUT	224b	1 1a
		נפל	FALL	657a	2 a
		רבה	BECOME MANY	915d	1 e5
1	5	איך	HOW	32c	1
		נגד	BE CONSPICUOUS	617a	5
1	6	בעל	LORD	127c	1 5b
		דבק	KEEP CLOSE	180a	2
		הר	MOUNTAIN	249c	1 a
		חנית	SPEAR	333d	1
		נגד	BE CONSPICUOUS	617a	5
		פרש	HORSEMAN	832a	
		קרה	ENCOUNTER	899d	2
		קשת	BOW	906c	2
		רכב	CHARIOT	939a	1
		שען	LEAN	1043d	
1	7	הנה	BEHOLD	244a	A
		פנה	TURN	815b	2 a
1	8	אנכי	I	59c	
		מי	WHO	566b	
		עמלקי	AMALEKITES	766a	
1	9	אחז	GRASP	28b	
		כל	ALL	482b	1 f
		מות	DIE	560a	
		נפש	SOUL	659d	3
		עוד	STILL	728d	1 aa
		על	UPON	756d	2 6c
		שבץ	CRAMP	990b	
1	10	הנה	HITHER	244c	A a
		זרוע	ARM	283d	1 a
		מות	DIE	560a	
		נזר	CROWN	634b	1 a
		עדות	TESTIMONY	730c	2
		אצעדה	ARMLET	858a	
1	11	חזק	BE FIRM	305a	6 a
		בכה	WEEP	113b	1
1	12	נפל	FALL	657b	2 a
		ספד	WAIL	704d	
		צום	FAST	847a	
1	13	אי	WHERE	32b	2 b
		גר	SOJOURNER	158b	2
		נגד	BE CONSPICUOUS	617a	5
		עמלקי	AMALEKITES	766a	
1	14	איך	HOW	32c	1
		ירא	FEAR	431b	1 d
		משיח	ANOINTED	603c	1
		שחת	GO TO RUIN	1008a	1
		שלח	SEND	1018c	3 a
1	15	נגש	DRAW NEAR	620d	1
		נכה	SMITE	645d	2 a

Ch	v.	Heb	Eng	Page	Sec
		פגע	MEET	803b	3
		קרא	CALL	895b	2
1	16	דם	BLOOD	197a	2 i
		מות	DIE	560a	
		משיח	ANOINTED	603c	1
		על	UPON	756c	2 7a b
		ענה	ANSWER	773a	3 a
1	17	פה	MOUTH	805a	2 a
		קינה	ELEGY	884b	
		קונן	CHANT	884b	
1	18	בן	SON	121a	1 jd
		ישר	STRAIGHT	449b	3 c2
		לא	NOT	*520c	4 bb
		למד	LEARN	540d	
		ספר	MISSIVE	707b	3 d
		ספר	MISSIVE	*707c	4
		קשת	BOW	906c	2
1	19	איך	HOW	32c	2
		במה	HIGH PLACE	119a	2
		במה	HIGH PLACE	*119a	2
		צדיק	BEAUTY	840a	1 b
		קינה	ELEGY	884b	
1	20	אשקלון	ASHKELON	80c	
		בת	DAUGHTER	123b	1 i
		בשר	BEAR TIDINGS	142b	1
		חוץ	THE OUTSIDE	300a	2 a
		עלז	EXULT	759c	
		ערל	HAVING FORESKIN	790c	
		פלשתי	PHILISTINE	814c	
		שמח	REJOICE	970b	1 b
1	21	אל	NOT	39b	A ba
		בלי	WEARING OUT	115c	2 b
		מגן	SHIELD	171c	
		געל	ABHOR	171d	
		הר	MOUNTAIN	249c	1 a
		טל	NIGHT-MIST	378c	
		משח	ANOINT	603a	1
		תרומה	OFFERING	929b	4 a
		שדה	FIELD	961c	1 d
		שדה	FIELD	961d	
		שם	THERE	1027a	1 a
		שמן	OIL	1032b	2 c
1	22	אחור	HINDER SIDE	30c	A
		דם	BLOOD	196c	2 c
		חלב	FAT	316d	1
		סוג	MOVE AWAY	690d	1 a
		קשת	BOW	906a	1 b
		ריקם	EMPTILY	938b	2
		שוב	TURN BACK	998a	7 a
1	23	ארי	LION	71d	1
		גבר	BE STRONG	149d	1
		חיים	LIFE	313b	1
		נעים	DELIGHTFUL	653d	1
		נשר	EAGLE	676d	
		פרד	DIVIDE	825c	2
		קלל	BE SLIGHT	886b	2
1	24	בכה	WEEP	113c	3
		לבש	CLOTHE	528b	1 a
		לבוש	CLOTHING	528c	
		עדי	ORNAMENTS	725d	1
		עדן	LUXURY	726c	
		עלה	GO UP	749d	4
		על	UPON	757a	2.7b
		עם	WITH	767b	1 a
		שני	SCARLET	1040c	
1	25	במה	HIGH PLACE	119a	2
1	26	אהבה	LOVE	13b	1
		אח	BROTHER	26b	1
		ל	TO	511a	1 e
		נעם	BE DELIGHTFUL	653c	
		על	UPON	754b	2 lf b
		פלא	BE SURPASSING	810c	3 a
		צרר	ADDENDA ET COR-RIGENDA	1126c	
1	27	אבד	PERISH	1c	1
		כלי	IMPLEMENT	479d	2 a
		מלחמה	WAR	536c	
2	1	אחר	AFTER	*30a	2 b
		אן	WHERE	33a	A
		דוד	DAVID	188a	
		חברון	HEBRON	289b	
		יהודה	JUDAH	397b	2
		עלה	GO UP	748b	1 c
		צקלג	ZIKLAG	862c	
		שאל	ASK	982a	2 b
2	2	אביגיל	ABIGAIL	4a	1
		אחינעם	AHINOAM	27b	2
		יזרעאלי	JEZREELITE	283c	2
		כרמלי	CARMELITE	502b	
		נבל	NABAL	615a	2
		צור	ROCK	849d	2 b
2	3	חברון	HEBRON	289b	
2	4	אשר	THAT	83c	8 ag
		בית	HOUSE	110a	5 de
		יבש	JABESH	386d	1
		יהודה	JUDAH	397b	1 2
		מלך	KING	573a	1
		מלך	KING	573c	5 c
		משח	ANOINT	603b	2
		קבר	BURY	868c	
2	5	אשר	THAT	83c	8 c
		אשר	THAT	84a	
		ברך	BLESS	138d	2 b
		ה	THE	208b	1 ha
		חסד	GOODNESS	338c	1 1
		יבש	JABESH	386d	1

Ch	v.	Heb	Eng	Page	Sec
		עשה	DO	794b	1 3
		קבר	BURY	868c	
2	6	אמת	FIRMNESS	54a	3 b
		חסד	GOODNESS	339b	2 2
		טובה	WELFARE	375d	3
		עשה	DO	794b	1 3
		עשה	DO	794b	1 3
2	7	בית	HOUSE	110a	5 de
		בן	SON	121d	8 a
		חזק	BE FIRM	304a	1 1a
		משח	ANOINT	603b	2
2	8	אישבשת	ISHBOSHETH	36b	1
		אשר	PARTICLE OF RE-LATION	83a	7 b
		בשת	SHAME	102b	2
		מחנים	MAHANAIM	334b	
		נר	NER	633a	1
		עבר	PASS OVER	718d	1 a
2	9	אל	TO	41a	B
		אשור	ASSHUR	78d	2
		אשורי	ASHURITE	79a	
		גשורי	GESHURITES	178c	2
		יזרעאל	JEZREEL	283c	1 b
		יזרעאל	JEZREEL	*283c	1 b
		חסד	KIND	339d	2 b
		כל	ALL	481d	1 da
		מלך	BE KING	574b	
		ישראל	ISRAEL	975c	2 a2
2	10	אישבשת	ISHBOSHETH	36b	1
		בית	HOUSE	110a	5 de
		היה	BECOME	225d	2 1b
		מלך	BE KING	574a	
		מלך	BE KING	574a	
		ישראל	ISRAEL	975c	2 a2
2	11	בית	HOUSE	110a	5 de
		חברון	HEBRON	289b	
		חדש	NEW MOON	294c	2 a
		מלך	KING	573b	5 b
2	12	אישבשת	ISHBOSHETH	36b	1
		גבעון	GIBEON	149c	
		מחנים	MAHANAIM	334b	
		נר	NER	633a	1
		עבד	SLAVE	714a	2
2	13	ברכה	POOL	140a	
		ברכה	POOL	140a	
		גבעון	GIBEON	149c	
		יואב	JOAB	222a	1
		יצא	GO OUT	423d	2 c
		ישב	SIT	442c	1 a
		על	UPON	756c	2 6c
		פגש	MEET	803d	
		צרויה	ZERUIAH	863b	
2	14	נער	RETAINER	655a	2 b
		פנה	FACE	816d	2 4
		קום	STAND	877d	1
		שחק	LAUGH	965d	1
2	15	אישבשת	ISHBOSHETH	36b	1
		מספר	NUMBER	709a	1 b
		עבר	PASS OVER	718b	5 g
		קום	STAND	877d	1
2	16	גבעון	GIBEON	149c	
		חזק	BE FIRM	305a	6 a
		חלקה	PORTION OF GROUND	324c	1 b
		הצצים	HAZZURIM	324d	
		יחדו	TOGETHER	403b	A
		צד	SIDE	841a	
		צר	HARD PEBBLE	866a	
		קרא	CALL	896a	6 e2
		רע	FRIEND	946b	3
		צר	ADDENDA ET COR-RIGENDA	1126c	
2	17	מלחמה	WAR	536d	
		מאד	EXCEEDINGLY	547c	2 b
		נגף	STRIKE	620a	
		קשה	SEVERE	904c	2 a
2	18	אבישי	ABISHAI	5a	
		עשהאל	ASAHEL	795c	1
		צבי	GAZELLE	840b	
		צרויה	ZERUIAH	863b	
		קל	LIGHT	886d	
		שדה	FIELD	961c	1 c
2	19	ימין	RIGHT HAND	412a	2 b
		נטה	BEND	640b	3 a
		על	UPON	757a	2 7c ab
		שמאל	LEFT	969d	1
2	20	זה	THIS	261c	4 f
		פנה	TURN	815b	2 a
2	21	אבה	BE WILLING	2c	
		אחז	GRASP	28b	
		אמר	SAY	56a	1
		חליצה	WHAT IS STRIPPED OFF	322d	
		ימין	RIGHT HAND	412a	2 b
		ל	TO	515d	5 ib
		נטה	BEND	640b	3 a
		סור	TURN ASIDE	693c	1
		שמאל	LEFT	969d	1
2	22	אחר	BEHIND	30b	4 aa
		איך	HOW	32c	1
		יסף	DO AGAIN	415c	2 a
		ל	TO	515d	5 ib
		מה	HOW	554a	4 d
		מה	HOW	554b	4 d
		נכה	SMITE	646a	2 a

Ch	v.	Heb	Eng	Page	Sec
		נשא	LIFT	670b	1 b 3
2	23	סור	TURN ASIDE	693c	1
		אחר	HINDER	30a	1
		אחר	BEHIND	30b	4 aa
		אל	TO	40c	8
		היה	COME TO PASS	224d	2 a1 am
		חמש	BELLY	332d	
		חנית	SPEAR	333d	1
		חנית	SPEAR	334a	2 c
		יצא	GO OUT	423b	1 f
		מאן	REFUSE	549a	
		נכה	SMITE	645d	2 a
		נפל	FALL	657a	2 a
		סור	TURN ASIDE	693c	1
		תחת	UNDERNEATH	1065a	2 2a
2	24	אבישי	ABISHAI	5a	
		אמה	AMMAH	52c	
		בוא	COME	98a	1 i
		גבעה	HILL	149a	4
		גבעון	GIBEON	149c	
		מדבר	WILDERNESS	185a	3 b
		דרך	WAY	202d	1
		פנה	FACE	818d	2 7a d
2	25	אגדה	BAND	8b	3
		בנימין	BENJAMIN	122d	1
		גבעה	HILL	149a	1
		עמד	STAND	763d	1 a
		קבץ	GATHER	868b	
		ראש	HEAD	910d	2 a
2	26	אחר	BEHIND	30b	4 aa
		אחרון	BEHIND	31a	B b
		אכל	EAT	37c	4
		חרב	SWORD	352d	1 g
		חרב	SWORD	*352d	1 f
		מר	BITTER	600c	1
		מתי	WHEN	607d	C
		שוב	TURN BACK	996d	1
2	27	אז	THEN	23b	2
		אחר	BEHIND	30b	4 aa
		אלהים	GOD	43d	3
		בקר	MORNING	134c	2
		חי	ALIVE	311d	1 a
		כי	THAT	472a	1 c
		כי	THAT	472c	1 db
		לולא	IF NOT	530c	A
		מן	FROM	581c	4 b
		עלה	GO UP	749b	2
2	28	יסף	ADD	414d	
		עמד	STAND	764a	2 a
2	29	בתרון	BITHRON	144c	
		הלך	WALK	230c	1 1d 1a
		הלך	WALK	230c	1 1d 2a
		מחנים	MAHANAIM	334b	
		לילה	NIGHT	539a	1
		ערבה	DESERT-PLAIN	787c	1 b
2	30	אחר	BEHIND	30b	4 aa
		נאם	UTTERANCE	610b	2
		עשר	TEN	797b	9 a
		פקד	ATTEND TO	823d	1
		קבץ	GATHER	867d	2
		שוב	TURN BACK	996d	1
		תשע	NINE	1077c	2
2	31	ב	IN	88c	1 2b
		מות	DIE	559d	1 a2
		נכה	SMITE	645d	2 a
2	32	אור	BECOME LIGHT	21b	
		הלך	WALK	230c	1 1d 1b
		חברון	HEBRON	289b	
		לילה	NIGHT	539a	1
		נשא	LIFT	670a	1 a
		קבר	BURY	868c	
		קצצר	GRAVE	868d	
3	1	ארך	LONG	74a	A
		בית	HOUSE	109d	5 c
		בית	HOUSE	109d	5 c
		דוד	DAVID	188a	B
		דל	WEAK	195d	
		הלך	WALK	233c	1 4d
		חזק	BE FIRM	304b	1 1c
		מלחמה	WAR	536a	
		מלחמה	WAR	536c	
3	2	אחינעם	AHINOAM	27b	2
		אמנון	AMNON	54c	1
		יזרעאלי	JEZREELITE	283c	2
		חברון	HEBRON	289b	
		ילד	BE BORN	408d	
		ילד	BE BORN	409a	
		ל	TO	512d	5 ac
3	3	אביגיל	ABIGAIL	4a	1
		אבשלום	ABSALOM	5a	2
		גשור	GESHUR	178a	2
		דניאל	DANIEL	193b	1
		כלאב	CHILEAB	476d	
		כרמלי	CARMELITE	502b	
		ל	TO	512d	5 ac
		מעכה	MAACAH	590d	2 a
		נבל	NABAL	615a	
		משנה	SECOND	1041d	3 b
		תלמי	TALMAI	1068d	1
3	4	אביטל	ABITAL	4b	
		אדניהו	ADONIJAH	11d	1
		חגית	HAGGITH	291b	1
		חמישי	FIFTH	332c	1
		רביעי	FOURTH	917d	1
		שפטיה	SHEPHATIAH	1049b	1 a

Ch	v.	Heb	Eng	Page	Sec
3	5	דוד	DAVID	188b	J
		חברון	HEBRON	289b	
		ילד	BE BORN	409a	
		יתרעם	ITHREAM	453c	
		ל	TO	512d	5 ac
		עגלה	EGLAH	722c	
3	6	בית	HOUSE	109d	5 c
		בית	HOUSE	109d	5 c
		דוד	DAVID	188a	B
		חזק	BE FIRM	305b	1
		מלחמה	WAR	536c	
3	7	איה	AIAH	17b	2
		אמר	SAY	56a	1
		מדוע	WHEREFORE	396c	
		פלגש	CONCUBINE	811c	1
		רצפה	RIZPAH	954c	
3	8	אישבשת	ISHBOSHETH	36b	1
		אל	TO	40a	3 c
		בית	HOUSE	109d	5 c
		ו	AND	254a	2 b
		חסד	GOODNESS	338c	11
		חרה	BURN	354a	1 b
		כלב	DOG	477a	B
		מצא	FIND	594b	3
		עון	INIQUITY	731a	1 c1
		על	UPON	754b	2 If b
		ראש	HEAD	910d	1 b
		מרע	FRIEND	946d	
3	9	יסף	ADD	415b	1
		כי	THAT	472a	1 c
		כן	SO	486c	2 cd
3	10	בארשבע	BEERSHEBA	92a	
		בית	HOUSE	109d	5 c
		דוד	DAVID	188b	E
		דן	DAN	193a	3
		כסא	THRONE	491a	3 a
		ממלכה	DOMINION	575b	2
		עבר	PASS OVER	719a	4
		קום	STAND	878d	2 a
		ישראל	ISRAEL	975c	2 a2
3	11	דבר	WORD	182b	1 1c
		ירא	FEAR	431b	1 b
		מן	ON ACCOUNT OF	583a	7 a
		שוב	TURN BACK	999c	3
3	12	ברית	COVENANT	136b	12
		ברית	COVENANT	136c	15
		חברון	HEBRON	289b	
		כרת	CUT	503d	4
		סבב	TURN ABOUT	686c	1 b
		עם	WITH	767c	1 a
3	13	אך	HOWBEIT	36c	2 a
		ברית	COVENANT	136b	12
		טוב	PLEASANT	374c	5
		כיאם	EXCEPT	474d	2 a
		כרת	CUT	503d	4
		מיכל	MICHAL	568a	
		פנה	FACE	816a	1 2b
3	14	אישבשת	ISHBOSHETH	36b	1
		ארש	BETROTH	77a	
		ב	IN	90a	3 3a
		מיכל	MICHAL	568a	
		ערלה	FORESKIN	790b	
3	15	אישבשת	ISHBOSHETH	36b	1
		ליש	LAISH	539d	
		מעם	FROM WITH	769a	C
		פלמיאל	PALTIEL	812d	2
		פלטי	PALTI	*812d	2
3	16	בחרים	BAHURIM	104c	
		בכה	WEEP	113b	1
		הלך	WALK	233a	1 4c 1g
		הלך	WALK	234b	1 5f 3
		שוב	TURN BACK	997d	3 a
3	17	בקש	SEEK	134d	2 a
		דבר	WORD	182a	1 1a
		היה	BE	227b	3 4d a
		זקן	OLD	278d	2 b
		ל	TO	512b	4 a
		מלך	KING	573c	5 c
		עם	WITH	767d	1 d
		שלשם	THREE DAYS AGO	1026b	
		תמול	YESTERDAY	1070a	2 ac
3	18	אמר	SAY	56b	1
		דוד	DAVID	188a	
		יד	HAND	391a	5 d
		ישע	DELIVER	446d	1 b
		עבד	SLAVE	714a	3
3	19	בית	HOUSE	110b	5 dt
		בנימין	BENJAMIN	122d	1
		דבר	SPEAK	181c	4 b
		חברון	HEBRON	289b	
		טוב	PLEASING	373b	5
3	20	עשרים	TWENTY	797d	1 1b
		חברון	HEBRON	289b	
		משתה	FEAST	1059d	1
3	21	אוה	DESIRE	16a	
		ברית	COVENANT	136b	12
		הלך	WALK	231d	1 d5 ta
		כרת	CUT	503d	4
		מלך	BE KING	574a	
		נפש	SOUL	660d	6 a
		קבץ	GATHER	867d	2
		שלח	SEND	1019a	3
3	22	גדוד	TROOP	151b	3
		הלך	WALK	231d	1 d5 ta
		חברון	HEBRON	289b	
		רב	MUCH	913a	1 a1

Ch	v.	Heb	Eng	Page	Sec
3	23	הלך	WALK	231d	1 d5 ta
		נר	NER	633a	1
		צבא	ARMY	839a	1 a
		שלח	SEND	1019a	3
3	24	הלך	WALK	233a	1 4b 2
		שלח	SEND	1019a	3
3	25	מבוא	ENTERING	99d	2
		מובא	ENTRANCE	100a	
		ידע	KNOW	393d	1 a
		מוצא	GOING FORTH	425d	1 a
		נר	NER	633a	1
3	26	פתח	BE SIMPLE	834d	2
		בוחסרה	WELL OF SIRAH	92d	
		מעם	FROM WITH	769a	A
3	27	ב	IN	90c	3 5
		דבר	SPEAK	181b	3 d
		דם	BLOOD	196d	2 f
		חברון	HEBRON	289b	
		חמש	BELLY	332d	
		נטה	INCLINE	640d	3 a
		נכה	SMITE	645d	2 a
		עשהאל	ASAHEL	795c	1
		שוב	TURN BACK	997b	3 a
		שלי	QUIETNESS	1017b	
		שער	GATE	1044d	1 a
		תוך	MIDST	1063d	
3	28	אחר	BEHIND	30b	4 ag
		דם	BLOOD	196d	2 f
		ממלכה	KINGDOM	575b	1
		מן	OUT OF	579d	2 d
		נר	NER	633a	1
		נקי	CLEAN	667c	1
		עולם	LONG DURATION	762b	2 b4
		מעם	FROM WITH	769b	D
3	29	אל	TO	41a	B
		זוב	FLOW	264d	1
		חול	WHIRL	297b	3
		חזק	BE FIRM	305a	6 b
		חסר	NEEDY	341c	
		כרת	BE CUT OFF	504b	4
		מעון	REFUGE	*733a	3
		על	UPON	756c	2 7a b
		פלך	WHIRL OF SPINDLE	813a	1
		צרע	BE STRUCK WITH LEPROSY	864a	
		ראש	HEAD	911b	8
3	30	גבעון	GIBEON	149c	
		הרג	KILL	247a	1 a
		הרג	KILL	247c	7
		ל	TO	512a	3 b
		על	UPON	758b	3 a
		עשהאל	ASAHEL	795c	1
3	31	חגר	GIRD	291d	2
		מטה	COUCH	642a	
		ספד	WAIL	704d	
		פנה	FACE	817c	2 4c a
		שק	SACK	974c	2
3	32	אל	TO	40c	8
		בכה	WEEP	113c	3
		בכה	WEEP	113c	1
		חברון	HEBRON	289b	
3	33	נבל	FOOLISH	615a	
		נבלה	SENSELESSNESS	615b	2
		קונן	CHANT	884b	
		קינה	ELEGY	884b	
3	34	אסר	TIE	63d	3
		בכה	WEEP	113c	3
		בן	SON	121d	8 b
		יסף	DO AGAIN	415c	2 a
		ך	LIKE	454d	3 a
		לא	NOT	519b	1 bc
		נגש	DRAW NEAR	621b	
		נחשת	COPPER	639a	2
		עולה	INJUSTICE	732c	1
3	35	אם	IF	50b	1 b2
		בוא	COME	98a	1 i
		ברה	EAT	136a	
		מעם	TASTE	381a	1
		יום	DAY	398b	1
		יסף	ADD	415b	1
		כי	THAT	472a	1 c
		כיאם	THAT IF	474c	1 a
		מאומה	ANYTHING	548d	
		עוד	STILL	729c	2 aa
		שבע	SWEAR	989a	1 a
3	36	טוב	PLEASING	373b	5
		יטב	BE PLEASING	405c	4
		נכר	REGARD	648a	1
3	37	מן	OUT OF	579d	2 d
		נר	NER	633a	1
3	38	גדול	GREAT	153b	6 b
		שר	CHIEFTAIN	978c	3 a
3	39	ך	LIKE	454a	1 b
		משח	ANOINT	603b	2
		צרויה	ZERUIAH	863b	
		קשה	SEVERE	904c	2 a
		רך	TENDER	940a	1
		שלם	BE COMPLETE	1022c	5
4	1	אישבשת	ISHBOSHETH	36b	1
		בהל	BE DISTURBED	96b	1
		חברון	HEBRON	289b	
		יד	HAND	389d	1 e1
		מריבבעל	MERIB-BAAL	937c	1
		רפה	SINK	951d	2
		ישראל	ISRAEL	975c	2 a2
4	2	אישבשת	ISHBOSHETH	36b	1

2 SAMUEL

Ch	v.	Heb	Eng	Page	Sec
		באדתי	BEEROTHITE	92a	
		באדות	BEEROTH	92a	
		בנימן	BENJAMIN	122a	1
		בענה	BAANAH	128d	1
		גדוד	BAND	151b	1
		חשב	THINK	363c	2
		מן	OUT OF	579c	2 cb
		על	UPON	755b	2 4a
		מריבבעל	MERIB-BAAL	937c	1
		רכב	RECHAB	939c	2
		רמון	RIMMON	942a	1
		שר	CHIEFTAIN	978a	1 b
4	3	באדתי	BEEROTHITE	92b	
		ברח	FLEE	138a	2
		גור	SOJOURN	157d	1
		גתים	GITTAIM	388a	
		יום	DAY	401b	71
4	4	אמן	CONFIRM	52d	3
		בן	SON	121d	9a
		בעל	BAAL	127d	2 1
		יזרעאל	JEZREEL	283b	1 b
		חפז	BE IN TREPIDATION	342a	1
		נכה	STRICKEN	646d	
		נפל	FALL	656d	1
		נשא	LIFT	670a	1 a
		מריבבעל	MERIB-BAAL	937c	1
		שמעתי	REPORT	1035b	1
4	5	אישבשת	ISHBOSHETH	36b	1
		באדתי	BEEROTHITE	92a	
		בענה	BAANAH	128d	1
		חם	HEAT	328d	1
		יום	DAY	398b	1
		צהר	MIDDAY	844a	1
		רכב	RECHAB	939c	2
		רמון	RIMMON	942a	1
		משכב	ACT OF LYING	1012d	2 a
4	6	בענה	BAANAH	128d	1
		הם	THEY	241d	7
		חמש	BELLY	332d	
		חטה	WHEAT	334d	
		ישן	SLEEP	445c	
		לקח	TAKE	542d	1
		מלט	SLIP AWAY	572b	1
		נום	BE DROWSY	630b	
		נכה	SMITE	645d	2 a
		סקל	STONE	709d	2
		רכב	RECHAB	939c	2
		שער	PORTER	1045b	
		תוך	MIDST	1063d	
4	7	דרך	WAY	202d	1
		הלך	WALK	230c	1 1d 1a
		חדר	CHAMBER	293d	
		לילה	NIGHT	539a	1
		מטה	COUCH	641d	
		נכה	SMITE	645d	2 a
		סור	TURN ASIDE	694b	1
		ערבה	DESERT-PLAIN	787c	1 c
		שכב	LIE DOWN	1012b	1 b
		משכב	ACT OF LYING	1012d	2 a
4	8	איב	BE HOSTILE TO	33c	
		אישבשת	ISHBOSHETH	36b	1
		בקש	SEEK	134d	2 a
		זרע	SOWING	282d	4 c
		חברון	HEBRON	289b	
		נפש	SOUL	659d	3 c
		נקמה	VENGEANCE	668c	1
		נתן	GIVE	678d	1 d
4	9	באדתי	BEEROTHITE	92a	
		בענה	BAANAH	128d	1
		חי	ALIVE	311d	1 a
		נפש	SOUL	660a	2
		פדה	RANSOM	804a	3 d
		צרה	DISTRESS	865b	
		רכב	BAND OF RIDERS	939c	2
		רמון	RIMMON	942a	1
4	10	אחז	GRASP	28b	
		אף	ALSO	65a	2
		בשר	BEAR TIDINGS	142b	1
		בשרה	TIDINGS	143a	3
		הרג	KILL	247a	1 a
		ו	AND	254d	5 b
		ל	TO	518a	7 bg
		צקלג	ZIKLAG	862c	
4	11	את	MARK OF THE ACCUSATIVE	85a	1 a
		בער	CONSUME	129b	3
		בקש	SEEK	135a	5 b
		דם	BLOOD	197b	2 k
		הרג	KILL	247a	1 a
		יד	HAND	391b	5 g3
		צדיק	JUST	843a	2
		רשע	WICKED	957b	1
		משכב	COUCH	1012d	1
4	12	אישבשת	ISHBOSHETH	36b	1
		ברכה	POOL	140a	
		הרג	KILL	247a	1 a
		חברון	HEBRON	289b	
		צוה	CHARGE	845d	2 b
		קבר	BURY	868c	
		קצץ	CUT OFF	893d	
		תלה	HANG	1068a	1
5	1	בשר	FLESH	142d	4
		הנה	BEHOLD	243d	
		חברון	HEBRON	289b	
		עצם	BONE	782d	1 a
5	2	יצא	BRING OUT	424d	1 c
		מלך	KING	573b	5 b
		רעה	TEND	945a	1 c
		שלשם	THREE DAYS AGO	1026b	
		תמול	YESTERDAY	*1070a	2 a
5	3	ברית	COVENANT	136b	12
		זקן	OLD	278d	2 b
		חברון	HEBRON	289b	
		חברון	HEBRON	289b	
		כרת	CUT	503d	4
		מלך	KING	573c	5 c
		משח	ANOINT	603b	2
		פנה	FACE	817b	2 4a h
5	4	שלשים	THIRTY	1026c	1
5	5	חדש	NEW MOON	294c	2 a
		ירושלים	JERUSALEM	437a	
		מלך	BE KING	574a	
		מלך	BE KING	574a	
		ישראל	ISRAEL	975c	2 a2
5	6	אמר	SAY	56b	2
		יבוסי	JEBUSITE	101a	1
		יבוסי	JEBUSITE	*101a	1
		ירושלים	JERUSALEM	437a	
		כיאם	BUT	475a	2 b
		עור	BLIND	734c	1 a
		פסח	LAME	820c	
5	7	דוד	DAVID	188a	A
		עיר	CITY	746c	2
		מצדה	FASTNESS	845a	
		ציון	ZION	851b	
5	8	יבוסי	JEBUSITE	101a	1
		ו	AND	253a	1 h
		כן	SO	487b	3 f
		נגע	REACH	619b	4
		עור	BLIND	734c	1 a
		פסח	LAME	820c	
		צנור	PIPE	857c	
		שנא	HATE	971c	1 a
5	9	בית	HOUSE	110c	7
		בנה	BUILD	124c	1 d
		דוד	DAVID	188a	A
		מלוא	MILLO	571c	2
		מן	FROM	581d	5 a
		עיר	CITY	746c	2
		מצדה	FASTNESS	845a	
		קרא	CALL	896a	6 e2
5	10	גדול	GREAT	153a	6 b
		הלך	WALK	233b	14c 3
		צבא	GOD OF WAR	839b	4 b
5	11	אבן	STONE	6c	2
		אבן	STONE	6c	2
		חירם	HIRAM	27c	1
		ארז	CEDAR	72c	2
		בנה	BUILD	124b	1 ab
		חרש	GRAVER	360d	1 b
		חרש	GRAVER	360d	1 c
		מלך	KING	573a	1
		עץ	TREE	781d	1 c
		צר	TYER	862d	
		קיר	WALL	885a	3
5	12	כן	ESTABLISH	466a	1
		כי	THAT	471d	1 a
		מלך	KING	573c	5 c
		מלך	KING	573c	5 c
		ממלכה	DOMINION	575b	2
		נשא	LIFT	672a	1
		עבור	FOR THE SAKE OF	721a	1 a
5	13	חברון	HEBRON	289b	
		ילד	BE BORN	408d	
		ירושלים	JERUSALEM	437a	
5	14	ילד	BORN	409c	
		ירושלים	JERUSALEM	437a	
		נתן	NATHAN	681d	1
		שובב	SHOBAB	1000a	1
		שלמה	SOLOMON	1024d	
		שמוע	SHAMMUA	1035b	1
5	15	אלישוע	ELISHUA	46a	
		יבחר	IBHAR	104d	
		יפיע	JAPHIA	422b	1 b
		נפג	NEPHEG	655d	2
5	16	אלידע	ELIADA	45a	A
		אליפלט	ELIPHELET	45d	A
		בעלידע	BEELIADA	128c	
5	17	בקש	SEEK	134d	2 a
		משח	ANOINT	603b	2
		מצדה	FASTNESS	845a	
5	18	נטש	FORSAKE	644a	3
		רפאים	REPHAIM	952b	
		רפאים	REPHAIM	952b	
5	19	שאל	ASK	982a	2 b
5	20	בעלפרצים	BAAL-PERAZIM	128b	
		כן	SO	487b	3 f
		מי	WATER	565d	4 b
		פנה	FACE	817b	2 4b c
		פרץ	BURSTING FORTH	829c	1
		פרץ	BREAK THROUGH	829c	6
5	21	עזב	LEAVE	737b	2 a2
		עצב	IDOL	781b	
5	22	יסף	DO AGAIN	415c	2 a
		נטש	FORSAKE	644a	3
		רפאים	REPHAIM	952b	
		רפאים	REPHAIM	952b	
5	23	אחר	BEHIND	30b	4 b
		אל	TO	40d	9
		בכא	BALSAM-TREE	113a	
		ל	TO	511c	1 gb
		מול	IN FRONT OF	557c	2 bb
		סבב	GO AROUND	685d	2 c
		סבב	GO AROUND	686c	2
		שאל	ASK	982a	2 b
5	24	אז	THEN	23a	1 d
		אז	THEN	23a	1 b
		בכא	BALSAM-TREE	113a	
		חרץ	CUT	358c	3
		יצא	GO OUT	424a	2 c
		צעדה	MARCHING	857d	
		קול	VOICE	877b	2 c
		ראש	HEAD	910d	2 a
5	25	בוא	COME	98c	2 e
		גבע	GEBA	*148d	
		גזר	GEZER	160c	
		כן	SO	486c	2 da
		מן	FROM	581d	5 a
6	1	בחר	CHOOSE	*104b	7
6	2	בעל	LORD	127c	1 5b
		בעלה	BAALAH	128b	
		ישב	SIT	442c	1 a
		כרוב	CHERUB	500d	3
		עלה	GO UP	749c	4
		צבא	GOD OF WAR	839c	4 c
		קרא	CALL	896b	2 d4
		קריתיערים	KIRIATH-JEARIM	900c	
6	3	אבינדב	ABINADAB	4c	1
		אחיו	AHIO	26d	1
		אל	TO	41a	A
		גבעה	HILL	149a	1
		גבעה	GIBEAH	149b	2
		חדש	NEW	294a	A
		נהג	DRIVE	624b	1
		עגלה	CART	722c	
		עזא	UZZAH	739b	1
		רכב	RIDE	938d	1
6	4	אבינדב	ABINADAB	4c	1
		אחיו	AHIO	26d	1
		גבעה	HILL	149a	1
		גבעה	GIBEAH	149b	2
6	5	ברוש	CYPRESS	*141c	1
		ברוש	CYPRESS	141c	3
		כנור	LYRE	490a	
		כנור	LYRE	490b	
		נבל	HARP	614c	
		מנענע	RATTLE	631c	
		עץ	TREE	781d	2 b
		צלצלים	CYMBALS	852d	
		מצלתים	CYMBALS	853a	
		שחק	LAUGH	966a	3
		שיר	SONG	1010c	3
		תף	TIMBREL	1074c	
6	6	אחז	GRASP	28b	
		בקר	CATTLE	133c	2
		גרן	THRESHING-FLOOR	175b	
		גרן	THRESHING-FLOOR	175b	
		יד	HAND	389b	1 c
		כון	BE FIRM	465d	1 c
		נבכון	NACON	467d	
		כידן	CHIDON	475d	
		עזא	UZZAH	739b	1
		שלח	SEND	1018c	3 a
		שמט	LET DROP	1030c	
6	7	אלהים	GOD	43d	3
		חרה	BURN	354a	2 a
		מות	DIE	560a	2 b
		נכה	SMITE	646a	2 c
		עזא	UZZAH	739b	1
		עם	WITH	768a	2
		של	IRREVERENCE	1016d	
6	8	חרה	BURN	354a	1 b
		יום	DAY	401b	71
		עזא	UZZAH	739b	1
		על	UPON	758a	3 a
		פרץ	BREAK THROUGH	829c	6
		פרץ	PEREZ	829d	2 a
		פרץ	BURSTING FORTH	829d	4
		קרא	CALL	896a	6 e2
6	9	היך	HOW	*228a	
		ירא	FEAR	431b	1 b
6	10	אבה	BE WILLING	2c	
		דוד	DAVID	188a	A
		גתי	GITTITE	388a	
		נטה	INCLINE	640d	3 a
		סור	TURN ASIDE	694c	2
		עבדאדם	OBED-EDOM	714d	1
		עיר	CITY	746c	2
		על	UPON	757b	2 7c ab
6	11	ברך	BLESS	139a	2 a
		חדש	NEW MOON	294c	2 a
		גתי	GITTITE	388a	
		ישב	REMAIN	442d	2 a
		עבדאדם	OBED-EDOM	714d	1
6	12	ברך	BLESS	139a	2 a
		דוד	DAVID	188a	A
		נגד	BE CONSPICUOUS	617a	
		עבדאדם	OBED-EDOM	714d	1
		עבור	FOR THE SAKE OF	721a	1 a
		עלה	GO UP	749c	4
		שמחה	JOY	970d	2
6	13	כי	WHEN	473a	2 a
		מריא	FATLING	597b	
		עפר	DRY EARTH	779c	1 a
		צעד	STEP	857c	
		שור	A HEAD OF CATTLE	1004b	
6	14	אפוד	EPHOD	65c	1 a

Ch	v.	Heb	Eng	Page	Sec
		בד	WHITE LINEN	94b	
		בוץ	BYSSUS	*101c	
		חגר	GIRD	291d	1
		כרר	DANCE	503a	
		עז	STRENGTH	739a	1
		רקד	SKIP ABOUT	*955a	
6	15	ב	IN	89c	3 1c
		תרועה	SHOUT OF WAR	930a	3
6	16	בזה	DESPISE	102c	
		בעד	AWAY FROM	126b	1a
		דוד	DAVID	188a	A
		חלון	WINDOW	319d	
		כרר	DANCE	503a	
		ל	TO	512a	3 b
		מיכל	MICHAL	568a	
		פזז	BE SUPPLE	808a	
		רקד	SKIP ABOUT	*955a	
		שקף	LOOK DOWN	1054c	
6	17	אהל	TENT	14b	3
		בוא	COME	99a	1
		יצג	SET	426c	
		נטה	SPREAD OUT	640a	2
		עלה	WHOLE BURNT OF-FERING	750d	
		שלם	PEACE-OFFERING	1023c	
6	18	ברך	BLESS	139a	3
		כלה	FINISH	478b	1 c
		עלה	WHOLE BURNT OF-FERING	750d	
		צבא	GOD OF WAR	839c	4 c
		שלם	PEACE-OFFERING	1023c	
		שם	NAME	1028b	3
6	19	אשפר	ASHPENAZ	80c	
		אשישה	RAISEN-CAKE	84b	
		המון	CROWD	242d	3 b
		חלה	A KIND OF CAKE	319c	1
		חלק	DIVIDE	323d	1
		לחם	FOOD	537a	1 a
		מן	FROM	583d	9 b1
6	20	אמה	MAID	51a	1
		אמה	MAID	51a	1
		ברך	BLESS	139a	3
		כבד	BE HONORED	457c	1 b
		מה	HOW	553c	2 b
		מיכל	MICHAL	568a	
		סבב	TURN ABOUT	*685c	1 a
		ריק	EMPTY	938a	2
		שוב	TURN BACK	997b	3 a
6	21	בחר	CHOOSE	104a	1 a
		מיכל	MICHAL	568a	
		צוה	GIVE CHARGE OVER	845d	1 d
		שחק	LAUGH	966a	3
6	22	אמה	MAID	51a	1
		אמה	MAID	51a	1
		אמר	SAY	56a	1
		כבד	BE HONORED	457c	1 b
		עם	WITH	768d	4 b
		קלל	BE SLIGHT	886c	1
		שפל	LOW	1050c	3
6	23	יום	DAY	398c	2 f
		יום	DAY	401b	7 l
		ילד	CHILD	409b	
		ילד	CHILD	409b	B
		מיכל	MICHAL	568a	
7		ברית	COVENANT	*136d	2 2f
7	1	ישב	SIT	442c	1 a
		כי	WHEN	473a	2 a
		נוח	REST	628c	A 1b 2
7	2	אנכי	I	59c	
		ארז	CEDAR	72c	2
		בית	HOUSE	108d	1 ag
		ה	INTERROG PART	209d	1 b
		יריעה	CURTAIN	438c	
		נביא	PROPHET	611d	1
		נתן	NATHAN	681d	2
7	3	לבב	HEART	523c	2 2
		נתן	NATHAN	681d	2
7	4	דבר	WORD	182c	12a
		נתן	NATHAN	681d	2
7	5	בית	HOUSE	*108c	1 a
		בנה	BUILD	124b	1 ab
		דוד	DAVID	188a	
		ה	INTERROG PART	209d	1 b
		עבד	SLAVE	714a	3
7	6	אהל	TENT	14b	3
		הלך	WALK	236c	2
		יום	DAY	400a	7 d1 z
		יום	DAY	401b	7 l
		ישב	DWELL	443a	3
		מן	FROM	583d	9 b2
		משכן	DWELLING-PLACE	1015d	2 c
7	7	ארז	CEDAR	72c	2
		אשר	PARTICLE OF RE-LATION	82c	4 bg
		בית	HOUSE	108d	1 ag
		בנה	BUILD	124b	1 ab
		דבר	SPEAK	181b	3 d
		ה	INTERROG PART	210a	1 b
		הלך	WALK	236c	2
		צוה	GIVE CHARGE OVER	845d	1 d
		רעה	TEND	945a	1 c
		שבט	TRIBE	987b	2 c
		שפט	JUDGE	*1047b	1 b
7	8	אחר	BEHIND	29d	2 a

Ch	v.	Heb	Eng	Page	Sec
		אחר	BEHIND	30b	4 a
		דוד	DAVID	188a	
		נוה	ABODE OF FLOCKS	627c	1 a
		עבד	SLAVE	714a	3
		צבא	GOD OF WAR	839c	4 c
7	9	גדול	GREAT	153b	6 b
		הלך	WALK	230d	1 1d 3a
		כרת	CUT OFF	504c	2 c
		עשה	DO	794c	2 1d
		שם	NAME	1028a	2 b1
7	10	בלה	BECOME OLD AND WORN OUT	*115a	A
		בן	SON	121d	8 b
		יסף	DO AGAIN	415c	2 c
		כאשר	AS	455b	1 a
		עולה	INJUSTICE	732c	1
		ענה	BE BOWED DOWN	776b	1
		ראשון	FIRST	911d	3 a1
		רגז	BE AGITATED	919b	
		שום	TO PLACE	963d	3 b
		שכן	SETTLE DOWN	1015a	1 a
		תחת	UNDERNEATH	1065d	2 ia
7	11	בית	HOUSE	109d	5 b
		דוד	DAVID	*187d	
		יום	DAY	401a	7 k
		מן	FROM	583d	9 b2
		נגד	BE CONSPICUOUS	616c	2
		נוח	REST	628c	A 1b 2
		עשה	DO	794c	2 1c
		צוה	GIVE CHARGE OVER	845d	1 d
		שבט	TRIBE	*987b	2 c
		שפט	JUDGE	1047b	1 b
7	12	אחר	AFTER	*30a	2 b
		דוד	DAVID	*187d	
		זרע	SOWING	282d	4 c
		מצא	FIND	394a	1 f
		יצא	GO OUT	423c	1 h
		כון	ESTABLISH	466a	1 a
		כי	WHEN	473b	2 a
		מלא	BE FULL	570b	1 b
		ממלכה	DOMINION	575b	2
		מעה	BELLY	589a	2
		קום	STAND	878d	3
		שכב	LIE DOWN	1012c	4 b
7	13	בנה	BUILD	124b	1 ab
		דוד	DAVID	*187d	
		כון	ESTABLISH	466d	1 b
		כסא	THRONE	491a	3 a
		ממלכה	DOMINION	575b	2
		עולם	LONG DURATION	762c	2 f
		שם	NAME	1028b	3
7	14	אב	FATHER	3b	2
		אדם	MAN	9c	2
		איש	MAN	35d	
		בן	SON	120b	1 c
		דוד	DAVID	*187d	
		יכח	CORRECT	407a	6
		נגע	STRIKE	619b	
		נגע	STROKE	619c	2
		עוה	COMMIT INIQUITY	731c	1
		שבט	ROD	987a	1 a
7	15	דוד	DAVID	*187d	
		דוד	DAVID	*188b	J
		חסד	GOODNESS	339a	2 1e
		סור	TURN ASIDE	693d	2
		סור	TURN ASIDE	694b	1
		מעם	FROM WITH	*769a	B
		מעם	FROM WITH	*769a	B
7	16	אמן	CONFIRM	52d	3
		כון	BE FIRM	465d	1 b
		כסא	THRONE	491a	3 a
		ממלכה	DOMINION	575b	2
		עולם	LONG DURATION	762c	2 f
7	17	חזון	VISION	303b	3
		כן	SO	486b	2 ac
		נתן	NATHAN	681d	2
		תשובה	RETURN	1000c	1
7	18	בוא	COME	99b	2
		יהוה	YAHWEH	*219a	2 1h
		הלם	HITHER	240d	
		ישב	SIT	442c	1 a
		מי	WHO	566d	F b
		פנה	FACE	817b	24a h
7	19	אדם	MAN	9b	2
		אל	TO	40c	6
		ה	INTERROG PART	209d	1 b
		יהוה	YAHWEH	*219a	2 1h
		זה	THIS	260c	1 a
		תורה	LAW	436b	3 b3
		מן	FROM	583d	9 b2
		מעלה	STEP	*752b	5
		קטן	BE SMALL	881d	
		ראה	TO SEE	*908a	8 c
		רחק	DISTANT	935c	2 b
		תור	PLAITS	1064c	
7	20	ידע	KNOW	394b	2
		יסף	DO AGAIN	415c	2 a
7	21	גדולה	GREATNESS	153c	B
		ידע	TEACH	395a	
		לב	HEART	524c	2 2
		עבור	FOR THE SAKE OF	721a	1 a
		אזן	EAR	24a	2 a
		גדל	BECOME GREAT	152b	2 f
		יהוה	YAHWEH	219a	2 1h
7	22	זולה	EXCEPT	265d	1

Ch	v.	Heb	Eng	Page	Sec
		ך	LIKE	453d	1 b
		כ	SO	487a	3 f
7	23	גדולה	GREATNESS	153c	B
		גוי	NATION	156d	1 c
		ירא	CAUSE FEAR	431d	2
		מי	WHO	566c	E b
		מצרים	EGYPT	595d	1 b2
		פדה	RANSOM	804a	3 a
		שום	TO PLACE	964c	5 b
		שם	NAME	1028a	2 b1
7	24	אלהים	GOD	44b	4 a
		כון	ESTABLISH	466d	2
		עולם	LONG DURATION	762d	2 f
7	25	יהוה	YAHWEH	219a	2 1h
		עולם	LONG DURATION	762c	2 f
7	26	בית	HOUSE	109d	5 c
		גדל	BECOME GREAT	152b	3 a
		כון	BE FIRM	465d	1 b
		עבד	SLAVE	714a	3
		עולם	LONG DURATION	762b	2 c
		צבא	GOD OF WAR	839c	4 c
7	27	אזן	EAR	24b	3
		בית	HOUSE	109d	5 b
		בנה	BUILD	124d	2 a
		כן	SO	487a	3 f
		לב	HEART	525d	20
		מצא	FIND	593d	4
		פלל	INTERVENE	813b	3
		תפלה	PRAYER	813c	1 b
		צבא	GOD OF WAR	839c	4 b
7	28	אלהים	GOD	43d	3
		אלהים	GOD	43d	3
		אמת	FIRMNESS	54b	4 c
		דבר	WORD	183a	2 2
		הוא	HE, SHE, IT	216b	4 ba
		טובה	WELFARE	375d	2 a
7	29	ברך	BLESS	139a	2 a
		ברך	BLESS	139a	2 a
		ברכה	BLESSING	139d	1 b
		יאל	SHOW-WILLING-NESS	384b	3
		מן	OUT OF	580a	2 eb
		עולם	LONG DURATION	762d	2 f
8	1	אחר	AFTER	*30a	2 b
		אמה	MOTHER-CITY	52a	
		בת	DAUGHTER	123d	4
		גת	GATH	387d	
		כנע	HUMBLE	488c	2
		לקח	TAKE	543d	8
		מתג	BRIDLE	607c	2
8	2	חבל	CORD	286d	2
		חיה	LIVE	311c	1
		מדד	MEASURE	551b	2
		מלא	FULNESS	571b	4
		מנחה	TRIBUTE	585a	2
		מנחה	OFFERING	585c	6
		נשא	LIFT	671b	2
		עבד	SLAVE	713d	2
		עבד	SLAVE	714c	7
		שכב	LIE DOWN	1012c	
8	3	הדדעזר	HADADEZER	*212d	1
		יד	HAND	390b	2
		מלך	KING	573a	1
		נהר	STREAM	625d	1
		נצה	STRUGGLE	*663c	
		פרת	EUPHRATES	832b	
		צובא	ZOBAH	844c	
		רחוב	REHOB	932b	2 a
8	4	אלף	THOUSAND	49a	1 b
		יתר	LEAVE OVER	451c	1 a
		לכד	CAPTURE	540a	1
		מאה	HUNDRED	547d	1 a1
		עקר	HAMSTRING	785d	
		פרש	HORSEMAN	832a	
		רגלי	ON FOOT	920b	
		רכב	CHARIOT	*939a	1
		רכב	CHARIOT	939a	1
		רכב	CHARIOT	939a	1
		רכב	CHARIOT	939b	1
8	5	ארם	ARAM	74b	A
		ארם	ARAM	74b	A
		דמשק	DAMASCUS	200a	
		ל	TO	*512a	3 b
		נצה	STRUGGLE	*663c	
		עזר	HELP	740b	
		צובא	ZOBAH	844c	
		שנים	TWO	1041b	3
		ארם	ARAM	74b	A
8	6	ארם	ARAM	74c	B
		דמשק	DAMASCUS	200a	
		הלך	WALK	230d	1 1d 3a
		ישע	DELIVER	446d	1 b
		ל	TO	*512a	3 b
		מנחה	TRIBUTE	585a	2
		מנחה	OFFERING	585c	6
		נציב	PREFECT	662d	1
		נשא	LIFT	671b	2 e
		עבד	SLAVE	713d	2
		עבד	SLAVE	714c	7
8	7	זהב	GOLD	263a	6
		ירושלים	JERUSALEM	437a	
		על	UPON	753a	2 1aa
		שלט	SHIELD	1020d	
		ברותי	BEROTHAI	92d	
8	8	בטח	BETAH	105c	

2 SAMUEL

Ch	v.	Heb	Eng	Page	Sec
		טבחת	TIBHATH	371a	
		כון	CUN	*467b	
		לקח	TAKE	543d	8
		נחשת	COPPER	639a	1
		רבה	BECOME MANY	915a	1 e4
8	9	חיל	STRENGTH	299a	4
		חמת	HAMATH	333a	1
		מלך	KING	573a	1
		נצה	STRUGGLE	*663c	
		תעו	TOI	1073d	
8	10	ברך	BLESS	139b	4 c
		הדורם	HADORAM	213b	2
		יהורם	JEHORAM	221b	4
		היה	BE	227a	3 4b
		זהב	GOLD	263a	6
		יד	HAND	391a	5 c4
		לחם	ENGAGE IN BATTLE	535c	
		מלחמה	WAR	536b	
		על	UPON	758b	3 a
		שאל	ASK	982a	2 a
		תעו	TOI	1073d	
8	11	זהב	GOLD	263c	1
		כבש	SUBDUE	461b	
		כסף	SILVER	494b	4
		קדש	BE SET APART	873b	1 b
8	12	ארם	ARAM	74c	A
		עמלק	AMALEK	766a	
		עמון	AMMON	770a	
		צובא	ZOBAH	844c	
		רחוב	REHOB	932b	2 a
8	13	אדום	EDOM	10c	2
		ארם	ARAM	74c	A
		גיא	VALLEY	161b	C
		דוד	DAVID	188b	J
		מלח	SALT	572a	
		נכה	SMITE	646b	3
		עשה	DO	794c	2 1d
		שוב	TURN BACK	997a	
		שם	NAME	1028a	2 b1
		שמנה	EIGHT	1033a	2 b
8	14	היה	BECOME	226a	2 2a
		הלך	WALK	230d	1 1d 3a
		ישע	DELIVER	446d	1 b
		נציב	PREFECT	662d	2
		עבד	SLAVE	713d	2
		עבד	SLAVE	714c	7
8	15	היה	BE	227c	3 5a
		צדקה	RIGHTEOUSNESS	842a	1 a
		ישראל	ISRAEL	975c	2 a1
8	16	אחילוד	AHILUD	27a	1
		אל	TO	41a	A
		יהושפט	JEHOSHAPHAT	221d	3
		זכר	REMEMBER	271a	4
		על	UPON	755a	2 3
		צבא	ARMY	839a	1 a
		צרויה	ZERUIAH	863b	
8	17	אביתר	ABIATHAR	5a	
		אחימלך	AHIMELECH	27a	1
		אחיטוב	AHITUB	27a	2
		כהן	PRIEST	463c	4
		ספר	ENUMERATOR	708b	1 b
		זדק	RIGHTEOUS	843b	1 a
		שריה	SERAIAH	976a	1
8	18	בן	SON	*120d	1 ja
		בניהו	BENAIAH	125c	1
		ה	THE	208b	1 g
		יהוידע	JEHOIADA	220b	1
		כהן	PRIEST-KING	463a	1
		כרתי	CHERETHITE	504d	
		פלתי	PELETHITES	814c	
9	1	בית	HOUSE	109d	5 c
		חסד	GOODNESS	338c	1 1
		יש	THERE IS	441d	2 b
		יתר	BE LEFT OVER	451b	
		כי	THAT	472b	1 da
		עבור	FOR THE SAKE OF	721a	1 a
		ש	WHO	*980b	4 d
9	2	בית	HOUSE	109d	5 c
		ציבא	ZIBA	850d	
		קרא	CALL	895c	5 a
9	3	אפס	NON-EXISTENCE	67b	3
		בית	HOUSE	109d	5 c
		חסד	GOODNESS	338c	1 1
		חסד	GOODNESS	338c	1 1
		ל	TO	512d	5 ac
		נכה	STRICKEN	646d	
9	4	איפה	WHERE	33a	1
		דביר	DEBIR	184c	2 b
		לאדבר	LO-DEBAR	520d	
		עמיאל	AMMIEL	770a	1
9	5	לאדבר	LO-DEBAR	520d	
		עמיאל	AMMIEL	770a	1
9	6	נפל	FALL	657b	3 b
		מריבבעל	MERIB-BAAL	937c	1
9	7	חסד	GOODNESS	338c	1 1
		ירא	FEAR	431a	1 a
		תמיד	CONTINUITY	556c	1 b
		עבור	FOR THE SAKE OF	721a	1 a
		על	UPON	756a	2 6b
		שדה	FIELD	961d	2 e
		שוב	TURN BACK	999a	1
		שלחן	TABLE	1020b	1
9	8	כ	LIKE	454b	1 d
		כלב	DOG	477a	B
		מות	DIE	559d	1 b
		פנה	TURN	815c	2 c1
		שחה	BOW DOWN	1005c	1 c
9	9	בית	HOUSE	109d	5 c
9	10	אדמה	GROUND	9c	1
		בוא	COME	99b	1 e
		תמיד	CONTINUITY	556c	1 b
		עבד	WORK	713a	1
		על	UPON	756a	2 6b
		מריבבעל	MERIB-BAAL	937c	1
		שלחן	TABLE	1020b	1
9	11	דוד	DAVID	188b	J
		כן	SO	486c	2 cc
		מריבבעל	MERIB-BAAL	937c	1
		שלחן	TABLE	1020b	1
		שלחן	TABLE	1020b	1
9	12	מושב	DWELLING	444b	5
		מיכא	MICA	567d	1
		מיכה	MICHA	567d	4
		קטן	SMALL	882a	1 a
		מריבבעל	MERIB-BAAL	937c	1
9	13	תמיד	CONTINUITY	556c	1 b
		פסח	LAME	820c	
		מריבבעל	MERIB-BAAL	937c	1
		שלחן	TABLE	1020b	1
10	1	אחר	AFTER	*30a	2 b
		חנון	HANUN	337a	1
		מות	DIE	559c	1 a1
		עמון	AMMON	770a	
10	2	אל	TO	40b	6
		חנון	HANUN	337a	1
		חסד	GOODNESS	338c	1 1
		חסד	GOODNESS	338c	1 1
		יד	HAND	391a	5 d
		נחם	CONSOLE ONESELF	637b	
		נחש	NAHASH	638b	1
		עבד	SLAVE	714a	2
		עם	WITH	767d	1 d
		עשה	DO	794b	1 3
10	3	הפך	TURN	245c	1 b
		חנון	HANUN	337a	1
		חקר	SEARCH	350c	2 a
		כבד	MAKE HONORABLE	457d	2 a
		נחם	CONSOLE ONESELF	637a	
		עבור	FOR THE SAKE OF	721a	1 b
		עין	EYE	744d	3 c
		רגל	GO ABOUT	920b	2
		שלח	SEND	1018b	1 a
10	4	זקן	BEARD	278b	2
		חנון	HANUN	337a	1
		חצי	HALF	345c	1
		חצי	HALF	345c	2
		כרת	CUT OFF	503d	1 a
		מדו	GARMENT	551d	
		מפשעה	STEPPING REGION	*832c	
		שת	BUTTOCKS	1059d	
10	5	זקן	BEARD	278b	2
		ישב	REMAIN	442d	2 a
		כלם	BE HUMILIATED	483d	1
		צמח	SPROUT	855c	
		שוב	TURN BACK	997b	3 b
10	6	איש	MAN	36a	
		ארם	ARAM	74b	A
		באש	STINK	93a	1
		באש	STINK	*93b	
		ביתרחוב	BETH-REHOB	112d	
		טוב	TOB	376a	
		מעכה	MAACAH	591a	3
		צובא	ZOBAH	844c	
		רגלי	ON FOOT	920b	
		שכר	HIRE	969a	
10	7	גבור	STRONG	150b	2
		צבא	ARMY	839a	1 a
		שלח	SEND	1018b	1 a
10	8	איש	MAN	36a	
		ארם	ARAM	74b	A
		בד	SEPARATION	94c	1 b
		ביתרחוב	BETH-REHOB	112d	
		טוב	TOB	376a	
		מעכה	MAACAH	591a	3
		ערך	ARRANGE	789c	1 d
		פתח	OPENING	836a	
		צובא	ZOBAH	844c	
		רחוב	REHOB	932b	1 a
		שדה	FIELD	961c	1 f
10	9	בחר	CHOOSE	104a	4
		בחר	CHOOSE	104b	7
		מן	FROM	578c	1 c
		ערך	ARRANGE	789c	1 d
		פנה	FACE	816b	1 6
		פנה	FACE	816b	1 5
		קרא	ENCOUNTER	897a	1
10	10	אבישי	ABISHAI	5a	
		יתר	REMAINDER	451d	1 b
		נתן	GIVE	679c	1 r
		ערך	ARRANGE	789c	1 d
		קרא	ENCOUNTER	897a	1
10	11	חזק	BE FIRM	304b	1 1b
		ישע	DELIVER	446c	1
		ישועה	DELIVERANCE	447b	2
10	12	אלהים	GOD	44d	4 c
		בעד	ON BEHALF OF	126c	2
		חזק	BE FIRM	304b	1 2c
		חזק	BE FIRM	305b	2
		טוב	PLEASANT	374a	2 f
10	13	מלחמה	WAR	536c	
		נגש	DRAW NEAR	620d	1
10	14	על	UPON	758d	4 2b
		שוב	TURN BACK	997a	2
10	15	יחד	UNION	403a	2 a2
		נגף	STRIKE	620a	
10	16	הדדעזר	HADADEZER	*212d	
		הדדעזר	HADADEZER	*212d	
		הדרעזר	HADADEZER	214c	
		חילם	HELAM	298a	
		יצא	BRING OUT	424c	1 c
		עבר	REGION ACROSS	719c	1 b
		שובך	SHOBACH	1000c	
10	17	אסף	GATHER	62b	1 a
		נגד	BE CONSPICUOUS	617a	
		ערך	ARRANGE	789c	1 d
		קרא	ENCOUNTER	897a	1
10	18	הרג	KILL	247b	1 b
		פנה	FACE	818a	2 5b
		פרש	HORSEMAN	832a	
		ארבעים	FORTY	91b	1 a
		רגלי	ON FOOT	920b	
		רכב	CHARIOT	939a	1
		שובך	SHOBACH	1000c	
10	19	הדדעזר	HADADEZER	*212d	
		הדרעזר	HADADEZER	214c	
		ירא	FEAR	431b	1 d
		ישע	DELIVER	446c	1
		נגף	STRIKE	620a	
		עבד	WORK	713a	3
		עבד	SLAVE	713d	2
		שלם	BE IN COVENANT OF PEACE	1023d	1
11	1	חנה	DECLINE	333c	2 c2
		ירושלים	JERUSALEM	437a	
		ל	TO	517a	6 a
		עת	TIME	773b	1 a
		עת	TIME	773c	2
		צור	CONFINE	848d	2
		צור	CONFINE	*848d	2
		רבה	RABBA	913d	1
		ישראל	ISRAEL	975c	2 a1
		תשובה	RETURN	1000c	2
		תשובה	RETURN	1000c	2
		שנה	YEAR	1040b	
11	2	גג	ROOF	150d	1
		הלך	WALK	235d	1 b
		טוב	PLEASANT	373c	1 a
		על	UPON	758c	4 2a
		על	UPON	758c	4 2a
		ערב	SUNSET	787d	1 a
		מראה	VISION	909d	1 b
		רחץ	WASH OFF	*934c	2
		על	UPON	*1106b	1 a
11	3	אוריה	URIAH	22c	1
		אליעם	ELIAM	45c	A
		בתשוע	BATH-SHUA	124a	
		בתשבע	BATHSHEBA	124a	
		דרש	SEEK	205c	4 b
		חתי	HITTITE	366d	1
		חתי	HITTITE	*367a	2 b
		ל	TO	514b	5 fa
		לא	NOT	520b	4 bb
		עמיאל	AMMIEL	770a	3
11	4	בוא	COME	98a	1 e
		טמאה	UNCLEANNESS	380a	1
		קדש	BE SET APART	873c	4
		שוב	TURN BACK	997a	3 a
		שכב	LIE DOWN	1012b	3
11	5	אנכי	I	59c	
		אשה	WOMAN	61a	1
		הרה	CONCEIVE	247d	1
11	6	חתי	HITTITE	366d	1
		שלח	SEND	1018b	1 c
		שלח	SEND	1018b	1 a
11	7	שאל	ASK	981d	2 a
		שלום	PEACE	1022d	3
11	8	יצא	GO OUT	422c	1 a
		יצא	GO OUT	423b	1 f
		משאת	PORTION	673a	4 a
		רחץ	WASH OFF	934c	2
11	9	ירד	GO DOWN	432d	1 c
11	10	מדוע	WHEREFORE	396c	
		ירד	GO DOWN	432d	1 c
11	11	אדון	LORD	11b	3 lj
		אם	IF	50a	1 b2
		ו	AND	252d	1 f
		חי	ALIVE	312a	1 b
		חיים	LIFE	313a	1
		חנה	DECLINE	333c	2 c2
		חנה	DECLINE	333d	2 2
		נפש	SOUL	659c	2
		סכה	THICKET	697c	2
		שדה	FIELD	961c	1 f
		שכב	LIE DOWN	1012b	3
11	12	בית	HOUSE	108d	1 ab
		מחר	TO-MORROW	564a	1 b
		מחרת	THE MORROW	564a	
		עת	TIME	773c	1 b
11	13	ירד	GO DOWN	432d	1 c
		עבד	SLAVE	713d	2
		שכר	BE DRUNK	1016b	
11	14	בקר	MORNING	134a	1 e
		יד	HAND	391a	5 d
		כתב	WRITE	507b	1 a
		כתב	WRITE	507d	1 c
		ספר	MISSIVE	707a	1 a
11	15	אחר	BEHIND	30b	4 aa

Ch	v.	Heb	Eng	Page	Sec
		חזק	STRONG	305c	1 d
		יהב	SET	396d	2
		מול	IN FRONT OF	557c	2 a
		נכה	SMITE	645a	
		ספר	MISSIVE	707a	1 a
		ספר	MISSIVE	707a	1 a
		שוב	TURN BACK	996d	1
11	16	אשר	PARTICLE OF RELATION	82d	4 d
		חיל	STRENGTH	298d	1 c
		מקום	STANDING PLACE	879d	1 b
		שם	THERE	1027b	1 b
		שמר	KEEP	1036c	1 b
11	17	חתי	HITTITE	366d	1
		לחם	ENGAGE IN BATTLE	535c	
		מן	FROM	580c	3 ba
		נפל	FALL	657a	2 a
11	18	מלחמה	WAR	536c	
11	19	כלה	FINISH	478b	1 c
		מלחמה	WAR	536c	
11	20	אשר	THAT	83b	8 aa
		חומה	WALL	327b	1
		חמה	RAGE	404c	2 a
		חמה	RAGE	*404d	2 c
		ירה	SHOOT	435b	2
		נגש	DRAW NEAR	621a	
		עלה	GO UP	749a	7
		על	UPON	758c	4 2a
11	21	אבימלך	ABIMELECH	4c	3
		בשת	SHAME	102b	2
		גדעון	GIDEON	154c	
		חומה	WALL	327b	1
		חתי	HITTITE	366d	1
		נגש	DRAW NEAR	621a	
		פלח	CLEAVAGE	812a	1
		ירבשת	JERUBBESHETH	937c	
		ירבעל	JERUBBAAL	937c	
		רכב	CHARIOT	939b	3
		רכב	CHARIOT	939b	3
		שלך	THROW	1021a	1 a
		תבץ	THEBEZ	1062a	
11	22	הלך	WALK	234a	1 5b
		חרה	BURN	354a	1 b
		מלחמה	WAR	536c	
11	23	גבר	BE STRONG	149d	2 b
		היה	BECOME	225d	1 b
		כי	THAT	472a	1 b
		על	UPON	757d	2 7d
		פתח	OPENING	836a	
		שדה	FIELD	961c	1 f
11	24	חתי	HITTITE	366d	1
		ירא	SHOOT	432b	
		מן	FROM	580c	3 ba
		על	UPON	758c	4 2a
11	25	אכל	EAT	37c	4
		את	MARK OF THE ACCUSATIVE	85a	1 c
		הרס	THROW DOWN	248c	1
		זה	THIS	262a	6 cb
		חזק	BE FIRM	305a	2
		חרב	SWORD	352d	1 g
		חרב	SWORD	*352d	1 f
		רעע	BE EVIL	949c	1
11	26	בעל	OWNER	127b	1 2
		ספד	WAIL	704d	
11	27	אבל	MOURNING	5d	
		אסף	GATHER	62b	2 b
		רעע	BE EVIL	949c	4
12	1	נתן	NATHAN	681d	2
		עשיר	RICH	799c	
		רוש	BE IN WANT	930d	
		שלח	SEND	1018c	2 a
12	2	עשיר	RICH	799c	
		רבה	BECOME MANY	915d	1 e4
12	3	גדל	GROW UP	152b	1 b
		חיק	BOSOM	300d	2
		חיה	LIVE	311c	1
		כבשה	EWE-LAMBS	461a	
		כוס	CUP	468a	
		כיאם	EXCEPT	474d	2 a
		כל	ALL	*482c	2 a
		ל	TO	513d	5 ad
		מן	OUT OF	579a	2 aa
		משיח	ANOINTED	603c	1
		פת	FRAGMENT	837d	
		מן	SMALL	882a	1 b
		רוש	BE IN WANT	930d	
		שכב	LIE DOWN	1012b	1 e
		שתה	DRINK	1059b	1 a
12	4	ארח	WANDER	72d	2
		ארח	WAY	73b	4
		ה	THE	209a	2 b
		הלך	TRAVELLER	237a	
		חמל	SPARE	328b	
		כבשה	EWE-LAMBS	461a	
		ל	TO	511c	1 gb
		לקח	TAKE	542d	3 a
		לקח	TAKE	543a	3 a
		עשה	DO	794d	2 3
		עשיר	RICH	799c	
		צרתן	SMALL CATTLE	838b	1 a1
		רוש	BE IN WANT	930d	
12	5	בן	SON	121d	8 e
		חי	ALIVE	311d	1 a
		חרה	BURN	354a	1 a
		מאד	EXCEEDINGLY	547b	2 a
		מות	DEATH	560d	2
		משיח	ANOINTED	603c	1
12	6	חמל	SPARE	328b	
		כבשה	EWE-LAMBS	461a	
		על	UPON	758b	3 a
		עקב	CONSEQUENCE	784d	1
12	7	מלך	KING	573c	5 c
		משח	ANOINT	603b	2
		ישראל	ISRAEL	975c	2 a2
12	8	הם	THEY	241d	8 c
		הם	THEY	241d	6 a
		ו	AND	254d	5 ca
		חיק	BOSOM	300d	3 a
		יסף	ADD	415b	1
12	9	בזה	DESPISE	102b	
		הרג	KILL	247a	1 a
		חתי	HITTITE	366d	1
		נכה	SMITE	646a	2 c
		רע	EVIL	948c	0 b
12	10	בזה	DESPISE	102c	
		חתי	HITTITE	366d	1
		סור	TURN ASIDE	693d	2
		עולם	LONG DURATION	762b	2 b4
		עקב	CONSEQUENCE	784d	1
12	11	קום	STAND	879a	3
		רע	FRIEND	946a	2
		שכב	LIE DOWN	1012b	3
		שמש	SUN	1039b	4 a
12	12	נגד	IN FRONT	617b	1 aa
		נגד	IN FRONT	617b	1 aa
		סתר	COVERING	712a	3
		שמש	SUN	1039b	4 a
12	13	גם	ALSO	169c	4
		חטא	MISS A GOAL OR WAY	307a	2 b
		חטאת	SIN	309a	1 d2
		מות	DIE	560a	2 b
		עבר	PASS OVER	719a	4
12	14	אפס	NON-EXISTENCE	67b	2 cb
		ילוד	BORN	409c	
		מות	DIE	560a	2 b
		נאץ	CONTEMN	611a	
12	15	אנש	BE SICK	60c	
		ילד	CHILD	409b	A
		נגף	STRIKE	619d	
12	16	אלהים	GOD	43d	3
		בעד	ON BEHALF OF	126c	2
		בקש	SEEK	134d	3 c
		לון	LODGE	533c	1 a
		צום	FAST	847a	
		צום	FASTING	847b	
		שכב	LIE DOWN	1012a	1 b
12	17	אבה	BE WILLING	2c	
		ברה	EAT	136a	
		זקן	OLD	278c	2 a
		מן	FROM	578a	1
		על	UPON	756b	2 6c
		קום	STAND	877d	1 e
		קום	STAND	878a	1 a
12	18	איך	HOW	32c	1
		חי	ALIVE	312a	1 b
		ילד	CHILD	409b	A
		ירא	FEAR	431b	1 d
		קול	VOICE	877b	3 a1
		רעה	MISERY	949b	2
12	19	בין	DISCERN	106d	2 c
		ילד	CHILD	409b	A
		לחש	WHISPER	538a	
12	20	בית	HOUSE	109b	1 ae 0
		חלף	PASS ON OR AWAY	322b	
		סוך	ANOINT	692a	1
		רחץ	WASH OFF	934c	2
		שום	TO PLACE	963b	1 c
		שמלה	WRAPPER	971a	
		שאל	ASK	981c	1 a
12	21	בכה	WEEP	113c	6
		חי	ALIVE	312a	1 b
		ילד	CHILD	409b	A
		כאשר	WHEN	455c	3
		עבור	FOR THE SAKE OF	721a	1 a
		צום	FAST	847a	
		קום	STAND	877c	1 a
12	22	אב	FATHER	3b	1
		אם	IF	50d	2 ba
		אמר	SAY	56b	2
		בכה	WEEP	113c	6
		חיה	LIVE	311a	1 b
		חיה	LIVE	311a	1 b
		חי	ALIVE	312a	1 b
		חנן	SHOW FAVOR	336a	2 a
		ילד	CHILD	409b	A
		מי	WHO	567a	F d
		עוד	STILL	729b	2 aa
		צום	FAST	847a	
12	23	הלך	WALK	234b	2 1
		הלך	WALK	234b	2 1
		צום	FAST	847a	
		שוב	TURN BACK	997c	4 b
		שוב	TURN BACK	999b	1 g
12	24	אהב	LOVE	13a	5 a
		בוא	COME	98a	1
		בתשבע	BATHSHEBA	124a	
		נחם	CONSOLE ONESELF	637a	
		שכב	LIE DOWN	1012b	3
		שלמה	SOLOMON	1024d	
12	25	יד	HAND	391a	5 d
		ידידיה	JEDIDIAH	392a	
12	26	לחם	ENGAGE IN BATTLE	535c	
		מלוכה	KINGSHIP	574d	
		עיר	CITY	746c	1 d
		עירשמש	CITY	746d	2
		רבה	RABBA	913d	1
12	27	לחם	ENGAGE IN BATTLE	535c	
		עיר	CITY	746d	2
		רבה	RABBA	913d	1
12	28	אני	I	59a	
		אנכי	I	59b	
		יתר	REMAINDER	451d	1 b
		על	UPON	755d	2 5
		קרא	CALL	896b	6 d4
		שם	NAME	1027d	2 a
12	29	אסף	GATHER	62b	1 a
		לחם	ENGAGE IN BATTLE	535c	
		רבה	RABBA	913d	1
12	30	אבן	STONE	6d	3
		היה	BECOME	225d	2 1b
		ו	AND	253a	1g
		זהב	GOLD	263c	9 c
		יצא	BRING OUT	425a	4 a
		יקר	PRECIOUS	430a	1 c
		כבר	ROUND	503b	3 b
		מלך	KING	573c	5 d
		מלכם	MILCOM	576a	
		עטרה	CROWN	742d	1
		על	UPON	758c	4 2a
		רבה	BECOME MANY	915d	1 e3
		שלל	SPOIL	1022a	2
		משקל	WEIGHT	1054a	
12	31	ברזל	IRON	137c	1 d
		ברזל	IRON	137c	1 d
		מגזרה	CUTTING INSTRUMENT	160d	
		מגרה	SAW	176b	
		חריץ	A CUT	358d	2
		יצא	CAUSE TO GO	424c	1 b
		מלבן	BRICK-MOLD	527c	1
		עבד	WORK	713c	1
		עבר	PASS OVER	719a	1
		שום	TO PLACE	963a	1 a
13	1	אבישלום	ABSALOM	5a	2
		אהב	LOVE	12d	1
		אחות	SISTER	27d	1
		אחר	AFTER	*30a	2 b
		אמנון	AMNON	54c	1
		יפה	BEAUTIFUL	421c	
		תמר	TAMAR	1071c	1 b
13	2	אחות	SISTER	27d	1
		בתולה	VIRGIN	143d	
		מאומה	ANYTHING	549a	
		פלא	BE SURPASSING	810c	1
		צרר	BIND	864d	B
		תמר	TAMAR	1071c	1 b
13	3	יהונדב	JEHONADAB	220d	2
		יהונתן	JONATHAN	220d	3
		חכם	WISE	314d	1
		רע	FRIEND	946a	1
		שמעא	SHIMEA	1035a	1
13	4	אהב	LOVE	12d	1
		אח	BROTHER	26b	1
		אחות	SISTER	27d	1
		בקר	MORNING	134b	1 f
		דל	WEAK	195d	
		ככה	THUS	462c	
13	5	ברה	FOOD	136a	
		ברה	EAT	136a	
		יהונדב	JEHONADAB	220d	2
		מען	PURPOSE	775c	2 a
		עשה	DO	794d	2 3
		ראה	TO SEE	907a	1 b
		ראה	TO SEE	907d	6 d
		שכב	LIE DOWN	1012a	1 b
13	6	ברה	EAT	136a	
		לבב	MAKE CAKES	525d	
		לבב	CAKES	525d	
		ראה	TO SEE	907d	6 d
13	7	אח	BROTHER	26b	1
		בריה	FOOD	136a	
		הלך	WALK	230d	1 1d 3a
		עשה	DO	794d	2 3
13	8	אח	BROTHER	26b	1
		בצק	DOUGH	130d	
		בשל	BOIL	143b	2
		הלך	WALK	230d	1 1d 3a
		לבב	CAKES	525d	
		לבב	MAKE CAKES	525d	
		לוש	KNEAD	534c	
		שכב	LIE DOWN	1012a	1 b
13	9	יצא	BRING OUT	424d	1 e
		יקק	POUR	427b	1
		מאן	REFUSE	549a	
		משרת	PAN	602a	
		על	UPON	759a	4 2c
13	10	בוא	COME	99a	1
		בריה	FOOD	136a	
		ברה	EAT	136a	
		חדר	CHAMBER	293c	
		לבב	CAKES	525d	

Ch	v.	Heb	Eng	Page	Sec
13	11	חזק	BE FIRM	305a	6 a
		נגש	APPROACH	621b	
		שכב	LIE DOWN	1012b	3
13	12	כן	SO	486a	1 ca
		נבלה	SENSELESSNESS	615a	1
		נבלה	SENSELESSNESS	615b	1
		ענה	BE BOWED DOWN	776b	2
		עשה	DO	795b	1
13	13	אן	WHERE	33a	A
		הלך	WALK	237a	3 a
		חרפה	REPROACH	358a	2 a
		מנע	WITHHOLD	586a	
		נבל	FOOLISH	615a	
13	14	אבה	BE WILLING	2c	
		חזק	BE FIRM	304a	1 1a
		ענה	BE BOWED DOWN	776b	2
		שכב	LIE DOWN	1012b	3
13	15	אהב	LOVE	12d	1
		אהבה	LOVE	13c	1
		שנא	HATE	971c	1 a
		שנאה	HATING	972a	1
13	16	אבה	BE WILLING	2c	
		אודה	CAUSE	15c	
		אל	NOT	39b	A bb
		רעה	MISERY	949b	2
		שלח	SEND	1019a	1 b
13	17	את	MARK OF THE ACCUSATIVE	84d	1 a
		בעד	BEHIND	*126c	1 b
		דלת	DOOR	195a	2
		זה	THIS	260c	1 a
		נעל	LOCK	653a	
		על	UPON	759a	4 2b
		שלח	SEND	1018b	1 a
		שרת	SERVE	1058a	1 a
13	18	בת	DAUGHTER	123a	1
		בעד	BEHIND	*126c	1 b
		בתולה	VIRGIN	144a	
		דלת	DOOR	195a	2
		חוץ	THE OUTSIDE	299c	1 a
		יצא	BRING OUT	424d	1 e
		כתנת	TUNIC	509a	
		לבש	PUT ON	528a	A
		מעיל	ROBE	591c	2
		נעל	LOCK	653a	
		על	UPON	753a	2 1 aa
		פס	FLAT OF HAND	821a	
		שרת	SERVE	1058a	1 a
13	19	אפר	ASHES	68a	1
		הלך	WALK	233b	14c 2
		זעק	CRY	277b	2 d
		חטב	VARICOLORED	310b	
		כתנת	TUNIC	509a	
		לקח	TAKE	543c	5
		פס	FLAT OF HAND	821a	
		קרע	TEAR	902c	1 a1
		קרע	TEAR	902c	1 a1
		שום	TO PLACE	963b	1 b
13	20	אמינון	AMNON	54c	
		אמינון	AMNON	54c	1
		היה	BE	227b	3 4d a
		ו	AND	252c	1 b
		חרש	BE SILENT	361b	1 a
		ישב	REMAIN	442d	2 a
		לב	HEART	524d	2 3c
		שית	PUT	1011b	2 b
		שמם	BE DESOLATED	1030d	1
13	21	אהב	LOVE	12d	1
		חרה	BURN	354a	1 b
		עצב	HURT	780c	
		שכב	LIE DOWN	1012b	1 b
13	22	דבר	SPEAK	181c	3 e
		דבר	WORD	184a	8
		טוב	PLEASANT	374a	2 f
		מן	FROM	583d	9 b1
		ענה	BE BOWED DOWN	776b	2
		רע	EVIL	948b	2
		שנא	HATE	971c	1 a
13	23	אפרים	EPHRAIM	68c	6
		בעלחצור	BAAL-HAZOR	128a	
		גזז	SHEAR	159c	
		היה	COME TO PASS	224c	2 a1 ad
		יום	TIME	399d	6 b
		ל	TO	517a	6 b
		עם	WITH	*768a	2
13	24	גזז	SHEAR	159c	
		נא	PART OF ENTREATY	609c	4 d
		עם	PEOPLE	*766b	1
13	25	אבה	BE WILLING	2c	
		אל	NOT	39a	A a
		ברך	BLESS	139a	3
		היה	COME TO PASS	224b	1 1b
		כבד	BE HEAVY	457b	1
		פרץ	PUSH	823a	
13	26	יש	BE	*442a	2 cf
		לא	NOT	520c	4 c
		מה	HOW	*554b	4 d
		מה	HOW	554b	4 d
13	27	אבישלום	ABSALOM	5a	2
		פרץ	PUSH	823a	
		משתה	FEAST	1059d	1
13	28	בן	SON	121d	4 a
		חזק	BE FIRM	304b	1 2c
		טוב	PLEASING	373b	2
		יין	WINE	406c	A
		ירא	FEAR	431a	1 a
		כ	LIKE	454d	3 b
		כי	THAT	472b	1 da
		לב	HEART	525c	2 9a
		ראה	TO SEE	907a	7 c
13	29	פרד	MULE	825d	
		רכב	RIDE	938c	1
13	30	היה	COME TO PASS	224d	2a 1b
		יתר	BE LEFT OVER	451b	
		שמועה	REPORT	1035b	1
13	31	נצב	STAND	662b	1 b
		קרע	TEAR	902c	1 a1
13	32	בד	SEPARATION	94c	1 b
		יהונדב	JEHONADAB	220d	
		היה	BE	227c	3 5a
		יום	DAY	400a	7 d1 e
		ענה	BE BOWED DOWN	776b	2
		פה	MOUTH	805d	6 d2
		שום	TO PLACE	964a	3 f
		שומה	SCOWL	965a	
		שמעא	SHIMEA	1035a	1
13	33	כאם	BUT	475b	2 b
		לב	HEART	525a	2 3d
		שום	TO PLACE	963b	1 b
13	34	ביתחורון	BETH-HORON	111c	
		ברח	FLEE	137d	2
		הר	MOUNTAIN	250d	1 m
		חרונים	HORONAIM	357b	
		מורד	DESCENT	434c	1
		צד	SIDE	841a	
		צפה	KEEP WATCH	859c	
		צפה	KEEP WATCH	859c	
		רב	MUCH	913a	1 a2
13	35	יהונדב	JEHONADAB	220d	1 a2
		כן	SO	486b	2 ab
13	36	בכה	WEEP	113b	1
		בכה	WEEP	113c	1
		בכה	WEEP	113c	2
		בכי	WEEPING	113d	
		היה	COME TO PASS	225a	2a 1c
13	37	אבל	MOURN	5c	
		ברח	FLEE	137d	2
		גשור	GESHUR	178a	2
		יום	DAY	400c	7 f
		עמיהוד	AMMIHUD	770a	1
		תלמי	TALMAI	1068d	1
13	38	ברח	FLEE	137d	2
		גשור	GESHUR	178a	2
13	39	אמנון	AMNON	54c	1
		דוד	DAVID	188b	J
		כלה	BE FINISHED	477d	2 b
		נחם	CONSOLE ONESELF	637a	3
14	1	אב	FATHER	3b	1
		על	UPON	757c	2 7 cc
		צרויה	ZERUIAH	863b	
14	2	אבל	MOURN	5c	
		אבל	MOURN	5c	
		אבל	MOURNING	5d	
		אשה	WOMAN	61b	1
		זה	THIS	261d	4 i
		חכם	WISE	314d	3
		לבש	PUT ON	527d	A
		סוך	ANOINT	692a	1
		שמן	OIL	1032b	2 c
		תקוע	TEKOA	1075d	
14	3	דבר	WORD	183d	4 7
		פה	MOUTH	805a	2 a
14	4	אף	NOSE	60b	2
		ה	THE	208d	1 i
		ישע	DELIVER	446c	1
		נפל	FALL	657c	3 b
		שחה	BOW DOWN	1005b	1 a
		תקועי	TEKOITE	1075d	
14	5	אבל	VERILY	6a	1
		אלמנה	WIDOW	48b	
		אשה	WOMAN	61b	1
		מה	WHAT	552d	1 ac
14	6	אמה	MAID	51a	2
		נכה	SMITE	645d	2 a
		נצה	STRUGGLE	663c	
		נצל	SNATCH AWAY	664d	1
		שדה	FIELD	961b	1 b
		שפחה	MAID	1046c	
14	7	אמה	GROUND	9d	4
		אמה	MAID	51a	2
		ב	IN	90c	3 5
		גחלת	COAL	161a	
		הרג	KILL	247a	1 a
		ירש	INHERIT	439d	2
		כבה	QUENCH	459d	
		מות	DIE	560b	1 b
		נפש	SOUL	659d	3 c
		נתן	GIVE	679c	1 s
		שום	TO PLACE	964c	5 b
		שאר	REMAIN	984a	1
		שארית	REST	984d	2
		שם	NAME	1028b	2 c
		שפחה	MAID	1046c	2
		משפחה	CLAN	1046d	1 a
14	8	על	UPON	754d	2 l f g
		צוה	COMMAND	845d	1 e
14	9	כסא	THRONE	491a	3 a
		נקי	FREE FROM	667c	2
		עון	INIQUITY	731c	3
		על	UPON	756c	2 7 a b
		תקועי	TEKOITE	1075d	
14	10	ו	AND	254c	5 a
		יסף	DO AGAIN	415c	2 a
		נגע	TOUCH	619a	3
14	11	גאל	ACT AS KINSMAN	145c	1 e
		דם	BLOOD	196d	2 e
		זכר	REMEMBER	270a	13 a
		חי	ALIVE	311d	1 a
		מן	FROM	581a	7 b
		מן	FROM	583b	7 ba
		נא	PART OF ENTREATY	609b	3 c
		נפל	FALL	657a	1
		רבה	BECOME MANY	*915b	
		רבה	BECOME MANY	915c	1 d1
		שערה	A HAIR	972b	1
		שחת	GO TO RUIN	1008a	1
14	12	אמה	MAID	51a	2
		נא	PART OF ENTREATY	609b	3 c
		שפחה	MAID	1046c	2
14	13	אשם	GUILTY	79d	
		דבר	SPEAK	181d	
		זה	THIS	262a	6 d
		חשב	THINK	363a	12
		מה	HOW	554a	4 d
		נדח	BANISH	623a	2
14	14	אסף	GATHER	62d	1 c
		בלת	NOT	117a	4 a
		חשב	THINK	363a	12
		מחשבה	THOUGHT	364c	2
		מות	DIE	560a	2 b
		נגר	POUR	620b	1
		נדח	BANISH	623a	2
		נדח	THRUST	623a	2
		נפש	SOUL	660d	6 a
		נשא	LIFT	671b	3 b
14	15	אמה	MAID	51a	2
		אמה	MAID	51a	2
		אשר	THAT	83b	8 aa
		דבר	WORD	182b	1 1e
		ירא	TERRIFY	431d	
		נא	PART OF ENTREATY	609b	3 a
		שפחה	MAID	1046c	2
14	16	שפחה	MAID	*1046c	2
		אמה	MAID	51a	2
		יחד	UNION	403a	2 a3
		כף	POWER	496d	2
		נחלה	PROPERTY	635b	1 e
		נצל	DELIVER	665a	3 a
		שפחה	MAID	*1046c	2
14	17	אלהים	GOD	44a	3 b
		אמה	MAID	51a	2
		טוב	A GOOD THING	375b	4
		כן	SO	486b	2 ad a
		ל	TO	514b	5 fb
		מלאך	MESSENGER	521d	2
		נא	PART OF ENTREATY	609b	3 c
		מנוחה	RESTING PLACE	630a	1
		רע	EVIL	948d	3
		שמע	HEAR	1033d	1 h
		שפחה	MAID	1046c	2
14	18	כחד	HIDE	470b	
14	19	שאל	ASK	981d	2 a
		אמה	MAID	51a	2
		אש	IS	78a	
		את	WITH	86a	1 a
		הוא	HE, SHE, IT	215d	2 a
		חי	ALIVE	312a	1 b
		יד	HAND	389d	1 e1
		ימן	GO TO THE RIGHT	412b	
		יש	CAN	442a	2 cc
		נפש	SOUL	659c	2
		פה	MOUTH	805a	2 a
		סמאל	TAKE THE LEFT	970a	2
		שפחה	MAID	1046c	2
14	20	אלהים	GOD	44a	3 b
		דבר	WORD	183c	4 3
		חכם	WISE	314d	2
		חכמה	WISDOM	315b	2
		סבב	TURN AROUND	685c	
		עבור	FOR THE SAKE OF	721a	1 b
		פנה	FACE	816b	1 5
14	22	ברך	BLESS	139b	4 g
		דבר	WORD	182b	1 1e
		חן	FAVOR	336b	2 b1
		נפל	FALL	657b	3 b
		עבד	SLAVE	714c	6
		שחה	BOW DOWN	1005b	1 a
14	23	גשור	GESHUR	178a	2
		הלך	WALK	230d	1 d 3b
14	24	סבב	TURN ABOUT	685c	1 a
		פנה	FACE	816a	1 2b
14	25	היה	BE	226d	3 1
		הלל	PRAISE	238a	1
		יפה	BEAUTIFUL	421c	
		כף	SOLE OF FOOT	496d	3
		ל	TO	514b	5 fb
		מום	BLEMISH	548c	1 a
		מן	FROM	581d	5 a
		קדקד	HEAD	869b	
		רגל	FOOT	919d	1 a
14	26	אבן	STONE	6d	5
		ב	IN	90d	3 8
		היה	COME TO PASS	225b	1 2b be

Ch	v.	Heb	Eng	Page	Sec
		יום	YEAR	399d	6 c
		כבד	HEAVY	458a	1 a
		ל	TO	517b	6 c
		מאה	HUNDRED	548a	1 b2
		מלך	KING	573c	5 d
		מן	FROM	582b	5 d2
		שער	HAIR	972b	2
		שקל	WEIGH	1053c	1
		שקל	SHEKEL	1053d	
		שקל	SHEKEL	1053d	
14	27	ילד	BE BORN	408d	
		יפה	BEAUTIFUL	421c	
		מראה	VISION	909d	1 b
		תמר	TAMAR	1071c	1 c
14	28	יום	TIME	399d	6 b
		פנה	FACE	816a	1 2b
14	29	אבה	BE WILLING	2c	
		שלח	SEND	1018b	1 c
14	30	אל	TO	40c	8
		אש	FIRE	77c	1
		חלקה	PORTION OF GROUND	324c	1 b
		יד	HAND	390d	5 a2
		יצת	KINDLE	428c	
		שערה	BARLEY	972d	1
14	31	אש	FIRE	77c	1
		אשר	PARTICLE OF RELATION	83a	7 b
		חלקה	PORTION OF GROUND	324c	1 b
		יצת	KINDLE	428c	
		מה	HOW	554a	4 d
14	32	גשור	GESHUR	178a	2
		טוב	PLEASING	373b	4
		מות	DIE	560b	1 b
		עוד	STILL	728d	1 aa
		עון	INIQUITY	731b	2 a
		פנה	FACE	816a	1 2b
14	33	אף	NOSE	60b	2
		נשק	KISS	676b	
		שחה	BOW DOWN	1005b	1 b
15	1	אחר	BEHIND	30b	4 ag
		ל	TO	515d	5 ia
		סוס	HORSE	692c	1
		עשה	DO	795a	2 7
		רוץ	RUN	930b	1
		רוץ	RUN	*930c	2 a
		מרכבה	CHARIOT	939d	1
15	2	אי	WHERE	32b	2 b
		דרך	WAY	202d	1
		היה	COME TO PASS	224d	2 a1 am
		יד	HAND	391c	5 h3
		ל	TO	515a	5 ha
		שכם	START EARLY	1014c	
		שער	GATE	1044d	1 a
		משפט	JUDGMENT	1048b	1 a
15	3	את	WITH	86d	4 b
		דבר	WORD	183d	4 5
		טוב	PLEASANT	374b	0 a
		נכח	STRAIGHTNESS	647c	
		שמע	HEAR	1033d	1 h
15	4	מי	WHO	566c	F a
		על	UPON	757b	2 7c aa
		שום	TO PLACE	964a	3 d
		שפט	JUDGE	1047c	2 b
		משפט	JUDGMENT	1048c	1 d
15	5	חזק	BE FIRM	304d	3
		חזק	BE FIRM	305a	6 a
		נשק	KISS	676b	
		קרב	COME NEAR	897c	1 g
15	6	גנב	STEAL	170c	
		דבר	WORD	183d	4 7
		לב	HEART	524d	2 3a
		משפט	JUDGMENT	1048b	1 a
15	7	חברון	HEBRON	289b	
		נדר	VOW	623d	
		נדר	VOW	624a	1
		נדר	VOW	624a	6
		שלם	BE COMPLETE	1022c	4
15	8	ארם	ARAM	74c	B
		גשור	GESHUR	178a	2
		נדר	VOW	623d	
		נדר	VOW	624a	1
		שוב	TURN BACK	998d	1 a
15	9	הלך	WALK	230d	1 1d 3b
		הלך	WALK	231d	1 d5 ta
		חברון	HEBRON	289b	
15	10	ו	AND	254d	5 a
		חברון	HEBRON	289b	
		רגל	GO ABOUT	920b	2
15	11	הלך	WALK	231d	1 1d 5a
		הלך	WALK	231d	1 d5 tc
		ידע	KNOW	393c	1 a
		ל	TO	516c	5 jb
		מאה	HUNDRED	548a	1 b1
		קרא	CALL	895d	5 c
		תם	INTEGRITY	1070d	2
15	12	אחיתפל	AHITHOPHEL	27c	
		אמיץ	MIGHTY	55c	
		הלך	WALK	233c	1 4d
		זבח	SACRIFICE	257c	1 1
		יעץ	ADVISE	419d	
		קרא	CALL	895d	5 c
		קשר	CONSPIRACY	905c	
15	13	לב	HEART	525a	2 4
		נגד	BE CONSPICUOUS	617a	5
15	14	ברח	FLEE	137d	2
		חרב	SWORD	352d	1 f
		מהר	HASTEN	555a	2
		מהר	HASTEN	555a	2
		נדה	THRUST	623b	1
		נכה	SMITE	646d	3
		נשג	OVERTAKE	673c	1 a
		על	UPON	756c	27a b
		פלישה	ESCAPE	812d	2 b
15	15	בחר	CHOOSE	104a	2 b
15	16	את	MARK OF THE ACCUSATIVE	85a	1 a
		עזב	LEAVE	737a	1 b
		רגל	FOOT	920a	1 f
		שמר	KEEP	1036c	1 b
15	17	ביתהמרחק	BETH-MERHAK	112a	1 f
		עם	PEOPLE	766c	2 c
		רגל	FOOT	920a	1 f
15	18	גת	GATH	387d	5 h3
		יד	HAND	391c	5 h3
		כרתי	CHERETHITE	504d	
		עבר	PASS OVER	718c	5 c
		פלתי	PELETHITES	814c	
		פנה	FACE	818c	27a a
		רגל	FOOT	920a	1 f
15	19	אתי	ITTAI	87b	1
		גתי	GITTITE	388a	
		נכרי	FOREIGN	648d	1 b
15	20	אמת	FIRMNESS	54a	3 a
		אשר	PARTICLE OF RELATION	82c	4 bg
		הלך	WALK	231a	1 d3 gb
		חסד	GOODNESS	339b	4
		נוע	WAVER	631c	4
		על	UPON	757b	2 7c ab
		תמול	YESTERDAY	1070a	1
15	21	אם	IF	50a	1 b1
		אתי	ITTAI	87b	1
		חי	ALIVE	311d	1 a
		חי	ALIVE	312a	1 b
		חיים	LIFE	313a	1
		כי	THAT	472a	1 c
		כיאם	SURELY	475b	2 c
		מות	DEATH	560c	1
		מקום	STANDING PLACE	880b	4
		שם	THERE	1027a	1 a
15	22	אתי	ITTAI	87b	1
		טף	CHILDREN	382a	1
		גתי	GITTITE	388a	
15	23	את	WITH	86b	2
		בכה	WEEP	113c	2
		דרך	WAY	202d	1
		זית	OLIVE TREE	268c	1
		נחל	WADY	636c	2
		עבר	PASS OVER	717a	1 a2
		עבר	PASS OVER	717c	3 b
		עבר	PASS OVER	718a	5 c
		פנה	FACE	818c	27a a
		קדרון	KEDRON	871b	
		קול	VOICE	877a	1 a
15	24	ארון	CHEST	75c	3 f
		יצק	POUR	427b	
		לוי	LEVITE	532a	3 1a
		עבר	PASS OVER	718a	5 a
		צדק	RIGHTEOUS	843b	1 a
		תמם	BE FINISHED	1070b	1
15	25	חן	FAVOR	336b	2 b2
		מצא	FIND	592d	1 a
		נוה	HABITATION	627c	2
		צדק	RIGHTEOUS	843b	1 a
15	26	שוב	TURN BACK	999a	1 a
		הנה	BEHOLD	244a	A
		חפץ	DELIGHT IN	342d	2 a
		טוב	PLEASING	373b	5
		כה	THUS	462b	1
15	27	אחימעץ	AHIMAAZ	27b	1
		יהונתן	JONATHAN	220d	2
		כהן	PRIEST	463c	4
		כהן	PRIEST	*464c	8
		ראה	SEER	909a	
		שוב	TURN BACK	997b	1 a
		שלום	PEACE	1023a	5 a
		דבר	WORD	182b	1 1c
15	28	מהה	LINGER	554c	
		עברה	FORD	720c	
		מעם	FROM WITH	768d	A
		ערבה	DESERT-PLAIN	787c	1 b
15	29	שוב	TURN BACK	999a	1 a
15	30	בכה	WEEP	113b	1
		הלך	WALK	231d	1 1d 5k
		זית	OLIVE TREE	268d	3
		זית	OLIVE TREE	*268d	3
		חפה	COVER	341d	
		יחף	BAREFOOT	405a	
		ל	TO	512d	5 aa
		מעלה	ASCENT	751c	1
15	31	אחיתפל	AHITHOPHEL	27c	
		ב	IN	88b	12
		עצה	ADVICE	420a	
		סכל	BE FOOLISH	698a	
		קשר	BIND	905b	2
15	32	אדמה	EARTH	9d	3
		ארכי	ARCHITE	74b	
		דוד	DAVID	188b	J
		היה	COME TO PASS	225a	1 2a 1c
		חושי	HUSHAI	302a	1
		כתנת	TUNIC	*509a	
		כתנת	TUNIC	509a	
		קרא	ENCOUNTER	897a	1
		קרע	TEAR	902c	1 a1
		רעה	FRIEND	946b	
15	33	אם	IF	49d	1 a3 a
		משא	LOAD	672c	1
		על	UPON	753a	2 1b
15	34	מאז	FROM THAT TIME	23b	A
		אחיתפל	AHITHOPHEL	27c	
		ו	AND	255a	5 cg
		עצה	ADVICE	420a	
		ל	TO	515c	5 hc
		מן	FROM	581d	4 c
		פרר	BREAK	830b	2 a
15	35	היה	COME TO PASS	225a	1 2b ag
		כהן	PRIEST	463c	4
		לא	NOT	520b	4 bb
		לא	NOT	520b	4 bb
15	36	אחימעץ	AHIMAAZ	27b	1
		יהונתן	JONATHAN	220d	2
15	37	חושי	HUSHAI	302a	1
		רעה	FRIEND	*946b	
		רעה	FRIEND	946b	
16	1	חבש	BIND	290a	1 c
		חמור	HE-ASS	331b	2 c
		חמור	HE-ASS	*331b	3
		יין	WINE	406c	D
		לחם	FOOD	537a	1 a
		מאה	HUNDRED	547d	1 a4
		מאה	HUNDRED	548a	1 b1
		מעט	A FEW	590a	1 d
		גבל	SKIN-BOTTLE	614b	1
		עבר	PASS OVER	717c	2
		צמד	COUPLE	855a	1
		צמוק	BUNCH OF RAISINS	856a	
		קיץ	SUMMER	884d	2
		קרא	ENCOUNTER	897a	1
		מריבבעל	MERIB-BAAL	937c	1
16	2	חמור	HE-ASS	331b	2 b
		יין	WINE	406c	A
		יעף	WEARY	419b	
		ל	TO	513a	5 ad
		קיץ	SUMMER	884d	2
		רכב	RIDE	938c	1
16	3	ממלכות	DOMINION	575c	2
		שוב	TURN BACK	999a	1 d
16	4	חן	FAVOR	336b	2 b1
		ציבא	ZIBA	850d	
		מריבבעל	MERIB-BAAL	937c	1
		שחה	BOW DOWN	1005c	1 c
16	5	בוא	COME	98b	2
		בחרים	BAHURIM	104c	
		בית	HOUSE	109d	5 c
		גרא	GERA	173a	
		יצא	GO OUT	424a	3
		קלל	BE SLIGHT	886c	1
		שמעי	SHIMEI	1035c	1 a
		משפחה	CLAN	1046d	1 a
16	6	אבן	STONE	6b	1
		ימין	RIGHT HAND	411d	2 a
		משיח	ANOINTED	603c	1
		סקל	STONE	709c	1
		שמאל	LEFT	969d	1
16	7	איש	MAN	36a	
		בליעל	WORTHLESSNESS	116a	1
		דם	BLOOD	197a	2 h
		קלל	BE SLIGHT	886c	1
		שמעי	SHIMEI	1035c	1 a
16	8	איש	MAN	36a	
		בית	HOUSE	109d	5 c
		דם	BLOOD	196d	2 f
		דם	BLOOD	197a	2 h
		ישב	REMAIN	442d	2 a
		מלך	BE KING	574a	
		מלוכה	KINGSHIP	574d	
		על	UPON	756c	2 7a b
		רעה	MISERY	949b	2
16	9	כלב	DOG	477a	B
		מה	HOW	554b	4 d
		מות	DIE	559d	1 b
		סור	TURN ASIDE	694b	1
		צרויה	ZERUIAH	863b	
		קלל	BE SLIGHT	886c	1
16	10	בן	SON	120c	1 g
		מה	WHAT	553b	1 dc
		מי	WHO	566d	F c
		קלל	BE SLIGHT	886c	1
16	11	אמר	SAY	56c	4
		אף	ALSO	65b	3
		בנימיני	BENJAMITE	122d	
		בקש	SEEK	134d	2 a
		יצא	GO OUT	423c	1 h
		מעה	BELLY	589a	2
		נוח	REST	629a	B 5
		נפש	SOUL	659d	3 c
		קלל	BE SLIGHT	886c	1
16	12	טובה	WELFARE	375d	3
		ל	TO	510d	1
		עני	AFFLICTION	777a	1
		קללה	CURSE	887a	
		ראה	TO SEE	908a	8 a2
		שוב	TURN BACK	999c	4 a
		תחת	INSTEAD	1066a	2 2b b

161

Ch	v.	Heb	Eng	Page	Sec
16	13	אבן	STONE	6b	1
		דרך	WAY	202c	1
		הלך	WALK	233b	14c 2
		הר	MOUNTAIN	250d	1 m
		ו	AND	*252b	1 b
		סקל	STONE	709c	1
		עמה	CLOSE BY	769c	A
		עפר	DUST	780a	
		צלע	RIB	854b	2
		קלל	BE SLIGHT	886c	1
		שמעי	SHIMEI	1035c	1 a
16	14	נפש	REFRESH ONESELF	661c	
		עיף	FAINT	746a	
16	15	אחתפל	AHITHOPHEL	27c	
16	16	ארכי	ARCHITE	74b	
		חושי	HUSHAI	302a	1
		חיה	LIVE	311b	1 d
		מלך	KING	573b	5 b
		רעה	FRIEND	946b	
16	17	את	WITH	86a	1 db
		הלך	WALK	231c	1 1d 5a
		חושי	HUSHAI	302a	1
		חסד	GOODNESS	338c	1 1
		רע	FRIEND	946a	1
16	18	בחר	CHOOSE	104a	2 a
		חושי	HUSHAI	302a	1
		כי	BUT	474c	3 e
		לא	NOT	519a	1 ad b
		לא	NOT	520c	1
16	19	כן	SO	486c	2 cd
		עבד	WORK	713a	2
		פנה	FACE	817b	2 4b a
		שני	SECOND	1041c	
16	20	אחתפל	AHITHOPHEL	27c	
		יהב	PROVIDE	396d	3
		עצה	ADVICE	420a	
16	21	אחתפל	AHITHOPHEL	27c	
		באש	STINK	93a	
		בוא	COME	98a	1 e
		חזק	BE FIRM	304a	1 a
		נוח	REST	629a	B 2
		שמר	KEEP	1036c	1 b
16	22	אהל	TENT	13d	1
		גג	ROOF	150d	1
		נטה	STRETCH OUT	640d	2
16	23	אחתפל	AHITHOPHEL	27c	
		אלהים	GOD	44a	3 b
		יעץ	ADVISE	419c	
		עצה	ADVICE	420a	
		כן	SO	485d	1 a
		שאל	ASK	982a	2 b
17	1	אחתפל	AHITHOPHEL	27c	
		בחר	CHOOSE	104b	5 b
		ל	TO	515d	5 ia
		לילה	NIGHT	539a	1
17	2	חרד	TREMBLE	353c	
		יגע	WEARY	388b	
		יד	HAND	389d	1 e1
		רפה	SLACK	952a	
17	3	בקש	SEEK	134c	1 b
		כל	ALL	482d	2 ba
		כלה	BRIDE	483c	2 b
		שוב	TURN BACK	997b	3 b
		שלון	PEACE	1023b	6
17	4	זקן	OLD	278d	2 b
		ישר	BE STRAIGHT	448c	2
17	5	ארכי	ARCHITE	74b	
		חושי	HUSHAI	302a	1
		מה	WHAT	552d	1 b
		פה	MOUTH	805a	2 a
17	6	אחתפל	AHITHOPHEL	27c	
		אין	NOT	34c	2 dd
		דבר	WORD	182b	1 b
		דבר	WORD	183d	4 7
17	7	אחתפל	AHITHOPHEL	27c	
		טוב	PLEASANT	374b	5
		יעץ	ADVISE	419c	
		עצה	ADVICE	420a	
17	8	דב	BEAR	179a	
		לון	LODGE	*533c	1 a
		לון	LODGE	533d	
		מלחמה	WAR	536b	
		מר	BITTER	600c	2 b
		נפש	SOUL	660d	6 c
		שדה	FIELD	961b	1
		שכל	BEREAVED	1014a	
17	9	חיה	COME TO PASS	224b	1 1b
		חבא	WITHDRAW	285b	
		תחלה	BEGINNING	321b	
		מגפה	SLAUGHTER	620a	2
		פחת	PIT	809b	
		מקום	STANDING PLACE	880a	4
17	10	אריה	LION	71d	
		בן	SON	121d	8 a
		גם	ALSO	169b	2
		לב	HEART	525c	29b
		לב	HEART	525d	2 0
		מסם	MELT	587d	2
		נמע	PLANT	642c	2
17	11	בארשבע	BEERSHEBA	92a	
		בארשבע	BEERSHEBA	92a	
		דן	DAN	193a	3
		הלך	WALK	231b	1 d3 ge
		חול	SAND	297d	A
		חול	SAND	297d	C
		יעץ	ADVISE	419d	
		על	UPON	757b	2 7c aa
		פנה	FACE	816a	1 2a
		קרב	BATTLE	898b	
		רב	MULTITUDE	914a	1
17	12	אדמה	GROUND	9d	4
		נחנו	WE	59d	
		גם	ALSO	169b	2
		טל	NIGHT-MIST	378c	
		יתר	BE LEFT OVER	451b	
		לא	NOT	518c	1 aa
		נפל	FALL	657a	1
		מקום	STANDING PLACE	880a	4
17	13	אסף	GATHER	62d	2 b
		גם	ALSO	*169b	2
		חבל	CORD	286c	1
		מצא	FIND	594b	2 d
		נחל	WADY	636c	2
		נשא	LIFT	672a	2
		סחב	DRAG	694d	
		עד	UNTIL	724d	2 1a a
		צרור	PEBBLE	866a	
17	14	אחתפל	AHITHOPHEL	27c	
		ארכי	ARCHITE	74b	
		חושי	HUSHAI	302a	1
		טוב	PLEASANT	374b	5
		טוב	PLEASANT	374c	6
		עצה	ADVICE	420a	
		עבור	FOR THE SAKE OF	721a	1 b
		פרר	BREAK	830b	2 a
		צוה	CHARGE	846a	5
		רעה	MISERY	949a	1
17	15	אחתפל	AHITHOPHEL	27c	
		אני	I	59a	
		אנכי	I	59b	
		זה	THIS	262a	6 d
		זקן	OLD	278d	2 b
		יעץ	ADVISE	419c	
		יעץ	ADVISE	419d	
		כהן	PRIEST	463c	4
17	16	בלע	SWALLOW UP	118c	
		ל	TO	511a	1 e
		לון	LODGE	533c	1 a
		לילה	NIGHT	539a	1
		מהרה	HASTE	555b	
		עבר	PASS OVER	717a	1 a2
		עברה	FORD	720c	
		ערבה	DESERT-PLAIN	787c	1 b
17	17	אחימעץ	AHIMAAZ	27b	1
		ה	THE	207c	1 d
		יהונתן	JONATHAN	220d	2
		ו	AND	*252b	1 b
		עין	SPRING	745b	C
		ראה	TO SEE	908c	1
		שפחה	MAID	1046c	1
17	18	באר	WELL	91c	1
		בחרים	BAHURIM	104c	
		הלך	WALK	232a	1 1d 5k
		חצר	ENCLOSURE	346d	2
		ירד	GO DOWN	433a	1 g
		ל	TO	513b	5 ba
		מהרה	HASTE	555b	
		ערש	COUCH	*793a	
17	19	באר	WELL	91d	1
		ידע	BE MADE KNOWN	394c	1
		לקח	TAKE	543c	4 g
		פרש	SPREAD OUT	831b	2
		ריפה	GRAIN	937d	
17	20	אחימעץ	AHIMAAZ	27b	1
		בקש	SEEK	134c	1 b
		יהונתן	JONATHAN	220d	2
		מיכל	STREAM	568a	
		מצא	FIND	593a	1 b
		עבר	PASS OVER	717a	1 al
17	21	אחתפל	AHITHOPHEL	27c	
		באר	WELL	91c	1
		יעץ	ADVISE	419d	
		ככה	THUS	462c	
		מהרה	HASTE	555b	
		עלה	GO UP	748b	1 b
17	22	אור	LIGHT	21c	2
		בקר	MORNING	133d	1 b
		עבר	PASS OVER	717a	1 al
		עד	AS FAR AS	724c	1 2a b
		עד	AS FAR AS	724d	1 3
		עדר	BE LACKING	727c	
17	23	אחתפל	AHITHOPHEL	27c	
		בית	HOUSE	110b	6
		חבש	BIND	289d	1 c
		חמור	HE-ASS	331b	2 b
		חנק	STRANGLE	338b	
		עצה	ADVICE	420a	
		מות	DIE	559c	1 al
		עשה	DO	795b	1 a
		צוה	GIVE CHARGE UNTO	845d	1 c
		קבר	BURY	868c	
17	24	אפרים	EPHRAIM	68c	5
		מחנים	MAHANAIM	334b	
		עבר	PASS OVER	717a	1 al
17	25	אביגיל	ABIGAIL	4a	2
		יתר	JETHER	452b	3
		יתרא	JITHRA	452b	
		נחש	NAHASH	638b	2
		עמשא	AMASA	772a	1
		צבא	ARMY	839a	1 a
		צרויה	ZERUIAH	863b	
		שום	TO PLACE	963d	3 d
		ישראלי	ISRAELITE	976a	
		ישמעאלי	ISHMAELITE	1035d	
17	26	חנה	DECLINE	333d	2 c2
17	27	אפרים	EPHRAIM	68c	5
		ברזלי	BARZILLAI	137d	1
		היה	COME TO PASS	224d	1 2a 1b
		מחנים	MAHANAIM	334b	
		לאדבר	LO-DEBAR	520d	
		נחש	NAHASH	638b	1
		עמון	AMMON	770a	
		עמיאל	AMMIEL	770a	
		רבה	RABBA	913d	1
		רגלים	ROGELIM	920c	
		שבי	SHOBI	986b	
17	28	ו	AND	252a	1
		חטה	WHEAT	334d	
		יצר	FORM	427d	1 a
		כלי	VESSEL	480b	3
		סף	BASIN	706b	
		עדשה	LENTILE	727d	
		עש	COUCH	793a	
		פול	BEANS	806d	
		קלי	PARCHED GRAIN	885d	
		קמח	FLOUR	887d	
		שערה	BARLEY	972d	2
		משכב	ACT OF LYING	1012d	2 a
17	29	בקר	CATTLE	*133a	
		בקר	CATTLE	133c	2
		דבש	HONEY	185b	
		חמאה	CURD	326a	
		נגש	APPROACH	621b	
		עיף	FAINT	746a	
		עם	PEOPLE	*766b	1
		צמא	THIRSTY	854a	
		רעב	HUNGRY	944a	
		רעב	HUNGRY	944c	
		שפות	CREAM	1046a	
18	2	אנכי	I	59b	
		אתי	ITTAI	87b	1
		גתי	GITTITE	388a	
		יד	HAND	391a	5 c3
		צרויה	ZERUIAH	863b	
		שלש	DO A THIRD TIME	1026a	
		שלישי	THIRD	1026b	
18	3	חצי	HALF	345c	1
		טוב	PLEASANT	374c	5
		כי	THAT	471d	1 a
		לב	HEART	524d	2 3c
		עור	HELP	740b	
		עור	HELP	740c	
		עתה	NOW	774c	2 gb
		עשר	TEN	796d	2 b
		שום	TO PLACE	963c	2 b
18	4	אל	TO	40c	8
		יד	HAND	390d	5 a2
		יטב	BE PLEASING	405c	4
		יצא	GO OUT	423d	2 c
		ל	TO	516b	5 ja
		מאה	HUNDRED	548a	1 cl
		מעיל	ROBE	591c	1
		שער	GATE	1044d	1 a
18	5	אב	FATHER	3b	1
		אט	GENTLENESS	31d	B
		אתי	ITTAI	87b	1
		ל	TO	515b	5 hb a
		ל	TO	516c	5 jb
		מי	WHO	*567b	H
		נער	YOUTH	655a	1
		צוה	COMMAND	845d	1 e
		שר	CHIEFTAIN	978c	1
			ADDENDA ET CORRIGENDA	1122a	
18	6	אפרים	EPHRAIM	68c	5
		היה	COME TO PASS	224b	1 1b
		יער	WOOD	420d	G
		שדה	FIELD	961c	1 f
18	7	נגף	STRIKE	620a	
		מגפה	SLAUGHTER	620a	2
18	8	אכל	EAT	37c	5
		אכל	EAT	37c	4
		אשר	PARTICLE OF RELATION	82a	1
		חרב	SWORD	352d	1 g
		יער	WOOD	420d	G
		מלחמה	WAR	536c	
		נפץ	DISPERSE	659a	
		פוץ	BE DISPERSED	807a	1
		רבה	BECOME MANY	915b	
		רבה	BECOME MANY	915c	1 d1
18	9	אלה	TEREBINTH	18c	
		גדול	GREAT	153a	1
		ה	THE	207c	1 d
		חזק	BE FIRM	304b	1 2a
		נתן	PUT	681d	1
		פרד	MULE	825d	
		קרא	ENCOUNTER	897a	
		רכב	RIDE	938c	2
		שובך	NETWORK OF BOUGHS	959a	
		שמי	HEAVENS	1029d	1 a
18	10	אלה	TEREBINTH	18c	
		ראה	TO SEE	907a	2 3
		תלה	HANG	1068a	1
		תלה	HANG	1068a	
18	11	חנה	IF	244c	D

Ch	v.	Heb	Eng	Page	Sec
		חגורה	GIRDLE	292b	
		ל	TO	517d	7 bd
		נגד	BE CONSPICUOUS	617a	5
		נכה	SMITE	646a	2 a
		על	UPON	753c	2 c
		עשר	TEN	797a	2 b
18	12	אתי	ITTAI	87b	1
		לי	IF	530a	
		לו	IF	530b	1 c
		מי	WHO	567b	H
		נער	YOUTH	655a	1 e
		שלח	SEND	1018c	1 a
		שמר	KEEP	1036c	1 b
		שקל	WEIGH	1053c	2
18	13	או	OR	15a	2
		יצב	STATION ONESELF	426b	A
		כחד	BE HIDDEN	470b	1
		נגד	IN FRONT	617d	2 ca
		שקר	DECEPTION	1055c	2
18	14	אלה	TEREBINTH	18c	
		חי	ALIVE	312a	1 b
		יחל	WAIT	404a	
		כן	SO	486b	1 cd
		לא	NOT	518c	1 aa
		לב	HEART	524b	1
		לב	HEART	524c	2 1
		לקח	TAKE	542d	1
		עוד	STILL	728d	1 aa
		שבט	ROD	987a	1 b
		תקע	THRUST	1075b	1
18	15	כלי	IMPLEMENT	479d	2 a
		נכה	SMITE	645d	2 a
		סבב	SURROUND	685d	2 d
18	16	חשך	WITHHOLD	362b	1 e
		חשך	WITHHOLD	362b	1 c
18	17	יער	WOOD	420d	G
		נצב	STAND	662c	2
		פחת	PIT	809b	
18	18	את	MARK OF THE AC-CUSATIVE	85a	1 a
		זכר	REMEMBER	270d	2
		חיים	LIFE	313b	1
		יד	MONUMENT	390c	4 a
		יום	DAY	401b	7 l
		לקח	TAKE	543c	4 g
		נצב	STAND	662c	2
		מצבה	PILLAR	663a	1 a
		עבור	FOR THE SAKE OF	721a	1 b
		על	UPON	754a	2 1f
		עמק	VALE	771a	
		קרא	CALL	896a	6 g
		קרא	CALL	896b	2 d1
		שם	NAME	1028b	2 c
18	19	אחימעץ	AHIMAAZ	27b	1
		איב	BE HOSTILE TO	33c	
		בשר	BEAR TIDINGS	142b	1
		יד	HAND	391b	5 g1
		רוץ	RUN	930b	1
		שפט	JUDGE	1047d	3 b1
18	20	איש	MAN	36a	
		בשר	BEAR TIDINGS	142b	2
		בשרה	TIDINGS	143a	2
		כעל־כן	FOR THEREFORE	475c	
		לא	NOT	519b	1 bb
18	21	כושי	CUSHITE	469a	C
		רוץ	RUN	930b	1
18	22	אחימעץ	AHIMAAZ	27b	1
		אכי	I	59b	
		בשרה	TIDINGS	143a	3
		זה	THIS	261c	4 c
		יסף	DO AGAIN	415c	2 a
		כושי	CUSHITE	469a	C
		מה	AUGHT	553d	3
		מצא	FIND	592d	1 a
		רוץ	RUN	930b	1
		רוץ	RUN	930b	1
18	23	אחימעץ	AHIMAAZ	27b	1
		דרך	WAY	202d	1
		כושי	CUSHITE	469a	C
		ככר	ROUND	503b	1
		מה	AUGHT	553d	3
		עבר	PASS OVER	*717d	4 a
		רוץ	RUN	930b	1
		רוץ	RUN	930b	1
18	24	בד	SEPARATION	94c	1 b
		גג	ROOF	151a	1
		רוץ	RUN	930b	1
		שער	GATE	1044d	1 a
		שער	GATE	1045a	2 a
18	25	בשרה	TIDINGS	143a	2
		הלך	WALK	233b	14 c 3
		הלך	WALK	*233c	14 d
		פה	MOUTH	805a	2 a
		קרא	CALL	895a	1 a
		קרב	APPROACHING	898b	1
18	26	בשר	BEAR TIDINGS	142b	1
		רוץ	RUN	930b	1
		שער	PORTER	*1045b	
18	27	אחימעץ	AHIMAAZ	27b	1
		בשרה	TIDINGS	143a	2
		טוב	PLEASANT	373d	2 d
		טוב	PLEASANT	374d	9 a
		ראה	TO SEE	907a	2 5
		ראשון	FIRST	911c	1 b
		מרוצה	RUNNING	930d	1
18	28	אחימעץ	AHIMAAZ	27b	1

Ch	v.	Heb	Eng	Page	Sec
		אף	NOSE	60b	2
		ברך	BLESS	138c	2 a
		נשא	LIFT	670b	1 b 1
		סגר	DELIVER UP	689b	1
		קרא	CALL	895a	1 b
		שחה	BOW DOWN	1005b	1 b
		שלום	PEACE	1022d	3
18	29	אחימעץ	AHIMAAZ	27b	1
		המון	TUMULT	242c	2
		ל	TO	517a	6 a
		מלך	KING	573b	
18	30	יצב	STATION ONESELF	426b	A
		כה	THUS	462b	2
		סבב	TURN ABOUT	685c	1 a
18	31	בשר	BEAR TIDINGS	142b	1
		כושי	CUSHITE	469a	C
		שפט	JUDGE	1047d	3 b1
18	32	כושי	CUSHITE	469a	C
		רעה	MISERY	949b	2
19	1	אב	FATHER	3b	1
		אנכי	I	59b	
		בכה	WEEP	113b	1
		בן	SON	120a	1
		נתן	GIVE	679a	1 f
		עליה	ROOF-CHAMBER	751a	
		על	UPON	757b	2 7c ab
		רגז	BE AGITATED	919b	
		שער	GATE	1044a	1
		תחת	INSTEAD	1065d	2 2b a
19	2	אב	FATHER	3b	1
		אבל	MOURN	5c	
		בכה	WEEP	113b	1
		נגד	BE CONSPICUOUS	617a	
19	3	אבל	MOURNING	5c	
		בן	SON	120a	1
		תשועה	DELIVERANCE	448b	1
		עצב	HURT	780c	
		שמע	HEAR	1033c	1 c
19	4	גנב	STEAL	170c	
		גנב	STEAL	170c	
		ה	THE	207b	1 ca
		כלם	BE HUMILIATED	483d	1
		ל	TO	517c	7 bb
19	5	בן	SON	120a	1
		זעק	CRY	277b	2 d
		לאט	COVER	521b	
		לוט	WRAP	532a	
		פנה	FACE	815d	1 la
19	6	בוש	BE ASHAMED	102a	2
		בוש	BE ASHAMED	102a	2 a
		מלט	SLIP AWAY	572c	3
		נפש	SOUL	660a	3 c
19	7	אהב	LOVE	13a	1
		אז	THEN	23b	2
		חי	ALIVE	312a	1 b
		ישר	STRAIGHT	449a	2 b
		כי	THAT	471d	1 a
		כי	THAT	472c	1 db
		ל	TO	517c	7 bb
		לו	IF	530a	1
		לו	IF	530a	1 a
		שר	CHIEFTAIN	978c	3 a
19	8	דבר	SPEAK	181d	5
		כי	IF	473b	2 b
		לב	HEART	525c	2 9a
		לון	LODGE	533c	1 a
		לילה	NIGHT	539a	1
		נערים	YOUTH	655c	
		עתה	NOW	774c	2 f
		רע	EVIL	948b	6
		שבע	SWEAR	989b	1 a
19	9	ישב	SIT	442d	1 b
		שער	GATE	1045a	2 a
19	10	ברח	FLEE	138a	2
		דין	JUDGE	192c	1
		כף	POWER	496d	2
		מלט	SLIP AWAY	572c	3
		נצל	DELIVER	665a	3 a
		על	UPON	759a	4 2b
19	11	חרש	BE SILENT	361b	1 a1
		מות	DIE	559c	1 a1
		משח	ANOINT	603b	2
		עתה	NOW	774b	2 b
		שוב	TURN BACK	999b	1 d
19	12	אחרון	BEHIND	30d	B
		זקן	OLD	278d	2 b
		כהן	PRIEST	463c	4
		שוב	TURN BACK	999b	1 d
19	13	אח	BROTHER	26b	2
		עצם	BONE	782d	1 a
		שוב	TURN BACK	999b	1 d
19	14	יום	DAY	400c	7 f
		יסף	ADD	415b	1
		עמשא	AMASA	772a	1
		עצם	BONE	782d	1 a
		פנה	FACE	817a	24a b
19	15	לבב	HEART	523c	2 2
		נטה	INCLINE	640d	3 c
19	16	הלך	WALK	233d	15 a
		עבר	PASS OVER	718d	1 a
		שוב	TURN BACK	997b	3 a
19	17	בחרים	BAHURIM	104c	
		בנימיני	BENJAMITE	122d	
		גרא	GERA	173a	
		מהר	HASTEN	555a	2
		שמעי	SHIMEI	1035c	1 a

Ch	v.	Heb	Eng	Page	Sec
19	18	בית	HOUSE	109d	5 c
		חמש	FIVE	332a	2 c
		עשר	TEN	797b	5 b
		צלח	RUSH	852b	
19	19	גרא	GERA	173a	
		טוב	PLEASANT	374b	2 f
		נפל	FALL	657b	3 b
		עבר	PASS OVER	717a	1 a1
		עבר	PASS OVER	717c	3 b
		עברה	FORD	720b	
		שמעי	SHIMEI	1035c	1 a
19	20	אל	TO	39d	2
		זכר	REMEMBER	269d	1 2 c
		חשב	THINK	363a	1 3
		לב	HEART	525a	2 3d
		עון	INIQUITY	731a	1 c5
		עוה	COMMIT INIQUITY	731c	
		שום	TO PLACE	963b	1 b
19	21	בית	HOUSE	110a	5 dz
		חטא	MISS A GOAL OR WAY	306d	2 a
		יוסף	JOSEPH	415d	1 b
		ל	TO	512d	5 ab
		ראשון	FIRST	911d	1 a
19	22	זה	THIS	260d	1 a
		מות	DIE	560c	2
		משיח	ANOINTED	603c	1
		צרויה	ZERUIAH	863b	
		שמעי	SHIMEI	1035c	1 a
		תחת	INSTEAD	1066a	2 2b b
19	23	לא	NOT	520b	4 ba
		מה	WHAT	553b	1 dc
		מות	DIE	560c	2
		צרויה	ZERUIAH	863b	
		שטן	ADVERSARY	966b	1
19	24	מות	DIE	559d	2 a
		שמעי	SHIMEI	1035c	1 a
19	25	אשר	PARTICLE OF RE-LATION	82c	4 ba
		בן	SON	120c	1 f
		יום	DAY	401b	7 k
		ישב	REMAIN	442d	2 a
		כבס	WASH	460a	1
		מן	FROM	583d	9 b2
		עשה	DO	794d	2 5
		קרר	BE DARK	*871a	
		שפם	MOUSTACHE	974a	
		שלום	PEACE	1023b	6
19	26	הלך	WALK	231c	1 1d 5b
		כי	WHEN	473a	2 a
		מריבעל	MERIB-BAAL	937c	1
19	27	ה	THE	207b	1 cb
		חבש	BIND	289d	1 c
		חמור	HE-ASS	331b	2 b
		חמור	HE-ASS	331c	6
		פסח	LAME	820c	
		רכב	RIDE	938c	1
		רמה	BEGUILE	941a	
19	28	אלהים	GOD	44a	3 b
		טוב	PLEASANT	374a	2 f
		מלאך	MESSENGER	521d	2
		רגל	GO ABOUT	920b	1
19	29	ו	AND	254a	2b
		זעק	CRY	277b	2 c
		כאם	EXCEPT	474d	2
		ל	TO	513a	5 d
		מה	WHAT	552c	1 aa
		מות	DEATH	560d	2
		צדקה	RIGHTEOUSNESS	842b	3
		שית	PUT	1011b	2 a
		שלחן	TABLE	1020b	1
19	30	דבר	SPEAK	180d	2
		חלק	DIVIDE	323c	1
		שדה	FIELD	961d	2 e
19	31	גם	ALSO	169b	2
		כל	ALL	*482d	2 ba
		מריבעל	MERIB-BAAL	937c	1
		שלון	PEACE	1023b	6
19	32	ברזלי	BARZILLAI	137d	1
		רגלים	ROGELIM	920c	
		שלח	SEND	1019a	1 d
19	33	בן	SON	121d	9 a
		ברזלי	BARZILLAI	137d	1
		גדול	GREAT	153a	6 b
		זקן	BE OLD	278b	
		מחנים	MAHANAIM	334b	
		שיבה	SOJOURN	444a	
		כול	SUSTAIN	465a	1
19	34	ברזלי	BARZILLAI	137d	1
		כול	SUSTAIN	465a	1
		עם	WITH	768b	3 a
		שיבה	OLD AGE	966d	2
19	35	ברזלי	BARZILLAI	137d	1
		חיים	LIFE	313a	1
		יום	DAY	399a	4 a
		מה	HOW	553d	4 ca
19	36	אם	IF	50d	2 ab a
		בין	INTERVAL	107c	1 d
		בין	INTERVAL	107c	1 b
		בן	SON	121d	9 a
		טוב	A GOOD THING	375b	4
		טעם	TASTE	381a	2
		ידע	KNOW	393d	1 d
		משא	LOAD	672c	1
		על	UPON	753a	2 1b
		קול	VOICE	876d	1

163

2 SAMUEL

Ch	v.	Heb	Eng	Page	Sec
		שׁיר	SING	1010d	
		שׁיר	SING	1010d	
		שׁמע	HEAR	1033d	1 e
19	37	מעט	A FEW	590b	2 b
19	38	אם	MOTHER	52a	1
		טוב	PLEASING	373b	5
		כמהם	CHIMHAM	484c	1
		עם	WITH	768a	2
19	39	בחר	CHOOSE	104b	6
		טוב	PLEASANT	374a	2 f
		כמהם	CHIMHAM	484c	1
		על	UPON	753b	2 1c
19	40	ברזלי	BARZILLAI	137d	1
		ברך	BLESS	139a	3
		נשׁק	KISS	676b	
19	41	חצי	HALF	345c	1
		כמהם	CHIMHAM	484c	1
		עבר	PASS OVER	718a	5 a
		עבר	PASS OVER	718a	5 a
		עבר	PASS OVER	719a	4
19	42	אח	BROTHER	26b	2
		גנב	STEAL	170b	
		עבר	PASS OVER	718d	1 a
19	43	חרה	BURN	354a	1 b
		כי	BECAUSE	473c	3 a
		ל	TO	514a	5 e
		נשׂא	LIFT	672a	4
		משׂאת	PORTION	673a	4 a
		על	UPON	757c	27c b
		ענה	ANSWER	772d	1 c
		קרב	NEAR	898c	2 c
19	44	דבר	WORD	182b	1 1d
		דוד	DAVID	188b	J
		יד	PART	390c	4 b
		קלל	BE SILENT	886d	2
		קשׁה	BE SEVERE	904b	2
		ראשׁון	FIRST	911d	2 a
		שׁוב	TURN BACK	999b	1 d
20	1	אהל	TENT	13d	1
		בכרי	BICHRI	114b	1
		בליעל	WORTHLESSNESS	116a	1
		בן	SON	120c	1g
		חלק	PORTION	324a	1 c
		ימיני	BENJAMITE	412b	
		ישׁי	JESSE	445b	
		ל	TO	511b	1 ga
		מה	WHAT	*553a	1 da
		מה	WHAT	553c	2 ab
		נחלה	PROPERTY	635b	2 b
		קרא	ENCOUNTER	897a	
		ישׂראל	ISRAEL	975c	2 a2
		שׁבע	SHEBA	989d	1
20	2	אחר	BEHIND	30b	4 aa
		בכרי	BICHRI	114b	1
		דבק	CLING	179d	2 a
		שׁבע	SHEBA	989d	1
20	3	אלמנה	WIDOW	48b	
		אלמנות	WIDOWHOOD	48c	
		בוא	COME	98a	1 e
		בית	HOUSE	109a	1 ae 2
		חיות	LIVING	313c	
		כל	SUSTAIN	465a	1
		נוח	REST	629a	B 2
		צרר	BIND	864d	A
		שׁמר	KEEP	1036d	1 b
		משׁמרת	GUARD	1038b	1
20	4	זעק	CRY	277c	1
20	5	אחר	DELAY	29c	1
		זעק	CRY	277c	1
		יעד	APPOINT	416d	
		מועד	APPOINTED TIME	417c	1 a
		מן	FROM	581c	4 b
20	6	אבישׁי	ABISHAI	5a	
		בכרי	BICHRI	114b	1
		בצר	MAKE INACCESSIBLE	131a	
		יואב	JOAB	*222a	1
		מן	THAN	582c	6 a
		מצא	FIND	592d	1 a
		נצל	SNATCH AWAY	664d	1
		עיר	CITY	746b	1 a
		עתה	NOW	774a	1 b
		פן	LEST	815a	2
		רדף	PURSUE	922c	1 a
		רעע	BE EVIL	949c	3
		שׁבע	SHEBA	989d	1
20	7	אבישׁי	ABISHAI	5a	
		בכרי	BICHRI	114b	1
		כרתי	CHERETHITE	504d	
		פלתי	PELETHITES	814c	
		רדף	PURSUE	922c	1 a
		שׁבע	SHEBA	989d	1
20	8	גבעון	GIBEON	149c	
		חגר	GIRD	292a	2
		חגור	BELT	292a	
		חרב	SWORD	352c	1 b
		חרב	SWORD	*352c	1 e
		יצא	GO OUT	423d	2 b
		לבושׁ	CLOTHING	528c	
		מד	GARMENT	551c	3
		מתנים	LOINS	608a	1 b
		נפל	FALL	657a	
		על	UPON	753a	2 1a a
		עם	WITH	*768a	2
		תער	RAZOR	789b	1
		צמד	BIND	855a	

Ch	v.	Heb	Eng	Page	Sec
20	9	אחז	GRASP	28b	
		אחר	DELAY	*29c	2
		זקן	BEARD	278b	1
		יד	HAND	389a	1 a
		ימין	RIGHT HAND	411d	1 a
		נשׁק	KISS	676b	
20	10	בכרי	BICHRI	114b	1
		ו	AND	253a	1 g
		חמשׁ	BELLY	332d	
		לחום	BOWELS	*536a	
		מעה	BELLY	588d	1 a
		נכה	SMITE	645d	2 a
		רדף	PURSUE	922c	1 a
		שׁבע	SHEBA	989d	1
		שׁמר	KEEP	1037b	1
		שׁנה	DO AGAIN	1040d	
		שׁפך	POUR OUT	1049c	1 a
20	11	חפץ	DELIGHT IN	342d	1 a
		ל	TO	515c	5 hc
		מי	WHO	567b	G
		על	UPON	756b	2 6c
20	12	דם	BLOOD	196d	2 f
		יגה	THRUST AWAY	*387c	
		סבב	TURN ABOUT	686c	1 a
		מסלה	HIGHWAY	700c	
		על	UPON	756b	27a a
		על	UPON	756b	2 6c
		ראה	TO SEE	907a	2 2
		שׂדה	FIELD	961c	1 f
20	13	בכרי	BICHRI	114b	1
		יגה	SUFFER	387b	
		יגה	THRUST AWAY	387c	
		מסלה	HIGHWAY	700c	
		עבר	PASS OVER	718a	5 d
		רדף	PURSUE	922c	1 a
		שׁבע	SHEBA	989d	1
20	14	אבל	ABEL	5d	2
		אחר	BEHIND	*30a	2 a
		אף	ALSO	64d	1
		ביתמעכה	BETH-MAACAH	112a	
		בכרי	BICHRI	114b	2
		ברים	BERITES	138c	
		עבר	PASS OVER	717c	3 a
		קהל	ASSEMBLE AS	874d	1 a
20	15	אבל	ABEL	6a	2
		ביתמעכה	BETH-MAACAH	112a	
		ביתמעכה	BETH-MAACAH	112a	
		חל	RAMPART	298a	1
		חומה	WALL	327c	1
		נפל	FALL	658a	1 b
		סללה	MOUND	700c	
		צור	CONFINE	848d	2
		שׁחת	GO TO RUIN	1008b	1
		שׁפך	POUR OUT	1049c	1 a
20	16	אשׁה	WOMAN	61b	1
		הנה	HITHER	244c	A a
		חכם	WISE	314d	2
		קרא	CALL	895a	1 b
		קרב	COME NEAR	897c	1 g
20	17	אמה	MAID	51a	2
		אנכי	I	59c	
		אנכי	I	59c	
20	18	אבל	ABEL	5d	2
		דן	DAN	193a	3
		ראשׁון	FIRST	911d	3 a1
		שׁאל	ASK	982b	1
		תמם	BE FINISHED	1070c	1
20	19	אם	MOTHER	52a	2
		אמה	MOTHER-CITY	52a	
		אמן	CONFIRM	52d	4 b
		בלע	SWALLOW UP	118c	2 b
		בקשׁ	SEEK	134d	2 d
		מה	HOW	554b	4 d
		מות	DIE	560b	1 a
		נחלה	PROPERTY	635b	
		שׁום	TO PLACE	963d	3 b
		שׁלם	BE IN COVENANT OF PEACE	1023d	
20	20	הוא	HE	*1090a	
		אם	IF	50b	1 b2
		בלע	SWALLOW UP	118c	2 b
		חלילה	FAR BE IT	321a	
		מות	DIE	*560b	1 a
20	21	בכרי	BICHRI	114b	1
		בעד	AWAY FROM	126b	1 a
		הר	MOUNTAIN	251a	2 b
		נשׂא	LIFT	670b	1 b 1
		נתן	GIVE	679c	1 s
		על	UPON	759a	4 2b
		שׁבע	SHEBA	989d	1
		שׁלך	THROW	1021c	1
20	22	בכרי	BICHRI	114b	1
		חכמה	WISDOM	315c	3
		כרת	CUT OFF	503d	1 a
		עיר	CITY	746c	1 h
		על	UPON	759a	4 2b
		פוץ	BE DISPERSED	807a	
		שׁבע	SHEBA	989d	1
		שׁוב	TURN BACK	997a	3 a
		שׁלך	THROW	1021a	1 a
20	23	אל	TO	41a	A
		בניהו	BENAIAH	125c	1
		יהוידע	JEHOIADA	220b	1
		יהוידע	JEHOIADA	*220b	1
		כרי	CARITES	501b	
		כרתי	CHERETHITE	504d	1

Ch	v.	Heb	Eng	Page	Sec
		על	UPON	755a	2 3
		פלתי	PELETHITES	814c	
		צבא	ARMY	839a	1 a
20	24	אדרם	ADORAM	12a	
		אדנירם	ADONIRAM	12a	
		אחילוד	AHILUD	27a	1
		יהושׁפט	JEHOSHAPHAT	221d	3
		זכר	REMEMBER	271a	4
		מס	LABOUR-GANG	587a	1
		על	UPON	755a	2 3
20	25	כהן	PRIEST	463c	4
		ספר	ENUMERATOR	708b	1 b
		שׂריה	SERAIAH	976a	1
		שׁוא	SHEVA	996a	2
		שׁיא	SHEVA	1009c	
20	26	יאירי	JAIRITE	22c	
		היה	BE	227a	3 4b
		כהן	PRIEST-KING	463a	1
		עירא	IRA	747a	1
21	1	בית	HOUSE	*109d	5 c
		בקשׁ	SEEK	134d	3 b
		גבעני	GIBEONITE	149c	
		דם	BLOOD	197a	2 i
		דם	BLOOD	197a	2 h
		היה	BECOME	225c	2 1a
		יום	DAY	399b	4 b
		רעב	FAMINE	944b	1
		שׁנה	YEAR	1040b	
21	2	אמרי	AMORITES	57c	2 b
		בקשׁ	SEEK	134d	2 d
		גבעני	GIBEONITE	149c	
		יתר	REMAINDER	451d	1 a
		לא	NOT	519b	1 bb
		מן	OUT OF	579c	2 cb
		על	UPON	756c	27a b
		קנא	BE ZEALOUS	888c	3 a
		שׁבע	SWEAR	989a	1 a
21	3	ברך	BLESS	139b	4 h
		גבעני	GIBEONITE	149c	
		ו	AND	254b	3
		כפר	COVER OVER	497c	2 a
		מה	HOW	553d	4 a
		נחלה	PROPERTY	635b	1 e
21	4	גבעני	GIBEONITE	149c	
		זהב	GOLD	262d	5
		זהב	GOLD	263c	1
		מה	WHAT	553b	1 ea
		מות	DIE	560b	1 b
		עם	WITH	767d	1 d
21	5	גבול	BOUNDARY	148a	2 a
		דמה	BE LIKE	198a	2
		יצב	STATION ONESELF	426b	A
		כלה	FINISH	478c	2 c1
		שׁמד	BE EXTERMINATED	1029b	1
21	6	בחיר	CHOSEN	104c	
		גבעה	GIBEAH	149b	2
		יקע	HANG	429c	
		נתן	GIVE	681d	1 c
		שׁאול	SAUL	*982c	1
21	7	בין	INTERVAL	107c	1 d
		חמל	SPARE	328b	
		מריבבעל	MERIB-BAAL	937c	1
		שׁבועה	OATH	989d	1 a
21	8	איה	AIAH	17b	2
		ארמני	ARMONI	74d	
		ברזלי	BARZILLAI	137d	3
		חמשׁ	FIVE	331d	1 d
		מחלתי	MEHOLATHITE	563b	
		מיכל	MICHAL	568a	
		מרב	MERAB	*597b	
		עדריאל	ADRIEL	727b	
		מריבבעל	MERIB-BAAL	937c	2
		רצפה	RIZPAH	954c	
21	9	גבעני	GIBEONITE	149c	
		תחלה	BEGINNING	321b	
		יום	TIME	399d	6 a
		יחד	UNION	403a	2 a3
		יקע	HANG	*429c	
		מות	DIE	560c	2
		נפל	FALL	657a	2 a
		פנה	FACE	817b	24a h
		קציר	HARVESTING	894d	3
		קציר	HARVESTING	894d	3
		ראשׁון	FIRST	911c	1 a
		שׂערה	BARLEY	972d	1
		שׁבעתים	SEVEN FOLD	988d	2
21	10	איה	AIAH	17b	2
		חיה	LIVING THING	312c	1 b
		יומם	BY DAY	401c	2
		מי	WATER	565c	1 g
		נוח	REST	628a	1
		נטה	STRETCH OUT	640d	2
		נתך	POUR FORTH	677d	
		עד	UNTIL	725a	2 1b a
		עוף	FLY	733d	1
		צור	ROCK	849c	1 b
		קציר	HARVESTING	894d	3
		רצפה	RIZPAH	954c	
		שׂק	SACK	974c	2 b
21	11	איה	AIAH	17b	2
		את	MARK OF THE ACCUSATIVE	85a	1 b
		ברח	FLEE	138a	2
		נגד	BE CONSPICUOUS	617a	
		רצפה	RIZPAH	954c	
21	12	ביתשׁאן	BETH-SHEAN	112d	

Ch	v.	Heb	Eng	Page	Sec
		בעל	OWNER	127c	1 3
		גגב	STEAL	170b	
		יבש	JABESH	386d	1
		עצם	BONE	782d	1 f
		רחוב	PLAZA	932b	
		תלא	HANG	1067d	
21	13	תלה	HANG	1068a	2
21	13	יקע	BE HANGED	429c	
21	14	עצם	BONE	782d	1 f
21	14	בנימין	BENJAMIN	122d	1
		עתר	PRAY	801c	
		צלע	ZELAH	854b	
		צלצח	ZELZEH	*854c	
		קיש	KISH	885c	1
21	15	ישבובנב	ISHBI-BENOB	444a	
		לחם	ENGAGE IN BATTLE	535c	
21	16	עיף	BE FAINT	746a	
21	16	אמר	SAY	56b	2
		גב	GOB	146c	
		חגר	GIRD	292a	2
		חדש	NEW	294b	A
		ילד	CHILDREN	409d	
		ישב	DWELL	*443a	3
		ישבובנב	ISHBI-BENOB	444a	
		קין	SPEAR	883d	
		רפה	HA-RAPHA	952a	
		שקל	SHEKEL	1053c	
		משקל	WEIGHT	*1054a	
		משקל	WEIGHT	1054a	
21	17	כבה	QUENCH	459d	
		נר	LAMP	632d	
		נכה	SMITE	645d	2 a
		פלשתי	PHILISTINE	814b	
		צרויה	ZERUIAH	863b	
		שבע	SWEAR	989b	1 a
21	18	אחר	AFTER	*30a	2 b
		גב	GOB	146c	
		גב	GOB	146c	
		חשתי	HASHATHITE	302a	
		ילד	CHILDREN	409d	
		מלחמה	WAR	536c	
		סבכי	SIBBECAI	687c	
		סף	SAPH	706c	
		רפה	HA-RAPHA	952a	
21	19	אלחנן	ELHANAN	45a	
		ארג	WEAVE	71a	
		ביתהלחמי	THE BETHLEHEMITE	112a	
		גב	GOB	146c	
		חנית	SPEAR	333d	1
		חץ	ARROW	346c	2
		גתי	GITTITE	388a	
		יעריארגים	JAARE-OREGIM	421a	
		מלחמה	WAR	536c	
		לחמי	LAHMI	*537c	
		מנור	BEAM	644d	
		יעור	JAIR	735d	
		עץ	TREE	781d	2 b
21	20	מדון	STRIFE	193c	
		גת	GATH	387d	
		ילד	BE BORN	409a	
		מד	MEASURE	551b	2
		מדה	SIZE	551c	2
		מספר	NUMBER	708d	1 a
		אצבע	FINGER	840c	1 d
		אצבע	FINGER	840c	2
		ארבע	FOUR	917b	2 b
		רגל	FOOT	919d	1 a
		רפה	HA-RAPHA	952a	
21	21	שש	SIX	995c	1 a
21	21	יהונתן	JONATHAN	220d	3
		יהונדב	JEHONADAB	*220d	2
		חרף	REPROACH	357d	
		שמעא	SHIMEA	1035a	1
		שמעי	SHIMEI	1035c	0
21	22	את	MARK OF THE ACCUSATIVE	85b	3 a
		גת	GATH	387d	
		ילד	BE BORN	409a	
		נפל	FALL	657b	2 a
		רפה	HA-RAPHA	952a	
22	1	דבר	SPEAK	181b	3 c
		דבר	WORD	*182d	2 1a
		יום	DAY	400b	7 d3 a
		כף	POWER	496d	2
		נצל	DELIVER	665a	3 a
		שירה	SONG	1010c	
22	2	חזק	STRENGTH	305d	
		סלע	CRAG	701a	2
		פלט	ESCAPE	812b	1
		מצודה	FASTNESS	845a	
		רחם	LOVE	933c	
22	3	אלהים	GOD	44d	
		מגן	SHIELD	*171c	
		חמס	VIOLENCE	329c	
		חסה	SEEK REFUGE	340b	
		ישע	DELIVER	446d	1 b
		ישע	DELIVER	446d	1 b
		ישע	DELIVERANCE	447a	2
		מנום	ESCAPE	631a	2
		צור	ROCK	849d	2 a
		קרן	HORN	901d	2
		משגב	SECURE HEIGHT	960d	1
22	4	הלל	PRAISE	239a	2
		ישע	BE DELIVERED	446b	1
		קרא	CALL	895d	5 c
22	5	אפף	SURROUND	67c	
		בליעל	WORTHLESSNESS	116b	3
		בעת	FALL UPON	130a	1
		חבל	CORD	286c	1
		נחל	TORRENT	636b	1
		משבר	BREAKER	991c	
22	6	חבל	CORD	286c	1
		מוקש	BAIT	430d	
		סבב	SURROUND	686a	2 d
		קדם	COME IN FRONT	869d	1 a
		שאול	SHEOL	983a	1
22	7	אזן	EAR	24b	2 b
		היכל	TEMPLE	*228b	2 a
		היכל	TEMPLE	228d	2 e
		צר	STRAITS	865a	
		קרא	CALL	895d	5 c
		שועה	CRY FOR HELP	1003a	
22	8	ארץ	EARTH	76a	1 b
		געש	SHAKE	172b	
		געש	SHAKE	172b	
		הר	MOUNTAIN	250d	1 m
		חרה	BURN	354b	2 b
		מוסד	FOUNDATION	414c	
		רגז	BE AGITATED	919a	
		רעש	SHAKE	950b	
		שמי	HEAVENS	1030a	1 b
22	9	אף	NOSE	60a	1
		בער	BURN	129a	1
		גחלת	COAL	160d	
		עשן	SMOKE	798c	2 b
		פה	MOUTH	804d	1 c
22	10	ירד	GO DOWN	433b	2
		נטה	BEND	640c	3 b
		ערפל	CLOUD	791d	
		רגל	FOOT	919d	1 b
22	11	שמי	HEAVENS	1030b	2 a
		ראה	FLY SWIFTLY	*178d	
		כנף	WING	489d	1 f
		כרוב	CHERUB	500c	1
		עוף	FLY	733c	1 a
		ראה	TO SEE	908b	1 a
		רוח	BREATH	924d	2
		רכב	RIDE	938d	2
22	12	חשך	DARKNESS	365a	1
		חשכה	DARKNESS	*365b	
		חשרה	COLLECTION	366b	
		סכה	THICKET	697d	2
		סתר	COVERING	*712a	2
		עב	DARK CLOUD	728a	2
		שחק	DUST	1007a	2
		שית	PUT	1011c	2
22	13	בער	BURN	*129a	1
		גחלת	COAL	160d	
		נגה	BRIGHTNESS	618b	
22	14	נתן	GIVE	679d	1 x
		עליון	HIGHEST	751b	1
		קול	VOICE	877a	2 b
		רעם	THUNDER	947b	
		שמי	HEAVENS	1030a	2 a
22	15	ברק	FLASH	140b	
		ברק	LIGHTNING	*140c	1
		ברק	LIGHTNING	140c	1
		המם	CONFUSE	243a	2
		חץ	ARROW	346c	
		פוץ	BE DISPERSED	807b	1 b
		רב	MUCH	*913b	1 g
		שלח	SEND	1018c	2 b
22	16	אף	NOSE	60a	1
		אפיק	CHANNEL	67d	
		גערה	REBUKE	172a	2
		תבל	WORLD	385d	
		מוסד	FOUNDATION	414c	
		נשמה	BREATH	675d	1
		ראה	TO SEE	908c	1 c
		רוח	BREATH	924d	1 d1
22	17	מי	WATER	565d	4 a
		משה	DRAW	602c	
		מרום	HEIGHT	928d	2
		מרום	HEIGHT	929a	3
22	18	אמץ	BE STRONG	55a	1
		עז	STRONG	738d	
22	19	איד	DISTRESS	15d	3
		איד	DISTRESS	15d	3
		קדם	COME	869d	1 a
		משען	SUPPORT	1044a	
22	20	חלץ	DRAW OFF OR OUT	322d	2
		חפץ	DELIGHT IN	342d	2 a
		יצא	BRING OUT	424d	2
		מרחב	ROOMY PLACE	932c	
22	21	בר	CLEANNESS	141b	
		צדקה	RIGHTEOUSNESS	842b	3
		שוב	TURN BACK	999c	4 a
22	22	דרך	WAY	204a	6 ec
		רשע	BE WICKED	957d	1
		שמר	KEEP	1037a	1
22	23	חקה	SOMETHING PRESCRIBED	350a	2 d
		סור	TURN ASIDE	*694b	1
22	24	ל	TO	511a	1 d
		עון	INIQUITY	731a	1 a
		שמר	KEEP	1037c	
		תמים	SOUND	1071a	4
22	25	בר	CLEANNESS	*141b	
		עין	EYE	744d	3 c
		צדקה	RIGHTEOUSNESS	842b	3
22	26	שוב	TURN BACK	999c	4 a
		גבר	MAN	*150a	
		חסד	BE GOOD	338c	
		חסיד	KIND	339c	1 a
		תמם	BE COMPLETE	1070d	
		תמים	COMPLETE	1071b	5
22	27	ברר	PURIFY	141a	B
		ברר	PURIFY	141a	2
		עקש	TWISTED	786a	
		פתל	TWIST	836d	
22	28	ישע	DELIVER	446d	1 b
		עין	EYE	744c	2 a
		עני	POOR	777a	4
		רום	BE HIGH	926d	2 b
22	29	שפל	BECOME LOW	1050b	1
		חשך	DARKNESS	365a	3 a
		נגה	SHINE	618b	1
		נר	LAMP	632d	
22	30	ב	IN	*88a	
		גדוד	BAND	151b	1
		דלג	LEAP	194c	
		רוץ	RUN	930b	1
		שור	WALL	1004b	
22	31	אל	GOD	42c	6 a
		אמרה	UTTERANCE	57b	
		מגן	SHIELD	*171c	
		דרך	WAY	204a	6 eb
		חסה	SEEK REFUGE	340b	
		צרף	SMELT	864b	1
		תמים	SOUND	1071a	4
22	32	אל	GOD	43a	6 f
		אלוהּ	GOD	44d	4 c
		בלעדי	APART FROM	116b	B b
		צור	ROCK	849d	2 b
22	33	אל	GOD	42c	6 a
		חיל	STRENGTH	298c	1 a
		נתן	GIVE	*681a	3 a
		נתר	BE FREE	684a	2
		מעוז	PLACE OF SAFETY	732a	1
		תמים	SOUND	1071a	4
22	34	אילה	HIND	19b	
		במה	HIGH PLACE	119b	2
		עמד	STAND	764d	2
		שוה	SET	1001b	
22	35	זרוע	ARM	284a	1 b
		מלחמה	WAR	536b	
		מלחמה	WAR	536c	
		למד	LEARN	540d	
		נחושה	COPPER	639a	2
		נחת	DESCEND	639c	
		קשת	BOW	906c	1 d
22	36	מגן	SHIELD	*171c	
		ימין	RIGHT HAND	*411d	1 c
		ישע	DELIVERANCE	447a	2
		סעד	SUPPORT	703c	2 b
		רבה	BECOME MANY	915d	1 e5
22	37	מעד	SLIP	588c	
		צעד	STEP	857d	1
		קרסל	ANKLE	902b	
22	38	רחב	BE LARGE	931c	2
		כלה	FINISH	478c	2 c1
		נשג	OVERTAKE	*673c	1 a
		שמד	BE EXTERMINATED	1029c	1
22	39	כלה	FINISH	478c	2 c1
		מחץ	SHATTER	563c	
		נפל	FALL	657b	2 a
		קום	STAND	877d	1 a
22	40	אזר	GIRD	25a	
		חיל	STRENGTH	298c	1 a
		כרע	CAUSE TO BOW DOWN	502d	2
22	41	ו	AND	254d	5 ca
		נתן	GIVE	681a	2
		ערף	BACK OF NECK	791b	1
		צמת	EXTERMINATE	856c	
		שן	HATE	971d	1
22	42	ישע	DELIVER	446c	1 a
		שעה	GAZE	1043a	
		שעע	BE BLINDED	*1044a	
22	43	דקק	PULVERISE	201a	3
		טיט	MUD	376c	1
		עפר	DRY EARTH	779d	1 d
		ריק	MAKE EMPTY	938a	3
		רקע	BEAT	956a	
		שחק	RUB AWAY	1007a	
22	44	עבד	WORK	713a	3
		פלט	ESCAPE	812b	1
		ריב	STRIFE	937a	2
22	45	אזן	EAR	23d	2 a
		בן	SON	121c	7 a
		כחש	DECEIVE	471b	
		כחש	DECEIVE	*471b	3
		נכר	FOREIGNNESS	648d	2
		שמע	HEAR	1034b	3
22	46	בן	SON	121c	7 a
		חגר	GIRD	292a	3
		חרג	QUAKE	353a	
		מן	OUT OF	579a	2 aa
		נבל	SINK	615b	1
		נכר	FOREIGNNESS	648d	2
		מסגרת	FASTNESS	689d	
22	47	אלהים	GOD	44c	4 bb
		ברך	BLESS	138d	2 a
		חי	ALIVE	311d	1 a
		ישע	DELIVERANCE	447a	2
		צור	ROCK	849d	2 a

Ch	v.	Heb	Eng	Page	Sec
		צור	ROCK	849d	2 a
22	48	רום	BE HIGH	927a	2 c
		אל	GOD	42c	6 a
		דבר	SPEAK	*182a	
		ירד	BRING DOWN	434a	1 c
		נקמה	VENGEANCE	668c	2
		נתן	GIVE	678d	1 d
22	49	חמס	VIOLENCE	329d	
		חמס	VIOLENCE	*329d	
		יצא	BRING OUT	424d	2
		פלט	ESCAPE	*812b	1
		רום	BE HIGH	927a	2 a
		תך	INJURY	*1067a	
22	50	זמר	MAKE MUSIC	274a	1
		ידה	PRAISE	392c	1 a2
		שם	NAME	1028d	3
22	51	גדל	GROW UP	*152c	
		מגדיל	TOWER	154a	
		דוד	DAVID	*188a	
		זרע	SOWING	282d	4 c
		חסד	GOODNESS	339a	2 Ie
		ישועה	VICTORY	447c	4
		משיח	ANOINTED	603c	1
		עולם	LONG DURATION	762c	2 f
		עשה	DO	794b	13
		גדל	ADDENDA ET COR-RIGENDA	1121d	
23	1	אלהים	GOD	44c	4 ba
		גבר	MAN	150a	1
		זמיר	SONG	274b	
		ישי	JESSE	445a	
		משיח	ANOINTED	603c	1
		נאם	UTTERANCE	610b	1
		נעים	DELIGHTFUL	653d	2
		נעים	SWEETLY SOUND-ING	654b	
		על	HEIGHT	752b	1
		יעקב	JACOB	785a	2
		קום	STAND	879b	
23	2	דבר	SPEAK	181c	4 a
		לשון	TONGUE	546b	1 b
		מלה	WORD	576b	
		על	UPON	753a	2 1
		יעקב	JACOB	785a	2
		רוח	BREATH	925d	9 b
23	3	דבר	SPEAK	181b	3 c
		ו	AND	255a	5 cg
		ירא	FEAR	432a	3
		משל	RULE	605d	1
		משל	RULE	605d	1
		צדיק	JUST	843a	1 a
		צור	ROCK	849d	2 a
23	4	אור	LIGHT	21c	3
		בקר	MORNING	133d	1 c
		דשא	GRASS	206a	
		זרח	RISE	280b	1 a
		לא	NOT	519d	2 e
		מטר	RAIN	564d	
		מן	ON ACCOUNT OF	580b	2 f
		מן	FROM	581c	4 b
		נגה	BRIGHTNESS	618b	
		עב	DARK CLOUD	728a	1 d
23	5	אל	GOD	43a	6 f
		ברית	COVENANT	137a	3 1
		ברית	COVENANT	137a	3 2
		חפץ	DELIGHT	343b	2
		ישע	SAFETY	447a	1
		כי	BECAUSE	473d	3 c
		כל	ALL	482d	2 ba
		לא	NOT	519a	1 a
		עולם	LONG DURATION	762c	2 d
		עם	WITH	767d	1 d
		ערך	ARRANGE	789d	1 g
		צמח	SPROUT	855c	1
		שום	TO PLACE	963b	1 c
		שמר	KEEP	1037b	4 b
23	6	בליעל	WORTHLESSNESS	116b	2
		נדד	RETREAT	622c	
		קוץ	THORN-BUSH	881a	2
23	7	ברזל	IRON	137c	2
		חנית	SPEAR	334a	2 a
		שבת	SEAT	444a	
		מלא	FILL	570b	1
		נגע	TOUCH	619a	1 a
		עץ	TREE	781d	2 b
		שרף	BURN	977a	
23	8	אישבשת	ISHBOSHETH	36b	2
		אשר	PARTICLE OF RE-LATION	83a	7 b
		תחכמני	HACHMONITE	315d	
		חלל	PIERCED	319c	1
		חנית	SPEAR	333d	1
		ישבבשבת	JOSHEB-BASSHE-BETH	444a	
		מאה	HUNDRED	548a	1 c2
		עדין	VOLUPTUOUS	726d	
		עור	ROUSE ONESELF	735a	
		פעם	OCCURRENCE	822a	3 a
		ישבעם	JASHOBEAM	1000b	
		שלש	THREE	*1025d	3
		שלשים	THIRTY	*1026c	2
		שליש	OFFICER	1026d	
		שמנה	EIGHT	1033a	3 a
23	9	אחוחי	AHOHITE	29a	1
		אלעזר	ELEAZAR	46c	C
		דודו	DODO	187d	2
		דודי	DODAI	*187d	
		היה	BE	227b	3 4da
		חרף	REPROACH	357d	
23	10	עלה	GO UP	748c	2 e
		דבק	CLING	179d	1 a
		חרב	SWORD	352c	1 c
		יגע	TOIL	388b	2
		יד	HAND	389c	1 d
		תשועה	DELIVERANCE	448b	1
		נכה	SMITE	646a	2 c
		עד	UNTIL	724d	2 Ia a
		עשה	DO	795a	29
		פשט	STRIP OFF	833a	
		שוב	TURN BACK	996d	1
23	11	אגא	AGEE	8a	1
		דבק	CLING	*179d	1 a
		הרי	HARARITE	251c	1 b
		חיה	COMMUNITY	312b	
		חלקה	PORTION OF GROUND	324c	1 a
		לחי	LEHI	534d	
		עדשה	LENTILE	727d	
		שמה	SHAMMAH	1031c	3 a
23	12	חלקה	PORTION OF GROUND	324c	1 b
		יצב	STATION ONESELF	426b	A
		תשועה	DELIVERANCE	448b	1
		עשה	DO	795a	29
23	13	חיה	COMMUNITY	312b	
		עדלם	ADULLAM	726b	
		מצודה	FASTNESS	845a	
		רפאים	REPHAIM	952b	
		רפאים	REPHAIM	952b	
		שלשים	THIRTY	1026c	2
23	14	אז	THEN	23a	1 a
		מצב	GARRISON	662d	3
		מצודה	FASTNESS	845a	
23	15	אוה	DESIRE	16b	
		בור	WELL	92b	2
		באר	WELL	92b	
		מי	WHO	566c	F a
		שער	GATE	1045a	2 a
		שקה	GIVE TO DRINK	1052c	2
23	16	אבה	BE WILLING	2c	
		באר	WELL	92b	
		בור	WELL	92b	2
		בקע	BREAK OPEN OR THROUGH	131d	2
		נסך	POUR OUT	650d	
		שאב	DRAW	980c	1
		שער	GATE	1045a	2 a
23	17	אבה	BE WILLING	2c	
		אלה	THESE	41c	A
		ב	IN	90a	3 3a
		דם	BLOOD	196c	2 c
		הלך	WALK	231d	1 d5 ta
		חלילה	FAR BE IT	321a	
		נפש	SOUL	659d	3 c
23	18	חלל	PIERCED	319c	2
		חנית	SPEAR	333d	1
		עור	ROUSE ONESELF	735a	
		עור	BE EXPOSED	*735d	
		עמשי	AMASAI	*772a	1
		צרויה	ZERUIAH	863b	
		שלישי	THIRD	1026b	
		שם	NAME	1028a	2 b1
23	19	בוא	COME	98d	2 f
		כבד	BE HONORED	457c	1 b
		כי	THAT	472b	1 da
		עד	AS FAR AS	724d	1 3
23	20	אחוחי	AHOHITE	*29a	
		ארי	LION	71d	
		אריה	LION	71d	
		אריאל	ARIEL	72a	3
		באר	WELL	92b	
		בור	PIT	92c	3
		בניה	BENAIAH	125c	1
		יהוידע	JEHOIADA	220b	1
		חיל	STRENGTH	298d	1 c
		חי	ALIVE	312b	2
		יום	DAY	398c	2 f
		מיכה	MICHA	567d	5
		מן	OUT OF	579c	2 cb
		פעל	DOING	821c	1 c
		קבצאל	KABZEEL	868b	
		רב	MUCH	913b	1 d
		שלג	SNOW	1017a	
		שנים	TWO	1041a	1 a
23	21	את	MARK OF THE AC-CUSATIVE	85a	1 a
		גזל	TEAR AWAY	159d	
		הרג	KILL	247a	1 a
		חנית	SPEAR	333d	1
		ירד	GO DOWN	432d	1 b
		מראה	VISION	909d	1 b
		שבט	ROD	987a	1 a
23	22	אלה	THESE	41c	A
		בניהו	BENAIAH	125c	1
		יהוידע	JEHOIADA	220b	1
		שם	NAME	1028a	2 b1
23	23	חנה	DECLINE	333c	2 c2
		כבד	BE HONORED	457c	1 b
		כבד	TO PLACE	964a	3 d
		משמעת	OBEDIENT BAND	1036a	1
23	24	אלחנן	ELHANAN	45a	
		דודו	DODO	187d	3
23	25	עשהאל	ASAHEL	795c	1
		אליקא	ELIKA	45d	
		הרורי	HARORITE	*248b	
		חרדי	HARODITE	353d	
		שמה	SHAMMAH	1031c	3 b
23	26	בית-פלט	BETH-PELET	112c	
		חלק	HELEZ	323b	1
		עירא	IRA	747a	2 a
		עקש	IKKESH	786a	
		פלני	PELONITE	813d	
		תקועי	TEKOITE	1075d	
23	27	אביעזר	ABIEZER	4c	2
		מבני	MEBUNNAI	125d	
		חשתי	HASHATHITE	302a	
		סבכי	SIBBECAI	687d	
23	28	ענתתי	ANATHOTHITE	779a	
		אחוחי	AHOHITE	29a	
		מהרי	MAHARAI	555b	
		נטפתי	NETOPHATHITE	643b	
		צלמון	ZALMON	854a	
23	29	אתי	ITTAI	87b	2
		בנימין	BENJAMIN	122d	1
		בענה	BAANAH	128d	2
		גבעה	GIBEAH	149b	2
		חלב	HELEB	317a	
		חלדי	HELDAI	*317c	1
		חלד	HELED	*317c	
		נטפתי	NETOPHATHITE	643b	
23	30	ריבי	RIBAI	937a	
		בניהו	BENAIAH	125c	2
		געש	GAASH	172b	
		הדי	HIDDAI	213b	
		יהוידע	JEHOIADA	*220b	1
		חורי	HURAI	301b	
		ירד	GO DOWN	433a	1 g
		מן	OUT OF	579c	2 cb
		מצרי	EGYPTIAN	596a	2
		מצרי	EGYPTIAN	596a	1
		נחל	WADY	636c	2
23	31	פרעתוני	PIRATHONITE	828a	
		אביעלבון	ABI-ALBON	3d	
		בחרומי	BAHARUMITE	104d	
		ביתהערבה	BETH-ARABAH	112c	
		ברחמי	BARHUMITE	138c	
		עזמות	AZMAVETH	740a	1 a
23	32	אליחבא	ELIAHBA	45b	
		גוני	GUNITES	157b	
		יהונתן	JONATHAN	221a	5
		חשם	HASHEM	251c	
		ישן	JASHEN	445a	
		שעלבני	SHAALBONITE	1043d	
23	33	אחיאם	AHIAM	26c	
		הררי	HARARITE	251b	1 a
		הררי	HARARITE	251c	2
		שכר	SACHAR	969b	2
		שמה	SHAMMAH	1031c	3 a
		שרר	SHARAR	1057b	
23	34	אחתפל	AHITHOPHEL	27c	
		אחסבי	AHASBAI	29b	
		אליעם	ELIAM	45c	B
		אליפל	ELIPHAL	45c	
		אליפלט	ELIPHELET	45d	B
		מעכתי	MAACATHITE	591a	
		פלני	PELONITE	813d	
23	35	אזבי	EZBAI	23c	
		ארבי	ARBITE	70c	
		חצרו	HEZRO	348a	
		כרמלי	CARMELITE	502b	
		נערי	NAARAI	*655c	
		פערי	PAARAI	822b	
23	36	בני	BANI	125b	1
		יגאל	IGAL	145d	2
		גדי	GADITE	151d	
		הגרי	HAGRITE	*212c	3
		חפר	HEPHER	*343d	3
		נתן	NATHAN	681d	3
		צובא	ZOBAH	844c	
23	37	בארתי	BEEROTHITE	92b	
		כלי	IMPLEMENT	479d	2 a
		נחרי	NAHARAI	638a	
		עמוני	AMMONITE	770a	
		צלק	ZELEK	854c	
		צרויה	ZERUIAH	863b	
23	38	גרב	GAREB	173a	1
		יתרי	ITHRITE	452b	
		עירא	IRA	747a	2 b
23	39	אוריה	URIAH	22c	1
		חתי	HITTITE	366a	
		כל	ALL	*482c	2 a
24	1	חרה	BURN	354a	2 a
		יסף	DO AGAIN	415c	2 a
		מנה	COUNT	584a	1
		סות	INCITE	694d	2
		שטן	SATAN	966c	2
24	2	ב	IN	88b	1 1
		בארשבע	BEERSHEBA	92a	
		דן	DAN	193a	3
		חיל	STRENGTH	299a	4
		ידע	KNOW	393c	1 a
		פקד	ATTEND TO	823a	A 4
		שר	CHIEFTAIN	978b	3 a
		שום	GO ABOUT	1002a	
24	3	הם	THEY	241d	8 b
		ו	AND	254c	4
		חפץ	DELIGHT IN	342d	1 a
		יסף	ADD	415b	1

Ch v.	Heb	Eng	Page	Sec
	ד	LIKE	*453b	1 a
	מאה	HUNDRED	547d	1 a2
	מה	HOW	554a	4 d
	פעם	OCCURRENCE	822a	3 a
	ראה	TO SEE	906d	1 b
24 4	חיל	STRENGTH	299a	4
	חזק	BE FIRM	304b	1 1d
	פקד	ATTEND TO	823c	A 4
24 5	גד	GAD	151c	1 b
	חלל	POLLUTE	320d	2
	חנה	DECLINE	333c	2 c2
	ימין	RIGHT HAND	411d	2 a
	ימין	RIGHT	412a	4
	מעיל	ROBE	591c	1
	נחל	WADY	636c	2
	יעזר	JAZER	741c	
	ערער	AROER	792d	1
24 6	דן	DAN	193a	
	חדשי	HODSHI	295d	
	חתי	HITTITE	366d	2 b
	סבב	TURN ABOUT	685c	1 a
	סביב	ROUND ABOUT	687a	1 d
	עיון	IJON	*743b	
	צידון	SIDON	851a	
	קדש	KADESH	874a	2
24 7	באר-שבע	BEERSHEBA	92a	
	מבצר	FORTIFICATION	131c	
	חוי	HIVITE	295d	2
	יהודה	JUDAH	397c	2
	כנעני	CANAANITE	489a	2 b
	נגב	SOUTH-COUNTRY	616b	1 a
	צר	TYER	862d	
24 8	חדש	NEW MOON	294c	2 a
	קצה	END	892b	4
	שוט	GO ABOUT	1002a	
	תשע	NINE	1077c	1 a
24 9	איש	MAN	35d	
	חיל	STRENGTH	298d	1 c
	חרב	SWORD	352c	1 c
	מאה	HUNDRED	548a	1 c2
	נתן	GIVE	679d	1 w
	מפקד	MUSTER	824c	1
	ישראל	ISRAEL	975c	2
24 10	שלף	DRAW OUT	1025c	1
	אחר	AFTER THAT	30b	3
	חטא	MISS A GOAL OR WAY	307a	2 b
	נכה	SMITE	645c	1 a
	סכל	BE FOOLISH	698a	
	ספר	COUNT	707d	1
	עבד	SLAVE	714c	6
	עבר	PASS OVER	719a	4
	עון	INIQUITY	731a	1 c2
24 11	בקר	MORNING	134b	1 h
	גד	GAD	151c	2
	דבר	WORD	182c	1 2a
	חזה	SEER	302d	1 b
24 12	בחר	CHOOSE	104a	3 b
	הלך	WALK	233c	14c 6
	הם	THEY	*241d	6 a
	הם	THEY	*241d	8 c
	מעיל	ROBE	591c	1
	נטה	STRETCH OUT	640a	1 c
	נטל	LIFT	642a	
	שלש	THREE	1025d	1 a
24 13	אם	IF	50d	2 ab b
	דבר	WORD	182b	1 1c
	דבר	PESTILENCE	184a	1
	חדש	NEW MOON	294c	2a
	ידע	KNOW	394a	1 g
	ל	TO	511c	1 gb
	מה	WHAT	552c	1 aa
	נגד	BE CONSPICUOUS	616c	2
	נוס	FLEE	630d	1
	ספה	SWEEP AWAY	*705a	1
	צר	ADVERSARY	865c	
	ראה	TO SEE	907c	5 b
	רעב	FAMINE	944b	1
	רעב	FAMINE	944b	1
	שבע	SEVEN	988a	1a
24 14	יד	HAND	390d	5 b3
	נפל	FALL	657c	2 a
	רחמים	COMPASSION	933c	1
	צרר	ADDENDA ET COR-RIGENDA	1126c	
24 15	באר-שבע	BEERSHEBA	92a	
	בקר	MORNING	133d	1 d
	דבר	PESTILENCE	184a	1
	דבר	PESTILENCE	*184a	1
	דוד	DAVID	188b	J
	דן	DAN	193a	3
	חלל	POLLUTE	320d	2
	חטה	WHEAT	334d	
	מועד	APPOINTED TIME	417c	1 a
	מגפה	PLAGUE	*620b	3
	עת	TIME	773d	2 c
	שבעים	HARVESTING	894c	2
	שבעים	SEVENTY	988c	2
24 16	אל	TO	40b	6
	ארונה	ARAUNAH	72c	
	ארנן	ORNAN	75a	
	יבוסי	JEBUSITE	101a	1
	גרן	THRESHING-FLOOR	175b	
	חיה	BE	227b	3 4d a
	יד	HAND	390a	1 e2
	מלאך	MESSENGER	521d	2

Ch v.	Heb	Eng	Page	Sec
	מסת	SUFFICIENCY	588b	2
	נחם	BE SORRY	637a	2
	עם	WITH	*768a	2
	עם	WITH	768a	2
	עתה	NOW	774a	1 a
	רב	MUCH	913b	1 f
	רעה	MISERY	949b	1
	רפה	SINK	951d	1
	שחת	GO TO RUIN	1008a	1
	שחת	GO TO RUIN	1008b	1
	שלח	SEND	1018d	3 c
24 17	חטא	MISS A GOAL OR WAY	307a	2 b
	מלאך	MESSENGER	521d	2
	נכה	SMITE	646c	4 a
	עוה	COMMIT INIQUITY	731c	2
	צאן	SMALL CATTLE	838c	3
	הוא	HE	*1090a	1
24 18	ארונה	ARAUNAH	72c	
	יבוסי	JEBUSITE	101a	1
	גרן	THRESHING-FLOOR	175b	
	מזבח	ALTAR	258d	8
	כי	THAT	*471d	1 a
	קום	STAND	878d	2 b
24 20	אף	NOSE	60b	2
	ארונה	ARAUNAH	72b	
	עבר	PASS OVER	717b	1 c
	שקף	LOOK DOWN	1054c	
24 21	ארונה	ARAUNAH	72b	
	גרן	THRESHING-FLOOR	175b	
	מגפה	PLAGUE	620a	3
	עבד	SLAVE	714c	6
	על	UPON	758d	4 2b
	מעם	FROM WITH	769a	C
	עצר	RESTRAIN	783d	
24 22	ארונה	ARAUNAH	72b	
	בקר	CATTLE	133c	2
	בקר	CATTLE	133c	2
	בקר	CATTLE	133c	2
	טוב	PLEASANT	374a	2 f
	כלי	EQUIPMENT	480a	2 d
	מורג	THRESHING-SLEDGE	558d	
	עלה	GO UP	749d	8
	עלה	WHOLE BURNT OF-FERING	750c	
	עץ	TREE	782a	2 d
	מצודה	FASTNESS	845a	
	ראה	TO SEE	907d	7 a
24 23	ארונה	ARAUNAH	72b	
	כל	ALL	482d	2 ba
	רצה	BE PLEASED WITH	953b	2
24 24	ארונה	ARAUNAH	72c	
	את	WITH	85c	
	ב	IN	90a	3 3a
	בקר	CATTLE	133c	2
	גרן	THRESHING-FLOOR	175b	
	יהוה	YAHWEH	218d	2 1f
	זהב	GOLD	*263b	9 a
	חמשים	FIFTY	332c	2 b
	חנם	OUT OF FAVOR	336c	A
	כי	BUT	474c	3 e
	כסף	SILVER	494b	8 a
	לא	NOT	519a	1 ad b
	מחיר	PRICE	564b	1
	מיכה	MICHA	567d	5
	עלה	WHOLE BURNT OF-FERING	750d	
24 25	שקל	SHEKEL	1053d	1
	מזבח	ALTAR	258b	1
	מיכה	MICHA	567d	5
	מגפה	PLAGUE	620a	3
	עלה	WHOLE BURNT OF-FERING	750d	
	על	UPON	758d	4 2b
	עצר	RESTRAIN	783d	
	עתר	PRAY	801c	
	שלם	PEACE-OFFERING	1023c	

1 KINGS

Ch v.	Heb	Eng	Page	Sec
1 1	בגד	GARMENT	94a	1
	דוד	DAVID	188a	
	זקן	BE OLD	278b	
	חמם	BE OR BECOME WARM	328c	1
	יום	DAY	399b	4 a
	כסה	COVER	491d	1
	ל	TO	511a	1 e
1 2	בקש	SEEK	134c	1 d
	בתולה	VIRGIN	143d	
	חיק	BOSOM	300d	3 a
	חמם	BE OR BECOME WARM	328c	1
	נערה	GIRL	655b	1
	סכן	BE OF USE	698b	1 e
	עמד	STAND	764a	1 e
	שכב	LIE DOWN	1012b	1 e
1 3	אבישג	ABISHAG	4d	
	בקש	SEEK	134c	1 b
	גבול	BOUNDARY	148a	2 a
	יפה	BEAUTIFUL	421c	
	מצא	FIND	593a	1 a
	נערה	GIRL	655b	1
	שונמית	SHUNAMMITE	1002d	1

Ch v.	Heb	Eng	Page	Sec
1 4	ידע	KNOW	394b	3
	יפה	BEAUTIFUL	421c	
	מאד	EXCEEDINGLY	547c	2 b
	נערה	GIRL	655b	1
	סכן	BE OF USE	698b	1
	שרת	SERVE	1058a	1 a
1 5	אדניהו	ADONIJAH	11d	1
	חגית	HAGGITH	291b	
	נשא	LIFT	672a	
	עשה	DO	795a	27
	פרש	HORSEMAN	832a	
	רוץ	RUN	930b	1
	רוץ	RUN	*930c	2 a
	רכב	CHARIOT	939a	1
1 6	אבשלום	ABSALOM	5a	2
	טוב	PLEASANT	373c	1 a
	יום	DAY	399b	4 a
	ככה	THUS	462c	
	מן	FROM	581c	4 a
	עצב	HURT	780c	
	תאר	FORM	1061c	
1 7	אדניהו	ADONIJAH	11d	1
	דבר	WORD	*182a	1 1a
	יואב	JOAB	222a	1
	היה	BE	227b	3 4d a
	כהן	PRIEST	463c	4
	עזר	HELP	740c	
	עם	WITH	767d	1 d
	צרויה	ZERUIAH	863b	
1 8	אדניהו	ADONIJAH	11d	1
	אשר	PARTICLE OF RE-LATION	83a	7 b
	בניהו	BENAIAH	125c	1
	גבור	STRONG	150b	2
	יהוידע	JEHOIADA	220b	1
	היה	BE	227b	3 4d a
	כהן	PRIEST	463c	4
	נתן	NATHAN	681d	2
	מרע	REI	946c	
	שמעי	SHIMEI	1035c	1 b
1 9	אבן	STONE	7a	9
	אצל	BESIDE	69b	A
	בקר	CATTLE	133b	1 a
	זחלת	CRAWLING THING	267b	
	מריא	FATLING	597b	
	עין	SPRING	745b	C
	עם	WITH	768a	2
	קרא	CALL	895d	5 c
	קרא	CALL	895d	5 a
1 10	בניהו	BENAIAH	125c	1
	גבור	STRONG	150b	2
	קרא	CALL	895d	5 c
1 11	אם	MOTHER	51d	1
	בת-שבע	BATHSHEBA	124a	
	חגית	HAGGITH	291b	
	שלמה	SOLOMON	1024d	
1 12	הלך	WALK	234b	1 5f 2
	עצה	ADVICE	420a	1
	מלט	SLIP AWAY	572c	3
	נא	PART OF EN-TREATY	609b	3 a
1 13	נפש	SOUL	660a	3 c
	אמה	MAID	51a	2
	הלך	WALK	234b	1 5f 3
	ישב	SIT	442b	1 a
	כי	THAT	472a	1 b
	כסא	THRONE	491a	3 a
	שבע	SWEAR	989b	1 a
1 14	דבר	SPEAK	181c	3 e
	מלא	FILL	570d	4
	עוד	STILL	729a	1 aa
1 15	אבישג	ABISHAG	4d	
	בת-שבע	BATHSHEBA	124a	
	זקן	BE OLD	278b	
	חדר	CHAMBER	293c	
	שרת	SERVE	1058a	1 a
1 16	בת-שבע	BATHSHEBA	124a	
	מה	WHAT	552d	1 ac
	קדד	BOW DOWN	869a	
1 17	אמה	MAID	51a	2
	ישב	SIT	442b	1 a
	כסא	THRONE	491a	3 a
	שבע	SWEAR	989b	1 a
1 18	אדניהו	ADONIJAH	11d	1
	עתה	NOW	774b	2
	עתה	NOW	774c	2 gb
1 19	כהן	PRIEST	463c	4
	רב	MULTITUDE	914a	1
	שור	A HEAD OF CATTLE	1004b	
1 20	ישב	SIT	442b	1 a
	כסא	THRONE	491a	3 a
	מי	WHO	566c	C
	על	UPON	757d	2 7 c c
	עתה	NOW	774c	2 gb
1 21	אב	FATHER	3c	4 a
	חטא	SINFUL	308b	1
	שכב	LIE DOWN	1012c	4 b
1 22	דבר	SPEAK	181c	3 e
	עוד	STILL	729a	1 aa
1 23	אף	NOSE	60b	2
	ל	TO	*511d	2
	נגד	BE CONSPICUOUS	616d	1
	שחה	BOW DOWN	1005b	1 b
1 24	כסא	THRONE	491a	3 a
1 25	חיה	LIVE	311b	1 d

Ch v.	Heb	Eng	Page	Sec
	ירד	GO DOWN	433a	1 e
	כהן	PRIEST	463c	4
	צבא	ARMY	839a	1 a
	רב	MULTITUDE	914a	1
	שר	CHIEFTAIN	978b	3 a
	שור	A HEAD OF CATTLE	1004b	
1 26	אנכי	I	59b	
	בניהו	BENAIAH	125c	1
	יהוידע	JEHOIADA	220b	1
	כהן	PRIEST	463c	4
	צדוק	RIGHTEOUS	*843b	
	קרא	CALL	895d	5 a
1 27	אם	IF	50c	2 aa
	את	WITH	86d	4 c
	היה	COME TO PASS	227d	2
	ידע	TEACH	395a	
	כסא	THRONE	491a	3 a
	מי	WHO	566c	C
1 28	בתשבע	BATHSHEBA	124a	
	ל	TO	515b	5 hb a
	קרא	CALL	895c	5 a
1 29	חי	ALIVE	311d	1 a
	נפש	SOUL	660a	3 c
	פדה	RANSOM	804a	3 d
	צרה	DISTRESS	865b	
	שבע	SWEAR	989a	1 a
1 30	כאשר	AS	455b	1 b
	כי	THAT	472b	1 c
	כן	SO	486c	2 cd
	כסא	THRONE	491a	3 a
	שבע	SWEAR	989b	1 a
	שלמה	SOLOMON	1024d	
1 31	אף	NOSE	60b	2
	בתשבע	BATHSHEBA	124a	
	היה	LIVE	311b	1 d
	עולם	LONG DURATION	762a	2 a
	קדד	BOW DOWN	869a	
	שחה	BOW DOWN	1005b	1 a
1 32	בניהו	BENAIAH	125c	1
	יהוידע	JEHOIADA	220b	1
	כהן	PRIEST	463c	4
	קרא	CALL	895d	5 a
1 33	אשר	PARTICLE OF RELATION	83a	7 b
	ירד	BRING DOWN	433d	1 a
	מלך	KING	573a	1
	על	UPON	757b	2 7c ab
	פרדה	SHE-MULE	825d	
	רכב	RIDE	938d	1
	שלמה	SOLOMON	1024d	
1 34	חיה	LIVE	311b	1 d
	כהן	PRIEST	463c	4
	מלך	KING	573a	1
	מלך	KING	573b	5 b
	מלך	KING	573c	5 c
	משח	ANOINT	603b	2
	שלמה	SOLOMON	1024d	
	שפר	HORN	1051d	
1 35	את	MARK OF THE ACCUSATIVE	85a	1 a
	כסא	THRONE	491a	3 a
	עלה	GO UP	748c	2 d
	צוה	GIVE CHARGE OVER	845d	1 d
	ישראל	ISRAEL	975a	2 a2
1 36	אלהים	GOD	44c	4 ba
	אמן	VERILY	53b	
	בניהו	BENAIAH	125c	1
	יהוידע	JEHOIADA	220b	1
	כן	SO	486a	1 ca
1 37	גדל	BECOME GREAT	152b	2
	דוד	DAVID	188b	E
	היה	BE	227b	3 4d a
	כן	SO	486c	2 cd
	כסא	THRONE	491b	3 a
	מן	THAN	582c	6 a
1 38	בניהו	BENAIAH	125c	1
	יהוידע	JEHOIADA	220b	1
	הלך	WALK	236d	1 d
	ירד	GO DOWN	433a	1 e
	כהן	PRIEST	463c	4
	כרתי	CHERETHITE	504d	
	על	UPON	757b	2 7c ab
	פלתי	PELETHITES	814c	
	פרדה	SHE-MULE	825d	
	רכב	RIDE	938d	1
1 39	אהל	TENT	14b	3
	היה	LIVE	311b	1 d
	כהן	PRIEST	463c	4
	מלך	KING	573b	5 b
	משח	ANOINT	603b	2
	קרן	HORN	901d	1 b
	שלמה	SOLOMON	1024d	
	שמן	OIL	1032b	2 d
	שפר	HORN	1051d	
1 40	בקע	BREAK OPEN OR THROUGH	132a	1
	חליל	FLUTE	319d	
	חלל	PLAY THE PIPE	320a	
	עלה	GO UP	748c	2 d
	קול	VOICE	876b	1 a
	שמח	JOYFUL	970c	1 b
	שמחה	JOY	970d	1
1 41	המה	ROAR	242b	4
	כלה	FINISH	478b	1 c
	קול	VOICE	877a	2 a

Ch v.	Heb	Eng	Page	Sec
	קול	VOICE	877b	2 d
	קרא	CALL	895d	5 c
	קריה	TOWN	900b	2
1 42	איש	MAN	35d	
	בא	COME	97d	1
	בשר	BEAR TIDINGS	142b	1
	יהונתן	JONATHAN	220d	2
	חיל	STRENGTH	298d	2
	טוב	A GOOD THING	375a	1
	כהן	PRIEST	463c	4
	עוד	STILL	729a	1 aa
1 43	אבל	VERILY	6a	1
	יהונתן	JONATHAN	220d	2
	מלך	BE KING	574b	
1 44	בניהו	BENAIAH	125c	1
	יהוידע	JEHOIADA	220b	1
	כהן	PRIEST	463c	4
	כרתי	CHERETHITE	504d	
	פלתי	PELETHITES	814c	
	פרדה	SHE-MULE	825d	
1 45	הום	MURMUR	223a	
	כהן	PRIEST	463c	4
	מלך	KING	573c	5 c
	משח	ANOINT	603b	2
	קריה	TOWN	900b	2
	שמח	JOYFUL	970c	1 a
1 46	כסא	THRONE	491b	3 a
	מלוכה	KINGSHIP	574d	
1 47	ברך	BLESS	139b	4 f
	גדל	BECOME GREAT	152b	2
	יטב	MAKE GOOD	406a	4
	כסא	THRONE	491b	3 a
	עבד	SLAVE	713d	2
	שחה	BOW DOWN	1005c	2 c
1 48	משכב	COUCH	1012d	1
	ברך	BLESS	138c	2 a
	כה	THUS	462c	1
	כסא	THRONE	491a	3 a
	נתן	PUT	680d	2 c
1 49	אשר	PARTICLE OF RELATION	83a	7 b
	דרך	JOURNEY	203a	2
	חרד	TREMBLE	353a	2
	קרא	CALL	895d	5 c
1 50	מזבח	ALTAR	258c	1
	חזק	BE FIRM	305a	6 a
	ירא	FEAR	431b	1 c
	קרן	HORN	902a	3
1 51	אחז	GRASP	28b	2
	אם	IF	50b	1 b2
	מזבח	ALTAR	258c	1
	יום	DAY	400d	7 h
	ירא	FEAR	431b	1 b
	מות	DIE	560b	1 b
	נגד	BE CONSPICUOUS	617a	1
	קרן	HORN	902a	3
	שבע	SWEAR	989b	1 a
1 52	אם	IF	49c	1 a1 a
	אם	IF	49c	1 a1 a
	בן	SON	121d	8 a
	חיל	STRENGTH	298d	2
	מצא	FIND	394a	1 g1
	מן	FROM	581a	3 bd
	נפל	FALL	657a	1
	שערה	A HAIR	972b	1
1 53	ירד	BRING DOWN	433d	1 a
	על	UPON	756d	2 7b
	על	UPON	759a	4 2c
2 1	אב	FATHER	3b	1
	דוד	DAVID	188a	A
	יום	DAY	399b	4 a
	קרב	COME NEAR	897c	2
2 2	איש	MAN	35d	
	ארץ	EARTH	76a	1 c
	דרך	WAY	203a	1
	דרך	WAY	*203b	4 a
	הלך	WALK	234b	2 1
	חזק	BE FIRM	304b	1 2c
2 3	דרך	WAY	204a	6 ec
	חקה	SOMETHING PRESCRIBED	350a	2
	חקה	SOMETHING PRESCRIBED	350b	2 e
	תורה	LAW	436b	2 b2
	ל	TO	517b	7 ba
	משה	MOSES	602d	
	עדות	TESTIMONY	730b	2
	פנה	TURN	815b	1
	מצוה	COMMANDMENT	846c	2 b2
	שכל	BE PRUDENT	968c	7
	שמר	KEEP	1037a	3 c
	משמרת	GUARD	1038c	3
2 4	אמת	FIRMNESS	54a	3 a
	דבר	SPEAK	181c	5
	דבר	WORD	182d	1 2b
	דרך	WAY	203c	6 a
	הלך	WALK	234d	2 3c
	כסא	THRONE	491b	3 a
	כרת	BE CUT OFF	504b	4
	ל	TO	512c	5 aa
	ל	TO	517b	7 ba
	לבב	HEART	523b	2
	נפש	SOUL	661b	0
	על	UPON	758a	4 2a
	פנה	FACE	817b	2 4a h
2 5	אבינר	ABNER	4c	

Ch v.	Heb	Eng	Page	Sec
	ב	IN	89a	2 2
	דם	BLOOD	196d	2 f
	חרג	KILL	247a	1 a
	חגורה	GIRDLE	292b	
	יתר	JETHER	452b	3
	מתנים	LOINS	608a	1 a
	נר	NER	633a	1
	נעל	SANDAL	653a	
	עמשא	AMASA	772a	1
	צבא	ARMY	839a	1 a
	צרויה	ZERUIAH	863b	
	שום	TO PLACE	963a	1 a
	שר	CHIEFTAIN	978b	3 a
	שלון	PEACE	1023b	6
2 6	ו	AND	254c	4
	חכמה	WISDOM	315c	2
	ירד	BRING DOWN	434a	1 d
	לא	NOT	518c	1 aa
	עשה	DO	794a	1 1a 7
	שיבה	OLD AGE	966d	1
	שאול	SHEOL	982d	1
	שלום	PEACE	1023a	4
2 7	אבישלום	ABSALOM	5a	2
	ברזלי	BARZILLAI	137d	1
	ברח	FLEE	138a	2
	היה	BE	227c	3 4d e
	חסד	GOODNESS	338c	1 1
	כן	SO	485d	1 b
	קרב	COME NEAR	897b	1 a
	שלחן	TABLE	1020b	1
2 8	בחרים	BAHURIM	104c	
	בנימיני	BENJAMITE	122d	
	גרא	GERA	173a	1
	הלך	WALK	230d	1 1d 3a
	מחנים	MAHANAIM	334b	
	מות	DIE	560b	1 b
	מרץ	BE SICK	599c	
	קלל	BE SLIGHT	886c	1
	קללה	CURSE	887a	
	קרא	ENCOUNTER	896d	1
	שבע	SWEAR	989b	1 a
	שמעי	SHIMEI	1035c	1 a
2 9	דם	BLOOD	197c	2 n
	חכם	WISE	314d	2
	ירד	BRING DOWN	434a	1 d
	נקה	BE CLEAN	667c	2
	שיבה	OLD AGE	966d	1
	שאול	SHEOL	982d	1
2 10	אב	FATHER	3c	4 a
	דוד	DAVID	188a	A
	קבר	BURY	868c	
	שכב	LIE DOWN	1012c	4 b
2 11	חברון	HEBRON	289b	
	שנה	YEAR	1040b	1
2 12	דוד	DAVID	188b	E
	כון	BE FIRM	465d	1 b
	כסא	THRONE	491a	3 a
	מלכות	ROYAL POWER	574d	1
	שלמה	SOLOMON	1024d	
2 13	אדניהו	ADONIJAH	11d	1
	אם	MOTHER	51d	1
	בתשבע	BATHSHEBA	124a	
	חגית	HAGGITH	291b	
	שלם	PEACE	1022d	3
2 15	מלוכה	KINGSHIP	574c	
	מן	OUT OF	579d	2 d
	סבב	TURNABOUT	685d	1 a
	על	UPON	757d	2 7c c
	שום	TO PLACE	963d	2 c
2 16	את	WITH	86d	4 a
	שאלה	REQUEST	982c	1
	שוב	TURN BACK	999d	5
2 17	אבישג	ABISHAG	4d	
	שוב	TURN BACK	999d	5
	שונמית	SHUNAMMITE	1002d	1
	שלמה	SOLOMON	1024d	
2 18	בתשבע	BATHSHEBA	124a	
	דבר	SPEAK	181d	5
	טוב	PLEASANT	374c	5
	על	UPON	754c	2 1f c
2 19	אם	MOTHER	51d	1
	בתשבע	BATHSHEBA	124a	
	דבר	SPEAK	181b	3 c
	דבר	SPEAK	181d	5
	ימין	RIGHT HAND	411d	2 a
	ישב	SIT	442c	1 a
	כסא	SEAT OF HONOR	490d	1 a
	ל	TO	510d	1 b
	על	UPON	754c	2 1f c
	שום	TO PLACE	964b	4 c
2 20	אם	MOTHER	51d	1
	מן	SMALL	882a	1 b
	שאל	ASK	981c	1 a
	שאלה	REQUEST	982c	1
	שוב	TURN BACK	999d	5
2 21	אבישג	ABISHAG	4d	
	נתן	GIVE	681d	1 b
	שונמית	SHUNAMMITE	1002d	1
2 22	אבישג	ABISHAG	4d	
	הוא	HE, SHE, IT	*216a	3 a
	ו	AND	252c	1 c
	כהן	PRIEST	463c	4
	מלוכה	KINGSHIP	574c	
	צרויה	ZERUIAH	863b	
	שאל	ASK	981c	1 a
	שונמית	SHUNAMMITE	1002d	1 a

Ch	v.	Heb	Eng	Page	Sec
2	23	ב	IN	90a	3 3a
		דבר	SPEAK	181c	4 e
		יסף	ADD	415b	1
		כי	THAT	472a	1 c
		נפש	SOUL	659d	1
		שבע	SWEAR	989b	1 a
2	24	בית	HOUSE	109d	5 b
		דוד	DAVID	188b	E
		חי	ALIVE	311d	1 a
		ישב	CAUSE TO SIT	443c	1
		כון	ESTABLISH	466a	1 a
		כסא	THRONE	491a	3 a
		מות	DIE	560c	2
		עשה	DO	794c	2 1c
2	25	בניהו	BENAIAH	125c	1
		יהוידע	JEHOIADA	220b	1
		מות	DIE	559d	2 a
		פגע	MEET	803b	3
2	26	אדון	LORD	11c	4 a
		איש	MAN	36a	
		ארון	CHEST	75c	3 e
		אשר	PARTICLE OF RELATION	82d	4 c
		הלך	WALK	231a	1 d3 gb
		ו	AND	252d	1 e
		כהן	PRIEST	463c	4
		כי	BECAUSE	474b	3 d
		מות	DIE	560b	1 b
		מות	DEATH	560d	2
		על	UPON	757a	2 7c a
		ענה	BE BOWED DOWN	776c	2
		ענתות	ANATHOTH	779a	1
2	27	גרש	DRIVE OUT	176d	
		דבר	SPEAK	181c	5
		כהן	PRIEST	463c	4
		כהן	PRIEST	463c	4
		מלא	FILL	570d	3
		עלי	ELI	750b	
		שלו	SHILOH	1017d	
2	28	אבשלום	ABSALOM	5a	2
		אדניהו	ADONIJAH	11d	1
		אהל	TENT	14b	3
		מזבח	ALTAR	258c	1
		חזק	BE FIRM	305a	6 a
		נוס	FLEE	630d	1
		נטה	BEND	640b	3 a
		קרן	HORN	902a	3
		שמועה	REPORT	1035b	1
2	29	אצל	BESIDE	69b	A
		בניהו	BENAIAH	125c	1
		יהוידע	JEHOIADA	220b	1
		הנה	BEHOLD	244a	A
		נגד	BE CONSPICUOUS	617a	
		נוס	FLEE	630d	1
		פגע	MEET	803b	3
2	30	אהל	TENT	14b	3
		בניהו	BENAIAH	125c	1
		דבר	WORD	182b	1 1c
		כה	THUS	462a	1
		כי	BUT	474c	3 e
2	31	דם	BLOOD	*196c	2 b
		דם	BLOOD	196d	2 d
		חנם	OUT OF FAVOR	336d	C
		סור	TURN ASIDE	694b	1
		על	UPON	758d	4 2b
		פגע	MEET	803b	3
2	32	אבינר	ABNER	4c	
		דם	BLOOD	197a	2 i
		הרג	KILL	247a	1 a
		טוב	PLEASANT	374c	6
		יתר	JETHER	452b	3
		נר	NER	633a	1
		על	UPON	756c	2 7a b
		עמשא	AMASA	772a	1
		פגע	MEET	803b	3
		צדיק	JUST	843a	2
		ראש	HEAD	911b	8
		שוב	TURN BACK	999c	4 a
2	33	ב	IN	89b	2 4b
		דם	BLOOD	197a	2 i
		זרע	SOWING	282d	4 c
		כסא	THRONE	491a	3 a
		עולם	LONG DURATION	762b	2 b4
		עולם	LONG DURATION	762c	2 f
		מעם	FROM WITH	769a	D
		ראש	HEAD	911b	8
		שוב	TURN BACK	998c	7 f
2	34	בניהו	BENAIAH	125c	1
		יהוידע	JEHOIADA	220b	1
		מות	DIE	560c	1 b
		פגע	MEET	803b	3
		קבר	BURY	868c	
		קבר	BURY	868c	
2	35	בניהו	BENAIAH	125c	1
		יהוידע	JEHOIADA	220b	1
		כהן	PRIEST	463c	4
		נתן	PUT	680d	2 c
		צבא	ARMY	839a	1 a
		צדק	RIGHTEOUS	843b	1 a
		תחת	INSTEAD	1065d	2 2b a
2	36	אן	WHERE	33a	C
		בנה	BUILD	124b	1 ab
2	37	דם	BLOOD	197a	2 i
		מות	DIE	559d	2 a
		נחל	WADY	636c	2
		קדרון	KEDRON	871b	
2	38	טוב	PLEASANT	374b	5
		כן	SO	486c	2 cd
2	39	אכיש	ACHISH	37a	
		ברח	FLEE	138a	2
		גת	GATH	387d	
		ל	TO	513c	5 cb a
		מעכה	MAACAH	590a	1 d
		מעוך	MAOCH	590d	
2	40	אכיש	ACHISH	37a	
		בקש	SEEK	134c	1 b
		חבש	BIND	290a	1 c
		חמור	HE-ASS	331b	2 b
		גת	GATH	387d	
		גת	GATH	387d	
2	41	הלך	WALK	231b	1 1d 4
		גת	GATH	387d	
		נגד	BE CONSPICUOUS	617a	
2	42	אן	WHERE	33a	C
		הלך	WALK	230d	1 1d 3b
		טוב	PLEASANT	374b	5
		מות	DIE	559d	2 a
		עוד	BEAR WITNESS	730a	3
		שבע	SWEAR	989c	1
2	43	צוה	LAY CHARGE UPON	845c	1 a
		מצוה	COMMANDMENT	846b	1
		שבועה	OATH	989d	1 a
		שמר	KEEP	1037a	3 c
2	44	ב	IN	89b	2 4b
		לבב	HEART	523a	2 3b
		ראש	HEAD	911b	8
		רעה	MISERY	949b	1
		שוב	TURN BACK	999c	4 a
2	45	ברך	BLESS	138d	2 b
		דוד	DAVID	188b	E
		כון	BE FIRM	465d	1 b
		כסא	THRONE	491a	3 a
		עולם	LONG DURATION	762c	2 f
2	46	בניהו	BENAIAH	125c	1
		יהוידע	JEHOIADA	220b	1
		כון	BE FIRM	465d	1 b
		מות	DIE	559d	2
		ממלכה	DOMINION	575b	2
		פגע	MEET	803b	3
		צוה	CHARGE	845c	2 b
3	1	את	WITH	86a	1 da
		בת	DAUGHTER	123b	1 h
		בנה	BUILD	124b	1 ab
		בנה	BUILD	124c	1 ad
		דוד	DAVID	188a	A
		חומה	WALL	327c	1
		חתן	MAKE ONESELF A SON IN LAW	368d	1
		מלך	KING	573a	1
		סביב	ROUND ABOUT	687a	1 b
		פרעה	PHARAOH	829a	
		פרעה	PHARAOH	829a	
3	2	במה	HIGH PLACE	119b	3
		בנה	BUILD	125a	1 a
		זבח	SLAUGHTER FOR SACRIFICE	257b	2
		כהן	PRIEST	463c	4
		רק	ONLY	956c	2 b
		במה	HIGH PLACE	119b	3
3	3	אהב	LOVE	13a	3
		במה	HIGH PLACE	119b	3
		הלך	WALK	234d	2 3a 1h
		זבח	SLAUGHTER FOR SACRIFICE	257b	2
		חקה	SOMETHING PRESCRIBED	350a	2 c
		חקה	SOMETHING PRESCRIBED	350b	2 e
		קטר	MAKE SACRAFICES SMOKE	883a	1 a
		רק	ONLY	956c	2 b
3	4	אלף	THOUSAND	48d	1 a
		במה	HIGH PLACE	119b	3
		גבעון	GIBEON	149c	
		הוא	HE, SHE, IT	*216a	3
		הלך	WALK	230d	1 1d 3b
		מזבח	ALTAR	258b	1
		עלה	GO UP	750a	8
		עלה	WHOLE BURNT OFFERING	750d	
3	5	גבעון	GIBEON	149c	
		חלום	DREAM	321d	2 a
		לילה	NIGHT	538d	1
		מה	WHAT	552d	1 b
		ראה	TO SEE	908b	1 a
		שאל	ASK	981c	1 a
3	6	אמת	FIRMNESS	54a	3 a
		גדול	GREAT	153b	6 c
		דוד	DAVID	*188b	J
		ה	THE	208b	1 ha
		הלך	WALK	234d	2 3c
		חסד	GOODNESS	339a	2 1e
		יום	DAY	400d	7 h
		ישרה	UPRIGHTNESS	449c	
		כסא	THRONE	491a	3 a
		לבב	HEART	523d	2 6a
		עם	WITH	767d	1 d
		צדקה	RIGHTEOUSNESS	842b	5
3	7	בוא	COME	97d	1 a
		יהוה	YAHWEH	218d	2 1f
		ידע	KNOW	394b	4 a
		יצא	GO OUT	424a	3
		מלך	BE KING	574b	
		נער	YOUTH	655a	1 c
		קטן	SMALL	882b	1 a
3	8	בחר	CHOOSE	104a	2 a
		מנה	COUNT	284a	1
		ספר	COUNT	708a	
		רב	MULTITUDE	914a	1
3	9	בין	DISCERN	107a	2
		בין	INTERVAL	107c	1 d
		בין	INTERVAL	107c	1 b
		טוב	A GOOD THING	375b	4
		כבד	MASSIVE	458a	1 b
		נתן	GIVE	678b	1 b
		שמע	HEAR	1033d	1 f
		שפט	JUDGE	1047b	
3	10	אדון	LORD	11c	3 2b
		יטב	BE PLEASING	405c	4
		שאל	ASK	981c	1 a
		שלמה	SOLOMON	1024d	
3	11	בין	DISCERN	107a	1 a
		ו	AND	252d	1 e
		יום	DAY	399a	4 a
		נפש	SOUL	659d	3 c
		יען	ON ACCOUNT OF	774d	2
		שאל	ASK	981c	1 a
		שמע	HEAR	1033d	1 a
		משפט	JUDGMENT	1048c	1 d
3	12	אשר	THAT	83c	8 b
		בין	DISCERN	107a	
		דבר	WORD	182b	1 b
		לב	HEART	524d	2 3b
		נתן	GIVE	678b	1 b
		קום	STAND	878a	4
3	13	אשר	THAT	83c	8 b
		כבד	HONOR	458c	2 a
		עשר	RICHES	799b	
3	14	ארך	BE LONG	73d	1 b
		דוד	DAVID	*187d	
		דרך	WAY	204a	6 ec
		חק	SOMETHING PRESCRIBED	349d	7 g
3	15	אדון	LORD	11c	3 2a
		חלום	DREAM	321d	2 a
		יקץ	AWAKE	429c	
		עלה	WHOLE BURNT OFFERING	750d	
		שלם	PEACE-OFFERING	1023c	
		משתה	FEAST	1059d	1
3	16	אז	THEN	23a	1 a
		אשה	WOMAN	61a	1
		זנה	COMMIT FORNICATION	275d	1
		עמד	STAND	763d	1 a
		שנים	TWO	1041b	1 b2
3	17	בי	I PRAY	106c	
		ילד	BEAR	408b	1 a
3	18	אשה	WOMAN	61a	1
		זולה	EXCEPT	266a	1
		זור	BE A STRANGER	266c	2 a
		ילד	BEAR	408b	1 a
3	19	אשר	THAT	83c	8 c
		שכב	LIE DOWN	1012b	1 d
3	20	אמה	MAID	51a	2
		אצל	BESIDE	69b	B
		חיק	BOSOM	300d	2
		ילד	CHILD	*409b	A
		ישן	SLEEPING	445d	
		לילה	NIGHT	538d	1
		שכב	LIE DOWN	1012c	
		שכב	LIE DOWN	1012c	
		תוך	MIDST	1063c	
3	21	בין	DISCERN	107a	3 c
		בקר	SEEK	*133a	
		בקר	MORNING	133d	1 b
		בקר	MORNING	134b	1 h
		ינק	NURSE	413c	
3	22	דבר	SPEAK	181c	3 f
		חי	ALIVE	312a	1 b
		כי	BUT	474c	3 e
		לא	NOT	519a	1 ad b
		זה	THIS	260d	1 b
3	23	חי	ALIVE	312a	1 b
3	24	ל	TO	515b	5 hb a
		גזר	CUT	160b	1
3	25	חי	ALIVE	312a	1 b
		ילד	CHILD	409b	A
3	26	בי	I PRAY	106c	
		בן	SON	120a	1
		גזר	CUT	160b	1
		חי	ALIVE	312a	1 b
		ילד	BEAR	408c	3
		כמר	GROW WARM	485b	1
		מות	DIE	560b	1 b
		על	UPON	756d	2 7a c
		רחמים	COMPASSION	933c	2
3	27	אם	MOTHER	51d	2
		היה	BECOME	225d	2 1b
		חי	ALIVE	312a	1 b
		ילד	BEAR	408c	3
		מות	DIE	560b	1 b
3	28	חכמה	WISDOM	315c	2
		ירא	FEAR	431b	2
		קרב	INWARD PART	899b	2 a
		שפט	JUDGE	1047c	2 b
		משפט	JUDGMENT	1048b	1 a
		משפט	JUDGMENT	1048b	1 a

1 KINGS

Ch	v.	Heb	Eng	Page	Sec
4	2	אשר	PARTICLE OF RE-LATION	83a	7 b
		עזריהו	AZARIAH	741b	5 a
		דך	RIGHTEOUS	843b	1 a
		שר	CHIEFTAIN	978b	2 a
4	3	אחיהו	AHIJAH	26d	2
		אחילוד	AHILUD	27a	1
		אליחרף	ELIHOREPH	45b	
		יהושפט	JEHOSHAPHAT	221d	3
		זכר	REMEMBER	271a	4
		ספר	ENUMERATOR	708b	1 b
		שריה	SERAIAH	976a	1
		שישא	SHISHA	1010d	
4	4	בניהו	BENAIAH	125c	1
		כהן	PRIEST	463c	4
		על	UPON	755a	2 3
		צבא	ARMY	839a	1 a
		דך	RIGHTEOUS	843b	1 a
4	5	זבוד	ZABUD	256b	
		כהן	PRIEST-KING	463a	1
		נצב	STAND	662b	3
		נתן	NATHAN	681d	4
		עזריהו	AZARIAH	741b	2
		על	UPON	755a	2 3
		רעה	FRIEND	946b	
4	6	אדנירם	ADONIRAM	12a	
		אחישר	AHISHAR	27c	
		בית	HOUSE	110b	6
		מס	LABOUR-GANG	587a	1
		עבדא	ABDA	715a	1
		על	UPON	755a	2 3
4	7	חדש	NEW MOON	294c	2 a
		כול	SUSTAIN	465a	1
		נצב	STAND	662b	3
		על	UPON	753c	2 1c
4	8	בנחור	BEN-HUR	122b	
		הר	MOUNTAIN	251a	2 b
		חור	HUR	301b	5
4	9	אלן	ELON	19a	4
		ביתחנן	BETH-HANAN	111c	
		ביתשמש	BETH-SHEMESH	112d	1
		בדקר	BEN-DEKER	122b	
		דקר	BEN-DEKER	201b	
		שעלבים	SHAALBIM	1043c	
4	10	ארבות	ARRUBBOTH	70d	
		בנחסד	BEN-HESED	122c	
		חפר	HEPHER	343d	2
		שוכה	SOCOH	962c	1
4	11	אבינדב	ABINADAB	4c	2
		בנאבינדב	BEN-ABINADAB	122a	
		דאר	DOR	190b	
		טפת	TAPHATH	382a	
		נפת	HEIGHT	632c	1
4	12	אבל	ABEL	6a	5
		אחילוד	AHILUD	27a	2
		אצל	BESIDE	69b	A
		ביתשאן	BETH-SHEAN	112d	
		בענא	BAANA	128d	1 a
		מגדו	MEGIDDO	152a	2
		יזראל	JEZREEL	283b	1 b
		עבר	REGION ACROSS	719d	1
		עד	AS FAR AS	724a	1 1a
		צרתן	ZERETHAN	866c	
		יקמים	JOKMEAM	880c	
		תחת	UNDERNEATH	1066b	3 2b
		תענך	TAANACH	1073d	
4	13	יאיר	JAIR	22c	1
		בנגבר	BEN-GEBER	122b	
		בריח	BAR	138b	2
		בריח	BAR	138b	1 b
		בשן	BASHAN	143c	
		גבר	GEBER	*150a	
		חבל	CORD	286d	3
		חוה	TENT-VILLAGE	295d	
		חומה	WALL	327c	1
		ארגב	ARGOB	*419a	1
		מנשה	MANASSEH	586d	1 b2 d
		נחשת	COPPER	638d	
		עיר	CITY	746b	1 a
		ארגב	ARGOB	918d	1
		רמות	RAMOTH	928b	1 a
4	14	אחינדב	AHINADAB	27b	
		מחנים	MAHANAIM	334b	
		עדו	IDDO	723b	1
4	15	אחימעץ	AHIMAAZ	27b	1
		בשמת	BASEMATH	142a	2
		נפתלי	NAPHTALI	837a	2 b
4	16	אשר	ASHER	81b	2
		בעלות	BEALOTH	128c	
		בענא	BAANA	128d	1 b
		חושי	HUSHAI	302a	2
4	17	יהושפט	JEHOSHAPHAT	221d	4
		ישכר	ISSACHAR	441a	1
		פרוה	PARUAH	827c	
4	18	אלא	ELA	41d	
		שמעי	SHIMEI	1035c	1 b
4	19	אורי	URI	22b	3
		אמרי	AMORITES	57c	2 a
		בשן	BASHAN	143c	
		גבר	GEBER	150a	
		נציב	PREFECT	662d	2
		סיחון	SIHON	695d	
		עוג	OG	728b	
4	20	חול	SAND	297d	C
		חול	SAND	297d	A
		רב	MUCH	913a	1 b
		שמח	JOYFUL	970d	1 b
4	34	בשר	FLESH	142c	1 b
5	1	גבול	BORDER	147d	1 a
		היה	BE	227c	3 5a
		חיים	LIFE	313b	1
		ממלכה	KINGDOM	575a	1
		מן	FROM	582b	5 d3
		מנחה	TRIBUTE	585a	2
		משל	RULE	605d	1
		נגש	APPROACH	621b	
		עבד	WORK	713a	3
		שלחן	TABLE	1020b	1
5	2	יום	DAY	400d	7 i
		כר	KOR	499d	
		סלת	FINE FLOUR	701c	
		קמח	FLOUR	887d	
5	3	אבס	FATTEN		7b
		איל	HART	19b	
		בקר	CATTLE	133c	2
		בקר	CATTLE	133c	2
		בריא	FAT	135d	
		ברברים	FATTENED FOWL	141b	
		יחמור	ROEBUCK	331c	
		מאה	HUNDRED	547d	1 a1
		עשר	TEN	796d	2 b
		עשרים	TWENTY	797d	1 1c
		צבי	GAZELLE	840b	
		רעי	PASTURE	945c	
5	4	עבר	REGION ACROSS	719d	2
		עבר	REGION ACROSS	719d	1 b
		עזה	GAZA	738b	
		תפסח	TIPHSAH	820c	
		רדה	HAVE DOMINION	922a	
5	5	באראשבע	BEERSHEBA	92a	1
		בטח	SECURITY	105b	
		גפן	VINE	172c	
		דן	DAN	193a	3
		ישראל	ISRAEL	975c	2 a2
		תאנה	FIG-TREE	1061a	1
5	6	אריה	MANGER	71d	
		היה	BE	227c	3 4d c
		סוס	HORSE	692c	2
		פרש	HORSEMAN	832b	
		ארבעים	FORTY	917b	1 a
		מרכב	CHARIOT	939c	1
5	7	דבר	WORD	183d	4 6
		חדש	NEW MOON	294c	2
		כול	SUSTAIN	465a	1
		נצב	STAND	662b	3
		עדר	BE LACKING	727c	
		קרב	APPROACHING	898b	1
5	8	ה	THE	207d	1 e
		סוס	HORSE	692c	2
		רכש	STEEDS	940d	
		שערה	BARLEY	972d	2
		משפט	JUDGEMNT	1049a	6 a
		תבן	STRAW	1062a	
5	9	תבונה	UNDERSTANDING	108b	3
		חול	SAND	297d	A
		חול	SAND	297d	2
		חכמה	WISDOM	315c	2
		ים	SEA	411a	8 a
		לב	HEART	524d	2 3a
		רבה	BECOME MANY	915d	1 e3
		רחב	WIDTH	931d	2
		שלמה	SOLOMON	1024d	
5	10	בן	SON	121b	1 jl
		בשר	FLESH	142c	1 b
		חכמה	WISDOM	315c	2
		חכמה	WISDOM	315c	3
		קדם	FRONT	869c	1 b
		רבה	BECOME MANY	915b	1 a1
		שלמה	SOLOMON	1024d	
5	11	הימן	HEMAN	54d	
		גוי	NATION	156d	1 c
		דרדע	DARDA	201c	
		אזרחי	EZRAHITE	280d	
		חכם	BE WISE	314c	
		איתן	ETHAN	451a	
		כלכל	CALCOL	465b	
		מחול	MAHOL	562d	
		סביב	ROUND ABOUT	687a	1 b
		אלף	THOUSAND	49a	1 b
5	12	דבר	SPEAK	181a	2
		חמש	FIVE	332b	5 f
		משל	PARABLE	605b	5
		שיר	SONG	1010b	1
		שלמה	SOLOMON	*1024d	
5	13	אזוב	HYSSOP	23c	
		ארז	CEDAR	72c	1 a
		בהמה	BEAST	97a	1
		דבר	SPEAK	181c	5
		דג	FISH	185c	
		ה	THE	207d	1 e
		יצא	GO OUT	423b	1 g
		לבנון	LEBANON	*526d	
		לבנון	LEBANON	527a	
		מן	FROM	582a	5 b
		עוף	FLY	733d	1
		על	UPON	754d	2 1f g
		קיר	WALL	885a	3
		רמש	CREEPING THINGS	943a	1
		שלמה	SOLOMON	*1024d	
5	14	את	WITH	86d	4 b
		בשר	FLESH	142c	1 b
		חכמה	WISDOM	315c	2
		שלמה	SOLOMON	1024d	
5	15	שמע	HEAR	1033c	1 a
		אהב	LOVE	13a	4 b
		חירם	HIRAM	27c	1
		היה	BE	227c	3 5a
		יום	DAY	400c	7 f
		ל	TO	513a	5 ad
		מלך	KING	573a	1
		משח	ANOINT	603b	2
		צידני	SIDONIANS	*851a	
		צר	TYER	862d	
5	16	חירם	HIRAM	27c	1
5	17	בנה	BUILD	124b	1 ab
		יהוה	YAHWEH	218d	2 1e
		כף	SOLE OF FOOT	496d	2
		סבב	SURROUND	686a	2 d
5	18	פנה	FACE	818c	2 6ca
		יהוה	YAHWEH	218d	2 1f
		נוח	REST	628c	A 1b 2
		מנוחה	REST	*630a	2
		פגע	OCCURRENCE	803c	
		רע	EVIL	948b	2
		שטן	ADVERSARY	966b	1
5	19	אמר	SAY	56b	2
		יהוה	YAHWEH	218d	2 1f
		כסא	THRONE	491a	3 a
5	20	אמר	SAY	56c	4
		ארז	CEDAR	72c	1 a
		ארז	CEDAR	72d	
		ידע	KNOW	394b	4 b
		כרת	HEW	503d	3
		ל	TO	517d	7 bc
		לבנון	LEBANON	527a	
		עץ	TREE	781d	1 c
		צוה	CHARGE	846a	2 d
		צידני	SIDONIANS	851a	
		שכר	HIRE	969a	1
5	21	חירם	HIRAM	27c	1
		ברך	BLESS	138c	2 a
		חכם	WISE	314d	2
5	22	חירם	HIRAM	27c	1
		ארז	CEDAR	72c	
		ברוש	CYPRESS	141c	3
		חפץ	DELIGHT	343b	2
		עץ	TREE	781d	1 c
		שלח	SEND	1018b	1 b
		שלמה	SOLOMON	1024d	
5	23	דברות	FLOATS	184a	
		חפץ	DELIGHT	343b	2
		ים	SEA	410d	1
		ירד	BRING DOWN	433d	1 a
		לבנון	LEBANON	527a	
		נשא	LIFT	671c	3 f
		רפסדה	RAFT	*952c	
		שום	TO PLACE	964c	5 a
		שלח	SEND	1018b	1 b
		נפץ	ADDENDA ET COR-RIGENDA	1125b	
5	24	חירם	HIRAM	27c	1
		ארז	CEDAR	72c	2
		ברוש	CYPRESS	141c	3
		היה	BE	227c	3 5a
		חפץ	DELIGHT	343b	2
		עץ	TREE	781d	1 c
5	25	חירם	HIRAM	27c	1
		מכלת	FOOD-STUFF	38c	
		חטה	WHEAT	334d	
		חטה	WHEAT	*334d	
		כה	THUS	462a	1
		כר	KOR	499d	
		כתית	BEATEN	510c	
		מכה	SLAUGHTER	647a	4
		שמן	OIL	1032b	2 b
5	26	חירם	HIRAM	27c	1
		בין	INTERVAL	107c	1 d
		ברית	COVENANT	136b	1 1
		חכמה	WISDOM	315c	2
		כרת	CUT	503d	4
		ל	TO	510d	5
		שלון	PEACE	1023b	6
5	27	מס	LABOUR-GANG	587a	1
		עלה	GO UP	749d	6
5	28	אדנירם	ADONIRAM	12a	
		אלף	THOUSAND	49a	1 c
		חדש	NEW MOON	294c	2 a
		חליפה	A CHANGE	322c	2
		לבנון	LEBANON	*527a	
		לבנון	LEBANON	527a	
		מס	LABOUR-GANG	587a	1
		שלח	SEND	1018b	1 a
5	29	חצב	HEW	345a	2 a
		סבל	BURDEN BEARER	688a	
		שאר	REMAIN	984b	1
5	30	ל	TO	513d	5 cb g
		מלאכה	WORK	522a	3 b
		מלאכה	WORK	522a	3 b
		נצב	STAND	662b	3
		על	UPON	755a	2 3
		רדה	HAVE DOMINION	922a	
		שר	CHIEFTAIN	978c	4 a
5	31	אבן	STONE	6c	1
		אבן	STONE	6c	2
		גזית	HEWING	159b	
		יסד	FOUND	414a	1
		יקר	PRECIOUS	430a	1 a

Ch	v.	Heb	Eng	Page	Sec
		נסע	PULL OUT	652c	2
5	32	חירם	HIRAM	27c	1
		בנה	BUILD	124b	1 ab
		בנה	BUILD	124c	1 e
		גבלי	GEBALITE	148c	
		כון	ESTABLISH	466b	2 a
		עץ	TREE	781d	1 c
		פסל	HEW	820a	
6	1	בנה	BUILD	124b	1 ab
		היכל	TEMPLE	228c	2 b
		זו	ZIV	264c	
		חדש	NEW MOON	294d	2 b1
		יצא	GO OUT	422d	1 a
		ירח	MONTH	437b	2
		מלך	BE KING	574a	
		רביעי	FOURTH	918a	2
		שלמה	SOLOMON	1024d	
		שמנים	EIGHTY	1033b	
6	2	אמה	CUBIT	52b	1
		ארך	LENGTH	73d	A
		בנה	BUILD	124b	1 ab
		היכל	TEMPLE	*228c	2 b
		היכל	TEMPLE	228c	2 b
		עשרים	TWENTY	797d	1 e
		קומה	HEIGHT	879b	3
		רחב	WIDTH	931d	
		רחב	WIDTH	931d	
		ששים	SIXTY	995d	
		שלמה	SOLOMON	1024d	
6	3	אמה	CUBIT	52b	1
		ארך	LENGTH	73d	A
		בית	HOUSE	109b	1 ae 0
		היכל	TEMPLE	228c	2 a
		עשר	TEN	796c	2 a
		פנה	FACE	818d	27 a d
		רחב	WIDTH	931d	
6	4	אטם	SHUT	32a	
		זו	ZIV	*264c	
		חלון	WINDOW	319d	
		שקוף	FRAME	1054d	
6	5	את	MARK OF THE ACCUSATIVE	85c	3 b
		בנה	BUILD	124b	1 ab
		דביר	HINDMOST CHAMBER	184b	
		היכל	TEMPLE	228c	2 b
		יציע	FLAT SURFACE	427a	
		סביב	ROUND ABOUT	687a	1 cb
		סביב	ROUND ABOUT	687a	1 cc
		על	UPON	752d	2 1
		צלע	RIB	854b	3
		קיר	WALL	885a	1 b
6	6	אחז	GRASP	*28b	
		אחז	GRASP	28b	
		אמה	CUBIT	52c	1
		מגרעה	RECESS	175d	
		חוץ	THE OUTSIDE	299d	1 a
		יציע	FLAT SURFACE	427a	
		נתן	PUT	680b	2 a
		צלע	RIB	854b	3
		קיר	WALL	885a	1 b
		רחב	WIDTH	931d	
		שבע	SEVEN	988a	1 a
		שש	SIX	995c	1 a
		תיכון	MIDDLE	1064a	
		תחתון	LOWER	1066b	
6	7	אבן	STONE	6c	2
		בנה	BUILD	125a	1 a
		ברזל	IRON	137c	1 d
		גרזן	AXE	173d	
		זהב	GOLD	263a	6
		כלי	INSTRUMENT	480a	2 c
		מסע	QUARRY	652d	
		מקבת	HAMMER	666c	
		שלם	COMPLETE	1024a	1 b
		שמע	HEAR	1034b	1
6	8	ימני	RIGHT	412b	
		יציע	FLAT SURFACE	427a	
		כתף	SIDE	509c	2 b
		לול	SHAFT	533b	
		על	UPON	757b	27 c ab
		פתח	OPENING	835d	
		תיכון	MIDDLE	1064a	
		תיכון	MIDDLE	*1064a	
		תחתון	LOWER	1066b	
6	9	ארז	CEDAR	72c	2
		גב	BEAM	155d	
		כלה	FINISH	478a	1 a
		שדרה	ROW	690c	
		ספן	COVER	706a	
6	10	אחז	GRASP	28b	
		אמה	CUBIT	52b	1
		ארז	CEDAR	72c	2
		בנה	BUILD	124b	1 ab
		יציע	FLAT SURFACE	427a	
6	11	דבר	WORD	182c	1 2a
6	12	אם	IF	49c	1 a1 a
		דבר	WORD	182d	1 2b
		הלך	WALK	234c	2 3a 1e
		חקה	SOMETHING PRESCRIBED	350a	2 d
		חקה	SOMETHING PRESCRIBED	350b	2 e
		מצוה	COMMANDMENT	846c	2 b2
		קום	STAND	879a	6 f
6	14	כלה	FINISH	478a	1 a
6	15	ארז	CEDAR	72c	2
		בית	HOUSE	110c	8 a
		בית	HOUSE	110c	8 a
		בנה	BUILD	124c	1 b
		ברוש	CYPRESS	141c	3
		ספן	CEILING	706a	
		צלע	RIB	854b	4
		צפה	LAY OUT	860a	
		צפה	LAY OUT	860b	
		קיר	WALL	885a	1 a
		קורה	RAFTER	900a	
		קרקע	FLOOR	903a	
6	16	ארז	CEDAR	72c	2
		בית	HOUSE	110c	8 a
		בנה	BUILD	124c	1 b
		בנה	BUILD	124c	1 d
		דביר	HINDMOST CHAMBER	184b	
		ירכה	EXTREME PARTS	438b	2
		צלע	RIB	854b	4
		קדש	APARTMENT	871d	2
		קיר	WALL	885a	1 a
		קרקע	FLOOR	903a	
6	17	היכל	TEMPLE	228c	2 b
		חר	NOBLE	359d	
		לפני	ANTERIOR	819b	
		ארבעים	FORTY	917b	1 a
6	18	ארז	CEDAR	72c	2
		כל	ALL	482d	2 ba
		על	UPON	752d	2 1
		פטר	SEPARATE	809d	2
		פנימה	WITHIN	819b	2
		פקעים	PEKAHIAH	825a	
		ציץ	BLOSSOM	847d	1
		מקלעת	CARVING	887c	
		ראה	TO SEE	908c	3
6	19	דביר	HINDMOST CHAMBER	184b	
		היכל	TEMPLE	*228c	2 b
		פנימה	WITHIN	819b	2
6	20	ארז	CEDAR	72c	2
		ארך	LENGTH	73d	A
		דביר	HINDMOST CHAMBER	184b	
		היכל	TEMPLE	*228c	2 b
		מזבח	ALTAR	258b	1
		מזבח	ALTAR	258d	4 b
		זהב	GOLD	263a	6
		זהב	GOLD	263d	2 c
		סגר	CLOSE	689b	4 b
		פנה	FACE	817d	24 d
		צפה	LAY OUT	860a	
		דביר	HINDMOST CHAMBER	184b	
6	21	זהב	GOLD	263a	6
		זהב	GOLD	263d	2 c
		סגר	CLOSE	689b	4 b
		עבר	PASS OVER	718c	2
		פנה	FACE	817d	24 d
		פנימה	WITHIN	819b	2
		פתוח	ENGRAVING	*836c	
		רתוק	CHAIN	958d	
		דביר	HINDMOST CHAMBER	184b	
6	22	מזבח	ALTAR	258d	4 b
		זהב	GOLD	263a	6
		זהב	GOLD	263d	2 c
		פתוח	ENGRAVING	*836c	
		תמן	BE FINISHED	1070b	1
		דביר	HINDMOST CHAMBER	184b	
6	23	כרוב	CHERUB	500d	5 a
		עץ	TREE	781d	2 a
		שמן	OIL	1032b	2 a
6	24	כנף	WING	489c	1 c
		כרוב	CHERUB	500d	5 a
		מן	FROM	581d	2 a
		קצה	END	892c	1
6	25	כרוב	CHERUB	500d	5 a
		מדה	SIZE	551c	2
		עשר	TEN	796d	2 a
		קצב	CUT	891d	1
		כן	SO	485d	1 a
		כרוב	CHERUB	500d	5 a
		עשר	TEN	796d	2 a
6	26	כרוב	CHERUB	500d	5 a
		עשר	TEN	796d	2 a
6	27	נגע	TOUCH	619a	1 a
		נגע	TOUCH	619a	1 a
		פנימי	INNER	819b	
		פרש	SPREAD OUT	831a	1
		קיר	WALL	885a	1 a
6	28	זהב	GOLD	263a	6
		זהב	GOLD	263d	2 c
		כרוב	CHERUB	500d	5 a
6	29	חיצון	OUTER	300b	1
		כרוב	CHERUB	500d	5 b
		מסב	THAT WHICH SURROUNDS	687b	1 b
		פטר	SEPARATE	809d	2
		פנימה	WITHIN	819b	2
		פתוח	ENGRAVING	836c	
		ציץ	BLOSSOM	847d	1
		קלע	CARVE	8870	
		מקלעת	CARVING	887c	
		תמרה	PALM-FIGURE	1071d	
6	30	בשר	FLESH	142c	1
		זהב	GOLD	263d	2 c
		חיצון	OUTER	300b	1
		כרוב	CHERUB	500d	5 b
		ל	TO	511d	2
		פנימה	WITHIN	819b	2
6	31	קרקע	FLOOR	903a	
		איל	PILASTER	18b	
		דביר	HINDMOST CHAMBER	184b	
		דלת	DOOR	*195a	1
		דלת	DOOR	195b	2
		מזוזה	DOOR-POST	265b	2 b
		חמישי	FIFTH	332d	3
		כרוב	CHERUB	500d	5 b
		עץ	TREE	781d	2 a
		פתח	OPENING	835d	
		שמן	OIL	1032b	2 a
6	32	דלת	DOOR	195b	2
		זהב	GOLD	263d	2 f
		זהב	GOLD	263d	2 g
		כרוב	CHERUB	500d	5 b
		עץ	TREE	781d	2 a
		פטר	SEPARATE	809d	2
		ציץ	BLOSSOM	847d	1
		צפה	LAY OUT	860b	
		קלע	CARVE	8870	
		מקלעת	CARVING	887c	
		רדד	BEAT OUT	921d	
		שמן	OIL	1032b	2 a
		תמרה	PALM-FIGURE	1071d	
6	33	את	WITH	87a	2
		היכל	TEMPLE	228c	2 b
		מזוזה	DOOR-POST	265b	2 b
		כן	SO	*486a	1 ca
		כרוב	CHERUB	500d	5 b
		עץ	TREE	781d	2 a
		פתח	OPENING	835d	
		רבע	SQUARED	*917c	
		רביעי	FOURTH	918a	2
		שמן	OIL	1032b	2 a
6	34	ברוש	CYPRESS	*141c	1
		ברוש	CYPRESS	141c	1
		דלת	DOOR	195a	1
		כרוב	CHERUB	500d	5 b
		צלע	RIB	854b	5
		קלע	CURTAIN	887c	
6	35	זהב	GOLD	263d	2 c
		חקה	CUT IN	348d	
		כרוב	CHERUB	500d	5 b
		פטר	SEPARATE	809d	2
		ציץ	BLOSSOM	847d	1
		צפה	LAY OUT	860b	
		קלע	CARVE	8870	
		תמרה	PALM-FIGURE	1071d	
6	36	ארז	CEDAR	72c	2
		בנה	BUILD	124b	1 ab
		בנה	BUILD	124c	1 b
		גזית	HEWING	159b	
		חצר	ENCLOSURE	347a	3 b
		טור	ROW	377a	1
		טור	ROW	377a	1
		כרת	HEW	503d	3
6	37	זו	ZIV	264c	
		חדש	NEW MOON	*294d	2 b1
		יסד	BE FOUNDED	414a	
		ירח	MONTH	437b	2
		רביעי	FOURTH	918a	2
6	38	בול	BUL	100d	
		דבר	WORD	183c	4 3
		חדש	NEW MOON	294d	2 b1
		ירח	MONTH	437b	2
		כלה	BE FINISHED	477c	1 b
		עשר	TEN	797a	1 b
		עשר	TEN	797c	
		שמיני	EIGHTH	1033b	
		שנה	YEAR	1040c	
		משפט	JUDGMENT	1049b	6 d
7	1	בנה	BUILD	124b	1 ab
		כלה	FINISH	478a	1 a
		עשר	TEN	797b	3 b
		שלש	THREE	1025d	1
7	2	ארז	CEDAR	72c	2
		בית	HOUSE	108d	1 ag
		בנה	BUILD	124b	1 ab
		יער	WOOD	420c	A
		כרת	HEW	503d	3
		לבנון	LEBANON	527b	
		מאה	HUNDRED	547d	1 a1
		עמוד	PILLAR	765b	1
7	3	ארז	CEDAR	72c	2
		חמש	FIVE	332b	5 e2
		ספן	COVER	706a	
		מעל	ABOVE	751c	1 a
		עמוד	PILLAR	765b	1
		צלע	RIB	854b	3
		ארבעים	FORTY	917c	2 a
7	4	מחזה	LIGHT	303d	
		טור	ROW	377a	1
		שקוף	FRAME	1054d	
7	5	מזוזה	DOOR-POST	265b	1
		מחזה	LIGHT	303d	
		מול	FRONT	557b	1
		פתח	OPENING	835d	
		רבע	SQUARED	917d	
		שקף	FRAME-WORK	1054d	
7	6	אולם	PORCH	17d	2
		עב	PROJECTING ROOF	712b	

Ch	v.	Heb	Eng	Page	Sec
		עמוד	PILLAR	765b	1
		פנה	FACE	818d	27 a d
7	7	רחב	WIDTH	931d	
		אולם	PORCH	17d	2
		ארז	CEDAR	72c	2
		ספן	COVER	706a	
		קורה	RAFTER	900a	
		קרקע	FLOOR	903a	
		שפט	JUDGE	1047c	1 b
		משפט	JUDGMENT	1048c	1 b
7	8	אולם	PORCH	17d	2
		אחר	ANOTHER	29c	
		בית	HOUSE	110c	8 b
		בת	DAUGHTER	123b	1 h
		ה	THE	209a	2 b
		היה	BECOME	226a	2 2c
		חצר	ENCLOSURE	346d	2
		מעשה	DEED	796a	2 a2
7	9	אבן	STONE	6c	2
		בית	HOUSE	110c	8 a
		גזית	HEWING	159b	
		גרר	DRAG	176a	
		מגרה	SAW	176b	
		חוץ	THE OUTSIDE	299d	1 bd
		חצר	ENCLOSURE	346d	2
		שפח	A SPAN	381c	2
		מסד	FOUNDATION	414c	
		יקר	PRECIOUS	430a	1 a
		מדה	SIZE	551c	2
7	10	אבן	STONE	6c	2
		יסד	BE FOUNDED	414a	
		יקר	PRECIOUS	430a	1 a
		שמנה	EIGHT	1032d	1 a
7	11	אבן	STONE	6c	2
		ארז	CEDAR	72c	2
		גזית	HEWING	159b	
		יקר	PRECIOUS	430a	1 a
		מדה	SIZE	551c	2
7	12	מעל	ABOVE	752a	2 d
		אולם	PORCH	17d	1
		ארז	CEDAR	72c	2
		בית	HOUSE	109a	1 ae 0
		גזית	HEWING	159b	
		ה	THE	209a	2 b
		חצר	ENCLOSURE	346d	2
		חצר	ENCLOSURE	347a	3 b
		טור	ROW	377a	1
		טור	ROW	377a	1
		כרת	HEW	503d	3
7	13	פנימי	INNER	819b	
		חירם	HIRAM	27c	2
		צר	TYER	862d	
7	14	אלמנה	WIDOW	48b	
		ב	IN	90c	3 6
		תבונה	UNDERSTANDING	108b	3
		ה	THE	208b	1 ha
		ה	THE	*208c	1 hb
		חכמה	WISDOM	315b	1
		חרש	CUT IN	360c	1
		דעת	SKILL	395c	1 b
		מלאכה	WORK	522b	4
		מלא	BE FULL	570c	1
		נחשת	COPPER	638d	1
		נחשת	COPPER	638d	1
		מטה	TRIBE	641d	3
		עשה	DO	794a	1 1b
		נפתלי	NAPHTALI	836d	2 a
		צרי	TYRIAN	863a	
7	15	אמה	CUBIT	52b	1
		חוט	THREAD	296c	3
		נחשת	COPPER	638d	1
		סבב	SURROUND	686a	2 d
		עמוד	PILLAR	765b	2
		עמוד	PILLAR	765b	2
		צור	FASHION	849b	
		שמנה	EIGHT	1033a	2 a
7	16	יצק	BE POURED	427c	2
		כתרת	CAPITAL	509d	
		ראש	HEAD	910d	2 a
7	17	מעשה	DEED	796a	2 a1
		ראש	HEAD	910d	2 a
		שבע	SEVEN	988a	1 b
		שרשרה	CHAIN	1057c	
		שבכה	ADDENDA ET COR-RIGENDA	1126d	
7	18	טור	ROW	377a	2
		כן	SO	*486a	1 ca
		כסה	COVER	491d	4
		רמון	POMEGRANATE	941d	3
		שבכה	LATTICE-WORK	959a	1
7	19	אולם	PORCH	17d	1
		מעשה	DEED	796a	2 a1
		שושן	LILY	1004c	
7	20	בטן	BELLY	106a	4
		טור	ROW	377a	2
		מאה	HUNDRED	548a	1 b3
		עבר	REGION ACROSS	719a	2
		מעל	ABOVE	751c	2 a
		עמה	CLOSE BY	769d	E
		רמון	POMEGRANATE	941d	3
		שבכה	LATTICE-WORK	959a	1
7	21	אולם	PORCH	17d	1
		בעז	BOAZ	*127a	2
		בעז	BOAZ	127a	2
		היכל	TEMPLE	228c	2 b
		ימני	RIGHT	412b	
		יכין	JACHIN	467c	2
		קום	STAND	878d	2 a
		שמאלי	LEFT	970a	
		שמאלי	LEFT	970a	
7	22	שושן	LILY	1004c	
		תמם	BE FINISHED	1070b	1
7	23	אמה	CUBIT	52c	1
		חוט	THREAD	*296c	3
		חמש	FIVE	331d	1 a
		ים	SEA	411a	7
		יצק	BE POURED	427c	2
		מן	FROM	581d	5 a
		סבב	SURROUND	686a	2 d
		עגל	ROUND	722c	
		עשר	TEN	796d	2 a
		קו	LINE	876a	
		קוה	CORNER	876a	
		שפה	SPEECH	974a	3
7	24	בקר	CATTLE	*133c	2
		טור	ROW	377a	2
		טור	ROW	*377a	2
		ים	SEA	411a	7
		יצק	CAST	427b	2
		יצקה	CASTING	427c	
		נקף	GO AROUND	669a	1 b
		סבב	SURROUND	686a	2 d
		עשר	TEN	796d	2 a
		פקעים	GOURDS	825a	
7	25	אחור	HINDER PART	30d	
		בית	HOUSE	110b	7
		בקר	CATTLE	133c	2
		מזרח	PLACE OF SUNRISE	281a	2 c1
		ים	SEA	411a	7
		ים	SEA	411b	9
		נגב	SOUTH-COUNTRY	616b	2
		מעל	ABOVE	752a	2 d
		פנה	TURN	815b	2 b
7	26	בת	BATH	144c	
		שפח	A SPAN	381c	1
		כול	CONTAIN	465b	1
		כוס	CUP	468a	
		עבי	THICKNESS	716a	
		פרח	BUD	827b	
		שושן	LILY	1004c	
7	27	מכונה	BASE	467d	
		עשר	TEN	796d	2 a
		ארבע	FOUR	*916d	1 a1
		רחב	WIDTH	931d	
		שלש	THREE	1025d	1 a
7	28	מסגרת	BORDER	689d	1
		שלב	BE BOUND	1016d	
		שלבים	JOININGS OF BASES	1016d	
7	29	ארי	LION	71d	
		בקר	CATTLE	133b	1 a
		מורד	DESCENT	434c	2
		כן	BASE	487c	1
		כרוב	CHERUB	501a	5 b
		ליה	WREATH	531b	
		מסגרת	BORDER	689d	1
		מעל	ABOVE	751c	1 a
		שלב	BE BOUND	1016d	
		שלבים	JOININGS OF BASES	1016d	
7	30	איש	MAN	36a	
		אופן	WHEEL	66c	C
		יצק	CAST	427b	2
		כיור	POT	468c	2
		כרוב	CHERUB	501a	5 b
		כתף	SUPPORT	509c	3
		ליה	WREATH	531b	
		סרן	AXLE	710d	
		עבר	REGION ACROSS	719d	2
		פנה	CORNER	819c	1 a
		פעם	FOOT	822a	1 c
7	31	אמה	CUBIT	52c	1
		בית	HOUSE	110c	8 b
		כן	BASE	487c	1
		כרוב	CHERUB	501a	5 b
		מסגרת	BORDER	689d	1
		עגל	ROUND	722c	
		מעל	ABOVE	751d	2 ba
		פה	MOUTH	805b	4
		מקלעת	CARVING	887c	
		רבע	SQUARED	917d	
7	32	אופן	WHEEL	66c	C
		יד	AXEL-TREES	390c	4 d
		כרוב	CHERUB	501a	5 b
		מן	FROM	583d	9 b1
		מסגרת	BORDER	689d	1
		ארבע	FOUR	917a	1 c1
		תחת	UNDERNEATH	1066b	3 2c
7	33	אופן	WHEEL	66c	C
		אופן	WHEEL	66d	A
		גב	BACK	146c	6
		חשוק	SPOKE OF A WHEEL	366b	
		חשור	NAVE	366b	
		יד	AXEL-TREES	390c	4 d
		יצק	BE POURED	427c	2
		כל	ALL	*482d	2 ba
		כרוב	CHERUB	501a	5 b
7	34	כרוב	CHERUB	501a	5 b
		כתף	SUPPORT	509c	3
		פנה	CORNER	819c	1 a
		פעם	FOOT	822a	1 c
7	35	יד	STAYS	390c	4 e
		כן	BASE	487c	1
		כרוב	CHERUB	501a	5 b
		מסגרת	BORDER	689d	1
		עגל	ROUND	722c	
7	36	ראש	HEAD	910d	2 a
		איש	MAN	36a	
		ארי	LION	71d	
		יד	STAYS	390c	4 e
		כרוב	CHERUB	501a	5 b
		ליה	WREATH	531b	
		לוח	BOARD	532a	3
		מסגרת	BORDER	689d	1
		מערה	BARE PLACE	789a	1
		פתח	ENGRAVE	836c	
		תמרה	PALM-FIGURE	1071d	
7	37	זה	THIS	262a	6 d
		מוצק	CASTING	427c	
		מדה	SIZE	551c	2
		קצב	CUT	891d	1
7	38	בת	BATH	144c	
		כול	CONTAIN	465b	1
		כיור	POT	468c	3 b
		ארבע	FOUR	*916d	1 a1
		ארבעים	FORTY	917b	1 a
		חמש	FIVE	331d	1 a
7	39	ימין	RIGHT HAND	411d	2 a
		ימני	RIGHT	412b	
		כתף	SIDE	509c	2 b
		מול	IN FRONT OF	557c	2 bb
		נגב	SOUTH-COUNTRY	616b	2
		נתן	PUT	680c	2 a
		קדם	EASTWARD	870a	
7	40	חירם	HIRAM	27c	2
		בית	HOUSE	109a	1 ae 0
		מזרק	BOWL	284d	2 a
		יע	SHOVEL	418b	
		כיור	POT	*468c	3 b
		סיר	POT	696c	2
7	41	כסה	COVER	491d	4
		שבכה	LATTICE-WORK	959a	1
7	42	טור	ROW	377a	2
		כסה	COVER	491d	4
		מאה	HUNDRED	548b	1 c4
		רמון	POMEGRANATE	941d	3
		שבכה	LATTICE-WORK	959a	1
7	43	כיור	POT	468c	3 b
		עשר	TEN	796d	2 b
		עשר	TEN	796d	2 a
7	44	בקר	CATTLE	133c	2
7	45	חירם	HIRAM	27c	2
		בית	HOUSE	109a	1 ae 0
		מזרק	BOWL	284d	2 a
		יע	SHOVEL	418b	
		כיור	POT	*468c	3 b
		כלי	UTENSIL	480a	2 f
		מרט	POLISH	599a	
		מרק	POLISH	*599d	
		נחשת	COPPER	638d	1
		סיר	POT	696c	2
7	46	אדמה	EARTH	9d	3
		יצק	CAST	427b	2
		ירדן	JORDAN	434d	
		ככר	ROUND	503b	1
		סכות	SUCCOTH	697d	1
		מעבה	THICKNESS	716b	
		מעברה	FORD	721b	1
		צרתן	ZERETHAN	866c	
7	47	חקר	SEARCH	350d	
		כלי	UTENSIL	480a	2 f
		מאד	EXCEEDINGLY	547b	2 f
		מאד	EXCEEDINGLY	547c	2 d
		נוח	REST	629a	B 2
		רב	MULTITUDE	914a	
		משקל	WEIGHT	1054a	
7	48	מזבח	ALTAR	258d	4 b
		זהב	GOLD	263a	6
		זהב	GOLD	263c	2 a
		כלי	UTENSIL	480a	2 f
		לחם	FOOD	537b	1 a
		שלחן	TABLE	1020b	3
7	49	דביר	HINDMOST CHAM-BER	184b	
		זהב	GOLD	*263c	2 a
		חמש	FIVE	331d	1 a
		ימין	RIGHT HAND	411d	2 a
		מלקחים	TONGS	544c	2
		נר	LAMP	632d	
		מנורה	LAMPSTAND	633a	2
		סגר	CLOSE	689b	4 b
		פנה	FACE	817d	2 4d
		פרח	BUD	827b	
7	50	דלת	DOOR	195a	1
		דלת	DOOR	195b	2
		היכל	TEMPLE	228c	2 b
		זהב	GOLD	*263c	2 a
		מזמרת	SNUFFERS	275a	
		מזרק	BOWL	284d	2 c
		מחתה	FIRE-HOLDER	367b	2
		פן	PAN	497a	4 b
		סגר	CLOSE	689b	4 b
		סף	BASIN	706b	
		פת	SOCKETS	834a	
7	51	קדש	APARTNESS	871d	2 d
		אוצר	TREASURE	70a	3 a
		בית	HOUSE	109a	1 ae 0
		זהב	GOLD	263c	1
		נתן	PUT	680b	2 a

Ch	v.	Heb	Eng	Page	Sec
		קדש	APARTNESS	872a	3 c
		שלם	BE COMPLETE	1022b	1
8	1	אב	FATHER	3c	2
		אז	THEN	23a	1 a
		דוד	DAVID	188a	A
		זקן	OLD	278d	2 b
		מטה	TRIBE	641d	3
		נשיא	PRINCE	672b	5
		עלה	GO UP	749c	4
		ציון	ZION	851b	
		קהל	ASSEMBLE AS	875a	2
8	2	חג	FESTIVAL-GATHERING	291a	1 b2
		חדש	NEW MOON	294d	2 b1
		ירח	MONTH	437b	2
		איתן	EVER-FLOWING	450d	1
		קהל	ASSEMBLE AS	875a	2
8	3	זקן	OLD	278d	2 b
		כהן	PRIEST	463b	4
		לוי	LEVITE	*532d	3 1a
8	4	אהל	TENT	14b	3
		מועד	TENT OF MEETING	418a	5
		כהן	PRIEST	*463d	5
		כלי	UTENSIL	480a	2 f
		לוי	LEVITE	532d	3 1a
8	5	בקר	CATTLE	133b	1 a
		זבח	SLAUGHTER FOR SACRIFICE	257a	1
		זבח	SLAUGHTER FOR SACRIFICE	257b	2
		מנה	COUNT	284a	1
		יעד	GATHER BY APPOINTMENT	417a	3
		עדה	CONGREGATION	417b	3
		ספר	COUNT	708a	1
		על	UPON	757c	2 7c aa
		רב	MULTITUDE	914a	1
8	6	אל	TO	40d	9
		דביר	HINDMOST CHAMBER	184b	
		כהן	PRIEST	463b	4
		כרוב	CHERUB	500d	5 a
		עזב	LEAVE	737a	1 a
		קדש	APARTNESS	871d	2 d
		תחת	UNDERNEATH	1066a	3 1a
8	7	בד	PART	94d	3 c
		כרוב	CHERUB	500d	5 a
		סכך	OVERSHADOW	697a	1
		מעל	ABOVE	752a	2 d
		פרש	SPREAD OUT	831a	1
		מקום	STANDING PLACE	879d	1 a
8	8	ארך	BE LONG	73d	2
		בד	PART	94d	3 c
		דביר	HINDMOST CHAMBER	184b	
		חוץ	THE OUTSIDE	299d	1 a
		פנה	FACE	818a	27a d
		ראה	TO SEE	908c	3
		ראש	HEAD	911a	2 a
8	9	אשר	PARTICLE OF RELATION	82c	4 bb
		חרב	HOREB	352a	
		יצא	GO OUT	422a	1 h
		כרת	CUT	503d	4
		לוח	TABLET	531d	1
		לוח	TABLET	*531d	1
		נוח	REST	628d	B 1
		רק	ONLY	956c	2 d
8	10	היה	COME TO PASS	224d	1 2a 1b
		כהן	PRIEST	463b	4
		מלא	FILL	570b	3
		ענן	CLOUD	778a	1 a
		קדש	APARTNESS	871d	2 d
8	11	כבוד	GLORY	458d	2 c1
		כהן	PRIEST	463b	4
		מלא	FILL	570b	3
		עמד	STAND	763d	1 a
		ענן	CLOUD	778a	1 a
		פנה	FACE	818c	2 6c a
		פנה	FACE	818c	2 6c b
		שרת	SERVE	1058a	2 a
8	12	ערפל	CLOUD	791d	2
		שכן	SETTLE DOWN	1015b	2 c
8	13	זבל	ELEVATION	259c	
		ישב	DWELL	443a	3
		מכון	FIXED PLACE	467c	1
		עולם	LONG DURATION	763a	21
8	14	ברך	BLESS	139a	3
		סבב	TURN ABOUT	686c	1 a
		קהל	ASSEMBLY	874d	2 a
8	15	את	WITH	86a	1 db
		ברך	BLESS	138c	2
		דבר	SPEAK	181b	3 d
		מלא	FILL	570d	3
		פה	MOUTH	805b	2 c
8	16	בחר	CHOOSE	104a	1 a
		בחר	CHOOSE	104a	1 a
		בנה	BUILD	124b	1 ab
		יצא	CAUSE TO GO	424c	1 ab
8	17	היה	BE	227b	3 4d a
		לבב	HEART	523c	22
		עם	WITH	768c	4 a
		שמנה	EIGHT	1033a	1 e
8	18	היה	BE	227b	3 4d a
		טוב	PLEASING	373c	
		לבב	HEART	523c	22
		עם	WITH	768c	4 a
		יען	ON ACCOUNT OF	774d	2 a
8	19	חלץ	LOINS	323b	1
		יצא	GO OUT	423c	1 h
		כיאם	BUT	*475a	2 b
		כיאם	BUT	*475a	2 b
		רק	ONLY	956c	2 b
8	20	דבר	WORD	182d	1 2b
		כסא	THRONE	491a	3 a
		קום	STAND	878a	4
		תחת	INSTEAD	1065d	2 2b a
8	21	יצא	CAUSE TO GO	424c	1 a
		כרת	CUT	503d	4
		שום	TO PLACE	963d	3 b
8	22	מזבח	ALTAR	259a	1
		עמד	STAND	763d	1 a
		פרש	SPREAD OUT	831b	1
8	23	קהל	ASSEMBLY	874d	2 a
		שמי	HEAVENS	1030a	1 b
		ברית	COVENANT	137b	3 2
		הלך	WALK	234a	2 3c
		חסד	GOODNESS	339a	2 1e
		לב	HEART	524c	22
		עבד	SLAVE	714a	3
		מעל	ABOVE	751c	1 a
		תחת	UNDENEATH	*1065b	1
8	24	דבר	SPEAK	181b	3 c
		דוד	DAVID	188a	
		יום	DAY	400d	7 h
		מלא	FILL	570d	3
		קרא	CALL	845b	2 c
8	25	דבר	SPEAK	181b	3 c
		דוד	DAVID	188a	
		דרך	WAY	203c	6 a
		הלך	WALK	234d	2 3c
		תורה	LAW	*436b	2 b2
		כסא	THRONE	491a	3 a
		כרת	BE CUT OFF	504b	4
		ל	TO	512c	5 aa
		פנה	FACE	818a	2 5a d
		קרא	CALL	845b	2 c
		רק	ONLY	956d	2 f
8	26	אמן	CONFIRM	53a	4
		דבר	SPEAK	181b	3 c
		דוד	DAVID	188a	
		קרא	CALL	845b	2 c
8	27	אמנם	VERILY	53d	
		אף	ALSO	65b	3
		ישב	DWELL	443a	3
		כול	CONTAIN	465a	2
		שמי	HEAVENS	1030b	2 a
8	28	יהוה	YAHWEH	219a	2 1f
		תחנה	FAVOR	337c	2
		פלל	INTERVENE	813b	3
		תפלה	PRAYER	813c	1 e
		תפלה	PRAYER	813c	1 b
		תפלה	PRAYER	813c	1 e
		פנה	TURN	815c	2 c1
		רנה	RINGING CRY	943c	1
		שמע	HEAR	1034b	2 f
8	29	אל	TO	39d	3 a
		אמר	SAY	56a	1
		יום	DAY	398b	1
		לילה	NIGHT	539a	1
		עין	EYE	744b	1 j
		פלל	INTERVENE	813b	3
		תפלה	PRAYER	813c	1 e
		תפלה	PRAYER	813c	1 b
		פתח	OPEN	835b	
		מקום	STANDING PLACE	880b	4
		יום	ADDENDA ET CORRIGENDA	1124a	
8	30	אל	TO	39d	3 a
		תחנה	FAVOR	337c	2
		תחנון	SUPPLICATION FOR FAVOR	*337d	2
		ישב	DWELL	443a	3
		סלח	FORGIVE	699b	
		פלל	INTERVENE	813b	3
		מקום	STANDING PLACE	880a	2 b2
		מקום	STANDING PLACE	880b	4
		שמי	HEAVENS	1030a	2 a
		שמע	HEAR	1034b	2 c
8	31	אלה	SWEAR	46d	1
		אלה	SWEAR	46d	1
		אלה	OATH	46d	1
		אשר	THAT	83d	8 d
		את	MARK OF THE ACCUSATIVE	85b	1 c
		חטא	MISS A GOAL OR WAY	306d	2 a
		נשא	LIFT	670a	1 a
		נשא	LIFT	670a	1 b 6
		נשא	BE A CREDITOR	673d	
		רע	FRIEND	946a	2
8	32	ב	IN	89b	2 4b
		דרך	WAY	203d	6 d
		ו	AND	254d	5 cb
		ל	LIKE	454a	1 b
		נתן	PUT	680d	2 b
		עשה	DO	794b	14
		צדקה	RIGHTEOUSNESS	842b	3
		צדק	DECLARE RIGHTEOUS	842d	2
		צדיק	JUST	843a	2
		רשע	WICKED	957b	1
		רשע	BE WICKED	957d	2
		שמי	HEAVENS	1030a	2 a
		שמע	HEAR	1034b	2 c
		שפט	JUDGE	1047c	2 a
8	33	אשר	THAT	83d	8 d
		חטא	MISS A GOAL OR WAY	307a	2 b
		חנן	SHOW FAVOR	336b	2
		ידה	CONFESS	392c	2 a
		כי	BECAUSE	*473c	3 a
		נגף	STRIKE	620a	
		פלל	INTERVENE	813b	3
		שוב	TURN BACK	997d	6 c
		שם	NAME	1028c	3
8	34	אדמה	LAND	10a	5
		חטאת	SIN	309a	1 d2
		סלח	FORGIVE	699b	
		פה	MOUTH	805b	2 c
		שוב	TURN BACK	998d	1 a
8	35	ה	THE	208d	1 i
		חטא	MISS A GOAL OR WAY	307a	2 b
		חטאת	SIN	308d	1 c
		ידה	CONFESS	392c	2 a
		כי	BECAUSE	473c	3 a
		מטר	RAIN	564d	
		עצר	RESTRAIN	783d	
		פלל	INTERVENE	813b	3
		מקום	STANDING PLACE	880b	4
		שוב	TURN BACK	997d	6 e
		שם	NAME	1028c	3
8	36	דרך	WAY	203c	6 c
		הלך	WALK	234c	2 3a 1a
		חטא	SIN	309a	1 d2
		טוב	PLEASANT	374d	0 a
		ירה	DIRECT	435c	5 c
		כי	BECAUSE	473c	3 a
		מטר	RAIN	564d	
		נתן	GIVE	678d	1 d
		סלח	FORGIVE	699b	
8	37	דבר	PESTILENCE	184a	1
		מחלה	SICKNESS	318b	
		חסיל	LOCUST	340c	
		ירקון	RUST	439a	1
		כי	IF	473b	2 b
		כל	ALL	482a	1 eb
		נגע	STROKE	619c	2
		צרר	BIND	864d	B
		ארבה	LOCUST	916a	
		שדפון	SMUT	995b	
		שער	GATE	1045a	2 c
8	38	אל	TO	39d	3 a
		תחנה	FAVOR	337c	2
		כף	HOLLOW OF THE HAND	496c	1 d4
		לבב	HEART	524b	2 9b
		נגע	STROKE	619c	2
		תפלה	PRAYER	813c	1 a
		פרש	SPREAD OUT	831b	1
8	39	דרך	WAY	203c	6 a
		ידע	KNOW	394a	2
		ישב	DWELL	443a	3
		מכון	FIXED PLACE	467d	22
		לבב	HEART	523c	22
		נתן	GIVE	679d	1 v
		סלח	FORGIVE	699b	
		עשה	DO	794b	14
8	40	אדמה	LAND	10a	5
		חי	ALIVE	312a	1 b
		יום	DAY	399a	4 a
		יום	DAY	399b	4 a
		ירא	FEAR	431c	3 b
8	41	אשר	PARTICLE OF RELATION	82b	2 b
		הוא	HE, SHE, IT	216b	3 c
		נכרי	FOREIGN	648d	1 b
		מען	PURPOSE	775a	1 a
		רחק	DISTANT	935b	1 a
		שם	NAME	1028b	3
8	42	גדול	GREAT	153b	6 c
		זרוע	ARM	284a	1 c
		חזק	STRONG	305c	1 b
		פלל	INTERVENE	813b	3
8	43	ירא	FEAR	431c	3 b
		ישב	DWELL	443a	3
		מכון	FIXED PLACE	467d	1
		נכרי	FOREIGN	648d	1 b
		קרא	CALL	896b	2 d4
8	44	בחר	CHOOSE	104a	1 a
		דרך	WAY	203b	3
		מלחמה	WAR	536c	
		פלל	INTERVENE	813b	3
8	45	תחנה	FAVOR	337c	2
		עשה	DO	794a	1 1a 6
		תפלה	PRAYER	813c	1 e
		שמע	HEAR	1034a	2 a
8	46	אדם	MAN	9b	2
		אנף	BE ANGRY	60a	
		חטא	MISS A GOAL OR WAY	307a	2 b
		חטא	MISS A GOAL OR WAY	307a	2 b
		קרב	NEAR	898b	1
		רחק	DISTANT	935b	1 a
		שבה	TAKE CAPTIVE	985c	1 c
8	47	ו	AND	252a	1

Ch v.	Heb	Eng	Page	Sec
10 2	שמע	REPORT	1034d	
	אבן	STONE	6d	3
	ב	IN	89b	3 1a
	בשם	SPICE	141d	1
	דבר	SPEAK	*181c	3 e
	היה	BE	227b	3 4d a
	זהב	GOLD	262d	5
	חיל	STRENGTH	299a	4
	יקר	PRECIOUS	430a	1 c
	כבד	MASSIVE	458b	2 b
	לבב	HEART	523c	2 2
	עם	WITH	768c	4 a
	רב	MUCH	913a	1 a1
	רב	MULTITUDE	914a	1
	שלמה	SOLOMON	1024d	
10 3	דבר	WORD	183d	4 6
	נגד	BE CONSPICUOUS	616d	2
	עלם	CONCEAL	761a	1
	שלמה	SOLOMON	1024d	
10 4	חכמה	WISDOM	315c	2
	מלכה	QUEEN	573c	
	שבא	SHEBA	985a	
	שלמה	SOLOMON	1024b	
10 5	מאכל	FOOD	38b	
	מושב	SEAT	444b	1 b
	מלבוש	RAIMENT	528b	
	עוד	STILL	729a	1 ab
	עלה	WHOLE BURNT OFFERING	750d	
	עליה	ROOF-CHAMBER	*751a	
	ממעמד	OFFICE	765b	3
	רוח	BREATH	925a	3 a
	שלחן	TABLE	1020b	1
	משקה	CUP-BEARER	1052d	
	שרת	SERVE	1058a	1 a
10 6	אמת	FIRMNESS	54b	4 a
	דבר	WORD	182b	1 1c
	היה	BE	227a	4 a
	חכמה	WISDOM	315c	2
	על	UPON	754d	2 1f g
10 7	אל	TO	40b	5
	אמן	CONFIRM	53a	2 b
	ו	AND	252d	1 e
	חכמה	WISDOM	315c	2
	טוב	A GOOD THING	375a	1
	יסף	ADD	415a	1
	נגד	BE CONSPICUOUS	617a	
	עד	UNTIL	724d	2 1a a
	שמועה	REPORT	1035b	1
10 8	אלה	THESE	41c	A
	אשר	HAPPINESS	80d	
	חכמה	WISDOM	315c	2
	תמיד	CONTINUITY	556b	1 a
	פנה	FACE	816c	2 2a
10 9	אהב	LOVE	13a	5 b
	ברך	BLESS	138c	2 a
	חפץ	DELIGHT IN	342d	2 a
	כסא	THRONE	491b	3 a
	כסא	THRONE	491b	3 a
	מלך	KING	573c	5 c
	עולם	LONG DURATION	762b	2 c
	צדקה	RIGHTEOUSNESS	842a	1 a
10 10	בשם	SPICE	141d	1
	בשם	SPICE	141d	1
	זהב	GOLD	262d	5
	יקר	PRECIOUS	430a	1 c
	מאד	EXCEEDINGLY	547b	2 a
	מלכה	QUEEN	573c	
	רב	MULTITUDE	*914a	1
	רב	MULTITUDE	914a	1
	רבה	BECOME MANY	915d	1 e3
	שבא	SHEBA	985a	
10 11	אופיר	OPHIR	20d	2
	חירם	HIRAM	27c	1
	אלמגים	A TREE	38d	
	אני	SHIPS	58b	
	זהב	GOLD	262c	1
	זהב	GOLD	263b	7
	יקר	PRECIOUS	430a	1 c
	רבה	BECOME MANY	915d	1 e3
10 12	אלמגים	A TREE	38d	
	בית	HOUSE	109a	1 ae 1
	כן	SO	485d	1 a
	כנור	LYRE	490a	
	נבל	HARP	614c	
	מסעד	SUPPORT	703c	
	ראה	TO SEE	908c	2 a
	שיר	SING	1010d	
10 13	בד	SEPARATION	94d	1 e
	הלך	WALK	231b	1 d3 gd
	חפץ	DELIGHT	343b	2
	יד	HAND	391d	5 e
	מלכה	QUEEN	573c	
	מלך	KING	573c	5 d
	פנה	TURN	815b	1 c
	שבא	SHEBA	985a	
10 14	בוא	COME	98b	1 j
	מאה	HUNDRED	548b	2 a1
	משקל	WEIGHT	1054a	
10 15	מסחר	MERCHANDISE	695c	
	ערב	MIXTURE	786b	
	ערב	STEPPE-DWELLERS	787b	
	פחה	GOVERNOR	808d	
	רכל	GO ABOUT	940b	
	תור	EXPLORE	1064c	3
10 16	זהב	GOLD	263b	9 a

Ch v.	Heb	Eng	Page	Sec
	זהב	GOLD	263b	8
	זהב	GOLD	263c	2 a
	מאה	HUNDRED	548a	1 b1
	עלה	GO UP	749d	4
	על	UPON	756d	2 7b
	צנה	LARGE SHIELD	857a	
	שחט	SLAUGHTER	1006b	4
10 17	מגן	SHIELD	171c	
	זהב	GOLD	263b	8
	זהב	GOLD	263b	9 b
	יער	WOOD	420c	A
	לבנון	LEBANON	527b	
	מנה	MANEH	584b	
	עלה	GO UP	749d	4
	על	UPON	756d	2 7b
	צנה	LARGE SHIELD	857a	
	שחט	SLAUGHTER	1006b	4
10 18	אופז	UPHAZ	20c	
	זהב	GOLD	263b	8
	זהב	GOLD	263d	2 c
	פז	BE REFINED	808a	
	צפה	LAY OUT	860a	
	שן	IVORY	1042b	2
	אופז	ADDENDA ET CORRIGENDA	1119d	
10 19	אחר	BEHIND	30b	4 ab
	ארי	LION	71c	
	זה	THIS	262a	6 e
	יד	STAYS	390c	4 e
	שבת	SEAT	443d	
	עגל	ROUND	722c	
	מעלה	STEP	752b	1
	מקום	STANDING PLACE	880a	4
	ראש	HEAD	910d	2 a
10 20	ארי	LION	71d	
	זה	THIS	262a	6 e
	כן	SO	485d	1 a
	ממלכה	KINGDOM	575a	1
	מעלה	STEP	752b	1
	עשה	DO	795b	2 a
10 21	חשב	THINK	363c	2
	יער	WOOD	420c	A
	כלי	UTENSIL	480a	2 f
	כלי	VESSEL	480b	3
	כסף	SILVER	494b	3
	לא	NOT	519b	1 bc
	לבנון	LEBANON	527b	
	סגר	CLOSE	689b	4 b
	משקה	DRINK	1052d	2
10 22	אופיר	OPHIR	20d	2
	חירם	HIRAM	27c	1
	אני	SHIPS	58b	
	אניה	A SHIP	58c	
	זהב	GOLD	263c	1
	כסף	SILVER	494b	5
	ל	TO	516b	5 ja
	קוף	APE	880c	
	שנהבים	IVORY	1042b	
	תכיים	PEACOCKS	1067a	
	תרשיש	TARSHISH	1077a	1
10 23	גדל	BECOME GREAT	152b	2 e
	חכמה	WISDOM	315c	2
	ל	TO	514c	5 fb
10 24	ארץ	EARTH	76a	1 c
	בקש	SEEK	134d	3 a
	חכמה	WISDOM	315c	2
	לב	HEART	524d	2 3b
	נתן	PUT	680c	2 b
	פחה	GOVERNOR	808d	
10 25	בשם	SPICE	141d	1
	דבר	WORD	183c	4 1
	זהב	GOLD	263a	6
	חרב	SWORD	352d	1 f
	מנחה	GIFT	585a	1
	נשק	EQUIPMENT	676d	1
	סוס	HORSE	692c	2
	פרד	MULE	825d	
	שלמה	GARMENT	971b	
10 26	אסף	GATHER	62b	1 c
	אריה	MANGER	71d	
	היה	BECOME	226c	2 2h
	נוח	REST	628d	B 1
	נחה	LEAD	635a	
	עיר	CITY	746c	1 e
	פרש	HORSEMAN	832a	
	רכם	CHARIOT	939b	1
10 27	אבן	STONE	7a	8
	ארז	CEDAR	72d	2
	כסף	SILVER	494b	3
	נתן	GIVE	681a	3 c
	שפלל	LOWLAND	1050d	1
	שקמה	SYCOMORE TREE	1054b	
10 28	אשר	PARTICLE OF RELATION	83a	7 b
	מוצא	GOING FORTH	425d	2 b
	מחיר	PRICE	564b	1
	מצרים	EGYPTIANS	596a	2 b
	סוס	HORSE	692c	2
	סחר	GO AROUND	695c	2
	מקוה	COLLECTION	876c	
10 29	ארם	ARAM	74c	C
	חתי	HITTITE	366d	2 b
	יצא	BRING OUT	424d	3
	כן	SO	485d	1 a
	סוס	HORSE	692c	2
	מרכבה	CHARIOT	939d	

Ch v.	Heb	Eng	Page	Sec
11 1	אדמי	EDOMITE	10c	
	אהב	LOVE	12d	1
	אשה	WOMAN	61b	1
	את	MARK OF THE ACCUSATIVE	85c	3 b
	בת	DAUGHTER	123b	1 h
	ו	AND	252b	1 a
	חתי	HITTITE	366d	1
	מואבי	MOABITISH	556a	
	נכרי	FOREIGN	648d	1 a
	עמוני	AMMONITE	770a	
	רב	MUCH	913a	1 b
11 2	אהב	LOVE	12d	1
	אכן	SURELY	38c	A
	אשר	PARTICLE OF RELATION	82d	4 d
	ב	IN	88c	1 4
	דבק	CLING	179d	2 a
	ל	TO	517b	7 ba
	לבב	HEART	523c	2 2
	נטה	INCLINE	640d	3 c
11 3	היה	BECOME	226c	2 2h
	לבב	HEART	523c	2 2
	לבב	HEART	525a	2 4
	מאה	HUNDRED	548b	1 c4
	נטה	INCLINE	640d	3 c
	פלגש	CONCUBINE	811c	1
	שרת	PRINCESS	979a	
11 4	אלהים	GOD	43c	1 d
	דוד	DAVID	*187d	
	יהוה	YAHWEH	218d	2 1e
	היה	COME TO PASS	224d	1 2a 1b
	זקנה	OLD AGE	279a	
	לבב	HEART	523c	2 2
	לבב	HEART	523d	2 6a
	נטה	INCLINE	640d	3 c
	עת	TIME	773c	1 b
	שלם	COMPLETE	1024a	3
11 5	מלכם	MILCOM		
	עמוני	AMMONITE	770a	
	עשתרת	ASTORETH	800a	
	צידני	SIDONIANS	851a	
11 6	מלא	FILL	570d	2
11 7	מלכם	MILCOM		
	ב	IN	88b	1 1
	במה	HIGH PLACE	119b	3
	בנה	BUILD	124c	1 ai
	הר	MOUNTAIN	249c	1 a
	זית	OLIVE TREE	*268d	3
	כמוש	CHEMOSH	484d	
	מלך	MOLECH	574c	
	עמון	AMMON	770a	
	פנה	FACE	819a	2 7a d
11 8	אשה	WOMAN	61b	1
	זבח	SLAUGHTER FOR SACRIFICE	257b	2
	כלי	IMPLEMENT	479d	2 a
	נכרי	FOREIGN	648d	1 a
	עשה	DO	793d	1 1a 3
	קטר	MAKE SACRAFICES SMOKE	883a	1 b
11 9	אנף	BE ANGRY	60a	
	ה	THE	209c	3
	לבב	HEART	523c	2 2
	נטה	BEND	640b	3 a
	מעם	FROM WITH	768d	A
	ראה	TO SEE	908b	1 a
11 10	אלהים	GOD	43c	1 d
	על	UPON	754d	2 1f g
11 11	ברית	COVENANT	137a	3 2
	חקה	SOMETHING PRESCRIBED	350a	2 d
	חקה	SOMETHING PRESCRIBED	350b	2 e
	כלי	IMPLEMENT	479d	2
	ממלכה	DOMINION	575b	2
	עם	WITH	768c	4 b
	צוה	LAY CHARGE UPON	845c	1 1
	קרע	TEAR	902c	2
	שמר	KEEP	1037a	3 c
11 12	יד	HAND	391b	5 gl
	מען	PURPOSE	775b	1
	קרע	TEAR	902c	2
	ש	WHO	*980b	4 d
11 13	בחר	CHOOSE	104a	2 a
	דוד	DAVID	188a	
	ממלכה	DOMINION	575b	2
	מען	PURPOSE	775b	1 a
	קרע	TEAR	902c	2
	רק	ONLY	956c	2 b
11 14	אדמי	EDOMITE	10c	
	הדד	HADAD	212d	2
	זרע	SOWING	282d	4 e
	קום	STAND	879a	4 b
	רזון	REZON	*931b	
	שטן	ADVERSARY	966c	1
	שטן	SATAN	966c	2
11 15	זכר	MALE	271c	11 b
	קבר	BURY	868d	
11 16	זכר	MALE	271c	11 b
	חדש	NEW MOON	294c	2 a
	ישב	REMAIN	442d	2 a
	כרת	CUT OFF	504c	2 b
	עד	UNTIL	725a	2 1b a
11 17	אדמי	EDOMITE	10c	

175

Ch v.	Heb	Eng	Page	Sec
	ברח	FLEE	138a	2
	הדד	HADAD	212d	2
	הדד	HADAD	212d	1 c
	נער	YOUTH	655a	1 c
	קטן	SMALL	882a	1 a
11 18	אמר	SAY	56c	4
	מדין	MIDIAN	193c	3
	מלך	KING	573a	1
	פארן	PARAN	803a	
	פרעה	PHARAOH	829a	
11 19	גבירה	LADY	150c	1
	הדד	HADAD	212d	2
	חן	FAVOR	336b	2 b1
	מאד	EXCEEDINGLY	547b	2 a
	מצא	FIND	592d	1 a
	תחפנים	TAHPENES	1065a	
11 20	גנבת	GENUBATH	170c	
	היה	BE	226d	3 2
	תחפנים	TAHPENES	1065a	
11 21	אב	FATHER	3c	4 a
	הדד	HADAD	212d	2
	כי	THAT	471d	1 a
11 22	בקש	SEEK	134d	2 d
	חסר	LACK	341b	1 a
	כי	THAT	*472a	1 a
	כי	BUT	474c	3 e
	עם	WITH	768b	3 a
11 23	אלידע	ELIADA	45a	B
	את	WITH	86d	4 a
	ברח	FLEE	138a	2
	הדדעזר	HADADEZER	212d	
	חזיון	HEZION	*303c	
	צובא	ZOBAH	844c	
	קום	STAND	879a	4 b
	רזון	REZON	931b	
	שטן	SATAN	966c	2 c
	שטן	ADVERSARY	966c	1
11 24	גדוד	BAND	151b	1
	דמשק	DAMASCUS	199d	
	הלך	WALK	230d	1 1d 3a
	הרג	KILL	247b	1 b
	מלך	BE KING	574a	
	על	UPON	757b	2 7c aa
	קבץ	GATHER	867d	2
	שר	CHIEFTAIN	978a	1 b
11 25	אשר	PARTICLE OF RELATION	83b	7 c
	את	MARK OF THE ACCUSATIVE	85c	3 b
	הדד	HADAD	212d	2
	היה	BECOME	226b	2 2d
	מלך	BE KING	574a	
	קוץ	FEEL A LOATHING	881a	1
	שטן	ADVERSARY	966b	1
11 26	צרתן	ZERETHAN		
	אלמנה	WIDOW	48b	
	אשה	WOMAN	61b	1
	אפרתי	EPHRATHITE	68d	1
	נבט	NEBAT	614a	
	עבד	SLAVE	714a	2
	צרדה	ZEREDAH	863a	
	צרועה	AERUAH	864a	
	ירבעם	JEROBOAM	*914c	1
	ירבעם	JEROBOAM	914c	1
	רום	BE HIGH	927b	1 a1
11 27	אשר	PARTICLE OF RELATION	82c	4 bd
	בנה	BUILD	124d	1 i
	דבר	WORD	184a	4 8
	דוד	DAVID	188a	A
	מלוא	MILLO	571c	2
	סגר	CLOSE	689a	2 b
	פרץ	BURSTING FORTH	829d	2
	רום	BE HIGH	927b	1 a1
11 28	בית	HOUSE	110a	5 dz
	גבור	STRONG	150b	2
	חיל	STRENGTH	298d	1 c
	יוסף	JOSEPH	415d	1 b
	מלאכה	WORK	522b	6 a
	סבל	BURDEN	687d	
	פקד	ATTEND TO	824a	1
	ראה	TO SEE	907a	2 1
11 29	אחיהו	AHIJAH	26d	3
	חדש	NEW	294a	A
	יצא	GO OUT	422d	1 a
	כסה	COVER	492b	
	שדה	FIELD	961c	1 f
	שלמה	GARMENT	971b	
	שילני	SHILONITE	1018a	
11 30	אחיהו	AHIJAH	26d	3
	חדש	NEW	294a	A
	על	UPON	753a	2 1aa
	קרע	TEAR	902c	1 a2
	קרע	TORN PIECES OF GARMENT	902d	
	שלמה	GARMENT	971b	
	תפש	LAY HOLD OF	1074d	1
11 31	יד	HAND	391b	5 g1
	ממלכה	DOMINION	575b	2
	קרע	TEAR	902c	2
	קרע	TORN PIECES OF GARMENT	902d	
11 32	בחר	CHOOSE	104a	1 a
	דוד	DAVID	188a	
	ו	AND	252d	1 e
	מען	PURPOSE	775b	1 a
11 33	מלכם	MILCOM		
	אלהים	GOD	43c	2 a
	דרך	WAY	204a	6 ec
	הלך	WALK	234c	2 3a 1b
	חקה	SOMETHING PRESCRIBED	350a	2 d
	חקה	SOMETHING PRESCRIBED	350b	2 e
	ישר	STRAIGHT	449a	2 a
	כמוש	CHEMOSH	484d	
	עמון	AMMON	770a	
	עשתרת	ASTORETH	800a	
	צידני	SIDONIANS	851a	
11 34	בחר	CHOOSE	104a	1
	דוד	DAVID	188a	2
	ו	AND	252d	1 e
	חיים	LIFE	313b	1
	חקה	SOMETHING PRESCRIBED	350b	2 e
	חקה	SOMETHING PRESCRIBED	350b	2 d
	יד	HAND	391b	5 g1
	לקח	TAKE	543a	3 a
	לקח	TAKE	543a	3 a
	ממלכה	DOMINION	575b	2
	נשיא	PRINCE	672b	2
	מען	PURPOSE	775b	1 a
	שית	PUT	1011c	3
11 35	יד	HAND	391b	5 g1
	מלוכה	KINGSHIP	574c	
11 36	בחר	CHOOSE	104a	2 a
	דוד	DAVID	*187d	
	דוד	DAVID	188a	
	יום	DAY	400c	7 f
	ניר	LAMP	633a	
11 37	אוה	DESIRE	16a	
	לקח	TAKE	543b	4 d
	מלך	KING	573a	5 b
	נפש	SOUL	660d	6 a
11 38	אמן	CONFIRM	52d	3
	בית	HOUSE	109d	5 b
	בנה	BUILD	124d	2 a
	בנה	BUILD	124d	2 a
	דוד	DAVID	188a	
	דרך	WAY	204a	6 ec
	הלך	WALK	234c	2 3a 1b
	חקה	SOMETHING PRESCRIBED	350b	2 d
	חקה	SOMETHING PRESCRIBED	350b	2 e
	ישר	STRAIGHT	449a	2 a
11 39	זה	THIS	260c	1 a
	זרע	SOWING	282d	4 c
	יום	DAY	400c	7 f
	מען	PURPOSE	775b	1 b
	ענה	BE BOWED DOWN	776b	3
	ש	WHO	*980b	4 d
11 40	בקש	SEEK	134d	2 d
	ברח	FLEE	138a	2
	ברח	FLEE	138a	2
	היה	BE	226d	3 2
	מות	DIE	560b	1 b
	מות	DEATH	560d	1
	מלך	KING	573a	1
	מצרים	EGYPT	595d	1 b1
	שישק	SHISHAK	1011a	
11 41	דבר	WORD	183c	4 2
	חכמה	WISDOM	315c	2
	יתר	REMAINDER	452a	1 b
	כתב	WRITE	507c	1 b1
	לא	NOT	520c	4 bb
	ספר	MISSIVE	707b	3 e
	שאר	REST	*984c	
11 42	מלך	BE KING	574a	
11 43	דוד	DAVID	188a	A
	רחבעם	REHOBOAM	932c	
	תחת	INSTEAD	1065d	2 2b a
12 1	הלך	WALK	230d	1 1d 3a
	מלך	BE KING	574b	
	רחבעם	REHOBOAM	932c	
12 2	בן	SON	120c	1 g
	ברח	FLEE	138a	2
	נבט	NEBAT	614a	
	עוד	STILL	*728d	1 aa
	ירבעם	JEROBOAM	914c	1
12 3	קהל	ASSEMBLY	874c	1 a
	קהל	ASSEMBLY	874d	2 a
	רחבעם	REHOBOAM	932c	
12 4	כבד	HEAVY	458a	1 ba
	מן	FROM	580d	3 ba
	נתן	PUT	680a	2 a
	עבדה	LABOR	715b	3
	על	YOKE	760d	
	עתה	NOW	774a	1 a
	קלל	BE SLIGHT	886d	1
	קשה	BE SEVERE	904c	1
	קשה	SEVERE	904c	2 a
12 5	אמר	SAY	56a	1
	עוד	STILL	729a	1 ab
12 6	איך	HOW	32c	1
	דבר	WORD	182b	1 1c
	זקן	OLD	278c	2 a
	חי	ALIVE	312a	1 b
	יעץ	CONSULT	419d	
	יעץ	CONSIDER	419d	
	פנה	FACE	816c	2 2a
	רחבעם	REHOBOAM	932c	
	שוב	TURN BACK	999c	3
12 7	טוב	PLEASANT	374d	9 a
	יום	DAY	400c	7 f
	עבד	WORK	713a	2
	ענה	ANSWER	772d	1 a
12 8	גדל	GROW UP	152b	1 a
	זקן	OLD	278c	2 a
	ילד	CHILD	409c	D
	יעץ	ADVISE	419c	
	יעץ	CONSULT	419d	
	עצה	ADVICE	420a	
	עצה	ADVICE	*420b	
	עזב	LEAVE	737c	2 d3
12 9	דבר	WORD	182b	1 1c
	יעץ	CONSIDER	419d	
	נתן	PUT	680a	2 a
	על	YOKE	760d	
	קלל	BE SLIGHT	886d	1
12 10	גדל	GROW UP	152b	1 a
	דבר	SPEAK	*181b	3 d
	ילד	CHILD	409c	D
	כבד	MAKE HEAVY	457d	1
	מתנים	LOINS	608b	2 a
	עבה	BE THICK	716a	
	על	YOKE	760d	
	קטן	LITTLE	882b	
	קלל	BE SLIGHT	886d	1
12 11	יסף	ADD	415b	1
	יסר	DISCIPLINE	416b	2 b
	כבד	HEAVY	458a	1 a
	על	YOKE	760d	
	עקרב	SCORPION	785d	
	שוט	SCOURGE	1002a	1
	עמם	ADDENDA ET CORRIGENDA	1126a	
12 13	זקן	OLD	278c	2 a
	יעץ	ADVISE	419c	
	עצה	ADVICE	420a	
	עזב	LEAVE	737c	2 d3
	קשה	SEVERE	904d	2 a
12 14	ילד	CHILD	409c	D
	יסף	ADD	415b	1
	יסר	DISCIPLINE	416b	2 b
	עצה	ADVICE	420a	
	כבד	MAKE HEAVY	457d	1
	על	YOKE	760d	
	עקרב	SCORPION	785d	
	שוט	SCOURGE	1002a	1
12 15	אחיהו	AHIJAH	26d	3
	בן	SON	120c	1 g
	דבר	SPEAK	*181c	4 a
	דבר	WORD	182d	1 2b
	נבט	NEBAT	614a	
	סבה	TURN OF AFFAIRS	686d	
	נסבה	TURN OF AFFAIRS	*687c	
	מעם	FROM WITH	769a	D
	שוב	TURN BACK	997b	3 b
12 16	אהל	TENT	13d	1
	דבר	WORD	182b	1 1c
	הלך	WALK	231b	1 d3 gd
	חלק	PORTION	324a	1 c
	ישי	JESSE	445b	
	ל	TO	511b	3 a
	מה	WHAT	552c	1 aa
	מה	WHAT	553c	2 ab
	נחלה	PROPERTY	635b	2 b
	ראה	TO SEE	907d	7 c
	ישראל	ISRAEL	975c	2 a2
12 17	יהודה	JUDAH	397b	2
	ישראל	ISRAEL	975d	2 a3
12 18	אבן	STONE	6b	1
	אדירם	ADONIRAM	12a	
	אדרם	ADORAM	12a	
	אמץ	BE STRONG	55b	3
	הדרם	HADORAM	214c	
	מות	DIE	559d	2 a
	מס	LABOUR-GANG	587a	1
	על	UPON	755b	2 3
	רגם	TO STONE	920c	1
	מרכבה	CHARIOT	939d	2
	ישראל	ISRAEL	975c	2 a2
	שילני	SHILONITE	1018a	
12 19	בית	HOUSE	109d	5 c
	פשע	REBEL	833b	1
	ישראל	ISRAEL	975c	2 a2
12 20	היה	BECOME	225d	2 1b
	זולה	EXCEPT	265d	1
	יהודה	JUDAH	397b	1 2
	עדה	CONGREGATION	417b	3
	מלך	BE KING	574b	
	קרא	CALL	895d	5 c
	ירבעם	JEROBOAM	914c	
12 21	אלף	THOUSAND	49a	1
	בחר	CHOOSE	104b	7
	בית	HOUSE	110a	5 de
	בנימן	BENJAMIN	122d	1
	מלוכה	KINGSHIP	574d	
	קהל	ASSEMBLE AS	875a	1 b
	שוב	TURN BACK	999a	1 d
12 22	איש	MAN	36a	
	אלהים	GOD	44a	3 b
	אלהים	GOD	44a	3 b
	דבר	WORD	*182c	12 a
	שמעיה	SHEMAIAH	1035c	1
12 23	אמר	SAY	56a	1

Ch	v.	Heb	Eng	Page	Sec
		אמר	SAY	56b	1
		בית	HOUSE	110a	5 de
		בית	HOUSE	110b	5 dt
		בנימין	BENJAMIN	122d	1
		יתר	REMAINDER	451d	1 b
12	24	את	WITH	86d	4 c
		היה	COME TO PASS	227d	2
12	25	שמע	HEAR	1034a	1 n
		הר	MOUNTAIN	251a	2 b
		פנל	PENVEL	819c	1
12	26	אמר	SAY	56b	2
		לב	HEART	525c	27
		ממלכה	DOMINION	575b	2
		שוב	TURN BACK	998a	7 b
12	27	הרג	KILL	247a	1 a
		זבח	SACRIFICE	257c	11
		זבח	SACRIFICE	258a	27
		שוב	TURN BACK	997c	5 a
12	28	אלהים	GOD	44d	4 c
		זהב	GOLD	263c	2 a
		יעץ	CONSIDER	419d	
		מן	THAN	583a	6 d
		עגל	CALF	722b	
		רב	MUCH	913b	1 f
		ישראל	ISRAEL	975d	2 a2
12	29	ביתאל	BETHEL	110d	1
		דן	DAN	193a	3
		שום	TO PLACE	964b	4 c
		דן	DAN	193a	3
12	30	הלך	WALK	231a	1 d3 gc
		חטא	SIN	308a	1 b
		פנה	FACE	817b	2 4b b
		הלך	ADDENDA ET CORRIGENDA	1122c	
12	31	בית	HOUSE	109b	1 ae 0
		במה	HIGH PLACE	119c	3
		בן	SON	*121a	1 jd
		בן	SON	121a	1 je
		כהן	PRIEST	463b	3 b
		לוי	LEVI	532c	1 c
		עשה	DO	795a	28
		קצה	END	892c	2
12	32	במה	HIGH PLACE	119c	3
		זבח	SLAUGHTER FOR SACRIFICE	257b	2
		מזבח	ALTAR	258b	1
		חג	FESTIVAL-GATHERING	291a	1 a
		חג	FESTIVAL-GATHERING	291b	1 b
		חדש	NEW MOON	294d	2 b2
		יום	DAY	398c	2 e
		כהן	PRIEST	463b	3 b
		עגל	CALF	722b	
		עלה	GO UP	750a	8
		עמד	STAND	764d	1
		עשה	DO	795a	28
12	33	ברא	DEVISE	94b	
		מזבח	ALTAR	259a	8
		מזבח	ALTAR	259a	1
		חג	FESTIVAL-GATHERING	291a	1 a
		חג	FESTIVAL-GATHERING	291b	1 b
		חדש	NEW MOON	294d	2 b2
		יום	DAY	398c	2 e
		לב	HEART	524c	2 3a
		מן	OUT OF	579c	2 cd
		עלה	GO UP	750a	8
		על	UPON	756d	2 7b
		עשה	DO	795a	28
		קטר	MAKE SACRAFICES SMOKE	883a	1 a
13	1	איש	MAN	36a	
		אלהים	GOD	44a	3 b
		את	WITH	86b	2
		ביתאל	BETHEL	110d	1
		מזבח	ALTAR	259a	1
		יהודה	JUDAH	397c	2
		על	UPON	756b	2 6c
		על	UPON	759a	4 2c
		קטר	MAKE SACRAFICES SMOKE	883a	1 a
		ירבעם	JEROBOAM	914c	1
13	2	יאשיהו	JOSIAH	78c	1
		במה	HIGH PLACE	119c	3
		זבח	SLAUGHTER FOR SACRIFICE	257a	3
		ילד	BE BORN	408d	
		כהן	PRIEST	463b	3 b
		קרא	CALL	895c	3 d
		שרף	BURN	976d	2 a
13	3	אמר	SAY	56b	1
		מופת	SIGN	69a	2
		מופת	SIGN	69a	2
		מופת	SIGN	69a	2
		דשן	FAT ASHES	206c	2
		נתן	GIVE	679b	1 m
		קרע	TEAR	902d	
		שפך	POUR OUT	1049d	
13	4	יבש	BE DRY	386c	1 e
		קרא	CALL	895b	3 a
		ירבעם	JEROBOAM	914c	1
		שוב	TURN BACK	999a	1 c
		שלח	SEND	1018c	3 a
		תפש	LAY HOLD OF	1074d	1
13	5	מופת	SIGN	69a	2
		מופת	SIGN	69a	2
		דשן	FAT ASHES	206c	2
		נתן	GIVE	679b	1 m
		קרע	TEAR	902d	
		שפך	POUR OUT	1049d	
13	6	חלה	MOLLIFY	318c	1 a
		כ	LIKE	455a	
		ראשון	FIRST	911d	3 a1
		שוב	TURN BACK	998b	7 i
13	7	בית	HOUSE	108d	1 a
		מתת	GIFT	682c	
		סעד	SUPPORT	703c	1
13	8	בית	HOUSE	110b	6
13	9	דרך	WAY	202c	1
		הלך	WALK	230c	1 1d 1a
13	10	דרך	WAY	202c	1
13	11	ביתאל	BETHEL	110d	1
		זקן	OLD	278c	1
		עמד	STANDING-PLACE	765a	
		מעשה	DEED	795c	1 a
13	12	אי	WHERE	32b	1 b
		דרך	WAY	202c	1
		הלך	WALK	230c	1 1d 1a
13	13	הלך	WALK	230b	1 1a
		חבש	BIND	290a	1 c
		חמור	HE-ASS	331b	2 b
		ל	TO	515b	5 hb a
		רכב	RIDE	938c	1
13	14	אלה	TEREBINTH	18c	
		אנכי	I	59c	
		מצא	FIND	593a	1 a
13	15	בית	HOUSE	108d	1 a
13	17	דרך	WAY	202c	1
		הלך	WALK	230c	1 1d 2a
		חר	NOBLE	359c	
		ל	TO	517c	7 bb
13	18	כחש	DECEIVE	471b	1
		מלאך	MESSENGER	521d	2
13	20	אל	TO	40d	8
		דבר	WORD	182c	1 2a
		היה	COME TO PASS	224d	2 a1 am
		שוב	TURN BACK	998d	1 a
		שלחן	TABLE	1020b	1
13	21	מרה	BE REBELLIOUS	598b	2
		יען	ON ACCOUNT OF	774d	2
		פה	MOUTH	805b	2 c
		מצוה	COMMANDMENT	846c	2 c
		קרא	CALL	895c	5 b
13	22	בוא	COME	98a	1 h
		נבלה	CARCASS	615c	1 a
		קבצר	GRAVE	868d	
		שוב	TURN BACK	997b	3 a
13	23	חבש	BIND	290a	1 c
		חמור	HE-ASS	331b	2 b
		שוב	TURN BACK	998a	1 a
13	24	אצל	BESIDE	69b	A
		אריה	LION	71d	
		דרך	WAY	202c	1
		היה	BE	227c	3 5a
		חמור	HE-ASS	331b	2 b
		מות	DIE	560c	3
		מצא	FIND	593b	3 a
		נבלה	CARCASS	615c	1 a
		שלך	THROW	1021c	1
13	25	אצל	BESIDE	69b	A
		אריה	LION	71d	
		דרך	WAY	202c	1
		זקן	OLD	278c	1
		נבלה	CARCASS	615c	1 a
		שלך	THROW	1021c	1
13	26	אריה	LION	71d	
		דרך	WAY	202c	1
		מות	DIE	560c	3
		מרה	BE REBELLIOUS	598b	2
		שבר	BREAK	990c	
13	27	חבש	BIND	290a	1 c
		חבש	BIND	*290a	1 c
		חמור	HE-ASS	331b	2 b
13	28	אכל	EAT	37b	1
		אכל	EAT	37c	2
		אריה	LION	71d	
		דרך	WAY	202c	1
		חמור	HE-ASS	331b	2 b
		מצא	FIND	593a	1 a
		נבלה	CARCASS	615c	1 a
		שבר	BREAK	990c	
		שלך	THROW	1021c	1
13	29	אל	TO	41a	A
		זקן	OLD	278c	1
		חמור	HE-ASS	331b	2 c
		נבלה	CARCASS	615c	1 a
		נוח	REST	628d	B 1
		נשא	LIFT	670a	1 a
		ספד	WAIL	704d	
		שוב	TURN BACK	999a	1 a
13	30	הוי	AH	222d	
		נבלה	CARCASS	615c	1 a
		נוח	REST	628d	B 1
		ספד	WAIL	704d	
13	31	אלהים	GOD	44a	3 b
		ו	AND	254d	5 a
		נוח	REST	628d	B 1
		קבר	BURY	868d	
		קבר	BURY	868d	
13	32	בית	HOUSE	109b	1 ae 0
		במה	HIGH PLACE	119c	3
		קרא	CALL	895b	3 a
		שמרון	SAMARIA	1038a	
13	33	במה	HIGH PLACE	119c	3
		דרך	WAY	203d	6 d
		ו	AND	254b	3
		חפץ	DELIGHTING IN	343a	1
		יד	HAND	389b	1 c
		כהן	PRIEST	463b	3 b
		מלא	FILL	570d	
		עשה	DO	795a	28
		קצה	END	892c	2
		ירבעם	JEROBOAM	914c	1
		רע	EVIL	948c	0 d
		שוב	TURN BACK	997d	6 e
		שוב	TURN BACK	998b	8
13	34	בית	HOUSE	110a	5 c
		חטאת	SIN	308d	1 b
		כחד	HIDE	470c	2
		פנה	FACE	819b	2 8b
		שמד	BE EXTERMINATED	1029b	1
14	1	ביתו	ABIJAM	4a	3
		חלה	BE WEAK	317d	2
14	2	אחיהו	AHIJAH	26d	3
		אמר	SAY	56a	1
		אתי	THOU	61c	
		דבר	SPEAK	181c	5
		הלך	WALK	230d	1 1d 3a
		ל	TO	512b	4 a
		מלך	KING	573b	5 b
		שלו	SHILOH	1017d	
		שנה	CHANGE	1040a	
14	3	בקבק	FLASK	132d	
		דבש	HONEY	185b	
		יד	HAND	391a	5 c4
		לחם	FOOD	537a	1 a
		לקח	TAKE	542d	2
		נקד	WHAT EASILY CRUMBLES	666d	2
14	4	עשר	TEN	796d	2 b
		אחיהו	AHIJAH	26d	3
		אחיהו	AHIJAH	26d	3
		הלך	WALK	230d	1 1d 3a
		מן	ON ACCOUNT OF	580b	2 f
		עין	EYE	744b	1 i
		קום	STAND	878c	7 j
		ראה	TO SEE	907b	4
		שיב	AGE	966c	
		שלו	SHILOH	1017d	
14	5	אחיהו	AHIJAH	26d	3
		אל	TO	40b	6
		דרש	SEEK	205b	2 a
		דרש	SEEK	205b	2 a
		זה	THIS	262a	6 cb
		חלה	BE WEAK	317d	2
		נכר	TREAT AS FOREIGN	649b	
14	6	עבר	REGION ACROSS	719c	1 b
		מעם	FROM WITH	769a	A
		אחיהו	AHIJAH	26d	3
		בוא	COME	97d	1
		נכר	TREAT AS FOREIGN	649b	
14	7	קול	VOICE	877b	2 c
		קשח	SEVERE	904d	2 a
		רום	BE HIGH	927c	1 f
14	8	דוד	DAVID	188a	
		הלך	WALK	235a	2 3d 1
		ישר	STRAIGHT	449a	2 a
		לבב	HEART	523c	22
		ממלכה	DOMINION	575b	2
		קרע	TEAR	902c	2
		רק	ONLY	956c	2 c
14	9	אלהים	GOD	43c	1 d
		את	MARK OF THE ACCUSATIVE	85a	1 a
		גו	BACK	156a	
		כעס	VEX	495a	2
		ל	TO	517c	7 bb
		מן	THAN	582c	6 a
		מסכה	MOLTEN IMAGE	651b	2
		רעע	BE EVIL	949d	2
		שלך	THROW	1021a	1 b
14	10	אל	TO	40b	4
		בית	HOUSE	110a	5 c
		בער	CONSUME	129b	2
		בער	BURN	129b	2
		כן	SO	486d	3 d
		כן	SO	487a	3 d
		כרת	CUT OFF	504e	2 c
		ל	TO	512b	5 aa
		עזב	LEAVE	737d	3
		קיר	WALL	885a	3
		שתן	URINATE	1010b	
		תמם	BE FINISHED	1070c	5
14	11	אכל	EAT	37c	2
		כלב	DOG	476d	A
		ל	TO	512d	5 ac
		עוף	FLY	733d	1
		שדה	FIELD	961c	1 f
14	12	הלך	WALK	231b	1 d3 gd
		ילד	CHILD	409b	4
14	13	אל	TO	40a	3 c
		בוא	COME	98a	1 h
		בית	HOUSE	110a	5 c

1 KINGS

Ch	v.	Heb	Eng	Page	Sec
		דבר	WORD	183d	4 6
		טוב	PLEASANT	374d	0 a
		ל	TO	512d	5 aa
		מצא	FIND	593d	1 c
		ספד	WAIL	704c	
		יען	ON ACCOUNT OF	774d	2 c
14	14	בית	HOUSE	110a	5 c
		זה	THIS	260d	2 a
		כרת	CUT OFF	504c	2 b
		מלך	KING	573c	5 c
		עתה	NOW	774b	2 d
14	15	אשרה	ASHERA	81c	B
		ה	THE	208a	1 f
		זרה	SCATTER	280a	1
		טוב	PLEASANT	374d	3 b
		כעס	VEX	495a	2
		נכה	SMITE	646c	4 b
		נתש	PLUCK UP	684c	
		קנה	STALK	889c	2
14	16	חטא	MISS A GOAL OR WAY	307b	2 b
		חטא	MISS A GOAL OR WAY	*307d	2
		חטא	MISS A GOAL OR WAY	307d	2
		חטאת	SIN	308d	1 b
		נתן	GIVE	679c	1 s
14	17	סף	THRESHOLD	706b	
		תרצה	TIRZAH	953d	2
14	18	אחיהו	AHIJAH	26d	3
		נביא	PROPHET	611d	1
		ספד	WAIL	704c	
		עבד	SLAVE	714b	4
14	19	אשר	PARTICLE OF RELATION	82d	4 c
		אשר	THAT	83b	8 aa
		יום	DAY	399b	4 c
		ל	TO	513d	5 cb g
		לא	NOT	520c	4 bb
		לחם	ENGAGE IN BATTLE	*535c	
		ספר	MISSIVE	707b	3 e
14	20	מלך	BE KING	574a	
		נדב	NADAB	621d	2
		עשרים	TWENTY	797d	12 a
		תחת	INSTEAD	1065d	2 2b a
14	21	אם	MOTHER	51d	1
		בחר	CHOOSE	104a	2 a
		מלך	BE KING	574a	
		מלך	BE KING	574a	
		נעמה	NAAMAH	653d	2
		עמוני	AMMONITE	770a	
		ארבעים	FORTY	917c	2 a
		שבע	SEVEN	988a	2 a
14	22	חטא	MISS A GOAL OR WAY	307b	2 b
		חטאת	SIN	308d	1 b
		קנא	BE ZEALOUS	888c	4
14	23	אשרה	ASHERA	81c	B
		במה	HIGH PLACE	119c	3 a
		בנה	BUILD	124c	1 ai
		גבה	HIGH	147b	1
		גבעה	HILL	149a	2
		מצבה	PILLAR	663b	1 c
		עץ	TREE	781c	1 a
		רענן	LUXURIANT	947d	
14	24	גוי	NATION	156d	1 c
		ירש	CAUSE TO POSSESS	440a	2 a
		קדש	TEMPLE-PROSTITUTE	873d	
		תועבה	ABOMINATION	1072d	1 b
14	25	חמישי	FIFTH	332c	2
		מלך	KING	573a	1
		עלה	GO UP	748c	2 c
		שישק	SHISHAK	1004d	
		שישק	SHISHAK	1011a	
14	26	אוצר	TREASURE	70a	1
		מגן	SHIELD	171c	
		זהב	GOLD	263c	2 a
		כל	ALL	*482d	2 ba
		לקח	TAKE	543d	9 a
14	27	מגן	SHIELD	171c	
		נחשת	COPPER	638d	1
		על	UPON	753b	2 1c
		פקד	ATTEND TO	824a	2 a
		רוץ	RUN	930c	2 a
		שר	CHIEFTAIN	978c	4 a
		שמר	KEEP	1036c	1 b
14	28	די	SUFFICIENCY	191d	2 ca
		היה	COME TO PASS	225a	12 a 1d
		רוץ	RUN	930c	2 a
		שוב	TURN BACK	998d	1 a
		תא	CHAMBER	1060b	
14	29	דבר	WORD	183c	4 2
		יום	DAY	399b	4 c
		ל	TO	513d	5 cb g
		לא	NOT	520c	4 bb
		ספר	MISSIVE	707b	3 e
14	30	יום	DAY	400c	7 f
14	31	אב	FATHER	3c	4 a
		ביהו	ABIJAM	4a	1
		אם	MOTHER	51d	1
		דוד	DAVID	188a	A
		מלך	BE KING	574a	
		נעמה	NAAMAH	653d	2
		עמוני	AMMONITE	770a	
15	1	קבר	BURY	*868c	
		ביהו	ABIJAM	4a	1
		מלך	BE KING	574a	
		נבט	NEBAT	614a	
		עשר	TEN	797b	8 b
		עשר	TEN	797c	
		ירבעם	JEROBOAM	914c	
		שמנה	EIGHT	1033a	2 a
15	2	אבשלום	ABSALOM	5a	1
		אם	MOTHER	51d	1
		מעכה	MAACAH	590d	2 b
15	3	אב	FATHER	3c	4 a
		יהוה	YAHWEH	218d	2 1e
		חלד	WALK	235a	23e 2
		חטאת	SIN	308d	1 b
		לבב	HEART	523d	26a
		שלם	COMPLETE	1024a	3
15	4	יהוה	YAHWEH	218d	2 1e
		ניר	LAMP	633a	
		עמד	STAND	764d	2
		מען	PURPOSE	775b	1 a
		קום	STAND	878d	3
15	5	אשר	THAT	83c	8 c
		דבר	WORD	183c	4 3
		חיים	LIFE	313b	1
		חתי	HITTITE	366d	1
		ישר	STRAIGHT	449a	2 a
		רק	ONLY	956c	2 d
		שפט	JUDGE	1047c	1 b
15	6	חיים	LIFE	313b	1
		רחבעם	REHOBOAM	932c	
15	7	ביהו	ABIJAM	4a	1
15	8	ביהו	ABIJAM	4a	1
		אסא	ASA	61d	
		דוד	DAVID	188a	A
15	9	אסא	ASA	61d	
		מלך	BE KING	574a	
		עשרים	TWENTY	798a	2 1
		אבשלום	ABSALOM	5a	1
		אם	MOTHER	51d	1
		מעכה	MAACAH	590d	2 b
		ארבעים	FORTY	917c	2 a
15	11	אב	FATHER	3c	4 a
		אסא	ASA	61d	
		ישר	STRAIGHT	449a	2 a
15	12	עבר	PASS OVER	719a	4
		קדש	TEMPLE-PROSTITUTE	873d	
15	13	אם	MOTHER	51d	1
		אשרה	ASHERA	81b	A
		גבירה	QUEEN-MOTHER	150c	2
		ו	AND	254d	5 b
		כרת	CUT OFF	503d	2
		מן	FROM	583b	7 bb
		נחל	WADY	636c	2
		סור	TURN ASIDE	694b	1
		מפלצת	HORRID THING	814a	
		קדרון	KEDRON	871b	
15	14	במה	HIGH PLACE	119c	3 b
		ו	AND	252d	1 e
		לבב	HEART	523d	26a
		סור	TURN ASIDE	694b	3
		רק	ONLY	956c	2 b
		שלם	COMPLETE	1024a	3
15	15	זהב	GOLD	263c	1
15	16	בעשא	BAASHA	129d	
15	17	בנה	BUILD	124c	1 b
		בעשא	BAASHA	129d	
		יצא	GO OUT	424a	3
		עמד	STAND	764d	5
		רמה	RAMA	928a	1
15	18	אוצר	TREASURE	70a	3 a
		בנהדד	BEN-HADAD	122b	1
		דמשק	DAMASCUS	199d	
		זהב	GOLD	263c	1
		חזיון	HEZION	303c	1
		טבמון	TABRIMMON	372a	
		כסף	SILVER	494b	6
		מלך	KING	573a	1
		רזון	REZON	931b	
15	19	בעשא	BAASHA	129d	
		ברית	COVENANT	136b	1 1
		זהב	GOLD	263c	1
		כסף	SILVER	494b	6
		עלה	GO UP	748c	2 e
		על	UPON	759a	4 2b
		פרר	BREAK	830b	1 c
		שחד	BRIBE	1005a	
15	20	אבל	ABEL	6a	2
		ארץ	EARTH	76a	2 c
		אשר	PARTICLE OF RELATION	83a	7 b
		ביתמעכה	BETH-MAACAH	112a	
		בנהדד	BEN-HADAD	122b	1
		דן	DAN	193a	3
		חיל	STRENGTH	299a	4
		כנרת	CHINNERETH	490b	2
		נכה	SMITE	646c	3
		עיון	IJON	743b	
		עיר	CITY	746a	1 e
		על	UPON	755c	24c
		נפתלי	NAPHTALI	837a	2 a
		שר	CHIEFTAIN	978c	3 a
15	21	חדל	CEASE	293a	2
		רמה	RAMA	928a	1
		תרצה	TIRZAH	953d	2
15	22	אבן	STONE	6c	2
		ב	IN	90c	3 6
		בנה	BUILD	124c	1 b
		גבע	GEBA	148d	
		נקי	FREE FROM	667c	3
		נשא	LIFT	671b	3 b
		עץ	TREE	781d	2 b
		מצפה	MIZPAH	860a	4
		רמה	RAMA	928a	1
		שמע	HEAR	1034c	1 a
		נקה	ADDENDA ET CORRIGENDA	1125b	
15	23	את	MARK OF THE ACCUSATIVE	85b	2 c
		גבורה	MIGHT	150c	2
		זקנה	OLD AGE	279a	
		חלא	BE SICK	*316a	
		חלה	BE WEAK	317d	2
		יתר	REMAINDER	452a	1 b
		עת	TIME	773c	1 b
		רק	ONLY	956c	2 b
15	24	אב	FATHER	3c	4 a
		אב	FATHER	3c	4 a
		דוד	DAVID	188a	A
		יהושפט	JEHOSHAPHAT	221d	1
		קבר	BURY	*868c	
15	25	ל	TO	513d	5 cb g
		מלך	BE KING	574b	
		נדב	NADAB	621d	2
15	26	שנים	TWO	1041b	1 b2
		דרך	WAY	*203d	6 d
		חלד	WALK	235a	23e 2
		חטא	MISS A GOAL OR WAY	*307d	2
		חטא	MISS A GOAL OR WAY	307d	2
		חטאת	SIN	308d	1 b
15	27	אחיהו	AHIJAH	26d	4
		אשר	PARTICLE OF RELATION	83a	7 c
		בית	HOUSE	110b	5 di
		גבתון	GIBBETHON	146d	
		יששכר	ISSACHAR	441a	1
		ל	TO	512d	5 ac
		נדב	NADAB	621d	2
		צור	CONFINE	848d	2
		קשר	BIND	905b	2
15	28	ל	TO	513d	5 cb g
		שלש	THREE	1025d	1 b
15	29	אחיהו	AHIJAH	26d	3
		בית	HOUSE	110a	5 c
		נשמה	BREATH	675d	3
		עבד	SLAVE	714b	4
		עד	AS FAR AS	*724d	12 a b
		שילני	SHILONITE	1018a	
15	30	חטא	MISS A GOAL OR WAY	307b	2 b
		חטא	MISS A GOAL OR WAY	307d	2
		חטא	MISS A GOAL OR WAY	*307d	2
		חטאת	SIN	308d	1 b
		כעס	VEX	495a	2
		כעס	ANGER	495b	2
15	31	נדב	NADAB	621d	2
15	33	אחיהו	AHIJAH	26d	4
		ארבע	FOUR	917d	2 b
		תרצה	TIRZAH	953d	2
15	34	דרך	WAY	203d	6 d
		חלד	WALK	235a	23e 2
		חטא	MISS A GOAL OR WAY	307d	2
		חטא	MISS A GOAL OR WAY	*307d	2
		חטאת	SIN	308d	1 b
16	1	דבר	WORD	182c	12a
		יהוא	JEHU	219d	2
		חנני	HANANI	337b	1
16	2	דרך	WAY	203d	6 d
		חלד	WALK	235a	23e 2
		חטא	MISS A GOAL OR WAY	307d	2
		חטא	MISS A GOAL OR WAY	*307d	2
		חטאת	SIN	308d	1 b
		כעס	VEX	495a	2
		עפר	DRY EARTH	780a	2 e
		ירבעם	JEROBOAM	914d	1
		רום	BE HIGH	927c	1 f
16	3	בית	HOUSE	110a	5 c
		בער	CONSUME	129b	2
		בער	CONSUME	129c	1
		נבט	NEBAT	614a	
16	4	נתן	GIVE	681a	3 c
		אכל	EAT	37c	2
		כלב	DOG	476d	A
		ל	TO	513a	5 ac
		שדה	FIELD	961c	1 f
16	5	גבורה	MIGHT	150c	2
16	6	אלה	ELAH	18d	2
		תרצה	TIRZAH	953d	2
16	7	דבר	WORD	182c	12a
		יהוא	JEHU	219d	2
		חנני	HANANI	337b	1
		יד	HAND	391a	5 d
		כעס	VEX	495a	2
		כעס	VEX	495a	2

Ch	v.	Heb	Eng	Page	Sec
		מעשה	DEED	795d	1 a2
16	8	ירבעם	JEROBOAM	914d	1
16	8	אלה	ELAH	18d	2
		ל	TO	513d	5 cb g
		תרצה	TIRZAH	953d	2
16	9	ארצא	ARZA	76c	
		בית	HOUSE	110b	6
		מחצית	HALF	346a	1
		קשר	BIND	905b	2
		תרצה	TIRZAH	953d	2
		שכר	DRUNKEN	1016c	
16	10	נכה	SMITE	645d	2 a
		עשרים	TWENTY	798a	2 2b
		שבע	SEVEN	988b	5 a3
16	11	כסא	THRONE	491a	3 a
		קיר	WALL	885a	3
		רע	FRIEND	946a	1
		שאר	REMAIN	984b	1
		שתן	URINATE	1010b	
16	12	דבר	SPEAK	181a	3 b
		יהוא	JEHU	219d	2
		יד	HAND	391a	5 d
		שמד	BE EXTERMINATED	1029c	1
16	13	אלה	ELAH	18d	2
		אל	TO	40c	6
		הבל	VAPOUR	211a	2
		חטא	MISS A GOAL OR WAY	307b	2 b
		חטא	MISS A GOAL OR WAY	*307d	2
		חטא	MISS A GOAL OR WAY	307d	2
		חטאת	SIN	308c	1 b
		כעס	VEX	495a	2
		שלם	PEACE-OFFERING	1023c	
16	14	אלה	ELAH	18d	2
16	15	אשר	PARTICLE OF RELATION	83a	7 c
		גבתון	GIBBETHON	146d	
		חנה	DECLINE	333c	2 c2
		תרצה	TIRZAH	953d	2
		שבע	SEVEN	988b	5 a3
16	16	מלך	BE KING	574b	
		עמרי	OMRI	771d	1
		קשר	BIND	905b	2
		שמע	HEAR	1033c	1 c
16	17	גבתון	GIBBETHON	146d	
		צור	CONFINE	848d	1
		תרצה	TIRZAH	953d	2
16	18	ארמון	CITADEL	74d	
		לכד	CAPTURE	540a	1
		שרף	BURN	976d	2 a
16	19	דרך	WAY	203d	6 d
		חטא	MISS A GOAL OR WAY	307b	2 b
		חטא	MISS A GOAL OR WAY	307d	2
		חטא	MISS A GOAL OR WAY	*307d	2
		חטאת	SIN	308a	1 b
		חטאת	SIN	308d	1 b
		ירבעם	JEROBOAM	914d	1
16	20	קשר	BIND	905b	2
		קשר	CONSPIRACY	905c	
16	21	גינת	GINATH	171b	
		חיה	BECOME	225d	2 1b
		חלק	DIVIDE	323c	
		חלק	DIVIDE	323d	2 b
		חצי	HALF	345c	1
		מלך	BE KING	574b	
		תבני	TIBNI	1062a	
16	22	גינת	GINATH	171b	
		חזק	BE FIRM	304b	1 1b
		מלך	BE KING	574a	
		תבני	TIBNI	1062a	
16	23	יהוא	JEHU	*219c	
		מלך	BE KING	574a	
		מלך	BE KING	574a	
		תרצה	TIRZAH	953d	2
		שלשים	THIRTY	1026c	2
16	24	אדון	LORD	11a	2 1a
		בנה	BUILD	124c	1 g
		כסף	SILVER	494c	8 c
		שמר	SHEMER	1037c	1
		שמרון	SAMARIA	1037d	
		שמרון	SAMARIA	1038a	
		שמרון	SAMARIA	1038a	
16	25	פנה	FACE	817d	2 4e
		רע	BE EVIL	949d	2
16	26	דרך	WAY	203d	6 d
		הבל	VAPOUR	211a	2
		הלך	WALK	235a	2 3e 2
		חטא	MISS A GOAL OR WAY	*307d	2
		חטא	MISS A GOAL OR WAY	307d	2
		חטאת	SIN	308d	1 b
		כעס	VEX	495a	2
		נבט	NEBAT	614a	
		ירבעם	JEROBOAM	914d	1
16	27	גבורה	MIGHT	150c	2
16	28	אחאב	AHAB	26c	1
		שמרון	SAMARIA	1037d	
16	29	אחאב	AHAB	26c	1
		מלך	BE KING	574b	
		שלשים	THIRTY	1026c	2

Ch	v.	Heb	Eng	Page	Sec
		שמנה	EIGHT	1033a	3 c
		שמרון	SAMARIA	1037d	
16	30	פנה	FACE	817d	2 4e
		פנה	FACE	818a	2 5b
16	31	איזבל	JEZEBEL	33b	
		אתבעל	ETHBAAL	87a	
		בעל	BAAL	127d	2 2
		ה	INTERROG PART	210a	1 c
		היה	COME TO PASS	224d	a1 am
		חטא	SIN	308d	1 b
		מן	THAN	583a	6 d
		נבט	NEBAT	614a	
		עבד	WORK	713b	4 b
		צידני	SIDONIANS	851a	
		קלל	BE SLIGHT	886c	2
		ירבעם	JEROBOAM	914d	1
		שחה	BOW DOWN	1005c	3
16	32	בנה	BUILD	124b	1 ab
		בעל	BAAL	127d	2 2
		מזבח	ALTAR	258d	7
		מזבח	ALTAR	258d	8
		קום	STAND	878d	2 b
		שמרון	SAMARIA	1037d	
16	33	אשרה	ASHERA	81c	B
		יסף	ADD	415b	1
		כעס	VEX	495a	2
16	34	אבירם	ABIRAM	4d	2
		חיאל	HIEL	27d	
		ביתהאלי	THE BETHELITE	111a	
		בנה	BUILD	124d	1 i
		דלת	DOOR	*195b	3
		יהושוע	JOSHUA	221c	1
		חיאל	HIEL	313c	
		יד	HAND	391a	5 d
		יום	DAY	399b	4 b
		יסד	FOUND	414a	1
		נון	NUN	630c	
		נצב	STAND	662c	2
		צעירו	YOUNG	859a	2
		שגוב	SEGUB	960d	1
17	1	אליה	ELIJAH	45b	A
		חי	ALIVE	311d	1 a
		טל	NIGHT-MIST	378c	
		תושב	SOJOURNER	444c	
		כי אם	EXCEPT	474d	2 a
		מטר	RAIN	564d	
		עמד	STAND	764a	1 e
		פה	MOUTH	805c	6 c1
		תשבי	TISHBITE	986c	
		תשבה	TISHBITE	986c	
17	2	דבר	WORD	182c	1 2a
17	3	כרית	CHERITH	504d	
		ל	TO	515d	5 ib
		נחל	WADY	636b	2
		סתר	HIDE	711b	1
		פנה	TURN	815b	1 a
		פנה	FACE	819a	2 7a e
		קדם	EASTWARD	870a	
17	4	כול	SUSTAIN	465a	1
		נחל	WADY	*636b	2
		נחל	WADY	*636b	2
		נחל	TORRENT	636b	1
		ערב	RAVEN	788b	
		שתה	DRINK	1059b	1 a
17	5	כרית	CHERITH	504d	
		נחל	WADY	636b	2
		פנה	FACE	819a	2 7a e
17	6	בוא	COME	99b	2
		בקר	MORNING	134a	1 e
		בשר	FLESH	142c	1 a
		לחם	FOOD	537a	1 a
		נחל	WADY	*636b	2
		נחל	TORRENT	636b	1
		נחל	WADY	*636b	2
		ערב	RAVEN	788b	
		שתה	DRINK	1059b	1 a
17	7	גשם	RAIN	177c	
		יבש	BE DRY	386c	2
		יום	DAY	399c	5 a
		נחל	WADY	*636b	2
		נחל	TORRENT	636b	1
		קץ	END	893d	1
17	8	דבר	WORD	182c	1 2a
17	9	אלמנה	WIDOW	48b	
		אשה	WOMAN	61b	1
		אשר	PARTICLE OF RELATION	83a	7 c
		כול	SUSTAIN	465a	1
		צידון	SIDON	851a	
		צרפת	ZAREPHATH	864c	
17	10	אלמנה	WIDOW	48b	
		אשה	WOMAN	61b	1
		כלי	VESSEL	480b	3
		ל	TO	515b	5 hb a
		לקח	TAKE	543c	6
		פתח	OPENING	836a	
		צרפת	ZAREPHATH	864c	
		קשש	GATHER STUBBLE	905d	
17	11	לחם	FOOD	537a	1 a
		פת	FRAGMENT	837d	
17	12	אם	IF	50b	1 b2
		חי	ALIVE	311d	1 a
		כד	JAR	461c	
		כף	HOLLOW OF THE HAND	496b	1 a

Ch	v.	Heb	Eng	Page	Sec
		מלא	FULNESS	571b	1
		מעוג	CAKE	728b	
		עשה	DO	794d	2 3
		צפחת	JAR	860b	
		קמח	FLOUR	888a	
		קשש	GATHER STUBBLE	905d	
		שמן	OIL	1032b	2 b
		שנים	TWO	1041b	1 b3
17	13	אחרון	BEHIND	31a	B b
		אך	HOWBEIT	36c	2 a
		דבר	WORD	182b	1 1b
		יצא	BRING OUT	425a	4 e
		ירא	FEAR	431a	1 a
		עגה	BREAD-CAKE	728b	
		מן	SMALL	882a	1 b
		ראשון	FIRST	912a	3 a1
		שם	THERE	1027c	4 d
17	14	אדמה	GROUND	9d	4
		גשם	RAIN	177c	
		חסר	LACK	341b	2
		כד	JAR	461c	
		כלה	BE FINISHED	477c	2 a
		צפחת	JAR	860b	
		קמח	FLOUR	888a	
		שמן	OIL	1032b	2 b
17	15	הוא	HE, SHE, IT	*214d	
		הוא	HE, SHE, IT	*215a	
		יום	DAY	399c	5 a
17	16	חסר	LACK	341b	2
		כד	JAR	461c	
		כלה	BE FINISHED	477c	2 a
		צפחת	JAR	860b	
		קמח	FLOUR	888a	
		שמן	OIL	1032b	2 b
17	17	אחר	AFTER	29d	2 b
		בעלה	MISTRESS	128b	1
		דבר	WORD	183c	4 4
		חזק	STRONG	305c	1 d
		חלה	BE WEAK	317d	2
		חלי	SICKNESS	318b	
		נשמה	BREATH	675d	2
		עד	UNTIL	724d	2 1a a
17	18	אלהים	GOD	44a	3 b
		זכר	REMEMBER	271a	3 b
		מה	WHAT	553b	1 dc
		עון	INIQUITY	731a	1 b
17	19	חיק	BOSOM	300d	2
		לקח	TAKE	542d	3 a
		מטה	COUCH	641d	
		עלה	GO UP	749c	1 c
		עליה	ROOF-CHAMBER	751a	
		שכב	LIE DOWN	1012c	
17	20	אלמנה	WIDOW	48b	
		גור	SOJOURN	158a	
		גם	ALSO	169b	2
		יהוה	YAHWEH	219a	2 1f
		על	UPON	757c	2 7c b
		רעע	BE EVIL	949d	1
17	21	יהוה	YAHWEH	219a	2 1f
		ילד	CHILD	409b	A
		מדד	MEASURE	551b	
		נא	PART OF ENTREATY	609b	3 c
		נפש	SOUL	659c	1 c
		נפש	SOUL	*661a	6 g
		על	UPON	757c	2 7c ab
		קרב	INWARD PART	899a	1 a
		שוב	TURN BACK	997b	3 b
17	22	חיה	LIVE	311b	2 d
		ילד	CHILD	409b	A
		נפש	SOUL	659c	1 c
		על	UPON	757c	2 7c ab
		קרב	INWARD PART	899a	1 a
		שוב	TURN BACK	997b	3 b
17	23	אם	MOTHER	51d	1
		חי	ALIVE	312a	1 b
		ילד	CHILD	409b	A
		ירד	BRING DOWN	433d	1
		עליה	ROOF-CHAMBER	751a	
17	24	אלהים	GOD	44a	3 b
		אמת	FIRMNESS	54b	4 c
		זה	THIS	261c	4 h
		עתה	NOW	774a	2
		עתה	NOW	774b	2 a
		פה	MOUTH	805a	2 a
17	32	אמה	CUBIT	52c	1
18	1	אדמה	GROUND	9d	4
		אחאב	AHAB	26c	1
		דבר	WORD	182c	1 2a
		מטר	RAIN	564d	
		ראה	TO SEE	908b	1 b
		שלישי	THIRD	1026a	
18	2	אחאב	AHAB	26c	1
		חזק	STRONG	305c	1 d
		ראה	TO SEE	908b	1 b
		רעב	FAMINE	944b	1
		שמרון	SAMARIA	1038a	
18	3	אחאב	AHAB	26c	1
		בית	HOUSE	110b	6
		היה	BE	227c	3 5a
		ירא	FEAR	431c	3 b
		עבדיהו	OBADIAH	715d	1 1
18	4	איזבל	JEZEBEL	33b	
		חבא	WITHDRAW	285b	
		כול	SUSTAIN	465a	1
		כרת	CUT OFF	504c	2 b

1 KINGS

Ch v.	Heb	Eng	Page	Sec
	לקח	TAKE	543c	4 g
	מאה	HUNDRED	547d	1 a2
	עבדיהו	OBADIAH	715c	1 1
	מערה	CAVE	792c	
18 5	היה	BE	226d	3 1
	חיה	LIVE	311c	1
	חציר	GREEN GRASS	348b	1
	כרת	CUT OFF	504d	5
	מן	FROM	581a	3 bc
	מצא	FIND	592c	1 a
	נחל	WADY	636b	2
	סוס	HORSE	692c	2
	עבדיהו	OBADIAH	715d	1 1
	מעין	SPRING	745d	1
	פרד	MULE	825d	
18 6	דרך	WAY	202c	1
	הלך	WALK	230c	1 1d 2a
	חלק	DIVIDE	323d	1
	עבדיהו	OBADIAH	715d	1 1
18 7	אדן	LORD	11b	3 1c
	דרך	WAY	202c	1
	זה	THIS	261c	4 f
	נכר	RECOGNIZE	648a	2
	נפל	FALL	657c	3 b
	עבדיהו	OBADIAH	715d	1 1
	קרא	ENCOUNTER	897a	1
18 8	אני	I	59a	
	אנכי	I	59c	
18 9	חמא	MISS 0A GOAL OR WAY0	306c	2 a
	כי	THAT	472d	1 f
18 10	אין	NOT	34c	2 dg
	אם	IF	50b	1 b2
	בקש	SEEK	134c	1 b
	ו	AND	254a	2 da
	יש	THERE IS	441d	2 b
	ממלכה	KINGDOM	575a	1
	מצא	FIND	593a	1 b
	שבע	SWEAR	989c	1
	שם	THERE	1027b	2
18 12	אשר	PARTICLE OF RELATION	82c	4 bg
	את	WITH	86c	4 a
	הרג	KILL	247a	1 a
	ירא	FEAR	431c	3 b
	מצא	FIND	593a	1 b
	נעורים	YOUTH	655b	
	נשא	LIFT	671a	2 a
	נשא	LIFT	671b	3 b
	על	UPON	757a	27 c a
	רוח	BREATH	925d	9 a
18 13	אדן	LORD	11b	3 1c
	איזבל	JEZEBEL	33b	
	את	MARK OF THE ACCUSATIVE	85a	1 b
	הרג	KILL	247a	1 a
	חבא	WITHDRAW	285b	
	כול	SUSTAIN	465a	1
	מאה	HUNDRED	547d	1 a1
	נגד	BE CONSPICUOUS	617a	
	מערה	CAVE	792c	
18 14	הרג	KILL	247a	1 a
	שום	TO PLACE	964a	3 f
18 15	חי	ALIVE	311d	1 a
	עמד	STAND	764a	1 e
	צבא	GOD OF WAR	839c	4 c
	ראה	TO SEE	908b	1 b
18 16	הלך	WALK	233d	1 5a
	עבדיהו	OBADIAH	715d	1 1
18 17	זה	THIS	261c	4 f
	עכר	STIR UP	747d	
18 18	ב	IN	91a	5 2
	בעל	BAAL	127d	2 3
	כיאם	BUT	475a	2 b
	עכר	STIR UP	747d	
	מצוה	COMMANDMENT	846c	2 b
18 19	איזבל	JEZEBEL	33b	
	אשרה	ASHERA	81b	A
	בעל	BAAL	127d	2 2
	הר	MOUNTAIN	249c	1 a
	כרמל	CARMEL	502a	1
	נביא	PROPHET	612a	3
	קבץ	GATHER	867d	2
	שלחן	TABLE	1020b	1
18 20	הר	MOUNTAIN	249c	1 a
	כרמל	CARMEL	502a	1
	נביא	PROPHET	612a	3
	קבץ	GATHER	867d	2
18 21	אלהים	GOD	43d	3
	אלהים	GOD	43d	3
	בעל	BAAL	127d	2 2
	דבר	WORD	182b	1 1c
	מתי	WHEN	607d	C
	סעפה	DIVISION	704a	
	פסח	LIMP	820c	
18 22	בעל	BAAL	127d	2 2
	יתר	BE LEFT OVER	451b	
	ל	TO	513c	5 cb a
	נביא	PROPHET	612a	3
18 23	בחר	CHOOSE	104a	3 b
	נתח	CUT IN PIECES	677c	
	נתן	PUT	680a	2 a
	עץ	TREE	782a	2 d
	עשה	DO	794d	2 3
	פר	YOUNG BULL	830d	2 b
	שום	TO PLACE	963c	1 d

Ch v.	Heb	Eng	Page	Sec
18 24	אלהים	GOD	43c	2 a
	אלהים	GOD	43d	3
	אלהים	GOD	43d	3
	אש	FIRE	77c	2
	ב	IN	90b	3 4
	היה	COME TO PASS	225b	1 2b f
	טוב	PLEASANT	374b	5
	ענה	ANSWER	772d	1 b
	קרא	CALL	845b	2 c
	שם	NAME	1028d	4
18 25	ב	IN	90b	3 4
	בחר	CHOOSE	104a	3 b
	בעל	BAAL	127d	2 2
	ברה	EAT	*136a	
	נביא	PROPHET	612a	3
	עשה	DO	794d	2 3
	פר	YOUNG BULL	830d	2 b
	ראשון	FIRST	912a	3 b1
	שום	TO PLACE	963c	1 d
	שם	NAME	1028d	4
18 26	ב	IN	90b	3 4
	בעל	BAAL	127d	2 2
	בקר	MORNING	134c	1 d
	ה	THE	208d	1 i
	מזבח	ALTAR	259a	8
	מן	FROM	582a	5 c
	עשה	DO	794d	2 3
	פסח	LIMP	820c	
	פר	YOUNG BULL	830d	2 b
	צהר	MIDDAY	843d	1
	שם	NAME	1028d	4
18 27	דרך	JOURNEY	203a	2
	התל	DECEIVE	251c	
	יקץ	AWAKE	429c	
	ישן	SLEEPING	445d	1
	כי	BECAUSE	473d	3 b
	סיג	A MOVING BACK	691a	1
	צהר	MIDDAY	843a	1
	קרא	CALL	895a	1 a
	שיח	COMPLAINT	967a	2
	שיג	ADDENDA ET CORRIGENDA	1125c	
18 28	גדד	CUT	151a	1
	דם	BLOOD	196c	2 b
	כשף	CUT	*506c	
	קרא	CALL	895a	1 a
	רמח	SPEAR	942b	
	משפט	JUDGMENT	1049a	6 b
	שפך	POUR OUT	1049c	1 a
18 29	מנחה	OFFERING	585a	3
	נבא	PROPHESY	612c	2
	עבר	PASS OVER	*717d	4 d
	עד	UNTIL	725c	3 2
	עלה	GO UP	749a	6
	עלה	GO UP	749d	8
	צהר	MIDDAY	843d	1
	קשב	ATTENTIVENESS	904a	
18 30	הרס	THROW DOWN	248c	1
	מזבח	ALTAR	258b	1
	רפא	HEAL	951a	1
18 31	אבן	STONE	6c	1
	דבר	WORD	182c	12a
	מזבח	ALTAR	258c	1
	מספר	NUMBER	709a	1 b
	ישראל	ISRAEL	975c	1
	שם	NAME	1027d	2 a
18 32	אבן	STONE	6c	1
	בית	HOUSE	109c	3
	בנה	BUILD	124c	1 b
	זרע	SOWING	282b	2 d
	סאה	SEAH	684b	
	סביב	ROUND ABOUT	687a	1 cb
	תעלה	WATER-COURSE	752b	C
18 33	ערך	ARRANGE	789c	1 b
	פר	YOUNG BULL	830d	2 b
18 34	בוא	COME	98a	1 i
	יצק	POUR	427b	1
	כד	JAR	461c	
	מלא	FILL	570b	2
	שלש	DO A THIRD TIME	1026a	
	שנה	DO AGAIN	1040d	
18 35	הלך	WALK	232b	1 3
	מלא	FILL	570c	1
	סביב	ROUND ABOUT	687a	1 cb
	תעלה	WATER-COURSE	752b	C
18 36	אלהים	GOD	44b	4 ba
	ידע	BE MADE KNOWN	394c	1
	מנחה	OFFERING	585a	3
	נביא	PROPHET	611d	1
	עלה	GO UP	749d	8
	יצחק	ISAAC	850c	
	ישראל	ISRAEL	975c	1
18 37	אחרנית	BACKWARDS	30d	
	אלהים	GOD	43d	3
	אלהים	GOD	43d	3
	סבב	TURN ABOUT	686c	1 a
	ענה	ANSWER	772d	1 b
18 38	אבן	STONE	6c	1
	אכל	EAT	37c	3
	אש	FIRE	77c	2
	לחך	LICK UP	535b	
	נפל	FALL	657a	1
	עלה	WHOLE BURNT OFFERING	750d	
	תעלה	WATER-COURSE	752b	C
	עפר	DRY EARTH	779d	1 a

Ch v.	Heb	Eng	Page	Sec
18 39	אלהים	GOD	43d	3
	אלהים	GOD	43d	3
	נפל	FALL	657c	3 b
18 40	בעל	BAAL	127d	2 2
	ירד	BRING DOWN	433d	1 a
	מלט	SLIP AWAY	572b	2
	נבא	PROPHET	612a	3
	קישון	KISHON	885c	
	שחט	SLAUGHTER	1006b	3
	תפש	LAY HOLD OF	1074d	1
	נחל	ADDENDA ET CORRIGENDA	1125a	
18 41	גשם	RAIN	177c	
18 42	חמון	SOUND	242c	1
	ברך	KNEE	139c	
	גהר	BEND	155c	
	כרמל	CARMEL	502a	1
18 43	דרך	WAY	203b	3
	מאומה	ANYTHING	548d	
	נבט	LOOK	613c	1 a
	נבט	LOOK	613c	1 a
	שוב	TURN BACK	997b	3 a
18 44	אסר	TIE	63d	2
	גשם	RAIN	177c	
	עב	DARK CLOUD	728a	1 a
	עלה	GO UP	748d	5
	עצר	RESTRAIN	783c	1
	מן	SMALL	882a	1 b
	שביעי	SEVENTH	988d	2
18 45	גדול	GREAT	153a	1
	גשם	RAIN	177c	
	היה	COME TO PASS	224c	2 a1 ak
	היה	BECOME	225c	2 1a
	הלך	WALK	230b	1 1a
	הלך	WALK	230d	1 1d 3b
	יזרעאל	JEZREEL	283c	1 b
	כה	THUS	462b	3
	עב	DARK CLOUD	728a	1 a
	קדרות	DARKNESS	*871d	
	קדר	BE DARK	871a	
	רוח	BREATH	924d	2 a
	רכב	RIDE	938c	1
	שמי	HEAVENS	1029d	1 a
18 46	אל	TO	41a	A
	בוא	COME	98c	2 e
	יזרעאל	JEZREEL	283c	1 b
	מתנים	LOINS	608a	1
	רוץ	RUN	930b	1
	רוץ	RUN	930b	1
	שנס	GIRD UP	1042b	
19 1	איזבל	JEZEBEL	33b	
	הרג	KILL	247a	1 a
	נביא	PROPHET	612a	3
	מערה	CAVE	792c	
19 2	איזבל	JEZEBEL	33b	
	יסף	ADD	415b	1
	מחר	TO-MORROW	564a	1 a
	עת	TIME	773c	1 a
	שום	TO PLACE	964a	1 e
19 3	אל	TO	40c	6
	אשר	PARTICLE OF RELATION	83a	7 c
	בארשבע	BEERSHEBA	92a	
	הלך	WALK	231d	1 d5 tb
	נוח	REST	629a	B 2
19 4	אב	FATHER	3c	4 a
	דרך	JOURNEY	203a	2
	הלך	WALK	230c	1 1d
	הלך	WALK	230c	1 1d 2a
	טוב	PLEASANT	374c	6
	יום	DAY	398b	2 b
	מות	DIE	560a	2 b
	נפש	SOUL	659d	3 c
	נפש	SOUL	659d	3 c
	עתה	NOW	774a	1 a
	רב	MUCH	913b	1 f
	רתם	BROOM-PLANT	958c	
	שאל	ASK	981c	1 a
19 5	חנח	BEHOLD	244b	C
	זה	THIS	261c	4 g
	ישן	SLEEP	445c	
	מלאך	MESSENGER	521d	2
	נגע	TOUCH	619a	1 a
	רתם	BROOM-PLANT	958c	
	שכב	LIE DOWN	1012a	1 b
19 6	נבט	LOOK	613c	1 a
	ענה	BREAD-CAKE	728b	
	צפחת	JAR	860b	
	מראשות	HEAD-PLACE	912b	
	רצפה	GLOWING STONE	954b	
	שוב	TURN BACK	998b	1 b
19 7	דרך	JOURNEY	203a	2
	מלאך	MESSENGER	521d	2
	מן	THAN	582d	6 d
	נגע	TOUCH	619a	1 a
	רב	GREAT	913c	2 d
	שוב	TURN BACK	997c	3 b
19 8	אכלה	A MEAL	38b	
	אלהים	GOD	44a	3 b
	הלך	WALK	231d	1 d5 ta
	הר	MOUNTAIN	249b	1 a
	הר	MOUNTAIN	249d	1 a
	חרב	HOREB	352a	
	יום	DAY	398b	1
	כח	STRENGTH	470c	1 a
	לילה	NIGHT	538d	1

Ch	v.	Heb	Eng	Page	Sec
19	9	ארבעים	FORTY	917b	1 a
		דבר	WORD	182c	12a
		מה	WHAT	552d	1 ad
		פה	HERE	806a	1 a
19	10	בד	SEPARATION	94c	1 b
		בקש	SEEK	134d	2 a
		ברית	COVENANT	137b	3 3
		הרג	KILL	247a	1
		הרס	THROW DOWN	248c	1
		מזבח	ALTAR	259c	0
		יתר	BE LEFT OVER	451b	
		לקח	TAKE	543a	3 d
		נפש	SOUL	659d	3 c
		עזב	LEAVE	737c	2 d2
		צבא	GOD OF WAR	839b	4 b
		קנא	BE ZEALOUS	888c	3 a
19	11	ב	IN	88b	1 1
		הנה	BEHOLD	244b	C
		הר	MOUNTAIN	249b	1 a
		חזק	STRONG	305c	1 c
		לא	NOT	519b	1 bb
		פרק	TEAR APART	830a	
		רעש	SHAKING	950b	1
		שבר	BREAK	991a	
19	12	דממה	WHISPER	199a	
		דק	SMALL	201a	2
		קול	VOICE	877a	1 b
		רעש	SHAKING	950b	1
19	13	אדרת	MANTLE	12b	2
		לוט	WRAP	532a	
		מערה	CAVE	792c	
		פה	HERE	806a	1 a
		פנה	FACE	815d	1 1a
		פתח	OPENING	835d	
		קול	VOICE	877a	1 b
19	14	בד	SEPARATION	94c	1 b
		בקש	SEEK	134d	2 a
		ברית	COVENANT	137b	3 3
		הרג	KILL	247a	1 a
		הרס	THROW DOWN	248c	1
		מזבח	ALTAR	259a	0
		יתר	BE LEFT OVER	451b	
		לקח	TAKE	543a	3 d
		נפש	SOUL	659d	3 c
		עזב	LEAVE	737c	2 d2
		צבא	GOD OF WAR	839b	4 b
		קנא	BE ZEALOUS	888c	3 a
19	15	דמשק	DAMASCUS	199c	
		הלך	WALK	234b	1 5f 3
		חזהאל	HAZAEL	303c	
		שוב	TURN BACK	997a	3 a
19	16	אבל	ABEL	6a	5
		אלישע	ELISHA	46a	
		יהוא	JEHU	219d	1
		משח	ANOINT	603a	2
		משח	ANOINT	603b	2
		נמשי	NIMSHI	650a	
		שפט	SHAPHAT	1048b	1
19	17	יהוא	JEHU	219d	1
		היה	COME TO PASS	225a	1 2b ag
		חזהאל	HAZAEL	303c	
		מות	DIE	560b	1 b
		מלט	SLIP AWAY	572c	2
19	18	בעל	BAAL	127d	2 2
		ברך	KNEE	139c	
		כרע	BOW DOWN	502c	1
		נשק	KISS	676b	
		פה	MOUTH	804d	1 b
		שאר	REMAIN	984b	1
19	19	אדרת	MANTLE	12b	2
		ב	IN	89c	3 1a
		בקר	CATTLE	*133c	
		הלך	WALK	231c	1 1d 4
		ו	AND	253c	1 k
		חרש	CUT IN	360c	2
		עבר	PASS OVER	718a	5 a
		עשר	TEN	797b	2 a
		צמד	COUPLE	855a	1
		שלך	THROW	1021a	1 a
		שפט	SHAPHAT	1048b	1
19	20	אב	FATHER	3b	1
		אם	MOTHER	51d	1
		אם	MOTHER	52a	1
		בקר	CATTLE	133c	
		הלך	WALK	234b	1 5f 3
		נשק	KISS	676b	
		עזב	LEAVE	737b	2 a2
		רוץ	RUN	930b	1
19	21	בקר	CATTLE	133c	2
		בקר	CATTLE	133c	2
		בשר	FLESH	142c	1 a
		בשל	BOIL	143a	2
		זבח	SLAUGHTER FOR SACRIFICE	257a	2
		כלי	EQUIPMENT	480a	2 d
		לקח	TAKE	543c	4 g
		צמד	COUPLE	855a	1
		שוב	TURN BACK	996d	1
		שרת	SERVE	1058a	1 c
20	1	בנהדד	BEN-HADAD	122b	2
		בנהדד	BEN-HADAD	*122b	
		הדדעזר	HADADEZER	*212d	
		לחם	ENGAGE IN BAT-TLE	535c	
		מלך	KING	573a	1

Ch	v.	Heb	Eng	Page	Sec
		סום	HORSE	692c	1
		צור	CONFINE	848d	2
		קבץ	GATHER	867d	2
		שמרון	SAMARIA	1037d	
20	2	אחאב	AHAB	26c	1
20	3	אמר	SAY	56a	1
		בנהדד	BEN-HADAD	122b	2
		זהב	GOLD	262c	
		טוב	PLEASANT	373c	1 a
		ל	TO	513b	5 ba
20	4	ל	TO	513b	5 ba
20	5	אמר	SAY	56a	1
		בנהדד	BEN-HADAD	122b	2
		זהב	GOLD	262c	
		כי	THAT	472a	1 b
		שוב	TURN BACK	997c	3 b
		שלח	SEND	1018b	1 c
20	6	היה	COME TO PASS	225a	1 2b ag
		מחמד	DESIRE	327a	
		חפש	SEARCH	344c	1
		כיאם	SURELY	475c	2 c
		מחר	TO-MORROW	564a	1 a
		עת	TIME	773c	1 a
		סום	TO PLACE	963a	1 a
20	7	בקש	SEEK	134d	2 b
		זהב	GOLD	262c	
		זקן	OLD	278d	2 b
		ידע	KNOW	394a	1 g
		ל	TO	514b	5 fa
		מנע	WITHHOLD	586a	
		ראה	TO SEE	907c	5 b
20	8	אבה	BE WILLING	2c	
		זקן	OLD	278d	2 b
20	9	בנהדד	BEN-HADAD	122b	2
		דבר	WORD	182b	1 c
		ראשון	FIRST	912a	3 a1
20	10	בנהדד	BEN-HADAD	122b	2
		יסף	ADD	415b	1
		עם	PEOPLE	766c	2 d
		עפר	DRY EARTH	779d	1 e
		רגל	FOOT	920a	1 f
		שפק	SUFFICE	974b	1
		שמרון	SAMARIA	1037d	
		שעל	HANDFUL	1043b	2
20	11	הלל	BE BOASTFUL	239a	1
		חגר	GIRD	292a	2
		פתח	OPEN	835c	2
20	12	דבר	WORD	182b	1 c
		סכה	THICKET	697c	2
		שום	TO PLACE	964b	4 a
20	13	אחאב	AHAB	26c	1
		ה	INTERROG PART	210a	1 c
		יהוה	YAHWEH	219a	2 2b a
		המון	CROWD	242c	3 a
		ידע	KNOW	393d	1 a
		נגש	DRAW NEAR	621a	
20	14	אחאב	AHAB	26c	1
		אסר	TIE	64a	5
		מדינה	PROVINCE	193d	1
		מלחמה	WAR	536a	
		מלחמה	WAR	536c	
		מי	WHO	566b	B
		נער	RETAINER	655a	2 b
		שר	CHIEFTAIN	978b	2 c
20	15	מדינה	PROVINCE	193d	1
		שר	CHIEFTAIN	978b	2 c
		שבע	SEVEN	988b	4
		שנים	TWO	1041b	3
20	16	בנהדד	BEN-HADAD	122b	2
		סכה	THICKET	697c	2
		עזר	HELP	740b	1
		צהר	MIDDAY	843d	1
		שכר	DRUNKEN	1016c	
20	17	בנהדד	BEN-HADAD	122b	2
		מדינה	PROVINCE	193d	1
		יצא	GO OUT	422d	1 a
		ראשון	FIRST	912a	3 a2
		שר	CHIEFTAIN	978b	2 c
		שלח	SEND	1018c	1 c
20	18	חי	ALIVE	312a	1 b
		יצא	GO OUT	423d	2 c
		מלחמה	WAR	536a	
		תפש	LAY HOLD OF	1074d	1
20	19	מדינה	PROVINCE	193d	1
		יצא	GO OUT	423d	2 c
		שר	CHIEFTAIN	978b	2 c
20	20	ארם	ARAM	74b	A
		בנהדד	BEN-HADAD	122b	2
		מלט	SLIP AWAY	572b	2
		סום	HORSE	*692c	1
		פרש	HORSEMAN	832a	1
20	21	ארם	ARAM	74b	A
		נכה	SMITE	646a	2
		מכה	SLAUGHTER	647a	2
20	22	חזק	BE FIRM	305b	1
		ידע	KNOW	394a	1 g
		ראה	TO SEE	907c	5 b
		תשובה	RETURN	1000c	1
20	23	אולם	BUT	19d	2
		אלהים	GOD	44d	4 a
		אם	IF	50b	1 b2
		את	WITH	85c	
		הר	MOUNTAIN	250b	1 e
		חזק	BE FIRM	304b	1 1b
		מישור	LEVEL PLACE	449d	1
		כן	SO	487b	3 f

Ch	v.	Heb	Eng	Page	Sec
		לחם	ENGAGE IN BAT-TLE	535c	
		עמק	VALE	771a	
20	24	מקום	STANDING PLACE	879d	1 c
		שום	TO PLACE	964a	3 d
20	25	את	WITH	85c	
		חזק	BE FIRM	304b	1 1b
		מישור	LEVEL PLACE	449d	1
		לחם	ENGAGE IN BAT-TLE	535c	
20	26	מנה	COUNT	584a	1
		אפק	APHEK	67d	1
		בנהדד	BEN-HADAD	122b	2
		היה	COME TO PASS	224c	2 a1 ad
		עמק	VALE	771a	
		תשובה	RETURN	1000c	2
		אפק	ADDENDA ET COR-RIGENDA	1120c	
20	27	הלך	WALK	233d	1 5a
		חנה	DECLINE	333d	2 c2
		חשיף	TWO LITTLE FLOCKS OF GOATS	362d	
		כול	BE SUPPORTED	465b	
		מלא	FILL	570c	1
		נגד	IN FRONT	617b	1 aa
		עז	SHE-GOAT	777c	5
		פקד	ATTEND TO	823d	
		קרא	ENCOUNTER	897a	1
20	28	אלהים	GOD	43c	2 a
		אלהים	GOD	44a	3 b
		יהוה	YAHWEH	219a	2 2b a
		המון	CROWD	242c	3 a
		הר	MOUNTAIN	250b	1 e
		ו	AND	254d	5 a
		ידע	KNOW	393d	1 a
		עמק	VALE	771a	
20	29	מלחמה	WAR	536a	
		מלחמה	WAR	536c	
		מאה	HUNDRED	547d	1 a1
		נכח	FRONT	647b	1
		קרב	COME NEAR	897c	1 h
		רגלי	ON FOOT	920b	
20	30	אפק	APHEK	67d	1
		בנהדד	BEN-HADAD	122b	2
		חדר	CHAMBER	293d	
		חומה	WALL	327c	1
		יתר	BE LEFT OVER	451c	
		נפל	FALL	657a	1
		שבע	SEVEN	988b	4
		אפק	ADDENDA ET COR-RIGENDA	1120c	
20	31	הנה	BEHOLD	244a	B a
		חבל	CORD	286c	1
		חיה	LIVE	311c	1
		חסד	GOODNESS	338d	1 2
		מתנים	LOINS	608b	1 e
		נפש	SOUL	659c	2
		שום	TO PLACE	963a	1 a
		שק	SACK	974c	2 a
20	32	אח	BROTHER	26b	2
		בנהדד	BEN-HADAD	122b	2
		חבל	CORD	286c	1
		חגר	GIRD	291d	2
		חיה	LIVE	311a	1 b
		חי	ALIVE	312a	1 b
		מתנים	LOINS	608b	1 e
		נפש	SOUL	659c	2
		עוד	STILL	728d	1 aa
		שק	SACK	974c	2 a
20	33	אח	BROTHER	26b	2
		בנהדד	BEN-HADAD	122b	2
		חלט	CATCH	319a	
		מהר	HASTEN	555a	2
		נחש	OBSERVE SIGNS	638c	2
		עלה	GO UP	749c	1 d
		על	UPON	757a	2 7b
		מרכבה	CHARIOT	939d	
20	34	בנהדד	BEN-HADAD	*122b	2
		ברית	COVENANT	136b	1 1
		דמשק	DAMASCUS	199d	
		חוץ	THE OUTSIDE	300a	2 a
		כרת	CUT	503d	4
		ל	TO	515b	5 hb a
		שום	TO PLACE	963d	3 b
		שוב	TURN BACK	999b	1 d
20	35	בן	SON	121c	7 a
		מאן	REFUSE	549a	
		נביא	PROPHET	611c	1
		נכה	SMITE	645c	1 b
		רע	FRIEND	946a	1
20	36	אצל	BESIDE	69b	B
		אריה	LION	71d	
		את	WITH	86c	4 a
		הלך	WALK	231c	1 1d 4
		הנה	BEHOLD	244b	B b
		מצא	FIND	593b	2 a
		נכה	SMITE	646a	2 c
20	37	נכה	SMITE	645c	1 b
		פצע	BRUISE	822d	
20	38	אפר	COVERING	68b	
		דרך	WAY	202c	1
		חפש	SEARCH	344c	
		ל	TO	511d	1 h
		על	UPON	758c	4 2a
		עמד	STAND	763d	1 a

Ch v.	Heb	Eng	Page	Sec
20 39	יצא	GO OUT	423d	2 c
	כסף	SILVER	494b	8 c
	כסף	SILVER	494c	9
	ככר	ROUND	503b	3 b
	מלחמה	WAR	536a	
	נפש	SOUL	659d	3 c
	פקד	ATTEND TO	823d	1
	צעק	CRY	858c	1 a
	קרב	INWARD PART	899b	1 f7
	שמר	KEEP	1036c	1 b
	שקל	WEIGH	1053c	2
	תחת	INSTEAD	1066a	2 2b b
20 40	אין	NOT	34b	2 b
	הנה	HITHER	244c	A a
	חרץ	CUT	358c	3
	כן	SO	485d	1 b
	משפט	JUDGMENT	1048c	1 e
20 41	אפר	COVERING	68b	
	מהר	HASTEN	555a	2
	ככר	RECOGNIZE	648a	2
	על	UPON	758c	4 2a
20 42	איש	MAN	36a	
	חרם	DEVOTED THING	356b	3
	נפש	SOUL	659d	3 c
	יען	ON ACCOUNT OF	774d	2 c
	תחת	INSTEAD	1066a	2 2b b
20 43	אל	TO	41b	
	הלך	WALK	231a	1 d3 gb
	זעף	VEXED	277a	
	סר	STUBBORN	711a	
	על	UPON	757b	2 7c ab
	שמרון	SAMARIA	1037d	
21 1	אחר	AFTER	29d	2 b
	אצל	BESIDE	69b	A
	דבר	WORD	183c	4 4
	היה	COME TO PASS	224d	1 2a 1b
	היכל	PALACE	228b	1
	יזרעאלי	JEZREELITE	283c	1
	יזראל	JEZREEL	283c	1 b
	כרם	VINEYARD	501d	
	נבות	NABOTH	613b	
	שמרון	SAMARIA	1038a	
21 2	גן	GARDEN	171a	
	הוא	HE, SHE, IT	*216a	3 a
	זה	THIS	260c	1 a
	טוב	PLEASING	373b	5
	טוב	PLEASANT	374c	6
	ירק	HERBS	438d	
	כסף	SILVER	494c	8 e
	מחיר	PRICE	564b	1
	נבות	NABOTH	613b	
	נתן	GIVE	679b	1 n
	נתן	GIVE	679c	1 p
	קרב	NEAR	898b	1
	תחת	INSTEAD	1066a	2 2b b
21 3	אב	FATHER	3c	4 a
	חלילה	FAR BE IT	321a	
	נבות	NABOTH	613b	
	נחלה	INHERITANCE	635c	3
21 4	אב	FATHER	3c	4 a
	אל	TO	41b	
	זעף	VEXED	277a	
	יזרעאלי	JEZREELITE	283c	1
	נחלה	INHERITANCE	635c	3
	מטה	COUCH	641d	
	סבב	TURN ABOUT	686c	1 a
	סר	STUBBORN	711a	
	על	UPON	754b	2 1f b
	על	UPON	754d	2 1f g
	על	UPON	757b	2 7c ab
	שכב	LIE DOWN	1012a	1 b
21 5	איזבל	JEZEBEL	33b	
	זה	THIS	261c	4 c
	מה	HOW	553c	2 aa
	סר	STUBBORN	711a	
	רוח	BREATH	925a	3 a
21 6	יזרעאלי	JEZREELITE	283c	1
	חפץ	DELIGHTING IN	343a	1
	כסף	SILVER	494d	9
	נתן	GIVE	679b	1 o
	נתן	GIVE	679c	1 p
21 7	יזרעאלי	JEZREELITE	283c	1
	יטב	BE GLAD	405c	1
	לב	HEART	525c	2 9a
	מלוכה	KINGSHIP	574d	
	נתן	GIVE	678d	1 b
	עשה	DO	793d	1 1a 1
21 8	ב	IN	90a	3 2d
	זן	OLD	279a	2 b
	חר	NOBLE	359d	
	חתם	SEAL	367d	1
	חתם	SEAL	368b	
	ספר	MISSIVE	707a	1 a
	ספר	MISSIVE	707a	1 a
	שם	NAME	1028a	2 a
21 9	ישב	CAUSE TO SIT	443c	1
	כתב	WRITE	507c	1 b3
	ספר	MISSIVE	707a	1 a
	ספר	MISSIVE	707a	1 a
	צום	FASTING	847b	
	קרא	CALL	895b	3 a
	ראש	HEAD	911a	3 d
21 10	בליעל	WORTHLESSNESS	116a	1
	ברך	BLESS	139b	5
	יצא	BRING OUT	424d	1 g
	ישב	CAUSE TO SIT	443c	1
	מות	DIE	559d	2 a
	סקל	STONE	709c	
	עוד	BEAR WITNESS	730a	1
21 11	זן	OLD	279a	2 b
	חר	NOBLE	359d	
	ספר	MISSIVE	707a	1 a
	ספר	MISSIVE	707a	1 a
21 12	ישב	CAUSE TO SIT	443c	1
	צום	FASTING	847b	
	קרא	CALL	895b	3 a
	ראש	HEAD	911a	3 d
21 13	אבן	STONE	6b	1
	בליעל	WORTHLESSNESS	116a	1
	בליעל	WORTHLESSNESS	116a	1
	ברך	BLESS	139b	5
	חוץ	THE OUTSIDE	300a	1 bd
	יצא	BRING OUT	424d	1 g
	מות	DIE	559d	2 a
	מות	DIE	559d	2 a
	נגד	IN FRONT	617b	1 aa
	סקל	STONE	709c	
	עוד	BEAR WITNESS	730a	1
21 14	מות	DIE	559d	2 a
21 15	יזרעאלי	JEZREELITE	283c	1
	חי	ALIVE	312a	1 b
	ירש	TAKE POSSESSION	439c	1 a
	כי	BUT	474b	3 e
	כסף	SILVER	494d	9
	מאן	REFUSE	549a	
	מות	DIE	559d	2 a
21 16	יזרעאלי	JEZREELITE	283c	1
	ירש	TAKE POSSESSION	439c	1 a
21 17	דבר	WORD	182c	1 2a
21 18	תשבי	TISHBITE	986c	
	ירש	TAKE POSSESSION	439c	1 a
	שם	THERE	1027b	2
21 19	שמרון	SAMARIA	1038c	
	אתה	THOU	61c	
	דם	BLOOD	196c	2 a
	ה	INTERROG PART	210a	1 c
	ירש	TAKE POSSESSION	439c	1 a
	כלב	DOG	476d	A
	לקק	LICK	545a	
	מקום	STANDING PLACE	880b	4
	רצח	MURDER	953d	
21 20	איב	BE HOSTILE TO	33c	
	מצא	FIND	593a	1 b
	יען	ON ACCOUNT OF	774d	1
21 21	בער	CONSUME	129b	3
	כרת	CUT OFF	504c	2 c
	עזב	LEAVE	737d	3
	קיר	WALL	885a	3
	שתן	URINATE	1010b	
21 22	אחיהו	AHIJAH	26d	4
	אל	TO	40c	6
	בית	HOUSE	110a	5 c
	חטא	MISS A GOAL OR WAY	*307d	2
	חטא	MISS A GOAL OR WAY	307d	2
	כעס	VEX	495a	2
	כעס	ANGER	495b	2
	נבט	NEBAT	614a	
21 23	אכל	EAT	37c	2
	יזראל	JEZREEL	283c	1 b
	חל	RAMPART	298a	1
	חלק	PORTION	324b	2 d
	כלב	DOG	476d	A
21 24	אכל	EAT	37c	2
	כלב	DOG	476d	A
	שדה	FIELD	961c	1 f
21 25	היה	BE	226d	3 1
	סות	INCITE	694d	2
	רק	ONLY	956d	2 e
21 26	אמרי	AMORITES	57c	2 b
	ירש	CAUSE TO POSSESS	440a	2 a
	תעב	BE ABHORRED	1073b	1
21 27	את	GENTLENESS	31d	A
	בשר	FLESH	142c	2
	הלך	WALK	235c	4
	צום	FAST	847a	
	שום	TO PLACE	963b	1 b
	שק	SACK	974c	2 a
	שק	SACK	974c	2 b
	שכב	LIE DOWN	1012a	1 b
21 28	דבר	WORD	182c	1 2a
	תשבי	TISHBITE	986c	
21 29	יום	DAY	399b	4 b
	כנע	BE HUMBLE	488c	1
	יען	ON ACCOUNT OF	774d	2 b
	פנה	FACE	818a	2 5b
	רעה	MISERY	949a	1
22 1	ישב	REMAIN	443a	2 b
	שמנה	EIGHT	1033a	1 a
22 2	יהושפט	JEHOSHAPHAT	221d	1
	ירד	GO DOWN	433a	1 e
22 3	חשה	BE SILENT	364d	2
	מלך	KING	573a	1
	מן	FROM	583b	7 ba
22 4	כ	LIKE	454b	2 a
	סוס	HORSE	692c	2
22 5	דרש	SEEK	205b	2 a
22 6	יום	DAY	400d	7 h
	אדון	LORD	11b	3 2a
	אם	IF	50d	2 ab a
	הלך	WALK	231a	1 d3 gb
	חדל	CEASE	293a	2
	יד	HAND	390d	5 b3
	נביא	PROPHET	612a	3
22 7	קבץ	GATHER	867d	2
	את	WITH	85c	
	את	WITH	86d	4 a
	דרש	SEEK	205b	2 a
	עוד	STILL	729b	1 c
22 8	את	WITH	85c	
	דרש	SEEK	205b	2 a
	דרש	SEEK	205b	2 a
	טוב	PLEASANT	374a	2 f
	כן	SO	486a	1 ca
	מיכיהו	MICAH	567c	2
	ימלה	IMLAH	571c	
	נבא	PROPHESY	612b	1 b
	עוד	STILL	729b	1
	רע	EVIL	948d	2
22 9	מהר	HASTEN	555a	3
	ימלה	IMLAH	571c	
	סרים	EUNUCH	710c	
22 10	גרן	THRESHING-FLOOR	175b	
	לבש	ARRAYED	528b	
	נביא	PROPHET	612a	3
	נבא	PROPHESY	612c	3
	פתח	OPENING	836a	
	שער	GATE	1045a	2 a
	אלה	THESE	41c	D
22 11	ברזל	IRON	137c	1 d
	כלה	FINISH	478c	2 c1
	כנענה	CHENAANAH	489b	1
	נגח	PUSH	618c	
	צדקיהו	ZEDEKIAH	843c	2 a
	קרן	HORN	901d	1 a
22 12	נביא	PROPHET	612a	3
	נבא	PROPHESY	612b	2
	צלח	ADVANCE	852c	2
22 13	דבר	SPEAK	181a	2
	הנה	BEHOLD	244a	B a
	טוב	PLEASANT	374a	2 f
	טוב	PLEASANT	374a	2 f
	נביא	PROPHET	612a	3
22 14	חי	ALIVE	311d	1 a
22 15	אם	IF	50d	2 ab a
	הלך	WALK	231a	1 d3 ga
	חדל	CEASE	293a	2
	צלח	ADVANCE	852c	2
22 16	אמת	FIRMNESS	54b	4 a
	אשר	THAT	83c	8 ab
	מה	HOW	553d	4 ca
	פעם	OCCURRENCE	822a	3 a
	רק	ONLY	956c	2 d
	שבע	SWEAR	989d	1
22 17	אלה	THESE	41c	D
	הר	MOUNTAIN	250c	1 g
	ל	TO	513b	5 ba
	לא	NOT	519b	1 bb
	פוץ	BE DISPERSED	807a	1
	צאן	SMALL CATTLE	838b	2
22 18	טוב	PLEASANT	374a	2 f
	נבא	PROPHESY	612b	1 b
	רע	EVIL	948d	2
22 19	ימין	RIGHT HAND	*411d	2 a
	ימין	RIGHT HAND	411d	2 a
	כן	SO	487a	3 da
	כסא	SEAT OF HONOR	490d	1 b
	על	UPON	756b	2 6c
	צבא	HOST	839a	1 b
22 20	בגד	GARMENT	94a	
	זה	THIS	260d	1 b
	כה	THUS	462b	1 b
	ככה	THUS	462c	
	נפל	FALL	657a	2 a
	פתה	BE SIMPLE	834d	2
22 21	עמד	STAND	764a	1 d
	פתה	BE SIMPLE	834d	2
	רוח	BREATH	925d	9 a
22 22	גם	ALSO	*169d	4
	יכל	PREVAIL	408a	2 a
	נביא	PROPHET	612a	3
	פתה	BE SIMPLE	834d	2
	רוח	BREATH	925d	9 a
22 23	אלה	THESE	41c	A
	דבר	SPEAK	181c	5
	נביא	PROPHET	612a	3
	נתן	PUT	680c	2
	רוח	BREATH	925d	9 a
22 24	אי	WHERE	32b	1 b
	את	WITH	85c	
	דבר	SPEAK	181b	3 d
	כנענה	CHENAANAH	489b	1
	לחי	CHEEK	534d	1
	נכה	SMITE	645b	1 a
	עבר	PASS OVER	717b	1 h
	צדקיהו	ZEDEKIAH	843c	2 a
	רוח	BREATH	925d	9 a
22 25	אשר	PARTICLE OF RELATION	82c	4 ba
	הנה	BEHOLD	244b	B b
	חבא	WITHDRAW	285d	
	חדר	CHAMBER	293d	
22 26	אמון	AMON	54c	B
	יהואש	JEHOASH	220a	4
	שר	CHIEFTAIN	978b	2 d
	שוב	TURN BACK	998d	1 a

Ch	v.	Heb	Eng	Page	Sec
22	27	אכל	EAT	38a	1
		את	MARK OF THE AC-CUSATIVE	84d	1a
		בית	HOUSE	109a	1 ae 2
		זה	THIS	260c	1 a
		כלא	CONFINEMENT	476c	
		לחם	FOOD	537c	3 a
		לחץ	OPPRESSION	537d	
		מי	WATER	565d	3
22	28	דבר	SPEAK	181c	4 a
		כל	ALL	481d	1 da
		שוב	TURN BACK	997b	3 b
22	30	חפש	SEARCH	344c	
		לבש	PUT ON	527d	A
22	31	אשר	PARTICLE OF RE-LATION	83a	7 b
		כיאם	EXCEPT	474d	2 a
		לחם	ENGAGE IN BAT-TLE	535c	
		קטן	SMALL	882b	2
		שר	CHIEFTAIN	978c	3 b
22	32	זעק	CRY	277b	2 d
		לחם	ENGAGE IN BAT-TLE	535c	
		שר	CHIEFTAIN	978c	3 b
22	33	היה	BE	*227a	3 4b
		לא	NOT	519b	1 bb
		שר	CHIEFTAIN	978c	3 b
22	34	שוב	TURN BACK	996d	1
		דבק	APPENDAGE	180a	2
		הפך	TURN	245b	1 a
		מחנה	ENCAMPMENT	334b	3 c
		יצא	CAUSE TO GO	424c	1 a
		ל	TO	*516c	5 jb
		משך	DRAW	604b	2
		נכה	SMITE	645c	1 a
		קשת	BOW	906c	1 d
		רכב	CHARIOTEER	939b	1
		שריון	BODY-ARMOUR	1056b	
		תם	INTEGRITY	1070d	2
22	35	דם	BLOOD	196c	2 a
		ה	THE	207b	1 cb
		היה	BE	227c	3 5a
		חיק	BOSOM	300d	3 b
		יצק	POUR	427b	4
		מכה	BLOW	646d	1 c
		נכח	FRONT	647b	1
		עלה	GO UP	748c	2 c
		עמד	STAND	765a	
		ערב	SUNSET	787d	1 a
		רכב	CHARIOT	939b	2
		מרכבה	CHARIOT	939d	
22	36	בוא	COME	98a	1 i
		רנה	RINGING CRY	943d	2
22	38	ברכה	POOL	140a	1
		דם	BLOOD	196c	2 a
		זנה	COMMIT FORNICA-TION	275d	1
		כלב	DOG	476d	A
		לקק	LICK	545a	2
		רחץ	WASH OFF	934c	2
		רכב	CHARIOT	939b	2
		שטף	OVERFLOW	1009b	3
22	39	בית	HOUSE	108d	1 ag
		בנה	BUILD	124b	1 ab
		שן	IVORY	1042b	2
22	40	אב	FATHER	3c	4 a
		אחזי	AHAZIAH	28d	1
22	41	ארבע	FOUR	917a	1 a4
		שנה	YEAR	1040c	
22	42	עזובה	AZUBAH	738a	1
		שלחי	SHILHI	1019d	
		שלשים	THIRTY	1026c	1
22	43	דרך	WAY	203d	6 c
		ישר	STRAIGHT	449a	2 a
22	44	במה	HIGH PLACE	119c	3 c
		במה	HIGH PLACE	119c	3
		זבח	SLAUGHTER FOR SACRIFICE	257b	2
		סור	TURN ASIDE	694a	3
		עוד	STILL	728d	1 aa
		קטר	MAKE SACRAFICES SMOKE	882d	
22	45	שלם	BE IN COVENANT OF PEACE	1023d	1
22	46	גבורה	MIGHT	150c	2
		לחם	ENGAGE IN BAT-TLE	*535c	
22	47	בער	CONSUME	129b	3
		יום	DAY	399b	4 b
		יתר	REMAINDER	451d	1 a
		קדש	TEMPLE-PROSTI-TUTE	873d	
22	49	אופיר	OPHIR	20c	2
		אופיר	OPHIR	20d	2
		אופיר	OPHIR	20d	2
		אניה	A SHIP	58b	
		אניה	A SHIP	58c	
		הלך	WALK	232b	1 3
		זהב	GOLD	262c	1
		זהב	GOLD	263b	7
		עציונגבר	EZION-GEBER	782b	
		עשר	BE RICH	799b	
		שבר	BREAK	990d	
		תרשיש	TARSHISH	1077a	1
22	50	אבה	BE WILLING	2c	

Ch	v.	Heb	Eng	Page	Sec
		אחזי	AHAZIAH	28d	1
		אניה	A SHIP	58b	
22	51	דוד	DAVID	188a	A
		אב	FATHER	3c	4a
22	52	יהורם	JEHORAM	221b	1
		אחזי	AHAZIAH	28d	1
		עשר	TEN	797b	7 b
		שבע	SEVEN	988b	2 a
		שמרון	SAMARIA	1038a	
22	53	דרך	WAY	203d	6 d
		חטא	MISS A GOAL OR WAY	*307d	2
		חטא	MISS A GOAL OR WAY	307d	2
22	54	נבט	NEBAT	614a	
		בעל	BAAL	127d	2 2
		כעס	VEX	495a	2
		עבד	WORK	713b	4 b

2 KINGS

Ch	v.	Heb	Eng	Page	Sec
1	1	פשע	REBEL	833b	1
1	2	אחזי	AHAZIAH	28d	1
		אם	IF	50d	2 ba
		בעד	AWAY FROM	126b	1 a
		בעל	BAAL	127d	2 4
		דרש	SEEK	205b	2 b
		זה	THIS	261a	2 ba
		חיה	LIVE	311b	2 a
		חלה	BE WEAK	317d	2
		חלי	SICKNESS	318b	
		נפל	FALL	656d	1
		עליה	ROOF-CHAMBER	751a	
		עקרון	EKRON	785d	
		שבכה	LATTICE-WORK	959a	1
1	3	אליה	ELIJAH	45b	
		בלי	WEARING OUT	115d	C a
		בעל	BAAL	127d	2 4
		דרש	SEEK	205b	2 b
		מלאך	MESSENGER	521d	2
		עלה	GO UP	748c	2 a
		עקרון	EKRON	785d	
		תשבי	TISHBITE	986c	
		שמרון	SAMARIA	1038a	
1	4	ירד	GO DOWN	433c	1 f
		כן	SO	*487a	3 da
		מות	DIE	560a	2 b
		מטה	COUCH	642a	
		עלה	GO UP	748b	1 c
		שם	THERE	1027b	2
1	5	זה	THIS	261c	4 c
		מה	HOW	553c	2 aa
		שוב	TURN BACK	997b	3 b
1	6	בלי	WEARING OUT	115d	C a
		בעל	BAAL	127d	2 4
		דרש	SEEK	205b	2 b
		ירד	GO DOWN	433c	1 f
		כן	SO	486d	3 d
		כן	SO	*487a	3 da
		מות	DIE	560a	2 b
		מטה	COUCH	642a	
		עלה	GO UP	748c	2 a
		עקרון	EKRON	785d	
		שוב	TURN BACK	997a	3 a
		שם	THERE	1027b	2
1	7	עלה	GO UP	748c	2 a
		משפט	JUDGMENT	1049b	6 c
1	8	אור	GIRD	25a	
		אזור	WAISTCLOTH	25b	
		בעל	LORD	127c	1 5a
		מתנים	LOINS	608a	1 a
		עור	SKIN	736b	2
		שער	HAIR	972b	1
		תשבי	TISHBITE	986c	
1	9	אלהים	GOD	44a	3 b
		הר	MOUNTAIN	249c	1 a
		הר	MOUNTAIN	250d	1 m
		חמשים	FIFTY	332b	1 a
		שר	CHIEFTAIN	978c	3 b
1	10	אכל	EAT	37c	3
		אש	FIRE	77c	2
		ירד	GO DOWN	433c	2
		ענה	ANSWER	773a	1 e
		שמי	HEAVENS	1029d	1 a
1	11	מהרה	HASTE	555b	
		ענה	ANSWER	773a	1 e
		ענה	ANSWER	773a	2 a
		שוב	TURN BACK	998b	8
1	12	אכל	EAT	37c	3
		אש	FIRE	77c	2
		ירד	GO DOWN	433c	2
		ענה	ANSWER	773a	1 e
1	13	אלה	THESE	41c	A
		אלהים	GOD	44a	3 b
		ברך	KNEE	139c	
		חנן	SHOW FAVOR	336b	1
		יקר	BE PRECIOUS	429d	1 b
		כרע	BOW DOWN	502c	1
		נגד	IN FRONT	617d	2 b
		שוב	TURN BACK	998b	8
		שלשי	THIRD	1026a	
1	14	אכל	EAT	37c	3
		אש	FIRE	77c	2
		חמשים	FIFTY	*332b	1 a
		יקר	BE PRECIOUS	429d	1 b

Ch	v.	Heb	Eng	Page	Sec
		ירד	GO DOWN	433c	3 a
		ראשון	FIRST	911c	1 a
		שר	CHIEFTAIN	978c	3 b
1	15	את	WITH	85c	
		ירא	FEAR	431b	1 c
		מלאך	MESSENGER	521d	2
1	16	בלי	WEARING OUT	115d	C a
		בעל	BAAL	127d	2 4
		דרש	SEEK	205b	2 b
		דרש	SEEK	205b	2 a
		ירד	GO DOWN	433a	1 f
		כן	SO	487a	3 d
		מות	DIE	560a	2 b
		מטה	COUCH	642a	
		עלה	GO UP	748b	1 c
		עקרון	EKRON	785d	
		שלח	SEND	1018c	1 a
		שם	THERE	1027b	2
1	17	יהורם	JEHORAM	221b	2
		יהורם	JEHORAM	221b	1
		יהושפט	JEHOSHAPHAT	221d	1
		מות	DIE	559c	1 a1
1	18	אחזי	AHAZIAH	28d	1
2	1	ב	IN	91a	5 1
		סערה	TEMPEST	704b	
		עלה	GO UP	749c	1 c
		שמי	HEAVENS	1030b	2 b
2	2	אם	IF	50b	1 b2
		חי	ALIVE	312a	1 b
		נפש	SOUL	659c	2
		עזב		737a	1 a
		שלח	SEND	1018c	2 a
2	3	אדון	LORD	11a	2 1d
		ביתאל	BETHEL	110d	1
		בן	SON	121c	7 a
		גם	ALSO	169c	4
		חשה	BE SILENT	364c	1
		לקח	TAKE	543a	3 a
		נביא	PROPHET	611c	1
2	4	חי	ALIVE	312a	1 b
		נפש	SOUL	659c	2
		עזב		737a	1 a
		שלח	SEND	1018c	2 a
2	5	אדון	LORD	11a	2 1d
		בן	SON	121c	7 a
		גם	ALSO	169c	4
		חשה	BE SILENT	364c	1
		נביא	PROPHET	611c	1
2	6	חי	ALIVE	312a	1 b
		נפש	SOUL	659c	2
		עזב		737a	1 a
		שלח	SEND	1018c	2 a
2	7	בן	SON	121c	7 a
		מן	FROM	580c	2
		נביא	PROPHET	611c	1
		נגד	IN FRONT	617d	2 ca
		על	UPON	756a	2 6a
		עמד	STAND	763d	1 a
		עמד	STAND	764a	1 f
		רחק	DISTANT	935c	2 a2
2	8	אדרת	MANTLE	12b	2
		הנה	HITHER	244c	A a
		חצה	DIVIDE	345c	
		חרבה	DRY GROUND	351c	
		נכה	SMITE	645b	1 a
2	9	היה	COME TO PASS	224d	1 2a 1b
		טרם	NOT YET	302c	2
		לקח	TAKE	544a	2
		מה	WHAT	552d	1 b
		נא	PART OF EN-TREATY	609b	3 c
		מעם	FROM WITH	768d	A
		פה	MOUTH	805c	5 b
		רוח	BREATH	925b	3 h
		שאל	ASK	981c	1 a
		שנים	TWO	1041a	1 b1
2	10	אין	NOT	34c	2 dd
		ל	TO	517c	7 bb
		לקח	TAKE	544a	4
		קשה	BE SEVERE	904b	1
		שאל	ASK	981c	1 a
2	11	היה	COME TO PASS	225a	1 2a 1c
		הלך	WALK	233b	1 4c 1g
		סוס	HORSE	692c	2
		סערה	TEMPEST	704b	
		עלה	GO UP	748b	1 c
		פרד	DIVIDE	825c	2
		רכב	CHARIOT	939b	1
		שמי	HEAVENS	1030b	2 b
2	12	אב	FATHER	3d	8
		חזק	BE FIRM	305a	6 a
		פרש	HORSEMAN	832b	
		קרע	TEAR	902c	1 a1
		קרע	TORN PIECES OF GARMENT	902d	
		רכב	CHARIOT	939b	1
2	13	אדרת	MANTLE	12b	2
		ירדן	JORDAN	434d	
		נפל	FALL	656d	1
		רום	BE HIGH	927c	1 c
2	14	אדרת	MANTLE	12b	2
		אלהים	GOD	44c	4 ba

Ch v.	Heb	Eng	Page	Sec
	אף	ALSO	64d	1
	הנה	HITHER	244c	A a
	חצה	DIVIDE	345c	
2 15	נפל	FALL	656d	1
	בן	SON	121c	7 a
	נביא	PROPHET	611c	1
	נגד	IN FRONT	617d	2 ca
	נוח	REST	628a	1
	רוח	BREATH	925b	1
2 16	אדון	LORD	11a	2 1d
	בן	SON	121d	8 a
	בקש	SEEK	134c	1 b
	גיא	VALLEY	161b	
	הר	MOUNTAIN	250b	1a
	נא	PART OF EN-TREATY	609c	4 d
	פן	LEST	815a	2
	רוח	BREATH	925b	9 a
	שלח	SEND	1018b	1 c
	שלך	THROW	1021b	2 b
2 17	בוש	BE ASHAMED	101d	3
	בקש	SEEK	134c	1 a
	מצא	FIND	593a	1 b
	פצר	PUSH	823a	
	שלח	SEND	1018b	1 c
	בוש	ADDENDA ET COR-RIGENDA	1121b	
2 19	אדון	LORD	11b	3 1c
	טוב	PLEASANT	373c	1 a
	מושב	SITUATION	444b	3
	נא	PART OF EN-TREATY	609c	4 d
	קום	STAND	877d	1 b
	ראה	TO SEE	907a	1 b
	רע	EVIL	948b	4
	שכל	BE BEREAVED	1013d	2 a
	משכלת	MISCARRIAGE	1014a	
2 20	חדש	NEW	294a	A
	לקח	TAKE	543c	6
	מלח	SALT	571d	
	צלחת	JAR	852d	
2 21	מוצא	GOING FORTH	425d	3 a
	מלח	SALT	571d	
	רפא	HEAL	951a	1
	שכל	BE BEREAVED	1013d	2 a
	משכלת	MISCARRIAGE	1014a	
2 22	רפא	HEAL	951a	1
2 23	דרך	WAY	202c	1
	ילד	CHILD	*409c	D
	נער	YOUTH	655a	1 c
	קטן	SMALL	882a	1 a
	קלס	MOCK	887b	
	קרח	BALD	901b	
2 24	בקע	CLEAVE	132b	
	דב	BEAR	179a	
	ילד	CHILD	409c	D
	יער	WOOD	420d	B
	מן	FROM	580c	3 a
	פנה	TURN	815b	2 a
	קלל	BE SLIGHT	886c	1
	ארבעים	FORTY	917c	2 a
	שם	NAME	1028b	3
2 25	הר	MOUNTAIN	249c	1 a
	כרמל	CARMEL	502a	1
	שוב	TURN BACK	997b	3 a
3 1	יהורם	JEHORAM	221b	2
	יהושפט	JEHOSHAPHAT	221d	1
	מלך	BE KING	574a	
	מלך	BE KING	574b	
3 2	בעל	BAAL	127d	2 2
	מצבה	PILLAR	663b	1 c
	רק	ONLY	956c	2 b
3 3	דבק	CLING	179a	1 b
	חטא	MISS A GOAL OR WAY	307d	2
	חטאת	SIN	308d	1 b
	נבט	NEBAT	614a	
	סור	TURN ASIDE	693d	1
3 4	איל	RAM	17d	1
	אלף	THOUSAND	49a	1 c
	היה	BE	227a	3 4b
	מישע	MESHA	448a	
	כר	LAMB	503a	
	מלך	KING	573a	1
	נקד	SHEEP-RAISER	667a	
	צמר	WOOL	856a	
	שוב	TURN BACK	999b	1 f
3 5	פשע	REBEL	833b	1
3 6	יהורם	JEHORAM	221b	2
3 7	יהושפט	JEHOSHAPHAT	221d	1
	הלך	WALK	234a	1 5b
	הלך	WALK	*234a	1 5f 2
	סוס	HORSE	692c	2
	פשע	REBEL	833b	1
3 8	אי	WHERE	32b	1 b
	מדבר	WILDERNESS	185a	3 c
	דרך	WAY	202c	1
	דרך	WAY	202d	1
	עלה	GO UP	748b	1 e
3 9	דרך	JOURNEY	203a	2
	מחנה	ENCAMPMENT	334b	3 c
	יום	DAY	398c	2 b
	סבב	GO AROUND	685d	2 c
	רגל	FOOT	920a	1 f
3 10	אהה	ALAS	13c	
3 11	את	WITH	85c	

Ch v.	Heb	Eng	Page	Sec
	דרש	SEEK	205b	2 a
	דרש	SEEK	205b	2 a
	יהושפט	JEHOSHAPHAT	221d	1
	יד	HAND	389a	1 a
	יצק	POUR	427b	1
	ל	TO	513c	5 cb a
	מי	WATER	565b	1 a
	פה	HERE	806a	1 a
3 12	שפט	SHAPHAT	1048b	1
	את	WITH	85c	
	את	WITH	86c	3 a
	דבר	WORD	182c	1 2a
	יהושפט	JEHOSHAPHAT	221d	1
3 13	אל	NOT	39b	A bb
	מה	WHAT	553b	1 dc
	נביא	PROPHET	612a	3
3 14	אם	IF	50b	1 b2
	אם	IF	50b	1 b2
	יהושפט	JEHOSHAPHAT	221d	1
	חי	ALIVE	311d	1 a
	לולא	IF NOT	530c	C
	נבט	LOOK	613d	2
	נשא	LIFT	670c	1 b 3
	עמד	STAND	764a	1 e
	צבא	GOD OF WAR	839c	4 c
3 15	אל	TO	41a	A
	היה	COME TO PASS	225a	1 2a 2
	היה	BECOME	*225d	2 1b
	יד	HAND	390a	1 e2
	לקח	TAKE	543c	6
	נגן	PLAY	618d	
3 16	גב	PIT	155d	
3 17	נחל	WADY	636c	2
	גשם	RAIN	177c	
	מי	WATER	565b	1 b
	מלא	FILL	570b	1
	נחל	WADY	636c	2
	מקנה	CATTLE	889b	2
3 18	זה	THIS	260c	1 a
	קלל	BE SLIGHT	886c	2
3 19	אבן	STONE	6b	1
	מבחור	CHOICE	104d	
	מבצר	FORTIFICATION	131c	
	חלקה	PORTION OF GROUND	324c	1 b
	טוב	PLEASANT	374b	3 c
	טוב	PLEASANT	374b	3 b
	כאב	MAR	456b	3
	נפל	FALL	658a	1 a
	סתם	STOP UP	711b	1
	מעין	SPRING	745d	
3 20	דרך	WAY	202d	1
	היה	COME TO PASS	225a	1 2a 1c
	מלא	FILL	570b	1
	מנחה	OFFERING	585a	3
	עלה	GO UP	749a	6
	עלה	GO UP	749d	8
3 21	גבול	BORDER	147d	1 a
	חגר	GIRD	291d	2
	חגורה	GIRDLE	292b	
	מן	FROM	582a	5 b
	מעל	ABOVE	751d	2 bb a
3 22	אדם	RED	10b	
	בקר	MORNING	133d	1 c
	בקר	MORNING	134b	1 h
	דם	BLOOD	197c	2
	זרח	RISE	280b	1 a
	נגד	IN FRONT	617d	2 ca
3 23	דם	BLOOD	197c	2 o
	זה	THIS	261a	3
	חרב	ATTACK	352b	
	חרב	ATTACK	352b	
	רע	FRIEND	946b	3
3 24	נכה	SMITE	646b	3
3 25	אבן	STONE	6b	1
	הרס	THROW DOWN	248c	1
	חלקה	PORTION OF GROUND	324c	1 b
	טוב	PLEASANT	374b	3 c
	טוב	PLEASANT	374b	3 b
	מלא	FILL	570c	1
	נכה	SMITE	645c	1 a
	נפל	FALL	658a	1 a
	סבב	SURROUND	685d	2 d
	סתם	STOP UP	711b	1
	עד	AS FAR AS	*724b	1 2a b
	מעין	SPRING	745d	
	קיר	KIR	885b	2
	קלע	SLINGER	887c	
	שאר	REMAIN	984b	1
	שנים	TWO	1041a	1 b1
3 26	את	WITH	85c	
	בקע	BREAK OPEN OR THROUGH	132b	
	חזק	BE FIRM	304c	1 4b
	חרב	SWORD	352c	1 c
	מלחמה	WAR	536d	
	שלף	DRAW OUT	1025c	1
3 27	ל	TO	511b	1 ga
	נסע	SET OUT	652b	2 b
	עלה	GO UP	749d	8
	עלה	WHOLE BURNT OF-FERING	750c	
	עלה	WHOLE BURNT OF-FERING	750d	
	על	UPON	759a	4 2b

Ch v.	Heb	Eng	Page	Sec
	קצף	WRATH	893c	1
4 1	בן	SON	121c	7 a
	היה	BE	227a	3 5a
	ילד	CHILD	409b	A
	ירא	FEAR	431c	3 b
	לקח	TAKE	543a	4 a
	נביא	PROPHET	611c	1
	נשה	LEND	674c	
	עבד	SLAVE	714c	7
	צעק	CRY	858c	
4 2	יש	HAVE	441d	2 cb
	אסוך	FLASK	692a	
	שפחה	MAID	1046c	2
	שמן	OIL	1032b	2 b
4 3	חוץ	THE OUTSIDE	299d	1
	כלי	VESSEL	480b	3
	ל	TO	515d	5 ia
	מעט	BE SMALL	589d	B
	נקף	GO AROUND	669a	1 b
	ריק	EMPTY	938a	1
	שאל	ASK	981d	1 b
	שכן	NEIGHBOUR	1015c	2
4 4	בעד	BEHIND	126b	1 b
	דלת	DOOR	195a	1
	יצק	POUR	427b	1
	כלי	VESSEL	480b	3
	מלא	FULL	571a	
	נסע	PULL OUT	652c	2
	סגר	SHUT	689a	1
4 5	בעד	BEHIND	126b	1 b
	דלת	DOOR	195a	1
	ילד	CHILD	*409b	A
	יצק	POUR	427b	
	נגש	APPROACH	621b	
	סגר	SHUT	689a	1
4 6	כלי	VESSEL	480b	3
	מלא	BE FULL	570a	1 a
	נגש	APPROACH	621b	
	עוד	STILL	729b	1 c
	עמד	STAND	764a	2 a
	שמן	OIL	1032b	2 b
4 7	אלהים	GOD	44a	3 b
	יתר	BE LEFT OVER	451c	
	מכר	SELL	569b	
	נשי	DEBT	674c	
	שלם	BE COMPLETE	1022c	3
	שמן	OIL	1032b	2 b
4 8	אכל	EAT	37b	1
	גדול	GREAT	153a	6 b
	די	SUFFICIENCY	191d	2 ca
	היה	COME TO PASS	225a	1 2a 1d
	היה	BECOME	225c	2 1a
	חזק	BE FIRM	305a	5
	יום	DAY	400a	7 b
	סור	TURN ASIDE	693c	1
	עבר	PASS OVER	717d	4 a
	עבר	PASS OVER	718a	5 a
	שונם	SHUNEM	1002a	
4 9	תמיד	CONTINUITY	556c	1 b
	נא	PART OF EN-TREATY	609c	4 d
	על	UPON	756a	2 6a
	קדוש	HOLY	872d	2 b
4 10	היה	COME TO PASS	225b	1 2b ae
	כסא	SEAT OF HONOR	490d	2
	מנורה	LAMPSTAND	633a	1
	מטה	COUCH	641d	
	סור	TURN ASIDE	693c	1
	עליה	ROOF-CHAMBER	751a	
	קטן	SMALL	882a	1 a
	קיר	WALL	885a	1 f
	שום	TO PLACE	964b	4 c
	שלחן	TABLE	1020b	
4 11	היה	BECOME	225c	2 1a
	יום	DAY	400a	7 b
	סור	TURN ASIDE	693c	1
	עליה	ROOF-CHAMBER	751a	
	שכב	LIE DOWN	1012b	2
	שם	THERE	1027c	1a
4 12	נער	RETAINER	655a	2 a
	שונמית	SHUNAMMITE	1002d	2
4 13	אל	TO	40a	3 c
	דבר	SPEAK	181b	3 c
	חרד	TREMBLE	353c	3
	חרדה	TREMBLING	353d	
	יש	CAN	442a	2 cc
	ל	TO	515c	5 hc
	ל	TO	518a	5 bf
	על	UPON	754c	2 lf c
	עם	KINSMAN	769c	
4 14	אבל	VERILY	6a	1
	בן	SON	120a	1
	זקן	BE OLD	278b	
4 16	אדון	LORD	11b	3 1c
	אל	NOT	39b	A bb
	אתי	THOU	61c	
	חבק	CLASP	287d	
	חי	ALIVE	312b	3
	מועד	APPOINTED TIME	417c	1 a
	כזב	LIE	469c	1
	שלה	BE QUIET	*1017b	
	שפחה	MAID	1046c	2
4 17	הרה	CONCEIVE	247d	1
	חי	ALIVE	312b	3
	מועד	APPOINTED TIME	417c	1 a
4 18	גדל	GROW UP	152b	1 a

Ch	v.	Heb	Eng	Page	Sec
		היה	BECOME	225c	2 1a
		יום	DAY	400a	7 b
		ילד	CHILD	409b	A
		קצר	HARVEST	894c	
4	19	ראש	HEAD	910d	1 a
4	20	ברך	KNEE	139c	
		ישב	SIT	442b	1 a
		צהר	MIDDAY	844a	1
4	21	בעד	BEHIND	126c	1 b
		מטה	COUCH	641d	
		סגר	SHUT	689a	1
		שכב	LIE DOWN	1012c	
4	22	אתון	SHE-ASS	87d	
		רוץ	RUN	930b	1
4	23	אתי	THOU	61c	
		חדש	NEW MOON	294c	1
		לא	NOT	519b	1 bb
		שבת	SABBATH	992b	1
4	24	אמר	SAY	56c	4
		אתון	SHE-ASS	87d	
		הלך	WALK	230b	1 1a
		חבש	BIND	290a	1 c
		ל	TO	515b	5 hb a
		ל	TO	517c	7 bb
		נהג	DRIVE	624b	1
		עצר	RESTRAIN	783c	1
		רכב	RIDE	938c	2
4	25	הלז	THIS	229c	
		הלך	WALK	234a	1 5b
		הר	MOUNTAIN	249c	1 a
		כרמל	CARMEL	502a	1
		נגד	IN FRONT	617d	2 ca
		נער	RETAINER	655a	2 a
		שונמית	SHUNAMMITE	1002d	2
4	26	ילד	CHILD	409b	A
		רוץ	RUN	930b	1
		שלום	PEACE	1022d	3
4	27	הדף	THRUST	213d	1
		הר	MOUNTAIN	249c	1 a
		חזק	BE FIRM	305a	6 a
		ל	TO	512b	5 aa
		מרר	BE BITTER	600a	2
		נגד	BE CONSPICUOUS	616d	2
		נגש	DRAW NEAR	620d	1
		עלם	CONCEAL	761a	
		רפה	SINK	952a	3
4	28	אדון	LORD	11b	3 1c
		בן	SON	120a	1
		שלה	BE QUIET	1017b	
4	29	ברך	BLESS	139b	4 a
		חגר	GIRD	291d	1
		כי	IF	473b	2 b
		לקח	TAKE	542d	1
		מצא	FIND	593b	3 a
		מתנים	LOINS	608a	1 c
		שום	TO PLACE	963b	1
		משענת	STAFF	1044a	
4	30	אם	MOTHER	51d	1
		חי	ALIVE	312a	1 b
		נפש	SOUL	659c	2
		עזב	AWAKE	737a	1 a
4	31	קיץ	AWAKE	884c	2
		קשב	ATTENTIVENESS	904a	
		משענת	STAFF	1044a	
		קשב	ADDENDA ET COR-RIGENDA	1126c	
4	32	מטה	COUCH	641d	
		שכב	LIE DOWN	1012c	
4	33	בעד	BEHIND	126c	1 b
		דלת	DOOR	195a	2
		סגר	SHUT	689a	1
		פלל	INTERVENE	813b	3
4	34	גהר	BEND	*155c	
		גהר	BEND	155c	
		חמם	BE OR BECOME WARM	328c	1
		ילד	CHILD	409b	A
		כף	HOLLOW OF THE HAND	496b	1 a
		עין	EYE	744a	1 a
		פה	MOUTH	804d	1 b
		שכב	LIE DOWN	1012b	1 d
4	35	גהר	BEND	155c	
		הלך	WALK	230b	1 1d 2a
		הלך	WALK	230d	1 1d 3b
		הנה	HITHER	244c	A a
		זרר	SNEEZE	284d	
		עד	AS FAR AS	724b	1 2a a
		עין	EYE	744b	1 j
		פקח	OPEN	824d	1 a
		זרר	ADDENDA ET COR-RIGENDA	1123a	
4	36	קרא	CALL	895b	2 a
		שונמית	SHUNAMMITE	1002d	2
4	37	נפל	FALL	657c	3 b
		שחה	BOW DOWN	1005b	1 a
4	38	בן	SON	121c	7 a
		בשל	BOIL	143a	1
		נזיד	THING BOILED	268a	
		נביא	PROPHET	611c	1
		סיר	POT	696c	1
		רעב	FAMINE	944b	1
		שפת	SET	1046a	1
4	39	ארה	HERB	21d	
		בגד	GARMENT	94a	1
		גפן	VINE	*172b	

Ch	v.	Heb	Eng	Page	Sec
		גפן	VINE	*172c	
		גפן	VINE	172c	
		נזיד	THING BOILED	268a	
		לקט	GATHER UP	544d	1
		מלא	FULNESS	571b	1
		סיר	POT	696c	1 a
		פלח	CLEAVE	812a	1
		פקעת	GOURDS	825a	
		שדה	FIELD	961c	1 d
		שדה	FIELD	961c	1 d
4	40	היה	COME TO PASS	224d	12a 1b
		נזיד	THING BOILED	268a	
		יצק	POUR	427b	1
		סיר	POT	696c	1 a
		צעק	CRY	858c	1 a
4	41	ו	AND	254c	4
		יצק	POUR	427b	1
		לקח	TAKE	543c	6
		סיר	POT	696c	1 a
		קמח	FLOUR	887d	1
		רע	EVIL	948a	1
4	42	אלהים	GOD	44a	3 b
		בכורים	FIRST-FRUITS	114c	
		בעל־שלשה	BAAL-SHALISHAH	128b	
		כרמל	GARDEN	502a	2
		לחם	FOOD	537a	1 a
		לחם	FOOD	537b	1 a
		צקלן	SACK	862d	1
		שערה	BARLEY	972d	2
		שלשה	SHALISHAH	1027a	
4	43	זה	THIS	260d	1 a
		יתר	SHOW EXCESS	*451c	3
		יתר	LEAVE OVER	451c	1
		מאה	HUNDRED	547d	1 a1
		מה	HOW	553c	2 aa
		נתן	PUT	680b	2 a
		שרת	SERVE	1058a	1 a
4	44	יתר	LEAVE OVER	451c	1
		נתן	PUT	680b	2 a
5	1	גבור	STRONG	150b	2
		גדול	GREAT	153a	6 b
		היה	BE	227a	3 4b
		חיל	STRENGTH	298d	1 c
		תשועה	DELIVERANCE	448b	1
		מלך	KING	573a	1
		נעמן	NAAMAN	654a	2
		נשא	LIFT	670c	1 b 3
		פנה	FACE	817a	2 4a g
		צרע	BE STRUCK WITH LEPROSY	864a	
5	2	ארץ	EARTH	76b	2 e
		גדוד	BAND	151b	1
		יצא	GO OUT	423a	2 c
		נעמן	NAAMAN	654a	2
		נערה	GIRL	655b	1
		פנה	FACE	817a	2 4b a
		קטן	SMALL	882a	1 a
		שבה	TAKE CAPTIVE	985c	1 a
5	3	אדון	LORD	11b	3 1a
		אז	THEN	23b	2
		אחלי	AH THAT	25b	
		אסף	GATHER	62c	4
		גברת	MISTRESS	150c	2
		צרעת	LEPROSY	863d	
5	4	ארץ	EARTH	76b	2 e
		זה	THIS	262a	6 d
		נערה	GIRL	655b	1
5	5	הלך	WALK	234a	1 5f 2
		זהב	GOLD	263b	9 a
		חליפה	A CHANGE	322c	1
		יד	HAND	391a	5 c4
		כסף	SILVER	494c	8 c
		ככר	ROUND	503b	3 b
		לקח	TAKE	542d	2
		ספר	MISSIVE	707a	1 a
		שלח	SEND	1018b	1 b
5	6	אסף	GATHER	62c	4
		נעמן	NAAMAN	654a	2
		ספר	MISSIVE	707a	1 a
		צרעת	LEPROSY	863d	
		שלח	SEND	1018b	1 a
		ענת	NOW	*1107b	
5	7	אנה	BE OPPORTUNE	58c	
		אסף	GATHER	62c	4
		חיה	LIVE	311d	2 a
		כי	THAT	472d	1 f
		ל	TO	510d	1 d
		מות	DIE	560b	2
		ספר	MISSIVE	707a	1 a
		ספר	MISSIVE	707a	1 a
		צרעת	LEPROSY	863d	
		קרא	CALL	895c	4 a
5	8	ראה	TO SEE	907c	5 b
		אלהים	GOD	44a	3 b
5	9	יש	THERE IS	441d	2 b
		ב	IN	89b	3 1a
		ל	TO	513d	5 cb g
		רכב	CHARIOT	939a	1
5	10	הלך	WALK	233c	1 4c 6
		טבל	DIP	*371b	2
		טהר	BE CLEAN	372a	1
		רחץ	WASH OFF	934c	2
		שוב	TURN BACK	998b	7 i
5	11	אמר	SAY	56b	2
		אסף	GATHER	62c	4
		יהוה	YAHWEH	218d	2 1e

Ch	v.	Heb	Eng	Page	Sec
		נוף	WAVE	632a	2 a
		קרא	CALL	845b	2 c
		צרע	BE STRUCK WITH LEPROSY	864a	
		מקום	STANDING PLACE	880b	4
5	12	קצף	BE WROTH	893b	2
		אמנה	AMANAH	53d	1
		דמשק	DAMASCUS	199d	
		הלך	WALK	231d	1 d5 ta
		טבל	DIP	*371b	2
		טהר	BE CLEAN	372a	1
		טוב	PLEASANT	374c	6
		חמה	RAGE	404c	2 a
		פרפר	PHARPAR	829b	
		רחץ	WASH OFF	934c	2
5	13	אב	FATHER	3d	8
		אף	ALSO	65a	1
		אף	ALSO	65b	3
		גדול	GREAT	153a	6 a
		טהר	BE CLEAN	372a	1
		רחץ	WASH OFF	934c	2
5	14	טבל	DIP	371b	2
		טהר	BE CLEAN	372a	1
		ירד	GO DOWN	433a	1 g
		נער	YOUTH	655a	1 c
		קטן	SMALL	882b	1
		שוב	TURN BACK	998b	7 i
5	15	ברכה	BLESSING	139d	5
		כיאם	EXCEPT	474d	2 a
		לקח	TAKE	543b	4 f
5	16	חי	ALIVE	311d	1
		לקח	TAKE	543b	4 f
		מאן	REFUSE	549b	
		עמד	STAND	764a	1 e
		פצר	PUSH	823a	
5	17	אדמה	EARTH	9d	3
		אלהים	GOD	43c	1 d
		זבח	SACRIFICE	257c	1 1
		זבח	SACRIFICE	258a	2 7
		יש	BE	442a	2 cf
		לא	NOT	520c	4 c
		משא	LOAD	672c	1
		נתן	GIVE	681d	1 a
		עלה	WHOLE BURNT OF-FERING	750d	
		עשה	DO	794d	2 4
		פרד	MULE	825d	
		צמד	COUPLE	855a	1
5	18	בית	HOUSE	109b	1 ae 0
		המון	HARMON	*248b	
		סלח	FORGIVE	699c	
		רמון	RIMMON	942a	
		שחה	BOW DOWN	1005c	3
		שען	LEAN	1043d	
5	19	ארץ	EARTH	76b	4 b
		הלך	WALK	231d	1 d5 tc
		כברה	DISTANCE	460c	
5	20	אדון	LORD	11b	3 1a
		אלהים	GOD	44a	3 b
		ארמי	ARAMEAN	74c	
		הנה	BEHOLD	244a	B a
		זה	THIS	*261a	2 bb
		חי	ALIVE	311d	1
		חשך	WITHHOLD	362b	1
		כיאם	SURELY	475b	2 c
		לקח	TAKE	543b	4 f
		מאומה	ANYTHING	549a	
		רוץ	RUN	930b	1
5	21	נפל	FALL	657d	6
		על	UPON	758c	4 2a
		רדף	PURSUE	922c	1 a
		רוץ	RUN	930b	1
		מרכבה	CHARIOT	939d	
5	22	אדון	LORD	11b	3 1a
		בן	SON	121c	7 a
		הר	MOUNTAIN	251a	2b
		זה	THIS	261c	4 h
		חליפה	A CHANGE	322c	1
		כסף	SILVER	494b	8 c
		ענה	NOW	774b	2 a
5	23	חליפה	A CHANGE	322c	1
		חרים	BAG	355a	
		יאל	SHOW-WILLING-NESS	384a	1
		כסף	SILVER	494c	8 c
		לקח	TAKE	543b	4 f
		פצר	PUSH	823a	
		צור	CONFINE	848d	1
5	24	עפל	MOUND	779b	
		פקד	ATTEND TO	823d	B 2
		שלח	SEND	1019a	1 d
5	25	אן	WHERE	33a	1
		אן	WHERE	33a	C
		הלך	WALK	230b	1 1b
		עמד	STAND	763d	1 a
5	26	הלך	WALK	235a	2 3f 1a
		הפך	TURN	245d	2 a
		זית	OLIVE TREE	268d	1
		כסף	SILVER	494d	9
		לא	NOT	519a	1 ae
		לקח	TAKE	543b	4 f
		עת	TIME	773d	2 b
		מרכבה	CHARIOT	939d	
		שפחה	MAID	1046c	1
5	27	דבק	CLING	179d	2 c
		זרע	SOWING	282a	4 c

Ch	v.	Heb	Eng	Page	Sec
		עולם	LONG DURATION	762b	2 b4
		פנה	FACE	817d	2 5a a
		צרעת	LEPROSY	863d	
		צרע	BE STRUCK WITH LEPROSY	864a	
		שלג	SNOW	1017a	
6	1	בן	SON	121c	7 a
		מן	THAN	582d	6 d
		צר	NARROW	865a	
6	2	הלך	WALK	231a	1 d3 gc
		קורה	RAFTER	900a	
6	3	יאל	SHOW-WILLINGNESS	384a	1
6	4	בוא	COME	98b	2
		גור	CUT	160b	3
		חיל	STRENGTH	299a	4
6	5	אדון	LORD	11b	3 1c
		אהה	ALAS	13c	
		את	MARK OF THE ACCUSATIVE	85b	3 a
		את	PLOUGHSHARE	88c	
		ברזל	IRON	137c	2
		היה	BE	227c	3 5a
		נפל	FALL	656d	1
		נפל	FALL	658a	1a
		צעק	CRY	858c	1a
		קורה	RAFTER	900a	
		שאל	ASK	981d	1 b
6	6	אן	WHERE	33a	A
		אלהים	GOD	44a	3 b
		ברזל	IRON	137c	2
		נפל	FALL	656d	1
		עץ	TREE	781c	1a
		צוף	FLOW	847b	2
		קצב	CUT OFF	891d	
		שלך	THROW	1021a	1a
6	7	ל	TO	515b	5 hb a
		רום	BE HIGH	927c	1 c
6	8	אלמני	SOME ONE	48c	
		תחנה	ENCAMPING	334c	
		יעץ	CONSULT	419d	
		לחם	ENGAGE IN BATTLE	*535c	
		פלני	A CERTAIN ONE	812a	
		מקום	STANDING PLACE	880a	4
6	9	נחת	DESCENDING	639c	
		עבר	PASS OVER	717d	4 a
		שמר	KEEP	1037b	1
6	10	זהר	ADMONISH	264b	
		לא	NOT	518d	1 ac
		שמר	KEEP	1037b	1
		שנים	TWO	1041b	1 b3
		שנים	TWO	1041b	1 b2
6	11	אל	TO	40a	3 c
		ל	TO	513c	5 ca
		לב	HEART	525c	2 9b
		מי	WHO	566c	D
		סער	STORM	704b	
		על	UPON	754b	2 1f b
		על	UPON	754d	2 1f g
		ש	WHO	980a	4 c
6	12	חדר	CHAMBER	293d	
		משכב	ACT OF LYING	1012d	2a
6	13	איכו	WHERE	32d	
		איכה	WHERE	32d	3
		דתן	DOTHAN	206d	
		לקח	TAKE	543c	6
		נגד	BE CONSPICUOUS	617a	
		ראה	TO SEE	907b	1a
6	14	כבד	MASSIVE	458a	1 b
		נקף	GO AROUND	669a	1 b
		שלח	SEND	1018b	1a
6	15	אדון	LORD	11b	3 1a
		אהה	ALAS	13c	
		איכה	IN WHAT MANNER	32d	1
		אלהים	GOD	44a	3 b
		חיל	STRENGTH	299a	4
		סבב	SURROUND	685d	2 d
		שכם	START EARLY	1014c	
		שרת	SERVE	1058a	1a
6	16	את	WITH	85c	
		את	WITH	85d	1a
		ירא	FEAR	431a	1 e
		רב	MUCH	913b	1 e
6	17	סביב	ROUND ABOUT	687b	2 bb
		סוס	HORSE	692c	2
		עין	EYE	744b	1 j
		פלל	INTERVENE	813b	3
		פקח	OPEN	824d	1 b
		ראה	TO SEE	907b	4
		רכב	CHARIOT	939b	1
6	18	נכה	SMITE	646b	4 a
		סנורים	SUDDEN BLINDNESS	703a	
		פלל	INTERVENE	813b	3
6	19	בקש	SEEK	134c	1 b
		דרך	WAY	202c	1
		הלך	WALK	236d	1 d
		הלך	WALK	236d	1 e
		זה	THIS	262b	
		לא	NOT	519b	1 bb
		שמרון	SAMARIA	1037d	
6	20	אלה	THESE	41c	A
		עין	EYE	744b	1 j
		פקח	OPEN	824d	1 b
		ראה	TO SEE	907b	4
6	21	אב	FATHER	3d	8
6	22	אשר	THAT	83d	8 f
		ה	INTERROG PART	209d	1 b
		הלך	WALK	231a	1 d3 ga
		קשת	BOW	906a	1 b
		שום	TO PLACE	963b	1 c
		שבה	TAKE CAPTIVE	985c	1a
6	23	גדוד	BAND	151b	1
		הלך	WALK	231a	1 d3 ga
		יסף	ADD	414d	
		כרה	GIVE A FEAST	500c	
		כרה	A FEAST	500c	
		שלח	SEND	1019a	1 d
6	24	אחר	AFTER	30a	2 b
		בנהדד	BEN-HADAD	122b	2
		צור	CONFINE	848d	2
		קבץ	GATHER	867d	2
6	25	דביונים	DOVE:S DUNG	179b	
		היה	BECOME	225c	2 1a
		חמור	HE-ASS	331b	5
		חרא	DUNG	*351a	
		חרא	DUNG	351a	
		יונה	DOVE	401d	
		צור	CONFINE	848d	2
		קב	KAB	866b	
		ראש	HEAD	910d	1 b
		רבע	FOURTH PART	917d	
		רעב	FAMINE	944a	1
		רעב	FAMINE	944b	1
		שמים	EIGHTY	1033b	
6	26	ישע	DELIVER	446c	1
		צעק	CRY	858c	1a
6	27	אין	WHENCE	32d	
		אל	NOT	39b	A bb
		גרן	THRESHING-FLOOR	175b	
		יקב	WINE-VAT	428c	
		ישע	DELIVER	446c	1
6	28	מה	WHAT	552d	1 ac
6	29	אחר	ANOTHER	29d	
		בשל	BOIL	143a	2
		חבא	WITHDRAW	285d	
6	30	בית	HOUSE	110c	8 a
		שק	SACK	974c	2 a
6	31	אם	IF	50b	1 b2
		יסף	ADD	415b	1
		עמד	STAND	764b	5 a
		עשה	DO	793d	1 1a 2
		שפט	SHAPHAT	1048b	1
6	32	בן	SON	120c	1 ia
		דלת	DOOR	195a	1
		ה	THE	*209a	2a
		ה	INTERROG PART	210a	1 c
		זקן	OLD	278d	2 b
		לחץ	PRESS	537d	1
		סגר	SHUT	688d	1
		סור	TURN ASIDE	694b	1
		פנה	FACE	817d	2 5a a
		קול	VOICE	877b	2 c
		ראה	TO SEE	907d	7 c
		רצח	MURDER	954a	
6	33	את	WITH	86d	4 c
		דבר	SPEAK	181c	3 e
		זה	THIS	260d	2b
		יחל	WAIT	404a	
		מה	WHAT	553c	2 ab
		עוד	STILL	729a	1 ab
		עוד	STILL	729a	1 aa
		מחר	TO-MORROW	564a	1
7	1	סאה	SEAH	684b	
		סלת	FINE FLOUR	701c	
		עת	TIME	773c	1 a
		שערה	BARLEY	972d	2
		שער	GATE	1045a	2 a
		שקל	SHEKEL	1053d	
7	2	אלהים	GOD	44a	3 b
		ארבה	LATTICE	70d	
		הנה	BEHOLD	243d	
		שליש	OFFICER	1026d	
		שם	THERE	1027c	4 d
		שמי	HEAVENS	1030a	1 b
		שען	LEAN	1043d	
7	3	מה	WHAT	553c	2 ab
		עד	UNTIL	725a	2 1b a
		פתח	OPENING	836a	
		צרע	BE STRUCK WITH LEPROSY	864a	
		רע	FRIEND	946b	3
7	4	אם	IF	49d	1 a3 a
		חיה	LIVE	311c	1
		ישב	REMAIN	442d	2a
		נפל	FALL	657c	4 b
7	5	נשף	TWILIGHT	676a	1
		קצה	END	892b	2
7	6	חתי	HITTITE	366d	2 b
		מצרים	EGYPTIANS	596a	2b
		רכב	CHARIOT	939b	1
		שכר	HIRE	969a	
		שמע	HEAR	1034c	2a
7	7	אל	TO	40c	6
		הוא	HE, SHE, IT	216b	3 d
		חמור	HE-ASS	331b	1
		נוס	FLEE	630d	1
		נשף	TWILIGHT	676a	1
		עזב	LEAVE	737b	2 a1
7	8	זהב	GOLD	262d	3
		זהב	GOLD	263c	1
		טמן	HIDE	380c	
		צרע	BE STRUCK WITH LEPROSY	864a	
		קצה	END	892b	2
7	9	אור	LIGHT	21c	2
		בקר	MORNING	133d	1 b
		בשרה	TIDINGS	142d	1
		הלך	WALK	234b	1 5f 3
		חכה	WAIT	314a	1
		חשה	BE SILENT	364c	1
		כן	RIGHT	467b	1
		מצא	FIND	593c	3 e
		עון	INIQUITY	731c	3
		רע	FRIEND	946b	3
7	10	אסר	TIE	63c	1 1
		הוא	HE, SHE, IT	*216b	1
		הם	THEY	241c	3 d
		חמור	HE-ASS	331b	1
		קול	VOICE	876d	1 a
		שער	PORTER	1045b	
7	11	פנימה	TOWARDS THE SIDE	819b	1
		קרא	CALL	895a	1 a
		שער	PORTER	1045b	
7	12	חבה	WITHDRAW	285d	1
		חי	ALIVE	312a	1 b
		יצא	GO OUT	422c	1 a
		נשף	TWILIGHT	676a	1
		עין	EYE	744b	1 f
		רעב	HUNGRY	944c	
		שדה	FIELD	961c	1 f
		תפש	LAY HOLD OF	1074d	1
7	13	המון	CROWD	242d	3 c
		תמם	BE FINISHED	1070c	5
7	14	רכב	CHARIOT	939b	4
		רכב	ADDENDA ET CORRIGENDA	1126d	
7	15	דרך	WAY	202c	1
		הלך	WALK	231a	1 d3 gc
		הלך	WALK	231c	1 1d 5z
		חפז	BE IN TREPIDATION	342a	
		חפז	BE IN TREPIDATION	342a	1
		מלא	FULL	571a	
		שלך	THROW	1021a	1 c
7	16	בזז	SPOIL	102d	
		מחנה	ENCAMPMENT	334b	2 b
		סאה	SEAH	684b	
		סלת	FINE FLOUR	701c	
		שערה	BARLEY	972d	2
		שקל	SHEKEL	1053d	
7	17	אלהים	GOD	44a	3 b
		מות	DIE	559d	2 a
		רמס	TRAMPLE	942d	
		שליש	OFFICER	1026d	
		שען	LEAN	1043d	
7	18	היה	COME TO PASS	224c	2 a1 aa
		מחר	TO-MORROW	564a	1 a
		סאה	SEAH	684b	
		סלת	FINE FLOUR	701c	1a
		עת	TIME	773c	1 a
		שערה	BARLEY	972d	2
		שער	GATE	1045a	2 a
		שקל	SHEKEL	1053d	
7	19	ארבה	LATTICE	70d	
		דבר	WORD	183d	4 7
		שליש	OFFICER	1026d	
		שם	THERE	1027c	4 d
		שמי	HEAVENS	1030a	1 b
7	20	היה	FALL OUT	224b	1 1a
		מות	DIE	559d	2 a
		רמס	TRAMPLE	942d	
8	1	אתי	THOU	61c	1
		אשר	PARTICLE OF RELATION	82c	4 bg
		גור	SOJOURN	157d	1
		חיה	LIVE	311d	2 c
8	2	אלהים	GOD	44a	3 b
		גור	SOJOURN	157d	1
		לחם	ENGAGE IN BATTLE	535c	
8	3	אל	TO	40b	6
		אל	TO	41a	B
		היה	COME TO PASS	224c	2 a1 az
		צעק	CRY	858c	1 a
		שוב	TURN BACK	997a	2
8	4	גדול	GREAT	153c	9
8	5	אדון	LORD	11b	3 1c
		אל	TO	40b	6
		אל	TO	41a	B
		חיה	LIVE	311d	2 c
		על	UPON	754d	2 1f g
		צעק	CRY	858c	1 a
8	6	תבואה	PRODUCT	100a	1
		יום	DAY	400a	7 d1 e
		ל	TO	512a	3 b
		סריס	EUNUCH	710c	
		עתה	NOW	774c	2 f
		שאל	ASK	981d	2 a
		שוב	TURN BACK	999a	1 d
8	7	בוא	COME	98b	2
		בנהדד	BEN-HADAD	122b	2
		חלה	BE WEAK	317d	2
		מלך	KING	573a	1
		נגד	BE CONSPICUOUS	617a	

Ch	v.	Heb	Eng	Page	Sec
8	8	את	WITH	85c	
		דרש	SEEK	205b	2 a
		זה	THIS	*261a	2 ba
		חזאל	HAZAEL	303c	
		חיה	LIVE	311b	2 a
		חלי	SICKNESS	318b	
		לקח	TAKE	542d	2
		מנחה	GIFT	585a	1
8	9	אב	FATHER	3d	8
		בן	SON	120b	1 c
		בנהדד	BEN-HADAD	122b	1
		זה	THIS	*261a	2 ba
		חזאל	HAZAEL	303c	
		חיה	LIVE	311b	2 a
		חלי	SICKNESS	318b	
		טוב	GOOD THINGS	375c	2
		לקח	TAKE	542d	2
		מנחה	GIFT	585a	1
		משא	LOAD	672c	1
		ארבעים	FORTY	917b	1 a
8	10	חיה	LIVE	311b	2 a
		לא	NOT	520c	
		מות	DIE	559d	2 a
		ראה	TO SEE	908d	1 a2
8	11	אלהים	GOD	44a	3 b
		בוש	BE ASHAMED	101d	3
		בכה	WEEP	113b	1
		עמד	STAND	764d	6 a
		שום	TO PLACE	964b	4 e
		בוש	ADDENDA ET COR-RIGENDA	1121b	
8	12	אש	FIRE	77c	1
		אשר	PARTICLE OF RE-LATION	82d	6 b
			THAT	83b	8 aa
		בחור	YOUNG MAN	104c	
		בכה	WEEP	113b	1
		מבצר	FORTIFICATION	131c	
		בקע	CLEAVE	132a	
		הרג	KILL	247b	1 b
		חזאל	HAZAEL	303c	
		עולל	CHILD	760c	
		רטש	DASH IN PIECES	936b	
		שלח	SEND	1019b	7
8	13	גדול	GREAT	153a	6 a
		חזאל	HAZAEL	303c	
		כי	THAT	*472a	1 b
		כי	THAT	472d	1 f
		כלב	DOG	477a	B
		מה	WHAT	553b	1 db
		עבד	SLAVE	714c	6
		ראה	TO SEE	908a	1 a2
8	14	חיה	LIVE	311b	2 a
8	15	חזאל	HAZAEL	303c	
		טבל	DIP	371b	1
		מכבר	CLOTH	460d	
		מות	DIE	559c	1 a1
		מחרת	THE MORROW	564a	
		מלך	BE KING	574a	
		מלך	BE KING	574a	
		פרש	SPREAD OUT	831b	2
8	16	יהורם	JEHORAM	221b	1
		יהורם	JEHORAM	221b	2
		יהושפט	JEHOSHAPHAT	221d	1
		חמש	FIVE	331d	1 e
		חמש	FIVE	331d	1 e
8	17	היה	BE	227a	3 4b
8	18	בית	HOUSE	110a	5 c
		דרך	WAY	203d	6 d
		חתן	MAKE ONESELF A SON IN LAW	*368d	1
		עשה	DO	793d	1 la1
8	19	אבה	BE WILLING	2c	
		דוד	DAVID	188a	
		יום	DAY	400c	7 f
		ניר	LAMP	633a	
		מען	PURPOSE	775b	1 a
		שחת	GO TO RUIN	1008b	1
		מלך	BE KING	574b	
8	20	פשע	REBEL	833b	1
		תחת	UNDERNEATH	1066a	3 2a
		יד	ADDENDA ET COR-RIGENDA	1123d	
8	21	יהורם	JEHORAM	221b	1
		היה	COME TO PASS	224d	2 a1 am
		ירד	GO DOWN	433a	1 e
		נכה	SMITE	646b	3
		סבב	SURROUND	686a	2 d
		עבר	PASS OVER	717a	1 b
		צעיר	ZAIR	859a	
8	22	לבנה	LIBNAH	526c	1
		פשע	REBEL	833b	1
		פשע	REBEL	833b	1
		תחת	UNDERNEATH	1066a	3 2a
		יד	ADDENDA ET COR-RIGENDA	1123d	
8	23	יהורם	JEHORAM	221b	1
8	24	אב	FATHER	3c	4 a
		אחזיה	AHAZIAH	28d	2
		דוד	DAVID	188a	A
		יהורם	JEHORAM	221b	1
8	25	אחזיה	AHAZIAH	28d	2
		יהורם	JEHORAM	221b	1
		יהורם	JEHORAM	221b	1
		עשר	TEN	797b	2 b
8	26	עמרי	OMRI	771d	1
		עתליה	ATHALIAH	801a	1
8	27	בית	HOUSE	110a	5 c
		דרך	WAY	204a	6 d
		חתן	DAUGHTER:S HUS-BAND	368c	1
		עשה	DO	793d	1 la 1
8	28	ארמי	ARAMEAN	74c	
		יהורם	JEHORAM	221b	2
		חזאל	HAZAEL	303c	
		מלחמה	WAR	536c	
		נכה	SMITE	645d	1 e
8	29	ארמי	ARAMEAN	74c	
		יהורם	JEHORAM	221b	2
		יהורם	JEHORAM	221b	2
		יזרעאל	JEZREEL	283c	1 b
		חזאל	HAZAEL	303c	
		חלה	BE WEAK	317d	2
		מחלוי	SICKNESS	*318c	
		מלך	KING	573a	1
		נכה	SMITE	645d	1 e
		מכה	BLOW	646d	1 c
		ראה	TO SEE	907d	6 d
		רמה	RAMA	928b	5
		רפא	HEAL	951a	
		מכה	ADDENDA ET COR-RIGENDA	1125a	
9	1	בן	SON	121c	7 a
		הלך	WALK	230d	1 ld 3a
		חגר	GIRD	291d	1
		יד	HAND	391a	5 c4
		לקח	TAKE	542d	2
		מתנים	LOINS	608a	1 c
		פך	PHIAL	810b	
		שמן	OIL	1032b	2 d
9	2	בוא	COME	99a	1
		יהוא	JEHU	*219c	
		יהוא	JEHU	219d	1
		יהושפט	JEHOSHAPHAT	221d	2
		חדר	CHAMBER	293d	
		חתר	SCEPTER	310c	
		נמשי	NIMSHI	650a	
		ספל	BOWL	705d	
		ראה	TO SEE	907d	6 g
9	3	אל	TO	41a	B
		דלת	DOOR	195a	2
		חכה	WAIT	314a	1
		יצק	POUR	427a	1
		משח	ANOINT	603b	2
		פך	PHIAL	810b	
		פתח	OPEN	835a	
		שמן	OIL	1032b	2 d
9	5	ה	THE	208d	1 i
		מי	WHO	566b	B
		שר	CHIEFTAIN	978c	3 a
		שר	CHIEFTAIN	978c	3 a
9	6	אל	TO	41a	B
		יצק	POUR	427b	1
		משח	ANOINT	603b	2
		שמן	OIL	1032b	2 d
9	7	איזבל	JEZEBEL	33b	
		בית	HOUSE	110a	5 c
		דם	BLOOD	196d	2 f
		יד	HAND	391b	5 g3
		נביא	PROPHET	611d	1
		נכה	SMITE	646b	2 c
		נקם	AVENGE	668a	1
		עבד	SLAVE	714a	3
		עבד	SLAVE	714b	4
9	8	אבד	PERISH	1c	1
		בית	HOUSE	110a	5 c
		כרת	CUT OFF	504c	3
		עזב	LEAVE	737d	3
		קיר	WALL	885a	3
		שתן	URINATE	1010b	
		אחיהו	AHIJAH	26d	4
9	9	בית	HOUSE	110a	5 c
		בית	HOUSE	110a	5 c
		בעשא	BAASHA	129d	
		נבט	NEBAT	614a	
9	10	דלת	DOOR	195a	2
		יזרעאל	JEZREEL	283c	1 b
		חלק	PORTION	324b	2 d
		כלב	DOG	476d	2
		פתח	OPEN	835a	
		קבר	BURY	868c	
		קבר	BURY	868c	
9	11	נבא	PROPHESY	*612b	1 a
		שיח	COMPLAINT	967a	4
		שגע	BE MAD	993d	
		שלום	PEACE	1022d	3
9	12	זה	THIS	262a	6 d
		משח	ANOINT	603b	2
		שקר	DECEPTION	1055c	3
9	13	גרם	SELF	175a	3
		מהר	HASTEN	555a	2
		מלך	BE KING	574a	
		מעלה	STEP	752b	1
9	14	יהורם	JEHORAM	221b	2
		יהושפט	JEHOSHAPHAT	221d	2
		היה	BE	227c	3 5a
		חזאל	HAZAEL	303c	
		מלך	KING	573a	1
		נמשי	NIMSHI	650a	
		קשר	BIND	905c	
9	15	שמר	KEEP	1036c	1 b
		ארמי	ARAMEAN	74c	
		את	WITH	86c	3 b
		יהורם	JEHORAM	221b	2
		יזרעאל	JEZREEL	283c	1 b
		חזאל	HAZAEL	303c	
		לחם	ENGAGE IN BAT-TLE	535c	
		מלך	KING	573a	1
		נכה	SMITE	645d	1 e
		מכה	BLOW	646d	1 c
		נפש	SOUL	661b	8
		פליט	ESCAPED ONE	812c	
		רפא	HEAL	951a	
		מכה	ADDENDA ET COR-RIGENDA	1125a	
9	16	אחזיה	AHAZIAH	28d	2
		יהורם	JEHORAM	221b	2
		הלך	WALK	230b	1 la
		יזרעאל	JEZREEL	283c	1 b
		ראה	TO SEE	907d	6 d
		רכב	RIDE	938c	1
		שכב	LIE DOWN	1012b	2
		שם	THERE	1027c	3 c
		רכב	ADDENDA ET COR-RIGENDA	1126d	
9	17	מגדל	TOWER	153d	1
		יהורם	JEHORAM	221b	2
		יזרעאל	JEZREEL	283c	1 b
		רכב	HORSEMAN	939b	2
		שלום	PEACE	1022d	3
9	18	אחר	BEHIND	30c	4 b
		אל	TO	40d	9
		הלך	WALK	230b	1 la
		הם	THEY	241d	7
		מה	WHAT	553b	1 dc
		סבב	TURN ABOUT	685c	1 a
		סוס	HORSE	692c	2
		רכב	RIDE	938d	3
		רכב	HORSEMAN	939b	2
		שלום	PEACE	1022d	3
9	19	אחר	BEHIND	30c	4 b
		אל	TO	40d	9
		מה	WHAT	553b	1 dc
		סבב	TURN ABOUT	685c	1 a
		סוס	HORSE	692c	2
		רכב	RIDE	938d	3
		רכב	HORSEMAN	939b	2
		שלום	PEACE	1022d	3
9	20	בוא	COME	98b	2
		בן	SON	120c	1 f
		נהג	DRIVE	624b	1
		מנהג	DRIVING	624c	
		נהג	DRIVE	*624c	3
		נמשי	NIMSHI	650a	
		עד	AS FAR AS	724c	1 la
		שגעון	MADNESS	993d	
9	21	אחזי	AHAZIAH	28d	2
		אסר	TIE	63d	2
		יהורם	JEHORAM	221b	2
		יזרעאלי	JEZREELITE	283c	1
		חלקה	PORTION OF GROUND	324c	1 b
		מצא	FIND	593a	1 c
		נבות	NABOTH	613b	
		רכב	CHARIOT	939b	2
9	22	יהורם	JEHORAM	221b	2
		זנונים	FORNICATION	276a	C
		כשף	SORCERY	506c	2
		מה	WHAT	553b	1 c
		עד	AS FAR AS	724c	1 b2
		שלום	PEACE	1022d	3
9	23	אחזי	AHAZIAH	28d	2
		יהורם	JEHORAM	221b	2
		הפך	TURN	245b	1 a
		מרמה	DECEIT	941b	
9	24	זרוע	ARM	284a	1 a
		חצי	ARROW	345d	2
		יד	HAND	389a	1 c
		יצא	GO OUT	423b	1 f
		כרע	BOW DOWN	502c	4
		לב	HEART	524c	2 1
		מלא	FILL	*570c	1
		מלא	FILL	570d	2
		נכה	SMITE	645c	1 a
		קשת	BOW	906c	1 d
		רכב	CHARIOT	939b	2
9	25	בדקר	BIDKAR	96a	
		זכר	REMEMBER	269c	1 1a
		יזרעאלי	JEZREELITE	283c	1
		חלקה	PORTION OF GROUND	324c	1 a
		נבות	NABOTH	613b	
		נשא	LIFT	670a	1 a
		נשא	LIFT	670d	1 b 6
		משא	UTTERANCE	672d	
		משא	UTTERANCE	*672d	
		צמד	COUPLE	855a	1
		שלך	THROW	1021a	1 a
		שליש	OFFICER	1026d	
9	26	אם	IF	50b	1 b2
		אמש	YESTERDAY	57d	
		דם	BLOOD	196d	2 f
		חלקה	PORTION OF GROUND	324c	1 b

Ch	v.	Heb	Eng	Page	Sec
		ירד	GO DOWN	433a	1 e
		נאם	UTTERANCE	610b	2
		נבות	NABOTH	613b	
		נשא	LIFT	670a	1 a
		שלך	THROW	1021a	1 a
9	27	אחזיה	AHAZIAH	28d	2
		את	WITH	86b	2
		בית	HOUSE	109a	1 ae 7
		ביתהגן	GARDEN HOUSE	111b	
		מגדו	MEGIDDO	152a	
		גור	GUR	158a	
		גן	GARDEN	171a	
		דרך	WAY	202d	1
		יבלעם	IBLEAM	385d	
		נוס	FLEE	630d	1
		רדף	PURSUE	922d	1 a
		מרכבה	CHARIOT	939d	
9	28	דוד	DAVID	188a	A
		קברה	GRAVE	869a	1
		רכב	RIDE	938d	1
9	29	אחזי	AHAZIAH	28d	2
		יהורם	JEHORAM	221b	2
		עשר	TEN	797a	1 b
		עשר	TEN	797c	
9	30	ה	THE	207c	1 e
		יזרעאל	JEZREEL	283c	1 b
		חלון	WINDOW	319d	
		יטב	MAKE GOOD	406a	4
		עין	EYE	744c	1 p
		פוך	ANTIMONY	806c	
		ראש	HEAD	910d	1 a
		שום	TO PLACE	963a	1 a
		שקף	LOOK DOWN	1054c	
9	31	הרג	KILL	247a	1 a
		שער	GATE	1045a	3 a
9	32	אל	TO	39d	3 a
		את	WITH	85d	1 a
		חלון	WINDOW	319d	
		ל	TO	*515c	5 hc
		נשא	LIFT	670a	1 b 3
		סרים	EUNUCH	710c	
		שנים	TWO	1041b	1 b3
		שקף	LOOK DOWN	1054c	
9	33	דם	BLOOD	196d	2 f
		מגר	CAST	*550d	
		נזה	SPURT	633b	
		סוס	HORSE	692c	2
		קיר	WALL	885a	1 b
		רמס	TRAMPLE	942d	
		שמט	LET DROP	1030c	
9	34	ארר	CURSE	76d	
		בת	DAUGHTER	123a	1
		פקד	ATTEND TO	823d	A 1b
9	35	יד	HAND	389a	1 b
		כיאם	EXCEPT	474d	2 a
		כף	HOLLOW OF THE HAND	496c	1 a
9	36	בשר	FLESH	142a	1 b
		הוא	HE, SHE, IT	216d	6 a
		יזרעאל	JEZREEL	283c	1 b
		חלק	PORTION	324b	2 d
		יד	HAND	391a	5 d
		כלב	DOG	476d	A
		עבד	SLAVE	714c	4
		תשבי	TISHBITE	986c	
		שוב	TURN BACK	997c	3 b
9	37	אשר	THAT	83c	8 b
		דמן	DUNG	199b	
		זה	THIS	261a	3
		יזרעאל	JEZREEL	283c	1 b
		חלק	PORTION	324b	2 d
		נבלה	CARCASS	615c	1 a
		שדה	FIELD	961c	1 f
10	1	אמן	CONFIRM	52d	1
		זקן	OLD	278d	2 b
		יזרעאל	JEZREEL	283c	1 b
		כתב	WRITE	507b	1 a
		כתב	WRITE	507d	1 c
		ספר	MISSIVE	707a	1 a
		ספר	MISSIVE	707a	1 a
		שר	CHIEFTAIN	978b	2 d
		שבעים	SEVENTY	988c	1 b
10	2	מבצר	FORTIFICATION	131c	
		נשק	EQUIPMENT	676d	1
		סוס	HORSE	692c	2
		ספר	MISSIVE	707a	1 a
		כענת	NOW	*1107b	
10	3	ה	THE	207b	1 b
		טוב	PLEASANT	374a	2 f
		ישר	STRAIGHT	449b	3 c2
		כסא	THRONE	491a	3 a
		לחם	ENGAGE IN BATTLE	535d	
		על	UPON	754b	2 lf c
		ראה	TO SEE	907a	6 g
10	4	אנחנו	WE	59d	
		ירא	FEAR	431a	1 a
		מאד	EXCEEDINGLY	547c	2 d
		עמד	STAND	764b	4
		עמד	STAND	764b	4
		פנה	FACE	817b	24b d
10	5	אמן	CONFIRM	52d	1
		בית	HOUSE	110b	6
		זקן	OLD	278d	2 b
		טוב	PLEASANT	374a	2 f
		מלך	BE KING	574b	
10	6	על	UPON	755b	2 3
		גדל	GROW UP	152b	1
		גדל	GREAT	153b	6 b
		כתב	WRITE	507d	1 c
		ל	TO	515c	5 hc
		מחר	TO-MORROW	564a	1 a
		ספר	MISSIVE	707a	1 a
		ספר	MISSIVE	707a	1 a
		עת	TIME	773c	1 a
		קול	VOICE	877b	3 a1
10	7	אגרמל	BASIN	*174a	
		דוד	POT	188c	B
		ספר	MISSIVE	707a	1 a
		שחט	SLAUGHTER	1006b	3
10	8	פתח	OPENING	836a	
		צבור	HEAP	840d	
		שום	TO PLACE	962d	1 a
10	9	הנה	BEHOLD	243d	
		הנה	IF	244c	D
		הרג	KILL	247a	1 a
		עמד	STAND	763d	1 b
		צדיק	JUST	843a	2
		קשר	BIND	905b	2
10	10	אזו	THEN	66b	2
		בית	HOUSE	110a	5 c
		דבר	SPEAK	181c	5
		מן	FROM	581a	3 bc
		נפל	FALL	657d	5
		עבד	SLAVE	714b	4
10	11	בית	HOUSE	110a	5 c
		בלת	NOT	117a	4 c
		גדל	GREAT	153b	6 b
		גדל	GREAT	*153b	6 b
		יזרעאל	JEZREEL	283c	1 b
		ידע	ACQUAINTANCE	394d	
		כהן	PRIEST	463b	2
		ל	TO	512d	5 ac
		שייד	SURVIVOR	975a	1
		שאר	REMAIN	984a	1
		שאר	REMAIN	984a	1
10	12	בית	HOUSE	109a	1 ae 8
		ס ביתעקדהרעי	BETH-EKED OF THE SHEPHERDS	112c	
		הלך	WALK	234a	1 5e
10	13	אחזיה	AHIZIAH	28d	2
		גבירה	QUEEN-MOTHER	150c	2
		מי	WHO	566b	
		מצא	FIND	593b	3 a
		שלום	PEACE	1022d	3
10	14	בור	PIT	92c	3
		בית	HOUSE	109a	1 ae 8
		ס ביתעקדהרעי	BETH-EKED OF THE SHEPHERDS	112c	
		חי	ALIVE	312a	1 b
		ארבעים	FORTY	917c	2 a
		שאר	REMAIN	984b	1
		שחט	SLAUGHTER	1006b	3
10	15	תפש	LAY HOLD OF	1074d	1
		את	WITH	86c	3 b
		ברך	BLESS	139b	4 a
		ה	THE	207b	1 cb
		יהונדב	JEHONADAB	220d	1
		יש	BE	441c	2 a
		ישר	STRAIGHT	449b	3 c1
		לבב	HEART	523d	2 6a
		מצא	FIND	593b	2
		נתן	GIVE	680a	1 z
		עלה	GO UP	749c	1
		עלה	GO UP	749c	1 d
		עם	WITH	768b	3 e
		קרא	ENCOUNTER	897a	1
		רכב	RECHAB	939c	1 a
		מרכבה	CHARIOT	939d	
10	16	קנאה	ZEAL	888b	2 a
		ראה	TO SEE	908a	8 a5
		רכב	RIDE	938d	1
		רכב	CHARIOT	939b	2
10	17	ל	TO	512d	5 ac
		עד	AS FAR AS	*724b	12 a b
		שאר	REMAIN	984a	1
10	18	בעל	BAAL	127d	2 2
		מעט	A FEW	590a	1 d
		עבד	WORK	713b	4 b
		קבץ	GATHER	867d	2
		רבה	BECOME MANY	915d	1 e3
		אבד	DESTROY	2b	1
10	19	בעל	BAAL	127d	2 2
		גדל	GREAT	153a	2
		זבח	SACRIFICE	257c	12
		כהן	PRIEST	463a	2
		ל	TO	513b	5 ba
		נביא	PROPHET	612a	3
		עבד	WORK	713b	4 b
		מען	PURPOSE	775b	1 c
		מקבה	INSIDIOUSNESS	784c	
		פקד	ATTEND TO	823d	1
10	20	בעל	BAAL	127d	2 2
		עצרה	ASSEMBLY	783d	1
		קדש	BE SET APART	873b	2
10	21	בית	HOUSE	109b	1 ae 0
		בעל	BAAL	127d	2 2
		מלא	FILL	570b	1
		עבד	WORK	713b	4 b
		פה	MOUTH	805c	5 a
10	22	בעל	BAAL	127d	2 2
		יצא	BRING OUT	425a	4 e
		לבש	CLOTHING	528c	
		מלבוש	RAIMENT	528d	
		מלתחה	WARDROBE	547a	
		עבד	WORK	713b	4 b
		על	UPON	755b	2 3
10	23	בית	HOUSE	109b	1 ae 0
		בעל	BAAL	127d	2 2
		יהונדב	JEHONADAB	220b	1
		חפש	SEARCH	344c	1
		כיאם	BUT	475a	2 b
		מן	FROM	581a	3 bc
		עבד	WORK	713b	4 b
		עבד	SLAVE	714a	3
		פן	LEST	814d	1
		ראה	TO SEE	907a	7 c
		רכב	RECHAB	939c	1 a
10	24	זבח	SACRIFICE	257c	12
		זבח	SACRIFICE	258a	27
		חוץ	THE OUTSIDE	299d	1 bb
		ל	TO	515b	5 hb a
		ל	TO	515b	5 ia
		מלט	SLIP AWAY	572b	2
		נפש	SOUL	659d	3 c
		עלה	WHOLE BURNT OFFERING	750d	
		שום	TO PLACE	964a	4 a
		שמנים	EIGHTY	1033b	
		תחת	INSTEAD	*1066a	2 2b b
10	25	בית	HOUSE	109b	1 ae 0
		בעל	BAAL	127d	2 2
		דביר	HINDMOST CHAMBER	184b	
		הלך	WALK	231a	1 d3 gc
		נכה	SMITE	646a	2 c
		עיר	CITY	746d	2
		עלה	WHOLE BURNT OFFERING	750d	
		רוץ	RUN	930c	2 a
		שליש	OFFICER	1026d	
10	26	בית	HOUSE	109b	1 ae 0
		בעל	BAAL	127d	2 2
		יצא	BRING OUT	425a	4 a
		מצבה	PILLAR	663b	1 c
10	27	בית	HOUSE	109b	1 ae 0
		בעל	BAAL	127d	2 2
		יום	DAY	401b	7 1
		מוצאה	GOING OUT	426a	B
		מצבה	PILLAR	663b	1 c
		נתץ	PULL DOWN	683b	1
		מחראה	ADDENDA ET CORRIGENDA	1123c	
10	28	בעל	BAAL	127d	2 2
		שמד	BE EXTERMINATED	1029c	1
10	29	ביאל	BETHEL	110d	1
		דן	DAN	193a	2
		חטא	MISS A GOAL OR WAY	307d	2
		חטא	SIN	308a	1 b
		נבט	NEBAT	614a	1
		סור	TURN ASIDE	693d	1
		עגל	CALF	722b	
10	30	בן	SON	120c	1 f
		טוב	PLEASING	373c	
		ישר	STRAIGHT	449b	2 a
		כסא	THRONE	491b	3 a
		ל	TO	512d	5 aa
		לבב	HEART	523c	2 2
		רביעי	FOURTH	918a	1
10	31	הלך	WALK	234c	2 3a 1d
		חטא	MISS A GOAL OR WAY	307d	2
		חטאת	SIN	308d	1 c
		תורה	LAW	436b	2 b2
		לבב	HEART	523c	2 2
		סור	TURN ASIDE	693d	1
		על	UPON	759d	4 2c
10	32	גבול	BOUNDARY	148a	2 a
		חזהאל	HAZAEL	303c	
		חלל	POLLUTE	320d	2
		קצה	CUT OFF	892a	
10	33	ארנון	ARNON	75a	
		בשן	BASHAN	143a	
		גדי	GADITE	151d	
		מזרח	PLACE OF SUNRISE	280d	1
		מנשי	MANASSITES	586d	
		נחל	WADY	636c	2
		ערער	AROER	792d	1
		ראובני	REUBENITE	910a	
10	34	גבורה	MIGHT	150c	2
10	35	יהואחז	JEHOAHAZ	219d	1
11	1	אבד	CAUSE TO PERISH	2a	1
		אחזי	AHAZIAH	28d	2
		דבר	SPEAK	181c	2
		זרע	SOWING	282d	4 e
		ממלכה	DOMINION	575c	2
		עתליה	ATHALIAH	801a	1
11	2	אחזי	AHAZIAH	28d	2
		גנב	STEAL	170b	
		יהואש	JEHOASH	220a	1
		יהורם	JEHORAM	221b	1
		יהושבע	JEHOSHEBA	221b	
		חדר	CHAMBER	293d	
		ינק	NURSE	413c	
		מות	DIE	560c	1
		ממות	DEATH	560d	
		מטה	COUCH	642a	

Ch v.	Heb	Eng	Page	Sec
	סתר	HIDE	711d	1
	עתליה	ATHALIAH	801a	1
11 3	היה	BE	226d	3 2
	חבא	WITHDRAW	285b	1
	מלך	BE KING	574a	
11 4	ברית	COVENANT	136c	1 3
	יהוידע	JEHOIADA	220c	2
	כרי	CARITES	501b	
	כרת	CUT	504a	4
	ל	TO	513d	5 cb g
	מאה	HUNDRED	548a	1 c1
	ראה	TO SEE	908a	
	ראה	TO SEE	908a	1 a1
	רוץ	RUN	930c	2 a
	שביעי	SEVENTH	988a	2
	שבע	SWEAR	989c	1
	שלח	SEND	1018b	1 c
11 5	בוא	COME	97d	1
	שבת	SABBATH	992b	1 a
	משמרת	GUARD	1038c	1
11 6	אחר	BEHIND	29d	2 a
	יסוד	FOUNDATION	*414b	1
	מסח	DEFENCE	587b	
	סור	SVR	694c	
	רוץ	RUN	930c	2 a
	משמרת	GUARD	1038c	1
	שער	GATE	1045b	3 a
	שער	GATE	1045b	3 a
11 7	יד	PART	390c	4 b
	שבת	SABBATH	992b	1 a
	משמרת	GUARD	1038c	1
11 8	בוא	COME	97d	1
	הרג	KILL	247b	1 b
	יד	HAND	390d	5 c1
	מות	DIE	560c	1
	נקף	GO AROUND	*669a	1 b
	נקף	GO AROUND	669a	1 b
	שדרה	ROW	690c	1
11 9	בוא	COME	97d	1
	בוא	COME	98a	1 c
	יהוידע	JEHOIADA	220c	2
	כהן	PRIEST	463c	4
	מאה	HUNDRED	548a	1 c1
	צוה	CHARGE	846a	3
	שבת	SABBATH	992b	1 a
11 10	אשר	PARTICLE OF RELATION	83a	7 b
	חנית	SPEAR	333d	1
	כהן	PRIEST	463c	4
	מאה	HUNDRED	548a	1 c1
	שלט	SHIELD	1020d	
11 11	יד	HAND	390d	5 c1
	ימני	RIGHT	412b	1
	כתף	SIDE	509c	2 b
	ל	TO	511d	1 h
	על	UPON	756a	2 6a
	רוץ	RUN	930c	2 a
	שמאלי	LEFT	970a	
11 12	חיה	LIVE	311b	1 d
	יצא	CAUSE TO GO	424c	1 b
	כף	HOLLOW OF THE HAND	496c	1 d1
	מלך	KING	573b	5 b
	מלך	BE KING	574b	
	משח	ANOINT	603b	2
	נזר	CROWN	634b	1 a
	נכה	SMITE	645d	1 c
	עדות	TESTIMONY	730c	2
	צעדה	ARMLET	857d	1
	אצעדה	ARMLET	*858a	
11 13	עתליה	ATHALIAH	801a	1
	קול	VOICE	877b	2 c
	רוץ	RUN	930c	2 a
11 14	אל	TO	40d	8
	חצצרה	CLARION	348c	1
	כ	LIKE	454a	1 c1
	עמוד	PILLAR	765b	2
	עם	PEOPLE	766c	5 c
	עתליה	ATHALIAH	801a	1
	קרא	CALL	895a	1 b
	קשר	CONSPIRACY	905c	2
	שמח	JOYFUL	970d	1 b
	משפט	JUDGMENT	1049a	6 b
11 15	אל	TO	40d	9
	בית	HOUSE	110c	8 b
	יהוידע	JEHOIADA	220c	2
	יצא	BRING OUT	424d	1 g
	כהן	PRIEST	463c	4
	מאה	HUNDRED	548a	1 c1
	מות	DIE	560c	1
	שדרה	ROW	690c	
	פקד	ATTEND TO	823c	B 1
11 16	מבוא	ENTRANCE	99d	1
	דרך	WAY	202d	1
	יד	HAND	389d	1
	מות	DIE	560c	1
	סוס	HORSE	692d	2
	שום	TO PLACE	963b	1 c
	שער	GATE	*1045b	3 a
11 17	ברית	COVENANT	136d	2 2g
	ברית	COVENANT	137a	3 1
	יהוידע	JEHOIADA	220c	2
	כרת	CUT	504a	4
11 18	ארץ	EARTH	76b	1 a
	בית	HOUSE	109b	1 ae 0
	בעל	BAAL	127d	2 2

Ch v.	Heb	Eng	Page	Sec
	מזבח	ALTAR	259a	0
	יטב	DO WELL	406a	3
	כהן	PRIEST	463a	2
	כהן	PRIEST	463c	4
	מתן	MATTAN	682b	1
	נתץ	PULL DOWN	683b	1
	עם	PEOPLE	766d	5 c
	פקדה	OVERSIGHT	824b	2 b
	צלם	IMAGE	853d	1
	שבר	BREAK	991d	
11 19	ארץ	EARTH	76b	4 a
	בוא	COME	97d	1
	דרך	WAY	202d	1
	ירד	BRING DOWN	433d	1 a
	כסא	THRONE	491b	3 a
	כרי	CARITES	501b	
	עם	PEOPLE	766d	5 c
	רוץ	RUN	930c	2 a
	שער	GATE	1045b	3 a
11 20	מות	DIE	560b	1 b
	עם	PEOPLE	766d	5 c
	עתליה	ATHALIAH	801a	1
	שקט	BE QUIET	1053a	1
12 1	יהואש	JEHOASH	220a	1
12 2	בארשבע	BEERSHEBA	92a	1
	יהוא	JEHU	219d	1
	יהואש	JEHOASH	220a	1
	צביה	ZIBIAH	840b	
12 3	שבע	SEVEN	988a	1 d
	אשר	THAT	83c	8 c
	יהואש	JEHOASH	220a	1
	יהוידע	JEHOIADA	220c	2
	ירה	DIRECT	435c	5 b
	ישר	STRAIGHT	449a	2 a
	כהן	PRIEST	463c	4
	עשה	DO	793d	1 1a 1
12 4	במה	HIGH PLACE	119c	3
	זבח	SLAUGHTER FOR SACRIFICE	257b	2
	סור	TURN ASIDE	694a	3
	עוד	STILL	*728d	1 aa
	קטר	MAKE SACRIFICES SMOKE	882d	
	רק	ONLY	956c	2 b
12 5	בוא	COME	99b	1
	בוא	COME	99c	A
	יהואש	JEHOASH	220a	1
	כהן	PRIEST	463c	4
	כסף	SILVER	494c	8 e
	נפש	SOUL	660c	4 c4
	עבר	PASS OVER	717d	4
	עלה	GO UP	749a	7
	ערך	ORDER	790a	2
12 6	אשר	PARTICLE OF RELATION	82d	6 b
	בדק	FISSURE	96a	
	בדק	FISSURE	96a	
	חזק	BE FIRM	304c	1 c
	כהן	PRIEST	463c	4
	ל	TO	514c	5 fd
	לקח	TAKE	543a	1
	מצא	FIND	593d	1 c
	מכר	ACQUAINTANCE	648c	
12 7	בדק	FISSURE	96a	
	יהואש	JEHOASH	220a	1
	היה	COME TO PASS	224d	1 2a 1b
	חזק	BE FIRM	304c	1 c
	כהן	PRIEST	463c	4
12 8	בדק	FISSURE	96a	
	יהואש	JEHOASH	220a	1
	יהוידע	JEHOIADA	220c	2
	חזק	BE FIRM	304c	1 c
	כהן	PRIEST	463c	4
	כסף	SILVER	494d	9
	מכר	ACQUAINTANCE	648c	
12 9	אות	CONSENT	23a	
	בדק	FISSURE	96a	
	בלת	NOT	116d	1 a
	חזק	BE FIRM	304c	1 c
	כהן	PRIEST	463c	4
	כסף	SILVER	494d	9
12 10	ארון	CHEST	75b	1
	בוא	COME	99c	A
	דלת	DOOR	195b	4
	יהוידע	JEHOIADA	220c	2
	חר	HOLE	359d	
	כהן	PRIEST	463c	4
	כהן	PRIEST	463c	4
	מצבה	PILLAR	663b	1 c
	נקב	PIERCE	666b	1
	נתן	PUT	680c	2 a
	סף	THRESHOLD	706c	
	שם	THERE	1027b	3 a
12 11	ארון	CHEST	75b	1
	כהן	PRIEST	464b	8
	מנה	COUNT	584a	1
	מצא	FIND	594a	2 c
	ספר	ENUMERATOR	708b	1 b
	צור	CONFINE	848d	1
	רב	MUCH	913a	1 a1
	חרש	GRAVER	360d	1 b
12 12	יצא	GO OUT	*423b	1 f
	יצא	BRING OUT	425a	4 g
	על	UPON	753b	2 1c
	פקד	ATTEND TO	824a	3

Ch v.	Heb	Eng	Page	Sec
12 13	תכן	MEASURE	1067c	
	אבן	STONE	6c	2
	אבן	STONE	6c	2
	אבן	STONE	6d	2
	בדק	FISSURE	96a	
	גדר	BUILD A WALL	154d	
	חזק	BE FIRM	304c	1 c
	חזקה	STRENGTH	306a	2
	חצב	HEW	345a	2 a
	מחצב	HEWING	345b	
	יצא	GO OUT	423b	1 f
	עץ	TREE	781d	2
12 14	בוא	COME	99c	A
	מזמרת	SNUFFERS	275a	
	מזרק	BOWL	284d	2 c
	חצצרה	CLARION	348c	2
	כלי	UTENSIL	480a	2 f
	סף	BASIN	706b	
	עשה	DO	795b	2 a
12 15	חזק	BE FIRM	304c	1 c
12 16	אמונה	FIRMNESS	53c	3 a
	חשב	THINK	363c	3
12 17	אשם	OFFENCE	80a	4
	בוא	COME	99c	A
	חטאת	SIN	309b	4
	כהן	PRIEST	463c	4
	כסף	SILVER	494c	8 e
12 18	חזהאל	HAZAEL	303c	
	גת	GATH	387d	
	לחם	ENGAGE IN BATTLE	535c	
12 19	שום	TO PLACE	963d	2 c
	אחזי	AHAZIAH	28d	2
	אוצר	TREASURE	70a	3 a
	יהואש	JEHOASH	220a	1
	יהורם	JEHORAM	221b	1
	יהרשפט	JEHOSHAPHAT	221d	1
	חזהאל	HAZAEL	303c	
	מצא	FIND	594a	2 c
	עלה	GO UP	748c	2 e
	קדש	BE SET APART	873b	1 b
12 20	יהואש	JEHOASH	220a	1
	מלוא	MILLO	571c	3
12 21	יהואש	JEHOASH	220a	1
	סלא	SILLA	698d	
	קום	STAND	878a	2
	קשר	BIND	905b	2
	קשר	BIND	905c	
	קשר	CONSPIRACY	905c	
	שמר	SHOMER	1037c	1
	שמרית	SHIMRITH	1037d	
12 22	אמציהו	AMAZIAH	55c	1
	דוד	DAVID	188a	A
	יהוזבד	JEHOZABAD	220a	1
	יוזכר	JOZACAR	222b	
	זבד	ZABAD	256b	4
	נכה	SMITE	645d	2 a
	קבר	BURY	868c	
	שמעת	SHIMEATH	1035a	
13 1	אחזי	AHAZIAH	28d	2
	יהוא	JEHU	219d	2
	יהואחז	JEHOAHAZ	219d	2
	יהואש	JEHOASH	220a	1
	מלך	BE KING	574b	
13 2	אחר	BEHIND	29d	2
	חטא	MISS A GOAL OR WAY	307d	1
	חטאת	SIN	308d	1 b
	נבט	NEBAT	614a	
13 3	חזהאל	HAZAEL	303c	
	חרה	BURN	354a	2 a
	יום	DAY	400c	7 f
13 4	יהואחז	JEHOAHAZ	219d	2
	חלה	MOLLIFY	318c	1 a
	לחץ	OPPRESS	537d	2
	לחץ	OPPRESSION	537d	
13 5	יצא	GO OUT	422d	1 c
	ישע	DELIVER	446c	1 a
	שלשם	THREE DAYS AGO	1026b	
	תחת	UNDERNEATH	1066b	3 2a
	תמול	YESTERDAY	1070a	2 b
	יד	ADDENDA ET CORRIGENDA	1123d	
13 6	אשרה	ASHERA	81c	B
	בית	HOUSE	110a	5 c
	הלך	WALK	235a	2 3e 2
	חטא	MISS A GOAL OR WAY	307d	2
	חטאת	SIN	308d	1 c
	עמד	STAND	764b	5 a
13 7	אבד	CAUSE TO PERISH	2a	1
	דוש	THRESH	190c	
	יהואחז	JEHOAHAZ	219d	2
	כיאם	EXCEPT	474d	2 a
	עפר	DRY EARTH	780a	2 c
	עשר	TEN	796d	2 b
	פרש	HORSEMAN	832b	
	רגלי	ON FOOT	920b	
	רכב	CHARIOT	*939a	1
	שאר	REMAIN	984b	1
13 8	גבורה	MIGHT	150c	2
	יהואחז	JEHOAHAZ	219d	2
13 9	יהואחז	JEHOAHAZ	219d	2
	יהואש	JEHOASH	220a	1
13 10	יהואחז	JEHOAHAZ	219d	2
	יהואש	JEHOASH	220a	1

Ch	v.	Heb	Eng	Page	Sec
		יהואש	JEHOASH	220a	2
		מלך	BE KING	574b	
		שבע	SEVEN	988b	5 a1
		שש	SIX	995c	2
13	11	הלך	WALK	235a	2 3e 2
		חטא	MISS 0A GOAL OR WAY0	307d	
		חטאת	SIN0	308d	1 c
		נבט	NEBAT	614a	
13	12	אמציהו	AMAZIAH	55c	1
		גבורה	MIGHT	150c	2
		יהואש	JEHOASH	220a	2
		לחם	ENGAGE IN BAT-TLE	535c	
13	13	יהואש	JEHOASH	220a	2
		כסא	THRONE	491a	3 a
		קבר	BURY	*868d	
		ירבעם	JEROBOAM	914d	2
13	14	אב	FATHER	3d	8
		בכה	WEEP	113c	3
		יהואש	JEHOASH	220a	2
		חלה	BE WEAK	317d	2
		חלי	SICKNESS	318b	
		פרש	HORSEMAN	832b	
		רכב	CHARIOT	939b	1
13	15	חץ	ARROW	346c	1
		קשת	BOW	906a	1 b
13	16	יד	HAND	389a	1
		קשת	BOW	906c	1 d
		רכב	RIDE	939a	3
13	17	אפק	APHEK	67d	1
		חלון	WINDOW	319d	
		חץ	ARROW	346c	1
		ירה	SHOOT	435a	3
		ירה	SHOOT	435b	2
		תשועה	DELIVERANCE	448b	1
		כלה	FINISH	478b	1
		נכה	SMITE	646b	3
		עד	AS FAR AS	724b	1 2a b
		פתח	OPEN	835a	
		קדם	EASTWARD	870a	
		אפק	ADDENDA ET COR-RIGENDA	1120c	
13	18	חץ	ARROW	346c	1
		נכה	SMITE	645b	1 a
		עמד	STAND	764a	2 d
13	19	אז	THEN	23b	2
		אלהים	GOD	44a	3 b
		כלה	FINISH	478b	1 d
		ל	TO	518a	7 bg
		נכה	SMITE	645b	1 a
		עד	AS FAR AS	724b	1 2a b
		פעם	OCCURRENCE	822a	3 a
		קצף	BE WROTH	893b	2
		שש	SIX	995d	5
13	20	גדוד	BAND	151b	1
		שנה	YEAR	1040b	
13	21	גדוד	BAND	151b	1
		היה	COME TO PASS	225a	1 2a 1c
		הלך	WALK	232d	1 3
		חיה	LIVE	311b	2 d
		נגע	TOUCH	619a	1 a
		קום	STAND	877d	1 a
		שלך	THROW	1021a	1 a
13	22	יהואחז	JEHOAHAZ	219d	2
		חזהאל	HAZAEL	303c	
		לחץ	OPPRESS	537d	2
		אפק	ADDENDA ET COR-RIGENDA	1120c	
13	23	אבה	BE WILLING	2c	
		ברית	COVENANT	136c	2 2b
		חנן	SHOW FAVOR	336a	2 b
		עתה	NOW	774c	2 f
		פנה	TURN	815c	2 c1
		פנה	FACE	819a	2 8a
		רחם	LOVE	933c	1
		שחת	GO TO RUIN	1008b	1
		שלך	THROW	1021b	2 b
13	24	בנהדד	BEN-HADAD	122b	
		חזהאל	HAZAEL	303c	
		מות	DIE	559c	1 a1
		מלך	BE KING	574a	
13	25	בנהדד	BEN-HADAD	122b	
		יהואחז	JEHOAHAZ	219d	2
		יהואש	JEHOASH	220a	2
		יהואש	JEHOASH	220a	2
		חזהאל	HAZAEL	303c	
		שוב	TURN BACK	998c	8
		שוב	TURN BACK	999b	1 d
14	1	אמציהו	AMAZIAH	55c	1
		יהואחז	JEHOAHAZ	219d	2
		יהואש	JEHOASH	220a	2
		יהואש	JEHOASH	220a	1
14	2	יהועדן	JEHOADDAN	221a	
		יהועדן	JEHOADDAN	221a	
		יהועדן	JEHOADDAN	221b	
		היה	BE	227a	3 4b
		תשע	NINE	1077c	4
14	3	אב	FATHER	3c	4 a
		יהואש	JEHOASH	220a	1
		ישר	STRAIGHT	449a	2 a
		רק	ONLY	956c	2 b
14	4	במה	HIGH PLACE	119c	3
		זבח	SLAUGHTER FOR SACRIFICE	257b	2
		סור	TURN ASIDE	694a	3

Ch	v.	Heb	Eng	Page	Sec
		קטר	MAKE SACRIFICES SMOKE	882d	
		רק	ONLY	956c	2 b
14	5	חזק	BE FIRM	304b	1 2b
		ממלכה	DOMINION	575b	2
14	6	תורה	LAW	436b	2 b2
		מות	DIE	560a	2 b
		מות	DIE	560a	2 b
		מות	DIE	560b	1 b
		מות	DIE	560c	2
		משה	MOSES	602d	
		ספר	MISSIVE	707b	3 c
14	7	גיא	VALLEY	161b	C
		הוא	HE, SHE, IT	215b	1 a
		יקתאל	JOKTHEEL	430d	1
		מלח	SALT	572a	
		תפש	LAY HOLD OF	1074d	1
		סלע	SELA	701aa	
14	8	אמציהו	AMAZIAH	55c	1
		יהואחז	JEHOAHAZ	219d	2
		יהוא	JEHU	219d	1
		יהואש	JEHOASH	220a	2
		פנה	FACE	815d	1 1c
		ראה	TO SEE	908c	
14	9	אמציהו	AMAZIAH	55c	1
		אמר	SAY	55d	1
		ארו	CEDAR	72c	1 a
		בת	DAUGHTER	123a	1
		יהואש	JEHOASH	220a	2
		חוח	BRIER	296b	1 a
		חיה	LIVING THING	312c	1 b
		לבנון	LEBANON	527a	
		לבנון	LEBANON	527b	
		רמס	TRAMPLE	942d	
14	10	גרה	ENGAGE IN STRIFE	173b	1
		כבד	BE HONORED	457c	1 b
		כבד	CAUSE TO BE HON-ORED	*458a	3
		מה	HOW	554b	4 d
		נשא	LIFT	670d	1 b 1
14	11	אשר	PARTICLE OF RE-LATION	83a	7 c
		ביתשמש	BETH-SHEMESH	113a	1
		יהואש	JEHOASH	220a	2
		פנה	FACE	816a	1 1c
		ראה	TO SEE	908c	
14	12	נגף	STRIKE	620a	
14	13	אחזי	AHAZIAH	28d	2
		אפרים	EPHRAIM	68c	7
		ביתשמש	BETH-SHEMESH	112d	1
		יהואש	JEHOASH	220a	2
		יהואש	JEHOASH	220a	1
		חומה	WALL	327c	1
		עשה	DO	793d	1 1a 1
		פנה	CORNER	819b	1 b
		פרץ	BREAK THROUGH	829b	2
		שער	GATE	1044b	1 b 6
		שער	GATE	1044d	1 b 1
14	14	אוצר	TREASURE	70a	3 a
		בן	SON	121d	8 d
		זהב	GOLD	263a	6
		מצא	FIND	594a	2 c
		תערבה	PLEDGE	787a	
		שמרון	SAMARIA	1037d	
		אשר	THAT	83b	8 aa
		גבורה	MIGHT	150c	2
		יהואש	JEHOASH	220a	2
		לחם	ENGAGE IN BAT-TLE	535c	
		נוד	FLUTTER	626d	1
14	16	יהואש	JEHOASH	220a	2
		חטא	SIN	308a	2
		קבר	BURY	*868d	
		ירבעם	JEROBOAM	914d	2
		שמד	BE EXTERMINATED	1029b	1
14	17	יהואחז	JEHOAHAZ	219d	2
		יהואש	JEHOASH	220a	2
		יהואש	JEHOASH	220a	1
		חיה	LIVE	311a	1 a
		חמש	FIVE	332a	2 a
		עשר	TEN	797b	5 c
14	19	לכיש	LACHISH	540c	
		קשר	BIND	905b	2
		קשר	CONSPIRACY	905c	
14	20	דוד	DAVID	188a	A
14	21	יהודה	JUDAH	397b	1 3
		מלך	BE KING	574b	
		עזריהו	AZARIAH	741b	1
14	22	אילאן	ELPARAN	18c	
		אילת	ELATH	19a	
		בנה	BUILD	124d	1 i
		הוא	HE, SHE, IT	215b	1 a
		שוב	TURN BACK	999b	1 d
14	23	יהואש	JEHOASH	220a	1
		יהואש	JEHOASH	220a	2
		חמש	FIVE	332a	2 a
		מלך	BE KING	574b	
		עשר	TEN	797b	5 c
		עשר	TEN	797c	
		ירבעם	JEROBOAM	914d	2
		ארבעים	FORTY	917c	2 a
14	24	חטא	MISS 0A GOAL OR WAY0	307d	2
		חטאת	SIN	308d	1 c
		נבט	NEBAT	614a	
14	25	אמתי	AMITTAI	54c	

Ch	v.	Heb	Eng	Page	Sec
		בוא	COME	98d	2 e
		גבול	BORDER	147d	1 a
		הוא	HE, SHE, IT	215b	1 a
		חמת	HAMATH	333a	
		חפר	HEPHER	343d	2
		גתהחפר	GATH-HEPHER	387d	
		יונה	JONAH	402a	
		ים	SEA	411a	3
		מן	FROM	581d	5 a
		נביא	PROPHET	611d	1
		עבד	SLAVE	714b	4
		ערבה	DESERT-PLAIN	787c	1 a
14	26	שוב	TURN BACK	999b	1 d
		אפס	NON-EXISTENCE	67b	2 b
		עזב	LEAVE	737d	1
		עזר	HELP	740c	
		עני	AFFLICTION	777a	1
		ראה	TO SEE	907a	2 1
14	27	דבר	SPEAK	181d	6
		יהואש	JEHOASH	220a	2
		יד	HAND	391a	5 d
		ישע	DELIVER	446d	1 b
		מחה	WIPE OUT	562a	2
		ירבעם	JEROBOAM	914d	2
		תחת	UNDERNEATH	1066a	3 2a
14	28	גבורה	MIGHT	150c	2
		דמשק	DAMASCUS	199d	
		חמת	HAMATH	333b	
		לחם	ENGAGE IN BAT-TLE	*535c	
		ירבעם	JEROBOAM	914d	2
		שוב	TURN BACK	999b	1 d
14	29	זכריהו	ZECHARIAH	272a	1
		ירבעם	JEROBOAM	914d	1
15	1	אמציהו	AMAZIAH	55c	1
		עזריהו	AZARIAH	741b	1
		ירבעם	JEROBOAM	914d	2
		שבע	SEVEN	988b	5 a1
15	2	היה	BE	227a	3 4b
		יכליה	JECOLIAH	408a	
15	3	אמציהו	AMAZIAH	55c	1
		ישר	STRAIGHT	449a	2 a
15	4	במה	HIGH PLACE	119c	3
		זבח	SLAUGHTER FOR SACRIFICE	257b	2
		סור	TURN ASIDE	694a	3
		קטר	MAKE SACRIFICES SMOKE	882d	
15	5	רק	ONLY	956c	2 b
		ארץ	EARTH	76b	4 a
		בית	HOUSE	109a	1 ae 9
		בית	HOUSE	110b	6
		יותם	JOTHAM	222d	1
		היה	BE	226d	3 2
		חפשית	FREEDOM	345a	
		יום	DAY	398c	2 f
		נגע	STRIKE	619b	
		עם	PEOPLE	766d	5 c
		צרע	BE STRUCK WITH LEPROSY	864a	
15	6	עזריהו	AZARIAH	741b	1
15	7	אב	FATHER	3c	4 a
		דוד	DAVID	188a	A
		יותם	JOTHAM	222d	1
		עזריהו	AZARIAH	741b	1
		קבר	BURY	868c	
15	8	זכריהו	ZECHARIAH	272a	1
		חדש	NEW MOON	294c	2 a
		עזריהו	AZARIAH	741b	1
		ירבעם	JEROBOAM	914d	2
		שמנה	EIGHT	1033a	3 c
15	9	חטא	MISS A GOAL OR WAY	307d	2
		חטאת	SIN	308d	1 c
		נבט	NEBAT	614a	
15	10	יבלעם	IBLEAM	385d	
		יביש	JABESH	386d	2
		קבל	SOMETHING IN FRONT	867b	2
		קשר	BIND	905b	2
		שלום	SHALLUM	1024b	1
15	11	זכריהו	ZECHARIAH	272a	1
		לא	NOT	520c	4 bb
15	12	יהוא	JEHU	219d	1
		היה	COME TO PASS	224b	1 1b
		כסא	THRONE	491b	3 a
		ל	TO	512d	5 aa
15	13	רביעי	FOURTH	918a	1
		חדש	NEW MOON	*294c	2 a
		יביש	JABESH	386d	2
		יום	TIME	399d	6 b
		ירח	MONTH	437b	1
		עזיהו	UZZIAH	739d	1 b
		שלום	SHALLUM	1024b	1
15	14	גדי	GADI	151d	
		יביש	JABESH	386d	2
		מנחם	MENAHEM	637c	
		תרצה	TIRZAH	953d	2
		שלום	SHALLUM	1024b	1
15	15	קשר	BIND	905b	2
		קשר	CONSPIRACY	905c	
		שלום	SHALLUM	1024b	1
15	16	בקע	CLEAVE	132a	
		גבול	BOUNDARY	148a	2 d
		מנחם	MENAHEM	637c	
		נכה	SMITE	646b	3

Ch	v	Heb	Eng	Page	Sec
		תפוח	TAPPUAH	656b	2
		פתח	OPEN	835a	
		תרצה	TIRZAH	953d	2
15	17	גדי	GADI	151d	
		מנחם	MENAHEM	637c	
		עזריהו	AZARIAH	741b	1
15	18	חטא	MISS A GOAL OR WAY	307d	2
		חטאת	SIN	308d	1 c
		נבט	NEBAT	614a	
		סור	TURN ASIDE	693d	1
		על	UPON	759a	4 2c
15	19	אלף	THOUSAND	48d	1 a
		אשור	ASSYRIA	78d	4
		את	WITH	86a	1 a
		חזק	BE FIRM	304d	1 b
		יד	HAND	389d	1 e1
		כסף	SILVER	494b	8 c
		מלך	KING	573a	1
		ממלכה	DOMINION	575b	2
		מנחם	MENAHEM	637c	
		פול	PUL	806d	
15	20	גבור	STRONG	150b	2
		חיל	STRENGTH	298d	1 c
		יצא	BRING OUT	425a	4 g
		כסף	SILVER	494b	8 a
		מלך	KING	573a	1
		מנחם	MENAHEM	637c	
		על	UPON	753b	2 1c
		עמד	STAND	764b	3 b
		שקל	SHEKEL	1053a	
15	21	מנחם	MENAHEM	637c	
15	22	מנחם	MENAHEM	637c	
		פקחיה	PEKAHIAH	824d	
15	23	חמשים	FIFTY	332c	5
		חמשים	FIFTY	332c	6
		מנחם	MENAHEM	637c	
		עזריהו	AZARIAH	741b	1
		פקחיה	PEKAHIAH	824d	
		שנה	YEAR	1040c	
15	24	חטא	MISS A GOAL OR WAY	307d	2
		חטאת	SIN	308d	1 c
		נבט	NEBAT	614a	
15	25	אריה	ARIEH	72a	
		ארמון	CITADEL	74d	
		ארגב	ARGOB	419a	2
		פקח	PEKAH	824d	
		קשר	BIND	905b	2
		רמליהו	REMILIAH	942b	
		שליש	OFFICER	1026d	
15	26	לא	NOT	520c	4 bb
		פקחיה	PEKAHIAH	824d	
15	27	חמשים	FIFTY	332c	5
		חמשים	FIFTY	332c	6
		עזריהו	AZARIAH	741b	1
		פקח	PEKAH	824d	
		רמליהו	REMILIAH	942b	
		שנים	TWO	1041b	3
15	28	חטא	MISS A GOAL OR WAY	307d	2
		חטאת	SIN	308d	1 c
		נבט	NEBAT	614a	
15	29	אבל	ABEL	6a	1
		אשור	ASSYRIA	78d	3
		ביתמעכה	BETH-MAACAH	112a	
		חצור	HAZOR	347d	1
		מלך	KING	573a	1
		ינוח	JANOAH	629c	
		עיון	IJON	743b	
		פקח	PEKAH	824d	
		נפתלי	NAPHTALI	837a	2 a
		קדש	KEDESH	873d	1
		תגלתפלאסר	TIGLATHPILESER	1062a	
		גליל	ADDENDA ET CORRIGENDA	1122a	
15	30	אלה	ELAH	18d	3
		יותם	JOTHAM	222d	1
		הושע	HOSHEA	448a	2
		נכה	SMITE	645d	2 a
		עזיהו	UZZIAH	739d	1 b
		פקח	PEKAH	824d	
		קשר	BIND	905b	2
		קשר	CONSPIRACY	905c	2
		רמליהו	REMILIAH	942b	
15	31	לא	NOT	520c	4 bb
		פקח	PEKAH	824d	
15	32	יותם	JOTHAM	222d	1
		עזיהו	UZZIAH	739d	1 a
		פקח	PEKAH	824d	
		רמליהו	REMILIAH	942b	
15	33	היה	BE	227a	3 4b
		ירושא	JERUSHA	440b	
		צדוק	ZADOK	843b	2
15	34	ישר	STRAIGHT	449a	2 a
		עזיהו	UZZIAH	739d	1 a
15	35	במה	HIGH PLACE	119c	3
		במה	HIGH PLACE	119c	3
		בנה	BUILD	124c	1 ae
		זבח	SLAUGHTER FOR SACRIFICE	257b	2
		סור	TURN ASIDE	694a	3
		עליון	HIGH	751b	2
		קטר	MAKE SACRIFICES SMOKE	882d	
		רק	ONLY	956c	2 b
		שער	GATE	1045b	3 b
15	36	יותם	JOTHAM	222d	1
15	37	חלל	POLLUTE	320d	2
		מלך	KING	573a	1
		פקח	PEKAH	824d	
		רמליהו	REMILIAH	942b	
		רצין	REZIN	954a	1
		שלח	SEND	1019c	
15	38	אב	FATHER	3c	4 a
		אב	FATHER	3c	4 a
		אחז	AHAZ	28c	1
		דוד	DAVID	188a	A
		יותם	JOTHAM	222d	1
16	1	אחז	AHAZ	28c	1
		יותם	JOTHAM	222d	1
		עשר	TEN	797b	7 b
		עשר	TEN	797c	
		פקח	PEKAH	824d	
		רמליהו	REMILIAH	942b	
16	2	שבע	SEVEN	988b	2 a
		אב	FATHER	3c	4 a
		אחז	AHAZ	28c	1
		יהוה	YAHWEH	218d	2 1e
		ישר	STRAIGHT	449a	2 a
16	3	אש	FIRE	77d	4
		דרך	WAY	203d	6 d
		ירש	CAUSE TO POSSESS	440a	1
		עבר	PASS OVER	718d	1 d
		תועבה	ABOMINATION	1072d	1 b
		במה	HIGH PLACE	119c	3 c
		גבעה	HILL	149a	2
16	4	זבח	SLAUGHTER FOR SACRIFICE	257b	2
		עץ	TREE	781c	1 a
		נפתלי	NAPHTALI	837a	2 a
		קטר	MAKE SACRIFICES SMOKE	883a	
16	5	רענן	LUXURIANT	947d	
		אחז	AHAZ	28c	1
		לחם	ENGAGE IN BATTLE	535d	
		מלך	KING	573a	1
		פקח	PEKAH	824d	
		צור	CONFINE	848d	2
		רמליהו	REMILIAH	942b	
		רצין	REZIN	954a	1
16	6	אדמי	EDOMITE	10c	
		אילפארן	ELPARAN	18c	
		אילת	ELATH	19a	
		אילות	ELOTH	19a	
		ארמי	ARAMEAN	74c	
		יהודי	JEW	397c	
		נשל	SLIP	675c	
		רצין	REZIN	954a	1
		שוב	TURN BACK	999b	1 d
16	7	אחז	AHAZ	28c	1
		בן	SON	120b	1 c
		ישע	DELIVER	446c	1 a
		כף	POWER	496d	2
		תגלתפלאסר	TIGLATHPILESER	1062a	
		אחז	AHAZ	28c	1
16	8	אוצר	TREASURE	70a	3 a
		זהב	GOLD	263c	1
		כסף	SILVER	494b	6
		מצא	FIND	594a	2 c
		שחד	BRIBE	1005a	
16	9	דמשק	DAMASCUS	199d	
		קיר	KIR	885b	
		רצין	REZIN	954a	1
		תפש	LAY HOLD OF	1074d	1
16	10	אוריה	URIAH	22c	2
		תבנית	PATTERN	125d	2
		דמות	LIKENESS	198b	1
		דמשק	DAMASCUS	199d	
		כהן	PRIEST	463c	4
		תגלתפלאסר	TIGLATHPILESER	1062a	
16	11	דמשק	DAMASCUS	199d	
		מזבח	ALTAR	*258c	4 a
		כהן	PRIEST	463c	4
		בן	SO	486c	2 cc
		עד	AS FAR AS	724c	1 2a b
16	12	דמשק	DAMASCUS	199d	
		עלה	GO UP	750a	8
		על	UPON	756d	2 7b
		על	UPON	757a	2 7c a
		קרב	COME NEAR	897c	1 b
16	13	אשר	PARTICLE OF RELATION	83a	7 b
		דם	BLOOD	197c	3 b
		זרק	TO TOSS	284c	1 b
		מנחה	OFFERING	585c	6
		נסך	POUR OUT	650d	
		נסך	DRINK-OFFERING	651a	1
		עלה	WHOLE BURNT OFFERING	751a	
		קטר	MAKE SACRIFICES SMOKE	883a	1 a
16	14	את	WITH	86d	4 a
		בין	INTERVAL	107d	D
		מזבח	ALTAR	*258c	4 a
		ירך	SIDE	438a	2
		נחשת	COPPER	638d	1
		צפון	NORTH	861a	
		קרב	COME NEAR	897d	1 a
16	15	ארץ	EARTH	76b	4 a
		בקר	SEEK	133a	
		דם	BLOOD	197c	3 b
		דם	BLOOD	*197d	3 b
		זבח	SACRIFICE	257c	1 1
		מזבח	ALTAR	*258c	4 a
		זרק	TO TOSS	284c	1 b
		כהן	PRIEST	463c	4
		מנחה	OFFERING	585b	4
		מנחה	OFFERING	585b	4
		מנחה	OFFERING	585c	6
		נחשת	COPPER	638d	1
		נסך	DRINK-OFFERING	651a	1
		עלה	WHOLE BURNT OFFERING	750b	
		עלה	WHOLE BURNT OFFERING	751a	
		עם	PEOPLE	766d	5 c
		ערב	SUNSET	788a	1 c
		קטר	MAKE SACRIFICES SMOKE	883a	1 a
16	16	כהן	PRIEST	463c	4
16	17	אבן	STONE	6c	2
		בקר	CATTLE	133c	2
		ירד	BRING DOWN	434a	2
		מכונה	BASE	467d	
		כיור	POT	468c	3 b
		מסגרת	BORDER	689d	1
		קצץ	CUT OFF	893d	1
		קצץ	CUT OFF	893d	1
		מרצפת	PAVEMENT	954b	
16	18	מבוא	ENTRANCE	99d	1
		בנה	BUILD	124c	1 am
		חיצון	OUTER	300b	1
		סבב	TURN ABOUT	686c	1 d
		מוסך	COVERED WAY	697b	
		שבת	SABBATH	992b	1 a
16	20	אב	FATHER	3c	4 a
		דוד	DAVID	188a	A
		חזקיהו	HEZEKIAH	306a	1
17	1	אלה	ELAH	18d	3
		הושע	HOSHEA	448a	2
		תשע	NINE	1077c	1 a
17	2	רק	ONLY	956c	2 b
17	3	הושע	HOSHEA	448a	2
		מלך	KING	573a	1
		מנחה	TRIBUTE	585a	2
		מנחה	OFFERING	585c	6
		עבד	SLAVE	714c	7
		על	UPON	757d	2 7d
		שוב	TURN BACK	999b	1 f
		שלמנאסר	SHALMANESER	1025b	
17	4	אסר	TIE	63d	3
		אשר	THAT	83c	8 c
		בית	HOUSE	109a	1 ae 2
		הושע	HOSHEA	448a	2
		כלא	CONFINEMENT	476c	
		מלך	KING	573a	1
		מנחה	TRIBUTE	585a	2
		מצא	FIND	593b	2 b
		סוא	SO	690c	
		עלה	GO UP	749d	6
		עצר	RESTRAIN	783c	1
		קשר	CONSPIRACY	905c	
17	5	צור	CONFINE	848d	2
17	6	אשור	ASSYRIA	78d	3
		גוזן	GOZAN	157a	
		גוזן	GOZAN	*157a	
		הרא	HARA	246d	
		חבור	HABOR	289c	
		חלח	HALAH	318d	1
		ישב	CAUSE TO SIT	443d	3 a
		הושע	HOSHEA	448a	2
		מדי	MEDIA	552a	2
		נהר	STREAM	625d	1
		נוח	REST	628d	B 1
		שנה	YEAR	1040c	
		תשיעי	NINTH	1077d	1
17	7	יהוה	YAHWEH	218d	2 1d
		היה	COME TO PASS	224b	1 1b
		חטא	MISS A GOAL OR WAY	307a	2 b
		ירא	FEAR	431c	3
		פרעה	PHARAOH	829a	
		תחת	UNDERNEATH	1066b	3 2a
		יד	ADDENDA ET CORRIGENDA	1123d	
17	8	גוי	NATION	156d	1 c
		הלך	WALK	234d	2 3a 2d
		חלח	HALAH	319a	
		חקה	SOMETHING PRESCRIBED	350a	2 b
		חקה	SOMETHING PRESCRIBED	350b	2 e
		ירש	CAUSE TO POSSESS	440a	2 a
17	9	במה	HIGH PLACE	119c	3 c
		בנה	BUILD	124c	1 ai
		מבצר	FORTIFICATION	131c	
		מגדל	TOWER	153d	1
		יהוה	YAHWEH	218d	2 1d
		חפא	DO SECRETLY	341d	
		כן	RIGHT	467b	1
		מן	FROM	582a	5 b
		נצר	WATCH	665d	1
		עיר	CITY	746d	3
17	10	אשרה	ASHERA	81c	B
		גבה	HIGH	147b	1
		גבעה	HILL	149a	1

Ch v.	Heb	Eng	Page	Sec
	נצב	STAND	662c	2
	מצבה	PILLAR	663b	1 c
	עץ	TREE	781c	1 a
	רענן	LUXURIANT	947d	
17 11	במה	HIGH PLACE	119c	3
	גוי	NATION	156d	1 c
	כעס	VEX	495a	2
	קטר	MAKE SACRAFICES SMOKE	882d	
	רע	EVIL	948c	0 d
17 12	אמר	SAY	56a	1
	אשר	PARTICLE OF RELATION	82d	4 d
	עבד	WORK	713b	4 b
17 13	דרך	WAY	203d	6 d
	חזה	SEER	302d	1 a
	חקה	SOMETHING PRESCRIBED	350b	2 e
	חקה	SOMETHING PRESCRIBED	350b	
	יד	HAND	391a	5 d
	תורה	LAW	436b	2 b2
	נביא	PROPHET	611d	1
	עבד	SLAVE	714b	4
	עוד	BEAR WITNESS	730a	3
	רע	EVIL	948c	0 d
17 14	אמן	CONFIRM	53b	2 c
	יהוה	YAHWEH	218d	2 1d
	ערף	BACK OF NECK	791c	2
	קשה	BE SEVERE	904c	3 a
17 15	בלת	NOT	116a	4 a
	ברית	COVENANT	137b	3 3
	גוי	NATION	156d	1 c
	הבל	VAPOUR	210d	2
	הבל	BECOME VAIN	211a	
	חק	SOMETHING PRESCRIBED	349d	7 g
	כרת	CUT	503d	4
	מאס	REJECT	549c	1 a
	עוד	BEAR WITNESS	730a	3
	עדות	TESTIMONY	730c	2
17 16	אשרה	ASHERA	81c	B
	בעל	BAAL	127d	2 2
	יהוה	YAHWEH	218d	2 1d
	מסכה	MOLTEN IMAGE	651b	2
	עבד	WORK	713b	4 b
	עגל	CALF	722b	
	צבא	HOST	839a	1 c
	מצוה	COMMANDMENT	846c	2 b
17 17	אש	FIRE	77d	4
	כעס	VEX	495a	2
	נחש	PRACTISE DIVINATION	638c	1
	עבר	PASS OVER	718d	1 d
	קסם	DIVINATION	890c	2
	קסם	PRACTICE OF DIVINATION	890d	3
17 18	אנף	BE ANGRY	60a	1
	יהודה	JUDAH	397b	1 2
	סור	TURN ASIDE	694b	1
	פנה	FACE	819a	2 8a
	רק	ONLY	956c	2 d
17 19	יהוה	YAHWEH	218d	2 1d
	הלך	WALK	234d	2 3a 2d
	חקה	SOMETHING PRESCRIBED	350a	2 b
	חקה	SOMETHING PRESCRIBED	350b	2 e
17 20	זרע	SOWING	283a	4 f
	מאס	REJECT	549c	1 b
	עד	UNTIL	724d	2 1a a
	ענה	BE BOWED DOWN	776b	1
	שלך	THROW	1021b	2 b
	שסה	PLUNDER	1042c	
17 21	בית	HOUSE	110a	5 c
	חטא	MISS A GOAL OR WAY	307d	2
	חטא	MISS A GOAL OR WAY	*307d	2
	חטאה	SIN	308b	1
	מלך	BE KING	574b	
	נבט	NEBAT	614a	
	נדא	DRIVE AWAY	621c	
	נדח	THRUST	623b	3
	על	UPON	759d	4 2c
	קרע	TEAR	902c	2
17 22	חטאה	SIN	308d	1 b
17 23	אדמה	LAND	10a	5
	אשור	ASSYRIA	78d	3
	יד	HAND	391a	5 d
	נביא	PROPHET	611d	1
	סור	TURN ASIDE	694b	1
	עבד	SLAVE	714b	4
	עד	UNTIL	724d	2 1a a
	פנה	FACE	819b	2 8a
17 24	בבל	BABEL	93c	
	חמת	HAMATH	*333a	
	חמת	HAMATH	333a	
	ירש	TAKE POSSESSION	439c	1 a
	ישב	CAUSE TO SIT	443d	3 a
	כותה	CUTHAH	469b	
	ספרוים	SEPHARVAIM	709b	
	עוה	AVVA	731d	
	שמרון	SAMARIA	1038a	
	שמרון	SAMARIA	1038a	
17 25	ארי	LION	71d	
	דלק	BURN	*196b	1

Ch v.	Heb	Eng	Page	Sec
	היה	COME TO PASS	224d	1 2a 1b
	הרג	KILL	247b	5
	הרג	KILL	247c	7
	תחלה	BEGINNING	321b	
	ירא	FEAR	431c	3 b
	שלח	SEND	1019a	2 d
17 26	אלהים	GOD	43c	2 a
	ארי	LION	71d	
	גוי	NATION	156d	1 c
	ישב	CAUSE TO SIT	443d	3 a
	כאשר	SINCE	455c	3
	מות	DIE	560c	3
	שלח	SEND	1019a	2 d
	שמרון	SAMARIA	1038a	
	משפט	JUDGEMNT	1049a	6 b
17 27	אלהים	GOD	43c	2 a
	הלך	WALK	236d	1 e
	ירה	DIRECT	435c	5 b
	כהן	PRIEST	463b	3 b
	משפט	JUDGMENT	1049a	6 b
17 28	איך	HOW	32c	1
	ביתאל	BETHEL	110d	1
	ירא	FEAR	431c	3 b
	ירה	DIRECT	435c	5 b
	כהן	PRIEST	463b	3 b
	שמרון	SAMARIA	1038a	
17 29	בית	HOUSE	109b	1 ae 0
	במה	HIGH PLACE	119c	3
	גוי	NATION	156d	1 c
	נוח	REST	628d	B 1
	שמרני	SAMARITANS	1038a	
17 30	אשימא	ASHIMA	79a	
	חמת	HAMATH	333a	
	חמת	HAMATH	*333a	
	כותה	CUTHAH	469b	
	נרגל	NERGAL	669c	
	סכות בנות	SUCCOTH-BENOTH	696d	
17 31	אדרמלך	ADRAM-MELECH	12c	1
	אלה	GOD	43a	1
	אש	FIRE	77d	4
	נבחז	NIBHAZ	613b	
	ספרוים	SEPHARVAIM	709b	
	ספרוי	OF SEPHARVAIM	709c	
	עוו	AVVITES	731d	
	ענמלך	ANAMMELECH	777d	
	שרף	BURN	977a	2 b2
	תרתק	TARTAK	1077b	
17 32	בית	HOUSE	109b	1 ae 0
	במה	HIGH PLACE	119c	3
	ירא	FEAR	431c	3 b
	כהן	PRIEST	463b	3 c
	עשה	DO	794d	2 4
	קצה	END	892c	2
17 33	ירא	FEAR	431c	3 b
	משפט	JUDGEMNT	1049a	6 b
17 34	בן	SON	120d	1 jb
	חקה	SOMETHING PRESCRIBED	350a	2 d
	חקה	SOMETHING PRESCRIBED	350b	2 e
	ירא	FEAR	431c	3 b
	תורה	LAW	436b	2 b2
	ראשון	FIRST	911c	1 a
	שום	TO PLACE	964c	5 b
	ישראל	ISRAEL	975c	1
	שם	NAME	1027d	2 a
	משפט	JUDGMENT	1049a	6 b
17 35	אלהים	GOD	43c	1 d
	ברית	COVENANT	137a	3 1
	ירא	FEAR	431c	3
	כרת	CUT	503d	4
	עבד	WORK	713b	4 b
17 36	זרוע	ARM	284a	1 c
	ירא	FEAR	431c	3 b
	כח	STRENGTH	470d	3
17 37	אלהים	GOD	43c	1 d
	חק	SOMETHING PRESCRIBED	349d	7 g
	יום	DAY	400c	7 f
	ירא	FEAR	431c	3
	תורה	LAW	436b	2 b2
	משפט	JUDGMENT	1049a	4
17 38	אלהים	GOD	43c	1 d
	ברית	COVENANT	137a	3 1
	ירא	FEAR	431c	3
	כרת	CUT	503d	4
	שכח	FORGET	1013b	1 c
17 39	יהוה	YAHWEH	218d	2 1b
	ירא	FEAR	431c	3 b
17 40	ראשון	FIRST	911c	1 a
17 41	בן	SON	120b	1 f
	ירא	FEAR	431c	3 b
	עבד	WORK	713b	4 b
18 1	אלה	ELAH	18d	1
	חזקיהו	HEZEKIAH	306a	1
	הושע	HOSHEA	448a	2
18 2	ביהו	ABIJAM	4a	8
	היה	BE	227a	3 4b
	זכריהו	ZECHARIAH	272b	2
18 3	אב	FATHER	3c	4 a
	ישר	STRAIGHT	449a	2 a
18 4	אשרה	ASHERA	81c	B
	במה	HIGH PLACE	119c	3 d
	מזבח	ALTAR	*258c	2
	כרת	CUT OFF	503d	2
	כתת	BEAT	510a	1

Ch v.	Heb	Eng	Page	Sec
	נחש	SERPENT	638b	2
	נחשת	COPPER	638d	1
	נחשתן	NEHUSHTAN	639b	
	מצבה	PILLAR	663b	1 c
	סור	TURN ASIDE	694b	1
	קטר	MAKE SACRAFICES SMOKE	883a	
18 5	ב	IN	88b	1 2
	במה	TRUST	105a	1 3a
18 6	דבק	CLING	179d	2 a
18 7	אשר	PARTICLE OF RELATION	82c	4 bg
	מרד	REBEL	597c	1
	עבד	WORK	713a	3
	שכל	BE PRUDENT	968c	6
18 8	מבצר	FORTIFICATION	131c	
	גבול	BOUNDARY	148a	2 d
	מגדל	TOWER	153d	1
	מן	FROM	582a	5 b
	נצר	WATCH	665d	1
	עזה	GAZA	738b	
	עיר	CITY	746d	3
18 9	אלה	ELAH	18d	3
	חזקיהו	HEZEKIAH	306a	1
	הושע	HOSHEA	448a	2
	צור	CONFINE	848d	2
	רביעי	FOURTH	918a	1
	שלמנאסר	SHALMANESER	1025b	
18 10	חזקיהו	HEZEKIAH	306a	1
	הושע	HOSHEA	448a	2
	לכד	CAPTURE	540a	1
	שש	SIX	995c	1 b
	חשע	NINE	1077c	1 b
18 11	אשור	ASSYRIA	78d	3
	גוזן	GOZAN	157a	
	חרא	HARA	246d	
	חבור	HABOR	289c	
	חלח	HALAH	318d	
	מדי	MEDIA	552a	1
	נהר	STREAM	625d	1
	נוח	REST	628d	B 1
	נחה	LEAD	635a	
18 12	ברית	COVENANT	137b	3 3
	יהוה	YAHWEH	218d	2 1d
	משה	MOSES	602d	
	עבד	SLAVE	714a	3
	עבר	PASS OVER	717c	1 i
	שמע	HEAR	1034a	1 j
18 13	בצר	MAKE INACCESSIBLE	131a	
	יהודה	JUDAH	397b	2
	מלך	KING	573a	1
	סנחריב	SENNACHERIB	703a	
	עשר	TEN	797b	4 b
	ארבע	FOUR	917a	2 a1 a
	שנה	YEAR	1040c	
	תפש	LAY HOLD OF	1074d	1
18 14	זהב	GOLD	263c	1
	חזקיהו	HEZEKIAH	306a	1
	חטא	MISS A GOAL OR WAY	306d	2 a
	כסף	SILVER	494b	8 c
	לכיש	LACHISH	540c	
	על	UPON	753b	2 1c
	על	UPON	759a	4 2b
	שוב	TURN BACK	997a	2
18 15	אוצר	TREASURE	70a	3 a
	חזקיהו	HEZEKIAH	306a	1
	כסף	SILVER	494b	6
	מצא	FIND	594a	2 c
18 16	אמן	CONFIRM	52d	4
	דלת	DOOR	195a	1
	היכל	TEMPLE	228c	2 b
	חזקיהו	HEZEKIAH	306a	1
	צפה	LAY OUT	860a	
	קצץ	CUT OFF	893c	
	קצץ	CUT OFF	893d	
18 17	ברכה	POOL	140a	
	חיל	STRENGTH	299a	4
	כבד	MASSIVE	458a	1 b
	כבס	WASH	460a	
	לכיש	LACHISH	540c	
	מסלה	HIGHWAY	700c	
	סרים	EUNUCH	710c	
	עליון	HIGH	751b	2
	תעלה	WATER-COURSE	752b	B
	רב	CHIEF	913c	
	רב	CHIEF	913c	
	רתרן	FIELD-MARSHAL	1077a	
18 18	אליקים	ELIAKIM	45d	A
	אסף	ASAPH	63a	1
	יואח	JOAH	222a	1
	זבר	REMEMBER	271a	4
	חלקיהו	HILKIAH	324d	1
	ספר	ENUMERATOR	708b	1 b
	קרא	CALL	895d	5 b
18 19	אמר	SAY	56b	3
	במה	TRUST	105a	1 2
	במחון	TRUST	105c	
	גדול	GREAT	153a	6 b
	מה	WHAT	553a	1 c
	מלך	KING	573b	5 a
	רב	CHIEF	913c	
18 20	במה	TRUST	105a	1 4b
	גבורה	MIGHT	150c	2
	דבר	WORD	*182a	1 1a

Ch	v.	Heb	Eng	Page	Sec
		עצה	ADVICE	420a	
		מי	WHO	566b	B
		מרד	REBEL	597c	1
		עתה	NOW	774b	1 d
		שפה	SPEECH	973d	1 a1
18	21	בוא	COME	97d	1
		בטח	TRUST	105a	1 4b
		בטח	TRUST	105a	1 4c
		ל	TO	516a	5 ic
		נקב	PIERCE	666b	1
		סמך	LEAN	702a	
		פרעה	PHARAOH	829a	
		קנה	STALK	889c	2
		רצץ	CRUSH	954c	1 a
		משענת	STAFF	1044a	
18	22	בטח	TRUST	105b	1 5a
		במה	HIGH PLACE	119c	3d
		הוא	HE, SHE, IT	*215c	1 e
		יהוה	YAHWEH	218d	2 1c
		מזבח	ALTAR	*258c	2
		מזבח	ALTAR	259a	0
		כי	IF	473b	2 b
		סור	TURN ASIDE	694b	1
		פנה	FACE	817a	2 4b b
		שחה	BOW DOWN	1005c	2 c
18	23	אלף	THOUSAND	48d	1 a
		אשור	ASSYRIA	78d	4
		ל	TO	515d	5 ia
		סוס	HORSE	692c	2
		ערב	TAKE ON PLEDGE	786a	1
		רכב	RIDE	938d	3
18	24	בטח	TRUST	105a	1 4b
		פחה	GOVERNOR	808a	
		מן	SMALL	882a	2 a
		שוב	TURN BACK	999c	5
18	25	בלעדי	APART FROM	116b	B a
		עלה	GO UP	748c	2 c
		עתה	NOW	774b	1 d
		מקום	STANDING PLACE	880a	3 a
		שחת	GO TO RUIN	1008b	1
18	26	אליקים	ELIAKIM	45d	A
		אנחנו	WE	59d	
		ארמית	ARAMAIC	74c	
		דבר	SPEAK	181c	3 e
		יואח	JOAH	222a	1
		חלקיהו	HILKIAH	324d	1
		חומה	WALL	327b	1
		יהודית	JEWISH	397c	
		רב	CHIEF	913d	
		שמע	HEAR	1033d	1 g
18	27	חומה	WALL	327b	1
		חרא	DUNG	351a	
		מי	WATER	565c	3
		על	UPON	757b	2 7c aa
		רב	CHIEF	913d	
		רגל	FOOT	920a	1 f
		שין	URINE	1010a	
		שתה	DRINK	1059b	1 a
18	28	גדול	GREAT	153a	6 b
		דבר	SPEAK	180d	1
		יהודית	JEWISH	397c	
		מלך	KING	573b	5 a
		עמד	STAND	763d	1 a
		קרא	CALL	895a	1 a
		רב	CHIEF	913d	
18	29	נשא	DECEIVE	674a	
18	30	בטח	TRUST	105b	
		יד	HAND	390d	5 b3
		נתן	GIVE	681c	1 e
18	31	אשור	ASSYRIA	78d	4
		בור	WELL	92b	1
		ברכה	BLESSING	139d	6
		גפן	VINE	172c	
		יצא	GO OUT	423d	2 a
		עשה	DO	794c	2 1e
		תאנה	FIG-TREE	1061a	1
18	32	ארץ	EARTH	76b	3 b
		דבש	HONEY	185b	
		דגן	CORN	186c	
		דגן	CORN	*186c	
		זית	OLIVE TREE	268d	1
		תירוש	NEW WINE	440d	
		לחם	FOOD	537d	1 b
		לקח	TAKE	543d	9 b
		סות	INCITE	694d	2
		יצהר	FRESH OIL	844a	
18	33	איש	MAN	36a	
		אלהים	GOD	43c	1 d
18	34	ארפד	ARPAD	75d	
		הנע	HENA	245a	
		חמת	HAMATH	333a	
		חמת	HAMATH	*333a	
		כי	THAT	*472c	1 da
		ספרוים	SEPHARVAIM	709b	
		עוה	AVVA	731d	
		פרש	HORSEMAN	832a	
18	35	ארץ	EARTH	76c	5
		כי	THAT	*472c	1 da
18	36	דבר	WORD	182b	1 1c
		הוא	HE, SHE, IT	216d	6 b
		חרש	BE SILENT	361b	1 a
		ענה	ANSWER	772d	1 a
		ענה	ANSWER	772d	1 a
		מצוה	COMMANDMENT	846b	1
18	37	אליקים	ELIAKIM	45d	A
		אסף	ASAPH	63a	1
		יואח	JOAH	222a	1
		זכר	REMEMBER	271a	4
		חלקיהו	HILKIAH	324d	1
		ספר	ENUMERATOR	708b	1 b
		קרע	TEAR	902c	1 a1
		רב	CHIEF	913d	
19	1	שבנא	SHEBNA	987d	
		כסה	COVER	492b	
19	2	אליקים	ELIAKIM	45d	A
		אמוץ	AMOZ	55b	
		זקן	OLD	278d	2 b
		ישעיהו	ISAIAH	447d	1
		כהן	PRIEST	464c	8
		כסה	COVER	492b	
		נביא	PROPHET	611d	1
		ספר	ENUMERATOR	708b	1 b
		שק	SACK	974c	2 a
19	3	אין	NOT	34c	2 c
		בוא	COME	98b	1
		יום	DAY	398d	2 f
		תוכחה	REBUKE	407b	
		ילד	BEAR	408b	1 a
		כח	STRENGTH	470c	1 b
		נאצה	CONTEMPT	611a	
		צרה	DISTRESS	865b	
		משבר	BREACH	991b	
19	4	אלהים	GOD	44b	4 a
		חי	ALIVE	311d	1 a
		חרף	REPROACH	357d	
		יכח	REPROVE	407a	5 a
		מצא	FIND	594b	2 d
		נשא	LIFT	670d	1 b 8
		תפלה	PRAYER	813c	1 b
		רב	CHIEF	913d	
		שארית	REST	984d	1
		שמע	HEAR	1034a	2 a
19	6	גדף	BLASPHEME	154c	2
		ירא	FEAR	431b	1 c
		נער	RETAINER	655a	2 b
19	7	נפל	FALL	658a	1 c
		רוח	BREATH	925b	3 g
		שמעה	REPORT	1035b	1
19	8	לבנה	LIBNAH	526c	1
		לחם	ENGAGE IN BATTLE	535c	
		לכיש	LACHISH	540c	
		מצא	FIND	593a	1 d
		נסע	SET OUT	652b	2 b
		רב	CHIEF	913d	
19	9	אמר	SAY	56b	1
		כוש	CUSH	469a	2 c
		לחם	ENGAGE IN BATTLE	535c	
		על	UPON	754d	2 1f g
		שוב	TURN BACK	998b	8
		שמע	HEAR	1033d	1 c
19	10	אלהים	GOD	44d	4 c
		בטח	TRUST	105a	1 3a
		יד	HAND	390d	5 b3
		נשא	DECEIVE	674a	
		נתן	GIVE	681c	1 e
19	11	ארץ	EARTH	76c	5
		אשור	ASSYRIA	78d	4
		חרם	BAN	355d	1 b
		נצל	DELIVER ONESELF	664c	1
		שמע	HEAR	1033d	1 d1
19	12	אב	FATHER	3c	4 a
		אלהים	GOD	43c	1 d
		ביתעדן	BETH-EDEN	112b	
		גוזן	GOZAN	157a	
		חרן	HARAN	357a	
		רצף	REZEPH	954c	
		שחת	GO TO RUIN	1008a	1
		שחת	GO TO RUIN	1008b	1
		תלאשר	TELASSAR	1067d	
19	13	אי	WHERE	32b	1 a
		הנע	HENA	245a	
		חמת	HAMATH	333a	
		ל	TO	513d	5 cb e
		ספרוים	SEPHARVAIM	709b	
		עוה	AVVA	731d	
		ספר	MISSIVE	707a	1 a
19	14	עלה	GO UP	748b	1 d
		פרש	SPREAD OUT	831b	1
		קרא	CALL	895c	4 b
19	15	אלהים	GOD	43d	3
		אלהים	GOD	43d	3
		ארץ	EARTH	76a	1 b
		ארץ	EARTH	76a	1 a
		ישב	SIT	442c	1 a
		כרוב	CHERUB	500d	3
		ל	TO	513d	5 ad
		ממלכה	KINGDOM	575b	1
19	16	אלהים	GOD	44b	4 a
		חי	ALIVE	311d	1 a
		חרף	REPROACH	357d	
		נטה	INCLINE	641a	3 e
		סנחריב	SENNACHERIB	703a	
		עין	EYE	744b	1 j
		פקח	OPEN	824d	1 a
		שמע	HEAR	1034a	2 a
19	17	אמנם	VERILY	54a	
		ארץ	EARTH	76c	5
		אשור	ASSYRIA	78d	4
19	18	חרב	BE WASTE	351d	
		אבד	CAUSE TO PERISH	2a	1
		אבן	STONE	6c	2
		לא	NOT	519b	1 bb
		נתן	PUT	680b	2 a
		עץ	TREE	782a	2 c
19	19	מעשה	DEED	796a	2 a3
		ארץ	EARTH	76a	1 a
		יהוה	YAHWEH	218d	2 1c
		ישע	DELIVER	446d	1 b
		ממלכה	KINGDOM	575b	1
19	20	אל	TO	40b	6
		אמוץ	AMOZ	55b	
		סנחריב	SENNACHERIB	703a	
		פלל	INTERVENE	813b	3
19	21	אחר	BEHIND	30a	2 a
		בוז	DESPISE	100b	
		בזה	DESPISE	*102c	
		בת	DAUGHTER	123c	3
		בת	DAUGHTER	123c	3
		בתולה	VIRGIN	144a	
		דבר	SPEAK	181c	5
		לעג	MOCK	541b	
		נוע	TOTTER	631c	2
19	22	גדף	BLASPHEME	154c	2
		חרף	REPROACH	357d	
		מי	WHO	566b	B
		נשא	LIFT	670a	1 b 4
		קדש	HOLY	872c	1 c
		רום	BE HIGH	927c	1 b
		מרום	HEIGHT	929a	2
19	23	אדון	LORD	11b	3 2a
		ארז	CEDAR	72c	1 a
		מבחור	CHOICE	104d	
		ברוש	CYPRESS	141c	1
		הר	MOUNTAIN	249c	1 a
		חרף	REPROACH	357d	
		יער	WOOD	420d	D
		ירכה	EXTREME PARTS	438a	2
		כרמל	GARDEN	502a	1
		כרת	CUT OFF	503d	2
		לבנן	LEBANON	*527a	
		לבנן	LEBANON	527b	1
		מלן	INN	533d	
		קומה	HEIGHT	879b	2
		קץ	END	894a	2
		רב	MULTITUDE	*914a	1
		מרום	HEIGHT	928d	1
		רכב	CHARIOT	939a	1
19	24	זור	BE A STRANGER	266c	2 c
		חרב	BE DRY	351b	
		יאר	STREAM	384c	2 a
		כף	SOLE OF FOOT	496d	3
		מצור	EGYPT	596a	
		פעם	BEAT	822a	1 b
		קור	BORE	881a	1
19	25	בוא	COME	99c	2 b
		בצר	MAKE INACCESSIBLE	131a	
		ו	AND	254b	3
		יום	DAY	401b	7 k
		יצר	FORM	428a	2 b
		מן	FROM	583d	9 b2
		מן	FROM	583d	9 b2
		נצה	FALL IN RUINS	663d	
		עתה	NOW	774a	1
		קדם	FRONT	869d	2 b
		רחק	DISTANT	935c	2 b
		שאה	MAKE A DIN	981a	
		שמע	HEAR	1033c	1 a
19	26	בוש	BE ASHAMED	101d	1
		גג	ROOF	150d	1
		דשא	GRASS	206a	
		חציר	GREEN GRASS	348b	2
		חתת	BE SHATTERED	369b	2 a
		יד	HAND	389d	1 e1
		ירק	HERBS	438d	
		ישב	SIT	*442d	1 b
		עשב	HERB	793c	
		קמה	STANDING GRAIN	879b	
		קצר	SHORT	894b	
		שדפה	BLIGHTED	995b	
		קמה	ADDENDA ET CORRIGENDA	1126c	
19	27	בוא	COME	97d	1 a
		יצא	GO OUT	424a	3
		ישב	SIT	442d	1 b
		רגז	BE AGITATED	919b	
19	28	אזן	EAR	24b	2 b
		אף	NOSE	60b	1 c
		דרך	WAY	202c	1
		חח	HOOK	296b	1
		מתג	BRIDLE	607c	1
		עלה	GO UP	749a	8
		יען	ON ACCOUNT OF	*774d	1
		רגז	BE AGITATED	919b	
		שום	TO PLACE	963a	1 a
		שפה	SPEECH	973d	1 f
		שאן	ROAR	981a	1
		שאנן	AT EASE	983c	4
19	29	אות	SIGN	16d	2
		אות	SIGN	16d	4
		אכל	EAT	37b	1
		ה	THE	207b	1 ca
		זרע	SOW	281c	1 a
		נטע	PLANT	642c	1

Ch	v.	Heb	Eng	Page	Sec
		שחיש	GRAIN	695a	
		ספיח	GROWTH	705c	
		פרי	FRUIT	826b	1
		קצר	HARVEST	894c	
		שחים	GRAIN THAT SHOOTS UP OF IT	*1006b	
19	30	בית	HOUSE	110a	5 de
		יסף	ADD	414d	
		מטה	DOWNWARDS	641b	2 a
		מעל	ABOVE	751d	2 ca
		עשה	DO	794d	2 2
		פליטה	ESCAPE	812d	2 c
		שרש	ROOT	1057c	1
19	31	פליטה	ESCAPE	812d	2 c
		צבא	GOD OF WAR	839c	4 c
		ציון	ZION	851b	
		קנאה	ZEAL	888c	2 b
		שארית	REST	984d	1
19	32	אמר	SAY	56a	1
		מגן	SHIELD	171c	
		חץ	ARROW	346b	1
		ירה	SHOOT	435b	2
		סללה	MOUND	700c	
		קדם	COME IN FRONT	869a	1 a
		שפך	POUR OUT	1049c	1 a
19	33	דרך	WAY	202c	1
		נאם	UTTERANCE	610b	2
19	34	גנן	DEFEND	170d	
		דוד	DAVID	188a	
		ישע	DELIVER	446d	1 b
		מען	PURPOSE	775b	1 a
19	35	אשור	ASSHUR	78d	1
		בקר	MORNING	134b	1 h
		מחנה	ENCAMPMENT	334b	3 a
		מלאך	MESSENGER	521d	2
		מות	DIE	560a	2 b
		נכה	SMITE	646c	4 a
		פגר	CORPSE	803d	1
19	36	הלך	WALK	234a	1 5e
		נינוה	NINEVEH	644b	
		נסע	SET OUT	652b	2 b
		סנחריב	SENNACHERIB	703a	
19	37	אדרמלך	ADRAM-MELECH	12c	2
		אסרחדן	ESARHADDON	64d	
		אררט	ARARAT	76d	
		היה	COME TO PASS	224d	1 2a 1b
		חרב	SWORD	352d	1 f
		מלט	SLIP AWAY	572c	2
		מלך	BE KING	574a	
		נסרך	NISROCK	652d	
		ענמלך	ANAMMELECH	777d	
		שראצר	SHAREZER	974d	1
		שחה	BOW DOWN	1005c	3
20	1	אמוץ	AMOZ	55b	
		בית	HOUSE	110b	6
		חיה	LIVE	311b	2a
		חלה	BE WEAK	317d	2
		ל	TO	517b	7 ba
		נביא	PROPHET	611d	1
		עד	UNTIL	725c	3 2
		צוה	GIVE CHARGE TO	845c	1 b
20	2	סבב	TURN ABOUT	686c	1 a
		פלל	INTERVENE	813b	3
20	3	אמת	FIRMNESS	54a	3 a
		אנא	AH, NOW	58a	
		בכה	WEEP	113c	2
		בכי	WEEPING	113d	
		הלך	WALK	236b	2
		זכר	REMEMBER	270b	2 2 b
		טוב	PLEASANT	374a	2 f
		לבב	HEART	523d	2 6a
		שלם	COMPLETE	1024a	3
20	4	בל	NOT	115c	
		דבר	WORD	182c	1 2a
		חצר	ENCLOSURE	347a	2
		תיכון	MIDDLE	1064a	
20	5	אלהים	GOD	44c	4 ba
		דוד	DAVID	188b	1
		דמעה	TEARS	199c	
		עלה	GO UP	748b	1 d
		רפא	HEAL	950d	1 a
20	6	גנן	DEFEND	170d	
		דוד	DAVID	188b	
		חמש	FIVE	332a	2 a
		יסף	ADD	415a	1
		כף	POWER	496d	2
		נצל	DELIVER	665a	3 a
		מען	PURPOSE	775b	1 a
20	7	דבלה	PRESSED FIG-CAKE	179b	
		חיה	LIVE	311b	2a
		מרח	RUB	*598d	
		שחין	BOIL	1006c	
		תאנה	FIG	1061a	1
20	8	אות	SIGN	16d	4
		עלה	GO UP	748b	1 d
		רפא	HEAL	950d	1 a
20	9	אות	SIGN	16d	4
		אשר	THAT	83c	8 ab
		הלך	WALK	232c	1 3
		מעלה	STEP	752b	2
		צל	SHADOW	853b	1
20	10	שוב	TURN BACK	998a	7 a
		אחרנית	BACKWARDS	30d	
		חזקיה	HEZEKIAH	*306a	1
		חזקיהו	HEZEKIAH	306a	1
		ל	TO	511a	1 e

Ch	v.	Heb	Eng	Page	Sec
		נטה	BEND	640b	3 a
		מעלה	STEP	752b	2
		צל	SHADOW	853b	2
		קלל	BE SLIGHT	886c	2
		שוב	TURN BACK	998a	7 a
20	11	אחרנית	BACKWARDS	30d	
		ירד	GO DOWN	433c	3 e
		נביא	PROPHET	611d	1
		מעלה	STEP	752b	2
		צל	SHADOW	853b	1
		שוב	TURN BACK	999a	1 a
20	12	בבל	BABEL	93c	
		בלאדן	BALADAN	*114d	
		בלאדן	BALADAN	114d	
		חלה	BE WEAK	317d	2
		מנחה	GIFT	585a	1
		מרדכבלאדן	MERODACH BALA-DAN	597d	
		ספר	MISSIVE	707a	1 a
		שלח	SEND	1018b	1 b
		שמע	HEAR	*1033c	1 a
20	13	אוצר	TREASURE	70a	1
		בית	HOUSE	109a	1 ae 6
		בשם	SPICE	141d	1
		זהב	GOLD	263c	1
		טוב	PLEASANT	374b	3 c
		כלי	IMPLEMENT	479d	1
		מצא	FIND	594a	2 c
		ממשלה	RULE	606a	1
		נכת	TREASURE	649b	
		על	UPON	757c	2 7 c b
		ראה	TO SEE	908d	1 a1
		שמח	REJOICE	970b	1 a
		שמן	OIL	1032b	2 b
		שמע	HEAR	1034a	1 k
20	14	אמר	SAY	55d	1
		נביא	PROPHET	611d	1
		רחק	DISTANT	935b	1 a
20	15	אוצר	TREASURE	70a	1
		ראה	TO SEE	908d	
		ראה	TO SEE	908d	1 a1
20	17	אב	FATHER	3c	4 a
		אצר	STORE UP	69d	
		בוא	COME	98c	2 B
		הנה	BEHOLD	244b	7 c
		יום	DAY	400a	
		יתר	BE LEFT OVER	451b	
		נשא	LIFT	671d	4
20	18	בבל	BABEL	93c	
		היכל	PALACE	*228a	
		היכל	PALACE	228b	1
		ילד	BEGET	409a	1
		יצא	GO OUT	423c	1 h
		סריס	EUNUCH	710c	
20	19	אם	IF	50c	1 cb
		אמת	FIRMNESS	54a	2
		טוב	PLEASANT	374b	5
		יום	DAY	399b	4 b
		שלון	PEACE	1023b	6
20	20	אשר	THAT	83b	8 aa
		בוא	COME	99a	1
		ברכה	POOL	140a	
		גבורה	MIGHT	150c	2
		הלך	WALK	*232d	1
		תעלה	WATER-COURSE	752b	B
20	21	מנשה	MANASSEH	586d	2
21	1	חפצי-בה	HEPHZIBAH	343b	1
		מנשה	MANASSEH	586d	2
21	2	ירש	CAUSE TO POSSESS	440a	2 a
		תועבה	ABOMINATION	1072d	1 b
21	3	אבד	CAUSE TO PERISH	2a	1
		אשרה	ASHERA	81c	B
		מה	HIGH PLACE	119d	3 d
		בנה	BUILD	124c	1 ai
		בנה	BUILD	124d	1 i
		בעל	BAAL	127d	2 2
		מזבח	ALTAR	258d	8
		עבד	WORK	713b	4 b
		צבא	HOST	839a	1 c
		קום	STAND	878d	2 b
		שוב	TURN BACK	998b	8
21	4	אמר	SAY	56a	1
		אשר	PARTICLE OF RELATION	82d	4 d
21	5	חצר	ENCLOSURE	347a	3 b
		צבא	HOST	839a	1 c
21	6	אוב	NECROMANCER	15b	2
		אש	FIRE	77d	4
		ידעני	FAMILIAR SPIRIT	396b	
		כעס	VEX	495a	2
		נחש	PRACTISE DIVINATION	638c	1
		עבר	PASS OVER	718d	1 d
		ענן	PRACTISE SOOTHSAYING	778b	
		עשה	DO	795a	2 8
		רבה	BECOME MANY	915c	1 d1
21	7	אשרה	ASHERA	81b	A
		בחר	CHOOSE	104a	2
		עולם	LONG DURATION	762c	2 e
		פסל	IDOL	820d	
		שום	TO PLACE	962a	1 a
		שום	TO PLACE	964b	2 c
21	8	יסף	DO AGAIN	415c	2 a
		תורה	LAW	436b	2 b2
		ל	TO	*514c	5 fd

Ch	v.	Heb	Eng	Page	Sec
		משה	MOSES	602d	
		נוד	WANDER	627a	1
		עבד	SLAVE	714a	3
		עמד	STAND	*764d	5
		רק	ONLY	956d	2 f
		ישראל	ISRAEL	975d	2 a3
21	9	רע	EVIL	948a	3
		תעה	ERR	1073c	3
21	10	נביא	PROPHET	611d	1
		עבד	SLAVE	714b	4
21	11	אמרי	AMORITES	57c	2 b
		חטא	MISS A GOAL OR WAY	*307d	2
		חטא	MISS A GOAL OR WAY	307d	1
		רעע	BE EVIL	949d	2
		תועבה	ABOMINATION	1072d	1 b
21	12	אזן	EAR	24a	2 a
		כן	SO	486d	3 d
		כן	SO	487a	3 d
		כן	SO	*487a	3 da
		צלל	TINGLE	852d	
		צלל	TINGLE	852d	
21	13	אבן	STONE	6d	6
		בית	HOUSE	109d	5 a
		בית	HOUSE	110a	5 c
		הפך	TURN	245b	1 a
		מחה	WIPE	562a	1
		נטה	STRETCH OUT	640a	1 b
		צלחת	DISH	852c	
		קו	LINE	876a	
		קו	LINE	876a	
		משקלת	LEVEL	1054a	
21	14	בז	SPOIL	103a	2
		נחלה	PROPERTY	635b	1 e
		נטש	FORSAKE	643d	2
		שארית	REST	984d	1
		משסה	PLUNDER	1042d	
21	15	יצא	GO OUT	422d	1 a
		כעס	VEX	495a	2
		רע	EVIL	948c	0 b
21	16	אל	TO	39d	1
		דם	BLOOD	196c	2 b
		דם	BLOOD	196d	2 d
		חטא	MISS 0A GOAL OR WAY0	*307d	
		חטא	MISS 0A GOAL OR WAY0	307d	1
		חטאת	SIN	308c	1 b
		מלא	FILL	570c	1
		נקי	CLEAN	667c	1
		עד	UNTIL	724d	2 1a a
		פה	MOUTH	805c	5 a
		רבה	BECOME MANY	915d	1 e3
21	17	חטא	MISS 0A GOAL OR WAY0	307b	2 b
		חטאת	SIN	308c	1 b
21	18	אמון	AMON	54c	A
		גן	GARDEN	171a	
		גן	GARDEN	171a	
		עזא	UZZAH	739c	2
		קבר	BURY	868c	
21	19	אמון	AMON	54c	A
		חרוץ	HARUZ	358d	
		יטבה	JOTBAH	406a	
		משלמת	MESHULLEMETH	1024c	
21	21	דרך	WAY	204a	6 d
		הלך	WALK	234d	2 3a
		הלך	WALK	234d	2 3a 2b
		עבד	WORK	713b	4 b
21	22	אלהים	GOD	44b	4 ba
		דרך	WAY	204a	6 ec
		הלך	WALK	234c	2 3a 1b
21	23	אמון	AMON	54c	A
21	24	אמון	AMON	54c	A
		ארץ	EARTH	76b	4 a
		יאשיהו	JOSIAH	78c	1
		מלך	BE KING	574d	
		עם	PEOPLE	766d	5 c
21	25	אמון	AMON	54c	A
21	26	יאשיהו	JOSIAH	78c	1
		גן	GARDEN	171a	
		עזא	UZZAH	739c	2
		קבר	BURY	868c	
		צברה	GRAVE	869a	1
22	1	בצקת	BOZKATH	130d	
		ידידה	JEDIDAH	392a	
		עדיהו	ADAIAH	726a	2
		שנה	YEAR	1040b	
22	2	אב	FATHER	3c	4 a
		דרך	WAY	203d	6 c
		ימין	RIGHT HAND	412a	2 b
		ישר	STRAIGHT	449a	2 a
		סור	TURN ASIDE	693c	1
22	3	אצליהו	AZALIAH	69d	
		ספר	ENUMERATOR	708c	1 b
		שלח	SEND	1018b	1 a
		משלם	MESHULLAM	1024c	1
		שמנה	EIGHT	1033a	2 a
		שפן	SHAPHAN	1051a	1
22	4	אסף	GATHER	62b	1 c
		בוא	COME	99c	A
		חלקיהו	HILKIAH	324d	2
		כהן	PRIEST	464b	8
		סף	THRESHOLD	706c	
		תמם	BE COMPLETE	1070c	3

Ch	v.	Heb	Eng	Page	Sec
22	5	ברק	FISSURE	96a	
		חזק	BE FIRM	304c	1 c
		על	UPON	753b	2 1c
		פקד	ATTEND TO	824a	3
22	6	אבן	STONE	6c	2
		אבן	STONE	6c	2
		גדר	BUILD A WALL	154d	
		חזק	BE FIRM	304c	1 c
		מחצב	HEWING	345b	
		חרש	GRAVER	360d	1 b
		עץ	TREE	781d	2 a
22	7	אמונה	FIRMNESS	53c	3 a
		חשב	THINK	363c	2
		נתן	GIVE	681c	1 d
22	8	חלקיהו	HILKIAH	324d	2
		חלקיהו	HILKIAH	324d	2
		תורה	LAW	436b	2 b2
		כהן	PRIEST	464b	8
		מצא	FIND	593b	3 a
		ספר	MISSIVE	707b	3 c
		ספר	ENUMERATOR	708c	1 b
		על	UPON	757c	27c b
		קרא	CALL	895c	4 b
		שפן	SHAPHAN	1051a	
22	9	דבר	WORD	182b	11c
		מצא	FIND	594a	2 c
		נתך	POUR FORTH	677d	
		ספר	ENUMERATOR	708c	1 b
		פקד	ATTEND TO	824a	3
		שפן	SHAPHAN	1051a	1
22	10	חלקיהו	HILKIAH	324d	2
		כהן	PRIEST	463c	4
		נתן	GIVE	678b	1 a
		ספר	ENUMERATOR	708c	1 b
		קרא	CALL	895c	4 a
		שפן	SHAPHAN	1051a	1
22	11	דבר	WORD	183a	2 2
		תורה	LAW	436b	2 b2
		ספר	MISSIVE	707b	3 c
22	12	אחיקם	AHIKAM	27b	
		חלקיהו	HILKIAH	324d	2
		כהן	PRIEST	463c	4
		מיכה	MICHA	*567d	7
		מיכיה	MICAH	567d	6
		ספר	ENUMERATOR	708c	1 b
		עבד	SLAVE	714a	2
		עכבור	ACHBOR	747b	2
		עשיה	ASAIAH	795c	1
		שפן	SHAPHAN	1051a	2
		שפן	SHAPHAN	1051a	1
22	13	אשר	PARTICLE OF RELATION	82b	2 a
		בעד	ON BEHALF OF	126c	2
		דרש	SEEK	205b	2 a
		חמה	RAGE	404c	2 c
		חמה	RAGE	*404d	2 c
		יצת	BE KINDLED	428b	
		כתב	WRITE	507c	1 b3
		מצא	FIND	593d	1 b
		על	UPON	753b	2 1c
		על	UPON	757c	27c b
		שמע	HEAR	1034a	1 k
		על־דבר	ADDENDA ET CORRIGENDA	1122a	
22	14	אחיקם	AHIKAM	27b	
		אשר	PARTICLE OF RELATION	83b	7 c
		הלך	WALK	231a	1 d3 ga
		חלדה	HULDAH	317c	
		חלקיהו	HILKIAH	324d	2
		חסרה	HARHAS	341c	
		חרחם	HARHAS	354d	
		כהן	PRIEST	463c	4
		נביאה	PROPHETESS	612c	1 b
		עכבור	ACHBOR	747b	2
		עשיה	ASAIAH	795c	1
		תקוה	TIKVAH	876b	1
		שלום	SHALLUM	1024b	1
		שמר	KEEP	1036c	1 a
		שמר	KEEP	1036d	1 b
		משנה	SECOND	1041d	3
		שפן	SHAPHAN	1051a	1
22	16	קרא	CALL	895c	4 c
22	17	אלהים	GOD	43c	1 d
		חמה	RAGE	404c	2 c
		חמה	RAGE	*404d	2 c
		יצת	BE KINDLED	428b	
		כבה	BE QUENCHED	459c	
		כעס	VEX	495a	2
		מעשה	DEED	795d	1 a2
		קטר	MAKE SACRAFICES SMOKE	883a	
		תחת	INSTEAD	1066a	2 3a b
22	18	דרש	SEEK	205b	2 a
22	19	בכה	WEEP	113c	6
		דבר	SPEAK	181d	5
		כנע	BE HUMBLE	488c	1
		לבב	HEART	524a	2 6a
		נאם	UTTERANCE	610b	2
		יען	ON ACCOUNT OF	774d	2 c
		פנה	FACE	818a	2 5b
		קללה	CURSE	887a	1
		רכך	BE TENDER	940a	1 b
		שמה	APPALMENT	1031c	1
		שמע	HEAR	1034b	2 h
22	20	אסף	GATHER	62b	2 a

Ch	v.	Heb	Eng	Page	Sec
		אסף	GATHER	62d	2 a
		דבר	WORD	182b	11c
		הנה	BEHOLD	244b	B b
		כן	SO	487a	3 d
		על	UPON	757b	27c aa
		קבצבר	GRAVE	868d	
		ראה	TO SEE	908a	8 a3
23	1	אסף	GATHER	62b	1 a
23	2	ברית	COVENANT	136d	2 2
		גדול	GREAT	153b	7
		כהן	PRIEST	463c	4
		מן	FROM	583d	9 b1
		מצא	FIND	593d	1 b
		נביא	PROPHET	611d	2
		ספר	MISSIVE	707b	3 c
		עלה	GO UP	748b	1 d
		קרא	CALL	895c	4 a
23	3	אחר	BEHIND	29d	2 a
		ברית	COVENANT	136d	2 2i
		ברית	COVENANT	136d	2 2c
		ברית	COVENANT	137a	3 1
		דבר	WORD	183a	2 2
		חקה	SOMETHING PRESCRIBED	350b	2 e
		חקה	SOMETHING PRESCRIBED	350b	2 d
		כרת	CUT	504a	4
		לבב	HEART	523b	2
		נפש	SOUL	661b	0
		עבר	PASS OVER	718b	5 e
		עדות	TESTIMONY	730b	2
		עמד	STAND	764c	7 b
		עמד	STAND	764d	6 c
		עמוד	PILLAR	765b	2
		מצוה	COMMANDMENT	846c	2 b2
23	4	אשרה	ASHERA	81c	A
		בעל	BAAL	127d	2 2
		דבר	WORD	183a	2 2
		היכל	TEMPLE	228c	2 b
		חלקיהו	HILKIAH	324d	2
		יצא	BRING OUT	425a	4 a
		כהן	PRIEST	464b	8
		כהן	PRIEST	464c	8
		כלי	UTENSIL	480a	2 f
		סף	THRESHOLD	706c	
		צבא	HOST	839a	1 c
		קדרון	KEDRON	871b	
		שדמה	FIELD	995b	
		משנה	SECOND	1041c	3 a
23	5	במה	HIGH PLACE	119c	3
		במה	HIGH PLACE	119d	3 e
		בעל	BAAL	127d	2 2
		דבר	WORD	183a	2 2
		יהודה	JUDAH	397b	2
		ירח	MOON	437a	
		כמר	PRIEST	485c	
		מזלות	CONSTELLATIONS	561b	
		נתן	PUT	680d	2 c
		מסב	THAT WHICH SURROUNDS	687b	1 a
		צבא	HOST	839a	1 c
		קטר	MAKE SACRAFICES SMOKE	882d	
		קטר	MAKE SACRAFICES SMOKE	883a	
		שבת	CEASE	992a	2
		שמש	SUN	1039b	3
23	6	אשרה	ASHERA	81c	B
		במה	HIGH PLACE	119c	3
		בן	SON	121b	3 jk
		דבר	WORD	183a	2 2
		דקק	PULVERISE	200d	
		חוץ	THE OUTSIDE	300a	1 bd
		יצא	BRING OUT	425a	4 a
		נחל	WADY	636c	1
		עם	PEOPLE	766d	5 b
		עפר	DRY EARTH	779d	1 d
		קבצבר	GRAVE	868d	
		קדרון	KEDRON	871b	
		שלך	THROW	1021a	1 a
23	7	ארג	WEAVE	70d	
		אשרה	ASHERA	81c	A
		בית	HOUSE	109b	1 ae 0
		במה	HIGH PLACE	119c	3
		דבר	WORD	183a	2 2
		נתן	PULL DOWN	683b	1
		קדש	TEMPLE-PROSTITUTE	873d	
		אשרה	ADDENDA ET CORRIGENDA	1121a	
23	8	בארשבע	BEERSHEBA	92a	
		במה	HIGH PLACE	119c	3
		במה	HIGH PLACE	119d	3 e
		גבע	GEBA	148d	
		דבר	WORD	183a	2 2
		יהושוע	JOSHUA	221c	4
		מזבח	ALTAR	258c	2
		טמא	BE UNCLEAN	379c	2
		יהודה	JUDAH	397b	2
		כהן	PRIEST	463d	5
		נתץ	PULL DOWN	683b	1
		פתח	OPENING	836a	
		קטר	MAKE SACRAFICES SMOKE	883a	
		שמאל	LEFT	969d	1

Ch	v.	Heb	Eng	Page	Sec
		שעיר	SATYR	972d	
		שר	CHIEFTAIN	978b	2 d
		שם	THERE	1027c	3 b
		שער	GATE	1045b	3 a
23	9	במה	HIGH PLACE	119c	3
		במה	HIGH PLACE	119d	3 e
		דבר	WORD	183a	2 2
		כהן	PRIEST	463d	5
		מצה	UNLEAVENED BREAD	695b	
		על	UPON	756d	27b
23	10	אש	FIRE	77d	4
		בלת	NOT	116d	4 a
		במה	HIGH PLACE	119c	3
		דבר	WORD	183a	2 2
		הנם	HINNOM	*245a	
		טמא	BE UNCLEAN	379c	2
		מלך	MOLECH	574c	
		עבר	PASS OVER	718d	1 d
		תפת	TOPHETH	1075a	
23	11	אש	FIRE	77c	1
		במה	HIGH PLACE	119c	3
		דבר	WORD	183a	2 2
		לשכה	ROOM	545d	1 b
		נתנמלך	NATHAN-MELECH	682a	
		סוס	HORSE	692c	2
		סרים	EUNUCH	710c	
		פרור	COLONNADE	826c	
		מרכבה	CHARIOT	939d	
		שרף	BURN	976d	2 a
		שבת	CEASE	992a	2
		שמש	SUN	1039b	3
23	12	במה	HIGH PLACE	119c	3
		גג	ROOF	151a	1
		דבר	WORD	183a	2 2
		מזבח	ALTAR	258d	7
		מזבח	ALTAR	259a	0
		חצר	ENCLOSURE	347a	3 b
		נחל	WADY	636c	2
		נתץ	PULL DOWN	683b	1
		עליה	ROOF-CHAMBER	751a	
		עפר	DRY EARTH	779d	1 d
		קדרון	KEDRON	871b	
		רוץ	RUN	930b	1
		רוץ	RUN	930c	1
		שלך	THROW	1021a	1 a
23	13	מלכם	MILCOM		
		במה	HIGH PLACE	119c	3
		בנה	BUILD	124c	1 ai
		דבר	WORD	183a	2 2
		הר	MOUNTAIN	249c	1 a
		זית	OLIVE TREE	*268d	3
		טמא	BE UNCLEAN	379c	2
		ימין	RIGHT HAND	411d	2
		ימין	RIGHT	412a	4
		כמוש	CHEMOSH	484d	
		עמון	AMMON	770a	
		עשתרת	ASTORETH	800a	
		פנה	FACE	819a	27a d
		צידני	SIDONIANS	851a	
		משחית	DESTRUCTION	1008c	
		שקוץ	DETESTED THING	1055a	
		תועבה	ABOMINATION	1073a	1 b
23	14	אשרה	ASHERA	81c	B
		במה	HIGH PLACE	119c	3
		דבר	WORD	183a	2 2
		כרת	CUT OFF	503d	1
		מלא	FILL	570c	1
		מצבה	PILLAR	663b	1 c
		מקום	STANDING PLACE	879d	1 a
23	15	אבן	STONE	6c	2
		אשרה	ASHERA	81c	B
		ביתאל	BETHEL	110d	1
		ביתאל	BETHEL	110d	1
		במה	HIGH PLACE	119c	3
		דבר	WORD	183a	2 2
		דקק	PULVERISE	200d	
		מזבח	ALTAR	*258b	1
		מזבח	ALTAR	259a	0
		חטא	MISS A GOAL OR WAY	307d	2
		חטא	MISS A GOAL OR WAY	*307d	2
		נבט	NEBAT	614a	
		נתץ	PULL DOWN	683b	1
		עפר	DRY EARTH	779d	1 d
23	16	אלהים	GOD	44a	3 b
		במה	HIGH PLACE	119c	3
		דבר	WORD	183a	2 2
		טמא	BE UNCLEAN	379c	2
		שרף	BURN	976d	2 a
23	17	אלהים	GOD	44a	3 b
		במה	HIGH PLACE	119c	3
		דבר	WORD	183a	2 2
		הלו	THIS	229c	
		ציון	SIGN POST	846b	
23	18	במה	HIGH PLACE	119c	3
		דבר	WORD	183a	2 2
		מלט	SLIP AWAY	572c	1
		נוח	REST	629a	B 5
		נוע	TREMBLE	631c	2
23	19	במה	HIGH PLACE	119c	3
		דבר	WORD	183a	2 2
		כעס	VEX	495a	2
		סור	TURN ASIDE	694b	1
		מעשה	DEED	795d	1 a3

Ch	v.	Heb	Eng	Page	Sec
23	20	שמרון	SAMARIA	1038a	
		במה	HIGH PLACE	119c	3
		דבר	WORD	183a	2 2
		זבח	SLAUGHTER FOR SACRIFICE	257a	3
		מזבח	ALTAR	258c	2
		כהן	PRIEST	463d	5
		שרף	BURN	976d	2 a
23	21	ברית	COVENANT	136d	2 2c
		דבר	WORD	183a	2 2
		יהוה	YAHWEH	218b	2 1b
		ספר	MISSIVE	707b	3 c
		פסח	PASSOVER	820b	3
23	22	דבר	WORD	183a	2 2
		יום	DAY	401a	7 j
		כי	THAT	472a	1 e
		עשה	DO	795b	3
		פסח	PASSOVER	820b	3
		ישראל	ISRAEL	975d	2 a3
		שפט	JUDGE	1047b	1 b
		שפט	JUDGE	1047b	1 b
23	23	דבר	WORD	183a	2 2
		כיאם	BUT	475a	2 b
		עשה	DO	795b	3
		פסח	PASSOVER	820b	3
23	24	אוב	NECROMANCER	15b	2
		בית	HOUSE	108d	1 a
		בער	CONSUME	129b	3
		דבר	WORD	183a	2 2
		חלקיהו	HILKIAH	324d	2
		ידעני	FAMILIAR SPIRIT	396b	
		יהודה	JUDAH	397b	2
		תורה	LAW	436b	2 b2
		כהן	PRIEST	463d	4
		מצא	FIND	593d	3 a
		ראה	TO SEE	908c	2 c
		שקוץ	DETESTED THING	1055a	
		תרפים	IDOL	1076d	
23	25	היה	BE	226d	3 1
		תורה	LAW	436b	2 b2
		לבב	HEART	523b	2 2
		מאד	FORCE	547b	1
		משה	MOSES	602d	
		נפש	SOUL	661b	0
		קום	STAND	878a	4
23	26	אשר	THAT	83c	8 c
		חרה	BURN	354a	2 a
		חרון	BURNING OF ANGER	354c	
		כעס	VEX	495a	2
		כעס	ANGER	495b	2
		שוב	TURN BACK	997c	6 f
23	27	בחר	CHOOSE	104a	2 a
		מאס	REJECT	549c	1 a
		סור	TURN ASIDE	694b	1
		סור	TURN ASIDE	694b	1
		פנה	FACE	819b	2 8a
		שם	THERE	1027b	1 b
23	29	מגדו	MEGIDDO	152a	
		הלך	WALK	233d	1 5a
		מלך	KING	573a	1
		נכו	NECO	647a	
		פרעה	PHARAOH	829a	
		פרת	EUPHRATES	832b	
		ראה	TO SEE	908c	
23	30	מגדו	MEGIDDO	152a	
		יהואחז	JEHOAHAZ	219d	1
		יהוחנן	JEHOHANAN	*220b	9
		הלך	WALK	*237a	3 a
		מלך	BE KING	574b	
		משח	ANOINT	603b	2
		צברה	GRAVE	869a	1
		רכב	RIDE	938d	1
23	31	יהואחז	JEHOAHAZ	219d	1
		חדש	NEW MOON	294c	2 a
		חמוטל	HAMUTAL	327d	
		לבנה	LIBNAH	526c	1
		פדיהו	PEDALAH	*804c	1
		ירמיה	JEREMIAH	941d	2
23	33	אסר	TIE	63d	3
		זהב	GOLD	*262d	5
		זהב	GOLD	263c	1
		חמת	HAMATH	333a	
		כסף	SILVER	494b	8 c
		מאה	HUNDRED	547d	1 a1
		נכו	NECO	647a	
		נתן	PUT	680c	2 b
		על	UPON	753b	2 1c
		ענש	FINE	*778d	
		ענש	INDEMNITY	778d	
		פרעה	PHARAOH	829a	
		רבלה	RIBLAH	916c	1
23	34	אליקים	ELIAKIM	45d	B
		יהואחז	JEHOAHAZ	219d	1
		יהויקים	JEHOIAKIM	220c	1
		יהויקים	JEHOIAKIM	220c	1
		לקח	TAKE	543d	9 b
		מלך	BE KING	574b	
		נכו	NECO	647a	
		סבב	TURN ABOUT	686c	1 c
		פרעה	PHARAOH	829a	
		שם	NAME	1028a	2 a
23	35	יהויקים	JEHOIAKIM	220c	1
		זהב	GOLD	262d	5
		זהב	GOLD	263c	1
		נגש	EXACT	620c	3
		נכו	NECO	647a	
		ערך	VALUE	790a	
		ערך	ORDER	790a	2
		פה	MOUTH	805d	6 d1 a
		פרעה	PHARAOH	829a	
23	36	ארומה	ARUMAH	72b	
		יהויקים	JEHOIAKIM	220c	1
		זבידה	ZEBIDAH	256b	
		עשר	TEN	797a	1 b
		פדיהו	PEDALAH	804c	1
		רומה	RUMAH	928a	
24	1	אליקים	ELIAKIM	45d	B
		בבל	BABEL	93c	
		יהויקים	JEHOIAKIM	220c	1
		מלך	KING	573a	1
		מרד	REBEL	597c	1
		נבוכדראצר	NEBUCHADNEZZAR	613b	
		עבד	SLAVE	714c	7
		שוב	TURN BACK	997c	5 e
24	2	אבד	DESTROY	2b	1
		גדוד	BAND	151b	1
		כשדים	CHALDEANS	505a	1 b
		נביא	PROPHET	611d	1
		עבד	SLAVE	714c	4
		עמון	AMMON	770a	
		שלח	SEND	1019a	2 d
24	3	חטאת	SIN	308d	1 b
		סור	TURN ASIDE	694b	1
		פנה	FACE	819b	2 8a
24	4	אבה	BE WILLING	2c	
		דם	BLOOD	196c	2 b
		דם	BLOOD	196d	2 d
		דם	BLOOD	196d	2 d
		נקי	CLEAN	667c	1
		נקי	CLEAN	667c	1
		סלח	FORGIVE	699b	
24	5	יהויקים	JEHOIAKIM	220c	1
		כשדים	CHALDEANS	*505a	1 b
24	6	יהויקים	JEHOIAKIM	220c	1
		יהויכין	JEHOIACHIN	220c	
24	7	בבל	BABEL	93c	
		יסף	DO AGAIN	415c	2 a
		נהר	STREAM	625d	1
		נחל	WADY	636c	2
		פרץ	BREAK THROUGH	829b	3
		פרת	EUPHRATES	832b	
24	8	אלנתן	ELNATHAN	46b	A
		יהויכין	JEHOIACHIN	220c	
		חדש	NEW MOON	294c	2 a
		נחשתא	NEHUSHTA	639a	
24	10	בוא	COME	98b	1 k
		כשדים	CHALDEANS	*505a	1 b
		נבוכדראצר	NEBUCHADNEZZAR	613b	
24	11	מצור	SIEGE	849a	1
		בבל	BABEL	93c	
		מלך	KING	573a	1
		נבוכדראצר	NEBUCHADNEZZAR	613b	
24	12	צור	CONFINE	848d	2
		בבל	BABEL	93c	
		יהויכין	JEHOIACHIN	220c	
		מלך	BE KING	574a	
		סרים	EUNUCH	710c	
		על	UPON	757b	2 7c aa
		שר	CHIEFTAIN	978b	2 a
		שמנה	EIGHT	1033a	1
24	13	אוצר	TREASURE	70a	1
		היכל	TEMPLE	228c	2 b
		זהב	GOLD	263c	6
		יצא	BRING OUT	425a	4 a
		קצץ	CUT OFF	893d	
24	14	גבור	STRONG	150b	2
		דלה	THE POOR	195d	
		זולה	EXCEPT	265d	1
		חיל	STRENGTH	298d	1 c
		חרש	GRAVER	360d	1 d
		מסגר	LOCKSMITH	689d	1
		עם	PEOPLE	766d	5 c
		עשר	TEN	796c	2 b
		שר	CHIEFTAIN	978b	2 a
		שאר	REMAIN	984a	1
24	15	אול	LEADING MAN	17c	
		אול	LEADER	18b	
		אל	GOD	42b	1
		יהויכין	JEHOIACHIN	220c	
		הלך	WALK	*236d	1 e
		הלך	WALK	236d	1 d
		סרים	EUNUCH	710c	
		גבור	STRONG	150b	2
24	16	חיל	STRENGTH	298d	1 c
		חרש	GRAVER	360d	1 d
		כל	ALL	482d	2 ba
24	17	דוד	UNCLE	187c	2
		מלך	BE KING	574b	
		מתניהו	MATTANIAH	682d	1
		סבב	TURN ABOUT	686c	1 c
		צדקיו	ZEDEKIAH	843b	1
		שם	NAME	1028a	2 a
24	18	חמוטל	HAMUTAL	327d	
		לבנה	LIBNAH	526c	1
		צדקיו	ZEDEKIAH	843b	1
		ירמיה	JEREMIAH	941d	2
24	19	יהויקים	JEHOIAKIM	220c	1
24	20	אף	NOSE	60b	3
		מרד	REBEL	597c	1
		עד	AS FAR AS	*724b	1 2a b
		פנה	FACE	819a	2 8a
		צדקיו	ZEDEKIAH	843b	1
		שלך	THROW	1021b	2 b
25	1	בנה	BUILD	124c	1 ah
		דיק	BULWARK	189b	
		חדש	NEW MOON	294d	2 b2
		חיל	STRENGTH	299a	4
		חנה	DECLINE	333c	2 c2
		יום	DAY	*398c	2 e
		ירושלים	JERUSALEM	437a	
		מלך	BE KING	574a	
		נבוכדראצר	NEBUCHADNEZZAR	613b	
		עשור	A TEN	797c	1 b
		שנה	YEAR	1040c	
		תשיעי	NINTH	1077d	
25	2	עשתי	ONE	799d	
		צדקיו	ZEDEKIAH	843b	1
		מצור	SIEGE	849a	1
25	3	חדש	NEW MOON	294d	2 b2
		חזק	BE FIRM	304c	1 4b
		יום	DAY	*398c	2 e
		רעב	FAMINE	944b	1
		תשע	NINE	1077c	1 b
25	4	בקע	BREAK OPEN OR THROUGH	132a	1
		גן	GARDEN	171a	
		דרך	WAY	202d	1
		דרך	WAY	202d	1
		חומה	WALL	327b	1
		כשדים	CHALDEANS	505a	1 b
		מלחמה	WAR	536b	
		לילה	NIGHT	539a	1
		על	UPON	756a	2 6a
		ערבה	DESERT-PLAIN	787c	1 b
		שער	GATE	1044d	1 b 6
25	5	חיל	STRENGTH	299a	4
		יריחו	JERICHO	437d	
		כשדים	CHALDEANS	505a	1 b
		נשג	OVERTAKE	673c	1 a
		על	UPON	759a	4 2c
		ערבה	DESERT-PLAIN	787c	3
		פוץ	BE DISPERSED	807a	1
		רדף	PURSUE	922c	1 a
25	6	דבר	SPEAK	*181b	3 d
		עלה	GO UP	749c	1
		רבלה	RIBLAH	916c	1
		משפט	JUDGMENT	1048c	1 c
25	7	אסר	TIE	63d	3
		נחשת	COPPER	639a	2
		עור	MAKE BLIND	734c	1
		צדקיו	ZEDEKIAH	843b	1
		שחט	SLAUGHTER	1006b	3
25	8	חדש	NEW MOON	294c	2 b2
		חמישי	FIFTH	332c	1
		טבח	COOK	371a	2
		נבוזראדן	NEBUZARADAN	613a	
		נבוכדראצר	NEBUCHADNEZZAR	613b	
		עבד	SLAVE	714a	2
		עשר	TEN	797b	9 b
		עשר	TEN	797c	
		עשור	A TEN	797d	1 b
		תשע	NINE	1077c	2
25	10	אשר	PARTICLE OF RELATION	83b	7 c
		חיל	STRENGTH	299a	4
		חומה	WALL	327c	1
		טבח	COOK	371a	2
		כשדים	CHALDEANS	505a	1 b
		נתץ	PULL DOWN	683b	1
25	11	המון	CROWD	242d	3 c
		טבח	COOK	371a	2
		יתר	REMAINDER	451d	1 a
		יתר	REMAINDER	451d	1 a
		נבוזראדן	NEBUZARADAN	613a	
		נפל	FALL	657c	4 b
25	12	גוב	DIG	155c	
		גב	PIT	*155d	
		גב	PIT	155d	
		דלה	THE POOR	195d	
		טבח	COOK	371a	2
		יגב	FIELD	387a	
		יגב	TILL	387a	
		כרם	DRESS VINES	501d	
		ל	TO	512c	4 a
		שאר	REMAIN	984b	1
25	13	ים	SEA	411a	7
		מכונה	BASE	467d	
		כשדים	CHALDEANS	505a	1 b
		נחשת	COPPER	639a	2
		עמוד	PILLAR	765b	2
		שבר	BREAK	991a	
25	14	מזמרות	SNUFFERS	275a	
		יע	SHOVEL	418b	
		כף	PAN	497a	4 b
		מנורה	LAMPSTAND	633a	2
		נחשת	COPPER	638d	1
		סיר	POT	696c	2
		שרת	SERVE	1057b	2 b
25	15	זהב	GOLD	263a	6
		זהב	GOLD	263c	1
		מזרק	BOWL	284d	2 c
		מחתה	FIRE-HOLDER	367b	2

Ch	v.	Heb	Eng	Page	Sec
		מבח	COOK	371a	2
		מנורה	LAMPSTAND	633a	2
25	16	מכונה	BASE	467d	
		עמוד	PILLAR	765b	2
		משקל	WEIGHT	1054a	
25	17	אלה	THESE	41d	D
		כל	ALL	*482d	2 ba
		כתרת	CAPITAL	509d	
		עמוד	PILLAR	765b	2
		קומה	HEIGHT	879b	3
		רמון	POMEGRANATE	942a	3
		סבכה	LATTICE-WORK	959a	2
25	18	מבח	COOK	371a	2
		כהן	PRIEST	464b	8
		כהן	PRIEST	464c	8
		סף	THRESHOLD	706c	
		צפניה	ZEPHANIAH	861b	1
		ראש	HEAD	911a	3 e
		ישראלי	ISARELITE	976a	2
		משנה	SECOND	1041c	3 a
25	19	אשר	PARTICLE OF RELATION	82b	2 a
		מצא	FIND	593d	1 c
		ספר	ENUMERATOR	708c	1 b
		סריס	EUNUCH	710c	
		פנה	FACE	816a	1 2b
		פקיד	COMMISSIONER	824b	
		צבא	SERVE	838d	
		ששים	SIXTY	995d	
25	20	הלך	WALK	236d	1 d
		מבח	COOK	371a	2
		נבוזראדן	NEBUZARADAN	613a	
		על	UPON	757b	2 7c aa
		רבלה	RIBLAH	916c	1
25	21	חמת	HAMATH	333a	
		נכה	SMITE	645d	2 a
		רבלה	RIBLAH	916c	1
25	22	אחיקם	AHIKAM	27b	
		גדליהו	GEDALIAH	153d	1
		נבוכדראצר	NEBUCHADNEZZAR	613b	
		שאר	REMAIN	984b	1
		שפן	SHAPHAN	1051a	2
25	23	יאזניהו	JAAZANIAH	24d	1
		גדליהו	GEDALIAH	153d	1
		יהוחנן	JEHOHANAN	220b	8
		חיל	STRENGTH	299a	4
		מעכתי	MAACATHITE	591a	
		תנחמת	TANHUMETH	637c	
		נטפתי	NETOPHATHITE	643b	
		נתניהו	NETHANIAH	682b	2
		פקד	ATTEND TO	823d	1
		מצפה	MIZPAH	860a	5
		קרח	KAREAH	901b	
		שריה	SERAIAH	976a	3
		שר	CHIEFTAIN	978c	3 a
		ישמעאל	ISHMAEL	1035d	2
25	24	גדליהו	GEDALIAH	153d	1
		יטב	BE WELL	405c	3
		ירא	FEAR	431b	1 c
		כשדים	CHALDEANS	505a	1 b
		עבד	WORK	713a	3
		שבע	SWEAR	989b	1 a
25	25	גדליהו	GEDALIAH	153d	1
		זרע	SOWING	282d	4 e
		חדש	NEW MOON	294d	2 b2
		יהודי	JEW	397c	
		כשדים	CHALDEANS	505a	1 b
		מלוכה	KINGSHIP	574d	
		נכה	SMITE	645d	2 a
		נתניהו	NETHANIAH	682b	2
		מצפה	MIZPAH	860a	4
		רב	CHIEF	*913c	
		ישמעאל	ISHMAEL	1035d	2
25	26	גדול	GREAT	153b	7
		ירא	FEAR	431b	1 c
		כשדים	CHALDEANS	505a	1 b
		שר	CHIEFTAIN	978c	3 a
25	27	אוילמרדך	EVIL-MERODACH	17b	
		בבל	BABEL	93c	
		בית	HOUSE	109a	1 ae 2
		יהויכין	JEHOIACHIN	220c	
		חדש	NEW MOON	294d	2 b2
		יצא	CAUSE TO GO	*424b	1 a
		מלך	BE KING	574a	
		מלכות	REIGN	575a	1 b
		נשא	LIFT	670b	1 b 2
		שלשים	THIRTY	1026c	2
25	28	דבר	SPEAK	181b	3 d
		מובה	WELFARE	375d	2 a
		כסא	SEAT OF HONOR	490d	2
		מעל	ABOVE	*751d	1 b
		על	UPON	759b	4 2d
25	29	חיים	LIFE	313b	1
		כלא	CONFINEMENT	476c	
		תמיד	CONTINUITY	556c	1 b
		שנה	CHANGE	1040a	
25	30	ארחה	MEAL	73c	
		דבר	WORD	183b	4 1
		חיים	LIFE	313b	1
		יום	DAY	400c	7 e3
		תמיד	CONTINUITY	556c	2 b
		נתן	GIVE	681c	1 c

1 CHRONICLES

Ch	v.	Heb	Eng	Page	Sec
1	1	אדם	ADAM	9c	3
		אנוש	ENOSH	60d	
		שת	SETH	1011d	
1	2	מהללאל	MAHALALEL	239d	1
		ירד	JARED	434b	1
		קנן	KENAN	884b	
1	3	חנוך	ENOCH	335c	3
		למך	LAMECH	541a	2
		מתושלח	METHUSELAH	607b	
1	4	חם	HAM	325d	1
		נח	NOAH	629b	
		יפת	JAPHETH	834d	
		שם	SHEM	1028d	
1	5	מגוג	MAGOG	156a	
		גמר	GOMER	170a	1
		יון	JAVAN	402a	
		יפת	JAPHETH	834d	
		תובל	TUBAL	1063a	
		תירס	TIRAS	1066d	
1	6	אשכנז	ASHKENAZ	79b	1
		גמר	GOMER	170a	1
		דיפת	DIPHATH	193d	
		ריפת	RIPHATH	937d	
1	7	אלישה	ELISHAH	47a	
		דדנים	DODANIM	187a	
		יון	JAVAN	402a	
		כתי	KITTIM	508c	
		רודנים	RHODIANS	922c	
		תרשיש	TARSHISH	1077a	1
1	8	חם	HAM	326a	1
		כוש	CUSH	469a	1
		כנען	CANAAN	488d	1
		מצרים	EGYPT	595d	2 a
1	9	דדן	DEDAN	187a	1
		חוילה	HAVILAH	296c	1
		כוש	CUSH	469a	1
		סבא	SEBA	685b	
		סבתה	SABTAH	688b	
		סבתכא	SABTECA	688b	
		רעמה	RAAMAH	947c	
		שבא	SHEBA	985b	
1	10	גבור	STRONG	150b	2
		חלל	POLLUTE	320d	2
		ילד	BEGET	408c	2 a
		כוש	CUSH	469a	3
		נמרד	NIMROD	650a	2
1	11	ילד	BEGET	408c	2 a
		להבים	LEHABIM	529c	
		לובים	LUBIM	530c	
		לוד	LUD	530d	2
		מצרים	EGYPT	595d	2 a
		נפתחים	NAPHTUHIM	661d	
		ענמים	ANAMIM	777d	
1	12	יצא	GO OUT	423c	1 h
		כסלחים	CASLUHIM	493b	
		כפתרי	CAPHTORIM	499c	
		פלשתי	PHILISTINE	814c	
		פתרסים	PATHRUSIM	837d	
1	13	חת	HETH	366c	
		ילד	BEGET	408c	2 a
		כנען	CANAAN	488d	1
		צידון	SIDON	851a	
1	14	אמרי	AMORITES	57c	1
		יבוסי	JEBUSITE	101a	1
		גרגשי	GIRGASHITE	173a	
		גרגשי	GIRGASHITE	173b	
1	15	חוי	HIVITE	295d	2
		סיני	SINITE	696b	
		ערקי	AKRITE	792b	
1	16	ארודי	ARVADITE	71c	
		חמתי	HAMATHITE	333b	
		צמרי	ZAMARITE	856b	
1	17	ארם	ARAM	74b	1
		ארפכשד	ARPACHSHAD	75d	
		אשור	ASSHUR	78d	1
		גתר	GETHER	178c	
		חול	HUL	299a	
		לוד	LUD	530d	2
		מש	MASH	602a	
		עוץ	UZ	734b	1 a
		עילם	ELAM	743d	
		שם	SHEM	1028d	
1	18	ילד	BEGET	408c	2 a
		עבר	EBER	720a	1
		שלח	SHELAH	1019d	
		שלח	SHELAH	1019d	
1	19	ילד	BE BORN	409a	
		יקטן	JOKTAN	429b	
		עבר	EBER	720a	1
		פלג	SPLIT	811a	
		פלג	PELEG	811b	
1	20	אלמודד	ALMODAD	38d	
		חצרמות	HAZARMAVETH	348a	
		ילד	BEGET	408c	2 a
		יקטן	JOKTAN	429b	
		ירח	JERAH	437b	
		שלף	SHELEPH	1025c	
1	21	אוזל	UZAL	23d	
		דקלה	DIKLAH	200d	
		הדורם	HADORAM	*213b	1
		הדורם	HADORAM	213b	1
1	22	אבימאל	ABIMAEL	4b	
		עיבל	EBAL	716c	

Ch	v.	Heb	Eng	Page	Sec
1	23	שבא	SHEBA	985b	
		אופיר	OPHIR	20c	1
		חוילה	HAVILAH	296d	
		יובב	JOBAB	384d	1
		יקטן	JOKTAN	429b	
1	24	שלח	SHELAH	1019d	
		שם	SHEM	1028d	
1	25	עבר	EBER	720a	1
		פלג	PELEG	811b	
		רעו	REU	946c	
1	26	נחור	NAHOR	637d	1
		תרח	TERAH	1076b	1
1	27	אברם	ABRAM	4d	
1	28	עוק	NECK	778c	
		יצחק	ISAAC	850c	
		ישמעאל	ISHMAEL	1035d	1
1	29	אדבאל	ADBEEL	9a	
		מבשם	MIBSAM	142a	1
		תולדות	GENERATIONS	410a	A
		נביות	NEBAIOTH	614a	
		קדר	KEDAR	871b	2
		ישמעאל	ISHMAEL	1035d	1
1	30	דומה	DUMAH	189a	1
		חדד	HADAD	292c	
		משא	BABYLON	601c	1
		משמע	MISHMA	1036a	1
		תימא	TEMA	1066d	
1	31	יטור	JETUR	377b	
		נודב	NODAB	*622a	
		נפיש	NAPHISH	661c	
		קדמה	KEDEMAH	870b	
		ישמעאל	ISHMAEL	1035d	1
1	32	דדן	DEDAN	187a	2
		מדן	MEDAN	193c	
		מדין	MIDIAN	193c	1
		זמרן	ZIMRAN	275b	
		יקשן	JOKSHAN	430d	
		פלגש	CONCUBINE	811c	1
		קטורה	KETURAH	882c	
		שבא	SHEBA	985b	
		ישבק	ISHBAK	990b	
		שוח	SHUAH	1001d	
1	33	אבידע	ABIDA	4a	
		אלדעה	ELDAAH	44d	
		מדין	MIDIAN	193c	1
		חנוך	ENOCH	335c	3
		עיפה	EPHAH	734a	1
		עפר	EPHER	780b	1
		קטורה	KETURAH	882c	
1	34	עשו	ESAU	796c	
		יצחק	ISAAC	850c	
		ישראל	ISRAEL	975c	1
1	35	אליפז	ELIPHAZ	45c	A
		יעוש	JEUSH	736c	1
		יעלם	JALAM	761c	
		עשו	ESAU	796c	
		קרח	KORAH	901b	1 a
		אליפז	ELIPHAZ	45c	A
1	36	אומר	OMAR	57b	
		געתם	GATTAM	172b	
		תמנע	TIMNA	286b	1 b
		תמן	TEMAN	412d	
		עמלק	AMALEK	766a	
		צפו	ZEPHO	859d	
		קנז	KENAZ	889d	
1	37	זרח	ZERAH	280c	2 a
		מזה	MIZZAH	561a	
		נחת	NAHATH	639c	1
		שמה	SHAMMAH	1031c	1
1	38	אצר	EZER	69d	
		דישן	DISHON	190d	1
		דישן	DISHAN	190d	
		לוטן	LOTAN	532b	
		ענה	ANAH	777b	1
		שעיר	SEIR	973a	1 d
		שובל	SHOBAL	987c	1
1	39	הומם	HOMAM	243a	
		תמנע	TIMNA	286b	2
		חרי	HORITE	360a	3 a
		לוטן	LOTAN	532b	
1	40	איה	AIAH	17b	1
		אונם	ONAM	20c	1
		מנחת	MANAHATH	630a	
		עיבל	EBAL	716c	
		עלון	ALVAN	759b	
		ענה	ANAH	777b	2
		שובל	SHOBAL	987c	1
		שפו	SHEPHO	1046a	
1	41	אשבן	ESHBAN	78b	
		דישן	DISHON	190d	2
		חמדן	HEMDAN	326d	
		חמרן	HAMRAN	331c	
		יתרן	ITHRAN	452d	1
		כרן	CHERAN	502b	
		ענה	ANAH	777b	1
1	42	אצר	EZER	69d	
		ארן	ARAN	75a	
		בלהן	BILHAN	117b	1
		בניעקן	BENE-JAAKAN	122c	
		דישן	DISHON	190d	2
		דישן	DISHAN	*190d	
		זעון	AZZVAN	266b	
		יען	ZAAVAN	276c	
		תמן	TEMAN	412d	
		עוץ	UZ	734b	1 c
		עקן	AKAN	785c	

1 CHRONICLES

Ch	v.	Heb	Eng	Page	Sec
1	43	ארץ	EARTH	76a	2 a
		בלע	BELA	118c	1
		בעור	BEOR	129d	2
		דנהבה	DINHABAH	200b	
		מלך	BE KING	574a	
1	44	בלע	BELA	118c	1
		בצרה	BOZRAH	131b	1
		זרח	ZERAH	280c	2 b
		יובב	JOBAB	384d	2
		מות	DIE	559c	1 a1
		מלך	BE KING	574a	
1	45	חשם	HUSHAM	302a	1
		יובב	JOBAB	384d	2
		תימני	TEMANITE	412d	1 a1
		מות	DIE	559c	1 a1
1	46	בדד	BEDAD	95a	
		מדין	MIDIAN	*193c	2
		הדד	HADAD	212d	1 a
		חשם	HUSHAM	302a	1
		מואב	MOAB	555d	2 b
		מות	DIE	559c	1 a1
		עוית	AVITH	732b	
1	47	הדד	HADAD	212d	1 a
		מות	DIE	559c	1 a1
		שמלה	SAMLAH	971a	
		משרקה	MASREKAH	977d	
1	48	מות	DIE	559c	1 a1
		נהר	STREAM	625d	1
		רחבות	REHOBOTH	932c	3
		שמלה	SAMLAH	971a	
		שאול	SAUL	982c	2
1	49	בעלחנן	BAAL-HANAN	128a	1
		מות	DIE	559c	1 a1
		עכבור	ACHBOR	747b	1
		שאול	SAUL	982c	2
1	50	בעלחנן	BAAL-HANAN	128a	1
		הדד	HADAD	212d	1 b
		הדר	HADAR	214c	
		מטרד	MATRED	382d	
		מהיטבאל	MEHETABEL	406b	1
		מות	DIE	559c	1 a1
		מיהזהב	ME-JARKON	566a	
		פעו	PAU	821b	
1	51	אלוף	CHIEF	49b	
		הדד	HADAD	212d	1 b
		תמנע	TIMNA	286b	1 a
		יתת	JETHETH	453c	
		עלוה	ALVAH	759b	
1	52	אהליבמה	OHOLIBAMA	14c	2
		אלה	ELAH	18d	1
		פינן	PINON	810a	
1	53	תמן	TEMAN	412d	1
		מבצר	MIBZAR	550b	
		קנז	KENAZ	889d	1
1	54	מגדיאל	MAGDIEL	550c	
		עירם	IRAM	747a	
2	1	זבולן	ZEBULUN	259d	1
		לוי	LEVI	532c	1 a
		ראובן	REUBEN	910a	1
		ישראל	ISRAEL	975c	1
2	2	אשר	ASHER	81b	1
		גד	GAD	151c	1 a
		דן	DAN	192d	1
		יוסף	JOSEPH	415d	1 a
		נפתלי	NAPHTALI	836a	1
2	3	בן	SON	*121a	1 jd
		בת	DAUGHTER	*123b	1 h
		בתשוע	BATH-SHUA	124a	2
		יהודה	JUDAH	397b	1 1
		ילד	BE BORN	408d	
		שוע	SHUA	447d	
		כנעני	CANAANITE	489a	2 a
		מות	DIE	560b	2
		ער	ER	735c	1
		רע	EVIL	948c	0 b
		שלה	SHELAH	1017c	
2	4	זרח	ZERAH	280b	1
		יהודה	JUDAH	397b	1 1
		כלה	DAUGHTER-IN-LAW	483c	1
		פרץ	PEREZ	829d	1
		תמר	TAMAR	1071c	1 a
2	5	חמול	HAMUL	328d	1
		חצרון	HEZRON	348a	2 b
		פרץ	PEREZ	829d	1
2	6	הימן	HEMAN	54d	1
		דרדע	DARDA	201d	
		זבדי	ZABDI	256c	1
		זרח	ZERAH	280b	1
		אזרחי	EZRAHITE	*280d	
		איתן	ETHAN	451a	
		כלכל	CALCOL	465b	
2	7	חרם	DEVOTED THING	356b	1 a
		כרמי	CARMI	501d	2
		מעל	ACT TREACHEROUSLY	591b	2 b
		עכן	ACHAN	747c	
		עכר	STIR UP	747d	
		ישראל	ISRAEL	975d	2 a4
2	8	איתן	ETHAN	451a	
		עזריהו	AZARIAH	741b	1 2a
2	9	את	MARK OF THE AC-CUSATIVE	85c	3 a
		חצרון	HEZRON	348a	2 b
		ילד	BE BORN	408d	
		כלב	CALEB	477a	
		כלובי	CHELUBAI	477b	
		כרמי	CARMI	*501d	2
		רם	RAM	928a	1 a
		ירחמאל	JERAHMEEL	934a	1
2	10	בן	SON	*121a	1 jd
		ילד	BEGET	409a	1
		נחשון	NAHSHON	638c	
		נשיא	PRINCE	672b	5
		עמינדב	AMMINADAB	770b	1
		רם	RAM	928a	1 a
2	11	בעז	BOAZ	127a	1
		ילד	BEGET	409a	1
		נחשון	NAHSHON	638c	
		שלמון	SALMON	969c	
2	12	בעז	BOAZ	127a	1
		ישי	JESSE	445a	
		עובד	OBED	714d	1
2	13	אליאב	ELIAB	45a	C
		שמעא	SHIMEA	1035a	1
2	14	חמישי	FIFTH	332c	1
		נתנאל	NETHANEL	682a	2
		רביעי	FOURTH	918a	1
2	15	רדי	RADDAI	921d	1
		אצם	OZEM	69d	1
2	16	שביעי	SEVENTH	988d	1
		אביגיל	ABIGAIL	4a	2
		יואב	JOAB	222a	1
		נחש	NAHASH	*638b	2
		עשהאל	ASAHEL	795c	1
		צרויה	ZERUIAH	863b	
		צרויה	ZERUIAH	863b	
2	17	אביגיל	ABIGAIL	4a	2
		יתר	JETHER	452b	3
		עמשא	AMASA	772a	1
		ישמעאלי	ISHMAELITE	1035d	
2	18	ארדון	ARDON	71b	
		חצרון	HEZRON	348a	2 b
		יריעות	JERIOTH	438c	
		ישר	JESHER	449c	
		כלב	CALEB	477a	
		כלובי	CHELUBAI	477b	
		עזובה	AZUBAH	738a	2
		שובב	SHOBAB	1000a	2
2	19	אפרתה	EPHRATH	68d	4
		חור	HUR	301b	2
		כלב	CALEB	477a	
		עזובה	AZUBAH	738a	2
		ישראלי	ISARELITE	976a	1
2	20	בצלאל	BEZALEL	130b	1
		חור	HUR	301b	2
2	21	בן	SON	121d	9 a
		חצרון	HEZRON	348a	2 b
		שגוב	SEGUB	960d	1
2	22	יאיר	JAIR	22c	1
		עשרים	TWENTY	797d	1 2b
		שגוב	SEGUB	960d	2
2	23	יאיר	JAIR	22c	1
		ארם	ARAM	74b	3
		גשור	GESHUR	178a	1
		חוה	TENT-VILLAGE	295d	
		קנת	KENATH	890b	
2	24	אב	FATHER	3d	9
		אביה	ABIJAM	4a	7
		אחר	AFTER	29d	1
		אפרתה	EPHRATH	68d	2
		חצרון	HEZRON	348a	2 b
		כלב	CALEB	477a	
		אשחור	ASHHUR	1007b	
		תקוע	TEKOA	1075d	
2	25	אחיה	AHIJAH	26d	5
		אצם	OZEM	69d	2
		ארן	OREN	75a	
		בונה	BUNAH	107b	
		חצרון	HEZRON	348a	2 b
		רם	RAM	928a	1 b
		ירחמאל	JERAHMEEL	934a	1
2	26	אונם	ONAM	20c	2
		עטרה	ATARAH	742d	1
		ירחמאל	JERAHMEEL	934a	1
2	27	ימין	JAMIN	412c	2
		מעץ	MAAZ	591d	1
		עקר	EKER	785d	
		רם	RAM	928a	1 b
		ירחמאל	JERAHMEEL	934a	1
2	28	אבישור	ABISHUR	4d	
		אונם	ONAM	20c	2
		ידע	JADA	395b	
		נדב	NADAB	621d	3
		שמי	SHAMMAI	1031d	1
2	29	אביחיל	ABIHAIL	4b	4
		אבישור	ABISHUR	4d	
		אחבן	AHBAN	26c	
		מוליד	MOLID	410a	
2	30	אפים	APPAIM	60b	
		לא	NOT	519d	2 e
		נדב	NADAB	621d	3
		סלד	SELED	699a	
2	31	אחלי	AHLAI	29a	1
		אפים	APPAIM	60b	
		ישי	ISHI	447d	1
		ששן	SHESHAN	1058a	
2	32	יהונתן	JOHATHAN	221a	2
		ידע	JADA	395b	
		יתר	JETHER	452b	4 a
		לא	NOT	519d	2 e
		שמי	SHAMMAI	1031d	1
2	33	יהונתן	JOHATHAN	221a	2
		זזא	ZAZA	265b	
		פלת	PELETH	814c	2
		ירחמאל	JERAHMEEL	934a	1
2	34	אחלי	AHLAI	29a	1
		מצרי	EGYPTIAN	596a	1
		ששן	SHESHAN	1058d	
2	35	ירחע	JARHA	437c	
		עתי	ATTAI	774c	1
		ששן	SHESHAN	1058b	
2	36	זבד	ZABAD	256b	1
		נתן	NATHAN	681d	5 a
		עתי	ATTAI	774c	1
2	37	זבד	ZABAD	256b	1
		עובד	OBED	714d	2 a
		אפלל	EPHLAL	813d	
2	38	יהוא	JEHU	219d	4
		עובד	OBED	714d	2 a
		עזריהו	AZARIAH	741b	1 2b
2	39	אלעשה	ELEASAH	46c	A
		חלץ	HELEZ	323b	2
2	40	עזריהו	AZARIAH	741b	1 2b
		אלעשה	ELEASAH	46c	A
		ססמי	SISMAI	703b	
2	41	שלום	SHALLUM	1024b	6
		יקמיה	JEKAMIAH	880c	1
		שלום	SHALLUM	1024b	6
2	42	אב	FATHER	3d	9
		זיף	ZIPH	268b	1 a
		זיף	ZIPH	*268b	2
		חברון	HEBRON	289c	2
		מישע	MESHA	448a	
		כלב	CALEB	477a	
		מרשה	MARESHAH	601c	
		ירחמאל	JERAHMEEL	934a	1
2	43	חברון	HEBRON	289c	2
		יקרעם	JORKEAM	*439a	
		תפח	TAPPUAH	656b	
		קרח	KORAH	901b	3
		רקם	REKEM	955d	1 b
		שמע	SHEMA	1034d	1
2	44	יקרעם	JORKEAM	439a	
		רחם	RAHAM	933d	
		רקם	REKEM	955d	1 b
		שמי	SHAMMAI	1031d	1
		שמע	SHEMA	1034d	1
2	45	ביתצור	BETH-ZUR	112d	1
		מעון	MAON	733a	2
		שמי	SHAMMAI	1031d	1
2	46	גזז	GAZEZ	159d	
		חרן	HARAN	357b	1
		מוצא	MOZA	426a	1
		כלב	CALEB	477a	
		עיפה	EPHAH	734a	3
		יהדי	JAHDAI	213a	1
2	47	יותם	JOTHAM	222d	3
		עיפה	EPHAH	734a	2
		פלט	PELET	812b	1
		רגם	RAGEM	920d	
		שעף	SHAAPH	1044c	2
2	48	כלב	CALEB	477a	
		מעכה	MAACAH	590d	2 d
		תרחנה	TIRHANAH	934b	
		שבר	SHEBER	991b	
2	49	גבעא	GIBEA	148d	1
		מדמנה	MADMANNAH	199c	2
		מכבנה	MACHBENA	460a	1
		כלב	CALEB	477a	
		עכסה	ACHSAH	747c	
		שוא	SHEVA	996a	1
		שעף	SHAAPH	1044c	1
2	50	אפרתה	EPHRATH	68d	4
		חור	HUR	301b	2
		כלב	CALEB	477a	
		קריתיערים	KIRIATH-JEARIM	900c	
		שובל	SHOBAL	987c	2 a
2	51	ביתגדר	BETH-GADER	111b	1
		ביתלחם	BETHLEHEM	111d	1
		גדר	GEDER	155a	
		חרף	HAREPH	358b	1
		שלמון	SALMON	969c	
2	52	חצי	HALF	345c	1
		חציהמנחות	HALF OF THE MANAHATHITES	345d	
		קריתיערים	KIRIATH-JEARIM	900c	
		ראה	HAROAH	909b	1
		ראיה	REAIAH	909d	1
		שובל	SHOBAL	987c	2 a
2	53	אשתאלי	ESHTAOLITE	84b	1
		יצא	GO OUT	423a	1 h
		יתרי	ITHRITE	452b	
		משרעי	MISHRAITES	606d	1
		פותי	PUTHITES	807d	
		צרעתי	ZORATHITES	864a	1
		קריתיערים	KIRIATH-JEARIM	900c	
		שמתי	SHUMATHITES	1029c	
2	54	ביתלחם	BETHLEHEM	111d	1
		חצי	HALF	345c	1
		חציהמנחות	HALF OF THE MANAHATHITES	345d	
		מנחתי	MANAHATHITES	630a	
		נטפתי	NETOPHATHITE	643b	
		יעבץ	JABEZ	716d	2
		עטרות	ATAROTH	743a	2 c
		צרעתי	ZORATHITES	864a	

Ch	v.	Heb	Eng	Page	Sec
2	55	שלמון	SALMON	969c	
		חמת	HAMMATH	329b	
		ספר	ENUMERATOR	708c	1 d
		יעבץ	JABEZ	716d	2
		קיני	KENITE	884b	
		רכב	RECHAB	939c	1 a
		שובתים	SHIMEATHITES	962c	
		שמעתים	SHIMEATHITES	1035b	
		תרעתים	TIRATHITES	1076c	
3	1	אביגיל	ABIGAIL	4a	1
		אחינעם	AHINOAM	27b	2
		אמנון	AMNON	54c	1
		בן	SON	*120d	1 ja
		דנאל	DANIEL	193b	1
		יזרעאלי	JEZREELITE	283c	2
		יזרעאלי	JEZREELITE	283c	2
		חברון	HEBRON	289b	
		ילד	BE BORN	408d	
		כלאב	CHILEAB	476d	
		כרמלי	CARMELITE	502b	
3	2	אבשלום	ABSALOM	5a	2
		אדניהו	ADONIJAH	11d	1
		חגית	HAGGITH	291b	
		ל	TO	514d	5 fe
		מעכה	MAACAH	590d	2 a
		רביעי	FOURTH	918a	1
		תלמי	TALMAI	1068d	1
3	3	אביטל	ABITAL	4b	
		חמשי	FIFTH	332c	1
		יתרעם	ITHREAM	453c	
		עגלה	EGLAH	722c	
		שפטיה	SHEPHATIAH	1049b	1 a
3	4	חברון	HEBRON	289b	
		חדש	NEW MOON	294c	2 a
		ילד	BE BORN	408d	
3	5	אליעם	ELIAM	45c	A
		בתשוע	BATH-SHUA	124a	1
		ילד	BE BORN	408d	
		עמיאל	AMMIEL	770a	3
		שובב	SHOBAB	1000a	1
		שלמה	SOLOMON	1024d	
		שמעא	SHIMEA	1035a	2
3	6	אליפלט	ELIPHELET	45d	A
		יבחר	IBHAR	104d	
3	7	יפיע	JAPHIA	422b	1 b
		נגה	NOGAH	618b	
		נפג	NEPHEG	655d	2
3	8	אלידע	ELIADA	45a	A
		אליפלט	ELIPHELET	45d	A
		תשע	NINE	1077c	1
3	9	בד	SEPARATION	94d	1 e
		בן	SON	*120d	1 ja
		כל	ALL	*482d	2 a
3	10	ביחו	ABIJAM	4a	1
		אסא	ASA	61d	
		יהושפט	JEHOSHAPHAT	221d	1
		רחבעם	REHOBOAM	932c	
3	11	אחזי	AHAZIAH	28d	1
		יהואש	JEHOASH	220a	1
		יהורם	JEHORAM	221b	1
3	12	אמציהו	AMAZIAH	55c	1
		יותם	JOTHAM	222d	1
		עזריהו	AZARIAH	741b	1
3	13	אחז	AHAZ	28c	1
		חזקיהו	HEZEKIAH	306a	1
3	14	אמון	AMON	54c	1
3	15	אליקים	ELIAKIM	45d	B
		יהואחז	JEHOAHAZ	*219d	1
		יהוחנן	JEHOHANAN	220b	9
		יהויקים	JEHOIAKIM	220c	1
		נתן	NATHAN	681d	1
		צדקיו	ZEDEKIAH	843b	1
		רביעי	FOURTH	918a	1
		שלום	SHALLUM	1024b	2
3	16	יהויקים	JEHOIAKIM	220c	1
		יהויכין	JEHOIACHIN	220c	
		צדקיהו	ZEDEKIAH	843c	5
3	17	אסר	PRISONERS	64b	
		יהויכין	JEHOIACHIN	220c	
		זרבבל	ZERUBBABEL	*279c	
		שמאלי	LEFT	970a	
		שאלתיאל	SHEALTIEL	982d	
3	18	יהושמע	HOSHAMA	221d	
		מלכירום	MALCHIRAM	575d	
		נדביה	NEDABIAH	622b	
		פדיהו	PEDALAH	804c	2
		יקמיה	JEKAMIAH	880c	2
		שנאצר	SHENAZZAR	1039c	
		ששבצר	SHESHBAZZAR	1058d	
3	19	זרבבל	ZERUBBABEL	279c	
		חנניהו	HANANIAH	337b	7
		פדיהו	PEDALAH	804c	2
		משלם	MESHULLAM	1024c	2
		שלמית	SHELOMITH	1025a	2
		שמעי	SHIMEI	1035c	4
3	20	אהל	OHEL	14b	
		יברכיהו	JEBERECHIAH	140a	1
		חמש	FIVE	331d	1 a
		חסדיה	HASADIAH	339d	
		חשבה	HASHUBAH	363d	
		יושב חסד	JUSHAB-HESED	1000a	
3	21	ארנן	ARNAN	75a	
		חנניהו	HANANIAH	337b	7
		ישעיה	JESHAIAH	447d	1
		עביהו	OBADIAH	715d	2 2
		פלטיהו	PELATIAH	812d	2
		רפיה	REPHAIAH	951b	1
		שכניה	SHECANIAH	1016a	1
3	22	בריח	BARIAH	138a	
		יגאל	IGAL	145d	3
		חטוש	HATTUSH	310d	1
		נעריה	NEARIAH	655d	1
		שכניה	SHECANIAH	1016a	1
		שמעיה	SHEMAIAH	1035d	4
		שפט	SHAPHAT	1048b	3
3	23	אליועיני	ELIOENAI	41b	1
		חזקיהו	HEZEKIAH	306b	1
		נעריה	NEARIAH	655d	1
		עזריקם	AZRIKAM	741b	1
3	24	אליועיני	ELIOENAI	41b	1
		אלישיב	ELIASHIB	46a	A
		דליהו	DELAIAH	195b	2 b
		יהוחנן	JEHOHANAN	220b	0
		ענני	ANANI	778b	
		עקוב	AKKUB	784d	1
		פלה	PELAIAH	811a	
4	1	בן	SON	*121a	1 jd
		חור	HUR	301b	2
		חצרון	HEZRON	348a	2 b
		יהודה	JUDAH	397b	1 1
		כלוב	CHELUB	*477b	1
		כרמי	CARMI	501d	2
		פרץ	PEREZ	829d	1
		שובל	SHOBAL	987c	2 b
4	2	אחומי	AHUMAI	26c	
		יחת	JAHATH	367a	1
		להד	LAHAD	529c	
		צרעתי	ZORATHITES	864a	
		ראיה	REAIAH	909d	1
		שובל	SHOBAL	987c	2 b
4	3	ידבש	IDBASH	185c	
		יזרעאל	JEZREEL	283c	1 a
		יזרעאל	JEZREEL	283c	1 a
		ישמא	ISHMA	445c	
		הצללפוני	HAZZELELPONI	853c	3
4	4	אפרתה	EPHRATH	68d	4
		בית לחם	BETHLEHEM	111d	1
		גדור	GEDOR	155b	1
		חור	HUR	301b	2
		חושה	HUSHAH	302a	1
		עזר	EZER	740d	2
		פנואל	PENVEL	819c	2
4	5	חלאה	HELAH	316a	
		נערה	NAARAH	655c	
		אשחור	ASHHUR	1007b	1
		תקוע	TEKOA	1075d	
4	6	אחזם	AHUZZAM	28d	
		האחשתרי	HAAHASHTARI	31c	
		חפר	HEPHER	343d	2
		תימני	TEMENI	412b	
		נערה	NAARAH	655c	
4	7	אתנן	ETHNAN	87d	
		חלאה	HELAH	316a	
		צחר	ZOHAR	850c	3
		צרת	ZERETH	866c	
4	8	אחרחל	AHARHEL	31c	
		חרם	HARUM	248b	
		ענוב	ANUB	772b	
		צבבה	ZOBEBAH	839d	
		קוץ	KOZ	881a	1
4	9	אם	MOTHER	51c	1
		כבד	BE HONORED	457c	1 b
		יעבץ	JABEZ	716d	1
		עצב	PAIN	780d	1
4	10	אם	IF	50b	1 b3
		בוא	COME	99c	2 b
		ברך	BLESS	139a	2 a
		גבול	BOUNDARY	148a	1 c
		יד	HAND	389d	1 e1
		יעבץ	JABEZ	716d	1
		עם	WITH	767c	1 a
		עצב	HURT	780c	
		קרא	CALL	895b	2 a
		רבה	BECOME MANY	916a	2
4	11	אשתון	ESHTON	84c	
		כלוב	CHELUB	477b	1
		מחיר	MEHIR	564b	
		שוחה	SHUHAH	1001d	2
4	12	אשתון	ESHTON	84c	
		בית רפא	BETH-RAPHA	112d	
		תחנה	TENINNAH	377c	
		נחש	NAHASH	638b	3
		פסח	PASEAH	820c	1
		רכה	RECAH	939d	
4	13	חתת	HATHATH	369d	
		עתניאל	OTHNIEL	801a	
		קנז	KENAZ	889d	
		שריה	SERAIAH	976a	4 a
4	14	גיא	VALLEY	161b	D
		יואב	JOAB	222a	1
		חרש	GRAVER	360d	1 d
		חרש	GRAVER	360d	1 d
		מעונתי	MEONOTHAI	733b	
		עפרה	OPHRAH	780b	2
		שריה	SERAIAH	976a	4 a
4	15	אלה	ELAH	18d	4
		כלב	CALEB	477a	
		ערו	IRU	747a	
		יפנה	JEPHUNNEH	819c	1
		קנז	KENAZ	889d	
4	16	אשראל	ASAREL	77b	
		יהללאל	JEHALLELEL	239c	1
		זיף	ZIPH	268b	2
		זיפה	ZIPHAH	268b	
		תיריא	TIRIA	432b	
		תיריא	TIRIA	1066d	
4	17	אשתמוע	ESHTEMOA	84c	
		אשתמוע	ESHTEMOA	84c	
		הרה	CONCEIVE	247d	1
		יתר	JETHER	452b	4 b
		מרד	MERED	597d	
		מרים	MIRIAM	599b	2
		עזרה	EZRAH	741a	
		עפר	EPHER	780b	2
		ישבח	ISHBAH	986d	
		שמי	SHAMMAI	1031d	3
		ילון	ADDENDA ET COR-RIGENDA	1124a	
4	18	בתיה	BITHIA	124a	
		גדור	GEDOR	155b	1
		חבר	HEBER	288c	3
		יהודי	JEW	397c	
		יקותיאל	JEKUTHIEL	429a	
		ירד	JARED	434b	1
		מרד	MERED	597d	
		פרעה	PHARAOH	829a	
		שובה	SOCOH	962c	1
4	19	אשתמוע	ESHTEMOA	84c	
		אשתמוע	ESHTEMOA	84c	
		גרמי	GARMITE	175a	
		הודיה	HODIAH	217c	1
		מעכתי	MAACATHITE	591a	
		נחם	NAHAM	637b	
4	20	אמנון	AMNON	54c	2
		בנזוחת	BEN-ZOHETH	122b	
		בנחנן	BENHANAN	122c	
		זוחת	ZOHETH	265d	
		ישעי	ISHI	447d	3
		רנה	RINNAH	943d	
		שימון	SHIMON	1010a	
		תילון	TILON	1066c	
4	21	בוץ	BYSSUS	101c	
		בית	HOUSE	109c	5 a
		לכה	LECAH	540b	
		לעדה	LAADAH	541d	
		מרשה	MARESHAH	601c	
		עבדה	LABOR	715b	1
		ער	ER	735c	2
		שבע	ASHBEA	990a	
		שלה	SHELAH	1017c	
4	22	בעל	RULE OVER	127b	2
		דבר	WORD	183a	2 1a
		יהואש	JEHOASH	220a	6
		יהויקים	JEHOIAKIM	220c	3
		כובא	COZEBA	469d	
		עתיק	OLD	801c	2
		שרף	SARAPH	977b	
		ישבי לחם	JASHUBI-LEHEM	1000b	1
4	23	גדרה	WALL	155a	
		יצר	FORM	427d	1 a
		נטעים	NETAIM	642d	
		שבע	SHEBA	989d	
4	24	זרח	ZERAH	280c	4
		ימואל	JEMUEL	410c	
		ימין	JAMIN	412c	1
		נמואל	NEMUEL	649c	1
		יריב	JARIB	937b	1
		שאול	SAUL	982c	3
4	25	מבשם	MIBSAM	142a	2
		שלום	SHALLUM	1024b	5
		משמע	MISHMA	1036a	2
4	26	זכור	ZACCUR	271d	2
		חמואל	HAMMUEL	329b	
		שמעי	SHIMEI	1035c	5
		משמע	MISHMA	1036a	2
4	27	בן	SON	121a	1 jd
		עד	AS FAR AS	724d	1 3
		שש	SIX	995c	1 a
		שש	SIX	995c	2
		שמעי	SHIMEI	1035c	5
4	28	בארשבע	BEERSHEBA	92a	1
		חצרשועל	HAZAR-SHUAL	347c	1
		מולדה	MOLADAH	409d	
4	29	אלתולד	ELTOLAD	39a	
		בלהה	BILHAH	117b	
		תולד	TOLAD	410a	
		עצם	EZEM	783a	
4	30	ביתאל	BETHEL	111a	2
		בתואל	BETHUEL	143d	
		חרמה	HORMAH	356c	
		צקלג	ZIKLAG	862c	
4	31	ביתלבאות	BETH-LEBAOTH	111d	
		ביתמרכבות	BETH-MARCABOTH	112b	
		חצרסוסה	HAZAR-SUSAH	347c	
		מלך	BE KING	574a	
		שערים	SHAARAIM	1045c	2
4	32	עיטם	ETAM	743c	3
		עין	AIN	745b	2 b
		עשן	ASHAN	798c	
		רמון	RIMMON	942a	2
		תכן	TOCHEN	1067c	
4	33	בעל	BAAL	127d	1
		התיחש	ENROLLMENT	405b	2
		מושב	DWELLING	444b	2 a
4	34	אמציהו	AMAZIAH	55c	1
		יושה	JOSHAH	444d	
		ימלך	JAMLECH	576a	

1 CHRONICLES

Ch	v.	Heb	Eng	Page	Sec
4	35	משובב	MESHOBAB	1000c	
		יהוא	JEHU	219d	5
		יואל	JOEL	222b	2
		ירושביה	JOSHIBIAH	444a	
		עשיאל	ASIEL	795c	
		שריה	SERAIAH	976a	4 b
4	36	אליועיני	ELIOENAI	41b	2
		בניה	BENAIAH	125c	3
		עדיאל	ADIEL	726a	1
		יעקבה	JAAKOBAH	785b	
		עשיה	ASAIAH	795c	2
		ישימאל	JESIMIEL	964d	
		ישוחיה	JESHOHAIAH	1006a	
4	37	אלון	ALLON	47d	
		זיזא	ZIZA	265b	1
		ידיה	JEDAIAH	393a	1
		שמעיה	SHEMAIAH	1035d	5
		שמרי	SHIMRI	1037c	1
		שפעי	SHIPHI	1051b	
4	38	בוא	COME	98d	2 g
		בית	HOUSE	110b	5 e
		נשיא	PRINCE	672b	5
		פרץ	BREAK THROUGH	829c	8
		רב	MULTITUDE	914a	1
		שם	NAME	1028a	2 a
4	39	מבוא	ENTRANCE	99d	1
		בקש	SEEK	134c	1 b
		גדור	GEDOR	155b	2
		גיא	VALLEY	161b	
		הלך	WALK	231b	1 d3 gd
		מזרח	PLACE OF SUNRISE	281a	2 d
		ל	TO	511b	1 ga
		עד	UNTIL	725c	3 l
		מרעה	PASTURAGE	945c	
4	40	חם	HAM	326a	1
		טוב	PLEASANT	374b	3 b
		יד	HAND	390c	3 d
		שלו	QUIET	1017c	2
		שמן	FAT	1032a	1
		שקט	BE QUIET	1053a	1
4	41	חזקיהו	HEZEKIAH	306a	1
		חרם	BAN	355d	1 a
		ישב	DWELL	443a	3
		כתב	WRITE	507d	3
		מעונים	MEUNITES	589b	
		מצא	FIND	594a	2 c
		נכה	SMITE	646b	3
		מרעה	PASTURAGE	945c	
		שם	THERE	1027c	3 b
		שם	NAME	1028a	2 a
4	42	הלך	WALK	231b	1 d3 gd
		הלך	WALK	231b	1 d3 gd
		ישעי	ISHI	447d	4
		ל	TO	511b	1 ga
		מאה	HUNDRED	548b	1 c4
		מן	FROM	580d	3 ba
		נעריה	NEARIAH	655d	2
		עזיאל	UZZIEL	739c	2
		פלטיהו	PELATIAH	812d	3
		ראש	HEAD	911a	3 d
		רפיה	REPHAIAH	951b	2
		שעיר	SEIR	973a	1 b
4	43	ל	TO	513d	5 cb g
		עמלק	AMALEK	766a	
		פליטה	ESCAPE	812c	2 b
		שארית	REST	984d	1
5	1	בכרה	RIGHT OF FIRST-BORN	114c	
		בכרה	RIGHT OF FIRST-BORN	114c	
		בן	SON	*120d	1 ja
		חלל	POLLUTE	320b	1 a
		התיחש	BE ENROLLED	405b	
		יוסף	JOSEPH	415d	1 a
		יצוע	BED	427a	
		לא	NOT	518d	1 ab
		נתן	GIVE	681b	1 a
		ראובן	REUBEN	910a	1
5	2	בכרה	RIGHT OF FIRST-BORN	114c	
		גבר	BE STRONG	149d	1
		יוסף	JOSEPH	415d	1 a
		ל	TO	514d	5 fe
5	3	חנוך	ENOCH	335c	4
		חצרון	HEZRON	348a	2 a
		כרמי	CARMI	501d	1
		פלוא	PALLU	811a	
		ראובן	REUBEN	910a	1
5	4	גוג	GOG	155d	1
		יואל	JOEL	222b	3
		שמעי	SHIMEI	1035c	6
		שמעיה	SHEMAIAH	1035d	6
5	5	בעל	BAAL	127d	2 a
		מיכה	MICHA	567d	3
5	6	ראיה	REAIAH	909d	2
		אשור	ASSYRIA	78d	4
		בארה	BEERAH	92a	
		נשיא	PRINCE	672b	5
		ראובני	REUBENITE	910a	
		תלפלאסר	TIGLATHPILESER	1062a	1
5	7	זכריה	ZECHARIAH	272b	4
		התיחש	ENROLLMENT	405b	
		תולדות	GENERATIONS	410a	A
		יעיאל	JEIEL	418b	2 b
		ראש	HEAD	911a	3 f
5	8	ביתבעלמעון	BETH-BAAL-MEON	111a	

Ch	v.	Heb	Eng	Page	Sec
		ביתבעלמעון	BETH-BAAL-MEON	111a	
		בלע	BELA	118c	3
		מעון	BAAL-MEON	128a	
		יואל	JOEL	222b	3
		נבו	NEBO	612d	1 a
		עזז	AZAZ	739b	5
		ערער	AROER	792d	2
		שמע	SHEMA	1034d	2
5	9	בוא	COME	98d	2 e
		מזרח	PLACE OF SUNRISE	281a	2 c3
		ל	TO	511d	1 h
		מן	FROM	583d	9 b1
		עד	UNTIL	725c	3 l
		פרת	EUPHRATES	832b	
		רבה	BECOME MANY	915a	1 b
5	10	הגרי	HAGRITE	212c	1
		מזרח	PLACE OF SUNRISE	281a	2 e
		ישב	DWELL	443a	3
		מלחמה	WAR	536c	
5	11	נפל	FALL	657b	2 a
		עמידב	AMMINADAB	770b	2 b
		עשה	DO	794c	2 le
		בשן	BASHAN	143c	
		גד	GAD	151c	1 b
		נגד	IN FRONT	617c	2 b
		סלכה	SALECAH	669c	
		עמידב	AMMINADAB	770b	2 b
5	12	בשן	BASHAN	143c	
		יואל	JOEL	222b	4
		יעני	JANAI	775a	
		ראש	HEAD	911a	3 f
		משנה	SECOND	1041d	3 b
		שפט	SHAPHAT	1048b	4
		שפם	SHAPHAM	1050d	
		יעני	ADDENDA ET CORRIGENDA	1126a	
5	13	אב	FATHER	3c	3
		בית	HOUSE	110b	5 e
		זיע	ZIA	266b	
		יורי	JORAI	436c	
		מיכאל	MICHAEL	567c	2
		עבר	EBER	720a	2
		יעכן	JACAN	747c	
		שבע	SHEBA	989d	2
		משלם	MESHULLAM	1024c	4
5	14	אביחיל	ABIHAIL	4b	2
		בוז	BUZ	100c	2
		חורי	HURI	301b	
		יחדי	JAHDO	403c	
		ירוח	JAROAH	437b	
		ישישי	JESHISHAI	450b	
		מיכאל	MICHAEL	567c	2
5	15	אב	FATHER	3c	3
		אחיהו	AHIJAH	26d	0
		גוני	GUNI	157b	2
		עבדיאל	ABDIEL	715d	
		ראש	HEAD	911a	3 f
5	16	בשן	BASHAN	143c	
		מגרש	OPEN LAND	177c	
		תוצאה	OUT GOING	426a	1
		שרון	SHARON	450a	2
		על	UPON	757c	2 7c ab
5	17	יותם	JOTHAM	222d	1
		התיחש	BE ENROLLED	405b	
		ירבעם	JEROBOAM	914d	2
5	18	אחז	GRASP	28c	
		גדי	GADITE	151d	
		מגן	SHIELD	171c	2
		דרך	TREAD	202b	4
		מלחמה	WAR	536c	
		למד	LEARN	540d	
		מן	FROM	581d	3 be
		מנשה	MANASSEH	586c	1 b2 d
		נשא	LIFT	671a	2 a
		צבא	WAR	839b	2
		קשת	BOW	906c	1 d
		ראובן	REUBEN	910a	2
		ארבע	FOUR	917b	2 c
5	19	הגרי	HAGRITE	212c	1
		יטור	JETUR	377b	
		מלחמה	WAR	536c	
		נודב	NODAB	622a	
		נפיש	NAPHISH	661c	
		עשה	DO	794c	2 le
5	20	בטח	TRUST	105a	1 3a
		הגרי	HAGRITE	212c	1
		זעק	CRY	277b	2 a
		עזר	HELP	740c	
		עתר	PRAY	801c	
5	21	אדם	MAN	9c	2
		אלף	THOUSAND	49a	1 c
		חמור	HE-ASS	331b	1
		חמשים	FIFTY	332c	3 b
		נפש	SOUL	660b	4 c1
		מקנה	CATTLE	889b	1
		שבה	TAKE CAPTIVE	985c	1 b
5	22	ישב	DWELL	443a	3
		לוי	LEVI	532c	1 a
		מן	OUT OF	579d	2 d
5	23	בן	SON	120d	1 ja
		בעלחרמון	BAAL-HERMON	128a	
		בשן	BASHAN	143c	
		הר	MOUNTAIN	249b	1 a
		חרמון	HERMON	356d	
		חרמון	HERMON	356d	
		חרמון	HERMON	356d	

Ch	v.	Heb	Eng	Page	Sec
		מנשה	MANASSEH	586c	1 b2 d
		רבה	BECOME MANY	915a	1 a
		שניר	SENIR	972a	
5	24	אליאל	ELIEL	45a	B
		גבור	STRONG	150b	2
		יחדיאל	JAHDIEL	292d	
		חיל	STRENGTH	298d	1 c
		ישעי	ISHI	447d	2
		עזריאל	AZRIEL	741a	2
		עפר	EPHER	780b	3
		ראש	HEAD	911a	3 f
		ראש	HEAD	911a	3 f
		ירמיה	JEREMIAH	941a	4
		שם	NAME	1028a	2 b1
		חודיה	ADDENDA ET CORRIGENDA	1124a	1
5	25	אלהים	GOD	43c	1 d
		זנה	COMMIT FORNICATION	275d	3
		מעל	ACT TREACHEROUSLY	591b	2 b
		עם	PEOPLE	766c	5 c
5	26	גדי	GADITE	151d	
		גוזן	GOZAN	157a	
		הרא	HARA	246d	
		חבור	HABOR	289c	
		חלח	HALAH	318d	
		ל	TO	511b	1 ga
		ל	TO	512a	3 b
		מנשה	MANASSEH	586c	1 b2 d
		עור	ROUSE ONESELF	735b	1
		פול	PUL	806d	
		ראובני	REUBENITE	910a	
		רוח	BREATH	925b	3 g
		שלמה	SOLOMON	1024d	
		תגלתפלאסר	TIGLATHPILESER	1062b	
5	27	בן	SON	*121a	1 je
		גרשון	GERSHON	177b	
		מררי	MERARI	601b	
		קהת	KOHATH	875b	
5	28	חברון	HEBRON	289b	1
		עזיאל	UZZIEL	739c	1 a
		עמרם	AMRAM	771d	1
		יצהר	IZHAR	844b	
5	29	אהרן	AARON	14d	
		איתמר	ITHAMAR	16a	
		אלעזר	ELEAZAR	46b	A
		בן	SON	*121a	1 jz
		מרים	MIRIAM	599b	1
		משה	MOSES	602c	
		נדב	NADAB	621c	1
		עמרם	AMRAM	771d	1
5	30	אבישוע	ABISHUA	4d	1
		אלעזר	ELEAZAR	46b	A
		כהן	PRIEST	*464c	8
5	31	אבישוע	ABISHUA	4d	1
		בקי	BUKKI	131c	2
		עזי	UZZI	739d	1 a
5	32	זרחיה	ZERAHIAH	280c	1
		מריות	MERAIOTH	599a	1
		עזי	UZZI	739d	1 a
5	33	אחיטוב	AHITUB	26d	1
		אמריה	AMARIAH	57c	1
		מריות	MERAIOTH	599a	1 a
5	34	אחיטוב	AHITUB	26d	1
		אחימעץ	AHIMAAZ	27b	1
		צדוק	ZADOK	843b	1 a
5	35	אחימעץ	AHIMAAZ	27b	1
		יהוחנן	JEHOHANAN	220b	1
		עזריהו	AZARIAH	741b	5 b
5	36	יהוחנן	JEHOHANAN	220b	1
		כהן	ACT AS PRIEST	464c	1
		עזריהו	AZARIAH	741b	5 a
5	37	אחיטוב	AHITUB	26d	1
		אמריהו	AMARIAH	57c	2
		עזריהו	AZARIAH	741b	5 a
5	38	אחיטוב	AHITUB	27a	2
		צדוק	ZADOK	843b	1 b
		שלום	SHALLUM	1024b	1
5	39	חלקיהו	HILKIAH	324d	2
		עזריהו	AZARIAH	741b	5 c
		שלום	SHALLUM	1024b	1
5	40	יהוצדק	JEHOZADAK	221b	
		עזריהו	AZARIAH	741b	5 c
5	41	יהוצדק	JEHOZADAK	221b	
		הלך	WALK	230b	1 1b
		כהן	PRIEST	*464c	8
		נבוכדראצר	NEBUCHADNEZZAR	613b	
6	1	בן	SON	*121a	1 je
		גרשון	GERSHON	*177a	
		גרשם	GERSHOM	177a	2
		לוי	LEVI	532c	1 a
		מררי	MERARI	601b	
		קהת	KOHATH	875b	
6	2	גרשון	GERSHON	*177a	
		גרשם	GERSHOM	177a	2
		לבני	LIBNI	526d	
		שמעי	SHIMEI	1035c	3 a
6	3	חברון	HEBRON	289b	1
		עזיאל	UZZIEL	739c	1 a
		יצהר	IZHAR	844b	
6	4	אב	FATHER	3c	3
		לוי	LEVI	532c	1 a
		מושי	MUSHI	559b	

Ch	v.	Heb	Eng	Page	Sec
		מחלי	MAHLI	563a	1
		מררי	MERARI	601b	
		משפחה	CLAN	1047a	1 d
6	5	גרשם	GERSHOM	177a	2
		גרשון	GERSHON	*177a	
		זמה	ZIMMAH	273c	1
		יחת	JAHATH	367a	2 a
		לבני	LIBNI	526d	
6	6	אתני	ETHNI	87d	
		יואח	JOAH	222a	2 a
		זרח	ZERAH	280c	3 a
		יאתרי	JEATHERAI	384d	
		עדו	IDDO	723b	3
6	7	אסיר	ASSIR	64b	
		עמינדב	AMMINADAB	770b	2 a
		קרח	KORAH	901b	2
6	8	אביאסף	ABIASAPH	4a	
		אלקנה	ELKANAH	46c	E a
		אסיר	ASSIR	64b	
6	9	אוריאל	URIEL	22c	1
		עזיהו	UZZIAH	739d	3
		צפניה	ZEPHANIAH	861b	
		שאול	SAUL	982c	4
		תחת	TAHATH	1066c	1 a
6	10	אחימות	AHIMOTH	27a	
		אלקנה	ELKANAH	46c	E a
		עמשי	AMASAI	772a	2 a
6	11	אלקנה	ELKANAH	46c	E b
		נחת	NAHATH	639c	2
		צוף	ZUPH	847c	
6	12	אליאב	ELIAB	45a	D
		אליאל	ELIEL	45a	E
		אליהו	ELIHU	45b	B
		אלקנה	ELKANAH	46c	A
6	13	ביחו	ABIJAM	4a	2
		יואל	JOEL	222b	1
		ושני	JOEL	255c	
		שמואל	SAMUEL	1028d	1
		שני	SECOND	*1041b	
6	14	לבני	LIBNI	526d	
		מחלי	MAHLI	563a	1
		מררי	MERARI	601b	
		עזה	UZZAH	739c	1
		שמעי	SHIMEI	1035c	3 b
6	15	חגיה	HAGGIAH	291b	
		עשיה	ASAIAH	795c	3 a
		שמעא	SHIMEA	1035a	3 a
6	16	יד	HAND	391c	5 h3
		מן	SINCE	583c	7 c
		מנוח	STATE OF REST	629d	3
		שיר	SONG	1010c	3
6	17	אהל	TENT	14a	3
		אהל	TENT	14b	3
		מועד	TENT OF MEETING	418a	5
		עבדה	LABOR	715b	4
		שיר	SONG	1010c	3
		משכן	DWELLING-PLACE	1015d	2 c
		משפט	JUDGMENT	1049a	6 b
		שרת	SERVE	1057b	2 b
6	18	הימן	HEMAN	54d	
		אסף	ASAPH	63a	2
		יואל	JOEL	222b	1
		קהתי	KOHATHITES	875c	
		שיר	SING	1010d	
		שמואל	SAMUEL	1028d	1
6	19	אליאב	ELIAB	45a	D
		אליאל	ELIEL	45a	E
		אליהו	ELIHU	45b	B
		אלקנה	ELKANAH	46c	A
		נחת	NAHATH	639c	2
		תוח	TOAH	1063c	
6	20	אלקנה	ELKANAH	46c	E b
		מחת	MAHATH	367b	A
		עמשי	AMASAI	772a	2 a
		צוף	ZUPH	847c	
6	21	אלקנה	ELKANAH	46c	E a
		יואל	JOEL	222b	1 a
		עזריהו	AZARIAH	741b	6
		צפניה	ZEPHANIAH	861b	4
6	22	אביאסף	ABIASAPH	4a	
		אסיר	ASSIR	64b	
		קרח	KORAH	901b	2
		רע	FRIEND	946a	2
		תחת	TAHATH	1066c	1 a
6	23	לוי	LEVI	532c	1 a
		יצהר	IZHAR	844b	
6	24	הימן	HEMAN	54d	
		אסף	ASAPH	63a	2
		יברכיהו	JEBERECHIAH	140a	5
		ימן	RIGHT HAND	411d	2 a
		שמעא	SHIMEA	1035a	3 b
6	25	בעשיה	BAASEIAH	129d	
		מיכאל	MICHAEL	567c	4
		מלכיה	MALCHIJAH	575d	5
		מעשיהו	MAASEIAH	796b	6
6	26	אתני	ETHNI	87d	
		זרח	ZERAH	280c	3 b
		יאתרי	JEATHERAI	384d	
		עדיהו	ADAIAH	726a	3
6	27	זמה	ZIMMAH	273c	2
		איתן	ETHAN	451a	
		שמעי	SHIMEI	1035c	3 c
6	28	גרשון	GERSHON	*177a	2
		גרשם	GERSHOM	177a	2
		יחת	JAHATH	367a	2 a
		לוי	LEVI	532c	1 a

Ch	v.	Heb	Eng	Page	Sec
6	29	קהת	KOHATH	875b	
		הימן	HEMAN	54d	
		אסף	ASAPH	63a	2
		איתן	ETHAN	451a	
		מלוך	MALLUCH	576a	1 a
		מררי	MERARI	601b	
		עבדי	ABDI	715d	1
		קושיהו	KUSHAIAH	881c	
		שמאל	LEFT	969d	1
6	30	אמציהו	AMAZIAH	55c	3
		חלקיהו	HILKIAH	324d	4 a
		חשביהו	HASHABIAH	364a	4
6	31	אמצי	AMZI	55c	1
6	32	בני	BANI	125b	2 a
		בקי	BUKKI	131c	2
		שמר	SHEMER	1037c	2 a
		לוי	LEVI	532c	1 a
		מושי	MUSHI	559b	
		מחלי	MAHLI	563a	2
		מררי	MERARI	601b	
6	33	לוי	LEVITE	533a	3 l d
		עבדה	LABOR	715c	4
		משכן	DWELLING-PLACE	1015d	2 c
6	34	אלהים	GOD	44a	3 b
		מזבח	ALTAR	258c	3 b
		כפר	COVER OVER	498a	3 j2
		ל	TO	518b	7 bh
		מלאכה	WORK	522b	6 b
		משה	MOSES	602d	
		עבד	SLAVE	714a	3
		עלה	WHOLE BURNT OF-FERING	750d	
		קדש	APARTNESS	871d	2 c
		קטר	MAKE SACRAFICES SMOKE	883b	3
6	35	אבישוע	ABISHUA	4d	1
		אלעזר	ELEAZAR	46b	A
		בן	SON	121a	1 jz
		כהן	PRIEST	*464c	8
6	36	זרחיה	ZERAHIAH	280c	1
		עזי	UZZI	739d	1 a
6	37	אמריהו	AMARIAH	57c	1
		מריות	MERAIOTH	599a	1 a
6	38	אחימעץ	AHIMAAZ	27b	1
		כהן	PRIEST	*464c	8
6	39	בן	SON	121a	1 jz
		גבול	BOUNDARY	147d	1
		גורל	LOT	174b	1
		טירה	ENCAMPMENT	377b	1
		מושב	DWELLING	444b	2 a
		מגרש	COMMON-LAND	177b	
6	40	חברון	HEBRON	289b	
6	41	חברון	HEBRON	*289b	
		חצר	SETTLED ABODE	347b	B
		כלב	CALEB	*477a	
		שדה	FIELD	961d	2 c
6	42	אהרן	AARON	14d	
		אשתמוע	ESHTEMOA	84c	
		בן	SON	121a	1 jz
		חברון	HEBRON	289b	
		יתיר	JATTIR	453a	
		לבנה	LIBNAH	526c	1
		מקלט	REFUGE	886a	
6	43	דביר	DEBIR	184c	2 c
		דביר	DEBIR	184c	2 c
		חלון	HOLON	298b	2
		חילן	HILEN	298b	
		יתיר	JATTIR	*453a	
6	44	ביתשמש	BETH-SHEMESH	113a	1
		עשן	ASHAN	798c	
6	45	בנימין	BENJAMIN	122d	1
		גבע	GEBA	148d	
		מטה	TRIBE	641d	3
		עלמת	ALEMETH	761b	2
		עלמון	ALMON	761b	
		ענתות	ANATHOTH	779a	1
		שלש	THREE	1025d	2
		משפחה	CLAN	1047a	1 d
6	46	גורל	LOT	174b	1
		מחצית	HALF	346a	1
		יתר	BE LEFT OVER	451b	
		מנשה	MANASSEH	586c	1 b1 g
		עשר	TEN	796d	2 a
6	47	אשר	ASHER	81b	2
		בשן	BASHAN	143c	
		גרשם	GERSHOM	177a	2
		גרשון	GERSHON	*177a	
		גרשון	GERSHON	*177b	
		יששכר	ISSACHAR	441a	1
		מנשה	MANASSEH	586c	1 b2 g
6	48	גד	GAD	151c	1 b
		גורל	LOT	174b	1
		זבולן	ZEBULUN	259d	3
		מררי	MERARI	601b	
		ראובן	REUBEN	910a	2
6	49	לוי	LEVITE	533a	3 l c
6	50	בן	SON	121a	1 jd
		בנימן	BENJAMIN	122d	1
		גורל	LOT	174b	1
		יהודה	JUDAH	397b	1 2
		קרא	CALL	896a	6 i
		שמעון	SIMEON	1035c	1
6	51	אפרים	EPHRAIM	68b	2
		גבול	BOUNDARY	147d	1 b
		קהת	KOHATH	875b	
6	52	גזר	GEZER	160c	

Ch	v.	Heb	Eng	Page	Sec
		הר	MOUNTAIN	251a	2 b
		מקלט	REFUGE	886a	
		שכם	SHECHEM	1014c	1
6	53	ביתחורון	BETH-HORON	111c	B
		קבצים	KIBZAIM	868b	
		יקמעם	JOKMEAM	880c	
6	54	אילון	AIJALON	19c	1
		גתרמון	GATH-RIMMON	387d	
6	55	בלעם	BILEAM	118d	
		מחצית	HALF	346a	1
		יבלעם	IBLEAM	*386a	
		יבלעם	IBLEAM	386a	
		יתר	BE LEFT OVER	451c	
		מנשה	MANASSEH	586c	1 b1 g
		ענר	ANER	778d	2
		קהת	KOHATH	875b	
6	56	בעשתרה	BE-ESHTERAH	129d	
		בשן	BASHAN	143c	
		גולן	GOLAN	157b	
		גרשם	GERSHOM	177a	2
		גרשון	GERSHON	*177a	
		גרשון	GERSHON	*177b	
		מנשה	MANASSEH	586c	1 b2 g
		פך	ASHTAROTH	800b	
6	57	דברת	DABERATH	184b	1
		יששכר	ISSACHAR	441a	1
		קדש	KEDESH	873d	2
		קישון	KISHION	*904d	1
6	58	עינגנים	EN-GANNIM	745c	2
		רמות	RAMOTH	928c	1 c
6	59	אשר	ASHER	81b	2
		משאל	MISHAL	602b	
		עבדון	ABDON	715c	2
6	60	חוקק	HUKOK	301a	1
		חוקק	HUKOK	350c	
		רחוב	REHOB	932b	1 b2
6	61	חמון	HAMMON	329a	2
		קדש	KEDESH	873d	1
		קריתים	KIRIATHIAM	900b	2
6	62	דמנה	DIMNAH	199b	2
		זבולן	ZEBULUN	259d	3
		יתר	BE LEFT OVER	451c	
		כסלות	CHESULLOTH	493b	
		מררי	MERARI	601b	
		רמון	RIMMON	942a	3
		תבור	TABOR	1061d	3
6	63	בצר	BEZER	131a	1
		מזרח	PLACE OF SUNRISE	281a	2 d
		יהץ	JAHAZ	397d	2
		ירדן	JORDAN	434c	
		ירדן	JORDAN	*434d	
		ל	TO	511d	1 h
		עבר	REGION ACROSS	719c	1 a
		ראובן	REUBEN	910a	2
6	64	מיפעת	MEPHAATH	422b	2
		קדמת	KEDEMOTH	870d	
6	65	גד	GAD	151c	1 b
		מחנים	MAHANAIM	334b	2
		רמות	RAMOTH	928b	1 a
6	66	חשבון	HESHBON	363d	
		יעזר	JAZER	*741d	
7	1	יוב	IOB	398a	
		יששכר	ISSACHAR	441a	1
		ל	TO	514c	5 fe
		פואה	PUAH	806a	
		ישוב	JASHUB	1000b	1
		שמרון	SHIMRON	1038a	1
		תולע	TOLA	1069a	
7	2	בית	HOUSE	110b	5 e
		יבשם	IBSAM	142a	
		חיל	STRENGTH	298d	1 c
		יחמי	JAHMAI	327d	1
		תולדות	GENERATIONS	410a	A
		יריאל	JERUEL	436c	
		עזי	UZZI	739d	2
		ראש	HEAD	911a	3 f
		רפיה	REPHAIAH	951b	3
		שמואל	SAMUEL	1028d	1
		תולע	TOLA	1069a	
7	3	יואל	JOEL	222b	1
		יזרחיה	IZRAHIAH	280c	1
		מיכאל	MICHAEL	567c	5
		ישיהו	ISSHIJAH	674c	2
		עבדיהו	OBADIAH	715d	2 3
		עזי	UZZI	739d	2
		ראש	HEAD	911a	3 f
7	4	גדוד	TROOP	151b	2
		תולדות	GENERATIONS	410a	A
		מלחמה	WAR	536b	
		צבא	ARMY	839a	1 a
		רבה	BECOME MANY	915c	1 a
7	5	גבור	STRONG	150b	2
		חיל	STRENGTH	298d	1 c
		התיחש	ENROLLMENT	405b	
		יששכר	ISSACHAR	441a	1
		כל	ALL	482d	2 ba
		ל	TO	512a	3 b
		ל	TO	514d	5 fe
		משפחה	CLAN	1047a	1 d
7	6	בכר	BECHER	114b	2
		בלע	BELA	118c	2
		ידיעאל	JEDIAEL	396a	1
7	7	אצבון	EZBON	69a	2
		בית	HOUSE	110b	5 e
		בלע	BELA	118c	2
		גבור	STRONG	150b	2

Ch	v.	Heb	Eng	Page	Sec
		חיל	STRENGTH	298d	1 c
		התיחש	BE ENROLLED	405b	
		ירימות	JEREMOTH	438b	1 a
		עזיאל	UZZIEL	739c	3
		עזי	UZZI	739d	3
		עירי	IRI	747a	
		ראש	HEAD	911a	3 f
		ארבע	FOUR	917b	2 c
7	8	ביהו	ABIJAM	4a	4
		אליעזר	ELIEZER	45c	C
		בכר	BECHER	114b	2
		יועש	JOASH	222c	1
		זמירה	ZEMIRAH	275b	
		ירימות	JEREMOTH	438b	1 b
		עלמת	ALEMETH	761b	1
		עמרי	OMRI	771d	2 a
		ענתות	ANATHOTH	779a	2 a
7	9	חיל	STRENGTH	298d	1 c
		התיחש	ENROLLMENT	405b	A
		תולדות	GENERATIONS	410a	a
		ראש	HEAD	911a	3 f
7	10	אהד	EHUD	13c	2
		אחישחר	AHISHAHAR	27c	
		בלהן	BILHAN	117b	2
		בנימן	BENJAMIN	122d	2
		זיתן	ZETHAN	268d	
		ידיעאל	JEDIAEL	396a	1
		כנענה	CHENAANAH	489b	2
		יעוש	JEUSH	736c	2 a
		תרשיש	TARSHISH	1077a	2 a
7	11	אב	FATHER	3c	3
		גבור	STRONG	150b	2
		חיל	STRENGTH	298d	1 c
		ידיעאל	JEDIAEL	396a	1
		מלחמה	WAR	536b	
		עשר	TEN	797b	7 a
		צבא	ARMY	839a	1 a
		צבא	WAR	839b	2
		שבע	SEVEN	*988b	2 b
7	12	אחי	EHI	*29a	
		אחר	AHER	31b	
		חופם	HUPHAM	*299c	
		חשם	HUSHIM	302a	
		מפים	MUPPIM	592b	
		עיר	IR	746a	
		שפופם	SHEPHUPHAM	*1051b	
		שפים	SHUPPIM	1051b	1
7	13	בלהה	BILHAH	117b	
		גוני	GUNI	157b	1
		יחצאל	JAHZEEL	345d	
		יצר	JEZER	428a	
7	14	שלום	SHALLUM	1024b	8
		ארמי	ARAMEAN	74c	
		אשריאל	ASRIEL	77b	
		מנשה	MANASSEH	586d	1 b2 d
		חופם	HUPHAM	*299c	
		חפים	HUPPIM	342c	1
		מעכה	MAACAH	591a	2 e
		צלפחד	ZELOPHEHAD	854c	
		שפים	SHUPPIM	1051b	1
7	16	אולם	ULAM	17d	1
		מעכה	MAACAH	591a	2 e
		פרש	PERESH	831d	
		רקם	REKEM	955d	1 c
		שרש	SHERESH	1058a	
7	17	אולם	ULAM	17d	1
		בדן	BEDAN	96a	2
		מנשה	MANASSEH	586d	1 b2 d
7	18	אביעזר	ABIEZER	4c	1
		אישהוד	ISHHOD	36b	
		אליעיני	ELIOENAI	41b	3
		מחלה	MAHLAH	563a	1
		מלכת	MOLECHETH	574c	
7	19	אחין	AHIAN	27b	
		אניעם	ANIAM	58b	
		לקחי	LIKHI	544b	
		שכם	SHECHEM	1014c	
		שמידע	SHEMIDA	1029a	
7	20	אלעדה	ELEADAH	46b	
		אפרים	EPHRAIM	68b	1
		בכר	BECHER	114b	1
		ברד	BERED	136a	2
		שותלח	SHUTHELAH	1004d	
		תחת	TAHATH	1066c	1 b
7	21	אלעד	ELEAD	46b	
		הרג	KILL	247a	1 a
		זבד	ZABAD	256b	2
		גת	GATH	387d	
		ילד	BE BORN	408d	
		עזר	EZER	740d	1
		שותלח	SHUTHELAH	1004d	
7	22	אבל	MOURN	5c	
		אפרים	EPHRAIM	68b	1
		נחם	CONSOLE ONESELF	637a	
7	23	ב	IN	91b	
		בריעה	BERIAH	140b	2
		הרה	CONCEIVE	247d	1
		רעה	MISERY	949b	1
7	24	אוזן-שארה	UZZEN-SHEERAH	25a	
		עליון	HIGH	751b	2
		שארה	SHEERAH	985a	
		תחתון	LOWER	1066b	
7	25	תחן	TAHAN	334c	
		רפה	REPHAH	952c	
		רשף	RESHEPH	958b	
		תלח	TELAH	1068b	
7	26	לעדן	LADAN	541d	1
		עמיהוד	AMMIHUD	770b	2
7	27	יהושע	JOSHUA	221c	1
		נון	NUN	630c	
7	28	אחזה	POSSESSION	28c	
		גזר	GEZER	160c	
		מזרח	PLACE OF SUNRISE	281a	2 c3
		מושב	DWELLING	444b	2 a
		ל	TO	511d	1 h
		נערן	NAARAN	655d	
		עי	AI	743b	1
		מערב	WEST	788a	
7	29	ביתשאן	BETH-SHEAN	112d	
		דאר	DOR	190b	1 b1 a
		מנשה	MANASSEH	286c	1 b1 a
		יד	HAND	391c	5 h3
		יוסף	JOSEPH	415d	1 b
		תענך	TAANACH	*1073d	
		תענך	TAANACH	1073d	
7	30	אשר	ASHER	81b	2
		בריעה	BERIAH	140b	1
		ימנה	IMNAH	412c	1
		שרח	SERAH	976b	
		ישוי	ISHVI	1001a	1
		ישוה	ISHVAH	1001a	
7	31	ברזות	BIRZAITH	137b	
		בריעה	BERIAH	140b	1
		חבר	HEBER	288c	2
		מלכיאל	MALCHIEL	575c	
7	32	חבר	HEBER	288c	2
		חותם	HOTHAM	368b	1
		שועא	SHUA	447d	
		יפלט	JAPHLET	812d	
		שמר	SHOMER	1037c	2
		שמר	SHEMER	1037c	2 b
7	33	במהל	BIMHAL	119d	
		עשות	ASHVATH	798b	
		יפלט	JAPHLET	812d	
		פסך	PASACH	820d	
7	34	אחיה	AHIJAH	26d	1
		ארם	ARAM	74b	4
		חבה	JEHUBBAH	285d	
		רנה	ROHGAH	923c	
		שמר	SHEMER	1037c	2 b
7	35	הלם	HELEM	240c	1
		חותם	HOTHAM	*368b	1
		ימנע	IMNA	586b	
		עמל	AMAL	765b	
		צופח	ZOPHAH	860a	
		שלש	SHELESH	1026d	
7	36	ברי	BERI	92d	
		חרנפר	HARNEPHER	357b	
		ימרי	IMRAH	598c	
		סוח	SUAH	691d	
		צופח	ZOPHAH	860a	
		שועל	SHUAL	1043c	1
7	37	בארא	BEERA	92a	
		בצר	BEZER	131a	2
		הוד	HOD	217b	
		יתר	JETHER	*452b	5
		יתרן	ITHRAN	452d	2
		שלשה	SHILSHAH	1027a	1
		שמא	SHAMMA	1031c	
7	38	ארא	ARA	70b	
		יתר	JETHER	452b	5
		יתרן	ITHRAN	*452d	2
		יפנה	JEPHUNNEH	819c	2
		פספה	PISPA	821a	
7	39	ארח	ARAH	73b	1
		חניאל	HANNIEL	337a	2
		יתר	JETHER	*452b	5
		עלא	ULLA	748a	
		רציא	RIZIA	954a	
7	40	אשר	ASHER	81b	2
		ברר	SELECT	141a	2
		גבור	STRONG	150b	2
		חיל	STRENGTH	298d	1 c
		התיחש	BE ENROLLED	405b	
		נשיא	PRINCE	672b	5
		צבא	WAR	839b	2
		ראש	HEAD	911a	3 f
8	1	אחירם	AHIRAM	*27c	
		אחי	EHI	*29a	
		אחרח	AHARAH	31b	
		אשבל	ASHBEL	78a	
		בלע	BELA	118c	2
		חמשי	FIFTH	332c	1
		נוחה	NOHAH	629b	
		רביעי	FOURTH	918a	1
		רפא	RAPHA	951b	
8	3	אביהוד	ABIHUD	4b	
		אדר	ADDAR	12b	1
		ארד	ARD	71b	
		בלע	BELA	118c	2
		גרא	GERA	173a	
8	4	אבישוע	ABISHUA	4d	2
		אחיהו	AHIJAH	26d	6
		אחוח	AHOAH	29a	
		נעמן	NAAMAN	654a	1
8	5	חירם	HIRAM	27c	3
		גרא	GERA	173a	
		שפופן	SHEPHUPHAN	1051b	
8	6	אחוד	EHUD	26a	
		גבע	GEBA	148d	2
		הם	THEY	241c	4 bg
		מנחת	MANAHATH	630a	
8	7	ראש	HEAD	911a	3 f
		אחיהו	AHIJAH	26d	6
		אחיחד	AHIHUD	26d	
		אחוח	AHOAH	29a	
		גרא	GERA	173a	
		נעמן	NAAMAN	654a	1
		עזא	UZZAH	739c	3
8	8	בערא	BAARA	129d	
		חדש	HODESH	*295a	
		חרשים	HUSHIM	302a	
		מואב	MOAB	555d	2 b
		מן	SINCE	583c	7 c
		שחרים	SHAHARAIM	1007d	
8	9	חדש	HODESH	295a	
		יובב	JOBAB	384d	4 a
		מישא	MESHA	568c	
		מלכם	MALCAM	575d	
		צביא	ZIBIA	840b	
8	10	מרמה	MIRMAH	599b	
		יעוץ	JEUZ	734b	
		ראש	HEAD	911a	3 f
		שכיה	SACHIA	967d	
8	11	אביטוב	ABITUB	4b	
		אלפעל	ELPAAL	46c	
		חרשים	HUSHIM	302a	
8	12	אונו	ONO	20c	
		אלפעל	ELPAAL	46c	
		לד	LOD	528d	
		משעם	MISHAM	606c	
		עבר	EBER	720a	3 a
		שמד	SHEMED	1029c	
		שמר	SHEMER	1037c	2 c
8	13	אילון	AIJALON	19c	1
		ברח	FLEE	138a	2
		בריעה	BERIAH	140b	3
		גת	GATH	387d	
		ל	TO	513d	5 cb g
		ראש	HEAD	911a	3 f
		שמע	SHEMA	1034d	3
		שמעי	SHIMEI	1035c	7
8	14	אחיו	AHIO	26d	2
		ירימות	JEREMOTH	438b	1 c
		ירחם	JEROHAM	*934a	2 a
		ששק	SHASHAK	1059a	
8	15	זבדיהו	ZEBADIAH	256c	3 a
		עדר	EDER	727d	
		ערד	ARAD	788c	
8	16	בריעה	BERIAH	140b	3
		יוחא	JOHA	398a	1
		מיכאל	MICHAEL	567c	6
		ישפה	ISHPAH	1046a	
8	17	זבדיה	ZEBADIAH	256c	3 b
		חבר	HEBER	288c	4
		חזקי	HIZKI	306a	
		משלם	MESHULLAM	1024c	3 a
8	18	אלפעל	ELPAAL	46c	
		יזליאה	IZLIAH	272c	
		יובב	JOBAB	384d	4 b
		ישמרי	ISHMERAI	1038b	
8	19	זבדי	ZABDI	256c	2
		זכרי	ZICHRI	271d	5 a
		אליאל	ELIEL	45a	C
8	20	צלתי	ZILLETHAI	853c	1
8	21	בראיה	BERAIAH	135c	
		עדיהו	ADAIAH	726a	4
		שמע	SHEMA	*1034d	3
		שמרת	SHIMRATH	1037d	
8	22	אליאל	ELIEL	45a	C
		עבר	EBER	720a	3 b
		ישפן	ISHPAN	1051a	
8	23	זכרי	ZICHRI	271d	5 b
		חנן	HANAN	336d	2
		עבדון	ABDON	715c	1 2
8	24	חנניהו	HANANIAH	337b	3
		עילם	ELAM	743d	3
		ענתתיה	ANTHOTHIJAH	779a	
8	25	יפדיה	IPHDEIAH	804c	
		פנל	PENVEL	819c	2 b
8	26	ששק	SHASHAK	1059a	
		עתליה	ATHALIAH	801a	2 a
		שחריה	SHEHARAIH	1007d	
		שמשרי	SHAMSHERAI	1039c	
8	27	אליה	ELIJAH	45b	B
		זכרי	ZICHRI	271d	5 c
		יערשיה	JAARESHIAH	793b	
		ירחם	JEROHAM	934a	2 a
8	28	תולדות	GENERATIONS	410a	A
		ראש	HEAD	911a	
		ראש	HEAD	911a	3 f
8	29	גבעון	GIBEON	149c	
		מעכה	MAACAH	591a	2 f
8	30	בעל	BAAL	127d	2 b
		נדב	NADAB	621d	4
		עבדון	ABDON	715c	1 3
		צור	ZUR	849d	1
8	31	קיש	KISH	885c	1
		אחיו	AHIO	26d	3
		גדור	GEDOR	155b	3
		זכר	ZECHER	271a	
		זכריהו	ZECHARIAH	272b	5
		מקלות	MIKLOTH	*596c	1
8	32	אף	ALSO	65a	1
		מקלות	MIKLOTH	596c	1
		שמאה	SHIMEAH	1029a	
8	33	אבינדב	ABINADAB	4c	3
		אישבשת	ISHBOSHETH	36b	1

Ch	v.	Heb	Eng	Page	Sec
		בשת	SHAME	102b	2
		יהונתן	JONATHAN	220d	1
		מלכישוע	MALCHI-SHUA	575d	1
		נר	NER	633a	2
		קיש	KISH	885c	1
		ישוי	ISHVI	1001a	2
8	34	יהונתן	JONATHAN	220d	1
		מיכה	MICHA	567d	4
		מריבבעל	MERIB-BAAL	937c	1
8	35	אחז	AHAZ	28c	2
		תחרע	TAHREA	357c	
		מלך	MELECH	574b	
		פיתון	PITHON	810b	
8	36	אחז	AHAZ	28c	2
		יהועדה	JEHOADDAH	221a	
		מוצא	MOZA	426a	2
		עזמות	AZMAVETH	740a	2
		עלמת	ALEMETH	761b	2
8	37	אלעשה	ELEASAH	46c	B
		אצל	AZEL	69c	
		בנעא	BINEA	126a	
		מוצא	MOZA	426a	2
		רפה	RAPHAH	951b	
8	38	אצל	AZEL	69c	
		בכרו	BOCHERU	114b	
		חנן	HANAN	336d	5
		עבדיהו	OBADIAH	716a	2 4
		עזריקם	AZRIKAM	741b	3
		ישמעאל	ISHMAEL	1035d	3
		שעריה	SHEARIAH	1045c	
8	39	אולם	ULAM	17d	2
		אליפלט	ELIPHELET	45d	C
		יעוש	JEUSH	736c	2 b
		עשק	ESHEK	799a	
8	40	אולם	ULAM	17d	2
		בן	SON	120b	1 f
		בנימין	BENJAMIN	122d	1
		דרך	TREAD	202b	4
		חיל	STRENGTH	298d	1 c
		חמשים	FIFTY	332c	4 a
		קשת	BOW	906c	1 d
		רבה	BECOME MANY	915c	1 a
9	1	התיחש	BE ENROLLED	405b	
		ל	TO	511b	1 ga
		מעל	UNFAITHFUL	591b	2
		ספר	MISSIVE	707c	3 e
9	2	אחזה	POSSESSION	28c	
		ישב	DWELL	443b	3
		כהן	PRIEST	464b	7
		לוי	LEVITE	533a	3 2b
		נתינים	NETHINIM	*682a	
		נתינים	NETHINIM	682a	
		ענק	NECK	778c	
		ישראל	ISRAEL	976a	2 e
9	3	אפרים	EPHRAIM	68b	2
		בנימין	BENJAMIN	122d	1
		מנשה	MANASSEH	586c	1 b1 a
9	4	אמרי	IMRI	57c	1
		בני	BANI	125b	3
		עותי	UTHAI	736d	1
		עמיהוד	AMMIHUD	770b	5
		עמרי	OMRI	771d	2 b
		עתיה	ATHAIAH	800d	
		פרץ	PEREZ	829d	1
9	5	עשיה	ASAIAH	795c	3 b
		שלני	SHELANITES	1017c	
		שלני	SHILONITE	1018a	
9	6	זרח	ZERAH	280b	1
		יעואל	JEUEL	418b	1
9	7	בנימין	BENJAMIN	122d	1
		סלוא	SALLU	699b	
		סנואה	HASSENUAH	703a	
		משלם	MESHULLAM	1024c	3 b
		הודויה	ADDENDA ET COR-RIGENDA	1124a	1
9	8	אלה	ELAH	18d	5
		יבניה	IBNIJAH	125d	
		יבניה	IBNEIAH	125d	
		גבאי סללי	GABBAI SALLAI	146c	
		מכרי	MACHRI	569d	
		עזי	UZZI	739d	3
		ירחם	JEROHAM	934a	2 b
		רעואל	REUEL	946c	4
		משלם	MESHULLAM	1024c	3 c
		שפטיה	SHEPHATIAH	1049b	1 e
9	9	תולדות	GENERATIONS	410a	A
		ראש	HEAD	911a	3 f
9	10	יהויריב	JEHOIARIB	220d	1
		ידעיה	JEDAIAH	396a	1
		לוי	LEVITE	*533a	3 2a
9	11	אחיטוב	AHITUB	27a	2
		בית	HOUSE	109a	1 ae 0
		חלקיהו	HILKIAH	324d	2
		מריות	MERAIOTH	599b	1 b
		נגיד	LEADER	618a	3
		עזריהו	AZARIAH	741b	5 c
		צדוק	ZADOK	843b	1 c
		משלם	MESHULLAM	1024c	7 a
9	12	אחזיה	AHAZIAH	28d	3
		אמצי	AMZI	55c	2
		אמר	IMMER	57b	2
		יחזרה	JAHZERAH	403d	
		מלכיהו	MALCHIJAH	575c	1
		עדיהו	ADAIAH	726a	5
		עדיאל	ADIEL	726a	B
		עמשסי	AMASHSAI	772a	0
		מעשיהו	MAASEIAH	796b	0
		פשחור	PASHHUR	832d	2
		ירחם	JEROHAM	934a	3 a
		משלם	MESHULLAM	1024c	7 b
		משלמות	MESHILLEMOTH	1024c	2
9	13	בית	HOUSE	109a	1 ae 0
		חיל	STRENGTH	298d	2
		מלאכה	WORK	522a	3 b
		עבדה	LABOR	715c	4
		ראש	HEAD	911a	3 f
9	14	חשוב	HASSHUB	363d	1
		חשביהו	HASHABIAH	364a	5
		לוי	LEVITE	533a	3 2a
		מררי	MERARI	601b	2
		עזריקם	AZRIKAM	741b	4
		שמעיה	SHEMAIAH	1035d	7 a
9	15	אסף	ASAPH	63b	2
		בקבקר	BAKBAKKAR	131c	
		זבדי	ZABDI	256c	4
		זכרי	ZICHRI	271d	3 c
		חרש	HERESH	361d	
		מיכא	MICA	*567d	2
		מתניהו	MATTANIAH	682d	3 a
9	16	אלקנה	ELKANAH	46c	Eg
		יברכיהו	JEBERECHIAH	140a	2
		חצר	SETTLED ABODE	347b	C
		ידותון	JEDUTHUN	s 393a	
		נטפתי	NETOPHATHITE	643b	1
		עבדיהו	OBADIAH	716a	2 5
		שמוע	SHAMMUA	1035b	3
		שמעיה	SHEMAIAH	1035d	7 b
		שער	GATE	1045a	2 a
		אסא	ADDENDA ET COR-RIGENDA	1120c	
9	17	אחימן	AHIMAN	27a	2
		טלמן	TALMON	379a	1
		עקוב	AKKUB	784d	3 a
		שלום	SHALLUM	1024b	2 a
		שער	PORTER	1045c	
9	18	בן	SON	121a	1 je
		הנה	HITHERTO	244d	B
		מזרח	PLACE OF SUNRISE	281a	2 cl
		מחנה	ENCAMPMENT	334b	1 b
		לוי	LEVI	532c	1 c
		שער	GATE	1045a	3 b
		שער	PORTER	1045c	
9	19	אביאסף	ABIASAPH	4a	
		אהל	TENT	14b	3
		אסף	ASAPH	63b	2
		מבוא	ENTRANCE	99d	1
		ל	TO	513d	5 cb g
		מלאכה	WORK	522a	3 b
		סף	THRESHOLD	706c	
		עבדה	LABOR	715c	4
		קורא	KORAHITES	896c	1
		קרח	KORAH	901b	1
		קרחי	KORAHITES	901c	
		שלום	SHALLUM	1024b	2 a
9	20	אלעזר	ELEAZAR	46b	A
		היה	BE	227a	3 4b
9	21	אהל	TENT	14b	3
		זכריהו	ZECHARIAH	272b	0 g
		מועד	TENT OF MEETING	418a	5
		ל	TO	513d	5 cb g
		פתח	OPENING	835d	2
		משלמיה	MESHELEMIAH	1024c	
		שער	PORTER	1045c	
9	22	אמונה	FIRMNESS	53c	3 a
		ברר	SELECT	141a	2
		חצר	SETTLED ABODE	347b	C
		התיחש	ENROLLMENT	405b	
		יסד	APPOINT	414a	2
		סף	THRESHOLD	706c	
		ראה	SEER	909a	
		שמואל	SAMUEL	1028d	1
		שער	PORTER	1045c	
9	23	אהל	TENT	14b	3
		בית	HOUSE	109a	1 ae 0
		ל	TO	513c	5 cb b
		על	UPON	755b	2 3
		משמרת	GUARD	1038c	1
		שער	GATE	1045b	3 b
9	24	מזרח	PLACE OF SUNRISE	281a	2 c2
		ים	SEA	411b	2
		ל	TO	511c	1 h
		נגב	SOUTH-COUNTRY	616b	2
		רוח	BREATH	924d	2 b
		שער	PORTER	1045c	
9	25	אל	TO	39d	1
		חצר	SETTLED ABODE	347b	C
		יום	DAY	398c	2 c
		ל	TO	516b	5 ja
		ל	TO	518a	7 bg
		מן	FROM	582b	5 d1
		עת	TIME	773c	1 a
9	26	אמונה	FIRMNESS	53c	3 a
		אוצר	TREASURE	70a	3 a
		בית	HOUSE	109a	1 ae 0
		גבור	STRONG	150b	2
		הם	THEY	241a	4 a
		לוי	LEVITE	533a	3 2b
		לשכה	ROOM	545d	1 b
		על	UPON	755b	2 3
9	27	בקר	MORNING	134b	1 f
		ו	AND	252c	1 b
		על	UPON	753c	2 1c
		מפתח	KEY	836b	
9	28	יצא	BRING OUT	425a	4 a
		כלי	UTENSIL	480a	2 f
		מן	FROM	580d	3 ba
		מספר	NUMBER	709a	1 b
		עבדה	LABOR	715b	2
9	29	בשם	SPICE	142a	1
		יין	WINE	406c	B
		כלי	UTENSIL	480a	2 f
		לבנה	FRANKINCENSE	526d	
		מנה	APPOINT	584b	
		סלת	FINE FLOUR	701c	
		שמן	OIL	1032c	2 h
9	30	בן	SON	121c	7 a
		בשם	SPICE	142a	1
		מן	FROM	580d	3 ba
		רקח	MIX OIL	955b	
		מרקחת	OINTMENT-POT	955c	1
9	31	אמונה	FIRMNESS	53c	3 a
		חבתים	FLAT CAKES	290a	
		לוי	LEVITE	533a	3 2b
		מתתיהו	MATTITHIAH	682d	2
		מעשה	DEED	796a	2 a1
		קרחי	KORAHITES	901c	
		שלום	SHALLUM	1024b	2 a
9	32	כון	ESTABLISH	466b	2
		לחם	FOOD	537b	1 a
		מן	FROM	580d	3 ba
		מערכת	ROW	790b	
		שבת	SABBATH	992c	1 d
9	33	ב	IN	91b	2
		לוי	LEVITE	533a	3 1c
		לשכה	ROOM	545d	1 b
		על	UPON	753c	2 1c
		פטר	SEPARATE	809c	2
		ראש	HEAD	911a	3 f
		שיר	SING	1010d	
9	34	תולדות	GENERATIONS	410a	A
		לוי	LEVITE	533a	3 1c
		ראש	HEAD	911a	3 f
9	35	גבעון	GIBEON	149c	
		יעיאל	JEIEL	418b	3 a
		מעכה	MAACAH	591a	2 f
9	36	בעל	BAAL	127d	2 b
		נדב	NADAB	621d	4
		נר	NER	633a	2
		עבדון	ABDON	715c	1 3
		צור	ZUR	849d	2
		קיש	KISH	885c	1
9	37	אחיו	AHIO	26d	3
		גדור	GEDOR	155b	3
		זכר	ZECHER	271a	
		זכריהו	ZECHARIAH	272b	5
		מקלות	MIKLOTH	596c	1
9	38	אף	ALSO	65a	1
		מקלות	MIKLOTH	596c	1
		שמאם	SHIMEAM	1029a	
9	39	אבינדב	ABINADAB	4c	3
		אישבשת	ISHBOSHETH	36b	1
		יהונתן	JONATHAN	220d	1
		מלכישוע	MALCHI-SHUA	575d	
		נר	NER	633a	2
		קיש	KISH	885c	1
		ישוי	ISHVI	1001a	2
9	40	יהונתן	JONATHAN	220d	1
		מיכה	MICHA	567d	4
		מריבבעל	MERIB-BAAL	937c	1
9	41	אחז	AHAZ	*28c	2
		תחרע	TAHREA	357c	
		מלך	MELECH	574b	
		פיתון	PITHON	810b	
9	42	אחז	AHAZ	28c	2
		יהועדה	JEHOADDAH	221a	
		יערה	JARAH	421a	
		מוצא	MOZA	426a	2
		עזמות	AZMAVETH	740a	2
		עלמת	ALEMETH	761b	1
9	43	אלעשה	ELEASAH	46c	B
		אצל	AZEL	69c	
		בנעא	BINEA	126a	
		מוצא	MOZA	426a	2
		רפיה	REPHAIAH	951b	4
9	44	אצל	AZEL	69c	
		בכרו	BOCHERU	114b	
		חנן	HANAN	336d	5
		עבדיהו	OBADIAH	716a	2 4
		עזריקם	AZRIKAM	741b	3
		ישמעאל	ISHMAEL	1035d	3
10	1	נפל	FALL	657a	2 a
10	2	אבינדב	ABINADAB	4c	3
		דבק	KEEP CLOSE	180a	2
		יהונתן	JONATHAN	220d	1
		מלכישוע	MALCHI-SHUA	575d	
10	3	חול	WHIRL	297a	2 b
		ירה	SHOOT	435a	3
		ירה	SHOOT	435b	2
		כבד	BE HEAVY	457b	1
		מלחמה	WAR	536d	
		מצא	FIND	593b	3 b
		קשת	BOW	906b	1 d
		קשת	BOW	906b	1 d
10	4	אבה	BE WILLING	2c	
		דקר	PIERCE	201b	2
		דקר	PIERCE	*201b	
		חרב	SWORD	352c	1 c

Ch v.	Heb	Eng	Page	Sec
	יָרֵא	FEAR	431a	1 a
	כְּלִי	IMPLEMENT	479d	2 a
	נפל	FALL	656d	1
	עלל	ACT ARBITRARILY	759d	1
	ערל	HAVING FORESKIN	790c	
	שלף	DRAW OUT	1025b	1
10 5	כלי	IMPLEMENT	479d	2 a
	נפל	FALL	656d	1
10 7	עזב	LEAVE	737b	2 a1
	עמק	VALE	771a	
10 8	מחרת	THE MORROW	564a	
	נפל	LIE	657d	7
	פשט	STRIP OFF	833a	
10 9	בית	HOUSE	109b	1 ae 0
	בשר	BEAR TIDINGS	142b	1
	כלי	IMPLEMENT	479d	2 a
	עצב	IDOL	781b	
	פשט	STRIP OFF	833a	1
10 10	גויה	CORPSE	*156b	2 a
	דגון	DAGON	186a	
	דגון	DAGON	186a	
	כלי	IMPLEMENT	479d	2 a
	תקע	THRUST	1075c	1
10 11	יבש	JABESH	386d	1
10 12	אלה	TEREBINTH	18c	
	גופה	BODY	157c	
	חיל	STRENGTH	298d	1 c
	יבש	JABESH	386d	1
	צום	FAST	847a	
10 13	קבר	BURY	868c	
	אוב	NECROMANCER	15b	4
	דרש	SEEK	205b	2 b
	ל	TO	518b	7 bh
	מות	DIE	560a	2 b
	מעל	ACT TREACHEROUSLY	591b	1 c
10 14	שאל	ASK	982a	2 b
	דרש	SEEK	205b	2 a
	ישי	JESSE	445a	
	מות	DIE	560b	2
	מלוכה	KINGSHIP	574c	
	סבב	TURN ABOUT	686c	1 b
11 1	בשר	FLESH	142d	4
	חברון	HEBRON	289b	
	עצם	BONE	782d	1 a
	קבץ	GATHER	867d	1
11 2	בוא	COME	99a	1 a
	יהוה	YAHWEH	218d	2 1a
	יצא	BRING OUT	424d	1 c
	רעה	TEND	945a	1 c
	שלשם	THREE DAYS AGO	1026b	
	תמול	YESTERDAY	1070a	2 ac
11 3	ברית	COVENANT	136b	12
	זקן	OLD	278d	2 b
	חברון	HEBRON	289b	
	חברון	HEBRON	289b	
	כרת	CUT	504a	4
	מלך	KING	573c	5 c
	משח	ANOINT	603b	2
	שמואל	SAMUEL	1028d	1
11 4	יבוסי	JEBUSITE	*101a	1
	יבוס	JEBUS	101a	
	הלך	WALK	230d	1 1d 3a
11 5	דוד	DAVID	188a	A
	מצדה	FASTNESS	845a	
	ציון	ZION	851b	
11 6	יבוסי	JEBUSITE	101a	1
	צרויה	ZERUIAH	863b	
	ראשון	FIRST	912a	3 a1
	שר	CHIEFTAIN	978c	3 a
11 7	דוד	DAVID	188a	A
	מצד	STRONGHOLD	844d	2
11 8	בנה	BUILD	124d	1 i
	חיה	LIVE	311c	3 c
	מלוא	MILLO	571c	2
	סביב	ROUND ABOUT	686d	1 a
	שאר	REST	984c	
11 9	הלך	WALK	233b	1 4c 3
	צבא	GOD OF WAR	839c	4 c
11 10	גבור	STRONG	150b	2
	חזק	BE FIRM	305b	4
	מלך	BE KING	574b	
	מלכות	ROYAL POWER	574d	1
	על	UPON	757c	2 7c b
	עם	WITH	767c	1
11 11	אישבשת	ISHBOSHETH	36b	2
	תחכמני	HACHMONITE	315d	
	חכמוני	HACHMONITE	315d	1
	חלל	PIERCED	319c	2
	חנית	SPEAR	333d	1
	ישבבשבת	JOSHEB-BASSHEBETH	*444a	
	עדין	VOLUPTUOUS	726a	
	עור	ROUSE ONESELF	735a	
	ישבעם	JASHOBEAM	1000b	
	שלש	THREE	*1025d	3
	שלשים	THIRTY	1026c	2
	שלש	OFFICER	1026d	
	שמנה	EIGHT	*1033a	3 a
11 12	אחוחי	AHOHITE	29a	
	אלעזר	ELEAZAR	46c	C
	דודו	DODO	187d	2
	היה	BE	227b	3 4d a
11 13	אגא	AGEE	8a	
	אפסדמים	EPHES-DAMMIM	67c	
	דבק	CLING	*179d	1 a
	היה	BE	227b	3 4d a
	חיה	COMMUNITY	*312d	
	חלקה	PORTION OF GROUND	324c	1 a
	חרב	SWORD	352c	1 c
	חרף	REPROACH	*357d	
	יגע	TOIL	*388b	2
	יד	HAND	389d	1 d
	מלא	FULL	571a	
	נכה	SMITE	*646a	2 c
	עלה	GO UP	748c	2 e
	עשה	DO	795a	2 9
	פשט	STRIP OFF	*833a	1
	שערה	BARLEY	972d	1
	שמה	SHAMMAH	*1031c	3 a
11 14	חלקה	PORTION OF GROUND	324c	1 b
	יצב	STATION ONESELF	426b	A
	ישע	GIVE VICTORY	447a	3 b
	תשועה	DELIVERANCE	448b	1
11 15	חיה	COMMUNITY	*312d	
	מחנה	ENCAMPMENT	334b	3 a
	עדלם	ADULLAM	726b	
	מצודה	FASTNESS	845a	
	צור	ROCK	849c	1 a
	רפאם	REPHAIM	952b	
	שקה	GIVE TO DRINK	1052c	2
11 16	נציב	PREFECT	662d	2
	מצודה	FASTNESS	845a	
11 17	אוה	DESIRE	16b	
	בור	WELL	92b	2
	שער	GATE	1045a	2 a
11 18	אבה	BE WILLING	2c	
	בור	WELL	92b	2
	בקע	BREAK OPEN OR THROUGH	131d	2
	נסך	POUR OUT	650d	
	שאב	DRAW	980c	
	שער	GATE	1045a	2 a
11 19	אבה	BE WILLING	2c	
	דם	BLOOD	196c	2 c
	הלך	WALK	231d	1 d5 ta
	חלילה	FAR BE IT	321a	
	נפש	SOUL	659d	3 c
	שתה	DRINK	1059b	1 a
11 20	הוא	HE, SHE, IT	215d	2 a
	היה	BE	227a	3 4b
	חלל	PIERCED	319c	2
	חנית	SPEAR	333d	1
	לא	NOT	520c	
	עור	ROUSE ONESELF	735a	
11 21	בוא	COME	98d	2 f
	כבד	BE HONORED	457c	1 b
	שר	CHIEFTAIN	978c	3 a
11 22	ארי	LION	71d	
	אריאל	ARIEL	72a	3
	בור	PIT	92c	3
	בניהו	BENAIAH	125c	1
	יהוידע	JEHOIADA	220b	1
	חיל	STRENGTH	298d	1 c
	יום	DAY	398c	2 f
	ירד	GO DOWN	433a	1 g
	קבצאל	KABZEEL	868b	
	רב	MUCH	913b	1 d
	שלג	SNOW	1017a	
	שנים	TWO	1041a	1 a
11 23	ארג	WEAVE	71a	
	גזל	TEAR AWAY	159d	
	הרג	KILL	247a	1 a
	חמש	FIVE	331d	1 a
	חנית	SPEAR	333d	1
	ירד	GO DOWN	432d	1 b
	מדה	SIZE	551c	2
	מצרי	EGYPTIAN	596a	2
	מצרי	EGYPTIAN	596a	1
	מנור	BEAM	644d	
	מראה	VISION	*909d	1 a
	שבט	ROD	987a	1 a
11 24	בניהו	BENAIAH	125c	1
	יהוידע	JEHOIADA	220b	1
11 25	הנה	BEHOLD	243d	
	כבד	BE HONORED	457c	1 b
	כי	THAT	472b	1 da
	שום	TO PLACE	964a	3 d
	משמעת	OBEDIENT BAND	1036a	1
11 26	אלחנן	ELHANAN	45a	
	גבור	STRONG	150b	2
	דודו	DODO	187d	3
	חיל	STRENGTH	298d	1 c
	עשהאל	ASAHEL	795c	1
11 27	אלקא	ELIKA	45d	
	ביתפלט	BETH-PELET	112c	
	הרורי	HARORITE	248b	
	הררי	HARARITE	251c	1 b
	חלץ	HELEZ	323b	1
	הרודי	HARODITE	353d	
	פלני	PELONITE	813d	
	שמה	SHAMMAH	1031c	3 b
11 28	אביעזר	ABIEZER	4c	
	עירא	IRA	747a	2 a
	ענתתי	ANATHOTHITE	779a	
	עקש	IKKESH	786a	
	תקועי	TEKOITE	1075d	
11 29	אחוחי	AHOHITE	29a	
	מבני	MEBUNNAI	125d	
	חשתי	HASHATHITE	302a	
	סבכי	SIBBECAI	687c	
	עילי	ILAI	743d	
	צלמון	ZALMON	854a	
11 30	בענה	BAANAH	128d	2
	חלב	HELEB	*317a	
	חלד	HELED	317c	
	חלדי	HELDAI	317c	1
	מהרי	MAHARAI	555b	
	נטפתי	NETOPHATHITE	643b	
11 31	אתי	ITTAI	87b	2
	בנימין	BENJAMIN	122d	1
	בניהו	BENAIAH	125c	2
	גבעה	GIBEAH	149b	2
	פרעתוני	PIRATHONITE	828d	
	ריבי	RIBAI	937a	
11 32	אביעלבון	ABI-ALBON	3d	
	ביתהערבה	BETH-ARABAH	112c	
	געש	GAASH	172b	
	הדי	HIDDAI	213b	
	חורי	HURAI	301b	
	נחל	WADY	636c	2
	פעל	DOING	821c	1 c
11 33	אליחבא	ELIAHBA	45b	
	בחרמי	BAHARUMITE	104d	
	ברחמי	BARHUMITE	138c	
11 34	עזמות	AZMAVETH	740a	1 a
	גוני	GUNITES	157b	
	גוני	GIZONITE	159b	
	יהונתן	JONATHAN	221a	5
	הררי	HARARITE	251b	1 a
	חשם	HASHEM	251c	
	ישן	JASHEN	445d	
	שגה	SHAGEE	993b	
11 35	אור	UR	22b	
	אחיאם	AHIAM	26c	
	אחסבי	AHASBAI	*29d	
	אליפל	ELIPHAL	45c	
	אליפלט	ELIPHELET	45d	B
	הררי	HARARITE	251c	
	שכר	SACHAR	969b	1
11 36	אחיהו	AHIJAH	26d	7
	חפר	HEPHER	343d	3
	מכרתי	MECHERATHITE	569d	
	פלני	PELONITE	813d	
11 37	אצבי	EZBAI	23c	
	חצרו	HEZRO	348a	
	כרמלי	CARMELITE	502b	
	נערי	NAARAI	655c	
11 38	מבחר	MIBHAR	104d	
	בני	BANI	*125b	1
	גרי	GADITE	*151d	
11 39	הגרי	HAGRITE	212c	3
	יואל	JOEL	222b	6
	נתן	NATHAN	681d	5 b
	צובא	ZOBAH	*844c	
	באארתי	BEEROTHITE	92b	1
	כלי	IMPLEMENT	479d	2 a
	נחרי	NAHARAI	638a	
	עמוני	AMMONITE	770a	
	צלק	ZELEK	854c	
	צרויה	ZERUIAH	863b	
11 40	גרב	GAREB	173a	1
	יתרי	ITHRITE	452b	
	עירא	IRA	747a	2 b
11 41	אחלי	AHLAI	29a	2
	זבד	ZABAD	256b	2
	חתי	HITTITE	366d	1
11 42	עדינא	ADINA	726d	
	ראובני	REUBENITE	910a	
	שיזא	SHIZA	1009d	
11 43	יהרשפט	JEHOSHAPHAT	221d	5
	חנן	HANAN	336d	1
	מעכה	MAACAH	590d	1 b
	מתני	MITHNITE	608c	
11 44	חותם	HOTHAM	368b	2
	יעיאל	JEIEL	418b	3 b
	עזיא	UZZIA	739d	
	ערערי	AROERITE	793a	
	עשתרתי	ASHTERATHITE	800c	
	שמע	SHAMA	1035a	
11 45	ידיעאל	JEDIAEL	396a	2
	יוחא	JOHA	398a	2
	שמרי	SHIMRI	1037c	2
	תיצי	TIZITE	1066d	
11 46	אליאל	ELIEL	45a	A
	אלנעם	ELNAAM	46b	
	מחוים	MAHAVITE	296a	
	ישויה	JOSHAVIAH	444d	
	יתמה	ITHMAH	450d	
	מואבי	MOABITISH	556a	
	יריבי	JERIBAI	937b	
11 47	אליאל	ELIEL	45a	A
	מצביה	MEZOBAITE	594b	
	עובד	OBED	714d	3
	יעשיאל	JAASIEL	795c	1
12 1	יהודה	JUDAH	397b	1 1
	ל	TO	511b	1 ga
	עזר	HELP	740c	
	עצר	RESTRAIN	783c	1
	צקלג	ZIKLAG	862c	
	קיש	KISH	885c	1
12 2	חץ	ARROW	346c	1
	ימן	GO TO THE RIGHT	412b	
	נשק	BE EQUIPPED WITH	676c	
	קשת	BOW	906a	1 b
	שמאל	TAKE THE LEFT	970a	3

Ch v.	Heb	Eng	Page	Sec
12 3	אחיעזר	AHIEZER	27b	2
	ברכה	BERACAH	139d	2
	גבעתי	GIBEATHITE	149b	
	יהוא	JEHU	219d	3
	יהואש	JEHOASH	220a	5
	יזיאל	JEZIEL	402b	
	עזמות	AZMAVETH	740a	1 b
	ענתתי	ANATHOTHITE	779a	
	פלט	PELET	812b	2
	שמעה	SHEMAAH	1035a	
12 4	גבעני	GIBEONITE	149c	
	גדרתי	GEDERATHITE	155b	
	יחזיאל	JAHAZIEL	303c	1
	ירמיה	JEREMIAH	941d	5
	ישמעיה	ISHMAIAH	1036a	1
12 5	אלעוזי	ELUZAI	46b	
	בעליה	BEALIAH	128c	
	יהוזבד	JEHOZABAD	220a	2 a
	יהוחנן	JEHOHANAN	220b	2 a
	חריפי	HARUPHITE	358b	
	שמריה	SHEMARIAH	*1037d	1
	שפטיה	SHEPHATIAH	1049b	2 b
12 6	אלקנה	ELKANAH	46c	D
	חריפי	HARUPHITE	358b	
	ישיהו	ISSHIJAH	674d	1
	קרחי	KORAHITES	*901c	
	שמריה	SHEMARIAH	1037d	1
12 7	גדור	GEDOR	155b	1
	יועזר	JOEZER	222c	
	יועאלה	JOELAH	*418d	
	ישיהו	ISSHIJAH	674d	1
	עזראל	AZAREL	741a	1
	קרחי	KORAHITES	901c	
	ירחם	JEROHAM	934a	2 a
	ישבעם	JASHOBEAM	1000b	
12 8	אריה	LION	71d	
	בדל	BE DIVIDED	95c	1 c
	גדי	GADITE	151d	
	הר	MOUNTAIN	250c	1 g
	זבדיהו	ZEBADIAH	256c	4
	יועאלה	JOELAH	418d	
	מלחמה	WAR	*536b	
	ערך	ARRANGE	789d	1 e
	פנה	FACE	816a	14
	צבי	GAZELLE	*840a	
	מצד	FASTNESS	844d	1
	צנה	LARGE SHIELD	*857a	
	רוח	BREATH	925d	9 b
	ירחם	JEROHAM	934a	4
	רמח	SPEAR	*942b	
12 9	אליאב	ELIAB	45a	E
	ל	TO	511b	1 ga
	ל	TO	514b	5 fb
	מלחמה	WAR	536b	
	מהר	HASTEN	555a	1
	נתן	PUT	680d	2 c
	עבדיהו	OBADIAH	716a	26
	ערך	ARRANGE	789d	1 e
	צבא	WAR	839b	2
	צבי	GAZELLE	840b	
	מצד	FASTNESS	844d	1
	צנה	LARGE SHIELD	857a	
	ראש	HEAD	911a	3 a
	רמח	SPEAR	942b	
12 10	עזר	EZER	740d	3
	ראש	HEAD	911a	3 a
	רביעי	FOURTH	918a	1
	ירמיה	JEREMIAH	941d	6
	משמנה	MISHMANNAH	*1032d	
12 11	אליאל	ELIEL	45a	A
	עתי	ATTAI	774c	2
	שביעי	SEVENTH	988d	1
	משמנה	MISHMANNAH	1032d	
12 12	אלזבד	ELZABAD	44d	A
	תשיעי	NINTH	1077d	
12 13	ביתעזמות	BETH-AZMAVETH	112b	
	יהוחנן	JEHOHANAN	220b	2 b
	עשירי	TENTH	798a	1
	עשתי	ONE	799d	
	קטן	SMALL	882a	2 b2
	ירמיה	JEREMIAH	941d	3
12 14	גד	GAD	151c	1 b
	מכבני	MACHBANNAI	460a	
	מאה	HUNDRED	548a	1 a5
	צבא	ARMY	839a	1 a
	קטן	SMALL	882a	2 b2
12 15	הם	THEY	241c	4 bg
	מורח	PLACE OF SUNRISE	*281a	2 c3
	חדש	NEW MOON	294d	2 b2
	ל	TO	511d	1 h
	עמק	VALE	*771a	
	ראשון	FIRST	911d	2 a
12 16	ברח	FLEE	138a	2
	גדיה	BANK OF RIVER	152a	
	גדיה	BANK OF RIVER	152a	
	מורח	PLACE OF SUNRISE	281a	2 c3
	ל	TO	511c	1 gb
	מלא	FILL	*570b	2
	מלא	FILL	570d	2
	עמק	VALE	771a	
	ענק	NECK	778c	
	מעב	WEST	788a	
	מצד	FASTNESS	844d	1
12 17	ראשון	FIRST	911d	2 a
	בנימן	BENJAMIN	122d	1
	חמס	VIOLENCE	329c	

Ch v.	Heb	Eng	Page	Sec
	יחד	UNION	403a	1
	יכח	DECIDE	406d	1
	לבב	HEART	523c	22
	עד	UNTIL	725c	3 1
	עדר	HELP	727b	
	על	UPON	757d	27c c
	מצד	FASTNESS	844d	1
	רמה	BEGUILE	941a	
12 18	ישי	JESSE	445b	
	כף	HOLLOW OF THE HAND	496d	1 d7
	לא	NOT	520a	4 aa
	לבש	PUT ON	528b	F
	עדר	HELP	727b	
	עזר	HELP	740b	
	רמה	BEGUILE	941a	
	שליש	OFFICER	*1026d	
12 19	גדוד	BAND	151b	1
	נפל	FALL	657c	4 b
	עם	WITH	767b	1
	עמשי	AMASAI	772a	1
	קבל	RECEIVE	867a	1
	שליש	OFFICER	1026d	
12 20	אליהו	ELIHU	45b	C
	עצה	ADVICE	420a	
	נפל	FALL	657c	4 b
	סרן	TYRANT	710c	
	עזר	HELP	740b	
	צלתי	ZILLETHAI	*853c	2
	צקלג	ZIKLAG	*862c	
12 21	יהוזבד	JEHOZABAD	220a	2 c
	יהוזבד	JEHOZABAD	220a	2 b
	ידיעאל	JEDIAEL	396a	2
	מיכאל	MICHAEL	567c	7
	נפל	FALL	657c	4 b
	עדנה	ADNAH	726d	2
	עזר	HELP	727b	
	עם	WITH	767c	1 a
	צלתי	ZILLETHAI	853c	2
	צקלג	ZIKLAG	862c	
	שר	CHIEFTAIN	978b	3 a
12 22	גדוד	BAND	151b	1
	גדול	GREAT	153a	2
	עדר	HELP	727b	
	עדר	HELP	*727b	
	עזר	HELP	740c	
	עת	TIME	773c	1 b
	צבא	ARMY	839a	1 a
	שר	CHIEFTAIN	978b	3 a
12 23	חברון	HEBRON	*289b	
	חלץ	EQUIP FOR WAR	*323a	2
	מלוכת	ROYAL POWER	574d	1
	עד	UNTIL	725c	3 3
	עדר	HELP	727b	
	עזר	HELP	740b	
	על	UPON	757b	27c aa
	פה	MOUTH	805c	6 ba
12 24	חברון	HEBRON	289b	
	חלץ	EQUIP FOR WAR	323a	2
	חלץ	EQUIP FOR WAR	*323a	2
	נשא	LIFT	671a	2 a
	סבב	TURN ABOUT	686c	1 b
	צנה	LARGE SHIELD	*857a	
	רמח	SPEAR	*942b	
12 25	חלץ	EQUIP FOR WAR	323a	2
	צבא	WAR	839b	2
	צנה	LARGE SHIELD	857a	
	רמח	SPEAR	942b	
12 26	לוי	LEVITE	*532b	2
12 27	אהרן	AARON	14d	
	בן	SON	121a	1 je
	לוי	LEVITE	532d	2
12 28	אהרן	AARON	14d	
	גבור	STRONG	150b	2
	יהוידע	JEHOIADA	220c	1
	נגיד	LEADER	618a	4
	עם	WITH	767b	1 a
	עשרים	TWENTY	797d	1 2c
	בית	HOUSE	109d	5 c
12 29	נער	YOUTH	655a	1 e
	עשרים	TWENTY	797d	1 2c
	מרבות	INCREASE	*916b	
	משמרת	GUARD	*1038d	1
12 30	אפרים	EPHRAIM	68b	2
	בנמין	BENJAMIN	122d	B
	הנה	HITHERTO	244d	B
	שם	NAME	*1028a	2 b1
	משמרת	GUARD	1038c	1
	משמרת	GUARD	1038c	4 a
12 31	אפרים	EPHRAIM	68b	2
	מנשה	MANASSEH	*586c	1 b1 g
	מטה	TRIBE	641d	3
	שם	NAME	1028a	2 b1
12 32	בינה	UNDERSTANDING	108a	3
	יששכר	ISSACHAR	*441a	1
	מאה	HUNDRED	548a	1 b5
	מלך	BE KING	574b	
	מנשה	MANASSEH	586c	1 b1 g
	עת	TIME	773d	2 b
12 33	ו	AND	253b	1 ia
	חמשים	FIFTY	332b	1 b2
	ידע	KNOW	394c	5
	יששכר	ISSACHAR	441a	1
	כלי	IMPLEMENT	*479d	2 a
	מלחמה	WAR	*536c	

Ch v.	Heb	Eng	Page	Sec
	מאה	HUNDRED	548a	1 b5
	ערך	ARRANGE	789c	1 d
	צבא	WAR	839b	2
12 34	זבולן	ZEBULUN	259d	2
	חמשים	FIFTY	332b	1 b2
	כלי	IMPLEMENT	479d	2 a
	לא	NOT	520a	4 aa
	מלחמה	WAR	536c	
	עדר	HELP	727b	
	עם	WITH	767b	1 a
	ערך	ARRANGE	789c	1 d
12 35	צנה	LARGE SHIELD	*857a	
	אלף	THOUSAND	48d	1 a
	דני	DANITES	193a	
	חנית	SPEAR	333d	1
	ערך	ARRANGE	789c	1 d
	צנה	LARGE SHIELD	857a	
12 36	שמנה	EIGHT	*1033a	3 b
	אשר	ASHER	81b	2
	ערך	ARRANGE	789c	1 d
	ערך	ARRANGE	789c	1 d
	צבא	WAR	839b	2
	ארבעים	FORTY	917b	1 a
	שמנה	EIGHT	1033a	3 b
12 37	גדי	GADITE	151d	
	ירדן	JORDAN	434c	
	כלי	IMPLEMENT	*479d	2 a
	מלחמה	WAR	*536c	
	מנשה	MANASSEH	*586c	1 b2 d
	עבר	REGION ACROSS	719c	1 a
	ערך	ARRANGE	789c	1 d
	צבא	WAR	839b	2
	ראובני	REUBENITE	910a	
	ארבעים	FORTY	917b	1 a
12 38	חברון	HEBRON	*289b	
	יחד	UNION	*403a	1
	כלי	IMPLEMENT	479d	2 a
	מלחמה	WAR	*536b	
	מלחמה	WAR	536c	
	מלך	BE KING	574b	
	מנשה	MANASSEH	586c	1 b2 d
	עדר	HELP	727b	
	מערכה	ROW	790a	1 a
	ראובני	REUBENITE	910a	
	שארית	REST	*984d	1
	שלם	COMPLETE	1024a	3
12 39	חברון	HEBRON	289b	
	כון	ESTABLISH	466b	2 a
	לבב	HEART	524a	2 6a
	מלחמה	WAR	536b	
	מלך	BE KING	574b	
	עדר	HELP	727b	
	מערכה	ROW	790a	1 a
	שארית	REST	984c	1
12 40	מאכל	FOOD	38b	
	בקר	CATTLE	133b	1 a
	בקר	CATTLE	133b	1 a
	יששכר	ISSACHAR	441a	1
	לחם	FOOD	537a	1 a
	פרד	MULE	825d	
	נפתלי	NAPHTALI	837a	2 b
	צמוק	BUNCH OF RAISINS	856a	
	קמח	FLOUR	*888a	
	קרב	NEAR	*898c	2 a
12 41	מאכל	FOOD	38b	
	דבלה	PRESSED FIG-CAKE	179b	
	חמור	HE-ASS	331b	3
	יששכר	ISSACHAR	441a	1
	נפתלי	NAPHTALI	837a	2 b
	צמוק	BUNCH OF RAISINS	856a	
	קמח	FLOUR	888a	
	קרב	NEAR	898c	2 a
13 1	יעץ	CONSULT	419d	
	ל	TO	514c	5 fd
	נגיד	LEADER	618a	4
	שר	CHIEFTAIN	978b	3 b
13 2	ארץ	EARTH	76c	5
	מגרש	COMMON-LAND	177b	
	יהוה	YAHWEH	218d	2 1c
	טוב	PLEASING	373c	5
	כהן	PRIEST	464a	7
	לוי	LEVITE	533a	2 a
	מן	OUT OF	579d	2 d
	על	UPON	757b	27c aa
	על	UPON	758a	28
	עם	WITH	767b	1 a
	פרץ	BREAK THROUGH	829c	
	קבץ	GATHER	867d	1
	קהל	ASSEMBLY	874d	2 a
13 3	ארון	CHEST	75c	3 d
	בנהדד	BEN-HADAD	122b	3
	דרש	SEEK	205b	2 a
	סבב	TURN ABOUT	686c	1 d
13 4	ישר	BE STRAIGHT	448c	2
	קהל	ASSEMBLY	874d	2 a
13 5	בוא	COME	98d	2 e
	חמת	HAMATH	333a	
	מצים	EGYPT	695c	1 a
	עד	UNTIL	725c	3 1
	קהל	ASSEMBLE AS	875a	1
	קריתיערים	KIRIATH-JEARIM	900c	
	שיחור	SHIHOR	1009d	
13 6	ארון	CHEST	75c	3 e
	בעלה	BAALAH	128b	
	בעלה	BAALAH	128c	
	דוד	DAVID	*187d	

1 CHRONICLES

206

Ch v.	Heb	Eng	Page	Sec
16 5	לוי	LEVITE	533a	3 ld
	שרת	SERVE	1057b	2 b
	אליאב	ELIAB	45a	F
	אסף	ASAPH	63a	2
	הלל	PRAISE	*238c	2 e
	זכריהו	ZECHARIAH	272b	0 a
	יחיאל	JEHIEL	313c	1
	יעיאל	JEIEL	418b	2 c1
	כלי	INSTRUMENT	479d	2 b
	כנור	LYRE	490a	
	נבל	HARP	614c	
	מתתיהו	MATTITHIAH	682d	1
	עבדאדם	OBED-EDOM	714d	2
	מצלתים	CYMBALS	853a	
	שמירמות	SHEMIRAMOTH	1029a	1
	שמע	HEAR	1034c	1 b
	משנה	SECOND	1041d	3 a
16 6	ארון	CHEST	75c	3 f
	יחזיאל	JAHAZIEL	303c	2
	חצצרה	CLARION	348c	2 c
	תמיד	CONTINUITY	556c	2 a
16 7	אז	THEN	23a	1 d
	אסף	ASAPH	63a	2
	ידה	PRAISE	392c	1 b
	נתן	GIVE	679d	1 x
	ראש	HEAD	911b	4 b
16 8	ידה	PRAISE	392c	1 b
	עלילה	WANTONNESS	760b	2
16 9	זמר	MAKE MUSIC	274a	1
	פלא	BE SURPASSING	810d	4
	שיח	MUSE	967b	3 a
	שיר	SING	1010d	
16 10	בקש	SEEK	134d	3 c
	הלל	BE BOASTFUL	239a	2
	לב	HEART	525c	2 9a
	קדש	APARTNESS	871c	1 c
	שמח	REJOICE	970b	2 a
	שם	NAME	1028c	3
16 11	בקש	SEEK	134d	3 b
	דרש	SEEK	205b	3 a
	תמיד	CONTINUITY	556b	1 a
	עז	STRENGTH	739d	3 c
16 12	מופת	WONDER	68d	1
	זכר	REMEMBER	269d	1 1 d
	משפט	JUDGMENT	1048c	1 f
16 13	בחור	CHOSEN	104c	
	זרע	SOWING	283a	4 f
	סור	TURN ASIDE	694b	1
	עבד	SLAVE	714a	3
16 14	משפט	JUDGMENT	1048c	1 f
16 15	ברית	COVENANT	136c	2 2b
	ברית	COVENANT	137a	3 2
	דבר	WORD	182d	12a
	דור	GENERATION	190a	2 c
	זכר	REMEMBER	270a	14 b
	עולם	LONG DURATION	762c	2 d
16 16	כרת	CUT	503d	4
	יצחק	ISAAC	850c	
	שבועה	OATH	990a	2
16 17	ברית	COVENANT	137a	3 2
	חק	SOMETHING PRE-SCRIBED	349c	6 c
	עולם	LONG DURATION	762c	2 d
	עמד	STAND	764d	5
16 18	חבל	CORD	286d	3
	כנען	CANAAN	488d	2 a
16 19	גור	SOJOURN	157d	1
	מעט	A FEW	590c	2
	מת	MALE	607b	2 a
	מספר	NUMBER	709a	1 a
16 20	גוי	NATION	156d	1 c
	הלך	WALK	236a	1 b
	ממלכה	KINGDOM	575a	1
16 21	יכח	REPROVE	407a	5 a
	נוח	REST	629a	B 6
	עשק	OPPRESS	798d	2
16 22	משיח	ANOINTED	603d	5
	נביא	PROPHET	611d	1
	נגע	TOUCH	619a	3
	רעע	BE EVIL	949c	1
16 23	אל	TO	39d	1
	בשר	BEAR TIDINGS	142b	3
	יום	DAY	400b	7 e1
	ישועה	DELIVERANCE	447b	3
	ל	TO	517b	6 c
	מן	FROM	582b	5 d1
	שיר	SING	1010d	
16 24	כבד	HONOR	459b	6 b
	ספר	COUNT	708a	1
	פלא	BE SURPASSING	810d	4
16 25	גדול	GREAT	153b	6 c
	הלל	PRAISE	239a	2
	ירא	BE REVERED	431d	3 a
16 26	אלהים	GOD	43c	1
	אליל	WORTHLESSNESS	47c	B
	הוד	SPLENDOUR	217a	2
16 27	הדר	SPLENDOUR	214b	2
	חדוה	JOY	292d	
	עז	STRENGTH	739a	3 a
16 28	יהב	ASCRIBE	396a	4
	כבוד	HONOR	459b	6 b
	עז	STRENGTH	739b	3 b
	עם	PEOPLE	766d	5 e
16 29	הדרה	ADORNMENT	214c	1
	יהב	ASCRIBE	396a	4
	כבוד	HONOR	459b	6 b
	נשא	LIFT	671b	2 e
	קדש	APARTNESS	872b	4 b
	שחה	BOW DOWN	1005c	2 b
16 30	בל	NOT	115b	
	חול	WHIRL	297a	2 b
	תבל	WORLD	*385d	
	תבל	WORLD	385d	
	כון	BE FIRM	465c	1 a
	מוט	SHAKE	557a	
16 31	מלך	BE KING	574a	
	שמח	REJOICE	970b	2 a
16 32	מלא	THAT WHICH FILLS	571b	3
	עלץ	REJOICE	763b	
	רעם	THUNDER	947b	
	שדה	FIELD	961d	3
16 33	יער	WOOD	420d	F
	פנה	FACE	818a	2 5b
	רנן	GIVE A RINGING CRY	943c	
16 34	שפט	JUDGE	1047d	3 d
	חסד	GOODNESS	339b	2 3c
	טוב	PLEASANT	374d	9 b
	ידה	PRAISE	392c	1 b
	עולם	LONG DURATION	762b	2 c
16 35	אלהים	GOD	44c	4 bb
	גוי	NATION	156d	1 c
	תהלה	PRAISE	240b	4
	ידה	PRAISE	392c	1 b
	ישע	DELIVER	446d	1 b
	ישע	DELIVERANCE	447a	2
	קבץ	GATHER	868a	1
	קדש	APARTNESS	871c	1 c
	שבח	PRAISE	986d	
16 36	אמן	VERILY	53b	
	ברך	BLESS	138c	2 a
	הלל	PRAISE	238c	2 e
	עולם	LONG DURATION	763a	2 m
16 37	הימן	HEMAN	54d	
	אסף	ASAPH	63a	2
	דבר	WORD	183b	4 1
	יום	DAY	400c	7 e3
	ל	TO	512a	3 b
	תמיד	CONTINUITY	556b	1 a
	עזב	LEAVE	737a	1 c
	שרת	SERVE	1057b	2 b
16 38	חסה	HOSAH	340b	1
	ידותון	JEDUTHUN	s 393a	
	עבדאדם	OBED-EDOM	714d	2
16 39	במה	HIGH PLACE	119b	3
	גבעון	GIBEON	149c	
	כהן	PRIEST	463c	4
	משכן	DWELLING-PLACE	1015d	2 c
16 40	בקר	MORNING	134a	1 e
	מזבח	ALTAR	258c	3 b
	תורה	LAW	436b	2 b3
	תמיד	CONTINUITY	556c	1 a
	עלה	GO UP	750a	8
	עלה	WHOLE BURNT OF-FERING	750d	
	עלה	WHOLE BURNT OF-FERING	750d	
16 41	ערב	SUNSET	787d	1 a
	הימן	HEMAN	54d	
	אסף	ASAPH	63a	2
	ברר	SELECT	141a	2
	חסד	GOODNESS	339b	2 3c
	ידה	PRAISE	392c	1 b
	ידותון	JEDUTHUN	s 393a	
	עולם	LONG DURATION	762b	2 c
	שאר	REST	984c	
	שם	NAME	1028a	2 a
16 42	הימן	HEMAN	54d	
	אסף	ASAPH	63a	2
	חצצרה	CLARION	348c	2 c
	ידותון	JEDUTHUN	s 393a	
	ידותון	JEDUTHUN	s 393a	
	כלי	INSTRUMENT	479d	2 b
	מצלתים	CYMBALS	853a	
	שער	GATE	1045b	3 b
16 43	ברך	BLESS	139a	2
	הלך	WALK	231b	1 d3 gd
	סבב	TURN ABOUT	685c	3
17 1	אני	I	59c	
	ארז	CEDAR	72d	2
	בית	HOUSE	108d	1 ag
	יריעה	CURTAIN	438c	
	נתן	NATHAN	681d	2
17 2	לבב	HEART	523c	2 2
	נתן	NATHAN	681d	2
17 3	דבר	WORD	*182c	12a
	היה	BECOME	226c	2 2f
	נתן	NATHAN	681d	2
17 4	אמר	SAY	56a	1
	דוד	DAVID	188a	
	ה	INTERROG PART	*209a	1 b
	לא	NOT	518d	1 ac
	אהל	TENT	14b	3
17 5	בית	HOUSE	109a	1 ae 0
	יום	DAY	401b	7 1
	מן	FROM	582b	5 d1
	משכן	DWELLING-PLACE	1015d	2 c
17 6	ארז	CEDAR	72d	2
	בית	HOUSE	108d	1 ag
	דבר	SPEAK	181b	3 d
	הלך	WALK	236c	
	צוה	GIVE CHARGE OVER	845d	1 d
	רעה	TEND	945a	1 c
	שבט	TRIBE	*987b	2 c
17 7	אחר	BEHIND	30b	4 a
	אחר	BEHIND	30b	4 aa
	דוד	DAVID	188a	
	צבא	GOD OF WAR	839c	4 c
17 8	גדול	GREAT	153b	6 b
	הלך	WALK	230d	1 1d 3a
	כרת	CUT OFF	504c	2 c
	עשה	DO	794c	2 1d
17 9	בלה	BECOME OLD AND WORN OUT	115a	A
	בן	SON	121d	8 b
	יסף	DO AGAIN	415c	2 a
	נטע	PLANT	642c	2
	עולה	INJUSTICE	732c	1
	ראשון	FIRST	912a	3 a1
	רגז	BE AGITATED	919b	
	שום	TO PLACE	963d	3 b
	שכן	SETTLE DOWN	1015a	1 a
17 10	בית	HOUSE	109d	5 b
	בנה	BUILD	124d	2 a
	כנע	HUMBLE	488c	2
	מן	FROM	583d	9 b2
	צוה	GIVE CHARGE OVER	845d	1 d
	שפט	JUDGE	1047b	1 b
17 11	זרע	SOWING	282d	4 c
	כון	ESTABLISH	466a	1 a
	כי	WHEN	473b	2 a
	מלא	BE FULL	570b	1 b
	מלכות	ROYAL POWER	574d	1
	קום	STAND	878d	3
17 12	כון	ESTABLISH	466a	1 b
	כסא	THRONE	*491a	3 a
	עולם	LONG DURATION	762c	2 f
17 13	בן	SON	120b	1 c
	חסד	GOODNESS	339a	2 1e
	סור	TURN ASIDE	693d	2
	מעם	FROM WITH	*769a	B
17 14	כון	BE FIRM	465c	1 b
	כסא	THRONE	491a	3 a
	מלכות	ROYAL POWER	574d	1
	עולם	LONG DURATION	762c	2 f
	עמד	STAND	764d	5
17 15	חזון	VISION	303a	3
	חזיון	VISION	*303b	3
	נתן	NATHAN	681d	2
17 16	בוא	COME	99b	2
	יהוה	YAHWEH	219a	2 1h
	הלם	HITHER	*240d	
	ישב	SIT	442c	1 a
	שפט	JUDGE	1047b	1 b
17 17	אדם	MAN	9b	2
	מגן	SHIELD	171c	
	יהוה	YAHWEH	219a	2 1h
	מן	FROM	583d	9 b2
	נוה	ABODE OF FLOCKS	627c	1 a
	מעלה	STEP	752b	5
	קטן	BE SMALL	881d	
	ראה	TO SEE	908a	8 c
	רחק	DISTANT	935c	2 b
	תאר	FORM	1061b	
	תור	PLAIT	1064c	
17 18	ידע	KNOW	394b	2
	יסף	DO AGAIN	*415c	2 a
	יסף	DO AGAIN	415c	2 a
	כבוד	HONOR	459b	6 a
17 19	גדולה	GREATNESS	153c	B
	ידע	MAKE KNOWN	395a	
	לב	HEART	*524c	2 2
17 20	יהוה	YAHWEH	*219a	2 1h
17 21	גדולה	GREATNESS	153c	B
	גוי	NATION	156d	1 c
	גרש	DRIVE OUT	177a	
	יהוה	YAHWEH	*219a	2 1h
	ירא	CAUSE FEAR	431d	2
	מי	WHO	566c	E b
	מצרים	EGYPT	595d	1 b2
	פדה	RANSOM	804a	3 a
	שום	TO PLACE	964c	5 b
	שם	NAME	1028a	2 b1
17 22	אלהים	GOD	44b	4 a
	יהוה	YAHWEH	*219a	2 1h
	עולם	LONG DURATION	762d	2 f
17 23	אמן	CONFIRM	53a	4
	יהוה	YAHWEH	*219a	2 1h
	עולם	LONG DURATION	762c	2 f
17 24	אמן	CONFIRM	52d	2
	בית	HOUSE	109d	5 c
	גדל	BECOME GREAT	*152a	3 b
	דוד	DAVID	188a	
	כון	BE FIRM	465d	1 b
	עולם	LONG DURATION	762c	2 f
	צבא	GOD OF WAR	839c	4 b
17 25	אזן	EAR	24b	3
	בית	HOUSE	109d	5 b
	בנה	BUILD	124d	2 a
	מצא	FIND	593c	4
17 26	אלהים	GOD	43d	3
	דוד	DAVID	188a	
	טובה	WELFARE	375d	2 a
17 27	ברך	BLESS	139a	2 a
	ברך	BLESS	139b	2 a

1 CHRONICLES

Ch	v.	Heb	Eng	Page	Sec
		יאל	SHOW-WILLING-NESS	384b	3
		עולם	LONG DURATION	762d	2f
18	1	בת	DAUGHTER	123d	4
		גת	GATH	387d	
		כנע	HUMBLE	488c	2
18	2	מנחה	TRIBUTE	585a	2
		עבד	SLAVE	713d	2
		עבד	SLAVE	714c	7
18	3	הדדעזר	HADADEZER	*212d	
		הדרעזר	HADADEZER	214c	
		חמת	HAMATH	333a	
		יד	HAND	390b	2
		יד	MONUMENT	390c	4a
		נהר	STREAM	625d	1
		נצב	STAND	662c	4
		נצב	STAND	662c	2
		פרת	EUPHRATES	832b	
		צובא	ZOBAH	844c	
18	4	אלף	THOUSAND	48d	1a
		אלף	THOUSAND	48d	1a
		יתר	LEAVE OVER	451c	1a
		לכד	CAPTURE	540a	1
		מאה	HUNDRED	547d	1a1
		עקר	HAMSTRING	785d	
		עשרים	TWENTY	797d	11a
		פרש	HORSEMAN	832a	
		רגלי	ON FOOT	920b	
		רכב	CHARIOT	939b	1
18	5	ארם	ARAM	74b	A
		דמשק	DAMASCUS	200a	
		הדדעזר	HADADEZER	*212d	
		הדרעזר	HADADEZER	214c	
		עזר	HELP	740b	
		צובא	ZOBAH	844c	
18	6	ארם	ARAM	74c	B
		דמשק	DAMASCUS	200a	
		היה	BECOME	226b	2 2d
		הלך	WALK	230d	1 1d 3a
		ישע	DELIVER	446d	1b
		ישע	GIVE VICTORY	447a	3b
		ל	TO	512a	3b
		מנחה	TRIBUTE	585a	2
		עבד	SLAVE	713d	2
		עבד	SLAVE	714c	7
18	7	הדדעזר	HADADEZER	*212d	
		הדרעזר	HADADEZER	214c	
		על	UPON	753a	2 1a a
		שלט	SHIELD	1020d	
18	8	בטח	BETAH	*105c	
		הדדעזר	HADADEZER	*212d	
		הדרעזר	HADADEZER	214c	
		טבחת	TIBHATH	371a	
		ידע	MAKE KNOWN	395a	
		ים	SEA	411a	7
		כון	CUN	467b	
		עמוד	PILLAR	765b	2
		רב	MUCH	913a	1a1
18	9	הדרעזר	HADADEZER	214c	
		חמת	HAMATH	333a	
		צובא	ZOBAH	844c	
		תעו	TOI	1073d	
18	10	ברך	BLESS	139b	4c
		הדדעזר	HADADEZER	*212d	
		הדורם	HADORAM	213b	2
		הדרעזר	HADADEZER	214c	
		הדרעזר	HADADEZER	214c	
		יהורם	JEHORAM	221b	4
		היה	BE	227a	3 4b
		זהב	GOLD	263c	1
		מלחמה	WAR	536b	
		שאל	ASK	982a	2a
		תעו	TOI	1073d	
18	11	אדום	EDOM	10c	2
		ארם	ARAM	74c	A
		כסף	SILVER	494b	4
		עמלק	AMALEK	766a	
		עמון	AMMON	770a	
		קדש	BE SET APART	873b	1b
18	12	אדום	EDOM	10c	2
		גיא	VALLEY	161b	C
		דוד	DAVID	188b	J
		מלח	SALT	572a	
		שמנה	EIGHT	1033a	2b
18	13	הלך	WALK	230d	1 1d 3a
		ישע	DELIVER	446d	1b
		ישע	GIVE VICTORY	447a	3b
		נציב	PREFECT	662d	2
		עבד	SLAVE	713d	2
		עבד	SLAVE	714c	7
18	14	היה	BE	227c	3 5a
		צדקה	RIGHTEOUSNESS	842a	1a
18	15	אחילוד	AHILUD	27a	1
		יהושפט	JEHOSHAPHAT	221d	3
		זכר	REMEMBER	271a	4
		צבא	ARMY	839a	1a
		צרויה	ZERUIAH	863b	
18	16	אבימלך	ABIMELECH	4c	4
		אחיטוב	AHITUB	*27a	2
		אחימלך	AHIMELECH	27a	1
		כהן	PRIEST	463c	4
		ספר	ENUMERATOR	708b	1b
		ידך	RIGHTEOUS	843b	1a
		שריה	SERAIAH	976a	1
		שושא	SHAVSHA	1004c	
18	17	בן	SON	*120d	1ja

Ch	v.	Heb	Eng	Page	Sec
		בניהו	BENAIAH	125c	1
		יהוידע	JEHOIADA	220b	1
		יד	HAND	391b	5f
		כרתי	CHERETHITE	504d	
		פלתי	PELETHITES	814c	
19	1	ראשון	FIRST	911d	2b
		מות	DIE	559c	1a1
		נחש	NAHASH	638b	1
19	2	חנון	HANUN	337a	1
		חסד	GOODNESS	*338d	11
		חסד	GOODNESS	338d	11
		מלאך	MESSENGER	521c	1a
		נחם	CONSOLE ONESELF	637a	
		נחם	CONSOLE ONESELF	637b	
		נחש	NAHASH	638b	1
		עם	WITH	767d	1d
		עשה	DO	794b	13
19	3	בלת	NOT	*116d	4a
		הפך	TURN	245c	1b
		חנון	HANUN	337a	1
		חקר	SEARCH	350c	2a
		כבד	MAKE HONORABLE	457d	2a
		נחם	CONSOLE ONESELF	637a	
		עבור	FOR THE SAKE OF	721a	1b
		עין	EYE	744d	3c
		מען	PURPOSE	775c	1c
		רגל	GO ABOUT	920b	2
19	4	חנון	HANUN	337a	1
		חצי	HALF	345d	2
		כרת	CUT OFF	503d	1a
		מדו	GARMENT	551d	
		מפשעה	STEPPING REGION	832c	
		שלח	SEND	1018b	1b
19	5	זקן	BEARD	278b	2
		כלם	BE HUMILIATED	483d	1
		צמח	SPROUT	855c	
19	6	אלף	THOUSAND	48d	1a
		באש	STINK	93b	
		חנון	HANUN	337a	1
		כסף	SILVER	494b	8c
		מעכה	MAACAH	591a	3
		עם	WITH	767d	1d
		פרש	HORSEMAN	832a	
		פתח	OPENING	836a	
		צובא	ZOBAH	844c	
19	7	שכר	HIRE	969a	
		מידבא	MEDEBA	568a	
		מעכה	MAACAH	591a	3
		פנה	FACE	817d	2 4d
		שכר	HIRE	969a	
19	8	גבור	STRONG	150b	2
		צבא	ARMY	839a	1a
19	9	ערך	ARRANGE	789c	1d
		שדה	FIELD	961c	1f
19	10	אחור	HINDER SIDE	30c	2
		ארם	ARAM	74b	A
		בחר	CHOOSE	*104a	7
		בחר	CHOOSE	*104b	7
		ערך	ARRANGE	789c	1d
		פנה	FACE	816b	16
		פנה	FACE	816b	15
19	11	יתר	REMAINDER	451d	1b
		ערך	ARRANGE	789c	1d
19	12	ארם	ARAM	74b	A
		חזק	BE FIRM	304b	1 1b
		ישע	DELIVER	446c	1
		ישועה	DELIVERANCE	447b	2
		תשועה	DELIVERANCE	448b	1 1
19	13	בשר	FLESH	142d	4
		חזק	BE FIRM	304b	1 2c
		חזק	BE FIRM	305b	2
		טוב	PLEASANT	374a	2f
19	14	בשר	FLESH	142d	4
		נגש	DRAW NEAR	620d	1
19	16	הדדעזר	HADADEZER	*212d	
		הדרעזר	HADADEZER	214c	
		יצא	BRING OUT	424c	1c
		מלאך	MESSENGER	521c	1a
		נגף	STRIKE	620a	
		עבר	REGION ACROSS	719c	1b
		שובך	SHOBACH	1000c	
19	17	נגד	BE CONSPICUOUS	617a	
		ערך	ARRANGE	789c	1d
		ערך	ARRANGE	789c	1d
19	18	הרג	KILL	247b	1b
		הרג	KILL	247c	7
		נום	FLEE	630d	1
		פנה	FACE	818a	2 5b
		פרש	HORSEMAN	*832a	
		ארבעים	FORTY	917b	1a
		רגלי	ON FOOT	920b	
		שובך	SHOBACH	1000c	
19	19	אבה	BE WILLING	2c	
		הדדעזר	HADADEZER	*212d	
		הדרעזר	HADADEZER	214c	
		ישע	DELIVER	446c	1
		נגף	STRIKE	620a	
		שלם	BE IN COVENANT OF PEACE	1023d	1
20	1	היה	COME TO PASS	224c	2 a1 ad
		חרם	THROW DOWN	248c	1
		חיל	STRENGTH	299a	4
		דרה	DRIVE	624b	1
		נכה	SMITE	646b	3
		עת	TIME	773c	2a
		צבא	ARMY	838d	1a

Ch	v.	Heb	Eng	Page	Sec
		צור	CONFINE	848d	2
		רבה	RABBA	913d	1
		תשובה	RETURN	1000c	2
20	2	ו	AND	*253a	1g
		יצא	BRING OUT	425a	4a
		יקר	PRECIOUS	430a	1c
		מלך	KING	573c	5d
		מלכם	MILCOM	576a	
		מצא	FIND	593a	1d
		עטרה	CROWN	742d	1
		רבה	BECOME MANY	915d	1e3
		שלל	SPOIL	1022a	2
20	3	ברזל	IRON	137c	1c
		מגזרה	CUTTING INSTRU-MENT	*160d	
		מגרה	SAW	176b	
		חריץ	A CUT	359a	2
		יצא	CAUSE TO GO	424c	1b
		שום	TO PLACE	963a	1a
		שור	SAW	965a	
20	4	גב	GOB	146c	
		גזר	GEZER	160c	
		חשתי	HASHATHITE	302a	
		ילד	CHILDREN	409d	
		כנע	BE HUMBLED	488c	2
		סבכי	SIBBECAI	687c	
		ספי	SIPPAI	706c	
		עמד	STAND	764c	6a
		רפה	HA-RAPHA	952a	
20	5	רפאים	REPHAIM	952b	
		אלחנן	ELHANAN	45a	
		ארג	WEAVE	71a	
		ביתהלחמי	THE BETHLEHEMITE	112a	
		גב	GOB	*146c	
		חנית	SPEAR	334a	2a
		גתי	GITTITE	388a	
		יערי ארגים	JAARE-OREGIM	*421a	
		לחמי	LAHMI	537c	
		מנור	BEAM	644d	
		יעור	JAIR	735d	
		עץ	TREE	781d	2b
20	6	גת	GATH	387d	
		ילד	BE BORN	408d	
		מדה	SIZE	551c	2
		ארבע	FOUR	917b	2b
		רפה	HA-RAPHA	952a	
		שש	SIX	995c	1a
20	7	יהונתן	JONATHAN	220d	3
		יהונדב	JEHONADAB	*220d	2
		חרף	REPROACH	357d	
		שמעא	SHIMEA	1035a	1
20	8	אל	THESE	41b	
		גת	GATH	387d	
		ילד	BE BORN	408d	
		נפל	FALL	657b	2a
		רפה	HA-RAPHA	952a	
21	1	אדם	ADAM	9c	3
		ה	THE	*207a	1a
		מנה	COUNT	584a	1
		סות	INCITE	694d	2
		עמד	STAND	764c	6c
		שמן	SATAN	966c	2c
21	2	בארשבע	BEERSHEBA	92a	
		דן	DAN	193a	3
		שר	CHIEFTAIN	978c	3a
21	3	אשמה	WRONG-DOING	80b	2
		בקש	SEEK	135a	4a
		הם	THEY	241d	8b
		יסף	ADD	415b	1
		מאה	HUNDRED	547d	1a2
		פעם	OCCURRENCE	822a	3a
21	4	דבר	WORD	182b	1 1b
		הלך	WALK	235d	1a
		חזק	BE FIRM	304b	1 1d
		שר	CHIEFTAIN	978c	3d
21	5	אלף	THOUSAND	49a	1c
		חרב	SWORD	352c	1c
		מפקד	MUSTER	824c	1
		מצודה	ISRAEL	845a	2
21	6	שלף	DRAW OUT	1025c	1
		דבר	WORD	182b	1 1b
		לוי	LEVI	532c	2
21	7	תעב	BE ABHORRED	1073a	2
		אלהים	GOD	44a	3
		נכה	SMITE	646c	4b
21	8	רעע	BE EVIL	949c	4
		חטא	MISS A GOAL OR WAY	307a	2b
		סכל	BE FOOLISH	698a	
		עבר	PASS OVER	719a	4
		עון	INIQUITY	731a	1c2
21	9	גד	GAD	151c	2
		חזה	SEER	302d	1b
21	10	הם	THEY	241d	8c
		הם	THEY	241d	6a
		נטל	LIFT	*642d	
21	11	קבל	RECEIVE	867a	1
21	12	גבול	BOUNDARY	148a	2a
		דבר	WORD	*182b	1 1c
		דבר	PESTILENCE	184a	1
		חדש	NEW MOON	294c	2a
		ל	TO	512c	4a
		מלאך	MESSENGER	521d	1
		נשג	OVERTAKE	673c	1b
		ספה	SWEEP AWAY	705a	1

Ch	v.	Heb	Eng	Page	Sec
		רעב	FAMINE	944b	1
		שבע	SEVEN	988a	1 a
		שחת	GO TO RUIN	1008b	1
21	13	אדם	MAN	9b	2
		נפל	FALL	657b	2 a
		רחמים	COMPASSION	933c	1
		צרר	ADDENDA ET COR-RIGENDA	1126c	
21	14	דבר	PESTILENCE	184a	1
21	15	ארונה	ARAUNAH	72c	
		ארנן	ORNAN	75a	
		יבוסי	JEBUSITE	101a	1
		גרן	THRESHING-FLOOR	175b	
		נחם	BE SORRY	637a	2
		עם	WITH	768a	2
		רב	MUCH	913b	1 f
		רפה	SINK	951d	1
		שחת	GO TO RUIN	1008b	1
21	16	ארץ	EARTH	76a	1 b
		זקן	OLD	278d	2 b
		חרב	SWORD	352c	1 c
		כסה	BE COVERED	492b	2
		נפל	FALL	657c	3 b
		שק	SACK	974c	2 a
		שלף	DRAW OUT	1025c	1
		שמי	HEAVENS	1029d	1 a
21	17	אמר	SAY	56c	4
		הוא	HE, SHE, IT	*216b	4 ba
		יהוה	YAHWEH	219a	2 lf
		חטא	MISS A GOAL OR WAY	307a	2 b
		מנה	COUNT	584a	1
		מגפה	PLAGUE	620b	3
		צאן	SMALL CATTLE	838a	3
21	18	אמר	SAY	56b	1
		אמר	SAY	56c	4
		ארנן	ORNAN	75a	
		יבוסי	JEBUSITE	101a	1
		גרן	THRESHING-FLOOR	175b	
		מזבח	ALTAR	258b	1
		מזבח	ALTAR	258d	8
		כי	THAT	471d	1
		קום	STAND	878d	2 b
21	19	דבר	SPEAK	181c	4 a
21	20	ארנן	ORNAN	75a	
		בחר	CHOOSE	*104a	3 b
		דוש	THRESH	190c	
		חבא	WITHDRAW	285b	1
		שוב	TURN BACK	997a	1
21	21	אף	NOSE	60b	2
		ארנן	ORNAN	75a	
		גרן	THRESHING-FLOOR	175b	
		חטה	WHEAT	334d	
		נבט	LOOK	613c	1 a
		שקף	LOOK DOWN	*1054c	
21	22	ארנן	ORNAN	75a	
		גרן	THRESHING-FLOOR	175b	
		כסף	SILVER	494c	8 e
		כסף	SILVER	494d	9
		מלא	FULL	571a	
		מגפה	PLAGUE	620b	3
		נתן	GIVE	679b	1 o
		עצר	RESTRAIN	783d	
		מקום	STANDING PLACE	880a	3 c
21	23	ארנן	ORNAN	75a	
		בקר	CATTLE	133c	2
		חטה	WHEAT	334d	
		טוב	PLEASANT	374a	2 f
		כל	ALL	*482d	2 ba
		מורג	THRESHING-SLEDGE	558d	
		מנחה	OFFERING	585b	4
		עלה	WHOLE BURNT OF-FERING	750c	
		עץ	TREE	782a	2 d
		ראה	TO SEE	*907d	7 a
21	24	ארנן	ORNAN	75a	
		חנם	OUT OF FAVOR	*336c	A
		חנם	OUT OF FAVOR	336c	A
		כסף	SILVER	494c	8 e
		מלא	FULL	571a	
		עלה	WHOLE BURNT OF-FERING	750d	
21	25	ארנן	ORNAN	75a	
		זהב	GOLD	263b	9 a
		מקום	STANDING PLACE	880a	3 c
		שקל	SHEKEL	1053d	
21	26	עלה	WHOLE BURNT OF-FERING	750d	
		עלה	WHOLE BURNT OF-FERING	750d	
		ענה	ANSWER	772d	1 b
		שלם	PEACE-OFFERING	1023c	
21	27	חרב	SWORD	352c	1 e
		נדן	SHEATH	623c	
		שוב	TURN BACK	999a	1 b
21	28	ארנן	ORNAN	75a	
		יבוסי	JEBUSITE	101a	1
		גרן	THRESHING-FLOOR	175b	
21	29	במה	HIGH PLACE	119b	3
		גבעון	GIBEON	149c	
		מזבח	ALTAR	258c	3 b
		עלה	WHOLE BURNT OF-FERING	750d	
		משכן	DWELLING-PLACE	1015d	2 c
21	30	בעת	TERRIFY	130a	
		דרש	SEEK	205b	2 a
		מלאך	MESSENGER	521d	2
		פנה	FACE	817b	24b b
		הלך	ADDENDA ET COR-RIGENDA	1122c	
22	1	אלהים	GOD	44a	3 b
		הוא	HE, SHE, IT	216c	4 bg
		מזבח	ALTAR	258b	1
		עלה	WHOLE BURNT OF-FERING	750d	
22	2	אבן	STONE	6c	2
		אבן	STONE	6d	2
		גר	SOJOURNER	158c	2
		גזית	HEWING	159b	
		חצב	HEW	345a	2 a
		כנס	GATHER	488a	
22	3	ברזל	IRON	137c	1 b
		דלת	DOOR	195a	1
		מחברה	BINDER	289c	
		כון	ESTABLISH	466b	2
		מסמר	NAIL	702c	
		משקל	WEIGHT	1054a	
22	4	אין	NOT	35a	6 cb
		ארז	CEDAR	72c	2
		מספר	NUMBER	708d	1 a
		צידני	SIDONIANS	851a	
		צרי	TYRIAN	863a	
22	5	גדל	BECOME GREAT	152c	1
		כון	ESTABLISH	466b	2 a
		ל	TO	518a	7 bg
		נער	YOUTH	655a	1 d
		מעל	ABOVE	752a	2 cb
		תפארה	BEAUTY	802d	2 b
22	7	רך	TENDER	940a	1
		יהוה	YAHWEH	219a	2 lf
		היה	BE	227b	3 4d a
		לב	HEART	523c	2 2
		עם	WITH	768a	4 a
22	8	דבר	WORD	182c	1 2a
		דם	BLOOD	*196c	2 b
		דם	BLOOD	196c	2 b
		מלחמה	WAR	536c	
		על	UPON	754d	2 lf g
		על	UPON	757c	27c b
		עשה	DO	794c	2 le
		שפך	POUR OUT	1049c	1 b
22	9	ילד	BE BORN	408d	2
		נוח	REST	628c	A 1b 2
		מנוחה	REST	630a	2
		על	UPON	756c	27a b
		שלום	PEACE	1023b	6
		שם	NAME	1027d	2 a
		שקט	QUIETNESS	1053b	
22	10	בן	SON	120b	1 c
		כון	ESTABLISH	466a	1 a
		כסא	THRONE	491a	3 a
		מלכות	ROYAL POWER	574d	1
		עולם	LONG DURATION	762c	2 f
22	11	דבר	SPEAK	181c	5
		יהוה	YAHWEH	218d	2 1a
		צלח	ADVANCE	852c	2
22	12	בינה	UNDERSTANDING	108a	3
		יהוה	YAHWEH	218d	2 1a
		תורה	LAW	436b	2 b2
		צוה	GIVE CHARGE OVER	845d	1 d
		שכל	PRUDENCE	968c	2
22	13	אמץ	BE STRONG	55a	2
		חזק	BE FIRM	304b	1 2c
		חתת	BE SHATTERED	369b	2 a
		ירא	FEAR	431a	1 a
		צוה	CHARGE	846a	4 c
		צלח	ADVANCE	852c	2
22	14	אלף	THOUSAND	49a	1 c
		ברזל	IRON	137c	1 b
		זהב	GOLD	263c	1
		יסף	ADD	415b	1
		כון	ESTABLISH	466b	2 a
		כסף	SILVER	494c	8 c
		עני	AFFLICTION	777z	2
		רב	MULTITUDE	914a	1
		משקל	WEIGHT	1054a	
22	15	אבן	STONE	6c	2
		אבן	STONE	6c	2
		חכם	WISE	314d	1 b
		חרש	GRAVER	360d	1 b
		חרש	GRAVER	360d	1 d
		מלאכה	WORK	522b	4
22	16	ברזל	IRON	137c	1 b
		זהב	GOLD	263c	1
		מספר	NUMBER	708d	1 a
22	17	צוה	GIVE CHARGE TO	845c	1 b
		שר	CHIEFTAIN	978b	2 a
22	18	יהוה	YAHWEH	218d	2 1b
		כבש	BE SUBDUED	461b	1
		ל	TO	511b	1 ga
		נחל	REFRESH	*625a	4
		נוח	REST	628c	A 1b 2
22	19	בנה	BUILD	125a	1
		דרש	SEEK	205b	3 a
		לב	HEART	523c	2 2
		לב	HEART	523d	2 4
		נפש	SOUL	661b	0
		מקדש	SACRED PLACE	874b	4
23	1	זקן	BE OLD	278b	
		מלך	BE KING	574b	
23	2	שבע	SATISFIED	959c	2 b
		כהן	PRIEST	464a	7
		לוי	LEVITE	533a	2 a
		עזיאל	UZZIEL	739c	1 a
23	3	בן	SON	122a	9 a
		בן	SON	122a	9 a
		גבר	MAN	150a	2
		ספר	COUNT	708a	
		מעל	ABOVE	751d	2 bb a
		שלשים	THIRTY	1026c	1
23	4	שמנה	EIGHT	1033a	3 b
		מלאכה	WORK	522b	6 b
		נצח	BE PRE-EMINENT	664a	2
		ארבע	FOUR	917b	2 b
		שטר	OFFICIAL	1009c	
23	5	שפט	JUDGE	1047d	2 b
		הלל	PRAISE	238c	2 e
		הלל	PRAISE	238d	2 g
		כלי	INSTRUMENT	479d	2 b
		שער	PORTER	1045c	
23	6	בן	SON	*121a	1 je
		גרשון	GERSHON	177b	
		חלק	DIVIDE	323c	
		חלק	DIVIDE	323d	3
		חלק	DIVIDE	323d	2
		מחלקת	DIVISION	325a	2
		ל	TO	512a	3 b
		לוי	LEVI	532c	1 a
		מררי	MERARI	601b	
		קהת	KOHATH	875b	
23	7	גרשני	GERSHONITES	177b	
		לעדן	LADAN	541d	3 a
		שמעי	SHIMEI	1035c	3 a
23	8	יואל	JOEL	222b	1 d
		זתם	ZETHAM	268d	
		זתן	ZETHAN	285c	
		יחיאל	JEHIEL	313c	2
		לעדן	LADAN	541d	2
		ראש	HEAD	911a	3 f
23	9	מגן	SHIELD	171c	
		הרן	HARAN	248c	2
		חזיאל	HAZIEL	303c	
		לעדן	LADAN	541d	2
		ראש	HEAD	911a	3 f
		שלמות	SHELOMOTH	1024d	1 b
		שמעי	SHIMEI	1035c	3 a
23	10	בריעה	BERIAH	140b	4
		זיזה	ZIZAH	265b	
		זינא	ZINA	268b	
		יחת	JAHATH	367a	2 b
		יעוש	JEUSH	736c	3
		ארבע	FOUR	917b	1 b2
		שמעי	SHIMEI	1035c	3 a
23	11	בית	HOUSE	110b	5 e
		כון	ESTABLISH	466a	1 a
		בריעה	BERIAH	140b	4
		זיזה	ZIZAH	265b	
		זינא	ZINA	268b	
		יחת	JAHATH	367a	2 b
		יעוש	JEUSH	736c	3
		פקדה	OVERSIGHT	824b	2 c
		ראש	HEAD	911a	3 f
		רבה	BECOME MANY	915c	1 a
23	12	חברון	HEBRON	289c	1
		יצהר	IZHAR	844b	
23	13	בדל	BE DIVIDED	95c	2 b
		ברך	BLESS	139a	1
		משה	MOSES	602c	
		עולם	LONG DURATION	762c	2 e
		קדש	APARTNESS	872b	6
		קדש	BE SET APART	873b	1 b
		קטר	MAKE SACRAFICES SMOKE	883b	3
23	14	שרת	SERVE	1058b	2 d
		אלהים	GOD	43d	3 b
		לוי	LEVITE	532d	2
		על	UPON	754a	2 1f
		קרא	CALL	896c	6 d5
23	15	אליעזר	ELIEZER	45c	B
		גרשם	GERSHOM	177a	1
23	16	גרשם	GERSHOM	177a	1
		שבואל	SHEBUEL	986c	
23	17	אליעזר	ELIEZER	45c	B
		מעל	ABOVE	751d	2 bb a
		מעל	ABOVE	752a	2 cb
		רבה	BECOME MANY	915a	1 a
		רחביה	REHABIAH	932c	
23	18	יצהר	IZHAR	844b	
		שלמות	SHELOMOTH	1024d	1 a
23	19	אמריהו	AMARIAH	57c	1
		חברון	HEBRON	289c	1
		יחזיאל	JAHAZIEL	303c	3
		יריהו	JERIAH	436c	
		יקמעם	JEKAMEAM	880c	
		ראש	HEAD	911a	3 f
23	20	רביעי	FOURTH	918a	1
		ישיהו	ISSHIJAH	674d	3 a
		עזיאל	UZZIEL	739c	1 a
		ראש	HEAD	911a	3 f
23	21	אלעזר	ELEAZAR	46c	D
		מושי	MUSHI	559b	
		מחלי	MAHLI	563a	1
		מררי	MERARI	601b	
		קיש	KISH	885c	2 a
23	22	אלעזר	ELEAZAR	46c	D
		קיש	KISH	885c	2 a
23	23	ירימות	JEREMOTH	438b	2 a

Ch	v.	Heb	Eng	Page	Sec
		מושי	MUSHI	559b	
23	24	עדר	EDER	727d	
		בן	SON	121a	1 je
		בן	SON	122a	9 a
		בן	SON	122a	9 a
		מלאכה	WORK	522a	3 b
		לוי	LEVI	532c	1 c
		עבדה	LABOR	715c	4
		מעל	ABOVE	751d	2 bb a
		פקד	ATTEND TO	823c	A 4
		ראש	HEAD	911a	3 f
23	25	נוח	REST	628c	A 1b 1
		עד	UNTIL	725c	3 2
		עולם	LONG DURATION	762c	2 c
23	26	אין	NOT	34d	5 b
		לוי	LEVITE	532d	3 1a
		עבדה	LABOR	715c	4
		משכן	DWELLING-PLACE	1015d	2 c
23	27	בן	SON	121a	1 je
		בן	SON	122a	9 a
		בן	SON	122a	9 a
		דבר	WORD	183c	4 2
		לוי	LEVI	532c	1 c
23	28	חצר	ENCLOSURE	347a	3 a
		מהרה	PURIFYING	372d	2
		יד	HAND	391b	5 f
		לוי	LEVI	*532c	1 c
		לשכה	ROOM	545d	1 b
		עבדה	LABOR	715c	4
		עבדה	LABOR	715c	4
		מעמד	OFFICE	765b	2
		מעשה	DEED	795d	1 b1
		קדש	APARTNESS	872b	6
23	29	מחבת	FLAT PLATE	290b	1
		לחם	FOOD	537b	1 a
		מדה	MEASURE	551c	1
		מנחה	OFFERING	585b	4
		משורה	MEASURE	601c	
		מצה	UNLEAVENED BREAD	695b	
		סלת	FINE FLOUR	701c	
		מערכת	ROW	790b	
		רבך	MIX	916c	
		רקק	A THIN CAKE	956d	
23	30	בקר	MORNING	134b	1 f
		הלל	PRAISE	238c	2 e
		ידה	PRAISE	392c	1 b
		כן	SO	485d	1 a
		ערב	SUNSET	787d	1 a
23	31	חדש	NEW MOON	294c	1
		מועד	APPOINTED TIME	417c	1 b
		כל	ALL	481b	1 a
		תמיד	CONTINUITY	556c	1 b
		עלה	WHOLE BURNT OFFERING	750d	
		על	UPON	753c	2 1c
		שבת	SABBATH	992c	1 d
23	32	אהל	TENT	14b	1
		מועד	TENT OF MEETING	418a	5
		עבדה	LABOR	715c	4
		משמרת	GUARD	1038c	4 a
		משמרת	GUARD	1038c	4 a
		משמרת	GUARD	1038c	4 a
24	1	איתמר	ITHAMAR	16a	
		אלעזר	ELEAZAR	46b	A
		בן	SON	*121a	1 jz
		בן	SON	121a	1 jz
		מחלקת	DIVISION	325a	2
		ל	TO	514d	5 fe
		נדב	NADAB	621c	1
24	2	איתמר	ITHAMAR	16a	
		אלעזר	ELEAZAR	46b	A
		כהן	ACT AS PRIEST	464c	1
		מות	DIE	560a	2 b
24	3	איתמר	ITHAMAR	16a	
		אלעזר	ELEAZAR	46b	A
		חלק	DIVIDE	323c	
		חלק	DIVIDE	323d	3
		חלק	DIVIDE	323d	2
		עבדה	LABOR	715c	4
		פקדה	OVERSIGHT	824b	2 c
24	4	איתמר	ITHAMAR	16a	
		אחימלך	AHIMELECH	27a	1
		אלעזר	ELEAZAR	46b	A
		גבר	MAN	150a	
		חלק	DIVIDE	323c	2
		ל	TO	514b	5 fb
		מצא	FIND	594b	2 f
		ראש	HEAD	911a	3 f
		רב	MUCH	913b	1 e
24	5	אדיר	MAJESTIC	12b	2
		איתמר	ITHAMAR	16a	
		אלעזר	ELEAZAR	46b	A
		גורל	LOT	174c	2 b
		חלק	DIVIDE	323c	2
		עם	WITH	767d	1 e
		קדש	APARTNESS	871d	2 d
		שר	CHIEFTAIN	978d	5
24	6	איתמר	ITHAMAR	16a	
		אחימלך	AHIMELECH	27a	1
		אחז	GRASP	28b	1
		אלעזר	ELEAZAR	46b	A
		כהן	PRIEST	463c	4
		כהן	PRIEST	464a	7
		כתב	WRITE	507d	3
		לוי	LEVITE	532d	
		לוי	LEVITE	533a	3 2a
		נתנאל	NETHANEL	682b	5 a
		ספר	ENUMERATOR	708c	1 b
		שמעיה	SHEMAIAH	1035d	7 d
24	7	גורל	LOT	174c	2 b
		יהויריב	JEHOIARIB	220d	1
		ידעיה	JEDAIAH	396a	1
24	8	גורל	LOT	*174c	2 b
		חרם	HARIM	356c	1
		רביעי	FOURTH	918a	1
		שערים	SEORIM	972d	1
24	9	גורל	LOT	*174c	2 b
		חמישי	FIFTH	332c	1
		מימן	MIJAMIN	568b	1 a
		מלכיהו	MALCHIJAH	575d	3 a
		משה	MOSES	602d	
24	10	אביהו	ABIJAM	4a	5
		גורל	LOT	*174c	2 b
		קוץ	KOZ	881a	2
		שביעי	SEVENTH	988d	1
		שמיני	EIGHTH	1033b	
24	11	גורל	LOT	*174c	2 b
		יהושוע	JOSHUA	221c	5
		עשירי	TENTH	798a	1
		שבניה	SHEBANIAH	987d	1 b
		שכניה	SHECANIAH	1016a	5 a
		תשיעי	NINTH	1077d	
24	12	אלישיב	ELIASHIB	46a	B
		גורל	LOT	*174c	2 b
		עשתי	ONE	799d	1
24	13	גורל	LOT	*174c	2 b
		חפה	HUPPAH	342c	1
		ישבאב	JESHEBEAB	444a	1
		שלש	THREE	1025d	2
24	14	אמר	IMMER	57b	1
		בלגה	BILGAH	114d	1
		גורל	LOT	*174c	2 b
		חזיר	HEZIR	*306c	1
		חמש	FIVE	332a	2 d
		עשר	TEN	797b	6 a
		שש	SIX	995c	2
24	15	גורל	LOT	*174c	2 b
		חזיר	HEZIR	306c	1
		עשר	TEN	797b	8 a
		פצץ	HAPPIZZEZ	823a	
		שבע	SEVEN	988b	2 b
		שמנה	EIGHT	1033a	2
24	16	גורל	LOT	*174c	2 b
		יחזקאל	EZEKIEL	306b	2
		עשר	TEN	797b	9 a
		פתחיה	PETHAHIAH	836a	1
		תשע	NINE	1077c	2
24	17	גורל	LOT	*174c	2 b
		שנים	TWO	1041b	3
24	18	גורל	LOT	174c	2 b
		דליהו	DELAIAH	195b	1 a
		מעזיהו	MAAZIAH	589b	1
		ארבע	FOUR	917b	2 b
24	19	ל	TO	511b	1 ga
		עבדה	LABOR	715b	4
		פקדה	OVERSIGHT	824b	2 c
		משפט	JUDGMENT	1048d	3
24	20	בן	SON	121a	1 je
		יחדיהו	JEHDEIAH	292d	1
		יתר	BE LEFT OVER	451c	
		ל	TO	512d	5 ac
		לוי	LEVI	532c	1 c
		שבואל	SHEBUEL	986c	
24	21	ל	TO	512d	5 ac
		ישיהו	ISSHIJAH	674d	3 b
		רחביה	REHABIAH	932c	1
24	22	יחת	JAHATH	367a	2 c
		יצהרי	IZHARITES	844b	1
		שלמות	SHELOMOTH	1024d	1 a
24	23	אמריהו	AMARIAH	57c	1
		יחזיאל	JAHAZIEL	303c	3
		יריהו	JERIAH	436c	1
		יקמעם	JEKAMEAM	880c	1
		רביעי	FOURTH	918a	1
24	24	עזיאל	UZZIEL	739c	1 a
		זכריהו	ZECHARIAH	272b	0 b
		שמיר	SHAMIR	1039a	
24	25	זכריהו	ZECHARIAH	272b	0 b
		ישיהו	ISSHIJAH	674d	3 a
24	26	בנו	BENO	122b	
		מושי	MUSHI	559b	
		מחלי	MAHLI	563a	1
		מררי	MERARI	601b	
24	27	בנו	BENO	122b	
		זכור	ZACCUR	271d	3 a
		מררי	MERARI	601b	
		עברי	IBRI	720b	
		יעזיהו	JAAZIAH	739d	
		שהם	SHOHAM	996a	
24	28	אלעזר	ELEAZAR	46c	D
		מחלי	MAHLI	563a	1
24	29	קיש	KISH	885c	2 a
		ירחמאל	JERAHMEEL	934a	3
24	30	בן	SON	121a	1 je
		ירמות	JEREMOTH	438b	2 c
		לוי	LEVITE	533b	3 2c
		מושי	MUSHI	559b	
		עדר	EDER	727d	
24	31	אחימלך	AHIMELECH	27a	1
		בן	SON	121a	1 jz
		גורל	LOT	174c	2 b
		כהן	PRIEST	464a	7
		לוי	LEVITE	533a	3 2a
		נפל	FALL	658a	3
		עמה	CLOSE BY	769d	C
		קטן	SMALL	882a	1 a
		שר	CHIEFTAIN	978d	6
25	1	הימן	HEMAN	54d	
		אסף	ASAPH	63b	2
		בדל	BE DIVIDED	95b	2
		ידותון	JEDUTHUN	*393a	
		איתן	ETHAN	*451a	
		כנור	LYRE	490a	
		כנור	LYRE	490b	
		ל	TO	512a	3 b
		נבא	PROPHESY	612a	1 a
		נבל	HARP	614c	
		עבדה	LABOR	715c	4
		צבא	ARMY	839a	1
		מצלתים	CYMBALS	853a	
25	2	אסף	ASAPH	63a	2
		אסף	ASAPH	63b	2
		אשראלה	ASHARELAH	77b	
		זכור	ZACCUR	271d	3 b
		יד	HAND	391c	5 h2
		יד	HAND	391c	5 h2
		יוסף	JOSEPH	415d	3
		ישראלה	JESHARELAH	441a	
		נבא	PROPHESY	612a	1 a
25	3	נתניהו	NETHANIAH	682b	3 b
		גדליהו	GEDALIAH	153d	3
		הלל	PRAISE	238c	2 e
		חשביהו	HASHABIAH	364a	1
		יד	HAND	391c	5 h2
		ידה	PRAISE	392c	1 b
		ידותון	JEDUTHUN	s 393a	
		ידותון	JEDUTHUN	s 393a	
		ישעיהו	JESHAIAH	447d	2
		כנור	LYRE	490a	
		כנור	LYRE	490b	
		נבא	PROPHESY	612a	1 a
		מתתיהו	MATTITHIAH	682d	1
		צרי	ZERI	863b	
25	4	רממתיעזר	ROMAMTI-EZER	928d	
		אליאתה	ELIATHAH	45a	
		הימן	HEMAN	54d	
		בקיהו	BUKKIAH	131c	
		גדלתי	GIDDALTI	153d	
		מחזיאות	MAHAZIOTH	303d	
		חנניהו	HANANIAH	337b	3
		חנני	HANANI	337b	3
		ירימות	JEREMOTH	438b	2 d
		ישבקשה	JOSHBEKASHAH	444a	
		הותיר	HOTHIR	452b	
		מלותי	MALLOTHI	576c	
		מתניהו	MATTANIAH	682d	2 a
		עזיאל	UZZIEL	739c	1 b
		רממתיעזר	ROMAMTI-EZER	928d	
		שבואל	SHEBUEL	986c	
25	5	הימן	HEMAN	54d	
		הימן	HEMAN	54d	
		דבר	WORD	183a	2 2
		חזה	SEER	302d	1 c
		קרן	HORN	902a	2
		רום	BE HIGH	927c	1 f
		שלש	THREE	1025d	1 a
25	6	הימן	HEMAN	54d	
		אסף	ASAPH	63a	2
		יד	HAND	391c	5 h2
		ידותון	JEDUTHUN	*393a	
		איתן	ETHAN	*451a	
		כנור	LYRE	490a	
		נבל	HARP	614c	
		עבדה	LABOR	715c	4
		מלתים	CYMBALS	853a	
		שיר	SONG	1010c	3
25	7	בין	DISCERN	107a	3 e
		למד	LEARN	540d	
		שיר	SONG	1010c	3
25	8	שמנים	EIGHTY	1033b	
		בין	DISCERN	107a	3 e
		גדול	GREAT	153b	7
		גורל	LOT	174c	2 b
		תלמיד	SCHOLAR	541a	
		נפל	FALL	658a	3
		עמה	CLOSE BY	769d	D
		משמרת	GUARD	1038d	4 a
25	9	אסף	ASAPH	63a	2
		גדליהו	GEDALIAH	153d	3
		גורל	LOT	*174c	2 b
		גורל	LOT	174c	2 b
25	10	יוסף	JOSEPH	415d	3
		גורל	LOT	*174c	2 b
		זכור	ZACCUR	271d	3 b
25	11	גורל	LOT	*174c	2 b
		יצרי	IZRI	428b	A
		צרי	ZERI	863b	
		רביעי	FOURTH	918a	1
25	12	גורל	LOT	*174c	2 b
		חמישי	FIFTH	332c	1
		נתניהו	NETHANIAH	682b	3 b
25	13	בקיהו	BUKKIAH	131c	
		גורל	LOT	*174c	2 b
25	14	אשראלה	ASHARELAH	77b	
		גורל	LOT	*174c	2 b
		ישראלה	JESHARELAH	441a	
		שביעי	SEVENTH	988d	1

Ch	v.	Heb	Eng	Page	Sec
25	15	גורל	LOT	*174c	2 b
		ישעיהו	JESHAIAH	447d	2
		שמנה	EIGHT	1033a	2 b
25	16	גורל	LOT	*174c	2 b
		תשיעי	NINTH	1077d	
25	17	גורל	LOT	*174c	2 b
		עשירי	TENTH	798a	1
		שמעי	SHIMEI	1035c	3 d
25	18	גורל	LOT	*174c	2 b
		עזראל	AZAREL	741a	2
		עשתי	ONE	799d	
25	19	גורל	LOT	*174c	2 b
		חשביהו	HASHABIAH	364a	1
25	20	גורל	LOT	*174c	2 b
		שבואל	SHEBUEL	986c	
		שלש	THREE	1025d	2
25	21	גורל	LOT	*174c	2 b
		מתתיהו	MATTITHIAH	682d	1
25	22	גורל	LOT	*174c	2 b
		ירמות	JEREMOTH	438b	2 b
25	23	גורל	LOT	*174c	2 b
		חנניהו	HANANIAH	337b	3
		שש	SIX	995c	2
25	24	גורל	LOT	*174c	2 b
		ישבקשה	JOSHBEKASHAH	444a	
		שבע	SEVEN	988b	2 b
25	25	גורל	LOT	174c	2 b
		חנני	HANANI	337b	3
		עשר	TEN	797b	8 a
25	26	גורל	LOT	*174c	2 b
		מלותי	MALLOTHI	576c	
		עשר	TEN	797b	9 a
		תשע	NINE	1077c	2
25	27	אליאתה	ELIATHAH	45a	
		גורל	LOT	*174c	2 b
25	28	גורל	LOT	*174c	2 b
		הותיר	HOTHIR	452d	
25	29	גדלתי	GIDDALTI	153d	
		גורל	LOT	*174c	2 b
25	30	גורל	LOT	*174c	2 b
		מחזיאות	MAHAZIOTH	303d	
25	31	גורל	LOT	*174c	2 b
		ארבע	FOUR	917b	2 b
26	1	אסף	ASAPH	63b	2
		מחלקת	DIVISION	325a	2
		ל	TO	514d	5 fe
		קורא	KORAHITES	896c	1
		קרחי	KORAHITES	901c	
		משלמיה	MESHELEMIAH	1024c	
26	2	זבדיהו	ZEBADIAH	256c	1 a
		זכריהו	ZECHARIAH	272b	0 c
		ידיעאל	JEDIAEL	396a	3
		רביעי	FOURTH	918a	1
		משלמיה	MESHELEMIAH	1024c	
		יתניאל	JATHNIEL	1072a	
26	3	אליהועיני	ELIEHOENAI	41b	1
		יהוחנן	JEHOHANAN	220b	4
		חמישי	FIFTH	332c	1
		עילם	ELAM	743a	4
		שביעי	SEVENTH	988d	1
26	4	יהוזבד	JEHOZABAD	220a	4 a
		יואח	JOAH	222a	4
		חמישי	FIFTH	332c	1
		נתנאל	NETHANE/L	682b	5 b
		עבדאדם	OBED-EDOM	714d	2
		רביעי	FOURTH	918a	1
		שכר	SACHAR	969b	2
		שמעיה	SHEMAIAH	1035d	7 e
26	5	ברך	BLESS	139a	2 a
		יששכר	ISSACHAR	441b	2
		עמיאל	AMMIEL	770a	4
		פעלתי	PEULLETHAI	821d	
		שביעי	SEVENTH	988b	1
26	6	ילד	BE BORN	408d	
		ממשל	RULER	606a	2
		שמעיה	SHEMAIAH	1035d	7 e
26	7	אלזבד	ELZABAD	44d	1
		אליהו	ELIHU	45b	D
		סמכיהו	SEMACHIAH	702b	
		עבד	OBED	714d	4
		עתני	OTHNI	801a	
		רפאל	REPHAEL	951b	
		שמעיה	SHEMAIAH	1035d	7 e
26	8	חיל	STRENGTH	298d	2
		כח	STRENGTH	470d	1 b
		עבדאדם	OBED-EDOM	714d	2
		עבדה	LABOR	715c	4
26	9	משלמיה	MESHELEMIAH	1024c	
		שמנה	EIGHT	1033a	2 a
26	10	היה	BE	227a	3 4b
		חסה	HOSAH	340b	1
		מררי	MERARI	601b	
		שמרי	SHIMRI	1037c	3 a
26	11	זכריהו	ZECHARIAH	272b	0 d
		חלקיהו	HILKIAH	324d	4 b
		חסה	HOSAH	340b	1
		טבליהו	TEBALIAH	371b	
		רביעי	FOURTH	918a	1
		שלש	THREE	1025d	2
26	12	גבר	MAN	150a	3
		מחלקת	DIVISION	325a	2
		עמה	CLOSE BY	769d	C
		משמרות	GUARD	1038d	4 a
		שרת	SERVE	1057d	4 b
26	13	גדול	GREAT	153b	7
		גורל	LOT	174c	2 b
		ו	AND	253b	1 ib
		נפל	FALL	658a	3
26	14	מגן	SHIELD	171c	
		גורל	LOT	174c	2 b
		גורל	LOT	174c	2 b
		גורל	LOT	174c	2 b
		זכריהו	ZECHARIAH	272b	0 c
		מזרח	PLACE OF SUNRISE	281a	2 c1
		יעץ	ADVISE	419d	
		נגב	SOUTH-COUNTRY	*616b	2
		נפל	FALL	657a	1
		נפל	FALL	658a	2
		סכל	PRUDENCE	968d	2
		שלמיה	SHELEMIAH	1025a	2
26	15	אסף	STORE	63b	
		נגב	SOUTH-COUNTRY	616b	2
		עבדאדם	OBED-EDOM	714d	2
26	16	חסה	HOSAH	340b	1
		ל	TO	511d	1 h
		נגב	SOUTH-COUNTRY	*616b	2
		מתניהו	MATTANIAH	682d	2 b
		מסלה	HIGHWAY	700c	
		עם	WITH	768a	2
		עמה	CLOSE BY	769d	B
		מערב	WEST	788a	
		שלכת	SHALLECHETH	1021c	
		משמר	GUARD	1038b	2
		שער	GATE	1045b	3 b
		שפים	SHUPPIM	1051b	2
26	17	אסף	STORE	63b	
		מזרח	PLACE OF SUNRISE	281a	2 c3
		מזרח	PLACE OF SUNRISE	281a	2 c1
		יום	DAY	401a	7 i
		ל	TO	511d	1 h
		לוי	LEVITE	533a	3 2b
		נגב	SOUTH-COUNTRY	616b	2
		שש	SIX	995c	1 a
26	18	ל	TO	511d	1 h
		נגב	SOUTH-COUNTRY	*616b	2
		מסלה	HIGHWAY	700c	
		מערב	WEST	788a	
26	19	פרור	COLONNADE	826c	
		ל	TO	513d	5 cb g
		מררי	MERARI	601b	
		קרחי	KORAHITES	901c	
26	20	אחיהו	AHIJAH	26d	8
		אוצר	TREASURE	70a	3 a
26	21	גרשני	GERSHONITES	177b	
		גרשני	GERSHONITES	177b	
		יחיאלי	JEHIELITES	313d	
		לעדן	LADAN	541d	2
26	22	אוצר	TREASURE	70a	3 a
		יואל	JOEL	222b	1 d
		זתם	ZETHAM	268d	
		זתם	ZETHAN	285c	
		יחיאלי	JEHIELITES	313d	
26	23	יחיאלי	JEHIELITES	*313d	
		חברוני	HEBRONITE	289c	
		ל	TO	512d	5 ac
		ל	TO	514d	5 fe
		עזיאלי	UZZIELITES	739c	
26	24	אוצר	TREASURE	70a	3 a
		גרשם	GERSHOM	177a	1
		נגיד	LEADER	618a	4
		שבואל	SHEBUEL	986c	
26	25	אליעזר	ELIEZER	45c	D
		יהורם	JEHORAM	221b	5
		זכרי	ZICHRI	271d	3 b
		ישעיהו	JESHAIAH	447d	3
		ל	TO	512d	5 ac
		ל	TO	514d	5 fe
		רחביה	REHABIAH	932c	
		שלמות	SHELOMOTH	1024d	1 a
26	26	אוצר	TREASURE	70a	3 a
		הוא	HE, SHE, IT	215c	1 e
		ל	TO	514d	5 fe
		צבא	ARMY	839a	1 a
		קדש	BE SET APART	873b	1 b
		שר	CHIEFTAIN	978c	3 b
		שלמות	SHELOMOTH	1024d	1 a
26	27	אוצר	TREASURE	70a	1
		חזק	BE FIRM	304c	1 c
		ל	TO	512a	3 b
		קדש	BE SET APART	873b	1 b
26	28	אבינר	ABNER	4c	
		ה	THE	209b	3
		נר	NER	633a	1
		צרויה	ZERUIAH	863b	
		קדש	BE SET APART	873b	1 b
		קיש	KISH	885c	1
		ראה	SEER	909a	1
		שלמות	SHELOMOTH	1024d	1 a
		שמואל	SAMUEL	1028d	1
26	29	חיצון	OUTER	300c	2
		כנניהו	CHENANIAH	487d	2
		ל	TO	512c	4 a
		מלאכה	WORK	522a	3 b
		שטר	OFFICIAL	1009c	
		שפט	JUDGE	1047d	2 b
26	30	חברוני	HEBRONITE	289c	
		חשביהו	HASHABIAH	364a	1
		ירדן	JORDAN	434c	
		מלאכה	WORK	522b	6 b
		עבדה	LABOR	715b	3
		עבר	REGION ACROSS	719c	1 b
		מערב	WEST	788b	
26	31	פקדה	OVERSIGHT	824a	2 a
		דרש	SEEK	205d	2
		חברוני	HEBRONITE	289c	
		מצא	FIND	394a	1 f
		תולדות	GENERATIONS	410a	A
		יריהו	JERIAH	436c	
		ל	TO	514d	5 fe
		מלכות	REIGN	575a	2
		יעזר	JAZER	*741b	
		ארבעים	FORTY	917c	3
26	32	גדי	GADITE	151d	
		דבר	WORD	183b	4 1
		ל	TO	*514c	5 fc
		מכשי	MANASSITES	586d	
		ראובני	REUBENITE	910a	
		ראש	HEAD	911a	3 f
27	1	ב	IN	90b	3 3b
		בוא	COME	98a	1 c
		דבר	WORD	183b	4 1
		ל	TO	*514c	5 fc
		מספר	NUMBER	709a	1 b
		ראש	HEAD	911a	3 f
		שר	CHIEFTAIN	978c	3 b
		שר	CHIEFTAIN	978d	6
		שטר	OFFICIAL	1009c	
		שרת	SERVE	1058a	1 b
27	2	אישבשת	ISHBOSHETH	36b	2
		זבדיאל	ZABDIEL	256c	1
		חדש	NEW MOON	294d	2 b2
		ישבעם	JASHOBEAM	1000b	
27	3	בן	SON	122a	9 a
		ל	TO	513c	5 cb b
		פרץ	PEREZ	829d	1
		צבא	ARMY	839a	1 a
		שר	CHIEFTAIN	978c	3 a
27	4	אחוחי	AHOHITE	29a	
		אלעזר	ELEAZAR	46c	C
		דודי	DODAI	187d	
		דודו	DODO	*187d	2
		מקלות	MIKLOTH	596c	2
		נגיד	LEADER	618a	4
27	5	בניהו	BENAIAH	125c	1
		יהוידע	JEHOIADA	220b	1
		כהן	PRIEST	464b	1
		ראש	HEAD	911a	3 e
27	6	בניהו	BENAIAH	125c	1
		הוא	HE, SHE, IT	215c	1 e
		עמיזבד	AMMIZABAD	770b	
27	7	זבדיה	ZEBADIAH	256c	5
		עשהאל	ASAHEL	795c	1
		רביעי	FOURTH	917d	1
		רביעי	FOURTH	918a	1
27	8	יזרח	IZRAHITE	280d	
		חמישי	FIFTH	332c	1
		חמישי	FIFTH	332c	1
		שמהות	SHAMHUTH	1030b	
		שמה	SHAMMAH	1031c	3 b
27	9	עירא	IRA	747a	2 a
		עקש	IKKESH	786a	
		תקועי	TEKOITE	1075d	
27	10	אפרים	EPHRAIM	68b	2
		ביתפלט	BETH-PELET	!12c	
		חלץ	HELEZ	323b	1
		פלני	PELONITE	813d	
		שביעי	SEVENTH	988d	1
27	11	זרחי	ZERAHITES	280c	1
		חשתי	HASHATHITE	302a	1
		סבכי	SIBBECAI	687d	
27	12	אביעזר	ABIEZER	4c	2
		בנימיני	BENJAMITE	122d	
		ענתתי	ANATHOTHITE	779a	
		תשיעי	NINTH	1077d	
		תשיעי	NINTH	1077d	
27	13	זרחי	ZERAHITES	280c	1
		עשירי	TENTH	798a	1
27	14	אפרים	EPHRAIM	68b	A
		בניהו	BENAIAH	125c	2
		עשתי	ONE	799d	
		פרעתוני	PIRATHONITE	828d	
27	15	חדש	NEW MOON	294d	2 b2
		חלב	HELEB	*317a	
		חלדי	HELDAI	317c	1
		חלד	HELED	*317c	
		עתניאל	OTHNIEL	801a	
27	16	אליעזר	ELIEZER	45c	E
		זכרי	ZICHRI	271d	1
		מעכה	MAACAH	590d	1 c
		נגיד	LEADER	618a	4
		ראובני	REUBENITE	910a	
		שמעוני	SIMEONITES	1035c	
		שפטיה	SHEPHATIAH	1049b	2 c
27	17	אהרן	AARON	14d	
		חשביהו	HASHABIAH	364a	2
		לוי	LEVI	532c	2
		קמואל	KEMUEL	887d	3
27	18	אליאב	ELIAB	45a	C
		אליהו	ELIHU	45b	E
		יששכר	ISSACHAR	441a	1
		מיכאל	MICHAEL	567c	8
		עמרי	OMRI	771d	2 c
27	19	ירמות	JEREMOTH	438b	1
		עבדיהו	OBADIAH	715d	12
		עזריאל	AZRIEL	741a	1
		ישמעיה	ISHMAIAH	1036a	2
27	20	אפרים	EPHRAIM	68b	2
		יואל	JOEL	222b	7

1 CHRONICLES

Ch v.	Heb	Eng	Page	Sec
	הושע	HOSHEA	448a	4
	מנשה	MANASSEH	586c	1 b1 d
	עזיהו	AZAZIAH	739c	2
	פדיהו	PEDALAH	804c	6
27 21	אבנר	ABNER	4c	
	זכריהו	ZECHARIAH	272b	6
	עדו	IDDO	392a	1
	מנשה	MANASSEH	586c	1 b2 b
	ישיאל	JAASIEL	795c	2
27 22	דן	DAN	192d	2
	עזראל	AZAREL	741a	3
	ירחם	JEROHAM	934a	5
	שר	CHIEFTAIN	978d	6
27 23	אמר	SAY	56b	3
	בן	SON	122a	9 a
	מן	FROM	583d	9 b1
	מטה	DOWNWARDS	641d	2 b b
	נשא	LIFT	671c	3 e
27 24	דבר	WORD	183c	4 2
	זה	THIS	262a	6 bd
	חלל	POLLUTE	320d	2
	יום	DAY	399b	4 c
	כלה	FINISH	478b	1 c
	מנה	COUNT	584a	1
	ספר	MISSIVE	707b	3 e
	מספר	NUMBER	708d	1 a
	עלה	GO UP	749a	6
	צרויה	ZERUIAH	863b	2
	קצף	WRATH	893c	1
27 25	אוצר	TREASURE	70a	3 b
	מגדל	TOWER	153d	1
	יהונתן	JONATHAN	221a	6
	כפר	VILLAGE	499a	
	עדיאל	ADIEL	726a	3
	עזיהו	UZZIAH	739d	2
	עזמות	AZMAVETH	740a	1 c
	על	UPON	755b	2 3
	שדה	FIELD	961c	1 f
27 26	אדמה	GROUND	9c	1
	כלוב	CHELUB	477b	2
	מלאכה	WORK	522a	3 b
	עבדה	LABOR	715a	1
	עזרי	EZRI	741b	
27 27	אוצר	TREASURE	70a	2
	זבדי	ZABDI	256c	3
	יין	WINE	406c	D
	רמתי	RAMATHITE	928b	2
	ש	WHO	979d	1
	שמעי	SHIMEI	1035c	2
	שפמי	SHIPHMITE	1050d	
27 28	אוצר	TREASURE	70a	2
	ביתגדר	BETH-GADER	111b	
	בעלחנן	BAAL-HANAN	128a	2
	גדרי	GEDERITE	155b	
	יועש	JOASH	222c	2
	זית	OLIVE TREE	268d	1
	שר	CHIEFTAIN	978c	4 a
	שפלה	LOWLAND	1050d	1
	שקמה	SYCOMORE TREE	1054b	
27 29	בקר	CATTLE	133b	1 a
	בקר	CATTLE	133b	1 a
	שרון	SHARON	450a	1
	עדלי	ADLAI	726b	
	עמק	VALE	771a	
	רעה	TEND	945b	2 a
	שמרי	SHITRAI	1009c	
	שפט	SHAPHAT	1048b	5
	שרון	SHARON	*1056c	
	שרוני	ADDENDA ET CORRIGENDA	1124b	
27 30	אוביל	OBIL	6b	
	אתון	SHE-ASS	87d	
	יחדיהו	JEHDEIAH	292d	1
	מרנתי	MEROTHONITE	599c	1
	ישמעאלי	ISHMAELITE	1035d	
27 31	הגרי	HAGRITE	212c	2
	יזיז	JAZIZ	265c	
	רכוש	PROPERTY	940d	1
	שר	CHIEFTAIN	978d	4 b
27 32	בין	DISCERN	107a	3 e
	דוד	UNCLE	187c	2
	יהונתן	JONATHAN	221a	4
	יחיאל	JEHIEL	313d	3
	חכמוני	HACHMONITE	315d	2
	יעץ	ADVISE	419d	
	כוכב	STAR	457a	
	ספר	ENUMERATOR	708c	1 d
27 33	אחיתפל	AHITHOPHEL	27c	
	ארכי	ARCHITE	74b	
	חושי	HUSHAI	302a	1
	יעץ	ADVISE	419d	
	רע	FRIEND	946a	1
	רעה	FRIEND	*946b	
27 34	אחיתפל	AHITHOPHEL	27c	
	בניהו	BENAIAH	125c	1
	יהוידע	JEHOIADA	220b	1
28 1	גבור	STRONG	150b	2
	חיל	STRENGTH	298d	1 c
	ל	TO	512a	3 b
	ל	TO	514d	5 fe
	סריס	EUNUCH	710c	
	קהל	ASSEMBLE AS	875a	2
	מקנה	CATTLE	889b	1
	רכוש	PROPERTY	940d	1
	שר	CHIEFTAIN	978c	4 a
	שר	CHIEFTAIN	978d	6
	שר	CHIEFTAIN	978d	4 b
	שרת	SERVE	1058a	1 b
	מחלקת	ADDENDA ET CORRIGENDA	1123b	
28 2	בית	HOUSE	109c	1 ae 0
	הדם	FOOTSTOOL	213c	
	כון	ESTABLISH	466b	2 a
	לבב	HEART	523c	2 2
	מנוחה	RESTING PLACE	629c	1
	עם	WITH	768c	4 a
	קום	STAND	877d	1 f
	רגל	FOOT	919d	1 b
	שמע	HEAR	1034a	1 i
28 3	דם	BLOOD	*196c	2 b
	מלחמה	WAR	536c	
	פך	POUR OUT	1049c	1 b
28 4	בחר	CHOOSE	103d	1 a
	בחר	CHOOSE	104a	1 a
	מלך	BE KING	574b	
28 5	נגיד	LEADER	618a	1
	עולם	LONG DURATION	762d	2 f
	רצה	BE PLEASED WITH	953b	3 b
	אלהים	GOD	43d	2 b
	בחר	CHOOSE	104a	1 a
	כסא	THRONE	491b	3 a
	מלכות	ROYAL POWER	574d	1
28 6	בן	SON	120b	1 c
28 7	חזק	BE FIRM	304b	1 2e
	יום	DAY	400d	7 h
	כון	ESTABLISH	466a	1 a
	מלכות	ROYAL POWER	574d	1
	עד	UNTIL	725c	3 2
	עולם	LONG DURATION	762d	2 f
	מצוה	COMMANDMENT	846c	2 b3
28 8	אזן	EAR	24b	2 b
	אחר	AFTER	30a	2 b
	טוב	PLEASANT	374b	1
	ירש	TAKE POSSESSION	439c	1 a
	נחל	GET AS A POSSESSION	636a	2
	עולם	LONG DURATION	762d	2 f
	קהל	ASSEMBLY	874d	2 a
28 9	בין	DISCERN	107a	1 b
	דרש	SEEK	205b	3 a
	דרש	SEEK	205c	4 b
	זנח	REJECT	276b	
	חפץ	DELIGHTING IN	343a	1
	מחשבה	THOUGHT	364b	1 a
	מצא	FIND	394a	1 f
	יצר	PURPOSE	428a	4
	לבב	HEART	523c	2 2
	לב	HEART	525b	2 6a
	נפש	SOUL	661b	0
	עד	PERPETUITY	723d	2 d
	שלם	COMPLETE	1024a	3
28 10	חזק	BE FIRM	304b	1 2c
28 11	אולם	PORCH	17d	1
	בית	HOUSE	109b	1 az
	תבנית	PATTERN	125d	2
	גגזך	TREASURY	170d	
	חדר	CHAMBER	293d	
	כפרת	PROPITIATORY	498c	
	עליה	ROOF-CHAMBER	751a	2
28 12	אוצר	TREASURE	70a	3 a
	תבנית	PATTERN	125d	2
	חצר	ENCLOSURE	347a	3 b
	לשכה	ROOM	545d	1 b
	עם	WITH	768c	4 b
	רוח	BREATH	925c	6
28 13	כהן	PRIEST	464a	7
	כלי	UTENSIL	480a	2 f
	מלאכה	WORK	522a	3 b
	עבדה	LABOR	715c	4
28 14	ו	AND	253b	1 ib
	זהב	GOLD	263a	6
	כלי	UTENSIL	480a	2 f
	עבדה	LABOR	715c	4
	משקל	WEIGHT	1054a	
	משקל	WEIGHT	1054a	
28 15	זהב	GOLD	263c	1
	מנורה	LAMPSTAND	633a	2
	עבדה	LABOR	715c	4
	משקל	WEIGHT	1054a	
28 16	זהב	GOLD	263c	1
	מערכת	ROW	790b	
	שלחן	TABLE	1020b	3
	משקל	WEIGHT	1054a	
28 17	זהב	GOLD	263b	8
	מזלג	THREE PRONGED FORK	272c	
	מזרק	BOWL	284d	2 c
	מהור	CLEAN	373a	2
	כפור	BOWL	499b	
	משקל	WEIGHT	1054a	
28 18	תבנית	PATTERN	125d	2
	מזבח	ALTAR	258d	4 b
	זקק	REFINE	279b	
	כרוב	CHERUB	500d	5 a
	ל	TO	512c	4 a
	סכך	OVERSHADOW	697a	1
	פרש	SPREAD OUT	831a	1
	קטרת	SMOKE	882d	2
	מרכבה	CHARIOT	939d	1
	משקל	WEIGHT	1054a	
28 19	תבנית	PATTERN	125d	2
	כל	ALL	482d	2 ba
28 20	כתב	WRITING	508b	5
	קשוה	JAR	903d	
	שכל	BE PRUDENT	968c	4
	אמץ	BE STRONG	55a	2
	יהוה	YAHWEH	219a	2 1h
	חזק	BE FIRM	304b	1 2c
	חתת	BE SHATTERED	369b	2 a
	ירא	FEAR	431a	1 a
	כלה	BE FINISHED	477c	1 b
	מלאכה	WORK	522a	3 b
	עבדה	LABOR	715c	4
	עד	UNTIL	725c	3 2
	רפה	SINK	952a	1
28 21	דבר	WORD	183b	4 1
	חכמה	WISDOM	315b	2
	כהן	PRIEST	464a	7
	ל	TO	514d	5 fe
	מלאכה	WORK	522b	4
	נדיב	INCLINED	622a	1
	עבדה	LABOR	715c	4
29 1	אדם	MAN	9b	2
	בחר	CHOOSE	104a	1 a
	בירה	CASTLE	108b	1
	יהוה	YAHWEH	219a	2 1h
	נער	YOUTH	655a	1 d
	רך	TENDER	940a	1
29 2	אבן	STONE	6c	2
	אבן	STONE	6d	3
	אבן	STONE	6d	3
	אבן	STONE	6d	3
	ברזל	IRON	137c	1 b
	כון	ESTABLISH	466b	2 a
	כח	STRENGTH	470d	1
	מלוא	SETTING	571b	1
	עץ	TREE	781d	2 b
	פוך	ANTIMONY	806c	
	רקמה	VARIEGATED STUFF	955d	
	שהם	CARNELIAN	996a	
	שיש	ALABASTER	1010d	
29 3	בית	HOUSE	109b	1 ae 0
	זהב	GOLD	263c	1
	יקר	PRECIOUS	430a	1 c
	כון	ESTABLISH	466b	2 a
	כל	ALL	481d	1 c
	סגלה	PROPERTY	688c	2
	עוד	STILL	729b	1 c
	מעל	ABOVE	752a	2 cb
	קדש	APARTNESS	871d	2 d
	רצה	BE PLEASED WITH	953b	1 b
29 4	אופיר	OPHIR	20d	3
	זהב	GOLD	263b	7
	זהב	GOLD	263c	1
	זקק	REFINE	279b	
	טוח	OVER-SPREAD	376b	
29 5	זהב	GOLD	263c	1
	חרש	GRAVER	360d	1 a
	יד	HAND	389b	1 c
	ל	TO	514d	5 fe
	מלאכה	WORK	522b	4
	מלא	FILL	570d	2
	נדב	INCITE	621c	1
29 6	ל	TO	514d	5 fe
	מלאכה	WORK	522b	6 a
	נדב	INCITE	621c	2
	שר	CHIEFTAIN	978c	3 b
	שר	CHIEFTAIN	978d	6
	שר	CHIEFTAIN	978d	4 b
29 7	אלף	THOUSAND	49a	1 c
	אלף	THOUSAND	49a	1 c
	ברזל	IRON	137c	1 b
	דרכמן	DRACHMA	204b	
	זהב	GOLD	263c	1
	חמש	FIVE	332a	4
	כסף	SILVER	494c	8 c
	ככר	ROUND	503b	3 b
	עבדה	LABOR	715c	4
	רבו	TEN THOUSAND	914b	
29 8	אוצר	TREASURE	70a	1
	גרשני	GERSHONITES	177b	
	ה	THE	209b	3
	יחיאל	JEHIEL	313c	2
	מצא	FIND	594a	2 b
29 9	לב	HEART	525b	2 6a
	נדב	INCITE	621c	
	שמח	REJOICE	970b	2 a
	שמח	REJOICE	970b	2 a
	שלם	COMPLETE	1024a	3
29 10	ברך	BLESS	138c	2
	ברך	BLESS	139a	1
	עולם	LONG DURATION	763a	2 m
29 11	ארץ	EARTH	76a	1 b
	גבורה	MIGHT	150c	3
	גדולה	GREATNESS	153c	B
	ה	THE	208b	1 ha
	הוד	SPLENDOUR	217b	3
	כל	ALL	481d	1 c
	כל	ALL	482c	2 a
	ממלכה	DOMINION	575b	2
	נצח	EMINENCE	664b	1
	נשא	LIFT	672a	
	תפארה	BEAUTY	802d	2 c
29 12	גבורה	MIGHT	150c	2
	גדל	BECOME GREAT	152b	2
	חזק	BE FIRM	304c	1 b
	יד	HAND	390a	1 e2

Ch	v.	Heb	Eng	Page	Sec
		כבוד	HONOR	458c	2a
		כח	STRENGTH	470d	3
		כל	ALL	*483a	2bb
		ל	TO	512a	3b
		ל	TO	517d	7bd
		משל	RULE	605d	3
29	13	פנה	FACE	818a	25ac
		הלל	PRAISE	238d	2e
		ידה	PRAISE	392c	1b
		תפארה	BEAUTY	802d	2c
		שם	NAME	1028c	3
29	14	זה	THIS	262a	6d
		כח	STRENGTH	470d	1b
		כי	THAT	472c	1da
		כל	ALL	483a	2bb
		מי	WHO	566d	F b
		נדב	INCITE	621c	2
		נתן	GIVE	679a	1k
		עצר	RESTRAIN	783d	2
29	15	גר	SOJOURNER	158b	1
		גר	SOJOURNER	*158c	2
		תושב	SOJOURNER	444c	3
		מקוה	HOPE	876a	
29	16	הוא	HE, SHE, IT	*215a	2
		המון	ABUNDANCE	242d	4
		כון	ESTABLISH	466b	2a
		כל	ALL	483a	2bb
		קדש	APARTNESS	871c	1c
29	17	בחן	TRY	103c	2b
		ה	THE	209b	3
		ישר	STRAIGHTNESS	449c	2
		מושר	LEVEL	449d	2
		לב	HEART	523d	26a
		לבב	HEART	523d	26
		מצא	FIND	594b	2e
		נדב	INCITE	621c	2
		רצה	BE PLEASED WITH	953a	1a
29	18	אלהים	GOD	44b	4ba
		מחשבה	THOUGHT	364d	1a
		יצר	PURPOSE	428a	4
		כון	ESTABLISH	466c	3
		ל	TO	512a	3b
		לבב	HEART	523c	23c
		לבב	HEART	523d	24
		עולם	LONG DURATION	762d	2g
		יצחק	ISAAC	850c	1
		ישראל	ISRAEL	975c	1
		שמר	KEEP	1036d	2a
29	19	בירה	CASTLE	108b	1
		חק	SOMETHING PRESCRIBED	349d	7g
		כון	ESTABLISH	466c	2b
		כל	ALL	482d	2ba
		לבב	HEART	524a	26a
		עדות	TESTIMONY	730b	2
		מצוה	COMMANDMENT	846c	2b1
		שלם	COMPLETE	1024a	3
29	20	ברך	BLESS	139a	1
		ברך	BLESS	139a	1
		ל	TO	512a	3b
		קדד	BOW DOWN	869a	
29	21	איל	RAM	18a	2g
		זבח	SACRIFICE	257c	11
		כבש	LAMB	461a	1
		ל	TO	*517a	6a
		מחרת	THE MORROW	564b	1
		נסך	DRINK-OFFERING	651a	1
		עלה	WHOLE BURNT OFFERING	750d	
		פר	YOUNG BULL	830d	2b
29	22	כהן	PRIEST	463c	4
		ל	TO	512a	3b
		מלך	BE KING	574b	
		משח	ANOINT	603b	2
		נגיד	LEADER	618a	1
		צדק	RIGHTEOUS	843b	1a
		שר	CHIEFTAIN	978d	6
29	23	כסא	THRONE	491a	3a
		ל	TO	512b	4a
		מלך	KING	573c	5c
		צלח	ADVANCE	852c	2
29	24	יד	HAND	389d	1d
		נתן	GIVE	680a	1z
29	25	גדל	BECOME GREAT	152b	1
		הוד	SPLENDOUR	217a	1
		מלך	KING	573b	5b
		מלכות	ROYALTY	574d	1
		נתן	PUT	680c	2b
		מעל	ABOVE	752a	2cb
29	26	ישי	JESSE	445a	
29	27	חברון	HEBRON	289b	
29	28	טוב	PLEASANT	374b	4a
		כבוד	HONOR	458c	2a
		מות	DIE	559c	1a1
		שבע	SATISFIED	960a	1b
		שיבה	OLD AGE	966d	1
		שלמה	SOLOMON	1024d	
29	29	גד	GAD	151c	2
		דבר	WORD	183a	21c
		דבר	WORD	183a	21c
		דבר	WORD	183c	42
		חזה	SEER	302d	1b
		נתן	NATHAN	681d	1
		ראה	SEER	909a	
		ראשון	FIRST	911c	1a
		שמואל	SAMUEL	1028d	1
29	30	גבורה	MIGHT	150c	2
		ממלכות	ROYAL POWER	574d	1
		ממלכה	KINGDOM	575b	1
		עבר	PASS OVER	717b	1g
		עת	TIME	773d	3

2 CHRONICLES

Ch	v.	Heb	Eng	Page	Sec
1	1	גדל	BECOME GREAT	152b	2
		יהוה	YAHWEH	218d	2le
		חזק	BE FIRM	305b	1
		מלכות	KINGDOM	575a	1
		מעל	ABOVE	752a	2cb
		על	UPON	752d	21
		שלמה	SOLOMON	1024d	
		על	UPON	*1106b	1a
1	2	נשיא	PRINCE	672b	5
		ראש	HEAD	911a	3f
		שר	CHIEFTAIN	978c	3b
		שפט	JUDGE	1047d	2b
1	3	אהל	TENT	14b	3
		במה	HIGH PLACE	119b	3
		גבעון	GIBEON	149c	
		הלך	WALK	231b	1d3 gd
		מועד	TENT OF MEETING	418a	5
		ל	TO	511b	1ga
		משה	MOSES	602d	
		עבד	SLAVE	714a	3
1	4	אבל	HOWBEIT	6a	2
		אהל	TENT	14b	3
		אלהים	GOD	44a	3b
		ה	THE	209b	3
		כון	ESTABLISH	466b	2a
		נטה	SPREAD OUT	640a	2
		קריתיערים	CHEPHIRAH	900c	
1	5	בצלאל	BEZALEL	130b	1
		דרש	RESORT TO	205a	3b
		מזבח	ALTAR	258c	3b
		חור	HUR	301b	2
		משכן	DWELLING-PLACE	1015d	2c
1	6	אהל	TENT	14b	3
		מזבח	ALTAR	258c	3b
		מועד	TENT OF MEETING	418a	5
		עלה	GO UP	750a	8
		עלה	GO UP	750a	8
		עלה	WHOLE BURNT OFFERING	750d	
		על	UPON	756d	27b
1	7	ראה	TO SEE	908b	1a
		שאל	ASK	981c	1a
		שלמה	SOLOMON	1024d	
1	8	גדול	GREAT	153b	6c
		דוד	DAVID	188b	J
		חסד	GOODNESS	339a	21e
		מלך	BE KING	574b	
1	9	אמן	CONFIRM	53a	4
		יהוה	YAHWEH	219a	21h
		מלך	BE KING	574b	
		עם	WITH	767d	1d
		עפר	DRY EARTH	780a	2a
1	10	בוא	COME	97d	1a
		זה	THIS	*261a	2bb
		חכמה	WISDOM	315c	2
		מדע	KNOWLEDGE	396b	1
		פנה	FACE	817c	24cb
		שפט	JUDGE	1047c	1b
1	11	חכמה	WISDOM	315c	2
		מדע	KNOWLEDGE	396b	1
		יום	DAY	399a	4a
		כבוד	HONOR	458c	2a
		לבב	HEART	523c	22
		מלך	BE KING	574b	
		נכס	RICHES	647d	
		נפש	SOUL	659d	3c
		עם	WITH	768c	4a
		שלמה	SOLOMON	1024d	
		שפט	JUDGE	1047c	1b
1	12	ה	THE	208b	1ha
		חכמה	WISDOM	315c	2
		מדע	KNOWLEDGE	396b	1
		כבוד	HONOR	458c	2a
		כן	SO	485d	1a
		נכס	RICHES	647d	
1	13	אהל	TENT	14b	3
		במה	HIGH PLACE	119b	3
		גבעון	GIBEON	149c	
		מועד	TENT OF MEETING	418a	5
		פנה	FACE	818a	25aa
1	14	אסף	GATHER	62b	1c
		נוח	REST	628c	B 1
		עיר	CITY	746c	1e
		פרש	HORSEMAN	832a	
1	15	אבן	STONE	7a	8
		ארז	CEDAR	72d	1
		זהב	GOLD	263c	1
		כסף	SILVER	494b	1
		נתן	GIVE	681a	3c
		שפלה	LOWLAND	1050d	1
		שקמה	SYCOMORE TREE	1054b	
1	16	מוצא	GOING FORTH	425d	2b
		מחיר	PRICE	564b	1
		מצרים	EGYPTIANS	596a	2b
		סחר	GO AROUND	695c	2
		קוה	KUE	875c	
1	17	מקוה	COLLECTION	876c	
		ארם	ARAM	74c	C
		חתי	HITTITE	366d	2b
		יד	HAND	391a	5d
		יצא	BRING OUT	424d	3
		מצרים	EGYPTIANS	596a	2b
		מרכבה	CHARIOT	939d	1
1	18	אמר	SAY	56c	4
		בית	HOUSE	109a	1ae1
		בית	HOUSE	109b	1ae0
		מלכות	ROYAL POWER	574d	1
2	1	הר	MOUNTAIN	251a	2a
		חצב	HEW	345a	2a
		נצח	BE PRE-EMINENT	663d	1
		סבל	BURDEN BEARER	688a	
		סבל	BURDEN BEARER	688a	
2	2	חירם	HIRAM	27c	1
		ארז	CEDAR	72d	2
		בנה	BUILD	124b	1ab
		עשה	DO	794b	12
		צר	TYER	862d	
2	3	בית	HOUSE	109b	1ae0
		בקר	MORNING	134a	1e
		יהוה	YAHWEH	219a	21f
		הנה	BEHOLD	243d	
		ו	AND	253a	1g
		חדש	NEW MOON	294c	2
		מועד	APPOINTED TIME	417c	1b
		תמיד	CONTINUITY	556c	2a
		סם	SPICE	702c	
		על	UPON	753c	21c
		עולם	LONG DURATION	762c	2e
		ערב	SUNSET	787d	1a
		מערכת	ROW	790b	
		קדש	BE SET APART	873b	1a
		קטר	MAKE SACRIFICES SMOKE	883b	2
2	4	אלהים	GOD	43c	1d
		גדול	GREAT	153b	6c
2	5	כול	CONTAIN	465a	2
		כח	STRENGTH	470d	1b
		כיאם	EXCEPT	475a	2a
		מי	WHO	566d	F b
		עצר	RESTRAIN	783d	2
		קטר	MAKE SACRIFICES SMOKE	883b	2
		שמי	HEAVENS	1030b	2a
2	6	ארגון	PURPLE	71a	
		ארגמן	PURPLE THREAD	71b	1
		ברזול	IRON	137c	1b
		זהב	GOLD	263c	2a
		זמרי	ZIMRI	275b	2
		ידע	KNOW	394b	4b
		כון	ESTABLISH	466c	2b
		כרמיל	CRIMSON	502b	
		עשה	DO	794a	11b
		פתוח	ENGRAVING	836c	
		פתח	ENGRAVE	836c	
		תבלת	VIOLET THREAD	1067b	1a
2	7	אלגומים	A TREE	38d	
		ארז	CEDAR	72c	2
		אשר	THAT	83c	8ab
		ברוש	CYPRESS	141c	3
		ידע	KNOW	394b	4b
		כרת	HEW	503d	3
		לבנון	LEBANON	527a	
		עץ	TREE	781c	1a
		ל	TO	518b	7bh
2	8	פלא	BE SURPASSING	810d	1
2	9	בת	BATH	144c	
		חטב	CUT OR GATHER WOOD	310a	
		חטה	WHEAT	334d	
		כר	KOR	499d	
		כרת	HEW	503d	3
		מכה	SLAUGHTER	647a	4
		שערה	BARLEY	972d	2
		שמן	OIL	1032b	2b
		מכלת	ADDENDA ET CORRIGENDA	1120a	
2	10	אהב	LOVE	13a	5b
		חירם	HIRAM	27c	1
		כתב	WRITING	508b	3
		מלך	KING	573c	5c
		צר	TYER	862d	
2	11	חירם	HIRAM	27c	1
		ארץ	EAXTH	76a	1b
		בינה	UNDERSTANDING	108a	1
		בית	HOUSE	109b	1ae0
		ברך	BLESS	138c	2a
		חכם	WISE	314d	2
		ידע	KNOW	394c	5
		מלכות	ROYAL POWER	574d	1
		עשה	DO	794d	21b
		שכל	PRUDENCE	968c	2
2	12	אב	FATHER	3d	8
		חירם	HIRAM	27c	1
		בינה	UNDERSTANDING	108a	3
		חכם	WISE	314d	1
		ידע	KNOW	394c	5
		ל	TO	512a	3b
2	13	ארגון	PURPLE	71a	
		ארגמן	PURPLE THREAD	71b	1a
		בוץ	BYSSUS	101c	
		בת	DAUGHTER	123b	1i
		ברזול	IRON	137c	1b

2 CHRONICLES

Ch	v.	Heb	Eng	Page	Sec
		דן	DAN	192d	2
		זהב	GOLD	263c	2 a
		חכם	WISE	314d	1
		חשב	THINK	363a	1 5
		מחשבה	THOUGHT	364c	3
		ידע	KNOW	394b	4 b
		כרמיל	CRIMSON	502b	
		נתן	GIVE	681c	1 d
		עשה	DO	794a	1 1b
		פתח	ENGRAVE	836c	
		פתוח	ENGRAVING	836c	
		צרי	TYRIAN	863a	
		תכלת	VIOLET THREAD	1067b	1 a
2	14	חטה	WHEAT	334d	
		שערה	BARLEY	972d	2
		שמן	OIL	1032b	2 b
		תכלת	VIOLET THREAD	1067b	1 a
2	15	ים	SEA	410d	1
		יפו	JOPPA	421d	
		כרת	HEW	503d	3
		לבנון	LEBANON	527a	
		עלה	GO UP	749c	4
		צרך	NEED	863c	
2	16	גר	SOJOURNER	158c	2
		חכם	WISE	314d	1
		מצא	FIND	594b	2 f
		ספר	COUNT	*707d	1
		ספר	ENUMERATION	708c	
		רפסדה	RAFT	952c	
2	17	הר	MOUNTAIN	251a	2 a
		חצב	HEW	345a	2 a
		נצח	PRE-EMINENT	663d	1
		סבל	BURDEN BEARER	688a	1
		עבד	WORK	713c	1
		עשה	DO	795a	2 8
3	1	ארנן	ORNAN	75a	
		יבוסי	JEBUSITE	101a	1
		גרן	THRESHING-FLOOR	175b	
		חלל	POLLUTE	320d	2
		כון	ESTABLISH	466b	2 a
		מריה	MORIAH	599a	
		מקום	STANDING PLACE	880a	3 c
		ראה	TO SEE	908b	1 a
3	2	חדש	NEW MOON	294d	2 b2
		חלל	POLLUTE	320d	2
		יום	DAY	*398c	2 e
		מלכות	REIGN	575a	2
		ארבע	FOUR	917a	1 a4
3	3	אמה	CUBIT	52b	1
		אמה	CUBIT	52b	1
		אמה	CUBIT	52c	1
		יסד	FOUNDING	414a	
		מדה	SIZE	551c	2
		עשרים	TWENTY	797d	1 1d
		ששים	SIXTY	995d	
3	4	אמה	CUBIT	52b	1
		גבה	HEIGHT	147b	1
		זהב	GOLD	263b	8
		זהב	GOLD	263d	2 c
		טהור	CLEAN	373a	1
		עשרים	TWENTY	797d	1 2d
		פנימה	WITHIN	819b	1
		צפה	LAY OUT	860a	
		רחב	WIDTH	931d	
3	5	ברוש	CYPRESS	*141c	1
		ברוש	CYPRESS	141c	1
		זהב	GOLD	263a	6
		זהב	GOLD	263b	8
		זהב	GOLD	263d	2 d
		חפה	COVER	342a	
		טוב	PLEASANT	374b	3 e
		עלה	GO UP	749d	4
		על	UPON	757a	2 7b
		שרשרה	CHAIN	1057c	
		תמרה	PALM-FIGURE	1071d	
3	6	זהב	GOLD	263a	6
		זהב	GOLD	263b	7
		יקר	PRECIOUS	430a	1 c
		תפארה	BEAUTY	802c	1
		פרוים	PARVAIM	826c	
		צפה	LAY OUT	860a	
3	7	דלת	DOOR	195a	1
		זהב	GOLD	263d	2 d
		חפה	COVER	342a	
		כרוב	CHERUB	500d	5 b
		סף	THRESHOLD	706b	
		פתח	ENGRAVE	836c	
		קורה	RAFTER	900a	
3	8	אמה	CUBIT	52b	1
		בית	HOUSE	109b	1 ae 0
		זהב	GOLD	263b	8
		זהב	GOLD	263d	2 d
		חפה	COVER	342a	
		טוב	PLEASANT	374b	3 e
		ל	TO	514c	5 fb
		קדש	APARTMENT	871d	
3	9	זהב	GOLD	263b	9 a
		זהב	GOLD	263d	2 d
		חפה	COVER	342a	
		ל	TO	514c	5 fb
		מסמר	NAIL	702d	
		עליה	ROOF-CHAMBER	751a	
		שקל	SHEKEL	1053d	
		תמר	TAMAR	1071c	1 b
3	10	בית	HOUSE	109b	1 ae 0
		זהב	GOLD	263d	2 c

Ch	v.	Heb	Eng	Page	Sec
		כרוב	CHERUB	500d	5 a
		מעשה	DEED	796a	2 a1
		צעצעים	IMAGES	847b	
		צפה	LAY OUT	860a	
		קדש	APARTMENT	871d	2 d
3	11	אמה	CUBIT	52c	1
		כנף	WING	*489b	
		כנף	WING	489c	1 c
		כרוב	CHERUB	500d	5 a
		ל	TO	514c	5 fb
		נגע	REACH	619c	2
3	12	דבק	CLINGING	180a	
		כרוב	CHERUB	500d	5 a
		נגע	REACH	619c	2
3	13	כנף	WING	*489b	
		כרוב	CHERUB	500d	5 a
		ל	TO	510d	1
		פנה	FACE	816a	13
		פרש	SPREAD OUT	831a	1
		רגל	FOOT	919d	1 c
3	14	ארגון	PURPLE	71a	
		ארגמן	PURPLE THREAD	71b	1 a
		בוץ	BYSSUS	101c	
		כרוב	CHERUB	501a	5 b
		כרמיל	CRIMSON	502b	
		עלה	GO UP	749d	4
		על	UPON	757a	2 7b
		פרכת	CURTAIN	827d	
3	15	חמש	FIVE	332a	5 b3
		עמוד	PILLAR	765b	2
		צפת	PLATED CAPITAL	860b	
		שרשרה	CHAIN	1057c	
3	16	דביר	HINDMOST CHAMBER	184b	
		מאה	HUNDRED	547b	1 a3
		עמוד	PILLAR	765b	2
		רמון	POMEGRANATE	942a	3
		שרשרה	CHAIN	1057c	
3	17	בעו	BOAZ	127a	2
		בעו	BOAZ	*127a	2
		היכל	TEMPLE	228c	2 b
		ימין	RIGHT HAND	411d	2 a
		ימיני	RIGHT	412a	
		ימני	RIGHT	412b	
		יכין	JACHIN	467c	2
		עמוד	PILLAR	765b	2
		פנה	FACE	818d	2 7ad
		קום	STAND	878d	2 a
		שמאל	LEFT	969d	1
4	1	מזבח	ALTAR	258d	4 a
		מזבח	ALTAR	259a	8
		קומה	HEIGHT	879b	3
4	2	אמה	CUBIT	52c	1
		חמש	FIVE	331d	1 a
		ים	SEA	411a	7
		יצק	BE POURED	427c	2
		סבב	SURROUND	686a	2 d
		עגל	ROUND	722c	
		קו	LINE	876a	
		קומה	HEIGHT	879b	3
4	3	בקר	CATTLE	133c	2
		בקר	CATTLE	*133c	2
		דמות	LIKENESS	198b	1
		מור	ROW	377a	2
		יצק	CAST	427b	2
		יצקה	CASTING	*427c	
		מוצקת	CASTING	427c	2
		סביב	SURROUND	686a	2 d
		סביב	ROUND ABOUT	687a	1 b
		תחת	UNDERNEATH	1065b	2 1
4	4	אחור	HINDER PART	*30d	
		בית	HOUSE	110b	7
		בקר	CATTLE	133c	2
		בקר	CATTLE	133c	2
		ים	SEA	411b	9
		נגב	SOUTH-COUNTRY	616b	2
		מעל	ABOVE	752a	2
		פנה	TURN	815b	2 b
4	5	בת	BATH	144c	
		חזק	BE FIRM	305b	6 e
		טפח	A SPAN	381c	1
		כל	CONTAIN	465b	1
		כום	CUP	468a	
		עבי	THICKNESS	716a	
		פרח	BUD	827b	
		שושן	LILY	1004c	
4	6	רוח	RINSE	188d	1
		ימין	RIGHT HAND	411d	2 a
		כיור	POT	468c	3 b
		מעשה	DEED	796a	2 a1
		עשר	TEN	796d	2 b
		רחץ	WASH OFF	934c	1
4	7	היכל	TEMPLE	228c	2 b
		זהב	GOLD	263c	2 a
		חמש	FIVE	331d	1 a
		ימין	RIGHT HAND	411d	2 a
		מנורה	LAMPSTAND	633a	2
		עשר	TEN	796d	2 b
		משפט	JUDGMENT	1048d	3
4	8	היכל	TEMPLE	228c	2 b
		זהב	GOLD	263c	2 a
		מזרק	BOWL	284d	2 c
		ימין	RIGHT HAND	411d	2 a
		מאה	HUNDRED	547d	1 a3
		נוח	REST	628d	B 1
		עשר	TEN	796d	2 b

Ch	v.	Heb	Eng	Page	Sec
		שלחן	TABLE	1020b	3
4	9	דלת	DOOR	195b	2
		חצר	ENCLOSURE	347a	3 b
		עזרה	ENCLOSURE	741c	2
		צפה	LAY OUT	860a	
4	10	ימני	RIGHT	412b	
		כתף	SIDE	509c	2 b
		מול	IN FRONT OF	557c	2 bb
		נגב	SOUTH-COUNTRY	616c	2
		קדם	EASTWARD	870a	
4	11	חירם	HIRAM	27c	3
		מזרק	BOWL	284d	2 c
		יע	SHOVEL	418b	
		כיור	POT	*468c	3 b
		סיר	POT	696c	2
4	12	כסה	COVER	491d	4
		כתרת	CAPITAL	509d	
		שבכה	LATTICE-WORK	959a	1
4	13	מור	ROW	377a	2
		כסה	COVER	491d	4
		כתרת	CAPITAL	509d	
		מאה	HUNDRED	548b	1 c4
		רמון	POMEGRANATE	942a	3
		שבכה	LATTICE-WORK	959a	1
		מכונה	BASE	467d	
4	14	כיור	POT	468c	3 b
4	15	בקר	CATTLE	133c	2
4	16	אב	FATHER	3d	8
		חירם	HIRAM	27c	3
		מזלגה	THREE PRONGED FORK	272c	
		יע	SHOVEL	418b	
		כיור	POT	*468c	3 b
		מרק	POLISH	599d	
		נחשת	COPPER	638d	1
		סיר	POT	696c	2
		צהב	GLEAM	843c	
4	17	אדמה	EARTH	9d	3
		יצק	CAST	427b	2
		ירדן	JORDAN	434d	
		כבר	ROUND	503b	1
		סכות	SUCCOTH	697d	2
		מעבה	THICKNESS	716b	
		מערה	FORD	721b	2
		צרתן	ZERETHAN	866c	
4	18	חקר	SEARCH	350d	
		מאד	EXCEEDINGLY	547b	2
4	19	מזבח	ALTAR	258d	4 b
		מזבח	ALTAR	259a	8
		זהב	GOLD	263c	2 a
		לחם	FOOD	537b	1 a
		קעילה	KEILAH	890d	
		שלחן	TABLE	1020b	3
4	20	בער	BURN	129b	1
		דביר	HINDMOST CHAMBER	184b	
		זהב	GOLD	263b	8
		מנורה	LAMPSTAND	633a	2
		סגר	CLOSE	689b	4 b
		משפט	JUDGMENT	1048d	3
		מכלה	PERFECTION	479a	
4	21	מלקחים	TONGS	544c	2
		פרח	BUD	827b	
4	22	דלת	DOOR	195a	1
		דלת	DOOR	195b	2
		היכל	TEMPLE	228c	2 b
		זהב	GOLD	263b	8
		מזמרת	SNUFFERS	275a	
		מזרק	BOWL	284d	2 c
		מחתה	FIRE-HOLDER	367b	2
		כף	PAN	497a	4 b
		סגר	CLOSE	689b	4 b
		פתח	OPENING	835d	
		קדש	APARTMENT	871d	2 d
		אוצר	TREASURE	70a	3 a
5	1	זהב	GOLD	263c	1
		שלם	BE COMPLETE	1022b	1
5	2	דוד	DAVID	188a	A
		זקן	OLD	278d	2 b
		מטה	TRIBE	641d	3
		נשיא	PRINCE	672b	5
		ציון	ZION	851b	
		קהל	ASSEMBLE AS	875a	2
5	3	חג	FESTIVAL-GATHERING	291a	1 b2
		קהל	ASSEMBLE AS	875a	2
5	4	זקן	OLD	278d	2 b
		לוי	LEVITE	532d	3 1a
5	5	אהל	TENT	14b	3
		מועד	TENT OF MEETING	418a	5
		כהן	PRIEST	463d	5
		לוי	LEVITE	532d	3 1a
5	6	בקר	CATTLE	133b	1 a
		זבח	SLAUGHTER FOR SACRIFICE	257a	1
		זבח	SLAUGHTER FOR SACRIFICE	257b	2
		מנה	COUNT	284a	1
		יעד	GATHER BY APPOINTMENT	417a	3
		עדה	CONGREGATION	*417b	3
		ספר	COUNT	708a	
		רב	MULTITUDE	914a	1
5	7	דביר	HINDMOST CHAMBER	184b	
		כרוב	CHERUB	500d	5 a

Ch v.	Heb	Eng	Page	Sec
	קדש	APARTNESS	871d	2 d
	תחת	UNDERNEATH	*1066a	3 1a
5 8	בד	PART	*94d	3 c
	כסה	COVER	492a	6
	כרוב	CHERUB	500d	5 a
	מעל	ABOVE	752a	2 d
	פרש	SPREAD OUT	831a	1
	מקום	STANDING PLACE	879d	1 a
5 9	ארך	BE LONG	73d	2
	בד	PART	*94d	3 c
	דביר	HINDMOST CHAMBER	184b	
	היה	BE	226d	3 2
	ראה	TO SEE	908c	3
	ראש	HEAD	911a	2 a
5 10	חרב	HOREB	352a	
	יצא	GO OUT	422d	1 a
	כרת	CUT	503d	4
	לוח	TABLET	*531d	1
	לוח	TABLET	531d	1
	רק	ONLY	956c	2 d
5 11	אין	NOT	34d	5 b
	ל	TO	512a	3 b
	מצא	FIND	594b	2 e
	קדש	APARTNESS	871d	2 d
	קדש	BE SET APART	873c	4
	שמר	KEEP	1037a	3 c
5 12	הימן	HEMAN	54d	
	אסף	ASAPH	63a	2
	בוץ	BYSSUS	101c	
	הלל	PRAISE	*238c	2 e
	מזרח	PLACE OF SUNRISE	281a	2 c2
	חצצרה	CLARION	348c	2 c
	חצצר	SOUND A TRUMPET	348d	
	ידותון	JEDUTHUN	s 393a	
	איתן	ETHAN	*451a	
	כנור	LYRE	490a	
	ל	TO	514c	5 fd
	ל	TO	514c	5 fe
	לבש	ARRAYED	528b	
	לוי	LEVITE	533a	3 2b
	נבל	HARP	614c	
	מצלתים	CYMBALS	853a	
5 13	הלל	PRAISE	238c	2 e
	הלל	PRAISE	238c	2 e
	חסד	GOODNESS	339d	2 3c
	חצצרה	CLARION	348c	2 c
	חצצרה	CLARION	348c	2 c
	חצצר	SOUND A TRUMPET	348d	
	טוב	PLEASANT	374d	9 b
	ידה	PRAISE	392c	1 b
	כלי	INSTRUMENT	479d	2 b
	מלא	BE FULL	570a	1 a
	עולם	LONG DURATION	762b	2 c
	ענן	CLOUD	778a	1 a
	מצלתים	CYMBALS	853a	
	קול	VOICE	877a	2 a
	קול	VOICE	877a	2 a
	רום	BE HIGH	927c	1 b
	שמע	HEAR	1034c	1 b
5 14	כבוד	GLORY	458d	2 c1
	מלא	FILL	570b	2
	עמד	STAND	763d	1 a
	ענן	CLOUD	778a	1 a
	שרת	SERVE	1058a	2 a
6 1	ערפל	CLOUD	791d	
	שכן	SETTLE DOWN	1015b	2 c
6 2	בית	HOUSE	109b	1 ae 0
	זבל	ELEVATION	259c	
	ישב	DWELL	443a	3
	מכון	FIXED PLACE	467c	1
	עולם	LONG DURATION	763b	2 1
6 3	ברך	BLESS	*139a	3
	סבב	TURN ABOUT	686c	1 a
	קהל	ASSEMBLY	874d	2 a
6 4	ברך	BLESS	138c	2 a
	דבר	SPEAK	181b	3 d
	מלא	FILL	570d	3
6 5	בחר	CHOOSE	*104a	1 a
	בחר	CHOOSE	104a	1 a
	בנה	BUILD	124b	1 ab
	יצא	CASUE TO GO	424c	1 a
6 6	בחר	CHOOSE	104a	1 a
	בחר	CHOOSE	*104a	1 a
6 7	היה	BE	227b	3 4d a
	לבב	HEART	*523c	2 2
6 8	עם	WITH	768c	4 a
	היה	BE	227b	3 4d a
	טוב	PLEASING	373c	
	לבב	HEART	*523c	2 2
	עם	WITH	768c	4 a
6 9	חלק	LOINS	323b	1
	יצא	GO OUT	423c	1 h
6 10	כסא	THRONE	491a	3 a
	קום	STAND	878a	4
6 11	כרת	CUT	503d	4
6 12	פרש	SPREAD OUT	831b	1
	קהל	ASSEMBLY	874d	2 a
6 13	אמה	CUBIT	52b	1
	ברך	KNEEL	138c	1
	ברך	KNEE	139c	
	כיור	STAGE	468c	4
	עזרה	ENCLOSURE	741c	2
	פרש	SPREAD OUT	831b	1
	קהל	ASSEMBLY	874d	2 a
	קומה	HEIGHT	879b	3
6 14	שמי	HEAVENS	1030a	1 b
	ברית	COVENANT	*137b	3 2
	חסד	GOODNESS	339a	2 1e
	לב	HEART	*524c	2 2
6 15	דבר	SPEAK	*181b	3 c
	דוד	DAVID	188a	
	יום	DAY	400d	7 h
	מלא	FILL	570d	3
6 16	דבר	SPEAK	*181b	3 c
	דוד	DAVID	188a	
	דרך	WAY	203c	6 a
	הלך	WALK	234c	2 3a 1d
	הלך	WALK	234d	2 3c
	תורה	LAW	436b	2 b2
	כסא	THRONE	491a	3 a
	כרת	BE CUT OFF	504b	4
	רק	ONLY	956c	2 f
6 17	אמן	CONFIRM	53a	4
	דבר	SPEAK	*181b	3 c
	דוד	DAVID	188a	
6 18	אדם	MAN	9b	2
	אמנם	VERILY	53d	
	אף	ALSO	65b	3
	ישב	DWELL	443a	3
	כול	CONTAIN	465a	2
	שמי	HEAVENS	1030b	2 a
6 19	יהוה	YAHWEH	219a	2 1f
	תחנה	FAVOR	337c	2
	תפלה	PRAYER	813c	1 b
	תפלה	PRAYER	813c	1 e
	תפלה	PRAYER	813c	1 e
	פנה	TURN	815c	2 c1
	רנה	RINGING CRY	943c	1
6 20	עין	EYE	744b	1 j
	פלל	INTERVENE	813b	3
	תפלה	PRAYER	813c	1 b
	תפלה	PRAYER	813c	1 e
	פתח	OPEN	835b	
	מקום	STANDING PLACE	880b	4
6 21	תחנה	FAVOR	*337c	2
	תחנון	SUPPLICATION FOR FAVOR	337d	2
	ישב	DWELL	443a	3
	סלח	FORGIVE	699b	
	פלל	INTERVENE	813b	3
	מקום	STANDING PLACE	880a	2 b2
	מקום	STANDING PLACE	880b	4
6 22	אלה	SWEAR	46d	
	אלה	OATH	46d	1
	אלה	SWEAR	46d	1
	חטא	MISS A GOAL OR WAY	306d	2 a
	נשא	LIFT	670a	1 a
	נשא	LIFT	670d	1 b 6
	נשא	BE A CREDITOR	673d	
6 23	דרך	WAY	203d	6 d
	נתן	PUT	680d	2 b
	צדקה	RIGHTEOUSNESS	842b	3
	צדק	DECLARE RIGHTEOUS	842d	3
	צדיק	JUST	843a	2
	רשע	WICKED	957b	1
	שוב	TURN BACK	999c	4 a
	שפט	JUDGE	1047c	2 a
6 24	איב	BE HOSTILE TO	33c	
	אשר	THAT	83d	8 d
	חטא	MISS A GOAL OR WAY	307a	2 b
	חנן	SHOW FAVOR	336b	2
	ידה	CONFESS	392c	2 a
	נגף	STRIKE	620a	3
	פלל	INTERVENE	813b	3
	שם	NAME	1028c	3
6 25	אדמה	LAND	10a	5
	חטאת	SIN	309a	1 d2
	סלח	FORGIVE	699b	
	שוב	TURN BACK	998b	1 a
6 26	חטא	MISS A GOAL OR WAY	307a	2 b
	חטאת	SIN	308d	1 c
	ידה	CONFESS	392c	2 a
	מטר	RAIN	564d	
	עצר	RESTRAIN	783d	
	פלל	INTERVENE	813b	3
	מקום	STANDING PLACE	880b	4
	שם	NAME	1028c	3
6 27	דרך	WAY	203c	6 c
	הלך	WALK	234c	2 3a 1a
	חטאת	SIN	309a	1 d2
	טוב	PLEASANT	374d	0 a
	ירה	DIRECT	*435c	5 c
	מטר	RAIN	564d	
	סלח	FORGIVE	699b	
6 28	דבר	PESTILENCE	184a	1
	מחלה	SICKNESS	318b	
	חסיל	LOCUST	340c	
	ירקון	RUST	439a	1
	נגע	STROKE	619c	2
	צרר	BIND	864d	B
	ארבה	LOCUST	916a	
	שדפון	SMUT	995b	
	שער	GATE	1045a	2 c
6 29	תחנה	FAVOR	337c	2
	מכאוב	PAIN	456b	1
	כף	HOLLOW OF THE HAND	496c	1 d4
	נגע	STROKE	619c	2
	תפלה	PRAYER	813c	1 a
	פרש	SPREAD OUT	831b	1
6 30	דרך	WAY	203c	6 a
	ידע	KNOW	394a	2
	ישב	DWELL	443a	3
	מכון	FIXED PLACE	467d	1
	לבב	HEART	*523c	2 2
	נתן	GIVE	679d	1 v
	סלח	FORGIVE	699b	
6 31	אדמה	LAND	10a	5
	דרך	WAY	204a	6 ec
	חי	ALIVE	312a	1 b
	ירא	FEAR	431c	3 b
6 32	גדול	GREAT	153b	6 c
	זרוע	ARM	284a	1 c
	חזק	STRONG	305c	1 b
	נכרי	FOREIGN	648d	1 b
	פלל	INTERVENE	813b	3
	רחק	DISTANT	935b	1 a
	שם	NAME	1028b	3
6 33	ירא	FEAR	431c	3 b
	ישב	DWELL	443a	3
	מכון	FIXED PLACE	467d	1
	נכרי	FOREIGN	648d	1 b
	קרא	CALL	896b	2 d4
	בחר	CHOOSE	*104a	1 a
6 34	דרך	WAY	203b	3
	מלחמה	WAR	536c	
	פלל	INTERVENE	813b	3
6 35	אשר	THAT	83d	8 d
	תחנה	FAVOR	337c	2
	תפלה	PRAYER	813c	1 e
6 36	אדם	MAN	9b	2
	אנף	BE ANGRY	60a	
	חטא	MISS A GOAL OR WAY	307a	2 b
	חטא	MISS A GOAL OR WAY	307a	2 b
	קרב	NEAR	898b	1
	רחק	DISTANT	935b	1 a
	שבה	TAKE CAPTIVE	985c	1 c
6 37	אשר	THAT	83d	8 d
	חטא	MISS A GOAL OR WAY	307a	2 b
	חנן	SHOW FAVOR	336b	2
	לבב	HEART	523d	2 3d
	עוה	COMMIT INIQUITY	731c	
	רשע	BE WICKED	957c	1
	שבה	TAKE CAPTIVE	985c	
	שבי	CAPTIVITY	985d	1
	שוב	TURN BACK	999d	8
6 38	בחר	CHOOSE	*104a	2 a
	דרך	WAY	203b	3
	לבב	HEART	523b	2 2
	נפש	SOUL	661b	0
	פלל	INTERVENE	813b	3
	שבי	CAPTIVITY	985d	1
6 39	חטא	MISS A GOAL OR WAY	307a	2 b
	תחנה	FAVOR	337c	2
	ישב	DWELL	443a	3
	מכון	FIXED PLACE	467d	1
	סלח	FORGIVE	699c	
	תפלה	PRAYER	813c	1 e
6 40	אזן	EAR	24b	2 b
	עין	EYE	744b	1 j
	תפלה	PRAYER	813c	1 e
	פתח	OPEN	835b	
	קשב	ATTENTIVE	904a	
6 41	ארון	CHEST	75c	3 j
	יהוה	YAHWEH	219a	2 1h
	חסיד	KIND	339d	2 b
	טוב	A GOOD THING	375a	1
	תשועה	DELIVERANCE	448b	2
	כהן	PRIEST	463d	4
	לבש	PUT ON	528a	B
	מנוחה	RESTING PLACE	629d	1
	עז	STRENGTH	739b	3 d
	קום	STAND	878b	6 a
	דוד	DAVID	188a	
6 42	דוד	DAVID	188b	J
	יהוה	YAHWEH	219a	2 1h
	זכר	REMEMBER	270b	2 3 b
	חסד	GOODNESS	339c	4
	ל	TO	512a	3 b
	משיח	ANOINTED	603c	1
	שוב	TURN BACK	999d	5
7 1	אכל	EAT	37c	1
	אש	FIRE	77c	4
	זבח	SACRIFICE	257c	1 1
	ירד	GO DOWN	433c	3 a
	כבוד	GLORY	458d	2 c1
	מלא	FILL	570b	2
	עלה	WHOLE BURNT OFFERING	750d	
7 2	פלל	INTERVENE	813b	3
	כבוד	GLORY	458d	2 c1
	מלא	FILL	570b	2
7 3	אף	NOSE	60b	2
	אש	FIRE	77c	4
	חסד	GOODNESS	339b	2x
	טוב	PLEASANT	374d	9 b
	ידה	PRAISE	392c	1 b
	ירד	GO DOWN	433c	3 a
	כבוד	GLORY	458d	2 c1

2 CHRONICLES

Ch v.	Heb	Eng	Page	Sec
	כרע	BOW DOWN	502c	1
	עולם	LONG DURATION	762b	2 c
	ראה	TO SEE	908a	8 a1
	רצפה	PAVEMENT	954b	
	שחה	BOW DOWN	1005c	2 a
7 4	זבח	SACRIFICE	257c	1 1
7 5	אלף	THOUSAND	49a	1 c
	בקר	CATTLE	133c	2
	זבח	SACRIFICE	257c	1 1
	חנך	TRAIN UP	335b	2
7 6	הלל	PRAISE	238d	2 g
	חסד	GOODNESS	339b	2 3c
	חצצר	SOUND A TRUMPET	348d	
	יד	HAND	391a	5 d
	ידה	PRAISE	392c	1 b
	כלי	INSTRUMENT	479d	2 b
	עולם	LONG DURATION	762b	2 c
	משמרת	GUARD	1038d	4 a
7 7	מזבח	ALTAR	258d	4 a
	מזבח	ALTAR	259a	8
	חלב	FAT	317a	2 b
	חצר	ENCLOSURE	347a	3 b
	כול	CONTAIN	465b	1
	מנחה	OFFERING	585b	4
	מנחה	OFFERING	585c	6
	עלה	WHOLE BURNT OF-FERING	750d	
	קדש	BE SET APART	873a	1 a
	שלם	PEACE-OFFERING	1023c	
7 8	בוא	COME	98d	2 e
	חג	FESTIVAL-GATHER-ING	291a	1 b2
	חג	FESTIVAL-GATHER-ING	291b	1 b
	חמת	HAMATH	333a	
	מן	FROM	581d	5 a
	נחל	WADY	636c	2
	קהל	ASSEMBLY	874d	1 d
7 9	מזבח	ALTAR	259a	9
	חג	FESTIVAL-GATHER-ING	291a	1 b2
	חג	FESTIVAL-GATHER-ING	291b	1 b
	חנכה	DEDICATION	335c	
	עצרה	ASSEMBLY	784a	1
7 10	טוב	PLEASANT	374c	7
	טובה	WELFARE	375d	3
	לב	HEART	*525c	2 9a
	עשרים	TWENTY	798a	2 2b
	שמח	JOYFUL	970c	1 a
7 11	בוא	COME	98c	2 d
	כלה	FINISH	478a	1 a
	לב	HEART	525a	2 3d
	צלח	ADVANCE	852c	1
7 12	בחר	CHOOSE	104a	1 a
	בית	HOUSE	109b	1 ae 0
	זבח	SACRIFICE	257c	1 1
	זבח	SACRIFICE	257c	1 1
	ראה	TO SEE	908b	1 a
7 13	אכל	EAT	37c	2
	דבר	PESTILENCE	184a	1
	הן	IF	243d	B
	חגב	LOCUST	290b	
	מטר	RAIN	564d	
	עצר	RESTRAIN	783c	1
	צוה	LAY CHARGE UPON	845c	1 a
7 14	בקש	SEEK	134d	3 b
	דרך	WAY	203d	6 d
	חטאת	SIN	309a	1 d2
	כנע	BE HUMBLE	488c	1
	סלח	FORGIVE	699b	
	פלל	INTERVENE	813b	3
	קרא	CALL	896b	2 d4
	רע	EVIL	948c	0 d
	רפא	HEAL	950d	2 a
7 15	אזן	EAR	24b	2 b
	עין	EYE	744b	1 j
	תפלה	PRAYER	813c	1 e
	פתח	OPEN	835b	
	קשב	ATTENTIVE	904b	
7 16	בחר	CHOOSE	104a	5 a
	יום	DAY	400c	7 f
	לב	HEART	*524c	2 1
	עולם	LONG DURATION	762b	2 e
	קדש	BE SET APART	873b	1 c
7 17	הלך	WALK	234d	2 3c
	חק	SOMETHING PRE-SCRIBED	349d	7 g
	ל	TO	518b	7 bh
7 18	כסא	THRONE	491a	3 a
	כרת	CUT	504a	4
	כרת	BE CUT OFF	504b	4
	מלכות	ROYAL POWER	574d	1
	משל	RULE	605d	1
	קום	STAND	879a	6 c
7 19	אלהים	GOD	43c	1 d
	חקה	SOMETHING PRE-SCRIBED	350b	2 d
	חקה	SOMETHING PRE-SCRIBED	*350b	2 e
	חקה	SOMETHING PRE-SCRIBED	350b	2 e
	עבד	WORK	713b	4 b
	שוב	TURN BACK	997d	6 a
7 20	אדמה	LAND	10a	5

Ch v.	Heb	Eng	Page	Sec
	אדמה	LAND	10a	5
	משל	PROVERB	605b	2
	נתש	PLUCK UP	684c	
	פנה	FACE	819a	2 8a
	קדש	BE SET APART	873c	1 c
	שנינה	SHARP WORD	1042b	
7 21	היה	BE	227a	3 4a
	ל	TO	514d	5 fe
	מה	HOW	553d	4a
	עליון	HIGH	751b	1
	שמם	BE DESOLATED	1031a	2
7 22	אלהים	GOD	43c	1 d
	בוא	COME	99c	2 a
	חזק	BE FIRM	305a	6 a
	יצא	CAUSE TO GO	424c	1 a
	עבד	WORK	713b	4 b
	רעה	MISERY	949a	1
8 1	היה	COME TO PASS	224d	2a 1b
8 2	חירם	HIRAM	27c	1
	בנה	BUILD	124d	1 i
	ישב	CAUSE TO SIT	443d	3 a
8 3	הלך	WALK	230d	1 1d 3a
	חזק	BE FIRM	304b	1 1b
	חמת	HAMATH	333a	
	צובא	ZOBAH	844c	
8 4	חמת	HAMATH	333a	
	חצצנתמר	HAZAZON-TAMAR	*346c	
	מסכנות	SUPPLY	698b	
	עיר	CITY	746c	1 e
	תמר	TAMAR	1071c	2
8 5	ביתחורן	BETH-HORON	111c	A
	ביתחורן	BETH-HORON	111c	B
	בריח	BAR	138b	2
	בריח	BAR	138b	1 b
	דלת	DOOR	195b	3
	חומה	WALL	327b	1
	חומה	WALL	327c	1
	עליון	HIGH	751b	2
	מצור	SIEGE	849a	2
	תחתון	LOWER	1066b	
	תחתון	LOWER	*1066b	
8 6	בנה	BUILD	124c	1 f
	בעלת	BAALATH	128c	
	חשק	BE ATTACHED TO	366a	
	חשק	DESIRE	366a	
	לבנון	LEBANON	527a	
	ממשלה	RULE	606a	1
	מסכנות	SUPPLY	698b	
	עיר	CITY	746c	1 e
	פרש	HORSEMAN	832a	
8 7	אמרי	AMORITES	57c	2 e
	יבוסי	JEBUSITE	101a	1
	חוי	HIVITE	295d	2
	חתי	HITTITE	366d	2 a
	יתר	BE LEFT OVER	451b	
8 8	יכל	BE ABLE	*407c	1 a
	יתר	BE LEFT OVER	451b	
	כלה	FINISH	478c	2 c1
	מס	LABOUR-GANG	587a	1
	עלה	GO UP	749d	6
8 9	תדמר	TADMOR	1062b	
	מלחמה	WAR	536b	
	פרש	HORSEMAN	832a	
	שר	CHIEFTAIN	978c	3 b
	שר	CHIEFTAIN	978c	3 b
8 10	נצב	STAND	662b	3
	נציב	PREFECT	662d	2
	רדה	HAVE DOMINION	922a	
	שר	CHIEFTAIN	978c	4 a
8 11	בת	DAUGHTER	123b	1 h
	דוד	DAVID	188a	A
	עלה	GO UP	749c	1 c
	פרעה	PHARAOH	829a	
	קדש	APARTNESS	871c	2 b
8 12	אולם	PORCH	17d	3
	עלה	GO UP	750a	8
	עלה	WHOLE BURNT OF-FERING	750d	
8 13	דבר	WORD	183b	4 1
	ו	AND	252c	1 b
	חג	FESTIVAL-GATHER-ING	291b	1 b2
	חג	FESTIVAL-GATHER-ING	291a	1 b2
	חג	FESTIVAL-GATHER-ING	291a	1 b2
	חדש	NEW MOON	294c	1
	יום	DAY	400b	7 e1
	מועד	APPOINTED TIME	417c	1 b
	ל	TO	518b	7 bh
	מצה	UNLEAVENED BREAD	695b	
	סכה	THICKET	697d	3
	עלה	GO UP	749d	8
	מצוה	COMMANDMENT	846b	2 a
	שבוע	PERIOD OF SEVEN	989a	1
8 14	אלהים	GOD	44a	3 b
	דבר	WORD	183b	4 1
	הלל	PRAISE	238d	2 g
	ו	AND	253b	1 ib
	מחלקת	DIVISION	325a	2
	יום	DAY	400c	7 e3
	ל	TO	516b	5 ja
	עבדה	LABOR	715b	4
	עמד	STAND	764d	5
	שלמה	SOLOMON	1024d	

Ch v.	Heb	Eng	Page	Sec
	משמרת	GUARD	1038d	4 a
	משפט	JUDGMENT	1048d	3
	שרת	SERVE	1057b	2 b
8 15	כהן	PRIEST	464a	1
	ל	TO	514c	5 fc
	סור	TURN ASIDE	693c	1
	על	UPON	753c	2 1c
8 16	מצוה	COMMANDMENT	846b	1
	יום	DAY	*401b	7 k
	מוסד	FOUNDATION	414c	
	כון	BE READY	466a	4
	כלה	BE FINISHED	477a	1 b
	שלם	COMPLETE	1024a	1 b
8 17	אילות	ELOTH	19a	
	הלך	WALK	231b	1 d3 gd
	הלך	WALK	231b	1 d3 gd
	ים	SEA	*411a	2
	ל	TO	511b	1 ga
	עציונגבר	EZION-GEBER	782b	
8 18	אופיר	OPHIR	20d	2
	חירם	HIRAM	27c	1
	אניה	A SHIP	58b	
	זהב	GOLD	263b	7
	ידע	KNOW	394b	4 b
9 1	בשם	SPICE	141d	1
	דבר	SPEAK	181c	3 e
	היה	BE	227b	3 4d a
	זהב	GOLD	262d	5
	חידה	RIDDLE	295c	3
	חיל	STRENGTH	299a	4
	יקר	PRECIOUS	430a	1 c
	כבד	MASSIVE	458b	2 b
	לב	HEART	*523c	2 2
	מלכה	QUEEN	573c	
	נסה	TEST	650b	1
	עם	WITH	768c	4 a
	רב	MULTITUDE	914a	1
	שבא	SHEBA	985a	
	שמע	REPORT	1034d	
9 2	נגד	BE CONSPICUOUS	616d	2
	עלם	CONCEAL	761a	
9 3	חכמה	WISDOM	315c	2
	מלכה	QUEEN	573c	
	שבא	SHEBA	985a	
9 4	מאכל	FOOD	38b	
	מושב	SEAT	444b	1 b
	מלבוש	RAIMENT	528d	
	עלה	WHOLE BURNT OF-FERING	750d	
	עליה	ROOF-CHAMBER	751a	
	מעמד	OFFICE	765b	3
	רוח	BREATH	925a	3 a
	שלחן	TABLE	1020b	1
	משקה	CUP-BEARER	1052d	
	שרת	SERVE	1058a	1 a
9 5	אמת	FIRMNESS	54b	4 a
	דבר	WORD	182b	1 1c
	חכמה	WISDOM	315c	2
9 6	אמן	CONFIRM	53a	2 b
	חכמה	WISDOM	315c	2
	יסף	ADD	414d	
	נגד	BE CONSPICUOUS	617a	
	עד	UNTIL	724d	2 1a a
	מרבי	INCREASE	916b	3
	שמועה	REPORT	1035b	1
9 7	אשר	HAPPINESS	80d	
	חכמה	WISDOM	315c	2
9 8	תמיד	CONTINUITY	556b	1 a
	אהב	LOVE	13a	5 b
	ברך	BLESS	138c	2 a
	יהוה	YAHWEH	218d	2 1a
	חפץ	DELIGHT IN	342d	2 a
	כסא	THRONE	491b	3 a
	מלך	KING	573c	5 c
	עמד	STAND	764d	5
	צדקה	RIGHTEOUSNESS	842a	1 a
9 9	בשם	SPICE	141d	1
	זהב	GOLD	262d	5
	יקר	PRECIOUS	430a	1 c
	מאד	EXCEEDINGLY	547b	2 a
	מלכה	QUEEN	573c	
	רב	MULTITUDE	914a	1
	שבא	SHEBA	985a	
9 10	אופיר	OPHIR	20d	2
	חירם	HIRAM	27c	1
	אלגומים	A TREE	38d	
	זהב	GOLD	263b	7
	יקר	PRECIOUS	430a	1 c
9 11	אלגומים	A TREE	38d	
	הם	THEY	241d	8 b
	כנור	LYRE	490a	
	נבל	HARP	614c	
	מסלה	HIGHWAY	700c	
	ראה	TO SEE	908c	2 a
9 12	בד	SEPARATION	94d	2 a
	חפץ	TURN	245d	2 a
	חפץ	DELIGHT	343b	2 a
	מלכה	QUEEN	573c	
	שבא	SHEBA	985a	
9 13	בוא	COME	98b	1 j
9 14	זהב	GOLD	263c	2
	כסף	SILVER	494b	6
	מסחר	MERCHANDISE	695c	
	סחר	GO AROUND	695c	2
	ערב	MIXTURE	*786b	
	ערב	STEPPE-DWELLERS	787b	

Ch	v.	Heb	Eng	Page	Sec
		פחה	GOVERNOR	808d	3
		תור	EXPLORE	1064c	
9	15	זהב	GOLD	263b	9 a
		מאה	HUNDRED	548a	1 b1
		עלה	GO UP	749d	4
		צנה	LARGE SHIELD	857a	
		שחט	SLAUGHTER	1006b	4
		שחט	SLAUGHTER	1006b	4
9	16	מגן	SHIELD	*171c	
		זהב	GOLD	263b	9 a
		יער	WOOD	420c	A
		לבנון	LEBANON	527b	
		עלה	GO UP	749d	4
		שחט	SLAUGHTER	1006b	4
9	17	אופז	UPHAZ	20c	
		גדול	GREAT	153a	1
		זהב	GOLD	263b	8
		זהב	GOLD	263d	2 c
		טהור	CLEAN	373a	2
		פזז	BE REFINED	808a	
		צפה	LAY OUT	860a	
		שן	IVORY	1042b	2
9	18	אחז	GRASP	28c	
		ארי	LION	71d	
		ב	IN	90c	3 6
		יד	STAYS	390c	4 e
		שבת	SEAT	443d	
		כבש	FOOTSTOOL	461c	
		מעלה	STEP	752b	1
		מקום	STANDING PLACE	880a	4
9	19	ארי	LION	71d	
		בשם	SPICE	141d	1
		ממלכה	KINGDOM	575a	1
		מעלה	STEP	752b	1
		עשה	DO	795b	2 a
9	20	בית	HOUSE	108d	1 ag
		חשב	THINK	363c	2
		יער	WOOD	420c	A
		כלי	UTENSIL	480a	2 f
		כלי	VESSEL	480b	3
		כסף	SILVER	494b	3
		לבנון	LEBANON	527b	
		נגיד	LEADER	618a	4
		סגר	CLOSE	689b	4 b
		משקה	DRINK	1052d	1
9	21	אופיר	OPHIR	20d	2
		חורם	HIRAM	27c	1
		אניה	A SHIP	58c	
		אניה	A SHIP	58c	
		הלך	WALK	232b	1 3
		זהב	GOLD	263b	8
		זהב	GOLD	263c	1
		כסף	SILVER	494b	5
		קוף	APE	880d	
		שנהבים	IVORY	1042b	
		תכיים	PEACOCKS	1067a	
		תרשיש	TARSHISH	1077a	1
9	22	גדל	BECOME GREAT	*152b	2 e
		חכמה	WISDOM	315c	2
9	23	בקש	SEEK	*134d	3 a
		חכמה	WISDOM	315c	2
		לב	HEART	*524d	2 3b
9	24	בשם	SPICE	141d	1
		דבר	WORD	183c	4 1
		זהב	GOLD	263a	6
		מנחה	GIFT	585a	1
		נשק	EQUIPMENT	676d	1
		שלמה	GARMENT	791b	
		פרד	MULE	825d	
9	25	אריה	MANGER	71d	
		אריה	MANGER	71d	
		נוח	REST	628d	B 1
		עיר	CITY	746c	1 e
		פרש	HORSEMAN	832b	
9	26	גבול	BORDER	147d	1 a
		היה	BE	227c	3 5a
		משל	RULE	605d	1
		נהר	STREAM	625d	1
9	27	ארז	CEDAR	72d	2
		כסף	SILVER	494b	3
		שפלה	LOWLAND	1050d	1
		שקמה	SYCOMORE TREE	1054b	
9	28	יצא	BRING OUT	424d	3
9	29	אחיהו	AHIJAH	26d	3
		דבר	WORD	183a	2 1c
		דבר	WORD	183c	4 2
		חזה	SEER	302d	1 b
		חזות	VISIONS	303a	
		כתב	WRITE	507c	1 b1
		נבואה	PROPHECY	612c	2
		נבט	NEBAT	614a	
		נתן	NATHAN	681d	2
		עדו	IDDO	723b	5
		ראשון	FIRST	911c	1 a
		שאר	REST	984c	
		שילני	SHILONITE	1018a	
9	31	דוד	DAVID	188a	A
		רחבעם	REHOBOAM	932c	
10	1	הלך	WALK	230d	1 1d 3b
		מלך	BE KING	574c	
		רחבעם	REHOBOAM	932c	
10	2	ברח	FLEE	138a	2
		מצרים	EGYPT	595d	1 b2
		נבט	NEBAT	614a	
		ירבעם	JEROBOAM	914c	1
		שוב	TURN BACK	997a	2

Ch	v.	Heb	Eng	Page	Sec
10	3	ירבעם	JEROBOAM	914c	1
		רחבעם	REHOBOAM	932c	
10	4	כבד	HEAVY	458a	1 a
		עבדה	LABOR	715b	3
		על	YOKE	760d	
		קלל	BE SILENT	886d	1
		קשה	BE SEVERE	904c	2
		קשה	SEVERE	904c	2 a
10	5	עוד	STILL	729a	1 ab
10	6	דבר	WORD	*182b	1 lc
		זקן	OLD	278c	2 a
		חי	ALIVE	312a	1 b
		יעץ	CONSIDER	419d	
		יעץ	CONSULT	419d	
		רחבעם	REHOBOAM	932c	
		שוב	TURN BACK	999c	3
10	7	טוב	PLEASANT	374d	9 a
		טוב	PLEASANT	374d	9 a
		יום	DAY	400c	7 f
		עבד	SLAVE	714c	7
		רצה	BE PLEASED WITH	953a	1 b
10	8	גדל	GROW UP	*152b	1 a
		זקן	OLD	278c	2 a
		ילד	CHILD	409c	D
		יעץ	ADVISE	419c	
		יעץ	CONSULT	419d	
		עצה	ADVICE	420a	
		עזב	LEAVE	737c	2 d3
10	9	דבר	WORD	*182b	1 lc
		יעץ	CONSULT	420a	
		על	YOKE	760d	
		קלל	BE SILENT	886d	1
10	10	גדל	GROW UP	*152b	1 a
		דבר	SPEAK	181b	3 d
		ילד	CHILD	409c	D
		כבד	MAKE HEAVY	457d	1
		מתנים	LOINS	608b	2 a
		על	YOKE	760d	
		קטן	LITTLE	882b	
		קלל	BE SLIGHT	886d	1
		יסף	ADD	415b	1
		יסר	DISCIPLINE	416b	2 b
		כבד	HEAVY	458a	1 a
		על	YOKE	760d	
		עקרב	SCORPION	785d	
		שוט	SCOURGE	1002a	1
		עמם	ADDENDA ET CORRIGENDA	1126a	
10	12	ירבעם	JEROBOAM	914c	1
		שוט	SCOURGE	1002a	1
10	13	זקן	OLD	278c	2 a
		עצה	ADVICE	420a	
		עזב	LEAVE	737c	2 d3
		קשה	SEVERE	904d	2 a
10	14	ילד	CHILD	409c	D
		יסף	ADD	415b	1
		יסר	DISCIPLINE	416b	2 b
		עצה	ADVICE	420a	
		כבד	MAKE HEAVY	457d	1
		על	YOKE	760d	
		עקרב	SCORPION	785d	
10	15	אחיהו	AHIJAH	26d	3
		דבר	SPEAK	181c	4 a
		יד	HAND	391a	5 d
		נבט	NEBAT	614a	
		סבה	TURN OF AFFAIRS	*686d	
		נסבה	TURN OF AFFAIRS	687c	
		מעם	FROM WITH	*769a	D
		שילני	SHILONITE	1018a	
10	16	אהל	TENT	13d	1
		הלך	WALK	231b	1 d3 gd
		חלק	PORTION	324a	1 c
		ישי	JESSE	445b	
		נחלה	PROPERTY	635c	2 b
		ראה	TO SEE	907d	7 c
		שוב	TURN BACK	999c	3
10	18	אבן	STONE	6b	1
		אדרם	ADORAM	12a	
		אמץ	BE STRONG	55b	3
		הדרם	HADORAM	214c	
		מות	DIE	559d	2 a
		מס	LABOUR-GANG	587a	1
		רגם	TO STONE	920c	
		מרכבה	CHARIOT	939d	
10	19	בית	HOUSE	110a	5 c
		פשע	REBEL	833b	1
11	1	בחר	CHOOSE	104b	7
		בית	HOUSE	110a	5 de
		בנימין	BENJAMIN	122d	1
		לחם	ENGAGE IN BATTLE	535c	
		ממלכה	DOMINION	575b	2
		עשה	DO	794c	2 1e
		קהל	ASSEMBLE AS	875a	1 b
		ישראל	ISRAEL	975d	2 a4
11	2	שוב	TURN BACK	999a	1 d
		אלהים	GOD	44a	3 b
		דבר	WORD	182c	1 2a
		שמעיה	SHEMAIAH	1035c	1
11	4	דבר	WORD	183b	3 2
		היה	COME TO PASS	227d	2
		שוב	TURN BACK	996d	1
		שמע	HEAR	1034a	1 n
11	5	מצור	SIEGE	849a	2
11	6	בנה	BUILD	124d	1 i

Ch	v.	Heb	Eng	Page	Sec
		עיטם	ETAM	743c	2
		תקוע	TEKOA	1075d	
11	7	ביתצור	BETH-ZUR	112d	
		עדלם	ADULLAM	726b	
		שוכה	SOCOH	962c	1
11	8	זיף	ZIPH	268b	1 a
		גת	GATH	387d	
		מרשה	MARESHAH	601c	
11	9	אדורים	ADORAIM	12a	
		לכיש	LACHISH	540c	
		עזקה	DIG ABOUT	740a	
11	10	אילון	AIJALON	19c	1
		חברון	HEBRON	289b	
		מצורה	SIEGE-WORKS	849a	2
		צרעה	ZORAH	864a	
11	11	מאכל	FOOD	38b	
		אוצר	TREASURE	70a	2
		חזק	BE FIRM	304c	1 c
		יין	WINE	406c	A
		נגיד	LEADER	618a	4
		מצורה	SIEGE-WORKS	849a	2
11	12	ו	AND	253b	1 ib
		חזק	BE FIRM	304c	1 c
		כל	ALL	481c	1 b
		מאד	EXCEEDINGLY	547b	2 a
		צנה	LARGE SHIELD	857a	
		רבה	BECOME MANY	915d	1 e5
		רמח	SPEAR	942b	
11	13	גבול	BOUNDARY	148a	1 b
		יצב	STATION ONESELF	426c	D
		כהן	PRIEST	464a	7
		על	UPON	757b	2 7c aa
11	14	אחזה	POSSESSION	28c	
		מגרש	COMMON-LAND	177b	
		זנח	REJECT	276b	
		כהן	ACT AS PRIEST	464c	1
		ל	TO	*511b	1 ga
		לוי	LEVITE	533a	3 1c
		עזב	LEAVE	737b	2 a1
11	15	במה	HIGH PLACE	119b	3
		כהן	PRIEST	463b	3 b
		עגל	CALF	722b	
		שעיר	SATYR	972d	
11	16	בקש	SEEK	134d	3 c
		התיחש	BE ENROLLED	*405b	
		לבב	HEART	523d	2 4
		נציב	PREFECT	*662d	2
11	17	אמץ	BE STRONG	55a	1
		דרך	WAY	203d	6 c
		הלך	WALK	234d	2 3a 1t
		חזק	BE FIRM	304c	1 d
		יהודה	JUDAH	397b	1 3
		ל	TO	517b	6 d
		מלכות	KINGDOM	575a	3
		שנה	YEAR	1040b	
11	18	ביחיל	ABIHAIL	4b	5
		אליאב	ELIAB	45a	C
		ירמות	JEREMOTH	438b	4
		ישי	JESSE	445a	
		מחלת	MAHALATH	563b	2
11	19	זהם	ZAHAM	263d	
		יעוש	JEUSH	736c	4
		שמריה	SHEMARIAH	1037d	2
11	20	ביהו	ABIJAM	4a	1
		אבישלום	ABSALOM	5a	1
		זיזא	ZIZA	265b	2
		מעכה	MAACAH	590d	2 b
		עתי	ATTAI	774c	3
		שלמות	SHELOMOTH	1025a	2
		אבישלום	ABSALOM	5a	1
11	21	אהב	LOVE	12d	1
		מעכה	MAACAH	590d	2 b
		נשא	LIFT	671c	3 d
		ששים	SIXTY	995d	
		ששים	SIXTY	995d	
		שמנה	EIGHT	1033a	2 a
11	22	ביהו	ABIJAM	4a	1
		ל	TO	518a	7 bg
		מלך	BE KING	574b	
		מעכה	MAACAH	590d	2 b
11	23	ארץ	EARTH	76c	5
		בין	DISCERN	107a	2
		המון	ABUNDANCE	242d	4
		מזון	FOOD	266a	
		כבר	MAKE MANY	*460b	
		פרץ	BREAK THROUGH	829c	
		מצורה	SIEGE-WORKS	849a	2
		שאל	ASK	981d	1 c
		המון	ADDENDA ET CORRIGENDA	1122c	
12	1	חזקה	STRENGTH	305d	2
		תורה	LAW	436b	2 b3
		ך	LIKE	454d	3 b
		כון	ESTABLISH	466a	1
		מלכות	ROYAL POWER	574d	1
12	2	חמישי	FIFTH	332c	2
		שישק	SHISHAK	1011a	
12	3	כושי	CUSHITE	469b	D
		לובים	LUBIM	530c	
		מעל	ACT TREACHEROUSLY	591b	2 b
		מצרים	EGYPT	595d	1 b2
		סכיים	SUKKIIM	696d	
		מספר	NUMBER	708d	1 a
		פרש	HORSEMAN	832a	
		ששים	SIXTY	995d	

Ch	v	Heb	Eng	Page	Sec
12	4	מצורה	SIEGE-WORKS	849a	2
12	5	אף	ALSO	65a	1
		עזב	LEAVE	737c	2e
		שׁישׁק	SHISHAK	1011a	
		שמעיה	SHEMAIAH	1035c	1
12	6	כנע	BE HUMBLE	488c	1
		צדיק	JUST	843a	1d
		ישראל	ISRAEL	975d	2a4
12	7	דבר	WORD	182c	12a
		חמה	RAGE	404d	2c
		חמה	RAGE	*405a	2c
		כנע	BE HUMBLE	488c	1
		מעט	A FEW	590b	2c
		נתך	POUR FORTH	677d	
		פליטה	ESCAPE	812c	2b
		שׁישׁק	SHISHAK	1011a	
		שמעיה	SHEMAIAH	1035c	1
12	8	ממלכה	KINGDOM	575b	1
		עבדה	LABOR	715b	4
		עבדה	LABOR	715b	3
12	9	מגן	SHIELD	*171c	
		זהב	GOLD	263c	2a
		כל	ALL	*482d	2ba
		שׁישׁק	SHISHAK	1011a	
12	10	מגן	SHIELD	*171c	
		פקד	ATTEND TO	824a	2a
		רוץ	RUN	930c	2a
		שר	CHIEFTAIN	978c	4a
		שמר	KEEP	1036c	1b
12	11	די	SUFFICIENCY	*191d	2ca
		היה	COME TO PASS	224d	12a 1b
		רוץ	RUN	930c	2a
		שוב	TURN BACK	998d	1a
		תא	CHAMBER	1060b	
12	12	דבר	WORD	183c	42
		טוב	PLEASANT	374d	0a
		יהודה	JUDAH	397b	13
		כלה	COMPLETE	478d	1
		כנע	BE HUMBLE	488c	1
		ל	TO	518a	7bg
		שוב	TURN BACK	997d	6f
12	13	בחר	CHOOSE	*104a	2a
		חזק	BE FIRM	305b	1
		נעמה	NAAMAH	653d	2
		עמוני	AMMONITE	770a	
12	14	דרש	SEEK	205b	3a
		כון	ESTABLISH	466c	3
		לב	HEART	525a	24
		רע	EVIL	948d	3
12	15	דבר	WORD	183a	21c
		דבר	WORD	183c	42
		חזה	SEER	302d	1b
		יום	DAY	400c	7f
		תחיש	BE ENROLLED	405b	
		עדו	IDDO	723b	5
		ראשון	FIRST	911c	1a
		שמעיה	SHEMAIAH	1035c	1
12	16	ביהו	ABIJAM	4a	1
		דוד	DAVID	188a	A
13	1	ביהו	ABIJAM	4a	1
13	2	ביהו	ABIJAM	4a	1
		אוריאל	URIEL	22c	2
		בית	HOUSE	110a	5c
		גבעה	GIBEAH	149b	2
		מעכה	MAACAH	590d	2b
13	3	ביהו	ABIJAM	4a	1
		אסר	TIE	64a	5
		בחר	CHOOSE	104b	7
		גבור	STRONG	150b	2
		גבור	STRONG	150b	2
		חיל	STRENGTH	298d	1c
		חיל	STRENGTH	299a	4
		מלחמה	WAR	536b	
		מלחמה	WAR	536c	
		ערך	ARRANGE	789c	1d
13	4	ביהו	ABIJAM	4a	1
		הר	MOUNTAIN	251a	2
		על	UPON	759b	42e a
		צמרים	ZEMARAIM	856b	2
		שמע	HEAR	1034a	1i
13	5	ברית	COVENANT	137b	32
		ל	TO	513b	5ba
		ל	TO	517d	7bd
		מלח	SALT	571d	
		ממלכה	DOMINION	575b	2
		עולם	LONG DURATION	762d	2f
13	6	מרד	REBEL	597c	1
		נבט	NEBAT	614a	
		קום	STAND	878a	2
13	7	אמץ	BE STRONG	55b	1
		בליעל	WORTHLESSNESS	116a	1
		היה	BE	227a	34b
		חזק	BE FIRM	305b	3
		לבב	HEART	524b	29b
		נער	YOUTH	655a	1d
		על	UPON	757b	27c aa
		קבץ	GATHER	867d	1
		רחבעם	REHOBOAM	932c	
		ריק	EMPTY	938a	2
		רך	TENDER	940a	2
13	8	אמר	SAY	56b	1
		בן	SON	120d	1ja
		המון	CROWD	242c	3a
		זהב	GOLD	263c	2a
		חזק	BE FIRM	305b	3
		ממלכה	DOMINION	575b	2
		עגל	CALF	722b	
13	9	אהרן	AARON	14d	
		איל	RAM	18a	2g
		בן	SON	121a	1jz
		בן	SON	121c	7b
		יד	HAND	389b	1c
		כהן	PRIEST	463b	3b
		כהן	PRIEST	464a	7
		כהן	PRIEST	464a	7
		לא	NOT	519d	2d
		לא	NOT	520c	4e
		מלא	FILL	570d	2
		נגח	THRUST	623b	2
		פר	YOUNG BULL	830d	2c
13	10	אהרן	AARON	14d	
		בן	SON	121a	1jz
		כהן	PRIEST	464a	7
		כהן	PRIEST	464a	7
		שרת	SERVE	1058b	2d
13	11	בער	BURN	129b	1
		בקר	MORNING	134a	1
		בקר	MORNING	134b	1f
		ו	AND	253a	1g
		מהור	CLEAN	373a	2
		לחם	FOOD	537b	1a
		מנורה	LAMPSTAND	633a	2
		סם	SPICE	702c	
		עלה	WHOLE BURNT OF-FERING	751a	
		ערב	SUNSET	787d	1a
		מערכת	ROW	790b	
		פרץ	PEREZ	829d	2a
		קטר	MAKE SACRIFICES SMOKE	883a	1a
		שלחן	TABLE	1020b	3
13	12	חצצרה	CLARION	348c	2b
		כהן	PRIEST	464b	7
		על	UPON	755d	25
		צלח	ADVANCE	852c	2
		ראש	HEAD	911a	3a
		רוע	RAISE A SHOUT	929c	2
		תרועה	SHOUT OF WAR	930a	2
		ישראל	ISRAEL	975d	2b2
13	13	אחר	BEHIND	30b	4ab
		מארב	AMBUSH	70d	2
		סבב	GO AROUND	686c	2a
13	14	אחור	HINDER SIDE	30c	A
		חצצרה	CLARION	*348c	2c
		חצצרה	CLARION	*348c	2b
		חצר	SOUND A TRUMPET	348d	
		פנה	TURN	815b	2a
		פנה	FACE	816b	16
		צעק	CRY	858c	1b
13	15	ביהף	ABIJAM	4a	1
		נגף	STRIKE	619d	
		רוע	RAISE A SHOUT	929c	1
13	17	ביהף	ABIJAM	4a	1
		בחר	CHOOSE	104b	7
		מאה	HUNDRED	548b	1c2
		נכה	SMITE	646a	2c
		מכה	SLAUGHTER	647a	1
13	18	אמץ	BE STRONG	55a	1
		יהודה	JUDAH	397b	13
		כנע	BE HUMBLED	488c	2
		שען	LEAN	1043d	
13	19	ביהף	ABIJAM	4a	1
		אפרים	EPHRAIM	68c	6
		ישנה	JESHANAH	446a	
		עפרון	EPHRON	780b	2
		עפרין	EPHRAIN	780b	
13	20	ביהף	ABIJAM	4a	1
		יום	DAY	399b	4b
		כח	STRENGTH	470d	1c
		מות	DIE	560a	2b
		נגף	STRIKE	619d	
		עצר	RESTRAIN	783c	2
13	21	חזק	BE FIRM	305b	1
		נשא	LIFT	671c	3d
		ארבע	FOUR	917a	2a1b
		שש	SIX	995c	2
13	22	ביהף	ABIJAM	4a	1
		דבר	WORD	183c	42
		דבר	WORD	183c	42
		דרך	WAY	203b	5
		מדרש	STUDY	205d	
		עדו	IDDO	723b	5
13	23	ביהף	ABIJAM	4a	1
		אסא	ASA	61d	
		דוד	DAVID	188a	A
		יצחק	ISAAC	850c	
		שקט	BE QUIET	1053a	1
14	1	טוב	PLEASANT	374a	2f
		ישר	STRAIGHT	449a	2a
14	2	אשרה	ASHERA	81c	B
		במה	HIGH PLACE	*119c	3b
		גדע	HEW	154b	
		מזבח	ALTAR	259a	0
		נכר	FOREIGNNESS	648d	3
		מצבה	PILLAR	663b	1c
		סור	TURN ASIDE	694b	1
14	3	אמר	SAY	56c	4
		דרש	SEEK	205b	3a
		תורה	LAW	436b	2b3
		נכה	SMITE	646b	3
		מצוה	COMMANDMENT	846b	2a
14	4	במה	HIGH PLACE	*119c	3b
		חמן	SUN-PILLAR	329a	1
		ממלכה	KINGDOM	575b	1
		סור	TURN ASIDE	694b	1
		שקט	BE QUIET	1053a	1
14	5	נוח	REST	628c	A 1b 2
		עם	WITH	767b	1a
		מצורה	SIEGE-WORKS	849a	2
		שקט	BE QUIET	1053a	1
14	6	בריח	BAR	138b	2
		בריח	BAR	138b	1b
		מגדל	TOWER	153d	1
		דלת	DOOR	195b	3
		דרש	SEEK	205b	3a
		חומה	WALL	327b	1
		נוח	REST	628c	A 1b 2
		סבב	SURROUND	686d	2b
		עוד	STILL	728d	1aa
		פנה	FACE	817a	24a f
		צלח	ADVANCE	852c	2
14	7	דרך	TREAD	202b	4
		חיל	STRENGTH	299a	4
		נשא	LIFT	671a	2a
		צנה	LARGE SHIELD	857a	
		קשת	BOW	906c	1d
		רמח	SPEAR	942b	
14	8	אלף	THOUSAND	49a	1c
		בית	HOUSE	110a	5c
		זרח	ZERAH	280c	5
		כושי	CUSHITE	469b	C
		מאה	HUNDRED	548b	1c4
		מרשה	MARESHAH	601c	
		מרכבה	CHARIOT	939d	
14	9	מרשה	MARESHAH	601c	
		ערך	ARRANGE	789c	1d
		פנה	FACE	817c	24b e
		צפתה	ZEPHATAH	862c	
14	10	אין	NOT	35a	6ca
		אנוש	MAN	60d	3
		בין	INTERVAL	107c	1d
		בין	INTERVAL	107c	1b
		המון	CROWD	242c	3a
		כח	STRENGTH	470d	1b
		עזר	HELP	740c	
		עם	WITH	768b	3d
		עצר	RESTRAIN	783d	2
		רב	GREAT	913c	2b
		שען	LEAN	1043d	
14	11	כושי	CUSHITE	469b	D
		נגף	STRIKE	619d	
14	12	אין	NOT	35a	6cb
		גרר	GERAR	176b	
		מחיה	PRESERVATION OF LIFE	313c	1
		כושי	CUSHITE	469b	D
		עד	UNTIL	725c	31
		רבה	BECOME MANY	915d	1e3
14	13	בז	SPOIL	102d	
		בז	SPOIL	103a	
		גרר	GERAR	176b	
		חיה	BECOME	225d	21b
		פחד	DREAD	808c	1
14	14	אהל	TENT	13d	1
		ל	TO	516c	5jb
		נכה	SMITE	646b	3
		שבה	TAKE CAPTIVE	985c	1
15	1	עדד	ODED	729c	1
		עזריהו	AZARIAH	741b	3
		רוח	BREATH	925d	9b
15	2	דרש	SEEK	205b	3a
		מצא	FIND	394a	1f
		שמע	HEAR	1034a	1i
15	3	אלהים	GOD	44c	4bb
		אמת	FIRMNESS	54b	3b
		ירה	DIRECT	435c	5b
		תורה	INSTRUCTION	436a	1e
		כהן	PRIEST	464b	7
		ל	TO	516d	5k
		לא	NOT	520c	4e
15	4	בקש	SEEK	134d	2
		מצא	FIND	394a	1f
		על	UPON	757b	27c aa
		צר	STRAITS	865b	
		שוב	TURN BACK	997d	6c
15	5	מהומה	TUMULT	223a	1
		יצא	GO OUT	424a	1
		על	UPON	753b	21b
		עת	TIME	773b	1a
15	6	מהומה	TUMULT	223a	1
		חמם	CONFUSE	243a	2
		כתת	BE BEATEN	510a	
15	7	חזק	BE FIRM	304b	1 2c
		פעלה	WORK	821d	1b
		רפה	SINK	951d	2
		שכר	HIRE	969b	2
15	8	אולם	PORCH	17d	1
		הר	MOUNTAIN	251a	2b
		מזבח	ALTAR	258d	4a
		חדש	RENEW	294a	2
		חזק	BE FIRM	305b	1
		נבואה	PROPHECY	612c	1
		עבר	PASS OVER	719a	4
		עדד	ODED	729c	1
15	9	גור	SOJOURN	157d	1
		נפל	FALL	657c	4b
		קבץ	GATHER	867d	1
15	10	חמש	FIVE	332a	2a

Ch v.	Heb	Eng	Page	Sec
	ל	TO	517a	6 a
	מלכות	REIGN	575a	2
	עשׂר	TEN	797b	5 c
	קבץ	GATHER	867d	1
15 11	בקר	CATTLE	133c	2
	שׁלל	SPOIL	1022a	2
15 12	ברית	COVENANT	137a	3 1
	דרשׁ	SEEK	205b	3 a
	לבב	HEART	523b	2 2
	נפשׁ	SOUL	661b	0
15 13	גדול	GREAT	153b	7
	דרשׁ	SEEK	205b	3 a
	מות	DIE	560c	1
	מן	FROM	583d	9 b1
	מן	FROM	583d	9 b1
15 14	חצצרה	CLARION	348c	2 c
	תרועה	SHOUT OF WAR	930a	3
	שׁבע	SWEAR	989b	1 a
	שׁפר	HORN	1051d	
15 15	בקשׁ	SEEK	134d	3 c
	מצא	FIND	394a	1 f
	לבב	HEART	523c	2 2
	נוח	REST	628c	A 1b 2
	רצון	GOODWILL	953c	3 b
	שׂמח	REJOICE	970b	1 a
	שׁבע	SWEAR	989b	1 a
	שׁבועה	OATH	990a	1 a
15 16	אשׁרה	ASHERA	81b	A
	גבירה	QUEEN-MOTHER	150c	2
	דקק	PULVERISE	200d	
	כרת	CUT OFF	503d	2
	מעכה	MAACAH	590d	2 c
	נחל	WADY	636c	2
	סור	TURN ASIDE	694b	1
	מפלצת	HORRID THING	814a	
	קדרון	KEDRON	871b	
15 17	במה	HIGH PLACE	119c	3
	לבב	HEART	*523d	2 6a
	סור	TURN ASIDE	694a	3
	שׁלם	COMPLETE	1024a	3
15 18	בוא	COME	99a	1
15 19	חמשׁ	FIVE	332a	5 b3
	מלכות	REIGN	575a	2
16 1	בוא	COME	97d	1 a
	בעשׁא	BAASHA	129d	
	יצא	GO OUT	424a	3
	מלכות	REIGN	575a	2
	רמה	RAMA	928a	1
16 2	אוצר	TREASURE	70a	3 a
	בנהדד	BEN-HADAD	122b	1
	דמשׂק	DAMASCUS	199d	
	חלה	BE WEAK	*317d	2
	כסף	SILVER	494b	6
16 3	בעשׁא	BAASHA	129d	
	ברית	COVENANT	136b	1 1
	ברית	COVENANT	136c	1 5
	כסף	SILVER	494b	6
	פרר	BREAK	830b	1 c
16 4	אבל	ABEL	6a	1
	בנהדד	BEN-HADAD	122b	1
	דן	DAN	193a	3
	חיל	STRENGTH	299a	4
	נכה	SMITE	646b	3
	מסכנות	SUPPLY	698b	
	עיון	IJON	743b	
	עיר	CITY	746c	1 e
	שׂר	CHIEFTAIN	978c	3 a
	שׁלח	SEND	1018b	1
16 5	בעשׁא	BAASHA	129d	
	חדל	CEASE	293a	2
	לקח	TAKE	543a	4 c
	עץ	TREE	781d	2 b
	רמה	RAMA	928a	1
	שׁבת	CEASE	992a	1
16 6	בנה	BUILD	124c	1 b
	בנה	BUILD	124c	1 b
	בעשׁא	BAASHA	129d	
	גבע	GEBA	148d	
	נשׂא	LIFT	671b	3 b
	מצפה	MIZPAH	860a	4
	רמה	RAMA	928a	1
16 7	יהוה	YAHWEH	218d	2 1a
	חיל	STRENGTH	299a	4
	חנני	HANANI	337b	1
	מלט	SLIP AWAY	572c	2
	ראה	SEER	909a	
	שׁען	LEAN	1043d	
	שׁען	LEAN	1043d	
16 8	כושׁי	CUSHITE	469b	D
	ל	TO	514c	5 fb
	לובים	LUBIM	530c	
	מאד	EXCEEDINGLY	547b	2 a
	פרשׁ	HORSEMAN	832a	
	רב	MULTITUDE	914a	1
	רבה	BECOME MANY	915d	1 e5
	שׁען	LEAN	1043d	
16 9	זה	THIS	262a	6 f
	חזק	BE FIRM	305b	4
	לבב	HEART	524b	2 6a
	סכל	BE FOOLISH	698a	
	עם	WITH	767b	1 a
	עם	WITH	767c	1 a
	עתה	NOW	774b	2 e
	שׁוט	GO ABOUT	1002a	3
	שׁלם	COMPLETE	1024a	3
16 10	בית	HOUSE	109a	1 ae 2

Ch v.	Heb	Eng	Page	Sec
	מהפכת	STOCKS	246c	
	זה	THIS	262c	6 f
	זעף	STORMING	277a	1
	כעס	BE ANGRY	495a	2
	עם	WITH	767d	1 d
	ראה	SEER	909a	
16 11	דבר	WORD	183c	4 2
	לא	NOT	520c	4 bb
	ספר	MISSIVE	707b	3 e
	ראשׁון	FIRST	911c	1 a
16 12	דרשׁ	SEEK	205b	3 a
	חלא	BE SICK	316a	
	חלי	SICKNESS	318b	
	מלכות	REIGN	575a	2
	עד	UNTIL	725c	3 3
	מעל	ABOVE	752a	2 cb
	רפא	HEAL	950d	1 b
16 13	מלך	BE KING	574a	
16 14	ארבעים	FORTY	917c	3
	בשׂם	SPICE	141d	1
	דוד	DAVID	188a	A
	זן	KIND	275b	
	כרה	DIG	500a	
	מאד	EXCEEDINGLY	547c	2 c
	מלא	FILL	570c	1
	עד	UNTIL	725c	3 3
	מעשׂה	DEED	796a	2 a1
	קצבר	GRAVE	868d	
	רקח	MIX OIL	955b	
	מרקחת	OINTMENT-MIX-TURE	955c	2
	שׂרף	BURN	977a	2 a
	שׂרף	BURN	977a	2 a
	שׂרפה	BURNING	977c	
	שׁכב	LIE DOWN	1012c	
	משׁכב	COUCH	1012d	1
17 1	יהושׁפט	JEHOSHAPHAT	221d	1
	חזק	BE FIRM	305b	1
17 2	אפרים	EPHRAIM	68c	4
	בצר	MAKE INACCESSI-BLE	131a	
	נציב	PREFECT	662d	2
	נציב	PREFECT	*662d	2
17 3	בעל	BAAL	127b	2 3
	דרך	WAY	203d	6 c
	דרשׁ	SEEK	205b	3 b
	היה	BE	227b	3 4d a
	הלך	WALK	234d	2 3a 1t
17 4	דרשׁ	SEEK	205b	2 3a 1t
	הלך	WALK	234c	2 3a 1g
	מעשׂה	DEED	795c	1 a2
17 5	כבוד	HONOR	458c	2 a
	כון	ESTABLISH	466a	1 a
	ממלכה	DOMINION	575b	2
	מנחה	TRIBUTE	585a	2
	סור	TURN ASIDE	694b	1
17 6	אשׁרה	ASHERA	81c	B
	גבה	BE HIGH	147a	3
	דרך	WAY	204a	6 ec
	לב	HEART	525b	2 6c
	עוד	STILL	729b	1 c
	בנחיל	BEN-HAIL	122c	
	זכריהו	ZECHARIAH	272b	8
	ל	TO	512a	3 b
	למד	LEARN	540d	
	מלך	BE KING	574a	
	נתנאל	NETHANE/L	682b	6
	עבדיהו	OBADIAH	716a	2 7
17 8	אדניהו	ADONIJAH	11d	2
	יהונתן	JONATHAN	221a	8 a
	יהורם	JEHORAM	221b	3
	זבדיהו	ZEBADIAH	256c	1 b
	טובאדוניה	TOBADONIJAH	375b	
	טוביהו	TOBIJAH	376a	1
	לוי	LEVITE	533b	3 2b
	נתניהו	NETHANIAH	682b	3 a
	עשׂהאל	ASAHEL	795c	2 a
	שׁמירמות	SHEMIRAMOTH	1029a	2
	שׁמעיה	SHEMAIAH	1035d	7 i
17 9	תורה	LAW	436b	2 b3
	למד	LEARN	540d	
	סבב	GO AROUND	685d	2 c
	ספר	MISSIVE	707b	3 e
17 10	היה	BECOME	225d	2 1b
	לחם	ENGAGE IN BAT-TLE	535c	
	ממלכה	KINGDOM	575b	1
	פחד	DREAD	808c	1
17 11	איל	RAM	17d	2
	כסף	SILVER	494b	6
	מן	FROM	580d	3 ba
	מנחה	TRIBUTE	585a	2
	משׂא	TRIBUTE	672a	4
	ערבי	ARABIAN	787b	
	צאן	SMALL CATTLE	838b	1 a4
	תישׁ	HE-GOAT	1067a	
17 12	בירנה	FORTRESS	108c	
	בנה	BUILD	124b	1 ag
	גדל	BECOMING GREAT	152d	1
	הלך	WALK	233c	1 4d
	מסכנות	SUPPLY	698a	
	עד	UNTIL	725c	3 3
	עיר	CITY	746c	1 e
	מעל	ABOVE	752a	2 cb
17 13	מלאכה	WORK	522a	2

Ch v.	Heb	Eng	Page	Sec
	מלחמה	WAR	536b	
17 14	עדנה	ADNAH	726d	1
	עם	WITH	767b	1 a
	פקדה	OVERSIGHT	824b	3
17 15	יהוחנן	JEHOHANAN	220b	5
	יד	HAND	391c	5 h3
	עם	WITH	767b	1 a
17 16	במה	HIGH PLACE	*119c	3 c
	גבור	STRONG	150b	2
	זכרי	ZICHRI	271d	2
	יד	HAND	391c	5 h3
	נדב	INCITE	621c	1
	עם	WITH	767b	1 a
	עמסיה	AMASIAH	770c	
17 17	אלידע	ELIADA	45a	C
	גבור	STRONG	150b	2
	נשׁק	BE EQUIPPED WITH	676c	
	עם	WITH	767b	1 a
	קשׁת	BOW	906c	1 d
17 18	יהוזבד	JEHOZABAD	220b	3
	חלץ	EQUIP FOR WAR	323a	2
	יד	HAND	391c	5 h3
	עם	WITH	767b	1 a
17 19	בד	SEPARATION	94d	1 e
	מבצר	FORTIFICATION	131c	
	שׁרת	SERVE	1058a	1 b
18 1	חתן	MAKE ONESELF A SON IN LAW	368d	1
	כבוד	HONOR	458c	2 a
18 2	בקר	CATTLE	133b	1 a
	זבח	SLAUGHTER FOR SACRIFICE	256d	1 1 ba
	זבח	SLAUGHTER FOR SACRIFICE	257a	1
	ירד	GO DOWN	433a	1 e
	ל	TO	511b	1 ga
	ל	TO	517a	6 a
	סות	INCITE	694d	2
	קץ	END	893d	1
18 4	דרשׁ	SEEK	*205b	2 a
	יום	DAY	400d	7 h
18 5	הלך	WALK	231a	1 d3 ga
	חדל	CEASE	293a	2
	נביא	PROPHET	612a	3
	קבץ	GATHER	867d	1
18 6	דרשׁ	SEEK	*205b	2 a
18 7	דרשׁ	SEEK	205b	2 a
	טובה	WELFARE	375d	1
	מיכיהו	MICAH	567c	2
	ימלה	IMLAH	571c	
	נבא	PROPHESY	612b	1 b
	רע	EVIL	*948d	2
18 8	מהר	HASTEN	555a	3
	ימלה	IMLAH	571c	
	סרים	EUNUCH	710c	
18 9	בגד	GARMENT	94a	1
	גרן	THRESHING-FLOOR	175b	
	לבשׁ	ARRAYED	528b	
	נביא	PROPHET	612a	3
	נבא	PROPHESY	612c	3
	נפל	FALL	657a	2 a
	פתח	OPENING	836a	
	שׁער	GATE	1045a	2 a
18 10	ברזל	IRON	137c	1 d
	כלה	FINISH	478c	2 c1
	כנענה	CHENAANAH	489b	1
	נגח	PUSH	618c	
	צדקיהו	ZEDEKIAH	843c	2 a
	קרן	HORN	901d	1 a
18 11	נביא	PROPHET	612a	3
	נבא	PROPHESY	612b	3
	צלח	ADVANCE	852c	2
18 12	טוב	PLEASANT	374a	2 f
	טוב	PLEASANT	374a	2 f
	מלאך	MESSENGER	521c	1 a
	נביא	PROPHET	612a	3
18 13	חי	ALIVE	311d	1 a
18 14	הלך	WALK	231a	1 d3 ga
	חדל	CEASE	293a	2
	מיכה	MICHA	567d	6
	צלח	ADVANCE	852c	2
18 15	אמת	FIRMNESS	54b	4 a
	מה	HOW	*553d	4 ca
	פעם	OCCURRENCE	822a	3 a
	רק	ONLY	956c	2 d
	שׁבע	SWEAR	989d	2
18 16	הר	MOUNTAIN	250c	1 g
	פוץ	BE DISPERSED	807a	1
	צאן	SMALL CATTLE	838b	2
18 17	שׁוב	TURN BACK	997b	3 a
	טוב	PLEASANT	374a	2 f
	נבא	PROPHESY	612b	1 b
	רע	EVIL	948d	2
18 18	ימין	RIGHT HAND	*411d	2 a
	ימין	RIGHT HAND	411d	2 a
	כסא	SEAT OF HONOR	490d	1 b
	צבא	HOST	839a	1 b
	שׂמאל	LEFT	969d	1
	שׁבנא	SHEBNA	987d	
18 19	כה	THUS	*462b	1 5
	ככה	THUS	462c	
	פתה	BE SIMPLE	834d	2
18 20	עמד	STAND	764a	1 d
	פתה	BE SIMPLE	834d	2
	רוח	BREATH	925d	9 a
18 21	יכל	PREVAIL	408a	1 a

2 CHRONICLES

Ch	v.	Heb	Eng	Page	Sec
		נביא	PROPHET	612a	3
		פתה	BE SIMPLE	834d	2
		רוח	BREATH	925d	9a
18	22	דבר	SPEAK	*181c	5
		נביא	PROPHET	612a	3
		רוח	BREATH	925d	9a
18	23	אי	WHERE	32b	1b
		אי	WHERE	32b	1b
		דבר	SPEAK	181b	3d
		כנענה	CHENAANAH	489b	1
		לחי	CHEEK	534d	2
		נכה	SMITE	645b	1a
		עבר	PASS OVER	717b	1h
		צדקיהו	ZEDEKIAH	843c	2a
		רוח	BREATH	925d	9a
18	24	חבא	WITHDRAW	285b	
		חדר	CHAMBER	293d	
18	25	אמון	AMON	54c	B
		יהואש	JEHOASH	220a	4
		שר	CHIEFTAIN	978b	2d
		שוב	TURN BACK	998d	1a
18	26	אכל	EAT	38a	1
		בית	HOUSE	109a	1ae 2
		כלא	CONFINEMENT	476c	
		לחם	FOOD	537c	3a
		לחץ	OPPRESSION	538a	
		מי	WATER	565d	3
		שבנא	SHEBNA	987d	
		שוב	TURN BACK	997b	3b
18	27	דבר	SPEAK	181c	1a
		שוב	TURN BACK	997b	3b
18	29	חפש	SEARCH	344c	
		לבש	PUT ON	527d	A
18	30	לחם	ENGAGE IN BATTLE	535c	
		קטן	SMALL	882b	2
		שר	CHIEFTAIN	978c	3b
18	31	זעק	CRY	277b	2d
		סבב	SURROUND	686a	2
		סות	INCITE	694d	1b
		עבדה	LABOR	715b	4
		שר	CHIEFTAIN	978c	3b
18	32	היה	BE	227a	3 4b
		שר	CHIEFTAIN	978c	3b
		שוב	TURN BACK	996d	1
		דבק	APPENDAGE	180b	2
18	33	הפך	TURN	245b	1a
		מחנה	ENCAMPMENT	334b	3c
		יצא	CAUSE TO GO	424c	1a
		משך	DRAW	604b	2
		נכה	SMITE	645c	1a
		קשת	BOW	906c	1d
		רכב	CHARIOTEER	939b	1
		שריון	BODY-ARMOUR	1056b	
		תם	INTEGRITY	1070d	2
18	34	חיה	BE	*227c	3 5a
		מלחמה	WAR	536c	
		נכח	FRONT	*647b	1
		עלה	GO UP	748c	2c
		עמד	STAND	765a	
		עת	TIME	773c	1c
		ערב	SUNSET	787d	1a
		מרכבה	CHARIOT	939d	
19	1	ל	TO	*511b	1ga
		שוב	TURN BACK	997a	3a
19	2	אהב	LOVE	13a	1
		יהוא	JEHU	219d	2
		זה	THIS	262a	6bd
		חזה	SEER	302d	1b
		חני	HANANI	337b	1
		ל	TO	512a	3b
		ל	TO	518a	7bg
		פנה	FACE	816c	21a
		פנה	FACE	817d	25aa
		קצף	WRATH	893c	2
		רשע	WICKED	957c	2
		שנא	HATE	971d	3
		שבנא	SHEBNA	987d	
19	3	אבל	HOWBEIT	6a	2
		אשרה	ASHERA	81c	B
		בער	CONSUME	129b	3
		דבר	WORD	183c	42
		דרש	SEEK	205b	3a
		טוב	PLEASANT	374d	0a
		כון	ESTABLISH	466c	3
		לבב	HEART	523d	24
		מצא	FIND	593d	1c
		עם	WITH	768b	3b
19	4	באר שבע	BEERSHEBA	92a	
		הר	MOUNTAIN	251a	2b
		שוב	TURN BACK	998b	8
		שוב	TURN BACK	999b	2a
19	5	בצר	MAKE INACCESSIBLE	131a	
		ו	AND	253b	1ib
		ל	TO	516b	5ja
		עמד	STAND	764d	1
		שפט	JUDGE	1047c	2b
19	6	דבר	WORD	183d	45
		שפט	JUDGE	1047c	2b
		שפט	JUDGE	1047c	2b
		משפט	JUDGMENT	1048b	1a
19	7	מקח	TAKING	544c	
		משא	LIFTING UP	673a	
		עולה	INJUSTICE	732d	3
		עם	WITH	768b	3b
19	8	שחד	BRIBE	1005a	7
		כהן	PRIEST	464a	7
		ישראל	ISRAEL	975d	2a4
		שוב	TURN BACK	997b	3b
		משפט	JUDGMENT	1048b	1a
19	9	אמונה	FIRMNESS	53c	3a
		ירא	FEAR	432a	3
		לבב	HEART	524a	26a
		שלם	COMPLETE	1024a	3
19	10	אשם	OFFEND	79c	1
		דם	BLOOD	197b	2j
		זהר	ADMONISH	264b	2
		חק	SOMETHING PRESCRIBED	349d	7g
		תורה	LAW	436a	2a
		קצף	WRATH	893c	1
19	11	אמריהו	AMARIAH	57c	4
		דבר	WORD	183b	41
		זבדיהו	ZEBADIAH	256c	2
		חזק	BE FIRM	304b	1 2c
		טוב	PLEASANT	374d	0a
		כהן	PRIEST	464b	8
		ל	TO	513c	5cb b
		ל	TO	*514c	5fc
		נגיד	LEADER	618a	4
		ראש	HEAD	911a	3e
		שטר	OFFICIAL	1009c	
		ישמעאל	ISHMAEL	1035d	4a
20	1	אחר	AFTER	30a	2b
		מעונים	MEUNITES	589b	
		עמוני	AMMONITE	*770a	
20	2	אדום	EDOM	10c	2
		ארם	ARAM	74c	B
		המון	CROWD	242c	3a
		חצצנתמר	HAZAZON-TAMAR	346c	1
		עבר	REGION ACROSS	719b	1
		עינגדי	ENGEDI	745b	
20	3	דרש	SEEK	205b	3a
		ירא	FEAR	431a	1a
		פנה	FACE	816a	11d
		צום	FASTING	847b	
20	4	בקש	SEEK	134d	3c
		בקש	SEEK	135a	6
		קבץ	GATHER	867d	1
20	5	חדש	NEW	294b	A
		חצר	ENCLOSURE	347a	3b
		קהל	ASSEMBLY	874d	1d
20	6	אין	NOT	34d	5a
		גבורה	MIGHT	150c	2
		יצב	STATION ONESELF	426c	D
		כח	STRENGTH	470d	3
		ממלכה	KINGDOM	575b	1
		משל	RULE	605d	3
		עם	WITH	768b	3d
		אצבע	FINGER	840c	2
20	7	אהב	LOVE	13a	4b
		זרע	SOWING	283a	4f
		ירש	CAUSE TO POSSESS	440a	2a
		עולם	LONG DURATION	762d	2f
20	8	בנה	BUILD	124b	1ab
20	9	דבר	PESTILENCE	184a	1
		זעק	CRY	277b	2a
		ישע	DELIVER	446d	1b
		שפוט	JUDGEMENT	1048a	
20	10	מצרים	EGYPT	595d	1 b2
		נתן	GIVE	679a	1g
		סור	TURN ASIDE	693c	1
		על	UPON	759a	42b
		שעיר	SEIR	973a	1b
20	11	גרש	DRIVE OUT	177a	
		ירש	CAUSE TO POSSESS	439d	1
		ירשה	POSSESSION	440b	
20	12	המון	CROWD	242c	3a
		כח	STRENGTH	470d	1b
		על	UPON	757d	27cc
		שפט	JUDGE	1047c	2a
20	13	טף	CHILDREN	382a	
		טף	CHILDREN	382a	
20	14	אסף	ASAPH	63b	2
		בניהו	BENAIAH	125c	4c
		זכריהו	ZECHARIAH	272b	0e
		יחזיאל	JAHAZIEL	303c	4
		יעיאל	JEIEL	418b	2c1
		לוי	LEVITE	532d	1
		מתניהו	MATTANIAH	682d	3b1
		קהל	ASSEMBLY	874d	1d
		רוח	BREATH	925d	9b
20	15	המון	CROWD	242c	3a
		חתת	BE SHATTERED	369b	2a
		ירא	FEAR	431b	1c
		מדבר	WILDERNESS	185a	3b
		ירד	GO DOWN	433a	1e
		ירואל	JERUEL	436c	
		מצא	FIND	593d	1c
		נחל	WADY	636c	2
		סוף	END	693a	
20	16	פנה	FACE	816b	16
		ציץ	ZIZ	851d	
20	17	זה	THIS	262a	6bd
		חתת	BE SHATTERED	369b	2a
		יצב	STATION ONESELF	426b	B
		ירא	FEAR	431a	1a
		ישועה	VICTORY	447a	4
		ל	TO	513b	5ba
		ל	TO	517d	7bd
		עמד	STAND	764a	2b
20	18	אף	NOSE	60b	2
		נפל	FALL	657b	3b
		קדד	BOW DOWN	869a	
		שחה	BOW DOWN	1005c	2a
20	19	הלל	PRAISE	238c	2e
		הלל	PRAISE	*238d	2e
		מעל	ABOVE	752a	2cb
		קהתי	KOHATHITES	875c	
		קום	STAND	878a	1g
		קרחי	KORAHITES	901c	
20	20	אמן	CONFIRM	53a	3
		אמן	CONFIRM	53b	2c
		אמן	CONFIRM	53b	2c
		בקר	MORNING	134b	1h
		מדבר	WILDERNESS	185a	3b
		צלח	ADVANCE	852c	2
		שמע	HEAR	1034a	1i
		תקוע	TEKOA	1075d	
20	21	הדרה	ADORNMENT	214c	1
		הלל	PRAISE	238d	2e
		חלץ	EQUIP FOR WAR	323a	2
		חסד	GOODNESS	339b	23c
		יעץ	CONSULT	419d	
		ל	TO	516d	5k
		עולם	LONG DURATION	762b	2c
		קדש	APARTNESS	872b	4b
		ארב	LIE IN WAIT	70c	
20	22	תהלה	PRAISE	240a	2
		חלל	POLLUTE	320d	2
		ידה	PRAISE	392c	1
		נגף	STRIKE	620a	
		עת	TIME	773c	1d
		רנה	RINGING CRY	943d	3
		שעיר	SEIR	973a	1b
20	23	חרם	BAN	355d	1b
		כלה	FINISH	478b	1d
		סור	TURN ASIDE	694a	3
		עזר	HELP	740c	
		עמד	STAND	764c	6c
		רע	FRIEND	946b	3
		שעיר	SEIR	973a	1a
		שעיר	SEIR	973a	1b
20	24	משחית	DESTRUCTION	1008c	
		בוא	COME	98b	2
		המון	CROWD	242c	3a
		ל	TO	511d	1h
		נפל	LIE	657d	7
		על	UPON	757a	27ca
		פגר	CORPSE	803d	1
		פליטה	ESCAPE	812c	2b
		פנה	TURN	815b	2a
		מצפה	WATCH TOWER	859d	2
20	25	אין	NOT	35a	6cb
		בז	SPOIL	102d	
		חמודה	DESIRABLENESS	326d	
		כלי	ARTICLE	479c	1
		מצא	FIND	592d	1a
		נצל	STRIP	664d	1
		משא	BEARING	672d	3
		פגר	CORPSE	803d	1
		רכוש	PROPERTY	940d	3
20	26	ברך	BLESS	139a	1
		ברכה	BERACAH	139d	1
		קהל	ASSEMBLE AS	875a	2
		רביעי	FOURTH	917d	1
20	27	מן	FROM	578a	1a
		ראש	HEAD	911b	4a
		שמח	REJOICE	970c	
		שוב	TURN BACK	997a	1
20	28	חצצרה	CLARION	348c	2c
		כנור	LYRE	490a	
		נבל	HARP	614a	
20	29	היה	BECOME	225d	2 1b
		ממלכה	KINGDOM	575b	1
		פחד	DREAD	808c	1
20	30	מלכות	KINGDOM	575a	3
		נוח	REST	628c	A 1b 2
		שקט	BE QUIET	1053a	1
20	31	עזובה	AZUBAH	738a	1
		שלחי	SHILHI	1019d	
20	32	דרך	WAY	203d	6c
		ישר	STRAIGHT	449a	2a
20	33	במה	HIGH PLACE	119c	3
		כון	ESTABLISH	466c	
		לבב	HEART	523d	24
		עוד	STILL	728d	1aa
20	34	דבר	WORD	183a	21c
		יהוא	JEHU	219d	2
		חני	HANANI	337b	1
		לא	NOT	*520c	4bb
		ספר	MISSIVE	707c	3e
		עלה	GO UP	750a	2
		על	UPON	757a	27b
		ראשון	FIRST	911c	1a
20	35	אחזיהו	AHAZIAH	28d	1
		חבר	UNITE	288c	
		רשע	BE WICKED	957d	3
20	36	אניה	A SHIP	58b	
		אניה	A SHIP	58c	
		הלך	WALK	232b	13
		חבר	UNITE	288b	1
		עציונגבר	EZION-GEBER	782b	
		תרשיש	TARSHISH	1077a	1
20	37	אחזיהו	AHAZIAH	28d	1
		אליעזר	ELIEZER	45c	F
		אניה	A SHIP	58b	

Ch v.	Heb	Eng	Page	Sec
	דודוהו	DODAVAHU	187d	
	הלך	WALK	232b	1 3
	חבר	UNITE	288c	
	מרשה	MARESHAH	601c	
	נבא	PROPHESY	612b	1 b
	עצר	RESTRAIN	783d	2
	מעשה	DEED	796a	2 a1
	פרץ	BREAK THROUGH	829c	5
	שבר	BREAK	990d	
	תרשיש	TARSHISH	1077a	1
21 1	דוד	DAVID	188a	A
21 1	יהורם	JEHORAM	221b	1
21 2	זכריהו	ZECHARIAH	272b	7
	יחיאל	JEHIEL	313d	4
	מיכאל	MICHAEL	567c	9
	עזריהו	AZARIAH	741b	4 a
	שפטיה	SHEPHATIAH	1049b	2 a
21 3	יהורם	JEHORAM	221b	1
	כסף	SILVER	494b	6
	ל	TO	514c	5 fb
	מגדנה	EXCELLENT THING	550c	
	ממלכה	DOMINION	575b	2
	מתנה	GIFT	682b	
	מצורה	SIEGE-WORKS	849a	2
21 4	יהורם	JEHORAM	221b	1
	הרג	KILL	247a	1 a
	חזק	BE FIRM	305b	1
	ממלכה	KINGDOM	575b	1
	קום	STAND	878a	4
21 5	יהורם	JEHORAM	221b	1
21 6	בית	HOUSE	110a	5 c
	דרך	WAY	203d	6 d
	חתן	MAKE ONESELF A SON IN LAW	*368d	1
21 7	אבה	BE WILLING	2c	
	אמר	SAY	56b	3
	בית	HOUSE	110a	5 c
	ברית	COVENANT	137a	3 1
	ברית	COVENANT	137b	3 2
	יום	DAY	400c	7 f
	כרת	CUT	504a	4
	ניר	LAMP	633a	
	שחת	GO TO RUIN	1008b	1
21 8	אין	NOT	35a	6 cb
	יד	HAND	*391b	5 g1
	מלך	BE KING	574b	
	פשע	REBEL	833b	1
	יד	ADDENDA ET CORRIGENDA	1123d	
21 9	יהורם	JEHORAM	221b	1
	היה	COME TO PASS	224d	2 a1 am
	נכה	SMITE	646b	3
	סבב	SURROUND	686a	2 d
	עבר	PASS OVER	717a	1 b
	עם	WITH	768a	1 g
21 10	יד	HAND	*391b	5 g1
	לבנה	LIBNAH	526c	1
	פשע	REBEL	833b	1
	יד	ADDENDA ET CORRIGENDA	1123d	
21 11	במה	HIGH PLACE	119c	3 c
	הר	MOUNTAIN	251a	2 b
	זנה	COMMIT FORNICATION	276a	1 b
	נדח	THRUST	623b	3
21 12	אלהים	GOD	44c	4 ba
	אליה	ELIJAH	45b	A
	דרך	WAY	203d	6 d
	הלך	WALK	234d	2 3a lt
	מכתב	WRITING	508c	2
	נביא	PROPHET	611d	1
	תחת	INSTEAD	1066a	2 3a b
21 13	בית	HOUSE	110a	5 c
	דרך	WAY	203d	6 d
	הרג	KILL	247a	1 a
	זנה	COMMIT FORNICATION	276a	1 b
21 14	טוב	PLEASANT	374c	6
	נגף	STRIKE	619d	
	מגפה	PLAGUE	620b	3
	רכוש	PROPERTY	940d	3
21 15	חלי	SICKNESS	318b	
	מחלה	SICKNESS	318b	
	יצא	GO OUT	423a	1 c
	מעה	BELLY	588d	1 a
	על	UPON	755b	2 4b
21 16	יהורם	JEHORAM	221b	1
	יד	HAND	391c	5 h3
	כושי	CUSHITE	469b	D
	עור	ROUSE ONESELF	735b	1
	ערבי	ARABIAN	787b	
	רוח	BREATH	925b	3 g
21 17	בקע	BREAK OPEN OR THROUGH	131d	2
	יהואחז	JEHOAHAZ	219d	3
	מצא	FIND	594a	2 c
	קטן	SMALL	882b	1 a
	רכוש	PROPERTY	940d	3
	שאר	REMAIN	984a	1
21 18	שבה	TAKE CAPTIVE	985c	1 b
	אחר	AFTER	30b	2 b
	זה	THIS	260d	1 a
	חלי	SICKNESS	318b	
	מעה	BELLY	588d	1 a
	נגף	STRIKE	619d	

Ch v.	Heb	Eng	Page	Sec
	מרפא	HEALING	951c	3
21 19	תחלאים	DISEASES	316a	
	חלי	SICKNESS	318b	
	יום	DAY	399d	6 c
	יום	DAY	401a	7 i
	יצא	GO OUT	423a	1 c
	יצא	GO OUT	423a	1 c
	ל	TO	517a	6 b
	מעה	BELLY	588d	1 a
	קץ	END	893d	1
	רע	EVIL	948a	1
	שרפה	BURNING	977c	
21 20	דוד	DAVID	188a	A
	היה	BE	227a	3 4b
	הלך	WALK	234b	2 1
	הלך	WALK	234d	2 3a 2a
	חמדה	DESIRE	326c	
	לא	NOT	520a	4 aa
22 1	אחזי	AHAZIAH	28d	2
	גדוד	BAND	151b	1
	יהורם	JEHORAM	221b	1
	הרג	KILL	247a	1 a
	מלך	BE KING	574b	
	ערבי	ARABIAN	787b	
	קטן	SMALL	882b	1 a
22 2	אם	MOTHER	51d	1
	חצב	HEW	345a	2 a
	עמרי	OMRI	771d	1
	עתליה	ATHALIAH	801a	1
	ארבעים	FORTY	917c	2
	שנים	TWO	1041b	3
22 3	אם	MOTHER	51d	1
	בית	HOUSE	110a	5 c
	דרך	WAY	204a	6 d
	הלך	WALK	234d	2 3a 2a
	יעץ	ADVISE	419d	
	רשע	BE WICKED	957d	3
22 4	בית	HOUSE	110a	5 c
	יעץ	ADVISE	419d	
	משחית	DESTRUCTION	1008c	
22 5	ארמי	ARAMEAN	74c	
	יהורם	JEHORAM	221b	2
	יהורם	JEHORAM	221b	2
	הלך	WALK	231a	1 d3 gb
	הלך	WALK	235a	2 3e 2
	חזהאל	HAZAEL	303c	
22 6	עצה	ADVICE	420a	
	יהורם	JEHORAM	221b	2
	יהורם	JEHORAM	221b	1
	יזרעאל	JEZREEL	283c	1 b
	חזהאל	HAZAEL	303c	
	חלה	BE WEAK	317d	2
	ירד	GO DOWN	433a	1 e
	לחם	ENGAGE IN BATTLE	535c	2
	נכה	SMITE	645d	1 e
	ראה	TO SEE	907d	6 d
	רמה	RAMA	928b	5
	רפא	HEAL	951a	
	מכה	ADDENDA ET CORRIGENDA	1125a	
22 7	תבוסה	RUIN	101b	
	בית	HOUSE	110a	5 c
	יהוא	JEHU	219d	1
	יהורם	JEHORAM	221b	2
	יהורם	JEHORAM	221b	2
	כרת	CUT OFF	504c	2 b
	מן	OUT OF	579d	2 d
	משח	ANOINT	603b	2
	נמשי	NIMSHI	650a	
	עזרי	AZARIAH	741b	2 b
22 8	בית	HOUSE	110a	5 c
	יהוא	JEHU	219d	1
	הרג	KILL	247a	1 a
	שפט	JUDGE	1048a	1
	שרת	SERVE	1058a	1 b
22 9	אין	NOT	34d	5 a
	בקש	SEEK	134c	1 b
	דרש	SEEK	205b	3 a
	יהוא	JEHU	219d	1
	חבא	WITHDRAW	285b	1
	כח	STRENGTH	470d	1 c
	ל	TO	517d	7 be
	לבב	HEART	523c	2 2
	לבד	CAPTURE	540a	1
	ממלכה	DOMINION	575b	2
	עצר	RESTRAIN	783c	2
22 10	דבר	SPEAK	181d	1
	זרע	SOWING	282d	4 e
	ל	TO	513d	5 cb g
	ממלכה	DOMINION	575c	1
	עתליה	ATHALIAH	801a	1
22 11	בת	DAUGHTER	123a	1
	גנב	STEAL	170b	
	יהואש	JEHOASH	220a	1
	יהוידע	JEHOIADA	220c	2
	יהורם	JEHORAM	221b	1
	יהושבע	JEHOSHEBA	221c	
	חדר	CHAMBER	293d	
	ינק	NURSE	413c	
	כהן	PRIEST	463c	4
	מות	DIE	560c	1
	מטה	COUCH	642d	1
	סתר	HIDE	711d	1
	עתליה	ATHALIAH	801a	1
22 12	היה	BE	226d	3 2

Ch v.	Heb	Eng	Page	Sec
	חבא	WITHDRAW	285b	1
	מלך	BE KING	574a	
	עתליה	ATHALIAH	801a	1
22 15	חצב	HEW	345a	2 a
22 16	עצה	ADVICE	420a	
	מכה	BLOW	646d	1 c
23 1	אלישפט	ELISHAPHAT	46a	
	ברית	COVENANT	136c	1 3
	יהוחנן	JEHOHANAN	220b	5
	יהוידע	JEHOIADA	220c	2
	זכרי	ZICHRI	271d	6
	חזק	BE FIRM	305b	1
	ל	TO	512a	3 b
	עובד	OBED	714d	2
	עדיהו	ADAIAH	726a	1
	עזריהו	AZARIAH	741b	7
	מעשיהו	MAASEIAH	796b	3 b
	ירחם	JEROHAM	934a	6
	ישמעאל	ISHMAEL	1035d	4 b
23 2	סבב	GO AROUND	685d	2 c
	קבץ	GATHER	867d	2
23 3	בן	SON	120d	1 ja
	ברית	COVENANT	136d	2 2g
	ברית	COVENANT	137a	3 1
	דבר	SPEAK	181c	5
	כרת	CUT	503d	4
23 4	בוא	COME	97d	1
	כהן	PRIEST	464a	7
	ל	TO	512c	4 a
	ל	TO	513d	5 cb g
	סף	THRESHOLD	706c	
	שבת	SABBATH	992b	1 a
	שער	PORTER	1045c	
23 5	חצר	ENCLOSURE	347a	3 b
	יסוד	FOUNDATION	414b	1
	שער	GATE	1045b	3 a
23 6	כאם	EXCEPT	474d	2 a
	קדש	APARTNESS	872b	4 a
	שרת	SERVE	1057b	2
23 7	בוא	COME	97d	1 a
	יד	HAND	390d	5 c1
	כלי	IMPLEMENT	479d	2 a
	מות	DIE	560c	1
	נקף	GO AROUND	669a	1 b
23 8	בוא	COME	97d	1
	בוא	COME	98a	1 c
	יהוידע	JEHOIADA	220c	2
	כהן	PRIEST	463c	4
	פטר	SEPARATE	809c	2
	צוה	CHARGE	846a	3
	שבת	SABBATH	992b	1 a
23 9	יהוידע	JEHOIADA	220c	2
	חנית	SPEAR	333d	1
	כהן	PRIEST	463c	4
	שלט	SHIELD	1020d	
23 10	ימני	RIGHT	412b	
	כתף	SIDE	509c	2 b
	שמאלי	LEFT	970a	
	שלח	MISSLE	1019c	1
23 11	יהוידע	JEHOIADA	220c	2
	חיה	LIVE	311b	1 d
	יצא	CAUSE TO GO	424c	1 b
	מלך	KING	573b	5 b
	מלך	BE KING	574b	
	משח	ANOINT	603b	2
	נזר	CROWN	634b	1 a
	עדות	TESTIMONY	730c	2
23 12	הלל	PRAISE	238a	1
	עתליה	ATHALIAH	801a	1
	קול	VOICE	877b	2 c
	רוץ	RUN	930b	1
	רוץ	RUN	*930c	2 a
23 13	מבוא	ENTRANCE	99d	1
	הלל	PRAISE	238d	2 g
	חצצרה	CLARION	348c	1
	ידע	MAKE KNOWN	395a	
	כלי	INSTRUMENT	479d	2 b
	עמוד	PILLAR	765b	2
	עתליה	ATHALIAH	801a	1
	קשר	CONSPIRACY	905c	
	שמח	JOYFUL	970d	1 b
23 14	בית	HOUSE	110c	8 b
	יהוידע	JEHOIADA	220c	2
	חיל	STRENGTH	299a	4
	יצא	CAUSE TO GO	424c	1 b
	יצא	BRING OUT	424d	1 c
	כהן	PRIEST	463c	4
	מות	DIE	560c	1
	שדרה	ROW	690c	
	פקד	ATTEND TO	823c	B 1
23 15	מבוא	ENTRANCE	99d	1
	יד	HAND	389a	1 a
	סוס	HORSE	692d	2
	שום	TO PLACE	963b	1 c
	שער	GATE	1045b	3 a
23 16	ברית	COVENANT	137a	3 1
	יהוידע	JEHOIADA	220c	2
	כרת	CUT	504a	2
23 17	בעל	BAAL	127d	2 2
	הרג	KILL	247b	1 b
	מזבח	ALTAR	259a	0
	כהן	PRIEST	463a	2
	מתן	MATTAN	682b	1
	נתץ	PULL DOWN	683b	1
	צלם	IMAGE	853d	1
23 18	יהוידע	JEHOIADA	220c	2

2 CHRONICLES

Ch v.	Heb	Eng	Page	Sec
	חלק	DIVIDE	323c	2
	יד	HAND	391c	5 h2
	תורה	LAW	436b	2 b3
	כהן	PRIEST	*464a	7
	לוי	LEVITE	533a	3 1b
	משה	MOSES	602d	
	עלה	WHOLE BURNT OF-FERING	750d	
	על	UPON	754c	2 1f d
	פקדה	OVERSIGHT	824a	2 a
	שום	TO PLACE	964a	3 d
	שיר	SONG	1010c	3
23 19	ממא	UNCLEAN	379d	2 a
	ל	TO	514d	5 g
23 20	אדיר	MAJESTIC	12b	2
	ירד	BRING DOWN	433d	1 a
	ישב	CAUSE TO SIT	443c	1
	כסא	THRONE	491b	3 a
	ממלכה	DOMINION	575b	2
	משל	RULE	605d	1
	עליון	HIGH	751b	2
	שער	GATE	1045b	3 b
23 21	מות	DIE	560b	1 b
	עתליה	ATHALIAH	801a	1
	שקט	BE QUIET	1053a	1
24 1	באר־שבע	BEERSHEBA	92a	1
	יהואש	JEHOASH	220a	1
	צביה	ZIBIAH	840b	
24 2	יהואש	JEHOASH	220a	1
	יהוידע	JEHOIADA	220c	2
	ישר	STRAIGHT	449a	2 a
	כהן	PRIEST	463c	4
24 3	יהוידע	JEHOIADA	220c	2
	נשא	LIFT	671c	3 d
	שנים	TWO	1041b	1 b2
24 4	אחר	AFTER	30a	2 b
	יהואש	JEHOASH	220a	1
	היה	BE	227b	3 4d a
	חדש	RENEW	294a	2
	לבב	HEART	*523c	22
	לב	HEART	524c	22
	עם	WITH	768c	4 a
24 5	די	SUFFICIENCY	191d	2 cb
	חזק	BE FIRM	304c	1 c
	כהן	PRIEST	464a	4
	ל	TO	512a	3 b
	מהר	HASTEN	555a	3
	קבץ	GATHER	867c	1
	קבץ	GATHER	867d	2
24 6	אהל	TENT	14a	3
	דרש	SEEK	205c	4 b
	יהוידע	JEHOIADA	220c	2
	משה	MOSES	602d	
	משאת	PORTION	673b	4 d
	עבד	SLAVE	714a	3
	עדות	TESTIMONY	730b	1
	ראש	HEAD	911a	3 e
24 7	בעל	BAAL	127d	2 3
	עתליה	ATHALIAH	801a	1
	מרשעת	WICKEDNESS	958a	
24 8	אמר	SAY	56c	4
	ארון	CHEST	75b	1
	חוץ	THE OUTSIDE	299d	1 a
24 9	אלהים	GOD	44a	3 b
	משאת	PORTION	673b	4 d
	עבד	SLAVE	714a	3
	על	UPON	753c	2 1c
	קול	VOICE	877b	3 a3
24 10	ארון	CHEST	75b	1
	כלה	FINISH	478b	1 a
	כלה	FINISH	478b	1 d
	עד	UNTIL	725c	3 2
	שלך	THROW	1021a	1 a
24 11	אסף	GATHER	62b	1 c
	ארון	CHEST	75b	1
	היה	COME TO PASS	225a	1 2a 1d
	יום	DAY	400b	7 e1
	כהן	PRIEST	464b	4
	ספר	ENUMERATOR	708c	1 b
	עת	TIME	773c	1 d
	ערה	BE NAKED	788d	2
	פקדה	OVERSIGHT	824a	2 b
	פקיד	COMMISSIONER	824b	
	ראש	HEAD	911a	3 e
	רב	MUCH	913a	1 a1
	שוב	TURN BACK	998d	1 a
24 12	ברזל	IRON	137c	1 b
	יהוידע	JEHOIADA	220c	2
	חדש	RENEW	294a	2
	חזק	BE FIRM	304c	1 c
	חצב	HEW	345a	2 a
	חרש	GRAVER	360d	1 a
	חרש	GRAVER	360d	1 a
	ל	TO	512a	3 b
	מלאכה	WORK	522a	3 b
	נחשת	COPPER	638d	1
	עבדה	LABOR	715c	4
	שכר	HIRE	969a	
24 13	אמץ	BE STRONG	55a	1
	ארוכה	HEALING	74b	B
	עלה	GO UP	749a	6
	עמד	STAND	764d	3
	מתכנת	MEASUREMENT	1067c	2
24 14	בוא	COME	99b	2
	יהוידע	JEHOIADA	220c	2
	זהב	GOLD	263c	1
	כלה	FINISH	478b	1 a
	כף	PAN	497a	4 b
	תמיד	CONTINUITY	556c	1 b
	עלה	WHOLE BURNT OF-FERING	750d	
	שאר	REST	984c	
	שרת	MINISTRY	1058b	
24 15	בן	SON	122a	9 a
	יהוידע	JEHOIADA	220c	2
	זקן	BE OLD	278b	
	שבע	SATISFIED	959c	2 b
24 16	דוד	DAVID	188a	A
	טובה	WELFARE	375d	2
24 17	יהוידע	JEHOIADA	220c	2
24 18	אשמה	WRONG-DOING	80a	1
	אשרה	ASHERA	81c	B
	זבידה	ZEBIDAH	*256c	
	זה	THIS	261a	2 ba
	עבד	WORK	713b	4 b
	עזב	LEAVE	737c	2 d2
	עצב	IDOL	781b	
	קצף	WRATH	893c	1
24 19	אזן	HEAR	24c	1
	עוד	BEAR WITNESS	730a	3
	שוב	TURN BACK	999b	2 a
24 20	יהוידע	JEHOIADA	220c	2
	זכריהו	ZECHARIAH	272b	1 c
	כהן	PRIEST	463c	4
	לבש	PUT ON	528b	F
	עבר	PASS OVER	717c	1 1
	על	UPON	759b	4 2e a
	צלח	ADVANCE	852c	2
	רוח	BREATH	925d	9 b
24 21	אבן	STONE	6b	1
	חצר	ENCLOSURE	347a	3 b
	קשר	BIND	905b	2
	רגם	TO STONE	920c	
24 22	דרש	SEEK	205c	5
	יהואש	JEHOASH	220a	1
	יהוידע	JEHOIADA	220c	2
	זכר	REMEMBER	269d	1 2c
	חסד	GOODNESS	338c	1 1
24 23	דמשק	DAMASCUS	200a	
	הרג	KILL	247a	1 a
	ל	TO	517a	6 a
	תקופה	COMING ROUND	880d	2
	שר	CHIEFTAIN	978d	6
	שחת	GO TO RUIN	1008b	1
	שנה	YEAR	1040b	
24 24	יהואש	JEHOASH	220a	1
	מאד	EXCEEDINGLY	547b	2 a
	עשה	DO	794a	1 1a 4
	מצער	SMALL THING	859b	1
	רב	MULTITUDE	914a	1
	שפט	JUDGEMENT	1048a	
24 25	דוד	DAVID	188a	A
	דם	BLOOD	196d	2 f
	יהוידע	JEHOIADA	220c	2
	הרג	KILL	247a	1 a
	מחלוי	SICKNESS	318c	1
	כהן	PRIEST	463c	4
	מטה	COUCH	641d	
	עזב	LEAVE	737a	1 e
	קשר	BIND	905c	
24 26	יהוזבד	JEHOZABAD	220a	1
	יוזכר	JOZACAR	222b	
	זבד	ZABAD	256b	4
	מואבי	MOABITISH	556a	
	עמוני	AMMONITE	770a	
	קשר	BIND	905c	
	שמעת	SHIMEATH	1035a	
	שמר	SHOMER	*1037c	1
	שמרית	SHIMRITH	1037d	
24 27	אמציהו	AMAZIAH	55c	1
	מדרש	STUDY	205d	
	יסד	FOUND	413d	
	כתב	WRITE	507c	1 b1
	משא	UTTERANCE	672d	
	ספר	MISSIVE	707c	3 e
	רבה	BECOME MANY	915b	2 b2
25 1	אמציהו	AMAZIAH	55c	1
	יהועדן	JEHOADDAN	221b	
25 2	ישר	STRAIGHT	449a	2 a
	לבב	HEART	524c	2 6a
	שלם	COMPLETE	1024a	1
25 3	הרג	KILL	247a	1 a
	חזק	BE FIRM	304b	1 2b
	ממלכה	DOMINION	575b	2
	על	UPON	753c	2 1c
25 4	חטא	SIN	308a	1
	תורה	LAW	436b	2 b2
	מות	DIE	560a	2 b
	מות	DIE	560a	2 b
	מות	DIE	560b	1 b
	משה	MOSES	602d	
	ספר	MISSIVE	707b	3 c
25 5	אחז	GRASP	28b	
	בחר	CHOOSE	104b	7
	בן	SON	122a	9 a
	בן	SON	122a	9 a
	ל	TO	512a	3 b
	ל	TO	514c	5 fd
	מן	FROM	583a	9 b1
	מצא	FIND	593a	1 d
	מעל	ABOVE	751a	2 bb a
	צבא	WAR	839b	2
	צנה	LARGE SHIELD	857a	2
	קבץ	GATHER	867d	2
	רמח	SPEAR	942b	
25 6	גבור	STRONG	150b	2
	כסף	SILVER	494b	8 c
	מאה	HUNDRED	547d	1 a1
	שכר	HIRE	969a	
25 7	אלהים	GOD	44a	3 b
	אפרים	EPHRAIM	68c	4
	צבא	ARMY	838d	1 a
25 8	חזק	BE FIRM	304b	1 2c
	כח	STRENGTH	470d	3
	כיאם	BUT	475b	2 b
	כשל	CAUSE TO STUM-BLE	506a	1 b
25 9	עזר	HELP	740c	
	אלהים	GOD	44a	3 b
	גדוד	TROOP	151b	2
	יש	CAN	442a	2 cc
	ל	TO	518a	7 bf
	מאה	HUNDRED	548b	1 d6
	רבה	BECOME MANY	915d	1 e5
25 10	אפרים	EPHRAIM	68c	4
	בדל	BE DIVIDED	95b	2
	גדוד	TROOP	151b	2
	חרה	BURN	354a	1 a
	חרי	BURNING	354c	
	ל	TO	512a	3 b
25 11	גיא	VALLEY	161b	C
	הלך	WALK	230d	1 1d 3a
	חזק	BE FIRM	305b	1
	מלח	SALT	572a	
	נהג	DRIVE	624b	1
	שעיר	SEIR	973a	1 d
25 12	בקע	BREAK OPEN OR THROUGH	132a	1
	חי	ALIVE	312a	1 b
	יהודה	JUDAH	397b	1 3
	יקע	HANG	*429c	1
	ראש	HEAD	910d	2 a
	שלך	THROW	1021b	1 e
25 13	בוז	SPOIL	102d	
	בזה	SPOIL	103a	
	ביתחורן	BETH-HORON	111c	B
	בן	SON	121c	7 a
	גדוד	TROOP	151b	2
	מן	FROM	583a	7 b
	נכה	SMITE	646a	2 c
	פשט	STRIP OFF	833a	2
	שוב	TURN BACK	998d	1 a
25 14	שמרון	SAMARIA	1038a	
	אדמי	EDOMITE	10c	
	עמד	STAND	764d	3.
	קטר	MAKE SACRAFICES SMOKE	883a	
	שעיר	SEIR	973a	1 d
	שחה	BOW DOWN	1005c	3
25 15	דרש	SEEK	205b	3 b
	חרה	BURN	354a	2 a
25 16	חדל	CEASE	293a	2
	יעץ	ADVISE	419d	
	יעץ	ADVISE	419d	
	ל	TO	516a	5 ic
	מה	HOW	554b	4 d
	נכה	SMITE	645c	1 b
25 17	יהוא	JEHU	219d	2
	יהואחז	JEHOAHAZ	219d	2
	יהואש	JEHOASH	220a	2
	יעץ	CONSIDER	419d	
	פנה	FACE	816a	1 1c
	ראה	TO SEE	908c	1
25 18	ארז	CEDAR	72c	1 a
	בת	DAUGHTER	123a	1
	יהואש	JEHOASH	220a	2
	חוח	BRIER	296b	1 a
	חיה	LIVING THING	312c	1 b
	לבנון	LEBANON	527a	
	לבנון	LEBANON	527b	
	רמס	TRAMPLE	942d	
25 19	גרה	ENGAGE IN STRIFE	173b	1
	כבד	CAUSE TO BE HON-ORED	458a	3
25 20	נשא	LIFT	670d	1 b1
	דרש	SEEK	205b	3 b
	הוא	HE, SHE, IT	216d	6 a
	מן	OUT OF	579d	2 d
25 21	ביתשמש	BETH-SHEMESH	113a	1
	יהואש	JEHOASH	220a	2
	פנה	FACE	816a	1 1c
	ראה	TO SEE	908c	1
25 22	נגף	STRIKE	620a	
25 23	אפרים	EPHRAIM	68c	7
	ביתשמש	BETH-SHEMESH	112d	1 1
	יהואחז	JEHOAHAZ	219d	3
	יהואש	JEHOASH	220a	1
	יהואש	JEHOASH	220a	1
	חומה	WALL	327b	1
	חומה	WALL	327c	1
	פנה	CORNER	819d	1 b
	פרץ	BREAK THROUGH	829b	2
	שער	GATE	1044d	1 b 6
	שער	GATE	1044d	1 b 1
25 24	אסף	STORE	63b	
	בן	SON	121d	8 d
	זהב	GOLD	263a	4
	זהב	GOLD	263c	1

Ch	v	Heb	Eng	Page	Sec
		מצא	FIND	594a	2 c
		עבדאדם	OBED-EDOM	714d	3
		תערבה	PLEDGE	787a	
25	25	יהואחז	JEHOAHAZ	219d	1
		יהואש	JEHOASH	220a	1
		יהואש	JEHOASH	220a	2
		חיה	LIVE	311a	1 a
		חמש	FIVE	332a	2 a
25	26	לא	NOT	520c	4 bb
		ספר	MISSIVE	707b	3 e
		ראשון	FIRST	911c	1 a
25	27	לכיש	LACHISH	540c	1
		קשר	BIND	905b	2
		קשר	CONSPIRACY	905c	
25	28	קבר	BURY	868c	
26	1	אמציהו	AMAZIAH	55c	1
		חיה	BE	227c	3 5a
		יהודה	JUDAH	397b	13
		מלך	BE KING	574b	
		עזיהו	UZZIAH	739d	1 a
26	2	אילות	ELOTH	19a	1
		בנה	BUILD	124c	1 i
		שוב	TURN BACK	999b	1 d
26	3	יכליהו	JECHILIAH	408a	1
		עזיהו	UZZIAH	739d	1 a
26	4	אמציהו	AMAZIAH	55c	1
		ישר	STRAIGHT	449a	2 a
26	5	בין	DISCERN	107a	2
		דרש	SEEK	205b	3 a
		דרש	SEEK	205b	3 a
		חיה	BE	227c	3 5b
		זכריהו	ZECHARIAH	272b	9
		יום	DAY	400b	7 d2 b
		ל	TO	518a	7 bg
26	6	צלח	ADVANCE	852c	1
		אשדוד	AHSDOD	78c	
		אשדוד	AHSDOD	78c	
		יבנה	JABNEH	125c	
		יבנאל	JABNEEL	125c	1
		חומה	WALL	327c	1
		חומה	WALL	327c	1
		גת	GATH	387d	
		פרץ	BREAK THROUGH	829b	2
26	7	גורבעל	GUR-BAAL	158a	
		מעונים	MEUNITES	*589b	
		מעונים	MEUNITES	589b	
		עזר	HELP	740b	
		ערבי	ARABIAN	787b	
26	8	בוא	COME	98d	2 e
		הלך	WALK	231a	1 d3 gc
		הלך	WALK	232d	1 3
		הלך	WALK	233d	1 5a
		חזק	BE FIRM	304d	1 c
		מנחה	TRIBUTE	585a	2
		עד	UNTIL	725b	3 1
		עד	UNTIL	725c	3 3
		עזיהו	UZZIAH	739d	1 a
		מעל	ABOVE	752a	2 cb
		עמונו	AMMONITE	770a	
		שם	NAME	1028a	2 b1
26	9	בנה	BUILD	124c	1 az
		מגדל	TOWER	153d	1
		גיא	VALLEY	161b	
		חזק	BE FIRM	304c	1 c
		עזיהו	UZZIAH	739d	1 a
		מקצע	CORNER-BUTRESS	893b	
		שער	GATE	1044d	1 b 6
		שער	GATE	1044d	1 b 4
26	10	אדמה	GROUND	9c	1
		אהב	LOVE	13a	2
		אכר	PLOUGHMAN	38d	
		בור	WELL	92b	1
		בנה	BUILD	124c	1 az
		מגדל	TOWER	153d	1
		הר	MOUNTAIN	250c	1 i
		חצב	HEW	345a	1
		מישור	LEVEL PLACE	449d	1
		כרם	DRESS VINES	501d	
		כרמל	GARDEN	502a	1
		שפלה	LOWLAND	1050c	1
26	11	גדוד	TROOP	151b	2
		חנניהו	HANANIAH	337b	2
		יעיאל	JEIEL	418b	3 c
		ל	TO	516b	5 ja
		מן	FROM	580d	3 bb
		ספר	ENUMERATOR	708c	1 d
		עזיהו	UZZIAH	739d	1 a
		עשה	DO	794c	2 1e
		מעשיהו	MAASEIAH	796b	4 a
		פקדה	OVERSIGHT	824b	1
		צבא	WAR	839b	2
		שטר	OFFICIAL	1009c	
		שטר	OFFICIAL	1009c	
26	13	חיל	STRENGTH	298c	1 a
		חיל	STRENGTH	299a	4
		יד	HAND	391c	5 h2
		כח	STRENGTH	470d	1 b
		עזר	HELP	740c	
		עשה	DO	794c	2 1e
		צבא	ARMY	838d	1 a
26	14	אבן	STONE	6b	1
		כובע	HELMET	464d	
		כון	ESTABLISH	466b	2 a
		ל	TO	512a	3 b
		עזיהו	UZZIAH	739d	1 a
		צבא	ARMY	839a	1 a
		קלע	SLING	887c	
		קשת	BOW	906a	1 b
		רמח	SPEAR	942b	
		שריון	BODY-ARMOUR	1056b	
26	15	אבן	STONE	6b	1
		מגדל	TOWER	153d	1
		חזק	BE FIRM	304b	1 1c
		חזקה	STRENGTH	*305d	2
		חץ	ARROW	346c	1
		חשב	THINK	363b	15
		חשבון	DEVICE	364a	
		מחשבה	THOUGHT	364c	3
		ירא	SHOOT	432b	1
		ל	TO	517c	7 bb
		מן	FROM	583d	9 b1
		עד	UNTIL	725a	2 1a a
		עד	UNTIL	725c	3 1
		עזר	HELP	740c	
		פלא	BE SURPASSING	810d	2
		פנה	CORNER	819d	1 b
		רחק	DISTANT	935c	2 a7
		שם	NAME	1028a	2 b1
26	16	גבה	BE HIGH	147a	3 b
		היכל	TEMPLE	228c	2 b
		מזבח	ALTAR	258d	4 b
		חזק	BE FIRM	304b	1 1c
		חזקה	STRENGTH	305d	2
		ל	LIKE	454d	3 b
		לב	HEART	525b	2 6c
		מעל	ACT TREACHEROUSLY	591b	1
		עד	UNTIL	725c	3 2
		קטר	MAKE SACRIFICES SMOKE	883b	2
26	17	כהן	PRIEST	464b	7
		כהן	PRIEST	464b	7
		עזריהו	AZARIAH	741b	5 e
		עם	WITH	767b	1 a
		שמנים	EIGHTY	1033b	
26	18	אהרן	AARON	14d	
		בן	SON	121a	1 jz
		יהוה	YAHWEH	219a	2 1h
		כבוד	HONOR	459b	4
		כהן	PRIEST	464a	1
		ל	TO	513b	5 ba
		ל	TO	517d	7 bd
		מעל	ACT TREACHEROUSLY	591b	2 b
		עזיהו	UZZIAH	739d	1 a
		עמד	STAND	763d	1 c
		קטר	MAKE SACRIFICES SMOKE	883b	2
26	19	זעף	BE VEXED	277a	2
		רוח	RISE	280b	2
		זרק	TO TOSS	*284c	2
		מצח	FOREHEAD	594d	
		עזיהו	UZZIAH	739d	1 a
		על	UPON	759b	4 2e b
		עם	WITH	767d	1 d
		יצהרי	IZHARITES	844b	
		צרעת	LEPROSY	863d	
		קטר	MAKE SACRIFICES SMOKE	883b	2
		מקטרת	CENSER	883b	
26	20	בהל	HASTEN	96d	2
		דחף	HASTEN	191b	
		יצא	GO OUT	422d	1 a
		כהן	PRIEST	464b	8
		מצח	FOREHEAD	594d	
		נגע	STRIKE	619b	
		פנה	TURN	815b	2 a
		צרע	BE STRUCK WITH LEPROSY	864a	
		ראש	HEAD	911a	3 e
		בית	HOUSE	109a	1 ae 9
		גזר	CUT	160c	1
		יותם	JOTHAM	222d	1
		היה	BE	226d	3 2
		חפשית	FREEDOM	345a	
		עזיהו	UZZIAH	739d	1 a
26	21	צרע	BE STRUCK WITH LEPROSY	864a	
26	22	שפט	JUDGE	1047c	1 b
		אמוץ	AMOZ	55b	
		ישעיהו	ISAIAH	447d	1
		נביא	PROPHET	611d	1
		עזיהו	UZZIAH	739d	1 a
		ראשון	FIRST	911c	1 a
26	23	יותם	JOTHAM	222d	1
		עזיהו	UZZIAH	739d	1 a
		יצהרי	IZHARITES	844b	
		צרע	BE STRUCK WITH LEPROSY	864a	
		קבר	BURY	868c	
		צברה	GRAVE	869a	1
		שדה	FIELD	961d	2 b
		יותם	JOTHAM	222d	1
27	1	ירושה	JERUSAH	440b	
		צדוק	ZADOK	843b	2
27	2	היכל	TEMPLE	228c	2 b
		ישר	STRAIGHT	449a	2 a
		עזיהו	UZZIAH	739d	1 a
		שחת	GO TO RUIN	1008c	2
27	3	בנה	BUILD	124c	1 ae
		בנה	BUILD	*124c	1 ad
		חומה	WALL	327c	1
		עפל	MOUND	779b	
		שער	GATE	1045b	3 b
		בירניות	FORTRESS	108c	
27	4	בנה	BUILD	124c	1 az
		בנה	BUILD	124c	1 ag
		מגדל	TOWER	153d	1
		הר	MOUNTAIN	251a	2 b
		חרש	WOOD	361c	
		יהודה	JUDAH	397c	2
		ו	AND	252c	1 c
27	5	חזק	BE FIRM	304b	1 1b
		חמה	WHEAT	334d	
		כסף	SILVER	494b	8 c
		כר	KOR	499d	
		לחם	ENGAGE IN BATTLE	535c	
		מאה	HUNDRED	547d	1 a1
		מנית	MINNITH	*586a	
		שעורה	BARLEY	972d	2
		שוב	TURN BACK	999b	1 f
27	6	דרך	WAY	203c	6 a
		יותם	JOTHAM	222d	1
		חזק	BE FIRM	305b	1
		כן	ESTABLISH	466c	3
27	7	דרך	WAY	203b	5
		יותם	JOTHAM	222d	1
		ספר	MISSIVE	707b	3 e
27	8	היה	BE	227a	3 4b
27	9	אחז	AHAZ	28c	1
		דוד	DAVID	188a	A
		יותם	JOTHAM	222d	1
28	1	ישר	STRAIGHT	449a	2 a
28	2	בעל	BAAL	127d	2 3
		דרך	WAY	203d	6 d
		מסכה	MOLTEN IMAGE	651b	2
28	3	אש	FIRE	77d	4
		בער	BURN	129c	1
		גוי	NATION	156d	1 c
		הנם	HINNOM	244d	
		הנם	HINNOM	245a	
		ירש	CAUSE TO POSSESS	440b	2 a
		קטר	MAKE SACRIFICES SMOKE	883a	1 a
28	4	תועבה	ABOMINATION	1072d	1 b
		במה	HIGH PLACE	119c	3 c
		גבעה	HILL	149a	2
		זבח	SLAUGHTER FOR SACRIFICE	257b	2
		מלך	KING	573b	5 b
		עץ	TREE	781c	1 a
		קטר	MAKE SACRIFICES SMOKE	883a	
28	5	רענן	LUXURIANT	947d	
		דמשק	DAMASCUS	199d	a
		מכה	SLAUGHTER	647a	3
		שבה	TAKE CAPTIVE	985c	2
		שביה	CAPTIVITY	986a	2
28	6	ב	IN	91a	5 2
		הרג	KILL	247b	1 b
		הרג	KILL	247c	7
		כל	ALL	482d	2 ba
		פקח	PEKAH	824d	
		רמליהו	REMILIAH	942b	
28	7	אלקנה	ELKANAH	46c	C
		הרג	KILL	247b	1 b
		זכרי	ZICHRI	271d	7
		עזריקם	AZRIKAM	741b	5
		מעשיהו	MAASEIAH	796b	5
		משנה	SECOND	1041c	3 a
28	8	בזז	SPOIL	102d	1
		ל	TO	511b	1 ga
		שבה	TAKE CAPTIVE	985c	1 a
28	9	הרג	KILL	247b	1 b
		הרג	KILL	247c	7
		זעף	STORMING	277a	1
		חמה	RAGE	*404d	2 c
		ל	TO	511b	1 ga
		נגע	REACH	619c	2
		עד	UNTIL	725c	3 1
		צבא	ARMY	838d	1 a
28	10	אמר	SAY	56b	2
		אשמה	WRONG-DOING	80a	1
		יהודה	JUDAH	397b	13
		כבש	SUBDUE	461b	1
		עבד	SLAVE	714c	1
		עם	WITH	767b	1 a
		רק	ONLY	956d	2 e
		שפחה	MAID	1046c	1
28	11	חרון	BURNING OF ANGER	354c	
		שבה	TAKE CAPTIVE	985c	2
		שביה	CAPTIVITY	986a	2
		שמע	HEAR	1034a	1 n
28	12	אפרים	EPHRAIM	68b	2
		יברכיהו	JEBERECHIAH	140a	6
		יהוחנן	JEHOHANAN	220b	6
		חדלי	HADLAI	293b	
		חזקיהו	HEZEKIAH	306b	5
		עזריהו	AZARIAH	741b	2
		עמשא	AMASA	772a	2
		צבא	WAR	839d	2
		שלום	SHALLUM	1024b	7
		משלמות	MESHILLEMOTH	1024c	1
28	13	אמר	SAY	56b	2
		אשמה	WRONG-DOING	80a	1
		חטאת	SIN	308d	1 b

Ch	v.	Heb	Eng	Page	Sec
		חרון	BURNING OF ANGER	354c	
		יסף	ADD	415b	1
		על	UPON	753b	2 1b
		שביה	CAPTIVITY	986a	2
28	14	בזה	SPOIL	103a	
		חלץ	EQUIP FOR WAR	323a	2
		עזב	LEAVE	737a	1 c
		שביה	CAPTIVITY	986a	2
28	15	אכל	EAT	38a	1
		אצל	BESIDE	69b	A
		חזק	BE FIRM	305a	6 a
		חמור	HE-ASS	331b	2 a
		יריחו	JERICHO	*437d	
		כשל	TOTTER	505c	2
		ל	TO	512a	3 b
		לבש	CLOTHE	528b	3
		נהל	BRING TO A STATION	625a	2
		נעל	FURNISH WITH SANDALS	653b	
		סוך	ANOINT	692a	2
		מערם	NAKED THING	736a	
		שביה	CAPTIVITY	986a	2
		שלל	SPOIL	1022a	2
		שם	NAME	1028a	2 a
		שקה	GIVE TO DRINK	1052c	2
		תמר	PALM-TREE	1071c	
28	16	אשור	ASSYRIA	78d	4
		עזר	HELP	740c	
		על	UPON	757b	2 7c aa
28	17	אדמי	EDOMITE	10c	
		שבה	TAKE CAPTIVE	985c	2
		שבי	CAPTIVITY	985d	3
28	18	אילון	AIJALON	19c	1
		בית שמש	BETH-SHEMESH	113a	1
		גדרות	GEDEROTH	155b	
		תמנה	TIMNAH	584d	2
		נגב	SOUTH-COUNTRY	616b	1 a
		פשט	STRIP OFF	833a	2
		שוכה	SOCOH	962c	1
		שפלל	LOWLAND	1050c	1
28	19	כנע	HUMBLE	488c	1
		מעל	ACT TREACHEROUSLY	591b	1 c
		פרע	LET GO	829a	2
28	20	חזק	BE FIRM	304c	2
		צרר	BIND	864d	B
		תגלתפלאסר	TIGLATHPILESER	1062b	
28	21	חלק	DIVIDE	323c	5
		עזרה	HELP	740d	1
		צרר	BIND	864d	B
28	22	הוא	HE, SHE, IT	215c	1 e
		יסף	DO AGAIN	415c	2 a
		מעל	ACT TREACHEROUSLY	591b	2 b
		צרר	BIND	864d	B
28	23	דמשק	DAMASCUS	200a	2
		זבח	SLAUGHTER FOR SACRIFICE	257d	2
		כשל	CAUSE TO STUMBLE	506a	1 b
		ל	TO	512a	3 b
		נכה	SMITE	646b	3
		עזר	HELP	740b	
		עזר	HELP	740b	
		עזר	HELP	740c	
28	24	דלת	DOOR	195a	1
		מזבח	ALTAR	259a	8
		כלי	UTENSIL	480a	2 f
		סגר	SHUT	688d	1
		פנה	CORNER	819c	1 a
		קצץ	CUT OFF	893d	
28	25	אלהים	GOD	43c	1 d
		במה	HIGH PLACE	119c	3 c
		ו	AND	253b	1 ib
		כל	ALL	481c	1 b
		כעם	VEX	495c	2
		קטר	MAKE SACRAFICES SMOKE	883a	
28	26	דבר	WORD	183c	4 2
		דרך	WAY	203c	5
		יתר	REMAINDER	452a	1 b
		ספר	MISSIVE	707b	3 a
		ראשון	FIRST	911c	1 a
28	27	חזקיהו	HEZEKIAH	306a	1
29	1	אביום	ABIJAM	4a	8
		זכריהו	ZECHARIAH	272b	
29	2	ישר	STRAIGHT	449a	2 a
29	3	דלת	DOOR	195a	1
		חזק	BE FIRM	304c	1 c
		מלך	BE KING	574a	
		פתח	OPEN	835a	
29	4	מזרח	PLACE OF SUNRISE	281a	2 e
		כהן	PRIEST	464a	7
		רחוב	PLAZA	932b	
29	5	יצא	BRING OUT	425a	4 a
		נדה	IMPURITY	622c	2
		קדש	APARTNESS	871d	2 d
		קדש	BE SET APART	873b	4 a
		קדש	BE SET APART	873c	4
29	6	מעל	ACT TREACHEROUSLY	591b	2 b
		נתן	GIVE	680a	1 z
		סבב	TURN ABOUT	686c	1 a
		ערף	BACK OF NECK	791c	1
29	7	משכן	DWELLING-PLACE	1015d	2 c
		אולם	PORCH	17d	1
		דלת	DOOR	195b	2
		כבה	QUENCH	459d	
		סגר	SHUT	688d	1
		עלה	WHOLE BURNT OFFERING	750d	
		קדש	APARTNESS	871d	2 d
		קטרת	SMOKE	882d	2
		קטר	MAKE SACRAFICES SMOKE	883b	2
29	8	זועה	A TREMBLING	266b	
		קצף	WRATH	893c	1
		ראה	TO SEE	907a	1 b
		שמה	APPALMENT	1031c	2
		שרקה	HISSING	1057a	
29	9	זה	THIS	262a	6 f
		שבי	CAPTIVITY	985d	1
29	10	ברית	COVENANT	136d	2 2h
		ברית	COVENANT	137a	3 1
		חרון	BURNING OF ANGER	354c	
		כרת	CUT	504a	4
		לבב	HEART	523c	2
		עם	WITH	768c	4 a
		שוב	TURN BACK	997d	6 f
29	11	בחר	CHOOSE	103d	1
		עמד	STAND	764a	1 e
		קטר	MAKE SACRAFICES SMOKE	883a	1 a
		שלה	BE QUIET	1017b	
		שרת	SERVE	1057b	2 b
		שרת	SERVE	1058b	2 b
29	12	אחימות	AHIMOTH	27a	
		גרשני	GERSHONITES	177b	
		יואח	JOAH	222a	2 b
		יואל	JOEL	222b	1 b
		יהללאל	JEHALLELEL	239c	2
		זמה	ZIMMAH	273c	3
		מחת	MAHATH	367b	B
		לוי	LEVITE	533b	3 2b
		מררי	MERARI	601b	
		עבדי	ABDI	715d	1
		עדן	EDEN	726c	
		עזריהו	AZARIAH	741b	6
		עמשי	AMASAI	772a	2 b
		קהתי	KOHATHITES	875c	
		קיש	KISH	885c	2 b
29	13	אליצפן	ELIZAPHAN	45d	A
		אסף	ASAPH	63b	2
		בן	SON	120d	1 ja
		זכריהו	ZECHARIAH	272b	0 f
		יעיאל	JEIEL	418b	3 d
		מתניהו	MATTANIAH	682d	2 c
		מתניהו	MATTANIAH	*682d	2 c
		שמרי	SHIMRI	1037c	3 b
29	14	הימן	HEMAN	54d	
		יחיאל	JEHIEL	313d	5
		ידותון	JEDUTHUN	s 393a	
		עזיאל	UZZIEL	739d	1 c
		שמעי	SHIMEI	1035c	3 e
		שמעיה	SHEMAIAH	1035d	7 f
29	15	טהר	BE CLEAN	372b	1 a
		קדש	BE SET APART	873c	4
29	16	היכל	TEMPLE	228c	2 b
		חוץ	THE OUTSIDE	299d	1 a
		חצר	ENCLOSURE	347a	3 b
		טהר	BE CLEAN	372b	1 a
		טמאה	UNCLEANNESS	380a	4
		יצא	BRING OUT	425a	4 a
		נחל	WADY	636c	2
		פנימה	TOWARDS THE SIDE	819b	1
		קבל	RECEIVE	867a	1
		קדרון	KEDRON	871b	
29	17	אולם	PORCH	17d	1
		בוא	COME	98b	2
		חלל	POLLUTE	320d	2
		יום	DAY	398c	2 e
		כלה	FINISH	478b	1 c
		ל	TO	517b	6 d
		עשר	TEN	797c	
		קדש	BE SET APART	873b	4 a
		שש	SIX	995c	2
		שמנה	EIGHT	1033a	1 b
29	18	מזבח	ALTAR	258d	4 a
		מזבח	ALTAR	259b	4
		חזקיהו	HEZEKIAH	306a	1
		טהר	BE CLEAN	372b	1 a
		עלה	WHOLE BURNT OFFERING	750d	
		מערכת	ROW	790b	
		פנימה	TOWARDS THE SIDE	819b	1
		שלחן	TABLE	1020b	3
29	19	זנח	REJECT	276b	
		כון	ESTABLISH	466c	4
		מלכות	REIGN	575a	2
		מעל	UNFAITHFUL	591b	2
		קדש	BE SET APART	873c	3
29	20	עלה	GO UP	748b	1 d
		שר	CHIEFTAIN	978b	2 d
29	21	אהרן	AARON	14d	
		איל	RAM	18a	2 g
		אמר	SAY	56c	4
		בן	SON	121a	1 jz
		בקר	CATTLE	*133c	2
		חמאת	SIN	309b	4
		כבש	LAMB	461a	1
		כהן	PRIEST	464a	7
		ממלכה	KINGDOM	575a	1
		עלה	GO UP	750a	8
		על	UPON	754c	2 1fc
		עז	SHE-GOAT	777c	3 f
		פר	YOUNG BULL	830d	2 c
		צפיר	HE-GOAT	862b	
29	22	איל	RAM	18a	2 g
		בקר	CATTLE	133c	2
		דם	BLOOD	197c	3 b
		זרק	TO TOSS	284c	1 b
		כבש	LAMB	461a	1
		קבל	RECEIVE	867a	1
		שחט	SLAUGHTER	1006a	2
29	23	חמאת	SIN	309b	4
		נגש	APPROACH	621b	
		סמך	LEAN	701d	1 a
		שעיר	HE-GOAT	972c	
29	24	אמר	SAY	56c	4
		דם	BLOOD	197c	3 b
		חטא	MISS A GOAL OR WAY	307c	2
		חמאת	SIN	309b	4
		כפר	COVER OVER	497d	3 b2
		שחט	SLAUGHTER	1006a	2
29	25	גד	GAD	151d	2
		חזה	SEER	302d	1 b
		כנור	LYRE	490a	
		לוי	LEVITE	533a	3 2b
		נבל	HARP	614c	
		נתן	NATHAN	681d	2
		מצוה	COMMANDMENT	846c	2 c
		מצלתים	CYMBALS	853a	
29	26	חצצרה	CLARION	348c	2 c
		כלי	INSTRUMENT	479d	2 b
29	27	אמר	SAY	56c	4
		ו	AND	252c	1 b
		חלל	POLLUTE	320d	2
		חצצרה	CLARION	348c	2 c
		יד	HAND	391c	5 h2
		כלה	BE FINISHED	*477c	1 a
		כלי	INSTRUMENT	479d	2 b
		עלה	GO UP	749d	8
		עלה	WHOLE BURNT OFFERING	750d	
		עת	TIME	773c	1 d
		שיר	SONG	1010b	2
29	28	חצצרה	CLARION	348c	2 c
		חצצר	SOUND A TRUMPET	348d	
		כלה	BE FINISHED	477c	1 a
		כל	ALL	482d	2 ba
		עד	UNTIL	725c	3 2
		שיר	SONG	1010c	3
		שיר	SING	1010d	
29	29	כלה	FINISH	478b	1 c
		כרע	BOW DOWN	502c	1
		מצא	FIND	594b	2 e
		עלה	GO UP	749d	8
		שחה	BOW DOWN	1005c	2 a
29	30	הימן	HEMAN	54d	
		אמר	SAY	56c	4
		אסף	ASAPH	63a	2
		דבר	WORD	182d	2 1a
		הלל	PRAISE	238c	2 e
		הלל	PRAISE	238d	2 g
		חזה	SEER	302d	1 c
		לוי	LEVITE	533a	3 2b
		עד	UNTIL	725c	3 3
		קדד	BOW DOWN	869a	
29	31	זבח	SACRIFICE	257c	2 4
		זבח	SACRIFICE	257d	2 5
		יד	HAND	389b	1 c
		יד	HAND	389b	1 c
		תודה	THANK-OFFERING	393a	4
		לב	HEART	525a	2 4
		מלא	FILL	570d	2
		נגש	DRAW NEAR	620d	1
		נדיב	INCLINED	622a	1
		עלה	WHOLE BURNT OFFERING	751a	
29	32	רוח	BREATH	*925c	7
		איל	RAM	18a	2 g
		בקר	CATTLE	133c	2
		כבש	LAMB	461a	1
		מאה	HUNDRED	547d	1 a3
		מאה	HUNDRED	548a	1 b3
		עלה	WHOLE BURNT OFFERING	750c	
		עלה	WHOLE BURNT OFFERING	751a	
29	33	שבעים	SEVENTY	988c	1 c
		בקר	CATTLE	133c	1
		קדש	APARTNESS	872a	3 b
29	34	חזק	BE FIRM	304d	1
		ישר	STRAIGHT	449b	1 a
		כלה	BE FINISHED	477c	1 a
		מלאכה	WORK	522a	3 b
		לבב	HEART	523d	2 6a
		מעט	A FEW	590a	1 a
		עד	UNTIL	725a	2 1b b
		עלה	WHOLE BURNT OFFERING	750d	
		פשט	STRIP OFF	833a	3

Ch	v.	Heb	Eng	Page	Sec
29	35	קדש	BE SET APART	873c	4
		חלב	FAT	317a	2 b
		כון	BE READY	466a	4
		נסך	DRINK-OFFERING	651a	1
		עבדה	LABOR	715c	4
		שלם	PEACE-OFFERING	1023c	
29	36	ה	THE	209c	3
		היה	COME TO PASS	224b	1 1b
		כון	ESTABLISH	466c	3
		פתאם	SUDDENNESS	837c	
		שמח	REJOICE	970b	2 a
30	1	אגרת	LETTER	8d	
		אפרים	EPHRAIM	68c	4
		כתב	WRITE	507b	1 a
		כתב	WRITE	507d	1 c
		על	UPON	757b	2 7c aa
		על	UPON	757c	2 7c b
		פסח	PASSOVER	820b	
30	2	יעץ	CONSIDER	419d	
		פסח	PASSOVER	820b	3
30	3	אסף	GATHER	62c	1 a
		די	SUFFICIENCY	191c	1
		ל	TO	*511b	1 ga
		ל	TO	516c	5 jb
		מה	WHAT	553b	1 ea
		קדש	BE SET APART	873c	4
30	4	ישר	BE STRAIGHT	448c	2
30	5	באר־שבע	BEERSHEBA	92a	
		דבר	WORD	182b	1 1b
		דן	DAN	193a	3
		עבר	PASS OVER	718d	2 a
		עמד	STAND	764d	5
		פסח	PASSOVER	820b	3
		קול	VOICE	877b	3 a3
		רב	MULTITUDE	914a	1
30	6	אגרת	LETTER	8d	
		אלהים	GOD	44b	4 ba
		אשור	ASSYRIA	78d	4
		הלך	WALK	230b	1 1a
		הלך	WALK	231c	1 1d 5g
		כף	POWER	496d	2
		פליטה	ESCAPE	812c	2 b
		יצחק	ISAAC	850c	
		רוץ	RUN	930c	2 b
		ישראל	ISRAEL	975c	1
		שאר	REMAIN	984a	1
		שוב	TURN BACK	998a	6 g
30	7	מעל	ACT TREACHEROUSLY	591b	1
		ראה	TO SEE	907a	1 b
		שמה	APPALMENT	1031c	2
30	8	חרון	BURNING OF ANGER	354c	
		יד	HAND	389d	1 d
		נתן	GIVE	680d	1 z
		עולם	LONG DURATION	762c	2 e
		ערף	BACK OF NECK	791c	2
		קדש	BE SET APART	873c	1 c
		קשה	BE SEVERE	904c	3 a
		שוב	TURN BACK	997d	6 f
30	9	חנן	GRACIOUS	337a	
		ל	TO	518b	7 bh
		על	UPON	757b	2 7c aa
		פנה	FACE	816a	1 1e
		רחמים	COMPASSION	933c	2
		רחון	COMPASSIONATE	933d	
		שוב	TURN BACK	997b	3 b
		שוב	TURN BACK	997d	6 c
30	10	אפרים	EPHRAIM	68b	4
		זבלון	ZEBULUN	259d	3
		לעג	MOCK	541c	
		מנשה	MANASSEH	586c	1 b1 b
		עבר	PASS OVER	718a	5 a
		רוץ	RUN	930c	2 b
		שחק	LAUGH	966a	
30	11	אשר	ASHER	81b	2
		זבלון	ZEBULUN	259d	2
		כנע	BE HUMBLE	488c	1
		ל	TO	*511b	1 ga
30	12	יד	HAND	390a	1 e2
30	13	אסף	GATHER	62c	1 a
		חג	FESTIVAL-GATHERING	291a	1 b2
		חג	FESTIVAL-GATHERING	291b	1 b
		מאד	EXCEEDINGLY	547b	2 a
		מצה	UNLEAVENED BREAD	695b	
		קהל	ASSEMBLY	874d	1 d
		רב	MULTITUDE	914a	1
30	14	מזבח	ALTAR	259a	0
		נחל	WADY	636c	2
		סור	TURN ASIDE	694b	1
		קדרון	KEDRON	871b	
		מקרה	INCENSE ALTER	883b	
		שלך	THROW	1021a	1 a
30	15	כהן	PRIEST	464a	7
		כלם	BE HUMILIATED	483d	1
		עלה	WHOLE BURNT OFFERING	751a	
		פסח	PASSOVER	820b	2
		קדש	BE SET APART	873c	4
		ארבע	FOUR	917b	2 a2 z
		שחט	SLAUGHTER	1006b	1
30	16	אלהים	GOD	43d	3 b
		דם	BLOOD	197c	3 b

Ch	v.	Heb	Eng	Page	Sec
		זרק	TO TOSS	284c	1 b
		תורה	LAW	436b	2 b3
		משה	MOSES	602d	
		עמד	STANDING-PLACE	765a	
30	17	כל	ALL	481d	1 c
		לא	NOT	519c	2 a
		על	UPON	755b	2 3
		פסח	PASSOVER	820b	
		קדש	BE SET APART	873c	4
		קדש	BE SET APART	873c	3
		רב	MUCH	913a	1 c
		שחיטה	SLAYING	1006b	
30	18	זבולן	ZEBULUN	259d	2
		טהר	BE CLEAN	372c	1 a
		טוב	PLEASANT	374d	9 b
		יששכר	ISSACHAR	441a	1
		ך	LIKE	454a	1 c1
		כל	ALL	481d	1 c
		כפר	COVER OVER	497c	2 b
		לא	NOT	520a	4 aa
		על	UPON	754c	2 1f c
		פלל	INTERVENE	813b	1
		פסח	PASSOVER	820b	1
		רב	MUCH	913a	1 c
30	19	דרש	SEEK	205b	3 a
		מטהרה	PURIFYING	372d	2
		כון	ESTABLISH	466c	3
		לבב	HEART	523d	2 4
30	20	רפא	HEAL	950d	2 a
30	21	הלל	PRAISE	238c	2 e
		חג	FESTIVAL-GATHERING	291a	1 b2
		חג	FESTIVAL-GATHERING	291b	1 b
		יום	DAY	400b	7 e1
		כהן	PRIEST	464a	7
		כלי	INSTRUMENT	480a	2 b
		מצא	FIND	594b	2 e
		מצה	UNLEAVENED BREAD	695b	
		עז	STRENGTH	739a	1
		שכל	BE PRUDENT	968c	4
30	22	דבר	SPEAK	181d	5
		זבח	SLAUGHTER FOR SACRIFICE	257a	1
		זבח	SLAUGHTER FOR SACRIFICE	257b	2
		זבח	SACRIFICE	257d	2 5
		טוב	PLEASANT	374d	8
		ידה	GIVE THANKS	392d	2
		מועד	APPOINTED TIME	417d	1 b
		לב	HEART	525c	29a
		שכל	BE PRUDENT	968c	4
		שכל	PRUDENCE	968c	2
		שלם	PEACE-OFFERING	1023c	
30	23	יעץ	CONSULT	420a	
		שמחה	JOY	970d	2
30	24	אלף	THOUSAND	48d	1 a
		עשר	TEN	796d	2 b
		פר	YOUNG BULL	830d	2 a
		קדש	BE SET APART	873c	4
		רב	MULTITUDE	914a	1
		רום	BE HIGH	927d	3 c
30	25	גר	SOJOURNER	158b	2
		גר	SOJOURNER	158c	2
		כהן	PRIEST	464a	7
		קהל	ASSEMBLY	874d	1 d
30	26	זה	THIS	*262a	6 d
30	27	ברך	BLESS	139a	3
		כהן	PRIEST	*464a	7
		לוי	LEVITE	533a	3 1b
		מעון	REFUGE	733a	2 a
		תפלה	PRAYER	813c	1 d
		קדש	APARTNESS	871c	2 a
		קום	STAND	877d	1 f
31	1	שמע	HEAR	1034b	4
		אחוזה	POSSESSION	28c	2
		אפרים	EPHRAIM	68c	4
		אשרה	ASHERA	81c	B
		במה	HIGH PLACE	119c	3 d
		גדע	HEW	154b	
		מזבח	ALTAR	259a	0
		כלה	FINISH	478a	1 a
		כלה	FINISH	478b	1 d
		מצא	FIND	594b	2 e
		מצבה	PILLAR	663b	1 c
		עד	UNTIL	725c	3 2
31	2	הלל	PRAISE	238d	2 g
		מחלקת	DIVISION	325a	2
		מחנה	ENCAMPMENT	334b	1 b
		ידה	PRAISE	392c	1 b
		כהן	PRIEST	464a	7
		עבדה	LABOR	715b	4
		עמד	STAND	764d	5
		פה	MOUTH	805c	6 bb
		שלם	PEACE-OFFERING	1023c	
		שער	GATE	1045b	3 b
		שרת	SERVE	1057b	2 b
31	3	בקר	MORNING	134a	1 e
		חדש	NEW MOON	294c	1
		מועד	APPOINTED TIME	417c	1 b
		תורה	LAW	436b	2 b3
		מן	FROM	580c	3 a
		מנת	PORTION	584c	
		רכוש	PROPERTY	940d	1
31	4	אמר	SAY	56c	4

Ch	v.	Heb	Eng	Page	Sec
		חזק	BE FIRM	304b	1 2d
		תורה	LAW	436b	2 b3
		כהן	PRIEST	464a	7
		מנת	PORTION	584c	
		עם	PEOPLE	766c	2 a
		קורא	KORAHITES	896c	2
31	5	בוא	COME	99b	2
		תבואה	PRODUCT	100a	1
		דבר	WORD	182b	1 1b
		דבש	HONEY	185b	
		דגן	CORN	186c	
		דגן	CORN	186c	
		תירוש	NEW WINE	440d	
		כל	ALL	482d	2 ba
		מעשר	TENTH PART	798b	2
		פרץ	BREAK THROUGH	829c	0
		יצהר	FRESH OIL	844a	
		ראשית	BEGINNING	912b	1 b
		רבה	BECOME MANY	915c	1 c
		ישראל	ISRAEL	975d	2 b3
31	6	יהוה	YAHWEH	218d	2 1d
		ערמה	HEAP	790d	
		מעשר	TENTH PART	798b	2
31	7	חלל	POLLUTE	320d	2
		יסד	FOUND	414a	
		כלה	FINISH	478b	1 a
		ערמה	HEAP	790d	
31	8	ברך	BLESS	139a	1
		ערמה	HEAP	790d	
31	9	דרש	SEEK	205c	4 b
		כהן	PRIEST	464a	7
		ערמה	HEAP	790d	
31	10	ברך	BLESS	139a	2 a
		המון	ABUNDANCE	242d	4
		חלל	POLLUTE	320d	2
		יתר	BE LEFT OVER	451c	
		יתר	LEAVE OVER	451c	1 a
		יתר	SHOW EXCESS	*451c	3
		כהן	PRIEST	464b	8
		מן	SINCE	583c	7 c
		עד	UNTIL	725c	3 3
		עזריהו	AZARIAH	741b	5
		צדוק	ZADOK	843b	1 a
		ראש	HEAD	911a	3 e
		תרומה	OFFERING	929a	4
31	11	אמר	SAY	56c	4
		כון	ESTABLISH	466b	2
		לשכה	ROOM	545d	1 b
31	12	אמונה	FIRMNESS	53c	3 a
		כוננהו	CONANIAH	467b	1
		לוי	LEVITE	532d	1
		נגיד	LEADER	618a	4
		על	UPON	755b	2 3
		מעשר	TENTH PART	798b	2
		תרומה	OFFERING	929a	4
		שמעי	SHIMEI	1035c	3 f
		משנה	SECOND	1041d	3 a
31	13	אליאל	ELIEL	45a	F
		בניהו	BENAIAH	125c	4 b
		יהוזבד	JEHOZABAD	220a	4 b
		יחיאל	JEHIEL	313d	6
		מחת	MAHATH	367b	B
		ירימות	JEREMOTH	438b	2
		כוננהו	CONANIAH	467b	1
		נגיד	LEADER	618a	3
		נחת	NAHATH	639d	3
		ישמכיהו	ISMACHIAH	702b	
		עזזיהו	AZAZIAH	739c	1 5
		עזריהו	AZARIAH	741b	5 e
		עשהאל	ASAHEL	795c	2 b
		פקיד	COMMISSIONER	824b	
		מפקד	MUSTER	824c	2
		שמעי	SHIMEI	1035c	3 f
31	14	מזרח	PLACE OF SUNRISE	281a	2 c3
		ימנה	IMNAH	412c	2
		ל	TO	511d	1 h
		לוי	LEVITE	532d	1
		נדבה	FREEWILL-OFFERING	621d	2 a
		קדש	APARTNESS	872a	3 b
		תרומה	OFFERING	929a	4
31	15	אמונה	FIRMNESS	53c	3 a
		אמריהו	AMARIAH	57d	5
		גדול	GREAT	153b	7
		יהושוע	JOSHUA	221d	6 b
		יד	HAND	391c	5 h3
		מימן	MIJAMIN	568b	1 c
		עדן	EDEN	726c	
		מן	SMALL	882a	1 a
		שכניה	SHECANIAH	1016a	5 b
		שמעיה	SHEMAIAH	1035d	7 j
31	16	בד	SEPARATION	94d	1
		בן	SON	122a	9 a
		בן	SON	122a	9 a
		דבר	WORD	183b	4 1
		זכר	MALE	271c	1 1b
		יום	DAY	400c	7 e3
		תחיום	ENROLLMENT	405b	
		ל	TO	512a	3 b
		ל	TO	514c	5 fd
		עבדה	LABOR	715b	4
		מעל	ABOVE	751d	2 bb a
31	17	את	MARK OF THE ACCUSATIVE	85c	3 a
		בן	SON	122a	9 a
		בן	SON	122a	9 a

2 CHRONICLES

Ch	v.	Heb	Eng	Page	Sec
		תתיחש	BE ENROLLED	405b	
		מעל	ABOVE	751d	2 bb a
31	18	אמונה	FIRMNESS	53c	3 a
		טף	CHILDREN	382a	
		טף	CHILDREN	382a	
		תתיחש	ENROLLMENT	405c	
		ל	TO	512a	3 b
		קדש	APARTNESS	872b	4 a
31	19	אהרן	AARON	14d	
		בן	SON	121a	1 jz
		מגרש	COMMON-LAND	177b	
		ו	AND	253b	1 ib
		תתיחש	ENROLLMENT	405c	
		כהן	PRIEST	464a	7
		כל	ALL	481c	1 b
		מנה	PORTION	584b	
		שם	NAME	1028a	2 a
31	20	אמת	FIRMNESS	54a	3 a
		זה	THIS	262a	6 d
		טוב	PLEASANT	374a	2 f
		ישר	STRAIGHT	449a	2 a
31	21	דרש	SEEK	205b	3 a
		חלל	POLLUTE	320d	2
		תורה	LAW	436b	2 b3
		לבב	HEART	523c	2 2
		עבדה	LABOR	715c	4
		עשה	DO	794b	14
		מעשה	DEED	795d	1 b1
		מצוה	COMMANDMENT	846b	2 a
		צלח	ADVANCE	852c	2
32	1	אמת	FIRMNESS	54a	3 a
		אמר	SAY	56b	3
		בצר	MAKE INACCESSIBLE	131a	
		בקע	BREAK OPEN OR THROUGH	131d	2
		בקע	BREAK OPEN OR THROUGH	*132b	
		דבר	WORD	183c	44
		חנה	DECLINE	333c	2 c2
		סנחריב	SENNACHERIB	703a	
32	2	ל	TO	510d	1 a
		סנחריב	SENNACHERIB	703a	
32	3	יעץ	CONSULT	419d	
		סתם	STOP UP	711b	1
		עור	HELP	740b	
		עין	SPRING	745b	
32	4	נחל	TORRENT	636b	1
		סתם	STOP UP	711b	1
		מעין	SPRING	746a	
		קבץ	GATHER	867a	1
		שטף	OVERFLOW	1009b	2
32	5	אחר	ANOTHER	29c	
		בנה	BUILD	124d	1 i
		מגדל	TOWER	153d	1
		מגן	SHIELD	171c	
		דוד	DAVID	188a	A
		חוץ	THE OUTSIDE	299d	1 bc
		חזק	BE FIRM	304c	1 c
		חזק	BE FIRM	305b	1 c
		חומה	WALL	327c	1
		מלוא	MILLO	571c	2
		עלה	GO UP	749c	1
		פרץ	BREAK THROUGH	829b	2
32	6	דבר	SPEAK	181d	5
		לבב	HEART	524b	2 9a
		מלחמה	WAR	536b	
		קבץ	GATHER	867a	2
		רחוב	PLAZA	932b	
		רחוב	PLAZA	932b	
		שר	CHIEFTAIN	978c	3 a
32	7	אמץ	BE STRONG	55a	2
		המון	CROWD	242a	3 a
		חזק	BE FIRM	304b	1 2c
		חתת	BE SHATTERED	369b	2 a
		ירא	FEAR	431b	1 c
		פנה	FACE	818a	2 5b
		רב	MUCH	913b	1 e
32	8	בשר	FLESH	142d	5
		זרוע	ARM	284a	2 a
		לחם	ENGAGE IN BATTLE	535d	
		מלחמה	WAR	536b	
		סמך	LEAN	702a	
32	9	אחר	AFTER	29d	2 b
		זה	THIS	260d	1 a
		לכיש	LACHISH	540c	
		ממשלה	RULE	606a	1
		סנחריב	SENNACHERIB	703a	
		על	UPON	757b	2 7c aa
32	10	בטח	TRUST	105a	1 4c
		מה	HOW	554b	4 f
		סנחריב	SENNACHERIB	703a	
		מצור	SIEGE	849a	2
32	11	כף	POWER	496d	2
		נצל	DELIVER	665a	3 a
		סות	INCITE	694d	2
		צמא	THIRST	854d	
		רעב	FAMINE	944b	2
32	12	במה	HIGH PLACE	119c	3 d
		הוא	HE, SHE, IT	215c	1 e
		מזבח	ALTAR	259a	0
		סור	TURN ASIDE	694b	1
		פנה	FACE	818a	2 5b
		שחה	BOW DOWN	1005c	2 c
32	13	אלהים	GOD	43c	1 d
		גוי	NATION	156d	1 c
		יכל	BE ABLE	407c	1
		עם	PEOPLE	766d	5 d
32	14	אלהים	GOD	43c	1 d
		חרם	BAN	355d	1 b
32	15	אלה	GOD	43a	1
		אמן	CONFIRM	53a	2 b
		אף	ALSO	65b	3
		זה	THIS	262a	6 d
		יכל	BE ABLE	407c	1
		כי	THAT	*472c	1 da
		ממלכה	KINGDOM	575a	1
		נשא	DECEIVE	674a	
		נשא	DECEIVE	*674a	
		סות	INCITE	694d	2
32	16	אלהים	GOD	43d	3
		דבר	SPEAK	181d	5
32	17	אלהים	GOD	43c	1 d
		אלהים	GOD	44c	4 ba
		חרף	REPROACH	357d	
		כתב	WRITE	507d	1 c
		ל	TO	512a	3 b
		ספר	MISSIVE	707a	1 a
		ספר	MISSIVE	707a	1 a
32	18	בהל	DISMAY	96c	1
		יהודית	JEWISH	397c	
		ירא	TERRIFY	431d	2
		על	UPON	757c	2 7c b
		קרא	CALL	895a	1 a
32	19	אלהים	GOD	43c	1 d
		דבר	SPEAK	*181d	5
		כ	LIKE	455a	B
		על	UPON	758b	4 1a
		עם	PEOPLE	766d	5 d
		מעשה	DEED	796a	2 a3
32	20	אמוץ	AMOZ	55b	
		זה	THIS	262a	6 f
		זעק	CRY	277b	2 a
		ישעיהו	ISAIAH	447d	1
		נביא	PROPHET	611d	1
		פלל	INTERVENE	813b	3
32	21	בשת	SHAME	102a	1
		גבור	STRONG	150b	2
		יצא	COMING FORTH	425c	
		כחד	HIDE	470c	2
		מלאך	MESSENGER	521d	2
		מן	FROM	580d	3 ba
		מעה	BELLY	589a	2
		נגיד	LEADER	618a	4
		נפל	FALL	658a	2
32	22	ישע	DELIVER	446d	1 b
		כל	ALL	482c	2 a
		נהל	REFRESH	625a	4
		נוח	REST	628c	A 1b 2
		סנחריב	SENNACHERIB	703a	
32	23	אחר	BEHIND	30b	4 ag
		מגרנה	EXCELLENT THING	550c	
		מנחה	GIFT	585a	1
		נשא	LIFT	671d	1 b
		פנה	FACE	818a	2 5b
32	24	מופת	SIGN	69a	2
		חלה	BE WEAK	317d	2
		עד	UNTIL	725d	3 2
		פלל	INTERVENE	813b	3
32	25	גבה	BE HIGH	147a	3 b
		לב	HEART	525b	2 6c
		קצף	WRATH	893c	1
		שוב	TURN BACK	999c	4 a
32	26	גבה	HEIGHT	147b	3
		כנע	BE HUMBLE	488c	1
		לב	HEART	525b	2 6c
		קצף	WRATH	893c	1
32	27	אוצר	TREASURE	70a	3 a
		בשם	SPICE	141d	1
		מגן	SHIELD	171c	
		חמדה	DESIRE	326d	
		יקר	PRECIOUS	430a	1 c
		כבוד	HONOR	458c	2
		כלי	ARTICLE	479c	1
		רבה	BECOME MANY	915d	1 e4
32	28	אריה	MANGER	71d	
		תבואה	PRODUCT	100a	1
		דגן	CORN	186c	
		ו	AND	253b	1 ib
		תירוש	NEW WINE	440d	
		כל	ALL	481c	1 b
		מסכנות	SUPPLY	698b	
		עדר	FLOCK	727c	1 a
		יצהר	FRESH OIL	844a	
		אריה	ADDENDA ET CORRIGENDA	1120d	
32	29	עשה	DO	795a	2 7
		מקנה	CATTLE	889b	2
		רב	MUCH	913a	1 a1
		רכוש	PROPERTY	940d	1
32	30	דוד	DAVID	188a	A
		הוא	HE, SHE, IT	215c	1 e
		מוצא	GOING FORTH	425d	3 a
		ישר	DIRECT	448d	2
		מי	WATER	565c	2
		מטה	DOWNWARDS	641b	2 a
		סתם	STOP UP	711b	1
		מערב	WEST	788b	
		מעשה	DEED	795d	1 b3
		צלח	ADVANCE	852c	2
32	31	מופת	SIGN	69a	2
		דרש	SEEK	205c	4 b
		היה	COME TO PASS	224b	1 1b
		כל	ALL	481c	1 c
		לב	HEART	523c	2 2
		ליץ	SCORN	539c	2
		נסה	TEST	650b	3 a
		עזב	LEAVE	737c	2 e
		על	UPON	757b	2 7c aa
		שר	CHIEFTAIN	978a	2 a
32	32	אמוץ	AMOZ	55b	
		חזון	VISION	303a	4
		חסד	GOODNESS	338d	1 3
		ישעיהו	ISAIAH	447d	1
		נביא	PROPHET	611d	1
		ספר	MISSIVE	707b	3 e
		על	UPON	757a	2 7c
32	33	בן	SON	120d	1 ja
		דוד	DAVID	188b	F
		כבוד	HONOR	459b	6 a
		מעלה	ASCENT	751c	1
33	2	ירש	CAUSE TO POSSESS	440a	2 a
		תועבה	ABOMINATION	1072d	1 b
33	3	אשרה	ASHERA	81c	B
		במה	HIGH PLACE	119c	3 d
		בנה	BUILD	124c	1 ai
		בנה	BUILD	124d	1 i
		בעל	BAAL	127d	2 3
		מזבח	ALTAR	258d	8
		עבר	WORK	713b	4 b
		צבא	HOST	839a	1 c
		קום	STAND	878d	2 b
		שוב	TURN BACK	998b	8
33	4	עולם	LONG DURATION	762c	2 e
33	5	חצר	ENCLOSURE	347a	3 b
		צבא	HOST	839a	1 c
33	6	אוב	NECROMANCER	15b	1
		אש	FIRE	77d	4
		הנם	HINNOM	244d	
		הנם	HINNOM	245a	
		ידעני	FAMILIAR SPIRIT	396b	
		כעס	VEX	495a	2
		כשף	PRACTICE SORCERY	506c	
		נחש	PRACTISE DIVINATION	638c	1
		עבר	PASS OVER	718d	1 d
		ענן	PRACTISE SOOTHSAYING	778b	
		עשה	DO	795c	2 8
		רבה	BECOME MANY	915c	1 d1
33	7	בחר	CHOOSE	104a	2 a
		סמל	IMAGE	702b	
		עולם	LONG DURATION	762b	2 c
		פסל	IDOL	820d	
		שום	TO PLACE	962d	1 a
		שום	TO PLACE	964b	4 c
33	8	אדמה	LAND	10a	5
		חק	SOMETHING PRESCRIBED	349d	7 g
		יד	HAND	391a	5 d
		יסף	DO AGAIN	415c	2 a
		תורה	LAW	436b	2 b
		ל	TO	514c	5 fd
		עמד	STAND	764d	5
		רק	ONLY	956d	2 f
		משפט	JUDGMENT	1049a	4
33	9	רע	EVIL	948d	3
		תעה	ERR	1073c	3
33	11	אסר	TIE	63d	3
		הלך	WALK	236d	1 e
		חוח	BRIER	296b	2 a
		חח	HOOK	*296b	1
		לכד	CAPTURE	540a	1
		נחשת	COPPER	639a	2
		צבא	ARMY	839a	1 a
33	12	חלה	MOLLIFY	318c	1
		כנע	BE HUMBLE	488c	1
		צרר	BIND	864d	B
33	13	אלהים	GOD	43d	3
		תחנה	FAVOR	337c	2
		מלכות	ROYAL POWER	574d	1
		עתר	PRAY	801c	
		שוב	TURN BACK	998d	1 a
33	14	בנה	BUILD	124c	1 ad
		בצר	MAKE INACCESSIBLE	131a	
		גבה	BE HIGH	147a	
		דג	FISH	185d	
		דוד	DAVID	188a	A
		חיצון	OUTER	300b	1
		ל	TO	511b	1 f
		נחל	WADY	636c	2
		סבב	SURROUND	686a	2 d
		עפל	MOUND	779b	
		מערב	WEST	788b	
		שום	TO PLACE	964a	3 d
		שר	CHIEFTAIN	978c	3 a
		שער	GATE	1044d	1 b5
33	15	אלהים	GOD	43c	1 d
		הר	MOUNTAIN	249c	1 a
		מזבח	ALTAR	259a	0
		חוץ	THE OUTSIDE	299d	1 a
		נכר	FOREIGNNESS	648c	1
		סמל	IMAGE	702b	
33	16	בנה	BUILD	124d	1 i

Ch	v	Heb	Eng	Page	Sec
		זבח	SACRIFICE	257d	2 5
		תודה	THANK-OFFERING	393a	4
		שלם	PEACE-OFFERING	1023c	
		שלם	PEACE-OFFERING	1023d	
33	17	אבל	HOWBEIT	6a	2
		במה	HIGH PLACE	119d	3 d
		יהוה	YAHWEH	218d	2 1d
		דבר	WORD	183a	2 1c
		דבר	WORD	183c	4 2
		חזה	SEER	302d	1 a
		תפלה	PRAYER	813c	1 c
33	18	אשרה	ASHERA	81c	B
		במה	HIGH PLACE	119d	3 d
		בנה	BUILD	124c	1 ai
		דבר	WORD	183a	2 1c
		חזה	SEER	302d	1 a
		חטא	SIN	308c	1 b
		כנע	BE HUMBLE	488c	1
		כתב	WRITE	507c	1 b1
		מעל	UNFAITHFUL	591b	2
		עמד	STAND	764d	3
		עתר	PRAY	801c	
		מקום	STANDING PLACE	880b	4
33	20	אמון	AMON	54c	A
		קבר	BURY	868c	
33	21	אמון	AMON	54c	A
33	22	אמון	AMON	54c	A
		זבח	SLAUGHTER FOR SACRIFICE	257b	2
33	23	עבד	WORK	713b	4 b
		אמון	AMON	54c	A
		אשמה	WRONG-DOING	80a	1
		הוא	HE, SHE, IT	215c	1 e
		כנע	BE HUMBLE	488c	1
		כנע	BE HUMBLE	488c	1
33	24	קשר	BIND	905b	2
33	25	אמון	AMON	54c	A
		מלך	BE KING	574b	
		קשר	BIND	905b	2
34	2	דרך	WAY	203d	6 c
		הלך	WALK	234d	2 3a 1t
		ימין	RIGHT HAND	412a	2 b
		ישר	STRAIGHT	449a	2 a
		סור	TURN ASIDE	693c	1
34	3	אלהים	GOD	44c	4 ba
		אשרה	ASHERA	81c	B
		במה	HIGH PLACE	119c	3
		דרש	SEEK	205b	3 a
		חלל	POLLUTE	320d	1
		טהר	BE CLEAN	372b	1 a
		מלך	BE KING	574a	
		מסכה	MOLTEN IMAGE	651b	2
		נער	YOUTH	655a	1 d
		עוד	STILL	*728d	1 aa
		פסיל	IDOL	821a	
		שמנה	EIGHT	1033a	1 a
34	4	אשרה	ASHERA	81c	B
		בעל	BAAL	127d	2 3
		גדע	HEW	154b	
		דקק	PULVERISE	200d	
		מזבח	ALTAR	259a	0
		זרק	TO TOSS	284c	1 a
		חמן	SUN-PILLAR	329a	
		מטה	DOWNWARDS	*641d	2 a
		מסכה	MOLTEN IMAGE	651b	2
		מעל	ABOVE	752a	2 ca
		על	UPON	759b	4 2d
		פסיל	IDOL	821a	
34	5	טהר	BE CLEAN	372b	1 a
		כהן	PRIEST	463b	2
		שרף	BURN	976d	2 a
34	6	אפרים	EPHRAIM	68c	4
		חרבה	WASTE	352a	1
		חרב	SWORD	353a	3
		נפתלי	NAPHTALI	837a	2 b
34	7	אשרה	ASHERA	81c	B
		גדע	HEW	154b	
		דקק	PULVERISE	200d	
		מזבח	ALTAR	259a	0
		חמן	SUN-PILLAR	329a	
		כתת	BEAT	510a	1
		פסיל	IDOL	821a	
34	8	אצליהו	AZALIAH	69d	
		יהואחז	JEHOAHAZ	219d	4
		יואח	JOAH	222a	3
		זכר	REMEMBER	271a	4
		חזק	BE FIRM	304c	1 c
		טהר	BE CLEAN	372b	1 a
		מלך	BE KING	574a	
		מעשיהו	MAASEIAH	796b	4 b
		שר	CHIEFTAIN	978b	2 d
		שפן	SHAPHAN	1051a	1
34	9	בוא	COME	99c	A
		חלקיהו	HILKIAH	324d	2
		כהן	PRIEST	464b	8
		סף	THRESHOLD	706c	
		שארית	REST	984d	1
34	10	בדק	MEND	96a	
		חזק	BE FIRM	304c	1 c
		פקד	ATTEND TO	824a	3
34	11	אבן	STONE	6c	1
		מחברה	BINDER	289c	
		מצב	HEWING	345b	
		חרש	GRAVER	360d	1 b
		עץ	TREE	781d	2 a

Ch	v	Heb	Eng	Page	Sec
		קרה	FURNISH WITH BEAMS	900a	
		שחת	GO TO RUIN	1008b	1
34	12	אמונה	FIRMNESS	53c	3 a
		בין	DISCERN	107a	2
		זכריהו	ZECHARIAH	272b	0 h
		יחת	JAHATH	367a	2 d
		כלי	INSTRUMENT	479d	2 b
		לוי	LEVITE	533a	3 2b
		לוי	LEVITE	533b	3 2b
		מררי	MERARI	601b	
		נצח	BE PRE-EMINENT	663d	1
		נתך	POUR FORTH	*677d	
		עבדיהו	OBADIAH	715d	1 3
		פקד	ATTEND TO	824a	3
		קהתי	KOHATHITES	875c	
		משלם	MESHULLAM	1024c	8 a
34	13	ו	AND	253b	1 ib
		ל	TO	512a	3 b
		נצח	BE PRE-EMINENT	663d	1
		סבל	BURDEN BEARER	688a	
		ספר	ENUMERATOR	708c	1 d
		עבדה	LABOR	715b	1
		שמר	OFFICIAL	1009c	
34	14	בוא	COME	99c	A
		חלקיהו	HILKIAH	324d	2
		יד	HAND	391a	5 d
		יצא	BRING OUT	425a	4 a
		תורה	LAW	436b	2 b3
		כהן	PRIEST	463c	4
		מצא	FIND	593d	1 b
		ספר	MISSIVE	707b	3 c
34	15	חלקיהו	HILKIAH	324d	2
		תורה	LAW	436b	2 b2
		מצא	FIND	593b	3 a
		ספר	MISSIVE	707b	3 c
		ספר	ENUMERATOR	708c	1 b
		שפן	SHAPHAN	1051a	1
34	16	דבר	WORD	*182b	1 1c
		נתן	GIVE	681c	1 d
		שפן	SHAPHAN	1051a	1
34	17	מצא	FIND	594a	2 c
		נתך	POUR FORTH	678a	
		פקד	ATTEND TO	824a	3
34	18	חלקיהו	HILKIAH	324d	2
		כהן	PRIEST	463c	4
		ספר	ENUMERATOR	708c	1 b
		קרא	CALL	895c	4 a
		שפן	SHAPHAN	1051a	1
34	19	דבר	WORD	*183a	2 2
		תורה	LAW	436b	2 b2
34	20	אחיקם	AHIKAM	27b	
		דבר	WORD	*183a	2 2
		חלקיהו	HILKIAH	324d	2
		מיכה	MICHA	567d	7
		מיכיה	MICAH	*567d	4
		ספר	ENUMERATOR	708c	1 b
		עבד	SLAVE	714a	2
		עבדון	ABDON	715c	1 4
		עשיה	ASAIAH	795c	1
		שפן	SHAPHAN	1051a	2
		שפן	SHAPHAN	1051a	1
34	21	אשר	PARTICLE OF RELATION	82b	2 a
		דבר	WORD	*183a	2 2
		דרש	SEEK	205b	2 a
		חמה	RAGE	404d	2 c
		חמה	RAGE	*405a	2 c
		מצא	FIND	593d	1 b
		נתך	POUR FORTH	677d	
		שאר	REMAIN	984a	1
		עלדבר	ADDENDA ET CORRIGENDA	1122a	
34	22	אשר	PARTICLE OF RELATION	83b	7 c
		דבר	WORD	*183a	2 2
		הלך	WALK	231a	1 d3 ga
		זה	THIS	262a	6 d
		חלדה	HULDAH	317c	
		חלקיהו	HILKIAH	324d	2
		חרחה	HARHAS	341c	
		נביאה	PROPHETESS	612c	1
		שלום	SHALLUM	1024b	3
		שמר	KEEP	1036c	1 a
		משנה	SECOND	1041d	3
34	23	דבר	WORD	*183a	2 2
34	24	אלה	OATH	46d	3
		דבר	WORD	*183a	2 2
		קרא	CALL	895c	4 a
34	25	אלהים	GOD	43c	1 d
		דבר	WORD	*183a	2 2
		חמה	RAGE	404d	2 c
		חמה	RAGE	*405a	2 c
		כבה	BE QUENCHED	459c	
		כעם	VEX	495a	2
		נתך	POUR FORTH	677d	
		מעשה	DEED	795d	1 a2
		קטר	MAKE SACRAFICES SMOKE	883a	1 b
		קטר	MAKE SACRAFICES SMOKE	883a	
		תחת	INSTEAD	1066a	2 3a b
34	26	דבר	WORD	*183a	2 2
		דרש	SEEK	205b	2 a
34	27	בכה	WEEP	113c	6
		דבר	WORD	*183a	2 2

Ch	v	Heb	Eng	Page	Sec
		כנע	BE HUMBLE	488c	1
		כנע	BE HUMBLE	488c	1
		לבב	HEART	524a	2 6a
		נאם	UTTERANCE	610b	2
		פנה	FACE	818a	2 5b
		רכך	BE TENDER	940a	1 b
34	28	אסף	GATHER	62b	2 a
		אסף	GATHER	62d	2 a
		דבר	WORD	*182b	1 1c
		דבר	WORD	*183a	2 2
		על	UPON	757b	2 7c aa
		קצבצר	GRAVE	868d	
		ראה	TO SEE	908a	8 a3
34	29	דבר	WORD	*183a	2 2
		זקן	OLD	278d	2 b
34	30	ברית	COVENANT	*136d	2 2c
		ברית	COVENANT	137a	3 1
		גדול	GREAT	153b	7
		דבר	WORD	*183a	2 2
		כהן	PRIEST	464a	7
		מצא	FIND	593d	1 b
		ספר	MISSIVE	707b	3 c
		עלה	GO UP	748b	1 d
		טן	SMALL	882a	1 a
		קרא	CALL	895c	4 a
34	31	ברית	COVENANT	136d	2 2c
		דבר	WORD	*183a	2 2
		חק	SOMETHING PRESCRIBED	349d	7 g
		כרת	CUT	504a	4
		לבב	HEART	523b	2 2
		נפש	SOUL	661b	0
		עדות	TESTIMONY	730b	2
		עמד	STANDING-PLACE	765a	
		מצוה	COMMANDMENT	846c	2 b1
34	32	ברית	COVENANT	136c	2 2c
		מצא	FIND	594b	2 e
		עמד	STAND	764d	6 c
34	33	יהוה	YAHWEH	218d	2 1d
		מצא	FIND	594b	2 e
		עבד	WORK	713c	3
		תועבה	ABOMINATION	1073a	1 b
35	1	פסח	PASSOVER	820b	3
		פסח	PASSOVER	820b	2
		שחט	SLAUGHTER	1006b	2
35	2	חזק	BE FIRM	304d	3
		עבדה	LABOR	715c	4
		משמרת	GUARD	1038d	4 a
35	3	ארון	CHEST	75c	3 h
		בין	DISCERN	107a	3 c
		כתף	SHOULDER	509b	1 a
		משא	BEARING	672d	3
		קדש	APARTNESS	872a	3 a
		קדוש	HOLY	872d	2 b
35	4	מחלקת	DIVISION	325a	1
		כון	BE READY	465d	3
		כון	ESTABLISH	466c	2 a
		כתב	WRITING	508b	4
		מכתב	WRITING	508c	2
		שלמה	SOLOMON	1024d	
35	5	בן	SON	121b	1 jk
		חלקה	PART	324c	
		לוי	LEVITE	533a	3 1c
		עם	PEOPLE	766d	5 b
		פלגה	DIVISION	811b	
35	6	יד	HAND	391a	5 d
		כון	ESTABLISH	466b	2
		פסח	PASSOVER	820b	2
		קדש	BE SET APART	873c	4
		שחט	SLAUGHTER	1006b	1 jk
35	7	בן	SON	121b	1 jk
		בקר	CATTLE	133c	2
		כבש	LAMB	461a	1
		כל	ALL	482d	2 ba
		מצא	FIND	594b	2 e
		עז	SHE-GOAT	777c	3 c
		פסח	PASSOVER	820b	2
		רום	BE HIGH	927d	3 c
		רכוש	PROPERTY	940d	2
35	8	בקר	CATTLE	133c	2
		זכריהו	ZECHARIAH	272b	1 b
		יחיאל	JEHIEL	313d	7
		חלקיהו	HILKIAH	324d	2
		כהן	PRIEST	464a	7
		ל	TO	516c	5 jb
		נגיד	LEADER	618a	3
		נדבה	FREEWILL-OFFERING	621d	2 c
		פסח	PASSOVER	820b	2
		רום	BE HIGH	927d	3 c
35	9	בקר	CATTLE	133c	2
		יהוזבד	JEHOZABAD	220a	4 c
		חמש	FIVE	332a	4
		חשביהו	HASHABIAH	364a	3
		יעיאל	JEIEL	418b	2 c2
		כונניהו	CONANIAH	467b	2
		לוי	LEVITE	533a	3 2b
		מאה	HUNDRED	548b	1 c4
		נתנאל	NETHANE/L	682b	5 c
		פסח	PASSOVER	820b	2
		רום	BE HIGH	927d	3 c
		שר	CHIEFTAIN	978d	5
		שמעיה	SHEMAIAH	1035d	7 k
35	10	מחלקת	DIVISION	325d	1
		כון	BE READY	466a	4
		עבדה	LABOR	715b	4

Ch	v.	Heb	Eng	Page	Sec
35	11	עמד	STANDING-PLACE	765a	
		זרק	TO TOSS	284c	1 b
		פסח	PASSOVER	820b	2
		פשט	STRIP OFF	833a	3
		שחט	SLAUGHTER	1006b	2
35	12	בן	SON	121b	1 jk
		בקר	CATTLE	*133c	2
		בן	SO	485d	1 a
		משה	MOSES	602d	
		ספר	MISSIVE	707b	3 c
		עם	PEOPLE	766d	5 b
		מפלגה	DIVISION	811b	
		קרב	COME NEAR	898a	2 b7
35	13	אש	FIRE	77c	3
		בשל	BOIL	143a	1
		דוד	POT	188c	A
		סיר	POT	696c	2
		פסח	PASSOVER	820b	2
		צלחה	POT	852c	1
		רוץ	RUN	930c	1
		משפט	JUDGMENT	1048d	3
35	14	אהרן	AARON	14d	
		בן	SON	121b	1 jz
		חלב	FAT	317a	2 b
		כהן	PRIEST	464a	7
		כון	ESTABLISH	466b	2 a
		לילה	NIGHT	538c	1
		עלה	WHOLE BURNT OFFERING	750d	
35	15	אין	NOT	34d	5 b
		הימן	HEMAN	54d	
		הימן	HEMAN	54d	
		אסף	ASAPH	63a	2
		אסף	ASAPH	63b	2
		ו	AND	253b	1 ib
		חזה	SEER	302d	1 c
		ידותון	JEDUTHUN	*393a	
		איתן	ETHAN	*451a	
		כון	ESTABLISH	466b	2 a
		ל	TO	511d	2
		עבדה	LABOR	715c	4
		על	UPON	759a	4 2c
		מעמד	OFFICE	765b	1
35	16	כון	BE READY	466a	4
		עבדה	LABOR	715b	4
		עלה	GO UP	750a	8
		עלה	WHOLE BURNT OFFERING	750d	
		פסח	PASSOVER	820b	3
35	17	חג	FESTIVAL-GATHERING	291a	1 b2
		חג	FESTIVAL-GATHERING	291b	1 b
		מצא	FIND	594b	2 e
		מצה	UNLEAVENED BREAD	695b	
		פסח	PASSOVER	820b	3
35	18	יום	DAY	399b	4 b
		כהן	PRIEST	464a	7
		מצא	FIND	594b	2 e
		עשה	DO	795b	2 e
		פסח	PASSOVER	820b	3
		שמואל	SAMUEL	1028d	1
35	19	מלכות	REIGN	575a	2
		עשה	DO	795b	2 e
		פסח	PASSOVER	820b	3
35	20	אחר	AFTER	30b	2 b
		אשר	PARTICLE OF RELATION	82c	4 ba
		זה	THIS	260d	1 a
		כון	ESTABLISH	466c	4
		כרכמיש	CARCHEMISH	501c	
		לחם	ENGAGE IN BATTLE	535c	
		נכו	NECO	647a	
		פרת	EUPHRATES	832c	
35	21	אמר	SAY	56b	1
		אמר	SAY	56c	4
		בהל	HASTEN	96c	2
		חדל	CEASE	293a	2
		ל	TO	516a	5 ic
		מלאך	MESSENGER	521c	1 a
		מה	WHAT	553b	1 dc
35	22	בקעה	PLAIN	132c	2
		מגדו	MEGIDDO	152a	
		חפש	SEARCH	344c	
		נכו	NECO	647a	
		סבב	TURN ABOUT	686c	1 a
35	23	ירה	SHOOT	435a	3
		ירה	SHOOT	435b	2
		עבר	PASS OVER	719a	4
35	24	אבל	MOURN	5c	
		הלך	WALK	237a	3 a
		עבר	PASS OVER	719a	4
		קברצבר	GRAVE	868d	
		רכב	RIDE	938d	1
		רכב	CHARIOT	939b	2
		מרכבה	CHARIOT	939d	
		משנה	SECOND	1041c	1
35	25	חק	SOMETHING PRESCRIBED	349c	6 a
		כתב	WRITE	507c	1 b1
		על	UPON	753b	2 1c
		קנן	CHANT	884b	
		קינה	ELEGY	884b	
		קינה	ELEGY	884b	

Ch	v.	Heb	Eng	Page	Sec
		ירמיה	JEREMIAH	941c	1
35	26	שיר	SING	1010d	
		חסד	GOODNESS	338d	1 3
		תורה	LAW	436b	2 b3
35	27	דבר	WORD	183c	4 2
		ספר	MISSIVE	707c	3 e
		ראשון	FIRST	911c	1 a
36	1	יהואחז	JEHOAHAZ	219d	1
		מלך	BE KING	574b	
36	2	יהואחז	JEHOAHAZ	219d	1
		חדש	NEW MOON	294c	2 a
36	3	כסף	SILVER	494b	8 c
		מאה	HUNDRED	547d	1 a1
		סור	TURN ASIDE	694b	1
		ענש	FINE	778d	
36	4	אליקים	ELIAKIM	45d	B
		יהואחז	JEHOAHAZ	219d	1
		יהויקים	JEHOIAKIM	220c	1
		יהויקים	JEHOIAKIM	220c	1
		לקח	TAKE	543d	9 b
		מלך	BE KING	574b	
		נכו	NECO	647a	
		סבב	TURN ABOUT	686c	1 c
		שם	NAME	1028a	2 a
36	5	יהויקים	JEHOIAKIM	220c	1
		זבידה	ZEBIDAH	*256b	
		זבידה	ZEBIDAH	256c	
36	6	אסר	TIE	63d	3
		הלך	WALK	236d	1 e
		נבוכדראצר	NEBUCHADNEZZAR	613b	
		נחשת	COPPER	639a	2
36	7	בוא	COME	99b	2
		היכל	PALACE	228b	1
		ל	TO	511b	1 ga
		נבוכדראצר	NEBUCHADNEZZAR	613b	
36	8	יהויכין	JEHOIACHIN	220c	
		יהויקים	JEHOIAKIM	220c	1
		מצא	FIND	394a	1 gl
		ספר	MISSIVE	707c	3 e
		על	UPON	753d	2 1d
36	9	יהויכין	JEHOIACHIN	220c	
		חדש	NEW MOON	294c	2 a
36	10	חמדה	DESIRE	326d	2
		כלי	UTENSIL	480a	2 f
		מלך	BE KING	574b	
		נבוכדראצר	NEBUCHADNEZZAR	613b	
		צדקיו	ZEDEKIAH	843b	1
		תשובה	RETURN	1000c	2
36	11	צדקיו	ZEDEKIAH	843b	1
36	12	כנע	BE HUMBLE	488c	1
		נביא	PROPHET	611d	1
		פנה	FACE	818a	2 5b
		ירמיה	JEREMIAH	941c	1
36	13	אמץ	BE STRONG	55b	3
		לבב	HEART	524a	2 6d
		מן	FROM	583b	7 ba
		מרד	REBEL	597c	1
		נבוכדראצר	NEBUCHADNEZZAR	613b	
		ערף	BACK OF NECK	791c	2
		קשה	BE SEVERE	904c	3 a
		שבע	SWEAR	989d	1
36	14	טמא	BE UNCLEAN	379c	2
		כהן	PRIEST	464c	8
		מסר	DELIVER UP	588b	
		מעל	ACT TREACHEROUSLY	591b	1 a
		קדש	BE SET APART	873a	1 c
		רבה	BECOME MANY	915c	1 d1
		שר	CHIEFTAIN	978d	5
		תועבה	ABOMINATION	1072d	1 b
36	15	חמל	SPARE	328b	1
		מלאך	MESSENGER	521c	1 b
		מעון	REFUGE	733a	2 b
		על	UPON	757c	27c aa
		שכם	START EARLY	1014d	1
36	16	אין	NOT	35a	6 cg
		בזה	DESPISE	102b	
		דבר	WORD	183a	2 2
		חמה	RAGE	*404d	2 c
		חמה	RAGE	404d	2 c
		מלאך	MESSENGER	521c	1 b
		לעג	JEST	541b	
		עד	UNTIL	725c	3 3
		עלה	GO UP	749a	1
		מרפא	HEALING	951b	1
		תעע	MOCK	1073d	
36	17	בחור	YOUNG MAN	104c	
		בחור	YOUNG MAN	104c	
		בית	HOUSE	109b	1 ae 0
		בתולה	VIRGIN	143d	
		הרג	KILL	247b	1 b
		זקן	OLD	278c	2 a
		חמל	SPARE	328b	
		ישש	AGED	450a	
		כל	ALL	482d	2 ba
		כשדים	CHALDEANS	505a	1 b
		עלה	GO UP	749c	2 b
		מקדש	SACRED PLACE	874b	4
36	18	בוא	COME	99b	2
		כלי	UTENSIL	480a	2 f
		כל	ALL	482d	2 ba
		קטן	SMALL	882a	1 b

Ch	v.	Heb	Eng	Page	Sec
36	19	שר	CHIEFTAIN	978b	2 a
		ארמון	CITADEL	74d	
		מחמד	DESIRE	327a	
		חומה	WALL	327c	1
		ל	TO	518a	7 bg
36	20	שחת	GO TO RUIN	1008b	1
		מלך	BE KING	574a	
		מלכות	REIGN	575a	2
		פרס	PERSIA	828a	
36	21	שארית	REST	984d	1
		יום	DAY	400b	7 d2 a
		מלא	FILL	570d	3
		מלא	FILL	570d	3
		פה	MOUTH	805a	2 a
		ירמיה	JEREMIAH	941c	1
		רצה	BE PLEASED WITH	953b	4
		שבת	CEASE	991d	2 c
		שבת	SABBATH	992c	3
		שבת	KEEP	992d	
		שמם	BE DESOLATED	1031b	
36	22	כורש	CYRUS	468d	
		כלה	BE FINISHED	477c	1 c
		מכתב	WRITING	508c	2
		מלכות	KINGDOM	575a	3
		עבר	PASS OVER	718d	2 a
		עור	ROUSE ONESELF	735b	1
		פה	MOUTH	805a	2 a
		פרס	PERSIA	828a	
		קול	VOICE	877b	3 a3
		רוח	BREATH	925b	3 g
		ירמיה	JEREMIAH	941c	1
36	23	אלהים	GOD	44c	4 bb
		כורש	CYRUS	468d	
		ממלכה	KINGDOM	575b	1
		פקד	ATTEND TO	823d	B 2
		פרס	PERSIA	828a	
		שמי	HEAVENS	1030b	2 a

EZRA

Ch	v.	Heb	Eng	Page	Sec
1	1	כורש	CYRUS	468d	
		כלה	BE FINISHED	477c	1 c
		מכתב	WRITING	508c	2
		מלך	KING	573a	1
		מלכות	KINGDOM	575a	3
		עבר	PASS OVER	718d	2 a
		עור	ROUSE ONESELF	735b	1
		פה	MOUTH	805a	2 a
		פרס	PERSIA	828a	
		קול	VOICE	877b	3 a3
		רוח	BREATH	925b	3 g
		ירמיה	JEREMIAH	941c	1
1	2	אלהים	GOD	44c	4 bb
		כורש	CYRUS	468d	
		ממלכה	KINGDOM	575b	1
		פקד	ATTEND TO	823d	B 2
		פרס	PERSIA	828a	
		שמי	HEAVENS	1030b	2 a
1	3	אלהים	GOD	43d	3
		בנה	BUILD	124d	1 i
		מי	WHO	567b	G
		עלה	GO UP	748b	1 c
1	4	בהמה	BEAST	97a	2
		גור	SOJOURN	157d	1
		זהב	GOLD	262d	2
		זהב	GOLD	263c	1
		נדבה	FREEWILL-OFFERING	621d	2 a
		נשא	LIFT	672a	1
		רכוש	PROPERTY	940d	3
1	5	כהן	PRIEST	464a	7
		כל	ALL	481d	1 c
		ל	TO	514c	5 fd
		עור	ROUSE ONESELF	735b	1
		רוח	BREATH	925b	3 g
1	6	בד	SEPARATION	94d	1 d
		בהמה	BEAST	97a	2
		זהב	GOLD	262d	2
		חזק	BE FIRM	304d	2
		יד	HAND	389d	1 e1
		כל	ALL	481d	1 c
		מגדנה	EXCELLENT THING	550c	
		נדב	INCITE	621c	2
		על	UPON	755a	2
		רכוש	PROPERTY	940d	3
1	7	יצא	BRING OUT	425a	4 a
		כורש	CYRUS	468d	
		כלי	UTENSIL	480a	2 f
		נבוכדראצר	NEBUCHADNEZZAR	613b	
1	8	גזבר	TREASURER	159d	
		יצא	BRING OUT	425b	4 a
		כורש	CYRUS	468d	
		מתרדת	MITHREDATH	609c	1
		נשיא	PRINCE	672c	7
		ספר	COUNT	707d	1
		ששבצר	SHESHBAZZAR	1058c	
1	9	אגרטל	BASIN	174a	1
		מחלף	KNIFE	322c	
		שלשים	THIRTY	1026c	1
1	10	כפור	BOWL	499b	
		עשר	TEN	797a	3 c
		שלשים	THIRTY	1026c	1
		משנה	SECOND	1041d	3 a
1	11	זהב	GOLD	263c	1

Ch	v.	Heb	Eng	Page	Sec
		חמש	FIVE	332a	4
		ירושלים	JERUSALEM	437a	
		כל	ALL	482d	2 ba
		עלה	GO UP	749a	1 a
		עם	WITH	768a	1 g
2	1	בן	SON	121b	1 jm
		מדינה	PROVINCE	193d	3
		ל	TO	511b	1 ga
		נבוכדראצר	NEBUCHADNEZ-ZAR	613b	
2	2	שבי	CAPTIVITY	985d	1
		בגוי	BIGVAI	94a	1
		בלשן	BILSHAN	119a	
		בענה	BAANAH	128d	3
		יהושע	JOSHUA	221c	3
		זרבבל	ZERUBBABEL	279c	
		נחום	NEHUM	637b	
		נחמיה	NEHEMIAH	637c	3
		מספר	MISPAR	709a	
		עזריהו	AZARIAH	*741b	9
		רחום	REHUM	933d	1 a
		רעליה	REELAIAH	947a	
		שריה	SERAIAH	976a	5 a
2	3	פרעש	PAROSH	829b	1
2	4	שבעים	SEVENTY	988c	3 c
2	4	שבעים	SEVENTY	988c	3 c
		שפטיה	SHEPHATIAH	1049b	1 d1
2	5	ארח	ARAH	73b	2
		חמש	FIVE	332b	5 h
		שבעים	SEVENTY	988c	3 c
2	6	יהושע	JOSHUA	221d	8
		יואב	JOAB	222a	3
		פחתמואב	PAHATH-MOAB	809b	
2	7	עילם	ELAM	743b	1 a
2	8	זתוא	ZATTU	285c	
		ארבעים	FORTY	917c	2 c
2	9	זבי	ZABBAI	*256a	
		זבי	ZACCAI	269b	
2	10	בנוי	BINNUI	*125a	1
		בני	BANI	125b	4
		ארבעים	FORTY	917c	2 c
		הודויה	ADDENDA ET COR-RIGENDA	1124a	3
2	11	בבי	BEBAI	93c	1
		ירושלים	JERUSALEM	437a	
2	12	עזגד	AZGAD	739d	1 a
2	13	אדניהו	ADONIJAH	11d	3
		אדניקם	ADONIKAM	12a	
2	14	בגוי	BIGVAI	94a	1
2	15	עדין	ADIN	726d	1
		ארבע	FOUR	917b	2 c
2	16	אטר	ATER	32a	
		חזקיהו	HEZEKIAH	306b	4
2	17	בצי	BEZAI	130a	
		ל	TO	1098b	1
2	18	חרף	HARIPH	358b	1
		יורה	JORAH	435c	
2	19	חשם	HASHUM	365c	
2	20	גבעון	GIBEON	*149c	
		גבר	GIBBAR	150a	
2	21	ביתלחם	BETHLEHEM	112a	1
2	22	נטפה	NETOPHAH	643b	
2	23	ענתות	ANATHOTH	779a	1
2	24	ביתעזמות	BETH-AZMAVETH	112b	
		ארבעים	FORTY	917c	2 a
2	25	בארות	BEEROTH	92a	
		כפירה	CHEPHIRAH	499a	
		קריתיערים	KIRIATH-JEARIM	900c	
		ארבעים	FORTY	917c	2 c
2	26	גבע	GEBA	148d	1
		רמה	RAMA	928a	1
2	27	מכמס	MICHMASH	485a	
2	28	עי	AI	743b	1
2	29	אחר	ANOTHER	*29c	
		גב	NOB	611b	1
		גבו	NEBO	612d	1 b
2	30	מגביש	MAGBISH	150d	
2	31	אחר	ANOTHER	29c	
		עילם	ELAM	743d	1 b
2	32	חרם	HARIM	356c	3 b
		עשרים	TWENTY	797d	1 2d
2	33	אונו	ONO	20c	
		חדיד	HADID	292c	
		לד	LOD	528d	
2	34	יריחו	JERICHO	437d	
		ארבעים	FORTY	917c	2 c
2	35	סנאה	SENAAH	702d	
		שלשים	THIRTY	1026c	1
		ל	IN REGARD TO	1098c	4 b
2	36	יהושע	JOSHUA	221d	5
		ידעיה	JEDAIAH	396a	2
		שבעים	SEVENTY	988c	3 c
2	37	אמר	IMMER	57b	2
2	38	פשחור	PASHHUR	832d	4
		ארבעים	FORTY	917c	2 c
2	39	חרם	HARIM	356c	3 b
		רחום	REHUM	933d	1 b
		שבע	SEVEN	988b	5 c
		שבע	SEVEN	*988b	5 c
2	40	בני	BANI	125b	2 b
		בנוי	BINNUI	125b	2
		הודוה	HODEVAH	217b	
		יהושע	JOSHUA	221d	6 a
		חגבה	HAGABAH	290c	
		לוי	LEVITE	533b	3 2b
		קדמיאל	KADMIEL	870d	

Ch	v.	Heb	Eng	Page	Sec
2	41	שבעים	SEVENTY	988c	3 a
		אסף	ASAPH	63b	2
		בן	SON	120d	1 ja
2	42	אטר	ATER	32a	
		בן	SON	121c	7 a
		טלמן	TALMON	379a	1
		כל	ALL	482d	2 ba
		עקוב	AKKUB	784d	2 a
		שבי	SHOBAI	986b	
		שלום	SHALLUM	1024b	2 a
		שער	PORTER	1045c	
2	43	גשפא	GISHPA	*178a	
		חשופא	HASUPHA	362d	
		טבעות	TABBAOTH	371d	
		נתינים	NETHINIM	682a	
		ציחא	ZIHA	851c	
2	44	סיעא	SIA	696b	
		פדון	PADON	804b	
		קרם	KEROS	902b	
2	45	לבנא	LEBANA	526c	
		עקוב	AKKUB	784d	2 b
2	46	חגב	HAGAB	290c	
		חנן	HANAN	336d	2
		שלמי	SHALMAI	969c	
2	47	גדל	GIDDEL	153c	1
		גחר	GAHAR	161a	
		ראיה	REAIAH	909d	3
2	48	גזם	GAZZAM	160b	
		נקודא	NEKODA	667a	
2	49	רצין	REZIN	954a	2
		בסי	BESAI	126a	
		עזא	UZZAH	739c	4
		פסח	PASEAH	820c	2
2	50	אסנה	ASNAH	62a	
		מעונים	MEUNITES	589b	
		נפיסים	NEPHESIM	656b	
2	51	בקבוק	BAKBUK	132d	
		חקופא	HAKUPHA	349a	
		חרחור	HARHUR	359c	
2	52	בצלות	BAZLUTH	130b	
		חרשא	HARSHA	361d	
		מחידא	MEHIDA	563a	
2	53	ברקום	BARKOS	140d	
		סיסרא	SISERA	696b	2
		תמח	TEMAH	1069c	
2	54	חטיפא	HATIPHA	310c	
		נציח	NEZIAH	664c	
2	55	סוטי	SOTAI	691d	
		ספרת	SOPHERETH	709b	
		פרודא	PERUDA	825c	
		קהלת	PREACHER	875b	
		שלמה	SOLOMON	1024d	
2	56	גדל	GIDDEL	153c	2
		דרקון	DARKON	204c	
		יעלה	JAALAH	419a	
2	57	אמי	AMI	51b	2
		אמון	AMON	54c	C
		חטיל	HATTIL	310b	
		פכרתהצבים	POCHERETH-HAZZEBAIM	810b	
		שפטיה	SHEPHATIAH	1049b	1 d2
2	58	נתינים	NETHINIM	682a	
		שלמה	SOLOMON	1024d	
2	59	אדן	ADDAN	11d	
		אם	IF	50d	2 ba
		אמר	IMMER	57b	5
		בית	HOUSE	110b	5 e
		זרע	SOWING	282d	4 e
		כרוב	CHERUB	500c	
		ישראל	ISRAEL	975d	2 a3
		תלחרשא	TEL-HARSHA	1068b	
		תלמלח	TEL-MELAH	1068b	
2	60	דליהו	DELAIAH	195b	2 a
		טוביהו	TOBIJAH	376a	3
		נקודא	NEKODA	667a	
2	61	בן	SON	121c	7 a
		ברזלי	BARZILLAI	137d	2
		ברזלי	BARZILLAI	137d	1
		חביה	HABAIAH	285d	
		חביה	HABAIAH	286a	
		קוץ	KOZ	881b	2
		קרא	CALL	896c	6 d5
2	62	בקש	SEEK	134c	1 b
		גאל	DEFILE	146a	
		מצא	FIND	394a	1 f
		התיחש	ENROLLMENT	405c	
		כהנה	PRIESTHOOD	464d	
		כתב	WRITING	508b	1
		מן	OUT OF	579a	2 aa
2	63	אורים	URIM	22a	
		אשר	THAT	83c	8 ab
		כהן	PRIEST	464b	7
		ל	TO	516d	5 k
		עמד	STAND	764b	6 a
		קדש	APARTNESS	872a	3 b
		תם	INTEGRITY	1070d	4
		תרשתא	TIRASHATHA	1077a	
2	64	אלף	THOUSAND	49a	1 b
		קהל	ASSEMBLY	874c	1 c
		רבו	TEN THOUSAND	914b	
		ארבע	FOUR	916d	1 a3
		חד	ONE	*1079c	1
2	65	אלה	THESE	41c	A
		אמה	MAID	51a	1
		בד	SEPARATION	94d	1 e
		מאה	HUNDRED	548a	1 b3

Ch	v.	Heb	Eng	Page	Sec
2	66	שיר	SING	1010d	
		סוס	HORSE	692d	2
		פרד	MULE	825d	
		ארבעים	FORTY	917c	2 c
2	67	חמור	HE-ASS	331b	1
2	68	מכון	FIXED PLACE	467c	1
		ל	TO	511b	1 ga
		מן	FROM	580d	3 ba
		נדב	INCITE	621c	
		עמד	STAND	764d	3
2	69	אוצר	TREASURE	70a	1
		דרכמון	DRACHMA	204b	
		זהב	GOLD	263c	9 d
		חמש	FIVE	332a	4
		כח	STRENGTH	470d	1 b
		כסף	SILVER	494c	8 d
		כתנת	TUNIC	509a	
		מאה	HUNDRED	547d	1 a3
		מנה	MANEH	584b	
		רבו	TEN THOUSAND	914c	
2	70	כהן	PRIEST	464a	7
		מן	FROM	580d	3 ba
		נתינים	NETHINIM	682a	
		ישראל	ISRAEL	975d	2 a3
		ישראל	ISRAEL	976a	1
3	1	אסף	GATHER	62c	1 a
		חרש	NEW MOON	294d	2 b2
		נגע	REACH	619b	4
		ישראל	ISRAEL	975d	2 b3
3	2	אלהים	GOD	43d	1 i
		בנה	BUILD	124d	1 i
		יהוצדק	JEHOZADAK	221b	
		יהושע	JOSHUA	221c	3
		מזבח	ALTAR	258d	6
		זרבבל	ZERUBBABEL	*279c	
		זרבבל	ZERUBBABEL	279c	
		תורה	LAW	436b	2 b3
		משה	MOSES	602d	2
		עלה	GO UP	750a	8
		עלה	WHOLE BURNT OF-FERING	750d	
3	3	אימה	TERROR	34a	
		ב	IN	91b	
		בקר	MORNING	134a	1 e
		מזבח	ALTAR	258d	8
		כון	ESTABLISH	466b	1 a
		מכונה	BASE	467d	
		עלה	GO UP	750a	8
		עלה	WHOLE BURNT OF-FERING	750d	
3	4	ערב	SUNSET	787d	1 a
		דבר	WORD	183b	4 l
		חג	FESTIVAL-GATHER-ING	291a	1 b2
		חג	FESTIVAL-GATHER-ING	291b	1 b
		יום	DAY	400b	7 e1
		יום	DAY	400c	7 e3
		סכה	THICKET	697d	3
		מספר	NUMBER	709a	1 b
3	5	מועד	APPOINTED TIME	417c	1 b
		תמיד	CONTINUITY	556c	2 b
		נדב	INCITE	621c	2
		נדבה	FREEWILL-OFFER-ING	621d	2 c
		עלה	WHOLE BURNT OF-FERING	750b	
3	6	היכל	TEMPLE	228c	2 d
		חלל	POLLUTE	320d	2
		יום	DAY	398c	2 e
		יסד	BE FOUNDED	414a	
		עלה	WHOLE BURNT OF-FERING	750d	
3	7	מאכל	FOOD	38b	
		ארז	CEDAR	72c	1 a
		ארז	CEDAR	72c	2
		חצב	HEW	345a	2 a
		חרש	GRAVER	360d	1 b
		ים	SEA	410d	1
		יפו	JOPPA	421d	
		לבנון	LEBANON	527b	
		צידני	SIDONIANS	851a	
		צרי	TYRIAN	863a	
		ראשון	FIRST	911d	2 a
		רשיון	PERMISSION	957a	
		משתה	DRINK	1059d	2
3	8	בן	SON	120d	1 ja
		בן	SON	122a	9 a
		בן	SON	122a	9 a
		יהוצדק	JEHOZADAK	221b	
		יהושע	JOSHUA	221c	3
		זרבבל	ZERUBBABEL	*279c	
		זרבבל	ZERUBBABEL	279c	
		חלל	POLLUTE	320d	2
		כהן	PRIEST	464a	7
		מלאכה	WORK	522b	6 b
		נצח	BE PRE-EMINENT	663d	1
		מעל	ABOVE	751d	2 bb a
		שאר	REST	984c	
		שבי	CAPTIVITY	985d	1
3	9	יהושע	JOSHUA	221d	6 a
		חנדד	HENADAD	337b	
		מלאכה	WORK	522b	3 b
		נצח	BE PRE-EMINENT	663d	1
		קדמיאל	KADMIEL	870d	

Ch v.	Heb	Eng	Page	Sec
	הודויה	ADDENDA ET COR- RIGENDA	*1124a	3
3 10	אסף	ASAPH	63b	2
	היכל	TEMPLE	228c	2 d
	הלל	PRAISE	238d	2 f
	חצצרה	CLARION	348c	2 c
	יד	HAND	391c	5 h2
	יסד	FOUND	414a	1
	לבש	ARRAYED	528b	
	מצלתים	CYMBALS	853a	
3 11	הלל	PRAISE	238c	2 e
	חסד	GOODNESS	339b	2 3c
	טוב	PLEASANT	374d	9 b
	ידה	PRAISE	392c	1 b
	יסד	FOUNDING	414a	
	על	UPON	756c	2 7a b
	עולם	LONG DURATION	762b	2 c
	ענה	SING	777b	
	רוע	RAISE A SHOUT	929a	5
	תרועה	SHOUT OF WAR	930a	3
	ישראל	ISRAEL	975d	2 a3
3 12	בכה	WEEP	113c	2
	זה	THIS	260d	2 a
	זקן	OLD	278c	1
	יסד	FOUND	413d	
	כהן	PRIEST	464a	7
	עין	EYE	745a	5
	ראשון	FIRST	911c	1 a
	רום	BE HIGH	927c	1 b
	תרועה	SHOUT OF WAR	930a	3
3 13	בכי	WEEPING	113d	
	ל	TO	516d	5 k
	מן	FROM	583d	9 b1
	נכר	RECOGNIZE	648b	5
	עד	UNTIL	725c	3 1
	קול	VOICE	876d	1 a
	קול	VOICE	876d	1 a
	רוע	RAISE A SHOUT	929d	5
	תרועה	SHOUT OF WAR	930a	3
	רחק	DISTANT	935c	2 a7
4 1	בן	SON	121c	7 a
	היכל	TEMPLE	228c	2 d
	צר	ADVERSARY	865d	
4 2	אסרחדן	ESARHADDON	64d	
	אשור	ASSYRIA	78d	4
	דרש	SEEK	205b	3 a
	זרבבל	ZERUBBABEL	279c	
	לא	NOT	520c	
	עלה	GO UP	749c	1 c
	פה	HERE	806a	2
4 3	יהושוע	JOSHUA	221c	3
	זרבבל	ZERUBBABEL	279c	
	יחד	UNION	403a	2 a1
	כורש	CYRUS	468d	
	ל	TO	513b	5 ba
	ל	TO	517d	7 bd
	מלך	KING	573a	5
	שאר	REST	984c	
4 4	בהל	DISMAY	96c	1
	בלה	BE TROUBLED	117a	
	היה	BE	227c	3 5a
	יהודה	JUDAH	397b	13
	עם	PEOPLE	766d	5 c
4 5	דריוש	DARIUS	201d	1
	יעץ	ADVISE	419d	
	עצה	ADVICE	420a	
	כורש	CYRUS	468d	
	מלכות	REIGN	575a	2
	סכר	HIRE	698d	
	פרר	BREAK	830b	2 a
	שכר	HIRE	969a	
4 6	אחשורוש	AHASUERUS	31c	
	תחלה	BEGINNING	321b	
	מלכות	REIGN	575a	2
	שטנה	ACCUSATION	966c	
4 7	ארמית	ARAMAIC	74c	
	ארתחששתא	ARTAXERXES	77a	
	בשלם	BISHLAM	143b	
	טבאל	TABEEL	370b	
	כנת	ASSOCIATE	490c	
	כתב	WRITE	507d	1 c
	כתב	WRITING	508b	2
	מתרדת	MITHREDATH	609c	2
	נשתון	LETTER	677a	
	על	UPON	757c	2 7c b
	שאר	REST	984c	
	תרגם	TRANSLATE	1076b	
	על	TO	1106b	4 a
	שמרין	SAMARIA	1116b	
4 8	שמשי	SHIMSHAI	1039c	
	אגרה	LETTER-MISSIVE	1078b	
	חד	A	1079c	2
	ארתחששתא	ARTAXERXES	1083a	
	בעל	OWNER	1085a	
	טעם	COMMAND	1094c	4
	ירושלם	JERUSALEM	1096b	
	כנמא	AS FOLLOWS	1097b	
	כתב	WRITE	1098a	
	ל	TO	1098b	1
	מלך	KING	1100b	
	ספר	SECRETARY	1104c	
	על	AGAINST	1106c	4 b
	רחום	REHUM	1113a	
	שמשי	SHIMSHAI	1116c	
4 9	ארך	ERECH	74b	
	שמשי	SHIMSHAI	1039c	
	אדין	THEN	1078d	
	אפרסיא	APHARSITES	1082b	
	ארכוי	ARCHEVITES	1083a	
	בעל	OWNER	1085a	
	דהיא	DEHAITES	1087a	
	דיניא	DINAITES	1088c	
	ו	AND	*1090d	
	טרפליא	TARPELITES	1094c	
	טעם	COMMAND	1094c	4
	כנת	ASSOCIATE	1097c	
	ספר	SECRETARY	1104c	
	עלמיא	ELAMITES	1106d	
	שאר	REMAINDER	1114b	
	שושנכיא	SUSIANS	1114d	
	שמשי	SHIMSHAI	1116c	
4 10	אמה	NATION	1081a	
	אסנפר	ASNAPPAR	1082a	
	גלא	REVEAL	1086c	
	המו	THEY	1090c	B
	יקיר	HONOURABLE	1096c	1
	יתב	DWELL	1096c	
	נהר	RIVER	1102c	
	עבר	BEYOND	1105b	
	כענת	NOW	1107b	
	קריה	CITY	1111d	
	רב	GREAT	1112b	2
	שאר	REMAINDER	1114b	
	שאר	REMAINDER	1114b	
	שמרין	SAMARIA	1116b	
4 11	אגרה	LETTER-MISSIVE	1078b	
	אנש	MAN	1081a	2
	דנה	THIS	1089a	A
	מלך	KING	1100b	
	נהר	RIVER	1102c	
	עבד	SLAVE	1105a	
	עבר	BEYOND	1105b	
	על	TO	1106b	4 a
	כענת	NOW	1107b	
	כענת	NOW	*1107b	
	פרשגן	COPY	1109a	
	שלח	SEND	1115c	
4 12	אש	FOUNDATION	1083b	
	אשרנא	WALL	*1083b	
	אתה	COME	1083c	
	באיש	BAD	1084a	
	בנה	BUILD	1084d	
	הוא	COME TO PASS	1090a	2
	חוט	REPAIR	1092b	
	ידע	KNOW	1095a	
	יהודי	JEW	1095c	
	ירושלם	JERUSALEM	1096b	
	כלל	COMPLETE	1097a	
	לות	BESIDE	1099a	
	סלק	COME UP	1104b	
	על	TO	1106b	4 a
	כענת	NOW	*1107b	
	קריה	CITY	1111d	
	שור	WALL	1114d	
4 13	אפתם	TREASURY	1082c	
	בלו	TRIBUTE	1084c	
	בנה	BUILD	1084d	
	די	THAT	1088a	3 a
	דך	THIS	1088c	
	הוא	COME TO PASS	1090a	2
	הלך	TOLL	1090b	
	הן	IF	1090c	1
	ידע	KNOW	1095a	
	כלל	COMPLETE	1097a	
	מלך	KING	1100b	
	מדה	TRIBUTE	1101b	
	נזק	SUFFER INJURY	1102c	
	נתן	GIVE	1103d	3
	כען	NOW	1107b	
	קריה	CITY	1111d	
	שור	WALL	1114d	
4 14	רוח	RESPITE	926c	2
	אריך	FITTING	1082d	
	דנה	THIS	1089a	D
	היכל	PALACE	1090b	1
	חזה	SEE	1092c	2 b
	ידע	KNOW	1095a	
	מלח	SALT	1100a	
	מלח	EAT SALT	1100b	
	כען	NOW	1107b	
	ערוה	DISHONOUR	1107d	
	קבל	BECAUSE THAT	1110b	2 b
	שלח	SEND	1115c	
4 15	אב	FATHER	1078b	2
	בקר	SEEK	1085b	
	גו	MIDST	1086a	A
	די	THAT	1088a	2
	די	THAT	1088b	3 c
	מדינה	DISTRICT	1088c	
	דך	THIS	1088c	
	דכרן	MEMORANDUM	1088d	
	דנה	THIS	1089a	D
	חרב	BE WASTE	1093d	
	ידע	KNOW	1095a	
	יום	DAY	1095c	
	מלך	KING	1100b	
	מן	FROM	1101a	4
	מרד	REBELLIOUS	1101d	
	נזק	SUFFER INJURY	1102d	
	ספר	BOOK	1104c	
	עבד	DO	1104d	2
	על	ON ACCOUNT OF	1106b	1 c
	עלם	PERPETUITY	1106d	
	קריה	CITY	1111d	
	קריה	CITY	1111d	
	אשתדור	REVOLT	1114c	
	שכח	FIND	1115b	
4 16	איתי	THERE IS	1080b	
	אנחנא	WE	1081c	
	אנחנא	WE	*1081c	
	ב	IN	1083d	1
	בנה	BUILD	1084d	
	דך	THIS	1088c	
	הן	IF	1090c	1
	חלק	POSSESSION	1093b	
	ידע	KNOW	1095a	
	כלל	COMPLETE	1097a	
	ל	IN REGARD TO	1098c	4 b
	נהר	RIVER	1102c	
	עבר	BEYOND	1105b	
	קבל	BEFORE	1110a	1 a
	קריה	CITY	1111d	
	שור	WALL	1114d	
4 17	שמשי	SHIMSHAI	1039c	
	בעל	OWNER	1085a	
	טעם	COMMAND	1094c	4
	יתב	DWELL	1096c	2
	כנת	ASSOCIATE	1097c	
	ספר	SECRETARY	1104c	
	עבר	BEYOND	1105b	
	על	TO	1106b	4 a
	כענת	NOW	1107b	
	כענת	NOW	*1107b	
	פתגם	WORD	1109b	
	שאר	REMAINDER	1114b	
	שאר	REMAINDER	1114b	
	שלח	SEND	1115c	
	שלם	PROSPERITY	1116a	
	שמשי	SHIMSHAI	1116c	
4 18	פרש	MAKE DISTINCT	*831d	
	נשתון	LETTER	1103c	
	על	TO	1106b	4 a
	פרש	MAKE DISTINCT	1109a	
	קדם	BEFORE	1110c	1
	קרא	CALL	1111c	
	שלח	SEND	1115c	
4 19	בקר	INQUIRE	1085b	
	דך	THIS	1088c	
	טעם	COMMAND	1094c	4
	יום	DAY	1095c	
	מן	FROM	1101a	2 a
	מן	FROM	1101a	4
	מרד	REBELLION	1101c	
	נשא	LIFT	1103c	
	עבד	DO	1105a	2
	עלם	PERPETUITY	1106d	
	קריה	CITY	1111d	
	שום	MAKE	1113d	
	אשתדור	REVOLT	1114c	
	שכח	FIND	1115b	
4 20	בלו	TRIBUTE	1084c	
	הלך	TOLL	1090b	
	יהב	GIVE	1095b	2
	מנדה	TRIBUTE	1101b	
	עבר	BEYOND	1105b	
	על	OVER	1106b	2
	שליט	HAVING MASTERY	1115d	1 b
	תקף	MIGHTY	1118c	
4 21	אלך	THESE	1080d	
	בטל	CEASE	1084b	
	בנה	BUILD	1084d	
	גבר	MAN	1086a	
	דך	THIS	1088c	
	טעם	COMMAND	1094c	4
	ל	TO	1098c	6
	עד	UNTIL	1105b	2 b
	כען	NOW	1107b	
	קריה	CITY	1111d	
	שום	MAKE	1113d	1
	שום	MAKE	1113d	
4 22	דנה	THIS	1089a	D
	זהר	WARN	1091a	
	חבל	HURT	1092a	
	ל	TO	1098c	6
	מה	WHAT	1099d	3 b
	נזק	SUFFER INJURY	1102d	
	עבד	DO	1104d	2
	על	ON ACCOUNT OF	1106b	1 c
	שגא	GROW GREAT	1113b	
	שלו	NEGLECT	1115c	
4 23	ארתחששתא	ARTAXERXES	77a	
	ארתחששתא	ARTAXERXES	77a	
	שמשי	SHIMSHAI	1039c	
	אדין	THEN	1078d	
	אזל	GO	1079b	1
	בטל	CEASE	1084b	
	בחלו	HASTE	1084b	
	די	THAT	1088b	4 bb
	אדרע	FORCE	1089b	
	המו	THEY	1090c	B
	חיל	POWER	1093a	1
	יהודי	JEW	1095c	
	כנת	ASSOCIATE	1097c	
	נשתון	LETTER	1103c	
	ספר	SECRETARY	1104c	
	על	TO	1106b	4 a
	פרשגן	COPY	1109a	
	קדם	BEFORE	1110c	1

Ch	v.	Heb	Eng	Page	Sec
4	24	קרא	CALL	1111c	
		שמשי	SHIMSHAI	1116c	
		אדין	THEN	1078d	
		אלה	GOD	1080c	2
		בטל	CEASE	1084b	
		בית	HOUSE	1084c	2
		די	WHO	1087d	1 a
		דריוש	DARIUS	1089a	1
		מלכו	REIGN	1100c	4
		עבידה	WORK	1105a	1
		עד	EVEN TO	1105b	1 c
		פרס	PERSIA	1108d	
		שנה	YEAR	1116d	
		תרין	TWO	1118b	
5	1	זכריהו	ZECHARIAH	*272b	1 f
		חגי	HAGGAI	291b	
		אלה	GOD	1080c	2
		בר	SON	1085b	1
		זכריה	ZECHARIAH	1091c	
		חגי	PROPHET	1092a	
		יהודי	JEW	1095c	
		יהוד	JUDAH	1095c	
		ישראל	ISRAEL	1096b	
		על	UPON	1106b	1 a
		על	TO	1106b	4 a
		שם	NAME	1116a	
		נבא	ADDENDA ET CORRIGENDA	1127c	
5	2	יהוצדק	JEHOZADAK	221b	
		יהושוע	JOSHUA	221c	3
		עם	WITH	767b	1 a
		אדין	THEN	1078d	
		אלה	GOD	1080c	2
		אלה	GOD	1080c	2
		בנה	BUILD	1084d	
		בר	SON	1085b	1
		די	THAT	1088a	2
		זרבבל	ZERUBBABEL	1091d	
		יוצדק	JOZADAK	1095c	
		ישוע	JESHUA	1096b	
		סעד	SUPPORT	1104b	
		עם	WITH	1107a	1 a
		קום	ARISE	1110d	3
5	3	אמר	SAY	1081b	1
		אשרנא	WALL	1083b	
		אתה	COME	1083c	
		בנה	BUILD	1084d	
		דנה	THIS	1089a	A
		זמן	TIME	1091c	
		כלל	COMPLETE	1097a	
		כן	THUS	1097b	
		כנת	ASSOCIATE	1097c	
		ל	TO	1098c	6
		מן	WHO	1100d	1
		עבר	BEYOND	1105b	
		פחה	GOVERNOR	1108b	
		שום	MAKE	1113d	1
		שתרבוזני	SHETHAR-BOZENAI	1117c	
		תתני	TATTENAI	1118d	
5	4	מי	WHO	566b	A
		אדין	THEN	1078d	
		אמר	SAY	1081b	1
		אנן	THEY	1081c	
		בנה	BUILD	1084d	
		בנין	A BUILDING	1084d	
		גבר	MAN	1086a	
		דנה	THIS	1089a	A
		הוא	HE	*1090a	
		כנמא	AS FOLLOWS	1097b	
		מן	WHO	1100d	1
		שם	NAME	1116a	
5	5	אדין	THEN	*1078d	
		בטל	CEASE	1084b	
		דנה	THIS	1089a	D
		הוא	COME TO PASS	1090a	2
		הלך	GO	1090b	
		המו	THEY	1090c	B
		מעם	JUDGMENT	1094c	3
		יהודי	JEW	1095c	
		יהודי	JEW	1095c	
		ל	TO	1098b	1
		נשתון	LETTER	1103c	
		עד	UNTIL	1105d	2 b
		עין	EYE	1105d	
		על	TO	1106b	4 a
		שיב	BE HOARY	1114a	
		תוב	RETURN	1117d	2
5	6	אגרה	LETTER-MISSIVE	1078b	
		אפרסכיא	APHARSACHITES	1082c	
		די	WHO	1087d	1 a
		כנת	ASSOCIATE	1097c	
		עבר	BEYOND	1105b	
		על	TO	1106b	4 a
		פחה	GOVERNOR	1108b	
		פרשגן	COPY	1109a	
		שלח	SEND	1115c	
		שתרבוזני	SHETHAR-BOZENAI	1117c	
		תתני	TATTENAI	1118d	
5	7	גו	MIDST	1086a	A
		גמר	COMPLETE	*1086c	
		דנה	THIS	1089a	C
		דנה	THIS	1089a	C
		כל	ALL	1097b	3
		כתב	WRITE	1098a	
		ל	TO	1098b	
		ל	TO	1098b	1
		פתגם	WORD	1109b	
		שלח	SEND	1115c	
		שלם	PROSPERITY	1116a	
5	8	אבן	STONE	1078b	2
		אזל	GO	1079b	1
		אספרנא	THOROUGHLY	1082a	
		אע	WOOD	1082b	1
		בנה	BUILD	1084d	
		גלל	ROLLING	1086c	
		מדינה	DISTRICT	1088c	
		דך	THIS	1088c	
		הוא	COME TO PASS	1090a	2
		הוא	HE	1090a	
		יד	HAND	1094d	1
		ידע	KNOW	1095a	
		יהוד	JUDAH	1095c	
		כתל	WALL	1098b	
		ל	IN REGARD TO	1098c	4 c
		עבד	DO	1105a	2
		עבידה	WORK	1105a	1
		צלח	PROSPER	1109d	2
		רב	GREAT	1112b	2
		שום	MAKE	1113d	
5	9	אדין	THEN	1078d	
		אלך	THESE	1080d	
		אמר	SAY	1081b	1
		אשרנא	WALL	1083b	
		בנה	BUILD	1084d	
		דנה	THIS	1089a	A
		כלל	COMPLETE	1097a	
		כנמא	AS FOLLOWS	*1097b	
		כנמא	AS FOLLOWS	1097b	
		מן	WHO	1100d	1
		שום	MAKE	1113d	1
		שיב	BE HOARY	1114a	
		שאל	ASK	1114a	2
5	10	אף	ALSO	1082b	
		ב	IN	1083d	1
		גבר	MAN	1086a	
		ידע	KNOW	1095a	
		כתב	WRITE	1098a	
		ראש	HEAD	1112a	3
		שאל	ASK	1114a	2
		שם	NAME	1116a	
5	11	ל	TO	*513d	5 cb e
		אלה	GOD	1080c	
		אמר	SAY	1081a	1
		אנחנא	WE	1081c	
		ארע	EARTH	1083a	
		בנה	BUILD	1084d	
		בנה	BUILD	1084d	
		המו	THEY	1090c	A
		ישראל	ISRAEL	1096b	
		כלל	COMPLETE	1097a	
		כנמא	AS FOLLOWS	1097b	
		ל	IN REGARD TO	1098c	4 c
		עבד	SLAVE	1105a	
		פתגם	WORD	1109b	
		קדמה	FORMER TIME	1110c	
		רב	GREAT	1112b	2
		שגיא	MUCH	1113c	2
		שמין	HEAVENS	1116b	2
		שנה	YEAR	1116d	
		תוב	RETURN	1117d	2
5	12	שתר	BURST	979c	
		אב	FATHER	1078b	2
		אלה	GOD	1080c	2
		ב	IN	1083d	2
		גלא	REVEAL	1086c	
		די	THAT	1088b	4 ba
		המו	THEY	1090c	B
		יד	HAND	1094d	2
		כשדי	CHALDEAN	1098a	1
		להן	BUT	1099a	2
		נבוכדנצר	NEBUCHADNEZZAR	1102a	
		סתר	DESTROY	1104d	
		עם	PEOPLE	1107a	
		רגז	ENRAGE	1112c	
		שמין	HEAVENS	1116b	2
5	13	חד	ONE	1079c	1
		בנה	BUILD	1084d	
		ברם	ONLY	1085c	
		כורש	CYRUS	1096d	
		ל	IN REGARD TO	1098c	4 c
		שום	MAKE	1113d	1
		שנה	YEAR	1116d	
5	14	אף	ALSO	1082b	
		דהב	GOLD	1087a	
		די	THAT	1088a	2
		היכל	TEMPLE	1090b	2 b
		היכל	TEMPLE	1090b	2 b
		המו	THEY	1090c	B
		יבל	BEAR ALONG	1094d	
		יהב	GIVE	1095b	
		כסף	SILVER	1097c	1
		מאן	VESSEL	1099c	
		נבוכדנצר	NEBUCHADNEZZAR	1102a	
		נפק	GO FORTH	1103b	
		פחה	GOVERNOR	1108b	
		שום	MAKE	1113d	2
		שם	NAME	1116a	
		ששבצר	ADDENDA ET CORRIGENDA	1127c	
5	15	אזל	GO	1079b	1
		אל	THESE	1080b	
		אלה	THESE	1080c	
		אמר	SAY	1081b	1
		אתר	PLACE	1083d	A
		בנה	BUILD	1084d	
		היכל	TEMPLE	1090b	2 a
		המו	THEY	1090c	B
		מאן	VESSEL	1099c	
		נחת	DESCEND	1102d	
		נשא	LIFT	1103c	
5	16	ששבצר	SHESHBAZZAR	*1058c	
		אדין	THEN	1078d	
		אשרנא	WALL	*1083b	
		אש	FOUNDATION	1083b	
		אתה	COME	1083c	
		בנה	BUILD	1084d	
		דך	THIS	1088c	
		חוט	REPAIR	1092c	
		יהב	GIVE	1095b	2
		עד	EVEN TO	1105b	1 c
		כען	NOW	1107b	
		שלם	BE COMPLETE	1115d	
		ששבצר	ADDENDA ET CORRIGENDA	1127c	
5	17	על	UPON	758a	2 8
		איתי	THERE IS	1080b	
		בית	HOUSE	1084c	1
		בנה	BUILD	1084d	
		בקר	INQUIRE	1085b	
		גנז	TREASURE	1086d	
		דך	THIS	1088c	
		דנה	THIS	1089a	D
		הן	IF	1090c	1
		הן	WHETHER	1090d	3
		טב	GOOD	1094b	
		מן	FROM	1101a	2 a
		על	ON ACCOUNT OF	1106b	1 c
		על	TO	1106c	5
		כען	NOW	1107b	
		רעו	GOOD PLEASURE	1113b	
		שום	MAKE	1113d	
		שלח	SEND	1115c	
		תמה	THERE	1118b	
6	1	אדין	THEN	1078d	
		בית	HOUSE	1084c	1
		בקר	INQUIRE	1085b	
		גנז	TREASURE	1086c	
		די	WHO	1087d	1 a
		נחת	DESCEND	1102d	
		ספר	BOOK	1104c	
		שום	MAKE	1113d	1
		תמה	THERE	1118b	
6	2	חד	A	1079c	2
		אחמתא	ECBATANA	1079c	
		בירתא	CASTLE	1084c	
		גו	MIDST	1086a	A
		מגלה	ROLL	1086c	
		די	WHO	1087d	1 a
		מדינה	DISTRICT	1088c	
		דכרון	MEMORANDUM	1088d	
		כן	THUS	1097b	
		כתב	WRITE	1098a	
		מדי	MEDIA	1099c	2
		שכח	FIND	1115b	
6	3	חד	ONE	1079c	1
		אמה	CUBIT	1081a	
		אש	FOUNDATION	1083b	
		אתר	PLACE	1083d	A
		בנה	BUILD	1084d	
		דבח	SACRIFICE	1087a	
		דבח	SACRIFICE	1087a	
		די	WHO	1087d	1 a
		ל	IN REGARD TO	1098c	4 c
		פתי	BREADTH	1109b	
		רום	HEIGHT	1112d	
		שום	MAKE	1113d	1
		שתין	SIXTY	1114d	
		שנה	YEAR	1116d	
6	4	אבן	STONE	1078b	2
		אע	WOOD	1082b	1
		בית	HOUSE	1084c	1
		גלל	ROLLING	1086c	
		די	THAT	1088a	2
		חדת	NEW	1092a	
		יהב	GIVE	1095b	2
		נדבך	ROW	1102b	
		נפקה	OUTLAY	1103b	
		תלת	THREE	1118a	
6	5	אף	ALSO	1082b	
		אתר	PLACE	1083d	A
		דהב	GOLD	1087a	
		היכל	TEMPLE	1090b	2 a
		הלך	GO	1090b	
		יבל	BEAR ALONG	1094d	
		כסף	SILVER	1097c	1
		ל	IN REGARD TO	1098c	4 b
		מאן	VESSEL	1099c	
		נבוכדנצר	NEBUCHADNEZZAR	1102a	
		נחת	DESCEND	1102d	
		נפק	GO FORTH	1103b	
		תוב	RETURN	1117d	1
6	6	אפרסתכיא	APHARSATHCHITES	1082c	
		די	WHO	1087d	1 a
		הוא	COME TO PASS	1090a	2
		כנת	ASSOCIATE	1097c	

EZRA

Ch	v.	Heb	Eng	Page	Sec
		ל	IN REGARD TO	1098c	4 b
		מן	FROM	1101a	1 a
		עבר	BEYOND	1105b	
		כען	NOW	1107b	
		פחה	GOVERNOR	1108b	
		רחיק	FAR	1113a	
		שתרבוזני	SHETHAR-BOZENAI	1117c	
		תמה	THERE	1118b	
		תתני	TATTENAI	1118d	
6	7	ל	TO	514d	5 fe
		אתר	PLACE	1083d	A
		בנה	BUILD	1084d	
		דך	THIS	1088c	
		יהודי	JEW	1095c	
		עבידה	WORK	1105a	1
		פחה	GOVERNOR	1108b	
		ארבע	FOUR	1112c	1
		שיב	BE HOARY	1114a	
		שבק	LEAVE	1114c	
6	8	לא	NOT	518a	1 ab
		אלך	THESE	1080d	
		אלך	THESE	1080d	
		אספרנא	THOROUGHLY	1082a	
		בטל	CEASE	1084d	
		בנה	BUILD	1084d	
		גבר	MAN	1086a	
		די	WHO	1087d	1 b
		די	WHO	1087d	1 a
		דך	THIS	1088c	
		הוא	COME TO PASS	1090a	2
		ו	AND	1091a	A
		יהב	GIVE	1095b	2
		יהודי	JEW	1095c	
		ל	IN REGARD TO	1098c	4 a
		ל	TO	1098c	6
		לא	NOT	1098d	
		מה	WHAT	*1099c	
		מה	WHAT	1099d	2
		מנדה	TRIBUTE	1101b	
		נכס	PROPERTY	1103a	
		נפקה	OUTLAY	1103b	
		עבר	DO	1104d	2
		עבר	BEYLOND	1105b	
		עם	WITH	1107a	1 b
		שום	MAKE	1113d	
		שיב	BE HOARY	1114a	
6	9	אלה	GOD	1080c	2
		מאמר	WORD	1081b	
		אמר	LAMB	1081b	
		ב	WITH	1083d	5
		בר	SON	1085b	2
		די	WHO	1087d	1 a
		דכר	RAM	1088d	
		הוא	COME TO PASS	1090a	2
		ו	AND	*1090d	
		ו	AND	1091a	A
		חנטה	WHEAT	1093b	
		חמר	WINE	1093b	
		חשחה	THING NEEDED	1093d	
		יהב	GIVE	1095b	1
		יום	DAY	1095c	
		ך	LIKE	1096c	
		כהן	PRIEST	1096d	
		ל	IN REGARD TO	1098c	4 d
		מה	WHAT	1099d	2
		מלח	SALT	1100a	
		משח	OIL	1101d	
		עלת	BURNT-OFFERING	1106a	
		שלו	NEGLECT	1115c	
		שמין	HEAVENS	1116b	2
		תור	BULLOCK	1117d	
6	10	אלה	GOD	1080c	2
		בר	SON	1085b	1
		די	THAT	1088b	3 c
		חי	LIVING	1092d	2
		ל	TO	1098b	1
		ל	IN REGARD TO	1098c	4 d
		ניחוח	SOOTHING	1102d	
		צלא	PRAY	1109d	
		קרב	APPROACH	1111c	1
		שמין	HEAVENS	1116b	2
6	11	אנש	MAN	1081d	1
		אע	WOOD	1082d	1
		בית	HOUSE	1084c	1
		דנה	THIS	1089d	D
		זקף	LIFT UP	1091d	
		כל	ALL	1097a	2
		מחא	SMITE	1099d	
		נולו	REFUSE-HEAP	1102c	
		נסח	PULL AWAY	1103a	
		עבד	MAKE	1105a	1
		פתגם	COMMAND	1109b	
		שום	MAKE	1113d	
		שנא	CHANGE	1116d	
6	12	אנה	I	1081c	
		אספרנא	THOROUGHLY	1082a	
		דך	THIS	1088c	
		חבל	DESTROY	1091d	
		יד	HAND	1094d	1
		כל	ALL	1097a	2
		מגר	OVERTHROW	1099c	
		עבר	DO	1105a	2
		עם	PEOPLE	1107a	
		שום	MAKE	1113d	1
		שכן	DWELL	1115b	
		שלח	SEND	1115c	
		שם	NAME	1116a	
		שנא	CHANGE	1116d	
		תמה	THERE	1118b	
6	13	אספרנא	THOROUGHLY	1082a	
		כנמא	ACCORDINGLY	1097b	
		כנת	ASSOCIATE	1097c	
		עבר	DO	1104d	2
		עבר	BEYLOND	1105b	
		פחה	GOVERNOR	1108b	
		קבל	BECAUSE THAT	1110b	1 b
		שלח	SEND	1115c	
		שתרבוזני	SHETHAR-BOZENAI	1117c	
		תתני	TATTENAI	1118d	
6	14	זכריהו	ZECHARIAH	*272b	1 f
		חגי	HAGGAI	291b	
		מן	ON ACCOUNT OF	580c	2 g
		אלה	GOD	1080c	2
		ב	THROUGH	1084a	6
		בנה	BUILD	1084d	
		בר	SON	1085b	1
		זכריה	ZECHARIAH	1091c	
		חגי	PROPHET	1092a	
		טעם	COMMAND	1094c	4
		טעם	COMMAND	1094c	4
		יהודי	JEW	1095c	
		ישראל	ISRAEL	1096b	
		כלל	COMPLETE	1097a	
		מן	AT	1101a	2 d
		נבואה	PROPHESYING	1102a	
		פרס	PERSIA	1108d	
		צלח	PROSPER	1109d	2
		שיב	BE HOARY	1114a	
6	15	אדר	ADAR	1078d	
		די	WHO	1087d	1 a
		הוא	HE	1090c	
		יום	DAY	1095c	
		ירח	MONTH	1096b	
		ל	IN REGARD TO	1098c	4 c
		מלכו	REIGN	1100c	4
		עד	EVEN TO	1105b	1 c
		שת	SIX	1114d	
		שיציא	FINISH	1115a	
		שנה	YEAR	1116d	
		תלת	THREE	1118a	
6	16	בר	SON	1085b	1
		בר	SON	1085b	1
		גלו	EXILE	1086c	
		חדוה	JOY	1092a	
		חנכה	DEDICATION	1093b	
		ישראל	ISRAEL	1096b	
		כהן	PRIEST	1096d	
		לוי	LEVITE	1099a	
		עבד	MAKE	1104d	1
		שאר	REMAINDER	1114b	
6	17	אמר	LAMB	1081b	
		דכר	RAM	1088d	
		חטיא	SIN-OFFERING	1092d	
		חנכה	DEDICATION	1093b	
		ל	IN REGARD TO	1098c	4 e
		ל	IN REGARD TO	1098c	4 d
		מאה	HUNDRED	1099b	
		מאה	HUNDRED	1099b	
		מאה	HUNDRED	1099b	
		מנין	NUMBER	1101b	
		על	ON ACCOUNT OF	1106b	1 d
		עז	GOAT	1107b	
		עשר	TEN	1108a	
		צפיר	HE-GOAT	1110a	
		קרב	APPROACH	1111c	1
		שבט	TRIBE	1114b	
		תור	BULLOCK	1117d	
		תרין	TWO	1118b	
6	18	אלה	GOD	1080c	2
		מחלקה	CLASS	1093b	
		טב	GOOD	*1094b	
		ך	LIKE	1096c	
		כהן	PRIEST	1096d	
		כתב	WRITING	1098a	2 b
		לוי	LEVITE	1099a	
		משה	MOSES	1101d	
		ספר	BOOK	1104c	
		עבידה	SERVICE	1105a	2
		על	OVER	1106b	2
		פלגה	DIVISION	1108c	
6	19	קום	ARISE	1111a	4
		בן	SON	121c	7 a
		יום	DAY	*398c	2 e
		פסח	PASSOVER	820b	3
6	20	בן	SON	121c	7 a
		מהר	BE CLEAN	372c	1 a
		כהן	PRIEST	464a	7
		פסח	PASSOVER	820b	2
		שחט	SLAUGHTER	1006b	2
		ל	TO	1098b	1
6	21	בדל	BE DIVIDED	95c	1 a
		גוי	NATION	156d	1 c
		דרש	SEEK	205b	3 a
		ממאה	UNCLEANNESS	380a	5
		שוב	TURN BACK	997a	1
6	22	אשור	ASSYRIA	78d	4
		חג	FESTIVAL-GATHERING	291a	1 b2
		חג	FESTIVAL-GATHERING	291b	1 b
		חזק	BE FIRM	304d	2
		יום	DAY	398c	2 c
		מלאכה	WORK	522b	6 b
		סבב	TURN ABOUT	686c	1 a
		מצה	UNLEAVENED BREAD	695b	
		על	UPON	757c	2 7c c
		שמח	REJOICE	970c	
		ל	IN REGARD TO	1098c	4 b
7	1	אחר	AFTER	29d	2 b
		ארתחששתא	ARTAXERXES	77a	
		ארתחששתא	ARTAXERXES	77a	
		דבר	WORD	183c	4 4
		חלקיהו	HILKIAH	324d	2
		מלכות	REIGN	575a	2
		עזרא	EZRA	740d	1
		עזריהו	AZARIAH	741b	5 c
		שריה	SERAIAH	976a	5 b
7	2	אחיטוב	AHITUB	27a	2
		שלום	SHALLUM	1024b	1
7	3	אמריהו	AMARIAH	57c	1
		מריות	MERAIOTH	599a	1 a
		עזריהו	AZARIAH	741b	5 a
7	4	בקי	BUKKI	131c	2
		זרחיה	ZERAHIAH	280c	1
7	5	אבישוע	ABISHUA	4d	1
		אלעזר	ELEAZAR	46b	A
		כהן	PRIEST	464c	8
		ראש	HEAD	911a	3 e
7	6	הוא	HE, SHE, IT	215c	1 e
		יד	HAND	390a	1 e2
		תורה	LAW	436b	2 b3
		מהיר	SKILLED	555b	
		משה	MOSES	602a	2
		נתן	GIVE	678d	1 e
		ספר	ENUMERATOR	708c	3
		עזרא	EZRA	740d	1
		עלה	GO UP	748b	1 a
		על	UPON	753a	2 la b
7	7	כהן	PRIEST	464a	7
		נתינים	NETHINIM	682a	
		עלה	GO UP	748b	1 c
7	8	חמישי	FIFTH	332c	1
		שביעי	SEVENTH	988d	2
		שנה	YEAR	1040c	
7	9	חמישי	FIFTH	332c	1
		טוב	PLEASANT	374d	9 b
		יד	HAND	390a	1 e2
		יסד	FOUND	413d	
		יסד	FOUNDATION	414b	1
		מעלה	STEP	752b	4
		על	UPON	753a	2 la b
7	10	דרש	SEEK	205c	6
		חק	SOMETHING PRESCRIBED	349c	6 d
		תורה	LAW	436b	2 b3
		כן	ESTABLISH	466c	3
		לב	HEART	523d	24
		למד	LEARN	540d	
		עזרא	EZRA	740d	1
		משפט	JUDGMENT	1048d	3
7	11	ארתחששתא	ARTAXERXES	77a	
		דבר	WORD	183a	2 2
		חק	SOMETHING PRESCRIBED	349c	7 g
		כהן	PRIEST	464b	7
		נשתון	LETTER	677a	
		ספר	ENUMERATOR	708c	3
		על	UPON	753c	2 1c
		פרשגן	COPY	832b	
		מצוה	COMMANDMENT	846c	2 b1
7	12	גמר	COMPLETE	1086c	
		דת	LAW	1089b	3
		כהן	PRIEST	1096d	
		ל	TO	1098b	1
		מלך	KING	*1100b	
		ספר	SCRIBE	1104c	
		עזרא	EZRA	1105d	
		כענת	NOW	1107b	
		שמין	HEAVENS	1116b	2
7	13	הלך	GO	1090b	
		הלך	GO	1090b	
		ישראל	ISRAEL	1096b	
		כהן	PRIEST	1096d	
		לוי	LEVITE	1099a	
		מלכו	KINGDOM	1100c	3
		נדב	VOLUNTEER	1102b	1
		עם	PEOPLE	1107a	
		שום	MAKE	1113d	
7	14	בקר	INQUIRE	1085b	
		דת	LAW	1089b	3
		יד	HAND	1094d	1
		יהוד	JUDAH	1095c	
		יעט	COUNSELLOR	1096a	
		ל	IN REGARD TO	1098c	4 a
		על	ON ACCOUNT OF	1106b	1 e
		קבל	BECAUSE THAT	1110b	2 b
		קדם	BEFORE	1110c	2
		שבע	SEVEN	1114b	
		שלח	SEND	1115c	
7	15	אלה	GOD	1080c	2
		דהב	GOLD	1087a	
		יבל	BEAR ALONG	1094d	
		יעט	COUNSELLOR	1096a	
		ישראל	ISRAEL	1096b	
		כסף	SILVER	1097c	2
		נדב	OFFER FREELY	1102b	2

Ch	v.	Heb	Eng	Page	Sec
7	16	משכן	ABODE	1115c	
		מדינה	DISTRICT	1088c	
		כהן	PRIEST	1096d	
		כסף	SILVER	1097c	2
		נדב	OFFER FREELY	1102b	2
		נדב	OFFER FREELY	1102b	2
		עם	PEOPLE	1107a	
7	17	שכח	FIND	1115b	
		אמר	LAMB	1081b	
		אספרנא	THOROUGHLY	1082a	
		ב	WITH	1083d	4
		מזבח	ALTAR	1087a	
		דכר	RAM	1088c	
		המו	THEY	1090c	B
		כסף	SILVER	1097c	2
		מנחה	OFFERING	1101c	2
		נסך	DRINK OFFERING	1103a	
		קבל	BECAUSE OF	1110b	2a
		קנא	BUY	1111b	
		קרב	APPROACH	1111c	
		תור	BULLOCK	1117d	
7	18	על	UPON	758a	28
		אח	BROTHER	1079c	
		ב	WITH	1083d	4
		ב	IN	1084a	8
		דהב	GOLD	1087a	
		די	WHO	1087d	1 b
		יוב	BE PLEASING	1095d	
		כסף	SILVER	1097c	2
		מה	WHAT	1099d	2
		עבד	DO	1104d	2
		על	TO	1106c	5
		רענ	GOOD PLEASURE	1113b	
		שאר	REMAINDER	1114b	
7	19	אלה	GOD	1080c	2
		ל	IN REGARD TO	1098c	4 d
		מאן	VESSEL	1099c	
		פלחן	SERVICE	1108c	
		שלם	BE COMPLETE	1116a	
7	20	בית	HOUSE	1084c	1
		גנז	TREASURE	1086d	
		חשחו	THINGS NEEDED	1093d	
		ל	TO	1098b	1
		נפל	FALL	1103a	3
		נתן	GIVE	1103d	3
		שאר	REMAINDER	1114b	
7	21	אנה	I	1081c	
		אנה	I	1081c	
		אספרנא	THOROUGHLY	1082a	
		ארתחששתא	ARTAXERXES	1083a	
		גזבר	TREASURER	1086b	
		דת	LAW	1089b	3
		כהן	PRIEST	1096d	
		ספר	SCRIBE	1104c	
		עבר	DO	1105a	2
		עבר	BEYLOND	1105b	
		עזרא	EZRA	1105d	
		שום	MAKE	1113d	
		שאל	ASK	1114a	1
		שמין	HEAVENS	1116b	2
7	22	בת	BATH	1085d	
		די	WHO	1087d	1 a
		חנטה	WHEAT	1093b	
		חמר	WINE	1093b	
		כור	KOR	1096d	
		כסף	SILVER	1097c	2
		ככר	TALENT	1098a	
		כתב	WRITING	1098a	2 b
		מאה	HUNDRED	1099b	
		מלח	SALT	1100a	
		משח	OIL	1101d	
		עד	EVEN TO	1105b	1 b
7	23	מה	HOW	554b	4 d
		אדרזדא	CORRECTLY	1079a	
		בר	SON	1085b	1
		די	WHO	1087d	1 a
		די	THAT	*1088b	3 c
		הוא	COME TO PASS	1089d	
		טעם	COMMAND	1094c	4
		כל	ALL	1097a	2
		ל	IN REGARD TO	1098c	4 d
		מה	WHAT	1099d	3 b
		מלכו	KINGDOM	1100c	3
		מן	AT	1101a	2 d
		עבר	DO	1105a	2
		על	AGAINST	1106c	4 b
		קצף	WRATH	1111c	
		שמין	HEAVENS	1116b	2
7	24	בלו	TRIBUTE	1084b	
		הלך	TOLL	1090b	
		זמר	SINGER	1091c	
		ידע	KNOW	1095a	
		כהן	PRIEST	1096d	
		לוי	LEVITE	1099a	
		מנדה	TRIBUTE	1101b	
		נתינין	NETHININ	1103c	
		על	UPON	1106b	1 a
		פלח	SERVE	1108c	2
		רמא	THROW	1113a	2
		שליט	RULING	1115d	3
		תרע	PORTER	1118d	
7	25	אנתה	THOU	1082a	
		די	WHO	1087d	1 a
		דין	JUDGE	1088b	
		דין	JUDGE	1088c	
		דת	LAW	1089b	3
		חכמה	WISDOM	1093a	
		יד	HAND	1094d	1
		ידע	KNOW	1095a	
		ידע	KNOW	1095a	
		ידע	KNOW	1095a	
		ל	MARK OF ACCUSA-TIVE	1098b	2
		מנה	NUMBER	1101b	
		עבר	BEYLOND	1105b	
		עזרא	EZRA	1105d	
		עם	PEOPLE	1107a	
7	26	שפט	JUDGE	1117a	
		אספרנא	THOROUGHLY	1082a	
		אסור	BOND	1082b	
		דין	JUDGEMENT	1088b	
		דת	LAW	1089b	3
		דת	DECREE	1089b	1
		הוא	COME TO PASS	1090a	2
		הן	WHETHER	1090d	2
		כל	ALL	1097a	2
		מות	DEATH	1099d	
		מן	FROM	1101a	1 d
		נכס	PROPERTY	1103a	
		עבד	DO	1104d	2
		עבר	DO	1105a	2
		ענש	CONFISCATION	1107b	
		שרשו	BANISHMENT	1117b	
7	27	ברך	BLESS	138c	2
		זה	THIS	262a	6 d
		לב	HEART	525a	2 4
7	28	גבור	STRONG	150b	2
		יהוה	YAHWEH	219a	2 1f
		חזק	BE FIRM	305b	1
		חסד	GOODNESS	339a	2 1a
		יד	HAND	390a	1 e2
		יעץ	ADVISE	419d	
		ל	TO	514d	5 fe
		נטה	BEND	641a	3 f
		על	UPON	758a	28
		קבץ	GATHER	867d	2
8	1	ארתחששתא	ARTAXERXES	77a	
		תיחיש	BE ENROLLED	405b	
		מלכות	REIGN	575a	2
		עלה	GO UP	748b	1 a
		ראש	HEAD	911a	3 f
8	2	איתמר	ITHAMAR	16a	
		גרשם	GERSHOM	177a	3
		דנאל	DANIEL	193b	2
		חטוש	HATTUSH	310d	1
8	3	זכר	MALE	271c	11 b
		זכריהו	ZECHARIAH	*272b	2a
		חמשים	FIFTY	332c	4 a
		תיחיש	ENROLLMENT	405c	
		עם	WITH	767b	1 a
		פרעש	PAROSH	829b	1
		שכניה	SHECANIAH	1016a	1
8	4	אליהועיני	ELIEHOENAI	41b	2
		זכר	MALE	271c	11 b
		זרחיה	ZERAHIAH	280c	2
		מאה	HUNDRED	548a	1 b2
		עם	WITH	767b	1 a
		עשר	TEN	796c	2 b
		פחתמואב	PAHATH-MOAB	809b	
8	5	זכר	MALE	271c	11 b
		יחזיל	JAHAZIEL	303c	5
		עם	WITH	767b	1 a
		שכניה	SHECANIAH	1016a	1
8	6	יהונתן	JOHATHAN	221a	3
		זכר	MALE	271c	11 b
		עבד	EBED	714d	2
		עדין	ADIN	726d	1
		עם	WITH	767b	1 a
8	7	זכר	MALE	271c	11 b
		ישעיה	JESHAIAH	447d	2
		עילם	ELAM	743d	1 c
		עם	WITH	767b	1 a
		עתליה	ATHALIAH	801a	2 b
		שבעים	SEVENTY	988c	1 b
		זבדיהו	ZEBADIAH	256c	6
8	8	זכר	MALE	271c	11 b
		מיכאל	MICHAEL	567c	0
		עם	WITH	767b	1 a
		שמנים	EIGHTY	1033b	
		שפטיה	SHEPHATIAH	1049b	1 d1
8	9	בכה	WEEP	113c	3
		יואב	JOAB	222a	3
		זכר	MALE	271c	11 b
		יחיאל	JEHIEL	313d	8
		עבדיהו	OBADIAH	716a	28
		עם	WITH	767b	1 a
		שמנה	EIGHT	1033a	2 b
8	10	זכר	MALE	271c	11 b
		יוספיה	JOSIPHIAH	415d	
		עם	WITH	767b	1 a
		ששים	SIXTY	995d	
		שלמות	SHELOMOTH	1025a	3
8	11	בבי	BEBAI	93c	
		זכר	MALE	271c	11 b
		זכריהו	ZECHARIAH	*272b	2 b
		עם	WITH	767b	1 a
8	12	יהוחנן	JEHOHANAN	220b	3
		זכר	MALE	271c	11 b
		עם	WITH	767b	1 a
		עשר	TEN	797a	3 c
		קטן	HAKKATAN	882a	
8	13	אדניהו	ADONIJAH	11d	3
		אדניקם	ADONIKAM	12a	D
		אליפלט	ELIPHELET	45d	7
		זכר	MALE	271c	11 b
		יעיאל	JEIEL	418b	2 a
		עם	WITH	767b	1 a
		שמעיה	SHEMAIAH	1035d	8 a
8	14	בגוי	BIGVAI	94a	1
		זבוד	ZABBUD	256b	
		זכר	MALE	271c	1 b
		זכור	ZACCUR	271d	4
		עותי	UTHAI	736d	2
		עם	WITH	767b	1 a
		שבעים	SEVENTY	988c	1 b
8	15	אהוא	AHAVA	13c	
		בין	DISCERN	106c	3 c
		בן	SON	121a	1 je
		חנה	DECLINE	333c	2 b
		חנה	DECLINE	333c	2 c2
		כהן	PRIEST	464b	7
		לוי	LEVI	532c	1 c
		קבץ	GATHER	867d	2
8	16	אליעזר	ELIEZER	45c	G
		אלנתן	ELNATHAN	46b	B
		אריאל	ARIEL	72a	2
		בין	DISCERN	107a	3 e
		יהויריב	JEHOIARIB	220d	2
		זכריהו	ZECHARIAH	*272b	2 a
		ל	TO	512a	3 b
		נתן	NATHAN	682a	6
		יריב	JARIB	937b	2
		משלם	MESHULLAM	1024c	8 b
		שמעיה	SHEMAIAH	1035d	7 g
8	17	אדו	IDDO	9a	
		יצא	BRING OUT	424d	1 h
		כספיא	CASIPHIA	494d	
		נתינים	NETHINIM	682a	
		נתינים	NETHINIM	682a	
		צוה	CHARGE	846a	4 c
		שרת	SERVE	1057b	2 b
8	18	טוב	PLEASANT	374d	9 b
		יד	HAND	390a	1 e2
		לוי	LEVI	532c	1 a
		מחלי	MAHLI	563a	1
		על	UPON	753a	2 la b
		סכל	PRUDENCE	968c	1
		שמנה	EIGHT	1033a	2 a
8	19	חשביהו	HASHABIAH	364a	6
		ישעיה	JESHAIAH	448a	3
		מררי	MERARI	601b	
8	20	לוי	LEVITE	533a	3 2b
		נתן	PUT	680d	2 c
		נתינים	NETHINIM	682a	
		עבדה	LABOR	715b	2
		שר	CHIEFTAIN	978b	2 a
		שם	NAME	1028a	2 a
8	21	אהוא	AHAVA	13c	
		טף	CHILDREN	382a	
		ישר	STRAIGHT	449a	1
		נהר	STREAM	625d	1
		ענה	BE BOWED DOWN	776c	3
		צום	FASTING	847b	
		רכוש	PROPERTY	940d	1
8	22	בוש	BE ASHAMED	101d	3
		בקש	SEEK	134d	3 c
		דרך	WAY	202d	1
		טובה	WELFARE	375d	3
		יד	HAND	390a	1 e2
		עז	STRENGTH	739b	2
		עזר	HELP	740b	
		על	UPON	753a	2 la b
		פרש	HORSEMAN	832b	
		שאל	ASK	981c	1
8	23	בקש	SEEK	135a	6
		זה	THIS	262a	6 f
		עתר	PRAY	801c	
		צום	FAST	847a	
8	24	בדל	BE DIVIDED	95b	2
		חשביהו	HASHABIAH	364a	6
		כהן	PRIEST	464b	7
		ל	TO	511d	1 i
		שר	CHIEFTAIN	978b	5
8	25	ה	THE	209c	3
		זהב	GOLD	263a	6
		זהב	GOLD	263c	1
		יעץ	ADVISE	419d	
		כסף	SILVER	494c	9
		מצא	FIND	594b	2 e
		רום	BE HIGH	927d	3 a
		תרומה	OFFERING	929b	1
		שקל	WEIGH	1053c	1
		שקל	WEIGH	1053c	1
8	26	חמשים	FIFTY	332c	4 a
		כסף	SILVER	494c	8
		ל	TO	514c	5 fb
		מאה	HUNDRED	547d	1 a4
		מאה	HUNDRED	547d	1 a1
		שקל	WEIGH	1053c	1
8	27	דרכמון	DRACHMA	204b	
		זהב	GOLD	263c	9 d
		חמודה	DESIRABLENESS	326d	
		טוב	PLEASANT	374b	3 e
		כפור	BOWL	499b	
		נחשת	COPPER	638d	1
		צהב	GLEAM	843c	
8	28	נדבה	FREEWILL-OFFER-ING	621d	2 a

EZRA

Ch	v	Heb	Eng	Page	Sec
		רביעי	FOURTH	918a	1
		שר	CHIEFTAIN	978d	6
		שוב	TURN BACK	999d	6 a
		שפט	JUDGE	1047d	2 b
10	15	יהונתן	JOHATHAN	221a	4
		יחזיה	JAHZEIAH	303c	
		לוי	LEVITE	532d	1
		עזר	HELP	740b	
		עמד	STAND	763d	1 c
		עשהאל	ASAHEL	795c	
		תקוה	TIKVAH	876b	2
		שבתי	SABBETHAI	992d	
		משלם	MESHULLAM	1024c	8 b
10	16	בדל	BE DIVIDED	95c	1 a
		בית	HOUSE	110b	5 e
		בן	SON	121c	7 a
		דרש	SEEK	205c	4 b
		כהן	PRIEST	464b	7
		שם	NAME	1028a	2 a
10	17	אשה	WOMAN	61b	1
		ה	THE	209c	3
		ישב	MARRY	443d	4
		כלה	FINISH	478b	1 d
		כל	ALL	482d	2 ba
		נכרי	FOREIGN	648d	1 a
10	18	אליעזר	ELIEZER	45c	D
		אשה	WOMAN	61b	1
		בן	SON	121c	7 a
		גדליה	GEDALIAH	153d	3
		יהוצדק	JEHOZADAK	221b	
		יהושוע	JOSHUA	221c	3
		מצא	FIND	394a	1 g2
		ישב	MARRY	443d	4
		נכרי	FOREIGN	648d	1 a
		מעשיהו	MAASEIAH	796b	9 a
		יריב	JARIB	937b	2 b
10	19	איל	RAM	18a	2 b
		אשם	OFFENCE	79d	4
		אשם	GUILTY	79d	
		אשמה	WRONG-DOING	80b	2
		יד	HAND	389d	1 d
		יצא	BRING OUT	424d	1 f
10	20	אמר	IMMER	57b	2
		זבדיהו	ZEBADIAH	256c	7
		חנני	HANANI	337b	5
10	21	אליה	ELIJAH	45b	C
		יחיאל	JEHIEL	313d	8
		חרם	HARIM	356c	3 a
		עזיהו	UZZIAH	739d	4
		מעשיהו	MAASEIAH	796b	9 b
		רחום	REHUM	933d	1 b
		שמעיה	SHEMAIAH	1035d	8 b
10	22	אליועיני	ELIOENAI	41b	4 a
		אלעשה	ELEASAH	46c	C
		יהוזבד	JEHOZABAD	220a	4 e
		נתנאל	NETHANEL	682a	4
		מעשיהו	MAASEIAH	796b	9 c
		פשחור	PASHHUR	832d	4
		ישמעאל	ISHMAEL	1035d	5
10	23	אליעזר	ELIEZER	45c	G
		יהוזבד	JEHOZABAD	220a	4 f
		יהודה	JUDAH	397b	14
		פתחיה	PETHAHIAH	836a	2
		קוליה	KOLAIAH	877c	3
		קליטא	KELITA	886b	
		שמעי	SHIMEI	1035c	3 g
10	24	אורי	URI	22b	2
		אלישיב	ELIASHIB	46a	D
		טלם	TELEM	379a	2
		שלום	SHALLUM	1024b	2 b
10	25	אלעזר	ELEAZAR	46c	F
		בניה	BENAIAH	125c	5 a
		מימן	MIJAMIN	568b	2
		מלכיהו	MALCHIJAH	575d	6 b
		מלכיהו	MALCHIJAH	575d	6 a
		יזיה	IZZIAH	633c	
		פרעש	PAROSH	829b	1
		רמיה	RAMAIH	941d	
		ישראל	ISRAEL	976a	2 e
10	26	אליה	ELIJAH	45b	C
		זכריהו	ZECHARIAH	*272b	2 c
		ירמות	JEREMOTH	438b	5 a
		מתניהו	MATTANIAH	682d	4 a
		עבדי	ABDI	715d	2
		עילם	ELAM	743d	1 c
10	27	אליועיני	ELIOENAI	41b	4 b
		אלישיב	ELIASHIB	46a	E
		זבד	ZABAD	256b	5 a
		זתוא	ZATTU	285c	
		ירמות	JEREMOTH	438c	5 b
		מתניהו	MATTANIAH	682d	4 b
		עזיזא	AZIZA	739c	
10	28	בבי	BEBAI	93c	
		יהוחנן	JEHOHANAN	220b	7
		זבי	ZABBAI	256a	
		חנניהו	HANANIAH	337b	9 a
		עתליה	ATHALIAH	801a	2 c
10	29	בני	BANI	125b	5 a
		ירמות	JEREMOTH	438c	5 c
		מלוך	MALLUCH	576a	2 a
		עדיהו	ADAIAH	726a	6 a
		רמות	RAMOTH	928c	2
		שאל	SHEAL	982b	
		ישוב	JASHUB	1000b	2
		משלם	MESHULLAM	1024c	9
10	30	בנוי	BINNUI	125b	3 a

Ch	v	Heb	Eng	Page	Sec
		בניהו	BENAIAH	125c	5 b
		בצלאל	BEZALEL	130b	2
		כלל	CHELAL	483c	
		מנשה	MANASSEH	586d	3 a
		מתניהו	MATTANIAH	682d	4 c
10	31	עדנא	ADNA	726c	1
		מעשיה	MAASEIAH	796b	9 d
		פתחמואב	PAHATH-MOAB	809b	
		אליעזר	ELIEZER	45c	H
		חרם	HARIM	356c	3 b
		מלכיה	MALCHIJAH	575d	6 c
		ישיהו	ISSHIJAH	674d	4
		שמעון	SIMEON	1035c	3
		שמעיה	SHEMAIAH	1035d	8 c
10	32	בנימן	BENJAMIN	122d	3
		מלוך	MALLUCH	576a	2 b
		שמריה	SHEMARIAH	1037d	3 a
10	33	אילפלט	ELIPHELET	45d	E
		זבד	ZABAD	256b	5 b
		חשם	HASHUM	365c	
		ירמי	JEREMAI	438b	
10	34	מנשה	MANASSEH	586d	3 b
		מתני	MATTENAI	682d	2 a
		מתתה	MATTATTAH	683a	
		שמעי	SHIMEI	1035c	8 a
		אואל	UEL	15a	
		בנוי	BINNUI	*125a	1
		בני	BANI	125b	5 c
10	35	מעדי	MAADAI	588c	2
		עמרם	AMRAM	771d	2
10	35	בדיה	BEDEIAH	95a	
		בניהו	BENAIAH	125c	5 c
		כלוהי	CHELUHI	479a	
10	36	אלישיב	ELIASHIB	46a	F
		וניה	VANIAH	255c	
		מרמות	MEREMOTH	599b	3
10	37	מתני	MATTENAI	682d	2 b
		מתניהו	MATTANIAH	682d	4 d
		יעשו	JAASU	795c	
10	38	בני	BANI	125b	6
		בנוי	BINNUI	125b	3 b
		שמעי	SHIMEI	1035c	8 b
10	39	נתן	NATHAN	682a	7
		עדיהו	ADAIAH	726a	6 b
		שלמיה	SHELEMIAH	1025a	3 c
10	40	מכנדבי	MACHNADEBAI	569a	
		ששי	SHASHAI	1058d	
10	41	עזראל	AZAREL	741a	4
		שלמיה	SHELEMIAH	1025a	3 d
		שמריה	SHEMARIAH	1037d	3 b
10	42	אמריהו	AMARIAH	57c	3
		יוסף	JOSEPH	415d	4
10	43	שלום	SHALLUM	1024b	3
		בניהו	BENAIAH	125c	5 d
		יואל	JOEL	222b	8
		זבד	ZABAD	256b	5 c
		זבינא	ZEBINA	259c	
		ידו	JADDAI	392a	2
		יעיאל	JEIEL	418b	2 d
		נב	NOB	611b	1
		נבו	NEBO	612d	1 b
		מתתיהו	MATTITHIAH	682d	4
10	44	אשה	WOMAN	61b	1
		נכרי	FOREIGN	648d	1 a
		נשא	LIFT	671c	3 d
		שום	TO PLACE	964d	5 b

NEHEMIAH

Ch	v	Heb	Eng	Page	Sec
1	1	אלול	ELUL	47a	
		ארתחששתא	ARTAXERXES	77a	
		בירה	CASTLE	108b	2
		בירה	CASTLE	*108b	1
		דבר	WORD	183a	2 b
		חדש	NEW MOON	294d	2 b1
		חכליה	HACALIAH	314b	
		טבת	TEBETH	372a	
		כסלו	CHISLEV	493b	
		נחמיה	NEHEMIAH	637c	1
		שושן	SUSA	1004d	
1	2	חנני	HANANI	337b	2
		יהודי	JEW	397c	
		פליטה	ESCAPE	812d	2 c
		שאל	ASK	981d	2 a
		שאר	REMAIN	984a	1
		שבי	CAPTIVITY	985d	1
1	3	אש	FIRE	77c	1
		מדינה	PROVINCE	193d	3
		חומה	WALL	327c	1
		חומה	WALL	327c	1
		חרפה	REPROACH	358a	2 e
		יצת	BE KINDLED	428b	
		פרץ	BREAK THROUGH	829c	
		רעה	MISERY	949b	1
		שאר	REMAIN	984a	1
		שבי	CAPTIVITY	985d	1
		שער	GATE	1044c	1
1	4	אבל	MOURN	5c	
		אלהים	GOD	44c	4 bb
		בכה	WEEP	113b	1
		היה	BE	227c	3 5a
		יום	DAY	399c	5 a
		ישב	SIT	442d	1 b
		צום	FAST	847a	
1	5	אהב	LOVE	13a	3

Ch	v	Heb	Eng	Page	Sec
		אל	GOD	42c	6 a
		אלהים	GOD	44c	4 bb
		אנא	AH, NOW	58a	
		ברית	COVENANT	137a	3 2
		ברית	COVENANT	137b	3 2
		גדול	GREAT	153b	6 c
		חסד	GOODNESS	339a	2 1e
1	6	ירא	BE REVERED	431d	3 a
		אזן	EAR	24b	2 b
		חטא	MISS A GOAL OR WAY	307a	2 b
		חטא	MISS A GOAL OR WAY	307a	2 b
		חטא	MISS A GOAL OR WAY	307b	2 b
		חטאת	SIN	308d	1 c
		ידה	CONFESS	392d	1 j
		עין	EYE	744b	1 j
		על	UPON	754c	2 lf c
		על	UPON	754d	2 lf g
		תפלה	PRAYER	813c	1 e
		פתח	OPEN	835b	
		קשב	ATTENTIVE	904a	
		ישראל	ISRAEL	975d	2 b3
1	7	חבל	ACT CORRUPTLY	287b	2
		חק	SOMETHING PRESCRIBED	349d	7 g
		מצוה	COMMANDMENT	846c	2 b1
1	8	דבר	WORD	182d	1 2a
		זכר	REMEMBER	270b	2 3 a
		מעל	ACT TREACHEROUSLY	591b	2 b
		משה	MOSES	602d	
		עבד	SLAVE	714a	3
		פוץ	BE DISPERSED	807a	1 a
1	9	בוא	COME	99b	2
		בחר	CHOOSE	104a	2 a
		נדח	BANISH	623a	2
		קבץ	GATHER	868a	1
		מקום	STANDING PLACE	880b	4
		קצה	END	892b	1
		שכן	SETTLE DOWN	1015b	1
		שמי	HEAVENS	1030a	1 a
1	10	חזק	STRONG	305c	1 b
		יד	HAND	390a	1 e2
		כח	STRENGTH	470d	3
		פדה	RANSOM	804a	3 a
1	11	אדון	LORD	11b	3 2a
		אזן	EAR	24b	2 b
		אנא	AH, NOW	58a	
		חפץ	DELIGHTING IN	343a	1
		ירא	FEAR	431c	3 b
		נתן	GIVE	681a	3 b
		תפלה	PRAYER	813c	1 e
		צלח	ADVANCE	852c	1
		קשב	ATTENTIVE	904a	
		רחמים	COMPASSION	933c	2
		שם	NAME	1028c	3
		משקה	CUP-BEARER	1052d	
2	1	ארתחששתא	ARTAXERXES	77a	
		חדש	NEW MOON	294d	2 b1
		ניסן	NISAN	644c	
		רע	EVIL	948b	7
2	2	בלת	EXCEPT	*116c	1
		זה	THIS	260d	1 a
		חלה	BE WEAK	317d	1
		ירא	FEAR	431a	1 a
		לב	HEART	525c	2 9b
		פנה	FACE	815d	1 la
		רבה	BECOME MANY	915d	1 e3
		רע	EVIL	948a	4
		רע	EVIL	948b	7
2	3	אכל	EAT	37d	
		אש	FIRE	77c	1
		בית	HOUSE	109c	2
		חיה	LIVE	311b	1 d
		חרב	WASTE	351d	
		עולם	LONG DURATION	762a	2 a
		פנה	FACE	815d	1 la
		רעע	BE EVIL	949c	1
		שער	GATE	1044c	1a
2	4	אלהים	GOD	44c	4 bb
		בקש	SEEK	135a	6
		זה	THIS	261c	4 c
		מה	HOW	554b	4 f
2	5	אשר	THAT	83c	3 8 ab
		בית	HOUSE	*109c	1 i
		בנה	BUILD	124d	1 i
		טוב	PLEASING	373c	5
		יטב	BE PLEASING	405c	3
		על	UPON	758a	2 8
		פנה	FACE	817a	24 a g
2	6	מלך	JOURNEY	237c	2
		זמן	APPOINTED TIME	273d	
		יטב	BE PLEASING	405c	4
		מתי	WHEN	607d	A
		נתן	GIVE	679d	1 w
		פנה	FACE	817a	24 a g
		שגל	CONSORT	993c	
2	7	אגרת	LETTER	8d	
		חרפה	REPROACH	358a	2 e
		טוב	PLEASING	373c	5
		עבר	PASS OVER	718d	2 a
		עבר	REGION ACROSS	719d	1 b
		על	UPON	757b	2 7c aa
		על	UPON	758a	2 8

Ch v.	Heb	Eng	Page	Sec
2 8	פחה	GOVERNOR	808d	
	אגרת	LETTER	8d	
	אסף	ASAPH	63b	3
	בירה	CASTLE	108b	1
	בירה	CASTLE	*108b	
	בירה	CASTLE	*108b	1
	טוב	PLEASANT	374d	9 b
	יד	HAND	390a	1
	על	UPON	753a	2 1a b
	עץ	TREE	781d	2 a
	פרדם	PRESERVE	825d	
	קרה	FURNISH WITH BEAMS	900a	
	שמר	KEEP	1036d	1 b
	שער	GATE	1045a	3 a
2 9	אגרת	LETTER	8d	
	עבר	REGION ACROSS	719d	1 b
	פחה	GOVERNOR	808d	
	פרש	HORSEMAN	832b	
	שר	CHIEFTAIN	978c	3 a
2 10	אדם	MAN	9b	1
	אשר	THAT	83c	8 ab
	ביתחרון	BETH-HORON	111c	
	בקש	SEEK	134d	2 b
	טובה	WELFARE	375d	1
	טוביהו	TOBIJAH	376a	2
	סנבלט	SANBALLAT	702d	
	עמוני	AMMONITE	770a	
	רעע	BE EVIL	949c	1
2 11	ירושלים	JERUSALEM	437d	
2 12	אדם	MAN	9b	1
	בהמה	BEAST	97a	2
	נגד	BE CONSPICUOUS	616d	1
	נתן	GIVE	678d	1 i
	רכב	RIDE	938d	2
	לב	ADDENDA ET CORRIGENDA	1124c	
2 13	אכל	EAT	37d	
	אש	FIRE	77c	1
	גיא	VALLEY	161b	
	היה	BE	227c	3 5a
	הם	THEY	241c	2 c
	חומה	WALL	327c	1
	יצא	GO OUT	422d	1 a
	עין	SPRING	7452	D
	פרץ	BREAK THROUGH	829c	
	שבר	INSPECT	960b	
	שער	GATE	1044c	1 a
	שער	GATE	1044d	1 b 2
	שער	GATE	1044d	1 b 4
	אשפת	REFUSE-HEAP	1046b	
	תנין	DRAGON	1072c	2
2 14	בהמה	BEAST	97a	2
	ברכה	POOL	140a	
	עבר	PASS OVER	718a	5 a
	עין	SPRING	7452	D
	מקום	STANDING PLACE	880a	4
	שער	GATE	1044d	1 b 4
2 15	גיא	VALLEY	161b	
	נחל	WADY	636d	2
	שבר	INSPECT	960b	
	שער	GATE	1044d	1 b 4
2 16	אן	WHERE	33a	A
	הלך	WALK	230d	1 1d 3b
	חר	NOBLE	359d	
	יהודי	JEW	397c	
	יתר	REMAINDER	451d	1 b
	כן	SO	487a	3 e
	מלאכה	WORK	522a	3 b
	סגן	RULER	688d	2
	סגן	RULER	*688d	2
	סגן	RULER	688d	2
2 17	אש	FIRE	77c	1
	בנה	BUILD	124d	1 i
	חומה	WALL	327c	1
	חרב	WASTE	351d	
	יצת	BE KINDLED	428b	
	ירושלים	JERUSALEM	437a	
	שער	GATE	1044c	1 a
2 18	אף	ALSO	65a	1
	אשר	PARTICLE OF RELATION	82b	2 a
	חזק	BE FIRM	304d	2
	טוב	PLEASANT	374d	9 b
	טובה	WELFARE	375d	3
	יד	HAND	390a	1 e2
	על	UPON	753a	2 1a b
2 19	בזה	DESPISE	102c	2
	ביתחרון	BETH-HORON	111c	
	גשם	GESHEM	177c	
	טוביהו	TOBIJAH	376a	2
	לעג	MOCK	541c	2
	מרד	REBEL	597c	1
	סנבלט	SANBALLAT	702d	
	עמוני	AMMONITE	770a	
	ערבי	ARABIAN	787b	
2 20	אלהים	GOD	44c	4 bb
	דבר	WORD	182b	1 1c
	זכרון	MEMORIAL	272a	1 d
	חלק	PORTION	324a	1 c
	עבד	SLAVE	714a	3
	צדקה	RIGHTEOUSNESS	*842b	3
	צלח	ADVANCE	852c	C
3 1	אלישיב	ELIASHIB	46a	C
	בנה	BUILD	124d	1 i
	מגדל	TOWER	154a	1
	מגדל	TOWER	154a	1
	דלת	DOOR	195b	3
	חננאל	HANANEL	337a	
	כהן	PRIEST	464b	8
	מאה	HUNDRED	548a	1 a5
	מאה	HUNDRED	548c	
	עמד	STAND	764d	3
	קדש	BE SET APART	873a	1 a
3 2	שער	GATE	1044d	1 b 7
	אמרי	IMRI	57c	3
	זכור	ZACCUR	271d	5
	יד	HAND	391c	5 h3
	יריחו	JERICHO	437d	
	רקד	SKIP ABOUT	955a	
3 3	בריח	BAR	138b	1 b
	בריח	BAR	138b	2
	דג	FISH	185d	
	דלת	DOOR	195b	3
	סלל	COVER OVER	*378d	
	מרמות	MEREMOTH	599b	2
	מנעול	BOLT	653b	
	סנאה	SENAAH	702d	
	קרה	FURNISH WITH BEAMS	900a	
3 4	שער	GATE	1044d	1 b5
	אוריה	URIAH	22c	3
	בענה	BAANAH	128d	3
	בננא	BAANA	128d	3
	ברכיהו	JEBERECHIAH	140a	3
	חזק	BE FIRM	305d	4
	מרמות	MEREMOTH	599b	2
	משיזבאל	MESHEZABEL	604a	
	צדוק	ZADOK	843b	3 a
	קוץ	KOZ	881b	2
	משלם	MESHULLAM	1024c	5 a
3 5	אדון	LORD	11a	2 1e
	אדיר	MAJESTIC	12b	2
	בוא	COME	99b	1 g
	עבדה	LABOR	715b	3
	צואר	NECK	848c	1
	תקועה	TEKOITE	1075d	
3 6	בסודיה	BESODEIAH	126a	
	בריח	BAR	138b	2
	בריח	BAR	138b	1 b
	דלת	DOOR	195b	3
	יהוידע	JEHOIADA	220c	3
	סלל	COVER OVER	*378d	
	ישן	OLD	446a	
	נבל	BE SENSELESS	614c	
	מנעול	BOLT	653b	
	פסח	PASEAH	820c	3
	קרה	FURNISH WITH BEAMS	900a	
	משלם	MESHULLAM	1024c	5 b
3 7	שער	GATE	1044d	1 b 8
	גבעון	GIBEON	149c	
	גבעני	GIBEONITE	149c	
	ידון	JADON	193d	
	כסא	SEAT OF HONOR	490d	2
	מלטיה	MELATIAH	572d	
	מרנתי	MEROTHONITE	599c	2
	עבר	REGION ACROSS	719d	1 b
	מצפה	MIZPAH	860a	4
3 8	בן	SON	121c	7 a
	חומה	WALL	327c	1
	חנניה	HANANIAH	337b	9 b
	חרחיה	HARHAIAH	354d	
	עזב	RESTORE	738a	
	עזיאל	UZZIEL	739c	4
	צרף	SMELT	864b	4
	רחב	WIDE	932a	
	רקח	OINTMENT-MAKER	955c	
3 9	חור	HUR	301b	4
	פלך	DISTRICT	813a	2
	רפיה	REPHAIAH	951b	5
	שר	CHIEFTAIN	978d	6
3 10	חטוש	HATTUSH	310d	1
	חרומף	HARUMAPH	354d	
	חשבניה	HASHABNEIAH	364b	1
	ידיה	JEDAIAH	393a	2
3 11	מגדל	TOWER	154a	1
	חרם	HARIM	356c	3 b
	חשוב	HASSHUB	363d	2 a
	מדה	MEASURE	551c	3
	מלכיהו	MALCHIJAH	575d	6 c
	פתחמואב	PAHATH-MOAB	809b	
	תנור	FIRE-POT	1072b	
3 12	לוחש	HALLOHESH	538a	
	פלך	DISTRICT	813a	2
	שר	CHIEFTAIN	978d	6
	שלם	SHALLUM	1024b	0
3 13	אלף	THOUSAND	48d	1 a
	בנה	BUILD	124d	1 i
	בריח	BAR	138b	2
	בריח	BAR	138b	1 b
	גיא	VALLEY	161b	
	דלת	DOOR	195b	3
	חנון	HANUN	337a	2 a
	מנעול	BOLT	653b	
	שער	GATE	1044d	1 b 2
	שער	GATE	1044d	1 b 4
	אשפת	REFUSE-HEAP	1046b	
3 14	ביתהכרם	BETH-HAKKEREM	111d	
	בנה	BUILD	124d	1 i
	בריח	BAR	138b	1 b
	בריח	BAR	138b	2
	דלת	DOOR	195b	3
	מלכיהו	MALCHIJAH	575d	6 d
	מנעול	BOLT	653b	
	פלך	DISTRICT	813a	2
	רכב	RECHAB	939c	1 b
	שר	CHIEFTAIN	978d	6
	שער	GATE	1044d	1 b 2
	אשפת	REFUSE-HEAP	1046b	
3 15	בנה	BUILD	124d	1 i
	בריח	BAR	138b	1 b
	בריח	BAR	138b	2
	ברכה	POOL	140a	
	גן	GARDEN	171a	
	דלת	DOOR	195b	3
	חומה	WALL	327c	1
	סלל	COVER OVER	378d	
	כלחזה	COL-HOZEH	480d	1
	ל	TO	511b	1 f
	מנעול	BOLT	653b	
	עין	SPRING	7452	D
	מעלה	STEP	752b	1
	פלך	DISTRICT	813a	2
	מצפה	MIZPAH	860a	4
	שר	CHIEFTAIN	978d	6
	שלח	SHELAH	1019d	
	שלון	SHALLUN	1024c	
	שער	GATE	1044d	1 b 4
3 16	ביתצור	BETH-ZUR	112d	
	ברכה	POOL	140a	
	גבור	STRONG	150b	2
	דוד	DAVID	188b	F
	נגד	IN FRONT	617d	2 d
	נחמיה	NEHEMIAH	637c	2
	עד	AS FAR AS	724a	1 1a
	עזבוק	AZBUK	739d	
	פלך	DISTRICT	813a	2
	קבצצר	GRAVE	868d	
	שר	CHIEFTAIN	978d	6
3 17	בני	BANI	125b	2 b
	חשביהו	HASHABIAH	364a	8
	לוי	LEVITE	533b	3 2b
	פלך	DISTRICT	813a	2
	קעילה	KEILAH	890d	
	קרה	COLD	903b	
	רחום	REHUM	933d	2 a
	שר	CHIEFTAIN	978d	6
3 18	בוי	BAVVAI	100c	
	בנוי	BINNUI	*125b	2
	חנדד	HENADAD	337b	
	פלך	DISTRICT	813a	2
	קעילה	KEILAH	890d	
	שר	CHIEFTAIN	978d	6
3 19	יהושוע	JOSHUA	221d	7
	חזק	BE FIRM	304c	1 c
	מדה	MEASURE	551c	3
	נגד	IN FRONT	617d	2 cb b
	נשק	ARMOURY	676d	2
	עזר	EZER	740d	1
	מקצע	CORNER-BUTTRESS	893a	
	מקצע	CORNER-BUTTRESS	893b	
	שר	CHIEFTAIN	978d	6
3 20	אלישיב	ELIASHIB	46a	C
	ברוך	BARUCH	140a	2
	זבי	ZABBAI	256a	
	זבי	ZACCAI	269b	
	חרה	BURN	354b	
	כהן	PRIEST	464b	8
	מדה	MEASURE	551c	3
	מקצע	CORNER-BUTTRESS	893a	
	מקצע	CORNER-BUTTRESS	893b	
3 21	אוריה	URIAH	22c	3
	אלישיב	ELIASHIB	46a	C
	תכלית	END	479b	1
	מדה	MEASURE	551c	3
	מרמות	MEREMOTH	599b	2
	קוץ	KOZ	881b	2
3 22	כבר	ROUND	503b	1
3 23	בנימין	BENJAMIN	122d	3
	חשוב	HASSHUB	363d	2 b
	נגד	IN FRONT	617d	1 aa
	עזריהו	AZARIAH	741b	1
	עניה	ANANIAH	778b	1
	מעשיהו	MAASEIAH	796b	7
3 24	בוי	BAVVAI	100c	
	בנוי	BINNUI	125b	2
	חנדד	HENADAD	337b	
	מדה	MEASURE	551c	3
	עזריהו	AZARIAH	741b	1
	פנה	CORNER	819c	1 b
	מקצע	CORNER-BUTTRESS	893b	
	שרף	BURN	976d	2 a
3 25	אחי	UZAI	17a	
	מגדל	TOWER	153d	1
	יצא	GO OUT	423d	1 h
	נגד	IN FRONT	617d	2 cb b
	מטרה	GUARD	643c	1
	עלה	GO UP	748d	3
	עליון	HIGH	751b	2
	פדיה	PEDALAH	804c	3 a
	פלל	PALAL	813c	
	פרעש	PAROSH	829b	1
	מקצע	CORNER-BUTTRESS	893b	
	שועל	FOX	1043c	
3 26	מגדל	TOWER	153d	1
	מזרח	PLACE OF SUNRISE	281a	2 c3
	יצא	GO OUT	423d	1 h

Ch	v.	Heb	Eng	Page	Sec
		ל	TO	511d	1 h
		נגד	IN FRONT	617d	2 d
		נתינים	NETHINIM	682a	
		עד	AS FAR AS	724a	1 1a
		עפל	MOUND	779b	
		שער	GATE	1044d	1 b 2
		ל	TO	1098b	1
3	27	מגדל	TOWER	153d	1
		חומה	WALL	327c	1
		יצא	GO OUT	423d	1 h
		מדה	MEASURE	551c	3
		נגד	IN FRONT	617d	2 cb b
		עפל	MOUND	779b	
		תקועי	TEKOITE	1075d	
3	28	סוס	HORSE	692c	2
		על	UPON	759b	4 2d
		שער	GATE	1044d	1 b 5
3	29	אמר	IMMER	57b	1
		מזרח	PLACE OF SUNRISE	281a	2 e
		נגד	IN FRONT	617b	1
		צדוק	RIGHTEOUS	843b	3 b
		צדוק	ZADOK	843b	3 b
		שכניה	SHECANIAH	1016a	3
		שער	GATE	1044d	1 b 9
3	30	יברכיהו	JEBERECHIAH	140a	3
		חנון	HANUN	337a	2 b
		חנניהו	HANANIAH	337b	9 c
		מדה	MEASURE	551c	3
		נשכה	CHAMBER	675b	
		צלף	ZALAPH	854c	
		משלם	MESHULLAM	1024c	5 a
		שלמיה	SHELEMIAH	1025a	3 a
		שני	SECOND	*1041b	
		שני	SECOND	*1041c	
3	31	מלכיהו	MALCHIJAH	575d	6 e
		נתינים	NETHINIM	682a	
		עליה	ROOF-CHAMBER	751a	
		פנה	CORNER	819d	1 b
		צרפי	GOLDSMITH	864c	
		רכל	GO ABOUT	940b	
		שער	GATE	1044d	1 b 3
3	32	עליה	ROOF-CHAMBER	751a	
		פנה	CORNER	819d	1 b
		צרף	SMELT	864b	4
		רכל	GO ABOUT	940b	
		שער	GATE	1044d	1 b 7
3	33	בנה	BUILD	124d	1 i
		היה	COME TO PASS	224c	2 a1 ah
		חרה	BURN	354a	1 b
		יהודי	JEW	397c	
		כעס	BE ANGRY	495a	1
		לעג	MOCK	541c	
		סנבלט	SANBALLAT	702d	
		רבה	BECOME MANY	915d	1 e3
3	34	אבן	STONE	6c	2
		אמלל	FEEBLE	51c	
		חיה	LIVE	311c	3 c
		יהודי	JEW	397c	
		כלה	FINISH	478b	1 a
		עזב	LEAVE	737b	1 h
		עפר	DRY EARTH	779d	1 e
		ערמה	HEAP	790d	
		שמרון	SAMARIA	1038a	
3	35	אבן	STONE	6c	2
		בנה	BUILD	124d	1 i
		גם	ALSO	169b	2
		חומה	WALL	327c	1
		חומה	WALL	327c	1
		טוביהו	TOBIJAH	376a	2
		עמוני	AMMONITE	770a	
		פרץ	BREAK THROUGH	829b	2
3	36	בוזה	CONTEMPT	100c	1
		בזה	SPOIL	103a	
		חרפה	REPROACH	357d	1
		חרפה	REPROACH	357d	1
		ראש	HEAD	911b	8
		שביה	CAPTIVITY	986a	1
		שוב	TURN BACK	999c	4 a
3	37	חטאת	SIN	309a	1 d4
		כסה	COVER	492a	6
		כעס	VEX	495a	2
		מחה	WIPE OUT	562b	2
		נגד	IN FRONT	617c	2 b
		עון	INIQUITY	731a	1 c3
		פנה	FACE	818a	25 a d
3	38	בנה	BUILD	124d	1 i
		חומה	WALL	327c	1
		עשה	DO	794b	1 1b
		קשר	BIND	905b	
3	39	שמעיה	SHEMAIAH	1035d	9 a
4	1	ארוכה	HEALING	74b	B
		אשדודי	ASHDODITE	78c	
		היה	COME TO PASS	224c	2 a1 ah
		חלל	POLLUTE	320d	2
		חומה	WALL	327c	1
		חרה	BURN	354a	1 b
		טוביהו	TOBIJAH	376a	2
		סנבלט	SANBALLAT	702d	
		סתם	STOP UP	711b	
		עלה	GO UP	749a	6
		עמוני	AMMONITE	770a	
		ערבי	ARABIAN	787b	
		פרץ	BREAK THROUGH	829b	2
4	2	לחם	ENGAGE IN BATTLE	535c	
		קשר	BIND	905b	2

Ch	v.	Heb	Eng	Page	Sec
		תועה	ERROR	1073c	2
4	3	עמד	STAND	764d	1
		משמר	GUARD	1038b	2
4	4	ב	IN	88c	1 2b
		בנה	BUILD	124c	1 ad
		יהודה	JUDAH	397b	13
		כח	STRENGTH	470c	1 a
		כשל	TOTTER	505c	2
		סבל	BURDEN BEARER	688a	
		עפר	DRY EARTH	779d	1 e
		רבה	BECOME MANY	915d	1 e4
4	5	הרג	KILL	247a	1 a
		מלאכה	WORK	522a	3 b
		צר	ADVERSARY	865d	
		ראה	TO SEE	907a	1 b
		שבת	CEASE	992a	1
4	6	אשר	THAT	83c	8 ag
		היה	COME TO PASS	224c	2 a1 ah
		יהודי	JEW	397c	
		על	UPON	757b	2 7c aa
		פעם	OCCURRENCE	822a	3 a
		מקום	STANDING PLACE	880a	4
		שוב	TURN BACK	997b	3 b
4	7	אחר	BEHIND	30b	4 ab
		עמד	STAND	*764d	1
		צחיח	SHINING	850a	
		מקום	STANDING PLACE	880a	4
		קשת	BOW	906a	1 b
		רמח	SPEAR	942b	1
		משפחה	CLAN	1046d	1 c
		תחתי	LOWER	1066c	
4	8	אדון	LORD	11b	3 2a
		גדול	GREAT	153b	6 c
		זכר	REMEMBER	270a	13 b
		חלקיהו	HILKIAH	324d	5
		חר	NOBLE	359d	
		ירא	FEAR	431b	1 c
		ירא	BE REVERED	431d	3 a
		יתר	REMAINDER	451d	1 b
		לחם	ENGAGE IN BATTLE	535d	
		סגן	RULER	688d	2
4	9	היה	COME TO PASS	224c	2 a1 ah
		ידע	BE MADE KNOWN	394c	1
		עצה	ADVICE	420a	
		ל	TO	514a	5 e
		פרר	BREAK	830b	2 a
		בבלי	BABYLONIANS	1084a	
4	10	מגן	SHIELD	171c	
		היה	COME TO PASS	224c	1 2a 1b
		חזק	BE FIRM	305a	6 a
		נער	RETAINER	655a	2 b
		עשה	DO	794a	1 1b
		קשת	BOW	906a	1 b
		רמח	SPEAR	942b	1
		שר	CHIEFTAIN	978d	6
		שריון	BODY-ARMOUR	1056b	
4	11	בנה	BUILD	124c	1 h
		חזק	BE FIRM	305a	6 a
		סבל	BURDEN	687d	
		עמס	LOAD	770c	1
		שלח	MISSLE	1019c	1
4	12	אסר	TIE	64a	4
		מתנים	LOINS	608a	1 b
4	13	חר	NOBLE	359d	
		יתר	REMAINDER	451d	1 b
		סגן	RULER	688d	2
		פרד	DIVIDE	825c	2
		רבה	BECOME MANY	915d	1 e4
		רחב	WIDE	932a	
		רחק	DISTANT	935b	1 a
4	14	לחם	ENGAGE IN BATTLE	535d	
		קבץ	GATHER	867d	1
		מקום	STANDING PLACE	880a	4
		מקום	STANDING PLACE	880b	4
4	15	חזק	BE FIRM	305a	6 b
		יצא	GO OUT	423b	1 f
		כוכב	STAR	456d	
		רמח	SPEAR	942b	1
		שחר	DAWN	1007b	
		יום	DAY	398b	1
		לילה	NIGHT	539a	1
4	16	משמר	GUARD	1038b	2
		יום	ADDENDA ET CORRIGENDA	1124a	
4	17	אין	NOT	34b	2
		נער	RETAINER	655a	2 b
		פשט	STRIP OFF	833a	1
		שלח	MISSLE	1019c	1
		משמר	GUARD	1038b	2
5	1	אח	BROTHER	26b	2
		יהודי	JEW	397c	
		עם	PEOPLE	766a	3
		צעקה	CRY	858d	1
5	2	דגן	CORN	186c	
		יש	BE	442a	2 cd
		לקח	TAKE	543a	4 b
5	3	דגן	CORN	186c	
		יש	BE	442a	2 cd
		ערב	TAKE ON PLEDGE	786d	2
5	4	יש	BE	442a	2 cd
		כסף	SILVER	494d	9
		לוה	BORROW	531a	
		מדה	TRIBUTE	551d	
5	5	אח	BROTHER	26b	2

Ch	v.	Heb	Eng	Page	Sec
		אל	GOD	43a	7
		בשר	FLESH	142d	4
		כבש	BE SUBDUED	461b	
		כבש	SUBDUE	461b	1
		מן	FROM	580d	3 ba
		עבד	SLAVE	714c	7
5	6	זעקה	CRY	277d	2
		חרה	BURN	354a	1 b
5	7	חר	NOBLE	359d	
		מלך	COUNSEL	576a	
		נשא	BE A CREDITOR	673d	
		משא	LENDING ON INTEREST	673d	
		נשה	LEND	674b	
		נתן	GIVE	681b	3 d
		סגן	RULER	688d	2
		על	UPON	753c	2 1d
		קהלה	ASSEMBLY	875a	
		ריב	STRIVE	936c	2
		מלך	REIGN	*1100c	
5	8	אח	BROTHER	26b	2
		גם	ALSO	169d	5
		די	SUFFICIENCY	191d	2 b
		חרש	BE SILENT	361b	1 a
		יהודי	JEW	397c	
		מכר	SELL	569b	
		מכר	SELL	569c	
		מצא	FIND	593a	1 b
5	9	חרפה	REPROACH	357d	1
		טוב	PLEASANT	375a	0 a
		יראה	FEAR	432a	3
5	10	דגן	CORN	186c	
		דגן	CORN	186c	
		משא	LENDING ON INTEREST	673d	
		נשה	LEND	674b	
		עזב	LEAVE	737b	2 d4
5	11	דגן	CORN	186c	
		דגן	CORN	186c	
		זית	OLIVE TREE	268d	1 h
		יום	DAY	400d	7 h
		תירוש	NEW WINE	440d	
		מאה	HUNDRED	548b	1 d6
		מאה	HUNDRED	548c	1
		נשה	LEND	674b	
		יצהר	FRESH OIL	844a	
5	12	שוב	TURN BACK	999a	1 d
		בקש	SEEK	135a	5 a
		דבר	WORD	182b	1 1b
		דבר	WORD	183d	47
		כן	SO	486c	2 db
		שבע	SWEAR	989c	1
		שוב	TURN BACK	999b	1 d
5	13	אמן	VERILY	53b	1
		דבר	WORD	182b	1 1b
		דבר	WORD	182b	1 1f
		דבר	WORD	183d	47
		הלל	PRAISE	238d	2 f
		חצן	BOSOM	346a	
		יגיע	TOIL	388c	2
		נער	SHAKE OUT	654c	
		קהל	ASSEMBLY	874d	1 d
		ריק	EMPTY	938a	1
5	14	ארתחששתא	ARTAXERXES	77a	
		יום	DAY	400b	7 d7
		מן	SINCE	583c	7 c
		שלשים	THIRTY	1026c	2
5	15	אחר	BESIDES	29d	2 c
		יראה	FEAR	432a	3
		כבד	MAKE HEAVY	457d	1
		כסף	SILVER	494b	8 a
		ראשון	FIRST	911c	1 a
		ארבעים	FORTY	917c	1 b
		שלט	DOMINEER	1020c	
		שקל	SHEKEL	1053d	
5	16	חזק	BE FIRM	305b	6 c
		קבץ	GATHER	867d	2
5	17	יהודי	JEW	397c	
		סגן	RULER	688d	2
		שלחן	TABLE	1020b	1
5	18	בין	INTERVAL	107c	1 d
		בקש	SEEK	135a	5 a
		ברר	SELECT	141a	2
		היה	BE	227c	3 5a
		זה	THIS	262a	6 g
		כבד	BE HEAVY	457b	1
		עבדה	LABOR	715b	3
		עם	WITH	768d	5
		עשה	DO	795b	2 c
		צאן	SMALL CATTLE	838b	1 b
		צאן	SMALL CATTLE	838b	1 a1
		צפור	BIRD	862a	1
		רבה	BECOME MANY	915d	1 e5
		שש	SIX	995c	1 a
5	19	זכר	REMEMBER	270b	2 1 a
		טובה	WELFARE	375d	3
		על	UPON	758a	2 8
		עשה	DO	794a	1 1a 3
6	1	בנה	BUILD	124c	1 ad
		גם	ALSO	169d	5
		גשם	GESHEM	177c	
		דלת	DOOR	195b	3
		היה	COME TO PASS	224c	2 a1 ah
		טוביהו	TOBIJAH	376a	2
		יתר	REMAINDER	451d	1 b
		ל	TO	514a	5 e

NEHEMIAH

Ch	v.	Heb	Eng	Page	Sec
		סנבלט	SANBALLAT	702d	
		עת	TIME	773c	1 a
		ערבי	ARABIAN	787b	
		פרץ	BURSTING FORTH	829d	2
		שמע	HEAR	1034b	1
6	2	אונו	ONO	20c	
		בקעה	PLAIN	132c	2
		גשם	GESHEM	177c	
		חשב	THINK	363a	1 2
		יסד	FIX THEMSELVES	414a	1
		יעד	MEET BY APPOINTMENT	416d	2
		כפירים	VILLAGES	499a	
		סנבלט	SANBALLAT	702d	
6	3	ירד	GO DOWN	433a	1 e
		מלאך	MESSENGER	521c	1 a
		מה	HOW	554b	4 d
		על	UPON	757b	27c aa
		רפה	SINK	952a	1
		שבת	CEASE	991d	1
6	4	דבר	WORD	183d	47
		דבר	WORD	183d	47
		פעם	OCCURRENCE	822a	3 a
		שוב	TURN BACK	999c	3
6	5	אגרת	LETTER	8d	
		דבר	WORD	183d	47
		חמישי	FIFTH	332c	2
		סנבלט	SANBALLAT	702d	
		פעם	OCCURRENCE	822a	3 a
		פתח	OPEN	835b	
		שלח	SEND	1018b	1 a
6	6	בנה	BUILD	124d	1 i
		גשם	GESHEM	177c	
		הוה	BECOME	217c	
		חשב	THINK	363a	12
		יהודי	JEW	397c	
		מרד	REBEL	597c	1
		שמע	HEAR	1034b	1
6	7	יחדו	TOGETHER	403b	A
		יעץ	CONSULT	420a	
		ל	TO	514a	5 e
		עמד	STAND	764d	
		קרא	CALL	895c	3 d
		שמע	HEAR	1034b	1
6	8	בדא	DEVISE	94b	
		היה	COME TO PASS	227d	2
		לב	HEART	524c	23a
6	9	חזק	BE FIRM	304d	2
		יד	HAND	389d	1e1
		ירא	TERRIFY	431d	
		עשה	DO	795a	1 a
		רפה	SINK	951d	2
6	10	דלת	DOOR	195a	1
		דליהו	DELAIAH	195b	2 c
		היכל	TEMPLE	228c	2 d
		הרג	KILL	247a	1 a
		מהיטבאל	MEHETABEL	406b	2
		יעד	MEET BY APPOINTMENT	416d	2
		סגר	SHUT	688d	1
		עצר	RESTRAIN	783c	1
		עצר	RESTRAIN	783d	
		שמעיה	SHEMAIAH	1035d	9 b
6	11	ברח	FLEE	137d	2
		היכל	TEMPLE	228c	2 d
6	12	דבר	SPEAK	181d	5
		ו	AND	253a	1 g
		טוביהו	TOBIJAH	376a	
		נבואה	PROPHECY	612c	1 b
		נכר	RECOGNIZE	648b	3
		סנבלט	SANBALLAT	702d	
		שכר	HIRE	969a	
6	13	חטא	MISS A GOAL OR WAY	306d	2 b
		חרף	REPROACH	357d	
		ירא	FEAR	431a	1 a
		מען	PURPOSE	775d	22
		רע	EVIL	948b	2
		שכר	HIRE	969a	
		שם	NAME	1028a	2 b2
6	14	אלה	THESE	41c	A
		זכר	REMEMBER	270b	2 1b
		טוביהו	TOBIJAH	376a	2
		נועדיה	NOADIAH	418a	2
		ירא	TERRIFY	431d	
		נביאה	PROPHETESS	612c	1
		סנבלט	SANBALLAT	702d	
		מעשה	DEED	795c	1 a2
6	15	אלול	ELUL	47a	
		חדש	NEW MOON	*294d	2 b1
		ל	TO	517a	6 b
		שלם	BE COMPLETE	1022b	1
6	16	את	WITH	86d	4 c
		היה	COME TO PASS	224c	2a1 ah
		נפל	FALL	657c	5
		עשה	DO	795a	1 a
6	17	אגרת	LETTER	8d	
		בא	COME	98b	2
		הלך	WALK	232c	13
		חר	NOBLE	359d	
		טוביהו	TOBIJAH	376a	2
		על	UPON	757b	27c aa
6	18	ארח	ARAH	73b	2
		בעל	LORD	127c	15b
		יברכיהו	JEBERECHIAH	140a	3
		יהוחנן	JEHOHANAN	220b	3
		חתן	DAUGHTER:S HUSBAND	368c	1
		ל	TO	513a	5 ad
		שבועה	OATH	989d	1
		שכניה	SHECANIAH	1016a	4
6	19	אגרת	LETTER	8d	
		אמר	SAY	56a	1
		טובה	WELFARE	375d	3
		טוביה	TOBIJAH	376a	2
		טוביהו	TOBIJAH	376a	
		יצא	BRING OUT	425b	4 k
		ירא	TERRIFY	431d	
7	1	ל	TO	511c	1 gb
		בנה	BUILD	125a	1
		דלת	DOOR	195b	3
		היה	COME TO PASS	224c	2a1 ah
		לוי	LEVITE	533a	3 2b
		פקד	ATTEND TO	823d	4
7	2	אמת	FIRMNESS	54a	3 a
		בירה	CASTLE	*108b	1
		בירה	CASTLE	108b	1
		חנניהו	HANANIAH	337b	9 d
		חנני	HANANI	337b	2
		ירא	FEAR	431c	3 b
		כ	LIKE	454b	1 d
		צוה	GIVE CHARGE OVER	845d	1 d
7	3	שר	CHIEFTAIN	978b	2 d
		אחז	GRASP	28b	
		גוף	CLOSE	157c	
		דלת	DOOR	195b	3
		חמם	BE OR BECOME WARM	328c	1
		עד	UNTIL	725b	22c
		עמד	STAND	764d	5
		פתח	OPEN	835d	
		משמר	GUARD	1038b	2
		משמרת	GUARD	1038c	1
		שמש	SUN	1039b	1
		שער	GATE	1044c	1 a
7	4	יד	HAND	390c	3 d
		מעט	A FEW	590a	1 a
7	5	חר	NOBLE	359d	
		התחש	BE ENROLLED	405b	
		יחש	GENEALOGY	405b	
		מצא	FIND	593a	1 d
		מצא	FIND	593b	3 a
		נתן	GIVE	679a	1 i
		סגן	RULER	688d	2
		ספר	MISSIVE	707b	3 b
		עם	PEOPLE	766d	3
		קבץ	GATHER	867d	2
		ראשון	FIRST	912a	3 a1
		לב	ADDENDA ET CORRIGENDA	1124c	
7	6	בן	SON	121b	1 jm
		מדינה	PROVINCE	193d	3
		נבוכדראצר	NEBUCHADNEZZAR	613b	
		שבי	CAPTIVITY	985d	1
7	7	רחום	REHUM	*	1 a
		אחר	ANOTHER	*29c	
		בגוי	BIGVAI	94a	1
		בלשן	BILSHAN	119a	
		בענה	BAANAH	128d	3
		יהושוע	JOSHUA	221c	3
		זרבבל	ZERUBBABEL	279c	
		מרדכי	MORDECAI	598a	1
		נחום	NEHUM	637b	
		נחמיה	NEHEMIAH	637c	3
		נחמני	NAHAMANI	637c	
		מספרת	MISPERETH	709a	
		עזריהו	AZARIAH	741b	9
		רעליה	REELAIAH	947a	
7	8	פרעש	PAROSH	829b	1
		שבעים	SEVENTY	988c	3 c
7	9	שבעים	SEVENTY	988c	3 c
		שפטיה	SHEPHATIAH	1049b	1 d1
7	10	ארח	ARAH	73b	2
7	11	יהושוע	JOSHUA	221c	8
		יואב	JOAB	222a	3
		פחתמואב	PAHATH-MOAB	809b	
		שמנה	EIGHT	1033a	2 a
7	12	אחר	ANOTHER	*29c	
		עילם	ELAM	743d	1 a
7	13	זתוא	ZATTU	285c	
		ארבעים	FORTY	917c	2 c
7	14	זבי	ZABBAI	*256a	
		זכי	ZACCAI	269b	
7	15	בנוי	BINNUI	125a	1
		בני	BANI	125b	4
		ארבעים	FORTY	917c	2 c
7	16	בבי	BEBAI	93c	
7	18	אדניהו	ADONIJAH	11d	3
		אדניקם	ADONIKAM	12a	
7	19	בגוי	BIGVAI	94a	1
7	20	עדין	ADIN	726d	1
7	21	אטר	ATER	32a	
7	22	חזקיהו	HEZEKIAH	306b	4
		חשם	HASHUM	365c	
7	23	בצי	BEZAI	130a	
		ארבע	FOUR	917b	2 b
7	24	חרף	HARIPH	358b	1
		חריפ	HARUPHITE	358b	
		מאה	HUNDRED	*548b	2 a1
7	25	גבעון	GIBEON	149c	
7	26	גבר	GIBBAR	150a	
		ביתלחם	BETHLEHEM	112a	1
		נטפה	NETOPHAH	643b	
7	27	ענתות	ANATHOTH	779a	1
7	28	ביתעזמות	BETH-AZMAVETH	112b	
		ארבעים	FORTY	917c	2 a
7	29	בארות	BEEROTH	92a	
		כפירה	CHEPHIRAH	499a	
		קריתיערים	KIRIATH-JEARIM	900c	
		ארבעים	FORTY	917c	2 c
7	30	גבע	GEBA	148d	1
		רמה	RAMA	928a	1
7	31	מכמס	MICHMASH	485a	
		מאה	HUNDRED	*548b	2 a1
7	32	עי	AI	743b	1
7	33	אחר	ANOTHER	29c	
		מגביש	MAGBISH	150d	
		נב	NOB	611b	1
7	34	אחר	ANOTHER	29c	
		נבו	NEBO	612d	1 b
		עילם	ELAM	743d	1 b
		חרם	HARIM	356c	3 b
7	35	עשרים	TWENTY	797d	12d
7	36	יריחו	JERICHO	437d	
		ארבעים	FORTY	917c	2 c
7	37	אונו	ONO	20c	
		חדיד	HADID	292c	
		לד	LOD	528d	
7	38	סנאה	SENAAH	702d	
		שלשים	THIRTY	1026c	1
7	39	יהושוע	JOSHUA	221d	5
		ידעיה	JEDAIAH	396a	2
7	40	שבעים	SEVENTY	988c	3 c
		אמר	IMMER	57b	2
7	41	פשחור	PASHHUR	832d	4
		ארבעים	FORTY	917c	2 c
7	42	חרם	HARIM	356c	3 a
		שבע	SEVEN	*988b	
		שבע	SEVEN	988b	5 c
7	43	בני	BANI	125b	2 b
		בנוי	BINNUI	125b	
		הודוה	HODEVAH	217b	
		יהושוע	JOSHUA	221d	6 a
		לוי	LEVITE	533b	3 2b
		קדמיאל	KADMIEL	870d	
		שבעים	SEVENTY	988c	3 a
7	44	אסף	ASAPH	63b	2
		ארבעים	FORTY	917c	2 c
7	45	אטר	ATER	32a	
		חטיטא	HATITA	310b	
		טלמן	TALMON	379a	1
		עקוב	AKKUB	784d	2 a
		שבי	SHOBAI	986b	
		שלום	SHALLUM	1024b	2 a
7	46	גשפא	GISHPA	178a	
		חשופא	HASUPHA	362d	
		טבעות	TABBAOTH	371d	
		נתינים	NETHINIM	682a	
		ציחא	ZIHA	851c	
7	47	סיעא	SIA	696b	
		פדון	PADON	804b	
		קרס	KEROS	902b	
7	48	חגבא	HAGABA	290c	
		חגב	HAGAB	*290c	
		לבנא	LEBANA	526c	
		שלמי	SHALMAI	969c	
7	49	גדל	GIDDEL	153c	1
		גחר	GAHAR	161a	
		חנן	HANAN	336d	2
7	50	נקודא	NEKODA	667a	
		ראיה	REAIAH	909d	3
		רצין	REZIN	954a	2
7	51	גזם	GAZZAM	160b	
		עזא	UZZAH	739c	4
		פסח	PASEAH	820c	2
7	52	אסנה	ASNAH	62a	
		בסי	BESAI	126a	
		מעונים	MEUNITES	589b	
		נפסים	NEPHESIM	656c	
7	53	בקבוק	BAKBUK	132d	
		חקופא	HAKUPHA	349a	
		חרחור	HARHUR	359c	
7	54	בצלות	BAZLUTH	130b	
		בצלות	BAZLUTH	130b	
		חרשא	HARSHA	361d	
7	55	ברקוס	BARKOS	140d	
		סיסרא	SISERA	696b	2
		תמח	TEMAH	1069c	
7	56	חטיפא	HATIPHA	310c	
7	57	סוטי	SOTAI	691d	
		ספרת	SOPHERETH	709b	
		פרודא	PERUDA	825d	
		שלמה	SOLOMON	1024d	
7	58	גדל	GIDDEL	153c	2
		דרקון	DARKON	204c	
		יעלא	JAALA	419a	
7	59	אמון	AMON	51b	
		אמון	AMON	54c	C
		חטיל	HATTIL	310b	
		פכרתהצבים	POCHERETH-HAZZEBAIM	810b	
		שפטיה	SHEPHATIAH	1049b	1 d2
7	60	נתינים	NETHINIM	682a	
		שלמה	SOLOMON	1024d	
7	61	אדון	ADDON	11d	

Ch	v.	Heb	Eng	Page	Sec
		אמר	IMMER	57b	5
		בית	HOUSE	110b	5 e
		זרע	SOWING	282d	4 e
		כרוב	CHERUB	500c	
		תלמלח	TEL-MELAH	1068b	
		תלחרשא	TEL-HARSHA	1068b	
7	62	דליהו	DELAIAH	195b	2 a
		טוביה	TOBIJAH	376a	3
		נקודא	NEKODA	667a	
		ארבעים	FORTY	917c	2 c
7	63	ברזלי	BARZILLAI	137d	1
		ברזלי	BARZILLAI	137d	2
		חביה	HABAIAH	285d	
		קוץ	KOZ	881b	2
		קרא	CALL	896c	6 d5
		ארבעים	FORTY	917c	2 c
7	64	בקש	SEEK	*134c	1 b
		גאל	DEFILE	146a	
		מצא	FIND	394a	1 f
		התיחש	ENROLLMENT	405c	
		כהנה	PRIESTHOOD	464d	
		כתב	WRITING	508b	1
7	65	אורים	URIM	22a	
		אשר	THAT	83c	8 ab
		כהן	PRIEST	464b	7
		ל	TO	516d	5 k
		עמד	STAND	764b	6 a
		קדש	APARTNESS	872a	3 b
		תם	INTEGRITY	1070d	4
		תרשתא	TIRASHATHA	1077a	
7	66	קהל	ASSEMBLY	874c	1 c
		רבו	TEN THOUSAND	914b	
		ארבע	FOUR	916d	1 a3
7	67	אמה	MAID	51a	1
		בד	SEPARATION	94d	1 e
		ארבעים	FORTY	917c	2 c
		שיר	SING	1010d	
7	68	חמור	HE-ASS	331b	1
		סוס	HORSE	692d	2
		פרד	MULE	825d	
		שבע	SEVEN	*988b	3
7	69	אוצר	TREASURE	70a	1
		דרכמון	DRACHMA	204b	
		זהב	GOLD	263c	9 d
		כתנת	TUNIC	509a	
		מן	FROM	580d	3 ba
		קצת	END	892c	2
7	70	תרשתא	TIRASHATHA	1077a	
		אוצר	TREASURE	70a	1
		אוצר	TREASURE	70a	1
		דרכמון	DRACHMA	204b	
		זהב	GOLD	263c	9 d
		מזרק	BOWL	284d	2 d
		כסף	SILVER	494c	8 d
		כתנת	TUNIC	*509a	
		רבו	TEN THOUSAND	914c	
		שר	CHIEFTAIN	978d	6
7	71	תרשתא	TIRASHATHA	1077a	
		אוצר	TREASURE	70a	1
		דרכמון	DRACHMA	204b	
		זהב	GOLD	263c	9 d
		כסף	SILVER	494c	8 d
		כתנת	TUNIC	509a	
		מנה	MANEH	584b	
		רבו	TEN THOUSAND	914c	
7	72	שארית	REST	984d	1
		שבע	SEVEN	988b	5 a2
		חדש	NEW MOON	294d	2 b2
		כהן	PRIEST	464a	7
		כתנת	TUNIC	*509a	
		מנה	MANEH	584b	
		נתינים	NETHINIM	682a	
		שארית	REST	*984d	1
		שבע	SEVEN	988b	5 a2
7	73	נגע	REACH	619b	4
		נתינים	NETHINIM	*682a	
8	1	אסף	GATHER	62c	1 a
		חצר	ENCLOSURE	347a	3 b
		תורה	LAW	436b	2 b3
		משה	MOSES	602a	
		ספר	MISSIVE	707b	3 c
		ספר	ENUMERATOR	708c	3
		עזר	EZRA	740d	1
		פנה	FACE	817d	2 4d
		רחוב	PLAZA	932b	
		רחוב	PLAZA	932b	
		שער	GATE	1044d	1 b 1
8	2	בין	DISCERN	107a	1 b
		חדש	NEW MOON	294d	2 b2
		יום	DAY	398c	2 e
		תורה	LAW	436b	2 b3
		כהן	PRIEST	464b	7
		קהל	ASSEMBLY	874c	2 b
8	3	אור	LIGHT	21c	2
		בין	DISCERN	107a	1 b
		מחצית	HALF	346a	2
		יום	DAY	398b	1
		תורה	LAW	436b	2 b3
		ספר	MISSIVE	707b	3 c
		פנה	FACE	817d	2 4d
		קרא	CALL	895c	4 a
		רחוב	PLAZA	932b	
		רחוב	PLAZA	932b	
		שער	GATE	1044d	1 b 1
8	4	אוריה	URIAH	22c	3
		מגדל	TOWER	154a	2
		זכריהו	ZECHARIAH	*272b	2 a
		חשבדנה	HASHBADDANAH	364c	
		חשם	HASHUM	365c	
		ימין	RIGHT HAND	411d	2 a
		מישאל	MISHAEL	567d	3
		מלכיה	MALCHIJAH	575d	4
		מתתיהו	MATTITHIAH	682d	3
		עזור	EZRA	740d	1
		עמד	STAND	763d	1 a
		עניה	ANAIAH	777d	
		עץ	TREE	781d	2 a
		מעשיהו	MAASEIAH	796b	8 a
		פדיהו	PEDALAH	804c	3 b
		שמע	SHEMA	1034d	4
8	5	עזר	EZRA	740d	1
		על	UPON	759b	4 2d
		עמד	STAND	764b	5 b
		פתח	OPEN	835b	
8	6	אלהים	GOD	43d	3
		אמן	VERILY	53b	
		אף	NOSE	60b	2
		ברך	BLESS	139a	2 a
		גדל	GREAT	153b	6 c
		חצר	ENCLOSURE	347a	3 b
		יד	HAND	389c	1 d
		עזר	EZRA	740d	1
		מעל	LIFTING	751b	
		ענה	ANSWER	772d	1 c
		קדד	BOW DOWN	869a	
		שחה	BOW DOWN	1005c	2 b
8	7	בין	DISCERN	107a	3 b
		בני	BANI	125b	2 b
		בנוי	BINNUI	*125b	2
		הודיה	HODIAH	217c	2 a
		יהוזבד	JEHOZABAD	220a	4 g
		יהושוע	JOSHUA	221d	6 a
		חנן	HANAN	336d	3
		ימין	JAMIN	412c	3
		תורה	LAW	436b	2 b3
		לוי	LEVITE	533b	3 2b
		עזריהו	AZARIAH	741b	6
		עמד	STANDING-PLACE	765a	
		עקוב	AKKUB	784d	3 b
		מעשיהו	MAASEIAH	796b	8 a
		פלאיה	PELAIAH	811a	
		קלימא	KELITA	886b	
		שבתי	SABBETHAI	992d	
8	8	בין	DISCERN	107a	3 d
		תורה	LAW	436b	2 b3
		ספר	MISSIVE	707b	3 c
		ספר	MISSIVE	*707c	4
		פרש	MAKE DISTINCT	831d	
		קרא	CALL	895c	4 a
		מקרא	CONVOCATION	896d	3
		שום	TO PLACE	964d	5 d
		שכל	PRUDENCE	968d	2
		פרש	MAKE DISTINCT	*1109a	
8	9	אבל	MOURN	5c	
		בין	DISCERN	107a	3 b
		בכה	WEEP	113b	1
		דבר	WORD	183a	2 2
		תורה	LAW	436b	2 b3
		כהן	PRIEST	464b	7
		נחמיה	NEHEMIAH	637c	1
		ספר	ENUMERATOR	708c	3
		קדוש	HOLY	872d	E
		תרשתא	TIRASHATHA	1077a	
8	10	אדון	LORD	11b	2 2
		אין	NOT	35a	6 ca
		ירוה	JOY	292d	
		כון	BE READY	466a	3
		מנה	PORTION	584b	
		ממתקים	SWEETNESS	609a	
		מעוז	PLACE OF SAFETY	732a	2 a
		עצב	HURT	780d	
		קדוש	HOLY	872d	E
		משמן	FAT PIECE	1032d	
		משנה	SECOND	*1041d	3 a
		שתה	DRINK	1059b	1 a
8	11	חס	HUSH	245a	
		חשה	BE SILENT	364d	3
		עצב	HURT	780d	
		קדוש	HOLY	872d	E
8	12	בין	DISCERN	107a	2
		ידע	MAKE KNOWN	395a	
		מנה	PORTION	584b	
		שמחה	JOY	970d	2
		שלח	SEND	1019a	1 e
8	13	אסף	GATHER	62c	1 a
		דבר	WORD	183a	2 2
		ו	AND	252c	1 b
		תורה	LAW	436b	2 b3
		כהן	PRIEST	464a	7
		ל	TO	518b	7 bh
		ספר	ENUMERATOR	708c	3
		עזר	EZRA	740d	1
		שכל	BE PRUDENT	968d	2
8	14	אשר	THAT	83c	8 ab
		חג	FESTIVAL-GATHER-ING	291a	1 b2
		חדש	NEW MOON	294d	2 b2
		יד	HAND	391a	5 d
		תורה	LAW	436b	2 b3
		מצא	FIND	593a	1 d
		סכה	THICKET	697d	3
		צוה	CHARGE	846a	4 b
8	15	משלם	MESHULLAM	1024c	8 b
		אשר	THAT	83c	8 ab
		הדס	MYRTLE	213c	
		הר	MOUNTAIN	251a	2 a
		זית	OLIVE TREE	268c	1
		זית	OLIVE TREE	*268d	3
		סכה	THICKET	697d	3
		עבר	PASS OVER	718d	2 a
		עבות	LEAFY	721c	
		עלה	LEAF	750a	
		עץ	TREE	781d	1 b
		קול	VOICE	877b	3 a3
		שמן	OIL	1032b	2
		תמר	PALM-TREE	1071c	
8	16	אפרים	EPHRAIM	68c	7
		גג	ROOF	150d	1
		חצר	ENCLOSURE	346d	2
		סכה	THICKET	697d	3
		רחוב	PLAZA	932b	
		רחוב	PLAZA	932b	
		שער	GATE	1044d	1 b 1
		שער	GATE	1044d	1 b 1
		שער	GATE	1045a	2 a
8	17	יהושוע	JOSHUA	221c	1
		יום	DAY	401b	7 l
		נון	NUN	630c	
		סכה	THICKET	697d	3
		קהל	ASSEMBLY	874d	2 b
		שבי	CAPTIVITY	985d	1
		שוב	TURN BACK	997a	2
8	18	אהרון	BEHIND	30d	B
		חג	FESTIVAL-GATHER-ING	291a	1 b2
		חג	FESTIVAL-GATHER-ING	291b	1 b
		יום	DAY	400b	7 e1
		תורה	LAW	436b	2 b3
		ספר	MISSIVE	707b	3
		ספר	MISSIVE	*707c	4
		עצרה	ASSEMBLY	783d	1
		קרא	CALL	895c	4 a
		ראשון	FIRST	911d	2 a
		משפט	JUDGMENT	1048d	3
9	1	אדמה	EARTH	9d	3
		אסף	GATHER	62c	1 a
		זרע	SOWING	*283a	4 f
		יום	DAY	398c	2 e
		צום	FASTING	847b	
		ארבע	FOUR	917b	2 b
		שק	SACK	974c	2
9	2	בדל	BE DIVIDED	95c	1 a
		בן	SON	121c	7 a
		זרע	SOWING	283a	4 f
		חטאת	SIN	308d	1 c
		ידה	CONFESS	392d	1
		נכר	FOREIGNNESS	648d	2
		עון	INIQUITY	731a	1 b
9	3	יהוה	YAHWEH	218d	2 1d
		ידה	CONFESS	392d	1
		תורה	LAW	436b	2 b3
		ספר	MISSIVE	707b	3 c
		ספר	MISSIVE	*707c	4
		עמד	STANDING-PLACE	765a	
		קום	STAND	877d	1 f
		קרא	CALL	895c	4 a
		רביעי	FOURTH	918a	4
9	4	בני	BUNNI	125b	1 a
		בני	BANI	125b	2 b
		בנוי	BINNUI	*125b	2
		יהוה	YAHWEH	218d	2 1d
		יהושוע	JOSHUA	221d	6 a
		זעק	CRY	277b	2 a
		כנני	CHENANI	487a	
		מעלה	ASCENT	751c	2
		קדמיאל	KADMIEL	870d	
		קום	STAND	878a	1 g
		שבניה	SHEBANIAH	987d	1 a1
9	5	בני	BANI	125b	2 b
		ברך	BLESS	139a	1
		ברך	BLESS	139a	1
		ברכה	BLESSING	139d	4
		הודיה	HODIAH	217c	2 a
		יהושוע	JOSHUA	221d	6 a
		תהלה	PRAISE	240a	1
		חשבניה	HASHABNEIAH	364b	1
		כבוד	GLORY	458d	2 c2
		לוי	LEVITE	533b	3 2b
		על	UPON	755a	2 3
		עולם	LONG DURATION	763a	2 m
		פתחיה	PETHAHIAH	836a	1
		קדמיאל	KADMIEL	870d	
		קום	STAND	878a	1 g
		רום	BE HIGH	927b	
		שבניה	SHEBANIAH	987d	1 a1
9	6	אתה	THOU	61c	
		חיה	LIVE	311c	1
		עשה	DO	794b	2 1b
		צבא	HOST	839a	1 b
		צבא	HOST	839b	1 c
		שמי	HEAVENS	1030b	2 a
9	7	אברם	ABRAM	4d	
		אור	UR	22d	
		אלהים	GOD	43d	3
		בחר	CHOOSE	103d	1 a
		כשדים	CHALDEANS	505a	1 a
		שום	TO PLACE	964c	5 b

NEHEMIAH

Ch	v.	Heb	Eng	Page	Sec
		שם	NAME	1027d	2 a
		אור	ADDENDA ET CORRIGENDA	1119d	
9	8	אמן	CONFIRM	53a	5
		אמרי	AMORITES	57c	2 e
		ובוסי	JEBUSITE	101a	1
		ברית	COVENANT	136c	2 2b
		ברית	COVENANT	137a	3 1
		גרגשי	GIRGASHITE	173a	
		דבר	WORD	183a	2 2
		זרע	SOWING	282c	4 b
		חתי	HITTITE	366d	2 a
		כנעני	CANAANITE	489a	2 b
		כרת	CUT	503d	4
		לבב	HEART	524a	2 6a
		מצא	FIND	593a	1 d
		צדיק	JUST	843a	1 d
9	9	זעקה	CRY	277d	2
		סוף	REEDS	693b	2 a
		עני	AFFLICTION	777a	1
9	10	אות	SIGN	16d	4
		מופת	WONDER	69a	1
		זיד	BOIL UP	267d	2
		יום	DAY	400d	7 h
		נתן	GIVE	681b	3 d
		עם	PEOPLE	766c	1
		פרעה	PHARAOH	829a	
		שם	NAME	1028a	2 b1
9	11	אבן	STONE	7a	8
		בקע	CLEAVE	131d	1
		ובשה	DRY LAND	387a	
		כמו	LIKE	*455d	1 a
		כמו	LIKE	455d	1
		עבר	PASS OVER	717c	3 b
		עז	STRONG	738c	
		מצולה	DEPTH	846d	
		רדף	PURSUE	922d	1 c
		שלך	THROW	1021b	2 b
		תוך	MIDST	1063d	
9	12	אור	BECOME LIGHT	21b	1
		אש	FIRE	77c	2
		נחה	LEAD	635a	
		עמוד	PILLAR	765b	4
		עמוד	PILLAR	765b	4
9	13	אמת	FIRMNESS	54b	4 c
		דבר	SPEAK	181c	3 e
		הר	MOUNTAIN	249b	1 a
		חק	SOMETHING PRESCRIBED	349d	7 g
		טוב	PLEASANT	375a	0 b
		ירד	GO DOWN	433b	2
		תורה	LAW	436a	2 a
		ישר	STRAIGHT	449a	3 a
		סיני	SINAI	696a	
		מצוה	COMMANDMENT	846c	2 b1
		משפט	JUDGMENT	1049a	4
9	14	חק	SOMETHING PRESCRIBED	349d	7 g
		יד	HAND	391d	5 d
		ידע	MAKE KNOWN	395a	
		תורה	LAW	436b	2 b3
		משה	MOSES	602d	
		עבד	SLAVE	714a	3
		צוה	GIVE CHARGE TO	845c	1 b
		מצוה	COMMANDMENT	846c	2 b1
		קדש	APARTNESS	872b	5
		שבת	SABBATH	992c	1 d
9	15	אמר	SAY	56b	3
		אמר	SAY	56c	4
		יד	HAND	389c	1 d
		יצא	BRING OUT	425a	4 i
		ירש	TAKE POSSESSION	439c	1 a
		ל	TO	515a	5 ha
		נשא	LIFT	670b	1 b1
		נתן	GIVE	678c	1 b
		סלע	CRAG	*701a	1
		צמא	THIRST	854d	
		שמי	HEAVENS	1030a	2 a
9	16	זיד	BOIL UP	267d	2
		ערף	BACK OF NECK	791c	2
		קשה	BE SEVERE	904c	3 a
9	17	אלה	GOD	43a	2
		אף	NOSE	60b	3
		ארך	LONG	74a	
		זכר	REMEMBER	269d	1 l d
		חנון	GRACIOUS	337a	
		חסד	GOODNESS	339a	2 3a
		מאן	REFUSE	549b	
		מרי	REBELLION	598b	
		סליחה	FORGIVENESS	669c	
		עבדות	SERVITUDE	715c	
		ערף	BACK OF NECK	791c	2
		קשה	BE SEVERE	904c	3 a
		רחון	COMPASSIONATE	933c	
		שוב	TURN BACK	997c	5 d
9	18	אף	ALSO	65b	3
		נאצה	CONTEMPT	611a	
		מסכה	MOLTEN IMAGE	651b	2
		עגל	CALF	722b	
9	19	אור	BECOME LIGHT	21b	1
		אש	FIRE	77c	2
		את	MARK OF THE ACCUSATIVE	85c	3 a
		יומם	DAYTIME	401c	1
		לילה	NIGHT	539a	1
		נחה	LEAD	635a	
		על	UPON	758c	4 2a
		עמוד	PILLAR	765b	4
		עמוד	PILLAR	765b	4
9	20	רחמים	COMPASSION	933c	1
		טוב	PLEASANT	374d	9 b
		מן	MANNA	577c	
		מנע	WITHHOLD	586a	
		נתן	GIVE	678c	1 b
		פה	MOUTH	804d	1 a
		צמא	THIRST	854d	
		רוח	BREATH	926a	9 f
		שכל	BE PRUDENT	968c	4
9	21	בלה	BECOME OLD AND WORN OUT	*115a	
		בצק	SWELL	130d	
		חסר	LACK	341b	1 b
		כול	SUSTAIN	465a	1
		שלמה	GARMENT	971b	
9	22	בשן	BASHAN	143c	
		חלק	DIVIDE	323c	1
		חשבון	HESHBON	363d	
		ירש	TAKE POSSESSION	439c	1 a
		ממלכה	KINGDOM	575a	1
		סיחון	SIHON	695d	
		עוג	OG	728b	
		פאה	CORNER	802a	1
9	23	אמר	SAY	56c	3
		ירש	TAKE POSSESSION	439c	1 a
		כוכב	STAR	457a	
9	24	ב	IN	89d	3 2b
		ירש	TAKE POSSESSION	439c	1 a
		כנע	HUMBLE	488c	2
		כנעני	CANAANITE	489a	2 b
		עשה	DO	794b	1 2
		רצון	GOODWILL	953c	3 b
9	25	אדמה	LAND	10a	5
		מאכל	FOOD	38b	
		בור	WELL	92b	1
		בצר	MAKE INACCESSIBLE	131a	
		גדול	GREAT	153b	6 c
		זית	OLIVE TREE	268d	1
		חצב	HEW	345a	1
		טוב	GOOD THINGS	375c	4 a
		טוב	GOOD THINGS	375c	2
		ירש	TAKE POSSESSION	439c	1 a
		מלא	FULL	571a	
		עדן	LUXURIATE	726c	
		עץ	TREE	781c	1 b
		רב	MULTITUDE	914a	1
		שמן	GROW FAT	1031d	
		שמן	FAT	1032a	1
9	26	גו	BACK	156a	1
		הרג	KILL	247a	1 a
		תורה	LAW	436b	2 b3
		מרד	REBEL	597c	1
		מרה	BE REBELLIOUS	598b	
		נאצה	CONTEMPT	611a	
		עוד	BEAR WITNESS	730a	3
		קשה	BE SEVERE	904c	3 a
		שוב	TURN BACK	999b	2 a
		שלך	THROW	1021a	1 b
9	27	ישע	DELIVER	446c	1 a
		ישע	DELIVER	446c	1 a
		צעק	CRY	858c	1 b
		צרר	BIND	864d	B
		צרה	DISTRESS	865b	
		רחמים	COMPASSION	933c	1
9	28	זעק	CRY	277b	2 a
		נוח	REST	628b	2
		עזב	LEAVE	737c	2 e
		עת	TIME	773d	4
		רב	MUCH	913a	1 b
		רדה	HAVE DOMINION	922a	
		רחמים	COMPASSION	933c	1
		רע	EVIL	948c	3
		שוב	TURN BACK	998b	8
9	29	זיד	BOIL UP	267d	2
		חטא	MISS A GOAL OR WAY	307b	2 b
		חיה	LIVE	311b	1 c
		תורה	LAW	436b	2 b3
		כתף	SHOULDER	509b	1 b
		נתן	GIVE	680a	1 z
		סרר	BE STUBBORN	711a	
		עוד	BEAR WITNESS	730a	3
		ערף	BACK OF NECK	791c	2
		מצוה	COMMANDMENT	846c	2 b3
		שוב	TURN BACK	999b	2 a
9	30	אזן	HEAR	24c	1
		יד	HAND	391a	5 d
		משך	DRAW	*604c	5
		עוד	BEAR WITNESS	730a	3
		על	UPON	758a	2 8
		עם	PEOPLE	766c	5 d
		רב	MUCH	913a	1 b
		רוח	BREATH	926a	9 b
9	31	אל	GOD	42d	6 d
		חנון	GRACIOUS	337a	
		כלה	COMPLETE	478d	2 a
		עשה	DO	794c	2 1g
		רחמים	COMPASSION	933c	1
		רחון	COMPASSIONATE	933d	
9	32	אל	GOD	42c	6 a
		אשור	ASSYRIA	78d	4
		את	MARK OF THE ACCUSATIVE	85b	1 c
		ברית	COVENANT	137a	3 2
		ברית	COVENANT	137b	3 2
		גבור	STRONG	150a	1
		גדול	GREAT	153b	6 c
		חסד	GOODNESS	339a	2 1e
		ירא	BE REVERED	431d	3 a
		כהן	PRIEST	464b	7
		ל	TO	512a	3 b
		תלאה	WEARINESS	521b	
		מעט	BE SMALL	589c	
		מצא	FIND	593b	3 e
		נביא	PROPHET	611d	2
		שר	CHIEFTAIN	978b	2 a
9	33	אמת	FIRMNESS	54a	3 b
		על	UPON	754d	2 1f h
		צדיק	JUST	843a	1 d
		רשע	BE WICKED	957d	3
9	34	את	MARK OF THE ACCUSATIVE	85c	3 a
		תורה	LAW	436b	2 b3
		כהן	PRIEST	464b	7
		עוד	BEAR WITNESS	730a	3
		עדות	TESTIMONY	730b	2
		מצוה	COMMANDMENT	846c	2 b3
		קשב	ATTEND	904a	
		שר	CHIEFTAIN	978c	2 a
9	35	ארץ	EARTH	76b	3 b
		טוב	GOOD THINGS	375c	1
		מלכות	KINGDOM	575a	3
		מעלל	DEED	760b	1
		רחב	WIDE	932a	
		רע	EVIL	948c	0 d
		שמן	FAT	1032a	1
9	36	טוב	GOOD THINGS	375c	1
9	37	בהמה	BEAST	97a	2
		תבואה	PRODUCT	100a	1
		גויה	BODY	156b	1
		חטאת	SIN	308d	1 b
		מלך	KING	573c	5 c
		משל	RULE	605d	1
		צרה	DISTRESS	865b	
		רבה	BECOME MANY	915c	1 c
		רצון	GOODWILL	953c	3 b
10	1	אמנה	FAITH	53d	1
		חתם	SEAL	367d	1
		כהן	PRIEST	464b	7
		כרת	CUT	504a	4
		לוי	LEVITE	532a	3
		שר	CHIEFTAIN	978d	6
		תרשתא	TIRASHATHA	1077a	
10	2	חכליה	HACALIAH	314b	
		חתם	SEAL	367d	1
		נחמיה	NEHEMIAH	637c	1
		צדקיהו	ZEDEKIAH	843c	4
10	3	עזריה	AZARIAH	741b	5
		ירמיה	JEREMIAH	941d	7 b
		ישראל	ISRAEL	975d	2 a3
		שריה	SERAIAH	976a	5 c
10	4	אמריהו	AMARIAH	57d	7
		מלכיהו	MALCHIJAH	575d	4
		פשחור	PASSHUR	832d	3
10	5	חטוש	HATTUSH	310d	3
		מלוך	MALLUCH	576a	2 c
		שבניה	SHEBANIAH	987d	1 b
		שכניה	SHECANIAH	1016a	5 a
10	6	חרם	HARIM	356c	2
		מרמות	MEREMOTH	599b	2
		עבדיהו	OBADIAH	716a	2 8
10	7	ברוך	BARUCH	140a	2
		גנתון	GINNETHON	171b	
		דניאל	DANIEL	193b	2
10	8	ביהו	ABIJAM	4a	6
		מימן	MIJAMIN	568b	1 b
		משלם	MESHULLAM	1024c	7 c
10	9	בלגי	BILGAI	114d	
		מזיזיהו	MAAZIAH	589b	2
		שמעיה	SHEMAIAH	1035d	0 a
10	10	אזניהו	AZANIAH	24c	
		בני	BANI	*125b	2 b
		בנוי	BINNUI	125b	2
		בני	BUNNI	125b	1 a
		יהושע	JOSHUA	221d	6 a
		חנדד	HENADAD	337b	
		לוי	LEVITE	533b	3 2b
		קמיאל	KADMIEL	870d	
10	11	הודיה	HODIAH	217c	2 a
		חנן	HANAN	336d	3
		פלאיה	PELAIAH	811a	
		קליטא	KELITA	886b	
		שבניה	SHEBANIAH	987d	1 a2
10	12	חשביהו	HASHABIAH	364a	6
		רחוב	REHOB	932b	2 b
10	13	זכור	ZACCUR	271d	3 c
		שבניה	SHEBANIAH	987d	1 a1
10	14	בנינו	BENINU	123a	
		בני	BANI	125b	2 b
		הודיה	HODIAH	217c	2 b
		בוני	BUNNI	125b	1
10	15	בני	BANI	125b	5 b
		זתוא	ZATTU	285c	
		עילם	ELAM	743d	2
		פחתמואב	PAHATH-MOAB	809b	
		פרעש	PAROSH	829b	2
10	16	בבי	BEBAI	93c	

Ch	v.	Heb	Eng	Page	Sec
		בני	BUNNI	125b	2
10	17	מיכא	MICA	567d	2
		אדניהו	ADONIJAH	11d	3
		אדניקם	ADONIKAM	12a	
		בגוי	BIGVAI	94a	2
		עדין	ADIN	726d	2
10	18	אטר	ATER	32a	
		חזקיהו	HEZEKIAH	306b	4
		עזור	AZZUR	741a	3
10	19	בצי	BEZAI	130a	
		הודיה	HODIAH	217c	3
		חשם	HASHUM	365c	
10	20	חרף	HARIPH	358b	2
		נובי	NOBAI	626c	
		ענתות	ANATHOTH	779a	2 b
10	21	חזיר	HEZIR	306c	2
		מגפיעש	MAGPIASH	550d	
		משלם	MESHULLAM	1024c	6
10	22	ידוע	JADDUA	396a	1
		משיזבאל	MESHEZABEL	604a	
		צדוק	ZADOK	843b	3 c
10	23	חנן	HANAN	336d	4 a
		עניה	ANAIAH	777d	
		פלטיהו	PELATIAH	812d	2
10	24	חנניהו	HANANIAH	337b	9 e
		חשוב	HASSHUB	363d	2 a
		הושע	HOSHEA	448a	5
10	25	לוחש	HALLOHESH	538a	
		פלחא	PILHA	812b	
		שובק	SHOBEK	990b	
10	26	חשבנה	HASHABNAH	364b	
		מעשיהו	MAASEIAH	796b	8 b
		רחום	REHUM	933d	2 b
10	27	אחיהו	AHIJAH	26d	9
		חנן	HANAN	336d	4 b
		ענן	ANAN	778b	
10	28	בענה	BAANAH	128d	4
		חרם	HARIM	356c	4
10	29	מלוך	MALLUCH	576a	2 d
		בדל	BE DIVIDED	95c	1 d
		בין	DISCERN	107a	1 b
		תורה	LAW	436b	2b3
		כהן	PRIEST	464b	7
		לוי	LEVITE	533a	3 2b
		נתינים	NETHINIM	682a	
		עם	PEOPLE	766d	5 d
		שאר	REST	984c	
10	30	אדון	LORD	11b	22
		אדיר	MAJESTIC	12b	2
		אלהים	GOD	44a	3 b
		אלה	OATH	46d	1
		הלך	WALK	234c	23a 1d
		חזק	BE FIRM	305b	6 c
		חק	SOMETHING PRE-SCRIBED	349d	7 g
		תורה	LAW	436b	2b3
		משה	MOSES	602d	
		נתן	GIVE	681c	1 h
		עבד	SLAVE	714a	3
		מצוה	COMMANDMENT	846c	2b1
		שבועה	OATH	990a	1a
10	31	אשר	THAT	83c	8 ab
		עם	PEOPLE	766d	5 d
10	32	יד	HAND	389c	1 d
		מקחה	WARE	544c	
		מכר	SELL	569b	
		נטש	LEAVE	643d	1
		משא	LENDING ON IN-TEREST	673d	
		קדש	APARTNESS	872b	5
		שבר	GRAIN	991c	
		שבת	SABBATH	992b	1 a
		שבת	SABBATH	992c	1 d
10	33	נתן	PUT	680c	2 b
		עבדה	LABOR	715c	4
		על	UPON	753b	2 1c
		עמד	STAND	764d	5
		מצוה	COMMANDMENT	846b	1
		שנה	YEAR	1040b	
		שקל	SHEKEL	1053d	
		שקל	SHEKEL	1053d	
10	34	חדש	NEW MOON	294c	1
		חטאת	SIN	309b	4
		מועד	APPOINTED TIME	417c	1 b
		כפר	COVER OVER	497d	3 b2
		מלאכה	WORK	522b	6 b
		לחם	FOOD	537b	1 a
		תמיד	CONTINUITY	556c	2 b
		מנחה	OFFERING	585b	4
		עלה	WHOLE BURNT OF-FERING	750b	
		מערכת	ROW	790b	
		ישראל	ISRAEL	975d	2 a3
		שבת	SABBATH	992c	1 d
10	35	בוא	COME	99b	2
		בית	HOUSE	110b	5 e
		בער	BURN	129b	2
		גורל	LOT	174c	2 d
		מזבח	ALTAR	259a	1
		זמן	BE FIXED	273d	
		תורה	LAW	436b	2b3
		כהן	PRIEST	464b	7
		ל	TO	511b	1 ga
		ל	TO	516d	6 a
		נפל	FALL	658a	3
		עת	TIME	773d	2 c

Ch	v.	Heb	Eng	Page	Sec
		קרבן	OFFERING	898d	
10	36	אדמה	GROUND	9c	1
		בכורים	FIRST-FRUITS	114c	
10	37	בהמה	BEAST	97a	2
		בוא	COME	99b	2
		בכור	FIRST-BORN	114b	1 c
		בכור	FIRST-BORN	114b	2 c
		בקר	HERD	133b	1 b
		תורה	LAW	436b	2b3
10	38	אדמה	GROUND	9c	1
		הוא	HE, SHE, IT	215c	1 e
		הם	THEY	241b	1 e
		תירוש	NEW WINE	440d	
		לשכה	ROOM	545b	1 d
		עבדה	LABOR	715b	1
		עריסה	COARSE MEAL	791b	
		עשר	TAKE THE TENTH OF	797c	
		מעשר	TENTH PART	798b	2
		יצהר	FRESH OIL	844a	
		ראשית	BEGINNING	912b	1 b
		תרומה	OFFERING	929b	4 a
10	39	אהרן	AARON	14d	
		אוצר	TREASURE	70a	3 a
		בן	SON	121b	1 jz
		היה	BE	227b	34d a
		כהן	PRIEST	464b	7
		ל	TO	513c	5 cb b
		לשכה	ROOM	545d	1 d
		עלה	GO UP	749d	6
		עשר	TAKE THE TENTH OF	797c	
		מעשר	TENTH PART	798b	2
		מעשר	TENTH PART	798b	2
10	40	בן	SON	121a	1 jg
		בן	SON	121a	1 je
		דגן	CORN	186c	
		דגן	CORN	186c	
		תירוש	NEW WINE	440d	
		כלי	UTENSIL	480a	2 f
		לוי	LEVITE	532d	1
		לשכה	ROOM	545d	1 d
		עזב	LEAVE	737c	2 d2
		יצהר	FRESH OIL	844a	
		תרומה	OFFERING	929b	4 a
		ישראל	ISRAEL	976a	2 e
11	1	גורל	LOT	174c	2 c
		יד	PART	390c	4 b
		עיר	CITY	746c	1 i
		עשר	TEN	797a	2 b
		קדש	APARTNESS	871d	2 e
		שר	CHIEFTAIN	978d	6
		שאר	REST	984c	
		תשע	NINE	1077c	1 a
11	2	ברך	BLESS	139b	4 d
		ל	TO	512a	3 b
		נדב	INCITE	621c	1
11	3	אחזה	POSSESSION	28c	
		כהן	PRIEST	464a	7
		נתינים	NETHINIM	682a	
		ישראל	ISRAEL	976a	2 e
		שלמה	SOLOMON	1024d	
11	4	אמריהו	AMARIAH	57d	8
		בנימן	BENJAMIN	122b	1
		מהללאל	MAHALALEL	239d	2
		זכריהו	ZECHARIAH	*272b	2 d
		מן	FROM	580d	3 ba
		עזיהו	UZZIAH	739d	5
		עתיה	ATHAIAH	800d	
		פרץ	PEREZ	829d	1
		שפטיה	SHEPHATIAH	1049b	1 c
11	5	ברוך	BARUCH	140a	3
		יהויריב	JEHOIARIB	220b	3
		זכריהו	ZECHARIAH	*272b	2 e
		חזיה	HAZAIAH	303c	
		כלחזה	COL-HOZEH	480d	2
		עדיה	ADAIAH	726a	7
		מעשיהו	MAASEIAH	796b	8 c
		שלני	SHELANITES	1017c	
		שילני	SHILONITE	1018a	
11	6	חיל	STRENGTH	298d	1 c
		פרץ	PEREZ	829d	1
11	7	איתיאל	ITHIEL	87b	2
		בנימן	BENJAMIN	122b	1
		יועד	JOED	222c	
		ישעיה	JESHAIAH	448a	4
		סלוא	SALLU	699b	
		מעשיהו	MAASEIAH	796b	8 d
		פדיהו	PEDALAH	804c	4
		קוליה	KOLAIAH	877c	2
11	8	גבסלי	GABBAI SALLAI	146c	
		סלי	SALLAI	699b	
11	9	יואל	JOEL	222b	9
		זכרי	ZICHRI	271d	5 d
		יהודה	JUDAH	397b	1 5
		פקיד	COMMISSIONER	824b	
		משנה	SECOND	1041d	3
11	10	יהויריב	JEHOIARIB	220d	1
		ידעיה	JEDAIAH	396a	1
11	11	אחיטוב	AHITUB	27a	2
		חלקיהו	HILKIAH	324d	1
		מריות	MERAIOTH	599b	1 b
		נגד	LEADER	618a	3
		צדוק	ZADOK	843b	1 c
		ירחם	JEROHAM	934a	3 b
		שריה	SERAIAH	976a	5 d

Ch	v.	Heb	Eng	Page	Sec
		משלם	MESHULLAM	1024c	7 a
11	12	אמצי	AMZI	55c	2
		זכריהו	ZECHARIAH	272b	1 d
		מלכיהו	MALCHIJAH	575c	1
		עדיהו	ADAIAH	726a	5
		פלליה	PELALIAH	813d	
		פשחור	PASHHUR	832d	2
11	13	אחזי	AHAZIAH	28d	3
		אמר	IMMER	57b	2
		יחזרה	JAHZERAH	403d	
		עזראל	AZAREL	741a	5 a
		עמשסי	AMASHSAI	772a	
		ראש	HEAD	911a	3 f
		ארבעים	FORTY	917c	2 c
		משלמות	MESHILLEMOTH	1024c	2
11	14	גבור	STRONG	150b	2
		גדול	GREAT	153b	6 b
		הגדולים	HAGGEDOLIM	153c	
		זבדיאל	ZABDIEL	256c	2
		פקיד	COMMISSIONER	824b	
11	15	בני	BUNNI	125b	1 b
		חשוב	HASSHUB	363d	1
		חשביהו	HASHABIAH	364a	3 1c
		לוי	LEVITE	533a	3 1c
		עזריקם	AZRIKAM	741b	4
		שמעיה	SHEMAIAH	1035d	7 h
11	16	יהוזבד	JEHOZABAD	220a	2
		זברי	ZICHRI	271d	3 c
		חיצון	OUTER	300c	2
		לוי	LEVITE	533a	3 1c
		שבתי	SABBETHAI	992d	1
11	17	אסף	ASAPH	63b	2
		בקבקיה	BAKBUKIAH	132d	1
		זבדי	ZABDI	256c	4
		ידה	PRAISE	392c	1 b
		ידותון	JEDUTHUN	s 393a	1
		ל	TO	511d	1 i
		מיכה	MICAH	*567d	3
		מיכא	MICA	567d	3
		מתניהו	MATTANIAH	682d	3 a
		מתניהו	MATTANIAH	*682d	3 a
		עבדא	ABDA	715a	2
		שמוע	SHAMMUA	1035b	3
		משנה	SECOND	1041d	3 a
11	18	עיר	CITY	746c	1 i
		קדש	APARTNESS	871d	2 e
11	19	טלמון	TALMON	379a	2
		עקוב	AKKUB	784d	3 c
		שבעים	SEVENTY	988c	3 c
11	20	כהן	PRIEST	464b	7
		ישראל	ISRAEL	976a	2 e
		שאר	REST	984c	
11	21	גשפא	GISHPA	177d	
		נתינים	NETHINIM	682a	
		עפל	MOUND	779b	
		ציחא	ZIHA	851c	
11	22	אסף	ASAPH	63b	2
		בני	BANI	125b	2 b
		חשביהו	HASHABIAH	364a	6
		מלאכה	WORK	522b	6 b
		מיכא	MICA	567d	3
		מיכה	MICAH	*567d	3
		נגד	IN FRONT	617c	2 b
		מתניהו	MATTANIAH	682d	3 a
		מתניהו	MATTANIAH	*682d	3 a
		עזי	UZZI	739d	1 b
		פקיד	COMMISSIONER	824b	
11	23	אמנה	FAITH	53d	2
		דבר	WORD	183b	4 l
		יום	DAY	400c	7 e3
		על	UPON	753c	2 1c
11	24	זרח	ZERAH	280b	1
		יד	HAND	391b	5 f
		ל	TO	514c	5 fc
		משיזבאל	MESHEZABEL	604a	
		פתחיה	PETHAHIAH	836a	3
11	25	בת	DAUGHTER	123d	4
		דיבן	DIBON	192a	2
		חנה	DECLINE	*333c	2 b
		חצר	SETTLED ABODE	347b	D
		חצר	SETTLED ABODE	*347b	B
		חצר	SETTLED ABODE	347b	B
		מן	FROM	580d	3 ba
		קבצאל	KABZEEL	868b	
		קריתארבע	FOURFOLD CITY	900c	
		שדה	FIELD	961d	2 c
11	26	ביתפלט	BETH-PELET	112c	
		בת	DAUGHTER	123d	4
		יהושוע	JOSHUA	221d	9
		מולדה	MOLADAH	409d	
11	27	בארשבע	BEERSHEBA	92a	
		בזיותיה	BIZIOTHIAH	103b	
		בת	DAUGHTER	123d	4
		חצר	SETTLED ABODE	*347b	B
		חצרשועל	HAZAR-SHUAL	347c	1
11	28	בת	DAUGHTER	123d	4
		מכנה	MECONAH	569a	
11	29	בת	DAUGHTER	123d	4
		ירמות	JARMUTH	438b	1
		עינרמון	EN-RIMMON	745c	
		צרעה	ZORAH	864a	
11	30	בארשבע	BEERSHEBA	92a	
		בת	DAUGHTER	123d	4
		הנם	HINNOM	245a	
		חנה	DECLINE	333c	2 b
		חצר	SETTLED ABODE	347b	B

241

Ch v.	Heb	Eng	Page	Sec
	ספר	MISSIVE	*707c	4
	עולם	LONG DURATION	762b	2 b4
	עמוני	AMMONITE	770a	
	קרא	CALL	896b	2 b
13 2	בלעם	BALAAM	118d	
	ברכה	BLESSING	*139d	1 b
	הפך	TURN	245c	1 c4
	קדם	COME IN FRONT	870a	1 b
	קללה	CURSE	887a	
	שכר	HIRE	969a	2
13 3	בדל	BE DIVIDED	95b	2
	חנן	HANAN	336d	3
	תורה	LAW	436b	2 b3
	ערב	MIXTURE	786b	1
13 4	אלישיב	ELIASHIB	46a	C
	טוביהו	TOBIJAH	376a	2
	כהן	PRIEST	464b	7
	לשכה	ROOM	545d	1 d
	נתן	PUT	680d	2 c
	פנה	FACE	817d	24e
	קרב	NEAR	898c	2 c
13 5	דגן	CORN	186c	
	דגן	CORN	186c	
	תירוש	NEW WINE	440d	
	לבנה	FRANKINCENSE	526d	
	לוי	LEVITE	533d	3 2b
	לשכה	ROOM	545d	1 d
	מנחה	OFFERING	585b	4
	מעשר	TENTH PART	798b	2
	יצהר	FRESH OIL	844a	
	מצוה	COMMANDMENT	846c	2 c
	תרומה	OFFERING	929b	4 a
13 6	ארתחששתא	ARTAXERXES	77a	
	בבל	BABEL	93c	
	זה	THIS	260d	1 a
	ל	TO	517a	6 a
	קץ	END	893d	1
	שאל	ASK	982b	
13 7	אלישיב	ELIASHIB	46a	C
	בין	DISCERN	106d	3 c
	חצר	ENCLOSURE	347a	3 b
	טוביהו	TOBIJAH	376a	2
	נשכה	CHAMBER	675b	
	עשה	DO	794d	23
13 8	חוץ	THE OUTSIDE	299c	1 a
	טוביהו	TOBIJAH	376a	2
	כלי	ARTICLE	479c	1
	לשכה	ROOM	545d	1 d
	רעע	BE EVIL	949c	1
13 9	אמר	SAY	56c	4
	טהר	BE CLEAN	372c	1 a
	כלי	UTENSIL	480d	2 f
	לבנה	FRANKINCENSE	526d	
	לשכה	ROOM	545d	1 d
	עד	AS FAR AS	724b	12a a
	עמד	STAND	764d	5
	שוב	TURN BACK	999a	1 a
13 10	ברח	FLEE	138a	2
	ל	TO	511b	1 ga
	לוי	LEVITE	533a	3 2b
	מנת	PORTION	584c	
	נתן	GIVE	681c	1 c
13 11	סגן	RULER	688d	2
	עזב	LEAVE	737d	2
	עמד	STAND	764d	1
	קבץ	GATHER	868a	2
	ריב	STRIVE	936c	2
13 12	אוצר	TREASURE	70a	3 b
	בוא	COME	99a	1
	דגן	CORN	186c	
	דגן	CORN	186c	
	תירוש	NEW WINE	440d	
	מעשר	TENTH PART	798b	2
	יצהר	FRESH OIL	844a	
13 13	אמן	CONFIRM	53a	5
	אצר	STORE UP	69d	
	אוצר	TREASURE	70a	3 b
	זכור	ZACCUR	271d	3 c
	חלק	DIVIDE	323c	1
	חשב	THINK	363c	1
	יד	HAND	391c	5 h3
	כהן	PRIEST	464b	7
	ל	TO	517d	7 bd
	מתניהו	MATTANIAH	682d	3 b3
	ספר	ENUMERATOR	708c	1 b
	על	UPON	753c	2 1c
	פדיהו	PEDALAH	804c	5
	צדוק	ZADOK	843b	3 d
	שלמיה	SHELEMIAH	1025a	3 b
13 14	זה	THIS	262a	6 f
	זכר	REMEMBER	270b	2 1 a
	חסד	GOODNESS	338d	1 3
	מחה	WIPE OUT	562b	1
	מחה	WIPE OUT	562b	3
	עשה	DO	794a	1 1a 5
	משמר	GUARD	1038b	3
13 15	אף	ALSO	65a	1
	בוא	COME	99b	1 e
	דרך	TREAD	202a	3
	חמור	HE-ASS	331b	3
	גת	WINE-PRESS	387c	1
	יין	WINE	406c	A
	מכר	SELL	569b	
	משא	LOAD	672c	1
	עוד	BEAR WITNESS	730a	3
	עמס	LOAD	770c	1
	ענב	GRAPE	772a	
	ערמה	HEAP	790d	
	ציד	PROVISION	845b	
	שבת	SABBATH	992c	1 d
	תאנה	FIG	1061a	2
13 16	דג	FISH	185c	
	דגה	FISH	185d	
	מכר	SELL	569b	
	צרי	TYRIAN	863a	
13 17	חלל	POLLUTE	320b	1 b
	חר	NOBLE	359d	
	ריב	STRIVE	936c	2
	רע	EVIL	948c	0 d
13 18	חלל	POLLUTE	320b	1 b
	חרון	BURNING OF AN-GER	354c	
	יסף	ADD	415a	1
	ל	TO	517c	7 bb
	שבת	SABBATH	992c	1 c
13 19	אחר	AFTER	29d	2 b
	אמר	SAY	56c	4
	אמר	SAY	56c	4
	אשר	THAT	83c	8 ab
	דלת	DOOR	195b	3
	היה	COME TO PASS	224c	2 a1 ah
	משא	LOAD	672c	1
	סגר	BE SHUT	689b	2
	פתח	OPEN	835a	
	צלל	BE DARK	853a	
13 20	מכר	SELL	569b	
	ממכר	WARE	569d	
	פעם	OCCURRENCE	822a	3 a
	רכל	GO ABOUT	940b	
	שנים	TWO	1041b	1 b3
13 21	עוד	BEAR WITNESS	730a	3
	עת	TIME	773c	1 a
	שבת	SABBATH	992c	1 d
	שנה	DO AGAIN	1040d	
13 22	אמר	SAY	56c	4
	אשר	THAT	83c	8 ab
	זכר	REMEMBER	270b	2 1 a
	חום	PITY	299b	B
	חסד	GOODNESS	339d	2 3a
	טהר	BE CLEAN	372c	1 a
	קדש	BE SET APART	873b	2
	רב	MULTITUDE	914a	2
	שמר	KEEP	1036c	1 b
13 23	אשה	WOMAN	61b	1
	אשדודי	ASHDODITE	78c	
	יהודי	JEW	397c	
	ישב	MARRY	443d	4
	מואבי	MOABITISH	556a	
	עמוני	AMMONITE	770a	
13 24	אשדודית	LANGUAGE OF ASHDOD	78c	
	דבר	SPEAK	181a	2
	ו	AND	253b	1 ib
	יהודית	JEWISH	397c	
	לשון	TONGUE	546c	2
	נכר	RECOGNIZE	648b	5
	עם	PEOPLE	766c	1
	עם	PEOPLE	767a	5 h
13 25	מרט	MAKE BARE	598d	1
	נכה	SMITE	645c	1 b
	נשא	LIFT	671c	3 d
	ריב	STRIVE	936c	2
	שבע	SWEAR	989d	1
13 26	אהב	LOVE	13a	5 a
	אשה	WOMAN	61b	1
	היה	BE	226d	3 1
	היה	BE	227c	3 5a
	חטא	MISS A GOAL OR WAY	307b	2 b
	חטא	MISS A GOAL OR WAY	307c	2
	ל	TO	514a	5 e
	מלך	KING	573a	5 c
	נכרי	FOREIGN	648d	1 a
	על	UPON	754d	2 1f h
13 27	אמר	SAY	56d	
	אשה	WOMAN	61b	1
	ה	INTERROG PART	210a	1 b
	ישב	MARRY	443d	4
	מעל	ACT TREACHER-OUSLY	591b	2 b
	נכרי	FOREIGN	648d	1 a
13 28	אלישיב	ELIASHIB	46a	C
	ביתחורן	BETH-HORON	111c	
	ברח	FLEE	138a	2
	יהוידע	JEHOIADA	220c	4
	חתן	DAUGHTER:S HUS-BAND	368c	1
	כהן	PRIEST	464b	8
	מן	FROM	580d	3 bb
	סנבלט	SANBALLAT	702d	
	על	UPON	759a	4 2b
13 29	ברית	COVENANT	136d	2 2d
	גאל	DEFILING	146a	
	זכר	REMEMBER	270b	2 1b
	כהנה	PRIESTHOOD	464d	
13 30	טהר	BE CLEAN	372c	1 a
	כהן	PRIEST	464a	7
	נכר	FOREIGNNESS	648d	3
	עמד	STAND	764d	5
13 31	בכורים	FIRST-FRUITS	114c	
	זכר	REMEMBER	270b	2 1 a
	זמן	BE FIXED	273d	3
	טובה	WELFARE	375d	3
	עת	TIME	773d	2 c
	קרבן	OFFERING	898d	

ESTHER

Ch v.	Heb	Eng	Page	Sec
1 1	אחשורוש	AHASUERUS	31c	
	מדינה	PROVINCE	193d	3
	הדו	INDIA	213a	
	כוש	CUSH	469a	2 a
	מלך	BE KING	574a	
1 2	אחשורוש	AHASUERUS	31c	
	בירה	CASTLE	108b	2
	מלך	KING	573a	1
	מלכות	ROYAL POWER	574d	1
	שושן	SUSA	1004d	1
1 3	מדי	MEDES	552a	1
	פרס	PERSIA	828a	1
	פרתמים	NOBLES	832c	
	שר	CHIEFTAIN	978b	2 c
	משתה	FEAST	1059d	1
1 4	גדולה	GREATNESS	153c	A
	יום	DAY	398c	2 c
	יקר	HONOUR	430b	3
	כבוד	HONOR	458c	2 b
	מאה	HUNDRED	548b	1 d6
	מלכות	ROYALTY	575a	1
	תפארה	BEAUTY	802c	2 a
	ראה	TO SEE	908d	1 a1
1 5	בירה	CASTLE	108b	2
	בית	HOUSE	113a	
	גדול	GREAT	153b	7
	גנה	GARDEN	171b	
	חצר	ENCLOSURE	347a	2
	מלא	BE FULL	570b	1 b
	מן	FROM	583d	9 b1
	מצא	FIND	594b	2 e
	קטן	SMALL	882a	2 b2
	שושן	SUSA	1004d	
1 6	אחז	GRASP	28b	
	ארגמן	PURPLE THREAD	71a	1
	ארגמן	PURPLE THREAD	71b	1
	בהט	PORPHYRY	96b	
	בוץ	BYSSUS	101c	
	דר	PEARL	204d	
	חבל	CORD	286c	1
	חור	WHITE STUFF	301a	
	כפס	BIND	*495d	1
	כרפס	COTTON	502d	
	מטה	COUCH	642a	
	סחרת	STONE	695c	
	עמוד	PILLAR	765b	1
	רצפה	PAVEMENT	954b	
	שש	ALABASTER	1010d	
	שש	ALABASTER	1010d	
	תכלת	VIOLET THREAD	1067b	1 b
1 7	יד	HAND	391b	5 e
	יין	WINE	406c	D
	מלכות	ROYAL POWER	574d	1
	מן	THAN	582c	6 a
	רב	MUCH	913a	1 a1
	שנה	CHANGE	1039d	
	שקה	GIVE TO DRINK	1052c	2
1 8	אנס	COMPEL	60a	
	דת	LAW	206d	2
	ו	AND	253b	1 ib
	יסד	APPOINT	414a	2
	על	UPON	753b	2 1c
	רב	CHIEF	913c	
	רצון	GOODWILL	953c	3 b
	שתיה	DRINKING	1059c	
1 9	אחשורוש	AHASUERUS	31c	
	ושתי	VASHTI	255d	
	מלכה	QUEEN	573c	
	מלכה	QUEEN	*573d	
	מלכות	ROYAL POWER	574d	1
1 10	אבגתא	ABAGTHA	1b	
	אחשורוש	AHASUERUS	31c	
	מהומן	MEHUMAN	54d	
	אמר	SAY	56c	4
	בגתא	BIGTHA	94a	
	בזתא	BIZTHA	103b	
	זתר	ZETHAR	285c	
	חרבונא	HARBONA	353a	
	טוב	PLEASING	373b	2
	יין	WINE	406c	A
	כרכס	CARKAS	501c	
	לב	HEART	525c	2 9a
	סרים	EUNUCH	710c	
	פנה	FACE	816c	22a
	שרת	SERVE	1058a	1 b
1 11	בוא	COME	99a	1
	ושתי	VASHTI	255d	
	טוב	PLEASANT	373c	1 a
	יפי	BEAUTY	421d	
	כתר	CROWN	509d	
	מלכות	ROYALTY	575a	1
	מראה	VISION	909d	1 a
1 12	בער	BURN	129a	4
	דבר	WORD	182b	1 1b
	ושתי	VASHTI	255d	
	חמה	RAGE	404c	2 a
	חמה	RAGE	*404c	2 c
	מאן	REFUSE	549a	

ESTHER

Ch	v.	Heb	Eng	Page	Sec
		נוח	REST	629a	B 5
		פזר	SCATTER	808b	
		פרד	DIVIDE	825c	
		שוה	AGREE WITH	1000d	
		שוה	AGREE WITH	1001a	
		שנה	CHANGE	1039d	
3	9	אבד	CAUSE TO PERISH	2a	1
		גנזים	TREASURY	170d	2
		טוב	PLEASING	373b	5
		כסף	SILVER	494b	8 c
		כתב	BE WRITTEN	508a	1
		מלאכה	WORK	522b	6 a
		על	UPON	758a	28
		שקל	WEIGH	1053c	2
3	10	המדתא	HAMMEDATHA	241a	
		טבעת	SIGNET	371d	1
		יד	HAND	389a	1 b
		יהודי	JEW	397c	
		סור	TURN ASIDE	694b	1
		צרר	SHEW HOSTILITY TOWARD	865d	
3	11	ב	IN	89d	3 2b
		טוב	PLEASANT	374a	2 f
		עשה	DO	794b	12
3	12	אחשורוש	AHASUERUS	31c	
		אחשדרפנים	SATRAPS	31c	
		ו	AND	253b	1 ib
		חדש	NEW MOON	294d	2 b2
		חתם	SEAL	368a	
		טבעת	SIGNET	371d	1
		יום	DAY	398c	2 e
		כתב	BE WRITTEN	508a	1
		כתב	WRITING	508b	2
		לשון	TONGUE	546c	2
		ספר	ENUMERATOR	708c	1 c
		עשר	TEN	797b	3 a
		פחה	GOVERNOR	808d	
		צוה	CHARGE	846a	4 a
		קרא	CALL	896b	2 c
		שר	CHIEFTAIN	978b	2 c
		שלש	THREE	1025d	2
		שם	NAME	1028a	2 a
3	13	אבד	CAUSE TO PERISH	2a	1
		אב	FATHER	3d	8
		אדר	ADAR	12c	
		בוז	SPOIL	102d	
		הרג	KILL	247a	1 a
		זקן	OLD	278c	2 a
		חדש	NEW MOON	294d	2 b1
		טף	CHILDREN	382a	
		יהודי	JEW	397c	
		יום	DAY	*398c	2 e
		נער	YOUTH	655a	1 d
		ספר	MISSIVE	707a	1 a
		עשר	TEN	797b	
		רוץ	RUN	930c	2 b
		שלח	SEND	1018d	
		שלש	THREE	1025d	2
		שמד	BE EXTERMINATED	1029b	1
3	14	דת	DECREE	206c	1
		דת	DECREE	*206c	1
		ו	AND	253b	1 ib
		כל	ALL	481c	1 b
		כתב	WRITING	508b	2
		נתן	GIVE	681c	1 h
		עתיד	READY	800c	1
		פתשגן	COPY	837d	
3	15	בוך	CONFUSE	100c	
		בירה	CASTLE	108b	2
		בירה	CASTLE	*108b	2
		דחף	DRIVE	191b	
		דת	DECREE	206c	1
		ישב	SIT	442d	1 b
		רוץ	RUN	930c	2 b
		שושן	SUSA	1004d	
		שושן	SUSA	1004d	
		שתה	DRINK	1059c	2
4	1	אפר	ASHES	68a	
		בגד	GARMENT	94a	1
		זעק	CRY	277c	2 d
		זעקה	CRY	277d	2
		לבש	PUT ON	527d	A
		מר	BITTER	600c	2 a
		עשה	DO	795a	1 a
		רחוב	PLAZA	932b	
		שק	SACK	974c	2 a
		עצב	PAIN	*1107d	
4	2	אין	NOT	34d	5 a
		לבוש	CLOTHING	528c	
		עד	AS FAR AS	724a	1 1a
		שק	SACK	974c	2 a
4	3	אבל	MOURNING	5d	
		אפר	ASHES	68a	
		בכי	WEEPING	113d	
		דת	DECREE	206c	1
		ו	AND	253b	1 ib
		יהודי	JEW	397c	
		יצע	BE LAID	426d	
		כל	ALL	481c	1 b
		ל	TO	514a	5 e
		נגע	REACH	619c	2
		מספד	WAILING	704d	2
		צום	FASTING	847b	
		מקום	STANDING PLACE	880a	3 b
		מקום	STANDING PLACE	880d	4
		שק	SACK	974c	2 b

Ch	v.	Heb	Eng	Page	Sec
4	4	בגד	GARMENT	94a	1
		חול	WHIRL	297c	
		לבש	CLOTHE	528b	3
		נערה	GIRL	655b	2
		קבל	RECEIVE	867b	2
		שק	SACK	974c	2 a
		שלח	SEND	1018b	1 b
4	5	התך	HATHACH	251c	
		מה	HOW	554b	4 f
		מן	FROM	580d	3 bb
		עמד	STAND	764d	6 e
		צוה	CHARGE	846a	4 c
4	6	התך	HATHACH	251c	
		רחוב	PLAZA	932b	
4	7	אבד	CAUSE TO PERISH	2a	1
		אמר	SAY	56b	3
		גנזים	TREASURY	170d	2
		יהודי	JEW	397c	
		על	UPON	755b	24a
		פרשה	EXACT STATEMENT	831d	
		קרה	ENCOUNTER	899c	2
		שקל	WEIGH	1053c	2
4	8	בקש	SEEK	135a	6
		דת	DECREE	206c	1
		חנן	SHOW FAVOR	336b	1
		כתב	WRITING	508b	4
		נתן	GIVE	681c	1 h
		על	UPON	754d	2 1fc
		פנה	FACE	818a	25 a c
		פתשגן	COPY	837d	
		ראה	TO SEE	908d	1 a1
		שושן	SUSA	1004d	
		קדם	BEFORE	*1110c	2
4	9	התך	HATHACH	251c	
4	10	התך	HATHACH	251c	
		צוה	CHARGE	846a	4 a
4	11	אשר	THAT	83c	8 ab
		מאשר	FROM THAT WHICH	84a	A
		דת	LAW	206c	2
		חצר	ENCLOSURE	347a	2
		ישט	HOLD OUT	445a	
		מות	DIE	560b	1 b
		קרא	CALL	896b	2 c
		שרביט	SCEPTRE	987b	
4	13	דמה	BE LIKE	198a	2
		יהודי	JEW	397c	
		מלט	SLIP AWAY	572c	2
		נפש	SOUL	661a	7
		שוב	TURN BACK	999c	3
4	14	אבד	PERISH	1c	1
		אם	IF	50d	2 ba
		חרש	BE SILENT	361b	1 a
		יהודי	JEW	397c	
		מי	WHO	567a	F d
		מלכות	ROYAL POWER	574d	1
		נגע	REACH	619c	2
		הצלה	DELIVERANCE	665a	
		עמד	STAND	764c	6 a
		עת	TIME	773b	1 a
		עת	TIME	773b	1 a
		מקום	STANDING PLACE	880b	6
		דנה	THIS	*1089a	C
4	15	אמר	SAY	56c	4
		שוב	TURN BACK	999c	3
4	16	אבד	PERISH	1c	1
		דת	LAW	206c	2
		ו	AND	253a	1 g
		יהודי	JEW	397c	
		יום	DAY	398c	2 c
		יום	DAY	*399a	3
		כאשר	WHEN	455c	3
		כן	SO	486d	3 b
		כנס	GATHER	488a	
		לילה	NIGHT	539a	1
		מצא	FIND	594b	2 e
		נערה	GIRL	655b	2
		על	UPON	754c	2 1fc
		צום	FAST	847b	
		שושן	SUSA	1004d	
5	1	בית	HOUSE	109a	1 ae 1
		חצר	ENCLOSURE	347a	2
		כסא	SEAT OF HONOR	490d	1 a
		לבש	PUT ON	527d	A
		מלכות	ROYAL POWER	574d	1
		מלכות	ROYAL POWER	574d	1
		מלכות	ROYALTY	575a	1
		נכח	FRONT	647b	1
5	2	חן	FAVOR	336c	2 b2
		חצר	ENCLOSURE	347a	2
		ישט	HOLD OUT	445a	
		נגע	TOUCH	619a	1 a
		נשא	LIFT	671c	3 f
		ראש	HEAD	911a	2 a
		שרביט	SCEPTRE	987b	
5	3	בקשה	REQUEST	135a	
		מה	WHAT	553b	1 ea
		מלכות	KINGDOM	575a	3
		נתן	GIVE	678d	1 e
		נתן	GIVE	681c	1 f
		עד	AS FAR AS	724d	13
5	4	טוב	PLEASING	373c	5
		על	UPON	758a	28
		עשה	DO	794c	2 1c
		דבר	WORD	182b	1 1d
5	5	מהר	HASTEN	555a	3

Ch	v.	Heb	Eng	Page	Sec
		עשה	DO	794c	2 1c
		עשה	DO	795b	1 a
5	6	יין	WINE	406c	D
		מה	WHAT	553b	1 ea
		מלכות	KINGDOM	575a	3
		נתן	GIVE	681c	1 f
		עד	AS FAR AS	724d	13
		שאלה	REQUEST	982c	1
		משתה	FEAST	1059d	1
5	7	בקשה	REQUEST	135a	
		שאלה	REQUEST	982c	1
5	8	בקשה	REQUEST	135a	
		חן	FAVOR	336b	2 b1
		טוב	PLEASING	373c	5
		מצא	FIND	592d	1 a
		על	UPON	758a	28
		שאלה	REQUEST	982c	1
5	9	זוע	TREMBLE	266b	
		טוב	PLEASANT	374c	7
		חמה	RAGE	404c	2 a
		לב	HEART	525c	29a
		מלא	BE FULL	570c	1
		מן	OUT OF	580b	2 ec
		ראה	TO SEE	907a	25
		שמח	JOYFUL	970c	1 a
5	10	אהב	LOVE	13a	4 b
		אפק	HOLD	67d	2
		בוא	COME	99c	2
		זרש	ZERESH	284d	
5	11	גדל	BECOME GREAT	152c	2
		כבוד	HONOR	458c	2 b
		נשא	LIFT	672a	1
5	12	אף	ALSO	64d	1
		בוא	COME	99c	2
		ל	TO	514a	5 e
		ל	TO	517a	6 a
		מחר	TO-MORROW	564a	1 a
		עשה	DO	794c	2 1c
		קרא	CALL	895d	5 c
5	13	יהודי	JEW	397c	
		עת	TIME	773b	1 a
		שוה	AGREE WITH	1000d	
5	14	אהב	LOVE	13a	4 b
		בבה	GATE	*93b	
		בקר	MORNING	134b	2
		גבה	HIGH	147b	1
		זרש	ZERESH	284d	
		יטב	BE PLEASING	405c	4
		פנה	FACE	817a	24a g
		משתה	FEAST	1059d	1
		תלה	HANG	1068a	2
6	1	אמר	SAY	56c	4
		זכרון	MEMORIAL	272a	1 d
		יום	DAY	399b	4 c
		שנה	SLEEP	446a	
		נדד	FLEE	622b	2
		ספר	MISSIVE	707c	
		קרא	CALL	896b	2 b
6	2	אשר	THAT	83c	8 ab
		בגתן	BIGTHAN	94b	
		בקש	SEEK	134d	2 d
		מצא	FIND	593d	1 d
		סף	THRESHOLD	706c	
		תרש	TERESH	1076d	
6	3	גדולה	GREATNESS	153c	A
		זה	THIS	262a	6 f
		יקר	HONOUR	430b	3
		מה	WHAT	552c	1 aa
		עשה	DO	795b	1 c
		שרת	SERVE	1058a	1 a
6	4	בוא	COME	97d	1
		חיצון	OUTER	300b	1
		חצר	ENCLOSURE	347a	2
		כון	ESTABLISH	466b	2
		ל	TO	511b	1 ga
		תלה	HANG	1068a	2
6	5	חצר	ENCLOSURE	347a	2
6	6	ב	IN	89d	3 2b
		חפץ	DELIGHT IN	342d	1 b
		חפץ	DELIGHT IN	342d	1 a
		יקר	HONOUR	430b	3
		יתר	ADVANTAGE	452c	
		לב	HEART	525c	27
6	7	חפץ	DELIGHT IN	342d	1 a
		יקר	HONOUR	430b	3
6	8	כתר	CROWN	509d	
		לבש	PUT ON	528a	D
		לבוש	CLOTHING	528c	
		מלכות	ROYALTY	575a	1
		מלכות	ROYALTY	575a	1
		נתן	PUT	681c	2 a
		רכב	RIDE	938d	2
6	9	חפץ	DELIGHT IN	342d	1 a
		יקר	HONOUR	430b	3
		לבש	CLOTHE	528b	3
		לבוש	CLOTHING	528c	
		פרתמים	NOBLES	832c	
		רחוב	PLAZA	932b	
		רכב	RIDE	938d	1
6	10	יהודי	JEW	397c	
		לבוש	CLOTHING	528c	
		מהר	HASTEN	555a	2
		מן	FROM	581a	3 bc
		נפל	FALL	658b	4
6	11	חפץ	DELIGHT IN	342d	1 a
		יקר	HONOUR	430b	3

Ch	v.	Heb	Eng	Page	Sec
		נתן	GIVE	681c	1 f
		עשה	DO	795b	1 a
		שאלה	REQUEST	982c	1
		שאר	REST	984c	1
9	13	שושן	SUSA	1004d	
		דת	DECREE	206c	1
		טוב	PLEASING	373c	5
		יהודי	JEW	397c	
		נתן	GIVE	681c	1 g
		על	UPON	758a	2 8
		שושן	SUSA	1004d	
		תלה	HANG	1068a	2
9	14	אמר	SAY	56c	4
		דת	DECREE	206c	1
		נתן	GIVE	681c	1 h
		עשה	DO	795a	1 a
		שושן	SUSA	1004d	
		תלה	HANG	1068a	2
9	15	אדר	ADAR	12c	
		בזה	SPOIL	103a	
		בירה	CASTLE	*108b	2
		הרג	KILL	247a	1 a
		חדש	NEW MOON	294d	2 b1
		יהודי	JEW	397c	
		תכריך	ROBE	501b	
		קהל	ASSEMBLE AS	874d	1 a
		ארבע	FOUR	917b	2 a2 d
		שושן	SUSA	1004d	
9	16	בזה	SPOIL	103a	
		הרג	KILL	247a	1 a
		יהודי	JEW	397c	
		נוח	REST	628b	2
		על	UPON	754c	2 lf c
		עמד	STAND	764b	4
		קהל	ASSEMBLE AS	874d	1 a
		שנא	HATE	971c	3
		שאר	REST	984c	1
		שבעים	SEVENTY	988c	3 b
9	17	אדר	ADAR	12c	
		חדש	NEW MOON	294d	2 b1
		נוח	REST	628b	2
		שמחה	JOY	970d	1
		שלש	THREE	1025d	2
		משתה	FEAST	1059d	1
9	18	בירה	CASTLE	*108b	2
		יהודי	JEW	397c	
		נוח	REST	628b	2
		פרזה	OPEN REGION	*826d	
		קהל	ASSEMBLE AS	874d	1 a
		שמחה	JOY	970d	1
		שושן	SUSA	1004d	
		שלש	THREE	1025d	2
		משתה	FEAST	1059d	1
9	19	אדר	ADAR	12c	
		חדש	NEW MOON	294d	2 b1
		טוב	PLEASANT	373c	2 a
		יהודי	JEW	397c	
		יום	DAY	*401b	7 m
		מנה	PORTION	584b	
		עיר	CITY	746b	1 b
		פרזה	OPEN REGION	826d	
		פרזי	HAMLET-DWELLER	826d	
		ארבע	FOUR	917b	2 a2 d
		שמחה	JOY	970d	1
		משלוח	SENDING	1020a	2
		משתה	FEAST	1059d	1
9	20	אגרת	LETTER	8d	
		יהודי	JEW	397c	
		כתב	WRITE	507d	1 c
		ספר	MISSIVE	707a	1 a
		קרב	NEAR	898a	2 b
		רחק	DISTANT	935b	1 a
9	21	אדר	ADAR	12c	
		ו	AND	253b	1 ib
		חדש	NEW MOON	294d	2 b1
		חמש	FIVE	332a	2 b1
		כל	ALL	481c	1 b
		על	UPON	753b	2 lc
		עשה	DO	795a	26
		קום	STAND	878c	2 c
		ארבע	FOUR	917b	2 a2 d
		שנה	YEAR	1040b	
9	22	אביון	NEEDY	2d	
		אבל	MOURNING	5d	
		הפך	TURN	246a	2 c
		טוב	PLEASANT	373c	2 a
		יגון	GRIEF	387b	
		יהודי	JEW	397c	
		יום	DAY	*401b	7 m
		מנה	PORTION	584b	
		נוח	REST	628b	2
		מתנה	GIFT	682c	
		שמחה	JOY	970d	1
		משלוח	SENDING	1020a	2
		משתה	FEAST	1059d	1
9	23	חלל	POLLUTE	320d	2
		יהודי	JEW	397c	
		כתב	WRITE	507d	1 c
		כתב	BE WRITTEN	508a	1
		קבל	RECEIVE	867b	3
9	24	אבד	CAUSE TO PERISH	2a	1
		אבד	CAUSE TO PERISH	2a	1
		אגגי	AGAGITE	8a	
		גורל	LOT	174d	2 i
		המדתא	HAMMEDATHA	241a	
		המם	CONFUSE	243a	2

Ch	v.	Heb	Eng	Page	Sec
		חשב	THINK	363a	12
		יהודי	JEW	397c	
		נפל	FALL	658a	3
		פור	LOT	807c	
		צרר	SHEW HOSTILITY TOWARD	865d	
9	25	אמר	SAY	56c	4
		חשב	THINK	363a	12
		מחשבה	THOUGHT	364c	2
		יהודי	JEW	397c	
		ספר	MISSIVE	707a	1 a
		עם	WITH	767b	1 a
		ראש	HEAD	911b	8
		רע	EVIL	948b	8
		שוב	TURN BACK	998b	7 f
		תלה	HANG	1068a	2
9	26	אגרת	LETTER	8d	
		דבר	WORD	183a	2 la
		ככה	THUS	462c	
		כן	SO	487b	3 f
		מה	WHAT	553b	1 ea
		נגע	REACH	619c	4
		על	UPON	758a	29
		פור	LOT	807c	
9	27	ו	AND	253b	1 ib
		זמן	APPOINTED TIME	274a	
		זרע	SOWING	283a	4 g
		יהודי	JEW	397c	
		כל	ALL	481c	1 b
		כתב	WRITING	508b	3
		לוה	BE JOINED	531a	
		עבר	PASS OVER	718b	6 d
		על	UPON	753b	2 lc
		עשה	DO	795a	26
		קבל	RECEIVE	867b	3
		קום	STAND	878c	2 c
		שנה	YEAR	1040b	
9	28	דור	PERIOD	189d	1 b
		דור	GENERATION	190a	2 c
		ו	AND	253b	1 ib
		זכר	REMEMBER	270d	3
		זכר	REMEMBRANCE	271b	1 d
		זרע	SOWING	283a	4 g
		יהודי	JEW	397c	
		כל	ALL	481c	1 b
		כל	ALL	481c	1 b
		כל	ALL	481c	1 b
		סוף	CEASE	692d	
		עבר	PASS OVER	718b	6 d
		עשה	DO	795b	2 e
		פור	LOT	807c	
		משפחה	CLAN	1046d	1 c
9	29	ביחיל	ABIHAIL	4b	3
		אגרת	LETTER	8d	
		את	WITH	86a	1 a
		יהודי	JEW	397c	
		פור	LOT	807c	
		קום	STAND	878c	2 c
		תקף	POWER	1076a	
9	30	אמת	FIRMNESS	54a	2
		יהודי	JEW	397c	
		מלכות	KINGDOM	575a	3
		ספר	MISSIVE	707a	1 a
9	31	זמן	APPOINTED TIME	274a	
		זעקה	CRY	277d	2
		זרע	SOWING	283a	4 g
		יהודי	JEW	397c	
		על	UPON	753b	2 lc
		פור	LOT	807c	
		צום	FASTING	847b	
		קום	STAND	878c	2 c
		קום	STAND	878c	2 c
9	32	מאמר	WORD	57d	
		פור	LOT	807c	
		קום	STAND	878c	2 c
10	1	אי	COAST	16a	
		אחשורוש	AHASUERUS	31c	
		מס	FORCED SERVICE	587a	4
10	2	גבורה	MIGHT	150c	2
		גדל	BECOME GREAT	152c	2
		גדולה	GREATNESS	153c	A
		יום	DAY	399b	4 c
		לא	NOT	520c	4 bb
		מדי	MEDES	552a	1
		ספר	MISSIVE	707b	3 e
		עשה	DEED	795d	1 b4
		פרס	PERSIA	828a	
		פרשה	EXACT STATEMENT	831d	
		תקף	POWER	1076a	
10	3	דבר	SPEAK	180c	
		דרש	SEEK	205c	6
		זרע	SOWING	282d	4 e
		טוב	A GOOD THING	375a	1
		יהודי	JEW	397c	
		יהודי	JEW	397c	
		ל	TO	513a	5 ad
		רב	MULTITUDE	914a	1
		רצה	BE PLEASED WITH	953b	1 b
		משנה	SECOND	1041c	3 a

JOB

Ch	v.	Heb	Eng	Page	Sec
1	1	איוב	JOB	33c	
		היה	BE	226d	3 1
		ירא	FEAR	431c	3 b

Ch	v.	Heb	Eng	Page	Sec
		ישר	STRAIGHT	449b	3 b
		סור	TURN ASIDE	693d	1
		עוץ	UZ	734b	2
		תם	COMPLETE	1071a	3
1	2	בן	SON	120a	1
		ילד	BE BORN	408d	
1	3	אלף	THOUSAND	49a	1 c
		אתון	SHE-ASS	87d	
		בן	SON	121b	1 jl
		בקר	CATTLE	133c	2
		גדול	GREAT	153a	6 b
		היה	BE	227a	3 4a
		מאה	HUNDRED	548b	1 c3
		עבדה	SERVICE	715c	
		צאן	SMALL CATTLE	838b	1 a4
		צאן	SMALL CATTLE	838b	1 b
		צמד	COUPLE	855a	1
		קדם	FRONT	869c	1 b
		מקנה	CATTLE	889b	1
		רב	MUCH	913a	1 a2
1	4	משתה	FEAST	1059d	1
1	5	אולי	PERADVENTURE	19c	1
		איוב	JOB	33c	
		בקר	MORNING	134b	1 h
		ברך	BLESS	139b	5
		חטא	MISS A GOAL OR WAY	306d	2 b
		יום	DAY	400c	7 f
		לב	HEART	524a	27
		נקף	GO AROUND	669a	2
		מספר	NUMBER	709a	1 b
		עלה	WHOLE BURNT OF-FERING	750d	
		קדש	BE SET APART	873b	4 b
		שלח	SEND	1018b	1 c
		משתה	FEAST	1059d	1
1	6	אדם	ADAM	9c	3
		אלהים	GOD	43b	1 c
		בן	SON	120b	1 d
		ה	THE	207a	1 a
		היה	BECOME	225c	2 la
		יום	DAY	400a	7 b
		יצב	STATION ONESELF	426c	C
		על	UPON	756b	2 6c
		שטן	SATAN	966c	2 a
		תוך	MIDST	1063d	1
		בר	SON	*1085b	1
1	7	אין	WHENCE	32d	
		הלך	WALK	235d	1 a
		שטן	SATAN	966c	2 a
			GO ABOUT	1002a	
1	8	איוב	JOB	33c	
		ה	INTERROG PART	209d	1 a
		ירא	FEAR	431c	3 b
		ישר	STRAIGHT	449b	3 b
		לב	HEART	524d	2 3c
		סור	TURN ASIDE	693d	1
		עבד	SLAVE	714a	3
		על	UPON	757d	2 7c c
		שום	TO PLACE	963c	2 b
		שטן	SATAN	966c	2 a
		תם	COMPLETE	1071a	3
1	9	איוב	JOB	33c	
		חנם	OUT OF FAVOR	336c	A
		ירא	FEAR	431c	3 b
		שטן	SATAN	966c	2 a
1	10	אתה	THOU	61c	
		בעד	ABOUT	126c	1 b
		ברך	BLESS	139a	2 b
		מעשה	DEED	795d	1 b3
		פרץ	BREAK THROUGH	829c	8
		שוך	FENCE UP	962b	
1	11	אולם	BUT	19d	
		אם	IF	50b	1 b2
		ברך	BLESS	139b	5
		נגע	TOUCH	619a	2
		פנה	FACE	818d	27a a
		שלח	SEND	1018d	3 b
1	12	יד	HAND	391a	5 c3
		יצא	GO OUT	422d	1 b
		מעם	FROM WITH	769a	A
		שטן	SATAN	966c	2 a
		שלח	SEND	1018d	3 c
1	13	היה	BECOME	225c	2 la
		זה	THIS	*260c	1 a
		יום	DAY	400a	7 b
		יין	WINE	406c	A
1	14	איוב	JOB	33c	
		אתון	SHE-ASS	87d	
		בקר	CATTLE	*133a	
		בקר	CATTLE	133c	2
		חרש	CUT IN	360c	2
		יד	HAND	391c	5 h3
		מלאך	MESSENGER	521c	1 a
		רעה	TEND	945b	2 a
1	15	חרב	SWORD	352d	1 f
		מלט	SLIP AWAY	572b	2
		נכה	SMITE	646a	2 c
		נער	RETAINER	655a	2 b
		נפל	FALL	657c	4 a
		רק	ONLY	956b	2 a
		שבא	SHEBA	985b	
1	16	אלהים	GOD	43d	2 c
		אש	FIRE	77c	2
		בער	BURN	129a	1
		דבר	SPEAK	180d	1

Ch v.	Heb	Eng	Page	Sec
	כחד	BE HIDDEN	470b	2
	מי	WHO	566d	F c
	נקי	CLEAN	667c	1
4 8	און	TROUBLE	20a	1
	זרע	SOW	281d	3 c
	חרש	CUT IN	360c	2
	עמל	TROUBLE	765d	2
	קצר	HARVEST	894c	
4 9	ראה	TO SEE	907a	1 b
	אבד	PERISH	1d	1
	כלה	BE FINISHED	477d	2 c
	מן	OUT OF	580a	2 eb
	מן	ON ACCOUNT OF	580b	2 f
	נשמה	BREATH	675d	1
	רוח	BREATH	924d	1 d1
4 10	אריה	LION	71d	
	כפיר	LION	498d	
	לביא	LION	522d	
	נתע	BREAK DOWN	683a	
	שאגה	ROARING	980d	1
	שחל	LION	1006c	
4 11	שן	TOOTH	1042a	1 b
	אבד	PERISH	1c	1
	בלי	WEARING OUT	116a	C b
	בן	SON	121b	4
	טרף	PREY	383c	1
	לביא	LION	522d	
	ליש	LION	539d	
	לקח	TAKE	543b	4 f
	פרד	DIVIDE	825c	
4 12	און	EAR	24a	2 a
	גנב	STEAL	170c	
	דבר	WORD	182c	1 2a
	שמץ	WHISPER	1036b	
4 13	חזיון	VISION	303b	2
	לילה	NIGHT	538d	1
	מן	OUT OF	579d	2 d
	נפל	FALL	657c	5
	תרדמה	DEEP SLEEP	922b	
	שעיפים	EXCITED THOUGHTS	972a	
4 14	פחד	DREAD	808b	
	פחד	DREAD	808c	1
	קרא	ENCOUNTER	897a	2
	רב	MULTITUDE	914a	1
	רעדה	TREMBLING	944d	1
4 15	בשר	FLESH	142c	1 b
	חלף	PASS ON OR AWAY	322a	1 a
	סמר	BRISTLE UP	702c	
	פנה	FACE	818d	27a a
	רוח	BREATH	925c	4 e
	שערה	A HAIR	972b	
4 16	דממה	WHISPER	199a	
	תמונה	LIKENESS	568c	
	נגד	IN FRONT	617c	2 b
	נכר	RECOGNIZE	648b	5
	עין	EYE	745a	5
4 17	אם	IF	50d	2 ab a
	אנוש	MAN	60d	3
	טהר	BE CLEAN	372b	3
	מן	OUT OF	579d	1
	צדק	BE JUST	842d	4
4 18	אמן	CONFIRM	53b	2 c
	הן	BEHOLD	243c	A
	מלאך	MESSENGER	521d	2
	עבד	SLAVE	714a	3
	שום	TO PLACE	963a	1 a
	תהלה	ERROR	1062d	
	תפלה	UNSEEMLINESS	1074b	
4 19	אף	ALSO	65a	2
	אשר	PARTICLE OF RELATION	82d	5
	בית	HOUSE	109c	1 c
	דכא	CRUSH	194a	
	חמר	CEMENT	330d	2 a
	יסוד	FOUNDATION	414b	1
	נתן	GIVE	*681d	3 c
	עפר	DRY EARTH	779d	1 b
	עש	MOTH	799c	
	פנה	FACE	817d	2 4f
	שכן	SETTLE DOWN	1015b	2 b
4 20	אבד	PERISH	1c	1
	בלי	WEARING OUT	116a	C b
	בקר	MORNING	134a	1 e
	כתת	BE BEATEN	510c	
	מן	FROM	582b	5 d2
	נצח	EVERLASTINGNESS	664b	4
	שום	TO PLACE	963c	2 b
	שום	TO PLACE	964d	
4 21	חכמה	WISDOM	315d	5 c
	יתד	PEG	450b	A
	יתר	CORD	452a	
	לא	NOT	520b	4 ba
	נסע	PULL OUT	652c	
5 1	יש	THERE IS	441d	2 b
	מן	FROM	580c	3 a
	ענה	ANSWER	772a	1 a
	פנה	TURN	815b	1 a
	קרא	CALL	845b	2 b
	קדוש	HOLY	872d	2 c
5 2	הרג	KILL	247b	7
	הרג	KILL	247c	7
	כי	BECAUSE	*473d	3 c
	כעש	ANGER	495b	1
	ל	TO	512a	3 b
	פתה	BE SIMPLE	834c	1

Ch v.	Heb	Eng	Page	Sec
5 3	כי	BECAUSE	*473d	3 c
	נוה	HABITATION	627c	2
	פתאם	SUDDENNESS	837c	
	קבב	CURSE	866d	
5 4	שרש	ROOT UP	1057d	2
	דכא	CRUSH	194a	1
	ישע	SAFETY	447a	1
	כי	BECAUSE	*473d	3 c
	נצל	DELIVER	664d	3 a
	רחק	BE DISTANT	935a	
5 5	שער	GATE	1045a	2 a
	אל	TO	39c	1
	אשר	PARTICLE OF RELATION	82d	5
	חיל	STRENGTH	299a	3
	כי	BECAUSE	*473d	3 c
	צמים	SNARE	855d	
	צן	THORN	856d	
	קציר	HARVESTING	894c	2
	רעב	HUNGRY	944b	2
	שאף	GASP	983c	2
5 6	אדמה	GROUND	9c	1
	און	TROUBLE	20a	1
	כי	BECAUSE	473d	3 c
	עמל	TROUBLE	765d	1
	עפר	DRY EARTH	779d	1 c
	צמח	SPROUT	855c	1
5 7	אדם	MAN	9b	2
	בן	SON	121b	6
	גבה	BE HIGH	147a	1
	ו	AND	253b	1 j
	ילד	BE BORN	409a	
	עוף	FLY	733c	1 a
	עמל	TROUBLE	765d	1
	קשת	BOW	906a	1 b
	רשף	FLAME	958b	1
5 8	אולם	BUT	19d	
	אל	GOD	42d	6 e
	אלהים	GOD	44b	4 a
	דברה	CAUSE	184b	1
	דרש	SEEK	205b	2 a
5 9	שום	TO PLACE	963c	1 d
	אין	NOT	35a	6 cg
	גדול	GREAT	153c	9
	ו	AND	253c	1 k
	חקר	SEARCHING	350d	
	מספר	NUMBER	708d	1 a
	עד	AS FAR AS	724c	1 2a d
	פלא	BE SURPASSING	810d	4
5 10	חוץ	THE OUTSIDE	300b	2 b
	מטר	RAIN	564d	
	מי	WATER	565c	1 g
	פנה	FACE	819a	2 7b
5 11	ישע	SAFETY	447a	1
	קדר	BE DARK	871a	
	מרום	HEIGHT	928d	1
	שגב	BE HIGH	960c	2
	שום	TO PLACE	963b	1 c
	שפל	LOW	1050c	1
5 12	מחשבה	THOUGHT	364b	2
	תושיה	SOUND WISDOM	444d	B
	ערום	CRAFTY	791a	1
	פרר	BREAK	830c	2 a
5 13	חכם	WISE	314b	3
	עצה	ADVICE	420b	
	לכד	CAPTURE	540a	2
	ערם	CRAFTINESS	791a	
	פתל	TWIST	836c	
5 14	חשך	DARKNESS	365b	3 d
	יומם	DAYTIME	*401c	1
	לילה	NIGHT	539a	1
	משש	GROPE	607a	2
	פגש	MEET	803d	
	צהר	MIDDAY	844a	2
5 15	אביון	NEEDY	2d	
	ישע	DELIVER	446d	1 b
	רל	POOR	195d	2
5 16	עולה	INJUSTICE	732d	2
	פה	MOUTH	805a	2 a
	תקוה	HOPE	876b	1
5 17	אנוש	MAN	60d	1
	אשר	HAPPINESS	81a	
	יכח	CORRECT	407a	6
	מוסר	DISCIPLINE	416c	2 a
	מאס	REJECT	549c	1 a
	שדי	ALMIGHTY	995a	1
5 18	הוא	HE, SHE, IT	*215b	1 a
	חבש	BIND	290a	2
	כאב	PAIN	456b	1
	מחץ	SHATTER	563c	
	רפא	HEAL	950d	3 a
	רפה	SINK	952a	3
5 19	ו	AND	252c	1
	נגע	TOUCH	619b	3
	צרה	DISTRESS	865b	
	רע	EVIL	948d	1
	שבע	SEVEN	988a	1 a
	שש	SIX	995d	5
5 20	יד	HAND	391b	5 g1
	פדה	RANSOM	804a	3 d
5 21	חבא	WITHDRAW	285b	
	ירא	FEAR	431b	1
	לשון	TONGUE	546c	1 b
	שד	VIOLENCE	994c	2
	שוט	SCOURGE	1002a	1
5 22	אל	NOT	39b	A c

Ch v.	Heb	Eng	Page	Sec
	חיה	LIVING THING	312c	1 b
	ירא	FEAR	431b	1 c
	כפן	HUNGER	495d	
	שחק	LAUGH	965d	1 a
	שד	VIOLENCE	994c	2
5 23	ברית	COVENANT	136b	11
	חיה	LIVING THING	312c	1 b
	שדה	FIELD	961b	1 c
	שדה	FIELD	961c	1 e
	שלם	BE IN COVENANT OF PEACE	1023d	
5 24	חטא	MISS A GOAL OR WAY	306d	1
	נוה	HABITATION	627c	1
	פקד	ATTEND TO	823c	A 4
	שלום	PEACE	1022d	2
5 25	זרע	SOWING	282d	4 c
	צאצא	OFFSPRING	425c	1
	עשב	HERB	793b	
5 26	גדיש	HEAP	155c	
	כלח	STRENGTH	480c	
	עלה	GO UP	748d	6
5 27	הוא	HE, SHE, IT	216d	6 a
	זה	THIS	261b	3
	חקר	SEARCH	350c	2 a
	כן	SO	485d	1 a
6 1	ל	TO	515a	5 ia
6 2	ענה	ANSWER	772d	1 d
	מאזן	BALANCES	24d	
	הוה	CHASM	*217d	2
	הוה	CHASM	217d	2
	היה	DESTRUCTION	217d	
	יחד	UNION	403a	2 a4
	כעש	ANGER	495b	1
	לו	IF	530b	2
	נשא	LIFT	670a	1 a
	עתה	NOW	774c	2 ga
	שקל	WEIGH	1053c	1
6 3	חול	SAND	297d	C
	חול	SAND	297d	C
	כבד	BE HEAVY	457b	1
	כי	THAT	*472c	1 db
	כי	BECAUSE	474b	3 d
	כן	SO	487b	3 f
	לוע	TALK WILDLY	534b	
	עתה	NOW	774c	2 ga
6 4	בעותים	TERRORS	130a	
	חץ	ARROW	346c	2
	חמה	POISON	404c	1 b
	עם	WITH	767b	1
	ערך	ARRANGE	789c	1 d
	רוח	BREATH	925b	3 e
	שתה	DRINK	1059b	1 a
6 5	אם	IF	50d	2 ab a
	בליל	FODDER	117d	
	געה	LOW	171d	
	דשא	GRASS	206a	
	מה	WHAT	553c	2 ab
	נהק	BRAY	625c	
	פרא	WILD ASS	825b	
6 6	שור	A HEAD OF CATTLE	1004a	
	אכל	EAT	37d	1
	אם	IF	50d	2 ab a
	בלי	WEARING OUT	116a	C b
	חלמות	WHITE OF AN EGG	321d	
	טעם	TASTE	381a	1
	מלח	SALT	571d	
	ריר	SPITTLE	938c	
	תפל	TASTELESS	1074a	
6 7	דוי	ILLNESS	188c	
	הם	THEY	241c	6 a
	מאן	REFUSE	549a	
	נגע	TOUCH	619a	1 a
	נפש	SOUL	661b	8
	חמר	ADDENDA ET CORRIGENDA	1122c	
6 8	בוא	COME	98c	2 c
	נתן	GIVE	678d	1 e
	נתן	GIVE	679a	1 f
	תקוה	HOPE	876b	1
	שאלה	REQUEST	982c	2
6 9	בצע	CUT OFF	130c	
	דכא	CRUSH	194a	1
	יאל	SHOW-WILLING-NESS	384b	3
	נתר	BE FREE	684a	2
6 10	אמר	WORD	57a	1
	חילה	ANGUISH	297d	
	חמל	SPARE	328b	
	כחד	HIDE	470h	
	נחמה	COMFORT	637c	
	סלד	SPRING	698d	
	קדוש	HOLY	872c	1 c
6 11	ארך	BE LONG	73d	1 c
	יחל	WAIT	404a	1
	כח	STRENGTH	470c	1 a
	כי	THAT	472d	1 f
	מה	WHAT	553a	1 db
	נפש	SOUL	661a	6 g
	קץ	END	893d	1
6 12	אבן	STONE	7a	8
	אם	IF	50c	2 aa
	בשר	FLESH	142c	1 a
	כח	STRENGTH	470c	1 a
	נחוש	OF BRONZE	639a	
6 13	אם	IF	50d	2 c

Ch	v.	Heb	Eng	Page	Sec
		תושיה	SOUND WISDOM	444d	B
		נדח	BANISH	623a	2
		עזרה	HELP	740d	1
6	14	חסד	GOODNESS	338d	1 2
		יראה	FEAR	432a	3
		מס	DESPAIRING	588a	1
		רע	FRIEND	946a	1
6	15	אפיק	CHANNEL	67d	1
		בגד	ACT TREACHEROUSLY	93d	A
		בגד	ACT TREACHEROUSLY	93d	A
		כמו	LIKE	455a	1 a
		אכזב	DECEPTIVE	*469d	1
		כי	BECAUSE	*473d	3 c
		לא	NOT	520a	3
		נחל	TORRENT	636b	1
		עבר	PASS OVER	*717d	4 a
		עבר	PASS OVER	718b	6 b
6	16	ה	THE	209a	2 a
		כי	BECAUSE	*473d	3 c
		עלם	CONCEAL	761b	
		קדר	BE DARK	871a	
		קרח	ICE	901c	2
		שלג	SNOW	1017a	
6	17	דער	BE EXTINGUISHED	200b	
		זרב	BE BURNT	279c	
		חמם	BE OR BECOME WARM	328c	1
		כי	BECAUSE	*473d	3 c
		עת	TIME	773d	1 d
		צמת	EXTERMINATE	856d	
		מקום	STANDING PLACE	879d	2 a
6	18	אבד	PERISH	1c	1
		ארח	WAY	73b	4
		ארח	WAY	73b	4
		כי	BECAUSE	*473d	3 c
		לפת	TWIST	542b	
		תהו	FORMLESSNESS	1062c	1
6	19	ארח	WAY	73b	4
		ארח	WAY	73b	4
		הליכה	TRAVELLING-COMPANY	237b	2
		כי	BECAUSE	*473d	3 c
		ל	TO	516a	5 ic
		נבט	LOOK	613c	1 a
		קוה	WAIT FOR	875d	1
		שבא	SHEBA	985b	
		תימא	TEMA	1066d	
6	20	בוש	BE ASHAMED	101d	3
		בוש	BE ASHAMED	101d	1
		בטח	TRUST	105b	2
		חפר	BE ABASHED	344a	
		כי	BECAUSE	*473d	3 c
6	21	חתת	TERROR	369d	
		ירא	FEAR	431a	1 a
		כי	BECAUSE	473d	3 c
		לא	NOT	520a	3
		עתה	NOW	774b	1 d
6	22	בעד	ON BEHALF OF	126d	2
		יהב	GIVE	396d	1
		כח	STRENGTH	471a	5
		כי	THAT	472b	1 da
		שחר	GIVE A BRIBE	1005a	
6	23	מלט	SLIP AWAY	572c	3
		עריץ	AWE-INSPIRING	792a	
		פדה	RANSOM	804a	2
6	24	בין	DISCERN	107a	3 c
		חרש	BE SILENT	361b	1 a
		ירה	POINT OUT	435b	4
		מה	WHAT	552d	1 b
		מה	WHAT	553b	1 ea
		שגה	GO ASTRAY	993a	3
		שמר	KEEP	1036c	1 b
6	25	אמר	WORD	57a	1
		יכח	REPROVE	407a	5 b
		ישר	STRAIGHTNESS	449c	2
		מן	OUT OF	579d	2 d
6	26	אמר	WORD	57a	1
		חשב	THINK	363a	1 2
		יאש	DESPAIR	384c	
		יכח	REPROVE	407a	5 b
		מלה	WORD	576b	
		רוח	BREATH	924c	1 b
6	27	יתום	ORPHAN	450c	
		כרה	TRADE	500b	
		נפל	FALL	658a	3
		על	UPON	756d	27 a c
6	28	אם	IF	50b	1 b2
		יאל	SHOW-WILLINGNESS	384a	1
		כזב	LIE	469c	1
		פנה	TURN	815c	2 e
		פנה	FACE	818d	27 a a
6	29	עולה	INJUSTICE	732d	3
		צדק	RIGHTEOUSNESS	841d	3
		שוב	TURN BACK	997c	5 e
6	30	בין	DISCERN	106d	1 d
		הוה	CHASM	217d	2
		חך	PALATE	335b	C
		יש	THERE IS	441d	2 b
		לשון	TONGUE	546b	1 b
		עולה	INJUSTICE	732c	2
7	1	אנוש	MAN	60d	1
		יום	DAY	399a	4 a
		לא	NOT	520b	4 ba
		צבא	HARD SERVICE	839b	3 b
		שכיר	HIRED	969b	2
7	2	פעל	DOING	821c	3
		צל	SHADOW	853b	2
		קוה	WAIT FOR	875d	1
		שכיר	HIRED	969b	2
7	3	ירח	MONTH	437b	1
		כן	SO	486b	2 ad g
		ל	TO	515d	5 ia
		לילה	NIGHT	538d	1
		מנה	APPOINT	584b	
		נחל	GET AS A POSSESSION	636a	
		עמל	TROUBLE	765d	1
		שוא	EMPTINESS	996a	1
7	4	אם	IF	49d	1 a3 a
		מדד	MEASURE	551b	1
		מתי	WHEN	607d	A
		נדד	TOSSING	622c	
		נשף	TWILIGHT	676a	2
		ערב	SUNSET	788a	1
		שבע	SATISFIED	959c	3 b
7	5	בשר	FLESH	142c	1 b
		גוש	CLOD	159a	
		לבש	PUT ON	528a	B
		מאס	RUN	549d	2
		עור	SKIN	736a	1
		עפר	DRY EARTH	779d	1 c
		רגע	HARDEN	921c	
		רמה	WORM	942c	
		שמר	KEEP	1036c	1 b
7	6	אפס	NON-EXISTENCE	67b	2 b
		ארג	LOOM	71a	
		יום	DAY	399a	4 a
		יום	DAY	399b	4 a
		ירד	GO DOWN	433b	1 i
		כלה	BE FINISHED	477d	2 b
		תקוה	HOPE	876b	1
		קלל	BE SLIGHT	886c	2
7	7	זכר	REMEMBER	270b	23 c
		חיים	LIFE	313a	1
		טוב	A GOOD THING	375a	1
		רוח	BREATH	925a	2 e
		שוב	TURN BACK	998b	8
7	8	ב	IN	*88d	14
		ראה	TO SEE	907d	6 d
		ראי	LOOKING	909b	3
		שור	BEHOLD	1003d	1
7	9	הלך	WALK	232c	13
		כלה	BE FINISHED	477d	2 b
		כן	SO	486c	2 db
		ענן	CLOUD	778a	1 c
		שאול	SHEOL	982d	1
		שאול	SHEOL	*983a	1
7	10	נכר	RECOGNIZE	648b	4
		שוב	TURN BACK	997c	4 b
7	11	גם	ALSO	169d	4
		חשך	WITHHOLD	362b	1 c
		מר	BITTER	600d	2 b
		נפש	SOUL	660d	6 c
		פה	MOUTH	805a	2 a
		צר	STRAITS	865a	
		רוח	BREATH	925c	5 b
		שיח	MUSE	967a	1
7	12	כי	THAT	472d	1 f
		משמר	GUARD	1038b	2
		תנין	SEA-MONSTER	1072c	3
7	13	כי	IF	473b	2 b
		נחם	CONSOLE ONESELF	637a	2
		נשא	LIFT	671a	2 a
		ערש	COUCH	793a	
		שיח	COMPLAINT	967a	1
7	14	בעת	TERRIFY	130a	2
		חזיון	VISION	303b	2
		חלום	DREAM	321c	1
		חתת	BE SHATTERED	369c	
		מן	OUT OF	580a	2 eb
7	15	בחר	CHOOSE	104b	5 b
		מחנק	STRANGLING	338b	
		מן	THAN	582c	6 a
		נפש	SOUL	661b	8
		עצבת	HURT	781a	
		עצם	BONE	783a	1
7	16	הבל	VAPOUR	210d	2
		חדל	CEASE	293a	2
		יום	DAY	399a	4 a
		יום	DAY	399b	4 a
		מאס	REJECT	549c	2
		עולם	LONG DURATION	762d	2 i
7	17	אנוש	MAN	60d	3
		גדל	BECOME GREAT	152c	3 a
		כי	THAT	472d	1 f
		לב	HEART	524d	23 c
		מה	WHAT	553d	1 db
		שית	PUT	1011b	2 b
7	18	בחן	EXAMINE	103c	1
		בקר	MORNING	*134a	1 f
		בקר	MORNING	134b	1 f
		פקד	ATTEND TO	823c	A 2
		רגע	A MOMENT	921b	BG
7	19	בלע	SWALLOW DOWN	118a	1
		מה	HOW	554a	4 cb
		עד	AS FAR AS	724c	1 2b
		רפה	SINK	952a	3
		רק	SPITTLE	956d	
		שית	PUT	*1011c	4
		שעה	GAZE	1043a	
		שעה	GAZE	*1043a	
7	20	חטא	MISS A GOAL OR WAY	306d	2 b
		מה	HOW	554a	4 d
		נצר	WATCH	665d	1
		משא	LOAD	672c	1
		על	UPON	753a	2 1b
		מפגע	THING HIT	803c	
		פעל	DO	821b	1 b
		שום	TO PLACE	964a	3 d
7	21	כי	THAT	*472c	1 db
		כי	BECAUSE	474a	2
		ל	TO	511c	1 ga
		נשא	LIFT	671b	2 c
		עבר	PASS OVER	719a	4
		עון	INIQUITY	731a	1 c2
		עפר	DRY EARTH	779d	1 f
		פשע	TRANSGRESSION	833c	3 d
		שבב	LOOK EARLY	1007c	
		שכב	LIE DOWN	1012c	4 c
8	1	בלדד	BILDAD	115a	
		שוחי	SHUHITE	1001d	
8	2	אן	WHERE	33a	
		אלה	THESE	41c	A
		אמר	WORD	57a	1
		כביר	GREAT	460b	
		כבר	MAKE MANY	460b	
		מלל	SPEAK	576b	
		פה	MOUTH	805a	2 a
8	3	אם	IF	50d	2 ab b
		עות	BE BENT	736c	1 a
		צדק	RIGHTEOUSNESS	841d	E
		משפט	JUDGEMNT	1048d	2 a
8	4	חטא	MISS 0A GOAL OR WAY0	307a	2 b
		יד	HAND	390d	5 b3
		פשע	TRANSGRESSION	833c	3 c
		שלח	SEND	1019b	7
8	5	חנן	SHOW FAVOR	336b	2
		שחר	LOOK EARLY	1007c	
8	6	זך	PURE	269b	2
		ישר	STRAIGHT	449b	3 b
		כי	THAT	472c	1 db
		נוה	HABITATION	627c	2
		נוה	PASTURE	627d	2 b
		עור	ROUSE ONESELF	735c	2
		על	UPON	756d	27 a c
		צדק	RIGHTEOUSNESS	841d	3
		שלם	BE COMPLETE	1022c	2
8	7	אחרית	END	31a	B
		מצער	SMALL THING	859b	1
		ראשית	BEGINNING	912a	1 a
		שגה	GROW	960d	
8	8	דור	GENERATION	190a	2 a
		חקר	SEARCHING	350d	
		כן	ESTABLISH	467a	4
		כי	BECAUSE	474b	3 d
		שאל	ASK	981d	2 a
8	9	יום	DAY	399a	4 a
		יום	DAY	399b	4 a
		כי	BECAUSE	474b	3 d
		צל	SHADOW	*853b	3
8	10	תמול	YESTERDAY	1070a	1
		יצא	BRING OUT	425b	4 k
		ירה	DIRECT	435b	5 a
		מלה	WORD	576b	
		מן	OUT OF	579c	2 cd
8	11	אחו	REEDS	28a	
		בלי	WEARING OUT	115c	2 b
		בצה	SWAMP	130c	
		גאה	RISE UP	144b	2
		ה	INTERROG PART	209d	1 b
		לא	NOT	520a	4 aa
		שגא	GROW GREAT	960c	
		שגה	GROW	960d	
8	12	אב	FRESHNESS	1a	
		חציר	GREEN GRASS	348b	2
		יבש	BE DRY	386b	1 d
		עוד	STILL	729a	1 aa
		קטף	PLUCK OFF	882c	
8	13	אבד	PERISH	1d	2
		ארח	WAY	73a	2
		חנף	PROFANE	338b	
		כן	SO	485d	1 a
		תקוה	HOPE	876b	3
		שכח	FORGETFUL	1013c	
8	14	מבטח	CONFIDENCE	105c	1
		בית	HOUSE	109b	1 b
		מוח	SPIN	*376a	
		כסל	CONFIDENCE	492d	3
		עכביש	SPIDER	747b	
8	15	בית	HOUSE	110b	6
		קוט	FEEL A LOATHING	876c	
		קוט	BREAK	876d	
		חזק	BE FIRM	305b	6 a
		עמד	STAND	764b	5 a
		קום	STAND	878b	7 c
		שען	LEAN	1043d	
8	16	גנה	GARDEN	171b	
		יונקת	TWIG	413c	
		יצא	GO OUT	423d	1 h
		רטב	MOIST	936a	
		שמש	SUN	1039b	1
8	17	אחז	GRASP	*28b	

Ch	v.	Heb	Eng	Page	Sec
		בית	BETWEEN	108a	
		בית	HOUSE	109c	2
		חזה	SEE	302c	
		סבך	INTERWEAVE	687c	1
		שרש	ROOT	1057d	1
8	18	בלע	SWALLOW UP	118c	2b
		כחש	DECEIVE	471b	2
8	19	הוא	HE, SHE, IT	216d	6a
		הן	BEHOLD	243b	
		עפר	DRY EARTH	779d	1b
		צמח	SPROUT	855c	1
		משוש	EXULTATION	965c	
8	20	הן	BEHOLD	243b	
		חזק	BE FIRM	305b	6c
		יד	HAND	389d	1e1
		מאס	REJECT	549c	
		תם	COMPLETE	1071a	3
8	21	עד	UNTIL	725a	2 1b b
		פה	MOUTH	805a	2b
		תרועה	SHOUT OF WAR	930a	4
		שחק	LAUGHTER	966a	1
		שפה	SPEECH	973d	1b
8	22	אהל	TENT	14a	2
		אין	NOT	34b	2b
		בשת	SHAME	102a	1
		לבש	PUT ON	528a	B
9	2	אמנם	VERILY	54a	
		אנוש	MAN	60d	3
		מה	HOW	553c	2aa
		עם	WITH	767c	1c
		עם	WITH	768a	4b
		צדק	BE JUST	842c	2
9	3	חפץ	DELIGHT IN	342d	1b
		ריב	STRIVE	936c	2
9	4	אמיץ	MIGHTY	55c	
		חכם	WISE	315a	6 b2
		כח	STRENGTH	471a	3
		לבב	HEART	523c	2 3b
		מי	WHO	566d	F c
		קשה	BE SEVERE	904c	3b
		שלם	BE COMPLETE	1022b	2
9	5	אשר	PARTICLE OF RELATION	82d	5
		אשר	THAT	83b	8 ab
		הפך	TURN	245c	1 a
		הר	MOUNTAIN	250a	1 c
		עמוד	PILLAR	765b	5 b
		עתק	MOVE	801b	2
9	6	ארץ	EARTH	76a	1 b
		פלץ	SHUDDER	814a	
		מקום	STANDING PLACE	879d	1a
		רגז	BE AGITATED	919b	
9	7	אמר	SAY	56c	4
		בעד	BEHIND	126c	1b
		זרח	RISE	280b	1a
		חרס	SUN	357b	
		חתם	SEAL	367d	2
		כוכב	STAR	456d	
9	8	במה	HIGH PLACE	119b	2b
		דרך	TREAD	202a	2
9	9	חדר	CHAMBER	293d	
		תימן	SOUTH	412c	1a
		כימה	PLEIADES	465b	
		כסיל	ORION	493a	
		עשה	DO	794b	2 1b
		עש	GREAT BEAR	798b	
9	10	גדול	GREAT	153c	9
		חקר	SEARCHING	350d	
		מספר	NUMBER	708d	1 a
		עד	AS FAR AS	724c	12a d
		פלא	BE SURPASSING	810d	4
9	11	בין	DISCERN	106d	1a
		הן	BEHOLD	243b	A
		חלף	PASS ON OR AWAY	322a	1 a
9	12	הן	BEHOLD	243c	A
		הן	IF	243d	B
		חתף	SEIZE	369a	
		מה	WHAT	552b	1 a
		מי	WHO	566d	F c
		מי	WHO	567a	F c
		שוב	TURN BACK	999d	5
9	13	עזר	HELP	740c	
		רהב	STORM	923c	1
		שוב	TURN BACK	999d	6a
		שחח	BOW	1005d	1
		תחת	UNDERNEATH	1065c	2 1c a
9	14	אף	ALSO	65b	3
		בחר	CHOOSE	104b	5 b
		עם	WITH	767c	1 c
		ענה	ANSWER	773a	3 b
9	15	אשר	PARTICLE OF RELATION	82d	5
		חנן	SHOW FAVOR	336b	2
		ענה	ANSWER	772a	1
		ענה	ANSWER	773a	3 b
		צדק	BE JUST	842c	1
		שפט	JUDGE	1048a	1
9	16	אזן	HEAR	24c	1
		אמן	CONFIRM	53b	2 d
		קרא	CALL	845b	2b
9	17	אשר	PARTICLE OF RELATION	82d	5
		חנם	OUT OF FAVOR	336d	C
		פצע	BRUISE	822d	
		שערה	TEMPEST	973b	
		שוף	BRUISE	1003a	

Ch	v.	Heb	Eng	Page	Sec
9	18	ממרור	BITTER THING	601b	
		נתן	GIVE	679a	1 g
		רוח	BREATH	924c	1 a
		שבע	SATISFIED	959d	
		שוב	TURN BACK	999a	1 c
9	19	אמיץ	MIGHTY	55c	
		יעד	MEET AT AN AP- POINTED PLACE	417a	
		כח	STRENGTH	470d	3
		ל	TO	514c	5 fc
		מי	WHO	567a	F c
		משפט	JUDGMENT	1048b	1a
9	20	עקש	TWIST	786a	
		פה	MOUTH	805a	2a
		צדק	BE JUST	842c	1
		רשע	BE WICKED	957d	2
		תם	COMPLETE	1071a	3
9	21	חיים	LIFE	313a	1
		ידע	KNOW	394b	2
		מאס	REJECT	549c	2
		נפש	SOUL	660a	4 b1
		תם	COMPLETE	1071a	3
9	22	הוא	HE, SHE, IT	216d	6a
		כלה	FINISH	478c	2 c2
		כן	SO	487b	3 f
		רשע	WICKED	957b	1
		תם	COMPLETE	1071a	3
9	23	לעג	MOCK	541b	
		מות	DIE	560b	1
		מסה	TRIAL	650b	
		נקי	CLEAN	667c	1
		פתאם	SUDDENNESS	837c	
		שוט	SCOURGE	1002a	1
9	24	אפו	THEN	66b	3
		כסה	COVER	491d	2
		לא	NOT	519a	1 ad a
		נתן	GIVE	681c	1 e
		רשע	WICKED	957b	1
		שפט	JUDGE	1047c	2 b
9	25	ברח	FLEE	138a	2
		טובה	WELFARE	375d	1
		קלל	BE SLIGHT	886c	2
		רוץ	RUN	930c	2 b
9	26	אבה	REED	3a	
		אכל	FOOD	38a	1
		אניה	A SHIP	58c	
		ה	THE	208a	1 f
		חלף	PASS ON OR AWAY	322a	1 b
		מוש	RUSH	377b	
	ד	LIKE	454a	1 c2
		נשר	EAGLE	676d	
		עם	WITH	768a	1 f
9	27	אם	IF	50a	1 a5
		בלג	SMILE	114d	1
		עזב	LEAVE	737d	3
		שיח	COMPLAINT	967a	1
9	28	יגר	BE AFRAID	388c	
		נקה	BE CLEAN	667c	1
		עצבת	HURT	781a	
9	29	הבל	VAPOUR	211a	2
		יגע	TOIL	388b	1
		רשע	BE WICKED	957d	2
9	30	אם	IF	49d	1 a3 a
		במו	IN	91b	
		בר	LYE	141b	
		זכך	BE BRIGHT	269b	
		כף	HOLLOW OF THE HAND	496d	1 d7
		מי	WATER	565d	3
		רחץ	WASH OFF	934d	
		שלג	SNOW	1017a	
9	31	אז	THEN	23b	2
		טבל	DIP	371b	1
		שלמה	GARMENT	971b	
		שחת	PIT	1001c	1
		תעב	BE ABHORRED	1073b	2
9	32	איש	MAN	35d	
		ה	THE	208c	1 hb
		יחדו	TOGETHER	403b	A
		לא	NOT	519b	1 bb
		משפט	JUDGMENT	1048c	1 c
9	33	יכח	DECIDE	407a	1
		יש	BE	442a	2 ch
		לא	NOT	520d	1
		לו	IF	530b	2
		שית	PUT	1011a	1
9	34	אימה	TERROR	34a	
		בעת	FALL UPON	130a	1
		על	UPON	758d	4 2b
		שבט	ROD	987a	1a
9	35	ירא	FEAR	431b	1
		כן	SO	486b	1 cd
		עם	WITH	768a	4 b
10	1	חיים	LIFE	313b	1
		מר	BITTER	600d	2 b
		נפש	SOUL	660d	6 c
		עזב	LEAVE	737d	3
		על	UPON	753d	2 1d
		קוט	FEEL A LOATHING	876c	
		שיח	COMPLAINT	967a	1
10	2	ידע	MAKE KNOWN	395a	
		מה	HOW	554b	4 f
		ריב	STRIVE	936c	3
		רשע	BE WICKED	957d	2
10	3	טוב	PLEASANT	374c	5
		יגיע	TOIL	388c	2

Ch	v.	Heb	Eng	Page	Sec
		עצה	ADVICE	420b	
		יפע	SHINE OUT	422a	1
		כף	HOLLOW OF THE HAND	496d	1 d7
		מאם	REJECT	549c	1 a
		על	UPON	757d	2 7c d
		עשק	OPPRESS	798d	1
		רשע	WICKED	957c	3
10	4	אם	IF	50d	2 ab a
		אנוש	MAN	60d	3
		בשר	FLESH	142d	5
10	5	אם	IF	50d	2 ab a
		אנוש	MAN	60d	3
		כי	THAT	472d	1 f
		שנה	YEAR	1040b	
10	6	בקש	SEEK	134d	1 c
		דרש	SEEK	205c	4 b
		חטאת	SIN	308d	1 d1
		עון	INIQUITY	731b	1 c5
10	7	דעת	KNOWLEDGE	395d	1 e
		נצל	DELIVER	664d	3 a
		על	UPON	754d	2 1ff
		רשע	BE WICKED	957d	2
10	8	בלע	SWALLOW UP	118c	2 a
	ו	AND	254a	2 b
		יחד	UNION	403a	2 a4
		יחד	ALTOGETHER	403b	2 b
		סבב	TURNABOUT	685d	1 c
		סביב	ROUND ABOUT	687a	1 d
		עצב	SHAPE	781a	
10	9	זכר	REMEMBER	270b	2 3 c
		חמר	CEMENT	330d	2 a
		עפר	DRY EARTH	779d	1 b
		שוב	TURN BACK	999b	1 g
10	10	גבינה	CURD	148c	2
		חלב	MILK	316b	A
		לא	NOT	520b	4 ba
		נתך	POUR FORTH	678a	
10	11	בשר	FLESH	142c	1 b
		לבש	CLOTHE	528b	1 b
		סך	WEAVE TOGETHER	697b	
		עור	SKIN	736a	1
		עצם	BONE	782d	1 a
		שכך	WEAVE	968a	
10	12	חיים	LIFE	313a	1
		חסד	GOODNESS	339a	2 1b
		פקד	ATTEND TO	823b	A 1a
		פקדה	OVERSIGHT	824a	1 b
		רוח	BREATH	925b	4 b
10	13	זה	THIS	260d	1 a
		לבב	HEART	523c	2 2
		עם	WITH	768c	4 b
		צפן	HIDE	860c	1
10	14	אם	IF	49d	1 a3 a
		חטא	MISS A GOAL OR WAY	306d	2 b
		נקה	BE CLEAN	667c	1
		עון	INIQUITY	731c	3
		שמר	KEEP	1036d	1 c
10	15	אללי	ALAS	47d	
		נשא	LIFT	670b	1 b 2
		עני	AFFLICTION	777a	1
		צדק	BE JUST	842d	4
		קלון	DISHONOUR	886a	2
		ראה	SEEING	909a	
		רוה	WATERED	924b	
		רשע	BE WICKED	957d	2
		שבע	SATISFIED	960b	2
10	16	גאה	RISE UP	144b	3
		צוד	HUNT	844c	
		שוב	TURN BACK	998b	8
		שחל	LION	1006c	
10	17	חדש	RENEW	294a	1
		חליפה	A CHANGE	322c	1
		כעש	ANGER	495b	2
		נגד	IN FRONT	617b	1 aa
		עם	WITH	767c	1 c
		עם	WITH	767d	1 d
		צבא	ARMY	839a	1 a
10	18	בטן	WOMB	*106a	1
		גוע	EXPIRE	157c	
		יצא	BRING OUT	424d	1 d
		רחם	WOMB	933b	1
10	19	בטן	WOMB	106a	3
		יבל	CONDUCT	385a	2
		כאשר	AS	455c	1 e
		ל	TO	511b	1 ga
10	20	קצבצר	GRAVE	868d	
		בלג	SMILE	114d	1
		לא	NOT	520b	4 ba
		מעט	A FEW	590a	1 d
		מעט	A FEW	590a	1 a
		שית	PUT	1011c	4
		שעה	GAZE	1043b	
		חדל	ADDENDA ET COR- RIGENDA	1123a	
10	21	ארץ	EARTH	76b	2 g
		טרם	NOT YET	*302c	1
		חשך	DARKNESS	365a	1
		צלמות	DEATH-SHADOW	853c	3
		שאול	SHEOL	*983a	1
		שאול	SHEOL	*983b	2 b
		שוב	TURN BACK	997c	4 b
10	22	אפל	DARKNESS	66c	1
		ארץ	EARTH	76b	2 g
		יפע	SHINE OUT	422b	1

Ch	v.	Heb	Eng	Page	Sec
		כמו	LIKE	455d	1 a
		לא	NOT	519d	2 d
		סדר	ARRANGEMENT	690b	
		עיפה	DARKNESS	734c	
		צלמות	DEATH-SHADOW	853c	3
11	1	נעמתי	NAAMATHITE	564b	
		צפר	ZOPHAR	862b	
11	2	אם	IF	50d	2 ab b
		דבר	WORD	183b	3 1
		ענה	ANSWER	773a	2 a
		צדק	BE JUST	842c	2
		רב	MULTITUDE	914a	1
		שפה	SPEECH	973c	1 a1
11	3	בד	EMPTY TALK	95a	A
		חרש	BE SILENT	361b	2
		כלם	HUMILIATE	484a	1
		לעג	MOCK	541c	
		מת	MALE	607b	3 a
11	4	בר	PURE	141a	1
		זך	PURE	269b	2
		לקח	TEACHING	544b	2
11	5	אולם	BUT	19d	
		נתן	GIVE	679a	1 f
		עם	WITH	767a	1 d
		פתח	OPEN	835d	
		שפה	SPEECH	973d	1 a1
11	6	חכמה	WISDOM	315c	5 a
		תושיה	SOUND WISDOM	444d	A
		כפל	DOUBLE	495d	
		ל	TO	514c	5 fb
		מן	FROM	580d	3 ba
		נגד	BE CONSPICUOUS	616c	2
		נשה	FORGET	674d	
		עון	INIQUITY	731a	1 c1
		תעלמה	HIDDEN THING	761b	1
11	7	אם	IF	50d	2 ab a
		חקר	SEARCHING	350d	1
		תכלית	END	479b	1
		מן	THAN	582d	6 c
		מצא	FIND	593a	2 a
		עד	AS FAR AS	724a	1 1a
11	8	גבה	HEIGHT	147b	1
		עמק	DEEP	771b	1
		פעל	DO	821b	1 b
		שאול	SHEOL	983a	1
11	9	ארך	LONG	74a	B
		מדה	SIZE	551c	2
		רחב	WIDE	932a	
11	10	חלף	PASS ON OR AWAY	322a	1 a
		מי	WHO	567a	F c
		סגר	SHUT UP	689c	2 a
		קהל	ASSEMBLE AS	875a	1 a
		שוב	TURN BACK	999d	5
11	11	און	TROUBLE	20a	3
		בין	DISCERN	107a	1 a
		הוא	HE, SHE, IT	*215a	1 a
		ידע	KNOW	394a	1
		מת	MALE	607b	3 b
		ראה	TO SEE	907b	3
		שוא	EMPTINESS	996b	3
11	12	ילד	BE BORN	408d	
		לבב	GET A MIND	525d	
		נבב	HOLLOW OUT	612c	
		עיר	MALE ASS	747a	
		פרא	WILD ASS	825b	
11	13	כון	ESTABLISH	466c	3
		לב	HEART	525a	2 4
		פרש	SPREAD OUT	831b	1
11	14	עולה	INJUSTICE	732d	3
		רחק	BE DISTANT	935b	2
		שכן	SETTLE DOWN	1015c	2
11	15	אז	THEN	23a	1 b
		יצק	BE POURED	427c	3
		ירא	FEAR	431a	1 a
		כי	BECAUSE	*473d	3 c
		מום	BLEMISH	548d	2 b
		מן	FROM	578c	1 b
		נשא	LIFT	670b	1 b 3
11	16	ה	THE	208a	1 f
		זכר	REMEMBER	269d	11 b
		כ	LIKE	454a	1 c2
		כי	BECAUSE	473d	3 c
		עבר	PASS OVER	717d	4 a
		עמל	TROUBLE	765d	1
11	17	בקר	MORNING	134b	1 f
		חלד	DURATION	317b	
		עוף	BE DARK	734a	
		תעפה	GLOOM	734a	
		צהר	MIDDAY	844a	2
		קום	STAND	878a	4
11	18	בטח	SECURITY	105b	
		בטח	TRUST	105b	2
		חפר	DIG	343a	2
		תקוה	HOPE	876b	1
		שכב	LIE DOWN	1012a	1 b
11	19	חלה	MOLLIFY	318d	1
		חרד	TREMBLE	353c	
		רבץ	LIE DOWN	918c	
11	20	אבד	PERISH	1d	2
		כלה	BE FINISHED	477d	2 b
		מנוס	ESCAPE	631a	2
		מפח	BREATHING OUT	656a	
		נפש	SOUL	659c	1 c
		תקוה	HOPE	876b	1
12	2	אמנם	VERILY	54a	
		חכמה	WISDOM	315d	5 c

Ch	v.	Heb	Eng	Page	Sec
		כי	THAT	472b	1 da
		מות	DIE	559d	1 a2
		עם	PEOPLE	766d	4
		די	THAT	*1088a	3 a
12	3	אלה	THESE	41d	D
		את	WITH	86c	3 b
		גם	ALSO	169d	4
		כמו	LIKE	455d	1 a
		כמו	LIKE	456a	1 a
		לא	NOT	519b	1 bc
		לבב	HEART	523c	23 a
		מי	WHO	566b	B
		מן	THAN	582c	6 a
		נפל	FALL	657d	6
12	4	ענה	ANSWER	772a	1 b
		צדיק	JUST	843b	3 b
		קרא	CALL	895b	2 a
		שחק	LAUGHTER	966a	2
		תמים	SOUND	1071b	4
12	5	בוז	CONTEMPT	100b	1
		כון	BE READY	466a	3
		כיד	DECAY	*475d	
		ל	TO	516c	5 jb
		לפיד	TORCH	542b	
		מעד	SLIP	588c	
		נכון	BLOW	646d	
		עשתות	THOUGHT	799d	
		פיד	RUIN	810a	
		רגל	FOOT	919d	1 a
		שאנן	AT EASE	983c	2
12	6	אלה	GOD	43a	1
		בוא	COME	99c	2
		בטחות	SECURITY	105c	
		ל	TO	512d	5 aa
		שדד	DEAL VIOLENTLY WITH	994b	
12	7	שלה	BE QUIET	1017b	2
		אולם	BUT	19d	
		בהמה	BEAST	97a	1
		ירה	DIRECT	435b	5 a
		נגד	BE CONSPICUOUS	616d	1
		שאל	ASK	981d	2
12	8	בהמה	BEAST	97a	1
		דג	FISH	185d	
		ירה	DIRECT	435b	5 a
		שיח	MUSE	967b	3 b
12	9	יהוה	YAHWEH	218c	1
		ידע	KNOW	*393d	1 a
		מי	WHO	567a	F c
12	10	איש	MAN	35d	
		בשר	FLESH	142d	6 c
		חי	ALIVE	312b	1 d
		נפש	SOUL	659c	2
		רוח	BREATH	925b	4 b
12	11	אזן	EAR	24a	2 a
		אכל	FOOD	38a	
		בחן	TRY	103c	2 d
		ו	AND	253b	1 j
		חך	PALATE	335b	C
		טעם	TASTE	381a	2
		ל	TO	515d	5 ia
		מלה	WORD	576b	
12	12	ארך	LENGTH	73d	B
		תבונה	UNDERSTANDING	108b	2
		חכמה	WISDOM	315c	5 c
12	13	ישיש	AGED	450b	
		תבונה	UNDERSTANDING	108b	2
		גבורה	MIGHT	150c	3
		חכמה	WISDOM	315c	5 a
		עצה	ADVICE	420b	
		ל	TO	513b	5 ba
		עם	WITH	768b	3 b
12	14	בנה	BUILD	125a	1 b
		הרס	THROW DOWN	248d	1
		סגר	CLOSE	689c	2 a
		על	UPON	753a	2 1a b
		פתח	OPEN	835c	
12	15	חפך	TURN	245c	1 b
		יבש	BE DRY	386c	2
		עצר	RESTRAIN	783c	1
		שלח	SEND	1019b	3
12	16	תושיה	SOUND WISDOM	444d	A
		ל	TO	513b	5 ba
		עז	STRENGTH	739a	1
		עם	WITH	768b	3 b
		שגג	GO ASTRAY	992d	1
		שנה	GO ASTRAY	993b	2
12	17	הלך	WALK	236d	2
		הלל	PRAISE	239a	
		יעץ	ADVISE	419d	2
		שלל	BAREFOOT	1021d	
		שפט	JUDGE	1047c	1 b
12	18	אזור	WAISTCLOTH	25b	
		אסר	TIE	63d	4
		מוסר	BAND	64c	
		מתנים	LOINS	608b	1 f
		פתח	OPEN	835c	2
12	19	הלך	WALK	236d	2
		איתן	ENDURING	451a	2
		כהן	PRIEST	463d	4
		סלף	TWIST	701b	2
		שולל	BAREFOOT	1021d	
12	20	אמן	CONFIRM	53a	5
		זקן	OLD	278c	2
		טעם	TASTE	381a	2
		ל	TO	515b	5 hb g

Ch	v.	Heb	Eng	Page	Sec
		לקח	TAKE	543a	3 a
		סור	TURN ASIDE	694b	1
		שפה	SPEECH	973d	1 a3
12	21	אפיק	CHANNEL	67d	
		בוז	CONTEMPT	100c	2
		מזיח	GIRDLE	561b	
		נדיב	NOBLE	622a	2
		רפה	SINK	951d	
		רפה	SINK	951d	
		פך	POUR OUT	1049d	2 a
		אפק	ADDENDA ET CORRIGENDA	1120c	
12	22	חשך	DARKNESS	365a	2
		יצא	BRING OUT	425b	5
		ל	TO	511b	1 ga
		עמק	DEEP	771b	2
		צלמות	DEATH-SHADOW	853c	1
12	23	אבד	CAUSE TO PERISH	2a	1
		גוי	NATION	156c	1
		ל	TO	511d	3 a
		ל	TO	512a	3 b
		נחה	LEAD	635a	
		שגא	GROW GREAT	960c	1
		שגה	GO ASTRAY	993b	3
		שטח	SPREAD	1009a	
		נחה	ADDENDA ET CORRIGENDA	1125a	
12	24	דרך	WAY	202d	1
		לא	NOT	519d	2 e
		תהו	FORMLESSNESS	1062c	1
		תעה	ERR	1073c	1
12	25	חשך	DARKNESS	365b	3 d
		משש	GROPE	607a	2
		שכר	DRUNKEN	1016c	
		תעה	ERR	1073c	2
13	1	אזן	EAR	24a	2 a
		בין	DISCERN	106d	1 b
		הן	BEHOLD	243b	
		כל	ALL	482c	2 a
		ל	TO	515d	5 ia
13	2	אנכי	I	59b	
		דעת	WISDOM	395d	2 a
		לא	NOT	519b	1 bc
		מן	THAN	582c	6 a
		נפל	FALL	657d	6
13	3	אולם	BUT	19d	
		חפץ	DELIGHT IN	342d	1 b
		יכח	PROVE	407a	3
13	4	אולם	BUT	19d	
		אליל	WORTHLESSNESS	47b	A
		טפל	SMEAR	381d	
		רפא	HEAL	950d	3 b
		שקר	DECEPTION	1055c	3
13	5	חכמה	WISDOM	315d	5 c
		חרש	BE SILENT	361b	1 a
13	6	תוכחת	ARGUMENT	407b	1
		קשב	ATTEND	904a	
		ריב	STRIFE	937a	4
		שפה	SPEECH	973c	1 a1
13	7	ל	TO	515c	5 hc
		עולה	INJUSTICE	732c	2
		רמיה	DECEIT	941b	
13	8	נשא	LIFT	670c	1 b 3
		ריב	STRIVE	936d	1
13	9	אנוש	MAN	60d	1
		חקר	SEARCH	350d	2 c
		טוב	PLEASANT	374a	2
		טוב	PLEASANT	*374c	5
		תלל	MOCK	1068b	
		תלל	MOCK	1068b	
13	10	יכח	CORRECT	407a	6
		נשא	LIFT	670c	1 b3
		סתר	COVERING	712a	3
13	11	בעת	FALL UPON	130a	1
		נפל	FALL	657c	2
		שאת	DIGNITY	673b	1
		פחד	DREAD	808c	1
13	12	אפר	ASHES	68a	
		גב	BACK	146c	4
		זכרון	MEMORIAL	272a	1 d
		חמר	CEMENT	330d	2 a
		ל	TO	512c	4 a
		זכרון	ADDENDA ET CORRIGENDA	1122d	
13	13	חרש	BE SILENT	361b	1 a
		מה	AUGHT	553d	3
		מה	HOW	*554d	4 f
		מן	FROM	578a	1 a
		עבר	PASS OVER	717b	1 h
13	14	בשר	FLESH	142c	1 b
		כף	HOLLOW OF THE HAND	496d	1 d6
		מה	HOW	554b	4 f
		נפש	SOUL	659c	3 c
		נשא	LIFT	670a	1 a
		שום	TO PLACE	963a	1 a
		שן	TOOTH	1042a	1 a
13	15	אך	HOWBEIT	36c	2 a
		דרך	WAY	203c	6 c
		הן	BEHOLD	243b	
		הן	IF	243b	B
		יכח	PROVE	407a	3
		לא	NOT	520c	1
		קטל	SLAY	881d	
13	16	הוא	HE, SHE, IT	216d	6 a
		חנף	PROFANE	338b	

Ch	v.	Heb	Eng	Page	Sec
		ישועה	DELIVERANCE	447b	3
		כי	THAT	471d	1 a
		לא	NOT	518d	1 ac
13	17	אזן	EAR	24a	2 a
		אחוה	DECLARATION	296a	
		מלה	WORD	576b	
13	18	נא	PART OF EN-TREATY	609c	4 d
		ערך	ARRANGE	789d	1 g
		צדק	BE JUST	842c	1
		משפט	JUDGMENT	1048c	1 d
13	19	גוע	EXPIRE	157c	
		הוא	HE, SHE, IT	216c	4 bb
		חרש	BE SILENT	361b	1 a
		מי	WHO	567a	F c
		עתה	NOW	774c	2 ga
		ריב	STRIVE	936a	2
13	20	אז	THEN	23a	1 b
		סתר	HIDE	711c	1
		שנים	TWO	1041b	1 b2
13	21	אימה	TERROR	34a	
		אכף	PRESSURE	38c	
		בעת	FALL UPON	130a	1
		כף	HOLLOW OF THE HAND	496c	1 b
		על	UPON	758d	4 2b
		רחק	BE DISTANT	935b	2
13	22	קרא	CALL	896a	5 d
		שוב	TURN BACK	999c	3
13	23	חטאת	SIN	308c	1 b
		ידע	KNOW	395a	
		מה	HOW	553d	4 ca
		עון	INIQUITY	730d	1
		פשע	TRANSGRESSION	833c	3 c
13	24	איב	BE HOSTILE TO	33c	
		חשב	THINK	363b	2 l
		ל	TO	512c	4 b
		סתר	HIDE	711d	2 a
13	25	יבש	DRY	386d	2
		כי	THAT	472a	1 f
		נדף	DRIVE	624a	
		עלה	LEAF	750a	
		ערץ	CAUSE TO TREMBLE	791d	1
		קש	STUBBLE	905d	
		רדף	PURSUE	922d	1 e
13	26	ירש	CAUSE TO POSSESS	439d	1
		כתב	WRITE	508a	4
		מרה	BITTER THING	601a	3
		נעורים	YOUTH	655c	
		עון	INIQUITY	730d	1
13	27	ארח	WAY	73a	2
		חקה	CUT IN	348d	
		סד	STOCKS	690a	
		על	UPON	753e	2 la b
		רגל	FOOT	919d	1 a
		שום	TO PLACE	963a	1 a
		שמר	KEEP	1036d	1 c
		שרש	ROOT	1057d	3
13	28	אכל	EAT	37c	2
		בגד	GARMENT	94a	1
		בלה	BECOME OLD AND WORN OUT	115a	
		עש	MOTH	799c	
		רקב	ROTTENNESS	955a	
13	29	מה	AUGHT	553d	3
14	1	אדם	MAN	9b	2
		אשה	WOMAN	61a	1
		זה	THIS	*261b	3
		חדל	CEASE	*293a	2
		קצר	SHORT	894b	
		רגז	AGITATION	919c	
		שבע	SATISFIED	960b	2
14	2	ברח	FLEE	138a	2
		ה	THE	208a	1 f
		זה	THIS	*261b	3
		יצא	GO OUT	423d	1 h
		מלל	WITHER	576d	
		ציץ	BLOSSOM	847d	1
		צל	SHADOW	853b	3
		מול	ADDENDA ET CORRIGENDA	1124d	
14	3	אף	ALSO	65a	1
		בוא	COME	99a	1 c
		זה	THIS	261b	3
		עין	EYE	744b	1 a
		על	UPON	757d	2 7c d
		עם	WITH	767c	1 c
		פקח	OPEN	824d	1 a
		משפט	JUDGMENT	1048c	1 c
		עין	ADDENDA ET CORRIGENDA	1125d	
14	4	טהור	CLEAN	373a	3
		טמא	UNCLEAN	379a	1
		לו	IF	530b	2
		נתן	GIVE	678d	1 f
14	5	את	WITH	86c	3 b
		חדש	NEW MOON	294c	2 a
		חק	SOMETHING PRESCRIBED	349c	5
		חרץ	CUT	358c	3
		עבר	PASS OVER	717b	1 b
		עבר	PASS OVER	717c	2
		עבר	PASS OVER	717c	1 i
14	6	חדל	CEASE	293a	2
		יום	TIME	399d	6 a
		כי	BECAUSE	*474a	3 c
		עד	UNTIL	725a	2 lb b
		עד	UNTIL	725b	2 3
		על	UPON	758d	4 2b
		עתה	NOW	774b	1 d
		רצה	BE PLEASED WITH	953a	1 b
		שכיר	HIRED	969b	2
		שעה	GAZE	1043a	
		שעה	GAZE	1043a	
14	7	ו	AND	255a	5 cb
		חדל	CEASE	293a	1
		חלף	PASS ON OR AWAY	322b	2
		יונקת	TWIG	413c	
		יש	HAVE	441d	2 cb
		כי	BECAUSE	474a	1 a
		כרת	BE CUT OFF	504b	2
		תקוה	HOPE	876b	1
14	8	גזע	STOCK	160b	
		זקן	BE OLD	278c	
		כי	BECAUSE	474a	3 c
		מות	DIE	559d	1 c
		עפר	DRY EARTH	779d	1 c
		שרש	ROOT	1057d	2
14	9	כמו	LIKE	455d	1 a
		כי	BECAUSE	474a	3 c
		מן	OUT OF	580a	2 eb
		נטע	PLANT	642a	3
		עשה	DO	794d	2 2
		פרח	BUD	827b	2
		קציר	BRANCHES	894d	
		ריח	SCENT	926b	1
14	10	אדם	MAN	9b	2
		אי	WHERE	32b	1 a
		גוע	EXPIRE	157c	
		חלש	BE WEAK	325d	1
		כי	BECAUSE	474a	3 c
14	11	אזל	GO	23c	
		ו	AND	253b	1 j
		חרב	BE DRY	351a	2
		יבש	BE DRY	386c	2
		כי	BECAUSE	474a	3 c
		נהר	STREAM	625d	1
14	12	בלתי	NOT	117a	4 c
		שנה	SLEEP	446a	
		כי	BECAUSE	474a	3 c
		עור	ROUSE ONESELF	735a	
		קום	STAND	877d	1 a
		קיץ	AWAKE	884c	2
		שכב	LIE DOWN	1012b	4 a
		שמי	HEAVENS	1030a	1 a
14	13	זכר	REMEMBER	270b	2 l a
		חק	SOMETHING PRESCRIBED	349c	5
		כי	BECAUSE	*473d	3 c
		נתן	GIVE	679a	1 f
		סתר	HIDE	711d	1
		צפן	HIDE	860d	1
		שאול	SHEOL	983b	2 b
		שוב	TURN BACK	997d	6 f
		שית	PUT	1011b	2 c
14	14	ה	INTERROG PART	209d	1 b
		חיה	LIVE	311b	2 d
		חליפה	A CHANGE	322c	3
		יחל	WAIT	404a	1
		כי	BECAUSE	*473d	2
		צבא	HARD SERVICE	839b	3 b
14	15	יד	HAND	389b	1 c
		כי	BECAUSE	*473d	3 c
		כסף	LONG	493d	
		מעשה	DEED	796b	2 b
		קרא	CALL	896a	5 d
		שום	TO PLACE	963c	1 d
14	16	חטאת	SIN	308d	1 d1
		כי	BECAUSE	473d	2
		לא	NOT	519b	1 a
		ספר	COUNT	707d	2
		צעד	STEP	857d	2
		שמר	KEEP	1036c	1 b
14	17	חתם	SEAL	367d	2
		טפל	SMEAR	381d	
		עון	INIQUITY	730d	1
		פשע	TRANSGRESSION	833d	4
		צרור	BUNDLE	865c	
14	18	אולם	BUT	19d	
		הר	MOUNTAIN	250a	1 c
		נבל	SINK	615c	1
		נפל	FALL	657a	1
		עתק	MOVE	801a	1
		צור	ROCK	849c	1 a
		מקום	STANDING PLACE	879d	1 a
14	19	אבד	DESTROY	2b	2
		אנוש	MAN	60d	3
		ו	AND	253b	1 j
		ספיח	OUTPOURING	705b	
		עפר	DRY EARTH	779d	1 c
		תקוה	HOPE	876b	1
		שחק	RUB AWAY	1007a	
		שטף	OVERFLOW	1009b	1
14	20	נצח	EVERLASTINGNESS	664b	4
		שנה	CHANGE	1040a	
		תקף	OVERPOWER	1075d	
14	21	בין	DISCERN	106d	1 a
		כבד	BE HONORED	457b	3
		צער	BE INSIGNIFICANT	858d	
		שאול	SHEOL	*983a	1
14	22	אבל	MOURN		5 c
		אך	ONLY	36d	2 ba
		בשר	FLESH	142c	2
		כאב	BE IN PAIN	456a	1
		נפש	SOUL	659b	1 b
		על	UPON	753c	2 ld
15	1	אליפז	ELIPHAZ	45c	B
		תימני	TEMANITE	412d	
15	2	בטן	BELLY	105d	1 a
		חכם	WISE	315a	6 b2
		דעת	KNOWLEDGE	395d	1 f
		ענה	ANSWER	772d	1 c
		קדים	EAST WIND	870b	1
		רוח	BREATH	925a	2 e
15	3	יכח	PROVE	407a	3
		יעל	PROFIT	418d	
		מלה	WORD	576b	
		סכן	BE OF USE	698d	2
15	4	אף	ALSO	65a	1
		גרע	RESTRAIN	175c	2
		יראה	FEAR	432a	3
		פרע	LET GO	828d	1
		פרר	BREAK	830c	2 c
		שיחה	COMPLAINT	967a	1
15	5	אלף	TEACH	48c	1
		בחר	CHOOSE	104b	5 b
		לשון	TONGUE	546c	1 b
		עון	INIQUITY	730d	1
		ערום	CRAFTY	791a	1
		פה	MOUTH	805a	2 a
15	6	ענה	ANSWER	773a	1
		פה	MOUTH	805a	2 a
15	7	גבעה	HILL	149a	3
		ה	INTERROG PART	209d	1 b
		חול	WHIRL	297c	2
		ילד	BE BORN	408d	
		פנה	FACE	817d	2 4e
15	8	גרע	RESTRAIN	175c	1
		ה	INTERROG PART	209d	1 b
		חכמה	WISDOM	315d	5 c
		סוד	COUNCIL	691c	1
		שמע	HEAR	1033c	1 a
15	9	בין	DISCERN	106d	2 b
		הוא	HE, SHE, IT	216c	6 a
		לא	NOT	519b	1 bb
		מה	WHAT	553c	1 da
		עם	WITH	768d	4 b
15	10	ישיש	AGED	450a	
		כביר	GREAT	460b	
		ל	TO	*514c	5 fb
		שיב	BE HOARY	966c	
15	11	אט	GENTLENESS	31d	B
		ה	INTERROG PART	209d	1 b
		מן	THAN	582d	6 d
		מעט	A FEW	590b	1 ea
		תנחום	CONSOLATION	637c	
		עם	WITH	767d	1 d
15	12	כי	THAT	472d	1 f
		לקח	TAKE	542d	3 a
		מה	WHAT	553c	1 db
		מה	WHAT	553c	2 ab
		עין	EYE	744c	1 m
		רום	WINK	931b	
15	13	יצא	BRING OUT	425b	4 k
		מלה	SPEECH	576b	
		רוח	BREATH	925a	2
		שוב	TURN BACK	999d	7
15	14	אנוש	MAN	60d	3
		אשה	WOMAN	61a	1
		זכה	BE CLEAR	269a	1
		זכך	BE BRIGHT	*269b	2
		כי	THAT	472d	1 f
		מה	WHAT	553c	1 db
		צדק	BE JUST	842d	4
15	15	אמן	CONFIRM	53b	2 c
		הן	BEHOLD	243c	A
		זכה	BE CLEAR	*269a	1
		זכך	BE BRIGHT	269b	2
		קדוש	HOLY	872d	2 c
		שמי	HEAVENS	1030b	3
15	16	אלח	BE CORRUPT	47a	3
		אף	ALSO	65b	3
		עולה	INJUSTICE	732d	3
		שתה	DRINK	1059c	1 g
		תעב	BE ABHORRED	1073a	1
15	17	ו	AND	254d	5 ca
		זה	THIS	260d	1 a
		זה	THIS	261d	5
		חוה	TELL	296a	
		חזה	SEE	302c	3 b
		ספר	COUNT	708a	1
		ראשון	FIRST	911d	2 a
		שמע	HEAR	1034a	1 j
15	18	חכם	WISE	315a	6 b2
		כחד	HIDE	470b	
15	19	זור	BE A STRANGER	266c	2 c
		נתן	GIVE	681b	1 j
15	20	עבר	PASS OVER	717c	3 a
		חול	WHIRL	297c	2
		עריץ	AWE-INSPIRING	792b	
		צפן	HIDE	860d	2
15	21	אזן	EAR	24a	2 a
		בוא	COME	98c	2 b
		ה	THE	208a	1 hb
		פחד	DREAD	808c	2
		שדד	DEAL VIOLENTLY WITH	994b	

Ch	v.	Heb	Eng	Page	Sec
15	22	שלום	PEACE	1023a	3
		אמן	CONFIRM	53b	2 e
		חשך	DARKNESS	365a	3 a
		צפה	KEEP WATCH	859c	
		צפן	HIDE	860c	1
		שוב	TURN BACK	997a	2
15	23	איה	WHERE	32c	
		חשך	DARKNESS	365a	3 a
		יד	HAND	391a	5 d
		כון	BE READY	466a	3
		ל	TO	515a	5 ha
		נדד	WANDER	622b	3
15	24	בעת	FALL UPON	130a	1
		כידור	ONSET	461d	
		מצוקה	STRAIGNESS	748b	
		עתיד	READY	800c	1
		צר	STRAITS	865a	
		תקף	OVERPOWER	1075d	
15	25	גבר	BE STRONG	149d	
		כי	BECAUSE	474b	3 d
		נטה	EXTEND	639d	1 a
15	26	גב	BACK	146c	3
		מגן	SHIELD	171c	
		עבי	THICKNESS	716a	
		צואר	NECK	848c	1
		רוץ	RUN	930b	1
15	27	חלב	FAT	316d	1
		כי	BECAUSE	474b	3 d
		כסה	COVER	491d	2
		כסל	LOINS	492d	1
		עשה	DO	794d	2 2
		פימה	SUPERABUNDANCE	810a	
15	28	ישב	DWELL	443a	3
		כחד	BE HIDDEN	470b	2
		ל	TO	516a	5 ic
		עתד	BE READY	800c	
15	29	חיל	STRENGTH	299a	3
		נטה	BEND	640b	3 a
		מנלה	ACQUISITION	649b	
		עשר	BE RICH	799b	
		קום	STAND	878b	7 c
15	30	חשך	DARKNESS	365a	3 a
		יבש	BE DRY	386c	
		יונקת	TWIG	413c	
		שלהבת	FLAME	529b	
		סור	TURN ASIDE	693d	2
		רוח	BREATH	924c	1 a
15	31	אמן	CONFIRM	53b	2 c
		תמורה	RECOMPENSE	558d	
		שוא	EMPTINESS	996b	3
		תעה	ERR	1073c	2
15	32	כפה	BRANCH	497a	
		לא	NOT	520b	4 ab
		מלא	BE FULL	570c	2
		רען	BE FRESH	947d	1
15	33	בסר	UNRIPE GRAPES	126a	
		גפן	VINE	172c	
		זית	OLIVE TREE	268c	1
		חמס	TREAT VIOLENTLY	329b	1
		נצה	BLOSSOM	665b	
		שלך	THROW	1021b	1 d
15	34	אהל	TENT	14a	2
		חנף	PROFANE	338b	
		עדה	CONGREGATION	417a	1
		כי	BECAUSE	473d	3 c
		שחד	BRIBE	1005a	
15	35	און	TROUBLE	20a	1
		בטן	BELLY	105d	1 a
		הרה	CONCEIVE	247d	2
		ילד	BEAR	408c	1 c
		כון	ESTABLISH	466b	2 a
		עמל	TROUBLE	765d	2
		מרמה	DECEIT	941b	
16	2	אלה	THESE	41d	D
		נחם	CONSOLE ONESELF	637b	
		עמל	TROUBLE	765d	1
16	3	או	OR	15a	1
		דבר	WORD	183b	3 l
		ה	INTERROG PART	210b	1 d
		כי	THAT	472d	1 f
		מה	WHAT	553a	1 db
		מרץ	BE SICK	599d	
		קץ	END	893d	1
		רוח	BREATH	924c	1 b
16	4	ב	IN	90b	3 4
		במו	IN	91b	
		גם	ALSO	169d	4
		חבר	UNITE	288b	
		לו	IF	530b	1 d
		מלה	WORD	576b	
		מן	OUT OF	579c	2 ca
		נוע	TOTTER	631c	2
		נפש	SOUL	660b	4 c1
		על	UPON	757d	2 7d
		תחת	INSTEAD	1065d	2 2b a
16	5	אמץ	BE STRONG	55a	1
		במו	IN	91b	
		חשך	WITHHOLD	362b	2
		ניד	QUIVERING MOTION	627a	
		שפה	SPEECH	973d	1 a2
16	6	חדל	CEASE	293a	1
		חשך	WITHHOLD	362b	
		כאב	PAIN	456b	
		מה	WHAT	553a	1 da
		מה	WHAT	553a	1 da

Ch	v.	Heb	Eng	Page	Sec
16	7	אך	SURELY	36c	1
		עדה	CONGREGATION	417a	1
		לאה	EXHAUST	521a	
		עתה	NOW	774b	1 d
		שמם	BE DESOLATED	1031b	1
16	8	היה	BECOME	226b	2 2e
		כחש	LEANNESS	471c	2
		עד	WITNESS	729c	1
		ענה	ANSWER	773a	3
		פנה	FACE	816d	2 3a
		קום	STAND	877d	1 f
16	9	ב	IN	90b	3 4
		חרק	GNASH	359b	
		שרף	TEAR	383a	
		ל	TO	*511a	1 d
		לטש	SHARPEN	538c	2
		עין	EYE	744c	1 n
		על	UPON	757d	2 7d
		שטם	BEAR A GRUDGE	966b	
		שן	TOOTH	1042a	1 a
16	10	ב	IN	90b	3 4
		חרפה	REPROACH	358c	1
		יחד	ALTOGETHER	403b	2 b
		לחי	CHEEK	534d	2
		מלא	FILL	570d	
		נכה	SMITE	645b	1 a
		על	UPON	757d	2 7d
		פה	MOUTH	804d	1 b
		פער	OPEN WIDE	822b	
16	11	ירט	PRECIPITATE	437c	
		סגר	DELIVER UP	689c	1
		עויל	UNJUST ONE	732d	
		על	UNJUST ONE	732d	
		רטה	WRING OUT	936a	
16	12	אחז	GRASP	28b	
		ל	TO	512c	4 b
		מטרה	TARGET	643c	2
		ערף	BACK OF NECK	791b	1
		פצץ	BREAK	823a	
		קום	STAND	879a	5
		שלו	QUIET	1017c	1
16	13	חמל	SPARE	328b	
		כליה	KIDNEYS	480b	1 a
		מררה	GALL	601a	
		מררה	GALL	*601a	1
		סבב	SURROUND	685d	2 d
		על	UPON	757d	2 7d
		פלח	CLEAVE	812a	1
		רבעם	ARCHER	914d	
		שפך	POUR OUT	1049c	1 a
16	14	גבור	STRONG	150b	2
		ה	THE	*207d	1 f
		על	UPON	755c	2 4b
		פנה	FACE	818d	2 7a c
		פרץ	BREAK THROUGH	829c	6
		פרץ	BURSTING FORTH	829d	4
		רוץ	RUN	930b	1
16	15	עלל	INSERT	760d	
		עפר	DRY EARTH	780a	2 e
		קרן	HORN	902a	2
		שק	SACK	974c	2 a
		תפר	SEW TOGETHER	1074c	
16	16	בכי	WEEPING	113d	
		חמר	FERMENT	330c	
		חמר	BE RED	331a	
		עפעף	EYELID	733d	
		פנה	FACE	815d	1 1a
		צלמות	DEATH-SHADOW	853c	1
16	17	זך	PURE	269b	2
		חמס	VIOLENCE	329c	
		כף	HOLLOW OF THE HAND	49c d	1 d7
		לא	NOT	519b	1 bb
		על	UPON	758b	3 cb
16	18	ארץ	EARTH	76a	1 b
		דם	BLOOD	196d	2 f
		זעקה	CRY	277d	2
		כסה	COVER	491d	2
		מקום	STANDING PLACE	880b	4
16	19	עד	WITNESS	729c	2 a
		עתה	NOW	774b	2 d
		מרום	HEIGHT	928d	2
		שהד	WITNESS	962a	
16	20	דלף	DROP	196a	
		כי	BECAUSE	*473d	3 c
		ליץ	SCORN	539c	1
		עין	EYE	744b	1 h
16	21	יכח	DECIDE	407a	1
		עם	WITH	767c	1 c
		רע	FRIEND	946a	2
16	22	ארח	WAY	73a	2 2
		אתה	COME	87c	
		כי	BECAUSE	473d	2
		מספר	NUMBER	709a	1 a
		שאול	SHEOL	*983a	1
		שוב	TURN BACK	997c	4 b
17	1	זעך	EXTINGUISH	276c	
		חבל	ACT CORRUPTLY	287c	
		קצבר	GRAVE	868d	
		רוח	BREATH	925c	4 d
17	2	תלים	MOCKERY	251d	
		לון	LODGE	533d	2
		מרה	BE REBELLIOUS	598b	
		עם	WITH	767b	1 a
17	3	הוא	HE, SHE, IT	216c	4 bb
		יד	HAND	389d	1 e1

Ch	v.	Heb	Eng	Page	Sec
		כף	HOLLOW OF THE HAND	*496c	1 d3
		מי	WHO	567a	F c
		עם	WITH	768b	3 c
		ערב	TAKE ON PLEDGE	786c	1
		ערבון	PLEDGE	786d	
		שום	TO PLACE	964d	5 d
		תקע	THRUST	1075c	
17	4	לב	HEART	524d	2 3b
		צפן	HIDE	860c	1
		רום	BE HIGH	927b	2 c
		שכל	PRUDENCE	968c	2
17	5	חלק	PORTION	324c	5
		כלה	BE FINISHED	477d	2 b
		נגד	BE CONSPICUOUS	617a	3
17	6	יצג	SET	426d	
		משל	BY-WORD	605c	2
		תפת	SPITTING	1064b	
17	7	יצרים	MEMBERS	428b	
		כהה	GROW DIM	462c	
		כעש	ANGER	495b	1
		מן	ON ACCOUNT OF	580b	2 f
		צל	SHADOW	853b	3
17	8	זה	THIS	*262a	6 f
		חנף	PROFANE	338b	
		ישר	STRAIGHT	449b	3 c2
		נקי	CLEAN	667c	1
		עור	ROUSE ONESELF	735b	
		שמם	BE DESOLATED	1031a	2
17	9	אחז	GRASP	28b	
		אחז	GRASP	*28b	
		אמץ	STRENGTH	55b	1
		טהור	CLEAN	373a	3
		יסף	ADD	415b	1
		צדיק	JUST	843b	3 b
17	10	אולם	BUT	19d	
		חכם	WISE	315b	6 b4
		שוב	TURN BACK	998b	8
17	11	זמה	PLAN	273c	1
		מורש	POSSESSION	440c	
		לבב	HEART	523d	2 3c
17	12	נתק	TEAR AWAY	683c	2
		חשך	DARKNESS	365a	1
		קרב	NEAR	898d	3
17	13	בית	HOUSE	109c	1 d
		חשך	DARKNESS	365a	1
		יצוע	BED	427a	
		קוה	WAIT FOR	875d	1
		רפד	SPREAD	951c	
		שאול	SHEOL	983a	1
		שאול	SHEOL	983b	2 b
17	14	אב	FATHER	3b	1
		אחות	SISTER	28a	4
		אם	MOTHER	52a	3
		קרא	CALL	896a	6 e2
		רמה	WORM	933d	
		שחת	PIT	1001c	2
17	15	אפו	THEN	66b	1
		מי	WHO	567a	F c
		תקוה	HOPE	876b	1
		תקוה	HOPE	876b	3
17	16	שור	BEHOLD	1003d	1
		בד	PART	94d	3 d
		יחד	UNION	403a	2 a4
		ירד	GO DOWN	433b	1 i
		נחת	REST	629b	2
		עפר	DRY EARTH	779d	1 f
		שאול	SHEOL	983a	1
		שאול	SHEOL	*983a	1
		בהמה	ADDENDA ET CORRIGENDA	1121b	
		נחת	ADDENDA ET CORRIGENDA	1125a	
18	1	בלדד	BILDAD	115a	
		שוחי	SHUHITE	1001d	
18	2	אן	WHERE	33a	D
		בין	DISCERN	106d	2 a
		מלה	SPEECH	576b	
		קנץ	SNARE	890b	
		שום	TO PLACE	963b	1 c
18	3	בהמה	BEAST	96d	1
		חשב	THINK	363b	1
		טמא	BE UNCLEAN	379b	4
		מטה	STUPID	380b	
18	4	מדוע	WHEREFORE	396c	
		טרף	TEAR	383a	
		עזב	LEAVE	737d	2
		מען	PURPOSE	775b	1
		עתק	MOVE	801b	1
		מקום	STANDING PLACE	879d	1 a
18	5	אש	FIRE	77d	6
		דעך	BE EXTINGUISHED	200b	
		נגה	SHINE	618b	
		שביב	BLAME	985b	
18	6	דעך	BE EXTINGUISHED	200b	
		חשך	GROW DARK	364d	1
		נר	LAMP	632d	
		על	UPON	755d	2 5
18	7	און	VIGOUR	20b	1
		עצה	ADVICE	420b	
		כי	BECAUSE	*473d	3 c
		צעד	STEP	857d	2
		צרר	BIND	864d	B
		שלך	THROW	1021b	1 e
18	8	רגל	WALK	236b	2
		רשת	NET	440c	1 b2

Ch	v.	Heb	Eng	Page	Sec
		כי	BECAUSE	473d	3 c
		רגל	FOOT	920a	1 f
		סבכה	LATTICE-WORK	959b	3
		שלח	SEND	1019c	
18	9	אחז	GRASP	28b	
		חזק	BE FIRM	305a	5
		עקב	HEEL	784a	A
		פח	BIRD-TRAP	809a	2 a
		צמים	SNARE	855d	
		צמים	SNARE	*855d	
18	10	חבל	CORD	286c	1
		טמן	HIDE	380c	2
		מלכדת	A SNARE	540b	
		נתיב	PATH	677b	
18	11	בלהה	TERROR	117a	1
		בעת	FALL UPON	130a	1
		פוץ	BE DISPERSED	807b	1 c
		רגל	FOOT	919d	1 f
18	12	צלע	RIB		6
		צלע	LIMPING		
		איד	DISTRESS	15d	3
		און	VIGOUR	20b	2
		כון	BE READY	466a	3
		רעב	HUNGRY	944c	
18	13	בד	PART	94d	3 a
		בכור	FIRST-BORN	114b	3
		מות	DEATH	560d	1
18	14	מבטח	CONFIDENCE	105c	2
		בלי	WEARING OUT	*116a	C g
		בלהה	TERROR	117a	1
		ל	TO	511c	1 gb
		מלך	KING	573b	4
		נתק	TEAR AWAY	683c	2
		צעד	STEP	857d	
18	15	בלי	WEARING OUT	116a	C g
		גפרית	BRIMSTONE	172d	
		זרה	SCATTER	280a	
		ל	TO	513d	5 cb d
		לא	NOT	*519d	2 d
		נוה	HABITATION	627c	2
		שכן	SETTLE DOWN	1015b	2 a
18	16	יבש	BE DRY	386c	1 d
		מלל	WITHER	576d	
		מעל	ABOVE	751c	1 a
		קציר	BRANCHES	894d	
		שרש	ROOT	1057d	1
		תחת	UNDERNEATH	1065b	1
		מול	ADDENDA ET COR-RIGENDA	1124d	
18	17	אבד	PERISH	1d	2
		זכר	REMEMBRANCE	271b	1 a
		חוץ	THE OUTSIDE	300b	2 b
		לא	NOT	519b	1 bb
		שם	NAME	1028b	2 c
18	18	הדף	THRUST	213d	2
		חשך	DARKNESS	365a	1
		תבל	WORLD	385d	
		נדד	FLUTTER	622c	
18	19	מגור	DWELLING PLACE	158c	
		לא	NOT	519b	1 bb
		נין	OFFSPRING	630c	
		נכד	PROGENY	645a	
		שריד	SURVIVOR	975a	1
18	20	אחז	GRASP	28b	
		אחרון	BEHIND	30d	A
		אחרון	BEHIND	31a	B
		יום	DAY	398d	2 h1
		קדמני	FORMER	870d	2
		שער	HORROR	972c	
		שמם	BE DESOLATED	1031a	2
18	21	אך	SURELY	36c	1
		אלה	THESE	41c	A
		זה	THIS	261b	3
		ידע	KNOW	394a	2
		עול	UNJUST ONE	732d	
		מקום	STANDING PLACE	880b	4
		משכן	DWELLING-PLACE	1015d	1a
19	2	אן	WHERE	33a	D
		דכא	CRUSH	194a	
		יגה	SUFFER	387b	
		מלה	WORD	576b	
19	3	בוש	BE ASHAMED	101d	3
		הכר	DEAL HARDLY WITH	229a	
		יד	HAND	390a	1 e2
		כלם	HUMILIATE	484a	1
		פעם	OCCURRENCE	822a	3 a
19	4	אמנם	VERILY	54a	
		אף	ALSO	65a	1
		לון	LODGE	533d	2
		שגה	GO ASTRAY	993a	3
		משוגה	ERROR	1000c	
19	5	אמנם	VERILY	54a	
		גדל	BECOME GREAT	152c	3 b
		חרפה	REPROACH	358a	2 c
		יכח	PROVE	407a	3
19	6	אפו	THEN	66b	2
		נקף	GO AROUND	669a	1 b
		עות	BE BENT	736c	1
		מצוד	HUNTING IMPLE-MENT	845a	
19	7	חמס	VIOLENCE	329c	
		ענה	ANSWER	773a	2 b
		צעק	CRY	858c	2
19	8	ארח	WAY	73a	2
		גדר	BUILD A WALL	154d	
		חשך	DARKNESS	365b	3 d
		נתיבה	PATH	677b	2 a
19	9	כבוד	HONOR	458c	2 a
		עטרה	CROWN	742d	3
		פשט	STRIP OFF	833a	2
19	10	נסע	PULL OUT	652c	2
		נתץ	PULL DOWN	683b	2 b
		תקוה	HOPE	876b	1
19	11	חרה	BURN	354b	
		חשב	THINK	363b	2 1
19	12	צר	ADVERSARY	865d	
		ארח	WAY	73b	3 c
		גדוד	BAND	151b	1
		חנה	DECLINE	333d	2 c2
		יחד	ALTOGETHER	403b	2 b
		סביב	ROUND ABOUT	687a	1 cb
		סלל	LIFT UP	699d	2
		על	UPON	757d	2 7d
19	13	אך	ONLY	36d	2 bb
		זור	BE A STRANGER	266c	1
		ידע	KNOW	394a	2
		על	UPON	759a	4 2c
		רחק	BE DISTANT	935b	1
19	14	חדל	CEASE	293a	1
		ידע	ACQUAINTANCE	394d	
		שכח	FORGET	1013a	1 b
19	15	אמה	MAID	51a	1
		אמה	MAID	51a	1
		גור	SOJOURN	157d	1
		זור	BE A STRANGER	266c	2 a
		חשב	THINK	363a	1 1
		נכרי	ALIEN	649a	3
19	16	במו	IN	91b	
		חנן	SHOW FAVOR	336b	1
		פה	MOUTH	805a	2 a
		קרא	CALL	895b	2 a
19	17	בטן	WOMB	106a	3
		זור	BE LOATHSOME	266d	
		חנן	SHOW FAVOR	336a	2 b
		חנן	BE LOATHSOME	337d	
		רוח	BREATH	924c	1 a
19	18	שוע	CRY OUT	1002d	
		דבר	SPEAK	181c	4 d
		מאס	REJECT	549c	2
		עויל	YOUNG BOY	732b	
19	19	אהב	LOVE	13a	1
		הפך	TURN	245d	1 a
		זה	THIS	260c	1 a
		זה	THIS	261d	5
		מת	MALE	607b	3 b
		סוד	COUNCIL	691c	1
		שו	WHO	979d	3 a
19	20	תעב	BE ABHORRED	1073b	1 a2
		בשר	FLESH	142c	1 b
		דבק	CLING	179c	1 a
		מלט	SLIP AWAY	572d	2
		עור	SKIN	736a	1
		עצם	BONE	782d	1 a
		שן	TOOTH	*1042a	1 a
19	21	חנן	SHOW FAVOR	336a	1 c
		יד	HAND	390a	1 e2
		נגע	TOUCH	619a	2
		אכל	EAT	37d	6
19	22	בשר	FLESH	142c	1 b
		רדף	PURSUE	922a	1 f
		שבע	SATISFIED	959c	1 c
19	23	אפו	THEN	66b	2
		ה	THE	*207c	1 d
		חקק	CUT IN	349b	
		כתב	BE WRITTEN	508a	1
		נתן	GIVE	679a	1 f
		ספר	MISSIVE	707a	3
		ספר	MISSIVE	*707c	4
19	24	ברזל	IRON	137c	1 d
		חצב	HEW	345b	
		עד	PERPETUITY	723c	2 b
		עט	STYLUS	741c	1
		עפרת	LEAD	780c	
		צור	ROCK	849c	1 a
19	25	אחרון	BEHIND	31a	B
		גאל	REDEEM	145c	3 a
		חי	ALIVE	311d	1 a
		עפר	DRY EARTH	779d	1 c
		קום	STAND	877d	1 f
		שאול	SHEOL	*983b	2 b
19	26	בשר	FLESH	142d	2
		זה	THIS	260c	1 a
		חזה	SEE	302b	1 a
		מן	FROM	578c	1 b
		נקף	STRIKE OFF	668d	
19	27	זור	BE A STRANGER	266c	2 b
		חיק	BOSOM	300d	3 b
		חזה	SEE	302b	1 a
		כלה	BE FINISHED	477d	2 b
		כליה	KIDNEYS	480c	2 b
19	28	דבר	WORD	183c	4 3
		מצא	FIND	394a	1 g1
		כי	IF	473b	2 b
		רדף	PURSUE	922a	1 f
		שרש	ROOT	1057d	1
19	29	גור	DREAD	159a	1
		דין	JUDGMENT	192d	
		חמה	RAGE	404d	2 c
		ל	TO	516a	5 ic
		עון	INIQUITY	730d	1 a
		שדי	ALMIGHTY	995a	1
20	1	נעמתי	NAAMATHITE	564b	
		צפר	ZOPHAR	862b	
20	2	חוש	HASTE	301d	
		כן	SO	487a	3 da
		עבור	FOR THE SAKE OF	721a	1 a
		ענה	ANSWER	772d	1 b
		שעפים	EXCITED THOUGHTS	972a	
20	3	שוב	TURN BACK	999c	3
		בינה	UNDERSTANDING	108a	2
		מוסר	DISCIPLINE	416c	1 a
		כלמה	INSULT	484a	1
		רוח	BREATH	925c	6
20	4	ה	INTERROG PART	210a	1 c
		מן	SINCE	583c	7 c
		עד	PERPETUITY	723c	1
		שום	TO PLACE	963b	1 b
20	5	חנף	PROFANE	338b	
		מן	FROM	581d	4 c
		עד	AS FAR AS	724c	1 2b
		קרב	NEAR	898d	3
		רגע	DISTURB	920d	
		רגע	A MOMENT	921a	BE
		רננה	JOYFUL	943c	
		שמחה	JOY	970d	1
20	6	ל	TO	511b	1 ga
		נגע	REACH	619c	2
		שיא	LOFTINESS	673b	
		עב	DARK CLOUD	728a	1 b
20	7	אבד	PERISH	1d	1
		אי	WHERE	32b	1 a
		נצח	EVERLASTINGNESS	664b	4
20	8	חלום	DREAM	321c	1
		לילה	NIGHT	538d	1
		מצא	FIND	593c	4
		נדד	RETREAT	622c	
20	9	עוף	FLY	733c	2
		יסף	DO AGAIN	415c	2 a
		שקר	OGLE	974c	
		שור	BEHOLD	1003d	1
		שזף	CATCH SIGHT OF	1004d	
20	10	און	VIGOUR	20b	3
		דל	POOR	195d	
		רצה	BE PLEASED WITH	953b	
		רצץ	CRUSH	954d	
20	11	שוב	TURN BACK	999b	1 e
		עלומים	YOUTH	761c	
		עפר	DRY EARTH	779d	1 f
		עצם	BONE	782d	1 b
20	12	שכב	LIE DOWN	1012c	4 c
		כחד	HIDE	470c	1
		לשון	TONGUE	546b	1 a
		פה	MOUTH	804d	1 a
		תחת	UNDERNEATH	1065c	2 1b
20	13	חמל	SPARE	328b	
		חך	PALATE	335b	C
		מנע	WITHHOLD	586a	
		עזב	LEAVE	737d	3
20	14	הפך	TURN	245d	1 b
		לחם	FOOD	537c	3 b
		מעה	BELLY	589a	1 b
		מרה	POISON	601a	2
		פתן	COBRA	837a	
20	15	קרב	INWARD PART	899a	1 a
		בטן	BELLY	105d	1 a
		בלע	SWALLOW UP	118b	2
		חיל	STRENGTH	299a	3
		ירש	CAUSE TO POSSESS	440a	2 b
		קיא	SPUE OUT	883c	
20	16	הרג	KILL	247b	5
		ינק	SUCK	413b	
		לשון	TONGUE	546d	3
		אפעה	VIPER	821b	
		פתן	COBRA	837a	
		ראש	VENOM	912c	2
20	17	דבש	HONEY	185b	
		חמאה	CURD	326a	
		נחל	TORRENT	636b	1
		פלגה	STREAM	811b	1
		ראה	TO SEE	908a	8 a5
		בלע	SWALLOW UP	118b	2
		ו	AND	255a	5 cb
		חיל	STRENGTH	299a	3
		יגע	GAIN	388b	
20	18	תמורה	EXCHANGE	559c	
		עלס	REJOICE	763a	
20	19	בנה	BUILD	124d	1 i
		גזל	TEAR AWAY	159d	
		דל	POOR	195d	
		כי	BECAUSE	474b	3 d
		עזב	LEAVE	737c	2 c
		רצץ	CRUSH	954d	2
20	20	בטן	BELLY	105d	1 a
		חמד	DESIRE	326c	C
		ידע	KNOW	394a	1 e
		מלט	SLIP AWAY	572c	3
		שלו	QUIET	1017c	3
20	21	אכל	EAT	37b	1
		חיל	BE FIRM	298c	
		טוב	GOOD THINGS	375c	2
		כן	SO	487b	3 f
		שריד	SURVIVOR	975a	2
20	22	בוא	COME	98c	2 b
		עמל	LABOURER	766a	1
		צרר	BIND	864d	B
		שפק	SUFFICIENCY	974b	

Ch	v.	Heb	Eng	Page	Sec
20	23	בטן	BELLY	105d	1 a
		חרון	BURNING OF ANGER	354c	
		לחום	BOWELS	536a	
		מטר	RAIN	565a	
20	24	מלא	FILL	570d	2
		ברזל	IRON	137c	1 d
		ברח	FLEE	138a	2
		חלף	PASS ON OR AWAY	322a	3 a
		נחושה	COPPER	639a	2
		נשק	EQUIPMENT	676d	1
		קשת	BOW	906c	1 f
20	25	אימה	TERROR	34a	
		ברק	LIGHTNING	140c	2
		גוה	BACK	156b	
		הלך	WALK	232c	1 3
		יצא	GO OUT	423b	1 f
		מררה	GALL	601a	1
		מררה	GALL	601b	
		שלף	DRAW OUT	1025b	1
20	26	חשך	DARKNESS	365a	3 a
		טמן	HIDE	380c	3
		לא	NOT	518d	1 ac
		נפח	BLOW	656a	
		צפן	HIDE	860d	1
		רעה	TEND	945b	2 d
		רעה	TEND	945c	
		שריד	SURVIVOR	975a	2
		אש	ADDENDA ET CORRIGENDA	1120d	
20	27	ל	TO	511a	1 d
		עון	INIQUITY	730d	1
		קום	STAND	878c	
20	28	יבול	PRODUCE	385b	
		נגר	RUN	620b	3
20	29	אדם	MAN	9b	1
		אלהים	GOD	44b	4 a
		אמר	WORD	57a	2
		זה	THIS	261b	3
		חלק	PORTION	324b	5
		מן	OUT OF	579d	2 d
		נחלה	PROPERTY	635b	2 a
		עם	WITH	768b	3 b
		רשע	WICKED	957c	3
21	2	מלה	WORD	576b	
		תנחום	CONSOLATION	637c	
21	3	אחר	AFTER	29d	2 b
		לעג	MOCK	541c	
		נשא	LIFT	671b	2 d
21	4	אם	IF	50d	2 ab b
		אנכי	I	59a	
		קצר	BE SHORT	894a	
		רוח	BREATH	925a	3 d
		שיח	COMPLAINT	967a	1
21	5	פה	MOUTH	804d	1 b
		פנה	TURN	815a	1 a
		שום	TO PLACE	963b	1
		שמם	BE DESOLATED	1031b	2 b
21	6	אחז	GRASP	28b	
		בהל	BE DISTURBED	96c	1
		בשר	FLESH	142c	1 b
		זכר	REMEMBER	270a	1 5
		פלצות	SHUDDERING	814a	
21	7	גבר	BE STRONG	149d	1
		גם	ALSO	169b	2
		גם	YEA	169c	3
		חיל	STRENGTH	298c	1 a
		עתק	MOVE	801b	2
21	8	זרע	SOWING	282d	4 c
		צאצא	OFFSPRING	425c	1
		כון	BE FIRM	465d	1 c
21	9	לא	NOT	519b	1 bb
		מן	FROM	578c	1 b
		על	UPON	753b	2 1b
		שבט	ROD	987a	1 a
		שלום	PEACE	1023a	4
21	10	געל	ABHOR	171d	
		עבר	PASS OVER	718c	1
		פלח	CLEAVE	*812a	2
		פלט	ESCAPE	812b	2
		פרה	HEIFER	831a	
		שור	A HEAD OF CATTLE	1004b	
		שכל	BE BEREAVED	1013d	2 b1
21	11	ילד	CHILD	409b	B
		עויל	YOUNG BOY	732b	
		צאן	SMALL CATTLE	838b	2
		רקד	SKIP ABOUT	955a	
21	12	כנור	LYRE	490a	
		ל	TO	516d	5 k
		עוגב	PIPE	721d	
		קול	VOICE	877a	2 a
		שמח	REJOICE	970b	1 a
		תף	TIMBREL	1074b	
21	13	בלה	BECOME OLD AND WORN OUT	115b	B
		טוב	A GOOD THING	375a	1
		כלה	FINISH	478b	1 b
		נחת	GO DOWN	639c	1
		רגע	A MOMENT	921a	BB
		שאול	SHEOL	982d	1
		נחת	ADDENDA ET CORRIGENDA	*1125a	
21	14	דרך	WAY	204a	6 ec
		חפץ	DELIGHT IN	342d	1 b
		דעת	KNOWLEDGE	395d	2 b
		סור	TURN ASIDE	693d	2
21	15	יעל	PROFIT	418d	
		כי	THAT	472c	1 f
		מה	WHAT	553a	1 db
		עבד	WORK	713b	4 a
		פגע	MEET	803b	4
21	16	טוב	GOOD THINGS	375c	3 c
		עצה	ADVICE	420b	
		רחק	BE DISTANT	934d	
		רשע	WICKED	957c	3
21	17	איד	DISTRESS	15d	3
		דעך	BE EXTINGUISHED	200b	
		חבל	CORD	286d	2
		חבל	PAIN	287a	2
		חלק	DIVIDE	323d	1
		מה	HOW	553d	4 ca
		נר	LAMP	632d	2
21	18	גנב	STEAL	170c	
		סופה	STORM-WIND	693a	
		תבן	STRAW	1062a	1
21	19	צפן	HIDE	860c	1
		שלם	BE COMPLETE	1022d	5
21	20	חמה	RAGE	404d	2 c
		כיד	DECAY	475d	
		מן	OUT OF	579d	2 bb
		פיד	RUIN	810a	
		שתה	DRINK	*1059b	1
		שתה	DRINK	1059c	1 e
21	21	אחר	AFTER	30a	2 b
		חדש	NEW MOON	294c	2 a
		חפץ	DELIGHT	343b	1
		חצץ	DIVIDE	346b	
		מה	WHAT	553a	1 da
		סכן	BE OF US	698b	
21	22	למד	LEARN	540d	
		למד	LEARN	540d	
		רום	BE HIGH	926d	1 a
		שפט	JUDGE	1047c	2 a
21	23	זה	THIS	260d	1 b
		כל	ALL	481b	1 a
		עצם	BONE	783a	3
		שאול	SHEOL	*983a	1
		שלאנן	AT EASE	1016d	
		שלו	QUIET	1017c	1
		תם	COMPLETENESS	1070d	1
21	24	חלב	MILK	316b	A
		מח	MARROW	562d	
		מלא	BE FULL	570a	1 a
		עטין	PAIL	742b	
		שקה	GIVE TO DRINK	1052c	
21	25	אכל	EAT	37b	1
		זה	THIS	260d	1 b
		טובה	WELFARE	375d	1
		מר	BITTER	600d	2 b
21	26	יחד	TOGETHER	403b	2 c
		כסה	COVER	492a	6
		עפר	DRY EARTH	779d	1 f
		רמה	WORM	933d	
		שאול	SHEOL	*983a	1
		שכב	LIE DOWN	1012c	4 c
21	27	מזמה	PURPOSE	273d	3 a
		חמס	TREAT VIOLENTLY	329b	2
		מחשבה	THOUGHT	364b	2
		על	UPON	757d	2 7d
21	28	איה	WHERE	32c	1
		נדיב	NOBLE	622a	2
		משכן	DWELLING-PLACE	1015d	3 a
21	29	אות	SIGN	16d	1
		נכר	REGARD	648a	
21	30	איד	DISTRESS	15d	3
		חשך	WITHHOLD	362c	
		יבל	CONDUCT	385a	3
		יום	DAY	401a	7 i
		ל	TO	516d	6 a
		עברה	OVERFLOW	720c	3 b
		רע	EVIL	948c	0 b
21	31	דרך	WAY	204a	6 eb
		מי	WHO	566d	F c
		פנה	FACE	818d	2 7 a a
21	32	גדיש	TOMB	155c	
		יבל	CONDUCT	385a	2
		קבר	GRAVE	868d	
		שקד	WATCH	1052a	2 b
21	33	אחר	AFTER	30b	2 b
		ו	AND	253b	1 j
		משך	DRAW	604b	3
		מתק	BE PLEASANT	608c	2
		נחל	WADY	636c	2
		מספר	NUMBER	708d	1 a
		רגב	CLOD OF EARTH	918d	
21	34	הבל	VAPOUR	211a	2
		היך	HOW	*228a	
		מעל	UNFAITHFUL	591b	1
		נחם	CONSOLE ONESELF	637a	
		תשובה	RETURN	1000c	3
22	1	אליפז	ELIPHAZ	45c	B
		תימני	TEMANITE	412d	
22	2	כי	BECAUSE	474b	3 c
		סכן	BE OF USE	698b	2
		על	UPON	758a	2 8
		שכל	BE PRUDENT	968c	5
22	3	אם	IF	50d	2 ab b
		בצע	PROFIT	130c	
		דרך	WAY	203c	6 c
		חפץ	DELIGHT	343b	1
		כי	THAT	471d	1 a
		צדק	BE JUST	842d	4
		תמם	BE COMPLETE	1070c	5
22	4	ה	THE	208c	1 hb
		יכח	REPROVE	407a	5 a
		יראה	FEAR	432a	3
		מן	ON ACCOUNT OF	580b	2 f
		משפט	JUDGMENT	1048c	1 c
22	5	עון	INIQUITY	730d	1
		קץ	END	894a	1
22	6	בגד	GARMENT	94a	1
		חבל	BIND	286b	2
		חנם	OUT OF FAVOR	336d	C
		ערום	NAKED	736a	
		פשט	STRIP OFF	833a	2
22	7	מנע	WITHHOLD	586a	
		עיף	FAINT	746a	
		רעב	HUNGRY	944c	
		שקה	GIVE TO DRINK	1052c	2
22	8	זרוע	ARM	284b	2 a
		ל	TO	513b	5 ba
22	9	נשא	LIFT	670c	1 b 3
		אלמנה	WIDOW	48b	
		דכא	CRUSH	194a	
		זרוע	ARM	284b	2 a
		יתום	ORPHAN	450c	
		ריקם	EMPTILY	938b	1
		שלח	SEND	1019a	1 c
22	10	בהל	DISMAY	96c	1
		פחד	DREAD	808c	2
		פח	BIRD-TRAP	809a	2 a
		פתאם	SUDDENNESS	837c	
22	11	או	OR	15a	1
		חשך	DARKNESS	365a	3 a
		כסה	COVER	491d	5
		לא	NOT	519a	1 ae
		מי	WATER	565d	4 a
		שפעה	ABUNDANCE	1051b	
22	12	גבה	HEIGHT	147b	1
		כוכב	STAR	457a	
		ראש	HEAD	911a	2 b
		רום	BE HIGH	926d	1 a
22	13	בעד	AWAY FROM	126b	1 a
		מה	WHAT	552c	1 a
		מה	WHAT	553a	1 da
		ערפל	CLOUD	791d	
		שפט	JUDGE	1047c	2 a
22	14	הלך	WALK	236a	1 b
		חוג	VAULT	295b	
		סתר	COVERING	712a	1
		עב	DARK CLOUD	728a	1 c
		שמי	HEAVENS	1030a	1 b
22	15	און	TROUBLE	20a	3
		ארח	WAY	73b	3 c
		דרך	TREAD	202a	2
		מת	MALE	607b	3 b
		עולם	LONG DURATION	762d	1 a
22	16	יסוד	FOUNDATION	414b	1
		יצק	BE POURED	427b	1
		לא	NOT	519b	1 bb
		עת	TIME	773d	2 b
		קמט	SEIZE	888a	
22	17	מה	WHAT	553a	1 da
		סור	TURN ASIDE	693d	2
		פעל	DO	821b	1 a
22	18	טוב	A GOOD THING	375b	2
		עצה	ADVICE	420b	
		מלא	FILL	570c	1
		רחק	BE DISTANT	934d	
		רשע	WICKED	957c	3
22	19	לעג	MOCK	541b	
		נקי	CLEAN	667c	1
		צדיק	JUST	843b	3 b
		שמח	REJOICE	970b	1 b
22	20	יתר	EXCESS	452a	2 c
		כחד	BE HIDDEN	470b	2
		קום	ADVERSARY	879c	
22	21	בוא	COME	98c	2 b
		טובה	WELFARE	375d	1
		שלם	BE IN COVENANT OF PEACE	1023d	
22	22	אמר	WORD	57a	1
		תורה	INSTRUCTION	435d	1 b
		לבב	HEART	523d	2 3d
		שום	TO PLACE	963a	1 a
22	23	בנה	BUILD	125a	1
		עולה	INJUSTICE	732d	3
		רחק	BE DISTANT	935b	2
		שוב	TURN BACK	997d	6 c
22	24	אופיר	OPHIR	20d	4
		בצר	PRECIOUS ORE	131a	
		נחל	WADY	636c	2
		עפר	DRY EARTH	780a	2 b
		צור	ROCK	849c	1 a
		צר	HARD PEBBLE	866a	
		שית	PUT	1011a	1
22	25	בצר	PRECIOUS ORE	131a	
		תועפה	EMINENCE	419c	
22	26	כי	BECAUSE	*473d	3 c
		אז	THEN	23a	1 b
		כי	BECAUSE	473d	3 c
		ענג	BE SOFT	772b	2
22	27	נדר	VOW	624a	2
		עתר	PRAY	801c	
22	28	אור	LIGHT	21d	8
		אמר	WORD	57a	2
		גזר	CUT	160c	6

Ch	v.	Heb	Eng	Page	Sec
		נגה	SHINE	618b	
		קום	STAND	878c	7 g
22	29	גוה	PRIDE	145b	2
		ישע	DELIVER	446d	1 b
		כי	THAT	474c	
		עין	EYE	744c	2 a
		שח	LOW	1006a	
		שפל	BECOME LOW	1050b	3
22	30	אי	NOT	33a	
		בר	CLEANNESS	141b	
		כף	HOLLOW OF THE HAND	496d	1 d7
		מלט	SLIP AWAY	572c	3
		מלט	SLIP AWAY	572c	3
		נקי	CLEAN	667c	1
		אי	ADDENDA ET COR-RIGENDA	1120a	
23	2	אנחה	SIGHING	58d	
		כבד	BE HEAVY	457b	1
		מרי	REBELLION	598b	
		שיח	COMPLAINT	967a	1
23	3	ו	AND	254a	2 a
		תכונה	ARRANGEMENT	467d	1
		מצא	FIND	593a	1 a
		נתן	GIVE	679a	1 f
23	4	תוכחת	ARGUMENT	407b	1
		ערך	ARRANGE	789d	1 g
		משפט	JUDGMENT	1048c	1 d
23	5	בין	DISCERN	106c	2 b
		מה	WHAT	552d	1 b
		מלה	WORD	576b	
		ענה	ANSWER	772d	1 c
23	6	כח	STRENGTH	471a	3
		לא	NOT	519a	1 ad b
		רב	MULTITUDE	914a	2
		ריב	STRIVE	936c	2
		שום	TO PLACE	963c	2 b
23	7	יכח	REASON	407a	
		ישר	STRAIGHT	449b	3 c2
		נצח	EVERLASTINGNESS	664b	4
		פלט	ESCAPE	812b	3
		שפט	JUDGE	1047c	2 a
23	8	אחור	HINDER SIDE	30c	A
		בין	DISCERN	106d	1 a
		כי	BECAUSE	*474a	3 c
		קדם	FRONT	869c	1 a
23	9	חזה	SEE	302c	3 a
		ימין	RIGHT HAND	411d	2 a
		עטף	TURN ASIDE	742b	
		שמאל	LEFT	969d	1
23	10	בחן	TRY	103c	2 a
		דרך	WAY	203c	6 c
		זהב	GOLD	262c	1
		יצא	GO OUT	423a	1 f
		כי	BECAUSE	474a	3 c
		עם	WITH	768d	4 b
23	11	אחז	GRASP	28b	
		אחז	GRASP	28b	
		אשור	STEP	81a	
		דרך	WAY	204a	6 ec
		כי	BECAUSE	474a	3 c
		נטה	INCLINE	640d	3 b
23	12	אמר	WORD	57a	1
		ו	AND	255a	5 cb
		חיק	BOSOM	300d	3 b
		חק	SOMETHING PRE-SCRIBED	349b	3
		כי	BECAUSE	474a	3 c
		מוש	REMOVE	559a	
		מצוה	COMMANDMENT	846c	2 c
		צפן	HIDE	860c	1
		שפה	SPEECH	974a	1 h
23	13	אוה	DESIRE	16a	
		ב	IN	88d	17a
		כי	BECAUSE	474a	3 c
		מי	WHO	567a	F c
		נפש	SOUL	660d	6 a
23	14	שוב	TURN BACK	999d	5
		הם	THEY	241d	8 c
		הם	THEY	241d	6 a
		חק	SOMETHING PRE-SCRIBED	349c	6 c
		כמו	LIKE	456a	1 a
		כי	BECAUSE	473d	3 c
		שלם	BE COMPLETE	1022c	1
23	15	בהל	BE DISTURBED	96b	1
		בין	DISCERN	107a	1 a
		פחד	DREAD	808b	1
		פנה	FACE	818b	2 6b
23	16	בהל	DISMAY	96c	1
		כי	BECAUSE	*474a	3 c
		רכך	BE TENDER	940a	
23	17	אפל	DARKNESS	66c	2
		חשך	DARKNESS	365a	3 a
		כי	BECAUSE	474a	3 c
		כסה	COVER	491c	1
		צמת	EXTERMINATE	856b	
24	1	חזה	SEE	302c	3 b
		ידע	KNOW	394a	2
		מן	OUT OF	580a	2 ea
		צפן	HIDE	860d	4 c
24	2	גבולה	BORDER	148b	1
		גזל	TEAR AWAY	159d	
		נשג	REACH	673d	3
		סוג	DISPLACE	691a	1
		עדר	FLOCK	727d	1 c
		רעה	TEND	944d	1 a
24	3	אלמנה	WIDOW	48b	
		חבל	BIND	286b	2
		חמור	HE-ASS	331b	1
		יתום	ORPHAN	450c	
		נהג	DRIVE	624b	1
		על	UPON	757d	2 7c d
		שור	A HEAD OF CATTLE	1004a	
24	4	אביון	NEEDY	2d	
		נבא	WITHDRAW	285b	
		יחד	ALTOGETHER	403b	2 b
		נטה	BEND	641a	3 g
		ענו	POOR	776c	2
		עני	POOR	776d	2
24	5	מדבר	WILDERNESS	184d	2
		טרף	PREY	383c	2
		לחם	FOOD	537b	2 b
		ערבה	DESERT-PLAIN	787c	5
		פעל	DOING	821c	1 c
		פרא	WILD ASS	825b	
		שחר	LOOK EARLY	1007c	
24	6	בליל	FODDER	117d	
		כרם	VINEYARD	501d	
		לקש	TAKE	545c	
		קצר	HARVEST	894b	
		קצר	HARVEST	894c	
24	7	בלי	WEARING OUT	116a	C b
		כסות	COVERING	492b	1
		לבוש	CLOTHING	528c	
		לון	LODGE	533c	1 a
		ערום	NAKED	736a	
		קרה	COLD	903b	
24	8	בלי	WEARING OUT	116a	C b
		הר	MOUNTAIN	250d	1 m
		זרם	FLOOD OF RAIN	281b	
		חבק	CLASP	287d	A
		מחסה	REFUGE	340b	1
		צור	ROCK	849c	1 a
24	9	רטב	BE MOIST	936a	
		גזל	TEAR AWAY	159d	
		חבל	BIND	286b	2
		יתום	ORPHAN	450c	
		שד	BREAST	994d	
24	10	בלי	WEARING OUT	115c	2 b
		הלך	WALK	235c	2
		לבוש	CLOTHING	528c	
		ערום	NAKED	736a	
		עמר	SHEAF	771c	
		רעב	HUNGRY	944c	
24	11	בין	INTERVAL	107b	1
		דרך	TREAD	202a	3
		יקב	WINE-PRESS	428c	
		צהר	PRESS OUT OIL	844b	
		צמא	BE THIRSTY	854d	
		שור	WALL	1004b	
		שורה	ROW	1004c	
24	12	חלל	PIERCED	319c	1
		מת	MALE	607b	3 a
		נאק	GROAN	611a	
		עני	POOR	776d	1
		ישוע	CRY OUT	1002d	
		מתם	SOUNDNESS	*1071b	
		תפלה	UNSEEMLINESS	1074b	
24	13	דרך	WAY	203c	6 c
		ישב	REMAIN	442d	2 a
		מרד	REBEL	597c	3
		נכר	RECOGNIZE	648b	4
		נתיבה	PATH	677b	2 b
24	14	אביון	NEEDY	2d	
		אור	LIGHT	21c	2
		גנב	THIEF	170c	
		ל	TO	517a	6 a
		עני	POOR	776d	2
		קטל	SLAY	881d	
		רצח	MURDER	954a	
24	15	נאף	COMMIT ADUL-TERY	610c	1 a
		נשף	TWILIGHT	676a	1
		סתר	COVERING	712a	1
		שום	TO PLACE	963b	1 b
		שור	BEHOLD	1003a	1
		שמר	KEEP	1036d	1 c
24	16	חשך	DARKNESS	365a	1
		חתם	SEAL	368a	
		חתר	DIG	369a	1
		יומם	BY DAY	401c	2
		ל	TO	515d	5 ia
24	17	בלהה	TERROR	117a	1
		בקר	MORNING	133d	1 b
		יחדו	TOGETHER	403c	B
		כי	BECAUSE	474a	3 c
		ל	TO	513a	5 ad
		נכר	RECOGNIZE	648b	4
		צלמות	DEATH-SHADOW	853c	1
		צלמות	DEATH-SHADOW	853c	1
24	18	דרך	WAY	203b	3
		חלקה	PORTION OF GROUND	324c	1 b
		פנה	TURN	815b	1 a
		קלל	BE SLIGHT	886d	
		קל	LIGHT	887a	
24	19	גזל	TEAR AWAY	159d	
		גם	ALSO	169b	1
		חטא	MISS A GOAL OR WAY	306d	2 b
		חם	HEAT	328d	
		מי	WATER	565d	3
		ציה	DRYNESS	851a	
		שאול	SHEOL	983a	2 a
		שלג	SNOW	1017a	
24	20	זכר	REMEMBER	270c	1 a
		מתק	BE SWEET	608c	3
		עולה	INJUSTICE	732d	3
		רחם	WOMB	933b	1
		רמה	WORM	933d	
		שבר	BREAK	990d	
		שכח	FORGET	1013a	1 b
24	21	יטב	DO GOOD TO	405d	2
		עקר	BARREN	785d	
		רעה	TEND	945b	2 d
24	22	אביר	MIGHTY	7d	1
		אמן	CONFIRM	53b	2 c
		חיים	LIFE	313a	1
		כח	STRENGTH	470d	3
		משך	DRAW	604c	5
		קום	STAND	877d	1 d
24	23	בטח	SECURITY	105b	
		שען	LEAN	1043d	
24	24	אין	NOT	34b	2 b
		כל	ALL	483a	2 bb
		מכך	BE LOW	568d	
		מלל	WITHER	576d	
		מעט	A FEW	590b	1 eb
		ראש	HEAD	910d	2 a
		רחום	BE EXALTED	933d	
		שבלת	EAR OF GRAIN	987c	
		מול	ADDENDA ET COR-RIGENDA	1124d	
24	25	אל	NOT	39b	C
		אפו	THEN	66b	3
		כזב	LIE	469c	
		לא	NOT	519a	1 ad a
		לא	NOT	520a	3
		מלה	WORD	576b	
25	1	בלדד	BILDAD	115a	
		שוחי	SHUHITE	1001d	
25	2	משל	RULE	605d	
		עם	WITH	768b	3 b
		מרום	HEIGHT	928d	2
		מרום	HEIGHT	928d	1
		שלון	PEACE	1023b	6
25	3	גדוד	BAND	*151b	1
		יש	HAVE	441b	2 cb
		מי	WHO	*567a	F c
		מספר	NUMBER	708d	1 a
		על	UPON	755d	2 5
		קום	STAND	878a	1 h
25	4	אהל	BE CLEAR	14c	
		אנוש	MAN	60d	3
		אשה	WOMAN	61a	1
		זכה	BE CLEAR	269a	1
		זכר	BE BRIGHT	*269d	2
		מה	HOW	553c	2 aa
		עם	WITH	767c	1 c
		עם	WITH	768d	4 b
		צדק	BE JUST	842c	2
25	5	אהל	BE CLEAR	14c	
		הן	BEHOLD	243c	A
		ו	AND	255a	5 cb
		זכה	BE CLEAR	*269a	1
		זכר	BE BRIGHT	269b	2
		ירח	MOON	437a	
		כוכב	STAR	457a	
25	6	עד	AS FAR AS	724d	13
		אדם	MAN	9b	2
		אנוש	MAN	60d	3
		אף	ALSO	65b	3
		רמה	WORM	933d	
		תולעה	WORM	1069a	1
26	2	זרוע	ARM	284a	1 b
		זרוע	ARM	284a	1 b
		ישע	DELIVER	446c	1 a
		כח	STRENGTH	470c	1 a
		לא	NOT	519d	2 d
		לא	NOT	520c	4 e
		מה	HOW	553c	2 b
		עז	STRENGTH	739a	1
26	3	חכמה	WISDOM	315d	5 c
		ידע	MAKE KNOWN	395a	
		יעץ	ADVISE	419d	
		תושיה	SOUND WISDOM	444d	A
		ל	TO	516c	5 jb
		לא	NOT	519d	2 d
		לא	NOT	520c	4 e
		מה	HOW	553c	2 b
		רב	MULTITUDE	914a	1
26	4	יצא	GO OUT	423c	1 g
		מי	WHO	566c	B
		מי	WHO	566d	F b
		מלה	SPEECH	576b	
		נשמה	BREATH	675d	4
26	5	חול	WHIRL	297c	1
		מי	WATER	565c	1 e
		רפאים	SHADES	952b	
		שאול	SHEOL	983a	1
		שכן	SETTLE DOWN	1015b	2
		תחת	UNDERNEATH	1066b	3 2a
26	6	אבדון	DESTRUCTION	2c	
		כסות	COVERING	492b	2
		נגד	IN FRONT	617b	1 aa
		ערום	NAKED	736a	
		שאול	SHEOL	983a	1

Ch	v.	Heb	Eng	Page	Sec
26	7	ארץ	EARTH	76a	1 b
		בלימה	NOTHINGNESS	116a	
		נטה	SPREAD OUT	640a	2
		תהו	FORMLESSNESS	1062c	1
		תלה	HANG	1068a	1
26	8	בקע	BREAK OPEN OR THROUGH	132a	1
		מי	WATER	565c	1 f
		ענן	CLOUD	778a	1 d
		צרר	BIND	864c	A
26	9	אחז	GRASP	28c	
		כסא	SEAT OF HONOR	490d	1 b
		על	UPON	753a	2 1a b
		ענן	CLOUD	778a	1 d
		פנה	FACE	816b	1 5
		פרשז	SPREADING	831c	
26	10	חוג	DRAW ROUND	295b	
		חק	SOMETHING PRESCRIBED	349c	5
		חשך	DARKNESS	365a	1
		תכלית	END	479b	1
26	11	גערה	REBUKE	172a	2
		עמוד	PILLAR	765b	5 b
		רפף	SHAKE	952c	
		שמי	HEAVENS	1030a	1 b
		תמה	BE ASTOUNDED	1069b	
26	12	תבונה	UNDERSTANDING	108b	1
		כח	STRENGTH	470d	3
		מחץ	SHATTER	563c	
		רגע	DISTURB	920d	
		רהב	STORM	923d	1
26	13	בריח	FLEEING	138a	
		חלל	BORE	319b	
		נחש	SERPENT	638b	3
		רוח	BREATH	924d	2 a
		שמי	HEAVENS	1029a	1 a
		שפרה	FAIRNESS	1051c	
26	14	בין	DISCERN	107a	2
		גבורה	MIGHT	150c	3
		דבר	WORD	183b	3 1
		דרך	WAY	204a	6 ea
		הן	BEHOLD	243b	
		מה	WHAT	552c	1 aa
		מי	WHO	567a	F c
		קצה	END	892c	1
		רעם	THUNDER	947b	
		שמע	HEAR	1033c	1 a
		שמע	HEAR	1034b	1
		שמץ	WHISPER	1036b	
27	1	יסף	DO AGAIN	415c	2 a
		משל	PARABLE	605b	3
		נשא	LIFT	670d	1 b 6
27	2	חי	ALIVE	311d	1 a
		מרר	BE BITTER	600b	1
		משפט	JUDGEMNT	1049a	5
27	3	אף	NOSE	60a	1
		כל	ALL	482b	1 f
		נפש	SOUL	659d	3 b
		נשמה	BREATH	675d	2
		עוד	STILL	728d	1 aa
		רוח	BREATH	925b	4 a
27	4	הגה	UTTER	211d	1 b
		לשון	TONGUE	546b	1 b
		עולה	INJUSTICE	732c	2
		רמיה	DECEIT	941b	
27	5	גוע	EXPIRE	157c	
		חלילה	FAR BE IT	321a	
		עד	UNTIL	725a	2 1b b
		צדק	DECLARE RIGHTEOUS	842d	2
		תמה	INTEGRITY	1070d	
27	6	חזק	BE FIRM	305a	6 a
		לבב	HEART	523d	2 5
		מן	FROM	581a	3 bc
		צדקה	RIGHTEOUSNESS	842b	3
		רפה	SINK	952a	2
27	7	איב	BE HOSTILE TO	33c	
		עול	UNJUST ONE	732d	
		קום	STAND	878c	
27	8	בצע	CUT OFF	130b	
		חנף	PROFANE	338b	
		כי	BECAUSE	474a	3 c
		תקוה	HOPE	876b	3
		שלה	BE QUIET	*1017b	2
		שלה	DRAW OUT	1017d	
27	9	כי	BECAUSE	474a	3 c
		צעקה	CRY	858d	2
		צרה	DISTRESS	865b	
27	10	כי	BECAUSE	474a	3 c
		ענג	BE SOFT	772b	2
		קרא	CALL	895d	5 c
27	11	יד	HAND	390b	2
		ירה	DIRECT	435b	5 a
		כחד	HIDE	470b	
		עם	WITH	768d	4 b
27	12	הבל	VAPOUR	211a	2
		הבל	BECOME VAIN	211a	
		חזה	SEE	302c	3 b
27	13	אדם	MAN	9b	1
		זה	THIS	261a	3
		חלק	PORTION	324b	5
		נחלה	PROPERTY	635b	2 a
		עם	WITH	768b	3 b
		עריץ	AWE-INSPIRING	792b	1
		רשע	WICKED	957c	1
27	14	צאצא	OFFSPRING	425c	1

Ch	v.	Heb	Eng	Page	Sec
		למו	TO	518b	
		למו	FOR	530c	
27	15	רבה	BECOME MANY	915a	1 a
		אלמנה	WIDOW	48b	
		ב	IN	89d	3 2c
		ב	IN	*89d	3 2a
		בכה	WEEP	113b	1
		שריד	SURVIVOR	975a	1
27	16	חמר	CEMENT	330d	2 b
		כון	ESTABLISH	466c	2 b
		מלבוש	RAIMENT	528d	
		עפר	DRY EARTH	780a	2 a
27	17	צבר	HEAP UP	840d	
		חלק	DIVIDE	323c	4
		כון	ESTABLISH	466c	2 b
		לבש	PUT ON	528d	C
		נקי	CLEAN	667c	1
		צדיק	JUST	843b	3 b
27	18	בית	HOUSE	*109d	1
		נצר	WATCH	665d	1
		סכה	THICKET	697c	2
		עכביש	SPIDER	747b	
		עש	MOTH	799c	
27	19	אין	NOT	34b	2 b
		עין	EYE	744b	1 j
		פקח	OPEN	824d	1 a
		אסף	ADDENDA ET CORRIGENDA	1120c	
27	20	בלהה	TERROR	117a	1
		גנב	STEAL	170c	
		מי	WATER	565d	4 d
		נשג	OVERTAKE	673c	1 b
		סופה	STORM-WIND	693a	
27	21	הלך	WALK	234a	1 5d
		קדים	EAST WIND	870b	1
		שער	SWEEP	973b	
27	22	ברח	FLEE	138a	2
		חמל	SPARE	328b	1
		שלך	THROW	1021b	2 a
27	23	כף	HOLLOW OF THE HAND	496c	1 d1
		מן	OUT OF	579a	2 ab
		ספק	SLAP	706c	1
		שרק	HISS	1056d	
28	1	זהב	GOLD	262c	1
		זקק	REFINE	279b	
		מוצא	GOING FORTH	425d	3 d
		יש	HAVE	441d	2 cb
		כי	THAT	472d	1 e
		כסף	SILVER	494a	1
28	2	אבן	STONE	6d	4
		ברזל	IRON	137c	1 a
		לקח	TAKE	544a	2
		נחושה	COPPER	639a	1
		צוק	POUR OUT	748b	
		עפר	DRY EARTH	779d	2 a
28	3	אבן	STONE	6d	4
		אפל	DARKNESS	66c	1
		חקר	SEARCH	350c	2 a
		חשך	DARKNESS	365a	1
		תכלית	END	479b	1
		ל	TO	511b	1 f
		צלמות	DEATH-SHADOW	853c	1
		קץ	END	893d	1
		שום	TO PLACE	963b	1
28	4	אנוש	MAN	60d	3
		גור	SOJOURN	158a	2
		דלל	HANG	195c	
		מן	FROM	578c	1 b
		מן	OUT OF	580a	2 eb
		נוע	WAVE	631b	1
		נחל	WADY	636c	3
		מעם	FROM WITH	769a	A
		פרץ	BREAK THROUGH	829d	4
		שכח	FORGET	1013b	
28	5	הפך	TURN	246a	2 e
		יצא	GO OUT	423g	1 b
		לחם	FOOD	537b	1 b
28	6	זהב	GOLD	262c	1
		ספיר	SAPPHIRE	705d	
		עפר	DRY EARTH	779d	2 a
28	7	איה	HAWK	17b	
		ידע	KNOW	393c	1 a
		נתיב	PATH	677b	
		עיט	BIRD OF PREY	743c	
		עין	EYE	744b	1 d
		שקר	OGLE	974c	
		שזף	CATCH SIGHT OF	1004d	
28	8	בן	SON	121b	4
		בן	SON	121b	8 n
		דרך	TREAD	202b	1
		עדה	PASS ON	723c	
		שחל	LION	1006c	
		שחץ	DIGNITY	1006d	
28	9	הפך	TURN	245c	1 b
		הר	MOUNTAIN	250c	1 f
		חלמיש	FLINT	321d	
		שלח	SEND	1018c	3 a
		שרש	ROOT	1057d	3
28	10	בקע	CLEAVE	132b	
		יאר	STREAM	384c	3
		יקר	PRECIOUSNESS	430a	1 a
		צור	ROCK	849c	1 a
28	11	בכי	WEEPING	113d	
		חבש	BIND	290a	
		יצא	BRING OUT	425a	4 h

Ch	v.	Heb	Eng	Page	Sec
		מן	FROM	583c	7 bb
		גבך	SPRING	614a	
		נהר	STREAM	625d	2
28	12	תעלמה	HIDDEN THING	761b	
		אין	WHENCE	32d	
		בינה	UNDERSTANDING	108a	3
		ה	THE	208b	1 ha
		זה	THIS	261b	4 a
		חכמה	WISDOM	315c	5 a
		מן	OUT OF	579c	2 cc
28	13	מצא	FIND	593d	1
		אנוש	MAN	60d	3
		חי	ALIVE	312a	1 b
		ידע	KNOW	393c	1 a
		מצא	FIND	593d	1 a
		ערך	ORDER	790a	2
28	14	אמר	SAY	55d	1
		לא	NOT	519b	1 bb
		עם	WITH	768b	3 b
		תהום	DEEP	1062d	1
28	15	כסף	SILVER	494d	9
		מחיר	PRICE	564b	1
		נתן	GIVE	681d	1 a
		סגר	CLOSE	689b	4 b
		סגור	ENCLOSURE	689c	1
		שקל	WEIGH	1053c	2
28	16	אופיר	OPHIR	20c	2
		אופיר	OPHIR	20d	3
		יקר	PRECIOUS	430a	1 c
		כתם	GOLD	508d	
		סלה	WEIGH	699a	
		ספיר	SAPPHIRE	705d	
		שהם	CARNELIAN	996a	
28	17	זהב	GOLD	262d	2
		זכוכית	GLASS	269b	
		כלי	ARTICLE	479c	1
		תמורה	EXCHANGE	558d	
		תמורה	EXCHANGE	558d	
		ערך	ARRANGE	789d	2 b
		פז	REFINED GOLD	808a	
28	18	גביש	CRYSTAL	150d	
		זכר	REMEMBER	270c	2
		חכמה	WISDOM	315d	5 c
		מן	THAN	582d	6 c
		משך	A DRAWING UP	605d	1
		משק	ACQUISITION	*606c	
		פנינים	CORALS	819d	
		ראמות	CORALS	910c	
28	19	טהור	CLEAN	373a	2
		כוש	CUSH	469a	2 a
		כתם	GOLD	508d	
		סלה	WEIGH	699a	
		ערך	ARRANGE	789d	2 b
		פטדה	TOPAZ	809c	
28	20	אין	WHENCE	32d	
		בינה	UNDERSTANDING	108a	3
		ה	THE	208b	1 ha
		זה	THIS	261b	4 a
		חכמה	WISDOM	315c	5 a
28	21	חי	ALIVE	312b	1 d
		סתר	HIDE	711c	2
		עין	EYE	744d	3 d
		עלם	CONCEAL	761a	
28	22	אבדון	DESTRUCTION	2c	
		אמר	SAY	55d	1
		מות	DEATH	560d	1
		שמע	REPORT	1034d	1
28	23	אלהים	GOD	44b	4 a
		בין	DISCERN	107a	1 b
		חכמה	WISDOM	315c	5 a
		ידע	KNOW	393c	1 a
28	24	הוא	HE, SHE, IT	*215b	1
		נבט	LOOK	613d	3
		קצה	END	892c	1
		תחת	UNDERNEATH	1065b	2 1
28	25	מדה	MEASURE	551c	1
		משקל	WEIGHT	1054a	
		תכן	MEASURE	1067b	
		דרך	WAY	203a	1
28	26	חזיז	THUNDER-BOLT	304a	
		חק	SOMETHING PRESCRIBED	349c	6 b
		מטר	RAIN	564d	
		קול	VOICE	877b	2 b
28	27	אז	THEN	23a	1 d
		חקר	SEARCH	350c	2 a
		כון	ESTABLISH	466b	1 c
		ספר	COUNT	708a	1
28	28	אדון	LORD	11b	3 2a
		בינה	UNDERSTANDING	108a	3
		חכמה	WISDOM	315c	5 c
		יראה	FEAR	432a	1
		סור	TURN ASIDE	693d	1
29	1	יסף	DO AGAIN	415c	2 a
		משל	PARABLE	605b	3
		נשא	LIFT	670d	1 b 6
29	2	יום	DAY	400b	7 d6
		ירח	MONTH	437b	1
		ד	LIKE	455a	B
		קדם	FRONT	869d	2 b
		שמר	KEEP	1037a	4 a
29	3	הלך	WALK	234c	2 2
		הלל	SHINE	237c	
		חשך	DARKNESS	365a	3 a
		ל	TO	516d	5 k
		נר	LAMP	632d	

Ch	v.	Heb	Eng	Page	Sec
29	4	על	UPON	755d	2 5
		אליחרף	ELIHOREPH	45b	
		חרף	HARVEST-TIME	358b	
		סוד	COUNSEL	691c	2 c
29	5	דין	JUDGMENT	*192d	
		עוד	STILL	729b	2 aa
		עם	WITH	767c	1 a
29	6	הליך	STEP	237b	
		חמאה	CURD	326a	
		חמה	WRATH	328a	
		צוק	POUR OUT	748b	
		עם	WITH	767b	1 a
		פלג	CHANNEL	811b	
		צור	ROCK	849c	1 a
		רחץ	WASH OFF	934c	2
		שמן	OIL	1032b	2 b
29	7	מושב	SEAT	444b	1 a
		קרת	TOWN	900d	
		רחוב	PLAZA	932b	
		רחוב	PLAZA	932b	
		שער	GATE	1045a	2 a
29	8	חבא	WITHDRAW	285b	
		ישיש	AGED	450b	
		עמד	STAND	764b	5 b
		קום	STAND	877d	1 a
29	9	חבא	WITHDRAW	285b	
		כף	HOLLOW OF THE HAND	496d	1 d5
		מלה	SPEECH	576b	
		עצר	RESTRAIN	783c	1
		פה	MOUTH	804d	1 b
		שום	TO PLACE	963b	1 b
		שר	CHIEFTAIN	978d	7
29	10	דבק	CLING	179d	1 a
		חבא	WITHDRAW	285b	
		חך	PALATE	335a	A
		לשון	TONGUE	546a	1 a
		נגיד	LEADER	618a	
29	11	אזן	EAR	24a	2 a
		אשר	GO STRAIGHT	80d	4
		כי	BECAUSE	474b	3 d
		עוד	BEAR WITNESS	730a	1
29	12	ו	AND	*253c	1 k
		יתום	ORPHAN	450c	
		לא	NOT	519b	1 bb
		מלט	SLIP AWAY	572c	3
		עני	POOR	776d	2
		שוע	CRY OUT	1002d	
29	13	אבד	PERISH	1c	1
		אלמנה	WIDOW	48b	
		ברכה	BLESSING	139d	1 d
		לב	HEART	525c	2 9a
		רנן	GIVE A RINGING CRY	943c	
29	14	לבש	PUT ON	528a	B
		לבש	PUT ON	528b	F
		מעיל	ROBE	591c	4
		צדק	RIGHTEOUSNESS	841d	3
		צניף	TURBAN	857b	
		משפט	JUDGEMNT	1048d	2 b
29	15	עור	BLIND	734c	1 a
		פסח	LAME	820c	
29	16	אביון	NEEDY	2d	
		אב	FATHER	3d	7
		אם	MOTHER	52a	2
		חקר	SEARCH	350d	2 d
29	17	טרף	PREY	383c	1
		עול	UNJUST ONE	732d	
		שבר	BREAK	991a	
		שלך	THROW	1021b	3
		שן	TOOTH	1042a	1 b
		מתלעות	TEETH	1069a	
29	18	גוע	EXPIRE	157c	
		חול	SAND	297d	A
		קן	NEST	890a	1
		רבה	BECOME MANY	915c	1 c
29	19	טל	NIGHT-MIST	378c	
		לון	LODGE	533d	1 c
		פתח	OPEN	835b	
		קציר	BRANCHES	894b	
		שרש	ROOT	1057d	1
29	20	חדש	NEW	294b	B
		חלף	PASS ON OR AWAY	322b	2
		יתר	CORD	*452a	
		כבוד	HONOR	458c	2 a
		עם	WITH	767b	1 a
		קשת	BOW	906c	1 e
29	21	דמם	BE SILENT	198d	2
		יחל	WAIT	404a	2
		עצה	ADVICE	420a	
		למו	TO	518b	
		למו	FOR	530c	
29	22	מלה	WORD	576b	
		נטף	DROP	643a	
		נתן	GIVE	678d	1 f
		על	UPON	756b	2 7a a
		שנה	DO AGAIN	1040d	
29	23	יחל	WAIT	404a	2
		ד	LIKE	455a	B
		מטר	RAIN	564d	
		פער	OPEN WIDE	822b	
29	24	אור	LIGHT	21d	0
		אמן	CONFIRM	53a	2 a
		נפל	FALL	658b	5
		שחק	LAUGH	965d	1 b
29	25	אבל	MOURNING	5d	

Ch	v.	Heb	Eng	Page	Sec
		בחר	CHOOSE	104b	5 b
		גדוד	TROOP	151b	2
		כאשר	WHEN	455d	3
		נחם	CONSOLE ONESELF	637a	
		שכן	SETTLE DOWN	1015a	1 a
30	1	כלב	DOG	476d	A
		ל	TO	514c	5 fb
		מאס	REJECT	549c	1 a
		עם	WITH	767d	1 e
		עת	NOW	774a	1 a
		צעיר	YOUNG	859a	2
		צעיר	YOUNG	859a	2
		שחק	LAUGH	965d	1 a
		שית	PUT	1011b	2 a
30	2	אבד	PERISH	1d	2
		כח	STRENGTH	470d	1 b
		כלח	STRENGTH	480c	
		ל	TO	513a	5 ad
		מה	HOW	554a	4 d
		על	UPON	753d	2 1d
30	3	אמש	YESTERDAY	57d	
		אמש	YESTERDAY	57d	
		חסר	WANT	341c	
		כפן	HUNGER	495d	
		ערק	GNAW	792b	
		ציה	DRYNESS	851b	
		שואה	DEVASTATION	996c	2
		משאה	DESOLATION	996c	1
30	4	מלוח	MALLOW	572a	
		על	UPON	756a	2 6a
		קטף	PLUCK OFF	882c	
		רתם	BROOM-PLANT	958c	
		שיח	BUSH	967b	
30	5	שרש	ROOT	1057d	2
		גו	MIDST	156b	
		גנב	THIEF	170c	
		גרש	DRIVE OUT	177a	
		ך	LIKE	455a	B
		על	UPON	756d	2 7a c
		רוע	RAISE A SHOUT	929c	2
30	6	חר	HOLE	359d	
		כף	ROCK	495b	
		ל	TO	518a	7 bg
		נחל	WADY	636c	2
		עפר	DRY EARTH	779d	1 c
		ערוץ	DREADFUL	792a	
		שכן	SETTLE DOWN	1015b	2
30	7	בין	INTERVAL	107b	1
		חרול	KIND OF WEED	355c	
		נהק	BRAY	625c	
		ספח	JOIN	705b	
		שיח	BUSH	967b	
30	8	בלי	WEARING OUT	115c	2 b
		בן	SON	120c	1 ia
		נבל	FOOLISH	614b	
		נכא	SCOURGE	644d	
		שם	NAME	1028a	2 b1
30	9	מלה	WORD	576b	
		נגינה	MUSIC	618d	2
30	10	חשך	WITHHOLD	362b	1 c
		רחק	BE DISTANT	934d	1
		רק	SPITTLE	956d	
		תעב	BE ABHORRED	1073c	1 a2
30	11	יתר	CORD	452a	
		ענה	BE BOWED DOWN	776b	1
		פתח	OPEN	835c	2
		רסן	HALTER	943d	1
		שלח	SEND	1019b	3
		שלח	SEND	1019b	7
30	12	איד	DISTRESS	15d	2
		ארח	WAY	73b	3 c
		ימין	RIGHT HAND	411d	2 a
		סלל	LIFT UP	699d	2
		על	UPON	757d	2 7d
		פרחה	BROOD	827b	
		קום	STAND	878a	1 f
		רגל	FOOT	920a	1
		שלח	SEND	1019b	7
30	13	הוה	CHASM	217d	2
		יעל	PROFIT	*418c	
		יעל	PROFIT	418d	
		לא	NOT	519b	1 bb
		נתיבה	PATH	677b	2 a
		נתם	BREAK DOWN	683a	
30	14	אתה	COME	87b	
		פרץ	BURSTING FORTH	829d	2
		רחב	WIDE	932a	
		רחב	WIDE	932a	
		שואה	DEVASTATION	996c	2
		תחת	UNDERNEATH	1065b	2 1
30	15	בלהה	TERROR	117a	1
		ישועה	DELIVERANCE	447b	1
		נדיבה	NOBILITY	622a	1
		עבר	PASS OVER	718a	6 c
		עב	DARK CLOUD	728a	1 e
		רדף	PURSUE	922a	1 f
		רדף	PURSUE	923a	1
30	16	אחז	GRASP	28b	2
		נפש	SOUL	659c	1 b
		על	UPON	753d	2 1d
		עני	AFFLICTION	777a	1
		שפך	POUR OUT	1049d	
30	17	נקר	DIG	669b	
		על	UPON	758d	4 2a
		עצם	BONE	782d	1 c
		ערק	GNAW	792b	

Ch	v.	Heb	Eng	Page	Sec
30	18	שכב	LIE DOWN	1012c	5
		אור	GIRD	25a	
		חפש	SEARCH	344c	
		כח	STRENGTH	470d	3
		כתנת	TUNIC	509a	
		לבוש	CLOTHING	528c	
		פה	MOUTH	805b	4
30	19	רב	MULTITUDE	914a	2
		אפר	ASHES	68a	
		חמר	CEMENT	330d	2 b
		ירה	THROW	435b	1
		משל	BE LIKE	605a	
		עפר	DRY EARTH	780a	2 e
30	20	בין	DISCERN	107b	1 f
		עמד	STAND	764a	1 h
		שפה	SPEECH	973d	1 a1
		שוע	CRY OUT	1002d	
30	21	הפך	TURN	246a	1 b
		אכזר	CRUEL	470a	
		ל	TO	*512c	4 b
		עצם	MIGHT	782c	1
		שטם	BEAR A GRUDGE	966b	
		שפה	SPEECH	973d	1 a1
30	22	תושיה	SOUND WISDOM	444d	B
		מוג	MELT	556b	
		רכב	RIDE	938d	1
		תשאה	NOISE	996c	
		שוה	AGREE WITH	1001a	
30	23	בית	HOUSE	109c	1 d
		חי	ALIVE	312b	1 d
		מועד	APPOINTED MEETING	417d	2
30	24	שוב	TURN BACK	999b	1 g
		שוע	OPULENCE	447b	
		ל	TO	514c	5 g
		עי	RUIN	730c	
		פיד	RUIN	810a	
		שוע	CRY FOR HELP	1002d	
30	25	שלח	SEND	1018c	3 a
		אביון	NEEDY	2d	
		בכה	WEEP	113c	3
		יום	DAY	399b	4 a
		נפש	SOUL	660d	6 c
		עגם	BE GRIEVED	723a	
		קשה	SEVERE	904c	2 a
30	26	אור	LIGHT	21d	8
		אפל	DARKNESS	66c	2
		טוב	A GOOD THING	375a	1
		יחל	WAIT	404a	2
		כי	BECAUSE	473d	3 c
		קוה	WAIT FOR	875d	1
		רע	EVIL	948d	1
30	27	רתם	BE STILL	198d	2
		מעה	BELLY	589a	5
		עני	AFFLICTION	777a	1
		קדם	COME IN FRONT	869d	1 a
		רתח	BOIL	958b	
30	28	הלך	WALK	235c	2
		הלך	WALK	*236a	1 b
		חמה	HEAT	329a	2
		לא	NOT	520a	4 aa
		קדר	BE DARK	871a	
		קהל	ASSEMBLY	874c	1 a
		קום	STAND	877d	1 f
		שוע	CRY OUT	1002d	
30	29	אח	BROTHER	26b	3
		בת	DAUGHTER	123d	6
		יענה	OSTRICH	419a	
		ל	TO	513a	5 ad
		רע	FRIEND	946a	1
		תן	JACKAL	1072b	
30	30	חרב	DRYNESS	351b	3
		חרר	BE HOT	359b	3
		עצם	BONE	782d	1 c
		שחר	BE BLACK	1007a	
30	31	אבל	MOURNING	5d	
		בכה	WEEP	113c	1
		כנור	LYRE	490a	
		עוגב	PIPE	721d	
31	1	בין	DISCERN	107b	1 d
		ברית	COVENANT	136c	1 3
		בתולה	VIRGIN	143d	
		כרת	CUT	504a	4
		מה	HOW	553c	2 aa
		מה	WHAT	553c	2 ab
		עין	EYE	744d	3 b
31	2	חלק	PORTION	324b	5
		נחלה	PROPERTY	635b	2 a
		מעל	ABOVE	751c	1
		מרום	HEIGHT	928d	2
31	3	איד	DISTRESS	15d	3
		און	TROUBLE	20a	3
		נכר	CALAMITY	648c	
		עול	UNJUST ONE	732d	
		פעל	DO	821b	1 b
31	4	ספר	COUNT	707d	2
		צעד	STEP	857d	2
31	5	אם	IF	50a	1 a4 a
		הלך	WALK	234d	2 3b
		חוש	HASTE	301d	2
		על	UPON	757c	2 7c db
		מרמה	DECEIT	941b	
		שוא	EMPTINESS	996b	2
31	6	מאזן	BALANCES	24d	2
		צדק	RIGHTNESS	841c	1
		שקל	WEIGH	1053b	1

Ch v.	Heb	Eng	Page	Sec
31 7	תמה	INTEGRITY	1070d	
	אחר	BEHIND	29d	2 a
	אם	IF	49c	1 a1 b
	אשר	STEP	81a	
	דבק	CLING	179d	1 a
	דרך	WAY	203c	6 b
	הלך	WALK	235a	2 3f 1b
	כף	HOLLOW OF THE HAND	496d	1 d7
	מאחם	BLEMISH	548c	2
	נטה	BEND	640b	3 a
	עין	EYE	744d	3 b
31 8	אחר	ANOTHER	*29c	
	זרע	SOW	281c	1 a
	צאצא	OFFSPRING	425c	1
	שרש	ROOT UP	1057d	1
31 9	אם	IF	50a	1 a4 a
	ארב	LIE IN WAIT	70b	
	על	UPON	756a	26 a
	פתה	BE SIMPLE	834c	
	פתח	OPENING	835d	
31 10	אחר	ANOTHER	29c	
	אחר	ANOTHER	*29c	
	טחן	GRIND	377c	
	כרע	BOW DOWN	502c	3
31 11	הוא	HE, SHE, IT	*214d	
	הוא	HE, SHE, IT	*215a	
	זמה	PLAN	273c	2 c
	כי	BECAUSE	474a	3 d
	עון	INIQUITY	730d	1 a
	פליל	JUDGE	813c	
31 12	אבדון	DESTRUCTION	2c	
	ב	IN	90b	3 4
	תבואה	REVENUE	100b	2 a
	שרש	ROOT UP	1057d	1
31 13	אם	IF	49c	1 a1 b
	אמה	MAID	51a	1
	ו	AND	252d	1 d
	מאס	REJECT	549c	1 a
	עבד	SLAVE	713d	1
31 14	פקד	ATTEND TO	823c	A 2
	קום	STAND	878b	6 a
	שוב	TURN BACK	999c	3
31 15	בטן	WOMB	106a	3
	כון	ESTABLISH	466d	2
	עשה	DO	794b	2 1b
	רחם	WOMB	933b	1
31 16	אלמנה	WIDOW	48b	
	אם	IF	49c	1 a1 b
	דל	WEAK	195d	
	ו	AND	252d	1 d
	חפץ	DELIGHT	343b	2
	כלה	FINISH	478c	2 b
	מנע	WITHHOLD	586a	
31 17	יתום	ORPHAN	450c	
	פת	FRAGMENT	837d	
31 18	אב	FATHER	3d	7
	אם	MOTHER	51d	1
	בטן	WOMB	106a	3
	גדל	GROW UP	152b	1 a
	כי	BECAUSE	474a	3 c
	נחה	LEAD	635a	
	נעורים	YOUTH	655b	
31 19	אבד	PERISH	1c	1
	אביון	NEEDY	2d	
	בלי	WEARING OUT	116a	C b
	כסות	COVERING	492b	1
	לבוש	CLOTHING	528c	
31 20	ברך	BLESS	139b	4 d
	גז	SHEARING	159c	
	חלץ	LOINS	323b	2
	חמם	BE OR BECOME WARM	328d	
	כבש	LAMB	461a	3
31 21	יתום	ORPHAN	450c	
	כי	WHEN	473a	2 a
	נוף	WAVE	632a	2 b
	עזרה	HELP	741a	2 a
	שער	GATE	1045a	2 a
31 22	אזרוע	ARM	284b	
	כתף	SHOULDER	509b	1 a
	נפל	FALL	657a	1
	קנה	STALK	889d	4 f
	שבר	BREAK	990d	
	שכם	SHOULDER	1014b	3
31 23	איד	DISTRESS	15d	2
	אל	TO	39c	1
	יכל	HAVE ABILITY	408a	3
	מן	OUT OF	580a	2 eb
	שאת	DIGNITY	673b	2
	פחד	DREAD	808c	2
31 24	מבטח	CONFIDENCE	105c	2
	זהב	GOLD	262d	2
	כסל	CONFIDENCE	492d	3
	כתם	GOLD	508d	
31 25	אם	IF	49c	1 a1 b
	חיל	STRENGTH	299a	3
	כביר	GREAT	460c	
	מצא	FIND	592d	1 a
31 26	אור	LIGHT	21c	3
	הלך	WALK	232b	1 3
	הלל	SHINE	237c	
	ו	AND	252d	1 d
	יקר	GLORIOUS	430a	3
	ירח	MOON	437a	
	כי	WHEN	473a	2 a
31 27	ראה	TO SEE	907c	6 a
	יד	HAND	389c	1 d
	נשק	KISS	676b	
	סתר	COVERING	712b	3
	פה	MOUTH	804d	1 b
31 28	פתה	BE SIMPLE	834c	2
	הוא	HE, SHE, IT	216d	6 a
	כחש	DECEIVE	471b	1
	עון	INIQUITY	730d	1 a
	מעל	ABOVE	751c	1 a
	פלילי	FOR A JUDGE	813d	
	פליל	JUDGE	813d	
31 29	כי	WHEN	473a	2 a
	מצא	FIND	593c	3 e
	עור	ROUSE ONESELF	735b	
	פיד	RUIN	810a	
	רע	EVIL	948d	1
	שמח	REJOICE	970b	1 b
	שנא	HATE	971d	1
31 30	אלה	OATH	46d	3 b
	חטא	MISS A GOAL OR WAY	307a	2 b
	חך	PALATE	335a	B
	שאל	ASK	981c	1
31 31	בשר	FLESH	142c	1 a
	לא	NOT	519d	2 d
	נתן	GIVE	679d	1 f
	שבע	SATISFIED	959d	
31 32	ארח	WAY	73b	4
	ארח	WAY	73b	4
	גר	SOJOURNER	158a	1
	דלת	DOOR	195a	1
	פתח	OPEN	835a	
31 33	אדם	MAN	9b	2
	חב	BOSOM	285c	
	ממן	HIDE	380c	1
	כסה	COVER	491d	2
	עון	INIQUITY	730d	1
	פשע	TRANSGRESSION	833c	3 b
31 34	בז	CONTEMPT	100b	1
	דמם	BE STILL	198d	2
	המון	CROWD	242d	3 c
	חתת	BE SHATTERED	369c	2 b
	יצא	GO OUT	422d	1 a
	ערץ	CAUSE TO TREMBLE	792a	2
	פתח	OPENING	835d	
31 35	נתן	GIVE	678d	1 f
	ספר	MISSIVE	707a	2
	ריב	STRIFE	937a	3
	שמע	HEAR	1033d	1 h
	תו	MARK	1063b	
31 36	נשא	LIFT	670a	1 a
	עטרה	CROWN	742d	2
	ענד	BIND AROUND	772c	
	שכם	SHOULDER	1014b	1 a
31 37	נגיד	LEADER	618a	
	צעד	STEP	857d	2
	קרב	COME NEAR	897d	1
31 38	אדמה	GROUND	9c	1
	בכה	WEEP	113b	1
	זעק	CRY	277c	2 e
	יחד	ALTOGETHER	403b	2 b
	תלם	FURROW	1068d	
31 39	בלי	WEARING OUT	115c	2 b
	בעל	OWNER	127b	11
	כח	STRENGTH	471a	5
	נפח	BREATHE	656a	
	מפח	BREATHING OUT	*656a	
	נפש	SOUL	659c	1 c
31 40	באשה	STINKING WEEDS	93b	
	דבר	WORD	183a	2 1b
	חוח	BRIER	296b	1 a
	חטה	WHEAT	334d	
	יצא	GO OUT	423d	1 h
	שערה	BARLEY	972d	1
	תמם	BE FINISHED	1070b	1
32 1	צדיק	JUST	843a	2
32 2	אלהים	GOD	44b	4 a
	אליהו	ELIHU	45b	A
	בוזי	BUZITE	100c	
	ברכאל	BARACHEL	140a	
	חרה	BURN	354a	1 a
	חרה	BURN	354a	1 a
	צדק	BE JUST	842d	1 d
	רם	RAM	928a	2
	משפחה	CLAN	1046d	1
32 3	חרה	BURN	354a	1 a
	מצא	FIND	593a	1 b
	מענה	ANSWER	775a	
	רשע	BE WICKED	957d	2
32 4	אליהו	ELIHU	45b	A
	זקן	OLD	278c	1
	חכה	WAIT	314a	1
	ל	TO	514c	5 fb
32 5	אליהו	ELIHU	45b	A
	חרה	BURN	354a	1 a
	מענה	ANSWER	775a	
32 6	אליהו	ELIHU	45b	A
	בוזי	BUZITE	100c	
	ברכאל	BARACHEL	140a	
	זחל	FEAR	267c	
	חוה	TELL	296a	
	דע	OPINION	395b	2
	ירא	FEAR	431b	1 d
	ישיש	AGED	450a	
	ל	TO	514c	5 fb
32 7	צעיר	YOUNG	859a	2
	אבן	PRESS	38c	B
	חכמה	WISDOM	315d	5 c
	ידע	MAKE KNOWN	395a	
32 8	אבן	SURELY	38c	B
	אנוש	MAN	60d	3
	בין	DISCERN	107a	3 b
	הוא	HE, SHE, IT	216d	6 b
	נשמה	BREATH	675d	1
	רב	MULTITUDE	914a	1
	רוח	BREATH	925a	3 d
	רוח	BREATH	926a	9 d
32 9	בין	DISCERN	106d	2 b
	זקן	OLD	278c	2 a
	חכם	BE WISE	314c	
	לא	NOT	518d	1 ac
	רב	GREAT	913c	2 c
	משפט	JUDGMENT	1048b	1 a
32 10	חוה	TELL	296a	
	דע	OPINION	395d	2
32 11	אזן	HEAR	24c	1
	תבונה	UNDERSTANDING	108b	3
	חקר	SEARCH	350c	1
	יחל	WAIT	404a	
	מלה	WORD	576b	
32 12	אמר	WORD	57a	1
	בין	DISCERN	107b	1 e
	יכח	CONVICT	407a	4
	עד	AS FAR AS	724a	1 la
	ענה	ANSWER	772d	1 a
32 13	איש	MAN	35d	
	חכמה	WISDOM	315d	5 c
	מצא	FIND	592d	1 a
	נדף	DRIVE	623c	
	פן	LEST	814d	1 b
32 14	אמר	WORD	57a	1
	ו	AND	255a	5 cb
	מלה	WORD	576b	
	ערך	ARRANGE	789d	1 f
	שוב	TURN BACK	999c	3
32 15	חתת	BE SHATTERED	369b	2 a
	מלה	SPEECH	576b	
	שוב	TURN BACK	999c	3
32 16	ו	AND	253a	1 f
	יחל	WAIT	404a	
	עמד	STAND	764a	1 g
	עתק	MOVE	801b	1
32 17	חוה	TELL	296a	
	חלק	PORTION	324a	1 d
	דע	OPINION	395b	2
32 18	בטן	BELLY	105d	1 a
	מלה	SPEECH	576b	
	צוק	CONSTRAIN	847d	
	רוח	BREATH	925a	3 d
32 19	אוב	SKIN-BOTTLE	15b	1
	בטן	BELLY	105d	1 a
	בקע	BREAK OPEN OR THROUGH	132a	1
	חדש	NEW	294a	A
	יין	WINE	406d	E
	פתח	OPEN	835c	
32 20	פתח	OPEN	835b	
	רוח	BE WIDE	926c	
32 21	כנה	GIVE TITLES TO	487b	
	נא	PART OF ENTREATY	609b	3 a
	נשא	LIFT	670a	1 b 3
	פתח	OPEN	*835b	
32 22	כנה	GIVE TITLES TO	487b	
	מעט	A FEW	590b	2 b
	נשא	LIFT	671b	3 b
	עשה	DO	794c	2 1b
32 23	עשה	DO	794c	2 1b
33 1	אולם	BUT	19d	
	אזן	HEAR	24c	1
	מלה	WORD	576b	
33 2	חך	PALATE	335a	B
	לשון	TONGUE	546b	1 b
	נא	PART OF ENTREATY	609c	4 d
	פה	MOUTH	805a	2 a
	פתח	OPEN	835b	
33 3	אמר	WORD	57a	1
	ברר	PURIFY	141a	1
	דעת	WISDOM	395d	2 a
	ישר	STRAIGHTNESS	449c	2
	לב	HEART	525a	26 a
	מלל	SPEAK	576b	
33 4	חיה	LIVE	311c	1
	נשמה	BREATH	675d	2
	נשמה	BREATH	675d	2
	רוח	BREATH	926a	9 e
33 5	יכל	BE ABLE	407c	1 b
	יצב	STATION ONESELF	426b	B
	ערך	ARRANGE	789d	1 f
	שוב	TURN BACK	999c	3
33 6	הן	BEHOLD	243b	
	חמר	CEMENT	330d	2 a
	ל	TO	513a	5 ad
	פה	MOUTH	805c	6 bb
	קרץ	PINCH	902d	
33 7	אימה	TERROR	34a	
	אכף	PRESSURE	38c	
	בעת	FALL UPON	130a	1
	כבד	BE HEAVY	457b	1

Ch	v.	Heb	Eng	Page	Sec
33	8	מלה	WORD	576b	
33	9	אנכי	I	59a	
		בלי	WEARING OUT	115c	2 b
		זך	PURE	269b	2
		חף	CLEAN	342c	
		לא	NOT	519b	1 bb
		עון	INIQUITY	731b	2 a
		פשע	TRANSGRESSION	833d	4
33	10	איב	BE HOSTILE TO	33c	
		חשב	THINK	363b	2 1
		מצא	FIND	592d	1 a
		תנואה	OPPOSITION	626b	
33	11	ארח	WAY	73a	2
		סד	STOCKS	690a	
		שום	TO PLACE	963a	1 a
		שמר	KEEP	1036d	1 c
33	12	אנוש	MAN	60d	3
		הן	BEHOLD	243b	
		זה	THIS	260c	1 a
		צדק	BE JUST	842c	1
		רבה	BECOME MANY	915b	2 a2
33	13	דבר	WORD	183c	4 2
		ענה	ANSWER	772d	1 a
		ריב	STRIVE	936d	4
33	14	שור	BEHOLD	1003d	3
		שנים	TWO	1041b	1 b2
		אחד	ADDENDA ET COR-RIGENDA	1120a	
33	15	חזיון	VISION	303b	2
		חלום	DREAM	321d	2 a
		לילה	NIGHT	538d	1
		תנומה	SLUMBER	630b	
		תרדמה	DEEP SLEEP	922b	
33	16	אז	THEN	23a	1 d
		חתם	SEAL	367d	1
		חתם	SEAL	368a	2
		מוסר	DISCIPLINE	416c	1 a
33	17	גוה	PRIDE	145b	1
		כסה	COVER	491d	2
		סור	TURN ASIDE	694b	1
		מעשה	DEED	795d	1 a2
33	18	חיה	LIVING THING	312d	2
		חשך	WITHHOLD	362b	1 b
		נפש	SOUL	659c	1 d
		עבר	PASS OVER	718c	6 c
		שחת	PIT	1001c	1
		שלח	MISSLE	1019c	1
33	19	יכח	BE CHASTENED	407a	
		איתן	ENDURING	450d	2
		מכאוב	PAIN	456b	1
		רב	MULTITUDE	914a	1
		ריב	STRIFE	936d	1
33	20	תאוה	DESIRE	16c	1
		מאכל	FOOD	38b	
		זהם	BE FOUL	263d	1
		חיה	LIVING THING	312d	1
33	21	בשר	FLESH	142c	1 b
		כלה	BE FINISHED	477d	2 b
		מן	FROM	583c	7 bb
		ראה	TO SEE	908c	1
		ראי	LOOKING	909b	2
		שפה	SWEEP BARE	1045d	
		שפי	BARENESS	1046a	1
33	22	חיה	LIVING THING	312d	2
		מות	DIE	560b	1 d
		נפש	SOUL	659c	1 d
		קרב	COME NEAR	897c	1 f
		שחת	PIT	1001c	2
33	23	ישר	STRAIGHTNESS	449c	3
		מלאך	MESSENGER	521c	1 d
		ליץ	SCORN	539c	2
		על	UPON	758a	2 8
33	24	חנן	SHOW FAVOR	336a	2 b
		ירד	GO DOWN	433b	1 i
		כפר	RANSOM	497b	1
		מצא	FIND	592d	1 a
		פדע	DELIVER	804c	
		שחת	PIT	1001c	2
33	25	בשר	FLESH	142c	1 b
		נער	YOUTH	655a	
		עלומים	YOUTH	761c	
		רטפש	GROW FRESH	936b	
		שוב	TURN BACK	997c	5 d
33	26	אנוש	MAN	60d	3
		עתר	PRAY	801c	
		פנה	FACE	816a	1 2b
		צדקה	RIGHTEOUSNESS	842b	1
		תרועה	SHOUT OF WAR	930a	3
		רצה	BE PLEASED WITH	953a	1 a
		שוב	TURN BACK	999d	1 d
33	27	חטא	MISS 0A GOAL OR WAY0	307a	2 b
		ישר	STRAIGHT	449c	3 c1
		עוה	BEND	730c	
		עוה	COMMIT INIQUITY	731c	
		על	UPON	757c	2 7c b
		שוה	AGREE WITH	1000d	1
		שור	BEHOLD	1003d	3
		שיר	SING	1010d	
33	28	חיה	LIVING THING	312d	2
		מי	WHO	566b	B
		נפש	SOUL	659c	1 d
		עבר	PASS OVER	718a	5 e
		פדה	RANSOM	804a	3 d
		ראה	TO SEE	908a	8 a5
		שחת	PIT	1001c	2
33	29	הן	BEHOLD	243b	
		עם	WITH	767d	1 d
		פעל	DO	821b	1 a
		פעם	OCCURRENCE	822a	3 a
33	30	אור	BECOME LIGHT	21b	
		אור	LIGHT	21c	7
		חי	ALIVE	312a	1 b
		נפש	SOUL	659c	1 d
		שוב	TURN BACK	999b	1 g
		שחת	PIT	1001c	2
33	31	חרש	BE SILENT	361b	1 a
33	32	חפץ	DELIGHT IN	342d	1 b
		מלה	SPEECH	576c	
		צדק	BE JUST	842d	3
		שוב	TURN BACK	999c	3
33	33	אין	NOT	34c	2 dd
		אלף	TEACH	48c	
		חכמה	WISDOM	315d	5 c
		חרש	BE SILENT	361b	1 a
34	1	אליהו	ELIHU	45b	A
34	2	אזן	HEAR	24c	1
		חכם	WISE	315a	6 b2
		מלה	WORD	576b	
34	3	אזן	EAR	24a	2 a
		בחן	TRY	103c	2 d
		חך	PALATE	335b	C
		טעם	TASTE	381a	1
		מלה	WORD	576b	
34	4	בחר	CHOOSE	104a	3 b
		טוב	PLEASANT	374d	0
		מה	WHAT	552d	1 b
		משפט	JUDGEMNT	1048d	2 b
34	5	צדק	BE JUST	842c	1
		משפט	JUDGEMNT	1049a	5
34	6	אנש	BE SICK	60c	
		בלי	WEARING OUT	115c	2 b
		חץ	ARROW	*346c	2
34	7	כזב	LIE	469c	1
		על	UPON	754d	2 l ff
		פשע	TRANSGRESSION	833d	4
		לעג	MOCKING	541d	1 a
		שתה	DRINK	1059c	1 g
34	8	און	TROUBLE	20a	3
		ארח	WANDER	72d	1
		הלך	WALK	234d	2 3b
		חברה	ASSOCIATION	288d	
		ל	TO	518b	7 bh
		פעל	DO	821b	1 b
		רשע	WICKEDNESS	957d	3
34	9	אלהים	GOD	44b	4 a
		סכן	BE OF USE	698b	2
		עם	WITH	767d	1 d
		רצה	BE PLEASED WITH	953b	1 b
34	10	חלילה	FAR BE IT	321a	
		לבב	HEART	523c	2 3a
		עול	INJUSTICE	732c	
		רשע	WICKEDNESS	957d	3
34	11	ארח	WAY	73b	3
		מצא	FIND	594b	1
		פעל	DOING	821c	1 c
		שלם	BE COMPLETE	1022c	5
34	12	אמנם	VERILY	54a	
		עות	BE BENT	736c	1 a
		רשע	BE WICKED	957d	3
		משפט	JUDGEMNT	1048d	2 a
34	13	תבל	WORLD	385d	
		כל	ALL	481d	1 da
		על	UPON	753b	2 1c
		פקד	ATTEND TO	823c	B 2
		שום	TO PLACE	964b	4 b
34	14	אסף	GATHER	62c	4
		לב	HEART	524d	2 3c
		נשמה	BREATH	675d	2
		רוח	BREATH	925c	4 d
		שום	TO PLACE	963c	2 b
34	15	בשר	FLESH	142d	6 a
		גוע	EXPIRE	157c	
		יחד	ALTOGETHER	*403b	2 b
		על	UPON	757c	2 7c ab
		עפר	DRY EARTH	779d	1 b
		רוח	BREATH	*925c	4 d
		שוב	TURN BACK	997c	4 a
34	16	אזן	HEAR	24c	1
		אם	IF	50b	1 b3
		בינה	UNDERSTANDING	108a	3
		מלה	WORD	576b	
34	17	אם	IF	50d	2 ab b
		אף	ALSO	65a	1
		חבש	BIND	290a	1 d
		כביר	GREAT	460c	
		צדיק	JUST	843a	1 d
		רשע	BE WICKED	957d	3
		שנא	HATE	971d	3
		משפט	JUDGEMNT	1048d	2 b
34	18	בליעל	WORTHLESSNESS	116b	1
		נדיב	NOBLE	622a	2
		רשע	WICKED	957c	3
		דל	WEAK	195d	1
34	19	נכר	REGARD	648a	
		נשא	LIFT	670c	1 b 3
		מעשה	DEED	796b	2 b
		פנה	FACE	817c	2 4c c
		שר	CHIEFTAIN	978d	7
34	20	אביר	MIGHTY	7d	2
		געש	SHAKE	172b	
		חצות	DIVISION	345c	
		לא	NOT	518d	1 ac
		לילה	NIGHT	538d	1
		סור	TURN ASIDE	694b	1
		עבר	PASS OVER	718b	6 c
		רגע	A MOMENT	921a	BB
		רגע	A MOMENT	921a	BA B
34	21	על	UPON	757d	2 7c d
		צעד	STEP	857d	2
34	22	און	TROUBLE	20a	3
		חשך	DARKNESS	365a	2
		סתר	HIDE	711b	1
		פעל	DO	821b	1 b
		צלמות	DEATH-SHADOW	853c	1
34	23	הלך	WALK	231a	1 d3 ga
		עוד	STILL	729a	1 ab
		שום	TO PLACE	963d	3 b
		משפט	JUDGMENT	1048c	1 c
34	24	חקר	SEARCHING	350d	
		כביר	GREAT	460c	
		לא	NOT	519d	2 e
		רעע	BREAK	949c	1
		דכא	CRUSH	194a	
34	25	הפך	TURN	245c	1 b
		כן	SO	487a	3 db
		לילה	NIGHT	538d	1
		נכר	REGARD	648a	1
		מעבד	WORK	716a	
		מעבד	WORK	*1105a	
34	26	ספק	SLAP	706d	2
		ראה	TO SEE	907a	1 b
		תחת	INSTEAD	1065d	2 2b a
34	27	אשר	THAT	83c	8 c
		דרך	WAY	204a	6 ec
		כי־עלכן	FOR THEREFORE	475d	
		שכל	BE PRUDENT	968b	2
34	28	בוא	COME	99c	2
		דל	WEAK	195d	
		עני	POOR	776d	2
		צעקה	CRY	858d	2
		צעקה	CRY	858d	2
34	29	גוי	NATION	156c	1
		ו	AND	253a	1 h
		יחד	TOGETHER	403b	2 c
		מי	WHO	567a	F c
		סתר	HIDE	711d	2 a
		רשע	BE WICKED	957d	2
		שקט	BE QUIET	1053b	2
34	30	חנף	PROFANE	338b	
		מוקש	BAIT	430d	
		מן	FROM	583b	7 ba
		מן	FROM	583c	7 bb
34	31	אמר	SAY	56d	
		ה	INTERROG PART	210a	1 b
		חבל	ACT CORRUPTLY	287b	
		נשא	LIFT	671d	2 d
34	32	בלעדי	APART FROM	116b	A
		חזה	SEE	302c	3 a
		יסף	DO AGAIN	415c	2 a
		ירה	DIRECT	435c	5 c
		ד	LIKE	*455a	A
		עול	INJUSTICE	732c	
		פעל	DO	821b	1 b
34	33	בחר	CHOOSE	104b	5 b
		מאס	REJECT	549c	2
		מה	WHAT	552d	1 b
		מן	OUT OF	579d	2 d
		מעם	FROM WITH	769b	D
34	34	חכם	WISE	315a	6 a
		לבב	HEART	523c	2 3a
34	35	דעת	WISDOM	395d	2
		שכל	BE PRUDENT	968b	3
34	36	און	TROUBLE	20a	3
		ב	IN	89a	1 7d
		בחן	TRY	103c	
		ביו	ENTREAT	106b	1
		נצח	ENDURING	664b	3
		תשובה	RETURN	1000c	3
34	37	אמר	WORD	57a	1
		בין	INTERVAL	107b	1
		חטאת	SIN	308d	1 b
		יסף	ADD	415a	1
		כבר	MAKE MANY	*460b	
		ל	TO	511a	1 d
		ספק	SLAP	706c	1
		פשע	TRANSGRESSION	833c	3 a
		רבה	BECOME MANY	*915c	1 c
		רבה	BECOME MANY	916a	2
35	1	אליהו	ELIHU	45b	A
35	2	חשב	THINK	363a	1 1
		צדק	RIGHTEOUSNESS	841d	5
35	3	חטאת	SIN	308d	1 b
		יעל	PROFIT	418d	
		סכן	BE OF USE	698b	2
35	4	מלה	SPEECH	576c	
		שוב	TURN BACK	999c	3
35	5	גבה	BE HIGH	147a	1
		נבט	LOOK	613c	1
		שחק	DUST	1007a	2
		שמי	HEAVENS	1030a	1 b
35	6	חטא	MISS A GOAL OR WAY	306d	2 b
		פעל	DO	821b	1 b
		פשע	TRANSGRESSION	833c	3 a
		רבב	BECOME MUCH	912d	1
35	7	צדק	BE JUST	842d	4

Ch	v.	Heb	Eng	Page	Sec
35	8	רשע	WICKEDNESS	957d	3
35	9	זעק	CRY	277c	2
		זרוע	ARM	284b	2 a
		עשוקים	OPPRESSION	799a	
		שוע	CRY OUT	1002d	
35	10	איה	WHERE	32c	
		זמיר	SONG	274b	
		לילה	NIGHT	538d	1
		לילה	NIGHT	539b	2
		עשה	DO	794c	2 1b
35	11	אלף	TEACH	48c	
		חכם	BE WISE	314c	
35	12	גאון	EXALTATION	145a	2
		צעק	CRY	858c	2
		רע	EVIL	948c	0 b
35	13	שוא	EMPTINESS	996b	2
		שוא	EMPTINESS	996b	1
		שור	BEHOLD	1003d	2
35	14	אף	ALSO	65b	3
		דין	JUDGMENT	192c	2
		חול	WHIRL	297c	3
		שור	BEHOLD	1003d	1
35	15	אין	NOT	34c	2 f
		פקד	ATTEND TO	823c	A 2
		פש	FOLLY	832d	
		פשע	TRANSGRESSION	833d	3 d
35	16	בלי	WEARING OUT	115d	A
		הבל	VAPOUR	211a	2
		דעת	WISDOM	395d	2 a
		כבר	MAKE MANY	460b	
		מלה	SPEECH	576c	
		פצה	PART	822c	1 b
36	1	אליהו	ELIHU	45b	A
		יסף	DO AGAIN	415c	2 b
36	2	זעיר	A LITTLE	277d	2
		חוה	TELL	296a	
		כתר	SURROUND	509c	
		מלה	WORD	576b	
36	3	דע	OPINION	395b	2
		מן	FROM	583d	9 b1
		נתן	GIVE	679a	1 h
		פעל	DO	821c	2 a
		צדק	RIGHTEOUSNESS	841d	E
		רחק	DISTANT	935c	2 a5
36	4	אמנם	VERILY	54a	
		דעה	KNOWLEDGE	395c	
		מלה	WORD	576b	
		שקר	DECEPTION	1055d	5
		תמים	COMPLETE	1071a	1
36	5	הן	BEHOLD	243b	
		כביר	GREAT	460c	
		כח	STRENGTH	471a	3
		לב	HEART	524d	2 3a
		מאס	REJECT	549c	2
36	6	חיה	LIVE	311c	1
		עני	POOR	776d	2
		רשע	WICKED	957c	3
		משפט	JUDGEMNT	1049a	5
36	7	גבה	BE EXALTED	147a	2
		גרע	WITHDRAW	175c	3
		ישב	CAUSE TO SIT	443c	1
		כסא	THRONE	491a	3 a
		ל	TO	511c	1 gb
		נצח	EVERLASTINGNESS	664b	4
		צדיק	JUST	843a	2
36	8	אסר	TIE	63d	3
		זק	FETTER	279b	
		חבל	CORD	286c	1
		לכד	CAPTURE	540b	2
		עני	AFFLICTION	777a	1
36	9	גבר	BE STRONG	149d	
		פעל	DOING	821c	1 c
		פשע	TRANSGRESSION	833c	3 c
36	10	אזן	EAR	24b	3
		אמר	SAY	56c	4
		מוסר	DISCIPLINE	416c	1 a
		כי	THAT	471d	1 a
36	11	בלה	BECOME OLD AND WORN OUT	*115b	B
		טוב	A GOOD THING	375a	1
		כלה	FINISH	478b	1 b
		נעים	DELIGHTFUL	653d	1
		שנה	YEAR	1040b	
36	12	בלי	WEARING OUT	115d	A
		גוע	EXPIRE	157c	
		דעת	WISDOM	395d	2 a
		עבר	PASS OVER	718b	6 c
		שלח	MISSLE	1019c	1
36	13	אסר	TIE	63d	1
		חנף	PROFANE	338b	
		לב	HEART	525b	2 6b
		שום	TO PLACE	963b	1 b
		שוע	CRY OUT	1002d	
36	14	ב	IN	89a	17 d
		חיה	LIVING THING	312d	2
		נער	YOUTH	655a	
		קדש	TEMPLE-PROSTI-TUTE	873d	
36	15	אזן	EAR	24b	3
		חלץ	DRAW OFF OR OUT	322d	2
		לחץ	OPPRESSION	537d	
		עני	POOR	776d	1
		עני	AFFLICTION	777a	1
36	16	דשן	FATNESS	206c	1
		נהר	STREAM	625d	2
			SOOTHING	629b	

Ch	v.	Heb	Eng	Page	Sec
		נחת	QUIETNESS	629b	1
		סות	INCITE	694d	1 b
		מוצק	CONSTRAINT	848a	
		צר	STRAITS	865a	
		רחב	BREADTH	931d	
		שלחן	TABLE	1020b	2
		תחת	UNDERNEATH	1065c	2 1a
36	17	דין	JUDGMENT	192c	3
		דין	JUDGMENT	192d	3
		מלא	BE FULL	570b	1 b
		רשע	WICKED	957c	3
		משפט	JUDGMENT	1048c	1 f
36	18	חמר	GRASP	1069d	1
		חמה	RAGE	404d	2 c
		כפר	RANSOM	497b	2
		נטה	INCLINE	640d	3 c
		סות	INCITE	694d	1 b
		שפק	HANDCLAPPING	706d	
		פן	LEST	814d	1 b
36	19	מאמץ	POWER	55c	
		שוע	OPULENCE	447d	2
		כח	STRENGTH	470d	1 d
		ערך	ARRANGE	789d	1 g
		צר	STRAITS	865a	
36	20	שוע	CRY FOR HELP	1002d	
		לילה	NIGHT	538d	1
		לילה	NIGHT	539b	2
		עלה	GO UP	749c	2 c
		שאא	GASP	983c	1
		תחת	UNDERNEATH	1065d	2 ia
36	21	בחר	CHOOSE	104b	6
		מן	THAN	582c	6 a
		עני	AFFLICTION	777a	1
		פנה	TURN	815b	1 a
		שמר	KEEP	1037b	1
36	22	הן	BEHOLD	243b	
		מורה	TEACHER	435d	
		כח	STRENGTH	470d	3
36	23	שגב	BE HIGH	960d	
		דרך	WAY	204a	6 eb
		עולה	INJUSTICE	732c	1
		פעל	DO	821b	1 b
		פקד	ATTEND TO	823c	B 2
36	24	אנוש	MAN	60d	3
		זכר	REMEMBER	270a	1 5
		כי	THAT	471d	1 a
		פעל	DOING	821c	1 a
		שגא	GROW GREAT	960c	2
		שיר	SING	1010d	
36	25	אנוש	MAN	60d	3
		חזה	SEE	302b	1 c
		נבט	LOOK	613d	1
		רחק	DISTANT	935c	2 a1
36	26	הן	BEHOLD	243b	
		ו	AND	255a	5 cg
		חקר	SEARCHING	350d	
		לא	NOT	519b	1 bb
		שגיא	GREAT	960c	
36	27	אד	MIST	15d	
		גרע	WITHDRAW	175d	
		זקק	REFINE	279b	
		מטר	RAIN	564d	
		נטף	DROP	643a	1
		אד	ADDENDA ET COR-RIGENDA	1119d	
		זקק	ADDENDA ET COR-RIGENDA	1123a	
36	28	נזל	FLOW	633d	1
		רעף	TRICKLE	950a	1
		שחק	DUST	1007a	2
36	29	בין	DISCERN	106d	2 b
		סכה	THICKET	697d	2
		עב	DARK CLOUD	728a	1 f
		מפרש	SWAYING	814a	
		מפרש	SPREADING OUT	831c	
		תשאה	NOISE	996c	
36	30	הן	BEHOLD	243b	
		כסה	COVER	492a	5
		פרש	SPREAD OUT	831b	1
		שרש	ROOT	1057d	3
		אד	ADDENDA ET COR-RIGENDA	1119d	
36	31	אכל	FOOD	38a	
		דין	JUDGE	192b	4
		כבר	MAKE MANY	460b	
		ל	TO	516c	5 jb
36	32	אור	LIGHT	21c	5
		ב	IN	89a	17 b
		כסה	COVER	492a	6
		כף	HOLLOW OF THE HAND	496c	1 b
		פגע	MEET	803c	4
		צוה	LAY CHARGE UPON	845c	1 a
36	33	עולה	INJUSTICE	732d	3
		עלה	GO UP	749a	0
		מקנה	CATTLE	889b	2
		רע	ROAR	929d	
37	1	חרד	TREMBLE	353c	2
		ל	TO	515a	5 g
		נתר	SPRING	684a	
		מקום	STANDING PLACE	879d	2 a
37	2	הגה	A RUMBLING	211d	2
		יצא	GO OUT	423c	1 g
		רגז	AGITATION	919c	

Ch	v.	Heb	Eng	Page	Sec
		שמע	HEAR	1033c	1 a
37	3	אור	LIGHT	21c	5
		ישר	DIRECT	448d	2
		כנף	EXTREMITY	489d	2 b
		שרה	LET LOOSE	1056a	
37	4	גאון	EXALTATION	145a	1 b
		עקב	FOLLOW AT THE HEEL	784c	
		קול	VOICE	877a	2 b
		רעם	THUNDER	947b	
		שאג	ROAR	980d	1
		תחת	UNDERNEATH	1065b	2 1
37	5	גדול	GREAT	153c	9
		פלא	BE SURPASSING	810d	3 a
		רעם	THUNDER	947b	
37	6	גשם	RAIN	177c	
		הוא	FALL	217a	
		מטר	RAIN	564d	
		עז	STRENGTH	739a	1
		שלג	SNOW	1017a	
37	7	חתם	SEAL	367d	1
		חתם	SEAL	368a	1
		מעשה	DEED	796b	2 b
37	8	ארב	LAIR	70c	2
		במו	IN	91b	
		חיה	LIVING THING	312c	1 b
		מענה	DEN	733b	1
		שכן	SETTLE DOWN	1015a	1 b
37	9	זרה	SCATTER	280a	1
		חדר	CHAMBER	293d	
		סופה	STORM-WIND	693a	
		קרה	COLD	903b	
37	10	ב	IN	88d	17a
		נשמה	BREATH	675d	1
		נתן	GIVE	680a	1 z
		נתן	GIVE	680a	1 z
		מוצק	CONSTRAINT	848a	1 z
		קרח	ICE	901c	2
		רחב	WIDTH	931d	
37	11	אור	LIGHT	21c	5
		טרח	TOIL	382b	
		ענן	CLOUD	778a	1 b
		פוץ	BE DISPERSED	807b	1 b
		רי	MOISTURE	924b	
37	12	ארץ	EARTH	76a	1
		הפך	TURN	246a	1
		תחבלה	DIRECTION	287b	
		תבל	WORLD	385d	
		תבל	WORLD	*385d	
		מסב	THAT WHICH SUR-ROUNDS	687b	1 b
		פעל	DO	821b	1 c
		צוה	CHARGE	846a	5
37	13	חסד	GOODNESS	339a	2 1a
		מצא	FIND	594b	2
		שבט	ROD	987a	1 a
37	14	אזן	HEAR	24c	1
		בין	DISCERN	107a	1 b
		עמד	STAND	764a	2 c
		פלא	BE SURPASSING	810d	3 a
37	15	אור	LIGHT	21c	5
		ידע	KNOW	393c	1 a
		יפע	SHINE	422b	2
		ענן	CLOUD	778a	1 d
		שום	TO PLACE	963b	1 b
37	16	ידע	KNOW	393c	1 a
		דע	KNOWLEDGE	395b	1
		עב	DARK CLOUD	728a	1 f
		מפלאה	WONDROUS WORK	811a	
		מפלש	SWAYING	814a	
		מפרש	SPREADING OUT	831c	
		תמים	COMPLETE	1071a	1
37	17	אשר	PARTICLE OF RE-LATION	82b	3
		בגד	GARMENT	94a	1
		דרום	SOUTH	205a	
		חם	HOT	328d	
37	18	שקט	BE QUIET	1053b	1
		חזק	STRONG	305d	1 e
		יצק	BE POURED	427c	2
		עם	WITH	768a	1 f
		ראי	MIRROR	909b	
		רקע	BEAT	956a	
37	19	שחק	DUST	1007a	2
		חשך	DARKNESS	365b	3 e
		ידע	MAKE KNOWN	395a	
		ערך	ARRANGE	789d	1 f
		פנה	FACE	818c	2 6b b
37	20	בלע	SWALLOW UP	118c	
		כי	THAT	471d	1 a
		ספר	COUNT	708b	
37	21	בהיר	BRIGHT	97c	
		טהר	BE CLEAN	372b	1 a
		עבר	PASS OVER	717d	4 a
		שחק	DUST	1007a	2
37	22	אתה	COME	87c	
		הוד	SPLENDOUR	217a	2
		זהב	GOLD	262c	1
		ירא	CAUSE FEAR	431d	2
		זהב	ADDENDA ET COR-RIGENDA	1122c	
37	23	כח	STRENGTH	471a	3
		מצא	FIND	593a	2 a
		מצא	FIND	*593a	1 a
		ענה	BE BOWED DOWN	776b	4
		צדקה	RIGHTEOUSNESS	842b	2

Ch	v.	Heb	Eng	Page	Sec
37	24	שגיא	GREAT	960c	
		משפט	JUDGEMNT	1048d	2 a
		חכם	WISE	314d	3
		ירא	FEAR	431b	1 b
		לב	HEART	524d	2 3b
		ראה	TO SEE	907c	6 b
38	1	סערה	TEMPEST	704b	
38	2	בלי	WEARING OUT	115c	2 b
		זה	THIS	261b	4 b
		חשך	GROW DARK	365a	3
		דעת	WISDOM	395d	2 a
		עצה	ADVICE	420b	
		מלה	SPEECH	576c	
38	3	אזר	GIRD	25a	
		חלץ	LOINS	323b	2
		ידע	ANSWER	395a	
38	4	איפה	WHERE	33a	1
		ארץ	EARTH	76a	1 b
		בינה	UNDERSTANDING	108a	3
		יסד	FOUND	413d	
38	5	כי	BECAUSE	473d	3 b
		ממד	MEASUREMENT	551d	
		מי	WHO	567a	F c
		נטה	STRETCH OUT	640a	1 b
		קו	LINE	876a	
		שום	TO PLACE	964a	3 f
38	6	אדן	STONE	6c	2
		אדן	BASE	10d	2
		טבע	SINK	371c	
		ירה	CAST	435a	2
		מה	HOW	554b	4 f
		מי	WHO	567a	F c
38	7	אלהים	GOD	43b	1 b
		אלהים	GOD	43b	1 c
		בן	SON	120b	1 d
		בקר	MORNING	133d	1 b
		יחד	UNION	403a	2 a1
		כוכב	STAR	457a	
		רוע	RAISE A SHOUT	929d	4
		רנן	GIVE A RINGING CRY	943b	1
38	8	דלת	DOOR	195b	4
		יצא	GO OUT	423c	1 h
		סוך	HEDGE	692a	
		רחם	WOMB	933b	1
38	9	חתלה	SWADDLING-BAND	367c	
		לבוש	CLOTHING	528c	
		ענן	CLOUD	778a	1 d
		ערפל	CLOUD	791d	
		פנה	CORNER	819c	1 a
38	10	בריח	BAR	138b	2
		דלת	DOOR	195b	4
		חק	SOMETHING PRE-SCRIBED	349c	5
		על	UPON	753b	2 1c
		שום	TO PLACE	964b	4 b
		שבר	BREAK	990d	
		שית	PUT	1011b	2 c
38	11	גאון	EXALTATION	145a	1 c
		יסף	DO AGAIN	415c	2 a
		פה	HERE	806a	1 b
		שית	PUT	1011b	2 c
38	12	בקר	MORNING	133d	1 b
		ה	INTERROG PART	209b	1 b
		ידע	CAUSE TO KNOW	394d	
		יום	DAY	399b	4 a
		מן	FROM	581c	4 a
		צוה	CHARGE	846a	4 d
		מקום	STANDING PLACE	879d	1 a
		שחר	DAWN	1007b	
38	13	אחז	GRASP	28b	
		כנף	EXTREMITY	489d	2 b
		נער	SHAKE OUT	654c	
38	14	הפך	TURN	246a	2
		חתם	SEAL	368b	
		יצב	STATION ONESELF	426b	B
		לבוש	CLOTHING	528c	
38	15	אור	LIGHT	21c	4
		זרוע	ARM	284a	1 b
		מנע	WITHHOLD	586b	
		רום	BE HIGH	926d	2 b
		שבר	BREAK	990d	
38	16	ה	INTERROG PART	209d	1 b
		הלך	WALK	235d	1 b
		חקר	SEARCHING	350d	
		מחקר	RANGE	*350d	
		נבך	SPRING	614a	
		תהום	DEEP	1062d	
38	17	ה	INTERROG PART	209d	1 b
		מות	DEATH	560d	3
		צלמות	DEATH-SHADOW	853c	3
		שער	GATE	1045b	4
		שער	GATE	1045b	4
38	18	בין	DISCERN	107b	1 e
		עד	AS FAR AS	724a	1 1a
		רחב	BREADTH	931d	
38	19	אור	LIGHT	21c	1
		אי	WHERE	32b	1 b
		דרך	WAY	203a	1
		זה	THIS	261b	4 a
		חשך	DARKNESS	365a	1
		מקום	STANDING PLACE	879d	1 a
		שכן	SETTLE DOWN	1015b	2 d
38	20	בין	DISCERN	106d	2 a
		בית	HOUSE	109c	1 e
		גבול	BOUNDARY	148a	2 e
		נתיבה	PATH	677b	1
38	21	ילד	BE BORN	408d	
38	22	אוצר	TREASURE	70a	3 d
		ה	INTERROG PART	209d	1 b
		שלג	SNOW	1017a	
38	23	חשך	WITHHOLD	362b	1 f
		יום	DAY	401a	7 i
		צר	STRAITS	865a	
		קרב	BATTLE	898b	
38	24	אי	WHERE	32b	1 b
		דרך	WAY	203a	1
		חלק	DIVIDE	323c	
		חלק	DIVIDE	323d	2 c
		פוץ	BE DISPERSED	807b	2
		קדים	EAST WIND	870a	2
38	25	דרך	WAY	203a	1
		חזיז	THUNDER-BOLT	304a	
		מי	WHO	567a	F c
		תעלה	WATER-COURSE	752b	A
		פלג	SPLIT	811b	1
		פלג	CHANNEL	*811b	
		קול	VOICE	877b	2 b
		שטף	FLOOD	1009b	
38	26	מדבר	WILDERNESS	184d	2
		לא	NOT	519b	1 bb
		לא	NOT	519d	2 e
		מטר	RAIN	565a	
		שואה	DEVASTATION	996c	2
38	27	דשא	GRASS	206a	
		מוצא	GOING FORTH	425d	3 d
		צמח	SPROUT	855c	1
		שבע	SATISFIED	959d	1 a
		שואה	DEVASTATION	996c	2
		משאה	DESOLATION	996c	1
38	28	אב	FATHER	3d	6
		אגל	DROP	8b	
		ה	INTERROG PART	210b	1 d
		טל	NIGHT-MIST	378c	
		ילד	BEGET	409a	1
		יש	HAVE	441d	2 cb
		מטר	RAIN	564d	
38	29	בטן	WOMB	106a	3
		ילד	BEAR	408c	1 c
		יצא	GO OUT	423c	1 h
		כפור	HOARFROST	499b	
		מי	WHO	567a	F c
		קרח	ICE	901c	2
38	30	אבן	STONE	7a	8
		חבא	WITHDRAW	285b	2
		לכד	CAPTURE	540b	
		פנה	FACE	816b	15
		תהום	SEA	1063a	2
38	31	ה	INTERROG PART	210b	1 d
		כימה	PLEIADES	465c	2
		כסיל	ORION	493a	
		מעדנות	BONDS	588d	2
		משכת	CORD	605d	
		מעדנות	BONDS	772c	
		פתח	OPEN	835c	2
		קשר	BIND	905c	2
38	32	בן	SON	121b	6
		יצא	BRING OUT	425a	4 h
		מזלות	CONSTELLATIONS	561b	2
		מזרות	A PARTICULAR STAR	561d	
		נחה	LEAD	635a	
		עיש	GREAT BEAR	747b	2
		על	UPON	755c	2 4c
38	33	חקה	SOMETHING PRE-SCRIBED	350a	2 a
		שום	TO PLACE	964a	3 f
		משטר	RULE	1009c	
38	34	כסה	COVER	491d	5
		רום	BE HIGH	927c	1 b
		שפעה	ABUNDANCE	1051d	
38	35	ברק	LIGHTNING	140c	1
		הלך	WALK	232c	13
		הלך	WALK	234a	15d
		הנה	BEHOLD	243d	
		הנה	BEHOLD	244a	A
38	36	בינה	UNDERSTANDING	108a	3
		חכמה	WISDOM	315c	5 a
		טחות	INWARD PARTS	376c	
		שכוי	APPEARANCE	967c	
		שית	PUT	1011a	1
38	37	חכמה	WISDOM	315c	5 a
		מי	WHO	567a	F c
		נבל	SKIN-BOTTLE	614b	1
		ספר	COUNT	707d	2
		ספר	COUNT	708b	3
		שחק	DUST	1007a	2
		שכב	LIE DOWN	1012c	
38	38	דבק	CLING	180a	1
		יצק	POUR	427b	4
		מוצק	CASTING	427c	
		עפר	DRY EARTH	779d	1 a
		רגב	CLOD OF EARTH	918d	
38	39	חיה	LIVING THING	312d	3
		טרף	PREY	383c	1
		כפיר	LION	498d	
		לביא	LION	522d	
		מלא	FILL	570d	2
		צוד	HUNT	844c	
38	40	ארב	LYING-IN-WAIT	70c	1
		למו	TO	518b	
		למו	FOR	530c	
		סכה	THICKET	697c	1
		מענה	DEN	733a	1
38	41	שחח	BOW	1005d	4
		אכל	FOOD	38a	
		בלי	WEARING OUT	115c	B
		ילד	CHILD	409b	A
		כון	ESTABLISH	466c	2 b
		ערב	RAVEN	788b	
		ציד	PROVISION	845b	
		שוע	CRY OUT	1002d	
		תעה	ERR	1073b	1
39	1	אילה	HIND	19b	
		חיל	WHIRL	297b	2
		ילד	BEAR	408b	1 a
		יעל	MOUNTAIN-GOAT	418d	
		עת	TIME	773c	2 a
		שמר	KEEP	1036d	1 d
39	2	ילד	BEAR	408b	1 a
		ירח	MONTH	437b	1
		מלא	FILL	570d	3
		עת	TIME	773c	2 a
39	3	חבל	PAIN	286d	1 a
		ילד	CHILD	409b	A
		כרע	BOW DOWN	502c	4
		פלח	CLEAVE	812a	2
		שלח	SEND	1019b	7
39	4	בן	SON	121b	4
		בר	FIELD	141b	
		חלם	BE HEALTHY	321b	
		ל	TO	516a	5 ib
		רבה	BECOME MANY	915b	2 b1
		שוב	TURN BACK	997b	3 b
39	5	מוסר	BAND	64c	
		מי	WHO	567a	F c
		ערוד	WILD ASS	789b	
		פרא	WILD ASS	825b	
		פתח	OPEN	835c	2
39	6	בית	HOUSE	109b	1 b
		מלחה	SALTNESS	572a	
		ערבה	DESERT-PLAIN	787c	5
		משכן	DWELLING-PLACE	1016a	3 a
39	7	המון	SOUND	242c	1
		נגש	DRIVE	620c	3
		קריה	TOWN	900b	4
		שחק	LAUGH	965d	1 a
		תשאה	NOISE	996c	
39	8	דרש	SEEK	205c	4 a
		הר	MOUNTAIN	250c	1 h
		ירוק	GREEN THING	438d	
		מרעה	PASTURAGE	945c	
		מרעה	PASTURAGE	945c	
		תור	SPY OUT	1064c	2
		יתור	SEARCHING	1064c	
39	9	אבה	BE WILLING	2c	
		אבוס	CRIB	7b	
		לון	LODGE	533c	1 b
		עבד	WORK	713a	2
		על	UPON	756a	2 6b
39	10	ראם	WILD OX	910b	
		עבת	CORD	721c	1 a
		עמק	VALE	771a	
		קשר	BIND	905b	1 a
		ראם	WILD OX	910b	
		שדד	HARROW	961a	
		תלם	FURROW	1068d	
39	11	בטח	TRUST	105a	1 3c
		יגיע	TOIL	388c	1
		כח	STRENGTH	471a	4
		עזב	LEAVE	737b	1 h
39	12	אמן	CONFIRM	53b	2 c
		אסף	GATHER	62b	1 c
		גרן	THRESHING-FLOOR	175b	
		זרע	SOWING	282b	2 d
		שוב	TURN BACK	997b	3 b
		שוב	TURN BACK	999a	1 a
39	13	אברה	PINION	7c	
		חסד	KIND	339c	1 b
		כי	BECAUSE	*474b	3 c
		כנף	WING	489c	1 a
		נצה	PLUMAGE	663b	
		עלס	REJOICE	763a	
		רננים	PIERCING CRY	943d	1
39	14	ביצה	EGG	101b	1
		חמם	BE OR BECOME WARM	328d	
		כי	BECAUSE	474b	3 c
		עזב	LEAVE	737b	1 i
		עפר	DRY EARTH	779d	1 a
39	15	דוש	TREAD	190c	
		זור	PRESS DOWN AND OUT	267a	
		חיה	LIVING THING	312c	1 b
		כי	THAT	471d	1 a
		רגל	FOOT	919d	1 d
		שבח	FORGET	1013a	1 a
39	16	בלי	WEARING OUT	115c	2 b
		בן	SON	121b	4
		יגיע	TOIL	388c	1
		ל	TO	512c	4 a
		ל	TO	513d	5 cb d
		לא	NOT	519d	2 d
		לא	NOT	520c	4 e
		קשח	TO TREAT HARDLY	905a	1
		ריק	EMPTINESS	938b	
39	17	ב	IN	88c	1 2b
		בינה	UNDERSTANDING	108a	3

Ch v.	Heb	Eng	Page	Sec
	ה	THE	208c	1 hb
	חכמה	WISDOM	315c	3
	חלק	DIVIDE	323c	3
39 18	נשה	FORGET	674d	
	מרא	BEAT	597a	
	מרום	HEIGHT	928d	1
	רכב	RIDE	938d	3
	שחק	LAUGH	965d	1 a
39 19	גבורה	STRENGTH	150b	1
	לבש	CLOTHE	528b	1 b
	סוס	HORSE	692d	2
	צואר	NECK	848c	2
	רעמה	VIBRATION	947c	
39 20	אימה	TERROR	34a	
	הוד	MAJESTY	217b	4
	נחר	A SNORTING	637d	
	ארבה	LOCUST	916a	
	רעש	SHAKE	950b	2
39 21	חפר	DIG	343c	1 a
	כח	STRENGTH	471a	4
	נשק	EQUIPMENT	676d	1
	עמק	VALE	771a	
	שוש	REJOICE	965b	
39 22	חתת	BE SHATTERED	369d	2 a
	שחק	LAUGH	965d	1 a
	שוב	TURN BACK	996d	1
39 23	אשפה	QUIVER	80c	
	חנית	SPEAR	334a	2 b
	כידון	JAVELIN	475d	
	להב	BLADE	529a	2
	רנה	RATTLE	943a	1
39 24	אמן	CONFIRM	53a	1
	מגמא	SWALLOW	170a	
	רגז	AGITATION	919c	
	רעש	SHAKING	950c	1
	רעש	ADDENDA ET CORRIGENDA	1126d	
39 25	אמר	SAY	55d	1
	די	SUFFICIENCY	1 191c	2 ab
	האח	AHA0	210c	
	ריח	SMELL	926b	
	תרועה	SHOUT OF WAR	930a	1
	רחק	DISTANT	935c	2 a1
	רעם	THUNDER	947b	
	שר	CHIEFTAIN	978c	3 a
	שפר	HORN	1051d	
39 26	אבר	FLY	7c	
	בינה	UNDERSTANDING	108a	2
	תימן	SOUTH	412c	1 a
	כנף	WING	489c	1 a
	מן	OUT OF	580a	2 eb
	מן	ON ACCOUNT OF	580c	2 g
	נץ	HAWK	665c	
	פרש	SPREAD OUT	831a	1
39 27	גבה	BE HIGH	147a	1
	כי	THAT	472b	1 da
	נשר	EAGLE	676d	
	נשר	EAGLE	*676d	
	קן	NEST	890a	1
	רום	BE HIGH	927c	1 e
39 28	לון	LODGE	533d	
	סלע	CRAG	701a	1
	מצודה	FASTNESS	845a	
	שכן	SETTLE DOWN	1015a	1 b
	שן	TOOTH	1042a	1 c
39 29	אכל	FOOD	38a	
	חפר	DIG	343d	
	מן	FROM	583d	9 b1
	נבט	LOOK	613c	1 b
	עין	EYE	744b	1 d
	רחק	DISTANT	935c	2 a5
	שם	THERE	1027c	4 a
39 30	אשר	PARTICLE OF RELATION	82c	4 bg
	דם	BLOOD	196c	2 c
	עלע	DRINK	763a	
	אפרח	YOUNG ONE	827b	
	שם	THERE	1027a	1 a
40 2	ה	INTERROG PART	209d	1 b
	יכח	REPROVE	407a	5 b
	יסור	REPROVER	416b	
	ענה	ANSWER	772a	1 a
	ריב	STRIVE	936c	2
40 4	יד	HAND	389c	1 d
	למו	TO	518b	
	למו	FOR	530c	
	פה	MOUTH	804d	1 b
	קלל	BE SLIGHT	886c	3
	שום	TO PLACE	963b	1 b
	שוב	TURN BACK	999c	3
40 5	יסף	DO AGAIN	415c	2 a
	שנה	DO AGAIN	1040d	
	שנים	TWO	1041b	1 b2
40 7	אזר	GIRD	25a	
	חלץ	LOINS	323b	2
	ידע	ANSWER	395a	
40 8	אם	IF	50d	2 ab b
	אף	ALSO	65a	1
	פרר	BREAK	830b	2 a
	צדק	BE JUST	842c	2
	רשע	BE WICKED	957d	2
	משפט	JUDGMENT	1048d	2 a
40 9	זרוע	ARM	284a	1 c
	ד	LIKE	455a	B
	רעם	THUNDER	947b	
	רעם	THUNDER	947b	
40 10	גאון	EXALTATION	145a	1 b
	גבה	HEIGHT	147b	2
	הדר	SPLENDOUR	214b	2
	הוד	SPLENDOUR	217a	2
	לבש	PUT ON	528a	B
	נא	PART OF ENTREATY	609b	1
40 11	עדה	ORNAMENT	725d	1 b
	גאה	PROUD	144b	
	עברה	OVERFLOW	720c	1
	פוץ	BE DISPERSED	807b	1 b
	שפל	BECOME LOW	1050b	1
40 12	גאה	PROUD	144b	
	הדך	CAST DOWN	213b	
	כנע	HUMBLE	488c	1
	תחת	UNDERNEATH	1065d	2 ia
40 13	חבש	BIND	289d	1 a
	טמן	HIDE	380c	1
	טמן	HIDE	380c	3
	יחד	ALTOGETHER	403b	2 b
	עפר	DRY EARTH	780a	2 e
40 14	ידה	PRAISE	392b	1 a1
	ישע	GIVE VICTORY	447a	3 a
40 15	בהמות	HIPPOPOTAMUS	97a	
	בהמות	HIPPOPOTAMUS	*97a	
	בקר	CATTLE	133b	1 a
	חציר	GREEN GRASS	348b	1
	נא	PART OF ENTREATY	609c	4 d
	עם	WITH	768a	1 f
40 16	און	VIGOUR	20b	2
	בטן	BELLY	105d	1 b
	כח	STRENGTH	471a	4
	מתנים	LOINS	608b	2 a
	נא	PART OF ENTREATY	609c	4 d
	שריר	MUSCLE	1057b	
40 17	ארז	CEDAR	72c	1 b
	זנב	TAIL	275c	1 a
	חפץ	DELIGHT IN	343a	2 c
	חפץ	BEND DOWN	343c	
	פחד	THIGH	808c	
40 18	אפיק	CHANNEL	67d	
	ברזל	IRON	137d	3
	גרם	BONE	175a	1
	ממיל	WROUGHT-METAL ROD	564c	
	נחושה	COPPER	639a	2
	נחוש	OF BRONZE	639a	
	עצם	BONE	782d	1
40 19	דרך	WAY	204a	6 ea
	נגש	APPROACH	621b	
	עשה	DO	794b	2 1b
	ראשית	BEGINNING	912b	1 a
40 20	הר	MOUNTAIN	250c	1 h
	חיה	LIVING THING	312d	1 b
	בול	PRODUCE	385b	
	נשא	LIFT	671b	2 g
	שחק	LAUGH	966a	3
40 21	בצה	SWAMP	130c	
	סתר	COVERING	712a	2 a
	צאלים	LOTUS	838a	
	קנה	STALK	889c	2
40 22	נחל	WADY	636c	2
	סבב	SURROUND	685d	2 d
	סכך	OVERSHADOW	697a	1
	ערבה	POPLAR	788b	
	צאלים	LOTUS	838a	
	צל	SHADOW	853b	2
40 23	בטח	TRUST	105b	2
	חן	IF	243d	B
	חפז	BE IN TREPIDATION	342a	2
	ירדן	JORDAN	434c	
	ירדן	JORDAN	434d	
	נהר	STREAM	625d	1
	עשק	OPPRESS	798d	3
	פה	MOUTH	805b	3
40 24	אף	NOSE	60b	1 c
	מוקש	BAIT	430c	
	לקח	TAKE	543d	8
	נקב	PIERCE	666b	1
	עין	EYE	744a	1 d
40 25	חבל	CORD	286c	1
	חכה	HOOK	335d	
	לויתן	LEVIATHAN	531b	
	לשון	TONGUE	546d	3
	משך	DRAW	604b	1
	שקע	SINK	1054b	
40 26	אגמן	BULRUSH	8c	1
	אף	NOSE	60b	1 c
	דוגה	FISHING	186a	
	חוח	BRIER	296b	2 a
	לחי	JAW	534d	1
	נקב	PIERCE	666b	1
	שום	TO PLACE	963a	1 a
40 27	תחנון	SUPPLICATION FOR FAVOR	337c	1
	רבה	BECOME MANY	915c	1 c
	רך	TENDER	940a	3
40 28	ברית	COVENANT	136c	1 3
	כרת	CUT	503d	4
	לקח	TAKE	543a	4 a
	עבד	SLAVE	713d	1
	עבד	SLAVE	714c	7
	עולם	LONG DURATION	762a	2 a
40 29	ב	IN	89d	3 2b
	נערה	GIRL	655b	1
	צפור	BIRD	862a	1
	קשר	BIND	905b	1 a
	שחק	LAUGH	966a	3
40 30	בין	INTERVAL	107b	1
	חבר	ASSOCIATE	289a	
	חצה	DIVIDE	345b	1
	כרה	TRADE	500b	
	על	UPON	756d	2 7a c
	כנעני	ADDENDA ET CORRIGENDA	1124c	
40 31	דג	FISH	185c	
	מלא	FILL	*570c	1
	עור	SKIN	736b	2
	צלצל	SPEAR	852d	
	ראש	HEAD	910d	1 b
	שכה	BARB	968a	
40 32	זכר	REMEMBER	270a	1 5
	יסף	DO AGAIN	415c	2 a
40 40	שום	TO PLACE	963b	1 b
41 1	גם	ALSO	169b	2
	ה	INTERROG PART	210a	1 c
	הן	BEHOLD	243b	
	טול	HURL	376d	1
	תוחלת	HOPE	404b	
	כזב	BE A LIAR	469c	
41 2	בן	SON	121b	6
	הוא	HE, SHE, IT	216c	4 bb
	יצב	STATION ONESELF	426c	D
	אכזר	CRUEL	470a	
	כי	THAT	473a	1 f
	לא	NOT	519b	1 bb
	מי	WHO	567a	F c
	עור	ROUSE ONESELF	735a	
	עור	ROUSE ONESELF	735c	1
	פנה	FACE	817b	2 4b d
	מראה	VISION	909c	1 b
41 3	מי	WHO	566d	F c
	קדם	COME IN FRONT	870a	2
	שלם	BE COMPLETE	1022c	3
	תחת	UNDERNEATH	1065b	2 1
41 4	בד	PART	94d	3 a
	גבורה	STRENGTH	150b	1
	דבר	WORD	182c	1 1i
	חין	GRACE	336d	
	חרש	BE SILENT	361b	1 a
	לא	NOT	520c	
	ערך	ORDER	789d	1
41 5	כפל	DOUBLE	495d	
	לבוש	CLOTHING	528c	
	מי	WHO	567a	F c
	פנה	FACE	816b	1 5
	רסן	JAW	944a	2
41 6	אימה	TERROR	34a	
	דלת	DOOR	195b	4
	מי	WHO	567a	F c
	פתח	OPEN	835c	3
	שן	TOOTH	1042a	1 b
41 7	אפיק	CHANNEL	67d	
	גאה	MAJESTY	144d	2
	מגן	SHIELD	171c	
	חתם	SEAL	368b	
	סגר	CLOSE	689b	3
	צר	NARROW	865a	
41 8	נגש	DRAW NEAR	621a	2
	רוח	BREATH	924d	2 c
41 9	אח	BROTHER	26c	4
	דבק	CLING	180a	1
	לכד	CAPTURE	540b	
	פרד	DIVIDE	825c	
41 10	אור	LIGHT	21c	6
	הלל	SHINE	237d	
	זרר	SNEEZE	284d	
	עפעף	EYELID	734a	
	עטישה	SNEEZING	743a	
	עין	EYE	744b	1 d
	שחר	DAWN	1007b	
41 11	אש	FIRE	77d	6
	הלך	WALK	232c	1 3
	כידוד	SPARK	461d	
	לפיד	TORCH	542b	
	מלט	SLIP AWAY	572d	1
	פה	MOUTH	805b	3
41 12	אגמן	BULRUSH	8c	1
	דוד	POT	188c	A
	ו	AND	253a	1 g
	נחיר	NOSTRIL	638a	
	נפח	BLOW	656a	
	עשן	SMOKE	798c	1 d
41 13	גחלת	COAL	160d	
	להב	FLAME	529a	1
	להט	SET ABLAZE	529b	
	נפש	SOUL	661c	0 b
	פה	MOUTH	805b	3
41 14	דאבה	DISMAY	178b	
	דוץ	DANCE	189b	
	לון	LODGE	533d	2
	עז	STRENGTH	739a	1
	צואר	NECK	848c	2
41 15	בל	NOT	115b	
	בשר	FLESH	142c	1 a
	דבק	CLING	179d	1 a
	יצק	CAST	427b	3
	מוט	SHAKE	557a	
	מפל	HANGING PART	658c	2

Ch	v.	Heb	Eng	Page	Sec
41	16	אבן	STONE	7a	8
		יצק	CAST	427b	3
		לב	HEART	525d	2 0
		פלח	CLEAVAGE	812a	1
		תחתי	LOWER	1066c	
41	17	איל	LEADER	18b	
		אל	GOD	42b	1
		גור	DREAD	159a	1
		חטא	MISS A GOAL OR WAY	307d	1
		מן	OUT OF	580a	2 ec
		שאת	UPRISING	673b	3
		שבר	BREAKING	991b	1
		משבר	BREAKER	991c	
41	18	בלי	WEARING OUT	115c	2 a
		קום	STAND	278b	7 a
		חנית	SPEAR	334a	1
		מסע	DART	652d	
		נשג	REACH	673c	2 a
41	19	שריה	JAVELIN	1056b	
		ברזל	IRON	137c	2
		חשב	THINK	363a	11
		נחושה	COPPER	639a	2
		רקבון	ROTTEN WOOD	955a	
		תבן	STRAW	1062a	
41	20	ברח	FLEE	138a	2
		הפך	TURN	246a	2 c
		קלע	SLING	887c	
		קש	STUBBLE	905d	
		קשת	BOW	906a	1 b
41	21	ה	THE	*207a	1 f
		חשב	THINK	363b	1
		תותח	CLUB	450c	
		כידון	JAVELIN	475d	
		קש	STUBBLE	905d	
		רעש	SHAKING	950c	3
		שחק	LAUGH	965d	1 a
41	22	חדוד	SHARPENED	292c	
		חרוץ	SHARP	358d	1
		חרש	EARTHENWARE	360b	2
		טיט	MUD	376c	1
		רפד	SPREAD	951c	
41	23	סור	POT	696c	1 a
		מצולה	DEPTH	847a	
		מרקחה	OINTMENT-POT	955c	1
		רתח	BOIL	958c	
41	24	אור	BECOME LIGHT	21b	2
		חשב	THINK	363a	11
		נתיב	PATH	677b	
		שיבה	OLD AGE	966d	1
		תהום	SEA	1063a	2
41	25	בלי	WEARING OUT	115d	B
		חת	TERROR	369c	
		משל	LIKENESS	605c	
		עפר	DRY EARTH	779d	1 c
41	26	בן	SON	121d	8 n
		גבה	HIGH	147b	1
		מלך	KING	573b	4
		שחץ	DIGNITY	1006d	
42	2	בצר	MAKE INACCESSIBLE	131a	
		מזמה	PURPOSE	273c	1
		יכל	BE ABLE	407d	1 g
		כל	ALL	482c	2 a
42	3	בין	DISCERN	106d	2 a
		בלי	WEARING OUT	115c	2 b
		זה	THIS	261b	4 b
		דעת	WISDOM	395d	2 a
		עצה	ADVICE	420b	
		כן	SO	487a	3 db
		עלם	CONCEAL	761a	
		פלא	BE SURPASSING	810c	2
42	4	ידע	ANSWER	395a	
42	5	אזן	EAR	23d	2 a
		ל	TO	*516b	5 jb
		שמע	HEAR	1033d	1 d2
		שמע	REPORT	1034d	
42	6	אפר	ASHES	68a	
		מאס	REJECT	549c	2
		נחם	BE SORRY	637a	2
		עפר	DRY EARTH	780a	2 d
42	7	אחר	BESIDES	30a	3
		אליפז	ELIPHAZ	45c	B
		דבר	WORD	183b	3 2
		היה	COME TO PASS	224c	2 a1 ai
		חרה	BURN	354a	2 a
		תימני	TEMANITE	412d	
		כון	BE FIRM	465d	2
		עבד	SLAVE	714a	3
42	8	איל	RAM	18a	2 g
		כון	BE FIRM	465d	2
		כיאם	BUT	475b	2 b
		כיאם	SURELY	475c	2 c
		נבלה	SENSELESSNESS	615b	2
		נשא	LIFT	670c	1 b3
		עבד	SLAVE	714a	3
		עלה	WHOLE BURNT OFFERING	750d	
		על	UPON	754c	2 lf c
		פלל	INTERVENE	813b	1
		פר	YOUNG BULL	830d	2 b
42	9	אליפז	ELIPHAZ	45c	B
		בלדד	BILDAD	115a	
		ו	AND	252a	1
		תימני	TEMANITE	412d	
		נעמתי	NAAMATHITE	564b	

Ch	v.	Heb	Eng	Page	Sec
		נשא	LIFT	670c	1 b 3
		צפר	ZOPHAR	862b	
		שוחי	SHUHITE	1001d	
42	10	יסף	ADD	415b	1
		שבית	CAPTIVITY	986b	2 d
		משנה	DOUBLE	1041c	1
42	11	איש	MAN	36a	
		בוא	COME	99c	2 a
		זהב	GOLD	263a	6
		ידע	KNOW	394a	2
		נוד	SHEW GRIEF	626d	2 b
		נזם	RING	634a	2
		קשיטה	WEIGHT	903d	
42	12	אחרית	END	31a	B
		אלף	THOUSAND	48d	1 a
		אלף	THOUSAND	48d	1 a
		אתון	SHE-ASS	87d	
		בקר	CATTLE	133c	2
		ברך	BLESS	139a	2 a
		צאן	SMALL CATTLE	838b	1 a4
		צאן	SMALL CATTLE	838b	1 b
		צמד	COUPLE	855a	1
		ראשית	BEGINNING	912a	1 a
		ארבע	FOUR	917a	2 a2 a
42	13	בן	SON	120a	1
		שבע	SEVEN	988a	1 b
42	14	ימימה	JEMIMAH	410d	
		קציאה	KAZIAH	893a	
		קרןהפוך	KEREN-HAPPUCH	902b	
42	15	מצא	FIND	394a	1 i
		יפה	BEAUTIFUL	421c	2
		נחלה	INHERITANCE	635c	3
42	16	אחר	AFTER	30a	2 b
		בן	SON	120b	1 f
		דור	GENERATION	190a	2 c
		זה	THIS	260d	1 a
		חיה	LIVE	311a	1 a
		ארבעים	FORTY	917c	2 c
42	17	זקן	OLD	278c	1
		יום	DAY	399b	4 a
		שבע	SATISFIED	960a	1 b

PSALMS

Ch	v.	Heb	Eng	Page	Sec
1	1	ארח	WANDER	72d	1
		אשר	HAPPINESS	81a	
		דרך	WAY	203d	6 d
		הלך	WALK	235a	2 3e 2
		חטא	SINFUL	308b	1
		עצה	ADVICE	420b	
		ישב	SIT	442c	1 a
		מושב	SEAT	444b	1 b
		ליץ	SCORN	539c	
		רשע	WICKED	957c	3
1	2	הגה	MUSE	211d	3 a
		חפץ	DELIGHT	343b	1
		יומם	BY DAY	401c	2
		תורה	LAW	436b	2 b2
		כיאם	BUT	475a	2 b
		לילה	NIGHT	538d	1
1	3	נבל	SINK	615c	2
		נתן	GIVE	679c	1 t
		עלה	LEAF	750a	
		על	UPON	756a	6a
		עת	TIME	773d	2 b
		עץ	TREE	781c	1 a
		פלג	CHANNEL	811b	
		צלח	ADVANCE	852c	1
		צלח	ADVANCE	852c	2
		שתל	TRANSPLANT	1060a	
1	4	אשר	PARTICLE OF RELATION	81d	2
		ה	THE	*208a	1 f
		כיאם	BUT	475a	2 b
		כן	SO	486b	1 cd
		מוץ	CHAFF	558b	
		נדף	DRIVE	623c	
1	5	קום	STAND	278b	7 a
		חטא	SINFUL	308b	2
		עדה	CONGREGATION	417a	1
		כן	SO	487b	3 f
		צדיק	JUST	843b	2
		משפט	JUDGMENT	1048c	1 g
1	6	אבד	PERISH	1d	1
		דרך	WAY	203c	6 c
		דרך	WAY	203d	6 d
		ידע	KNOW	394b	2
		רשע	WICKED	957c	3
2	1	הגה	MUSE	211d	3 b
		לאם	PEOPLE	522c	
		רגש	BE IN TUMULT	921c	
		ריק	EMPTINESS	938b	1
2	2	ה	THE	208d	1 i
		יחד	UNION	403a	2 a2
		יסד	FIX THEMSELVES	414a	1
		יצב	STATION ONESELF	426b	B
		משיח	ANOINTED	603c	1
		רזן	BE WEIGHTY	931b	
2	3	מוסר	CORD	64c	
		בר	SON	*135a	
		נתק	TEAR APART	683d	1
		עבת	CORD	721c	1 a
		שלך	THROW	1021a	1 c
2	4	אדון	LORD	11c	3 2b
		ישב	SIT	442c	1 a

Ch	v.	Heb	Eng	Page	Sec
		ל	TO	510d	1 d
		לעג	MOCK	541b	
		שחק	LAUGH	965d	1 a
		שמי	HEAVENS	1030a	2 a
2	5	אז	THEN	23a	1 c
		בהל	DISMAY	96c	1
		חרון	BURNING OF ANGER	354c	
2	6	הר	MOUNTAIN	249d	1 a
		מלך	KING	573b	2
		נסך	INSTALL	651c	
		ציון	ZION	851c	
2	7	אל	TO	40c	6
		בן	SON	120b	1 a
		ברא	CREATE	*135c	2
		חק	SOMETHING PRESCRIBED	349c	6 c
		ילד	BEGET	408c	2 b
		ספר	COUNT	708a	1
2	8	אחזה	POSSESSION	28d	
		אפס	END	67a	1
		ה	THE	208d	1 i
		נחלה	PROPERTY	635b	1 c
		שאל	ASK	981c	1 a
2	9	ברזל	IRON	137d	3
		יצר	FORM	427d	1 a
		כלי	VESSEL	480b	3
		נפץ	SHATTER	658d	
		רעע	BREAK	949d	1
		שבט	ROD	987a	1 d
		הא	DEMONSTRATIVE PARTICLE	*1089c	B
		הא	DEMONSTRATIVE PARTICLE	*1089c	A
2	10	ה	THE	208d	1 i
		ו	AND	254c	4
		יסר	BE CORRECTED	416a	
		עתה	NOW	774b	2 b
		שכל	BE PRUDENT	968c	5
		שפט	JUDGE	1047c	1 b
2	11	ירא	FEAR	432a	1
		רעדה	TREMBLING	944d	
2	12	אבד	PERISH	1c	1
		אנף	BE ANGRY	60a	
		אשר	HAPPINESS	81a	
		בער	BURN	129a	1
		בר	SON	135a	
		בר	PURE	141b	3
		חסה	SEEK REFUGE	340b	
		מעט	A FEW	590b	2 b
		נשק	KISS	676c	
		פן	LEST	814d	1
3	1	אבישלום	ABSALOM	5a	2
		ברח	FLEE	138a	2
		מזמור	MELODY	274c	
		ל	TO	513c	5 bb
3	2	מה	HOW	553c	2 b
		צר	ADVERSARY	865d	
		רבב	BECOME MUCH	912d	1
3	3	אלהים	GOD	44a	4 a
		אמר	SAY	56a	1
		ישועה	DELIVERANCE	447b	3
		ל	TO	514b	5 fa
		סלה	LIFT UP	700a	
3	4	בעד	ABOUT	126c	1 b
		מגן	SHIELD	171c	
		כבוד	GLORY	459c	7
		ראש	HEAD	911b	8
		רום	BE HIGH	927c	1 a1
3	5	הר	MOUNTAIN	249d	1 a
		סלה	LIFT UP	700a	
		קול	VOICE	877a	1 a
		קרא	CALL	895b	2 a
3	6	ישן	SLEEP	445c	
		סמך	LEAN	702a	2
		קיץ	AWAKE	884c	1 a
		שכב	LIE DOWN	1012a	1 b
3	7	ירא	FEAR	431b	1 c
		מן	OUT OF	580a	2 ec
		סביב	ROUND ABOUT	687a	1 b
		רבבה	MULTITUDE	914b	
		שית	PUT	1011c	4
3	8	ישע	DELIVER	446d	1 b
		לחי	CHEEK	534d	2
		נכה	SMITE	645b	1 a
		קום	STAND	878b	6 a
		רשע	WICKED	957b	3
		שן	TOOTH	1042a	1 b
3	9	ברכה	BLESSING	139d	1 b
		ישועה	DELIVERANCE	447b	3
		ל	TO	513b	5 ba
		סלה	LIFT UP	700a	
		על	UPON	756c	27 a b
4	1	מזמור	MELODY	274c	
		נגינה	MUSIC	618d	1
4	2	אלהים	GOD	44d	4 bb
		חנן	SHOW FAVOR	336a	2 b
		תפלה	PRAYER	813c	1
		צדק	RIGHTEOUSNESS	841d	E
		קרא	CALL	845b	2 b
		צר	STRAITS	865a	
		רחב	BE LARGE	931c	2
4	3	אהב	LOVE	13a	2
		בן	SON	120b	1 a
		בקש	SEEK	134d	2 b
		כבוד	HONOR	459b	4

Ch v.	Heb	Eng	Page	Sec
	כזב	LIE	469c	
	כלמה	IGNOMINY	484a	2
	מה	HOW	554b	4 e
	מה	HOW	*554b	4 e
	סלה	LIFT UP	700a	
	ריק	EMPTY	938b	2
	ריק	EMPTINESS	938b	
4 4	חסיד	KIND	339d	2 b
	פלה	BE SEPARATED	811d	2
	קרא	CALL	895b	2 a
4 5	דמם	BE SILENT	198d	1
	חטא	MISS A GOAL OR WAY	306d	2 b
	לבב	HEART	524a	27
	סלה	LIFT UP	700a	
	רגז	BE AGITATED	919b	
4 6	בטח	TRUST	105c	1 5 a
	זבח	SACRIFICE	257c	11
	צדק	RIGHTNESS	841c	1
4 7	אור	BECOME LIGHT	21c	5
	אור	LIGHT	21d	0
	טוב	A GOOD THING	375a	1
	מי	WHO	566c	F a
	נשא	LIFT	670b	1 b 3
	ראה	TO SEE	908c	1 a1
4 8	דגן	CORN	186c	
	תירוש	NEW WINE	440d	
	לב	HEART	525a	29a
	מן	THAN	582d	6 c
	נתן	PUT	680c	2 b
	רבב	BECOME MUCH	912d	1
	שמחה	JOY	970d	2
4 9	בדד	ISOLATION	95a	
	בטח	SECURITY	105b	
	יחדו	TOGETHER	403c	A
	ישב	CAUSE TO SIT	443d	3 a
	ישן	SLEEP	445c	
	שכב	LIE DOWN	1012a	1 b
	שלום	PEACE	1023a	4
5 1	אל	TO	40c	7
	מזמור	MELODY	274c	
	נחל	WADY	636a	2
5 2	אמר	WORD	57a	1
	בין	DISCERN	106d	3 a
	הגיג	MURMURING	211c	1
5 3	מלך	KING	573b	3
	קשב	ATTEND	904a	
	שוע	CRY OUT	1002d	
5 4	בקר	MORNING	134a	1 d
	בקר	MORNING	134b	1 f
	ערך	ARRANGE	789d	1 f
	צפה	KEEP WATCH	859c	
5 5	אל	GOD	42d	6 d
	גור	SOJOURN	157d	1
	חפץ	DELIGHTING IN	343a	2
	רע	EVIL	949a	3
	רשע	WICKEDNESS	957d	3
5 6	און	TROUBLE	20a	3
	הלל	BE BOASTFUL	238a	
	יצב	STATION ONESELF	426c	D
	נגד	IN FRONT	617c	2 b
	פעל	DO	821b	1 b
	שנא	HATE	971c	2
5 7	אבד	CAUSE TO PERISH	2a	1
	דבר	SPEAK	180c	1
	דם	BLOOD	197a	2 h
	כזב	LIE	469c	
	מרמה	DECEIT	941b	
	תעב	BE ABHORRED	1073b	1 b1
5 8	ב	IN	90c	3 5
	היכל	TEMPLE	228c	2 d
	היכל	TEMPLE	*228c	2 d
	חסד	GOODNESS	339b	2 3a
	יראה	FEAR	432a	3
	קדש	APARTNESS	871d	2 d
	רב	MULTITUDE	914a	1
	שחה	BOW DOWN	1005c	2 b
5 9	דרך	WAY	203c	6 a
	נחה	LEAD	634d	
	מען	PURPOSE	775b	1 b
	צדקה	RIGHTEOUSNESS	842c	6 a
	שורר	WATCHER	1004a	
5 10	גרון	THROAT	173c	
	הוה	CHASM	217d	2
	חלק	BE SMOOTH	325b	2
	כון	BE FIRM	465d	2
	לשון	TONGUE	546b	1 b
	פתח	OPEN	835a	
	קבר	GRAVE	868d	
	קרב	INWARD PART	899b	2 b
	הא	DEMONSTRATIVE PARTICLE	*1089c	A
5 11	אלהים	GOD	44a	4 a
	אשם	OFFEND	79c	
	ב	IN	90c	3 5
	מועצה	PLAN	420b	
	מן	ON ACCOUNT OF	580b	2 f
	מרה	BE REBELLIOUS	598a	2
	נדח	THRUST	623b	2
	נפל	FALL	657b	2 b
	פשע	TRANSGRESSION	833d	4
5 12	אהב	LOVE	13a	3
	חסה	SEEK REFUGE	340b	1
	סכך	OVERSHADOW	697a	2
	עולם	LONG DURATION	762b	2 a
	עלץ	REJOICE	763b	

Ch v.	Heb	Eng	Page	Sec
	רנן	GIVE A RINGING CRY	943b	
	שם	NAME	1028c	3
5 13	ברך	BLESS	139a	2 a
	עטר	SURROUND	742c	
	צדיק	JUST	843a	3 b
	צנה	LARGE SHIELD	857a	
	רצון	GOODWILL	953c	1 a
	הא	DEMONSTRATIVE PARTICLE	*1089c	A
6 1	מזמור	MELODY	274c	
	נגינה	MUSIC	618d	1
	על	UPON	754a	2 1f a
	שמיני	EIGHTH	1033b	
6 2	חמה	RAGE	404d	2 c
	יכח	CORRECT	407a	6
	יסר	DISCIPLINE	416b	2 a
6 3	אמלל	FEEBLE	51c	
	בהל	BE DISTURBED	*96b	1
	בהל	BE DISTURBED	96b	1
	חנן	SHOW FAVOR	336a	2 b
	כי	BECAUSE	473d	3 b
	עצם	BONE	782d	1 d
	רפא	HEAL	950d	2 a
6 4	אתה	THOU	61c	
	בהל	BE DISTURBED	96b	1
	בהל	BE DISTURBED	*96b	1
	מתי	WHEN	607d	C
	עצם	BONE	782d	1 d
6 5	חלץ	DRAW OFF OR OUT	322d	2
	חסד	GOODNESS	339a	2 1b
	ישע	DELIVER	446d	1 b
	מען	PURPOSE	775b	1 a
	שוב	TURN BACK	998a	6 g
6 6	זכר	REMEMBRANCE	271b	2
	ידה	PRAISE	392c	1
	מות	DEATH	560d	3
	מי	WHO	567a	F c
	שאול	SHEOL	983c	2 a
6 7	אנחה	SIGHING	58d	1
	דמעה	TEARS	199c	
	יגע	TOIL	388b	2
	לילה	NIGHT	538d	1
	לילה	NIGHT	539d	1
	מסה	MELT	587b	
	מטה	COUCH	641d	
	ערש	COUCH	793a	
	שחה	SWIM	965c	
6 8	שיח	MUSE	967a	1
	כעס	ANGER	495b	3
	מן	ON ACCOUNT OF	580b	2 f
	עין	EYE	744b	1 i
	עשש	WASTE AWAY	799c	
	עתק	MOVE	801b	2
	צרר	SHEW HOSTILITY TOWARD	865d	
6 9	בכי	WEEPING	113d	
6 10	תחנה	FAVOR	337c	2
	תפלה	PRAYER	813c	1 e
	שמע	HEAR	1034a	1
6 11	בהל	BE DISTURBED	96b	1
	בוש	BE ASHAMED	101d	1
	רגע	A MOMENT	921a	BA B
	שוב	TURN BACK	996d	1
7 1	בנימיני	BENJAMITE	122d	
	כוש	CUSH	469a	
	שגיון	DIRGE	993c	
	שיר	SING	1010c	
	עלדבר	ADDENDA ET CORRIGENDA	1122a	
7 2	יהוה	YAHWEH	219a	2 1f
	חסה	SEEK REFUGE	340b	
	ישע	DELIVER	446d	1 b
	רדף	PURSUE	922d	1 f
7 3	אין	NOT	34d	4 c
	אריה	LION	71d	
	ה	THE	*207d	1 f
	טרף	TEAR	382d	
	כ	LIKE	454a	1 c2
	נצל	DELIVER	664d	3 a
	פן	LEST	814d	1
	פרק	TEAR APART	830a	
7 4	יהוה	YAHWEH	219a	2 1f
	יש	THERE IS	441d	2 b
	כף	HOLLOW OF THE HAND	496d	1 d7
7 5	עול	INJUSTICE	732c	
	חלץ	DRAW OFF OR OUT	322d	2
	צרר	SHEW HOSTILITY TOWARD	865d	
	ריקם	EMPTILY	938b	2
	רע	EVIL	948d	2
	שלם	BE IN COVENANT OF PEACE	1023d	
7 6	חיים	LIFE	313a	1
	כבוד	HONOR	459b	5
	ל	TO	511c	1 ga
	ל	TO	511c	1 ga
	נשג	OVERTAKE	673c	1
	סלה	LIFT UP	700a	
	עפר	DRY EARTH	780a	2 e
	רדף	PURSUE	922d	1 e
	רדף	PURSUE	*923a	
	רמס	TRAMPLE	942d	
	שכן	SETTLE DOWN	1015c	1 a
7 7	עברה	OVERFLOW	720c	3 a

Ch v.	Heb	Eng	Page	Sec
	עור	ROUSE ONESELF	734d	
	צוה	CHARGE	846a	5
	צרר	SHEW HOSTILITY TOWARD	865d	
7 8	משפט	JUDGMENT	1048c	1 e
	עדה	CONGREGATION	417a	1
	ל	TO	511b	1 ga
	לאם	PEOPLE	522c	
	סבב	SURROUND	686b	2
	על	UPON	755d	2 5
	מרום	HEIGHT	928d	1
7 9	שוב	TURN BACK	997b	3 a
	דין	JUDGE	192b	1
	כ	LIKE	454a	1 c1
	על	UPON	753d	2 1
	צדק	RIGHTEOUSNESS	841d	3
	שפט	JUDGE	1047d	3 b1
	תם	INTEGRITY	1070d	3
7 10	אלהים	GOD	44b	4 a
	בחן	TRY	103c	2 b
	גמר	COME TO AN END	170a	1
	כון	ESTABLISH	466d	1
	כליה	KIDNEYS	480c	2 b
	לב	HEART	525a	26
	נא	PART OF ENTREATY	609b	3 c
	צדיק	JUST	843a	3 b
	צדיק	JUST	843a	1 d
	רע	EVIL	949a	3
	רשע	WICKED	957b	2
7 11	אלהים	GOD	44a	4 a
	מגן	SHIELD	171c	
	ישע	DELIVER	446d	1 b
	ישר	STRAIGHT	449b	3 b
	לב	HEART	525a	26a
	על	UPON	753c	2 1c
	אל	GOD	42d	6 e
	אלהים	GOD	44a	4 a
7 12	זעם	BE INDIGNANT	276d	1
	יום	DAY	400c	7 g
	כל	ALL	481c	1
	צדיק	JUST	843a	1 d
	שפט	JUDGE	1047c	2 a
7 13	דרך	TREAD	202b	1
	חרב	SWORD	352c	1 d
	כון	ESTABLISH	467a	2
	לטש	SHARPEN	538c	2
	קשת	BOW	906c	1 d
	שוב	TURN BACK	998b	8
7 14	דלק	BURN	196b	1
	חץ	ARROW	346c	2
	כון	ESTABLISH	466b	2 a
	כלי	IMPLEMENT	479d	2 a
	ל	TO	511a	1 a
	ל	TO	512b	1 d
	פעל	DO	821c	2 a
7 15	און	TROUBLE	20a	1
	הרה	CONCEIVE	247d	2
	חבל	BIND	286c	
	ילד	BEAR	408a	1 c
	עמל	TROUBLE	765d	2
	שקר	DECEPTION	1055c	1
	שקר	DECEPTION	1055c	2
7 16	בור	PIT	92c	3
	חפר	DIG	343c	1 a
	כרה	DIG	500a	
	נפל	FALL	656d	1
	פעל	DO	821c	2 b
	שחת	PIT	1001c	1
7 17	חמס	VIOLENCE	329c	
	ירד	GO DOWN	433c	3 i
	על	UPON	756c	27 a b
	עמל	TROUBLE	765d	2
	קדקד	HEAD	869b	
	ראש	HEAD	911b	8
	שוב	TURN BACK	998b	7 f
7 18	זמר	MAKE MUSIC	274a	1
	ידה	PRAISE	392c	1 a2
	עליון	HIGHEST	751b	1
	צדק	RIGHTEOUSNESS	841d	2 c
8 1	מזמור	MELODY	274c	
	גתית	GITTITH	388a	1
	על	UPON	754a	2 1f a
8 2	אדון	LORD	11b	2 2
	אדיר	MAJESTIC	12b	
	הוד	SPLENDOUR	217b	2
	מה	HOW	553c	2 b
	נתן	PUT	680c	2
	שם	NAME	1028c	3
	תנה	HIRE	1071d	
8 3	ינק	SUCK	413b	
	יסד	FOUND	414a	2
	נקם	AVENGE	668d	
	עז	STRENGTH	739b	5
	עולל	CHILD	760c	
	מען	PURPOSE	775b	1 b
	צרר	SHEW HOSTILITY TOWARD	865d	
8 4	שבת	CEASE	992a	2
	ירח	MOON	437a	
	כוכב	STAR	456d	
	כון	ESTABLISH	466d	1
	מעשה	DEED	796b	2 b
	אצבע	FINGER	840c	1 d
	שמי	HEAVENS	1030a	1 a

Ch	v.	Heb	Eng	Page	Sec
8	5	שמי	HEAVENS	1030b	2 a
		אנוש	MAN	60d	3
		זכר	REMEMBER	270b	2 1 e
		כי	THAT	472d	1 f
		מה	WHAT	553a	1 db
		פקד	ATTEND TO	823b	A 1a
8	6	אלהים	GOD	43b	1 b
		הדר	SPLENDOUR	214b	2
		חסר	LACK	341b	
		כבוד	HONOR	458c	2 a
		מן	FROM	583b	7 bb
		מעט	A FEW	589d	1 a
		עטר	CROWN	743a	
8	7	כל	ALL	482c	2 a
		משל	RULE	605d	
		מעשה	DEED	796b	2 b
		שית	PUT	1011b	1
		תחת	UNDERNEATH	1065c	2 1e
8	8	אלף	CATTLE	48c	
		כל	ALL	481d	1 da
		צנה	FLOCKS	856c	
		שדי	FIELD	961b	2
8	9	ארח	WAY	73a	1
		בהמה	BEAST	97a	1
		דג	FISH	185c	
		ה	THE	208d	1 i
		עבר	PASS OVER	718b	5 h
		צפור	BIRD	862a	2
		שמי	HEAVENS	1029d	1 a
8	10	אדון	LORD	11b	2 2
		אדיר	MAJESTIC	12b	1
		שם	NAME	1028c	3
9	1	מזמור	MELODY	274c	
		לבן	LABBEN	527c	
		מות	DIE	560a	2 d
		על	UPON	754a	2 1f a
		עלמה	YOUNG WOMAN	761c	
9	2	ידה	PRAISE	392c	1 a2
		ספר	COUNT	708a	1
		פלא	BE SURPASSING	810d	4
9	3	אמר	MAKE MUSIC	274a	1
		עליון	HIGHEST	751b	1
		עלץ	REJOICE	763b	
		שמח	REJOICE	970b	2 a
9	4	אבד	PERISH	1c	1
		אחור	HINDER SIDE	30c	A
		כשל	STUMBLE	505d	1 b
		פנה	FACE	818b	2 6b
		שוב	TURN BACK	997a	1
9	5	דין	JUDGMENT	192c	1
		ישב	SIT	442c	1 a
		ישב	SIT	442c	1 a
		כסא	SEAT OF HONOR	490d	1 b
		ל	TO	511c	1 b
		עשה	DO	794a	1 1a 6
		צדק	RIGHTEOUSNESS	841d	E
		שפט	JUDGE	1047c	2 a
		משפט	JUDGMENT	1048c	1 f
9	6	אבד	CAUSE TO PERISH	2a	1
		גער	REBUKE	172a	2
		ה	THE	208d	1 i
		מחה	WIPE OUT	562a	2
		עד	PERPETUITY	723d	2 e
		רשע	WICKED	957b	2
9	7	אבד	PERISH	1d	2
		זכר	REMEMBRANCE	271b	1 a
		חרבה	WASTE	352b	2
		נצח	EVERLASTINGNESS	664b	4
		נתש	PLUCK UP	684c	
		תמם	BE FINISHED	1070c	5
9	8	ה	THE	208c	1 hb
		ישב	SIT	442c	1 a
		כון	ESTABLISH	466d	1 b
		כסא	SEAT OF HONOR	490d	1 b
		עולם	LONG DURATION	762c	2 c
		משפט	JUDGMENT	1048b	1 a
9	9	דין	JUDGE	192b	1
		תבל	WORLD	385d	
		מישר	LEVEL	449d	2
		לאם	PEOPLE	522c	
		צדק	RIGHTEOUSNESS	841d	E
		שפט	JUDGE	1047d	3 d
9	10	בצרה	DEARTH	131b	
		דך	CRUSHED	194c	
		ל	TO	516d	6 a
		עת	TIME	773c	1 b
		צרה	DISTRESS	865b	
		משגב	SECURE HEIGHT	960d	2
9	11	במח	TRUST	105a	1 3a
		דרש	SEEK	205b	3 a
		עזב	LEAVE	737c	2 e
		שם	NAME	1028c	3
9	12	זמר	MAKE MUSIC	274a	1
		נגד	BE CONSPICUOUS	617a	4
		עלילה	WANTONNESS	760a	2 b
9	13	דם	BLOOD	197b	2 k
		דרש	SEEK	205c	5
		זכר	REMEMBER	270b	2 1 c
		ענו	POOR	776c	3
		עני	POOR	777a	3
		צעקה	CRY	858d	1
		שכח	FORGET	1013b	2 b
9	14	חנן	SHOW FAVOR	336a	2 b
		מות	DEATH	560d	1
		מן	OUT OF	579d	2 d
		עני	AFFLICTION	777a	1

Ch	v.	Heb	Eng	Page	Sec
		רום	BE HIGH	927a	2 a
9	15	שער	GATE	1045b	4
		בת	DAUGHTER	123c	3
		תהלה	PRAISE	240b	4
		ישועה	DELIVERANCE	447b	3
		ספר	COUNT	708a	1
		מען	PURPOSE	775c	2 b
		תהלה	ADDENDA ET COR-RIGENDA	1122c	
9	16	זו	THIS	262b	2
		זו	THIS	262c	2
		טבע	SINK	371c	
		טמן	HIDE	380c	2
		רשת	NET	440c	1 b2
		לכד	CAPTURE	540b	1
		לכד	CAPTURE	540b	
		שחת	PIT	1001c	1
9	17	ה	THE	208d	1 i
		הגיון	RESOUNDING MU-SIC	212a	1
		ידע	MAKE ONESELF KNOWN	394d	2
		כף	HOLLOW OF THE HAND	496c	1 d7
		נקש	STRIKE	669c	
		סלה	LIFT UP	*699d	
		פעל	DOING	821c	1 c
		רשע	WICKED	957b	2
		משפט	JUDGMENT	1048c	1 f
9	18	אלהים	GOD	44a	4 a
		רשע	WICKED	957b	2
		שאול	SHEOL	983a	2 a
		שוב	TURN BACK	997c	4 a
		שכח	FORGETFUL	1013c	
9	19	אבד	PERISH	1d	2
		אביון	NEEDY	2d	
		לא	NOT	518c	1 aa
		לא	NOT	*518d	1 ac
		נצח	EVERLASTINGNESS	664b	4
		עד	PERPETUITY	723c	2 e
		ענו	POOR	776c	3
		עני	POOR	777a	3
		תקוה	HOPE	876b	3
9	20	אנוש	MAN	60d	3
		עזז	BE STRONG	738c	
		פנה	FACE	818d	2 7a a
		שפט	JUDGE	1048a	2
9	21	אנוש	MAN	60d	3
		מורה	FEAR	432b	2
		סלה	LIFT UP	700a	
		שית	PUT	1011b	1
10	1	בצרה	DEARTH	131b	
		ל	TO	513c	5 bb
		ל	TO	516d	6 a
		עלם	CONCEAL	761a	
		עמד	STAND	764a	1 f
		עת	TIME	773c	1 b
		צרה	DISTRESS	865b	
		רחק	DISTANT	935c	2 a4
		עולם	ADDENDA ET COR-RIGENDA	1125d	
10	2	גאוה	PRIDE	144d	3
		דלק	HOTLY PURSUE	196b	2
		זו	THIS	262b	2
		מזמה	PURPOSE	273d	3 a
		חשב	THINK	363a	12
		עני	POOR	776d	3
		רשע	WICKED	957b	2
		תפש	LAY HOLD OF	1075a	
10	3	תאוה	DESIRE	16c	1
		בצע	GAIN BY VIOLENCE	130b	
		ברך	BLESS	139b	5
		הלל	PRAISE	238d	3
		נפש	SOUL	660d	6 a
10	4	אלהים	GOD	44a	4 a
		בל	NOT	115b	
		גבה	HEIGHT	147b	3
		דרש	SEEK	205c	5
		מזמה	PURPOSE	273d	3 a
10	5	חול	BE FIRM	298c	1
		כל	ALL	481c	1 b
		נגד	IN FRONT	*617d	2 b
		נגד	IN FRONT	617d	2 cb b
		פוח	BREATHE	806b	2 a
		צרר	SHEW HOSTILITY TOWARD	865d	
		מרום	HEIGHT	929a	2
		משפט	JUDGMENT	1048c	1 f
10	6	אמר	SAY	56b	2
		אשר	THAT	83c	8 ag
		בל	NOT	115b	
		בל	NOT	115b	
		דור	PERIOD	189d	1 b
		לב	HEART	525c	2 7
		מוט	SHAKE	*557a	
		רע	EVIL	948d	1
10	7	און	TROUBLE	20a	1
		אלה	OATH	46d	3 b
		לשון	TONGUE	546b	1 a
		עמל	TROUBLE	765d	2
		מרמה	DECEIT	941b	
		תחת	UNDERNEATH	1065c	2 1b
		תך	INJURY	1067a	
10	8	מארב	AMBUSH	70d	1 b
		הרג	KILL	247a	1 a
		חלכה	HAPLESS	319a	

Ch	v.	Heb	Eng	Page	Sec
		חצר	SETTLED ABODE	347b	A
		נקי	CLEAN	667c	1
		מסתר	SECRET PLACE	712c	2 b
		צפן	HIDE	860d	2
10	9	ארב	LIE IN WAIT	70b	
		ארב	LIE IN WAIT	70b	
		אריה	LION	71d	
		חטף	CATCH	310c	
		רשת	NET	440c	1 b2
		משך	DRAW	604b	1
		סך	THICKET	697c	
		מסתר	SECRET PLACE	712c	2 b
		עני	POOR	776d	3
10	10	דכה	CRUSH	194b	2
		חלכה	HAPLESS	319a	
		כאה	COWED	456c	
		עצום	MIGHTY	783a	1
		שחח	BOW	1005d	1
10	11	אל	GOD	42d	6 e
		אמר	SAY	56b	2
		בל	NOT	115b	
		לב	HEART	525c	2 7
		נצח	EVERLASTINGNESS	664b	4
		סתר	HIDE	711d	2 b
		שכח	FORGET	1013b	2 b
10	12	אל	GOD	42d	6 e
		יד	HAND	389c	1 d
		נשא	LIFT	670b	1 b 1
		ענו	POOR	776c	3
		עני	POOR	777a	3
		שכח	FORGET	1013b	2 a
10	13	אלהים	GOD	44a	4 a
		אמר	SAY	56b	2
		דרש	SEEK	205c	5
		לב	HEART	525c	2 7
		מה	HOW	554b	4 f
		נאץ	CONTEMN	611a	
10	14	אף	NOSE	60b	2
		חלכה	HAPLESS	319a	
		יתום	ORPHAN	450c	
		כי	BECAUSE	473d	3 b
		כעס	ANGER	495b	3
		נבט	LOOK	613d	3
		עזב	LEAVE	737b	1 h
		עזר	HELP	740b	
		על	UPON	753b	2 1c
		עמל	TROUBLE	765d	1
10	15	בל	NOT	115b	
		דרש	SEEK	205c	5
		זרוע	ARM	284a	1 b
		מצא	FIND	593b	2 b
		רע	EVIL	948c	0 b
		רשע	WICKEDNESS	957d	3
		שבר	BREAK	990c	
10	16	אבד	PERISH	1c	1
		מלך	KING	573b	2
		עד	PERPETUITY	723d	2 e
		עולם	LONG DURATION	762c	2 c
10	17	תאוה	DESIRE	16c	1
		אזן	EAR	24b	2 b
		כון	ESTABLISH	466b	1 b
		לב	HEART	525a	2 4
		ענו	POOR	776c	3
		קשב	ATTEND	904a	
10	18	אנוש	MAN	60d	3
		בל	NOT	115b	
		דך	CRUSHED	194c	
		יסף	DO AGAIN	415c	2 a
		יתום	ORPHAN	450c	
		מן	OUT OF	579c	2 cc
		ערץ	CAUSE TO TREM-BLE	791d	1
		שפט	JUDGE	1047d	3 b1
11	1	איך	HOW	32c	1
		הר	MOUNTAIN	250c	1 g
		הר	MOUNTAIN	250c	1 f
		חסה	SEEK REFUGE	340b	
		נוד	FLUTTER	626d	1 b
		צפור	BIRD	862a	2
11	2	אפל	DARKNESS	66c	1
		במו	IN	91b	
		דרך	TREAD	202b	4
		חץ	ARROW	346c	2
		ירה	SHOOT	435a	3
		ישר	STRAIGHT	449b	3 b
		יתר	CORD	452a	
		כון	ESTABLISH	467a	3
		לב	HEART	525b	2 6a
		קשת	BOW	906c	1 d
11	3	הרס	THROW DOWN	248d	
		פעל	DO	821b	1 b
		צדיק	JUST	843a	3 b
		שת	FOUNDATION	1011d	
11	4	בחן	EXAMINE	103c	1
		היכל	TEMPLE	228d	2 e
		חזה	SEE	302b	1 b
		כסא	SEAT OF HONOR	490d	1 b
		עפעף	EYELID	733d	
		עין	EYE	744b	1 f
		קדש	APARTNESS	871c	2 a
11	5	אהב	LOVE	13a	2
		בחן	EXAMINE	103c	1
		חמס	VIOLENCE	329c	
		נפש	SOUL	661a	6 f
		צדיק	JUST	843a	3 b
		רשע	WICKED	957c	3

Ch v.	Heb	Eng	Page	Sec
11 6	שנא	HATE	971c	2
	גפרית	BRIMSTONE	172d	
	זלעפה	RAGING HEAT	273a	2
	כוס	CUP	468a	
	מטר	RAIN	565a	
	מנת	PORTION	584c	
	פחם	COAL	809b	
11 7	אהב	LOVE	13b	5 c
	חזה	SEE	302b	1 a
	ישר	STRAIGHT	449b	3 c2
	פנה	FACE	816a	1 2b
	צדקה	RIGHTEOUSNESS	842c	7 b
	צדיק	JUST	843a	1 d
	שפה	SPEECH	974a	2
12 1	מזמור	MELODY	274c	
	על	UPON	754a	2 1fa
	שמיני	EIGHTH	1033b	
12 2	אמן	CONFIRM	52d	4 b
	גמר	COME TO AN END	170a	1
	חסיד	KIND	339d	2 b
	ישע	DELIVER	446d	1 b
	פסס	DISAPPEAR	821a	
12 3	דבר	SPEAK	181a	1 a
	ו	AND	253b	1 ia
	חלקה	SMOOTH PART	325c	3
	לב	HEART	525b	2 6b
	שפה	SPEECH	973d	1 a1
	שוא	EMPTINESS	996b	2
12 4	גדול	GREAT	153c	9
	חלקה	SMOOTH PART	325c	3
	כרת	CUT OFF	504c	1
	לשון	TONGUE	546b	1 b
	שפה	SPEECH	973d	1 a1
12 5	אדון	LORD	11a	1 1b
	את	WITH	86a	1 a
	את	WITH	86c	3 a
	גבר	BE STRONG	149d	
	ל	TO	513a	5 ad
	לשון	TONGUE	546c	1 b
	מי	WHO	567a	F c
	שפה	SPEECH	973c	1 a1
12 6	אביון	NEEDY	2d	
	אנקה	CRYING	60c	
	ישע	SAFETY	447a	1
	מן	ON ACCOUNT OF	580b	2f
	עתה	NOW	774a	1 b
	עני	POOR	776d	3
	פוח	BREATHE	806b	2 d
	שד	VIOLENCE	994c	1
	שית	PUT	1011b	2a
12 7	אמרה	UTTERANCE	57b	
	זקק	REFINE	279b	
	מהור	CLEAN	373a	3
	כסף	SILVER	494a	1
	כסף	SILVER	494c	9
	עליל	FURNACE	760d	
	שבעתים	SEVEN FOLD	988d	2
12 8	דור	GENERATION	190a	3
	זו	THIS	262b	1
	נצר	GUARD	665d	2
12 9	הלך	WALK	236a	1 b
	זלת	WORTHLESSNESS	273a	
	סביב	ROUND ABOUT	687a	1 b
	רום	BE HIGH	927a	2 c
	רשע	WICKED	957c	3
13 1	מזמור	MELODY	274c	
13 2	אן	WHERE	33a	D
	יהואדן	JEHOADDAN	221a	
	נצח	EVERLASTINGNESS	664b	4
	סתר	HIDE	711d	2 c
	שכח	FORGET	1013b	2a
13 3	אן	WHERE	33a	D
	יגון	GRIEF	387b	
	יום	DAY	400b	7 e1
	יומם	BY DAY	401c	2
	עצה	ADVICE	420a	
	לבב	HEART	524b	2 9b
	נפש	SOUL	661b	0
	רום	BE HIGH	927a	2 c
	שית	PUT	1011b	1
13 4	אור	BECOME LIGHT	21b	4
	יהוה	YAHWEH	219a	2 1f
	ישן	SLEEP	445d	
	נבט	LOOK	613d	3
13 5	יכל	PREVAIL	408a	2 c
	מוט	SHAKE	557a	
	צר	ADVERSARY	865d	
13 6	בטח	TRUST	105a	1 3d
	חסד	GOODNESS	339a	2 1a
	ישועה	DELIVERANCE	447b	3
	לב	HEART	525c	2 9a
	שיר	SING	1010d	
14 1	אלהים	GOD	44a	4 a
	אמר	SAY	56b	2
	טוב	A GOOD THING	375b	4
	ל	TO	513c	5 bb
	לב	HEART	525c	2 7
	נבל	FOOLISH	614d	
	שחת	GO TO RUIN	1008c	2
	תעב	BE ABHORRED	1073b	2
14 2	אלהים	GOD	44a	4 a
	דרש	SEEK	205b	3 a
	יש	THERE IS	441d	2
	מן	OUT OF	579a	2 ab
	עול	INJUSTICE	732c	
	ראה	TO SEE	907b	5 a
	שכל	BE PRUDENT	968c	5
	שקף	LOOK DOWN	1054d	
14 3	אין	NOT	34c	2 c
	אלח	BE CORRUPT	47a	
	גם	ALSO	169b	2
	טוב	A GOOD THING	375b	4
	יחדו	TOGETHER	403c	B
	כל	ALL	482a	1 db
	כל	ALL	482d	2 ba
	סור	TURN ASIDE	693c	1
	על	UPON	757d	2 7c d
	תעב	BE ABHORRED	*1073a	1
14 4	אכל	EAT	37d	6
14 5	ידע	KNOW	394a	1 e
	אלהים	GOD	44a	4 a
	דור	GENERATION	190b	3
	פחד	DREAD	808b	1
	פחד	DREAD	808c	1
	שם	THERE	1027a	1
14 6	בוש	BE ASHAMED	101d	1
	מחסה	REFUGE	340c	B
	עצה	ADVICE	420a	
	עני	POOR	776d	3
	עצם	BONE	*783a	3
14 7	ישועה	DELIVERANCE	447b	3
	נתן	GIVE	678d	1 f
	יעקב	JACOB	785a	1
	ציון	ZION	851c	
	ישראל	ISRAEL	975d	2 a3
	שבות	CAPTIVITY	986b	2 a
15 1	אהל	TENT	14b	3
	גור	SOJOURN	157d	1
	הר	MOUNTAIN	249d	1 a
	מזמור	MELODY	274c	
	מי	WHO	*566c	F
	מי	WHO	567a	F e
15 2	אמת	FIRMNESS	54b	4 a
	דבר	SPEAK	180c	
	הלך	WALK	235a	2 3e 1
	לבב	HEART	524a	2 7
	מי	WHO	*567a	F e
	פעל	DO	821b	1 b
	צדק	RIGHTEOUSNESS	841d	5
	רגל	GO-ABOUT	*920b	
	תמים	SOUND	1071b	4
15 3	חרפה	REPROACH	357d	1
	לשון	TONGUE	546c	1 b
	מי	WHO	*567a	F e
	נשא	LIFT	670d	1 b 6
	על	UPON	752d	2 1
	קרב	NEAR	898c	2 c
	רגל	GO-ABOUT	920b	
	רע	FRIEND	946a	2
15 4	בזה	DESPISE	102c	1
	ירא	FEAR	431c	3 b
	כבד	MAKE HONORABLE	457d	2 a
	מאס	REJECT	549c	2
	מור	CHANGE	558c	1
	מי	WHO	*567a	F e
	רעע	BE EVIL	949d	1
	שבע	SWEAR	989b	1 a
15 5	אלה	THESE	41c	A
	אלה	THESE	41c	A
	אלה	THESE	41c	A
	ב	IN	90b	3 3b
	כסף	SILVER	494d	9
	לקח	TAKE	543b	4 f
	מוט	SHAKE	557a	
	מי	WHO	*567a	F e
	נקי	CLEAN	667c	1
	נשך	INTEREST	675b	
	נתן	GIVE	679c	1 q
	עולם	LONG DURATION	762a	2 a
	שחד	BRIBE	1005a	
16 1	אל	GOD	42d	6 e
	חסה	SEEK REFUGE	340b	
	שמר	KEEP	1037a	4 a
16 2	אדון	LORD	11b	3 2a
	בל	NOT	115b	
	טובה	WELFARE	375d	1
	על	UPON	755a	2 2
16 3	אדיר	MAJESTIC	26a	2
	אשר	PARTICLE OF RE-LATION	82b	2 b
	חפץ	DELIGHT	343b	1
	ל	TO	*514d	5 fe
	קדוש	HOLY	872d	2 b
16 4	בל	NOT	115b	
	דם	BLOOD	197d	3 b
	מהר	ACQUIRE BY PAYING PURCHASE	555c	
	מן	OUT OF	579b	2 ba
	נסך	POUR OUT	650d	
	נסך	DRINK-OFFERING	651a	1
	נשא	LIFT	670d	1 b7
	על	UPON	753a	2 1
	עצבת	HURT	781a	
	רבה	BECOME MANY	915b	1
	שם	NAME	1028d	4
16 5	גורל	LOT	174d	3
	חבל	CORD	286d	2
	חלק	PORTION	324b	3 b
	כוס	CUP	468a	
	תמיד	CONTINUITY	*556b	1 a
	מנת	PORTION	584c	
	תמך	GRASP	1069d	1
16 6	אף	ALSO	64d	1
	נעים	DELIGHTFUL	653d	1
	נפל	FALL	657a	1
	על	UPON	758a	2 8
	שפר	BE BEAUTIFUL	1051c	
16 7	אף	ALSO	64d	1
	ברך	BLESS	139a	1
	יסר	DISCIPLINE	416b	1 b
	יעץ	ADVISE	419c	
	כליה	KIDNEYS	480c	2 b
	לילה	NIGHT	538d	1
	לילה	NIGHT	539a	1
16 8	בל	NOT	115b	
	בל	NOT	115b	
	ימין	RIGHT HAND	411d	2 a
	תמיד	CONTINUITY	556b	1 a
	מוט	SHAKE	557a	
	נגד	IN FRONT	617c	2 b
	שוה	AGREE WITH	1001a	
	שוה	SET	1001b	
16 9	אף	ALSO	64d	1
	בטח	SECURITY	105b	
	בשר	FLESH	142c	2
	כבוד	HONOR	459b	5
	כן	SO	486d	3 d
	ל	TO	510d	1 c
	לב	HEART	525c	2 9a
	שמח	REJOICE	970b	2 a
	שכן	SETTLE DOWN	1015a	1 a
16 10	חסיד	KIND	339d	2 b
	נפש	SOUL	659c	1 0
	עזב	LEAVE	737c	2 e
	ראה	TO SEE	907b	3
	שאול	SHEOL	983a	2 b
	שחת	PIT	1001c	2
16 11	ארח	WAY	73b	3 b
	חיים	LIFE	313b	1
	ידע	KNOW	395a	
	ימין	RIGHT HAND	411d	1 c
	נעים	DELIGHTFUL	653d	1
	נצח	EVERLASTINGNESS	664b	4
	פנה	FACE	816a	2 2a
	שבע	ABUNDANCE	960a	2
	שאול	SHEOL	*983b	2 b
16 14	אחר	ANOTHER	29d	
	שפה	SPEECH	973d	1 a1
17 1	לא	NOT	520a	4 aa
	תפלה	PRAYER	813c	1 e
	תפלה	PRAYER	813c	
	צדק	RIGHTEOUSNESS	841d	3
	קשב	ATTEND	904a	
	מרמה	DECEIT	941b	
	רנה	RINGING CRY	943c	1
	שפה	SPEECH	973d	1 a1
17 2	חזה	SEE	302b	1 b
	יצא	GO OUT	423b	1 f
	מישר	LEVEL	449d	3
	פנה	FACE	818a	2 5a c
	משפט	JUDGMENT	1048c	1 e
17 3	בחן	TRY	103c	2 b
	בל	NOT	115b	
	זמם	CONSIDER	273b	2 b
	לב	HEART	525a	2 6
	לילה	NIGHT	538d	1
	מצא	FIND	593b	2 b
	עבר	PASS OVER	717c	1 i
	פקד	ATTEND TO	823c	A 2
	צרף	SMELT	864b	2
	שחת	CORRUPT	*1115a	
17 4	ארח	WAY	73b	3 c
	דבר	WORD	*182a	1 1a
	כן	SO	487d	3 f
	ל	TO	514d	5 fe
	פעלה	WORK	821d	1 b
	פריץ	VIOLENT ONE	829d	
	שפה	SPEECH	974a	1 h
	שמר	KEEP	1036d	1 d
	שמר	KEEP	*1037a	3 c
17 5	אשור	STEP	81a	
	בל	NOT	115b	
	מוט	SLIP	556d	
	מעגל	ENTRENCHMENT	723a	2 b
	פעם	BEAT	822a	1 a
	תמך	GRASP	1069d	3
17 6	אזן	EAR	24b	2 b
	אל	GOD	42d	6 e
	אמרה	UTTERANCE	57b	
	נמה	INCLINE	641a	3 e
17 7	חסד	GOODNESS	339c	4
	חסה	SEEK REFUGE	340b	
	ישע	DELIVER	446d	1 b
	פלה	BE SEPARATED	811d	2
17 8	קום	STAND	878c	
	אישון	PUPIL	36b	
	כנף	WING	489d	1 h
	סתר	HIDE	711d	1
	צל	SHADOW	853b	2
17 9	זו	THIS	262b	2
	נפש	SOUL	660c	5 c
	נקף	GO AROUND	669a	1 b
	שדד	DEAL VIOLENTLY WITH	994b	
17 10	גאות	MAJESTY	145b	3
	חלב	FAT	316d	1
	סגר	SHUT	689a	1
17 11	נמה	BEND	640b	3 a

Ch	v.	Heb	Eng	Page	Sec
		סבב	SURROUND	686a	2 d
		עין	EYE	744d	3 b
		שית	PUT	1011b	2 a
17	12	אריה	LION	71d	
		דמין	LIKENESS	198b	
		טרף	TEAR	382d	
		כסף	LONG	493d	
		כפיר	LION	498d	
		מסתר	SECRET PLACE	712c	2 b
		שחק	LION	*1006d	
17	13	כרע	CAUSE TO BOW DOWN	502d	2
		פלט	ESCAPE	812b	1
		קדם	COME IN FRONT	869d	1 a
		רשע	WICKED	957b	2
17	14	בטן	BELLY	105d	1 a
		חיים	LIFE	313a	1
		חלד	DURATION	317b	
		חלק	PORTION	324b	4
		יתר	EXCESS	452a	2 c
		כ	LIKE	453d	1 b
		מלא	FILL	570d	2
		מת	MALE	607b	3 a
		נוח	REST	629a	B 2
		עולל	CHILD	760c	
		צפון	TREASURE	860d	
		צפן	HIDE	860d	1
		שבע	SATISFIED	959c	2 b
17	15	חזה	SEE	302b	1 a
		תמונה	LIKENESS	568c	
		פנה	FACE	816a	1 2b
		צדק	RIGHTEOUSNESS	841d	5
		קיץ	AWAKE	884c	4
		שבע	SATISFIED	959c	2 b
		שאול	SHEOL	*983b	2 b
18	1	דבר	SPEAK	*181b	3 c
		דבר	WORD	182d	2 1a
		דוד	DAVID	188a	
		ו	AND	252c	1 a
		יום	DAY	400b	7 d3 a
		כף	POWER	496d	2
		נצל	DELIVER	665a	3 a
		שאול	SAUL	982b	1
		שירה	SONG	1010c	
18	2	חזק	STRENGTH	305d	
		רחם	LOVE	933c	
18	3	אל	GOD	42c	6 b
		אלהים	GOD	44d	
		מגן	SHIELD	171c	
		חמס	VIOLENCE	*329c	
		חסה	SEEK REFUGE	340b	
		ישע	DELIVERANCE	447a	2
		מנוס	ESCAPE	631a	2
		סלע	CRAG	701a	2
		פלט	ESCAPE	812b	1
		מצודה	FASTNESS	845a	
		צור	ROCK	849d	2
		קרן	HORN	902a	2
		משגב	SECURE HEIGHT	960d	2
18	4	הלל	PRAISE	239a	2
		ישע	BE DELIVERED	446b	1
		עפר	DRY EARTH	779d	1 d
		קרא	CALL	895d	5 c
18	5	אפף	SURROUND	67c	
		בליעל	WORTHLESSNESS	116b	3
		בעת	FALL UPON	130a	1
		חבל	CORD	286c	1
		נחל	TORRENT	636b	1
		משבר	BREAKER	991c	
18	6	חבל	CORD	286c	1
		מוקש	BAIT	430d	
		סבב	SURROUND	686a	2 d
		קדם	COME IN FRONT	869d	1 a
		שאול	SHEOL	983a	1
18	7	אזן	EAR	24b	2 b
		היכל	TEMPLE	*228b	2 a
		היכל	TEMPLE	228d	2 e
		צר	STRAITS	865a	
		קרא	CALL	895d	5 c
		שוע	CRY OUT	1002d	
		שועה	CRY FOR HELP	1003a	
18	8	ארץ	EARTH	76a	1 b
		געש	SHAKE	172b	
		געש	SHAKE	172b	
		הר	MOUNTAIN	250d	1 m
		חרה	BURN	354b	2 b
		מוסד	FOUNDATION	414c	
		רגז	BE AGITATED	919a	
		רעש	SHAKE	950b	1
		שמי	HEAVENS	1030a	1 b
18	9	אף	NOSE	60a	1
		בער	BURN	129a	1
		גחלת	COAL	160d	
		מן	OUT OF	580a	2 ea
		מן	THAN	582b	6 a
		עשן	SMOKE	798c	2 b
		פה	MOUTH	804d	1 c
18	10	ה	THE	208d	1 i
		ירד	GO DOWN	433b	2
		נטה	BEND	640c	3 b
		ערפל	CLOUD	791d	
		רגל	FOOT	919d	1 b
		שמי	HEAVENS	1030b	2 a
18	11	דאה	FLY SWIFTLY	178d	1
		כנף	WING	489d	1 f
		כרוב	CHERUB	500c	1

Ch	v.	Heb	Eng	Page	Sec
		עוף	FLY	733c	1 a
		ראה	TO SEE	*908b	1 a
		רוח	BREATH	924d	2
18	12	רכב	RIDE	938d	2
		חביון	HIDING	*285d	
		חשך	DARKNESS	365a	1
		חשכה	DARKNESS	365b	
		חשרה	COLLECTION	*366b	
		סביב	ROUND ABOUT	687b	2 bb
		סכה	THICKET	697d	2
		סתר	COVERING	712a	1
		עב	DARK CLOUD	728a	2
		שחק	DUST	1007a	2
		שית	PUT	1011c	3
18	13	אש	FIRE	77c	2
		גחלת	COAL	160d	
		נגד	IN FRONT	617b	1 aa
		נגה	BRIGHTNESS	618b	
		עבר	PASS OVER	718c	6 f
		עב	DARK CLOUD	728a	2
18	14	אש	FIRE	77c	2
		גחלת	COAL	*160d	
		נתן	GIVE	679d	1 x
		עליון	HIGHEST	751b	1
		קול	VOICE	877a	2 b
		רעם	THUNDER	947b	
		שמי	HEAVENS	1030a	2 a
18	15	ברק	FLASH	140b	
		ברק	LIGHTNING	*140c	1
		ברק	LIGHTNING	140c	1
		המם	CONFUSE	243a	2
		חץ	ARROW	346c	2
		פוץ	BE DISPERSED	807b	1 b
		רב	MUCH	913b	1 g
		רבם	SHOOT	914d	
		שלח	SEND	1018c	2
18	16	אף	NOSE	60a	1
		אפיק	CHANNEL	67d	
		גערה	REBUKE	172a	2
		תבל	WORLD	385d	
		מוסד	FOUNDATION	414c	
		מן	OUT OF	580a	2 eb
		נשמה	BREATH	675d	1
		ראה	TO SEE	908c	1 c
		רוח	BREATH	924d	1 d1
18	17	מי	WATER	565d	4 a
		משה	DRAW	602c	
		מרום	HEIGHT	928d	2
18	18	מן	THAN	582d	6 d
		עז	STRONG	738d	
18	19	איד	DISTRESS	15d	2
		איד	DISTRESS	15d	2
		קדם	COME IN FRONT	869d	1 a
		משען	SUPPORT	1044a	
18	20	חלק	DRAW OFF OR OUT	322d	2
		חפץ	DELIGHT IN	342d	2 a
		יצא	BRING OUT	424d	2
		ל	TO	511b	1 ga
18	21	בר	CLEANNESS	*141b	
		צדק	RIGHTEOUSNESS	841d	3
		שוב	TURN BACK	999c	4 a
18	22	דרך	WAY	204a	6 ec
		מן	FROM	578a	1 a
		רשע	BE WICKED	957d	1
		שמר	KEEP	1037a	3
18	23	חקה	SOMETHING PRE-SCRIBED	350a	2 d
		נגד	IN FRONT	617c	2 b
		סור	TURN ASIDE	694b	1
		משפט	JUDGMENT	1049a	4
18	24	ל	TO	*511a	1 d
		עון	INIQUITY	731a	1 a
		עם	WITH	767d	1 d
		שמר	KEEP	1037c	
18	25	תמים	SOUND	1071a	4
		בר	CLEANNESS	141b	
		כ	LIKE	454a	1 b
		נגד	IN FRONT	617c	2 b
		עין	EYE	744d	3
		צדק	RIGHTEOUSNESS	841d	3
		שוב	TURN BACK	999c	4 a
18	26	גבר	MAN	150a	
		חסד	BE GOOD	338c	
		חסיד	KIND	339c	1 a
		תמם	BE COMPLETE	1070d	
		תמים	COMPLETE	1071b	5
18	27	ברר	PURIFY	141a	B
		ברר	PURIFY	141a	2
		עקש	TWISTED	786a	
		פתל	TWIST	836d	
18	28	ישע	DELIVER	446d	1 b
		עין	EYE	744c	2 a
		עני	POOR	777a	4
		רום	BE HIGH	926d	2 b
		שפל	BECOME LOW	1050b	1
18	29	אור	BECOME LIGHT	21b	3
		יהוה	YAHWEH	219a	2 1f
		חשך	DARKNESS	365a	3 a
		נגה	SHINE	618b	1
		נר	LAMP	632d	
18	30	ב	IN	89d	3 2c
		גדוד	BAND	151b	1
		דלג	LEAP	194c	
		רוץ	RUN	930b	1
		שור	WALL	1004b	

Ch	v.	Heb	Eng	Page	Sec
18	31	אל	GOD	42c	6 a
		אמרה	UTTERANCE	57b	
		מגן	SHIELD	171c	
		דרך	WAY	204a	6 eb
		חסה	SEEK REFUGE	340b	
		ל	TO	513a	5 ad
		צרף	SMELT	864b	1
		תמים	SOUND	1071a	4
18	32	אלה	GOD	43a	2
		בלעדי	APART FROM	*116c	B b
		בלעדי	APART FROM	116c	B b
		זולה	EXCEPT	*265d	1
		זולה	EXCEPT	265d	1
		מי	WHO	*566c	F
		מי	WHO	566d	F
		צור	ROCK	849d	2 b
18	33	אזר	GIRD	25a	
		אל	GOD	42c	6 a
		חיל	STRENGTH	298c	1 a
		נתן	GIVE	681a	3 a
		נתר	BE FREE	*684a	2
		תמים	SOUND	1071b	4
18	34	אילה	HIND	19b	
		במה	HIGH PLACE	119b	2 a
		ך	LIKE	453d	1 b
		ך	LIKE	455a	B
		עמד	STAND	764d	2
		שוה	SET	1001b	
18	35	זרוע	ARM	284a	1 b
		מלחמה	WAR	536b	
		למד	LEARN	540d	
		נחושה	COPPER	639a	2
		נחת	DESCEND	639c	
		קשת	BOW	906c	1 d
18	36	מגן	SHIELD	171c	
		ימין	RIGHT HAND	411d	1 c
		ישע	DELIVERANCE	447a	2
		סעד	SUPPORT	703c	2 b
		ענוה	HUMILITY	776d	2
		רבה	BECOME MANY	915d	2
18	37	מעד	SLIP	588c	
		צעד	STEP	857d	1
		קרסל	ANKLE	902b	
		רחב	BE LARGE	931c	2
		תחת	UNDERNEATH	1065c	1
18	38	כלה	FINISH	478c	2 cl
		נשג	OVERTAKE	673c	1 a
18	39	יכל	BE ABLE	407c	1 b
		נפל	FALL	657b	2 a
		קום	STAND	877d	1 a
		תחת	UNDERNEATH	1065c	2 1e
18	40	אזר	GIRD	25a	
		חיל	STRENGTH	298c	1 a
		כרע	CAUSE TO BOW DOWN	502d	2
		תחת	UNDERNEATH	1065c	2 1c a
18	41	נתן	GIVE	681a	3 a
		ערף	BACK OF NECK	791b	1
		צמת	EXTERMINATE	856c	
		שן	HATE	971d	1
		שית	PUT	*1011c	3
		שכם	SHOULDER	*1014b	2
18	42	ישע	DELIVER	446c	1 a
		על	UPON	757c	27c b
		שוע	CRY OUT	1002d	
		שעה	GAZE	1043a	
18	43	דקק	PULVERISE	*200d	
		דקק	PULVERISE	*201a	
		חוץ	THE OUTSIDE	300b	2 a
		טיט	MUD	376c	1
		עפר	DRY EARTH	779d	1 d
		פנה	FACE	818d	27a a
		ריק	MAKE EMPTY	938a	1
		שחק	RUB AWAY	1007a	
18	44	ה	THE	208d	1 i
		עבד	WORK	713a	3
		פלט	ESCAPE	812b	1
		ריב	STRIFE	937a	2
18	45	אזן	EAR	23d	2 a
		בן	SON	121c	7 a
		כחש	DECEIVE	*471b	
		כחש	DECEIVE	471b	1
		נכר	FOREIGNNESS	648d	2
		שמע	HEAR	1034b	3
		שמע	REPORT	1034d	
18	46	בן	SON	121c	7 a
		חגר	GIRD	292a	3
		חרג	QUAKE	353a	2
		מן	OUT OF	579a	2 aa
		נבל	SINK	615b	1
		נכר	FOREIGNNESS	648d	2
		מסגרת	FASTNESS	689d	2
18	47	אלהים	GOD	44c	4 bb
		ברך	BLESS	*138d	2 a
		חי	ALIVE	311d	1 a
		ישע	DELIVERANCE	447a	2
		צור	ROCK	*849d	2 a
		צור	ROCK	849d	2 a
		רום	BE HIGH	927a	2 c
18	48	אל	GOD	42c	6 a
		דבר	SPEAK	182a	
		ירד	BRING DOWN	*434a	1 c
		נקמה	VENGEANCE	668c	1
		נתן	GIVE	678d	1 d
		תחת	UNDERNEATH	1065c	2 1c a

269

Ch	v.	Heb	Eng	Page	Sec
22	17	שפת	SET	1046b	1
		ארי	LION	71d	
		עדה	CONGREGATION	417a	1
		כור	PIERCE	468c	
		כלב	DOG	477a	B
		כרה	DIG	500b	
		נקף	GO AROUND	669a	1 b
		סבב	SURROUND	686a	2 d
		רעע	BE EVIL	949d	2
		הא	DEMONSTRATIVE PARTICLE	*1089c	A
22	18	נבט	LOOK	613c	1
		ספר	COUNT	708b	3
		ראה	TO SEE	908a	8 a6
22	19	בגד	GARMENT	94a	1
		גורל	LOT	174d	2 h
		חלק	DIVIDE	323d	1
		לבוש	CLOTHING	528c	
		נפל	FALL	658a	3
22	20	אילות	HELP	33d	
		חוש	HASTE	301d	1
		עזרה	HELP	741a	1
		רחק	BE DISTANT	934d	
22	21	יד	HAND	391b	5 g1
		יחיד	ONLY ONE	402d	1
		כלב	DOG	477a	B
22	22	אריה	LION	71d	
		ישע	DELIVER	446d	1 b
		מן	FROM	578a	1 a
		פה	MOUTH	805b	3
		קרן	HORN	901d	1 a
		ראם	WILD OX	910b	
22	23	הלל	PRAISE	*238b	2 c
		הלל	PRAISE	238b	2 c
		קהל	ASSEMBLY	874d	1 d
22	24	גור	DREAD	159a	2
		הלל	PRAISE	238b	2 c
		זרע	SOWING	283a	4 f
		ירא	FEAR	431c	3 b
		כבד	MAKE HONORABLE	457d	2 c
22	25	בזה	DESPISE	102c	
		הלל	PRAISE	*238b	2 c
		סתר	HIDE	711d	2 c
		ענות	AFFLICTION	776d	
		עני	POOR	777a	3
		שוע	CRY OUT	1002d	
		שמע	HEAR	1034b	2 h
		שקץ	DETEST	1055a	1
22	26	את	WITH	87a	4 c
		תהלה	PRAISE	240a	2
		ירא	FEAR	431c	3 b
		נגד	IN FRONT	617b	1 aa
		נדר	VOW	624a	2
		קהל	ASSEMBLY	874d	1 d
22	27	דרש	SEEK	205b	3 a
		הלל	PRAISE	238b	2 b
		חיה	LIVE	311b	1 d
		לבב	HEART	524a	27
		עד	PERPETUITY	723c	2 a
		ענו	POOR	776c	3
22	28	אפס	END	67a	1
		זכר	REMEMBER	270a	13 b
		עם	PEOPLE	766d	5 e
22	29	מלוכה	KINGSHIP	574d	
		משל	RULE	605d	3
22	30	דשן	FAT	206c	
		חיה	LIVE	311c	1
		ירד	GO DOWN	433b	1 i
		כרע	BOW DOWN	502c	1
		נפש	SOUL	659c	2
		עפר	DRY EARTH	779d	1 f
22	31	דור	GENERATION	190a	2 c
		דור	GENERATION	*190b	3
		זרע	SOWING	282d	4 c
		ל	TO	514b	5 fa
		ספר	COUNT	708b	
		עבד	WORK	713b	4 a
22	32	ברא	CREATE	*135c	2
		דור	GENERATION	190a	2 c
		דור	GENERATION	*190b	3
		ילד	BE BORN	408d	
		נגד	BE CONSPICUOUS	617a	4
		עשה	DO	794b	1 4
		צדקה	RIGHTEOUSNESS	842c	6 a
23	1	מזמור	MELODY	274c	
		חסר	LACK	341b	1 b
		רעה	TEND	945a	1 d3
23	2	דשא	GRASS	206a	
		נהג	DRIVE	*624b	2
		נהל	BRING TO A PLACE OF REST	625a	1
		נוה	PASTURE	627d	1
		מנוחה	REST	630a	2
		רבץ	LIE DOWN	918c	
23	3	נחת	LEAD	635a	
		נפש	SOUL	661a	1 d
		מעגל	ENTRENCHMENT	722d	2 b
		מען	PURPOSE	775b	1 a
		צדק	RIGHTNESS	841c	1
		שוב	TURN BACK	998c	2 a
23	4	גיא	VALLEY	161b	
		גם	YEA	169d	6
		הלך	WALK	234c	2 2
		הם	THEY	241b	2 2
		ירא	FEAR	431b	1 b
		כי	THOUGH	473c	2 ca
		נחם	CONSOLE ONESELF	637a	
		עם	WITH	767c	1 a
		צלמות	DEATH-SHADOW	853c	2 b
		רע	EVIL	948d	1
		שבט	ROD	987a	1 c
		משענת	STAFF	1044a	
23	5	דשן	BE FAT	206b	
		כוס	CUP	468a	
		נגד	IN FRONT	617b	1 aa
		ערך	ARRANGE	789c	1 c
		צרר	SHEW HOSTILITY TOWARD	865d	
		רויה	SATURATION	924b	
		שלחן	TABLE	1020b	2
		שמן	OIL	1032b	2 c
23	6	אך	SURELY	36c	1
		אך	ONLY	36d	
		ארך	LENGTH	73d	B
		חיים	LIFE	313b	1
		חסד	GOODNESS	339b	22
		טוב	A GOOD THING	375a	1
		יום	DAY	399a	4 a
		רדף	PURSUE	922d	1 g
24	1	מזמור	MELODY	274c	
		תבל	WORLD	*385d	
		תבל	WORLD	385d	
		ל	TO	513c	5 bb
		מלא	THAT WHICH FILLS	571b	3
24	2	הוא	HE, SHE, IT	*215b	1 a
		ים	SEA	411a	5
		יסד	FOUND	413d	
		כון	ESTABLISH	466d	1 b
24	3	הר	MOUNTAIN	249d	1 a
		מי	WHO	567a	F e
		עלה	GO UP	748b	1 d
		קדש	APARTNESS	871d	2 f
		מקום	STANDING PLACE	880b	4
24	4	אשר	PARTICLE OF RELATION	82d	5
		בר	PURE	141a	1 d
		כף	HOLLOW OF THE HAND	496d	1 d7
		לבב	HEART	524a	26 a
		נפש	SOUL	660d	6 a
		נקי	CLEAN	667c	1
		נשא	LIFT	670d	1 b 9
		מרמה	DECEIT	941b	
		שבע	SWEAR	989b	1 a
		שוא	EMPTINESS	996a	1
24	5	אלהים	GOD	44c	4 bb
		את	WITH	86c	4 a
		ברכה	BLESSING	139d	1 b
		ישע	DELIVERANCE	447a	2
		נשא	LIFT	671c	3 f
24	6	בקש	SEEK	134d	3 b
		דור	GENERATION	190b	3
		דרש	SEEK	205b	2 a
		זה	THIS	261b	3
		סלה	LIFT UP	700a	
		יעקב	JACOB	785a	2
		צדקה	RIGHTEOUSNESS	842b	6 a
24	7	כבד	GLORY	458d	2 c3
		מלך	KING	573b	3
		נשא	LIFT	670b	1 b 2
		נשא	LIFT	671a	1 a
		עולם	LONG DURATION	762d	1 a
		פתח	OPENING	836a	
		ראש	HEAD	910d	1 a
		שער	GATE	1044d	1 a
24	8	גבור	STRONG	150a	1
		זה	THIS	261b	4 b
		כבוד	GLORY	458d	2 c3
		מלחמה	WAR	536b	
		מי	WHO	567a	F e
		מלך	KING	573b	3
		עזוז	MIGHTY	739b	5
24	9	כבד	GLORY	458d	2 c3
		מלך	KING	573b	3
		נשא	LIFT	670b	1 b 2
		נשא	LIFT	671a	1 a
		עולם	LONG DURATION	762d	1 a
		פתח	OPENING	836a	
		ראש	HEAD	910d	1 a
		שער	GATE	1044d	1 a
24	10	הוא	HE, SHE, IT	216c	4 bb
		זה	THIS	*261b	4 b
		כבוד	GLORY	458d	2 c3
		מי	WHO	566c	E a
		מי	WHO	567a	F e
		מלך	KING	573b	3
		סלה	LIFT UP	700a	
		צבא	GOD OF WAR	839c	4 c
25	1	אל	TO	40a	3 c
		נפש	SOUL	660d	6 a
		נשא	LIFT	670d	1 b 9
25	2	אל	NOT	39a	A a
		בטח	TRUST	105a	1 3a
		ל	TO	510d	1 d
		עלץ	REJOICE	763b	
25	3	בגד	ACT TREACHEROUSLY	93d	D
		קוה	WAIT FOR	875d	
		ריקם	EMPTILY	938b	2
25	4	ארח	WAY	73b	3 b
		דרך	WAY	204a	6 ec
		ידע	KNOW	395a	
25	5	למד	LEARN	540d	
		אלהים	GOD	44c	4 bb
		אמת	FIRMNESS	54a	3 a
		דרך	TREAD	202c	3
		יום	DAY	400c	7 f
		ישע	DELIVERANCE	447a	2
		למד	LEARN	540d	
		קוה	WAIT FOR	875d	1
25	6	זכר	REMEMBER	270b	23 b
		חסד	GOODNESS	339c	4
		עולם	LONG DURATION	762a	1 c
		רחמים	COMPASSION	933c	1
25	7	זכר	REMEMBER	270b	21 a
		זכר	REMEMBER	270c	24
		חטאת	SIN	308c	1 b
		חסד	GOODNESS	339a	21 d
		טוב	GOOD THINGS	375c	4 b
		נעורים	YOUTH	655c	
		מען	PURPOSE	775b	1 a
		פשע	TRANSGRESSION	833d	3 d
25	8	דרך	WAY	203c	6 b
		חטא	SINFUL	308b	2
		טוב	PLEASANT	375a	0 b
		ישר	DIRECT	435b	5 a
		ישר	STRAIGHT	449a	3 a
25	9	דרך	TREAD	202c	3
		דרך	WAY	204a	6 ec
		למד	LEARN	540d	
		ענו	POOR	776c	3
		משפט	JUDGMENT	1048d	3
25	10	אמת	FIRMNESS	54b	3 a
		ארח	WAY	73b	3 a
		ברית	COVENANT	136c	2 2c
		ברית	COVENANT	137a	1
		חסד	GOODNESS	339a	22
		נצר	KEEP	665d	1
		עדה	TESTIMONIES	730a	
25	11	סלה	FORGIVE	699b	
		עון	INIQUITY	731a	1 c2
		מען	PURPOSE	775b	1 a
		שם	NAME	1028c	3
25	12	בחר	CHOOSE	104a	2 a
		דרך	WAY	203c	6 b
		זה	THIS	261b	4 b
		ירא	FEAR	431c	3 b
		ירה	DIRECT	435c	5 c
		מי	WHO	567b	G
25	13	זרע	SOWING	282d	4 c
		טוב	A GOOD THING	375a	1
		ירש	TAKE POSSESSION	439c	1 a
		לון	LODGE	533d	2
		נפש	SOUL	660a	4 a3
25	14	ברית	COVENANT	136c	21
		ידע	KNOW	395a	
		ירא	FEAR	431c	3 b
		ל	TO	518b	7 bh
		סוד	COUNSEL	691c	2
25	15	הוא	HE, SHE, IT	*215b	1 a
		יצא	BRING OUT	424d	2
		רשת	NET	440c	1 b2
		תמיד	CONTINUITY	556b	1
25	16	חנן	SHOW FAVOR	336a	2 b
		יחיד	ONLY ONE	402d	3
		כי	BECAUSE	473d	3 b
		ענו	POOR	776d	3
		פנה	TURN	815c	2 c1
25	17	יצא	BRING OUT	424d	2
		לבב	HEART	524b	29 b
		מצוקה	STRAIGNESS	748b	3
		צרה	DISTRESS	865b	
25	18	חטאת	SIN	309a	1 d2
		נשא	LIFT	671c	3 c
		עמל	TROUBLE	765d	1
		עני	AFFLICTION	777a	1
25	19	חמס	VIOLENCE	329c	
		רבב	BECOME MUCH	912d	1
		שנאה	HATING	971d	1
25	20	חסה	SEEK REFUGE	340b	
		נפש	SOUL	660a	3 c
25	21	ישר	STRAIGHTNESS	449c	2
		נצר	GUARD	665d	2
		קוה	WAIT FOR	875d	1
		תם	INTEGRITY	1070d	3
25	22	אלהים	GOD	44a	4 a
		פדה	RANSOM	804a	3 c
		צרה	DISTRESS	865b	
26	1	בטח	TRUST	105a	1 3a
		מעד	SLIP	588c	
		שפט	JUDGE	1047d	3 b1
		תם	INTEGRITY	1070d	3
26	2	בחן	TRY	103c	2 b
		כליה	KIDNEYS	480c	2 b
		לב	HEART	525a	26
		נסה	TEST	650b	3 a
		צרף	SMELT	864b	2
26	3	אמת	FIRMNESS	54a	3 a
		הלך	WALK	236b	2
		חסד	GOODNESS	339b	22
		נגד	IN FRONT	617c	3
26	4	בוא	COME	98d	3
		ישב	DWELL	443a	3
		מת	MALE	607b	3 b
		עלם	CONCEAL	761a	3
		שוא	EMPTINESS	996b	3
26	5	קהל	ASSEMBLY	874c	1 a
		רעע	BE EVIL	949d	

Ch v.	Heb	Eng	Page	Sec
	רשע	WICKED	957c	3
26 6	שנא	HATE	971c	1a
	כף	HOLLOW OF THE HAND	496d	1d7
	נקיון	INNOCENCY	667d	1
	סבב	GO AROUND	686b	3
	רחץ	WASH OFF	934c	1
26 7	תודה	THANKSGIVING	392d	2
	פלא	BE SURPASSING	810d	4
	קול	VOICE	876d	1a
	שמע	HEAR	1034c	1a
26 8	אהב	LOVE	13a	3
	כבוד	GLORY	458d	2c1
	משכן	DWELLING-PLACE	1015d	2a
26 9	אסף	GATHER	62c	4
	דם	BLOOD	197a	2h
	חטא	SINFUL	308b	2
	חיים	LIFE	313a	1
	משך	DRAW	*604b	1
	עם	WITH	767d	1e
26 10	זמה	PLAN	273c	2a
	ימין	RIGHT HAND	411c	1a
	מלא	BE FULL	570a	1b
	שחד	BRIBE	1005a	
26 11	הלך	WALK	235a	23e1
	חנן	SHOW FAVOR	336a	2b
	פדה	RANSOM	804a	3d
	תם	INTEGRITY	1070d	3
26 12	ברך	BLESS	139a	1
	מישור	LEVEL PLACE	449d	2
	עמד	STAND	764a	1i
	מקהל	ASSEMBLY	875b	
27 1	אור	LIGHT	21d	1
	חיים	LIFE	313b	2
	ירא	FEAR	431b	1c
	ישע	DELIVERANCE	447a	2
	מי	WHO	566b	B
	מן	OUT OF	580a	2ec
	מעוז	PLACE OF SAFETY	732a	2a
	פחד	DREAD	808b	1
27 2	אכל	EAT	37d	6
	בשר	FLESH	142c	1b
	המה	THEY	241b	2a
	כשל	STUMBLE	505c	1
	נפל	FALL	657b	2b
	צר	ADVERSARY	865d	
	קרב	COME NEAR	897b	1a
	רעע	BE EVIL	949d	2
27 3	אם	IF	49d	1a1c
	ב	IN	90c	37
	בטח	TRUST	105a	13c
	זה	THIS	261d	6bg
	חנה	DECLINE	333c	2c2
	מחנה	ENCAMPMENT	334b	3a
	ירא	FEAR	431a	1a
	מלחמה	WAR	536c	
	על	UPON	757d	27d
	קום	STAND	878a	2
27 4	את	WITH	86d	4a
	בקר	SEEK	133a	
	בקש	SEEK	134d	2a
	היכל	TEMPLE	228c	2d
	חזה	SEE	302b	1c
	חיים	LIFE	313b	1
	נעם	DELIGHTFULNESS	653c	1
	שאל	ASK	981c	1a
27 5	אהל	TENT	14b	3
	סכה	THICKET	697c	2
	סך	THICKET	697c	
	סתר	HIDE	711d	1
	סתר	COVERING	712a	2a
	צור	ROCK	849c	1a
	צפן	HIDE	860c	1
	רום	BE HIGH	927a	2a
27 6	אהל	TENT	14b	3
	ב	IN	89a	21
	זבח	SACRIFICE	257c	24
	זמר	MAKE MUSIC	274a	1
	סביב	ROUND ABOUT	687b	2bb
	ראש	HEAD	911b	8
	רום	BE HIGH	927a	2b
	תרועה	SHOUT OF WAR	930a	3
	שיר	SING	1010d	
27 7	חנן	SHOW FAVOR	336a	2b
	קול	VOICE	877a	1a
27 8	בקש	SEEK	134d	3b
27 9	אלהים	GOD	44c	4bb
	ישע	DELIVERANCE	447a	2
	נטה	EXTEND	641a	3h
	נטש	FORSAKE	643d	1
	סתר	HIDE	711d	2c
	עבד	SLAVE	714c	6
	עזרה	HELP	741a	2b
27 10	אם	MOTHER	51d	1
	אסף	GATHER	62b	2c
	כי	BECAUSE	473d	3b
	עזב	LEAVE	737b	2b1
27 11	ארח	WAY	73a	2
	ארץ	EARTH	76b	4c
	דרך	WAY	204a	6ec
	ירה	DIRECT	435c	5c
	מישור	LEVEL PLACE	449d	2
	נחה	LEAD	634d	3
	מען	PURPOSE	775b	1b
	שורר	WATCHER	1004a	
27 12	חמס	VIOLENCE	329c	
	יפח	BREATHING	422a	
	עד	WITNESS	729d	2c
	עד	WITNESS	729d	2c
	קום	STAND	877d	1f
	קום	STAND	878a	2
	שקר	DECEPTION	1055c	3
27 13	אמן	CONFIRM	53b	2e
	ארץ	EARTH	76b	4d
	חי	ALIVE	312a	1b
	טוב	GOOD THINGS	375c	1
	לולא	IF NOT	530c	A
	לולא	IF NOT	*530c	D
	אל	TO	40a	3c
27 14	אמץ	BE STRONG	55b	
	חזק	BE FIRM	304d	12c
	לב	HEART	525d	2O
	קוה	WAIT FOR	875d	1
28 1	בור	PIT	92c	5
	חרש	BE SILENT	361a	2
	חשה	BE SILENT	364c	
	ירד	GO DOWN	433b	1i
	מן	FROM	578a	1a
	משל	BE LIKE	605a	
	עם	WITH	768a	1f
28 2	צור	ROCK	849c	2a
	אל	TO	39d	3a
	דביר	HINDMOST CHAMBER	184b	
	דביר	DEBIR	*184c	2a
	תחנון	SUPPLICATION FOR FAVOR	337d	2
	יד	HAND	389c	1d
	נשא	LIFT	670b	1b1
	קדש	APARTNESS	871d	2d
	קול	VOICE	877a	1a
	שוע	CRY OUT	1002d	
28 3	דבר	SPEAK	180c	
	דבר	SPEAK	180c	
	לב	HEART	523b	21
	משך	DRAW	604b	1
	משך	DRAW	604c	5
	עם	WITH	767d	1e
	רע	FRIEND	946a	2
	שלום	PEACE	1023a	5a
28 4	כ	LIKE	454a	1b
	נתן	GIVE	679d	1v
	מעשה	DEED	795d	1b3
	פעל	DOING	821c	1c
	רע	EVIL	948a	3
28 5	בין	DISCERN	106c	3d
	בנה	BUILD	124d	2b
	הרס	THROW DOWN	248d	1
	מעשה	DEED	796a	1c
	פעלה	WORK	821d	1a
28 6	ברך	BLESS	138c	2a
	תחנון	SUPPLICATION FOR FAVOR	337d	2
	קול	VOICE	877a	1a
28 7	בטח	TRUST	105a	13a
	מגן	SHIELD	171c	
	ידה	PRAISE	392c	1a2
	לב	HEART	525c	29a
	עז	STRENGTH	739a	2c
	עזר	HELP	740c	
	עלז	EXULT	759c	
	שיר	SONG	1010b	2
28 8	ישועה	VICTORY	447c	4
	ל	TO	513a	5ad
	משיח	ANOINTED	603c	1
	מעוז	PLACE OF SAFETY	732a	2a
	עז	STRENGTH	739a	2c
28 9	ברך	BLESS	139a	2a
	ישע	DELIVER	446d	1b
	נחלה	PROPERTY	635b	1e
	נשא	LIFT	672a	3
	עולם	LONG DURATION	762d	2g
	רעה	TEND	944d	1b
29 1	אל	GOD	42b	2
	בן	SON	120b	1d
	מזמור	MELODY	274c	
	יהב	ASCRIBE	396d	4
	כבוד	HONOR	459b	6b
	עז	STRENGTH	739b	3b
29 2	הדרה	ADORNMENT	214c	1
	יהב	ASCRIBE	396d	4
	כבוד	HONOR	459b	6b
	ל	TO	*516d	5k
	קדש	APARTNESS	872b	4b
	שחה	BOW DOWN	1005c	2b
	שם	NAME	1028c	3
29 3	אל	GOD	42c	2c
	כבוד	GLORY	458d	2c2
	מי	WATER	565c	1f
	קול	VOICE	877a	2b
	רעם	THUNDER	947b	
	רעם	THUNDER	947b	
29 4	ב	IN	89c	31c
	הדר	SPLENDOUR	214b	2
	כח	STRENGTH	470d	3
	כח	STRENGTH	471a	3
29 5	ארז	CEDAR	72c	1a
	לבנון	LEBANON	527a	
	קול	VOICE	877a	2b
	שבר	BREAK	990a	
	שבר	BREAK	991a	
29 6	בן	SON	121c	7b
	כמו	LIKE	455d	1a
	לבנון	LEBANON	*527a	
	לבנון	LEBANON	527b	
	עגל	CALF	722a	
	ראם	WILD OX	910b	
	רקד	SKIP ABOUT	955b	
	שרין	SIRION	976b	
29 7	אש	FIRE	77d	6
	חצב	HEW	345a	3
	להבה	FLAME	*529b	1
	להבה	FLAME	529b	1
	קול	VOICE	877a	2b
29 8	מדבר	WILDERNESS	185a	3a
	חול	WHIRL	297c	
	קדש	KADESH	873d	1
29 9	אילה	HIND	19b	
	היכל	TEMPLE	228d	2e
	חול	WHIRL	297b	2
	יער	WOOD	420d	C
	כבוד	HONOR	459b	6b
	כל	ALL	482a	1db
	קול	VOICE	877a	2b
29 10	ישב	SIT	442c	1a
	ישב	SIT	442c	1a
	מבול	FLOOD	550a	
	מלך	KING	573b	3
	עולם	LONG DURATION	762c	2c
29 11	ברך	BLESS	139a	2a
	ה	THE	208c	1hb
	עז	STRENGTH	739a	2b
	שלום	PEACE	1023a	5b
30 1	מזמור	MELODY	274c	
	חנכה	DEDICATION	335c	
	שיר	SONG	*1010b	2
30 2	דלה	DRAW	194d	
	ל	TO	510d	1d
	רום	BE HIGH	927b	3
	שמח	REJOICE	970c	
30 3	יהוה	YAHWEH	219a	21f
	רפא	HEAL	950d	2a
	שוע	CRY OUT	1002d	
30 4	בור	PIT	92c	5
	דלה	DRAW	*194d	
	חיה	LIVE	311c	1
	ירד	GO DOWN	433b	1i
	מן	FROM	578a	1a
	מן	FROM	583b	7ba
	נפש	SOUL	659c	1
	עלה	GO UP	749b	1b1
	שאול	SHEOL	983a	2a
30 5	זכר	REMEMBRANCE	271b	1c
	זמר	MAKE MUSIC	274a	1
	חסיד	KIND	339d	2b
	ידה	PRAISE	392c	1a
	קדש	APARTNESS	871c	1c
30 6	בכי	WEEPING	113d	
	בקר	MORNING	134a	1e
	בקר	MORNING	134b	1g
	חיים	LIFE	313b	2
	ל	TO	517a	6a
	לון	LODGE	533d	1d
	רגע	A MOMENT	921a	A
	רנה	RINGING CRY	943d	3
	רצון	GOODWILL	953c	1a
30 7	אני	I	59c	
	בל	NOT	115b	
	מוט	SHAKE	557a	
	עולם	LONG DURATION	762a	2a
	שלו	EASE	1017b	
	שלוה	QUIETNESS	1017d	
30 8	בהל	BE DISTURBED	96b	1
	סתר	HIDE	711d	2a
	עז	STRENGTH	738d	1
	עמד	STAND	765a	
	רצון	GOODWILL	953c	1a
30 9	חנן	SHOW FAVOR	336b	2
30 10	אמת	FIRMNESS	54b	4a
	בצע	PROFIT	130c	
	דם	BLOOD	196d	2d
	ידה	PRAISE	392c	1a2
	ירד	GO DOWN	433b	1i
	מה	WHAT	552c	1aa
	מה	WHAT	553a	1da
	עפר	DRY EARTH	779d	1f
	שחת	PIT	1001c	2
30 11	חנן	SHOW FAVOR	336a	2b
	עזר	HELP	740c	
30 12	אזר	GIRD	25a	
	הפך	TURN	245c	1c4
	מחול	DANCE	298b	
	ספד	WAIL	*704d	
	מספד	WAILING	704d	4
	פתח	OPEN	835c	2
	שק	SACK	974c	2a
30 13	דמם	BE SILENT	198d	1
	יהוה	YAHWEH	219a	21f
	זמר	MAKE MUSIC	274a	1
	ידה	PRAISE	392c	1a2
	כבוד	HONOR	459b	5
	עולם	LONG DURATION	762a	2a
	מען	PURPOSE	775c	2b
31 1	מזמור	MELODY	274c	
31 2	ב	IN	89c	31c
	חסה	SEEK REFUGE	340b	
	עולם	LONG DURATION	762b	2a
	פלט	ESCAPE	812b	1

Ch	v.	Heb	Eng	Page	Sec
31	3	צדקה	RIGHTEOUSNESS	842c	6 a
		אזן	EAR	24b	2 b
		ישע	DELIVER	446d	1 b
		מהרה	HASTE	555b	
		נטה	INCLINE	641a	3 e
		מעוז	PLACE OF SAFETY	732a	2 a
		מצודה	FASTNESS	845a	
		צור	ROCK	849d	2 a
31	4	נהל	LEAD,GUIDE	625a	3
		נחה	LEAD	635a	
		סלע	CRAG	701a	2
		מען	PURPOSE	775b	1 a
		מצודה	FASTNESS	845a	
		שם	NAME	1028c	3
31	5	זו	THIS	262b	2
		טמן	HIDE	380c	2
		יצא	BRING OUT	424d	2
		רשת	NET	440c	1 b2
		מעוז	PLACE OF SAFETY	732a	2
31	6	אל	GOD	42d	6 c
		אמת	FIRMNESS	54b	3 b
		פדה	RANSOM	804a	3 d
		פקד	ATTEND TO	824a	2 a
		רוח	BREATH	925c	4 d
31	7	בטח	TRUST	105b	15 a
		הבל	VAPOUR	211a	2
		שנא	HATE	971c	1 a
		שוא	EMPTINESS	996a	1
		שמר	KEEP	1036d	1 b
		שמר	KEEP	1037a	3 d
		שמר	KEEP	*1037c	
31	8	חסד	GOODNESS	339a	2 la
		ידע	KNOW	393b	1 b
		ידע	KNOW	394b	1
		עני	AFFLICTION	777a	1
		צרה	DISTRESS	865b	
31	9	ה	THE	208d	2 a
		סגר	DELIVER UP	689c	1
		עמד	STAND	764d	6 b
		מרחב	ROOMY PLACE	932c	
		שפה	SPEECH	973d	1 a1
31	10	ב	IN	90c	3 5
		בטן	BELLY	105d	2
		חנן	SHOW FAVOR	336a	2 b
		כעס	ANGER	495b	2
		מן	ON ACCOUNT OF	580b	2 f
		נפש	SOUL	659b	1 a
		עין	EYE	744b	1 i
		עשש	WASTE AWAY	799c	
		צרר	ADDENDA ET COR- RIGENDA	1126c	
31	11	אנחה	SIGHING	58d	
		חיים	LIFE	313a	1
		יגון	GRIEF	387b	
		כח	STRENGTH	470c	1 a
		כלה	BE FINISHED	477d	2
		כשל	TOTTER	505c	2
		עון	INIQUITY	731c	3
		עצם	BONE	782d	1 c
		עשש	WASTE AWAY	799c	
		שנה	YEAR	1040b	
31	12	חוץ	THE OUTSIDE	299d	1 bb
		חרפה	REPROACH	358a	3
		ידע	ACQUAINTANCE	394d	
		מאד	EXCEEDINGLY	547b	2 a
		מן	ON ACCOUNT OF	580b	2 f
		נדד	RETREAT	622b	1
		פחד	DREAD	808c	2
		צרר	SHEW HOSTILITY TOWARD	865d	
		שכן	NEIGHBOUR	1015c	2
31	13	אבד	PERISH	1d	1
		לב	HEART	525a	2 3d
		מן	OUT OF	579a	2 aa
		דבה	WHISPERING	179b	1
31	14	זמם	CONSIDER	273d	2 b
		יחד	UNION	403a	2 a2
		יסד	FIX THEMSELVES	414a	1
		לקח	TAKE	543a	3 d
		נפש	SOUL	659d	3 c
		סביב	ROUND ABOUT	687a	1 d
31	15	בטח	TRUST	105a	14 a
31	16	עת	TIME	773d	3
		רדף	PURSUE	922d	1 f
31	17	אור	BECOME LIGHT	21c	5
		חסד	GOODNESS	339a	2 la
		ישע	DELIVER	446d	1 b
		עבד	SLAVE	714c	6
		על	UPON	757d	2 7c d
31	18	אלם	BIND	47d	2
		דמם	BE STILL	198d	2
		שאול	SHEOL	983a	2 a
31	19	אלם	BIND	47d	2
		בוז	CONTEMPT	100b	1
		גאוה	PRIDE	144d	3
		דבר	SPEAK	180c	2
		עתק	FORWARD	801b	
		שקר	DECEPTION	1055c	3
31	20	חסה	SEEK REFUGE	340b	
		טוב	GOOD THINGS	375d	4 c
		ירא	FEAR	431c	3 b
		נגד	IN FRONT	617b	1 aa
		פעל	DO	821b	1 a
		צפן	HIDE	860c	1
		רב	GREAT	913c	2 a
31	21	לשון	TONGUE	546c	1 b
		סבה	THICKET	697c	2
		סתר	HIDE	711d	1
		סתר	COVERING	712a	2 a
		צפן	HIDE	860c	1
		ריב	STRIFE	936d	1
31	22	רכס	SNARE	940d	
		ברך	BLESS	138c	2 a
		חסד	GOODNESS	339a	2 a
		עיר	CITY	746b	1 a
		פלא	BE SURPASSING	810d	2
		פלה	BE SEPARATED	*811d	2
		מצור	SIEGE	849a	2
31	23	אכן	SURELY	38c	B
		אנכי	I	59c	
		גרז	CUT OFF	173d	
		תחנון	SUPPLICATION FOR FAVOR	337d	2
		חפז	BE IN TREPIDA- TION	342a	1
		נגד	IN FRONT	617d	2 cb a
		עין	EYE	745a	5
		קול	VOICE	877a	1 a
		שוע	CRY OUT	1002d	2
31	24	אהב	LOVE	13a	3
		אמן	CONFIRM	52d	4 b
		אמן	TRUSTING	53c	2
		גאוה	PRIDE	144d	2
		חסיד	KIND	339d	2 b
		יתר	EXCESS	452a	2 b
		נצר	GUARD	665d	2
		על	UPON	754d	2 1f e
31	25	שלם	BE COMPLETE	1022c	5
		אמץ	BE STRONG	55b	
		חזק	BE FIRM	304b	1 2c
		יחל	WAIT	404a	2
		לבב	HEART	524b	2 0b
32	1	אשר	HAPPINESS	81a	
		חטאה	SIN	308b	1
		חטאת	SIN	*309a	1 d3
		כסה	COVER	491c	2
		כסה	COVER	492a	5
		נשא	LIFT	671c	3 c
		פשע	TRANSGRESSION	833c	3 d
32	2	אשר	HAPPINESS	81a	
		חשב	THINK	363a	1 3
		חשב	THINK	363b	2 3
		מלאך	MESSENGER	521d	2
		עון	INIQUITY	731b	1 c5
		רוח	BREATH	925d	8
		רמיה	DECEIT	941b	1
32	3	ב	IN	90c	3 5
		בלה	BECOME OLD AND WORN OUT	115a	
		חרש	BE SILENT	361b	1 a
		יום	DAY	400c	7 f
		כי	WHEN	473a	2 a
		שאגה	ROARING	980d	1
32	4	הפך	TURN	246a	2 c
		חרבון	DROUGHT	351c	
		יומם	BY DAY	401c	2
		כבד	BE HEAVY	457b	1
		לשד	JUICE	545c	
		לשד	SUCK	545c	
		לשן	LICK	546a	
		סלה	LIFT UP	700a	
		קיץ	SUMMER	884d	1
32	5	חטאת	SIN	308c	1 b
		חטאת	SIN	308d	1 d2
		ידה	CONFESS	392c	2 b
		ידע	KNOW	395a	
		כסה	COVER	491d	2
		נשא	LIFT	671b	3 c
		סלה	LIFT UP	700a	
		עון	INIQUITY	731a	1 b
		עון	INIQUITY	731a	1 c2
		על	UPON	754d	2 1f g
		פשע	TRANSGRESSION	833c	3 b
32	6	זה	THIS	262a	6 f
		חסיד	KIND	339d	2 b
		ל	TO	517a	6 a
		מי	WATER	565d	4 a
		מצא	FIND	593a	1 a
		נגע	REACH	619c	4
		פלל	INTERVENE	813b	3
		מצוק	STRAITNESS	848a	
		רק	ONLY	956d	2 e
		שטף	FLOOD	1009b	
32	7	מן	FROM	578b	1 a
		נצר	GUARD	665d	2
		סבב	SURROUND	686b	1
		סלה	LIFT UP	700a	
		סתר	COVERING	712a	2 a
		פלט	DELIVERANCE	812c	
		צר	STRAITS	865a	
		רן	RINGING CRY	943c	
32	8	דרך	WAY	203c	6 b
		זו	THIS	262c	2
		יעץ	ADVISE	419d	
		ירה	DIRECT	435b	5 a
		שכל	BE PRUDENT	968c	4
32	9	אין	NOT	34d	4 a
		בין	DISCERN	107a	1 a
		בל	NOT	115c	
		בלם	CURB	117d	
		ל	TO	518a	7 bg
		מתג	BRIDLE	607c	1
		סוס	HORSE	692d	2
		עדי	ORNAMENTS	726a	4
		פרד	MULE	825d	
32	10	רסן	HALTER	943d	1
		בטח	TRUST	105a	1 3a
		חסד	GOODNESS	339a	2 la
		מכאוב	PAIN	456b	1
		סבב	SURROUND	686b	1
		רשע	WICKED	957c	3
32	11	ישר	STRAIGHT	449b	3 b
		לב	HEART	525b	2 6a
		צדיק	JUST	843b	3 b
		רנן	GIVE A RINGING CRY	943c	
		שמח	REJOICE	970b	2 a
33	1	תהלה	PRAISE	*240a	2
		יאה	BEFIT	*383b	
		נאוה	SEEMLY	610a	2
		ישר	STRAIGHT	779b	3 c2
		צדיק	JUST	843b	4
		רנן	GIVE A RINGING CRY	943c	
33	2	זמר	MAKE MUSIC	274b	2
		ידה	PRAISE	392c	1 b
		כנור	LYRE	490b	
		כנור	LYRE	490b	
		נבל	HARP	614c	
		עשור	A TEN	797d	2
33	3	חדש	NEW	294a	A
		יטב	DO WELL	405d	3
		נגן	PLAY	618d	
		תרועה	SHOUT OF WAR	930a	3
		שיר	SING	1010c	
33	4	אמונה	FIRMNESS	53c	3 b
		ישר	STRAIGHT	449b	3 a
		מעשה	DEED	795d	
33	5	אהב	LOVE	13b	5 c
		חסד	GOODNESS	339a	2 3b
		מלא	BE FULL	570a	1 b
		משפט	JUDGMENT	1048d	2
33	6	דבר	WORD	182d	1 2b
		ה	THE	208d	1 i
		פה	MOUTH	805b	2
		צבא	HOST	839b	1 c
33	7	רוח	BREATH	924c	1 c
		אוצר	TREASURE	70a	3 d
		כנס	GATHER	488a	
		נד	HEAP	622d	
		תהום	DEEP	1062d	1
33	8	ארץ	EARTH	76a	1 c
		גור	DREAD	159a	2
		תבל	WORLD	385d	
		ירא	FEAR	431b	2
33	9	הוא	HE, SHE, IT	*215b	1
		עמד	STAND	764c	6 b
		צוה	CHARGE	846a	5
33	10	גוי	NATION	156d	1 c
		מחשבה	THOUGHT	364b	2
		עצה	ADVICE	420a	
		נוא	RESTRAIN	626b	1 a
		פרר	BREAK	830b	2 a
33	11	דור	PERIOD	189d	1 b
		מחשבה	THOUGHT	364b	1 a
		עצה	ADVICE	420b	
		לב	HEART	524d	2 3c
		עולם	LONG DURATION	762c	2 c
		עמד	STAND	764b	3 c
33	12	אשר	HAPPINESS	81a	
		בחר	CHOOSE	104a	2 a
		גוי	NATION	156c	1 b
		גוי	NATION	156d	1 c
		יהוה	YAHWEH	218d	2 1e
		ל	TO	512c	4 b
		נחלה	PROPERTY	635b	1 e
33	13	נבט	LOOK	613d	3
33	14	ה	THE	*209a	2 a
		ישב	DWELL	443a	3
		מכון	FIXED PLACE	467d	1
		שגח	GAZE	993b	
33	15	בין	DISCERN	107a	2
		ה	THE	209a	2 a
		יחד	ALTOGETHER	403b	2 b
		יצר	FORM	427d	2 a
		לב	HEART	524c	2 2
		מעשה	DEED	795d	1 a3
33	16	גבור	STRONG	150b	2
		ישע	BE DELIVERED	446b	2
		תשועה	DELIVERANCE	*448b	1 d
		כח	STRENGTH	470d	1 d
		נצל	BE DELIVERED	664c	2
		רב	MULTITUDE	914a	2
33	17	חיל	STRENGTH	298c	1 a
		תשועה	DELIVERANCE	448b	1
		מלט	SLIP AWAY	572c	3
		שקר	DECEPTION	1055c	
33	18	אל	TO	40a	3 a
		חסד	GOODNESS	339a	2 la
		יחל	WAIT	404a	2
		ירא	FEAR	431c	3 b
		ל	TO	510d	1 a
		עין	EYE	744a	1 f
		עין	EYE	744d	3 a
33	19	חיה	LIVE	311c	1
		נפש	SOUL	660a	3 c
		נצל	DELIVER	665a	3 b
33	20	מגן	SHIELD	171c	

Ch	v.	Heb	Eng	Page	Sec
		חכה	WAIT	314a	3
		עזר	HELP	740d	2
33	21	בטח	TRUST	105a	1 3d
		לב	HEART	525c	2 9a
33	22	חסד	GOODNESS	339d	2 1a
		יחל	WAIT	404a	2
		על	UPON	756c	2 7a b
34	1	אבימלך	ABIMELECH	4b	2
		גרש	DRIVE OUT	176d	
		הלך	WALK	234a	1 5d
		טעם	TASTE	381b	2
		שנה	CHANGE	1040a	
34	2	ברך	BLESS	139a	1
		תהלה	PRAISE	240a	1
		תמיד	CONTINUITY	556b	1a
		עת	TIME	773b	1a
34	3	הלל	BE BOASTFUL	239a	2
		ענו	POOR	776c	3
34	4	גדל	BECOME GREAT	152c	3 b
		יחדו	TOGETHER	403b	A
		ל	TO	512a	3 b
		רום	BE HIGH	927b	3
34	5	מגורה	FEAR	159a	
		דרש	SEEK	205b	3 a
		הלך	WALK	234b	1 5f 2
34	6	אל	NOT	39b	A c
		חפר	BE ABASHED	344a	
		נבט	LOOK	613d	2
		נהר	BEAM	626a	
34	7	זה	THIS	260d	2 a
		ישע	DELIVER	446d	1 b
		עני	POOR	777a	3
		שמע	HEAR	1034b	2 h
34	8	חלץ	DRAW OFF OR OUT	322d	2
		חנה	DECLINE	333d	2 c2
		ירא	FEAR	431c	3 b
		מלאך	MESSENGER	521d	2
		סביב	ROUND ABOUT	687a	1 cb
		סביב	ROUND ABOUT	687a	1 b
34	9	אשר	HAPPINESS	81a	
		חסה	SEEK REFUGE	340b	
		טוב	PLEASANT	374d	9 b
		טעם	TASTE	381a	3
34	10	מחסור	NEED	341d	2
		ירא	FEAR	431c	3 b
		ירא	FEAR	431c	3 b
		קדוש	HOLY	872d	2 b
34	11	דרש	SEEK	205b	3 a
		חסר	LACK	341b	1a
		טוב	A GOOD THING	375a	1
		כפיר	LION	498d	
		רוש	BE IN WANT	930d	
		רעב	BE HUNGRY	945b	
34	12	יראה	FEAR	432a	3
		למד	LEARN	540d	
34	13	אהב	LOVE	13a	2
		חיים	LIFE	313a	1
		חפץ	DELIGHTING IN	343a	1
		טוב	A GOOD THING	375a	1
		מי	WHO	567b	G
34	14	לשון	TONGUE	546c	1 b
		נצר	WATCH	665d	1
		מרמה	DECEIT	941b	
34	15	בקש	SEEK	134d	2 b
		טוב	A GOOD THING	375b	4
		סור	TURN ASIDE	693d	1
		רדף	PURSUE	923a	2
		רע	EVIL	949a	3
		שלום	PEACE	1023a	5 a
34	16	אזן	EAR	24b	2 b
		אל	TO	40a	3 a
		עין	EYE	744a	1 b
		עין	EYE	744a	3 a
		שועה	CRY FOR HELP	1003a	
		על	TO	1106b	4 a
34	17	זכר	REMEMBRANCE	271b	1 a
		כרת	CUT OFF	504c	2 c
		כתב	BE WRITTEN	*508a	2
		פנה	FACE	816a	1 1e
		צרה	DISTRESS	865b	
34	18	צעק	CRY	858c	1 b
		צרה	DISTRESS	865b	
		שמע	HEAR	1034b	2 h
34	19	דבא	CONTRITE	194b	
		ישע	DELIVER	446d	1 b
		לב	HEART	525b	2 6a
		קרב	NEAR	898c	2 f
		רוח	BREATH	925c	8
		רוח	BREATH	*925d	8
		שבר	BREAK	990d	
34	20	צדיק	JUST	843b	4
		רעה	MISERY	949a	1
34	21	הם	THEY	241d	8 c
		מן	FROM	580c	3 a
		שבר	BREAK	990d	
34	22	אשם	OFFEND	79c	3
		מות	DIE	560d	
		צדיק	JUST	843b	4
34	23	אשם	OFFEND	79c	3
		חסה	SEEK REFUGE	340b	
		נפש	SOUL	660a	3 c
		עבד	SLAVE	714a	3
		פדה	RANSOM	804a	3 d
35	1	את	WITH	86b	1 dd
		לחם	FIGHT	535b	
		ריב	STRIVE	936c	2
		יריב	OPPONENT	937a	
35	2	ב	IN	89a	1 7b
		מגן	SHIELD	171c	
		חזק	BE FIRM	305a	6 a
		עזרה	HELP	741a	2 b
		צנה	LARGE SHIELD	857a	
35	3	חנית	SPEAR	334a	1
		ישועה	DELIVERANCE	447b	3
		סגר	CLOSE	689a	2 b
		קרא	ENCOUNTER	897a	1
		רדף	PURSUE	922d	1 f
		ריק	MAKE EMPTY	938a	3
35	4	אחור	HINDER SIDE	30c	A
		בוש	BE ASHAMED	101d	3
		בקש	SEEK	134d	2 a
		חפר	BE ABASHED	344a	
		חשב	THINK	363a	1 2
		כלם	BE HUMILIATED	483d	2
		נפש	SOUL	659d	3 c
		סוג	MOVE AWAY	691a	2
35	5	דחה	PUSH	191a	
		דחה	THRUST	191a	
		מלאך	MESSENGER	521d	2
		מוץ	CHAFF	558b	
		פנה	FACE	818d	2 7a a
35	6	דחה	PUSH	*191a	
		חלקלקות	SMOOTHNESS	325c	1
		חשך	DARKNESS	365b	3 d
		מלאך	MESSENGER	521d	2
		רדף	PURSUE	922d	1 e
35	7	חנם	OUT OF FAVOR	336d	C
		חפר	DIG	343c	1 a
		טמן	HIDE	380c	2
		רשת	NET	440c	1 b2
		ל	TO	515b	5 hb g
		שואה	DEVASTATION	996c	1
		שחת	PIT	1001c	1
35	8	טמן	HIDE	380c	2
		ידע	KNOW	394a	1 h
		רשת	NET	440c	1 b2
		לכד	CAPTURE	540a	2
		נפל	FALL	656d	1
		שואה	DEVASTATION	996c	1
		שואה	DEVASTATION	996c	1
		שחת	PIT	1001c	1
35	9	ישועה	DELIVERANCE	447b	3
		נפש	SOUL	660d	6 d
		עצם	BONE	782d	1 d
		שוש	REJOICE	965b	
35	10	אביון	NEEDY	2d	
		גזל	TEAR AWAY	159d	
		חזק	STRONG	305d	2
		מי	WHO	566d	F c
		עני	POOR	776d	3
		עני	POOR	777a	3
		עצם	BONE	782d	1 d
35	11	חמס	VIOLENCE	329c	
		עד	WITNESS	729d	2 c
		עד	WITNESS	729d	2 c
		קום	STAND	877d	1 f
35	12	טובה	WELFARE	375d	3
		רעה	MISERY	949b	2
		שכל	BEREAVEMENT	1013d	
		שלם	BE COMPLETE	1022c	5
		תחת	INSTEAD	1066a	2 2b b
35	13	חזק	BOSOM	300d	1
		חלה	BE WEAK	317d	2
		לבוש	CLOTHING	528c	
		על	UPON	757c	2 7c ab
		ענה	BE BOWED DOWN	776b	4
		תפלה	PRAYER	813c	1 a
		צום	FASTING	847b	
		שק	SACK	974c	2 a
		שוב	TURN BACK	998a	7 d2
		אבל	MOURNING	5d	
35	14	אם	MOTHER	51d	1
		הלך	WALK	236b	2
		ל	TO	513a	5 ad
		קדר	BE DARK	871a	
		רע	FRIEND	946a	1
		שחח	BOW	1005d	3
35	15	דמם	BE SILENT	198d	1
		נכה	SMITTEN ONES	646d	
		צלע	LIMPING	854c	
		קרע	TEAR	902d	4
		שמח	REJOICE	970b	1 b
		ב	IN	89a	1 7b
		ב	IN	*90b	3 4
35	16	חנף	PROFANE	338b	
		חרק	GNASH	359b	
		לעג	MOCKING	541d	
		מעוג	CAKE	728b	
		שוא	RAVAGE	996b	
		שן	TOOTH	1042a	1 a
35	17	יחיד	ONLY ONE	402d	2
		כפיר	LION	498d	
		מה	HOW	554a	4 cb
		ראה	TO SEE	907b	5 a
		שוא	RAVAGE	996b	
		שוב	TURN BACK	998d	1 a
35	18	הלל	PRAISE	238b	2 b
		ידה	PRAISE	392c	1 a2
		עצום	MIGHTY	783a	2
35	19	חנם	OUT OF FAVOR	336d	C
		ל	TO	510d	1 d
		עין	EYE	744c	11
		קרץ	PINCH	902d	
		שמח	REJOICE	970b	1 b
		שקר	DECEPTION	1055c	2
35	20	חשב	THINK	363a	1 2
		רגע	RESTFUL	921b	
		מרמה	DECEIT	941b	
		שלום	PEACE	1023a	5 a
35	21	האח	AHA	210c	
		פה	MOUTH	804d	1 b
		רחב	BE LARGE	931d	2
35	22	חפץ	DELIGHTING IN	343a	1
		חרש	BE SILENT	361a	1
35	23	רחק	BE DISTANT	934d	
		אדון	LORD	11c	3 2a
		עור	ROUSE ONESELF	735c	2
		קיץ	AWAKE	884c	1 b
		משפט	JUDGMENT	1048b	1a
35	24	יהוה	YAHWEH	219a	2 1f
		צדק	RIGHTEOUSNESS	841d	E
		שמח	REJOICE	970b	1 b
		שפט	JUDGE	1047d	3 b1
35	25	אמר	SAY	56b	2
		האח	AHA0	210c	
		לב	HEART	525c	2 7
		נפש	SOUL	660d	6 a
35	26	בוש	BE ASHAMED	101d	3
		בשת	SHAME	102a	1
		גדל	BECOME GREAT	152c	3 b
		חפר	BE ABASHED	344a	
		יחדו	TOGETHER	403c	B
		כלמה	IGNOMINY	484b	2
		לבש	PUT ON	528a	B
		שמחה	JOYFUL	970d	2
35	27	גדל	BECOME GREAT	152b	3 b
		חפץ	DELIGHTING IN	343a	1
		תמיד	CONTINUITY	556b	1 a
		עבד	SLAVE	714c	6
		צדק	RIGHTEOUSNESS	841d	3
		רנן	GIVE A RINGING CRY	943b	1
		שלון	PEACE	1023a	5 b
35	28	הגה	UTTER	211d	2
		תהלה	PRAISE	240b	4
		יום	DAY	400c	7 f
		לשון	TONGUE	546b	1 b
		צדק	RIGHTEOUSNESS	841d	E
36	1	דוד	DAVID	188a	
36	2	אלהים	GOD	44b	4 a
		לב	HEART	525c	2 7
		נאם	UTTERANCE	610b	1
		גגד	IN FRONT	617c	2 b
		פחד	DREAD	808c	2
		פשע	TRANSGRESSION	833c	3 a
		קרב	INWARD PART	899b	2 a
36	3	חלק	BE SMOOTH	325b	2
		ל	TO	517c	7 bb
		מצא	FIND	593b	2 b
		עון	INIQUITY	731b	2
		על	UPON	757c	2 7c b
36	4	חדל	CEASE	293a	1
		יטב	DO RIGHT	406a	5 a
		פה	MOUTH	805a	2 a
		מרמה	DECEIT	941b	
		שכל	BE PRUDENT	968c	5
36	5	און	TROUBLE	20a	3
		דרך	WAY	203d	6 d
		חשב	THINK	363a	1 2
		טוב	PLEASANT	374d	0 a
		יצב	STATION ONESELF	426b	A
		לא	NOT	519c	2 a
		מאס	REJECT	549c	1 a
		רע	EVIL	948d	3
36	6	אמונה	FIRMNESS	53d	3 b
		חסד	GOODNESS	339b	2 3b
		עד	AS FAR AS	724a	1 1a
		שחק	DUST	1007a	1
		שמי	HEAVENS	1030b	2 a
36	7	אל	GOD	42c	5
		אלף	THOUSAND	49a	1 c
		בהמה	BEAST	96d	1
		הר	MOUNTAIN	*249d	1 a
		ישע	DELIVER	446c	1
		צדקה	RIGHTEOUSNESS	842b	2
		רב	GREAT	913c	2
		משפט	JUDGEMNT	1048d	2 a
		תהום	DEEP	1062d	1
36	8	אלהים	GOD	44b	4 a
		חסד	GOODNESS	339a	2 1a
		חסה	SEEK REFUGE	340b	
		יקר	PRECIOUS	430a	1 b
		כנף	WING	489d	1 h
		מה	HOW	553c	2
		צל	SHADOW	853b	2
36	9	דשן	FATNESS	206c	1
		מן	OUT OF	579b	2 bb
		נחל	TORRENT	636b	1
		עדן	LUXURY	726c	
		רוה	BE SATURATED	924a	
		שקה	GIVE TO DRINK	1052c	2
36	10	חיים	LIFE	313b	2
		משך	DRAW	604c	5
		עם	WITH	768b	3 b
		מקור	SPRING	881b	1 a
36	11	חסד	GOODNESS	339a	2 1a
		חסד	GOODNESS	339b	2 2
		ישר	STRAIGHT	449b	3 b

Ch v.	Heb	Eng	Page	Sec
	לב	HEART	525b	2 6a
36 12	צדקה	RIGHTEOUSNESS	842b	6 a
	בוא	COME	98c	2 b
	גאוה	PRIDE	144d	3
	נוד	WANDER	627a	1
	רגל	FOOT	919d	1 a
36 13	דחה	THRUST	191a	
	יכל	BE ABLE	407c	1 b
	שם	THERE	1027a	1 a
37 1	חרה	BURN	354b	
	עולה	INJUSTICE	732c	1
	קנא	BE ZEALOUS	888c	2
37 2	דשא	GRASS	206a	
	חציר	GREEN GRASS	348b	2
	ירק	GREEN	438d	
	מהרה	HASTE	555b	
	מלל	WITHER	576d	
	מול	ADDENDA ET COR-RIGENDA	1124d	
37 3	אמונה	FIRMNESS	53c	3 a
	בטח	TRUST	105a	1 3a
	טוב	A GOOD THING	375b	4
	רעה	ASSOCIATE WITH	945d	
37 4	לב	HEART	525c	2 9a
	נתן	GIVE	678d	1 e
	ענג	BE SOFT	772b	2
	משאלה	REQUEST	982c	
37 5	בטח	TRUST	105a	1 4a
	יהב	LOT	*396d	
	על	UPON	753b	2 1c
	עשה	DO	794b	1 4
37 6	יצא	BRING OUT	425b	5
	צדק	RIGHTEOUSNESS	841d	3
	צהר	MIDDAY	844a	2
37 7	דמם	BE SILENT	198d	2
	דרך	WAY	203b	5
	מזמה	PURPOSE	273d	3 b
	חול	WHIRL	297c	3
	חרה	BURN	354b	
	צלח	ADVANCE	852c	1
37 8	אך	ONLY	36d	2 ba
	חרה	BURN	354b	
	חמה	RAGE	404c	2 a
	עזב	LEAVE	737b	1 g
	רפה	SINK	952a	3
37 9	הם	THEY	241c	2 a
	ירש	TAKE POSSESSION	439c	1 a
	כרת	BE CUT OFF	504b	1 b
	קוה	WAIT FOR	875d	
37 10	אין	NOT	34b	2 b
	בין	DISCERN	107b	1 d
	מעט	A FEW	590b	1 eb
	עוד	STILL	729a	1 ab
37 11	ירש	TAKE POSSESSION	439c	1 a
	ענג	BE SOFT	772b	2
	ענו	POOR	776c	3
	שלום	PEACE	1023a	3
37 12	זמם	CONSIDER	273d	2 b
	חרק	GNASH	359b	
	ל	TO	511a	1 d
37 13	אדון	LORD	11c	3 2b
	יום	DAY	398d	2 h1
	ל	TO	510d	1 d
	שחק	LAUGH	965d	1 a
37 14	אביון	NEEDY	2d	
	דרך	TREAD	202b	4
	דרך	WAY	203c	6 c
	חרב	SWORD	352c	1 c
	טבח	SLAUGHTER	370d	2
	ישר	STRAIGHT	449b	3 b
	נפל	FALL	658a	1
	עני	POOR	776d	3
	פתח	OPEN	835b	
	פתיחה	DRAWN SWORD	*836a	
	קשת	BOW	906c	1 d
37 15	לב	HEART	524c	2 l
	קשת	BOW	906a	1 b
	קשת	BOW	906c	1 e
	שבר	BREAK	990d	
37 16	המון	ABUNDANCE	242d	5
	טוב	PLEASANT	374c	6
	ל	TO	513d	5 cb e
	מעט	A FEW	589d	1 a
37 17	זרוע	ARM	284a	1 b
	סמך	LEAN	702a	2
	שבר	BREAK	990d	
37 18	ידע	KNOW	394b	2
	נחלה	PROPERTY	635b	2 a
	עולם	LONG DURATION	762d	2 f
	תמים	SOUND	1071b	4
37 19	רעבון	HUNGER	944c	
	שבע	SATISFIED	959b	1 a
37 20	אבד	PERISH	1d	1
	איב	BE HOSTILE TO	33c	
	ב	IN	89a	17d
	יקר	GLORY	430a	3
	כלה	BE FINISHED	477d	2 c
	כר	PASTURE	*499d	
	כר	PASTURE	499d	
	עשן	SMOKE	798c	1 c
37 21	חנן	SHOW FAVOR	336a	1 b
	לוה	BORROW	531a	
	שלם	BE COMPLETE	1022c	3
37 22	ברך	BLESS	139b	2 a
	ירש	TAKE POSSESSION	439c	1 a
	כרת	BE CUT OFF	504b	1 b
	קלל	BE SLIGHT	886d	
37 23	דרך	WAY	203b	5
	חפץ	DELIGHT IN	343a	2 a
	כון	BE ESTABLISHED	467a	
	מצעד	STEP	857d	
37 24	טול	HURL	376d	1
	כי	THOUGH	473c	2 ca
	סמך	LEAN	702a	2
37 25	בקש	SEEK	134c	1 b
	זקן	BE OLD	278b	
	זרע	SOWING	282d	4 c
	נער	YOUTH	655a	1 d
37 26	עזב	LEAVE	737d	2
	ברכה	BLESSING	139d	2
	זרע	SOWING	282d	4 c
	חנן	SHOW FAVOR	336a	1 b
	יום	DAY	400c	7 f
	לוה	BORROW	531a	
37 27	טוב	A GOOD THING	375b	4
	סור	TURN ASIDE	693d	1
	עולם	LONG DURATION	762a	2 a
	רע	EVIL	949a	3
	שכן	SETTLE DOWN	1015a	2 a
37 28	אהב	LOVE	13b	5 c
	זרע	SOWING	282d	4 c
	חסיד	KIND	339d	2 b
	כרת	BE CUT OFF	504b	1 b
	עולם	LONG DURATION	762a	2 a
	רשע	WICKED	957c	3
	שמר	KEEP	1037b	3
	משפט	JUDGMENT	1048d	2 a
37 29	ירש	TAKE POSSESSION	439c	1 a
	עד	PERPETUITY	723d	2 d
	שכן	SETTLE DOWN	1015b	3
37 30	הגה	UTTER	211d	2
	חכמה	WISDOM	315c	4
	לשון	TONGUE	546b	1 b
	פה	MOUTH	805a	2 a
	משפט	JUDGMENT	1048d	2 b
37 31	אשור	STEP	81a	
	תורה	INSTRUCTION	436a	1 c
	מעד	SLIP	588c	2
37 32	בקש	SEEK	134d	2 d
	צפה	KEEP WATCH	859c	
37 33	עזב	LEAVE	737c	2 e
	רשע	BE WICKED	957d	2
	שפט	JUDGE	1048a	2
37 34	דרך	WAY	204a	6 ec
	ירש	TAKE POSSESSION	439c	1 a
	כרת	BE CUT OFF	504b	1 b
	נפל	FALL	657b	2 c
	קוה	WAIT FOR	875d	1
	רום	BE HIGH	927b	2 c
37 35	אזרח	A NATIVE	280c	2
	ערה	BE NAKED	788d	2
	עריץ	AWE-INSPIRING	792b	
	רענן	LUXURIANT	947d	
37 36	בקש	SEEK	134c	1 b
	מצא	FIND	594a	2 c
	עבר	PASS OVER	718b	6 c
37 37	אחרית	END	31b	D
	ישר	STRAIGHT	449b	3 b
	שלום	PEACE	1023a	4
	שמר	KEEP	1036d	1 d
	תם	COMPLETE	1071a	2
37 38	אחרית	END	31b	D
	יחדו	TOGETHER	403c	B
	כרת	BE CUT OFF	504b	1 b
	פשע	REBEL	833b	2
	שמד	BE EXTERMINATED	1029b	1
37 39	תשועה	DELIVERANCE	448b	1
	מן	OUT OF	579d	2 d
	מעוז	PLACE OF SAFETY	732a	2 a
	צרה	DISTRESS	865b	
37 40	חסה	SEEK REFUGE	340b	
	ישע	DELIVER	446d	1 b
	עזר	HELP	740b	
	פלט	ESCAPE	812b	1
	פלט	ESCAPE	812b	1
38 1	זכר	REMEMBER	271a	3 d
	מזמור	MELODY	274c	
38 2	חמה	RAGE	404d	2 c
	יכח	CORRECT	407a	6
	יסר	DISCIPLINE	416b	2 a
	קצף	WRATH	893c	1
38 3	חץ	ARROW	346c	2
	נחת	DESCEND	639c	
	נחת	DESCEND	639c	2
	בשר	FLESH	142c	1 b
	זעם	INDIGNATION	276d	
38 4	חטאת	SIN	308d	1 b
	פנה	FACE	818c	26c a
	שלום	PEACE	1022d	2
	מתם	SOUNDNESS	1071b	
38 5	כבד	BE HEAVY	457b	1
	כבד	HEAVY	458a	1 a
	מן	THAN	582d	6 d
	משא	LOAD	672c	1
	עבר	PASS OVER	717b	1 f
	עון	INIQUITY	731b	2 b
38 6	באש	STINK	93a	1
	חבורה	STRIPE	289a	
	מקק	FESTER	596d	1
	פנה	FACE	818c	26c a
38 7	הלך	WALK	235c	2
	הלך	WALK	*236a	1 b
	יום	DAY	400c	7 f
	מאד	EXCEEDINGLY	547c	2 b
	עוה	BEND	730c	
	קדר	BE DARK	871a	
	שחח	BOW	1005d	3
38 8	בשר	FLESH	142c	1 b
	כסל	LOINS	492d	1
	קלה	ROAST	885d	
	מתם	SOUNDNESS	1071b	
38 9	דכה	CRUSH	194b	
	מאד	EXCEEDINGLY	547c	2 b
	נהמה	GROANING	625c	2
	פוג	GROW NUMB	806a	
	שאג	ROAR	980d	2
38 10	תאוה	DESIRE	16c	1
	אנחה	SIGHING	58d	
	נגד	IN FRONT	617b	1 aa
	סתר	HIDE	711c	2
38 11	אור	LIGHT	21d	0
	את	WITH	86c	3 a
	כח	STRENGTH	470c	1 a
	עזב	LEAVE	737c	2 g
38 12	אהב	LOVE	13a	4 b
	נגד	IN FRONT	617d	2cb b
	סלה	LIFT UP	*700a	
	עמד	STAND	764a	1 f
	עמד	STAND	764a	1 f
	קרב	NEAR	898c	2 c
	רחק	DISTANT	935c	2a2
38 13	בקש	SEEK	134d	2 a
	דרש	SEEK	205c	6
	הגה	UTTER	211d	2
	הוה	CHASM	217d	2
	יום	DAY	400c	7 f
	נפש	SOUL	659d	3 c
	נקש	STRIKE	669c	
	מרמה	DECEIT	941b	
38 14	אלם	DUMB	48a	1
	חרש	DEAF	361c	
	פתח	OPEN	835b	
	שמע	HEAR	1033d	1 f
38 15	תוכחת	ARGUMENT	407b	1
	לא	NOT	519b	1 bc
	שמע	HEAR	1033d	1 e
38 16	אדון	LORD	11c	3 2b
	יחל	WAIT	404a	
38 17	גדל	BECOME GREAT	152c	3 b
	מוט	SLIP	556d	
	פן	LEST	814d	1 a
38 18	שמח	REJOICE	970b	1 5
	מכאוב	PAIN	456b	2
	כון	BE READY	466a	3
	תמיד	CONTINUITY	556b	1 a
	נגד	IN FRONT	617b	1 b
	צלע	LIMPING	854c	
38 19	דאג	BE ANXIOUS	178b	1
	חטאת	SIN	308d	1 c
	מן	ON ACCOUNT OF	580b	2 f
	נגד	BE CONSPICUOUS	617a	5
	עון	INIQUITY	731a	1 b
38 20	חי	ALIVE	312b	2
	עצם	BE VAST	782c	2
	רבב	BECOME MUCH	912d	1
	שקר	DECEPTION	1055c	2
38 21	טוב	A GOOD THING	375b	4
	טובה	WELFARE	375d	3
	רדף	PURSUE	923a	2
	רעה	MISERY	949b	2
	שטן	ACT AS ADVER-SARY	966c	
	שלם	BE COMPLETE	1022c	5
	תחת	INSTEAD	1066a	2 2b b
	תחת	INSTEAD	1066a	2 2b b
38 22	רחק	BE DISTANT	934d	
38 23	חוש	HASTE	301d	
	תשועה	DELIVERANCE	448b	1
	עזרה	HELP	741a	1
39 1	מזמור	MELODY	274c	
	ידותון	JEDUTHUN	393a	
39 2	דרך	WAY	203c	6 a
	חטא	MISS A GOAL OR WAY	307a	2 b
	מחסום	MUZZLE	340d	
	לשון	TONGUE	546c	1 b
	מן	FROM	583b	7 ba
	נגד	IN FRONT	617c	2 b
	עוד	STILL	729b	2 aa
	פה	MOUTH	805a	2 a
	שמר	KEEP	1036d	2
39 3	אלם	BIND	47d	1
	דומיה	SILENCE	189b	
	חשה	BE SILENT	364c	1
	טוב	A GOOD THING	375a	1
	כאב	PAIN	456b	
	מן	FROM	583c	7 bb
	עכר	STIR UP	747d	
39 4	אש	FIRE	77d	5
	בער	BURN	129a	1
	הגיג	MUSING	211c	2
	חמם	BE OR BECOME WARM	328d	2
39 5	קרב	INWARD PART	899b	2 a
	הוא	HE, SHE, IT	216a	3 b
	חדל	FORBEARING	293b	
	ידע	KNOW	395a	
	יום	DAY	399c	4 a

Ch v.	Heb	Eng	Page	Sec
	מדה	SIZE	551c	2
	מה	WHAT	552d	1 b
	מה	HOW	553c	2 aa
39 6	קץ	END	893d	1
	אין	NOTHING	34a	1
	אך	ONLY	36d	
	הבל	VAPOUR	210d	2
	חלד	DURATION	317b	
	מפח	A SPAN	381c	1
	יום	DAY	399a	4 a
	כל	ALL	481b	1 a
	כל	ALL	481c	1 b
	נגד	IN FRONT	617b	1 b
	נצב	STAND	662b	4
	נתן	GIVE	681a	3 a
	סלה	LIFT UP	700a	
	סלה	LIFT UP	700a	
39 7	לא	NOT	*1098d	
	אך	ONLY	36d	
	אסף	GATHER	62b	1 c
	ב	IN	89a	1 7b
	הבל	VAPOUR	211a	1
	הלך	WALK	236a	1 b
	המה	ROAR	242b	4
	מי	WHO	566c	C
	צבר	HEAP UP	840d	
	צלם	IMAGE	854a	3
39 8	תוחלת	HOPE	404b	
	ל	TO	510d	1 a
	עתה	NOW	774b	2 b
	קוה	WAIT FOR	875d	1
39 9	חרפה	REPROACH	358a	3
	נצל	DELIVER	665a	4
	פשע	TRANSGRESSION	833d	3 d
	שום	TO PLACE	964c	5 a
39 10	אלם	BIND	47d	1
	פתח	OPEN	835b	
39 11	תגרה	CONTENTION	173d	
	כלה	BE FINISHED	477d	2 c
	מן	OUT OF	580a	2 eb
	על	UPON	758d	4 2b
39 12	אך	ONLY	36d	
	הבל	VAPOUR	210d	2
	חמד	DESIRE	326b	C
	תוכחת	REBUKE	407b	3
	יסר	DISCIPLINE	416b	2 a
	כל	ALL	*481b	1 a
	מסה	DISSOLVE	587b	
	סלה	LIFT UP	700a	
	עון	INIQUITY	731a	1 c1
	על	UPON	754b	2 lf b
	עש	MOTH	799c	
39 13	אזן	LISTENING	24c	2
	גר	SOJOURNER	158b	1
	גר	SOJOURNER	*158c	2
	דמעה	TEARS	199c	
	חרש	BE SILENT	361a	1
	תושב	SOJOURNER	444c	
	עם	WITH	768b	3 a
	תפלה	PRAYER	813c	1 e
	שועה	CRY FOR HELP	1003a	
39 14	אין	NOT	34b	2 b
	בלג	SMILE	114d	1
	הלך	WALK	234b	2 1
	טרם	NOT YET	*382c	2
	שעה	GAZE	1043a	
	שעע	BE BLINDED	1044b	
40 1	מזמור	MELODY	274c	
40 2	נטה	BEND	640b	3 a
	קוה	WAIT FOR	875d	1
	שועה	CRY FOR HELP	1003a	
40 3	אשור	STEP	81a	
	בור	PIT	92c	3
	טיט	MUD	376c	1
	יון	MIRE	401c	
	כון	ESTABLISH	466d	1 b
	מן	OUT OF	579a	2 aa
	סלע	CRAG	701a	2
	עלה	GO UP	749b	1 b1
	קום	STAND	879d	6 a
	שאון	ROAR	981a	1
40 4	במה	TRUST	105a	1 3a
	תהלה	PRAISE	240a	1
	חדש	NEW	294a	A
	ירא	FEAR	431b	1 a
40 5	אשר	HAPPINESS	81a	
	מבטח	CONFIDENCE	105c	2
	כזב	LIE	469d	
	פנה	TURN	815c	2 c1
	רהב	PROUD	923b	
	שוט	SWERVE	962b	
40 6	אין	NOT	34d	5 a
	אל	TO	40a	3 a
	יהוה	YAHWEH	219a	2 lf
	מחשבה	THOUGHT	364b	1 b
	מן	THAN	582d	6 d
	ספר	COUNT	708a	1
	עצם	BE VAST	782c	2
	ערך	ARRANGE	789d	2 a
40 7	אזן	EAR	24b	3
	זבח	SACRIFICE	257c	11
	חטאה	SIN	308b	2
	חפץ	DELIGHT IN	342d	2 a
	כרה	DIG	500a	
	ל	TO	512d	5 aa
	מנחה	OFFERING	585b	4

Ch v.	Heb	Eng	Page	Sec
	עלה	WHOLE BURNT OFFERING	750d	
40 8	כתב	WRITE	507c	1 b3
	ספר	MISSIVE	707b	3 a
	על	UPON	753b	2 1c
40 9	בטן	BELLY	105d	1 a
	חפץ	DELIGHT IN	342d	1 b
	תורה	INSTRUCTION	436a	1 c
	מעה	BELLY	589a	4
	רצון	GOODWILL	953c	3 a
	תוך	MIDST	1063d	
40 10	בשר	BEAR TIDINGS	142b	3
	כלא	RESTRAIN	476b	2
	צדק	RIGHTEOUSNESS	842a	6 a
	שפה	SPEECH	973d	1 a1
40 11	אמת	FIRMNESS	54a	3 b
	אמר	SAY	56a	1
	חסד	GOODNESS	339a	2 2
	תשועה	DELIVERANCE	448b	1
	כחד	HIDE	470b	
	כסה	COVER	491d	2
	ל	TO	515b	5 hb g
	צדקה	RIGHTEOUSNESS	842c	6 a
	תוך	MIDST	1063d	
40 12	אמת	FIRMNESS	54a	3 b
	חסד	GOODNESS	339a	2 2
	כלא	RESTRAIN	476b	3
	תמיד	CONTINUITY	556b	1 a
	נצר	GUARD	665d	2
	רחמים	COMPASSION	933c	1
40 13	אין	NOT	35a	6 cg
	אפס	NON-EXISTENCE	67b	2 b
	אפף	SURROUND	67c	
	נשג	OVERTAKE	673d	1 b
	מספר	NUMBER	708d	1 a
	עד	AS FAR AS	724c	1 2a d
	עון	INIQUITY	731b	2 b
	עצם	BE VAST	782c	2
	ראה	TO SEE	907b	4
	רעה	MISERY	949a	1
	שערה	A HAIR	972b	
40 14	חוש	HASTE	301d	1
	עזרה	HELP	741a	1
	רצה	BE PLEASED WITH	953b	3 a
40 15	אחור	HINDER SIDE	30c	A
	בוש	BE ASHAMED	101d	3
	בקש	SEEK	134d	2 a
	חפץ	DELIGHTING IN	343b	1
	חפר	BE ABASHED	344a	
	יחד	ALTOGETHER	*403a	2 b
	כלם	BE HUMILIATED	483d	2
	נפש	SOUL	659d	3 c
	סוג	MOVE AWAY	691a	1
	ספה	SWEEP AWAY	705a	2
40 16	בשת	SHAME	102a	1
	האח	AHA	210c	
	עקב	CONSEQUENCE	784d	1
	שמם	BE DESOLATED	1031a	2
40 17	אהב	LOVE	13a	3
	בקש	SEEK	134d	3 c
	גדל	BECOME GREAT	152b	3 b
	ישועה	DELIVERANCE	*447b	1
	תשועה	DELIVERANCE	448b	1
	תמיד	CONTINUITY	556b	1 a
	שוש	REJOICE	965b	
	שרג	BE INTERTWINED	974d	1
40 18	אביון	NEEDY	2d	
	אחר	DELAY	29b	1
	חשב	THINK	363b	2 2
	עזרה	HELP	741a	2 b
	עני	POOR	776d	3
	עשה	THINK	*799d	
	פלט	ESCAPE	812b	1
41 1	מזמור	MELODY	274c	
41 2	אשר	HAPPINESS	81a	
	דל	WEAK	195d	
	מלט	SLIP AWAY	572c	3
	שכל	BE PRUDENT	968b	2
41 3	אל	NOT	39b	A c
	אשר	GO STRAIGHT	80d	2
	חיה	LIVE	311c	1
	חסיד	KIND	339d	2 a
41 4	דוי	ILLNESS	188c	
	הפך	TURN	245c	1 c1
	חלי	SICKNESS	318b	
	סעד	SUPPORT	703c	2 b
	ערש	COUCH	793b	
41 5	אני	I	59c	
	חטא	MISS A GOAL OR WAY	307a	2 b
	חנן	SHOW FAVOR	336a	2 b
	רפא	HEAL	950d	3 a
41 6	אבד	PERISH	1d	2
	ל	TO	514b	5 fa
	מתי	WHEN	607d	A
	רע	EVIL	948d	2
41 7	אם	IF	49d	1 a3 a
	חוץ	THE OUTSIDE	299d	1 bc
	ל	TO	511c	1 h
	קבץ	GATHER	867c	1
	שוא	EMPTINESS	996b	2
41 8	חשב	THINK	363a	1 2
	יחד	ALTOGETHER	*403b	2 b
	יחד	ALTOGETHER	403b	2 b
	לחש	WHISPER	538a	

Ch v.	Heb	Eng	Page	Sec
41 9	אשר	PARTICLE OF RELATION	82b	3
	בליעל	WORTHLESSNESS	116a	1
	בליעל	WORTHLESSNESS	116b	3
	יסף	DO AGAIN	415c	2 a
	יצק	POUR	427b	1
	שכב	LIE DOWN	1012a	1 b
41 10	בטח	TRUST	105a	1 3b
	גדל	BECOME GREAT	152c	1
	גם	YEA	169c	3
	לחם	FOOD	537a	1 a
	עקב	HEEL	784a	A
	שלום	PEACE	1023a	5 a
	שלם	BE IN COVENANT OF PEACE	1023d	
41 11	חנן	SHOW FAVOR	336a	2 b
	קום	STAND	878d	1
41 12	זה	THIS	261d	6 bb
	חפץ	DELIGHT IN	342d	2 a
	ידע	KNOW	*393d	1 a
	כי	THAT	471d	1 a
41 13	רוע	RAISE A SHOUT	929c	3
	נצב	STAND	662c	1
	עולם	LONG DURATION	762a	2 a
	תמך	SUPPORT	1069d	1
	תם	INTEGRITY	1070d	3
41 14	אלהים	GOD	44c	4 ba
	אמן	VERILY	53b	
	ברך	BLESS	138c	2 a
	עולם	LONG DURATION	763a	2 m
	ל	TO	*513c	5 bb
42 1	קרח	KORAH	901b	2
42 2	איל	HART	19b	
	אפיק	CHANNEL	67d	
	ה	THE	208a	1 f
	כ	LIKE	454a	1 c2
	כ	LIKE	454d	2 d
	כן	SO	486b	2 ad g
	ערג	LONG FOR	788b	
42 3	אל	GOD	42d	6 d
	חי	ALIVE	311d	1 a
	ל	TO	*510b	1 a
	מתי	WHEN	607d	A
	נפש	SOUL	660c	5 b
	פנה	FACE	816c	2 2a
	צמא	BE THIRSTY	854d	
42 4	איה	WHERE	32c	
	בכי	WEEPING	*113d	
	דמעה	TEARS	199d	
	יום	DAY	400c	7 f
	לחם	FOOD	537c	3 b
42 5	אלה	THESE	41c	A
	דדה	MOVE SLOWLY	186d	
	דדה	MOVE SLOWLY	186d	
	המון	CROWD	242d	3 c
	זכר	REMEMBER	269d	11 a
	זכר	REMEMBER	271d	5
	חגג	MAKE PILGRIMAGE	290d	1
	תודה	THANKSGIVING	392d	2
	כי	THAT	471d	1 a
	נפש	SOUL	659a	1 b
	סך	THRONG	697c	
	על	UPON	753d	2 1d
	רגש	THRONG	*921c	
	רנה	RINGING CRY	943d	3
	שפך	POUR OUT	1049d	2 b
42 6	המה	MURMUR	242a	2
	יחה	PRAISE	392c	1 a2
	יחל	WAIT	404a	
	ישועה	DELIVERANCE	447b	3
	מה	WHAT	553c	2 ab
	עוד	STILL	729a	1 ab
	על	UPON	753c	2 1d
	שחח	BOW	1006a	
42 7	ארץ	EARTH	76a	2 b
	זכר	REMEMBER	270a	13 b
	חרמון	HERMON	356d	
	ירדן	JORDAN	434c	
	ירדן	JORDAN	434d	
	כן	SO	487b	3 f
	זן	OUT OF	579a	2 ab
	נפש	SOUL	659c	1 b
	על	UPON	753c	2 1d
	מצער	MIZAR	859b	
	מצער	SMALL THING	859b	2
	שחח	BOW	1006a	
42 8	ל	TO	515a	5 g
	עבר	PASS OVER	717b	1 f
	צנור	PIPE	857c	
	קול	VOICE	877b	2 f
	משבר	BREAKER	991c	
	תהום	DEEP	1063a	4
	תהום	SEA	1063a	2
42 9	אל	GOD	42d	6 c
	חיים	LIFE	313b	2
	חסד	GOODNESS	339a	2 1a
	יומם	BY DAY	401c	2
	לילה	NIGHT	538d	1
	עם	WITH	767b	1 a
	תפלה	PRAYER	813c	1 c
	צוה	CHARGE	846a	4 d
	שיר	SONG	1010b	2
42 10	אל	GOD	42c	6 c
	ב	IN	90c	3 5
	הלך	WALK	234c	2 2
	הלך	WALK	*235c	2

Ch v.	Heb	Eng	Page	Sec
	הלך	WALK	*236a	1 b
	לחץ	OPPRESSION	537d	
	מה	HOW	554a	4 d
	סלע	CRAG	701a	2
	קדר	BE DARK	871a	
	שכח	FORGET	1013b	2 a
42 11	איה	WHERE	32c	
	חרף	REPROACH	357d	
	יום	DAY	400c	7 f
	צרר	SHEW HOSTILITY TOWARD	865d	
	רצח	SHATTERING	954a	
42 12	המה	MURMUR	242a	2
	ידה	PRAISE	392c	1 a2
	יחל	WAIT	404b	
	ישועה	DELIVERANCE	447b	3
	על	UPON	753c	2 1d
	פנה	FACE	816a	1 2a
	שחח	BOW	1006a	
43 1	לא	NOT	519c	2 a
	מן	FROM	578a	1 a
	עולה	INJUSTICE	732c	1
	פלט	ESCAPE	812b	1
	ריב	STRIVE	936c	3
	מרמה	DECEIT	941b	
	שפט	JUDGE	1047d	3 b1
43 2	אלהים	GOD	44d	
	הלך	WALK	236b	1 b
	זנח	REJECT	276b	
	לחץ	OPPRESSION	537d	
	מה	HOW	554a	4 d
	מעוז	PLACE OF SAFETY	732a	2 a
	קדר	BE DARK	871a	
	הוא	HE	*1090a	
43 3	אור	LIGHT	21d	1
	אמת	FIRMNESS	54b	3 b
	הר	MOUNTAIN	249d	1 a
	נחה	LEAD	635a	
	משכן	DWELLING-PLACE	1016a	3 b
	שלח	SEND	1018c	2 b
43 4	אל	GOD	42c	6 c
	ידה	PRAISE	392c	1 a2
	כנור	LYRE	490b	
	כנור	LYRE	490b	
43 5	המה	MURMUR	242a	2
	ידה	PRAISE	392c	1 a2
	יחל	WAIT	404a	
	ישועה	DELIVERANCE	447b	3
	על	UPON	753c	2 1d
	פנה	FACE	816a	1 2a
	שחח	BOW	1006a	
44 1	קרח	KORAH	901b	2
44 2	ספר	COUNT	*708a	1
	פעל	DO	821b	1 a
	פעל	DOING	821c	1 a
	קדם	FRONT	869d	2 b
44 3	ירש	CAUSE TO POSSESS	440a	2 a
	לאם	PEOPLE	522c	
	נטע	PLANT	642c	2
44 4	אור	LIGHT	21d	0
	זרוע	ARM	284a	1 c
	זרוע	ARM	284b	2 a
	ירש	TAKE POSSESSION	439c	1 a
	ישע	GIVE VICTORY	447a	3 a
	רצה	BE PLEASED WITH	953a	1 a
44 5	הוא	HE, SHE, IT	216b	4 ba
	הוא	HE, SHE, IT	216c	4 ba
	ישועה	VICTORY	447c	4
	מלך	KING	573b	3
	יעקב	JACOB	785a	2
	צוה	CHARGE	846a	5
44 6	ב	IN	89d	3 2c
	ב	IN	90a	3 2d
	בוס	TRAMPLE	100d	
	נגח	PUSH	618c	
44 7	בטח	TRUST	105a	1 3c
	ישע	DELIVER	446d	1 c
	קשת	BOW	906a	1 b
44 8	בוש	BE ASHAMED	101d	1
	ישע	DELIVER	446d	1 b
	כי	BUT	474b	3 e
	שנא	HATE	971d	1
44 9	ב	IN	90d	4 e
	הלל	PRAISE	238d	3
	ידה	PRAISE	392b	1 a2
	יום	DAY	400c	7 f
	סלה	LIFT UP	700a	
	סלה	LIFT UP	700b	
	עולם	LONG DURATION	762a	2 a
44 10	אף	ALSO	65a	1
	זנח	REJECT	276b	
	כלם	HUMILIATE	484a	1
	צבא	ARMY	839a	1 a
44 11	אחור	HINDER SIDE	30c	A
	ל	TO	515d	5 ia
	שן	HATE	971d	1
	שוב	TURN BACK	999c	5
	שסה	PLUNDER	1042c	
44 12	מאכל	FOOD	38b	
	זרה	SCATTER	280a	1
	צאן	SMALL CATTLE	838b	1 a1
	הון	WEALTH	223c	2
	לא	NOT	519d	2 d
	לא	NOT	520b	4 ac
	מחיר	PRICE	564b	1
	מכר	SELL	569b	
	מכר	SELL	*569b	
	רבה	BECOME MANY	915b	
44 14	חרפה	REPROACH	358a	3
	לעג	MOCKING	541d	1
	מגוד	SHAKING	*627b	
	קלם	DERISION	887b	
44 15	שכן	NEIGHBOUR	1015c	2
	לאם	PEOPLE	522c	
	משל	PROVERB	605b	2
	מגוד	SHAKING	627b	
44 16	ראש	HEAD	911b	8
	בשת	SHAME	102a	1
	יום	DAY	400c	7 f
	כלמה	IGNOMINY	484a	2
	כסה	COVER	492a	5
	נגד	IN FRONT	617b	1 b
44 17	גדף	REVILE	154c	1
	חרף	REPROACH	357d	
	נקם	AVENGE	668d	
44 18	בוא	COME	98c	2 b
	ברית	COVENANT	136c	2 c
	ברית	COVENANT	137b	3 3
	שקר	DEAL FALSELY	1055d	
44 19	אחור	HINDER SIDE	30c	A
	אחר	WAY	73b	3 b
	אשור	STEP	81a	
	כי	THAT	473a	1 f
	לא	NOT	518c	1 aa
	נמה	BEND	640b	3 a
	סביב	ROUND ABOUT	687b	2 ba b
	סוג	MOVE AWAY	690d	1 b2
44 20	דכה	CRUSH	194b	
	כסה	COVER	492a	6
	צלמות	DEATH-SHADOW	853c	2 b
	מקום	STANDING PLACE	880a	4
	תן	JACKAL	1072b	
44 21	אל	GOD	42c	3
	זור	BE A STRANGER	266c	2 c
	ל	TO	510c	1 a
	פרש	SPREAD OUT	831b	
	שכח	FORGET	1013b	1 c
44 22	חקר	SEARCH	350c	2 a
	לב	HEART	524c	2 2
	תעלמה	HIDDEN THING	761b	
44 23	חשב	THINK	363b	1
	טבחה	THING SLAUGHTERED	371a	2
	יום	DAY	400c	7 f
	ך	LIKE	453d	1 b
	כי	BECAUSE	*474b	3 c
	על	UPON	754b	2 1f b
	צאן	SMALL CATTLE	*838c	3
	צאן	SMALL CATTLE	838c	2
44 24	זנח	REJECT	276b	
	ישן	SLEEP	445c	
	כי	BECAUSE	474b	3 c
	מה	HOW	554a	4 da
	נצח	EVERLASTINGNESS	664b	4
	עור	ROUSE ONESELF	734d	
	קיץ	AWAKE	884c	1 b
44 25	לחץ	OPPRESSION	537d	
	מה	HOW	554a	4 da
	סתר	HIDE	711d	2 a
	עני	AFFLICTION	777a	1
	שכח	FORGET	1013b	2 b
44 26	במן	BELLY	106a	2
	דבק	CLING	179d	1 a
	ל	TO	511a	1 f
	עפר	DRY EARTH	780a	2 e
	שוח	SINK DOWN	1001b	
	שוח	SINK DOWN	1001b	
44 27	חסד	GOODNESS	339d	2 1a
	עזרה	HELP	741a	2 b
	מען	PURPOSE	775b	1 a
	פדה	RANSOM	804a	3 d
45 1	אל	TO	40c	7
	ידיד	LOVE	391d	3
	עט	STYLUS	741d	2
	על	UPON	754a	2 1f a
	קרח	KORAH	901b	2
	שושן	LILY	1004c	
	שיר	SONG	1010b	2
	שיר	SONG	1010b	2
45 2	דבר	WORD	182c	1 1i
	טוב	PLEASANT	373d	2 d
	לב	HEART	524c	1
	לשון	TONGUE	546b	1 b
	מהיר	READY	555b	
	ספר	ENUMERATOR	708c	2
	מעישה	DEED	796a	2 a1
	רחש	KEEP MOVING	935d	
45 3	ברך	BLESS	139a	2 a
	חן	FAVOR	336b	1 b
	יפה	BE BEAUTIFUL	421b	
	יצק	BE POURED	427c	1
	כן	SO	487b	3 f
	מן	THAN	582c	6 b
	עולם	LONG DURATION	762a	2 h
45 4	גבור	STRONG	150b	2
	הדר	SPLENDOUR	214b	2
	הוד	SPLENDOUR	217a	1
	חגר	GIRD	291d	2
	חרב	SWORD	352c	1 b
	ירך	THIGH	437d	1 a
45 5	אמת	FIRMNESS	54a	3 a
	בשת	SHAME	102b	1
	דבר	WORD	184a	4 8
	הדר	SPLENDOUR	214b	2
	ירא	CAUSE FEAR	431d	2
	ירה	POINT OUT	435b	4
	ענוה	HUMILITY	776d	1
	צדק	RIGHTEOUSNESS	841d	2 c
45 6	רכב	RIDE	938d	2
	חץ	ARROW	346c	2
	שנן	SHARPEN	1041d	
45 7	תחת	UNDERNEATH	1065c	2 lc a
	אלהים	GOD	43d	2h
	מישור	UPRIGHTNESS	449d	3
	כסא	THRONE	491b	3 a
	מלכת	ROYAL POWER	574d	1
	עד	PERPETUITY	723d	2 e
	עולם	LONG DURATION	762d	2 h
	שנא	HATE	971c	1 b
	שבט	ROD	987a	1 d
45 8	אהב	LOVE	13b	5 c
	חבר	UNITED	288d	2 b
	כן	SO	487b	3 f
	מן	THAN	582c	6 a
	משח	ANOINT	603b	2
	צדק	RIGHTEOUSNESS	841d	5
	רשע	WICKEDNESS	957d	3
	ששון	REJOICING	965b	
	שמן	OIL	1032b	2 e
45 9	אהל	ALOE	14d	2
	בגד	GARMENT	94a	1
	היכל	PALACE	228b	1
	ו	AND	252a	1
	מן	STRING	577c	
	מר	MYRRH	600d	
	קציעה	CASSA	893a	
	שמח	REJOICE	970c	
	שן	IVORY	1042b	2
45 10	אופיר	OPHIR	20d	3
	בת	DAUGHTER	123a	1
	ימין	RIGHT HAND	411d	2a
	יקר	PRECIOUS	430a	1 b
	כתם	GOLD	508d	
	נצב	STAND	662b	1 b
	שגל	CONSORT	993c	
45 11	אזן	EAR	24a	2 a
	בת	DAUGHTER	123b	1 f
	נטה	INCLINE	641a	3 e
	עם	PEOPLE	766c	1
	ראה	TO SEE	907d	7 c
	שכח	FORGET	1013a	1
45 12	אדון	LORD	11a	2 1c
	אוה	DESIRE	16b	
	הוא	HE, SHE, IT	*216a	3 a
	יפי	BEAUTY	421d	
45 13	בת	DAUGHTER	123c	3
	חלה	MOLLIFY	318d	2
	מנחה	GIFT	585a	1
	עשיר	RICH	799b	
	עשיר	RICH	799c	
	צר	TYER	862d	
45 14	דמה	ONE SILENCED	*199a	
	ה	THE	208d	1 i
	כבוד	GLORIOUS	458c	
	כל	ALL	481b	1 a
	לבוש	CLOTHING	528c	
	מן	OUT OF	579b	2 ba
	פנימה	WITHIN	819b	2
	פנינים	CORALS	819d	
	משבצות	CHEQUERED WORK	990b	
	כבוד	ADDENDA ET CORRIGENDA	1124b	
45 15	בוא	COME	99c	B
	בתולה	VIRGIN	144a	
	יבל	CONDUCT	385a	3
	ל	TO	511c	1 gb
	ל	TO	516d	5 k
	רעה	COMPANION	946b	
	רקמה	VARIEGATED STUFF	955d	
45 16	ה	THE	208d	1 i
	היכל	PALACE	228b	1
	יבל	CONDUCT	385a	3
	שמחה	JOY	970d	1
45 17	ל	TO	512b	4 a
	שר	CHIEFTAIN	978d	7
	שית	PUT	1011c	3
	תחת	INSTEAD	1065d	2 2b a
45 18	דור	PERIOD	189d	1 b
	ו	AND	253b	1 ib
	זכר	REMEMBER	270d	2
	ידה	PRAISE	392b	1 a1
	כל	ALL	481c	1 b
	עד	PERPETUITY	723d	2 e
	עולם	LONG DURATION	762d	2 g
	שם	NAME	1028c	3
46 1	על	UPON	754a	2 1f a
	עלמה	YOUNG WOMAN	761c	
	קרח	KORAH	901b	2
	שיר	SONG	1010b	2
46 2	מחסה	REFUGE	340c	B
	מאד	EXCEEDINGLY	547b	2 a
	מצא	FIND	594b	2 f
	עז	STRENGTH	739a	2 c
	עזרה	HELP	741a	2 b
	צרה	DISTRESS	865b	
46 3	ארץ	EARTH	76a	1 b

PSALMS

Ch v.	Heb	Eng	Page	Sec
50 5	על	HEIGHT	752c	1
	ברית	COVENANT	136c	2 2c
	ברית	COVENANT	137a	3 1
	זבח	SACRIFICE	257c	1 1
	חסיד	KIND	339d	2 b
	כרת	CUT	503d	4
	על	UPON	754c	2 1f e
50 6	נגד	BE CONSPICUOUS	617a	4
	סלה	LIFT UP	700a	
	צדק	RIGHTEOUSNESS	841d	E
	שמי	HEAVENS	1030b	3
	שפט	JUDGE	1047d	3 d
50 7	עוד	BEAR WITNESS	730a	3
50 8	זבח	SACRIFICE	257c	1 1
	יכח	REPROVE	407a	5 a
	תמיד	CONTINUITY	556b	1 a
	נגד	IN FRONT	617c	2 b
50 9	על	UPON	754b	2 1f b
	מכלה	FOLD	476c	
	עתוד	HE/GOAT	800d	
	פר	YOUNG BULL	830a	2 b
50 10	אל	GOD	42c	5
	אלף	THOUSAND	49a	1 c
	בהמה	BEAST	97a	2
	הר	MOUNTAIN	250c	1 h
	זיז	MOVING THINGS	*265b	
	חיה	LIVING THING	312d	1 b
	יער	WOOD	420d	B
	ל	TO	513b	5 ba
50 11	הר	MOUNTAIN	250c	1 g
	זיז	MOVING THINGS	265b	
	ידע	KNOW	393c	1 a
	עוף	FLY	733d	1
	עם	WITH	768c	4 b
	שדי	FIELD	961b	2
50 12	תבל	WORLD	385d	
	ל	TO	513b	5 ba
	מלא	THAT WHICH FILLS	571b	3
	רעב	BE HUNGRY	945b	
50 13	אביר	MIGHTY	7d	3
	בשר	FLESH	142c	1 a
	דם	BLOOD	197c	3 b
	ה	INTERROG PART	209d	1 b
	עתוד	HE/GOAT	800d	
	שתה	DRINK	1059b	1 c
50 14	זבח	SLAUGHTER FOR SACRIFICE	256d	1 1 a
	זבח	SLAUGHTER FOR SACRIFICE	257a	1 3
	תודה	THANK-OFFERING	393a	4
	נדר	VOW	624a	5
	עליון	HIGHEST	751b	1
	שלם	BE COMPLETE	1022c	4
50 15	חלץ	DRAW OFF OR OUT	322c	2
	כבד	MAKE HONORABLE	457d	2 c
	צרה	DISTRESS	865b	
	קרא	CALL	895b	5 c
50 16	ברית	COVENANT	136c	2 2c
	ברית	COVENANT	137a	3 1
	חק	SOMETHING PRE-SCRIBED	349d	7 g
	ל	TO	513b	5 ba
	מה	WHAT	553b	1 dc
	נשא	LIFT	670d	1 b 7
	על	UPON	753a	2 1
	רשע	WICKED	957c	3
50 17	דבר	WORD	183a	2 2
	מוסר	DISCIPLINE	416c	1 a
	שלך	THROW	1021a	1 b
50 18	גנב	THIEF	170c	
	חלק	PORTION	324b	4
	נאף	COMMIT ADUL-TERY	610d	1 a
	עם	WITH	767d	1 d
	רצה	BE PLEASED WITH	953b	1 b
50 19	לשון	TONGUE	546c	1 b
	צמד	BIND	855a	
	מרמה	DECEIT	941b	
	שלח	SEND	1018d	5
50 20	אם	MOTHER	51d	1
	בן	SON	120b	1 a
	דבר	SPEAK	181c	4 d
	דפי	FAULT	200c	
	נתן	PUT	680d	2 b
50 21	אלה	THESE	41c	A
	דמה	BE LIKE	198a	2
	ו	AND	252d	1 f
	חרש	BE SILENT	361b	1 b
	יכח	CONVICT	407a	4
	ערך	ARRANGE	789d	1 g
50 22	אלה	GOD	43a	2
	בין	DISCERN	106d	3 a
	טרף	TEAR	383a	
	נצל	DELIVER	664d	3 a
	שכח	FORGETFUL	1013c	
50 23	דרך	WAY	203c	6 a
	זבח	SLAUGHTER FOR SACRIFICE	256d	1 1 a
	תודה	THANK-OFFERING	393a	4
	ישע	DELIVERANCE	447a	2
	כבד	MAKE HONORABLE	457d	2 c
	ראה	TO SEE	909a	2 a
	שום	TO PLACE	964c	5 b
51 1	מזמור	MELODY	274c	
51 2	נביא	PROPHET	611d	1
	נתן	NATHAN	681d	2

Ch v.	Heb	Eng	Page	Sec
51 3	חנן	SHOW FAVOR	336a	2 b
	חסד	GOODNESS	339a	2 1d
	כ	LIKE	454a	1 c1
	מחה	WIPE OUT	562b	2
	פשע	TRANSGRESSION	833d	3 d
	רחמים	COMPASSION	933c	1
51 4	חטאת	SIN	309a	1 d4
	טהר	BE CLEAN	372c	1 c
	כבס	WASH	460b	2
	עון	INIQUITY	731a	1 c4
	רבה	BECOME MANY	915b	
	רבה	BECOME MANY	915d	1 d2
	רבה	BECOME MANY	915d	1 e3
51 5	חטאת	SIN	308c	1 b
	ידע	KNOW	394b	1 f
	תמיד	CONTINUITY	556b	1 a
	נגד	IN FRONT	617b	1 b
	פשע	TRANSGRESSION	833c	3 b
51 6	בד	SEPARATION	94c	1 b
	דבר	SPEAK	180c	
	זכה	BE CLEAR	269a	2
	חטא	MISS A GOAL OR WAY	307a	2 b
	מען	PURPOSE	775d	2 1
	צדק	BE JUST	842d	3
	רע	EVIL	948c	0 b
	שפט	JUDGE	1047d	3 c1
51 7	אם	MOTHER	51c	1
	הן	BEHOLD	243c	A
	חול	WHIRL	297c	2
	חטא	SIN	308a	2
	יחם	CONCEIVE	404b	
	עון	INIQUITY	731b	2 c
51 8	אמת	FIRMNESS	54a	3 a
	הן	BEHOLD	243c	A
	חכמה	WISDOM	315c	4
	חפץ	DELIGHT IN	343a	2 a
	מחות	INWARD PARTS	376c	
	ידע	KNOW	395a	
	סתם	STOP UP	711b	2
51 9	אזוב	HYSSOP	23c	
	חטא	MISS A GOAL OR WAY	307c	4
	טהר	BE CLEAN	372b	3
	כבס	WASH	460b	2
	לבן	MAKE WHITE	526b	2
	שלג	SNOW	1017a	
51 10	דכה	CRUSH	194b	2
	ששון	REJOICING	965b	
51 11	חטא	SIN	308a	1 b
	מחה	WIPE OUT	562b	2
	סתר	HIDE	711d	2 b
	עון	INIQUITY	731a	1 c4
51 12	ברא	CREATE	135c	4
	חדש	RENEW	294a	1
	טהור	CLEAN	373a	2
	כון	BE FIRM	465d	2
	ל	TO	512b	5 aa
	לב	HEART	525b	26 a
	קרב	INWARD PART	899b	2 a
	רוח	BREATH	925c	7
51 13	לקח	TAKE	543a	3 a
	פנה	FACE	818a	2 5a d
	קדש	APARTNESS	871c	1 d
	רוח	BREATH	926a	9 f
	שלך	THROW	1021b	2 b
51 14	ישע	DELIVERANCE	447a	2
	נדיב	INCLINED	622a	1
	סמך	LEAN	702a	2
	רוח	BREATH	925c	7
	ששון	REJOICING	965b	
	שוב	TURN BACK	999b	1 d
51 15	דרך	WAY	204a	6 ec
	חטא	SINFUL	308b	2
	למד	LEARN	540d	
	פשע	REBEL	833b	2
	שוב	TURN BACK	997b	6 c
51 16	אלהים	GOD	44c	4 bb
	דם	BLOOD	197a	2 g
	תשועה	DELIVERANCE	448b	2
	לשון	TONGUE	546c	1 c
	נצל	DELIVER	665a	4
	צדקה	RIGHTEOUSNESS	842c	6 a
	רנן	GIVE A RINGING CRY	943c	
51 17	תהלה	PRAISE	240a	1
	נגד	BE CONSPICUOUS	617a	4
	פתח	OPEN	835b	
	שפה	SPEECH	973b	1 a1
51 18	ו	AND	254b	3
	זבח	SACRIFICE	257c	1 1
	חפץ	DELIGHT IN	342d	2 a
	עלה	WHOLE BURNT OF-FERING	750d	
	רצה	BE PLEASED WITH	953b	2
51 19	בזה	DESPISE	102c	
	דכה	CRUSH	194b	2
	זבח	SACRIFICE	257c	1 1
	לב	HEART	525b	26 a
	רוח	BREATH	925d	8
	שבר	BREAK	990d	
51 20	בנה	BUILD	124d	1 i
	חומה	WALL	327c	1
	יטב	DO GOOD TO	405d	2
	ציון	ZION	851b	
	רצון	GOODWILL	953c	1 a

Ch v.	Heb	Eng	Page	Sec
51 21	אז	THEN	23a	1 b
	זבח	SACRIFICE	257c	1 1
	חפץ	DELIGHT IN	342d	2 a
	כליל	WHOLE	483a	2 b
	עלה	GO UP	749d	8
	עלה	GO UP	750a	8
	פר	YOUNG BULL	830d	2 b
52 2	צדק	RIGHTNESS	841c	1
	אדמי	EDOMITE	10c	
	אחימלך	AHIMELECH	27a	1
	דאג	DOEG	178c	
	שאול	SAUL	982b	1
52 3	אל	GOD	42d	6 e
	גבור	STRONG	150b	2
	הלל	BE BOASTFUL	239a	1
	חסד	GOODNESS	339d	2 3c
	יום	DAY	400c	7 f
52 4	הוה	CHASM	217d	2
	חשב	THINK	363a	12
	לטש	SHARPEN	538c	
	לשון	TONGUE	546c	1 b
	תער	RAZOR	789b	1 a
	רמיה	DECEIT	941b	
52 5	אהב	LOVE	13a	2
	טוב	A GOOD THING	375b	4
	מן	THAN	582c	6 a
	סלה	LIFT UP	700a	
	צדק	RIGHTEOUSNESS	841d	4
	רע	EVIL	948d	3
52 6	אהב	LOVE	13a	2
	בלע	SWALLOWING	118c	1
	לשון	TONGUE	546c	1 b
	מרמה	DECEIT	941b	
52 7	אל	GOD	42d	6 e
	גם	ALSO	169d	4
	חי	ALIVE	312a	1 b
	חתה	SNATCH UP	367a	
	מן	FROM	583c	7 bb
	נסח	TEAR AWAY	650c	
	נצח	EVERLASTINGNESS	664b	4
	נתץ	PULL DOWN	683b	2 b
	סלה	LIFT UP	700a	
	שרש	ROOT UP	1057d	1
52 8	ירא	FEAR	431b	1 a
	שחק	LAUGH	965d	1 a
52 9	בטח	TRUST	105a	1 3c
	הוה	DESIRE	217d	1
	מעוז	PLACE OF SAFETY	732a	2 a
	עזז	BE STRONG	738c	
52 10	בטח	TRUST	105a	1 3d
	זית	OLIVE TREE	268c	1
	חסד	GOODNESS	339a	2 1a
	עד	PERPETUITY	723d	2 e
	עולם	LONG DURATION	762a	2 a
	רענן	LUXURIANT	947d	
52 11	חתה	TELL	296a	
	חסיד	KIND	339d	2 b
	טוב	PLEASANT	374d	9 b
	ידה	PRAISE	392c	1 a2
	נגד	IN FRONT	617b	1 aa
	עולם	LONG DURATION	762a	2 a
	עשה	DO	794b	14
	קוה	WAIT FOR	875d	1
53 1	מחלת	MAHALATH	318d	
	על	UPON	754a	2 1f a
53 2	טוב	A GOOD THING	375b	4
	לב	HEART	*525c	27
	עול	INJUSTICE	732c	
	שחת	GO TO RUIN	1008c	2
	תעב	BE ABHORRED	1073b	2
53 3	ראש	SEEK	*205b	3 a
	ראה	TO SEE	907b	5 a
	שכל	BE PRUDENT	968c	5
	שקק	LOOK DOWN	1054d	
53 4	אלה	BE CORRUPT	47a	
	גם	ALSO	*169b	2
	טוב	A GOOD THING	375b	4
	כל	ALL	482a	1 db
	תעב	BE ABHORRED	*1073a	
53 6	בוש	BE ASHAMED	101d	1
	חנה	DECLINE	333d	2 c2
	מאס	REJECT	549c	1
	עני	POOR	*776d	3
	עצם	BONE	783a	3
	פזר	SCATTER	808b	
	פחד	DREAD	808b	1
53 7	ישועה	DELIVERANCE	447b	3
	נתן	GIVE	678d	1 f
	ציון	ZION	851c	
	ישראל	ISRAEL	975d	2 a3
	שבית	CAPTIVITY	986b	2 a
54 1	נגינה	MUSIC	618d	1
54 2	זיפי	ZIPHITES	268b	
	סתר	HIDE	711c	
	שאול	SAUL	982b	1
54 3	גבורה	MIGHT	150c	3
	דין	JUDGE	192b	3
	ישע	DELIVER	446d	1 b
	שם	NAME	1028c	3
54 4	אזן	LISTENING	24c	2
	אמר	WORD	57a	1
	פה	MOUTH	805a	2 a
54 5	בקש	SEEK	134d	2 a
	זור	BE A STRANGER	266c	2
	נגד	IN FRONT	617c	2 b
	נפש	SOUL	659d	3 c

PSALMS

Ch v.	Heb	Eng	Page	Sec
	סלה	LIFT UP	700a	
	עריץ	AWE-INSPIRING	792a	
54 6	שום	TO PLACE	963c	1 c
	ב	IN	89a	17a
	סמך	LEAN	702a	2
	עזר	HELP	740c	
54 7	אמת	FIRMNESS	54a	3 b
	צמת	EXTERMINATE	856c	
	צמת	EXTERMINATE	856c	
	רע	EVIL	948d	2
	שוב	TURN BACK	998b	7 f
	שרור	WATCHER	1004a	
54 8	טוב	PLEASANT	374d	9 b
	ידה	PRAISE	392b	1 a2
	נדבה	VOLUNTARINESS	621d	1
54 9	איב	BE HOSTILE TO	33c	
	ראה	TO SEE	908a	8 a6
	ראה	TO SEE	908a	8 a5
55 1	נגינה	MUSIC	618d	1
55 2	אזן	LISTENING	24c	2
	תחנה	FAVOR	337c	2
	עלם	CONCEAL	761b	
	תפלה	PRAYER	813c	1 e
55 3	אזן	LISTENING	24c	2
	הום	MURMUR	223a	
	הום	MURMUR	223a	
	קשב	ATTEND	904a	
	רוד	ROAM	923d	1
	שיח	COMPLAINT	967a	1
55 4	עקה	PRESSURE	734b	
	שטם	BEAR A GRUDGE	966b	
55 5	אימה	TERROR	34a	
	חול	WHIRL	297a	2 b
	לב	HEART	525c	29b
	נפל	FALL	657c	5
	קרב	INWARD PART	899b	2 a
55 6	אימה	TERROR	34a	
	יראה	FEAR	432a	1
	כסה	COVER	492a	5
	פלצות	SHUDDERING	814a	
55 7	רעד	TREMBLING	944d	
	אבר	PINIONS	7c	
	יונה	DOVE	401d	
	נתן	GIVE	678d	1 f
	עוף	FLY	733c	2
	שכן	SETTLE DOWN	1015a	1 b
55 8	נדד	WANDER	622b	3
	סלה	LIFT UP	700b	
	רחק	BE DISTANT	935a	1
55 9	חוש	HASTE	301d	2
	סעה	RUSH	703c	
	סער	TEMPEST	704b	
	מפלט	ESCAPE	812d	
	רוח	BREATH	924d	2 a
55 10	בלע	SWALLOW UP	118b	2 a
	בלע	SWALLOW UP	*118b	2 a
	חמס	VIOLENCE	329c	
	לשון	TONGUE	546c	1 b
	פלג	SPLIT	811b	2
	ריב	STRIFE	937a	2
55 11	און	TROUBLE	20a	1
	סבב	GO AROUND	686b	3
	עמל	TROUBLE	765d	2
55 12	הוה	CHASM	217d	2
	מוש	REMOVE	559b	
	רחוב	PLAZA	932b	
	מרמה	DECEIT	941b	
	תך	INJURY	1067a	
55 13	איב	BE HOSTILE TO	33c	
	גדל	BECOME GREAT	152c	3 b
	ו	AND	254b	3
	חרף	REPROACH	357d	2
	סתר	HIDE	711c	1
55 14	איב	BE HOSTILE TO	33c	
	אלוף	TAME	48d	2
	אנוש	MAN	60d	1
	ידע	ACQUAINTANCE	394d	
	ערך	ORDER	790a	2
55 15	הלך	WALK	235b	1
	סוד	COUNSEL	691c	2 a
	רגש	THRONG	921c	
55 16	מגור	DWELLING PLACE	158c	
	חי	ALIVE	312a	1 b
	ירד	GO DOWN	433a	1 i
	ישימה	DESOLATION	445b	
	נשא	DECEIVE	674a	
	על	UPON	756c	27 a b
	קרב	INWARD PART	899b	1 f5
	רע	EVIL	948d	0 d
	שאול	SHEOL	983a	1
55 17	ישע	DELIVER	446d	1 b
55 18	בקר	MORNING	134a	1 d
	בקר	MORNING	134b	1 f
	הום	MURMUR	*223a	
	חמה	MURMUR	242a	2
	ערב	SUNSET	787d	1 a
	צהר	MIDDAY	844a	1
	שיח	MUSE	967a	1
55 19	ב	IN	89a	17b
	ל	TO	513d	5 cb e
	נפש	SOUL	660a	3 c
	עם	WITH	767c	1 c
	פדה	RANSOM	804a	3 d
	קרב	COME NEAR	897c	1 a
	קרב	BATTLE	898b	
55 20	אל	GOD	42d	6 e
	אשר	PARTICLE OF RELATION	82d	5
	חליפה	A CHANGE	322c	4
	ירא	FEAR	431c	3 b
	ישב	SIT	442a	1 a
	סלה	LIFT UP	700b	
	קדם	FRONT	869d	2 d
	שמע	HEAR	1034b	2 c
55 21	ברית	COVENANT	136c	14
	חלל	POLLUTE	320c	3
	יד	HAND	389b	1 c
	שלון	PEACE	1023b	7
55 22	חלק	BE SMOOTH	325b	
	לב	HEART	524c	21
	מחמאת	CURD-LIKE	563b	
	פתיחה	DRAWN SWORD	836a	
	קרב	BATTLE	898b	
	רכך	BE TENDER	940a	2
	שמן	OIL	1032b	2 e
	מחמאת	ADDENDA ET COR-RIGENDA	1123c	
55 23	יהב	LOT	396d	
	כל	SUSTAIN	465a	1
	מוט	SHAKING	557a	1
	על	UPON	753b	21c
	עולם	LONG DURATION	762a	2 a
	שלך	THROW	1021b	1 f
55 24	באר	WELL	91d	2
	בטח	TRUST	105a	13a
	דם	BLOOD	197a	2 h
	חצה	DIVIDE	345b	2
	ירד	BRING DOWN	434a	1 d
	מרמה	DECEIT	941b	
	שחת	PIT	1001c	2
56 1	אחז	GRASP	28b	
	אלם	SILENCE	48a	
	גת	GATH	387d	
	יונה	DOVE	401d	
	על	UPON	754a	21fa
	רחק	DISTANT	935b	1 a
56 2	אנוש	MAN	60d	3
	חנן	SHOW FAVOR	336a	2 b
	יום	DAY	400c	7 f
	לחם	FIGHT	535b	
	לחץ	OPPRESS	537d	2
	שאף	CRUSH	983d	
56 3	יום	DAY	400c	7 f
	ל	TO	511a	1 d
	לחם	FIGHT	535b	
	מרום	HEIGHT	929a	3
	שאף	CRUSH	983d	
	שורר	WATCHER	1004a	
56 4	בטח	TRUST	105a	15a
	יום	DAY	400b	7 d4
	ירא	FEAR	431a	1 a
	מרום	HEIGHT	929a	3
56 5	ב	IN	89d	32c
	בטח	TRUST	105a	13a
	בשר	FLESH	142d	5
	הלל	PRAISE	238b	2 b
	ירא	FEAR	431a	1 a
	מה	WHAT	553a	1 da
56 6	מחשבה	THOUGHT	364b	2
	יום	DAY	400c	7 f
	עצב	HURT	780d	
	רע	EVIL	948d	2
56 7	גרד	PENETRATE	*151a	1
	גור	STIR UP STRIFE	158a	1
	גור	STIR UP STRIFE	*158d	1
	עקב	HEEL	784b	B
	צפן	HIDE	860d	2
	צפן	HIDE	860d	
	קוה	WAIT FOR	875b	2
	שמר	KEEP	1036d	1 c
56 8	ירד	BRING DOWN	434a	1 c
	פלט	DELIVERANCE	812c	
56 9	דמעה	TEARS	199c	2
	נאד	SKIN BOTTLE	609d	
	נוד	WANDERING	627a	
	ספר	COUNT	707d	2
	ספרה	BOOK	707d	
56 10	אחור	HINDER SIDE	30c	A
	זה	THIS	260d	1 a
	יום	DAY	400b	7 d4
	כי	THAT	471d	1 a
	ל	TO	515c	5 hc
	שוב	TURN BACK	996d	1
56 11	ב	IN	89d	32c
	הלל	PRAISE	238b	2 b
	הלל	PRAISE	238b	2 b
56 12	בטח	TRUST	105a	13a
	ירא	FEAR	431a	1 a
56 13	תודה	THANK-OFFERING	393a	4
	נדר	VOW	624a	5
	על	UPON	753b	21c
	שלם	BE COMPLETE	1022c	4
56 14	אור	LIGHT	21c	7
	דחי	STUMBLING	191a	2
	הלך	WALK	236b	2
	חי	ALIVE	312a	1 b
	לא	NOT	520c	4 bb
	נפש	SOUL	660a	3 c
	נצל	DELIVER	665a	3 b
57 1	אמת	FIRMNESS	54b	3 b
	ברח	FLEE	138a	2
	מכתם	MIKHTAM	508d	
	מערה	CAVE	792c	1
	שאול	SAUL	982b	1
57 2	שחת	GO TO RUIN	1008c	2
	הוה	CHASM	217d	2
	חנן	SHOW FAVOR	336a	2 b
	חסה	SEEK REFUGE	340b	
	חסה	SEEK REFUGE	340b	
	כנף	WING	489d	1 h
	עד	UNTIL	725a	21bb
	צל	SHADOW	853b	2
57 3	אל	GOD	42d	6 e
	גמר	COMPLETE	170a	2
	עליון	HIGHEST	751b	1
	קרא	CALL	895b	2 a
57 4	אמת	FIRMNESS	54b	3 b
	חסד	GOODNESS	339a	22
	חרף	REPROACH	357d	
	ישע	DELIVER	446d	1 b
	סלה	LIFT UP	700b	
	שאף	CRUSH	983d	
	שלח	SEND	1018c	2 b
57 5	חד	SHARP	292b	1
	חנית	SPEAR	334a	3
	חץ	ARROW	346c	1
	חרב	SWORD	353a	1 k
	לבי	LION	522d	
	להט	FLAME	529d	
	שכב	LIE DOWN	1012a	1 b
	שן	TOOTH	1042a	1 b
57 6	כבוד	GLORY	458d	2 c2
	לשון	TONGUE	546b	1 b
	על	UPON	755a	23
	רום	BE HIGH	927a	2 c
57 7	רשת	NET	440c	1 b2
	כון	ESTABLISH	466b	2 a
	כפף	BEND DOWN	496a	
	כרה	DIG	500a	
	ל	TO	515b	5 hb g
	נפל	FALL	656d	1
	סלה	LIFT UP	700b	
	פעם	BEAT	822a	1 b
	שוחה	PIT	1001c	
57 8	זמר	MAKE MUSIC	274b	1
	כון	BE FIRM	465d	2
	לב	HEART	525a	24
	רוח	BREATH	*925c	7
	שיר	SING	1010d	
57 9	כבוד	HONOR	459b	5
	כנור	LYRE	490d	
	נבל	HARP	614c	
	עור	ROUSE ONESELF	734d	
	עור	ROUSE ONESELF	735a	
	עור	ROUSE ONESELF	735c	1
	שחר	DAWN	1007b	
57 10	זמר	MAKE MUSIC	274a	1
	ידה	PRAISE	392c	1 a2
	לאם	PEOPLE	522c	
57 11	גדול	GREAT	153b	6 c
	חסד	GOODNESS	339b	23b
	על	UPON	759b	42d
	שחק	DUST	1007a	1
57 12	כבוד	GLORY	458d	2 c2
	על	UPON	755a	23
	רום	BE HIGH	927a	2 c
58 1	מכתם	MIKHTAM	508d	
	שחת	GO TO RUIN	1008c	2
58 2	אלם	SILENCE	48a	
	אמנם	VERILY	53d	
	מישר	LEVEL	449d	2
	צדק	RIGHTEOUSNESS	841c	2 a
	שפט	JUDGE	1047d	3 a
58 3	אף	ALSO	65a	1
	חמס	VIOLENCE	329c	
	עולה	INJUSTICE	732c	1
	פלס	WEIGH	814a	1
	פעל	DO	821b	1 b
58 4	בטן	WOMB	106a	3
	דבר	SPEAK	180c	
	זור	BE A STRANGER	266c	1
	כזב	LIE	469c	
	רחם	WOMB	933b	1
	תעה	ERR	1073c	3
58 5	אזן	EAR	24a	2 a
	אטם	SHUT	32a	
	בית	HOUSE	*109c	3
	דמות	LIKENESS	198b	2
	חרש	DEAF	361c	
	חמה	POISON	404c	1 b
	כ	LIKE	453d	1 b
	כמו	LIKE	*455d	1 b
	ל	TO	513d	5 cb e
	נחש	SERPENT	638b	1 a
	פתן	COBRA	837a	
58 6	חבר	UNITE	288a	2
	חבר	COMPANY	288c	3 a
	חכם	BE WISE	314c	
	לחש	WHISPER	538a	
58 7	הרס	THROW DOWN	248d	2
	כפיר	LION	498d	
	נתץ	PULL DOWN	683b	2 c
	שן	TOOTH	1042a	1 b
	מלתעות	TEETH	1069a	
58 8	דרך	TREAD	202b	4
	הלך	WALK	235d	1 a
	חץ	ARROW	346c	2
	כמו	LIKE	*455d	1 a

Ch	v.	Heb	Eng	Page	Sec
		כמו	LIKE	456a	1 a
		ל	TO	516a	5 ib
		מאס	FLOW	549d	2
		מול	CIRCUMCIZE	558a	
		מלל	CIRCUMCIZE	576d	
58	9	שבלול	SNAIL	117d	
		חזה	SEE	302b	1 a
		כמו	LIKE	*455d	1 a
		תמס	MELTING	588a	
		נפל	MISCARRIAGE	658b	
		שמש	SUN	1039b	4 b
58	10	אטד	BRAMBLE	31d	
		בין	DISCERN	106d	1 c
		חי	ALIVE	312b	1 e
		חרון	BURNING OF AN-GER	354c	
		כמו	LIKE	456a	1 a
		סור	POT	696c	1 a
		שער	SWEEP	973b	
58	11	דם	BLOOD	197b	2 n
		חזה	SEE	302b	1 a
		כי	BECAUSE	473d	3 b
		מחץ	SHATTER	*563d	
		נקם	VENGEANCE	668b	1
		פעם	BEAT	822a	1 b
		רחץ	WASH OFF	934c	1
58	12	אך	SURELY	36c	1
		יש	THERE IS	441a	2 b
		פרי	FRUIT	826a	3
		שפט	JUDGE	1047a	3 b1
59	1	מכתם	MIKHTAM	508d	1
		שאול	SAUL	982b	1
		שחת	GO TO RUIN	1008c	2
		שמר	KEEP	1036d	1 c
59	2	קום	STAND	878c	
		שגב	BE HIGH	960c	1
59	3	דם	BLOOD	197a	2 h
		ישע	DELIVER	446d	1 b
59	4	ארב	LIE IN WAIT	70b	
		בלי	WEARING OUT	115c	2 b
		גדר	PENETRATE	*151a	
		גור	STIR UP STRIFE	*158d	1
		גור	STIR UP STRIFE	158d	1
		חטאת	SIN	308c	1 b
		לא	NOT	519d	2 e
		עז	STRONG	738d	
		פשע	TRANSGRESSION	833d	4
59	5	בלי	WEARING OUT	115c	2 b
		כון	BE ESTABLISHED	467a	
		סגר	CLOSE	*689b	
		עור	ROUSE ONESELF	734d	
		קרא	ENCOUNTER	897a	1
		רוץ	RUN	930b	1
59	6	אלהים	GOD	44c	4 ba
		בגד	ACT TREACHER-OUSLY	93d	A
		בגד	ACT TREACHER-OUSLY	93d	D
		חנן	SHOW FAVOR	336a	2 b
		סלה	LIFT UP	700a	
		פקד	ATTEND TO	823c	A 2
		צבא	GOD OF WAR	839c	4 b
		קיץ	AWAKE	884c	1 b
59	7	ה	THE	208d	1 i
		חמה	GROWL	242a	1
		כלב	DOG	476b	A
		סבב	GO AROUND	686b	3
		ערב	SUNSET	787d	1 a
59	8	חרב	SWORD	353a	1 k
		מי	WHO	567a	F c
		נבע	BUBBLE UP	616a	3
59	9	לעג	MOCK	541b	
		שחק	LAUGH	965d	1 a
59	10	עז	STRENGTH	739a	2 c
		משגב	SECURE HEIGHT	960d	2
		שמר	KEEP	*1036c	1 b
		שמר	KEEP	1037a	3 d
59	11	אלהים	GOD	44d	4 bb
		חסד	GOODNESS	339a	2
		קדם	COME IN FRONT	870a	1 b
		ראה	TO SEE	908a	
		ראה	TO SEE	909a	2 b
		שורר	WATCHER	1004a	
59	12	מגן	SHIELD	171c	
		הרג	KILL	247b	2
		חיל	STRENGTH	298c	1 a
		ירד	BRING DOWN	434a	1 c
		נוד	WANDER	627a	1
		נוע	WAVER	631c	4
		שכח	FORGET	1013b	1 c
59	13	אלה	OATH	46d	3 b
		גאון	EXALTATION	145a	2
		דבר	WORD	182a	1 1a
		חטאת	SIN	308c	1 b
		כחש	LYING	471c	1
		לכד	CAPTURE	540b	2
		ספר	COUNT	708b	2
		שפה	SPEECH	973d	1 a1
59	14	אין	NOT	34b	2
		אפס	END	67a	1
		אפס	END	67a	1
		חמה	RAGE	404d	2 c
		כלה	FINISH	478c	2 c2
		ל	TO	511b	1 f
		משל	RULE	605d	3
		סלה	LIFT UP	700a	

Ch	v.	Heb	Eng	Page	Sec
59	15	ה	THE	208d	1 i
		חמה	GROWL	242a	1
		כלב	DOG	476b	A
		סבב	GO AROUND	686b	3
		ערב	SUNSET	787d	1 a
59	16	ו	AND	254d	5 b
		לון	LODGE	533c	1 a
		לון	MURMUR	534a	
		נוע	TOTTER	631b	2
		שבע	SATISFIED	959b	1 a
59	17	בקר	MORNING	134a	1 d
		בקר	MORNING	134b	1 g
		חסד	GOODNESS	339a	2 1a
		מנוס	ESCAPE	631a	2
		עז	STRENGTH	739b	3 b
		צר	STRAITS	865b	
		רנן	GIVE A RINGING CRY	943c	
		משגב	SECURE HEIGHT	960d	2
		שיר	SING	1010d	
		צרר	ADDENDA ET COR-RIGENDA	1126c	
59	18	אלהים	GOD	44d	
		זמר	MAKE MUSIC	274a	1
		חסד	GOODNESS	339a	2
		עז	STRENGTH	739a	2 c
		משגב	SECURE HEIGHT	960d	2
60	1	דוד	DAVID	188b	J
		למד	LEARN	540d	
		עדות	TESTIMONY	730b	2
		על	UPON	754a	2 1f a
		שושן	LILY	1004c	
60	2	אדום	EDOM	10c	2
		ארם	ARAM	74b	A
		ארם	ARAM	74b	A
		ארם	ARAM	74c	B
		גיא	VALLEY	161b	C
		יואב	JOAB	222a	1
		מלח	SALT	572a	
		נצה	STRUGGLE	663c	
		צובא	ZOBAH	844c	
		שוב	TURN BACK	997c	3 b
		שמנה	EIGHT	1033a	2 b
60	3	אנף	BE ANGRY	60a	
		זנח	REJECT	276b	
		פרץ	BREAK THROUGH	829c	6
		שוב	TURN BACK	998c	1
60	4	ארץ	EARTH	76a	1 b
		מוט	SLIP	556d	
		פצם	SPLIT OPEN	822d	
		רעש	SHAKE	950b	1
		רפא	HEAL	950d	2 a
		רפה	SINK	952a	3
		שבר	BREAKING	991a	1
60	5	יין	WINE	406d	E
		קשה	SEVERE	904c	2 a
		ראה	TO SEE	909a	1 b
		תרעלה	REELING	947a	2
60	6	ירא	FEAR	431c	3 b
		נוס	ESCAPE	631a	
		נסס	BE CONSPICUOUS	651c	
		נס	STANDARD	651d	1 a
		סלה	LIFT UP	700b	
		קשט	BOW	905a	
60	7	חלץ	DRAW OFF OR OUT	322d	
		ידיד	BELOVED	391d	1
		ישע	DELIVER	446d	1 b
60	8	חלק	DIVIDE	323d	1
		מדד	MEASURE	551b	2
		סכות	SUCCOTH	697d	1
		עלז	EXULT	759c	
60	9	אפרים	EPHRAIM	68c	4
		חקק	CUT IN	349b	B
		מנשה	MANASSEH	586c	1 b2 b
		מעוז	PLACE OF SAFETY	732a	3
		ראש	HEAD	910d	1 a
60	10	נעל	SANDAL	653b	
		סור	POT	696c	1 b
		פלשת	PHILISTIA	814b	
		רוע	RAISE A SHOUT	929a	1
		רוע	RAISE A SHOUT	929a	1
		רחץ	WASHING	934b	
		שלך	THROW	1021b	2 a
60	11	מבצר	FORTIFICATION	*131c	
		יבל	CONDUCT	385a	3
		מי	WHO	566c	F a
		נחה	LEAD	634d	
		מצור	SIEGE	849a	2
60	12	אדום	EDOM	10c	2
		זנח	REJECT	276b	
		צבא	ARMY	839a	1 a
60	13	יהב	GIVE	396d	1
		תשועה	DELIVERANCE	448b	1
		מן	FROM	578b	1 a
		עזרה	HELP	741a	1
		צר	STRAITS	865a	
		שוא	EMPTINESS	996a	1
60	14	ב	IN	89d	3 2c
		בוס	TRAMPLE	100d	
		חיל	STRENGTH	298d	1 b
61	1	נגינה	MUSIC	618d	1
61	2	תפלה	PRAYER	813c	1 e
		קשב	ATTEND	904a	
		רנה	RINGING CRY	943c	1
61	3	מן	THAN	582d	6 d

Ch	v.	Heb	Eng	Page	Sec
		נחה	LEAD	635a	
		עטף	BE FEEBLE	742c	
		צור	ROCK	849c	1 a
		רום	BE HIGH	926d	1 a
61	4	מגדל	TOWER	153d	1
		מחסה	REFUGE	340c	B
		עז	STRENGTH	738d	1
61	5	אהל	TENT	14b	3
		גור	SOJOURN	157d	1
		חסה	SEEK REFUGE	340b	
		כנף	WING	489d	1 h
		סלה	LIFT UP	700a	
		סתר	COVERING	712a	2 a
		עולם	LONG DURATION	763a	2 l
61	6	ירא	FEAR	431c	3 b
		ירשה	POSSESSION	440b	
		כן	SO	*486a	1 b
		נדר	VOW	624a	2
		נתן	GIVE	678c	1 b
		שם	NAME	1028c	3
		שמע	HEAR	1034b	2 g
61	7	דור	PERIOD	189d	1 b
		ה	THE	208d	1 i
		יום	DAY	399b	4 a
		יסף	ADD	415a	1
		כמו	LIKE	455d	1 a
		מלך	KING	573b	2
		על	UPON	755b	2 4a
61	8	אמת	FIRMNESS	54a	3 b
		חסד	GOODNESS	339a	2 2
		ישב	SIT	442c	1 a
		כן	SO	*486a	1 b
		מנה	APPOINT	584b	
		נצר	GUARD	665d	2
		עולם	LONG DURATION	762a	2 a
		עולם	LONG DURATION	762a	2 a
		פנה	FACE	817a	2 4a b
61	9	זמר	MAKE MUSIC	274a	1
		יום	DAY	400b	7 e1
		כן	SO	486a	1 b
		נדר	VOW	624a	2
		עד	PERPETUITY	723c	2 a
62	1	מזמור	MELODY	274c	
		ידותון	JEDUTHUN	393a	
		על	UPON	753d	2 1c
62	2	אך	ONLY	36d	2 ba
		דומיה	SILENCE	189b	
		ישועה	DELIVERANCE	447b	3
		מן	OUT OF	579d	2 d
62	3	ישועה	DELIVERANCE	447b	3
		מוט	SHAKE	557a	
		צור	ROCK	849a	2 a
		רב	MUCH	913b	1 g
		משגב	SECURE HEIGHT	960d	2
62	4	אן	WHERE	33a	D
		גדר	WALL	155a	
		גדרה	WALL	155b	
		דחה	PUSH	191a	
		ה	THE	209b	2 b
		הות	SHOUT AT	223d	
		הות	SHOUT AT	*223d	
		נטה	BEND	640b	3 b
		קיר	WALL	885a	3
		רצח	MURDER	954a	
62	5	ברך	BLESS	139b	4 f
		יעץ	ADVISE	419d	
		כזב	LIE	469c	
		ל	TO	517d	7 bc
		נדח	THRUST	623b	2
		שאת	DIGNITY	673b	1
		סלה	LIFT UP	700a	
		קלל	BE SLIGHT	886c	1
		קרב	INWARD PART	899b	2 a
		רצה	BE PLEASED WITH	953a	1 b
62	6	דומיה	SILENCE	*189b	
		דמם	BE SILENT	198d	2
		תקוה	HOPE	876b	2
		תקוה	HOPE	876b	1
62	7	ישועה	DELIVERANCE	447b	3
		מוט	SHAKE	557a	
		צור	ROCK	849d	2 a
		משגב	SECURE HEIGHT	960d	2
62	8	מחסה	REFUGE	340c	B
		ישע	DELIVERANCE	447a	2
		כבוד	HONOR	459b	6 a
		עז	STRENGTH	738d	1
		על	UPON	753c	2 1c
		צור	ROCK	849d	2 a
62	9	בטח	TRUST	105a	1 3a
		מחסה	REFUGE	340c	B
		לבב	HEART	523c	2 2
		סלה	LIFT UP	700a	
		שפך	POUR OUT	1049d	2 b
62	10	אדם	MAN	9c	2
		מאזן	BALANCES	24d	
		איש	MAN	35d	
		אך	ONLY	36d	
		בן	SON	120b	1 e
		הבל	VAPOUR	210d	2
		יחד	ALTOGETHER	403a	2 b
		כזב	LIE	*469d	
		כזב	LIE	469d	
		ל	TO	518a	7 bg
		לב	HEART	524d	2 3c
		מן	OUT OF	579b	2 ba
		עלה	GO UP	749a	1

281

Ch	v.	Heb	Eng	Page	Sec
		את	WITH	86b	1 dg
		ברך	BLESS	139a	2 a
		חנן	SHOW FAVOR	336a	2 b
		סלה	LIFT UP	700b	
67	3	דרך	WAY	204a	6 ec
67	3	ישועה	DELIVERANCE	447c	3
67	4	ידה	PRAISE	392c	1 a2
		כל	ALL	481d	1 da
67	5	מישור	UPRIGHTNESS	449d	3
		לאם	PEOPLE	522c	
		נחה	LEAD	635a	
		סלה	LIFT UP	700a	
		רנן	GIVE A RINGING CRY	943c	
67	6	שפט	JUDGE	1047d	3 d
		ידה	PRAISE	392c	1 a2
		כל	ALL	481d	1 da
67	7	ברך	BLESS	139a	2 a
		יבול	PRODUCE	385b	
		נתן	GIVE	679c	1 t
67	8	אפס	END	67a	1
		ברך	BLESS	139a	2 a
		ירא	FEAR	431c	3 b
68	1	איב	BE HOSTILE TO	33c	
		מזמור	MELODY	274c	
68	2	פוץ	BE DISPERSED	807a	
		שן	HATE	971d	1
68	3	אבד	PERISH	1d	1
		דונג	WAX	200a	
		כ	LIKE	454d	3 a
		מסס	MELT	587d	1
		נדף	DRIVE	623c	
		נדף	DRIVE	623c	
		עשן	SMOKE	798c	1 c
		פנה	FACE	818c	2 6b
68	4	עלץ	REJOICE	763b	
		שוש	REJOICE	965b	
68	5	ב	IN	88d	1 7a
		יה	YAH	*219c	
		זמר	MAKE MUSIC	274a	1
		סלל	LIFT UP	699d	3
		עלו	EXULT	759c	
		ערבה	DESERT-PLAIN	787c	5
		רכב	RIDE	938d	2
		שיר	SING	1010d	
68	6	אב	FATHER	3b	2
		אלמנה	WIDOW	48b	
		דין	JUDGE	193a	
		יתום	ORPHAN	450c	
		מעון	REFUGE	733a	2 a
		קדש	APARTNESS	871c	2 a
68	7	אסיר	PRISONER	64a	
		בית	HOUSE	108a	1 a
		יחיד	ONLY ONE	402d	3
		יצא	BRING OUT	424d	
		ישב	CAUSE TO SIT	443d	3 a
		כושרה	PROSPERITY	507a	
		סרר	BE STUBBORN	711a	
		צחיחה	SCORCHED LAND	850b	
68	8	יצא	GO OUT	424a	2 c
		ישימון	WASTE	445c	B
		סלה	LIFT UP	700b	
68	9	אף	ALSO	64d	1
		זה	THIS	*260d	2 a
		נטף	DROP	643a	
		סיני	SINAI	696a	
		רעש	SHAKE	950b	
68	10	גשם	RAIN	177c	
		ו	AND	252c	1 b
		כון	ESTABLISH	466d	1 b
		לאה	BE WEARY	521a	
		נדבה	VOLUNTARINESS	621d	1
		נוף	BESPRINKLE	632b	5
		נחלה	PROPERTY	635b	1 e
68	11	חיה	COMMUNITY	312d	
		חיה	COMMUNITY	312d	
		טובה	WELFARE	375d	3
		כון	ESTABLISH	466b	2 a
		עני	POOR	777a	3
68	12	אמר	WORD	57a	2
		בשר	BEAR TIDINGS	142b	1
		נתן	GIVE	679d	1 x
		צבא	ARMY	839a	1 a
68	13	חלק	DIVIDE	323d	1
		נדד	RETREAT	622b	1
		נוה	ABIDING	627d	
		צבא	ARMY	839a	1 a
68	14	אברה	PINION	7c	
		חפה	COVER	341d	
		חרוץ	GOLD	359a	
		יונה	DOVE	401d	
		ירקרק	GREENISH	439a	
		כנף	WING	489c	1 a
		כסף	SILVER	494a	2
		צלמון	ZALMON	854a	2
		שוש	REJOICE	965b	
		שכב	LIE DOWN	1012a	1 b
		שפתים	PACK-SADDLES	1046b	
68	15	פרש	SPREAD OUT	831c	2
		שדי	ALMIGHTY	995a	1
		שלג	SNOW	1017a	
68	16	אלהים	GOD	43d	2 c
		בשן	BASHAN	143c	
		גבנן	PEAK	148d	
		הר	MOUNTAIN	*249d	1 a
		הר	MOUNTAIN	250a	1 b

Ch	v.	Heb	Eng	Page	Sec
68	17	אף	ALSO	64d	1
		גבנן	PEAK	148d	
		הר	MOUNTAIN	249d	1 a
		הר	MOUNTAIN	250a	1 b
		חמד	DESIRE	326b	C
		נצח	EVERLASTINGNESS	664b	4
		רצד	WATCH STEALTHILY	953a	
68	18	שכן	SETTLE DOWN	1015b	2 c
		אלף	THOUSAND	49a	1 c
		קדש	APARTNESS	871c	1 a
		רבו	TEN THOUSAND	914c	
		רכם	CHARIOT	939b	1
		שנאן	REPETITION	1041d	
68	19	אף	ALSO	65a	1
		יה	YAH	219c	
		ל	TO	511b	1 ga
		מתנה	GIFT	682c	
		סרר	BE STUBBORN	711a	
		מרום	HEIGHT	928d	2
		מרום	HEIGHT	929a	2
		שבה	TAKE CAPTIVE	985c	2
		שבי	CAPTIVITY	985d	3
68	20	שכן	SETTLE DOWN	1015b	2 c
		אל	GOD	42c	6 a
		ברך	BLESS	138d	2 a
		יום	DAY	400b	7 el
		ישועה	VICTORY	447c	4
		סלה	LIFT UP	700a	
		עמס	CARRY A LOAD	770c	2
68	21	אדון	LORD	11d	5
		אל	GOD	42c	6 a
		תוצאה	OUT GOING	426a	3
		מושעה	DELIVERANCE	448a	
68	22	איב	BE HOSTILE TO	33c	
		אשם	OFFENCE	79d	1
		הלך	WALK	236b	2
		מחץ	SHATTER	563c	2
		קדקד	HEAD	869b	
		שער	HAIR	972b	2
68	23	בשן	BASHAN	143c	
		מצולה	DEPTH	846d	
68	24	דם	BLOOD	197b	2 n
		חמץ	BE RED	330a	
		כלב	DOG	476d	A
		לשון	TONGUE	546d	3
		מחץ	SHATTER	563d	
		מנת	PORTION	584c	
		מן	PORTION	585d	1
68	25	אל	GOD	42c	6 b
		הליכה	A GOING	237b	1 b
		מלך	KING	573b	2
		קדש	APARTNESS	871d	2 f
		אחר	BEHIND	29d	1 a
68	26	נגן	PLAY	618d	
		עלמה	YOUNG WOMAN	761c	
		קדם	COME IN FRONT	870a	2 a
		תף	SOUND THE TIMBREL	1074c	
68	27	ברך	BLESS	139a	1
		מן	OUT OF	579c	2 cb
		מקהל	ASSEMBLY	875b	
		מקור	SPRING	881b	1 d
68	28	בנימן	BENJAMIN	122d	2
		זבולן	ZEBULUN	259d	2
		צעיר	YOUNG	859a	1 a
		רגמה	HEAP-CROWD	920c	
		רגש	THRONG	921c	
		רדה	HAVE DOMINION	922a	
		שר	CHIEFTAIN	978d	6
68	29	זו	THIS	262c	2
		ל	TO	515a	5 hb a
		עזז	BE STRONG	738c	
		עז	STRENGTH	739b	3 c
		פעל	DO	821b	1 a
		צוה	CHARGE	846a	5
68	30	היכל	TEMPLE	228c	2 d
		יבל	CONDUCT	385a	1
		שי	GIFT	1009c	
68	31	אביר	MIGHTY	7d	3
		בזר	SCATTER	103b	
		בצר	PRECIOUS ORE	131a	
		גער	REBUKE	172a	2
		חיה	LIVING THING	312c	1 b
		חפץ	DELIGHT IN	342d	1 a
		עדה	CONGREGATION	417b	2
		כסף	SILVER	494c	8 e
		עגל	CALF	722b	
		פתרום	PATHROS	837d	
		קנה	STALK	889c	2
		קרב	BATTLE	898b	
		קרב	BATTLE	898b	
		רפם	STAMP	952c	
		רץ	PIECE	954d	
68	32	אתה	COME	87b	
		חשמן	AMBASSADOR	365c	
		יד	HAND	389c	1 d
		כוש	CUSH	469a	2 b
		מצרים	EGYPT	595d	1 b2
		רוץ	RUN	930c	2
68	33	זמר	MAKE MUSIC	274a	1
		ממלכה	KINGDOM	575b	1
		סלה	LIFT UP	700b	
		שיר	SING	1010d	
68	34	ב	IN	90b	3 4
		הן	BEHOLD	243c	A

Ch	v.	Heb	Eng	Page	Sec
		נתן	GIVE	679d	1 x
		עז	STRENGTH	739a	1
		קדם	FRONT	869d	2 a
		רכב	RIDE	938d	2
		שמי	HEAVENS	1030a	2 a
		שמי	HEAVENS	1030b	2 a
68	35	גאה	MAJESTY	144d	2
		נתן	GIVE	679a	1 h
		עז	STRENGTH	739a	3 a
		עז	STRENGTH	739b	3 b
		על	UPON	755d	2 5
		שחק	DUST	1007a	2
68	36	אל	GOD	42c	6 c
		ברך	BLESS	138d	2 a
		הוא	HE, SHE, IT	215d	2 a
		ירא	CAUSE FEAR	431d	2 ab
		מן	OUT OF	579a	2 ab
		נתן	GIVE	678c	1 b
		עז	STRENGTH	739a	2 b
		תעצמה	MIGHT	783b	
		מקדש	SACRED PLACE	874b	4
69	1	על	UPON	754a	2 lf a
		שושן	LILY	1004c	
69	2	ישע	DELIVER	446d	1 b
		מי	WATER	565d	4 a
		נפש	SOUL	659d	3 b
69	3	עד	AS FAR AS	724a	1 la
		טבע	SINK	371c	
		יון	MIRE	401c	
		מי	WATER	565d	4 a
		מעמד	STANDING-GROUND	765c	
		מעמקים	DEPTHS	771b	
		מצולה	DEPTH	847a	
		שאון	ROAR	981a	2
		שבלת	FLOWING STREAM	987c	
		שטף	OVERFLOW	1009a	1
69	4	גרון	THROAT	173c	2
		חרר	BE HOT	359c	2
		יגע	TOIL	388b	2
		יחל	WAIT	404a	2
		כלה	BE FINISHED	477d	2 b
69	5	גזל	TEAR AWAY	159d	
		חנם	OUT OF FAVOR	336c	C
		עצם	BE VAST	782c	2
		עצם	BONE	783a	3
		צמת	EXTERMINATE	856c	
		צמת	EXTERMINATE	856c	
		רבב	BECOME MUCH	912d	1
		שערה	A HAIR	972b	
		שוב	TURN BACK	999b	1 d
		שקר	DECEPTION	1055c	2
69	6	אשמה	WRONG-DOING	80a	1
		ידע	KNOW	393d	1 a
		כחד	BE HIDDEN	470b	1 b
		ל	TO	512a	3 b
69	7	אדון	LORD	11d	6 a
		אלהים	GOD	44c	4 ba
		בוש	BE ASHAMED	101d	3
		בקש	SEEK	134d	3 c
		כלם	BE HUMILIATED	483d	2
		קוה	WAIT FOR	875d	
69	8	חרפה	REPROACH	357d	1
		כלמה	IGNOMINY	484b	2
		כסה	COVER	492a	5
		נשא	LIFT	671b	2 d
		על	UPON	754b	2 lf b
		פנה	FACE	815d	1 la
69	9	אם	MOTHER	51d	1
		בן	SON	120b	1 a
		זור	BE A STRANGER	266d	
		נכרי	ALIEN	649a	3
69	10	חרפה	REPROACH	357d	1
		חרפה	REPROACH	357d	1
		נפל	FALL	657c	5
		קנאה	ZEAL	888b	2 a
69	11	בכה	WEEP	113b	1
		חרפה	REPROACH	358a	3
		צום	FASTING	847b	
69	12	לבוש	CLOTHING	528c	
		משל	PROVERB	605b	2
		נתן	GIVE	681a	3 a
		שק	SACK	974c	2 a
69	13	ב	IN	90d	4 e
		נגינה	MUSIC	618d	2
		שיח	MUSE	967b	3 a
		שכר	INTOXICATING DRINK	*1016b	
		שכר	INTOXICATING DRINK	1016c	
69	14	שתה	DRINK	1059b	1 b
		אמת	FIRMNESS	54b	3 b
		חסד	GOODNESS	339b	23 a
		ישע	DELIVERANCE	447a	1 a
		תפלה	PRAYER	813c	1 c
		רב	MULTITUDE	914a	2
		רצון	GOODWILL	953c	1 a
69	15	טבע	SINK	371c	
		טיט	MUD	376c	1
		מי	WATER	565d	4
		נצל	BE DELIVERED	664c	2
69	16	מעמקים	DEPTHS	771b	
		אטר	SHUT UP	32a	
		באר	WELL	91d	2
		בלע	SWALLOW UP	118b	2
		מי	WATER	565d	4 a

Ch	v.	Heb	Eng	Page	Sec
		פה	MOUTH	804d	1 a
		שבלת	FLOWING STREAM	987c	
		שטף	OVERFLOW	1009a	1
69	17	חסד	GOODNESS	339b	2 3d
		טוב	PLEASANT	374d	9 b
		פנה	TURN	815c	2 c1
		רחמים	COMPASSION	933c	1
69	18	מהר	HASTEN	555a	2
		מהר	QUICKLY	*555b	
		סתר	HIDE	711d	2 c
		עבד	SLAVE	714c	6
		צרר	ADDENDA ET CORRIGENDA	1126c	
69	19	גאל	REDEEM	145c	3 a
		מען	PURPOSE	775b	1 b
		פדה	RANSOM	804a	3 d
		קרב	COME NEAR	897b	1 a
69	20	בשת	SHAME	102a	1
		חרפה	REPROACH	357d	1
		כלמה	IGNOMINY	484b	1
		נגד	IN FRONT	617b	1 aa
		צרר	SHEW HOSTILITY TOWARD	865d	
69	21	אין	NOT	34c	2 da
		אנש	BE SICK	60c	
		חרפה	REPROACH	357d	1
		נוד	SHEW GRIEF	626d	2 b
		נוש	BE SICK	633b	
		נחם	CONSOLE ONESELF	637a	
		קוה	WAIT FOR	875d	1
		שבר	BREAK	990c	
69	22	ברות	FOOD	136a	1
		חמץ	VINEGAR	330a	
		ל	TO	515c	5 ha
		נתן	GIVE	678c	1 b
		צמא	THIRST	854d	
		ראש	VENOM	912c	1
		שקה	GIVE TO DRINK	1052c	2
69	23	מוקש	BAIT	430d	
		פח	BIRD-TRAP	809a	2 b
		שלחן	TABLE	1020b	2
		שלום	PEACE	1023a	4
69	24	חשך	GROW DARK	364d	3
		תמיד	CONTINUITY	556b	1 a
		מן	FROM	583b	7 ba
		מעד	TOTTER	588c	
		מתנים	LOINS	608b	2 a
		ראה	TO SEE	907a	4
69	25	זעם	INDIGNATION	276d	
		זעם	INDIGNATION	277a	
		חרון	BURNING OF ANGER	354c	
69	26	נשג	OVERTAKE	673c	1 b
		אהל	TENT	14a	2
		טירה	ENCAMPMENT	377b	1
		שמם	BE DESOLATED	1031a	1
69	27	אל	TO	40c	6
		חלל	PIERCED	319c	1
		מכאוב	PAIN	456b	2
		ספר	COUNT	708b	1
		רדף	PURSUE	922d	1 f
69	28	עון	INIQUITY	731c	3
		על	UPON	755c	2 4a
		צדקה	RIGHTEOUSNESS	842c	6 a
69	29	חי	ALIVE	312a	1 b
		כתב	BE WRITTEN	508a	1
		מחה	WIPE OUT	562b	1
		ספר	MISSIVE	*707c	4
		ספר	MISSIVE	*707c	3 g
		עם	WITH	767d	1 e
69	30	ישועה	DELIVERANCE	447b	1
		כאב	BE IN PAIN	456a	2
		עני	POOR	776d	3
		שגב	BE HIGH	960c	1
69	31	גדל	BECOME GREAT	152c	3 b
		הלל	PRAISE	238b	2 b
		תודה	THANKSGIVING	392d	2
		מן	OUT OF	579b	2 bb
		שיר	SONG	1010b	2
69	32	יטב	BE PLEASING	405c	4
		פרס	BREAK IN TWO	828b	2
		פר	YOUNG BULL	830d	2 d
		קרן	SEND OUT RAYS	902a	2
		שור	A HEAD OF CATTLE	1004b	
69	33	דרש	SEEK	205b	3 a
		ו	AND	254d	5 ca
		חיה	LIVE	311b	1 d
		לבב	HEART	524a	2 7
		ענו	POOR	776c	3
69	34	אביון	NEEDY	2d	
		אסיר	PRISONER	64a	
		בוה	DESPISE	102c	
69	35	הלל	PRAISE	238a	2 b
		רמש	CREEP	943a	2 b
69	36	בנה	BUILD	124d	1 i
		יהודה	JUDAH	397b	2
		ירש	TAKE POSSESSION	439b	1 a
		ישע	DELIVER	446b	1 a
69	37	אהב	LOVE	13a	3
		זרע	SOWING	282d	4 c
		נחל	TAKE AS A POSSESSION	635c	1 a
		עבד	SLAVE	714a	3
		שכן	SETTLE DOWN	1015b	1
		שם	NAME	1028d	3
70	1	זכר	REMEMBER	271a	3 d

Ch	v.	Heb	Eng	Page	Sec
70	2	חוש	HASTE	301d	
		עזרה	HELP	741a	1
70	3	בוש	BE ASHAMED	101d	3
		בקש	SEEK	134d	2 a
		חפץ	DELIGHTING IN	343a	1
		חפר	BE ABASHED	344a	
		כלם	BE HUMILIATED	483d	2
		נפש	SOUL	659d	3 c
70	4	בשת	SHAN'E	102a	1
		האח	AHA	*210c	
		עקב	CONSEQUENCE	*784d	1
		שוב	TURN BACK	996d	1
70	5	אהב	LOVE	13a	3
		בקש	SEEK	134d	3 c
		גדל	BECOME GREAT	152b	3 b
		ישועה	DELIVERANCE	447b	3
		תמיד	CONTINUITY	556b	1 a
		שוש	REJOICE	965b	
70	6	אביון	NEEDY	2d	
		אחר	DELAY	29b	1
		חוש	HASTE	301d	
		עזר	HELP	740d	2
		עני	POOR	776d	3
71	1	חסה	SEEK REFUGE	340b	
		עולם	LONG DURATION	762b	2 a
71	2	אזן	EAR	24b	2 b
		ישע	DELIVER	446d	1 b
		נמה	INCLINE	641a	3 e
		פלט	ESCAPE	812b	1
		צדקה	RIGHTEOUSNESS	842c	6 a
71	3	ישע	DELIVER	446d	1 b
		תמיד	CONTINUITY	556c	1 b
		סלע	CRAG	701a	2
		מעון	REFUGE	733a	3
		מצודה	FASTNESS	845a	
		צוה	CHARGE	846a	5
		צור	ROCK	849d	4
71	4	חמץ	BE RUTHLESS	330b	
		כף	POWER	496d	2
		עול	ACT WRONGFULLY	732c	
		פלט	ESCAPE	812b	1
71	5	אדון	LORD	11c	4 a
		מבטח	CONFIDENCE	105c	2
		נעורים	YOUTH	655c	
		תקוה	HOPE	876b	2
71	6	אם	MOTHER	51c	1
		ב	IN	90d	4 e
		בטן	WOMB	106a	3
		גזה	CUT	159b	
		תהלה	PRAISE	240a	1
		תמיד	CONTINUITY	556b	1 a
		סמך	LEAN	702a	
71	7	מופת	WONDER	69a	1
		מחסה	REFUGE	340c	1 B
		עז	STRENGTH	738d	
71	8	תהלה	PRAISE	240a	1
		יום	DAY	400c	7 f
		מלא	BE FULL	570c	1
		תפארה	BEAUTY	802d	2 c
71	9	זקנה	OLD AGE	279a	
		כח	STRENGTH	470c	1 a
		כלה	BE FINISHED	477d	2 b
		עת	TIME	773c	1 b
		שלך	THROW	1021b	2 b
71	10	אמר	SAY	56a	1
		יחדו	TOGETHER	403b	A
		יעץ	CONSULT	420a	
		שמר	KEEP	1036d	1 c
71	11	נצל	DELIVER	664d	3 a
		רדף	PURSUE	922d	1 e
		תפש	LAY HOLD OF	1074d	1
71	12	חוש	HASTE	301d	
		עזרה	HELP	741a	1
		רחק	BE DISTANT	934d	
71	13	בקש	SEEK	134d	2 b
		חרפה	REPROACH	357d	1
		כלה	BE FINISHED	477d	2 c
		כלמה	IGNOMINY	484b	2
		עטה	WRAP ONESELF	741d	
		שטן	ACT AS ADVERSARY	966c	1
71	14	יחל	WAIT	404a	2
		יסף	ADD	415b	1
		תמיד	CONTINUITY	556b	1 a
71	15	יום	DAY	400c	7 f
		תשועה	DELIVERANCE	448b	1
		ספרה	NUMBER	708d	
71	16	אדן	LORD	11c	4 a
		ב	IN	89c	3 b
		בד	SEPARATION	94c	1 b
		בוא	COME	98c	2 a
		גבורה	MIGHT	150c	3
		זכר	REMEMBER	271a	3 b
		צדקה	RIGHTEOUSNESS	842c	6 a
71	17	הגה	HITHERTO	244d	B
		למד	LEARN	540d	
		נעורים	YOUTH	655c	
71	18	גבורה	MIGHT	150c	3
		דור	GENERATION	190a	2 c
		זקנה	OLD AGE	279a	
		זרוע	ARM	284b	2 b
		כל	ALL	481d	1 c
		עד	UNTIL	725a	2 lb
		עד	UNTIL	725a	2 lb b
		שיבה	OLD AGE	966d	1

Ch	v.	Heb	Eng	Page	Sec
71	19	אשר	PARTICLE OF RELATION	82b	3
		גדול	GREAT	153c	9
		צדקה	RIGHTEOUSNESS	842b	2
		מרום	HEIGHT	928d	2
71	20	אשר	PARTICLE OF RELATION	82b	3
		חיה	LIVE	311c	3 a
		צרה	DISTRESS	865b	
		ראה	TO SEE	909a	1 b
		שוב	TURN BACK	998c	8
		תהום	ABYSS	1063a	5
		תחתי	LOWER	*1066c	
71	21	גדולה	GREATNESS	153c	A
		נחם	CONSOLE ONESELF	637a	
		סבב	TURNABOUT	685d	1 c
71	22	אמת	FIRMNESS	54a	3 b
		גם	ALSO	169d	4
		זמר	MAKE MUSIC	274b	2
		ידה	PRAISE	392c	1 a2
		כלי	INSTRUMENT	479d	2 b
		כבור	LYRE	490b	
		כבור	LYRE	490b	
		נבל	HARP	614c	
		קדוש	HOLY	872c	1 c
71	23	זמר	MAKE MUSIC	274a	1
		נפש	SOUL	660a	3 c
		פדה	RANSOM	804a	3 d
		רנן	GIVE A RINGING CRY	943b	
		רנן	GIVE A RINGING CRY	943c	
71	24	בוש	BE ASHAMED	101d	3
		בקש	SEEK	134d	2 b
		הגה	UTTER	211d	2
		חפר	BE ABASHED	344a	
		יום	DAY	400c	7 f
		לשון	TONGUE	546b	1 b
		צדקה	RIGHTEOUSNESS	842c	6 a
72	1	בן	SON	120c	1 ib
		צדקה	RIGHTEOUSNESS	842a	1 c
		שלמה	SOLOMON	1024d	
72	2	דין	JUDGE	192b	1
		עני	POOR	777a	3
		צדק	RIGHTEOUSNESS	841d	2 c
72	3	גבעה	HILL	149a	3
		הר	MOUNTAIN	250c	1 i
		נשא	LIFT	671b	2 g
		צדקה	RIGHTEOUSNESS	842a	1 c
		שלום	PEACE	1023a	5 a
72	4	אביון	NEEDY	2d	
		דכא	CRUSH	194a	
		ישע	DELIVER	446c	1
		עני	POOR	777a	3
		עשק	OPPRESS	798d	1
		שפט	JUDGE	1047d	3 b2
72	5	דור	PERIOD	189d	1 b
		ירא	FEAR	431c	3 b
		ירח	MOON	437a	
		עם	WITH	768a	1 g
		פנה	FACE	817a	2 4a e
		שמש	SUN	1039b	1
72	6	ארץ	EARTH	76b	3 b
		גז	MOWING	159c	
		זרזיף	DROP	284b	
		זרף	DRIP	284b	
		ירד	GO DOWN	433c	3 a
		מטר	RAIN	564d	
72	7	בלי	WEARING OUT	116a	D
		בלת	NOT	*117a	4 c
		די	SUFFICIENCY	*191b	1
		ירח	MOON	437a	
		פרח	BUD	827a	
		שלום	PEACE	1023a	3
72	8	אפס	END	67a	1
		ה	THE	208d	1 i
		ים	SEA	411b	8 d
		מן	FROM	581d	5 A
		נהר	STREAM	625d	1
		רדה	HAVE DOMINION	922a	
72	9	כרע	BOW DOWN	502c	1
		לחך	LICK UP	535b	
		עפר	DRY EARTH	780a	2 e
		צי	YELPER	850d	
72	10	אי	COAST	16a	
		מנחה	TRIBUTE	585a	2
		מנחה	OFFERING	585c	6
		סבא	SEBA	685b	
		קרב	COME NEAR	897d	1 a
		שבא	SHEBA	985a	
		שוב	TURN BACK	999b	1 f
		אשכר	GIFT	1016d	
		תרשיש	TARSHISH	1077a	1
72	12	אביון	NEEDY	2d	
		ו	AND	253c	1 k
		ל	TO	*512a	3 b
		עני	POOR	777a	3
		שוע	CRY OUT	1002d	
72	13	אביון	NEEDY	2d	
		דל	POOR	195d	
		חוס	PITY	299c	C
		ישע	DELIVER	446c	1
72	14	גאל	REDEEM	145c	3 a
		דם	BLOOD	196c	1
		חמס	VIOLENCE	329c	
		יקר	BE PRECIOUS	429d	1 b

Ch v.	Heb	Eng	Page	Sec
72 15	תר	INJURY	1067a	2
	בעד	ON BEHALF OF	126c	2
	ברך	BLESS	139b	4 g
	זהב	GOLD	263b	7
	יום	DAY	400c	7 f
	תמיד	CONTINUITY	556b	1 a
	מן	FROM	580d	3 ba
	שבא	SHEBA	985b	
72 16	ארץ	EARTH	76b	3 b
	ב	IN	88b	11
	בר	GRAIN	141b	
	הר	MOUNTAIN	250d	1 m
	לבנון	LEBANON	527b	
	מן	OUT OF	579c	2 cc
	עשב	HERB	793b	
	פסה	ABUDANCE	821a	
	פרי	FRUIT	826b	1
	צוץ	BLOSSOM	847c	1
	רעש	SHAKE	950b	
72 17	אשר	GO STRAIGHT	80d	4
	ברך	BLESS	139c	
	נון	INCREASE	630c	
	עולם	LONG DURATION	762d	2 h
	פנה	FACE	817a	24a e
	שמש	SUN	1039b	1
72 18	ברך	BLESS	138c	2a
	יהוה	YAHWEH	219a	2 1h
72 19	אמן	VERILY	53b	
	ברך	BLESS	138d	2 a
	כבוד	GLORY	458d	2 c2
	כבוד	GLORY	459a	2 c3
	מלא	BE FULL	570c	1
	עולם	LONG DURATION	762b	2 c
72 20	דוד	DAVID	188a	
	ישי	JESSE	445a	
	כלה	BE FINISHED	478d	
	תפלה	PRAYER	813c	2
73 1	אך	SURELY	36c	1
	אך	ONLY	36d	
	בר	PURE	141a	1
	מזמור	MELODY	274c	
	טוב	PLEASANT	374d	9 b
	ל	TO	511a	1 d
	לבב	HEART	524a	26a
73 2	אין	NOTHING	34a	1
	אשור	STEP	81a	
	כי	BECAUSE	*474a	3 c
	מעט	A FEW	590b	2 a
	נטה	BEND	640c	3 b
	שפך	POUR OUT	1049b	
73 3	הלל	BE BOASTFUL	238a	
	קנא	BE ZEALOUS	888c	2
	שלום	PEACE	1023a	3
73 4	אל	BODY	17c	
	בריא	FAT	135d	
	חרצבה	BOND	359a	2
	תם	COMPLETE	1071a	1
	מותם	ADDENDA ET CORRIGENDA	1124d	
73 5	אדם	MAN	9c	2
	אין	NOT	34b	2
	אנוש	MAN	60d	2
	נגע	STRIKE	619b	
	עמל	TROUBLE	765d	1
	עם	WITH	767d	1 e
73 6	גאוה	PRIDE	144d	3
	חמס	VIOLENCE	329c	
	כן	SO	486d	3 d
	ל	TO	513d	5 cb e
	נוה	PASTURE	*627d	2
	עטף	ENVELOP ONESELF	742b	
	ענק	SERVE AS NECKLACE	778d	
	שית	GARMENT	1011c	
73 7	חלב	FAT	316d	1
	יצא	GO OUT	423a	1 g
	לבב	HEART	523c	2 3c
	עבר	PASS OVER	717b	1 e
	עין	EYE	744c	2 b
	משכית	SHOW-PIECE	967d	2
73 8	ב	IN	89c	3 1c
	מוק	MOCK	558b	
	עשק	OPPRESSION	799a	1
	מרום	HEIGHT	929c	2
	רע	EVIL	948d	2
73 9	הלך	WALK	232c	1 3
	הלך	WALK	*232c	1 3
	לשון	TONGUE	546b	1 b
	שתת	APPOINT	1060c	
73 10	הלם	HITHER	240d	
	כן	SO	486d	3 d
	ל	TO	514a	5 e
	מלא	FULL	571a	
	מצה	DRAIN	594d	
	שוב	TURN BACK	997c	5 d
	שוב	TURN BACK	997c	5 d
73 11	איכה	IN WHAT MANNER	32d	1
	אל	GOD	42d	6 e
	היך	HOW	*228a	
	דעה	KNOWLEDGE	395c	
	יש	THERE IS	441d	2 b
	עליון	HIGHEST	751b	1
73 12	אלה	THESE	41c	A
	זה	THIS	*261b	3
	חיל	STRENGTH	299a	3
	עולם	LONG DURATION	762a	2 a
73 13	שגה	GROW	960d	
	שלו	QUIET	1017c	1
	אך	SURELY	36c	1
	אך	ONLY	36d	
	זכה	BE CLEAR	269a	
	כף	HOLLOW OF THE HAND	496d	1 d7
	לבב	HEART	523b	2 1
	נקיון	INNOCENCY	667d	1
	רחץ	WASH OFF	934c	1
	ריק	EMPTINESS	938b	
73 14	בקר	MORNING	134b	1 f
	ו	AND	254a	2 b
	יום	DAY	400c	7 f
	תוכחת	REBUKE	407b	3
	כי	BECAUSE	*474a	3
	ל	TO	516b	5 ja
	נגע	TOUCH	619a	2
73 15	אם	IF	50a	1 a4 c
	בגד	ACT TREACHEROUSLY	93d	C
	דור	GENERATION	190b	3
	כמו	LIKE	456a	1 a
	ספר	COUNT	708a	1
	ספר	COUNT	708b	2
73 16	הוא	HE, SHE, IT	*215a	
	חשב	THINK	363c	B
73 17	אחרית	END	31a	B
	אל	GOD	42d	6 e
	בין	DISCERN	106d	3 b
	עד	UNTIL	725a	2 1b b
	מקדש	SACRED PLACE	874b	4
73 18	אך	ONLY	36d	
	חלקה	SMOOTH PART	325c	2
	ל	TO	512a	3 b
	נפל	FALL	658a	2
	משואות	DECEPTIONS	674b	
	משאה	DESOLATION	996c	2
	משאה	PUT	1011b	2 a
73 19	בלהה	CALAMITY	117a	1
	מן	OUT OF	580a	2 eb
	סוף	CEASE	692d	
	רגע	A MOMENT	921a	BC
	רגע	A MOMENT	921a	BB
	משואה	DESOLATION	996c	B
	שמה	WASTE	1031c	1
	תמם	BE FINISHED	1070b	1
73 20	בזה	DESPISE	102c	
	חלום	DREAM	321c	1
	כי	BECAUSE	*474a	3 c
	מן	SINCE	583c	7 c
	עור	ROUSE ONESELF	735c	2
	צלם	IMAGE	854a	3
	קיץ	AWAKE	884c	1 a
73 21	חמץ	BE SOUR	329d	
	כי	BECAUSE	474a	3 c
	כליה	KIDNEYS	480c	2 b
	לבב	HEART	524d	2 9b
	שנן	SHARPEN	1042a	
73 22	בהמה	BEAST	97a	3
	בהמות	HIPPOPOTAMUS	97a	
	בער	BRUTISHNESS	129d	
	עם	WITH	767d	1 d
73 23	אחז	GRASP	28b	
	יד	HAND	389a	1 a
	ימין	RIGHT HAND	411d	1 b
	תמיד	CONTINUITY	556b	1 a
	עם	WITH	768c	4 b
	שאול	SHEOL	*983b	2 b
73 24	עצה	ADVICE	420b	
	כבוד	HONOR	459a	3
	נחה	LEAD	635a	
73 25	חפץ	DELIGHT IN	342d	1 a
	עם	WITH	768b	3 d
	שאול	SHEOL	*983b	2 b
73 26	חלק	PORTION	324b	3 b
	כלה	BE FINISHED	477d	2 b
	לבב	HEART	523b	2 1
	עולם	LONG DURATION	762a	2 a
	צור	ROCK	849d	2 a
	שאר	FLESH	985a	1 b
73 27	אבד	PERISH	1d	1
	זנה	COMMIT FORNICATION	276a	3
	מן	FROM	578a	1 a
	צמת	EXTERMINATE	856c	
	צמת	EXTERMINATE	856c	
	רחק	REMOVING	935b	
73 28	אדון	LORD	11c	4 a
	מחסה	REFUGE	340c	B
	טוב	PLEASANT	374c	5
	מלאכה	WORK	522a	3 a
	ספר	COUNT	*708a	1
	קרבה	APPROACH	898b	
	שית	PUT	1011b	1
74 1	זנח	REJECT	276b	
	נצח	EVERLASTINGNESS	664b	4 da
	מה	HOW	554a	
	עשן	SMOKE	798c	1 b
	צאן	SMALL CATTLE	838c	3
	מרעית	PASTURING	945c	1
74 2	גאל	REDEEM	145c	3 b
	הר	MOUNTAIN	249c	1 a
	זה	THIS	261d	5
	זכר	REMEMBER	270b	2 1 c
	עדה	CONGREGATION	417b	3
	נחלה	PROPERTY	635b	1 e
	קדם	FRONT	869d	2 d
	קנה	ACQUIRE	889a	1 b
	שבט	TRIBE	987b	2 b
74 3	כל	ALL	*481d	1 c
	כל	ALL	482c	2 a
	ל	TO	511b	1 ga
	נצח	ENDURING	664b	3
	משאות	DECEPTIONS	674b	
	פעם	BEAT	822a	1 b
	רום	BE HIGH	927b	1 a1
	רעע	BE EVIL	949d	1
	משאה	DESOLATION	996c	2
74 4	אות	SIGN	17a	7
	מועד	APPOINTED MEETING	417d	2
	צרר	SHEW HOSTILITY TOWARD	865d	
	קרב	INWARD PART	899a	1 d
	שום	TO PLACE	964b	4 c
	שאג	ROAR	980c	1
74 5	ידע	BE PERCEIVED	394d	3
	כילפות	AXE	*476a	
	סבך	THICKET	687c	
	מעל	ABOVE	752a	2 ca
	עץ	TREE	781d	1 b
	קרדם	AXE	899c	
74 6	יהוה	YAHWEH	218a	1
	הלם	SMITE	240c	
	יחד	ALTOGETHER	403b	2 b
	כילפות	AXE	476a	
	כשיל	AXE	506a	
	פתוח	ENGRAVING	836c	
74 7	חלל	POLLUTE	320b	1 b
	ל	TO	511c	1 ga
	מקדש	SACRED PLACE	874b	4
	משכן	DWELLING-PLACE	1015d	2 a
	שלח	SEND	1019b	7
74 8	אל	GOD	42d	6 e
	יחד	ALTOGETHER	403b	2 b
	ינה	SUPPRESS	413a	
	מועד	APPOINTED PLACE	418a	3 b
	לב	HEART	525c	2 7
74 9	אות	SIGN	16d	4
	לא	NOT	519b	1 bb
	מה	HOW	554b	4 e
	נביא	PROPHET	611d	1
	עוד	STILL	729a	1 ab
74 10	חרף	REPROACH	357d	
	מתי	WHEN	607d	C
	נאץ	CONTEMN	611a	
	נצח	EVERLASTINGNESS	664b	4
	שם	NAME	1028c	3
74 11	חוק	BOSOM	300c	
	חיק	BOSOM	300d	1
	כלא	RESTRAIN	476b	2
	כלה	FINISH	478c	2 c2
	מה	HOW	554a	4 da
	מן	OUT OF	579a	2 aa
	קרב	INWARD PART	899b	1 g
	שוב	TURN BACK	999a	1 c
74 12	ישועה	VICTORY	447c	4
	מלך	KING	573b	3
	מן	FROM	581c	4 a
	פעל	DO	821b	1 a
	קדם	FRONT	869d	2 c
74 13	לויתן	LEVIATHAN	*531b	
	עז	STRENGTH	739b	3 c
	פרר	SPLIT	830d	
	ראש	HEAD	910d	1 b
	שבר	BREAK	991a	
	תנין	SEA-MONSTER	1072c	3
74 14	מאכל	FOOD	38b	
	לויתן	LEVIATHAN	531b	
	עם	PEOPLE	766c	1
	צי	YELPER	*850d	
	ראש	HEAD	910d	1 b
	רצץ	CRUSH	954d	1
74 15	בקע	CLEAVE	131d	1
	יבש	BE DRY	386c	1
	איתן	EVER-FLOWING	450d	1
	נחל	TORRENT	636b	1
	נתן	GIVE	*679c	1 t
	מעין	SPRING	746a	
74 16	מאור	LUMINARY	22c	
	אף	ALSO	64d	1
	כון	ESTABLISH	466c	2 b
	שמש	SUN	1039b	1
74 17	גבולה	BORDER	148b	
	חרף	HARVEST-TIME	358b	
	יצר	FORM	427d	2 a
	נצב	STAND	662b	4
	קיץ	SUMMER	884d	1
74 18	זכר	REMEMBER	270c	2 4
	חרף	REPROACH	357d	
	נאץ	CONTEMN	611a	
	שם	NAME	1028c	3
74 19	חיה	LIVING THING	312d	2
	חיה	COMMUNITY	313a	
	נצח	EVERLASTINGNESS	664b	4
	עני	POOR	777a	3
	תר	TURTLE-DOVE	1076a	
74 20	ברית	COVENANT	136c	2 2c
	גאות	MAJESTY	145b	3
	חמס	VIOLENCE	329c	
	מחשך	DARK PLACE	365b	A

Ch	v.	Heb	Eng	Page	Sec
		נבט	LOOK	613d	3
74	21	נוה	PASTURE	627d	2
		אביון	NEEDY	2d	
		דך	CRUSHED	194c	
		הלל	PRAISE	238b	2 b
		כלם	BE HUMILIATED	483d	1
		עני	POOR	776d	3
74	22	שוב	TURN BACK	997a	1
		זכר	REMEMBER	270c	24
		חרפה	REPROACH	358a	1
		יום	DAY	400c	7 f
		מן	OUT OF	579d	2 d
		ריב	STRIVE	936c	3
74	23	תמיד	CONTINUITY	556b	1 a
		עלה	GO UP	749a	8
		צרר	SHEW HOSTILITY TOWARD	865d	
		שאון	ROAR	981a	1
		שכח	FORGET	1013b	2 c
75	1	מזמור	MELODY	274c	
		שחת	GO TO RUIN	1008c	2
75	2	ידה	PRAISE	392c	1 b
		קרב	NEAR	898c	2 f
		שם	NAME	1028d	3
75	3	מועד	APPOINTED TIME	417c	1 a
		מישר	LEVEL	449d	2
		שפט	JUDGE	1048a	3 d
75	4	מוג	MELT	556a	
		סלה	LIFT UP	700b	
		עמוד	PILLAR	765b	5 b
		תכן	MEASURE	1067c	
75	5	הלל	BE BOASTFUL	237d	
		הלל	BE BOASTFUL	238a	
		קרן	HORN	902a	2
		רום	BE HIGH	927c	1 f
75	6	עתק	FORWARD	801b	
		צואר	NECK	848c	1
		צור	ROCK	849d	2 a
		קרן	HORN	902a	2
		רום	BE HIGH	927c	1 f
		מרום	HEIGHT	928d	
75	7	הר	MOUNTAIN	250c	1 e
		מוצא	GOING FORTH	425d	3 c
		מערב	WEST	788b	
		רום	BE HIGH	927c	1 f
75	8	זה	THIS	260d	1 b
		רום	BE HIGH	927c	1 f
		שפט	JUDGE	1047d	3 d
		שפל	BECOME LOW	1050b	1
75	9	חמר	FERMENT	330b	
		יין	WINE	406d	E
		כוס	CUP	468a	
		מלא	FULL	571a	
		מסך	MIXTURE	587c	
		מצה	DRAIN	594c	
		נגר	POUR	620b	
		רשע	WICKED	957c	3
		שמר	LEES	1038d	1
		שתה	DRINK	1059c	1 e
75	10	אלהים	GOD	44c	4 ba
		זמר	MAKE MUSIC	274a	
		עולם	LONG DURATION	762b	2
75	11	גדע	HEW	154c	
		צדיק	JUST	843b	4
		קרן	HORN	902a	2
		קרן	HORN	902a	2
		רום	BE HIGH	927b	
76	1	מזמור	MELODY	274c	
		נגינה	MUSIC	618d	1
76	2	גדול	GREAT	153b	6 c
		ידע	BE MADE KNOWN	394c	1
76	3	סך	THICKET	697c	
		מעונה	DEN	733b	1
		ציון	ZION	851c	
		שלם	SALEM	1024a	
76	4	מגן	SHIELD	171c	
		סלה	LIFT UP	700a	
		קשת	BOW	906a	1 b
		שבר	BREAK	991a	
		שם	THERE	1027c	3 c
76	5	אדיר	MAJESTIC	12b	1
		אור	BECOME LIGHT	21b	
		הר	MOUNTAIN	250b	1 c
		טרף	PREY	383c	1
76	6	אביר	MIGHTY	7d	1
		חיל	STRENGTH	298d	1 c
		יד	HAND	390b	2
		שנה	SLEEP	446a	
		לב	HEART	525d	20
		מצא	FIND	593c	4
		נום	BE DROWSY	630b	
		שלל	SPOIL	1021d	
76	7	אלהים	GOD	44c	4 ba
		גערה	REBUKE	172a	2
		ו	AND	253a	1 h
		מן	OUT OF	580a	2 eb
		רדם	BE IN HEAVY SLEEP	922b	
76	8	מאז	FROM THAT TIME	23b	B
		ירא	CAUSE FEAR	431d	2
		מי	WHO	566a	F c
		פנה	FACE	817b	24 bd
76	9	דין	JUDGMENT	192c	1
		ירא	FEAR	431a	1 a
		שקט	BE QUIET	1053a	1
76	10	ישע	DELIVER	446d	1 b
		סלה	LIFT UP	700a	
		ענו	POOR	776c	2
		קום	STAND	878b	6 a
		משפט	JUDGMENT	1048b	1 a
76	11	חגר	GIRD	292a	3
		ידה	PRAISE	392c	1 a2
		חמה	RAGE	404c	2 a
		כי	THAT	472d	1 e
		שארית	REST	984c	1
76	12	יהוה	YAHWEH	218d	2 1b
		יבל	CONDUCT	385a	1
		מורא	FEAR	432b	3
		נדר	VOW	623d	
		סביב	ROUND ABOUT	687a	2 aa
		שי	GIFT	1009c	
		שלם	BE COMPLETE	1022c	4
76	13	בצר	CUT OFF	131a	
		ירא	CAUSE FEAR	431d	2
		נגיד	LEADER	617d	
		רוח	BREATH	925a	3 b
77	1	מזמור	MELODY	274c	
		ידותון	JEDUTHUN	393a	
		על	UPON	753c	2 1c
77	2	אזן	LISTENING	24c	2
		צעק	CRY	858c	1 b
77	3	דרש	SEEK	205b	3 a
		יד	HAND	389c	1 d
		לילה	NIGHT	538d	1
		מאן	REFUSE	549a	
		נגר	FLOW	620b	
		נחם	CONSOLE ONESELF	637a	3
		נפש	SOUL	661b	8
		פוג	GROW NUMB	806a	
		צרה	DISTRESS	865b	
77	4	הום	MURMUR	*223a	
		המה	MURMUR	242a	2
		זכר	REMEMBER	270a	13 b
		סלה	LIFT UP	700a	
		עטף	BE FEEBLE	742c	
		רוח	BREATH	925a	3 b
		שיח	MUSE	967a	1
77	5	אחז	GRASP	28b	
		פעם	THRUST	821d	
		שמרה	EYE-LID	1037d	
77	6	חשב	THINK	363c	1
		יום	DAY	399c	5 c
		מן	FROM	581d	4 c
		עולם	LONG DURATION	762a	1 e
		קדם	FRONT	869d	2 c
77	7	זכר	REMEMBER	269d	11 a
		חפש	SEARCH	344c	2 b
		לבב	HEART	*523d	23 c
		לבב	HEART	523c	22
		לילה	NIGHT	538d	1
		עם	WITH	768c	4 a
		רוח	BREATH	925c	6
		שיח	MUSE	967b	1
77	8	זנח	REJECT	276b	
		יסף	DO AGAIN	415c	2 a
		עולם	LONG DURATION	763a	21
		רצה	BE PLEASED WITH	953a	1 a
77	9	אמר	WORD	57a	2
		אפס	CEASE	67a	
		גמר	COME TO AN END	170a	1
		דור	PERIOD	189d	1 b
		חסד	GOODNESS	339b	22
		נצח	EVERLASTINGNESS	664b	4
77	10	אל	GOD	42d	6 e
		אם	IF	50d	2 ab a
		הוא	HE, SHE, IT	216d	6 a
		חנן	SHOW FAVOR	336a	2 b
		סלה	LIFT UP	700a	
		רחמים	COMPASSION	933c	1
		שכח	FORGET	1013b	2 d
77	11	חלה	BE WEAK	317d	1
		חלל	BORE	319b	
		ימין	RIGHT HAND	411d	1 c
		עליון	HIGHEST	751b	1
		שנה	CHANGE	1039d	
77	12	יה	YAH	219c	
		זכר	REMEMBER	269d	11 d
		זכר	REMEMBER	271a	3 b
		כי	THAT	472d	1 e
		מעלל	DEED	760b	2
		פלא	WONDER	810c	2
		קדם	FRONT	869d	2 c
77	13	הגה	MUSE	211d	3 a
		עלילה	WANTONNESS	760b	2 b
		פעל	DOING	821c	1 a
		שיח	MUSE	967b	2
77	14	אל	GOD	42d	6 d
		אלהים	GOD	44b	4 a
		גדול	GREAT	153b	6 c
		דרך	WAY	204a	6 eb
		קדש	APARTNESS	871c	1 a
77	15	אל	GOD	42c	6 a
		ידע	MAKE KNOWN	395a	
		עז	STRENGTH	739b	3 c
		פלא	WONDER	810c	2
77	16	בן	SON	120d	1 ja
		בן	SON	120d	1 jb
		גאל	REDEEM	145c	3 b
		זרוע	ARM	284a	1 c
		יוסף	JOSEPH	415d	1 c
		סלה	LIFT UP	700a	
77	17	חול	WHIRL	297a	2 b
		רגז	BE AGITATED	919a	
		תהום	SEA	1063a	2
77	18	הלך	WALK	*235c	1
		הלך	WALK	235d	1 a
		זרם	POUR FORTH IN FLOODS	281b	
		חץ	ARROW	346c	2
		נתן	GIVE	679d	1 x
		קול	VOICE	877a	2 b
		שחק	DUST	1007a	1
77	19	אור	BECOME LIGHT	21b	2
		ארץ	EARTH	76a	1 b
		ברק	LIGHTNING	140c	1
		תבל	WORLD	385d	2
		קול	VOICE	877a	2 b
		רגז	BE AGITATED	919a	
		רעם	THUNDER	947b	
		רעש	SHAKE	950b	
77	20	דרך	WAY	203a	1
		ידע	BE MADE KNOWN	394c	1
		עקב	HEEL	784b	B
		שביל	WAY	987c	
77	21	אהרן	AARON	14d	
		משה	MOSES	602c	
		נחה	LEAD	634d	
		צאן	SMALL CATTLE	838b	2
78	1	אזן	HEAR	24c	1
		אמר	WORD	57a	1
		תורה	INSTRUCTION	435d	1 a
		נטה	INCLINE	641a	3 e
78	2	חידה	RIDDLE	295c	1
		מן	OUT OF	579d	2 d
		משל	PARABLE	605b	5
		נבע	BUBBLE UP	616a	3
		פתח	OPEN	835b	
		קדם	FRONT	869d	2 c
		ספר	COUNT	*708a	1
78	3	ספר	COUNT	*708a	1
78	4	אחרון	BEHIND	30d	B
		דור	GENERATION	190a	2 c
		תהלה	PRAISE	240b	4
		כחד	HIDE	470b	
		ספר	COUNT	*708a	1
		עזוז	STRENGTH	739b	5
		ידע	MAKE KNOWN	395a	
78	5	תורה	LAW	436a	2 b1
		עדות	TESTIMONY	730b	2
		קום	STAND	878d	2 c
		שום	TO PLACE	963d	3 b
78	6	אחרון	BEHIND	30d	B
		דור	GENERATION	190a	2 c
		ילד	BE BORN	408d	
78	7	אל	GOD	42d	6 e
		כסל	CONFIDENCE	492d	3
		נצר	GUARD	665d	3
		מעלל	DEED	760b	2
		שום	TO PLACE	963a	1 a
		שכח	FORGET	1013b	1 c
78	8	אל	GOD	42d	6 e
		אמן	CONFIRM	53a	5
		את	WITH	86b	1 dg
		דור	GENERATION	190a	3
		כון	ESTABLISH	466c	3
		לב	HEART	525a	24
		מרה	BE REBELLIOUS	598a	2
		סרר	BE STUBBORN	710d	
		רוח	BREATH	925d	8
78	9	אפרים	EPHRAIM	68c	4
		הפך	TURN	245d	2 a
		נשק	BE EQUIPPED WITH	676c	
		קרב	BATTLE	898b	
		קשת	BOW	906c	1 d
		רמה	SHOOT	941a	
78	10	ברית	COVENANT	136c	2 2c
		ברית	COVENANT	137a	3 2
		תורה	LAW	436a	2 b1
		מאן	REFUSE	549b	
78	11	עלילה	WANTONNESS	760b	2 b
		פלא	BE SURPASSING	810d	4
		שכח	FORGET	1013b	1 c
78	12	ארץ	EARTH	76a	2 a
		נגד	IN FRONT	*617b	1 aa
		פלא	WONDER	810c	2
		צען	ZOAN	858b	
78	13	שדה	FIELD	961d	2 c
		בקע	CLEAVE	131d	1
		כמו	LIKE	*455d	1 a
		נד	HEAP	622d	
		נצב	STAND	662c	3
		עבר	PASS OVER	718d	2 a
78	14	אש	FIRE	77d	6
		לילה	NIGHT	539a	1
		נחה	LEAD	635a	
		ענן	CLOUD	778a	1 a
78	15	בקע	CLEAVE	132b	
		גזל	FLOW	633d	1
		צור	ROCK	849c	1 a
		רב	MUCH	913b	1 g
		שקה	GIVE TO DRINK	1052c	1
		תהום	SEA	1063a	2
78	16	יצא	BRING OUT	425a	4 i
		ירד	BRING DOWN	434a	1 b
		גזל	FLOW	633d	1
		סלע	CRAG	*701a	1
78	17	חטא	MISS A GOAL OR WAY	307a	2 b
		יוסף	DO AGAIN	415c	2 a

Ch	v.	Heb	Eng	Page	Sec
		מרה	BE REBELLIOUS	598b	
		עליון	HIGHEST	751b	1
		ציה	DRYNESS	851b	
78	18	אכל	FOOD	38a	
		אל	GOD	42d	6 e
		ל	TO	517c	7 bb
		לבב	HEART	523b	2 1
		נסה	TEST	650b	3 b
		נפש	SOUL	660d	6 a
78	19	אל	GOD	42d	6 e
		דבר	SPEAK	181c	4 d
		ערך	ARRANGE	789c	1 c
		שלחן	TABLE	1020b	1
78	20	אם	IF	50d	2 ab a
		גם	ALSO	169b	2
		הן	BEHOLD	243c	A
		זוב	FLOW	264c	1
		יכל	BE ABLE	407c	1 b
		כון	ESTABLISH	466b	2 a
		לחם	FOOD	537a	1 a
		נחל	TORRENT	636b	1
		נכה	SMITE	645b	1 a
		צור	ROCK	849c	1 a
		שאר	FLESH	985a	1 a
		שטף	OVERFLOW	1009b	2
78	21	עבר	BE ARROGANT	720d	2 a
		שלק	KINDLE	969c	
78	22	אמן	CONFIRM	53b	2 c
		בטה	TRUST	105a	1 3 d
		ישועה	DELIVERANCE	447b	3
78	23	דלת	DOOR	195b	4
		מעל	ABOVE	751c	1 a
		פתח	OPEN	835a	1
		צוה	CHARGE	846a	5
		שחק	DUST	1007a	2
		שמי	HEAVENS	1030a	1 b
78	24	דגן	CORN	186c	
		מטר	RAIN	565a	
		מן	MANNA	577c	
		שמי	HEAVENS	1030a	1 b
78	25	אביר	MIGHTY	7d	2
		ל	TO	516c	5 jb
		צידה	PROVISION	845b	
		שבע	ABUNDANCE	960a	1
78	26	תימן	SOUTH	412d	2
		נהג	DRIVE	624c	2
		נסע	SET OUT	652c	1
		עז	STRENGTH	739d	3 c
		קדים	EAST WIND	870b	1
78	27	חול	SAND	297d	C
		חול	SAND	297d	A
		כנף	WING	489c	1 a
		מטר	RAIN	565a	
		עוף	FLY	733d	1
		עפר	DRY EARTH	780a	2 a
		שאר	FLESH	985a	1 a
78	28	נפל	FALL	658a	1 g
		סביב	ROUND ABOUT	687a	1 cb
78	29	תאוה	DESIRE	16c	2
		בוא	COME	99c	2 b
78	30	תאוה	DESIRE	16c	1
		אכל	FOOD	38a	
		זור	BE A STRANGER	266c	1
		עוד	STILL	729a	1 aa
78	31	ב	IN	88c	1 2b
		בחר	CHOOSE	104b	7
		הרג	KILL	247b	2
		הרג	KILL	247c	1
		כרע	CAUSE TO BOW DOWN	502d	2
		משמן	FATNESS	1032d	
78	32	אמן	CONFIRM	53b	2 c
		ב	IN	90c	3 7
		זה	THIS	262a	6 bg
		חטא	MISS A GOAL OR WAY	306d	2 b
78	33	ב	IN	89a	1 7d
		בהלה	DISMAY	96d	
		הבל	VAPOUR	210d	2
		כלה	FINISH	478c	2 a
78	34	אל	GOD	42d	6 e
		אם	IF	50c	1 b4 a
		דרש	SEEK	205b	1 a
		הרג	KILL	247b	2
		שחר	LOOK EARLY	1007c	
78	35	גאל	REDEEM	145c	3 b
		זכר	REMEMBER	269d	1 1 d
		כי	THAT	471d	1 a
		עליון	HIGHEST	751b	1
		צור	ROCK	849d	2 a
78	36	כזב	LIE	469c	1
		לשון	TONGUE	546b	1 b
		פתה	BE SIMPLE	834d	2
78	37	אמן	CONFIRM	53a	5
		את	WITH	86b	1 dg
		ברית	COVENANT	136c	2 2c
		כון	BE FIRM	465d	2
		לב	HEART	525a	2 4
		עם	WITH	767d	1 d
78	38	המה	RAGE	404d	2 c
		כפר	COVER OVER	497c	2 b
		עון	INIQUITY	731a	1 c3
		עור	ROUSE ONESELF	735b	1
		רבה	BECOME MANY	915c	1 d1
		רחום	COMPASSIONATE	933d	1
		שוב	TURN BACK	999d	6 a

Ch	v.	Heb	Eng	Page	Sec
78	39	בשר	FLESH	142d	5
		הלך	WALK	232b	13
		זכר	REMEMBER	270b	21
		רוח	BREATH	925a	2 e
		רוח	BREATH	925c	4 d
		שוב	TURN BACK	998b	7 a
78	40	ישימון	WASTE	445c	B
		מה	HOW	554a	4 ca
		מרה	BE REBELLIOUS	598b	
		עצב	HURT	780d	
78	41	אל	GOD	42d	6 e
		נסה	TEST	650b	3 b
		קדוש	HOLY	872c	1 c
		שוב	TURN BACK	997d	6 a
		תוה	PAIN	1063c	
78	42	זכר	REMEMBER	269d	1 1 d
		יד	HAND	390b	2
		פדה	RANSOM	804a	3 a
		צר	ADVERSARY	865d	
78	43	אות	SIGN	16d	4
		מופת	WONDER	69a	1
		נתן	GIVE	*681b	3 d
		צען	ZOAN	858b	
		שדה	FIELD	961d	2 c
		שום	TO PLACE	964d	5 c
78	44	דם	BLOOD	197c	2 o
		הפך	TURN	245c	1 c4
		יאר	STREAM	384c	2 a
		נזל	FLOW	633d	1
78	45	אכל	EAT	37c	2
		ערב	SWARM	786c	
		צפרדע	FROGS	862c	
		חסיל	LOCUST	340c	
		יבול	PRODUCE	385b	
78	46	יגיע	TOIL	388c	2
		ארבה	LOCUST	916a	
78	47	גפן	VINE	172c	
		הרג	KILL	247b	4
		חנמל	FROST	335d	
		שקמה	SYCOMORE TREE	1054b	
78	48	בעיר	BEASTS	129c	
		סגר	DELIVER UP	689c	1
		מקנה	CATTLE	889b	1
		רשף	FLAME	958b	1
78	49	זעם	INDIGNATION	276d	
		חרון	BURNING OF AN-GER	354c	
		מלאך	MESSENGER	521c	1 e
		עברה	OVERFLOW	720c	3 b
		רע	EVIL	948a	1
		משלחת	DEPUTATION	1020a	2
78	50	דבר	PESTILENCE	184a	2
		חיה	LIVING THING	312d	2
		חשב	WITHHOLD	362b	1 b
		נתיב	PATH	677b	
		סגר	DELIVER UP	689c	1
78	51	פלס	WEIGH	814a	1
		און	VIGOUR	20b	1
		בכור	FIRST-BORN	114b	1 d
		חם	HAM	326a	2
		נכה	SMITE	646a	2 c
		ראשית	BEGINNING	912b	1 a
78	52	נהג	DRIVE	624b	2
		נסע	SET OUT	652c	1
		עדר	FLOCK	727d	1 a
		צאן	SMALL CATTLE	838b	2
78	53	בטח	SECURITY	105b	
		כסה	COVER	491d	5
		נחה	LEAD	635a	
		פחד	DREAD	808b	1
78	54	גבול	BOUNDARY	148a	2 e
		זה	THIS	261d	5
		ימין	RIGHT HAND	411d	1 c
		קדש	APARTNESS	871c	2 e
		קנה	ACQUIRE	889a	1 b
78	55	ב	IN	89a	17c
		גרש	DRIVE OUT	177a	
		חבל	CORD	286d	2
		נפל	FALL	658b	3
		שכן	SETTLE DOWN	1015c	2
78	56	מרה	BE REBELLIOUS	598b	
		נסה	TEST	650b	3 b
		עדה	TESTIMONIES	730a	
		עליון	HIGHEST	751b	1
78	57	בגד	ACT TREACHER-OUSLY	93d	A
		הפך	TURN	245d	1 a
		סוג	MOVE AWAY	690d	1 b2
		קשת	BOW	906a	1 b
		רמיה	DECEIT	941b	
78	58	במה	HIGH PLACE	119c	3
		כעס	VEX	495a	2
		קנא	BE ZEALOUS	888d	
78	59	מאס	REJECT	549c	1 b
		עבר	BE ARROGANT	720d	2 a
		שמע	HEAR	1034b	2 1
78	60	אהל	TENT	14b	3
		נטש	FORSAKE	643d	2
		שכן	SETTLE DOWN	1015b	1
		משכן	DWELLING-PLACE	1015d	2 b
		שלו	SHILOH	1017d	
78	61	עז	STRENGTH	739b	3 d
		תפארה	BEAUTY	802d	2 c
		שבי	CAPTIVITY	985d	1
78	62	נחלה	PROPERTY	635b	1 e
		סגר	DELIVER UP	689c	1

Ch	v.	Heb	Eng	Page	Sec
		עבר	BE ARROGANT	720d	2 a
78	63	בחור	YOUNG MAN	104c	
		בתולה	VIRGIN	144a	
		הלל	PRAISE	238d	1
78	64	אלמנה	WIDOW	48b	
		בכה	WEEP	113b	1
		כהן	PRIEST	463d	4
78	65	אדון	LORD	11c	3 2b
		גבור	STRONG	150b	2
		יין	WINE	406d	E
		יקץ	AWAKE	429c	
		ישן	SLEEPING	445d	
		מן	OUT OF	580a	2 eb
		רן	OVERCOME	929c	
		רנן	GIVE A RINGING CRY	943c	
78	66	חרפה	REPROACH	358a	3
		עולם	LONG DURATION	762b	2 b4
		צר	ADVERSARY	865d	
78	67	אהל	TENT	14b	3
		אפרים	EPHRAIM	68b	2
		בחר	CHOOSE	103d	1 a
		יוסף	JOSEPH	415d	1 c
		מאס	REJECT	549c	1 b
78	68	אהב	LOVE	13b	5 b
		בחר	CHOOSE	104a	5 a
		הר	MOUNTAIN	249c	1 a
		יהודה	JUDAH	397b	12
		ציון	ZION	851c	
78	69	בנה	BUILD	124b	1 ab
		יסד	FOUND	413d	
		כמו	LIKE	455d	1 a
		עולם	LONG DURATION	762b	2 b1
		רום	BE HIGH	926d	1
78	70	בחר	CHOOSE	104a	1
		דוד	DAVID	188a	
		מכלה	FOLD	476c	
78	71	אחר	BEHIND	29d	2 a
		בוא	COME	99c	2 d
		נחלה	PROPERTY	635b	1 e
		עול	GIVE SUCK	732b	
		רעה	TEND	945a	1 c
78	72	תבונה	UNDERSTANDING	108b	1
		כף	HOLLOW OF THE HAND	496d	1 d7
		לבב	HEART	523d	2 6a
		נחה	LEAD	635a	
		רעה	TEND	945a	1 c
		רעה	TEND	945c	
		תם	INTEGRITY	1070d	3
79	1	היכל	TEMPLE	228c	2 d
		מזמור	MELODY	274c	
		טמא	BE UNCLEAN	379c	2
		נחלה	PROPERTY	635b	1 e
		עי	RUIN	730d	
		קדש	APARTNESS	871d	2 d
79	2	מאכל	FOOD	38b	
		בשר	FLESH	142c	1 b
		חיה	LIVING THING	312c	1 b
		חסיד	KIND	339d	2 b
		נבלה	CARCASS	615c	1 a
		עבד	SLAVE	714a	1
79	3	דם	BLOOD	196c	2 b
		פך	POUR OUT	1049c	1 b
79	4	חרפה	REPROACH	358a	3
		לעג	MOCKING	541d	1 b
		סביב	ROUND ABOUT	687b	2 ba b
		קלס	DERISION	887b	
		רשף	FLAME	958b	1
		שכן	NEIGHBOUR	1015c	2
79	5	אנף	BE ANGRY	60a	
		אש	FIRE	77d	5
		בער	BURN	129a	4
		כמו	LIKE	455d	1 a
		מה	HOW	554a	4 e
		נצח	EVERLASTINGNESS	664b	1
		קנאה	ZEAL	888c	3 b
79	6	אל	TO	41a	B
		ידע	KNOW	394a	2
		חמה	RAGE	404d	2 c
		חמה	RAGE	*405a	2 c
		ממלכה	KINGDOM	575a	1
		קרא	CALL	845b	2 c
		פך	POUR OUT	1049d	2 a
79	7	נוה	HABITATION	627c	1
		שמם	BE DESOLATED	1031b	1
79	8	דלל	BE LOW	195c	
		זכר	REMEMBER	270b	24
		מהר	HASTEN	555a	2
		מהר	QUICKLY	*555b	
		עון	INIQUITY	731b	1 c5
		קדם	COME IN FRONT	870a	1 b
		ראשון	FIRST	911c	1 a
		רחמים	COMPASSION	933c	1
79	9	אלהים	GOD	44c	4 bb
		דבר	WORD	184a	4 8
		חטאת	SIN	309a	1 d3
		ישע	DELIVERANCE	447a	2
		כבוד	HONOR	459b	6 b
		כפר	COVER OVER	497c	2 b
		נצל	DELIVER	665a	4
		מען	PURPOSE	775b	1 a
79	10	איה	WHERE	32c	
		דם	BLOOD	196c	2 b
		דם	BLOOD	*196d	2 f
		ידע	BE MADE KNOWN	394c	1

Ch v.	Heb	Eng	Page	Sec
	מה	HOW	554b	4 d
79 11	נקמה	VENGEANCE	668c	1
	עבד	SLAVE	714a	3
	שפך	POUR OUT	*1049c	1 b
	אנקה	CRYING	60c	
	אסיר	PRISONER	64a	
	בן	SON	121d	8 e
	גדל	GREATNESS	152d	1
	זרוע	ARM	284a	1 c
	יתר	SAVE OVER	451c	1 c
	תמותה	DEATH	560d	
	גדל	ADDENDA ET CORRIGENDA	1121d	
79 12	שבעתים	SEVEN FOLD		1
	חיק	BOSOM	300d	1
	חרף	REPROACH	357d	1
	חרפה	REPROACH	357d	1
	חרפה	REPROACH	358a	1
	על	UPON	757c	2 7c ab
	שכן	NEIGHBOUR	1015c	1
79 13	דור	PERIOD	189d	1 b
	תהלה	PRAISE	240b	4
	ידה	PRAISE	392c	1 b
	ספר	COUNT	*708a	1
	עולם	LONG DURATION	762a	2 a
	צאן	SMALL CATTLE	838c	3
	מרעית	PASTURING	945c	1
80 1	אל	TO	40c	7
	מזמור	MELODY	274c	
	עדות	TESTIMONY	730b	2
	שושן	LILY	1004c	
80 2	אזן	EAR	24b	2 b
	אזן	LISTENING	24c	2
	יוסף	JOSEPH	415d	1 d
	ישע	SHINE OUT	422a	1
	כרוב	CHERUB	500d	3
	נהג	DRIVE	624b	1
	צאן	SMALL CATTLE	838b	2
	רעה	TEND	945a	1 d3
80 3	בנימין	BENJAMIN	122d	1
	גבורה	MIGHT	150c	3
	הלך	WALK	230b	1 1c
	ישועה	DELIVERANCE	447b	3
	מנשה	MANASSEH	586c	1 b1 b
	עור	ROUSE ONESELF	735a	
80 4	אור	BECOME LIGHT	21c	5
	ישע	BE DELIVERED	446b	1
	שוב	TURN BACK	999b	1 d
80 5	מתי	WHEN	607d	C
	עשן	SMOKE	798c	2
	תפלה	PRAYER	813c	1 a
80 6	אכל	EAT	37c	1
	אכל	EAT	37d	1
	בכי	WEEPING	*113d	
	דמעה	TEARS	199d	
	דמעה	TEARS	199d	
	לחם	FOOD	537c	3 b
	שליש	THIRD	1026c	
	שקה	GIVE TO DRINK	1052c	2
80 7	מדון	STRIFE	193b	2
	ל	TO	516a	5 ic
	לעג	MOCK	541c	
	שכן	NEIGHBOUR	1015c	2
80 8	אור	BECOME LIGHT	21c	5
	ישע	BE DELIVERED	446b	1
	צבא	GOD OF WAR	839c	4 c
	שוב	TURN BACK	999b	1 d
80 9	גפן	VINE	172c	
	גרש	DRIVE OUT	177a	
	נטע	PLANT	642b	1
	נסע	SET OUT	652c	1
80 10	פנה	TURN	815c	
	שרש	ROOT	1057d	2
	שרש	ROOT UP	1057d	2
80 11	אל	GOD	42c	5
	ארז	CEDAR	72c	1 b
	כסה	BE COVERED	492b	1
	ענף	BRANCH	778c	
	צל	SHADOW	853b	2
80 12	יונקת	TWIG	413c	
	קציר	BRANCHES	894d	
	שלח	SEND	1019b	4
	שלח	SPROUT	*1019c	2
80 13	ארה	PLUCK	71c	
	גדר	WALL	155a	
	עבר	PASS OVER	*717d	4 a
	פרץ	BREAK THROUGH	829b	2
80 14	זיז	MOVING THINGS	265b	
	חזיר	SWINE	306c	2
	יער	WOOD	420d	B
	כרסם	TEAR OFF	493c	
	מן	OUT OF	579c	2 cc
	רעה	TEND	945b	2 c
	שדי	FIELD	961b	2
80 15	גפן	VINE	172c	
	זה	THIS	261a	2 ba
	פקד	ATTEND TO	823b	A 1a
	צבא	GOD OF WAR	839c	4 c
	שוב	TURN BACK	998a	6 g
80 16	אמץ	BE STRONG	55b	2
	בן	SON	120b	1 c
	בן	SON	121b	5
	כנה	ROOT	488a	
	נטע	PLANT	642b	1
80 17	אבד	PERISH	1c	1
	גערה	REBUKE	172a	2

Ch v.	Heb	Eng	Page	Sec
	כסח	CUT OFF	492d	
	פנה	FACE	816a	1 1e
	שרף	BURN	976d	2a
80 18	אמץ	BE STRONG	55b	2
	היה	BECOME	225d	2 1b
80 19	חיה	LIVE	311c	3 d
	שוב	TURN BACK	999b	1 d
80 20	אור	BECOME LIGHT	21c	5
	ישע	BE DELIVERED	446b	1
81 1	גתית	GITTITH	388a	2
	על	UPON	754b	2 1fa
81 2	אלהים	GOD	44c	4 ba
	עז	STRENGTH	739a	2 c
	רוע	RAISE A SHOUT	929d	5
	רנן	GIVE A RINGING CRY	943c	
81 3	זמרה	MELODY	274b	3
	כנור	LYRE	490b	
	נעים	SWEETLY SOUNDING	564b	
	נבל	HARP	614c	
	נעים	DELIGHTFUL	653d	2
	עם	WITH	767b	1 a
	תף	TIMBREL	1074c	
81 4	חג	FESTIVAL-GATHERING	291a	1 b2
	חדש	NEW MOON	294c	1
	יום	DAY	398d	2 i
	כסא	FULL MOON	490c	
	ל	TO	516d	6 a
	שפר	HORN	1051d	
	תקע	GIVE A BLOW	1075c	2
81 5	אלהים	GOD	44c	4 ba
	חק	SOMETHING PRESCRIBED	349c	6 a
	משפט	JUDGMENT	1048d	3
81 6	חק	SOMETHING PRESCRIBED	349c	6 a
	יוסף	JOSEPH	415d	1 d
	עדות	TESTIMONY	730b	2
	על	UPON	752d	2 1
	שום	TO PLACE	963d	3 b
	שפה	SPEECH	974a	2
81 7	דוד	POT	188c	B
	סבל	BURDEN	687d	
	סבלה	BURDEN	*688a	
	סור	TURN ASIDE	694b	1
	עבר	PASS OVER	718b	6 e
	שכם	SHOULDER	1014b	1 a
81 8	ב	IN	88d	1 6
	בחן	TRY	103c	2 b
	חלץ	DRAW OFF OR OUT	322d	2
	מי	WATER	565b	1 a
	סלה	LIFT UP	700a	
	סלה	LIFT UP	700b	
	סתר	COVERING	712a	1
	צרה	DISTRESS	865b	
	מריבה	MERIBAH	937b	2
	רעם	THUNDER	947b	
81 9	אם	IF	50b	1 b3
	עוד	BEAR WITNESS	730a	3
81 10	אל	GOD	42c	3
	זור	BE A STRANGER	266c	2 c
	נכר	FOREIGNNESS	648c	1
81 11	יהוה	YAHWEH	218d	2 1a
	יהוה	YAHWEH	219b	2 d
	רחב	BE LARGE	931d	2
81 12	אבה	BE WILLING	2c	
81 13	מועצה	PLAN	420b	
	לב	HEART	525c	2 6d
	שלח	SEND	1019a	2 b
	שרירות	STUBBORNNESS	1057b	
81 14	דרך	WAY	204a	6 ec
	הלך	WALK	235c	4
	חטה	WHEAT	*334d	
81 15	לו	IF	530b	1 c
	כנע	HUMBLE	488c	2
	לו	IF	530b	1 c
81 16	מעט	A FEW	590b	2 b
	שוב	TURN BACK	999a	1 a
	כחש	DECEIVE	471b	3
	לו	IF	530b	1 c
	עולם	LONG DURATION	762b	2 b2
	שן	HATE	971d	2
81 17	אכל	EAT	38a	1
	דבש	HONEY	185b	
	חלב	FAT	317a	3
	חטה	WHEAT	334d	
	לו	IF	530b	1 c
	מן	OUT OF	579b	2 bb
	צור	ROCK	849c	1 a
	שבע	SATISFIED	959d	1 b
82 1	אל	GOD	42d	6 e
	אלהים	GOD	43b	1 a
	מזמור	MELODY	274c	
	עדה	CONGREGATION	417a	1
	נצב	STAND	662a	1 a
	קרב	INWARD PART	899b	1 f6
	שפט	JUDGE	1047c	2
82 2	מתי	WHEN	607d	C
	נשא	LIFT	670c	1 b 3
	סלה	LIFT UP	700a	
	עול	INJUSTICE	732c	
	שפט	JUDGE	1047d	3 a
82 3	דל	WEAK	195d	
	עני	POOR	776d	3

Ch v.	Heb	Eng	Page	Sec
	צדק	DECLARE RIGHTEOUS	842d	2
	צדק	DECLARE RIGHTEOUS	842d	1
	רוש	BE IN WANT	930d	
82 4	שפט	JUDGE	1047d	3 b2
	אביון	NEEDY	2d	
	דל	POOR	195d	
	פלט	ESCAPE	812b	1
82 5	ארץ	EARTH	76a	1 b
	בן	DISCERN	106d	2 a
	הלך	WALK	236b	2
	חשכה	DARKNESS	365b	
	מוסד	FOUNDATION	414c	
	מוט	SHAKE	557a	
82 6	אכן	SURELY	38c	B
	אלהים	GOD	43b	1 a
	אנכי	I	59c	
	בן	SON	120b	1 c
	עליון	HIGHEST	751b	2
82 7	אדם	MAN	9b	2
	אכן	SURELY	38c	B
	שר	CHIEFTAIN	978d	7
82 8	נחל	TAKE AS A POSSESSION	635c	1 c
	שפט	JUDGE	1047d	3 d
83 1	מזמור	MELODY	274c	
83 2	אל	NOT	39b	A ba
	אל	GOD	42d	6 e
	דמי	QUIET	198c	1
	חרש	BE SILENT	361a	1
	שקט	BE QUIET	1053a	2
83 3	המה	ROAR	242b	3
	נשא	LIFT	670b	1 b 2
	שן	HATE	971d	2
83 4	יעץ	CONSPIRE	420a	
	סוד	COUNSEL	691c	2 a
	ערם	BE SHREWD	791a	
	צפן	HIDE	860d	1
83 5	גוי	NATION	156c	1 b
	זכר	REMEMBER	270d	2
	כחד	HIDE	470c	2
	מן	FROM	583b	7 bb
83 6	ברית	COVENANT	136b	1
	יחדו	TOGETHER	403b	A
	יעץ	CONSULT	420a	
	כרת	CUT	504a	4
83 7	אהל	TENT	14a	1
	הגרי	HAGRITE	212c	1
	ישמעאלי	ISHMAELITE	1035d	
83 8	גבל	GEBAL	148c	
	עמלק	AMALEK	766a	
	עם	WITH	767b	1 a
	עמון	AMMON	*769d	
	פלשת	PHILISTIA	814b	
	צר	TYER	862d	
83 9	בן	SON	120d	1 ja
	זרוע	ARM	284b	2 a
	לוה	BE JOINED	531a	
	לוט	LOT	532b	1
	סלה	LIFT UP	700a	
83 10	יבין	JABIN	108a	2
	מדין	MIDIAN	193c	2
	כ	LIKE	455a	B
	נחל	TORRENT	636a	1
	סיסרא	SISERA	696b	1
	קישון	KISHON	885c	
83 11	אדמה	GROUND	9c	1
	דמן	DUNG	199b	
	עין־דר	EN-DOR	745c	
	שמד	BE EXTERMINATED	1029b	1
83 12	זאב	ZEEB	256a	
	זבח	ZEBAH	258a	
	כ	LIKE	453d	1 b
	נדיב	NOBLE	622a	2
	נסיך	PRINCE	651c	
	צלמנע	ZALMUNNA	854a	
	שית	PUT	1011c	3
	ערב	ADDENDA ET CORRIGENDA	1126a	
83 13	ירש	TAKE POSSESSION	439c	1 a
	ל	TO	515d	5 ia
	נוה	PASTURE	627d	1
	פנה	FACE	818d	2 7a a
83 14	קש	STUBBLE	905b	
	שית	PUT	1011c	3
83 15	בער	BURN	129a	3
	ה	THE	208a	1 f
	הר	MOUNTAIN	250c	1 j
	יער	WOOD	420d	C
	כ	LIKE	454a	1 c2
	כ	LIKE	454d	2 d
	להבה	FLAME	529b	
	להט	SET ABLAZE	529d	
83 16	בהל	DISMAY	96c	1
	כן	SO	486b	2 ad g
	סופה	STORM-WIND	693a	
	סער	TEMPEST	704b	
	רדף	PURSUE	922d	1 e
83 17	בקש	SEEK	135a	3 c
	פנה	FACE	815d	1 1a
	קלון	DISHONOUR	886a	1
	שם	NAME	1028b	1
83 18	אבד	PERISH	1c	1
	בהל	BE DISTURBED	96b	1
	חפר	BE ABASHED	344a	

Ch	v	Heb	Eng	Page	Sec
		עד	PERPETUITY	723c	2 c
83	19	עליון	HIGHEST	751b	1
84	1	מזמור	MELODY	274c	
		גתית	GITTITH	388a	2 lf a
		על	UPON	754b	2 lf a
		קרח	KORAH	901b	2
84	2	ידיד	LOVELY	391d	2
		משכן	DWELLING-PLACE	1016a	3 b
84	3	אל	GOD	42d	6 d
		בשר	FLESH	142c	2
		חי	ALIVE	311d	1 a
		חצר	ENCLOSURE	347a	3 b
		כלה	BE FINISHED	477d	2 b
		ל	TO	*510b	1 a
		לב	HEART	524c	2 1
		רנן	GIVE A RINGING CRY	943c	
84	4	אשר	PARTICLE OF RELATION	82c	4 bb
		בית	HOUSE	109b	1 b
		גם	YEA	169c	3
		דרור	SWALLOW	204d	
		כסף	LONG	494a	
		מלך	KING	573b	3
		מצא	FIND	592c	1 a
		אפרח	YOUNG ONE	827b	
		צפור	BIRD	862a	1
		קן	NEST	890a	1
		שית	PUT	1011b	1
84	5	אשר	HAPPINESS	81a	
		הלל	PRAISE	238b	2 b
		סלה	LIFT UP	700a	
		עוד	STILL	729a	1 ab
84	6	אשר	HAPPINESS	81a	
		לבב	HEART	523c	2 2
		מסלה	HIGHWAY	700c	
		עז	STRENGTH	739a	2 b
		עז	STRENGTH	739a	2 c
		מעלה	STEP	752b	5
84	7	בכא	BALSAM-TREE	113a	
		ברכה	BLESSING	139d	3
		גם	YEA	169c	3
		מורה	RAIN	435c	
		עבר	PASS OVER	717c	3 b
		עטה	WRAP ONESELF	742a	
		מעין	SPRING	746a	
		מקום	STANDING PLACE	880a	3 d
		שית	PUT	1011c	3
84	8	הלך	WALK	234c	2 2
		חיל	STRENGTH	298c	1 a
		מן	FROM	582c	5 d1
		ראה	TO SEE	908b	1 b
84	9	אזן	LISTENING	24c	2
		אלהים	GOD	44c	4 ba
		סלה	LIFT UP	700a	
84	10	מגן	SHIELD	171c	
		משיח	ANOINTED	603c	2
		נבט	LOOK	613d	3
84	11	אהל	TENT	14a	2
		בחר	CHOOSE	104a	1 b
		דור	DWELL	189c	
		חצר	ENCLOSURE	347a	3 b
		טוב	PLEASANT	374c	6
		מן	THAN	582c	6 a
		ספף	STAND AT THE THRESHOLD	706c	
		רשע	WICKEDNESS	957d	3
84	12	מגן	SHIELD	171c	
		יהוה	YAHWEH	219a	2 1h
		הלך	WALK	235a	2 3e 1
		חן	FAVOR	336c	2 b1
		טוב	A GOOD THING	375a	1
		כבוד	HONOR	458d	2 b
		ל	TO	515b	5 hb g
		מנע	WITHHOLD	586a	
		שמש	SUN	1039c	5
		תמים	COMPLETE	1071b	5
84	13	אשר	HAPPINESS	81a	
		בטח	TRUST	105a	1 3a
85	1	מזמור	MELODY	274c	
		קרח	KORAH	901b	2
85	2	רצה	BE PLEASED WITH	953a	1 a
		שבית	CAPTIVITY	986b	2 a
85	3	חטאת	SIN	309a	1 d3
		כסה	COVER	492a	5
		סלה	LIFT UP	700b	
		עון	INIQUITY	731a	1 c2
85	4	אסף	GATHER	62c	4
		חרון	BURNING OF ANGER	354c	
		עברה	OVERFLOW	720c	3 b
		פרר	BREAK	830c	2 c
		שוב	TURN BACK	999d	0
85	5	אלהים	GOD	44c	4 bb
		ישע	DELIVERANCE	447a	2
		כעס	ANGER	495b	2
		עם	WITH	767d	1 d
		שוב	TURN BACK	998c	9
85	6	אנף	BE ANGRY	60a	
		דור	PERIOD	189d	1 b
		משך	DRAW	604c	5
		עולם	LONG DURATION	762d	2 g
85	7	חיה	LIVE	311c	3 d
		שוב	TURN BACK	998c	8
85	8	חסד	GOODNESS	339a	2 1a
		ישע	DELIVERANCE	447a	2
85	9	ראה	TO SEE	909a	1 b
		אל	GOD	42c	6 a
		חסיד	KIND	339d	2 b
		כסלה	CONFIDENCE	493a	
		מה	WHAT	*552d	1 b
		שוב	TURN BACK	997c	5 d
		שלום	PEACE	1023b	5 b
85	10	ירא	FEAR	431c	3 b
		ישע	DELIVERANCE	447a	2
		כבוד	GLORY	459a	2 c3
		קרב	NEAR	898c	2 f
		שכן	SETTLE DOWN	1015b	2 c
85	11	אמת	FIRMNESS	54b	3 b
		חסד	GOODNESS	339a	2 2
		נשק	KISS	676c	2
		פגש	MEET	803d	
		צדק	RIGHTEOUSNESS	841d	E
85	12	שלום	PEACE	1023b	5 b
		אמת	FIRMNESS	54b	3 b
		מן	OUT OF	579a	2 ab
		צדק	RIGHTEOUSNESS	841d	E
		צמח	SPROUT	855c	1
		שמי	HEAVENS	1030b	2 a
		שקף	LOOK DOWN	1054c	
85	13	טוב	A GOOD THING	375a	1
		יבול	PRODUCE	385b	
85	14	נתן	GIVE	679c	1 t
		דרך	WAY	204a	6 eb
		הלך	WALK	235b	1
		פעם	BEAT	822a	1 a
		צדק	RIGHTEOUSNESS	841d	E
		שום	TO PLACE	964c	5 a
86	1	אביון	NEEDY	2d	
		אזן	EAR	24b	2 b
		נטה	INCLINE	641a	3 e
		עני	POOR	776d	3
		תפלה	PRAYER	813c	2
86	2	בטח	TRUST	105b	1 5a
		חסיד	KIND	339d	2 b
		ישע	DELIVER	446d	1 b
86	3	חנן	SHOW FAVOR	336a	2 b
		יום	DAY	400c	7 f
86	4	נפש	SOUL	660d	6 a
		נפש	SOUL	660d	6 d
		נשא	LIFT	670d	1 b 9
		שמח	REJOICE	970c	
		סמח	REJOICE	970c	
86	5	חסד	GOODNESS	339b	2 3a
		טוב	PLEASANT	374d	9 b
		סלה	READY TO FORGIVE	669c	
		קרא	CALL	895d	5 c
86	6	אזן	LISTENING	24c	2
		תחנון	SUPPLICATION FOR FAVOR	337d	2
		תפלה	PRAYER	813c	1 e
86	7	קשב	ATTEND	904a	
		צרה	DISTRESS	865b	
86	8	אלהים	GOD	43c	1 d
86	9	כבד	MAKE HONORABLE	457d	2 c
		ל	TO	512a	3 b
86	10	גדול	GREAT	153b	6 c
86	11	אמת	FIRMNESS	54a	3 a
		דרך	WAY	204a	6 ec
		הלך	WALK	235c	4
		יחד	UNITE	402d	
		ירא	FEAR	431c	4
		ירה	DIRECT	435c	5 c
		לבב	HEART	523c	2 2
86	12	אדון	LORD	11c	3 2b
		ידה	PRAISE	392c	1 a2
		כבד	MAKE HONORABLE	457d	2 c
		לבב	HEART	523c	2 2
		עולם	LONG DURATION	762b	2
86	13	גדול	GREAT	153b	6 c
		חסד	GOODNESS	339a	2 1b
		נפש	SOUL	659c	1 d
		נצל	DELIVER	665a	3 b
		על	UPON	756c	2 7a b
		שאול	SHEOL	983a	2 a
		תחתי	LOWER	1066c	
86	14	בקש	SEEK	134d	2 a
		זד	INSOLENT	267d	
		עדה	CONGREGATION	417a	1
		נגד	IN FRONT	*617c	2 b
		נפש	SOUL	659d	3 c
		עריץ	AWE-INSPIRING	792a	
		שום	TO PLACE	963c	1 c
86	15	אל	GOD	42d	6 d
		אמת	FIRMNESS	54a	3 b
		ארך	LONG	74a	
		חנן	GRACIOUS	337a	
		חסד	GOODNESS	*339b	2 3a
		חסד	GOODNESS	339b	2 2
		רחום	COMPASSIONATE	933d	
86	16	אמה	MAID	51a	2
		בן	SON	120c	1 ib
		חנן	SHOW FAVOR	336a	2 b
		ישע	DELIVER	446d	1 b
		עבד	SLAVE	714a	3
		עז	STRENGTH	739a	2 b
		פנה	TURN	815c	2 c1
86	17	אות	SIGN	16d	1
		טובה	WELFARE	375d	3
		נחם	CONSOLE ONESELF	637a	
		עם	WITH	767d	1 d
87	1	עשה	DO	794a	1 la 3
		עם	WITH	*1107a	1 b
		מזמור	MELODY	274c	
		יסודה	FOUNDATION	414b	
		קדש	APARTNESS	871d	2 e
		קרח	KORAH	901b	2
87	2	אהב	LOVE	13b	5 b
		שער	GATE	1045a	2 b
87	3	אלהים	GOD	44a	3 b
		ב	IN	90d	4 e
		דבר	SPEAK	181d	
		כבד	BE HONORED	457c	1 b
		סלה	LIFT UP	700b	
		עיר	CITY	746c	1 g
87	4	בבל	BABEL	93c	
		זכר	REMEMBER	271a	3 b
		ילד	BE BORN	409a	
		כוש	CUSH	469a	2 c
		ל	TO	512c	4 a
		עם	WITH	767b	1 a
		פלשת	PHILISTIA	814b	
		צר	TYER	862d	
		רהב	STORM	923c	2
87	5	אמר	SAY	56c	
		הוא	HE, SHE, IT	215c	1 e
		ו	AND	253b	1 ib
		ילד	BE BORN	409a	
		כון	ESTABLISH	466d	1 b
		עליון	HIGHEST	751b	1
87	6	ילד	BE BORN	409a	
		כתב	WRITE	507d	3
		סלה	LIFT UP	700b	
		ספר	COUNT	707d	1
87	7	חול	WHIRL	297b	1
		הלל	PLAY THE PIPE	320a	
		מעין	SPRING	746a	
88	1	הימן	HEMAN	54d	
		מזמור	MELODY	274c	
		אזרחי	EZRAHITE	280d	
		מחלת	MAHALATH	318d	
		על	UPON	754b	2 lf a
		ענה	SING	777b	
		קרח	KORAH	901b	2
88	2	אלהים	GOD	44c	4 bb
		ישועה	DELIVERANCE	447b	3
		לילה	NIGHT	538d	1
		צעק	CRY	858c	1 b
		שוע	CRY OUT	1002d	
88	3	אזן	EAR	24b	2 b
		נטה	INCLINE	641a	3 e
		תפלה	PRAYER	813c	1 c
		רנה	RINGING CRY	943c	1
88	4	חיים	LIFE	313a	1
		נגע	REACH	619c	3
		רעה	MISERY	949a	1
		שבע	SATISFIED	959c	3 c
		שאול	SHEOL	982d	1
		שאול	SHEOL	*983d	3 b
88	5	אל	HELP	33d	
		אין	NOT	34d	4 a
		בור	PIT	92c	5
		חשב	THINK	363b	1
		עם	WITH	768a	1 f
88	6	גזר	CUT	160c	1
		זכר	REMEMBER	270b	2 1 a
		חפשי	FREE	344d	1
		יד	HAND	391b	5 g2
		כמו	LIKE	455d	1 a
		קבצר	GRAVE	868d	
		שאול	SHEOL	*983d	2 a
		שכב	LIE DOWN	1012c	4 c
		בור	PIT	92c	3
88	7	משך	DARK PLACE	365b	C
		מצולה	DEPTH	847a	
		שית	PUT	1011b	2 a
		תחתי	LOWER	1066c	
88	8	חמה	RAGE	404d	2 c
		סלה	LIFT UP	700b	
		סמך	LEAN	702a	1 b
		על	UPON	753b	2 1b
		ענה	BE BOWED DOWN	776b	3
		משבר	BREAKER	991c	
88	9	ידע	ACQUAINTANCE	394d	
		כלא	SHUT UP	476b	1
		רחק	BE DISTANT	935b	2
		שית	PUT	1011c	3
		תועבה	ABOMINATION	1072d	1 a
88	10	דאב	BECOME FAINT	178b	
		יום	DAY	400c	7 g
		עין	EYE	744b	1 i
		עני	AFFLICTION	777a	1
		שטח	SPREAD	1009a	
		ידה	PRAISE	392c	1 a2
88	11	נשיה	OBLIVION	*674d	
		פלא	WONDER	810c	2
		קום	STAND	877d	1 a
		רפאם	SHADES	952b	
88	12	אבדון	DESTRUCTION	2c	
		אמונה	FIRMNESS	53c	3 b
		חסד	GOODNESS	339b	2 2
		נשיה	OBLIVION	*674d	
		ספר	COUNT	708b	
		קבר	GRAVE	868d	
88	13	חשך	DARKNESS	365a	1
		ידע	BE MADE KNOWN	394c	1
		נשיה	OBLIVION	674d	

Ch v.	Heb	Eng	Page	Sec
	פלא	WONDER	810c	2
	צדקה	RIGHTEOUSNESS	842c	6 d
88 14	בקר	MORNING	134a	1 d
	תפלה	PRAYER	813c	1 c
	קדם	COME IN FRONT	870a	1 b
	שוע	CRY OUT	1002d	
88 15	זנח	REJECT	276b	
	סתר	HIDE	711d	2 c
88 16	אימה	TERROR	34a	
	אפונה	OVERCOME	67a	
	גוע	EXPIRE	157c	
	נער	YOUTH	655a	
	נשא	LIFT	671b	2 d
	עני	POOR	777a	3
	פוג	GROW NUMB	806a	
	פון	GROW NUMB	806d	
88 17	אימה	TERROR	34a	
	בעותים	TERRORS	130a	
	חרון	BURNING OF ANGER	354c	
	עבר	PASS OVER	717c	1 f
	צמת	EXTERMINATE	856c	
88 18	יום	DAY	400c	7 f
	יחד	UNION	403a	2 a2
	מי	WATER	565d	4 d
	נקף	GO AROUND	669a	1 b
	סבב	SURROUND	686a	2 d
88 19	אהב	LOVE	13a	4 b
	מחשך	DARK PLACE	365b	C
	ידע	ACQUAINTANCE	394d	
	רחק	BE DISTANT	935b	2
89 1	אזרחי	EZRAHITE	280d	
	איתן	ETHAN	451a	
89 2	אמונה	FIRMNESS	53c	3 b
	דור	PERIOD	189d	1 b
	חסד	GOODNESS	339c	4
	ידע	MAKE KNOWN	395a	
	עולם	LONG DURATION	762a	2 a
	עולם	LONG DURATION	762b	2 c
	שיר	SING	1010d	
89 3	אמונה	FIRMNESS	53c	3 b
	בנה	BUILD	125a	2 b
	חסד	GOODNESS	339b	2 2
	כון	ESTABLISH	466b	1 b
	שמי	HEAVENS	1030b	2 a
89 4	בחיר	CHOSEN	104c	
	ברית	COVENANT	136d	2 2f
	ברית	COVENANT	137a	3 1
	דוד	DAVID	188a	
	כרת	CUT	504a	4
	שבע	SWEAR	989c	2
89 5	בנה	BUILD	124d	2 a
	דור	PERIOD	189d	1 b
	זרע	SOWING	282d	4 c
	כון	ESTABLISH	466a	1 a
	כסא	THRONE	491a	3 a
	סלה	LIFT UP	700b	
	עולם	LONG DURATION	762c	2 f
89 6	אמונה	FIRMNESS	53c	3 b
	ידה	PRAISE	392c	1 a2
	פלא	WONDER	810c	2
	קדוש	HOLY	872d	2 c
	קהל	ASSEMBLY	874d	2 c
	קול	VOICE	877a	1 a
	שמי	HEAVENS	1030b	3
89 7	אל	GOD	42b	2
	בן	SON	120b	1 d
	דמה	BE LIKE	198a	
	מי	WHO	566d	F c
	ערך	ARRANGE	789d	2 b
	שחק	DUST	1007a	1
89 8	ירא	BE REVERED	431d	3 a
	סביב	ROUND ABOUT	687a	2 aa
	סוד	ASSEMBLY	691c	1 b
	על	UPON	755a	2 3
	ערץ	CAUSE TO TREMBLE	792a	
	קדוש	HOLY	872d	2 c
	רב	MUCH	913b	1 g
89 9	אמונה	FIRMNESS	53c	3 b
	יה	YAH	219c	
	חסן	STRONG	340d	
89 10	צבא	GOD OF WAR	839b	4 b
	גאות	MAJESTY	145a	1
	משל	RULE	605d	3
	נשא	LIFT	671a	1 b 1
	שבח	SOOTHE	986c	
89 11	דכא	CRUSH	194a	
	זרוע	ARM	284a	1 c
	חצב	HEW	*345b	
	עז	STRENGTH	739a	1
	פזר	SCATTER	808a	
	רהב	STORM	923c	1
89 12	תבל	WORLD	*385d	
	תבל	WORLD	385d	
	יסד	FOUND	413d	
	מלא	THAT WHICH FILLS	571b	3
	ברא	CREATE	135b	1
89 13	חרמון	HERMON	356d	
	ימין	RIGHT	412a	4
	רנן	GIVE A RINGING CRY	943c	
	תבור	TABOR	1061d	1
89 14	גבורה	MIGHT	150c	3
	זרוע	ARM	284a	1 c
	עזז	BE STRONG	738c	
	עם	WITH	767b	1 a
89 15	רום	BE HIGH	926d	2 b
	אמת	FIRMNESS	54b	3 b
	חסד	GOODNESS	339a	2 2
	מכון	FIXED PLACE	467d	1
	כסא	THRONE	491b	3 b
	צדק	RIGHTEOUSNESS	841d	E
	קדם	COME IN FRONT	870a	1 b
	משפט	JUDGMENT	1048d	2 a
89 16	אור	LIGHT	21d	0
	אשר	HAPPINESS	81a	
	הלך	WALK	235c	2
	תרועה	SHOUT OF WAR	930a	3
89 17	יום	DAY	400c	7 f
	צדקה	RIGHTEOUSNESS	842c	6 a
	רום	BE HIGH	927a	2 c
89 18	עז	STRENGTH	739a	2 c
	תפארה	BEAUTY	802d	2 c
	קרן	HORN	902a	2
	רום	BE HIGH	927a	2 b
	רום	BE HIGH	927c	1 f
	רצון	GOODWILL	953c	1 a
89 19	מגן	SHIELD	171c	
	מלך	KING	573b	2
	קדוש	HOLY	872c	1 c
89 20	בחר	CHOOSE	104b	7
	גבור	STRONG	150b	2
	חזון	VISION	303a	1
	חסד	KIND	339d	2 b
	עזר	HELP	740c	1
	רום	BE HIGH	927a	1 f
89 21	שוה	SET	1001b	
	דוד	DAVID	188a	
	מצא	FIND	593b	3 a
	משח	ANOINT	603b	2
	קדש	APARTNESS	872a	3 d
	שמן	OIL	1032b	2 d
89 22	אמץ	BE STRONG	55a	1
	זרוע	ARM	284a	1 c
	כון	BE FIRM	465c	1 a
	עם	WITH	767b	1 a
89 23	בן	SON	121d	8 b
	נשא	BE A CREDITOR	673d	
	עולה	INJUSTICE	732c	1
	ענה	BE BOWED DOWN	776b	1
89 24	כתת	BEAT	510a	1
	נגף	STRIKE	619d	
	פנה	FACE	818b	2 6a
	שן	HATE	971d	1
89 25	אמונה	FIRMNESS	53d	3 b
	ב	IN	90a	3 2d
	חסד	GOODNESS	339b	2 2
	עם	WITH	767b	1 a
	קרן	HORN	902a	2
	רום	BE HIGH	927a	2 b
89 27	אב	FATHER	3b	2
	אל	GOD	42c	6 b
	ישועה	DELIVERANCE	447b	3
	צור	ROCK	849d	2 a
	קרא	CALL	896a	6 d
89 28	אף	ALSO	64d	1
	בכור	FIRST-BORN	114b	3
	ל	TO	513a	5 ad
	עליון	HIGH	751b	3
89 29	אמן	CONFIRM	53a	4
	ברית	COVENANT	136d	2 2f
	ברית	COVENANT	137a	3 2
	חסד	GOODNESS	339a	2 1e
	ל	TO	511a	1 d
	עולם	LONG DURATION	762d	2 f
89 30	זרע	SOWING	282d	4 c
	ד	LIKE	453d	1 b
	כסא	THRONE	491a	3 a
	שום	TO PLACE	963d	3 c
	שמי	HEAVENS	1030a	1 a
89 31	אם	IF	49c	1 a1a
	הלך	WALK	234d	2 3a 1z
	תורה	INSTRUCTION	436a	1 c
	משפט	JUDGMENT	1049a	4
89 32	חלל	POLLUTE	320c	3
	חקה	SOMETHING PRESCRIBED	350a	2 d
	חק	SOMETHING PRESCRIBED	350b	2 e
89 33	מצוה	COMMANDMENT	846b	2 b2
	אם	IF	49c	1 a1a
	עון	INIQUITY	731a	1 c1
	פקד	ATTEND TO	823c	A 2
	פשע	TRANSGRESSION	833c	3 c
	שבט	ROD	987a	1 a
89 34	אמונה	FIRMNESS	53d	3 b
	ברית	COVENANT	136d	2 2f
	ברית	COVENANT	137b	3 3
	חסד	GOODNESS	339a	2 1e
	מעם	FROM WITH	*769a	B
	פרר	BREAK	830c	2 c
89 35	שקר	DEAL FALSELY	1055d	
	חלל	POLLUTE	320c	3
	מוצא	GOING FORTH	425d	2 a
	שפה	SPEECH	973d	1 a1
	שנה	CHANGE	1040a	
89 36	אם	IF	50b	1 b2
	דוד	DAVID	188a	
	כזב	LIE	469c	1
	קדש	APARTNESS	871c	1 b
	קדש	APARTNESS	*871d	2 d
89 37	שבע	SWEAR	989b	2
	זרע	SOWING	282d	4 c
	ד	LIKE	*453d	1 b
	כסא	THRONE	491a	3 a
	נגד	IN FRONT	617b	1 aa
	עולם	LONG DURATION	762d	2 f
	שמש	SUN	1039b	1
89 38	אמן	CONFIRM	53a	5
	ו	AND	253d	1 k
	ירח	MOON	437a	
	כון	BE FIRM	465c	1 b
	סלה	LIFT UP	700b	
	עד	WITNESS	729c	1
	עולם	LONG DURATION	762d	2 h
	שחק	DUST	1007a	1
89 39	ברית	COVENANT	136d	2 2f
	ברית	COVENANT	137b	3 3
	זנח	REJECT	276b	
	מאס	REJECT	549c	1 a
	משיח	ANOINTED	603c	1
	עבר	BE ARROGANT	720d	2 a
89 40	חלל	POLLUTE	320c	1
	ל	TO	511c	1 ga
	נאר	ABHOR	611b	
	נזר	CROWN	634b	1 a
89 41	מבצר	FORTIFICATION	131c	
	גדרה	WALL	155a	
	מחתה	TERROR	370a	2
	פרץ	BREAK THROUGH	829b	2
89 42	היה	BECOME	226b	2 2d
	חרף	REPROACH	358a	3
	עבר	PASS OVER	*717d	4 a
	שכן	NEIGHBOUR	1015c	2
89 43	רום	BE HIGH	927a	1 a1
	שמח	REJOICE	970c	
89 44	חרב	SWORD	352c	1 a
	צור	ROCK	849d	2 b
	צר	HARD PEBBLE	866a	
	קום	STAND	879a	6 b
	שוב	TURN BACK	999c	1
89 45	מטהר	CLEARNESS	372d	
	כסא	THRONE	491a	3 a
	מגר	CAST	550d	
	שבת	CEASE	992a	4
89 46	בושה	SHAME	102a	
	סלה	LIFT UP	700b	
	עטה	WRAP ONESELF	742a	1
	עלומים	YOUTH	761c	
	קצר	BE SHORT	894b	2
89 47	אש	FIRE	77d	5
	בער	BURN	129a	4
	חמה	RAGE	404d	2 c
	חמה	RAGE	*404d	2 c
	מה	HOW	554b	4 e
	נצח	EVERLASTINGNESS	664b	4
	סתר	HIDE	711b	1
89 48	ברא	CREATE	135b	1
	זכר	REMEMBER	270c	2 3 c
	חלד	DURATION	317b	
	מה	WHAT	552c	1 a
	על	UPON	754c	2 1fd
	שוא	EMPTINESS	996a	1
89 49	יד	HAND	391b	5 g1
	מלט	SLIP AWAY	572c	3
	נפש	SOUL	659c	1 d
	נפש	SOUL	660a	3 c
	סלה	LIFT UP	700b	
	ראה	TO SEE	907b	3
	שאול	SHEOL	982d	1
89 50	אמונה	FIRMNESS	53d	3 b
	דוד	DAVID	188a	
	דוד	DAVID	188b	J
	חסד	GOODNESS	339c	4
	שבע	SWEAR	989c	2
89 51	זכר	REMEMBER	270c	2 4
	חיק	BOSOM	300d	2
	חרפה	REPROACH	357d	1
	חרפה	REPROACH	357d	1
	כלמה	IGNOMINY	484b	2
	עבד	SLAVE	714a	3
89 52	חרף	REPROACH	357d	
	משיח	ANOINTED	603c	1
	עקב	HEEL	784b	B
89 53	אמן	VERILY	53b	
	ברך	BLESS	138d	2 a
	עולם	LONG DURATION	762b	2 c
90 1	אהל	TENT	14b	3
	אלהים	GOD	43d	3 b
	דור	PERIOD	189d	1 a
	משה	MOSES	602d	
	מעון	REFUGE	733a	3
	תפלה	PRAYER	813c	2
90 2	אל	GOD	42d	6 e
	דור	PERIOD	*189d	1 a
	הר	MOUNTAIN	250a	1 c
	חול	WHIRL	297b	2
	טרם	NOT YET	382c	2
	תבל	WORLD	385d	
	ילד	BE BORN	409a	
	מן	FROM	582a	5 c
	עולם	LONG DURATION	763a	2 m
	אנוש	MAN	60d	3
90 3	דכא	DUST	194b	
	עד	AS FAR AS	724a	1 1a
	שוב	TURN BACK	997c	4 a

Ch	v.	Heb	Eng	Page	Sec
90	4	שוב	TURN BACK	999b	1 g
		אלף	THOUSAND	48d	1 a
		יום	DAY	400a	7 a3
		לילה	NIGHT	538d	1
		אשמורה	WATCH	1038a	
		שנה	YEAR	1040b	
		תמול	YESTERDAY	1070a	1
90	5	בקר	MORNING	134a	1 e
		זרם	POUR FORTH IN FLOODS	281b	
		חלף	PASS ON OR AWAY	322a	2
		חציר	GREEN GRASS	348b	2
		שנה	SLEEP	446a	
		שלף	DRAW OUT	1025c	3
90	6	בקר	MORNING	134a	1 e
		חלף	PASS ON OR AWAY	322a	2
		יבש	BE DRY	386b	1 d
		מלל	WITHER	576d	
		ציץ	BLOSSOM	847c	1
		שלף	DRAW OUT	1025c	3
		מול	ADDENDA ET CORRIGENDA	1124d	
90	7	בהל	BE DISTURBED	96b	1
		חמה	RAGE	404d	2 c
		כלה	BE FINISHED	477d	2 c
90	8	מאור	LUMINARY	22d	
		נגד	IN FRONT	617c	2 b
		עון	INIQUITY	731a	1 c1
		עלם	CONCEAL	761a	
		שית	PUT	1011b	2 a
90	9	ב	IN	90c	3 5
		הגה	A MOANING	212a	3
		יום	DAY	399a	4 a
		כמו	LIKE	455d	1 a
		כלה	FINISH	478b	1 b
		עברה	OVERFLOW	720c	3 b
		פנה	TURN	815b	1 d
90	10	און	TROUBLE	20a	1
		ב	IN	89c	3 1c
		גבורה	STRENGTH	150b	1
		גוז	PASS AWAY	157a	
		חיש	QUICKLY	301d	
		יום	DAY	399a	4 a
		יום	DAY	399a	4 a
		עוף	FLY	733c	2
		עמל	TROUBLE	765d	1
		רהב	PRIDE	923b	
		שמנים	EIGHTY	1033d	
90	11	יראה	FEAR	432a	3
		כן	SO	*486a	1 b
		מי	WHO	*567a	F d
		עברה	OVERFLOW	720c	3 b
		עז	STRENGTH	739b	3 c
90	12	בוא	COME	99b	1 g
		בוא	COME	99c	2 e
		חכמה	WISDOM	315c	4
		ידע	MAKE KNOWN	395a	
		יום	DAY	399a	4 a
		כן	SO	486a	1 b
		לבב	HEART	523b	2 3b
		מנה	COUNT	584a	1
90	13	מתי	WHEN	607d	C
		נחם	BE SORRY	637a	1
		עבד	SLAVE	714a	3
		שוב	TURN BACK	998a	6 g
90	14	בקר	MORNING	134b	1 g
		חסד	GOODNESS	339a	2 1a
		יום	DAY	399a	4 a
		רנן	GIVE A RINGING CRY	943c	
		שבע	SATISFIED	959b	
		שמח	REJOICE	970b	1 a
90	15	יום	DAY	400b	7 d5
		ענה	BE BOWED DOWN	776a	3
		רעה	MISERY	949a	1
		שמח	REJOICE	970c	
90	16	הדר	SPLENDOUR	214b	2
		עבד	SLAVE	714a	3
		על	UPON	757c	27c ab
		ראה	TO SEE	908c	1 c
90	17	אדון	LORD	11c	3 2b
		יהוה	YAHWEH	218d	2 1c
		כון	ESTABLISH	466d	1
		נעם	DELIGHTFULNESS	653c	1
		על	UPON	753d	2 1d
		על	UPON	756c	27a b
		מעשה	DEED	795d	1 b3
91	1	לון	LODGE	533d	
		סתר	COVERING	712a	2 a
		עליון	HIGHEST	751b	1
		צל	SHADOW	853b	2
		שדי	ALMIGHTY	995a	1
91	2	בטח	TRUST	105a	13a
		מחסה	REFUGE	340c	B
		מצודה	FASTNESS	845a	
91	3	דבר	PESTILENCE	184a	1
		הוא	HE, SHE, IT	*215b	1 a
		הוה	CHASM	217d	2
		יקוש	FOWLER	430c	
		פח	BIRD-TRAP	809a	2 a
91	4	אברה	PINION	7c	
		אמת	FIRMNESS	54b	3 b
		חסה	SEEK REFUGE	340b	
		כנף	WING	489d	1 h
		סחרה	BUCKLER	695c	
		סכך	OVERSHADOW	697a	2

Ch	v.	Heb	Eng	Page	Sec
		צנה	LARGE SHIELD	857a	
91	5	חץ	ARROW	346c	2
		יומם	BY DAY	401c	2
		ירא	FEAR	431b	1 c
		עוף	FLY	733c	1 a
91	6	אפל	DARKNESS	66c	1
		דבר	PESTILENCE	184a	1
		הלך	WALK	232c	13
		צהר	MIDDAY	844a	1
		קטב	DESTRUCTION	881c	
91	7	ימין	RIGHT HAND	411d	2 a
		מן	FROM	578d	1 c
		נגש	DRAW NEAR	620d	1
		צד	SIDE	841a	
		רבבה	MULTITUDE	914b	
91	8	נבט	LOOK	613d	1
		רק	ONLY	956b	2 a
91	9	שלמה	REQUITAL	1024b	
		מחסה	REFUGE	340c	B
		מעון	REFUGE	733a	3
		עליון	HIGHEST	751b	1
91	10	אהל	TENT	13d	2
		אנה	BE OPPORTUNE	58c	
		נגע	STROKE	619c	2
91	11	קרב	COME NEAR	897c	1 e
		דרך	WAY	203b	5
		ל	TO	514b	5 fa
		מלאך	MESSENGER	521d	
		צוה	COMMAND	845d	1 e
		שמר	KEEP	1037a	4 a
91	12	נגף	STRIKE	619d	
		נגף	STRIKE	*620a	
		נשא	LIFT	671b	2 c
91	13	דרך	TREAD	202a	2
		כפיר	LION	498d	
		פתן	COBRA	837a	
		רמס	TRAMPLE	942d	
		שחל	LION	1006c	
		תנין	SERPENT	1072c	1
91	14	חשק	BE ATTACHED TO	366a	
		פלט	ESCAPE	812b	1
		שגב	BE HIGH	960c	1
91	15	ב	IN	88d	3 16
		חלץ	DRAW OFF OR OUT	322d	2
		כבד	MAKE HONORABLE	457d	2 a
		צרה	DISTRESS	865d	
91	16	ארך	LENGTH	73d	B
		ישועה	DELIVERANCE	447b	3
		ראה	TO SEE	909a	2 a
		שבע	SATISFIED	959d	1 b
92	1	מזמור	MELODY	274c	
		שיר	SONG	*1010b	1
92	2	זמר	MAKE MUSIC	274a	1
		טוב	PLEASANT	374c	1
		ידה	PRAISE	392c	1 b
		עליון	HIGHEST	751b	1
92	3	אמונה	FIRMNESS	53d	3 b
		בקר	MORNING	133d	1 a
		בקר	MORNING	134a	1 d
		חסד	GOODNESS	339b	2 2
		לילה	NIGHT	538d	1
		לילה	NIGHT	539a	1
92	4	נגד	BE CONSPICUOUS	617a	4
		הגיון	RESOUNDING MUSIC	212a	1
		כנור	LYRE	490b	
		נבל	HARP	614c	
		על	UPON	754c	2 If e
		עשור	A TEN	797d	2
92	5	מעשה	DEED	796a	1 c
		רנן	GIVE A RINGING CRY	943c	
		שמח	REJOICE	970c	
92	6	גדל	BECOME GREAT	152b	2 f
		מחשבה	THOUGHT	364b	1 b
		מאד	EXCEEDINGLY	547c	2 a
		עמק	BE DEEP	770d	
92	7	בין	DISCERN	106d	2 b
		בער	BRUTISHNESS	129c	
		זה	THIS	260c	1a
		כסיל	FOOL	493a	
92	8	עד	PERPETUITY	723c	2 c
		עשב	HERB	793b	
		פרח	BUD	827a	
		ציץ	BLOSSOM	847c	1
		שמד	BE EXTERMINATED	1029b	1
92	9	עולם	LONG DURATION	762c	2 c
		מרום	HEIGHT	929a	1
92	10	אבד	PERISH	1d	1
		איב	BE HOSTILE TO	33c	
		פרד	DIVIDE	825c	
92	11	בלל	MIX	117c	2
		קרן	HORN	*901d	1 a
		קרן	HORN	902a	2
		ראם	WILD OX	910b	
		רום	BE HIGH	927c	1 f
		רענן	LUXURIANT	947d	
		שמן	OIL	1032b	2 c
92	12	אזן	EAR	24a	2 a
		נבט	LOOK	613d	2
		שורר	WATCHER	1004a	
		שור	WALL	1004a	
		שמע	HEAR	1033d	1 d2
92	13	ארז	CEDAR	72c	1 b
		ארז	CEDAR	72c	1 a
		לבנון	LEBANON	527b	

Ch	v.	Heb	Eng	Page	Sec
		פרח	BUD	827a	
		שגה	GROW	960d	
		תמר	PALM-TREE	1071c	
92	14	פרח	BUD	827b	2
		שתל	TRANSPLANT	1060a	
92	15	דשן	FAT	206c	
		נוב	BEAR FRUIT	626b	
		עוד	STILL	729a	1 ab
		רענן	LUXURIANT	947d	
		שיבה	OLD AGE	966d	2
		רענן	FLOURISHING	*1113b	
92	16	ישר	STRAIGHT	449a	3 a
		נגד	BE CONSPICUOUS	617a	4
		צור	ROCK	849d	2 a
93	1	אזר	GIRD	25a	
		אף	ALSO	64d	1
		בל	NOT	115b	
		גאות	MAJESTY	145a	2
		תבל	WORLD	385d	
		כון	BE FIRM	465c	1 a
		לבש	PUT ON	528a	B
		מוט	SHAKE	557a	
		מלך	BE KING	574a	
		עז	STRENGTH	739a	3 a
93	2	מאז	FROM THAT TIME	23b	A
		כון	BE FIRM	465d	1 b
		כסא	THRONE	491b	3 b
		עולם	LONG DURATION	762a	1 c
93	3	דכי	POUNDING	194b	
		נשא	LIFT	670c	1 b 5
		קול	VOICE	877b	2 f
93	4	אדיר	MAJESTIC	12b	1
		אדיר	MAJESTIC	12b	1
		קול	VOICE	877b	2 f
		מרום	HEIGHT	928d	2
		משבר	BREAKER	991c	
93	5	אמן	CONFIRM	53a	4
		ארך	LENGTH	73d	B
		נאה	BE BEFITTING	610a	2
		נאוה	SEEMLY	610a	2
		עדה	TESTIMONIES	730a	
		קדש	APARTNESS	872b	6
94	1	אל	GOD	42d	6 c
		יפע	SHINE OUT	422a	1
		נקמה	VENGEANCE	668c	1
94	2	גאה	PROUD	144b	
		נשא	LIFT	671d	2
		על	UPON	756c	27a b
		שפט	JUDGE	1047d	3 d
94	3	מתי	WHEN	607d	C
		עלז	EXULT	759c	
94	4	אמר	SAY	56d	
		נבע	BUBBLE UP	616a	3
		עתק	FORWARD	801b	
94	5	דכא	CRUSH	194a	
		נחלה	PROPERTY	635d	1 e
		ענה	BE BOWED DOWN	776b	1
94	6	אלמנה	WIDOW	48b	
		גר	SOJOURNER	158b	2
		הרג	KILL	247a	1 a
		יתום	ORPHAN	450c	
		רצח	MURDER	954a	
94	7	אלהים	GOD	44c	4 ba
		בין	DISCERN	106d	3 a
		יה	YAH	219c	
94	8	בין	DISCERN	106d	3 a
		בער	BE BRUTISH	129c	
		כסיל	FOOL	493a	
		מתי	WHEN	607d	A
		שכל	BE PRUDENT	968b	3
94	9	אזן	EAR	24a	2 a
		יצר	FORM	427d	2 a
		נבט	LOOK	613d	2
		נטע	PLANT	642c	3
		שמע	HEAR	1034b	2 d
94	10	דעת	KNOWLEDGE	395d	1 e
		יכח	DECIDE	406d	1
		יסר	DISCIPLINE	416a	3
		למד	LEARN	540d	
94	11	הבל	VAPOUR	210d	2
		מחשבה	THOUGHT	364b	1 a
94	12	אשר	HAPPINESS	81a	
		יה	YAH	219c	
		יסר	DISCIPLINE	416a	1 a
		תורה	LAW	436b	2 b2
		למד	LEARN	540d	
		מן	OUT OF	579c	2 bb
94	13	כרה	BE DUG	500b	
		מן	FROM	578a	1 a
		רע	EVIL	948d	1
		שחת	PIT	1001c	1
		שקט	BE QUIET	1053b	2
94	14	נחלה	PROPERTY	635b	1 e
		נטש	FORSAKE	643d	2
94	15	ישר	STRAIGHT	449b	3 b
		לב	HEART	525b	26a
		צדק	RIGHTEOUSNESS	841c	2
		שוב	TURN BACK	998b	7 g
94	16	יצב	STATION ONESELF	426c	7
		ל	TO	515c	5 hc
		מי	WHO	566c	F a
		עם	WITH	767c	1 c
		קום	STAND	878a	2
94	17	דומה	SILENCE	189a	
		לולא	IF NOT	530c	D
		מעט	A FEW	590b	2 a

Ch	v.	Heb	Eng	Page	Sec
		עזרה	HELP	741a	2 b
94	18	שכן	SETTLE DOWN	1015b	2 b
		אם	IF	49d	1 a3 a
		חסד	GOODNESS	339a	2 1a
		מוט	SLIP	556d	1
		סעד	SUPPORT	703c	2 b
94	19	תנחום	CONSOLATION	637c	1
		נפש	SOUL	660d	6 d
		קרב	INWARD PART	899b	2 a
		שרעפים	DISQUIETING THOUGHTS	972a	1
		שעע	TAKE DELIGHT IN	1044b	1
94	20	הוה	CHASM	217d	2
		חבר	UNITE	288b	1 a
		חק	SOMETHING PRESCRIBED	349c	6 d
		יצר	FORM	427d	1 c
		כסא	SEAT OF HONOR	490d	2
		על	UPON	754a	2 1f
		עמל	TROUBLE	765d	1
94	21	גדד	PENETRATE	151a	1
		גוד	ATTACK	156a	1
		גור	STIR UP STRIFE	*158d	1
		דם	BLOOD	196d	2 d
		נקי	CLEAN	667c	1
		צדיק	JUST	843b	3 b
		רשע	BE WICKED	957d	1
94	22	מחסה	REFUGE	340c	B
		ל	TO	512c	4 b
		צור	ROCK	849d	2 a
		משגב	SECURE HEIGHT	960d	2
94	23	ב	IN	90c	3 5
		יהוה	YAHWEH	218d	2 1c
		על	UPON	756c	2 7a b
		צמת	EXTERMINATE	856c	
		צמת	EXTERMINATE	856c	
95	1	ישע	DELIVERANCE	447a	2
		צור	ROCK	849d	2 a
		רוע	RAISE A SHOUT	929d	5
		רנן	GIVE A RINGING CRY	943c	
95	2	זמיר	SONG	274c	
		תודה	THANKSGIVING	392d	2
		קדם	COME IN FRONT	870a	1 b
		רוע	RAISE A SHOUT	929d	5
		הלך	ADDENDA ET CORRIGENDA	*1122c	
95	3	אל	GOD	42d	6 d
		גדול	GREAT	153b	6 c
		גדול	GREAT	153b	6 c
		מלך	KING	573b	5 a
		מלך	KING	573b	3
		על	UPON	755a	2 3
95	4	אשר	PARTICLE OF RELATION	82d	5
		הר	MOUNTAIN	250d	1 m
		מחקר	RANGE	350d	
		תועפה	EMINENCE	419c	2
95	5	אשר	PARTICLE OF RELATION	82d	5
		יבשת	DRY LAND	387a	
		יצר	FORM	427d	2 a
		עשה	DO	794b	2 1b
95	6	ברך	KNEEL	138c	1
		כרע	BOW DOWN	502c	1
		עשה	DO	794c	2 1b
		שחה	BOW DOWN	1005c	2 b
95	7	אם	IF	50b	1 b3
		צאן	SMALL CATTLE	838c	3
		מרעית	PASTURING	945c	1
95	8	כ	LIKE	455a	B
		לבב	HEART	524a	2 6d
		מסה	MASSAH	650c	
		קשה	BE SEVERE	904c	3 a
		מריבה	MERIBAH	937b	2
95	9	בחן	TRY	103c	2 c
		גם	ALSO	169d	5
		נסה	TEST	650b	3 b
		פעל	DOING	821c	1 a
95	10	דור	GENERATION	190a	2a
		דרך	WAY	204a	6 ec
		לבב	HEART	524a	2 6b
		קוט	FEEL A LOATHING	876c	
		תעה	ERR	1073c	3
95	11	אם	IF	50b	1 b2
		מנוחה	RESTING PLACE	629d	1
		שבע	SWEAR	989c	2
96	1	חדש	NEW	294a	A
		שיר	SING	1010d	
96	2	אל	TO	39d	1
		ברך	BLESS	139a	1
		בשר	BEAR TIDINGS	142b	3
		יום	DAY	400b	7 e1
		ישועה	DELIVERANCE	447b	3
		ל	TO	517b	6 c
		מן	FROM	582b	5 d1
		מן	FROM	582b	5 d2
		שיר	SING	1010d	
96	3	כבוד	HONOR	459b	6 b
		ספר	COUNT	708a	1
96	4	גדול	GREAT	153b	6 c
		הלל	PRAISE	239a	2
		ירא	BE REVERED	431d	3 a
		על	UPON	755a	2 3
96	5	אלהים	GOD	43c	1 d
		אליל	WORTHLESSNESS	47c	B
96	6	הדר	SPLENDOUR	214b	2
		הוד	SPLENDOUR	217a	2
		עז	STRENGTH	739a	3 a
		תפארה	BEAUTY	802d	2 c
96	7	יהב	ASCRIBE	396d	4
		כבוד	HONOR	459b	6 b
		עז	STRENGTH	739b	3 b
		עם	PEOPLE	766d	5 e
96	8	חצר	ENCLOSURE	347a	3 b
		יהב	ASCRIBE	396d	4
		כבוד	HONOR	459b	6 b
		ל	TO	511b	1 ga
		מנחה	OFFERING	585a	3
		מנחה	OFFERING	585c	6
		נשא	LIFT	671b	2 e
		שם	NAME	1028c	3
96	9	הדרה	ADORNMENT	214c	1
		חול	WHIRL	*297a	1
		ל	TO	*516d	5 k
		פנה	FACE	818a	2 5b
		קדש	APARTNESS	872b	4 b
		שחה	BOW DOWN	1005c	2 b
96	10	בל	NOT	*115b	
		בל	NOT	115b	
		דין	JUDGE	192b	1
		תבל	WORLD	*385d	
		תבל	WORLD	385d	
		מישר	LEVEL	449d	2
		כון	BE FIRM	465c	1 a
		מוט	SHAKE	557a	
		מלך	BE KING	574a	
96	11	מלא	THAT WHICH FILLS	571b	3
		רעם	THUNDER	947b	
		שמח	REJOICE	970b	2 a
96	12	אז	THEN	23a	1 c
		יער	WOOD	420d	F
		עלו	EXULT	759c	
		רנן	GIVE A RINGING CRY	943c	
		שדי	FIELD	961b	4
		שדה	FIELD	961d	3
96	13	אמונה	FIRMNESS	53d	3 b
		תבל	WORLD	385d	
		תבל	WORLD	*385d	
		פנה	FACE	818a	2 5b
		צדק	RIGHTEOUSNESS	841d	E
		שפט	JUDGE	1047d	3 d
		שפט	JUDGE	1047d	3 d
97	1	אי	COAST	16a	
		מלך	BE KING	574a	
97	2	מכן	FIXED PLACE	467d	1
		כסא	THRONE	491b	3 b
		סביב	ROUND ABOUT	687b	2 ab
		ענן	CLOUD	778a	1 a
		ערפל	CLOUD	791d	
		צדק	RIGHTEOUSNESS	841d	E
		משפט	JUDGEMNT	1048d	2 a
97	3	הלך	WALK	232c	1 3
		להט	SET ABLAZE	529d	
		צר	ADVERSARY	865d	
97	4	ברק	LIGHTNING	140c	1
		חול	WHIRL	297a	2 b
		תבל	WORLD	385d	
97	5	ארון	LORD	11a	1 2
		דונג	WAX	200a	
		הר	MOUNTAIN	250a	1 c
		מסס	MELT	587d	1
		פנה	FACE	818a	2 5b
97	6	כבוד	GLORY	459a	2 c3
		נגד	BE CONSPICUOUS	617a	4
		צדק	RIGHTEOUSNESS	841d	E
		שמי	HEAVENS	1030b	3
97	7	אלהים	GOD	43b	1 c
		אליל	WORTHLESSNESS	47c	B
		הלל	BE BOASTFUL	239a	1
		עבד	WORK	713b	4 b
97	8	בת	DAUGHTER	123b	1 i
		מען	PURPOSE	775b	1 b
		משפט	JUDGMENT	1048c	1 f
97	9	מאד	EXCEEDINGLY	547c	2 a
		עלה	GO UP	749b	3
		עליון	HIGH	751b	1
97	10	אהב	LOVE	13a	3
		חסיד	KIND	339d	2 b
		נפש	SOUL	660a	3 c
		רע	EVIL	948d	3
		רשע	WICKED	957c	3
97	11	אור	LIGHT	21d	8
		זרע	SOW	281d	3 f
		ישר	STRAIGHT	449b	3 b
		לב	HEART	525b	2 6a
		צדיק	JUST	843b	3 b
97	12	זכר	REMEMBRANCE	271d	1 c
		ידה	PRAISE	392c	1 b
		קדש	APARTNESS	871c	1 c
98	1	מזמור	MELODY	274c	
		זרוע	ARM	284a	1 c
		חדש	NEW	294a	A
		ימין	RIGHT HAND	411d	1 c
		ישע	GIVE VICTORY	447a	3 b
		קדש	APARTNESS	871c	1 a
98	2	ידע	MAKE KNOWN	395a	
		ישועה	DELIVERANCE	447c	3
		צדקה	RIGHTEOUSNESS	842d	6 a
98	3	אמונה	FIRMNESS	53d	3 b
		אפס	END	67a	1
		זכר	REMEMBER	270b	2 3 b
		חסד	GOODNESS	339b	2 2
		ישועה	DELIVERANCE	447c	3
98	4	זמר	MAKE MUSIC	274b	1
		פצח	CAUSE TO BREAK FORTH	822d	
		רוע	RAISE A SHOUT	929d	5
		רנן	GIVE A RINGING CRY	943c	
98	5	זמר	MAKE MUSIC	274b	2
		זמרה	MELODY	274b	3
		כנור	LYRE	490b	
		כנור	LYRE	490b	
98	6	חצצרה	CLARION	348c	2 c
		מלך	KING	573b	3
		רוע	RAISE A SHOUT	929d	5
		שפר	HORN	1051d	
98	7	תבל	WORLD	385d	3
		מלא	THAT WHICH FILLS	571b	3
		רעם	THUNDER	947b	
98	8	שדי	FIELD	961b	4
		יחד	ALTOGETHER	403b	2 b
		כף	HOLLOW OF THE HAND	496c	1 d1
		מחא	CLAP	561d	
		רנן	GIVE A RINGING CRY	943c	
98	9	תבל	WORLD	385d	
		מישר	LEVEL	449d	2
		צדק	RIGHTEOUSNESS	841d	E
		שפט	JUDGE	1047d	3 d
		שפט	JUDGE	1047d	3 d
99	1	ארץ	EARTH	76a	1 b
		ישב	SIT	442c	1 a
		כרוב	CHERUB	500d	3
		מלך	BE KING	574a	
		נוט	DANGLE	630a	
		רגז	BE AGITATED	919b	
99	2	גדול	GREAT	153b	6 c
		רום	BE HIGH	926d	1 b
99	3	גדול	GREAT	153b	6 c
		ידה	PRAISE	392b	1 a2
		ירא	BE REVERED	431d	3 b
		קדוש	HOLY	872c	1 a
99	4	אהב	LOVE	13b	5 c
		מישר	LEVEL	449d	2
		כון	ESTABLISH	466d	1 b
		מלך	KING	573b	2
		עז	STRENGTH	739a	3 a
		צדקה	RIGHTEOUSNESS	842b	2
		משפט	JUDGMENT	1048d	2 a
99	5	הדם	FOOTSTOOL	213c	2
		יהוה	YAHWEH	218d	2 1c
		ל	TO	*510b	1 a
		קדוש	HOLY	872c	1 a
		רגל	FOOT	919d	1 b
		רום	BE HIGH	927b	3
		שחה	BOW DOWN	1005c	2 b
99	6	אהרן	AARON	14d	
		כהן	PRIEST	463d	4
		משה	MOSES	602e	
		קרא	CALL	895c	3 b
		שמואל	SAMUEL	1028c	1
99	7	חק	SOMETHING PRESCRIBED	349c	6 d
		עדה	TESTIMONIES	730a	
		עמוד	PILLAR	765b	4
99	8	אל	GOD	42d	6 d
		יהוה	YAHWEH	218d	2 1c
		ל	TO	513a	5 ad
		נקם	AVENGE	668a	1
		נשא	LIFT	671c	3 c
99	9	יהוה	YAHWEH	218d	2 1c
		קדוש	HOLY	872c	1 a
		רום	BE HIGH	927b	3
		שחה	BOW DOWN	1005c	2 c
100	1	מזמור	MELODY	274c	
		תודה	THANK-OFFERING	393a	4
		רוע	RAISE A SHOUT	929d	5
100	2	רננה	JOYFUL	943c	
100	3	אלהים	GOD	44b	4 a
		לא	NOT	520c	
		עשה	DO	794b	2 1b
		צאן	SMALL CATTLE	838c	3
		מרעית	PASTURING	945c	1
100	4	בוא	COME	97d	1
		ברך	BLESS	139a	1
		תהלה	PRAISE	240a	2
		חצר	ENCLOSURE	347a	3 b
		ידה	PRAISE	392c	1 b
		תודה	THANKSGIVING	392d	2
		שער	GATE	1045b	3 b
100	5	אמונה	FIRMNESS	53d	3 b
		דור	PERIOD	189d	1 b
		חסד	GOODNESS	339b	2 3c
		טוב	PLEASANT	374d	9 b
		עולם	LONG DURATION	762b	2 c
101	1	זמר	MAKE MUSIC	274a	1
		מזמור	MELODY	274c	
		חסד	GOODNESS	339b	2 2
		שיר	SING	1010d	
101	2	דרך	WAY	203c	6 c
		הלך	WALK	236b	2
		לב	HEART	523d	2 6a
		מתי	WHEN	607d	A
		קרב	INWARD PART	899a	1 d

Ch v.	Heb	Eng	Page	Sec
	שכל	BE PRUDENT	968b	2
	תם	INTEGRITY	1070d	3
	תמים	SOUND	1071a	4
101 3	בליעל	WORTHLESSNESS	116a	1
	דבק	CLING	180a	2 c
	נגד	IN FRONT	617c	1 b
	שם		962b	
	שית	PUT	1011b	1
101 4	לבב	HEART	524a	2 6b
	עקש	TWISTED	786a	1
101 5	גבה	HIGH	147b	3
	יכל	BE ABLE	407d	1 h
	לבב	HEART	524a	2 6c
	לשן	SLANDER	546d	1
	סתר	COVERING	712b	3
	עין	EYE	744c	2 a
	צמת	EXTERMINATE	856c	
	רחב	WIDE	932a	
	רע	FRIEND	946a	1
101 6	אמן	CONFIRM	53a	5
	ב	IN	*88d	1 4
	דרך	WAY	203c	6 c
	הלך	WALK	234c	2 3a 1a
	שרת	SERVE	1057b	2
	תמים	SOUND	1071b	4
101 7	דבר	SPEAK	180c	
	כון	BE FIRM	465d	1 c
	נגד	IN FRONT	*617c	2 b
	קרב	INWARD PART	899a	1 d
	רמיה	DECEIT	941b	
	שקר	DECEPTION	1055b	5
101 8	בקר	MORNING	134b	1 f
	כרת	CUT OFF	504c	2 b
	כתב	BE WRITTEN	*508a	2
	ל	TO	516b	5 ja
	ל	TO	517c	7 bb
	מן	OUT OF	579a	2 aa
	עיר	CITY	746c	1 g
	צמת	EXTERMINATE	856c	
	רשע	WICKED	957c	3
102 1	כי	WHEN	473a	2 a
	עטף	BE FEEBLE	742c	
	עני	POOR	776d	3
	תפלה	PRAYER	813c	2
	שיח	COMPLAINT	967a	1
	שפך	POUR OUT	1049d	2 b
102 2	שועה	CRY FOR HELP	1003a	
102 3	אזן	EAR	24b	2 b
	יום	DAY	400b	7 d4
	מהר	HASTEN	555a	2
	מהר	QUICKLY	*555b	
	נטה	INCLINE	641a	3 e
	סתר	HIDE	711d	2 a
	צר	STRAITS	865b	
	צרר	ADDENDA ET COR-RIGENDA	1126c	
102 4	ב	IN	89a	17d
	חרר	BE HOT	359c	2
	מוקד	BURNING MASS	428d	2
	כלה	BE FINISHED	477d	2 b
	עצם	BONE	782d	1 c
	עשן	SMOKE	798c	1 c
102 5	יבש	BE DRY	386b	1 d
	לב	HEART	524c	2
	מן	FROM	583b	7 ba
	נכה	SMITE	646d	7
	עשב	HERB	793b	
	שכח	FORGET	1013a	1 a
102 6	אנחה	SIGHING	58d	1
	בשר	FLESH	142c	1 b
	דבק	CLING	179d	1 a
	עצם	BONE	782d	1 a
	קול	VOICE	876d	1 a
102 7	מדבר	WILDERNESS	184d	2
	דמה	BE LIKE	198a	
	חרבה	WASTE	352a	1
	כוס	OWL	468b	
	קאת	PELICAN	866b	
102 8	בדד	BE SEPARATE	94b	1
	גג	ROOF	150d	1
	צפור	BIRD	862a	1
	שקד	WATCH	1052b	2
102 9	ב	IN	90a	3 2d
	הות	SHOUT AT	223d	
	הלל	PRAISE	239b	
	חרף	REPROACH	357d	
	יום	DAY	400c	7 f
	שבע	SWEAR	989b	1 b
102 10	אכל	EAT	37c	1
	אכל	EAT	38a	1
	אפר	ASHES	68a	
	בכי	WEEPING	113d	
	מסך	MIX	587c	2
	שקוי	DRINK	1052d	
102 11	זעם	INDIGNATION	276d	
	זעם	INDIGNATION	276d	
	קצף	WRATH	893c	1
	שלך	THROW	1021b	2 c
102 12	ה	THE	208a	1 f
	יבש	BE DRY	386b	1 d
	נטה	BEND	640b	3 a
	עשב	HERB	793b	
	צל	SHADOW	853b	3
102 13	דור	PERIOD	189d	1 b
	זכר	REMEMBRANCE	271b	1 b
	ישב	SIT	442c	1 a
	עולם	LONG DURATION	762c	2 c
102 14	חנן	SHOW FAVOR	336a	2 b
	מועד	APPOINTED TIME	417c	1 a
	עת	TIME	773d	2 c
	רחם	LOVE	933c	1
102 15	עבד	SLAVE	714a	3
	עפר	DRY EARTH	779d	1 e
	רצה	BE PLEASED WITH	953a	1 b
102 16	ירא	FEAR	431c	3 b
	כבוד	GLORY	459a	2 c3
102 17	בנה	BUILD	124d	2 b
	כבוד	GLORY	459a	2 c3
102 18	בזה	DESPISE	102c	
	ערער	STRIPPED	792d	
	תפלה	PRAYER	813c	1 e
	תפלה	PRAYER	813c	1 e
	פנה	TURN	815c	2 c1
102 19	אחרון	BEHIND	30d	B
	ברא	CREATE	135c	2
	דור	GENERATION	190a	2 c
	יה	YAH	219c	
	הלל	PRAISE	238c	2 d2
	זה	THIS	260d	1 a
	כתב	BE WRITTEN	508a	1
102 20	נבט	LOOK	613d	3
	קדש	APARTNESS	871c	2 a
	מרום	HEIGHT	928d	2
	שקף	LOOK DOWN	1054d	
102 21	אנקה	CRYING	60c	
	אסיר	PRISONER	64a	
	בן	SON	121d	8 e
	תמותה	DEATH	560d	
	פתח	OPEN	835c	1
102 22	תהלה	PRAISE	240b	4
	ספר	COUNT	708a	1
	ציון	ZION	851c	
102 23	ממלכה	KINGDOM	575a	1
	קבץ	GATHER	867d	1
	דרך	WAY	203b	5
102 24	כח	STRENGTH	470c	1 a
	ענה	BE BOWED DOWN	776b	4
	קצר	BE SHORT	894b	
102 25	אל	GOD	42c	6 b
	דור	PERIOD	189d	1 b
	דור	PERIOD	190a	1 c
	חצי	HALF	345d	2
	עלה	GO UP	749c	2 c
	שנה	YEAR	1040b	
102 26	יסד	FOUND	413d	
	מעשה	DEED	796b	2 b
	אבד	PERISH	1d	1
	בגד	GARMENT	94a	1
	בלה	BECOME OLD AND WORN OUT	115a	
	חלף	PASS ON OR AWAY	322a	1 b
	חלף	PASS ON OR AWAY	322b	1
102 28	לבוש	CLOTHING	528c	
	עמד	STAND	764b	3 c
	הוא	HE, SHE, IT	216c	5
	שנה	YEAR	1040b	
	תמם	BE FINISHED	1070b	2
102 29	בן	SON	120c	1 ib
	זרע	SOWING	282d	4 c
	כון	BE FIRM	465b	1 c
	עבד	SLAVE	714a	3
	פנה	FACE	817a	24a b
	שכן	SETTLE DOWN	1015a	1 a
103 1	ברך	BLESS	139a	1
	קרב	INWARD PART	899b	2 b
	שם	NAME	1028c	3
103 2	ברך	BLESS	139a	1
	שכח	FORGET	1013b	1 c
103 3	תחלאים	DISEASES	316a	
	סלח	FORGIVE	699b	
	עון	INIQUITY	731a	1 c2
	רפא	HEAL	950d	2 a
103 4	גאל	REDEEM	145c	3 a
	חיים	LIFE	313a	1
	חסד	GOODNESS	339b	2 2
	עטר	CROWN	743a	
	רחמים	COMPASSION	933c	1
	שחת	PIT	1001c	2
103 5	חדש	RENEW	294a	
	טוב	A GOOD THING	375b	2
	נעורים	YOUTH	655c	
	נשר	EAGLE	677a	
	עדי	ORNAMENTS	725d	1
	שבע	SATISFIED	959d	1 a
103 6	עשק	OPPRESS	798d	1
	צדקה	RIGHTEOUSNESS	842c	7 a
	משפט	JUDGMENT	1048c	1 f
103 7	דרך	WAY	204a	6 eb
	ידע	MAKE KNOWN	395a	
	עלילה	WANTONNESS	760b	2 b
	ישראל	ISRAEL	975d	2 a3
103 8	ארך	LONG	74a	
	חנון	GRACIOUS	337a	
	חסד	GOODNESS	339b	2 3a
	רחום	COMPASSIONATE	933d	
103 9	שטף	TEAR	383a	
	לא	NOT	*518d	1 ac
	נטר	KEEP	643c	1
	נצח	EVERLASTINGNESS	664b	4
	עולם	LONG DURATION	762d	2 g
	ריב	STRIVE	936c	3
103 10	חטא	SIN	308a	2
	עון	INIQUITY	731a	1 c1
103 11	גבה	BE HIGH	147a	1
	גבר	BE STRONG	149d	2 b
	חסד	GOODNESS	339b	2 3b
	ירא	FEAR	431c	3 b
	על	UPON	756c	2 7a b
103 12	מזרח	PLACE OF SUNRISE	280d	2 a
	מערב	WEST	788a	
	פשע	TRANSGRESSION	833c	3 d
	רחק	BE DISTANT	935a	
	רחק	BE DISTANT	935b	2
103 13	אב	FATHER	3b	1
	אב	FATHER	3b	2
	ירא	FEAR	431c	3 b
	רחם	LOVE	933c	1
	רחם	LOVE	933d	2
103 14	הוא	HE, SHE, IT	*215b	1 a
	זכר	REMEMBER	270b	2 3 c
	יצר	FORM	428a	3
	עפר	DRY EARTH	779d	1 b
103 15	אנוש	MAN	60d	3
	חציר	GREEN GRASS	348b	2
	יום	DAY	399a	4 a
	כן	SO	486b	2 ad b
	ציץ	BLOSSOM	847c	1
	ציץ	BLOSSOM	847d	1
	שדה	FIELD	961c	1 d
103 16	אין	NOT	34b	3
	נכר	RECOGNIZE	648b	4
	עבר	PASS OVER	*717d	4 b
103 17	חסד	GOODNESS	339d	2 3c
	ירא	FEAR	431c	3 b
	על	UPON	756c	2 7a b
	עולם	LONG DURATION	763a	2 m
	צדקה	RIGHTEOUSNESS	842b	6 a
103 18	ברית	COVENANT	136c	2 2c
	ברית	COVENANT	137a	3 2
	זכר	REMEMBER	270a	1 4 b
	פקוד	PRECEPT	824c	
103 19	כון	ESTABLISH	466a	1 a
	כל	ALL	483a	2 bb
	כסא	THRONE	491b	3
	מלכות	ROYAL POWER	574d	1
	משל	RULE	605d	3
103 20	אביר	MIGHTY	7d	2
	ברך	BLESS	139a	1
	גבור	STRONG	150b	2
	דבר	WORD	182d	1 2b
	כח	STRENGTH	470d	2
	ל	TO	517c	7 bb
	מלאך	MESSENGER	521d	2
103 21	ברך	BLESS	139a	1
	צבא	HOST	839a	3 b
	רצון	GOODWILL	953c	3 a
	שרת	SERVE	1058a	1 d
103 22	ברך	BLESS	139a	1
	ברך	BLESS	139a	1
	ממשלה	RULE	606b	3
	מעשה	DEED	796b	2 b
104 1	ברך	BLESS	139a	1
	גדל	BECOME GREAT	152b	2 f
	הדר	SPLENDOUR	214b	2
	הוד	SPLENDOUR	217a	2
	יהוה	YAHWEH	219a	2 1f
	לבש	PUT ON	528a	B
104 2	יריעה	CURTAIN	438c	
	עטה	WRAP ONESELF	741d	
	שלמה	GARMENT	971b	
104 3	הלך	WALK	235b	1
	כנף	WING	489d	1 f
	מי	WATER	565c	1 f
	עב	DARK CLOUD	728a	1 c
	עליה	ROOF-CHAMBER	751a	
	קרה	FURNISH WITH BEAMS	900a	
	רוח	BREATH	924d	2 a
	רכוב	CHARIOT	939c	
104 4	אש	FIRE	77d	6
	מלאך	MESSENGER	521d	1 e
	להט	FLAME	529c	
	עשה	DO	794c	2 1g
	רוח	BREATH	924d	2 a
	שרת	SERVE	1058a	1 d
	אש	ADDENDA ET COR-RIGENDA	1120d	
104 5	ארץ	EARTH	76a	1 b
	בל	NOT	115b	
	יסד	FOUND	413d	
	מכון	FIXED PLACE	467d	2
	מוט	SHAKE	557a	
	עד	PERPETUITY	723d	2 e
	עולם	LONG DURATION	762b	2 b1
104 6	הר	MOUNTAIN	250a	1 c
	כסה	COVER	491c	2
	לבוש	CLOTHING	528c	
	עמד	STAND	764a	1 j
	תהום	DEEP	1063a	3
104 7	גערה	REBUKE	172a	2
	חפז	BE IN TREPIDATION	342a	
	נוס	FLEE	630d	1
	קול	VOICE	877a	2 b
	רעם	THUNDER	947b	
104 8	בקעה	VALLEY	132c	1
	הר	MOUNTAIN	250b	1 e

PSALMS

Ch v.	Heb	Eng	Page	Sec
	זה	THIS	261d	5
	יסד	FOUND	413d	
	ירד	GO DOWN	433a	1 h
104 9	מקום	STANDING PLACE	880b	4
	גבול	BOUNDARY	148a	1 e
	כסה	COVER	491d	5
	עבר	PASS OVER	717c	2
	שום	TO PLACE	964a	3 f
	שוב	TURN BACK	998a	7 a
104 10	הלך	WALK	235b	1
	הר	MOUNTAIN	250b	1 e
	נחל	WADY	636b	2
	מעין	SPRING	746a	
	שלח	SEND	1019a	2 d
	שלח	SHILOAH	1019d	
104 11	חיה	LIVING THING	312d	1 b
	פרא	WILD ASS	825b	
	צמא	THIRST	854a	
	שדי	FIELD	961b	2
	שבר	BREAK	990d	
	שקה	GIVE TO DRINK	1052c	2
104 12	בין	INTERVAL	107d	D
	נתן	GIVE	679d	1 x
	עפאים	FOLIAGE	779b	
	קול	VOICE	877a	1 e
	שכן	SETTLE DOWN	1015a	1 b
104 13	עליה	ROOF-CHAMBER	751b	
	פרי	FRUIT	826c	3
	שבע	SATISFIED	959c	1 c
	שקה	GIVE TO DRINK	1052c	1
104 14	חציר	GREEN GRASS	348b	1
	יצא	BRING OUT	425b	4 j
	לחם	FOOD	537b	1 b
	עבדה	LABOR	715b	1
	עשב	HERB	793c	
	צמח	SPROUT	855c	1
104 15	אנוש	MAN	60d	3
	יין	WINE	406c	A
	לבב	HEART	524a	2 8
	לב	HEART	525c	2 8
	מן	OUT OF	580a	2 eb
	סעד	SUPPORT	703c	1
	צהל	MAKE SHINING	843d	
	שמח	REJOICE	970c	
	שמח	REJOICE	970c	
	שמן	OIL	1032b	2 c
104 16	ארז	CEDAR	72c	1 a
	לבנון	LEBANON	527a	
	עץ	TREE	781c	1 a
	שבע	SATISFIED	959c	1 b
104 17	בית	HOUSE	109c	1 b
	ברוש	CYPRESS	141c	1
	ברוש	CYPRESS	*141c	1
	חסידה	STORK	339d	
	צפור	BIRD	862a	1
104 18	גבה	HIGH	147a	1
	ה	THE	209a	2 b
	הר	MOUNTAIN	250b	1 d
	מחסה	REFUGE	340c	B
	יעל	MOUNTAIN-GOAT	418d	1
	סלע	CRAG	701a	1
	שפן	ROCK-BADGER	1051a	
104 19	מבוא	ENTERING	99d	2
	ידע	CAUSE TO KNOW	394d	
	מועד	APPOINTED TIME	417d	1 b
	ירח	MOON	437a	
	שמש	SUN	1039b	1
104 20	חיה	LIVING THING	312d	1 b
	חשך	DARKNESS	365a	
	יער	WOOD	420d	B
	רמש	CREEP	943a	2 c
	שית	PUT	1011c	3
104 21	אכל	FOOD	38a	
	אל	GOD	42d	6 e
	בקש	SEEK	135a	6
	טרף	PREY	383c	1
	כפיר	LION	498d	
	ל	TO	518b	7 bh
	שאג	ROAR	980c	1
104 22	זרח	RISE	280b	1 a
	מעונה	DEN	733a	1
	רבץ	LIE DOWN	918c	
104 23	עבדה	LABOR	715a	1
	עד	AS FAR AS	724b	12 a a
	פעל	DOING	821c	1 c
104 24	חכמה	WISDOM	315c	5 a
	מלא	BE FULL	570a	1 b
	מעשה	DEED	796b	2 b
	קנין	ACQUISITION	889b	2
	רבב	BECOME MUCH	912d	1
104 25	אין	NOT	34d	4 b
	ו	AND	253c	1 k
	זה	THIS	260d	2 a
	חיה	LIVING THING	312c	1 a
	יד	HAND	390c	3 d
	ים	SEA	410d	1
	מספר	NUMBER	708d	1 a
	עם	WITH	767b	1 a
	מן	SMALL	882a	1 b
	רמש	CREEPING THINGS	943a	2
104 26	אניה	A SHIP	58b	
	הלך	WALK	235b	1
	זה	THIS	261d	5
	יצר	FORM	427d	2 a
	לויתן	LEVIATHAN	531b	
	שחק	LAUGH	966a	3
	שם	THERE	1027a	1 a
104 27	אכל	FOOD	38a	
	עת	TIME	773d	2 b
	שבר	HOPE	960b	
104 28	טוב	A GOOD THING	375b	2
	לקט	GATHER UP	544d	1
	פתח	OPEN	835c	
104 29	אסף	GATHER	62c	4
	בהל	BE DISTURBED	96b	1
	גוע	EXPIRE	157c	
	נפש	SOUL	659c	2
	סתר	HIDE	711d	2 a
	עפר	DRY EARTH	779d	1 b
	רוח	BREATH	925c	4 d
	שוב	TURN BACK	997c	4 a
104 30	ברא	CREATE	135c	4
	חדש	RENEW	294a	1
	נפש	SOUL	659c	2
	פנה	FACE	816b	1 5
	רוח	BREATH	925c	4 d
104 31	כבוד	GLORY	458d	2 c2
	עולם	LONG DURATION	762b	2 c
	סמח	REJOICE	970c	2 b
104 32	הר	MOUNTAIN	250a	1 c
	נבט	LOOK	613d	3
	נגע	TOUCH	619a	1 b
	עשן	SMOKE	798c	1 a
	רעד	TREMBLE	944c	
104 33	זמר	MAKE MUSIC	274a	1
	חיים	LIFE	313b	1
	עוד	STILL	729c	2 aa
	שיר	SING	1010d	
104 34	על	UPON	758a	2 8
	ערב	BE SWEET	787a	1
	שיח	COMPLAINT	967a	2
	ברך	BLESS	139a	1
104 35	יה	YAH	219c	
	הלל	PRAISE	238c	2 d2
	הלל	PRAISE	238c	2 d
	חטא	SINFUL	308b	2
	תמם	BE FINISHED	1070c	5
105 1	ידה	PRAISE	392c	1 b
	ידע	MAKE KNOWN	395b	
	עלילה	WANTONNESS	760a	2 b
105 2	זמר	MAKE MUSIC	274a	1
	שיח	MUSE	967b	3 a
	שיר	SING	1010d	
105 3	בקש	SEEK	*134d	3 c
	הלל	BE BOASTFUL	239a	2
	לב	HEART	*525c	2 9a
105 4	בקש	SEEK	134d	3 b
	דרש	SEEK	*205b	1
	תמיד	CONTINUITY	556b	1 a
	עז	STRENGTH	739b	3 c
105 5	מופת	WONDER	68d	1
	זכר	REMEMBER	269d	11 d
	משפט	JUDGMENT	1048c	1 f
105 6	בחיר	CHOSEN	104c	
	בן	SON	120d	1 jb
	זרע	SOWING	283a	4 f
	עבד	SLAVE	714a	3
105 7	יהוה	YAHWEH	218d	2 1c
	משפט	JUDGMENT	1048c	1 f
105 8	ברית	COVENANT	136c	2 2b
	ברית	COVENANT	137a	3 2
	דבר	WORD	*182d	12 a
	דור	GENERATION	190a	2 c
	זכר	REMEMBER	270b	2 3 a
	עולם	LONG DURATION	762c	2 d
	צוה	GIVE CHARGE TO	845c	1 b
105 9	כרת	CUT	503d	4
	יצחק	ISAAC	850c	
	שבועה	OATH	990a	2
105 10	ברית	COVENANT	136c	2 2b
	ברית	COVENANT	137b	3 2
	חק	SOMETHING PRESCRIBED	349c	6 c
	עולם	LONG DURATION	762c	2 d
	עמד	STAND	764d	5
105 11	חבל	CORD	286d	3
	כנען	CANAAN	488d	2 a
	גור	SOJOURN	157d	1
105 12	מעט	A FEW	590c	2 e
	מת	MALE	607b	2 a
	מספר	NUMBER	709a	1 a
105 13	הלך	WALK	236b	1 b
	ממלכה	KINGDOM	575a	1
	מן	FROM	582b	5 d1
105 14	יכח	REPROVE	407a	5 a
	עשק	OPPRESS	798d	2
105 15	משיח	ANOINTED	603d	5
	נביא	PROPHET	611d	1
	נגע	TOUCH	619a	1 b
	רעע	BE EVIL	949c	1
105 16	לחם	FOOD	537a	1 a
	מטה	STAFF	641c	1
105 17	יוסף	JOSEPH	415d	1 a
	מכר	SELL	569c	
105 18	בוא	COME	98b	1 k
	ברזל	IRON	137d	3
	כבל	FETTER	459d	
	ענה	BE BOWED DOWN	776b	1
105 19	אמרה	UTTERANCE	57b	
	צרף	SMELT	864b	3
105 20	משל	RULE	605d	1
	נתר	BE FREE	684a	2
	פתח	OPEN	835c	1
105 21	אדון	LORD	11a	1 1a
	משל	RULE	605d	1
	קנין	ACQUISITION	889a	1
	שום	TO PLACE	964a	3 d
105 22	אסר	TIE	63d	3
	זקן	OLD	279a	2 b
	חכם	BE WISE	314c	
	נפש	SOUL	660d	6 a
	שר	CHIEFTAIN	978a	2 a
105 23	גור	SOJOURN	157d	1
	חם	HAM	326a	2
	ישראל	ISRAEL	975c	1
105 24	עצם	BE VAST	782c	
	פרה	BEAR FRUIT	826b	2
105 25	הפך	TURN	245c	1 c3
	נכל	KNAVISH	647d	
	עבד	SLAVE	714a	3
105 26	אהרן	AARON	14d	1
	בחר	CHOOSE	103d	1 a
	משה	MOSES	602d	
	עבד	SLAVE	714a	3
105 27	אות	SIGN	16d	4
	מופת	WONDER	69a	1
	דבר	WORD	183c	4 2
	חם	HAM	*326a	1
	חם	HAM	326a	1
	שום	TO PLACE	964d	5 c
105 28	חשך	GROW DARK	365a	1
	חשך	DARKNESS	365a	1
	מרה	BE REBELLIOUS	598b	2
	שלח	SEND	1018b	1 b
105 29	דגה	FISH	185d	
	דם	BLOOD	197c	2 o
	הפך	TURN	245c	1 c4
	מות	DIE	560b	1
105 30	חדר	CHAMBER	293d	
	צפרדע	FROGS	862c	
	שרץ	SWARM	1056c	1
105 31	אמר	SAY	56c	4
	גבול	BOUNDARY	148a	2 a
	כן	GNAT	487d	
	כן	GNAT	488a	
	ערב	SWARM	786c	
105 32	אש	FIRE	77d	6
	גשם	RAIN	177c	
	גבול	BOUNDARY	148a	2 a
	להבה	FLAME	529b	1
105 33	גבול	BOUNDARY	148a	2 a
	גפן	VINE	172c	
	נכה	SMITE	646c	4 a
	שבר	BREAK	991a	1
	תאנה	FIG-TREE	1061a	1
105 34	אמר	SAY	56c	4
	ו	AND	253c	1 k
	ילק	LOCUST	410c	A
	מספר	NUMBER	708d	1 a
	ארבה	LOCUST	916a	1
105 35	אדמה	GROUND	9c	1
	עשב	HERB	793b	
105 36	און	VIGOUR	20b	1
	בכור	FIRST-BORN	114b	1 d
	ל	TO	513d	5 cb e
	נכה	SMITE	646a	2 c
	ראשית	BEGINNING	912b	1 a
105 37	זהב	GOLD	263a	6
	זהב	GOLD	263c	
	יצא	CAUSE TO GO	424c	1 a
	כשל	TOTTER	505c	1
105 38	פחד	DREAD	808c	1
105 39	אור	BECOME LIGHT	21b	1
	מסך	COVERING	697b	1
	ענן	CLOUD	778a	1 a
	פרש	SPREAD OUT	831b	2
105 40	שבע	SATISFIED	959d	1 b
	שלו	QUAIL	969c	
	שאל	ASK	981c	1 a
	שמי	HEAVENS	1030a	1 b
105 41	הלך	WALK	232b	1 3
	זוב	FLOW	264c	1
	נהר	STREAM	625d	1
	פתח	OPEN	835b	
	צור	ROCK	849c	1
	ציה	DRYNESS	851a	
	ציה	DRYNESS	851b	
105 42	דבר	WORD	182d	1 2b
	זכר	REMEMBER	270b	2 3 a
	עבד	SLAVE	714a	3
	קדש	APARTNESS	871c	1 b
105 43	בחיר	CHOSEN	104c	
	יצא	CAUSE TO GO	424c	1 a
	רנה	RINGING CRY	943d	3
	ששון	REJOICING	965b	
105 44	ארץ	EARTH	76c	5
	ירש	TAKE POSSESSION	439c	1 a
	לאם	PEOPLE	522c	
	עמל	TROUBLE	765b	
105 45	יה	YAH	219c	
	הלל	PRAISE	238c	2 d2
	חק	SOMETHING PRESCRIBED	349d	7 g
	תורה	LAW	436a	2 a
	נצר	GUARD	665d	3
	עבור	FOR THE SAKE OF	721b	2
106 1	יה	YAH	219c	
	הלל	PRAISE	238c	2 d1

294

Ch v.	Heb	Eng	Page	Sec
	חסד	GOODNESS	339b	2 3c
	טוב	PLEASANT	374d	9 b
	ידה	PRAISE	392c	1 b
	עולם	LONG DURATION	762b	2 c
106 2	גבורה	MIGHT	150c	3
	תהלה	PRAISE	240b	4
	מלל	SPEAK	576b	
106 3	אשר	HAPPINESS	81a	
	צדקה	RIGHTEOUSNESS	842b	5
	משפט	JUDGEMNT	1048d	2 b
106 4	זכר	REMEMBER	270d	2 1 a
	ישועה	DELIVERANCE	447b	3
	פקד	ATTEND TO	823d	A 2
	רצון	GOODWILL	953c	1 a
106 5	בחיר	CHOSEN	104c	
	גוי	NATION	156d	1 b
	הלל	BE BOASTFUL	239a	2
	טובה	WELFARE	375d	1
	נחלה	PROPERTY	635b	1 e
	ראה	TO SEE	908a	8 a5
	שמחה	JOY	970d	4
106 6	חטא	MISS A GOAL OR WAY	307a	2 b
	עוה	COMMIT INIQUITY	731c	
	עם	WITH	768a	1 e
	רשע	BE WICKED	957d	3
106 7	זכר	REMEMBER	269d	1 1 d
	חסד	GOODNESS	339b	2 3a
	מרה	BE REBELLIOUS	598b	
	סוף	REEDS	693b	2 a
	שכל	BE PRUDENT	968b	2
106 8	גבורה	MIGHT	150c	3
	ידע	MAKE KNOWN	395a	
	ישע	DELIVER	446d	1 b
	מען	PURPOSE	775b	1 a
106 9	גער	REBUKE	172a	2
	הלך	WALK	236c	1 a
	חרב	BE DRY	351a	2
	סוף	REEDS	693b	2 a
	תהום	SEA	1063a	1
106 10	גאל	REDEEM	145c	3 b
	ישע	DELIVER	446d	1 b
106 11	יתר	BE LEFT OVER	451b	1
	כסה	COVER	491d	5
106 12	אמן	CONFIRM	53b	2 c
	תהלה	PRAISE	240a	1
	תהלה	PRAISE	*240a	2
	שיר	SING	1010c	
106 13	חכה	WAIT	314a	3
	עצה	ADVICE	420b	
	מהר	HASTEN	555a	2
	שכח	FORGET	1013b	1 c
106 14	אוה	DESIRE	16b	
	תאוה	DESIRE	16c	1
	אל	GOD	42d	6 e
	ישימון	WASTE	445c	B
	נסה	TEST	650b	3 b
106 15	נתן	GIVE	678d	1 e
	רזון	LEANNESS	931a	2
	שאלה	REQUEST	982c	2
106 16	אהרן	AARON	14d	
	ל	TO	511a	1 d
	נטע	PLANT	642b	1
	קדוש	HOLY	872d	2 b
	קנא	BE ZEALOUS	888c	2
106 17	אבירם	ABIRAM	4d	1
	בלע	SWALLOW UP	118a	2
	דתן	DATHAN	206d	
	עדה	CONGREGATION	417b	1
	כסה	COVER	492a	6
	פתח	OPEN	835b	
106 18	בער	BURN	129a	1
	עדה	CONGREGATION	417b	1
	להבה	FLAME	529b	1
	להט	SET ABLAZE	529d	
106 19	הר	MOUNTAIN	250a	1 a
	חרב	HOREB	352a	
	מסכה	MOLTEN IMAGE	651b	2
	עגל	CALF	722b	
106 20	ב	IN	90a	3 3b
	תבנית	FIGURE	125d	3
	כבוד	GLORY	459c	7
	מור	CHANGE	558c	2
	עשב	HERB	793b	
	שור	A HEAD OF CATTLE	1004a	
106 21	אל	GOD	42d	6 e
	גדול	GREAT	153c	9
	ישע	DELIVER	446d	1 b
106 22	חם	HAM	326a	2
	ירא	CAUSE FEAR	431d	2
	סוף	REEDS	693b	2 a
106 23	אמר	SAY	56c	4
	בחיר	CHOSEN	104c	
	חמה	RAGE	*404d	2 c
	חמה	RAGE	404d	2 c
	לולא	IF NOT	530c	A
	לולא	IF NOT	*530c	D
	מן	FROM	583b	7 ba
	פרץ	BURSTING FORTH	829d	2
	שוב	TURN BACK	999d	6 a
106 24	אמן	CONFIRM	53a	2 b
	חמדה	DESIRE	326d	
	מאס	REJECT	549c	1 a
106 25	רגן	MURMUR	920d	1
106 26	יד	HAND	389c	1 d
	נפל	FALL	658a	2

Ch v.	Heb	Eng	Page	Sec
	נשא	LIFT	670b	1 b 1
106 27	ארץ	EARTH	76c	5
	זרה	SCATTER	280a	1
	זרע	SOWING	283a	4 g
	נפל	FALL	658a	2
106 28	בעלפעור	BAAL-PEOR	128b	
	זבח	SACRIFICE	257c	12
106 29	מות	DIE	559d	1 d
	צמד	BIND	855a	
	כעס	VEX	495a	2
	מנפע	PLAGUE	620b	3
	מעלל	DEED	760b	1
	פרץ	BREAK THROUGH	829c	6
106 30	מנפה	PLAGUE	620b	3
	עמד	STAND	764b	6 a
	עצר	RESTRAIN	783d	
	פלל	INTERVENE	813b	
106 31	דור	PERIOD	189d	1 b
	חשב	THINK	363c	3
	עולם	LONG DURATION	762b	2 b4
	צדקה	RIGHTEOUSNESS	842b	5
106 32	ל	TO	511a	1 e
	מי	WATER	565b	1 a
	עבור	FOR THE SAKE OF	721a	1 a
	קצף	BE WROTH	893b	2
	מריבה	MERIBAH	937b	2
106 33	רעע	BE EVIL	949c	3
	בטה	SPEAK RASHLY	104d	1
	מרה	BE REBELLIOUS	598b	
	רוח	BREATH	926a	9 f
106 34	אמר	SAY	56c	4
	אשר	THAT	83d	8 e
106 35	למד	LEARN	540d	1
	ערב	TAKE ON PLEDGE	786d	2 a
106 36	מוקש	BAIT	430d	1
	עבד	WORK	713d	4 b
	עצב	IDOL	781b	
106 37	זבח	SLAUGHTER FOR SACRIFICE	256d	1 1 bb
	זבח	SLAUGHTER FOR SACRIFICE	257a	13
	שד	DEMON	994a	
	דם	BLOOD	196d	2 d
106 38	דם	BLOOD	197b	21
	זבח	SLAUGHTER FOR SACRIFICE	257b	2
	זבח	SLAUGHTER FOR SACRIFICE	257b	2
	חנף	BE POLLUTED	338a	1
	כנען	CANAAN	488d	2 a
	נקי	CLEAN	667c	1
	עצב	IDOL	781b	
106 39	זנה	COMMIT FORNICATION	276a	3
	טמא	BE UNCLEAN	379a	2
	מעלל	DEED	760b	1
106 40	חרה	BURN	354a	2 a
	נחלה	PROPERTY	635b	1 e
	תעב	BE ABHORRED	1073b	1 a1
106 41	משל	RULE	605d	1
106 42	כנע	BE HUMBLED	488c	2
	לחץ	OPPRESS	537d	2
	תחת	UNDERNEATH	*1065c	2 1 d
106 43	עצה	ADVICE	420b	
	מכך	HUMILIATED	568d	
	מרה	BE REBELLIOUS	598b	
	עון	INIQUITY	731c	3
	פעם	OCCURRENCE	822a	3 a
	רב	MUCH	913a	1 b
	צר	STRAITS	865b	
106 44	ראה	TO SEE	908a	8 a2
	רנה	RINGING CRY	943c	1
106 45	ברית	COVENANT	136c	2 2c
	ברית	COVENANT	137a	3 2
	זכר	REMEMBER	270b	2 3 a
	חסד	GOODNESS	339b	2 3a
	נחם	BE SORRY	637a	2
	רב	MULTITUDE	914a	1
106 46	נתן	GIVE	681a	3 b
	רחמים	COMPASSION	933c	2
106 47	יהוה	YAHWEH	218d	2 1c
	תהלה	PRAISE	240b	4
	ידה	PRAISE	392c	1 b
	ישע	DELIVER	446d	1 b
	קבץ	GATHER	868a	1
	שבח	PRAISE	986d	2
106 48	אלהים	GOD	44c	4 ba
	אמן	VERILY	53b	
	אמן	VERILY	53b	
	ברך	BLESS	138d	2 a
	יה	YAH	219c	
	הלל	PRAISE	238c	2 d2
	עולם	LONG DURATION	763a	2 m
107 1	חסד	GOODNESS	339b	2 3c
	טוב	PLEASANT	374d	9 b
	ידה	PRAISE	392c	1 b
	עולם	LONG DURATION	762b	2 c
107 2	גאל	REDEEM	145c	3 c
	גאל	REDEEM	145c	3 c
107 3	ארץ	EARTH	76c	5
	מזרח	PLACE OF SUNRISE	281a	2 b
	ים	SEA	411b	9
	ימין	RIGHT	412a	4
	מערב	WEST	788a	
	קבץ	GATHER	868a	1
107 4	מושב	DWELLING	444b	2 a

Ch v.	Heb	Eng	Page	Sec
	ישימון	WASTE	445c	B
	מצא	FIND	592d	1 a
	עיר	CITY	746c	1 i
	תעה	ERR	1073c	1
107 5	גם	ALSO	169b	1
	עטף	BE FEEBLE	742c	
	צמא	THIRSTY	854d	
107 6	רעב	HUNGRY	944c	
	מצוקה	STRAIGNESS	748b	
	צעק	CRY	858c	1 b
	צר	STRAITS	865b	
107 7	דרך	TREAD	202b	3
	מושב	DWELLING	444b	2 a
	ישר	STRAIGHT	449a	1
107 8	עיר	CITY	746c	1 i
	חסד	GOODNESS	339a	2 1a
	ידה	PRAISE	392c	1 b
107 9	טוב	A GOOD THING	375b	2
	מלא	FILL	570c	1
	נפש	SOUL	660c	5 a
	נפש	SOUL	660c	5 a
	רעב	HUNGRY	944c	
	רעב	HUNGRY	944d	
	שבע	SATISFIED	959d	1 a
	שקק	RUN	1055b	
107 10	אסר	PRISONER	64a	
	ברול	IRON	137c	3
	חשך	DARKNESS	365a	3 a
	עני	AFFLICTION	777a	1
	צלמות	DEATH-SHADOW	853c	2 a
107 11	אל	GOD	42d	6 e
	אמר	WORD	57a	1
	עצה	ADVICE	420b	
	מרה	BE REBELLIOUS	598b	
	נאץ	CONTEMN	610d	
	עליון	HIGHEST	751b	1
107 12	כנע	HUMBLE	488c	1
	כשל	STUMBLE	505c	1
	עזר	HELP	740c	
	עמל	TROUBLE	765b	
107 13	זעק	CRY	277b	2 a
	ישע	DELIVER	446d	1 b
	מצוקה	STRAITNESS	748b	
	צר	STRAITS	865b	
107 14	מוסר	BAND	64c	
	חשך	DARKNESS	365a	3 a
	יצא	BRING OUT	424d	2
	נתק	TEAR APART	683d	1
	צלמות	DEATH-SHADOW	853c	2 a
107 15	חסד	GOODNESS	339a	2 1a
	ידה	PRAISE	392c	1 b
107 16	ברול	IRON	137c	3
	בריח	BAR	138b	2
	גדע	HEW	154c	
	דלת	DOOR	195b	3
	שבר	BREAK	991a	
107 17	דרך	WAY	203d	6 d
	מן	ON ACCOUNT OF	580b	2 f
	עון	INIQUITY	730d	1
	ענה	BE BOWED DOWN	776c	2
	פשע	TRANSGRESSION	833c	3 a
107 18	אכל	FOOD	38a	
	מות	DEATH	560d	3
	נגע	REACH	619c	2
	שער	GATE	1045b	4
	תעב	BE ABHORRED	1073b	1 c
107 19	זעק	CRY	277b	2 a
	ישע	DELIVER	446d	1 b
	מצוקה	STRAITNESS	748b	
	צר	STRAITS	865b	
107 20	דבר	WORD	182d	1 2a
	מלט	SLIP AWAY	572c	3
	רפא	HEAL	950c	1 a
	שחת	PIT	1005d	
	שלח	SEND	1018c	2b
107 21	חסד	GOODNESS	339a	2 1a
	ידה	PRAISE	392c	1 b
107 22	זבח	SACRIFICE	257c	2 4
	תודה	THANK-OFFERING	393a	4
	רנה	RINGING CRY	943d	3
107 23	אניה	A SHIP	58b	
	ירד	GO DOWN	433a	1 g
	מלאכה	WORK	522a	3 b
107 24	הם	THEY	241c	2
	מצולה	DEPTH	847a	
107 25	אמר	SAY	56c	4
	סערה	TEMPEST	704c	
	עמד	STAND	765a	6 f
	רוח	BREATH	924d	2a
	רום	BE HIGH	927b	2 b
107 26	ירד	GO DOWN	433a	1 h
	מוג	MELT	556b	
	רעה	MISERY	949b	1
	תהום	SEA	1063a	2
107 27	בלע	SWALLOW UP	*118b	2 a
	בלע	SWALLOW UP	118c	
	חגג	MAKE PILGRIMAGE	290d	3
	חכמה	WISDOM	315b	1
	נוע	WAVE	631b	1
	שכר	DRUNKEN	1016c	
107 28	יצא	BRING OUT	424d	2
	מצוקה	STRAITNESS	748b	
	צעק	CRY	858c	1 b
	צר	STRAITS	865b	
107 29	דממה	WHISPER	199a	
	חשה	BE SILENT	364c	

Ch v.	Heb	Eng	Page	Sec
	סערה	TEMPEST	704c	
107 30	קום	STAND	879a	5
	חפץ	DELIGHT	343b	2
	מחוז	CITY	562c	
	נחה	LEAD	635a	
	שתק	BE QUIET	1060c	
107 31	חסד	GOODNESS	339a	2 1a
	ידה	PRAISE	392c	1 b
107 32	הלל	PRAISE	238b	2 b
	זן	OLD	279a	2 b
	מושב	SEAT	444b	1 b
	עם	PEOPLE	766c	1
	קהל	ASSEMBLY	874d	1 d
	רום	BE HIGH	927b	3
107 33	מוצא	GOING FORTH	425d	3 a
	צמאון	THIRSTY GROUND	855a	
107 34	ארץ	EARTH	76b	3 b
	מלחה	SALTNESS	572a	
	פרי	FRUIT	826b	1
	רעה	MISERY	949b	3
107 35	אגם	POOL	8c	2
	ארץ	EARTH	76b	3 b
	מוצא	GOING FORTH	425d	3 a
	ציה	DRYNESS	851a	
107 36	ישב	CAUSE TO SIT	443d	3 a
	מושב	DWELLING	444b	2 a
	כון	ESTABLISH	466d	1 a
	עיר	CITY	746c	1 i
	רחם	WOMB	*933b	1
	רעב	HUNGRY	944c	
107 37	תבואה	PRODUCT	100a	1
	זרע	SOW	281c	1 b
	נטע	PLANT	642c	1
	עשה	DO	795a	2 7
	פרי	FRUIT	826b	1
107 38	ברך	BLESS	139a	2 a
	מעט	BE SMALL	589c	A
	רבה	BECOME MANY	915a	1 a
107 39	יגון	GRIEF	387b	1
	מן	OUT OF	580a	2 eb
	מעט	BE SMALL	589c	
	עצר	RESTRAINT	783d	
	שחח	BOW	1005d	1
107 40	בוז	CONTEMPT	100c	2
	דרך	WAY	202d	1
	נדיב	NOBLE	622a	2
	פך	POUR OUT	1049d	2 a
	תהו	FORMLESSNESS	1062c	1
	תעה	ERR	1073c	1
107 41	אביון	NEEDY	2d	
	עני	AFFLICTION	777a	1
	צאן	SMALL CATTLE	838b	2
	שגב	BE HIGH	960c	1
107 42	עולה	INJUSTICE	732d	2
	ישר	STRAIGHT	779b	3 c2
	פה	MOUTH	805a	2 a
107 43	אלה	THESE	41c	A
	בין	DISCERN	107a	1 b
	חכם	WISE	314c	5
	חסד	GOODNESS	339c	4
	מי	WHO	567b	G
	שמר	KEEP	1036d	1 d
108 1	מזמור	MELODY	274c	
	שיר	SONG	*1010b	2
108 2	אלהים	GOD	44b	4 a
	זמר	MAKE MUSIC	274b	1
	כבוד	HONOR	459b	5
	כון	BE FIRM	465d	2
	לב	HEART	*525a	2 4
	שיר	SING	1010d	
108 3	זמר	MAKE MUSIC	*274b	1
	כנור	LYRE	490b	
	נבל	HARP	614c	
	עור	ROUSE ONESELF	735a	
	עור	ROUSE ONESELF	735c	1
	שחר	DAWN	1007b	
108 4	זמר	MAKE MUSIC	274a	1
	זמר	MAKE MUSIC	*274b	1
	ידה	PRAISE	392c	1 a2
	לאם	PEOPLE	522c	
108 5	אמת	FIRMNESS	54b	3 b
	גדול	GREAT	153b	6 c
	חסד	GOODNESS	339b	2 3b
	על	UPON	759b	4 2d
	שחק	DUST	1007a	2
108 6	אלהים	GOD	44b	4 a
	כבוד	GLORY	458b	2 c2
	רום	BE HIGH	927a	2 c
108 7	חלץ	DRAW OFF OR OUT	322d	
	ידיד	BELOVED	391d	1
	ישע	DELIVER	446d	1 b
108 8	אלהים	GOD	44b	4 a
	חלק	DIVIDE	323d	1
	מדד	MEASURE	551b	2
	סכות	SUCCOTH	697d	1
	עלז	EXULT	759c	
108 9	קדש	APARTNESS	871d	2 d
	אפרים	EPHRAIM	68c	4
	חקק	CUT IN	349b	B
	מנשה	MANASSEH	586c	1 b2 b
	מעוז	PLACE OF SAFETY	732a	2
	ראש	HEAD	910d	1 a
108 10	נעל	SANDAL	653b	
	סיר	POT	696c	1 b
	פלשת	PHILISTIA	814b	
	רחץ	WASHING	934d	
	שלך	THROW	1021b	2 a
108 11	מבצר	FORTIFICATION	131c	
	יבל	CONDUCT	385a	3
	נחה	LEAD	634d	
	מעור	SIEGE	849a	2
108 12	אלהים	GOD	44b	4 a
	זנח	REJECT	276b	
	יצא	GO OUT	424a	2 c
	צבא	ARMY	839a	1 a
108 13	יהב	GIVE	396d	1
	תשועה	DELIVERANCE	448b	1
	עזרה	HELP	741a	1
	צר	STRAITS	865a	
	שוא	EMPTINESS	996a	1
108 14	אלהים	GOD	43d	3
	אלהים	GOD	44b	4 a
	בוס	TRAMPLE	100d	
	חיל	STRENGTH	298d	1 b
109 1	אלהים	GOD	44d	
	תהלה	PRAISE	240a	1
	מזמור	MELODY	274c	
	חרש	BE SILENT	361a	1
109 2	את	WITH	86a	1 db
	לשון	TONGUE	546c	1 b
	פתח	OPEN	835b	
	מרמה	DECEIT	941b	1
	שקר	DECEPTION	1055d	5
109 3	חנם	OUT OF FAVOR	336d	C
	לחם	ENGAGE IN BATTLE	535c	
	סבב	SURROUND	686a	2 d
	שנאה	HATING	971d	1
109 4	אהבה	LOVE	13b	1
	שטן	ACT AS ADVERSARY	966c	
	תחת	INSTEAD	1066a	2 2b b
109 5	אהבה	LOVE	13b	1
	טובה	WELFARE	375d	3
	על	UPON	756c	27a b
	שום	TO PLACE	963b	1
	שנאה	HATING	971d	1 b
	תחת	INSTEAD	1066a	2 2b b
109 6	ימין	RIGHT HAND	411d	2
	שטן	ADVERSARY	966c	1
109 7	חטאה	SIN	308b	1
	יצא	GO OUT	422d	1 c
	שפט	JUDGE	1048a	2
109 8	אחר	ANOTHER	*29c	
	לקח	TAKE	543a	4 c
	מעט	A FEW	590a	1 c
	פקדה	OVERSIGHT	824b	4
109 9	אלמנה	WIDOW	48b	
	יתום	ORPHAN	450c	
109 10	דרש	SEEK	205d	2
	חרבה	WASTE	352a	1
	חרב	SWORD	353a	3
	מן	OUT OF	579a	2 ab
	נוע	TOTTER	631b	2
	שאל	ASK	982b	2
109 11	בז	SPOIL	102d	
	זור	BE A STRANGER	266c	2 a
	יגיע	TOIL	388c	2
	נקש	STRIKE	669c	
	נשה	LEND	674c	
109 12	אל	NOT	39a	A a
	חנן	SHOW FAVOR	336a	1 b
	חסד	GOODNESS	338d	1 2
	יתום	ORPHAN	450c	
	משך	DRAW	604c	5
109 13	אחר	ANOTHER	29d	
	אחרית	END	31b	D
	דור	GENERATION	190a	2 c
	כרת	CUT OFF	504c	2 b
	ל	TO	518a	7 bf
	מחה	WIPE OUT	562b	2
109 14	זכר	REMEMBER	270d	1 d
	חטאת	SIN	309a	1 d4
	מחה	WIPE OUT	562b	2
	עון	INIQUITY	731b	1 c5
109 15	זכר	REMEMBRANCE	271b	1 a
	כרת	CUT OFF	504c	2 c
	תמיד	CONTINUITY	556b	1 a
	נגד	IN FRONT	617b	1 b
109 16	ש	NEEDY	2d	
	אביון	NEEDY	2d	
	זכר	REMEMBER	269d	1 2 d
	חסד	GOODNESS	338d	1 2
	כאה	BE COWED	456c	
	ל	TO	518a	7 bh
	מות	DIE	560a	
	עני	POOR	776d	3
	עשה	DO	794b	1 3
	רדף	PURSUE	922d	1 f
109 17	אהב	LOVE	13a	1
	ברכה	BLESSING	139d	1 c
	חפץ	DELIGHT IN	342d	1 a
	קללה	CURSE	887a	
	רחק	BE DISTANT	934d	2
109 18	לבש	PUT ON	528a	B
	מד	GARMENT	551c	3
	קללה	CURSE	887a	
	קרב	INWARD PART	899a	1 a
	שמן	OIL	1032b	2 e
109 19	בגד	GARMENT	94a	1
	חגר	GIRD	291d	2
	תמיד	CONTINUITY	556b	1 a
	מזח	GIRDLE	561b	
109 20	עטה	WRAP ONESELF	741d	
	את	WITH	87a	4 c
	דבר	SPEAK	180c	2
	דבר	SPEAK	180c	2
	זה	THIS	261b	3
	פעלה	WORK	821d	2
	רע	EVIL	948d	2
	שטן	ACT AS ADVERSARY	966c	
109 21	אדון	LORD	11d	5
	את	WITH	86b	1 db
	חסד	GOODNESS	339b	2 3d
	טוב	PLEASANT	374d	9 b
	מען	PURPOSE	775b	1 a
	עשה	DO	794b	1 2
109 22	אביון	NEEDY	2d	
	חלל	BORE	319b	2
	לב	HEART	525c	2 9b
	עני	POOR	776d	3
	קרב	INWARD PART	899b	2 a
109 23	הלך	WALK	235a	2
	נטה	BEND	640b	3 a
	נער	SHAKE OUT	654c	
	צל	SHADOW	853b	3
	ארבה	LOCUST	916a	
109 24	ברך	KNEE	139c	
	בשר	FLESH	142c	1 b
	כחש	GROW LEAN	471a	
	כחש	LEANNESS	*471c	2
	כשל	TOTTER	505c	2
	מן	FROM	583c	7 bb
	צום	FASTING	847b	
	שמן	FAT	1032a	1
109 25	ב	IN	90b	3 4
	חרפה	REPROACH	358a	3
	נוע	TOTTER	631c	2
109 26	יהוה	YAHWEH	219a	2 1f
	חסד	GOODNESS	339a	2 1c
	ישע	DELIVER	446d	1 b
	עזר	HELP	740b	
109 28	ברך	BLESS	139a	2 a
	הם	THEY	241b	1 c
	עבד	SLAVE	714c	6
	קום	STAND	878a	2
	קלל	BE SLIGHT	886c	1
109 29	בשת	SHAME	102a	1
	כלמה	IGNOMINY	484b	2
	לבש	PUT ON	528a	B
	מעיל	ROBE	591c	4
	עטה	WRAP ONESELF	741d	
	שמן	ACT AS ADVERSARY	966c	
109 30	הלל	PRAISE	238b	2 b
	ידה	PRAISE	392c	1 a2
109 31	אביון	NEEDY	2d	
	ימין	RIGHT HAND	411d	2 a
	ישע	DELIVER	446d	1 b
	שפט	JUDGE	1047d	3 c2
	שפט	JUDGE	1048a	
110 1	הדם	FOOTSTOOL	213c	
	מזמור	MELODY	274c	
	ימין	RIGHT HAND	411d	2
	ישב	SIT	442c	1 a
	מן	OUT OF	579a	2 ab
	נאם	UTTERANCE	610c	2
	עד	UNTIL	725a	2 1b b
	רגל	FOOT	919d	1 a
	שית	PUT	1011c	1
110 2	ר	STAFF	641d	1
	עז	STRENGTH	739a	1
	קרב	INWARD PART	899b	1 f5
	רדה	HAVE DOMINION	922a	
110 3	הדר	ORNAMENT	214b	1
	חיל	STRENGTH	298c	1 a
	טל	NIGHT-MIST	*378c	
	טל	NIGHT-MIST	378d	
	ילדות	YOUTH	409c	
	ל	TO	512b	5 aa
	נדבה	VOLUNTARINESS	621d	1
	קדש	APARTNESS	871d	2 e
	קדש	APARTNESS	872b	4 b
	רחם	WOMB	933b	1
	שחר	DAWN	1007b	
	משחר	DAWN	1007d	
110 4	דברה	MANNER	184b	1
	כהן	PRIEST-KING	463a	1
	מלכיצדק	MELCHIZEDEK	575d	
	נחם	BE SORRY	637a	2
	על	UPON	754a	2 1f a
	עולם	LONG DURATION	762d	2 h
	שבע	SWEAR	989c	2
110 5	אדון	LORD	11c	3 2b
	ימין	RIGHT HAND	411d	2
	מחץ	SHATTER	563c	
	על	UPON	756a	2 6a
	על	UPON	759a	4 2c
110 6	גויה	CORPSE	156c	2 a
	דין	JUDGE	192b	3
	על	UPON	752c	21
110 7	דרך	WAY	202d	1
	כן	SO	487b	3 f
	נחל	TORRENT	636b	1
	ראש	HEAD	911b	8
	רום	BE HIGH	927b	1 a1
	ש	DRINK	1059b	1 a

Ch v.	Heb	Eng	Page	Sec
111 1	יה	YAH	219c	
	הלל	PRAISE	238c	2 d1
	ידה	PRAISE	392c	1 a2
	עדה	CONGREGATION	417a	1
	לבב	HEART	523c	2 2
	סוד	ASSEMBLY	691c	1 b
	ישר	STRAIGHT	779b	3 c2
111 2	גדול	GREAT	153b	6 c
	דרש	SEEK	205c	6
	חפץ	DELIGHTING IN	343a	1
	ל	TO	514a	5 e
111 3	הדר	SPLENDOUR	214b	2
	הוד	SPLENDOUR	217b	2
	עד	PERPETUITY	723c	2 d
	עמד	STAND	764b	3 c
	צדקה	RIGHTEOUSNESS	842c	6 a
111 4	זכר	REMEMBRANCE	271b	1 c
	חנון	GRACIOUS	337a	
	רחום	COMPASSIONATE	933d	
111 5	ברית	COVENANT	136c	2 2c
	ברית	COVENANT	137a	3 2
	זכר	REMEMBER	270b	2 3 a
	טרף	TEAR	*383a	
	טרף	PREY	383c	2
	ירא	FEAR	431c	3 b
	עולם	LONG DURATION	762c	2 d
111 6	כח	STRENGTH	471a	3
	נחלה	PROPERTY	635b	1 c
111 7	אמן	CONFIRM	53a	4
	אמת	FIRMNESS	54b	3 b
	פקוד	PRECEPT	824c	
	משפט	JUDGMENT	1048d	2 a
111 8	אמת	FIRMNESS	54b	3 b
	ישר	STRAIGHTNESS	449c	2
	סמך	LEAN	702a	2
	עד	PERPETUITY	723d	2 e
	ישר	STRAIGHT	779b	4
111 9	ברית	COVENANT	136c	2 2c
	ברית	COVENANT	137a	3 1
	ירא	BE REVERED	431c	3 b
	פדות	RANSOM	804b	
	צוה	CHARGE	845d	2 d
	קדוש	HOLY	872c	1 a
111 10	תהלה	PRAISE	239d	1
	חכמה	WISDOM	315d	5 c
	טוב	PLEASANT	374d	8
	יראה	FEAR	432a	3
	עד	PERPETUITY	723c	2 d
	עמד	STAND	764b	3 c
	ראשית	BEGINNING	912a	1 a
	שכל	PRUDENCE	968c	2
112 1	אשר	HAPPINESS	81a	
	יה	YAH	219c	
	הלל	PRAISE	238c	2 d1
	חפץ	DELIGHT IN	342d	1 a
	ירא	FEAR	431c	3 b
112 2	ברך	BLESS	139d	2 a
	גבור	STRONG	150a	1
	דור	GENERATION	190b	3
	זרע	SOWING	282d	4 c
	ישר	STRAIGHT	779b	3 c2
112 3	הון	WEALTH	223c	1
	עד	PERPETUITY	723c	2 d
	עמד	STAND	764b	3 c
112 4	חנון	GRACIOUS	337a	
	חשך	DARKNESS	365a	3 a
	ישר	STRAIGHT	779b	3 c2
	רחום	COMPASSIONATE	933d	
112 5	חנן	SHOW FAVOR	336a	1 b
	טוב	PLEASANT	374c	7
	כול	SUPPORT	465b	3
	לוה	BORROW	531a	
	משפט	JUDGMENT	1048c	1 c
112 6	זכר	REMEMBRANCE	271b	1 a
	מוט	SHAKE	557a	
112 7	בטח	TRUST	105a	1 3a
	ירא	FEAR	431b	1 c
	כון	BE FIRM	465d	2
	לב	HEART	525a	2 4
	רע	EVIL	948b	1
	שמועה	REPORT	1035b	1
112 8	ירא	FEAR	431a	1 a
	סמך	LEAN	702a	2
	עד	UNTIL	725a	2 1b b
	ראה	TO SEE	908a	8 a6
112 9	אביון	NEEDY	2d	
	כבוד	HONOR	459a	3
	עד	PERPETUITY	723c	2 d
	עמד	STAND	764b	3 c
	פזר	SCATTER	808b	
	קרן	HORN	902a	2
	רום	BE HIGH	927a	2 b
112 10	אבד	PERISH	1d	2
	תאוה	DESIRE	16c	1
	חרק	GNASH	359b	
	כעס	BE ANGRY	495a	1
	מסס	MELT	587d	1
	שן	TOOTH	1042a	1 a
113 1	יה	YAH	219c	
	הלל	PRAISE	238c	2 d1
	עבד	SLAVE	714b	4
113 2	ברך	BLESS	139b	1
	עולם	LONG DURATION	763a	2 m
	עתה	NOW	774a	1 a
113 3	מבוא	ENTERING	100a	1
	הלל	PRAISE	239a	2
113 4	מזרח	PLACE OF SUNRISE	280d	1
	כבוד	GLORY	458d	2 c2
	רום	BE HIGH	926d	1 b
113 5	גבה	BE HIGH	147a	
	יהוה	YAHWEH	218d	2 1c
	ל	TO	517c	7 bb
	שפל	BECOME LOW	*1050b	3
113 6	ל	TO	517c	7 bb
	שפל	BECOME LOW	1050b	3
113 7	אביון	NEEDY	2d	
	דל	POOR	195d	
	עפר	DRY EARTH	780a	2 e
	קום	STAND	878d	1 a
	רום	BE HIGH	927c	1 a2
	אשפת	REFUSE-HEAP	1046b	
113 8	ישב	CAUSE TO SIT	443d	3 a
	נדיב	NOBLE	622a	2
113 9	אם	MOTHER	51c	1
	יה	YAH	219c	
	הלל	PRAISE	238c	2 d2
	ישב	MARRY	*443d	4
	ישב	CAUSE TO SIT	443d	3 a
	עקר	BARREN	785d	
	שמח	JOYFUL	970c	1 a
114 1	בית	HOUSE	110a	5 dg
	יצא	GO OUT	422d	1 a
	לעז	TALK INDISTINCTLY	541d	
114 2	עם	PEOPLE	767a	5 h
	יהודה	JUDAH	397b	2
	ממשלה	RULE	606b	3
	קדש	APARTNESS	872b	4 b
114 3	אחור	HINDER SIDE	30c	C a
	נום	FLEE	630d	1
	סבב	TURN ABOUT	685c	1 a
114 4	איל	RAM	17d	1
	בן	SON	121c	7 b
	גבעה	HILL	149a	3
	הר	MOUNTAIN	250b	1 c
	רקד	SKIP ABOUT	955a	
114 5	אחור	HINDER SIDE	30c	C a
	מה	WHAT	552d	1 ac
	נום	FLEE	630d	1
	סבב	TURNABOUT	685c	1 a
114 6	איל	RAM	17d	1
	בן	SON	121c	7 b
	גבעה	HILL	149a	3
	הר	MOUNTAIN	250b	1 c
	רקד	SKIP ABOUT	955a	
114 7	אדון	LORD	11a	1 2
	אלה	GOD	43a	2
	ארץ	EARTH	76a	1 b
	חול	WHIRL	297a	2 b
	יעקב	JACOB	785a	2
	פנה	FACE	818a	2 5b
114 8	אגם	POOL	8c	2
	הפך	TURN	245c	1 c4
	חלמיש	FLINT	321d	
	מעין	SPRING	745d	
	צור	ROCK	849c	1 a
115 1	אמת	FIRMNESS	54a	3 b
	חסד	GOODNESS	339a	2 2
	כבוד	HONOR	459b	6 b
	נתן	GIVE	679a	1 h
115 2	איה	WHERE	32c	
	מה	HOW	554b	4 d
	נא	PART OF ENTREATY	609d	4 f
115 3	חפץ	DELIGHT IN	343a	2 a
115 4	זהב	GOLD	263a	6
	זהב	GOLD	263c	1
	כסף	SILVER	494b	7
	עצב	IDOL	781b	
	מעשה	DEED	796a	2 a3
115 5	עין	EYE	744a	1 c
	פה	MOUTH	805b	2 d
	ראה	TO SEE	907b	4
115 6	אזן	EAR	24a	2 a
	אף	NOSE	60a	1 a
	ריח	SMELL	926b	
	שמע	HEAR	1033d	1 e
115 7	גרון	THROAT	173c	2
	הגה	UTTER	211d	2
	הלך	WALK	235b	1
	מוש	FEEL	559b	
	רגל	FOOT	919d	1 c
115 8	בטח	TRUST	105a	1 3c
115 9	בטח	TRUST	105a	1 3a
	מגן	SHIELD	171c	
	עזר	HELP	740d	2
115 10	אהרן	AARON	14d	
	בטח	TRUST	105a	1 3a
	בית	HOUSE	110b	5 dl
	מגן	SHIELD	171c	
	עזר	HELP	740d	2
115 11	בטח	TRUST	105a	1 3a
	מגן	SHIELD	171c	
	ירא	FEAR	431c	3 b
	עזר	HELP	740d	2
115 12	אהרן	AARON	14d	
	בית	HOUSE	110b	5 dl
	ברך	BLESS	139a	2 a
	זכר	REMEMBER	270b	2 1 c
115 13	ברך	BLESS	139a	2 a
	ירא	FEAR	431c	3 b
	קטן	SMALL	882a	2 b2
115 14	יסף	ADD	415b	1
115 15	ברך	BLESS	138d	2 b
115 17	דומה	SILENCE	189a	
	יה	YAH	219c	
	הלל	PRAISE	*238d	2 b
	הלל	PRAISE	238c	2 d2
	ירד	GO DOWN	433b	1 i
115 18	לא	NOT	518d	1 ac
	ברך	BLESS	139a	1
	יה	YAH	219c	
	יה	YAH	219c	
	הלל	PRAISE	238c	2 d2
	עולם	LONG DURATION	762a	2 a
	עולם	LONG DURATION	763a	2 m
	עתה	NOW	774a	1 a
116 1	אהב	LOVE	13a	3
116 2	אזן	EAR	24b	2 b
	תחנון	SUPPLICATION FOR FAVOR	337d	2
	נטה	INCLINE	641a	3 e
	קרא	CALL	845b	2 d
116 3	אפף	SURROUND	67c	
	חבל	CORD	286c	1
	יגון	GRIEF	387b	
	מצא	FIND	593a	1 f
	מצא	FIND	593a	3 e
	מר	STRAITS	865c	
	שאול	SHEOL	983a	1
116 4	אנא	AH, NOW	58a	
	מלט	SLIP AWAY	572c	3
	נפש	SOUL	660a	3 c
116 5	חנן	GRACIOUS	337a	
	צדיק	JUST	843a	1 d
	רחם	LOVE	933c	1
116 6	דלל	BE LOW	195c	
	ישע	DELIVER	446c	1
	ל	TO	*512a	3 b
	פתי	SIMPLE	834c	
116 7	מנוח	CONDITION OF REST	629d	2
116 8	שוב	TURN BACK	997d	6 c
	דחי	STUMBLING	191a	
	דמעה	TEARS	199c	
	חלץ	DRAW OFF OR OUT	322d	2
	לא	NOT	*520d	4 bb
	עין	EYE	744b	1 h
116 9	ארץ	EARTH	76c	5
	הלך	WALK	236b	2
	חי	ALIVE	312a	1 b
116 10	אמן	CONFIRM	53a	2 a
	ענה	BE BOWED DOWN	776a	3
116 11	חפז	BE IN TREPIDATION	342a	1
	כזב	LIE	469b	
	כזב	LIE	*469d	
116 12	על	UPON	756c	27 a b
	שוב	TURN BACK	999c	4 a
116 13	ישועה	DELIVERANCE	447b	3
	כוס	CUP	468a	
	ל	TO	514a	5 d
	נא	PART OF ENTREATY	609d	4 g
	נגד	IN FRONT	*617b	1 aa
	נדר	VOW	624a	1
	שלם	BE COMPLETE	1022c	4
116 15	חסיד	KIND	*339d	2 b
	חסיד	KIND	339d	2 b
	יקר	PRECIOUS	430a	1 b
	ל	TO	513d	5 cb e
116 16	אמה	MAID	51a	2
	אנא	AH, NOW	58a	
	מוסר	BAND	64c	
	ל	TO	512a	3 b
	עבד	SLAVE	714a	3
	פתח	OPEN	835c	2
116 17	זבח	SACRIFICE	257c	24
	תודה	THANK-OFFERING	393a	4
	ל	TO	514a	5 d
	נא	PART OF ENTREATY	609d	4 g
	נגד	IN FRONT	*617b	1 aa
	נדר	VOW	624a	1
	שלם	BE COMPLETE	1022c	4
116 19	יה	YAH	219c	
	הלל	PRAISE	238c	2 d2
	חצר	ENCLOSURE	347a	3 b
117 1	אמה	TRIBE	52c	
	הלל	PRAISE	238b	2 c
	שבח	PRAISE	986d	1
117 2	אמת	FIRMNESS	54b	3 b
	גבר	BE STRONG	149d	2 b
	יה	YAH	219c	
	הלל	PRAISE	238c	2 d2
	חסד	GOODNESS	339b	2 2
	על	UPON	756c	27 a b
	עולם	LONG DURATION	762b	2 c
118 1	חסד	GOODNESS	339b	2 3c
	טוב	PLEASANT	374d	9 b
	ידה	PRAISE	392c	1 b
	עולם	LONG DURATION	762b	2 c
118 2	חסד	GOODNESS	339b	2 3c
	נא	PART OF ENTREATY	609b	3 c
	עולם	LONG DURATION	762b	2 c
118 3	אהרן	AARON	14d	
	בית	HOUSE	110b	5 dl

Ch	v.	Heb	Eng	Page	Sec
		חסד	GOODNESS	339b	2 3c
		נא	PART OF EN-TREATY	609b	3 c
118	4	עולם	LONG DURATION	762b	2 c
		חסד	GOODNESS	339b	2 3c
		ירא	FEAR	431c	3 b
		עולם	LONG DURATION	762b	2 c
118	5	יה	YAH	219c	
		מצר	STRAITS	865c	
		מרחב	ROOMY PLACE	932c	
118	6	ירא	FEAR	431a	1 a
		ל	TO	515c	5 hc
118	7	ב	IN	88d	17 a
		ל	TO	515c	5 hc
		ראה	TO SEE	908a	8 a6
118	8	בטח	TRUST	105a	13 b
		חסה	SEEK REFUGE	340b	
		טוב	PLEASANT	374c	6
		ל	TO	517c	7 bd
		מן	THAN	582c	6 a
118	9	בטח	TRUST	105a	13 b
		חסה	SEEK REFUGE	340b	
		טוב	PLEASANT	374c	6
		ל	TO	517c	7 bd
		נדיב	NOBLE	622a	2
118	10	כי	THAT	472b	1 da
		מול	CIRCUMCIZE	558a	
		סבב	SURROUND	686a	2 d
118	11	גם	ALSO	169b	2
		כי	THAT	472b	1 da
		מול	CIRCUMCIZE	558a	
		סבב	SURROUND	686a	2 d
118	12	דבורה	BEE	184b	
		דונג	WAX	200a	
		דעך	BE EXTINGUISHED	200b	
		כי	THAT	472b	1 da
		מול	CIRCUMCIZE	558a	
		סבב	SURROUND	686a	2 d
		קוץ	THORN-BUSH	881a	1
118	13	דחה	PUSH	191a	
118	14	יה	YAH	219c	
		יה	YAH	219c	
		זמרה	MELODY	274b	2
		ישועה	VICTORY	447c	4
		עז	STRENGTH	739a	2 c
118	15	אהל	TENT	14a	2
		חיל	STRENGTH	298d	1 b
		ישועה	VICTORY	447c	4
		צדיק	JUST	843b	4
		רנה	RINGING CRY	943d	3
118	16	חיל	STRENGTH	298d	1 b
		רום	BE HIGH	927b	2 c
118	17	יה	YAH	219c	
		כי	BUT	474b	3 e
118	18	יה	YAH	219c	
		יסר	DISCIPLINE	416a	1 a
		נתן	GIVE	679c	1 s
118	19	יה	YAH	219c	
		ידה	PRAISE	392c	1 a2
		פתח	OPEN	835a	
		צדק	RIGHTEOUSNESS	842a	6 c
		שער	GATE	1045c	3 b
118	20	זה	THIS	260d	2 a
		שער	GATE	1045c	3 b
118	21	ידה	PRAISE	392c	1 a2
		ישועה	VICTORY	447c	4
118	22	אבן	STONE	6c	2
		בנה	BUILD	124c	1 e
		מאס	REJECT	549c	1 a
		פנה	CORNER	819c	1 a
		ראש	HEAD	910d	2 a
118	23	את	WITH	86d	4 c
		הוא	HE, SHE, IT	216d	6 a
		זה	THIS	*260c	1 a
118	24	פלא	BE SURPASSING	810c	3 a
		יום	DAY	398d	2 f
		עשה	DO	795a	2 8
118	25	אנא	AH, NOW	58a	
		ישע	DELIVER	446d	1 b
		צלח	ADVANCE	852c	1
118	26	ברך	BLESS	138d	2 b
		ברך	BLESS	139a	3
118	27	אור	BECOME LIGHT	21c	5
		אל	GOD	42d	6 e
		אסר	TIE	63c	1 1
		מזבח	ALTAR	259b	2
		חג	FESTIVAL-GATHER-ING	291b	2
		עבת	CORD	721c	1 a
		עד	AS FAR AS	724a	1 1a
		קרן	HORN	902a	3
118	28	אל	GOD	42c	6 b
		ידה	PRAISE	392c	1 a2
		רום	BE HIGH	927b	3
118	29	חסד	GOODNESS	339b	2 3c
		טוב	PLEASANT	374d	9 b
		ידה	PRAISE	392c	1 b
		עולם	LONG DURATION	762b	2 c
119	1	אשר	HAPPINESS	81a	
		דרך	WAY	203c	6 b
		דרך	WAY	203c	6 c
		תורה	LAW	436b	2 b3
		תמים	SOUND	1071a	4
119	2	אשר	HAPPINESS	81a	
		דרש	SEEK	205b	3 a
		נצר	GUARD	665d	3
		עדה	TESTIMONIES	730a	
119	3	דרך	WAY	204a	6 ec
		הלך	WALK	234c	2 3a 1b
		עולה	INJUSTICE	732c	1
		פעל	DO	821b	1 b
119	4	פקוד	PRECEPT	824c	
119	5	אחלי	AH THAT	25b	
		דרך	WAY	203c	6 a
		חק	SOMETHING PRE-SCRIBED	349d	7 g
		כון	BE FIRM	465d	2
		לילה	NIGHT	538d	1
119	6	אז	THEN	23b	2
		נבט	LOOK	613d	2
119	7	ידה	PRAISE	392c	1 a2
		ישר	STRAIGHTNESS	449c	2
		לבב	HEART	523d	26 a
		למד	LEARN	540d	
		צדק	RIGHTEOUSNESS	841c	2 b
		משפ	JUDGMENT	1048d	3
119	8	מאד	EXCEEDINGLY	547c	2 b
		שמר	KEEP	1037a	3 c
119	9	ארח	WAY	73b	3
		זכה	BE CLEAR	269a	
119	10	דרש	SEEK	205b	3 a
		לב	HEART	524c	2 2
		נתן	PUT	680c	2 a
		שגה	GO ASTRAY	993b	3
119	11	אמרה	UTTERANCE	57b	
		חוק	BOSOM	*300d	3 b
		חטא	MISS A GOAL OR WAY	307a	2 b
		מען	PURPOSE	775c	2 cb
		צפן	HIDE	860c	1
119	12	ברך	BLESS	138d	2 a
		למד	LEARN	540d	
119	13	ספר	COUNT	708a	1
119	14	דרך	WAY	204a	6 ec
		הון	WEALTH	223c	1
		כ	LIKE	455a	B
		עדות	TESTIMONY	730c	1
		על	UPON	758b	4 1a
		שוש	REJOICE	965b	
119	15	ארח	WAY	73b	3 b
		נבט	LOOK	613d	2
		פקוד	PRECEPT	824c	
		שיח	MUSE	967b	2
119	16	חקה	SOMETHING PRE-SCRIBED	350b	2 e
		שכח	FORGET	1013b	1 c
		שעע	TAKE DELIGHT IN	1044b	
119	17	שמר	KEEP	1037a	3 c
119	18	תורה	LAW	436b	2 b3
		נבט	LOOK	613d	2
		פלא	BE SURPASSING	810c	3 a
119	19	גר	SOJOURNER	158b	1
		סתר	HIDE	711d	1
119	20	גרס	BE CRUSHED	176c	
		תאבה	LONGING	1060b	
119	21	ארר	CURSE	76d	
		גער	REBUKE	172a	2
		זד	INSOLENT	267d	
		שגה	GO ASTRAY	993b	3
119	22	בוז	CONTEMPT	100b	1
		חרפה	REPROACH	357d	1
		נצר	GUARD	665d	3
		עדה	TESTIMONIES	730a	
		על	UPON	758b	4 2b
119	23	דבר	SPEAK	180d	1
		שר	CHIEFTAIN	978d	7
119	24	עצה	ADVICE	420b	
		עדה	TESTIMONIES	730a	
		שעשעים	DELIGHT	1044b	
119	25	דבק	CLING	179d	1 a
		חיה	LIVE	311c	3 d
		עפר	DRY EARTH	780a	2 e
119	26	דרך	WAY	203c	6 a
		למד	LEARN	540d	
		ספר	COUNT	708a	1
119	27	בין	DISCERN	107a	3 e
		דרך	WAY	204a	6 ec
		פקוד	PRECEPT	824c	
		שיח	MUSE	967b	2
119	28	דלף	DROP	196a	
		תוגה	GRIEF	387b	
		קום	STAND	878c	2 b
119	29	דרך	WAY	203d	6 d
		חנן	SHOW FAVOR	336a	
		תורה	LAW	436b	2 b3
		שקר	DECEPTION	1055c	1
119	30	אמונה	FIRMNESS	53c	3 a
		בחר	CHOOSE	104b	5 b
		דרך	WAY	203c	6 c
		פתי	SIMPLE	834c	
		שוה	AGREE WITH	1000d	
119	31	בוש	BE ASHAMED	101d	1
		דבק	CLING	179d	2 a
		עדות	TESTIMONY	730c	1
119	32	דרך	WAY	204a	6 ec
		רחב	BE LARGE	931c	2
119	33	דרך	WAY	204a	6 ec
		ירה	DIRECT	435c	5 c
		נצר	GUARD	665d	3
		עקב	CONSEQUENCE	784d	3
119	34	בין	DISCERN	107a	3 b
		תורה	LAW	436b	2 b3
		לב	HEART	524c	2 2
		נצר	GUARD	665d	3
		שמר	KEEP	1037a	3
119	35	דרך	TREAD	202b	3
		חפץ	DELIGHT IN	342d	1 a
		נתיב	PATH	677b	
119	36	בצע	UNJUST GAIN	130c	
		ירד	GO DOWN	433c	3 c
		לב	HEART	525a	2 4
		נטה	INCLINE	640d	3 d
		עדות	TESTIMONY	730c	2
119	37	דרך	WAY	203b	5
		חיה	LIVE	311c	3 d
		עבר	PASS OVER	719a	4
		שוא	EMPTINESS	996b	1
119	38	אמרה	UTTERANCE	57b	
		יראה	FEAR	432a	3
119	39	חרפה	REPROACH	357d	1
		טוב	PLEASANT	375a	0 b
		יגר	BE AFRAID	388c	
119	40	עבר	PASS OVER	719a	4
		חיה	LIVE	311c	3 d
		צדקה	RIGHTEOUSNESS	842c	6 a
		תאב	LONG FOR	1060b	
119	41	אמרה	UTTERANCE	57b	
		בוא	COME	98c	2 b
		חסד	GOODNESS	339a	2 1c
		תשועה	DELIVERANCE	448c	2
119	42	בטח	TRUST	105a	13 d
		דבר	WORD	182b	1 1c
		עולם	LONG DURATION	762b	2 c
119	43	יחל	WAIT	404a	1
		מאד	EXCEEDINGLY	547c	2 b
		נצל	SNATCH AWAY	664d	1
		משפ	JUDGMENT	1048d	3
119	44	תורה	LAW	436b	2 b3
		תמיד	CONTINUITY	556b	1 a
		עד	PERPETUITY	723d	2 c
		עולם	LONG DURATION	762b	2 a
119	45	דרש	SEEK	205c	6
		הלך	WALK	236b	2
		פקוד	PRECEPT	824c	
		רחב	WIDE	932a	
119	46	דבר	SPEAK	181c	4 c
		עדה	TESTIMONIES	730a	
119	47	אהב	LOVE	13a	3
		שעע	TAKE DELIGHT IN	1044b	
119	48	נשא	LIFT	670b	1 b1
119	49	אשר	PARTICLE OF RE-LATION	82a	2
		זכר	REMEMBER	270b	2 3a
		על	UPON	758b	3 a
		יחל	ADDENDA ET COR-RIGENDA	1124a	
119	50	זה	THIS	260d	1 a
		חיה	LIVE	311c	3 d
		נחמה	COMFORT	637c	
		עני	AFFLICTION	777a	1
119	51	זד	INSOLENT	267d	
		תורה	LAW	436b	2 b3
		ליץ	SCORN	539c	1
		מאד	EXCEEDINGLY	547c	2 b
		נטה	BEND	640d	3 a
119	52	זכר	REMEMBER	270a	14 b
		נחם	CONSOLE ONESELF	637b	3
		עולם	LONG DURATION	762a	1 c
119	53	אחז	GRASP	28b	
		זלעפה	RAGING HEAT	273a	3
		תורה	LAW	436b	2 b3
		מן	ON ACCOUNT OF	580b	2 f
		רשע	WICKED	957c	3
119	54	בית	HOUSE	109c	1 c
		מגור	SOJOURNING PLACE	158c	
		זמר	SONG	274c	
119	55	זכר	REMEMBER	270a	13 b
		תורה	LAW	436b	2 b3
119	56	זה	THIS	260d	1 a
		נצר	GUARD	665d	3
119	57	דבר	WORD	183a	2 2
		חלק	PORTION	324b	3 b
		חלה	MOLLIFY	318c	1 b
119	58	חנן	SHOW FAVOR	336a	2 b
		ל	TO	*516c	5 jb
		לב	HEART	524c	2 2
119	59	דרך	WAY	203c	6 a
		חשב	THINK	363c	1
		עדה	TESTIMONIES	730a	
		שוב	TURN BACK	999d	6 b
119	60	חוש	HASTE	301d	
		מהה	LINGER	554d	
119	61	חבל	CORD	286c	1
		תורה	LAW	436b	2 b3
		עוד	RETURN	728c	
119	62	עות	BE BENT	736c	1 a
		רשע	WICKED	957c	3
		חצות	DIVISION	345c	
		ידה	PRAISE	392c	1 b
		צדק	RIGHTEOUSNESS	841c	2 b
119	63	חבר	UNITED	288d	2 f
		ירא	FEAR	431c	3 b
119	64	חסד	GOODNESS	339b	2 3b
		למד	LEARN	540d	
		מלא	BE FULL	570a	1 b
119	65	טוב	A GOOD THING	375b	3
119	66	אמן	CONFIRM	53b	2 c

Ch v.	Heb	Eng	Page	Sec
	טוב	GOOD THINGS	375c	3 d
	טעם	TASTE	381a	2
	דעת	KNOWLEDGE	395d	1 e
119 67	למד	LEARN	540d	
	טרם	NOT YET	382c	1
	ענה	BE BOWED DOWN	776a	3
	שגג	GO ASTRAY	993a	2
119 68	טוב	PLEASANT	375a	0 b
	יטב	DO RIGHT	406a	5 b
	למד	LEARN	540d	
119 69	זד	INSOLENT	267d	
	טפל	SMEAR	381d	
	לב	HEART	524c	2 2
	נצר	GUARD	665d	3
	שקר	DECEPTION	1055c	3
119 70	חלב	FAT	316d	1
	תורה	LAW	436b	2 b3
	שעע	TAKE DELIGHT IN	1044b	
119 71	טוב	PLEASING	373b	4
	למד	LEARN	540d	
	ענה	BE BOWED DOWN	776b	1
119 72	אלף	THOUSAND	48d	1 a
	זהב	GOLD	262d	2
	זהב	GOLD	263b	9 a
	זהב	GOLD	263c	1
	טוב	PLEASANT	374c	6
	תורה	LAW	436b	2 b3
	מן	THAN	582b	6 a
119 73	בין	DISCERN	107a	3 b
	כון	ESTABLISH	466d	2
	למד	LEARN	540d	
	עשה	DO	794b	2 1b
119 74	יחל	WAIT	404a	2
	ירא	FEAR	431c	3 b
	שמח	REJOICE	970b	2 a
119 75	אמונה	FIRMNESS	53d	3 b
	ענה	BE BOWED DOWN	776b	3
	צדק	RIGHTEOUSNESS	841c	2 b
119 76	חסד	GOODNESS	339a	2 1c
	נחם	CONSOLE ONESELF	637a	
119 77	בוא	COME	98c	2 b
	תורה	LAW	436b	2 b3
	רחמים	COMPASSION	933c	1
	שעשעים	DELIGHT	1044b	
	שעע	TAKE DELIGHT IN	*1044b	
119 78	זד	INSOLENT	267d	
	עות	BE BENT	736c	1 a
	שיח	MUSE	967b	2
	שקר	DECEPTION	1055c	2
119 79	ירא	FEAR	431c	3 b
	ל	TO	511c	1 gb
	עדה	TESTIMONIES	730a	
	שוב	TURN BACK	997c	5 c
119 80	מען	PURPOSE	775c	2 cb
	תמים	SOUND	1071b	4
119 81	יחל	WAIT	404a	2
	תשועה	DELIVERANCE	448c	3
	כלה	BE FINISHED	477d	2 b
119 82	כלה	BE FINISHED	477d	2 b
	מתי	WHEN	607d	A
	נחם	CONSOLE ONESELF	637a	
119 83	כי	THOUGH	473c	2 cb
	נאד	SKIN	609d	
	קיטור	SMOKE	882c	
119 84	מה	HOW	553d	4 ca
	מתי	WHEN	607d	A
	רדף	PURSUE	922d	1 f
	משפט	JUDGMENT	1048c	1 f
119 85	זד	INSOLENT	267d	
	תורה	LAW	436b	2 b3
	כרה	DIG	500a	
	שיחה	PIT	1001c	
119 86	אמונה	FIRMNESS	53d	3 b
	רדף	PURSUE	922d	1 f
	שקר	DECEPTION	1055c	2
119 87	כלה	FINISH	478c	2 c1
	מעט	A FEW	590b	2 a
119 88	חיה	LIVE	311c	3 d
	חסד	GOODNESS	339a	2 1c
	עדות	TESTIMONY	730b	2
119 89	דבר	WORD	182d	1 2b
	נצב	STAND	662b	4
	עולם	LONG DURATION	762c	2 e
	שמי	HEAVENS	1030b	2 a
119 90	אמונה	FIRMNESS	53d	3 b
	דור	PERIOD	189d	1 b
	כון	ESTABLISH	466d	1 b
	עמד	STAND	764c	6 b
119 91	כל	ALL	483a	2 bb
	ל	TO	516c	5 jb
	עבד	SLAVE	714a	3
119 92	אבד	PERISH	1c	1
	אז	THEN	23b	2
	אזי	THEN	23b	
	תורה	LAW	436b	2 b3
	לולא	IF NOT	530c	D
	עני	AFFLICTION	777a	1
	שעשעים	DELIGHT	1044b	
119 93	חיה	LIVE	311c	3 d
	עולם	LONG DURATION	762b	2 a
119 94	דרש	SEEK	205c	6
	ישע	DELIVER	446d	1 b
119 95	אבד	CAUSE TO PERISH	2a	1
	בין	DISCERN	107a	1 b
	עדה	TESTIMONIES	730a	
	קוה	WAIT FOR	875d	2

Ch v.	Heb	Eng	Page	Sec
119 96	תכלה	PERFECTION	479a	1
	קץ	END	894a	1
	רחב	WIDE	932a	
119 97	יום	DAY	400c	7 f
	תורה	LAW	436b	2 b3
	שיחה	COMPLAINT	967a	2
119 98	חכם	BE WISE	314c	
	עולם	LONG DURATION	762b	2 a
119 99	למד	LEARN	540d	
	עדות	TESTIMONY	730c	2
	שיחה	COMPLAINT	967a	2
	שכל	BE PRUDENT	968b	3
119 100	בין	DISCERN	107b	3
	זקן	OLD	278c	2 a
	נצר	GUARD	665d	3
119 101	ארח	WAY	73b	3 c
	כלא	RESTRAIN	476b	1
	רע	EVIL	949a	3
119 102	ירה	DIRECT	435c	5 c
119 103	דבש	HONEY	185c	
	חך	PALATE	335b	C
	מלץ	BE SMOOTH	576d	
	מרץ	BE SICK	*599d	
	פה	MOUTH	804d	1 a
119 104	ארח	WAY	73b	3 c
	בין	DISCERN	107b	2
	שקר	DECEPTION	1055c	1
119 105	דבר	WORD	182d	1 2b
	נר	LAMP	632d	
	נתיבה	PATH	677b	2 a
119 106	צדק	RIGHTEOUSNESS	841c	2 b
	קום	STAND	878c	1
	שבע	SWEAR	989b	1 a
119 107	חיה	LIVE	311c	3 d
	מאד	EXCEEDINGLY	547c	2 b
	ענה	BE BOWED DOWN	776a	3
119 108	למד	LEARN	540d	
	נדבה	FREEWILL-OFFER-ING	621d	2 b
	רצה	BE PLEASED WITH	953b	2
119 109	תורה	LAW	436b	2 b3
	כף	HOLLOW OF THE HAND	496d	1 d6
	תמיד	CONTINUITY	556b	1 a
119 110	פח	BIRD-TRAP	809a	1
	תעה	ERR	1073c	3
119 111	לב	HEART	525c	2 9a
	נחל	TAKE AS A POSSES-SION	635c	2
	עדות	TESTIMONY	730c	2
	עולם	LONG DURATION	762b	2 a
	ששון	REJOICING	965b	
119 112	לב	HEART	525a	2 4
	נטה	BEND	640c	3 b
	עולם	LONG DURATION	762b	2 a
	עקב	CONSEQUENCE	784d	3
119 113	תורה	LAW	436b	2 b3
	סעף	DIVIDED	704a	
119 114	מגן	SHIELD	171c	
	יחל	WAIT	404a	2
	סתר	COVERING	712a	2 a
119 115	נצר	GUARD	665d	3
119 116	בוש	BE ASHAMED	101d	1
	ל	TO	*516c	5 jb
	סמך	LEAN	702a	2
	שבר	HOPE	960b	
119 117	ישע	BE DELIVERED	446b	1
	תמיד	CONTINUITY	556b	1 a
	סעד	SUPPORT	703c	2 b
	שעה	GAZE	1043a	
119 118	סלה	MAKE LIGHT OF	699a	
	רמיות	DECEITFULNESS	941c	
	שגה	GO ASTRAY	993b	3
	שקר	DECEPTION	1055c	1
119 119	סיג	DROSS	691b	2
	עדה	TESTIMONIES	730a	
	רשע	WICKED	957c	3
	שבת	CEASE	992a	2
119 120	בשר	FLESH	142d	2
	ירא	FEAR	431b	1 c
	סמר	BRISTLE UP	702c	
	פחד	DREAD	808c	1
119 121	נוח	REST	629a	B 4
	עשק	OPPRESS	798d	2
	צדק	RIGHTEOUSNESS	841d	5
	זד	INSOLENT	267d	
119 122	טוב	A GOOD THING	375b	3
	ערב	TAKE ON PLEDGE	786c	1
	עשק	OPPRESS	798d	2
119 123	ישועה	DELIVERANCE	447b	3
	כלה	BE FINISHED	477d	2 b
	צדק	RIGHTEOUSNESS	842a	6 a
119 124	חסד	GOODNESS	339a	2 1c
	למד	LEARN	540d	
	עם	WITH	767d	1
119 125	בין	DISCERN	107a	3 b
	עבד	SLAVE	714a	3
	עדה	TESTIMONIES	730a	
119 126	תורה	LAW	436b	2 b3
	עת	TIME	773d	2 b
	פרר	BREAK	830b	1 e
119 127	זהב	GOLD	262d	2
	פז	REFINED GOLD	808a	
119 128	ארח	WAY	73b	3 c
	ישר	APPROVE	448d	3
	כל	ALL	482d	2 a

Ch v.	Heb	Eng	Page	Sec
	פקוד	PRECEPT	824c	
	שקר	DECEPTION	1055c	1
119 129	נצר	GUARD	665d	3
	עדות	TESTIMONY	730c	2
	פלא	WONDER	810c	1
119 130	אור	BECOME LIGHT	21b	1
	בין	DISCERN	107a	3 b
	דבר	WORD	183a	2 2
	פתח	OPENING	836a	
119 131	יאב	LONG	383b	1
	פה	MOUTH	805b	2 b
	פער	OPEN WIDE	822b	
119 132	שאף	GASP	983c	2
	חנן	SHOW FAVOR	336a	2 b
	פנה	TURN	815c	2 c1
	רוץ	RUN	930b	1
	שם	NAME	1028c	3
	משפט	JUDGMENT	1049a	6 b
119 133	כון	ESTABLISH	466c	3
	פעם	BEAT	822a	1 a
	שלט	DOMINEER	1020c	2
119 134	עשק	OPPRESSION	799a	1
	פדה	RANSOM	804b	3 d
119 135	אור	BECOME LIGHT	21c	5
	למד	LEARN	540d	
119 136	תורה	LAW	436b	2 b3
	על	UPON	758b	3 ca
	פלג	CHANNEL	811b	
119 137	ישר	STRAIGHT	449a	3 a
	צדיק	JUST	843a	1 d
119 138	אמונה	FIRMNESS	53d	3 b
	עדה	TESTIMONIES	730b	
	צדק	RIGHTEOUSNESS	841c	2 b
119 139	דבר	WORD	183a	2 2
	צמת	EXTERMINATE	856b	
	קנאה	ZEAL	888c	3 a
	שכח	FORGET	1013b	1 c
119 140	צרף	SMELT	864b	1
119 141	בזה	DESPISE	102c	1
	צעיר	YOUNG	859a	1 b
119 142	אמת	FIRMNESS	54b	4 c
	תורה	LAW	436b	2 b3
	צדק	RIGHTEOUSNESS	841d	E
	צדקה	RIGHTEOUSNESS	842c	6 a
119 143	מצא	FIND	593c	3 e
	מצוק	STRAITNESS	848a	
	צר	STRAITS	865a	
	שעשעים	DELIGHT	1044b	
119 144	בין	DISCERN	107a	3 b
	עדות	TESTIMONY	730c	2
	עולם	LONG DURATION	762c	2
	צדק	RIGHTEOUSNESS	841c	2 b
119 145	לב	HEART	524c	2 2
	נצר	GUARD	665d	3
119 146	ישע	DELIVER	446d	1 b
	עדה	TESTIMONIES	730b	
119 147	יחל	WAIT	404a	2
	נשף	TWILIGHT	676a	2
	קדם	COME IN FRONT	870a	1
	שוע	CRY OUT	1002d	
119 148	קדם	COME IN FRONT	870a	1
	שיח	MUSE	967b	2
	אשמורה	WATCH	1038a	
119 149	חיה	LIVE	311c	3 d
	חסד	GOODNESS	339a	2 1c
	משפט	JUDGEMNT	1048d	2 a
119 150	זמה	PLAN	273c	2 a
	תורה	LAW	436b	2 b3
	רדף	PURSUE	923d	2
	רחק	BE DISTANT	935a	
119 151	אמת	FIRMNESS	54b	4 c
	קרב	NEAR	898c	2 f
119 152	ידע	KNOW	393d	1 a
	יסד	FOUND	413d	
	עדה	TESTIMONIES	730b	
	עולם	LONG DURATION	762c	2
	קדם	FRONT	869d	2 d
119 153	חלק	DRAW OFF OR OUT	322d	2
	תורה	LAW	436b	2 b3
	עני	AFFLICTION	777a	1
119 154	גאל	REDEEM	145c	3 a
	חיה	LIVE	311c	3 d
	ל	TO	516c	5 jb
	ריב	STRIVE	936c	3
119 155	דרש	SEEK	205c	6
	ישועה	DELIVERANCE	447b	3
	רחק	DISTANT	935c	1 a
119 156	חיה	LIVE	311c	3 d
	רחמים	COMPASSION	933c	1
119 157	נטה	BEND	640b	3 a
	עדות	TESTIMONY	730c	2
	רדף	PURSUE	922d	1 f
119 158	בגד	ACT TREACHER-OUSLY	93d	D
	קוט	FEEL A LOATHING	876c	
119 159	חיה	LIVE	311c	3 d
	חסד	GOODNESS	339a	2 1c
119 160	אמת	FIRMNESS	54b	4 c
	עולם	LONG DURATION	762c	2
	צדק	RIGHTEOUSNESS	841c	2 b
	ראש	HEAD	911b	7
	משפט	JUDGMENT	1048d	2
119 161	חנם	OUT OF FAVOR	336d	C
	פחד	DREAD	808c	1
	רדף	PURSUE	922d	1 f
	שר	CHIEFTAIN	978d	1

Ch v.	Heb	Eng	Page	Sec
	קצץ	CUT OFF	893c	
	קצץ	CUT OFF	893d	
129 6	גג	ROOF	150d	1
	חציר	GREEN GRASS	348b	2
	יבש	BE DRY	386b	1 d
	קדמה	ANTIQUITY	870b	3
	שלף	DRAW OUT	1025c	3
129 7	חצן	BOSOM	346a	
	כף	HOLLOW OF THE HAND	496b	1 a
	מלא	FILL	570c	1
	עמר	BIND SHEAVES	771c	
	קצר	HARVEST	894c	
129 8	ברך	BLESS	139a	3
	ברכה	BLESSING	139d	1 b
130 1	מן	OUT OF	579a	2 ab
	מעמקים	DEPTHS	771b	
130 2	אזן	EAR	24b	2 b
	תחנון	SUPPLICATION FOR FAVOR	337d	2
	קשב	ATTENTIVE	904b	
130 3	יה	YAH	219c	
	מי	WHO	566d	F c
	עון	INIQUITY	731a	1 c1
	שמר	KEEP	1036d	1 d
130 4	ה	THE	208b	1 ha
	ירא	BE REVERED	431d	2 c
	כי	BECAUSE	474b	3 c
	סליחה	FORGIVENESS	669c	
130 5	יחל	WAIT	404a	
	קוה	WAIT FOR	875d	1
130 6	בקר	MORNING	134a	1 f
	ל	TO	510d	1 a
	שמר	KEEP	1036d	1 c
130 7	חסד	GOODNESS	339a	2
	יחל	WAIT	404a	2
	עם	WITH	768b	3 b
	פדות	RANSOM	804b	
	רבה	BECOME MANY	915d	1 e4
130 8	עון	INIQUITY	731b	1 c6
	פדה	RANSOM	804a	3 c
131 1	גבה	BE HIGH	147a	3 b
	גדול	GREAT	153c	9
	הלך	WALK	235c	4
	לב	HEART	525b	2 6c
	מן	THAN	582d	6 d
	עין	EYE	744c	2 a
	פלא	BE SURPASSING	810c	2
	רום	BE HIGH	926d	2 b
131 2	אם	IF	50b	1 b2
	אם	IF	50c	1 ce
	אם	MOTHER	51d	1
	דמם	BE SILENT	199a	
	נפש	SOUL	659c	1 b
	על	UPON	753c	2 1d
	שוה	AGREE WITH	1000d	
131 3	יחל	WAIT	404a	2
	עולם	LONG DURATION	763a	2 m
	עתה	NOW	774a	1 a
132 1	דוד	DAVID	188a	
	זכר	REMEMBER	270b	2 2 b
	ענה	BE BOWED DOWN	776b	1
132 2	אביר	STRONG	7d	
	נדר	VOW	623d	4
	שבע	SWEAR	989b	1 a
132 3	אהל	TENT	13d	2
	יצוע	BED	427a	
	עלה	GO UP	748c	1 f
	ערש	COUCH	793a	
132 4	שנה	SLEEP	446a	
	תנומה	SLUMBER	630b	1
	נתן	GIVE	679a	1 g
	עפעף	EYELID	733d	
132 5	אביר	STRONG	7d	
	מצא	FIND	592d	1 a
	משכן	DWELLING-PLACE	1016a	3 b
132 6	אפרתה	EPHRATH	68d	3
	יער	WOOD	421a	G
	מצא	FIND	593b	3 a
	קריתיערים	KIRIATH-JEARIM	900c	
132 7	הדם	FOOTSTOOL	213c	
	ל	TO	511b	1 ga
	רגל	FOOT	919d	1 b
	שחה	BOW DOWN	1005c	2 b
	משכן	DWELLING-PLACE	1016a	3 b
132 8	ארון	CHEST	75c	3 i
	יהוה	YAHWEH	*219a	2 1h
	מנוחה	RESTING PLACE	629d	1
	עז	STRENGTH	739b	3 d
	קום	STAND	878b	6 a
132 9	חסיד	KIND	339d	2 b
	כהן	PRIEST	463d	4
	לבש	PUT ON	528a	B
	צדק	RIGHTEOUSNESS	842a	6 c
	רנן	GIVE A RINGING CRY	943c	
132 10	דוד	DAVID	188a	
	משיח	ANOINTED	603c	1
	עבור	FOR THE SAKE OF	721a	1 a
	שוב	TURN BACK	999d	5
132 11	אמת	FIRMNESS	54b	5
	בטן	WOMB	106a	3
	דוד	DAVID	188a	
	כסא	THRONE	491a	3 a
	ל	TO	511c	1 gb
	ל	TO	512d	5 aa
	מן	FROM	580d	3 bb
	שוב	TURN BACK	998a	6 h
132 12	שית	PUT	1011b	2 a
	אם	IF	49c	1 a1 a
	ברית	COVENANT	136d	2 2f
	ברית	COVENANT	137a	3 2
	גם	ALSO	169b	2
	זו	THIS	262b	
	כסא	THRONE	491a	3 a
	ל	TO	511c	1 gb
	ל	TO	512d	5 aa
	למד	LEARN	540d	
	עדה	TESTIMONIES	730a	
132 13	אוה	DESIRE	16a	
	בחר	CHOOSE	104a	1 a
	מושב	DWELLING	444b	2 a
	ל	TO	512c	4 b
132 14	אוה	DESIRE	16a	
	מנוחה	RESTING PLACE	629d	1
	עד	PERPETUITY	723c	2 d
132 15	אביון	NEEDY	2d	
	ברך	BLESS	139a	2 b
	ציד	PROVISION	845b	
	שבע	SATISFIED	959d	1 b
132 16	חסיד	KIND	339d	2 b
	ישע	DELIVERANCE	447a	2
	תשועה	DELIVERANCE	*448c	2
	כהן	PRIEST	463d	4
	לבש	CLOTHE	528b	1 b
	רנן	GIVE A RINGING CRY	943b	
	רנן	GIVE A RINGING CRY	943c	
132 17	דוד	DAVID	188a	
	משיח	ANOINTED	603c	1
	נר	LAMP	632d	
	ערך	ARRANGE	789c	1 b
	צמח	SPROUT	855d	3
	קרן	HORN	902a	2
	שם	THERE	1027a	1 a
132 18	בשת	SHAME	102a	1
	לבש	CLOTHE	528b	1 b
	נזר	CROWN	634b	1
	צוץ	BLOSSOM	847c	2
133 1	גם	ALSO	169a	4
	טוב	PLEASANT	374a	2 e
	יחד	UNION	403a	2 a2
	ישב	DWELL	443a	3
	נעים	DELIGHTFUL	653d	1
133 2	זקן	BEARD	278b	1
	טוב	PLEASANT	374b	3 c
	ירד	GO DOWN	433c	3 d
	מדה	GARMENT	551c	4
	פה	MOUTH	805b	4
	שמן	OIL	1032b	2 c
133 3	ברכה	BLESSING	139d	1 b
	חיים	LIFE	313b	2
	חרמון	HERMON	356d	
	טל	NIGHT-MIST	378c	
	ירד	GO DOWN	433c	3 a
	עולם	LONG DURATION	762d	2 f
	צוה	CHARGE	846a	4 d
	ציון	ZION	851c	
134 1	ברך	BLESS	139a	1
	לילה	NIGHT	538d	1
	לילה	NIGHT	539a	1
	עבד	SLAVE	714b	4
134 2	ברך	BLESS	139a	1
	נשא	LIFT	670b	1 b 1
	קדש	APARTNESS	872b	6
134 3	ברך	BLESS	139a	2 a
135 1	יה	YAH	219c	
	הלל	PRAISE	238c	2 d1
	עבד	SLAVE	714b	4
135 2	חצר	ENCLOSURE	347a	3 b
135 3	יה	YAH	219c	
	הלל	PRAISE	238b	2 d
	זמר	MAKE MUSIC	274a	1
	טוב	PLEASANT	374d	9 b
	נעים	DELIGHTFUL	653d	1
135 4	בחר	CHOOSE	104a	3 a
	יה	YAH	219c	
	סגלה	PROPERTY	688c	1
135 5	אדון	LORD	11b	2 2
	בחר	CHOOSE	104a	3 a
	גדול	GREAT	153c	6 c
135 6	חפץ	DELIGHT IN	343a	2 a
	תהום	DEEP	1062d	1
	תהום	SEA	1063a	2
135 7	אוצר	TREASURE	70a	3 d
	ארץ	EARTH	76b	4 e
	ברק	LIGHTNING	140c	1
	יצא	BRING OUT	425b	5
	מטר	RAIN	564d	
	רוח	BREATH	924d	2 a
135 8	בהמה	BEAST	96d	1
	בכור	FIRST-BORN	114b	1 c
	נכה	SMITE	646a	2 c
135 9	אות	SIGN	16d	4
	מופת	WONDER	69a	1
	פרעה	PHARAOH	829a	
135 10	הרג	KILL	247b	2
	עצום	MIGHTY	783a	1
135 11	אמרי	AMORITES	57c	2 a
	בשן	BASHAN	143c	
	הרג	KILL	247c	7
	כנען	CANAAN	488d	2 a
	ל	TO	512a	3 b
	ל	TO	512a	3 b
	ממלכה	KINGDOM	575a	1
	סיחון	SIHON	695d	
	עוג	OG	728b	
135 12	נתן	GIVE	681a	3 a
135 13	דור	PERIOD	189d	1 b
	זכר	REMEMBRANCE	271b	2 a
	עולם	LONG DURATION	762b	2 c
135 14	דין	JUDGE	*192b	1
	נחם	BE SORRY	637b	1
	עבד	SLAVE	714a	3
135 15	זהב	GOLD	263a	6
	זהב	GOLD	263c	1
	כסף	SILVER	494b	7
	עצב	IDOL	781b	
135 16	מעשה	DEED	796a	2 a3
	עין	EYE	744a	1 c
	ראה	TO SEE	907b	4
135 17	אזן	EAR	24a	2 a
	אזן	HEAR	24b	1
	אין	NOT	34b	2 c
	אין	NOT	35b	
	יש	BE	442a	2 cg
	רוח	BREATH	924c	1 a
135 18	בטח	TRUST	105a	1 3c
135 19	אהרן	AARON	14d	
	בית	HOUSE	110b	5 dl
	ברך	BLESS	139a	1
135 20	בית	HOUSE	110b	5 dk
	ברך	BLESS	139a	1
	ה	THE	208b	1 g
	ירא	FEAR	431c	3 b
	לוי	LEVITE	532d	1
135 21	ברך	BLESS	138d	2 a
	יה	YAH	219c	
	הלל	PRAISE	238c	2 d2
	ציון	ZION	851c	
136 1	שכן	SETTLE DOWN	1015b	2 c
	חסד	GOODNESS	339b	23 c
	טוב	PLEASANT	374d	9 b
	ידה	PRAISE	392c	1 b
	ידה	PRAISE	392c	1 b
	עולם	LONG DURATION	762b	2 c
136 2	אלהים	GOD	43c	1 d
136 3	אדון	LORD	11a	2
	אדון	LORD	11b	2 2
	ידה	PRAISE	392c	1 b
136 5	תבונה	UNDERSTANDING	108b	1
136 6	מי	WATER	565c	1 e
	רקע	BEAT	956a	
136 7	אור	LIGHT	21c	3
136 8	ממשלה	RULE	606a	2
	שמש	SUN	1039b	1
136 9	ירח	MOON	437a	
	כוכב	STAR	456d	
	ממשלה	RULE	606a	2
136 10	בכור	FIRST-BORN	114b	1 c
	נכה	SMITE	646c	4 a
136 11	יצא	CAUSE TO GO	424c	1 a
	זרוע	ARM	284a	1 c
136 12	חזק	STRONG	305c	1 b
136 13	גזר	CUT	160b	2
	גזר	PART	160c	
	סוף	REEDS	693b	2 a
136 14	עבר	PASS OVER	718d	2 a
136 15	נער	SHAKE OUT	654d	
	סוף	REEDS	693b	2 a
	פרעה	PHARAOH	829a	
136 16	הלך	WALK	236c	1 a
	פה	MOUTH	805b	2 d
136 17	פה	MOUTH	805b	2 d
136 18	אדיר	MAJESTIC	12b	1
136 19	הרג	KILL	247b	1
	אמרי	AMORITES	57c	2 a
	הרג	KILL	247c	7
	ל	TO	512a	3 b
	ל	TO	512a	3 b
	סיחון	SIHON	695d	
136 20	בשן	BASHAN	143c	
	הרג	KILL	247c	7
	ל	TO	512a	3 b
	ל	TO	512a	3 b
	עוג	OG	728b	
136 22	עבד	SLAVE	714b	5
136 23	זכר	REMEMBER	270b	2 1 c
	שפל	LOW ESTATE	1050c	
136 24	פרק	TEAR APART	830a	
136 25	בשר	FLESH	142d	6 a
	לחם	FOOD	537b	2 a
136 26	אל	GOD	42c	6 c
	חסד	GOODNESS	339b	23 c
	ידה	PRAISE	392c	1 b
	שמי	HEAVENS	1030b	2 a
137 1	בבל	BABEL	93c	
	בכה	WEEP	113c	3
	גם	ALSO	169b	2
	זכר	REMEMBER	269d	1 1 a
	נהר	STREAM	625d	1
137 2	כנור	LYRE	490b	
	ערבה	POPLAR	788b	
	תלה	HANG	1068a	1
137 3	דבר	WORD	182d	1 a
	מן	FROM	580d	3 ba
	שמחה	JOY	970d	1

Ch v.	Heb	Eng	Page	Sec
	שאל	ASK	981c	1 a
	שאלתיאל	SHEALTIEL	*982d	
	שיר	SONG	1010b	1
	שיר	SING	1010c	
	תלל	BE WASTED	1064a	
137 4	איך	HOW	32c	1
	נכר	FOREIGNNESS	648d	3
	על	UPON	752d	21
	שיר	SONG	1010b	2
137 5	זכר	REMEMBER	269d	11 a
	ימין	RIGHT HAND	411c	1 a
	שכח	FORGET	1013a	1 b
	שכח	FORGET	1013a	1 b
137 6	דבק	CLING	179d	1 a
	זכר	REMEMBER	269d	11 a
	חך	PALATE	335a	A
	לשון	TONGUE	546a	1
	עלה	GO UP	749d	7
	על	UPON	757a	27b
	ראש	HEAD	911b	5
	שמחה	JOY	970d	1
137 7	אדום	EDOM	10c	4
	הלך	WALK	231c	11d4
	זכר	REMEMBER	270c	24
	יום	DAY	398d	2g
	יסוד	FOUNDATION	414b	1
	ל	TO	515b	5 hb g
	ערה	BE NAKED	788c	1
137 8	אשר	HAPPINESS	81a	
	בבל	BABEL	93c	
	בת	DAUGHTER	123c	3
	ש	WHO	979d	1
	שדד	DEAL VIOLENTLY WITH	994a	
137 9	אחז	GRASP	28b	
	אשר	HAPPINESS	81a	
	נפץ	SHATTER	658d	
	עולל	CHILD	760c	
	ש	WHO	979d	1
138 1	אלהים	GOD	43b	1 a
	זמר	MAKE MUSIC	274a	1
	ידה	PRAISE	392c	1 a2
	לב	HEART	524c	22
	נגד	IN FRONT	617b	1 aa
138 2	אמת	FIRMNESS	54a	3 b
	אמרה	UTTERANCE	57b	
	גדל	BECOME GREAT	152c	2
	היכל	TEMPLE	228c	2 d
	חסד	GOODNESS	339a	22
	ידה	PRAISE	392b	1 a2
	על	UPON	755a	22
	קדש	APARTNESS	871d	2 d
	שחה	BOW DOWN	1005c	2 b
138 3	יום	DAY	400b	7 d3a
	נפש	SOUL	660d	6 d
	עז	STRENGTH	739a	2 b
	רהב	ACT STORMILY	923b	
138 4	אמר	WORD	57a	1
	ידה	PRAISE	392d	1 a2
138 5	גדול	GREAT	153b	6 c
	דרך	WAY	204a	6 eb
	כבוד	GLORY	458d	2 c2
	שיר	SING	1010d	
138 6	גבה	HIGH	147b	3
	ראה	TO SEE	907c	6 b
	רום	BE HIGH	926d	1 b
	מרחק	DISTANT PLACE	935d	2
	שפל	LOW	1050c	4
138 7	הלך	WALK	234c	22
	חיה	LIVE	311c	1
	ישע	DELIVER	446d	1 b
	קרב	INWARD PART	899b	1 f7
	שלח	SEND	1018d	3 b
138 8	בעד	ON BEHALF OF	126d	2
	גמר	COMPLETE	170a	2
	חסד	GOODNESS	339b	23c
	עולם	LONG DURATION	762b	2 c
	רפה	SINK	952a	1
139 1	מזמור	MELODY	274c	
	חקר	SEARCH	350d	2 c
139 2	בין	DISCERN	106d	3 b
	ישב	SIT	442d	1 b
	רחק	DISTANT	935c	2 a1
	רע	PURPOSE	946d	2
	רחק	ADDENDA ET CORRIGENDA	1126d	
139 3	ארח	WAY	73a	2
	דרך	WAY	203b	5
	זרה	SCATTER	280a	2
	סכן	BE OF USE	698b	
	רבע	LIE DOWN	918a	1
	ארח	ADDENDA ET CORRIGENDA	1120d	
139 4	הן	BEHOLD	243c	A
	ידע	KNOW	394a	2
	לשון	TONGUE	546b	1 b
	מלה	WORD	576b	
139 5	כף	HOLLOW OF THE HAND	496c	1 b
	צור	CONFINE	848d	3
	קדם	FRONT	869c	1 a
	שית	PUT	1011a	1
139 6	דעת	KNOWLEDGE	395d	1 e
	יכל	BE ABLE	407d	1 i
	מן	THAN	582d	6 d
	פלאי	WONDERFUL	811a	

Ch v.	Heb	Eng	Page	Sec
	שגב	BE HIGH	960c	1
139 7	אן	WHERE	33a	A
	ברח	FLEE	138a	2
	פנה	FACE	816a	12a
	רוח	BREATH	926a	9 f
139 8	אם	IF	49d	1 a1 c
	הנה	BEHOLD	243d	
	יצע	LAY	426d	
	יצוע	BED	*427a	
	סלק	ASCEND	701c	
	רוח	BREATH	926a	9 f
	שאול	SHEOL	983a	1
139 9	אחרית	END	31a	A
	כנף	WING	489d	1 g
	שחר	DAWN	1007b	
139 10	אחז	GRASP	28b	
	גם	YEA	*169c	3
	נחה	LEAD	635a	
	שם	THERE	1027a	1 a
139 11	אך	SURELY	36c	1
	אך	ONLY	36d	
	בעד	ABOUT	126c	1 b
	חשך	DARKNESS	365a	2
	עוף	CLOUD	*791d	
	שוף	BRUISE	1003a	
139 12	אור	BECOME LIGHT	21b	2
	אורה	LIGHT	21d	1
	גם	YEA	169c	3
	חשך	DARKNESS	365a	2
	חשך	GROW DARK	365a	2
	חשכה	DARKNESS	365b	
	יום	DAY	400d	7 h
	כ	LIKE	454c	2 a
139 13	בטן	WOMB	106a	3
	כליה	KIDNEYS	480b	1 a
	סכך	WEAVE TOGETHER	697b	
	קנה	ACQUIRE	889a	1 a
	רקם	VARIEGATE	*955d	
139 14	ידה	PRAISE	392c	1 a2
	ירא	CAUSE FEAR	431d	2
	נפש	SOUL	661a	7
	על	UPON	758a	3 b
	פלא	BE SURPASSING	810c	3 a
	פלה	BE SEPARATED	811d	2
139 15	ארץ	EARTH	76b	2 g
	אשר	PARTICLE OF RELATION	82b	3
	כחד	BE HIDDEN	470b	1
	סתר	COVERING	712a	2 b
	עצם	BONES	782c	2
	עשה	DO	795b	
	רקם	VARIEGATE	955d	
	תחתי	LOWER	1066c	
139 16	יצר	BE FORMED	428a	
	כתב	BE WRITTEN	508a	1
	לא	NOT	520c	
	ספר	MISSIVE	707c	3 g
139 17	אל	GOD	42d	6 e
	יקר	BE PRECIOUS	429d	1 a
	עצם	BE VAST	782c	2
	ראש	HEAD	911b	7
	רע	PURPOSE	946d	
139 18	חול	SAND	297d	B
	עם	WITH	768c	4 b
	קיץ	AWAKE	884c	1 a
	רבה	BECOME MANY	915b	1 c
139 19	אלה	GOD	43a	2
	אם	IF	50b	1 b3
	דם	BLOOD	197a	2 h
	קטל	SLAY	881d	
139 20	אמר	SAY	56a	1
	מזמה	PURPOSE	273d	3 b
	מרה	BE REBELLIOUS	598b	
	נשא	LIFT	670d	1 b7
	עיר	ADVERSARY	786b	
	שוא	EMPTINESS	996a	1
139 21	קוט	FEEL A LOATHING	876c	2
	קום	STAND	878c	
	שנא	HATE	971c	1 a
	שן	HATE	971d	2
139 22	תכלית	END	479b	2
	ל	TO	512c	4 b
	שנאה	HATING	971d	1
139 23	אל	GOD	42d	6 e
	בחן	EXAMINE	103c	1
	חקר	SEARCH	350d	2 c
	לב	HEART	523c	22
	שרעפים	DISQUIETING THOUGHTS	972a	
139 24	אם	IF	50d	2 ba
	דרך	WAY	203b	6 c
	דרך	WAY	203d	6 d
	נחה	LEAD	634d	
	עולם	LONG DURATION	762d	2 f
	עצב	PAIN	780d	
	ראה	TO SEE	907b	5 a
140 1	מזמור	MELODY	274c	
140 2	חלץ	DRAW OFF OR OUT	322d	2
	חמס	VIOLENCE	329d	
	נצר	GUARD	665d	2
	רע	EVIL	948c	0 b
	חך	INJURY	*1067a	
140 3	גור	STIR UP STRIFE	158d	1
	חשב	THINK	363a	12
	לב	HEART	524d	23c
140 4	חמה	POISON	404c	1 b

Ch v.	Heb	Eng	Page	Sec
	לשון	TONGUE	546b	1 b
	נחש	SERPENT	638b	1 a
	סלה	LIFT UP	700b	
	עכשוב	ASP	748a	
	שפה	SPEECH	973d	1 a1
	שנן	SHARPEN	1041d	
	שנינה	SHARP WORD	*1042b	
	תחת	UNDERNEATH	*1065c	2 1b
140 5	דחה	PUSH	191a	
	חמס	VIOLENCE	329d	
	חשב	THINK	363a	12
	נצר	GUARD	665d	2
	פעם	BEAT	822a	1 b
	חך	INJURY	*1067a	
140 6	גאה	PROUD	144b	
	מחמרה	FLOOD	*243b	
	חבל	CORD	286c	1
	טמן	HIDE	380c	2
	יד	HAND	391b	5 f
	מוקש	BAIT	430d	
	רשת	NET	440c	1 b2
	סלה	LIFT UP	700b	
	מעגל	ENTRENCHMENT	722d	2 a
	פח	BIRD-TRAP	809a	2 a
	פרש	SPREAD OUT	831b	1
	שית	PUT	1011b	2 a
140 7	אזן	LISTENING	24c	2
	אל	GOD	42d	6 b
	תחנון	SUPPLICATION FOR FAVOR	337d	2
140 8	אדון	LORD	11d	5
	ישועה	DELIVERANCE	447b	3
	נשק	EQUIPMENT	676d	1
	סכך	OVERSHADOW	691a	1
	עז	STRENGTH	739a	2 c
140 9	מאוי	DESIRE	16c	
	ממם	PLAN	273b	
	נתן	GIVE	678d	1 e
	סלה	LIFT UP	700b	
	פוק	BRING OUT	807c	3
	רום	BE HIGH	927a	2 b
	רום	BE HIGH	927b	1 a1
140 10	כסה	COVER	492a	5
	סבב	SURROUND	686d	2
	מסב	THAT WHICH SURROUNDS	687b	2
	עמל	TROUBLE	765d	2
	ראש	HEAD	911b	8
	רום	BE HIGH	927a	2 b
140 11	גחלת	COAL	161a	
	מחמרה	FLOOD	243b	
	מכמר	NET	485c	
	מוט	SLIP	557a	
	נפל	FALL	658a	1 e
	על	UPON	756c	27 a b
140 12	איש	MAN	36a	
	מדחפה	THRUST	191b	
	חמס	VIOLENCE	329d	
	כון	BE FIRM	465d	1 c
	ל	TO	516b	5 ja
	לשון	TONGUE	546c	1 b
	צוד	HUNT	844c	
	רע	EVIL	948d	1
140 13	אביון	NEEDY	2d	
	דין	JUDGMENT	192c	2
	עני	POOR	777a	3
	משפט	JUDGEMNT	1049a	5
140 14	אך	SURELY	36c	1
	ידה	PRAISE	392c	1 a2
	ישב	DWELL	443a	3 c2
	ישר	STRAIGHT	779b	3 c2
	פנה	FACE	816d	22a
141 1	אזן	LISTENING	24c	2
	מזמור	MELODY	274c	
	חוש	HASTE	301d	
	קרא	CALL	895b	2 a
141 2	כון	BE READY	466a	4
	מנחה	OFFERING	585b	4
	משאת	UPRISING	673a	1 c
	ערב	SUNSET	788a	1 c
	תפלה	PRAYER	813c	1 c
	קטרת	SMOKE	882d	1
141 3	דל	DOOR	194d	2
	נצר	WATCH	665d	1
	שפה	SPEECH	973c	1 a1
	שית	PUT	1011b	2 a
	שמרה	GUARD	1037c	
141 4	דבר	WORD	183d	46
	לב	HEART	525a	24
	לחם	EAT	536d	
	מנעמים	DELICACIES	564b	
	נטה	INCLINE	640d	3 d
	עלל	ACT ARBITRARILY	760a	
	רע	EVIL	948c	0 d
	רשע	WICKEDNESS	957c	1
141 5	הלם	SMITE	240c	
	חסד	GOODNESS	338c	11
	יכח	CORRECT	407a	6
	נוא	RESTRAIN	626b	1
	רעה	MISERY	949b	1
	שמן	OIL	1032b	2 c
141 6	דבר	WORD	57a	1
	יד	HAND	391a	5 d
	נעם	BE DELIGHTFUL	653c	
	שמט	LET DROP	1030c	
	שפט	JUDGE	1047d	3 c2

Ch v.	Heb	Eng	Page	Sec
141 7	בקע	CLEAVE	131d	1
	ל	TO	511d	2
	פה	MOUTH	805b	4
	פלח	CLEAVE	812a	
	שאול	SHEOL	983a	1
141 8	אדון	LORD	11d	5
	ב	IN	*88a	
	חסה	SEEK REFUGE	340b	
	ערה	BE NAKED	788d	3
141 9	יד	HAND	391b	5 g1
	יקש	LAY SNARES	430c	
	מוקש	BAIT	430d	
	פח	BIRD-TRAP	809a	2 a
141 10	יחד	UNION	403a	2 a4
	מכמר	NET	485c	
	נפל	FALL	656d	1
	עד	UNTIL	725b	2 2b
142 1	מערה	CAVE	792c	
	תפלה	PRAYER	813c	2
142 2	זעק	CRY	277b	2 a
	חנן	SHOW FAVOR	336b	2
	קול	VOICE	877a	1 a
142 3	רוח	BREATH	925a	3 b
	נגד	BE CONSPICUOUS	616d	1
	שיח	COMPLAINT	967a	1
	שפך	POUR OUT	1049d	2 b
142 4	ארח	WAY	73a	2
	הלך	WALK	235c	4
	זו	THIS	262c	2
	טמן	HIDE	380c	2
	נתיבה	PATH	677b	2 a
	עטף	BE FEEBLE	742c	
	על	UPON	753c	2 1d
	פח	BIRD-TRAP	809a	2 a
142 5	אבד	PERISH	1d	2
	אין	NOT	34d	3
	דרש	SEEK	205d	7
	דרש	SEEK	205d	7
	ימין	RIGHT HAND	412a	2 b
	ל	TO	*512a	3 b
	ל	TO	*512a	3 b
	נבט	LOOK	613d	2
	מנוס	ESCAPE	631a	2
	נכר	RECOGNIZE	648b	3
142 6	ארץ	EARTH	76b	4 d
	זעק	CRY	277b	2 a
	חי	ALIVE	312a	1b
	חלק	PORTION	324b	3 b
	מחסה	REFUGE	340c	B
142 7	אמץ	BE STRONG	55a	1
	דלל	BE LOW	195c	
	קשב	ATTEND	904a	
	רדף	PURSUE	922d	1 f
	רנה	RINGING CRY	943d	1
142 8	ידה	PRAISE	392c	1 a2
	יצא	BRING OUT	424d	2
	כתר	SURROUND	509c	
	מסגר	DUNGEON	689d	2
143 1	אזן	LISTENING	24c	2
	אמונה	FIRMNESS	53d	3 b
	מזמור	MELODY	274c	
	תחנון	SUPPLICATION FOR FAVOR	337d	2
	צדקה	RIGHTEOUSNESS	842c	6 a
143 2	את	WITH	86b	1 dd
	ה	THE	*208c	1 hb
	חי	ALIVE	312b	1 d
	כל	ALL	482b	1 ec
	עבד	SLAVE	714a	3
	עבד	SLAVE	714c	6
	פנה	FACE	817a	24a g
	צדק	BE JUST	842c	2
	משפט	JUDGMENT	1048c	1 c
143 3	דכא	CRUSH	194a	
	חיה	LIVING THING	312d	2
	מחשך	DARK PLACE	365b	C
	ישב	CAUSE TO SIT	443d	3 a
	עולם	LONG DURATION	762a	1 b
	רדף	PURSUE	922d	1 f
143 4	עטף	BE FEEBLE	742c	
	על	UPON	753c	2 1d
	שמם	BE DESOLATED	1031b	1
143 5	הגה	MUSE	211d	3 a
	זכר	REMEMBER	269d	11 d
	יום	DAY	399c	5 c
	קדם	FRONT	869d	2 c
	שיח	MUSE	967b	
143 6	כף	HOLLOW OF THE HAND	496c	1 d4
	ל	TO	510d	1 a
	נפש	SOUL	660c	5 b
	סלה	LIFT UP	700b	
	עיף	FAINT	746b	
	פרש	SPREAD OUT	831c	1 a
143 7	בור	PIT	92c	5
	כלה	BE FINISHED	477d	2 b
	מהר	HASTEN	555a	1
	מהר	QUICKLY	*555b	
	משל	BE LIKE	605a	
	סתר	HIDE	711d	2 a
	עם	WITH	768a	1 f
	רוח	BREATH	925b	3 f
143 8	בטח	TRUST	105a	1 3a
	בקר	MORNING	134b	1
	דרך	WAY	203c	6 b
	זו	THIS	262c	2

Ch v.	Heb	Eng	Page	Sec
	חסד	GOODNESS	339a	2 1a
	ידע	KNOW	395a	
	נפש	SOUL	660d	6 a
143 9	נשא	LIFT	670d	1 b 9
	כסה	COVER	492a	
143 10	ארץ	EARTH	76b	4 c
	טוב	PLEASANT	374d	9 b
	מישור	LEVEL PLACE	449d	2
	למד	LEARN	540d	
	נחה	LEAD	635a	
	רוח	BREATH	926a	9 f
	רצון	GOODWILL	953c	3 a
143 11	חיה	LIVE	311c	3 d
	יצא	BRING OUT	424d	2
	מען	PURPOSE	775b	1 a
	צדקה	RIGHTEOUSNESS	842c	6 a
143 12	אבד	DESTROY	2b	1
	חסד	GOODNESS	339a	2 1a
	צמת	EXTERMINATE	856c	
	צמת	EXTERMINATE	856c	
	צרר	SHEW HOSTILITY TOWARD	865d	
144 1	ברך	BLESS	138d	2 a
	מלחמה	WAR	536b	
	למד	LEARN	540d	
	אצבע	FINGER	840c	1 d
	צור	ROCK	849d	2
	קרב	BATTLE	898b	
144 2	מגן	SHIELD	171c	
	חסד	GOODNESS	339a	2
	חסה	SEEK REFUGE	340b	
	פלט	ESCAPE	812b	1
	מצודה	FASTNESS	845a	
	רדד	BEAT OUT	921d	
	משגב	SECURE HEIGHT	960d	2
	תחת	UNDERNEATH	*1065c	2 l c a
144 3	אדם	MAN	9b	2
	אנוש	MAN	60d	3
	ו	AND	254a	2 b
	חשב	THINK	363c	1
144 4	אדם	MAN	9b	2
	דמה	BE LIKE	198a	
	הבל	VAPOUR	210d	2
	עבר	PASS OVER	718b	6 b
	צל	SHADOW	853b	3
144 5	ירד	GO DOWN	*433b	2
	נגע	TOUCH	619a	1 b
	נטה	BEND	641a	3 f
	עשן	SMOKE	798c	1 a
	שמי	HEAVENS	1030b	2 a
	שמי	HEAVENS	1030b	2 a
144 6	ברק	FLASH	140b	
	ברק	LIGHTNING	140c	1
	המם	CONFUSE	243a	2
	חץ	ARROW	346c	2
	פוץ	BE DISPERSED	807b	1 b
	שלח	SEND	1018c	2 b
144 7	בן	SON	121c	7 a
	מי	WATER	565d	4 a
	נכר	FOREIGNNESS	648d	2
	פצה	PART	822c	2
	מרום	HEIGHT	928d	2
	שלח	SEND	1018d	3 b
144 8	ימין	RIGHT HAND	411d	1 a
	שוא	EMPTINESS	996b	2
144 9	זמר	MAKE MUSIC	274b	2
	חדש	NEW	294a	A
	נבל	HARP	614c	
	עשור	A TEN	797d	2
144 10	דוד	DAVID	188a	
	תשועה	DELIVERANCE	448b	1
	פצה	PART	822c	2
	רע	EVIL	948a	1
144 11	בן	SON	121c	7 a
	ימין	RIGHT HAND	411d	1 a
	נכר	FOREIGNNESS	648d	2
	פצה	PART	822c	2
	שוא	EMPTINESS	996b	2
144 12	אשר	PARTICLE OF RELATION	82b	3
	תבנית	CONSTRUCTION	125d	1
	גדל	GROW UP	152c	
	היכל	PALACE	228b	1
	זוית	CORNER	265a	
	חטב	CUT OR GATHER WOOD	310a	
	חמבות	DARK-HUED STUFFS	310b	
	נטיע	PLANT	642d	
	נעורים	YOUTH	655c	
144 13	מזו	GARNER	265a	
	זן	KIND	275b	
	חוץ	THE OUTSIDE	300b	2 b
	מלא	FULL	571a	
	מן	FROM	582a	5 d1
	פוק	BRING OUT	807c	1
	קרה	COLD	*903b	
	אלף	ADDENDA ET CORRIGENDA	1120b	
	רבב	ADDENDA ET CORRIGENDA	1126c	
144 14	אלוף	TAME	48d	3
	יצא	GO OUT	423d	2 a
	סבל	BEAR	687d	
	פרץ	BURSTING FORTH	829d	2
	צוחה	OUTCRY	846d	

Ch v.	Heb	Eng	Page	Sec
	רחוב	PLAZA	932b	
144 15	אשר	HAPPINESS	81a	
	יהוה	YAHWEH	218d	2 1e
	ככה	THUS	462c	
145 1	ברך	BLESS	139a	1
	תהלה	PRAISE	240a	1
	מלך	KING	573b	3
	עד	PERPETUITY	723d	2 e
	עולם	LONG DURATION	762a	2 a
	רום	BE HIGH	927b	3
145 2	ברך	BLESS	139a	1
	הלל	PRAISE	238b	2 b
	יום	DAY	400c	7 g
	עד	PERPETUITY	723d	2 e
	עולם	LONG DURATION	762a	2 a
145 3	גדול	GREAT	153b	6 c
	גדולה	GREATNESS	153c	B
	הלל	PRAISE	239a	1
	חקר	SEARCHING	350d	
145 4	גבורה	MIGHT	150c	3
	דור	GENERATION	190a	2 c
	הוד	SPLENDOUR	217b	2
	נגד	BE CONSPICUOUS	617a	4
	שבח	PRAISE	986d	1
145 5	דבר	WORD	183c	4 2
	הדר	SPLENDOUR	214b	2
	כבוד	GLORY	458d	2 c2
	שיח	MUSE	967b	2
145 6	גדולה	GREATNESS	153c	B
	ירא	CAUSE FEAR	431d	2
	נבע	BUBBLE UP	*616a	3
	ספר	COUNT	708a	1
	עזוז	STRENGTH	739b	5
145 7	זכר	REMEMBRANCE	271b	1 c
	טוב	GOOD THINGS	375c	4 b
	נבע	BUBBLE UP	616a	3
	צדקה	RIGHTEOUSNESS	842c	6 a
	קשב	ATTENTIVENESS	904a	
	רב	MUCH	913b	1 c
	רב	MULTITUDE	914a	2
	רנן	GIVE A RINGING CRY	943c	
145 8	ארך	LONG	74a	
	גדול	GREAT	153c	8
	חנן	GRACIOUS	337a	
	חסד	GOODNESS	339b	2 3b
	רחום	COMPASSIONATE	933d	
145 9	טוב	PLEASANT	374d	9 b
	כל	ALL	483a	2 bb
	על	UPON	756c	27 a b
	רחמים	COMPASSION	933c	1
145 10	ברך	BLESS	139a	1
	חסד	KIND	339d	2 b
	ידה	PRAISE	392c	1 a2
145 11	גבורה	MIGHT	150c	3
	כבוד	HONOR	459b	6 b
	מלכות	ROYAL POWER	574d	1
145 12	גבורה	MIGHT	150c	3
	ידע	MAKE KNOWN	395a	
	כבוד	GLORY	458d	2 c2
	מלכות	ROYAL POWER	574d	1
145 13	דור	PERIOD	190a	1 c
	ו	AND	253b	1 ib
	כל	ALL	481c	1 b
	מלכות	ROYAL POWER	574d	1
	ממשלה	RULE	606a	3
	עולם	LONG DURATION	763a	21
145 14	זקף	RAISE UP	279a	
	כפף	BEND DOWN	496a	
	נפל	FALL	657b	2 c
	סמך	LEAN	702a	2
145 15	אכל	FOOD	38a	
	כל	ALL	482c	2 a
	עת	TIME	773d	2 b
	שבר	HOPE	960b	
145 16	חי	ALIVE	312b	1 d
	פתח	OPEN	835b	
	רצון	GOODWILL	953c	3 b
	שבע	SATISFIED	959d	1 c
145 17	דרך	WAY	204a	6 eb
	חסד	KIND	339c	1 c
	צדיק	JUST	843a	1 d
145 18	אמת	FIRMNESS	54c	5
	קרב	NEAR	898c	2 f
145 19	ירא	FEAR	431c	3 b
	ישע	DELIVER	446d	1 b
	רצון	GOODWILL	953c	3 b
	שועה	CRY FOR HELP	1003a	
145 20	אהב	LOVE	13a	3
	רשע	WICKED	957c	3
	שמד	BE EXTERMINATED	1029c	1
145 21	ברך	BLESS	139a	1
	בשר	FLESH	142d	6 c
	דבר	SPEAK	180d	1
	תהלה	PRAISE	240a	1
	עד	PERPETUITY	723d	2 e
	עולם	LONG DURATION	762d	2 g
146 1	יה	YAH	219c	
	הלל	PRAISE	238c	2 d1
146 2	הלל	PRAISE	238b	2 b
	זמר	MAKE MUSIC	274a	1
	חיים	LIFE	313b	1
	עוד	STILL	729c	2 aa
146 3	בטח	TRUST	105a	1 3b
	תשועה	DELIVERANCE	448b	1
	נדיב	NOBLE	622a	2

PROVERBS

Ch v.	Heb	Eng	Page	Sec
146 4	אבד	PERISH	1c	1
	אדמה	EARTH	9d	3
	יצא	GO OUT	423a	1 e
	ל	TO	511b	1 ga
	עזר	HELP	740d	2
	עשתן	THOUGHT	799d	
	רוח	BREATH	925c	4 d
	שוב	TURN BACK	997c	4 a
146 5	אל	GOD	42c	6 c
	אשר	HAPPINESS	81a	
	ב	IN	88d	17a
	יהוה	YAHWEH	218d	2 1e
	על	UPON	757d	27c c
	יעקב	JACOB	785a	
	שבר	HOPE	960b	
	ש	WHO	979d	1
146 6	אמת	FIRMNESS	54b	3 b
	ארץ	EARTH	76a	1 b
	עולם	LONG DURATION	762b	2 c
	שמר	KEEP	1037b	4 b
146 7	אסר	TIE	63d	3
	נתר	BE FREE	684a	2
	עשק	OPPRESS	798d	1
	רעב	HUNGRY	944c	
	משפט	JUDGMENT	1048c	1 f
146 8	אהב	LOVE	13a	5 a
	זקף	RAISE UP	279a	
	כפף	BEND DOWN	496a	
	עור	BLIND	734c	2 a
	עין	EYE	744b	1 j
	פקח	OPEN	824d	1 b
146 9	אלמנה	WIDOW	48b	
	גר	SOJOURNER	158b	2
	דרך	WAY	203b	5
	יתום	ORPHAN	450c	
	עוד	RETURN	728c	
	עות	BE BENT	736c	2
	רשע	WICKED	957c	3
146 10	דור	PERIOD	189d	1 b
	יה	YAH	219c	
	הלל	PRAISE	238c	2 d2
	מלך	BE KING	574a	
	עולם	LONG DURATION	762c	2 c
147 1	יה	YAH	219c	
	הלל	PRAISE	238c	2 d1
	תהלה	PRAISE	240a	
	זמר	MAKE MUSIC	274a	1
	טוב	PLEASANT	374c	5
	נאוה	SEEMLY	610a	2
	נעים	DELIGHTFUL	653d	1
147 2	בנה	BUILD	124b	1 ab
	נדח	BANISH	623a	2
	ישראל	ISRAEL	975d	2 a3
147 3	חבש	BIND	290a	
	לב	HEART	525b	2 6a
	עצבת	HURT	781a	
	רפא	HEAL	950a	3 a
	שבר	BREAK	990d	
147 4	כוכב	STAR	457a	
	מנה	COUNT	584a	1
	מספר	NUMBER	708d	1 a
	קרא	CALL	896a	6 f
147 5	אדון	LORD	11b	2 2
	תבונה	UNDERSTANDING	108b	3
	גדול	GREAT	153b	6 c
	כח	STRENGTH	471a	3
	מספר	NUMBER	708d	1 a
	רב	MUCH	913b	1 d
147 6	עוד	RETURN	728c	
	ענו	POOR	776c	3
	שפל	BECOME LOW	1050b	1
147 7	זמר	MAKE MUSIC	274b	2
	תודה	THANKSGIVING	392d	2
	כנור	LYRE	490b	
	כנור	LYRE	490b	
	ענה	SING	777b	
147 8	הר	MOUNTAIN	250c	1 i
	חציר	GREEN GRASS	348b	1
	כון	ESTABLISH	466c	2 b
	כסה	COVER	491d	1
	מטר	RAIN	564d	
	צמח	SPROUT	855c	1
147 9	בן	SON	121d	7 b
	לחם	FOOD	537b	2 b
	ערב	RAVEN	788b	
	קרא	CALL	845b	2 b
147 10	גבורה	STRENGTH	150b	1
	חפץ	DELIGHT IN	342d	2 a
	סוס	HORSE	692d	2
	רצה	BE PLEASED WITH	953a	1 a
	שוק	LEG	1003b	1
147 11	חסד	GOODNESS	339a	2 1a
	ירא	FEAR	431c	3 b
	רצה	BE PLEASED WITH	953a	1 a
	יחל	ADDENDA ET COR-RIGENDA	1124a	
147 12	הלל	PRAISE	238b	2 c
	ציון	ZION	851c	
	שבח	PRAISE	986d	1
147 13	בריח	BAR	138b	2
	בריח	BAR	138b	1 b
	ברך	BLESS	139a	2 a
	חזק	BE FIRM	304c	1 c
	שער	GATE	1044c	1
147 14	גבול	BOUNDARY	148a	2 a
	חלב	FAT	317a	3
	חמה	WHEAT	334d	
	חמה	WHEAT	*334d	
	שבע	SATISFIED	959d	1 b
147 15	אמרה	UTTERANCE	57b	
	מהרה	HASTE	555b	
	עד	AS FAR AS	724d	1 3
	רוץ	RUN	930b	1
	שלח	SEND	1018c	2 b
147 16	אפר	ASHES	68a	
	כפור	HOARFROST	499b	
	פזר	SCATTER	808b	
	צמר	WOOL	856a	
	קרח	ICE	*901c	2
	שלג	SNOW	1017a	
147 17	מי	WHO	567a	F c
	פנה	FACE	817b	2 4b d
	פת	FRAGMENT	837d	
	קרח	ICE	901c	2
	קרח	COLD	903b	
	שלך	THROW	1021b	2 a
147 18	דבר	WORD	182d	1 2a
	מסה	MELT	587b	
	נזל	FLOW	633d	1
	נשב	BLOW	674b	
147 19	חק	SOMETHING PRE-SCRIBED	349d	7 g
	נגד	BE CONSPICUOUS	616d	2
	משפט	JUDGMENT	1049a	4
147 20	יה	YAH	219c	
	הלל	PRAISE	238c	2 d2
	משפט	JUDGMENT	1048d	3
148 1	יה	YAH	219c	
	הלל	PRAISE	238c	2 d1
	מן	FROM	578a	1 a
	מרום	HEIGHT	928d	2
	הלל	PRAISE	238b	2 c
148 2	מלאך	MESSENGER	521d	2
	צבא	HOST	839a	1 b
148 3	אור	LIGHT	21c	2
	הלל	PRAISE	238b	2 c
	ירח	MOON	437a	
	כוכב	STAR	457a	
	שמש	SUN	1039b	1
148 4	הלל	PRAISE	238b	2 c
	מי	WATER	565c	1 f
	על	UPON	759b	4 2d
	שמי	HEAVENS	1029c	1 a
	שמי	HEAVENS	1030b	2
	שמי	HEAVENS	1030b	3
148 5	ברא	CREATE	135c	1
	הוא	HE, SHE, IT	*215b	1 a
	הלל	PRAISE	238a	2 b
	הלל	PRAISE	238b	2 b
	צוה	CHARGE	846a	5
148 6	חק	SOMETHING PRE-SCRIBED	349c	5
	נתן	GIVE	681b	3 d
	עבר	PASS OVER	717c	1 i
	עד	PERPETUITY	723d	2
	עולם	LONG DURATION	762b	2 b1
	עמד	STAND	764d	5
148 7	הלל	PRAISE	238b	2 c
	תהום	SEA	1063a	2
	תנין	SEA-MONSTER	1072c	3
148 8	אש	FIRE	77c	2
	דבר	WORD	182d	1 2b
	סערה	TEMPEST	704c	
	קיטור	SMOKE	882c	
	רוח	BREATH	924d	2 a
	שלג	SNOW	1017a	
148 9	ארז	CEDAR	72c	1 a
	גבעה	HILL	149a	3
	הר	MOUNTAIN	250b	1 c
	עץ	TREE	781c	1 b
	פרי	FRUIT	826b	1
148 10	בהמה	BEAST	97a	2
	חיה	LIVING THING	312c	1 b
	כנף	WING	489c	1 a
	צפור	BIRD	862a	2
	רמש	CREEPING THINGS	943a	1
148 11	לאם	PEOPLE	522c	
	שר	CHIEFTAIN	978d	7
	שפט	JUDGE	1047c	1 b
148 12	בחור	YOUNG MAN	104c	
	בתולה	VIRGIN	144a	
	זקן	OLD	278c	2 a
	נער	YOUTH	655a	1 d
148 13	הוד	SPLENDOUR	217b	2
	הלל	PRAISE	238a	2 c
	שגב	BE HIGH	960c	3
	יה	YAH	219c	
148 14	הלל	PRAISE	238c	2 d2
	תהלה	PRAISE	240a	1
	תהלה	PRAISE	240b	5 ca
	חסיד	KIND	339d	2 b
	קרב	NEAR	898c	2 d
	קרן	HORN	*902a	2
	קרן	HORN	902a	2
	רום	BE HIGH	927c	1 f
149 1	יה	YAH	219c	
	הלל	PRAISE	238c	2 d1
	תהלה	PRAISE	240a	2
	חדש	NEW	294a	A
	חסיד	KIND	339d	2 b
	חסיד	KIND	339d	2 b
	קהל	ASSEMBLY	874d	2 b
149 2	בן	SON	121b	1 jt
	מלך	KING	573b	3
	ציון	ZION	851b	
	ישראל	ISRAEL	975d	2 a3
149 3	הלל	PRAISE	238b	2 b
	זמר	MAKE MUSIC	274b	2
	מחול	DANCE	298b	
	מחול	DANCE	298b	
	כנור	LYRE	490b	
	כנור	LYRE	490b	
	תף	TIMBREL	1074c	
149 4	מחול	DANCE	298b	
	ישועה	VICTORY	447c	4
	ענו	POOR	776c	3
	רצה	BE PLEASED WITH	953a	1 a
149 5	חסיד	KIND	339d	2 b
	חסיד	KIND	339d	2 b
	כבוד	HONOR	459c	6 b
	עלז	EXULT	759c	
	רנן	GIVE A RINGING CRY	943c	
149 6	אל	GOD	42d	6 e
	גרון	THROAT	173c	2
	חרב	SWORD	352c	1 a
	פה	MOUTH	805b	3
	רומם	EXTOLLING	928c	
	תחת	UNDERNEATH	*1065c	2 1b
149 7	תוכחה	REBUKE	407b	
	לאם	PEOPLE	522c	
	נקמה	VENGEANCE	668c	2
	עשה	DO	794a	1 la 5
149 8	אסר	TIE	63d	3
	ברזל	IRON	137c	1 d
	זק	FETTER	279b	
	כבד	BE HONORED	457c	1 b
	כבל	FETTER	460a	
149 9	הדר	HONOUR	214b	3
	יה	YAH	219c	
	הלל	PRAISE	238c	2 d2
	חסיד	KIND	339d	2 b
	חסיד	KIND	339d	2 b
	עשה	DO	794a	1 la 5
	משפט	JUDGMENT	1048c	1 f
150 1	אל	GOD	42d	6 e
	יה	YAH	219c	
	הלל	PRAISE	238b	2 c
	הלל	PRAISE	238c	2 d1
	עז	STRENGTH	738d	1
	קדש	APARTNESS	871c	2 a
	רקיע	ADDENDA ET COR-RIGENDA	1126d	
150 2	גבורה	MIGHT	150c	3
	גדל	GREATNESS	152d	2 b
	הלל	PRAISE	238b	2 c
	הלל	PRAISE	238b	2 c
150 3	כנור	LYRE	490b	
	כנור	LYRE	490b	
	נבל	HARP	614c	
	שפר	HORN	1051d	
	שפר	HORN	1051d	
	תקע	BLAST	1075d	
150 4	הלל	PRAISE	238b	2 c
	מחול	DANCE	298b	
	מן	STRING	577c	
	עוגב	PIPE	721d	
	תף	TIMBREL	1074c	
150 5	הלל	PRAISE	238b	2 c
	צלצלים	CYMBALS	853a	
	תרועה	SHOUT OF WAR	930a	2
	שמע	HEAR	1034c	1
150 6	יה	YAH	219c	
	יה	YAH	219c	
	הלל	PRAISE	238c	2 d2
	הלל	PRAISE	238c	2 d2
	כל	ALL	482c	
	נשמה	BREATH	675d	3

PROVERBS

Ch v.	Heb	Eng	Page	Sec
1 1	משל	PROVERB	605b	6
	שלמה	SOLOMON	1024d	
1 2	אמר	WORD	57a	1
	בין	DISCERN	107a	1 b
	בינה	UNDERSTANDING	108a	3
	חכמה	WISDOM	315d	5 c
	ידע	KNOW	394c	5
	מוסר	DISCIPLINE	416c	1 c
1 3	מוסר	DISCIPLINE	416c	1 c
	מישר	LEVEL	449d	2
	צדק	RIGHTEOUSNESS	841d	5
	שכל	BE PRUDENT	968b	3
1 4	מזמה	PURPOSE	273d	2
	דעת	WISDOM	395d	2 a
	ערמה	CRAFTINESS	791a	2
	פתי	SIMPLE	834c	
1 5	בין	DISCERN	106d	
	תחבלה	DIRECTION	287b	
	חכם	WISE	315a	6 b1
	יסף	ADD	415b	1
	לקח	LEARNING	544b	1
	קנה	ACQUIRE	889a	1 d
1 6	בין	DISCERN	107a	1 b
	דבר	WORD	182d	2 1a
	חידה	RIDDLE	295c	1

Ch	v.	Heb	Eng	Page	Sec
		חכם	WISE	315a	6 b2
		מליצה	SATIRE	539c	
1	7	בוז	DESPISE	100b	
		חכמה	WISDOM	315d	5 c
		דעת	KNOWLEDGE	395d	2 b
		מוסר	DISCIPLINE	416c	1 c
		יראה	FEAR	432a	3
		משל	PROVERB	605b	6
1	8	ראשית	BEGINNING	912a	1 a
		אב	FATHER	3b	1
		אם	MOTHER	51d	1
		בן	SON	120b	1
		מוסר	DISCIPLINE	416c	1 c
		תורה	INSTRUCTION	435d	1 a
		משל	PROVERB	605b	6
1	9	נטש	FORSAKE	643d	2
		גרגרות	NECK	176b	
		חן	FAVOR	336b	1 a
		לויה	WREATH	531b	
		משל	PROVERB	605b	6
		ענק	NECKLACE	778d	
1	10	אבה	BE WILLING	2c	
		בן	SON	120b	1 c
		חטא	SINFUL	308b	2
		פתה	BE SIMPLE	834d	1
1	11	ארב	LIE IN WAIT	70b	
		דם	BLOOD	197a	2f
		חנם	OUT OF FAVOR	336d	C
		נקי	CLEAN	667c	1
		צפן	HIDE	860d	2
1	12	בור	PIT	92c	5
		בלע	SWALLOW UP	118b	2
		חי	ALIVE	312a	1 b
		שאול	SHEOL	983a	1
		תמים	SOUND	1071a	2
1	13	הון	WEALTH	223c	1
		יקר	PRECIOUS	430a	1 a
		מצא	FIND	592d	1 a
		שלל	SPOIL	1022a	3
1	14	גורל	LOT	174d	3
		כיס	BAG	476a	B
		נפל	FALL	658a	3
1	15	דרך	WAY	203d	6 d
		מנע	WITHHOLD	586a	
		נתיבה	PATH	677b	2 b
1	16	דם	BLOOD	196c	2 b
		מהר	HASTEN	555a	1
		רוץ	RUN	930b	1
		רע	EVIL	948d	2
1	17	בעל	LORD	127c	1 5a
		זרה	SCATTER	280c	
		חנם	OUT OF FAVOR	336c	B
		רשת	NET	440b	1 a
		כנף	WING	489c	1 a
		עין	EYE	744b	1 d
1	18	ארב	LIE IN WAIT	70b	
		דם	BLOOD	197a	2f
		צפן	HIDE	860d	2
1	19	ארח	WAY	73b	3 c
		בעל	OWNER	127b	1 1
		בצע	GAIN BY VIOLENCE	130b	
		בצע	UNJUST GAIN	130c	
		לקח	TAKE	543a	3 d
		נפש	SOUL	659d	3 c
1	20	חוץ	THE OUTSIDE	300a	2 a
		חכמה	WISDOM	315c	
		נתן	GIVE	679d	1 x
		רחוב	PLAZA	932b	
		רנן	GIVE A RINGING CRY	943b	3
1	21	אמר	WORD	57a	1
		המה	ROAR	242b	4
		פתח	OPENING	836a	
		ראש	HEAD	910d	2 a
1	22	אהב	LOVE	13a	2
		חמד	DESIRE	326b	B
		דעת	KNOWLEDGE	395d	2 b
		כסיל	FOOL	493a	
		ל	TO	515d	5 ia
		ליץ	SCORN	539b	
		לצון	SCORNING	539c	
		מתי	WHEN	607d	C
		פתי	SIMPLE	834c	
		פתי	SIMPLICITY	834c	
		שנא	HATE	971c	1 b
1	23	חכמה	WISDOM	315c	5 b
		ידע	KNOW	395a	
		תוכחת	REPROOF	407b	2
		נבע	FLOW	615d	1
		רוח	BREATH	926a	9 d
		שוב	TURN BACK	997d	6 c
1	24	מאן	REFUSE	549b	
		נטה	EXTEND	640a	1 a
1	25	אבה	BE WILLING	2c	
		תוכחת	REPROOF	407b	2
		עצה	ADVICE	420b	
		פרע	LET GO	829a	2
1	26	איד	DISTRESS	15d	3
		גם	ALSO	169d	4
		לעג	MOCK	541b	
		פחד	DREAD	808c	1
		שחק	LAUGH	965d	1 a
1	27	איד	DISTRESS	15d	3
		אתה	COME	87c	
		סופה	STORM-WIND	693a	
		פחד	DREAD	808c	

Ch	v.	Heb	Eng	Page	Sec
		צוקה	PRESSURE	848a	
		צרה	DISTRESS	865b	
		שאוה	STORM	981a	
		שואה	DEVASTATION	996c	1
1	28	מצא	FIND	593a	1a
		קרא	CALL	895d	5 c
		שחר	LOOK EARLY	1007c	
1	29	בחר	CHOOSE	104b	5 b
		דעת	KNOWLEDGE	395d	2 b
		יראה	FEAR	432a	3
		תחת	INSTEAD	1066a	2 3b
1	30	אבה	BE WILLING	2c	
		תוכחת	REPROOF	407b	2
		עצה	ADVICE	420b	
		נאץ	CONTEMN	610d	
1	31	אכל	EAT	37c	1
		דרך	WAY	203d	6 d
		מועצה	PLAN	420b	
		פרי	FRUIT	826c	3
		שבע	SATISFIED	959c	1 c
1	32	אבד	CAUSE TO PERISH	2a	1
		הרג	KILL	247b	7
		פתי	SIMPLE	834c	
		משובה	TURNING BACK	1000b	
		שלוה	QUIETNESS	1017c	
1	33	בטח	SECURITY	105b	
		מן	FROM	578a	1b
		פחד	DREAD	808c	1
		רעה	MISERY	949a	1
		שאן	BE AT EASE	983b	
		שכן	SETTLE DOWN	1015a	1a
2	1	אמר	WORD	57a	1
		את	WITH	86c	3b
		בן	SON	120b	1c
		מצוה	COMMANDMENT	846c	3
		צפן	HIDE	860c	1
2	2	אזן	EAR	24a	2a
		תבונה	UNDERSTANDING	108b	3
		ה	THE	208c	1 hb
		ה	THE	208c	1 hb
		חכמה	WISDOM	315d	5 c
		לב	HEART	524d	2 3b
		לב	HEART	525a	24
		נטה	INCLINE	640d	3 d
2	3	קשב	ATTEND	904a	1
		אם	IF	50a	1b1
		תבונה	UNDERSTANDING	108b	3
		ה	THE	208c	1 hb
		ה	THE	208c	1 hb
		נתן	GIVE	679d	1 x
		קרא	CALL	895d	2 a
2	4	בקש	SEEK	134c	1 b
		חפש	SEARCH	344b	1
		מממון	HIDDEN TREASURE	380c	
		כסף	SILVER	494a	1
2	5	אז	THEN	23b	2
		אלהים	GOD	44b	4 a
		בין	DISCERN	106d	2 b
		דעת	KNOWLEDGE	395d	2 b
		יראה	FEAR	432a	3
		מצא	FIND	592d	1 a
2	6	תבונה	UNDERSTANDING	108b	2
		חכמה	WISDOM	315c	5 a
		דעת	KNOWLEDGE	395d	1 e
2	7	מגן	SHIELD	171c	
		הלך	WALK	235a	2 3e 1
		תושיה	SOUND WISDOM	444d	B
		ישר	STRAIGHT	449b	3 c2
		צפן	HIDE	860c	1
		תם	INTEGRITY	1070d	3
2	8	ארח	WAY	73b	3 b
		בינה	UNDERSTANDING	108a	4
		דרך	WAY	203b	5
		חסיד	KIND	339d	2 b
		נצר	GUARD	665d	2
2	9	בין	DISCERN	106d	2 b
		טוב	A GOOD THING	375b	4
		מישר	LEVEL	449d	2
		מעגל	ENTRENCHMENT	722d	2 b
		צדק	RIGHTEOUSNESS	841d	5
2	10	חכמה	WISDOM	315d	5 c
		דעת	KNOWLEDGE	395d	2 b
		לב	HEART	524d	2 3b
		נעם	BE DELIGHTFUL	653c	
		נפש	SOUL	661b	0
2	11	תבונה	UNDERSTANDING	108b	2
		מזמה	PURPOSE	273d	2
		נצר	GUARD	665d	2
2	12	דרך	WAY	203d	6 d
		תהפכה	PERVERSITY	246c	
2	13	ארח	WAY	73b	3b
		דרך	WAY	203d	6 d
		חשך	DARKNESS	365b	3 f
		ישר	STRAIGHTNESS	449c	1
		עזב	LEAVE	737c	2 d3
2	14	תהפכה	PERVERSITY	246c	
		רע	EVIL	949a	3
		שמח	JOYFUL	970d	2
2	15	ארח	WAY	73b	3 c
		לוז	BE CROOKED	531b	
		מעגל	ENTRENCHMENT	722d	2 b
		עקש	TWISTED	786a	
2	16	אמר	WORD	57a	1
		אשה	WOMAN	61a	1
		זור	BE A STRANGER	266c	2 b
		חלק	BE SMOOTH	325b	2

Ch	v.	Heb	Eng	Page	Sec
2	17	נכרי	FOREIGN	649a	2
		אלהים	GOD	44d	4 c
		אלוף	TAME	48d	2
		ברית	COVENANT	136c	1 5
		נעורים	YOUTH	655c	
		עזב	LEAVE	737b	2 b1
2	18	שכח	FORGET	1013b	1 c
		מעגל	ENTRENCHMENT	722d	2 b
		רפאים	SHADES	952b	
		שוח	SINK DOWN	1001b	
		שוח	SINK DOWN	1001b	
2	19	ארח	WAY	73b	3 b
		בוא	COME	98a	1 e
		חיים	LIFE	313b	2
		נשג	REACH	673c	2
2	20	שוב	TURN BACK	997c	4 b
		דרך	WAY	203c	6 c
		טוב	PLEASANT	374d	0 a
		צדיק	JUST	843a	3 b
		שמר	KEEP	1037a	3 c
2	21	ישר	STRAIGHT	449b	3 c2
		שכן	SETTLE DOWN	1015b	2 a
		תמים	SOUND	1071b	4
2	22	בגד	ACT TREACHEROUSLY	93d	D
		כרת	BE CUT OFF	504b	1 b
		נסח	TEAR AWAY	650c	
3	1	תורה	INSTRUCTION	435d	1 a
		נצר	GUARD	666a	3
		מצוה	COMMANDMENT	846c	3
		שכח	FORGET	1013b	1 c
3	2	ארך	LENGTH	73d	B
		חיים	LIFE	313b	1
		יום	DAY	399b	4 a
		יסף	ADD	415a	1
		שלום	PEACE	1023a	1
3	3	אמת	FIRMNESS	54a	3 a
		גרגרות	NECK	176b	
		חסד	GOODNESS	338d	1 2
		כתב	WRITE	507c	1 b1
		לב	HEART	525a	2 3d
		לוח	TABLET	*531d	1
		לוח	TABLET	531d	1
		קשר	BIND	905b	1 b
3	4	אלהים	GOD	44b	4 a
		חן	FAVOR	336b	2 b2
		טוב	PLEASANT	374d	8
		מצא	FIND	592d	1 a
		שכל	PRUDENCE	968c	2
3	5	בטח	TRUST	105b	1 5a
		בינה	UNDERSTANDING	108a	2
		לב	HEART	524c	2 2
		שען	LEAN	1043d	
3	6	ארח	WAY	73a	2
		דרך	WAY	203b	5
		ישר	MAKE STRAIGHT	448d	1
3	7	חכם	WISE	314d	3
		ירא	FEAR	431c	3 b
		סור	TURN ASIDE	693d	1
		רע	EVIL	949a	3
3	8	כישור	DISTAFF	*507a	
		עצם	BONE	782d	1 d
		רפאות	HEALING	951b	
		שקוי	DRINK	1052d	
		שר	NAVEL-STRING	1057a	
3	9	תבואה	PRODUCT	100a	1
		הון	WEALTH	223c	1
		ו	AND	254c	3
		כבד	MAKE HONORABLE	457d	2 c
		ראשית	BEGINNING	912b	1 b
3	10	אסם	STOREHOUSE	62a	
		יקב	WINE-VAT	428c	
		תירוש	NEW WINE	440d	
		מלא	FILL	570b	1
		פרץ	BREAK THROUGH	829c	9
		שבע	PLENTY	960a	1
3	11	תוכחת	REPROOF	407b	2
		מוסר	DISCIPLINE	416c	2 a
		מאס	REJECT	549c	1 a
		קוץ	FEEL A LOATHING	881a	1
3	12	אהב	LOVE	13a	5 a
		בן	SON	120a	1
		ו	AND	252c	1 b
		יכח	CORRECT	407a	6
		רצה	BE PLEASED WITH	953a	1 b
3	13	אשר	HAPPINESS	81a	
		תבונה	UNDERSTANDING	108b	3
		חכמה	WISDOM	315d	5 c
		מצא	FIND	593a	1 a
3	14	תבואה	REVENUE	100b	2 b
		חרוץ	GOLD	359a	
		טוב	PLEASANT	374c	6
		כסף	SILVER	494b	5
		סחר	TRAFFIC	695c	
3	15	חפץ	DELIGHT	343b	2
		יקר	PRECIOUS	*430a	1 c
		יקר	PRECIOUS	430a	1 b
		פנינים	CORALS	819d	
		שוה	AGREE WITH	1000d	
3	16	ארך	LENGTH	73d	B
		יום	DAY	399b	4 a
		ימין	RIGHT HAND	*411d	1 c
		כבוד	HONOR	458c	2 a
		עשר	RICHES	799b	
		שמאל	LEFT	969d	2

PROVERBS

Ch	v.	Heb	Eng	Page	Sec
		יקש	BE ENSNARED	430c	2
		לכד	CAPTURE	540b	2
6	3	אזו	THEN	66b	2
		כף	POWER	496d	2
		נצל	DELIVER ONESELF	664c	1
		רהב	ACT STORMILY	923b	
		רפס	STAMP	952c	
6	4	שנה	SLEEP	446a	
		תנומה	SLUMBER	630b	
		נתן	GIVE	679a	1 g
		עפעף	EYELID	733d	
6	5	יקוש	FOWLER	430c	
		נצל	DELIVER ONESELF	664c	1
		צבי	GAZELLE	840b	
		צפור	BIRD	862a	1
6	6	דרך	WAY	203d	6 d
		חכם	BE WISE	314c	
		נמלה	ANT	649c	
		עצל	SLUGGISH	782b	
6	7	משל	RULE	605d	1
		קצין	CHIEF	892d	3
		שטר	OFFICIAL	1009c	
		שטר	OFFICIAL	1009c	
6	8	אגר	GATHER	8d	
		מאכל	FOOD	38b	
		כון	ESTABLISH	466b	2 a
		לחם	FOOD	537b	2 b
		קיץ	SUMMER	884d	1
		קציר	HARVESTING	894d	3
6	9	שנה	SLEEP	446a	
		מתי	WHEN	607d	A
		עצל	SLUGGISH	782b	
		שכב	LIE DOWN	1012a	1 b
6	10	חבק	CLASPING	287d	
		שנה	SLEEP	446a	
		מעט	A FEW	590a	1 b
		תנומה	SLUMBER	630b	
6	11	מגן	SHIELD	171c	
		הלך	WALK	235b	1
		הלך	WALK	*236a	1 b
		מחסור	NEED	341d	3
		ריש	POVERTY	930d	
6	12	אדם	MAN	9b	1
		און	TROUBLE	20a	3
		בליעל	WORTHLESSNESS	116b	2
		הלך	WALK	234d	2 3a 2g
		עקשות	CROOKEDNESS	786a	
		פה	MOUTH	805a	2 a
6	13	ב	IN	90b	3 4
		ירה	POINT OUT	435b	4
		מלל	RUB	576c	
		עין	EYE	744c	11
		אצבע	FINGER	840c	1 d
		קרץ	PINCH	902d	1
6	14	מדון	STRIFE	193b	1
		תהפכה	PERVERSITY	246c	
		חרש	CUT IN	360c	3
		רע	EVIL	948d	2
		שלח	SEND	1019b	3
6	15	איד	DISTRESS	15d	3
		פתע	SUDDENNESS	837b	
		פתאם	SUDDENNESS	837c	
		מרפא	HEALING	951c	2
		שלוה	QUIETNESS	1017d	
6	16	הם	THEY	*241c	4 a
		ו	AND	252c	1 c
		שבע	SEVEN	988a	1 a
		שש	SIX	995d	5
		תועבה	ABOMINATION	1073a	2 b
6	17	דם	BLOOD	*196c	2 b
		דם	BLOOD	196d	2 d
		לשון	TONGUE	546c	1 b
		נקי	CLEAN	667c	1
		עין	EYE	744c	2 a
		רום	BE HIGH	926c	2 b
		רום	WINK	*931b	
		שקר	DECEPTION	1055c	5
6	18	און	TROUBLE	20a	3
		חרש	CUT IN	360c	3
		מחשבה	THOUGHT	364c	2
		לב	HEART	524d	2 3c
		מהר	HASTEN	555a	2
		רוץ	RUN	930b	1
		רעה	MISERY	949b	2
6	19	בין	INTERVAL	107c	1 d
		מדון	STRIFE	193b	1
		כזב	LIE	469c	
		עד	WITNESS	729d	2 c
		פוח	BREATHE	806b	1
		שלח	SEND	1019b	3
		שקר	DECEPTION	1055c	3
6	20	אב	FATHER	3b	1
		אם	MOTHER	51d	1
		בן	SON	120a	1
		תורה	INSTRUCTION	435d	1 a
		נטש	FORSAKE	643d	2
		נצר	GUARD	666a	3
6	21	גרגרות	NECK	176b	
		לב	HEART	525a	2 3d
		תמיד	CONTINUITY	556b	1 a
		ענד	BIND AROUND	772c	
		קשר	BIND	905b	1 b
6	22	הלך	WALK	235d	1 b
		נחה	LEAD	635a	
		קיץ	AWAKE	884c	1 a
		שיח	MUSE	967b	3 b
		שכב	LIE DOWN	1012a	1 b
		שמר	KEEP	1036c	1 b
6	23	אור	LIGHT	21d	9
		דרך	WAY	203c	6 c
		חיים	LIFE	313b	2
		תוכחת	REPROOF	407b	2
		מוסר	DISCIPLINE	416c	1 c
		תורה	INSTRUCTION	435d	1 a
		נר	LAMP	632d	
		מצוה	COMMANDMENT	846c	3
6	24	אשה	WOMAN	61b	1
		חלקה	SMOOTH PART	325c	3
		לשון	TONGUE	546b	1 b
		נכרי	FOREIGN	649a	2
		רע	EVIL	949a	3
6	25	חמד	DESIRE	326b	A
		יפי	BEAUTY	421d	
		לבב	HEART	524a	2 9a
		לקח	TAKE	543d	8
6	26	עפעף	EYELID	733d	
		אשה	WOMAN	61a	1
		אשה	WOMAN	61b	1
		בעד	ON BEHALF OF	126d	2
		זנה	COMMIT FORNICATION	275d	1
		יקר	PRECIOUS	430a	1 b
		ככר	ROUND	503b	2
		צוד	HUNT	844c	
6	27	בגד	GARMENT	94a	1
		חיק	BOSOM	300d	1
		חתה	SNATCH UP	367a	
		כוה	BE BURNED	*464d	
		שרף	BURN	977a	
6	28	גחלת	COAL	160d	
		הלך	WALK	235b	1
		כוה	BE BURNED	464d	
6	29	בא	COME	98a	1 e
		כן	SO	485d	1 a
		נגע	TOUCH	619a	3
		נקה	BE CLEAN	667b	3
6	30	בוז	DESPISE	100b	
		גנב	THIEF	170c	
		גנב	STEAL	170c	
		מלא	FILL	570d	2
6	31	רעב	BE HUNGRY	944b	1
		הון	WEALTH	223c	1
		מצא	FIND	394a	1 g2
		שבעתים	SEVEN FOLD	988d	1
6	32	חסר	NEEDY	341c	
		לב	HEART	524c	2 3a
		נאף	COMMIT ADULTERY	610c	1 a
		שחת	GO TO RUIN	1008b	2
6	33	חרפה	REPROACH	358a	2 a
		מחה	WIPE OUT	562b	2
		מצא	FIND	592d	1 a
		נגע	STROKE	619c	1
		קלון	DISHONOUR	886a	2
6	34	גבר	MAN	150a	
		חמל	SPARE	328b	
		חמה	RAGE	404c	2 a
		נקם	VENGEANCE	668b	3
		קנאה	ZEAL	888b	1
6	35	אבה	BE WILLING	2c	
		כפר	RANSOM	497b	1
		נשא	LIFT	670c	1 b 3
		שחד	BRIBE	1005a	
		שחד	GIVE A BRIBE	1005a	
7	1	אמר	WORD	57a	1
		מצוה	COMMANDMENT	846c	3
		צפן	HIDE	860c	1
		שמר	KEEP	1037a	3 d
7	2	אישון	PUPIL	36b	
		תורה	INSTRUCTION	435d	1 a
		מצוה	COMMANDMENT	846c	3
		שמר	KEEP	1037a	3 d
7	3	לב	HEART	525a	2 3d
		לוח	TABLET	*531d	1
		לוח	TABLET	531d	1
		אצבע	FINGER	840c	1 d
		קשר	BIND	905b	1 b
7	4	אחות	SISTER	28a	4
		בינה	UNDERSTANDING	108a	4
		ה	THE	208c	1 hb
		ה	THE	208c	1 hb
		חכמה	WISDOM	315d	5 c
		מודע	KINSMAN	396b	
7	5	אמר	WORD	57a	1
		אשה	WOMAN	61a	1
		זור	BE A STRANGER	266c	2 b
		חלק	BE SMOOTH	325b	1
		נכרי	FOREIGN	649a	2
7	6	חלון	WINDOW	319d	
		אשנב	WINDOW-LATTICE	1039d	
		שקף	LOOK DOWN	1054c	
7	7	בין	DISCERN	106d	1 a
		בן	SON	121b	3
		חסר	NEEDY	341c	
		לב	HEART	524c	2 3a
		פתי	SIMPLE	834c	
7	8	דרך	WAY	202d	1
		עבר	PASS OVER	718b	5 h
		צעד	STEP	857c	
		שוק	STREET	1003b	
7	9	אישון	PUPIL	36b	
		אפלה	DARKNESS	66c	1
		לילה	NIGHT	538d	1
		נשף	TWILIGHT	676a	1
		ערב	SUNSET	788a	2
7	10	זנה	COMMIT FORNICATION	275d	1
		נצר	GUARD	666a	4
		קרא	ENCOUNTER	897a	1
		שית	GARMENT	1011c	
7	11	המה	ROAR	242b	5
		סרר	BE STUBBORN	711a	
		שכן	SETTLE DOWN	1015a	1 a
7	12	ארב	LIE IN WAIT	70b	
		חוץ	THE OUTSIDE	*300a	2 a
		פנה	CORNER	819c	1 a
		פעם	OCCURRENCE	822b	3 e
		רחוב	PLAZA	932b	
7	13	חזק	BE FIRM	305a	6 a
		נשק	KISS	676b	
		עזז	BE STRONG	738c	
7	14	זבח	SACRIFICE	257d	2 5
		על	UPON	753b	2 1c
		שלם	PEACE-OFFERING	1023c	
7	15	יצא	GO OUT	423d	2 c
		מצא	FIND	593a	1 b
		פנה	FACE	816a	1 2a
7	16	שחר	LOOK EARLY	1007c	
		אטון	THREAD	32a	
		חטבות	DARK-HUED STUFFS	310b	
		מצרים	EGYPT	595c	1 a
		ערש	COUCH	793a	
		ירבעם	BE-SPREAD	914d	
7	17	אהל	ALOE	14d	2
		מר	MYRRH	600d	
		נוף	BESPRINKLE	631d	
		קנמון	CINNAMON	890a	
		משכב	COUCH	1012d	1
7	18	אהב	LOVE	13b	1
		דד	BREAST	186d	
		דוד	LOVE	187c	3
		עלס	REJOICE	763a	
		רוה	BE SATURATED	924a	
7	19	הלך	WALK	230c	1 1d 1a
		רחק	DISTANT	935c	2 a3
7	20	כסא	FULL MOON	490c	
		ל	TO	516d	6 a
		לקח	TAKE	542d	1
		צרור	BUNDLE	865c	
7	21	חלק	SMOOTHNESS	325b	
		לקח	TEACHING	544b	2
		נדח	THRUST	623b	4
		נטה	INCLINE	640d	3 c
		שפה	SPEECH	973d	1 a1
7	22	טבח	SLAUGHTERING	370d	1
		מוסר	DISCIPLINE	416c	2 b
		עכס	ANKLET	747c	
		פתאם	SUDDENNESS	837c	
		שור	A HEAD OF CATTLE	1004b	
7	23	ב	IN	90a	3 3a
		הוא	HE, SHE, IT	216d	6 a
		חץ	ARROW	346c	2
		כבד	LIVER	458b	
		מהר	HASTEN	555a	1
		נפש	SOUL	659d	3 c
		פח	BIRD-TRAP	809a	1
		פלח	CLEAVE	812a	1
		צפור	BIRD	862a	1
7	24	אחרי	BACKWARDS	30c	1
		אמר	WORD	57a	1
		קשב	ATTEND	904a	
7	25	דרך	WAY	203d	6 d
		נתיבה	PATH	677b	2 b
		שטה	TURN ASIDE	966b	
		שטה	TURN ASIDE	966b	
		תעה	ERR	1073c	1
7	26	הרג	KILL	247b	7
		נפל	FALL	658a	2
		עצום	MIGHTY	783a	
7	27	חדר	CHAMBER	293d	
		ירד	GO DOWN	433b	1 i
		מות	DEATH	560d	3
		שאול	SHEOL	982d	1
8	1	תבונה	UNDERSTANDING	108b	4
		חכמה	WISDOM	*315c	5 b
		חכמה	WISDOM	315c	5 b
		נתן	GIVE	679d	1 x
8	2	בית	BETWEEN	108a	
		בית	HOUSE	109c	2
		דרך	WAY	202d	1
		נצב	STAND	662a	1 a
		נתיבה	PATH	677b	1
		ראש	HEAD	910d	2 a
		מרום	HEIGHT	928d	1
8	3	מבוא	ENTRANCE	99d	1
		יד	HAND	391b	5 f
		ל	TO	511d	2
		פה	MOUTH	805b	4
		קרת	TOWN	900d	1
		רנן	GIVE A RINGING CRY	943b	3
		שער	GATE	1044d	1 a
8	4	אדם	MAN	9c	2
8	5	בין	DISCERN	107a	1 b
		חכמה	WISDOM	315c	5 b
		לב	HEART	524d	2 3b
		ערמה	CRAFTINESS	791a	

Ch	v.	Heb	Eng	Page	Sec
8	6	פתי	SIMPLE	834c	
		מושר	LEVEL	449d	2
		נגיד	LEADER	618b	5
		מפתח	OPENING	836b	
8	7	שפה	SPEECH	973d	1 a1
		אמת	FIRMNESS	54b	4 a
		הגה	UTTER	211d	2
		חך	PALATE	335a	B
		רשע	WICKEDNESS	957d	1
		תועבה	ABOMINATION	1073a	2 a
8	8	אמר	WORD	57a	1
		נכח	STRAIGHTNESS	647c	
		עקש	TWISTED	786a	
		פתל	TWIST	836c	
		צדק	RIGHTEOUSNESS	841d	4
8	9	בין	DISCERN	107a	1 b
		דעת	WISDOM	395d	2 a
		ישר	STRAIGHT	449a	3 a
		מצא	FIND	592d	1 a
		נכח	STRAIGHTNESS	647c	
8	10	אל	NOT	39b	A bg
		בחר	CHOOSE	104b	A
		חרוץ	GOLD	359a	
		דעת	WISDOM	395d	2 a
		מוסר	DISCIPLINE	416c	1 c
8	11	חכמה	WISDOM	315c	5 b
		חכמה	WISDOM	315c	5 c
		חפץ	DELIGHT	343b	2
		טוב	PLEASANT	374c	6
		פנינים	CORALS	819d	
		שוה	AGREE WITH	1000d	
8	12	מזמה	PURPOSE	273d	2
		חכמה	WISDOM	315c	5 c
		דעת	WISDOM	395d	2 a
		מצא	FIND	593b	2 c
		ערמה	CRAFTINESS	791a	2
		שכן	SETTLE DOWN	1015b	2 e
8	13	גאה	PRIDE	144d	
		גאון	EXALTATION	145a	2
		דרך	WAY	203d	6 d
		תהפכה	PERVERSITY	246c	
		יראה	FEAR	432a	3
		כן	SO	485d	1 a
		פה	MOUTH	805a	2 a
		רע	EVIL	948d	3
8	14	בינה	UNDERSTANDING	108a	4
		גבורה	MIGHT	150b	2
		חכמה	WISDOM	315c	5 b
		עצה	ADVICE	420b	
		תושיה	SOUND WISDOM	444d	A
8	15	מלך	BE KING	574a	
		צדק	RIGHTEOUSNESS	841c	2 a
		רזן	BE WEIGHTY	931b	2
8	16	נדיב	NOBLE	622a	2
		שר	CHIEFTAIN	978b	2 b
		שרר	ACT AS PRINCE	979a	
		שפט	JUDGE	1047c	1 b
8	17	אהב	LOVE	13a	2
		מצא	FIND	593a	1 a
		שחר	LOOK EARLY	1007c	
8	18	את	WITH	86c	3 a
		הון	WEALTH	223c	1
		כבוד	HONOR	458c	2 a
		עתק	VALUABLE	801b	
		צדקה	RIGHTEOUSNESS	842c	6 b
8	19	תבואה	REVENUE	100b	2 b
		בחר	CHOOSE	104b	A
		חרוץ	GOLD	359a	
		טוב	PLEASANT	374c	6
		כסף	SILVER	494b	3
		פז	REFINED GOLD	808a	
		פרי	FRUIT	826c	3
8	20	ארח	WAY	73b	3 b
		הלך	WALK	235b	1
		נתיבה	PATH	677b	2 b
		צדקה	RIGHTEOUSNESS	842b	5
8	21	אהב	LOVE	13a	2
		אוצר	TREASURE	70a	3 b
		חכמה	WISDOM	*315c	5 b
		יש	SUBSTANCE	441b	1
		נחל	TAKE AS A POSSESSION	635d	1 b
8	22	מאז	FROM THAT TIME	23b	A
		דרך	WAY	204a	6 ea
		חכמה	WISDOM	*315c	5 b
		מפעל	WORK	821d	
		קדם	FRONT	869d	2 e
		קנה	ACQUIRE	889a	1 a
		ראשית	BEGINNING	912b	1 a
8	23	נסך	INSTALL	651c	
		עולם	LONG DURATION	762a	1 c
		קדם	FRONT	869d	2 e
		ראש	HEAD	911b	4 b
8	24	אין	NOT	35a	6 ab
		חול	WHIRL	297c	2
		כבד	BE MADE HEAVY	457d	1 a
		מעין	SPRING	746a	
		תהום	DEEP	1062d	1
8	25	גבעה	HILL	149a	3
		הר	MOUNTAIN	250a	1 c
		חול	WHIRL	297c	2
		טבע	SINK	371c	
		טרם	NOT YET	382c	2
		פנה	FACE	817d	24 e
8	26	חוץ	THE OUTSIDE	300b	2 b
		תבל	WORLD	385d	
		עד	UNTIL	725b	2 2d
		עפר	DRY EARTH	779d	2 a
		עשה	DO	794b	2 1b
		ראש	HEAD	911b	4 c
8	27	חוג	DRAW ROUND	*295b	
		חוג	VAULT	295b	
		חקק	CUT IN	349a	3
		כן	ESTABLISH	466b	1 a
		שמים	HEAVENS	1030a	1
		תהום	DEEP	1063b	3
8	28	אמץ	BE STRONG	55a	1
		עזז	BE STRONG	738c	
		עין	SPRING	745b	
		מעין	SPRING	*746a	
8	29	מעל	ABOVE	751c	1 a
		שחק	DUST	1007a	2
		תהום	DEEP	1062d	1
		חקק	CUT IN	349a	3
		חק	SOMETHING PRESCRIBED	349c	5
		מוסד	FOUNDATION	414c	
		עבר	PASS OVER	717c	2
		פה	MOUTH	805b	2 c
		שום	TO PLACE	963d	3 b
		שמי	HEAVENS	*1030a	1 a
8	30	אמון	ARCHITECT	54c	
		אצל	BESIDE	69b	A
		יום	DAY	400b	7 e1
		עת	TIME	773b	1 a
		שחק	LAUGH	965d	1
		שעשעים	DELIGHT	1044b	
8	31	ארץ	EARTH	76a	1 c
		חכמה	WISDOM	*315c	5 b
		תבל	WORLD	385d	
		שחק	LAUGH	965d	1
		שעשעים	DELIGHT	1044b	
8	32	אשר	HAPPINESS	81a	
		דרך	WAY	203c	6 b
		שמר	KEEP	1037a	3 c
8	33	חכם	BE WISE	314c	
		מוסר	DISCIPLINE	416c	1 c
		פרע	LET GO	829a	2
8	34	אשר	HAPPINESS	81a	
		דלת	DOOR	195a	1
		מזוזה	DOOR-POST	265b	1
		יום	DAY	400b	7 e1
		שקד	WATCH	1052a	1
8	35	חיים	LIFE	313b	2
		מצא	FIND	592d	1 a
		מצא	FIND	593a	1 a
		פוק	BRING OUT	807c	2
		רצון	GOODWILL	953c	1 a
		אהב	LOVE	13a	2
8	36	חטא	MISS A GOAL OR WAY	306d	1
		חמס	TREAT VIOLENTLY	329b	3
		שן	HATE	971d	3
9	1	בנה	BUILD	124b	1 ab
		חכמה	WISDOM	315c	5 b
		חצב	HEW	345a	2 a
		עמוד	PILLAR	765b	5 c
9	2	חכמה	WISDOM	*315c	5 b
		טבח	SLAUGHTER	370c	1
		טבח	SLAUGHTERING	370d	1
		יין	WINE	406d	E
		מסך	MIX	587c	2
		ערך	ARRANGE	789c	1 c
		שלחן	TABLE	1020b	2
9	3	גף	HEIGHT	172d	2
		נערה	GIRL	655b	2
		קרת	TOWN	900d	
9	4	חסר	NEEDY	341c	
		לב	HEART	524c	2 3a
		מי	WHO	567b	G
		סור	TURN ASIDE	693c	1
		פתי	SIMPLE	834b	
9	5	ב	IN	88c	1 2b
		חכמה	WISDOM	*315c	5 b
		יין	WINE	406d	E
		לחם	EAT	536d	1
		מסך	MIX	587c	2
		שתה	DRINK	1059b	1 a
9	6	בינה	UNDERSTANDING	108a	3
		דרך	WAY	203c	6 b
		עזב	LEAVE	737b	1 k
		פתי	SIMPLE	834c	
9	7	יכח	REPROVE	407a	5 b
		יסר	ADMONISH	416a	1
		ליץ	SCORN	539b	
		לקח	TAKE	543a	4 b
		מום	BLEMISH	548d	2 b
		קלון	DISHONOUR	886a	2
		רשע	WICKED	957c	3
9	8	אהב	LOVE	13a	1
		חכם	WISE	315a	6 b1
		יכח	REPROVE	407a	5 b
		יכח	REPROVE	407a	5 b
		ליץ	SCORN	539b	
9	9	חכם	BE WISE	314c	
		חכם	WISE	315a	6 b1
		ידע	MAKE KNOWN	395a	
		יסף	ADD	415b	1
		לקח	LEARNING	544b	1
		עוד	STILL	729b	1 c
		צדיק	JUST	843a	3 b
9	10	בינה	UNDERSTANDING	108a	3
		חכמה	WISDOM	315d	5 c
		תחלה	BEGINNING	321a	
		דעת	KNOWLEDGE	395d	2 b
		יראה	FEAR	432a	3
		קדוש	HOLY	872c	1 c
9	11	חיים	LIFE	313b	1
		יסף	ADD	415a	1
		רבה	BECOME MANY	915b	1 c
9	12	חכם	BE WISE	314c	
		ליץ	SCORN	539b	
9	13	נשא	LIFT	671a	2 b
		אשה	WOMAN	61b	1
		בל	NOT	115b	
		המה	ROAR	242b	5
		כסילות	FOLLY	493a	
		מה	AUGHT	553d	3
		פתיות	SIMPLICITY	834c	
9	14	ישב	SIT	442c	1 a
		כסא	SEAT OF HONOR	490d	2
		קרת	TOWN	900d	
9	15	מרום	HEIGHT	928d	1
		ארח	WAY	73a	1
		ישר	MAKE STRAIGHT	448d	1
		עבר	PASS OVER	*717d	4 a
9	16	חסר	NEEDY	341c	
		לב	HEART	524c	2 3a
		מי	WHO	567b	G
		סור	TURN ASIDE	693c	1
		פתי	SIMPLE	834b	
9	17	גנב	STEAL	170b	
		מתק	BE SWEET	608c	1
		נעם	BE DELIGHTFUL	653c	
		סתר	COVERING	712a	3
9	18	עמק	DEPTH	771b	
		קרא	CALL	895d	5 c
		רפאם	SHADES	952b	
		שאול	SHEOL	983b	3 a
		שחת	PIT	1001d	2
10	1	אב	FATHER	3b	1
		אם	MOTHER	51d	1
		בן	SON	120a	1
		ו	AND	252d	1 e
		חכם	WISE	315a	6 a
		תוגה	GRIEF	387b	
		ל	TO	513a	5 ad
		משל	PROVERB	605b	6
		שמח	REJOICE	970c	
		שלמה	SOLOMON	1024d	
10	2	אוצר	TREASURE	70a	2
		ו	AND	252d	1 e
		יעל	PROFIT	418d	
		צדקה	RIGHTEOUSNESS	842b	5
		רשע	WICKEDNESS	957c	1
10	3	הדף	THRUST	213d	1
		הוה	DESIRE	217d	1
		ו	AND	252d	1 e
		רעב	BE HUNGRY	944b	
		רשע	WICKED	957c	3
10	4	ו	AND	252d	1 e
		חרוץ	SHARP	358d	2
		עשר	BE RICH	799b	2
		רוש	BE IN WANT	930d	
		רמיה	LAXNESS	941c	
10	5	אגר	GATHER	8d	
		בוש	BE ASHAMED	101d	1
		פרד	DIVIDE	825c	1
		קיץ	SUMMER	884d	1
		קציר	HARVESTING	894d	3
		רדם	BE IN HEAVY SLEEP	922b	
10	6	שכל	BE PRUDENT	968c	5
		ברכה	BLESSING	139d	1 c
		חמס	VIOLENCE	329c	
		כסה	COVER	492a	5
10	7	ברכה	BLESSING	139d	2
		זכר	REMEMBRANCE	271b	2 a
		רקב	ROT	955a	
		שם	NAME	1028b	2 c
10	8	חכם	WISE	315a	6 a
		לב	HEART	524d	2 3b
		לבט	BE THRUST DOWN	526a	
		מצוה	COMMANDMENT	846b	1
		שפה	SPEECH	973c	1 a1
10	9	בטח	SECURITY	105b	
		דבר	WORD	183b	3 1
		דרך	WAY	203c	6 a
		הלך	WALK	234c	2 2
		הלך	WALK	235a	2 3e1
		ידע	BE MADE KNOWN	394c	1
		עקש	TWIST	786a	
		תם	INTEGRITY	1070d	3
10	10	ב	IN	*90b	3 4
		לבט	BE THRUST DOWN	526a	
		עין	EYE	744c	11
		עצבת	HURT	781a	
		קרץ	PINCH	902d	
		שפה	SPEECH	973c	1 a1
10	11	חיים	LIFE	313b	2
		חמס	VIOLENCE	329c	
		כסה	COVER	492a	5
		מקור	SPRING	881b	1 a
10	12	אהבה	LOVE	13b	1
		כסה	COVER	492a	5
		נצל	DELIVER	665a	3 b
		עור	ROUSE ONESELF	735a	

Ch	v.	Heb	Eng	Page	Sec
		פשע	TRANSGRESSION	833c	1
		שנא	HATING	971d	1
10	13	בין	DISCERN	106d	
		גו	BACK	156b	
		חכמה	WISDOM	315d	5 c
		חסר	NEEDY	341c	
		לב	HEART	524c	2 3a
10	14	שבט	ROD	987a	1 a
		חכם	WISE	315a	6 b1
		מחתה	TERROR	370c	2
		דעת	WISDOM	395d	2 a
		צפן	HIDE	860c	1
		קרב	NEAR	898d	3
10	15	דל	POOR	195d	
		הון	WEALTH	223c	1
		מחתה	TERROR	370c	2
		עז	STRENGTH	738d	1
		עשיר	RICH	799c	
		קריה	TOWN	900b	4
		ריש	POVERTY	930d	
10	16	תבואה	REVENUE	100b	2 a
		חטאת	SIN	308d	1 b
		חיים	LIFE	313b	2
		פעלה	WORK	821d	2
10	17	ארח	WAY	73b	3 b
		חיים	LIFE	313b	2
		תוכחת	REPROOF	407b	2
		מוסר	DISCIPLINE	416c	1 c
		עזב	LEAVE	737c	2 d3
		תעה	ERR	*1073c	3
		תעה	ERR	1073c	1
10	18	דבה	DEFAMATION	179b	2
		הוא	HE, SHE, IT	215d	2 a
		יצא	BRING OUT	425b	4 k
		כסה	COVER	491d	2
		שנא	HATING	971d	1
		שקר	DECEPTION	1055c	3
10	19	חדל	CEASE	293a	1 c
		חשך	WITHHOLD	362b	1 c
		פשע	TRANSGRESSION	833c	1
		רב	MULTITUDE	914a	1
		שכל	BE PRUDENT	968c	5
		שפה	SPEECH	973d	1 a1
10	20	בחר	CHOOSE	104b	A
		כסף	SILVER	494b	3
		לשון	TONGUE	546c	1 b
		מעט	A FEW	590b	2 d
		חסר	LACK	341b	1 a
		לב	HEART	524c	2 3a
		מות	DIE	560a	2 d
		רעה	TEND	945a	1 c
10	22	ברכה	BLESSING	139d	1 b
		הוא	HE, SHE, IT	215d	2 a
		יסף	ADD	415b	1
		עצב	PAIN	780d	1
		עשר	BE RICH	799b	1
10	23	תבונה	UNDERSTANDING	108b	2
		זמה	PLAN	273c	2 b
		חכמה	WISDOM	315d	5 c
		כסיל	FOOL	493a	
		שחק	LAUGHTER	966a	3
10	24	תאוה	DESIRE	16c	2
		בוא	COME	98c	2 b
		מגורה	FEAR	159a	
		הוא	HE, SHE, IT	215d	2 a
		נתן	GIVE	678d	1 e
		נתן	GIVE	680a	1 z
10	25	ו	AND	255a	5 cg
		יסוד	FOUNDATION	414b	1
		סופה	STORM-WIND	693a	
		עבר	PASS OVER	717c	4 a
10	26	חמץ	VINEGAR	330a	
		כ	LIKE	454c	2 d
		כן	SO	486b	2 ad a
		עצל	SLUGGISH	782b	
		עשן	SMOKE	798c	1 c
		שן	TOOTH	1042a	1 a
10	27	יסף	ADD	415b	1
		יראה	FEAR	432a	3
		קצר	BE SHORT	894a	
		קצר	BE SHORT	894b	
10	28	אבד	PERISH	1d	2
		תוחלת	HOPE	404b	
		תקוה	HOPE	876b	3
		שמחה	JOY	970d	4
10	29	און	TROUBLE	20a	3
		דרך	WAY	204a	6 eb
		מחתה	TERROR	370c	2
		מעוז	PLACE OF SAFETY	732a	2 a
		פעל	DO	821b	1 b
		תם	INTEGRITY	1070d	3
10	30	בל	NOT	115b	
		מוט	SHAKE	557a	
		עולם	LONG DURATION	762a	2 a
10	31	תהפכה	PERVERSITY	246c	
		חכמה	WISDOM	315c	4
		כרת	BE CUT OFF	504a	1 a
		לשון	TONGUE	546c	1 b
		נוב	BEAR FRUIT	626c	
10	32	תהפכה	PERVERSITY	246c	
		פרד	DIVIDE	825c	1
		רצון	GOODWILL	953c	1 b
11	1	אבן	STONE	6d	5
		מאזן	BALANCES	24d	
		מרמה	DECEIT	941b	
		רצון	GOODWILL	953c	1 a

Ch	v.	Heb	Eng	Page	Sec
11	2	שלם	COMPLETE	1024a	1 a
		את	WITH	86c	3 a
		זדון	INSOLENCE	268a	2
		חכמה	WISDOM	315d	5 c
		צנוע	MODEST	857a	
		קלון	DISHONOUR	886a	2
11	3	ישר	STRAIGHT	449b	3 c2
		נחה	LEAD	635a	
		סלף	CROOKEDNESS	701b	
		שדד	DEAL VIOLENTLY WITH	994b	
		תמה	INTEGRITY	1070d	
11	4	הון	WEALTH	223c	1
		יום	DAY	399a	3
		יעל	PROFIT	418d	
		יעץ	ADVISE	419d	
		נצל	DELIVER	665a	3 b
		עברה	OVERFLOW	720c	3 b
		צדקה	RIGHTEOUSNESS	842b	5
11	5	דרך	WAY	203b	5
		ישר	MAKE STRAIGHT	448d	1
		נפל	FALL	657b	2 b
		צדקה	RIGHTEOUSNESS	842b	5
		רשעה	WICKEDNESS	958a	1
		תמים	SOUND	1071b	4
11	6	חוה	DESIRE	217d	1
		ישר	STRAIGHT	449b	3 c2
		לכד	CAPTURE	540b	2
		נצל	DELIVER	665a	3 b
		צדקה	RIGHTEOUSNESS	842b	5
11	7	אבד	PERISH	1d	2
		אבד	PERISH	1d	2
		און	VIGOUR	20b	2
		תוחלת	HOPE	404b	
		תקוה	HOPE	876b	3
		רשע	WICKED	957c	3
11	8	חלץ	DRAW OFF OR OUT	322d	
11	9	חלץ	DRAW OFF OR OUT	322d	
		חנף	PROFANE	338b	
		דעת	WISDOM	395d	2 a
		שחת	GO TO RUIN	1008b	1
11	10	אבד	PERISH	1c	1
		טוב	GOOD THINGS	375c	3 c
		עלץ	REJOICE	763b	
		קריה	TOWN	900b	4
		רנה	RINGING CRY	943d	3
11	11	ברכה	BLESSING	139d	3
		הרס	THROW DOWN	248d	
		ישר	STRAIGHT	449b	3 c2
		קרת	TOWN	900d	
		רום	BE HIGH	927a	2 c
11	12	בוז	DESPISE	100b	
		תבונה	UNDERSTANDING	108b	2
		חסר	NEEDY	341c	
		חרש	BE SILENT	361b	1 a
		לב	HEART	524c	2 3a
		תמים	SOUND	1071a	4
11	13	אמן	CONFIRM	53a	5
		הלך	WALK	232a	1 1d 5k
		כסה	COVER	491d	2
		סוד	COUNSEL	691c	2 b
		רוח	BREATH	925d	8
		רכיל	SLANDER	940c	
11	14	אין	NOT	35a	6 aa
		תחבלה	DIRECTION	287b	
		תשועה	DELIVERANCE	448b	1
		בטח	TRUST	105b	2
11	15	זור	BE A STRANGER	266c	2 a
		כי	WHEN	473a	2 a
		ערב	TAKE ON PLEDGE	786c	1
		רוע	RAISE A SHOUT	929d	6
		רע	EVIL	948d	2
		רעע	BE EVIL	949c	
		שנא	HATE	971d	3
		תקע	CLAP	1075c	3
11	16	אשה	WOMAN	61b	1
		חן	FAVOR	336b	1 a
		כבוד	HONOR	458c	2 a
		עריץ	AWE-INSPIRING	792b	
		תמך	GRASP	1069d	1
11	17	חסד	GOODNESS	338d	1 2
		אכזרי	CRUEL	470a	
		נפש	SOUL	659b	1 a
		עכר	STIR UP	747d	
		שאר	FLESH	985a	3
11	18	אמת	FIRMNESS	54a	1
		זרע	SOW	281d	3 c
		פעלה	WORK	821d	1 b
		צדקה	RIGHTEOUSNESS	842b	5
		שכר	HIRE	969a	
		שקר	DECEPTION	1055c	2
11	19	חיים	LIFE	313b	2
		כן	TRUE	467b	2
		צדקה	RIGHTEOUSNESS	842b	5
		רדף	PURSUE	923a	
11	20	דרך	WAY	203c	6 c
		לב	HEART	525b	2 6b
		עקש	TWISTED	786a	
		רצון	GOODWILL	953c	1 a
11	21	זרע	SOWING	283b	5
		יד	HAND	391b	5 f
		מלט	SLIP AWAY	572c	3
		נקה	BE CLEAN	667b	3
		רע	EVIL	948c	0 b
11	22	אף	NOSE	60b	1 c
		זהב	GOLD	263a	6

Ch	v.	Heb	Eng	Page	Sec
11	23	חזיר	SWINE	306c	1
		טעם	TASTE	381a	2
		יפה	BEAUTIFUL	421c	
		נזם	RING	633d	1
		סור	TURN ASIDE	693d	1
		תאוה	DESIRE	16c	1
		טוב	A GOOD THING	375b	3
		עברה	OVERFLOW	720d	3 b
		תקוה	HOPE	876b	3
11	24	אך	ONLY	36d	2 ba
		מחסור	NEED	341d	3
		חשך	WITHHOLD	362b	1 a
		יסף	BE JOINED	415a	2
		יש	THERE IS	441d	2 b
		ישר	STRAIGHTNESS	449c	3
		זור	SCATTER	808b	
11	25	ברכה	BLESSING	139d	5
		דשן	BE FAT	206b	
		ירא	BE WATERED	432c	
		נפש	SOUL	660b	4 c1
		רוה	BE SATURATED	924b	
		רוה	BE SATURATED	924b	
11	26	ברכה	BLESSING	139d	1 c
		בר	GRAIN	141b	
		לאם	PEOPLE	522c	
		מנע	WITHHOLD	586a	
		קבב	CURSE	866d	
		שבר	BUY GRAIN	991d	
11	27	בקש	SEEK	134d	2 b
		דרש	SEEK	205c	6
		טוב	A GOOD THING	375b	3
		רצון	GOODWILL	953c	1 b
		שחר	LOOK EARLY	1007c	
11	28	בטח	TRUST	105a	1 3c
		הוא	HE, SHE, IT	215d	2 a
		עלה	LEAF	750a	
		פרח	BUD	827a	
11	29	חכם	WISE	314d	5
		לב	HEART	524d	2 3b
		נחל	TAKE AS A POSSES-SION	635d	2
		עבד	SLAVE	714c	7
		עכר	STIR UP	747d	
11	30	חיים	LIFE	313b	2
		חכם	WISE	315b	6 b4
		נפש	SOUL	660c	4 c4
		עץ	TREE	781c	1 a
		פרי	FRUIT	826c	3
11	31	אף	ALSO	65b	3
		הן	BEHOLD	243c	A
		חטא	MISS A GOAL OR WAY	307a	2 b
12	1	שלם	BE COMPLETE	1022c	2
		אהב	LOVE	13a	2
		בער	BRUTISHNESS	129d	
		דעת	WISDOM	395d	2 a
		תוכחת	REPROOF	407b	2
		מוסר	DISCIPLINE	416c	1 c
12	2	מזמה	PURPOSE	273d	3 b
		טוב	PLEASANT	374d	0 a
		פוק	BRING OUT	807c	2
		רצון	GOODWILL	953c	1 a
		רשע	BE WICKED	957d	2
12	3	בל	NOT	115b	
		כן	BE FIRM	465d	1 c
		מוט	SHAKE	557a	
		רשע	WICKEDNESS	957c	1
		שרש	ROOT	1057d	1
12	4	אשה	WOMAN	61b	1
		בוש	BE ASHAMED	102a	1
		בעל	OWNER	127b	1 2
		חיל	STRENGTH	298d	2
		עטרה	CROWN	742d	3
		רקב	ROTTENNESS	955a	
12	5	תחבלה	DIRECTION	287b	
		משבה	THOUGHT	364b	2
		מרמה	DECEIT	941b	
		משפט	JUDGEMNT	1048d	2 b
12	6	ארב	LIE IN WAIT	70b	
		דם	BLOOD	197a	2 f
		ישר	STRAIGHT	449b	3 c2
		צל	DELIVER	665a	3 b
12	7	הפך	TURN	245c	1 b
		עמד	STAND	764b	5 a
12	8	בוז	CONTEMPT	100b	1
		הלל	PRAISE	238d	1
		עוה	BEND	730c	
		פה	MOUTH	805d	6 c1
		סכל	PRUDENCE	968d	2
12	9	חסר	NEEDY	341c	
		טוב	PLEASANT	374c	6
		כבד	HONOR ONESELF	458a	2
		עבד	SLAVE	714c	7
		קלה	DISHONOURED	885d	
12	10	אכזרי	CRUEL	470a	
		נפש	SOUL	659d	3 c
		רחמים	COMPASSION	933c	2
12	11	אדמה	GROUND	9c	1
		חסר	NEEDY	341c	
		לב	HEART	524c	2 3a
		עבד	WORK	713a	1
		רדף	PURSUE	923a	
		ריק	EMPTY	938a	2
12	12	חמד	DESIRE	326b	A
		נתן	GIVE	679c	1 t

Ch v.	Heb	Eng	Page	Sec
	מצוד	HUNTING IMPLE-MENT	845a	
12 13	רע	EVIL	948c	0 b
	שרש	ROOT	1057d	1
	מוקש	BAIT	430d	
	פשע	TRANSGRESSION	833c	1
	רע	EVIL	948c	0 b
	שפה	SPEECH	973d	1 a1
12 14	טוב	A GOOD THING	375b	2
	פרי	FRUIT	826c	
	שבע	SATISFIED	959c	1 c
	שוב	TURN BACK	998b	7 f
12 15	דרך	WAY	203d	6 d
	חכם	WISE	315a	6 b1
	עצה	ADVICE	420b	
	ישר	STRAIGHT	449a	2 b
	שמע	HEAR	1034a	1 j
12 16	ידע	BE MADE KNOWN	394c	1
	כסה	COVER	491c	1
	כעס	ANGER	495b	1
	כעס	ANGER	495b	1
	ערום	CRAFTY	791a	2
	קלון	DISHONOUR	886a	2
12 17	אמונה	FIRMNESS	53c	3 a
	עד	WITNESS	729d	2 c
	פוח	BREATHE	806b	3
	צדק	RIGHTEOUSNESS	841d	4
	מרמה	DECEIT	941b	
	שקר	DECEPTION	1055d	3
12 18	בטה	SPEAK RASHLY	104d	
	מדקרה	THRUST	201b	
	חכם	WISE	315a	6 b2
	יש	THERE IS	441a	1
	לשון	TONGUE	546c	1 b
	מרפא	HEALING	951b	2
12 19	אמת	FIRMNESS	54b	4 a
	כון	BE FIRM	465d	1 c
	לשון	TONGUE	546c	1 b
	עד	PERPETUITY	723c	2 a
	רגע	DISTURB	920d	
	שפה	SPEECH	973d	1 a1
	שקר	DECEPTION	1055d	5
12 20	חרש	CUT IN	360c	3
	יעץ	ADVISE	419d	
	מרמה	DECEIT	941b	
	רע	EVIL	948d	2
	שמחה	JOY	970d	4
	שלום	PEACE	1023a	5 a
12 21	און	TROUBLE	20a	1
	אנה	BE OPPORTUNE	58c	
	רע	EVIL	948d	1
12 22	אמונה	FIRMNESS	53c	3 a
	רצון	GOODWILL	953c	1 a
	שקר	DECEPTION	1055d	5
12 23	אולת	FOLLY	17c	
	דעת	KNOWLEDGE	395d	2 c
	כסה	COVER	491c	1
	כסיל	FOOL	493a	
	לב	HEART	524d	2 3b
	ערום	CRAFTY	791a	2
12 24	חרוץ	SHARP	358d	2
	מס	LABOUR-GANG	587a	3
	משל	RULE	605d	1
	רמיה	LAXNESS	941c	
12 25	דאגה	ANXIETY	178d	
	דבר	WORD	182d	2 1a
	טוב	PLEASANT	373d	2 d
	שמח	REJOICE	970c	
	שחה	BOW DOWN	1005b	
12 26	רע	FRIEND	946a	1
	מרע	FRIEND	946d	
	רשע	WICKED	957c	3
	תור	SPY OUT	1064c	
	תעה	ERR	1073c	1
12 27	הון	WEALTH	223c	1
	חרך	SET IN MOTION	355b	
	חרוץ	SHARP	358d	2
	יקר	PRECIOUS	430a	1 a
	ציד	GAME	844d	2
	רמיה	LAXNESS	941c	
12 28	ארח	WAY	73b	3 b
	דרך	WAY	203c	6 c
	חיים	LIFE	313b	2
	נתיב	PATH	677b	
	נתיבה	PATH	677c	2 b
	צדקה	RIGHTEOUSNESS	842b	5
13 1	בן	SON	120a	1
	גערה	REBUKE	172a	1
	חכם	WISE	315a	6a
	מוסר	DISCIPLINE	416c	1 c
	לץ	SCORN	539b	
13 2	חמס	VIOLENCE	329c	
	טוב	A GOOD THING	375b	2
	פרי	FRUIT	826c	
13 3	מחתה	TERROR	370c	
	נפש	SOUL	660a	1
	נצר	WATCH	665d	1
	פה	MOUTH	805a	2 a
	פשק	PART WIDE	832d	
	שפה	SPEECH	973d	1 a1
	שמר	KEEP	1036c	1 b
13 4	אוה	DESIRE	16b	
	אין	NOT	34c	2 da
	דשן	BE FAT	206b	
	חרוץ	SHARP	358d	2
	נפש	SOUL	660d	6 a

Ch v.	Heb	Eng	Page	Sec
13 5	באש	STINK	93a	2
	דבר	WORD	183b	3 1
	חפר	BE ABASHED	344a	
	שקר	DECEPTION	1055d	5
13 6	דרך	WAY	203c	6 c
	חטאה	SIN	308c	1 b
	נצר	GUARD	665d	2
	סלף	TWIST	701b	2
	רשעה	WICKEDNESS	958a	1
	תם	INTEGRITY	1070d	3
13 7	הון	WEALTH	223c	1
	יש	THERE IS	441d	2 b
	כל	ALL	*482c	2 a
	עשר	BE RICH	799b	
	רוש	BE IN WANT	930d	
13 8	גערה	REBUKE	172a	1
	כפר	RANSOM	497b	1
	רוש	BE IN WANT	930d	
13 9	אור	LIGHT	21c	6
	דעך	BE EXTINGUISHED	200b	
	נר	LAMP	632d	
	שמח	REJOICE	970b	1 a
13 10	את	WITH	86c	3 a
	זדון	INSOLENCE	268a	2
	חכמה	WISDOM	315d	5 c
	יעץ	CONSULT	420a	
	מצה	STRIFE	663c	
	נתן	GIVE	680a	1 z
	רק	ONLY	956c	2
13 11	הבל	VAPOUR	210d	2
	הון	WEALTH	223c	1
	יד	HAND	391c	5 h2
	מן	OUT OF	579b	2 ba
	מעט	BE SMALL	589c	
	קבץ	GATHER	867c	1
	רבה	BECOME MANY	915c	1 c
13 12	תאוה	DESIRE	16c	1
	בוא	COME	98c	2 c
	חיים	LIFE	313b	2
	חלה	BE WEAK	318a	2
	תוחלת	HOPE	404b	
	משך	DRAW	604c	
	עץ	TREE	781c	4
13 13	בוז	DESPISE	100b	
	דבר	WORD	183c	4 3
	הוא	HE, SHE, IT	215d	2 a
	חבל	BIND	286b	
	חבל	ACT CORRUPTLY	287b	
	ירא	FEAR	431c	3
	ל	TO	514a	5 e
	מצוה	COMMANDMENT	846c	
	שלם	BE COMPLETE	1022c	2
13 14	חיים	LIFE	313b	2
	חכם	WISE	315a	6 b2
	מוקש	BAIT	430d	
	תורה	INSTRUCTION	435d	1 a
	סור	TURN ASIDE	693c	1
	מקור	SPRING	881b	1 a
13 15	דרך	WAY	203d	6 d
	חן	FAVOR	336b	2 a
	טוב	PLEASANT	374b	8
	איתן	ENDURING	451a	2
	נתן	GIVE	679d	1 u
	שכל	PRUDENCE	968c	2
13 16	דעת	KNOWLEDGE	395d	2 c
	ערום	CRAFTY	791a	2
	פרש	SPREAD OUT	831b	1
13 17	אמן	TRUSTING	53c	1 a
	מלאך	MESSENGER	521c	1 a
	נפל	FALL	657b	2 b
	ציר	ENVOY	851d	
	רע	EVIL	948d	1
	מרפא	HEALING	951b	2
	רשע	WICKED	957c	3
13 18	תוכחת	REPROOF	407b	2
	מוסר	DISCIPLINE	416c	1 c
	כבד	BE HONORED	457d	
	פרע	LET GO	829a	2
	קלון	DISHONOUR	886a	2
	רוש	POVERTY	930d	
13 19	תאה	DESIRE	16c	1
	היה	COME TO PASS	227d	2
	סור	TURN ASIDE	693d	1
	ערב	BE SWEET	787a	
	תועבה	ABOMINATION	1073a	2 a
13 20	בוא	COME	*98d	2
	הלך	WALK	234d	2 3b
	חכם	BE WISE	314c	
	חכם	WISE	315a	6 b2
	רעה	ASSOCIATE WITH	945d	
	רעע	BE EVIL	949c	
13 21	חטא	SINFUL	308b	2
	טוב	A GOOD THING	375b	2
	רדף	PURSUE	923a	
13 22	בן	SON	120b	1 f
	חיל	STRENGTH	299a	3
	חטא	MISS A GOAL OR WAY	307a	2 b
	טוב	PLEASANT	374b	0 a
	נחל	GET AS A POSSES-SION	63 d	2
13 23	אכל	FOOD	38a	
	יש	THERE IS	441d	2 b
	לא	NOT	519d	2 d
	לא	NOT	520b	4 ac

Ch v.	Heb	Eng	Page	Sec
	ניר	UNTILLED GROUND	644c	
	ספה	SWEEP AWAY	705a	1
	רוש	BE IN WANT	930d	
	רוש	BE IN WANT	930d	
13 24	אהב	LOVE	12d	1
	בן	SON	120a	1
	חשך	WITHHOLD	362b	1 a
	מוסר	DISCIPLINE	416d	2 b
	שנא	HATE	971c	3
	שחר	LOOK EARLY	1007c	
13 25	בטן	BELLY	105d	1 a
	חסר	LACK	341b	1 b
	נפש	SOUL	660c	5 a
	שבע	ABUNDANCE	960a	1
14 1	אולת	FOLLY	17c	
	בנה	BUILD	124d	2 a
	הרס	THROW DOWN	248c	1
	חכמה	WISDOM	315d	5 c
14 2	בוז	DESPISE	102c	
	דרך	WAY	203c	6 a
	ירא	FEAR	431c	3 b
	ישר	STRAIGHTNESS	449c	2
	לוז	BE CROOKED	531b	
14 3	גאוה	PRIDE	144d	3
	חטר	BRANCH	310d	
	חכם	WISE	315b	6 b3
14 4	אבוס	CRIB	7b	
	אין	NOT	35a	6 aa
	אלף	CATTLE	48c	
	תבואה	REVENUE	100b	2 a
	בר	CLEAN	141a	2
	כח	STRENGTH	471a	4
	שור	A HEAD OF CATTLE	1004b	
14 5	אמן	TRUSTING	53c	1
	כזב	LIE	469c	
	כזב	LIE	469c	1
	עד	WITNESS	729d	1
	עד	WITNESS	729d	2 c
	פוח	BREATHE	806b	3
	שקר	DECEPTION	1055c	3
14 6	אין	NOT	34c	2 da
	בין	DISCERN	106d	1
	בקש	SEEK	134d	2 b
	חכמה	WISDOM	315d	5 c
	דעת	WISDOM	395d	2
	ליץ	SCORN	539c	
	קלל	BE SLIGHT	886c	2
	בל	NOT	115b	
14 7	דעת	KNOWLEDGE	396a	2 d
	נגד	IN FRONT	617d	2 cb g
	שפה	SPEECH	973d	1 a1
14 8	בין	DISCERN	107a	1 b
	דרך	WAY	203c	6 a
	חכמה	WISDOM	315d	5 c
	ערום	CRAFTY	791a	2
	מרמה	DECEIT	941b	
14 9	אשם	OFFENCE	79d	2
	בין	INTERVAL	107c	1 d
	ישר	STRAIGHT	449b	3 c2
	ליץ	SCORN	539b	
	רצון	GOODWILL	953c	1 b
14 10	זור	BE A STRANGER	266c	2
	לב	HEART	524d	2 3b
	מרה	BITTERNESS	601a	
	ערב	TAKE ON PLEDGE	786d	2 b
	שמחה	JOY	970d	1
14 11	אהל	TENT	14a	2
	ישר	STRAIGHT	779b	3 c2
	פרח	BUD	827b	2
	שמד	BE EXTERMINATED	1029b	2
14 12	אחרית	END	31a	B
	דרך	WAY	203c	6 a
	דרך	WAY	203d	6 d
	יש	THERE IS	441d	2 b
	ישר	STRAIGHT	449a	2 b
	פנה	FACE	817a	24a g
14 13	גם	ALSO	169b	2
	תוגה	GRIEF	387b	
	כאב	BE IN PAIN	456a	2
	לב	HEART	525c	2 9b
	שחק	LAUGHTER	966a	1
	שמחה	JOY	970d	1
14 14	דרך	WAY	203d	6 d
	טוב	PLEASANT	374d	0 a
	על	UPON	759b	4 2d
	שבע	SATISFIED	959c	1 c
14 15	אמן	CONFIRM	53b	2 b
	אשור	STEP	81a	
	בין	DISCERN	106d	1 a
	ערום	CRAFTY	791b	2
	פתי	SIMPLE	834c	
14 16	בטח	TRUST	105b	2
	חכם	WISE	315a	6 b1
	ירא	FEAR	431a	1 a
	עבר	BE ARROGANT	720d	1
14 17	מזמה	PURPOSE	273d	3 b
	קצר	SHORT	894b	
	שן	HATE	971d	
14 18	אולת	FOLLY	17c	
	דעת	KNOWLEDGE	395d	2 c
	כתר	SURROUND	509c	
	נחל	TAKE AS A POSSES-SION	635d	2
	ערום	CRAFTY	791b	2
	פתי	SIMPLE	834c	

Ch	v.	Heb	Eng	Page	Sec
14	19	טוב	PLEASANT	374d	0 a
		על	UPON	756a	2 c
		רע	EVIL	948c	0 b
		שחה	BOW	1005d	2
		שער	GATE	1045a	2 c
14	20	אהב	LOVE	13a	4 b
		גם	ALSO	169b	2
		ל	TO	514a	5 e
		נפש	SOUL	660b	4 b5
		עשיר	RICH	799c	
		שן	HATE	971d	
14	21	אשר	HAPPINESS	81a	
		בוז	DESPISE	100b	
		חטא	MISS A GOAL OR WAY	307a	2 b
		חנן	SHOW FAVOR	336b	
		ענו	POOR	776c	1
		עני	POOR	776d	1
		תעה	ERR	*1073c	3
		חנן	SHEW FAVOUR	*1093b	
14	22	אמת	FIRMNESS	54a	3 a
		חסד	GOODNESS	338d	12
		חרש	CUT IN	360c	3
		טוב	A GOOD THING	375b	3
		רע	EVIL	948d	2
		תעה	ERR	1073c	3
14	23	אך	ONLY	36d	2 ba
		דבר	WORD	182a	1 1a
		מחסור	NEED	341d	3
		מותר	ABUNDANCE	452d	1
		עצב	PAIN	780d	3
		שפה	SPEECH	973d	1 a1
14	24	אולת	FOLLY	17c	
		חכם	WISE	315b	6 b3
		עטרה	CROWN	742d	3
		עשר	RICHES	799b	
14	25	אמת	FIRMNESS	54b	4 b
		כזב	LIE	469c	
		נפש	SOUL	660c	4 c4
		עד	WITNESS	729d	2 c
		פוח	BREATHE	806b	3
		מרמה	DECEIT	941b	
14	26	מבטח	CONFIDENCE	105c	3
		מחסה	REFUGE	340c	B
		יראה	FEAR	432a	3
		עז	STRENGTH	739a	2 c
14	27	חיים	LIFE	313b	2
		מוקש	BAIT	430d	
		יראה	FEAR	432a	3
		מקור	SPRING	881b	1 a
14	28	אפס	NON-EXISTENCE	67b	2 b
		בצרה	DEARTH	*131b	
		הדרה	GLORY	214c	2
		מחתה	TERROR	370d	2
		לאם	PEOPLE	522c	
		רב	MULTITUDE	914a	1
		רזון	POTENTATE	931b	
14	29	אולת	FOLLY	17c	
		אף	NOSE	60b	3
		ארך	LONG	74a	
		תבונה	UNDERSTANDING	108b	3
		קצר	SHORT	894b	
		רב	MUCH	913b	1 d
		רוח	BREATH	925a	3 d
		רום	BE HIGH	927c	1 f
14	30	בשר	FLESH	142a	2
		חיים	LIFE	313b	1
		לב	HEART	524c	2 l
		עצם	BONE	782d	1 d
		קנאה	ZEAL	888c	3 a
		מרפא	HEALING	951c	2
		רקב	ROTTENNESS	955a	
14	31	אביון	NEEDY	2d	
		דל	POOR	195d	
		חנן	SHOW FAVOR	336a	1 b
		חרף	REPROACH	357d	
		כבד	MAKE HONORABLE	457d	2 c
		עשה	DO	794b	2 1b
		עשק	OPPRESS	798d	1
14	32	ארח	WAY	73b	3 b
		דחה	THRUST	191a	
		חסה	SEEK REFUGE	340b	
		רעה	MISERY	949b	1
14	33	בין	DISCERN	106d	
		חכמה	WISDOM	315d	5 c
		ידע	BE MADE KNOWN	394c	1
		לב	HEART	524d	2 3b
		נוח	REST	628b	1
		קרב	INWARD PART	899b	2 a
14	34	גוי	NATION	156c	1
		חטאת	SIN	308c	1 b
		חסד	GOODNESS	339c	4
		חסד	SHAME	340a	
		לאם	PEOPLE	522c	
		רום	BE HIGH	927c	2 c
14	35	בוש	BE ASHAMED	101d	1
		עבד	SLAVE	713d	2
		עברה	OVERFLOW	720c	3 a
		רצון	GOODWILL	953c	1 b
		שכל	BE PRUDENT	968c	5
15	1	חמה	RAGE	404c	2 a
		חמה	RAGE	*404d	2 c
		עלה	GO UP	749d	5
		מענה	ANSWER	775a	
		עצב	PAIN	780d	2
		רך	TENDER	940a	3
15	2	שוב	TURN BACK	999d	6 a
		חכם	WISE	315a	6 b2
		דעת	KNOWLEDGE	395d	2 c
		יטב	DO WELL	405d	3
		כסיל	FOOL	493a	
		לשון	TONGUE	546c	1 b
		נבע	BUBBLE UP	616a	3
15	3	טוב	PLEASANT	374d	0 a
		צפה	KEEP WATCH	859c	
		מקום	STANDING PLACE	880a	4
		רע	EVIL	948c	0 b
15	4	חיים	LIFE	313b	2
		לשון	TONGUE	546c	1 b
		סלף	CROOKEDNESS	701b	
		עץ	TREE	781c	1 a
		רוח	BREATH	925b	3 f
		מרפא	HEALING	951c	2
		שבר	BREAKING	991b	1
15	5	תוכחת	REPROOF	407b	2
		מוסר	DISCIPLINE	416d	2 b
		נאץ	CONTEMN	610d	
		ערם	BE SHREWD	791a	
15	6	תבואה	REVENUE	100b	2 a
		חסן	WEALTH	340d	
		עכר	STIR UP	747d	
15	7	זרה	SCATTER	280a	1
		חכם	WISE	315a	6 b2
		דעת	KNOWLEDGE	396a	2 c
		כן	RIGHT	467b	1
		לב	HEART	524d	2 3b
15	8	זבח	SACRIFICE	257c	1 1
		ישר	STRAIGHT	779b	3 c2
		רצון	GOODWILL	953c	1 a
		תועבה	ABOMINATION	*1073a	2 b
15	9	דרך	WAY	203d	6 d
		צדקה	RIGHTEOUSNESS	842b	5
		רדף	PURSUE	923a	
		רשע	WICKED	957c	3
15	10	ארח	WAY	73b	3 b
		תוכחת	REPROOF	407b	2
		מוסר	DISCIPLINE	416d	2 b
		מות	DIE	560a	2 d
		עזב	LEAVE	737c	2 d3
		רע	EVIL	948b	2
15	11	אבדון	DESTRUCTION	2c	
		אף	ALSO	65b	3
		נגד	IN FRONT	617b	1 aa
		שאול	SHEOL	983b	3 b
15	12	אהב	LOVE	13a	1
		חכם	WISE	315b	6 b4
		יכח	REPROVE	407a	5 b
		ליץ	SCORN	539b	
15	13	יטב	MAKE GLAD	405d	1
		לב	HEART	525c	2 9a
		נכא	A STRICKEN SPIRIT	644d	
		עצבה	HURT	781a	
		פנה	FACE	815d	1 1a
		רוח	BREATH	925b	3 f
		שמח	JOYFUL	970c	1
15	14	בין	DISCERN	106d	
		בקש	SEEK	134d	2 b
		דעת	KNOWLEDGE	396a	2 c
		כסיל	FOOL	493a	
		לב	HEART	524d	2 3b
		רעה	TEND	945b	2 b
15	15	טוב	PLEASANT	374c	7
		לב	HEART	525c	2 9a
		תמיד	CONTINUITY	556b	1
		עני	POOR	776d	1
		רע	EVIL	948a	2
		משתה	FEAST	1059d	1
15	16	אוצר	TREASURE	70a	1
		מהומה	TUMULT	223a	1
		טוב	PLEASANT	374c	6
		יראה	FEAR	432a	3
		מעט	A FEW	590a	1 a
15	17	אבס	FATTEN	7b	
		אהבה	LOVE	13b	1
		ארחה	MEAL	73c	
		טוב	PLEASANT	374c	6
		ירק	HERBS	438d	
		שנא	HATING	971d	1
		שור	A HEAD OF CATTLE	1004b	
15	18	אף	NOSE	60b	3
		ארך	LONG	74a	
		גרה	STIR UP STRIFE	173b	
		מדון	STRIFE	193b	1
		חמה	RAGE	404c	2 a
		ריב	STRIFE	936d	1
		שקט	BE QUIET	1053b	2
15	19	משכה	HEDGE		
		ארח	WAY	73a	2
		דרך	WAY	203d	6 d
		חדק	BRIER	293c	
		סלל	LIFT UP	699d	1
		ישר	STRAIGHT	779b	3 c2
15	20	אב	FATHER	3b	1
		אדם	MAN	9b	2
		אם	MOTHER	51d	1
		בזה	DESPISE	102c	
		חכם	WISE	315a	6 a
		שמח	REJOICE	970c	
15	21	אולת	FOLLY	17c	
		תבונה	UNDERSTANDING	108b	2
		הלך	WALK	234c	2 3
		חסר	NEEDY	341c	
		ישר	MAKE STRAIGHT	448d	1
		לב	HEART	524c	1
		שמחה	JOY	970d	1
15	22	אין	NOT	35a	6 aa
		מחשבה	THOUGHT	364c	2
		יעץ	ADVISE	419d	
		סוד	COUNSEL	691c	2 a
		פרר	BREAK	830c	2 a
		קום	STAND	878c	7
15	23	דבר	WORD	182d	2 1a
		טוב	PLEASANT	373d	2 d
		עת	TIME	773d	2 b
		מענה	ANSWER	775a	
		שמחה	JOY	970d	1
15	24	ארח	WAY	73b	3 b
		חיים	LIFE	313b	2
		מטה	DOWNWARDS	641b	1
		מעל	ABOVE	752a	2 ca
		שכל	BE PRUDENT	968c	5
		שאול	SHEOL	982d	1
15	25	אלמנה	WIDOW	48b	
		גאה	PROUD	144b	
		גבול	BOUNDARY	148a	1 c
		נסח	TEAR AWAY	650c	
		נצב	STAND	662c	4
15	26	אמר	WORD	57a	1
		מחשבה	THOUGHT	364c	2
		מהור	CLEAN	373a	3
		נעם	PLEASANTNESS	653d	3
		רע	EVIL	949a	3
15	27	בצע	GAIN BY VIOLENCE	130b	
		בצע	UNJUST GAIN	130c	
		מתנה	GIFT	682c	
		עכר	STIR UP	747d	
		שנא	HATE	971d	3
15	28	הגה	MUSE	211d	3 b
		לב	HEART	524d	2 3c
		נבע	BUBBLE UP	615d	
		רע	EVIL	948c	0 c
15	29	רחק	DISTANT	935b	1 a
15	30	מאור	LUMINARY	22d	
		דשן	BE FAT	206b	
		טוב	PLEASANT	373d	2 d
		לב	HEART	525c	2 9a
		עין	EYE	744c	1 s
		עצם	BONE	782d	1 d
		שמח	REJOICE	970c	
		שמועה	REPORT	1035b	1
15	31	אזן	EAR	24a	2 a
		חיים	LIFE	313b	2
		חכם	WISE	315a	6 b1
		תוכחת	REPROOF	407b	2
		לון	LODGE	533d	2
		קרב	INWARD PART	899b	1 f5
15	32	תוכחת	REPROOF	407b	2
		מוסר	DISCIPLINE	416c	1 c
		לב	HEART	524d	2 3a
		מאס	REJECT	549c	2
		פרע	LET GO	829a	2
		קנה	ACQUIRE	889a	1 d
15	33	חכמה	WISDOM	315d	5 c
		מוסר	DISCIPLINE	416c	1 c
		יראה	FEAR	432a	3
		כבוד	HONOR	459a	3
		ענוה	HUMILITY	776d	1
16	1	לשון	TONGUE	546b	1 b
		מן	OUT OF	579d	2 d
		מענה	ANSWER	775a	
		מערך	ARRANGEMENT	790a	
16	2	דרך	WAY	203c	6 a
		זך	PURE	269b	2
		כל	ALL	482c	
		רוח	BREATH	925b	4 b
		תכן	ESTIMATE	1067b	
16	3	מחשבה	THOUGHT	364c	2
		כון	BE FIRM	465d	1 c
		מעשה	DEED	795d	1 b5
16	4	חמה	RAGE	404c	2 a
		כל	ALL	482c	2 a
		מענה	ANSWER	775a	
		פעל	DO	821c	2 a
16	5	גבה	HIGH	147b	3
		לב	HEART	525b	2 6c
		נקה	BE CLEAN	667b	1
		רוח	BREATH	*925d	8
16	6	אמת	FIRMNESS	54a	3 a
		ה	THE	*208c	1 hb
		חסד	GOODNESS	338d	12
		יראה	FEAR	432a	3
		כפר	BE COVERED OVER	498b	1
		סור	TURN ASIDE	693d	1
		עון	INIQUITY	731a	1 c3
16	7	איב	BE HOSTILE TO	33c	
		דרך	WAY	203c	6 a
		רצה	BE PLEASED WITH	953a	1 a
		שלם	BE IN COVENANT OF PEACE	1023d	2
16	8	תבואה	REVENUE	100b	2 a
		טוב	PLEASANT	374c	6
		לא	NOT	*520a	4 aa
		מעט	A FEW	590a	1 a
16	9	דרך	WAY	203c	6 a
		חשב	THINK	363c	2
		כון	ESTABLISH	466c	1
		לב	HEART	524d	2 3c
		צעד	STEP	857d	2

PROVERBS

Ch	v	Heb	Eng	Page	Sec
16	10	מעל	UNFAITHFUL	*591b	1
		מעל	ACT TREACHEROUSLY	591b	2 a
		קסם	DIVINATION	890c	3
		משפט	JUDGMENT	1048b	1 a
16	11	אבן	STONE	6d	5
		מאזן	BALANCES	24d	
		כיס	BAG	476a	A
		מעשה	DEED	796b	2 b
		פלס	BALANCE	813d	
16	12	כון	BE FIRM	465d	1 b
		כסא	THRONE	491a	3 a
		צדקה	RIGHTEOUSNESS	842a	1 a
		רשע	WICKEDNESS	957c	1
		תועבה	ABOMINATION	1073a	2 a
16	13	אהב	LOVE	13a	1
		דבר	SPEAK	180c	
		ישר	STRAIGHT	449b	3 c1
		צדק	RIGHTEOUSNESS	841d	4
		רצון	GOODWILL	953c	1 b
		שפה	SPEECH	973d	1 a1
16	14	חכם	WISE	314d	5
		כפר	COVER OVER	497c	1
		מלאך	MESSENGER	521c	1 e
		מות	DEATH	560d	2
16	15	חיים	LIFE	313b	2
		מלקש	SPRING-RAIN	545b	
		רצון	GOODWILL	953c	1 b
16	16	בחר	CHOOSE	104b	B
		בינה	UNDERSTANDING	108a	2
		חכמה	WISDOM	315d	5 c
		חרוץ	GOLD	359a	
		טוב	PLEASANT	374c	6
		קנה	ACQUIRE	889a	1 d
16	17	בזה	DESPISE	*102c	
		דרך	WAY	203d	6 a
		נפש	SOUL	660a	3 c
		נצר	WATCH	665d	1
		סור	TURN ASIDE	693d	1
		מסלה	HIGHWAY	700c	
		ישר	STRAIGHT	779b	3 c2
		שמר	KEEP	1036c	1 b
16	18	גאון	EXALTATION	145a	1
		גבה	HEIGHT	147b	3
		כשלון	STUMBLING	506a	
		רוח	BREATH	925d	8
		שבר	BREAKING	991b	1
16	19	גאה	PROUD	144b	
		חלק	DIVIDE	323d	1
		טוב	PLEASANT	374c	6
		ענו	POOR	776c	4
		עני	POOR	777a	4
		רוח	BREATH	925d	8
		שלל	SPOIL	1022a	3
		שפל	BECOME LOW	1050a	2
		שפל	LOW	1050c	4
16	20	אשר	HAPPINESS	81a	
		בטח	TRUST	105a	1 3a
		דבר	WORD	183c	4 3
		טוב	A GOOD THING	375a	1
		שכל	BE PRUDENT	968b	2
16	21	בין	DISCERN	106d	
		חכם	WISE	315a	6 a
		יסף	ADD	415b	1
		לב	HEART	524d	2 3b
		לקח	TEACHING	544b	2
		מתק	SWEETNESS	608d	
		קרא	CALL	896b	2 d1
16	22	אולת	FOLLY	17c	
		בעל	OWNER	127b	1 1
		חיים	LIFE	313b	
		מוסר	DISCIPLINE	416c	1 c
		מקור	SPRING	881b	1 a
		שכל	PRUDENCE	968d	2
16	23	חכם	WISE	315a	6 b2
		יסף	ADD	415a	1
		לב	HEART	524d	2 3b
		לקח	TEACHING	544b	2
		על	UPON	753a	2 1
		שכל	BE PRUDENT	968c	4
16	24	אמר	WORD	57a	1
		דבש	HONEY	185b	
		דבש	HONEY	*185c	
		מתוק	SWEET	608d	1
		נעם	PLEASANTNESS	653d	3
		נפש	SOUL	660c	5 a
		עצם	BONE	782d	1 d
		צוף	HONEY COMB	847b	
		מרפא	HEALING	951b	2
16	25	דרך	WAY	203c	6 a
		דרך	WAY	203d	6 d
		יש	THERE IS	441d	2 b
		ישר	STRAIGHT	449a	2 b
16	26	אכף	PRESS	38c	
		ל	TO	515c	5 hc
		עמל	LABOUR	765c	
		עמל	LABOURER	766a	1
16	27	בליעל	WORTHLESSNESS	116a	1
		כרה	LIKE	453d	1 b
		כרה	DIG	500a	
		על	UPON	753a	2 1
		צרב	SCORCHING	863a	
16	28	אלוף	TAME	48d	2
		מדון	STRIFE	193b	1
		תהפכה	PERVERSITY	246c	
		פרד	DIVIDE	825c	1

Ch	v	Heb	Eng	Page	Sec
		רגן	MURMUR	920d	2
		שלח	SEND	1019b	3
16	29	דרך	WAY	203d	6 d
		הלך	WALK	237a	4
		חמס	VIOLENCE	329d	
		טוב	PLEASANT	374d	0 a
		לא	NOT	519c	2 a
		פתה	BE SIMPLE	834d	1
16	30	תהפכה	PERVERSITY	246c	
		חשב	THINK	363a	1 2
		כלה	FINISH	478c	1 f
		עצה	SHUT	781b	
		קרץ	PINCH	902d	
		שפה	SPEECH	973d	1 a1
16	31	דרך	WAY	203d	6 c
		עטרה	CROWN	742d	3
		תפארה	BEAUTY	802c	2
		צדקה	RIGHTEOUSNESS	842b	5
		שיבה	OLD AGE	966d	1
16	32	אף	NOSE	60b	3
		ארך	LONG	74a	
		גבור	STRONG	150b	2
		טוב	PLEASANT	374c	6
		משל	RULE	605d	1
		רוח	BREATH	925a	3 c
16	33	גורל	LOT	174b	
		חיק	BOSOM	300d	1
		טול	HURL	376d	2
		משפט	JUDGMENT	1048b	1 a
17	1	זבח	SACRIFICE	257c	1 1
		חרב	DRY	351b	
		טוב	PLEASANT	374c	6
		מלא	FULL	571a	
		פת	FRAGMENT	837d	
		ריב	STRIFE	936d	1
		שלוה	QUIETNESS	1017c	
17	2	בוש	BE ASHAMED	102a	1
		חלק	DIVIDE	323c	4
		משל	RULE	605d	1
		שכל	BE PRUDENT	968c	5
17	3	בחן	TRY	103c	2 b
		י	AND	253b	1 j
		זהב	GOLD	262c	1
		כור	FURNACE	468b	
		כסף	SILVER	494a	1
		מצרף	CRUCIBLE	864c	
17	4	און	TROUBLE	20a	3
		אזן	HEAR	24c	1
		הוה	CHASM	*217d	2
		לשון	TONGUE	546c	1 b
		קשב	ATTEND	904a	
		רעע	BE EVIL	949d	2
		שפה	SPEECH	973d	1 a1
		שקר	DECEPTION	1055d	5
17	5	חרף	REPROACH	357d	
		לעג	MOCK	541c	
		נקה	BE CLEAN	667b	3
		עשה	DO	794b	2 1b
		שמח	JOYFUL	970d	2
17	6	בן	SON	120b	1 f
		זקן	OLD	278c	2 a
		עטרה	CROWN	742d	3
		תפארה	BEAUTY	802d	3 b
17	7	אף	ALSO	65b	3
		יתר	EXCESS	452a	2 a
		נאוה	SEEMLY	610a	2
		נבל	FOOLISH	614d	
		נדיב	NOBLE	622a	3
		שפה	SPEECH	973d	1 a1
		שקר	DECEPTION	1055c	3
17	8	אבן	STONE	6d	3
		אל	TO	40d	
		אשר	PARTICLE OF RELATION	82c	4 bg
		בעל	OWNER	127b	1 1
		חן	FAVOR	336b	1 a
		פנה	TURN	815b	1 a
		שכל	BE PRUDENT	968c	6
		שחד	BRIBE	1005a	
17	9	אהבה	LOVE	13b	1
		אלוף	TAME	48d	2
		בקש	SEEK	134d	2 b
		כסה	COVER	491d	2
		פרד	DIVIDE	825c	1
		פשע	TRANSGRESSION	833c	1
		שנה	DO AGAIN	1040d	
17	10	בין	DISCERN	107a	1 b
		גערה	REBUKE	172a	1
		מאה	HUNDRED	548a	1 a5
		נחת	DESCEND	639c	2
		נכה	SMITE	645c	1 b
17	11	בקש	SEEK	134d	2 b
		אכזרי	CRUEL	470a	
		מלאך	MESSENGER	521c	1 a
		מרי	REBELLION	598c	
		רע	EVIL	948d	2
		שלח	SEND	1019b	
17	12	אל	NOT	39b	A bg
		דב	BEAR	179a	
		פגש	MEET	803d	
		שכול	BEREAVED	1014a	
17	13	טובה	WELFARE	375d	3
		מוש	DEPART	559a	
		מוש	REMOVE	559b	
		על	UPON	756c	2 7a b
		תחת	INSTEAD	1066a	2 2b b

Ch	v	Heb	Eng	Page	Sec
17	14	מדון	STRIFE	193b	1
		נטש	FORSAKE	643d	2
		פטר	SEPARATE	809c	2
		ראשית	BEGINNING	912a	1 a
		ריב	STRIFE	936d	1
17	15	גם	ALSO	169c	2
		צדק	DECLARE RIGHTEOUS	842d	2
		צדיק	JUST	843a	2
		רשע	WICKED	957b	1
		רשע	BE WICKED	957d	1
17	16	חכמה	WISDOM	315d	5 c
		לב	HEART	524d	2 3b
		לב	HEART	524d	2 3a
		מחיר	PRICE	564b	1
		קנה	ACQUIRE	889a	1 d
17	17	אהב	LOVE	13a	1
		ילד	BE BORN	408d	
		רע	FRIEND	946a	1
17	18	חסר	NEEDY	341c	
		כף	HOLLOW OF THE HAND	496c	1 d3
		לב	HEART	524c	2 3a
		ערבה	THING EXCHANGED	786d	
		ערב	TAKE ON PLEDGE	786d	2
		פנה	FACE	816d	2 4
		תקע	CLAP	1075c	3
17	19	אהב	LOVE	13a	1
		בקש	SEEK	134d	2 b
		גבה	BE HIGH	147a	
		מצה	STRIFE	663c	
		פשע	TRANSGRESSION	833c	1
		פתח	OPENING	835d	
		שבר	BREAKING	991b	1
17	20	הפך	TURN	246a	1 c
		טוב	A GOOD THING	375a	1
		לב	HEART	525b	2 6b
		לשון	TONGUE	546c	1 b
		נפל	FALL	657b	2 b
		עקש	TWISTED	786a	
		רעה	MISERY	949b	1
17	21	תוגה	GRIEF	387b	
		ילד	BEGET	408c	2 a
		ל	TO	513a	5 ad
17	22	גהה	HEALING	155c	
		גרם	BONE	175a	1
		יבש	BE DRY	386c	
		יטב	MAKE GOOD	406a	4
		לב	HEART	525c	2 9a
		נכא	A STRICKEN SPIRIT	644d	
		רוח	BREATH	925b	3 f
		שמח	JOYFUL	970c	1 a
17	23	ארח	WAY	73b	3 b
		חיק	BOSOM	300d	1
		נטה	BEND	641a	3 g
		רשע	WICKED	957b	1
		שחד	BRIBE	1005a	
17	24	ארץ	EARTH	76b	4 e
		בין	DISCERN	107a	1 b
		חכמה	WISDOM	315d	5 c
		פנה	FACE	816c	2 2a
		קצה	END	892b	1
17	25	כעס	ANGER	495b	1
		ממר	BITTERNESS	601b	
17	26	טוב	PLEASANT	375a	0 a
		ישר	STRAIGHTNESS	449c	2
		ל	TO	512a	3 b
		נדיב	NOBLE	622a	3
		ענש	FINE	778d	
		צדיק	JUST	843a	2
17	27	אמר	WORD	57a	1
		תבונה	UNDERSTANDING	108b	2
		חשך	WITHHOLD	362b	1 c
		ידע	KNOW	394c	5
		דעת	WISDOM	395d	2 a
		יקר	COOL	430a	4
		קר	COOL	903b	
		רוח	BREATH	925b	3 g
17	28	אטם	SHUT	32a	
		בין	DISCERN	106d	
		גם	ALSO	169b	2
		חכם	WISE	315a	6 b1
		חרש	BE SILENT	361b	1 a
		חשב	THINK	363b	
		שפה	SPEECH	973d	1 a1
18	1	תאוה	DESIRE	16c	1
		בקש	SEEK	134d	2 b
		תושיה	SOUND WISDOM	444d	A
		לעג	MOCK	541c	
		פרד	DIVIDE	825c	1
18	2	תבונה	UNDERSTANDING	108b	3
		חפץ	DELIGHT IN	342d	1 a
		כסיל	FOOL	493a	
18	3	בוז	CONTEMPT	100b	1
		חרפה	REPROACH	357d	1
		קלון	DISHONOUR	886a	2
18	4	חכמה	WISDOM	315d	5 c
		נחל	TORRENT	636b	1
		עמק	DEEP	771b	1
		מקור	SPRING	881b	1 a
18	5	ה	THE	208c	1 hb
		טוב	PLEASANT	375a	0 a
		נטה	BEND	641a	3 g
		נשא	LIFT	670c	1 b 3
		צדיק	JUST	843a	2

Ch	v.	Heb	Eng	Page	Sec
		רשע	WICKED	957b	1
		משפט	JUDGEMNT	1049a	5
18	6	בוא	COME	98c	2 a
		מהלמות	BLOWS	240d	
		קרא	CALL	895d	5 b
		ריב	STRIFE	936d	1
18	7	מחתה	TERROR	370c	2
		מוקש	BAIT	430d	
18	8	בטן	BELLY	105d	1 a
		חדר	CHAMBER	293d	
		ירד	GO DOWN	433c	3 j
		לחם	SWALLOW GREEDILY	529d	
18	9	רגן	MURMUR	920d	2
		אח	BROTHER	26b	3
		בעל	LORD	127c	15a
		בריח	BAR	138b	2
		מלאכה	WORK	522a	1
		רפה	SINK	952a	
		שחת	GO TO RUIN	*1008c	2
		משחית	DESTRUCTION	1008c	
18	10	מגדל	TOWER	153d	1
		עז	STRENGTH	738d	1
		רוץ	RUN	930b	1
		שגב	BE HIGH	960c	2
18	11	הון	WEALTH	223c	1
		חומה	WALL	327d	3
		עז	STRENGTH	738d	1
		קריה	TOWN	900b	4
		שגב	BE HIGH	960c	1
		משכית	SHOW-PIECE	967d	1
18	12	גבה	BE HIGH	147a	3 b
		כבוד	HONOR	459a	1
		לב	HEART	525b	26c
		ענוה	HUMILITY	776d	1
		שבר	BREAKING	991b	1
18	13	דבר	WORD	182b	11c
		הוא	HE, SHE, IT	216d	6 a
		טרם	NOT YET	382d	2
		כלמה	IGNOMINY	484b	2
		שוב	TURN BACK	999c	3
18	14	מחלה	SICKNESS	318d	
		כול	SUPPORT	465b	3
		מי	WHO	567a	F c
		נכא	A STRICKEN SPIRIT	644d	
		נשא	LIFT	671b	2
		רוח	BREATH	925a	3 b
		רוח	BREATH	925b	3 f
18	15	אזן	EAR	24a	2 a
		בין	DISCERN	106d	
		בקש	SEEK	134d	2 b
		חכם	WISE	315a	6 b1
		דעת	WISDOM	395d	2 a
		לב	HEART	524d	23b
		קנה	ACQUIRE	889a	1 d
18	16	גדול	GREAT	153d	6 b
		נחה	LEAD	635a	
		מתן	GIFTS	682b	
		פנה	FACE	817a	2 4
		רחב	BE LARGE	931c	2
18	17	חקר	SEARCH	350d	2 d
		צדיק	JUST	843a	2
		ריב	STRIFE	937a	4
18	18	גורל	LOT	174b	
		עצום	MIGHTY	783a	1
		פרד	DIVIDE	825c	2
		שבת	CEASE	992a	1
18	19	ארמון	CITADEL	74d	
		בריח	BAR	138b	2
		מדון	STRIFE	193b	1
		עז	STRENGTH	738d	1
		פשע	REBEL	833b	
		קריה	TOWN	900b	4
18	20	תבואה	REVENUE	100b	2 b
		בטן	BELLY	105d	1 a
		מן	OUT OF	579b	2 bb
		פרי	FRUIT	826c	
		שבע	SATISFIED	959c	1 b
		שפה	SPEECH	973d	1 a1
18	21	אהב	LOVE	13a	2
		אכל	EAT	37c	1
		חיים	LIFE	313a	1
		יד	HAND	391a	5 c3
		לשון	TONGUE	546b	1 b
		פרי	FRUIT	826c	
18	22	טוב	A GOOD THING	375a	1
		מצא	FIND	592c	1 a
		פוק	BRING OUT	807c	2
		רצון	GOODWILL	953c	1 a
18	23	תחנון	SUPPLICATION FOR FAVOR	337c	1
		עז	STRONG	738d	
		ענה	ANSWER	772c	1 c
18	24	אהב	LOVE	13a	4 b
		איש	MAN	36a	
		דבק	CLINGING	180a	
		יש	THERE IS	441d	2 b
		ל	TO	518a	7 bg
		רע	ASSOCIATE WITH	945d	
		רע	FRIEND	946a	1
		רעע	BREAK	950a	
19	1	טוב	PLEASANT	374c	6
		עקשות	CROOKEDNESS	*786a	
		עקש	TWISTED	786a	
		שפה	SPEECH	973d	1 a1
		תם	INTEGRITY	1070d	3

Ch	v.	Heb	Eng	Page	Sec
19	2	און	HASTEN	21a	3
		חטא	MISS A GOAL OR WAY	306d	1
		טוב	PLEASANT	374c	5
		דעת	WISDOM	395d	2 a
		לא	NOT	520a	4 aa
		נפש	SOUL	661a	7
19	3	דרך	WAY	203c	6 a
		זעף	BE VEXED	277a	1
		סלף	TWIST	701b	2
19	4	דל	POOR	195d	
		הון	WEALTH	223c	1
		יסף	ADD	415b	1
		פרד	DIVIDE	825c	2
19	5	כזב	LIE	469c	
		מלט	SLIP AWAY	572b	2
		נקה	BE CLEAN	667b	3
		עד	WITNESS	729d	2 c
		פוח	BREATHE	806b	3
		שקר	DECEPTION	1055c	3
19	6	חלה	MOLLIFY	318d	2
		כל	ALL	482a	1 db
		נדיב	NOBLE	622a	2
		מתן	GIFTS	682b	
19	7	אמר	WORD	57a	1
		אף	ALSO	65b	3
		הם	THEY	*241c	3 d
		לא	NOT	519b	1 bb
		לא	NOT	520c	
		רדף	PURSUE	923a	
		רחק	BE DISTANT	934d	
		מרע	FRIEND	946d	
19	8	אהב	LOVE	13a	2
		תבונה	UNDERSTANDING	108b	3
		טוב	A GOOD THING	375a	1
		ל	TO	518a	7 bg
		לב	HEART	524d	23a
		נפש	SOUL	660d	6 a
		קנה	ACQUIRE	889a	1 d
19	9	אבד	PERISH	1d	3
		כזב	LIE	469c	
		נקה	BE CLEAN	667b	3
		עד	WITNESS	729d	2 c
		פוח	BREATHE	806b	3
		שקר	DECEPTION	1055c	3
19	10	אף	ALSO	65b	3
		משל	RULE	605d	1
		נאוה	SEEMLY	610a	2
		עבד	SLAVE	714a	2
		תענוג	DAINTINESS	772c	1
		שר	CHIEFTAIN	978d	7
19	11	ארך	BE LONG	73d	1 c
		עבר	PASS OVER	717c	1 j
		תפארה	BEAUTY	802d	3 b
		פשע	TRANSGRESSION	833c	1
		פשע	TRANSGRESSION	833c	3 d
		שכל	PRUDENCE	968d	2
19	12	זעף	STORMING	277a	1
		טל	NIGHT-MIST	378d	
		כפיר	LION	498d	
		נהם	GROWLING	625b	
		עשב	HERB	793b	
		רצון	GOODWILL	953c	1 b
19	13	דלף	A DROPPING	196a	
		הוה	CHASM	217d	2
		טרד	PURSUE	382b	
		הון	WEALTH	223c	1
19	14	נחלה	INHERITANCE	635c	3
		שכל	BE PRUDENT	968d	5
19	15	נפל	FALL	658b	5
		נפש	SOUL	660b	4 c1
		עצלה	SLUGGISHNESS	782b	
		תרדמה	DEEP SLEEP	922b	
		רמיה	LAXNESS	941c	
		רעב	BE HUNGRY	944b	
19	16	בזה	DESPISE	102c	
		דרך	WAY	203c	6 a
		מות	DIE	560a	2 d
		מות	DIE	560c	4
		נפש	SOUL	660a	3 c
		מצוה	COMMANDMENT	846c	3
		שמר	KEEP	1036c	1 b
19	17	דל	WEAK	195d	
		חנן	SHOW FAVOR	336a	1 b
		לוה	BORROW	531a	
19	18	בן	SON	120a	1
		יסר	DISCIPLINE	416a	1 b
		מות	DIE	560c	4
		נשא	LIFT	670a	1 b 9
		תקוה	HOPE	876b	1
19	19	גדול	GREAT	153d	8
		גרל	GREAT	175a	
		חמה	RAGE	404c	2 a
		יסף	DO AGAIN	415c	2 a
		נצל	DELIVER	664d	3 a
		נשא	LIFT	671a	2 b
19	20	ענש	INDEMNITY	778d	
		חכם	BE WISE	314c	
		מוסר	DISCIPLINE	416c	1 c
		עצה	ADVICE	420b	
		קבל	RECEIVE	867b	2
19	21	הוא	HE, SHE, IT	215d	2 a
		מחשבה	THOUGHT	364b	2
		עצה	ADVICE	420b	
		לב	HEART	524d	23c
		קום	STAND	878c	7 g

Ch	v.	Heb	Eng	Page	Sec
19	22	תאוה	DESIRE	16c	2
		תאוה	DESIRE	16c	1
		חסד	GOODNESS	338c	1 1
		טוב	PLEASANT	374c	6
		כזב	LIE	469c	
19	23	בל	NOT	115b	
		חיים	LIFE	313b	3
		יראה	FEAR	432a	3
		לון	LODGE	533d	2
		פקד	ATTEND TO	823d	3
		רע	EVIL	948d	1
		שבע	SATISFIED	960a	1 a
19	24	טמן	HIDE	380b	1
		פה	MOUTH	804d	1 a
		צלחת	DISH	852c	
		שוב	TURN BACK	998d	1 a
19	25	בין	DISCERN	106d	1
		דעת	WISDOM	395d	2 a
		יכח	REPROVE	407a	5 b
		ליץ	SCORN	539c	
		נכה	SMITE	645c	1 b
		ערם	BE SHREWD	791a	
		פתי	SIMPLE	834c	
19	26	בוש	BE ASHAMED	102a	1
		ברח	FLEE	138a	2
		חפר	BE ABASHED	344a	
		שדד	DEAL VIOLENTLY WITH	994b	
19	27	אמר	WORD	57a	1
		חדל	CEASE	293a	2
		דעת	WISDOM	395d	2 a
		מוסר	DISCIPLINE	416c	1 c
		שגה	GO ASTRAY	993b	3
19	28	און	TROUBLE	20a	3
		בליעל	WORTHLESSNESS	116a	1
		בלע	SWALLOW UP	118c	2 c
		ליץ	SCORN	539b	
		עד	WITNESS	729d	2 c
		רשע	WICKED	957b	1
		משפט	JUDGEMNT	1048d	2 b
19	29	גו	BACK	156b	
		מהלמות	BLOWS	240d	
		כון	BE READY	466a	4
		ליץ	SCORN	539c	
		שפט	JUDGEMENT	1048a	
20	1	ה	THE	207d	1 e
		חמה	ROAR	242b	5
		חכם	BE WISE	314c	
		ליץ	SCORN	539c	
		שגה	GO ASTRAY	993a	2
		שכר	INTOXICATING DRINK	1016b	
20	2	אימה	TERROR	34a	
		חטא	MISS A GOAL OR WAY	306d	1
		חטא	MISS A GOAL OR WAY	307b	3
		כפיר	LION	498d	
		נהם	GROWLING	625b	
		עבר	BE ARROGANT	720d	2 b
20	3	כבוד	HONOR	459b	2
		ריב	STRIFE	936d	1
		שבת	CESSATION	992a	
20	4	אין	NOT	34c	2 da
		חרף	HARVEST-TIME	358b	
		חרש	CUT IN	360c	2
		מן	ON ACCOUNT OF	580b	2 f
		קציר	HARVESTING	894d	3
		שאל	ASK	981d	1 c
20	5	דלה	DRAW	194d	
		עצה	ADVICE	420b	
		עמק	DEEP	771b	1
20	6	אמן	TRUSTING	53c	2
		חסד	GOODNESS	338c	1 1
		מי	WHO	567a	F c
		רב	MULTITUDE	914a	1
20	7	אחר	AFTER	30a	2 b
		אשר	HAPPINESS	81a	
		הלך	WALK	236b	2
		תם	INTEGRITY	1070d	3
20	8	דין	JUDGMENT	192c	1
		זרה	SCATTER	280a	1
		כסא	THRONE	491b	3 a
		מלחמה	WAR	536c	
		מלך	KING	573c	5 c
20	9	זכה	BE CLEAR	269a	
		חטאת	SIN	308d	1 b
		טהר	BE CLEAN	372b	3
		מי	WHO	566d	F c
20	10	אבן	STONE	6d	5
		איפה	EPHAH	35b	2
		גם	ALSO	169c	2
20	11	גם	ALSO	169b	2
		זך	PURE	269b	2
		ישר	STRAIGHT	449b	3 b
		מעלל	DEED	760b	3
		פעל	DOING	821c	1 c
20	12	אזן	EAR	24a	2 a
		גם	ALSO	169c	2
		שמע	HEAR	1033d	1 e
20	13	אהב	LOVE	13a	2
		ירש	BE IMPOVERISHED	439d	
		שנה	SLEEP	446a	
		עין	EYE	744b	1 j
		פקח	OPEN	824d	1 a

PROVERBS

Ch	v.	Heb	Eng	Page	Sec
20	14	אול	GO	23c	
		הלל	BE BOASTFUL	239a	1
		ל	TO	516a	5 ib
		קנה	ACQUIRE	889a	2
		רע	EVIL	948b	5
20	15	דעת	KNOWLEDGE	396a	2 d
		יקר	PRECIOUSNESS	430b	1 b
		יש	THERE IS	441d	2 b
		כלי	ARTICLE	479c	1
		פנינים	CORALS	819d	
		שפה	SPEECH	973d	1 a1
20	16	בגד	GARMENT	94a	1
		בעד	ON BEHALF OF	126d	2
		חבל	BIND	286b	2
		נכרי	FOREIGN	649a	2
		נכרי	ALIEN	649a	3
		ערב	TAKE ON PLEDGE	786c	1
20	17	חצץ	GRAVEL	346b	
		לחם	FOOD	537b	3 a
		מי	WATER	565d	3
		מלא	BE FULL	570c	1
		ערב	SWEET	787a	
		שקר	DECEPTION	1055c	2
20	18	תחבלה	DIRECTION	287b	
		מחשבה	THOUGHT	364c	2
		עצה	ADVICE	*420a	
		עצה	ADVICE	420b	
20	19	כון	BE FIRM	465d	1 c
		הלך	WALK	232a	1 1d 5k
		סוד	COUNSEL	691c	2 b
		ערב	TAKE ON PLEDGE	786c	2 a
		פתה	BE SPACIOUS	834b	
		פתה	BE SIMPLE	834c	1
		רכיל	SLANDER	940c	
		שפה	SPEECH	973d	1 a1
20	20	אישון	PUPIL	36b	
		דעך	BE EXTINGUISHED	205a	1
		חשך	DARKNESS	365a	1
		נר	LAMP	632d	
20	21	בהל	HASTEN	96c	
		בחל	GOTTEN BY GREED	103c	
		ברך	BLESS	139b	2 a
		חבל	VAPOUR	210d	2
		ראשון	FIRST	912a	3 a1
20	22	ישע	DELIVER	446d	1 b
		קוה	WAIT FOR	875d	1
		רע	EVIL	948d	2
		שלם	BE COMPLETE	1022c	5
20	23	אבן	STONE	6d	5
		מאזן	BALANCES	24d	
		ו	AND	253b	1 ia
		טוב	PLEASANT	375a	0 a
		מרמה	DECEIT	941b	
20	24	בין	DISCERN	106d	2 b
		דרך	WAY	203b	5
		מה	HOW	553c	2 aa
		מן	OUT OF	579d	2 d
		מן	OUT OF	580a	2 ea
		מצעד	STEP	857d	
20	25	בקר	SEEK	133a	
		מוקש	BAIT	430d	
		ל	TO	518a	7 bg
		לוע	TALK WILDLY	534c	
		נדר	VOW	624a	2
		עולם	LONG DURATION	762a	2 a
		קדש	APARTNESS	872a	3 c
20	26	אופן	WHEEL	66d	A
		זרה	SCATTER	280a	1
		חכם	WISE	314d	2
		רשע	WICKED	957b	1
		שוב	TURN BACK	998d	1 a
20	27	בטן	BELLY	105d	1 a
		חדר	CHAMBER	293d	
		חפש	SEARCH	344b	3
		נר	LAMP	632d	
		נשמה	BREATH	675d	4
20	28	אמת	FIRMNESS	54a	3 a
		ה	THE	208c	1 hb
		חסד	GOODNESS	338d	1 2
		חסד	GOODNESS	338d	1 2
		כסא	THRONE	491a	3 a
		נצר	GUARD	665d	2
		סעד	SUPPORT	703c	2 a
20	29	בחור	YOUNG MAN	104c	
		הדר	ORNAMENT	214b	1
		זקן	OLD	278c	2 a
		כח	STRENGTH	470c	1 a
		מי	WHO	566b	B
		תפארה	BEAUTY	802d	3 b
		שיבה	OLD AGE	966d	1
20	30	ב	IN	90b	3 4
		בטן	BELLY	105d	1 a
		חבורה	STRIPE	289a	
		חדר	CHAMBER	293d	
		מרק	POLISH	599d	
		תמרוק	RUBBING	600a	
		מכה	BLOW	646d	1 a
		פצע	BRUISE	822d	
21	1	חפץ	DELIGHT IN	343a	2 a
		נטה	INCLINE	640d	3 d
		על	UPON	757b	2 7c ab
		פלג	CHANNEL	811b	
21	2	דרך	WAY	203c	6 a
		ישר	STRAIGHT	449a	2 b
		תכן	ESTIMATE	1067b	
21	3	בחר	CHOOSE	104b	B
		זבח	SACRIFICE	257c	1 1
		ל	TO	*514a	5 e
		צדקה	RIGHTEOUSNESS	842b	5
21	4	חטאת	SIN	308c	1 b
		לב	HEART	525b	2 6c
		ניר	LAMP	633a	
		עין	EYE	744c	2
		רום	HEIGHT	927d	1
		רחב	WIDE	932a	
21	5	אוץ	HASTEN	21a	3
		אך	ONLY	36d	2 ba
		מחסור	NEED	341d	3
		חרוץ	SHARP	358c	1
		מחשבה	THOUGHT	364b	2
		מותר	ABUNDANCE	452d	1
21	6	אוצר	TREASURE	70a	1
		בקש	SEEK	134c	1 b
		הבל	VAPOUR	210d	1
		לשון	TONGUE	546c	1 b
		נדף	DRIVE	623c	
		פעל	DOING	821c	4
		שקר	DECEPTION	1055d	5
		גרר	DRAG AWAY	176a	
21	7	מאן	REFUSE	549b	
		שד	VIOLENCE	994c	1
		משפט	JUDGMENT	1048d	2 b
21	8	דרך	WAY	203d	6 d
		הפכפך	CROOKED	246b	
		זור	CRIMINAL	255c	
		זך	PURE	269b	2
		ישר	STRAIGHT	449b	3 b
		פעל	DOING	821c	1 c
21	9	אשה	WOMAN	61b	1
		גג	ROOF	150d	1
		מדון	STRIFE	193b	1
		חבר	COMPANY	288c	2
		טוב	PLEASANT	374c	6
		ל	TO	517d	7 bd
		מן	THAN	582b	6 a
21	10	פנה	CORNER	819c	1 a
		אוה	DESIRE	16a	
		חנן	SHOW FAVOR	336b	
		ירש	INHERIT	439d	2
		נפש	SOUL	660d	6 a
		רע	EVIL	948d	2
21	11	חכם	BE WISE	314c	
		חכם	WISE	315a	6 b1
		דעת	WISDOM	395d	2 a
		ליץ	SCORN	539c	
		ענש	FINE	778d	
		פתי	SIMPLE	834c	
		שכל	BE PRUDENT	968c	4
21	12	דעת	KNOWLEDGE	395d	1 e
		סלף	TWIST	701b	2
		רע	EVIL	948d	2
		שכל	BE PRUDENT	968b	2
21	13	אזן	EAR	24a	2 a
		אטם	SHUT	32a	
		דל	WEAK	195d	
		זעקה	CRY	277d	2
		ענה	ANSWER	773a	2 b
		קרא	CALL	845b	2 b
21	14	חיק	BOSOM	300d	1
		חמה	RAGE	404c	2 a
		מתן	GIFTS	682b	
		סתר	COVERING	712b	3
		עז	STRONG	738d	
		שחד	BRIBE	1005a	
21	15	און	TROUBLE	20a	3
		מחתה	TERROR	370a	1 b
		פעל	DO	821b	1 b
		שמחה	JOY	970d	1
		משפט	JUDGMENT	1048d	2 b
21	16	אדם	MAN	9b	1
		דרך	WAY	203c	6 b
		נוח	REST	628b	1
		קהל	ASSEMBLY	874d	2 d
		רפאים	SHADES	952b	
		שכל	BE PRUDENT	968b	3
		תעה	ERR	1073c	3
21	17	אהב	LOVE	13a	2
		מחסור	NEED	341d	3
		יין	WINE	406c	C
		עשר	BE RICH	799b	2
		שמחה	JOY	970d	1
		שמן	OIL	1032b	2 b
21	18	כפר	RANSOM	497b	1
		ישר	STRAIGHT	779b	3 c2
21	19	אשה	WOMAN	61b	1
		מדבר	WILDERNESS	184d	1
		מדון	STRIFE	193b	1
		טוב	PLEASANT	374c	6
		כעס	ANGER	495b	1
		ל	TO	*517d	7 bd
		מן	THAN	582b	6 a
21	20	אדם	MAN	9b	1
		אוצר	TREASURE	70a	1
		בלע	SWALLOW UP	118c	2 c
		חכם	WISE	315a	6 b3
		חמד	DESIRE	326c	
		נוה	HABITATION	627c	2
21	21	חיים	LIFE	313b	2
		חסד	GOODNESS	338d	1 2
		כבוד	HONOR	459d	4
		מצא	FIND	592d	1 a
		צדקה	RIGHTEOUSNESS	842b	5
		צדקה	RIGHTEOUSNESS	842b	5
		רדף	PURSUE	923a	2
21	22	מבטח	CONFIDENCE	105c	1
		גבור	STRONG	150b	2
		חכם	WISE	315b	6 b4
		ירד	BRING DOWN	434a	1 c
		עז	STRENGTH	738d	1
21	23	לשון	TONGUE	546b	1 b
		פה	MOUTH	805a	2 a
		שמר	KEEP	1036c	1 b
21	24	זד	INSOLENT	267d	
		זדון	INSOLENCE	268a	2
		יהיר	PROUD	397d	
		ליץ	SCORN	539b	
		עברה	OVERFLOW	720c	1
		שם	NAME	1027d	2 a
21	25	תאוה	DESIRE	16c	1
		מאן	REFUSE	549a	
		מות	DIE	560c	4
21	26	אוה	DESIRE	16b	
		תאוה	DESIRE	16c	1
		חשך	WITHHOLD	362b	1 a
		יום	DAY	400c	7 f
21	27	אף	ALSO	65a	2
		זבח	SACRIFICE	257c	1 1
		זמה	PLAN	273c	2 b
		תועבה	ABOMINATION	1073a	2 b
21	28	אבד	PERISH	1d	1
		כזב	LIE	469d	
		נצח	ENDURING	664b	3
		עד	WITNESS	729d	2 c
		שמע	HEAR	1033d	1 f
		שמע	HEAR	1033d	1 e
21	29	בין	DISCERN	106d	3 a
		דרך	WAY	203c	6 a
		ישר	STRAIGHT	449b	3 c2
		כון	ESTABLISH	466c	3
		עזז	BE STRONG	738c	
		רשע	WICKED	957c	3
21	30	תבונה	UNDERSTANDING	108b	1
		חכמה	WISDOM	315d	5 c
		עצה	ADVICE	420b	
21	31	נגד	IN FRONT	617c	2 b
		יום	DAY	401a	7 i
		תשועה	DELIVERANCE	448b	1
		כון	BE ESTABLISHED	466d	2
		ל	TO	*517a	6 a
		סוס	HORSE	692c	2
22	1	בחר	CHOOSE	104b	B
		זהב	GOLD	262d	2
		זהב	GOLD	263c	1
		חן	FAVOR	336b	2 a
		טוב	PLEASANT	374c	6
22	2	פגש	MEET	803d	
22	3	סתר	HIDE	711b	1
		ענש	FINE	779a	
		ערום	CRAFTY	791b	2
		פתי	SIMPLE	834c	
		רעה	MISERY	949a	1
22	4	חיים	LIFE	313b	2
		יראה	FEAR	432a	3
		כבוד	HONOR	458c	2 a
		ענוה	HUMILITY	776d	1
		עקב	CONSEQUENCE	784d	2
22	5	דרך	WAY	203d	6 d
		נפש	SOUL	660d	3 c
		עקש	TWISTED	786a	
		פח	BIRD-TRAP	809a	2 a
		צן	THORN	856d	
		רחק	BE DISTANT	935a	
		שמר	KEEP	1036c	1 b
22	6	גם	YEA	169d	6
		דרך	WAY	203c	6 b
		זקן	BE OLD	278c	
		חנך	TRAIN UP	335b	1
		נער	YOUTH	655a	1 d
		פה	MOUTH	805d	6 d2
22	7	לוה	BORROW	531a	
		לוה	BORROW	531a	
		משל	PROVERB	605b	6
		משל	RULE	605d	1
		עבד	SLAVE	713d	1
		עבד	SLAVE	714c	7
		רוש	BE IN WANT	930d	1
22	8	און	TROUBLE	20a	1
		זרע	SOW	281d	3 1
		כלה	BE FINISHED	477d	2 c
		עברה	OVERFLOW	720c	3 a
		עולה	INJUSTICE	732d	3
		קצר	HARVEST	894b	
		קצר	HARVEST	894c	
		שבט	ROD	987a	1 d
22	9	ברך	BLESS	139b	4
		דל	POOR	195d	
		הוא	HE, SHE, IT	215d	2 a
		טוב	PLEASANT	374d	9 a
		לחם	FOOD	537b	2 a
		עין	EYE	744c	3 b
22	10	גרש	DRIVE OUT	176d	
		דין	JUDGMENT	192d	4
		מדון	STRIFE	193b	1
		ליץ	SCORN	539c	
		קלון	DISHONOUR	886a	2
22	11	אהב	LOVE	13a	2
		חן	FAVOR	336b	1 b
		טהור	CLEAN	373a	3

Ch	v.	Heb	Eng	Page	Sec
22	12	שפה	SPEECH	973d	1 a1
		דעת	WISDOM	395d	2 a
		נצר	GUARD	665d	2
22	13	סלף	TWIST	701b	2
		ארי	LION	71d	
		חוץ	THE OUTSIDE	*300a	2 a
		רחוב	PLAZA	932b	
		רצח	MURDER	954a	
22	14	זור	BE A STRANGER	266c	2 b
		זעם	BE INDIGNANT	276d	1
		נפל	FALL	656d	1
		עמק	DEEP	771b	1
		שוחה	PIT	1001c	
22	15	אולת	FOLLY	17c	
		מוסר	DISCIPLINE	416d	2 b
		קשר	BIND	905b	1 b
		רחק	BE DISTANT	935b	2
22	16	שבט	ROD	987a	1 a
		אך	ONLY	36d	2 ba
		דל	POOR	195d	
		מחסור	NEED	341d	3
		משל	PROVERB	605b	6
		עשק	OPPRESS	798d	1
		רבה	BECOME MANY	915c	1 c
22	17	אזן	EAR	24a	2 a
		דבר	WORD	182d	2 1a
		חכם	WISE	315a	6 b2
		דעת	WISDOM	395d	2 a
		לב	HEART	524c	2 1
		לב	HEART	524d	2 3c
		לב	HEART	524d	2 3b
		נטה	INCLINE	641a	3 e
		שית	PUT	1011b	2 b
22	18	בטן	BELLY	105d	1 a
		כון	BE READY	465d	3
		נעים	DELIGHTFUL	653d	1
		על	UPON	752d	2 1
		שמר	KEEP	1036d	2 a
22	19	אתה	THOU	61c	1
		אף	ALSO	64d	1
		מבטח	CONFIDENCE	105c	1
		ידע	ANSWER	395a	
22	20	דעת	WISDOM	395d	2 a
		מועצה	PLAN	420b	
		שלשם	THREE DAYS AGO	1026b	
		שליש	OFFICER	1026d	
22	21	אמת	FIRMNESS	54b	4 a
		אמר	WORD	57a	1
		ידע	KNOW	395a	
		קשט	TRUTH	905a	
		שוב	TURN BACK	999c	3
22	22	גזל	TEAR AWAY	159d	
		דכא	CRUSH	194a	
		דכא	CRUSH	*194a	
		דל	WEAK	195d	
		עני	POOR	776d	2
22	23	קבע	ROB	867b	
		קבע	ROB	867c	
		ריב	STRIVE	936c	3
22	24	אף	NOSE	60b	3
		בוא	COME	98d	3
		בעל	LORD	127c	15a
		חמה	RAGE	404c	2 a
		רעה	ASSOCIATE WITH	945d	
22	25	אלף	LEARN	48c	
		ארח	WAY	73b	3 c
		מוקש	BAIT	430d	
		לקח	TAKE	543b	4 f
22	26	היה	BE	227c	3 4d e
		כף	HOLLOW OF THE HAND	496c	1 d3
		משאה	LOAN	673d	
		ערב	TAKE ON PLEDGE	786c	1
		תקע	CLAP	1075c	3
22	27	שלם	BE COMPLETE	1022d	3
		תחת	UNDERNEATH	1066b	3 2a
22	28	גבול	BOUNDARY	148a	1 c
		סוג	DISPLACE	691a	1
		עולם	LONG DURATION	761d	1 a
22	29	בל	NOT	115b	
		חזה	SEE	302b	1 a
		חשך	OBSCURE	365b	
		יצב	STATION ONESELF	426c	C
		מלאכה	WORK	522a	1
		מהיר	SKILLED	555b	
23	1	בין	DISCERN	106d	3 a
		לחם	EAT	536d	
		משל	RULE	605b	1
23	2	אזן	EAR	24a	2 a
		בעל	LORD	127c	15a
		לע	THROAT	534b	
		נפש	SOUL	660c	5 c
		שום	TO PLACE	963a	1 a
		שכין	KNIFE	967d	
23	3	אוה	DESIRE	16b	
		מטעם	TASTY	381b	
		כוב	LIE	469d	
		לחם	FOOD	537b	3 a
23	4	בינה	UNDERSTANDING	108a	2
		חדל	CEASE	293a	2
		יגע	TOIL	388b	1
		עשר	BE RICH	799b	2
23	5	כנף	WING	489c	1 a
		נשר	EAGLE	676d	
		עוף	FLY	733c	1
		שמי	HEAVENS	1030a	1 b
23	6	אוה	DESIRE	16b	
		מטעם	TASTY	381b	
		לחם	EAT	536d	
		עין	EYE	744d	3 b
		רע	EVIL	948b	9
23	7	בל	NOT	115b	
		כמו	LIKE	456a	1 bb
		כן	SO	486b	2 aa
		נפש	SOUL	661a	7
		עם	WITH	768a	3 e
		שער	CALCULATE	1045c	
23	8	נעים	DELIGHTFUL	653d	1
		פת	FRAGMENT	837d	
		קיא	SPUE OUT	883c	
		קיא	SPUE OUT	883c	
		שחת	GO TO RUIN	1008a	1
23	9	בז	DESPISE	100b	
		דבר	SPEAK	181c	4 b
		מלה	WORD	576b	
		סכל	PRUDENCE	968d	2
23	10	גבול	BOUNDARY	148a	1 c
		יתום	ORPHAN	450c	
		סוג	DISPLACE	691a	1
		עולם	LONG DURATION	761d	1 a
23	11	את	WITH	86b	1 dd
		גאל	REDEEM	145c	3 a
		חזק	STRONG	305c	1
		ריב	STRIVE	936c	3
23	12	אמר	WORD	57a	1
		בוא	COME	99b	1 g
		דעת	WISDOM	395d	2 a
		מוסר	DISCIPLINE	416c	1 c
		לב	HEART	524c	2 1
23	13	בין	INTERVAL	*107b	1
		מוסר	DISCIPLINE	416d	2 b
		מות	DIE	560a	2 d
		מנע	WITHHOLD	586a	
		נכה	SMITE	645c	1 b
23	14	נכה	SMITE	645c	1 b
		נפש	SOUL	659c	1 d
		נצל	DELIVER	665a	3 b
		שאול	SHEOL	983a	2 a
23	15	אנכי	I	59b	
		חכם	BE WISE	314c	
		לב	HEART	524d	2 3b
		שמח	REJOICE	970b	1 a
23	16	מישר	LEVEL	449d	2
		כליה	KIDNEYS	480c	2 b
		עלז	EXULT	759c	
23	17	חטא	SINFUL	308b	2
		יום	DAY	400c	7 f
		יראה	FEAR	432a	3
		כיאם	BUT	475a	2 b
		קנא	BE ZEALOUS	888c	2
23	18	אחרית	END	31a	B
		כיאם	SURELY	475c	2
		כרת	BE CUT OFF	504b	4
		תקוה	HOPE	876b	3
23	19	אשר	GO STRAIGHT	80d	2
		דרך	WAY	203c	6 b
		חכם	BE WISE	314c	
23	20	בשר	FLESH	142c	1 a
		היה	BE	227c	3 4d e
		זלל	BE LIGHT	272d	2
		יין	WINE	406c	D
		ל	TO	515d	5 ia
		סבא	DRINK LARGELY	685a	
23	21	זלל	BE LIGHT	272d	2
		ירש	BE IMPOVERISHED	439d	
		לבש	CLOTHE	528b	2
		נומה	SOMNOLENCE	630b	
		סבא	DRINK LARGELY	685a	
		קרע	TORN PIECES OF GARMENT	902d	
23	22	אב	FATHER	3b	1
		בז	DESPISE	100b	
		זה	THIS	261d	5
		זקן	BE OLD	278b	
		ילד	BEGET	408c	2 a
		כי	WHEN	473a	2 a
23	23	בינה	UNDERSTANDING	108a	3
		חכמה	WISDOM	315d	5 c
		מוסר	DISCIPLINE	416c	1 c
		מכר	SELL	569b	
		קנה	ACQUIRE	889d	1 d
23	24	ו	AND	254d	5 ca
		חכם	WISE	315a	6 a
		ילד	BEGET	408c	2 a
23	26	דרך	WAY	203c	6 b
		לב	HEART	525a	2 4
		רצה	BE PLEASED WITH	953a	1 b
		לב	ADDENDA ET CORRIGENDA	1124c	
23	27	באר	WELL	91d	2
		זנה	COMMIT FORNICATION	275d	1
		נכרי	FOREIGN	649a	2
		עמק	DEEP	771b	1
		צר	NARROW	865a	
		שוחה	PIT	1001c	
23	28	אף	ALSO	64d	1
		ארב	LIE IN WAIT	70b	
		חתף	PREY	369a	
		יסף	ADD	415b	1
23	29	אבוי	OH	5a	
		אוי	WOE	17a	
		מדון	STRIFE	193b	1
		חנם	OUT OF FAVOR	336d	C
		עין	EYE	744c	1 s
		פצע	BRUISE	822d	
		שיח	COMPLAINT	967a	1
23	30	אחר	DELAY	29b	1
		חכללות	DULNESS	*314b	
		חקר	SEARCH	350c	1
		יין	WINE	406c	C
		ממסך	MIXED DRINK	587c	
		על	UPON	756a	2 6b
23	31	אדם	BE RED	10a	
		הלך	WALK	236a	1 b
		יין	WINE	406c	C
		מישר	LEVEL	449d	1
		כוס	CUP	468a	
		ל	TO	*516c	5 jb
		נתן	GIVE	679b	1 m
		עין	EYE	745a	4 c
23	32	אחרית	END	31a	B
		נחש	SERPENT	638b	1 a
		נשך	BITE	675a	
		פרש	PIERCE	831d	
		צפעוני	VIPER	861c	
23	33	תהפכה	PERVERSITY	246c	
		זור	BE A STRANGER	266c	2 b
23	34	חבל	MAST	287a	
		לב	HEART	524b	1
		ראש	HEAD	910d	2 a
		שכב	LIE DOWN	1012a	1 b
23	35	בל	NOT	115b	
		בקש	SEEK	134c	1 b
		הלם	SMITE	240c	
		חלה	BE WEAK	317d	2
		חלה	BE WEAK	317d	2
		יסף	DO AGAIN	415c	2 c
		מתי	WHEN	607d	A
		קיץ	AWAKE	884c	3
24	1	אוה	DESIRE	16b	
		יקר	PRECIOUS	430a	1 a
		קנא	BE ZEALOUS	888c	2
		רעה	MISERY	949b	3
24	2	הגה	MUSE	211d	3 b
		לב	HEART	524d	2 3c
		עמל	TROUBLE	765d	2
		שפה	SPEECH	973d	1 a1
		שד	VIOLENCE	994c	1
24	3	תבונה	UNDERSTANDING	108b	1
		בנה	BUILD	125a	2 b
		חכמה	WISDOM	315d	5 c
		כון	BE ESTABLISHED	467a	
24	4	חון	WEALTH	223c	1
		חדר	CHAMBER	293d	
		דעת	WISDOM	395d	2 a
		מלא	FILL	570b	1
		נעים	DELIGHTFUL	653d	1
24	5	אמץ	BE STRONG	55a	1
		חכם	WISE	315a	6 b3
		דעת	KNOWLEDGE	396a	1
		כח	STRENGTH	470d	1 b
		עז	STRONG	738c	
24	6	תחבלה	DIRECTION	287b	
		יעץ	ADVISE	419d	
		תשועה	DELIVERANCE	448b	1
		מלחמה	WAR	536c	
		עשה	DO	794c	2 1e
24	7	חכמה	WISDOM	315d	5 c
		פתח	OPEN	835b	
		ראמות	CORALS	910c	
		רום	BE HIGH	927a	3
		שער	GATE	1045a	2 a
24	8	בעל	LORD	127c	15a
		מזמה	PURPOSE	273d	2
		חשב	THINK	363c	2
24	9	רעע	BE EVIL	949c	1
		זמה	PLAN	273c	2 a
		חטאת	SIN	308c	1 b
		ליץ	SCORN	539c	
		תועבה	ABOMINATION	1073a	2 a
24	10	יום	DAY	*398d	2 f
		כח	STRENGTH	470d	1 b
		צר	NARROW	865a	
		צרה	DISTRESS	865b	
		רפה	SINK	952a	
24	11	אם	IF	50b	1 b3
		הרג	SLAUGHTER	247c	
		חשך	WITHHOLD	362b	1 a
		לקח	TAKE	543d	7
		מוט	SLIP	556d	
24	12	בין	DISCERN	106d	2 a
		הוא	HE, SHE, IT	215d	2 a
		הן	BEHOLD	243c	A
		זה	THIS	260d	1 a
		נפש	SOUL	661b	0
		נצר	GUARD	665d	2
		פעל	DOING	821c	1 c
		שוב	TURN BACK	999c	4 a
		תכן	ESTIMATE	1067b	
24	13	דבש	HONEY	185b	
		חך	PALATE	335b	C
		טוב	PLEASANT	373d	1 b
		כן	SO	*486a	1 b
		מתוק	SWEET	608d	1
		נפת	HONEY FROM THE COMB	661d	
24	14	אחרית	END	31a	B

Ch v.	Heb	Eng	Page	Sec
	חכמה	WISDOM	315d	5 c
	ידע	KNOW	394c	5
	כן	SO	486a	1 b
	כרת	BE CUT OFF	504b	4
	מצא	FIND	592d	1 a
	נפש	SOUL	661a	7
	תקוה	HOPE	876b	3
24 15	ארב	LIE IN WAIT	70b	
	נוה	HABITATION	627c	2
	רבץ	RESTING PLACE	918c	
	שדד	DEAL VIOLENTLY WITH	994b	
24 16	כשל	STUMBLE	505d	1 b
	נפל	FALL	657b	2 c
	רעה	MISERY	949b	1
	שבע	SEVEN	988a	1 a
24 17	אויב	BE HOSTILE TO	33c	
	כשל	STUMBLE	505d	1 a
	לב	HEART	525c	29a
	נפל	FALL	657b	2 b
	שמח	REJOICE	970b	1 b
24 18	על	UPON	758d	4 2b
	רעע	BE EVIL	949c	1
	שוב	TURN BACK	999d	6 a
24 19	חרה	BURN	354b	
	קנא	BE ZEALOUS	888c	2
24 20	אחרית	END	31a	B
	אחרית	END	31b	D
	דעך	BE EXTINGUISHED	200b	
	נר	LAMP	632d	
	רע	EVIL	948c	0 b
24 21	ירא	FEAR	431c	3 b
	ערב	TAKE ON PLEDGE	786d	2 a
	שנה	CHANGE	1040a	
24 22	איד	DISTRESS	15d	3
	מי	WHO	*567a	F d
	מי	WHO	567a	F c
	משל	PROVERB	605b	6
	פיד	RUIN	810a	
	פתאם	SUDDENNESS	837c	
	קום	STAND	878a	4
	שנים	TWO	1041a	1 a
24 23	בל	NOT	115b	
	ה	THE	208c	1 hb
	חכם	WISE	*315a	6 b2
	טוב	PLEASANT	375a	0 a
	משל	PROVERB	605b	6
	נכר	REGARD	648a	1
	משפט	JUDGMENT	1048b	1 a
24 24	זעם	BE INDIGNANT	276d	2
	לאם	PEOPLE	522c	
	צדיק	JUST	843a	2
	קבב	CURSE	866d	
	רשע	WICKED	957b	1
24 25	ברכה	BLESSING	139d	1 c
	טוב	A GOOD THING	375b	2
	יכח	REPROVE	407a	5 b
	נעם	BE DELIGHTFUL	653c	
24 26	דבר	WORD	182b	1 1c
	נכח	STRAIGHTNESS	647c	
	נשק	KISS	676c	
	שפה	SPEECH	974a	1 g
	שוב	TURN BACK	999c	1
24 27	בנה	BUILD	124b	1 ab
	חוץ	THE OUTSIDE	300b	2 b
	כון	ESTABLISH	466b	2 a
	מלאכה	WORK	522a	3 b
	עתד	BE READY	800c	
24 28	חנם	OUT OF FAVOR	336d	C
	עד	WITNESS	729d	2 c
	פתה	BE SPACIOUS	834b	
	פתה	BE SIMPLE	834d	2
24 29	כן	SO	486c	2 cd
	פעל	DOING	821c	1 a
	שוב	TURN BACK	999d	4 a
24 30	אדם	MAN	9b	1
	חסר	NEEDY	341c	
	לב	HEART	524c	2 3a
	עצל	SLUGGISH	782b	
24 31	חרם	THROW DOWN	248d	
	חרול	KIND OF WEED	355b	
	כל	ALL	481b	1 a
	כסה	BE COVERED	492b	4
	עלה	GO UP	748d	4
	פנה	FACE	816b	15
	קמוש	THISTLES	888b	
24 32	חזה	SEE	302c	3 a
	מוסר	DISCIPLINE	416c	1 c
	לב	HEART	524d	2 3c
	לקח	TAKE	543b	4 f
	שית	PUT	1011b	2 b
24 33	חבק	CLASPING	287d	
	שנה	SLEEP	446a	
	תנומה	SLUMBER	630b	
24 34	מגן	SHIELD	171c	
	הלך	WALK	*235d	1
	הלך	WALK	236a	1 b
	מחסור	NEED	341d	3
	משל	PROVERB	605b	6
	ריש	POVERTY	*930d	
	ריש	POVERTY	930d	
25 1	חזקיהו	HEZEKIAH	306a	1
	משל	PROVERB	605b	6
	עתק	MOVE	801b	3
	שלמה	SOLOMON	1024d	
25 2	אלהים	GOD	44b	4 a
	חקר	SEARCH	350c	2 a
	כבוד	HONOR	459b	4
	סתר	HIDE	711d	1
25 3	ו	AND	253b	1 j
	חקר	SEARCHING	350d	
	ל	TO	514b	5 fb
	לב	HEART	524c	2 2
	עמק	DEPTH	771b	
	רום	HEIGHT	927d	1
25 4	הגה	REMOVE	212a	
	כלי	VESSEL	480b	3
	כסף	SILVER	494a	1
	סיג	DROSS	691b	2
	צרף	SMELT	864b	4
25 5	ה	THE	208c	1 hb
	הגה	REMOVE	212a	
	כון	BE FIRM	465d	1 b
	כסא	THRONE	491a	3 a
	צדק	RIGHTEOUSNESS	841c	2 a
	רשע	WICKED	957b	1
25 6	גדול	GREAT	153d	6 b
	הדר	HONOUR	214a	
25 7	טוב	PLEASANT	374c	6
	מן	THAN	582b	6 a
	נדיב	NOBLE	622a	2
	שפל	BECOME LOW	1050b	2
25 8	אחרית	END	31a	B
	כלם	HUMILIATE	484a	1
	מה	AUGHT	553d	3
	מהר	QUICKLY	555b	
	ריב	STRIVE	936d	3
	פן	ADDENDA ET CORRIGENDA	1126b	
25 9	סוד	COUNSEL	691c	2 b
	ריב	STRIVE	936d	3
25 10	דבה	EVIL REPORT	179b	3
	חסד	BE GOOD	338c	
	חסד	BE REPROACHED	340a	
	שוב	TURN BACK	998b	7 e
25 11	אפן	CIRCUMSTANCE	67a	
	דבר	SPEAK	180c	
	זהב	GOLD	263a	6
	תפוח	APPLES	656b	2
	על	UPON	754a	2 1fa
	משכית	SHOW-PIECE	967d	1
25 12	אזן	EAR	24a	2 a
	זהב	GOLD	263a	6
	חכם	WISE	315a	6 a
	חלי	ORNAMENT	318d	
	יכח	REPROVE	407a	5 b
	כתם	GOLD	508d	1
	נזם	RING	634a	2
25 13	אדון	LORD	11a	2 1b
	אמן	CONFIRM	53a	5
	יום	TIME	399c	6 a
	נפש	SOUL	661a	6 g
	ציר	ENVOY	851d	
	צנה	COOLNESS	856d	
	קציר	HARVESTING	894d	3
	שוב	TURN BACK	999b	2 b
	שלג	SNOW	1017a	
25 14	גשם	RAIN	177c	
	הלל	BE BOASTFUL	239a	1
	מתת	GIFT	682c	
	שקר	DECEPTION	1055c	1
25 15	אף	NOSE	60b	1
	ארך	LENGTH	73d	C
	ארך	LONG	74a	1
	גרם	BONE	175a	1
	לשון	TONGUE	546b	1 b
	פתה	BE SIMPLE	834d	1
	קצין	CHIEF	892d	3
	רך	TENDER	940a	3
	שבר	BREAK	990c	
25 16	דבש	HONEY	185b	
	די	SUFFICIENCY	191c	1
	מצא	FIND	593b	3 a
	קיא	SPUE OUT	883c	
	שבע	SATISFIED	959c	3 a
25 17	יקר	MAKE RARE	429d	
	מן	FROM	578a	1 a
	שבע	SATISFIED	959c	3 b
25 18	חץ	ARROW	346c	2
	עד	WITNESS	729d	2 c
	ענה	ANSWER	773a	3 a
	מפיץ	SCATTERER	807b	
	שנן	SHARPEN	1041d	
	שקר	DECEPTION	1055c	3
25 19	מבטח	CONFIDENCE	105c	1
	יום	DAY	*398c	2 f
	מעד	SLIP	588c	
	צרה	DISTRESS	865b	
	רעע	BREAK	949d	2
	שן	TOOTH	1042a	1 a
25 20	בגד	GARMENT	94a	1
	ו	AND	253b	1 j
	חמץ	VINEGAR	330a	
	יום	DAY	398c	2 f
	נתר	CARBONATE OF SODA	684c	
	עדה	PASS ON	723c	
	על	UPON	757c	2 7c b
	קרה	COLD	903b	
	רע	EVIL	948b	7
	שיר	SONG	1010b	1
	שיר	SING	1010c	
25 21	אכל	EAT	38a	1
	צמא	THIRSTY	854d	
	רעב	HUNGRY	944c	
25 22	גחלת	COAL	161a	
	חתה	SNATCH UP	367a	
25 23	גשם	RAIN	177c	
	חול	WHIRL	297b	2
	לשון	TONGUE	546c	1 b
	סתר	COVERING	712a	3
	צפון	NORTH	861a	
	רוח	BREATH	924d	2 a
25 24	אשה	WOMAN	61b	1
	גג	ROOF	150d	1
	מדין	STRIFE	193b	1
	חבר	COMPANY	288c	2
	טוב	PLEASANT	374c	6
	ל	TO	*517d	7 bd
	פנה	CORNER	819c	1 a
25 25	ו	AND	253b	1 j
	טוב	PLEASANT	373d	2 d
	נפש	SOUL	660c	5 b
	עיף	FAINT	746a	
	קר	COOL	903b	
	מרחק	DISTANT PLACE	935d	
	שמועה	REPORT	1035b	1
25 26	מוט	SLIP	556d	
	מעין	SPRING	746a	
	מקור	SPRING	881b	1 c
	רפס	STAMP	952c	
	שחת	GO TO RUIN	1008c	
25 27	דבש	HONEY	185b	
	טוב	PLEASANT	374c	5
	כבוד	HONOR	459b	4
	רבה	BECOME MANY	*915c	
	רבה	BECOME MANY	915d	1 e4
25 28	חומה	WALL	327c	1
	חומה	WALL	327d	3
	מעצר	RESTRAINT	784a	
	פרץ	BREAK THROUGH	829b	2
	רוח	BREATH	925b	3 c
26 1	כבוד	HONOR	459a	3
	כן	SO	486b	2 ad b
	מטר	RAIN	564d	
	נאוה	SEEMLY	610a	2
	קין	SUMMER	884d	1
	קציר	HARVESTING	894d	3
	שלג	SNOW	1017a	
26 2	דרור	SWALLOW	204d	
	חנם	OUT OF FAVOR	336c	C
	כן	SO	486b	2 ad b
	ל	TO	514b	5 fb
	לא	NOT	520c	
	נוד	FLUTTER	626d	1 b
	עוף	FLY	733c	1
	צפור	BIRD	862a	1
	קללה	CURSE	887a	
26 3	גו	BACK	156b	
	ו	AND	253b	1 j
	חמור	HE-ASS	331b	1
	מתג	BRIDLE	607c	1
	שוט	WHIP	1002a	2
26 4	שוה	AGREE WITH	1000d	
26 5	חכם	WISE	314d	3
26 6	חמס	VIOLENCE	329c	
	קצה	CUT OFF	892a	
	שתה	DRINK	1059c	1 g
26 7	דלה	DRAW	194d	
	פסח	LAME	820d	
	שוק	LEG	1003b	1
26 8	כבוד	HONOR	459b	6 a
	כן	SO	486b	2 ad a
	צרר	BIND	864d	A
	מרגמה	SLING	920d	
26 9	ו	AND	253b	1 j
	חוח	BRIER	296b	1 a
	עלה	GO UP	748d	4
	שכר	DRUNKEN	1016c	
26 10	חול	WHIRL	297b	2
	חלל	BORE	319b	
	כל	ALL	482c	2 a
	עבר	PASS OVER	*717d	2 a
	רב	GREAT	913c	2 d
	ירבעם	ARCHER	914d	
	שכר	HIRE	969a	
26 11	כלב	DOG	476d	A
	על	UPON	757c	2 7c ab
	קא	VOMIT	883c	
	שוב	TURN BACK	997a	3 a
	שנה	DO AGAIN	1040d	
26 12	חכם	WISE	314d	3
	תקוה	HOPE	876b	1
26 13	ארי	LION	71d	
	בין	INTERVAL	107b	1
	דרך	WAY	202d	1
	רחוב	PLAZA	932b	
	רחוב	PLAZA	932b	
	שחל	LION	1006c	
26 14	דלת	DOOR	195b	4
	ו	AND	253b	1 j
	מטה	COUCH	641d	
	סבב	TURN ABOUT	685c	1 a
	ציר	PIVOT	852a	
26 15	טמן	HIDE	380b	1
	לאה	BE WEARY	521a	
	פה	MOUTH	804d	1 a
	צלחת	DISH	852c	

Ch	v.	Heb	Eng	Page	Sec
26	16	שוב	TURN BACK	999a	1 a
		חכם	WISE	314d	3
		טעם	TASTE	381a	2
		שוב	TURN BACK	999c	3
		טעם	JUDGMENT	*1094c	2
26	17	אזן	EAR	23d	1
		חזק	BE FIRM	305a	6 a
		כלב	DOG	476d	A
		ל	TO	513d	5 cb d
		לא	NOT	519c	2c
		עבר	BE ARROGANT	720d	2 a
		ריב	STRIFE	936d	1
26	18	ה	THE	209b	2 b
		זק	MISSILE	278a	
		חץ	ARROW	346c	2
		ירה	SHOOT	435a	3
		ללהלה	AMAZE	529c	
26	19	כן	SO	486b	2 ad a
		רמה	BEGUILE	941a	
		שחק	LAUGH	965d	2
26	20	אין	NOT	35a	6 aa
		אפס	NON-EXISTENCE	67b	2 b
		מדון	STRIFE	193b	1
		ו	AND	253b	1 j
		כבה	BE QUENCHED	459c	
		רגן	MURMUR	920d	2
26	21	גחלת	COAL	160d	
		מדון	STRIFE	193b	1
		חרר	BE HOT	359c	
		פחם	COAL	809b	
		ריב	STRIFE	936d	1
26	22	בטן	BELLY	105d	1 a
		חדר	CHAMBER	293d	
		ירד	GO DOWN	433c	3 j
		לחם	SWALLOW GREEDILY	530a	
26	23	רגן	MURMUR	920d	2
		דלק	BURN	196b	1
		חרש	EARTHENWARE	360a	1
		חרש	EARTHENWARE	*360b	1
		כסף	SILVER	494a	1
		לב	HEART	525b	2 6b
		סוג	DROSS	691b	2
		צפה	LAY OUT	860b	
		רע	EVIL	948b	9
26	24	נכר	DISGUISE	649a	
		קרב	INWARD PART	899b	2 a
		מרמה	DECEIT	941b	
		שנא	HATE	971d	3
		שית	PUT	1011b	1
26	25	אמן	CONFIRM	53b	2 c
		חנן	SHOW FAVOR	336a	
		תועבה	ABOMINATION	1073a	2 b
26	26	כסה	COVER	492b	
		משאון	GUILE	674b	
		קהל	ASSEMBLY	874c	1 a
		שנאה	HATING	971d	1
26	27	גומץ	PIT	170a	
		כרה	DIG	500a	1
		נפל	FALL	656d	1
		שוב	TURN BACK	998a	7 a
		שחת	PIT	1001c	1
26	28	מדחה	MEANS OF STUMBLING	191a	
		דך	CRUSHED	194c	
		חלק	SMOOTH	325c	2
		לשון	TONGUE	546c	1 b
		פה	MOUTH	805a	2 a
		שקר	DECEPTION	1055d	5
27	1	הלל	BE BOASTFUL	239a	1
		יום	DAY	400a	7 a2
		ילד	BEAR	408c	1 c
		מחר	TO-MORROW	564a	1 a
27	2	אל	NOT	39b	A bg
		הלל	PRAISE	238a	1
		זור	BE A STRANGER	266c	2 b
		נכרי	ALIEN	649a	3
27	3	אבן	STONE	6d	5
		חול	SAND	297d	C
		כבד	HEAVY	458a	1
		כבד	HEAVINESS	458c	1
		כעש	ANGER	495b	1
		כעש	ANGER	495b	1
		נטל	BURDEN	642b	
		סוס	HORSE	692d	2
27	4	חמה	RAGE	404c	2 a
		אכזריות	FIERCENESS	470a	
		קנאה	ZEAL	888b	1
		שטף	FLOOD	1009b	
27	5	אהבה	LOVE	13b	1
		טוב	PLEASANT	374c	6
		תוכחת	REPROOF	407b	2
		סתר	HIDE	711c	
27	6	אהב	LOVE	13a	1 a
		אמן	CONFIRM	53a	5
		נשיקה	KISS	676c	
		עתר	BE ABUNDANT	801d	
		פצע	BRUISE	822d	
		שנא	HATE	971d	3
27	7	בוס	TRAMPLE	100d	1
		מר	BITTER	600c	1
		מתוק	SWEET	608d	1
		נפש	SOUL	660c	5 a
		נפש	SOUL	660c	5 a
		נפת	HONEY FROM THE COMB	661d	

Ch	v.	Heb	Eng	Page	Sec
		רעב	HUNGRY	944c	
		רעב	HUNGRY	944c	
		שבע	SATISFIED	960a	1 a
27	8	כן	SO	486b	2 ad a
		נדד	WANDER	622b	3
		צפור	BIRD	862a	1
		קן	NEST	890a	1
27	9	עצה	ADVICE	420b	
		לב	HEART	525c	29a
		מתק	SWEETNESS	608d	
		נפש	SOUL	661c	0 a
		קטרת	SMOKE	882d	3
		רע	FRIEND	946a	1
		שמח	REJOICE	970c	
		שמן	OIL	1032b	2 b
27	10	איד	DISTRESS	15d	3
		טוב	PLEASANT	374c	6
		יום	DAY	*398c	2 f
		עזב	LEAVE	737c	2 d3
		קרב	NEAR	898c	2 b
		רחק	DISTANT	935b	1 a
		רעה	FRIEND	946b	
		שכן	NEIGHBOUR	1015c	2
27	11	דבר	WORD	182b	1 1c
		חכם	BE WISE	314c	
		לב	HEART	525c	29a
		שמח	REJOICE	970c	
27	12	סתר	HIDE	711b	1
		ערום	FINE	779a	
		ערום	CRAFTY	791b	2
		פתי	SIMPLE	834c	
		רעה	MISERY	949b	1
27	13	בגד	GARMENT	94a	1
		בעד	ON BEHALF OF	126d	2
		זור	BE A STRANGER	266c	2 a
		חבל	BIND	286b	2
		נכרי	ALIEN	649a	3
		נכרי	FOREIGN	649a	2
		עבט	TAKE ON PLEDGE	786c	1
27	14	בקר	MORNING	134b	1 h
		ברך	BLESS	139b	4 e
		חשב	THINK	363c	3
		קללה	CURSE	887a	
27	15	אשה	WOMAN	61b	1
		מדון	STRIFE	193b	1
		דלף	A DROPPING	196a	
		טרד	PURSUE	382b	
		יום	DAY	398c	2 f
		סגריר	STEADY RAIN	690a	
		שוה	AGREE WITH	1001a	
		שתה	DRINK	1059c	2
27	16	צפן	HIDE	860c	1
		קרא	CALL	895d	5 b
		שמן	OIL	1032b	2 b
27	17	ברזל	IRON	137c	2
		חדד	BE SHARP	292c	
27	18	אדון	LORD	11a	2 1b
		בנה	BUILD	124d	2 a
		כבד	BE HONORED	457d	
		נצר	WATCH	665d	1
		תאנה	FIG-TREE	1061a	1
27	19	כן	SO	486b	2 ad a
27	20	אבדה	LOST THING	2b	
		אבדון	DESTRUCTION	2c	
		שבע	SATISFIED	959c	2a
		שאול	SHEOL	983a	1
27	21	מהלל	PRAISE	239c	
		ו	AND	253b	1j
		זהב	GOLD	262c	1
		כור	FURNACE	468b	
		כסף	SILVER	494a	1
		פה	MOUTH	805d	6 c1
		מצרף	CRUCIBLE	864c	
27	22	אולת	FOLLY	17c	
		כתש	POUND	509d	
		מכתש	MORTAR	509d	
		עלי	PESTLE	750a	
		ריפה	GRAIN	937d	
27	23	לב	HEART	524d	2 3c
		עדר	FLOCK	727c	1 a
		פנה	FACE	816b	15
		שית	PUT	1011b	2 b
27	24	אם	IF	50d	2 ab b
		דור	PERIOD	189d	1 b
		חסן	WEALTH	340d	
		נזר	CROWN	634b	1 a
		עולם	LONG DURATION	762d	2 i
27	25	אסף	GATHER	62d	1 c
		דשא	GRASS	206a	
		הר	MOUNTAIN	250c	1 h
		חציר	GREEN GRASS	348b	1
		עשב	HERB	793c	
		ראה	TO SEE	908c	1 c
27	26	כבש	LAMB	461a	3
		לבוש	CLOTHING	528c	
		מחיר	PRICE	564b	1
		עתוד	HE-GOAT	800d	
27	27	די	SUFFICIENCY	191c	1
		חיים	LIFE	313b	3
		חלב	MILK	316c	A 1
		לחם	FOOD	537b	2 a
		נערה	GIRL	655b	2
		עז	SHE-GOAT	777c	2
		צאן	SMALL CATTLE	*838b	1 a3
28	1	בטח	TRUST	105b	2

Ch	v.	Heb	Eng	Page	Sec
		כפיר	LION	498d	
		רדף	PURSUE	922d	1 c
		שנא	HATE	971d	3
28	2	ארך	BE LONG	73d	2
		בין	DISCERN	107a	1 b
		כן	RIGHT	467a	1
		פשע	TRANSGRESSION	833c	2
		שר	CHIEFTAIN	978b	2 b
28	3	דל	WEAK	195d	
		לחם	FOOD	537b	1 b
		מטר	RAIN	564d	
		סחף	PROSTRATE	695a	
		עשק	OPPRESS	798d	1
		רוש	BE IN WANT	930d	
28	4	גרה	ENGAGE IN STRIFE	173c	1
		הלל	PRAISE	238a	1
		תורה	INSTRUCTION	435d	1 a
		רשע	WICKED	957b	1
28	5	בין	DISCERN	106d	2 b
		בין	DISCERN	106d	2 b
		בקש	SEEK	134d	3 c
		כל	ALL	482c	2 a
		רע	EVIL	949a	3
		משפט	JUDGMENT	1048d	2 b
28	6	ב	IN	88d	16
		דרך	WAY	203d	6 d
		טוב	PLEASANT	374c	6
		עקש	TWISTED	786a	
		תם	INTEGRITY	1070d	3
28	7	בין	DISCERN	107a	1 b
		דלל	BE LIGHT	272d	2
		תורה	INSTRUCTION	435d	1 a
		כלם	HUMILIATE	484a	1
		נצר	GUARD	666a	3
		רעה	ASSOCIATE WITH	945d	
28	8	דל	WEAK	195d	
		הון	WEALTH	223c	1
		חנן	SHOW FAVOR	336a	1 b
		נשך	INTEREST	675b	
		קבץ	GATHER	868a	2
		תרבית	INTEREST	916b	
28	9	אזן	EAR	24a	2 a
		תורה	INSTRUCTION	435d	1 a
		סור	TURN ASIDE	694b	1
		תועבה	ABOMINATION	1073a	2 b
28	10	דרך	WAY	203d	6 d
		טוב	A GOOD THING	375a	1
		נחל	TAKE AS A POSSESSION	635c	2
		נפל	FALL	656d	1
		ישר	STRAIGHT	779b	3 c2
		שגה	GO ASTRAY	993b	3
		שחות	PIT	1005c	
		תמים	SOUND	1071b	4
28	11	בין	DISCERN	107a	1 b
		דל	POOR	195d	
		חכם	WISE	314d	3
		חקר	SEARCH	350d	2 d
28	12	חפש	SEARCH	344c	
		עלץ	REJOICE	763b	
		תפארה	BEAUTY	802d	3 b
28	13	קום	STAND	878a	3
		ידה	CONFESS	392c	2 b
		כסה	COVER	491d	
		פשע	TRANSGRESSION	833c	1
		צלח	ADVANCE	852c	2
		רחם	LOVE	933d	
28	14	אשר	HAPPINESS	81a	
		לב	HEART	525b	2 6d
		תמיד	CONTINUITY	556b	1 a
		נפל	FALL	657b	2 b
		פחד	DREAD	808b	
		קשה	BE SEVERE	904c	3 a
		רעה	MISERY	949b	1
28	15	ארי	LION	71d	
		דב	BEAR	179a	
		דל	POOR	195d	
		משל	RULE	605d	1
		נהם	GROWL	625b	1
		רשע	WICKED	957b	1
		שקק	RUN	1055b	
28	16	ארך	BE LONG	73d	1
		תבונה	UNDERSTANDING	108b	2
		בצע	UNJUST GAIN	130c	
		חסר	NEEDY	341c	
		נגיד	LEADER	617d	
		מעשקה	EXTORTIONATE ACT	799a	
28	17	בור	PIT	92c	5
		דם	BLOOD	197b	21
		נוס	FLEE	630d	1
		נפש	SOUL	660b	4 c2
		עשק	OPPRESS	799a	3
		תמך	GRASP	1069d	1
28	18	דרך	WAY	203d	6 d
		ישע	BE DELIVERED	446b	1
		עקש	TWIST	786a	
		תמים	SOUND	1071b	4
		אחר	ADDENDA ET CORRIGENDA	1120a	
28	19	אדמה	GROUND	9c	1
		עבד	WORK	713a	1
		רדף	PURSUE	923a	
		ריש	POVERTY	930d	
		ריק	EMPTY	938a	2
		שבע	SATISFIED	959c	3 b

PROVERBS

Ch v.	Heb	Eng	Page	Sec
28 20	אוץ	HASTEN	21a	3
	אמונה	FIRMNESS	53c	3 a
	ברכה	BLESSING	139d	1 c
	נקה	BE CLEAN	667b	3
	עשר	BE RICH	799b	2
	רב	MUCH	913b	1 d
28 21	טוב	PLEASANT	375a	0 a
	לחם	FOOD	537a	1 a
	נכר	REGARD	648a	1
	על	UPON	754b	2 1f b
	פשע	REBEL	833b	2
	פת	FRAGMENT	837d	
28 22	בהל	BE IN HASTE	96c	2
	בוא	COME	98c	2 b
	הון	WEALTH	223c	1
	חסר	WANT	341c	
	עין	EYE	744d	3 b
	רע	EVIL	948b	9
28 23	אחרי	BACKWARDS	30c	
	חלק	BE SMOOTH	325b	2
	חן	FAVOR	336c	2 b2
	יכח	REPROVE	407a	5 b
	לשון	TONGUE	546b	1 b
	מצא	FIND	592d	1 a
28 24	גזל	TEAR AWAY	159d	
	חבר	UNITED	288d	2 f
	פשע	TRANSGRESSION	833c	1
	שחת	GO TO RUIN	1008c	1
28 25	בטח	TRUST	105a	1 4a
	גרה	STIR UP STRIFE	173b	
	מדון	STRIFE	193b	1
	דשן	BE FAT	206b	
	רחב	WIDE	932a	
28 26	בטח	TRUST	105a	1 3c
	חכמה	WISDOM	315d	5 c
	מלט	SLIP AWAY	572c	3
28 27	מארה	CURSE	76d	
	מחסור	NEED	341d	3
	עין	EYE	744d	3 d
	עלם	CONCEAL	761a	
	רב	MUCH	913b	1 d
28 28	אבד	PERISH	1c	1
	סתר	HIDE	711b	1
	קום	STAND	878a	3
	רבה	BECOME MANY	915a	1 a
29 1	תוכחת	REPROOF	407b	2
	ערף	BACK OF NECK	791c	2
	פתע	SUDDENNESS	*837b	
	קשה	BE SEVERE	904b	1
	קשה	BE SEVERE	904c	3 a
	מרפא	HEALING	951c	2
29 2	אנח	SIGN	58d	1
	משל	RULE	605d	1
	צדיק	JUST	843a	1 b
	רבה	BECOME MANY	915a	1 a
	רשע	WICKED	957b	1
29 3	אבד	CAUSE TO VANISH	2a	2
	אב	FATHER	3b	1
	אהב	LOVE	13a	2
	הון	WEALTH	223c	1
	זנה	COMMIT FORNICA-TION	275d	1
	חכמה	WISDOM	315d	5 c
	רעה	ASSOCIATE WITH	945d	
	שמח	REJOICE	970c	
29 4	הרס	THROW DOWN	248d	1
	עמד	STAND	764d	2
	תרומה	OFFERING	929b	7
	משפט	JUDGEMNT	1048d	2 b
29 5	חלק	BE SMOOTH	325b	2
	רשת	NET	440c	1 b2
	על	UPON	754c	2 1f d
	על	UPON	757c	2 7c b
	פעם	BEAT	822a	1 b
	פרש	SPREAD OUT	831b	1
29 6	מוקש	BAIT	430d	
	פשע	TRANSGRESSION	833c	1
	רון	OVERCOME	929c	
	רוץ	RUN	930c	2 a
	רנן	GIVE A RINGING CRY	943b	1
29 7	רע	EVIL	949a	3
	בין	DISCERN	106d	2 b
	דין	JUDGMENT	192c	2
	דל	WEAK	195d	
	דעת	WISDOM	395d	2 a
29 8	חכם	WISE	314d	5
	לצון	SCORNING	539c	
	פוח	BREATHE	806b	2 c
	קריה	TOWN	900b	4
	שוב	TURN BACK	999d	6 a
29 9	אויל	FOOLISH	17b	
	ו	AND	252d	1 d
	חכם	WISE	314d	5
	נחת	QUIETNESS	629b	1
	רגז	BE AGITATED	919a	
	שחק	LAUGH	965a	1 a
	שפט	JUDGE	1048a	1
29 10	בקש	SEEK	134d	2 a
	דם	BLOOD	197a	2 h
	נפש	SOUL	659d	3 c
	ישר	STRAIGHT	779b	3 c2
	תם	COMPLETE	1071a	3
29 11	אחור	HINDER SIDE	30c	B
	חכם	WISE	314d	5
	יצא	BRING OUT	425b	4 k

Ch v.	Heb	Eng	Page	Sec
	רוח	BREATH	925a	3 c
29 12	שבח	SOOTHE	986c	
	דבר	WORD	183b	3 1
	משל	RULE	605d	1
	קשב	ATTEND	904a	
	רשע	WICKED	957b	1
	שרת	SERVE	1058a	1 b
29 13	אור	BECOME LIGHT	21b	4
	פגש	MEET	803d	
	תך	INJURY	1067a	
29 14	אמת	FIRMNESS	54a	3 a
	דל	WEAK	195d	
	כון	BE FIRM	465d	1 b
	כסא	THRONE	491a	3 a
	עד	PERPETUITY	723c	2 a
	שפט	JUDGE	1047d	3 b2
29 15	בוש	BE ASHAMED	102a	1
	חכמה	WISDOM	315d	5 c
	תוכחת	REBUKE	407b	3
	נתן	GIVE	679d	1 u
	שבט	ROD	987a	1 a
	שלח	SEND	1019c	
29 16	מפלת	OVERTHROW	658c	2 b
	פשע	TRANSGRESSION	833c	1
	רבה	BECOME MANY	915a	1 a
	רבה	BECOME MANY	915b	1 c
29 17	בן	SON	120a	1
	יסר	DISCIPLINE	416a	1 b
	נוח	REST	628c	A 1c
	נפש	SOUL	660d	6 d
	מעדן	DAINTY	726d	
29 18	אין	NOT	35a	6 aa
	אשר	HAPPINESS	81a	
	חזון	VISION	303a	3
	תורה	INSTRUCTION	435d	1 a
	פרע	LET GO	829a	
29 19	בין	DISCERN	106d	1 b
	יסר	BE CORRECTED	416a	
	מענה	ANSWER	775a	
29 20	אוץ	HASTEN	21a	3
	חזה	SEE	302b	1 a
	תקוה	HOPE	876b	1
29 21	מנן	THANKLESS ONE	584d	
	נער	YOUTH	655a	
	פנק	INDULGE	819d	
29 22	בעל	LORD	127c	1 5a
	גרה	STIR UP STRIFE	173b	
	מדון	STRIFE	193b	1
	חמה	RAGE	404c	2 a
	פשע	TRANSGRESSION	833c	1
	רב	MUCH	913b	1 d
29 23	גאוה	PRIDE	144d	3
	כבוד	HONOR	459a	3
	רוח	BREATH	925d	8
	שפל	BECOME LOW	1050b	4
	שפל	LOW	1050c	4
	תמך	SUPPORT	1069d	2
29 24	אלה	OATH	46d	1
	גנב	THIEF	170c	
	חלק	DIVIDE	323c	4
	נגד	BE CONSPICUOUS	617a	3
	שנא	HATE	971c	1 a
29 25	בטח	TRUST	105a	1 3a
	חרדה	TREMBLING	353d	1
	מוקש	BAIT	430d	
	נתן	GIVE	679d	1 u
	שגב	BE HIGH	960d	
29 26	בקש	SEEK	134d	3 a
	משל	RULE	605d	1
	משפט	JUDGMENT	1048b	1 a
29 27	דרך	WAY	203b	5
	ישר	STRAIGHT	449b	3 b
	עול	INJUSTICE	732c	
	תועבה	ABOMINATION	1073a	2 a
	תועבה	ABOMINATION	1073a	2 a
30 1	אגור	AGUR	8d	
	דבר	WORD	183a	2 1b
	יקה	JAKEH	429a	
	משל	PROVERB	605b	6
	נאם	UTTERANCE	610b	1
	מצא	UTTERANCE	672d	
30 2	בינה	UNDERSTANDING	108a	2
	בער	BRUTISHNESS	129d	
	כי	THAT	472d	1 e
	מן	FROM	583b	7 bb
30 3	חכמה	WISDOM	315d	5 c
	ידע	KNOW	394c	3
	דעת	KNOWLEDGE	395d	2 b
	למד	LEARN	540d	
	קדוש	HOLY	872c	1 c
30 4	אסף	GATHER	62b	1 c
	אסם	END	67a	1
	ארץ	EARTH	76b	4 e
	חפן	HOLLOW OF HAND	342b	
	ירד	GO DOWN	433b	2
	כי	BECAUSE	473d	3 b
	מי	WHO	566d	F c
	צרר	BIND	864c	A
	קום	STAND	879a	6 c
	שמלה	WRAPPER	971a	
	שם	NAME	1028a	2 a
	שמי	HEAVENS	1030a	1 a
30 5	אלה	GOD	43a	2
	אמרה	UTTERANCE	57b	
	מגן	SHIELD	171c	
	חסה	SEEK REFUGE	340b	

Ch v.	Heb	Eng	Page	Sec
	צרף	SMELT	864b	1
30 6	דבר	WORD	183b	3 2
	יכח	CONVICT	407a	4
	יסף	ADD	415b	1
	כזב	BE A LIAR	469c	
30 7	מנע	WITHHOLD	586a	
	שנים	TWO	1041b	1 b2
	שנים	TWO	*1041b	1 b2
30 8	דבר	WORD	182a	1 1a
	חק	SOMETHING PRE-SCRIBED	349b	2
	טרף	TEAR	383a	
	כזב	LIE	469c	
	לחם	FOOD	537c	3 a
	ריש	POVERTY	930d	
	רחק	BE DISTANT	935b	2
	שוא	EMPTINESS	996b	2
30 9	אלהים	GOD	44d	4 c
	גנב	STEAL	170c	
	ירש	BE IMPOVERISHED	439d	
	כחש	DECEIVE	471b	2
	מי	WHO	566d	F b
	שבע	SATISFIED	959c	2 a
	שם	NAME	1028b	3
30 10	תפש	LAY HOLD OF	1074d	1
	אדון	LORD	11a	2 1b
	אשם	OFFEND	79c	3
	לשן	SLANDER	546d	
30 11	ברך	BLESS	139b	4 d
	דור	GENERATION	190a	3
30 12	דור	GENERATION	190a	3
	טהור	CLEAN	373a	3
	צאה	FILTH	844b	
	רחץ	WASH OFF	934c	
30 13	דור	GENERATION	190a	3
	נשא	LIFT	671d	1 a
	עפעף	EYELID	734a	
	רום	BE HIGH	926d	2 b
	רום	WINK	*931b	
30 14	אביון	NEEDY	2d	
	אכל	EAT	37d	6
	מאכלת	KNIFE	38c	
	דור	GENERATION	190a	3
	משל	PROVERB	605b	6
	עני	POOR	776d	2
	שן	TOOTH	1042a	1 b
	מלתעות	TEETH	1069a	
30 15	בת	DAUGHTER	123d	7
	הון	SUFFICIENCY	223c	3
	הם	THEY	*241c	4 a
	יהב	GIVE	396d	1
	משל	PROVERB	605b	6
	עלוקה	LEECH	763c	
	ארבע	FOUR	917a	1 a5
	שבע	SATISFIED	959c	2 a
	הון	SUFFICIENCY	223c	3
30 16	מי	WATER	565c	1 b
	עצר	RESTRAINT	783d	
	רחם	WOMB	933b	1
	שבע	SATISFIED	959b	1 b
	שאול	SHEOL	983a	1
30 17	בוז	DESPISE	100b	
	בן	SON	121d	7 b
	יקהת	OBEDIENCE	429b	
	לעג	MOCK	541c	
	נחל	WADY	636b	2
	נקר	DIG	669b	
	נשר	EAGLE	676d	
	עין	EYE	744c	2 a
	ערב	RAVEN	788b	
30 18	הם	THEY	*241c	4 a
	ו	AND	252c	1 c
	פלא	BE SURPASSING	810c	2
	ארבע	FOUR	917a	1 a5
30 19	אניה	A SHIP	58b	
	דרך	WAY	203a	1
	לב	HEART	524b	1
	נחש	SERPENT	638b	1 b
	נשר	EAGLE	677a	
	עלמה	YOUNG WOMAN	761c	
	צור	ROCK	849c	1 b
	שמי	HEAVENS	1029d	1 a
30 20	און	TROUBLE	20a	3
	אכל	EAT	37b	1
	אשה	WOMAN	61b	1
	דרך	WAY	203a	1
	מחה	WIPE	562a	1
	נאף	COMMIT ADUL-TERY	610d	1 b
	פה	MOUTH	804d	1 b
	פעל	DO	821b	1 b
30 21	ו	AND	252c	1 c
	יכל	BE ABLE	407c	1 b
	נשא	LIFT	671b	2 d
	ארבע	FOUR	917a	1 a5
	רגז	BE AGITATED	919a	
	תחת	UNDERNEATH	1065c	2 1c c
30 22	מלך	BE KING	574a	
	עבד	SLAVE	714a	2
	תחת	UNDERNEATH	1065c	2
30 23	גברת	MISTRESS	150c	2
	ירש	INHERIT	439c	2
	שנא	HATE	971c	1
	שפחה	MAID	1046b	1
	תחת	UNDERNEATH	1065c	2 1c c
30 24	הם	THEY	241c	4 a

Ch	v.	Heb	Eng	Page	Sec
		חכם	BE WISE	314c	
		חכם	WISE	314d	3
		מן	SMALL	882a	1 b
30	25	כון	ESTABLISH	466b	2 a
		לא	NOT	519c	2 a
		לחם	FOOD	537b	2 b
		נמלה	ANT	649c	
		עז	STRONG	738c	
		עם	PEOPLE	766c	1
		קיץ	SUMMER	884d	1
30	26	בית	HOUSE	109c	1 b
		לא	NOT	519c	2 a
		סלע	CRAG	701a	1
		עם	PEOPLE	766c	1
		עצום	MIGHTY	783a	1
		שפן	ROCK-BADGER	1051a	
30	27	חצץ	DIVIDE	346b	
		מלך	KING	573b	4
		ארבה	LOCUST	916a	
30	28	היכל	PALACE	228b	1
		שממית	LIZARD	791b	
		תפש	LAY HOLD OF	1075a	
30	29	הלך	WALK	232a	1 2
		הם	THEY	241c	4 a
		ו	AND	252c	1 c
		יטב	DO WELL	405d	3
		יטב	DO WELL	406a	3
		צעד	STEP	857d	1
30	30	ב	IN	88b	1 2a
		בהמה	BEAST	97a	3
		גבור	STRONG	150a	1
		ה	THE	207b	1 b
		הלך	WALK	*232a	1 2
		כל	ALL	482c	2 a
		ליש	LION	539d	
		שוב	TURN BACK	996d	1
30	31	אלקום	BAND OF SOLDIERS	39a	
		הלך	WALK	*232a	1 2
		זרזיר	GIRDED	267d	
		מתנים	LOINS	608b	1 d
		תיש	HE-GOAT	1067a	
30	32	זמם	CONSIDER	273b	2 b
		נבל	BE SENSELESS	614c	
		נשא	LIFT	672a	
		פה	MOUTH	804d	1 b
		זמם	ADDENDA ET COR-RIGENDA	1122d	
		נבל	ADDENDA ET COR-RIGENDA	1125a	
30	33	אף	NOSE	60a	1
		דם	BLOOD	196c	2 a
		חלב	MILK	316b	A
		חמאה	CURD	326a	
		יצא	BRING OUT	425b	4 j
		מיץ	SQUEEZING	568c	
		משל	PROVERB	605b	6
		ריב	STRIFE	936d	1
31	1	אם	MOTHER	51d	1
		דבר	WORD	183a	2 1b
		יסר	DISCIPLINE	416b	1 b
		למואל	LEMUEL	541a	
		משא	BABYLON	601c	2
		משל	PROVERB	605b	6
		משא	UTTERANCE	672d	
31	2	בטן	WOMB	106a	3
		בר	SON	135a	
		נדר	VOW	624a	1
31	3	דרך	WAY	203b	5
		חיל	STRENGTH	298c	1 a
		מחה	WIPE OUT	562b	3
31	4	או	OR	15a	4
		או	DESIRE	16b	
		אי	WHERE	32b	1 a
		יין	WINE	406c	C
		למואל	LEMUEL	541a	
		רזן	BE WEIGHTY	931b	
		שכר	INTOXICATING DRINK	1016c	
31	5	שתה	DRINK	1059b	1 a
		בן	SON	121d	8 h
		דין	JUDGMENT	192c	2
		חקק	CUT IN	349b	
		עני	AFFLICTION	777a	1
		שנה	CHANGE	1040a	
31	6	אבד	PERISH	1c	1
		יין	WINE	406c	A
		מר	BITTER	600c	2 b
		נפש	SOUL	660d	6 c
		שכר	INTOXICATING DRINK	1016c	
31	7	זכר	REMEMBER	269d	1 1 b
		עמל	TROUBLE	765d	1
		ריש	POVERTY	930d	
31	8	אלם	DUMB	48a	
		בן	SON	121d	8 t
		דין	JUDGMENT	192c	2
		חלוף	A PASSING AWAY	322b	
		ל	TO	515c	5 hc
		פתח	OPEN	835b	
31	9	אביון	NEEDY	2d	
		דין	JUDGE	192b	2 a
		משל	PROVERB	605b	6
		עני	POOR	776d	2
		פתח	OPEN	835b	
		צדק	RIGHTEOUSNESS	841c	2 a
		שפט	JUDGE	1047d	3 a

Ch	v.	Heb	Eng	Page	Sec
31	10	אשה	WOMAN	61b	1
		חיל	STRENGTH	298d	2
		מי	WHO	567a	F c
		משל	PROVERB	605b	6
		פנינים	CORALS	819d	
31	11	רחק	DISTANT	935c	1 a
		במח	TRUST	105a	1 3b
		בעל	OWNER	127b	1 2
		חסר	LACK	341b	1 a
		שלל	SPOIL	1022a	4
31	12	חיים	LIFE	313b	1
		טוב	A GOOD THING	375b	3
		יום	DAY	399a	4 a
		רע	EVIL	948d	2
31	13	דרש	SEEK	205c	7
		חפץ	DELIGHT	343b	4
		כף	HOLLOW OF THE HAND	496d	1 d7
		עשה	DO	794b	1 1b
		פשת	FLAX	833d	
31	14	אניה	A SHIP	58c	
		לחם	FOOD	537c	3 a
		מרחק	DISTANT PLACE	935d	
31	15	חק	SOMETHING PRE-SCRIBED	349b	2
		טרף	TEAR	*383a	
		טרף	PREY	383c	2
		נערה	GIRL	655b	2
		עוד	STILL	729c	2 aa
31	16	זמם	CONSIDER	273b	1
		כף	HOLLOW OF THE HAND	496d	1 d7
		לקח	TAKE	543a	4 b
		נטע	PLANT	642c	1
		פרי	FRUIT	826c	3
31	17	אמץ	BE STRONG	55a	1
		זרוע	ARM	284a	2 a
		חגר	GIRD	291d	1
		מתנים	LOINS	608b	2 a
		עז	STRENGTH	739a	1
31	18	טוב	PLEASANT	374b	4 b
		טעם	TASTE	381a	3
		כבה	BE QUENCHED	459c	
		נר	LAMP	632d	
		סחר	TRAFFIC	695c	
		צמר	WOOL	856a	
31	19	כף	HOLLOW OF THE HAND	496b	1 a
		כישור	DISTAFF	507a	
		פלך	WHIRL OF SPINDLE	813a	1
		שלח	SEND	1019b	7
		תמך	GRASP	1069c	1
31	20	אביון	NEEDY	2d	
		עני	POOR	776d	1
		פרש	SPREAD OUT	831b	1
		שלח	SEND	1019b	7
31	21	ירא	FEAR	431b	1 c
		לבש	PUT ON	528a	E
		שלג	SNOW	1017a	
		שני	SCARLET	1040c	
31	22	ארגמן	PURPLE THREAD	71b	2
		ישב	SIT	442c	1 a
		לבוש	CLOTHING	528c	2
		שש	BYSSUS	1058c	
31	23	בעל	OWNER	127b	1 2
		זקן	OLD	278d	2 b
		ידע	BE MADE KNOWN	394c	1
		שער	GATE	1045a	2 a
31	24	חגור	BELT	292a	
		כנעני	TRADER	489b	
		מכר	SELL	569b	
		נתן	GIVE	678b	1 a
		סדין	LINEN WRAPPER	690b	
31	25	אחרון	BEHIND	30d	B
		הדר	SPLENDOUR	214b	2
		יום	DAY	399c	5 c
		לבוש	CLOTHING	528c	2
		עז	STRENGTH	739a	1
31	26	שחק	LAUGH	965d	1 a
		חכמה	WISDOM	315d	5 c
		חסד	GOODNESS	338c	1 1
		תורה	INSTRUCTION	435d	1 a
		לשון	TONGUE	546b	1 b
		על	UPON	753a	2 1
		פתח	OPEN	835b	
31	27	הליכה	A GOING	237b	1 c
		לחם	FOOD	537b	3 a
		עצלות	SLUGGISHNESS	782c	
		צפה	KEEP WATCH	859c	
31	28	אשר	GO STRAIGHT	80d	4
		בעל	OWNER	127b	1 2
		הלל	PRAISE	238a	1
		קום	STAND	877d	1 f
31	29	בת	DAUGHTER	123c	1
		חיל	STRENGTH	298d	2
		עלה	GO UP	749a	0
		על	UPON	755a	2 3
		עשה	DO	793d	1 1a 1
31	30	ה	THE	208b	1 ha
		הבל	VAPOUR	210d	2
		הלל	PRAISE	239a	3
		חן	FAVOR	336b	1 a
		יפי	BEAUTY	421d	
		ירא	FEAR	431c	3 b
		שקר	DECEPTION	1055c	1
31	31	הלל	PRAISE	238a	1

Ch	v.	Heb	Eng	Page	Sec
		משל	PROVERB	605b	6
		מעשה	DEED	795d	1 a3
		פרי	FRUIT	826c	3
		שער	GATE	1045a	2 a

ECCLESIASTES

Ch	v.	Heb	Eng	Page	Sec
1	1	דבר	WORD	183a	2 1b
		מלך	KING	573b	5 b
		קהלת	PREACHER	875b	
1	2	הבל	VAPOUR	210d	2
		הבל	VAPOUR	*210d	2
		הבל	VAPOUR	211a	2
		כל	ALL	483a	2 bb
		קהלת	PREACHER	875b	
1	3	יתרון	ADVANTAGE	452c	
		מה	WHAT	552c	1 aa
		עמל	LABOUR	765c	
		עמל	TROUBLE	765d	3
		שמש	SUN	1039b	4 c
		תחת	UNDERNEATH	1065b	2 1
1	4	ארץ	EARTH	76a	1 b
		דור	GENERATION	190a	2
		הלך	WALK	234b	2 1
		עולם	LONG DURATION	762b	2 b1
		עמד	STAND	764b	3 c
1	5	בוא	COME	98a	1 i
		זרח	RISE	280b	1 a
		מקום	STANDING PLACE	879b	2 a
		שאף	GASP	983c	1
1	6	דרום	SOUTH	205a	
		הלך	WALK	232b	1 3
		הלך	WALK	233d	1 4d
		סבב	TURN ABOUT	685c	1 a
		סבב	TURN ABOUT	685c	1 a
		סביב	ROUND ABOUT	687b	2 ba a
		על	UPON	757c	2 7c ab
		עמל	TROUBLE	765d	3
		צפון	NORTH	861a	
		שוב	TURN BACK	998a	7 a
1	7	הלך	WALK	232b	1 3
		הלך	WALK	232b	1 3
		הלך	WALK	233d	1 5a
		מלא	FULL	571a	
		נחל	TORRENT	636b	1
		מקום	STANDING PLACE	880b	4
		ש	WHO	979d	2
		שוב	TURN BACK	998b	8
		שם	THERE	1027a	1 a
1	8	אזן	EAR	24a	2 a
		יגע	WEARY	388b	
		מלא	FILL	*570b	1
		מלא	BE FULL	570c	1
		עין	EYE	744d	3 b
		שבע	SATISFIED	959c	2 d
1	9	היה	COME TO PASS	224b	1 1b
		חדש	NEW	294b	A
		מה	WHAT	553b	1 eb
		עשה	DO	795b	1 a
		ש	WHO	979d	1
1	10	תחת	UNDERNEATH	1065b	2 1
		היה	COME TO PASS	224b	1 1b
		חדש	NEW	294b	B
		כבר	ALREADY	460c	
		ל	TO	516c	5 jb
		עולם	LONG DURATION	762a	1 e
		פנה	FACE	818a	2 5c
1	11	אחרון	BEHIND	31a	B g
		אחרון	BEHIND	31a	B
		זכרון	MEMORIAL	272a	2
		ראשון	FIRST	911c	1 a
		ש	WHO	979d	1
1	12	מלך	KING	573b	5 b
1	13	בור	MAKE CLEAR	101c	
		דרש	SEEK	205c	6
		חכמה	WISDOM	315d	5 c
		נתן	GIVE	679a	1 i
		ענה	BE OCCUPIED	775d	
		ענין	OCCUPATION	775d	
		עשה	DO	795b	1 a
		רע	EVIL	948a	2
		שמי	HEAVENS	1029d	1 a
		תור	SPY OUT	1064c	2
		תחת	UNDERNEATH	1065b	2 1
		לב	ADDENDA ET COR-RIGENDA	1124c	
1	14	הבל	VAPOUR	210d	2
		כל	ALL	483a	2 bb
		עשה	DO	795b	1 a
		מעשה	DEED	795d	1 b5
		רוח	BREATH	925a	2 e
		רעות	LONGING	946d	1
1	15	מנה	COUNT	284a	1
		חסרון	THING LACKING	341c	1
		יכל	BE ABLE	407c	1
		עות	BE BENT	736c	
		תקן	BECOME STRAIGHT	1075b	
1	16	גדל	BECOME GREAT	152c	1
		דבר	SPEAK	181c	3 e
		חכמה	WISDOM	315d	5 c
		דעת	WISDOM	395d	2 a
		יסף	ADD	415b	1
		לב	HEART	524d	2 3b
		לב	HEART	525c	2 7
		על	UPON	755a	2 2

Ch v.	Heb	Eng	Page	Sec
	עם	WITH	768c	4 a
	ראה	TO SEE	907d	7 d
	רבה	BECOME MANY	915d	1 e3
1 17	הוא	HE, SHE, IT	216c	4 bg
	הוללה	MADNESS	239c	
	ו	AND	254a	2 c
	זה	THIS	260d	1 a
	חכמה	WISDOM	315d	5 c
	ידע	KNOW	393d	1 a
	לב	HEART	524d	
	נתן	GIVE	679a	1 i
	סכלות	FOLLY	698a	
	רוח	BREATH	925a	2 e
	רעיון	STRIVING	946d	
	סכלות	MADNESS	968d	
	ש	WHO	979d	3 a
	לב	ADDENDA ET COR-RIGENDA	1124c	
1 18	חכמה	WISDOM	315d	5 c
	דעת	WISDOM	395d	2 a
	יסף	ADD	415b	1
	מכאוב	PAIN	456c	2
	כעס	ANGER	495b	3
2 1	אמר	SAY	56b	2
	הבל	VAPOUR	210d	2
	הוא	HE, SHE, IT	216d	6 a
	טוב	A GOOD THING	375a	1
	לב	HEART	525c	27
	נסה	TEST	650b	1
	נסה	TEST	650a	1
	ראה	TO SEE	908a	8 a5
	שמחה	JOY	970d	1
2 2	הלל	PRAISE	239b	
	זה	THIS	262b	
	שחק	LAUGHTER	966a	1
	שמחה	JOY	970d	1
2 3	אחז	GRASP	28b	
	אי	WHERE	32b	2 a
	בור	MAKE CLEAR	101c	
	בשר	FLESH	142c	2
	חיים	LIFE	313b	1
	חכמה	WISDOM	315d	5 c
	טוב	PLEASANT	374a	2 e
	יום	DAY	399a	4 a
	יום	DAY	399a	4 a
	לב	HEART	524c	2 1
	לב	HEART	524d	2 3b
	משך	DRAW	604c	7
	נהג	DRIVE	624b	2
	סכלות	FOLLY	698a	
	מספר	NUMBER	709a	1 a
	עד	UNTIL	725a	2 1a b
	ראה	TO SEE	907b	5 a
	תור	SEEK OUT	1064c	1
2 4	בנה	BUILD	124b	1 ab
	גדל	BECOME GREAT	152c	1
	נטע	PLANT	642c	1
	מעשה	DEED	795d	1 b2
2 5	גנה	GARDEN	171b	1
	נטע	PLANT	642b	1
	עץ	TREE	781c	1 b
	פרדס	PRESERVE	825d	
	פרי	FRUIT	826b	1
2 6	ברכה	POOL	140a	1
	יער	WOOD	420c	A
	צמח	SPROUT	855c	1
	שקה	GIVE TO DRINK	1052c	1
2 7	בית	HOUSE	109d	4
	בן	SON	120c	1 h
	מקנה	CATTLE	889b	2
	רבה	BECOME MANY	915d	1 e4
	שפחה	MAID	1046c	1
2 8	מדינה	PROVINCE	193d	4
	זהב	GOLD	263c	1
	כנס	GATHER	488a	1
	סגלה	PROPERTY	688c	2
	תענוג	DAINTINESS	772c	1
	עשה	DO	795a	27
	שדה	LADY	994d	
	שיר	SING	1010d	
2 9	גדל	BECOME GREAT	152b	2 e
	חכמה	WISDOM	315d	5 c
	יסף	ADD	415b	1
	עמד	STAND	764b	3 c
	עמד	STAND	764b	3 c
2 10	אצל	LAY ASIDE	69b	
	חלק	PORTION	324b	5
	לב	HEART	525c	29a
	מן	OUT OF	580b	2 ec
	מנע	WITHHOLD	586a	
	עין	EYE	744d	3 b
	עמל	TROUBLE	765d	3
	שמח	JOYFUL	970d	1 b
	שמחה	JOY	970d	1
	שאל	ASK	981d	1 c
2 11	אני	I	59a	
	ו	AND	*252b	1 b
	יתרון	ADVANTAGE	452c	
	כל	ALL	483a	2 bb
	עמל	LABOUR	765c	
	עמל	TROUBLE	765d	3
	מעשה	DEED	795d	1 b2
	פנה	TURN	815c	2 e
	רוח	BREATH	925a	2 e
	רעות	LONGING	946d	
2 12	הוללה	MADNESS	239c	
	ו	AND	*252b	1 b
	חכמה	WISDOM	315d	5 c
	כבר	ALREADY	460c	
	סכלות	FOLLY	698a	
2 13	פנה	TURN	815c	1 c
	ה	THE	208b	1 ha
	ה	THE	208b	1 ha
	ו	AND	*252b	1 b
	חכמה	WISDOM	315d	5 c
	חשך	DARKNESS	365a	1
	יתרון	ADVANTAGE	452c	
	סכלות	FOLLY	698a	
	ראה	TO SEE	907b	5 a
	ש	WHO	979d	3 a
2 14	הבל	VAPOUR	210d	2
	חכם	WISE	315b	6 b3
	חשך	DARKNESS	365b	3 e
	קרה	ENCOUNTER	899d	2
	מקרה	ACCIDENT	900a	2
	ש	WHO	979d	3 a
2 15	אז	THEN	23b	2
	אמר	SAY	56b	2
	אני	I	59a	
	דבר	SPEAK	181c	4 b
	הבל	VAPOUR	210d	2
	ו	AND	*252b	1 b
	זה	THIS	260d	1 a
	חכם	BE WISE	314c	
	יתר	ADVANTAGE	452c	
	לב	HEART	525c	27
	לב	HEART	525c	27
	מה	HOW	554a	4 d
	קרה	ENCOUNTER	899d	2
	מקרה	ACCIDENT	900a	2
	ש	WHO	979d	3 a
2 16	איך	HOW	32c	2
	בא	COME	98c	2
	זכרון	MEMORIAL	272a	2
	חכם	WISE	315b	6 b3
	יום	DAY	399c	5 c
	כבר	ALREADY	460c	
	כל	ALL	483a	2 bb
	עולם	LONG DURATION	762d	2 j
	עם	WITH	768a	1 e
	ש	WHO	980a	4 a
2 17	ה	THE	208b	1 ha
	חיים	LIFE	313a	1
	כל	ALL	483a	2 bb
	על	UPON	758a	2 8
	עשה	DO	795b	1 a
	מעשה	DEED	795d	1 b5
	רוח	BREATH	925a	2 e
	רעות	LONGING	946d	
	רע	EVIL	948a	2
	שנא	HATE	971c	1 b
2 18	אני	I	59a	
	נוח	REST	629a	B 2
	עמל	TROUBLE	765d	3
	עמל	TOILING	766a	
	שנא	HATE	971c	1 b
	ש	WHO	980a	3 b
2 19	ה	INTERROG PART	210b	2 b
	זה	THIS	*260d	1 a
	חכם	BE WISE	314c	
	חכם	WISE	315a	6 a
	סכל	FOOL	698a	
	עמל	LABOUR	765c	
	עמל	TROUBLE	765d	3
	שלט	DOMINEER	1020c	
2 20	אני	I	59a	
	יאש	DESPAIR	384c	
	סבב	TURNABOUT	685d	1 c
	עמל	LABOUR	765c	
	עמל	TROUBLE	765d	3
2 21	זה	THIS	*260d	1 a
	חכמה	WISDOM	315d	5 c
	חלק	PORTION	324b	5
	דעת	WISDOM	395d	2 a
	יש	THERE IS	441d	2 b
	כשרון	SKILL	507a	1
	עמל	LABOUR	765c	
	עמל	TROUBLE	765d	3
	רעה	MISERY	949b	2
2 22	הוה	BECOME	217c	2
	עמל	TROUBLE	765b	3
	עמל	TOILING	766a	
	רעיון	STRIVING	946d	
2 23	זה	THIS	*260d	1 a
	מכאוב	PAIN	456c	2
	כעס	ANGER	495b	3
	ענין	OCCUPATION	775d	
	שכב	LIE DOWN	1012c	5
2 24	הוא	HE, SHE, IT	216d	6 a
	זה	THIS	262b	
	טוב	PLEASANT	374c	6
	טוב	A GOOD THING	375a	1
	נפש	SOUL	660c	5 c
	עמל	TROUBLE	765d	3
	ראה	TO SEE	907a	2 1
	ראה	TO SEE	908a	1 a1
	שתה	DRINK	1059b	1 a
2 25	חוץ	THE OUTSIDE	300a	1 bf
	חוש	FEEL	302a	
2 26	חטא	MISS A GOAL OR WAY	307a	2 b
	חכמה	WISDOM	315d	5 c
	טוב	PLEASANT	373d	2 c
	דעת	WISDOM	395d	2 a
	כנס	GATHER	488b	
	ענין	OCCUPATION	775d	
	פנה	FACE	817a	2 4a g
	רוח	BREATH	925a	2 e
	רעות	LONGING	946d	
3 1	זמן	APPOINTED TIME	273d	
	חפץ	DELIGHT	343b	4
	כל	ALL	483a	2 bb
	ל	TO	517b	7 a
3 2	נטע	PLANT	642c	1
	עת	TIME	773d	2 b
	עקר	PLUCK	785c	
3 3	בנה	BUILD	124c	1 d
	הרג	KILL	247b	6
	הרג	KILL	247b	7
	עת	TIME	773d	2 b
	פרץ	BREAK THROUGH	829b	2
	רפא	HEAL	950d	1 b
3 4	בכה	WEEP	113b	1
	מספד	WAILING	*704d	4
	ספד	WAIL	704d	
	עת	TIME	773d	2 b
	רקד	SKIP ABOUT	955a	
	שחק	LAUGH	965d	1 b
3 5	חבק	CLASP	287d	
	כנס	GATHER	488b	
	עת	TIME	773d	2 b
	רחק	BE DISTANT	935a	
	שלך	THROW	1021a	1 c
3 6	אבד	CAUSE TO STRAY	2a	3
	בקש	SEEK	134c	1 a
	עת	TIME	773d	2 b
	שלך	THROW	1021a	1 c
	שמר	KEEP	1036d	2 a
3 7	חשה	BE SILENT	364c	
	עת	TIME	773d	2 b
	קרע	TEAR	902c	1 a3
	תפר	SEW TOGETHER	1074c	
3 8	אהב	LOVE	12d	1
	עת	TIME	773d	2 b
	עת	TIME	773d	2 b
	שנא	HATE	971c	1 a
	שלון	PEACE	1023b	6
3 9	אשר	PARTICLE OF RELATION	82d	4 c
	באשר	IN WHICH	84a	A
	יתרון	ADVANTAGE	452c	
	עמל	TOILING	766a	
3 10	ענה	BE OCCUPIED	775d	
	ענין	OCCUPATION	775d	
3 11	בלי	WEARING OUT	115d	C b
	יפה	BEAUTIFUL	421c	
	כל	ALL	483a	2 bb
	לב	HEART	525a	24
	מצא	FIND	593a	2 a
	נתן	PUT	680c	2 b
	סוף	END	693a	
	עולם	LONG DURATION	762d	2 k
	עת	TIME	773d	2 b
	עשה	DO	793d	1 1a l
	מעשה	DEED	796a	1 c
	ראש	HEAD	911b	4 b
3 12	חיים	LIFE	313b	1
	טוב	PLEASANT	374c	6
	טוב	A GOOD THING	375b	4
	שמח	REJOICE	970b	1 a
3 13	גם	ALSO	169d	5
	הוא	HE, SHE, IT	216d	6 a
	טוב	A GOOD THING	375a	1
	מתת	GIFT	682c	
	עמל	TROUBLE	765d	3
	ראה	TO SEE	907d	7 d
	ש	WHO	980a	3 a
3 14	אין	NOT	34d	5 a
	גרע	DIMINISH	175c	1
	היה	BE	226d	3 2
	יסף	ADD	415b	1
	ירא	FEAR	431c	2
	עולם	LONG DURATION	762c	2 c
	עשה	DO	795a	29
	פנה	FACE	818a	2 5b
3 15	בקש	SEEK	134c	1 b
	כבר	ALREADY	460c	
	ל	TO	518a	7 bg
	מה	WHAT	553a	1 eb
	רדף	PURSUE	923a	
3 16	ה	THE	208b	1 ha
	ה	THE	208b	1 ha
	צדק	RIGHTEOUSNESS	841d	D
	מקום	STANDING PLACE	880b	4
	ראה	TO SEE	907b	5 a
	רשע	WICKEDNESS	957c	1
	שם	THERE	1027c	3 c
	משפט	JUDGMENT	1048c	1 b
3 17	אמר	SAY	56b	2
	חפץ	DELIGHT	343b	4
	לב	HEART	525c	27
	על	UPON	754c	2 1f d2
	מעשה	DEED	795d	1 b2
	צדיק	JUST	843a	3 b
	שם	THERE	1027b	1
	שפט	JUDGE	1047c	2 a
3 18	אמר	SAY	56b	2
	בהמה	BEAST	96d	1

Ch	v.	Heb	Eng	Page	Sec
		ברר	PURIFY	141a	4
		דברה	CAUSE	184b	2 7
		לב	HEART	525c	2 7
		ראה	TO SEE	907b	5 a
		ש	WHO	979d	3 a
3	19	בהמה	BEAST	96d	1
		מותר	SUPERIORITY	452d	2
		כל	ALL	483a	2 bb
		כל	ALL	483a	2 bb
		מקרה	ACCIDENT	900a	2
		רוח	BREATH	924d	1 e
3	20	היה	BECOME	226a	2 1
		הלך	WALK	234b	2 1
		כל	ALL	483a	2 bb
		עפר	DRY EARTH	779d	1 b
		מקום	STANDING PLACE	880b	4
		שוב	TURN BACK	997c	4 a
3	21	בהמה	BEAST	96d	1
		ה	INTERROG PART	210b	2 a
		ירד	GO DOWN	433b	1 i
		מטה	DOWNWARDS	641b	2 a
		מעל	ABOVE	752a	2 ca
		רוח	BREATH	925c	4 d
3	22	אשר	THAT	83c	3
		מאשר	FROM THAT WHICH	84a	A
		הוא	HE, SHE, IT	216d	6 a
		היה	COME TO PASS	224b	1 1b
		חלק	PORTION	324b	5
		טוב	PLEASANT	374c	6
		מה	WHAT	553b	1 eb
		מעשה	DEED	795d	1 b2
		ראה	TO SEE	908a	8 a1
		שמח	REJOICE	970b	1 a
		ש	WHO	*980a	4 c
4	1	דמעה	TEARS	199c	
		ו	AND	254a	2 c
		כח	STRENGTH	470d	1 b
		נחם	CONSOLE ONESELF	637a	
		עשה	DO	795b	1 a
		עשק	OPPRESS	798d	1
		עשק	OPPRESS	798d	1
		עשוקים	OPPRESSION	799a	
		שוב	TURN BACK	998b	8
4	2	הם	THEY	241c	2 c
		הנה	HITHERTO	244d	B
		חי	ALIVE	312a	1 b
		כבר	ALREADY	460c	
		עדנה	HITHERTO	725c	
		שבח	PRAISE	986d	2
4	3	את	MARK OF THE AC-CUSATIVE	85c	3 a
		הנה	HITHERTO	244d	B
		טוב	PLEASANT	374c	6
		עדנה	HITHERTO	725c	
		עשה	DO	795b	1 a
		מעשה	DEED	795d	1 a2
		רע	EVIL	948a	2
4	4	כשרון	SKILL	507a	1
		עמל	TROUBLE	765d	3
		מעשה	DEED	795d	1 a3
		קנאה	ZEAL	888b	1
		ראה	TO SEE	907a	2 1
		רוח	BREATH	925a	2 e
		רע	FRIEND	946a	2
		רעות	LONGING	946d	
4	5	אכל	EAT	37b	1
		בשר	FLESH	142c	2
		חבק	CLASP	287d	
4	6	חפן	HOLLOW OF HAND	342b	
		טוב	PLEASANT	374c	6
		כף	HOLLOW OF THE HAND	496b	1 a
		מלא	FULNESS	571b	1
		נחת	QUIETNESS	629b	1
		רוח	BREATH	925a	2 e
		רעות	LONGING	946d	
4	7	ו	AND	254a	2 c
		שוב	TURN BACK	998b	8
4	8	גם	ALSO	169d	5
		חסר	LACK	341b	
		טובה	WELFARE	375d	1
		יש	THERE IS	441d	2 b
		נפש	SOUL	660c	5 c
		עין	EYE	744d	3 b
		עמל	TROUBLE	765d	3
		עמל	TOILING	766a	
		ענין	OCCUPATION	775d	
		קץ	END	894a	1
		רע	EVIL	948a	2
		שבע	SATISFIED	959c	2 b
4	9	טוב	PLEASANT	374b	4 b
		טוב	PLEASANT	374c	6
		עמל	TROUBLE	765d	3
		שכר	HIRE	969b	2
4	10	אי	ALAS	33a	
		חבר	UNITED	288d	3
		נפל	FALL	656d	1
		קום	STAND	878d	1 a
4	11	חמם	BE OR BECOME WARM	328c	1
		שלמה	GARMENT	971b	
		שכב	LIE DOWN	1012a	1 b
4	12	חוט	THREAD	296c	2
		מהרה	HASTE	555b	
		נתק	TEAR AWAY	683c	2

Ch	v.	Heb	Eng	Page	Sec
		שלש	DO A THIRD TIME	1026a	
		תקף	OVERPOWER	1075d	
4	13	זהר	ADMONISH	264b	
		זקן	OLD	278c	1
		חכם	WISE	315a	6 a
		טוב	PLEASANT	374c	6
		ידע	KNOW	394b	4 a
		ילד	CHILD	409c	D
		מסכן	POOR	587d	
		אסר	TIE	63d	3
4	14	בית	HOUSE	109a	1 ae 2
		גם	YEA	169d	6
		ילד	BE BORN	408d	
		מלכות	ROYAL POWER	574d	1
		רוש	BE IN WANT	930d	
4	15	הלך	WALK	235c	2
		חי	ALIVE	312a	1 b
		ילד	CHILD	409c	D
		עמד	STAND	764c	6 a
4	16	אחרון	BEHIND	31a	B
		גם	ALSO	169d	5
		כי	THAT	472d	1 e
		פנה	FACE	817c	2 4c b
		קץ	END	894a	2
		רוח	BREATH	925a	2 e
		רעיון	STRIVING	946d	
4	17	אלהים	GOD	44a	3 b
		הלך	WALK	231a	1 d3 ga
		זבח	SACRIFICE	257c	1 1
		זבח	SACRIFICE	258a	2 7
		ידע	KNOW	394b	4 a
		כאשר	WHEN	455c	3
		מן	THAN	582d	6 c
		קרב	COME NEAR	897c	1 g
		שמר	KEEP	1036d	2 b
		מן	ADDENDA ET COR-RIGENDA	1124a	
5	1	בהל	HASTEN	96c	2
		הלך	WALK	230b	1 1a
		יצא	BRING OUT	425b	4 k
		מהר	HASTEN	555a	
		מעט	A FEW	590a	1 c
		על	UPON	753a	2 1
5	2	דבר	WORD	183b	3 1
		ו	AND	253b	1 j
		חלום	DREAM	321c	1
		ענין	OCCUPATION	775d	
5	3	אחר	DELAY	29b	2
		חפץ	DELIGHT	343b	1
		כאשר	WHEN	455c	3
		נדר	VOW	623d	
		נדר	VOW	623d	
		נדר	VOW	624a	2
5	4	אשר	THAT	83c	8 ab
		טוב	PLEASANT	*374b	4
		טוב	PLEASANT	374c	6
		נדר	VOW	623d	
		ש	WHO	980a	4 c
5	5	בשר	FLESH	142c	2
		הוא	HE, SHE, IT	*216d	6 a
		חבל	ACT CORRUPTLY	287b	
		חטא	MISS A GOAL OR WAY	307d	3
		מלאך	MESSENGER	521c	1 c
		מה	HOW	554b	4 d
		מעשה	DEED	795d	1 b1
		קצף	BE WROTH	893b	1
		שגגה	SIN OF ERROR	993a	
5	6	הבל	VAPOUR	211a	2
		ו	AND	252c	1 c
		חלום	DREAM	321c	1
		ירא	FEAR	431c	3 b
		רבה	BECOME MANY	915d	1 e4
5	7	גבה	HIGH	147b	2
		גזל	ROBBERY	160a	
		מדינה	PROVINCE	193d	4
		חפץ	DELIGHT	343b	4
		על	UPON	759b	4 2d
		עשק	OPPRESSION	799a	1
		צדק	RIGHTEOUSNESS	841c	2 a
		רוש	BE IN WANT	930d	
		שמר	KEEP	1036c	1 b
		תמה	BE ASTOUNDED	1069b	
5	8	הוא	HE, SHE, IT	*215a	
		יתרון	ADVANTAGE	452c	
		כל	ALL	482d	2 ba
		עבד	WORK	713c	2
5	9	אהב	LOVE	13a	2
		תבואה	REVENUE	100b	2 a
		המון	ABUNDANCE	242d	5
		מי	WHO	567b	G
		שבע	SATISFIED	959c	2
5	10	בעל	OWNER	127b	1 1
		טובה	WELFARE	375d	2
		כיאם	EXCEPT	475a	2 a
		כשרון	SUCCESS	507a	2
		מה	WHAT	552c	1 aa
		ראות	LOOK	909b	
		רבב	BECOME MUCH	912d	1
		רבה	BECOME MANY	915b	1 c
		יתב	ADDENDA ET COR-RIGENDA	1124a	
5	11	ישן	SLEEP	445c	
		שנה	SLEEP	446a	
		ל	TO	513d	5 cb e
		מתוק	SWEET	609a	2

Ch	v.	Heb	Eng	Page	Sec
		נוח	REST	629a	B 6
		עבד	WORK	713a	1
		רבה	BECOME MANY	915d	1 e5
		שבע	PLENTY	960a	1
		בעל	OWNER	127b	1 1
5	12	חלה	BE WEAK	317d	
		יש	THERE IS	441d	2 b
		ל	TO	514a	5 e
		רעה	MISERY	949b	1
5	13	אבד	PERISH	1d	1
		ילד	BEGET	409a	1
		ענין	OCCUPATION	775d	
		רע	EVIL	948a	2
5	14	אם	MOTHER	51c	1
		בוא	COME	98b	2
		בטן	WOMB	106a	3
		הלך	WALK	233d	1 5a
		הלך	WALK	237a	3 b
		יצא	GO OUT	423c	1 h
		מאומה	ANYTHING	548d	
		ערום	NAKED	736a	
		עמל	TROUBLE	765d	3
		ש	WHO	980a	4 b a
		שוב	TURN BACK	997c	3 b
		שוב	TURN BACK	997c	4 a
5	15	בוא	COME	98b	2
		זה	THIS	262b	
		חלה	BE WEAK	317d	2
		יתרון	ADVANTAGE	452c	1 f
		כל	ALL	482b	1
		כן	SO	486c	2 cd
		מה	WHAT	552c	1 aa
		עמל	LABOUR	765c	
		עמה	CLOSE BY	769d	D
		רוח	BREATH	925a	2 e
		רעה	MISERY	949b	2
		ש	WHO	980a	3 ab
		ש	WHO	980a	3 a
5	16	אכל	EAT	37b	1
		חלי	SICKNESS	318b	
		חשך	DARKNESS	365a	1 a
		כעס	BE ANGRY	495a	3
		כעס	ANGER	495b	3
		קצף	WRATH	893c	2
		רבה	BECOME MANY	915d	1 e4
5	17	חיים	LIFE	313b	1
		חלק	PORTION	324c	5
		טוב	PLEASANT	374b	5
		טובה	WELFARE	375d	1
		יום	DAY	399a	4 a
		יפה	BEAUTIFUL	421c	
		מספר	NUMBER	709a	1 a
		עמל	LABOUR	765c	
		עמל	TROUBLE	765d	3
		ראה	TO SEE	907b	3
5	18	גם	ALSO	169d	5
		זה	THIS	262b	
		חלק	PORTION	324c	5
		נכס	RICHES	647d	
		מתת	GIFT	682c	
		עמל	TROUBLE	765d	3
		שלט	DOMINEER	1020c	1
5	19	זכר	REMEMBER	270a	1 5
		חיים	LIFE	313b	1
		יום	DAY	399a	4 a
		לב	HEART	525c	2 9a
		ענה	ANSWER	773a	
		רבה	BECOME MANY	915d	1 e3
		שמחה	JOY	970d	1
6	1	יש	THERE IS	441d	2 b
		על	UPON	753b	2 1b
6	2	אוה	DESIRE	16b	
		חלי	SICKNESS	318b	
		חסר	NEEDY	341c	
		כבוד	HONOR	458c	2 a
		נכס	RICHES	647d	
		נכרי	ALIEN	649a	3
		נפש	SOUL	660c	5 c
		רע	EVIL	948a	2
		שלט	DOMINEER	1020c	1
6	3	איש	MAN	35d	
		טוב	PLEASANT	374c	6
		טובה	WELFARE	375d	1
		יום	DAY	399a	4 a
		ילד	BEGET	409a	1
		מאה	HUNDRED	548a	1 a5
		נפל	MISCARRIAGE	658b	
		נפש	SOUL	660c	5 c
		צברה	GRAVE	869a	1 b
		רב	MUCH	913a	1 b
		רב	MUCH	913a	1 a1
		שבע	SATISFIED	959c	2 c
		ש	WHO	979d	1
6	4	הבל	VAPOUR	210d	2
		חשך	DARKNESS	365a	3 g
		כסה	BE COVERED	492b	1
6	5	נחת	REST	629a	2
6	6	אלו	IF	47a	
		אלף	THOUSAND	48d	1 a
		אלף	THOUSAND	49a	1 a
		הלך	WALK	234b	2 1
		טובה	WELFARE	375d	1
		כל	ALL	483a	2 bb
		מקום	STANDING PLACE	880b	4
		שנה	YEAR	1040c	

Ch v.	Heb	Eng	Page	Sec
6 7	גם	ALSO	169d	5
	מלא	BE FULL	570c	1
	נפש	SOUL	660c	5 c
	עמל	TROUBLE	765d	3
6 8	הלך	WALK	235a	2 3c
	חי	ALIVE	312a	1 b
	חכם	WISE	315d	6 b3
	יותר	ADVANTAGE	452c	
	מה	WHAT	552c	1 aa
	עני	POOR	776d	2
6 9	הלך	WALK	235a	2 3f 2
	טוב	PLEASANT	374c	6
	נפש	SOUL	660c	5 c
	עין	EYE	744b	1 f
	מראה	VISION	909d	4
	רוח	BREATH	925a	2 e
	רעות	LONGING	946d	
6 10	דין	JUDGE	192c	6
	הוא	HE, SHE, IT	216b	4 a
	ידע	BE MADE KNOWN	394c	1
	כבר	ALREADY	460c	
	מה	WHAT	553b	1 eb
	קרא	CALL	896c	6 d9
	ש	WHO	979d	1
	תקיף	MIGHTY	1076a	
6 11	הבל	VAPOUR	210d	2
	יש	THERE IS	441d	2 b
	יותר	ADVANTAGE	452c	
	מה	WHAT	552c	1 aa
	ראה	TO SEE	907b	5 a
	רבה	BECOME MANY	915d	1 e4
6 12	חיים	LIFE	313a	1
	חיים	LIFE	313b	1
	טוב	PLEASANT	374a	2 e
	יום	DAY	399a	4 a
	מספר	NUMBER	709a	1 a
	עשה	DO	795a	2 1
	צל	SHADOW	853b	3
7 1	ו	AND	253b	1 j
	טוב	PLEASANT	374b	6
	טוב	PLEASANT	374c	6
	יום	DAY	398c	2 f
	יום	DAY	400a	7 d1 a
	ילד	BE BORN	408d	
	שמן	OIL	1032b	2 b
7 2	אבל	MOURNING	5d	
	באשר	IN THAT	84a	C
	בית	HOUSE	108d	1 ad
	הלך	WALK	231a	1 d3 ga
	חי	ALIVE	312a	1 b
	טוב	PLEASANT	374c	6
	ל	TO	517d	7 bd
	לב	HEART	525a	24
	נתן	GIVE	679a	1 i
	סוף	END	693a	
	משתה	FEAST	1059d	1
	לב	ADDENDA ET CORRIGENDA	1124c	
7 3	טוב	PLEASANT	374c	6
	יטב	BE GLAD	405c	1
	כעס	ANGER	495b	1
	לב	HEART	525c	29a
	פנה	FACE	815d	1 1a
	רע	EVIL	948a	4
	שחוק	LAUGHTER	966a	1
7 4	אבל	MOURNING	5d	
	בית	HOUSE	108d	1 ad
	חכם	WISE	315d	6 b4
	לב	HEART	524d	2 3b
	שמחה	JOY	970d	1
7 5	גערה	REBUKE	172a	1
	חכם	WISE	315d	6 b2
	טוב	PLEASANT	374c	6
	ל	TO	517d	7 bd
	שיר	SONG	1010b	1
7 6	סיר	POT	696c	1 a
	סיר	THORN	696c	1
	קול	VOICE	877b	21
	שחק	LAUGHTER	966a	1
7 7	אבד	CAUSE TO VANISH	2a	2
	הלל	PRAISE	239b	
	חכם	WISE	315d	6 b4
	כי	THAT	472d	1 e
	מתנה	GIFT	682c	
	עשק	OPPRESSION	799a	3
7 8	אחרית	END	31a	B
	ארך	LONG	74a	
	גבה	HIGH	147b	3
	טוב	PLEASANT	374c	6
	טוב	PLEASANT	374c	6
	ראשית	BEGINNING	912a	1a
	רוח	BREATH	925a	3 d
	רוח	BREATH	925d	8
7 9	בהל	HASTEN	96c	2
	חיק	BOSOM	300d	3 b
	כעס	BE ANGRY	495a	2
	כעס	ANGER	495b	1
	נוח	REST	628b	1
	רוח	BREATH	925a	3 c
7 10	חכמה	WISDOM	315d	5 c
	טוב	PLEASANT	374c	6
	יום	DAY	399c	5 c
	מן	OUT OF	579c	2 bb
	ראשון	FIRST	911c	1 a
	ש	WHO	980a	3 aa
	שאל	ASK	981d	2 a
7 11	חכמה	WISDOM	315d	5 c
	טוב	PLEASANT	374b	5
	יותר	ADVANTAGE	452c	
	עם	WITH	767b	1 a
	עם	WITH	768a	1 f
	ראה	TO SEE	907a	1 b
7 12	בעל	LORD	127c	1 5a
	ה	THE	207d	1 e
	ה	THE	208b	1 ha
	חיה	LIVE	311c	3 d
	חכמה	WISDOM	315d	5 c
	דעת	WISDOM	395d	2 a
	יתרון	ADVANTAGE	452c	
	צל	SHADOW	853b	2
7 13	חיים	LIFE	313a	1
	עת	BE BENT	736c	2
	מעשה	DEED	796a	1 c
	ראה	TO SEE	907b	5 a
	תקן	BECOME STRAIGHT	1075b	
7 14	דברה	CAUSE	184b	
	טוב	A GOOD THING	375a	1
	טובה	WELFARE	375d	1
	מצא	FIND	593a	1 f
	עמה	CLOSE BY	769d	C
	ראה	TO SEE	907d	7 f
	ש	WHO	980a	3 ab
7 15	אבד	PERISH	1c	1
	ארך	BE LONG	73d	1 a
	הבל	VAPOUR	211a	2
	יש	THERE IS	441d	2 b
	צדק	RIGHTEOUSNESS	841d	5
7 16	חכם	BE WISE	314c	
	יותר	ADVANTAGE	452c	4 d
	מה	HOW	554b	4 d
	רבה	BECOME MANY	*915d	1 e3
	רבה	BECOME MANY	915d	1 e3
	שמם	BE DESOLATED	1031b	2
7 17	לא	NOT	520b	4 ab
	מה	HOW	554b	4 d
	מות	DIE	560a	2 d
	סכל	FOOL	698a	
	עת	TIME	773d	2 b
	רבה	BECOME MANY	915d	1 e3
	רשע	BE WICKED	957d	1
7 18	אחז	GRASP	28b	1
	אשר	THAT	83c	8 ab
	זה	THIS	260d	1 a
	טוב	PLEASANT	374b	5
	יצא	GO OUT	*422d	1 b
	יצא	GO OUT	423a	1 d
	ירא	FEAR	431c	3 b
	נוח	REST	628d	B 1
7 19	ה	THE	208b	1 ha
	חכם	WISE	315b	6 b3
	חכמה	WISDOM	315d	5 c
	עזז	BE STRONG	738c	
	שליט	HAVING MASTERY	1020c	1
7 20	אדם	MAN	9b	1
	חטא	MISS A GOAL OR WAY	307a	2 b
	טוב	A GOOD THING	375b	4
	כי	THAT	472d	1 e
7 21	נתן	GIVE	679a	1 i
	שמע	HEAR	1033c	1 b
	לב	ADDENDA ET CORRIGENDA	1124c	
7 22	אתה	THOU	61c	1
	אשר	THAT	83c	8 ab
	לב	HEART	524d	2 3b
	לב	HEART	525a	25
	פעם	OCCURRENCE	822a	3 a
	רב	MUCH	913a	1 b
7 23	זה	THIS	262b	
	חכם	BE WISE	314c	
	חכמה	WISDOM	315d	5 c
	נסה	TEST	650b	1
	רחק	DISTANT	935c	1 a
7 24	מה	WHAT	553b	1 eb
	מצא	FIND	593b	2 a
	עמק	DEEP	771b	2
	רחק	DISTANT	935c	1 a
7 25	בור	MAKE CLEAR	101c	
	בקש	SEEK	134d	2 b
	הוללה	MADNESS	239c	
	חכמה	WISDOM	315d	5 c
	חשבון	RECKONING	363d	
	כסל	FOLLY	492d	2
	ל	TO	518b	7 bh
	לב	HEART	524d	2 3b
	סבב	TURNABOUT	685d	1 c
	סכלות	FOLLY	698a	
	רשע	WICKEDNESS	957d	3
	רשע	WICKEDNESS	957d	3
	תור	SPY OUT	1064c	2
7 26	אסור	BAND	64a	
	אשר	PARTICLE OF RELATION	82b	2 a
	ה	THE	208b	1 g
	חטא	MISS A GOAL OR WAY	307a	2 b
	חרם	NET	357a	
	טוב	PLEASANT	373d	2 c
	לכד	CAPTURE	540b	2
	מלט	SLIP AWAY	572c	2
	מצא	FIND	593a	1 d
7	מר	BITTER	*600c	1
	מר	BITTER	600d	2 b
	פנה	FACE	817a	24 a g
	מצוד	HUNTING IMPLEMENT	845a	
7 27	חשבון	RECKONING	363d	
	ל	TO	511d	1 i
	מצא	FIND	593a	1 e
	קהלת	PREACHER	875b	
7 28	אדם	MAN	9b	1
	אשה	WOMAN	61a	1
	נפש	SOUL	660c	5 c
7 29	אדם	MAN	9b	2
	אשר	THAT	83c	8 ab
	בד	SEPARATION	94c	1 c
	בקש	SEEK	134d	2 b
	חשבון	DEVICE	364a	
	ישר	STRAIGHT	449a	3 b
	מצא	FIND	593a	1 e
8 1	אור	BECOME LIGHT	21c	5
	חכם	WISE	315d	6 b3
	חכמה	WISDOM	315d	5 c
	עז	STRONG	738d	
	עז	STRENGTH	739b	4
	פשר	SOLUTION	833d	
	שנה	CHANGE	1040a	
8 2	דברה	CAUSE	184b	
	ו	AND	252c	1 b
	שבועה	OATH	990a	1 a
8 3	בהל	BE IN HASTE	96c	2
	חפץ	DELIGHT IN	342d	1 a
	עמד	STAND	764b	3 f
	רע	EVIL	948c	0 d
8 4	באשר	IN THAT	84a	C
	דבר	WORD	182b	1 1b
	מה	WHAT	552c	1 aa
	מי	WHO	566d	F c
	שלטון	MASTERY	1020d	
	מלא	SMITE	*1099d	
8 5	חכם	WISE	315a	6 a
	לב	HEART	524d	2 3b
	לב	HEART	524d	2 3b
	עת	TIME	773d	2 b
	רע	EVIL	948c	0 d
	משפט	JUDGMENT	1048c	1 e
8 6	חפץ	DELIGHT	343b	4
	על	UPON	753b	2 1b
	עת	TIME	773d	2 c
	משפט	JUDGMENT	1048c	1 e
8 7	היה	COME TO PASS	224b	1 1b
	מה	WHAT	553b	1 eb
8 8	בעל	LORD	127c	1 5a
	ו	AND	253b	1 j
	כלא	RESTRAIN	476b	2
	מלט	SLIP AWAY	572c	3
	רוח	BREATH	925c	4 d
	רשע	WICKEDNESS	957d	3
	משלחת	DISCHARGE	1020a	1
	שלט	HAVING MASTERY	1020c	1
	שלטון	MASTERY	1020d	
8 9	נתן	GIVE	679a	1 i
	עשה	DO	795b	1 a
	מעשה	DEED	795d	1 b2
	רע	EVIL	948c	0 d
	שלט	DOMINEER	1020c	
	לב	ADDENDA ET CORRIGENDA	1124c	
8 10	הלך	WALK	235c	3
	כן	RIGHT	467a	1
	כן	SO	486d	3 b
	קבר	BURY	868c	
	קבר	BURY	868c	
	קדוש	HOLY	872d	2 a
	מקום	STANDING PLACE	880b	4
	רשע	WICKED	957c	3
	שכח	FORGET	1013b	
8 11	אין	NOT	34c	2 f
	אשר	THAT	83c	8 c
	לב	HEART	*525d	20
	מהרה	HASTE	555b	
	מלא	FILL	*570b	2
	מלא	BE FULL	570b	1 b
	עשה	DO	795b	1 a
	מעשה	DEED	795d	1 a2
	פתגם	EDICT	834b	
8 12	רעה	MISERY	949b	3
	ארך	BE LONG	73d	1 a
	אשר	THAT	83b	8 ab
	אשר	THAT	83c	8 c
	אשר	THAT	83c	8 c
	גם	YEA	169d	6
	חטא	MISS A GOAL OR WAY	307a	2 b
	טוב	PLEASANT	374a	2 e
	ירא	FEAR	431c	2
	ירא	FEAR	431c	3 b
	ל	TO	515d	5 ia
	מאה	HUNDRED	548a	1 d1
	מאה	HUNDRED	548b	1 d6
	פנה	FACE	818a	2 5b
8 13	ארך	BE LONG	73d	1 a
	טוב	PLEASANT	374a	2 e
	ירא	FEAR	431c	2
	פנה	FACE	818a	2 5b
	צל	SHADOW	853b	3
8 14	אשר	THAT	83c	8 ab

Ch	v.	Heb	Eng	Page	Sec
		יש	THERE IS	441d	2 b
		ך	LIKE	453d	1 b
		נגע	REACH	619c	4
		עשה	DO	795b	1 a
		מעשה	DEED	795d	1 a3
		מעשה	DEED	795d	1 a2
		ש	WHO	980a	3 a
8	15	חיים	LIFE	313b	1
		טוב	PLEASANT	374c	6
		לוה	BE JOINED	530d	
		עמל	TROUBLE	765d	3
		עשה	DO	795b	1 a
		שמחה	JOY	970d	1
		שבח	PRAISE	986d	2
8	16	חכמה	WISDOM	315c	5 c
		ידע	KNOW	394c	5
		יום	DAY	398b	1
		שנה	SLEEP	446a	
		לב	HEART	524d	2 3b
		נתן	GIVE	679a	1 i
		ענין	OCCUPATION	775d	
		ראה	TO SEE	907b	3
		ראה	TO SEE	907d	6 e
		לב	ADDENDA ET COR-RIGENDA	1124c	
8	17	בקש	SEEK	134c	1 a
		גם	YEA	*169d	6
		חכם	WISE	315b	6 b3
		מצא	FIND	593b	2 a
		עמל	LABOUR	765c	
		עשה	DO	795b	1 a
		מעשה	DEED	795d	1 b5
		מעשה	DEED	796a	1 c
		ש	WHO	980b	4 c
9	1	אהבה	LOVE	13b	1
		אלהים	GOD	44a	3 b
		אשר	THAT	83c	8 ab
		בור	MAKE CLEAR	101c	
		ברר	PURIFY	141a	4
		חכם	WISE	315b	6 b3
		כל	ALL	483a	2 bb
		ל	TO	518b	7 bh
		לב	HEART	525a	2 4
		נתן	GIVE	679a	1 i
		עבד	WORK	714d	1
		שנאה	HATING	971d	1
		תור	SPY OUT	1064c	2
		לב	ADDENDA ET COR-RIGENDA	1124c	
9	2	חטא	MISS A GOAL OR WAY	307a	2 b
		טהור	CLEAN	373d	3
		טוב	PLEASANT	374d	0 a
		טמא	UNCLEAN	379d	2 a
		ירא	FEAR	431c	3
		כל	ALL	483a	2 bb
		מקרה	ACCIDENT	900a	1
		שבועה	OATH	990a	1 a
9	3	הוללה	MADNESS	239c	1
		חיים	LIFE	313b	1
		כל	ALL	483a	2 bb
		לבב	HEART	523c	2 3a
		מלא	BE FULL	570a	1 b
		עשה	DO	795b	1 a
		מקרה	ACCIDENT	900a	2
		רע	EVIL	948a	2
9	4	אריה	LION	71d	1
		בחר	CHOOSE	104b	
		בטחון	TRUST	105c	
		חבר	UNITE	288b	1 b
		חי	ALIVE	312a	1 b
		חי	ALIVE	312b	1 c
		טוב	PLEASANT	374c	6
		כלב	DOG	477a	A
		ל	TO	514d	5 fe
		מות	DIE	559d	1 b
		מי	WHO	567b	G
		מעט	A FEW	590a	1 b
9	5	זכר	REMEMBRANCE	271b	2 a
		חי	ALIVE	312a	1 b
		שכר	HIRE	969b	2
		ש	WHO	979d	3 a
		שאול	SHEOL	983a	1
		שכח	FORGET	1013b	
9	6	אבד	PERISH	1c	1
		אהבה	LOVE	13b	1
		חלק	PORTION	324a	1 c
		כבר	ALREADY	460c	
		עולם	LONG DURATION	762d	2 j
		עשה	DO	795b	1 a
		קנאה	ZEAL	888b	1
		שנאה	HATING	971d	1
		שאול	SHEOL	983a	1
9	7	טוב	PLEASANT	374c	7
		יין	WINE	406c	A
		כבר	ALREADY	460c	
		לב	HEART	525c	2 9a
		מעשה	DEED	795d	1 b2
		רצה	BE PLEASED WITH	953a	1 a
		שמחה	JOY	970d	1
9	8	בגד	GARMENT	94a	1
		חסר	LACK	341b	2
		לבן	WHITE	526b	
		שמן	OIL	1032b	2 c
9	9	אהב	LOVE	12d	1
		הבל	VAPOUR	211a	2

Ch	v.	Heb	Eng	Page	Sec
		הוא	HE, SHE, IT	216d	6 a
		חיים	LIFE	313a	1
		חיים	LIFE	313b	1
		חלק	PORTION	324c	5
		עמל	TROUBLE	765b	
		עמל	TOILING	766a	
9	10	הלך	WALK	234b	2 1
		חכמה	WISDOM	315d	5 c
		חשבון	RECKONING	363d	
		דעת	WISDOM	395d	2 a
		כח	STRENGTH	470d	1 b
		מצא	FIND	593b	3 c
		מצא	FIND	593c	4
		מעשה	DEED	795d	1 b2
		שאול	SHEOL	983a	1
9	11	בין	DISCERN	106d	1
		גבור	STRONG	150b	2
		ו	AND	253b	1 j
		חכם	WISE	315b	6 b3
		חן	FAVOR	336b	2 a
		ידע	KNOW	394c	5
		עת	TIME	773d	2 d
		פגע	OCCURRENCE	803c	2
		קל	LIGHT	887a	
		קרה	ENCOUNTER	899d	2
		שוב	TURN BACK	998b	8
9	12	אחז	GRASP	28b	1
		אחז	GRASP	28c	
		דג	FISH	185d	
		הם	THEY	241d	8 b
		יקש	ENTRAPPED	430c	
		נפל	FALL	657c	5
		עת	TIME	773d	2 c
		פח	BIRD-TRAP	809a	1
		פתאם	SUDDENNESS	837c	
		מצודה	NET	845a	
		צפור	BIRD	862a	1
		רע	EVIL	948b	2
		ש	WHO	980a	4 bb
9	13	זה	THIS	262b	
		חכמה	WISDOM	315d	5 c
9	14	בנה	BUILD	124c	1 ah
		גדול	GREAT	153a	6 b
		מלך	KING	573b	5 a
		סבב	SURROUND	685d	2 d
		עיר	CITY	746b	1
		מצוד	SIEGEWORKS	844d	1
9	15	מן	SMALL	882a	2 a
		חכם	WISE	315b	6 b4
		חכמה	WISDOM	315d	5 c
		מלט	SLIP AWAY	572c	3
		מסכן	POOR	587d	1
		מצא	FIND	593c	4
9	16	בזה	DESPISE	102c	
		גבורה	STRENGTH	150b	1
		חכמה	WISDOM	315d	5 c
		טוב	PLEASANT	374c	6
		מסכן	POOR	587d	
9	17	דבר	WORD	183a	2 1a
		זעקה	CRY	277d	3
		חכם	WISE	315a	6 b2
		מן	THAN	582d	6 c
		משל	RULE	605d	1
		נחת	QUIETNESS	629b	1
		שמע	HEAR	1034b	3
9	18	אבד	CAUSE TO VANISH	2a	2
		חטא	MISS A GOAL OR WAY	307a	2 b
		חכמה	WISDOM	315d	5 c
		טוב	PLEASANT	374c	6
		טובה	WELFARE	375d	1
		כלי	IMPLEMENT	479d	2 a
		קרב	BATTLE	898b	
		רבה	BECOME MANY	915d	1 e4
10	1	באש	STINK	93a	2
		זבוב	FLY	256a	
		חכמה	WISDOM	315d	5 c
		יקר	WEIGHTY	430a	4
		כבוד	HONOR	459b	4
		מות	DEATH	560d	1
		מעט	A FEW	590a	1 b
		נבע	BUBBLE UP	615d	2
		סכלות	FOLLY	698a	1
		רקח	MIX OIL	955b	
		שמן	OIL	1032b	2 b
10	2	חכם	WISE	315b	6 b3
		ימין	RIGHT HAND	412a	2
		ל	TO	*511d	2
		לב	HEART	524d	2 3b
		שמאל	LEFT	969d	
10	3	דרך	WAY	202d	1
		חסר	LACK	341b	2
		כל	ALL	483a	2 bb
		לב	HEART	524d	2 3a
		סכל	FOOL	698a	
		ש	WHO	980a	4 bb
10	4	חטא	SIN	308a	1 a
		מה	WHAT	553b	1 eb
		משל	RULE	605d	1
		נוח	REST	629a	B 3
		נוח	REST	629a	B 5
		עלה	GO UP	749a	7
		מקום	STANDING PLACE	879d	1 c
		רוח	BREATH	925a	3 c
		מרפא	HEALING	951c	2
10	5	יצא	GO OUT	422d	1 b

Ch	v.	Heb	Eng	Page	Sec
		יש	THERE IS	441d	2 b
		ך	LIKE	454b	1 d
		פנה	FACE	818a	2 5a c
		שגגה	SIN OF ERROR	993a	
		שליט	HAVING MASTERY	1020c	1
10	6	ה	THE	208b	1 ha
		נתן	PUT	681c	2 a
		סכל	FOLLY	698a	
		עשיר	RICH	799b	
		מרום	HEIGHT	928d	1
		שפל	LOW ESTATE	1050c	
10	7	הלך	WALK	230b	1 1a
		עבד	SLAVE	714a	2
		ראה	TO SEE	907a	2 5
		שר	CHIEFTAIN	978d	7
10	8	גדר	WALL	155a	
		גומץ	PIT	170a	
		חפר	DIG	343c	1 a
		נחש	SERPENT	638a	1 a
		נפל	FALL	656d	1
		נשך	BITE	675a	
		פרץ	BREAK THROUGH	829b	2
10	9	בקע	CLEAVE	131d	1
		נסע	PULL OUT	652c	2
		סכן	INCUR DANGER	698c	
		עצב	HURT	780c	
10	10	ברזל	IRON	137c	2
		גבר	BE STRONG	149d	
		חיל	STRENGTH	298c	1 a
		חכמה	WISDOM	315d	5 c
		יתרון	ADVANTAGE	452d	
		כשר	SUCCEED	506d	1
		פנה	FACE	816b	1 5
		קהה	BE BLUNT	874b	
		קלל	BE SILENT	886d	2
10	11	בעל	LORD	127c	1 5a
		יתרון	ADVANTAGE	452c	
		לא	NOT	520a	4 aa
		לחש	CHARMING	538a	1
		לשון	TONGUE	546c	1 b
		נחש	SERPENT	638a	1 a
		נשך	BITE	675a	
10	12	בלע	SWALLOW UP	118c	2 a
		חכם	WISE	315a	6 b2
		חן	FAVOR	336b	1 b
		פה	MOUTH	805a	2 a
10	13	הוללות	MADNESS	239c	
		תחלה	BEGINNING	321a	
		סכלות	FOLLY	698a	
		פה	MOUTH	805a	2 a
		פה	MOUTH	805a	2 a
10	14	אחר	BEHIND	30b	4 ag
		היה	COME TO PASS	224b	1 1b
		כסל	FOOL	698a	
		רבה	BECOME MANY	915c	1 c
		יגע	TOIL	388b	1
10	15	ידע	KNOW	394b	4 a
		עמל	TROUBLE	765d	3
10	16	אי	ALAS	33a	1
		ארץ	EARTH	76a	2 a
		נער	YOUTH	655a	1 d
		שר	CHIEFTAIN	978b	1
10	17	ארץ	EARTH	76a	2 a
		אשר	HAPPINESS	81a	
		בן	SON	120c	1 ib
		גבורה	STRENGTH	150b	1
		חר	NOBLE	359d	
		שר	CHIEFTAIN	978b	2 a
		שתי	DRINKING	1059c	
10	18	דלף	DRIP	196a	1
		מכך	BE LOW	568d	
		עצלה	SLUGGISHNESS	782b	
		מקרה	BEAM-WORK	900a	
		שפלות	SINKINA	1050d	
10	19	חיים	LIFE	313a	1
		יין	WINE	406c	A
		כל	ALL	482d	2 b
		כל	ALL	483a	2 bb
		לחם	FOOD	537a	1 a
		ענה	ANSWER	773a	2 b
		שחק	LAUGHTER	966a	1
		שמח	REJOICE	970c	
10	20	בעל	LORD	127c	1 5a
		הלך	WALK	237a	3 b
		חדר	CHAMBER	293d	
		מדע	THOUGHT	396b	2
		כנף	WING	489c	1 a
		עוף	FLY	733d	1
		קול	VOICE	877b	3 a2
		משכב	ACT OF LYING	1012d	2 a
11	1	מצא	FIND	*394a	1 h
		לחם	FOOD	537a	3 a
		מצא	FIND	592d	1 a
		רב	MULTITUDE	914a	1
		שלח	SEND	1019b	7
11	2	חלק	PORTION	324a	1 b
		מה	WHAT	552c	1 aa
11	3	אם	IF	50a	1 b1
		גשם	RAIN	177c	
		דרום	SOUTH	205a	
		הוה	BECOME	217c	
		מלא	FILL	570b	1
		נפל	FALL	657a	1
		ריק	MAKE EMPTY	938a	2
		ש	WHO	979d	2
		שם	THERE	1027a	1

323

SONG OF SOLOMON

Ch v.	Heb	Eng	Page	Sec
11 4	זרע	SOW	281c	1 a
	קצר	HARVEST	894b	
	ראה	TO SEE	908a	8 a4
	שמר	KEEP	1036d	1 d
11 5	בטן	WOMB	106a	3
	ככה	THUS	462c	
	כל	ALL	483a	2 bb
	מלא	FULL	571a	
	עצם	BONE	782d	1 a
	מעשה	DEED	796a	1 c
	רוח	BREATH	925c	4 d
11 6	אי	WHERE	32b	2 a
	בקר	MORNING	134a	1 e
	ה	INTERROG PART	210b	2 b
	זרע	SOW	281c	1 c
	זרע	SOWING	282b	2 b
	טוב	PLEASANT	374b	3 c
	כשר	SUCCEED	506d	
	נוח	REST	628d	B 1
	ערב	SUNSET	787d	1 a
11 7	טוב	PLEASANT	373c	1 a
	מתוק	SWEET	609a	2
11 8	זכר	REMEMBER	270a	1 5
	חשך	DARKNESS	365a	3 a
	רבה	BECOME MANY	915c	1 e4
	רבה	BECOME MANY	915c	1 e4
	שמח	REJOICE	970b	1 a
11 9	בוא	COME	99a	1 c
	בחור	YOUNG MAN	104c	
	בחורים	YOUTH	104c	
	דרך	WAY	203c	6 a
	הלך	WALK	235c	4
	יטב	MAKE GLAD	405d	1
	ילדות	YOUTH	409c	
	לב	HEART	525c	2 9a
	מראה	VISION	909d	4
	משפט	JUDGMENT	1048c	1 c
11 10	בשר	FLESH	142c	2
	ה	THE	208b	1 ha
	ילדות	YOUTH	409c	
	כעס	ANGER	495b	2
	לב	HEART	525c	2 9b
	עבר	PASS OVER	719a	4
	שחרות	BLACKNESS	1007b	
12 1	בחורים	YOUTH	104c	
	ברא	CREATE	135b	2
	זכר	REMEMBER	270a	1 3 b
	חפץ	DELIGHT	343b	1
	נגע	REACH	619c	3
	עד	UNTIL	725b	2 2d
	רעה	MISERY	949a	1
12 2	גשם	RAIN	177c	
	חשך	GROW DARK	364d	1
	ירח	MOON	437a	
	כוכב	STAR	456d	
	עד	UNTIL	725b	2 2d
	שוב	TURN BACK	998a	7 a
12 3	ארבה	LATTICE	70c	
	בטל	CEASE	105d	
	בית	HOUSE	109c	1 c
	זוע	TREMBLE	266b	
	חיל	STRENGTH	298d	1 c
	חשך	GROW DARK	364d	3
	טחן	GRIND	377c	
	טחנה	MILL	*377d	
	מעט	BE SMALL	589c	
	עות	BE BENT	736c	
	שמר	KEEP	1036c	1 b
12 4	בת	DAUGHTER	123d	5
	דלת	DOOR	195b	4
	טחנה	MILL	377d	
	סגר	BE SHUT UP	689c	3
	קול	VOICE	877a	1 e
	קול	VOICE	877b	2 m
	קום	STAND	877c	1 a
	שוק	STREET	1003b	
	שחח	BOW	1005d	
	שיר	SONG	1010b	1
	שפל	BECOME LOW	1050a	3
12 5	אביונה	CAPER-BERRY	3a	
	אדם	MAN	9b	2
	בית	HOUSE	109c	1 d
	גבה	HIGH	147b	1
	דרך	WAY	202d	1
	הלך	WALK	234b	2 1
	חגב	LOCUST	290b	
	חתחת	TERROR	369d	
	ירא	FEAR	431b	1 c
	כחש	LEANNESS	*471c	2
	נצץ	BLOSSOM	665b	
	סבב	GO AROUND	685d	2 c
	סבל	BEAR	687d	
	ספד	WAIL	704d	
	עולם	LONG DURATION	762d	2 j
	פרר	BREAK	830c	2 d
	שוק	STREET	1003b	
	שקד	ALMOND-TREE	1052b	2
12 6	בור	WELL	92c	2
	זהב	GOLD	263a	6
	חבל	CORD	286c	1
	כד	JAR	461c	
	מבוע	SPRING OF WATER	616a	
	עד	UNTIL	725b	2 2d
	רחק	BE DISTANT	935a	
	רצץ	CRUSH	954c	1 b
	רצץ	CRUSH	954d	

Ch v.	Heb	Eng	Page	Sec
	רצץ	CRUSH	954d	
	רתק	BIND	958d	
	שבר	BREAK	990d	
12 7	נתן	GIVE	678c	1 b
	עפר	DRY EARTH	779d	1 b
	רוח	BREATH	925c	4 d
	ש	WHO	980a	4 ba
	שוב	TURN BACK	997c	4 a
12 8	הבל	VAPOUR	*210d	2
	הבל	VAPOUR	211a	2
	כל	ALL	483a	2 bb
	קהלת	PREACHER	875b	
12 9	אזן	WEIGH	24d	
	חכם	WISE	315a	6 b2
	חקר	SEARCH	350d	
	דעת	WISDOM	395d	2 a
	יותר	ADVANTAGE	452c	
	למד	LEARN	540d	
	עוד	STILL	729b	1 c
	קהלת	PREACHER	875b	
	רבה	BECOME MANY	915c	1 e4
	תקן	BECOME STRAIGHT	1075b	
12 10	אמת	FIRMNESS	54b	4 a
	בקש	SEEK	134d	2 d
	חפץ	DELIGHT	343a	1
	ישר	STRAIGHTNESS	449c	2
	מצא	FIND	593a	1 b
	קו	LINE UPON LINE	875b	
	קהלת	PREACHER	875b	
12 11	אספה	COLLECTION	63b	
	בעל	LORD	127c	1 5b
	דבר	WORD	183a	2 1a
	דרבנה	GOAD	201c	
	חכם	WISE	315a	6 b2
	מן	OUT OF	580a	2 ea
	נטע	PLANT	642c	2
	נתן	GIVE	681c	1 c
	מסמר	NAIL	702d	
	מסמר	NAIL	791b	
	קהלת	PREACHER	875b	
	רעה	TEND	945b	1 d3
12 12	בשר	FLESH	142c	2
	הם	THEY	241d	8 a
	זהר	ADMONISH	264b	
	יגעה	WEARYING	388b	
	יותר	ADVANTAGE	452c	
	להג	STUDY	529c	
	קץ	END	894a	1
	רבה	BECOME MANY	915c	1 e4
12 13	ירא	FEAR	431c	3 b
	כל	ALL	482d	2 ba
	סוף	END	693a	
12 14	אם	IF	50a	1 b1
	בוא	COME	99a	1
	טוב	PLEASANT	374d	0 a
	עלם	CONCEAL	761a	1
	מעשה	DEED	795d	1 a3
	רע	EVIL	948c	0 a
	משפט	JUDGMENT	1048c	1 c

SONG OF SOLOMON

Ch v.	Heb	Eng	Page	Sec
1 1	שיר	SONG	1010b	1
	שלמה	SOLOMON	1024d	
1 2	דוד	LOVE	187c	3
	טוב	PLEASANT	374c	6
	יין	WINE	406d	E
	ל	TO	514c	5 fb
	מן	FROM	580d	3 ba
	נשק	KISS	676b	
	נשיקה	KISS	676c	
	פה	MOUTH	804d	1 b
1 3	אהב	LOVE	12d	1
	טוב	PLEASANT	373d	1 c
	כן	SO	487b	3 f
	עלמה	YOUNG WOMAN	761c	
	ריק	MAKE EMPTY	938a	
	שמן	OIL	1032b	2 b
	שמן	OIL	1032b	2 b
1 4	אהב	LOVE	12d	1
	בוא	COME	99a	1
	דוד	LOVE	187c	3
	זכר	REMEMBER	271a	3 b
	חדר	CHAMBER	293c	
	מישר	LEVEL	449d	3
	רוץ	RUN	930b	1
1 5	אהל	TENT	13d	1
	בת	DAUGHTER	123c	1 i
	יריעה	CURTAIN	438c	
	נאוה	COMELY	610a	1
	קדר	KEDAR	871b	1
	שחר	BLACK	1007b	
	שלמה	SOLOMON	1024d	
1 6	אם	MOTHER	51d	1
	חרה	BURN	354b	
	חרר	BE HOT	359c	2
	כרם	VINEYARD	501d	1
	ל	TO	513c	5 ca
	נטר	KEEP	643c	2
	שום	TO PLACE	964a	3 d
	ש	WHO	980a	4 d
	ש	WHO	980a	3 b
	שזף	CATCH SIGHT OF	1004d	
	שחרחר	BLACKISH	1007b	
	שמש	SUN	1039b	1

Ch v.	Heb	Eng	Page	Sec
1 7	אהב	LOVE	12d	1
	איכה	WHERE	32d	3
	חבר	UNITED	288d	2 c
	טעה	WANDER	380d	
	מה	HOW	554b	4 d
	נפש	SOUL	660d	6 e
	עדר	FLOCK	727d	1 c
	עטה	WRAP ONESELF	742a	
	עטה	GRASP	*742a	
	צהר	MIDDAY	843d	1
	רבץ	LIE DOWN	918c	
	רעה	TEND	944d	1 a
	ש	WHO	979d	1
	ש	WHO	980a	3 b
1 8	ב	IN	88b	1 2a
	גדיה	KIDS	152a	
	ה	THE	207b	1 b
	יפה	BEAUTIFUL	421c	
	ל	TO	515d	5 ia
	ל	TO	516a	5 ib
	עקב	HEEL	784b	B
	רעה	TEND	944d	1 a
	משכן	DWELLING-PLACE	1016a	3 a
1 9	דמה	BE LIKE	198a	1
	סוסה	MARE	692d	
	פרעה	PHARAOH	829a	
	רכב	CHARIOT	939b	2
	רעיה	COMPANION	946b	
1 10	חרוז	STRING OF BEADS	354d	
	לחי	CHEEK	534c	2
	נאה	BE COMELY	610a	1
	צואר	NECK	848c	1
	תור	PLAIT	1064c	
1 11	ה	THE	207d	1 e
	זהב	GOLD	263c	1
	נקדה	POINT	667a	
	עם	WITH	767b	1 a
	תור	PLAIT	1064c	
1 12	נרד	NARD	669d	
	נתן	GIVE	679c	1 t
	מסב	THAT WHICH SUR-ROUNDS	687b	2
	עד	UNTIL	725b	2 2d
	ריח	SCENT	926b	1
	ש	WHO	980a	3 a
1 13	דוד	BELOVED	187c	1
	לון	LODGE	533d	1 c
	מר	MYRRH	600d	
	צרור	BUNDLE	865c	
	ריח	SCENT	926b	1
	שד	BREAST	994c	1
1 14	אשכול	CLUSTER	79b	2
	דוד	BELOVED	187c	1
	כפר	HENNA	499a	
	עינגדי	ENGEDI	745b	
1 15	יונה	DOVE	401d	
	יפה	BEAUTIFUL	421c	
	עין	EYE	744c	1 p
	רעיה	COMPANION	946b	
1 16	דוד	BELOVED	187c	1
	יפה	BEAUTIFUL	421c	
	נעים	DELIGHTFUL	653d	2
	ערש	COUCH	793b	
	רענן	LUXURIANT	947c	
1 17	ארז	CEDAR	72c	1 a
	בית	HOUSE	108d	1 ab
	ברות	CYPRESS	141d	
	קורה	RAFTER	900a	
	רחיט	BOARDS	923d	
2 1	חבצלת	MEADOW-SAFFRON	287c	
	שרון	SHARON	450a	1
	עמק	VALE	771a	
	ש	WHO	980a	4 d
	שושן	LILY	1004c	
2 2	בין	INTERVAL	107b	1
	בת	DAUGHTER	123c	2
	חוח	BRIER	296b	1 a
	כן	SO	486b	2 ad a
	רעיה	COMPANION	946b	
	ש	WHO	980a	4 d
	שושן	LILY	1004c	
2 3	בין	INTERVAL	107b	1
	בן	SON	121b	3
	דוד	BELOVED	187c	1
	ו	AND	254a	2 a
	חמד	DESIRE	326c	
	חך	PALATE	335b	C
	יער	WOOD	420d	F
	ישב	SIT	442c	1 a
	כן	SO	486b	2 ad a
	מתוק	SWEET	608d	1
	תפוח	APPLE-TREE	656b	1
	צל	SHADOW	853b	2
	ריח	SCENT	926b	1
2 4	אהבה	LOVE	13b	1
	בוא	COME	99a	1
	בית	HOUSE	109a	1 ae 4
	דגל	STANDARD	186b	
	יין	WINE	406c	D
	על	UPON	755d	2 5
2 5	אהבה	LOVE	13b	1
	אשישה	RAISEN-CAKE	84b	
	חלה	BE WEAK	317d	2
	תפוח	APPLES	656b	2
	סמך	LEAN	702b	
2 6	חבק	CLASP	287d	

Ch	v.	Heb	Eng	Page	Sec
		שמאל	LEFT	969d	2
		תחת	UNDERNEATH	1065b	2 1
		אהבה	LOVE	13b	1
2	7	אילה	HIND	19b	
		אם	IF	50b	1 b2
		בת	DAUGHTER	123b	1 i
		ה	THE	208b	1 ha
		חפץ	DELIGHT IN	342d	1 c
		מה	WHAT	553c	2 ab
		עד	UNTIL	725a	2 1 a b
		עור	ROUSE ONESELF	735a	
		עור	ROUSE ONESELF	735c	1
		צבי	GAZELLE	840b	
2	8	שדה	FIELD	961b	1 c
		שבע	SWEAR	989d	2
		גבעה	HILL	149a	3
		דוד	BELOVED	187c	1
		דלג	LEAP	194c	
		זה	THIS	261c	4 g
		קול	VOICE	877a	1 f
2	9	קפץ	DRAW TOGETHER	891d	1
		או	OR	14d	1
		איל	HART	19b	
		אחר	BEHIND	29d	2 a
		דוד	BELOVED	187c	1
		דמה	BE LIKE	198a	
		זה	THIS	261c	4 g
		חלון	WINDOW	319d	
		חרכים	LATTICE	355b	
		כתל	WALL	508c	
		מן	OUT OF	579b	2 ab
		צבי	GAZELLE	840b	
		צוץ	GAZE	847d	
		שגח	GAZE	993b	
		אשיח	ADDENDA ET CORRIGENDA	1121a	
2	10	אמר	SAY	56b	1
		דוד	BELOVED	187c	1
		הלך	WALK	231d	1 1d 5h
		יפה	BEAUTIFUL	421c	
		ל	TO	516a	5 ib
		רעיה	COMPANION	946b	
2	11	גשם	RAIN	177c	
		הלך	WALK	231d	1 1d 5h
		הלך	WALK	232c	1 3
		חלף	PASS ON OR AWAY	322a	1 b
		ל	TO	516a	5 ib
		סתו	WINTER	711a	
		עבר	PASS OVER	*717d	4 d
2	12	זמיר	SONG	274c	
		זמיר	TRIMMING	274d	
		נגע	REACH	619c	3
		נצן	BLOSSOM	665b	
		עת	TIME	773c	1 b
		קול	VOICE	877a	1 e
		ראה	TO SEE	908c	1 c
		תר	TURTLE-DOVE	1076a	
2	13	גפן	VINE	172c	
		הלך	WALK	231d	1 1d 5h
		חנט	SPICE	334c	1
		יפה	BEAUTIFUL	421c	
		ל	TO	516a	5 ib
		נתן	GIVE	679c	1 s
		סמדר	BLOSSOM OF GRAPE	701d	
		פגה	EARLY FIG	803a	
		רעיה	COMPANION	946b	
		תאנה	SINKING	1061a	1
2	14	מדרגה	STEEP PLACE	201c	
		חגוים	PLACES OF CONCEALMENT	291c	
		יונה	DOVE	401d	
		נאוה	COMELY	610a	1
		סלע	CRAG	701a	
		סתר	COVERING	712a	2 a
		ערב	SWEET	787a	
		קול	VOICE	876d	1 a
		מראה	VISION	909c	1 b
		שמע	HEAR	1034c	1 a
2	15	אחז	GRASP	28b	
		חבל	ACT CORRUPTLY	287c	
		כרם	VINEYARD	501d	
		ל	TO	515b	5 hb a
		סמדר	BLOSSOM OF GRAPE	701d	
		שועל	FOX	1043c	
2	16	דוד	BELOVED	187c	1
		ל	TO	513b	5 ba
		רעה	TEND	945b	2 b
		שושן	LILY	1004c	
2	17	איל	HART	19b	
		בתר	PART	144b	2
		דוד	BELOVED	187c	1
		דמה	BE LIKE	198a	
		ל	TO	516a	5 ic
		נום	ESCAPE	630d	3
		סבב	TURN ABOUT	685c	1 a
		עד	UNTIL	725a	2 1 a b
		פוח	BREATHE	806b	
		צבי	GAZELLE	840b	
		צל	SHADOW	853b	1
		רוח	BREATH	*924c	2 a
3	1	אהב	LOVE	12d	1
		בקש	SEEK	134c	1 b
		לילה	NIGHT	539a	1
		מצא	FIND	593a	1 b-
		נפש	SOUL	660d	6 e
		ש	WHO	979d	1
		משכב	COUCH	1012d	1
3	2	אהב	LOVE	12d	1
		בקש	SEEK	134c	1 b
		מצא	FIND	593a	1 b
		נא	PART OF ENTREATY	609b	3 a
		נפש	SOUL	660d	6 e
		סבב	GO AROUND	686b	3
		רחב	PLAZA	932b	
		רחב	PLAZA	932b	
		ש	WHO	980a	4 d
		שוק	STREET	1003b	
3	3	אהב	LOVE	12d	1
		מצא	FIND	593b	3 a
		נפש	SOUL	660d	6 e
		שמר	KEEP	1036c	1 b
3	4	אהב	LOVE	12d	1
		אחז	GRASP	28b	
		אם	MOTHER	51d	1
		אשר	THAT	83b	8 aa
		בוא	COME	99a	1
		הרה	CONCEIVE	247d	1
		חדר	CHAMBER	293d	
		מעט	A FEW	590b	2 a
		מצא	FIND	593a	1 b
		נפש	SOUL	660d	6 e
		עבר	PASS OVER	717c	2
		עד	UNTIL	724d	2 1 aa
		רפה	SINK	952a	2
3	5	אהבה	LOVE	13b	1
		אילה	HIND	19b	
		אם	IF	50b	1 b2
		בת	DAUGHTER	123b	1 i
		ה	THE	208b	1 ha
		חפץ	DELIGHT IN	342d	1 c
		מה	WHAT	553c	2 ab
		סבב	GO AROUND	685d	2 c
		עד	UNTIL	725a	2 1 a b
		עור	ROUSE ONESELF	735a	
		עור	ROUSE ONESELF	735c	1
		צבי	GAZELLE	840b	
		שדה	FIELD	961b	1 c
		שבע	SWEAR	989d	2
3	6	אבקה	POWDERS	7c	
		מדבר	WILDERNESS	185a	3
		זה	THIS	261c	4 b
		לבנה	FRANKINCENSE	526d	
		מי	WHO	566b	A
		מי	WHO	567b	F e
		מר	MYRRH	600d	
		עלה	GO UP	748b	1 a
		עשן	SMOKE	798c	1 c
		קטר	MAKE SACRIFICES SMOKE	883a	
		רכל	GO ABOUT	940b	
		תמורה	COLUMN	1071d	
3	7	גבור	STRONG	150b	2
		מטה	COUCH	641d	
		סביב	ROUND ABOUT	687a	1 cb
		ששים	SIXTY	995d	
		שלמה	SOLOMON	1024d	
3	8	אחז	GRASP	28b	
		ירך	THIGH	437d	1 a
		מלחמה	WAR	536b	
		לילה	NIGHT	539a	1
		למד	LEARN	540d	
		מן	ON ACCOUNT OF	580b	2 f
		על	UPON	753a	2 1 aa
3	9	אפריון	SEDAN	68b	
		לבנון	LEBANON	527b	
		מן	OUT OF	579b	2 ba
		עשה	DO	794d	2 1g
		שלמה	SOLOMON	1024d	
3	10	אהבה	LOVE	13c	1
		ארגמן	PURPLE THREAD	71b	2
		בת	DAUGHTER	123b	1 i
		עמוד	PILLAR	765b	3
		עשה	DO	794c	2 1g
		מרכב	CHARIOT	939c	3
		רפידה	SUPPORT	951c	
3	11	אם	MOTHER	51d	1
		בת	DAUGHTER	123b	1 i
		חתנה	MARRIAGE	368d	
		יום	DAY	398d	2 f
		לב	HEART	525c	2 9a
		עטר	CROWN	742d	
		עטרה	CROWN	742d	1
		ציון	ZION	851b	
		ראה	TO SEE	908a	8 a5
		שמחה	JOY	970d	1
		שלמה	SOLOMON	1024d	
4	1	בעד	BEHIND	126d	2
		יונה	DOVE	401d	
		יפה	BEAUTIFUL	421c	
		מן	FROM	578b	1 a
		עדר	FLOCK	727d	1 b
		עין	EYE	744c	1 p
		עז	SHE-GOAT	777c	5
		צמה	WOMANS VEIL	855d	
		רעיה	COMPANION	946b	
		שער	HAIR	972b	2
4	2	עדר	FLOCK	727c	1 a
		עלה	GO UP	748d	3
		קצב	CUT OFF	891d	
		רחצה	WASHING	934d	
		שכול	BEREAVED	1014a	
		שן	TOOTH	1042a	1 a
4	3	בעד	BEHIND	126d	2
		מדבר	MOUTH	184c	1
		חוט	THREAD	296c	1
		נאוה	COMELY	610a	1
		נאוה	SEEMLY	*610a	2
		פלח	CLEAVAGE	812a	2
		צמה	WOMANS VEIL	855d	
		רמון	POMEGRANATE	941d	2
		רקה	THE TEMPLE	956d	
		שפה	SPEECH	973d	1 e
		שני	SCARLET	1040c	
4	4	אלף	THOUSAND	48d	1 a
		בנה	BUILD	124c	1 az
		גבור	STRONG	150b	1
		מגדל	TOWER	154a	1
		מגדל	TOWER	154a	1
		מגן	SHIELD	171c	
		דוד	DAVID	188b	G
		צואר	NECK	848c	1
		שלט	SHIELD	1020d	
		תלה	HANG	1068a	1
		תלפיות	COURSES OF STONES	1069b	
4	5	צביה	GAZELLE	840b	
		רעה	TEND	945b	2 b
		שד	BREAST	994c	1
		שושן	LILY	1004c	
		תואם	TWIN	1060d	
4	6	גבעה	HILL	149a	4
		גבעה	HILL	149a	3
		הלך	WALK	231d	1 1d 5h
		הר	MOUNTAIN	250c	1
		ל	TO	516a	5 ib
		לבנה	FRANKINCENSE	526d	
		מר	MYRRH	600d	
		נום	ESCAPE	630d	3
		עד	UNTIL	725a	2 1 a b
		פוח	BREATHE	806b	
		צל	SHADOW	853b	1
		רוח	BREATH	924c	2 a
4	7	יפה	BEAUTIFUL	421c	
		כל	ALL	481b	1 a
		מום	BLEMISH	548c	1 a
		רעיה	COMPANION	946b	
4	8	אמנה	AMANAH	53d	2
		ארי	LION	71d	
		הר	MOUNTAIN	250c	1 g
		חרמון	HERMON	356d	
		חרמון	HERMON	356d	
		כלה	BRIDE	483c	2 a
		לבנון	LEBANON	527a	
		לבנון	LEBANON	*527a	
		נמר	LEOPARD	649d	
		מענה	DEN	733a	1
		שניר	SENIR	972a	
		שור	BEHOLD	1003d	1
4	9	אחות	SISTER	27d	2
		כלה	BRIDE	483c	2 a
		לבב	ENCOURAGE	525d	
		עין	EYE	744c	1 p
		ענק	NECKLACE	778d	
		צורון	NECKLACE	848d	
4	10	אחות	SISTER	27d	2
		בשם	SPICE	142a	2
		דוד	LOVE	187c	3
		טוב	PLEASING	373b	1
		יין	WINE	406d	E
		יפה	BE BEAUTIFUL	421b	
		כלה	BRIDE	483c	2 a
		מה	HOW	553c	2 b
		ריח	SCENT	926b	1
		שמן	OIL	1032b	2 b
4	11	דבש	HONEY	185c	
		כלה	BRIDE	483c	2 a
		לבנון	LEBANON	*527a	
		לבנון	LEBANON	527b	
		לשון	TONGUE	546b	1 a
		נטף	DROP	643a	
		נפת	HONEY FROM THE COMB	661d	
		ריח	SCENT	926b	1
		ריח	SCENT	926b	1
		שפה	SPEECH	974a	1 e
		תחת	UNDERNEATH	1065c	2 1b
4	12	אחות	SISTER	27d	2
		גן	GARDEN	171a	
		חלב	MILK	316c	A 4
		חתם	SEAL	367d	2
		יונה	DOVE	401d	
		כלה	BRIDE	483c	2 a
		נעל	LOCK	653a	
		מעין	SPRING	746a	
		פרי	FRUIT	826b	1
4	13	כפר	HENNA	499a	
		מגד	EXCELLENCE	550c	
		נרד	NARD	669d	
		עם	WITH	767b	1 a
		פרדס	PRESERVE	825d	
		רמון	POMEGRANATE	941d	1
		שלח	SPROUT	1019c	2
4	14	אהל	ALOE	14d	2
		בשם	SPICE	142a	2
		כרכם	SAFFRON	501b	

Ch	v.	Heb	Eng	Page	Sec
		לבנה	FRANKINCENSE	526d	
		מר	MYRRH	600d	
		נרד	NARD	669d	
		עם	WITH	767b	1 a
		עץ	TREE	781c	1 a
		קנה	STALK	889d	3
		קנמון	CINNAMON	890a	
		ראש	HEAD	911b	5
4	15	באר	WELL	91d	1
		גן	GARDEN	171a	
		חי	ALIVE	312b	1 f
		לבנן	LEBANON	*527a	
		לבנן	LEBANON	527a	
		נזל	FLOW	633d	1
		מעין	SPRING	746a	
4	16	בשם	BALSAM	142a	2
		גן	GARDEN	171a	
		דוד	BELOVED	187c	1
		תימן	SOUTH	412d	2
		ל	TO	511b	1 ga
		מגד	EXCELLENCE	550c	
		נזל	DISTIL	633d	2
		עור	ROUSE ONESELF	735a	
		פוח	BREATHE	806b	1
		פרי	FRUIT	826b	1
		צפון	NORTH	861a	
		רוח	BREATH	*924d	2 a
5	1	אחות	SISTER	27d	2
		ארה	PLUCK	71c	
		בשם	BALSAM	142a	2
		גן	GARDEN	171a	
		דבש	HONEY	*185b	
		דבש	HONEY	185c	
		דוד	LOVE	*187c	3
		דוד	LOVE	187c	3
		חלב	MILK	316c	A 3
		יין	WINE	406d	E
		יער	HONEYCOMB	421a	
		כלה	BRIDE	483c	2 a
		ל	TO	511b	1 ga
		מר	MYRRH	600d	
		עם	WITH	767b	1
		רע	FRIEND	946a	1
		שכר	BE DRUNK	1016b	
		שתה	DRINK	1059b	1 a
5	2	אחות	SISTER	27d	2
		דוד	BELOVED	187c	1
		דפק	KNOCK	200c	
		טל	NIGHT-MIST	378c	
		יונה	DOVE	401d	
		ישן	SLEEPING	445d	
		לב	HEART	524c	2 1
		מלא	FILL	570b	1
		עור	ROUSE ONESELF	735a	
		פתח	OPEN	835a	
		קול	VOICE	877a	1 f
		קוצות	LOCKS OF HAIR	881b	
		רסיס	DROP	944a	
		רעיה	COMPANION	946b	
		ש	WHO	980a	3 b
		תאם	BE DOUBLE	1061a	
		תם	COMPLETE	1071a	1
5	3	איככה	HOW	32d	
		טנף	SOIL	380d	
		כתנת	TUNIC	509a	
		לבש	PUT ON	527d	A
		פשט	STRIP OFF	833a	1
		רחץ	WASH OFF	934c	1
5	4	דוד	BELOVED	187c	1
		המה	MURMUR	242b	2
		חר	HOLE	359d	
		ל	TO	*515a	5 g
		מן	OUT OF	579b	2 ab
		מעה	BELLY	589a	4
		על	UPON	756d	2 7 a c
		שלח	SEND	1018a	3 a
5	5	דוד	BELOVED	187c	1
		כף	HOLLOW	497a	4 e
		מר	MYRRH	600d	
		מר	MYRRH	600d	
		נטף	DROP	643a	
		מנעול	BOLT	653b	
		עבר	PASS OVER	717d	4 a
		פתח	OPEN	835a	
		אצבע	FINGER	840c	1 d
5	6	בקש	SEEK	134c	1 b
		דוד	BELOVED	187c	1
		חמק	TURN AWAY	330b	
		לבב	ENCOURAGE	*525d	
		מצא	FIND	593a	1 b
		נפש	SOUL	660d	4 a
		עבר	PASS OVER	718b	6 b
		פתח	OPEN	835a	
		קרא	CALL	895d	5 c
5	7	מצא	FIND	593b	3 a
		נכה	SMITE	645c	1 b
		סבב	GO AROUND	685d	2 c
		פצע	BRUISE	822d	
		רדיד	WIDE WRAPPER	921d	
		שמר	KEEP	1036c	1 b
5	8	אהבה	LOVE	13b	1
		בת	DAUGHTER	123b	1 i
		דוד	BELOVED	187c	1
		חלה	BE WEAK	317d	2
		מה	WHAT	553c	2 ab
		מצא	FIND	593b	3 a
5	9	שבע	SWEAR	989d	2
		דוד	BELOVED	187c	1
		יפה	BEAUTIFUL	421c	
		מה	WHAT	553a	1 da
		ש	WHO	980a	3 aa
		שבע	SWEAR	989d	2
5	10	אדם	RED	10b	
		דגל	LOOK	186b	
		דוד	BELOVED	187c	1
		מן	THAN	582c	6 b
		צח	DAZZLING	850a	
		רבבה	MULTITUDE	914b	
5	11	כתם	GOLD	508d	1
		ערב	RAVEN	788b	
		פז	REFINED GOLD	808a	
		קוצות	LOCKS OF HAIR	881b	
		שחר	BLACK	1007b	
		תלתלים	DATE-PANICLE	1068b	
5	12	אפיק	CHANNEL	67d	
		חלב	MILK	316c	B
		ישב	SIT	442d	1 d
		מלאת	SETTING	571c	
		עין	EYE	744c	1 p
		רחץ	WASH OFF	934c	2
5	13	בשם	BALSAM	142a	2
		גדל	GROW UP	152b	1
		מגדל	TOWER	154a	3
		לחי	CHEEK	534d	2
		מר	MYRRH	600d	
		נטף	DROP	643a	
		עבר	PASS OVER	717d	4 a
		ערוגה	GARDEN TERRACE	788c	
		מרקח	SPICE	955c	
		שושן	LILY	1004c	
5	14	מלא	FILL	570d	
		מעה	BELLY	589a	6
		ספיר	SAPPHIRE	705d	
		עלף	COVER	763b	
		עשת	PLATE	799d	
		שן	IVORY	1042b	2
		תרשיש	YELLOW JASPAR	1076d	
5	15	אדן	BASE	10d	1
		ארז	CEDAR	72c	1 a
		בחר	CHOOSE	104b	7
		יסד	BE FOUNDED	414a	
		לבנן	LEBANON	527b	
		עמוד	PILLAR	765b	1
		פז	REFINED GOLD	808a	
		מראה	VISION	909c	1 b
		שוק	LEG	1003b	1
		שש	ALABASTER	1010d	
5	16	בת	DAUGHTER	123b	1 i
		דוד	BELOVED	187c	1
		זה	THIS	261b	3
		מחמד	DESIRE	327a	
		חך	PALATE	335b	D
		כל	ALL	481b	1 a
		ממתקים	SWEETNESS	609c	
		רע	FRIEND	946a	1
6	1	אגוז	NUTS	8b	
		בקש	SEEK	134c	1 b
		דוד	BELOVED	187c	1
		הלך	WALK	230d	1 1 d 3 b
		יפה	BEAUTIFUL	421c	
		פנה	TURN	815b	1 a
6	2	בשם	BALSAM-TREE	142a	2
		גן	GARDEN	171a	
		דוד	BELOVED	187c	1
		ל	TO	511b	1 ga
		לקט	GATHER UP	544d	1
		ערוגה	GARDEN TERRACE	788c	
		רעה	TEND	945b	2 b
		שושן	LILY	1004c	
6	3	דוד	BELOVED	187c	1
		ל	TO	513b	5 ba
		רעה	TEND	945b	2 b
		שושן	LILY	1004c	
6	4	אים	TERRIBLE	33d	
		דגל	SET UP STANDARD	186b	
		יפה	BEAUTIFUL	421c	
		נאוה	COMELY	610a	1
		רעיה	COMPANION	946b	
		תרצה	TIRZAH	953d	2 cb a
		נגד	IN FRONT	617d	2 cb a
6	5	סבב	TURN ABOUT	686c	1 a
		עדר	FLOCK	727d	1 b
		עז	SHE-GOAT	777c	5
		רהב	ACT STORMILY	923b	
		רהב	BE LARGE	931c	2
		שער	HAIR	972b	2
6	6	עדר	FLOCK	727c	1 a
		עלה	GO UP	748d	3
		רחל	EWE	932d	
		רחצה	WASHING	954d	
		שכל	BEREAVED	1014a	
		שן	TOOTH	1042a	1
		תאם	BE DOUBLE	1061a	2
6	7	בעד	BEHIND	126d	2
		פלח	CLEAVAGE	812a	2
		צמה	WOMANS VEIL	855d	
		רמן	POMEGRANATE	941d	2
		רקה	THE TEMPLE	956d	
6	8	חם	THEY	241c	4 a
		מלכה	QUEEN	573d	
		מספר	NUMBER	708d	1 a
		עלמה	YOUNG WOMAN	761c	
		פלגש	CONCUBINE	811c	1
		שמנים	EIGHTY	1033b	
6	9	אם	MOTHER	51c	1
		אשר	GO STRAIGHT	80d	4
		בת	DAUGHTER	123c	2
		בר	PURE	141a	1
		הוא	HE, SHE, IT	216b	4 a
		חלל	PRAISE	238a	1
		יונה	DOVE	401d	
		מלכה	QUEEN	573d	
		פלגש	CONCUBINE	811c	1
		תם	COMPLETE	1071a	1
6	10	אים	TERRIBLE	33d	
		בר	PURE	141a	1
		דגל	SET UP STANDARD	186b	
		זה	THIS	261c	4 b
		חמה	HEAT	329a	2
		יפה	BEAUTIFUL	421c	
		כ	LIKE	454a	1 c2
		כמו	LIKE	455d	1 a
		לבנה	MOON	526b	
		מי	WHO	567b	F e
		שחר	DAWN	1007c	
		שקף	LOOK DOWN	1054c	
6	11	אב	FRESHNESS	1a	
		גנה	GARDEN	171b	
		גפן	VINE	172c	
		ה	INTERROG PART	210b	2 a
		נחל	WADY	636c	2
		נצץ	BLOSSOM	665b	
		פרח	BUD	827a	
		ראה	TO SEE	908a	8 a5
		רמון	POMEGRANATE	941d	1
6	12	נדיב	NOBLE	622a	3
		נפש	SOUL	660a	4 b1
		עם	PEOPLE	*766c	
		מרכבה	CHARIOT	939d	
7	1	מחולה	DANCING	298b	1
		חזה	SEE	302b	1 c
		מחנים	MAHANAIM	334b	
		שוב	TURN BACK	997a	1
		שולמית	SHULAMMITE	1002c	
7	2	בת	DAUGHTER	123a	4
		חלי	ORNAMENT	318d	
		חמוק	CURVING	330b	
		יפה	BE BEAUTIFUL	421b	
		ירך	THIGH	437d	1 a
		כמו	LIKE	455d	1 a
		מה	HOW	553c	2 b
		נדיב	NOBLE	622a	1
		נעל	SANDAL	653a	
		מעשה	DEED	796a	2 1
		פעם	BEAT	822a	1 b
7	3	אגן	BASIN	8c	2
		בטן	BELLY	105d	1 a
		חסר	LACK	341b	2
		מזג	MIXTURE	561a	
		סהר	ROUNDNESS	690c	
		סוג	FENCE ABOUT	691b	
		ערמה	HEAP	790d	
		שושן	LILY	1004c	
		שר	NAVEL-STRING	1057a	
7	4	צביה	GAZELLE	840b	
		שד	BREAST	994c	1
		תואם	TWIN	1060d	
7	5	אף	NOSE	60a	1
		בתרבים	BATH-RABBIM	123d	
		ברכה	POOL	140a	
		מגדל	TOWER	154a	1
		מגדל	TOWER	154a	1
		דמשק	DAMASCUS	199d	
		חשבון	HESHBON	364a	
		לבנן	LEBANON	527a	
		עין	EYE	744c	1 p
		פנה	FACE	816b	16
		צואר	NECK	848c	1
		צפה	KEEP WATCH	859c	
		רב	MUCH	913b	1 c
		שן	IVORY	1042b	2
7	6	אסר	TIE	63d	3
		ארגמן	PURPLE THREAD	71b	2
		דלה	HAIR	195d	
		כרמל	CARMEL	502b	1
		כרמיל	CRIMSON	502b	
		רהט	LOCK	923d	
7	7	אהבה	LOVE	13b	1
		יפה	BE BEAUTIFUL	421b	
		נעם	BE DELIGHTFUL	653c	
		תענוג	DAINTINESS	772c	3
7	8	אשכול	CLUSTER	79a	1
		דמה	BE LIKE	198a	2
		זה	THIS	260d	2 a
		קומה	HEIGHT	879b	1
		שד	BREAST	994c	1
		תמר	PALM-TREE	1071c	
7	9	אחז	GRASP	28b	
		אף	NOSE	60a	1
		אשכול	CLUSTER	79a	1
		גפן	VINE	172c	
		תפוח	APPLES	656b	2
		סנסנים	FRUIT-STALK	703b	
		ריח	SCENT	926b	1
		שד	BREAST	994c	1
		תמר	PALM-TREE	1071c	
7	10	דבב	GLIDE OVER	179a	
		דוד	BELOVED	187c	1

Ch	v.	Heb	Eng	Page	Sec
		הלך	WALK	232c	1 3
		הלך	WALK	*236a	1 b
		חך	PALATE	335b	D
		טוב	PLEASANT	373d	1 b
		יין	WINE	406c	D
		יין	WINE	406d	E
		ישן	SLEEPING	445d	
		מישר	LEVEL	449d	1
		ל	TO	516c	5 jb
		שפה	SPEECH	974a	1 g
7	11	דוד	BELOVED	187c	1
		על	UPON	757c	2 7 c c
		תשוקה	LONGING	1003c	
7	12	דוד	BELOVED	187c	1
		כפר	VILLAGE	499a	1
7	13	אם	IF	50d	2 ba
		גפן	VINE	172c	1
		ל	TO	511b	1 ga
		נצץ	BLOSSOM	665b	
		סמדר	BLOSSOM OF GRAPE	701d	
		פרח	BUD	827a	
		פתח	OPEN	835c	3
		רמון	POMEGRANATE	941d	1
		שכם	START EARLY	1014c	
7	14	גם	ALSO	169b	1
		דוד	BELOVED	187c	1
		חדש	NEW	294b	A
		ישן	OLD	446a	
		מגד	EXCELLENCE	550c	
		נתן	GIVE	679c	1 s
		פתח	OPENING	835c	
		צפן	HIDE	860c	1
		ריח	SCENT	926b	1
8	1	אם	MOTHER	51d	1
		אם	MOTHER	51d	1
		בוז	DESPISE	100b	
		גם	YEA	169c	3
		ינק	SUCK	413b	
		מצא	FIND	593b	3 a
		נשק	KISS	676b	
		נתן	GIVE	678d	1 f
		שד	BREAST	994c	1
8	2	אם	MOTHER	51d	1
		יין	WINE	406c	D
		למד	LEARN	540d	
		מן	OUT OF	579b	2 bb
		נהג	DRIVE	624b	1
		עסיס	SWEET WINE	779b	
		רמון	POMEGRANATE	941d	2
		רקח	SPICE	955c	
		שקה	GIVE TO DRINK	1052c	2
8	3	חבק	CLASP	287d	1
		מי	WHO	567b	F e
		שמאל	LEFT	969d	2
		תחת	UNDERNEATH	1065b	2 1
8	4	אהבה	LOVE	13b	1
		בת	DAUGHTER	123b	1 i
		ה	THE	208b	1 ha
		חפץ	DELIGHT IN	342d	1 c
		מה	WHAT	553c	2 ab
		מה	WHAT	553c	2 ab
		עד	UNTIL	725a	2 1a b
		עור	ROUSE ONESELF	735a	
		עור	ROUSE ONESELF	735c	1
		שבע	SWEAR	989d	2
8	5	אם	MOTHER	51c	1
		מדבר	WILDERNESS	185a	3
		דוד	BELOVED	187c	1
		זה	THIS	261c	4 b
		זית	OLIVE TREE	*268d	3
		חבל	BIND	286c	
		תפוח	APPLE-TREE	656b	1
		עור	ROUSE ONESELF	735a	
		עלה	GO UP	748b	1 a
		רפק	SUPPORT ONESELF	952d	
		שם	THERE	1027b	3
8	6	אהבה	LOVE	13b	1
		מאפליה	DEEP DARKNESS	66d	
		אש	FIRE	77d	6
		יה	YAH	219c	
		זרוע	ARM	283d	1 a
		חתם	SEAL	368b	
		לב	HEART	524c	2 1
		שלהבת	FLAME	529b	
		מות	DEATH	560d	3
		עז	STRONG	738c	
		קנאה	ZEAL	888b	1
		קשה	SEVERE	904d	2 b
		רשף	FLAME	958a	1
		שום	TO PLACE	963b	1 b
		שאול	SHEOL	982d	1
8	7	אהבה	LOVE	13b	1
		ב	IN	90b	3 3b
		בוז	DESPISE	100b	
		ה	THE	208b	1 ha
		הון	WEALTH	223c	1
		יכל	BE ABLE	407c	1
		כבה	QUENCH	459d	
		נתן	GIVE	679b	1 n
		שטף	OVERFLOW	1009a	1
8	8	אחות	SISTER	27d	1
		דבר	SPEAK	*181c	4 c
		דבר	SPEAK	181d	1
		קטן	SMALL	882a	1 a
		שד	BREAST	994c	1

Ch	v.	Heb	Eng	Page	Sec
8	9	ארז	CEDAR	72d	2
		בנה	BUILD	124c	1 az
		דלת	DOOR	*195a	2
		דלת	DOOR	195b	4
		חומה	WALL	327d	1 3
		טירה	ENCAMPMENT	377b	2
		לוח	BOARD	531d	2
		צור	CONFINE	848d	3
8	10	מגדל	TOWER	154a	1
		חומה	WALL	327d	1
		כ	LIKE	454b	1 d
		מצא	FIND	592d	1 a
		שד	BREAST	994c	1
		שלום	PEACE	1023b	6
8	11	ב	IN	90b	3 3b
		בעלהמן	BAAL-HAMON	128a	
		כסף	SILVER	494b	8 b
		נצר	KEEP	643c	2
		נתן	GIVE	679c	1 r
		פרי	FRUIT	826b	1
		שלמה	SOLOMON	1024d	
8	12	כרם	VINEYARD	501d	
		ל	TO	513c	5 ca
		נצר	KEEP	643c	2
		פנה	FACE	817a	24 a f
		פרי	FRUIT	826b	1
		שלמה	SOLOMON	1024d	
8	13	גן	GARDEN	171a	
		חבר	UNITED	288d	2 e
		קול	VOICE	876d	1 a
		קשב	ATTEND	904a	1
		שמע	HEAR	1034c	1 a
8	14	איל	HART	19b	
		ברח	FLEE	138a	3
		בשם	BALSAM-TREE	142a	2
		דוד	BELOVED	187c	1
		דמה	BE LIKE	198a	
		הר	MOUNTAIN	250c	1 h
		ל	TO	516a	5 ic
		צבי	GAZELLE	840b	

ISAIAH

Ch	v.	Heb	Eng	Page	Sec
1	1	אחז	AHAZ	28c	1
		אמוץ	AMOZ	55b	
		יותם	JOTHAM	222d	1
		ו	AND	252b	1 a
		חזה	SEE	302c	2
		חזון	VISION	303a	4
		חזקיהו	HEZEKIAH	306a	1
		ישעיהו	ISAIAH	447d	1
		עזיהו	UZZIAH	739d	1 a
		על	UPON	754d	2 1f g
1	2	אזן	HEAR	24b	1
		ארץ	EARTH	76a	1 h
		בן	SON	120b	1 c
		גדל	GROW UP	152b	1
		דבר	SPEAK	180d	1
		ה	THE	208d	1 i
		ו	AND	252b	1 a
		פשע	REBEL	833b	1
		רוח	BE WIDE	927a	
		שמי	HEAVENS	1030b	3
1	3	אבס	CRIB	7b	
		בין	DISCERN	107a	1 a
		בעל	OWNER	127b	1 1
		חמור	HE-ASS	331b	1
		ידע	KNOW	394a	2
		ידע	KNOW	394c	5
		קנה	ACQUIRE	889d	2
		ישראל	ISRAEL	975d	2 a3
		שור	A HEAD OF CATTLE	1004a	
1	4	אחור	HINDER SIDE	30c	A
		בן	SON	120b	1 c
		גוי	NATION	156d	1 b
		הוי	AH	222d	
		זור	BE A STRANGER	266d	
		זרע	SOWING	283b	5
		חטא	MISS A GOAL OR WAY	307a	2 b
		כבד	HEAVY	458a	1 a
		נאץ	CONTEMN	611a	
		עון	INIQUITY	731b	2 b
		קדוש	HOLY	872c	1 c
		רעע	BE EVIL	949d	2
		שחת	GO TO RUIN	1008c	2
1	5	דוי	FAINT	188d	
		חלי	SICKNESS	318b	
		יסף	ADD	415b	1
		ל	TO	516d	5 k
		לבב	HEART	524b	2 9b
		לב	HEART	524c	2 1
		מה	HOW	554b	4 f
		נכה	SMITE	646c	1
		סרה	A TURNING ASIDE	694c	2
		עוד	STILL	729a	1 ab
		ה	THE	208d	1 i
1	6	מזור	WOUND	*267a	
		זור	PRESS DOWN AND OUT	267a	
		חבורה	STRIPE	289a	
		חבש	BIND	290a	
		טרי	FRESH	382b	
		כף	SOLE OF FOOT	496d	3
		מן	FROM	581d	5 a

Ch	v.	Heb	Eng	Page	Sec
		מכה	BLOW	646d	1 c
		פצע	BRUISE	822d	
		רגל	FOOT	919d	1 a
1	7	רכך	BE TENDER	940a	
		שמן	OIL	1032b	2 c
		מתם	SOUNDNESS	1071b	
1	7	אדמה	GROUND	9c	1
		אכל	EAT	37c	4
		אש	FIRE	77c	1
		מהפכה	OVERTHROW	246b	
		זור	BE A STRANGER	266c	2 c
		נגד	IN FRONT	617c	2 b
		שרף	BURN	976d	2 a
		שממה	WASTE	1031b	
1	8	בת	DAUGHTER	123c	3
		יתר	BE LEFT OVER	451b	
		מלונה	LODGE	534a	
		נצר	GUARD	666a	5
		סכה	THICKET	697c	2
		מקשה	FIELD OF CUCUMBERS	903d	
1	9	דמה	BE LIKE	198a	
		היה	BECOME	226a	2 2c
		יתר	LEAVE OVER	451c	1 a
		לולא	IF NOT	530c	A
		מעט	A FEW	590c	2 e
		סדם	SODOM	690a	
		עמרה	GOMORRAH	771d	
		צבא	GOD OF WAR	839c	4 c
		שריד	SURVIVOR	975a	1
1	10	אזן	HEAR	24c	1
		אלהים	GOD	44d	4 c
		חרב	SWORD	352d	1 g
		תורה	INSTRUCTION	435d	1 b
		סדם	SODOM	690a	
		עמרה	GOMORRAH	771d	
		קצין	CHIEF	892c	3
1	11	איל	RAM	18a	2 g
		דם	BLOOD	197c	3 b
		זבח	SACRIFICE	257c	1 1
		חלב	FAT	317a	2 b
		חפץ	DELIGHT IN	342d	2 a
		כבש	LAMB	461a	1
		ל	TO	513a	5 ad
		מה	HOW	554a	4 d
		מריא	FATLING	597b	
		עלה	WHOLE BURNT OFFERING	750c	
		עתוד	HE-GOAT	800d	
		פר	YOUNG BULL	830d	2 d
		רב	MULTITUDE	914a	1
		שבע	SATISFIED	959c	3 b
1	12	בקש	SEEK	135a	5 a
		זה	THIS	260d	1 a
		חצר	ENCLOSURE	347a	3 b
		כי	WHEN	473a	2 a
		מי	WHO	566d	F c
		פנה	FACE	816d	2 2
		פנה	FACE	816d	2 2a
		ראה	TO SEE	908b	1 b
		רמס	TRAMPLE	942d	
1	13	און	TROUBLE	20a	3
		ו	AND	252a	1
		חדש	NEW MOON	294c	1
		יכל	BE ABLE	407d	1 h
		יסף	DO AGAIN	415c	2 a
		ל	TO	513a	5 ad
		מנחה	OFFERING	585a	3
		מנחה	OFFERING	585c	6
		עצרה	ASSEMBLY	783d	1
		קטרת	SMOKE	882d	1
		קרא	CALL	895c	3 a
		מקרא	CONVOCATION	896d	1
		שבת	SABBATH	992b	1 a
		שוא	EMPTINESS	996a	1
		תועבה	ABOMINATION	1073a	2 b
1	14	חדש	NEW MOON	294c	1
		טרח	BURDEN	382b	
		מועד	APPOINTED TIME	417c	1 b
		לאה	BE WEARY	521a	1
		נפש	SOUL	661a	6 f
		נשא	LIFT	671a	2 a
		על	UPON	753a	2 1b
		שנא	HATE	971c	2
1	15	אדם	BE RED	10b	
		אין	NOT	34b	2 c
		ב	IN	91a	5 3
		גם	YEA	169d	6
		דם	BLOOD	196d	2 f
		דם	BLOOD	197b	21
		כי	THOUGH	473c	2 ca
		כף	HOLLOW OF THE HAND	*496d	1 d7
		מלא	BE FULL	570a	1 b
		עין	EYE	744d	3 d
		עלם	CONCEAL	761a	
		תפלה	PRAYER	813c	1 a
		פרש	SPREAD OUT	831c	1 a
		רבה	BECOME MANY	915c	1 c
1	16	זכה	BE CLEAR	269a	
		חדל	CEASE	293a	2
		נגד	IN FRONT	617d	2 cb a
		מעלל	DEED	760b	1
		רחץ	WASH OFF	934c	2
		רע	EVIL	948a	3
1	17	אלמנה	WIDOW	48b	

Ch	v.	Heb	Eng	Page	Sec
		אשר	GO STRAIGHT	80d	3
		דרש	SEEK	205c	6
		חמוץ	THE RUTHLESS	330b	
		יטב	DO RIGHT	406a	5 a
		יתום	ORPHAN	450c	
		למד	LEARN	540d	
		ריב	STRIVE	936d	3
		שפט	JUDGE	1047d	3 b2
		שפט	JUDGE	1047d	3 b2
		משפט	JUDGEMNT	1048d	2 b
1	18	אדם	BE RED	10b	
		אם	IF	49d	1 a1 c
		ה	THE	207d	1 f
		חטא	SIN	308a	2
		חטאת	SIN	*308c	1 b
		יכח	REASON	407a	
		כתם	BE STAINED	*508d	
		לבן	MAKE WHITE	526b	2
		נא	PART OF EN-TREATY	609a	1
		צמר	WOOL	856a	
		שלג	SNOW	1017a	
		שני	SCARLET	1040c	
		תולע	SCARLET STUFF	1068d	2
1	19	אבה	BE WILLING	2c	
		טוב	GOOD THINGS	375c	1
		שמע	HEAR	1034a	1 o
1	20	אכל	EAT	37d	
		דבר	SPEAK	180d	1
		מאן	REFUSE	549b	
		מרה	BE REBELLIOUS	598a	2
		פה	MOUTH	805b	2 c
1	21	איכה	HOW	32d	2
		אמן	CONFIRM	53a	5
		ה	THE	208d	1 i
		זנה	COMMIT FORNICATION	276a	4
		לון	LODGE	533d	2
		מלא	FULL	571a	
		מלא	FULL	571a	
		עתה	NOW	774a	1 a
		צדק	RIGHTEOUSNESS	841d	D
		קריה	TOWN	900b	2
		רצח	MURDER	954a	
1	22	היה	BECOME	226b	2 2e
		כסף	SILVER	494a	1
		מהל	WEAKEN	554c	
		סבא	LIQUOR	685a	
		סיג	DROSS	691b	2
1	23	אהב	LOVE	13a	2
		אלמנה	WIDOW	48b	
		גנב	THIEF	170c	
		חבר	UNITED	288d	2 f
		יתום	ORPHAN	450c	
		כל	ALL	482a	1 db
		סרר	BE STUBBORN	710d	
		רדף	PURSUE	922d	2
		שר	CHIEFTAIN	978b	2 b
		שחד	BRIBE	1005a	
		שלמן	REWARD	1024b	
		שפט	JUDGE	1047d	3 b2
1	24	אביר	STRONG	7d	
		אדון	LORD	11a	1 2
		הוי	AH	222d	
		כן	SO	486d	3 d
		נאם	UTTERANCE	610b	2
		נוח	REST	628b	2
		נחם	CONSOLE ONESELF	637a	4
		נקם	AVENGE	668b	1 a
		צבא	GOD OF WAR	839c	4 c
		צר	ADVERSARY	865d	
1	25	בדיל	TIN	95d	1
		בר	LYE	141b	
		כ	LIKE	455c	B
		סיג	DROSS	691b	2
		צרף	SMELT	864b	1
		שוב	TURN BACK	999a	1 a
		בר	ADDENDA ET CORRIGENDA	1121d	
		נקה	ADDENDA ET CORRIGENDA	1125b	
1	26	ה	THE	208b	1 ha
		תחלה	BEGINNING	321b	
		יעץ	ADVISE	419d	
		כ	LIKE	455a	
		עיר	CITY	746c	1 i
		צדק	RIGHTEOUSNESS	841d	D
		קרא	CALL	896b	2 d1
		קריה	TOWN	900b	2
		ראשון	FIRST	911d	3 a1
		שוב	TURN BACK	999b	1 d
		שפט	JUDGE	1047c	1 b
1	27	פדה	RANSOM	804b	
		צדקה	RIGHTEOUSNESS	842b	2
		שוב	TURN BACK	997d	6 d
1	28	חטא	SINFUL	308b	2
		יחדו	TOGETHER	403c	B
		כלה	BE FINISHED	477d	2 c
		פשע	REBEL	833b	2
		שבר	BREAKING	991a	1
1	29	איל	TEREBINTH	18b	
		בוש	BE ASHAMED	101d	2
		בחר	CHOOSE	104a	2 b
		גנה	GARDEN	171b	
		חמד	DESIRE	326b	B
		חפר	BE ABASHED	344a	
1	30	מן	OUT OF	580b	2 ec
		אלה	TEREBINTH	18c	
		גנה	GARDEN	171b	
		כי	BECAUSE	473d	3 c
		מי	WATER	565c	1
		נבל	SINK	615c	2
		עלה	LEAF	750a	
1	31	אין	NOT	34d	4 c
		בער	BURN	129a	2
		חסן	STRONG	340d	
		יחדו	TOGETHER	403c	B
		כבה	QUENCH	459d	
		נעורת	TOW	654a	
		ניצוץ	SPARK	665b	
		פעל	DOING	821c	2 b
2	1	אמוץ	AMOZ	55b	
		דבר	WORD	182d	12a
		ו	AND	252c	1 a
		חזה	SEE	302c	2
2	2	אחרית	END	31b	B
		גבעה	HILL	149a	3
		גוי	NATION	156c	1
		גוי	NATION	156c	1
		חיה	BE	227c	3 5a
		הר	MOUNTAIN	249c	1a
		הר	MOUNTAIN	250d	1 m
		כון	BE FIRM	465c	2
		כל	ALL	481b	1a
		נהר	FLOW	625c	
		נשא	LIFT	671d	1a
		על	UPON	757b	2 7c ab
2	3	אלהים	GOD	44c	4 ba
		ארח	WAY	73b	3 b
		דרך	WAY	204d	6 ec
		הלך	WALK	233d	1 5b
		הלך	WALK	234a	1 5f 2
		הלך	WALK	234c	2 3a 1b
		הר	MOUNTAIN	249d	1a
		יצא	GO OUT	423c	1 g
		ירה	DIRECT	435c	5 c
		תורה	INSTRUCTION	436a	1
		מן	OUT OF	579b	2 bb
		עלה	GO UP	748b	1 c
		יעקב	JACOB	785a	2
		ציון	ZION	851c	
2	4	אל	TO	40b	4
		את	PLOUGHSHARE	88c	
		בין	INTERVAL	107c	1 d
		גוי	NATION	156c	1
		גוי	NATION	156c	1 c
		מזמרה	PRUNING-KNIFE	275a	
		חנית	SPEAR	333d	1
		יכח	DECIDE	407a	1
		כתת	BEAT	510a	2
		מלחמה	WAR	536b	
		למד	LEARN	540d	
		נשא	LIFT	670a	1a
		עוד	STILL	729a	1 ab
		שפט	JUDGE	1047c	2 a
2	5	אור	LIGHT	21d	1
		כי	BECAUSE	*474a	3
2	6	ילד	CHILD	409c	C
		כי	BECAUSE	473d	3 c
		כי	BECAUSE	474b	3 d
		נטש	FORSAKE	643d	2
		נכרי	FOREIGN	648d	1 b
		ספק	SLAP	706d	
		ענן	PRACTISE SOOTHSAYING	778b	
		צלמות	DEATH-SHADOW	853c	2 b
		קדם	FRONT	869c	1 b
		קסם	DIVINATION	890c	1
		קסם	PRACTICE OF DIVINATION	890d	1
2	7	אוצר	TREASURE	70a	1
		זהב	GOLD	262d	2
		זהב	GOLD	263c	1
		מלא	FILL	570b	1
		סוס	HORSE	692c	2
		קצה	END	892c	
		מרכבה	CHARIOT	939c	
2	8	אליל	WORTHLESSNESS	47c	B
		יד	HAND	389b	1 c
		מלא	FILL	570b	1
		מעשה	DEED	796a	2 a3
		אצבע	FINGER	840c	1 d
2	9	אדם	MAN	9c	2
		אל	NOT	39b	A c
		נשא	LIFT	671c	3 c
		שחח	BOW	1005d	
		שפל	BECOME LOW	1050a	1
2	10	גאון	EXALTATION	145a	1 b
		הדר	SPLENDOUR	214b	2
		טמן	HIDE	380c	
		עפר	DRY EARTH	779d	1 c
		ערץ	CAUSE TO TREMBLE	*791d	1
		פחד	DREAD	808c	1
		פנה	FACE	818b	26a
		צור	ROCK	849c	1a
2	11	אדם	MAN	9c	2
		גבהות	HAUGHTINESS	147b	
		ו	AND	252b	1 a
		יום	DAY	400d	7 g
		עין	EYE	744c	2 a
		רום	HEIGHT	927d	2
		שגב	BE HIGH	960c	3
		שחח	BOW	1005d	1
		שפל	BECOME LOW	1050a	1
2	12	גאה	PROUD	144b	
		יום	DAY	399a	3
		כל	ALL	*481c	1 b
		ל	TO	513b	5 ba
		נשא	LIFT	671d	1 a
		צבא	GOD OF WAR	839c	4 c
		רום	BE HIGH	926d	1 a
		שפל	BECOME LOW	1050a	1
2	13	אלון	OAK	47c	1 a
		ארז	CEDAR	72c	1 a
		בשן	BASHAN	143c	
		לבנון	LEBANON	527a	
		נשא	LIFT	671d	1 a
		רום	BE HIGH	926d	1 a
2	14	גבעה	HILL	149a	3
		הר	MOUNTAIN	250b	1 d
		נשא	LIFT	671d	1 a
		רום	BE HIGH	926d	1 a
2	15	בצר	MAKE INACCESSIBLE	131a	
		בצר	MAKE INACCESSIBLE	131a	
		גבה	HIGH	147a	1
		מגדל	TOWER	153d	1
		חומה	WALL	327b	1
		חומה	WALL	327c	1
2	16	אניה	A SHIP	58c	
		חמדה	DESIRE	326d	
		כל	ALL	*481c	1 b
		שכיה	SHIPS	967c	
		תרשיש	TARSHISH	1077a	1
2	17	אדם	MAN	9c	2
		גבהות	HAUGHTINESS	147b	
		יום	DAY	400d	7 g
		רום	HEIGHT	927d	2
		שגב	BE HIGH	960c	3
		שחח	BOW	1005d	1
		שפל	BECOME LOW	1050a	1
2	18	אליל	WORTHLESSNESS	47c	B
		חלף	PASS ON OR AWAY	322a	1 b
		כליל	WHOLE	483a	2 a
2	19	ארץ	EARTH	76a	1 b
		גאון	EXALTATION	145a	1 b
		הדר	SPLENDOUR	214b	2
		מחלה	HOLE	320a	
		עפר	DRY EARTH	779d	1 c
		ערץ	CAUSE TO TREMBLE	791d	1
		מערה	CAVE	792c	
		פחד	DREAD	808c	1
		פנה	FACE	818b	26a
		צור	ROCK	849c	1 a
		קום	STAND	878b	6 a
2	20	אליל	WORTHLESSNESS	47c	B
		זהב	GOLD	263a	6
		חפר	DIG	343d	2
		חפרפרה	MOLE	344a	
		יום	DAY	400d	7 g
		כסף	SILVER	494b	7
		עטלף	BAT	742b	
		שחה	BOW DOWN	1005c	3
		שלך	THROW	1021a	1 a
2	21	ארץ	EARTH	76a	1 b
		גאון	EXALTATION	145a	1 b
		הדר	SPLENDOUR	214b	2
		נקרה	HOLE	669b	
		סלע	CRAG	701a	1
		ערץ	CAUSE TO TREMBLE	791d	1
		פחד	DREAD	808c	1
		פנה	FACE	818b	26a
		צור	ROCK	849c	1a
		קום	STAND	878b	6 a
2	22	אף	NOSE	60a	1
		ב	IN	90b	3 3b
		חדל	CEASE	293a	2
		חשב	THINK	363b	1
		ל	TO	516a	5 ic
		מה	HOW	553d	4 a
		נשמה	BREATH	675d	2
3	1	אדון	LORD	11a	1 2
		הנה	BEHOLD	244b	B b
		לחם	FOOD	537a	1 a
		סור	TURN ASIDE	694b	1
		על	UPON	753d	2 1e
		משען	SUPPORT	1044a	
		משען	SUPPORT	1044a	
3	2	גבור	STRONG	150b	2
		זקן	OLD	278d	2 b
		מלחמה	WAR	536b	
		נביא	PROPHET	611d	2
		קסם	PRACTICE OF DIVINATION	890d	2
		שפט	JUDGE	1047c	1 b
3	3	בין	DISCERN	106d	
		חכם	WISE	314d	1
		חמשים	FIFTY	332b	1 a
		חרש	MAGIC ART	361d	
		יעץ	ADVISE	419d	
		לחש	CHARMING	538a	1
		נשא	LIFT	670c	1 b 3
		קסם	PRACTICE OF DIVINATION	890d	2

Ch	v.	Heb	Eng	Page	Sec
3	4	שר	CHIEFTAIN	978c	3 b
		משל	RULE	605d	1
		נער	YOUTH	655a	1 d
		נתן	GIVE	681a	3 a
		תעלולים	WANTONNESS	760c	
		שר	CHIEFTAIN	978b	2 b
3	5	זקן	OLD	278c	2 a
		כבד	BE HONORED	457c	1 b
		נער	YOUTH	655a	1 d
		קלה	DISHONOURED	885d	
		רהב	ACT STORMILY	923b	
		מרהבה	BOISTEROUS	923c	
		רע	FRIEND	946b	3
3	6	יד	HAND	391c	5 i
		יד	HAND	391c	5 i
		מכשלה	RUIN	506b	1
		נצח	JUICE	664c	
		קצין	CHIEF	892d	2
		שמלה	WRAPPER	971a	
		תחת	UNDERNEATH	1065c	2 1d
		תפש	LAY HOLD OF	1074d	1
3	7	חבש	BIND	290a	2
		יום	DAY	400d	7 g
		נשא	LIFT	670c	1 b 5
		קצין	CHIEF	892d	2
		שום	TO PLACE	964c	5 b
		שמלה	WRAPPER	971a	
3	8	אל	TO	40b	4
		כבוד	GLORY	458d	2 c2
		כי	BECAUSE	473c	3 c
		כי	BECAUSE	474b	3 d
		כשל	STUMBLE	505c	1
		לשון	TONGUE	546b	1 b
		מרה	BE REBELLIOUS	598b	
		נפל	FALL	657b	2
		מעלל	DEED	760b	1
3	9	אוי	WOE	17a	
		חטאת	SIN	308c	1 b
		כחד	HIDE	470b	
		ל	TO	510d	1 d
		נגד	BE CONSPICUOUS	617a	5
		הכרה	LOOK	648b	
		נפש	SOUL	660a	4 a5
		סדם	SODOM	690a	
		ענה	ANSWER	773a	3 a
		רעה	MISERY	949b	2
3	10	אמר	SAY	56a	1
		ה	THE	208d	1 i
		טוב	PLEASING	373b	4
		מעלל	DEED	760b	1
		פרי	FRUIT	826b	3
		צדיק	JUST	843a	3 b
3	11	אוי	WOE	17a	
		ה	THE	208d	1 i
		עשה	DO	795b	1 c
		רע	EVIL	948b	2
		רשע	WICKED	957c	3
3	12	ארח	WAY	73a	2
		אשר	GO STRAIGHT	80d	2
		בלע	SWALLOW UP	*118b	
		דרך	WAY	203c	5
		משל	RULE	605d	1
		נגש	DRIVE	620c	3
		עלל	ACT THE CHILD	760c	
		תעה	ERR	1073c	3
3	13	דין	JUDGE	192b	1
		נצב	STAND	662a	1 a
		קדש	APARTNESS	872b	4 b
		ריב	STRIVE	936c	3
3	14	את	WITH	86b	1 dd
		בער	CONSUME	129b	3
		גזלה	PLUNDER	160a	
		כרם	VINEYARD	501d	
		עם	WITH	767c	1 c
		עני	POOR	776d	2
		שר	CHIEFTAIN	978b	2 b
		משפט	JUDGMENT	1048c	1 c
3	15	אדון	LORD	11d	6 c
		דכא	CRUSH	194a	
		מחן	GRIND	377c	
		מה	WHAT	552d	1 ac
		נאם	UTTERANCE	610b	2
		עני	POOR	776d	2
		צבא	ARMY	839c	4 c
		שאא	CRUSH	*983d	
3	16	בת	DAUGHTER	123b	1 i
		גבה	BE HIGH	147a	3 b
		גרון	NECK	173c	3
		הלך	WALK	231d	1 1d 5k
		הלך	WALK	233a	14c 1a
		ו	AND	254d	5 a
		טפף	TRIP	381d	
		נטה	EXTEND	640a	1 a
		עכס	SHAKE BANGLES	747c	
		יען	ON ACCOUNT OF	774d	2 b
		ציון	ZION	851b	
		שקר	OGLE	974c	
3	17	אדון	LORD	11c	3 2b
		בת	DAUGHTER	123b	1 i
		שפח	CAUSE A SCAB UPON	705c	
		ערה	BE NAKED	788c	1
		פת	SECRET PARTS	834a	
		ציון	ZION	851b	
		קדקד	HEAD	869b	
3	18	יום	DAY	400d	7 g
		עכס	ANKLET	747c	
		תפארה	BEAUTY	802c	1
		שהרון	MOON	962a	
3	19	נטיפה	DROP	643b	
		רעלה	VEIL	947a	
		שרה	BRACELET	1057b	
3	20	בית	HOUSE	109c	3
		לחש	CHARMS	538a	2
		נפש	SOUL	661c	0 c
		פאר	HEAD-DRESS	802c	
		צעדה	ARMLET	857d	
		קשרים	BANDS	905c	
3	21	אף	NOSE	60a	1 b
		טבעת	SIGNET	371d	2
		נזם	RING	633d	1
3	22	מחלצה	ROBE OF STATE	323a	
		חרוט	BAG	355a	
		משפחת	CLOAK	381c	
		מעטפה	OVERTUNIC	742c	
3	23	סדין	LINEN WRAPPER	690b	
		צניף	TURBAN	857b	
		רדיד	WIDE WRAPPER	921d	
3	24	בשם	SPICE	141d	1
		מחגרת	A GIRDING	292b	
		חגורה	GIRDLE	292b	
		יפי	BEAUTY	421d	
		כי	BRANDING	465a	
		מק	DECAY	597a	
		נקפה	ENCIRCLING ROPE	669a	
		מעשה	DEED	796a	2 a1
		פתיגיל	RICH ROBE	836c	
		קרחה	BALD SPOT	901b	2
		קרחה	BALD SPOT	901b	
		מקשה	TURNERS WORK	904d	
		שק	SACK	974c	2 a
		תחת	INSTEAD	1065d	2 2b a
3	25	גבורה	MIGHT	150b	2
		מת	MALE	607a	1
		נפל	FALL	657b	2 a
3	26	אבל	MOURN	5c	
		אנה	MOURN	58b	
		ישב	SIT	442c	1 a
		ל	TO	511c	1 ga
		נקה	BE CLEAN	667b	1
		פתח	OPENING	836a	
4	1	איש	MAN	35d	
		אסף	GATHER	62c	4
		חזק	BE FIRM	305a	6 a
		חרפה	REPROACH	358a	2 b
		יום	DAY	400d	7 g
		לבש	PUT ON	528a	A
		קרא	CALL	896b	6 d4
		רק	ONLY	956c	2 b
		שמלה	WRAPPER	971a	
		שבע	SEVEN	988a	1 a
		שם	NAME	*1027d	2 a
4	2	גאון	EXALTATION	145a	1 a
		יום	DAY	400d	7 g
		כבוד	HONOR	458d	2 b
		תפארה	BEAUTY	802d	2 c
		פליטה	ESCAPE	812d	2 c
		צדיק	BEAUTY	840a	1 a
		צמח	SPROUT	855c	1
4	3	אמר	SAY	56c	
		היה	COME TO PASS	225a	1 2b ag
		חיים	LIFE	313b	2
		כתב	WRITE	507d	3
		ל	TO	515a	5 ha
		ציון	ZION	851b	
		קרוש	HOLY	872d	2 b
		שאר	REMAIN	984a	1
4	4	אם	IF	50c	1 b4 b
		בת	DAUGHTER	123b	1 i
		בער	CONSUME	129b	3
		דוח	CLEANSE AWAY BY RINSING	188d	2
		דם	BLOOD	196d	2 f
		צאה	FILTH	844b	
		ציון	ZION	851b	
		רחץ	WASH OFF	934c	1
		משפט	JUDGMENT	1048c	1 f
4	5	אש	FIRE	77d	6
		ברא	CREATE	135b	2
		הר	MOUNTAIN	249c	1 a
		חפת	CANOPY	342c	1
		כבוד	HONOR	458d	2 b
		מכון	FIXED PLACE	467c	1
		להבה	FLAME	529b	1
		נגה	BRIGHTNESS	618b	
		על	UPON	755d	2 5
		ענן	CLOUD	778a	1 a
		עשן	SMOKE	798c	2 a
		ציון	ZION	851c	
		מקרא	CONVOCATION	896c	1
4	6	זרם	FLOOD OF RAIN	281b	
		מחסה	REFUGE	340b	A
		חרב	DRYNESS	351b	3
		יומם	BY DAY	401c	2
		מטר	RAIN	564d	1
		מן	FROM	578b	1 a
		סכה	THICKET	697c	2
		מסתור	PLACE OF SHELTER	712c	
		צל	SHADOW	853b	2
5	1	בן	SON	121d	8 o
		דוד	BELOVED	187c	1
		היה	BE	227b	3 4d c
		ידיד	BELOVED	391d	1
		כרם	VINEYARD	501d	
		נא	PART OF EN-TREATY	609b	3 a
		קרן	HORN	902a	4
		שירה	SONG	1010c	
		שיר	SING	1010c	
		שמן	FAT	1032a	1
5	2	באשים	STINKING THINGS	93b	
		בנה	BUILD	124c	1 az
		מגדל	TOWER	153d	1
		חצב	HEW	345a	1
		יקב	WINE-VAT	428c	
		ל	TO	517d	7 bc
		נטע	PLANT	642c	1
		סקל	STONE	709d	2
		עזק	DIG ABOUT	740a	
		ענב	GRAPE	772a	
		עשה	DO	794d	2 2
		קוה	WAIT FOR	875d	1
		שרק	VINE	977d	
5	3	בין	INTERVAL	107c	1 d
		נא	PART OF EN-TREATY	609a	1
		עתה	NOW	774b	2 b
		שפט	JUDGE	1047c	2 b
5	4	באשים	STINKING THINGS	93b	
		מדוע	WHEREFORE	396c	
		ל	TO	518a	7 bf
		עוד	STILL	729b	1 c
		ענב	GRAPE	772a	
		עשה	DO	794d	2 2
		קוה	WAIT FOR	875d	1
5	5	בער	CONSUME	129b	3
		גדר	WALL	155a	
		היה	BE	227c	3 5b
		ידע	KNOW	395a	2
		ל	TO	518a	7 bf
		נא	PART OF EN-TREATY	609b	3 a
		עתה	NOW	774b	2 b
		פרץ	BREAK THROUGH	829b	2
		מרמס	TRAMPLING-PLACE	942d	2
		משכה	HEDGE	968a	
5	6	בתה	END	144d	1
		זמר	TRIM	274d	
		מטר	RAIN	564d	
		מטר	RAIN	565a	
		מן	FROM	583b	7 ba
		עדר	HOE	727c	
		עב	DARK CLOUD	728a	1
		עלה	GO UP	748d	4
		צוה	LAY CHARGE UPON	845c	1 a
		שית	PUT	1011c	3
		שית	THORN-BUSHES	1011d	
		שמיר	THORN	1039a	1
5	7	און	TROUBLE	20a	3
		בית	HOUSE	110a	5 dd
		ה	THE	*208b	1 hb
		כי	BECAUSE	473d	3 c
		נטע	PLANTATION	642c	1
		משפח	OUTPOURING	705c	
		צבא	GOD OF WAR	839c	4 c
		צדקה	RIGHTEOUSNESS	842a	1 a
		צעקה	CRY	858d	2
		קוה	WAIT FOR	875d	1
		שעשעים	DELIGHT	1044b	1
5	8	אפס	NON-EXISTENCE	67b	2 b
		בד	SEPARATION	94c	1 b
		הוי	AH	223a	
		ישב	BE MADE TO DWELL	443d	
		נגע	TOUCH	619c	1
		עד	AS FAR AS	724c	1 2a d
		מקום	STANDING PLACE	880b	5 a
		קרב	COME NEAR	897d	1 a
		קרב	INWARD PART	899a	1 e
		שדה	FIELD	961d	2 b
5	9	אזן	EAR	24a	2 a
		אין	NOT	35a	6 db
		אם	IF	50b	1 b2
		אמר	SAY	56a	1
		טוב	PLEASANT	373c	1 a
		ישב	DWELL	443b	3
		כי	BECAUSE	*474a	3 c
		מן	FROM	583c	7 bb
		צבא	GOD OF WAR	839c	4 c
		שמה	WASTE	1031c	1
5	10	איפה	EPHAH	35b	1
		איפה	EPHAH	35b	1
		בת	BATH	144c	
		זרע	SOWING	282b	2
		חמר	HOMER	331a	
		כי	BECAUSE	474a	3 c
		עשה	DO	794d	2
		עשה	DO	794d	2 2
		צמד	COUPLE	855b	2
5	11	אחר	DELAY	29b	1
		בקר	MORNING	134b	1 h
		דלק	BURN	196b	
		הוי	AH	223a	
		יין	WINE	406c	C
		נשף	TWILIGHT	676a	1
		רדף	PURSUE	922d	2
		שכם	START EARLY	1014d	

Ch v.	Heb	Eng	Page	Sec
5 12	שכר	INTOXICATING DRINK	1016b	
	חליל	FLUTE	319d	
	כנור	LYRE	490a	
	נבט	LOOK	613d	2
	נבט	LOOK	613d	3
	נבל	HARP	614c	
	מעשה	DEED	796a	1 c
	פעל	DOING	821c	1 a
	משתה	FEAST	1059d	1
5 13	תף	TIMBREL	1074b	
	בלי	WEARING OUT	115d	C a
	המון	CROWD	242a	3 b
	דעת	KNOWLEDGE	395c	1 a
	כבוד	HONOR	459a	3
	כן	SO	486d	3 d
	מזה	EMPTY	561a	
	מת	MALE	607b	3 b
	צחה	PARCHED	850a	
	צמא	THIRST	854d	
	רעב	FAMINE	944b	1
5 14	בלי	WEARING OUT	115d	B
	הדר	SPLENDOUR	214b	2
	המון	SOUND	242c	1
	ו	AND	252b	1 a
	חק	SOMETHING PRE-SCRIBED	349c	5
	חקה	SOMETHING PRE-SCRIBED	350b	2 e
	ירד	GO DOWN	433b	1 i
	כן	SO	486d	3 d
	ל	TO	516c	5 k
	נפש	SOUL	660c	5 c
	עלז	EXULTANT	759c	
	פה	MOUTH	804d	1 a
	פער	OPEN WIDE	822b	
	רחב	BE LARGE	931d	2
	שאון	ROAR	981a	2
	שאול	SHEOL	983a	1
5 15	אדם	MAN	9c	2
	גבה	HIGH	147b	3
	עין	EYE	744c	2 a
	שחח	BOW	1005d	
	שפל	BECOME LOW	1050a	1
	שפל	BECOME LOW	1050a	1
5 16	אל	GOD	42c	6 a
	גבה	BE EXALTED	147a	2
	צבא	GOD OF WAR	839c	4 c
	צדקה	RIGHTEOUSNESS	842b	2
	קדוש	HOLY	872c	1 a
	קדש	BE SET APART	873a	1
5 17	גור	SOJOURN	158a	2
	דבר	PASTURE	184a	
	חרבה	WASTE	352b	2
	כ	LIKE	455a	B
	כבש	LAMB	461a	2
	מח	FATLING	562d	
	קציר	HARVESTING	894c	2
	רעה	TEND	945b	2 a
5 18	הוי	AH	223a	
	חבל	CORD	286c	1
	חטאה	SINFUL THING	308b	
	משך	DRAW	604b	1
	עבת	CORD	721c	1 b
	עגלה	CART	722c	
	עון	INIQUITY	730d	1
	שוא	EMPTINESS	996b	3
5 19	חוש	HASTE	301d	1
	עצה	ADVICE	420b	
	מהר	HASTEN	555a	1
	מען	PURPOSE	775c	2 b
	קדוש	HOLY	872c	1 c
	קרב	COME NEAR	897c	1 h
5 20	אמר	SAY	56a	1
	חשך	DARKNESS	365b	3 f
	טוב	A GOOD THING	375b	4
	ל	TO	512b	4 a
	מר	BITTER	600c	1
	מתוק	SWEET	608d	1
	רע	EVIL	948d	3
5 21	בין	DISCERN	106d	1
	חכם	WISE	314d	2
	נגד	IN FRONT	617c	1 b
5 22	בין	DISCERN	106d	1
	גבור	STRONG	150b	2
	חיל	STRENGTH	298d	1 c
	יין	WINE	406c	C
	מסך	MIX	587c	2
	שכר	INTOXICATING DRINK	1016b	
5 23	שחה	DRINK	1059b	1
	עקב	CONSEQUENCE	784d	1
	צדקה	RIGHTEOUSNESS	842b	5
	צדק	DECLARE RIGHTEOUS	842d	2
	צדיק	JUST	843a	2
	רשע	WICKED	957b	1
	שחד	BRIBE	1005a	
5 24	אבק	DUST	7c	
	אכל	EAT	37c	3
	אמרה	UTTERANCE	57b	
	אש	FIRE	77d	6
	ה	THE	207d	1 f
	חשש	CHAFF	366b	
	תורה	INSTRUCTION	435d	1 b
	כ	LIKE	454d	3 a
	כן	SO	486d	3 d
	לשון	TONGUE	546d	4
	מאס	REJECT	549c	1 a
	מק	DECAY	597a	
	נאץ	CONTEMN	611a	
	פרח	BUD	827b	
5 25	צבא	GOD OF WAR	839c	4 c
	קדוש	HOLY	872c	1 c
	רפה	SINK	951d	1
	שרש	ROOT	1057c	1
	ב	IN	90c	3 7
	הר	MOUNTAIN	250a	1 c
	זה	THIS	262a	6 bg
	חוץ	THE OUTSIDE	300b	2 a
	חרה	BURN	354a	2 a
	כן	SO	487b	3 f
	נבלה	CARCASS	615c	1 a
	נטה	EXTEND	640a	1 a
	נטה	EXTEND	640a	1 a
	נכה	SMITE	646c	4 b
	סוחה	OFFAL	691d	
5 26	עוד	STILL	728d	1 aa
	קרב	INWARD PART	899a	1 c
	רגז	BE AGITATED	919a	
	שוב	TURN BACK	997d	6 f
	מהרה	HASTE	555b	
	נס	STANDARD	651d	1 a
	נשא	LIFT	670a	1 a
	קל	LIGHT	887a	
	קצה	END	892a	1
	רחק	DISTANT	935c	2 a2
	שרק	HISS	1056d	
5 27	אזור	WAISTCLOTH	25b	
	חלץ	LOINS	323b	2
	ישן	SLEEP	445c	
	כשל	STUMBLE	505c	1
	נום	BE DROWSY	630b	
	נעל	SANDAL	653b	
	נתק	TEAR AWAY	683c	2
	עיף	FAINT	746a	
	פתח	OPEN	835c	
	שרוך	THONG	976c	
5 28	דרך	TREAD	202b	4
	ה	THE	207d	1 f
	חץ	ARROW	346c	1
	חשב	THINK	363b	1
	סוס	HORSE	692c	1
	סופה	STORM-WIND	693a	
	פרסה	HOOF	828b	2
	צר	HARD PEBBLE	866a	
	קשת	BOW	906c	1 d
	שנן	SHARPEN	1041d	
	הא	DEMONSTRATIVE PARTICLE	*1089c	A
5 29	אחז	GRASP	28b	
	אין	NOT	34d	4 c
	ה	THE	*207d	1 f
	ו	AND	*252b	1 b
	טרף	PREY	383c	1
	כפיר	LION	498d	
	לביא	LION	522d	
	נהם	GROWL	625b	1
	נצל	DELIVER	664d	3 a
	שאג	ROAR	980d	1
	שאגה	ROARING	980d	1
5 30	חשך	GROW DARK	364d	1
	חשך	DARKNESS	365a	3 a
	נהם	GROWL	625b	1
	נהמה	GROWLING	625c	1
	על	UPON	756c	2 7 a c
	עריף	CLOUD	791d	
	צ	STRAITS	865a	
6 1	היכל	TEMPLE	*228b	2
	היכל	TEMPLE	228b	2 e
	ו	AND	254d	5 b
	כסא	SEAT OF HONOR	490d	1 b
	מות	DEATH	560c	1
	מלא	FILL	570b	2
	נשא	LIFT	671d	1 a
	עזיהו	UZZIAH	739d	1 a
	רום	BE HIGH	926d	1 a
	שול	SKIRT	1002c	
	שנה	YEAR	1040b	
6 2	כנף	WING	489c	1 d
	כסה	COVER	491c	1
	כרוב	CHERUB	501a	6 b
	עוף	FLY	733c	1
	מעל	ABOVE	751c	1 b
	על	UPON	756b	2 6 c
	פנה	FACE	816a	1 3
	רגל	FOOT	919d	1 c
	שרף	SERAPHIM	977b	
6 3	זה	THIS	260d	1 b
	כבוד	GLORY	458d	2 c2
	כרוב	CHERUB	501a	6 b
	מלא	THAT WHICH FILLS	571b	3
	קדוש	HOLY	872c	1 a
	קדוש	HOLY	872c	1 c
	קרא	CALL	895b	2 a
6 4	אמה	PIVOT	52c	
	ה	THE	208b	1 g
	ישב	DWELL	443b	3
	כרוב	CHERUB	501a	6 b
	מלא	FILL	570b	1
	מן	OUT OF	580a	2 eb
	נוע	WAVE	631b	1
	עשן	SMOKE	798c	2 a
	קול	VOICE	877a	1 c
	קרא	CALL	895a	1 a
6 5	אוי	WOE	17a	
	אנכי	I	59c	
	דמה	CUT OFF	198c	
	טמא	UNCLEAN	379d	1
	כי	BECAUSE	474b	3 d
	כי	BECAUSE	474b	3 d
	כרוב	CHERUB	501a	6 b
	נהר	BEAM	626a	
	ראה	TO SEE	906d	1 a
	שפה	SPEECH	973c	1 a1
6 6	יד	HAND	390d	5 c1
	כרוב	CHERUB	501a	6 b
	מלקחים	TONGS	544c	1
	עוף	FLY	733c	1
	על	UPON	758c	4 2 a
	רצפה	GLOWING STONE	954b	
	שרף	SERAPHIM	977b	
6 7	חטאת	SIN	309a	1 d3
	כפר	BE COVERED OVER	498b	1
	נגע	TOUCH	619a	1 a
	נגע	TOUCH	619b	1
	סור	TURN ASIDE	694a	3
	על	UPON	757b	2 7 c aa
	שפה	SPEECH	973c	1 a1
6 8	את	MARK OF THE AC-CUSATIVE	84d	1 a
	הנה	BEHOLD	244a	A
	ל	TO	515c	5 hc
	מי	WHO	566b	B
	קול	VOICE	877a	1 b
	שלח	SEND	1018c	2 a
6 9	בין	DISCERN	106d	2 a
6 10	אזן	EAR	24b	3
	בין	DISCERN	106d	2 a
	כבד	MAKE HEAVY	458a	2
	לב	HEART	523c	2 3b
	לב	HEART	525b	2 6d
	עין	EYE	744b	1 i
	פן	LEST	814d	1
	רפא	HEAL	950d	2 a
	שוב	TURN BACK	997d	6 d
	שמן	GROW FAT	1031d	
	שעע	BE BLINDED	1044b	
6 11	אדמה	LAND	10a	5
	אין	NOT	35a	6 db
	אם	IF	50c	1 ce
	משאה	BE GROSS	*382a	
	מתי	WHEN	607d	C
	עד	UNTIL	725a	2 1 aa
	שאה	MAKE A DIN	980d	
6 12	עזובה	FORSAKENNESS	737d	
	רבב	BECOME MUCH	912b	2
	רחק	BE DISTANT	935a	
6 13	אלה	TEREBINTH	18c	
	אלון	OAK	47c	
	בער	CONSUME	129b	3
	זרע	SOWING	283b	5
	ל	TO	518a	7 bf
	מצבה	STUMP	663b	2
	עשירי	TENTH	798a	2
	שוב	TURN BACK	998b	8
	שלכת	FELLING	1021c	
7 1	אחז	AHAZ	28c	1
	ארם	ARAM	74c	C
	יותם	JOTHAM	222d	1
	לחם	ENGAGE IN BATTLE	535c	
	לחם	ENGAGE IN BATTLE	535d	
	עזיהו	UZZIAH	739d	1 a
	פקח	PEKAH	824d	
	רמליהו	REMILIAH	942b	
	רצין	REZIN	954a	1
7 2	אפרים	EPHRAIM	68c	4
	אפרים	EPHRAIM	68c	4
	ארם	ARAM	74b	A
	בית	HOUSE	110a	5 c
	יער	WOOD	420d	F
	לבב	HEART	523c	2 2
	נגד	BE CONSPICUOUS	617a	
	נוח	REST	628a	1
	נוע	WAVE	631b	1
	נוע	WAVE	631b	1
	עץ	TREE	781c	1 a
7 3	אחז	AHAZ	28c	1
	ברכה	POOL	140a	
	כבס	WASH	460a	
	נא	PART OF EN-TREATY	609a	1
	מסלה	HIGHWAY	700c	
	עליון	HIGH	751b	2
	תעלה	WATER-COURSE	752b	B
	קצה	END	892a	1
	קרא	ENCOUNTER	896d	1
	שאריושוב	SHEARJASHUB	984c	
	ישוב	JASHUB	1000b	1
7 4	אוד	BRAND	15c	
	ארם	ARAM	74b	A
	ב	IN	90c	3 5
	בן	SON	120c	1 g
	זנב	TAIL	275c	2
	חרי	BURNING	354c	
	ירא	FEAR	431a	1 a

Ch	v.	Heb	Eng	Page	Sec
		לבב	HEART	524b	2 9b
		עשן	SMOKING	798c	
		רכך	BE TENDER	940a	1 a
		רמליהו	REMILIAH	942b	
		רצין	REZIN	954a	1
		שמר	KEEP	1037b	1
		שקט	BE QUIET	1053b	1
7	5	אפרים	EPHRAIM	68c	4
		בן	SON	120c	1 g
		יעץ	ADVISE	419c	
		יען	ON ACCOUNT OF	774d	2 b
7	6	בן	SON	120c	1 g
		בקע	BREAK OPEN OR THROUGH	132b	
		טבאל	TABEEL	370b	
		יהודה	JUDAH	397b	2
		ל	TO	*512a	3 b
		מלך	BE KING	574b	
		עלה	GO UP	748c	2 c
		צוק	CONSTRAIN	848a	
		קוץ	FEEL A LOATHING	881a	
		רמליהו	REMILIAH	942b	
		תוך	MIDST	1063d	
7	7	אדון	LORD	11c	4 c
		היה	COME TO PASS	224b	1 1b
		כה	THUS	462a	1 a
		קום	STAND	878c	7 g
7	8	אפרים	EPHRAIM	68c	4
		ארם	ARAM	74b	A
		דמשק	DAMASCUS	199d	
		חתת	BE SHATTERED	369b	1
		חתת	BE SHATTERED	*369b	1
		כי	BECAUSE	473d	3 c
		מן	FROM	583b	7 bb
		עוד	STILL	729c	2 ab
		ראש	HEAD	911a	3 b
		רצין	REZIN	954a	1
		ששים	SIXTY	995d	
7	9	אמן	CONFIRM	53a	3
		אמן	CONFIRM	53a	2 a
		אפרים	EPHRAIM	68c	4
		בן	SON	120c	1 g
		כי	THAT	472c	1 db
		ראש	HEAD	911a	3 b
		רמליהו	REMILIAH	933d	
7	10	אחז	AHAZ	28c	1
		יסף	DO AGAIN	415c	2 a
7	11	אות	SIGN	16d	2
		גבה	BE HIGH	147a	
		יהוה	YAHWEH	218d	2 la
		ל	TO	*515d	5 ia
		מעל	ABOVE	751d	2 ca
		מעם	FROM WITH	769a	A
		עמק	BE DEEP	770d	
		שאל	ASK	981c	1 a
		שאל	SHEOL	983a	1
7	12	אחז	AHAZ	28c	1
		נסה	TEST	650d	3 b
		שאל	ASK	981c	1 a
7	13	אלהים	GOD	44d	4 c
		בית	HOUSE	110a	5 c
		כי	THAT	472d	1 f
		לאה	EXHAUST	521a	
		מן	THAN	582d	6 d
		מעט	A FEW	590b	1 ea
7	14	אות	SIGN	16d	2
		אל	GOD	42d	6 e
		הוא	HE, SHE, IT	215c	1 c
		הנה	BEHOLD	244a	B b
		כן	SO	486d	3 d
		עלמה	YOUNG WOMAN	761c	
		עמנואל	IMMANUEL	769b	
		עת	TIME	773c	1 b
		קרא	CALL	896a	6 a
7	15	בחר	CHOOSE	104a	1 b
		דבש	HONEY	185b	
		חמאה	CURD	326a	
		טוב	A GOOD THING	375b	4
		ידע	KNOW	394b	4 a
		כי	BECAUSE	*474a	3 c
		ל	TO	517a	6 a
		מאס	REJECT	549c	1 b
		רע	EVIL	948d	3
7	16	אדמה	LAND	10a	5
		בחר	CHOOSE	104a	1 b
		טוב	A GOOD THING	375b	4
		טרם	NOT YET	382c	2
		ידע	KNOW	394b	4 a
		כי	BECAUSE	474a	3 c
		מאס	REJECT	549c	1 b
		נער	YOUTH	654d	1 a
		עזב	LEAVE	737d	2
		קוץ	FEEL A LOATHING	881a	2
		רע	EVIL	948d	3
7	17	אפרים	EPHRAIM	68c	4
		אשור	ASSYRIA	78d	4
		יום	DAY	400a	7 d1 z
		כי	BECAUSE	*474a	3 c
		מן	FROM	583d	9 b2
		סור	TURN ASIDE	693d	2
		על	UPON	759b	4 2c
7	18	ארץ	EARTH	76a	2 a
		אשור	ASSYRIA	78d	4
		דבורה	BEE	184b	
		זבוב	FLY	256a	
		יאר	STREAM	384c	2 a

Ch	v.	Heb	Eng	Page	Sec
		מצרים	EGYPT	595c	1 a
		מצרים	EGYPT	695c	1 a
		קצה	END	892a	1
		שרק	HISS	1056d	
7	19	בתה	PRECIPICE	144c	
		כל	ALL	481b	1 a
		נחל	PASTURE	625b	
		נחח	REST	628a	1
		נחל	WADY	636c	2
		נעצוץ	THORN BUSH	654c	
		נקק	CLEFT	669b	
		סלע	CRAG	701a	1
7	20	אשור	ASSYRIA	78d	4
		ה	THE	209b	2 b
		זקן	BEARD	278b	2
		נהר	STREAM	625d	1
		ספה	SWEEP AWAY	705a	2
		עבר	REGION ACROSS	719d	1 b
		תער	RAZOR	789b	1
		רגל	FOOT	920a	1 f
		שכיר	HIRED	969b	1
		שער	HAIR	972b	1
7	21	בקר	CATTLE	133b	1 a
		חיה	LIVE	311c	1
		עגלה	HEIFER	722b	
		צאן	SMALL CATTLE	838a	1 b
7	22	דבש	HONEY	185b	
		חלב	MILK	316b	1
		חמאה	CURD	326a	
		עשה	DO	794d	2 2
7	23	אלף	THOUSAND	48d	1 a
		ב	IN	90b	3 3b
		גפן	VINE	172c	
		מקום	STANDING PLACE	880a	3 c
		שית	THORN-BUSHES	1011d	
		שמיר	THORN	1039a	1
7	24	ב	IN	89c	3 lb
		חץ	ARROW	346c	1
		קשת	BOW	906a	1 b
		שית	THORN-BUSHES	1011d	
		שמיר	THORN	1039a	1
		הר	MOUNTAIN	250c	1 i
7	25	יראה	FEAR	432a	1
		עדר	HOE	727c	
		מעדר	HOE	727c	
		מרמס	TRAMPLING-PLACE	942d	1
		שה	A SHEEP	962a	1
		שור	A HEAD OF CATTLE	1004a	
		שית	THORN-BUSHES	1011d	
		משלח	PLACE OF LETTING LOOSE	1020a	2
		שמיר	THORN	1039a	1
8	1	איש	MAN	35d	
		אמה	CUBIT	52b	1
		אנוש	MAN	60d	2
		בן	SON	103a	2
		חוש	HASTE	301d	
		חרט	GRAVING-TOOL	355a	2
		כתב	WRITE	507c	1 b1
		כתב	WRITE	507c	1 c
		ל	TO	513a	5 bb
		מהר	HASTEN	555a	1
		שלל	SPOIL	1022a	2
8	2	אוריה	URIAH	22c	2
		אמן	CONFIRM	53a	5
		יברכיהו	JEBERECHIAH	140a	
		זכריהו	ZECHARIAH	272b	3
		כהן	PRIEST	463c	4
		ל	TO	*512a	3 b
		עוד	BEAR WITNESS	730a	2
		את	MARK OF ACCUSATIVE	*1098b	2
8	3	בו	SPOIL	103a	2
		הרה	CONCEIVE	247d	1
		חוש	HASTE	301d	
		מהר	HASTEN	555a	1
		נביאה	PROPHETESS	612c	3
		קרא	CALL	896a	6 a
		קרב	COME NEAR	897b	1 a
		שלל	SPOIL	1022a	2
8	4	אם	MOTHER	51d	1
		אשור	ASSYRIA	78d	4
		דמשק	DAMASCUS	199d	
		חיל	STRENGTH	299a	3
		נער	YOUTH	654d	1 a
		נשא	LIFT	671a	2 a
		פנה	FACE	817c	2 4c a
		שלל	SPOIL	1022a	2
8	5	יסף	DO AGAIN	415c	2 a
8	6	אט	GENTLENESS	31d	B
		הלך	WALK	232b	1 3
		מאס	REJECT	549c	1 a
		מי	WATER	565c	2
		יען	ON ACCOUNT OF	774d	2 b
		רחום	REMILIAH	933d	
		רצין	REZIN	954a	1
		משוש	EXULTATION	965c	
		שלח	SHILOAH	1019d	
8	7	אפיק	CHANNEL	67d	
		אשור	ASSYRIA	78d	4
		גדה	BANK OF RIVER	152a	
		הלך	WALK	232b	1 3
		ו	AND	254d	5 cb
		כבוד	HONOR	459a	3
		כן	SO	487a	3 d
		מי	WATER	565c	1 b

Ch	v.	Heb	Eng	Page	Sec
8	8	עלה	GO UP	748d	5
		עלה	GO UP	749c	4
		על	UPON	755a	2 2
		עצום	MIGHTY	783a	1
		רב	MUCH	913a	1 b
		אל	GOD	42d	6 e
		ו	AND	252b	1 a
		חלף	PASS ON OR AWAY	322a	1 a
		כנף	WING	489c	1 a
		מלא	THAT WHICH FILLS	571b	3
		מטה	OUTSPREADING	642a	
		עבר	PASS OVER	717b	1 e
		עד	AS FAR AS	724a	1 1a
		עמנואל	IMMANUEL	769b	
		צואר	NECK	848c	1
		רחב	WIDTH	931d	
		שטף	OVERFLOW	1009a	1
8	9	אזן	HEAR	24c	1
		אזר	GIRD	25a	
		חתת	BE SHATTERED	369b	1
		מרחק	DISTANT PLACE	935d	
		רעע	BREAK	949d	2
8	10	אל	GOD	42d	6 e
		עצה	ADVICE	420a	
		עוץ	COUNSEL	734a	
		עם	WITH	767c	1 a
		עמנואל	IMMANUEL	769b	
		פרר	BREAK	830c	1
		קום	STAND	878c	7 g
8	11	דרך	WAY	204a	6 d
		חזקה	STRENGTH	305d	1
		יד	HAND	390a	1 e2
		יסר	ADMONISH	416a	1
		כה	THUS	462a	1 a
		מן	FROM	583b	7 ba
8	12	אמר	SAY	56a	1
		אשר	PARTICLE OF RELATION	82d	4 c
		ירא	FEAR	431b	1 b
		מורא	FEAR	432b	3
		ערץ	CAUSE TO TREMBLE	792a	1
8	13	אלה	GOD	41d	1 b
		מורא	FEAR	432b	3
		ערץ	CAUSE TO TREMBLE	792a	2
		קדש	BE SET APART	873c	2
8	14	אבן	STONE	6b	1
		בית	HOUSE	110a	5 dd
		מוקש	BAIT	430d	
		מכשול	STUMBLING	506b	1
		נגף	STRIKING	620a	2
		פח	BIRD-TRAP	809a	2 b
		צור	ROCK	849c	1 c
		מקדש	SACRED PLACE	874b	5
		ישראל	ISRAEL	975d	2 c
8	15	יקש	BE ENSNARED	430c	1
		כשל	STUMBLE	505c	1
		לכד	CAPTURE	540b	2
		נפל	FALL	657b	2 b
		שבר	BREAK	990d	
8	16	ב	IN	89c	3 la
		בן	SON	120c	1 g
		חתם	SEAL	367d	2
		תורה	INSTRUCTION	435d	1 b
		כשל	STUMBLE	505c	1
		למד	TAUGHT	541a	
		תעודה	TESTIMONY	730c	1 A
		צרר	BIND	864c	1
8	17	בית	HOUSE	110a	5 dg
		חכה	WAIT	314a	3
		סתר	HIDE	711d	2 c
		צפעוני	VIPER	861c	
		קוה	WAIT FOR	875d	1
8	18	אות	SIGN	16d	3
		מופת	SIGN	69a	2
		הר	MOUNTAIN	249c	1 a
		ילד	CHILD	409b	A
		מעם	FROM WITH	769a	D
		ישראל	ISRAEL	975d	2 a3
		שכן	SETTLE DOWN	1015b	2 c
8	19	אוב	NECROMANCER	15b	1
		אוב	NECROMANCER	15b	2
		אטי	MUTTERER	31d	
		אל	TO	39c	1
		אלהים	GOD	44d	4 c
		בעד	ON BEHALF OF	126c	2
		דרש	SEEK	205b	2 b
		דרש	SEEK	205b	2 b
		הגה	UTTER	211d	2
		חי	ALIVE	312a	1 b
		ידעני	FAMILIAR SPIRIT	396b	
		כי	WHEN	473b	2 a
		לא	NOT	520b	4 ba
		צפף	CHIRP	861d	2
8	20	אשר	THAT	84a	
		דבר	WORD	183d	4 7
		תורה	INSTRUCTION	435d	1 b
		תעודה	TESTIMONY	730c	1
		שחר	DAWN	1007c	
8	21	אלהים	GOD	44d	4 c
		היה	COME TO PASS	225b	1 2b ba
		כי	WHEN	473b	2
		מעל	ABOVE	751d	2 ca
		פנה	TURN	815b	2 a
		קלל	BE SLIGHT	886c	1

Ch	v.	Heb	Eng	Page	Sec
		קצף	BE WROTH	893b	
		קשה	BE SEVERE	904b	
		רעב	HUNGRY	944c	
		רעב	BE HUNGRY	945b	
		רעב	BE HUNGRY	945b	
8	22	אפלה	DARKNESS	66c	2
		חשכה	DARKNESS	365b	
		כי	THAT	*474c	
		נבט	LOOK	613c	1 a
		נדח	THRUST	623b	
		מעוף	GLOOM	734a	
		צוקה	PRESSURE	848a	
		צרה	DISTRESS	865b	
8	23	אחרון	BEHIND	30d	B
		ארץ	EARTH	76a	2 c
		גוי	NATION	156d	1 c
		דרך	WAY	202d	1
		זבולן	ZEBULUN	259d	3
		ירדן	JORDAN	434d	
		כ	LIKE	453c	1 a
		כבד	CAUSE TO BE HONORED	458a	3
		כי	THAT	474c	
		עבר	REGION ACROSS	719c	1 a
		מועף	GLOOM	734a	
		עת	TIME	773c	1 a
		נפתלי	NAPHTALI	837a	2 a
		מוצק	CONSTRAINT	848d	
		קלל	BE SILENT	886d	2
		ראשון	FIRST	911c	1 a
9	1	אור	LIGHT	21d	9
		חשך	DARKNESS	365a	3 a
		נגה	SHINE	618b	
		צלמות	DEATH-SHADOW	853c	2 a
9	2	גדל	BECOME GREAT	152c	1
		חלק	DIVIDE	323d	1
		כאשר	AS	455c	1 d
		לא	NOT	520c	
		פנה	FACE	817b	24 a h
		קציר	HARVESTING	894d	3
		רבה	BECOME MANY	915b	
		רבה	BECOME MANY	915c	1 a
		שמח	REJOICE	970b	2 a
		שמחה	JOY	970d	1
9	3	מדין	MIDIAN	193c	2
		חתת	BE SHATTERED	369c	1
		יום	DAY	398d	2 g
		כ	LIKE	455a	B
		נגש	DRIVE	620c	3
		מטה	STAFF	641c	1
		סבל	BURDEN	688a	
		על	YOKE	760d	
		שכם	SHOULDER	1014b	2
9	4	מאכלת	FUEL	38c	
		דם	BLOOD	196d	2 f
		ו	AND	254d	5 a
		כי	BECAUSE	473c	3 c
		סאן	TREAD	684d	1
		סאון	SANDAL	684d	
		רעש	SHAKING	950c	1
		שמלה	WRAPPER	971a	
		שרפה	BURNING	977b	
		שרפה	BURNING	977b	
		הא	DEMONSTRATIVE PARTICLE	*1089c	A
9	5	אב	FATHER	3d	7
		אל	GOD	42b	1
		גבור	STRONG	150a	1
		ילד	BE BORN	409a	
		ילד	CHILD	409b	A
		יעץ	ADVISE	419d	
		נתן	GIVE	681d	1 a
		עד	BOOTY	723d	
		על	UPON	753c	2 1c
		פלא	WONDER	810c	1
		קרא	CALL	896a	6 a
		משרה	RULE	976a	
		שר	CHIEFTAIN	978c	3 a
		שכם	SHOULDER	1014b	1 a
		שלון	PEACE	1023b	6
9	6	דוד	DAVID	188b	E
		כסא	THRONE	491b	3 a
		ממלכה	KINGDOM	575b	1
		מן	FROM	582a	5 c
		סעד	SUPPORT	703c	2 a
		על	UPON	752d	2 1
		עולם	LONG DURATION	762d	2 h
		עולם	LONG DURATION	763a	2 m
		צדקה	RIGHTEOUSNESS	842a	1 a
		צדקה	RIGHTEOUSNESS	842b	1 c
		קנאה	ZEAL	888d	2 b
		קץ	END	894a	1
		מרבה	INCREASE	916a	2
		משרה	RULE	976a	
9	7	דבר	WORD	182d	12a
		ו	AND	252c	1 a
		נפל	FALL	657d	5
		יעקב	JACOB	785a	2
		שלח	SEND	1018c	2 b
9	8	גאוה	PRIDE	144d	3
		גדל	GREATNESS	152d	3
		ידע	KNOW	394a	1 e
		כל	ALL	481d	1 da
		לבב	HEART	524a	26c
9	9	ארז	CEDAR	72d	2
		בנה	BUILD	124c	1 d

Ch	v.	Heb	Eng	Page	Sec
		גדע	HEW DOWN	154c	
		גזית	HEWING	159b	
		חלף	PASS ON OR AWAY	322b	1
		לבנה	BRICK	527c	1
		נפל	FALL	656d	1
		שקמה	SYCOMORE TREE	1054b	
9	10	צר	ADVERSARY	865d	
		רצין	REZIN	954a	1
		שגב	BE HIGH	960c	2
		שכך	ADDENDA ET CORRIGENDA	1127a	
9	11	אחור	HINDER SIDE	39c	D
		ארם	ARAM	74b	A
		ב	IN	90c	3 7
		זה	THIS	262a	6 bg
		יד	HAND	390a	1 e2
		נטה	EXTEND	640a	1 a
		קדם	FRONT	869c	1 a
		שוב	TURN BACK	997d	6 f
9	12	דרש	SEEK	205b	3 a
		נכה	SMITE	646c	4 b
		שוב	TURN BACK	997d	6 f
9	13	אגמן	BULRUSH	8c	2
		זנב	TAIL	275c	1 b
		יום	DAY	400a	7 a6
		כפה	BRANCH	497a	
		כרת	CUT OFF	504c	2 c
		ראש	HEAD	910d	1 b
9	14	הוא	HE, SHE, IT	215d	2 b
		זנב	TAIL	*275c	1 b
		זקן	OLD	278d	2 b
		ירה	DIRECT	435b	5 a
		נביא	PROPHET	611d	2
		נשא	LIFT	670c	1 b 3
		ראש	HEAD	910d	1 b
		שקר	DECEPTION	1055c	4
9	15	אשר	GO STRAIGHT	80d	1
		אשר	GO STRAIGHT	80d	2
		בלע	SWALLOW UP	118c	
		תעה	ERR	1073c	3
9	16	אלמנה	WIDOW	48b	
		ב	IN	90c	3 7
		דבר	SPEAK	180c	
		זה	THIS	262a	6 bg
		חנף	PROFANE	338b	
		יד	HAND	390a	1 e2
		יתום	ORPHAN	450c	
		כל	ALL	481c	1 b
		כל	ALL	482a	1 db
		כן	SO	487b	3 f
		נבלה	SENSELESSNESS	615b	1
		נטה	EXTEND	640a	1 a
		פה	MOUTH	805a	2 a
		רחם	LOVE	933c	1
		רעע	BE EVIL	949d	2
		שמח	REJOICE	970c	2 b
		שוב	TURN BACK	997d	6 f
9	17	אבך	TURN	5b	
		אש	FIRE	77d	5
		בחור	YOUNG MAN	104c	
		בער	BURN	129a	4
		גאות	MAJESTY	145a	1
		ה	THE	208a	1 f
		יער	WOOD	420d	C
		יצת	KINDLE	428b	
		סבך	THICKET	687c	
		עשן	SMOKE	798c	1 b
		רשעה	WICKEDNESS	958a	1
		שית	THORN-BUSHES	1011d	
		שמיר	THORN	1039a	1
9	18	מאכלת	FUEL	38c	
		היה	BECOME	226a	2 2c
		חמל	SPARE	328b	
		עברה	OVERFLOW	720c	3 b
		עתם	BURN	801a	
9	19	בשר	FLESH	142c	1 b
		גזר	CUT	160b	4
		זרוע	ARM	283d	1 a
		רעב	BE HUNGRY	945b	
		שבע	SATISFIED	959b	1 a
9	20	ב	IN	90c	3 7
		זה	THIS	262a	6 bg
		יד	HAND	390a	1 e2
		יחדו	TOGETHER	403c	B
		מנשה	MANASSEH	586c	1 b1 b
		נטה	EXTEND	640a	1 a
		על	UPON	758a	2 7d
		שמאל	LEFT	969d	1
		שוב	TURN BACK	997d	6 f
10	1	און	TROUBLE	20a	1
		חקק	CUT IN	349b	4
		חקק	SOMETHING PRESCRIBED	349d	7 e
		כתב	WRITE	508a	
		עמל	TROUBLE	765d	2
10	2	אלמנה	WIDOW	48b	
		בז	SPOIL	102d	
		גזל	TEAR AWAY	159d	
		גזל	ROBBERY	*160a	
		דין	JUDGMENT	192c	2
		דל	WEAK	195d	
		יתום	ORPHAN	450c	
		נטה	BEND	641a	3 g
		עני	POOR	776d	1
		שלל	SPOIL	1022a	3
		משפט	JUDGEMNT	1049a	5

Ch	v.	Heb	Eng	Page	Sec
		עד	ADDENDA ET CORRIGENDA	1125d	
10	3	אן	WHERE	33a	B
		יום	DAY	400d	7 i
		כבוד	RICHES	458c	1
		ל	TO	515a	5 ha
		ל	TO	516d	6 a
		מי	WHO	566d	F c
		נוס	FLEE	630d	1
		עזב	LEAVE	737a	1 d
		עזרה	HELP	740d	1
		על	UPON	757b	27c aa
		פקדה	OVERSIGHT	824a	1 a
		מרחק	DISTANT PLACE	935d	
		שואה	DEVASTATION	996c	1
10	4	אסיר	PRISONERS	64b	
		ב	IN	90c	3 7
		בלת	EXCEPT	116c	3
		בלת	EXCEPT	*116d	3
		הרג	KILL	247b	1 b
		זה	THIS	262a	6 bg
		יד	HAND	390a	1 e2
		כרע	BOW DOWN	502c	4
		נטה	EXTEND	640a	1 a
		נפל	FALL	657a	2 a
		שוב	TURN BACK	997d	6 f
10	5	אשור	ASSHUR	78d	2
		אשור	ASSHUR	78d	2
		הוי	AH	223a	
		זעם	INDIGNATION	276d	
		מטה	STAFF	641c	1
		שבט	ROD	987a	1 a
10	6	בזז	SPOIL	102d	
		בז	SPOIL	103a	2
		גוי	NATION	156d	1 b
		חוץ	THE OUTSIDE	*300b	2
		חמר	CEMENT	330d	2 b
		חנף	PROFANE	338b	
		עברה	OVERFLOW	720c	3 b
		עם	PEOPLE	767a	5 i
		צוה	COMMAND	845d	1 e
		מרמס	TRAMPLING-PLACE	942d	2
		שלל	SPOIL	1021d	
10	7	דמה	BE LIKE	198a	1
		חשב	THINK	363a	1 1
		כי	BUT	474b	3 e
		כן	SO	486b	1 cd
		כרת	CUT OFF	504c	2 b
		ל	TO	517d	7 bd
		לא	NOT	519c	2 a
		לבב	HEART	523c	2 3c
		מעט	A FEW	590a	1 b
10	8	יחדו	TOGETHER	403c	B
		כי	BECAUSE	473d	3 c
		לא	NOT	520b	4 ba
		שר	CHIEFTAIN	978a	2 a
10	9	ארפד	ARPAD	75d	
		דמשק	DAMASCUS	199d	
		חמת	HAMATH	*333a	
		כי	BECAUSE	473c	3 c
		כלנה	CALNEH	484c	
		כרכמיש	CARCHEMISH	501c	
		לא	NOT	520b	4 ba
10	10	אליל	WORTHLESSNESS	47c	b
		כי	BECAUSE	473c	3 c
		ל	TO	511a	1 f
		ממלכה	KINGDOM	575a	1
		מן	THAN	582d	6 c
		מצא	FIND	593b	3 c
		פסיל	IDOL	820d	
10	11	אליל	WORTHLESSNESS	47c	b
		כאשר	AS	455b	1 b
		כי	BECAUSE	473d	3 c
		כן	SO	486c	2 cd
		כן	SO	486c	2 cd
		לא	NOT	520b	4 ba
		עצב	IDOL	781b	
10	12	אשור	ASSYRIA	78d	4
		בצע	CUT OFF	130c	
		גדל	GREATNESS	152d	3
		הר	MOUNTAIN	249c	1 a
		כי	WHEN	473b	2 a
		לבב	HEART	524a	26c
		עין	EYE	744c	2 a
		תפארה	BEAUTY	802d	3 b
		פקד	ATTEND TO	823c	A 3
		פרי	FRUIT	826c	
		ציון	ZION	851c	
		רום	HEIGHT	927d	1
10	13	אביר	MIGHTY	7d	1
		בין	DISCERN	106d	
		גבולה	BORDER	148b	
		חכמה	WISDOM	315b	1
		ירד	BRING DOWN	434a	1 c
		ישב	SIT	442c	1 a
		כ	LIKE	454b	1 d
		כביר	GREAT	460b	
		כח	STRENGTH	470d	1 d
		עתיד	READY	800c	4
		שסה	PLUNDER	1042c	
10	14	אסף	GATHER	62b	1 c
		ביצה	EGG	101b	
		ביצה	EGG	101b	
		ה	THE	207d	1 f
		חיל	STRENGTH	299a	3
		כנף	WING	489c	1 a

Ch	v	Heb	Eng	Page	Sec
		ל	TO	511a	1 f
		מצא	FIND	593b	3 c
		נדד	FLUTTER	622b	4
		עזב	LEAVE	737b	2 a2
		פה	MOUTH	805b	3
		פצה	PART	822c	1 b
		צפף	CHIRP	861d	1
		צפף	CHIRP	861d	1
		קן	NEST	890a	1
10	15	אם	IF	50d	2 ab a
		גדל	BECOME GREAT	152c	
		גרזן	AXE	173d	
		ה	INTERROG PART	*210a	1 d
		חצב	HEW	345a	2
		כ	LIKE	454d	3 a
		לא	NOT	519c	2 d
		נוף	MOVE TO AND FRO	632a	1
		מטה	STAFF	641c	1
		משור	SAW	673d	
		פאר	BEAUTIFY	802b	1
		רום	BE HIGH	927c	1 a1
		שבט	ROD	987a	1 a
10	16	אדון	LORD	11a	1 2
		יקד	BE KINDLED	428d	
		יקד	BURNING	428d	
		כבוד	HONOR	459a	3
		כן	SO	486d	3 d
		צבא	GOD OF WAR	*839c	4 c
		רזון	LEANNESS	931a	1
		משמן	FATNESS	1032a	
10	17	אור	LIGHT	21d	1
		אכל	EAT	37c	3
		בער	BURN	129a	4
		יום	DAY	400a	7 a6
		להבה	FLAME	529b	1
		קדש	HOLY	872c	1 c
		שית	THORN-BUSHES	1011d	
		שמיר	THORN	1039a	1
10	18	בשר	FLESH	142c	2
		יער	WOOD	420d	C
		כבוד	HONOR	458d	2 b
		כלה	FINISH	478c	2 c2
		כרמל	GARDEN	502a	5 b
		מן	FROM	582a	5 b
		מסס	MELT	587d	
		נסס	BE SICK	651c	
		נפש	SOUL	659b	1 a
10	19	יער	WOOD	420d	F
		כתב	WRITE	507d	3
		נער	YOUTH	655a	1 d
		מספר	NUMBER	709a	1 a
		עץ	TREE	781d	1 b
		שאר	REST	984b	
10	20	אמת	FIRMNESS	54a	3 a
		בית	HOUSE	110a	5 dg
		יסף	DO AGAIN	415c	2 a
		נכה	SMITE	646b	3
		פליטה	ESCAPE	812d	2 c
		קדוש	HOLY	872c	1 c
		שאר	REST	984c	
		שען	LEAN	1043d	
		שען	LEAN	1043d	
10	21	גבור	STRONG	150a	1
		יעקב	JACOB	785a	2
		שאר	REST	984c	
		שארישוב	SHEARJASHUB	984c	
10	22	שוב	TURN BACK	997d	6 c
		חול	SAND	297c	C
		חול	SAND	297c	A
		חרץ	CUT	358c	3
		ים	SEA	411b	8 b
		כי	BECAUSE	474b	3 d
		כאם	FOR IF	474d	1 b
		כליון	FAILING	479a	2
		צדקה	RIGHTEOUSNESS	842b	2
		שאר	REST	984c	
		שוב	TURN BACK	997d	6 d
		שטף	OVERFLOW	1009a	1
10	23	אדון	LORD	11d	6 a
		חרץ	CUT	358c	
		כלה	COMPLETE	478d	2 a
10	24	אדון	LORD	11d	6 c
		ב	IN	90d	3 8
		ירא	FEAR	431b	1 c
		כן	SO	486d	3 d
		מטה	STAFF	641c	1
		נכה	SMITE	645c	1 b
		נשא	LIFT	670a	1 a
		שבט	ROD	987a	1 a
10	25	תבלית	DESTRUCTION	115b	
		זעם	INDIGNATION	276d	
		מזער	A LITTLE	277d	1
		כלה	BE FINISHED	477c	1 a
		מעט	A FEW	590b	1 eb
		עוד	STILL	729a	1 ab
		על	UPON	757d	2 7c c
10	26	ב	IN	90d	3 8
		מדין	MIDIAN	193c	2
		מטה	STAFF	641c	1
		מכה	BLOW	646d	1 b
		נשא	LIFT	670a	1 a
		עור	ROUSE ONESELF	735a	
		צור	ROCK	849d	1 d
		שוט	SCOURGE	1002a	1
		ערב	ADDENDA ET CORRIGENDA	1126a	
10	27	חבל	ACT CORRUPTLY	287c	
		סבל	BURDEN	687d	
		סור	TURN ASIDE	694a	3
		על	UPON	758c	4 2a
		על	YOKE	760d	
		פנה	FACE	818c	26c a
		צואר	NECK	848c	1
		שכם	SHOULDER	1014b	1 a
		שמן	FAT	1032a	1
10	28	מכמם	MICHMASH	485a	
		ל	TO	*511d	2
		מגרון	MIGRON	550d	2
		עי	AI	743b	1
		פקד	ATTEND TO	824a	2 b
		שמן	FAT	1032a	1
10	29	גבע	GEBA	148d	
		גבעה	GIBEAH	149b	2
		חרד	TREMBLE	353c	2
		מלון	INN	533d	
		עבר	PASS OVER	717c	3 a
		מעברה	FORD	721b	2
		רמה	RAMA	928a	1
		שאול	SAUL	982b	1
10	30	בת	DAUGHTER	123c	3
		ליש	LAISHAH	539d	
		ענתות	ANATHOTH	779a	1
		צהל	CRY SHRILLY	843c	2
		קשב	ATTEND	904a	
10	31	גבים	GEBIM	155d	
		מדמנה	MADMENAH	199b	
		נדד	RETREAT	622b	1
		עוז	TAKE REFUGE	731d	
10	32	בת	DAUGHTER	123c	3
		גבעה	HILL	149a	4
		הר	MOUNTAIN	249d	1 a
		יד	HAND	389c	1 d
		ל	TO	518a	7 bg
		נב	NOB	611b	2
		נוף	WAVE	631d	
		עוד	STILL	728d	1 aa
		ציון	ZION	851b	
10	33	אדון	LORD	11a	1 2
		גבה	HIGH	147b	3
		גדע	HEW DOWN	154b	
		הנה	BEHOLD	244b	B b
		סעף	LOP OFF BOUGHS	703b	
		מערצה	AWFUL SHOCK	792b	
		פארה	BOUGHS	802d	
		קומה	HEIGHT	879b	2
		רום	BE HIGH	926d	1 a
		שפל	BECOME LOW	1050a	1
10	34	אדיר	MAJESTIC	12b	2
		ברזל	IRON	137c	2
		יער	WOOD	420d	A
		לבנון	LEBANON	527b	
		נפל	FALL	657a	1
		נקף	STRIKE OFF	668d	
		סבך	THICKET	687c	
11	1	גזע	STOCK	160b	
		חטר	BRANCH	310d	
		יצא	GO OUT	423d	1 h
		ישי	JESSE	445b	
		נצר	SPROUT	666a	
		פרה	BEAR FRUIT	826a	2
		שרש	ROOT	1057d	1
11	2	בינה	UNDERSTANDING	108a	3
		גבורה	MIGHT	150c	2
		חכמה	WISDOM	315c	2
		דעת	KNOWLEDGE	395d	2 b
		עצה	ADVICE	420b	
		יראה	FEAR	432a	3
		נוח	REST	628a	1
		רוח	BREATH	925d	9 b
		רוח	BREATH	926a	9 c2
11	3	אזן	EAR	24a	2 a
		יכח	DECIDE	406d	1
		יראה	FEAR	432a	3
		ל	TO	516b	5 jb
		מראה	VISION	909d	2
		ריח	SMELL	926b	
		משמע	THING HEARD	1036a	
		שפט	JUDGE	1047c	2 b
11	4	יכח	DECIDE	407a	1
		מישור	UPRIGHTNESS	449d	3
		מות	DIE	560b	1 b
		נכה	SMITE	645b	1 a
		ענו	POOR	776c	1
		עריץ	AWE-INSPIRING	792b	
		פה	MOUTH	805b	2 c
		צדק	RIGHTEOUSNESS	841d	2 c
		רוח	BREATH	924c	1 c2
		רשע	WICKED	957b	2
		שפה	SPEECH	973d	1 a1
		שפט	JUDGE	1047d	3 b2
11	5	אזור	WAISTCLOTH	25b	
		אמונה	FIRMNESS	53d	3 b
		ה	THE	208b	1 ha
		חלץ	LOINS	323b	2
		מתנים	LOINS	608a	1 a
		צדק	RIGHTEOUSNESS	841d	2 c
11	6	גור	SOJOURN	158a	2
		ה	THE	208d	1 i
		זאב	WOLF	255d	
		כבש	LAMB	461a	2
		כפיר	LION	498d	
		מריא	FATLING	597b	
		נהג	DRIVE	624b	1
		נמר	LEOPARD	649d	
		נער	YOUTH	655a	1 c
		עגל	CALF	722a	
		קטן	SMALL	882b	1 a
		רבץ	LIE DOWN	918c	
11	7	אריה	LION	71d	
		בקר	CATTLE	133b	1 a
		דב	BEAR	179a	
		ה	THE	207d	1 f
		ה	THE	208d	1 i
		יחדו	TOGETHER	403c	B
		ילד	CHILD	409b	A
		פרה	HEIFER	831a	
		רבץ	LIE DOWN	918c	
		רעה	TEND	945b	2 a
		רעה	ASSOCIATE WITH	945d	
		תבן	STRAW	1062a	
11	8	ה	THE	208d	1 i
		הדה	STRETCH OUT THE HAND	213a	
		חר	HOLE	359d	
		ינק	SUCK	413b	
		פתן	COBRA	837a	
		צפעוני	VIPER	861c	
		שעע	TAKE DELIGHT IN	1044b	1
11	9	הר	MOUNTAIN	249d	1 a
		דעה	KNOWLEDGE	395c	
		כסה	COVER	492a	6
		ל	TO	513a	5 ad
		מלא	BE FULL	570a	1
		קדש	APARTNESS	871d	2 e
		רעע	BE EVIL	949c	1
		שחת	GO TO RUIN	1008b	1
11	10	אל	TO	39c	1
		גוי	NATION	156d	1 c
		גוי	NATION	156d	1 c
		דרש	SEEK	205b	2 a
		ישי	JESSE	445b	
		כבוד	GLORY	459a	2 c3
		ל	TO	512b	4 a
		מנוחה	RESTING PLACE	629d	1
		נס	STANDARD	651d	1
		שרש	ROOT	1057d	1
11	11	אי	COAST	16a	1
		אשור	ASSYRIA	78d	3
		חמת	HAMATH	333a	
		כוש	CUSH	469a	2 a
		מצרים	EGYPT	595d	1 a
		עילם	ELAM	743d	
		פתרום	PATHROS	837d	
		קנה	ACQUIRE	889a	1 b
		שאר	REMAIN	984a	1
		שאר	REST	984c	
		שנער	SHINAR	1042c	
11	12	אסף	GATHER	62b	1 a
		גוי	NATION	156d	1 c
		כנף	EXTREMITY	489d	2 b
		נדח	BANISH	623a	1
		נס	STANDARD	651d	1 a
		נפץ	DISPERSE	659a	
		נשא	LIFT	670a	1 a
		קבץ	GATHER	868a	1
11	13	כרת	BE CUT OFF	504a	1 b
		סור	TURN ASIDE	694a	4
		צרר	SHEW HOSTILITY TOWARD	865c	
		צרר	SHEW HOSTILITY TOWARD	865d	
		קנאה	ZEAL	888b	1
		קנא	BE ZEALOUS	888c	1
11	14	בזז	SPOIL	102d	
		בן	SON	121b	1 jl
		יד	HAND	389c	1 d
		יחדו	TOGETHER	403c	B
		כתף	SHOULDER	509b	1 a
		עוף	FLY	733c	1 a
		עמון	AMMON	770a	
		קדם	FRONT	869c	1 b
		משלוח	OUTSTRECHING	1020a	1
		משמעת	OBEDIENT BAND	1036a	2
11	15	דרך	TREAD	202b	3
		חרב	BE DRY	351b	
		חרם	BAN	356a	1 c
		יד	HAND	389c	1 d
		ים	SEA	411a	2
		ים	SEA	411b	8 c
		ל	TO	512b	4 a
		לשון	TONGUE	546d	6
		נוף	WAVE	632a	2 b
		נחל	TORRENT	636b	1
		נכה	SMITE	645b	1 a
		נעל	SANDAL	653a	
		מצרים	EGYPT	695c	1 a
		עים	GLOW	744a	
		על	UPON	755d	2 5
		עצם	MIGHT	782c	1
		רוח	BREATH	924d	2 a
11	16	אשור	ASSYRIA	78d	3
		מסלה	HIGHWAY	700c	
		שאר	REMAIN	984a	1
		שאר	REST	984c	
12	1	אנף	BE ANGRY	60a	1
		ידה	PRAISE	392c	1 a2
		כי	BECAUSE	474a	3 c
		נחם	CONSOLE ONESELF	637a	

Ch	v.	Heb	Eng	Page	Sec
12	2	שוב	TURN BACK	997d	6 f
		אל	GOD	42d	6 c
		בטח	TRUST	105a	1 1
		יה	YAH	219c	
		זמרה	MELODY	274b	2
		ישועה	DELIVERANCE	447b	3
		ישועה	VICTORY	447c	4
		עז	STRENGTH	739a	2 c
		פחד	DREAD	808b	1
12	3	ישועה	DELIVERANCE	447b	3
		מעין	SPRING	746a	
		ששון	REJOICING	965b	
		שאב	DRAW	980c	
12	4	ב	IN	90b	3 4
		זכר	REMEMBER	271a	3 c
		ידה	PRAISE	392d	1 b
		ידע	MAKE KNOWN	395a	
		עלילה	WANTONNESS	760a	2 b
		שגב	BE HIGH	960c	3
12	5	גאות	MAJESTY	145a	2
		זמר	MAKE MUSIC	274a	1
		ידע	KNOWN	394d	
		ידע	BE MAKE KNOWN	395b	
		קציר	HARVESTING	894d	2
12	6	גדול	GREAT	153b	6 c
		ישב	DWELL	443b	3
		צהל	CRY SHRILLY	843d	2
		קדוש	HOLY	872c	1 c
		רנן	GIVE A RINGING CRY	943b	1
13	1	אמוץ	AMOZ	55b	
		בבל	BABEL	93c	
		חזה	SEE	302c	2
		משא	UTTERANCE	672d	
13	2	הר	MOUNTAIN	*250d	1 m
		נדיב	NOBLE	622a	2
		נוף	WAVE	632a	2 c
		נס	STANDARD	651d	1 a
		פתח	OPENING	836a	
		רום	BE HIGH	927c	1 b
		שפה	SWEEP BARE	1045d	
13	3	גאוה	PRIDE	144d	3
		גבור	STRONG	150b	2
		גם	YEA	169c	3
		עליז	EXULTANT	759c	
		צוה	GIVE CHARGE TO	845c	1 b
		קרא	CALL	895d	5 c
13	4	דמות	LIKENESS	198b	2
		המון	SOUND	242c	1
		הר	MOUNTAIN	250a	1 a
		מלחמה	WAR	536b	
		ממלכה	KINGDOM	575b	1
		פקד	ATTEND TO	823d	
		קול	VOICE	877a	1 f
		קול	VOICE	877b	2 i
		שאון	ROAR	981a	1
13	5	זעם	INDIGNATION	277a	
		חבל	ACT CORRUPTLY	287c	
		כלי	IMPLEMENT	479d	2 a
		קצה	END	892b	1
		מרחק	DISTANT PLACE	935d	
13	6	יום	DAY	399a	3
		ילל	HOWL	410b	
		כ	LIKE	454b	1 d
		קרב	NEAR	898d	3
		שד	VIOLENCE	994c	2
		שדי	ALMIGHTY	995a	1
13	7	אנוש	MAN	60d	3
		כל	ALL	481b	1 a
		כן	SO	487b	3 f
		לבב	HEART	524b	2 9b
		מסס	MELT	587d	2
		רפה	SINK	951d	2
13	8	אחז	GRASP	28b	
		אל	TO	40a	3 a
		בהל	BE DISTURBED	96b	1
		ה	THE	207d	1 f
		חבל	PAIN	287a	1 b
		חול	WHIRL	297a	2 b
		ילד	BEAR	408c	1 b
		להב	FLAME	529a	1
		פנה	FACE	815a	1 1a
		ציר	PANG	852a	
		צמים	SNARE	*855d	
		רע	FRIEND	946b	3
		תמה	BE ASTOUNDED	1069b	
13	9	ו	AND	253a	1 g
		חטא	SINFUL	308b	2
		חרון	BURNING OF ANGER	354c	
		יום	DAY	399a	3
		אכזרי	CRUEL	470a	
		כי	BECAUSE	*473d	3 c
		ל	TO	512b	4 a
		עברה	OVERFLOW	720c	3 b
		שמד	BE EXTERMINATED	1029b	1
		שמה	WASTE	1031c	1
13	10	חלל	SHINE	237c	
		חשך	GROW DARK	364d	1
		יצא	GO OUT	423b	1 f
		ירח	MOON	437a	
		כוכב	STAR	457a	
		כי	BECAUSE	473d	3 c
		כסיל	ORION	493a	
		נגה	SHINE	618b	2
		שמש	SUN	1039a	1

Ch	v.	Heb	Eng	Page	Sec
13	11	גאוה	PRIDE	144d	3
		גאון	EXALTATION	144d	1 a
		זד	INSOLENT	267d	
		תבל	WORLD	385d	
		עון	INIQUITY	731a	1 c1
		עריץ	AWE-INSPIRING	792b	
		רשע	WICKED	957b	2
		שאון	ROAR	*981a	1
		שבת	CEASE	992d	1
		שפל	BECOME LOW	1050b	1
13	12	אדם	MAN	9b	1
		אופז	UPHAZ	20c	
		אופיר	OPHIR	20d	3
		אנוש	MAN	60d	1
		יקר	MAKE RARE	429d	
		יקר	RARE	*430a	2
		כתם	GOLD	508d	
		פז	REFINED GOLD	808a	
13	13	חרון	BURNING OF ANGER	354c	
		יום	DAY	399a	3
		כן	SO	487b	3 f
		עברה	OVERFLOW	720c	3 b
		מקום	STANDING PLACE	879d	1 a
		רעש	SHAKE	950b	
13	14	נדח	BANISH	624a	4
		נוס	FLEE	630d	1
		פנה	TURN	815a	1 a
		צאן	SMALL CATTLE	838c	2
		צבי	GAZELLE	840b	
		קבץ	GATHER	868a	2
13	15	דקר	PIERCE	201b	
		מצא	FIND	593d	1 c
		ספה	SWEEP AWAY	705a	2
13	16	עולל	CHILD	760c	
		רטש	DASH IN PIECES	936b	
		שגל	VIOLATE	993b	
		שסס	PLUNDER	1042d	
13	17	הנה	BEHOLD	244b	B b
		חפץ	DELIGHT IN	342d	1 a
		חשב	THINK	363a	1 4
		מדי	MEDES	552a	1
		עור	ROUSE ONESELF	735b	1
13	18	בטן	WOMB	106a	3
		חוס	PITY	299b	A
		עין	EYE	744c	2 a
		קשת	BOW	906a	1 b
		רחם	LOVE	933d	2
		רטש	DASH IN PIECES	936b	
13	19	אלהים	GOD	44b	4 a
		את	MARK OF THE ACCUSATIVE	85b	1 d
		בבל	BABEL	93c	
		גאון	EXALTATION	144d	1 a
		מהפכה	OVERTHROW	246b	
		כשדים	CHALDEANS	505a	1 b
		ממלכה	KINGDOM	575b	1
		סדם	SODOM	690a	
		עמרה	GOMORRAH	771d	
		תפארה	BEAUTY	802d	3 b
		צבי	BEAUTY	840a	1 b
13	20	אהל	MOVE TENT	14b	
		דור	PERIOD	189d	1 b
		ו	AND	*253b	1 ib
		ישב	SIT	443b	4
		לא	NOT	*518d	1 ac
		נצח	EVERLASTINGNESS	664b	4'
		עד	AS FAR AS	724b	12 a a
		ערבי	STEPPE-DWELLER	787b	
		רבץ	LIE DOWN	918c	
		שכן	SETTLE DOWN	1015a	1 a
13	21	אח	JACKAL	28d	
		בת	DAUGHTER	123d	6
		יענה	OSTRICH	419a	
		מלא	BE FULL	570a	1 a
		עון	DWELL	*732d	
		צי	YELPER	850d	
		רבץ	LIE DOWN	918c	
		רקד	SKIP ABOUT	955a	
		שעיר	SATYR	972d	
		שכן	SETTLE DOWN	1015a	1 b
13	22	אי	JACKAL	17b	
		אלמנה	WIDOW	48b	
		ארמון	CITADEL	74d	
		היכל	PALACE	228b	1
		משך	DRAW	604c	
		עון	DWELL	732d	
		ענג	DAINTINESS	772b	
		עת	TIME	773d	2 c
		צי	WILD BEAST	*850d	
		קרב	NEAR	898d	3
		תן	JACKAL	1072b	
13	23	קסם	DIVINATION	890c	2
14	1	אדמה	LAND	10a	5
		בחר	CHOOSE	104a	1 a
		בית	HOUSE	110a	5 dg
		גר	SOJOURNER	158b	2
		לוה	BE JOINED	531d	
		נוח	REST	628d	B 1
		ספח	JOIN	705b	
		על	UPON	755b	2 4a
		יעקב	JACOB	785a	2
		רחם	LOVE	933c	1
14	2	אדמה	LAND	10a	5
		בוא	COME	99b	2
		בית	HOUSE	110a	5 dd

Ch	v.	Heb	Eng	Page	Sec
		ל	TO	512c	4 a
		ל	TO	513a	5 ad
		נגש	DRIVE	620c	3
		נחל	TAKE AS A POSSESSION	635d	
		עבד	SLAVE	713d	1
		על	UPON	752d	2 1
		רדה	HAVE DOMINION	922a	
		שבה	TAKE CAPTIVE	985c	1 c
		שבה	TAKE CAPTIVE	985c	1 c
		שפחה	MAID	1046c	1
14	3	לבב	HEART	524a	2 7
		נוח	REST	628c	A 1b 3
		עבד	WORK	713c	
		עבדה	LABOR	715b	3
		עצב	PAIN	780d	
		קשה	SEVERE	904c	2 a
		רגז	AGITATION	919c	
14	4	איך	HOW	32c	2
		בבל	BABEL	93c	
		משל	PARABLE	605b	3
		נגש	DRIVE	620c	3
		נשא	LIFT	670d	1 b 6
		מרהבה	BOISTEROUS	923c	
		שבת	CEASE	991d	1
14	5	משל	RULE	605b	1
		מטה	STAFF	641c	1
		רשע	WICKED	957b	2
		שבר	ROD	987a	1 d
		שבר	BREAK	990c	
14	6	בלי	WEARING OUT	115c	2 a
		בלת	NOT	116c	1
		חשך	WITHHOLD	362b	1 b
		נכה	SMITE	646b	3
		מכה	SLAUGHTER	647a	3
		סרה	A TURNING ASIDE	694c	3
		עברה	OVERFLOW	720c	3 a
		רדה	HAVE DOMINION	922a	
		מרדה	DOMINION	922a	
		מרדף	PERSECUTION	923b	
14	7	נוח	REST	628c	2
		פצה	CAUSE TO BREAK FORTH	822c	
		רנה	RINGING CRY	943d	3
		שקט	BE QUIET	1053a	1
14	8	מאז	FROM THAT TIME	23b	B
		ארז	CEDAR	72c	1 a
		ברוש	CYPRESS	141c	1
		גם	YEA	169c	3
		כרת	HEW	503d	3
		לבנון	LEBANON	527a	1
		לבנון	LEBANON	*527a	
		שמח	REJOICE	970b	1 a
		שכב	LIE DOWN	1012b	4 a
14	9	כסא	SEAT OF HONOR	490d	1 a
		עור	ROUSE ONESELF	735a	
		עתוד	HE-GOAT	800d	
		קום	STAND	878d	1 b
		קרא	ENCOUNTER	897a	1
		רגז	BE AGITATED	919b	
		רפאים	SHADES	952b	
		שאול	SHEOL	982d	1
		שאול	SHEOL	*983a	1
		תחת	UNDERNEATH	1065b	1
14	10	ו	AND	252b	1
		משל	BE LIKE	605a	
14	11	גאון	EXALTATION	144d	1 a
		המיה	SOUND	242d	
		יצע	BE LAID	426d	
		ירד	BE BROUGHT DOWN	434b	1
		מכסה	COVERING	492c	
		נבל	HARP	614c	
		רחום	WORM	933d	
		שאול	SHEOL	982d	1
		תולעה	WORM	1069a	1
14	12	איך	HOW	32c	2
		בן	SON	121d	8 m
		גדע	HEW OFF	154b	
		הילל	SHINING ONE	237d	
		חלש	BE WEAK	325d	2
		ילל	HOWL	410b	
		ל	TO	511c	1 ga
		מן	FROM	577d	1 a
		נפל	FALL	657b	2 b
		שחר	DAWN	1007c	
14	13	אל	GOD	42c	5
		אמר	SAY	56b	2
		הר	MOUNTAIN	249d	1 a
		מועד	APPOINTED MEETING	417d	2
		ירכה	EXTREME PARTS	438b	1
		כוכב	STAR	457a	
		כסא	THRONE	491b	3 a
		מעל	ABOVE	751c	1 b
		צפון	NORTH	861a	
		רום	BE HIGH	927c	1 e
14	14	במה	HIGH PLACE	119b	2 b
		דמה	BE LIKE	198a	
		עב	DARK CLOUD	728a	1 b
		עלה	GO UP	748c	1 f
		עליון	HIGHEST	751b	1
		על	UPON	756d	2 7b
14	15	אך	HOWBEIT	36c	2 a
		בור	PIT	92c	5

Ch	v.	Heb	Eng	Page	Sec
		ירד	BE BROUGHT DOWN	434b	1
		ירכה	EXTREME PARTS	438b	2
		שאול	SHEOL	982d	1
14	16	בין	DISCERN	107b	3 c
		זה	THIS	261a	3
		ממלכה	KINGDOM	575a	1
		רגז	BE AGITATED	919b	
		רעש	SHAKE	950a	1
		שגח	GAZE	993b	
14	17	אסיר	PRISONER	64a	
		בית	HOUSE	108d	1 a
		הרס	THROW DOWN	248c	1
		תבל	WORLD	385d	
		פתח	OPEN	835a	
14	18	כל	ALL	481d	1 da
		שכב	LIE DOWN	1012c	4 c
14	19	אבן	STONE	6c	2
		בור	PIT	92c	5
		בוס	TRAMPLE	101a	
		הרג	KILL	247b	1 b
		טען	PIERCE	381b	
		ירד	GO DOWN	433b	1 i
		נצר	SPROUT	666a	
		פגר	CORPSE	803d	1
		שלך	THROW	1021c	2
		תעב	BE ABHORRED	1073a	1
14	20	הרג	KILL	247a	1 a
		זרע	SOWING	283b	5
		יחד	BE UNITED	402d	
		עולם	LONG DURATION	762b	2 b3
		צברה	GRAVE	869a	
		קרא	CALL	896c	6 d8
		רעע	BE EVIL	949d	1
14	21	בל	NOT	115b	
		מטבח	SLAUGHTERING-PLACE	371a	
		תבל	WORLD	385d	
		כון	ESTABLISH	466a	2 a
		עון	INIQUITY	731a	1 c1
		פנה	FACE	816b	15
		שבר	BREAK	990d	
14	22	בבל	BABEL	93c	
		כרת	CUT OFF	504c	2 c
		נאם	UTTERANCE	610b	2
		נאם	UTTERANCE	610b	2
		נין	OFFSPRING	630c	
		נכד	PROGENY	645a	
		קום	STAND	878a	2
		שאר	REST	*984c	
		שם	NAME	1028b	2 c
14	23	אגם	TROUBLED POOL	8b	1
		מאטא	SWEEP	370a	
		ממאטא	BROOM	370a	
		מורש	POSSESSION	440c	
		נאם	UTTERANCE	610b	2
		שמד	BE EXTERMINATED	1029c	1
14	24	אם	IF	50b	1 b2
		דמה	BE LIKE	198a	1
		הוא	HE, SHE, IT	216d	6 a
		יעץ	ADVISE	419d	
		כאשר	AS	455b	1 b
		כן	SO	486c	2 cd
		עמד	STAND	764b	3 c
		קום	STAND	878a	7 g
		שבע	SWEAR	989c	1
14	25	אשור	ASSHUR	78d	2
		בוס	TRAMPLE	100d	
		סבל	BURDEN	688a	
		סור	TURN ASIDE	694a	3
		סרה	A TURNING ASIDE	*694c	3
		על	YOKE	760d	
		שבר	BREAK	990c	
		שכם	SHOULDER	1014b	1 a
14	26	זה	THIS	261b	3
		יעץ	ADVISE	419c	
		עצה	ADVICE	420b	1
		נטה	EXTEND	640a	1 a
		על	UPON	756d	27 a c
14	27	ה	THE	209b	2 c
		יעץ	ADVISE	419d	
		מי	WHO	567a	F c
		נטה	EXTEND	640a	1 a
		פרר	BREAK	830b	2 a
		שוב	TURN BACK	999d	5
14	28	אחז	AHAZ	28c	1
		היה	BECOME	226a	2 1b
		מות	DEATH	560c	1
		משא	UTTERANCE	672d	
		שנה	YEAR	1040b	
14	29	יצא	GO OUT	423a	1 h
		כי	BECAUSE	473d	3 b
		כל	ALL	481d	1 da
		נחש	SERPENT	638b	1 a
		נכה	SMITE	645b	1 a
		עוף	FLY	733c	1
		פלשת	PHILISTIA	814b	
		פרי	FRUIT	826b	2
		צפע	SERPENT	861c	
		שמח	REJOICE	970b	1 a
		שרף	FIERY SERPENT	977b	
		שבט	ROD	987a	1 a
		שרש	ROOT	1057d	1 a
14	30	אביון	NEEDY	2d	
		בטח	SECURITY	105b	
		בכור	FIRST-BORN	114b	3
		דל	POOR	195d	2
		הרג	KILL	247b	2
		מות	DIE	560b	2
		רבץ	LIE DOWN	918c	
		רעה	TEND	945b	2 c
		שארית	REST	984d	1
		שרש	ROOT	1057c	1
14	31	בדד	BE SEPARATE	94b	
		זעק	CRY	277c	2 d
		ילל	HOWL	410b	
		מועד	RANK	418a	
		כל	ALL	481d	1 da
		מוג	MELT	556a	
		עשן	SMOKE	798c	1 a
		פלשת	PHILISTIA	814b	
		צפון	NORTH	861a	
		שער	GATE	1045a	2 b
		מוג	ADDENDA ET CORRIGENDA	1124d	
14	32	חסה	SEEK REFUGE	340a	
		יסד	FOUND	414a	1
		מלאך	MESSENGER	521c	1 a
		ציון	ZION	851b	
15	1	דמה	CUT OFF	198c	
		כי	THAT	474c	
		לילה	NIGHT	538d	1
		לילה	NIGHT	539a	1
		משא	UTTERANCE	672d	
		ער	AR	786b	
		קיר	KIR	885b	1
		שדד	DEAL VIOLENTLY WITH	994b	
15	2	בית	BETH	110c	
		בכי	WEEPING	113d	
		במה	HIGH PLACE	119b	3
		גרע	HEW OFF	154b	
		גרע	DIMINISH	175c	1
		דיבן	DIBON	192a	1
		זקן	BEARD	278b	2
		כל	ALL	481c	1 b
		מידבא	MEDEBA	567d	
		נבו	NEBO	612d	1 a
		קרחה	BALD SPOT	901b	
		בכי	WEEPING	113d	
15	3	גג	ROOF	150d	1
		חגר	GIRD	291d	2
		חוץ	THE OUTSIDE	300b	2 a
		ירד	GO DOWN	433b	1 j
		ירד	GO DOWN	433c	2
		כל	ALL	482a	1 db
		רחוב	PLAZA	932b	
		שק	SACK	974c	2 a
15	4	אלעלא	ELEALEH	46c	
		זעק	CRY	277c	2 d
		חלץ	EQUIP FOR WAR	323a	2
		חשבון	HESHBON	363d	
		יהץ	JAHAZ	397d	
		ירע	QUIVER	438c	
		כן	SO	487b	3 f
		ל	TO	*512d	5 aa
		נפש	SOUL	660d	6 c
		עד	AS FAR AS	724a	1 1a
		רוע	RAISE A SHOUT	929d	6
15	5	בכי	WEEPING	113d	
		בכי	WEEPING	113d	
		בליח	FLEEING	138a	
		בריח	BAR	138b	1 b
		דרך	WAY	202b	1
		זעק	CRY	277c	2 d
		זעקה	CRY	277d	2
		חרונים	HORONAIM	357b	
		כי	BECAUSE	474b	3 d
		ל	TO	514d	5 g
		לוחית	LUHITH	532a	
		עגלת	EGLATH	722c	
		עור	ROUSE ONESELF	735a	
		צער	ZOAR	858d	
		שבר	BREAKING	991b	1
		שלישי	THIRD	1026b	
		יעערו	ADDENDA ET CORRIGENDA	1124b	
15	6	בית נמרה	BETH-NIMRAH	112b	
		דשא	GRASS	206a	
		חציר	GREEN GRASS	348a	1
		יבש	BE DRY	386b	1 d
		ירק	GREEN	438d	
		כי	BECAUSE	474b	3 d
		כלה	BE FINISHED	477c	2 b
		מי	WATER	565c	2
		נמרים	NIMRIM	649d	
		משמה	DEVASTATION	1031d	1
15	7	זרד	ZERED	*279d	
		יתרה	ABUNDANCE	452b	2
		כן	SO	487b	3 f
		נחל	WADY	636c	2
		ערבה	POPLAR	788b	1
		עשה	DO	795a	27
		פקדה	OVERSIGHT	824b	4
15	8	אגלים	EGLAIM	8b	
		באר	BEER	91d	3 a
		גבול	BORDER	147d	1 a
		זעקה	CRY	277d	2
		כי	BECAUSE	474b	3 d
		נקף	GO AROUND	669a	1 a
15	9	אריה	LION	71d	1
		דיבן	DIBON	192a	1
		דם	BLOOD	197c	2 o
		יסף	BE JOINED	415a	2
		כי	BECAUSE	474b	3 d
		מי	WATER	565c	2
		פליטה	ESCAPE	812c	2 b
		שארית	REST	984c	1
		שית	PUT	1011a	1
16	1	בת	DAUGHTER	123c	3
		הר	MOUNTAIN	249d	1 a
		כר	LAMB	503a	
		משל	RULE	605d	1
		ציון	ZION	851b	
		סלע	SELA	701aa	
		ארנון	ARNON	75b	
16	2	בת	DAUGHTER	123b	1 i
		ל	TO	513d	5 cb e
		נדד	WANDER	622b	3
		מעברה	FORD	721b	1
		עוף	FLY	733d	1
		קן	NEST	890a	1
		שלח	SEND	1019c	
16	3	עצה	ADVICE	420a	
		לילה	NIGHT	539b	2
		נדד	RETREAT	622b	1
		נדח	BANISH	623a	2
		סתר	HIDE	711c	
		פלילה	OFFICE OF JUDGE	813d	
		צהר	MIDDAY	844a	2
		צל	SHADOW	853b	2
		שית	PUT	1011c	3
16	4	אפס	CEASE	67a	2
		גור	SOJOURN	157d	1
		הוה	BECOME	217c	
		כלה	BE FINISHED	477d	2 c
		מץ	EXTORTIONER	568c	
		נדח	BANISH	623a	2
		ספס	DISAPPEAR	821a	
		רמס	TRAMPLE	942d	
		שדד	DEAL VIOLENTLY WITH	994b	
		שד	VIOLENCE	994c	2
		תמם	BE FINISHED	1070c	5
16	5	אהל	TENT	14a	2
		אמת	FIRMNESS	54a	3 b
		דוד	DAVID	188a	C
		דרש	SEEK	205c	6
		ה	THE	208c	1 hb
		ו	AND	253a	1 h
		חסד	GOODNESS	338d	12
		כון	BE ESTABLISHED	466d	1
		כסא	THRONE	491a	3 a
		מהר	PROMPT	555b	
		צדק	RIGHTEOUSNESS	841d	2 c
		שפט	JUDGE	1047c	1 b
16	6	בד	EMPTY TALK	95a	A
		גא	PROUD	144b	
		גאוה	MAJESTY	144d	2
		גאון	EXALTATION	145a	2
		כן	TRUE	467b	2
		סתר	COVERING	712a	2 a
		עברה	OVERFLOW	720c	2
		שוה	AGREE WITH	1000d	
16	7	אך	ONLY	36d	2 bb
		אשישה	RAISEN-CAKE	84b	
		הגה	MOAN	211d	1 b
		ילל	HOWL	410b	
		ילל	HOWL	410b	
		כום	CUP	468a	
		כל	ALL	482a	1 db
		כן	SO	486d	3
		ל	TO	515a	5 g
		נכא	STRICKEN	644d	
		קיר	KIR	885b	2
16	8	אמל	BE WEAK	51b	
		בעל	LORD	127c	14
		גפן	VINE	172c	
		חלם	SMITE	240c	
		חשבון	HESHBON	363d	
		ים	SEA	411a	3
		נגע	REACH	619b	4
		נטש	FORSAKE	644a	3
		עבר	PASS OVER	717a	1 a1
		יעזר	JAZER	741c	
		שבם	SEBAM	959b	
		שרק	VINE-TENDRILS	977d	
		שדמה	FIELD	995b	
		שלוחה	SHOOT	1020a	2
		תעה	ERR	1073c	1
16	9	אלעלא	ELEALEH	46c	
		בכה	WEEP	113c	2
		בכה	WEEP	113c	4
		בכי	WEEPING	113d	
		בכי	WEEPING	113d	
		גפן	VINE	172c	
		דמעה	TEARS	199c	2
		הידד	SHOUT	212c	2
		חשבון	HESHBON	363d	
		כן	SO	487b	3 f
		נפל	FALL	657c	4 a
		יעזר	JAZER	741c	
		קיץ	SUMMER	884d	2
		קציר	HARVESTING	894c	2
		רוה	BE SATURATED	924b	2
		שבם	SEBAM	959b	
16	10	אסף	GATHER	62d	3
		דרך	TREAD	202a	3

Ch v.	Heb	Eng	Page	Sec
	הידד	SHOUTING	212c	1
	יקב	WINE-PRESS	428c	
	כרמל	GARDEN	502a	1
	רוע	RAISE A SHOUT	929d	
	רנן	GIVE A RINGING CRY	943c	
	שמחה	JOY	970d	1
16 11	המה	MURMUR	242b	2
	כן	SO	487b	3 f
	כנור	LYRE	490a	
	ל	TO	515a	5 g
	מעה	BELLY	589a	5
	קיר	KIR	885b	2
	קרב	INWARD PART	899b	2 b
16 12	במה	HIGH PLACE	119b	3
	יכל	PREVAIL	408a	2 a
	כי	WHEN	473b	2 a
	לאה	BE WEARY	521a	1
	פלל	INTERVENE	813b	2
	מקדש	SACRED PLACE	874a	2
	ראה	TO SEE	908b	1 b
16 13	מאז	FROM THAT TIME	23b	A
	דבר	SPEAK	181a	3 b
	זה	THIS	261b	3
	מן	FROM	581d	4 c
16 14	המון	CROWD	242d	3 b
	מועד	A LITTLE	277d	2
	כבוד	HONOR	459a	3
	כבוד	GREAT	460c	
	לא	NOT	519c	2 a
	מעט	A FEW	590a	1 a
	עתה	NOW	774a	1 a
	קלה	DISHONOURED	885d	
	שכור	HIRED	969b	2
	שאר	REST	984c	
	שנה	YEAR	1040b	
17 1	דמשק	DAMASCUS	199d	
	הנה	BEHOLD	244b	B b
	מן	FROM	583b	7 bb
	מעי	RUIN-HEAP	590c	
	מפלה	RUIN	658d	
	משא	UTTERANCE	672d	
	סור	TURN ASIDE	694c	
	מעי	RUIN	730d	
17 2	חרד	TREMBLE	353c	
	עדר	FLOCK	727c	1 a
	עזב	LEAVE	737b	2 l
	רבץ	LIE DOWN	918b	
17 3	ארם	ARAM	74b	A
	מבצר	FORTIFICATION	131c	
	דמשק	DAMASCUS	199d	
	כבוד	HONOR	459a	3
	ממלכה	DOMINION	575b	2
	נאם	UTTERANCE	610b	2
	שאר	REST	984c	
	שבת	CEASE	991d	
17 4	בשר	FLESH	142c	1 b
	דלל	BE LOW	195c	
	כבוד	HONOR	459a	3
	יעקב	JACOB	785a	2
	רוה	GROW LEAN	931a	
	משמן	FATNESS	1032c	
17 5	אסף	GATHER	62b	1 c
	זרוע	ARM	283d	1 a
	לקט	GLEAN	544d	3
	קמה	STANDING GRAIN	879b	
	קצר	HARVEST	894b	
	קצר	HARVEST	894b	
	קציר	HARVESTING	894d	3
	רפאים	REPHAIM	952b	
	שבלת	EAR OF GRAIN	987c	
17 6	אלהים	GOD	44c	4 ba
	אמיר	TOP	57b	
	גרגר	BERRY	176b	
	זית	OLIVE TREE	268d	1
	ך	LIKE	455a	B
	נאם	UTTERANCE	610b	2
	נקף	STRIKING OFF	668d	
	סעיף	BRANCH	703d	2
	עוללות	GLEANING	760a	
	פרה	BEAR FRUIT	826a	2
	ראש	HEAD	910d	2 a
	שאר	REMAIN	984a	1
	שנים	TWO	1041b	1 b3
17 7	על	UPON	757d	27 c c
	עשה	DO	794b	2 1b
	קדוש	HOLY	872c	1 c
	ראה	TO SEE	908a	8 b
	שעה	GAZE	1043a	
17 8	אשרה	ASHERA	81c	B
	חמן	SUN-PILLAR	329a	
	מעשה	DEED	796a	2 a3
	אצבע	FINGER	840c	1 d
	שעה	GAZE	1043a	
17 9	אמיר	TOP	57b	
	חרש	WOOD	361c	
	מעוז	PLACE OF SAFETY	732a	1
	עזב	LEAVE	737b	2 a1
	עזובה	FORSAKENNESS	738a	
	עיר	CITY	746b	1 a
	פנה	FACE	818b	26 a
	ישראל	ISRAEL	975d	2 a3
17 10	אלהים	GOD	44c	4 bb
	זור	BE A STRANGER	266c	2 c
	זכר	REMEMBER	270a	13 b
	זמורה	BRANCH	274d	
	זרע	SOW	281d	3 d
	ישע	DELIVERANCE	447a	2
	כן	SO	487b	3 f
	נטע	PLANT	642c	1
	נטע	PLANTATION	642c	
	נעמן	PLEASANTNESS	654a	
	מעוז	PLACE OF SAFETY	732a	2 a
	צור	ROCK	849d	2 a
	שכח	FORGET	1013b	1 c
17 11	אנש	BE SICK	60c	
	זרע	SOWING	282c	2 e
	חלה	BE WEAK	318a	2
	כאב	PAIN	456b	
	נד	HEAP	622d	
	נוד	WANDER	626d	1 a
	נטע	PLANTING	642c	2
	סוג	FENCE ABOUT	691b	
	פרח	BUD	827b	1
	קציר	HARVESTING	894c	2
	קציר	HARVESTING	894d	2
17 12	הוי	AH	223a	
	המה	ROAR	242b	3
	המון	SOUND	242c	1
	כביר	GREAT	460b	
	לאם	PEOPLE	522c	
	מי	WATER	565d	4 c
	רגש	BE IN TUMULT	921c	
	שאה	MAKE A DIN	980d	
	שאון	ROAR	981a	1
17 13	גער	REBUKE	172a	2
	הר	MOUNTAIN	250d	1 m
	לאם	PEOPLE	522c	
	מץ	CHAFF	558b	
	מי	WATER	565d	4 c
	מן	FROM	578d	1 c
	נוס	FLEE	630d	1
	סופה	STORM-WIND	693a	
	רדף	PURSUE	923a	
	מרחק	DISTANT PLACE	935d	
	שאה	MAKE A DIN	980d	
	שאון	ROAR	981a	1
17 14	אין	NOT	34b	2 b
	בזז	SPOIL	102d	
	בלהה	CALAMITY	117a	2
	בקר	MORNING	134a	1 e
	גורל	LOT	174d	4
	זה	THIS	261b	3
	חלק	PORTION	324b	5
	טרם	NOT YET	382d	2
	ערב	SUNSET	787d	1 a
	שסה	PLUNDER	1042c	
18 1	הוי	AH	223a	
	כוש	CUSH	469a	2 a
	כנף	WING	489c	1 b
	עבר	REGION ACROSS	719b	1
18 2	צלצל	WHIRRING	852d	
	אבה	REED	3a	
	מבוסה	SUBJUGATION	101b	
	בוא	DIVIDE	102b	
	הוא	HE, SHE, IT	216b	3 d
	הלאה	ONWARDS	229c	B
	ירא	BE FEARFUL	431d	1
	כלי	VESSEL	480b	4
	כנף	WING	*489c	1
	מלאך	MESSENGER	521c	1 a
	מן	FROM	581d	4 a
	מרט	POLISH	599a	
	משך	DRAW	604c	
	פנה	FACE	819a	27 b
	ציר	ENVOY	851d	
	ציר	ENVOY	851d	
	קוקו	MIGHT	876a	
	קו	LINE	876a	
	קל	LIGHT	886d	
	קל	LIGHT	887a	
	הר	MOUNTAIN	*250d	1 m
	תבל	WORLD	385d	
18 3	ישב	DWELL	443b	3
	נס	STANDARD	651d	1 a
	שכן	SETTLE DOWN	1015b	2 a
	תקע	GIVE A BLOW	1075c	2
18 4	אור	LIGHT	21c	3
	חם	HEAT	328d	
	טל	NIGHT-MIST	*378c	
	טל	NIGHT-MIST	378d	
	כה	THUS	462a	1 a
	מכון	FIXED PLACE	467d	3
	נבט	LOOK	613d	3
	עב	DARK CLOUD	728a	1 g
	על	UPON	754c	2 lf e
	צח	DAZZELING	850a	
	קציר	HARVESTING	894d	3
	שקט	BE QUIET	1053a	2
18 5	בסר	UNRIPE GRAPES	126a	
	זלזל	TENDRILS	272d	
	מזמרה	PRUNING-KNIFE	275a	
	כי	BECAUSE	474a	3 c
	כרת	CUT OFF	503d	1 a
	נטישה	TENDRIL	644a	
	נצה	BLOSSOM	665b	
	פרח	BUD	827b	
	קציר	HARVESTING	894d	3
	תזז	STRIKE AWAY	1064d	
	תמם	BE FINISHED	1070c	2
18 6	בהמה	BEAST	97a	3
	חרף	REMAIN IN HARVEST-TIME	358b	
	יחדו	TOGETHER	403c	B
	ל	TO	510d	1 c
	עיט	LEAVE	737d	1
	עיט	BIRD OF PREY	743c	
	עיט	BIRD OF PREY	743c	
	קיץ	SPENT THE SUMMER	884d	
18 7	מבוסה	SUBJUGATION	101b	
	בוא	DIVIDE	102b	
	הוא	HE, SHE, IT	216b	3 d
	הלאה	ONWARDS	229c	B
	הר	MOUNTAIN	249c	1 a
	יבל	CONDUCT	385a	1
	ירא	BE FEARFUL	431d	1
	מן	FROM	581b	4 a
	מרט	POLISH	599a	
	משך	DRAW	604c	
	קוקו	MIGHT	876a	
	קו	LINE	876a	
	מקום	STANDING PLACE	880b	4
	שי	GIFT	1009c	
19 1	אליל	WORTHLESSNESS	47c	B
	הנה	BEHOLD	244b	B b
	לבב	HEART	524b	2 9b
	משא	UTTERANCE	672d	
	עב	DARK CLOUD	728a	1 c
	פנה	FACE	818c	26 b
	קל	LIGHT	887a	
	קרב	INWARD PART	899a	1 a
	רכב	RIDE	938d	2
19 2	אח	BROTHER	26b	4
	ממלכה	KINGDOM	575a	1
	רע	FRIEND	946b	3
	שכך	ADDENDA ET CORRIGENDA	1127a	
19 3	אוב	NECROMANCER	15b	2
	אטי	MUTTERER	31d	
	אליל	WORTHLESSNESS	47c	B
	בלע	SWALLOW UP	*118b	2 a
	בלע	SWALLOW UP	118b	2 a
	בקק	EMPTY	132d	
	דרש	SEEK	205b	2 b
	ידעני	FAMILIAR SPIRIT	396b	
	עצה	ADVICE	420a	
	קרב	INWARD PART	899b	2 a
	רוח	BREATH	925a	3 b
19 4	אדון	LORD	11a	1 2
	משל	RULE	605d	1
	נאם	UTTERANCE	610b	2
	נכר	TREAT AS FOREIGN	*649d	
	סכר	SHUT UP	698c	
	עז	STRONG	738d	
	קשה	SEVERE	904c	2 a
19 5	חרב	BE DRY	351a	2
	יבש	BE DRY	386c	2
	ים	SEA	411a	6
	נהר	STREAM	625d	1
	נשת	BE DRY	677a	
19 6	דלל	BE LOW	195c	
	ו	AND	252b	1 a
	זנח	REJECT	276b	
	זנח	STINK	276c	
	חרב	BE DRY	351a	2
	יאר	STREAM	384c	2 a
	מצור	EGYPT	596a	
	סוף	REEDS	693a	1
	קמל	BE DECAYED	888a	
	קנה	STALK	889c	2
19 7	מערו	PLACE OF SOWING	283c	
	יאר	STREAM	384b	1
	יבש	BE DRY	386b	1 d
	נדף	DRIVE	623d	
	על	UPON	756a	26 a
	ערה	BARE PLACE	788d	
	פה	MOUTH	805b	4
19 8	אבל	MOURN	5b	
	אמל	BE WEAK	51b	
	אנה	MOURN	58b	
	דוג	FISHER	186a	
	חכה	HOOK	335d	
	יאר	STREAM	384b	1
	מכמרת	FISHERMAN	485c	
	פנה	FACE	819a	27 b
	פרש	SPREAD OUT	831b	
	שלך	THROW	1021b	3
19 9	ארג	WEAVE	70d	
	בוש	BE ASHAMED	101d	1
	חורי	WHITE STUFF	301a	
	עבד	WORK	713a	1
	פשת	FLAX	833d	
	שריק	CARDED	977c	
19 10	אגם	SAD	8c	
	דכא	CRUSH	194a	
	נפש	SOUL	660d	6 c
	שכר	HIRE	969a	
	שת	FOUNDATION	1011d	
19 11	איך	HOW	32c	1
	אך	ONLY	36d	2 bb
	בן	SON	120c	1 ib
	בער	BE BRUTISH	129c	
	חכם	WISE	314d	2
	חכם	WISE	*314d	4
	יאל	BE FOOLISH	*383d	2

Ch	v.	Heb	Eng	Page	Sec
		יעץ	ADVISE	419d	
		עצה	ADVICE	420a	
		פרעה	PHARAOH	829a	
		צען	ZOAN	858a	
19	12	קדם	FRONT	869d	2 a
		אי	WHERE	32b	1 a
		אפו	THEN	66b	1
		חכם	WISE	314d	2
		חכם	WISE	*314d	4
		יעץ	ADVISE	419c	
		נא	PART OF EN-TREATY	609b	3 c
19	13	נגד	BE CONSPICUOUS	616d	1
		יאל	BE FOOLISH	383d	2
		מף	MEMPHIS	592a	
		נשא	DECEIVE	674a	
		פנה	CORNER	819d	2
		צען	ZOAN	858a	
		תעה	ERR	1073c	2
19	14	מסך	MIX	587c	1
		עועים	DISTORTING	730c	
		מעשה	DEED	795d	1 b3
		קיא	VOMIT	883c	
		קרב	INWARD PART	899b	2 a
		רוח	BREATH	*925b	3 h
		רוח	BREATH	925b	3 g
		שכר	DRUNKEN	1016c	
		תעה	ERR	1073c	2
		תעה	ERR	1073c	1
19	15	אגמן	BULRUSH	8c	2
		זנב	TAIL	275c	1 b
		כפה	BRANCH	497a	
		עיר	CITY	746b	1 c
		מעשה	DEED	795d	1 b3
		ראש	HEAD	910d	1 b
19	16	חרד	TREMBLE	353c	2
		יד	HAND	389c	1 d
		מצרים	EGYPTIANS	595d	2 b
		נוף	WAVE	632a	2 b
		תנופה	SWINGING	632b	1
		על	UPON	755d	2 5
		פחד	DREAD	808b	1
19	17	אדמה	LAND	9d	5
		זכר	REMEMBER	271a	3 b
		חגג	MAKE PILGRIMAGE	*290d	3
		חגא	REELING	291b	
		יהודה	JUDAH	397b	2
		יעץ	ADVISE	419c	
19	18	עצה	ADVICE	420a	
		פחד	DREAD	808b	1
		אלישבע	ELISHEBA	45d	
		אמר	SAY	56c	
		הרס	OVERTHROW	249a	
		כנען	CANAAN	488d	2 a
		שפה	SPEECH	974a	2
		שבע	SWEAR	989b	1 a
19	19	גבול	BORDER	147d	1 a
		מזבח	ALTAR	258b	1
		מצבה	PILLAR	663b	1 c
19	20	אות	SIGN	17a	5
		ישע	DELIVER	446c	1 a
		לחץ	OPPRESS	537d	2
		עד	WITNESS	729c	1
		צעק	CRY	858a	1 b
19	21	זבח	SACRIFICE	257c	1 1
		זבח	SACRIFICE	258a	2 7
		ידע	MAKE ONESELF KNOWN	394c	1
		מנחה	OFFERING	585b	3
		מצרים	EGYPTIANS	595d	2 b
		נדר	VOW	623d	
		נדר	VOW	624a	2
		עבד	WORK	713b	4 a
		שלם	BE COMPLETE	1022c	4
19	22	נגף	STRIKE	619d	
		עתר	PRAY	801c	
		רפא	HEAL	950d	2 a
		רפא	HEAL	950d	2 a
19	23	אשור	ASSYRIA	78d	3
		אשור	ASSYRIA	78d	3
		אשור	ASSHUR	78d	2
		ב	IN	88c	1 4
		מצרים	EGYPTIANS	595d	2 b
		מצרים	EGYPT	595d	1 b1
		מסלה	HIGHWAY	700c	
19	24	אשור	ASSHUR	78d	2
		ברכה	BLESSING	139d	2
		שלישי	THIRD	1026b	
19	25	אשור	ASSHUR	78d	2
		ברך	BLESS	138d	2 b
		ברך	BLESS	139a	2 a
		מצרים	EGYPTIANS	595d	2 b
		נחלה	PROPERTY	635b	1 e
		מעשה	DEED	796b	2 b
20	1	אשדוד	AHSDOD	78c	
		אשדוד	AHSDOD	78c	
		אשור	ASSYRIA	78d	4
		לחם	ENGAGE IN BAT-TLE	535c	
		סרגון	SARGON	710a	
		שנה	YEAR	1040b	
		תרתן	FIELD-MARSHAL	1077a	
20	2	אמוץ	AMOZ	55b	
		דבר	SPEAK	181c	4 a
		הלך	WALK	232d	1 4a
		חלץ	DRAW OFF OR OUT	322d	1
		יחף	BAREFOOT	405a	
		מתנים	LOINS	608b	1 e
		נעל	SANDAL	653d	
		ערום	NAKED	736a	
		פתח	OPEN	835c	2
		שק	SACK	974c	2 a
20	3	אות	SIGN	16d	4
		מופת	SIGN	69a	2
		הלך	WALK	231d	1 1d 5k
		יחף	BAREFOOT	405a	
		כוש	CUSH	469a	2 c
		מצרים	EGYPT	595c	1 a
		עבד	SLAVE	714b	4
		ערום	NAKED	736a	
20	4	זקן	OLD	278c	2 a
		חשף	STRIP OFF	362c	2
		יחף	BAREFOOT	405a	
		כוש	CUSH	469a	2 b
		כן	SO	486c	2 cd
		מצרים	EGYPT	595c	1 a
		נהג	DRIVE	624b	1
		נער	YOUTH	655a	1 d
		ערום	NAKED	736a	
		ערוה	NAKEDNESS	789a	1
		שבי	CAPTIVITY	985d	3
		שת	BUTTOCKS	1059d	
20	5	בוש	BE ASHAMED	101d	2
		חתת	BE SHATTERED	369b	2 a
		כוש	CUSH	469a	2 c
		מצרים	EGYPT	595c	1 a
		מבט	EXPECTATION	614a	
		תפארה	BEAUTY	802d	3 b
20	6	אי	COAST	15d	2
		איך	HOW	32c	1
		אנחנו	WE	59d	
		אשור	ASSYRIA	78d	4
		כה	THUS	462a	1
		מלט	SLIP AWAY	572b	2
		מבט	EXPECTATION	614a	
		נוס	FLEE	630d	1
		נצל	BE DELIVERED	664c	2
		עזרה	HELP	740d	1
		שם	THERE	1027b	2
21	1	חלף	PASS ON OR AWAY	322a	1 a
		ים	SEA	411a	6
		ירא	BE FEARFUL	431d	1
		כי	BECAUSE	*474a	3
		ל	TO	514b	5 fb
		נגב	SOUTH-COUNTRY	616b	1 b
		משא	UTTERANCE	672d	
		סופה	STORM-WIND	693a	
		אנחה	SIGHING	58d	
21	2	בגד	ACT TREACHER-OUSLY	93d	D
		חזות	VISION	303b	1
		כי	BECAUSE	*474a	3 c
		מדי	MEDES	552a	1
		נגד	BE CONSPICUOUS	617a	
		נגד	BE CONSPICUOUS	617a	
		עילם	ELAM	743d	
		צור	CONFINE	848d	2
		קשה	SEVERE	904d	2 a
		שדד	DEAL VIOLENTLY WITH	994a	
		שדד	DEAL VIOLENTLY WITH	994b	
21	3	אחז	GRASP	28b	
		בהל	BE DISTURBED	96b	1
		חלחלה	ANGUISH	298b	
		ילד	BEAR	408c	1 b
		כי	BECAUSE	*474a	3 c
		כן	SO	487b	3 f
		מתנים	LOINS	608b	2 b
		עוה	BEND	730c	
		צור	PANG	852a	
		צור	PANG	852a	
		שמע	HEAR	1033d	1 e
21	4	בעת	FALL UPON	130a	1
		חרדה	TREMBLING	353d	1
		חשק	DESIRE	366a	
		כי	BECAUSE	*474a	3 c
		ל	TO	512c	4 b
		לבב	HEART	524b	2 9b
		נשף	TWILIGHT	676a	1
		פלצות	SHUDDERING	814a	1
		תעה	ERR	1073c	2
21	5	מגן	SHIELD	171c	
		כי	BECAUSE	*474a	3 c
		משח	ANOINT	603a	1
		ערך	ARRANGE	789c	1 c
		צפה	LAY OUT	860a	
		צפית	CARPET	860b	
		שר	CHIEFTAIN	978a	2 a
		שלחן	TABLE	1020b	1
21	6	כי	BECAUSE	474a	3 c
		עמד	STAND	764d	1
		צפה	KEEP WATCH	859d	1
21	7	חמור	HE-ASS	331b	2 b
		פרש	HORSEMAN	832b	
		צמד	COUPLE	855a	1
		קשב	ATTENTIVENESS	904a	
		קשב	ATTEND	904a	
		רב	MUCH	913b	1 c
		רכב	CHARIOT	939b	4
		אריה	LION	71d	
21	8	יומם	BY DAY	401c	2
		לילה	NIGHT	539a	1
		תמיד	CONTINUITY	556b	1 a
		נצב	STAND	662a	1 b
		מצפה	WATCH TOWER	859d	1
		משמרת	GUARD	1038c	1
21	9	בבל	BABEL	93c	
		זה	THIS	261c	4 g
		ל	TO	511c	1 ga
		פסיל	IDOL	821a	
		פרש	HORSEMAN	832b	
		צמד	COUPLE	855a	1
		רכב	CHARIOT	939b	2
21	10	אלהים	GOD	44c	4 ba
		את	WITH	86d	4 c
		בן	SON	121c	6
		גרן	THRESHING-FLOOR	175c	
		מדשה	THAT WHICH IS THRESHED	190d	
		צבא	GOD OF WAR	839c	4 b
21	11	דומה	DUMAH	189a	1
		דומה	SILENCE	189a	
		דומה	DUMAH	189a	3
		לילה	NIGHT	539b	2
		מה	WHAT	552b	1
		מן	FROM	580c	3 a
		משא	UTTERANCE	672d	
		שעיר	SEIR	973a	1 a
		שמר	KEEP	1036c	1 b
21	12	אתה	COME	87b	
		אתה	COME	87c	
		בעה	INQUIRE	126d	1
		בקר	MORNING	133d	1 a
		לילה	NIGHT	539b	2
		שוב	TURN BACK	997b	3 b
		שמר	KEEP	1036c	1 b
21	13	ארחה	TRAVELLING COM-PANY	73c	
		דדני	DEDANITES	187a	
		יער	WOOD	420d	E
		משא	UTTERANCE	672d	
		ערב	DESRT-PLATEAU	787a	
		צור	ROCK	849c	1 a
21	14	אתה	COME	87c	
		נדד	RETREAT	622b	1
		צמא	THIRSTY	854d	
		קדם	COME IN FRONT	870a	1 b
		קרא	ENCOUNTER	897a	1
		תימא	TEMA	1066d	
21	15	דרך	TREAD	202b	4
		חרב	SWORD	352c	1 c
		חרב	SWORD	*352c	1 d
		כבד	VEHEMENCE	458c	3
		מלחמה	WAR	536d	
		נדד	RETREAT	622b	1
		נטש	PERMIT	644a	3
		קשת	BOW	906c	1 d
21	16	כבוד	HONOR	459a	1 d
		כלה	BE FINISHED	477d	2 c
		עוד	STILL	729a	1 ab
		עוד	STILL	729c	2 ab
		קדר	KEDAR	871a	1
		שכיר	HIRED	969b	2
		שנה	YEAR	1040b	
21	17	אלהים	GOD	44c	4 ba
		גבור	STRONG	150b	2
		דבר	SPEAK	180d	1
		מעט	BE SMALL	589c	
		קדר	KEDAR	871b	1
		קשת	BOW	906a	1 c
		שאר	REST	984c	
22	1	אפו	THEN	66b	1
		גג	ROOF	150d	1
		גיא	VALLEY	161b	
		חזיון	VISION	303b	1
		כי	THAT	472d	1 f
		ל	TO	511b	1 ga
		מה	WHAT	552d	1 ac
		משא	UTTERANCE	672d	
22	2	המה	ROAR	242b	4
		חלל	PIERCED	319c	2
		מלא	FULL	571a	
		עיר	CITY	746c	1 h
		עליז	EXULTANT	759c	
		תשאה	NOISE	996c	
22	3	אסר	TIE	64a	
		ברח	FLEE	137d	2
		יחד	ALTOGETHER	403b	2 b
		יחדו	TOGETHER	*403c	B
		מן	FROM	578c	1 b
		מן	FROM	578d	1 c
		מן	OUT OF	580a	2 eb
		מצא	FIND	593d	1 c
		נדד	RETREAT	622b	1
		קצין	CHIEF	892d	3
		קשת	BOW	906a	1 b
		רחק	DISTANT	935c	2 a3
22	4	בכי	WEEPING	113d	
		בת	DAUGHTER	123c	3
		מרר	BE BITTER	600b	1
		תמרור	BITTERNESS	*601b	
		נחם	CONSOLE ONESELF	637a	
		עם	PEOPLE	767a	5 f
		שד	VIOLENCE	994c	2
		שעה	GAZE	*1043a	
		שעה	GAZE	1043a	
22	5	אדון	LORD	11d	6 a

337

ISAIAH

Ch	v.	Heb	Eng	Page	Sec
		מבוכה	CONFUSION	100d	
		מבוסה	SUBJUGATION	101b	
		גיא	VALLEY	161b	2
		מהומה	DISCOMFITURE	223a	2
		הר	MOUNTAIN	249c	1 a
		חזיון	VISION	303b	1
		יום	DAY	398d	2 f
		ל	TO	513b	5 ba
		קיר	WALL	885b	3
		קרר	TEAR DOWN	903b	
		שוע	CRY	1003a	
22	6	אדם	MAN	9b	2
		אשפה	QUIVER	80c	
		מגן	SHIELD	171c	
		עילם	ELAM	743d	
		ערה	BE NAKED	788c	1
		פרש	HORSEMAN	832b	
		קיר	KIR	885b	
		רכב	CHARIOT	939b	4
22	7	היה	COME TO PASS	224d	2 / a1 am
		עמק	VALE	771a	
		פרש	HORSEMAN	832b	
		רכב	CHARIOT	*939b	4
		שית	PUT	1011c	4
22	8	בית	HOUSE	108d	1 ag
		יער	WOOD	420c	A
		נבט	LOOK	613d	2
		נשק	EQUIPMENT	676d	1
		מסך	COVERING	697b	1
22	9	בקיע	FISSURE	132c	
		ברכה	POOL	140a	
		דוד	DAVID	188a	A
		קבץ	GATHER	868a	2
		ראה	TO SEE	907a	2 1
		רבב	BECOME MUCH	912d	1
		תחתון	LOWER	1066b	
22	10	בצר	MAKE INACCESSIBLE	131a	
		חומה	WALL	327b	1
		חומה	WALL	327c	1
		נתץ	PULL DOWN	683b	1
22	11	בין	INTERVAL	107b	1
		ברכה	POOL	140a	
		חומה	WALL	327b	1
		חומה	WALL	327b	1
		יצר	FORM	427d	2 b
		ישן	OLD	446a	
		נבט	LOOK	613d	2
		מקוה	RESERVOIR	876c	
		רחק	DISTANT	935c	2 b
22	12	אדון	LORD	11d	6 a
		בכי	WEEPING	113d	
		חגר	GIRD	291d	2
		מספד	WAILING	704d	3
		קרא	CALL	895d	5 d
		שק	SACK	974c	2
22	13	בקר	CATTLE	133b	1 a
		בשר	FLESH	142c	1 a
		הרג	KILL	247b	4
		מחר	TO-MORROW	564a	1 b
		ששון	REJOICING	965b	
		שמחה	JOY	970d	1
		שחט	SLAUGHTER	1006a	1
22	14	אדון	LORD	11d	6 c
		אם	IF	50b	1 b2
		כפר	BE COVERED OVER	498b	1
		עד	UNTIL	725a	2 1b b
		עד	UNTIL	725b	2 3
		עון	INIQUITY	731a	1 c3
22	15	אדון	LORD	11d	6 c
		אל	TO	41b	
		בוא	GO	98d	4
		בית	HOUSE	110b	6
		הלך	WALK	234b	1 5f 2
		סכן	BE OF USE	698b	1
		על	UPON	755b	2 3
		על	UPON	757b	2 7c aa
		שבנא	SHEBNA	987d	
22	16	חצב	HEW	345a	1
		חקק	CUT IN	349a	1
		כי	THAT	472d	1 f
		כל	ALL	*481d	1 da
		מה	WHAT	552d	1 ad
		סלע	CRAG	701a	1
		פה	HERE	806a	1 a
		קברצר	GRAVE	868a	
		מרום	HEIGHT	928d	1
		משכן	DWELLING-PLACE	1015d	1
22	17	גבר	MAN	150a	
		הנה	BEHOLD	244b	B b
		טלטלה	A HURLING	376d	
		טול	HURL	376d	
		עטה	GRASP	742a	
22	18	אספה	A GATHERING	63b	
		דור	BALL	189c	1
		יד	HAND	390c	3 d
		כבוד	HONOR	458c	2 b
		כדור	BALL	462a	
		צנף	WRAP	857b	
		צנפה	WINDING	857b	
		קלון	DISHONOUR	886a	2
		מרכבה	CHARIOT	939d	
		שם	THERE	1027c	3 c
22	19	הדף	THRUST	213d	3
		הרס	THROW DOWN	248d	1
		מצב	STATION	662d	2
		מעמד	OFFICE	765b	1
22	20	אליקים	ELIAKIM	45d	A
		חלקיהו	HILKIAH	324d	1
		עבד	SLAVE	714a	3
22	21	אב	FATHER	3d	7
		אם	MOTHER	52a	2
		בית	HOUSE	110a	5 de
		אבנט	GIRDLE	126a	
		חזק	BE FIRM	304d	4 a
		כתנת	TUNIC	509a	
		לבש	CLOTHE	528b	1 a
		ממשלה	RULE	606a	1
22	22	בית	HOUSE	109d	5 a
		בית	HOUSE	110a	5 c
		סגר	SHUT	689a	1
		על	UPON	753c	2 1c
		פתח	OPEN	835a	
		מפתח	KEY	836b	
		שכם	SHOULDER	1014b	1 a
22	23	אמן	CONFIRM	52d	2
		יתד	PEG	450b	B
		כבוד	HONOR	458c	2 b
		כסא	SEAT OF HONOR	490d	2
		מקום	STANDING PLACE	880b	4
		תקע	THRUST	1075c	1
22	24	אגן	BASIN	8c	3
		צאצא	OFFSPRING	425c	1
		יתד	PEG	450b	B
		כבוד	HONOR	459c	3
		כלי	VESSEL	480b	3
		נבל	JAR	614b	2
		צפיעה	OFF SHOOT	861c	
		קטן	SMALL	882a	1 b
		תלה	HANG	1068a	1
22	25	אמן	CONFIRM	52d	2
		גדע	HEW OFF	154b	
		דבר	SPEAK	180d	1
		כרת	BE CUT OFF	504a	1 a
		מוש	DEPART	559a	
		נאם	UTTERANCE	619b	2
		נפל	FALL	657a	1
		משא	LOAD	672c	1
		מקום	STANDING PLACE	880b	4
		תקע	THRUST	1075c	1
23	1	אניה	A SHIP	58c	3
		ארץ	EARTH	76a	2 a
		דמם	WAIL	199b	
		ילל	HOWL	410b	
		כתי	KITTIM	508c	
		מן	FROM	583b	7 ba
		מן	FROM	583c	7 bb
		משא	UTTERANCE	672d	
		מעוז	PLACE OF SAFETY	732a	2 b
		צר	TYER	862d	
		שדד	DEAL VIOLENTLY WITH	994b	
		תרשיש	TARSHISH	1077a	1
		תרשיש	TARSHISH	*1077a	1
23	2	אי	COAST	15d	
		דמם	BE DUMB	199a	3
		דמם	WAIL	199b	
		מלא	FILL	570c	1
		סחר	GO AROUND	695c	2
		פקד	ATTEND TO	823b	A 1b
		צידון	SIDON	851a	
23	3	תבואה	REVENUE	100b	2 a
		זרע	SOWING	282b	2 d
		יאר	STREAM	384c	1
		סחר	TRAFFIC	695c	
		קציר	HARVESTING	894c	2
		שיחור	SHIHOR	1009d	
23	4	בוש	BE ASHAMED	101d	1
		בחור	YOUNG MAN	104c	
		בתולה	VIRGIN	144a	
		גדל	GROW UP	152b	1
		חול	WHIRL	297a	2 a
		ילד	BEAR	408c	1 a
		לא	NOT	518c	1 aa
		מעוז	PLACE OF SAFETY	732a	1
		צידון	SIDON	851a	
		רוח	BE WIDE	927a	
		רום	BE HIGH	927a	1 a
23	5	חול	WHIRL	297a	2 b
		כ	LIKE	453d	1 a
		כ	LIKE	454d	3 b
		כאשר	WHEN	455c	3
		ל	TO	511b	1 ga
		צידון	SIDON	851a	
		צר	TYER	862d	
		שמע	REPORT	1034d	
		שמע	REPORT	1034d	
23	6	אי	COAST	15d	
		דמם	WAIL	199b	
		ילל	HOWL	410b	
		עבר	PASS OVER	717a	1 a2
		תרשיש	TARSHISH	1077a	1
23	7	זה	THIS	261a	3
		יבל	CONDUCT	385a	2
		ל	TO	512d	5 aa
		מן	FROM	578d	1 c
		מן	FROM	581c	4 a
		עליו	EXULTANT	759c	
		קדם	FRONT	869d	2 b
		קדמה	ANTIQUITY	870b	1
		רחק	DISTANT	935c	2 a3
23	8	יעץ	ADVISE	419c	
		כבד	BE HONORED	457c	1 b
		מי	WHO	567a	F e
		סתר	GO AROUND	695c	2
		עטר	CROWN	743a	
		צר	TYER	862d	
		שר	CHIEFTAIN	978d	7
		כנעני	ADDENDA ET CORRIGENDA	1124c	
23	9	גאון	EXALTATION	145a	1 a
		חלל	POLLUTE	320c	2
		יעץ	ADVISE	419c	
		כבד	BE HONORED	457c	1 b
		מי	WHO	*567a	F e
		צדיק	BEAUTY	840a	1 b
		קלל	BE SILENT	886d	2
23	10	בת	DAUGHTER	123c	3
		יאר	STREAM	384c	1
23	11	אל	TO	40c	6
		כנען	CANAAN	488d	2 b
		ממלכה	KINGDOM	575a	1
		נטה	EXTEND	640a	1 a
		מעוז	PLACE OF SAFETY	732a	1
		על	UPON	755b	2 5
		צוה	COMMAND	845d	1 e
		שמד	BE EXTERMINATED	1029c	1
23	12	בת	DAUGHTER	123c	3
		בתולה	VIRGIN	144a	
		גם	YEA	169c	3
		יסף	DO AGAIN	415c	2 a
		כתי	KITTIM	508c	
		נוח	REST	628b	2
		עבר	PASS OVER	717a	1 a2
		עלז	EXULT	759c	
		עשק	OPPRESS	799a	
		צידון	SIDON	851a	
		שם	THERE	1027a	1 a
23	13	ארמון	CITADEL	74d	
		ארץ	EARTH	76a	2
		אשור	ASSHUR	78d	2
		בחון	SEIGE-TOWER	103d	
		היה	BE	226d	3 1
		הן	BEHOLD	243c	A
		זה	THIS	260d	2 a
		יסד	FOUND	413d	
		כשדים	CHALDEANS	505a	1 b
		מפלה	RUIN	658c	
		ערר	STRIP ONESELF	792d	
		צי	YELPER	850d	
		קום	STAND	878d	2 b
23	14	אניה	A SHIP	58c	
		ילל	HOWL	410b	
		מעוז	PLACE OF SAFETY	732a	1
		שדד	DEAL VIOLENTLY WITH	994b	
		תרשיש	TARSHISH	*1077a	1
		תרשיש	TARSHISH	1077a	1
23	15	זנה	COMMIT FORNICATION	275d	
		ך	LIKE	453d	1 b
		צר	TYER	862d	
		שירה	SONG	1010c	
		שכח	FORGET	1013b	
23	16	זכר	REMEMBER	270c	1 a
		זנה	COMMIT FORNICATION	275d	
		יטב	DO WELL	405d	2
		כנור	LYRE	490a	
		נגן	PLAY	618d	
		סבב	GO AROUND	685d	2 c
		מען	PURPOSE	775c	2 b
		רבה	BECOME MANY	915b	
		רבה	BECOME MANY	915c	1 c
		שיר	SONG	1010b	1
		שכח	FORGET	1013b	
23	17	היה	COME TO PASS	225b	1 2b ae
		זנה	COMMIT FORNICATION	275d	
		ל	TO	511b	1 ga
		ממלכה	KINGDOM	575b	1
		פקד	ATTEND TO	823b	A 2
		צר	TYER	862d	
		שוב	TURN BACK	997c	5 d
		אתנן	HIRE	1072d	
23	18	אצר	STORE UP	69d	
		חסן	STRONG	340d	
		מכסה	COVERING	492c	
		ל	TO	515b	5 hb b
		סחר	TRAFFIC	695c	
		עתיק	EMINENT	801b	
		פנה	FACE	817b	2 4a h
		קדש	APARTNESS	872b	4 b
		שבעה	SATIETY	960a	1
		אתנן	HIRE	1072d	
		חסן	ADDENDA ET CORRIGENDA	1123c	
24	1	בלק	WASTE	118d	
		בקק	EMPTY	132d	
		הנה	BEHOLD	244b	B b
		עוה	DISTORTION	*730c	
		עוה	BEND	730c	
		פוץ	BE DISPERSED	807b	1 a

Ch	v.	Heb	Eng	Page	Sec
		פנה	FACE	816b	1 5
		קבב	CURSE	*866d	
24	2	אדון	LORD	11a	2 1b
		אשר	PARTICLE OF RELATION	82a	1
		גברת	MISTRESS	150c	2
		היה	BECOME	226b	2 2c
		כ	LIKE	454c	2 a
		כהן	PRIEST	463d	4
		לוה	BORROW	531a	
		לוה	BORROW	531a	
		מכר	SELL	569b	
		נשא	BE A CREDITOR	673d	
		נשה	LEND	674c	
		עבד	SLAVE	713d	1
		קנה	ACQUIRE	889a	2
		שפחה	MAID	1046c	1
24	3	בזז	SPOIL	103a	
		בלק	WASTE	118d	
		בקק	EMPTY	132d	
		דבר	SPEAK	180d	1
		קבב	CURSE	*866d	
24	4	אבל	MOURN	5c	
		אמל	BE WEAK	51b	
		תבל	WORLD	385d	
		נבל	SINK	615c	2
		מרום	HEIGHT	929a	4
24	5	ברית	COVENANT	137b	3 3
		ברית	COVENANT	137b	3 2
		חלף	PASS ON OR AWAY	322a	3 b
		חנף	BE POLLUTED	338a	1
		חק	SOMETHING PRESCRIBED	349c	6 d
		חקה	SOMETHING PRESCRIBED	350b	2 e
		תורה	LAW	436a	2 a
		עבר	PASS OVER	717c	1 i
		עולם	LONG DURATION	762c	2 d
		פרר	BREAK	830b	1 b
		תחת	UNDERNEATH	1065c	2 1c c
24	6	אלה	OATH	46d	3 a
		אנוש	MAN	60d	2
		אשם	OFFEND	79c	3
		מזער	A LITTLE	277d	2
		חרר	BE HOT	359b	2
24	7	אמל	BE WEAK	51c	
		אנח	SIGN	58d	1
		גפן	VINE	172a	
		תירוש	NEW WINE	440d	
		ל	TO	511a	1 e
		לב	HEART	525c	2 9a
		שמח	JOYFUL	970a	1
24	8	חדל	CEASE	293a	1
		כנור	LYRE	490a	
		עליז	EXULTANT	759c	
		משוש	EXULTATION	965c	2
		שאון	ROAR	981a	2
		תף	TIMBREL	1074b	
24	9	יין	WINE	406c	C
		מרר	BE BITTER	600a	1
		שיר	SONG	1010b	1
24	10	כל	ALL	481c	1 b
		מן	FROM	583b	7 ba
		סגר	BE SHUT UP	689c	1
		קריה	TOWN	900b	3
		תהו	FORMLESSNESS	1062c	2 a
24	11	חוץ	THE OUTSIDE	300b	2 a
		ערב	BECOME EVENING	788a	
		צוחה	OUTCRY	846d	
		משוש	EXULTATION	965c	
24	12	כתת	BE BEATEN	510c	
		שאיה	RUIN	981a	
		שמה	WASTE	1031c	1
24	13	אם	IF	50c	1 b4 b
		בציר	VINTAGE	131b	
		זית	OLIVE TREE	268d	1
		כה	THUS	462a	1
		כלה	BE FINISHED	477c	1 a
		נקף	STRIKING OFF	668d	
		עוללות	GLEANING	760a	
		קרב	INWARD PART	899a	1 e
24	14	גאון	EXALTATION	145a	1 b
		הם	THEY	241b	1 a
		מן	FROM	578a	1 a
		נשא	LIFT	670c	1 b 5
		צהל	CRY SHRILLY	843d	2
		רנן	GIVE A RINGING CRY	943b	1
24	15	אי	COAST	16a	
		אורים	EAST	22a	
		אלהים	GOD	44c	4 ba
		כבד	MAKE HONORABLE	457d	2 c
24	16	אוי	WOE	17a	
		בגד	ACT TREACHEROUSLY	93d	D
		בגד	TREACHERY	93d	
		בגד	ACT TREACHEROUSLY	93d	A
		בגד	ACT TREACHEROUSLY	93d	A
		בגד	GARMENT	94a	1
		זמיר	SONG	274b	
		כנף	EXTREMITY	489d	2 b
		צבי	HONOUR	840a	2
		צדיק	JUST	843b	4
		רזי	LEANNESS	931a	

Ch	v.	Heb	Eng	Page	Sec
24	17	על	UPON	756c	2 7a b
		פח	BIRD-TRAP	809a	2 a
		פחת	PIT	809b	
24	18	ארבה	LATTICE	70d	
		ארץ	EARTH	76a	1 b
		ארץ	EARTH	76a	1 b
		היה	COME TO PASS	225a	1 2b ag
		מוסד	FOUNDATION	414c	
		לכד	CAPTURE	540b	2
		נפל	FALL	656d	1
		עלה	GO UP	748b	1 b
		פחד	DREAD	808c	2
		פח	BIRD-TRAP	809a	2 a
		פחת	PIT	809b	
		פתח	OPEN	835c	
		מרום	HEIGHT	928d	2
24	19	ארץ	EARTH	76a	1 b
		מוט	SLIP	556d	
		מוט	SHAKE	557a	
		פרר	SPLIT	830c	
		רעע	BREAK	950a	
24	20	ארץ	EARTH	76a	1 b
		יסף	DO AGAIN	415c	2
		כבד	BE HEAVY	457b	1
		מלונה	LODGE	534a	
		לוע	SWALLOW	*534b	
		נוד	MOVE TO AND FRO	627a	1
		נפל	FALL	657b	2 b
		פשע	TRANSGRESSION	833d	4
		שכר	DRUNKEN	1016c	
24	21	אדמה	GROUND	9d	4
		אדמה	EARTH	10a	6
		צבא	HOST	839a	1 b
		מרום	HEIGHT	928d	2
		מרום	HEIGHT	929a	2
24	22	אסף	GATHER	63a	
		אספה	A GATHERING	63b	
		אסיר	PRISONERS	64b	
		בור	PIT	92c	4
		מן	FROM	581c	4 b
		סגר	BE SHUT UP	689c	2
		מסגר	DUNGEON	689d	2
		על	UPON	757c	2 7c ab
		פקד	ATTEND TO	823d	2
24	23	הר	MOUNTAIN	249c	1 a
		זקן	OLD	278d	2 b
		חמה	HEAT	329a	1
		חפר	BE ABASHED	344a	
		כבוד	GLORY	459a	2 c3
		לבנה	MOON	526b	
		מלך	BE KING	574a	
		ציון	ZION	851c	
25	1	אמן	FAITHFULNESS	53b	
		אמונה	FIRMNESS	53c	3 b
		אמונה	FIRMNESS	53d	3
		יהוה	YAHWEH	219a	2 1f
		ידה	PRAISE	392b	1 a2
		עצה	ADVICE	420b	1
		פלא	WONDER	810c	2
		רום	BE HIGH	927b	3
		רחק	DISTANT	935c	2 b
25	2	ארמון	CITADEL	74d	
		בנה	BUILD	125a	1 b
		בצר	MAKE INACCESSIBLE	131a	
		זור	BE A STRANGER	266c	2 c
		מן	FROM	583b	7 bb
		מפלה	RUIN	658c	
		עולם	LONG DURATION	762b	2 b1
		קריה	TOWN	900b	3
25	3	שום	TO PLACE	964c	5 a
		ירא	FEAR	431c	3 b
		כבד	MAKE HONORABLE	457d	2 c
		עז	STRONG	738d	
		קריה	TOWN	900b	3
25	4	אביון	NEEDY	2d	
		דל	POOR	195d	
		זרם	FLOOD OF RAIN	281b	
		מחסה	REFUGE	340b	A
		חרב	DRYNESS	351b	3
		מן	FROM	578b	1 a
		מעוז	PLACE OF SAFETY	732a	2 a
		עריץ	AWE-INSPIRING	792b	
		צל	SHADOW	853b	2
		צל	SHADOW	853b	2
		צר	STRAITS	865b	
		קיר	WALL	885a	1 b
		רוח	BREATH	924d	1 d2
25	5	זור	BE A STRANGER	266c	2 c
		זמיר	SONG	274c	
		חרב	DRYNESS	351b	3
		כנע	HUMBLE	488c	1
		עב	DARK CLOUD	728a	1 d
		ענה	BE BOWED DOWN	776a	1
		עריץ	AWE-INSPIRING	792b	
		ציה	DRYNESS	851b	
		שאון	ROAR	981a	1
25	6	זקק	REFINE	279b	
		מחה	FULL OF MARROW	562d	
		עשה	DO	794c	2 1c
		שמן	FAT	1032a	1
		שמר	LEES	1038d	
		משתה	FEAST	1059d	1

Ch	v.	Heb	Eng	Page	Sec
		זקק	ADDENDA ET CORRIGENDA	1123a	
25	7	בלע	SWALLOW UP	118c	2 a
		לוט	WRAP	532a	
		לוט	COVERING	532b	
		נסך	WEAVE	651b	
		מסכה	WEB	651b	
		פנה	FACE	816b	1 5
25	8	אדון	LORD	11c	4 b
		בלע	SWALLOW UP	118c	2
		דבר	SPEAK	180d	1
		דמעה	TEARS	199c	
		ה	THE	208b	1 ha
		חרפה	REPROACH	357d	1
		כל	ALL	481b	1 a
		מחה	WIPE	562a	1
		נצח	EVERLASTINGNESS	664b	4
		סור	TURN ASIDE	694b	1
		על	UPON	758c	4 2a
		על	UPON	758d	4 2b
		פנה	FACE	815d	1 1a
25	9	ו	AND	254b	3
		זה	THIS	261d	5
		ישע	DELIVER	446d	1 b
		ישועה	DELIVERANCE	447b	3
		קוה	WAIT FOR	875d	1
25	10	במו	IN	91b	
		דוש	THRESH	190c	
		מדמנה	DUNG-PLACE	199b	
		מדמן	MADMEN	*199b	
		מי	WATER	565c	3
		נוח	REST	628b	1
		מתבן	STRAW/HEAP	1062a	
		תחת	UNDERNEATH	1065d	2 ia
25	11	ארבה	ARTIFICE	70c	
		גאוה	PRIDE	144d	3
		עם	WITH	767b	1 a
		פרש	SPREAD OUT	831c	1 b
		קרב	INWARD PART	899a	1 c
		שחה	SWIM	965c	
		שוט	GO ABOUT	*1001d	
		שפל	BECOME LOW	1050b	1
25	12	מבצר	FORTIFICATION	131c	1
		חומה	WALL	327b	1
		נגע	TOUCH	619b	1
		עד	AS FAR AS	724a	1 1a
		עפר	DRY EARTH	779d	1 c
		משגב	SECURE HEIGHT	960d	1 a
		שחח	BOW	1005d	
		שפל	BECOME LOW	1050b	1
26	1	חל	RAMPART	298a	1
		חומה	WALL	327d	3
		ישועה	DELIVERANCE	447b	3
		עז	STRENGTH	738d	1
		עיר	CITY	746b	1 a
		שיר	SONG	1010b	2
		שיר	SING	1010d	
		שית	PUT	1011c	3
26	2	אמן	TRUSTING	53c	1
		גוי	NATION	156d	1 b
		פתח	OPEN	835a	
26	3	בטח	TRUST	105a	1 3a
		יצר	PURPOSE	428a	4
		נצר	GUARD	665d	1
		סמך	LEAN	702a	2
26	4	ב	IN	89a	1 7c
		בטח	TRUST	105a	1 3a
		יה	YAH	219c	
		עד	PERPETUITY	723d	2 c
		עולם	LONG DURATION	763a	2 1
		צור	ROCK	849d	2 a
26	5	נגע	TOUCH	619b	1
		עד	AS FAR AS	724a	1 1a
		עפר	DRY EARTH	779d	1 c
		קריה	TOWN	900b	3
		מרום	HEIGHT	928d	1
		שגב	BE HIGH	960c	1
		שחח	BOW	1006a	
		שפל	BECOME LOW	1050b	1
		שפל	BECOME LOW	*1050b	1
26	6	דל	WEAK	195d	
		עני	POOR	777a	3
		פעם	BEAT	822a	1 b
		רמס	TRAMPLE	942d	1
26	7	ארח	WAY	73a	2
		ישר	STRAIGHT	449a	1
		מישר	LEVEL	449d	1
		ל	TO	513d	5 cb e
		מעגל	ENTRENCHMENT	722d	2 b
		פלס	WEIGH	814a	1
		צדיק	JUST	843b	4
26	8	תאוה	DESIRE	16c	1
		ארח	WAY	73b	3 b
		זכר	REMEMBRANCE	271b	2 a
		ל	TO	*510d	1
		נפש	SOUL	660d	6 a
		קוה	WAIT FOR	875d	1
		משפט	JUDGMENT	1048c	1 f
26	9	אוה	DESIRE	16a	
		תבל	WORLD	385d	
		ל	TO	511c	1 ga
		לילה	NIGHT	538d	1
		למד	LEARN	540d	
		צדק	RIGHTEOUSNESS	841d	5
		קרב	INWARD PART	899b	2 a
		רוח	BREATH	925c	5 a

Ch	v.	Heb	Eng	Page	Sec
		שחר	LOOK EARLY	1007c	
		משפט	JUDGMENT	1048c	1 f
26	10	בל	NOT	115b	
		גאות	MAJESTY	145a	2
		חנן	SHOW FAVOR	336b	
		למד	LEARN	540d	
		נכח	STRAIGHTNESS	647c	
		עול	ACT WRONGFULLY	732c	
		צדק	RIGHTEOUSNESS	841d	5
		רשע	WICKED	957b	2
26	11	בל	NOT	115b	
		חזה	SEE	302c	3 a
		צר	ADVERSARY	865d	
		קנאה	ZEAL	888c	3 b
		רום	BE HIGH	926d	2
26	12	גם	ALSO	169b	2
		מעשה	DEED	795c	1 a1
		פעל	DO	821b	1 a
		שפת	SET	1046b	2
26	13	אדון	LORD	11a	2
		ב	IN	89d	3 2c
		בד	SEPARATION	94c	1 c
		בעל	RULE OVER	127b	2
		יהוה	YAHWEH	218d	2 1c
		זולה	EXCEPT	265d	1
		זכר	REMEMBER	270d	3 a
		שם	NAME	1028c	3
26	14	אבד	CAUSE TO VANISH	2a	2
		בל	NOT	115b	
		זכר	REMEMBRANCE	271b	1 a
		חיה	LIVE	311b	2 d
		כן	SO	487a	3 db
		ל	TO	512b	5 aa
		פקד	ATTEND TO	823c	A 2
		קום	STAND	877d	1 a
		רפאים	SHADES	952b	
		שמד	BE EXTERMINATED	1029b	1
26	15	גוי	NATION	156d	1 b
		יסף	ADD	414d	
		כבד	BE HONORED	457c	2
		קצה	END	*892b	1
		קצו	BOUNDRY	892c	
26	16	מוסר	DISCIPLINE	416c	2 a
		לחש	WHISPER	538a	3
		צוק	POUR OUT	748b	
		צוק	POUR OUT	748b	
		פקד	ATTEND TO	823d	A 1c
		צר	STRAITS	865a	
26	17	זעק	CRY	277b	2 d
		חבל	PAIN	286d	1 b
		חול	WHIRL	297a	2 a
		כמו	LIKE	455d	1 a
		כמו	LIKE	456a	1
		כן	SO	486b	2 ad g
		פנה	FACE	818c	26b
		קרב	COME NEAR	898a	1 b
26	18	בל	NOT	115b	
		הרה	CONCEIVE	247d	2
		חול	WHIRL	297a	2 a
		תבל	WORLD	385d	
		ילד	BEAR	408c	1 c
		ישועה	VICTORY	447c	4
		כמו	LIKE	455d	1 a
		נפל	FALL	657d	6
		רוח	BREATH	925a	2 d
26	19	אורה	LIGHT	21d	2
		אורה	HERB	21d	
		חיה	LIVE	311b	2 d
		טל	NIGHT-MIST	378d	
		נבלה	CARCASS	615c	1 a
		נפל	FALL	657d	6
		נפל	FALL	658b	6
		עפר	DRY EARTH	779d	1 f
		קום	STAND	877d	1 a
		קיץ	AWAKE	884c	2
		רנן	GIVE A RINGING CRY	943b	
		רפאים	SHADES	952b	
		שאול	SHEOL	*983b	4
		שכן	SETTLE DOWN	1015b	2 b
26	20	בעד	BEHIND	126b	1 b
		דלה	DOOR	194d	1
		הלך	WALK	234b	1 5f 2
		זעם	INDIGNATION	276d	
		חבה	WITHDRAW	285d	
		חדר	CHAMBER	293c	
		מעט	A FEW	590c	2 e
		סגר	SHUT	689a	1
		עד	UNTIL	725a	2 1b b
		רגע	A MOMENT	921a	BF
26	21	דם	BLOOD	196d	2 f
		הרג	KILL	247b	1
		כסה	COVER	492a	6
		עון	INIQUITY	731a	1 c1
		מקום	STANDING PLACE	880a	2 b2
27	1	בריח	FLEEING	138a	
		הרג	KILL	247b	4
		חזק	STRONG	305c	1 c
		ים	SEA	411a	6
		לויתן	LEVIATHAN	531b	
		נחש	SERPENT	638b	3
		עקלתון	CROOKED	785c	
		קשה	SEVERE	904c	2 a
		תנין	SEA-MONSTER	1072c	3
27	2	חמד	DESIRE	326c	
		חמר	WINE	330c	
27	3	ענה	SING	777b	
		יהוה	YAHWEH	219b	2 2d
		ל	TO	516b	5 ja
		לילה	NIGHT	539a	1
		נצר	WATCH	665d	1
		פן	LEST	814d	1
		פקד	ATTEND TO	823c	A 3
		רגע	A MOMENT	921a	BG
		שקה	GIVE TO DRINK	1052b	1
		יום	ADDENDA ET CORRIGENDA	1124a	
		פן	ADDENDA ET CORRIGENDA	1126b	
27	4	יחד	ALTOGETHER	403b	2 b
		חמה	RAGE	404c	2 c
		נתן	GIVE	678d	1 f
		פשע	STEP	832c	
		שית	THORN-BUSHES	1011d	
		שמיר	THORN	1039a	1
27	5	או	OR	15a	4
		חזק	BE FIRM	305a	2 a
		מעוז	PLACE OF SAFETY	732a	2 a
		שלום	PEACE	1023b	5 b
27	6	בא	COME	98c	2
		תבל	WORLD	385d	
		תנובה	FRUIT	626c	
		פנה	FACE	816b	15
		פרח	BUD	827a	
		צוץ	BLOSSOM	847c	1
		שרש	ROOT UP	1057d	2
27	7	הרג	KILL	*247b	2
		הרג	SLAUGHTER	247c	
		נכה	SMITE	646c	4 b
27	8	הגה	REMOVE	212a	1
		סאה	SEAH	684b	
		סאסא	WHENCE	684d	
		קדים	EAST WIND	870b	1
		קשה	SEVERE	904c	2 a
		ריב	STRIVE	936c	3
27	9	אבן	STONE	7a	7
		אשרה	ASHERA	81c	B
		אשרא	ASHERA	81c	B
		ב	IN	90a	3 2e
		מזבח	ALTAR	258c	1
		זה	THIS	261d	6 ba
		חמאת	SIN	309a	1 d2
		חמן	SUN-PILLAR	329a	
		כן	SO	486d	3 d
		כפר	BE COVERED OVER	498b	1
		נפץ	SHATTER	658b	2
		עון	INIQUITY	731a	1 c3
		פרי	FRUIT	826c	3
		קום	STAND	877d	1 a
27	10	בדד	ISOLATION	94d	2
		בצר	MAKE INACCESSIBLE	131a	
		כלה	FINISH	478d	2 c2
		נוח	HABITATION	627c	2
		סעיף	BRANCH	703d	2
		עגל	CALF	722a	
		עזב	LEAVE	737d	2
		רבץ	LIE DOWN	918b	
		רעה	TEND	945b	2 a
		שלח	SEND	1019c	
		שם	THERE	1027a	1 a
27	11	אור	BECOME LIGHT	21b	3
		אור	GIRD	25a	
		בינה	UNDERSTANDING	108a	2
		חנן	SHOW FAVOR	336a	2 b
		יבש	BE DRY	386b	1 d
		יצר	FORM	427d	2
		לא	NOT	519b	1 bb
		עם	PEOPLE	767a	5 i
		קצור	BRANCHES	894d	
		רחם	LOVE	933c	1
		שבר	BREAK	990d	
27	12	חבט	BEAT OFF	286a	2
		ל	TO	516b	5 ja
		נחל	WADY	636c	2
		שבלת	FLOWING STREAM	987c	
27	13	אבד	PERISH	1c	1
		ארץ	EARTH	76a	2 a
		הר	MOUNTAIN	249d	1 a
		נדח	BANISH	623a	2
		שחה	BOW DOWN	1005c	2 c
		תקע	GIVE A BLOW	1075c	1
28	1	גאות	MAJESTY	145a	2
		גיא	VALLEY	161b	
		הוי	AH	223a	
		הלם	SMITE	240c	
		עטרה	CROWN	742d	3
		תפארה	BEAUTY	802c	1
		צדיק	BEAUTY	840a	1 b
		צוץ	BLOSSOM	847d	1
		ראש	HEAD	910d	2 a
		שכר	DRUNKEN	1016c	
		שמן	FAT	1032a	1
28	2	אמיץ	MIGHTY	55c	
		זרם	FLOOD OF RAIN	281b	
		זרם	FLOOD OF RAIN	281b	
		חזק	STRONG	305d	2
		כביר	GREAT	460b	
		ל	TO	511c	1 ga
		ל	TO	513b	5 ba
		מו	WATER	565d	4 d
		נוח	REST	628c	B 1
		קטב	DESTRUCTION	881d	
		שער	STORM	973b	
		שטף	OVERFLOW	1009a	1
28	3	ב	IN	89d	3 2a
		גאות	MAJESTY	145a	2
		עטרה	CROWN	742d	3
		רגל	FOOT	919d	1 d
		רמס	TRAMPLE	942d	
		שכר	DRUNKEN	1016c	
28	4	בכורה	FIRST RIPE FIG	114c	
		בלע	SWALLOW DOWN	118a	1
		גיא	VALLEY	161b	
		טרם	NOT YET	382d	2
		עוד	STILL	729b	2 aa
		תאארה	BEAUTY	802c	1
		צדיק	BEAUTY	840a	1 b
		צוץ	BLOSSOM	847d	1
		קיץ	SUMMER	884d	1
		ראש	HEAD	910d	2 a
		שמן	FAT	1032b	1
28	5	עטרה	CROWN	742d	3
		תאארה	BEAUTY	802c	1
		צדיק	BEAUTY	840a	1 b
		צפירה	DIADEM	862a	
		שאר	REST	984c	
28	6	גבורה	MIGHT	150b	2
		ישב	SIT	442c	1 a
		על	UPON	756a	2 6b
		רוח	BREATH	925b	3 g
		שוב	TURN BACK	999c	5
		שער	GATE	1044c	1 a
		משפט	JUDGMENT	1048b	1 a
		משפט	JUDGMENT	1048c	1 b
28	7	ב	IN	90c	3 5
		בלע	SWALLOW UP	*118b	2 a
		בלע	SWALLOW UP	118b	
		ה	THE	207d	1 e
		חזה	SEER	*302d	2
		יין	WINE	406c	C
		כהן	PRIEST	463c	4
		כי	BECAUSE	*474a	3 c
		מן	OUT OF	580a	2 eb
		מן	OUT OF	580a	2 eb
		נביא	PROPHET	611d	2
		פוק	REEL	807b	
		פליליה	THE GIVING A DECISION	813d	
		ראה	VISION	909b	
		שגה	GO ASTRAY	993a	2
		שגה	GO ASTRAY	993a	2
		שכר	INTOXICATING DRINK	1016b	
		תעה	ERR	1073c	2
28	8	בלי	WEARING OUT	115c	2 b
		כי	BECAUSE	474a	3 c
		כל	ALL	481b	1 a
		צאה	FILTH	844b	
		מקום	STANDING PLACE	880b	5 a
		קיא	VOMIT	883c	
		שלחן	TABLE	1020b	2
28	9	בין	DISCERN	107a	3 e
		חלב	MILK	316c	A 2
		דעה	KNOWLEDGE	395c	
		ירה	DIRECT	435b	5 a
		מי	WHO	*566c	F
		מי	WHO	566c	F b
		עתיק	REMOVED	801c	1
		שד	BREAST	994d	1
		שמועה	REPORT	1035b	1
28	10	זעיר	A LITTLE	277d	1
		כי	BECAUSE	*474a	3 c
		ל	TO	511d	1 i
		צו	WORD	846c	
		קר	LINE ON LINE	875c	
		קו	LINE	876a	
		שם	THERE	1027a	1 a
28	11	אחר	ANOTHER	29c	
		כי	BECAUSE	474a	3 c
		לעג	MOCKING	541d	
		לעג	MOCKING	541d	2
		לשון	TONGUE	546c	2
		שפה	SPEECH	974a	2
28	12	אבה	BE WILLING	2c	
		אשר	THAT	84a	
		נוח	REST	628c	A 1b 2
		מנוחה	REST	630a	2
		עוף	FAINT	746a	
		ארגעה	REST	921c	
28	13	זעיר	A LITTLE	277d	1
		יקש	BE ENSNARED	430c	
		כי	BECAUSE	*474a	3 c
		כשל	STUMBLE	505c	1
		ל	TO	511d	1 i
		לכד	CAPTURE	540b	2
		צו	WORD	846d	
		קו	LINE UPON LINE	875c	
		קו	LINE	876a	
		שבר	BREAK	990d	
		שם	THERE	1027a	1 a
28	14	כן	SO	487a	3 d
		לצון	SCORNING	539c	
		משל	RULE	605d	1
28	15	ברית	COVENANT	136b	11
		ה	THE	208c	1 hb
		חזה	SEER	302d	2
		מחסה	REFUGE	340c	B

Ch v.	Heb	Eng	Page	Sec
	כזב	LIE	469d	
	כי	BECAUSE	473c	3 a
	כרת	CUT	503d	4
	מות	DEATH	560d	3
	סתר	HIDE	711b	1
	עבר	PASS OVER	*717c	4 c
	שאול	SHEOL	983a	1
	שוט	SCOURGE	1002a	1
	שיט	ROWING	1002b	
	שטף	OVERFLOW	1009a	1
	שקר	DECEPTION	1055c	
28 16	אבן	STONE	6c	2
	אדון	LORD	11c	4 c
	אמן	CONFIRM	53a	2 a
	בחן	TESTING	103d	
	הנה	BEHOLD	244b	B b
	חוש	HASTE	301d	1
	יסד	FOUND	414a	1
	מוסד	FOUNDATION	414b	
	יסד	FOUNDING	414b	
	יקר	PRECIOUS	430a	1 a
	כן	SO	486d	3 d
	כן	SO	487a	3 d
	פנה	CORNER	819c	1 a
28 17	מחסה	REFUGE	340c	B
	יעה	SWEEP AWAY	418a	
	כזב	LIE	469d	
	ל	TO	512b	4 a
	מי	WATER	565d	4 d
	סתר	COVERING	712a	2 a
	צדקה	RIGHTEOUSNESS	842b	2
	קו	LINE	876a	
	שום	TO PLACE	964b	5 a
	שטף	OVERFLOW	1009a	1
	משקלת	LEVEL	1054a	
28 18	ברית	COVENANT	136b	1 1
	חזות	VISION	303b	1
	כי	IF	473b	2 b
	ל	TO	512c	4 b
	מות	DEATH	560d	3
	עבר	PASS OVER	*717c	4 c
	פרר	BREAK	830c	2
	קום	STAND	878c	7 g
	מרמס	TRAMPLING-PLACE	942d	2
	שאול	SHEOL	983a	1
	שוט	SCOURGE	1002a	1
	שטף	OVERFLOW	1009a	1
28 19	בין	DISCERN	107a	1 b
	בקר	MORNING	134b	1 f
	די	SUFFICIENCY	191d	2 ca
	זועה	A TREMBLING	266b	
	כי	BECAUSE	*474a	3 c
	עבר	PASS OVER	*717d	4 c
	רק	ONLY	956c	2 c
	שמועה	REPORT	1035b	1
28 20	מצע	BED	427a	
	ל	LIKE	454d	3 b
	כי	BECAUSE	474a	3 c
	כנס	GATHER	488b	
	מן	THAN	582d	6 d
	מסכה	WEB	651b	
	צרר	BIND	864d	B
	קצר	BE SHORT	894a	
	קצר	BE SHORT	894a	
	שרע	EXTEND	976d	
28 21	גבעון	GIBEON	149c	
	זור	BE A STRANGER	266c	2 c
	נכרי	ALIEN	649a	3
	עבד	WORK	713a	1
	עבדה	LABOR	715b	1
	עמק	VALE	771a	
	פרץ	PEREZ	829d	2 b
	קום	STAND	878b	6 a
	רגז	BE AGITATED	919b	
28 22	אדון	LORD	11d	6 a
	מוסר	BAND	64c	
	את	WITH	86d	4 c
	חזק	BE FIRM	304b	1 1e
	חרץ	CUT	358c	
	כלה	COMPLETE	478d	2 a
	ליץ	SCORN	539c	2
	פן	LEST	814d	1
28 23	אזן	HEAR	24c	1
	אמרה	UTTERANCE	57b	
	קשב	ATTEND	904a	
	שמע	HEAR	1033d	1 f
28 24	אדמה	GROUND	9c	1
	ה	INTERROG PART	209d	1 b
	זרע	SOW	281c	1 a
	חרש	CUT IN	360c	2
	חרש	CUT IN	360c	2
	יום	DAY	400c	7 f
	פתח	OPEN	835c	2
	שדד	HARROW	961a	
28 25	אם	IF	50c	1 b4 b
	גבולה	BORDER	148b	
	זרק	TO TOSS	284c	1 a
	חטה	WHEAT	334d	
	כמן	CUMMIN	485a	
	כסמת	SPELT	493c	
	לא	NOT	520b	4 ba
	סמן	PLACE	702c	
	פוץ	BE DISPERSED	807b	1 b
	קצח	BLACK CUMIN	892d	
	שום	TO PLACE	964b	4 d
	שורה	IN ROWS	965a	

Ch v.	Heb	Eng	Page	Sec
	שערה	BARLEY	972d	1
	שרה	PERSIST	975b	
	ישוה	AGREE WITH	1000d	
28 26	יסר	DISCIPLINE	416a	1 a
	ירה	DIRECT	435c	5 c
	ל	TO	516b	5 jb
	משפט	JUDGEMNT	1049a	6 a
28 27	אופן	WHEEL	66d	A
	דוש	THRESH	190c	
	חבט	BEAT OFF	286a	
	חרוץ	SHARP	358d	1
	כי	BUT	474b	3 e
	כמן	CUMMIN	485a	
	מטה	STAFF	641d	1
	עגלה	CART	722c	
	קצח	BLACK CUMIN	892d	
	שבט	ROD	987a	1 a
28 28	דוש	THRESH	190c	
	דקק	CRUSH	200d	1
	דקק	CRUSH	201a	
	המם	MOVE NOISILY	243a	1
	כי	BECAUSE	474b	3 c
	לא	NOT	518d	1 ac
	לחם	FOOD	537b	1 b
	נצח	EVERLASTINGNESS	664b	4
	עגלה	CART	722c	
	פרש	HORSE	832a	
28 29	גדל	BECOME GREAT	152c	1
	עצה	ADVICE	420b	
	יצא	GO OUT	423b	1 g
	תושיה	SOUND WISDOM	444d	A
	מעם	FROM WITH	769a	D
	פלא	BE SURPASSING	810d	2
29 1	אריאל	ARIEL	72a	1
	אריאל	HEARTH	72b	
	דוד	DAVID	188a	A
	חג	FESTIVAL-GATHER-ING	291a	1 b1
	נקה	DECLINE	333d	2 c2
	יסף	ADD	414d	
	כת	LIKE	*454b	1 d
	נקף	GO AROUND	668d	
	קריה	TOWN	900b	2
29 2	אניה	MOURNING	58b	
	אריאל	ARIEL	72a	1
	כת	LIKE	454b	1 d
	ל	TO	513a	5 ad
	צוק	CONSTRAIN	848a	
29 3	דור	CIRCLE	189c	1
	נקה	DECLINE	333c	2 c2
	מצב	PALISADE	663a	
	צור	CONFINE	*848d	3
	צור	CONFINE	848d	2
	מצורה	SIEGE-WORKS	849a	1
	קום	STAND	878d	2 b
29 4	אוב	NECROMANCER	15b	3
	אטי	MUTTERER	31d	
	אמרה	UTTERANCE	57b	
	אמרה	UTTERANCE	57b	
	ל	LIKE	455a	B
	מן	FROM	578a	1 a
	עפר	DRY EARTH	780a	2 e
	צפף	CHIRP	861d	2
	שחח	BOW	1005d	
	שפל	BECOME LOW	1050a	1
29 5	אבק	DUST	7c	
	דק	SMALL	201a	2
	ה	THE	208a	1 f
	היה	COME TO PASS	224b	1 1b
	המון	CROWD	242c	3 a
	זור	BE A STRANGER	266c	2 c
	ל	TO	516d	5 k
	מוץ	CHAFF	558b	
	עבר	PASS OVER	718b	6 b
	עריץ	AWE-INSPIRING	792b	
	פתע	SUDDENNESS	837b	
29 6	להב	FLAME	529a	1
	סופה	STORM-WIND	693a	
	סערה	TEMPEST	704b	
	מעם	FROM WITH	769a	D
	פקד	ATTEND TO	823a	2
	רעם	THUNDER	947b	
	רעש	SHAKING	950c	1
29 7	אריאל	ARIEL	72a	1
	המון	CROWD	242d	3 c
	חזון	VISION	303a	2
	חלום	DREAM	321c	1
	לילה	NIGHT	538d	1
	צבא	WAGE WAR	838d	1
	צבא	WAGE WAR	838d	1
	צבה	SWELL	839d	
	מצודה	FASTNESS	845a	
	צוק	CONSTRAIN	848a	
	ציון	ZION	851b	
29 8	היה	COME TO PASS	225a	1 2b ad
	המון	CROWD	242d	3 c
	הנה	BEHOLD	244b	C
	הר	MOUNTAIN	249c	1 a
	חלם	DREAM	321c	A
	כאשר	AS	455c	1 d
	עיף	FAINT	746a	
	צבא	WAGE WAR	838d	1
	ציון	ZION	851b	
	צמא	THIRSTY	854d	
	קיץ	AWAKE	884c	1 a
	ריק	EMPTY	938d	1

Ch v.	Heb	Eng	Page	Sec
	רעב	HUNGRY	944c	
	שקק	RUN	1055b	
29 9	לוע	SWALLOW	*534b	
	מהה	LINGER	554c	
	נוע	WAVE	631b	1
	שכר	INTOXICATING DRINK	1016b	
	שכר	BE DRUNK	1016b	
	שעע	BE BLINDED	1044a	
	תמה	BE ASTOUNDED	1069b	
29 10	חזה	SEER	302d	1 a
	כסה	COVER	491d	2
	נביא	PROPHET	611d	2
	נסך	POUR OUT	650d	1
	עצה	SHUT	*781b	
	עצם	SHUT THE EYES	783b	
	תרדמה	DEEP SLEEP	922b	
29 11	רוח	BREATH	925b	3 h
	דבר	WORD	183a	2 1a
	חזות	VISION	303b	1
	חתם	SEAL	367d	2
	ידע	KNOW	394b	4 b
	יכל	BE ABLE	407d	1 c
	כל	ALL	482d	2 ba
	ספר	MISSIVE	707a	3
	ספר	MISSIVE	*707c	4
	על	UPON	757b	2 7c ab
	קרא	CALL	895c	4 a
	שלום	PEACE	1023b	5 b
29 12	ידע	KNOW	394b	4 b
	ספר	MISSIVE	707a	3
	ספר	MISSIVE	*707c	4
	על	UPON	757b	2 7c ab
	קרא	CALL	895c	4 a
29 13	ירא	FEAR	431c	3 b
	כבד	MAKE HONORABLE	457d	2 c
	לב	HEART	524c	2 1
	למד	LEARN	540d	
	נגש	DRAW NEAR	621a	
	יען	ON ACCOUNT OF	774d	2 b
	פה	MOUTH	805a	2 a
	מצוה	COMMANDMENT	846b	1
	רחק	BE DISTANT	935a	
	שפה	SPEECH	973c	1 al
	תהו	FORMLESSNESS	1062d	2
29 14	אבד	PERISH	1d	2
	בין	DISCERN	106a	
	בינה	UNDERSTANDING	108a	3
	הנה	BEHOLD	244b	B b
	הנה	BEHOLD	244b	B b
	חכם	WISE	314d	2
	חכמה	WISDOM	315b	2
	יסף	ADD	414d	
	כן	SO	486d	3 d
	כן	SO	487a	3 d
	סתר	HIDE	711c	
	פלא	BE SURPASSING	810d	2
29 15	הוי	AH	223a	
	מחשך	DARK PLACE	365b	D
	עצה	ADVICE	420b	
	ל	TO	517c	7 bb
	מי	WHO	*566c	F
	סתר	HIDE	711d	1
	עמק	BE DEEP	770d	
	מעשה	DEED	795d	1 b2
29 16	אם	IF	50c	2 aa
	בין	DISCERN	107a	1 a
	הפך	THE CONTRARY	246b	2
	חמר	CEMENT	330d	2 a
	חשב	THINK	363b	1
	יצר	FORM	427d	1 a
	יצר	FORM	427d	1 a
	יצר	FORM	428a	1
	כי	THAT	472d	1 f
	מעשה	DEED	796a	2 al
29 17	מזער	A LITTLE	277d	1
	חשב	THINK	363b	1
	יער	WOOD	420d	D
	כרמל	GARDEN	502a	1
	לא	NOT	520b	4 ba
	לבנון	LEBANON	*527a	
	לבנון	LEBANON	527b	
	מעט	A FEW	590b	1 eb
	עוד	STILL	729a	1 ab
	שוב	TURN BACK	998a	7 c
29 18	אפל	DARKNESS	66c	1
	דבר	WORD	183a	2 1a
	חרש	DEAF	361c	
	חשך	DARKNESS	365a	3 a
	מן	OUT OF	579b	2 ab
	מן	FROM	581c	4 b
	עור	BLIND	734c	2 a
	ראה	TO SEE	907b	4
29 19	אביון	NEEDY	2d	
	יסף	ADD	414d	
	ענו	POOR	776c	2
	קדוש	HOLY	872c	1 c
29 20	און	TROUBLE	20a	3
	אפס	CEASE	67a	
	ו	AND	252b	1 a
	כלה	BE FINISHED	477d	2 c
	כרת	BE CUT OFF	504a	1 b
	ליץ	SCORN	539c	
	עריץ	AWE-INSPIRING	792b	
	שקד	WATCH	1052a	1
29 21	ה	THE	208c	1 hb

ISAIAH

Ch v.	Heb	Eng	Page	Sec
	חטא	MISS A GOAL OR WAY	307d	3
	חטא	SINFUL	*308b	1 b
	יכח	REPROVE	407a	5 b
	נטה	BEND	641a	3 g
	צדיק	JUST	843a	2
	קוש	LAY BAIT	881c	
	שער	GATE	1045a	2 a
	תהו	FORMLESSNESS	1062c	2
29 22	אל	TO	40c	6
	בוש	BE ASHAMED	101d	
	בית	HOUSE	110a	5 dg
	חור	BE WHITE	301a	
	כן	SO	486d	3 d
	עתה	NOW	774a	1 c
	פדה	RANSOM	804a	3 d
	פנה	FACE	815d	1 a
29 23	אלהים	GOD	44c	4 ba
	ילד	CHILD	409c	C
	כי	BUT	474b	3 e
	יעקב	JACOB	785a	2
	ערץ	CAUSE TO TREMBLE	792a	1
	קדוש	HOLY	872c	1 c
	קדש	BE SET APART	873c	2
29 24	בינה	UNDERSTANDING	108a	3
	ידע	KNOW	394c	5
	למד	LEARN	540d	
	לקח	LEARNING	544b	1
	רגן	MURMUR	920d	
	רוח	BREATH	925c	6
	תעה	ERR	1073c	3
30 1	את	WITH	87a	4 c
	בן	SON	120b	1 c
	חטאת	SIN	308c	1 b
	חטאת	SIN	308d	1 b
	יסף	ADD	414d	
	עצה	ADVICE	420a	
	מן	OUT OF	579d	2 d
	נאם	UTTERANCE	610b	2
	נסך	POUR OUT	650d	2
	מסכה	WEB	651b	
	נסך	WEAVE	651b	
	מסכה	LIBATION	651b	1
	ספה	SWEEP AWAY	705a	2
	סרר	BE STUBBORN	710d	
	מען	PURPOSE	775c	2 1
	רוח	BREATH	925a	9 a
30 2	חסה	SEEK REFUGE	340a	
	ירד	GO DOWN	433a	1 d
	עוז	TAKE REFUGE	731d	
	מעוז	PLACE OF SAFETY	732a	3
	צל	SHADOW	853b	2
	שאל	ASK	982a	2 b
30 3	בשת	SHAME	102a	1
	חסות	REFUGE	340b	
	כלמה	IGNOMINY	484a	2
	מעוז	PLACE OF SAFETY	732a	3
	צל	SHADOW	853b	2
30 4	חנם	HANES	337d	
	מלאך	MESSENGER	521c	1 a
	נגע	REACH	619c	2
	צען	ZOAN	858a	
	שר	CHIEFTAIN	978a	2 a
30 5	בשת	SHAME	102a	1
	בוש	BE ASHAMED	102a	2 d
	בוש	BE ASHAMED	102a	2
	חרפה	REPROACH	358a	3
	יעל	PROFIT	418d	
	כי	BUT	474b	3 e
	כל	ALL	482c	2 a
30 6	עזר	HELP	740c	1
	אוצר	TREASURE	70a	1
	בהמות	HIPPOPOTAMUS	97a	
	בהמות	HIPPOPOTAMUS	*97a	
	דבשת	HUMP	185c	1
	חיל	STRENGTH	299a	3
	יעל	PROFIT	418d	
	כתף	SHOULDER	509b	1 b
	לביא	LION	522d	
	ליש	LION	539d	
	נגב	SOUTH-COUNTRY	616b	1 a
	משא	UTTERANCE	672d	2
	עוף	FLY	733c	1
	עיר	MALE ASS	747a	
	על	UPON	757b	2 7c aa
	אפעה	VIPER	821b	
	צוקה	PRESSURE	848a	
	צרה	DISTRESS	865b	
	שרף	FIERY SERPENT	977b	
30 7	הבל	VAPOUR	211a	2
	הם	THEY	241c	2 b
	עזר	HELP	740c	
	רהב	STORM	923c	2
	ריק	EMPTINESS	938b	
	שבת	CESSATION	992a	
30 8	אחרון	BEHIND	30d	B
	את	WITH	86a	1 c
	חקק	CUT IN	349a	2
	לוח	TABLET	531d	1
	לוח	TABLET	*531d	1
	ספר	MISSIVE	707a	3
	ספר	MISSIVE	*707c	4
	עד	PERPETUITY	723d	2 e
	עולם	LONG DURATION	762b	2 b1
	עתה	NOW	774b	1 e
30 9	אבה	BE WILLING	2c	
	בן	SON	120b	1 c
	תורה	INSTRUCTION	435d	1 b
	כחש	FALSE	471c	
	מרי	REBELLION	598b	
30 10	דבר	SPEAK	181b	3 c
	חזה	SEE	302c	2
	חזה	SEE	302c	2
	חזה	SEER	302d	1 a
	חלקה	SMOOTH PART	325c	3
	נכח	STRAIGHTNESS	647c	
	ראה	TO SEE	907a	1 b
	ראה	SEER	909b	
	מהתלות	ADDENDA ET CORRIGENDA	1122c	
30 11	ארח	WAY	73b	3 b
	דרך	WAY	203c	5
	נטה	INCLINE	640d	3 a
	סור	TURN ASIDE	693d	2
	פנה	FACE	818b	2 6
	קדוש	HOLY	872c	1 c
	שבת	CEASE	992a	4
30 12	בטח	TRUST	105a	1 3c
	כן	SO	486d	3 d
	לוז	BE CROOKED	531c	
	מאס	REJECT	549c	1 b
	יען	ON ACCOUNT OF	774d	1
	עשק	OPPRESSION	799a	
	קדוש	HOLY	872c	1 c
	שען	LEAN	1043d	
30 13	בקע	CAUSE TO SWELL	126d	
	חומה	WALL	327d	3
	כן	SO	487a	3 d
	ל	TO	516d	5 k
	נפל	FALL	656d	1
	עון	INIQUITY	731c	3
	פרץ	BURSTING FORTH	829d	3
	פתע	SUDDENNESS	837b	
	שגב	BE HIGH	960c	1
	שבר	BREAKING	991a	1
30 14	גבא	CISTERN	146b	1
	חמל	SPARE	328b	
	חרש	EARTHENWARE	360b	2
	חשף	STRIP OFF	362c	3
	חתה	SNATCH UP	367a	
	יצר	FORM	427d	1 a
	יקד	BE KINDLED	428d	
	כתת	BEAT	510a	1
	מכתה	CRUSHED	510c	
	מצא	FIND	594b	2 d
	נבל	JAR	614b	2
	שבר	BREAK	990c	
	שבר	BREAKING	991a	1
30 15	אבה	BE WILLING	2c	
	אדון	LORD	11c	4 c
	בטח	SECURITY	105b	
	בטחה	TRUSTING	105c	
	גבורה	MIGHT	150b	2
	ישע	BE DELIVERED	446b	1
	נחת	QUIETNESS	629b	1
	קדוש	HOLY	872c	1 c
	שובה	WITHDRAWAL	1000a	
	שקט	BE QUIET	1053b	1
30 16	אכל	EAT	37d	3
	כי	BUT	474c	3 e
	נוס	ESCAPE	630d	4
	קלל	BE SLIGHT	886c	1
	קל	LIGHT	887a	1
	רדף	PURSUE	922b	1 c
	רכב	RIDE	938d	2
30 17	אם	IF	50c	1 cd
	גבעה	HILL	149a	3
	גערה	REBUKE	172a	1
	הר	MOUNTAIN	250d	1 m
	יתר	BE LEFT OVER	451b	
	נס	STANDARD	651d	1 a
	עד	UNTIL	725a	2 1b a
	תרן	MAST	1076c	
30 18	אלהים	GOD	44c	4 bb
	אשר	HAPPINESS	81a	
	חכה	WAIT	314a	3
	חנן	SHOW FAVOR	336a	2 b
	רום	BE HIGH	927a	2 c
	רחם	LOVE	933c	1
	משפט	JUDGMENT	1048d	2 a
30 19	בכה	WEEP	113b	1
	בכה	WEEP	113c	2
	זעק	CRY	277b	2 a
	חנן	SHOW FAVOR	336a	2 b
	כ	LIKE	454d	3 b
	ציון	ZION	851b	
	צער	BE INSIGNIFICANT	858d	
	שמע	HEAR	1034a	1
30 20	היה	BE	227c	3 5a
	מורה	TEACHER	435d	
	כנף	BE CORNERED	489d	
	לחץ	OPPRESSION	538a	
	עוד	STILL	729a	1 ab
	צר	STRAITS	865a	
	ראה	TO SEE	906d	1
30 21	אזן	EAR	23d	2 a
	אחר	BEHIND	30b	4 aa
	דרך	WAY	203c	6 b
	הלך	WALK	234c	2 3a 1a
	ימן	GO TO THE RIGHT	412b	
	כי	WHEN	473a	2 a
	שמאל	TAKE THE LEFT	970a	2
30 22	אפוד	EPHOD	65d	3 a
	אפדה	EPHOD	66a	2
	דוה	UNWELL	188c	2
	זהב	GOLD	263a	6
	זרה	SCATTER	279d	1
	טמא	BE UNCLEAN	379c	2
	כמו	LIKE	455d	1 a
	מסכה	MOLTEN IMAGE	651b	2
	פסיל	IDOL	821a	
	צפוי	METAL PLATING	860b	
30 23	אדמה	GROUND	9c	1
	תבואה	PRODUCT	100a	1
	דשן	FAT	206c	
	זרע	SOW	281c	1 d
	זרע	SOWING	282b	2 b
	כר	PASTURE	499d	
	כר	PASTURE	*499d	
	לחם	FOOD	537b	1 b
	מטר	RAIN	564d	
	מקנה	CATTLE	889b	2
	רחב	BE LARGE	931c	
	רעה	TEND	945b	2 a
	שמן	FAT	1032a	1
30 24	אדמה	GROUND	9c	1
	אלף	CATTLE	48c	
	בליל	FODDER	117d	
	זרה	SCATTER	279d	2
	מזרה	PITCH-FORK	280a	
	חמיץ	SEASONED	330a	
	עבד	WORK	713a	1
	עיר	MALE ASS	747a	
	רחת	WINNOWING-SHOVEL	935d	
	נגד	STREAM	*1102a	
30 25	גבה	HIGH	147b	1
	גבעה	HILL	149a	3
	מגדל	TOWER	153d	1
	היה	BE	227a	3 3
	הרג	SLAUGHTER	247c	
	הר	MOUNTAIN	250b	1 d
	יבל	WATERCOURSE	385a	
	נפל	FALL	656d	1
	נשא	LIFT	671d	1 a
	פלג	CHANNEL	811b	
30 26	שבעתים	SEVEN FOLD		
	אור	LIGHT	21c	3
	חבש	BIND	290a	2
	חמה	HEAT	329a	2
	לבנה	MOON	526b	
	מחץ	SEVERE WOUND	563d	
	מכה	BLOW	647a	1 c
	רפא	HEAL	950d	2 a
	שבר	BREAKING	991a	1
30 27	אכל	EAT	37c	3
	בער	BURN	129a	4
	זעם	INDIGNATION	276d	
	זעב	INDIGNATION	276d	
	כבד	VEHEMENCE	458c	3
	לשון	TONGUE	546d	4
	משאה	THE UPLIFTED	673a	
	מרחק	DISTANT PLACE	935d	
	שפה	SPEECH	973d	1 a1
30 28	חצה	DIVIDE	345c	2
	לחי	JAW	534d	1
	נוף	WAVE	632a	3
	נפה	SIEVE	632b	
	נחל	TORRENT	636b	1
	צואר	NECK	848c	1
	רוח	BREATH	924d	1 d1
	רסן	HALTER	943d	1
	שאון	ROAR	*981b	2
	שוא	EMPTINESS	996b	3
	שטף	OVERFLOW	1009a	1
	תעה	ERR	1073c	1
30 29	הר	MOUNTAIN	249d	1 a
	חג	FESTIVAL-GATHERING	291a	1 b1
	חג	FESTIVAL-GATHERING	291b	1 b
	חליל	FLUTE	319d	
	לבב	HEART	524a	2 9a
	לילה	NIGHT	538c	1
	צור	ROCK	849d	2 a
	קדש	BE SET APART	873c	3
	שמחה	JOY	970d	2
	שיר	SONG	1010b	1
30 30	אבן	STONE	6d	7
	אכל	EAT	37c	3
	הוד	SPLENDOUR	217b	2
	זעם	STORMING	277a	1
	זרם	FLOOD OR RAIN	281b	
	זרוע	ARM	284a	1 c
	להב	FLAME	529a	1
	נחת	DESCENT	639c	
	נפץ	DRIVING STORM	658d	
	קול	VOICE	877a	2 b
	ראה	TO SEE	908a	1
	ראה	TO SEE	908d	1 a2
	שמע	HEAR	1034c	2 a
30 31	אשור	ASSHUR	78d	1
	חתת	BE SHATTERED	369b	1
	מן	OUT OF	580a	2
	נכה	SMITE	646c	4 b
	קול	VOICE	877a	2 b
	שבט	ROD	987a	1 a

Ch	v.	Heb	Eng	Page	Sec
30	32	מוסדה	FOUNDATION	414c	
		כנור	LYRE	490a	
		נוח	REST	628c	A 2
		תנופה	SWINGING	632b	1
		מטה	STAFF	641c	1
		מעבר	FORD	721b	3
		תף	TIMBREL	1074c	
30	33	בער	BURN	129a	1
		גפרית	BRIMSTONE	172d	
		מדורה	PILE	190b	
		הוא	HE, SHE, IT	*214d	
		כון	BE ESTABLISHED	466d	2
		נחל	TORRENT	636b	1
		נשמה	BREATH	675d	1
		עמק	BE DEEP	770d	
		עץ	TREE	782a	2 d
		ערך	ARRANGE	789c	1 b
		רבה	BECOME MANY	915d	1 e4
		רחב	BE LARGE	931c	1
		תמול	YESTERDAY	1070a	3
		תפתה	TOPHETH	1075b	
31	1	בטח	TRUST	105a	1 4c
		דרש	SEEK	205b	3 a
		הוי	AH	223a	
		ירד	GO DOWN	433a	1 d
		סוס	HORSE	692c	1
		עזרה	HELP	740d	1
		על	UPON	757d	27 c c
		עצם	BE VAST	782c	1
		פרש	HORSEMAN	832a	
		קדוש	HOLY	872c	1 c
		שעה	GAZE	1043a	
		שען	LEAN	1043d	
31	2	און	TROUBLE	20a	3
		גם	ALSO	169c	4
		דבר	WORD	183b	3 2
		חכם	WISE	314d	2
		סור	TURN ASIDE	694b	2
		עזרה	HELP	740d	1
		פעל	DO	821b	1 b
		קום	STAND	878a	2
		רע	EVIL	948a	1
		רעע	BE EVIL	949d	1
31	3	אדם	MAN	9b	2
		אל	GOD	42d	6 d
		בשר	FLESH	142d	5
		יחדו	TOGETHER	*403d	B
		יחדו	TOGETHER	403c	B
		כלה	BE FINISHED	477d	2 c
		כל	ALL	481b	1 a
		כשל	STUMBLE	505c	1
		נטה	STRETCH OUT	640d	1
		נפל	FALL	657b	2 b
		סוס	HORSE	692c	1
		עזר	HELP	740c	
		עזר	HELP	740c	
		רוח	BREATH	926a	9 e
31	4	אריה	LION	71d	
		אשר	THAT	83d	8 d
		גבעה	HILL	149a	4
		גבעה	HILL	149a	3
		הגה	GROWL	211d	1 a
		המון	SOUND	242c	1
		הר	MOUNTAIN	249c	1 a
		חתת	BE SHATTERED	369d	2 b
		טרף	PREY	383c	1
		ירד	GO DOWN	433b	2
		כאשר	AS	455c	1 d
		כפיר	LION	498d	1
		מלא	FULNESS	571b	2
		על	UPON	756d	27 a c
		ענה	BE BOWED DOWN	776a	2
		צבא	WAGE WAR	838d	1
		ציון	ZION	851c	
		קרא	CALL	896b	2 c
		רעה	TEND	945a	1 d1
31	5	גנן	DEFEND	171a	
		כן	SO	486b	2 ad b
		מלט	SLIP AWAY	572d	2
		עוף	FLY	733c	1 b
		פסח	PASS OVER	820a	
		ציון	ZION	*851c	
		ציון	ZION	851c	4 c
		צפור	BIRD	862a	1
31	6	אשר	PARTICLE OF RE-LATION	82d	4 c
		כי	BECAUSE	*474a	3 c
		ל	TO	511c	1 gb
		סרה	A TURNING ASIDE	694c	2
		עמק	BE DEEP	770d	
31	7	אליל	WORTHLESSNESS	47c	B
		זהב	GOLD	263a	6
		חטא	SIN	308a	1 b
		כי	BECAUSE	474a	3 c
		מאס	REJECT	549c	1 a
31	8	איש	MAN	35d	
		אשור	ASSHUR	78d	2
		בחור	YOUNG MAN	104c	
		ל	TO	515d	5 ib
		לא	NOT	519c	2 d
		מס	LABOUR-GANG	587a	2 b
31	9	אור	FLAME	22a	
		מגור	FEAR	159a	
		חתת	BE SHATTERED	369b	2 b
		מן	OUT OF	580a	2 eb
		נאם	UTTERANCE	610b	2

Ch	v.	Heb	Eng	Page	Sec
		נס	STANDARD	651d	1 a
		סלע	CRAG	701a	2
		עבר	PASS OVER	718b	6 c
		ציון	ZION	851c	
		שר	CHIEFTAIN	978a	2 a
		תנור	FIRE-POT	1072b	
32	1	הן	BEHOLD	243c	A
		ל	TO	514d	5 fe
		ל	TO	516b	5 jb
		מלך	KING	573b	2
		מלך	BE KING	574a	
		צדק	RIGHTEOUSNESS	841c	2 a
		שרר	ACT AS PRINCE	979a	
32	2	זרם	FLOOD OF RAIN	281b	
		מחבא	HIDING-PLACE	285c	
		כבד	HEAVY	458a	1 a
		סלע	CRAG	701a	2
		סתר	COVERING	712a	2 a
		עיף	FAINT	746b	
		פלג	CHANNEL	811b	
		ציה	DRYNESS	851b	
		צל	SHADOW	853b	2
32	3	אזן	EAR	24a	2 a
		עין	EYE	744b	1 i
		ראה	TO SEE	907a	1 b
		שמע	HEAR	1033d	1 e
		שעה	GAZE	1043a	
		שעע	BE BLINDED	1044a	
32	4	בין	DISCERN	106d	2 d
		דעת	WISDOM	395d	2 a
		לבב	HEART	523c	2 3b
		לשון	TONGUE	546b	1 b
		מהר	HASTEN	555a	2
		עלג	SPEAKING IN-ARTICULATELY	748a	
		צח	DAZZELING	850a	
32	5	אמר	SAY	56c	
		כי	BECAUSE	*473d	3 c
		נבל	FOOLISH	614d	
		נדיב	NOBLE	622a	3
		כילי	KNAVE	647d	
		קרא	CALL	896b	2 d1
32	6	און	TROUBLE	20a	3
		אל	TO	40b	4
		חנף	PROFANENESS	338a	
		חסר	LACK	341b	
		כי	BECAUSE	473d	3 c
		נבל	FOOLISH	614d	
		נבלה	SENSELESSNESS	*615b	1
		נבלה	SENSELESSNESS	615b	1
		צמא	THIRSTY	854d	
		ריק	EMPTY	938a	1
		ריק	MAKE EMPTY	938a	1
		ריק	EMPTY	*938a	1
		רעב	HUNGRY	944c	
		משקה	DRINK	1052d	2
		תועה	ERROR	1073c	1
32	7	אביון	NEEDY	2d	
		הוא	HE, SHE, IT	215b	1 a
		ו	AND	252c	1 b
		זמה	PLAN	273c	2
		חבל	ACT CORRUPTLY	287c	
		יעץ	ADVISE	419c	
		כלי	IMPLEMENT	479d	2 a
		כילי	KNAVE	647d	
		ענו	POOR	776c	2
		עני	POOR	776d	2
		רע	EVIL	948b	2
		שקר	DECEPTION	1055c	3
32	8	יעץ	ADVISE	419c	
		נדיב	NOBLE	622a	3
		נדיבה	NOBILITY	622a	2
		קום	STAND	878c	7 h
32	9	אזן	HEAR	24c	1
		אמרה	UTTERANCE	57b	
		בטח	TRUST	105b	2
		בת	DAUGHTER	123c	2
		קום	STAND	878a	1 g
		שאנן	AT EASE	983c	3
32	10	אסף	GATHERING	63a	
		בטח	TRUST	105b	2
		בלי	WEARING OUT	115c	2 a
		בציר	VINTAGE	131b	
		כלה	BE FINISHED	477d	2 b
		על	UPON	755a	2 2
		על	UPON	755b	2 4b
		רגז	BE AGITATED	919b	2
32	11	בטח	TRUST	105b	2
		חגר	GIRD	291d	1
		חגורה	GIRDLE	292b	
		חלץ	LOINS	323b	2
		חרד	TREMBLE	353c	2
		ערר	STRIP ONESELF	792c	
		פשט	STRIP OFF	833a	1
		רגז	BE AGITATED	919b	2
		שאנן	AT EASE	983c	3
32	12	גפן	VINE	172c	
		חמד	DESIRE	326c	
		ספד	WAIL	704d	
		פרה	BEAR FRUIT	826a	2
		שד	BREAST	994d	1
32	13	בית	HOUSE	109a	1 ae 4
		כי	THAT	472d	1 e
		עלה	GO UP	748d	4
		עליז	EXULTANT	759c	
		קוץ	THORN-BUSH	881a	1

Ch	v.	Heb	Eng	Page	Sec
		קריה	TOWN	900b	2
		משוש	EXULTATION	965c	
		שמיר	THORN	1039a	1
32	14	ארמון	CITADEL	74d	
		בחן	WATCH-TOWER	103d	
		בעד	ON BEHALF OF	126d	2
		המון	SOUND	242c	1
		נטש	FORSAKE	644a	
		עדר	FLOCK	727c	1 a
		עזב	LEAVE	737d	
		עולם	LONG DURATION	762b	2 b1
		עפל	MOUND	779b	
		מערה	CAVE	792c	
		פרא	WILD ASS	825b	
		מרעה	PASTURAGE	945c	
		מרעה	PASTURAGE	945c	
		מרעה	PASTURAGE	945c	
		משוש	EXULTATION	965c	
32	15	חשב	THINK	363b	1
		יער	WOOD	420d	D
		כרמל	GARDEN	502a	1
		עד	UNTIL	725a	2 1b b
		ערה	BE NAKED	788d	2
		רוח	BREATH	926a	9 c1
		מרום	HEIGHT	928d	2
32	16	ה	THE	*208b	1 ha
		ישב	DWELL	443a	3
		כרמל	GARDEN	502a	1
		שכן	SETTLE DOWN	1015b	2 e
32	17	בטח	SECURITY	105b	
		בטחה	TRUSTING	105c	
		ה	THE	208b	1 ha
		עבדה	LABOR	715b	1
		עולם	LONG DURATION	762b	2 b4
		מעשה	DEED	796b	2 c
		צדקה	RIGHTEOUSNESS	842a	1 a
		שלום	PEACE	1023a	4
		שקט	BE QUIET	1053b	1
32	18	מבטח	CONFIDENCE	105c	3
		נוה	HABITATION	627c	2
		מנוחה	RESTING PLACE	629d	1
		שאנן	AT EASE	983b	1
		שלום	PEACE	1023a	4
32	19	ברד	HAIL	136a	
		ה	THE	208c	1 hb
		יער	WOOD	420c	A
		ירד	GO DOWN	433b	1 k
		שפל	BECOME LOW	1050a	1
		שפלה	HUMILIATION	1050c	
32	20	אשר	HAPPINESS	81a	
		זרע	SOW	281c	1 a
		חמור	HE-ASS	331c	4
		שור	A HEAD OF CATTLE	1004a	
33	1	בגד	ACT TREACHER-OUSLY	93d	D
		בגד	ACT TREACHER-OUSLY	93d	A
		בגד	ACT TREACHER-OUSLY	93d	B
		תהלה	PRAISE	240a	1
		נלה	OBTAIN	649b	
		שדד	DEAL VIOLENTLY WITH	994a	
		שדד	DEAL VIOLENTLY WITH	994b	
		שדד	DEAL VIOLENTLY WITH	994b	
		תמם	BE FINISHED	1070c	2
33	2	בקר	MORNING	134b	1 f
		זרוע	ARM	284b	2
		חנן	SHOW FAVOR	336a	2 b
		ישועה	DELIVERANCE	447b	3
		ל	TO	516b	5 ja
		ל	TO	*517a	6 a
		צרה	DISTRESS	865b	
		קוה	WAIT FOR	875d	1
33	3	המון	SOUND	242c	1
		מן	OUT OF	580a	2 eb
		נפץ	DISPERSE	659a	
		רוממה	EXTOLLING	928c	
33	4	אסף	GATHERING	63a	
		אסף	GATHER	63a	
		גבה	LOCUST	146d	
		חסיל	LOCUST	340c	
		שקק	RUN	1055b	
		משק	RUNNING	1055b	
33	5	מלא	FILL	570c	1
		צדקה	RIGHTEOUSNESS	842b	5
		ציון	ZION	851b	
		מרום	HEIGHT	929a	2
		שגב	BE HIGH	960c	3
		שכן	SETTLE DOWN	1015b	2 c
33	6	אמונה	FIRMNESS	53c	2
		אוצר	TREASURE	70c	2
		הוא	HE, SHE, IT	215d	2 b
		חכמה	WISDOM	315c	4
		חסן	WEALTH	340d	
		דעת	WISDOM	395d	2 a
		יראה	FEAR	432a	3
		ישועה	VICTORY	447c	4
		עת	TIME	773d	3
33	7	אראל	HEROES	72a	
		בכה	WEEP	113c	2
		בכי	WEEPING	*113d	
		הן	BEHOLD	243c	A
		חוץ	THE OUTSIDE	299d	1 a

343

Ch v.	Heb	Eng	Page	Sec
	מלאך	MESSENGER	521c	1 a
	מר	BITTER	600c	2 a
	צעק	CRY	858c	2
	שלון	PEACE	1023b	6
33 8	אנוש	MAN	60d	2
	ארח	WAY	73a	1
	ברית	COVENANT	136b	11
	חשב	THINK	363a	14
	מאס	REJECT	549c	2
	נדד	RETREAT	622b	1
	מסלה	HIGHWAY	700c	
	עבר	PASS OVER	*717d	4 a
	פרר	BREAK	830b	1 c
	שמם	BE DESOLATED	1031a	1
33 9	אבל	MOURN	5c	
	אמל	BE WEAK	51c	
	בשן	BASHAN	143c	
	חפר	BE ABASHED	344a	
	שרון	SHARON	450a	1
	כרמל	CARMEL	502b	1
	לבנון	LEBANON	*527a	
	לבנון	LEBANON	527b	
	נער	SHAKE OUT	654c	
	ערבה	DESERT-PLAIN	787c	5
	קמל	BE DECAYED	888d	
33 10	נשא	LIFT	671d	2
	עתה	NOW	774a	1 b
	רום	BE HIGH	927d	
	רחום	BE EXALTED	933d	
33 11	יהוה	YAHWEH	218a	1
	הרה	CONCEIVE	247d	2
	חשש	CHAFF	366b	
	ילד	BEAR	408c	1 c
	רוח	BREATH	925a	2 d
33 12	יצת	KINDLE	428b	1
	כסח	CUT OFF	492d	
	סבך	INTERWEAVE	*687c	
	קוץ	THORN-BUSH	881a	1
	שיד	WHITEWASH	966d	
	משרפה	A BURNING	977c	
33 13	גבורה	MIGHT	150c	3
	קרב	NEAR	898c	2
	רחק	DISTANT	935b	1 a
33 14	אחז	GRASP	28b	
	אכל	EAT	37c	3
	גור	SOJOURN	157d	1
	חטא	SINFUL	308b	2
	חנף	PROFANE	338b	
	מוקד	BURNING MASS	428d	
	ל	TO	512d	5 aa
	מי	WHO	567a	F e
	עולם	LONG DURATION	762c	2 c
	פחד	DREAD	808b	1
	רעדה	TREMBLING	944d	
33 15	אזן	EAR	24a	2 a
	אטם	SHUT	32a	
	בצע	UNJUST GAIN	130c	
	דבר	SPEAK	180c	1
	דם	BLOOD	197a	2 f
	הוא	HE, SHE, IT	215d	2 a
	הלך	WALK	*234d	2 3a 2g
	מישר	LEVEL	449d	2
	מאס	REJECT	549c	1 b
	מן	FROM	583b	7 ba
	נכח	STRAIGHTNESS	647c	
	נער	SHAKE OUT	654c	
	עצם	SHUT THE EYES	783b	
	מעשקה	EXTORTIONATE ACT	799a	
	צדקה	RIGHTEOUSNESS	842c	7 b
	שחד	BRIBE	1005a	
	תמך	GRASP	1069d	1
33 16	אמן	CONFIRM	52d	2
	אמנה	AMANAH	53d	1
	הוא	HE, SHE, IT	215d	2 a
	נתן	GIVE	681c	1 c
	סלע	CRAG	701a	2
	מצד	FASTNESS	844d	1
	מרום	HEIGHT	928d	1
	מרום	HEIGHT	928d	1
	משגב	SECURE HEIGHT	960d	1 b
	שכן	SETTLE DOWN	1015a	1 a
33 17	חזה	SEE	302b	1 b
	יפי	BEAUTY	421d	
	מרחק	DISTANT PLACE	935d	
33 18	איה	WHERE	32c	
	אימה	TERROR	34a	
	מגדל	TOWER	153d	1
	הגה	MUSE	211d	3 a
	לב	HEART	524d	2 3c
	ספר	COUNT	707d	1
	שקל	WEIGH	1053a	1
33 19	את	MARK OF THE ACCUSATIVE	85a	1 a
	בינה	UNDERSTANDING	108a	1
	יעז	FIERCE	418c	
	לעג	MOCK	541c	
	לשון	TONGUE	546c	2
	מן	THAN	582d	6 d
	עמק	DEEP	771b	
	שפה	SPEECH	974a	2
	שמע	HEAR	1033d	1 g
33 20	בל	NOT	115b	
	חבל	CORD	286c	1
	חזה	SEE	302b	1 a
	מועד	APPOINTED TIME	417c	1 b
	יתד	PEG	450b	A
	נוה	HABITATION	627c	2
	נסע	PULL OUT	652a	1
	נצח	EVERLASTINGNESS	664b	4
	נתק	TEAR AWAY	683c	2
33 21	צען	WANDER	858a	
	קריה	TOWN	900b	2
	שאנן	AT EASE	983b	1
	אדיר	MAJESTIC	12b	1
	אדיר	MAJESTIC	12b	2
	אני	SHIPS	58b	
	בל	NOT	115b	
	הלך	WALK	232b	1 3
	יאר	STREAM	384c	2 b
	יד	HAND	390c	3 d
	כי אם	BUT	475a	2 b
	ל	TO	515c	5 hc
	עבר	PASS OVER	717d	3 e
	צי	SHIP	850d	
	מקום	STANDING PLACE	880c	7 b
	רחב	WIDE	932a	
	שוט	ROWING	1002b	
33 22	הוא	HE, SHE, IT	215b	1 a
	חקק	CUT IN	349b	A
	ישע	DELIVER	446d	1 b
	שפט	JUDGE	1047b	1 a
33 23	אז	THEN	23a	1 c
	אז	THEN	23a	1 b
	בזז	SPOIL	102d	
	בז	SPOIL	103a	2
	בל	NOT	115b	
	חבל	CORD	286c	1
	חזק	BE FIRM	304c	1 c
	חלק	DIVIDE	324a	
	כן	RIGHT	*467b	1
	כן	BASE	487c	1
	נטש	FORSAKE	644a	2
	נס	ENSIGN	652a	3 b
	עד	BOOTY	723d	
	פסח	LAME	820d	
	פרש	SPREAD OUT	831b	1
	מפרש	SPREADING OUT	*831c	
	מרבה	ABUNDANCE	916a	1
	תרן	MAST	1076c	
	עד	ADDENDA ET CORRIGENDA	1125d	
33 24	בל	NOT	115b	
	חלה	BE WEAK	317d	2
	נשא	LIFT	671c	2
	עון	INIQUITY	731a	1 c2
	שכן	NEIGHBOR	1015c	1
34 1	תבל	WORLD	385d	2
	צאצא	PRODUCE	425c	2
	לאם	PEOPLE	522c	
	מלא	THAT WHICH FILLS	571b	3
	קרב	COME NEAR	897c	1 g
	קשב	ATTEND	904a	
34 2	חרם	BAN	355d	1 c
	טבח	SLAUGHTERING	370d	2
	חמה	RAGE	404d	2 c
	חמה	RAGE	*404d	2 c
	ל	TO	513b	5 ba
	צבא	ARMY	838d	1 a
	קצף	WRATH	893c	1
34 3	באש	STENCH	93b	
	דם	BLOOD	196d	2 f
	הר	MOUNTAIN	250c	1 k
	מן	OUT OF	580a	2 eb
	מסס	MELT	587d	1
	עלה	GO UP	748d	5
	פגר	CORPSE	803d	1
	שלך	THROW	1021c	2
34 4	גפן	VINE	172c	
	מקק	ROT	596d	3
	נבל	SINK	615c	2
	ספר	MISSIVE	707a	3
	ספר	MISSIVE	707b	3 a
	עלה	LEAF	750a	
	צבא	HOST	839b	1 c
	צבא	HOST	839b	1 c
	תאנה	FIG-TREE	1061a	1
34 5	חרם	DEVOTED THING	356c	3
	ירד	GO DOWN	433c	3 i
	רוה	BE SATURATED	924a	1
	שמי	HEAVENS	1030b	2 a
	משפט	JUDGMENT	1048b	1 a
34 6	איל	RAM	18a	2 g
	בצרה	BOZRAH	131b	1
	דם	BLOOD	196d	2 f
	דשן	BE FAT	206b	
	זבח	SACRIFICE	258a	2 6
	חלב	FAT	317a	2 b
	חלב	FAT	*317a	2 b
	חרב	SWORD	352d	1 j
	טבח	SLAUGHTERING	370d	2
	כליה	KIDNEYS	480c	1 b
	כר	LAMB	503a	
	ל	TO	513b	5 ba
	עתוד	HE/GOAT	800d	
	עתוד	HE-GOAT	800d	
34 7	אביר	MIGHTY	7d	3
	דם	BLOOD	196d	2 f
	דשן	BE FAT	206b	
	חלב	FAT	317a	2 b
	ירד	GO DOWN	433b	1 k
	מן	OUT OF	579b	2 bb
	עם	WITH	767b	1 a
	עפר	DRY EARTH	779d	1 a
	פר	YOUNG BULL	831a	2 f
	ראם	WILD OX	910b	
	רוה	BE SATURATED	924a	1
34 8	יום	DAY	399a	3
	ל	TO	513b	5 ba
	נקם	VENGEANCE	668b	2
	שלום	REQUITAL	1024b	1
34 9	בער	BURN	129a	2
	גפרית	BRIMSTONE	172d	
	הפך	TURN	246a	2 c
	זפת	PITCH	278a	
	נחל	TORRENT	636b	1
	עפר	DRY EARTH	779d	1 a
34 10	דור	PERIOD	189d	1 b
	חרב	BE WASTE	351c	
	יומם	BY DAY	401c	2
	כבה	BE QUENCHED	459c	
	נצח	EVERLASTINGNESS	664b	4
	עולם	LONG DURATION	762b	2 b4
	עשן	SMOKE	798c	1 b
34 11	אבן	STONE	6d	6
	בהו	EMPTINESS	96a	
	ירש	TAKE POSSESSION	439c	1 a
	ירש	TAKE POSSESSION	*439d	
	נטה	STRETCH OUT	640a	1 b
	ינשוף	OWL	676b	
	עם	PEOPLE	767a	5 i
	ערב	RAVEN	788b	
	קאת	PELICAN	866b	
	קו	LINE	876a	
	שכן	SETTLE DOWN	1015a	1 b
	תהו	FORMLESSNESS	1062c	1
34 12	אפס	NON-EXISTENCE	67b	2 a
	ו	AND	255a	5 cg
	חר	NOBLE	359d	
	מלוכה	KINGSHIP	574c	
	שר	CHIEFTAIN	978a	2 a
34 13	ארמון	CITADEL	74d	
	בת	DAUGHTER	123d	6
	מבצר	FORTIFICATION	131c	
	חוח	BRIER	296b	1 a
	חציר	SETTLED ABODE	347d	
	יענה	OSTRICH	419a	
	נוה	HABITATION	627d	2
	סיר	THORN	696c	1
	עלה	GO UP	748d	4
	קמוש	THISTLES	888b	
	תן	JACKAL	1072b	
34 14	אי	JACKAL	17b	
	אך	SURELY	36c	1
	לילית	LILITH	539b	
	מצא	FIND	592c	1 a
	מנוח	RESTING PLACE	629d	1
	על	UPON	757c	2 7cb
	פגש	MEET	803d	
	צי	YELPER	850d	
	קרא	CALL	895b	2 a
	רגע	BE AT REST	921b	B
	רע	FRIEND	946a	2
	שעיר	SATYR	972d	
	שם	THERE	1027a	1 a
34 15	אך	SURELY	36c	1
	אשה	WOMAN	61b	4
	בקע	CLEAVE	131d	2
	דיה	KITE	178d	
	דגר	GATHER TOGETHER AS A BROOD	186c	
	מלט	SLIP AWAY	572c	1
	צל	SHADOW	853b	2
	קבץ	GATHER	867d	1
	רעות	FELLOW	946c	
	שם	THERE	1027a	1 a
	שם	THERE	1027c	3 c
34 16	אשה	WOMAN	61b	4
	דרש	SEEK	205b	2 a
	הוא	HE, SHE, IT	215d	2 a
	הם	THEY	241d	8 c
	מן	FROM	580c	2 a
	ספר	MISSIVE	*707c	4
	עדר	BE LACKING	727c	
	על	UPON	758c	4 2a
	פקד	ATTEND TO	823b	A 1d
	צוה	CHARGE	846a	5
	קבץ	GATHER	868a	1
	קרא	CALL	895c	a
	רוח	BREATH	924c	1 c1
	רעות	FELLOW	946c	
34 17	גורל	LOT	174b	1
	דור	PERIOD	189d	1 b
	חלק	DIVIDE	323d	1
	ירש	TAKE POSSESSION	439c	1 a
	נפל	FALL	658a	3
	עולם	LONG DURATION	762d	2 f
	קו	LINE	876a	
	קו	LINE	876a	
35 1	חבצלת	MEADOW-SAFFRON	287c	
	ערבה	DESERT-PLAIN	787c	5
	פרח	BUD	827a	
	ציה	DRYNESS	851b	
	שוש	REJOICE	965b	
35 2	הדר	SPLENDOUR	214b	2
	שרון	SHARON	450a	1
	כבוד	HONOR	458d	2 b

Ch v.	Heb	Eng	Page	Sec
	כבוד	GLORY	459a	2 c3
	כרמל	CARMEL	502b	1
	לבנון	LEBANON	527b	
	נתן	GIVE	681b	1 a
	פרח	BUD	827a	
	רנן	GIVE A RINGING CRY	943b	
35 3	אמץ	BE STRONG	55a	1
	ברך	KNEE	139c	
	חזק	BE FIRM	304d	2
	כשל	TOTTER	505c	2
	רפה	SLACK	952a	
35 4	אלהים	GOD	44b	4 a
	חזק	BE FIRM	304b	1 2c
	ירא	FEAR	431a	1 a
	ישע	DELIVER	446d	1 b
	נקם	VENGEANCE	668b	1
35 5	אז	THEN	23a	1 b
	אזן	EAR	24b	3
	חרש	DEAF	361c	
	עור	BLIND	734c	2 a
	עין	EYE	744b	1 j
	פקח	OPEN	824d	
	פתח	OPEN	835c	
35 6	איל	HART	19b	2
	אז	THEN	23a	1 b
	אלם	DUMB	48a	1
	בקע	BREAK OPEN OR THROUGH	132a	1
	דלג	LEAP	194c	
	ה	THE	208a	1 f
	לשון	TONGUE	546c	1 c
	נחל	TORRENT	636b	1
	ערבה	DESERT-PLAIN	787c	5
	פסח	LAME	820d	
	רנן	GIVE A RINGING CRY	943b	
35 7	לא	NOT	*1098d	
	חציר	SETTLED ABODE	347d	
	חציר	GREEN GRASS	348b	1
	מבוע	SPRING OF WATER	616a	
	נוה	HABITATION	627d	2
	צמאון	THIRSTY GROUND	855a	
	קנה	STALK	889c	2
	רבץ	RESTING PLACE	918c	
	שרב	BURNING HEAT	1055d	
	תן	JACKAL	1072b	
35 8	אויל	FOOLISH	17b	
	הלך	WALK	230c	1 1d 1a
	טמא	UNCLEAN	380a	2 d
	מסלול	HIGHWAY	700c	
	עבר	PASS OVER	718b	5 h
	קדש	APARTNESS	872b	6
	קרא	CALL	896b	2 d1
	תעה	ERR	1073b	1
35 9	אריה	LION	71d	
	בל	NOT	115b	
	גאל	REDEEM	145c	3 c
	חיה	LIVING THING	312d	1 b
	מצא	FIND	594a	2 c
	עלה	GO UP	748d	3
	פריץ	VIOLENT ONE	829a	
35 10	יגון	GRIEF	387b	
	נוס	ESCAPE	630d	3
	נשג	REACH	673c	2 a
	עולם	LONG DURATION	762d	2 f
	פדה	RANSOM	804a	3 b
	רנה	RINGING CRY	943b	1
	ששון	REJOICING	965b	
	שמחה	JOY	970d	2
36 1	בצר	MAKE INACCESSIBLE	131a	
	חזקיהו	HEZEKIAH	306a	1
	סנחריב	SENNACHERIB	703a	
	ארבע	FOUR	917a	2 a1 a
	תפש	LAY HOLD OF	1074d	1
36 2	ברכה	POOL	*140a	
	חיל	STRENGTH	299a	4
	כבד	MASSIVE	458a	1 b
	כבס	WASH	460a	
	לכיש	LACHISH	540c	
	מסלה	HIGHWAY	700c	
	עליון	HIGH	751b	2
	תעלה	WATER-COURSE	752b	B
	רב	CHIEF	913d	
	רב	CHIEF	913d	
	תרתן	FIELD-MARSHAL	*1077a	
36 3	אליקים	ELIAKIM	45d	A
	אסף	ASAPH	63a	1
	בית	HOUSE	110b	6
	יואח	JOAH	222a	1
	זכר	REMEMBER	271a	4
	חלקיהו	HILKIAH	324d	1
	ספר	ENUMERATOR	708b	1 b
	שבנא	SHEBNA	987d	
36 4	בטח	TRUST	105a	1 2
	בטחון	TRUST	105c	
	גדול	GREAT	153a	6 b
	מלך	KING	573b	5 a
	רב	CHIEF	913d	
36 5	בטח	TRUST	105a	1 4b
	גבורה	MIGHT	150c	2
	דבר	WORD	182a	1 1a
	עצה	ADVICE	420a	
	עצה	ADVICE	*420b	
	כי	THAT	472d	1 f

Ch v.	Heb	Eng	Page	Sec
	מרד	REBEL	597c	1
	שפה	SPEECH	973d	1 a1
36 6	בטח	TRUST	105a	1 4c
	בטח	TRUST	105a	1 4b
	כן	SO	485d	1 a
	נקב	PIERCE	666b	1
	סמך	LEAN	702a	
	פרעה	PHARAOH	829a	
	קנה	STALK	889c	2
	רצץ	CRUSH	954c	1 a
	משענת	STAFF	1044a	
36 7	בטח	TRUST	*105b	1 5a
	במה	HIGH PLACE	119d	3 d
	יהוה	YAHWEH	218d	2 1c
	מזבח	ALTAR	259a	0
	כי	WHEN	473b	2 a
	סור	TURN ASIDE	694b	1
	שחה	BOW DOWN	1005a	2 c
36 8	אלף	THOUSAND	48d	1 a
	אשור	ASSYRIA	78d	4
	סוס	HORSE	692c	2
	עתה	NOW	774b	2 b
	ערב	TAKE ON PLEDGE	786d	1
	רכב	RIDE	938a	3
36 9	בטח	TRUST	105a	1 4b
	עבד	SLAVE	714a	2
	פחה	GOVERNOR	808d	
	פרש	HORSEMAN	832a	
	קטן	SMALL	882a	2 a
	שוב	TURN BACK	999c	5
36 10	בלעדי	APART FROM	*116b	B a
	חוץ	THE OUTSIDE	*300a	1 b
	עלה	GO UP	748c	2 c
	שחת	GO TO RUIN	1008b	1
36 11	אליקים	ELIAKIM	45d	A
	ארמית	ARAMAIC	74c	
	יואח	JOAH	222a	1
	חומה	WALL	327b	1
	יהודית	JEWISH	397c	
	עבד	SLAVE	714c	6
	רב	CHIEF	913d	
	שבנא	SHEBNA	987d	
	שמע	HEAR	1033d	1 g
	ה	INTERROG PART	209d	1 b
36 12	חומה	WALL	327b	1
	חרא	DUNG	351a	
	מי	WATER	565c	3
	על	UPON	757b	2 7c aa
	רב	CHIEF	913d	
	רגל	FOOT	920a	1 f
	שין	URINE	1010a	
	שתה	DRINK	1059b	1 a
	גדול	GREAT	153a	6 b
36 13	יהודית	JEWISH	397c	
	מלך	KING	573b	5 a
	עמד	STAND	763d	1 a
	קרא	CALL	895a	1 a
	רב	CHIEF	913d	
36 14	נשא	DECEIVE	674a	
36 15	בטח	TRUST	105b	
	נתן	GIVE	681c	1 e
	אשור	ASSYRIA	78d	4
36 16	בור	WELL	92b	1
	ברכה	BLESSING	139d	6
	גפן	VINE	172c	
	יצא	GO OUT	423d	2 a
	תאנה	FIG-TREE	1061a	1
36 17	ארץ	EARTH	76b	3 b
	דגן	CORN	186c	
	דגן	CORN	*186c	
	תירוש	NEW WINE	440d	
	לחם	FOOD	537b	1 b
	לקח	TAKE	543d	9 b
36 18	איש	MAN	36a	
	אלהים	GOD	43c	1 d
	סות	INCITE	694d	2
	פן	LEST	814d	1 b
36 19	איה	WHERE	32c	
	ארפד	ARPAD	75d	
	חמת	HAMATH	333a	
	כי	THAT	472b	1 da
	ספרוים	SEPHARVAIM	709b	
36 20	ארץ	EARTH	76c	5
	מי	WHO	566c	D
	מי	WHO	566d	F c
	דבר	WORD	182b	1 1c
	הוא	HE, SHE, IT	216d	6 b
36 21	חרש	BE SILENT	361b	1 a
	ענה	ANSWER	772a	1 a
	ענה	ANSWER	772a	1 c
	מצוה	COMMANDMENT	846b	1
36 22	אליקים	ELIAKIM	45d	A
	אסף	ASAPH	63a	1
	בגד	GARMENT	94a	1
	יואח	JOAH	222a	1
	זכר	REMEMBER	271a	4
	חלקיהו	HILKIAH	324d	1
	ספר	ENUMERATOR	708b	1 b
	קרע	TEAR	902c	1 a1
	רב	CHIEF	913d	
	שבנא	SHEBNA	987d	
37 1	בגד	GARMENT	94a	1
	כסה	COVER	492b	
	שק	SACK	974c	2 a
	אליקים	ELIAKIM	45d	A
37 2	אמוץ	AMOZ	55b	

Ch v.	Heb	Eng	Page	Sec
	זקן	OLD	278d	2 b
	כהן	PRIEST	464c	8
	כסה	COVER	492b	
	נביא	PROPHET	611d	1
	ספר	ENUMERATOR	708b	1 b
	שק	SACK	974c	2 a
	שבנא	SHEBNA	987d	
37 3	בוא	COME	98b	2
	יום	DAY	398d	2 f
	תוכחה	REBUKE	407b	
	ילד	BEAR	408b	1 a
	כח	STRENGTH	470c	1 b
	נאצה	CONTEMPT	611a	
	צרה	DISTRESS	865b	
	משבר	BREACH	991b	
37 4	אלהים	GOD	44b	4 a
	בעד	ON BEHALF OF	126c	2
	יהוה	YAHWEH	218d	2 1a
	חי	ALIVE	311d	1 a
	חרף	REPROACH	357d	
	יכח	REPROVE	407a	5 a
	מצא	FIND	594b	2 d
	נשא	LIFT	670d	1 b 8
	תפלה	PRAYER	813c	1 b
	רב	CHIEF	913d	
	שארית	REST	984d	1
37 6	גדף	BLASPHEME	154c	2
	ירא	FEAR	*431b	1 c
	נער	RETAINER	655a	2 b
37 7	נפל	FALL	658a	2
	רוח	BREATH	925b	3 g
	שמועה	REPORT	1035b	1
37 8	לבנה	LIBNAH	526c	1
	לחם	ENGAGE IN BATTLE	535c	
	לכיש	LACHISH	540c	
	מצא	FIND	593a	1 d
	נסע	SET OUT	652b	2 b
	רב	CHIEF	913d	
37 9	אמר	SAY	56b	1
	כוש	CUSH	469a	2 c
	מלאך	MESSENGER	521c	1 a
	לחם	ENGAGE IN BATTLE	535c	
	על	UPON	754d	2 1f g
	שמע	HEAR	1033c	1 c
	תרהקה	TIRHAKAH	1076b	
37 10	בטח	TRUST	105a	1 3a
	נשא	DECEIVE	674a	
37 11	נתן	GIVE	681c	1 e
	ארץ	EARTH	76c	5
	אשור	ASSYRIA	78d	4
	חרם	BAN	355d	1 b
	נצל	DELIVER ONESELF	664c	1
37 12	אלהים	GOD	43c	1 d
	גוזן	GOZAN	157a	
	חרן	HARAN	357a	
	עדן	EDEN	727a	
	רצף	REZEPH	954c	
	שחת	GO TO RUIN	1008a	1
	שחת	GO TO RUIN	1008b	1
	תלאשר	TELASSAR	1067d	
37 13	אי	WHERE	32b	1 a
	הנע	HENA	245a	
	חמת	HAMATH	333a	
	ספרוים	SEPHARVAIM	709b	
	עוה	AVVA	731d	
37 14	מלאך	MESSENGER	521c	1 a
	ספר	MISSIVE	707a	1 a
	עלה	GO UP	748d	1 d
	פרש	SPREAD OUT	831b	1
	קרא	CALL	895c	4 b
37 16	אלהים	GOD	43d	3
	אלהים	GOD	43d	3
	אלהים	GOD	44c	4 ba
	ארץ	EARTH	76a	1 b
	ארץ	EARTH	76a	1 a
	הוא	HE, SHE, IT	216b	4 ba
	הוא	HE, SHE, IT	216c	4 ba
	כרוב	CHERUB	500d	3
	ממלכה	KINGDOM	575b	1
	צבא	GOD OF WAR	839c	4 b
37 17	אזן	EAR	24b	2 b
	אלהים	GOD	44b	4 a
	חי	ALIVE	311d	1 a
	חרף	REPROACH	357d	
	נטה	INCLINE	641a	3 e
	סנחריב	SENNACHERIB	703a	
	עין	EYE	744b	1 j
	פקח	OPEN	824d	1 a
37 18	אמנם	VERILY	54a	
	ארץ	EARTH	76c	5
	אשור	ASSYRIA	78d	4
	חרב	BE WASTE	351d	
37 19	אבד	CAUSE TO PERISH	2a	1
	אבן	STONE	6c	2
	עץ	TREE	782a	2 c
	מעשה	DEED	796a	2 a3
37 20	ארץ	EARTH	76a	1 a
	יהוה	YAHWEH	218d	2 1c
	ישע	DELIVER	446d	1 b
	ממלכה	KINGDOM	575b	1
37 21	אל	TO	40b	6
	אלהים	GOD	44c	4 ba
	אמוץ	AMOZ	55b	
	סנחריב	SENNACHERIB	703a	

Ch v.	Heb	Eng	Page	Sec
37 22	פלל	INTERVENE	813b	3
	אחר	BEHIND	*30a	2 a
	ב	IN	*90b	3 4
	בזה	DESPISE	*102c	
	בת	DAUGHTER	123c	3
	בת	DAUGHTER	123c	3
	בתולה	VIRGIN	*144a	
37 23	דבר	SPEAK	181c	5
	לעג	MOCK	541b	
	נוע	TOTTER	631c	2
	גדף	BLASPHEME	154c	2
	חרף	REPROACH	357d	
	מי	WHO	567b	F e
	נשא	LIFT	670c	1 b 4
	קדוש	HOLY	872c	1 c
	רום	BE HIGH	927c	1
	מרום	HEIGHT	929a	2
37 24	אדון	LORD	11b	3 2a
	ארז	CEDAR	72c	1 a
	מבחור	CHOICE	104d	
	ברוש	CYPRESS	141c	1
	הר	MOUNTAIN	249c	1 a
	חרף	REPROACH	357d	
	יער	WOOD	420d	D
	ירכה	EXTREME PARTS	438a	2
	כרמל	GARDEN	502a	1
	כרת	CUT OFF	503d	2
	לבנון	LEBANON	*527a	
	לבנון	LEBANON	527b	
	מלון	INN	534a	
	קומה	HEIGHT	879b	2
	קץ	END	894a	2
	רב	MULTITUDE	*914a	1
	מרום	HEIGHT	928d	1
	רכב	CHARIOT	939a	1
37 25	חרב	BE DRY	351b	
	יאר	STREAM	384c	2 a
	כף	SOLE OF FOOT	496d	3
	מצור	EGYPT	596a	
	פעם	BEAT	822a	1 b
	קור	BORE	881b	
37 26	בוא	COME	99c	2 b
	בצר	MAKE INACCESSI-BLE	131a	
	יצר	FORM	428a	2 b
	ל	TO	518a	7 bf
	מן	FROM	583d	9 b2
	מן	FROM	583d	9 b2
	נצה	FALL IN RUINS	663d	
	רחק	DISTANT	935c	2 b
	שאה	MAKE A DIN	981a	
	שמע	HEAR	1033c	1 a
37 27	בוש	BE ASHAMED	101d	1
	גג	ROOF	150d	1
	דשא	GRASS	206a	
	חציר	GREEN GRASS	348b	2
	חתת	BE SHATTERED	369b	2 a
	יד	HAND	389d	1 e1
	ירק	HERBS	438d	
	עשב	HERB	793c	
	קמה	STANDING GRAIN	879b	
	קצר	SHORT	894b	
	שדפה	BLIGHTED	995b	
	שממה	FIELD	995b	
	קמה	ADDENDA ET COR-RIGENDA	1126c	
37 28	בוא	COME	97d	1 a
	יצא	GO OUT	424a	3
	ישב	SIT	442d	1 b
	רגז	BE AGITATED	919b	
	קמה	ADDENDA ET COR-RIGENDA	1126c	
37 29	אזן	EAR	24b	2 b
	אף	NOSE	60b	1 c
	דרך	WAY	202c	1
	חח	HOOK	296b	1
	מתג	BRIDLE	607c	1
	עלה	GO UP	749a	8
	יען	ON ACCOUNT OF	774d	1
	רגז	BE AGITATED	919b	
	שום	TO PLACE	963a	1 a
	שפה	SPEECH	973d	1 f
	שאון	ROAR	981a	1
	שאנן	AT EASE	983c	4
37 30	אות	SIGN	16d	4
	זרע	SOW	281c	1 a
	נטע	PLANT	642c	1
	סחיש	GRAIN	*695a	
	ספיח	GROWTH	705c	
	פרי	FRUIT	826b	1
	קצר	HARVEST	894c	
	שחיס	GRAIN THAT SHOOTS UP OF IT	1006b	
37 31	בית	HOUSE	110a	5 de
	יסף	ADD	414d	
	מטה	DOWNWARDS	641b	2 a
	מעל	ABOVE	751d	2 ca
	עשה	DO	794d	2 2
	פליטה	ESCAPE	812d	2 c
	שרש	ROOT	1057c	1
37 32	הר	MOUNTAIN	249c	1 a
	פליטה	ESCAPE	812d	2 c
	ציון	ZION	851b	
	קנאה	ZEAL	888c	2 b
	שארית	REST	984d	1
37 33	אל	TO	40c	6
	מגן	SHIELD	171c	1
	חץ	ARROW	346c	1
	ירה	SHOOT	435b	2
	כן	SO	486d	3 d
	סללה	MOUND	700c	
	על	UPON	757d	2 7d
	קדם	COME IN FRONT	869d	1 a
	שפך	POUR OUT	1049c	1 a
37 34	דרך	WAY	202c	1
	נאם	UTTERANCE	610b	2
37 35	גנן	DEFEND	170d	
	דוד	DAVID	188a	
	ישע	DELIVER	446d	1 b
	מען	PURPOSE	775b	1 a
37 36	אשור	ASSHUR	78d	2
	בקר	MORNING	134b	1 h
	מחנה	ENCAMPMENT	334b	3 a
	מלאך	MESSENGER	521d	2
	מות	DIE	560a	2 b
	נכה	SMITE	646c	4 a
	פגר	CORPSE	803d	
	קדם	FRONT	869d	2 b
37 37	הלך	WALK	234a	1 5e
	נינוה	NINEVEH	644b	
	נסע	SET OUT	652b	2 b
	סנחריב	SENNACHERIB	703a	
37 38	אדרמלך	ADRAM-MELECH	12c	2
	אסרחדן	ESARHADDON	64d	
	אררט	ARARAT	76d	
	היה	COME TO PASS	224d	12a 1b
	חרב	SWORD	352d	1 f
	יצא	COMING FORTH	*425c	
	מלט	SLIP AWAY	572c	2
	נסרך	NISROCK	652d	
	שראצר	SHAREZER	974d	1
	שחה	BOW DOWN	1005c	3
38 1	אמוץ	AMOZ	55b	
	בית	HOUSE	110b	6
	חיה	LIVE	311b	2 a
	חלה	BE WEAK	317d	2
	נביא	PROPHET	611d	
38 2	צוה	GIVE CHARGE TO	845c	1 b
	סבב	TURN ABOUT	686c	1 a
	פלל	INTERVENE	813b	3
38 3	אמת	FIRMNESS	54a	3 a
	אנא	AH, NOW	58a	
	אשר	THAT	83b	8 aa
	בכה	WEEP	113c	2
	בכי	WEEPING	113d	
	גדול	GREAT	153a	3
	הלך	WALK	236b	2
	זכר	REMEMBER	270b	2 2 b
	טוב	PLEASANT	374a	2 f
	לבב	HEART	*523b	2 6a
	לב	HEART	525b	2 6a
	שלם	COMPLETE	1024a	3
38 4	דבר	WORD	182c	1 2a
38 5	אלהים	GOD	44c	4 ba
	דמעה	TEARS	199c	
	הלך	WALK	233c	1 4c 6
	הנה	BEHOLD	*244b	B b
	חמש	FIVE	332a	2 a
	יסף	ADD	414d	
38 6	גנן	DEFEND	170d	
	כף	POWER	496d	2
	נצל	DELIVER	665a	3 a
38 7	אות	SIGN	16d	4
	אשר	THAT	83c	8 ab
	את	WITH	86d	4 c
	חשך	WITHHOLD	362b	1 b
38 8	אחז	AHAZ	28c	1
	אחרנית	BACKWARDS	30d	
	הלך	WALK	*232d	1 3
	ירד	GO DOWN	433c	3 e
	מעלה	STEP	752b	2
	צל	SHADOW	853b	1
	שוב	TURN BACK	998a	7 a
	שוב	TURN BACK	999a	1 a
	שמש	SUN	1039b	1
38 9	חיה	LIVE	311b	2 a
	חלה	BE WEAK	317d	2
	חלי	SICKNESS	318b	
	חלי	SICKNESS	318b	
	מכתב	WRITING	508c	3
	ל	TO	513b	5 bb
38 10	אנכי	I	59c	
	בד	PART	*94d	3 d
	דמי	QUIET	198c	2
	יתר	REMAINDER	451d	1 b
	פקד	ATTEND TO	823d	
	שאול	SHEOL	983a	1
	שער	GATE	1045b	1
	פקד	ADDENDA ET COR-RIGENDA	1126b	
38 11	דמי	QUIET	198d	2
	יה	YAH	219c	
	חדל	CESSATION	293b	
	חי	ALIVE	312a	1 b
	חלד	DURATION	317b	
	ישב	DWELL	443b	3
	נבט	LOOK	613c	1 a
	עם	WITH	767d	1 e
38 12	ארג	WEAVE	70d	
	בצע	CUT OFF	130c	
	דור	DWELLING	190b	1 a
	דלה	THRUM	195d	
	חיים	LIFE	313a	1
	לילה	NIGHT	538c	1
	נסע	PULL OUT	652c	
	רעה	TEND	945a	1 d1
	שלם	BE COMPLETE	1022c	2
38 13	ארי	LION	71d	
	ה	THE	*207d	1 f
	לילה	NIGHT	538c	1
	שבר	BREAK	991a	
	שוה	AGREE WITH	1000d	
	שוה	SET	1001b	
	שוע	CRY OUT	1002d	
	שלם	BE COMPLETE	1022c	2
38 14	דלל	LANGUISH	195c	
	הגה	MOAN	211d	1 b
	יונה	DOVE	401d	
	ך	LIKE	454d	2 d
	כן	SO	486b	2 ad b
	ל	TO	510c	1 a
	סוס	SWALLOW	692b	
	עגור	CRANE	723a	
	עין	EYE	744b	1 i
	ערב	TAKE ON PLEDGE	786c	1
	עשקה	OPPRESSION	799a	
	צפף	CHIRP	861d	1
	מרום	HEIGHT	929a	2
38 15	דדה	MOVE SLOWLY	186d	
	דדה	MOVE SLOWLY	186d	
	ו	AND	253a	1 h
	מר	BITTER	600d	2 b
	נפש	SOUL	660d	6 c
38 16	אדון	LORD	11b	3 2a
	ב	IN	88a	
	חיה	LIVE	311b	1 c
	חיה	LIVE	311d	2 a
	חיים	LIFE	313b	1
	חלם	BE HEALTHY	321b	
	כל	ALL	481d	1 c
	על	UPON	753d	2 1e
	רוח	BREATH	925c	4 d
	בלי	WEARING OUT	115c	1
38 17	גו	BACK	156b	
	חטא	SIN	308a	1 b
	חשק	BE ATTACHED TO	366a	
	מן	OUT OF	579a	2 aa
	מרר	BE BITTER	600b	2
	מר	BITTER	600d	2 b
	נפש	SOUL	659c	1 d
	שחת	PIT	1001c	2
	שלך	THROW	1021b	2
	שלום	PEACE	1022d	2
38 18	אמת	FIRMNESS	54a	3 b
	בור	PIT	92c	5
	הלל	PRAISE	238a	1
	ידה	PRAISE	392c	1 a2
	שבר	HOPE	960b	1
	שאול	SHEOL	983a	2 a
38 19	אמת	FIRMNESS	54a	3 b
	הוא	HE, SHE, IT	215d	2 a
	חי	ALIVE	312a	1 b
	ידה	PRAISE	392c	1 a2
	ידע	MAKE KNOWN	395a	
38 20	חיים	LIFE	313b	1
	ישע	DELIVER	446d	1 b
	ל	TO	518a	7 bg
	גנן	PLAY	618d	
	נגינה	MUSIC	618d	1
	על	UPON	756a	2 6a
38 21	דבלה	PRESSED FIG-CAKE	179b	
	חיה	LIVE	311b	2 a
	מרח	RUB	598d	
	שחין	BOIL	1006c	
	תאנה	FIG	1061a	2
38 22	אות	SIGN	16d	4
	עלה	GO UP	748b	1 d
39 1	בבל	BABEL	93c	
	בלאדן	BALADAN	114d	
	חזק	BE FIRM	304a	1 a
	חלה	BE WEAK	317d	2
	מנחה	GIFT	585a	1
	מרדכבלאדן	MERODACH BALA-DAN	597d	
	נביא	PROPHET	611d	1
	ספר	MISSIVE	707a	1 a
	שמע	HEAR	1033c	1
39 2	אוצר	TREASURE	70a	1
	בית	HOUSE	109a	1 ae 6
	בשם	SPICE	141d	1
	דבר	WORD	183d	4 6
	טוב	PLEASANT	374b	3 c
	כלי	IMPLEMENT	479d	1
	מצא	FIND	594a	2 c
	ממשלה	RULE	606a	1
	נכת	TREASURE	649b	
	על	UPON	757c	2 7c b
	ראה	TO SEE	908d	1 a1
	שמח	REJOICE	970b	1 a
	שמן	OIL	1032b	2 b
39 3	בבל	BABEL	93c	
	רחק	DISTANT	935b	1 a
39 4	אוצר	TREASURE	70a	1
	ראה	TO SEE	908d	
	ראה	TO SEE	908d	1 a1
39 6	אצר	STORE UP	69d	
	בבל	BABEL	93c	
	בוא	COME	98c	2

Ch v.	Heb	Eng	Page	Sec
	הנה	BEHOLD	244b	B b
	יום	DAY	400a	7 c
	יתר	BE LEFT OVER	451b	
	נשא	LIFT	671d	4
39 7	בבל	BABEL	93c	
	היכל	PALACE	228b	1
	ילד	BEGET	409a	1
	יצא	GO OUT	423c	1 h
	מן	FROM	580d	3 ba
	סרים	EUNUCH	710c	
39 8	אם	IF	50c	1 cb
	אמת	FIRMNESS	54a	2
	טוב	PLEASANT	374c	5
	כי	THAT	474c	
	שלון	PEACE	1023b	6
40 1	נחם	CONSOLE ONESELF	637a	
40 2	דבר	SPEAK	181d	5
	חטאת	SIN	308d	1 b
	כפל	DOUBLE	495d	
	לב	HEART	525c	2 9a
	לקח	TAKE	543b	4 f
	מלא	BE FULL	570b	1 b
	עון	INIQUITY	731c	3
	צבא	HARD SERVICE	839b	3 b
	רצה	BE PLEASED WITH	953b	2
40 3	דרך	WAY	203a	1
	ישר	MAKE STRAIGHT	448d	1
	מסלה	HIGHWAY	700c	
	ערבה	DESERT-PLAIN	787c	4
	פנה	TURN	815c	
	קול	VOICE	877a	1 f
	קרא	CALL	895c	3 d
40 4	בקעה	PLAIN	132c	2
	גבעה	HILL	149a	3
	גיא	VALLEY	161b	
	הר	MOUNTAIN	250b	1 e
	מישור	LEVEL PLACE	449d	1
	נשא	LIFT	671d	1 a
	עקב	STEEP	784c	
	רכס	ROUGHNESS	940c	
	שפה	SWEEP BARE	*1045d	
	שפל	BECOME LOW	1050a	1
40 5	בשר	FLESH	142d	6 c
	דבר	SPEAK	180d	1
	יחדו	TOGETHER	403c	B
	כבוד	GLORY	459a	2 c3
	פה	MOUTH	805b	2 c
40 6	בשר	FLESH	142d	6 c
	חסד	GOODNESS	338d	1 4
	חציר	GREEN GRASS	348b	2
	ציץ	BLOSSOM	847d	1
	קרא	CALL	895c	3 d
40 7	אכן	SURELY	38c	A
	חציר	GREEN GRASS	348b	2
	יבש	BE DRY	386b	1 d
	נבל	SINK	615c	2
	נשב	BLOW	674b	
	ציץ	BLOSSOM	847d	1
	רוח	BREATH	924d	2 a
40 8	דבר	WORD	182d	1 2b
	חציר	GREEN GRASS	348b	2
	יבש	BE DRY	386b	1 d
	נבל	SINK	615c	2
	עולם	LONG DURATION	762c	2 f
	ציץ	BLOSSOM	847d	1
	קום	STAND	878b	7 g
40 9	בשר	BEAR TIDINGS	142b	3
	גבה	HIGH	147a	1
	הר	MOUNTAIN	250b	1 d
	יהודה	JUDAH	397b	2
	ירא	FEAR	431a	1 a
	כח	STRENGTH	470c	1 a
	ל	TO	515c	5 ib
	על	UPON	756d	27b
	ציון	ZION	851c	
	רום	BE HIGH	927c	1 b
40 10	אדון	LORD	11c	4 b
	ב	IN	89a	17b
	זרוע	ARM	284b	2 b
	חזק	STRONG	305d	2
	משל	RULE	605d	3
	פנה	FACE	817c	24c a
	פעלה	WORK	821d	2
	תרומה	OFFERING	*929b	7
	שכר	HIRE	969b	1
40 11	אסף	GATHER	62c	2 c
	זרוע	ARM	284a	1 c
	חיק	BOSOM	300d	2
	טלה	LAMB	378b	
	נהל	BRING TO A PLACE OF REST	625a	1
	עדר	FLOCK	727d	1 a
	עול	GIVE SUCK	732b	1
	קבץ	GATHER	868a	1
	רעה	TEND	944d	1 b
40 12	מאזן	BALANCES	24d	
	גבעה	HILL	149a	3
	הר	MOUNTAIN	250a	1 c
	זרת	SPAN	285a	
	כל	COMPREHEND	465a	
	מדד	MEASURE	551a	3
	מדד	MEASURE	551a	
	מי	WHO	567a	F c
	עפר	DRY EARTH	779d	2 a
	פלס	BALANCE	813d	
	שליש	THIRD	1026c	

Ch v.	Heb	Eng	Page	Sec
	שעל	HOLLOW HAND	1043b	1
	שקל	WEIGH	1053c	1
	תכן	MEASURE	1067b	
40 13	איש	MAN	36a	
	ידע	MAKE KNOWN	395a	
	ידע	TEACH	395a	
	עצה	ADVICE	420b	
	מי	WHO	566d	F c
	רוח	BREATH	925c	6
	תכן	MEASURE	1067b	
40 14	ארח	WAY	73b	3 b
	בין	DISCERN	107a	3 b
	תבונה	UNDERSTANDING	108b	2
	דרך	WAY	203c	6 b
	ידע	KNOW	395a	
	דעת	SKILL	395c	1 b
	יעץ	CONSULT	419c	
	למד	LEARN	540d	
	למד	LEARN	540d	
	מי	WHO	566d	F c
	משפט	JUDGEMNT	1049a	6 a
40 15	אי	COAST	16a	
	מאזן	BALANCES	24d	
	דלי	BUCKET	194d	
	דק	SMALL	201a	1
	הן	BEHOLD	243c	A
	חשב	THINK	363b	1
	מן	FROM	578b	1 a
	מר	DROP	601c	
	נטל	LIFT	642a	
	שדה	FIELD	961c	1 d
	שחק	DUST	1007a	1
40 16	בער	BURN	129b	2
	די	SUFFICIENCY	191c	1
	חיה	LIVING THING	312c	1 b
	לבנן	LEBANON	*527a	
	לבנן	LEBANON	527b	
40 17	אין	NOTHING	34a	1
	אפס	NON-EXISTENCE	67b	2 a
	חשב	THINK	363c	1
	ל	TO	*514a	5 e
	מן	OUT OF	579b	2 ba
	נגד	IN FRONT	617b	1 b
	תהו	FORMLESSNESS	1062c	2
40 18	אל	GOD	42d	6 e
	דמה	BE LIKE	198a	1
	דמות	LIKENESS	198b	1
	מה	WHAT	552c	1 aa
	מי	WHO	566d	F c
40 19	ערך	ARRANGE	789d	2 a
	זהב	GOLD	263d	2 f
	חרש	GRAVER	360d	1 a
	נסך	POUR OUT	650d	3
	פסל	IDOL	820d	
	צרף	SMELT	864b	4
	רקע	BEAT	956a	
	רתקה	CHAIN	958d	
40 20	בחר	CHOOSE	104b	5 b
	בקש	SEEK	134d	1 d
	חכם	WISE	314d	1
	חרש	GRAVER	360d	1 b
	כון	ESTABLISH	466b	1 c
	לא	NOT	518c	1 aa
	מוט	SHAKE	557a	
	סכן	BE POOR	698c	
	עץ	TREE	782a	2 c
	פסל	IDOL	820d	
	תרוה	OFFERING	929b	7
	רקב	ROT	955a	
40 21	בין	DISCERN	107a	1 a
	מוסד	FOUNDATION	414c	
	לא	NOT	520b	4 ba
	נגד	BE CONSPICUOUS	617a	
	ראש	HEAD	911b	4 b
40 22	חגב	LOCUST	290b	
	חוג	VAULT	295b	
	ישב	SIT	442c	1 a
	מתח	SPREAD OUT	607c	
	אין	NOTHING	34a	1
	לא	NOT	520b	4 ba
40 23	רזן	BE WEIGHTY	931b	
	שפט	JUDGE	1047c	1 b
	תהו	FORMLESSNESS	1062c	2
40 24	אף	ALSO	*64d	1
	בל	NOT	115c	
	גזע	STOCK	160b	
	ה	THE	208a	1 f
	זרע	SOW	282a	
	יבש	BE DRY	386c	1 d
	נטע	PLANT	642c	
	נשא	LIFT	671d	3 b
	נשף	BLOW	676a	
	סערה	TEMPEST	704b	
	קש	STUBBLE	*905d	1
	שרש	ROOT UP	1057d	2
40 25	דמה	BE LIKE	198a	1
	קדוש	HOLY	872c	1 c
	שוה	AGREE WITH	1000d	1
	שוה	AGREE WITH	1001a	
40 26	און	VIGOUR	20b	2
	אמיץ	MIGHTY	55c	
	ברא	CREATE	135b	1
	יצא	BRING OUT	425a	4 h
	כח	STRENGTH	471a	3
	נשא	LIFT	670c	1 b 4
	עדר	BE LACKING	727c	

Ch v.	Heb	Eng	Page	Sec
	צבא	HOST	839b	1 c
	קרא	CALL	896a	6 f
	ראה	TO SEE	907b	5 a
	מרום	HEIGHT	929a	2
	אמץ	ADDENDA ET CORRIGENDA	1120b	
40 27	את	WITH	86c	3 a
	דרך	WAY	203b	5
	סתר	HIDE	711c	2
	עבר	PASS OVER	718b	6 c
	ישראל	ISRAEL	975d	2 a3
	משפט	JUDGEMNT	1049a	5
40 28	אלהים	GOD	44c	4 bb
	ארץ	EARTH	76c	4 e
	תבונה	UNDERSTANDING	108b	3
	ברא	CREATE	135b	1
	חקר	SEARCHING	350d	
	יגע	TOIL	388b	2
	יעף	BE WEARY	419b	
	עולם	LONG DURATION	762b	2 c
	קצה	END	892c	1
	שמע	HEAR	1033c	1 a
40 29	און	VIGOUR	20b	2
	אין	NOT	35a	6 ca
	יעף	WEARY	419b	
	כח	STRENGTH	470d	1 e
	עצמה	MIGHT	782c	
40 30	בחור	YOUNG MAN	104c	2
	ו	AND	252b	1 b
	יגע	TOIL	388b	2
	יעף	BE WEARY	419b	
	כשל	BE FEEBLE	505d	2
40 31	אבר	PINIONS	7c	
	הלך	WALK	230b	1 1a
	חלף	PASS ON OR AWAY	322b	1
	יגע	TOIL	388b	2
	יעף	BE WEARY	419b	
	כח	STRENGTH	470d	1 e
	כשל	BE FEEBLE	*505d	2
	נשר	EAGLE	676d	
	עלה	GO UP	748d	3
	קוה	WAIT FOR	875d	
	רוץ	RUN	930b	1
41 1	אי	COAST	16a	
	אז	THEN	23a	1 c
	חלף	PASS ON OR AWAY	322b	1
	חרש	BE SILENT	361b	1 a
	יחדו	TOGETHER	403b	A
	כח	STRENGTH	470d	1 e
	לאם	PEOPLE	522c	
	קרב	COME NEAR	897c	1 g
	משפט	JUDGMENT	1048b	1
41 2	ה	THE	208a	1 f
	מזרח	PLACE OF SUNRISE	280d	2 b
	מי	WHO	567a	F c
	מי	WHO	567b	F e
	נדף	DRIVE	623d	
	עור	ROUSE ONESELF	735b	1
	עפר	DRY EARTH	780a	2 c
	צדק	RIGHTEOUSNESS	842a	6 d
	קשת	BOW	906a	1 b
	רגל	FOOT	919d	1 f
	רדד	BEAT OUT	921d	
	רדה	HAVE DOMINION	922a	
41 3	ארח	WAY	73a	1
	הלך	WALK	230b	1 1a
	רדף	PURSUE	922d	1 b
41 4	אחרון	BEHIND	30d	3
	אחרון	BEHIND	31a	B
	דור	GENERATION	190a	2 a
	הוא	HE, SHE, IT	216c	5
	יהוה	YAHWEH	219b	2 2d
	מי	WHO	567b	F e
	פעל	DO	821b	1 a
	ראש	HEAD	911b	4 b
	ראשון	FIRST	911d	2 a
41 5	אי	COAST	16a	
	ארץ	EARTH	76c	4 e
	אתה	COME	87c	
	חרד	TREMBLE	353b	1
	ירא	FEAR	431b	1 a
	קצה	END	892c	1
	קרב	COME NEAR	897c	1 h
41 6	חזק	BE FIRM	304b	1 2c
	עזר	HELP	740b	
	רע	FRIEND	946b	3
41 7	את	MARK OF THE AC-CUSATIVE	85a	1 a
	דבק	JOINING	180a	1
	הלם	SMITE	240c	
	חזק	BE FIRM	304c	1 c
	חזק	BE FIRM	304d	3
	חלק	BE SMOOTH	325b	1
	חרש	GRAVER	360d	1 a
	טוב	PLEASANT	374b	5
	ל	TO	514b	5 fa
	לא	NOT	518c	1 aa
	מוט	SHAKE	557a	
	מסמר	NAIL	702c	
	פטיש	FORGE-HAMMER	809c	
	פעם	ANVIL	822a	2
	צרף	SMELT	864b	4
41 8	אהב	LOVE	13a	4 b
	בחר	CHOOSE	104a	2 a
	זרע	SOWING	283a	4 f
	עבד	SLAVE	714b	5

Ch v.	Heb	Eng	Page	Sec
41 9	ישראל	ISRAEL	975d	2 a3
	אציל	SIDE	69c	1
	ארץ	EARTH	76c	4 e
	בחר	CHOOSE	104b	5 a
	חזק	BE FIRM	305a	6 a
	מאס	REJECT	549c	1 a
	עבד	SLAVE	714b	5
	קצה	END	892c	1
41 10	אמץ	BE STRONG	55a	1
	אף	ALSO	64d	1
	ימין	RIGHT HAND	411d	1 b
	ימין	RIGHT HAND	411d	1 c
	ירא	FEAR	431a	1 a
	עזר	HELP	740b	
	צדק	RIGHTEOUSNESS	842a	6 a
	שעה	GAZE	1043a	
	תמך	SUPPORT	1069d	2
41 11	אבד	PERISH	1c	1
	אין	NOTHING	34a	1
	בוש	BE ASHAMED	101d	3
	הן	BEHOLD	243c	A
	חרה	BURN	354b	
	חרר	BE HOT	359c	2
	כלם	BE HUMILIATED	483d	2
	ריב	STRIFE	937a	2
41 12	אין	NOTHING	34a	1
	אפס	NON-EXISTENCE	67b	2 a
	בקש	SEEK	134c	1 b
	מלחמה	WAR	536b	
	מצא	FIND	593c	4
	מצות	STRIFE	663d	
41 13	יהוה	YAHWEH	218d	2 1a
	יהוה	YAHWEH	219b	2 2c
	חזק	BE FIRM	305a	6 a
	ימין	RIGHT HAND	411d	1 b
	ירא	FEAR	431a	1 a
	עזר	HELP	740b	
41 14	גאל	REDEEM	145c	3 c
	ירא	FEAR	431a	1 a
	מת	MALE	607b	3 a
	עזר	HELP	740b	
	קדוש	HOLY	872c	1 c
	תולעה	WORM	1069a	1
41 15	בעל	LORD	127c	15a
	גבעה	HILL	149a	3
	דוש	THRESH	190c	
	דקק	CRUSH	200d	1
	ה	THE	208a	1 f
	הר	MOUNTAIN	250d	1 n
	חדש	NEW	294a	A
	חרוץ	SHARP	358d	1
	מוץ	CHAFF	558b	
	מורג	THRESHING-SLEDGE	558b	
41 16	פה	MOUTH	805a	3
	הלל	BE BOASTFUL	239a	2
	זרה	SCATTER	279d	2
	נשא	LIFT	671b	3 b
	סערה	TEMPEST	704b	
	פוץ	BE DISPERSED	807a	1 a
	קדוש	HOLY	872c	1 c
41 17	אביון	NEEDY	2d	
	אין	NOT	34c	2 da
	אלהים	GOD	44c	4 ba
	בקש	SEEK	134c	1 b
	יהוה	YAHWEH	219b	2 2d
	לשון	TONGUE	546a	1 a
	נשת	BE DRY	677a	
	עזב	LEAVE	737c	2 e
	ענה	ANSWER	772a	1 b
	עני	POOR	776d	3
	צמא	THIRST	854d	
41 18	אגם	POOL	8c	2
	בקעה	VALLEY	132c	1
	מוצא	GOING FORTH	425d	3 a
	מעין	SPRING	746a	
	פתח	OPEN	835b	
	ציה	DRYNESS	851d	
	מקום	STANDING PLACE	880a	3 d
	שפי	BARE HEIGHT	1046a	2
41 19	ארז	CEDAR	72c	1 a
	תאשור	BOX-TREE	81b	
	ברוש	CYPRESS	141c	1
	תדהר	ELM	*187b	
	תדהר	ELM	187b	
	תדהר	ELM	*187b	
	הדס	MYRTLE	213c	
	יחדו	TOGETHER	403c	A
	עץ	TREE	781d	1 b
	ערבה	DESERT-PLAIN	787c	4
	שום	TO PLACE	964b	4 d
	שטה	ACACIA	1008d	
	שמן	OIL	1032a	2 a
41 20	ברא	CREATE	135c	4
	ו	AND	252b	1 b
	יחדו	TOGETHER	403c	B
	קדוש	HOLY	872c	1 c
	שום	TO PLACE	963c	2 b
	שכל	BE PRUDENT	968d	2
41 21	מלך	KING	573b	3
	נגש	APPROACH	621b	
	עצמה	DEFENCE	783b	
	יעקב	JACOB	785a	2
	קרב	COME NEAR	897d	1
41 22	אחרית	END	31a	B
	בוא	COME	98c	2
	הוא	HE, SHE, IT	216a	3 b
	הם	THEY	241c	3 b
	לב	HEART	524d	2 3c
	מה	WHAT	552d	1 b
	נגש	APPROACH	621b	
	קרה	ENCOUNTER	899c	2
	ראשון	FIRST	911c	1 a
	שום	TO PLACE	963c	2 b
41 23	אחור	HINDER SIDE	30c	C b
	אתה	COME	87c	
	יחדו	TOGETHER	403c	B
	יטב	DO GOOD TO	405d	2
	ל	TO	517a	6 a
	רעע	BE EVIL	949c	1
	שעה	GAZE	1043b	
41 24	אין	NOTHING	34a	1
	אפס	NON-EXISTENCE	67b	2 a
	אפע	NON-EXISTENCE	67c	
	בחר	CHOOSE	104a	1 b
	הן	BEHOLD	243c	A
	מן	OUT OF	579b	2 ba
	פעל	DOING	821c	1 b
	תועבה	ABOMINATION	1072d	1 b
41 25	אתה	COME	87b	
	מזרח	PLACE OF SUNRISE	280d	1
	חמר	CEMENT	330d	2 b
	טיט	MUD	376c	2
	יצר	FORM	427d	1 a
	כמו	LIKE	*455d	1 a
	סגן	PREFECT	688d	1
	עור	ROUSE ONESELF	735b	1
	צפון	NORTH	861a	
41 26	אמר	WORD	57a	1
	אף	ALSO	64d	1
	מי	WHO	566d	F c
	פנה	FACE	816b	1 6
	פנה	FACE	818b	2 5c
	צדיק	JUST	843b	5
	ראש	HEAD	911b	4 b
	שמע	HEAR	1034c	1 c
41 27	בשר	BEAR TIDINGS	142b	3
	ציון	ZION	851b	
41 28	ראשון	FIRST	911d	2 a
	דבר	WORD	182b	1 1c
	יעץ	ADVISE	419d	
41 29	און	TROUBLE	20a	2
	אפס	NON-EXISTENCE	67b	2 a
	הן	BEHOLD	243c	A
	נסך	MOLTEN IMAGE	651d	1
	מעשה	DEED	796a	2 a3
	רוח	BREATH	925a	2 e
	תהו	FORMLESSNESS	1062c	1
42 1	בחיר	CHOSEN	104c	
	יצא	BRING OUT	425b	5
	נפש	SOUL	661b	8
	נתן	PUT	680c	2
	עבד	SLAVE	714b	5
	רוח	BREATH	926a	9 c2
	רצה	BE PLEASED WITH	953a	1 a
	תמך	SUPPORT	1069d	2
42 2	נשא	LIFT	670c	1 b 5
	עבד	SLAVE	*714b	5
	צעק	CRY	858c	3
	שמע	HEAR	1034c	1 a
42 3	אמת	FIRMNESS	54a	3
	יצא	BRING OUT	425b	5
	כבה	QUENCH	459d	
	כהת	DIM	462d	
	ל	TO	516c	5 jb
	עבד	SLAVE	*714b	5
	פשתה	FLAX	834a	2
	קנה	STALK	889c	2
	רצץ	CRUSH	954c	1 a
	שבר	BREAK	990c	
42 4	אי	COAST	16a	
	יחל	WAIT	404a	2
	תורה	INSTRUCTION	436a	1 d
	כהת	GROW DIM	462c	
	עבד	SLAVE	*714b	5
	עד	UNTIL	725a	2 1b b
	רגע	BE AT REST	*921b	A
	רצץ	CRUSH	954c	1 a
	רצץ	CRUSH	954d	
	שום	TO PLACE	963d	3 b
	משפ	JUDGMENT	1048d	3
42 5	אל	GOD	42c	6 a
	ברא	CREATE	135b	1
	ו	AND	253a	1 g
	צאצא	PRODUCE	425c	2
	נשמה	BREATH	675d	2
	עבד	SLAVE	*714b	5
	רגע	BE AT REST	*921b	A
	רוח	BREATH	925b	4 a
	רקע	BEAT	956a	
42 6	אור	LIGHT	21d	9
	ברית	COVENANT	137a	2 2k
	ברית	COVENANT	137a	2 2k
	יהוה	YAHWEH	219b	2 2d
	חזק	BE FIRM	305b	6 c
	ל	TO	512b	4
	נצר	GUARD	665d	2
	עבד	SLAVE	*714b	5
	צדק	RIGHTEOUSNESS	841d	E
42 7	אסור	PRISONERS	64b	
	בית	HOUSE	109a	1 ae 2
	חשך	DARKNESS	365a	3 a
	יצא	CAUSE TO GO	424b	1 a
	כלא	CONFINEMENT	476c	
	מסגר	DUNGEON	689d	2
	עור	BLIND	734d	2 a
	עין	EYE	744b	1 j
	עין	EYE	744c	3 a
	פקח	OPEN	824d	1 b
42 8	אחר	ANOTHER	29d	
	יהוה	YAHWEH	219b	2 2d
	תהלה	PRAISE	240a	1
	כבוד	HONOR	459b	6 b
42 9	בוא	COME	98c	2 c
	חדש	NEW	294b	A
	טרם	NOT YET	382c	2
	צמח	SPROUT	855c	1
	ראשון	FIRST	911c	1 a
	שמע	HEAR	1034d	2 b
42 10	אי	COAST	16a	
	ארץ	EARTH	76b	4 e
	תהלה	PRAISE	240a	1
	חדש	NEW	294a	A
	ירד	GO DOWN	433a	1 g
	מלא	THAT WHICH FILLS	571b	3
	מן	FROM	578a	1 a
	קצה	END	892c	1
	שיר	SONG	1010b	2
	שיר	SING	1010c	
42 11	מדבר	WILDERNESS	184d	3
	הר	MOUNTAIN	250d	1 m
	חצר	SETTLED ABODE	347b	A
	חצר	SETTLED ABODE	*347b	C
	מן	FROM	578a	1 a
	נשא	LIFT	670c	1 b 5
	סלע	CRAG	701a	1
	צוח	CRY ALOUD	846d	
	קדר	KEDAR	871a	1
	רנן	GIVE A RINGING CRY	943b	1
42 12	אי	COAST	16a	
	תהלה	PRAISE	240a	2
	כבוד	HONOR	459b	6 b
	נגד	BE CONSPICUOUS	617a	4
	שום	TO PLACE	963b	1 c
42 13	אף	ALSO	64d	1
	גבר	BE STRONG	149d	
	גבור	STRONG	150b	2
	ה	THE	*207d	1 f
	כ	LIKE	454a	1 c2
	מלחמה	WAR	536b	
	עור	ROUSE ONESELF	735b	1
	צרח	CRY	863c	
	קנאה	ZEAL	888c	2 b
	רוע	RAISE A SHOUT	929c	1
42 14	אפק	HOLD	67d	2
	ה	THE	*207d	1 f
	חרש	BE SILENT	361b	1 b
	חשה	BE SILENT	364c	1
	יחד	UNION	403a	2 a4
	ילד	BEAR	408c	1 b
	מן	FROM	581c	4 a
	נשם	PANT	675c	
	עולם	LONG DURATION	762a	1 c
	פעה	GROAN	821a	
	שאף	GASP	983c	1
	שמם	BE DESOLATED	1031a	2
42 15	אגם	POOL	8c	2
	אי	COAST	16a	
	גבעה	HILL	149a	3
	הר	MOUNTAIN	250a	1 c
	חרב	BE WASTE	351d	
	יבש	BE DRY	386c	1
	יבש	BE DRY	386c	2
	עשב	HERB	793b	
	שום	TO PLACE	964c	5 a
42 16	דבר	WORD	183d	4 6
	דרך	TREAD	202b	3
	הלך	WALK	236c	1 a
	מחשך	DARK PLACE	365b	B
	מישור	LEVEL PLACE	449d	1
	נתיבה	PATH	677b	2 a
	עור	BLIND	734c	2 a
	מעקש	TWISTED PLACE	786a	
	שום	TO PLACE	964c	5 a
42 17	בוש	SHAME	102a	1
	בטח	TRUST	105a	1 3c
	מסכה	MOLTEN IMAGE	651b	2
	סוג	MOVE AWAY	691a	2
	פסל	IDOL	820d	
42 18	ה	THE	208d	1 i
	חרש	DEAF	361c	
	נבט	LOOK	613d	2
	עור	BLIND	734d	2 b
	ראה	TO SEE	907b	4
42 19	חרש	DEAF	361c	
	כיאם	EXCEPT	475a	2 a
	מלאך	MESSENGER	521c	1 b
	מי	WHO	566d	F c
	עבד	SLAVE	714b	5
	עור	BLIND	734d	2 b
	שלם	BE IN COVENANT OF PEACE	1023d	
42 20	אזן	EAR	24a	2
	פקח	OPEN	824d	2
	שמע	HEAR	1033d	1 e
	שמר	KEEP	1036d	1 d
42 21	אדר	WIDE	12a	

Ch	v.	Heb	Eng	Page	Sec
		גדל	BECOME GREAT	152c	2
		חפץ	DELIGHT IN	343a	2c
		תורה	INSTRUCTION	435d	1c
		מען	PURPOSE	775b	1a
		צדק	RIGHTEOUSNESS	842a	6a
42	22	בזז	SPOIL	102d	
		בז	SPOIL	103a	2
		בית	HOUSE	109a	1ae2
		חבא	WITHDRAW	285b	
		חר	HOLE	359d	
		כלא	CONFINEMENT	476c	
		נצל	DELIVER	664d	3a
		פחח	ENSNARE	809a	
		שוב	TURN BACK	999b	1d
		שסה	PLUNDER	1042c	
		משסה	PLUNDER	1042d	
42	23	אזן	HEAR	24c	1
		אחור	HINDER SIDE	30c	Cb
		ל	TO	517a	6a
		מי	WHO	566c	D
		מי	WHO	566c	Fa
42	24	אבה	BE WILLING	2c	
		בזז	SPOIL	102d	
		דרך	WAY	204a	6ec
		הלך	WALK	232d	14a
		זו	THIS	262b	2
		חטא	MISS A GOAL OR WAY	307a	2b
		תורה	INSTRUCTION	435d	1c
		לא	NOT	520b	4ba
		מי	WHO	567b	Fe
		נתן	GIVE	681a	3b
		ישראל	ISRAEL	975d	2a3
		שסה	PLUNDER	1042c	
		משסה	PLUNDER	*1042d	
42	25	בער	BURN	129a	3
		חמה	RAGE	404d	2c
		חמה	RAGE	*405a	2c
		לב	HEART	525d	23d
		לחם	SET ABLAZE	529d	
		מלחמה	WAR	536d	
		סביב	ROUND ABOUT	687a	1d
		עזוז	STRENGTH	739b	5
		שום	TO PLACE	963b	1b
		פך	POUR OUT	1049a	2a
43	1	ב	IN	90b	34
		ברא	CREATE	135b	2
		גאל	REDEEM	145c	3c
		יצר	FORM	427d	2a
		ירא	FEAR	431a	1a
		ל	TO	513b	5ba
		קרא	CALL	896a	5e
43	2	אנכי	I	59b	
		במו	IN	91b	
		בער	BURN	129a	3
		כוה	BE BURNED	464d	
		להבה	FLAME	529b	1
		מי	WATER	565d	4a
		עבר	PASS OVER	717c	3b
		שטף	OVERFLOW	1009a	1
43	3	יהוה	YAHWEH	218d	21a
		יהוה	YAHWEH	219b	22c
		ישע	DELIVER	446d	1b
		כוש	CUSH	469a	2c
		כפר	RANSOM	497b	1
		כפר	COVER OVER	*497c	1
		סבאים	SABEANS	*685b	
		סבא	SEBA	685b	
		קדוש	HOLY	872c	1c
		תחת	INSTEAD	1066a	22bb
43	4	אהב	LOVE	13b	5b
		מאשר	FROM THAT	84a	C
		ו	AND	254d	5ca
		יקר	BE PRECIOUS	429d	1a
		כבד	BE HONORED	457c	1b
		לאם	PEOPLE	522c	
		נפש	SOUL	660a	4a2
		נתן	GIVE	679d	1p
		תחת	INSTEAD	1066a	22bb
		די	THAT	*1088b	4ba
43	5	אנכי	I	59b	
		את	WITH	86a	1a
		מזרח	PLACE OF SUNRISE	280d	2b
		זרע	SOWING	283a	4f
		ירא	FEAR	431a	1a
		עם	WITH	767c	1a
		מערב	WEST	788a	
		קבץ	GATHER	868a	1
43	6	ארץ	EARTH	76b	4e
		בת	DAUGHTER	123b	1f
		תימן	SOUTH	412c	1a
		כלא	RESTRAIN	476b	3
		צפון	NORTH	861a	
		קצה	END	892a	1
		רחק	DISTANT	935c	2a1
43	7	אף	ALSO	64d	1
		ברא	CREATE	135b	2
		יצר	FORM	427d	2a
		כבד	HONOR	459b	6b
		קרא	CALL	896c	6d6
43	8	אזן	EAR	24a	2a
		חרש	DEAF	361c	
		יצא	CAUSE TO GO	424c	1b
		יש	BE	442a	2c
		עור	BLIND	734d	2b
43	9	אמת	FIRMNESS	54b	4a
		אסף	GATHER	62c	1a
		לאם	PEOPLE	522c	
		מי	WHO	566c	D
		מי	WHO	566d	Fc
		צדק	BE JUST	842c	2
		צדיק	JUST	843b	5
		קבץ	GATHER	867d	1
		ראשון	FIRST	911c	1a
43	10	אל	GOD	42b	3
		אמן	CONFIRM	53a	2b
		בחר	CHOOSE	104a	2a
		בין	DISCERN	106d	2c
		הוא	HE, SHE, IT	216c	5
		יצר	BE FORMED	428a	
		כסא	SEAT OF HONOR	490d	1a
		עבד	SLAVE	714b	5
43	11	פנה	FACE	817d	24e
		אפס	NON-EXISTENCE	67b	2b
		בלעדי	APART FROM	116c	Bb
		יהוה	YAHWEH	219b	22d
		ישע	DELIVER	446d	1b
43	12	אל	GOD	42d	6e
		זור	BE A STRANGER	266c	2c
		ישע	DELIVER	446d	1b
		שמע	HEAR	1034d	2c
43	13	גם	YEA	169c	3
		הוא	HE, SHE, IT	216c	5
		יום	DAY	401a	7j
		מי	WHO	567a	Fc
		מן	FROM	581c	4a
		נצל	DELIVER	664d	3a
		פעל	DO	821b	1a
		שוב	TURN BACK	999d	1
43	14	אניה	A SHIP	58b	
		בבל	BABEL	93c	
		בריח	FLEEING	138a	
		גאל	REDEEM	145c	3c
		ירד	BRING DOWN	434a	1a
		כשדים	CHALDEANS	505a	1b
		מען	PURPOSE	775a	1a
		קדוש	HOLY	872c	1c
		רנה	RINGING CRY	943d	3
43	15	ברא	CREATE	135b	2
		יהוה	YAHWEH	219b	22d
		מלך	KING	573b	3
		קדוש	HOLY	872c	1c
43	16	דרך	WAY	202d	1
		דרך	WAY	203a	1
		נתיבה	PATH	677b	1
		עז	STRONG	738c	
		בל	NOT	115b	
43	17	דעך	BE EXTINGUISHED	200b	
		יחדו	TOGETHER	403c	B
		יצא	BRING OUT	424c	1c
		כבה	BE QUENCHED	459c	
		עזוז	MIGHTY	739b	5
		פשתה	FLAX	834a	2
		קום	STAND	877d	1a
		שכב	LIE DOWN	1012b	4a
43	18	בין	DISCERN	107a	1b
		זכר	REMEMBER	269d	11d
		קדמני	FORMER	870d	1
		ראשון	FIRST	911c	1a
43	19	אף	ALSO	64d	1
		דרך	WAY	202d	1
		דרך	WAY	203a	1
		הנה	BEHOLD	244b	Bb
		חדש	NEW	294b	A
		ישימון	WASTE	445c	B
		לא	NOT	520b	4ba
		עתה	NOW	774a	*b
		שום	TO PLACE	964c	5b
43	20	בחיר	CHOSEN	104c	
		בת	DAUGHTER	123d	6
		חיה	LIVING THING	312c	1
		יענה	OSTRICH	419a	
		ישימון	WASTE	445c	B
		כבד	MAKE HONORABLE	457d	2c
		שקה	GIVE TO DRINK	1052c	2
		תן	JACKAL	1072b	
43	21	תהלה	PRAISE	240b	4
		זו	THIS	262b	2
		יצר	FORM	427d	2a
		ספר	COUNT	708a	1
43	22	את	MARK OF THE ACCUSATIVE	85a	1a
		יגע	TOIL	388b	2
		כי	THAT	473a	1f
		לא	NOT	518d	1ac
		קרא	CALL	845b	2d
43	23	זבח	SACRIFICE	257c	11
		יגע	TOIL	388b	
		כבד	MAKE HONORABLE	457d	2c
		לבנה	FRANKINCENSE	526d	
		מנחה	OFFERING	585b	4
		עבד	WORK	713c	1
		עלה	WHOLE BURNT OFFERING	751a	
		שה	A SHEEP	962a	1
43	24	אך	HOWBEIT	36c	2a
		זבח	SACRIFICE	257c	11
		חטאת	SIN	308d	1b
		חלב	FAT	317a	2b
		יגע	TOIL	388b	
		כסף	SILVER	494d	9
		עבד	WORK	713c	1
		עון	INIQUITY	730d	1
		קנה	STALK	889d	3
		רוה	BE SATURATED	924b	
43	25	הוא	HE, SHE, IT	216b	4ba
		זכר	REMEMBER	270c	24
		חטאת	SIN	309a	1d5
		מחה	WIPE OUT	562b	2
		מען	PURPOSE	775b	1a
		פשע	TRANSGRESSION	833d	3d
43	26	אתה	THOU	61c	
		זכר	REMEMBER	270d	1
		יחד	UNION	403a	2a1
		ספר	COUNT	708a	1
		צדק	BE JUST	842c	2
		שפט	JUDGE	1048a	1
43	27	אב	FATHER	3c	4b
		חטא	MISS A GOAL OR WAY	306d	2b
		ליץ	SCORN	539c	2
		פשע	REBEL	833b	2
		ראשון	FIRST	911d	2a
43	28	גדופים	REVILINGS	154d	
		חלל	POLLUTE	320c	1d
		חרם	DEVOTED THING	356c	3
		קדש	APARTNESS	871d	2d
		שר	CHIEFTAIN	978d	5
44	1	בחר	CHOOSE	103d	1a
		עבד	SLAVE	714b	5
		ישראל	ISRAEL	975d	2a5
44	2	בחר	CHOOSE	103d	1a
		בטן	WOMB	106a	3
		יצר	FORM	427d	2a
		ירא	FEAR	431a	1a
		ישרון	JESHURUN	449c	
		עבד	SLAVE	714b	5
44	3	ברכה	BLESSING	139d	1b
		זרע	SOWING	283a	4g
		יבשה	DRY LAND	387a	
		צאצא	OFFSPRING	425c	1
		יצק	POUR	427b	1
		יצק	POUR	427b	1
		נזל	FLOW	633d	1
		צמא	THIRSTY	854d	
		צמא	THIRST	*854d	
		רוח	BREATH	926a	9e
44	4	בין	INTERVAL	107d	B
		חציר	GREEN GRASS	348b	1
		יבל	WATERCOURSE	385a	
		ערבה	POPLAR	788b	
		צמח	SPROUT	855c	1
		נגד	STREAM	*1102a	
44	5	ב	IN	90b	34
		זה	THIS	260d	1b
		כנה	TITLE	487b	
		כנה	BE TITLED	487c	
		כתב	WRITE	507b	1a
		ל	TO	513b	5ba
		קרא	CALL	895c	3
44	6	אחרון	BEHIND	30d	B
		אין	NOT	34b	2a
		בלעדי	APART FROM	116c	Bb
		גאל	REDEEM	145c	3c
		מלך	KING	573b	3
		צבא	GOD OF WAR	839c	4c
		ראשון	FIRST	911d	2a
44	7	אתה	COME	87c	
		ל	TO	515d	5ia
		מן	SINCE	583c	7c
		עולם	LONG DURATION	762d	1a
		עם	PEOPLE	767a	5i
		ערד	ARRANGE	789d	1f
		שום	TO PLACE	963d	1a
44	8	מאז	FROM THAT TIME	23b	A
		אלה	GOD	43a	2
		בל	NOT	115b	
		בלעדי	APART FROM	116c	Bb
		ירה	BE AFRAID	436c	
		יש	THERE IS	441d	2b
		פחד	DREAD	808b	1
		צור	ROCK	849d	2b
44	9	רתה	FEAR	923c	
		שמע	HEAR	1034c	2a
		בל	NOT	115b	
		חמד	DESIRE	326b	B
		יעל	PROFIT	418c	
		יצר	FORM	427d	1b
		פסל	IDOL	820d	
		תהו	FORMLESSNESS	1062c	2
44	10	אל	GOD	42b	3
		בלת	NOT	116d	4a
		יעל	PROFIT	418c	
		יצר	FORM	427d	1b
		מי	WHO	566d	Fb
		נסך	POUR OUT	650d	3
		פסל	IDOL	820d	
44	11	חם	THEY	241c	2b
		חבר	UNITE	*288a	1a
		חבר	UNITED	288d	2d
		חמד	DESIRE	326b	B
		חרש	GRAVER	360d	1d
		יחד	ALTOGETHER	403a	2b
		פחד	DREAD	808b	1
		קבץ	GATHER	868b	
44	12	ברזל	IRON	137c	1b
		גם	YEA	169c	3
		זרוע	ARM	283d	1a

Ch	v.	Heb	Eng	Page	Sec
		חדד	BE SHARP	292b	
		חרש	GRAVER	*360d	1 d
		חרש	GRAVER	360d	1 a
		יעף	BE WEARY	419b	
		יצר	FORM	427d	1 b
		כח	STRENGTH	470c	1 a
		מקבת	HAMMER	666c	
		מעצד	AXE	781b	
		פחם	COAL	809b	
		פעל	DO	821c	2 b
		רעב	BE HUNGRY	945b	
44	13	תבנית	FIGURE	125d	3
		מחוגה	CIRCLE-INSTRUMENT	295b	
		חרש	GRAVER	*360d	1 d
		חרש	GRAVER	360d	1 b
		נטה	STRETCH OUT	640a	1 b
		תפארה	BEAUTY	802c	1
		קו	LINE	876a	
		מקצעה	SCRAPING TOOL	893a	
		שרד	STYLUS	975b	
		תאר	DRAW IN OUTLINE	1061c	
44	14	אלון	OAK	47c	
		אמץ	BE STRONG	55b	2
		ארז	CEDAR	72c	1 a
		ארז	CEDAR	72d	2
		ארן	FIR	75a	
		גדל	GROW UP	152b	1
		גשם	RAIN	177c	
		יער	WOOD	420d	F
		כרת	CUT OFF	503d	2
		ל	TO	518d	7 bg
		נטע	PLANT	642b	1
		עץ	TREE	781c	1 a
		תרזה	CYPRESS	1076b	
44	15	אל	GOD	42b	3
		אפה	BAKE	66a	
		בער	BURN	129b	2
		חמם	BE OR BECOME WARM	328c	1
		לחם	FOOD	537a	1 a
		סגד	PROSTRATE ONESELF	688c	
		פסל	IDOL	820d	
		פעל	DO	821c	2 b
		שלק	KINDLE	969d	
		שחה	BOW DOWN	1005c	3
44	16	אור	FLAME	22a	
		אש	FIRE	77c	3
		במו	IN	91b	
		בשר	FLESH	142c	1 a
		האח	AHA	210c	4
		חמם	BE OR BECOME WARM	328c	1
		צלי	ROASTED	852a	
		צלה	ROAST FLESH	852a	
		שבע	SATISFIED	959b	1 a
		שרף	BURN	976d	2 a
44	17	אל	GOD	42b	3
		אל	GOD	42c	6 b
		יתר	REMAINDER	*451d	1
		ל	TO	512b	4 a
		סגד	PROSTRATE ONESELF	688b	
		עשה	DO	794c	2 1g
		פלל	INTERVENE	813b	2
		פסל	IDOL	820d	
		שארית	REST	984c	1
		שחה	BOW DOWN	1005c	3
44	18	בין	DISCERN	106d	2
		שחח	BE BESMEARED	377c	
		מן	FROM	583b	7 ba
		עין	EYE	744c	3 a
		ראה	TO SEE	907b	4
		שכל	BE PRUDENT	968b	2
44	19	אפה	BAKE	66a	
		אש	FIRE	77c	3
		במו	IN	91b	
		תבונה	UNDERSTANDING	108b	2
		בשר	FLESH	142c	1 a
		נחלת	COAL	160d	
		בול	PRODUCE	385b	
		דעת	WISDOM	395d	2 a
		יתר	REMAINDER	451d	1
		ל	TO	512b	4 a
		לא	NOT	519b	1 bb
		לב	HEART	524d	2 3d
		לחם	FOOD	537a	1 a
		סגד	PROSTRATE ONESELF	688c	
		עץ	TREE	782a	2 c
		עשה	DO	794d	2 1g
		צלה	ROAST FLESH	852a	
		שרף	BURN	976d	2 a
		שוב	TURN BACK	999d	8
		תועבה	ABOMINATION	1073a	1 b
44	20	אפר	ASHES	68a	
		נטה	INCLINE	640d	3 c
		נצל	DELIVER	665a	3 c
		רעה	TEND	945b	2 b
		תלל	DECEIVE	1068b	
44	21	אלה	THESE	41c	A
		זכר	REMEMBER	270a	1 4 a
		יצר	FORM	427d	2 a
		נשה	FORGET	674c	
		עבד	SLAVE	714b	5
		ישראל	ISRAEL	975d	2 a5
44	22	גאל	REDEEM	145c	3 c
		חטאת	SIN	309a	1 d4
		מחה	WIPE OUT	562b	2
		עב	DARK CLOUD	728a	1 e
		ענן	CLOUD	778a	1 c
		פשע	TRANSGRESSION	833d	3 d
44	23	ארץ	EARTH	76b	2 g
		גאל	REDEEM	145c	3 c
		הר	MOUNTAIN	250b	1 c
		יער	WOOD	420d	F
		עץ	TREE	781d	1 b
		פאר	BEAUTIFY	802c	2
		פצח	CAUSE TO BREAK FORTH	822c	
		רוע	RAISE A SHOUT	929d	5
		רנן	GIVE A RINGING CRY	943b	1
		רנה	RINGING CRY	943d	3
44	24	תחתי	LOWER	1066c	
		את	WITH	87a	4 c
		בד	SEPARATION	94c	1 b
		בטן	WOMB	106a	3
		גאל	REDEEM	145c	3 c
		יהוה	YAHWEH	219b	2 2d
		יצר	FORM	427d	2 a
		כל	ALL	482c	2 a
		רקע	BEAT	956a	
44	25	אות	SIGN	16d	2
		אחור	HINDER SIDE	30c	3
		בד	EMPTY TALKERS	95a	B
		הלל	PRAISE	239b	
		חכם	WISE	314d	4
		דעת	WISDOM	395d	2 a
		סכל	BE FOOLISH	698a	
		פרר	BREAK	830c	2 a
		קסם	PRACTICE OF DIVINATION	890c	1
		שוב	TURN BACK	999c	5
44	26	בנה	BUILD	125a	1 b
		חרבה	WASTE	352a	1
		יהודה	JUDAH	397b	2
		עצה	ADVICE	420b	
		ישב	SIT	*443b	4
		ישב	BE INHABITED	443d	
		מלאך	MESSENGER	521c	1 b
		עבד	SLAVE	714b	4
		קום	STAND	878c	
		שלם	BE COMPLETE	1022c	1
		שלם	BE IN COVENANT OF PEACE	1023d	
44	27	חרב	BE DRY	351a	2
		יבש	BE DRY	386c	1
		צולה	OCEAN DEEP	846d	
44	28	בנה	BUILD	125a	1 b
		היכל	TEMPLE	*228a	2
		היכל	TEMPLE	228c	2 d
		ו	AND	*252c	1 b
		חפץ	DELIGHT	343b	3
		יסד	BE FOUNDED	414a	2
		כורש	CYRUS	468d	
		ל	TO	518b	7 bh
		רעה	TEND	945a	1 d2
		שלם	BE COMPLETE	1022c	1
45	1	דלת	DOOR	195b	3
		חזק	BE FIRM	305b	6 c
		כורש	CYRUS	468d	
		משיח	ANOINTED	603c	3
		מתנים	LOINS	608a	1 b
		סגר	BE SHUT	689b	2
		פנה	FACE	817b	2 4b c
		פתח	OPEN	835a	
		פתח	OPEN	835c	1
		רדד	BEAT OUT	921d	
		שער	GATE	1044c	1 a
45	2	ברזל	IRON	137c	1 d
		בריח	BAR	138b	2
		בריח	BAR	138b	1 b
		גדע	HEW	154c	
		דלת	DOOR	195b	3
		הדר	SWELL	213d	1
		הלך	WALK	231c	1 1d 5e
		ישר	MAKE STRAIGHT	448d	1
		נחושה	COPPER	639a	2
		שבר	BREAK	991a	1
45	3	אוצר	TREASURE	70a	1
		ב	IN	90b	3 4
		יהוה	YAHWEH	219b	2 2b d
		חשך	DARKNESS	365a	2
		ממון	HIDDEN TREASURE	380c	
		מסתר	SECRET PLACE	712c	1
		קרא	CALL	896a	5 e
45	4	בחיר	CHOSEN	104c	
		ו	AND	254d	5 b
		כנה	TITLE	487b	
		עבד	SLAVE	714b	5
		מען	PURPOSE	775a	1 a
		קרא	CALL	895d	5 a
45	5	אזר	GIRD	25a	
		אין	NOT	34b	2 a
		אפס	NON-EXISTENCE	67b	2 b
		יהוה	YAHWEH	219b	2 2d
		זולה	EXCEPT	265d	1
		עוד	STILL	729b	1 c
45	6	אין	NOT	34b	2 a
		אפס	NON-EXISTENCE	67b	2 b
		אפס	NON-EXISTENCE	67b	2 b
		בלעדי	APART FROM	116b	A
		יהוה	YAHWEH	219b	2 2d
		מזרח	PLACE OF SUNRISE	280d	1
		עוד	STILL	729b	1 c
		מערב	WEST	788a	
45	7	ברא	CREATE	135b	3
		יהוה	YAHWEH	219b	2 2d
		חשך	DARKNESS	365a	1
		יצר	FORM	427d	2 a
		רע	EVIL	948d	2
45	8	ברא	CREATE	135b	3
		יהוה	YAHWEH	219b	2 2d
		יחד	UNION	403a	2 a4
		ישע	DELIVERANCE	447a	1
		נזל	FLOW	633d	1
		מעל	ABOVE	751c	1 a
		פרה	BEAR FRUIT	826a	2
		פתח	OPEN	835b	
		צדק	RIGHTEOUSNESS	842a	6 a
		צדקה	RIGHTEOUSNESS	842b	6 a
		צמח	SPROUT	855c	1
		רעף	TRICKLE	950a	
45	9	אדמה	EARTH	9d	3
		את	WITH	85d	1
		את	WITH	86b	1 dd
		הוי	AH	223a	
		חמר	CEMENT	330d	2 a
		חרש	EARTHENWARE	360b	1
		יצר	FORM	427d	2 a
		מה	WHAT	552c	1 a
		פעל	DOING	821c	2
		ריב	STRIVE	936c	2
		אב	FATHER	3b	1
45	10	הוי	AH	223a	
		חול	WHIRL	297a	2
		ילד	BEGET	409a	1
		מה	WHAT	552c	1
45	11	אתה	COME	87c	
		יצר	FORM	427d	2 a
		פעל	DOING	821c	2 a
		שאל	ASK	981d	2 a
45	12	ברא	CREATE	135b	3
		צבא	HOST	839b	1 c
		צוה	COMMAND	845d	1 a
		צוה	CHARGE	846a	5
45	13	ב	IN	90b	3 3b
		בנה	BUILD	124d	1 i
		דרך	WAY	203b	5
		ישר	MAKE STRAIGHT	448d	1
		לא	NOT	518d	1 ac
		מחיר	HIRE	564b	2
		עור	ROUSE ONESELF	735b	1
		צבא	GOD OF WAR	839c	4 c
		צדק	RIGHTEOUSNESS	841d	E
		שחד	BRIBE	1005a	
45	14	אך	ONLY	36d	2 ba
		אך	ONLY	36d	
		אל	GOD	42d	6 e
		אפס	NON-EXISTENCE	67b	2 b
		זק	FETTER	279b	
		יגיע	TOIL	388c	2
		כוש	CUSH	469a	2 c
		מדה	SIZE	551c	2
		מצרים	EGYPT	595c	1 a
		סבאים	SABEANS	685b	
		סחר	TRAFFIC	695c	
		עבר	PASS OVER	717b	1 c
		עוד	STILL	729b	1 c
		על	UPON	755b	2 4a
		פלל	INTERVENE	813b	2
		שחה	BOW DOWN	1005b	1 c
45	15	אכן	SURELY	38c	A
		אל	GOD	42d	6 d
		ישע	DELIVER	446d	1 b
		סתר	HIDE	711c	
45	16	בוש	BE ASHAMED	101d	1
		בוש	BE ASHAMED	101d	3
		ה	THE	208c	1 hb
		הלך	WALK	231b	1 d3 ge
		הלך	WALK	235a	2 4
		חרש	GRAVER	360d	1 d
		יחדו	TOGETHER	403c	B
		יחדו	TOGETHER	403c	B
		כלם	BE HUMILIATED	483d	2
		כלמה	IGNOMINY	484a	2
		ציר	IMAGE	849c	
45	17	ב	IN	89d	3 2c
		בוש	BE ASHAMED	101d	3
		ישע	BE DELIVERED	446b	2
		תשועה	DELIVERANCE	448b	1
		כלם	BE HUMILIATED	483d	1
		עד	PERPETUITY	723d	2 e
		עולם	LONG DURATION	762d	2 1
45	18	אין	NOT	34b	2 a
		אלהים	GOD	43d	3
		אלהים	GOD	43d	3
		אפס	NON-EXISTENCE	67b	2 b
		ברא	CREATE	135b	3
		יהוה	YAHWEH	219b	2 2d
		יצר	FORM	427d	2 a
		ישב	DWELL	443a	3
		כון	ESTABLISH	466d	1 b
		עוד	STILL	729b	1 c
		תהו	FORMLESSNESS	1062c	1

Ch	v.	Heb	Eng	Page	Sec
45	19	בקש	SEEK	134d	3 c
		דבר	SPEAK	180c	
		יהוה	YAHWEH	219b	2 2d
		זרע	SOWING	283a	4 f
		חשך	DARKNESS	365a	1
		מושר	LEVEL	449d	2
		סתר	COVERING	712a	1
		צדק	RIGHTEOUSNESS	841d	E
		תהו	FORMLESSNESS	1062d	2
45	20	אל	GOD	42d	6 e
		ישע	DELIVER	446d	1 c
		נגש	DRAW NEAR	621b	
		עץ	TREE	782a	2 c
		פליט	ESCAPED ONE	812c	
		פלל	INTERVENE	813b	2
		פסל	IDOL	820d	
		קבץ	GATHER	867d	1
45	21	מאז	FROM THAT TIME	23b	A
		אל	GOD	42d	6 d
		אפס	NON-EXISTENCE	67b	2 b
		בד	SEPARATION	*94d	1
		בלעדי	APART FROM	116c	B b
		יהוה	YAHWEH	219b	2 2d
		זולה	EXCEPT	265d	1
		זולה	EXCEPT	*265d	1
		יחדו	TOGETHER	403b	A
		יעץ	CONSULT	420a	
		ישע	DELIVER	446d	1 b
		מי	WHO	567b	F e
		נגש	APPROACH	621b	
		עוד	STILL	729d	1 c
		צדיק	JUST	843a	1 d
		קדם	FRONT	869d	2 c
45	22	אין	NOT	34b	2 a
		אפס	END	67a	1
		ישע	BE DELIVERED	446b	1
		עוד	STILL	729b	1 c
		פנה	TURN	815b	1 a
45	23	ברך	KNEE	139c	
		יצא	GO OUT	423c	1 g
		כרע	BOW DOWN	502c	1
		לשון	TONGUE	546b	1 b
		פה	MOUTH	805b	2 c
		צדקה	RIGHTEOUSNESS	842b	4
		שבע	SWEAR	989b	1 a
		שבע	SWEAR	989b	2
		שוב	TURN BACK	998a	7 d1
45	24	חרה	BURN	354b	
		חרר	BE HOT	359c	2
		עד	AS FAR AS	724c	1 la
		עז	STRENGTH	739a	2 c
		צדקה	RIGHTEOUSNESS	842c	7 a
45	25	ב	IN	89d	3 2c
		הלל	BE BOASTFUL	239a	2
		זרע	SOWING	283a	4 f
		צדק	BE JUST	842c	2
46	1	בהמה	BEAST	97a	2
		בל	BEL	128c	
		חיה	LIVING THING	312c	1 a
		כרע	BOW DOWN	502c	4
		נבו	NEBO	612d	
		נשואה	WHAT IS BORNE ABOUT	672b	
		משא	LOAD	672c	1
		עיף	FAINT	746b	
		עמס	CARRY A LOAD	770c	
		עצב	IDOL	781b	
		קרס	BEND DOWN	902b	
46	2	ה	THE	208c	1 hb
		הלך	WALK	231b	1 d3 ge
		יחדו	TOGETHER	403c	B
		יכל	BE ABLE	407c	1 b
		כרע	BOW DOWN	502c	4
		מלט	SLIP AWAY	572c	3
		נפש	SOUL	660a	4 a5
		משא	LOAD	672c	1
		קרס	BEND DOWN	902b	
		שבי	CAPTIVITY	985d	1
46	3	בטן	WOMB	106a	3
		בית	HOUSE	110a	5 dd
		בית	HOUSE	110a	5 dg
		עמס	CARRY A LOAD	770c	
		רחם	WOMB	933b	1
		שארית	REST	984d	1
46	4	הוא	HE, SHE, IT	216c	5
		זקנה	OLD AGE	279a	
		מלט	SLIP AWAY	572c	3
		סבל	BEAR	687d	
		שיבה	OLD AGE	966d	1
46	5	דמה	BE LIKE	198a	
		דמה	BE LIKE	198a	1
		משל	BE LIKE	605a	
		שוה	AGREE WITH	1001a	
46	6	אל	GOD	42b	3
		ה	THE	209a	2 a
		זהב	GOLD	263c	9 d
		זול	LAVISH	266a	
		כיס	BAG	476a	B
		כסף	SILVER	494d	9
		סגר	PROSTRATE ONE-SELF	688c	
		צרף	SMELT	864b	4
		קנה	STALK	889d	4 c
		שכר	HIRE	969c	
		שחה	BOW DOWN	1005c	3
		שקל	WEIGH	1053c	1

Ch	v.	Heb	Eng	Page	Sec
46	7	ישע	DELIVER	446d	1 c
		כתף	SHOULDER	509b	1 a
		מוש	REMOVE	559a	
		נוח	REST	628d	B 1
		נשא	LIFT	671a	2 a
		סבל	BEAR	687d	
		צעק	CRY	858c	1 c
		מקום	STANDING PLACE	879d	2 a
		תחת	UNDERNEATH	1065d	2 ia
46	8	אשש	SHEW YOURSELVES FIRM	84b	
		זכר	REMEMBER	270a	14 a
		לב	HEART	524d	2 3d
		פשע	REBEL	833b	2
		שוב	TURN BACK	999d	8
46	9	אל	GOD	42d	6 e
		אפס	NON-EXISTENCE	67b	2 b
		זכר	REMEMBER	269d	11 d
		עוד	STILL	729d	1 c
		עולם	LONG DURATION	762a	1 c
		ראשון	FIRST	911c	1 a
46	10	אחרית	END	31a	B
		חפץ	DELIGHT	343b	3
		עצה	ADVICE	420b	
		עשה	DO	795b	1 a
		קדם	FRONT	869d	2 c
		קום	STAND	878c	7 g
		ראשית	BEGINNING	912a	1 a
46	11	אף	ALSO	64d	1
		מזרח	PLACE OF SUNRISE	280d	2 b
		עצה	ADVICE	420b	
		יצר	FORM	428a	2 b
		עיט	BIRD OF PREY	743c	
		קרא	CALL	895d	5 c
		מרחק	DISTANT PLACE	935d	2
46	12	אביר	MIGHTY	7d	1
		לב	HEART	525d	2 0
		רחק	DISTANT	935c	1 a
46	13	אחר	DELAY	29b	1
		תשועה	DELIVERANCE	448b	1
		תפארה	BEAUTY	802d	2 c
		צדקה	RIGHTEOUSNESS	842b	6 a
		קרב	COME NEAR	897d	2
		רגע	BE AT REST	*921b	A
		רחק	BE DISTANT	935a	
47	1	אין	NOT	34d	4 a
		בבל	BABEL	93c	
		בבל	BABEL	93c	
		בת	DAUGHTER	123c	3
		בת	DAUGHTER	123c	3
		בתולה	VIRGIN	144a	
		יסף	DO AGAIN	415c	2 c
		ירד	GO DOWN	433a	1 f
		ישב	SIT	442c	1 a
		ישב	SIT	442c	1 a
		כסא	SEAT OF HONOR	490d	1 a
		כשדים	CHALDEANS	505a	1 b
		ל	TO	511c	1 ga
		ענג	DAINTY	772b	
		עפר	DRY EARTH	780a	2 e
		רך	TENDER	940a	1
47	2	חשף	STRIP OFF	362c	1
		מחן	GRIND	377c	
		צמה	WOMANS VEIL	855d	
		קמח	FLOUR	888a	
		שבל	FLOWING SKIRT	987c	
		שוק	LEG	1003b	1
47	3	גם	YEA	169c	3
		חרפה	REPROACH	358a	2 a
		לקח	TAKE	543d	0
		נקם	VENGEANCE	668b	1
		ערוה	NAKEDNESS	789a	1
		פגע	MEET	803b	2
		ראה	TO SEE	908c	3
47	4	גאל	REDEEM	145c	3 c
		צבא	GOD OF WAR	839c	4 b
		קדוש	HOLY	872c	1 c
47	5	בוא	GO	98d	4
		בת	DAUGHTER	123c	3
		גברת	LADY	150c	1
		דומם	SILENTLY	189b	
		ה	THE	208c	1 hb
		חשך	DARKNESS	365a	3 c
		יסף	DO AGAIN	415c	2 c
		כשדים	CHALDEANS	505a	1 b
		ממלכה	KINGDOM	575b	1
47	6	אחרית	END	31a	B
		זקן	OLD	278c	2 a
		חלל	POLLUTE	320b	1 d
		כבד	MAKE HEAVY	457d	1
		נחלה	PROPERTY	635b	1 e
		על	YOKE	760d	
		קצף	BE WROTH	893b	1
		רחמים	COMPASSION	933c	2
		שום	TO PLACE	963c	2 a
47	7	אחרית	END	31a	B
		אלה	THESE	41c	A
		גברת	LADY	150c	1
		זכר	REMEMBER	270a	15
		לב	HEART	525a	2 3d
		עד	PERPETUITY	723c	2
		עד	UNTIL	725b	2 3
		עולם	LONG DURATION	762b	2 b2
		שום	TO PLACE	963b	1 b
47	8	אלמן	WIDOWHOOD	48a	
		אלמנה	WIDOW	48b	

Ch	v.	Heb	Eng	Page	Sec
		אמר	SAY	56b	2
		אפס	NON-EXISTENCE	67b	2 b
		במח	SECURITY	105b	
		זה	THIS	260c	1 a
		לבב	HEART	524a	2 7
		עדין	VOLUPTUOUS	726d	
		עוד	STILL	729b	1 c
		שכול	BEREAVEMENT	1013d	
47	9	אלה	THESE	41c	A
		אלמן	WIDOWHOOD	48a	
		ב	IN	90c	3 7
		בוא	COME	98c	2 b
		חבר	COMPANY	288c	3 b
		יום	DAY	400a	7 a6
		כשף	SORCERY	506c	1
		ל	TO	511c	1 gb
		מאד	EXCEEDINGLY	547b	2
		עצמה	MIGHT	782c	
		עצם	BE VAST	782c	2
		רגע	A MOMENT	921a	BA B
		שכול	BEREAVEMENT	1013d	
		שנים	TWO	1041a	1 a
		תם	COMPLETENESS	1070d	1
47	10	אין	NOT	34b	2 a
		אמר	SAY	56b	2
		אפס	NON-EXISTENCE	67b	2 b
		במח	TRUST	105a	1 3c
		הוא	HE, SHE, IT	215d	2 a
		חכמה	WISDOM	315c	3
		דעת	WISDOM	395d	2 a
		לב	HEART	525c	2 7
		עוד	STILL	729d	1 c
		רעה	MISERY	949b	3
		שוב	TURN BACK	998b	3
47	11	הוה	DISASTER	217d	1
		ידע	KNOW	394b	1 h
		יכל	BE ABLE	407c	1 b
		כפר	COVER OVER	497c	1
		נפל	FALL	657c	5
		פתאם	SUDDENNESS	837c	
		רעה	MISERY	949a	1
		שואה	DEVASTATION	996c	1
		שחד	GIVE A BRIBE	1005a	
		שחר	DAWN	1007c	
47	12	אולי	PERADVENTURE	19c	1
		אשר	PARTICLE OF RE-LATION	82a	1
		באשר	IN WHICH	84a	A
		חבר	COMPANY	288c	3 b
		יגע	TOIL	388b	1
		יכל	BE ABLE	407c	1 b
		יעל	PROFIT	*418d	
		יעל	PROFIT	418d	
		כשף	SORCERY	506c	1
		נא	PART OF EN-TREATY	609a	1
		נעורים	YOUTH	655b	
		ערץ	CAUSE TO TREM-BLE	791d	1
47	13	פנה	FACE	817a	2 4a c
		מאשר	FROM THAT WHICH	84a	A
		חבר	DIVIDE	211b	
		חדש	NEW MOON	294c	1
		חזה	SEE	302c	1 c
		ידע	MAKE KNOWN	395b	
		עצה	ADVICE	420a	
		ישע	DELIVER	446d	1 c
		כוכב	STAR	456d	
		ל	TO	516b	5 ja
		לאה	BE WEARY	521a	
		מן	FROM	580d	3 ba
		נא	PART OF EN-TREATY	609b	1
47	14	שמי	HEAVENS	1029d	1 a
		אור	FLAME	22a	
		גחלת	COAL	161a	
		ה	THE	*207d	1 f
		חמם	BE OR BECOME WARM	328c	1
		יד	HAND	391b	5 g1
		ישב	SIT	442c	1 a
		לא	NOT	*519a	1 ac
		להבה	FLAME	529b	1
		נפש	SOUL	660b	4 b5
		שרף	BURN	977a	2 b1
47	15	אשר	PARTICLE OF RE-LATION	82d	4 c
		יגע	TOIL	388b	1
		ישע	DELIVER	446c	1 a
		כן	SO	485d	1 a
		נעורים	YOUTH	655b	
		סחר	GO AROUND	695c	2
		עבר	REGION ACROSS	719d	2
		תעה	ERR	1073c	1
48	1	אמת	FIRMNESS	54a	3 a
		בית	HOUSE	110a	5 dg
		זה	THIS	260c	1 a
		זכר	REMEMBER	270d	3 a
		זכר	REMEMBER	271a	3 a
		יצא	GO OUT	423c	1 h
		כל	ALL	*481d	1 da
		לא	NOT	518d	1 ac
		מן	OUT OF	579c	2 cb
		צדקה	RIGHTEOUSNESS	842b	4
		קרא	CALL	896c	6 d

Ch v.	Heb	Eng	Page	Sec
	קריתים	KIRIATHIAM	900b	1
48 2	שבע	SWEAR	989b	1 a
	מן	OUT OF	579c	2 cb
	סמך	LEAN	702a	
	עיר	CITY	746c	1 i
	צבא	GOD OF WAR	839c	4 b
	קדש	APARTNESS	871d	2 e
	קרא	CALL	896b	1
48 3	מאז	FROM THAT TIME	23b	A
	יצא	GO OUT	423c	1 g
	פתאם	SUDDENNESS	837c	
	ראשון	FIRST	911c	1 a
	שמע	HEAR	1034d	2 b
48 4	ברזל	IRON	137d	3
	מן	ON ACCOUNT OF	583a	7 a
	מצח	FOREHEAD	594d	
	נחושה	COPPER	639a	2
	ערף	BACK OF NECK	791c	2
	קשה	SEVERE	904d	3
48 5	מאז	FROM THAT TIME	23b	A
	טרם	NOT YET	382c	2
	נסך	MOLTEN IMAGE	651d	2
	עצב	IDOL	781b	
	פן	LEST	814d	1
	פסל	IDOL	820d	
	שמע	HEAR	1034c	2 a
48 6	ברא	CREATE	135c	3
	חדש	NEW	294b	A
	חזה	SEE	302c	3 a
	נגד	BE CONSPICUOUS	617a	5
	נצר	GUARD	666a	4
	עתה	NOW	774b	2 e
48 7	מאז	FROM THAT TIME	23b	A
	ו	AND	255a	5 cb
	יום	DAY	401a	7 i
	פן	LEST	814d	1
	פנה	FACE	817d	2 4e
48 8	מאז	FROM THAT TIME	23b	A
	אזן	EAR	24a	2 a
	בגד	ACT TREACHER-OUSLY	93d	A
	בטן	WOMB	106a	3
	גם	YEA	169c	3
	מצח	FOREHEAD	595a	
	פשע	REBEL	833b	2
	פתח	OPEN	835c	3
	קרא	CALL	896c	
48 9	ארך	BE LONG	73d	1 c
	תהלה	PRAISE	240a	1
	חטם	HOLD IN	310c	
	כרת	CUT OFF	504c	2 c
	מצח	FOREHEAD	595a	
	מען	PURPOSE	775b	1 a
	שם	NAME	1028c	3
48 10	בחר	CHOOSE	104b	8
	כור	FURNACE	468b	
	כסף	SILVER	494a	1
	כסף	SILVER	494c	9
	עני	AFFLICTION	777a	1
	צרף	SMELT	864b	2
	בר	ADDENDA ET COR-RIGENDA	*1121d	
48 11	איך	HOW	32c	1
	הלך	WALK	231b	1 d3 ge
	חלל	POLLUTE	320b	2
	כבוד	HONOR	459b	6 b
	מען	PURPOSE	775b	1 a
48 12	אחרון	BEHIND	30d	B
	אף	ALSO	65a	1
	הוא	HE, SHE, IT	216c	5
	קרא	CALL	896c	
	ראשון	FIRST	911d	2 a
48 13	ארץ	EARTH	76a	1 b
	טפח	EXTEND	381b	1
	יחדו	TOGETHER	403c	B
	יסד	FOUND	413d	
	עמד	STAND	764c	6 b
48 14	אהב	LOVE	13b	5 b
	אלה	THESE	41c	A
	בבל	BABEL	93c	
	חפץ	DELIGHT	343b	3
	כשדים	CHALDEANS	505a	1 b
	מי	WHO	566c	D
	מי	WHO	566d	F c
	עשה	DO	794a	1 1a 5
	קבץ	GATHER	867d	1
48 15	אף	ALSO	65a	1
	דרך	WAY	203b	5
	צלח	ADVANCE	852c	1
	קרא	CALL	896a	5 e
48 16	ו	AND	253a	1 g
	זה	THIS	260c	1 a
	סתר	COVERING	712a	3
	קרב	COME NEAR	897b	1 a
	ראש	HEAD	911b	4
	רוח	BREATH	925d	9 b
48 17	גאל	REDEEM	145c	3 c
	דרך	TREAD	202c	3
	דרך	WAY	203c	6 b
	יהוה	YAHWEH	219b	2 2d
	יעל	PROFIT	*418c	
	יעל	PROFIT	418d	
	למד	LEARN	540d	
	קדוש	HOLY	872c	1 c
48 18	לו	IF	*530a	
	לו	IF	530b	2

Ch v.	Heb	Eng	Page	Sec
	נהר	STREAM	625d	1
	צדקה	RIGHTEOUSNESS	842b	5
	צמא	THIRST	854d	
	קשב	ATTEND	904a	
	שלום	PEACE	1023b	5 b
48 19	זרע	SOWING	283a	4 g
	חול	SAND	297d	A
	צאצא	OFFSPRING	425c	1
	כרת	BE CUT OFF	504b	4
	מעה	BELLY	589a	2
	מעה	GRAIN	589a	
	פנה	FACE	818a	2 5a d
	שמד	BE EXTERMINATED	1029b	1
48 20	בבל	BABEL	93c	
	ברח	FLEE	138a	2
	גאל	REDEEM	145c	3 c
	יצא	BRING OUT	425b	4 k
	כשדים	CHALDEANS	505a	1 b
	עבד	SLAVE	714b	5
	קצה	END	892b	1
	רנה	RINGING CRY	943d	3
48 21	בקע	CLEAVE	131d	1
	הלך	WALK	236c	1 a
	זוב	FLOW	264c	1
	חרבה	WASTE	352b	2
	נזל	FLOW	633d	
	צור	ROCK	849c	1 a
	צמא	BE THIRSTY	854d	
48 22	רשע	WICKED	957b	2
	שלום	PEACE	1022d	3
48 23	קריתים	KIRIATHIAM	900b	1
49 1	אי	COAST	16a	1
	אם	MOTHER	51d	1
	בטן	WOMB	106a	3
	לאם	PEOPLE	522c	
	מעה	BELLY	589a	3
	קרא	CALL	896a	5 e
	קשב	ATTEND	904a	
	רחק	DISTANT	935c	2 a1
49 2	אשפה	QUIVER	80c	
	ברר	PURIFY	141a	3
	חבא	WITHDRAW	285b	
	חד	SHARP	292b	
	חץ	ARROW	346c	2
	יד	HAND	390a	1 e2
	סתר	HIDE	711d	1
	צל	SHADOW	853b	2
49 3	עבד	SLAVE	714b	5
	פאר	BEAUTIFY	802c	2
	ישראל	ISRAEL	975d	2 a5
49 4	אכן	SURELY	38c	B
	אנכי	I	59c	
	את	WITH	86c	3 a
	הבל	VAPOUR	211a	2
	יגע	TOIL	388b	1
	כח	STRENGTH	470d	1 c
	כלה	FINISH	478c	2 b
	פעלה	WORK	821d	2
	ריק	EMPTINESS	938b	
	משפט	JUDGEMNT	1049a	5
	תהו	FORMLESSNESS	1062c	2
49 5	בטן	WOMB	106a	3
	יצר	FORM	427d	2 a
	כבד	BE HONORED	457c	1 b
	ל	TO	512c	4 b
	לא	NOT	520c	
	עבד	SLAVE	714b	5
	עז	STRENGTH	739a	2 c
	שוב	TURN BACK	998c	1
49 6	אור	LIGHT	21d	9
	ו	AND	254c	4
	ישועה	DELIVERANCE	447c	3
	מן	THAN	583a	6 d
	נצר	GUARD	665d	2
	עבד	SLAVE	714b	5
	קום	STAND	878d	1 d
	קלל	BE SLIGHT	886c	2
	קצה	END	892b	1
49 7	אמן	CONFIRM	53a	5
	בזה	DESPISE	102c	
	בחר	CHOOSE	104b	5 a
	גאל	REDEEM	145c	3 c
	משל	RULE	605d	1
	עבד	SLAVE	714b	5
	קדוש	HOLY	872c	1 c
	קדוש	HOLY	872c	1 c
	קום	STAND	877d	1 a
	שר	CHIEFTAIN	978a	2
	שחה	BOW DOWN	1005c	1 c
	תעב	BE ABHORRED	1073b	2
49 8	ברית	COVENANT	137a	2 2k
	ברית	COVENANT	137a	2 2k
	ישועה	DELIVERANCE	447b	3
	נחל	TAKE AS A POSSES-SION	635d	1 b
	נצר	GUARD	665d	2
	ענה	ANSWER	772a	1 b
	קום	STAND	878d	1 a
	רצון	GOODWILL	953c	1 a
	שמם	BE DESOLATED	1030d	1
49 9	אסר	TIE	63d	3
	דרך	WAY	202d	1
	חשך	DARKNESS	365a	3 a
	רעה	TEND	945b	2 c
	מרעית	PASTURING	945c	2
	שפי	BARE HEIGHT	1046a	2

Ch v.	Heb	Eng	Page	Sec
49 10	מבוע	SPRING OF WATER	616a	
	נהג	DRIVE	624b	2
	נהל	BRING TO A PLACE OF REST	625a	1
	נכה	SMITE	645d	1 f
	צמא	BE THIRSTY	854d	
	רחם	LOVE	933c	1
	רעב	BE HUNGRY	945b	
	שמש	SUN	1039b	1
	שרב	BURNING HEAT	1055d	
49 11	דרך	WAY	202d	1
	זרוע	ARM	*284b	2 b
	מסלה	HIGHWAY	700c	
	רום	BE HIGH	926d	2 a
49 12	אלה	THESE	41c	B
	סונים	SYENITES	692b	
	סינים	SINIM	696b	
	צפון	NORTH	861a	
	רחק	DISTANT	935c	2 al
49 13	הר	MOUNTAIN	250b	1 c
	נחם	CONSOLE ONESELF	637b	
	עני	POOR	777a	3
	פצח	CAUSE TO BREAK FORTH	822c	
	רחם	LOVE	933c	1
	רנן	GIVE A RINGING CRY	943b	1
	רנה	RINGING CRY	943d	3
49 14	אדון	LORD	11b	3 2a
	עזב	LEAVE	737c	2
	שכח	FORGET	1013b	2 a
49 15	אשה	WOMAN	61a	1
	בטן	WOMB	106a	3
	בן	SON	120a	1
	גם	YEA	169c	3
	מן	FROM	583b	7 ba
	עול	SUCKING CHILD	732b	
	רחם	LOVE	933d	2
	שכח	FORGET	1013a	1 b
49 16	חקק	CUT IN	349a	2
	תמיד	CONTINUITY	556b	1 a
49 17	הרס	THROW DOWN	248d	
	חרב	BE WASTE	351d	
	מהר	HASTEN	555a	1
49 18	חי	ALIVE	311d	1 a
	כי	THAT	472a	1 c
	כלה	BRIDE	483c	2 a
	ל	TO	511b	1 ga
	לבש	PUT ON	528a	B
	נאם	UTTERANCE	610c	2
	נשא	LIFT	670c	1 b 4
	עדי	ORNAMENTS	725d	1
	קבץ	GATHER	867d	1
	קשרים	BANDS	*905c	
	קשר	BIND	905c	1
49 19	הריסות	OVERTHROW	249a	
	חרבה	WASTE	352a	1
	ישב	DWELL	443b	3
	כי	BECAUSE	473d	3 b
	מן	THAN	582d	6 d
	עתה	NOW	774a	1 b
	עתה	NOW	774a	1 b
	צרר	BIND	864d	B
	רחק	BE DISTANT	934d	
	שמם	BE DESOLATED	1031a	1
49 20	אמר	SAY	56a	1
	ל	TO	515b	5 hb a
	נגש	DRAW NEAR	621a	1
	עוד	STILL	729a	1 ab
	צר	NARROW	865a	
	שכלים	BEREAVEMENT	1014a	
49 21	איפה	WHERE	33a	1
	אמר	SAY	56b	2
	את	MARK OF THE AC-CUSATIVE	84d	1 a
	בד	SEPARATION	94c	1 b
	גדל	GROW UP	152b	1
	הם	THEY	241c	3 b
	לבב	HEART	524a	2
	מי	WHO	566d	F b
	סור	TURN ASIDE	693d	2
	שאר	REMAIN	984a	2
	שכול	CHILDLESS	1014a	
49 22	אדון	LORD	11c	4 c
	בוא	COME	99c	2
	בת	DAUGHTER	123b	1 i
	חצן	BOSOM	346a	
	יד	HAND	389c	1 d
	כתף	SHOULDER	509b	1 a
	נס	STANDARD	651d	1 a
	נשא	LIFT	670b	1 b 1
	נשא	LIFT	671d	3
	על	UPON	757a	2 7c a
	רום	BE HIGH	927c	1
49 23	אמן	CONFIRM	52d	2
	אף	NOSE	60b	2
	אשר	PARTICLE OF RE-LATION	82b	3
	יהוה	YAHWEH	219a	2 2b d
	ינק	NURSE	413c	
	לחך	LICK UP	535b	
	עפר	DRY EARTH	780a	2 e
	קוה	WAIT FOR	875d	
	שרה	PRINCESS	979a	
49 24	אם	IF	50d	2 ab b
	גבור	STRONG	150b	1

Ch	v.	Heb	Eng	Page	Sec
		כי	BECAUSE	*474b	3 c
		לקח	TAKE	544a	3
		מלקוח	BOOTY	544b	
		מלט	SLIP AWAY	572b	2
		עריץ	AWE-INSPIRING	*792b	
		צדיק	JUST	843b	5
		שבי	CAPTIVITY	985d	3
49	25	גבור	STRONG	150b	2
		גם	YEA	169c	3
		ישע	DELIVER	446d	1 b
		כי	BECAUSE	474b	3 c
		מלט	SLIP AWAY	572b	2
		עריץ	AWE-INSPIRING	792b	
		ריב	STRIVE	936c	2
		יריב	OPPONENT	937a	
		שבי	CAPTIVITY	985d	3
49	26	אביר	STRONG	7d	
		אכל	EAT	37d	1
		בשר	FLESH	142c	1 a
		בשר	FLESH	142d	6 c
		גאל	REDEEM	145c	3 c
		דם	BLOOD	197b	2 n
		יהוה	YAHWEH	219a	2 2b d
		ינה	OPPRESS	413b	
		ישע	DELIVER	446d	1 b
		עסיס	SWEET WINE	779b	
		שכר	BE DRUNK	1016b	
50	1	אי	WHERE	32b	1 b
		אם	MOTHER	52a	
		ב	IN	90c	3 5
		הן	BEHOLD	243c	A
		כריתות	DIVORCEMENT	504d	
		מי	WHO	566c	D
		מי	WHO	566c	F c
		מכר	SELL	569b	
		מכר	SELL	569c	
		מן	FROM	580c	3 a
		נשה	LEND	674c	
		ספר	MISSIVE	707a	2
		עון	INIQUITY	730d	1
		פשע	TRANSGRESSION	833a	3 c
		שלח	SEND	1019a	
50	2	אין	NOT	35a	6 da
		אם	IF	50d	2 ab b
		באש	STINK	93a	
		גערה	REBUKE	172a	2
		דגה	FISH	185d	
		הן	BEHOLD	243c	A
		חרב	BE DRY	351b	
		יד	HAND	390a	1 e2
		מדוע	WHEREFORE	396c	
		כח	STRENGTH	470d	3
		מן	THAN	582d	6 d
		נצל	DELIVER	664d	3 a
		פדות	RANSOM	804b	
		צמא	THIRST	854d	
		קצר	BE SHORT	894a	
		קצר	BE SHORT	894a	
		קרא	CALL	896a	5 d
50	3	כסות	COVERING	492b	1
		לבש	CLOTHE	528b	1 b
		קדרות	DARKNESS	871a	
		שק	SACK	974c	2 a
50	4	אזן	EAR	24b	3
		בקר	MORNING	134b	1 f
		ידע	KNOW	394b	4 a
		יעף	WEARY	419b	
		ל	TO	512b	5 aa
		למד	TAUGHT	541a	
		לשון	TONGUE	546c	1 b
		עור	ROUSE ONESELF	735b	1
		עות	HELP	*736c	
50	5	אזן	EAR	24b	3
		אחור	HINDER SIDE	30c	A
		ל	TO	512b	5 aa
		מרה	BE REBELLIOUS	598a	1
		סוג	MOVE AWAY	690d	1 b2
		פתח	OPEN	835b	
50	6	גו	BACK	156b	
		כלמה	IGNOMINY	484b	2
		לחי	CHEEK	534d	2
		מרט	MAKE BARE	598d	1
		נכה	SMITE	645c	1 b
		נתן	GIVE	680a	1 z
		סתר	HIDE	711d	2 a
		רק	SPITTLE	956d	
50	7	חלמיש	FLINT	321d	
		כלם	BE HUMILIATED	483d	1
		עזר	HELP	740c	
50	8	את	WITH	86b	1 dd
		בעל	LORD	127c	1 5a
		יחד	UNION	403a	2 a2
		מי	WHO	567b	G
		מי	WHO	567b	G
		עמד	STAND	763d	1 c
		צדק	JUSTIFY	842d	1 a
		קרב	NEAR	898c	2 f
		ריב	STRIVE	936c	3
		משפט	JUDGMENT	1048c	1 d
50	9	בגד	GARMENT	94a	1
		בלה	BECOME OLD AND WORN OUT	115a	
		הוא	HE, SHE, IT	216c	4 bb
		הן	BEHOLD	243c	A
		מי	WHO	567a	F c
		עזר	HELP	740c	
		עש	MOTH	799c	
50	10	רשע	BE WICKED	957d	2
		בטח	TRUST	105a	1 3d
		הלך	WALK	234c	2 2
		חשכה	DARKNESS	365b	
		ירא	FEAR	431c	3 b
		מי	WHO	566c	D
		נגה	BRIGHTNESS	618b	
		נכח	STRAIGHTNESS	647c	
		עבד	SLAVE	714b	4
		שען	LEAN	1043d	
50	11	אור	FLAME	22a	
		אזר	GIRD	25a	
		בער	BURN	129b	1
		הן	BEHOLD	243c	A
		זק	MISSILE	278a	
		ל	TO	516d	5 k
		מן	OUT OF	579d	2 d
		מעצבה	PLACE OF PAIN	781a	
		קדח	KINDLE	869b	2
		שכב	LIE DOWN	1012c	4 c
51	1	בור	PIT	92c	3
		בקש	SEEK	134d	3 c
		חצב	HEW	345b	
		נבט	LOOK	613d	2
		מקבת	EXCAVATION	666c	
		נקר	DIG	669b	
		צדק	RIGHTEOUSNESS	841d	5
		צור	ROCK	849c	1 a
		רדף	PURSUE	923a	2
51	2	אב	FATHER	3c	4 b
		ברך	BLESS	139a	2 a
		חול	WHIRL	297b	2
		נבט	LOOK	613d	2
		קרא	CALL	896a	5 f
		שרה	SARAH	979a	
51	3	גן	GARDEN	171a	
		זמרה	MELODY	274b	2
		חרבה	WASTE	352b	2
		תודה	THANKSGIVING	392d	2
		מצא	FIND	594a	2 c
		נחם	CONSOLE ONESELF	637a	
		עדן	EDEN	727a	
		ערבה	DESERT-PLAIN	787b	1 a
		ששון	REJOICING	965b	
51	4	אור	LIGHT	21d	9
		אזן	HEAR	24c	1
		את	WITH	86d	4 c
		יצא	GO OUT	423c	1 g
		תורה	INSTRUCTION	436a	1 d
		לאם	PEOPLE	522c	
		קשב	ATTEND	904a	
		רגע	BE AT REST	921b	A
		משפט	JUDGMENT	1048d	3
51	5	אי	COAST	16a	
		אל	TO	40a	3 c
		זרוע	ARM	284b	2 b
		יחל	WAIT	404a	2
		יצא	GO OUT	423c	1 g
		ישע	DELIVERANCE	447a	2
		צדק	RIGHTEOUSNESS	842a	6 a
		קוה	WAIT FOR	875d	1
		קרב	NEAR	898c	2 f
		שפט	JUDGE	1047d	3 c1
51	6	בלה	BECOME OLD AND WORN OUT	115a	
		ה	THE	208a	1 f
		חתת	BE SHATTERED	369b	1
		ישועה	DELIVERANCE	447c	3
		כמו	LIKE	455d	1 a
		כן	SO	486d	3 c
		כן	GNAT	487d	
		כן	GNAT	488a	
		ל	TO	510c	1 a
		מלח	DISSIPATE	571d	
		נבט	LOOK	613c	1 a
		נשא	LIFT	670c	1 b 4
		עולם	LONG DURATION	762c	2 c
		עשן	SMOKE	798c	2
		צדקה	RIGHTEOUSNESS	842b	6 a
		תחת	UNDERNEATH	*1065b	1
51	7	אנוש	MAN	60d	2
		גדופים	REVILINGS	154d	
		חרפה	REPROACH	357d	!
		חתת	BE SHATTERED	369b	2 b
		ירא	FEAR	431b	1 b
		תורה	INSTRUCTION	435d	1 c
51	8	דור	PERIOD	190a	1 b
		ישועה	DELIVERANCE	447c	3
		סס	MOTH	703b	
		עולם	LONG DURATION	762c	2 c
		עש	MOTH	799c	
		צמר	WOOL	856a	
51	9	דור	PERIOD	189d	1 a
		הוא	HE, SHE, IT	216b	4 ba
		זרוע	ARM	284a	1 c
		חלל	BORE	319b	
		חצב	HEW	345b	
		ך	LIKE	455a	B
		לבש	PUT ON	528a	B
		עור	ROUSE ONESELF	734d	
		עז	STRENGTH	739a	1
		עולם	LONG DURATION	762a	1 e
		קדם	FRONT	869d	2 b
		רהב	STORM	923c	1
		תנין	SEA-MONSTER	1072c	3
51	10	גאל	REDEEM	145c	3 c
		דרך	WAY	202d	1
		דרך	WAY	203a	1
		ה	THE	209c	3
		הוא	HE, SHE, IT	216b	4 ba
		חרב	BE DRY	351b	
		ים	SEA	411a	2
		עבר	PASS OVER	718b	5 h
		מעמקים	DEPTHS	771b	
		רב	GREAT	913c	2
		תהום	DEEP	1062d	1
51	11	אנחה	SIGHING	58d	
		יגון	GRIEF	387b	
		נוס	ESCAPE	630d	3
		נשג	REACH	673c	2 a
		עולם	LONG DURATION	762d	2 f
		פדה	RANSOM	804a	3 b
		רנה	RINGING CRY	943d	3
		ששון	REJOICING	965b	
		שמחה	JOY	970d	2
51	12	אנוש	MAN	60d	3
		הוא	HE, SHE, IT	216b	4 ba
		ו	AND	254a	2 b
		חציר	GREEN GRASS	348b	2
		ירא	FEAR	431b	1 c
		מי	WHO	566b	
		נחם	CONSOLE ONESELF	637a	
		נתן	PUT	681d	2 c
51	13	איה	WHERE	32c	
		ארץ	EARTH	76a	1 b
		יום	DAY	400c	7 f
		חמה	RAGE	404c	2 a
		יסד	FOUND	413d	
		כון	ESTABLISH	467a	3
		תמיד	CONTINUITY	556b	1 a
		עשה	DO	794c	2 1b
		פחד	DREAD	808b	
		צוק	CONSTRAIN	848a	
		שחת	GO TO RUIN	1008b	1
51	14	חסר	LACK	341b	2
		ל	TO	511b	1 ga
		מהר	HASTEN	555a	2
		פתח	OPEN	835c	
		צעה	STOOP	858a	1
		שחת	PIT	1001c	2
51	15	תבונה	UNDERSTANDING	*108b	1
		יהוה	YAHWEH	218d	2 1a
		יהוה	YAHWEH	219b	2 2d
		המה	ROAR	242b	3
		ו	AND	253d	1 k
		צבא	GOD OF WAR	839c	4 b
		רגע	DISTURB	920d	
51	16	ארץ	EARTH	76a	1 b
		יסד	FOUND	413d	
		כסה	COVER	491d	3
		נטע	PLANT	642c	2
		צל	SHADOW	853b	2
51	17	חמה	RAGE	404d	2 c
		כוס	CUP	468a	
		מצה	DRAIN	594c	
		עור	ROUSE ONESELF	735b	
		קבעת	CUP	867c	
		תרעלה	REELING	947a	
		שתה	DRINK	1059c	1 e
51	18	גדל	GROW UP	152b	1
		חזק	BE FIRM	305a	6 a
		ילד	BEAR	408c	1 c
		ל	TO	*512a	3 b
		מן	FROM	580c	3 a
		נהל	LEAD,GUIDE	625a	3
51	19	הם	THEY	241c	4 a
		מי	WHO	566b	
		נוד	SHEW GRIEF	626d	2 a
		נחם	CONSOLE ONESELF	637a	
		קרא	ENCOUNTER	897a	2
		שבר	BREAKING	991a	1
		שד	VIOLENCE	994c	2
		שנים	TWO	1041b	1 b2
51	20	גערה	REBUKE	172a	2
		ה	THE	209a	2 a
		חוץ	THE OUTSIDE	300b	2 a
		חמה	RAGE	404d	2 c
		כל	ALL	481b	1 a
		מכמר	NET	485b	
		מלא	FULL	571a	
		עלף	COVER	763b	
		שכב	LIE DOWN	1012b	4 a
		תאו	ANTELOPE	1060d	
51	21	זה	THIS	260c	1 a
		כן	SO	487a	3 d
		מן	OUT OF	579b	2 bb
		עני	POOR	776d	3
51	22	אדון	LORD	11b	2 2
		אדון	LORD	11b	3 2a
		חמה	RAGE	404d	2 c
		יסף	DO AGAIN	415c	2 a
		כוס	CUP	468a	
		קבעת	CUP	867c	
		תרעלה	REELING	947a	
		שתה	DRINK	1059c	1 e
51	23	גו	BACK	156b	
		חוץ	THE OUTSIDE	300a	2 a
		יגה	SUFFER	387b	
		נפש	SOUL	660a	4 a2
		עבר	PASS OVER	717b	1 d
		שחה	BOW DOWN	1005b	

Ch v.	Heb	Eng	Page	Sec
52 1	טמא	UNCLEAN	380a	2 d
	יסף	DO AGAIN	415c	2 c
	לבש	PUT ON	528a	B
	עור	ROUSE ONESELF	734d	
	עז	STRENGTH	739a	2 b
	עיר	CITY	746c	1 i
	ערל	HAVING FORESKIN	790c	
	תפארה	BEAUTY	802c	1
	ציון	ZION	851b	
	קדש	APARTNESS	871a	2 e
52 2	מוסר	BAND	64c	
	בת	DAUGHTER	123c	3
	ישב	SIT	442d	1 b
	נער	SHAKE OUT	654d	
	עפר	DRY EARTH	780a	2 e
	פתח	OPEN	835c	
	צואר	NECK	848c	1
	ציון	ZION	851b	
	שבי	CAPTIVITY	985d	3
	שבוה	CAPTIVE	986a	
52 3	גאל	REDEEM	145d	2 c
	חנם	OUT OF FAVOR	336c	A
	מכר	SELL	569c	
52 4	אדון	LORD	11c	4 c
	אפס	NON-EXISTENCE	67b	2 a
	אשור	ASSHUR	78d	2
	גור	SOJOURN	157d	1
	ירד	GO DOWN	433a	1 d
	עשק	OPPRESS	798d	2
	ראשון	FIRST	911d	3 a1
52 5	חנם	OUT OF FAVOR	336c	A
	יום	DAY	400c	7 f
	ילל	HOWL	410b	
	כי	THAT	472d	1 f
	לקח	TAKE	544a	3
	תמיד	CONTINUITY	556b	1 a
	משל	RULE	605d	1
	נאץ	CONTEMN	611a	
	עתה	NOW	774b	2 b
	פה	HERE	806a	1a
52 6	הוא	HE, SHE, IT	216b	4 ba
	הנה	BEHOLD	244a	A
	שם	NAME	1028c	3
52 7	בשר	BEAR TIDINGS	142b	3
	הר	MOUNTAIN	250b	1 d
	טוב	A GOOD THING	375a	1
	טוב	A GOOD THING	375a	1
	ישועה	DELIVERANCE	447b	3
	מה	HOW	553c	2 b
	מלך	BE KING	574a	
	נאה	BE COMELY	610a	1
	שמע	HEAR	1034c	1 a
52 8	ב	IN	88d	14
	יחדו	TOGETHER	403c	B
	נשא	LIFT	670c	1 b 5
	עין	EYE	745a	5
	צפה	KEEP WATCH	859c	
	צפה	KEEP WATCH	859c	
	קול	VOICE	876d	1 a
	קול	VOICE	877a	1 f
	ראה	TO SEE	908a	8 a5
	ראה	TO SEE	908b	1 a
	רנן	GIVE A RINGING CRY	943b	
52 9	שוב	TURN BACK	998c	9
	גאל	REDEEM	145c	3 c
	חרבה	WASTE	352a	1
	יחדו	TOGETHER	403c	A
	נחם	CONSOLE ONESELF	637b	
	פצח	CAUSE TO BREAK FORTH	822d	
	רנן	GIVE A RINGING CRY	943b	
52 10	אפס	END	67a	1
	זרוע	ARM	284a	1 c
	חשף	STRIP OFF	362c	2
	ישועה	DELIVERANCE	447b	3
	קדש	APARTNESS	871c	1a
52 11	ברר	PURIFY	141a	A
	טמא	UNCLEAN	379d	2 c
	כלי	UTENSIL	480a	2 f
	נגע	TOUCH	619a	1 a
	סור	TURN ASIDE	693d	1
	פקדה	OVERSIGHT	824a	1 a
52 12	אסף	GATHER	62c	3
	אסף	GATHER	63a	3
	הלך	WALK	231c	1 1d 5e
	הלך	WALK	231d	1 d5 ta
	חפזון	TREPIDATION	342a	
	מנוסה	FLIGHT	631a	
	פנה	FACE	817c	2 4c a
52 13	גבה	BE EXALTED	147a	2
	נשא	LIFT	671d	1
	עבד	SLAVE	714b	5
	רום	BE HIGH	927a	2 c
	שכל	BE PRUDENT	968c	6
52 14	כאשר	AS	455b	1 b
	כן	SO	486c	2 cd
	מן	FROM	583b	7 bb
	מראה	VISION	909c	1 b
	משחת	DISFIGUREMENT	1008c	
	שמם	BE DESOLATED	1031a	2
	תאר	FORM	1061b	
	מן	FROM	*1101b	5
52 15	בין	DISCERN	107a	1 b
	נזה	LEAP	633c	

Ch v.	Heb	Eng	Page	Sec
	נזה	SPURT	633c	
	ספר	COUNT	708b	
	פה	MOUTH	805a	2 a
53 1	אמן	CONFIRM	53b	2 b
	זרוע	ARM	284b	2 b
	מי	WHO	566d	F c
	על	UPON	757a	2 7c a
	שמועה	REPORT	1035b	1
53 2	הדר	SPLENDOUR	214b	2
	ו	AND	254b	3
	חמד	DESIRE	326b	C
	חמודה	DESIRABLENESS	*326d	
	ינק	SUCK	413c	
	ינק	SAPLING	413c	
	ל	TO	513b	5 ba
	עלה	GO UP	748d	4
	פנה	FACE	817a	2 4a b
	ציה	DRYNESS	851a	
	מראה	VISION	909d	1 b
	שרש	ROOT	1057d	1
	תאר	FORM	1061b	
53 3	אכן	SURELY	38c	B
	בוז	DESPISE	102c	1
	חדל	FORBEARING	293b	
	חלי	SICKNESS	318b	
	חשב	THINK	363a	14
	ידע	KNOW	394a	1
	מכאוב	PAIN	456c	2
	מסתר	HIDING	712c	
	לא	NOT	*1098c	1
53 4	אכן	SURELY	38c	B
	חלי	SICKNESS	318b	
	חשב	THINK	363a	11
	מכאוב	PAIN	456c	2
	נגע	TOUCH	619a	1
	נכה	SMITE	646d	6
	נשא	LIFT	671b	2 b
	סבל	BEAR	687d	
	ענה	BE BOWED DOWN	776b	1
53 5	ב	IN	90c	3 5
	דכא	CRUSH	194a	1
	חבורה	STRIPE	289a	
	חלל	BORE	319b	
	מוסר	DISCIPLINE	416c	2 a
	ל	TO	511a	1 e
	מן	ON ACCOUNT OF	580b	2 f
	עון	INIQUITY	730d	1
	על	UPON	753b	2 1b
	פשע	TRANSGRESSION	833c	3 c
	רפא	HEAL	951a	2 a
	שלון	PEACE	1023b	5 b
53 6	דרך	JOURNEY	203b	2
	דרך	WAY	203d	6 d
	כל	ALL	481b	1 a
	עון	INIQUITY	731c	3
	פגע	MEET	803c	1
	פנה	TURN	815b	1 a
	צאן	SMALL CATTLE	838b	2
	תעה	ERR	1073b	1
53 7	אלם	BIND	47d	1
	גזז	SHEAR	159c	
	טבח	SLAUGHTERING	370d	1
	יבל	CONDUCT	385a	3
	ענה	BE BOWED DOWN	776a	2
	פתח	OPEN	835c	
	רחל	EWE	932d	
	שה	A SHEEP	962a	1
53 8	את	MARK OF THE ACCUSATIVE	85b	3 a
	גזר	CUT	160c	1
	דור	GENERATION	190a	2 a
	חי	ALIVE	312a	1 b
	לקח	TAKE	544a	4
	מן	ON ACCOUNT OF	580b	2 f
	נגע	STROKE	619d	2
	עצר	RESTRAINT	783d	
	פשע	TRANSGRESSION	833c	3 c
	שיח	MUSE	967b	
	משפט	JUDGMENT	1048c	1 f
53 9	במה	HIGH PLACE	119d	4
	חמס	VIOLENCE	329c	
	מות	DEATH	560d	2
	על	UPON	758b	3 cb
	עשיר	RICH	799c	
	מרמה	DECEIT	941b	
	רשע	WICKED	957c	3
53 10	ארך	BE LONG	73d	1 a
	אשם	OFFENCE	80a	4
	דכא	CRUSH	194a	
	זרע	SOWING	283b	5
	חלה	BE WEAK	318a	1
	חפץ	DELIGHT IN	343a	2 b
	חפץ	DELIGHT	343b	4
	דעת	WISDOM	395d	2 a
53 11	ל	TO	511d	3 a
	מן	FROM	581c	4 b
	סבל	BEAR	687d	
	עבד	SLAVE	714b	5
	עון	INIQUITY	731c	3
	עמל	TROUBLE	765d	1
	צדק	JUSTIFY	842d	3
	צדיק	JUST	843b	4
	ראה	TO SEE	907c	6 b
	שבע	SATISFIED	959c	2 a
53 12	מנה	RECKON	284a	2
	חטא	SIN	308a	3

Ch v.	Heb	Eng	Page	Sec
	חלק	DIVIDE	323d	1
	חלק	DIVIDE	323d	1
	נשא	LIFT	671b	1 b
	עם	WITH	767c	1 b
	עצום	MIGHTY	783a	2
	ערה	BE NAKED	788d	2
	פגע	MEET	803c	3
	פשע	REBEL	833b	2
54 1	רב	GREAT	913c	2 b
	שלל	SPOIL	1022a	2
	תחת	INSTEAD	1066a	2 3a b
	בעט	MARRY	127a	1
	חול	WHIRL	297a	2 a
	ילד	BEAR	408c	1 c
	כל	ALL	*481d	1 da
	עקר	BARREN	785d	
	פצח	CAUSE TO BREAK FORTH	822c	
	צהל	CRY SHRILLY	843d	2
	רב	MUCH	913b	1 e
	רנן	GIVE A RINGING CRY	943b	1
	רנה	RINGING CRY	943d	3
	שמם	BE DESOLATED	1030d	1
54 2	אהל	TENT	14a	2
	ארך	BE LONG	73d	1 d
	חשך	WITHHOLD	362b	1 d
	יריעה	CURTAIN	438c	
	יתד	PEG	450b	A
	מיתר	CORD	452d	
	נטה	STRETCH OUT	640d	2
	מקום	STANDING PLACE	879d	2 b1
	רחב	BE LARGE	931c	2
	משכן	DWELLING-PLACE	1015d	3 a
54 3	זרע	SOWING	283a	4 g
	ימין	RIGHT HAND	412a	2
	ירש	TAKE POSSESSION	439c	1 b
	ישב	CAUSE TO SIT	443d	3 b
	פרץ	BREAK THROUGH	829c	8
	שמם	BE DESOLATED	1031a	1
54 4	אלמנות	WIDOWHOOD	48c	
	בשת	SHAME	102a	1
	זכר	REMEMBER	269d	1 1 b
	חזק	BE FIRM	304c	1 c
	חפר	BE ABASHED	344a	
	חרפה	REPROACH	358a	2 b
	ירא	FEAR	431a	1 a
	כלם	BE HUMILIATED	483d	1
	עלומים	YOUTH	761c	
54 5	אלהים	GOD	44c	4 bb
	בעט	MARRY	127a	1
	גאל	REDEEM	145c	3 c
	עשה	DO	794c	2 1b
	צבא	GOD OF WAR	839c	4 b
	קדוש	HOLY	872c	1 c
	קרא	CALL	896c	6 d5
54 6	מאס	REJECT	549c	2
	נעורים	YOUTH	655c	
	עזב	LEAVE	737b	2 b1
	עצב	HURT	780c	
	קרא	CALL	896a	3
54 7	רוח	BREATH	925b	3 e
	גדול	GREAT	153b	6 c
	עזב	LEAVE	737c	2 e
	קבץ	GATHER	868a	1
	קטן	SMALL	882b	1 b
	רגע	A MOMENT	921a	A
	רחמים	COMPASSION	933c	1
54 8	גאל	REDEEM	145c	3 c
	חסד	GOODNESS	339b	2 3c
	סתר	HIDE	711d	2
	עולם	LONG DURATION	762b	2 c
	קצף	WRATH	893c	1
	רגע	A MOMENT	921a	BA A
	רחם	LOVE	933c	1
54 9	שטף	FLOOD	1009b	
	אשר	PARTICLE OF RELATION	82d	6 c
	אשר	THAT	83d	8 e
	גער	REBUKE	172a	2
	כן	SO	486c	2 db
	כן	SO	*486d	2 db
	ל	TO	513a	5 ad
	מבול	FLOOD	*550a	
	מי	WATER	565c	1 d
	מן	FROM	583b	7 ba
	נח	NOAH	629b	
	עבר	PASS OVER	717b	1 f
	קצף	BE WROTH	893b	1
	שבע	SWEAR	989c	2
54 10	את	WITH	86d	4a
	ברית	COVENANT	136c	2 2a
	ברית	COVENANT	137b	3 2
	גבעה	HILL	149a	3
	הר	MOUNTAIN	250d	1 n
	חסד	GOODNESS	339a	2 1e
	מוש	SLIP	556d	
	מוש	DEPART	559a	
	רחם	LOVE	933c	1
	שלום	PEACE	1023a	5 b
54 11	יסד	FOUND	413d	
	לא	NOT	*519c	2 b
	נחם	CONSOLE ONESELF	637b	
	סער	STORM	704a	
	ספיר	SAPPHIRE	705d	
	עני	POOR	776d	3

Ch v.	Heb	Eng	Page	Sec
	פוך	ANTIMONY	806c	
	רבץ	LIE DOWN	918c	
	שום	TO PLACE	963a	1 a
54 12	אבן	STONE	6d	3
	גבול	BOUNDARY	148a	1 fg
	חפץ	DELIGHT	343a	1
	כדכד	RUBY	461d	
	אקדח	SPARKLE	869b	
	שום	TO PLACE	964c	5 b
	שמש	SUN	1039c	5
54 13	למד	TAUGHT	541a	
	שלון	PEACE	1023b	5 b
54 14	מחתה	TERROR	370a	1 a
	ירא	FEAR	431a	1 a
	כון	BE ESTABLISHED	467a	
	עשק	OPPRESSION	799a	2
	צדקה	RIGHTEOUSNESS	842a	1 a
	רחק	BE DISTANT	935a	
54 15	אפס	NON-EXISTENCE	67b	2 b
	את	WITH	87a	4 c
	גור	STIR UP STRIFE	158d	2
	גור	QUARREL	158d	2
	הן	IF	243d	B
	מי	WHO	567b	G
54 16	ברא	CREATE	135b	2
	חבל	ACT CORRUPTLY	287c	
	חרש	GRAVER	360d	1 a
	יצא	BRING OUT	425a	4 j
	כלי	IMPLEMENT	479d	2 a
	ל	TO	516c	5 jb
	נפח	BREATHE	656a	
	מעשה	DEED	795d	1 b2
	פחם	COAL	809b	
	שחת	GO TO RUIN	1008b	1
54 17	את	WITH	87a	4 c
	זה	THIS	261b	3
	יצר	BE FORMED	428a	
	כלי	IMPLEMENT	479d	2 a
	לשון	TONGUE	546b	1 b
	נאם	UTTERANCE	610c	2
	נחלה	PROPERTY	635b	2 a
	עבד	SLAVE	714a	3
	צדקה	RIGHTEOUSNESS	842b	6 a
	קום	STAND	878b	6 a
	רשע	BE WICKED	957d	2
	משפט	JUDGMENT	1048b	1 a
55 1	הוי	AH	223a	
	הלך	WALK	230b	1 lc
	הלך	WALK	230c	1 l
	חלב	MILK	316c	A 3
	יין	WINE	406d	E
	כסף	SILVER	494d	9
	לא	NOT	520a	4 aa
	מחיר	PRICE	564b	1
	צמא	THIRSTY	854d	
	שבר	BUY GRAIN	991c	
55 2	דשן	FATNESS	206c	1
	ו	AND	254c	3
	טוב	A GOOD THING	375b	2
	יגע	TOIL	388c	2
	כסף	SILVER	494c	9
	לא	NOT	519d	2 d
	לא	NOT	520b	4 ac
	ענג	BE SOFT	772b	2
	שבעה	SATIETY	960a	1
	שקל	WEIGH	1053c	2
55 3	אמן	CONFIRM	52d	2
	ברית	COVENANT	137b	3 1
	ברית	COVENANT	137a	2 2k
	ברית	COVENANT	137b	3 2
	דוד	DAVID	188b	J
	הלך	WALK	230b	1 lc
	חיה	LIVE	311a	1 b
	חסד	GOODNESS	339c	4
	כרת	CUT	504a	4
	נטה	INCLINE	641a	3 e
	נפש	SOUL	659c	2
	עולם	LONG DURATION	762c	2 d
55 4	לאם	PEOPLE	522c	
	עד	WITNESS	729a	2 b
55 5	יהוה	YAHWEH	218d	2 1a
	ל	TO	514d	5 g
	לאם	PEOPLE	*522c	
	מען	PURPOSE	775b	1 a
	קדוש	HOLY	872c	1 c
	קרא	CALL	896a	5 f
	רוץ	RUN	930b	1
55 6	דרש	SEEK	205b	3 a
	מצא	FIND	*394a	1 i
	מצא	FIND	394a	1 f
	קרא	CALL	895d	5 c
	קרב	NEAR	898a	2 f
55 7	דרך	WAY	203d	6 d
	מחשבה	THOUGHT	364b	2
	ל	TO	517c	7 bb
	סלח	FORGIVE	699b	
	עזב	LEAVE	737c	2 d4
	רבה	BECOME MANY	915c	1 d1
	רחם	LOVE	933c	1
55 8	דרך	WAY	203b	5
	דרך	WAY	204a	6 eb
	מחשבה	THOUGHT	364b	1 b
55 9	גבה	BE HIGH	147a	1
	גבה	BE EXALTED	147a	2
	דרך	WAY	203b	5
	דרך	WAY	204a	6 eb
	מחשבה	THOUGHT	364b	1 b
	כן	SO	486c	2 db
55 10	גשם	RAIN	177c	
	זרע	SOW	281c	1 e
	זרע	SOWING	282b	2 a
	זרע	SOWING	282c	2 e
	ילד	BEGET	409a	1
	ירד	GO DOWN	433c	3 a
	כאשר	AS	455c	1 d
	כיאם	BUT	475a	2 b
	לחם	FOOD	537b	1 b
	נתן	GIVE	679c	1 t
	צמח	SPROUT	855c	2
	רוח	BE SATURATED	924b	1
	שוב	TURN BACK	998a	7 a
	שלג	SNOW	1017a	
55 11	אשר	PARTICLE OF RELATION	82c	4 bb
	חפץ	DELIGHT IN	343a	2 a
	יצא	GO OUT	423c	1 g
	כיאם	BUT	475a	2 b
	צלח	ADVANCE	852c	2
	ריקם	EMPTILY	938b	2
	שוב	TURN BACK	998a	7 d1
	שלח	SEND	1018c	2 b
55 12	גבעה	HILL	149a	3
	הר	MOUNTAIN	250b	1 c
	יבל	CONDUCT	385a	3
	כף	HOLLOW OF THE HAND	496c	1 d1
	מחא	CLAP	561d	
	עץ	TREE	781c	1 a
	פצה	CAUSE TO BREAK FORTH	822c	
	רנה	RINGING CRY	943d	3
	שדה	FIELD	961c	1 d
	שלון	PEACE	1023b	5 b
55 13	אות	SIGN	16d	5
	ברוש	CYPRESS	*141c	1
	ברוש	CYPRESS	141c	1
	הדם	MYRTLE	213c	
	כרת	BE CUT OFF	504b	4
	נעצוץ	THORN-BUSH	654c	
	סרפד	NETTLE	710d	
	עלה	GO UP	748d	4
	עולם	LONG DURATION	762d	2 f
	שם	NAME	1028d	5
	תחת	INSTEAD	1065d	2 2b a
56 1	ישושעה	DELIVERANCE	447c	3
	צדקה	RIGHTEOUSNESS	842b	5
	קרב	NEAR	898d	2
	שמר	KEEP	1037a	3 d
	משפט	JUDGEMNT	1048d	2 b
56 2	אנוש	MAN	60d	1
	אשר	HAPPINESS	81a	
	זה	THIS	260d	1 a
	חזק	BE FIRM	305a	6 a
	חלל	POLLUTE	320b	1 b
	שבת	SABBOTH	992c	1 c
	שמר	KEEP	1036d	2 b
	שמר	KEEP	1036d	3 b
56 3	בדל	BE DIVIDED	95b	2
	בן	SON	121c	7 a
	ה	THE	209c	3
	יבש	DRY	386d	2
	לוה	BE JOINED	531a	
	נכר	FOREIGNNESS	648d	2
	סריס	EUNUCH	710c	
	על	UPON	759b	4 2c
56 4	באשר	IN WHICH	84a	A
	בחר	CHOOSE	104a	1 b
	ברית	COVENANT	136c	2 2c
	ברית	COVENANT	137a	3 2
	חזק	BE FIRM	305a	6 a
	חפץ	DELIGHT IN	342d	2 a
	סריס	EUNUCH	710c	
	שבת	SABBOTH	992c	1 c
	שבת	SABBOTH	992c	1 c
	שמר	KEEP	1036d	3 b
56 5	ב	IN	88c	1 3
	טוב	PLEASANT	374c	6
	יד	MONUMENT	390c	4 a
	כרת	BE CUT OFF	504b	4
	עולם	LONG DURATION	762d	2 f
	שם	NAME	1028a	2 a
	שם	NAME	1028d	5
56 6	אהב	LOVE	13a	3
	בן	SON	121c	7 a
	ברית	COVENANT	136c	2 2c
	ברית	COVENANT	137a	3 2
	ו	AND	254d	5 a
	חזק	BE FIRM	305a	6 a
	חלל	POLLUTE	320b	1 b
	ל	TO	518b	7 bh
	לוה	BE JOINED	531a	
	מן	FROM	583b	7 ba
	נכר	FOREIGNNESS	648d	2
	עבד	SLAVE	714a	3
	שבת	SABBATH	992c	1 c
	שם	NAME	1028c	3
	שמר	KEEP	1036d	3 b
	שרת	SERVE	1058b	2 a
56 7	בוא	COME	99b	2
	בית	HOUSE	109b	1 ae 0
	הר	MOUNTAIN	249d	1
	זבח	SACRIFICE	257c	1 1
	עלה	WHOLE BURNT OFFERING	750d	
	על	UPON	757b	2 7c ab
	תפלה	PRAYER	813c	1 d
	קרא	CALL	896b	2 d3
	רצון	GOODWILL	953c	2
	שמח	REJOICE	970c	
56 8	אדון	LORD	11c	4 c
	ל	TO	511d	1 i
	נאם	UTTERANCE	610b	2
	נאם	UTTERANCE	610c	2
	נדח	BANISH	623a	2
	עוד	STILL	729a	1 ab
	על	UPON	755b	2 4a
	קבץ	GATHER	867d	2
	קבץ	GATHER	868a	1
	קבץ	GATHER	868a	1
56 9	אתה	COME	87c	
	חיה	LIVING THING	312d	1 b
	חיה	LIVING THING	312d	1 b
	יער	WOOD	420d	B
	שדי	FIELD	961b	2
56 10	אהב	LOVE	13a	2
	אלם	DUMB	48a	
	חזה	DREAM	223d	
	ידע	KNOW	394c	5
	כלב	DOG	477a	B
	נבח	BARK	613b	
	נום	BE DROWSY	630b	
	עור	BLIND	734d	2 b
	צפה	KEEP WATCH	859d	
	צפה	KEEP WATCH	859c	
56 11	בין	DISCERN	107a	1 a
	בצע	UNJUST GAIN	130c	
	דרך	JOURNEY	*203b	2
	דרך	WAY	203b	5
	ידע	KNOW	394b	4 a
	כלב	DOG	477a	B
	נפש	SOUL	660c	5 a
	עז	STRONG	738d	
	פנה	TURN	815b	1 a
	קצה	END	892b	3
	רעה	TEND	945a	1 d2
	שבעה	SATIETY	960a	1
56 12	אתה	COME	87b	
	זה	THIS	262a	6 ca
	יום	DAY	400a	7 a2
	יין	WINE	406c	C
	יתר	EXCESS	452a	2 b
	מחר	TO-MORROW	564a	1
	סבא	DRINK LARGELY	685a	
	שכ־	INTOXICATING DRINK	1016b	
57 1	אבד	PERISH	1c	1
	אין	NOT	35a	6 aa
	בין	DISCERN	107a	2
	חסד	GOODNESS	338d	13
	לב	HEART	525a	2 3d
	צדיק	JUST	843a	3 b
	שאול	SHEOL	*983b	2 b
57 2	נוח	REST	628b	2
	נכח	STRAIGHTNESS	647c	
	שאול	SHEOL	*983b	2 b
	משכב	COUCH	1012d	1
	שלום	PEACE	1023a	4
57 3	בן	SON	120c	1 ia
	הנה	HITHER	244c	A a
	זנה	COMMIT FORNICATION	276a	3
	זרע	SOWING	283b	5
	נאף	COMMIT ADULTERY	610d	2
	ענן	PRACTISE SOOTHSAYING	778b	
57 4	קרב	COME NEAR	897c	1 f
	ארך	BE LONG	73d	1 d
	זרע	SOWING	283b	5
	ילד	CHILD	409c	E
	לשון	TONGUE	546b	1 b
	מי	WHO	566b	B
	ענג	BE SOFT	772b	2
	פה	MOUTH	804d	1 b
	פשע	TRANSGRESSION	833c	3 a
	רחב	BE LARGE	931d	2
	שקר	DECEPTION	1055c	2
57 5	איל	TEREBINTH	18b	
	חמם	BE OR BECOME WARM	328d	
	ילד	CHILD	409c	B
	נחל	WADY	636c	2
	סעיף	CLEFT	703d	1
	עץ	TREE	781c	1 a
	רענן	LUXURIANT	947d	2
	שחט	SLAUGHTER	1006b	3
57 6	אלה	THESE	41d	D
	גם	YEA	169c	3
	גורל	LOT	174d	3
	ה	INTERROG PART	209d	1 b
	חלק	PORTION	324d	4
	חלק	SMOOTH	325b	1
	מנחה	OFFERING	585b	4
	מנחה	OFFERING	585c	6
	נחל	WADY	636b	2
	נחם	CONSOLE ONESELF	637a	4
	נסך	DRINK-OFFERING	651a	2
	נסך	MOLTEN IMAGE	651a	

Ch	v.	Heb	Eng	Page	Sec
		עלה	GO UP	749d	8
57	7	שפך	POUR OUT	1049c	1 a
		נבה	HIGH	147a	1
		גם	YEA	169c	3
		הר	MOUNTAIN	250d	11
		זבח	SACRIFICE	257c	12
		נשא	LIFT	671d	1 a
		משכב	COUCH	1012d	1
57	8	שם	THERE	1027a	1 a
		אהב	LOVE	12d	1
		אחר	BEHIND	29d	2 a
		את	WITH	86d	4 a
		דלת	DOOR	195a	1
		מזוזה	DOOR-POST	265b	1
		זכרון	MEMORIAL	272a	1 c
		חזה	SEE	302b	1 a
		יד	HAND	390c	4 g
		כרת	CUT	504a	
		רחב	BE LARGE	931c	1
		שום	TO PLACE	964b	4 c
57	9	משכב	COUCH	1012d	1
		ל	TO	511c	1 gb
		מן	FROM	578d	1 c
		עד	AS FAR AS	724a	1 1a
		ציר	ENVOY	851d	
		ציר	ENVOY	851d	
		רחק	DISTANT	935c	2 a6
		רקוח	PERFUMERY	955c	
		שאול	SHEOL	983b	4
		שור	TRAVEL	1003d	
		שמן	OIL	1032c	2 k
		שפל	BECOME LOW	1050b	2
57	10	חיה	LIVING THING	312d	4
		חלה	BE WEAK	317d	1
		יאש	DESPAIR	384c	
		יגע	TOIL	388b	2
		מצא	FIND	593c	4
		רב	MULTITUDE	914a	2
57	11	אסף	GATHER	62d	3
		את	MARK OF THE AC-CUSATIVE	85a	1 a
		דאג	FEAR	178b	2
		ו	AND	252c	1 b
		זכר	REMEMBER	270a	13 b
		חשה	BE SILENT	364c	1
		חשה	BE SILENT	*364c	
		ירא	FEAR	431b	1 b
		ירא	FEAR	431b	1 b
		כזב	LIE	469c	1
		לב	HEART	525a	23 d
		עולם	LONG DURATION	762a	1 c
		עולם	ADDENDA ET COR-RIGENDA	1125d	
57	12	את	MARK OF THE AC-CUSATIVE	85b	3 a
		יעל	PROFIT	418c	
		נגד	BE CONSPICUOUS	617a	4
		מעשה	DEED	796a	2 a3
		צדקה	RIGHTEOUSNESS	842b	3
57	13	הבל	VAPOUR	210d	1
		הר	MOUNTAIN	249d	11
		זעק	CRY	277b	2 d
		חסה	SEEK REFUGE	340b	
		ירש	TAKE POSSESSION	439c	1 a
		נחל	TAKE AS A POSSES-SION	635c	1 a
57	14	קבוץ	ASSEMBLAGE	868b	
		דרך	WAY	202d	1
		מכשול	STUMBLING	506b	2 b
		סלל	LIFT UP	699d	1
		פנה	TURN	815c	
		רום	BE HIGH	927c	2
57	15	דכא	CRUSH	194a	
		דכא	CONTRITE	194b	
		חיה	LIVE	311d	2 b
		לב	HEART	525b	26 a
		נשא	LIFT	671d	1 b
		עד	PERPETUITY	723c	2 d
		קדוש	HOLY	872c	1 a
		קדוש	HOLY	872c	2 a
		רוח	BREATH	*925c	8
		רוח	BREATH	925d	8
		רום	BE HIGH	926d	1 b
		מרום	HEIGHT	928d	2
		שכן	SETTLE DOWN	1015b	2 c
		שכן	SETTLE DOWN	1015b	2 c
		שם	NAME	1028d	3
		שפל	LOW	1050c	4
57	16	לא	NOT	*518d	1 ac
		נצח	EVERLASTINGNESS	664b	4
		נשמה	BREATH	675d	3
		עטף	BE FEEBLE	742c	1
		עולם	LONG DURATION	762d	2 g
		פנה	FACE	818a	25 b
		קצף	BE WROTH	893b	1
		רוח	BREATH	925c	4 d
		ריב	STRIVE	936c	3
57	17	ב	IN	90c	3 5
		בצע	UNJUST GAIN	130c	
		דרך	WAY	203c	6 a
		נכה	SMITE	646c	4 b
		סתר	HIDE	711d	2 a
		עון	INIQUITY	731b	2
		קצף	BE WROTH	893b	1
		שובב	BACKTURNING	1000a	
57	18	אבל	MOURNING	5d	
		דרך	WAY	203c	5
		נחה	LEAD	635a	
		נחום	COMFORT	637b	1
57	19	רפא	HEAL	950d	2 a
		ברא	CREATE	135b	3
		נוב	FRUIT	626c	
		ניב	FRUIT	626c	
		קרב	NEAR	898a	2 b
		רחק	DISTANT	935b	1 a
		רפא	HEAL	950d	2 a
57	20	שפה	SPEECH	973d	1 a1
		גרש	CAST OUT	176c	
		גרש	DRIVE OUT	176d	
		טיט	MUD	376c	1
		יכל	BE ABLE	407c	1 b
		רפש	MIRE	952d	
		רשע	WICKED	957b	2
		שקט	BE QUIET	1053b	1
57	21	רשע	WICKED	957b	2
		שלום	PEACE	1022d	3
58	1	ב	IN	89d	3 2a
		בית	HOUSE	110a	5 dg
		גרון	THROAT	173c	2
		חטאת	SIN	308c	1 b
		חשך	WITHHOLD	362b	1 d
		נגד	BE CONSPICUOUS	616d	2
		פשע	TRANSGRESSION	833c	3 a
		רום	BE HIGH	927c	1 b
		שפר	HORN	1051d	
58	2	גוי	NATION	156d	1 b
		דרך	WAY	204a	6 ec
		דרש	SEEK	205b	3 a
		חפץ	DELIGHT IN	342d	1 a
		חפץ	DELIGHT IN	342d	1 b
		דעת	KNOWLEDGE	395d	2 b
		צדק	RIGHTEOUSNESS	841c	2 b
		צדקה	RIGHTEOUSNESS	842b	5
		קרבה	APPROACH	898b	
		משפט	JUDGMENT	1048d	3
		משפ	JUDGMENT	1048d	3
58	3	חפץ	DELIGHT	343b	4
		מצא	FIND	592d	1 a
		נגש	PRESS	620c	1
		ענה	BE BOWED DOWN	776b	4
		עצב	TOILER	780d	
		צום	FAST	847a	
		צום	FASTING	847b	
58	4	אגרף	FIST	175d	
		יום	DAY	400d	7 h
		ל	TO	515a	5 ha
		נכה	SMITE	645b	1 a
		מצה	STRIFE	663c	
		צום	FAST	847a	
		מרום	HEIGHT	928d	2
		ריב	STRIFE	936d	1
		רשע	WICKEDNESS	957c	1
		שמע	HEAR	1034c	1 a
58	5	אמן	BULRUSH	8c	1
		אפר	ASHES	68a	
		בחר	CHOOSE	104a	2 a
		ה	INTERROG PART	209d	1
		זה	THIS	262a	6 ca
		יום	DAY	398d	2 f
		יום	DAY	400a	7 d1 a
		יצע	LAY	426d	
		כפף	BEND DOWN	496a	
		ענה	BE BOWED DOWN	776b	4
		צום	FASTING	847b	
		קרא	CALL	896a	6 c
		רצון	GOODWILL	953c	1 a
		שק	SACK	974c	2 b
58	6	אגדה	BAND	8a	1
		בחר	CHOOSE	104a	2 a
		זה	THIS	261a	3
		חפשי	FREE	344d	1
		חרצבה	BOND	359a	1
		מומה	BAR OF YOKE	557b	1
		נתק	TEAR APART	683d	1
		נתר	BE FREE	684a	1
		פתח	OPEN	835c	2
		צום	FASTING	847b	
		רצץ	CRUSH	954c	2
		רשע	WICKEDNESS	957c	1
58	7	בשר	FLESH	142d	4
		כסה	COVER	491c	1
		ערום	NAKED	736a	
		עלם	CONCEAL	761b	1
		עני	POOR	776d	2
		פרס	BREAK IN TWO	828a	
		מרוד	RESTLESSNESS	924a	
		רעב	HUNGRY	944c	
58	8	אז	THEN	23a	1 b
		אסף	GATHER	62c	3
		ארוכה	HEALING	74a	A
		בקע	BREAK OPEN OR THROUGH	132a	1
		הלך	WALK	231c	1 1d 5e
		כבוד	GLORY	459a	2 c3
		מהרה	HASTE	555b	
		פנה	FACE	817c	24c a
		צדק	RIGHTEOUSNESS	842a	6 c
		צמח	SPROUT	855c	1
		שחר	DAWN	1007c	
58	9	און	TROUBLE	20a	3
		אז	THEN	23a	1 b
		הנה	BEHOLD	244a	A
		מומה	BAR OF YOKE	557b	2
		סור	TURN ASIDE	694b	1
		אצבע	FINGER	840c	1 b
		קרא	CALL	895b	2 b
		שוע	CRY OUT	1002d	
		שלח	SEND	1018d	3 a
58	10	אפלה	DARKNESS	66c	2
		חשך	DARKNESS	365a	3 a
		נפש	SOUL	660c	5 a
		ענה	BE BOWED DOWN	776a	2
		פוק	BRING OUT	807c	1
		צהר	MIDDAY	844a	2
		רעב	HUNGRY	944c	
		שבע	SATISFIED	959d	1 a
58	11	חלץ	EQUIP FOR WAR	323b	
		מוצא	GOING FORTH	425d	3 a
		כוב	FAIL	469c	2
		אזב	DECEPTIVE	*469d	
		תמיד	CONTINUITY	556b	1 a
		נחה	LEAD	634d	
		צחצחה	SCORCHED REGION	850b	
		רוה	WATERED	924b	
		שבע	SATISFIED	959d	1 a
58	12	בנה	BUILD	124d	1 i
		גדר	BUILD A WALL	154d	
		דור	PERIOD	189d	1 a
		חרבה	WASTE	352a	1
		מוסד	FOUNDATION	414c	
		מן	OUT OF	579c	2 cb
		נתיבה	PATH	677b	1
		עולם	LONG DURATION	762d	1 a
		פרץ	BURSTING FORTH	829d	2
		קום	STAND	878c	
		קרא	CALL	896c	
58	13	שוב	TURN BACK	998c	2 b
		דבר	SPEAK	181a	2
		דרך	WAY	203c	5
		חפץ	DELIGHT	343b	4
		יום	DAY	398d	2 i
		כבד	BE HONORED	457b	
		כבד	MAKE HONORABLE	457d	2 b
		מן	FROM	583b	7 ba
		מצא	FIND	592d	1 a
		ענג	DAINTINESS	772b	
		עשה	DO	793d	1 1a 1
		קדש	APARTNESS	872b	5
		קדוש	HOLY	872d	E
		שבת	SABBOTH	992c	1 c
58	14	שוב	TURN BACK	999a	1 c
		אז	THEN	23b	2
		אכל	EAT	37d	1
		במה	HIGH PLACE	119b	2 a
		דבר	SPEAK	180d	1
		נחלה	PROPERTY	635a	1 a
		ענג	BE SOFT	772b	2
		רכב	RIDE	938d	1
59	1	אזן	EAR	24b	2 b
		יד	HAND	390a	1 e2
		ישע	DELIVER	446d	1 b
		כבד	BE HEAVY	457b	
		מן	THAN	582d	6 d
		קצר	BE SHORT	894a	
		שמע	HEAR	1034b	2 d
59	2	בדל	BE DIVIDED	95b	1
		בין	INTERVAL	107c	1 d
		חטאת	SIN	308c	1 b
		כיא	BUT	475a	2 b
		סתר	HIDE	711d	2 a
		עון	INIQUITY	730d	1
		שמע	HEAR	1034b	2 c
59	3	גאל	DEFILE	146a	
		דבר	SPEAK	181a	2
		דם	BLOOD	197b	21
		הגה	UTTER	211d	2
		כף	HOLLOW OF THE HAND	496d	1 d7
		לשון	TONGUE	546b	1 b
		עון	INIQUITY	731b	2
		עולה	INJUSTICE	732c	2
		אצבע	FINGER	840c	1 d
		שפה	SPEECH	973d	1 a1
59	4	און	TROUBLE	20a	1
		אמונה	FIRMNESS	53c	3 a
		במח	TRUST	105a	14 c
		הרה	CONCEIVE	247d	2
		ילד	BEAR	409a	2
		עמל	TROUBLE	765d	2
		צדק	RIGHTEOUSNESS	841d	3
		קרא	CALL	895a	1 a
		שוא	EMPTINESS	996b	2
		שפט	JUDGE	1048a	1
		תהו	FORMLESSNESS	1062c	2
59	5	ארג	WEAVE	70d	
		ביצה	EGG	101b	
		בקע	BREAK OPEN OR THROUGH	132a	1
		בקע	BREAK OPEN OR THROUGH	132b	
		זור	PRESS DOWN AND OUT	267a	
		עון	INIQUITY	731b	2 a
		עכביש	SPIDER	747b	
		אפעה	VIPER	821b	
		צפעוני	VIPER	861c	
		קור	THREAD	881c	
59	6	און	TROUBLE	20a	3

Ch v.	Heb	Eng	Page	Sec
	חמס	VIOLENCE	329c	
	כסה	COVER	492b	
	כף	HOLLOW OF THE HAND	496d	1 d7
	מעשה	DEED	795d	1 a2
	פעל	DOING	821c	1 c
	קור	THREAD	881c	
59 7	און	TROUBLE	20a	3
	דם	BLOOD	196d	2 d
	מחשבה	THOUGHT	364b	2
	מחשבה	THOUGHT	364b	2
	מהר	HASTEN	555a	1
	נקי	CLEAN	667c	1
	מסלה	HIGHWAY	700c	
	רוץ	RUN	930b	1
	רע	EVIL	948d	2
	שבר	BREAKING	991a	1
	שד	VIOLENCE	994d	1
59 8	דרך	TREAD	202a	2
	דרך	WAY	203c	6 c
	ל	TO	515b	5 ia
	נתיבה	PATH	677b	2
	מעגל	ENTRENCHMENT	723a	2 b
	עקש	TWIST	786a	
	שלום	PEACE	1023a	5 a
59 9	אפלה	DARKNESS	66c	2
	הלך	WALK	235c	2
	חשך	DARKNESS	365a	3 a
	נגהה	BRIGHTNESS	618c	
	נשג	OVERTAKE	673c	1 b
	קוה	WAIT FOR	875d	1
	רחק	BE DISTANT	934d	
59 10	אין	NOT	35a	6 b
	גשש	FEEL WITH THE HAND	178c	
	כשל	STUMBLE	505c	1
	כשף	TWILIGHT	676a	1
	עור	BLIND	734c	1 a
	צהר	MIDDAY	844a	2
	קיר	WALL	885a	1 b
	אשמנים	LUSTY	1032c	
59 11	אין	NOT	34c	2 da
	דב	BEAR	179a	
	ה	THE	208c	1 hb
	הגה	MOAN	211d	1 b
	המה	GROWL	242a	1
	יונה	DOVE	401d	
	ישועה	DELIVERANCE	447b	3
	קוה	WAIT FOR	875d	1
	רחק	BE DISTANT	934d	
59 12	משפט	JUDGMENT	1048b	1 a
	את	WITH	86c	1
	חטאת	SIN	308c	1 b
	ידע	KNOW	394a	1 f
	נגד	IN FRONT	617b	1 aa
	עון	INIQUITY	731a	1 b
	ענה	ANSWER	773a	3 a
	פשע	TRANSGRESSION	833c	3 a
	פשע	TRANSGRESSION	833c	3 a
	רבב	BECOME MUCH	912d	1
59 13	אחר	BEHIND	29d	2 a
	דבר	WORD	183b	3 l
	הגה	UTTER	211d	
	הרה	CONCEIVE	247d	2
	הרה	CONCEIVE	248a	
	כחש	DECEIVE	471b	2
	לב	HEART	524d	2 3c
	מן	OUT OF	579c	2 cd
	סוג	MOVE AWAY	690d	1 b2
	סרה	A TURNING ASIDE	694c	1
	עשק	OPPRESSION	799a	
	פשע	REBEL	833c	2
59 14	אמת	FIRMNESS	54b	4 a
	ה	THE	*208b	1 ha
	כשל	STUMBLE	505c	1
	נכח	STRAIGHTNESS	647c	
	סוג	BE DRIVEN BACK	691a	
	עמד	STAND	764a	1 f
	רחוב	PLAZA	932b	
	רחק	DISTANT	935c	2 a2
59 15	אמת	FIRMNESS	54b	4 a
	ה	THE	208b	1 ha
	סור	TURN ASIDE	693d	1
	עדר	BE LACKING	727c	
	רע	EVIL	949a	3
	רעע	BE EVIL	949c	4
	שלל	SPOIL	1021d	
59 16	הוא	HE, SHE, IT	215d	2 a
	זרוע	ARM	284b	2 b
	ישע	GIVE VICTORY	447a	3 b
	סמך	LEAN	702a	2
	פגע	MEET	803c	3
	שמם	BE DESOLATED	1031d	
59 17	ב	IN	89a	2 2
	ישועה	VICTORY	447c	4
	כובע	HELMET	464d	
	לבש	PUT ON	528a	B
	תלבשת	RAIMENT	528d	
	מעיל	ROBE	591c	4
	נקם	VENGEANCE	668d	1
	עטה	WRAP ONESELF	741d	
	קנאה	ZEAL	888c	2 b
	שריון	BODY-ARMOUR	1056b	
59 18	אי	COAST	16a	
	חמה	RAGE	404d	2 c
	ל	LIKE	454c	2 a

Ch v.	Heb	Eng	Page	Sec
	ל	LIKE	455a	A
	על	UPON	758b	4 1b
	צר	ADVERSARY	865d	
	שלם	BE COMPLETE	1022c	5
	שלם	RECOMPENCE	1024a	
59 19	מזרח	PLACE OF SUNRISE	280d	1
	ירא	FEAR	431c	3 b
	כבוד	GLORY	459a	2 c3
	נהר	STREAM	625d	1
	נוס	ESCAPE	630d	
	מערב	WEST	788a	
	צר	NARROW	865a	
	רוח	BREATH	924d	1 d1
59 20	גאל	REDEEM	145c	3 c
	ל	TO	511b	1 ga
	פשע	TRANSGRESSION	833c	3 b
	שוב	TURN BACK	997d	6 e
59 21	את	WITH	85c	
	את	WITH	86a	1 da
	ברית	COVENANT	137a	2 2k
	זרע	SOWING	283a	4 g
	מוש	DEPART	559a	
	עולם	LONG DURATION	762c	2 e
	עולם	LONG DURATION	763a	2 m
	עתה	NOW	774a	1 a
	פה	MOUTH	805a	2 a
	רוח	BREATH	925c	8
60 1	אור	BECOME LIGHT	21b	
	כבוד	GLORY	459a	2 c3
	על	UPON	755d	2 5
	ה	THE	208b	1 ha
60 2	זרח	RISE	280b	1 b
	חשך	DARKNESS	365a	3 a
	כבוד	GLORY	459a	2 c3
	כסה	COVER	492a	5
	לאם	PEOPLE	522a	
	על	UPON	755d	2 5
	ערפל	CLOUD	791d	
	ראה	TO SEE	908b	1 a
60 3	הלך	WALK	231b	1 d3 gd
	זרח	DAWNING	280b	
	נגה	BRIGHTNESS	618c	
	מקום	STANDING PLACE	880b	4
60 4	אמן	CONFIRM	52d	1
	בת	DAUGHTER	123b	1 i
	ל	TO	511b	1 ga
	נשא	LIFT	670c	1 b 4
	צד	SIDE	841a	
	קבץ	GATHER	867d	1
	רחק	DISTANT	935c	2 a1
60 5	אז	THEN	23a	1 b
	המון	ABUNDANCE	242d	5
	הפך	TURN	245d	1 a
	חיל	STRENGTH	299a	3
	ל	TO	511b	1 ga
	לבב	HEART	524a	2 6c
	על	UPON	755b	2 4a
	פחד	DREAD	808b	2
	רחב	BE LARGE	931c	
60 6	בכרה	YOUNG CAMEL	114c	
	בשר	BEAR TIDINGS	142b	3
	מדין	MIDIAN	193c	2
	תהלה	PRAISE	240b	4
	כסה	COVER	491d	4
	לבנה	FRANKINCENSE	526d	
	עיפה	EPHAH	734a	1
	שבא	SHEBA	985b	
	שפעה	ABUNDANCE	1051b	
60 7	איל	RAM	18a	2 g
	בית	HOUSE	109b	1 ae 0
	ל	TO	511b	1 ga
	נביות	NEBAIOTH	614a	
	עלה	GO UP	749a	6
	עלה	GO UP	749a	8
	על	UPON	754d	2 1f e
	תפאהה	BEAUTY	802d	2 c
	קבץ	GATHER	867d	2
	קדר	KEDAR	871a	1
	רצון	GOODWILL	953c	2
	שרת	SERVE	1058b	2 a
60 8	ארבה	LATTICE	70c	
	יונה	DOVE	401d	
	מי	WHO	566b	
	מי	WHO	567b	F e
	עב	DARK CLOUD	728a	1 e
	עוף	FLY	733c	1 a
60 9	אי	COAST	16a	
	אניה	A SHIP	58c	
	יהוה	YAHWEH	219a	2 1g
	זהב	GOLD	263c	1
	כי	THAT	472d	1 e
	כסף	SILVER	494b	6
	קדוש	HOLY	872c	1 c
	קוה	WAIT FOR	875d	1
	קוה	COLLECT	876b	
	ראשון	FIRST	912a	3 a2
	רחק	DISTANT	935c	2 a1
	שם	NAME	1028b	3
	שמש	SUN	1039b	1
	תרשיש	TARSHISH	1077a	1
60 10	בן	SON	121c	7 a
	בנה	BUILD	124c	1 ad
	נכה	SMITE	646c	4 b
	נכר	FOREIGNNESS	648d	2
	קצף	WRATH	893c	1
	רחם	LOVE	933c	1

Ch v.	Heb	Eng	Page	Sec
	רצון	GOODWILL	953c	1 a
	שרת	SERVE	1058a	1 e
60 11	חיל	STRENGTH	299a	3
	תמיד	CONTINUITY	556b	1 a
	נהג	DRIVE	624b	1
	סגר	BE SHUT	689b	2
	פתח	OPEN	835c	3
	שער	GATE	1044c	1
60 12	אבד	PERISH	1c	1
	חרב	BE WASTE	351c	
	ממלכה	KINGDOM	575a	1
60 13	ברוש	BOX-TREE	81b	
	ברוש	CYPRESS	141c	1
	תדהר	ELM	187b	
	הדם	FOOTSTOOL	*213b	
	כבד	MAKE HONORABLE	457d	2 b
	כבוד	HONOR	458d	2 b
	לבנון	LEBANON	527b	
	רגל	FOOT	919d	1 b
60 14	הלך	WALK	231a	1 d3 ga
	הלך	WALK	232a	1 ld 5k
	נאץ	CONTEMN	611a	
	עיר	CITY	746c	1 g
	על	UPON	757c	2 7c ab
	ענה	BE BOWED DOWN	776b	1
	קדוש	HOLY	872c	1 c
	שחה	BOW DOWN	1005b	1 b
	שחה	BOW	1005d	2
60 15	גאון	EXALTATION	145a	1 a
	דור	PERIOD	189d	1 b
	ו	AND	254d	5 a
	עזב	LEAVE	737b	2 b1
	עולם	LONG DURATION	762d	2 f
	משוש	EXULTATION	965c	
	שנא	HATE	971c	1 a
	תחת	INSTEAD	1065d	2 2b a
60 16	אביר	STRONG	7d	
	גאל	REDEEM	145c	3 c
	יהוה	YAHWEH	219a	2 2b d
	חלב	MILK	316c	A 2
	ינק	SUCK	413b	
	ישע	DELIVER	446d	1 b
	שד	BREAST	994d	
60 17	ברזל	IRON	137c	1 d
	ה	THE	207d	1 e
	נגש	DRIVE	620c	3
	נחשת	COPPER	639a	3
	פקדה	OVERSIGHT	824b	2 b
	צדקה	RIGHTEOUSNESS	842a	1 a
	שום	TO PLACE	964c	5 b
	שלון	PEACE	1023b	5 b
60 18	גבול	BOUNDARY	148a	2 d
	תהלה	PRAISE	240b	5 cb
	חמס	VIOLENCE	329c	
	ישועה	DELIVERANCE	447b	3
	שבר	BREAKING	991a	1
	שד	VIOLENCE	994d	1
60 19	אור	BECOME LIGHT	21b	
	אור	LIGHT	21d	1
	ירח	MOON	437a	
	נגה	BRIGHTNESS	618d	
	עולם	LONG DURATION	762c	2 c
	תפאהה	BEAUTY	802d	2 c
60 20	אבל	MOURNING	5d	
	אור	LIGHT	21d	1
	אסף	GATHER	62d	3
	בא	COME	98a	1 i
	עולם	LONG DURATION	762c	2 c
	שלם	BE COMPLETE	1022b	1
60 21	מטע	PLANTING	642d	2
	נצר	SPROUT	666a	
	עולם	LONG DURATION	762d	2 f
	מעשה	DEED	796b	2
	פאר	BEAUTIFY	802c	2
	צדיק	JUST	843b	4
60 22	גוי	NATION	156d	1 b
	יהוה	YAHWEH	219b	2 2d
	חוש	HASTE	301d	3
	עת	TIME	773d	2 b
	עצום	MIGHTY	783a	4
	צעיר	YOUNG	859a	1 a
	קטן	SMALL	882b	2
61 1	אדון	LORD	11c	4 b
	אסר	TIE	63d	3
	בשר	BEAR TIDINGS	142b	3
	דרור	LIBERTY	204d	2
	חבש	BIND	290a	2
	לב	HEART	525b	2 6a
	משח	ANOINT	603a	2
	יען	ON ACCOUNT OF	774d	2 c
	ענו	POOR	776c	3
	פקחקוח	OPENING	824d	
	קרא	CALL	895b	3 a
	רוח	BREATH	925d	9 b
	רוח	BREATH	*925d	8
	שבה	TAKE CAPTIVE	985c	1 c
	שבר	BREAK	990d	
61 2	אבל	MOURNING	5d	
	יום	DAY	399a	3
	נחם	CONSOLE ONESELF	637a	
	נקם	VENGEANCE	668b	1
	רצון	GOODWILL	953c	1 a
	שנה	YEAR	1040b	
61 3	אבל	MOURNING	5d	
	אבל	MOURNING	5d	
	איל	TEREBINTH	18b	

ISAIAH

Ch v.	Heb	Eng	Page	Sec
	אפר	ASHES	68a	
	ה	THE	208b	1 ha
	תהלה	PRAISE	240b	5 a
	כהה	DIM	462d	
	מטע	PLANTATION	642d	3
	נתן	GIVE	679c	1 p
	מעטפה	WRAP	742a	
	פאר	BEAUTIFY	802c	2
	פאר	HEAD-DRESS	802c	
	צדק	RIGHTEOUSNESS	842a	6 c
	קרא	CALL	896c	
	רוח	BREATH	925b	3 f
	רפא	HEAL	*950d	3 a
	שום	TO PLACE	964d	5 d
	ששון	REJOICING	965b	
	שמן	OIL	1032b	2 e
	תחת	INSTEAD	1065d	2 2b a
61 4	בנה	BUILD	124d	1 i
	דור	PERIOD	189d	1 a
	חדש	RENEW	294a	2
	חרב	DESOLATION	351d	
	חרבה	WASTE	352b	2
	עולם	LONG DURATION	762d	1 a
	קום	STAND	878c	
	שמם	BE DESOLATED	1031a	1
	שמם	BE DESOLATED	1031a	1
61 5	אכר	PLOUGHMAN	38d	
	בן	SON	121c	7 a
	זור	BE A STRANGER	266c	2 c
	כרם	DRESS VINES	501d	
	נכר	FOREIGNNESS	648d	2
	רעה	TEND	944d	1 a
61 6	אמר	SAY	56c	
	אמר	SAY	56d	
	חיל	STRENGTH	299a	3
	ימר	BOAST	413a	
	כבוד	RICHES	458c	1
	כהן	PRIEST-KING	463a	1
	קרא	CALL	896c	6 d5
	שרת	SERVE	1058b	2 a
61 7	בשת	SHAME	102a	1
	חלק	PORTION	324b	2 c
	ירש	TAKE POSSESSION	439b	1 a
	כלמה	IGNOMINY	484a	2
	כן	SO	487a	3 db
	עולם	LONG DURATION	762d	2 f
	רנן	GIVE A RINGING CRY	943b	1
	שמחה	JOY	970d	2
	משנה	DOUBLE	1041c	1
	תחת	INSTEAD	1065d	2 2b a
61 8	אהב	LOVE	13b	5 c
	אמת	FIRMNESS	54a	3 b
	ברית	COVENANT	137a	3 1
	ברית	COVENANT	137a	2 2k
	ברית	COVENANT	137b	3 2
	גזל	ROBBERY	160a	
	יהוה	YAHWEH	219b	2 2c
	כרת	CUT	504a	4
	נתן	GIVE	679b	1 n
	עולה	INJUSTICE	732c	1
	עולם	LONG DURATION	762c	2 d
	פעלה	WORK	821d	2
	שנא	HATE	971c	3
	שנא	HATE	971c	2
	משפט	JUDGEMNT	1048d	2 b
61 9	ברך	BLESS	139b	2 a
	הם	THEY	*241c	3 a
	זרע	SOWING	283a	4 g
	זרע	SOWING	283b	5
	ידע	BE MADE KNOWN	394c	1
	צאצא	OFFSPRING	425c	1
	נכר	RECOGNIZE	648b	3
61 10	ה	THE	*208a	1 f
	חתן	DAUGHTER:S HUS-BAND	368d	2
	יעט	COVER	418c	
	ישע	DELIVERANCE	447a	1
	ך	LIKE	454a	1 c2
	כהן	ACT AS PRIEST	464c	3
	כלי	ARTICLE	479c	1
	כלה	BRIDE	483c	2 a
	לבש	CLOTHE	528b	1 b
	מעיל	ROBE	591c	4
	נפש	SOUL	660d	6 d
	עדה	ORNAMENT	725d	1 a
	עטה	WRAP ONESELF	742a	
	פאר	HEAD-DRESS	802c	
	שוש	REJOICE	965b	
61 11	אדון	LORD	11c	4 b
	גנה	GARDEN	171b	
	תהלה	PRAISE	240b	5 ca
	זרוע	SOWING	283b	
	יצא	BRING OUT	425b	4 j
	כן	SO	486b	2 ad g
	צמח	SPROUT	855c	1
	צמח	SPROUT	855c	1
	צמח	SPROUT	855c	1
62 1	בער	BURN	129a	2
	ה	THE	208a	1 f
	חשה	BE SILENT	364c	
	יצא	GO OUT	423b	1 f
	ישועה	DELIVERANCE	447c	3
	ך	LIKE	454a	1 c2
	לפיד	TORCH	542b	
	נגה	BRIGHTNESS	618b	

Ch v.	Heb	Eng	Page	Sec
	עד	UNTIL	725a	2 1b b
	מען	PURPOSE	775a	1 a
	צדק	RIGHTEOUSNESS	842a	6 c
	ציון	ZION	851b	
	שקט	BE QUIET	1053a	2
62 2	אחר	ANOTHER	*29c	
	חדש	NEW	294a	A
	כבוד	HONOR	458d	2 b
	נקב	PIERCE	666b	2
	צדק	RIGHTEOUSNESS	842a	6 c
	קרא	CALL	896c	
62 3	מלוכה	KINGSHIP	574d	
	עטרה	CROWN	742d	3
	תפארה	BEAUTY	802c	2 a
	צניף	TURBAN	857b	
	צנף	WRAP	857b	
62 4	אמר	SAY	56d	
	ארץ	EARTH	76a	2 a
	בעל	MARRY	127b	1
	בעל	MARRY	127b	
	חפץ	DELIGHT IN	342d	2 a
	חפצי-בה	HEPHZIBAH	343b	2
	עוד	STILL	729a	1 ab
	עזב	LEAVE	737b	2 b1
	קרא	CALL	896b	2 d1
	שמם	BE DESOLATED	*1031a	1
62 5	בחור	YOUNG MAN	104c	
	בעל	MARRY	127b	1
	בתולה	VIRGIN	143d	1
	חתן	DAUGHTER:S HUS-BAND	368d	2
	כלה	BRIDE	483c	2 a
	שוש	REJOICE	965b	
	משוש	EXULTATION	965c	
	שמר	KEEP	1036c	1 b
62 6	אל	NOT	39b	A ba
	דמי	QUIET	198c	1
	זכר	REMEMBER	270d	3 a
	חשה	BE SILENT	364c	
	לילה	NIGHT	539a	1
	תמיד	CONTINUITY	556b	1 a
	נתן	GIVE	679a	1 g
62 7	דמי	QUIET	198c	1
	תהלה	PRAISE	240b	5 cb
	כן	ESTABLISH	466d	1 b
	עד	UNTIL	725a	2 1b b
62 8	מאכל	FOOD	38b	
	אם	IF	50b	1 b2
	ב	IN	90a	3 2d
	בן	SON	121c	7 a
	דגן	CORN	186c	
	זרוע	ARM	284a	1 c
	יגע	TOIL	388b	1
	ימין	RIGHT HAND	411d	1 c
	תירוש	NEW WINE	440d	
	נכר	FOREIGNNESS	648d	2
	עז	STRENGTH	739a	1
	שבע	SWEAR	989c	2
	שתה	DRINK	1059b	1 a
62 9	אסף	GATHER	63a	1
	הלל	PRAISE	238b	2 b
	חצר	ENCLOSURE	347a	3 b
	קבץ	GATHER	868a	2
	קדש	APARTNESS	871d	2 d
	שתה	DRINK	1059b	1 a
62 10	ב	IN	88b	1 1
	נס	STANDARD	651d	1 a
	סלל	LIFT UP	699d	1
	מסלה	HIGHWAY	700c	
	סקל	STONE	709d	2
	עבר	PASS OVER	717c	3 b
	על	UPON	757c	2 7c a
	פנה	TURN	815c	
	רום	BE HIGH	927c	1 d
	שער	GATE	1044c	1 a
62 11	בת	DAUGHTER	123c	3
	ישע	DELIVERANCE	447a	1
	פנה	FACE	817c	2 4c a
	פעלה	WORK	821d	2
	קצה	END	892b	1
	שכר	HIRE	969b	2
	שמע	HEAR	1034d	2 c
62 12	גאל	REDEEM	145c	3 c
	דרש	SEEK	205d	7
	לא	NOT	*519c	2 b
	עזב	LEAVE	737d	2
	עם	PEOPLE	767a	5 g
	קדש	APARTNESS	872b	4 b
	קרא	CALL	896c	2 d1
63 1	בצרה	BOZRAH	131b	2
	הדר	ADORN	214a	3
	זה	THIS	261b	4 b
	חמק	BE RED	330a	
	ישע	DELIVER	446d	1 b
	כח	STRENGTH	471a	3
	לבוש	CLOTHING	528c	
	מי	WHO	567b	F e
	צדקה	RIGHTEOUSNESS	842b	4
	צעה	STOOP	858a	1
	רב	GREAT	913c	2 b
	רב	MULTITUDE	914a	2
63 2	אדם	RED	10b	
	דרך	TREAD	202a	3
	גת	WINE-PRESS	387c	
	מדוע	WHEREFORE	396c	
	ך	LIKE	455a	B

Ch v.	Heb	Eng	Page	Sec
	ל	TO	513b	5 ba
	לבוש	CLOTHING	528c	
63 3	את	WITH	86a	1 a
	בד	SEPARATION	94c	1 b
	גאל	DEFILE	146a	
	דרך	TREAD	202a	3
	דרך	TREAD	202a	3
	חמה	RAGE	404d	2 c
	מלבוש	RAIMENT	528d	
	נזה	SPURT	633b	
	פורה	WINE PRESS	807d	
	רמס	TRAMPLE	942d	
63 4	גאל	REDEEM	145c	3 c
	גאולים	REDEMPTION	145d	
	יום	DAY	399a	3
	נקם	VENGEANCE	668b	1
	הוא	HE, SHE, IT	215d	2 a
63 5	זרוע	ARM	284b	2 b
	חמה	RAGE	404c	2 c
	ישע	GIVE VICTORY	447a	3 b
	נבט	LOOK	613d	2
	סמך	LEAN	702a	2
	עזר	HELP	740c	
63 6	שמם	BE DESOLATED	1031b	1
	בוס	TRAMPLE	100d	
	חמה	RAGE	404d	2 c
	ירד	BRING DOWN	434a	1 c
	שכר	BE DRUNK	1016b	
63 7	בית	HOUSE	110a	5 dd
	תהלה	PRAISE	240b	4
	זכר	REMEMBER	271a	3 b
	חסד	GOODNESS	339c	4
	חסד	GOODNESS	339c	4
	טוב	GOOD THINGS	375c	4 b
	ך	LIKE	455a	A
	על	UPON	758b	4 1b
	קשב	ATTENTIVENESS	904a	
	רב	MUCH	913b	1 c
	רב	MULTITUDE	914a	2
	רחמים	COMPASSION	933c	1
63 8	ישע	DELIVER	446d	1 b
	ל	TO	512c	4 b
	שקר	DEAL FALSELY	1055d	
63 9	גאל	REDEEM	145c	3 c
	חמלה	COMPASSION	328b	
	יום	DAY	399c	5 c
	ישע	DELIVER	446d	1 b
	לא	NOT	520c	
	מלאך	MESSENGER	521d	3
	נטל	BEAR	642a	
	נשא	LIFT	672a	3
	עולם	LONG DURATION	762d	1 a
	פנה	FACE	816a	1 2a
	צר	STRAITS	865a	
	רוח	BREATH	926a	9 f
	תמך	SUPPORT	1069d	2
63 10	איב	BE HOSTILE TO	33c	
	הפך	TURN	246a	1 b
	ל	TO	512c	4 b
	מרה	BE REBELLIOUS	598a	2
	עצב	HURT	780d	
	קדש	APARTNESS	871c	1 d
	רוח	BREATH	926a	9 f
63 11	איה	WHERE	32c	
	זכר	REMEMBER	269d	11 d
	יום	DAY	399c	5 c
	ים	SEA	411a	2
	משה	MOSES	602c	
	עולם	LONG DURATION	762d	1 a
	קדש	APARTNESS	871c	1 d
	רוח	BREATH	926a	9 f
	רעה	TEND	945a	1 d2
	שום	TO PLACE	963a	1 a
63 12	בקע	CLEAVE	131d	2
	הלך	WALK	237a	5 a
	זרוע	ARM	284a	1 c
	משה	MOSES	602c	
	עולם	LONG DURATION	762d	2 f
	תפארה	BEAUTY	802d	2 c
	פנה	FACE	818b	2 6a
	שם	NAME	1028a	2 b1
63 13	הלך	WALK	236c	1 a
	כשל	STUMBLE	505d	2
	סוס	HORSE	692d	2
	תהום	SEA	1063a	2
63 14	בקעה	VALLEY	132c	1
	כן	SO	486b	2 ad g
	נהג	DRIVE	624b	1
	נוח	REST	628c	A 1b 1
	תפארה	BEAUTY	802d	2 c
	רוח	BREATH	926a	9 f
	שם	NAME	1028a	2 b1
63 15	איה	WHERE	32c	
	אל	TO	40a	3 c
	אפק	HOLD	67d	2
	גבורה	MIGHT	150c	3
	היכל	TEMPLE	*228d	2 e
	המון	SOUND	242c	1
	זבל	ELEVATION	259c	
	מעה	BELLY	589a	5
	נבט	LOOK	613d	3
	תפארה	BEAUTY	802d	2 c
	קדש	APARTNESS	871c	2a
	קנאה	ZEAL	888c	2 b
	רחמים	COMPASSION	933c	1
63 16	אב	FATHER	3b	2

Ch	v.	Heb	Eng	Page	Sec
		גאל	REDEEM	145c	3 c
		נכר	RECOGNIZE	648b	3
		עולם	LONG DURATION	762a	1 c
63	17	דרך	WAY	204a	6 ec
		ירא	FEAR	432a	3
		מן	FROM	578a	1 a
		נחלה	PROPERTY	635b	1 e
		עבד	SLAVE	714a	3
		מען	PURPOSE	775b	1 a
		קשח	TO MAKE HARD	905a	1
		שבט	TRIBE	987b	2 a
		שוב	TURN BACK	998a	6 g
		תעה	ERR	1073c	3
63	18	בוס	TRAMPLE	100d	
		ירש	TAKE POSSESSION	439c	1 a
		ל	TO	517c	6 d
		עם	PEOPLE	767a	5 g
		מצער	SMALL THING	859b	4
		קדש	APARTNESS	872b	4 b
		מקדש	SACRED PLACE	874b	4
63	19	הר	MOUNTAIN	250a	1 c
		זלל	SHAKE	272d	
		ירד	GO DOWN	433b	2
		לו	IF	*530a	1
		לו	IF	530b	2
		משל	RULE	605d	3
		עולם	LONG DURATION	762a	1 c
		פנה	FACE	818c	2 6b
		קרא	CALL	896b	2 d4
		קרע	TEAR	902d	3 c
		שמי	HEAVENS	1030b	2 a
64	1	בעה	CAUSE TO BOIL UP	126d	1
		חמס	BRUSHWOOD	243b	
		ידע	MAKE KNOWN	395a	
		מי	WATER	565c	1 a
		צר	ADVERSARY	865d	
		קדח	KINDLE	869b	2
		רגז	BE AGITATED	919b	
64	2	הר	MOUNTAIN	250a	1 c
		זלל	SHAKE	272d	
		ירא	CAUSE FEAR	431d	2
		ירד	GO DOWN	433b	2
		קוה	WAIT FOR	875d	1
64	3	אזן	HEAR	24b	1
		זולה	EXCEPT	265d	1
		חכה	WAIT	314a	3
		ל	TO	515a	5 hb a
		עולם	LONG DURATION	761d	1 a
64	4	דרך	WAY	204a	6 ec
		זכר	REMEMBER	270a	13 b
		חמא	MISS A GOAL OR WAY	306d	2 b
		רשע	BE DELIVERED	446b	1
		עולם	LONG DURATION	762a	1 a
		פגע	MEET	803b	2
		צדק	RIGHTEOUSNESS	841d	5
		קצף	BE WROTH	893b	1
		שוש	REJOICE	965b	
64	5	בלל	MIX	117c	
		טמא	UNCLEAN	379d	2 a
		נבל	SINK	615c	2
		עדה	MENSTRUATION	723b	
		עון	INIQUITY	731c	3
		עלה	LEAF	750a	1
		צדקה	RIGHTEOUSNESS	842d	7 b
64	6	מגן	DELIVER UP	171c	
		חזק	BE FIRM	305a	6 a
		יד	HAND	390d	5 b3
		מוג	MELT	556a	2
		סתר	HIDE	711d	2 c
		עון	INIQUITY	731c	3
		עור	ROUSE ONESELF	735b	
64	7	אב	FATHER	3b	2
		חמר	CEMENT	330d	2 a
		יצר	FORM	427d	2 a
		מעשה	DEED	796b	2 b
64	8	זכר	REMEMBER	270c	2 4
		מאד	EXCEEDINGLY	547c	3
		נבט	LOOK	613d	3
		עד	PERPETUITY	723d	2 d
		עון	INIQUITY	731b	1 c5
		קצף	BE WROTH	893b	1
64	9	ציון	ZION	851b	
		קדש	APARTNESS	872a	2 g
64	10	אשר	PARTICLE OF RELATION	82c	4 bb
		בית	HOUSE	109b	1 ae 0
		הלל	PRAISE	238b	2 b
		מחמד	DESIRE	327a	
		חרבה	WASTE	352b	2
		כל	ALL	482c	
		תפארה	BEAUTY	802d	2 c
		קדש	APARTNESS	871d	2 d
		שרפה	BURNING	977b	
64	11	אלה	THESE	41d	D
		אפק	HOLD	67d	2
		חשה	BE SILENT	364c	
		מאד	EXCEEDINGLY	547c	2 b
		על	UPON	754c	2 lf e
		ענה	BE BOWED DOWN	776b	3
65	1	בקש	SEEK	134d	3 c
		דרש	SEEK	205b	1
		הנה	BEHOLD	243d	
		הנה	BEHOLD	244a	A
		מצא	FIND	394a	1 f
		ל	TO	514a	5 e

Ch	v.	Heb	Eng	Page	Sec
		לא	NOT	519a	2 d
		לא	NOT	520c	4 e
		קרא	CALL	845b	2 c
		קרא	CALL	896c	
65	2	שאל	ASK	982a	2 b
		אחר	BEHIND	29d	2 a
		דרך	WAY	203d	6 d
		מחשבה	THOUGHT	364b	2
		טוב	PLEASANT	374d	0 a
		יום	DAY	400c	7 f
		סרר	BE STUBBORN	710d	
		פרש	SPREAD OUT	831c	1 a
65	3	גנה	GARDEN	171b	
		ה	THE	208d	2 a
		כעס	VEX	495a	2
		לבנה	BRICK	527c	1
		תמיד	CONTINUITY	556b	1 a
		קטר	MAKE SACRAFICES SMOKE	882d	
		קטר	MAKE SACRAFICES SMOKE	883a	
65	4	בשר	FLESH	142c	1 a
		ה	THE	208d	2 a
		חזיר	SWINE	306b	1
		מרק	BROTH	600a	
		נצר	GUARD	666a	4
		פגול	FOUL THING	803b	
		פרק	FRAGMENT	830a	
		קבצאר	GRAVE	868a	
65	5	אף	NOSE	60a	1
		אש	FIRE	77d	6
		דת	LAW	206d	
		ה	THE	208d	2 a
		חשה	BE SILENT	*364c	1
		יום	DAY	400c	7 f
		יקד	BE KINDLED	428a	1
		נגש	DRAW NEAR	620d	1
		עשן	SMOKE	798c	2 b
		קדש	BE SET APART	872d	1
		קרב	COME NEAR	897b	1 a
65	6	חיק	BOSOM	300d	1
		חשה	BE SILENT	364c	
		כיא	EXCEPT	474d	2 a
		על	UPON	757c	27c ab
		פנה	FACE	817a	24 c
		שלם	BE COMPLETE	1022c	5
		שלם	BE COMPLETE	1022c	5
65	7	גבעה	HILL	149a	3
		הר	MOUNTAIN	250d	11
		חיק	BOSOM	300d	1
		חרף	REPROACH	357d	
		יחדו	TOGETHER	403c	A
		מדד	MEASURE	551a	
		מדד	MEASURE	551a	3
		עון	INIQUITY	731a	1 c1
		על	UPON	757c	27c ab
		פעלה	WORK	821d	1 b
		קטר	MAKE SACRAFICES SMOKE	883a	
65	8	ראשון	FIRST	912a	3 b1
		אשכול	CLUSTER	79a	1
		ברכה	BLESSING	139d	2
		תירוש	NEW WINE	440d	
		כאשר	AS	455c	1 d
		כל	ALL	482d	2 ba
		כן	SO	486c	2 cf
		מצא	FIND	594a	2 c
		עבד	SLAVE	714a	3
		מען	PURPOSE	775b	1 a
		שחת	GO TO RUIN	1008b	1
65	9	בחיר	CHOSEN	104c	
		זרע	SOWING	283b	5
		ירש	TAKE POSSESSION	439b	1 a
		עבד	SLAVE	714a	3
		יעקב	JACOB	785a	2
		שכן	SETTLE DOWN	1015b	2 a
		שם	THERE	1027c	3 c
65	10	דרש	SEEK	205b	3 a
		שרון	SHARON	450a	1
		נוה	ABODE OF FLOCKS	627c	1 a
		עבור	DISTURBANCE	747d	
		רבץ	RESTING PLACE	918c	
65	11	גד	GOD OF FORTUNE	151c	2
		הר	MOUNTAIN	249d	1 a
		מלא	FILL	570c	1
		מני	MENI	584c	
		ממסך	MIXED DRINK	587c	
		ערך	ARRANGE	789c	1 c
		קרא	CALL	896a	6 f
		שכח	FORGETFUL	1013c	
		שלחן	TABLE	1020c	3
65	12	באשר	IN WHICH	84a	A
		בחר	CHOOSE	104a	1 b
		חפץ	DELIGHT IN	342d	2 a
		טבח	SLAUGHTERING	370d	1
		כרע	BOW DOWN	502c	4
		ל	TO	511b	1 ga
		מנה	RECKON	584a	2
		יען	ON ACCOUNT OF	774d	2 c
		קרא	CALL	896a	5 d
		רע	EVIL	948c	0 b
65	13	אדון	LORD	11c	4 c
		עבד	SLAVE	714a	3
		צמא	BE THIRSTY	854d	
65	14	טוב	GOOD THINGS	375c	3 b
		ילל	HOWL	410b	

Ch	v.	Heb	Eng	Page	Sec
		כאב	PAIN	456b	
		לב	HEART	525c	29a
		לב	HEART	525c	29b
		מן	ON ACCOUNT OF	580b	2 f
		עבד	SLAVE	714a	3
		צעק	CRY	858c	2
		רוח	BREATH	925c	8
		רנן	GIVE A RINGING CRY	943b	1
65	15	שבר	BREAKING	991b	1
		אחר	ANOTHER	29c	
		בחיר	CHOSEN	104c	
		מות	DIE	560b	2
		נוח	REST	629a	B 2
		עבד	SLAVE	714a	3
		שבועה	OATH	990a	1 b
65	16	אלהים	GOD	44c	4 bb
		אמן	VERILY	53b	
		ברך	BLESS	139c	
		כי	BECAUSE	474b	3 d
		סתר	HIDE	711c	2
		עין	EYE	744d	3 d
		שבע	SWEAR	989b	1 a
65	17	ברא	CREATE	135c	4
		זכר	REMEMBER	270c	1 a
		חדש	NEW	294a	A
		לב	HEART	524d	2 3d
		עלה	GO UP	749a	7
		על	UPON	756c	27b
		שמי	HEAVENS	1030a	1 a
65	18	ברא	CREATE	135c	4
		כיאם	BUT	475b	2 b
		עד	PERPETUITY	723c	2 c
		שוש	REJOICE	965b	
		משוש	EXULTATION	965c	
65	19	בכי	WEEPING	113d	
		זעקה	CRY	277d	2
		שוש	REJOICE	965b	
65	20	בן	SON	122a	9 a
		זקן	OLD	278c	2 a
		חמא	MISS A GOAL OR WAY	307a	2 b
		יום	DAY	399c	5 a
		מאה	HUNDRED	547a	1 a1
		מלא	FILL	570d	3
		נער	YOUTH	655a	1 d
		עול	SUCKING CHILD	732b	
		קלל	BE SLIGHT	886d	
		שם	THERE	1027c	4 c
65	21	בנה	BUILD	124b	1 ab
		כרם	VINEYARD	*501d	1
		נטע	PLANT	642c	1
		פרי	FRUIT	826b	1
65	22	אחר	ANOTHER	*29c	
		בחיר	CHOSEN	104c	
		בלה	BECOME OLD AND WORN OUT	115a	B
		בנה	BUILD	124c	1 d
		נטע	PLANT	642c	1
		עץ	TREE	781d	1 b
		מעשה	DEED	795d	1 b1
65	23	בהלה	DISMAY	96d	
		ברך	BLESS	138d	2 b
		זרע	SOWING	283b	5
		יגע	TOIL	388b	1
		צאצא	OFFSPRING	425c	1
		ריק	EMPTINESS	938b	
65	24	היה	COME TO PASS	225b	1 2b ae
		טרם	NOT YET	382c	1
		עוד	STILL	729a	1 aa
		קרא	CALL	895b	2 b
65	25	אריה	LION	71d	
		בקר	CATTLE	133b	1 a
		הר	MOUNTAIN	249d	1 a
		זאב	WOLF	255d	
		טלה	LAMB	378b	
		לחם	FOOD	537b	2 b
		נחש	SERPENT	638b	1 c
		עפר	DRY EARTH	779d	1 a
		רעה	TEND	945b	2 a
		רעע	BE EVIL	949c	1
		שחת	GO TO RUIN	1008b	1
		תבן	STRAW	1062a	
66	1	אי	WHERE	32b	1 b
		בנה	BUILD	124b	1 ab
		הדם	FOOTSTOOL	213b	
		כסא	SEAT OF HONOR	490d	1 b
		מנוחה	RESTING PLACE	629d	1
		רגל	FOOT	919d	1 b
		שמי	HEAVENS	1030a	2 a
66	2	אלה	THESE	41c	A
		זה	THIS	260c	1 a
		חרד	TREMBLING	353d	
		נבט	LOOK	613d	3
		נכה	STRICKEN	646d	
		ענו	POOR	*776c	3
		עני	POOR	777a	3
		רוח	BREATH	925c	8
66	3	און	TROUBLE	20a	2
		בחר	CHOOSE	104a	1 b
		ברך	BLESS	139a	4
		גם	ALSO	169c	4
		דם	BLOOD	197d	3 b
		דרך	WAY	203d	6 d
		זכר	REMEMBER	271a	5
		חזיר	SWINE	306b	1

Ch v.	Heb	Eng	Page	Sec
	חפץ	DELIGHT IN	342d	1 a
	כלב	DOG	476a	A
	לבנה	FRANKINCENSE	526d	
	מנחה	OFFERING	585b	4
	מנחה	OFFERING	585c	6
	נפש	SOUL	661b	8
	עלה	GO UP	749d	8
	ערף	BREAK THE NECK	791c	
	שה	A SHEEP	962a	1
	שור	A HEAD OF CATTLE	1004b	
	שחט	SLAUGHTER	1006a	2
	שקוץ	DETESTED THING	1055a	
66 4	באשר	IN WHICH	84a	A
	בחר	CHOOSE	104a	1 a
	בחר	CHOOSE	104a	1 b
	מגורה	FEAR	159a	
	גם	ALSO	169c	2
	חפץ	DELIGHT IN	342d	2 a
	ל	TO	*511c	1 gb
	תעלולים	WANTONNESS	760c	
	יען	ON ACCOUNT OF	774d	2 c
	קרא	CALL	896a	5
	רע	EVIL	948c	0 b
66 5	חרד	TREMBLING	353d	
	כבד	BE HONORED	457b	3
	נדח	PUT AWAY	622d	
	שמחה	JOY	970d	2
	שנא	HATE	971c	3
	שם	NAME	1028c	3
66 6	איב	BE HOSTILE TO	33c	
	היכל	TEMPLE	228c	2 d
	שאון	ROAR	981a	1
	שלם	BE COMPLETE	1022c	5
66 7	זכר	MALE	271c	11 b
	חבל	PAIN	287a	1 b
	חול	WHIRL	297a	2 a
	ילד	BEAR	408c	1 c
	ל	TO	*511c	1 gb
	מלט	SLIP AWAY	572c	1
66 8	אלה	THESE	41d	D
	אם	IF	50d	2 ab a
	גם	YEA	169c	3
	גם	ALSO	169d	4
	זה	THIS	262a	6 d
	חול	WHIRL	297a	2 a
	חול	WHIRL	297c	
	ילד	BEAR	408c	1 c
	ילד	BE BORN	408d	
	כי	BECAUSE	474b	3 c
	מי	WHO	566d	F c
	ציון	ZION	851b	
	ראה	TO SEE	907a	1 b
	שמע	HEAR	1033d	1 d1
66 9	אני	I	59a	
	ה	THE	209b	2 c
	ו	AND	252d	1 f
	ילד	BEGET	409a	1
	עצר	RESTRAIN	783c	1
	שבר	BREAK	991a	
66 10	אבל	MOURN	5c	
	אהב	LOVE	13a	3
	שוש	REJOICE	965b	
	משוש	EXULTATION	965c	
	שמח	REJOICE	970b	1 a
66 11	זיז	ABUNDANCE	265c	
	ינק	SUCK	413b	
	כבוד	RICHES	458c	1
	מצץ	DRAIN OUT	595a	
	תנחום	CONSOLATION	637c	
	ענג	BE SOFT	772b	2
	שבע	SATISFIED	959c	1 c
	שד	BREAST	994d	
66 12	ברך	KNEE	139c	
	ינק	SUCK	413b	
	כבוד	RICHES	458c	1
	נחל	TORRENT	636b	1
	נטה	BEND	640c	3 b
	נשא	LIFT	671d	3
	צד	SIDE	841a	
	שטף	OVERFLOW	1009b	1
	שלום	PEACE	1023b	5 b
	שעע	TAKE DELIGHT IN	1044b	
66 13	אם	MOTHER	51d	1
	נחם	CONSOLE ONESELF	637a	
	נחם	CONSOLE ONESELF	637b	
66 14	את	WITH	86b	1 dg
	דשא	GRASS	206a	
	זעם	BE INDIGNANT	276a	1
	ידע	BE MADE KNOWN	394c	1
	לב	HEART	525c	2 9a
	עבד	SLAVE	714a	3
	עצם	BONE	782d	1 d
	פרח	BUD	827a	
	שוש	REJOICE	965b	
66 15	אש	FIRE	77d	5
	אש	FIRE	77d	6
	גערה	REBUKE	172a	2
	חמה	RAGE	404d	2 c
	חמה	RAGE	*404d	2 c
	להב	FLAME	529a	1
	סופה	STORM-WIND	693a	
	מרכבה	CHARIOT	939d	
	שוב	TURN BACK	999c	4 b
66 16	בשר	FLESH	142d	6 c
	חלל	PIERCED	319c	2
	רבב	BECOME MUCH	912d	1
66 17	שפט	JUDGE	1048a	1
	אל	TO	39c	1
	בשר	FLESH	142c	1 a
	גנה	GARDEN	171b	
	חזיר	SWINE	306b	1
	טהר	BE CLEAN	372c	1 a
	יחדו	TOGETHER	403c	B
	סוף	CEASE	692d	
	עכבר	MOUSE	747b	
	קדש	BE SET APART	873a	4
	שקץ	DETESTATION	1055a	
	תוך	MIDST	1063c	
66 18	מחשבה	THOUGHT	364b	2
	כבוד	GLORY	459a	2 c3
	לשון	TONGUE	546c	2
	מעשה	DEED	795d	1 a3
	קבץ	GATHER	868a	1
	לשון	TONGUE	*1099b	
66 19	אי	COAST	16a	
	אות	SIGN	16d	4
	יון	JAVAN	402a	
	כבוד	GLORY	459a	2 c3
	לוד	LUD	530d	2
	מן	FROM	580c	3 a
	משך	DRAW	604b	2
	פוט	LIBYANS	806c	
	פול	PUL	806c	
	פליט	ESCAPED ONE	812c	
	קשת	BOW	906c	1 d
	רחק	DISTANT	935b	1 a
	שום	TO PLACE	964d	5 c
	שמע	REPORT	1034d	1
	תובל	TUBAL	1063a	
	תרשיש	TARSHISH	1077a	1
66 20	אח	BROTHER	26b	2
	הר	MOUNTAIN	249d	1 a
	טהור	CLEAN	373a	1
	כאשר	AS	455c	1 d
	כלי	VESSEL	480b	3
	מנחה	OFFERING	585b	4
	מנחה	OFFERING	585c	6
	על	UPON	757b	2 7c ab
	פרד	MULE	825d	
	צב	LITTER	839d	
	רכב	CHARIOT	939a	1
66 21	כהן	PRIEST	463d	5
	לוי	LEVITE	532b	3
	לוי	LEVITE	533a	3 2a
66 22	זרע	SOWING	283a	4 g
	חדש	NEW	294a	A
	כאשר	AS	455c	1 d
	עמד	STAND	764b	3 c
	פנה	FACE	817a	24 a b
	שם	NAME	1028b	2 c
	שמי	HEAVENS	1030a	1 a
66 23	בשר	FLESH	142d	6 c
	די	SUFFICIENCY	191d	2 cb
	היה	COME TO PASS	225b	1 2b ae
	חדש	NEW MOON	294c	1
	חדש	NEW MOON	295a	2 b3
	שבת	SABBATH	992b	1 a
	שבת	SABBATH	992c	1 d
	שבת	SABBATH	992c	4
66 24	שחה	BOW DOWN	1005c	2 c
	בשר	FLESH	142d	6 c
	דראון	ABHORRENCE	201b	
	ה	THE	208d	2 a
	הנם	HINNOM	245a	
	כבה	BE QUENCHED	459c	
	מות	DIE	559d	1 b
	פגר	CORPSE	803d	1
	פשע	REBEL	833b	2
	ראה	TO SEE	908a	8 a3
	תולעה	WORM	1069a	1

JEREMIAH

Ch v.	Heb	Eng	Page	Sec
1 1	בנימין	BENJAMIN	122d	1
	דבר	WORD	183a	2 1b
	חלקיהו	HILKIAH	324d	3
	כהן	PRIEST	463d	4
	מן	OUT OF	579c	2 cb
	ענתת	ANATHOTH	779a	1
	ירמיה	JEREMIAH	941c	1
1 2	אמון	AMON	54c	A
	ברית	COVENANT	136c	2 2c
	דבר	WORD	182c	1 2a
	שלש	THREE	1025d	2
1 3	אליקים	ELIAKIM	45d	B
	ברית	COVENANT	136c	2 2c
	יהויקים	JEHOIAKIM	220c	1
	חדש	NEW MOON	294d	2 b2
	חמישי	FIFTH	332c	1
	עשר	TEN	797a	1 d
	עשתי	ONE	799d	
	צדקיהו	ZEDEKIAH	843b	1
	תמם	BE FINISHED	1070b	2
1 4	דבר	WORD	182c	1 2a
	היה	BECOME	226a	2 1b
1 5	בטן	WOMB	106a	3
	טרם	NOT YET	382c	2
	יצא	GO OUT	423c	1 h
	יצר	FORM	427d	2 a
	נביא	PROPHET	611d	1
	נתן	PUT	680d	2 c
	צור	FASHION	849b	
	קדש	BE SET APART	873c	1 c
	רחם	WOMB	933b	1
1 6	אדון	LORD	11c	4 a
	אהה	ALAS	13c	
	אנכי	I	59c	
	ברית	COVENANT	136c	2 2c
	ידע	KNOW	394b	4 a
	נער	YOUTH	655a	1 d
1 7	אשר	PARTICLE OF RE-LATION	82c	4 bg
	הלך	WALK	231a	1 d3 gb
	נער	YOUTH	655a	1 d
	על	UPON	757b	2 7c ab
1 8	אנכי	I	59b	
	את	WITH	86a	1 a
	ברית	COVENANT	136c	2 2c
	ירא	FEAR	431b	1 c
1 9	נגע	TOUCH	619b	1
	נתן	PUT	680c	2 b
	על	UPON	757b	2 7c aa
	שלח	SEND	1018d	3 b
1 10	בנה	BUILD	124c	1 d
	ברית	COVENANT	136c	2 2c
	הרס	THROW DOWN	248d	1
	ממלכה	KINGDOM	575a	1
	נטע	PLANT	642c	2
	נתץ	PULL DOWN	683b	2 a
	נתש	PLUCK UP	684c	
	פקד	ATTEND TO	823d	1
1 11	היה	BECOME	226a	2 1b
	מה	WHAT	552b	1 a
	מקל	ROD	596c	
	ירמיה	JEREMIAH	941c	1
	שקד	ALMOND-TREE	1052b	2
1 12	אני	I	59a	
	יטב	DO WELL	405d	3
	ל	TO	517c	7 bb
	שקד	WATCH	1052a	1
1 13	היה	BECOME	226a	2 1b
	נפח	BLOW	656a	
	סיר	POT	696c	1 a
	פנה	FACE	816b	1 5
1 14	פתח	OPEN	835c	
	צפון	NORTH	861a	1
1 15	חומה	WALL	327b	1
	כסא	SEAT OF HONOR	490d	1 a
	ממלכה	KINGDOM	575b	1
	פתח	OPENING	836a	
	צפון	NORTH	861a	1
	שער	GATE	1045a	2 a
	רמא	CAST	*1113b	1
1 16	אלהים	GOD	43c	1 d
	את	WITH	86a	1 db
	דבר	SPEAK	181b	3 d
	דבר	SPEAK	181c	5
	עזב	LEAVE	737c	2 d1
	על	UPON	754b	2 1f b
	מעשה	DEED	796a	2 a3
	קטר	MAKE SACRAFICES SMOKE	883a	
	רעה	MISERY	949b	3
	משפט	JUDGMENT	1048c	1 c
1 17	אור	GIRD	25a	
	חתת	BE SHATTERED	369b	2 b
	מתנים	LOINS	608a	1 c
	פנה	FACE	817b	24 b c
	פנה	FACE	818b	26 b
	קום	STAND	877d	1 f
1 18	מבצר	FORTIFICATION	131c	
	ברזל	IRON	137c	3
	חומה	WALL	327d	3
	כהן	PRIEST	463d	4
	עמוד	PILLAR	765b	5 a
	שר	CHIEFTAIN	978b	2 a
1 19	אנכי	I	59b	
	את	WITH	86a	1 a
	יכל	PREVAIL	408a	2 b
	לחם	ENGAGE IN BAT-TLE	535c	
2 1	היה	BECOME	226a	2 1b
2 2	אהבה	LOVE	13c	1
	הלך	WALK	233c	14 c 6
	הלך	WALK	235a	23 d 1
	זכר	REMEMBER	270b	2 2b
	זרע	SOW	281c	1 b
	חסד	GOODNESS	338d	1 3
	חסיד	KIND	339c	2
	כה	THUS	462a	1 a
	כלולה	BETROTHAL	483c	
	ל	TO	515b	5 hb g
	לא	NOT	519c	2 b
	נעורים	YOUTH	655c	
2 3	אשם	OFFEND	79c	3
	תבואה	REVENUE	100b	2 b
	קדש	APARTNESS	872b	4 b
	ראשית	BEGINNING	912b	1 b
	רעה	MISERY	949a	1
	ישראל	ISRAEL	975d	2 a3
2 4	בית	HOUSE	110a	5 dd
	בית	HOUSE	110a	5 dg
	משפחה	CLAN	1046d	1 c
2 5	הבל	VAPOUR	210d	2
	הבל	BECOME VAIN	211a	

Ch v.	Heb	Eng	Page	Sec
	כה	THUS	462a	1 a
	מה	WHAT	552c	1 aa
	מצא	FIND	593b	2 b
	עול	INJUSTICE	732c	
	על	UPON	759a	4 2c
	רחק	BE DISTANT	934d	
2 6	אדם	MAN	9b	1
	איה	WHERE	32c	
	הלך	WALK	236c	1 a
	ערבה	DESERT-PLAIN	787c	5
	ציה	DRYNESS	851a	
	שוחה	PIT	1001c	
2 7	טוב	GOOD THINGS	375c	1
	טמא	BE UNCLEAN	379c	2
	כרמל	GARDEN	502a	1
	נחלה	PROPERTY	635b	1 e
	שום	TO PLACE	964c	5 a
	תועבה	ABOMINATION	1072d	1 b
2 8	איה	WHERE	32c	
	בעל	BAAL	127d	2 2
	הלך	WALK	235a	2 3d 3
	יעל	PROFIT	418c	
	תורה	INSTRUCTION	436d	1 e
	כהן	PRIEST	463d	4
	לא	NOT	519d	2 d
	נביא	PROPHET	611d	2
	נבא	PROPHESY	612b	3
	פשע	REBEL	833b	1
	רעה	TEND	945a	1 d2
	תפש	LAY HOLD OF	1074d	
2 9	כן	SO	486d	3 d
	ריב	STRIVE	936c	3
2 10	אי	COAST	16a	
	בין	DISCERN	107a	1 a
	חם	IF	243d	C
	זה	THIS	*262a	6 d
	כתי	KITTIM	508c	
	עבר	PASS OVER	717a	1 a2
	קדר	KEDAR	871a	1
2 11	ימר	CHANGE	413a	
	יעל	PROFIT	418d	4
	כבוד	GLORY	459c	7
	לא	NOT	519b	1 bb
	לא	NOT	519d	2 d
	לא	NOT	520b	4 ac
	מור	CHANGE	558c	2
2 12	זה	THIS	262a	6 f
	חרב	BE WASTE	351c	
	שער	BRISTLE	972c	
	שמי	HEAVENS	1030b	3
	שמם	BE DESOLATED	1031a	2
2 13	באר	WELL	92b	
	חי	ALIVE	312b	1 f
	חצב	HEW	345a	1
	כול	CONTAIN	465b	1
	ל	TO	515d	5 ia
	מי	WATER	565d	3
	מקור	SPRING	881b	1 a
	שבר	BREAK	990d	
2 14	בז	SPOIL	103a	2
	בז	SPOIL	103a	2
	בית	HOUSE	109c	4
	מדוע	WHEREFORE	396c	
	יליד	BORN	409d	
	עבד	SLAVE	713d	1
	ישראל	ISRAEL	975d	2 a3
2 15	בלי	WEARING OUT	115d	C b
	יצת	BE KINDLED	428b	
	ישב	DWELL	443b	3
	כפיר	LION	498d	
	נצה	FALL IN RUINS	663d	
	נתן	GIVE	679d	1 x
	קול	VOICE	877a	1 e
	שאג	ROAR	980c	1
	שית	PUT	1011c	3
	שמה	WASTE	1031c	1
2 16	מף	MEMPHIS	592a	
	קדקד	HEAD	869b	
	רעה	TEND	945b	2 c
	תחפנחס	TAHPANHES	1064d	
2 17	יהוה	YAHWEH	219a	2 lg
	הלך	WALK	236c	1 a
2 18	אשור	ASSYRIA	78d	3
	דרך	WAY	202d	1
	מה	WHAT	553b	1 dc
	מי	WATER	565c	1 b
	מי	WATER	565c	1 b
	מצרים	EGYPT	595c	1 a
	נהר	STREAM	625d	1
	שיחור	SHIHOR	1009d	
2 19	אדן	LORD	11d	6 c
	אל	TO	39c	1
	יהוה	YAHWEH	219a	2 lg
	יכח	REPROVE	407a	5 b
	יסר	DISCIPLINE	416b	2 c
	לא	NOT	519b	1 bb
	מר	BITTER	600c	1
	פחדה	DREAD	808c	
	ראה	TO SEE	907c	5 b
	רע	EVIL	948b	2
	רעה	MISERY	949b	3
	משובה	TURNING BACK	1000b	
2 20	מוסר	BAND	64c	
	גבה	HIGH	147b	1
	גבעה	HILL	149a	2
	זנה	COMMIT FORNICA-TION	276a	3
	נתק	TEAR APART	683d	1
	עבד	WORK	713b	4 a
	עבר	PASS OVER	718b	6 f
	על	YOKE	760d	
	עולם	LONG DURATION	761d	1 a
	עץ	TREE	781c	1 a
	צעה	STOOP	858a	1
	רענן	LUXURIANT	947d	
	שבר	BREAK	990c	
2 21	איך	HOW	32c	2
	אמת	FIRMNESS	54a	1
	גפן	VINE	172c	
	הפך	TURN	245d	1 b
	זרע	SOWING	283b	5
	כל	ALL	481b	1 a
	ל	TO	512d	5 aa
	נטע	PLANT	642b	1
	נכרי	ALIEN	649a	3
	סור	TURN ASIDE	693d	1
	שרק	VINE	977d	
2 22	אדן	LORD	11c	4 c
	ברית	LYE	141b	
	כבס	WASH	460b	2
	כתם	BE STAINED	*508d	
	נאם	UTTERANCE	610b	2
	נתר	CARBONATE OF SODA	684a	
	עון	INIQUITY	731b	2
	פנה	FACE	817a	2 4ac c
2 23	איך	HOW	32c	1
	בכרה	YOUNG CAMEL	114c	
	בעל	BAAL	127d	2 3
	בעל	BAAL	*127d	2 1
	גיא	VALLEY	161b	
	דרך	WAY	203a	1
	דרך	WAY	203d	6 d
	הלך	WALK	235a	2 3d 2
	טמא	BE UNCLEAN	379b	2
	קל	LIGHT	886d	
	קל	LIGHT	887a	1
	שרך	TWIST	976c	1
	אוה	DESIRE	16b	
	תאנה	OCCASION	58c	1
	בקש	SEEK	134c	1 b
	מדבר	WILDERNESS	184d	1
	חדש	NEW MOON	295a	2 b3
2 24	יעף	BE WEARY	419b	
	למד	TAUGHT	541a	
	מי	WHO	567a	F c
	מי	WHO	567a	F c
	נפש	SOUL	660d	6 a
	פרא	WILD ASS	825b	
	שאף	GASP	983c	1
	שוב	TURN BACK	999d	5
2 25	אהב	LOVE	12d	1
	גרון	THROAT	173c	2
	זור	BE A STRANGER	266c	2 c
	יאש	DESPAIR	384c	1
	יחף	BAREFOOT	405c	
	מן	FROM	583b	7 bb
	מנע	WITHHOLD	586a	
	צמאה	PARCHED CONDITION	854d	
2 26	רגל	FOOT	919d	1 a
	בוש	BE ASHAMED	102a	2 c
	בשת	SHAME	102a	1
	בוש	BE ASHAMED	102a	2
	בית	HOUSE	110a	5 dd
	גנב	THIEF	170c	
	מצא	FIND	394a	1 g2
	כהן	PRIEST	463d	4
	כן	SO	486b	2 ad d
	נביא	PROPHET	611d	2
2 27	אב	FATHER	3b	2
	ישע	DELIVER	446d	1 b
	עץ	TREE	782d	2 c
	ערף	BACK OF NECK	791b	1
	פנה	TURN	815b	1 b
	פנה	FACE	816a	1 ld
	קום	STAND	878b	1
	רעה	MISERY	949a	1
2 28	איה	WHERE	32c	
	יהודה	JUDAH	397b	1 3
	ישע	DELIVER	446d	1 c
	מספר	NUMBER	709a	1
	קום	STAND	878b	6 a
	רעה	MISERY	949a	1
2 29	פשע	REBEL	833b	2
	ריב	STRIVE	936d	4
2 30	אכל	EAT	37c	4
	אריה	LION	71d	
	חרב	SWORD	352d	1 g
	מוסר	DISCIPLINE	416c	2 a
	לקח	TAKE	543b	4 f
	נביא	PROPHET	611d	2
	נכה	SMITE	646c	4 b
	שוא	EMPTINESS	996b	1
	שחת	GO TO RUIN	1008b	1
2 31	מאפליה	DEEP DARKNESS	66d	
	מאפלי	DEEP DARKNESS	66d	
	דבר	WORD	182d	12a
	מדבר	WILDERNESS	185a	4
	דור	GENERATION	190a	2
	ה	THE	208d	1 i
	מדוע	WHEREFORE	396c	
	ראה	TO SEE	907d	7 c
	רוד	ROAM	923d	
2 32	ישראל	ISRAEL	975d	2 a3
	אין	NOT	34d	4 a
	בתולה	VIRGIN	143d	
	כלה	BRIDE	483c	2 a
	מספר	NUMBER	708d	1 a
	עדי	ORNAMENTS	725d	1
	קשרים	BANDS	905c	
2 33	אהבה	LOVE	13c	1
	בקש	SEEK	134c	1 b
	גם	ALSO	169b	2
	דרך	WAY	203c	6 a
	דרך	WAY	203d	6 d
	יטב	MAKE GOOD	406a	4
	כן	SO	487b	3 db
	למד	LEARN	540c	
	מה	HOW	553c	2 b
	רע	EVIL	948c	0 b
2 34	אביון	NEEDY	2d	
	דם	BLOOD	196d	2 d
	מחתרת	BREAKING IN	369a	
	מצא	FIND	394a	1 gl
	כנף	EXTREMITY	489d	2 a
	מצא	FIND	593b	2 b
	נפש	A LIVING BEING	659d	3 a
	נקי	CLEAN	667c	1
2 35	את	WITH	85c	
	חטא	MISS A GOAL OR WAY	306d	2 b
	נקה	BE CLEAN	667b	2
	על	UPON	754d	2 lf b
	שוב	TURN BACK	997d	6 f
	שפט	JUDGE	1048a	1
2 36	אזל	GO	23c	
	אשור	ASSYRIA	78d	3
	בוש	BE ASHAMED	101d	2
	גם	ALSO	169c	4
	דרך	WAY	203b	5
	מה	HOW	553c	2 b
	שנה	CHANGE	1040a	
2 37	את	WITH	86d	4 a
	מבטח	CONFIDENCE	105c	2
	יצא	GO OUT	422d	1 b
	ל	TO	514c	5 fc
	מאס	REJECT	549c	1 b
	צלח	ADVANCE	852c	1
	שום	TO PLACE	963b	1 b
3 1	אחר	ANOTHER	29c	
	את	WITH	86d	4 a
	ה	INTERROG PART	209d	1 b
	היה	BECOME	226d	2 2h
	הלך	WALK	231c	1 d4
	הן	IF	243d	B
	זנה	COMMIT FORNICATION	275d	2
	זנה	COMMIT FORNICA-TION	276a	3
	חנף	BE POLLUTED	338a	1
	רע	FRIEND	946a	1
	שוב	TURN BACK	997c	5 a
	שלח	SEND	1019a	1 b
3 2	איפה	WHERE	33a	1
	זנות	FORNICATION	276b	C
	חנף	BE POLLUTED	338a	1
	ל	TO	515a	5 ha
	נשא	LIFT	670c	1 b4
	ערבי	STEPPE-DWELLER	787b	1
	ראה	TO SEE	907b	5 a
	שגל	VIOLATE	993c	
	שפי	BARE HEIGHT	1046a	2
3 3	אשה	WOMAN	61a	1
	זנה	COMMIT FORNICA-TION	275d	2
	כלם	BE HUMILIATED	483d	1
	מלקש	SPRING-RAIN	545b	
	מאן	REFUSE	549b	
	מנע	WITHHOLD	586a	
	מצח	FOREHEAD	595a	
3 4	אב	FATHER	3b	2
	אלוף	TAME	48d	2
	מן	FROM	581c	4 a
	נעורים	YOUTH	655c	
	עתה	NOW	774b	2 e
	קרא	CALL	895b	2 a
3 5	אם	IF	50d	2 ab a
	יכל	PREVAIL	408a	2 a
	נצר	KEEP	643c	1
	נצח	EVERLASTINGNESS	664b	4
	עולם	LONG DURATION	762d	2 g
	רע	EVIL	948c	0 d
	שמר	KEEP	1036d	2 a
3 6	גבה	HIGH	147b	1
	הלך	WALK	231a	1 d3 gb
	הר	MOUNTAIN	250d	11
	זנה	COMMIT FORNICA-TION	276a	3
	עץ	TREE	781c	1 a
	רענן	LUXURIANT	947d	
	משובה	TURNING BACK	1000b	
	תחת	UNDERNEATH	1066a	3 1a
3 7	אחות	SISTER	28a	3
	בגוד	TREACHEROUS	93d	
	שוב	TURN BACK	·997d	6 d
	שוב	TURN BACK	997d	6 c

Ch	v.	Heb	Eng	Page	Sec
3	8	אודה	CAUSE	15c	
		אחות	SISTER	28a	3
		בגד	ACT TREACHEROUSLY	93d	D
		זנה	COMMIT FORNICATION	276a	3
		ירא	FEAR	431a	1 a
		כריתות	DIVORCEMENT	504d	
		נאף	COMMIT ADULTERY	610d	2
		נתן	GIVE	678b	1 a
		ספר	MISSIVE	707a	2
		משובה	TURNING BACK	1000b	
3	9	אבן	STONE	6c	2
		היה	COME TO PASS	225a	1 2a 2
		זנות	FORNICATION	276b	C
		חנף	BE POLLUTED	338a	2
		חנף	BE POLLUTED	338a	1
		נאף	COMMIT ADULTERY	610c	2
		עץ	TREE	782a	2 c
		קול	VOICE	877b	3 b
		קל	LIGHTNESS	887a	1
3	10	אחות	SISTER	28a	3
		בגוד	TREACHEROUS	93d	1 hb
		ה	THE	*208c	1
		זה	THIS	262a	6 bg
		כיאם	BUT	475a	2 b
		לב	HEART	524c	2 2
		שקר	DECEPTION	1055c	3
3	11	בגד	ACT TREACHEROUSLY	93d	D
		נפש	SOUL	660a	4 b4
		צדק	BE JUST	842d	1
		משובה	TURNING BACK	1000b	
3	12	דבר	WORD	183b	3 2
		הלך	WALK	233c	14c 6
		חסד	KIND	339c	1 c
		נצר	KEEP	643d	1
		נפל	FALL	658b	5
		עולם	LONG DURATION	762d	2 g
		שוב	TURN BACK	997d	6 d
		משובה	TURNING BACK	1000b	
3	13	דרך	JOURNEY	203b	2
		יהוה	YAHWEH	219a	2 1g
		זור	BE A STRANGER	266c	2 c
		ידע	KNOW	394a	1 f
		עון	INIQUITY	731a	1 b
		עץ	TREE	781c	1 a
		פזר	SCATTER	808b	
		פשע	REBEL	833b	2
		קול	VOICE	877b	3 b
		רענן	LUXURIANT	947d	
		שמע	HEAR	1034a	1 m
3	14	בן	SON	120b	1 c
		בעל	MARRY	127b	1
		שוב	TURN BACK	997d	6 d
		שובב	BACKTURNING	1000a	
		שנים	TWO	1041d	1 b3
		משפחה	CLAN	1046d	1 c
		בחל	ADDENDA ET CORRIGENDA	1121b	
		בעל	ADDENDA ET CORRIGENDA	1121c	
		בעל	ADDENDA ET CORRIGENDA	*1121c	
3	15	דעה	KNOWLEDGE	395c	
		כ	LIKE	454a	1 c1
		לב	HEART	524c	2 2
		רעה	TEND	945a	1 c
		רעה	TEND	945a	1 d2
		שכל	BE PRUDENT	968b	3
3	16	ארון	CHEST	75b	3
		ארון	CHEST	75c	3f
		ב	IN	90d	4 e
		זכר	REMEMBER	269d	1 1 a
		לב	HEART	524d	2 3d
		עוד	STILL	729a	1 ab
		עשה	DO	795b	2 a
		פקד	ATTEND TO	823b	A 1d
		פרה	BEAR FRUIT	826a	1
		רבה	BECOME MANY	915a	1
		רוח	BREATH	*925c	6
3	17	כסא	SEAT OF HONOR	490d	1 b
		ל	TO	511b	1 ga
		ל	TO	514d	5 g
		לב	HEART	525b	2 6d
		קוה	COLLECT	876b	
		רע	EVIL	948c	0 c
		שרירות	STUBBORNNESS	1057b	
3	18	בית	HOUSE	110a	5 de
		יהודה	JUDAH	397b	13
		יחדו	TOGETHER	403b	A
		נחל	TAKE AS A POSSESSION	635d	1 a
		על	UPON	755c	2 4c
		על	UPON	757a	2 7c a
		צפון	NORTH	861a	
3	19	אב	FATHER	3b	2
		איך	HOW	32c	2
		אכן	SURELY	38c	B
		חמדה	DESIRE	326d	
		צבא	HOST	839b	1 c
		צבי	BEAUTY	840a	1 b
		קרא	CALL	896a	6 e1
		שוב	TURN BACK	997b	6 a
3	20	שית	PUT	1011b	2 a
		אכן	SURELY	38c	B
		בגד	ACT TREACHEROUSLY	93d	D
		בגד	ACT TREACHEROUSLY	93d	B
		כן	SO	486c	2 db
		מן	FROM	578a	1 a
		רע	FRIEND	946a	1
3	21	בכי	WEEPING	*113d	
		בכי	WEEPING	113d	
		דרך	WAY	203c	6 a
		יהוה	YAHWEH	218d	2 1d
		תחנון	SUPPLICATION FOR FAVOR	337d	2
		עוה	BEND	730c	
		שפי	BARE HEIGHT	1046a	2
3	22	אתה	COME	87b	1 c
		בן	SON	120b	1 c
		יהוה	YAHWEH	218d	2 1c
		הנה	BEHOLD	243d	
		הנה	BEHOLD	244a	A
		ל	TO	511c	1 gb
		רפא	HEAL	950d	2 a
		רפה	SINK	952a	3
		שוב	TURN BACK	997d	6 d
		שובב	BACKTURNING	1000a	
		משובה	TURNING BACK	1000b	
3	23	אכן	SURELY	38c	A
		גבעה	HILL	149a	3
		המון	CROWD	242c	3 a
		תשועה	DELIVERANCE	448b	1
		שקר	DECEPTION	1055c	1
3	24	אכל	EAT	37c	5
		בשת	SHAME	102b	2
		יגיע	TOIL	388c	2
		נעורים	YOUTH	655b	
3	25	בשת	SHAME	102a	1
		הר	MOUNTAIN	250d	11
		חטא	MISS A GOAL OR WAY	307a	2 b
		כלמה	IGNOMINY	484a	2
		כסה	COVER	492a	5
		מן	FROM	582a	5 c
		נעורים	YOUTH	655c	
		קול	VOICE	877b	3 b
		שכב	LIE DOWN	1012a	1 b
4	1	גוד	WANDER	626d	1
		ישראל	ISRAEL	975d	2a3
		שוב	TURN BACK	997d	6 d
		שקוץ	DETESTED THING	1055a	
4	2	אמת	FIRMNESS	54b	3 b
		ברך	BLESS	139c	
		הלל	BE BOASTFUL	239a	2
		חי	ALIVE	311d	1 a
		צדקה	RIGHTEOUSNESS	842b	4
		שבע	SWEAR	989b	1 a
4	3	אל	TO	39d	2
		זרע	SOW	281d	3 c
		ניר	UNTILLED GROUND	644c	
		ניר	BREAK UP	644c	
		קוץ	THORN-BUSH	881a	1
4	4	בער	BURN	129a	4
		חמה	RAGE	404c	2 c
		חמה	RAGE	*404d	2 c
		יצא	GO OUT	423c	1 g
		כבה	QUENCH	459d	
		לבב	HEART	524a	2 6d
		מול	CIRCUMCIZE	557d	
		מעלל	DEED	760b	1
		ערלה	FORESKIN	790c	
		פנה	FACE	818c	2 6c a
		רע	EVIL	948a	3
4	5	מבצר	FORTIFICATION	131c	
		מלא	FULL	*571a	
		קרא	CALL	895a	1 a
		שמע	HEAR	1034c	1 c
		שפר	HORN	1051d	
		תקע	GIVE A BLOW	1075c	2
4	6	נס	SIGNAL	651d	1 b
		עוז	TAKE REFUGE	731d	
		צפון	NORTH	861a	
		רעה	MISERY	949a	1
		שבר	BREAKING	991a	1
4	7	אריה	LION	71d	
		ישב	DWELL	443b	3
		ל	TO	512b	4 a
		נסע	SET OUT	652a	2 a
		נצה	FALL IN RUINS	663d	
		סבך	THICKET	687c	
		סך	THICKET	697c	
		עלה	GO UP	748d	3
		מקום	STANDING PLACE	880a	2 b3
		שחת	GO TO RUIN	1008b	1
		שמה	WASTE	1031c	1
4	8	זה	THIS	262a	6 f
		חגר	GIRD	291d	2
		חרון	BURNING OF ANGER	354c	
		ילל	HOWL	410b	
		ספד	WAIL	704d	1
		שק	SACK	974c	2 a
		שוב	TURN BACK	997d	6 f
4	9	אבד	PERISH	1d	2
		כהן	PRIEST	463d	4
		נביא	PROPHET	611d	2
		שמם	BE DESOLATED	1031a	2
		תמה	BE ASTOUNDED	1069b	
4	10	אדון	LORD	11c	4 a
		אהה	ALAS	13c	
		אכן	SURELY	38c	A
		נגע	REACH	619b	4
		נפש	SOUL	659d	3 b
		נשא	DECEIVE	674a	
		עד	AS FAR AS	724a	1 1a
4	11	אמר	SAY	56c	
		בת	DAUGHTER	123c	3
		ברר	PURIFY	141a	1
		דרך	WAY	203d	6 d
		זרה	SCATTER	279d	2
		לא	NOT	518d	1 ac
		עם	PEOPLE	767a	5 f
		צח	DAZZELING	850a	
		שפי	BARE HEIGHT	1046a	2
4	12	את	WITH	86a	1 db
		גם	ALSO	169c	4
		דבר	SPEAK	181b	3 d
		ל	TO	511c	1 gb
		מלא	FULL	571a	
		עתה	NOW	774a	1 a
		עתה	NOW	774a	1 a
		משפט	JUDGMENT	1048c	1 c
4	13	אוי	WOE	17a	
		נשר	EAGLE	676d	
		סוס	HORSE	692c	1
		סופה	STORM-WIND	693a	
		עלה	GO UP	748d	5
		ענן	CLOUD	778a	1 c
		קלל	BE SLIGHT	886b	2
		מרכבה	CHARIOT	939d	
		שדד	DEAL VIOLENTLY WITH	994b	
4	14	און	TROUBLE	20a	1
		מחשבה	THOUGHT	364c	2
		ישע	BE DELIVERED	446b	2
		כבס	WASH	460b	2
		לון	LODGE	533d	2
		מתי	WHEN	607d	C
		קרב	INWARD PART	899b	2 a
4	15	און	TROUBLE	20a	1
		דן	DAN	193a	3
		הר	MOUNTAIN	251a	2 b
		קול	VOICE	877a	1 f
		שמע	HEAR	1034c	1 a
4	16	זכר	REMEMBER	271a	2
		נצר	GUARD	666a	5
		נתן	GIVE	679d	1 x
		על	UPON	755c	2 5
4	17	מרחק	DISTANT PLACE	935d	
		מרה	BE REBELLIOUS	598b	2
		סביב	ROUND ABOUT	687a	1 d
		שדי	FIELD	961b	1
4	18	דרך	WAY	203d	6 d
		מר	BITTER	600c	1
		נגע	REACH	619b	4
		עד	AS FAR AS	724a	1 1a
4	19	חמה	MURMUR	242b	1
		חול	WHIRL	297a	2 b
		חרש	BE SILENT	361b	1
		יחל	WAIT	404a	
		ל	TO	*512d	5 aa
		לב	HEART	524c	2 1
		מעה	BELLY	589a	5
		קיר	WALL	885b	5
		תרועה	SHOUT OF WAR	929d	1
4	20	יריעה	CURTAIN	438c	
		על	UPON	755b	2 4b
		פתאם	SUDDENNESS	837c	
		קרא	CALL	896b	2 a
		רגע	A MOMENT	921a	BA B
		שבר	BREAKING	991a	1
		שדד	DEAL VIOLENTLY WITH	994b	
		שדד	DEAL VIOLENTLY WITH	994b	
4	21	מתי	WHEN	607d	C
		נס	STANDARD	651d	1 a
4	22	בין	DISCERN	106d	1
		בן	SON	120b	1 c
		חכם	WISE	314d	1
		יטב	DO RIGHT	406a	5 a
		סכל	FOOL	698d	
		רעע	BE EVIL	949d	2
4	23	בהו	EMPTINESS	96a	
		ראה	TO SEE	908a	8 b
		תהו	FORMLESSNESS	1062c	1
4	24	גבעה	HILL	149a	3
		הר	MOUNTAIN	250a	1 c
		קלל	BE SILENT	886d	
		רעש	SHAKE	950b	
4	25	אדם	MAN	9b	1
		נדד	RETREAT	622b	1
4	26	חרון	BURNING OF ANGER	354c	
		כרמל	GARDEN	502a	1
		פנה	FACE	818c	2 6b
4	27	כה	THUS	462a	1 a
		כלה	COMPLETE	478d	2 a
		שממה	WASTE	1031b	
4	28	אבל	MOURN	5c	1
		זה	THIS	262a	6 f

JEREMIAH

Ch	v.	Heb	Eng	Page	Sec
6	4	תקע	THRUST	1075c	1
		אוי	WOE	17a	
		מלחמה	WAR	536c	
		נטה	STRETCH OUT	640c	
		ערב	SUNSET	788a	1 c
		פנה	TURN	815b	1 d
		צהר	MIDDAY	843d	1
		צל	SHADOW	853b	1
		קדש	BE SET APART	873b	4 c
6	5	ארמון	CITADEL	74d	
		לילה	NIGHT	538d	1
		לילה	NIGHT	539a	1
		שחת	GO TO RUIN	1008b	1
6	6	כרת	CUT OFF	503d	2
		סללה	MOUND	700c	
		עצה	TREES	782a	
		עשק	OPPRESSION	799a	1
		פקד	ATTEND TO	824a	1
		צבא	GOD OF WAR	839c	4 c
		שפך	POUR OUT	1049c	1 a
6	7	בור	WELL	92c	2
		חלה	BE WEAK	317d	2
		חלי	SICKNESS	318b	
		חמס	VIOLENCE	329c	
		כן	SO	486b	2 add
		תמיד	CONTINUITY	556b	1 a
		מכה	BLOW	646d	1 c
		פנה	FACE	818d	27 a a
		קרר	BE COLD	903b	
		שד	VIOLENCE	994c	1
6	8	יסר	BE CORRECTED	416a	
		יקע	TORN AWAY	429c	
		ישב	BE INHABITED	443d	
		לא	NOT	*519c	2 b
		נפש	SOUL	661a	6 f
6	9	בצר	CUT OFF	131a	1
		גפן	VINE	172c	
		סללה	SHOOT	700d	
		עלל	GLEAN	760a	
		צבא	GOD OF WAR	839c	4 c
		שארית	REST	984d	1
		שוב	TURN BACK	999a	1 a
6	10	אזן	EAR	24a	2 a
		דבר	SPEAK	*181d	5
		חפץ	DELIGHT IN	342d	1 a
		חרפה	REPROACH	358a	3
		יכל	BE ABLE	407c	1 a
		עוד	BEAR WITNESS	730a	3
		על	UPON	757c	27 c b
		ערל	HAVING FORESKIN	790d	
6	11	בחור	YOUNG MAN	104c	
		גם	ALSO	169b	2
		זקן	OLD	278c	2 a
		יחדו	TOGETHER	403c	A
		כול	CONTAIN	465b	1
		לאה	BE WEARY	521a	
		לכד	CAPTURE	540b	2
		מלא	FULL	571a	
		סוד	COUNCIL	691c	1 a
		עולל	CHILD	760c	
		עם	WITH	767b	1 a
		שפך	POUR OUT	1049d	2 a
6	12	אחר	ANOTHER	*29c	
		יחדו	TOGETHER	403c	A
		נטה	STRETCH OUT	640d	1
		סבב	TURN AROUND	686b	2
6	13	בצע	GAIN BY VIOLENCE	130b	
		בצע	UNJUST GAIN	130c	
		גדול	GREAT	153b	7
		כהן	PRIEST	463c	4
		כל	ALL	482a	1 db
		מן	FROM	581d	5 b
		קטן	SMALL	882a	2 b2
		שקר	DECEPTION	1055c	2
6	14	בת	DAUGHTER	123c	3
		על	UPON	754b	2 1fe
		עם	PEOPLE	767a	5 f
		קלל	BE SLIGHT	886c	2
		רפא	HEAL	951a	2
		שבר	BREAKING	991a	1
		שלום	PEACE	1022d	3
		שלום	PEACE	1022d	3
6	15	בוש	BE ASHAMED	101d	2
		בוש	BE ASHAMED	102a	2
		בוש	BE ASHAMED	102a	2 c
		גם	ALSO	169d	5
		ידע	KNOW	394b	4 a
		כלם	HUMILIATE	484a	2
		כן	SO	486d	3 d
		כשל	STUMBLE	505a	1 b
		עת	TIME	773d	2
		פקד	ATTEND TO	823c	A 2
		פקדה	OVERSIGHT	824a	1 a
		תועבה	ABOMINATION	1073a	2 b
6	16	אי	WHERE	32b	1 b
		דרך	WAY	203c	6 c
		הלך	WALK	234c	23a 1a
		טוב	PLEASANT	374d	0 a
		כה	THUS	462a	1 a
		מצא	FIND	592d	1
		נתיבה	PATH	677b	2 b
		עולם	LONG DURATION	761d	1 a
		מרגוע	REST	921b	
		שאל	ASK	981d	2 a
6	17	צפה	KEEP WATCH	859c	
		קום	STAND	879a	6 a
6	18	קשב	ATTEND	904a	
		גוי	NATION	156d	1 c
		עדה	CONGREGATION	417b	3
		כן	SO	487a	3 d
6	19	ארץ	EARTH	76a	1 b
		מחשבה	THOUGHT	364b	2
		תורה	INSTRUCTION	436a	1 c
		מאס	REJECT	549c	1 b
		פרי	FRUIT	826c	3
		קשב	ATTEND	904a	
6	20	ה	THE	209a	2 b
		זבח	SACRIFICE	257c	11
		טוב	PLEASANT	373d	1 c
		ל	TO	513a	5 ad
		לבנה	FRANKINCENSE	526d	
		מה	HOW	554a	4 d
		עלה	WHOLE BURNT OF-FERING	750d	
		ערב	BE SWEET	787a	
		קנה	STALK	889c	3
		מרחק	DISTANT PLACE	935d	3
		רצון	GOODWILL	953c	2
		שבאי	SABEANS	985b	
		שבא	SHEBA	985b	
6	21	אבד	PERISH	1c	1
		יחדו	TOGETHER	403c	A
		כן	SO	486d	3 d
		כשל	STUMBLE	505c	1
		מכשול	STUMBLING	506b	2 b
		רע	FRIEND	946a	2
		שכן	NEIGHBOUR	1015c	2
6	22	אציל	SIDE	69c	1
		ירכה	EXTREME PARTS	438b	2
		עור	ROUSE ONESELF	735a	
		צפון	NORTH	861a	
6	23	בת	DAUGHTER	123c	3
		חמה	ROAR	242b	3
		חזק	BE FIRM	305a	6 a
		אכזרי	CRUEL	470a	
		כידון	JAVELIN	475d	
		ערך	ARRANGE	789c	1 d
		קשת	BOW	906a	1 b
		רחם	LOVE	933d	2
		רכב	RIDE	938d	2
6	24	חיל	A WRITHING	297d	2
		חזק	BE FIRM	305a	6 a
		ילד	BEAR	408c	1 b
		רפה	SINK	951d	2
		שמע	REPORT	1035a	
6	25	מגור	FEAR	159a	
		דרך	WAY	202d	1
		סביב	ROUND ABOUT	687a	1 d
		שדה	FIELD	961c	1 f
6	26	אבל	MOURNING	5c	
		אפר	ASHES	68a	
		בת	DAUGHTER	123c	3
		חגר	GIRD	291d	2
		יחיד	ONLY ONE	402d	1
		תמרור	BITTERNESS	601b	
		מספד	WAILING	704d	2
		פלש	ROLL IN	814b	
		פתאם	SUDDENNESS	837c	
		שק	SACK	974c	2 a
		שדד	DEAL VIOLENTLY WITH	994b	
6	27	בחן	TRY	103c	2 b
		בחן	ASSAYER	103d	
		מבצר	FORTIFICATION	131c	
		דרך	WAY	203c	6 a
6	28	ברזל	IRON	137d	3
		הלך	WALK	232a	1 1d 5k
		נחשת	COPPER	639a	3
		סור	TURN ASIDE	694a	4
		סרר	BE STUBBORN	710d	
		סר	STUBBORN	711a	
		רכיל	SLANDER	940c	
		שחת	GO TO RUIN	1008c	2
6	29	אש	FIRE	77c	3
		אשה	FIRE	77d	
		חרר	BE HOT	359c	1
		כסף	SILVER	*494a	1
		נחר	NOSTRIL	637d	
		מפח	BELLOWS	656b	
		נתק	TEAR AWAY	683c	3
		עפרת	LEAD	780c	
		צרף	SMELT	864b	1
		רע	EVIL	948c	0 b
		שוא	EMPTINESS	996b	1
		תמם	BE FINISHED	1070c	4
		חרר	ADDENDA ET COR-RIGENDA	1123d	
6	30	כסף	SILVER	494a	1
		מאס	REJECT	549c	2
		מאס	REJECT	549c	1 b
7	1	את	WITH	86d	4
		דבר	WORD	182c	1 2a
7	2	היכל	TEMPLE	*228c	2 b
		שחה	BOW DOWN	1005c	2 c
		שער	GATE	1045b	3 b
7	3	דרך	WAY	203c	6 a
		יטב	MAKE GOOD	406a	4
		צבא	GOD OF WAR	839c	4 b
		שכן	SETTLE DOWN	1015c	2
7	4	בטח	TRUST	105a	1 5c
		דבר	WORD	183b	3 1
		ה	THE	208b	1 ha
		היכל	TEMPLE	228c	2 b
		הם	THEY	241c	6 a
		ל	TO	516a	5 ic
7	5	דרך	WAY	203c	6 a
		יטב	MAKE GOOD	406a	4
		כי אם	FOR IF	474d	1 b
		רע	FRIEND	946a	2
		משפט	JUDGMENT	1048c	1 f
7	6	אלמנה	WIDOW	48b	
		גר	SOJOURNER	158b	2
		דם	BLOOD	196d	2 d
		הלך	WALK	235a	23d 2
		טוב	A GOOD THING	375a	1
		יתום	ORPHAN	450c	
		נקי	CLEAN	667c	1
		עשק	OPPRESS	798d	1
		רע	EVIL	948d	2
7	7	מן	FROM	583d	9 b2
		עולם	LONG DURATION	763a	2 m
		שכן	SETTLE DOWN	1015c	2
7	8	בטח	TRUST	*105b	1 5c
		בלת	NOT	116d	4 a
		דבר	WORD	183b	3 1
		ה	THE	208b	1 ha
		יעל	PROFIT	418d	
		ל	TO	516a	5 ic
7	9	בעל	BAAL	*127d	2 1
		בעל	BAAL	127d	2 2
		גנב	STEAL	170c	
		ה	INTERROG PART	209d	1 b
		הלך	WALK	232d	1 4a
		ידע	KNOW	394a	2
		נאף	COMMIT ADUL-TERY	610c	1 a
		רצח	MURDER	953d	
		שבע	SWEAR	989b	1 a
7	10	נצל	BE DELIVERED	664c	2
		עמד	STAND	763d	1 d
		מען	PURPOSE	775b	1 c
		קרא	CALL	896b	6 d4
		שם	NAME	1028b	3
		תועבה	ABOMINATION	1072d	1 b
7	11	גם	ALSO	169c	4
		מערה	CAVE	792c	
		פריץ	VIOLENT ONE	829d	
		קרא	CALL	896b	6 d4
7	12	פנה	FACE	818c	26c a
		ראשון	FIRST	911d	3 a1
		רעה	MISERY	949b	3
		שכן	SETTLE DOWN	1015b	1
		שלו	SHILOH	1017d	1
7	13	דבר	SPEAK	180d	1
		יען	ON ACCOUNT OF	774d	1
		שכם	START EARLY	1014d	
		שמע	HEAR	1034a	1 j
7	14	בטח	TRUST	105a	1 3c
		קרא	CALL	896b	6 d4
		שלו	SHILOH	1017d	
7	15	אפרים	EPHRAIM	68c	4
		זרע	SOWING	283a	4 g
		פנה	FACE	819a	28a
		שלך	THROW	1021b	2 b
7	16	אין	NOT	34b	2 c
		בעד	ON BEHALF OF	126c	2
		נשא	LIFT	670d	1 b8
		פגע	MEET	803b	4
		תפלה	PRAYER	813c	1 b
		רנה	RINGING CRY	943c	1
7	17	חוץ	THE OUTSIDE	300a	2 a
		מה	WHAT	552d	1
		ראה	TO SEE	907b	5 a
7	18	בער	BURN	129b	1
		בצק	DOUGH	130d	
		כון	CAKE	468a	
		כעס	VEX	495a	2
		לוש	KNEAD	534c	
		לקט	GATHER UP	544d	1
		מלכת	QUEEN	573d	
		נסך	POUR OUT	650d	
		נסך	DRINK-OFFERING	651a	1
		מען	PURPOSE	775b	1 c
		מען	PURPOSE	775c	2 1
7	19	את	MARK OF THE AC-CUSATIVE	85a	1 a
		את	MARK OF THE AC-CUSATIVE	85a	1 a
		בשת	SHAME	102a	1
		כעס	VEX	495a	2
		מען	PURPOSE	775c	2 1
7	20	אדמה	GROUND	9c	2
		אדון	LORD	11c	4 c
		בער	BURN	129a	4
		חמה	RAGE	*405a	2 c
		כבה	BE QUENCHED	459c	
		נתך	POUR FORTH	677d	
7	21	בשר	FLESH	142c	1
		זבח	SACRIFICE	257c	11
		יסף	ADD	414d	
		צבא	GOD OF WAR	839c	4 b
7	22	דבר	SPEAK	181b	3 d
		זבח	SACRIFICE	257c	11
		יצא	CASUE TO GO	424c	1 a
		צוה	COMMAND	845d	1 e
		עלדבר	ADDENDA ET COR-RIGENDA	1122a	
7	23	דבר	WORD	182d	1 2a

Ch v.	Heb	Eng	Page	Sec
	דרך	WAY	203c	6 b
	יטב	BE WELL	405c	3
	כיאם	BUT	475a	2 b
	קול	VOICE	877b	3 b
7 24	אחור	HINDER SIDE	30c	C a
	מועצה	PLAN	420b	
	ל	TO	511c	1 h
	לב	HEART	525b	26d
	נטה	INCLINE	641a	3 e
	פנה	FACE	816b	1 c
	רע	EVIL	948c	0 c
	ששון	REJOICING	965b	
	שרירות	STUBBORNNESS	1057b	
7 25	יום	DAY	400b	7 e1
	יום	DAY	401b	7 k
	יצא	GO OUT	422d	1 a
	מן	FROM	583d	9 b2
	נביא	PROPHET	611d	4
	עבד	SLAVE	714b	4
	שכם	START EARLY	1014d	
	שלח	SEND	1018c	2 a
7 26	ערף	BACK OF NECK	791c	2
	קשה	BE SEVERE	904c	3 a
	רעע	BE EVIL	949d	2
	שמע	HEAR	*1034a	1 k
7 28	אבד	PERISH	1d	2
	אמונה	FIRMNESS	53c	3 a
	גוי	NATION	156d	1 b
	ה	THE	208b	1 ha
	יהוה	YAHWEH	218d	2 1e
	מוסר	DISCIPLINE	416c	2 a
	כרת	BE CUT OFF	504b	4
	פה	MOUTH	805a	2 a
7 29	גזז	SHEAR	159c	
	דור	GENERATION	190a	3
	מאס	REJECT	549c	1 a
	נזר	CONSECRATION	634b	3 b
	נזר	NAZIRITESHIP	634b	2
	נטש	FORSAKE	643d	2
	נשא	LIFT	670d	1 b 6
	עברה	OVERFLOW	720c	3 b
	קינה	ELEGY	884b	
	שלך	THROW	1021a	1 c
	שפי	BARE HEIGHT	1046a	2
7 30	בן	SON	121a	1 jd
	טמא	BE UNCLEAN	379c	3
	יהודה	JUDAH	397b	13
	קרא	CALL	896c	6 d4
	קרא	CALL	896b	6 d4
	רע	EVIL	948c	0 b
	שום	TO PLACE	964b	4 c
	שקוץ	DETESTED THING	1055a	
7 31	במה	HIGH PLACE	119d	3 e
	בנה	BUILD	124c	1 ai
	הנם	HINNOM	245a	
	לב	HEART	524d	2 3d
	שרף	BURN	977a	2 b2
	תפת	TOPHETH	1075a	
7 32	אין	NOT	35a	6 da
	אמר	SAY	56d	
	בוא	COME	98c	2
	גיא	VALLEY	161b	
	הנם	HINNOM	245a	
	הרגה	SLAUGHTER	247c	
	יום	DAY	400a	7 e
	כיאם	BUT	475a	2 b
	כן	SO	486d	3 d
	מקום	STANDING PLACE	880b	5 a
	תפת	TOPHETH	1075a	
	תפת	TOPHETH	1075a	
7 33	מאכל	FOOD	38b	
	בהמה	BEAST	97a	3
	חרד	TREMBLE	353c	
	נבלה	CARCASS	615c	1 a
7 34	חוץ	THE OUTSIDE	300a	2 a
	חרבה	WASTE	352b	2
	חתן	DAUGHTER:S HUSBAND	368d	2
	כלה	BRIDE	483c	2 a
	קול	VOICE	876d	1 a
	שמחה	JOY	970d	1
	שבת	CEASE	992a	1
8 1	יצא	BRING OUT	425a	4 a
	כהן	PRIEST	463d	4
	נביא	PROPHET	611d	2
8 2	אהב	LOVE	13a	2
	אסף	GATHER	62d	1 c
	דמן	DUNG	199b	
	דרש	SEEK	205b	3 b
	הלך	WALK	235a	2 3d 2
	ירח	MOON	437a	
	עבד	WORK	713b	4 b
	צבא	HOST	839b	1 c
	קבר	BURY	868c	
	שמי	HEAVENS	1029d	1 a
	שמש	SUN	1039b	3
8 3	בחר	CHOOSE	104b	B
	ל	TO	514a	5 e
	מן	THAN	582c	6 a
	נאם	UTTERANCE	610b	2
	נדח	THRUST	623b	2
	צבא	GOD OF WAR	839c	4 c
	רע	EVIL	948c	0 b
	שאר	REMAIN	984a	1
	שארית	REST	984d	1
8 4	נפל	FALL	656d	1
	קום	STAND	877d	1 a
	שוב	TURN BACK	997d	6 a
8 5	חזק	BE FIRM	305a	6 a
	מדוע	WHEREFORE	396c	
	מאן	REFUSE	549b	
	נצח	BE ENDURING	663d	
	עם	PEOPLE	766c	2 a
	תרמית	DECEITFULNESS	941c	
	שוב	TURN BACK	998c	4
	משובה	TURNING BACK	1000b	
	משובה	TURNING BACK	1000b	
8 6	כן	RIGHT	467b	1
	כל	ALL	482a	1 db
	נחם	BE SORRY	637a	2
	סוס	HORSE	692d	2
	מרוצה	RUNNING	930d	2
	רעה	MISERY	949b	1
	שוב	TURN BACK	997c	5 d
	שוט	GO ABOUT	1002a	
	שטף	OVERFLOW	1009b	1
8 7	חסידה	STORK	339d	2
	ידע	KNOW	*394a	2
	מועד	APPOINTED TIME	417c	1 a
	סוס	SWALLOW	692d	2
	עגור	CRANE	723a	
	שמי	HEAVENS	1029d	1 a
	שמר	KEEP	1036d	1 d
	משפט	JUDGMENT	1048d	3
	תר	TURTLE-DOVE	1076a	
8 8	איך	HOW	32c	1
	איכה	IN WHAT MANNER	32d	1
	אכן	SURELY	38c	A
	את	WITH	86c	3 a
	חכם	WISE	314d	5
	תורה	INSTRUCTION	435d	1 b
	ספר	ENUMERATOR	708c	2
	עט	STYLUS	741d	2
	שקר	DECEPTION	1055c	2
	שקר	DECEPTION	1055c	2
8 9	בוש	BE ASHAMED	102a	2 d
	בוש	BE ASHAMED	102a	2
	חכם	WISE	314d	5
	חכמה	WISDOM	315c	4
	חתת	BE SHATTERED	369b	2 a
	לכד	CAPTURE	540b	2
	מאס	REJECT	549c	1 b
	מה	WHAT	552d	1 ae
8 10	אחר	ANOTHER	*29c	
	בצע	GAIN BY VIOLENCE	130b	
	בצע	UNJUST GAIN	130c	
	גדול	GREAT	153b	7
	ירש	TAKE POSSESSION	439c	1 a
	כהן	PRIEST	463c	4
	כל	ALL	482a	1 db
	כן	SO	486d	3 d
	נביא	PROPHET	611d	2
	קטן	SMALL	882b	2
	שקר	DECEPTION	1055c	2
8 11	בת	DAUGHTER	123c	3
	עבד	WORK	713b	5
	על	UPON	754d	2 1f e
	קלל	BE SLIGHT	886c	1
	רפא	HEAL	951a	2
	שבר	BREAKING	991a	1
8 12	בוש	BE ASHAMED	101d	1
	בוש	BE ASHAMED	102a	2 d
	בוש	BE ASHAMED	102a	2
	גם	ALSO	169d	5
	כלם	BE HUMILIATED	483d	1
	כשל	STUMBLE	505d	J b
	נפל	FALL	657b	2 b
	עת	TIME	773d	2 c
	פקדה	OVERSIGHT	824a	1 a
	קשר	CONSPIRACY	905c	2
	תועבה	ABOMINATION	1073a	2 b
8 13	אסף	GATHER	62c	4
	גפן	VINE	172c	
	גבל	SINK	615c	2
	סוף	CEASE	692d	2
	עבר	PASS OVER	718b	6 f
	עלה	LEAF	750a	2
	ענב	GRAPE	772a	
	תאנה	FIG-TREE	1061a	1
	תאנה	FIG	1061a	2
8 14	מבצר	FORTIFICATION	131c	
	דמם	BE STILL	198d	2
	דמם	BE SILENT	199a	1
	חטא	MISS A GOAL OR WAY	307a	2 b
	מה	HOW	554b	4 f
	מי	WATER	565d	4 a
	שקה	GIVE TO DRINK	1052c	2
	בעתה	TERROR	130a	
8 15	טוב	A GOOD THING	375a	1
	נגש	BE SICK	*633b	
	קוה	WAIT FOR	875d	1
	מרפא	HEALING	951b	1
8 16	אביר	MIGHTY	7d	3
	אכל	EAT	37c	4
	דן	DAN	193a	3
	מלא	THAT WHICH FILLS	571b	3
	מן	OUT OF	580a	2 eb
	נחרת	A SNORTING	637d	
	מצהלה	NEIGHING	843d	2
	קול	VOICE	877a	1 e
	ראש	HEAD	911b	8
	רעש	SHAKE	950b	
8 17	גם	YEA	169c	3
	הנה	BEHOLD	244b	B b
	לחש	CHARMING	538a	1
	נחש	SERPENT	638a	1 a
	נשך	BITE	675a	
8 18	מבליגיה	SOURCE OF BRIGHTENING	114d	
	דוי	FAINT	188d	
	יגון	GRIEF	387b	
	על	UPON	753c	2 1d
	על	UPON	754c	2 1f e
8 19	בת	DAUGHTER	123c	3
	הבל	VAPOUR	211a	2
	מדוע	WHEREFORE	396c	
	כעם	VEX	495a	2
	נכר	FOREIGNNESS	648d	3
	קול	VOICE	876d	1 a
	מרחוק	DISTANT PLACE	935d	
	שועה	CRY FOR HELP	1003a	
8 20	ישע	BE DELIVERED	446b	1
	כלה	BE FINISHED	477c	1 a
	קיץ	SUMMER	884d	1
	קציר	HARVESTING	894d	3
8 21	בת	DAUGHTER	123c	3
	חזק	BE FIRM	305a	6 a
	קדר	BE DARK	871a	
	שבר	BREAKING	991a	1
	שבר	BREAK	991a	1
	שמה	APPALMENT	1031c	2
8 22	ארוכה	HEALING	74a	A
	בת	DAUGHTER	123c	3
	מדוע	WHEREFORE	396c	
	עלה	GO UP	749a	6
	צרי	BALM	863b	
	רפא	HEAL	950d	2 a
8 23	בכה	WEEP	113c	4
	בת	DAUGHTER	123c	3
	דמעה	TEARS	199c	
	חיים	LIFE	313a	1
	נתן	GIVE	678d	1 f
	סוס	HORSE	692c	1
	עין	EYE	744b	1 h
	מקור	SPRING	881b	2
9 1	ארח	WANDER	72d	2
	את	WITH	86c	4 a
	בגד	ACT TREACHEROUSLY	93d	D
	מדבר	WILDERNESS	184d	2
	מלון	INN	533d	
	נתן	GIVE	678d	1 f
	עזב	LEAVE	737a	1 a
	עצרה	ASSEMBLY	784a	2
9 2	אמונה	FIRMNESS	53c	3 a
	את	MARK OF THE ACCUSATIVE	85a	1 a
	גבר	BE STRONG	149d	2 a
	דרך	TREAD	202b	2
	יצא	GO OUT	423d	2 b
	ל	TO	516c	5 jb
	לשון	TONGUE	546b	1 b
	מן	FROM	582b	5 d1
	נאף	COMMIT ADULTERY	610d	1 a
9 3	קשת	BOW	906c	1 d
	שקר	DECEPTION	1055c	2
	בטח	TRUST	105a	14 b
	הלך	WALK	232a	1 1d 5k
	רכיל	SLANDER	940c	
	רע	FRIEND	946a	1
	שמר	KEEP	1037b	1
9 4	אמת	FIRMNESS	54b	4 a
	דבר	SPEAK	181a	2
	לאה	BE WEARY	521a	
	למד	LEARN	540d	
	לשון	TONGUE	546b	1 b
	עוה	COMMIT INIQUITY	731c	
	תלל	MOCK	1068b	
9 5	מאן	REFUSE	549b	
	מרמה	DECEIT	941b	
9 6	איך	HOW	32c	1
	בחן	TRY	103c	2 b
	בת	DAUGHTER	123c	3
	צבא	GOD OF WAR	839c	4 c
	צרף	SMELT	864b	2
9 7	ארב	AMBUSCADE	70c	A
	דבר	SPEAK	181b	3 d
	לשון	TONGUE	*546b	1 b
	לשון	TONGUE	546c	1 b
	קרב	INWARD PART	899c	2 a
	מרמה	DECEIT	941b	
	רע	FRIEND	946a	2
	שום	TO PLACE	964a	4 a
	שחט	SLAUGHTER	1006b	4
	שלום	PEACE	1023a	5 a
9 8	גוי	NATION	156d	1 b
	זה	THIS	*262a	6 ca
	חץ	ARROW	346c	2
	נקם	AVENGE	668b	
	פקד	ATTEND TO	823c	A 2
	בלי	WEARING OUT	115d	C b
9 9	מדבר	WILDERNESS	184d	1
	הלך	WALK	232a	12

Ch v.	Heb	Eng	Page	Sec
	הר	MOUNTAIN	250a	1 c
	יצת	BE KINDLED	428b	
	מן	FROM	582a	5 b
	נדד	RETREAT	622b	1
	נהי	WAILING	624c	
	נוה	PASTURE	627d	1
	נצה	FALL IN RUINS	663d	
	נשא	LIFT	670d	1 b 6
	קול	VOICE	877a	1 e
	מקנה	CATTLE	889b	1
9 10	בכי	WEEPING	113d	
	בלי	WEARING OUT	115d	C b
	ישב	DWELL	443b	3
	נתן	GIVE	681a	3 b
	מעון	REFUGE	732d	1
	תן	JACKAL	1072b	
9 11	אבד	PERISH	1d	
	בין	DISCERN	106d	2 b
	בלי	WEARING OUT	115d	C b
	זה	THIS	260c	1 a
	חכם	WISE	314d	5
	יצת	BE KINDLED	428b	
	מה	HOW	554b	4 f
	מי	WHO	567b	G
	נצה	FALL IN RUINS	663d	
	פה	MOUTH	805b	2 c
9 12	הלך	WALK	234c	2 3a 1d
	תורה	INSTRUCTION	435d	1 c
	על	UPON	754b	2 If b
	פנה	FACE	817c	2 4b g
9 13	בעל	BAAL	127d	2 3
	לב	HEART	525b	2 6d
	למד	LEARN	540d	
	שרירות	STUBBORNNESS	1057b	
9 14	אכל	EAT	37d	1
	כן	SO	487a	3 d
	לענה	WORMWOOD	542a	
	מי	WATER	565d	4 a
	שקה	GIVE TO DRINK	1052c	2
9 15	ידע	KNOW	394a	2
	כלה	FINISH	478c	2 c2
	עד	AS FAR AS	724b	1 2a b
	פוץ	BE DISPERSED	807a	1 a
9 16	בין	DISCERN	107a	1 a
	חכם	WISE	314d	1
	פנה	FACE	818c	2 6c a
	צבא	GOD OF WAR	839c	4 c
	קונן	CHANT	884b	
9 17	בכי	WEEPING	*113d	
	דמעה	TEARS	199c	
	ירד	GO DOWN	433c	3 c
	מהר	HASTEN	555a	2
	נהי	WAILING	624c	
	נזל	FLOW	633d	1
	נשא	LIFT	670d	1 b 6
	עפעף	EYELID	733d	
9 18	איך	HOW	32c	2
	נהי	WAILING	624d	
	עזב	LEAVE	737b	2 a1
	קול	VOICE	876d	1 a
	שדד	DEAL VIOLENTLY WITH	994b	
9 19	שלך	THROW	1021b	1 e
	אזן	EAR	24a	2 a
	אשה	WOMAN	61b	4
	למד	LEARN	540d	
	נהי	WAILING	624d	
	קינה	ELEGY	884b	
	רעות	FELLOW	946c	
9 20	ארמון	CITADEL	74d	
	בחור	YOUNG MAN	104c	
	חוץ	THE OUTSIDE	300a	2 a
	חלון	WINDOW	319d	
	כרת	CUT OFF	504c	2 b
	עולל	CHILD	760c	
	רחוב	PLAZA	932b	
9 21	אחר	BEHIND	30b	4 aa
	אסף	GATHER	63a	1
	דמן	DUNG	199b	
	כה	THUS	462a	1
	נבלה	CARCASS	615c	1 a
	נפל	FALL	657b	2 a
	עמיר	SWATH	771c	
	קצר	HARVEST	894b	
	קצר	HARVEST	894c	
9 22	גבורה	MIGHT	150b	2
	הלל	BE BOASTFUL	239a	1
	חכם	WISE	314d	3
	חכמה	WISDOM	315c	3
	עשר	RICHES	799b	
	עשיר	RICH	799c	
	שדה	FIELD	961c	1 f
9 23	יהוה	YAHWEH	219b	2 2c
	הלל	BE BOASTFUL	239a	1
	הלל	BE BOASTFUL	239a	2
	חסד	GOODNESS	339d	2 2
	חפץ	DELIGHT IN	342d	2 a
	כי אם	BUT	475a	2 b
	צדקה	RIGHTEOUSNESS	842b	2
	שכל	BE PRUDENT	968b	3
9 24	בוא	COME	98c	2
	מול	CIRCUMCIZE	557d	
	ערלה	FORESKIN	790c	
	פקד	ATTEND TO	823c	A 3
9 25	לב	HEART	525b	2 6d
	עמון	AMMON	770a	
	ערל	HAVING FORESKIN	790c	
	ערל	HAVING FORESKIN	790d	
	פאה	CORNER	802b	1
	קצץ	CUT OFF	893c	
10 1	דבר	SPEAK	181d	5
	על	UPON	757c	2 7c b
10 2	אות	SIGN	17a	8
	אל	TO	40a	3 c
	דרך	WAY	204a	6 d
	הם	THEY	241d	8 a
	חתת	BE SHATTERED	369b	2 b
	למד	LEARN	540d	
	שמי	HEAVENS	1029d	1 a
10 3	הבל	VAPOUR	210d	2
	חקה	SOMETHING PRESCRIBED	350a	2 b
	חרש	GRAVER	360d	1 b
	יער	WOOD	420c	A
	כרת	CUT OFF	503d	1
	מעצד	AXE	781b	
	מעשה	DEED	796a	2 a3
10 4	זהב	GOLD	263c	1
	חזק	BE FIRM	304c	1 c
	יפה	BEAUTIFY	421b	
	כסף	SILVER	494b	7
	כסף	SILVER	494c	9
	מקבת	HAMMER	666c	
	מסמר	NAIL	702d	
	פוק	REEL	807c	1
10 5	את	WITH	85c	
	את	WITH	86c	3 a
	הלך	WALK	*235b	1
	יוב	DO GOOD TO	405a	2
	ירא	FEAR	431b	1 c
	נשא	LIFT	671a	2 a
	נשא	LIFT	671d	3
	צעד	STEP	857c	
	מקשה	FIELD OF CUCUMBERS	903d	
	רעע	BE EVIL	949c	1
	תמר	PALM-TREE	1071c	
10 6	אין	NOT	35b	6 dg
	גבורה	MIGHT	150c	3
	גדול	GREAT	153b	6 c
	גדול	GREAT	153b	6 c
	חלק	PORTION	324b	3 b
	מן	FROM	581b	3 be
10 7	אין	NOT	35b	6 dg
	חכם	WISE	314a	1
	יאה	BEFIT	383b	
	ירא	FEAR	431c	3 b
	מי	WHO	567a	F c
	מלך	KING	573b	3
	מלכות	ROYAL POWER	574d	1
	מן	FROM	581b	3 be
10 8	בער	BE BRUTISH	129c	
	הבל	VAPOUR	211a	2
	מוסר	DISCIPLINE	416c	1 b
	כסל	BE STUPID	492d	
	עץ	TREE	782a	2 f
	אחר	ADDENDA ET CORRIGENDA	1120a	
10 9	אופז	UPHAZ	20c	
	אחור	HINDER SIDE	30c	D
	ארגמן	PURPLE THREAD	71b	2
	בוא	COME	99d	B
	זהב	GOLD	262c	1
	זהב	GOLD	263b	7
	חכם	WISE	314a	1
	חרש	GRAVER	360d	1 a
	מעשה	DEED	796a	2 a3
	מעשה	DEED	796a	2 a3
	רקע	BEAT	956a	
	תכלת	VIOLET THREAD	1067b	2
	תרשיש	TARSHISH	1077a	1
	אופז	ADDENDA ET CORRIGENDA	1119d	
	אופז	ADDENDA ET CORRIGENDA	1119d	
10 10	אלהים	GOD	44a	4
	אלהים	GOD	44b	4 a
	אלהים	GOD	44b	4 a
	אמת	FIRMNESS	54c	5
	זעם	INDIGNATION	276d	
	חי	ALIVE	311d	1 a
	כל	SUSTAIN	465b	2
	מלך	KING	573b	5 a
	מלך	KING	573b	3
	מן	OUT OF	580a	2 b
	עולם	LONG DURATION	762c	2 c
	קצף	WRATH	893c	1
	רעש	SHAKE	950b	
10 11	אבד	PERISH	1078b	
	אלה	THESE	1080c	
	אלה	GOD	1080c	
	אמר	SAY	1081b	1
	ארק	EARTH	1083a	
	ארע	EARTH	1083a	
	ארע	EARTH	1083a	
	די	WHO	1087d	1 a
	דנה	THIS	1089a	C
	לא	NOT	1098b	
	מן	FROM	1101a	1 c
	עבד	MAKE	1104d	1
	שמין	HEAVENS	1116a	1
	שמין	HEAVENS	1116a	1
10 12	תחות	UNDER	1117d	
	תבונה	UNDERSTANDING	108b	1
	חכמה	WISDOM	315c	5 a
	תבל	WORLD	385d	
	כון	ESTABLISH	466a	1 a
	כח	STRENGTH	470d	3
	נטה	SPREAD OUT	640a	2
10 13	אוצר	TREASURE	70a	3 d
	ברק	LIGHTNING	140c	1
	המון	SOUND	242c	1
	יצא	BRING OUT	425b	5
	מטר	RAIN	564d	
	מי	WATER	565c	1 f
	נתן	GIVE	679d	1 x
	קול	VOICE	877a	2 a
	רוח	BREATH	924d	2 a
	בער	ADDENDA ET CORRIGENDA	*1121c	
10 14	אדם	MAN	9b	2
	בוש	BE ASHAMED	102a	2
	בוש	BE ASHAMED	102a	2 d
	בער	BE BRUTISH	129c	
	דעת	WISDOM	395d	2 a
	לא	NOT	519b	1 bb
	מן	FROM	583b	7 ba
	נסך	MOLTEN IMAGE	651a	2
	פסל	IDOL	820d	
	רוח	BREATH	924c	1 a
	שקר	DECEPTION	1055c	1
	בער	ADDENDA ET CORRIGENDA	1121c	
10 15	אבד	PERISH	1c	1
	הבל	VAPOUR	210d	2
	עת	TIME	773d	2 c
	מעשה	DEED	796a	2 a3
	פקדה	OVERSIGHT	824a	1 a
	תעתעים	MOCKERY	1074a	
10 16	אלה	THESE	41d	D
	יצר	FORM	427d	2 a
	כל	ALL	482d	2 bb
	לא	NOT	519b	1 bb
	נחלה	PROPERTY	635b	1 e
	צבא	GOD OF WAR	839c	4 b
	שבט	TRIBE	987b	2
	שם	NAME	1028c	3
10 17	אסף	GATHER	62c	4
	ישב	DWELL	443b	3
	כנעה	BUNDLE	488c	
	מצור	SIEGE	849a	1
10 18	מצא	FIND	593a	1 a
	צרר	BIND	864d	B
	קלע	SLING	887c	
10 19	אוי	WOE	17a	
	אנכי	I	59c	
	חלה	BE WEAK	317a	2
	חלה	BE WEAK	318a	2
	חלי	SICKNESS	318b	
	מכה	BLOW	647a	1 c
	על	UPON	754b	2 If b
	שבר	BREAKING	991a	1
10 20	יצא	GO OUT	422d	1 b
	יצא	GO OUT	423d	2 a
	יריעה	CURTAIN	438c	
	מיתר	CORD	452d	
	נטה	SPREAD OUT	640a	2
	נתק	TEAR AWAY	683c	2
	עוד	STILL	729a	1 ab
	קום	STAND	878d	2 b
	שדד	DEAL VIOLENTLY WITH	994b	
10 21	בער	BE BRUTISH	129c	
	דרש	SEEK	205b	3 a
	כן	SO	487b	3 f
	פוץ	BE DISPERSED	807a	1
	מרעית	PASTURING	945c	3
	שכל	BE PRUDENT	968b	6
10 22	מעון	REFUGE	732d	1
	צפון	NORTH	861a	2
	קול	VOICE	877a	1 f
	רעש	SHAKING	950c	1
	שמועה	REPORT	1035b	1
	תן	JACKAL	1072b	
10 23	דרך	WAY	203b	5
	כון	ESTABLISH	466c	1
	ל	TO	513b	5 ba
10 24	צעד	STEP	857d	2
	אך	HOWBEIT	36c	2 a
	יסר	DISCIPLINE	416b	2 a
	ל	TO	*516c	5 jb
	מעט	BE SMALL	589a	A
10 25	אכל	EAT	37c	1
	אל	TO	41a	B
	חמה	RAGE	*405a	2 c
	כלה	FINISH	478c	2 c1
	נוה	HABITATION	627c	2
	יעקב	JACOB	785a	2
	קרא	CALL	845b	2 c
	שמם	BE DESOLATED	1031b	1
	פך	POUR OUT	1049d	2 a
11 1	את	WITH	86d	4 c
11 2	אל	TO	41b	
	ברית	COVENANT	136d	2 2c
	דבר	WORD	183a	2 2
	על	UPON	757c	2 7c b
11 3	אר	CURSE	76d	
	ברית	COVENANT	136d	2 2c

Ch v.	Heb	Eng	Page	Sec
	דבר	WORD	183a	2 2
11 4	שמע	HEAR	1034a	1 n
	אנכי	I	59c	
	ברית	COVENANT	136d	2 2c
	ברזל	IRON	137c	3
	דבר	WORD	183a	2 2
	יצא	CAUSE TO GO	424c	1 a
	כור	FURNACE	468d	
11 5	אמן	VERILY	53b	
	ברית	COVENANT	136d	2 2c
	דבר	WORD	183a	2 2
	דבש	HONEY	185b	
	זוב	FLOW	264d	2
	חלב	MILK	316c	A 4
	יום	DAY	400d	7 h
	מען	PURPOSE	775b	1 c
	שבע	SWEAR	989c	2
	שבועה	OATH	990a	1 a
11 6	ברית	COVENANT	136d	2 2c
	דבר	WORD	183a	2 2
11 7	ברית	COVENANT	136d	2 2c
	דבר	WORD	183a	2 2
	עוד	BEAR WITNESS	730a	3
	שכם	START EARLY	1014d	
11 8	ברית	COVENANT	136d	2 2c
	דבר	WORD	183a	2 2
	לב	HEART	525b	2 6d
	רע	EVIL	948c	0 c
	שרירות	STUBBORNNESS	1057b	
11 9	קשר	CONSPIRACY	905c	
11 10	ברית	COVENANT	137a	3 1
	ברית	COVENANT	137b	3 3
	הלך	WALK	235a	2 3d 2
	כרת	CUT	503d	4
	מאן	REFUSE	549b	
	עבד	WORK	713b	4 b
	עון	INIQUITY	730d	
	על	UPON	757c	2 7c ab
	פרר	BREAK	830b	1 b
	שוב	TURN BACK	997c	5 d
	שוב	TURN BACK	997c	5 d
11 11	זעק	CRY	277b	2 a
	יכל	BE ABLE	407c	1 a
	יצא	GO OUT	423a	1 d
11 12	אלהים	GOD	43d	3
	בעד	ON BEHALF OF	*126d	2
	הלך	WALK	233d	1 5b
	זעק	CRY	277b	2 b
	ישע	DELIVER	446c	1
11 13	בשת	SHAME	102b	2
	בעל	BAAL	127d	2 2
	בעל	BAAL	*127d	2 1
	בעל	BAAL	127d	2 1
	מזבח	ALTAR	258d	8
	מספר	NUMBER	709a	1 b
	שום	TO PLACE	964b	4 c
11 14	בעד	ON BEHALF OF	126c	2
	בעד	ON BEHALF OF	126d	2
	נשא	LIFT	670d	1 b 8
	עת	TIME	773c	1 c
	תפלה	PRAYER	813c	1 b
	רנה	RINGING CRY	943c	1
	שכן	NEIGHBOUR	1015c	2
	שמע	HEAR	1034b	2 h
11 15	אז	THEN	23a	1 b
	בשר	FLESH	142c	1 a
	מזמה	PURPOSE	273d	3 b
	ידיד	BELOVED	391d	4
	עבר	PASS OVER	718c	6 f
	עבר	PASS OVER	719a	4
	עלז	EXULT	759c	
	קדש	APARTNESS	872b	6
	מזמה	ADDENDA ET CORRIGENDA	1122d	
11 16	דליות	BRANCH	194d	
	חמלה	TUMULT	242d	
	זית	OLIVE TREE	268c	1
	יפה	BEAUTIFUL	421c	
	יצת	KINDLE	428c	
	רענן	LUXURIANT	947d	
	רעע	BREAK	949d	2
	תאר	FORM	1061c	
11 17	בעל	BAAL	*127d	2 1
	בעל	BAAL	127d	2 2
	דבר	SPEAK	181d	5
	כעס	VEX	495a	2
	ל	TO	515d	5 ia
	נטע	PLANT	642b	5 d
	על	UPON	756d	2 7a c
	רעה	MISERY	949b	3
11 18	ידע	ANSWER	395a	
	מעלל	DEED	760b	1
11 19	אלוף	TAME	48d	1
	ב	IN	89c	3 1a
	זכר	REMEMBER	270d	2
	חי	ALIVE	312a	1 b
	חשב	THINK	363a	1 2
	מחשבה	THOUGHT	364c	2
	טבח	SLAUGHTER	370c	1
	יבל	CONDUCT	385a	3
	כבש	LAMB	461a	1
	כרת	CUT OFF	503d	1 b
	לח	FRESHNESS	535a	
	לחם	FOOD	537c	3 b
	על	UPON	757d	2 7d
	שחת	GO TO RUIN	1008b	1

Ch v.	Heb	Eng	Page	Sec
11 20	בחן	TRY	103c	2 b
	כליה	KIDNEYS	480c	2 b
	לב	HEART	525a	2 6
	נקמה	VENGEANCE	668c	1
	צדק	RIGHTEOUSNESS	841d	E
	שפט	JUDGE	1047c	2 a
11 21	ב	IN	90a	3 2d
	בקש	SEEK	134d	2 a
	נבא	PROPHESY	612b	1 b
	נפש	SOUL	659d	3 c
11 22	עתתות	ANATHOTH	779a	1
	בחור	YOUNG MAN	104c	
	הנה	BEHOLD	244b	B b
	מות	DIE	559c	1 a1
	פקד	ATTEND TO	823c	A 3
	רעב	FAMINE	944b	1
11 23	עתתות	ANATHOTH	779a	1
	שארית	REST	984d	1
	שנה	YEAR	1040b	
12 1	את	WITH	86a	1 db
	בגד	ACT TREACHEROUSLY	93d	D
	בגד	TREACHERY	93d	1
	בגד	GARMENT	94a	1
	דבר	SPEAK	181b	3 d
	דבר	SPEAK	*181b	3 d
	דרך	WAY	203b	5
	צדיק	JUST	843a	1 d
	ריב	STRIVE	936a	4
	רשע	WICKED	957c	3
	שלה	BE QUIET	1017b	2
	משפט	JUDGMENT	1048c	1 c
12 2	גם	YEA	169c	3
	הלך	WALK	232d	1 3
	כליה	KIDNEYS	480c	2 b
	נטע	PLANT	642c	2
	עשה	DO	794d	2 2
	קרב	NEAR	898c	2
	רחק	DISTANT	935b	1 a
	שרש	ROOT UP	1057d	2
12 3	את	WITH	86c	3 b
	בחן	TRY	103c	2 b
	הרגה	SLAUGHTER	247c	
	טבחה	THING SLAUGHTERED	371a	2
	לב	HEART	525a	2 6
	נתק	PULL	683d	2
	צאן	SMALL CATTLE	838c	2
	קדש	BE SET APART	873c	1 c
12 4	אבל	MOURN	5c	
	אחרית	END	31a	ß
	יבש	BE DRY	386b	1 d
	מן	ON ACCOUNT OF	580b	2 f
	ספה	SWEEP AWAY	705a	1
	רעה	MISERY	949b	3
12 5	בטח	TRUST	105a	1 3c
	גאון	EXALTATION	145a	1 c
	חרה	BURN	354b	
	ירדן	JORDAN	434d	
	לאה	EXHAUST	521a	
	סוס	HORSE	692d	2
	רגלי	ON FOOT	920b	
	רוץ	RUN	930b	1
	שלום	PEACE	1023a	4
12 6	אמן	CONFIRM	53b	2 c
	בגד	ACT TREACHEROUSLY	93d	B
	גם	ALSO	169b	2
	דבר	SPEAK	181a	2
	טובה	WELFARE	375d	2 a
	מלא	FULL	571a	
	קרא	CALL	895a	1 a
12 7	ידדות	LOVE	392a	
	כף	POWER	496d	2
	נחלה	PROPERTY	635b	1 e
	נטש	FORSAKE	643d	2
	נפש	SOUL	660d	6 e
	עזב	LEAVE	737c	2 e
12 8	אריה	LION	71d	
	ב	IN	90b	3 4
	יער	WOOD	420d	B
	כן	SO	487b	3 f
	נחלה	PROPERTY	635b	1 e
	נתן	GIVE	679d	1 x
	שנא	HATE	971a	2
12 9	אסף	GATHER	62b	1 b
	אתה	COME	87c	
	חיה	LIVING THING	312b	1 b
	ל	TO	513a	5 ad
	נחלה	PROPERTY	635b	1 e
	עיט	BIRD OF PREY	743c	
	צבוע	COLORED	840c	
12 10	בוס	TRAMPLE	100d	
	חלקה	PORTION OF GROUND	324c	1 b
	חמדה	DESIRE	326d	
	כרם	VINEYARD	501d	
	שחת	GO TO RUIN	1008a	1
12 11	אבל	MOURN	5c	
	לב	HEART	525a	2 3d
	על	UPON	753b	2 1b
	שמם	BE DESOLATED	1031a	1
	שמם	DEVASTATED	1031b	
12 12	אכל	EAT	37c	4
	בשר	FLESH	142d	6 c
	חרב	SWORD	352d	1 j

Ch v.	Heb	Eng	Page	Sec
	מן	FROM	581d	5 a
	קצה	END	892b	1
	שפי	BARE HEIGHT	1046a	2
12 13	תבואה	REVENUE	100b	2 b
	בוש	BE ASHAMED	101d	2
	זרע	SOW	281c	1 c
	חלה	BE WEAK	317d	1
	חמה	WHEAT	334d	
	חרון	BURNING OF ANGER	354c	
	יעל	PROFIT	418d	
	קוץ	THORN-BUSH	881a	1
	קצר	HARVEST	894b	
	קצר	HARVEST	894c	
12 14	נגע	TOUCH	619a	3
	נחלה	PROPERTY	635b	1 a
	נחל	TAKE AS A POSSESSION	635d	1 a
	נתש	PLUCK UP	684c	
	נתש	PLUCK UP	684c	
	עשב	HERB	793b	
	רע	EVIL	948c	0 b
12 15	נתש	PLUCK UP	684c	
	רחם	LOVE	933c	1
	שוב	TURN BACK	998a	6 g
	שוב	TURN BACK	998a	1
12 16	בנה	BUILD	125a	2 a
	בעל	BAAL	127d	2 2
	דרך	WAY	203d	6 c
	חי	ALIVE	311d	1 a
	ל	TO	517d	7 bc
	למד	LEARN	540d	
	למד	LEARN	540d	
	שבע	SWEAR	989b	1 a
	שבע	SWEAR	989b	1 a
12 17	אבד	CAUSE TO PERISH	2a	1
	גוי	NATION	156d	1 b
	נתש	PLUCK UP	684c	
	שמע	HEAR	1034a	1 o
13 1	אזור	WAISTCLOTH	25b	
	בוא	COME	99b	1 f
	הלך	WALK	233c	14c 6
	מתנים	LOINS	608a	1
	פשת	FLAX	833d	1
	קנה	ACQUIRE	889a	2
	שום	TO PLACE	963b	1 b
13 2	אזור	WAISTCLOTH	25b	
	מתנים	LOINS	608a	1 a
	שום	TO PLACE	963b	1 b
13 4	אזור	WAISTCLOTH	25b	
	הלך	WALK	230d	1 1d 3b
	טמן	HIDE	380b	1
	מתנים	LOINS	608a	1 a
	נקק	CLEFT	669b	
	סלע	CRAG	701a	1
	פרת	EUPHRATES	832b	
13 5	טמן	HIDE	380b	1
	פרת	EUPHRATES	832b	
13 6	אזור	WAISTCLOTH	25b	
	הלך	WALK	230d	1 1d 3b
	טמן	HIDE	380b	1
	פרת	EUPHRATES	832b	
	קץ	END	893d	1
13 7	אזור	WAISTCLOTH	25b	
	הלך	WALK	230d	1 1d 3b
	חפר	DIG	343d	1 b
	טמן	HIDE	380b	1
	כל	ALL	482d	2 ba
	פרת	EUPHRATES	832b	
	שחת	GO TO RUIN	1007d	
	שם	THERE	1027b	3
13 8	היה	BECOME	226a	2 1b
13 9	גאון	EXALTATION	145a	1 c
	ככה	THUS	462c	
	שחת	GO TO RUIN	1008b	1
13 10	אזור	WAISTCLOTH	25b	
	כל	ALL	482d	2 ba
	לב	HEART	525b	2 6d
	מאן	REFUSING	549b	
	עבד	WORK	713b	4 b
	רע	EVIL	948c	0 b
	שרירות	STUBBORNNESS	1057b	
13 11	אזור	WAISTCLOTH	25b	
	דבק	CLING	179d	1 a
	דבק	CLING	180a	1
	תהלה	PRAISE	240b	5 ca
	כן	SO	486c	2 cf
	מתנים	LOINS	608a	1 a
	תפארה	BEAUTY	802d	2 b
13 12	דבר	WORD	182a	1 1a
	יין	WINE	406c	D
	מלא	FILL	570b	
	נבל	SKIN-BOTTLE	614b	1
13 13	דוד	DAVID	188b	E
	כהן	PRIEST	463d	4
	כסא	THRONE	491a	3 a
	ל	TO	512d	5 aa
	נביא	PROPHET	611d	2
	שכרון	DRUNKENNESS	1016c	
13 14	ו	AND	253a	1 h
	חום	PITY	299b	B
	חמל	SPARE	328b	
	יחדו	TOGETHER	403c	A
	מן	FROM	583b	7 ba
	נפץ	SHATTER	658d	
	רחם	LOVE	933c	1

Ch v.	Heb	Eng	Page	Sec
13 15	אזן	HEAR	24c	1
	גבה	BE HIGH	147a	3 b
	דבר	SPEAK	180d	1
13 16	יהוה	YAHWEH	218d	2 1b
	הר	MOUNTAIN	250d	1 n
	חשׁך	GROW DARK	365a	1
	טרם	NOT YET	382c	2
	כבוד	HONOR	459b	6 b
	נגף	STRIKE	620a	
	נשׁף	TWILIGHT	676a	1
	נתן	GIVE	679a	1 h
	ערפל	CLOUD	791d	
	צלמות	DEATH-SHADOW	853c	2 a
	קוה	WAIT FOR	875d	1
	שׁות	PUT	1011c	3
13 17	בכה	WEEP	113c	3
	גוה	PRIDE	145b	1
	דמעה	TEARS	199c	
	דמע	WEEP	199c	
	ירד	GO DOWN	433c	3 c
	נפשׁ	SOUL	660d	6 c
	מסתר	SECRET PLACE	712c	1
	עדר	FLOCK	727d	1 a
	פנה	FACE	818c	26c a
	שׁבה	TAKE CAPTIVE	985c	
13 18	גבירה	QUEEN-MOTHER	150c	2
	ירד	GO DOWN	433c	3 g
	עטרה	CROWN	742d	1
	עמק	BE DEEP	770d	
	תפארה	BEAUTY	802c	2 a
	מראשׁות	HEAD-PLACE	912c	
	שׁפל	BECOME LOW	1050b	3
13 19	כל	ALL	481d	1da
	נגב	SOUTH-COUNTRY	616b	1 a
	סגר	BE SHUT UP	689b	1
	פתח	OPEN	835a	
	שׁלום	PEACE	1022d	1
13 20	נתן	GIVE	681c	1 d
	עדר	FLOCK	727d	1
	תפארה	BEAUTY	802c	1
	צאן	SMALL CATTLE	838c	3
	צפון	NORTH	861a	
13 21	אחז	GRASP	28b	
	אלוף	TAME	48d	2
	אשׁה	WOMAN	61a	1
	חבל	PAIN	287a	1 b
	ילד	BEAR	408c	1 a
	כמו	LIKE	455d	1 a
	למד	LEARN	540d	
	פקד	ATTEND TO	823c	A 3
13 22	אלה	THESE	41c	A
	חמס	TREAT VIOLENTLY	329b	
	כי	WHEN	473b	2 a
	לבב	HEART	524a	2 7
	עון	INIQUITY	731b	2 b
	עקב	HEEL	784a	A
	קרא	ENCOUNTER	897a	2
	שׁול	SKIRT	1002c	
13 23	הפך	TURN	245c	1 c1
	חברברה	STRIPE	289a	
	יטב	DO RIGHT	406a	5 a
	יכל	BE ABLE	407c	1 a
	כושׁי	CUSHITE	469a	B
	למד	TAUGHT	541a	
	נמר	LEOPARD	649d	
	עור	SKIN	736a	1
	רעע	BE EVIL	949d	2
13 24	עבר	PASS OVER	718b	6 b
	פוץ	BE DISPERSED	807b	1 a
13 25	את	WITH	87a	4 c
	בטח	TRUST	105a	13c
	גורל	LOT	174d	4
	ה	THE	208c	1 hb
	זה	THIS	261b	3
	מד	MEASURE	551b	1
	מנת	PORTION	584c	
	שׁקר	DECEPTION	1055c	1
13 26	חשׂף	STRIP OFF	362c	1
	פנה	FACE	818d	27a a
	קלון	DISHONOUR	886a	1
	ראה	TO SEE	908c	3
	שׁול	SKIRT	1002c	
13 27	אוי	WOE	17a	
	גבעה	HILL	149a	2
	זמה	PLAN	273c	2 c
	זנות	FORNICATION	276b	C
	טהר	BE CLEAN	372b	3
	מתי	WHEN	607d	D
	נאף	ADULTERY	610d	
	עוד	STILL	729a	1 ab
	מצהלה	NEIGHING	843d	
	שׂדה	FIELD	961c	1f
	שׁקוץ	DETESTED THING	1055a	
14 1	אשׁר	PARTICLE OF RE-LATION	82d	6 a
	בצרה	DEARTH	131b	
	דבר	WORD	182c	12a
	דבר	WORD	184a	4 8
14 2	אבל	MOURN	5c	
	אמל	BE WEAK	51c	
	עלה	GO UP	749a	8
	צוחה	OUTCRY	846d	
	קדר	BE DARK	871a	
	שׁער	GATE	1045a	2 c
14 3	אדיר	MAJESTIC	12b	2
	בושׁ	BE ASHAMED	101d	3
	גב	PIT	155d	
	חפה	COVER	341d	
	כלם	BE HUMILIATED	484a	2
	על	UPON	757b	27c ab
	צעיר	YOUNG	859a	1 b
	צעירה	YOUTH	859a	
	ריק	EMPTY	938a	1
	ריקם	EMPTILY	938b	2
	שׁלח	SEND	1018b	1 a
14 4	אדמה	GROUND	9c	1
	אכר	PLOUGHMAN	38d	
	גשׁם	RAIN	177c	
	חפה	COVER	341d	
	חתת	BE SHATTERED	369b	2 a
	עבור	FOR THE SAKE OF	721a	1 a
	חתת	ADDENDA ET COR-RIGENDA	1123d	
	עבור	ADDENDA ET COR-RIGENDA	1125d	
14 5	גם	ALSO	169b	2
	דשׁא	GRASS	206a	
	ילד	BEAR	408b	1 a
	עזב	LEAVE	737b	2 b2
	שׂדה	FIELD	961b	1 c
14 6	כלה	BE FINISHED	477d	2 b
	עשׂב	HERB	793c	
	פרא	WILD ASS	825b	
	רוח	BREATH	924d	2 c
	שׁאף	GASP	983c	1
	שׁפי	BARE HEIGHT	1046a	2
	תן	JACKAL	1072c	
14 7	חטא	MISS A GOAL OR WAY	307a	2 b
	עון	INIQUITY	730d	1
	ענה	ANSWER	773a	3 a
	מען	PURPOSE	775b	1 a
	עשׂה	DO	794b	1 4
	רבב	BECOME MUCH	912d	1
	משׁובה	TURNING BACK	1000b	
	שׁם	NAME	1028c	3
14 8	ארח	WANDER	72d	2
	גר	SOJOURNER	158b	1
	ישׁע	DELIVER	446d	1 b
	לון	LODGE	533c	1 a
	נטה	BEND	640b	3 a
	צרה	DISTRESS	865b	
	מקוה	HOPE	876b	
14 9	דהם	ASTONISH	187a	
	ישׁע	DELIVER	446c	1 a
	כן	SO	*486a	1 b
	נוח	REST	629a	B 4
	נכה	SMITE	646c	4 b
	קרא	CALL	896b	2 d4
	נחה	ADDENDA ET COR-RIGENDA	*1125a	
14 10	אהב	LOVE	13a	2
	זכר	REMEMBER	270c	2 4
	חטאת	SIN	308d	1 d1
	חשׂך	WITHHOLD	362b	1 c
	כן	SO	485d	1 b
	נוע	TOTTER	631b	2
	עון	INIQUITY	731b	1 c5
	עתה	NOW	774a	1 b
	פקד	ATTEND TO	823b	A 1a
	רצה	BE PLEASED WITH	953b	2
	טובה	WELFARE	375d	1
14 11				
14 12	דבר	PESTILENCE	184a	1
	כי	WHEN	473a	2
	כי	THOUGH	473c	2 ca
	כלה	FINISH	478c	2 c2
	מנחה	OFFERING	585b	3
	מנחה	OFFERING	585c	6
	עלה	WHOLE BURNT OF-FERING	750d	
	צום	FAST	847a	
	רנה	RINGING CRY	943d	1
	רעב	FAMINE	944b	1
	רצה	BE PLEASED WITH	953b	2
14 13	אדון	LORD	11c	4 a
	אהה	ALAS	13c	
	אמת	FIRMNESS	54a	1
	נביא	PROPHET	612a	2
	ראה	TO SEE	907b	3
14 14	אליל	WORTHLESSNESS	47b	A
	חזון	VISION	303a	3
	לב	HEART	525b	26b
	נביא	PROPHET	612a	2
	נבא	PROPHESY	612b	2
	נבא	PROPHESY	612c	3
	קסם	DIVINATION	890c	2
	תרמית	DECEITFULNESS	941c	
	שׁלח	SEND	1018c	2 a
	שׁקר	DECEPTION	1055c	4
	שׁקר	DECEPTION	1055c	4
14 15	נביא	PROPHET	612a	2
	נבא	PROPHESY	612b	1 b
	שׁלח	SEND	1018c	2
	שׁמנה	EIGHT	1033a	1
	תמם	BE FINISHED	1070c	5
14 16	אין	NOT	34d	3
	המ	THEY	241d	8 a
	ל	TO PROPHESY	*512a	3 b
	נבא	PROPHESY	612b	2
	על	UPON	756c	27a b
	פנה	FACE	818c	26c a
	קבר	BURY	868d	
	שׁלך	THROW	1021c	1
	שׁפך	POUR OUT	1049d	2 a
14 17	אמר	SAY	55d	1
	בת	DAUGHTER	123c	3
	בתולה	VIRGIN	144a	
	דבר	WORD	182a	1 1a
	דומה	SILENCE	*189b	
	דמה	CEASE	198c	1
	דמעה	TEARS	199c	
	חלה	BE WEAK	318a	2
	יומם	BY DAY	401c	2
	ירד	GO DOWN	433c	3 c
	מרץ	BE SICK	*599c	
	מכה	BLOW	647a	1 c
	עם	PEOPLE	767a	5 f
	שׁבר	BREAK	990d	
	שׁבר	BREAKING	991a	1
14 18	תחלאים	DISEASES	316a	
	חלל	PIERCED	319c	2
	ידע	KNOW	394a	2
	יצא	GO OUT	423d	2 a
	כהן	PRIEST	463c	4
	נביא	PROPHET	611d	2
	סחר	GO AROUND	695b	1
	רעב	FAMINE	944b	1
	שׂדה	FIELD	961c	1 f
14 19	בעתה	TERROR	130a	
	געל	ABHOR	171d	
	טוב	A GOOD THING	375a	1
	מדוע	WHEREFORE	396c	
	מאס	REJECT	549c	1 a
	נפשׁ	SOUL	660d	6 b
	קוה	WAIT FOR	875d	1
	מרפא	HEALING	951b	1
14 20	חטא	MISS A GOAL OR WAY	307a	2 b
	ידע	KNOW	394a	1 f
	עון	INIQUITY	731a	1 b
	רשׁע	WICKEDNESS	957d	3
14 21	ברית	COVENANT	136c	2 2c
	ברית	COVENANT	137b	3 3
	זכר	REMEMBER	270b	2 3 a
	כבוד	HONOR	458c	2 5
	כסא	THRONE	491b	3 b
	נאץ	CONTEMN	610d	
	נבל	BE SENSELESS	614d	
	מען	PURPOSE	775b	1 a
	פרר	BREAK	830b	1
	שׁם	NAME	1028c	3
14 22	אם	IF	50d	2 ab b
	גשׁם	CAUSE RAIN	177d	
	הבל	VAPOUR	211a	2
	הוא	HE, SHE, IT	216b	4 ba
	ישׁ	THERE IS	441d	2 b
	קוה	WAIT FOR	875d	1
15 1	אל	TO	40a	3 c
	משׁה	MOSES	602c	
	עמד	STAND	763d	1 a
	פנה	FACE	819a	28a
	שׁמואל	SAMUEL	1028d	1
15 2	שׁבי	CAPTIVITY	985d	1
15 3	בהמה	BEAST	97a	3
	הרג	KILL	247b	7
	הרג	KILL	247b	2
	כלב	DOG	476d	A
	סחב	DRAG	694d	
	פקד	ATTEND TO	823c	B 1
	ארבע	FOUR	916d	1 a1
15 4	זועה	A TREMBLING	266b	
	חזקיהו	HEZEKIAH	306a	1
	ל	TO	512c	4 b
	ממלכה	KINGDOM	575b	1
	מנשׁה	MANASSEH	586d	2
	נתן	GIVE	681a	3 b
15 5	גור	DREAD	*159a	1
	חמל	SPARE	328d	
	נוד	SHEW GRIEF	626d	2 a
	סור	TURN ASIDE	693c	1
	קמה	STANDING GRAIN	879b	
	שׁאל	ASK	982a	2 a
15 6	לאה	BE WEARY	521a	1
	נחם	BE SORRY	637a	1
	נטה	STRETCH OUT	640d	1
	נטשׁ	FORSAKE	643d	2
15 7	אבד	CAUSE TO PERISH	2a	1
	דרך	WAY	203d	6 d
	זרה	SCATTER	279d	2
	מזרה	PITCH-FORK	280a	
	שׁוב	TURN BACK	997d	6 e
	שׁכל	BE BEREAVED	1013d	1
	שׁער	GATE	1045a	2 c
15 8	אלמנה	WIDOW	48b	1
	אם	MOTHER	51c	1
	בהלה	DISMAY	96d	
	בחור	YOUNG MAN	104c	
	חול	SAND	297d	C
	חול	SAND	297d	B
	יומם	DAYTIME	*401c	2
	ל	TO	513a	5 ad
	נפל	FALL	658b	5
	עיר	AGITATION	735c	
	עצם	BE VAST	782c	2
	פתאם	SUDDENNESS	837c	
	צהר	MIDDAY	843d	1
15 9	איב	BE HOSTILE TO	33c	
	אמל	BE WEAK	51b	

Ch v.	Heb	Eng	Page	Sec
	בוא	COME	98a	1 i
	בוש	BE ASHAMED	101d	3
	חפר	BE ABASHED	344a	
	יומם	DAYTIME	401c	1
	נפח	BLOW	656a	
	מפח	BREATHING OUT	*656a	
	נפש	SOUL	659c	1 c
	עוד	STILL	729c	2 aa
	שארית	REST	984d	1
15 10	אוי	WOE	17a	
	איש	MAN	36a	
	אם	MOTHER	51c	1
	מדון	STRIFE	193c	
	כל	ALL	482a	1 db
	ל	TO	513a	5 ad
	נשה	LEND	674b	
	ריב	STRIFE	937a	1
15 11	אם	IF	50b	1 b2
	בעד	ON BEHALF OF	*126d	2
	טוב	A GOOD THING	375a	1
	פגע	MEET	803c	2
	צרה	DISTRESS	865b	
	שרה	LET LOOSE	1056a	
15 12	ברזל	IRON	137c	3
	ה	INTERROG PART	209d	1 b
	צפון	NORTH	861a	
	רעע	BREAK	949d	1
15 13	אוצר	TREASURE	70a	1
	בז	SPOIL	103a	2
	גבול	BOUNDARY	148a	2 d
	ו	AND	252c	1 b
	חיל	STRENGTH	299a	3
	חטאת	SIN	308d	1 b
	מחיר	PRICE	564b	1
15 14	יקד	BE BURNING	428d	
	עבד	WORK	713c	2
	עבר	PASS OVER	719a	4
	קדח	KINDLE	869b	1
15 15	ארך	LONG	74a	
	זכר	REMEMBER	270b	2 1 a
	חרפה	REPROACH	357d	1
	ל	TO	516c	1
	נקם	AVENGE	668b	1 a
	נשא	LIFT	671b	2 d
	על	UPON	754b	2 1f b
	פקד	ATTEND TO	823c	A 2
	רדף	PURSUE	922d	1 f
15 16	אכל	EAT	37b	1
	לבב	HEART	524a	2 9a
	מצא	FIND	594a	1 e
	צבא	GOD OF WAR	839b	4 b
	קרא	CALL	896b	2 d4
	ששון	REJOICING	965b	
	שמחה	JOY	970d	2
15 17	בדד	ISOLATION	94d	
	זעם	INDIGNATION	276d	
	ישב	SIT	442c	1 a
	מלא	FILL	570c	1
	סוד	COUNCIL	691c	1 a
	עלז	EXULT	759c	
	פנה	FACE	818c	2 6c a
	שחק	LAUGH	966a	3
15 18	אמן	CONFIRM	52d	2
	אנש	BE SICK	60c	
	כאב	PAIN	456b	
	אכזב	DECEPTIVE	469d	
	לא	NOT	*519c	2 b
	מאן	REFUSE	549a	
	מה	HOW	554a	4 d
	מכה	BLOW	647a	1 c
	נצח	EVERLASTINGNESS	664b	4
	רפא	HEAL	951a	2 b
15 19	הם	THEY	241b	1 c
	זלל	BE LIGHT	272d	1
	יצא	BRING OUT	425b	5
	יקר	PRECIOUS	430a	1 b
	עמד	STAND	764a	1 e
	שוב	TURN BACK	997c	5 b
	שוב	TURN BACK	998d	1 a
15 20	בצר	MAKE INACCESSIBLE	131a	
	חומה	WALL	327d	3
	יכל	PREVAIL	408a	2 b
	ישע	DELIVER	446d	1 b
	ל	TO	512c	4 b
	לחם	ENGAGE IN BATTLE	535c	
15 21	כף	POWER	496d	2
	עריץ	AWE-INSPIRING	792a	
	פדה	RANSOM	804b	3 d
	רע	EVIL	948c	0 b
16 2	מקום	STANDING PLACE	880a	3 b
16 3	אם	MOTHER	51d	1
	טול	HURL	376d	
	ילד	BEGET	409a	1
	ילד	BORN	409c	
	על	UPON	754d	2 1f g
	מקום	STANDING PLACE	880a	3 b
16 4	מאכל	FOOD	38b	
	בהמה	BEAST	97a	3
	דמן	DUNG	199b	
	תחלאים	DISEASES	316a	
	כלה	BE FINISHED	477d	2 c
	ממות	DEATH	560d	
	נבלה	CARCASS	615c	1 a
	ספד	WAIL	704d	
16 5	קבר	BURY	868c	4
	אסף	GATHER	62c	4
	בית	HOUSE	108d	1 ad
	ה	THE	208b	1 ha
	חסד	GOODNESS	339b	2 2
	ל	TO	515b	5 hb a
	נוד	SHEW GRIEF	626d	2 a
	ספד	WAIL	704d	
	מרוח	CRY	931a	1
	רחמים	COMPASSION	933c	1
	שלום	PEACE	1023c	5 b
16 6	גדד	CUT	151a	1
	ל	TO	512a	3 b
	ל	TO	514d	5 g
	ל	TO	515b	5 hb a
	ספד	WAIL	704c	
	קבר	BURY	868c	
	טן	SMALL	882a	1 a
	קרח	MAKE BALD	901a	
16 7	אבל	MOURNING	5c	
	אם	MOTHER	51d	1
	לחם	FOOD	537c	3 a
	נחם	CONSOLE ONESELF	637b	
	תנחום	CONSOLATION	637c	
16 8	את	WITH	85c	
	בית	HOUSE	108d	1 ad
	ישב	SIT	442c	1 a
	משתה	FEAST	1059d	1
16 9	חתן	DAUGHTER:S HUSBAND	368d	2
	כלה	BRIDE	483c	2 a
	קול	VOICE	876d	1 a
	ששון	REJOICING	965b	
	שמחה	JOY	970d	2
	שבת	CEASE	992a	1
16 10	דבר	SPEAK	181d	5
	חטא	MISS A GOAL OR WAY	307b	2 b
	חטאת	SIN	308c	1 b
	מה	HOW	554b	4 f
	עון	INIQUITY	730d	1
16 11	הלך	WALK	235a	2 3d 2
	תורה	INSTRUCTION	435d	1 c
	עבד	WORK	713b	4 b
	על	UPON	758b	3 a
16 12	בלת	NOT	*116d	4 a
	הנה	BEHOLD	243d	
	לב	HEART	525b	2 6d
	רע	EVIL	948c	0 c
	רעע	BE EVIL	949d	1
	רעע	BE EVIL	949d	2
	שרירות	STUBBORNNESS	1057b	
16 13	אשר	THAT	83c	8 c
	חנינה	FAVOR	337a	
	ידע	KNOW	394a	2
	נבא	PROPHET	611d	2
	נתן	GIVE	678c	1 b
	עבד	WORK	713b	4 b
	על	UPON	757a	2 7c a
16 14	אמר	SAY	56c	
	בוא	COME	98c	2
	חי	ALIVE	311d	1 a
	כן	SO	486d	3 d
16 15	אדמה	LAND	10a	5
	ארץ	EARTH	76c	5
	חי	ALIVE	311d	1 a
	כיאם	BUT	475a	2 b
	נדח	THRUST	623b	2
	עלה	GO UP	749b	1 a
	על	UPON	757a	2 7c a
	צפון	NORTH	861a	
	שוב	TURN BACK	998d	1 a
16 16	גבעה	HILL	149a	3
	דוג	FISH FOR	185d	
	דוג	FISHER	186a	
	דוג	FISHER	186a	
	הנה	BEHOLD	244b	B b
	הר	MOUNTAIN	250c	1 f
	נקיק	CLEFT	669b	
	צוד	HUNT	844c	
	ציד	HUNTER	844d	
	שלח	SEND	1018b	1 a
16 17	דרך	WAY	203c	6 a
	נגד	IN FRONT	617d	2 cb a
	סתר	HIDE	711c	2
	עון	INIQUITY	730d	1
	פנה	FACE	818a	2 5a d
	צפן	HIDE	860d	
16 18	חטאת	SIN	308c	1 b
	חלל	POLLUTE	320b	1 b
	מלא	FILL	570b	2
	נבלה	CARCASS	615c	1 b
	נחלה	PROPERTY	635b	1 e
	עון	INIQUITY	731a	1 c1
	על	UPON	754b	2 1f b
	ראשון	FIRST	912a	3 b1
	שלם	BE COMPLETE	1022c	5
	משנה	DOUBLE	1041c	1
	שקוץ	DETESTED THING	1055a	
	תועבה	ABOMINATION	1073a	1 b
16 19	אך	ONLY	36d	2 bb
	אפס	END	67a	1
	הבל	VAPOUR	210d	2
	יעל	PROFIT	418d	
	מנוס	ESCAPE	631a	2
	נחל	TAKE AS A POSSESSION	635d	2
	מעוז	PLACE OF SAFETY	732a	2 a
	עז	STRENGTH	739a	2 c
	צרה	DISTRESS	865b	
	שקר	DECEPTION	1055c	1
16 20	ה	INTERROG PART	209d	1 b
	לא	NOT	519b	1 bb
16 21	גבורה	MIGHT	150c	3
	ידע	KNOW	395a	
	ידע	ANSWER	395a	
	כן	SO	486d	3 d
17 1	ברזל	IRON	137c	1 d
	מזבח	ALTAR	259b	2
	חטאת	SIN	309a	2
	חרש	CUT IN	360c	1
	חרת	GRAVE	*362a	
	כתב	WRITE	507c	1 c
	לב	HEART	525a	2 3d
	לוח	TABLET	531d	1
	לוח	TABLET	*531d	1
	עט	STYLUS	741c	1
	צפרן	STYLUS POINT	862b	2
	קרן	HORN	902a	3
	שמיר	ADAMANT	1039a	2
17 2	אשרה	ASHERA	81c	B
	גבה	HIGH	147b	1
	גבעה	HILL	149a	2 b
	ה	THE	209a	2
	זכר	REMEMBER	269c	1 1 a
	על	UPON	756a	2 6a
	על	UPON	756b	2 6c
	עץ	TREE	781c	1 a
	רענן	LUXURIANT	947d	
17 3	אוצר	TREASURE	70a	1
	בז	SPOIL	103a	2
	במה	HIGH PLACE	119d	3 e
	גבול	BOUNDARY	148a	2 d
	הר	MOUNTAIN	249c	3
	חיל	STRENGTH	299a	3
	חטאת	SIN	308d	1 b
	שדה	FIELD	961c	1 g
17 4	ידע	KNOW	394a	2
	יקד	BE BURNING	428d	
	עבד	WORK	713c	2
	קדח	KINDLE	869b	1
	שמט	LET DROP	1030c	
17 5	ארר	CURSE	76d	
	בטח	TRUST	105a	1 3b
	בשר	FLESH	142d	5
	גבר	MAN	150a	
	זרוע	ARM	284a	2 a
17 6	חרר	PARCHED PLACE	359c	
	טוב	A GOOD THING	375a	1
	ישב	SIT	443b	4
	מלחה	SALTNESS	572a	
	ערבה	DESERT-PLAIN	787c	5
	ערוער	JUNIPER	792d	
	שכן	SETTLE DOWN	1015b	2 a
17 7	במה	TRUST	105a	1 3a
	מבטח	CONFIDENCE	105c	2
	ברך	BLESS	138d	2 b
17 8	בצרת	DEARTH	131b	
	דאג	BE ANXIOUS	178b	1
	חם	HEAT	328d	
	יבל	STREAM	385b	
	מוש	REMOVE	559b	
	עלה	LEAF	750a	
	על	UPON	756a	2 6a
	עץ	TREE	781c	1 a
	עשה	DO	794d	2 2
	רענן	LUXURIANT	947d	
	שלח	SEND	1019b	4
	שלח	SPROUT	*1019c	2
	שרש	ROOT	1057d	2
	שתל	TRANSPLANT	1060a	
17 9	אנש	BE SICK	60c	
	כל	ALL	482c	2 a
	מי	WHO	567a	F c
	מן	THAN	582c	6 b
	נרש	BE SICK	*633b	
	עקב	INSIDIOUS	784c	1
17 10	בחן	TRY	103c	2 b
	דרך	WAY	203c	6 a
	יהוה	YAHWEH	219b	2 2d
	ו	AND	*252c	1 b
	חקר	SEARCH	350d	2 c
	כליה	KIDNEYS	480c	2 b
	ל	TO	518b	7 bh
	לב	HEART	525b	2 6
	נתן	GIVE	679d	1 v
	מעלל	DEED	760b	1
	פרי	FRUIT	826c	3
	רוח	BREATH	924d	2 a
17 11	דגר	GATHER TOGETHER AS A BROOD	186c	
	חצי	HALF	345d	2
	ילד	BEAR	408b	1 a
	נבל	FOOLISH	615a	
	עשה	DO	795a	2 7
	עשר	RICHES	799b	
	קרא	PARTRIDGE	896c	
17 12	כבוד	HONOR	458c	2 b

Ch v.	Heb	Eng	Page	Sec
19 11	אין	NOT	35a	6 da
	חרסות	POTSHERD	*360b	
	יכל	BE ABLE	407c	1 a
	יצר	FORM	427d	1 a
	כבה	THUS	462c	
	כלי	VESSEL	480b	3
	קבר	BURY	868c	
	מקום	STANDING PLACE	880b	5 a
	רפא	HEAL	951a	1
	שבר	BREAK	990d	
	תפת	TOPHETH	1075a	
19 12	ו	AND	*252c	1 b
	ל	TO	518b	7 bh
	תפת	TOPHETH	1075a	
19 13	גג	ROOF	150d	1
	טמא	UNCLEAN	379d	2 c
	ל	TO	514c	5 fd
	נסך	POUR OUT	650d	
	נסך	DRINK-OFFERING	651a	1
	צבא	HOST	839b	1 c
	קטר	MAKE SACRAFICES SMOKE	883a	
	קטר	MAKE SACRAFICES SMOKE	883a	
	תפת	TOPHETH	1075a	
19 14	חצר	ENCLOSURE	347a	3 b
	נבא	PROPHESY	612b	1 b
	שלח	SEND	1018c	2 a
	תפת	TOPHETH	1075a	
19 15	אל	TO	41a	B
	דבר	SPEAK	181d	5
	ערף	BACK OF NECK	791c	2
	קשה	BE SEVERE	904c	3 a
	רעה	MISERY	949a	1
20 1	אמר	IMMER	57b	3
	כהן	PRIEST	463c	4
	נבא	PROPHESY	612b	1 b
	נגיד	LEADER	618a	3
	פקיד	COMMISSIONER	824b	
	פשחור	PASSHUR	832d	1
	שמע	HEAR	1033c	1 b
20 2	בנימין	BENJAMIN	122d	1
	מהפכת	STOCKS	246b	
	חדש	NEW	*294b	A
	נכה	SMITE	645c	1 b
	נתן	PUT	680b	2 a
	פשחור	PASSHUR	832d	1
	שער	GATE	1045b	3 b
20 3	מגור	FEAR	159a	
	מהפכת	STOCKS	246c	
	יצא	CAUSE TO GO	424b	1 a
	כיאם	BUT	475a	2 b
	מחרת	THE MORROW	564a	
	סביב	ROUND ABOUT	687a	1 d
	פשחור	PASSHUR	832d	1
20 4	אהב	LOVE	13a	4 b
	בבל	BABEL	93c	
	מגור	FEAR	159a	
	הנה	BEHOLD	244b	B b
	ל	TO	512c	4 b
20 5	אוצר	TREASURE	70a	1
	בבל	BABEL	93c	
	בוא	COME	99b	2
	בז	SPOIL	102d	
	חסן	WEALTH	340d	
	יגע	TOIL	388c	2
	יקר	PRECIOUSNESS	430b	1 a
20 6	אהב	LOVE	13a	4 b
	בבל	BABEL	93c	
	ה	THE	208c	1 hb
	הלך	WALK	231b	1 d3 ge
	נבא	PROPHESY	612b	2
	פשחור	PASSHUR	832d	1
	שבי	CAPTIVITY	985d	1
	שקר	DECEPTION	1055c	4
20 7	חזק	BE FIRM	304b	1 1b
	יום	DAY	400c	7 f
	יכל	PREVAIL	408a	2 a
	כל	ALL	482a	1 db
	לעג	MOCK	541c	
	פתה	BE SIMPLE	834c	
	פתה	BE SIMPLE	834d	2
	פתה	BE SIMPLE	834d	2
	שחק	LAUGHTER	966a	2
	פתה	ADDENDA ET CORRIGENDA	1126b	
20 8	די	SUFFICIENCY	191d	2 cg
	זעק	CRY	277d	2 d
	חמס	VIOLENCE	329c	
	חרפה	REPROACH	358a	3
	יום	DAY	400c	7 f
	קלס	DERISION	887b	
	קרא	CALL	895a	1 b
	שד	VIOLENCE	994c	1
20 9	בער	BURN	129a	1
	דבר	SPEAK	181c	4 a
	ו	AND	254a	2 da
	זכר	REMEMBER	270a	1 7
	יכל	BE ABLE	407d	1 c
	כול	CONTAIN	465b	2
	לאה	BE WEARY	521a	
	עצם	BONE	782d	1 b
	עצר	RESTRAIN	783c	1
	אש	ADDENDA ET CORRIGENDA	1120d	
20 10	צלע	LIMPING		
	אולי	PERADVENTURE	19c	1
	אנוש	MAN	60d	1
	מגור	FEAR	159a	
	דבה	WHISPERING	179b	1
	יכל	PREVAIL	408a	2 b
	לקח	TAKE	543d	0
	נגד	BE CONSPICUOUS	617a	3
	נקם	AVENGE	*668a	1 a
	נקמה	VENGEANCE	668c	3
	סביב	ROUND ABOUT	687a	1 d
	פתה	BE SIMPLE	834d	2
	צלע	RIB	854b	6
	שלום	PEACE	1023a	5 a
	שמר	KEEP	1036d	1 c
	פתה	ADDENDA ET CORRIGENDA	1126b	
20 11	את	WITH	85c	
	את	WITH	85d	1 a
	יכל	PREVAIL	408a	2 a
	כלמה	IGNOMINY	484b	2
	כן	SO	487b	3 f
	כשל	STUMBLE	505d	1 b
	עולם	LONG DURATION	762a	2 a
	עריץ	AWE-INSPIRING	792a	
	רדף	PURSUE	922d	1 e
	שכל	BE PRUDENT	968c	6
	שוב	TURN BACK	997b	3 b
20 12	בחן	TRY	*103c	2 b
	כליה	KIDNEYS	480c	2 b
	לב	HEART	525a	26
	נקמה	VENGEANCE	668c	1
	צדיק	JUST	843a	3 b
20 13	אביון	NEEDY	2d	
	הלל	PRAISE	238b	2 c
	רעע	BE EVIL	949d	2
	שיר	SING	1010d	
	אם	MOTHER	51c	1
	ארר	CURSE	76d	
	אשר	PARTICLE OF RELATION	82c	4 ba
	ברך	BLESS	138d	2 b
	יום	DAY	398d	2 f
	ילד	BE BORN	409a	
	ארר	CURSE	76d	
20 15	בן	SON	121b	2
	בשר	BEAR TIDINGS	142b	1
	זכר	MALE	271c	2
	ילד	BE BORN	409a	
	שמח	REJOICE	970c	
	שמח	REJOICE	970c	
	שמח	REJOICE	970c	
20 16	בקר	MORNING	134a	1 d
	הפך	TURN	245c	1 b
	זעקה	CRY	277d	2
	נחם	BE SORRY	637a	2
	עת	TIME	773c	1 b
	צהר	MIDDAY	843d	1
	תרועה	SHOUT OF WAR	930a	1
20 17	אם	MOTHER	51d	1
	מות	DIE	560a	
	עולם	LONG DURATION	762a	2 a
	קבצר	GRAVE	868d	
	רחם	WOMB	933b	1
	רחם	WOMB	933b	1
20 18	בשת	SHAME	102a	1
	יגון	GRIEF	387b	
	יצא	GO OUT	423c	1 h
	כלה	BE FINISHED	477d	2 b
	מה	HOW	554a	4 d
	עמל	TROUBLE	765d	1
	ראה	TO SEE	907b	3
	רחם	WOMB	933b	1
21 1	כהן	PRIEST	463c	4
	מלכיהו	MALCHIJAH	575c	1
	מעשיהו	MAASEIAH	796b	1
	פשחור	PASSHUR	832d	2
	צדקיו	ZEDEKIAH	843b	1
	צפניה	ZEPHANIAH	861b	1
21 2	את	WITH	86b	1 db
	בעד	ON BEHALF OF	126c	2
	דרש	SEEK	205b	2 a
	לחם	ENGAGE IN BATTLE	535c	
	נבוכדראצר	NEBUCHADNEZZAR	613a	
	עלה	GO UP	748c	2 e
	על	UPON	759a	4 2b
	עשה	DO	794b	12
	פלא	BE SURPASSING	810d	4
21 3	ירמיה	JEREMIAH	*941c	1
	צדקיו	ZEDEKIAH	843b	1
21 4	חוץ	THE OUTSIDE	300a	1 bd
	כלי	IMPLEMENT	479d	2 a
	כשדים	CHALDEANS	505a	1 b
	לחם	ENGAGE IN BATTLE	535c	
	מלחמה	WAR	536c	
	סבב	TURN ABOUT	686c	1 a
	צור	CONFINE	848d	2
	תוך	MIDST	1063d	
21 5	אני	I	59b	
	גדול	GREAT	153a	3
	זרוע	ARM	284a	1 c
	חזק	STRONG	305c	1 b
	חמה	RAGE	404d	2 c
	לחם	ENGAGE IN BATTLE	535c	
21 6	קצף	WRATH	893c	1
	אדם	MAN	9b	2
	ו	AND	253a	1 h
	מות	DIE	559c	1 a1
21 7	בקש	SEEK	134d	2 a
	חוס	PITY	299c	C
	חמל	SPARE	328b	1
	נבוכדראצר	NEBUCHADNEZZAR	613a	
	נכה	SMITE	646a	2 c
	נפש	SOUL	659d	3 c
	עם	PEOPLE	766c	1
	צדקיהו	ZEDEKIAH	843b	1
	רחם	LOVE	933d	2
	רעב	FAMINE	944b	1
	שאר	REMAIN	984a	1
21 8	דרך	WAY	203c	6 c
	דרך	WAY	203d	6 d
	ה	THE	*208b	1 ha
	חיים	LIFE	313b	2
	פנה	FACE	817c	2 4b g
21 9	ב	IN	89d	3 2a
	כשדים	CHALDEANS	505a	1 b
	ל	TO	512c	4 b
	נפל	FALL	657c	4 b
	על	UPON	755b	4 2a
	צור	CONFINE	848d	2
	רעב	FAMINE	944b	1
	שלל	SPOIL	1022a	2
21 10	טובה	WELFARE	375d	1
	ל	TO	515a	5 ha
	נתן	GIVE	681c	1 e
	רעה	MISERY	949b	1
	שום	TO PLACE	963d	2
21 11	בית	HOUSE	110a	5 de
	מחשבה	THOUGHT	364c	2
21 12	בית	HOUSE	110a	5 c
	בער	BURN	129a	4
	בקר	MORNING	*134b	1 f
	גזל	TEAR AWAY	159d	
	דין	JUDGE	192b	4
	חמה	RAGE	*404d	2 c
	יצא	GO OUT	423c	1 g
	כבה	QUENCH	459d	1
	מעלל	DEED	760b	1
	עשק	OPPRESS	798d	1
	עשוק	OPPRESSOR	*799a	
	רע	EVIL	948a	3
	משפט	JUDGMENT	1048c	1 f
21 13	אל	TO	40b	4
	ישב	DWELL	443b	3
	מישור	LEVEL PLACE	449d	1
	מי	WHO	567a	F c
	נחשתן	NEHUSHTAN	639c	1
	מענה	DEN	733b	1
	עמק	VALE	771a	
21 14	יער	WOOD	420d	C
	יצת	KINDLE	*428c	
	סביב	ROUND ABOUT	687b	2 ab
	סביב	ROUND ABOUT	*687b	2 ba b
	מעלל	DEED	760b	1
	פקד	ATTEND TO	823c	A 3
	פרי	FRUIT	826c	1
22 1	ירד	GO DOWN	432d	1 c
22 2	דוד	DAVID	188b	E
	כסא	THRONE	491a	3 a
	שער	GATE	1045a	3 a
22 3	אלמנה	WIDOW	48b	
	גר	SOJOURNER	158b	2
	גזל	TEAR AWAY	159d	
	דם	BLOOD	*196c	2 b
	דם	BLOOD	196d	2
	חמס	TREAT VIOLENTLY	329b	1
	ינה	OPPRESS	413b	
	יתום	ORPHAN	450c	
	נקי	CLEAN	667c	1
	עשוק	OPPRESSOR	799a	
	צדקה	RIGHTEOUSNESS	842a	1 a
22 4	דוד	DAVID	188b	E
	ל	TO	512d	5 aa
	עם	PEOPLE	766c	3
	רכב	RIDE	938d	2
	רכב	CHARIOT	939a	1 1
	שער	GATE	1045a	3 a
22 5	חרבה	WASTE	352a	1
	כי	THAT	471d	1 a
	שבע	SWEAR	989b	2
22 6	אם	IF	50b	1 b2
	בית	HOUSE	110a	5 de
	ישב	BE INHABITED	443c	
	ל	TO	513a	5 ad
	לא	NOT	*519c	2 b
	לבנון	LEBANON	527a	
	על	UPON	757c	2 7c b
	שית	PUT	1011c	3
22 7	ארז	CEDAR	72c	1 b
	ו	AND	253a	1 g
	כלי	IMPLEMENT	479d	2 a
	כרת	CUT OFF	503d	2
	נפל	FALL	658a	1 e
	קדש	BE SET APART	873b	4 c
	שחת	GO TO RUIN	1008b	1
22 8	כבה	THUS	*462c	
	מה	HOW	*554b	4 f

JEREMIAH

Ch	v.	Heb	Eng	Page	Sec
		תחת	INSTEAD	*1066a	2 2b b
22	9	אמר	SAY	56a	1
		ברית	COVENANT	136c	2 2c
		ברית	COVENANT	137b	3 3
		יהוה	YAHWEH	218d	2 1
		עבד	WORK	713b	4 b
		על	UPON	758b	3 a
22	10	בכה	WEEP	113c	2
		בכה	WEEP	113c	3
		הלך	WALK	230b	1 1b
		מולדת	KINDRED	409d	1
		ל	TO	515b	5 hb a
		נוד	SHEW GRIEF	626d	2 a
22	11	יצא	GO OUT	423d	2 a
		מלך	BE KING	574a	
		שלום	SHALLUM	1024b	2
22	12	שם	THERE	1027a	1 a
22	13	ב	IN	89d	3 2b
		בנה	BUILD	124c	1 d
		הוי	AH	223a	
		חנם	OUT OF FAVOR	336c	A
		לא	NOT	520a	4 aa
		נתן	GIVE	679d	1 n
		עבד	WORK	713a	1
		עליה	ROOF-CHAMBER	751a	
		פעל	DOING	821c	3
		צדק	RIGHTEOUSNESS	841d	5
		רע	FRIEND	946a	2
22	14	ארז	CEDAR	72d	2
		בית	HOUSE	108d	1 ab
		בנה	BUILD	124b	1 ab
		חלון	WINDOW	319d	
		ל	TO	515d	5 ia
		מדה	SIZE	551c	2
		משח	ANOINT	603a	1
		ספן	COVER	706a	
		עליה	ROOF-CHAMBER	751a	
		פצם	SPLIT OPEN	822d	
		קרע	TEAR	902d	3 b
		רוח	BE WIDE	926c	
		ששר	VERMILION	1059a	
22	15	אמר	SAY	56d	
		ארז	CEDAR	72d	2
		ה	INTERROG PART	210a	1 b
		חרה	BURN	354b	
		טוב	PLEASING	373b	4
		טוב	PLEASING	*373b	4
		צדקה	RIGHTEOUSNESS	842a	1 a
22	16	אביון	NEEDY	2d	
		דין	JUDGE	192b	2 a
		דין	JUDGMENT	192c	2
		הוא	HE, SHE, IT	216d	6 a
		טוב	PLEASING	373b	4
		דעת	KNOWLEDGE	395d	2 b
		עני	POOR	776d	2
22	17	בצע	UNJUST GAIN	130c	
		דם	BLOOD	*196c	2 b
		דם	BLOOD	196d	2 d
		כיאם	EXCEPT	474d	2 a
		לב	HEART	524a	2 1
		נקי	CLEAN	667c	1
		על	UPON	757d	2 7c c
		עשק	OPPRESSION	799a	1
		מרוצה	RUNNING	930d	2
		מרוצה	CRUSHING	954d	
22	18	אדון	LORD	11a	1 1c
		אחות	SISTER	27d	1
		אמר	SAY	56a	1
		הוד	SPLENDOUR	217a	1
		יהויקים	JEHOIAKIM	220c	1
		הוי	AH	222d	
		ספד	WAIL	704c	2
22	19	הלאה	OUT THERE	229b	A
		חמור	HE-ASS	331c	6
		סחב	DRAG	695a	
		קבר	BURY	868c	
		צבחה	GRAVE	869a	2
		שלך	THROW	1021a	1 a
22	20	אהב	LOVE	13b	2
		בשן	BASHAN	143c	
		לבנן	LEBANON	527a	
		נתן	GIVE	679d	1 x
		עברים	ABARIM	720d	
		צעק	CRY	858c	2
		שבר	BREAK	990d	
22	21	דרך	WAY	203d	6 d
		זה	THIS	260d	1 a
		נעורים	YOUTH	655c	
		מקום	STANDING PLACE	880b	4
		שלוה	QUIETNESS	1017d	
		שמע	HEAR	1034b	2 c
22	22	אהב	LOVE	13b	2
		בוש	BE ASHAMED	101d	3
		הלך	WALK	231b	1 d3 ge
		כי	THAT	472d	1 e
		כלם	BE HUMILIATED	483d	1
		רעה	TEND	945b	2 d
		שבי	CAPTIVITY	985d	1
22	23	ארז	CEDAR	72c	1 a
		חבל	PAIN	287a	1 b
		חיל	A WRITHING	297d	1
		חנן	SHOW FAVOR	336a	
		ילד	BEAR	408c	1 b
		ישב	DWELL	443b	3
		לבנן	LEBANON	527b	
		קנן	MAKE A NEST	890b	
22	24	יהויכין	JEHOIACHIN	220c	
		יהויקים	JEHOIAKIM	220c	1
		חי	ALIVE	311d	1 a
		חתם	SEAL	368b	
		יד	HAND	389a	1 a
		כי	THAT	472b	1 c
		כיאם	THAT IF	474c	1 a
22	25	נתק	PULL OFF	683c	2
		בקש	SEEK	134d	2 a
		יגור	FEARING	388d	
		כשדים	CHALDEANS	505a	1 b
		נבוכדראצר	NEBUCHADNEZ-ZAR	613a	
		נפש	SOUL	659d	3 c
		צפניה	ZEPHANIAH	861b	1
22	26	אחר	ANOTHER	29c	
		אם	MOTHER	51c	1
		טול	HURL	376d	
		ילד	BE BORN	409a	
		על	UPON	757a	2 7c a
22	27	נפש	SOUL	660d	6 a
		נשא	LIFT	672a	2
		על	UPON	757a	2 7c a
		שוב	TURN BACK	997b	3 b
		שוב	TURN BACK	997b	3 a
		שם	THERE	1027b	2
22	28	בזה	DESPISE	102c	1
		יהויכין	JEHOIACHIN	220c	
		זרע	SOWING	282d	4 c
		חפץ	DELIGHT	343b	1
		טול	HURL	376d	1
		ידע	KNOW	394a	2
		מדוע	WHEREFORE	396c	
		כלי	ARTICLE	479c	1
		נפץ	SHATTER	658d	
		עצב	VESSEL	781a	
		שלך	THROW	1021c	2
22	29	ארץ	EARTH	76a	1 b
		צפניה	ZEPHANIAH	861b	1
22	30	דוד	DAVID	188b	E
		זרע	SOWING	282d	4 c
		כתב	WRITE	507d	3
		משל	RULE	605d	1
		ערירי	STRIPPED	792d	
22	33	ל	TO	511c	1 gb
23	1	אבד	CAUSE TO STRAY	2a	3
		פוץ	BE DISPERSED	807b	1 a
		צאן	SMALL CATTLE	838c	3
		מרעית	PASTURING	945c	1
23	2	הנה	BEHOLD	*244b	B b
		נדח	THRUST	623b	2
		על	UPON	757c	2 7c b
		פוץ	BE DISPERSED	807b	1 a
		צאן	SMALL CATTLE	838c	3
		רעה	TEND	945a	1 c
		רע	EVIL	948a	3
23	3	נדח	THRUST	623b	2
		נוה	ABODE OF FLOCKS	627c	1 a
		על	UPON	757a	2 7c a
		פרה	BEAR FRUIT	826a	1
		צאן	SMALL CATTLE	838c	3
		קבץ	GATHER	868a	1
		רבה	BECOME MANY	915a	1 a
		שארית	REST	984d	1
		שוב	TURN BACK	998d	1 a
		שם	THERE	1027b	2
23	4	חתת	BE SHATTERED	369b	2 a
		ירא	FEAR	431a	1 a
		פקד	ATTEND TO	823d	1
		קום	STAND	879a	6 a
		רעה	TEND	945a	1 c
23	5	מלך	KING	573b	2
		מלך	BE KING	574a	
		צדקה	RIGHTEOUSNESS	842b	1 c
		צדיק	JUST	843a	1 a
		צמח	SPROUT	855d	3
		קום	STAND	879a	3
		שכל	BE PRUDENT	968c	6
23	6	במח	SECURITY	105b	2
		יהוה	YAHWEH	*219b	2 3
		יהודה	JUDAH	397b	2
		ישע	BE DELIVERED	446b	1
		צדק	RIGHTEOUSNESS	842a	6 b
		קרא	CALL	896a	6 c
		שכן	SETTLE DOWN	1015a	1 a
23	7	חי	ALIVE	311d	1 a
23	8	בית	HOUSE	110a	5 dd
		זרע	SOWING	283a	4 f
		חי	ALIVE	311d	1 a
		נדח	THRUST	623b	2
		עלה	GO UP	749b	1 a
		צפון	NORTH	861a	
		שם	THERE	1027b	2
23	9	דבר	WORD	*182d	1 2b
		יין	WINE	406d	E
		ל	TO	514b	5 fa
		נביא	PROPHET	612a	2
		עבר	PASS OVER	717b	1 f
		פנה	FACE	818c	2 6c a
		קדש	APARTNESS	871c	1 b
		קרב	INWARD PART	899a	1 a
		רחף	GROW SOFT	934b	
		שבר	BREAK	990d	
		שבר	DRUNKEN	1016c	
23	10	אבל	MOURN	5c	1
		אלה	OATH	46d	3 a
		גבורה	MIGHT	150b	2
		מדבר	WILDERNESS	184d	1
		יבש	BE DRY	386b	1 b
		כן	RIGHT	467b	1
		מלא	BE FULL	570a	1 b
		נאף	COMMIT ADUL-TERY	610d	1 a
		נוה	PASTURE	627d	1
		מרוצה	RUNNING	930d	2
		רע	EVIL	948c	0 d
23	11	גם	YEA	169c	3
		חנף	BE POLLUTED	338a	2
		כהן	PRIEST	463c	4
		מצא	FIND	593b	2 b
		נביא	PROPHET	611d	2
23	12	אפלה	DARKNESS	66c	1
		דחה	PUSH	*191a	
		דחה	THRUST DOWN	191a	
		דחה	THRUST	*191a	
		דרך	WAY	203b	5
		חלקלקות	SMOOTHNESS	325c	1
23	13	נבא	PROPHESY	612c	2
		ראה	TO SEE	907a	2 5
		שמרון	SAMARIA	1038a	
		תעה	ERR	1073c	3
		תפלה	UNSEEMLINESS	1074b	
23	14	בלת	NOT	117a	4 a
		ה	THE	208c	1 ha
		הלך	WALK	232d	1 4a
		חזק	BE FIRM	304d	2
		נאף	COMMIT ADUL-TERY	610c	1 a
		סדם	SODOM	690a	
		עמרה	GOMORRAH	771d	
		ראה	TO SEE	907a	2 5
		רעה	MISERY	949b	3
		רעע	BE EVIL	949d	2
		שערורה	HORRIBLE THING	1045d	
23	15	אכל	EAT	37d	1
		חנפה	PROFANENESS	338b	
		יצא	GO OUT	423b	1 g
		לענה	WORMWOOD	542a	
		מי	WATER	565d	4 a
		שקה	GIVE TO DRINK	1052c	2
23	16	הבל	BECOME VAIN	211a	
		חזון	VISION	303a	3
		נבא	PROPHESY	612b	2
		על	UPON	757c	2 7c b
23	17	לב	HEART	525b	2 6d
		נאץ	CONTEMN	611a	
		שרירות	STUBBORNNESS	1057b	
23	18	מי	WHO	566d	F c
		סוד	COUNCIL	691c	1
		עמד	STAND	764c	7 d
		קשב	ATTEND	904a	
23	19	גרר	DRAG	*176a	
		חול	WHIRL	297b	3
		חול	WHIRL	297c	1
		חמה	RAGE	404d	2 c
		יצא	GO OUT	423c	1 g
		סער	TEMPEST	704b	
		סערה	TEMPEST	704b	
		רשע	WICKED	957c	3
		שוב	TURN BACK	997d	6 f
23	20	אחרית	END	31b	B
		בין	DISCERN	107b	1
		בינה	UNDERSTANDING	108a	1
		מזמה	PURPOSE	273c	1
		קום	STAND	879a	6 f
		שוב	TURN BACK	997d	6 f
23	21	נבא	PROPHESY	612b	2
		רוץ	RUN	930b	1
23	22	דרך	WAY	203d	6 d
		סוד	COUNCIL	691c	1 a
		עמד	STAND	764c	7 d
		רע	EVIL	948a	3
		רע	EVIL	948c	0 d
		שוב	TURN BACK	999b	2 a
23	23	אלהים	GOD	44c	4 bb
		מן	FROM	581d	4 c
		קרב	NEAR	898c	2 f
		רחק	DISTANT	935c	2 a2
23	24	מלא	FILL	570b	2
		סתר	HIDE	711b	1
		מסתר	SECRET PLACE	712c	2 a
23	25	חלם	DREAM	321c	C
		נבא	PROPHESY	612b	2
		נבא	PROPHESY	612b	2
		שקר	DECEPTION	1055c	4
23	26	אמר	SAY	56d	
		ה	THE	208c	1 ha
		ה	INTERROG PART	210a	1 b
		זכר	REMEMBER	270a	1 7
		יש	BE	441c	2
		לב	HEART	525b	2 6b
		נבא	PROPHESY	612b	2
		תרמית	DECEITFULNESS	941c	
		שקר	DECEPTION	1055c	4
23	27	חלום	DREAM	321c	2 b
		חשב	THINK	363a	1 2
		שבח	FORGET	1013b	
		שבח	FORGET	1013b	1 c
23	28	אמת	FIRMNESS	54c	5
		את	WITH	85d	1
		את	WITH	86c	3 a
		בר	GRAIN	141b	

Ch	v.	Heb	Eng	Page	Sec
		דבר	WORD	182c	1 2a
		חלום	DREAM	321d	2 b
		מה	WHAT	553b	1 dc
		ספר	COUNT	708a	1
		תבן	STRAW	1062a	
23	29	אש	FIRE	77d	5
		כה	THUS	462a	1
		כה	THUS	*462a	1
		פטיש	FORGE-HAMMER	809c	
		פצץ	BREAK	823a	1
23	30	אל	TO	40b	4
		גנב	STEAL	170c	
23	31	לקח	TAKE	543c	4 g
		לשון	TONGUE	546b	1 b
		נאם	UTTER A PROPHECY	610c	
23	32	אל	TO	40b	4
		חלום	DREAM	321d	2 b
		יעל	PROFIT	418d	1
		ספר	COUNT	708a	1
		פחזות	RECKLESSNESS	808d	1
		תעה	ERR	1073c	3
23	33	את	MARK OF THE ACCUSATIVE	85b	3 a
		כהן	PRIEST	463c	4
		נביא	PROPHET	611d	2
		נטש	FORSAKE	643d	2
		משא	UTTERANCE	672d	
		נשה	FORGET	*674d	
23	34	כהן	PRIEST	463c	4
		נביא	PROPHET	611d	2
		משא	UTTERANCE	672d	
23	35	אל	TO	41b	
		על	UPON	757c	2 7c b
23	36	אלהים	GOD	44b	4 a
		אלהים	GOD	44d	4 c
		הפך	TURN	245c	1 c2
		חי	ALIVE	311d	1 a
		משא	UTTERANCE	672d	
23	38	דבר	WORD	182a	1 1a
		כן	SO	487a	3 d
		משא	UTTERANCE	672d	
		יען	ON ACCOUNT OF	774d	1
23	39	נטש	FORSAKE	643d	2
		נשה	FORGET	674c	
		נשה	FORGET	674c	
		פנה	FACE	819a	2 8a
23	40	חרפה	REPROACH	357d	1
		כלמות	IGNOMINY	484b	
		נתן	PUT	680c	2 b
		עולם	LONG DURATION	762a	2 b
24	1	דוד	POT	188c	B
		יהויקים	JEHOIAKIM	220c	1
		יהויכין	JEHOIACHIN	220c	
		היכל	TEMPLE	228c	2 b
		חרש	GRAVER	360d	1 d
		יעד	BE SET	417a	
		מסגר	LOCKSMITH	689d	1
		ראה	TO SEE	908d	1 a2
		תאנה	FIG	1061a	2
24	2	אכל	EAT	37d	1
		בכורה	FIRST RIPE FIG	114c	
		דוד	POT	188c	B
		טוב	PLEASANT	373d	1 b
		מן	ON ACCOUNT OF	580b	2 f
		רע	EVIL	947d	1
		רע	EVIL	948b	4
		תאנה	FIG	1061a	2
		תאנה	FIG	1061a	2
		בכורה	ADDENDA ET CORRIGENDA	1121c	
24	3	אכל	EAT	37d	1
		טוב	PLEASANT	373d	1 b
		רע	EVIL	947d	1
		רע	EVIL	948b	4
		תאנה	FIG	1061a	2
24	5	טוב	PLEASANT	373d	1 b
		טובה	WELFARE	375d	3
		כשדים	CHALDEANS	505a	1 b
		נכר	REGARD	648a	1
		שלח	SEND	1019a	1 a
		תאנה	FIG	1061a	2
24	6	בנה	BUILD	124d	2 b
		הרס	THROW DOWN	248d	1
		טובה	WELFARE	375d	3
		נטע	PLANT	642c	2
		נתש	PLUCK UP	684c	
		על	UPON	757c	2 7c a
		שום	TO PLACE	963d	2 c
		שוב	TURN BACK	998d	1 a
		עין	ADDENDA ET CORRIGENDA	1125d	
24	7	אנכי	I	59c	
		יהוה	YAHWEH	219a	2 2b a
		לב	HEART	524c	2 2
		לב	HEART	524d	2 3b
24	8	אכל	EAT	37d	1
		רע	EVIL	947d	1
		רע	EVIL	948b	4
		שארית	REST	984d	1
		תאנה	FIG	1061a	2
24	9	זועה	A TREMBLING	266b	
		חרפה	REPROACH	358a	3
		ממלכה	KINGDOM	575b	1
		משל	PROVERB	605b	2
		נדח	THRUST	623b	2
		נתן	GIVE	681a	3 b
		קללה	CURSE	887a	
		שנינה	SHARP WORD	1042b	
24	10	אדמה	LAND	10a	5
		תמם	BE FINISHED	1070c	5
25	1	יהודה	JUDAH	397b	1 3
		נבוכדראצר	NEBUCHADNEZZAR	613a	
		על	UPON	757c	2 7c b
		ראשני	FIRST	912a	2
		רביעי	FOURTH	918a	2
25	2	אל	TO	41a	B
		דבר	SPEAK	*181d	1
		יהודה	JUDAH	397b	1 3
		על	UPON	757c	2 7c b
25	3	אמון	AMON	54c	A
		דבר	SPEAK	180d	1
		דבר	WORD	182c	1 2a
		שכם	START EARLY	1014d	
		שלש	THREE	1025d	2
25	4	נביא	PROPHET	611d	1
		נטה	INCLINE	641a	3 e
		עבד	SLAVE	714b	4
		שכם	START EARLY	1014d	
		שלח	SEND	1018c	2 a
25	5	אדמה	LAND	10a	5
		דרך	WAY	203d	6 d
		מן	FROM	583d	9 b2
		עולם	LONG DURATION	763a	2 m
		רע	EVIL	948a	3
25	6	הלך	WALK	235a	2 3d 2
		כעס	VEX	495a	2
		עבד	WORK	713b	4 b
		מעשה	DEED	795d	1 a2
25	7	טוב	A GOOD THING	375a	1
		כעס	VEX	495a	2
		מעשה	DEED	795d	1 a2
		רע	EVIL	948a	2
25	8	יען	ON ACCOUNT OF	774d	2 a
25	9	בוא	COME	99c	2 a
		חרבה	WASTE	352b	2
		חרם	BAN	355d	1 c
		נבוכדראצר	NEBUCHADNEZZAR	613a	
		עבד	SLAVE	713d	1
		עולם	LONG DURATION	762b	2 b1
		צפון	NORTH	861a	
		שמה	APPALMENT	1031c	2
		שרקה	HISSING	1056d	
25	10	אבד	DESTROY	2b	2
		אור	LIGHT	21c	6
		חתן	DAUGHTER:S HUSBAND	368d	1
		כלה	BRIDE	483c	2 a
		נר	LAMP	632d	
		קול	VOICE	876d	1 a
		קול	VOICE	877b	2 m
		ששון	REJOICING	965b	
		שמחה	JOY	970d	1
25	11	חרבה	WASTE	352b	2
		שמה	APPALMENT	1031c	2
25	12	היה	COME TO PASS	225b	1 2b ae
		כשדים	CHALDEANS	505a	1 b
		מלא	BE FULL	570b	1
		עון	INIQUITY	731a	1 c1
		עולם	LONG DURATION	762b	2 b1
25	13	בוא	COME	99c	2 a
		דבר	SPEAK	181d	5
		דבר	WORD	183a	2 2
		גבא	PROPHESY	612b	1 b
		ספר	MISSIVE	707b	3 a
25	14	עבד	WORK	713b	3
		מעשה	DEED	795d	1 a3
		פעל	DOING	821c	1 c
25	15	חמה	RAGE	404d	2 c
		יין	WINE	406d	E
		כוס	CUP	468a	
		שקה	GIVE TO DRINK	1052c	2
25	16	געש	SHAKE	172b	
		הלל	PRAISE	239b	
		שלח	SEND	1018c	2 b
		שתה	DRINK	1059b	1 e
25	17	כוס	CUP	468a	
		שקה	GIVE TO DRINK	1052c	2
25	18	חרבה	WASTE	352b	2
		יום	DAY	400d	7 h
		קללה	CURSE	887a	
		שמה	APPALMENT	1031c	2
		שרקה	HISSING	1056d	
25	19	פרעה	PHARAOH	829a	
25	20	ארץ	EARTH	76a	2 a
		אשדוד	AHSDOD	78c	
		אשקלון	ASHKELON	80c	
		כשל	STUMBLE	505c	1
		עוץ	UZ	734b	2
		עזה	GAZA	738b	
		עקרון	EKRON	785d	
		ערב	MIXTURE	786b	
		שארית	REST	984d	1
25	22	אי	COAST	16a	
		עבר	REGION ACROSS	719b	1
		צידון	SIDON	851a	
		צר	TYER	862d	
25	23	בוז	BUZ	100c	1
		דדן	DEDAN	187a	1
		פאה	CORNER	802b	1
		קצץ	CUT OFF	893c	
		תימא	TEMA	1066d	
25	24	דדן	ADDENDA ET CORRIGENDA	1122a	
		ערב	MIXTURE	786b	
		ערב	STEPPE-DWELLERS	787b	
		פלש	ROLL IN	814b	
25	25	מדי	MEDES	552a	1
		עילם	ELAM	743d	
25	26	אל	TO	40b	5
		ארץ	EARTH	76a	1 a
		ממלכה	KINGDOM	575b	1
		צפון	NORTH	861a	
		קרב	NEAR	898c	2 b
		רחק	DISTANT	935b	1 a
		ששך	SHESHACH	1058d	
		שתה	DRINK	1059c	1 e
25	27	נפל	FALL	656d	1
		קום	STAND	877d	1 a
		קיה	VOMIT	883d	
		שכר	BE DRUNK	1016b	
		שתה	DRINK	1059c	1 e
25	28	כוס	CUP	468a	
		מאן	REFUSE	549b	
25	29	ארץ	EARTH	76a	1 a
		ו	AND	252d	1 f
		חלל	POLLUTE	320d	2
		נאם	UTTERANCE	610b	2
		נקה	BE CLEAN	667b	3
		קרא	CALL	896b	6 d4
		רעע	BE EVIL	949d	1
25	30	ארץ	EARTH	76a	1 a
		דרך	TREAD	202a	3
		הידד	SHOUT	212c	2
		הידד	SHOUTING	212c	1
		נבא	PROPHESY	612b	1 b
		נוה	HABITATION	627c	2
		נתן	GIVE	679d	1 x
		מעון	REFUGE	733a	2
		ענה	SING	777b	
		קדש	APARTNESS	871c	2 a
		מרום	HEIGHT	928d	2
		שאג	ROAR	980d	1
		שאג	ROAR	980d	1
25	31	בשר	FLESH	142d	6 c
		ל	TO	511a	1 d
		קצה	END	892b	1
		ריב	STRIFE	937a	3
		רשע	WICKED	957b	2
		שאון	ROAR	981a	1
		שפט	JUDGE	1048a	1
25	32	ירכה	EXTREME PARTS	438b	2
		סער	TEMPEST	704b	
		עור	ROUSE ONESELF	735a	
25	33	אדמה	GROUND	9c	1
		אסף	GATHER	62d	1 c
		דמן	DUNG	199b	
		חלל	PIERCED	319c	2
		ספד	WAIL	704d	
		קבר	BURY	868c	
		קצה	END	892b	1
25	34	אדיר	MAJESTIC	12b	2
		זעק	CRY	277c	2 d
		חמדה	DESIRE	326d	
		טבח	SLAUGHTER	370c	1
		ילל	HOWL	410b	
		כלי	ARTICLE	479c	1
		מלא	BE FULL	570b	1 b
		תפוצה	DISPERSION	807b	
		צאן	SMALL CATTLE	838c	3
25	35	אבד	PERISH	1d	2
		אדיר	MAJESTIC	12b	2
		מנוס	ESCAPE	631a	2
		פליטה	ESCAPE	812c	1
		צאן	SMALL CATTLE	838c	3
25	36	אדיר	MAJESTIC	12b	2
		יללה	HOWLING	410b	
		צאן	SMALL CATTLE	838c	3
		צעקה	CRY	858d	2
		מרעית	PASTURING	945c	2
		שדד	DEAL VIOLENTLY WITH	994a	
25	37	דמם	BE SILENT	199a	
		חרון	BURNING OF ANGER	354c	
		נוה	PASTURE	627d	1
		שלום	PEACE	1023a	4
25	38	חרון	BURNING OF ANGER	354c	
		חרון	BURNING OF ANGER	354c	
		כפיר	LION	498d	
		סך	THICKET	697c	
		שמה	APPALMENT	1031c	2
26	1	ממלכות	REIGN	575c	3
		ראשית	BEGINNING	912a	1 a
26	2	גרע	DIMINISH	175c	1
		דבר	SPEAK	*181d	1
		חצר	ENCLOSURE	347a	3 b
		על	UPON	757c	2 7c b
		שחה	BOW DOWN	1005c	2 c
26	3	דרך	WAY	203d	6 d
		חשב	THINK	363b	2 2
		נחם	BE SORRY	637a	2
		רע	EVIL	948a	3

Ch	v.	Heb	Eng	Page	Sec
26	4	רעה	MISERY	949b	1
		תורה	INSTRUCTION	436a	1 c
		נתן	PUT	680d	2 b
		פנה	FACE	817c	2 4b g
26	5	נביא	PROPHET	611d	4
		עבד	SLAVE	714b	4
		על	UPON	757c	2 7c b
		שכם	START EARLY	1014d	
26	6	ארץ	EARTH	76a	1 a
		זה	THIS	260a	
		שלו	SHILOH	1017d	
26	7	כהן	PRIEST	463c	4
		נביא	PROPHET	611d	2
		שמע	HEAR	1033c	1 b
26	8	כהן	PRIEST	463c	4
		מות	DIE	559d	2 a
		נביא	PROPHET	611d	2
		תפש	LAY HOLD OF	1074d	1
26	9	חרב	BE WASTE	351c	
		ישב	DWELL	443b	3
		נבא	PROPHESY	612b	1 b
		קהל	ASSEMBLE AS	875a	2
		שלו	SHILOH	1017d	
26	10	חדש	NEW	294b	A
		ישב	SIT	442c	1 a
		עלה	GO UP	748b	1 d
		פתח	OPENING	836a	
		שער	GATE	1045b	3 b
26	11	כהן	PRIEST	463c	4
		מות	DEATH	560d	2
		נביא	PROPHET	611d	2
		נבא	PROPHESY	612b	1 b
		משפט	JUDGMENT	1048c	1 e
26	12	נבא	PROPHESY	612b	1 b
26	13	דבר	SPEAK	181d	5
		דרך	WAY	203c	6 a
		יטב	MAKE GOOD	406a	4
		נחם	BE SORRY	637a	2
		רעה	MISERY	949b	1
26	14	טוב	PLEASANT	374a	2 f
		ישר	STRAIGHT	449a	2 b
26	15	אל	TO	41a	B
		אמת	FIRMNESS	54c	5
		דבר	SPEAK	181c	4 b
		דם	BLOOD	*196d	2 d
		דם	BLOOD	197a	2 i
		כי	THAT	471d	1 a
		כיאם	THAT IF	474c	1 a
		מות	DIE	560b	1 b
		נקי	CLEAN	667c	1
		על	UPON	756c	2 7a b
		על	UPON	757b	2 7c aa
		שום	TO PLACE	*963a	
26	16	דבר	SPEAK	181c	4 a
		כהן	PRIEST	463c	4
		מות	DEATH	560d	2
		נביא	PROPHET	611d	2
		משפט	JUDGMENT	1048c	1 e
26	17	זקן	OLD	278d	2 b
		קהל	ASSEMBLY	874c	1 d
26	18	במה	HIGH PLACE	119a	1
		הר	MOUNTAIN	249c	1 a
		חזקיהו	HEZEKIAH	306a	1
		חרש	CUT IN	360c	
		יער	WOOD	420d	E
		מורשתי	MORESHETH	440d	
		מיכה	MICAH	567c	1
		מכה	MICHA	*567d	2
		נבא	PROPHESY	612b	1 b
		עי	RUIN	730d	
		ציון	ZION	851b	
26	19	דבר	SPEAK	181d	5
		חזקיהו	HEZEKIAH	306a	1
		חלה	MOLLIFY	318c	1 a
		ירא	FEAR	431c	3 b
		מות	DIE	560b	1 b
		נחם	BE SORRY	637a	2
		נפש	SOUL	660b	4 b7
		עשה	DO	793d	1 1a 2
		רעה	MISERY	949b	1
		רעה	MISERY	949b	1
26	20	אוריהו	URIAH	22c	
		נבא	PROPHESY	612b	1 b
		נבא	PROPHESY	612b	1 b
		קריתיערים	KIRIATH-JEARIM	900c	
		שמעיה	SHEMAIAH	1035d	3
26	21	בקש	SEEK	134d	2 c
		ברח	FLEE	137d	2
		ירא	FEAR	431a	4
		מות	DIE	560b	1 b
26	22	אלנתן	ELNATHAN	46b	A
		מצרים	EGYPT	595d	1 b1
		עכבור	ACHBOR	747b	2
26	23	בן	SON	121b	1 jk
		יצא	CAUSE TO GO	424c	1 a
		נבלה	CARCASS	615c	1 a
		עם	PEOPLE	766d	5 b
		קבצער	GRAVE	868d	
26	24	אחיקם	AHIKAM	27b	
		את	WITH	86a	1 a
		יד	HAND	389d	1 e1
		מות	DIE	560b	1 b
		שפן	SHAPHAN	1051a	2
27	1	יאשיהו	JOSIAH	78c	1
		ממלכה	REIGN	575c	3
		ראשית	BEGINNING	912a	1 a

Ch	v.	Heb	Eng	Page	Sec
		ירמיה	JEREMIAH	941c	1
27	2	מוסר	BAND	64c	
		מוטה	BAR OF YOKE	557b	2
		נתן	PUT	680a	2 a
		צואר	NECK	848c	1
27	3	ה	THE	209b	2 b
		מלאך	MESSENGER	521c	1 a
		צידון	SIDON	851a	
		צר	TYER	862d	
		שלח	SEND	1019a	1 e
27	4	צוה	CHARGE	846a	4 a
27	5	זרוע	ARM	284a	1 c
		ישר	BE STRAIGHT	448c	2
		כח	STRENGTH	471c	3
27	6	חיה	LIVING THING	312c	1 b
		נבוכדראצר	NEBUCHADNEZ-ZAR	613b	
		עבד	WORK	713a	2
		עבד	SLAVE	713d	1
27	7	ב	IN	89d	3 2b
		בן	SON	120b	1 f
		גדול	GREAT	153a	6 b
		עבד	WORK	713a	3
		עבד	WORK	713b	3
		עת	TIME	773d	2 c
27	8	את	MARK OF THE ACCUSATIVE	85b	3 a
		היה	COME TO PASS	225a	1 2b ag
		מוטה	BAR OF YOKE	*557b	2
		ממלכה	KINGDOM	575a	1
		נבוכדראצר	NEBUCHADNEZ-ZAR	613b	
		נתן	PUT	680d	2 a
		על	YOKE	760d	
		צואר	NECK	848c	1
		תמם	BE COMPLETE	1070c	7
		תמם	BE FINISHED	1070c	5
27	9	אשר	PARTICLE OF RELATION	82b	2 a
		הם	THEY	241c	2 c
		חלום	DREAM	321d	2 b
		כשף	SORCERER	506d	1
		נביא	PROPHET	612a	2
		ענן	PRACTISE SOOTH-SAYING	778b	
		קסם	PRACTICE OF DIVINATION	890d	2
27	10	אבד	PERISH	1c	1
		נבא	PROPHESY	612b	2
		נדח	THRUST	623b	2
		מען	PURPOSE	775c	2 1
		רחק	BE DISTANT	935b	2
		שקר	DECEPTION	1055c	4
27	11	מוטה	BAR OF YOKE	*557b	2
		גוח	REST	628d	B 2
		עבד	WORK	713a	1
		על	YOKE	760d	
		צואר	NECK	848c	1
27	12	בוא	COME	99b	1 g
		מוטה	BAR OF YOKE	*557b	
		על	YOKE	760d	
		צדקיה	ZEDEKIAH	843b	1
		צואר	NECK	848c	1
27	13	דבר	SPEAK	181a	3 b
27	14	נביא	PROPHET	612a	2
		נבא	PROPHESY	612b	2
		שקר	DECEPTION	1055c	4
27	15	אבד	PERISH	1c	1
		נביא	PROPHET	612a	2
		נבא	PROPHESY	612b	2
		נבא	PROPHESY	612b	2
		נדח	THRUST	623b	2
		מען	PURPOSE	775c	2 1
		שקר	DECEPTION	1055c	4
27	16	כהן	PRIEST	463d	4
		כלי	UTENSIL	480a	2 f
		מהרה	HASTE	555b	
		נביא	PROPHET	612a	2
		נבא	PROPHESY	612b	2
		נבא	PROPHESY	612b	2
		שוב	TURN BACK	1000a	
		שקר	DECEPTION	1055c	4
27	17	חרבה	WASTE	352a	1
27	18	את	WITH	86c	3 a
		בלת	NOT	117a	4 a
		דבר	WORD	182c	1 2a
		יש	BE	441c	2 a
		כלי	UTENSIL	480a	2 f
		נביא	PROPHET	612a	2
		פגע	MEET	803c	4
27	19	אל	TO	41a	B
		אמר	SAY	56a	1
		יתר	REMAINDER	451d	1 a
		מכונה	BASE	467d	
		כלי	UTENSIL	480a	2 f
		על	UPON	754d	2 1f g
		עמוד	PILLAR	765b	2
27	20	יהויכין	JEHOIACHIN	220c	
		חר	NOBLE	359d	
		נבוכדראצר	NEBUCHADNEZ-ZAR	613b	
27	21	יתר	BE LEFT OVER	451b	
		כלי	UTENSIL	480a	2 f
27	22	בוא	COME	99d	B
		על	UPON	757a	2 7c a
		פקד	ATTEND TO	823c	A 2

Ch	v.	Heb	Eng	Page	Sec
		מקום	STANDING PLACE	880b	4
		שוב	TURN BACK	998d	1 a
		שם	THERE	1027c	3 c
28	1	גבעון	GIBEON	149c	1
		חמישי	FIFTH	332c	1
		חנניהו	HANANIAH	337b	4
		כהן	PRIEST	463d	4
		ממלכה	REIGN	575c	3
		נביא	PROPHET	612a	2
		עזור	AZZUR	741a	1
		צדקיהו	ZEDEKIAH	843b	1
		ראשית	BEGINNING	912a	1 a
		רביעי	FOURTH	918a	2
		שנה	YEAR	1040c	
28	2	על	YOKE	760d	
		שבר	BREAK	990c	
28	3	יום	TIME	399d	6 b
		כלי	UTENSIL	480a	2 f
		נבוכדראצר	NEBUCHADNEZ-ZAR	613b	
		עוד	STILL	729c	2 ab
		שוב	TURN BACK	998d	1 a
28	4	יהויכין	JEHOIACHIN	220c	
		על	YOKE	760d	
		שבר	BREAK	990c	
28	5	חנניה	HANANIAH	337b	4
		כהן	PRIEST	463d	4
		נביא	PROPHET	612a	2
		ירמיה	JEREMIAH	941c	1
28	6	אמן	VERILY	53b	
		כלי	UTENSIL	480a	2 f
		כן	SO	*486a	1 ca
		נבא	PROPHESY	612b	1 b
		ירמיה	JEREMIAH	941c	1
		שוב	TURN BACK	998d	1 a
28	7	דבר	SPEAK	180c	
28	8	אל	TO	41a	B
		ממלכה	KINGDOM	575b	1
		נביא	PROPHET	611d	1
		נבא	PROPHESY	612b	1 b
		עולם	LONG DURATION	761d	1 a
28	9	אמת	FIRMNESS	54c	5
		בוא	COME	98c	2
		ידע	BE MADE KNOWN	394c	1
		נביא	PROPHET	611d	1
		נבא	PROPHESY	612b	1 b
		עדד	ODED	729c	2
28	10	חנניהו	HANANIAH	337b	4
		מוטה	BAR OF YOKE	557b	2
		נביא	PROPHET	612a	2
		על	UPON	758c	4 2a
		ירמיה	JEREMIAH	941c	1
		שבר	BREAK	990c	
28	11	אמר	SAY	56a	1
		דרך	JOURNEY	203b	1
		חנניהו	HANANIAH	337b	4
		יום	TIME	399d	6 b
		ככה	THUS	462c	
		מוטה	BAR OF YOKE	*557b	2
		נבוכדראצר	NEBUCHADNEZ-ZAR	613b	
		עוד	STILL	729c	2 ab
		על	UPON	758c	4 2a
		על	YOKE	760d	
		ירמיה	JEREMIAH	941c	1
		שבר	BREAK	990c	
28	12	חנניהו	HANANIAH	337b	4
		מוטה	BAR OF YOKE	557b	2
		נביא	PROPHET	612a	2
		ירמיה	JEREMIAH	941c	1
		שבר	BREAK	990c	
28	13	בעל	BAAL	127d	2 2
		ברזל	IRON	137c	3
		הלך	WALK	233c	1 4c 6
		חנניהו	HANANIAH	337b	4
		מוטה	BAR OF YOKE	557b	2
		עץ	TREE	781d	2 a
		שבר	BREAK	990c	
28	14	ברזל	IRON	137c	3
		חיה	LIVING THING	312c	1 b
		מוטה	BAR OF YOKE	*557b	2
		נבוכדראצר	NEBUCHADNEZ-ZAR	613b	
		נתן	PUT	680a	2 a
		עבד	WORK	713a	3
		על	YOKE	760d	
28	15	בטח	TRUST	105b	
		חנניהו	HANANIAH	337b	4
		נביא	PROPHET	612a	2
		ירמיה	JEREMIAH	941c	1
28	16	דבר	SPEAK	181a	1
		ה	THE	207b	1 ca
		סרה	A TURNING ASIDE	694c	2
		פנה	FACE	819b	2 8b
		שלח	SEND	1019a	2 c
28	17	חנניהו	HANANIAH	337b	4
		נביא	PROPHET	612a	2
29	1	דבר	WORD	183a	2 1a
		זקן	OLD	278d	2 b
		יתר	REMAINDER	451d	1 b
		כהן	PRIEST	463c	4
		נביא	PROPHET	611d	2
		נבוכדראצר	NEBUCHADNEZ-ZAR	613b	
		ספר	MISSIVE	707a	1 b
		ירמיה	JEREMIAH	941c	1

Ch	v.	Heb	Eng	Page	Sec
29	2	גבירה	QUEEN-MOTHER	150c	2
		יהויכין	JEHOIACHIN	220c	
		חרש	GRAVER	360d	1 d
		מסגר	LOCKSMITH	689d	1
		סריס	EUNUCH	710c	
29	3	אלעשה	ELEASAH	46c	D
		גמריהו	GEMARIAH	170b	2
		חלקיהו	HILKIAH	324d	6
		נבוכדראצר	NEBUCHADNEZZAR	613b	
		צדקיהו	ZEDEKIAH	843b	1
		שפן	SHAPHAN	1051a	3
29	5	בנה	BUILD	124b	1 ab
		גנה	GARDEN	171b	
		נטע	PLANT	642c	1
		פרי	FRUIT	826b	1
29	6	איש	MAN	35d	
		ילד	BEGET	409a	1
		לקח	TAKE	543b	4 e1
		מעט	BE SMALL	589c	
29	7	דרש	SEEK	205c	6
		פלל	INTERVENE	813b	1
29	8	חלם	DREAM	321c	
		חלום	DREAM	321d	2 b
		נביא	PROPHET	612a	2
		נשא	DECEIVE	674a	
		קסם	PRACTICE OF DIVINATION	890d	2
29	9	ה	THE	*208c	1 hb
		נבא	PROPHESY	612b	2
		שקר	DECEPTION	1055c	4
29	10	דבר	WORD	182d	1 2b
		טוב	PLEASANT	374d	9 b
		מלא	BE FULL	570b	1 b
		על	UPON	756d	27 a c
		פה	MOUTH	805c	6 c1
		פקד	ATTEND TO	823c	A 2
29	11	אחרית	END	31a	B
		חשב	THINK	363b	2 2
		מחשבה	THOUGHT	364c	1
		על	UPON	756d	27 a c
		תקוה	HOPE	876b	3
29	12	קרא	CALL	895d	5 c
29	13	בקש	SEEK	134d	3 a
		דרש	SEEK	205b	3 a
		לבב	HEART	523c	2 2
		מצא	FIND	593a	1 a
		מצא	FIND	394a	1 f
29	14	נדח	THRUST	623b	2
		קבץ	GATHER	868a	1
		שבית	CAPTIVITY	986b	2 a
29	15	נביא	PROPHET	612a	2
		קום	STAND	879a	3
29	16	דוד	DAVID	188b	E
		יצא	GO OUT	423d	2 a
		עם	PEOPLE	766c	2 a
29	17	אכל	EAT	37d	1
		רע	EVIL	947d	1
		שער	HORRID	1045d	
29	18	אלה	OATH	46d	4
		זועה	A TREMBLING	266b	
		חרפה	REPROACH	358a	3
		ממלכה	KINGDOM	575b	1
		נדח	THRUST	623b	2
		נתן	GIVE	681a	3 b
		רדף	PURSUE	922d	1 e
		שמה	APPALMENT	1031c	2
		שרקה	HISSING	1057a	
29	19	נביא	PROPHET	611d	1
		עבד	SLAVE	714b	4
		שכם	START EARLY	1014d	
		שמע	HEAR	1034a	1 k
		תחת	INSTEAD	1066a	23 a b
29	20	שלח	SEND	1019a	1 a
29	21	אחאב	AHAB	26c	2
		נבא	PROPHESY	612b	2
		נבוכדראצר	NEBUCHADNEZZAR	613a	
		מעשיהו	MAASEIAH	796b	2
		צדקיהו	ZEDEKIAH	843c	2 b
		שקר	DECEPTION	1055c	4
29	22	אחאב	AHAB	26c	2
		ב	IN	90a	32 d
		ל	TO	514a	5 e
		לקח	TAKE	544a	1
		צדקיהו	ZEDEKIAH	843c	2 b
		קלה	ROAST	885d	2
		קללה	CURSE	887a	
		שוה	SET	1001b	
29	23	דבר	SPEAK	181c	4 a
		הוא	HE, SHE, IT	*214d	
		הוא	HE, SHE, IT	216b	4 ba
		ו	AND	253d	1 k
		נאף	COMMIT ADULTERY	610d	1 a
		נבלה	SENSELESSNESS	615a	1
		עד	WITNESS	729d	2 a
		יען	ON ACCOUNT OF	774d	2 a
		רע	FRIEND	946a	2
29	24	נחלמי	NEHELAMITE	636d	
		שמעיה	SHEMAIAH	1035c	2 a
29	25	כהן	PRIEST	463c	4
		כהן	PRIEST	463d	4
		ספר	MISSIVE	707a	1 b
		עם	PEOPLE	766c	2 a
		מעשיהו	MAASEIAH	796b	1
		שם	NAME	1028a	2 a
29	26	יהוידע	JEHOIADA	220c	2
		מהפכת	STOCKS	246b	
		כהן	PRIEST	463c	4
		כהן	PRIEST	463c	4
		נבא	PROPHESY	612b	1 a
		נגיד	LEADER	618a	3
		נתן	PUT	680b	2 a
		פקיד	COMMISSIONER	824b	
		צינק	PILLORY	857b	
		שגע	BE MAD	993d	
29	27	גער	REBUKE	172a	1
		נבא	PROPHESY	612b	1 b
		ענתתי	ANATHOTHITE	779a	
		ירמיה	JEREMIAH	941c	1
29	28	בנה	BUILD	124b	1 ab
		גנה	GARDEN	171b	
		כיעלכן	FOR THEREFORE	475c	
		נטע	PLANT	642c	1
		פרי	FRUIT	826b	1
		שלח	SEND	1018b	1 c
29	29	כהן	PRIEST	463c	4
		ספר	MISSIVE	707b	1 b
		קרא	CALL	895c	4 a
29	31	בטח	TRUST	105b	
		נבא	PROPHESY	612b	2
		נחלמי	NEHELAMITE	636d	
		על	UPON	757b	27 c aa
		שמעיה	SHEMAIAH	1035c	2 a
29	32	דבר	SPEAK	181a	2
		זרע	SOWING	282d	4 c
		טוב	A GOOD THING	375a	1
		נחלמי	NEHELAMITE	636d	
		סרה	A TURNING ASIDE	694c	2
		ראה	TO SEE	908a	8 a5
		שמעיה	SHEMAIAH	1035c	2 a
30	2	ספר	MISSIVE	707b	3 a
		ספר	MISSIVE	*707c	4
		על	UPON	757a	27 c a
30	3	שבית	CAPTIVITY	986b	2 a
30	4	דבר	SPEAK	181a	3 b
30	5	חרדה	TREMBLING	353d	1
		פחד	DREAD	808c	1
30	6	אם	IF	50d	2 ba
		הפך	TURN	246a	1
		זכר	MALE	271c	11 b
		חלץ	LOINS	323b	3
		מדוע	WHEREFORE	396c	
		ילד	BEAR	*408b	1 a
		ילד	BEAR	408c	1 b
		ירקון	PALENESS	439a	2
		פנה	FACE	815d	1 a
		פנה	FACE	815d	11
		ראה	TO SEE	907b	5 a
		ראה	TO SEE	907b	26
		שאל	ASK	982a	2 a
30	7	אין	WHENCE	32d	
		אין	NOT	35b	6 dg
		גדול	GREAT	153a	6 a
		הוי	AH	223a	
		ישע	BE DELIVERED	446b	1
		יעקב	JACOB	785a	2
		צרה	DISTRESS	865b	
30	8	מוסר	BAND	64c	
		זור	BE A STRANGER	266c	2 c
		נאם	UTTERANCE	610b	2
		נתק	TEAR APART	683d	1
		עבד	WORK	713a	2
		על	YOKE	760d	
		צואר	NECK	848c	1
30	9	דוד	DAVID	188a	
		יהוה	YAHWEH	218d	2 1d
		קום	STAND	879a	3
30	10	זרע	SOWING	283a	4 g
		חרד	TREMBLE	353c	
		חתת	BE SHATTERED	369b	2 a
		ירא	FEAR	431a	1 a
		ישע	DELIVER	446d	1 b
		ל	TO	513b	5 ba
		עבד	SLAVE	714b	5
		שאן	BE AT EASE	983b	
		שבי	CAPTIVITY	985d	1
		שקט	BE QUIET	1053a	1
30	11	אנכי	I	59b	
		יסר	DISCIPLINE	416b	2 a
		ישע	DELIVER	446d	1 b
		כי	BECAUSE	474a	3 c
		כלה	COMPLETE	478d	2 a
		כלה	COMPLETE	478d	2 a
		ל	TO	516c	5 jb
		נקה	BE CLEAN	667c	2
		פוץ	BE DISPERSED	807b	1 a
30	12	אנש	BE SICK	60c	
		חלה	BE WEAK	318a	2
		מכה	BLOW	647a	1 c
		שבר	BREAKING	991a	1
30	13	דין	JUDGE	192b	2 a
		דין	JUDGMENT	192c	2
		מזור	WOUND	267a	
		תעלה	HEALING	752b	
		רפאה	REMEDY	951b	
30	14	אהב	LOVE	13b	2
		איב	BE HOSTILE TO	33c	
		דרש	SEEK	205c	7
		חטאת	SIN	308c	1 b
		מוסר	DISCIPLINE	416c	2 a
		אכזרי	CRUEL	470a	
		נכה	SMITE	645d	1 e
		מכה	BLOW	647a	1 c
		עון	INIQUITY	731b	2 b
		עצם	BE VAST	782c	2
30	15	אנש	BE SICK	60c	
		שכח	FORGET	1013a	1 b
		זעק	CRY	277c	2 d
		חטאת	SIN	308c	1 b
		מכאוב	PAIN	456c	2
		עון	INIQUITY	731b	2 b
		עצם	BE VAST	782c	2
		שבר	BREAKING	991a	1
30	16	אכל	EAT	37c	1
		בזו	SPOIL	102d	
		בז	SPOIL	103a	1
		הלך	WALK	231b	1 d3 ge
		כל	ALL	481d	1 da
		שבי	CAPTIVITY	985d	1
		שסה	PLUNDER	1042c	
		שסס	PLUNDER	1042d	
		משסה	PLUNDER	1042d	
30	17	אין	NOT	34d	3
		ארוכה	HEALING	74a	A
		דרש	SEEK	205c	7
		ל	TO	*512a	3 b
		מכה	BLOW	647a	1 c
		עלה	GO UP	749d	4
		קרא	CALL	896a	6 e1
		רפא	HEAL	950d	2 a
30	18	אהל	TENT	14a	2
		בנה	BUILD	125a	1 b
		ישב	SIT	443b	4
		על	UPON	754a	2 1f
		רחם	LOVE	933c	1
		שבית	CAPTIVITY	986b	2 a
		משכן	DWELLING-PLACE	1015d	3 a
		משפט	JUDGMENT	1049b	6 d
		תל	MOUND	1068b	2
30	19	תודה	THANKSGIVING CHOIR	392d	3
		כבד	CAUSE TO BE HONORED	458a	3
		קול	VOICE	876d	1 a
		שחק	LAUGH	966a	3
30	20	עדה	CONGREGATION	417b	3
		כון	BE FIRM	465c	1 a
		לחץ	OPPRESS	537d	2
		פנה	FACE	817a	24a b
		קדם	FRONT	869d	2 d
30	21	אדיר	MAJESTIC	12b	2
		הוא	HE, SHE, IT	216c	4 bb
		חיה	BECOME	226a	2 1b
		זה	THIS	*261b	4 b
		מי	WHO	566c	E a
		מי	WHO	566c	F c
		מן	OUT OF	579c	2 cb
		משל	RULE	605d	1
		נגש	DRAW NEAR	620d	1
		נגש	DRAW NEAR	621a	
		ערב	TAKE ON PLEDGE	786d	2
		קרב	COME NEAR	898a	2 a1
30	22	אנכי	I	59c	
30	23	גרר	DRAG	176a	
		חול	WHIRL	297b	3
		חול	WHIRL	*297c	1
		חמה	RAGE	404d	2 c
		יצא	GO OUT	423c	1 g
		סערה	TEMPEST	704b	
		סער	TEMPEST	704b	
		רשע	WICKED	957c	3
30	24	אחרית	END	31b	B
		בין	DISCERN	107b	1 f
		מזמה	PURPOSE	273c	1
		חרון	BURNING OF ANGER	354c	
		שוב	TURN BACK	997d	6 f
31	1	משפחה	CLAN	1046d	1 c
31	2	חן	FAVOR	336c	2 b2
		מצא	FIND	592d	1 a
		רגע	BE AT REST	921b	A
		שריד	SURVIVOR	975a	1
31	3	אהב	LOVE	13b	5 b
		אהבה	LOVE	13c	2
		חסד	GOODNESS	339a	2 1a
		כן	SO	487b	3 f
		משך	DRAW	604b	1
		משך	DRAW	*604c	5
		עולם	LONG DURATION	762b	2 c
		ראה	TO SEE	908b	1 a
		רחק	DISTANT	935c	2 a2
31	4	בנה	BUILD	124d	2 b
		בנה	BUILD	125a	1 b
		בתולה	VIRGIN	144a	
		מחול	DANCE	298b	
		עדה	ORNAMENT	725d	1 a
		עוד	STILL	729b	1 b
		שחק	LAUGH	966a	3
		תף	TIMBREL	1074c	
31	5	חלל	POLLUTE	320c	4
		כרם	VINEYARD	501d	
		נטע	PLANT	642c	1
		עוד	STILL	729b	1 b
		שמרון	SAMARIA	1038a	
31	6	הר	MOUNTAIN	251a	2 b

Ch v.	Heb	Eng	Page	Sec
	נצר	WATCH	665d	1
	עלה	GO UP	748b	1 c
31 7	קרא	CALL	895b	3 a
	הלל	PRAISE	238b	2 b
	ישע	DELIVER	446d	1 b
	צהל	CRY SHRILLY	843d	2
	ראש	HEAD	911a	3 c
	רנן	GIVE A RINGING CRY	943b	1
	שארית	REST	984d	1
31 8	גדול	GREAT	153a	2
	הנה	HITHER	244c	A a
	יחדו	TOGETHER	403c	A a
	ילד	BEAR	408b	1 a
	ירכה	EXTREME PARTS	438b	2
	עור	BLIND	734c	1 a
	פסח	LAME	820c	
	צפון	NORTH	861a	
	צפון	NORTH	861a	
	קבץ	GATHER	868a	1
	קהל	ASSEMBLY	874c	1 c
	שוב	TURN BACK	997b	3 b
31 9	אב	FATHER	3b	2
	אפרים	EPHRAIM	68c	4
	בכי	WEEPING	113d	
	בכור	FIRST-BORN	114b	3
	הלך	WALK	236d	1 d
	תחנון	SUPPLICATION FOR FAVOR	337d	
	יבל	CONDUCT	385a	3
	ישר	STRAIGHT	449a	1
	כשל	STUMBLE	505d	1
	נחל	TORRENT	636b	1
	שמר	KEEP	1037a	4 a
31 10	אי	COAST	16a	
	זרה	SCATTER	280a	1
	עדר	FLOCK	727d	1 a
	קבץ	GATHER	868a	1
	מרחק	DISTANT PLACE	935d	2
31 11	אל	TO	41b	
	גאל	REDEEM	145c	3 c
	חזק	STRONG	305d	2
	פדה	RANSOM	804a	3 b
31 12	אל	TO	41b	
	דאב	BECOME FAINT	178b	
	דגן	CORN	186c	
	טוב	GOOD THINGS	375c	1
	יסף	DO AGAIN	415c	2 a
	תירוש	NEW WINE	440d	
	נהר	FLOW	625c	
	על	UPON	757b	2 7c ab
	יצהר	FRESH OIL	844a	
	ציון	ZION	851c	
	רוה	WATERED	924b	
	מרום	HEIGHT	928d	1
	רנן	GIVE A RINGING CRY	943b	
31 13	אבל	MOURNING	5d	
	בחור	YOUNG MAN	104c	
	בתולה	VIRGIN	143d	
	הפך	TURN	245c	1 c4
	זקן	OLD	278c	2 a
	מחול	DANCE	298b	
	מחול	DANCE	298b	
	יגון	GRIEF	387b	
	יחדו	TOGETHER	403c	A
	מן	FROM	578a	1 a
	נחם	CONSOLE ONESELF	637b	
	ששון	REJOICING	965b	
	שמח	REJOICE	970c	
31 14	דשן	FATNESS	206c	1
	טוב	GOOD THINGS	375c	1
	כהן	PRIEST	463d	4
	רוה	BE SATURATED	924b	2
	שבע	SATISFIED	959c	2 b
31 15	בכי	WEEPING	113d	
	בכי	WEEPING	113d	
	מאן	REFUSE	549a	
	תמרור	BITTERNESS	601b	
	נהי	WAILING	624d	
	נחם	CONSOLE ONESELF	637a	3
	רמה	RAMA	928a	1
	רחל	RACHEL	933a	
31 16	בכי	WEEPING	113d	
	דמעה	TEARS	199c	
	מנע	WITHHOLD	586a	
	עין	EYE	744b	1 h
	פעלה	WORK	821d	1
	שכר	HIRE	969a	2
	שוב	TURN BACK	997a	2
31 17	אחרית	END	31a	B
	גבול	BOUNDARY	148a	2
	ל	TO	511b	1 ga
	תקוה	HOPE	876b	1
31 18	אפרים	EPHRAIM	68c	4
	יהוה	YAHWEH	219a	2 1f
	יסר	BE CORRECTED	416a	
	יסר	DISCIPLINE	416b	2 a
	לא	NOT	*519c	2 b
	נוד	SHEW GRIEF	627a	3
	עגל	CALF	722b	
	שוב	TURN BACK	999b	2 a
	שמע	HEAR	1034b	2 h
31 19	בוש	BE ASHAMED	101d	
	חרפה	REPROACH	357d	1
	ידע	BE PERCEIVED	394d	4
	ירך	THIGH	438a	1 a
	כי	THAT	472d	1 e
	כלם	BE HUMILIATED	483d	2
	נחם	BE SORRY	637a	2
	נעורים	YOUTH	655c	
31 20	נשא	LIFT	671b	2 d
	ספק	SLAP	706c	1
	אפרים	EPHRAIM	68c	4
	בן	SON	120b	1 c
	די	SUFFICIENCY	191d	2 ca
	ה	INTERROG PART	210a	1 c
	חמה	MURMUR	242b	2
	זכר	REMEMBER	270b	2 1 c
	ילד	CHILD	409c	E
	יקור	VERY PRECIOUS	430b	
	כן	SO	487b	3 f
	ל	TO	515a	5 g
	מעה	BELLY	589a	5
	על	UPON	756d	2 7a c
	רחם	LOVE	933c	1
	שעשעים	DELIGHT	1044b	
31 21	אלה	THESE	41c	A
	בתולה	VIRGIN	144a	
	ל	TO	515d	5 ia
	לב	HEART	524d	2 3c
	נצב	STAND	662c	2
	מסלה	HIGHWAY	700c	
	ציון	SIGN POST	846b	
	שום	TO PLACE	964b	4 c
	שית	PUT	1011b	2 b
	תמרור	SIGN-POST	1071d	
31 22	בת	DAUGHTER	123c	3
	ברא	CREATE	135b	3
	חדש	NEW	294b	A
	חמק	TURN AWAY	330b	
	נקבה	FEMALE	666c	1
	סבב	SURROUND	686b	1
	שובב	BACKTURNING	1000a	
31 23	אכר	PLOUGHMAN	38d	
	ברך	BLESS	139a	2 a
	דבר	WORD	182a	1 1a
	הר	MOUNTAIN	249d	1 a
	נוה	HABITATION	627d	2
	עוד	STILL	729b	1 b
	צדק	RIGHTEOUSNESS	841d	D
	קדש	APARTNESS	871d	2 e
	שבית	CAPTIVITY	986b	2
31 24	אכר	PLOUGHMAN	38d	
	נסע	JOURNEY	652b	3
31 25	בכה	WEEP	113c	
	דאב	BECOME FAINT	178b	
	נפש	SOUL	660c	5 b
	עיף	FAINT	746a	
	רוה	BE SATURATED	924b	
	שמש	SUN	1039b	1
31 26	שנה	SLEEP	446a	
	ערב	BE SWEET	787a	
	קיץ	AWAKE	884c	1 c
31 27	אדם	MAN	9b	2
	זרע	SOW	281d	3 b
	זרע	SOWING	282c	3
31 28	בנה	BUILD	124c	1 d
	היה	COME TO PASS	225a	1 2b ad
	הרס	THROW DOWN	248d	1
	כאשר	AS	*455b	1 b
	כן	SO	486c	2 cd
	נטע	PLANT	642c	2
	נתץ	PULL DOWN	683b	2 a
	נתש	PLUCK UP	684c	1
	רעע	BE EVIL	949c	1
	שקד	WATCH	1052a	1
31 29	בסר	SOUR GRAPES	126a	
	קהה	BE BLUNT	874b	
	שן	TOOTH	1042a	1 a
31 30	ב	IN	*90c	3 5
	בסר	SOUR GRAPES	126a	
	מות	DIE	560a	2 b
	עון	INIQUITY	731b	2 c
	קהה	BE BLUNT	874b	
	שן	TOOTH	1042a	1 a
31 31	ברית	COVENANT	137a	3 1
	ברית	COVENANT	137a	2 2k
	ברית	COVENANT	137a	2 2k
	חדש	NEW	294a	A
	כרת	CUT	503d	4
31 32	אשר	PARTICLE OF RELATION	82b	3
	בעט	MARRY	127b	1
	ברית	COVENANT	136c	2 2c
	ברית	COVENANT	137a	3 1
	ברית	COVENANT	137b	3 3
	חזק	BE FIRM	305a	6 a
	יצא	CAUSE TO GO	424c	1 a
	כרת	CUT	503d	4
	פרר	BREAK	830b	1 b
	בהל	ADDENDA ET CORRIGENDA	1121b	
	בעל	ADDENDA ET CORRIGENDA	1121c	
	בעל	ADDENDA ET CORRIGENDA	1121c	
31 33	ברית	COVENANT	137a	3 1
	ברית	COVENANT	137a	2 2k
	תורה	INSTRUCTION	436a	1 d
	כרת	CUT	503d	4
	כתב	WRITE	507c	1 b1
	לב	HEART	525a	2 3d
	קרב	INWARD PART	899b	2 a
31 34	גדול	GREAT	153b	7
	זכר	REMEMBER	270c	24
	חטאת	SIN	309a	1 d5
	למד	LEARN	540d	
	מן	FROM	583d	9 b1
	סלח	FORGIVE	699b	
	עון	INIQUITY	731a	1 c2
	קטן	SMALL	882a	2 b2
31 35	חמה	ROAR	242b	3
	חקה	SOMETHING PRESCRIBED	350a	2 a
	יומם	BY DAY	401c	2
	ירח	MOON	437a	
	כוכב	STAR	456d	
	צבא	GOD OF WAR	839c	4 b
	רגע	DISTURB	920d	
31 36	גוי	NATION	156c	1 b
	גם	ALSO	169d	4
	זרע	SOWING	283a	4 f
	חק	SOMETHING PRESCRIBED	349c	7 a
	יום	DAY	400c	7 f
	מוש	DEPART	559a	
	מן	FROM	583a	7 b
	פנה	FACE	817a	24 a b
	פנה	FACE	818a	2 5a d
31 37	גם	ALSO	169d	4
	זרע	SOWING	283a	4 f
	חקר	SEARCH	350d	
	מוסד	FOUNDATION	414c	
	מאס	REJECT	549d	1 b
	מדד	MEASURE	551a	
	מטה	DOWNWARDS	641b	2 a
	מעל	ABOVE	752a	2 d
31 38	בנה	BUILD	125a	1 b
	מגדל	TOWER	154a	1
	חננאל	HANANEL	337a	
	מן	FROM	581d	5 a
	מן	FROM	582b	5 d3
	שער	GATE	1044d	1 b 6
31 39	גבעה	HILL	149a	4
	געה	GOAH	171d	
	גרב	GAREB	173a	2
	יצא	GO OUT	423d	1 h
	מדה	MEASURE	551c	1
	נגד	IN FRONT	617b	1 ab
	סבב	TURN AROUND	686b	1 c
	על	UPON	757c	2 7c ab
	קו	LINE	876a	
	קוה	CORNER	876a	
	קו	LINE	876a	
31 40	דשן	FAT ASHES	206c	2
	הרס	THROW DOWN	248d	1
	מזרח	PLACE OF SUNRISE	281a	2 c1
	נחל	WADY	636c	2
	נתש	PLUCK UP	684c	
	סוס	HORSE	692b	2
	עולם	LONG DURATION	762d	2 f
	עמק	VALE	771a	
	פגר	CORPSE	803d	1
	קדרון	KEDRON	871b	
	קדש	APARTNESS	871d	2 e
	שדמה	FIELD	995b	
	שער	GATE	1044d	1 b 5
32 1	נבוכדראצר	NEBUCHADNEZZAR	613a	
	עשר	TEN	797c	
	עשירי	TENTH	798a	1
	שמנה	EIGHT	1033a	2 a
	שנה	YEAR	1040c	
32 2	חיל	STRENGTH	299a	4
	חצר	ENCLOSURE	347a	2
	כלא	SHUT UP	476b	1
	מורה	GUARD	643c	1
	צור	CONFINE	848d	2
32 3	אמר	SAY	56b	1
	כלא	SHUT UP	476b	1
	נבא	PROPHESY	612b	1 b
32 4	דבר	SPEAK	181c	3 e
	כשדים	CHALDEANS	505a	1 b
	מלט	SLIP AWAY	572c	2
	עין	EYE	745a	5
	פה	MOUTH	805a	2 a
	ראה	TO SEE	906d	1 b
32 5	הלך	WALK	236d	1 d
	כשדים	CHALDEANS	505a	1 b
	לחם	ENGAGE IN BATTLE	535c	
	פקד	ATTEND TO	823c	A 2
	צלח	ADVANCE	852c	2
32 7	גאלה	REDEMPTION	145d	3
	דוד	UNCLE	187c	2
	חנמאל	HANAMEL	335d	
	ל	TO	513b	5 ba
	ל	TO	515d	5 ia
	ענתות	ANATHOTH	779a	1
	שלום	SHALLUM	1024b	4
	משפט	JUDGMENT	1049a	5
32 8	בנימין	BENJAMIN	122d	1
	גאלה	REDEMPTION	145d	3
	דוד	UNCLE	187c	2
	חנמאל	HANAMEL	335d	
	חצר	ENCLOSURE	347a	2
	ירשה	POSSESSION	440b	

Ch v.	Heb	Eng	Page	Sec
	ל	TO	513b	5 ba
	מטרה	GUARD	643c	1
	ענתות	ANATHOTH	779a	1
	משפט	JUDGMENT	1049a	5
32 9	דוד	UNCLE	187c	2
	חנמאל	HANAMEL	335d	
	כסף	SILVER	494b	8 a
	כסף	SILVER	494c	9
	ענתות	ANATHOTH	779a	1
	עשר	TEN	797a	3 d
	שקל	WEIGH	1053c	2
	שקל	SHEKEL	1053d	
32 10	מאזן	BALANCES	24d	
	חתם	SEAL	367d	2
	כסף	SILVER	494c	9
	ספר	MISSIVE	707a	2
	עד	WITNESS	729d	2 c
	עוד	BEAR WITNESS	730a	2
	שקל	WEIGH	1053c	2
32 11	חק	SOMETHING PRE-SCRIBED	349c	7 c
	חתם	SEAL	367d	2
	ספר	MISSIVE	707a	2
	מקנה	PURCHASE	889c	1
32 12	ברוך	BARUCH	140a	1
	דוד	UNCLE	187c	2
	חנמאל	HANAMEL	335d	
	מחסיה	MAHSEIAH	340c	
	חצר	ENCLOSURE	347a	2
	יהודי	JEW	397c	
	נריהו	NERIAH	633a	
	מטרה	GUARD	643c	1
	ספר	MISSIVE	707a	2
	עד	WITNESS	729d	2 c
	עין	EYE	745a	5
	מקנה	PURCHASE	889c	1
32 13	ברוך	BARUCH	140a	1
32 14	ו	AND	253a	1 h
	חרש	EARTHENWARE	360a	1
	חתם	SEAL	367d	2
	כלי	VESSEL	480a	3
	ספר	MISSIVE	707a	2
	עמד	STAND	764b	3 c
	מקנה	PURCHASE	889c	1
32 15	עוד	STILL	729b	1 b
	קנה	ACQUIRE	889a	
32 16	ברוך	BARUCH	140a	1
	נריהו	NERIAH	633a	
	ספר	MISSIVE	707a	2
	מקנה	PURCHASE	889c	1
32 17	אדון	LORD	11c	4 a
	אהה	ALAS	13c	
	דבר	WORD	183d	4 6
	זרוע	ARM	284a	1 c
	כח	STRENGTH	*470d	3
	כח	STRENGTH	471a	3
	כל	ALL	*482b	1 ec
	פלא	BE SURPASSING	810c	1
32 18	אחר	AFTER	30a	2 b
	אל	GOD	42c	6 a
	אלף	THOUSAND	49a	1 a
	גבור	STRONG	150a	1
	גדול	GREAT	153b	6 c
	חיק	BOSOM	300d	1
	חסד	GOODNESS	339b	2 3b
	עון	INIQUITY	731a	1 c1
	על	UPON	757c	7 c ab
	שלם	BE COMPLETE	1022c	5
32 19	אשר	PARTICLE OF RE-LATION	82b	3
	גדול	GREAT	153c	8
	דרך	WAY	203c	6 a
	ה	THE	208b	1 ha
	עצה	ADVICE	420b	
	נתן	GIVE	679d	1 v
	עין	EYE	744b	1 j
	מעלל	DEED	760b	1
	עליליה	DEED	760b	
	פקח	OPEN	824d	1 a
	פרי	FRUIT	826c	
	רב	MUCH	913b	1 d
32 20	אדם	MAN	9c	2
	אות	SIGN	16d	4
	מופת	WONDER	69a	1
	מופת	SIGN	69a	2
	ו	AND	253a	1 h
	יום	DAY	400d	7 h
	שום	TO PLACE	964d	5 c
	שם	NAME	1028a	2 b1
32 21	אות	SIGN	16d	4
	מופת	WONDER	69a	1
	זרוע	ARM	284a	1 c
	אזרוע	ARM	284b	
	חזק	STRONG	305c	1 b
	יצא	CAUSE TO GO	424c	1 a
	מורא	FEAR	432b	4
	נטה	EXTEND	640a	1 a
32 22	דבש	HONEY	185b	
	זוב	FLOW	264d	2
	חלב	MILK	316c	A 4
	שבע	SWEAR	989c	2
32 23	תורה	LAW	436a	2
	צוה	GIVE CHARGE TO	845c	1 b
	קרא	ENCOUNTER	897a	
32 24	בוא	COME	98b	2
	כשדים	CHALDEANS	505a	1 b

Ch v.	Heb	Eng	Page	Sec
	לחם	ENGAGE IN BAT-TLE	535c	
	סללה	MOUND	700c	
32 25	אדון	LORD	11c	4 a
	כסף	SILVER	494d	9
	כשדים	CHALDEANS	505a	1 b
	עד	WITNESS	729d	2 c
	עוד	BEAR WITNESS	730a	2
32 27	אלהים	GOD	44c	4 bb
	בשר	FLESH	142d	6 c
	דבר	WORD	183d	4 6
	ה	INTERROG PART	209d	1 b
	יהוה	YAHWEH	219b	2 2d
	הנה	BEHOLD	243d	
	פלא	BE SURPASSING	810c	1
32 28	כשדים	CHALDEANS	505a	1 b
	נבוכדראצר	NEBUCHADNEZ-ZAR	613a	
32 29	בעל	BAAL	127d	2 2
	גג	ROOF	150d	1
	י	AND	253a	1 g
	יצת	KINDLE	428c	
	כעס	VEX	495a	2
	כשדים	CHALDEANS	505a	1 b
	לחם	ENGAGE IN BAT-TLE	535c	
	נסך	POUR OUT	650d	
	נסך	DRINK-OFFERING	651a	1
	מען	PURPOSE	775c	2 1
	קטר	MAKE SACRAFICES SMOKE	883a	
	קטר	MAKE SACRAFICES SMOKE	883a	
32 30	אך	ONLY	36d	2 bb
	כעס	VEX	495a	2
	כעס	VEX	495a	2
	נעורות	YOUTH	655c	
	מעשה	DEED	795d	1 a2
	רע	EVIL	948c	0 b
32 31	בנה	BUILD	124b	1 aa
	יום	DAY	401b	7 k
	מן	FROM	583d	9 b2
	סור	TURN ASIDE	694b	1
	על	UPON	757d	2 7 c c
	פנה	FACE	819b	2 8a
32 32	כהן	PRIEST	463d	4
	כעס	VEX	495a	2
	נביא	PROPHET	611d	2
	רעה	MISERY	949b	3
32 33	מוסר	DISCIPLINE	416c	1 a
	למד	LEARN	540d	
	ערף	BACK OF NECK	791b	1
	פנה	TURN	815b	1 b
	פנה	FACE	816a	1 1d
	שכם	START EARLY	1014d	
32 34	טמא	BE UNCLEAN	379a	2
	קרא	CALL	896b	6 d4
	שום	TO PLACE	964b	4 c
	שקוץ	DETESTED THING	1055a	
32 35	במה	HIGH PLACE	119b	3
	בנה	BUILD	124c	1 ai
	בעל	BAAL	127d	2 2
	הנם	HINNOM	245a	
	חטא	MISS A GOAL OR WAY	*307d	2
	חטא	MISS A GOAL OR WAY	307d	2
	לב	HEART	525a	2 3d
	מלך	MOLECH	574c	
	עבר	PASS OVER	718d	1 d
	במה	SECURITY	105b	
32 37	חמה	RAGE	404d	2 c
	ישב	CAUSE TO SIT	443d	3 a
	נדח	THRUST	623b	2
	קבץ	GATHER	868a	1
	קצף	WRATH	893c	1
32 39	אחר	AFTER	30a	2 b
	דרך	WAY	*203c	6 a
	דרך	WAY	203c	6 c
	טוב	A GOOD THING	375a	1
	יום	DAY	400c	7 f
	יחד	UNITE	*402d	
	ירא	FEAR	431c	3 b
32 40	ברית	COVENANT	137a	2 2k
	ברית	COVENANT	137a	3 1
	ברית	COVENANT	137b	3 2
	יטב	DO GOOD TO	405d	2
	יראה	FEAR	432a	3
	כרת	CUT	504a	4
	לבב	HEART	524a	2 6a
	סור	TURN ASIDE	693c	1
	על	UPON	759a	4 2c
	עולם	LONG DURATION	762c	2 d
	שוב	TURN BACK	998a	6 h
32 41	אמת	FIRMNESS	54c	5
	יטב	DO GOOD TO	405d	2
	לבב	HEART	523b	2 2
	נטע	PLANT	642c	2
	נפש	SOUL	661b	0
	שוש	REJOICE	965b	
32 42	בוא	COME	99c	2 a
	דבר	SPEAK	180c	
	טובה	WELFARE	375d	1
	כן	SO	486c	2 cd
	על	UPON	756d	2 7 a c
32 43	אין	NOT	35a	6 db

Ch v.	Heb	Eng	Page	Sec
	כשדים	CHALDEANS	505a	1 b
	קנה	ACQUIRE	889a	
	שממה	WASTE	*1031b	
32 44	בנימן	BENJAMIN	122d	1
	הר	MOUNTAIN	251a	2 b
	חתם	SEAL	367d	2
	כסף	SILVER	494d	9
	נגב	SOUTH-COUNTRY	616b	1 a
	סביב	ROUND ABOUT	687b	2 ab
	ספר	MISSIVE	*707a	2
	עד	WITNESS	729d	2 c
	עוד	BEAR WITNESS	730a	2
	שבית	CAPTIVITY	986b	2
	שבית	CAPTIVITY	986b	2 a
	שוב	TURN BACK	999d	9
	שפלה	LOWLAND	1050c	1
33 1	חצר	ENCLOSURE	347a	2
	מטרה	GUARD	643c	1
	עוד	STILL	*728d	1 aa
	עצר	RESTRAIN	783c	1
33 2	יצר	FORM	428a	2 b
	כון	ESTABLISH	466b	1 c
	שם	NAME	1028c	3
33 3	בצר	MAKE INACCESSI-BLE	131a	
33 4	ענה	ANSWER	772d	1 b
	נתץ	PULL DOWN	683b	1
	סללה	MOUND	700c	
	על	UPON	754d	2 1f g
33 5	כשדים	CHALDEANS	505a	1 b
	לחם	ENGAGE IN BAT-TLE	535c	
	סתר	HIDE	711d	2 c
	פגר	CORPSE	803d	1
	רעה	MISERY	949b	3
33 6	אמת	FIRMNESS	54a	2
	ארוכה	HEALING	74a	A
	עלה	GO UP	749d	4
	עתרת	ABUNDANCE	801d	
	רפא	HEAL	950d	2 a
	מרפא	HEALING	951b	1
33 7	בנה	BUILD	124d	2 b
	כ	LIKE	455a	
	ראשון	FIRST	911d	3 a1
	שבית	CAPTIVITY	986b	2 a
	שוב	TURN BACK	999d	9
33 8	חטא	MISS A GOAL OR WAY	307a	2 b
	טהר	BE CLEAN	372c	1 c
	סלח	FORGIVE	699b	
	עון	INIQUITY	731a	1 c2
	עון	INIQUITY	731a	1 c4
	פשע	REBEL	833b	2
33 9	את	WITH	86b	1 db
	תהלה	PRAISE	240b	5 ca
	טובה	WELFARE	375d	2
	טובה	WELFARE	375d	1
	תפארה	BEAUTY	802d	2 b
	פחד	DREAD	808b	1
	רגז	BE AGITATED	919b	
	ששון	REJOICING	965b	
	שלום	PEACE	1023a	5 b
33 10	אין	NOT	35a	6 db
	חרב	WASTE	351d	
	ישב	DWELL	443b	3
	שמם	BE DESOLATED	1031a	1
33 11	חסד	GOODNESS	339d	2 3c
	חתן	DAUGHTER:S HUS-BAND	368d	2
	טוב	PLEASANT	374d	9 b
	ידה	PRAISE	392c	1 b
	תודה	THANK-OFFERING	393a	4
	כ	LIKE	455a	
	כלה	BRIDE	483c	2 a
	עולם	LONG DURATION	762b	2 c
	קול	VOICE	876d	1 a
	ראשון	FIRST	911d	3 a1
	ששון	REJOICING	965b	
	שמחה	JOY	970d	1
	שבית	CAPTIVITY	986b	2 a
	שוב	TURN BACK	999d	9
33 12	אין	NOT	35a	6 db
	חרב	WASTE	351d	
	נוה	ABODE OF SHEP-HERD	627c	1 b
	עוד	STILL	729b	1 b
	רבץ	LIE DOWN	918c	1
33 13	בנימן	BENJAMIN	122d	1
	הר	MOUNTAIN	251a	2 b
	יד	HAND	391c	5 h2
	מנה	COUNT	584a	1
	נגב	SOUTH-COUNTRY	616b	1 a
	סביב	ROUND ABOUT	687b	2 ab
	עבר	PASS OVER	718b	5 g
	עוד	STILL	729b	1 b
	על	UPON	754a	2 1f a
	שבט	ROD	*987a	1 c
	שפלה	LOWLAND	1050c	1
33 14	אל	TO	41a	B
	דבר	SPEAK	181a	3 b
	דבר	WORD	182d	1 2b
	טוב	PLEASANT	374d	9 b
33 15	צדקה	RIGHTEOUSNESS	842a	1 a
	צדקה	RIGHTEOUSNESS	842b	1 c
	צמח	SPROUT	855c	1
	צמח	SPROUT	855d	3

JEREMIAH

Ch v.	Heb	Eng	Page	Sec
33 16	במח	SECURITY	105b	
	יהוה	YAHWEH	219b	2 3
	זה	THIS	261b	2
	יהודה	JUDAH	397b	2
	ישע	BE DELIVERED	446b	1
	צדק	RIGHTEOUSNESS	842a	6 b
	קרא	CALL	896a	6 e1
	שכן	SETTLE DOWN	1015a	1 a
33 17	כסא	THRONE	491b	3 a
	כרת	BE CUT OFF	504b	4
33 18	זבח	SACRIFICE	257c	1 1
	זבח	SACRIFICE	258a	7 f
	יום	DAY	400c	7 f
	כהן	PRIEST	463b	5
	כרת	BE CUT OFF	504b	4
	לוי	LEVITE	533a	3 1b
	מנחה	OFFERING	585b	4
	מנחה	OFFERING	585c	6
	עלה	WHOLE BURNT OF-FERING	750d	
	עשה	DO	794d	2 4
	פנה	FACE	818a	2 5a d
	קמר	MAKE SACRIFICES SMOKE	883a	1 a
33 20	ברית	COVENANT	136c	2 2a
	ברית	COVENANT	137b	3 3
	יומם	DAYTIME	401c	1
	לילה	NIGHT	538c	1
	פרר	BREAK	830b	1 b
33 21	ברית	COVENANT	136d	2 2f
	ברית	COVENANT	137b	3 3
	גם	ALSO	169d	4
	דוד	DAVID	188a	
	זרע	SOWING	282d	4 c
	כהן	PRIEST	463b	5
	לוי	LEVITE	533a	3 1b
	מן	FROM	583b	7 ba
	פרר	BREAK	830c	2
	שרת	SERVE	1058b	2 a
33 22	אשר	THAT	83d	8 e
	דוד	DAVID	188a	
	זרע	SOWING	282d	4 c
	חול	SAND	297d	A
	חול	SAND	297d	C
	כן	SO	486d	2 db
	לוי	LEVITE	533a	3 1b
	מדד	MEASURE	551a	
	ספר	COUNT	708a	
	צבא	HOST	839b	1 c
	שרת	SERVE	1058b	2 a
33 24	בחר	CHOOSE	103d	1 a
	גוי	NATION	156c	1 b
	מאס	REJECT	549c	1 a
	מה	WHAT	552d	1 b
	מן	FROM	583b	7 ba
	נאץ	CONTEMN	610d	
	ראה	TO SEE	907b	5 a
33 25	אם	IF	50a	1a4 a
	ברית	COVENANT	136c	2 2a
	חקה	SOMETHING PRE-SCRIBED	350a	2 a
	יומם	DAYTIME	401c	1
	לילה	NIGHT	538c	1
	שום	TO PLACE	963d	3 b
33 26	גם	ALSO	169d	4
	דוד	DAVID	188a	
	זרע	SOWING	282d	4 c
	זרע	SOWING	283a	4 f
	זרע	SOWING	283a	4 f
	מאס	REJECT	549c	1 a
	מן	FROM	583b	7 ba
	משל	RULE	605d	1
	יצחק	ISAAC	850c	
	רחם	LOVE	933c	1
	שבות	CAPTIVITY	986b	2 a
	שוב	TURN BACK	999d	9
34 1	חיל	STRENGTH	299a	4
	לחם	ENGAGE IN BAT-TLE	535c	
	ממלכה	KINGDOM	575b	1
	ממשלה	RULE	606a	1
	נבוכדראצר	NEBUCHADNEZ-ZAR	613a	
34 2	אמר	SAY	56b	1
	הלך	WALK	233c	14c 6
34 3	מלט	SLIP AWAY	572c	2
	עין	EYE	745a	5
	פה	MOUTH	805a	2 a
	ראה	TO SEE	906d	1 b
	תפש	LAY HOLD OF	1074d	2
	תפש	LAY HOLD OF	1075a	
34 4	חומה	WALL	327b	1
34 5	אדון	LORD	11a	1 1c
	הוי	AH	222d	
	כן	SO	486b	2 ad d
	ספד	WAIL	704d	
	שרף	BURN	977a	2 a
	משרפה	A BURNING	977c	
34 7	אל	TO	41a	B
	מבצר	FORTIFICATION	131c	
	הוא	HE, SHE, IT	*215b	1 a
	הם	THEY	241b	1 a
	יתר	BE LEFT OVER	451d	
	לחם	ENGAGE IN BAT-TLE	535c	
	לכיש	LACHISH	540c	
	עזקה	DIG ABOUT	740a	
	שאר	REMAIN	984a	1
34 8	ברית	COVENANT	136b	1 2
	דרור	LIBERTY	204d	2
	כרת	CUT	503d	4
	לחם	ENGAGE IN BAT-TLE	535c	
	קרא	CALL	895b	3 a
34 9	ברית	COVENANT	136b	1 2
	חפשי	FREE	344d	1
	יהודי	JEWISH	397c	
	עבד	WORK	713a	2
	עברי	HEBREW	720b	1 b
	שפחה	MAID	1046c	1
34 10	ברית	COVENANT	136b	1 2
	ברית	COVENANT	136c	1 5
	חפשי	FREE	344d	1
	עבד	WORK	713a	2
	שפחה	MAID	1046c	1
34 11	ברית	COVENANT	136b	1 2
	חפשי	FREE	344d	1
	כבש	SUBDUE	461b	1
	כבש	SUBDUE	461b	1
	ל	TO	512c	4 a
	עבד	SLAVE	713d	1
	עבד	SLAVE	714c	7
	שוב	TURN BACK	997c	5 e
	שוב	TURN BACK	998d	1 a
	שפחה	MAID	1046c	1
34 12	ברית	COVENANT	136b	1 2
34 13	בית	HOUSE	109a	1ae 9
	ברית	COVENANT	136b	1 2
	ברית	COVENANT	137a	3 1
	יצא	CAUSE TO GO	424c	1 a
	כרת	CUT	503d	4
	עבד	SLAVE	713d	1
34 14	אח	BROTHER	26b	4
	ברית	COVENANT	136b	1 2
	חפשי	FREE	344d	1
	מכר	SELL	569c	
	עבד	WORK	713a	2
	עברי	HEBREW	720b	1 b
	מעם	FROM WITH	*769a	C
	אח	BROTHER	26b	4
34 15	אתם	YOU	61d	
	ברית	COVENANT	136b	1 2
	דרור	LIBERTY	204d	2
	ישר	STRAIGHT	449a	2 a
	כרת	CUT	504a	4
	קרא	CALL	895b	3 a
	קרא	CALL	896b	6 d4
	שוב	TURN BACK	997c	5 e
34 16	ברית	COVENANT	136b	1 2
	חלל	POLLUTE	320b	1 c
	חפשי	FREE	344d	1
	כבש	SUBDUE	461b	1
	נפש	SOUL	660d	6 a
	עבד	SLAVE	714c	7
	שוב	TURN BACK	997c	5 e
	שוב	TURN BACK	998d	1 a
	שפחה	MAID	1046c	1
34 17	אח	BROTHER	26b	4
	ברית	COVENANT	136b	1 2
	דרור	LIBERTY	204d	2
	דרור	LIBERTY	204d	2
	זועה	A TREMBLING	266b	
	ממלכה	KINGDOM	575b	1
	נתן	GIVE	681a	3 b
	קרא	CALL	895b	3 a
34 18	ברית	COVENANT	136b	1 2
	ברית	COVENANT	136c	2 2b
	בתר	PART	144a	1
	דבר	WORD	183a	2 2
	כרת	CUT	503d	4
	כרת	CUT	504a	4
	עבר	PASS OVER	717c	1 i
	עבר	PASS OVER	717d	3 d
	עגל	CALF	722b	
	שנים	TWO	1041a	1 b1
34 19	בתר	PART	144a	1
	כהן	PRIEST	463b	4
	סרים	EUNUCH	710c	
	עבר	PASS OVER	717d	3 d
	עגל	CALF	722b	
	עם	PEOPLE	766d	5 c
34 20	איב	BE HOSTILE TO	33c	
	מאכל	FOOD	38b	
	בהמה	BEAST	97a	3
	בקש	SEEK	134d	2 a
	נבלה	CARCASS	615c	1 a
	נפש	SOUL	659d	3 c
34 21	איב	BE HOSTILE TO	33c	
	בקש	SEEK	134d	2 a
	נפש	SOUL	659d	3 c
	שר	CHIEFTAIN	978b	2 a
34 22	לחם	ENGAGE IN BAT-TLE	535c	
	שממה	WASTE	*1031b	
34 23	ישב	DWELL	443b	3
34 24	עדר	FLOCK	727d	1 a
35 2	דבר	SPEAK	181b	3 d
	הלך	WALK	233c	14c 6
	יין	WINE	406c	C
	לשכה	ROOM	545d	1 b
	רכבי	RECHABITES	939c	2
35 3	יאזניהו	JAAZANIAH	24d	3
	חבצניה	HABAXZINIAH	287c	
	רכבי	RECHABITES	939c	2
35 4	אלהים	GOD	44a	3 b
	יגדליהו	IGDALIAH	153d	
	חנן	HANAN	337a	6
	לשכה	ROOM	545d	1 b
	סף	THRESHOLD	706c	
	מעל	ABOVE	751c	1 b
	מעשיהו	MAASEIAH	796b	1
	שלום	SHALLUM	1024b	9
	שמר	KEEP	1036c	1 b
35 5	גביע	CUP	149b	
	יין	WINE	406c	C
	כוס	CUP	468a	
	מלא	FULL	571a	
	רכבי	RECHABITES	939c	2
35 6	אב	FATHER	3b	1
	יהונדב	JEHONADAB	220d	1
	עולם	LONG DURATION	762b	2 b4
	צוה	LAY CHARGE UPON	845c	1 a
	רכב	RECHAB	939c	1 a
35 7	בנה	BUILD	124b	1 ab
	גור	SOJOURN	157d	1
	זרע	SOW	281c	1 c
	זרע	SOWING	282b	2 b
	זרע	SOWING	282c	2 e
	ישב	DWELL	443a	3
	נטע	PLANT	642c	1
35 8	בלת	NOT	116d	4 a
	יהונדב	JEHONADAB	220d	1
	צוה	CHARGE	846a	3
	רכב	RECHAB	939c	1 a
35 9	בנה	BUILD	124b	1 ab
	זרע	SOWING	282b	2 b
35 10	יהונדב	JEHONADAB	220d	1
	ישב	DWELL	443a	3
35 11	ארם	ARAM	74b	A
	כשדים	CHALDEANS	505a	1 b
	נבוכדראצר	NEBUCHADNEZ-ZAR	613a	
35 13	פנה	FACE	818b	2 6a
	הלך	WALK	233c	14c 6
	מוסר	DISCIPLINE	416c	1 a
35 14	את	MARK OF THE AC-CUSATIVE	85a	1 b
	בלת	NOT	116d	4 a
	דבר	SPEAK	180d	1
	יהונדב	JEHONADAB	220d	1
	מצוה	COMMANDMENT	846b	1
	קום	STAND	879b	
	רכב	RECHAB	939c	1 a
35 15	אדמה	LAND	10a	5
	אל	TO	41a	A
	דרך	WAY	203d	6 d
	יטב	MAKE GOOD	406a	4
	נביא	PROPHET	611d	1
	עבד	WORK	713b	4 b
	עבד	SLAVE	714b	1
	שכם	START EARLY	1014d	
	שכם	START EARLY	1014d	
35 16	יהונדב	JEHONADAB	220d	1
	מצוה	COMMANDMENT	846b	1
	רכב	RECHAB	939c	1 a
35 17	אלהים	GOD	44c	4 ba
	דבר	SPEAK	181d	5
	כן	SO	487a	3 d
	צבא	GOD OF WAR	839c	4 b
	קרא	CALL	895b	2 a
35 18	יהונדב	JEHONADAB	220d	1
	על	UPON	757c	27c b
	מצוה	COMMANDMENT	846b	1
	מצוה	COMMANDMENT	846b	1
	רכבי	RECHABITES	939c	2
	שמר	KEEP	1037a	3 c
35 19	יהונדב	JEHONADAB	220d	1
	יום	DAY	400c	7 f
	כרת	BE CUT OFF	504b	4
	רכב	RECHAB	939c	1 a
36 1	רביעי	FOURTH	918a	2
	ירמיה	JEREMIAH	941c	1
36 2	דרך	WAY	203d	6 d
	יום	DAY	400b	7 d3 b
	כתב	WRITE	507c	1 b2
	כתב	WRITE	507c	1 b1
	כתב	WRITE	507d	1 c
	מן	FROM	581c	4 a
	ספר	MISSIVE	707b	3 a
	עט	STYLUS	*741c	
36 3	חטאת	SIN	309a	1 d2
	חשב	THINK	363b	2 2
	סלח	FORGIVE	699b	
	עון	INIQUITY	731a	1 c2
	רעה	MISERY	949b	1
36 4	ברוך	BARUCH	140a	1
	דבר	WORD	183a	2 2
	נריהו	NERIAH	633a	
	ספר	MISSIVE	707b	3 a
	ירמיה	JEREMIAH	941c	1
36 5	ברוך	BARUCH	140a	1
	דבר	WORD	183a	2 2
	עצר	RESTRAIN	783c	1
36 6	ברוך	BARUCH	140a	1
	דבר	WORD	183a	2 2
	צום	FASTING	847b	
	קרא	CALL	895c	4 a

Ch	v.	Heb	Eng	Page	Sec
36	7	קרא	CALL	895c	4 a
		ברוך	BARUCH	140a	1
		דבר	SPEAK	181a	3 b
		דבר	WORD	183a	2 2
		דרך	WAY	203d	6 d
		תחנה	FAVOR	337c	2
		נפל	FALL	657d	6
36	8	ברוך	BARUCH	140a	1
		דבר	WORD	183a	2 2
		נריהו	NERIAH	633a	
		ספר	MISSIVE	*707c	4
		קרא	CALL	895c	4 a
		קרא	CALL	895c	4 a
36	9	ברוך	BARUCH	140a	1
		דבר	WORD	183a	2 2
		חמישי	FIFTH	332c	2
		יתר	REMAINDER	451d	1 a
		עם	PEOPLE	766d	4
		צום	FASTING	847b	
		קרא	CALL	895b	3 a
		תשיעי	NINTH	1077d	
36	10	ברוך	BARUCH	140a	1
		גמריהו	GEMARIAH	170b	1
		דבר	WORD	183a	2 2
		חדש	NEW	294b	A
		חצר	ENCLOSURE	347a	3 b
		לשכה	ROOM	545d	1 b
		ספר	MISSIVE	*707c	4
		ספר	ENUMERATOR	708b	1 b
		פתח	OPENING	836a	
		קרא	CALL	895c	4 a
		שער	GATE	1045b	3 b
		שפן	SHAPHAN	1051a	4
36	11	ברוך	BARUCH	140a	1
		גמריהו	GEMARIAH	170b	1
		דבר	WORD	183a	2 2
		מיכיהו	MICAH	567c	3
		ספר	MISSIVE	*707c	4
		על	UPON	758d	4 2a
		שפן	SHAPHAN	1051a	4
36	12	אלנתן	ELNATHAN	46b	A
		ברוך	BARUCH	140a	1
		גמריהו	GEMARIAH	170b	1
		דבר	WORD	183a	2 2
		דליהו	DELAIAH	195b	1 b
		חנניהו	HANANIAH	337b	1
		ירד	GO DOWN	432d	1 c
		לשכה	ROOM	545d	2
		ספר	ENUMERATOR	708b	1 b
		עכבור	ACHBOR	747b	2
		על	UPON	757b	27c ab
		צדקיהו	ZEDEKIAH	843c	3
		שמעיה	SHEMAIAH	1035c	2 b
		שפן	SHAPHAN	1051a	4
36	13	ברוך	BARUCH	140a	1
		דבר	WORD	183a	2 2
		מיכיהו	MICAH	567c	3
		ספר	MISSIVE	*707c	4
36	14	ברוך	BARUCH	140a	1
		דבר	WORD	183a	2 2
		יהודי	JEHUDI	397c	
		כושי	CUSHI	469b	1
		נריהו	NERIAH	633a	
		נתניהו	NETHANIAH	682b	1
		קרא	CALL	895c	4 a
		שלמיהו	SHELEMIAH	1025a	1 a
36	15	ברוך	BARUCH	140a	1
		דבר	WORD	183a	2 2
		ישב	SIT	442d	1 b
		קרא	CALL	895c	4 a
36	16	אל	TO	40a	3 a
		ברוך	BARUCH	140a	1
		דבר	WORD	183a	2 2
		פחד	DREAD	808b	1
36	17	איך	HOW	32c	1
		ברוך	BARUCH	140a	1
		דבר	WORD	183a	2 2
36	18	ברוך	BARUCH	140a	1
		דבר	WORD	183a	2 2
		דיו	INK	188d	
		ספר	MISSIVE	*707c	4
		פה	MOUTH	805a	2 a
		קרא	CALL	895a	1 b
36	19	איפה	WHERE	33a	1
		ברוך	BARUCH	140a	1
		דבר	WORD	183a	2 2
		סתר	HIDE	711b	1
36	20	ברוך	BARUCH	140a	1
		דבר	WORD	183a	2 2
		חצר	ENCLOSURE	347a	2
		לשכה	ROOM	545d	2
		ספר	ENUMERATOR	708b	1 b
		פקד	ATTEND TO	824a	2 b
36	21	ברוך	BARUCH	140a	1
		דבר	WORD	183a	2 2
		יהודי	JEHUDI	397c	
		לשכה	ROOM	545d	2
		ספר	ENUMERATOR	708b	1 b
		על	UPON	759a	4 2c
		קרא	CALL	895c	4 a
36	22	אח	FIRE-POT	29a	
		את	MARK OF THE AC-CUSATIVE	85b	3 a
		בית	HOUSE	109a	1 ae 5
		בער	BURN	129b	
		ברוך	BARUCH	140a	1
		דבר	WORD	183a	2 2
		חרף	HARVEST-TIME	358b	
		את	ADDENDA ET COR-RIGENDA	1120a	
36	23	אח	FIRE-POT	29a	
		ברוך	BARUCH	140a	1
		דבר	WORD	183a	2 2
		דלת	DOOR	195b	4
		היה	COME TO PASS	225a	12a 1d
		יהודי	JEHUDI	397c	
		ספר	ENUMERATOR	708c	2
		עט	STYLUS	*741c	2
		תער	RAZOR	789b	1 b
		קרא	CALL	895c	4 a
		קרע	TEAR	902c	3 a
		תמם	BE FINISHED	1070c	5
36	24	ברוך	BARUCH	140a	1
		דבר	WORD	183a	2 2
		פחד	DREAD	808b	1
36	25	אלנתן	ELNATHAN	46b	A
		בלת	NOT	116d	4 a
		ברוך	BARUCH	140a	1
		גמריהו	GEMARIAH	170b	1
		דבר	WORD	183a	2 2
		דליהו	DELAIAH	195b	1 b
		פגע	MEET	803c	3
		שרף	BURN	976d	1
36	26	ברוך	BARUCH	140a	1
		דבר	WORD	183a	2 2
		ספר	ENUMERATOR	708c	2
		סתר	HIDE	711d	1
		עבדאל	ABDEEL	715a	
		עזריאל	AZRIEL	741a	1
		ירחמאל	JERAHMEEL	934a	2
		שריה	SERAIAH	976a	6
		שלמיה	SHELEMIAH	1025a	1 b
36	27	ברוך	BARUCH	140a	1
		דבר	WORD	183a	2 2
		שרף	BURN	976d	2 a
36	28	ברוך	BARUCH	140a	1
		דבר	WORD	183a	2 2
		כתב	WRITE	507c	1 b1
		שרף	BURN	976d	2 a
		שוב	TURN BACK	998b	8
		שוב	TURN BACK	998b	8
36	29	ברוך	BARUCH	140a	1
		דבר	WORD	183a	2 2
		על	UPON	757c	27c b
		שרף	BURN	976d	2 a
		שבל	SHOBAL	987c	1
		שבת	CEASE	992a	2
		שחת	GO TO RUIN	1008b	1
36	30	ברוך	BARUCH	140a	1
		דבר	WORD	183a	2 2
		דוד	DAVID	188b	E
		זרע	SOWING	*282d	4 c
		חרב	DRYNESS	351b	3
		נבלה	CARCASS	615c	1 a
		תנובה	FRUIT	626c	
		קרח	FROST	901c	1
		שלך	THROW	1021c	1
36	31	אל	TO	41a	B
		בוא	COME	99c	2 a
		ברוך	BARUCH	140a	1
		דבר	SPEAK	181a	3 b
		דבר	WORD	183a	2 2
		זרע	SOWING	282d	4 c
		עון	INIQUITY	731a	1 c1
		רעה	MISERY	949a	1
36	32	ברוך	BARUCH	140a	1
		דבר	WORD	183a	2 2
		הם	THEY	241d	8 a
		יסף	BE JOINED	415a	2
		כתב	WRITE	507c	1 b1
		כתב	WRITE	507d	1 c
		נריהו	NERIAH	633a	
		ספר	MISSIVE	*707c	4
		ספר	ENUMERATOR	708c	2
		עוד	STILL	729b	1 c
		שרף	BURN	976d	2 a
		תשיעי	NINTH	1077d	
37	1	יהויכין	JEHOIACHIN	220c	
		מלך	BE KING	574b	
		נבוכדראצר	NEBUCHADNEZ-ZAR	613a	
37	2	דבר	SPEAK	181c	4 a
		עם	PEOPLE	766d	5 c
37	3	יהוכל	JEHUCAL	220d	
		כהן	PRIEST	463a	4
		מעשיהו	MAASEIAH	796b	1
		צפניה	ZEPHANIAH	861b	1
		שלמיה	SHELEMIAH	1025a	1 c
37	4	בית	HOUSE	109a	1 ae 2
		נתן	PUT	680c	2 a
37	5	יצא	GO OUT	423d	2 c
		כשדים	CHALDEANS	505a	1 b
		עלה	GO UP	749b	1 c2
		על	UPON	759a	4 2b
		צור	CONFINE	848d	2
		שמע	REPORT	1034d	1
37	7	דרש	SEEK	205b	2 a
		מצרים	EGYPT	595d	1 b1
		עזרה	HELP	740d	1
37	8	כשדים	CHALDEANS	505a	1 b
		שוב	TURN BACK	997c	3 b
37	9	אמר	SAY	56b	1
		הלך	WALK	233a	1 4b 1
		כשדים	CHALDEANS	505a	1 b
		נפש	SOUL	660b	4 b6
		נשא	DECEIVE	674a	
37	10	אהל	TENT	13d	1
		דקר	PIERCE	201b	1
		כשדים	CHALDEANS	505a	1 b
		לחם	ENGAGE IN BAT-TLE	535c	
		נכה	SMITE	646b	3
		שאר	REMAIN	984a	1
37	11	היה	COME TO PASS	225a	12a 2
		כשדים	CHALDEANS	505a	1 b
		עלה	GO UP	749b	1 c2
		על	UPON	759a	4 2b
		פנה	FACE	818b	26a
37	12	בנימן	BENJAMIN	122a	1
		הלך	WALK	230d	1 1d 3a
		חלק	DIVIDE	324a	
		עם	PEOPLE	766c	2 b
		שם	THERE	1027c	4 a
37	13	אל	TO	41a	B
		בנימן	BENJAMIN	122a	1
		בעל	LORD	127c	1 5a
		חנניהו	HANANIAH	337b	6
		כשדים	CHALDEANS	505a	1 b
		נפל	FALL	657c	4 b
		פקדת	OVERSIGHT	824b	
		יראיה	IRIJAH	909d	
		שאל	ASK	981d	2 a
		שלמיה	SHELEMIAH	1025a	1 d
		שם	NAME	1027d	2 a
		שער	GATE	1044d	1 b 3
37	14	אל	TO	41a	B
		כשדים	CHALDEANS	505a	1 b
		נפל	FALL	657c	4 b
		יראיה	IRIJAH	909d	
		שקר	DECEPTION	1055c	3
		תפש	LAY HOLD OF	1074d	1
37	15	אסור	BAND	64a	
		בית	HOUSE	109a	1 ae 2
		בית	HOUSE	109a	1 ae 2
		יהונתן	JONATHAN	221a	7
		כלא	CONFINEMENT	476c	
		נכה	SMITE	645c	1 b
		נתן	PUT	680c	2 a
		ספר	ENUMERATOR	708b	1 b
		עשה	DO	794d	2 1g
		קצף	BE WROTH	893b	2
37	16	בור	PIT	92c	4
		בית	HOUSE	109a	1 ae 2
		חנות	CELL	333d	
37	17	את	WITH	86d	4 c
		יש	BE	441c	2 a
		סתר	COVERING	712a	3
37	18	בית	HOUSE	109a	1 ae 2
		חטא	MISS A GOAL OR WAY	306d	2 a
		כלא	CONFINEMENT	476c	
		נתן	PUT	680b	2 a
37	19	אי	WHERE	32b	1 a
		איה	WHERE	32c	
		נביא	PROPHET	612a	2
		נבא	PROPHESY	612b	2
37	20	יהונתן	JONATHAN	221a	7
		תחנה	FAVOR	337c	2
		כיאם	FOR IF	474d	1 b
		נפל	FALL	657d	6
		ספר	ENUMERATOR	708b	1 b
37	21	אפה	BAKE	66a	
		חוץ	THE OUTSIDE	300a	2 a
		חצר	ENCLOSURE	347a	2
		יום	DAY	401a	7 i
		ככר	ROUND	503b	2
		לחם	FOOD	*537a	1 a
		משרה	GUARD	643c	1
		פקד	ATTEND TO	824a	2 b
		תמם	BE FINISHED	1070c	4
38	1	גדליהו	GEDALIAH	153d	2
		יהוכל	JEHUCAL	220d	
		מלכיהו	MALCHIJAH	575c	1
		מתן	MATTAN	682b	2
		פשחור	PASSHUR	832d	4
		פשחור	PASSHUR	832d	2
		שלמיה	SHELEMIAH	1025a	1 c
		שפטיה	SHEPHATIAH	1049b	1 b
38	2	חיה	LIVE	311a	1 b
		כשדים	CHALDEANS	505a	1 b
		שלל	SPOIL	1022a	2
38	4	את	MARK OF THE AC-CUSATIVE	85a	1 b
		דרש	SEEK	205c	6
		כיעלכן	FOR THEREFORE	475c	
		מלחמה	WAR	536b	
		מות	DIE	560c	2
		רפה	SINK	951d	
		שלום	PEACE	1022d	3
38	5	אין	NOT	34c	2 f
		הנה	BEHOLD	243d	
		יכל	BE ABLE	407d	1 g
38	6	בור	PIT	*92c	4
		בור	PIT	92c	4
		חבל	CORD	286c	1
		חצר	ENCLOSURE	347a	2
		טבע	SINK	371c	
		טיט	MUD	376c	1

Ch	v.	Heb	Eng	Page	Sec
40	14	שר	CHIEFTAIN	978c	3 a
		אחיקם	AHIKAM	27b	
		אמן	CONFIRM	53a	2 b
		בעליס	BAALIS	128d	
		גדליהו	GEDALIAH	153d	1
		נכה	SMITE	645d	2 a
		נפש	SOUL	659d	3 c
		נתניהו	NETHANIAH	682b	2
		שלח	SEND	1018b	1 a
		ישמעאל	ISHMAEL	1035d	2
40	15	אבד	PERISH	1c	1
		גדליהו	GEDALIAH	153d	1
		יהוחנן	JEHOHANAN	220b	8
		מה	HOW	554b	4 d
		נכה	SMITE	645d	2 a
		נפש	SOUL	659d	3 c
		נתניהו	NETHANIAH	682b	2
		סתר	COVERING	712a	3
		פוץ	BE DISPERSED	807a	1
		קבץ	GATHER	867d	1
		שארית	REST	984d	1
		ישמעאל	ISHMAEL	1035d	2
40	16	אחיקם	AHIKAM	27b	
		אל	TO	40c	6
		גדליהו	GEDALIAH	153d	1
		דבר	SPEAK	180c	
		דבר	SPEAK	180c	
		יהוחנן	JEHOHANAN	220b	8
		ישמעאל	ISHMAEL	1035d	2
41	1	אחיקם	AHIKAM	27b	
		אכל	EAT	37b	1
		גדליהו	GEDALIAH	153d	1
		זרע	SOWING	282d	4 e
		יחדו	TOGETHER	403b	A
		מלוכה	KINGSHIP	574d	
		מן	FROM	580d	3 bb
		נתניהו	NETHANIAH	682b	2
		רב	CHIEF	913c	
41	2	אחיקם	AHIKAM	27b	
		גדליהו	GEDALIAH	153d	1
		נכה	SMITE	645d	2 a
		שפן	SHAPHAN	1051a	2
41	3	גדליהו	GEDALIAH	153d	1
		יהודי	JEW	397c	
		כשדים	CHALDEANS	505a	1 b
		מלחמה	WAR	536b	
		מצא	FIND	594b	2 c
41	4	גדליהו	GEDALIAH	153d	1
41	5	גדד	CUT	151a	1
		גדליהו	GEDALIAH	153d	1
		זקן	BEARD	278b	2
		לבנה	FRANKINCENSE	526d	
		מנחה	OFFERING	585b	4
		מנחה	OFFERING	585b	4
		קרע	TEAR	902c	1 a1
		שלו	SHILOH	1017d	
		שמנים	EIGHTY	1033b	
41	6	אחיקם	AHIKAM	27b	
		בכה	WEEP	113b	1
		גדליהו	GEDALIAH	153d	1
		הלך	WALK	233b	14c 1g
		פגש	MEET	803d	
41	7	אל	TO	39c	1
		בור	PIT	92c	3
		גדליהו	GEDALIAH	153d	1
		שחט	SLAUGHTER	1006b	3
41	8	גדליהו	GEDALIAH	153d	1
		דבש	HONEY	185b	
		חדל	CEASE	293a	2
		חטה	WHEAT	334d	
		מטמון	HIDDEN TREASURE	380c	
		מצא	FIND	593d	1 c
		שערה	BARLEY	972d	1
41	9	אסא	ASA	61d	
		בור	PIT	92c	3
		בעשא	BAASHA	129d	1
		גדליהו	GEDALIAH	153d	1
		יד	HAND	391a	5 c3
		מלא	FILL	570c	1
		נתניהו	NETHANIAH	682b	2
		פגר	CORPSE	803d	1
		פנה	FACE	818b	26a
41	10	אחיקם	AHIKAM	27b	
		בת	DAUGHTER	123a	1
		גדליהו	GEDALIAH	153d	1
		נבוזראדן	NEBUZARADAN	613a	
		פקד	ATTEND TO	824a	1
		שארית	REST	984d	1
		שבה	TAKE CAPTIVE	985c	1 a
41	11	גדליהו	GEDALIAH	153d	1
		יהוחנן	JEHOHANAN	220b	8
		חיל	STRENGTH	299a	4
		רעה	MISERY	949b	2
41	12	אל	TO	40d	8
		גבעון	GIBEON	149c	
		גדליהו	GEDALIAH	153d	1
		מצא	FIND	593a	1 c
41	13	גדליהו	GEDALIAH	153d	1
		יהוחנן	JEHOHANAN	220b	8
		חיל	STRENGTH	299a	4
		עם	PEOPLE	766c	2 c
		שמח	REJOICE	970b	1 a
41	14	גדליהו	GEDALIAH	153d	1
		יהוחנן	JEHOHANAN	220b	8
		הלך	WALK	231a	1 d3 ga
		סבב	TURN ABOUT	685c	1 a

Ch	v.	Heb	Eng	Page	Sec
		עם	PEOPLE	766c	2 c
		שבה	TAKE CAPTIVE	985c	1 a
41	15	ב	IN	89b	3 1a
		גדליהו	GEDALIAH	153d	1
		יהוחנן	JEHOHANAN	220b	8
		מלט	SLIP AWAY	572c	2
41	16	אחיקם	AHIKAM	27b	
		אחר	BESIDES	30a	3
		גבעון	GIBEON	149c	
		גבר	MAN	150a	
		גדליהו	GEDALIAH	153d	1
		גדליהו	GEDALIAH	153d	1
		יהוחנן	JEHOHANAN	220b	8
		חיל	STRENGTH	299a	4
		טף	CHILDREN	382a	
		מלחמה	WAR	536b	
		סריס	EUNUCH	710c	
		שארית	REST	984d	1
		שוב	TURN BACK	998d	1 a
		שוב	TURN BACK	998d	1 a
41	17	אצל	BESIDE	69b	A
		גדליהו	GEDALIAH	153d	1
		גרות	LODGING-PLACE	158c	2
		הלך	WALK	233d	1 5a
		כמהם	CHIMHAM	484c	2
41	18	אחיקם	AHIKAM	27b	
		גדליהו	GEDALIAH	153d	1
		ירא	FEAR	431b	1 c
		כשדים	CHALDEANS	505a	1 b
42	1	יאזניה	JAAZANIAH	24d	5
		גדול	GREAT	153b	7
		יהוחנן	JEHOHANAN	220b	8
		חיל	STRENGTH	299a	4
		הושעיה	HOSHAIAH	448a	2
		עזריה	ADDENDA ET COR-RIGENDA	1125d	
42	2	תחנה	FAVOR	337c	1
		מעט	A FEW	589d	1 a
		נפל	FALL	657d	6
		ראה	TO SEE	906d	1
		רבה	BECOME MANY	915d	1 e5
		שאר	REMAIN	984a	1
		שארית	REST	984d	1
42	3	נגד	BE CONSPICUOUS	616d	2
42	4	דבר	WORD	183d	4 6
		היה	COME TO PASS	225a	1 2b ag
		מנע	WITHHOLD	586a	
42	5	אמן	CONFIRM	53a	5
		אמת	FIRMNESS	54b	4 b
		דבר	WORD	182d	1 2a
		כן	SO	486b	2 ac
		עד	WITNESS	729d	2 a
		עד	WITNESS	729d	2 a
42	6	אם	IF	50a	1 b1
		אנו	WE	59a	
		טוב	A GOOD THING	375a	1
		יטב	BE WELL	405c	3
		מען	PURPOSE	775c	2 a
		רע	EVIL	948d	1
42	7	יום	DAY	398c	2 c
42	8	גדול	GREAT	153b	7
		יהוחנן	JEHOHANAN	220b	8
		חיל	STRENGTH	299a	4
		מן	FROM	583d	9 b1
		קרא	CALL	895d	5 b
42	9	תחנה	FAVOR	337c	1
		נפל	FALL	658b	6
		שלח	SEND	1018b	1 a
42	10	בנה	BUILD	124d	2 b
		הרם	THROW DOWN	248d	1
		נחם	BE SORRY	637a	2
		נטע	PLANT	642c	2
		נתש	PLUCK UP	684c	
		רעה	MISERY	949b	1
		שוב	TURN BACK	997b	3 a
42	11	ירא	FEAR	431b	1 c
		ירא	FEAR	431b	1 c
		ישע	DELIVER	446d	1 b
		נחם	CONSOLE ONESELF	637b	
42	12	נתן	GIVE	678c	1 b
		רחמים	COMPASSION	933c	1
		רחם	LOVE	933d	2
42	13	בלת	NOT	*116d	4 a
42	14	ראה	TO SEE	907b	3
		רעב	BE HUNGRY	945b	
42	15	גור	SOJOURN	158a	1
		כן	SO	487a	3 d
		שום	TO PLACE	963d	2
		שארית	REST	984d	1
42	16	דאג	BE ANXIOUS	178b	1
		דבק	CLING	180a	2 c
		ירא	FEAR	431b	1 c
		מצרים	EGYPT	595d	1 b1
		נשג	OVERTAKE	673c	1 b
42	17	גור	SOJOURN	158a	1
		פליט	ESCAPED ONE	812c	
		שום	TO PLACE	963d	2
		שריד	SURVIVOR	975a	1
42	18	אלה	OATH	46d	4
		חרפה	REPROACH	358a	3
		חמה	RAGE	*405a	2 c
		ירא	FEAR	431c	3 b
		כן	SO	486c	2 cd
		נתך	POUR FORTH	677d	
		נתך	POUR FORTH	677d	
		שמה	APPALMENT	1031c	2

Ch	v.	Heb	Eng	Page	Sec
42	19	דבר	SPEAK	181d	5
		עוד	BEAR WITNESS	730a	3
		שארית	REST	984d	1
42	20	כן	SO	486c	2 cc
		נפש	SOUL	660b	4 b6
		תעה	ERR	1073c	3
42	22	גור	SOJOURN	158a	1
		חפץ	DELIGHT IN	342d	1 b
43	1	יהוה	YAHWEH	218d	2 1d
43	2	יאזניהו	JAAZANIAH	24d	5
		גור	SOJOURN	158a	1
		יהוחנן	JEHOHANAN	220b	8
		זד	INSOLENT	267d	1
		הושעיה	HOSHAIAH	448a	2
		עזריה	ADDENDA ET COR-RIGENDA	1125d	
43	3	ברוך	BARUCH	140a	1
		כשדים	CHALDEANS	505a	1 b
		נריהו	NERIAH	633a	
		סות	INCITE	694d	2
43	4	יהוחנן	JEHOHANAN	220b	8
		חיל	STRENGTH	299a	4
43	5	גור	SOJOURN	158a	2
		יהוחנן	JEHOHANAN	220b	8
		חיל	STRENGTH	299a	4
		שארית	REST	984d	1
		שוב	TURN BACK	997a	2
43	6	אחיקם	AHIKAM	27b	
		בת	DAUGHTER	123a	1
		ברוך	BARUCH	140a	1
		גדליהו	GEDALIAH	153d	1
		טף	CHILDREN	382a	
		טף	CHILDREN	382a	
		נבוזראדן	NEBUZARADAN	613a	
		נוח	REST	629a	B 2
		נריהו	NERIAH	633a	
		נפש	SOUL	660b	4 c3
		שפן	SHAPHAN	1051a	
43	7	תחפנחס	TAHPANHES	1064d	
43	8	תחפנחס	TAHPANHES	1064d	
43	9	טמן	HIDE	380b	1
		יהודי	JEWISH	397c	
		מלבן	QUADRANGLE	527c	2
		מלט	MORTAR	572d	
		תחפנחס	TAHPANHES	1064d	
43	10	טמן	HIDE	380b	1
		נבוכדראצר	NEBUCHADNEZ-ZAR	613a	
		נטה	SPREAD OUT	640a	2
		עבד	SLAVE	713d	1
		מעל	ABOVE	751c	1 b
		שום	TO PLACE	964b	4 b
		שפריר	CARPET	1051d	
43	11	נכה	SMITE	646b	3
		שבי	CAPTIVITY	985d	1
43	12	אלהים	GOD	43c	1 d
		יצת	KINDLE	*428c	
		עטה	WRAP ONESELF	741d	
		עטה	GRASP	742a	
		שבה	TAKE CAPTIVE	985c	1 a
43	13	אלהים	GOD	43c	1 d
		און	ON	58a	
		בית שמש	BETH-SHEMESH	113a	4
		מצבה	PILLAR	663b	1 c
		מגדל	MIGDOL	154b	
44	1	יהודי	JEW	397c	
		מף	MEMPHIS	592a	
		מצרים	EGYPT	595d	1 a
		פתרום	PATHROS	837d	
		תחפנחס	TAHPANHES	1064d	
44	2	בוא	COME	99c	2 a
		חרבה	WASTE	352a	1
44	3	ידע	KNOW	394a	2
		כעס	VEX	495a	2
		עבד	WORK	713b	4 b
		רעה	MISERY	949b	3
44	4	נביא	PROPHET	611d	1
		עבד	SLAVE	714b	4
		שנא	HATE	971c	2
		שכם	START EARLY	1014d	1
		תועבה	ABOMINATION	1072d	1 b
44	5	נטה	INCLINE	641a	3 e
		רעה	MISERY	949b	3
44	6	בער	BURN	129a	1
		חרבה	WASTE	352a	1
		יום	DAY	400d	7 h
		חמה	RAGE	*404d	2 c
		חמה	RAGE	*405a	2 c
		נתך	POUR FORTH	677d	
44	7	ינק	SUCK	413b	
		יתר	LEAVE OVER	451c	1 a
		כרת	CUT OFF	504c	2 c
		נפש	SOUL	660b	4 b6
		עולל	CHILD	760c	
		צבא	GOD OF WAR	839c	4 b
		רעה	MISERY	949b	3
		שארית	REST	984d	1
44	8	גור	SOJOURN	158a	1
		חרפה	REPROACH	358a	3
		כעס	VEX	495a	2
		כרת	CUT OFF	504c	2 c
		מעשה	DEED	795d	1 a2
44	10	דכא	CRUSH	194a	1
		הלך	WALK	234c	2 3a 1e
		חקה	SOMETHING PRE-SCRIBED	350b	2 d

Ch v.	Heb	Eng	Page	Sec
	חקה	SOMETHING PRE-SCRIBED	350b	2 e
	ירא	FEAR	431c	3 a
	תורה	INSTRUCTION	436a	1 c
	נתן	PUT	680d	2 b
	פנה	FACE	817c	2 4b g
44 11	כרת	CUT OFF	504c	2 c
	שום	TO PLACE	963d	2 c
44 12	אלה	OATH	46d	4
	גדול	GREAT	153b	7
	גור	SOJOURN	158a	1
	חרפה	REPROACH	358a	3
	כל	ALL	482c	2 a
	שום	TO PLACE	963d	2 c
	שארית	REST	984d	1
	שמח	APPALMENT	1031c	2
	תמם	BE FINISHED	1070d	5
44 14	גור	SOJOURN	158a	1
	כיאם	EXCEPT	474d	2 a
	ל	TO	518b	7 bh
	נפש	SOUL	660d	6 a
	נשא	LIFT	672a	2
	פלט	ESCAPED ONE	812c	
	פלט	ESCAPED ONE	812c	
	שריד	SURVIVOR	975a	1
	שארית	REST	984d	1
44 15	מצרים	EGYPT	595d	1 a
	פתרום	PATHROS	837d	
	קהל	ASSEMBLY	874c	1 d
44 16	דבר	SPEAK	181c	4 a
44 17	טוב	PLEASANT	374c	7
	יצא	SATISFIED	423c	1 g
	מלכת	QUEEN	573d	
	נסך	POUR OUT	650d	
	נסך	DRINK-OFFERING	651a	1
	רעה	MISERY	949a	1
	שבע	SATESFIED	959b	1 b
44 18	מאז	FROM THAT TIME	23b	B
	חדל	CEASE	293a	2
	חסר	LACK	341b	1 a
	כל	ALL	*482c	2 a
	ל	TO	517c	7 bb
	מלכת	QUEEN	573d	
	נסך	POUR OUT	650d	
	נסך	DRINK-OFFERING	651a	1
	תמם	BE FINISHED	1070c	5
44 19	בלעדי	APART FROM	116b	B a
	כון	CAKE	468a	
	כי	WHEN	473a	2 a
	ל	TO	518b	7 bh
	מלכת	QUEEN	573d	
	נסך	POUR OUT	650d	
	נסך	DRINK-OFFERING	651a	1
	עצב	SHAPE	781a	
44 20	דבר	WORD	182b	1 1c
	על	UPON	757c	27c b
44 21	זכר	REMEMBER	270c	2 4
	עם	PEOPLE	766c	5 c
	קטר	MAKE SACRAFICES SMOKE	882d	
	קטר	INCENSE	883b	
44 22	חרבה	WASTE	352b	2
	יום	DAY	400d	7 h
	יכל	BE ABLE	407c	1
	ישב	DWELL	443b	3
	רע	EVIL	948a	3
	שמה	APPALMENT	1031c	2
	תועבה	ABOMINATION	1072d	1 b
44 23	הלך	WALK	234c	2 3a 1d
	הלך	WALK	234c	2 3a 1e
	חטא	MISS A GOAL OR WAY	307a	2 b
	חקה	SOMETHING PRE-SCRIBED	350b	2 e
	חקה	SOMETHING PRE-SCRIBED	350b	2 d
	יום	DAY	400d	7 h
	תורה	INSTRUCTION	436a	1 c
	עדות	TESTIMONY	730b	2
	פנה	FACE	818c	26c c
	קטר	MAKE SACRAFICES SMOKE	882d	
44 25	קרא	ENCOUNTER	897a	2
	מלא	FILL	570d	3
	מלכת	QUEEN	573d	
	נדר	VOW	623d	
	נדר	VOW	624a	6
	נדר	VOW	624a	6
	נסך	POUR OUT	650d	
	נסך	DRINK-OFFERING	651a	1
44 26	אדון	LORD	11c	4 b
	גדול	GREAT	153b	6 c
	חי	ALIVE	311d	1 a
	כן	SO	487a	3 d
	קרא	CALL	896b	2
	שבע	SWEAR	989c	1
44 27	טובה	WELFARE	375d	1
	כלה	BE FINISHED	477d	2 c
	שקד	WATCH	1052a	1
	תמם	BE FINISHED	1070c	5
44 28	גור	SOJOURN	158a	1
	מי	WHO	566b	B
	מן	FROM	581b	3 be
	מצרים	EGYPT	595d	1 b2
	מצרים	EGYPT	595d	1 b1
	מת	MALE	607b	2 a

Ch v.	Heb	Eng	Page	Sec
	מספר	NUMBER	709a	1 a
	פליט	ESCAPED ONE	812c	
	קום	STAND	878c	7 g
	שארית	REST	984d	1
	שוב	TURN BACK	997a	2
44 29	אות	SIGN	16d	2
	אני	I	59a	
	קום	STAND	878b	7 g
	מקום	STANDING PLACE	880a	3 b
44 30	בקש	SEEK	134d	2
	חפרע	HOPHRA	344b	
	נבוכדראצר	NEBUCHADNEZ-ZAR	613a	
	נפש	SOUL	659d	3 c
	פרעה	PHARAOH	829a	
45 1	ברוך	BARUCH	140a	1
	כתב	WRITE	507d	1 c
	נריהו	NERIAH	633a	
	רביעי	FOURTH	918a	2
45 2	ברוך	BARUCH	140a	1
45 3	אוי	WOE	17a	
	אנחה	SIGHING	58d	
	יגון	GRIEF	387b	
	יגע	TOIL	388b	2
	יסף	ADD	414d	
	מכאוב	PAIN	456b	2
	מצא	FIND	592c	1 a
	מנוחה	REST	630a	2
45 4	את	MARK OF THE AC-CUSATIVE	85b	3 a
	בנה	BUILD	124d	2 b
	הרם	THROW DOWN	248d	1
	נטע	PLANT	642c	2
	נתש	PLUCK UP	684c	
45 5	בקש	SEEK	134d	2 a
	בשר	FLESH	142d	6 c
	גדול	GREAT	153c	9
	הלך	WALK	230d	1 1d 3b
	ו	AND	252d	1 f
	נתן	GIVE	678d	1 d
	על	UPON	752d	2 1
	שלל	SPOIL	1022a	2
	שם	THERE	1027b	2
46 1	אשר	PARTICLE OF RE-LATION	82d	6 a
	דבר	WORD	182c	1 2a
46 2	כרכמיש	CARCHEMISH	501c	
	ל	TO	514b	5 fa
	נבוכדראצר	NEBUCHADNEZ-ZAR	613a	
	נכו	NECO	647a	
	פרעה	PHARAOH	829a	
	פרת	EUPHRATES	832b	
	רביעי	FOURTH	918a	2
	שנה	YEAR	1040c	
46 3	מגן	SHIELD	171c	
	מלחמה	WAR	536c	
	נגש	DRAW NEAR	620d	1
	ערך	ARRANGE	789d	1 e
	צנה	LARGE SHIELD	857a	
46 4	אסר	TIE	63d	2
	יצב	STATION ONESELF	426b	B
	כובע	HELMET	464d	
	לבש	PUT ON	527d	A
	מרק	POLISH	599d	
	סוס	HORSE	692c	1
	סרין	ARMOR	710b	
	פרש	HORSE	832a	
	רמח	SPEAR	942b	
46 5	חת	SHATTERED	369c	2
	כתת	BE BEATEN	510c	
	נוס	FLEE	630d	1
	מנוס	FLIGHT	631a	1
	סביב	ROUND ABOUT	687a	1 d
	סוג	MOVE AWAY	691a	2
	פנה	TURN	815c	2
	ראה	TO SEE	*907a	2 3
46 6	אל	NOT	39b	A c
	יד	HAND	391c	5 h3
	כשל	STUMBLE	505c	1
	מלט	SLIP AWAY	572b	2
	נוס	ESCAPE	630d	2
	פרת	EUPHRATES	832b	
46 7	קל	LIGHT	887a	
	געש	SHAKE	172b	
	זה	THIS	261b	4 b
	יאר	STREAM	384c	1
	מי	WHO	567b	F e
	עלה	GO UP	748d	5
46 8	אבד	DESTROY	2b	1
	געש	SHAKE	172b	
	געש	SHAKE	*172b	
	יאר	STREAM	384c	1
	כסה	COVER	491d	5
	מצרים	EGYPTIANS	595d	2 b
	עלה	GO UP	748d	5
46 9	מגן	SHIELD	171c	
	הלל	PRAISE	239b	
	כוש	CUSH	469a	2 b
	לובים	LUBIM	530c	
	לוד	LUD	530d	2
	סוס	HORSE	692c	1
	פוט	LIBYANS	806c	
	קשת	BOW	*906c	1 d
	קשת	BOW	906c	1 d
	תפש	LAY HOLD OF	1074d	2

Ch v.	Heb	Eng	Page	Sec
46 10	תפש	LAY HOLD OF	*1074d	2
	אדון	LORD	11d	6 b
	אל	TO	40d	8
	דם	BLOOD	197b	2 n
	זבח	SACRIFICE	258a	2 6
	חרב	SWORD	352d	1 g
	יום	DAY	399a	3
	יום	DAY	399a	3
	נקם	AVENGE	668b	1 a
	נקמה	VENGEANCE	668c	1
	פרת	EUPHRATES	832b	
	צר	ADVERSARY	865d	
	רוה	BE SATURATED	924a	
	שבע	SATISFIED	959b	1 a
46 11	בת	DAUGHTER	123c	3
	בתולה	VIRGIN	144a	
	מצרים	EGYPTIANS	596a	2 b
	תעלה	HEALING	752b	
	צרי	BALM	863b	
	רבה	BECOME MANY	915c	1 c
	רפאה	REMEDY	951b	
46 12	שוא	EMPTINESS	996b	1
	יחדו	TOGETHER	403c	B
	כשל	STUMBLE	505c	1
	נפל	FALL	657b	2 b
	צוחה	OUTCRY	846d	
	קלון	DISHONOUR	885d	1
46 13	נבוכדראצר	NEBUCHADNEZ-ZAR	613a	
	נכה	SMITE	646b	3
46 14	מגדל	MIGDOL	*154a	
	מגדל	MIGDOL	154b	
	חרב	SWORD	352d	1 g
	יצב	STATION ONESELF	426b	B
	כון	ESTABLISH	466c	2 a
	ל	TO	515d	5 ia
	מף	MEMPHIS	592a	
	סביב	ROUND ABOUT	687b	2 ab
	תחפנחס	TAHPANHES	1064d	
46 15	אביר	MIGHTY	7d	1
	סחף	PROSTRATE	695b	
	אבביר	ADDENDA ET COR-RIGENDA	1119b	
	אבביר	ADDENDA ET COR-RIGENDA	*1119b	
46 16	גם	YEA	169c	3
	ח	THE	209b	2 b
	חרון	BURNING OF AN-GER	*354c	
	מולדת	KINDRED	409d	1
	כשל	STUMBLE	505c	1
	נפל	FALL	657b	4 a
	עם	PEOPLE	766c	1
	רבה	BECOME MANY	915c	1 a
	שוב	TURN BACK	997a	3 a
46 17	מועד	APPOINTED TIME	417c	1 a
	עבר	PASS OVER	719a	3 b
	פרעה	PHARAOH	829a	
	קרא	CALL	896a	6 a
	שאון	ROAR	981a	1
46 18	אנכי	I	59b	
	ב	IN	88b	12a
	הר	MOUNTAIN	249c	1 a
	חי	ALIVE	311d	1 a
	כרמל	CARMEL	502b	1
	מלך	KING	573b	3
	נאם	UTTERANCE	610b	2
	שם	NAME	1028c	3
	תבור	TABOR	1061d	1
46 19	בת	DAUGHTER	123c	3
	יצת	BE KINDLED	428b	
	ישב	DWELL	443b	3
	ישב	DWELL	443b	1
	כלי	ARTICLE	479c	1
	מף	MEMPHIS	592a	
	מצרים	EGYPTIANS	596a	2 b
	נצה	FALL IN RUINS	663d	
	שמה	WASTE	1031c	1
46 20	יפהפיה	PRETTY	421d	
	עגלה	HEIFER	722b	
	צפון	NORTH	861a	
	קרץ	NIPPING	903a	
	תאר	FORM	*1061c	
46 21	איד	DISTRESS	15d	3
	איד	DISTRESS	15d	1
	עגל	CALF	722a	
	עת	TIME	773d	2 c
	פנה	TURN	815c	2
	קרב	INWARD PART	899b	1 fl
	מרבק	STALL	918d	
	שכיר	HIRED	969b	2 1
46 22	הלך	WALK	232b	1 2
	חטב	CUT OR GATHER WOOD	310a	
	כשיל	AXE	*506a	
	ל	TO	511c	1 gb
	נחש	SERPENT	638b	1 c
	קול	VOICE	877a	1 e
	קרדם	AXE	899c	
46 23	חקר	SEARCH	350d	
	יער	WOOD	420c	A
	כי	THOUGH	473c	2 ca
	כרת	CUT OFF	503d	1
	מספר	NUMBER	708d	1
	רבב	BECOME MUCH	912d	1
	ארבה	LOCUST	916a	

Ch	v.	Heb	Eng	Page	Sec
46	24	בוש	BE ASHAMED	102a	2 c
		בת	DAUGHTER	123c	3
		מצרים	EGYPTIANS	596a	2 b
		צפון	NORTH	861a	
46	25	אמון	AMON	51b	
		בטח	TRUST	105a	1 3b
		מן	OUT OF	579c	2 cb
		נא	THEBES	609d	
		פקד	ATTEND TO	823a	A 3
		אמון	ADDENDA ET CORRIGENDA	1120b	
46	26	בקש	SEEK	134c	2 a
		נבוכדראצר	NEBUCHADNEZZAR	613a	
		נפש	SOUL	659d	3 c
		קדם	FRONT	869a	2 b
		שכן	SETTLE DOWN	1015a	1 a
46	27	זוע	SOWING	283a	4 g
		חרד	TREMBLE	353c	
		חתת	BE SHATTERED	369b	2 a
		ירא	FEAR	431a	1 a
		ישע	DELIVER	446d	1 b
		עבד	SLAVE	714b	5
		רחק	DISTANT	935c	2 a1
		שאן	BE AT EASE	983b	
		שבי	CAPTIVITY	985d	1
		שקט	BE QUIET	1053a	1
46	28	יסר	DISCIPLINE	416b	2
		ירא	FEAR	431a	1 a
		כלה	COMPLETE	478d	2 a
		כלה	COMPLETE	478d	2 a
		ל	TO	*516c	5 jb
		נדח	THRUST	623b	2
		נקה	BE CLEAN	667c	2
		עבד	SLAVE	714b	5
47	1	אשר	PARTICLE OF RELATION	82d	6 a
		דבר	WORD	182c	1 2a
		טרם	NOT YET	382c	2
		נכה	SMITE	646b	3
		עזה	GAZA	738b	
		רכב	CHARIOT	939a	1
47	2	זעק	CRY	277c	2 d
		ילל	HOWL	410b	
		מלא	THAT WHICH FILLS	571b	3
		נחל	TORRENT	636b	1
		עלה	GO UP	748d	5
		צפון	NORTH	861a	
		שטף	OVERFLOW	1009a	1
		שטף	OVERFLOW	1009a	1
47	3	אביר	MIGHTY	7d	3
		המון	SOUND	242c	1
		ל	TO	513c	5 cb e
		פנה	TURN	815c	2
		פרסה	HOOF	828b	2
		קול	VOICE	877b	2 d
		רכב	CHARIOT	939a	1
		רעש	SHAKING	950c	1
		רפיון	SINKING	952a	1
		שעטה	STAMPING	1043b	
47	4	אי	COAST	16a	
		בוא	COME	98c	2
		כפתור	CAPHTOR	499c	
		כרת	CUT OFF	504c	2 c
		עזר	HELP	740c	
		צידון	SIDON	851a	
		צר	TYER	862d	
		שריד	SURVIVOR	975a	1
		שארית	REST	984c	1
		שדד	DEAL VIOLENTLY WITH	994c	
47	5	אשקלון	ASHKELON	80c	
		גדד	CUT	151a	1
		דמה	CUT OFF	198c	
		עזה	GAZA	738b	
		עמק	VALE	771a	
		ענק	NECK	778c	
		קרחה	BALD SPOT	901b	
		שארית	REST	984c	1
47	6	אן	WHERE	33a	D
		אסף	GATHER	62d	2 b
		דמם	BE STILL	198d	2
		הוי	AH	223a	
		חרב	SWORD	*352c	1 e
		חרב	SWORD	352d	1 j
		תער	RAZOR	789b	2
		רגע	BE AT REST	921b	
		שקט	BE QUIET	1053a	2
47	7	אשקלון	ASHKELON	80c	
		חוף	SHORE	342b	
		יעד	APPOINT	416d	
		צוה	COMMAND	845d	1 e
		שקט	BE QUIET	1053a	2
48	1	בוש	BE ASHAMED	102a	2 c
		הוי	AH	223a	
		חתת	BE SHATTERED	369b	2 a
		ל	TO	514b	5 fa
		לכד	CAPTURE	540a	1
		מואב	MOAB	555d	2 a
		נבו	NEBO	612d	1 a
		משגב	MISGAB	960d	
		שדד	DEAL VIOLENTLY WITH	994b	
48	2	גם	YEA	169c	3
		דמם	BE STILL	198d	2
		מדמן	MADMEN	199b	

Ch	v.	Heb	Eng	Page	Sec
		הלך	WALK	232c	1 3
		תהלה	PRAISE	240c	5 cd
		חשב	THINK	363a	1 2
		חשבון	HESHBON	364a	
		כרת	CUT OFF	504c	2 b
		מואב	MOAB	555d	2 a
		מן	FROM	583b	7 bb
		עוד	STILL	729a	1 ab
		רעה	MISERY	949b	2
48	3	חרונים	HORONAIM	357b	
		צעקה	CRY	858d	2
		שבר	BREAKING	991a	1
		שד	VIOLENCE	994c	
48	4	זעקה	CRY	277d	2
		צער	ZOAR	858d	
		צעיר	YOUNG	859a	1 b
		צעוריה	YOUTH	859a	
		שבר	BREAK	990d	
48	5	בכי	WEEPING	113d	
		חרונים	HORONAIM	357b	
		מורד	DESCENT	434c	1
		לוחית	LUHITH	532a	
		עלה	GO UP	748d	1 e
		צעקה	CRY	858d	2
		צר	ADVERSARY	865a	
		שבר	BREAKING	991b	1
48	6	מלט	SLIP AWAY	572c	3
		נפש	SOUL	660a	3 c
		ערוער	JUNIPER	792d	
48	7	אוצר	TREASURE	70a	1
		בטח	TRUST	105a	1 3c
		יחדו	TOGETHER	*403c	A
		יצא	GO OUT	423d	2 a
		כהן	PRIEST	463b	1
		כמוש	CHEMOSH	484d	1
		לכד	CAPTURE	540b	2
		יען	ON ACCOUNT OF	774d	1
		מעשה	DEED	795c	1 b4
		שר	CHIEFTAIN	978a	1 a
48	8	אבד	PERISH	1d	1
		אשר	THAT	83d	8 e
		מישור	LEVEL PLACE	449d	1
		מלט	SLIP AWAY	572b	2
		נתניהו	NETHANIAH	682b	2
		עמק	VALE	771a	
		שמד	BE EXTERMINATED	1029b	2
48	9	הם	THEY	242a	8 d
		יצא	GO OUT	423a	1 d
		ישב	DWELL	443b	3
		נצא	FLY	661d	
		ציץ	WINGS	851c	
		שמה	WASTE	1031c	1
48	10	ארר	CURSE	76d	1
		דם	BLOOD	196d	2 f
		מנע	WITHHOLD	586a	
		רמיה	LAXNESS	941c	
48	11	הלך	WALK	231b	1 d3 ge
		טעם	TASTE	381a	1
		כלי	VESSEL	480b	3
		מן	FROM	582b	5 d1
		נעורים	YOUTH	655b	
		עמד	STAND	764c	7 g
		ריח	SCENT	926b	1
		ריק	MAKE EMPTY	938a	
		שאן	BE AT EASE	983b	
		שמר	LEES	1038d	
		שקט	BE QUIET	1053a	1
48	12	כלי	VESSEL	480b	3
		נבל	JAR	614b	2
		נפץ	SHATTER	658d	
		צעה	STOOP	858a	
		צעה	STOOP	858a	2
		ריק	MAKE EMPTY	937a	1
		שלח	SEND	1019a	1 a
48	13	בוש	BE ASHAMED	101d	2
		מבטח	CONFIDENCE	105c	2
		ביתאל	BETHEL	110d	1
		כמוש	CHEMOSH	484d	1
48	14	איך	HOW	32c	1
		חיל	STRENGTH	298d	1 c
		מלחמה	WAR	536b	
48	15	בחור	YOUNG MAN	104c	2
		טבח	SLAUGHTERING	370d	1
		ירד	GO DOWN	433b	1 k
		ל	TO	511b	1 ga
		מלך	KING	573b	3
		נאם	UTTERANCE	610b	2
		שדד	DEAL VIOLENTLY WITH	994b	
48	16	איד	DISTRESS	15d	1
		מהר	HASTEN	555a	1
		קרב	NEAR	898d	3
48	17	איכה	HOW	32d	2
		מקל	ROD	596c	1
		נוד	SHEW GRIEF	626d	2 a
		מטה	STAFF	641d	1
		סביב	ROUND ABOUT	687a	2 aa
		עז	STRENGTH	739a	1
		תפארה	BEAUTY	802d	3 b
		שבר	BREAK	990d	
		שם	NAME	1028c	3
48	18	בת	DAUGHTER	123c	3
		מבצר	FORTIFICATION	131c	
		דיבן	DIBON	192a	1
		ירד	GO DOWN	433a	1 f
		ישב	DWELL	443b	3

Ch	v.	Heb	Eng	Page	Sec
		כבוד	HONOR	459a	3
		עלה	GO UP	748c	2 c
		עמק	BE DEEP	770d	
		שחת	GO TO RUIN	1008a	1
48	19	חיה	COME TO PASS	227d	2
		ישב	DWELL	443b	3
		מלט	SLIP AWAY	572b	2
		עמד	STAND	763d	1 a
		ערוער	AROER	792d	1
		צפה	KEEP WATCH	859c	
48	20	ארנון	ARNON	75b	
		בוש	BE ASHAMED	102a	2 c
		זעק	CRY	277c	2 d
		חתת	BE SHATTERED	369b	2 a
		חתת	BE SHATTERED	*369b	2 a
		ילל	HOWL	410b	
		שדד	DEAL VIOLENTLY WITH	994b	
48	21	ארץ	EARTH	76b	4 c
		חלון	HOLON	298b	1
		יהץ	JAHAZ	397d	
		מיפעת	MEPHAATH	422b	
		מישור	LEVEL PLACE	449d	1
		משפט	JUDGMENT	1048c	1 f
48	22	בית	BETH-DIBLATHIAM	110c	
		ביתבלתים	BETH-DIBLATHIAM	111b	
		דבלתים	DIBLATHAIM	179c	
		דיבן	DIBON	192a	1
		נבו	NEBO	612d	1 a
48	23	ביתבעלמעון	BETH-BAAL-MEON	111a	
		ביתבעלמעון	BETH-BAAL-MEON	111a	
		ביתגמול	BETH-GAMUL	111b	
48	24	בצרה	BOZRAH	131b	2
		מואב	MOAB	555d	2 b
		קרב	NEAR	898b	1
		קריות	KERIOTH-HEZRON	901a	1
		רחק	DISTANT	935c	1 a
48	25	גדע	HEW OFF	154b	1
		זרוע	ARM	284a	1 b
		קרן	HORN	902a	2
		שבר	BREAK	990d	
48	26	גדל	BECOME GREAT	152c	3 b
		ספק	SLAP	706d	3
		קיא	VOMIT	883c	
		שחק	LAUGHTER	966a	2
		שבר	BE DRUNK	1016b	
48	27	אם	IF	50c	2 aa
		גנב	THIEF	170c	
		די	SUFFICIENCY	191d	2 cb
		מצא	FIND	394a	1 g2
		נוד	MOVE TO AND FRO	627a	2
		שחק	LAUGHTER	966a	2
48	28	יונה	DOVE	401d	1
		סלע	CRAG	701a	1
		עבר	REGION ACROSS	719b	2
		עזב	LEAVE	737b	2 a1
		פה	MOUTH	805b	4
		פחת	PIT	809b	
		קנן	MAKE A NEST	890b	
		שבר	BREAK	990c	
		שכן	SETTLE DOWN	1015b	2 a
48	29	גאה	PROUD	144b	
		גא	PROUD	*144b	
		גאה	MAJESTY	144d	2
		גאון	EXALTATION	145a	2
		גבה	HEIGHT	147b	3
		לב	HEART	525b	2 6c
		רום	HEIGHT	927d	1
48	30	בד	EMPTY TALK	95a	A
		כן	RIGHT	467b	1
		כן	TRUE	467b	2
		עברה	OVERFLOW	720c	2
48	31	הגה	MOAN	211d	1 b
		זעק	CRY	277c	2 d
		ילל	HOWL	410b	
		כל	ALL	481d	1 da
		קיר	KIR	885b	2
48	32	בכה	WEEP	113c	2
		בכה	WEEP	113c	3
		בכי	WEEPING	113d	
		בכי	WEEPING	113d	
		בציר	VINTAGE	131b	2
		גפן	VINE	172c	
		ים	SEA	411a	3
		נגע	REACH	619b	4
		נטישה	TENDRIL	644b	
		נפל	FALL	657c	4 a
		יעזר	JAZER	741c	
		קיץ	SUMMER	884d	2
		קציר	HARVESTING	*894d	2
48	33	שבם	SEBAM	959b	
		אסף	GATHER	62d	3
		דרך	TREAD	202a	3
		הידד	SHOUTING	212c	1
		הידד	SHOUT	212c	2
		יקב	WINE-PRESS	*428c	
		כרמל	GARDEN	502a	1
		מואב	MOAB	555d	2 b
		שבת	CEASE	992a	1
48	34	אלעלא	ELEALEH	46c	
		זעקה	CRY	277d	2
		חרונים	HORONAIM	357b	
		חשבון	HESHBON	364a	
		יהץ	JAHAZ	397d	
		מי	WATER	565c	2
		נמרים	NIMRIM	649d	

Ch	v.	Heb	Eng	Page	Sec
		נתן	GIVE	679d	1 x
48	35	עגלת	EGLATH	722c	
		צער	ZOAR	858d	
		צער	ZOAR	858d	
		שלישי	THIRD	1026b	
		משמה	DEVASTATION	1031d	1
48	35	במה	HIGH PLACE	119b	3
		ל	TO	512c	5 aa
		עלה	GO UP	749d	8
		קטר	MAKE SACRAFICES SMOKE	883a	1 b
		שבת	CEASE	992a	5
48	36	אבד	PERISH	1d	1
		המה	MURMUR	242b	2
		חליל	FLUTE	319d	
		יתרה	ABUNDANCE	452b	
		עשה	DO	795a	27
		קיר	KIR	885b	2
48	37	גדוד	CUTTING	151b	2
		גדע	HEW	154b	
		גרע	DIMINISH	175c	1
		זקן	BEARD	278b	2
		כל	ALL	481b	1 a
		מתנים	LOINS	608b	1 e
		קרחה	BALD SPOT	901b	
		שק	SACK	974c	2 a
48	38	גג	ROOF	150d	1
		חפץ	DELIGHT	343b	1
		כלי	ARTICLE	*479c	1
		כל	ALL	482a	1 db
		מספד	WAILING	704d	2
		רחוב	PLAZA	932b	
		שבר	BREAK	990c	
48	39	איך	HOW	32c	2
		בוש	BE ASHAMED	101d	1
		חתת	BE SHATTERED	369b	2 a
		חתת	BE SHATTERED	*369b	2 a
		מחתה	TERROR	370a	1 a
		ילל	HOWL	410b	
		סביב	ROUND ABOUT	687a	2 aa
		ערף	BACK OF NECK	791b	1
		פנה	TURN	815c	1
		שחק	LAUGHTER	966a	2
48	40	דאה	FLY SWIFTLY	178d	1
		כנף	WING	489c	1 a
		נשר	EAGLE	676d	
		פרש	SPREAD OUT	831a	1
48	41	לכד	CAPTURE	540a	1
		מצד	STRONGHOLD	844d	2
		צרר	SUFFER DISTRESS	865b	
		קריות	KERIOTH-HEZRON	901a	2
		תפש	LAY HOLD OF	1075a	
48	42	גדל	BECOME GREAT	152c	3 b
		מן	FROM	583b	7 bb
		שמד	BE EXTERMINATED	1029b	1
48	43	על	UPON	756c	27 a b
		פח	BIRD-TRAP	809a	2 a
		פחת	PIT	809b	
48	44	לכד	CAPTURE	540b	2
		נוס	FLEE	630d	1
		נפל	FALL	656d	
		עלה	GO UP	748b	1 b
		פחד	DREAD	808c	2
		פח	BIRD-TRAP	809a	2 a
		פחת	PIT	809b	
48	45	בין	INTERVAL	107d	D
		בן	SON	121d	8 i
		חשבון	HESHBON	363d	
		חשבון	HESHBON	364a	
		יצא	GO OUT	423b	1 g
		כח	STRENGTH	470c	1 a
		להבה	FLAME	529b	1
		מן	FROM	578c	1 b
		סיחון	SIHON	695d	
		פאה	CORNER	802b	1
		צל	SHADOW	853b	2
		שאון	ROAR	981a	1
		שאת	DIN OF BATTLE	*981b	
		אש	ADDENDA ET CORRIGENDA	1120d	
48	46	אבד	PERISH	1c	1
		אוי	WOE	17a	
		כמוש	CHEMOSH	484d	1
		לקח	TAKE	544a	3
		עם	PEOPLE	766c	1
		שבי	CAPTIVITY	985d	1
		שביה	CAPTIVITY	986a	1
		שבית	CAPTIVITY	986b	2 b
		שבית	CAPTIVITY	*986b	1
48	47	אחרית	END	31b	B
		הנה	HITHER	244c	A a
		שבית	CAPTIVITY	986b	2 b
		משפט	JUDGMENT	1048d	1 f
		כה	HERE	*1096d	1
49	1	גד	GAD	151c	1 b
		מדוע	WHEREFORE	396c	
		ירש	TAKE POSSESSION	439c	1 b
		ירש	INHERIT	439d	2
		ל	TO	514b	5 fa
		מלכם	MALCAM	575d	
		מלכם	MILCOM	576a	
49	2	בת	DAUGHTER	123d	4
		יצת	KINDLE	428b	
		ירש	TAKE POSSESSION	439c	1 b
		רבה	RABBA	913d	1
		תרועה	SHOUT OF WAR	930a	1
49	3	תל	MOUND	1068b	1
		בת	DAUGHTER	123b	1 i
		גדרה	WALL	155a	
		חגר	GIRD	291d	2
		חשבון	HESHBON	364a	
		יחדו	TOGETHER	*403c	A
		ילל	HOWL	410b	
		כהן	PRIEST	463a	2
		מלכם	MALCAM	575d	
		מלכם	MILCOM	576a	
		ספד	WAIL	704d	
49		עי	AI	743b	2
		רבה	RABBA	913d	1
		ספדנה	LAMENT	973c	
		שק	SACK	974c	2 a
		שר	CHIEFTAIN	978a	1 a
		שדד	DEAL VIOLENTLY WITH	994b	
49	4	שוט	GO ABOUT	1002a	
		אוצר	TREASURE	70a	1
		בטח	TRUST	105a	1 3c
		בת	DAUGHTER	123c	1
		הלל	BE BOASTFUL	239a	1
		זוב	FLOW	264d	2
		מי	WHO	567a	F c
		עמק	VALE	771a	
		שובב	BACKTURNING	1000a	
49	5	אדון	LORD	11d	6 c
		אין	NOT	34d	3
		ל	TO	*512a	3 b
		נאם	UTTERANCE	610b	2
		נדד	WANDER	622b	3
		סביב	ROUND ABOUT	687b	2 ab
		קבץ	GATHER	868a	
49	6	שבית	CAPTIVITY	986b	2 b
		שוב	TURN BACK	999d	9
49	7	אבד	PERISH	1d	2
		בין	DISCERN	106d	4
		חכמה	WISDOM	315b	2
		תימן	TEMAN	412d	
		עצה	ADVICE	420b	
		ל	TO	514b	5 fa
		סרח	GO FREE	710b	
49	8	איד	DISTRESS	15d	1
		בוא	COME	99c	2 a
		דדן	DEDAN	187a	2
		עמק	BE DEEP	770d	
		עת	TIME	773d	2 c
		עשו	ESAU	796c	
		פנה	TURN	815c	
		פקד	ATTEND TO	823c	A 2
		פקדה	OVERSIGHT	824a	1 a
49	9	בצר	CUT OFF	131a	
		גנב	THIEF	170c	
		די	SUFFICIENCY	191c	1
		הלל	PRAISE	239b	
		ל	TO	511c	1 gb
		לא	NOT	519a	1 ae
		עוללות	GLEANING	760a	
		שאר	REMAIN	984b	1
		שחת	GO TO RUIN	1008b	1
49	10	זרע	SOWING	283a	4 f
		חבה	WITHDRAW	285d	
		חשף	STRIP OFF	362c	2
		יכל	BE ABLE	407c	1 b
		מסתר	SECRET PLACE	712c	2 a
		שדד	DEAL VIOLENTLY WITH	994b	
		שכן	NEIGHBOUR	1015c	2
49	11	אלמנה	WIDOW	48b	
		בטח	TRUST	105a	1 4a
		חיה	LIVE	311c	1
		יתום	ORPHAN	450c	
		עזב	LEAVE	737b	2 b1
49	12	הוא	HE, SHE, IT	216b	4 ba
		כוס	CUP	468a	
		נקה	BE CLEAN	667b	3
49	13	בצרה	BOZRAH	131b	1
		חרבה	DESOLATION	351d	
		חרבה	WASTE	352b	2
		חרפה	REPROACH	358a	3
		עולם	LONG DURATION	762b	2 b1
		שבע	SWEAR	989b	2
		שמה	APPALMENT	1031c	2
49	14	את	WITH	86d	4 c
		קום	STAND	278b	6 b
		ציר	ENVOY	851d	
		קבץ	GATHER	868b	
		שמועה	REPORT	1035b	1
49	15	ב	IN	88b	1 2a
		בזה	DESPISE	102c	
		קטן	SMALL	882b	2
49	16	גבה	BE HIGH	147a	
		גבעה	HILL	149a	3
		זדון	INSOLENCE	268a	2
		חגוים	PLACES OF CONCEALMENT	291c	
		ירד	BRING DOWN	434a	1 a
		כי	THOUGH	473c	2 ca
		לב	HEART	525b	2 6c
		נשא	DECEIVE	674a	
		נשר	EAGLE	676d	
		סלע	CRAG	701a	1
		תפלצת	SHUDDERING	814a	
		קן	NEST	890a	1
		מרום	HEIGHT	928d	1
		תפש	LAY HOLD OF	1074d	1
49	17	מכה	BLOW	647a	1 c
		שמם	BE DESOLATED	1031a	2
		שמה	APPALMENT	1031c	2
		שרק	HISS	1056d	
49	18	גור	SOJOURN	158a	2
		מהפכה	OVERTHROW	246b	
		סדם	SODOM	690a	
		עמרה	GOMORRAH	771d	
		שכן	NEIGHBOUR	1015c	2
49	19	אריה	LION	71d	
		בחר	CHOOSE	104b	7
		גאון	EXALTATION	145a	1 c
		זה	THIS	261b	4 b
		יעד	MEET AT AN APPOINTED PLACE	417a	
		ירדן	JORDAN	434d	
		איתן	ENDURING	450d	2
		מי	WHO	567a	F c
		מי	WHO	567b	G
		נוה	HABITATION	627c	2
		עלה	GO UP	748d	3
		פנה	FACE	817b	2 4b d
		פקד	ATTEND TO	823c	B 1
		רגע	DISTURB	921a	
		רוץ	RUN	930c	2
49	20	אם	IF	50b	1 b2
		חשב	THINK	363b	2 2
		מחשבה	THOUGHT	364c	2
		תימן	TEMAN	412d	
		יעץ	ADVISE	419c	
		עצה	ADVICE	420b	
		נוה	ABODE OF FLOCKS	627c	1 a
		סחב	DRAG	695a	
		על	UPON	753d	2 1d
		צאן	SMALL CATTLE	838c	3
		צעיר	YOUNG	859a	1 a
		שמם	BE DESOLATED	1031b	2 a
49	21	סוף	REEDS	693b	2 b
		צעקה	CRY	858d	2
		קול	VOICE	877b	2 h
		רעש	SHAKE	950b	
		רעש	SHAKE	950b	
49	22	בצרה	BOZRAH	131b	1
		דאה	FLY SWIFTLY	178d	
		כנף	WING	489c	1 a
		לב	HEART	524c	2 1
		נשר	EAGLE	676d	
		עלה	GO UP	748d	3
		פרש	SPREAD OUT	831a	1
		צרר	SUFFER DISTRESS	865b	
49	23	ארפד	ARPAD	75d	
		אנחה	ANXIETY	178d	
		דמשק	DAMASCUS	199d	
		חמת	HAMATH	333a	
		יכל	BE ABLE	407c	1 b
		ל	TO	514b	5 fa
		מוג	MELT	556a	
		רע	EVIL	948b	2
		שמועה	REPORT	1035b	1
		שקט	BE QUIET	1053b	1
49	24	אחז	GRASP	28b	
		דמשק	DAMASCUS	199d	
		חבל	PAIN	287a	1 b
		חזק	BE FIRM	305a	6 a
		ילד	BEAR	408c	1 b
		פנה	TURN	815c	2
		צרה	DISTRESS	865b	
		צרר	SUFFER DISTRESS	865b	
		רטט	TREMBLING	936a	
		רפה	SINK	951d	2
49	25	תהלה	PRAISE	240b	5 a
		עזב	LEAVE	737d	
		עיר	CITY	746c	1 i
		קריה	TOWN	900b	2
49	26	בחור	YOUNG MAN	104c	
		דמם	BE SILENT	199a	
		מלחמה	WAR	536b	
		נאם	UTTERANCE	610b	2
		רחוב	PLAZA	932b	
49	27	ארמון	CITADEL	74d	
		בנהדר	BEN-HADAD	122b	
		דמשק	DAMASCUS	199d	
		חומה	WALL	327d	1
		יצת	KINDLE	*428c	
49	28	בן	SON	121b	1 jl
		חצור	HAZOR	347d	4
		ל	TO	514b	5 fa
		ממלכה	KINGDOM	575b	2
		נבוכדראצר	NEBUCHADNEZZAR	613a	
		נבוכדראצר	NEBUCHADNEZZAR	613b	
		קדם	FRONT	869c	1 b
		קדר	KEDAR	871a	1
		שדד	DEAL VIOLENTLY WITH	994b	
49	29	אהל	TENT	13d	1
		יריעה	CURTAIN	438c	
		נשא	LIFT	671b	3 b
		סביב	ROUND ABOUT	687a	1 d
		קרא	CALL	895b	3 a
49	30	חצור	HAZOR	347d	4
		חשב	THINK	363a	12
		מחשבה	THOUGHT	364c	2

Ch	v	Heb	Eng	Page	Sec
		יעץ	ADVISE	419c	
		עצה	ADVICE	420a	
		נבוכדראצר	NEBUCHADNEZ-ZAR	613a	
49	31	נוד	WANDER	626d	1 a
		עמק	BE DEEP	770d	
		בדד	ISOLATION	95a	
		בטח	SECURITY	105b	
		בריח	BAR	138b	1
		בריח	BAR	138b	1 b
		דלת	DOOR	195b	3
		לא	NOT	519b	1 bb
		שכן	SETTLE DOWN	1015a	1 a
		שלו	QUIET	1017c	1
49	32	איד	DISTRESS	15d	1
		בז	SPOIL	103a	2
		המון	ABUNDANCE	242d	4
		זרה	SCATTER	280a	1
		ל	TO	511c	1 h
		מן	FROM	578d	1 c
		עבר	REGION ACROSS	719d	2
		פאה	CORNER	802b	2
		קצץ	CUT OFF	893c	
		שלל	SPOIL	1022a	2
49	33	גור	SOJOURN	158a	2
		חצור	HAZOR	347d	4
		מעון	REFUGE	732d	1
		עולם	LONG DURATION	762b	2 b1
		תן	JACKAL	1072b	
49	34	אשר	PARTICLE OF RELATION	82d	6 a
		דבר	WORD	182c	1 2a
		מלכות	REIGN	575a	2
		עילם	ELAM	743d	
		צדקיהו	ZEDEKIAH	843b	1
		ראשית	BEGINNING	912a	1 a
49	35	גבורה	MIGHT	150b	2
		עילם	ELAM	743d	
		קשת	BOW	906c	1 e
		ראשית	BEGINNING	912b	2
		שבר	BREAK	990c	
49	36	בוא	COME	99c	2 a
		זרה	SCATTER	280a	1
		ל	TO	511c	1 h
		נדח	BANISH	623a	2
		עילם	ELAM	743d	
		קצה	END	892c	1
		רוח	BREATH	924d	2 a
49	37	בוא	COME	99c	2 a
		בקש	SEEK	134d	2 a
		חרון	BURNING OF ANGER	354c	
		חתת	BE SHATTERED	369c	2 a
		כלה	FINISH	478c	2 c2
		נפש	SOUL	659d	3 c
		עילם	ELAM	743d	
49	38	אבד	DESTROY	2b	1
		כסא	SEAT OF HONOR	490d	1 a
		עילם	ELAM	743d	
		שר	CHIEFTAIN	978a	2 a
49	39	אחרית	END	31b	B
		עילם	ELAM	743d	
		שבית	CAPTIVITY	986b	2 b
		שוב	TURN BACK	999d	9
50	1	דבר	SPEAK	181a	3 b
		דבר	SPEAK	181c	4 a
		כשדים	CHALDEANS	505a	1 b
50	2	בוש	BE ASHAMED	102a	2 c
		בל	BEL	128c	
		חתת	BE SHATTERED	*369b	2 a
		חתת	BE SHATTERED	369b	2 a
		כחד	HIDE	470b	1
		לכד	CAPTURE	540a	1
		מרדך	MERODACH	597d	
		נס	STANDARD	651d	1 a
		עצב	IDOL	781b	
50	3	אדם	MAN	9b	2
		בהמה	BEAST	96d	1
		בחור	YOUNG MAN	104c	
		הלך	WALK	232a	1 2
		ישב	DWELL	443b	3
		נוד	WANDER	626d	1 a
		צפון	NORTH	861a	
		שית	PUT	1011c	3
		שמה	WASTE	1031c	1
50	4	בכה	WEEP	113b	1
		בקש	SEEK	134d	3 c
		יהוה	YAHWEH	218d	2 1d
		הלך	WALK	233a	1 4c 1a
		יחדו	TOGETHER	403c	A
50	5	ברית	COVENANT	137a	2 2k
		ברית	COVENANT	137b	3 2
		ברית	COVENANT	137b	3 3
		דרך	WAY	202b	1 2
		הנה	HITHER	244c	A a
		לוה	BE JOINED	531a	1
		עולם	LONG DURATION	762c	2 d
		שאל	ASK	981d	2 c2
50	6	אבד	BE LOST	1d	3
		הלך	WALK	232a	1 2
		הר	MOUNTAIN	250c	1 g
		צאן	SMALL CATTLE	838c	3
		רבץ	RESTING PLACE	918c	1
		שה	A SHEEP	962a	1
		שוב	TURN BACK	998c	3
		שובב	BACKTURNING	1000a	
		תעה	ERR	1073c	1
50	7	אכל	EAT	37c	1
		אכל	EAT	37c	2
		אשם	OFFEND	79c	2
		גבעה	HILL	149a	3
		חטא	MISS A GOAL OR WAY	307a	2 b
		מצא	FIND	593b	3 a
		נוה	HABITATION	627c	2
		צדק	RIGHTEOUSNESS	841d	D
		מקוה	HOPE	876b	
		תחת	INSTEAD	1066a	23a b
50	8	כשדים	CHALDEANS	505a	1 b
		נוד	WANDER	626d	1 a
		עתוד	HE-GOAT	800d	
		צאן	SMALL CATTLE	838b	1 a
50	9	חץ	ARROW	346c	1
		כ	LIKE	455a	B
		ל	TO	511a	1 d
		לכד	CATPURE	540b	1
		עור	ROUSE ONESELF	735b	1
		עלה	GO UP	749c	2 b
		ערך	ARRANGE	789c	1 d
		צפון	NORTH	861a	
		קהל	ASSEMBLY	874c	1 b
		ריקם	EMPTILY	938b	2
		שכל	BE PRUDENT	968c	5
		שוב	TURN BACK	998a	7 a
		שכל	BE BEREAVED	1013d	
50	10	כשדים	CHALDEA	505b	2
		שבע	SATISFIED	959b	2 a
		שלל	SPOIL	1021d	
		שלל	SPOIL	1022a	2
50	11	אביר	MIGHTY	7d	3
		דוש	THRESH	190c	
		דשא	SPROUT	206a	
		כי	THOUGH	473c	2 ca
		נחלה	PROPERTY	635b	1 e
		עגלה	HEIFER	722b	
		עלז	EXULT	759c	
		פוש	SPRING ABOUT	807d	
		צהל	NEIGH	843c	1
		שסה	PLUNDER	1042c	
50	12	אחרית	END	31b	C
		אם	MOTHER	51c	1
		חפר	BE ABASHED	344a	1 c
		ילד	BEAR	408c	1 c
		ערבה	DESERT-PLAIN	787c	5
		ציה	DRYNESS	851a	
50	13	ישב	SIT	443b	4
		מן	ON ACCOUNT OF	580b	2 f
		מכה	BLOW	647a	1 c
		קצף	WRATH	893c	1
		שמם	BE DESOLATED	1031a	2
		שרק	HISS	1056d	
50	14	דרך	TREAD	202b	4
		חטא	MISS A GOAL OR WAY	307a	2 b
		חמל	SPARE	328b	
		חץ	ARROW	346c	1
		ידה	CAST	392b	
		ערך	ARRANGE	789c	1 d
		קשת	BOW	906c	1 d
50	15	אשיה	BUTTRESS	78c	
		הוא	HE, SHE, IT	216d	6 b
		הרס	THROW DOWN	248d	
		חומה	WALL	327c	1
		נפל	FALL	656d	1
		נקם	AVENGE	668b	1 a
		נקמה	VENGEANCE	668c	1
		נתן	GIVE	680a	1 z
		רוע	RAISE A SHOUT	929c	3
		אשיה	ADDENDA ET CORRIGENDA	1121a	
50	16	ה	THE	209b	2 b
		זרע	SOW	281c	1 e
		חרון	BURNING OF ANGER	*354c	
		ינה	OPPRESS	*413a	
		כרת	CUT OFF	503d	1 b
		מגל	SICKLE	618c	
		עת	TIME	773c	1 b
		פנה	TURN	815a	1 a
		פנה	FACE	818b	2 6a
		קציר	HARVESTING	894d	3
		תפש	LAY HOLD OF	1074d	2
50	17	אכל	EAT	37c	2
		ארי	LION	71d	
		אשור	ASSYRIA	78d	4
		זה	THIS	261d	4 i
		נבוכדראצר	NEBUCHADNEZ-ZAR	613a	
		נדח	THRUST	623b	2
		עצם	BREAK BONES	783a	
		פזר	SCATTER	808a	
		ראשון	FIRST	911a	2 a
		שה	A SHEEP	962a	1
		ישראל	ISRAEL	975d	2 a3
		עצם	ADDENDA ET CORRIGENDA	1126a	
50	18	אשור	ASSYRIA	78d	4
		פקד	ATTEND TO	823c	A 3
50	19	בשן	BASHAN	143c	2
		הר	MOUNTAIN	251a	2 b
		כרמל	CARMEL	502a	1
		נוה	ABODE OF FLOCKS	627c	1 a
		נפש	SOUL	660c	5 a
		רעה	TEND	945b	2 c
		שבע	SATISFIED	959b	1 a
		ישראל	ISRAEL	975d	2 a3
		שוב	TURN BACK	998c	1
50	20	את	MARK OF THE ACCUSATIVE	85a	1 b
		חטאת	SIN	308c	1 b
		סלח	FORGIVE	699c	
		עון	INIQUITY	731b	1 c5
		שאר	REMAIN	984b	1
50	21	חרב	ATTACK	352b	
		חרם	BAN	355d	1 b
		מרתים	BABYLON	601c	
		פקוד	PEKOD	824c	
50	22	קול	VOICE	877b	2 j
		שבר	BREAKING	991b	2
50	23	גדע	HEW OFF	154b	2
		פטיש	FORGE-HAMMER	809c	
		שבר	BREAK	990d	
		שמה	APPALMENT	1031c	2
50	24	גם	ALSO	*169d	4
		גרה	ENGAGE IN STRIFE	173b	1
		מצא	FIND	394a	1 g2
		יקש	LAY SNARES	430c	
		לכד	CAPTURE	540a	1
		תפש	LAY HOLD OF	1075a	
50	25	אדון	LORD	11d	6 b
		אוצר	TREASURE	70a	3 c
		הוא	HE, SHE, IT	216d	6 b
		זעם	INDIGNATION	277a	
		יצא	BRING OUT	425a	4 a
		כלי	IMPLEMENT	479d	2 a
		כשדים	CHALDEANS	505a	1 b
		מלאכה	WORK	522a	3 a
		פתח	OPEN	835a	
50	26	מאבוס	GRANARY	7b	
		חרם	BAN	355d	1 b
		כמו	LIKE	455d	1 a
		ל	TO	511c	1 gb
		סלל	LIFT UP	699d	2
		ערמה	HEAP	790d	
		פתח	OPEN	835a	
		קצה	END	892b	3
		קץ	END	894a	2
		שארית	REST	984d	1
50	27	הוי	AH	223a	
		חרב	ATTACK	352b	
		טבח	SLAUGHTERING	370d	1
		יום	DAY	398d	2 g
		יום	DAY	398d	2 h1
		ירד	GO DOWN	433b	1 k
		ל	TO	511b	1 ga
		על	UPON	756c	2 7 a b
		עת	TIME	773d	2 c
		פר	YOUNG BULL	831a	2 f
50	28	בבל	BABEL	93c	
		היכל	TEMPLE	228c	2 b
		נגד	BE CONSPICUOUS	616d	2
		נקמה	VENGEANCE	668c	1
		פליט	ESCAPED ONE	812c	
		קול	VOICE	877a	1 f
50	29	דרך	TREAD	202b	4
		זיד	BOIL UP	267c	
		חנה	DECLINE	333c	2 c2
		פליטה	ESCAPE	812c	2 b
		פעל	DOING	821c	1 c
		קדוש	HOLY	872c	1 c
		קשת	BOW	906c	1 d
		ירבעם	ARCHER	914d	
		שמע	HEAR	1034a	1 d
50	30	דמם	BE SILENT	199a	
		מלחמה	WAR	536b	
		רחוב	PLAZA	932b	
50	31	אדון	LORD	11d	6 c
		אל	TO	40b	4
		זדון	INSOLENCE	268a	2
		יום	DAY	398d	2 g
		יום	DAY	398d	2 h1
		עת	TIME	773d	2 c
		פקד	ATTEND TO	823c	A 2
		פקדה	OVERSIGHT	824a	1 c
50	32	אין	NOT	34d	3
		זדון	INSOLENCE	268a	2
		יצת	KINDLE	*428c	
		כשל	STUMBLE	505c	1
		ל	TO	*512a	3 b
		נפל	FALL	657b	2 b
		סביב	ROUND ABOUT	687b	2 ba b
		קום	STAND	878d	1 a
50	33	חזק	BE FIRM	305a	6 b
		יחדו	TOGETHER	403c	A
		מאן	REFUSE	549a	
		עשק	OPPRESS	798d	2
		שבה	TAKE CAPTIVE	985c	1 c
50	34	גאל	REDEEM	145c	3 a
		חזק	STRONG	305c	1 a
		מען	PURPOSE	775b	1 c
		רגע	BE AT REST	921b	A
		ריב	STRIVE	936c	3
		ריב	STRIFE	937a	1
50	35	חכם	WISE	314d	1
		כשדים	CHALDEANS	505a	1 b
50	36	בד	EMPTY TALKERS	95a	B
		חתת	BE SHATTERED	369b	2 a
		יאל	BE FOOLISH	383d	2

Ch v.	Heb	Eng	Page	Sec
	שמה	APPALMENT	1031c	2
	שרקה	HISSING	1057a	
	תן	JACKAL	1072b	
51 38	ארי	LION	71d	
	גור	WHELP	158d	
	יחדו	TOGETHER	403c	B
	כפיר	LION	498d	
	נער	GROWL	654c	
	שאג	ROAR	980d	1
51 39	חמם	BE OR BECOME WARM	328d	2
	ישן	SLEEP	445c	
	שנה	SLEEP	446a	
	עולם	LONG DURATION	762d	2j
	קיץ	AWAKE	884c	2
	שית	PUT	1011c	3
	שכר	BE DRUNK	1016b	
	משתה	FEAST	1059d	1
51 40	איל	RAM	18a	2g
	טבח	SLAUGHTER	370c	1
	ירד	BRING DOWN	434a	1c
	כר	LAMB	503a	
	עם	WITH	767b	1a
	עתוד	HE/GOAT	800d	
51 41	איך	HOW	32c	2
	תהלה	PRAISE	240c	5cc
	לכד	CAPTURE	540a	1
	שמה	APPALMENT	1031c	2
	ששך	SHESHACH	1058d	
	תפש	LAY HOLD OF	1075a	
51 42	המון	CROWD	242d	3c
	ים	SEA	411a	5
	כסה	BE COVERED	491c	
51 43	הם	THEY	242a	8d
	ציה	DRYNESS	851a	
	שמה	WASTE	1031c	1
51 44	בלע	THING SWOLLOWED	118c	2
	בל	BEL	128c	
	גם	YEA	169c	3
	נהר	FLOW	625c	
	נפל	FALL	656d	1
51 45	חרון	BURNING OF ANGER	354c	
	מלט	SLIP AWAY	572c	3
	נפש	SOUL	660a	3c
51 46	ב	IN	90c	3 5
	חמס	VIOLENCE	329c	
	ירא	FEAR	431b	1c
	לבב	HEART	524b	29b
	משל	RULE	605d	1
	פן	LEST	814d	1b
	רכך	BE TENDER	940a	1a
	שמועה	REPORT	1035b	1
51 48	ל	TO	511c	1gb
	רנן	GIVE A RINGING CRY	943b	
51 49	גם	ALSO	169c	4
	חלל	PIERCED	319c	2
	ל	TO	518a	7bg
51 50	זכר	REMEMBER	270a	13b
	לבב	HEART	523b	23d
	עלה	GO UP	749a	7
	פליט	ESCAPED ONE	812c	
	רחק	DISTANT	935c	2a1
51 51	זור	BE A STRANGER	266c	2c
	חרפה	REPROACH	357d	1
	כלמה	IGNOMINY	484b	2
	כסה	COVER	492a	5
	על	UPON	757b	27c ab
	פנה	FACE	815d	1 1a
	מקדש	SACRED PLACE	874b	4
51 52	אנק	CRY	60b	
	חלל	PIERCED	319c	1
51 53	את	WITH	86d	4c
	בצר	MAKE INACCESSIBLE	131a	
	כי	THOUGH	473c	2ca
	ל	TO	511c	1gb
	עז	STRENGTH	738d	1
	מרום	HEIGHT	928d	1
51 54	זעקה	CRY	277d	2
	כשדים	CHALDEANS	505a	1b
	שבר	BREAKING	991b	2
51 55	אבד	CAUSE TO VANISH	2a	2
	אבד	DESTROY	2b	2
	המה	ROAR	242b	3
	נתן	GIVE	681c	1i
	קול	VOICE	877b	2j
	שאון	ROAR	981a	1
	שדד	DEAL VIOLENTLY WITH	994a	
51 56	אל	GOD	42d	6c
	חתת	BE SHATTERED	369b	1
	חתת	BE SHATTERED	369c	
	לכד	CAPTURE	540a	1
	קשת	BOW	906a	1b
	שלם	BE COMPLETE	1022c	5
51 57	חכם	WISE	314d	4
	ישן	SLEEP	445c	
	שנה	SLEEP	446a	
	מלך	KING	573b	3
	סגן	PREFECT	688d	1
	עולם	LONG DURATION	762d	2j
	פחה	GOVERNOR	808d	
	קיץ	AWAKE	884c	2

Ch v.	Heb	Eng	Page	Sec
	שכר	BE DRUNK	1016b	
51 58	גבה	HIGH	147b	1
	די	SUFFICIENCY	191c	2aa
	חומה	WALL	327c	1
	יגע	TOIL	388b	1
	יעף	BE WEARY	419b	
	יצת	KINDLE	428b	
	לאם	PEOPLE	522c	
	ערר	STRIP ONESELF	792d	
	רחב	WIDE	932a	
	ריק	EMPTINESS	938b	
	שער	GATE	1044c	1a
51 59	מחסיה	MAHSEIAH	340c	
	מנחה	RESTING PLACE	630a	1
	נריה	NERIAH	633a	
	רביעי	FOURTH	918a	2
	שריה	SERAIAH	976a	3
	שר	CHIEFTAIN	978c	4a
	שנה	YEAR	1040c	
51 60	כתב	WRITE	507c	1b2
	ספר	MISSIVE	*707c	4
	רעה	MISERY	949a	1
51 61	דבר	WORD	183a	2 2
	קרא	CALL	895c	4a
	שריה	SERAIAH	976a	3
51 62	אדם	MAN	9b	2
	דבר	SPEAK	181a	3 b
	ישב	DWELL	443b	3
	כרת	CUT OFF	504c	2
	מן	FROM	583d	9b1
	עולם	LONG DURATION	762b	2d
51 63	היה	COME TO PASS	225b	1 2b ae
	ספר	MISSIVE	*707c	4
	ספר	MISSIVE	*707c	4
	פרת	EUPHRATES	832c	
	קרא	CALL	895c	4a
	קשר	BIND	905b	1a
	דבר	WORD	183a	2 1b
51 64	הנה	HITHER	244c	A a
	יעף	BE WEARY	419b	
	ככה	THUS	462c	
	שקע	SINK	1054b	
	כה	HERE	*1096d	
52 1	בן	SON	122a	9 a
	חמוטל	HAMUTAL	327d	
	לבנה	LIBNAH	526c	1
	ירמיה	JEREMIAH	941d	2
52 3	מרד	REBEL	597c	1
	עד	AS FAR AS	*724b	12a b
	פנה	FACE	819a	2b
	שלך	THROW	1021b	2b
52 4	בנה	BUILD	124c	1ah
	דיק	BULWARK	189b	
	חנה	DECLINE	333c	2c2
	נבוכדראצר	NEBUCHADNEZZAR	613a	
	עשור	A TEN	797c	1b
52 5	עשתי	ONE	799d	
	מצור	SIEGE	849a	1
52 6	חזק	BE FIRM	304c	14b
	רביעי	FOURTH	917d	1
	רעב	FAMINE	944b	1
52 7	בקע	BREAK OPEN OR THROUGH	132a	2
	ברח	FLEE	137d	2
	גן	GARDEN	171a	
	דרך	WAY	202d	1
	דרך	WAY	202d	1
	הלך	WALK	230c	1 1d 1a
	חומה	WALL	327b	1
	כשדים	CHALDEANS	505a	1b
	מלחמה	WAR	536b	
	לילה	NIGHT	539a	1
	ערבה	DESERT-PLAIN	787c	1b
	שער	GATE	1044d	1 b 6
52 8	ירחו	JERICHO	437d	
	כשדים	CHALDEANS	505a	1b
	נשג	OVERTAKE	673c	1a
	ערבה	DESERT-PLAIN	787c	3
	פוץ	BE DISPERSED	807a	1
52 9	את	WITH	86a	1db
	דבר	SPEAK	181b	3d
	חמת	HAMATH	333a	
	עלה	GO UP	749c	2a
	רבלה	RIBLAH	916c	1
	משפט	JUDGMENT	1048c	1c
	תפש	LAY HOLD OF	1074d	1
52 10	רבלה	RIBLAH	916c	1
	שחט	SLAUGHTER	1006b	3
	שחט	SLAUGHTER	1006b	3
52 11	אסר	TIE	63d	3
	נחשת	COPPER	639a	2
	עור	MAKE BLIND	734c	
52 12	חמישי	FIFTH	332c	1
	נבוזראדן	NEBUZARADAN	613a	
	נבוכדראצר	NEBUCHADNEZZAR	613a	
	עשר	TEN	797b	9 b
	עשר	A TEN	797c	1 b
	עשר	TEN	797c	
	תשע	NINE	1077c	2
52 13	גדול	GREAT	153a	1
52 14	אשר	PARTICLE OF RELATION	83b	7c
	חומה	WALL	327c	1
	כשדים	CHALDEANS	505a	1b

Ch v.	Heb	Eng	Page	Sec
52 15	נתץ	PULL DOWN	683b	1
	אמון	ARCHITECT	54c	
	דלה	THE POOR	*195d	
	המון	CROWD	*242d	3 c
	יתר	REMAINDER	451a	1a
	יתר	REMAINDER	451a	1a
	נבוזראדן	NEBUZARADAN	613a	
	נפל	FALL	657c	4 b
52 16	גוב	DIG	155c	
	גב	PIT	155d	
	דלה	THE POOR	*195d	
	יגב	FIELD	387a	
	יגב	TILL	387a	
	כרם	DRESS VINES	501d	
	נבוזראדן	NEBUZARADAN	613a	
52 17	שאר	REMAIN	984b	1
	אשר	PARTICLE OF RELATION	83a	7 b
	ים	SEA	411a	7
	מכונה	BASE	467d	
	כשדים	CHALDEANS	505a	1 b
	נחשת	COPPER	639a	1
	עמוד	PILLAR	765b	2
	שבר	BREAK	991a	
52 18	מזמרת	SNUFFERS	275a	
	מזרק	BOWL	284d	2 a
	יע	SHOVEL	418b	
	כף	PAN	497a	4 b
	נחשת	COPPER	638d	1
	סיר	POT	696c	2
	שרת	SERVE	1057b	2 b
52 19	זהב	GOLD	263a	2
	מזרק	BOWL	284d	2 c
	מחתה	FIRE-HOLDER	367b	2
	כף	PAN	497a	4 b
	מנורה	LAMPSTAND	633a	2
	מנקיה	SACRIFICIAL BOWL	667d	
	סיר	POT	696c	2
	סף	BASIN	706b	
52 20	בקר	CATTLE	133c	2
	ים	SEA	411a	7
	מכונה	BASE	467d	
	נחשת	COPPER	639a	1
	עמוד	PILLAR	765b	2
	שלמה	SOLOMON	1024d	
	משקל	WEIGHT	1054a	
52 21	אמה	CUBIT	52b	1
	חוט	THREAD	296c	3
	נבב	HOLLOW OUT	612c	
	סבב	SURROUND	686a	2 d
	עבי	THICKNESS	716a	
	עמ ד	PILLAR	765b	2
	אצבע	FINGER	840c	1 d
	קומה	HEIGHT	879b	3
52 22	אלה	THESE	41d	D
	אמה	CUBIT	52b	1
	כל	ALL	*482d	2 ba
	כתרת	CAPITAL	509d	
	קומה	HEIGHT	879b	3
	רמון	POMEGRANATE	942a	3
	שבכה	LATTICE-WORK	959b	2
52 23	מאה	HUNDRED	547d	1 a3
	רוח	BREATH	924d	2 b
	רמון	POMEGRANATE	942a	3
	שבכה	LATTICE-WORK	959b	2
52 24	כהן	PRIEST	464b	8
	כהן	PRIEST	464c	8
	סף	THRESHOLD	706c	
	צפניה	ZEPHANIAH	861b	1
	ראש	HEAD	911a	3 e
	שריה	SERAIAH	976a	2
	משנה	SECOND	1041c	3 a
52 25	אשר	PARTICLE OF RELATION	82b	2 a
	מלחמה	WAR	536b	
	מצא	FIND	593d	1 c
	ספר	ENUMERATOR	708c	1 b
	סרים	EUNUCH	710c	
	פנה	FACE	816a	1 2b
	פקיד	COMMISSIONER	824b	
	צבא	SERVE	838d	
	ששים	SIXTY	995d	
52 26	הלך	WALK	236d	1 d
	נבוזראדן	NEBUZARADAN	613a	
	רבלה	RIBLAH	916c	1
52 27	חמת	HAMATH	333a	
	נכה	SMITE	645d	2 a
	רבלה	RIBLAH	916c	1
52 28	יהודי	JEW	397c	
	נבוכדראצר	NEBUCHADNEZZAR	613a	
52 29	נבוכדראצר	NEBUCHADNEZZAR	613a	
	נפש	SOUL	660a	4 c3
52 30	חמש	FIVE	332b	5 e2
	יהודי	JEW	397c	
	נבוזראדן	NEBUZARADAN	613a	
	נבוכדראצר	NEBUCHADNEZZAR	613a	
	נפש	SOUL	660a	4 c3
	ארבעים	FORTY	917c	2 c
52 31	אוילמרדך	EVIL-MERODACH	17b	
	בבל	BABEL	93c	
	בית	HOUSE	109a	1 ae 2
	בית	HOUSE	109a	1 ae 2
	יהויכין	JEHOIACHIN	220c	

LAMENTATIONS

Ch v.	Heb	Eng	Page	Sec
	יצא	CAUSE TO GO	424b	1 a
	מלכות	REIGN	575d	2
	נשא	LIFT	670b	1 b 2
	שלשים	THIRTY	1026c	2
52 32	דבר	SPEAK	181b	3 d
	טובה	WELFARE	375d	2
	כסא	SEAT OF HONOR	490d	2
	מעל	ABOVE	751b	1 b
	על	UPON	759b	4 2 d
52 33	חיים	LIFE	313b	1
	כלא	CONFINEMENT	476c	1
	תמיד	CONTINUITY	556c	1 b
	שנה	CHANGE	1040a	
52 34	ארחה	MEAL	73c	
	בבל	BABEL	93c	
	דבר	WORD	183c	4 1
	חיים	LIFE	313b	1
	יום	DAY	400c	7 e3
	תמיד	CONTINUITY	556c	2 b
	נתן	GIVE	681c	1 c

LAMENTATIONS

Ch v.	Heb	Eng	Page	Sec
1 1	איכה	HOW	32d	2
	אלמנה	WIDOW	48b	
	ב	IN	88b	1 2a
	בדד	ISOLATION	94d	
	מדינה	PROVINCE	193d	2
	מס	LABOUR-GANG	587a	2 b
	רב	MUCH	913b	1 d
	רב	GREAT	913c	2 a
	שרה	PRINCESS	979a	
1 2	אהב	LOVE	13a	4 a
	אין	NOT	34d	3
	בגד	ACT TREACHEROUSLY	93d	B
	בכה	WEEP	113b	1
	בכה	WEEP	113c	2
	דמעה	TEARS	199c	
	ל	TO	*512a	3 b
	לחי	CHEEK	534d	2
	נחם	CONSOLE ONESELF	637b	
	רע	FRIEND	946a	1
1 3	מצא	FIND	592c	1 a
	מנוח	RESTING PLACE	629d	1
	נשג	OVERTAKE	673c	1 a
	עבדה	LABOR	715b	1
	עני	AFFLICTION	777a	1
	מצר	STRAITS	865c	
	רדף	PURSUE	922a	1 e
1 4	אבל	MOURNING	5d	
	אנה	SIGN	58d	1
	בוא	COME	98b	2
	בלי	WEARING OUT	115d	C a
	בתולה	VIRGIN	144a	
	יגה	SUFFER	387b	
	מועד	APPOINTED TIME	417c	1 b
	כהן	PRIEST	463d	4
	מרר	BE BITTER	600b	2
	שמם	BE DESOLATED	1031a	1
1 5	דרך	WAY	202d	1
	הלך	WALK	*231b	1 d3 ge
	יגה	SUFFER	387b	
	עולל	CHILD	760c	
	פנה	FACE	817c	2 4c a
	פשע	TRANSGRESSION	833c	3 c
	שבי	CAPTIVITY	985d	1
	שלה	BE QUIET	1017b	2
1 6	איל	HART	19b	
	בת	DAUGHTER	123c	3
	הדר	SPLENDOUR	214b	2
	יצא	GO OUT	423a	1 e
	כח	STRENGTH	470c	1 a
	לא	NOT	520a	4 aa
	פנה	FACE	817c	2 4c a
	רדף	PURSUE	922d	1 c
	מרעה	PASTURAGE	945c	
1 7	זכר	REMEMBER	269d	1 1 a
	מחמד	DESIRABLE	327a	
	יום	DAY	398c	2 f
	ל	TO	*512a	3 b
	נפל	FALL	657c	4 c
	עני	AFFLICTION	777a	1
	קדם	FRONT	869d	2 b
	מרוד	RESTLESSNESS	924a	
	שחק	LAUGH	965d	1 a
	שבית	CAPTIVITY	986b	1
	משבת	CESSATION	992d	
1 8	אנה	SIGN	58d	1
	דלל	BE LIGHT	273a	
	חטא	MISS A GOAL OR WAY	307b	2 b
	חטא	SIN	308a	1 b
	כבד	MAKE HONORABLE	457d	2 a
	נידה	IMPURITY	622c	
	ערוה	NAKEDNESS	788d	1
	שוב	TURN BACK	996d	1
1 9	אין	NOT	34d	3
	זכר	REMEMBER	270a	1 5
	טמאה	UNCLEANNESS	380a	1
	ירד	GO DOWN	433b	1 k
	ל	TO	*512a	3 b
	נחם	CONSOLE ONESELF	637b	
	עני	AFFLICTION	777a	1
	פלא	WONDER	810c	1

Ch v.	Heb	Eng	Page	Sec
1 10	שול	SKIRT	1002c	
	מחמד	DESIRE	327a	
	ל	TO	512c	5 aa
	פרש	SPREAD OUT	831b	1
	ראה	TO SEE	907b	5 a
1 11	אכל	FOOD	38a	
	אנח	SIGN	58d	2
	ב	IN	90b	3
	בקש	SEEK	134c	1 b
	זלל	BE LIGHT	272d	1
	מחמד	DESIRABLE	327a	
	מחמד	DESIRE	327d	1
	נבט	LOOK	613d	3
	נפש	SOUL	661a	6 g
	שוב	TURN BACK	999d	2 b
1 12	אם	IF	50d	2 ba
	חרון	BURNING OF ANGER	354c	
	יגה	SUFFER	387b	
	יום	DAY	399a	3
	יש	THERE IS	441d	2 b
	מכאוב	PAIN	456c	2
	לא	NOT	519a	1 a
	נבט	LOOK	613d	3
1 13	עבר	PASS OVER	*717d	4 a
	ראה	TO SEE	907b	5 a
	רוח	FAINT	188c	1
	יום	DAY	400c	7 f
	רשת	NET	440c	1 b1
	עצם	BONE	782d	1 c
	פרש	SPREAD OUT	831b	1
	רדה	HAVE DOMINION	922a	1
	מרום	HEIGHT	928d	3
	שוב	TURN BACK	999d	5
	שמם	BE DESOLATED	1030d	1
1 14	אדון	LORD	11c	3 2b
	קום	STAND	278b	7 a
	יכל	BE ABLE	407c	1 b
	כח	STRENGTH	470d	1 c
	כשל	MAKE FEEBLE	506a	2
	על	YOKE	760d	2
	פשע	TRANSGRESSION	833c	3 c
	צואר	NECK	848c	1
	שקד	BIND ON	974b	
	שרג	BE INTERTWINED	974d	
	שקד	WATCH	1052b	2
1 15	אביר	MIGHTY	7d	1
	בחור	YOUNG MAN	104c	
	בת	DAUGHTER	123c	3
	בתולה	VIRGIN	144a	
	דרך	TREAD	202a	3
	גת	WINE-PRESS	387c	
	יהודה	JUDAH	397b	1 3
	מועד	APPOINTED MEETING	417d	2
	סלה	MAKE LIGHT OF	699a	
	קרא	CALL	895c	3 a
	שבר	BREAK	990c	
1 16	בכה	WEEP	113c	3
	גבר	BE STRONG	149d	2 a
	ירד	GO DOWN	433c	3 c
	נחם	CONSOLE ONESELF	637a	
	רחק	BE DISTANT	934d	
	שוב	TURN BACK	999d	2 b
	שמם	BE DESOLATED	1030d	1
1 17	אין	NOT	34d	3
	ב	IN	90b	3 4
	כף	HOLLOW OF THE HAND	496c	1 d4
	ל	TO	*512a	3 b
	נדה	IMPURITY	622c	2
	נחם	CONSOLE ONESELF	637b	
	סביב	ROUND ABOUT	687b	2 ab
	פרש	SPREAD OUT	831c	1 a
	צוה	COMMAND	845d	1 e
1 18	בחור	YOUNG MAN	104c	
	בתולה	VIRGIN	144a	
	הוא	HE, SHE, IT	216b	4 a
	הלך	WALK	231b	1 d3 ge
	מכאוב	PAIN	456c	2
	מרה	BE REBELLIOUS	598b	2
	צדיק	JUST	843a	1
	שבי	CAPTIVITY	985d	1
1 19	אהב	LOVE	13b	2
	אכל	FOOD	38a	
	בקש	SEEK	134d	1 d
	גוע	EXPIRE	157c	
	ו	AND	254b	3
	זקן	OLD	278d	2b
	כהן	PRIEST	463c	4
	נפש	SOUL	661a	6 g
	רמה	BEGUILE	941a	
	שוב	TURN BACK	999b	2 b
1 20	הפך	TURN	245d	1 b
	חוץ	THE OUTSIDE	300a	1 bd
	חמר	FERMENT	330c	
	חמר	BE RED	331a	
	כ	LIKE	453d	1 b
	כ	LIKE	*454b	1 d
	מעה	BELLY	589a	5
	מרה	BE REBELLIOUS	598a	2
	קרב	INWARD PART	899b	2 a
	שכל	BE BEREAVED	1013d	1
	צרר	ADDENDA ET CORRIGENDA	1126c	
1 21	אנח	SIGN	58d	1

Ch v.	Heb	Eng	Page	Sec
	בוא	COME	99c	2
	ל	TO	*512a	3 b
	נחם	CONSOLE ONESELF	637b	
	שוש	REJOICE	965b	
1 22	אנחה	SIGHING	58d	
	בוא	COME	98b	2
	בוא	COME	98c	2 d
	דוי	FAINT	188d	2
	עלל	ACT ARBITRARILY	759d	
	עלל	ACT ARBITRARILY	759d	
	פנה	FACE	817c	2 4a c
	פשע	TRANSGRESSION	833c	3 c
2 1	איכה	HOW	32d	2
	ארץ	EARTH	76a	1 b
	בת	DAUGHTER	123c	3
	הדם	FOOTSTOOL	213b	
	זכר	REMEMBER	270b	2 1 d
	יום	DAY	399a	3
	עוב	BECLOUD	728a	
	תפארה	BEAUTY	802d	3 a
	רגל	FOOT	919d	1 b
	שלך	THROW	1021b	2 c
2 2	בלע	SWALLOW UP	118b	2 a
	בת	DAUGHTER	123c	3
	מבצר	FORTIFICATION	131c	
	הרס	THROW DOWN	248c	1
	חלל	POLLUTE	320c	2
	חמל	SPARE	328b	
	יהודה	JUDAH	397b	1 3
	ממלכה	KINGDOM	575b	1
	נגע	TOUCH	619b	1
	נוה	PASTURE	627d	1
	עברה	OVERFLOW	720c	3 b
2 3	בער	BURN	129a	3
	גדע	HEW OFF	154b	
	חרי	BURNING	354c	
	להבה	FLAME	529b	1
	שוב	TURN BACK	999a	1 c
2 4	אהל	TENT	14a	1
	איב	BE HOSTILE TO	33c	
	אש	FIRE	77d	5
	בת	DAUGHTER	123c	3
	דרך	TREAD	202b	4
	הרג	KILL	247b	1
	מחמד	DESIRE	327a	
	חמה	RAGE	404c	2 c
	חמה	RAGE	*405a	2 c
	נצב	STAND	662a	1 a
	קשת	BOW	906c	1 d
	פך	POUR OUT	1049d	2 a
2 5	איב	BE HOSTILE TO	33c	
	אניה	MOURNING	58b	
	ארמון	CITADEL	74d	
	בלע	SWALLOW UP	118b	2 a
	מבצר	FORTIFICATION	131c	
	יהודה	JUDAH	397b	1 3
	רבה	BECOME MANY	915b	
	שחת	GO TO RUIN	1008a	1
2 6	גן	GARDEN	171a	
	זעם	INDIGNATION	277a	
	חמס	TREAT VIOLENTLY	329b	1
	מועד	APPOINTED TIME	417c	1 b
	מועד	APPOINTED PLACE	417d	3 a
	כהן	PRIEST	463d	4
	נאץ	CONTEMN	610d	
	שך	BOOTH	968a	
	שבת	SABBOTH	992c	1 c
	שחת	GO TO RUIN	1008a	1
	שכח	FORGET	1013b	
2 7	ארמון	CITADEL	74d	
	זנח	REJECT	276b	
	חומה	WALL	327d	2 a
	מועד	APPOINTED TIME	417c	1 b
	נאר	ABHOR	611b	
	נתן	GIVE	679d	1 x
	סגר	DELIVER UP	689c	1
	קול	VOICE	877b	2 j
2 8	אבל	MOURN	5c	
	אמל	BE WEAK	51c	
	בלע	SWALLOW UP	118b	2 a
	בת	DAUGHTER	123c	3
	חל	RAMPART	298a	1
	חומה	WALL	327c	1
	חשב	THINK	363b	2 2
	יחדו	TOGETHER	403c	B
	נטה	STRETCH OUT	640a	1 b
	קו	LINE	876a	
	שוב	TURN BACK	999a	1 c
	שחת	GO TO RUIN	1008b	1
2 9	אבד	CAUSE TO PERISH	2a	1
	בריח	BAR	138b	2
	בריח	BAR	138b	1 b
	חזון	VISION	303a	1
	טבע	SINK	371c	
	תורה	INSTRUCTION	435d	1 b
	מצא	FIND	593a	1 b
	נביא	PROPHET	612a	1
	שבר	BREAK	991a	
2 10	בת	DAUGHTER	123c	3
	בתולה	VIRGIN	144a	
	דמם	BE SILENT	198d	1
	זקן	OLD	278d	2 b
	חגר	GIRD	291d	2
	ירד	LET DOWN	434b	3
	ישב	SIT	442c	1 a
	עלה	GO UP	749c	4

Ch	v.	Heb	Eng	Page	Sec
		עפר	DRY EARTH	779c	1 a
		שק	SACK	974c	2 a
2	11	דמעה	TEARS	199c	
		חמר	FERMENT	330c	
		חמר	BE RED	331a	
		ינק	SUCK	413b	
		כבד	LIVER	458b	
		כלה	BE FINISHED	477d	2 b
		מעה	BELLY	589a	5
		עטף	BE FEEBLE	742c	
		עולל	CHILD	760c	
		עם	PEOPLE	767a	5 f
		קריה	TOWN	900b	2
		רחוב	PLAZA	932b	
		שבר	BREAKING	991a	1
		שפך	POUR OUT	1049d	
2	12	דגן	CORN	186c	
		חיק	BOSOM	300d	2
		חלל	PIERCED	319c	1
		עטף	BE FEEBLE	742c	
		רחוב	PLAZA	932b	
		שפך	POUR OUT	1050a	
2	13	בת	DAUGHTER	123c	3
		בת	DAUGHTER	123c	3
		בתולה	VIRGIN	144a	
		דמה	BE LIKE	198a	1
		מה	WHAT	553a	1 da
		נחם	CONSOLE ONESELF	637a	
		עוד	BEAR WITNESS	729d	
		עוד	BEAR WITNESS	730a	1
		ציון	ZION	851b	
		רפא	HEAL	950d	2 b
		שביה	CAPTIVE	986a	
		שבר	BREAKING	991a	1
		שוה	AGREE WITH	1001a	
2	14	חזה	SEE	302c	2
		חזה	SEE	302c	2
		חזה	SEE	302c	2
		נביא	PROPHET	612a	2
		מדוח	ENTICEMENT	623c	
		עון	INIQUITY	730d	1
		שבית	CAPTIVITY	986b	2 a
		שוא	EMPTINESS	996b	2
		שוא	EMPTINESS	996b	2
		שוב	TURN BACK	999d	9
		תפל	TASTELESS	1074a	
2	15	אמר	SAY	56a	1
		ב	IN	*90b	3 4
		בת	DAUGHTER	123c	3
		זה	THIS	261a	3
		יפי	BEAUTY	421d	
		כליל	WHOLE	483a	1
		נוע	TOTTER	631c	2
		ספק	SLAP	706c	1
		עבר	PASS OVER	*717d	4 a
		משוש	EXULTATION	965c	
		שרק	HISS	1056d	
2	16	בלע	SWALLOW UP	118c	2 a
		חרק	GNASH	359b	
		פה	MOUTH	805b	3
		פצה	PART	822c	1 a
		קוה	WAIT FOR	875d	1
		שן	TOOTH	1042a	1 a
		שרק	HISS	1056d	
2	17	אמרה	UTTERANCE	57b	
		בצע	CUT OFF	130c	
		הרס	THROW DOWN	248d	1
		זמם	CONSIDER	273b	2 a
		חמל	SPARE	328b	
		קדם	FRONT	869d	2 b
		קרן	HORN	902a	2
		רום	BE HIGH	927c	1 f
		שמח	REJOICE	970c	
2	18	בת	DAUGHTER	123c	3
		בת	DAUGHTER	123d	6
		דמם	BE STILL	199a	2
		דמעה	TEARS	199c	
		ירד	BRING DOWN	434a	1 b
		נחל	TORRENT	636b	1
		נתן	GIVE	679a	1 g
		פוגת	BENUMBING	806b	
		צעק	CRY	858c	1 b
2	19	חוץ	THE OUTSIDE	300b	2 a
		כל	ALL	481b	1 a
		נכח	FRONT	647b	2
		נשא	LIFT	670b	1 b 1
		עטף	BE FEEBLE	742c	
		עולל	CHILD	760c	
		ראש	HEAD	911b	4 b
		רנן	GIVE A RINGING CRY	943b	1
		אשמורה	WATCH	1038a	
		פך	POUR OUT	1049d	2 b
2	20	הרג	KILL	247c	1
		מפחים	DANDLING	381c	
		כהן	PRIEST	463c	4
		נביא	PROPHET	611d	2
		נבט	LOOK	613d	3
		עלל	ACT ARBITRARILY	759d	
		עולל	CHILD	760c	
		פרי	FRUIT	826b	2
		ראה	TO SEE	907b	5 a
2	21	בחור	YOUNG MAN	104c	
		בתולה	VIRGIN	144a	
		הרג	KILL	247b	7
		הרג	KILL	247b	2
		זקן	OLD	278c	2 a
		חמל	SPARE	328b	
		טבח	SLAUGHTER	370d	2
		נער	YOUTH	655a	1 d
		שכב	LIE DOWN	1012b	4 a
2	22	מטפח	EXTEND	381b	2
		יום	DAY	399a	3
		מועד	APPOINTED TIME	417c	1 b
		כלה	FINISH	478c	2 c1
		סביב	ROUND ABOUT	687a	1 d
		פליט	ESCAPED ONE	812c	
		רבה	BECOME MANY	915b	2
		שריד	SURVIVOR	975a	1
3	1	גבר	MAN	150a	
		עברה	OVERFLOW	720c	3 b
		עני	AFFLICTION	777a	1
3	2	שבט	ROD	987a	1 a
		אור	LIGHT	21d	8
		הלך	WALK	236d	1 d
		חשך	DARKNESS	365a	3 a
		נהג	DRIVE	624b	1
3	3	הפך	TURN	245b	1 a
		יום	DAY	400c	7 f
		שוב	TURN BACK	998b	8
3	4	בלה	BECOME OLD AND WORN OUT	115a	A
		בשר	FLESH	142c	1 b
		שבר	BREAK	991a	1
3	5	בנה	BUILD	124c	1 ah
		תלאה	WEARINESS	521b	1
		נקף	GO AROUND	669a	1 b
		ראש	VENOM	912c	۱
3	6	מחשך	DARK PLACE	365b	C
		ישב	CAUSE TO SIT	443d	3 a
		עולם	LONG DURATION	762a	1 b
3	7	בעד	ABOUT	126c	1 b
		גדר	BUILD A WALL	154d	
		כבד	MAKE HEAVY	457d	1
		נחשת	COPPER	639c	2
3	8	גם	YEA	169d	6
		זעק	CRY	277b	2 d
		עור	SKIN	736a	1
		שתם	STOP UP	979c	
		שוע	CRY OUT	1002d	
		שתם	OPEN	*1060c	
3	9	גדר	BUILD A WALL	154d	
		גזית	HEWING	159b	
		דרך	WAY	203b	5
		נתיבה	PATH	677b	2 a
		עוה	BEND	730c	
3	10	ארב	LIE IN WAIT	70b	
		אריה	LION	71d	
		ארי	LION	71d	
		דב	BEAR	179a	
		מסתר	SECRET PLACE	712c	2 b
3	11	דרך	WAY	203b	5
		סור	TURN ASIDE	694a	
		פשח	TEAR IN PIECES	832d	
		שמם	BE DESOLATED	1030d	1
		שסע	DIVIDE	*1042d	
3	12	אשפה	QUIVER	80c	
		דרך	TREAD	202b	4
		חץ	ARROW	346c	2
		מטרה	TARGET	643c	2
		נצב	STAND	662c	1
		קשת	BOW	906c	1 d
3	13	אשפה	QUIVER	80c	
		בוא	COME	99a	1
		בן	SON	121c	6
		כליה	KIDNEYS	480b	1 a
		קשת	BOW	906a	1 b
3	14	יום	DAY	400c	7 f
		נגינה	MUSIC	618d	2
		שחק	LAUGHTER	966a	2
3	15	לענה	WORMWOOD	542a	
		מר	BITTER THING	601a	
		ממרור	BITTER THING	*601b	C
		רוה	BE SATURATED	924b	1
3	16	שבע	SATISFIED	959d	3
		אפר	ASHES	68a	
		גרס	BE CRUSHED	176c	
		חצץ	GRAVEL	346b	
		כפש	MAKE BENT	499b	
3	17	זנח	REJECT	276b	
		טובה	WELFARE	375d	1
		נשה	FORGET	674c	
3	18	אבד	PERISH	1d	2
		תוחלת	HOPE	404b	
		נצח	ENDURING	664b	2
3	19	זכר	REMEMBER	270b	2 2 a
		עני	AFFLICTION	777a	1
		ראש	VENOM	912c	1
		מרוד	RESTLESSNESS	924a	
3	20	זכר	REMEMBER	269d	1 1 b
		נפש	SOUL	659c	1 b
		על	UPON	753c	2 1d
		שוח	SINK DOWN	1001b	
		שוח	SINK DOWN	1001c	
3	21	יחל	WAIT	404a	
		לב	HEART	524d	2 3d
		שוב	TURN BACK	999d	8
3	22	חסד	GOODNESS	339a	4
		כי	THAT	472d	1
		כלה	BE FINISHED	477d	2 b
		רחמים	COMPASSION	933c	1
		תמם	BE FINISHED	1070c	2
3	23	אמונה	FIRMNESS	53c	3 b
		בקר	MORNING	134b	1 f
		חדש	NEW	294b	B
3	24	אמר	SAY	56b	2
		חלק	PORTION	324b	3 b
		יחל	WAIT	404a	
		יחיל	WAITING	404b	
		נפש	SOUL	660a	4 a1
3	25	דרש	SEEK	205b	3 a
		טוב	PLEASANT	374d	9 b
		קוה	WAIT FOR	875d	
3	26	דומם	SILENTLY	189b	1
		ו	AND	252c	1 b
		ו	AND	254a	2 a
		טוב	PLEASANT	374c	5
		יחיל	WAITING	404a	
		תשועה	DELIVERANCE	448b	1
3	27	גבר	MAN	150a	
		טוב	PLEASANT	374c	5
		נעורים	YOUTH	655c	
		נשא	LIFT	671a	2 a
		על	YOKE	760d	
3	28	בדד	ISOLATION	94d	
		דמם	BE SILENT	198d	1
		נטל	LIFT	642d	
3	29	אנן	COMPLAIN	59d	
		נתן	PUT	680b	2 a
		עפר	DRY EARTH	780a	2 d
		תקוה	HOPE	876b	1
3	30	חרפה	REPROACH	358a	2 e
		לחי	CHEEK	534d	2
		נכה	SMITE	645b	1 a
		נתן	GIVE	680a	1 z
		שבע	SATISFIED	959d	3 c
3	31	זנח	REJECT	276b	
		עולם	LONG DURATION	762a	2 g
3	32	חסד	GOODNESS	339b	2 3 a
		יגה	SUFFER	387b	
		רחם	LOVE	933c	1
3	33	בן	SON	120b	1 e
		יגה	SUFFER	387b	
		ענה	BE BOWED DOWN	776b	3
3	34	אסיר	PRISONER	64a	
		דכא	CRUSH	194a	
		תחת	UNDERNEATH	1065c	2 1e
3	35	גבר	MAN	150a	
		נטה	BEND	641a	3 g
		עליון	HIGHEST	751b	1
		משפט	JUDGEMNT	1049a	5
3	36	לא	NOT	519a	1 a
		עות	BE BENT	736c	1 a
		ריב	STRIFE	937a	3
3	37	זה	THIS	261b	4 b
		מי	WHO	566d	2 e
		צוה	CHARGE	846a	2
3	38	טוב	PLEASANT	375a	0 b
		לא	NOT	519a	1 a
		עליון	HIGHEST	751b	1
3	39	גבר	MAN	150a	
		חטא	SIN	308a	3
		חי	ALIVE	312a	1 b
3	40	דרך	WAY	203c	6 a
		חפש	SEARCH	344b	3
		חקר	SEARCH	350d	2 d
3	41	אל	TO	40b	5
		אל	GOD	42d	6 e
		לב	HEART	523b	2 1
		נשא	LIFT	670d	1 b 9
3	42	נחנו	WE	59d	
		מרה	BE REBELLIOUS	598a	2
		סלח	FORGIVE	699b	
		פשע	REBEL	833b	2
3	43	הרג	KILL	247b	7
		הרג	KILL	247b	2
		חמל	SPARE	328b	
		סכך	OVERSHADOW	697a	2
		רדף	PURSUE	922d	1 e
3	44	מן	FROM	583b	7 ba
		סכך	OVERSHADOW	697a	1
		עבר	PASS OVER	717c	2
		ענן	CLOUD	778a	1 a
3	45	מאס	REFUSE	549d	2
		סחי	OFFSCOURING	695a	
		קרב	INWARD PART	899b	1 f8
3	46	פה	MOUTH	805b	3
		פצה	PART	822c	1 a
3	47	פחת	PIT	809b	
		שאת	DIN OF BATTLE	981b	
		שבר	BREAKING	991a	1
		שת	SETH	*1011d	
3	48	בת	DAUGHTER	123c	3
		ירד	GO DOWN	433c	3 c
		עם	PEOPLE	767a	5 f
		פלג	CHANNEL	811b	
		שבר	BREAKING	991a	1
3	49	אין	NOT	35a	6 db
		דמה	CEASE	198c	1
		גרה	POUR	620b	2
		עין	EYE	744b	1 h
3	50	הפוגה	BENUMBING	806b	
		ראה	TO SEE	907c	6 c
		שקף	LOOK DOWN	1054d	
3	51	בת	DAUGHTER	123c	1 i
		עלל	ACT ARBITRARILY	759d	
3	52	חנם	OUT OF FAVOR	336d	C
		צוד	HUNT	844c	

Ch	v.	Heb	Eng	Page	Sec
3	53	צפור	BIRD	862a	1
		בור	PIT	92c	4
		חיים	LIFE	313a	1
		ירה	CAST	392b	
		צמת	EXTERMINATE	856b	
3	54	גזר	CUT	160c	2
		מי	WATER	565d	4 a
		צוף	FLOW	847b	1
3	55	בור	PIT	92c	4
		קרא	CALL	895d	5 c
		תחתי	LOWER	1066c	
3	56	אזן	EAR	24b	2 b
		עלם	CONCEAL	761a	
		רוחה	RESPITE	926c	
		שועה	CRY FOR HELP	1003a	
3	57	יום	DAY	400b	7 d4
		ירא	FEAR	431b	1 a
		קרא	CALL	895d	5 c
		קרב	COME NEAR	897c	1 h
3	58	גאל	REDEEM	145c	3 a
		חיים	LIFE	313a	1
		ריב	STRIVE	936c	3
		ריב	STRIFE	937a	3
3	59	עותה	SUBVERSION	736c	
		שפט	JUDGE	1047d	3 b1
		משפט	JUDGMENT	1048c	1 d
3	60	מחשבה	THOUGHT	364b	2
		ל	TO	511a	2
		נקמה	VENGEANCE	668c	3
3	61	הגיון	MEDITATION	*212a	2
		חרפה	REPROACH	357d	1
		מחשבה	THOUGHT	364b	2
		ל	TO	*511a	1 d
3	62	הגיון	MEDITATION	212a	2
		יום	DAY	400c	7 f
3	63	נבט	LOOK	613d	3
		מנגינה	SONG	618d	
		קימה	RISING UP	879c	
3	64	מעשה	DEED	795d	1 a2
3	65	תאלה	CURSE	46d	
		מגנה	COVERING	171c	
3	66	רדף	PURSUE	*922d	1 e
		שמי	HEAVENS	1030b	2 a
		תחת	UNDERNEATH	1066a	3 2a
4	1	איכה	HOW	32d	2
		זהב	GOLD	262d	2
		חוץ	THE OUTSIDE	300b	2 a
		טוב	PLEASANT	374b	3 e
		כתם	GOLD	508d	
		עמם	DARKEN	770b	
		שנה	CHANGE	1039d	
		שפך	POUR OUT	1050a	
4	2	איכה	HOW	32d	2
		בן	SON	121b	1 jt
		זהב	GOLD	*262d	2
		חרש	EARTHENWARE	360a	1
		יצר	FORM	427d	1 a
		יקר	PRECIOUS	430a	1 c
		נבל	JAR	614b	2
		סלא	WEIGH	698d	
		מעשה	DEED	796a	2 a1
		פז	REFINED GOLD	808a	
		ציון	ZION	851b	
		שוש	REJOICE	965b	
4	3	בת	DAUGHTER	123c	3
		גור	YOUNG	158d	2
		מדבר	WILDERNESS	184d	2
		חלץ	DRAW OFF OR OUT	322d	1
		ינק	NURSE	413c	
		יען	OSTRICH	419a	
		אכזר	CRUEL	470a	
		ל	TO	512c	4 a
		עם	PEOPLE	767a	5 f
		רננים	PIERCING CRY	943d	1
		שד	BREAST	994d	2
		תן	JACKAL	1072c	
4	4	דבק	CLING	179d	1 a
		דרש	SEEK	205d	7
		חך	PALATE	335a	A
		ינק	SUCK	413b	
		ל	TO	*512a	3 b
		לשון	TONGUE	546a	1 a
		עולל	CHILD	760c	
		פרם	BREAK IN TWO	828b	
		צמא	THIRST	854d	
4	5	אמן	CONFIRM	52d	4 a
		חבק	CLASP	287d	
		ל	TO	512a	3 b
		מעדן	DAINTY	726d	
		שמם	BE DESOLATED	1031a	2
		אשפת	REFUSE-HEAP	1046b	
		תולע	SCARLET STUFF	1068d	1
4	6	בת	DAUGHTER	123c	3
		גדל	BECOME GREAT	152b	2 c
		הפך	TURN	245c	1 b
		חול	WHIRL	297b	3
		חטאת	SIN	308a	1 b
		כמו	LIKE	455d	1 a
		סדם	SODOM	690a	
		עון	INIQUITY	730d	1
		עם	PEOPLE	767a	5 f
		רגע	A MOMENT	921a	BD
4	7	אדם	BE RED	10a	
		גזרה	CUTTING	160d	1
		זכך	BE BRIGHT	269a	1
		חלב	MILK	316c	B

Ch	v.	Heb	Eng	Page	Sec
		נזיר	CONSECRATED	634c	1
		ספיר	SAPPHIRE	705d	
		עם	WITH	*768d	5
		עצם	BONE	782d	1 e
		פנינים	CORALS	819d	
		צחח	BE DAZZLING	*850a	
		צח	DAZZLING	850a	
		שלג	SNOW	1017a	
4	8	חשך	GROW DARK	364d	2
		יבש	BE DRY	386c	1 e
		נכר	RECOGNIZE	648a	
		עצם	BONE	782d	1 a
		צפד	DRAW TOGETHER	859b	
		שחור	BLACKNESS	1007a	
		תאר	FORM	1061c	
4	9	דקר	PIERCE	201b	1
		זוב	FLOW	264d	3
		חלל	PIERCED	319c	2
		טוב	PLEASANT	374c	6
		תנובה	FRUIT	626c	2
		שדי	FIELD	961b	1
4	10	בת	DAUGHTER	123c	3
		ברה	EAT	136a	
		בשל	BOIL	143a	2
		ילד	CHILD	409c	B
		עם	PEOPLE	767a	5 f
		רחמני	COMPASSIONATE WOMAN	933d	
		שבר	BREAKING	991a	1
4	11	חרון	BURNING OF ANGER	354c	
		חמה	RAGE	404d	2 c
		חמה	RAGE	*405a	2 c
		יסוד	FOUNDATION	414b	1
		יצת	KINDLE	428c	
		כלה	FINISH	478c	1 e
		פך	POUR OUT	1049d	2 a
4	12	אמן	CONFIRM	53b	2 d
		תבל	WORLD	385d	
		כי	THAT	471d	1 a
		שער	GATE	1044c	1 a
4	13	דם	BLOOD	*196c	2 b
		דם	BLOOD	196d	2 d
		חטאת	SIN	308d	1 b
		כהן	PRIEST	463c	4
		נביא	PROPHET	612a	2
		עון	INIQUITY	730d	1
		צדיק	JUST	843b	3 b
4	14	גאל	DEFILE	146a	
		דם	BLOOD	197b	21
		יכל	BE ABLE	407d	1 e
		לא	NOT	520a	4 aa
		לבוש	CLOTHING	528c	
		נגע	TOUCH	619a	1 a
		נוע	TOTTER	631b	2
		עור	BLIND	734c	1 a
4	15	גור	SOJOURN	158a	2
		גם	ALSO	169b	1
		טמא	UNCLEAN	379d	2 a
		יסף	DO AGAIN	415c	2 a
		נגע	TOUCH	619a	1 a
		נוע	TOTTER	631b	2
		נצה	FLY	663b	
		סור	TURN ASIDE	693d	2
		קרא	CALL	895b	2 a
4	16	זקן	OLD	278d	2 b
		חלק	DIVIDE	323d	3
		חנן	SHOW FAVOR	336a	1 c
		יסף	DO AGAIN	415c	2 a
		כהן	PRIEST	463c	4
		נבט	LOOK	613d	3
		נשא	LIFT	670c	1 b 3
		פנה	FACE	816a	12 a
		אל	TO	40a	3 c
4	17	הבל	VAPOUR	210d	2
		ישע	DELIVER	446d	1 c
		כלה	BE FINISHED	477d	2 b
		עוד	STILL	728d	1 aa
		עזרה	HELP	740d	1
		צפה	KEEP WATCH	859c	
		צפיה	OUTLOOK-POST	859d	
4	18	הלך	WALK	230d	1 1d 2a
		מלא	BE FULL	570b	1 b
		מן	FROM	583b	7 ba
		צוד	HUNT	844c	
		צעד	STEP	857d	1
		קץ	END	893d	1
		קרב	COME NEAR	897c	1 h
		רחוב	PLAZA	932b	
4	19	ארב	LIE IN WAIT	70b	1
		דלק	HOTLY PURSUE	196b	2
		הר	MOUNTAIN	250b	1 e
		נשר	EAGLE	676d	
		קל	LIGHT	887a	
		רדף	PURSUE	922d	1 e
		שמי	HEAVENS	1029d	1 a
4	20	אמר	SAY	56a	1
		אף	NOSE	60a	1
		חיה	LIVE	311a	1 b
		לכד	CAPTURE	540a	1
		משיח	ANOINTED	603c	1
		צל	SHADOW	853b	2
		רוח	BREATH	924c	1 a
		שחת	PIT	1005d	
4	21	אדום	EDOM	10c	2
		בת	DAUGHTER	123c	3

Ch	v.	Heb	Eng	Page	Sec
		ישב	DWELL	443b	3
		כוס	CUP	468a	
		עבר	PASS OVER	718a	5 a
		עבר	PASS OVER	718a	5 d
		עוץ	UZ	734b	2
		על	UPON	755b	2 4a
		ערה	BE NAKED	788d	1
		שוש	REJOICE	965b	
		שכר	BE DRUNK	1016b	
4	22	אדום	EDOM	10c	2
		בת	DAUGHTER	123c	3
		בת	DAUGHTER	123c	3
		חטאת	SIN	308c	1 b
		יסף	DO AGAIN	415c	2 a
		סבב	TURN ABOUT	*685c	1 a
		עון	INIQUITY	731a	1 cl
		עון	INIQUITY	731c	3
		פקד	ATTEND TO	823b	A 1a
		תמם	BE FINISHED	1070c	2
5	1	זכר	REMEMBER	270b	2 2 a
		חרפה	REPROACH	358a	2 e
		נבט	LOOK	613d	3
5	2	הפך	TURN	246a	2 a
		זור	BE A STRANGER	266c	2 c
		נכרי	FOREIGN	648d	1 b
5	3	אלמנה	WIDOW	48b	
		יתום	ORPHAN	450c	
5	4	מחיר	PRICE	564b	1
5	5	יגע	TOIL	388b	1
		ל	TO	511a	1 e
		נוח	REST	629a	A
		צואר	NECK	848c	1
		רדף	PURSUE	923a	1
5	6	אשור	ASSHUR	78d	2
		נתן	GIVE	680a	1 z
		שבע	SATISFIED	959b	1 b
5	7	חטא	MISS A GOAL OR WAY	306d	2 b
		סבל	BEAR	687d	
5	8	עון	INIQUITY	731c	3
		משל	RULE	605d	1
5	9	פרק	TEAR APART	830a	
		ב	IN	90a	3 3a
		בוא	COME	99c	2 e
		נפש	SOUL	659d	3 c
5	10	רעב	FAMINE	944b	1
		ולעפה	RAGING HEAT	273a	1
		כמר	GROW WARM	485b	2
		רעב	FAMINE	944b	1
5	11	תנור	FIRE-POT	1072b	
		בתולה	VIRGIN	144a	
		יהודה	JUDAH	397b	2
5	12	ענה	BE BOWED DOWN	776b	2
		הדר	HONOUR	214a	
		זקן	OLD	278d	2 b
5	13	תלה	HANG	1068a	
		בחור	YOUNG MAN	104c	
		טחון	GRINDING-MILL	377c	
		כשל	STUMBLE	505c	1
5	14	נשא	LIFT	*671b	3 b
		בחור	YOUNG MAN	104c	
		זקן	OLD	278d	2 b
5	15	נגינה	MUSIC	618d	1
		אבל	MOURNING	5d	
		הפך	TURN	246a	1 b
		מחול	DANCE	298b	2
		לב	HEART	525c	2 9a
		משוש	EXULTATION	965c	
5	16	אוי	WOE	17a	1
		חטא	MISS A GOAL OR WAY	307a	2 b
		נא	PART OF ENTREATY	609c	4 e
5	17	נפל	FALL	657a	1
		עטרה	CROWN	742d	3
		דוה	FAINT	188c	1
		זה	THIS	260d	1 a
		זה	THIS	262a	6 f
		חשך	GROW DARK	364d	3
		לב	HEART	525c	2 9b
5	18	הלך	WALK	235b	1
		הר	MOUNTAIN	249c	1 a
		ציון	ZION	851c	
		שמם	BE DESOLATED	1031a	1
		שועל	FOX	1043c	
5	19	דור	PERIOD	190a	1 c
		ישב	SIT	442b	1 a
		כסא	THRONE	491b	3 b
		עולם	LONG DURATION	762c	2 c
5	20	ארך	LENGTH	73d	B
		נצח	EVERLASTINGNESS	664b	4
		שכח	FORGET	1013b	2 a
5	21	חדש	RENEW	294a	1
		כיאם	EXCEPT	474d	2 a
		קדם	FRONT	869d	2 d
		שוב	TURN BACK	999b	2
5	22	מאד	EXCEEDINGLY	*547c	2 b
		מאס	REJECT	549c	1 a
		קצף	BE WROTH	893b	1

EZEKIEL

Ch	v.	Heb	Eng	Page	Sec
1	1	חדש	NEW MOON	294d	2 b2
		חמש	FIVE	332a	1 e
		יום	DAY	*398c	2 e

Ch	v.	Heb	Eng	Page	Sec
		כבר	CHEBAR	460d	
		נהר	STREAM	625d	1
		פתח	OPEN	835c	
		מראה	VISION	909b	
		רביעי	FOURTH	918a	1
		שלשים	THIRTY	1026c	2
		שמי	HEAVENS	1030b	2 a
1	2	יהויכין	JEHOIACHIN	220c	
		חמש	FIVE	332a	1 e
		חמישי	FIFTH	332c	2
		יום	DAY	*398c	2 e
1	3	ב	IN	*89a	2 1
		בוזי	BUZI	100c	
		דבר	WORD	182c	1 2a
		יחזקאל	EZEKIEL	306b	1
		יד	HAND	390a	1 e2
		כבר	CHEBAR	460d	
		כהן	PRIEST	463c	4
		כשדים	CHALDEANS	505a	1 b
		נהר	STREAM	625d	1
1	4	חשמל	SHINING SUB-STANCE	365c	
		ך	LIKE	*453d	1 b
		לקח	TAKE	544a	
		נגה	BRIGHTNESS	618b	
		סערה	TEMPEST	704b	
		עין	EYE	745a	4 c
		ענן	CLOUD	778a	1 a
		רוח	BREATH	924d	2 a
1	5	אדם	MAN	9b	2
		דמות	LIKENESS	198b	1
		דמות	LIKENESS	198b	1
		הם	THEY	241d	8 c
		חיה	LIVING THING	312d	1 c
		כרוב	CHERUB	501a	6 a
		מראה	VISION	909c	1 b
1	6	כנף	WING	489c	1 c
		כרוב	CHERUB	501a	6 a
		פנה	FACE	815d	1 1
1	7	ישר	STRAIGHT	449a	1
		כף	SOLE OF FOOT	496d	3
		כרוב	CHERUB	501a	6 a
		נחשת	COPPER	639a	1
		נצץ	SHINE	665b	
		עגל	CALF	722a	
		עין	EYE	745a	4 c
		קלל	BURNISHED	887a	
		רגל	FOOT	919d	1 c
		רגל	FOOT	919d	1 d
1	8	אדם	MAN	9b	2
		כרוב	CHERUB	501a	6 a
		פנה	FACE	816a	1 3
		ארבע	FOUR	917d	1 c4
		רבע	FOURTH PART	917d	2
		תחת	UNDERNEATH	1066a	3 2a
1	9	אחות	ANOTHER	28a	5
		אשה	WOMAN	61c	4
		הלך	WALK	230b	1 1a
		חבר	UNITE	288a	1 b
		חבר	UNITE	288a	1 b
		כרוב	CHERUB	501a	6 a
		סבב	TURN AROUND	686a	1 b
		עבר	REGION ACROSS	719d	2
		על	UPON	758a	2 9
1	10	אדם	MAN	9b	2
		אריה	LION	71d	
		דמות	LIKENESS	198b	1
		ימין	RIGHT HAND	412a	2 b
		כרוב	CHERUB	501a	6 a
		נשר	EAGLE	677a	
		פנה	FACE	816a	1 4
		ארבע	FOUR	917d	1 c4
		שמאל	LEFT	969d	1
		שור	A HEAD OF CATTLE	1004b	
1	11	גויה	BODY	156b	1
		חבר	UNITE	288a	1 b
		כסה	COVER	491c	1
		כרוב	CHERUB	501a	6 a
		מעל	ABOVE	752a	2 d
		פנה	FACE	816a	1 3
		פרד	DIVIDE	825b	
1	12	הלך	WALK	230b	1 1a
		הלך	WALK	231a	1 d3 gb
		כרוב	CHERUB	501a	6 a
		סבב	TURN AROUND	686a	1 b
		עבר	REGION ACROSS	719d	2
		על	UPON	757b	2 7c ab
		על	UPON	758a	2 9
		רוח	BREATH	926a	9 e
1	13	אש	FIRE	77d	6
		בער	BURN	129a	3
		ברק	LIGHTNING	140c	1
		גחלת	COAL	160d	
		דמות	LIKENESS	198b	2
		הלך	WALK	235d	1 a
		חיה	LIVING THING	312d	1 c
		יצא	GO OUT	423b	1 f
		כרוב	CHERUB	501a	6 a
		לפיד	TORCH	542b	
		נגה	BRIGHTNESS	618b	
		מראה	VISION	909c	1 b
1	14	בזק	LIGHTENING FLASH	103b	
		חיה	LIVING THING	312d	1 c
		כרוב	CHERUB	501a	6 a
		רצא	RUN	952d	

Ch	v.	Heb	Eng	Page	Sec
1	15	שוב	TURN BACK	997a	2
		אופן	WHEEL	66d	B
		אצל	BESIDE	69b	A
		חיה	LIVING THING	312d	1 c
		כרוב	CHERUB	501a	6 a
1	16	אופן	WHEEL	66d	B
		דמות	LIKENESS	198b	2
		דמות	LIKENESS	198b	2
		כרוב	CHERUB	501a	6 a
		עין	EYE	745a	4 c
		מעשה	DEED	796a	2 a2
		תרשיש	YELLOW JASPAR	1076d	
1	17	הלך	WALK	232b	1 3
		כרוב	CHERUB	501a	6 a
		סבב	TURN AROUND	686a	1 b
		רבע	FOURTH PART	917d	
1	18	גב	BACK	146c	6
		גבה	HEIGHT	147b	1
		יראה	FEAR	432a	2
		כרוב	CHERUB	501a	6 a
		מלא	FULL	571a	
		עין	EYE	744b	1 e
1	19	אופן	WHEEL	66d	B
		אצל	BESIDE	69b	A
		הלך	WALK	230b	1 1a
		הלך	WALK	232b	1 3
		חיה	LIVING THING	312d	1 c
		כרוב	CHERUB	501a	6 a
		נשא	LIFT	671d	1 a
		על	UPON	758c	4 2a
1	20	אופן	WHEEL	66d	B
		הלך	WALK	230b	1 1a
		הלך	WALK	*231a	1 d3 gb
		חיה	LIVING THING	312d	1 c
		כרוב	CHERUB	501a	6 a
		נשא	LIFT	671d	1 a
		על	UPON	757b	2 7c ab
		עמה	CLOSE BY	769c	a
		רוח	BREATH	926a	9 e
1	21	אופן	WHEEL	66d	B
		הלך	WALK	230b	1 1a
		הלך	WALK	232b	1 3
		חיה	LIVING THING	312d	1 c
		כרוב	CHERUB	501a	6 a
		נשא	LIFT	671d	1 a
		על	UPON	758c	4 2a
		עמה	CLOSE BY	769c	a
		רוח	BREATH	926a	9 e
1	22	דמות	LIKENESS	198b	1
		חיה	LIVING THING	312d	1 c
		יראא	BE FEARFUL	431d	1
		כרוב	CHERUB	501a	6 a
		נטה	SPREAD OUT	640a	2
		עין	EYE	745a	4 c
		מעל	ABOVE	752a	2 d
		קרח	ICE	901c	2
		ראש	HEAD	910d	1 b
		רקיע	EXTENDED SURFACE	956a	1
1	23	אחות	ANOTHER	28a	5
		אשה	WOMAN	61c	4
		גויה	BODY	156b	1
		הם	THEY	241d	8 c
		ישר	STRAIGHT	449a	1
		כסה	COVER	491c	1
		כרוב	CHERUB	501a	6 a
		רקיע	EXTENDED SURFACE	956a	1
1	24	הלך	WALK	230b	1 1a
		המלה	TUMULT	243a	
		כרוב	CHERUB	501a	6 a
		קול	VOICE	877b	2 f
		קול	VOICE	877b	2 k
		רפה	SINK	951d	
		שדי	ALMIGHTY	995a	1
1	25	היה	BECOME	225c	2 1a
		כרוב	CHERUB	501a	6 a
		על	UPON	759b	4 2e a
		רפה	SINK	951d	
		רפה	SINK	951d	
		רקיע	EXTENDED SURFACE	956a	1
1	26	אבן	STONE	6d	3
		אדם	MAN	9b	2
		דמות	LIKENESS	198b	1
		דמות	LIKENESS	198b	1
		דמות	LIKENESS	198b	1
		ך	LIKE	*453d	1 b
		כסא	SEAT OF HONOR	490d	1 b
		כרוב	CHERUB	501a	6 a
		ספיר	SAPPHIRE	705d	
		מעל	ABOVE	751c	1 b
		מעל	ABOVE	752a	1 b
		על	UPON	759b	4 2e a
		מראה	VISION	909c	1 b
		ראש	HEAD	910d	1 b
		רקיע	EXTENDED SURFACE	956a	1
1	27	בית	HOUSE	109c	3
		זהר	SHINING	*264a	
		חשמל	SHINING SUB-STANCE	365c	
		ך	LIKE	*453d	1 b
		כרוב	CHERUB	501a	6 a
		מתנים	LOINS	608b	1 g
		נגה	BRIGHTNESS	618b	

Ch	v.	Heb	Eng	Page	Sec
		מטה	DOWNWARDS	641b	2 b a
		עין	EYE	745a	4 c
		מעל	ABOVE	751d	2 b a
		ראה	TO SEE	907a	1 b
		מראה	VISION	909c	1 b
1	28	גשם	RAIN	177c	
		דמות	LIKENESS	198b	1
		כבוד	GLORY	458d	2 c1
		כרוב	CHERUB	501a	6 a
		נגה	BRIGHTNESS	618b	
		נגה	BRIGHTNESS	*618b	
		ענן	CLOUD	778a	1 b
		קשת	BOW	906c	2
2	1	אדם	MAN	9b	2
		את	WITH	86a	1 db
		דבר	SPEAK	181b	3 d
		עמד	STAND	764b	5 b
2	2	בוא	COME	97d	1
		דבר	SPEAK	182a	
		עמד	STAND	764d	3
		רוח	BREATH	925d	9 a
		שמע	HEAR	1033c	1 b
2	3	אדם	MAN	9b	2
		בן	SON	120d	1 jg
		גוי	NATION	156d	1 b
		ה	THE	209b	2 b
		יום	DAY	401b	7 1
		מרד	REBEL	597c	2
		עצם	BONE	783a	3
		פשע	REBEL	833b	2
		ישראל	ISRAEL	975d	2 b3
2	4	חזק	STRONG	305d	1 e
		לב	HEART	525b	2 6d
		פנה	FACE	816a	1 1d
		קשה	SEVERE	904d	3
2	5	אם	IF	50a	1 b1
		בית	HOUSE	110a	5 dd
		חדל	CEASE	293a	2
		מרי	REBELLION	598b	
		נביא	PROPHET	611d	1
		שמע	HEAR	1034a	1 j
2	6	אדם	MAN	9b	2
		אל	TO	41a	B
		את	WITH	85c	
		את	WITH	86b	1 dg
		בית	HOUSE	110a	5 dd
		חתת	BE SHATTERED	369b	2 a
		ירא	FEAR	431b	1 c
		מרי	REBELLION	598b	
		סלון	BRIER	699b	
		סרב	REBEL	709d	
		עקרב	SCORPION	785d	
2	7	דבר	WORD	183b	3 2
		חדל	CEASE	293a	2
		מרי	REBELLION	598b	
2	8	אדם	MAN	9b	2
		בית	HOUSE	110a	5 dd
		מרי	REBELLION	598b	
		מרי	REBELLION	598c	
2	9	פצה	PART	822c	1 a
		ספר	MISSIVE	707b	3 a
		שלח	SEND	1018d	3 b
2	10	אחור	HINDER SIDE	30c	A
		הגה	A MOANING	211d	2
		חי	LAMENTATION	223d	
		כתב	WRITE	507b	1 a
		כתב	WRITE	507b	1 a
		כתב	WRITE	507c	1 b2
		חי	WAILING	624d	
		נהי	WAILING	624d	
		פנה	FACE	816a	1 6
		פרש	SPREAD OUT	831b	1
		קינה	ELEGY	884b	1
3	1	בית	HOUSE	110a	5 dd
		בן	SON	120d	1 jg
		מצא	FIND	593b	3 a
3	2	אכל	EAT	37d	1
		פתח	OPEN	835b	
		שאלתיאל	SHEALTIEL	982d	
3	3	אכל	EAT	38a	1
		בטן	BELLY	105d	1 a
		דבש	HONEY	185b	
		ל	TO	514b	5 fb
		מלא	FILL	570c	1
		מעה	BELLY	589a	1 b
		מתוק	SWEET	608d	1
		שאלתיאל	SHEALTIEL	982d	
3	4	בוא	GO	98d	4
		בית	HOUSE	110a	5 dd
		הלך	WALK	234b	1 5f z
3	5	בית	HOUSE	110a	5 dd
		חדש	NEW MOON	294c	1
		כבד	HEAVY	458b	1 d
		לשון	TONGUE	546c	2
		עם	PEOPLE	767a	5 h
		עמק	DEEP	771b	
		שפה	SPEECH	974a	2
3	6	אם	IF	50c	1 ce
		כבד	HEAVY	458b	1 d
		לשון	TONGUE	546c	2
		עם	PEOPLE	767a	5 h
		עמק	DEEP	771b	
		שפה	SPEECH	974a	2
		שלח	SEND	1018c	2 a
		שמע	HEAR	1033d	1 g
3	7	אבה	BE WILLING	2c	

Ch	v.	Heb	Eng	Page	Sec
		בית	HOUSE	110a	5 dd
		חזק	STRONG	305d	1 e
		לב	HEART	525b	2 6d
		מצח	FOREHEAD	594d	
		צפה	KEEP WATCH	859c	
3	8	הוא	HE, SHE, IT	215c	1 e
		חזק	STRONG	305d	1 e
		מצח	FOREHEAD	594d	
3	9	עמה	CLOSE BY	769c	A
		בית	HOUSE	110a	5 dd
		חזק	STRONG	305d	1 e
		תחת	BE SHATTERED	369b	2 a
		ירא	FEAR	431b	1 b
		מרי	REBELLION	598b	
		צר	HARD PEBBLE	866a	
		שמיר	ADAMANT	1039a	2
3	10	לבב	HEART	523b	2 1
3	11	בוא	GO	98d	4
		בן	SON	121b	1 ji
		הלך	WALK	234b	1 5f 2
		חדל	CEASE	293a	2
3	12	ברך	BLESS	138d	2 a
		כבוד	GLORY	458d	2 c1
		נשא	LIFT	670a	1 a
		רוח	BREATH	925b	9 a
		רעש	SHAKING	950c	1
3	13	אחוה	ANOTHER	28a	5
		אשה	WOMAN	61c	4
		אופן	WHEEL	66d	B
		חיה	LIVING THING	312d	1 c
		נשק	KISS	676c	
		עמה	CLOSE BY	769c	A k
		קול	VOICE	877b	2 k
		קול	VOICE	877b	2 e
		רעש	SHAKING	950c	1
3	14	הלך	WALK	234c	2 2
		חזק	BE FIRM	304c	1 1a
		חזק	BE FIRM	304b	1 3
		חזק	STRONG	305c	1 a
		חזקה	STRENGTH	*305d	1
		יד	HAND	390a	1 e2
		חמה	RAGE	404c	2 a
		לקח	TAKE	542d	3 a
		מר	BITTER	600d	2 b
		נשא	LIFT	670a	1 a
		רוח	BREATH	925b	3 e
		רוח	BREATH	925d	9 a
3	15	אל	TO	40d	8
		כבר	CHEBAR	460d	
		שמם	BE DESOLATED	1031b	2 b
		תלאביב	TEL-ABIB	1068b	
3	16	דבר	WORD	182c	1 2a
		היה	COME TO PASS	224c	2 a1 az
		היה	BECOME	226a	2 1b
3	17	בית	HOUSE	110a	5 dd
		זהר	ADMONISH	264b	
3	18	מן	OUT OF	579d	2 d
		ב	IN	*90c	3 5
		בקש	SEEK	135a	5 b
		דבר	SPEAK	181d	6
		דם	BLOOD	197b	2 k
		דרך	WAY	203d	6 d
		זהר	ADMONISH	264b	
		זהר	ADMONISH	264b	
		חיה	LIVE	311c	1
		מות	DIE	560a	2 b
		מות	DIE	560a	2 b
		נזר	SEPARATE	634b	
		עון	INIQUITY	731b	2 c
		רשע	WICKED	957c	3
		רשע	WICKED	957c	3
3	19	דרך	WAY	203d	6 d
		זהר	ADMONISH	264b	
		כי	WHEN	473a	2 a
		כי	IF	473b	2 b
		מות	DIE	560a	2 b
		נצל	DELIVER	665a	3 a
		עון	INIQUITY	731b	2 c
		רשע	WICKED	957c	3
		רשע	WICKEDNESS	957d	3
		שוב	TURN BACK	997d	6 e
3	20	בקש	SEEK	135a	5 b
		דם	BLOOD	197b	2 k
		זהר	ADMONISH	264b	
		זכר	REMEMBER	270d	1 c 1
		חטאת	SIN	309a	2
		כי	WHEN	473a	2 a
		מכשול	STUMBLING	506b	2 b
		מות	DIE	560a	2 b
		מות	DIE	560a	2 b
		נתן	PUT	680c	2 a
		עול	INJUSTICE	732c	
		צדק	RIGHTEOUSNESS	841d	5
		צדק	RIGHTEOUSNESS	842c	7 b
		צדיק	JUST	843b	3 b
		שוב	TURN BACK	997d	6 e
3	21	זהר	ADMONISH	264b	
		זהר	ADMONISH	264b	
		חטא	MISS A GOAL OR WAY	306d	2 b
		כי	WHEN	473a	2 a
		נצל	DELIVER	665a	3 a
		צדיק	JUST	843b	3 b
3	22	את	WITH	86a	1 db
		בקעה	PLAIN	132c	2
		דבר	SPEAK	181b	3 d

Ch	v.	Heb	Eng	Page	Sec
		היה	BECOME	*225d	2 1b
		יד	HAND	390a	1 e2
		יצא	GO OUT	423d	2 a
3	23	בקעה	PLAIN	132c	2
		כבוד	GLORY	458d	2 c1
		כבוד	GLORY	458d	2 c1
		כבר	CHEBAR	460d	
		נפל	FALL	657c	3 b
3	24	את	WITH	86a	1 db
		דבר	SPEAK	181b	3 d
		סגר	BE SHUT UP	689b	1
		עמד	STAND	764d	3
		רוח	BREATH	925d	9 a
3	25	אסר	TIE	63d	3
		עבת	CORD	721c	1 a
3	26	אלם	BIND	47d	1
		בית	HOUSE	110a	5 dd
		דבק	CLING	180a	1
		חך	PALATE	335a	A
		יכח	REPROVE	407c	5 b
		לשון	TONGUE	546a	1 a
		מרי	REBELLION	598b	
3	27	את	WITH	86a	1 db
		בית	HOUSE	110a	3 d
		דבר	SPEAK	181b	3 d
		חדל	CEASE	293a	2
		חדל	FORBEARING	293b	
		מרי	REBELLION	598b	
		פתח	OPEN	835b	
4	1	חקק	CUT IN	349a	2
		לבנה	BRICK	527c	2
4	2	בנה	BUILD	124c	1 ah
		דיק	BULWARK	189b	1
		כר	LAMB	503a	
		נתן	PUT	680c	2 b
		סללה	MOUND	700c	
		מצור	SIEGE	849a	1
		שום	TO PLACE	963b	1 b
		שפך	POUR OUT	1049c	1 a
4	3	אות	SIGN	16d	3
		ברזל	IRON	137c	1 d
		מחבת	FLAT PLATE	290b	2
		כון	ESTABLISH	466c	3
		צור	CONFINE	848d	2
		מצור	SIEGE	849a	1
		קיר	WALL	885a	3
4	4	נשא	LIFT	671b	2 b
		עון	INIQUITY	731b	3
		עון	INIQUITY	731c	3
		עון	INIQUITY	731c	3
		צד	SIDE	841a	
		שמאלי	LEFT	970a	
		שכב	LIE DOWN	1012b	1 c
4	5	יום	DAY	398c	2
		נשא	LIFT	671b	2 b
		מספר	NUMBER	709a	1 b
		עון	INIQUITY	730d	1
		עון	INIQUITY	731c	3
		תשעים	NINETY	1077d	
		תשעים	NINETY	1077d	
4	6	בית	HOUSE	110a	5 de
		יהודה	JUDAH	397b	1 3
		יום	DAY	398c	2
		יום	DAY	399d	6 c
		ימיני	RIGHT	412a	
		ימיני	RIGHT	412c	
		כלה	FINISH	478b	1 b
		נשא	LIFT	671b	2 b
		עון	INIQUITY	731c	3
		צד	SIDE	841a	
		שכב	LIE DOWN	1012b	1 c
		שני	SECOND	1041c	
4	7	זרוע	ARM	283d	1 a
		חשף	STRIP OFF	362c	2
		כון	ESTABLISH	466c	3
		נבא	PROPHESY	612b	1 b
		מצור	SIEGE	849a	1
4	8	הפך	TURN	245d	1 a
		כלה	FINISH	478b	1 b
		עבת	CORD	721c	1 a
		צד	SIDE	841a	2 b
		מצור	SIEGE	849a	1
4	9	דחן	MILLET		
		חטה	WHEAT	335a	
		כסמת	SPELT	493c	
		לחם	FOOD	537a	1 a
		עדשה	LENTILE	727d	
		עשה	DO	794d	2 1g
		פול	BEANS	806d	
		צד	SIDE	841a	
		שערה	BARLEY	972d	2
		שכב	LIE DOWN	1012b	1 c
		תשעים	NINETY	1077d	
		תשעים	NINETY	1077d	
4	10	מאכל	FOOD	38b	
		ב	IN	90c	3 8
		יום	DAY	401a	7 i
		מן	FROM	582a	5 c
		עת	TIME	773c	1 a
		שקל	SHEKEL	1053d	
		משקול	WEIGHT	1054a	
4	11	הין	HIN	228d	1
		מן	FROM	582a	5 c
		משורה	MEASURE	601c	
		עת	TIME	773c	1 a
		שׁשׁי	SIXTH	995d	

Ch	v.	Heb	Eng	Page	Sec
		שתה	DRINK	1059b	1 a
4	12	עגה	BREAD-CAKE	728b	
		עוג	BAKE	728b	
		צאה	FILTH	844b	
		שערה	BARLEY	972d	2
4	13	גוי	NATION	156d	1 c
		טמא	UNCLEAN	379d	2 a
		נדח	THRUST	623b	2
		שם	THERE	1027b	2
4	14	אדון	LORD	11c	4 a
		אהה	ALAS	13c	
		בשר	FLESH	142c	1 a
		טמא	BE UNCLEAN	379c	
		טרפה	ANIMAL TORN	383c	1
		לא	NOT	519b	1 bc
		נבלה	CARCASS	615d	2
		נעורים	YOUTH	655c	
		נפש	SOUL	661b	9
		עתה	NOW	774c	2 f
		פגול	FOUL THING	803b	
4	15	אדם	MAN	9b	2
		בקר	CATTLE	133c	2
		צפיע	DUNG OF CATTLE	861c	
4	16	דאגה	ANXIETY	178d	
		לחם	FOOD	537a	1 a
		משורה	MEASURE	601c	
		מטה	STAFF	641c	1
		שממון	APPLMENT	1031d	
		משקל	WEIGHT	1054a	
4	17	שתה	DRINK	1059b	1 a
		חסר	LACK	341b	1 a
		מקק	PINE AWAY	596d	4
		עון	INIQUITY	731c	3
		שמם	BE DESOLATED	1031a	1
5	1	מאזן	BALANCES	24d	
		בן	SON	120c	1 f
		זקן	BEARD	278b	1
		חד	SHARP	292b	
		חלק	DIVIDE	323d	1
		חרב	SWORD	353a	2
		עבר	PASS OVER	718d	1 b
		תער	RAZOR	789b	1 a
		משקל	WEIGHT	1054a	
5	2	אור	FLAME	22a	
		בער	BURN	129c	2
		זרה	SCATTER	279d	1
		חרב	SWORD	352c	1 c
		מלא	BE FULL	570b	1 b
		מצור	SIEGE	849a	1
		ריק	MAKE EMPTY	938a	3
		רעב	FAMINE	944b	1
5	3	כנף	EXTREMITY	489d	2 a
		מעט	A FEW	589d	1 a
		מספר	NUMBER	709a	1 b
		צור	CONFINE	848d	1
		שם	THERE	1027c	4 d
5	4	שרף	BURN	976d	2 a
		שלך	THROW	1021a	1 a
5	5	זה	THIS	261a	3
5	6	גוי	NATION	156d	1 c
		הלך	WALK	234c	23a 1e
		חקה	SOMETHING PRE-SCRIBED	350a	2 d
		חקה	SOMETHING PRE-SCRIBED	350b	2 e
		ל	TO	517b	7 ba
		מאס	REJECT	549c	1
		מן	THAN	582c	6 a
		מרה	BE REBELLIOUS	598b	
		רשעה	WICKEDNESS	958a	2
5	7	הלך	WALK	234c	23a 1e
		המון	RAGE	243a	
		חקה	SOMETHING PRE-SCRIBED	350a	2 d
		חקה	SOMETHING PRE-SCRIBED	350b	2 e
		יען	ON ACCOUNT OF	774d	1
		אל	TO	40b	4
		גם	ALSO	169c	4
		כן	SO	487a	3 d
5	8	משפט	JUDGMENT	1048c	1 f
		תוך	MIDST	1063d	
5	9	יען	ON ACCOUNT OF	774d	1
		תועבה	ABOMINATION	1072d	1 b
5	10	זרה	SCATTER	280a	1
		ל	TO	511c	1 h
		שארית	REST	984d	1
		שפט	JUDGEMENT	1048a	
		תוך	MIDST	1063d	
5	11	גם	ALSO	169c	4
		גרע	WITHDRAW	175c	3
		חום	PITY	299b	A
		חי	ALIVE	311d	1 a
		חמל	SPARE	328b	
		טמא	BE UNCLEAN	379c	2
		כן	SO	486d	3 d
		עין	EYE	744c	2
		יען	ON ACCOUNT OF	774d	2 c
		שקוץ	DETESTED THING	1055a	
		תועבה	ABOMINATION	1073a	1 b
5	12	דבר	PESTILENCE	184a	1
		זרה	SCATTER	280a	1
		חרב	SWORD	352c	1 c
		כלה	BE FINISHED	477d	2 c
		נפל	FALL	657b	2 a

Ch	v	Heb	Eng	Page	Sec
		ריק	MAKE EMPTY	938a	3
		שלישי	THIRD	1026b	
5	13	דבר	SPEAK	180d	1
		יהוה	YAHWEH	219b	2 2b z
		חמה	RAGE	404c	2 c
		*חמה	RAGE	*405a	2 c
		חמה	RAGE	*405a	2 c
		כלה	BE FINISHED	477c	1 c
		כלה	FINISH	478c	1 e
		נוח	REST	628c	A 1a
		נחם	CONSOLE ONESELF	637b	4
		קנאה	ZEAL	888c	3 b
5	14	חרבה	WASTE	352a	2
		חרפה	REPROACH	358a	3
		עבר	PASS OVER	717c	4 a
5	15	גדופה	TAUNT	154d	
		יהוה	YAHWEH	219b	2 2d
		חרפה	REPROACH	358a	3
		חמה	RAGE	404c	2 c
		תוכחת	REBUKE	407b	3
		מוסר	DISCIPLINE	416c	1 b
		משמה	HORROR	1031d	c
		שפט	JUDGEMENT	1048a	
5	16	חץ	ARROW	346c	2
		יסף	ADD	415a	1
		לחם	FOOD	537a	1 a
		מטה	STAFF	641c	1
		רעב	FAMINE	944b	1
		רע	EVIL	948a	1
		שחת	GO TO RUIN	1008a	1
		משחית	DESTRUCTION	1008c	
5	17	בוא	COME	99c	2 a
		דם	BLOOD	196d	2 f
		חיה	LIVING THING	312c	1 b
		רע	EVIL	948a	1
		שכל	BE BEREAVED	1013d	1
6	1	היה	BECOME	226a	2 1b
6	2	הר	MOUNTAIN	251a	2 b
		נבא	PROPHESY	612b	1 b
		שום	TO PLACE	963a	2 c
6	3	אבד	PERISH	1d	1
		אבד	CAUSE TO PERISH	2a	1
		אדן	LORD	11c	4 c
		אפיק	CHANNEL	67d	
		במה	HIGH PLACE	119d	3 e
		גבעה	HILL	149a	3
		גיא	VALLEY	161b	
		הנה	BEHOLD	244a	A
		הר	MOUNTAIN	250b	1 c
6	4	חמן	SUN-PILLAR	329a	
		נפל	FALL	658a	2
		שבר	BREAK	990d	
		שמם	BE DESOLATED	1031a	1
6	5	זרה	SCATTER	280a	1
		פגר	CORPSE	803d	1
6	6	אשם	OFFEND	79c	3
		במה	HIGH PLACE	119d	3 e
		גדע	HEW OFF	154b	
		חמן	SUN-PILLAR	329a	
		חרב	BE WASTE	351c	
		חרב	BE WASTE	351c	
		מושב	DWELLING	444b	2 a
		ישם	BE DESOLATE	445b	
		מחה	WIPE OUT	562b	3
		מעשה	DEED	796a	2 a3
		שבר	BREAK	990d	
		שבת	CEASE	991d	
6	7	יהוה	YAHWEH	219b	2 2b a
		חלל	PIERCED	319c	2
		ידע	KNOW	393d	1 a
6	8	זרה	SCATTER	279d	
		יתר	LEAVE OVER	451c	1 b
		פליט	ESCAPED ONE	812c	
6	9	זכר	REMEMBER	270a	13 b
		זנה	COMMIT FORNICA-TION	275d	3
		זנה	COMMIT FORNICA-TION	276a	3
		סור	TURN ASIDE	693c	1
		עין	EYE	744d	3 b
		על	UPON	759a	4 2c
		פליט	ESCAPED ONE	812c	
		פנה	FACE	816d	2 3a
		קוט	FEEL A LOATHING	876c	
		שבה	TAKE CAPTIVE	985c	
		שבר	BREAK	990c	
		שבר	BREAK	990d	
		תועבה	ABOMINATION	1073a	1 b
6	10	דבר	SPEAK	181d	6
		חנם	OUT OF FAVOR	336c	B
		ידע	KNOW	393d	1 a
6	11	אח	ALAS	25b	
		כף	HOLLOW OF THE HAND	496c	1 d1
		נכה	SMITE	645d	1 c
		נפל	FALL	657d	1
		רעב	FAMINE	944b	1
		רע	EVIL	948c	0 d
		רקע	BEAT	956a	
6	12	חמה	RAGE	*405a	2 c
		כלה	FINISH	478c	1 e
		קרב	NEAR	898c	2 b
		רחק	DISTANT	935b	1
		רעב	FAMINE	944b	1
6	13	אלה	TEREBINTH	18c	
		גבעה	HILL	149a	3
		הר	MOUNTAIN	250d	1 m
		ידע	KNOW	393d	1 a
		ניחח	SOOTHING	629c	
		נתן	GIVE	679a	1 k
		עבת	LEAFY	721c	
		עץ	TREE	781c	1 a
		מקום	STANDING PLACE	880b	4
		מקום	STANDING PLACE	880b	4
		ריח	SCENT	926b	2
		רום	BE HIGH	926d	1 a
		רענן	LUXURIANT	947d	
6	14	דבלה	DIBLAH	179c	
		מושב	DWELLING	444b	2 a
		מן	FROM	582b	5 d3
		נטה	EXTEND	640a	1 a
		משממה	DEVASTATION	1031d	1
7	1	היה	BECOME	226a	2 1b
7	2	טור	ROW	377a	1
		כנף	WING	*489b	
		כנף	EXTREMITY	489d	2 b
		קץ	END	893d	1
		ארבע	FOUR	917a	1 c1
7	3	דרך	WAY	203c	6 a
		טור	ROW	377a	1
		נתן	GIVE	679d	1 v
		על	UPON	756c	2 7a b
		קץ	END	893d	1
		שפט	JUDGE	1047d	3 c1
7	4	דרך	WAY	203d	6 d
		חום	PITY	299b	A
		חמל	SPARE	328b	
		נתן	GIVE	679d	1 v
		על	UPON	756c	2 7a b
7	5	רעה	MISERY	949a	1
7	6	קיץ	AWAKE	884c	4
		קץ	END	893d	1
7	7	בוא	COME	98c	2
		הר	SHOUT	212d	
		מהומה	TUMULT	223a	1
		עת	TIME	773d	2 c
		צפירה	DIADEM	862a	
		קרב	NEAR	898d	2
7	8	דרך	WAY	203c	6 a
		חמה	RAGE	*405a	2 c
		כלה	FINISH	478c	1 e
		מן	FROM	581d	4 c
		נתן	GIVE	679d	1 v
		על	UPON	756c	2 7a b
		על	UPON	756c	2 7a b
		קרב	NEAR	898a	3
		שפט	JUDGE	1047d	3 c1
7	9	דרך	WAY	203c	6 a
		יהוה	YAHWEH	219a	2 2b d
		חום	PITY	299b	A
		חמל	SPARE	328b	
		חמל	SPARE	*328b	
		נתן	GIVE	679d	1 v
7	10	זדון	INSOLENCE	268a	2
		מטה	STAFF	641c	1
		פרח	BUD	827a	
		ציץ	BLOSSOM	847c	1
		צפירה	DIADEM	862a	
7	11	חם	WEALTH	241a	
		המון	CROWD	242d	3 b
		חמס	VIOLENCE	329c	
		נה	EMINENCY	627b	
		מטה	STAFF	641c	1
		קום	STAND	878a	5
		רשע	WICKEDNESS	957c	1
7	12	אבל	MOURN	5c	
		המון	CROWD	242d	3 a
		חרון	BURNING OF AN-GER	354c	
		חרון	BURNING OF AN-GER	354c	
		מכר	SELL	569b	
		נגע	REACH	619c	3
		עת	TIME	773d	2 c
		קנה	ACQUIRE	889a	2
7	13	המון	CROWD	242d	3 a
		חזון	VISION	303a	3
		חזק	BE FIRM	305b	6 d
		חיה	LIVING THING	312c	2
		חיים	LIFE	313a	1
		מכר	SELL	569b	
		ממכר	WARE	569d	
		עון	INIQUITY	730d	1
		שוב	TURN BACK	997b	3 a
		שוב	TURN BACK	997b	3 b
7	14	הלך	WALK	231b	1 d3 gd
		המון	CROWD	242d	3 b
		חרון	BURNING OF AN-GER	354c	
		חרון	BURNING OF AN-GER	354c	
		כון	ESTABLISH	466c	2 a
		כל	ALL	482d	2 ba
		תקע	GIVE A BLOW	1075c	2
		תקוע	A BLAST INSTRU-MENT	1075d	
7	15	אכל	EAT	37c	5
		בית	HOUSE	110c	8 a
		חוץ	THE OUTSIDE	299d	1 bb
		חוץ	THE OUTSIDE	300a	1 bd
		רעב	HUNGRY	*944c	
		שדה	FIELD	961c	1 f
7	16	גיא	VALLEY	161b	
		המה	GROWL	242a	1
		יונה	DOVE	401d	
		עון	INIQUITY	731c	3
		פלט	ESCAPE	812b	
		פליט	ESCAPED ONE	812c	
7	17	ברך	KNEE	139c	
		הלך	WALK	232b	1 3
		רפה	SINK	951d	2
7	18	אל	TO	41a	A
		בושה	SHAME	102a	
		חגר	GIRD	291d	2
		כסה	COVER	492a	5
		פלצות	SHUDDERING	814a	
		פנה	FACE	815d	1 1a
		קרחה	BALD SPOT	901b	
		שק	SACK	974c	2 a
7	19	זהב	GOLD	263c	1
		מכשול	STUMBLING	506b	2 c
		מלא	FILL	570c	1
		מעה	BELLY	589a	1 b
		נדה	IMPURITY	622c	2
		נפש	SOUL	660c	5 a
		עברה	OVERFLOW	720c	3 b
		עון	INIQUITY	731a	1 a
		שבע	SATISFIED	959d	
		שלך	THROW	1021a	1 a
7	20	ב	IN	90c	3 6
		גאון	EXALTATION	145a	2
		כן	SO	487b	3 f
		נדה	IMPURITY	622c	2
		עדי	ORNAMENTS	726a	3
		צבי	BEAUTY	840a	1 a
		צלם	IMAGE	853d	1
		שקוץ	DETESTED THING	1055a	
		תועבה	ABOMINATION	1073a	1 b
7	21	בז	ROBBERY	103a	1
		זור	BE A STRANGER	266c	2 c
		חלל	POLLUTE	320b	1 b
		רשע	WICKED	957c	1
		שלל	SPOIL	1022a	2
7	22	חלל	POLLUTE	320b	1 b
		סבב	TURN ABOUT	686c	1 a
		פריץ	VIOLENT ONE	829d	
		צפן	HIDE	860d	1
		דם	BLOOD	197a	2 f
7	23	חמס	VIOLENCE	329c	
		מלא	BE FULL	570a	1 b
		מטה	THAT WHICH IS PERVERTED	*642a	
		רתוק	CHAIN	958d	
		משפט	JUDGMENT	1048c	1 e
7	24	גאון	EXALTATION	145a	1 a
		חלל	POLLUTE	320b	1 a
		ירש	TAKE POSSESSION	439c	1 a
		עז	STRONG	738c	
		קדש	BE SET APART	873a	1 a
		רע	EVIL	948b	6
		שבת	CEASE	992a	1
7	25	אין	NOT	34c	2 da
		בקש	SEEK	134c	1
		שלום	PEACE	1023b	6
7	26	אבד	PERISH	1d	1
		אל	TO	40b	5
		בקש	SEEK	135a	4 b
		הוה	DISASTER	217d	
		זקן	OLD	278d	2 b
		חזון	VISION	303a	3
		עצה	ADVICE	420b	
		תורה	INSTRUCTION	436a	1 e
		כהן	PRIEST	463d	4
		נביא	PROPHET	611b	2
		על	UPON	755b	2 4b
		שמעה	REPORT	1035b	1
7	27	אבל	MOURN	5c	
		ארץ	EARTH	76b	4 a
		את	WITH	86b	1 db
		בהל	BE DISTURBED	96b	1
		בהל	BE DISTURBED	*96b	1
		דרך	WAY	203c	6 a
		לבש	PUT ON	528a	B
		מן	ON ACCOUNT OF	580b	2 f
		מן	ON ACCOUNT OF	580b	2 f
		נשיא	PRINCE	672b	6 a
		שפט	JUDGE	1047d	3 c1
8	1	אדן	LORD	11c	4 a
		זקן	OLD	278d	2 b
		חדש	NEW MOON	294d	2 b2
		חמש	FIVE	332a	1 e
		נפל	FALL	657a	1
		ששי	SIXTH	995d	
8	2	דמות	LIKENESS	198b	1
		זהר	SHINING	264a	
		חשמל	SHINING SUB-STANCE	365c	
		מתנים	LOINS	608b	1 g
		מטה	DOWNWARDS	641b	2 ba
		עין	EYE	745a	4 c
		מעל	ABOVE	751d	2 ba
		מראה	VISION	909c	1 b
8	3	תבנית	FIGURE	125d	3
		יד	HAND	388d	1
		מושב	LOCATION	444b	4
		נשא	LIFT	670a	1 a
		סמל	IMAGE	702b	1
		פנה	TURN	815c	2 b

Ch v.	Heb	Eng	Page	Sec
	פנימי	INNER	819b	
	פתח	OPENING	836a	
	ציצת	TASSEL	851d	
	קנאה	ZEAL	888c	3 b
	קנא	BE ZEALOUS	888d	
	מראה	VISION	909b	
	רוח	BREATH	925d	9 a
	שלח	SEND	1018d	3 b
	שמי	HEAVENS	1029d	1 a
	שער	GATE	1045b	3 b
8 4	אלהים	GOD	44c	4 ba
	בקעה	PLAIN	132c	2
	כבוד	GLORY	458d	2 c1
	מראה	VISION	909d	3
8 5	באה	ENTRANCE	99d	
	דרך	WAY	203b	3
	נשא	LIFT	670c	1 b 4
	סמל	IMAGE	702b	
	צפון	NORTH	861a	
	קנאה	ZEAL	888c	3 b
	שער	GATE	1045b	3 b
8 6	הם	THEY	241d	7
	על	UPON	759a	4 2c
	ראה	TO SEE	907b	5 a
	רחק	BE DISTANT	935a	
	שוב	TURN BACK	998b	8
	תועבה	ABOMINATION	1072d	1 b
8 7	חצר	ENCLOSURE	347a	3 b
	חר	HOLE	359d	
	פתח	OPENING	835d	
	קיר	WALL	885a	2
8 8	חתר	DIG	369a	1
	פתח	OPENING	835d	
	קיר	WALL	885a	2
8 9	רע	EVIL	948c	0 d
8 10	תבנית	FIGURE	125d	3
	חקה	CUT IN	348d	
	סביב	ROUND ABOUT	687a	1 b
	רמש	CREEPING THINGS	943a	1
	שקץ	DETESTATION	1055a	
8 11	זקן	OLD	278d	2 b
	עלה	GO UP	748d	5
	ענן	CLOUD	778a	2
	עתר	ODOUR	801d	
	קטרת	SMOKE	882d	2
	מקטרת	CENSER	883b	
	שפן	SHAPHAN	1051a	5
8 12	ה	INTERROG PART	210a	1 c
	זקן	OLD	278d	2 b
	חדר	CHAMBER	293d	
	חשך	DARKNESS	365a	2
	עזב	LEAVE	737c	2 f
	משכית	SHOW-PIECE	967d	1
8 13	עוד	STILL	729a	1 ab
	שוב	TURN BACK	998b	8
8 14	בכה	WEEP	113c	
	פתח	OPENING	836a	
	צפון	NORTH	861a	
	ראש	VENOM	912c	1
	שער	GATE	1045b	3 b
	תמוז	TAMMUZ	1069c	
8 15	ה	INTERROG PART	210a	1 c
	עוד	STILL	729a	1 ab
	שוב	TURN BACK	998b	8
8 16	אולם	PORCH	17d	1
	אחור	HINDER PART	30d	
	גבול	BOUNDARY	*148a	2 a
	היכל	TEMPLE	228c	2 b
	חצר	ENCLOSURE	347a	3 b
	פנימי	INNER	819b	
	פתח	OPENING	835d	
	קדם	EASTWARD	870a	
	שמש	SUN	1039b	3
8 17	אף	NOSE	60a	1
	גבול	BOUNDARY	*148a	2 a
	ה	INTERROG PART	210a	1 c
	זמורה	BRANCH	274d	
	חמס	VIOLENCE	329c	
	כעס	VEX	495a	2
	מלא	FILL	570b	2
	מן	THAN	583a	6 d
	קלל	BE SLIGHT	886c	2
	שוב	TURN BACK	998b	8
	שלח	SEND	1018d	3 e
8 18	אזן	EAR	24b	2 b
	חום	PITY	299b	A
	חמל	SPARE	328b	
	עשה	DO	794a	1 1a 7
	קרא	CALL	845b	2 b
9 1	כלי	IMPLEMENT	479d	2 a
	פקדה	OVERSIGHT	824a	1 a
	קול	VOICE	877b	1 b
	קרא	CALL	895a	1 a
	קרב	COME NEAR	897c	1 h
	משחת	DESTRUCTION	1008c	
9 2	בד	WHITE LINEN	94b	
	דרך	WAY	202d	1
	דרך	WAY	*203b	3
	מזבח	ALTAR	258d	4 a
	כלי	IMPLEMENT	479d	2 a
	לבש	PUT ON	528a	E
	מתנים	LOINS	608a	1 b
	מפץ	SHATTERING	658d	
	ספר	ENUMERATOR	708c	2
	עמד	STAND	763d	1 a
	פנה	TURN	815d	

Ch v.	Heb	Eng	Page	Sec
	קסת	POT	903c	
	שער	GATE	1045b	3 b
9 3	בגד	GARMENT	94a	
	בד	WHITE LINEN	94b	
	כבוד	GLORY	458d	2 c1
	כרוב	CHERUB	501a	6 a
	לבש	PUT ON	528a	E
	מתנים	LOINS	608a	1 b
	ספר	ENUMERATOR	708c	2
	עלה	GO UP	749b	1 c1
	מפתן	THRESHOLD	837b	
	קסת	POT	903d	
9 4	אות	SIGN	58d	1
	אנק	CRY	60c	
	מצח	FOREHEAD	594d	
	עבר	PASS OVER	717c	3 a
	תו	MARK	1063b	
	תוה	MAKE A MARK	1063b	
	תוך	MIDST	1063d	
	תוך	MIDST	1063d	
9 5	חום	PITY	299b	A
	חמל	SPARE	328b	
9 6	בוש	BE ASHAMED	101d	1
	בוש	BE ASHAMED	101d	3
	בחור	YOUNG MAN	104c	
	בתולה	VIRGIN	144a	
	הרג	KILL	247b	3
	זקן	OLD	278c	2 a
	זקן	OLD	278d	2 b
	חלל	POLLUTE	320d	2
	חלל	POLLUTE	320d	2
	טף	CHILDREN	382a	
	טף	CHILDREN	382a	
	נגש	DRAW NEAR	620d	1
	על	UPON	757b	2 7c aa
	משחית	DESTRUCTION	1008c	
	תו	MARK	1063b	
9 7	גדול	GREAT	153a	3
	חצר	ENCLOSURE	347a	3 b
	טמא	BE UNCLEAN	379c	3
	מלא	FILL	570b	1
9 8	אדון	LORD	11c	4 a
	אהה	ALAS	13c	
	ב	IN	91a	5 2
	ה	INTERROG PART	210a	1 c
	זעק	CRY	277b	2 d
	חמה	RAGE	*405a	2 c
	נפל	FALL	657c	3 b
	עבדות	SERVITUDE	715c	
	שאר	REMAIN	984a	1
	שארית	REST	984d	1
9 9	בית	HOUSE	110a	5 de
	בית	HOUSE	110a	5 dd
	דם	BLOOD	196d	2 f
	מאד	MUCHNESS	547c	2 e
	מלא	BE FULL	570c	1
	מטה	THAT WHICH IS PERVERTED	642a	
	עבדות	SERVITUDE	715c	
	עוון	INIQUITY	731b	2
	עזב	LEAVE	737c	2 f
9 10	ב	IN	89b	2 4b
	דרך	WAY	203d	6 d
	חום	PITY	299b	A
	חמל	SPARE	328b	
	נתן	PUT	680d	2 b
	מצוה	COMMANDMENT	846c	2 b
9 11	בד	WHITE LINEN	94b	
	דבר	WORD	182b	1 1c
	לבש	PUT ON	528a	E
	מתנים	LOINS	608a	1 b
	קסת	POT	903d	
	שוב	TURN BACK	999c	3
9 14	ראש	VENOM	912c	1
9 15	צדיק	JUST	843a	1 d
10 1	אבן	STONE	6d	3
	דמות	LIKENESS	198b	1
	כסא	SEAT OF HONOR	490d	1 b
	כרוב	CHERUB	501a	6 a
	ספיר	SAPPHIRE	705d	
	ראה	TO SEE	908c	2 a
	ראש	HEAD	910d	1 b
	רקיע	EXTENDED SURFACE	956a	1
10 2	אל	TO	40d	9
	אש	FIRE	77d	6
	בד	WHITE LINEN	94b	
	בין	INTERVAL	107d	A
	בין	INTERVAL	107d	E
	גחלת	COAL	160d	
	זרק	TO TOSS	284c	1 a
	חפן	HOLLOW OF HAND	342b	
	כרוב	CHERUB	501a	6 a
	לבש	PUT ON	528a	E
	מלא	FILL	570c	1
	תחת	UNDERNEATH	1066a	3 1a
10 3	חצר	ENCLOSURE	347a	3 b
	ימין	RIGHT HAND	411d	2 a
	כרוב	CHERUB	501a	6 a
	מלא	FILL	570b	2
	ענן	CLOUD	778a	1 a
	פנימי	INNER	819b	
10 4	חצר	ENCLOSURE	347a	3 b
	כבוד	GLORY	458d	2 c1
	כרוב	CHERUB	501a	6 a
	מלא	BE FULL	570a	1 a

Ch v.	Heb	Eng	Page	Sec
	מלא	FILL	570b	1
	נגה	BRIGHTNESS	618b	
	נשר	EAGLE	677a	
	ענן	CLOUD	778a	1 a
	מפתן	THRESHOLD	837b	
10 5	רום	BE HIGH	927a	3
	חיצון	OUTER	300b	1
	חצר	ENCLOSURE	347a	3 b
	כרוב	CHERUB	501a	6 a
	קול	VOICE	877a	1 b
	קול	VOICE	877b	2 k
	שדי	ALMIGHTY	995a	2
10 6	אופן	WHEEL	66d	B
	בד	WHITE LINEN	94b	
	בין	INTERVAL	107d	E
	כרוב	CHERUB	501a	6 a
	לבש	PUT ON	528a	E
	עמד	STAND	763d	1 a
10 7	בד	WHITE LINEN	94b	
	בין	INTERVAL	107d	E
	חפן	HOLLOW OF HAND	342b	
	כרוב	CHERUB	501a	6 a
	לבש	PUT ON	528a	E
	שלח	SEND	1018d	3 c
10 8	אדם	MAN	9b	2
	תבנית	FIGURE	125d	3
	יד	HAND	389a	1
	כרוב	CHERUB	501a	6 a
	ראה	TO SEE	908c	2 c
10 9	אופן	WHEEL	66d	B
	כרוב	CHERUB	501a	6 a
	עין	EYE	745a	4 c
	צרף	SMELT	864b	4
	תרשיש	YELLOW JASPAR	1076d	
10 10	אופן	WHEEL	66d	B
	דמות	LIKENESS	198b	2
	דמות	LIKENESS	198b	1
	כרוב	CHERUB	501a	6 a
10 11	הלך	WALK	232b	13
	כרוב	CHERUB	501a	6 a
	סבב	TURN AROUND	686a	1 b
	פנה	TURN	815b	1 a
	מקום	STANDING PLACE	880b	6
	ראש	HEAD	910d	1 b
	רבע	FOURTH PART	917d	
10 12	אופן	WHEEL	66d	B
	גב	BACK	146b	1
	גב	BACK	146c	6
	כרוב	CHERUB	501a	6 a
	מלא	FULL	571a	
	עין	EYE	744b	1 e
10 13	אופן	WHEEL	66d	B
	כרוב	CHERUB	501a	6 a
	קרא	CALL	896c	
10 14	אדם	MAN	9b	2
	אריה	LION	71d	
	כרוב	CHERUB	501a	6 a
	פנה	FACE	815d	1 1
	פנה	FACE	816a	1 4
	צרף	SMELT	864b	4
10 15	ב	IN	89a	2 1
	חיה	LIVING THING	312d	1 c
	כבר	CHEBAR	460d	
	כרוב	CHERUB	501a	6 a
	רום	BE EXALTED	933d	
10 16	אופן	WHEEL	66d	B
	אצל	BESIDE	69b	B
	הלך	WALK	230a	1 1a
	כרוב	CHERUB	501a	6 a
	נשא	LIFT	670a	1 a
	סבב	TURN AROUND	686a	1 b
	רום	BE HIGH	927a	3
10 17	את	WITH	85c	
	חיה	LIVING THING	312d	1 c
	כרוב	CHERUB	501a	6 a
	רוח	BREATH	926a	9 e
	רום	BE HIGH	927a	3
	רום	BE EXALTED	933d	
10 18	יצא	GO OUT	423a	1 e
	כבוד	GLORY	458d	2 c1
	כרוב	CHERUB	501a	6 a
	מפתן	THRESHOLD	837b	
10 19	אופן	WHEEL	66d	B
	כבוד	GLORY	458d	2 c1
	כרוב	CHERUB	501a	6 a
	נשא	LIFT	670a	1 a
	מעל	ABOVE	752a	2 d
	עמה	CLOSE BY	769c	A
	פתח	OPENING	836a	
	קדמני	FORMER	870d	2
	רום	BE EXALTED	933d	
	שער	GATE	1045b	3 b
10 20	ב	IN	89a	2 1
	חיה	LIVING THING	312d	1 c
	כבר	CHEBAR	460d	
	כרוב	CHERUB	501a	6 a
10 21	אדם	MAN	9b	2
	דמות	LIKENESS	198b	1
	יד	HAND	389a	1
	פנה	FACE	815d	1 1
	ארבע	FOUR	917a	1 b1
10 22	דמות	LIKENESS	198b	1
	כבר	CHEBAR	460d	
	עבר	REGION ACROSS	719d	2
11 1	יאזניהו	JAAZANIAH	24d	4
	בניהו	BENAIAH	125c	5 e

Ch v.	Heb	Eng	Page	Sec
	סערה	TEMPEST	704b	
	רוח	BREATH	924d	2 a
	שטף	OVERFLOW	1009b	1
13 14	הרס	THROW DOWN	248c	1
	מחה	OVER-SPREAD	376b	
	יסוד	FOUNDATION	414b	1
	כלה	BE FINISHED	477d	2 c
	נגע	TOUCH	619b	1
	נפל	FALL	656d	1
	קיר	WALL	885a	3
	תפל	WHITEWASH	1074b	
13 15	מחה	OVER-SPREAD	376b	
	מחה	OVER-SPREAD	376b	
	חמה	RAGE	*405a	2 c
	כלה	FINISH	478c	1 e
	קיר	WALL	885a	3
	תפל	WHITEWASH	1074b	
13 16	חזה	SEE	302c	2
	חזון	VISION	303a	1
	נביא	PROPHET	612a	2
	נבא	PROPHESY	612b	2
	ישראל	ISRAEL	975d	2 a3
13 17	בת	DAUGHTER	123c	1 i
	לב	HEART	524c	2 3a
	נבא	PROPHESY	612a	1 b
	נבא	PROPHESY	612c	3
	על	UPON	756d	2 7a c
13 18	אציל	JOINT	69c	
	הוי	AH	223a	
	חיה	LIVE	311c	1
	יד	HAND	389a	1 b
	כסת	BAND	492c	
	נפש	SOUL	660c	4 c4
	מספחה	LONG VEIL	705b	
	צוד	HUNT	844c	
	קומה	HEIGHT	879b	1
	תפר	SEW TOGETHER	1074c	
13 19	אל	TO	40a	3 b
	חיה	LIVE	311c	1
	חלל	POLLUTE	320b	1 c
	כזב	LIE	469c	1
	כזב	LIE	469c	
	לחם	FOOD	537a	1 a
	נפש	SOUL	660c	4 c4
	פתות	FRAGMENT	837d	
	שעורה	BARLEY	972d	2
	שעל	HANDFUL	1043b	2
13 20	אל	TO	40b	4
	אתם	YOU	61d	
	אתן	YOU	61d	
	כסת	BAND	492c	
	ל	TO	512c	2
	נפש	SOUL	660c	4 c4
	נפש	SOUL	660c	4 c4
	פרח	FLY	827c	
	צוד	HUNT	844c	
	קרע	TEAR	902c	1 b
13 21	מספחה	LONG VEIL	705d	
	מצודה	PREY	845a	2
	קרע	TEAR	902c	1 b
13 22	דרך	WAY	203d	6 d
	חזק	BE FIRM	304d	2
	חיה	LIVE	311c	1
	כאב	PAIN	456b	2
	כאה	BE COWED	456c	
	ל	TO	518b	7 bh
	יען	ON ACCOUNT OF	774d	1
	שוב	TURN BACK	997b	6 e
13 23	חזה	SEE	302c	2
	כן	SO	487a	3 d
	קסם	PRACTICE OF DIVI-NATION	890d	2
	שוא	EMPTINESS	996b	2
13 30	זרוע	ARM	283d	1 a
14 1	זקן	OLD	278d	2 b
	ישראל	ISRAEL	975d	2 a3
14 3	דרש	SEEK	205d	1
	מכשול	STUMBLING	506b	2 c
	לב	HEART	524c	2 1
	נכח	FRONT	647b	1
	עון	INIQUITY	731a	1 a
	עלה	GO UP	749d	5
14 4	איש	MAN	36a	
	את	WITH	86a	1 db
	דבר	SPEAK	181b	3 d
	יהוה	YAHWEH	219b	2 2d
	כן	SO	487a	3 d
	מכשול	STUMBLING	506b	2 c
	ל	TO	514a	5 e
	לב	HEART	524c	2 1
	נביא	PROPHET	612a	2
	נכח	FRONT	647b	1
	עון	INIQUITY	731a	1 a
	ענה	ANSWER	773a	1
	שום	TO PLACE	963c	1 c
14 5	זור	BE A STRANGER	266d	
	כל	ALL	481d	1 da
	על	UPON	759a	4 2c
	מען	PURPOSE	775b	1
	תפש	LAY HOLD OF	1074d	1
14 6	כן	SO	487a	3 d
	על	UPON	759a	4 2c
	שוב	TURN BACK	997b	6 e
	שוב	TURN BACK	999b	6 a
	שוב	TURN BACK	999b	0
	תועבה	ABOMINATION	1073a	1 b
14 7	איש	MAN	36a	
	גור	SOJOURN	157d	1
	גר	SOJOURNER	158b	2
	דרש	SEEK	205b	2 a
	יהוה	YAHWEH	219b	2 2d
	מכשול	STUMBLING	506b	2 c
	ל	TO	514a	5 e
	לב	HEART	524c	2 1
	נביא	PROPHET	612a	2
	נזר	DEDICATE	634a	
	נכח	FRONT	647b	1
	עון	INIQUITY	731a	1 a
	עלה	GO UP	749a	7
	עלה	GO UP	749d	5
	ענה	ANSWER	773a	1
	שום	TO PLACE	963c	1 c
	ישראל	ISRAEL	975d	2 a3
14 8	אות	SIGN	16d	5
	כרת	CUT OFF	504c	2 c
	משל	PROVERB	605b	2
	נתן	PUT	680d	2 b
	שום	TO PLACE	964d	1
	שמם	BE DESOLATED	1031b	1
14 9	יהוה	YAHWEH	219b	2 2d
	כי	IF	473b	2
	נביא	PROPHET	612a	2
	פתה	BE SIMPLE	834d	2
	פתה	BE SIMPLE	834d	2
	ישראל	ISRAEL	975d	2 a3
14 10	דרש	SEEK	205b	2 b
	נביא	PROPHET	612a	2
	נשא	LIFT	671a	2 b
	עון	INIQUITY	731c	3
	עון	INIQUITY	731c	3
14 11	טמא	BE UNCLEAN	379d	
	מען	PURPOSE	775c	2 cb
	פשע	TRANSGRESSION	833d	4
	תעה	ERR	1073c	3
14 13	אדם	MAN	9b	2
	ארץ	EARTH	76b	2 f
	חטא	MISS A GOAL OR WAY	307a	2 b
	כי	IF	473b	2 b
	כרת	CUT OFF	504c	2 c
	ל	TO	*512d	5 aa
	לחם	FOOD	537a	1 a
	מעל	ACT TREACHER-OUSLY	591b	1 a
	מטה	STAFF	641c	1
	שלח	SEND	1019c	
14 14	איוב	JOB	33c	
	דנאל	DANIEL	193b	3
	נח	NOAH	629b	
	נפש	SOUL	660b	4 b5
	נצל	DELIVER	664d	1
	צדקה	RIGHTEOUSNESS	842b	5
14 15	בלי	WEARING OUT	115d	C b
	חיה	LIVING THING	312c	1 b
	חיה	LIVING THING	312c	1 b
	לו	IF	530a	1 b
	עבר	PASS OVER	717c	3 a
	עבר	PASS OVER	718d	2 a
	רע	EVIL	948a	1
	שכל	BE BEREAVED	1013d	1
14 16	אם	IF	50b	1 b2
	חי	ALIVE	311d	1 a
	נצל	DELIVER ONESELF	664c	1
14 17	אדם	MAN	9b	2
	או	OR	15a	2
	בוא	COME	99c	2 a
	כרת	CUT OFF	504c	2 c
	לו	IF	*530a	1 b
	חי	ALIVE	311d	1 a
14 18	נצל	DELIVER ONESELF	664c	1
14 19	אדם	MAN	9b	2
	או	OR	15a	2
	דם	BLOOD	197b	2 n
	חמה	RAGE	*405a	2 c
	כרת	CUT OFF	504c	2 c
	לו	IF	*530a	1 b
	שפך	POUR OUT	1049c	2 a
14 20	אויב	JOB	33c	
	דנאל	DANIEL	193b	3
	חי	ALIVE	311d	1 a
	נח	NOAH	629b	
	נצל	DELIVER	665a	3 a
	צדקה	RIGHTEOUSNESS	842b	5
14 21	אדם	MAN	9b	2
	אף	ALSO	65a	2
	חיה	LIVING THING	312c	1 b
	כרת	CUT OFF	504c	2 c
	רע	EVIL	948a	1
	רע	EVIL	948a	1
	שפט	JUDGEMENT	1048a	
14 22	את	MARK OF THE AC-CUSATIVE	85c	3 b
	בוא	COME	99c	2 a
	דרך	WAY	203c	6 a
	ה	THE	209b	2 b
	יצא	CAUSE TO GO	424b	1 a
	יצא	BE BROUGHT FORTH	425c	
	נחם	CONSOLE ONESELF	637a	3
	עלילה	WANTONNESS	760b	2 c
	פליטה	ESCAPE	812d	2 c
14 23	דרך	WAY	203c	6 a
	חנם	OUT OF FAVOR	336d	C
	נחם	CONSOLE ONESELF	637a	
	עלילה	WANTONNESS	760b	2 c
15 2	גפן	VINE	172c	
	גפן	VINE	172c	
	זמורה	BRANCH	274d	
	יער	WOOD	420d	F
	מן	THAN	582d	6 c
	עץ	TREE	781c	1 a
	עץ	TREE	781c	1 a
15 3	יתד	PEG	450b	B
	מלאכה	WORK	522b	5
	לקח	TAKE	544a	2
	תלה	HANG	1068a	1
15 4	אכלה	FOOD	38b	3
	ה	THE	207d	1 e
	חרר	BE HOT	359c	1
	נתן	PUT	681d	2 b
	קצה	END	892c	1
	תוך	MIDST	1063c	
15 5	אף	ALSO	65a	2
	חרר	BE HOT	359c	1
	עשה	DO	795b	2 f
	תמם	SOUND	1071a	2
15 6	אכלה	FOOD	38b	3
	גפן	VINE	172c	
	גפן	VINE	172c	
	יער	WOOD	420d	F
	עץ	TREE	781c	1 a
	עץ	TREE	781d	1 b
15 7	ה	THE	207d	1 e
	נתן	PUT	680d	2 b
	שום	TO PLACE	963d	2 c
15 8	מעל	ACT TREACHER-OUSLY	591b	1 a
16 2	ידע	KNOW	395a	
16 3	אב	FATHER	3c	4 b
	אם	MOTHER	52a	2
	אמרי	AMORITES	57c	2 e
	חתי	HITTITE	366d	1
	חתית	TERROR	369d	
	מולדת	BIRTH	409d	2
	מכורה	ORIGIN	468d	
	כנעני	CANAANITE	489a	2 b
16 4	את	MARK OF THE AC-CUSATIVE	85a	1 b
	חתל	ENTWINE	367c	
	ילד	BE BORN	409b	
	מולדת	BIRTH	409d	2
	כרת	BE CUT OFF	504b	1
	מלח	SALT	572a	
	משעי	CLEANSING	606b	
	רחץ	WASH OFF	934c	
	שר	NAVEL-STRING	*1057a	
	שר	NAVEL-STRING	1057a	
16 5	את	MARK OF THE AC-CUSATIVE	85a	1 b
	געל	LOATHING	172a	
	חוס	PITY	299b	A
	חמל	SPARE	328b	
	ילד	BE BORN	409b	
	פנה	FACE	816c	2 1d
	שדה	FIELD	961c	1 f
	שלך	THROW	1021c	2
16 6	בוס	TRAMPLE	101a	
	דם	BLOOD	196c	2 a
	דם	BLOOD	196d	2 f
	דם	BLOOD	*196d	2 f
16 7	גדל	BECOME GREAT	152b	2 e
	כון	BE FIRM	465c	1 a
	עדי	ORNAMENTS	725d	1
	עים	NAKEDNESS	736a	2
	עריה	NAKEDNESS	789a	1
	צמח	SPROUT	855c	
	צמח	SPROUT	855c	1
	רבבה	MULTITUDE	914b	
	רבה	BECOME MANY	915b	2 b1
	שדה	FIELD	961c	1 d
	שער	HAIR	972b	2
	שד	BREAST	994c	1
16 8	ברית	COVENANT	136c	2 2c
	ברית	COVENANT	137a	3 1
	דוד	LOVE	187c	3
	היה	BECOME	226d	2 2h
	כנף	EXTREMITY	489d	2 a
	כסה	COVER	491c	2
	ערוה	NAKEDNESS	789a	1
	פרש	SPREAD OUT	831b	2
	שבע	SWEAR	989c	2
16 9	דם	BLOOD	196d	2 f
	סוך	ANOINT	692a	2
	רחץ	WASH OFF	934c	1
	שטף	OVERFLOW	1009b	3
	שמן	OIL	1032b	2
16 10	חבש	BIND	289d	1 a
	כסה	COVER	491c	2
	לבש	CLOTHE	528b	1 a
	נעל	FURNISH WITH SANDALS	653b	
	רקמה	VARIEGATED STUFF	955d	
	שש	BYSSUS	1058c	
	תחש	SEALSKIN	1065a	
16 11	נתן	PUT	680a	2 a
	עדה	ORNAMENT	725d	2
	עדי	ORNAMENTS	725d	1

Ch v.	Heb	Eng	Page	Sec
	צמיד	BRACELET	855b	
	ירבעם	CHAIN	914d	
16 12	אזן	EAR	23d	1
	אף	NOSE	60a	1 b
	נום	RING	633d	1
	עגיל	HOOP	722d	
	עטרה	CROWN	742d	2
	תפארה	BEAUTY	802c	2 a
16 13	דבש	HONEY	185b	
	יפה	BE BEAUTIFUL	421b	
	מלבש	RAIMENT	528d	
	מאד	MUCHNESS	547c	2 e
	מלוכה	KINGSHIP	574d	
	משי	SILK	603d	
	סלת	FINE FLOUR	701c	
	עדה	ORNAMENT	725d	1 a
	צלח	ADVANCE	852b	
	רקמה	VARIEGATED STUFF	955d	
	שמן	OIL	1032b	2 b
	שש	BYSSUS	*1058c	
16 14	הדר	ORNAMENT	214b	1
	יפי	BEAUTY	421d	
	כליל	WHOLE	483a	1
	ל	TO	512d	5 aa
	שם	NAME	1028a	2 b1
16 15	בטח	TRUST	105a	1 3c
	זנה	COMMIT FORNICA-TION	275d	1
	תזנות	FORNICATION	276b	
	יפי	BEAUTY	421d	
	על	UPON	753d	2 1f
	שפך	POUR OUT	*1049d	
	שפך	POUR OUT	1049d	2 b
16 16	בגד	GARMENT	94a	1
	במה	HIGH PLACE	119b	3
	זנה	COMMIT FORNICA-TION	276a	3
	טלא	PATCH	378a	
16 17	זכר	MALE	271c	11 a
	זנה	COMMIT FORNICA-TION	276a	3
	כלי	ARTICLE	479c	1
	כסף	SILVER	494b	7
	תפארה	BEAUTY	802c	1
	צלם	IMAGE	853d	1
16 18	כסה	COVER	491c	1
	קטרת	SMOKE	882d	3
	רקמה	VARIEGATED STUFF	955d	
16 19	שמן	OIL	1032c	2 k
	אכל	EAT	37d	1
	דבש	HONEY	185b	
	לחם	FOOD	537b	2 c
	ניחח	SOOTHING	629c	
	סלת	FINE FLOUR	701c	
	ריח	SCENT	926b	2
	שמן	OIL	1032c	2 k
16 20	זבח	SLAUGHTER FOR SACRIFICE	256d	11 bb
	תזנות	FORNICATION	276b	
	תזנות	FORNICATION	276b	
	ילד	BEAR	408c	1 c
	מן	THAN	582d	6 d
	מעט	A FEW	590b	1 ea
	עבר	PASS OVER	718d	1 d
	שמן	OIL	1032b	2 b
16 21	בן	SON	120b	1 c
	עבר	PASS OVER	718d	1 d
	שחט	SLAUGHTER	1006b	3
16 22	את	MARK OF THE AC-CUSATIVE	85c	3 a
	בוס	TRAMPLE	101a	
	דם	BLOOD	196c	2 a
	זכר	REMEMBER	269d	11 d
	תזנות	FORNICATION	276b	
	נעורים	YOUTH	655c	
	עירם	NAKEDNESS	736a	2
16 23	אוי	WOE	17a	
16 24	בנה	BUILD	124c	1 ai
	גב	BACK	146c	2
	רמה	HEIGH-PLACE	928a	
	רחוב	PLAZA	932b	
16 25	בנה	BUILD	124c	1 ai
	תזנות	FORNICATION	276b	
	תזנות	FORNICATION	276b	
	יפי	BEAUTY	421d	
	פשק	PART WIDE	832d	
	רגל	FOOT	920a	1 f
	רמה	HEIGH-PLACE	928a	
	תעב	BE ABHORRED	1073b	2
16 26	אל	TO	39c	1
	בן	SON	121b	1 jt
	בשר	FLESH	142d	3
	גדל	GREAT	152d	
	זנה	COMMIT FORNICA-TION	275d	2
	תזנות	FORNICATION	276b	
	כעס	VEX	495a	2
	מצרים	EGYPTIANS	595d	2 b
	שכן	NEIGHBOUR	1015c	2
16 27	בת	DAUGHTER	123c	3
	גרע	DIMINISH	175c	1
	גרע	WITHDRAW	*175c	3
	דרך	WAY	203d	6 d
	זמה	PLAN	273c	2 c

Ch v.	Heb	Eng	Page	Sec
	זמה	PLAN	273c	2 c
	חק	SOMETHING PRE-SCRIBED	349b	2
	כלם	BE HUMILIATED	483d	1
	נפש	SOUL	660d	6 a
16 28	אל	TO	39c	1
	אשור	ASSHUR	78d	2
	בלת	NOT	117a	4 b
	בן	SON	121b	1 jt
	גם	ALSO	169d	5
	זנה	COMMIT FORNICA-TION	275d	2
	זנה	COMMIT FORNICA-TION	275d	2
	שבע	SATISFIED	959c	2 a
	שבעה	SATIETY	960a	2
16 29	אל	TO	39c	1
	תזנות	FORNICATION	276b	
	כנען	MERCHANT	488d	
	כשדים	CHALDEA	505b	2
	שבע	SATISFIED	959c	2 a
16 30	אמל	BE WEAK	51b	
	אשה	WOMAN	61a	1
	זנה	COMMIT FORNICA-TION	275d	1
	לבה	ANGER	525d	
	מעשה	DEED	795d	1 a2
	שליט	HAVING MASTERY	1020d	2
16 31	בנה	BUILD	124c	1 ai
	גב	BACK	146c	2
	זנה	COMMIT FORNICA-TION	275d	1
	קבץ	GATHER	867c	1
	קלם	MOCK	887b	
	רמה	HEIGH-PLACE	928a	
	רחוב	PLAZA	932b	
	אתנן	HIRE	1072c	
16 32	זור	BE A STRANGER	266c	2
	נאף	COMMIT ADUL-TERY	610d	1 b
16 33	אהב	LOVE	13b	2
	זנה	COMMIT FORNICA-TION	275d	1
	תזנות	FORNICATION	276b	
	נדה	GIFT	622d	
	נדן	GIFT	623c	
	סביב	ROUND ABOUT	687a	1 d
	שחד	GIVE A BRIBE	1005a	
16 34	היה	COME TO PASS	224d	1 1b
	הפך	THE CONTRARY	246b	1
	תזנות	FORNICATION	276b	
	נתן	GIVE	681b	1 a
	אתנן	HIRE	1072c	
16 35	זנה	COMMIT FORNICA-TION	276a	3
16 36	אהב	LOVE	13b	2
	דם	BLOOD	196d	2 f
	תזנות	FORNICATION	276b	
	נחשת	COPPER	639a	3
	נחשתן	NEHUSHTAN	639b	
	ערוה	NAKEDNESS	789a	1
	שפך	POUR OUT	1049d	
	תועבה	ABOMINATION	1073a	1 b
16 37	אהב	LOVE	12d	1
	אהב	LOVE	13b	2
	כן	SO	486d	3 d
	סביב	ROUND ABOUT	687a	1 d
	על	UPON	755b	24b
	ערב	BE SWEET	787a	
	ערוה	NAKEDNESS	788d	1
	ערוה	NAKEDNESS	789a	1
	קבץ	GATHER	868a	1
	שנא	HATE	971c	1 a
16 38	דם	BLOOD	196c	2 b
	דם	BLOOD	197b	2 n
	חמה	RAGE	404d	2 c
	חמה	RAGE	*405a	2 c
	נאף	COMMIT ADUL-TERY	610c	1 b
	קנאה	ZEAL	888c	3 b
	שפט	JUDGE	1047d	3 c1
	משפט	JUDGMENT	1048c	1 e
16 39	גב	BACK	146c	2
	הרם	THROW DOWN	248c	1
	כלי	ARTICLE	479c	1
	נוח	REST	629a	B 2
	עירם	NAKEDNESS	736a	2
	תפארה	BEAUTY	802c	1
	פשט	STRIP OFF	833a	1
	רמה	HEIGH-PLACE	928a	
16 40	אבן	STONE	6b	1
	בתק	CUT	144a	
	עלה	GO UP	749c	2 b
	קהל	ASSEMBLY	874c	1 b
	רגם	TO STONE	920c	
16 41	זנה	COMMIT FORNICA-TION	276a	3
	מן	FROM	583d	7 bb
	שבת	CEASE	992a	3
	שפט	JUDGEMENT	1048a	
	שפט	JUDGEMENT	1048a	
	אתנן	HIRE	1072c	
16 42	חמה	RAGE	*405a	2 c
	כעס	BE ANGRY	495a	2
	נוח	REST	628c	A 1a
	סור	TURN ASIDE	693d	2

Ch v.	Heb	Eng	Page	Sec
	קנאה	ZEAL	888c	3 b
	שקט	BE QUIET	1053a	1 c
16 43	גם	ALSO	169c	4
	דרך	WAY	203d	6 d
	לא	LO	210c	
	זכר	REMEMBER	269d	11 d
	זמה	PLAN	273c	2 c
	זמה	PLAN	273c	2 c
	נעורים	YOUTH	655c	
	נתן	PUT	680d	2 b
	על	UPON	755b	24b
	על	UPON	755c	24b
	רגז	BE AGITATED	919b	
16 44	אם	MOTHER	52a	2
	בת	DAUGHTER	123c	3
	משל	USE A PROVERB	605c	
16 45	אב	FATHER	3c	4 b
	אחות	SISTER	28a	3
	איש	MAN	35d	
	אם	MOTHER	52a	2
	אמרי	AMORITES	57c	2 e
	בת	DAUGHTER	123c	3
	געל	ABHOR	171d	
	חתי	HITTITE	366d	1
	חתית	TERROR	369d	
16 46	בת	DAUGHTER	123c	3
	גדול	GREAT	153a	5
	ימין	RIGHT	412a	4
	סדם	SODOM	690a	
	קטן	SMALL	882a	1 a
	שמאל	LEFT	969d	3
	שמאל	LEFT	969d	1
	שמרון	SAMARIA	1037d	
16 47	דרך	WAY	203d	6 d
	הלך	WALK	234d	2 3a 2a
	הם	THEY	242a	8 d
	מעט	A FEW	590b	2 a
	קוט	FEEL A LOATHING	876c	
	קט	MERELY	881c	
	שחת	GO TO RUIN	1008c	2
16 48	חי	ALIVE	311d	1 a
	סדם	SODOM	690a	
16 49	אביון	NEEDY	2d	
	גאון	EXALTATION	145a	2
	חזק	BE FIRM	305a	3
	סדם	SODOM	690a	
	עון	INIQUITY	731b	2
	עני	POOR	776d	2
	שלוה	QUIETNESS	1017c	1
	שקט	BE QUIET	1053b	1
16 50	גבה	BE HIGH	147a	3 b
	ראה	TO SEE	907a	1 b
	תועבה	ABOMINATION	1072d	1 b
16 51	הם	THEY	241d	8 c
	חטא	MISS A GOAL OR WAY	306d	2 b
	חטאת	SIN	308c	1 b
	צדק	BE JUST	842d	3
	שמרון	SAMARIA	1037d	
16 52	אחות	SISTER	28a	3
	בוש	BE ASHAMED	101d	3
	הם	THEY	242a	8 d
	חטאת	SIN	308d	1 b
	כלמה	IGNOMINY	484b	2
	נשא	LIFT	671a	2 b
	פלל	INTERVENE	813a	
	צדק	BE JUST	842d	3
	צדק	BE JUST	842d	4
	תעב	BE ABHORRED	1073b	1
16 53	בת	DAUGHTER	123c	3
	סדם	SODOM	690a	
	שבות	CAPTIVITY	986b	2 c
	שבות	CAPTIVITY	986b	2
	שבות	CAPTIVITY	986b	2 a
	שמרון	SAMARIA	1037d	
16 54	כלם	BE HUMILIATED	483d	1
	כלמה	IGNOMINY	484b	2
	נחם	CONSOLE ONESELF	637a	
16 55	בת	DAUGHTER	123d	3
	סדם	SODOM	690a	
	קדמה	ANTIQUITY	870b	2
	שוב	TURN BACK	997c	5 d
	שמרון	SAMARIA	1037d	
16 56	גאון	EXALTATION	145a	1 a
	סדם	SODOM	690a	
	שמועה	REPORT	1035b	2
16 57	ארם	ARAM	74b	A
	בת	DAUGHTER	123c	3
	חרפה	REPROACH	358a	2 a
	טרם	NOT YET	382c	2
	כמו	LIKE	455d	1 a
	סביב	ROUND ABOUT	687b	2 ba b
	עתה	NOW	774c	2 gb
	שוט	TREAT WITH DE-SPITE	1002b	
16 58	זמה	PLAN	273c	2 c
	נאם	UTTERANCE	610b	2
16 59	אלה	OATH	46d	1
	את	WITH	86b	1 db
	בזה	DESPISE	102b	
	ברית	COVENANT	136c	2 2c
	ברית	COVENANT	137b	3 3
	פרר	BREAK	830b	1 b
16 60	את	WITH	86a	1 da
	ברית	COVENANT	136c	2 2c
	ברית	COVENANT	137a	3 2

397

Ch	v.	Heb	Eng	Page	Sec
		ברית	COVENANT	137a	2 2k
		ברית	COVENANT	137a	3 1
		ברית	COVENANT	137b	3 2
		זכר	REMEMBER	270b	2 3 a
		נעורים	YOUTH	655c	
		עולם	LONG DURATION	762c	2 d
		קום	STAND	879a	6 d
16	61	ברית	COVENANT	136b	11
		דרך	WAY	203d	6 d
		זכר	REMEMBER	269d	11 c1
		כלם	BE HUMILIATED	483d	1
		מן	ON ACCOUNT OF	580b	2 f
		קטן	SMALL	882a	1a
16	62	ברית	COVENANT	137a	3 1
		ברית	COVENANT	137a	2 2k
		קום	STAND	879a	6 d
16	63	בוש	BE ASHAMED	101d	1
		זכר	REMEMBER	269d	11 c1
		כלמה	IGNOMINY	484b	2
		כפר	COVER OVER	497c	2 b
		פתחון	OPENING	836a	
17	2	חידה	RIDDLE	295c	1
		חוד	PROPOUND A RIDDLE	295c	
		משל	PARABLE	605b	4
		משל	USE A PROVERB	605c	
17	3	אבר	PINIONS	7c	
		ארז	CEDAR	72c	1a
		ארך	LONG	74a	
		גדול	GREAT	153a	1
		גדול	GREAT	153b	8
		כנף	WING	489c	1a
		לבנון	LEBANON	527b	
		מלא	FULL	571a	
		נוצה	PLUMAGE	663b	
		נשר	EAGLE	676d	
		צמרת	TREE-TOP	856a	
		רקמה	VARIEGATED STUFF	955d	
17	4	יניקה	TWIG	413c	
		כנען	MERCHANT	488d	1
		עיר	CITY	746c	1 i
		קטף	PLUCK OFF	882c	
		ראש	HEAD	910d	2a
		רכל	GO ABOUT	940b	
17	5	זרע	SOWING	282a	1 a
		זרע	SOWING	282b	2 b
		זרע	SOWING	282c	2 e
		מן	FROM	580d	3 bb
		צפצפה	WILLOW	861d	
		שדה	FIELD	961d	2 a
		שום	TO PLACE	964b	4 d
17	6	בד	PART	94d	3 b
		גפן	VINE	172c	
		דליות	BRANCH	194d	
		חיה	BECOME	226b	2 2e
		סרח	GO FREE	710b	1
		עשה	DO	794d	2 2
		פארה	BOUGH	802d	
		פנה	TURN	815a	1 a
		צמח	SPROUT	855b	1
		קומה	HEIGHT	879b	2
		שפל	LOW	1050c	1
		שרש	ROOT	1057d	2
17	7	גדול	GREAT	153b	8
		גפן	VINE	172c	
		דליות	BRANCH	194d	
		כנף	WING	489c	1 a
		כפן	BE HUNGRY	495d	
		נוצה	PLUMAGE	663b	
		נשר	EAGLE	676d	
		ערוגה	GARDEN TERRACE	788c	
		רב	MUCH	913b	1 d
		שקה	GIVE TO DRINK	1052c	1
		שרש	ROOT	1057d	2
17	8	אדיר	MAJESTIC	12b	1
		אדרת	GLORY	12b	1
		אל	TO	40d	8
		גפן	VINE	172c	
		טוב	PLEASANT	374b	3 b
		ענף	BRANCH	778c	
		עשה	DO	794d	2 2
		שדה	FIELD	961d	2 a
		שתל	TRANSPLANT	1060a	
17	9	את	MARK OF THE ACCUSATIVE	85b	1 d
		זרוע	ARM	284b	2 a
		טרף	PREY	383c	3
		יבש	BE DRY	386c	1 d
		נשא	LIFT	671c	3 f
		נתק	PULL	683d	1
		צמח	SPROUT	855c	1
		קסם	STRIP OFF	890d	1
		שרש	ROOT	1057d	2
17	10	ה	INTERROG PART	209d	1 b
		יבש	BE DRY	386c	1 d
		נגע	TOUCH	619a	2
		ערוגה	GARDEN TERRACE	788c	
		צמח	SPROUT	855c	1
		קדים	EAST WIND	870c	2 a
		שתל	TRANSPLANT	1060a	
17	12	בית	HOUSE	110a	5 dd
		מרי	REBELLION	598b	
		שר	CHIEFTAIN	978b	2 a
17	13	איל	LEADER	18b	
		אל	GOD	42b	1
		אלה	OATH	46d	1
		ברית	COVENANT	136b	11
		זרע	SOWING	282d	4 e
		כרת	CUT	503d	4
		מלוכה	KINGSHIP	574d	
		מן	FROM	580d	3 bb
17	14	ברית	COVENANT	136b	11
		ממלכה	KINGDOM	575b	1
		נשא	LIFT	672a	
		פרי	FRUIT	826b	1
		שמר	KEEP	1036d	3 c
		שפל	LOW	1050c	2
17	15	ברית	COVENANT	136b	11
		מלאך	MESSENGER	521c	1 a
		מלט	SLIP AWAY	572b	2
		מרד	REBEL	597c	1
		סוס	HORSE	692c	1
		פרר	BREAK	830b	1 c
17	16	אלה	OATH	46d	1
		בזה	DESPISE	102b	
		ברית	COVENANT	136b	11
		חי	ALIVE	311d	1 a
		מלך	BE KING	574b	
		פרר	BREAK	830b	1 c
17	17	את	WITH	86b	1 db
		בנה	BUILD	124c	1 ah
		ברית	COVENANT	136b	11
		גדול	GREAT	153a	2
		דיק	BULWARK	189b	
		חיל	STRENGTH	299a	4
		כרת	CUT OFF	504c	2 b
		נפש	SOUL	660c	4 c4
		סללה	MOUND	700c	
		עשה	DO	794d	1 2
		פרעה	PHARAOH	829a	
		קהל	ASSEMBLY	874c	1 b
		שפך	POUR OUT	1049c	1 a
17	18	אלה	OATH	46d	2
		בזה	DESPISE	102b	
		ברית	COVENANT	136b	11
		ברית	COVENANT	137b	3 3
		מלט	SLIP AWAY	572b	2
		פרר	BREAK	830b	1 c
17	19	אלה	OATH	46d	2
		בזה	DESPISE	102b	
		ברית	COVENANT	136b	11
		ברית	COVENANT	137b	3 3
		חי	ALIVE	311d	1 a
		נתן	PUT	680d	2 b
		פרר	BREAK	830b	1 c
17	20	רשת	NET	440b	1 a1
		מעל	ACT TREACHEROUSLY	591b	1 b
		פרש	SPREAD OUT	831b	1
		מצודה	PREY	845a	1
		שפט	JUDGE	1048a	1
		תפש	LAY HOLD OF	1075a	
17	21	אגף	BAND	8d	
		את	MARK OF THE ACCUSATIVE	85c	3 a
		מברח	FUGITIVE	138b	
		יהוה	YAHWEH	219b	2 2b z
		פרש	SPREAD OUT	831b	1
		שאר	REMAIN	984a	1
17	22	אנכי	I	59b	
		ארז	CEDAR	72c	1 b
		גבה	HIGH	147b	1
		הר	MOUNTAIN	250b	1 d
		יונקת	TWIG	413c	
		צמרת	TREE-TOP	856a	
		ראש	HEAD	910d	2 a
		רום	BE HIGH	926d	1 a
		רך	TENDER	940a	1
		שתל	TRANSPLANT	1060a	
		תלול	EXALTED	1068a	
17	23	אדיר	MAJESTIC	12b	1
		ארז	CEDAR	72c	1 b
		דליות	BRANCH	194d	
		הר	MOUNTAIN	249d	1 a
		הר	MOUNTAIN	251a	2 b
		כל	ALL	*481c	1 b
		כנף	WING	489c	1 a
		נשא	LIFT	671b	2 g
		ענף	BRANCH	778c	
		עשה	DO	794d	2 2
		פרי	FRUIT	826b	1
		צל	SHADOW	853b	2
		צפור	BIRD	862a	2
		מרום	HEIGHT	928c	1
		שכן	SETTLE DOWN	1015a	1 b
		שכן	SETTLE DOWN	1015a	1 b
		שתל	TRANSPLANT	1060a	
17	24	גבה	BE HIGH	147a	
		גבה	HIGH	147a	1
		יהוה	YAHWEH	219b	2 2b d
		יבש	BE DRY	386c	2
		יבש	DRY	386d	2
		לח	FRESH	535a	1
		עץ	TREE	781c	1 a
		פרח	BUD	827b	1
		שפל	BECOME LOW	1050b	1
		שפל	LOW	1050c	1
18	2	בסר	SOUR GRAPES	126a	
		מה	WHAT	552d	1 ac
		מה	WHAT	552d	1 ac
		משל	PROVERB	605a	1
		משל	USE A PROVERB	605c	
		קהה	BE BLUNT	874c	
		שן	TOOTH	1042a	1 a
18	3	חי	ALIVE	311d	1 a
		משל	PROVERB	605a	1
		משל	USE A PROVERB	605c	
18	4	הן	BEHOLD	*243d	A
		חטא	MISS A GOAL OR WAY	307a	2 b
		כ	LIKE	454c	2 c
		מות	DIE	560a	2 b
		נפש	SOUL	660b	4 c2
		נפש	SOUL	660c	4 c4
18	5	כי	IF	473b	2 b
		צדקה	RIGHTEOUSNESS	842b	5
18	6	אכל	EAT	37b	1
		אל	TO	41a	8
		הר	MOUNTAIN	250d	11
		טמא	BE UNCLEAN	379c	1
		נדה	IMPURITY	622c	1
		נשא	LIFT	670c	1 b 4
		קרב	COME NEAR	897b	1 a
		רע	FRIEND	946a	2
18	7	גזל	TEAR AWAY	159d	
		גזלה	PLUNDER	160a	
		חבלה	PLEDGE	287a	
		חוב	DEBT	295a	
		ינה	OPPRESS	413b	
		כסה	COVER	491c	1
		עירם	NAKED	736a	1
		רעב	HUNGRY	944c	
		שוב	TURN BACK	999a	1 d
18	8	אמת	FIRMNESS	54b	4 b
		נשך	INTEREST	675b	
		נתן	GIVE	679c	1 q
		עול	INJUSTICE	732c	
		תרבית	INTEREST	916b	
		שוב	TURN BACK	999a	1 c
		משפט	JUDGMENT	1048c	1 f
18	9	אמת	FIRMNESS	54a	3 b
		הלך	WALK	234d	2 3a 1e
		הלך	WALK	235c	1
		חקה	SOMETHING PRESCRIBED	350a	2 d
		חקה	SOMETHING PRESCRIBED	350b	2 e
18	10	אח	ALAS	25b	
		דם	BLOOD	196c	2 b
		ילד	BEGET	409a	1
		מן	FROM	581a	3 bd
		פריץ	VIOLENT ONE	829d	
		אח	ADDENDA ET CORRIGENDA	1119d	
18	11	אכל	EAT	37b	1
		אל	TO	41a	8
		טמא	BE UNCLEAN	379c	1
		רע	FRIEND	946a	2
18	12	אביון	NEEDY	2d	
		גזל	TEAR AWAY	159d	
		גזלה	PLUNDER	160a	
		חבל	PLEDGE	287a	
		ינה	OPPRESS	413b	
		נשא	LIFT	670c	1 b 4
		עני	POOR	776d	2
		שוב	TURN BACK	999a	1 c
		תועבה	ABOMINATION	1072d	1 b
18	13	דם	BLOOD	197a	2 i
		דם	BLOOD	197a	2 g
		לקח	TAKE	543b	4 f
		מות	DIE	560a	2 b
		נשך	INTEREST	675b	
		נתן	GIVE	679c	1 q
		תרבית	INTEREST	916b	
18	14	הם	THEY	242a	8 d
		חטאת	SIN	308c	1 b
		ילד	BEGET	409a	1
18	15	אכל	EAT	37b	1
		אל	TO	41a	8
		הר	MOUNTAIN	250d	11
		טמא	BE UNCLEAN	379c	1
		נשא	LIFT	670c	1 b 4
		רע	FRIEND	946a	2
18	16	גזל	TEAR AWAY	159d	
		גזלה	PLUNDER	160a	
		חבל	BIND	286b	2
		חבל	PLEDGE	287a	
		ינה	OPPRESS	413b	
		כסה	COVER	491c	1
		עירם	NAKED	736a	1
		רעב	HUNGRY	944b	1
18	17	ב	IN	*90c	3 5
		הלך	WALK	234d	2 3a 1e
		חקה	SOMETHING PRESCRIBED	350a	2 d
		חקה	SOMETHING PRESCRIBED	350b	2 e
		לקח	TAKE	543b	4 f
		מות	DIE	560a	2 b
		נשך	INTEREST	675b	
		עון	INIQUITY	731b	2 c
		עני	POOR	776d	2
		תרבית	INTEREST	916b	
		שוב	TURN BACK	999a	1 c
18	18	גזל	TEAR AWAY	159d	
		גזל	ROBBERY	160a	
		טוב	PLEASANT	375a	0 a

Ch	v.	Heb	Eng	Page	Sec
		כי	IF	473b	2 b
		מות	DIE	560a	2 b
		עון	INIQUITY	731b	2 c
		עם	KINSMAN	769c	
		עשק	OPPRESS	798d	1
		עשק	OPPRESSION	799a	1
18	19	חקה	SOMETHING PRE-SCRIBED	350b	2 e
		נשא	LIFT	671b	2 b
		עון	INIQUITY	731c	3
18	20	חטא	MISS A GOAL OR WAY	307a	2 b
		מות	DIE	560a	2 b
		נשא	LIFT	671b	2 b
		עון	INIQUITY	731c	3
		על	UPON	753d	2 1d
		צדקה	RIGHTEOUSNESS	842b	5
		רשעה	WICKEDNESS	958a	3
18	21	חטאת	SIN	308a	1 c
		חקה	SOMETHING PRE-SCRIBED	350b	2 e
		כי	IF	473b	2 b
		מות	DIE	560a	2 b
18	22	זכר	REMEMBER	270d	1 c 2
		פשע	TRANSGRESSION	833c	3 a
		צדקה	RIGHTEOUSNESS	842b	5
18	23	דרך	WAY	203d	6 d
		חפץ	DELIGHT IN	342d	2 a
18	24	זכר	REMEMBER	270d	1 c 1
		חטא	MISS A GOAL OR WAY	307b	2 b
		חטאת	SIN	309a	2
		מות	DIE	560a	2 b
		מעל	ACT TREACHEROUSLY	591b	1 a
		עול	INJUSTICE	732c	
		צדקה	RIGHTEOUSNESS	842c	7 b
		שוב	TURN BACK	997d	6 e
18	25	אדן	LORD	11c	3 2b
		דרך	WAY	203c	6 a
		דרך	WAY	204a	6 eb
		תכן	MEASURE	1067b	2
		תכן	MEASURE	1067b	2
18	26	מות	DIE	560a	2 b
		מות	DIE	560a	2 b
		עול	INJUSTICE	732c	
		על	UPON	754b	2 1f b
		שוב	TURN BACK	997d	6 e
18	27	חיה	LIVE	311c	1
		נפש	SOUL	659c	1
		רשעה	WICKEDNESS	958a	3
18	28	מות	DIE	560a	2 b
		פשע	TRANSGRESSION	833c	3 a
18	29	אדן	LORD	11c	3 2b
		דרך	WAY	203c	6 a
		דרך	WAY	204a	6 eb
		תכן	MEASURE	1067b	2
		תכן	MEASURE	1067b	2
18	30	דרך	WAY	203c	6 a
		מכשול	STUMBLING	506b	2 c
		עון	INIQUITY	731a	1 a
		פשע	TRANSGRESSION	833c	3 b
		שוב	TURN BACK	997d	6 e
		שוב	TURN BACK	999d	0
		שפט	JUDGE	1047d	3 c1
18	31	חדש	NEW	294b	A
		לב	HEART	525b	2 6a
		מות	DIE	560a	2 b
		על	UPON	758d	4 2b
		עשה	DO	794c	2 1d
		פשע	REBEL	833b	1
		פשע	TRANSGRESSION	833c	3 b
		רוח	BREATH	925c	8
		רוח	BREATH	925c	8
		שלך	THROW	1021b	1 c
18	32	ו	AND	254c	4
		חפץ	DELIGHT IN	342d	2 a
19	1	נשא	LIFT	670d	1 b 6
		נשיא	PRINCE	672b	6 a
		קינה	ELEGY	884b	
19	2	אם	MOTHER	52a	2
		ארי	LION	71d	
		בין	INTERVAL	107b	1
		גור	WHELP	158d	1
		כפיר	LION	498d	
		לביא	LIONESS	522d	
		קינה	ELEGY	884b	
		רבה	BECOME MANY	915b	
		רבץ	LIE DOWN	918c	
19	3	אכל	EAT	37c	2
		גור	WHELP	158d	1
		טרף	TEAR	382d	
		טרף	PREY	383c	1
		כפיר	LION	498d	
		למד	LEARN	540d	
		עלה	GO UP	749c	3
19	4	אל	TO	40c	6
		חח	HOOK	*296b	1
		חח	HOOK	296b	1
		שחת	PIT	1001c	1
		שמע	HEAR	1033d	1 d2
		תפש	LAY HOLD OF	1075a	
19	5	אבד	PERISH	1d	2
		גור	WHELP	158d	1
		יחל	WAIT	403d	
		כפיר	LION	498d	
		תקוה	HOPE	876b	3
		שום	TO PLACE	964c	5 b
19	6	אכל	EAT	37c	2
		ארי	LION	71d	
		הלך	WALK	236a	1 b
		טרף	TEAR	382d	
		טרף	PREY	383c	1
		כפיר	LION	498d	
		למד	LEARN	540d	
19	7	אלמנה	WIDOW	48b	
		ארמון	CITADEL	74d	
		חרב	BE WASTE	351d	
		ישם	BE DESOLATE	445b	
		מלא	THAT WHICH FILLS	571b	3
		שאגה	ROARING	980d	1
19	8	מדינה	PROVINCE	193d	2
		רשת	NET	440c	1 a2
		פרש	SPREAD OUT	831b	1
		שחת	PIT	1001c	1
		תפש	LAY HOLD OF	1075a	
19	9	הר	MOUNTAIN	251a	2 b
		חח	HOOK	296b	1
		חח	HOOK	*296b	1
		סגר	CAGE	689d	1
		מען	PURPOSE	775c	2 cb
		מצד	STRONGHOLD	844d	2
		מצודה	NET	845d	
		מצודה	FASTNESS	845a	
19	10	אם	MOTHER	52a	2
		גפן	VINE	172c	
		דם	BLOOD	197d	4
		מן	OUT OF	580a	2 eb
		ענף	FULL OF BRANCHES	778c	
		פרה	BEAR FRUIT	826a	2
		שתל	TRANSPLANT	1060a	
19	11	בין	INTERVAL	107d	C
		גבה	BE HIGH	147a	1
		גבה	HEIGHT	147b	1
		דליות	BRANCH	195a	
		משל	RULE	605d	1
		מטה	BRANCH	641d	2
		עבת	CORD	721c	2
		עב	DARK CLOUD	728a	1 b
		עז	STRENGTH	739a	1
		על	UPON	758a	2 9
		קומה	HEIGHT	879b	2
		ראה	TO SEE	908c	2 a
		שבט	ROD	987a	1 d
19	12	יבש	BE DRY	386c	1
		יבש	BE DRY	386c	1 d
		מטה	BRANCH	641d	2
		נתש	PLUCK UP	684c	
		עז	STRENGTH	739a	1
		פרק	TEAR APART	830a	
		קדים	EAST WIND	870c	2 a
		רוח	BREATH	924d	2 a
		שלך	THROW	1021c	3
19	13	ציה	DRYNESS	851b	
		צמא	THIRST	854d	
		שתל	TRANSPLANT	1060a	
19	14	בד	PART	94d	3 b
		משל	RULE	605d	1
		מטה	BRANCH	641d	2
		עז	STRENGTH	739a	1
		קינה	ELEGY	884b	
		שבט	ROD	987a	1 d
19	49	שבעה	SATIETY	960a	1 d
20	1	דרש	SEEK	205b	2 a
		זקן	OLD	278d	2 b
		חדש	NEW MOON	294d	2 b2
		עשור	A TEN	797c	1 b
20	3	דבר	SPEAK	181b	3 d
		דרש	SEEK	205b	2 a
		דרש	SEEK	205d	1
		זקן	OLD	278d	2 b
		חי	ALIVE	311d	1 a
20	4	ה	INTERROG PART	210a	1 c
		ידע	KNOW	395a	
		שפט	JUDGE	1047c	2 b
20	5	בחר	CHOOSE	103d	1 a
		בית	HOUSE	110a	5 dg
		יהוה	YAHWEH	218d	2 1b
		יהוה	YAHWEH	219a	2 2a
		זרע	SOWING	283a	4 f
		יד	HAND	389c	1 d
		ידע	MAKE ONESELF KNOWN	394c	2
		ל	TO	510d	1 b
		נשא	LIFT	670b	1 b 1
20	6	דבש	HONEY	185b	
		זוב	FLOW	264d	2
		חלב	MILK	316c	A 4
		יד	HAND	389c	1 d
		יצא	CAUSE TO GO	424c	1 a
		ל	TO	510d	1 b
		נשא	LIFT	670b	1 b 1
		צבי	BEAUTY	840a	1 b
		תור	SEEK OUT	1064b	1
20	7	יהוה	YAHWEH	218d	2 1b
		יהוה	YAHWEH	219b	2 2d
		טמא	BE UNCLEAN	379d	
		עין	EYE	744c	2 b
		שלך	THROW	1021a	1 c
		שקוץ	DETESTED THING	1055a	
20	8	אבה	BE WILLING		2 c
		חמה	RAGE	*405a	2 c
		כלה	FINISH	478c	1 e
		מרה	BE REBELLIOUS	598b	
		עזב	LEAVE	737c	2 d4
		עין	EYE	744c	2 b
		שלך	THROW	1021a	1 c
20	9	שקוץ	DETESTED THING	1055a	
		חלל	POLLUTE	320b	2
		חלל	POLLUTE	320c	1 a
		ידע	MAKE ONESELF KNOWN	394d	2
		יצא	CAUSE TO GO	424c	1 a
		מען	PURPOSE	775b	1 a
		עשה	DO	794b	1 4
		שם	NAME	1028c	3
20	10	יצא	CAUSE TO GO	424c	1 a
20	11	חיה	LIVE	311b	1
		חקה	SOMETHING PRE-SCRIBED	350a	2 d
20	12	ידע	KNOW	395a	
		אות	SIGN	17a	6
		יהוה	YAHWEH	219b	2 2be
		נתן	GIVE	678c	1 b
		קדש	BE SET APART	873b	4 d
		שבת	SABBOTH	992b	2
20	13	הלך	WALK	234d	2 3a 1e
		חיה	LIVE	311b	1
		חלל	POLLUTE	320b	1 b
		חקה	SOMETHING PRE-SCRIBED	350a	2 d
		חקה	SOMETHING PRE-SCRIBED	350b	2 e
		חמה	RAGE	*405a	2 c
		כלה	FINISH	478c	2 c2
		מאס	REJECT	549c	1 b
		מרה	BE REBELLIOUS	598b	
		שבת	SABBATH	992c	1 c
		חלל	POLLUTE	320b	2
20	14	יצא	CAUSE TO GO	424c	1 a
		מען	PURPOSE	775b	1 a
		עשה	DO	794b	1 4
		שם	NAME	1028c	3
20	15	בלת	NOT	116d	4 a
		גם	ALSO	169d	5
		דבש	HONEY	185b	
		זוב	FLOW	264d	2
		חלב	MILK	316c	A 4
		יד	HAND	389c	1 d
		נשא	LIFT	670b	1 b 1
		צבי	BEAUTY	840a	1 b
20	16	את	MARK OF THE AC-CUSATIVE	85c	3 a
		הלך	WALK	234d	2 3a 1e
		הלך	WALK	235a	2 3f 1b
		חלל	POLLUTE	320b	1 b
		חקה	SOMETHING PRE-SCRIBED	350a	2 d
		חקה	SOMETHING PRE-SCRIBED	350b	2 e
		מאס	REJECT	549d	1 b
		יען	ON ACCOUNT OF	774d	2 c
		חום	PITY	299b	A
20	17	כלה	COMPLETE	478d	2 a
		מן	FROM	583b	7 ba
		עשה	DO	794c	2 1g
		שחת	GO TO RUIN	1008a	1
20	18	הלך	WALK	234d	2 3a 2d
		חקה	SOMETHING PRE-SCRIBED	349c	7 d
		טמא	BE UNCLEAN	379d	
		שמר	KEEP	1037a	3 c
20	19	יהוה	YAHWEH	218d	2 1b
		יהוה	YAHWEH	219b	2 2d
		הלך	WALK	234d	2 3a 1e
		חקה	SOMETHING PRE-SCRIBED	350a	2 d
		חקה	SOMETHING PRE-SCRIBED	350b	2 e
20	20	אות	SIGN	17a	6
		יהוה	YAHWEH	218d	2 1b
		יהוה	YAHWEH	219a	2 2b b
		קדש	BE SET APART	873b	4 d
		שבת	SABBATH	992b	1 c
20	21	הלך	WALK	234d	2 3a 1e
		חיה	LIVE	311b	1 c
		חלל	POLLUTE	320b	1 b
		חקה	SOMETHING PRE-SCRIBED	350a	2 d
		חקה	SOMETHING PRE-SCRIBED	350b	2 e
20	22	חמה	RAGE	*405a	2 c
		כלה	FINISH	478c	1 e
		מרה	BE REBELLIOUS	598b	
		חלל	POLLUTE	320b	2
		יצא	CAUSE TO GO	424c	1 a
		מען	PURPOSE	775b	1 a
		עשה	DO	794b	1 4
20	23	שוב	TURN BACK	999a	1 c
		גם	ALSO	169d	5
		זרה	SCATTER	280a	1
		יד	HAND	389c	1 d
		ל	TO	510d	1 b
		נשא	LIFT	670b	1 b 1
20	24	פוץ	BE DISPERSED	807a	1 a
		חלל	POLLUTE	320b	1 b
		חקה	SOMETHING PRE-SCRIBED	350a	2 d

Ch v.	Heb	Eng	Page	Sec
	חקה	SOMETHING PRE-SCRIBED	350b	2 e
	מאם	REJECT	549c	1 a
	יען	ON ACCOUNT OF	774d	2 c
	מען	PURPOSE	775b	1 a
20 25	חיה	LIVE	311b	1 c
	חק	SOMETHING PRE-SCRIBED	349c	7 d
	טוב	PLEASANT	375a	0 b
	לא	NOT	519c	2 a
20 26	אשר	THAT	83b	8 ab
	יהוה	YAHWEH	219b	2 2b z
	טמא	BE UNCLEAN	379c	2
	מתנה	GIFT	682c	
	עבר	PASS OVER	718d	1 d
	עבר	PASS OVER	718d	1 d
	פטר	THAT WHICH SEPA-RATES	809d	
	רחם	WOMB	933b	1
	שמם	BE DESOLATED	1031b	1
20 27	גדף	BLASPHEME	154c	2
	זה	THIS	260c	1 a
	כן	SO	487a	3 d
	מעל	ACT TREACHER-OUSLY	591b	1 b
	עוד	STILL	729b	1 c
20 28	זבח	SACRIFICE	257c	12
	יד	HAND	389c	1 d
	כעס	ANGER	495b	2
	ניחח	SOOTHING	629c	
	נסך	POUR OUT	650d	
	נסך	DRINK-OFFERING	651a	1
	נשא	LIFT	670b	1 b 1
	עבות	LEAFY	721c	
	עץ	TREE	781c	1 a
	ראה	TO SEE	907d	6 d
	רוח	SCENT	926b	2
	רום	BE HIGH	926d	1 a
20 29	במה	HIGH PLACE	119d	3 e
	קרא	CALL	896c	2 d2
20 30	דרך	WAY	204a	6 d
	זנה	COMMIT FORNICA-TION	275d	3
20 31	טמא	BE UNCLEAN	379b	2
	כן	SO	487a	3 d
	שקוץ	DETESTED THING	1055a	
20 31	דרש	SEEK	205d	1
	ו	AND	252d	1 f
	חי	ALIVE	311d	1 a
	טמא	BE UNCLEAN	379b	2
	יום	DAY	401b	7 l
	ל	TO	514d	5 g
	נשא	LIFT	671b	2 e
	מתנה	GIFT	682c	
	עבר	PASS OVER	718d	1 d
20 32	אבן	STONE	6c	2
	ארץ	EARTH	76c	5
	גוי	NATION	156d	1 c
	עלה	GO UP	749a	7
	עץ	TREE	782a	2 c
	רוח	BREATH	925c	6
	שרת	SERVE	1058b	2 e
20 33	זרוע	ARM	284a	1 c
	חזק	STRONG	305c	1 b
	חי	ALIVE	311d	1 a
	חמה	RAGE	*405a	2 c
	פך	POUR OUT	1049d	2 a
20 34	זרוע	ARM	284a	1 c
	חזק	STRONG	305c	1 b
	חמה	RAGE	*405a	2 c
	יצא	CAUSE TO GO	424c	1 a
	פוץ	BE DISPERSED	807a	1
	פך	POUR OUT	1049d	2 a
20 35	פנה	FACE	815d	11 c
	שפט	JUDGE	1048a	1
20 36	כן	SO	486c	2 cd
	שפט	JUDGE	1048a	1
20 37	מסרת	BOND OF THE COV-ENANT	64b	
	ברית	COVENANT	137a	2 2k
	ברית	COVENANT	137b	3 2
	מספר	NUMBER	709a	1 b
	עבר	PASS OVER	719a	3 d
	שבט	ROD	987a	1 c
20 38	ברר	PURIFY	141a	1
	מגור	SOJOURNING PLACE	158c	
	יצא	CAUSE TO GO	424c	1 a
	מרד	REBEL	597c	2
	פשע	REBEL	833b	2
20 39	אדון	LORD	11c	4 a
	חלל	POLLUTE	320b	1 c
	מתנה	GIFT	682c	
	עבד	WORK	713b	4 b
20 40	דרש	SEEK	205c	5
	הר	MOUNTAIN	249d	1 a
	הר	MOUNTAIN	249d	1 a
	הר	MOUNTAIN	251a	2 b
	כל	ALL	*481d	1 da
	משאת	PORTION	673b	4 e
	קדש	APARTNESS	871d	2 c
	קדש	APARTNESS	872a	3 c
	ראשית	BEGINNING	912b	2
	מרום	HEIGHT	928d	1
	תרומה	OFFERING	929a	1
	רצה	BE PLEASED WITH	953b	2
20 41	ב	IN	89a	17 c
	יצא	CAUSE TO GO	424c	1 a
	ניחח	SOOTHING	629c	
	פוץ	BE DISPERSED	807a	1
	קדש	BE SET APART	873a	1
	ריח	SCENT	926b	2
	רצה	BE PLEASED WITH	953b	2
20 42	יד	HAND	389c	1 d
	נשא	LIFT	670b	1 b 1
20 43	דרך	WAY	203d	6 d
	זכר	REMEMBER	269d	11 c1
	טמא	BE UNCLEAN	379b	2
	עלילה	WANTONNESS	760b	2 c
	פנה	FACE	816d	2 3a
	קוט	FEEL A LOATHING	876c	
20 44	את	WITH	86b	1 db
	דרך	WAY	203d	6 d
	עלילה	WANTONNESS	760b	2 c
	עשה	DO	794b	12
	רע	EVIL	948c	0 d
	שחת	GO TO RUIN	1007d	
21 2	דרך	WAY	203b	3
	דרום	SOUTH	205a	
	תימן	SOUTH	412d	1 b
	יער	WOOD	420d	C
	יער	WOOD	420d	G
	נבא	PROPHESY	612b	1 b
	נגב	SOUTH-COUNTRY	616c	2
	נטף	DRIP	643a	2
	שדה	FIELD	961c	1 d
	שום	TO PLACE	963d	2 c
21 3	יבש	DRY	386d	1
	יער	WOOD	420d	G
	יער	WOOD	420d	C
	יצת	KINDLE	428c	
	כבה	BE QUENCHED	459c	
	להבה	FLAME	529b	1
	שלהבת	FLAME	529b	
	לח	FRESH	535a	1
	מן	FROM	582b	5 d3
	נגב	SOUTH-COUNTRY	616b	1
	נגב	SOUTH-COUNTRY	616b	2
	פנה	FACE	815d	1 1a
	צרב	SCORCH	863a	1
21 4	בער	BURN	129b	1
	בשר	FLESH	142d	6 c
	יהוה	YAHWEH	219b	2 2c
	כבה	BE QUENCHED	459c	
21 5	משל	PARABLE	605b	4
	משל	SPEAK IN PAR-ABLES	605c	
	אהה	ALAS	854c	
21 7	נבא	PROPHESY	612b	1 b
	נטף	DRIP	643a	2
	מקדש	SACRED PLACE	874b	4
21 8	אל	TO	40b	1
	חרב	SWORD	*352c	1 e
	חרב	SWORD	352c	1 c
	יצא	BRING OUT	425a	4 c
	כרת	CUT OFF	504c	2 c
	תער	RAZOR	789b	2
21 9	בשר	FLESH	142d	6 c
	כרת	CUT OFF	504c	2 c
	נגב	SOUTH-COUNTRY	616b	2
	תער	RAZOR	789b	2
21 10	בשר	FLESH	142d	6 c
	יהוה	YAHWEH	219b	2 2b d
	חרב	SWORD	352c	1 c
	יצא	BRING OUT	425a	4 c
	לב	HEART	525c	2 9b
	תער	RAZOR	789b	2
	שוב	TURN BACK	998a	7 a
	אח	ADDENDA ET COR-RIGENDA	1119d	
21 11	אנח	SIGN	58d	1
	ינון	GRIEF	*387b	
	מרירות	BITTERNESS	601b	
	מתנים	LOINS	608b	2 a
	שברון	BREAKING	991b	
21 12	אדון	LORD	11c	3 2b
	אל	TO	41a	B
	אנח	SIGN	58d	1
	ברך	KNEE	139c	
	חיה	COME TO PASS	*227d	2
	חיה	COME TO PASS	227d	2
	הלך	WALK	232b	13
	יד	HAND	389c	1 a
	כהה	GROW DIM	462c	
	כל	ALL	481b	1 a
	מה	HOW	554b	4 f
	מסס	MELT	588a	2
	רוח	BREATH	925b	3 f
	רפה	SINK	951d	2
	שמועה	REPORT	1035b	1
21 14	חדד	BE SHARP	292b	
	חרב	SWORD	352c	1 d
	מרט	POLISH	599a	2
	נבא	PROPHESY	612b	1 b
21 15	או	OR	15a	1
	ברק	LIGHTNING	140c	2
	חדד	BE SHARP	292b	
	מבח	SLAUGHTERING	370d	2
	מבח	SLAUGHTER	370d	2
	מאם	REJECT	549c	1 a
	מרט	POLISH	599a	
	מען	PURPOSE	775c	1 c
	עץ	TREE	782a	2 f
	שוש	REJOICE	965b	
21 16	הוא	HE, SHE, IT	216b	4 a
	הרג	KILL	247b	7
	הרג	KILL	247b	1 b
	חדד	BE SHARP	292b	
	חרב	SWORD	352c	1 d
	כף	HOLLOW OF THE HAND	496b	1 a
	מרט	POLISH	599a	2
	מרט	POLISH	599a	
	תפש	LAY HOLD OF	1074d	2
21 17	זעק	CRY	277c	2 d
	ילל	HOWL	410b	
	ירך	THIGH	438a	1 a
	מגר	CAST	550d	
	נשיא	PRINCE	672c	6 b
	ספק	SLAP	706c	1
21 18	בחן	TRY	103c	
	בחן	TESTING	103d	
	מאם	REJECT	549c	2
21 19	חדר	SURROUND	293c	
	כפל	BE DOUBLED	495c	
	כף	HOLLOW OF THE HAND	496c	1 d1
	נבא	PROPHESY	612b	1 b
	נכה	SMITE	645d	1 c
	שכל	BE BEREAVED	1013d	1
	שלישי	THIRD	1026b	
	חדר	ADDENDA ET COR-RIGENDA	1123a	
21 20	אבחה	SLAUGHTER	5b	
	אח	ALAS	25b	
	בלת	NOT	*116d	4 a
	ברק	LIGHTNING	140c	2
	מבח	SLAUGHTERING	370d	2
	כשל	STUMBLE	506a	
	מכשול	STUMBLING	506b	1
	מוג	MELT	556a	1
	מרט	POLISH	599a	2
	מען	PURPOSE	775c	1 c
	רבה	BECOME MANY	915d	1 e2
	שער	GATE	1044c	1 a
21 21	חדד	BE SHARP	292b	
	ימן	GO TO THE RIGHT	412b	
	יעד	BE SET	417a	
	פנה	FACE	816d	15
	שום	TO PLACE	964d	
	שמאל	TAKE THE LEFT	970a	1
	אחד	ADDENDA ET COR-RIGENDA	1119d	
21 22	כף	HOLLOW OF THE HAND	496c	1 d1
	נוח	REST	628c	A 1a
	נכה	SMITE	645d	1 c
21 24	ברא	CREATE	135c	2
	דרך	WAY	202d	1
	יד	SIGN	390c	4 a
	שום	TO PLACE	964c	5 b
21 25	את	MARK OF THE AC-CUSATIVE	85b	2 a
	בצר	MAKE INACCESSI-BLE	131a	
	דרך	WAY	202d	1
	עמון	AMMON	770a	
	רבה	RABBA	913d	1
	שום	TO PLACE	964c	5 b
21 26	אם	MOTHER	52a	4
	חץ	ARROW	346c	
	כבד	LIVER	458b	
	עמד	STAND	763d	1 a
	קלל	BE SILENT	886d	1
	קסם	PRACTICE OF DIVI-NATION	890c	1
	קסם	DIVINATION	890c	1
	ראה	TO SEE	908a	8 a1
	שאל	ASK	982a	2 b
	תרפים	IDOL	1076d	
21 27	בנה	BUILD	124c	1 ah
	דיק	BULWARK	189b	
	ימין	RIGHT HAND	411c	1 a
	כר	LAMB	503a	
	סללה	MOUND	700c	
	פה	MOUTH	805b	3
	פתח	OPEN	835b	
	קסם	DIVINATION	890c	1
	רום	BE HIGH	927c	1 b
	תרועה	SHOUT OF WAR	930a	1
	רצח	SHATTERING	954a	
	שום	TO PLACE	964a	3 d
	שום	TO PLACE	964b	4 b
	שער	GATE	1044c	1 a
	שפך	POUR OUT	1049c	1 a
21 28	זכר	REMEMBER	271a	3 b
	עון	INIQUITY	731a	1 b
	קסם	PRACTICE OF DIVI-NATION	890c	1
	שבע	SWEAR	989a	1
	שבוע	PERIOD OF SEVEN	989a	2
	שבועה	OATH	990a	2
	שוא	EMPTINESS	996b	2
	תפש	LAY HOLD OF	1075a	
21 29	זכר	REMEMBER	270c	1 b 2
	זכר	REMEMBER	271a	3 b
	חמאת	SIN	308c	1 b
	עון	INIQUITY	731a	1 b

Ch	v.	Heb	Eng	Page	Sec
		עלילה	WANTONNESS	760b	2 c
		פשע	TRANSGRESSION	833c	3 a
		ראה	TO SEE	908c	2 a
21	30	תפש	LAY HOLD OF	1075a	
		חלל	PROFANED	321a	
		יום	DAY	398d	2 h1
		נשיא	PRINCE	672b	6 a
		עון	INIQUITY	731c	3
		עת	TIME	773d	2 c
		קץ	END	893d	1
		רשע	WICKED	957c	3
21	31	גבה	BE HIGH	147a	
		גבה	EXALTED	147b	2
		עטרה	CROWN	742d	1
		מצנפת	TURBAN	857b	
		רום	BE HIGH	927c	2
		שפל	BECOME LOW	1050b	1
		שפל	LOW	1050c	2
21	32	ל	TO	513b	5 ba
		עוה	DISTORTION	730c	
21	33	אכל	EAT	38a	2
		ברק	LIGHTNING	140c	2
		חרב	SWORD	352a	1 c
		חרפה	REPROACH	357d	1
		טבח	SLAUGHTERING	370d	2
		כול	CONTAIN	465b	1
		מרט	POLISH	599a	1
		נבא	PROPHESY	612b	1 b
		עמון	AMMON	770a	
		פתח	OPEN	835b	2
		פתיחה	DRAWN SWORD	*836a	
21	34	חזה	SEE	302c	2
		חלל	PROFANED	321a	
		יום	DAY	398d	2 h1
		כזב	LIE	469c	2
		עון	INIQUITY	731c	3
		עת	TIME	773d	2 c
		צואר	NECK	848c	1
		קסם	DIVINATION	890c	2
		קסם	PRACTICE OF DIVI-NATION	890d	1
21	35	קץ	END	893d	1
		רשע	WICKED	957b	2
		שוא	EMPTINESS	996b	2
		ברא	CREATE	135c	2
		מכורה	ORIGIN	468d	
		תער	RAZOR	789b	2
		מקום	STANDING PLACE	880b	4
		שוב	TURN BACK	999a	1 b
		שפט	JUDGE	1047d	3 c1
21	36	אש	FIRE	77d	5
		בער	BE BRUTISH	129c	
		זעם	INDIGNATION	276d	
		זעם	INDIGNATION	277a	
		חרש	GRAVER	360d	2
		פוח	BREATHE	806b	2 b
		משחית	DESTRUCTION	1008c	
		שפך	POUR OUT	1049d	2 a
21	37	אכלה	FOOD	38b	3
		דם	BLOOD	196d	2 f
		זכר	REMEMBER	270d	2
22	2	דם	BLOOD	197a	2 h
		ה	INTERROG PART	210a	1 c
		ידע	KNOW	395a	
		עיר	CITY	746c	1 i
		שפט	JUDGE	1047c	2
22	3	דם	BLOOD	196c	2 b
		טמא	BE UNCLEAN	379a	2
		על	UPON	753d	2 1d
		תוך	MIDST	1063d	
22	4	ארץ	EARTH	76c	5
		אשם	OFFEND	79c	2
		דם	BLOOD	196c	2 b
		דם	BLOOD	196c	2 i
		חרפה	REPROACH	358a	3
		טמא	BE UNCLEAN	379a	2
		כן	SO	487b	3 f
		קלסה	MOCKING	887b	
		קרב	COME NEAR	898a	1 b
		שפך	POUR OUT	1049a	1 b
22	5	מהומה	TUMULT	223a	1
		טמא	UNCLEAN	379d	1
		קלס	MOCK	887b	
		קרב	NEAR	898c	2 b
		רב	MUCH	913b	1 d
		רחק	DISTANT	935b	1 a
		שם	NAME	1028a	2 b2
22	6	דם	BLOOD	196c	2 b
		זרוע	ARM	284a	2 a
		ל	TO	516c	2
		נשיא	PRINCE	672c	6 b
		מען	PURPOSE	775c	1 c
22	7	אם	MOTHER	51d	3
		גר	SOJOURNER	158b	2
		ינה	OPPRESS	413b	
		יתום	ORPHAN	450c	
		עשק	OPPRESSION	799a	1
		קלל	BE SILENT	886d	2
		תוך	MIDST	1063d	
22	8	בזה	DESPISE	102c	
		חלל	POLLUTE	320b	1 b
		קדש	APARTNESS	872a	3 c
22	9	אכל	EAT	37b	1
		דם	BLOOD	196c	2 b
		דם	BLOOD	196c	2 b

Ch	v.	Heb	Eng	Page	Sec
		זמה	PLAN	273c	2 c
		רכיל	SLANDER	940c	
		תוך	MIDST	1063d	
22	10	טמא	UNCLEAN	379d	2 a
		נדה	IMPURITY	622c	1
		ענה	BE BOWED DOWN	776b	2
22	11	אחות	SISTER	27d	1
		בת	DAUGHTER	123a	1 d
		זמה	PLAN	273c	2 c
		טמא	BE UNCLEAN	379c	1
		כלה	DAUGHTER-IN-LAW	483c	1
		ענה	BE BOWED DOWN	776b	2
		רע	FRIEND	946a	2
		תועבה	ABOMINATION	1073a	2 b
22	12	בצע	GAIN BY VIOLENCE	130c	
		דם	BLOOD	196c	2 b
		לקח	TAKE	543b	4 f
		נשך	INTEREST	675b	
		עשק	OPPRESSION	799a	1
		תרבית	INTEREST	916d	2
		רע	FRIEND	946a	2
		שחד	BRIBE	1005a	
22	13	בצע	UNJUST GAIN	130c	
		דם	BLOOD	196d	2 f
		כף	HOLLOW OF THE HAND	496c	1 d1
		נכה	SMITE	645d	1 c
		על	UPON	756d	27 a c
		עשה	DO	795a	27
		תוך	MIDST	1063d	
22	14	את	WITH	86b	1 db
		חזק	BE FIRM	304a	1 1a
		ל	TO	517a	6 a
		לב	HEART	524c	21
		עמד	STAND	764b	3 d
		עשה	DO	794b	12
22	15	זרה	SCATTER	280a	1
		טמאה	UNCLEANNESS	380a	3
		פוץ	BE DISPERSED	807a	1 a
		תמם	BE COMPLETE	1070c	4
22	16	חלל	POLLUTE	320b	2
22	18	בדיל	TIN	95d	2
		בדיל	IRON	137d	3
		כור	FURNACE	468b	
		כסף	SILVER	494a	1
		נחשת	COPPER	639a	3
		סיג	DROSS	691b	2
		עפרת	LEAD	780c	
22	19	כן	SO	486d	3 d
		כנס	GATHER	*488b	
		סיג	DROSS	691b	2
		קבץ	GATHER	867d	2
		בדיל	TIN	95d	2
22	20	ברזל	IRON	137d	3
		כור	FURNACE	468b	
		כן	SO	*486b	2 ad d
		כן	SO	486d	2 db
		כנס	GATHER	*488b	
		כסף	SILVER	494a	1
		כסף	SILVER	494a	1
		כסף	SILVER	*494a	9
		נוח	REST	628d	B 1
		נפח	BLOW	656a	
		נתך	POUR FORTH	677d	2
		עפרת	LEAD	780c	
		קבץ	GATHER	867d	2
		קבצה	A GATHERING	868b	
22	21	כנס	GATHER	488b	
		כסף	SILVER	*494a	9
		נפח	BLOW	656a	
		נתך	POUR FORTH	677d	2
		עברה	OVERFLOW	720c	3 b
22	22	יהוה	YAHWEH	219b	2 2b d
		חמה	RAGE	*405a	2 c
		כ	LIKE	454d	2 d
		כור	FURNACE	468b	
		כן	SO	486b	2 ad d
		כסף	SILVER	494a	1
		כסף	SILVER	*494c	9
		נתך	POUR FORTH	678a	
		התוך	A MELTING	678a	
22	24	גשם	BE RAINED UPON	177d	
		גשם	BE RAINED UPON	177d	
		זעם	INDIGNATION	277a	
		מהר	BE CLEAN	372c	
		לא	NOT	519b	1 bc
22	25	אכל	EAT	37c	2
		אלמנה	WIDOW	48b	
		ארי	LION	71d	
		חסן	WEALTH	340d	
		טרף	TEAR	382d	
		טרף	PREY	383c	1
		יקר	PRECIOUSNESS	430b	1 a
		נביא	PROPHET	612a	2
		נפש	SOUL	660c	4 c3
		קשר	CONSPIRACY	905c	1
		שאג	ROAR	980d	1
22	26	בדל	BE DIVIDED	95c	3
		חלל	POLLUTE	320b	1 b
		חלל	POLLUTE	320b	2
		חל	PROFANENESS	320d	
		חמם	TREAT VIOLENTLY	329b	2
		מהור	CLEAN	373a	1
		טמא	UNCLEAN	380a	2 d
		ידע	MAKE KNOWN	395b	

Ch	v.	Heb	Eng	Page	Sec
		תורה	INSTRUCTION	436a	1 e
		כהן	PRIEST	463d	4
		עין	EYE	744d	3 d
		עלם	CONCEAL	761a	
22	27	קרש	APARTNESS	872b	6
		שבת	SABBOTH	992c	1 c
		אבד	CAUSE TO PERISH	2a	1
		בצע	GAIN BY VIOLENCE	130b	
		בצע	UNJUST GAIN	130c	
		דם	BLOOD	196c	2 b
		זאב	WOLF	255d	
		טרף	TEAR	382d	
		טרף	PREY	383c	1
		נפש	SOUL	660c	4 c4
		שר	CHIEFTAIN	978b	2 b
22	28	חזה	SEE	302c	2
		מוח	OVER-SPREAD	376b	2
		כזב	LIE	469c	
		נביא	PROPHET	612a	2
		קסם	DIVINATION	890c	2
		קסם	PRACTICE OF DIVI-NATION	890d	2
		שוא	EMPTINESS	996b	2
		תפל	WHITEWASH	1074a	
22	29	אביון	NEEDY	2d	
		גר	SOJOURNER	158b	2
		גזל	TEAR AWAY	159d	
		גזל	ROBBERY	160a	
		ינה	OPPRESS	413b	
		לא	NOT	*520a	4 aa
		עני	POOR	776a	2
		עשק	OPPRESS	798d	1
		עשק	OPPRESS	798d	1
		עשק	OPPRESSION	799a	1
22	30	בעד	ON BEHALF OF	126d	2
		בקש	SEEK	134c	1 b
		גדר	BUILD A WALL	154d	
		גדר	WALL	155a	
		מצא	FIND	593a	1 b
		פרץ	BURSTING FORTH	829d	2
		שחת	GO TO RUIN	1008a	1
22	31	אש	FIRE	77d	5
		דרך	WAY	203a	6 d
		זעם	INDIGNATION	276d	
		זעם	INDIGNATION	277a	
		כלה	FINISH	478c	2 c2
		נתן	PUT	680d	2 b
		עברה	OVERFLOW	720c	3 b
23	2	אם	MOTHER	52a	2
		בת	DAUGHTER	123d	3
		נעורים	YOUTH	655c	
23	3	בתולים	VIRGINITY	144a	
		דד	BREAST	186d	
		דד	BREAST	186d	
		זנה	COMMIT FORNICA-TION	276a	3
		מעך	PRESS	590d	
		עשה	PRESS	796c	
		שד	BREAST	994c	1
		שם	THERE	1027c	3 c
23	4	אהליבה	OHOLIBA	14c	
		אחות	SISTER	28a	3
		עולם	LONG DURATION	762b	2 b4
		שמרון	SAMARIA	1037d	
23	5	אהב	LOVE	13b	2
		אשור	ASSHUR	78d	2
		זנה	COMMIT FORNICA-TION	275d	2
		עגב	LUST	721d	
		קרב	NEAR	898c	2 b
		תחת	UNDERNEATH	1065c	2 1c b
23	6	חמד	DESIRE	326c	
		לבש	PUT ON	528a	E
		סגן	PREFECT	688d	1
		פחה	GOVERNOR	808d	
		פרש	HORSEMAN	832b	
		רכב	RIDE	938d	3
		תכלת	VIOLET THREAD	1067b	2
23	7	אשור	ASSHUR	78d	2
		בן	SON	121b	1 jt
		זנות	FORNICATION	276b	
		טמא	BE UNCLEAN	379b	2
		עגב	LUST	721d	
23	8	בתולים	VIRGINITY	144a	
		דד	BREAST	186d	
		זנות	FORNICATION	276b	
		זנות	FORNICATION	276b	
		נעורים	YOUTH	655c	
		עזב	LEAVE	737c	2 d4
		עשה	PRESS	796c	
		שכב	LIE DOWN	1012b	3
		שפך	POUR OUT	1049d	2 b
23	9	אהב	LOVE	13b	2
		אשור	ASSHUR	78d	2
		בן	SON	121b	1 jt
		עגב	LUST	721d	
23	10	הרג	KILL	247b	1 b
		ערוה	NAKEDNESS	789a	1
		שם	NAME	1028a	2 b2
		שפוט	JUDGEMENT	1048b	
23	11	אהליבה	OHOLIBA	14c	
		אחות	SISTER	28a	3
		זנונים	FORNICATION	276a	C
		זנות	FORNICATION	276b	
		עגבה	LUSTFULNESS	721d	
		שחת	GO TO RUIN	1008b	2

Ch	v.	Heb	Eng	Page	Sec
23	12	אשור	ASSHUR	78d	2
		בן	SON	121b	1 jt
		חמד	DESIRE	326c	
		מכלל	PERFECTION	483b	
		לבש	PUT ON	528a	E
		סגן	PREFECT	688d	1
		עגב	LUST	721d	
		פחה	GOVERNOR	808d	
		פרש	HORSEMAN	832b	
		קרב	NEAR	898c	2 b
		רכב	RIDE	938d	3
23	13	דרך	WAY	203d	6 d
		טמא	BE UNCLEAN	379b	
		שנים	TWO	1041a	1 a
23	14	תזנות	FORNICATION	276b	
		חקה	CUT IN	348d	
		חקק	CUT IN	349a	2
		יסף	ADD	415b	1
		כשדים	CHALDEANS	505a	1 b
		צלם	IMAGE	853d	1
		קיר	WALL	885a	1 d
		ששר	VERMILION	1059a	
23	15	אזור	WAISTCLOTH	25b	
		בן	SON	121b	1 jt
		דמות	LIKENESS	198b	2
		חגור	GIRT	292a	
		טבול	TURBAN	371b	
		מולדת	CHALDEA	409d	1
		כשדים	LOINS	505b	2
		מתנים	LOINS	608a	1 a
		סרח	GO FREE	710b	2
		ראש	VENOM	912c	1
		שליש	OFFICER	1026d	
23	16	כשדים	CHALDEA	505b	2
		מלאך	MESSENGER	521c	1 a
		עגב	LUST	721d	
		מראה	VISION	909d	
23	17	בן	SON	121b	1 jt
		דוד	LOVE	187c	3
		תזנות	FORNICATION	276b	
		טמא	BE UNCLEAN	379a	1
		טמא	BE UNCLEAN	379c	1
		יקע	TORN AWAY	429c	
		משכב	ACT OF LYING	1012d	2 b
23	18	תזנות	FORNICATION	276b	
		יקע	TORN AWAY	429c	
		נפש	SOUL	661a	6 f
		נקע	BE ESTRANGED	668c	
		על	UPON	759a	4 2c
23	19	זכר	REMEMBER	269d	1 1 c2
		זנה	COMMIT FORNICA-TION	276a	3
		תזנות	FORNICATION	276b	
		נעורים	YOUTH	655c	
23	20	בשר	FLESH	142d	3
		זרמה	ISSUE	281b	
		חמור	HE-ASS	331c	5
		סוס	HORSE	692d	2
		עגב	LUST	721d	
		פלגש	CONCUBINE	811c	2
23	21	דד	BREAST	186d	
		דד	BREAST	186d	
		זמה	PLAN	273c	2 c
		נעורים	YOUTH	655c	
		עשה	PRESS	796c	
		פקד	ATTEND TO	823b	A 1c
		שד	BREAST	994c	1
23	22	אהב	LOVE	13b	2
		אהליבה	OHOLIBA	14c	
		בוא	COME	99c	2 a
		נפש	SOUL	661a	6 f
		סביב	ROUND ABOUT	687a	1 d
		עור	ROUSE ONESELF	735b	1
23	23	אשור	ASSHUR	78d	2
		את	WITH	85c	
		בן	SON	121b	1 jt
		בן	SON	121b	1 jt
		חמד	DESIRE	326c	
		כשדים	CHALDEANS	505a	1 b
		סגן	PREFECT	688d	1
		פחה	GOVERNOR	808d	
		פקוד	PEKOD	824c	
		קוע	KOA	880c	
		קרא	CALL	895c	3 c
		רכב	RIDE	938d	3
		שוע	SHOA	1003a	
		שליש	OFFICER	1026d	
23	24	מגן	SHIELD	171c	
		הצן	WEAPONS	246c	
		עם	PEOPLE	766c	1
		פנה	FACE	817c	2 4b g
		צנה	LARGE SHIELD	857a	
		רכב	CHARIOT	939a	1
		שום	TO PLACE	963b	1
		שפט	JUDGE	1047d	3 c1
23	25	אזן	EAR	23d	1
		אחרית	END	31b	D
		אכל	EAT	37d	2
		אף	NOSE	60a	1
		את	WITH	86b	1 db
		חמה	RAGE	404c	2 a
		עשה	DO	794b	12
		קנאה	ZEAL	888c	3 b
23	26	כלי	ARTICLE	479c	1
		תפארה	BEAUTY	802c	1
		פשט	STRIP OFF	833a	1
23	27	זכר	REMEMBER	269d	1 1 c2
		זמה	PLAN	273c	2 c
		זנות	FORNICATION	276b	B
		נשא	LIFT	670c	1 b 4
		שבת	CEASE	992a	4
23	28	נפש	SOUL	661a	6 f
23	29	את	WITH	86b	1 db
		זמה	PLAN	273c	2 c
		זנונים	FORNICATION	276a	C
		תזנות	FORNICATION	276b	
		יגע	TOIL	388c	2
		עירם	NAKEDNESS	736a	2
		עזב	LEAVE	737a	1 e
		ערוה	NAKEDNESS	789a	1
		עשה	DO	794b	12
		שנאה	HATING	971d	1
23	30	זנה	COMMIT FORNICA-TION	275d	2
		טמא	BE UNCLEAN	379b	
23	31	דרך	WAY	203d	6 d
		הלך	WALK	234d	2 3a 2a
		כוס	CUP	468a	
23	32	כול	CONTAIN	465b	1
		כוס	CUP	468a	
		לעג	MOCKING	541d	1 b
		עמק	DEEP	771b	1
		רחב	WIDE	932a	
		שתה	DRINK	1059c	1 e
23	33	יגון	GRIEF	387b	
		כוס	CUP	468a	
		מלא	FULL	570c	1
		שברון	BREAKING	991b	
		שברון	DRUNKENNESS	1016b	
		שמה	WASTE	1031c	1
		שמרון	SAMARIA	1037d	
23	34	גרם	BREAK BONES	175a	
		חרש	EARTHENWARE	360b	2
		מצה	DRAIN	594c	
		נתק	PULL	683d	2
		קהל	ASSEMBLY	874b	1 b
		שד	BREAST	994c	1
		שתה	DRINK	1059c	1 e
23	35	גו	BACK	156a	
		גם	ALSO	169c	4
		זמה	PLAN	273c	2 c
		תזנות	FORNICATION	276b	
		שלך	THROW	1021a	1 b
23	36	אהליבה	OHOLIBA	14c	
		שפט	JUDGE	1047c	2 b
23	37	אכלה	FOOD	38b	3
		דם	BLOOD	197b	21
		ילד	BEAR	408a	1 c
		נאף	COMMIT ADUL-TERY	610d	1 b
		נאף	COMMIT ADUL-TERY	610d	2
23	38	עבר	PASS OVER	718d	1 d
		חלל	POLLUTE	320b	1 b
		טמא	BE UNCLEAN	379c	2
		עוד	STILL	729b	1 c
23	39	חלל	POLLUTE	320b	1 b
		שחט	SLAUGHTER	1006b	3
23	40	אף	ALSO	65a	1
		אשר	PARTICLE OF RE-LATION	82a	2
		כחל	PAINT	471a	
		מלאך	MESSENGER	521c	1 a
		עדי	ORNAMENTS	725d	1
		עדה	ORNAMENT	725d	1 a
		עין	EYE	744c	1 p
		רחץ	WASH OFF	934c	2
		מרחק	DISTANT PLACE	935d	
23	41	דמה	ONE SILENCED	*199a	
		ישב	SIT	442b	1 a
		כבוד	GLORIOUS	458c	
		מטה	COUCH	642a	
		ערך	ARRANGE	789c	1 c
		קטרת	SMOKE	882d	3
		שלחן	TABLE	1020b	3
		שמן	OIL	1032c	2 k
23	42	אדם	MAN	9c	2
		בוא	COME	99c	B
		המון	CROWD	242d	3 c
		סבא	DRINK LARGELY	685a	
		סבא	DRUNKARDS	685a	
		סבאים	SABEANS	685b	
		עטרה	CROWN	742d	2
		תפארה	BEAUTY	802c	2 a
		צמיד	BRACELET	855b	
		קל	VOICE	877b	2 i
		שלו	QUIET	1017c	1
23	43	בלה	WORN OUT	115b	
		זנה	COMMIT FORNICA-TION	275d	2
		תזנות	FORNICATION	276b	
23	44	נאף	ADULTERY	610d	
		אהליבה	OHOLIBA	14c	
		אשה	WOMAN	61a	1
		אשה	WOMAN	61a	1
		בוא	COME	98a	1 e
		זמה	PLAN	273c	2 c
		זנה	COMMIT FORNICA-TION	275d	1
23	45	כן	SO	486b	2 ad d
		דם	BLOOD	196c	2 b
		נאף	COMMIT ADUL-TERY	610c	1 b
		צדיק	JUST	843a	1 b
		שפט	JUDGE	1047d	3 c2
		שפט	JUDGE	*1047d	3 c1
		משפט	JUDGMENT	1048c	1 e
23	46	בז	ROBBERY	103a	1
		זועה	A TREMBLING	266b	
		עלה	GO UP	749c	2 b
23	47	אבן	STONE	6b	1
		ברא	CREATE	135c	1
		הרג	KILL	247b	1 b
		רגם	TO STONE	920c	
23	48	זמה	PLAN	273c	2 c
		יסר	BE DISCIPLINED	416b	
		שבת	CEASE	992a	4
23	49	אדון	LORD	11c	2
		זמה	PLAN	273c	2 c
		חטא	SIN	308a	3
		נשא	LIFT	671a	2 b
		נתן	GIVE	679d	1 v
		על	UPON	756c	2 7 b
24	1	חדש	NEW MOON	*294d	2 b2
		חדש	NEW MOON	294d	2 b2
		עשור	A TEN	797c	1 b
		עשירי	TENTH	798a	1
24	2	סמך	LEAN	702a	1 b
		עצם	BONE	783a	3
		שם	NAME	1027d	1
24	3	בית	HOUSE	110a	5 dd
		יצק	POUR	427b	1
		מי	WATER	565c	1 a
		מרי	REBELLION	598b	
		משל	PARABLE	605b	4
		משל	USE A PROVERB	605c	
		סיר	POT	696c	1 a
		שפת	SET	1046a	1
24	4	טוב	PLEASANT	374b	3 d
		כתף	SHOULDER	509b	1 b
		מלא	FILL	570c	1
		נתח	PIECE OF A DI-VIDED CARCASS	677c	
		עצם	BONE	782d	2
		רתח	BOILING	*958c	
24	5	מבחר	CHOICEST	*104d	3
		בשל	BOIL	143a	
		גם	YEA	169c	3
		דור	BALL	*189c	3
		דור	HEAP UP	189c	
		עץ	TREE	782a	2 d
		עצם	BONE	782d	2
		עצם	BONE	783a	3
		צאן	SMALL CATTLE	838c	3
		רתח	BOIL	958b	
		רתח	BOILING	958c	
		נתח	ADDENDA ET COR-RIGENDA	1125c	
24	6	אוי	WOE	17a	
		גורל	LOT	174c	2 f
		דם	BLOOD	197a	2 h
		חלאה	RUST	316a	
		יצא	BRING OUT	425a	4 a
		ל	TO	516b	5 ja
		נפל	FALL	657a	1
		נתח	PIECE OF A DI-VIDED CARCASS	677c	
		סיר	POT	696c	1 a
		עיר	CITY	746c	1 i
		רתח	BOILING	*958c	
24	7	כסה	COVER	492a	6
		סלע	CRAG	701a	1
		עפר	DRY EARTH	779d	1 a
		צחיח	SHINING	850a	
		שפך	POUR OUT	1049c	1
24	8	דם	BLOOD	196d	2 f
		חמה	RAGE	*404d	2 c
		כסה	BE COVERED	491c	
		נקם	AVENGE	668a	1 a
		נקם	VENGEANCE	668b	1
		סלע	CRAG	701a	2
		עלה	GO UP	749d	5
		צחיח	SHINING	850a	
24	9	אוי	WOE	17a	
		גדל	BECOME GREAT	152c	1
		דור	BALL	*189c	3
		מדורה	PILE	190b	
		דם	BLOOD	197a	2 h
		עיר	CITY	746c	1 i
24	10	דלק	BURN	196b	
		חרר	BE HOT	359c	1
		עצם	BONE	783a	3
		רבה	BECOME MANY	915b	
		רקח	MIX OIL	955b	
		תמם	BE FINISHED	1070c	1
24	11	גחלת	COAL	161a	
		חלאה	RUST	316a	
		חמם	BE OR BECOME WARM	328c	1
		חרר	BE HOT	359b	1
		טמאה	UNCLEANNESS	380a	2
		נתך	POUR FORTH	677d	
		ריק	EMPTY	938a	1
		תמם	BE FINISHED	1070c	4
24	12	תאנים	TOIL	20b	
		חלאה	RUST	316a	
		לאה	EXHAUST	521c	

Ch	v.	Heb	Eng	Page	Sec
24	13	רב	MUCH	913b	1 c
		זמה	PLAN	273c	2 c
		זמה	PLAN	273c	2 c
		טהר	BE CLEAN	372b	3
		טהר	BE CLEAN	372c	1 c
		טמאה	UNCLEANNESS	380a	3
		טמאה	UNCLEANNESS	380a	3
		חמה	RAGE	*405a	2 c
		נוח	REST	628c	1 a
24	14	דרך	WAY	203c	6 a
		חום	PITY	299b	B
		נחם	BE SORRY	637a	2
		עלילה	WANTONNESS	760b	2 c
		פרע	LET GO	829a	2
		שפט	JUDGE	1047d	3 c1
24	16	בכה	WEEP	113b	1
		דמעה	TEARS	199d	
		מחמד	DESIRE	327a	
		יצא	GO OUT	423a	1 e
		מגפה	BLOW	620a	1
		ספד	WAIL	704d	
		עין	EYE	744c	2 b
24	17	אבל	MOURNING	5c	
		איש	MAN	35d	
		אנק	CRY	60c	
		דמם	BE SILENT	198d	1
		חבש	BIND	289d	1 a
		לחם	FOOD	537c	3 a
		נעל	SANDAL	653a	
		עטה	WRAP ONESELF	741d	
		פאר	HEAD-DRESS	802c	
		שום	TO PLACE	963a	1 a
		שפם	MOUSTACHE	974a	
		איש	ADDENDA ET COR-RIGENDA	1120a	
24	18	בקר	MORNING	134a	1 e
		צוה	CHARGE	846b	4 c
24	19	כי	THAT	472d	1 f
		ל	TO	513a	5 ad
		נגד	BE CONSPICUOUS	616d	1
24	20	דבר	WORD	182c	1 2a
24	21	גאון	EXALTATION	145a	1 a
		חלל	POLLUTE	320b	1 b
		מחמד	DESIRE	327a	
		מחמל	THING PITIED	328c	
		נפש	SOUL	661a	6 g
		עזב	LEAVE	737a	1 b
		עז	STRENGTH	739a	2 a
		עין	EYE	744c	2 b
24	22	איש	MAN	35d	
		לחם	FOOD	537c	3 a
		עטה	WRAP ONESELF	741d	
		שפם	MOUSTACHE	974a	
		איש	ADDENDA ET COR-RIGENDA	1120a	
24	23	בכה	WEEP	113b	1
		דמעה	TEARS	199d	
		מקק	PINE AWAY	596d	4
		נחם	GROAN	625b	2
		נעל	SANDAL	653a	
		ספד	WAIL	704d	
		עון	INIQUITY	731c	3
		פאר	HEAD-DRESS	802c	
24	24	אדון	LORD	11c	4 a
		מופת	SIGN	69a	2
		יחזקאל	EZEKIEL	306b	1
24	25	מחמד	DESIRE	327a	
		משא	LIFTING	672c	2
		מעוז	PLACE OF SAFETY	732a	1
		עין	EYE	744c	2 b
		תפארה	BEAUTY	802d	3 b
24	26	אזן	EAR	24a	2 a
		ה	THE	208b	1 g
		פליט	ESCAPED ONE	812c	
		השמעות	CAUSING TO HEAR	1036a	
24	27	אלם	BIND	47d	1
		מופת	SIGN	69a	2
		פליט	ESCAPED ONE	812c	
		פתח	OPEN	835c	
25	2	נבא	PROPHESY	612b	1 b
25	3	אדון	LORD	11c	4 c
		האח	AHA	210c	
		הלך	WALK	231b	1 d3 ge
		חלל	POLLUTE	320b	1
		יען	ON ACCOUNT OF	774d	1
		שמם	BE DESOLATED	1031a	1
25	4	בן	SON	121b	1 jl
		חלב	MILK	316b	A
		מורה	ENCAMPMENT	377b	1
		מורשה	POSSESSION	440c	
		ישב	SET	443c	
		כן	SO	486d	3 d
		פרי	FRUIT	826b	1
		קדם	FRONT	869c	1 b
		משכן	DWELLING-PLACE	1015d	3 a
		שתה	DRINK	1059b	1 a
25	5	נוח	ABODE OF FLOCKS	627c	1 a
		רבה	RABBA	913d	1
		מרבץ	PLACE OF WILD BEASTS	918c	
25	6	כף	HOLLOW OF THE HAND	*496c	1 d1
		מחא	CLAP	561d	
		יען	ON ACCOUNT OF	774d	1
		רקע	BEAT	956a	
		שמח	REJOICE	970b	1 b

Ch	v.	Heb	Eng	Page	Sec
25	7	שאט	DESPITE	1002b	1
		אבד	DESTROY	2b	1
		בג	SPOIL	93c	
		בז	SPOIL	103a	2
		כן	SO	486d	3 d
		כרת	CUT OFF	504c	2 c
25	8	בית	HOUSE	110a	5 dd
		גוי	NATION	156d	1 c
		יען	ON ACCOUNT OF	774d	1
		שעיר	SEIR	973a	1 c
25	9	ביתבעלמעון	BETH-BAAL-MEON	111a	
		ביתבעלמעון	BETH-BAAL-MEON	111a	
		ביתהשימות	BETH-JESHIMOTH	111d	
		מעון	BAAL-MEON	128a	
		כן	SO	486d	3 d
		כתף	SHOULDER	509b	1
		מן	FROM	583c	7 bb
		פתח	OPEN	835a	
		צבי	BEAUTY	840a	1 b
		קצה	END	892a	1
		קריתים	KIRIATHIAM	900b	1
25	10	בן	SON	121b	1 jl
		זכר	REMEMBER	270d	2
		מורשה	POSSESSION	440c	
		על	UPON	755b	24 b
		מען	PURPOSE	775c	2 cb
		קדם	FRONT	869c	1 b
25	11	עשה	DO	794a	1 1a 5
		שפט	JUDGEMENT	1048a	
25	12	אשם	OFFEND	79c	1
		נקם	AVENGE	668a	1 c
		נקם	AVENGE	668b	1
		נקם	VENGEANCE	668b	3
		יען	ON ACCOUNT OF	774d	1
		עשה	DO	794b	1 2
25	13	אדם	MAN	9b	2
		חרבה	WASTE	352b	2
		תימן	TEMAN	412d	1
		כרת	CUT OFF	504c	2 c
		מן	FROM	582b	5 d3
		ידע	KNOW	394a	1 e
25	14	נקמה	VENGEANCE	668c	1
		נקמה	VENGEANCE	668c	1
25	15	איבה	ENMITY	33c	
		נקם	AVENGE	668b	1 c
		נקם	VENGEANCE	668b	3
		נקמה	VENGEANCE	668c	3
		עולם	LONG DURATION	762b	2 b4
		עשה	DO	794a	1 1a 7
		שאט	DESPITE	1002b	
		משחית	DESTRUCTION	1008c	
25	16	אבד	DESTROY	2b	1
		חוף	SHORE	342b	1
		ים	SEA	411b	8 a
		כרת	CUT OFF	504c	2 c
		כרתי	CHERETHITE	504d	1
		שארית	REST	984c	1
25	17	חמה	RAGE	404d	2 c
		תוכחת	REBUKE	407b	3
		נקמה	VENGEANCE	668c	1
26	1	דמה	ONE SILENCED	*199a	
		חדש	NEW MOON	294d	2 b2
		עשתי	ONE	799d	
26	2	דלת	DOOR	195b	4
		האח	AHA	210c	
		חרב	BE WASTE	351d	
		מלא	BE FULL	570c	1
		סבב	TURN ABOUT	*685c	1 a
		סבב	TURN AROUND	686a	1 b
		צר	TYER	862d	
26	3	אל	TO	40b	4
		עלה	GO UP	749c	2 b
		צר	TYER	862d	
26	4	מגדל	TOWER	153d	1
		חרם	THROW DOWN	248d	1
		חומה	WALL	327c	1
		סחה	SCRAPE	695a	
		סלע	CRAG	701a	
		עפר	DRY EARTH	779d	1 e
		צר	TYER	862d	
26	5	שחת	GO TO RUIN	1008a	1
		בז	SPOIL	103a	2
		חרם	NET	357a	
		משטח	SPREADING-PLACE	1009a	
26	6	הרג	KILL	247c	2
		שדה	FIELD	961d	3
26	7	הצן	WEAPONS	*246c	
		מלך	KING	573b	5 a
		נבוכדראצר	NEBUCHADNEZ-ZAR	613a	
		פרש	HORSEMAN	832b	
		צפון	NORTH	861a	
		צר	TYER	862d	
26	8	דיק	BULWARK	189b	
		הרג	KILL	247b	1 b
		נתן	PUT	680b	2 a
		סללה	MOUND	700c	
		צנה	LARGE SHIELD	857a	
		קום	STAND	878d	1
		שדה	FIELD	961d	3
		שפך	POUR OUT	1049c	1 a
26	9	מגדל	TOWER	153d	1
		חומה	WALL	327b	1
		חרב	SWORD	353a	3
		מחי	STROKE	562c	
		נתץ	PULL DOWN	683b	1

Ch	v.	Heb	Eng	Page	Sec
26	10	קבל	SOMETHING IN FRONT	867b	1
		אבק	DUST	7c	
		מבוא	ENTERING	99d	2
		בקע	BREAK OPEN OR THROUGH	132b	
		כ	LIKE	454b	1 d
		כסה	COVER	492a	5
		פרש	HORSEMAN	832b	
		קול	VOICE	877b	2 d
		רעש	SHAKE	950b	
		רעש	SHAKE	950b	
		שער	GATE	1044c	1 a
		שפעה	ABUNDANCE	1051b	
26	11	הרג	KILL	247b	1 b
		ירד	GO DOWN	433b	1 k
		ל	TO	511c	1 ga
		מצבה	PILLAR	663b	1 c
		עז	STRENGTH	738d	1
		פרסה	HOOF	828b	2
		רגל	FOOT	919d	1 d
26	12	בז	SPOIL	102d	
		בית	HOUSE	108d	1 ad
		הרס	THROW DOWN	248c	1
		חיל	STRENGTH	299a	3
		חמדה	DESIRE	326d	1
		חומה	WALL	327c	1
		נתץ	PULL DOWN	683b	1
		עפר	DRY EARTH	779d	1 e
		עץ	TREE	781d	2 b
		רכלה	MERCHANDIS	940b	2
		שום	TO PLACE	963a	1 a
		שלל	SPOIL	1021d	
26	13	המון	SOUND	242c	1
		כנור	LYRE	490a	
		קול	VOICE	877a	2 a
		שיר	SONG	1010b	1
26	14	בנה	BUILD	125a	1 b
		חרם	NET	357a	
		סלע	CRAG	701a	
		צחיח	SHINING	850a	
		משטח	SPREADING-PLACE	1009a	
		אי	COAST	16a	
26	15	אנק	CRY	60b	
		הרג	KILL	247c	2
		הרג	SLAUGHTER	247c	
		חלל	PIERCED	319c	1
		מפלת	OVERTHROW	658c	2 b
		צר	TYER	862d	
		קול	VOICE	877b	2 h
		רעש	SHAKE	950b	
26	16	חרד	TREMBLE	353c	2
		חרדה	TREMBLING	353d	1
		ירד	GO DOWN	433a	1 f
		ישב	SIT	442c	1 a
		כסא	SEAT OF HONOR	490d	1 a
		לבש	PUT ON	528a	B
		מעיל	ROBE	591c	1
		נשיא	PRINCE	672c	6 d
		סור	TURN ASIDE	694b	1
		פשט	STRIP OFF	833a	1
		רגע	A MOMENT	921a	BG
		רקמה	VARIEGATED STUFF	955d	
26	17	שמם	BE DESOLATED	1031a	2
		אבד	PERISH	1d	1
		ה	THE	209b	3
		הלל	PRAISE	238d	1
		חזק	STRONG	305c	1 a
		חתת	TERROR	369d	
		ישב	BE INHABITED	443c	
		נשא	LIFT	670d	1 b 6
		עיר	CITY	746c	1 i
		קינה	ELEGY	884b	
		קינה	ELEGY	884b	
		אי	COAST	16a	
26	18	בהל	BE DISTURBED	96b	1
		חרד	TREMBLE	353d	1
		מן	OUT OF	580a	2 ec
		מפלת	OVERTHROW	658c	2 b
26	19	חרב	BE WASTE	351c	
		ישב	BE INHABITED	443c	
		כסה	COVER	491d	5
		תהום	SEA	1063a	1
26	20	בור	PIT	92c	5
		בור	PIT	92c	5
		חי	ALIVE	312a	1 b
		חרבה	WASTE	352b	2
		ירד	GO DOWN	433b	1 i
		ירד	BRING DOWN	434a	1 d
		ישב	SIT	443b	4
		ישב	CAUSE TO SIT	443d	3 a
		עולם	LONG DURATION	762a	1 b
		עולם	LONG DURATION	762d	1 a
		עם	PEOPLE	766d	4
		מען	PURPOSE	775c	2 cb
		צבי	HONOUR	840a	2
		שתק	BE QUIET	1060c	
		תחתי	LOWER	1066c	
26	21	בלהה	CALAMITY	117a	2
		מצא	FIND	594a	2 c
		עולם	LONG DURATION	762b	2 b1
27	2	נשא	LIFT	670d	1 b 6
		צר	TYER	862d	
		קינה	ELEGY	884b	
27	3	אי	COAST	16a	

Ch	v.	Heb	Eng	Page	Sec
		יפי	BEAUTY	421d	
		יפעה	SPLENDOUR	422b	
		עריץ	AWE-INSPIRING	792b	3
28	8	ריק	MAKE EMPTY	938a	3
		ירד	BRING DOWN	434a	1 d
		ל	TO	511c	1 ga
		לב	HEART	524b	1
		ממות	DEATH	560d	
		שחת	PIT	1001c	2
28	9	אדם	MAN	9b	2
		אל	GOD	42d	6 d
		אמר	SAY	56a	1
		הרג	KILL	247b	1 b
		חלל	BORE	319b	
28	10	זור	BE A STRANGER	266c	2 c
		ערל	HAVING FORESKIN	790c	
28	12	חכמה	WISDOM	315b	2
		חתם	SEAL	368a	2
		יפי	BEAUTY	421d	
		כליל	WHOLE	483a	1
		מלא	FULL	571a	
		נשא	LIFT	670d	1 b 6
		צידון	SIDON	*851a	
		צר	TYER	862d	
		קינה	ELEGY	884b	
		קינה	ELEGY	884b	
		תבנית	MEASUREMENT	1067c	
28	13	אדם	CARNELIAN	10b	
		אלהים	GOD	43d	2 c
		ברקת	EMERALD	140d	
		גן	GARDEN	171a	
		יהלם		240d	
		יקר	PRECIOUS	430a	1 c
		ישפה	JASPER	448c	
		כון	BE ESTABLISHED	467a	
		מלאכה	WORK	522b	5
		נפך	EMERALD	656c	
		נקב	JEWELLER:S WORK	666b	
		מסכה	COVERING	697b	
		ספיר	SAPRHIRE	705d	
		עדן	EDEN	727a	
		פטדה	TOPAZ	809c	
		שהם	CARNELIAN	996a	
		תף	TIMBREL	1074c	
		תרשיש	YELLOW JASPAR	1076d	
28	14	אבן	STONE	6d	3
		אלהים	GOD	43d	2 c
		את	THOU	61d	
		אש	FIRE	77d	6
		הלך	WALK	236a	1 b
		הר	MOUNTAIN	249d	1 a
		כרוב	CHERUB	501a	6 a
		ממשח	ANOINTED CHERUB	603d	
		סכך	OVERSHADOW	697a	1
		קדש	APARTNESS	871d	2 b
28	15	ברא	CREATE	135c	2
		דרך	WAY	203c	6 a
		מצא	FIND	394a	1 g1
		יום	DAY	400a	7 d1 e
		עד	UNTIL	725a	2 1b a
		עול	INJUSTICE	732c	
		עלה	INJUSTICE	732d	3
		תמים	SOUND	1071a	4
28	16	אבד	CAUSE TO PERISH	2a	1
		אבן	STONE	6d	3
		אלהים	GOD	43d	2 c .
		אש	FIRE	77d	6
		הר	MOUNTAIN	249d	1 a
		חטא	MISS A GOAL OR WAY	306d	2 b
		חלל	POLLUTE	320b	1 b
		חמס	VIOLENCE	329c	
		כרוב	CHERUB	501a	6 a
		מלא	FILL	570b	2
		מן	OUT OF	579a	2 aa
		סכך	OVERSHADOW	697a	1
		רכלה	TRAFFIC	940b	1
28	17	גבה	BE HIGH	147a	3 b
		חכמה	WISDOM	315b	2
		יפי	BEAUTY	421d	
		יפעה	SPLENDOUR	422b	
		לב	HEART	525b	2 6c
		על	UPON	753d	2 1f
		ראה	TO SEE	908a	8 a6
		שחת	GO TO RUIN	1008a	2
		שלך	THROW	1021b	2 b
28	18	אפר	ASHES	68a	
		חלל	POLLUTE	320b	1 b
		יצא	BRING OUT	425b	5
		עון	INIQUITY	731b	2 b
		עול	INJUSTICE	732c	
		מקדש	SACRED PLACE	874a	2
		רכלה	TRAFFIC	940b	1
28	19	בלהה	CALAMITY	117a	2
		עולם	LONG DURATION	762b	2 b1
		שמם	BE DESOLATED	1031a	2
28	21	נבא	PROPHESY	612b	1 b
		צידון	SIDON	851a	
28	22	אל	TO	40b	4
		כבד	BE HONORED	457c	2
		צידון	SIDON	851a	
		קדש	BE SET APART	873a	1
		שפט	JUDGEMENT	1048a	
28	23	דם	BLOOD	196d	2 f
		חוץ	THE OUTSIDE	300b	2 a

Ch	v.	Heb	Eng	Page	Sec
		נפל	FALL	658b	
		שלח	SEND	1019a	2 d
28	24	אדון	LORD	11c	4 a
		כאב	PAIN	456b	1
		מאר	PAIN	549d	2
		סביב	ROUND ABOUT	687b	2 ba b
		סלון	BRIER	699b	
		קוץ	THORN-BUSH	881a	2
		שוט	TREAT WITH DESPITE	1002b	
28	25	אדמה	LAND	10a	5
		עבד	SLAVE	714a	3
		פוץ	BE DISPERSED	807a	1
		קדש	BE SET APART	873a	1
28	26	בטה	SECURITY	105b	
		בנה	BUILD	124b	1 ab
		יהוה	YAHWEH	218d	2 1d
		יהוה	YAHWEH	219a	2 2b g
		נטע	PLANT	642c	1
		סביב	ROUND ABOUT	687b	2 bb
		שוט	TREAT WITH DESPITE	1002b	
		שפט	JUDGEMENT	1048a	
28	27	איל	RAM	18a	2 d
28	28	איל	RAM	18a	2 d
29	1	חדש	NEW MOON	294d	2 b2
		עשירי	TENTH	798a	1
29	2	כל	ALL	481d	1 da
		נבא	PROPHESY	612b	1 b
		פרעה	PHARAOH	829a	
		שום	TO PLACE	963d	2 c
29	3	אל	TO	40b	4
		יאר	STREAM	384c	2 a
		יאר	STREAM	384c	1
		ל	TO	513b	5 ba
		לחי	JAW	*534d	1
		פרעה	PHARAOH	829a	
		רבץ	LIE DOWN	918c	
		תנין	SEA-MONSTER	1072c	3
29	4	את	MARK OF THE ACCUSATIVE	85c	3 a
		דבק	CLING	179d	1 a
		דבק	CLING	180a	1
		דגה	FISH	185d	
		דוגה	FISHING	186a	
		חח	HOOK	296b	1
		יאר	STREAM	384c	2 a
		לחי	JAW	534d	1
		קשקשת	SCALE OF FISH	903d	
29	5	אכלה	FOOD	38b	2
		אסף	GATHER	62d	1 c
		דגה	FISH	185d	
		חיה	LIVING THING	312c	1 b
		יאר	STREAM	384c	2 a
		נטש	FORSAKE	643d	2
		קבץ	GATHER	867d	2
		קבץ	GATHER	868a	2
		קבר	BURY	868c	
		שדה	FIELD	961c	1 f
29	6	קנה	STALK	889c	2
		משענת	STAFF	1044a	
29	7	בקע	CLEAVE	131d	1
		כף	HOLLOW OF THE HAND	496c	1 d2
		כתף	SHOULDER	509b	1 a
		ל	TO	512d	5 aa
		מעד	SHAKE	588c	
		מתנים	LOINS	608b	2 a
		עמד	STAND	765a	
		רצץ	CRUSH	954d	
		שבר	BREAK	990d	
		שען	LEAN	1043d	
		תפש	LAY HOLD OF	1074d	1
29	8	אדם	MAN	9b	2
		איל	RAM	18a	2 d
		כרת	CUT OFF	504c	2
29	9	חרבה	WASTE	352a	1
		יאר	STREAM	384c	1
29	10	אל	TO	40b	4
		מגדל	MIGDOL	154b	
		חרב	DESOLATION	351d	
		חרבה	WASTE	352a	1
		חרבה	WASTE	*352a	1
		יאר	STREAM	384c	1
		כוש	CUSH	469a	2 a
		כוש	CUSH	*469a	2
		מצרים	EGYPT	595c	1 a
		סונה	SYENE	692b	
29	11	אדם	MAN	9b	2
		ישב	SIT	443b	4
29	12	זרה	SCATTER	280a	1
		חרב	BE WASTE	351d	
		פוץ	BE DISPERSED	807b	1 a
		שמם	BE DESOLATED	1031a	1
29	13	בן	SON	121c	7 b
		פוץ	BE DISPERSED	807a	1
		קבץ	GATHER	868a	1
		שבית	CAPTIVITY	986b	2 b
29	14	מכורה	ORIGIN	468d	
		ממלכה	KINGDOM	575b	1
		על	UPON	757a	2 7c a
		פתרוס	PATHROS	837d	
		שבית	CAPTIVITY	986b	2 b
		שוב	TURN BACK	998d	1
		שפל	LOW	1050c	2
29	15	ממלכה	KINGDOM	575b	1

Ch	v.	Heb	Eng	Page	Sec
		מעט	BE SMALL	589c	A
		נשא	LIFT	672a	
		רדה	HAVE DOMINION	922a	
		שפל	LOW	1050c	2
29	16	אדון	LORD	11c	4 a
		מבטח	CONFIDENCE	105c	2
		זכר	REMEMBER	271a	3 b
		נתה	LAMENT	*624c	
		עון	INIQUITY	731a	1 b
		פנה	TURN	815b	2 a
29	17	חדש	NEW MOON	294d	2 b2
		עשרים	TWENTY	798a	2 a
		ראשון	FIRST	911d	2 a
		שבע	SEVEN	988b	5 a1
29	18	כתף	SHOULDER	509b	1
		מרט	MAKE BARE	598a	1
		נבוכדראצר	NEBUCHADNEZZAR	613a	
		עבד	WORK	713a	1
		עבד	WORK	713c	1
		עבדה	LABOR	715b	3
		צר	TYER	862d	
		קרח	MAKE BALD	901a	
		שכר	HIRE	969a	1
29	19	בזז	SPOIL	102d	
		בז	SPOIL	103a	2
		המון	CROWD	242d	3 b
		נבוכדראצר	NEBUCHADNEZZAR	613a	
		שכר	HIRE	969a	1
		שלל	SPOIL	1021d	
29	20	עבד	WORK	713a	2
		עשה	DO	794a	1 1b
		פעלה	WORK	821d	2
29	21	פתחון	OPENING	836a	
		צמח	SPROUT	855c	1
		קרן	HORN	902a	2
30	2	הה	ALAS	214c	
		יום	DAY	401a	7 i
		ילל	HOWL	*410b	
		נבא	PROPHESY	612b	1 b
		רבע	SQUARED	917c	
30	3	יום	DAY	399a	3
		עת	TIME	773d	2 c
		ענן	CLOUD	778a	1 e
		קרב	NEAR	898d	3
30	4	המון	CROWD	242c	3 a
		חרם	THROW DOWN	248d	
		חלחלה	ANGUISH	298b	
		יסוד	FOUNDATION	414b	1
		כוש	CUSH	469a	2 c
		מצרים	EGYPT	595c	1 a
30	5	בן	SON	121b	1 jt
		ברית	COVENANT	136b	1 1
		כוש	CUSH	469a	2 c
		לוד	LUD	530d	2
		לובים	LUBIM	530d	
		ערב	MIXTURE	786b	
		ערב	STEPPE-DWELLERS	787b	
		פוט	LIBYANS	806c	
30	6	גאון	EXALTATION	145a	1 a
		מגדל	MIGDOL	154b	
		ירד	GO DOWN	433c	3 h
		מצרים	EGYPT	595d	1 a
		סונה	SYENE	692b	
		סמך	LEAN	702a	2
		עז	STRENGTH	739a	2
30	7	חרב	BE WASTE	351c	
		שמם	BE DESOLATED	1031a	1
		שמם	BE DESOLATED	1031a	2
30	8	עור	HELP	740c	
30	9	בטה	SECURITY	105b	
		חלחלה	ANGUISH	298b	
		חרד	TREMBLE	353c	
		יום	DAY	398d	2 g
		כוש	CUSH	469a	2 c
		מלאך	MESSENGER	521c	1 a
		מצרים	EGYPT	595c	1 a
		צי	SHIP	850d	
30	10	המון	CROWD	242d	3 b
		נבוכדראצר	NEBUCHADNEZZAR	613a	
30	11	בוא	COME	99d	B
		חלל	PIERCED	319c	2
		מלא	FILL	570b	2
		עריץ	AWE-INSPIRING	792b	2
		ריק	MAKE EMPTY	938a	3
		שחת	GO TO RUIN	1008a	1
30	12	זור	BE A STRANGER	266c	2 c
		חרבה	DRY GROUND	351c	
		יאר	STREAM	384c	2 a
		מכר	SELL	569b	
		מלא	THAT WHICH FILLS	571b	3
		רע	EVIL	948c	0 b
		שמם	BE DESOLATED	1031b	1
30	13	אבד	DESTROY	2b	1
		אליל	WORTHLESSNESS	47c	B
		יראה	FEAR	432a	1
		מף	MEMPHIS	592a	
		נשיא	PRINCE	672c	6 d
		שבת	CEASE	992a	2
		נא	THEBES	609d	
30	14	פתרוס	PATHROS	837d	
		צען	ZOAN	858a	
		שמם	BE DESOLATED	1031b	1
		שפט	JUDGEMENT	1048a	

Ch	v.	Heb	Eng	Page	Sec
30	15	המון	CROWD	242d	3 b
		חמה	RAGE	*405a	2 c
		כרת	CUT OFF	504c	2 c
		מף	MEMPHIS	592a	
		נא	THEBES	609d	
		סין	SIN	695d	
		מעוז	PLACE OF SAFETY	732a	1
30	16	בקע	BREAK OPEN OR THROUGH	132a	2
		חול	WHIRL	297a	2 b
		יומם	DAYTIME	401c	1
		ל	TO	518a	7 bf
		מף	MEMPHIS	592a	
		נא	THEBES	609d	
		סונה	SYENE	692b	
		סין	SIN	695d	
		צר	ADVERSARY	865d	
30	17	און	TROUBLE	20a	2
		אן	ON	58a	
		בחור	YOUNG MAN	104c	
		הלך	WALK	231b	1 d3 ge
		הם	THEY	241b	1 b
		פיבסת	PI-BESETH	809d	
		שבי	CAPTIVITY	985d	1
30	18	גאון	EXALTATION	145a	1 a
		הלך	WALK	231b	1 d3 ge
		חשך	WITHHOLD	362b	2
		חשך	GROW DARK	364d	1
		כסה	COVER	492a	5
		מוטה	BAR OF YOKE	557b	2
		מצרים	EGYPTIANS	595d	2 b
		עז	STRENGTH	739a	2 a
		ענן	CLOUD	778a	1 e
		שבי	CAPTIVITY	985d	1
		שבת	CEASE	991d	
		תחפנחס	TAHPANHES	1064d	
30	19	שפט	JUDGEMENT	1048a	
30	20	חדש	NEW MOON	294d	2 b2
		ראשון	FIRST	911d	2 a
		שבע	SEVEN	988a	1
30	21	זרוע	ARM	284a	1 b
		חבש	BIND	290a	
		חבש	BIND	290a	2
		חזק	BE FIRM	304a	1 1a
		חתל	BANDAGE	367c	
		פרעה	PHARAOH	829a	
		רפאה	REMEDY	951b	
		שום	TO PLACE	963c	1 d
		שבר	BREAK	990c	
		תפש	LAY HOLD OF	1074d	2
30	22	אל	TO	40b	4
		זרוע	ARM	284a	1 b
		חזק	STRONG	305c	1 b
		נפל	FALL	658a	1 f
		פרעה	PHARAOH	829a	
		שבר	BREAK	990c	
		שבר	BREAK	990d	
30	23	זרה	SCATTER	280a	1
		פוץ	BE DISPERSED	807b	1 a
30	24	זרוע	ARM	284a	1 b
		זרוע	ARM	284a	1 b
		חזק	BE FIRM	304c	1 b
		חזק	BE FIRM	*305a	3
		חלל	PIERCED	319c	1
		נאק	GROAN	611a	
		נאקה	GROANING	611a	
		שבר	BREAK	990c	
30	25	זרוע	ARM	284a	1 b
		זרוע	ARM	284a	1 b
		חזק	BE FIRM	*304c	1 b
		חזק	BE FIRM	305a	3
		נטה	EXTEND	640a	1 a
		נפל	FALL	657b	3 a
30	26	זרה	SCATTER	280a	1
		פוץ	BE DISPERSED	807b	1 a
31	1	חדש	NEW MOON	294d	2 b2
31	2	גדל	GREATNESS	152d	2 a
		דמה	BE LIKE	198a	
		המון	CROWD	242d	3 b
		פרעה	PHARAOH	829a	
31	3	ארז	CEDAR	72c	1 b
		אשור	ASSHUR	78d	2
		בין	INTERVAL	107b	1
		גבה	HIGH	147b	1
		חרש	WOOD	361c	
		יפה	BEAUTIFUL	421c	
		לבנון	LEBANON	527b	
		עבת	CORD	721d	2
		עב	DARK CLOUD	728a	1 b
		ענף	BRANCH	778c	
		צלל	BE DARK	853a	
		צמרת	TREE-TOP	856a	
		קומה	HEIGHT	879b	2
31	4	גדל	GROW UP	152b	1
		הלך	WALK	232b	1 3
		מטע	PLACE OF PLANTING	642d	1
		תעלה	WATER-COURSE	752b	A
		רום	BE HIGH	927a	1 b
		רוח	BE WIDE	927a	
		תהום	DEEP	1063a	4
31	5	ארך	BE LONG	73c	
		ארך	LENGTH	73d	C
		גבה	BE HIGH	147a	1
		כן	SO	487b	3 f
		מן	OUT OF	580a	2 eb
		סרעפה	BOUGH	704a	
		פארה	BOUGH	802d	
		קומה	HEIGHT	879b	2
		רבה	BECOME MANY	915b	1 c
		שלח	SEND	1019b	4
		שלח	SPROUT	1019c	2
		סרעפה	ADDENDA ET CORRIGENDA	1125c	
31	6	חיה	LIVING THING	312a	1 b
		ילד	BEAR	408b	1 a
		ישב	SIT	442c	1 a
		סתעפה	BOUGH	703d	
		פארה	BOUGH	802d	
		צל	SHADOW	853b	2
31	7	שלח	SPROUT	*1019c	2
		אל	TO	40d	8
		ארך	LENGTH	73d	C
		גדל	GREATNESS	152d	1
		דליות	BRANCH	195a	
		יפה	BE BEAUTIFUL	421b	
		שרש	ROOT	1057d	2
31	8	אלהים	GOD	43d	2 c
		ארז	CEDAR	72c	1 a
		ברוש	CYPRESS	141c	2
		גן	GARDEN	171a	
		דמה	BE LIKE	198a	
		יפי	BEAUTY	421d	
		סעפה	BOUGH	703d	
		עמם	DARKEN	770b	
		ערמון	PLANE-TREE	790d	
		פארה	BOUGH	802d	
31	9	אלהים	GOD	43d	2 c
		גן	GARDEN	171a	
		דליות	BRANCH	195a	
		יפה	BEAUTIFUL	421c	
		עדן	EDEN	727a	
		עץ	TREE	781c	1 a
		קנא	BE ZEALOUS	888c	1
31	10	אל	TO	40d	9
		בין	INTERVAL	107d	A
		גבה	BE HIGH	147a	1
		גבה	HEIGHT	147b	1
		לבב	HEART	524a	2 6c
		נתן	GIVE	680a	1 y
		עבת	CORD	721d	2
		עב	DARK CLOUD	728a	1 b
		על	UPON	758a	2 9
		צמרת	TREE-TOP	856a	
		קומה	HEIGHT	879b	2
		רום	BE HIGH	926d	2 b
31	11	איל	LEADER	18b	
		אל	GOD	42b	1
		גרן	AXE	*173d	
		גרש	DRIVE OUT	177a	
		עשה	DO	794b	1 4
		רשע	WICKEDNESS	957c	2
31	12	אפיק	CHANNEL	67d	2
		גיא	VALLEY	161b	
		דליות	BRANCH	195a	
		הר	MOUNTAIN	250b	1 e
		זור	BE A STRANGER	266c	2 c
		כרת	CUT OFF	503d	2
		נטש	FORSAKE	644a	2
		נפל	FALL	657a	1
		עריץ	AWE-INSPIRING	792b	
		פארה	BOUGH	802d	
		צל	SHADOW	853b	2
		שבר	BREAK	990d	
31	13	חיה	LIVING THING	312a	1 b
		מפלת	RUIN	658c	2 a
		פארה	BOUGH	802d	
		שכן	SETTLE DOWN	1015a	1 b
31	14	איל	LEADER	18b	
		איל	TEREBINTH	18b	
		אל	TO	40d	9
		אל	TO	40d	
		בור	PIT	92c	5
		בור	PIT	*92c	5
		בין	INTERVAL	107d	A
		גבה	BE HIGH	147a	1
		גבה	HEIGHT	147b	1
		נתן	GIVE	680a	1 y
		נתן	GIVE	681c	1 e
		עבת	CORD	721d	2
		עב	DARK CLOUD	728a	1 b
		על	UPON	758a	2 9
		מען	PURPOSE	775c	2 ca
		עץ	TREE	781c	1 a
		צמרת	TREE-TOP	856a	
		קומה	HEIGHT	879b	2
		שחת	DRINK	1059b	1 b
		תחתי	LOWER	1066c	
31	15	אבל	MOURN	5c	
		ירד	GO DOWN	433a	1 i
		כלא	BE RESTRAINED	476c	
		כסה	COVER	492a	
		לבנון	LEBANON	*527a	
		לבנון	LEBANON	527b	
		מנע	WITHHOLD	586a	
		עלף	COVER	763b	
		עלף	COVER	763b	
		קדר	BE DARK	871a	2
		שאול	SHEOL	983a	2 a
		תהום	DEEP	1063a	4
31	16	בור	PIT	92c	5
		בור	PIT	*92c	5
		מבחר	CHOICEST	104d	
		טוב	PLEASANT	374b	3 c
		ירד	BRING DOWN	434a	1 d
		לבנון	LEBANON	*527a	
		לבנון	LEBANON	527b	
		נחם	CONSOLE ONESELF	637a	3
		מפלת	OVERTHROW	658c	2 b
		עדן	EDEN	727a	
		עץ	TREE	781c	1 a
		קול	VOICE	877b	2 h
		רעש	SHAKE	950b	1
		שאול	SHEOL	983a	2 a
		שתה	DRINK	1059b	1 b
		תחתי	LOWER	1066c	
31	17	זרוע	ARM	284a	2 a
		חלל	PIERCED	319c	2
		חרב	SWORD	352d	1 h
		ירד	GO DOWN	433a	1 i
		ישב	SIT	442c	1 a
		צל	SHADOW	853b	2
		שאול	SHEOL	983a	2 a
31	18	גדל	GREATNESS	152d	2 a
		דמה	BE LIKE	198a	
		המון	CROWD	242d	3 b
		חלל	PIERCED	319c	2
		חרב	SWORD	352d	1 h
		ירד	BE BROUGHT DOWN	434b	2
		כבוד	HONOR	458d	2 b
		עדן	EDEN	727a	
		עץ	TREE	781c	1 a
		ערל	HAVING FORESKIN	790c	
		ערל	HAVING FORESKIN	790c	
		שכב	LIE DOWN	1012b	4 a
		תחתי	LOWER	1066c	
32	1	חדש	NEW MOON	*294d	2 b2
		חדש	NEW MOON	294d	2 b2
		שנים	TWO	1041b	2
		שנים	TWO	1041b	2
32	2	דלח	MAKE TURBID	*195c	
		דלח	MAKE TURBID	195c	
		דמה	CUT OFF	198c	2
		ים	SEA	411a	6
		כפיר	LION	498d	
		נשא	LIFT	670d	1 b 6
		קינה	ELEGY	884b	
		קינה	ELEGY	884b	
		רגל	FOOT	919d	1 d
		רפס	STAMP	952c	
		תנין	SEA-MONSTER	1072c	3
32	3	חרם	NET	357a	
		רשת	NET	440b	1 a1
		עלה	GO UP	749c	1 b2
		עם	PEOPLE	766c	1
		פרש	SPREAD OUT	831b	1
		קהל	ASSEMBLY	874c	1 b
32	4	חיה	LIVING THING	312c	1 b
		טול	HURL	376d	
		נטש	FORSAKE	643d	2
		פנה	FACE	819a	2 7b
		שבע	SATISFIED	959d	1 d
		שדה	FIELD	961c	1 f
		שכן	SETTLE DOWN	1015c	1 b
32	5	בשר	FLESH	142c	1 b
		גיא	VALLEY	161b	
		הר	MOUNTAIN	250b	1 e
		רמות	HEIGHT	928c	
32	6	אפק	CHANNEL	67d	
		דם	BLOOD	196c	2 a
		דם	BLOOD	197c	2 o
		מלא	FILL	570b	1
		מלא	FILL	*570b	1
		צף	OUT-FLOW	847a	3 g
		שקה	GIVE TO DRINK	1052c	1
32	7	ירח	MOON	437a	
		כוכב	STAR	456d	
		כוכב	STAR	457a	
		כבה	BE QUENCHED	459c	
		כבה	QUENCH	459d	
		כסה	COVER	491d	2
		כסה	COVER	491d	1
		ענן	CLOUD	778a	1 e
		קדר	BE DARK	871a	1
		שמש	SUN	1039b	1
32	8	אור	LIGHT	21c	3
		מאור	LUMINARY	22c	
		חשך	DARKNESS	365a	3 b
		קדר	BE DARK	871a	1
32	9	כעס	VEX	495a	1
		על	UPON	757a	2 7c a
		שבי	CAPTIVITY	985d	3
		שבר	BREAKING	991b	4
32	10	חרד	TREMBLE	353c	2
		מפלת	OVERTHROW	658c	2 b
		עוף	FLY	733c	1
		פנה	FACE	819a	2 7a e
		רגע	A MOMENT	*921b	BG
		שער	BRISTLE	972c	
		שער	HORROR	972c	
		שמם	BE DESOLATED	1031b	2 a
32	11	בוא	COME	98c	2 b
32	12	גאון	EXALTATION	144d	1 a
		גבור	STRONG	150b	2
		המון	CROWD	242d	3 b
		כל	ALL	481d	1 da
		נפל	FALL	658a	2

Ch v.	Heb	Eng	Page	Sec
	עריץ	AWE-INSPIRING	792b	
	שדד	DEAL VIOLENTLY WITH	994a	
32 13	שמד	BE EXTERMINATED	1029b	1
	אבד	DESTROY	2b	1
	אדם	MAN	9b	2
	דלח	MAKE TURBID	195c	
	דלח	MAKE TURBID	*195c	
	פרסה	HOOF	828b	1
32 14	הלך	WALK	237a	5 b
	שמן	OIL	1032b	2 e
	שקע	SINK	1054b	
	משקע	WHAT IS SETTLED	*1054b	
32 15	מלא	THAT WHICH FILLS	571b	3
	מן	FROM	583c	7 bb
	נכה	SMITE	646c	4 b
	שמם	BE DESOLATED	1031a	1
32 16	בת	DAUGHTER	123c	3
	המון	CROWD	242d	3 b
	קונן	CHANT	884b	
	קונן	CHANT	884b	
	קינה	ELEGY	884b	
32 17	חדש	NEW MOON	294d	2 b2
	שנים	TWO	1041b	2
32 18	אדיר	MAJESTIC	12b	1
	בור	PIT	92c	5
	בת	DAUGHTER	123c	3
	המון	CROWD	242d	3 b
	ירד	BRING DOWN	434a	1 d
	נהה	LAMENT	624c	
	תחתי	LOWER	1066c	
32 19	ירד	GO DOWN	433b	1 i
	מי	WHO	566b	B
	נעם	BE DELIGHTFUL	653c	
	ערל	HAVING FORESKIN	790c	
	שכב	LIE DOWN	1012c	
32 20	המון	CROWD	242d	3 b
	חלל	PIERCED	319c	2
	חרב	SWORD	352d	1 h
	משך	DRAW	604b	1
	נפל	FALL	657a	2 a
	נתן	GIVE	681c	1 e
32 21	אל	GOD	42b	1
	דבר	SPEAK	181b	3 c
	חלל	PIERCED	319c	2
	חרב	SWORD	352d	1 h
	ירד	GO DOWN	433b	1 i
	שאול	SHEOL	983a	2 a
	שכב	LIE DOWN	1012b	4 c
32 22	אשור	ASSHUR	78d	2
	ה	THE	209b	2
	חרב	SWORD	352d	1 h
	נפל	LIE	657d	7
	קבר	GRAVE	868d	
	שם	THERE	1027a	1 a
	שם	THERE	*1027c	3 c
32 23	בור	PIT	92c	5
	חי	ALIVE	312a	1 b
	חתית	TERROR	369d	
	ירכה	EXTREME PARTS	438b	2
	נפל	LIE	657d	7
	נתן	PUT	681d	2 b
	קבר	GRAVE	868d	
	צרה	GRAVE	869a	1
32 24	בור	PIT	92c	5
	ה	THE	209b	2 b
	המון	CROWD	242d	3 b
	חי	ALIVE	312a	1 b
	חתית	TERROR	369d	
	ירד	GO DOWN	433b	1 i
	כלמה	IGNOMINY	484b	2
	נפל	LIE	657d	7
	עילם	ELAM	743d	
	צרה	GRAVE	869a	1
	שם	THERE	1027a	1 a
	שם	THERE	*1027c	3 c
	תחתי	LOWER	1066c	
32 25	בור	PIT	92c	5
	המון	CROWD	242d	3 b
	חי	ALIVE	312a	1 b
	חלל	PIERCED	319c	2
	חרב	SWORD	352d	1 h
	חתית	TERROR	369d	
	כלמה	IGNOMINY	484b	2
	נתן	PUT	681d	2 b
	נתן	PUT	681d	2 b
	קבר	GRAVE	868d	
	משכב	COUCH	1012d	1
32 26	המון	CROWD	242d	3 b
	חי	ALIVE	312a	1 b
	חלל	BORE	319b	
	חתית	TERROR	369d	
	קבר	GRAVE	868d	
	שם	THERE	*1027c	3 c
	תובל	TUBAL	1063a	
32 27	חי	ALIVE	312a	1 b
	חתית	TERROR	369d	
	ירד	GO DOWN	433a	1 i
	כלי	IMPLEMENT	479d	2 a
	מלחמה	WAR	536c	1
	נפל	LIE	657d	7
	עון	INIQUITY	731c	3
	עולם	LONG DURATION	762a	1 a
	ערל	HAVING FORESKIN	790c	
	שאול	SHEOL	983a	2 a
	שכב	LIE DOWN	1012b	4 a

Ch v.	Heb	Eng	Page	Sec
32 28	חלל	PIERCED	319c	2
	חרב	SWORD	352d	1 h
	שכב	LIE DOWN	1012b	4 a
32 29	אדום	EDOM	10c	3
	בור	PIT	92c	5
	גבורה	MIGHT	150b	2
	חלל	PIERCED	319c	2
	חרב	SWORD	352d	1 h
	נשיא	PRINCE	672c	6 d
	נתן	PUT	681d	2 b
	שכב	LIE DOWN	1012b	4 a
	שם	THERE	1027c	3 c
32 30	בור	PIT	92c	5
	בוש	BE ASHAMED	101d	2
	גבורה	MIGHT	150b	2
	חלל	PIERCED	319c	2
	חרב	SWORD	352d	1 h
	חת	SHATTERED	369c	1
	חתית	TERROR	369d	
	ירד	GO DOWN	433b	1 i
	כל	ALL	481d	1 da
	כלמה	IGNOMINY	484b	2
	נסיך	PRINCE	651c	
	צידני	SIDONIANS	851a	
	צידני	SIDONIANS	851a	
	צפון	NORTH	861a	
	שכב	LIE DOWN	1012b	4 a
	שם	THERE	1027c	3 c
32 31	המון	CROWD	242d	3 b
	חיל	STRENGTH	299a	4
	חלל	PIERCED	319c	2
	חרב	SWORD	352d	1 h
	נחם	CONSOLE ONESELF	637a	3
32 32	המון	CROWD	242d	3 b
	חי	ALIVE	312a	1 b
	חלל	PIERCED	319c	2
	חרב	SWORD	352d	1 h
	חתית	TERROR	369d	
	שכב	LIE DOWN	1012c	
33 1	מות	DIE	560a	2 c
33 2	בוא	COME	99c	2 a
	בן	SON	121b	1 ji
	כי	IF	*473b	2 b
	עם	PEOPLE	766d	5 a
	צפה	KEEP WATCH	859c	
	קצה	END	892b	3
33 3	ו	AND	254b	2 db
	זהר	ADMONISH	264b	
	ראה	TO SEE	907a	2 3
33 4	דם	BLOOD	197a	2 i
	זהר	ADMONISH	264b	
	לקח	TAKE	543a	3 c
33 5	דם	BLOOD	197a	2 i
	זהר	ADMONISH	264b	
	זהר	ADMONISH	264b	
	מלט	SLIP AWAY	572c	3
	נפש	SOUL	660a	3 c
33 6	בחור	YOUNG MAN	104c	
	דם	BLOOD	197b	2 k
	דרש	SEEK	205c	5
	זהר	ADMONISH	264b	
	יד	HAND	391b	5 g3
	כי	IF	473b	2 b
	לקח	TAKE	543a	3 c
	לקח	TAKE	544a	2
	נפש	SOUL	660b	4 c2
	עון	INIQUITY	731b	2 b
	צפה	KEEP WATCH	859c	
	ראה	TO SEE	907a	2 3
33 7	זהר	ADMONISH	264b	
	מן	OUT OF	579d	2 d
	בקש	SEEK	135a	5 b
33 8	דבר	SPEAK	181d	6
	דם	BLOOD	197b	2 k
	דרך	WAY	203d	6 d
	הוא	HE, SHE, IT	215c	1 e
	זהר	ADMONISH	264b	
	יד	HAND	391b	5 g3
	מות	DIE	560a	2 b
	מות	DIE	560a	2 b
	נזר	SEPARATE	634b	
	עון	INIQUITY	731b	2 c
	רשע	WICKED	957c	3
33 9	דרך	WAY	203d	6 d
	זהר	ADMONISH	264b	
	כי	WHEN	473a	2 a
	מות	DIE	560a	2 b
	נזר	SEPARATE	634b	
	עון	INIQUITY	731b	2 c
33 10	חטאת	SIN	308c	1 b
	כן	SO	486a	1 ca
	מקק	PINE AWAY	596d	4
	על	UPON	753c	2 1b
	פשע	TRANSGRESSION	833d	4
33 11	דרך	WAY	203d	6 d
	דרך	WAY	203d	6 d
	חי	ALIVE	311d	1 a
	חפץ	DELIGHT IN	342d	2 a
	רע	EVIL	948c	0 d
33 12	בחור	YOUNG MAN	104c	
	בן	SON	121b	1 ji
	חטא	MISS A GOAL OR WAY	306d	2 b
	כשל	STUMBLE	505d	1 b
	עם	PEOPLE	766d	5 a
	פשע	TRANSGRESSION	833c	3 a

Ch v.	Heb	Eng	Page	Sec
	צדקה	RIGHTEOUSNESS	842b	5
	רשע	WICKEDNESS	957d	3
	רשעה	WICKEDNESS	958a	3
33 13	בטח	TRUST	105a	1 4c
	זכר	REMEMBER	270d	1 c 1
	מות	DIE	560a	2 b
	עול	INJUSTICE	732c	
	צדקה	RIGHTEOUSNESS	842c	7 b
33 14	חטאת	SIN	308d	1 c
	מות	DIE	560a	2 b
33 15	גזלה	PLUNDER	160a	
	הלך	WALK	234d	2 3a 1e
	חבל	PLEDGE	287a	
	חיים	LIFE	313b	2
	חקה	SOMETHING PRE-SCRIBED	350b	2 d
	חקה	SOMETHING PRE-SCRIBED	350b	2 e
	מות	DIE	560a	2 b
	עול	INJUSTICE	732c	
	שוב	TURN BACK	999a	1 d
33 16	זכר	REMEMBER	270d	1 c 2
	חטא	MISS A GOAL OR WAY	307b	2 b
	חטאת	SIN	308c	1 b
33 17	אדון	LORD	11c	3 2b
	בן	SON	121b	1 ji
	דרך	WAY	203c	6 a
	דרך	WAY	204a	6 eb
	תכן	MEASURE	1067b	2
33 18	מות	DIE	560a	2 b
	עול	INJUSTICE	732c	
	על	UPON	754b	2 1f b
	שוב	TURN BACK	997d	6 e
33 19	חיה	LIVE	311b	1 c
	נצל	DELIVER	665a	3 d
	על	UPON	753d	2 1e
	רשעה	WICKEDNESS	958a	3
33 20	אדון	LORD	11c	3 2b
	דרך	WAY	203c	6 a
	דרך	WAY	204a	6 a
	שפט	JUDGE	1047d	3 c1
	תכן	MEASURE	1067b	2
33 21	ה	THE	208b	1 g
	חדש	NEW MOON	294d	2 b2
	חמש	FIVE	332a	1 c
	נכה	SMITE	646d	5
	עשירי	TENTH	798a	1
	פליט	ESCAPED ONE	812c	
	שנים	TWO	1041b	2
33 22	אלם	BIND	47d	1
	בקר	MORNING	134a	1 e
	עד	AS FAR AS	724c	12a b
	פליט	ESCAPED ONE	812c	
	פתח	OPEN	835b	
	פתח	OPEN	835c	
33 23	בחור	YOUNG MAN	104c	
33 24	חרבה	WASTE	352b	2
	ירש	TAKE POSSESSION	439c	1 a
	מורשה	POSSESSION	440c	
	נתן	GIVE	681b	1 a
33 25	אכל	EAT	37b	1
	דם	BLOOD	196c	1
	דם	BLOOD	196c	1
	הר	MOUNTAIN	250d	11
	ו	AND	252d	1 f
	ירש	TAKE POSSESSION	439c	1 a
	כן	SO	487a	3 d
	נשא	LIFT	670c	1 b 4
	על	UPON	755c	2 4c
33 26	חרב	SWORD	352d	1 h
	טמא	BE UNCLEAN	379c	1
	ירש	TAKE POSSESSION	439c	1 a
	על	UPON	753d	2 1e
	עמד	STAND	764c	7 c
	רע	FRIEND	946b	3
	תועבה	ABOMINATION	1073a	2 b
33 27	חי	ALIVE	311d	1 a
	חיה	LIVING THING	312c	1 b
	חרבה	WASTE	352b	2
	מערה	CAVE	792c	
	מצד	FASTNESS	844d	1
	שדה	FIELD	961b	1 b
33 28	אין	NOT	35a	6 db
	גאון	EXALTATION	145a	1
	הר	MOUNTAIN	251a	2 b
	עבר	PASS OVER	717c	3 a
	עז	STRENGTH	739d	2 a
	שבת	CEASE	991d	
	שמם	BE DESOLATED	1030d	1
	משמה	DEVASTATION	1031d	1
33 29	משמה	DEVASTATION	1031d	1
33 30	אצל	BESIDE	69b	A
	את	WITH	86d	4 c
	בן	SON	121b	1 ji
	דבר	SPEAK	180d	
	דבר	SPEAK	181b	3 d
	יצא	GO OUT	423c	1 g
	קיר	WALL	885a	1 b
33 31	מבוא	ENTERING	99d	2
	בצע	UNJUST GAIN	130c	
	הלך	WALK	235a	2 3f 1b
	עגב	SENSUOUS LOVE	721d	
33 32	יטב	DO WELL	405d	3
	יפה	BEAUTIFUL	421c	
	נגן	PLAY	618d	

Ch v.	Heb	Eng	Page	Sec
	עגב	SENSUOUS LOVE	721d	
	קול	VOICE	876d	1 a
	שיר	SONG	1010b	1
33 33	נביא	PROPHET	611d	1
34 2	את	MARK OF THE AC-CUSATIVE	85a	1 a
	נבא	PROPHESY	612b	1 b
	נבא	PROPHESY	612b	1 b
	צאן	SMALL CATTLE	838c	3
	רעה	TEND	945a	1 c
	רעה	TEND	945a	1 c
	רעה	TEND	945a	1 d2
34 3	בריא	FAT	135d	
	זבח	SLAUGHTER FOR SACRIFICE	256d	1 1 ba
	זבה	SLAUGHTER FOR SACRIFICE	257a	1
	חלב	MILK	316b	A
	חלב	FAT	316d	2 a
	לבש	PUT ON	528a	A
	צאן	SMALL CATTLE	838c	3
	צמר	WOOL	856a	
	רעה	TEND	945a	1 c
34 4	אבד	BE LOST	1d	3
	בקש	SEEK	134c	1 b
	חבש	BIND	290a	2
	חזק	BE FIRM	304c	1 b
	חזקה	STRENGTH	306a	1
	חלה	BE WEAK	317d	1
	חלה	BE WEAK	318a	2
	נדח	BANISH	623a	2
	פרך	HARSHNESS	827d	
	רדה	HAVE DOMINION	922a	
	שבר	BREAK	990d	
	שוב	TURN BACK	999a	1 a
34 5	אכלה	FOOD	38b	2
	בלי	WEARING OUT	115d	C a
	חיה	LIVING THING	312d	1 b
	פוץ	BE DISPERSED	807a	
34 6	בקש	SEEK	134c	1 a
	גבעה	HILL	149a	3
	דרש	SEEK	205c	4 a
	הר	MOUNTAIN	250c	1 g
	פוץ	BE DISPERSED	807a	1
	רום	BE HIGH	926d	1
	שגה	GO ASTRAY	993a	1
34 8	אין	NOT	35a	6 da
	אכלה	FOOD	38b	2
	בז	SPOIL	103a	2
	דרש	SEEK	205c	4 a
	חי	ALIVE	311d	1 a
	חיה	LIVING THING	312d	1 b
	רעה	TEND	945a	1 c
	רעה	TEND	945a	1 c
34 10	אכלה	FOOD	38b	2
	אל	TO	40b	4
	דרש	SEEK	205c	4
	יד	HAND	391b	5 g3
	נצל	SNATCH AWAY	664d	1
	פה	MOUTH	805b	3
	רעה	TEND	945a	1 c
	רעה	TEND	945a	1 c
	שבת	CEASE	992a	3
34 11	בקר	SEEK	133a	
	דרש	SEEK	205c	4 a
	הנה	BEHOLD	244a	A
34 12	בקר	SEEK	133a	
	בקרה	A SEEKING	134c	
	כן	SO	486b	2 ad d
	עדר	FLOCK	727c	1 a
	ענן	CLOUD	778a	1 e
	ערפל	CLOUD	791d	
	פוץ	BE DISPERSED	807a	1
	פרש	SPREAD OUT	831b	
	פרש	MAKE DISTINCT	831c	
	צאן	SMALL CATTLE	838b	2
34 13	אדמה	LAND	10a	5
	אפיק	CHANNEL	67d	
	הר	MOUNTAIN	251a	2 b
	יצא	CAUSE TO GO	424c	1 a
	מושב	DWELLING	444b	2 a
	רעה	TEND	944d	1 b
34 14	הר	MOUNTAIN	251a	2 b
	טוב	PLEASANT	374b	3 b
	טוב	PLEASANT	374b	3 b
	נוה	ABODE OF FLOCKS	627c	1 a
	רבץ	LIE DOWN	918b	
	רבץ	LIE DOWN	918c	
	מרום	HEIGHT	928d	1
	רעה	TEND	944d	1
	רעה	TEND	945b	2 c
	מרעה	PASTURAGE	945c	
	רפא	HEAL	951a	2
	שמן	FAT	1032a	1
34 15	רבץ	LIE DOWN	918c	
	רעה	TEND	944d	1 b
34 16	בקש	SEEK	134c	1 b
	חבש	BIND	290a	2
	חזק	BE FIRM	304c	1 b
	חזק	STRONG	305d	2
	חלה	BE WEAK	317d	1
	נדח	BANISH	623a	2
	שבר	BREAK	990d	
	שוב	TURN BACK	999a	1 a
	שמד	BE EXTERMINATED	1029c	1
	שמן	ROBUST	1032a	2
34 17	משנה	SECOND	*1041d	3 a
	משפט	JUDGMENT	1048c	1 c
	איל	RAM	17d	1
	אתן	YOU	61d	
	עתוד	HE/GOAT	800d	
	שה	A SHEEP	962a	1
	שפט	JUDGE	1047c	2 a
34 18	טוב	PLEASANT	374b	3 b
	יתר	BE LEFT OVER	451c	
	יתר	REMAINDER	451a	1 a
	מן	THAN	582d	6 d
	מעט	A FEW	590b	1 ea
	רמס	TRAMPLE	942d	
	רעה	TEND	945b	2 c
	מרעה	PASTURAGE	945c	
	מרעה	PASTURAGE	945c	
	מרעה	PASTURAGE	945c	
	רפס	STAMP	952c	
	משקע	WHAT IS SETTLED	1054b	
	שתה	DRINK	1059c	1 d
34 19	מרמס	TRAMPLING-PLACE	942d	1
	רעה	TEND	945b	2 c
	מרפש	BEFOULED	952c	
	שתה	DRINK	1059c	1 d
34 20	בריא	FAT	135d	
	בריה	FOOD	136a	
	הנה	BEHOLD	244a	A
	רוח	LEAN	931a	
	שה	A SHEEP	962a	1
	שפט	JUDGE	1047c	2 a
34 21	הדף	THRUST	213d	1
	חוץ	THE OUTSIDE	299d	1 ba
	חלה	BE WEAK	318a	2
	כתף	SHOULDER	509b	1 b
	נגח	PUSH	618c	
	עד	UNTIL	724d	2 1a a
	יען	ON ACCOUNT OF	774d	2 c
	יען	ON ACCOUNT OF	774d	2 c
	פוץ	BE DISPERSED	807b	1 a
	צד	SIDE	841a	
	קרן	HORN	901d	1 a
	הלא	ADDENDA ET CORRIGENDA	*1122b	
34 22	בז	SPOIL	103a	2
	ישע	DELIVER	446d	1 b
	שה	A SHEEP	962a	1
	שפט	JUDGE	1047c	2 a
34 23	דוד	DAVID	188a	
	קום	STAND	879a	6 a
	רעה	TEND	945a	1 c
34 24	דוד	DAVID	188a	
	יהוה	YAHWEH	219b	2 2d
	נשיא	PRINCE	672c	6 c
34 25	בטח	SECURITY	105b	
	ברית	COVENANT	137a	3 1
	ברית	COVENANT	137a	2 2k
	ברית	COVENANT	137b	3 2
	חיה	LIVING THING	312c	1 b
	יער	WOOD	420d	B
	יער	WOOD	421a	G
	ישן	SLEEP	445c	
	כרת	CUT	504a	4
	רע	EVIL	948a	1
	שבת	CEASE	992a	2
	שלון	PEACE	1023a	5 b
34 26	ברכה	BLESSING	139d	2
	ברכה	BLESSING	139d	1 b
	גבעה	HILL	149a	4
	גשם	RAIN	177c	
	גשם	RAIN	177c	
	ירד	BRING DOWN	434a	1 b
34 27	אדמה	LAND	10a	5
	בטח	SECURITY	105b	
	יבול	PRODUCE	385b	
	מוטה	BAR OF YOKE	557b	2
	נתן	GIVE	679c	1 t
	עבד	WORK	713b	3
	על	YOKE	760d	
34 28	בז	SPOIL	103a	2
	בטח	SECURITY	105b	
	חיה	LIVING THING	312c	1 b
	חרד	TREMBLE	353c	
34 29	אסף	GATHER	62c	4
	כלמה	IGNOMINY	484b	1
	מטע	PLACE OF PLANTING	642d	1
	קום	STAND	879a	3
	רעב	FAMINE	944b	1
	שם	NAME	1028a	2 b1
34 30	יהוה	YAHWEH	218d	2 1d
	יהוה	YAHWEH	219a	2 2b g
34 31	אלהים	GOD	44d	4 c
	אתן	YOU	61d	
	צאן	SMALL CATTLE	838c	3
	מרעית	PASTURING	945c	1
35 1	קהל	ASSEMBLE AS	875a	2
35 2	נבא	PROPHESY	612b	1 b
	שום	TO PLACE	963d	2 c
35 3	אל	TO	40b	4
	שממה	DEVASTATION	1031d	1
35 4	חרבה	WASTE	352a	1
35 5	איד	DISTRESS	15d	1
	איבה	ENMITY	33c	
	יד	HAND	391c	5 h1
	נגר	POUR	620b	
	עון	INIQUITY	731c	3
	עולם	LONG DURATION	762b	2 b4
	עת	TIME	773d	2 c
35 6	קץ	END	893d	1
	דם	BLOOD	197b	2 k
	חי	ALIVE	311d	1 a
	כן	SO	486d	3 d
	עשה	DO	794d	2 3
	רדף	PURSUE	922d	1 g
	שנא	HATE	971c	1 b
35 7	כרת	CUT OFF	504c	2 c
	עבר	PASS OVER	717c	3 a
	שוב	TURN BACK	997a	2
	שממה	WASTE	1031c	
	משמה	DEVASTATION	1031d	1
35 8	אפיק	CHANNEL	67d	
	גבעה	HILL	149a	3
	גיא	VALLEY	161b	
	הר	MOUNTAIN	250b	1 e
	חרב	SWORD	352d	1 h
	נפל	FALL	657a	2 a
35 9	ישב	SIT	443b	4
	ישב	BE INHABITED	443c	
	ישב	BE INHABITED	443d	
	עולם	LONG DURATION	762b	2 b1
	שוב	TURN BACK	998a	7 b
35 10	את	MARK OF THE AC-CUSATIVE	85b	3 a
	גוי	NATION	156c	1 b
	ירש	TAKE POSSESSION	439c	1 b
35 11	חי	ALIVE	311d	1 a
	ידע	MAKE ONESELF KNOWN	394d	2
	כן	SO	486d	3 d
	מן	ON ACCOUNT OF	580b	2 f
	קנאה	ZEAL	888c	3 a
	שנאה	HATING	971d	1
	שפט	JUDGE	1047d	3 c1
35 12	אכלה	FOOD	38b	2
	יהוה	YAHWEH	219b	2 2b d
	הר	MOUNTAIN	251a	2 b
	נאצה	CONTEMPT	611a	
	נתן	GIVE	681c	1 e
	שמם	BE DESOLATED	1030d	1
35 13	גדל	BECOME GREAT	152c	3 b
	עתר	BE ABUNDANT	801d	
	פה	MOUTH	805a	2 a
35 15	אדום	EDOM	10c	3
	כל	ALL	481d	1 da
	כן	SO	486d	2 ad d
	ל	TO	510d	1 d
	שמחה	JOY	970d	1
	שלם	PEACE-OFFERING	1023c	
	שמם	BE DESOLATED	1030d	1
36 1	הר	MOUNTAIN	250b	1 c
	נבא	PROPHESY	612b	1 b
36 2	במה	HIGH PLACE	119a	1
	האח	AHA	210c	
	מורשה	POSSESSION	440c	
	על	UPON	756d	2 7a c
	עולם	LONG DURATION	761d	1 a
36 3	דבה	EVIL REPORT	179b	3
	מורשה	POSSESSION	440c	
	כן	SO	487a	3 d
	לשון	TONGUE	546c	1 b
	נבא	PROPHESY	612b	1 b
	עלה	GO UP	749a	1 b
	על	UPON	753a	2 1
	יען	ON ACCOUNT OF	775a	3
	שפה	SPEECH	973d	1 a3
	שאף	CRUSH	983d	
	שארית	REST	984c	1
	שמם	BE DESOLATED	1030d	1
36 4	אדון	LORD	11c	4 c
	אפיק	CHANNEL	67d	
	בז	SPOIL	103a	2
	גבעה	HILL	149a	3
	גיא	VALLEY	161b	
	הר	MOUNTAIN	250b	1 c
	הר	MOUNTAIN	250b	1 e
	חרבה	WASTE	352b	1
	לעג	MOCKING	541d	1 b
	עזב	LEAVE	737d	2
	שארית	REST	984c	1
	שמם	BE DESOLATED	1030d	1
36 5	אדום	EDOM	10c	3
	אש	FIRE	77d	5
	בז	SPOIL	103a	2
	גרש	CAST OUT	176c	
	דבר	SPEAK	181d	5
	מורשה	POSSESSION	440c	
	כל	ALL	481d	1 da
	לב	HEART	524a	2 9a
	מען	PURPOSE	775c	1 c
	קנאה	ZEAL	888c	3 b
	שמחה	JOY	970d	1
	שארית	REST	984c	1
	שאט	DESPITE	1002b	
	שמם	BE DESOLATED	1030d	1
36 6	אפיק	CHANNEL	67d	
	גבעה	HILL	149a	3
	גיא	VALLEY	161b	
	חמה	RAGE	404d	2 c
	כלמה	IGNOMINY	484b	1
	כן	SO	487a	3 d
	נבא	PROPHESY	612b	1 b
	נשא	LIFT	671b	2 d

Ch	v.	Heb	Eng	Page	Sec
		יען	ON ACCOUNT OF	774d	2 c
		קנאה	ZEAL	888c	3 b
36	7	הם	THEY	241c	2 a
		יד	HAND	389c	1 d
		כלמה	IGNOMINY	484b	2
		נשא	LIFT	670b	1 b 1
36	8	הר	MOUNTAIN	250b	1 b
		נשא	LIFT	671b	2 g
		נתן	GIVE	679c	1 t
		ענף	BRANCH	778c	
		קרב	COME NEAR	897d	2
36	9	אל	TO	40a	3 c
		אל	TO	40b	4
		זרע	SOW	281d	1 a
		ל	TO	517c	7 bb
		עבד	WORK	713c	1
		פנה	TURN	815c	2 c1
36	10	בנה	BUILD	125a	1 b
		חרבה	WASTE	352a	1
		ישב	SIT	*443b	4
		ישב	BE INHABITED	443c	
		כל	ALL	*481d	1 da
		רבה	BECOME MANY	915a	1 a
36	11	אדם	MAN	9b	2
		ישב	DO GOOD TO	405d	2
		ישב	CAUSE TO SIT	443d	3 a
		פרה	BEAR FRUIT	826a	1
		קדמה	ANTIQUITY	870b	2
		ראשה	EARLY TIME	911c	
		רבה	BECOME MANY	915a	1 a
		רבה	BECOME MANY	915a	1 b
		רבה	BECOME MANY	*915c	1 a
		רבה	BECOME MANY	915c	1 b
36	12	הלך	WALK	237a	5 a
		יסף	DO AGAIN	415c	2 a
		ירש	TAKE POSSESSION	439c	1 b
		שכל	BE BEREAVED	1013d	1
36	13	אתי	THOU	61c	
		גוי	NATION	156d	1 b
		יען	ON ACCOUNT OF	774d	1
		שכל	BE BEREAVED	1013d	1
36	14	גוי	NATION	156d	1 b
		כשל	STUMBLE	505d	
		שכל	BE BEREAVED	1013d	1
36	15	חרפה	REPROACH	357d	1
		כלמה	IGNOMINY	484b	2
		כשל	CAUSE TO STUMBLE	506a	1 b
36	17	שמע	HEAR	1034d	2 b
		דרך	WAY	203d	6 d
		טמא	BE UNCLEAN	379c	2
		טמאה	UNCLEANNESS	380a	4
		נדה	IMPURITY	622c	1
		עלילה	WANTONNESS	760b	2 c
36	18	דם	BLOOD	196c	2 b
		טמא	BE UNCLEAN	379c	2
		חמה	RAGE	*405a	2 c
		שפך	POUR OUT	1049c	1 b
36	19	דרך	WAY	203d	6 a
		זרה	SCATTER	279d	
		עלילה	WANTONNESS	760b	2 c
		פוץ	BE DISPERSED	807a	1 a
		שפט	JUDGE	1047d	3 c1
36	20	חלל	POLLUTE	320b	1 c
		שם	THERE	1027b	2
36	21	זכר	REMEMBER	269d	11 c1
		חלל	POLLUTE	320b	1 c
		חמל	SPARE	328b	
36	22	חלל	POLLUTE	320b	1 c
		כי אם	BUT	475a	2 b
		כן	SO	487a	3 d
		ל	TO	514a	5 g
		מען	PURPOSE	775b	1 a
		שם	THERE	1027b	2
36	23	גדול	GREAT	153b	6 c
		חלל	POLLUTE	320b	1 c
		חלל	POLLUTE	320c	
		קדש	BE SET APART	873a	1
		קדש	BE SET APART	873b	3 a
36	24	מן	OUT OF	579a	2 aa
36	25	זרק	TO TOSS	284c	1 c
		טהר	BE CLEAN	372b	3
		טהר	BE CLEAN	372c	1 c
		טהרו	CLEAN	373a	2
		טמאה	UNCLEANNESS	380a	3
		מי	WATER	565c	1 a
36	26	אבן	STONE	7a	8
		בשר	FLESH	142c	1 b
		חדש	NEW	294b	A
		לב	HEART	525b	26 d
		לב	HEART	525b	26 a
		קרב	INWARD PART	899b	2 a
		רוח	BREATH	925c	8
		רוח	BREATH	925c	8
36	27	הלך	WALK	234d	23 a 1e
		זה	THIS	260c	1 a
		חק	SOMETHING PRESCRIBED	349d	7 g
		קרב	INWARD PART	899b	2 a
		רוח	BREATH	925c	8
36	28	אנכי	I	59c	
		מקצע	SET IN CORNERS	893b	
36	29	דגן	CORN	186c	1
		טמאה	UNCLEANNESS	380a	3
		ישע	DELIVER	447a	2
		על	UPON	756c	27 a b
36	30	חרפה	REPROACH	358a	2 c
		על	UPON	753a	21 a b
		מען	PURPOSE	775c	2 ca
		עץ	TREE	781c	1 b
36	31	דרך	WAY	203d	6 d
		טוב	PLEASANT	374d	0 a
		עון	INIQUITY	731b	2
		מעלל	DEED	760b	1
		פנה	FACE	816d	23 a
		קוט	FEEL A LOATHING	876c	
		רע	EVIL	948c	0 d
36	32	בוש	BE ASHAMED	101d	2
		בוש	BE ASHAMED	101d	3
		דרך	WAY	203d	6 d
		ידע	BE MADE KNOWN	394c	1
		כלם	BE HUMILIATED	483d	2
		ל	TO	514a	5 e
36	33	בנה	BUILD	125a	1 b
		חרבה	WASTE	352a	1
		טהר	BE CLEAN	372c	1 c
		יום	DAY	399a	3
		ישב	CAUSE TO SIT	443d	3 b
		עון	INIQUITY	731a	1 c4
36	34	עבד	WORK	713c	1
		עבר	PASS OVER	717d	4 a
		שמם	BE DESOLATED	1031a	1
		תחת	INSTEAD	1066a	23 a a
36	35	בצר	MAKE INACCESSIBLE	131a	
		גן	GARDEN	171a	
		הלזה	THIS	229d	
		הרס	THROW DOWN	248d	
		חרב	WASTE	351d	2
		ישב	SIT	443b	4
		עדן	EDEN	727a	
		שמם	BE DESOLATED	1031a	1
		שמם	BE DESOLATED	1031a	1
36	36	בנה	BUILD	124d	1 i
		יהוה	YAHWEH	219b	2 2b d
		הרס	THROW DOWN	248d	
		נטע	PLANT	642c	2
		שמם	BE DESOLATED	1031a	1
36	37	דרש	SEEK	205d	1 c
		עוד	STILL	729b	1 c
		צאן	SMALL CATTLE	838b	2
36	38	מועד	APPOINTED TIME	417c	1 b
		מלא	FULL	571a	
		צאן	SMALL CATTLE	838b	2
		צאן	SMALL CATTLE	838c	3
		קדש	APARTNESS	872a	3 b
37	1	בקעה	PLAIN	132c	2
		יד	HAND	390a	1 e2
		יצא	CAUSE TO GO	424c	1 b
		מלא	FULL	571a	
		נוח	REST	628c	A 2
		עצם	BONE	782d	1 f
		רוח	BREATH	925d	9 a
37	2	בקעה	PLAIN	132c	2
		יבש	DRY	386d	2
		סביב	ROUND ABOUT	687a	1 b
		עבר	PASS OVER	718d	3 a
37	3	אדון	LORD	11c	4 a
		חיה	LIVE	311b	2 d
37	4	ה	THE	208d	1 i
		יבש	DRY	386d	2
		נבא	PROPHESY	612b	1 b
37	5	בוא	COME	99a	1
		הנה	BEHOLD	243d	
		חיה	LIVE	311b	2 d
		רוח	BREATH	924d	1 e
37	6	בשר	FLESH	142c	1 b
		חיה	LIVE	311b	2 d
		עור	SKIN	736a	1
		עלה	GO UP	749c	4
		על	UPON	757a	27 b
		קרם	SPREAD OVER	901c	
		רוח	BREATH	924d	1 e
37	7	חיה	BECOME	225d	21 a
		נבא	PROPHESY	612b	1 b
		צוה	CHARGE	846b	
		קול	VOICE	877b	2 g
		רעש	SHAKING	950c	1
37	8	בשר	FLESH	142c	1 b
		עור	SKIN	736a	1
		עלה	GO UP	748d	6
		מעל	ABOVE	752a	2 d
		קרם	SPREAD OVER	901c	
		רוח	BREATH	924d	1 e
37	9	הרג	KILL	247b	1 b
		חיה	LIVE	311b	2 d
		נבא	PROPHESY	612b	1 b
		נפח	BREATHE	656a	
		רוח	BREATH	924d	2 a
		רוח	BREATH	924d	1 e
37	10	אמה	CUBIT	52b	1
		בוא	COME	97d	1
		חיה	LIVE	311b	2 d
		מאד	EXCEEDINGLY	547c	2 d
		נבא	PROPHESY	612b	1 b
		על	UPON	752d	21
		עמד	STAND	764b	5 b
		רוח	BREATH	924d	1 e
37	11	אבד	PERISH	1d	1
		גזר	CUT	160c	2
		יבש	BE DRY	386c	1 e
		ל	TO	516a	5 ic
		תקוה	HOPE	876b	3
37	12	הנה	BEHOLD	243d	
		כן	SO	487a	3 d
		נבא	PROPHESY	612b	1 b
		עלה	GO UP	749b	1 b1
		פתח	OPEN	835a	
		קבר	GRAVE	868d	
37	13	עלה	GO UP	749b	1 b1
		פתח	OPEN	835a	
		קבר	GRAVE	868d	
37	14	חיה	LIVE	311b	2 d
		נאם	UTTERANCE	610b	2
		נוח	REST	628d	B 1
		רוח	BREATH	924d	1 e
37	16	אפרים	EPHRAIM	68c	4
		חבר	UNITED	288d	2 a
		יוסף	JOSEPH	415d	1 c
		כתב	WRITE	507c	1 b1
37	17	קרב	COME NEAR	897d	2
37	18	בן	SON	121b	1 ji
		ל	TO	513a	5 ad
37	19	אפרים	EPHRAIM	68c	4
		את	MARK OF THE AC-CUSATIVE	85c	3 b
		הנה	BEHOLD	243d	
		חבר	UNITED	288d	2 a
		יוסף	JOSEPH	415d	1 c
37	21	בין	INTERVAL	107d	D
		הלך	WALK	230b	1 1b
		הנה	BEHOLD	243d	
		סביב	ROUND ABOUT	687a	1 d
		קבץ	GATHER	868a	1
37	22	גוי	NATION	156c	1 b
		גוי	NATION	156d	1 b
		הר	MOUNTAIN	250b	1 c
		חצה	DIVIDE	345c	
		מלך	KING	573b	2
		ממלכה	KINGDOM	575b	1
37	23	חטא	MISS A GOAL OR WAY	307a	2 b
		טהר	BE CLEAN	372c	1 c
		טמא	BE UNCLEAN	379d	
		מושב	DWELLING	444c	5
		ישע	DELIVER	447a	2
		פשע	TRANSGRESSION	833d	4
		משובה	TURNING BACK	1000b	
		שקוץ	DETESTED THING	1055a	
37	24	דוד	DAVID	188a	
		הלך	WALK	234d	2 3a 1z
		חקה	SOMETHING PRE-SCRIBED	350a	2 d
		חקה	SOMETHING PRE-SCRIBED	350b	2 e
37	25	מלך	KING	573b	2
		אמה	CUBIT	52b	1
		בן	SON	120b	1 f
		דוד	DAVID	188a	
		נשיא	PRINCE	672c	6 c
		עבד	SLAVE	714a	3
		עולם	LONG DURATION	762d	2 f
37	26	את	WITH	85c	
		ברית	COVENANT	137a	3 1
		ברית	COVENANT	137a	2 2k
		ברית	COVENANT	137b	3 2
		ברית	COVENANT	137b	3 2
		כרת	CUT	504a	4
		עולם	LONG DURATION	762c	2 d
		מקדש	SACRED PLACE	874b	6
		שלון	PEACE	1023a	5 b
		תוך	MIDST	1063d	
37	27	חיה	BE	227a	3 3
		משכן	DWELLING-PLACE	1016a	3 b
37	28	יהוה	YAHWEH	219b	2 2b e
		עולם	LONG DURATION	762c	2 c
		קדש	BE SET APART	873b	4 d
		מקדש	SACRED PLACE	874b	6
		תוך	MIDST	1063d	
38	2	גוג	GOG	155d	2
		גוג	GOG	155d	2
		מגוג	MAGOG	156a	
		נבא	PROPHESY	612b	1 b
		נשיא	PRINCE	672c	6 c
		ראש	ROSH	912c	
		תובל	TUBAL	1063a	
38	3	אל	TO	40b	4
		גוג	GOG	155d	2
		נשיא	PRINCE	672c	6 d
		ראש	ROSH	912c	
		תובל	TUBAL	1063a	
38	4	מגן	SHIELD	171c	
		חח	HOOK	296b	1
		יצא	CAUSE TO GO	424c	1 b
		מכלל	PERFECTION	483b	
		לבש	PUT ON	528a	E
		לחי	JAW	534d	1
		סוס	HORSE	692c	1
		פרש	HORSEMAN	832b	
		צנה	LARGE SHIELD	857a	
		קהל	ASSEMBLY	874c	1 b
		שוב	TURN BACK	998c	3
		תפש	LAY HOLD OF	1074d	2
38	5	מגן	SHIELD	171c	
		כובע	HELMET	464d	
		כוש	CUSH	469a	2 b
		פוט	LIBYANS	806c	
		פרס	PERSIA	828a	

Ch v.	Heb	Eng	Page	Sec
38 6	אגף	BAND	8d	
	אגף	BAND	8d	
	גמר	GOMER	170a	1
	ירכה	EXTREME PARTS	438b	2
	צפון	NORTH	861a	
	צפון	NORTH	861a	
	תגרמה	TOGARMAH	1062b	
38 7	כון	BE READY	465d	3
	כון	ESTABLISH	466c	2 a
	קהל	ASSEMBLY	874c	1 b
	קהל	ASSEMBLE AS	874d	1 a
	משמר	GUARD	1038b	2
38 8	אחרית	END	31b	B
	בטח	SECURITY	105b	
	הר	MOUNTAIN	250b	1 c
	חרב	DESOLATION	351d	
	יום	DAY	401a	7 j
	יצא	BE BROUGHT FORTH	425c	
	תמיד	CONTINUITY	556b	1 a
	מן	FROM	581c	4 b
	פקד	ATTEND TO	823d	2
	קבץ	GATHER	868a	3
	שוב	TURN BACK	998c	
38 9	אגף	BAND	8d	
	כסה	COVER	492a	5
	ל	TO	514b	5 fb
	ענן	CLOUD	778a	1 c
	שואה	DEVASTATION	996c	1
38 10	חשב	THINK	363a	12
	מחשבה	THOUGHT	364c	2
	לבב	HEART	523d	2 3d
	עלה	GO UP	749a	7
	רע	EVIL	948b	8
38 11	אין	NOT	35a	6 aa
	בטח	SECURITY	105b	
	בריח	BAR	138b	2
	בריח	BAR	138b	1 b
	דלת	DOOR	195b	3
	פרזה	OPEN REGION	826d	
	שקט	BE QUIET	1053a	1
38 12	אסף	GATHER	63a	
	בזז	SPOIL	102d	
	בז	SPOIL	103a	2
	טבור	HIGHEST PART	371d	
	ישב	BE INHABITED	443c	
	עשה	DO	795a	2 7
	קנין	ACQUISITION	889a	1
	מקנה	CATTLE	889b	2
	שוב	TURN BACK	999a	1 a
	שלל	SPOIL	1021d	
38 13	בזז	SPOIL	102d	
	בז	SPOIL	103a	2
	דדן	DEDAN	187a	1
	זהב	GOLD	263c	1
	כפיר	LION	498d	
	סחר	GO AROUND	695c	2
	קהל	ASSEMBLE AS	875a	1 b
	קנין	ACQUISITION	889a	1
	מקנה	CATTLE	889b	2
	שבא	SHEBA	985b	
	שלל	SPOIL	1021d	
	תרשיש	TARSHISH	1077a	1
38 14	בטח	SECURITY	105b	
	גוג	GOG	155d	2
	כן	SO	487a	3 d
	נבא	PROPHESY	612b	1 b
38 15	ירכה	EXTREME PARTS	438b	2
	סוס	HORSE	692c	1
	צפון	NORTH	861a	
	צפון	NORTH	861a	
	קהל	ASSEMBLY	874c	1 b
	רכב	RIDE	938a	3
38 16	אחרית	END	31b	B
	גוג	GOG	155d	2
	כסה	COVER	492a	5
	ל	TO	513c	5 bb
	ל	TO	514b	5 fb
	ענן	CLOUD	778a	1 c
	קדש	BE SET APART	873a	1
38 17	דבר	SPEAK	181c	4 a
	הוא	HE, SHE, IT	*216b	4 ba
	ל	TO	513c	5 bb
	נביא	PROPHET	611d	1
	נבא	PROPHESY	612b	1 b
	עבד	SLAVE	714b	4
	קדמני	FORMER	870d	1
	שנה	YEAR	1040b	
	קדמה	FORMER TIME	1110c	1
38 18	אף	NOSE	60a	1
	גוג	GOG	155d	2
38 19	אש	FIRE	77d	5
	עברה	OVERFLOW	720c	3
	קנאה	ZEAL	888c	3 b
	רעש	SHAKING	950c	1
38 20	אדמה	GROUND	9d	4
	דג	FISH	185d	
	מדרגה	STEEP PLACE	201c	
	הרס	THROW DOWN	248d	
	הר	MOUNTAIN	250b	1 c
	חיה	LIVING THING	312c	1 b
	חומה	WALL	327c	1
	נפל	FALL	656d	1
	נפל	FALL	657a	1
	רמש	CREEPING THINGS	943a	1
	רמש	CREEP	943a	2 a
	רעש	SHAKE	950b	
38 21	אח	BROTHER	26b	4
38 22	חרדה	TREMBLING	353d	1
	אבן	STONE	6d	7
	אגף	BAND	8d	
	אלגביש	HAIL	38d	
	גפרית	BRIMSTONE	172d	
	גשם	RAIN	177c	
	דם	BLOOD	196d	2 f
	מטר	RAIN	565a	
	שטף	OVERFLOW	1009b	1
	שפט	JUDGE	1048a	1
38 23	גדל	BECOME GREAT	152c	
	ידע	MAKE ONESELF KNOWN	394d	2
	קדש	BE SET APART	873c	1
39 1	אל	TO	40b	4
	גוג	GOG	155d	2
	גוג	GOG	155d	2
	נבא	PROPHESY	612b	1 b
	נשיא	PRINCE	672c	6 d
	ראש	ROSH	912c	
	תובל	TUBAL	1063a	
39 2	הר	MOUNTAIN	250b	1 c
	ירכה	EXTREME PARTS	438b	2
	צפון	NORTH	861a	
	ששה	GIVE SIXTH PART OF	995d	
	שוב	TURN BACK	998c	3
	נשא	LEAD ON	1058c	
39 3	יד	HAND	389a	1 a
	יד	HAND	389a	1 a
	נכה	SMITE	645c	1 a
	נפל	FALL	658a	1 f
	קשת	BOW	906a	1 b
	שמאל	LEFT	969d	2
39 4	אגף	BAND	8d	
	אלה	FOOD	38b	2
	הר	MOUNTAIN	250b	1 c
	חיה	LIVING THING	312c	1 b
	כנף	WING	489c	1 a
	עיט	BIRD OF PREY	743c	
	צפור	BIRD	862a	1
	שדה	FIELD	961c	1 f
39 5	אי	COAST	16a	
39 6	בטח	SECURITY	105b	
	מגוג	MAGOG	156a	
	שלח	SEND	1019b	7
39 7	יהוה	YAHWEH	219a	2 2b e
	חלל	POLLUTE	320c	1
	ידע	MAKE KNOWN	395a	
	קדוש	HOLY	872c	1 b
	שם	NAME	1028c	3
39 8	היה	COME TO PASS	*227d	2
	היה	COME TO PASS	227d	2
	חץ	ARROW	346c	1
	יום	DAY	399a	3
39 9	בער	BURN	129b	1
	מגן	SHIELD	171c	
	חץ	ARROW	346c	1
	יד	HAND	389d	1 c
	מקל	STAFF	596c	1
	נשק	EQUIPMENT	676d	1
	צנה	LARGE SHIELD	857a	
	קשת	BOW	906a	1 b
	רבע	SQUARED	917c	
	רמח	SPEAR	942b	
	שלק	KINDLE	969c	
39 10	בז	SPOIL	102d	
	בער	BURN	129b	1
	חטב	CUT OR GATHER WOOD	310a	
	יער	WOOD	420c	A
	נשק	EQUIPMENT	676d	1
	שדה	FIELD	961c	1 d
	שלל	SPOIL	1021d	
39 11	גוג	GOG	155d	2
	גיא	VALLEY	161b	
	המון	CROWD	242a	3 a
	המון	CROWD	242a	3 a
	חסם	STOP UP	340c	
	יום	DAY	399a	3
	עבר	PASS OVER	717d	3 c
	קדמה	EAST	870b	2
	קרא	CALL	896a	6 b
	שם	THERE	1027b	1
39 12	חדש	NEW MOON	294c	2 a
	טהר	BE CLEAN	372b	1 a
39 13	יום	DAY	399a	3
	יום	DAY	400a	7 d1 a
	כבד	BE HONORED	457c	2
	שם	NAME	1028a	2 b1
39 14	בדל	BE DIVIDED	95b	2
	חדש	NEW MOON	294c	2 a
	חקר	SEARCH	350c	1
	טהר	BE CLEAN	372b	1 a
	יתר	BE LEFT OVER	451b	
	תמיד	CONTINUITY	556c	2 a
	עבר	PASS OVER	717d	3 c
	קבר	BURY	868d	
39 15	אצל	BESIDE	69b	A
	בנה	BUILD	124c	1 ak
	גוג	GOG	155d	2
	המון	CROWD	242a	3 a
	ו	AND	254b	2 db
	עבר	PASS OVER	717d	4 a
	עד	UNTIL	725a	2 1b a
	ציון	SIGN POST	846b	
	קבר	BURY	868c	
	קבר	BURY	868d	
39 16	המונה	HAMONAH	242d	
	טהר	BE CLEAN	372b	1 a
39 17	בשר	FLESH	142c	1 b
	דם	BLOOD	196c	2 c
	זבח	SLAUGHTER FOR SACRIFICE	257a	3
	זבח	SACRIFICE	258a	26
	חיה	LIVING THING	312d	1 b
	כנף	WING	489c	1 a
	צפור	BIRD	862a	2
	קבץ	GATHER	867d	1
	שתה	DRINK	1059c	1 f
39 18	איל	RAM	18a	2 g
	בשר	FLESH	142c	1 b
	בשן	BASHAN	143c	
	דם	BLOOD	196c	2 c
	זבח	SLAUGHTER FOR SACRIFICE	257a	3
	כר	LAMB	503a	
	מריא	FATLING	597b	
	נשיא	PRINCE	672c	6 d
	עתוד	HE/GOAT	800d	
	פר	YOUNG BULL	831a	2 f
	שתה	DRINK	1059c	1 f
39 19	דם	BLOOD	196c	2 c
	דם	BLOOD	197b	2 n
	זבח	SLAUGHTER FOR SACRIFICE	257a	3
	זבח	SACRIFICE	258a	26
	חלב	FAT	316d	2 a
	שבע	SATIETY	9600	1
	שכרון	DRUNKENNESS	1016c	
	שתה	DRINK	1059c	1 f
39 20	מלחמה	WAR	536b	
	שבע	SATISFIED	959b	1 b
	שלחן	TABLE	1020c	3
39 21	כבוד	HONOR	459b	6 b
	משפט	JUDGMENT	1048c	1 f
39 22	יהוה	YAHWEH	218d	2 1d
	יהוה	YAHWEH	219a	2 2b g
	הלאה	ONWARDS	229c	B
39 23	מן	FROM	581b	4 a
	מעל	ACT TREACHEROUSLY	591b	2 b
	סתר	HIDE	711d	2 c
	עון	INIQUITY	731c	3
39 24	את	WITH	86b	1 db
	טמאה	UNCLEANNESS	380a	3
	סתר	HIDE	711d	2 c
	פשע	TRANSGRESSION	833c	3
39 25	קנא	BE ZEALOUS	888c	3 b
	רחם	LOVE	933c	1
	שבית	CAPTIVITY	986b	2 a
	שוב	TURN BACK	999d	9
39 26	בטח	SECURITY	105b	
	חרד	TREMBLE	353c	
	כלמה	IGNOMINY	484b	2
	מעל	ACT TREACHEROUSLY	591b	1 b
39 27	קדש	BE SET APART	873a	1
	שוב	TURN BACK	998c	1
39 28	יהוה	YAHWEH	218d	2 1d
	יהוה	YAHWEH	219a	2 2b g
	יתר	LEAVE OVER	451c	1 a
39 29	סתר	HIDE	711d	2 c
	רוח	BREATH	926a	9 e
	שפך	POUR OUT	1049d	1
40 1	אחר	BESIDES	30a	3
	יד	HAND	390a	1 e2
	נכה	SMITE	646d	5
	עצם	BONE	783a	3
	עצם	BONE	783a	3
	עשור	A TEN	797c	1 b
	ארבע	FOUR	917a	2 a1 b
40 2	מבנה	STRUCTURE	125d	
	גבה	HIGH	147b	1
	הר	MOUNTAIN	250b	1 d
	נגב	SOUTH-COUNTRY	616b	2
	נוח	REST	628c	A 2
	מראה	VISION	909b	
40 3	יד	HAND	390a	5 c1
	מדה	MEASURE	551c	1
	פשת	FLAX	833d	1
	פתיל	CORD	836d	
	קנה	STALK	889d	4 a
	שער	GATE	1045b	3 c
40 4	בוא	COME	99d	B
	לב	HEART	524d	2 3c
	פתח	OPENING	836a	
	ראה	TO SEE	907c	6 c
	ראה	TO SEE	908d	1 a1
	ראה	TO SEE	908d	
	ראה	TO SEE	908d	
	שום	TO PLACE	963c	2 b
40 5	אמה	CUBIT	52b	1
	אמה	CUBIT	52b	1
	בנין	STRUCTURE	125c	A
	חומה	WALL	327d	2 b
	טפח	SPAN	381c	
	יד	HAND	390d	5 c1
	מדד	MEASURE	551a	1
	מדה	MEASURE	551c	1

Ch	v.	Heb	Eng	Page	Sec
		סביב	ROUND ABOUT	687a	1 b
		קומה	HEIGHT	879b	3
		קנה	STALK	889d	4 b
		קנה	STALK	889d	4 a
		רחב	WIDTH	931a	
40	6	דרך	WAY	203b	3
		מדד	MEASURE	551a	1
		סף	THRESHOLD	706c	
		עלה	GO UP	748c	1 f
		מעלה	STEP	752a	1
		פנה	FACE	816a	1 5
		קדים	EAST WIND	870c	2 b
		שער	GATE	1045b	3 c
40	7	אולם	PORCH	17d	3
		אמה	CUBIT	52b	1
		אצל	BESIDE	69b	B
		ארך	LENGTH	73d	A
		מן	FROM	578d	1 c
		מן	FROM	578d	1 c
		סף	THRESHOLD	706c	
		תא	CHAMBER	1060b	
40	8	אולם	PORCH	17d	3
		מדד	MEASURE	551a	1
		מן	FROM	578d	1 c
40	9	אולם	PORCH	17d	3
		איל	PILASTER	18b	
		אמה	CUBIT	52b	1
		אמה	CUBIT	52b	1
		מן	FROM	578d	1 c
40	10	איל	PILASTER	18b	
		דרך	WAY	203b	3
		מדה	SIZE	551c	2
		פה	HERE	806a	1 c
		קדים	EAST WIND	870c	2 a
		שלש	THREE	1025d	
		תא	CHAMBER	1060b	
40	11	אמה	CUBIT	52b	1
		ארך	LENGTH	73d	A
		פתח	OPENING	836a	
		רחב	WIDTH	932a	1
		שלש	THREE	1025d	2
40	12	אמה	CUBIT	52b	1
		גבל	BOUNDARY	148a	1 fa
		פה	HERE	806a	1 c
		תא	CHAMBER	1060b	
40	13	אמה	CUBIT	52b	1
		גג	ROOF	151a	1
		מן	FROM	582b	5 d2
		פתח	OPENING	835d	
		תא	CHAMBER	1060b	
40	14	איל	PILASTER	18b	
		חצר	ENCLOSURE	347a	3 c
		ששים	SIXTY	995d	
40	15	אולם	PORCH	17d	3
		איתון	ENTRANCE	87c	
		על	UPON	758a	2 9
40	16	איל	PILASTER	18b	
		אולם	PORCH	19b	
		אטם	SHUT	32a	
		חלון	WINDOW	319d	
		חלון	WINDOW	319d	
		כן	SO	485d	1 a
		ל	TO	511d	2
		פנימה	WITHIN	819b	2
		תא	CHAMBER	1060b	
		תמרה	PALM-FIGURE	1071d	
40	17	חצון	OUTER	300b	1
		לשכה	ROOM	545d	1 c
		רצפה	PAVEMENT	954b	
		שלשים	THIRTY	1026c	1
40	18	אל	TO	40d	8
		ארך	LENGTH	73d	A
		כתף	SIDE	509c	2 b
		עמה	CLOSE BY	769d	B
		רצפה	PAVEMENT	954b	
		תחתון	LOWER	1066b	
40	19	חוץ	THE OUTSIDE	299d	1 bd
		חצר	ENCLOSURE	347a	3 c
		מאה	HUNDRED	547d	1 a1
		קדים	EAST WIND	870c	2 c
		תחתון	LOWER	1066b	
40	20	דרך	WAY	203b	3
		חצון	OUTER	300b	1
		מדד	MEASURE	551a	1
		פנה	FACE	816b	1 5
		צפון	NORTH	861a	1
		שבע	SEVEN	988a	1 a
40	21	אולם	PORCH	19b	
		אמה	CUBIT	52c	1
		חמש	FIVE	332a	5 a3
		מדה	SIZE	551c	2
		עשרים	TWENTY	797d	1 2a
		פה	HERE	806a	1 c
		תא	CHAMBER	1060b	
40	22	אולם	PORCH	19a	
		דרך	WAY	203b	3
		חלון	WINDOW	319d	
		מדה	SIZE	551c	2
		עלה	GO UP	748c	1 f
		פנה	FACE	816b	1 5
		תמרה	PALM-FIGURE	1071d	
40	23	ל	TO	511d	1 h
		מן	FROM	582a	5 d1
		צפון	NORTH	861a	1
		קדים	EAST WIND	870c	2 a
40	24	דרך	WAY	203b	3

Ch	v.	Heb	Eng	Page	Sec
		דרום	SOUTH	205a	
		הלך	WALK	236d	1 c
		מדה	SIZE	551c	2
40	25	אמה	CUBIT	52b	1
		חלון	WINDOW	319d	
40	26	בן	SON	121b	1 jh
		עלה	ASCENT	751a	
		שבע	SEVEN	988a	1 a
		תמרה	PALM-FIGURE	1071d	
40	27	אמה	CUBIT	52b	1
		דרום	SOUTH	*204d	
		דרום	SOUTH	205a	
		דרום	SOUTH	205a	
40	28	מן	FROM	582a	5 d1
		דרום	SOUTH	*204d	
		דרום	SOUTH	205a	
		ה	THE	209a	2 b
		מדה	SIZE	551c	2
40	29	איל	PILASTER	18b	
		אמה	CUBIT	52b	1
		חלון	WINDOW	319d	
		מדה	SIZE	551c	2
		תא	CHAMBER	1060b	
40	30	אולם	PORCH	19b	
		אמה	CUBIT	52b	1
40	31	חיצון	OUTER	300b	1
		מעלה	ASCENT	751c	2
		שמנה	EIGHT	1033a	1 a
40	32	חצר	ENCLOSURE	347a	3 c
		מדה	SIZE	551c	2
40	33	אמה	CUBIT	52b	1
		חלון	WINDOW	319d	
		מדה	SIZE	551c	2
		תא	CHAMBER	1060b	
40	34	חיצון	OUTER	300b	1
		מעלה	ASCENT	751c	2
40	35	מדד	MEASURE	551a	
		מדה	SIZE	551c	2
40	36	צפון	NORTH	861a	
		אמה	CUBIT	52b	1
		חלון	WINDOW	319d	
		תא	CHAMBER	1060b	
40	37	אלם	PORCH	19a	
		חיצון	OUTER	300b	1
		מעלה	ASCENT	751c	2
40	38	איל	PILASTER	18b	
		דוח	RINSE	188d	1
		לשכה	ROOM	545d	1 c
		עלה	WHOLE BURNT OFFERING	750d	
40	39	אולם	PORCH	17d	3
		אשם	OFFENCE	79d	4
		חטאת	SIN	309b	4
		חטאת	SIN	310a	4 c
		עלה	WHOLE BURNT OFFERING	750d	
		שחט	SLAUGHTER	1006b	2
		שלחן	TABLE	1020b	3
40	40	אולם	PORCH	17d	3
		חוץ	THE OUTSIDE	300a	1 be
		כתף	SIDE	509c	2 b
		כתף	SIDE	509c	2 b
40	41	שחט	SLAUGHTER	1006a	
40	42	אבן	STONE	6c	2
		אמה	CUBIT	52b	1
		גבה	HEIGHT	147b	1
		גזית	HEWING	159b	
		זבח	SACRIFICE	257c	1 1
		זבח	SACRIFICE	258a	2 7
		כלי	IMPLEMENT	479d	2 a
		נוח	REST	628d	B 1
		עלה	WHOLE BURNT OFFERING	750d	
		רחב	WIDTH	931d	
		שחט	SLAUGHTER	1006b	2
		שלחן	TABLE	1020b	3
40	43	שפח	SPAN	381c	
		כן	BE ESTABLISHED	466d	1
		שפתים	HOOKS	1052a	
40	44	דרום	SOUTH	205a	
		חוץ	THE OUTSIDE	300a	1 be
		כתף	SIDE	509c	2 b
		לשכה	ROOM	545d	1 c
		פנה	FACE	816b	1 5
		קדים	EAST WIND	870c	2 a
		שיר	SING	*1010d	
40	45	דרום	SOUTH	205a	
		זה	THIS	262b	
		כהן	PRIEST	464a	6
		לשכה	ROOM	545d	1 c
		פנה	FACE	816b	1 5
		משמרת	GUARD	1038c	4 a
40	46	בן	SON	121a	1 je
		מזבח	ALTAR	259a	1
		כהן	PRIEST	464a	6
		לוי	LEVI	532c	1 c
		לשכה	ROOM	545d	1 c
		פנה	FACE	816b	1 5
		צדק	RIGHTEOUS	843b	1 a
		קרב	APPROACHING	898b	2
		משמרת	GUARD	1038c	4 a
		שרת	SERVE	1058b	2 c
40	47	רבע	SQUARED	917a	
40	48	אולם	PORCH	17d	3
		איל	PILASTER	18b	
40	49	אולם	PORCH	17d	3

Ch	v.	Heb	Eng	Page	Sec
		אמה	CUBIT	52b	1
		עלה	GO UP	748c	1 f
		מעלה	STEP	752b	1
		עמוד	PILLAR	765b	2
		עשתי	ONE	799d	
41	1	אהל	TENT	14a	3
		היכל	TEMPLE	228c	2 c
41	2	כתף	SIDE	509c	2 b
		ארבעים	FORTY	917b	1 a
		רחב	WIDTH	932a	
41	3	איל	PILASTER	18b	
		אמה	CUBIT	52b	1
		פנימה	TOWARDS THE SIDE	819b	1
41	4	רחב	WIDTH	932a	
		היכל	TEMPLE	228c	2 c
		פנה	FACE	816a	2 1c
		קדש	APARTNESS	871d	2 d
41	5	יציע	FLAT SURFACE	427a	
		צלע	RIB	854b	3
		קיר	WALL	885a	1 e
		רחב	WIDTH	931d	
41	6	אחז	GRASP	28c	
		יציע	FLAT SURFACE	427a	
		קיר	WALL	885a	1 b
		שלשים	THIRTY	1026c	
41	7	כן	SO	485d	1 a
		מוסב	ENCOMPASSING	687c	
		עליון	HIGH	751b	2
		מעל	ABOVE	751d	2 ca
		על	UPON	757b	2 7c ab
		רחב	BE LARGE	931c	
		רחב	WIDTH	931d	
		תיכון	MIDDLE	1064a	
		תחתון	LOWER	1066b	
41	8	אמה	CUBIT	52b	1
		אצל	JOINT	69c	
		גבה	HEIGHT	147b	1
		מוסדה	FOUNDATION	414c	
		מוסד	FOUNDATION	414c	
		מלא	FULNESS	571b	4
		קנה	STALK	889d	4 b
41	9	בית	BETWEEN	108a	
		חוץ	THE OUTSIDE	299d	1 ba
		נוח	REST	629a	B
		קיר	WALL	885a	1 e
		רחב	WIDTH	932a	
41	10	בית	BETWEEN	*108a	
		לשכה	ROOM	545d	1 c
		סביב	ROUND ABOUT	687a	1 cb
41	11	דרום	SOUTH	205a	
		ל	TO	511d	1 h
		נוח	REST	629a	B
		פתח	OPENING	835d	
		מקום	STANDING PLACE	880a	4
41	12	בנין	STRUCTURE	125c	B
		גזרה	SEPARATION	160d	2
		דרך	WAY	203b	3
		ים	SEA	411b	9
		ים	SEA	411b	9
		פאה	CORNER	802b	2 a
		פנה	FACE	816c	2 1c
		קיר	WALL	885a	1 e
		רחב	WIDTH	932a	
		תשעים	NINETY	1077d	
41	13	גזרה	SEPARATION	160d	2
		קיר	WALL	885a	1 e
41	14	גזרה	SEPARATION	160d	2
		ל	TO	511d	1 h
		פנה	FACE	816b	1 5
		קדים	EAST WIND	870c	2 a
41	15	אולם	PORCH	17d	3
		אלם	PORCH	19a	
		אחר	BEHIND	30c	4 c
		אתיק	GALLERY	87d	
		אתוק	GALLERY	87d	
		בנין	STRUCTURE	125c	B
		גזרה	SEPARATION	160d	2
		היכל	TEMPLE	228c	2 c
		חצר	ENCLOSURE	347a	3 c
		על	UPON	758a	2 9
		פנה	FACE	816c	2 1c
41	16	אטם	SHUT	32a	
		חלון	WINDOW	319d	
		חלון	WINDOW	319d	
		כסה	BE COVERED	492b	1
		סביב	ROUND ABOUT	687a	1 cb
		סף	THRESHOLD	706b	
		שחף	PANELLED	965d	
		שלש	THREE	1025d	
		שקוף	FRAME	1054d	
41	17	חוץ	THE OUTSIDE	299d	1 bc
		חיצון	OUTER	300b	1
		מדה	MEASURE	551c	1
		על	UPON	758a	2 9
		על	UPON	759b	4 2d
		פנימי	INNER	819b	
		קיר	WALL	885a	1 c
41	18	בין	INTERVAL	107c	1 5
		כרוב	CHERUB	*501a	6 b
41	19	אדם	MAN	9b	2
		גרון	NECK	173c	1
		כפיר	LION	498d	
		כרוב	CHERUB	*501a	6 b
		פנה	FACE	816a	14
41	20	היכל	TEMPLE	*228c	2 c

EZEKIEL

Ch v.	Heb	Eng	Page	Sec
	כרוב	CHERUB	*501a	6 b
	עד	AS FAR AS	724a	1 1a
	על	UPON	758a	2 9
	על	UPON	759b	4 2d
	קיר	WALL	885a	1 c
41 21	רבע	SQUARED	917d	
	את	WITH	87a	4d
	היכל	TEMPLE	228c	2 c
	מזוזה	DOOR-POST	265b	2 c
	כרוב	CHERUB	*501a	6 b
	פנה	FACE	816b	15
	קדש	APARTNESS	871d	2 d
	רבע	SQUARED	917d	
41 22	ארן	BASE	10d	3
	אמה	CUBIT	52b	1
	ארך	LENGTH	73d	C
	גבה	HIGH	147b	1
	מזבח	ALTAR	258d	5 a
	כרוב	CHERUB	*501a	6 b
	קיר	WALL	885d	4
	מקצע	CORNER-BUTRESS	893a	
	שלחן	TABLE	1020b	3
41 23	דלת	DOOR	195a	1
	דלת	DOOR	195b	2
	היכל	TEMPLE	228c	2 c
	כרוב	CHERUB	*501a	6 b
	קדש	APARTNESS	871d	2 d
41 24	אחר	ANOTHER	29c	
	דלת	DOOR	195a	1
	דלת	DOOR	*195a	
	כרוב	CHERUB	*501a	6 b
	סבב	TURN ABOUT	686d	1
41 25	אולם	PORCH	17d	3
	דלת	DOOR	195a	1
	היכל	TEMPLE	228c	2 c
	חוץ	THE OUTSIDE	300a	1 bd
	כרוב	CHERUB	*501a	6 b
	עב	PROJECTING ROOF	712b	
	פנה	FACE	816c	2 1c
	קיר	WALL	885a	1 c
41 26	אולם	PORCH	17d	3
	אטם	SHUT	32a	
	חלון	WINDOW	319d	
	כתף	SIDE	509c	2 b
	עב	PROJECTING ROOF	712b	
42 1	בנין	STRUCTURE	125c	C
	בנין	STRUCTURE	125c	C
	גזרה	SEPARATION	160d	2
	חיצון	OUTER	300b	1
	יצא	BRING OUT	424d	1 g
	לשכה	ROOM	545d	1 c
	צפון	NORTH	861a	
42 2	אמה	CUBIT	52b	1
	אמה	CUBIT	52b	1
	מאה	HUNDRED	547d	1 a3
	פנה	FACE	816c	2 1c
	צפון	NORTH	861a	
42 3	אתק	GALLERY	87d	
	חיצון	OUTER	300b	1
	לשכה	ROOM	545d	1 c
	פנה	FACE	816c	2 1c
	רצפה	PAVEMENT	954b	
	שלישי	THIRD	1026d	
42 4	אמה	CUBIT	52b	1
	דרך	WAY	*203b	3
	מהלך	WALK	237c	3
	ל	TO	511d	1 h
	לשכה	ROOM	545d	1 c
	פנימי	INNER	819b	
42 5	אתק	GALLERY	87d	
	בנין	STRUCTURE	125c	C
	הם	THEY	241d	8 c
	לשכה	ROOM	545d	1 c
	עליון	HIGH	751b	2
	קצר	BE SHORT	894a	
	קצר	BE SHORT	894a	
	תיכון	MIDDLE	1064a	
	תחתון	LOWER	1066b	
42 6	אצל	LAY ASIDE	69b	
	חצר	ENCLOSURE	347a	3 c
	עמוד	PILLAR	765b	1
	שלש	DO A THIRD TIME	1026a	
	תיכון	MIDDLE	1064a	
	תחתון	LOWER	1066b	
		ADDENDA ET COR-RIGENDA	1123c	
42 7	גדר	WALL	155a	
	דרך	WAY	203b	3
	חוץ	THE OUTSIDE	299d	1 bc
	חיצון	OUTER	300b	1
	לשכה	ROOM	545d	1 c
	עמה	CLOSE BY	769c	A
	פנה	FACE	816c	2 1c
42 8	היכל	TEMPLE	228c	2 c
	חיצון	OUTER	300b	1
	לשכה	ROOM	545d	1 c
	פנה	FACE	818d	2 7a d
42 9	אלה	THESE	41c	C
	מבוא	ENTRANCE	99d	1
	הם	THEY	241d	8 c
	חיצון	OUTER	300b	1
	קדים	EAST WIND	870c	2 a
	תחת	UNDERNEATH	1066b	3 2a
42 10	בנין	STRUCTURE	125c	C
	גזרה	SEPARATION	160d	2
	דרום	SOUTH	205a	

Ch v.	Heb	Eng	Page	Sec
	פנה	FACE	816c	2 1c
	רחב	WIDTH	931d	
	רחב	WIDTH	*932a	
	רחב	WIDTH	932a	
42 11	דרך	WAY	202d	1
	מוצא	GOING FORTH	425d	1 c
	כן	SO	486b	2 aa
	לשכה	ROOM	545d	1 c
	משפט	JUDGMENT	1049a	6 b
42 12	גדרה	WALL	155a	
	דרך	WAY	202d	1
	דרום	SOUTH	205a	
	הגן	APPROPRIATE	212b	
	לשכה	ROOM	545d	1 c
	פנה	FACE	816d	2 3b
	אשם	OFFENCE	79d	4
42 13	גזרה	SEPARATION	160d	2
	דרום	SOUTH	205a	
	חטאת	SIN	309b	4
	כהן	PRIEST	464a	6
	לשכה	ROOM	545d	1 c
	מנחה	OFFERING	585b	4
	נוח	REST	628d	B 1
	פנה	FACE	816c	2 1c
	קדש	APARTNESS	871d	2 d
	קדש	APARTNESS	872a	3 b
	קדוש	HOLY	872c	2 a
	קרוב	NEAR	898c	2 e
42 14	אחר	ANOTHER	29c	
	ב	IN	88a	3
	בגד	GARMENT	*94a	
	חיצון	OUTER	300b	1
	כהן	PRIEST	464a	6
	לבש	PUT ON	527d	A
	נוח	REST	628d	B 1
	קדש	APARTNESS	871d	2 d
	קדש	APARTNESS	872b	4 a
	קרב	COME NEAR	897c	1 b
	שרת	SERVE	1057b	2 c
42 15	יצא	BRING OUT	424d	1 g
	כלה	FINISH	478a	1 c
	מדד	MEASURE	551a	
	מדה	MEASURE	551c	1
	פנה	FACE	816b	15
42 16	אמה	CUBIT	52b	1
	חמש	FIVE	331d	1 c
	חמש	FIVE	332a	3
	מדה	MEASURE	551c	1
	קדים	EAST WIND	870c	2 a
	קנה	STALK	889d	4 a
	רוח	BREATH	924d	2 b
42 17	מדה	MEASURE	551c	1
	צפון	NORTH	861a	
	קנה	STALK	889d	4 a
	רוח	BREATH	924d	2 b
42 18	דרום	SOUTH	204d	
	מדה	MEASURE	551c	1
	קנה	STALK	889d	4 a
	רוח	BREATH	924d	2 b
42 19	ים	SEA	411b	9
	מדד	MEASURE	551a	
	מדה	MEASURE	551c	1
	סבב	TURN ABOUT	685c	1 a
	קנה	STALK	889d	4 a
	רוח	BREATH	924d	2 b
42 20	בדל	BE DIVIDED	95c	3
	בין	INTERVAL	107c	1 b
	חל	PROFANENESS	320d	
	חומה	WALL	327d	2 b
	ל	TO	511c	1 h
	מדד	MEASURE	551a	
	קדש	APARTNESS	872b	6
	רוח	BREATH	924d	2 b
43 1	דרך	WAY	203b	3
	הלך	WALK	236d	1 d
	פנה	TURN	815c	2 b
	אור	BECOME LIGHT	21b	2
43 2	דרך	WAY	*203b	3
	כבוד	GLORY	458d	2 c1
	כבוד	GLORY	459a	2 c3
	קדים	EAST WIND	870c	2 a
	קול	VOICE	877b	2 f
43 3	אל	TO	40d	8
	כבר	CHEBAR	460d	
	נפל	FALL	657b	3 b
	מראה	VISION	909b	
	מראה	VISION	909d	3
	שחת	GO TO RUIN	1008a	1
43 4	דרך	WAY	202d	1
	כבוד	GLORY	458d	2 c1
	פנה	FACE	816b	15
43 5	כבוד	GLORY	458d	2 c1
	מלא	FILL	570b	2
	רוח	BREATH	925d	9 a
43 6	דבר	SPEAK	182a	
	שמע	HEAR	1033c	1 b
43 7	את	MARK OF THE AC-CUSATIVE	85c	3 a
	במה	HIGH PLACE	119d	4
	זנות	FORNICATION	276b	C
	טמא	BE UNCLEAN	379c	2
	כסא	SEAT OF HONOR	490d	1 b
	כף	SOLE OF FOOT	496c	3
	עולם	LONG DURATION	762c	2 c
	פגר	CORPSE	803d	1
	מקום	STANDING PLACE	880b	4

Ch v.	Heb	Eng	Page	Sec
	רגל	FOOT	919d	1 b
	שם	NAME	1028c	3
	תוך	MIDST	1063d	
43 8	את	WITH	86b	2
	ב	IN	91a	5 2
	מזוזה	DOOR-POST	265b	1
	מזוזה	DOOR-POST	265b	2 c
	טמא	BE UNCLEAN	379c	1
	כלה	FINISH	478c	2 c2
	סף	THRESHOLD	706b	
	קיר	WALL	885a	1 f
43 9	זנות	FORNICATION	276b	C
	עולם	LONG DURATION	762c	2 c
	פגר	CORPSE	803d	1
	שכן	SETTLE DOWN	1015b	2 c
	תוך	MIDST	1063d	
43 10	את	MARK OF THE AC-CUSATIVE	85a	1 a
	כלם	BE HUMILIATED	483d	1
	מדד	MEASURE	551a	
	עון	INIQUITY	731a	1 b
	צור	FASHION	*849b	
	תכנית	MEASUREMENT	1067c	
43 11	מובא	ENTRANCE	100a	
	חקה	SOMETHING PRE-SCRIBED	350b	2 d
	חקה	SOMETHING PRE-SCRIBED	350b	2 e
	חקה	SOMETHING PRE-SCRIBED	350b	2 d
	ידע	KNOW	395a	
	מוצא	GOING FORTH	425d	1 c
	תורה	LAW	436a	2 a
	תכונה	ARRANGEMENT	467d	1
	כלם	BE HUMILIATED	483d	1
	צורה	FASHION	849b	
	צור	FASHION	849b	
43 12	גבול	BOUNDARY	148a	2 c
	תורה	LAW	436a	2 a
	קדש	APARTNESS	872a	2 f
43 13	אמה	CUBIT	52b	1
	גב	BACK	146c	6
	גבה	HEIGHT	147b	1
	גבול	BOUNDARY	148a	1 fb
	מזבח	ALTAR	258d	5 b
	זרת	SPAN	285a	
	חיק	BOSOM	301a	3 b
	טפח	SPAN	381c	
	מדה	SIZE	551c	2
	שפה	SPEECH	974a	3
43 14	אמה	CUBIT	52b	1
	אמה	CUBIT	52b	1
	אמה	CUBIT	52b	1
	חיק	BOSOM	301a	3 b
	עזרה	ENCLOSURE	741c	1
	מן	SMALL	882a	1 b
	תחתון	LOWER	1066b	
43 15	אריאל	ARIEL	72a	4
	אריאל	HEARTH	72b	
	מעל	ABOVE	751d	2 ba
	קרן	HORN	902a	3
43 16	אריאל	ARIEL	72a	4
	אריאל	HEARTH	72b	
	רבע	SQUARED	917c	
	רבע	FOURTH PART	917d	2
43 17	את	MARK OF THE AC-CUSATIVE	85c	3 b
	גבול	BOUNDARY	148a	1 fb
	מזבח	ALTAR	258d	5 b
	חיק	BOSOM	301a	3 b
	סבב	ROUND ABOUT	687a	1 cc
	עזרה	ENCLOSURE	741c	1
	מעלה	STEP	752b	1
	פנה	TURN	815c	2 b
	קדם	EAST WIND	870c	2 c
	רבע	FOURTH PART	917d	2
43 18	דם	BLOOD	197c	3 b
	זרק	TO TOSS	284c	1 b
	חקה	SOMETHING PRE-SCRIBED	350b	2 d
	עלה	GO UP	750a	8
	עלה	WHOLE BURNT OF-FERING	750d	
	עשה	DO	795b	2 a
43 19	אשר	PARTICLE OF RE-LATION	82b	2 a
	בן	SON	121c	7 b
	הם	THEY	241d	8 c
	זרע	SOWING	282d	4 c
	חטאת	SIN	309b	4
	כהן	PRIEST	463d	5
	כהן	PRIEST	464a	6
	לוי	LEVITE	533a	3 1b
	פר	YOUNG BULL	830d	2 c
	זדך	RIGHTEOUS	843b	1 a
	קרב	NEAR	898c	2 e
	שרת	SERVE	1058b	2 c
43 20	גבול	BOUNDARY	148a	1 fb
	דם	BLOOD	197d	3 b
	חמא	MISS A GOAL OR WAY	307c	1
	כפר	COVER OVER	497d	3 a
	עזרה	ENCLOSURE	741c	1
	פנה	CORNER	819c	1 a
	קרן	HORN	902a	3

Ch	v	Heb	Eng	Page	Sec
43	21	חטא	SIN	309b	4
		מפקד	MUSTER	824c	3
		שרף	BURN	977a	2 a
43	22	מזבח	ALTAR	259b	4
		חטא	MISS A GOAL OR WAY	307c	3
		חטאת	SIN	309b	4
		עז	SHE-GOAT	777c	3 f
		שעיר	HE-GOAT	972c	
		תמים	SOUND	1071a	2
43	23	איל	RAM	18a	2 f
		בן	SON	121c	7 b
		חטא	MISS A GOAL OR WAY	307c	3
		כלה	FINISH	478b	1 c
		פר	YOUNG BULL	830d	2 b
43	24	כהן	PRIEST	464a	6
		מלח	SALT	571d	
		עלה	WHOLE BURNT OF-FERING	750d	
43	25	איל	RAM	18a	2 f
		בן	SON	121c	7 b
		חטאת	SIN	309b	4
		יום	DAY	401a	7 i
		עשה	DO	794d	2 4
		שעיר	HE-GOAT	972c	
43	26	מזבח	ALTAR	259b	4
		מהר	BE CLEAN	372c	1 b
		יד	HAND	389d	1 c
		כפר	COVER OVER	497d	3 a
		מלא	FILL	570d	2
43	27	הלאה	ONWARDS	229c	B
		כהן	PRIEST	464a	6
		עלה	WHOLE BURNT OF-FERING	750d	
		רצה	BE PLEASED WITH	953b	2
		שלם	PEACE-OFFERING	1023c	
44	1	דרך	WAY	202d	1
		חיצון	OUTER	300b	1
		חיצון	OUTER	300b	1
		סגר	SHUT	689a	1
		פנה	TURN	815c	2 b
44	2	היה	BE	227d	3 5a
		סגר	SHUT	689a	1
		פתח	OPEN	835c	
44	3	אולם	PORCH	17d	3
		את	MARK OF THE AC-CUSATIVE	85c	3 a
		דרך	WAY	202d	1
		דרך	WAY	*203b	3 a
		נשיא	PRINCE	672c	6 c
44	4	דרך	WAY	202d	1
		כבוד	GLORY	458d	2 c1
		מלא	FILL	570b	2
		נפל	FALL	657d	3 b
44	5	את	WITH	86a	1 db
		מבוא	ENTERING	99d	2
		דבר	SPEAK	181b	3 d
		חקה	SOMETHING PRE-SCRIBED	350b	2 d
		חקה	SOMETHING PRE-SCRIBED	350b	2 d
		מוצא	GOING FORTH	425d	1 c
		תורה	LAW	436a	2 a
		ל	TO	514b	5 fa
		לב	HEART	524d	2 3c
		לב	HEART	524d	2 3c
		ראה	TO SEE	907c	6 c
		שום	TO PLACE	963c	2 b
		שום	TO PLACE	963c	2 b
44	6	בית	HOUSE	*110a	5 dd
		מן	THAN	583a	6 d
		מרי	REBELLION	598b	
		רב	MUCH	913b	1 f
44	7	אל	TO	40b	5
		ב	IN	91a	5 2
		בן	SON	121c	7 a
		ברית	COVENANT	136c	2 2c
		ברית	COVENANT	137b	3 3
		בשר	FLESH	142d	3
		דם	BLOOD	197c	3 b
		חלב	FAT	317a	2 b
		חלל	POLLUTE	320b	1 b
		לב	HEART	525b	2 6d
		לחם	FOOD	537b	2 c
		נכר	FOREIGNNESS	648c	2
		על	UPON	755c	2 4b
		ערל	HAVING FORESKIN	790c	
		ערל	HAVING FORESKIN	790d	
		פרר	BREAK	830b	1 b
44	8	שום	TO PLACE	964d	1
		משמרת	GUARD	1038c	4 a
		משמרת	GUARD	1038c	4 a
44	9	בן	SON	121c	7 a
		בשר	FLESH	142d	3
		ל	TO	514c	5 fd
		לב	HEART	525b	2 6d
		נכר	FOREIGNNESS	648c	2
		ערל	HAVING FORESKIN	790c	
		ערל	HAVING FORESKIN	790d	
44	10	כי אם	BUT	475a	2 b
		לוי	LEVITE	533a	3 2a
		עון	INIQUITY	731c	3
		על	UPON	759a	4 2c
		על	UPON	759a	4 2c
		רחק	BE DISTANT	934d	

Ch	v	Heb	Eng	Page	Sec
		תעה	ERR	1073c	3
		תעה	ERR	1073c	3
44	11	זבח	SACRIFICE	257c	11
		זבח	SACRIFICE	258a	27
		עלה	WHOLE BURNT OF-FERING	750d	
		עמד	STAND	764a	1 e
		פקדה	OVERSIGHT	824b	2 b
		שחט	SLAUGHTER	1006b	2
		שער	GATE	1045b	3 c
		שרת	SERVE	1057b	2 b
44	12	מכשול	STUMBLING	506b	2 c
		נשא	LIFT	670b	1 b 1
		נשא	LIFT	671a	2 b
		עון	INIQUITY	731a	1 a
		עון	INIQUITY	731c	3
		יען	ON ACCOUNT OF	774d	2 a
		שרת	SERVE	1057b	2 b
44	13	כהן	ACT AS PRIEST	*464c	1
		כהן	ACT AS PRIEST	464c	1
		כלמה	IGNOMINY	484b	2
		נגש	DRAW NEAR	620d	1
		נגש	DRAW NEAR	620d	1
		על	UPON	757b	27c ab
		קדש	APARTNESS	872a	3 c
44	14	ל	TO	514c	5 fc
		עבדה	LABOR	715c	4
		עשה	DO	795a	1a
		משמרת	GUARD	1038c	4 a
44	15	בן	SON	121b	1 jh
		דם	BLOOD	197c	3 b
		הם	THEY	241c	2 a
		חלב	FAT	317a	2 b
		כהן	PRIEST	463d	5
		כהן	PRIEST	464a	6
		לוי	LEVITE	533a	3 1b
		על	UPON	759a	4 2c
		עמד	STAND	764a	1 e
		צדק	RIGHTEOUS	843b	1 a
		קרב	COME NEAR	897b	1 a
		משמרת	GUARD	1038c	4 a
		שרת	SERVE	1058b	2 c
44	16	קרב	COME NEAR	897c	1 b
		שלחן	TABLE	1020b	3
		משמרת	GUARD	1038c	4 a
		שרת	SERVE	1058b	2 c
44	17	בית	HOUSE	110c	7
		היה	COME TO PASS	225b	12b ae
		לבש	PUT ON	527d	A
		עלה	GO UP	748d	6
		על	UPON	753a	2 1a a
		פשת	FLAX	833d	1
		צמר	WOOL	856a	
		שער	GATE	1045b	3 c
		שרת	SERVE	1057b	2 c
44	18	חגר	GIRD	292a	3
		יזע	SWEAT	402c	
		מכנס	BREECH	488b	
		מתנים	LOINS	608b	1 f
		על	UPON	753a	2 1a a
		פאר	HEAD-DRESS	802c	
		פשת	FLAX	833d	
44	19	אחר	ANOTHER	29c	
		חיצון	OUTER	300b	1
		לבש	PUT ON	527d	A
		לשכה	ROOM	545d	1 c
		נוח	REST	628d	B 1
		פשט	STRIP OFF	833a	1
		קדש	APARTNESS	871d	2 d
		קדש	BE SET APART	873b	4 b
		שרת	SERVE	1058b	2 c
44	20	כסם	SHEAR	493c	
		פרע	LONG HAIR	828d	
		שלח	SEND	1019b	4
44	21	יין	WINE	406c	C
		כהן	PRIEST	464a	6
44	22	אלמנה	WIDOW	48b	
		בית	HOUSE	110a	5 dd
		בתולה	VIRGIN	144a	
		גרש	CAST OUT	176c	
		זרע	SOWING	283a	4 f
		כהן	PRIEST	464a	6
		כי אם	BUT	475a	2 b
		מן	FROM	578a	1 a
44	23	בין	INTERVAL	107c	1 d
		בין	INTERVAL	107c	1 b
		חל	PROFANENESS	320d	
		מהור	CLEAN	373a	1
		טמא	UNCLEAN	380a	2 d
		ידע	MAKE KNOWN	395b	
		ירה	DIRECT	435c	5 b
		קדש	APARTNESS	872b	6
44	24	חקה	SOMETHING PRE-SCRIBED	350b	2 e
		חקה	SOMETHING PRE-SCRIBED	350b	2 d
		מועד	APPOINTED TIME	417c	1 b
		תורה	LAW	436a	2 a
		על	UPON	754c	2 1f e
		קדש	BE SET APART	873b	
		ריב	STRIFE	937a	3
		שבת	SABBATH	992b	1 b
		שפט	JUDGE	1047c	2 b
		שפט	JUDGE	1047c	2 b
		משפט	JUDGMENT	*1048b	1 a

Ch	v	Heb	Eng	Page	Sec
		משפט	JUDGMENT	1048d	3
44	25	אם	MOTHER	51d	1
		טמא	BE UNCLEAN	379b	3
		טמא	BE UNCLEAN	379d	
44	26	מהרה	PURIFYING	372d	2
		ספר	COUNT	707d	1
44	27	חטא	SIN	309c	4
		חטאת	SIN	310a	4 c
		קדש	APARTNESS	871d	2 d
		שרת	SERVE	1058b	2 c
44	28	אחזה	POSSESSION	28c	
		אחזה	POSSESSION	28d	
44	29	אשם	OFFENCE	79d	4
		חטאת	SIN	309b	4
		חרם	DEVOTED THING	356b	2
		מנחה	OFFERING	585b	4
44	30	בכורים	FIRST-FRUITS	114c	
		ברכה	BLESSING	139d	1 b
		כהן	PRIEST	464a	6
		כל	ALL	482d	2 a
		נוח	REST	628c	A 2
		עריסה	COARSE MEAL	791b	
		ראשית	BEGINNING	912b	1 b
		ראשית	BEGINNING	912b	1 b
		תרומה	OFFERING	929a	4
		תרומה	OFFERING	929b	7
44	31	בהמה	BEAST	96d	1
		טרפה	ANIMAL TORN	383c	1
		כהן	PRIEST	464a	6
		נבלה	CARCASS	615d	2
45	1	ב	IN	89a	1 7c
		גבול	BORDER	147d	1 a
		נחלה	PROPERTY	635b	1 b
		נפל	FALL	658b	3
		עשר	TEN	796d	2 b
		עשרים	TWENTY	797d	1 1a
		קדש	APARTNESS	872a	2 g
		רום	BE HIGH	927d	3 a
		תרומה	OFFERING	929a	3
		תרומה	OFFERING	929b	7
		רחב	WIDTH	931d	
45	2	מגרש	OPEN LAND	177c	
		רבע	SQUARED	917a	
45	3	חמש	FIVE	332a	5 a2
		מדד	MEASURE	551d	
		מדה	MEASURE	551c	3
		קדש	APARTNESS	872a	2 g
		רחב	WIDTH	931d	
45	4	כהן	PRIEST	464a	6
		לוי	LEVITE	*533a	3 2a
		מקדש	SACRED PLACE	874b	4
		קרב	APPROACHING	898b	2
		שרת	SERVE	1058b	2 c
		שרת	SERVE	1058b	2 c
45	5	אחזה	POSSESSION	28c	
		לוי	LEVITE	533a	3 2a
		לשכה	ROOM	545d	1 c
		רחב	WIDTH	931d	
		שרת	SERVE	1058b	2 c
45	6	אחזה	POSSESSION	28c	
		חמש	FIVE	332a	4
		עמה	CLOSE BY	769c	A
		תרומה	OFFERING	929a	3
		רחב	WIDTH	931d	
45	7	אחזה	POSSESSION	28c	
		זה	THIS	262a	6 e
		חלק	PORTION	324b	2 c
		עמה	CLOSE BY	769c	A
		פאה	CORNER	802b	2 a
		פנה	FACE	816c	2 1c
		קדם	EASTWARD	870a	
		קדים	EAST WIND	870c	2 b
		תרומה	OFFERING	929a	3
45	8	אחזה	POSSESSION	28c	
		ינה	OPPRESS	413b	
		נשיא	PRINCE	672c	6 b
45	9	גרשה	EXPULSION	177a	
		חמס	VIOLENCE	329c	
		נשיא	PRINCE	672c	6 b
		צדקה	RIGHTEOUSNESS	842a	1 a
		רב	MUCH	913b	1 f
		רום	BE HIGH	927c	3
		שד	VIOLENCE	994c	1
45	10	מאזן	BALANCES	24d	
		איפה	EPHAH	35b	2
		בת	BATH	144c	
		צדק	RIGHTNESS	841c	1
45	11	איפה	EPHAH	35b	1
		איפה	EPHAH	35b	1
		בת	BATH	144c	
		חמר	HOMER	331a	
		נשא	LIFT	671b	2 f
		עשרון	TENTH	798a	2
		מעשר	TENTH PART	798b	1
		תכן	MEASUREMENT	1067c	
		מתכנת	MEASUREMENT	1067c	2
45	12	גרה	GERAH	176a	
		חמש	FIVE	332a	2 d
		מנה	MANEH	584b	
		עשר	TEN	797a	3 d
		שקל	SHEKEL	1053d	
		שקל	SHEKEL	1053d	
		שקל	SHEKEL	1053d	
45	13	איפה	EPHAH	35b	1
		חמר	HOMER	330d	
		חמר	HOMER	331a	

Ch	v.	Heb	Eng	Page	Sec
		חטה	WHEAT	334d	
		רום	BE HIGH	927d	3 a
		תרומה	OFFERING	929a	2
		שערה	BARLEY	972d	2
		ששי	SIXTH	995d	
		ששי	SIXTH	995d	
		ששה	GIVE SIXTH PART OF	995d	
45	14	בת	BATH	*144c	
		בת	BATH	144c	
		חמר	HOMER	*331a	
		חמר	HOMER	331a	
		חק	SOMETHING PRE-SCRIBED	349c	4
		כר	KOR	499d	1
		מעשר	TENTH PART	798b	2
		שמן	OIL	1032c	2 i
45	15	כפר	COVER OVER	498a	3 b2
		מנחה	OFFERING	585b	4
		שה	A SHEEP	962a	1
		משקה	IRRIGATION	1052d	1
45	16	תרומה	OFFERING	929a	2
45	17	חג	FESTIVAL-GATHER-ING	291a	1 b1
		חדש	NEW MOON	294c	1
		חטאת	SIN	309b	4
		חטאת	SIN	309b	4
		חטאת	SIN	310a	4 c
		מועד	APPOINTED TIME	417d	1 b
		כפר	COVER OVER	498a	3 e
		מנחה	OFFERING	585b	4
		עלה	WHOLE BURNT OF-FERING	750d	
		על	UPON	753c	2 lc
		עשה	DO	794d	24
		שלם	PEACE-OFFERING	1023c	
		שלם	PEACE-OFFERING	1023c	
45	18	בן	SON	121c	7 b
		חדש	NEW MOON	294d	2 b2
		חטא	MISS A GOAL OR WAY	307c	3
		חטאת	SIN	*309b	4
		ראשון	FIRST	911d	2 a
45	19	דם	BLOOD	*197d	3 b
		דם	BLOOD	197d	3 b
		מזוזה	DOOR-POST	265b	2 c
		חטאת	SIN	309b	4
		כהן	PRIEST	464a	6
		ל	TO	513d	5 cb g
		עזרה	ENCLOSURE	741c	1
		פנה	CORNER	819c	1 a
45	20	חדש	NEW MOON	294d	2 b2
		חטאת	SIN	*309b	4
		כפר	COVER OVER	497d	3 a
		מן	ON ACCOUNT OF	580b	2 f
		פתי	SIMPLE	834c	
		שבע	SEVEN	988a	1 d
		שגה	GO ASTRAY	993b	4
45	21	אכל	EAT	37d	1
		חג	FESTIVAL-GATHER-ING	291a	1 b2
		חדש	NEW MOON	294d	2 b2
		יום	DAY	398c	2 e
		מצה	UNLEAVENED BREAD	695b	
		פסח	PASSOVER	820b	3
		ראשון	FIRST	911d	2 a
		שבע	SEVEN	988a	1 c
45	22	בעד	ON BEHALF OF	126c	2
		חטאת	SIN	309c	4
		עם	PEOPLE	766d	5 c
		אל	RAM	18a	2 d
45	23	חג	FESTIVAL-GATHER-ING	291a	1 b2
		חטאת	SIN	309c	4
		יום	DAY	401a	7 i
		עלה	WHOLE BURNT OF-FERING	750c	
		עלה	WHOLE BURNT OF-FERING	750c	
		עז	SHE-GOAT	777c	3 f
		שעיר	HE-GOAT	972c	
		שבע	SEVEN	988a	1 c
45	24	אל	RAM	18a	2 d
		איפה	EPHAH	35b	1
		הין	HIN	229a	1 a
		מנחה	OFFERING	585b	4
		מנחה	OFFERING	585c	6
45	25	אלה	THESE	41d	D
		חדש	NEW MOON	294d	2 b2
		חטאת	SIN	309b	4
		יום	DAY	398c	2 e
		מנחה	OFFERING	585b	4
		שביעי	SEVENTH	988d	1
46	1	חדש	NEW MOON	294c	1
		יום	DAY	398b	2 a
		סגר	SHUT	689a	1
		מעשה	DEED	795d	1 b1
		פנה	TURN	815c	2 b
		פתח	OPEN	835c	
		קדים	EAST WIND	870c	2 c
		שבת	SABBATH	992b	1 a
46	2	אולם	PORCH	17d	3
		דרך	WAY	202d	1
		מזוזה	DOOR-POST	265b	2 c
		חוץ	THE OUTSIDE	299d	1 bd
		כהן	PRIEST	464a	6
		סגר	BE SHUT	689b	2
		עלה	WHOLE BURNT OF-FERING	750d	
		על	UPON	756a	2 6a
		עשה	DO	794d	24
		מפתן	THRESHOLD	837b	
		שחה	BOW DOWN	1005d	2 c
		שלם	PEACE-OFFERING	1023c	
46	3	עם	PEOPLE	766d	5 c
		פתח	OPENING	836a	
		שחה	BOW DOWN	1005c	2 c
46	4	איל	RAM	18a	2 c
		כבש	LAMB	461a	1
		עלה	WHOLE BURNT OF-FERING	750c	
		עלה	WHOLE BURNT OF-FERING	750d	
46	5	שבת	SABBATH	992b	1 a
		איל	RAM	18a	2 c
		איפה	EPHAH	35b	1
		הין	HIN	229a	1 a
		יד	HAND	390b	2
		מנחה	OFFERING	585b	4
		מתת	GIFT	682c	
46	6	איל	RAM	18a	2 c
		בן	SON	121c	7 b
		הין	HIN	229a	1 a
		חדש	NEW MOON	294c	1
46	7	איל	RAM	18a	2 c
		איפה	EPHAH	35b	1
		יד	HAND	390b	2
		מנחה	OFFERING	585b	4
		מנחה	OFFERING	585c	6
		נשג	REACH	673d	3
46	8	אולם	PORCH	17d	3
		דרך	WAY	202d	1
46	9	דרך	WAY	202d	1
		חיצון	OUTER	300b	1
		מועד	APPOINTED TIME	417c	1 b
		נגב	SOUTH-COUNTRY	616b	2
		נכח	FRONT	647b	1
		עם	PEOPLE	766d	5 c
		שוב	TURN BACK	997b	3 a
46	11	איל	RAM	18a	2 c
		איפה	EPHAH	35b	1
		הין	HIN	229a	1 a
		חג	FESTIVAL-GATHER-ING	291a	1 b1
		יד	HAND	390b	2
		מועד	APPOINTED TIME	417c	1 b
		מנחה	OFFERING	585b	4
		מתת	GIFT	682c	
46	12	נדבה	FREEWILL-OFFER-ING	621d	2 b
		נדבה	FREEWILL-OFFER-ING	621d	2 c
		סגר	SHUT	688d	1
		עלה	WHOLE BURNT OF-FERING	750d	
		פנה	TURN	815c	2 b
		פתח	OPEN	835a	
		קדים	EAST WIND	870c	2 c
		שלם	PEACE-OFFERING	1023c	
		שלם	PEACE-OFFERING	1023c	
		שלם	PEACE-OFFERING	1023d	
46	13	בן	SON	122a	9 b
		בקר	MORNING	134b	1 f
		יום	DAY	401a	7 i
		עלה	WHOLE BURNT OF-FERING	750b	
		עלה	WHOLE BURNT OF-FERING	750d	
46	14	איפה	EPHAH	35b	1
		בקר	MORNING	134b	1 f
		הין	HIN	229a	1 a
		הין	HIN	229a	1 a
		חקה	SOMETHING PRE-SCRIBED	350b	2 d
		תמיד	CONTINUITY	556c	1 a
		מנחה	OFFERING	585b	4
		מנחה	OFFERING	585c	6
		סלת	FINE FLOUR	701c	
		רסס	MOISTEN	944a	
		ששי	SIXTH	995d	
46	15	בקר	MORNING	134b	1 f
		תמיד	CONTINUITY	556c	2 b
		מנחה	OFFERING	585b	4
		מנחה	OFFERING	585c	6
		עלה	WHOLE BURNT OF-FERING	750b	
46	16	עשה	DO	794d	24
		אחזה	POSSESSION	28d	2
		ב	IN	89a	17b
		נחלה	INHERITANCE	635c	3
		מתנה	GIFT	682c	
46	17	דרור	LIBERTY	204d	2
		מתנה	GIFT	682c	
		שוב	TURN BACK	998a	7 b
46	18	אחזה	POSSESSION	28c	2
		ינה	OPPRESS	413b	
		נחל	GET AS A POSSES-SION	635d	2
		מען	PURPOSE	775c	2 ca
		פוץ	BE DISPERSED	807a	
46	19	מבוא	ENTRANCE	99d	1
		ירכה	EXTREME PARTS	438b	2
		כהן	PRIEST	464a	6
		כתף	SIDE	509c	2 b
		לשכה	ROOM	545d	1 c
		פנה	TURN	815c	2 b
		קדש	APARTNESS	871d	2 d
46	20	אפה	BAKE	66a	
		אשם	OFFENCE	79d	4
		בשל	BOIL	143a	1
		חיצון	OUTER	300b	1
		חטאת	SIN	309b	4
		יצא	BRING OUT	425a	4 d
		כהן	PRIEST	464a	6
		מנחה	OFFERING	585b	4
		קדש	BE SET APART	873b	4 b
46	21	חיצון	OUTER	300b	1
		יצא	BRING OUT	424d	1 g
		עבר	PASS OVER	718d	2 a
		מקצע	CORNER-BUTTRESS	893a	
		מקצע	CORNER-BUTTRESS	893a	
		מקצע	CORNER-BUTTRESS	893b	
46	22	מדה	SIZE	551c	2
		מן	SMALL	882a	1 b
		קטר	ENCLOSE	883c	
		מקצע	CORNER-BUTTRESS	893a	
		מקצע	CORNER-BUTTRESS	893b	
		מקצע	SET IN CORNERS	893b	
46	23	ארבעים	FORTY	917b	1 a
		מבשלות	COOKING-PLACES	143a	1
		טור	ROW	377a	1
		טירה	ENCAMPMENT	377b	3
		תחת	UNDERNEATH	1066b	3 2a
46	24	בית	HOUSE	109b	1 az
		בשל	BOIL	143a	1
		מבשלות	COOKING-PLACES	*143b	
		זבח	SACRIFICE	258a	2 7
		שרת	SERVE	1058b	2 c
47	1	ימני	RIGHT	412b	
		יצא	GO OUT	423a	1 f
		ירד	GO DOWN	433c	3 b
		כתף	SIDE	509c	2 b
		מי	WATER	565c	1 b
		פנה	FACE	816b	15
		פתח	OPENING	835d	
		מפתן	THRESHOLD	837b	
		קים	EAST WIND	870c	2 c
		תחת	UNDENEATH	1065b	1
		תחת	UNDERNEATH	1066a	3 2a
47	2	דרך	WAY	202d	1
		חוץ	THE OUTSIDE	299d	1 a
		ימני	RIGHT	412b	
		יצא	BRING OUT	424d	1 g
		כתף	SIDE	509c	2 b
		מי	WATER	565c	1 b
		סבב	GO AROUND	686c	2 a
		פנה	TRICKLE	810b	
		פנה	TURN	815c	2 b
		קים	EAST WIND	870c	2 c
47	3	אלף	THOUSAND	48d	1 a
		אמה	CUBIT	52c	1
		אפס	THE TWO EXTREM-ITIES	67c	
		יד	HAND	390b	5 c1
		מדד	MEASURE	551a	
		עבר	PASS OVER	718d	2 a
		קים	EAST WIND	870c	2 c
		קו	LINE	876a	
		קו	LINE	876a	
47	4	אפס	THE TWO EXTREM-ITIES	67c	
		ברך	KNEE	139c	
		מדד	MEASURE	551a	
		מתנים	LOINS	608b	1 g
		עבר	PASS OVER	718d	2 a
47	5	גאה	RISE UP	144b	1
		מדד	MEASURE	551a	
		נחל	TORRENT	636b	1
		עבר	PASS OVER	718c	
		שחו	SWIMMING	965c	
47	6	נחל	TORRENT	636b	1
		שוב	TURN BACK	998d	1 a
47	7	אל	TO	40d	8
		נחל	TORRENT	636b	1
47	8	יצא	GO OUT	423a	1 f
		יצא	BE BROUGHT FORTH	425c	
		ירד	GO DOWN	433c	3 b
		על	UPON	757a	2 7 c a
		ערבה	DESERT-PLAIN	787b	1 a
		קדמון	EASTERN	870c	
		רפא	HEAL	951a	1
47	9	דגה	FISH	185d	
		היה	COME TO PASS	225a	1 2 b ag
		חי	ALIVE	312b	1 d
		נחל	TORRENT	636b	1
		נפש	SOUL	659c	2
		רפא	HEAL	951a	1
		שרץ	SWARM	1056c	2
47	10	דגה	FISH	185d	
		דגה	FISH	185d	
		דוג	FISHER	186a	
		חרם	NET	357a	
		ים	SEA	410d	1
		מין	KIND	568b	
		עינגדי	ENGEDI	745b	
		עינעגלים	ENEGLAIM	745c	

414

Ch	v.	Heb	Eng	Page	Sec
47	11	משטוח	SPREADING-PLACE	1009a	
		בצה	SWAMP	130c	
		גבא	POOL	146b	2
		מלח	SALT	571d	
		נתן	GIVE	681c	1 j
		רפא	HEAL	951a	1
47	12	מאכל	FOOD	38b	
		בכר	BEAR NEW FRUIT	114a	1
		היה	BECOME	226b	2 2e
		יצא	GO OUT	423a	1 f
		ל	TO	516b	5 ja
		נבל	SINK	615c	2
		נחל	TORRENT	636b	1
		עלה	GO UP	748d	4
		עלה	LEAF	750a	
		עץ	TREE	781c	1 b
		תרופה	HEALING	930a	
		תמם	BE FINISHED	1070c	4
47	13	גה	THIS	155c	
		חבל	CORD	286d	3
		יוסף	JOSEPH	415d	1 c
		נחל	TAKE AS A POSSES-SION	635d	1 a
47	14	ב	IN	89a	17b
		יד	HAND	389d	1 d
		נחל	TAKE AS A POSSES-SION	635c	1 a
		נפל	FALL	*657a	1
		נשא	LIFT	670b	1 b 1
47	15	בוא	COME	98d	2 e
		דרך	WAY	202d	1
		חיל	STRENGTH	*299a	4
		חתלן	HETHLON	367c	
		ים	SEA	410d	1
		ל	TO	*511c	1 h
		פאה	CORNER	802b	2 a
		צדד	ZEDAD	841b	
47	16	ברותה	BEROTHAH	92d	
		גבול	BOUNDARY	148a	2 b
		דמשק	DAMASCUS	199d	
		חילם	HELAM	298a	
		חורן	HAURAN	301c	
		חמת	HAMATH	333b	
		חצרהתיכן	HAZER-HATTICON	347c	
		סברים	SIBRAIM	688a	
		תיכון	MIDDLE	1064a	
47	17	את	MARK OF THE AC-CUSATIVE	85c	3 b
		גבול	BOUNDARY	148a	2 b
		דמשק	DAMASCUS	199d	
		חמת	HAMATH	333b	
		חצרעינון	HAZAR-ENAN	347c	
47	18	את	MARK OF THE AC-CUSATIVE	85c	3 b
		בין	INTERVAL	107d	D
		גבל	BOUND	148b	
		דמשק	DAMASCUS	199d	
		חורן	HAURAN	301c	
		ים	SEA	411a	3
		מדד	MEASURE	551a	
		מדד	MEASURE	551a	
		מדד	MEASURE	551a	
		על	UPON	757c	27c ab
		פאה	CORNER	802b	2 a
		קדים	EAST WIND	870c	2 b
		קדים	EAST WIND	870c	2 a
		קדמני	FORMER	870d	2
47	19	את	MARK OF THE AC-CUSATIVE	85c	3 b
		חצצנתמר	HAZAZON-TAMAR	346c	
		ים	SEA	410d	1
		תימן	SOUTH	412d	1 b
		תימן	SOUTH	412d	1 b
		מי	WATER	565b	
		נגב	SOUTH-COUNTRY	616b	2
		נחל	WADY	636c	2
		פאה	CORNER	802b	2 a
		קדש	KADESH	873d	1
		מריבה	MERIBAH	937b	2
		תמר	TAMAR	1071c	2
47	20	את	MARK OF THE AC-CUSATIVE	85c	3 b
		בוא	COME	98d	2 e
		חמת	HAMATH	333b	
		ים	SEA	410d	1
47	21	חלק	DIVIDE	323d	1
47	22	ב	IN	89a	17c
		גור	SOJOURN	157d	1
		גר	SOJOURNER	158b	2
		גר	SOJOURNER	*158c	2
		אורח	A NATIVE	280c	1
		ילד	BEGET	409a	1
		נחלה	PROPERTY	635b	1 b
		נחלה	PROPERTY	635b	1 b
		נפל	FALL	657a	1
		נפל	FALL	658b	3
47	23	גבול	BORDER	147d	1 a
		גור	SOJOURN	157d	1
		גר	SOJOURNER	158b	2
		גר	SOJOURNER	*158c	2
		היה	COME TO PASS	225a	1 2b ab
48	1	בוא	COME	98d	2 e
		גבול	BOUNDARY	148a	1 b
		גבול	BOUNDARY	148a	2
		דן	DAN	192d	1
		דמשק	DAMASCUS	199d	

Ch	v.	Heb	Eng	Page	Sec
		דרך	WAY	202d	1
		חיל	STRENGTH	*299a	4
		חמת	HAMATH	333b	
		חצרעינון	HAZAR-ENAN	347c	
		חתלן	HETHLON	367c	
		יד	HAND	390d	4 2
		פאה	CORNER	802b	2 a
		קדים	EAST WIND	870c	2 a
		קצה	END	892a	1
48	2	אשר	ASHER	81b	2
		דן	DAN	192d	2
48	3	אשר	ASHER	81b	2
		נפתלי	NAPHTALI	837a	2 a
		קדים	EAST WIND	870c	2 b
48	4	מנשה	MANASSEH	586d	1 b 3 b
		נפתלי	NAPHTALI	837a	2 a
48	5	מנשה	MANASSEH	586d	1 b 3 b
48	6	קדים	EAST WIND	870c	2 a
48	7	ראובן	REUBEN	910a	2
		קדים	EAST WIND	870c	2 a
		ראובן	REUBEN	910a	2
48	8	חלק	PORTION	324b	2 c
		קדים	EAST WIND	870c	2 a
		רום	BE HIGH	927d	3 a
		תרומה	OFFERING	929a	3
48	9	רום	BE HIGH	927d	3 a
		תרומה	OFFERING	929a	3
48	10	כהן	PRIEST	464a	6
		נגב	SOUTH-COUNTRY	616c	2
		קדים	EAST WIND	870c	2 c
		תרומה	OFFERING	929a	3
48	11	בן	SON	121b	1 jh
		כהן	PRIEST	464a	6
		לוי	LEVITE	533a	3 2a
		צדק	RIGHTEOUS	843b	1 a
		משמרת	GUARD	1038c	4 a
		תעה	ERR	1073c	3
48	12	אל	TO	40d	8
		לוי	LEVITE	533a	3 2a
		קדש	APARTNESS	872a	2 g
		תרומה	OFFERING	929a	3
		תרומיה	SUBDIVISION	929c	
48	13	כהן	PRIEST	464a	6
		לוי	LEVITE	533a	3 2a
		עמה	CLOSE BY	769c	A
48	14	לא	NOT	518c	1 aa
		מור	CHANGE	558c	2
		מכר	SELL	569b	
		עבר	PASS OVER	718b	6 f
		עבר	PASS OVER	719a	4
		קדש	APARTNESS	872a	2 g
		ראשית	BEGINNING	912b	1 b
48	15	מגרש	COMMON-LAND	177c	
		חל	PROFANENESS	320d	
		חמש	FIVE	332a	4
		מושב	DWELLING	444b	2 a
		יתר	BE LEFT OVER	451b	
48	16	מדה	SIZE	551c	2
		נגב	SOUTH-COUNTRY	616b	2
		קדים	EAST WIND	870c	2 a
48	17	מגרש	COMMON-LAND	177c	
		נגב	SOUTH-COUNTRY	616c	2
		קדים	EAST WIND	870c	2 c
48	18	תבואה	PRODUCT	100a	1
		יתר	BE LEFT OVER	451b	
		לחם	FOOD	537b	1 b
		עבד	WORK	713a	1
		עמה	CLOSE BY	769c	A
		תרומה	OFFERING	929a	3
48	19	עבד	WORK	713a	1
		עבד	WORK	713a	1
48	20	אחזה	POSSESSION	28c	
		רביעי	FOURTH	918a	3
		רום	BE HIGH	927d	3 a
		תרומה	OFFERING	929a	3
		אחזה	POSSESSION	28c	
48	21	זה	THIS	262a	6 e
		חלק	PORTION	324b	2 c
		יתר	BE LEFT OVER	451c	
		על	UPON	757c	27c ab
		עמה	CLOSE BY	769c	A
		פנה	FACE	816c	2 1c
		קדים	EAST WIND	870c	2 b
		מקדש	SACRED PLACE	874b	4
		תרומה	OFFERING	929a	3
48	22	אחזה	POSSESSION	28c	
		בנימין	BENJAMIN	122d	1
		גבול	BOUNDARY	148a	1 b
		לוי	LEVITE	533a	3 2a
48	23	בנימין	BENJAMIN	122d	1
		יתר	REMAINDER	451d	1 b
48	24	בנימין	BENJAMIN	122d	1
		על	UPON	756a	26a
48	25	יששכר	ISSACHAR	441b	1
48	26	זבולן	ZEBULUN	259d	2
		יששכר	ISSACHAR	441b	1
48	27	גד	GAD	151c	1 b
		זבולן	ZEBULUN	259d	3
48	28	גד	GAD	151c	1 b
		חצצנתמר	HAZAZON-TAMAR	346c	
		ים	SEA	410d	1
		תימן	SOUTH	412d	1 b
		מי	WATER	565b	1 a
		נגב	SOUTH-COUNTRY	616b	2
		נחל	WADY	636c	2
		על	UPON	757c	27c ab

Ch	v.	Heb	Eng	Page	Sec
		קדש	KADESH	873d	1
		מריבה	MERIBAH	937b	2
		תמר	TAMAR	1071c	2
48	29	ב	IN	89a	17c
		מחלקת	DIVISION	325a	1
		נפל	FALL	658b	3
48	30	אלף	THOUSAND	49a	1 c
		תוצאה	OUT GOING	426a	1
		מדה	MEASURE	551c	2
48	31	לוי	LEVI	532a	2
		ראובן	REUBEN	910a	2
		שער	GATE	1045a	1 c
48	32	בנימין	BENJAMIN	122d	1
		דן	DAN	192d	2
		יוסף	JOSEPH	415d	1 c
		קדים	EAST WIND	870c	2 b
48	33	זבולן	ZEBULUN	259d	2
		יששכר	ISSACHAR	441a	1
		מדה	MEASURE	551c	2
		נגב	SOUTH-COUNTRY	616b	2
48	34	אשר	ASHER	81b	2
		גד	GAD	151c	1 b
		נפתלי	NAPHTALI	837a	2 a
48	35	יהוה	YAHWEH	219c	2 3
		יום	DAY	401a	7 j
		מן	FROM	581c	4 a
		שם	THERE	1027c	3 c

DANIEL

Ch	v.	Heb	Eng	Page	Sec
1	1	בבל	BABEL	93c	
		דנאל	DANIEL	193b	4
		יהויקים	JEHOIAKIM	220c	1
		מלכת	REIGN	575a	2
		נבוכדראצר	NEBUCHADNEZ-ZAR	613b	
1	2	צור	CONFINE	848d	2
		אדון	LORD	11c	3 2b
		אלהים	GOD	43c	2 a
		אלהים	GOD	44a	3 b
		אוצר	TREASURE	70a	2
		בוא	COME	99b	2
		בית	HOUSE	109b	1 ae 0
		דנאל	DANIEL	193b	4
		יהויקים	JEHOIAKIM	220c	1
		כלי	UTENSIL	480a	2 f
		מן	FROM	580d	3 ba
		קצת	END	892c	2
		שנער	SHINAR	1042c	
1	3	אשפנז	ASHPENAZ	80c	
		דנאל	DANIEL	193b	4
		ו	AND	252c	1 b
		זרע	SOWING	282d	4 e
		מלוכה	KINGSHIP	574d	
		סרים	EUNUCH	710c	
		פרתמים	NOBLES	832c	
1	4	בין	DISCERN	107a	1 b
		דנאל	DANIEL	193b	4
		היכל	PALACE	228b	1
		חכמה	WISDOM	315c	3
		טוב	PLEASANT	373c	1 a
		ידע	KNOW	394c	5
		דעת	WISDOM	395d	2 a
		מדע	KNOWLEDGE	396b	1
		ילד	CHILD	409c	D
		כח	STRENGTH	470d	1 b
		כשדים	CHALDEANS	505b	1 b
		למד	LEARN	540d	
		לשון	TONGUE	546d	2
		מאום	BLEMISH	548c	1
		ספר	MISSIVE	*707c	2
		עמד	STAND	764a	1 d
		מראה	VISION	909d	1 b
		שכל	BE PRUDENT	968b	3
1	5	גדל	GROW UP	152b	1
		דבר	WORD	183c	4 1
		דנאל	DANIEL	193b	4
		יום	DAY	400c	7 e3
		יין	WINE	406c	A
		מנה	APPOINT	584b	
		מנה	PORTION	*584b	
		פתבג	PORTION	834a	
		קצת	END	892d	3
		שנה	YEAR	1040b	
		משתה	DRINK	1059d	2
1	6	דנאל	DANIEL	193b	4
		דנאל	DANIEL	193b	4
		חנניהו	HANANIAH	337b	5
		מישאל	MISHAEL	567d	1
		עזריה	AZARIAH	*1105d	
		עזריה	ADDENDA ET COR-RIGENDA	1125d	
1	7	בלטשאצר	BELTESHAZZAR	117b	
		בלטשאצר	BELTESHAZZAR	*117b	
		חנניהו	HANANIAH	337b	5
		מדע	KNOWLEDGE	396b	1
		מישאל	MISHAEL	567d	2
		מישך	MESHACH	568d	
		סרים	EUNUCH	710c	
		עבדנגו	ABED-NEGO	715a	
		שום	TO PLACE	964c	5 b
		שר	CHIEFTAIN	978c	4 a
		שדרך	SHADRACH	995b	
		שם	NAME	1027d	2 a

Ch	v.	Heb	Eng	Page	Sec
		עזריה	ADDENDA ET COR-RIGENDA	1125d	
1	8	אשר	THAT	83c	8 ab
		בקש	SEEK	135a	6
		גאל	DEFILE	146a	
		לב	HEART	525a	23d
		סריס	EUNUCH	710c	
		פתבג	PORTION	834a	
		שום	TO PLACE	963c	2b
		שר	CHIEFTAIN	978c	4a
		משתה	DRINK	1059d	2
1	9	אלהים	GOD	43d	3
		חסד	GOODNESS	338d	12
		נתן	GIVE	681a	3b
		סריס	EUNUCH	710c	
		רחמים	COMPASSION	933c	2
		שר	CHIEFTAIN	978c	4a
1	10	מאכל	FOOD	38b	
		אשר	THAT	83c	8c
		זעף	BE VEXED	277a	1
		חוב	BE GUILTY	295a	
		ילד	CHILD	409c	D
		ירא	FEAR	431b	1b
		מה	HOW	554b	4d
		מנה	PORTION	*584b	
		מנה	APPOINT	584b	
		סריס	EUNUCH	710c	
		ראה	TO SEE	907a	23
		ראש	HEAD	911b	8
		שר	CHIEFTAIN	978c	4a
		משתה	DRINK	1059d	2
1	11	חנניהו	HANANIAH	337b	5
		מישאל	MISHAEL	567d	2
		מלצר	GUARDIAN	576d	
		מנה	APPOINT	584b	
		סריס	EUNUCH	710c	
		שר	CHIEFTAIN	978c	4a
		עזריה	ADDENDA ET COR-RIGENDA	1125d	
1	12	זרע	VEGETABLE	283b	
		נסה	TEST	650b	1
		עשר	TEN	796d	2b
1	13	ילד	CHILD	409c	D
		עשה	DO	794b	12
		פתבג	PORTION	834a	
		ראה	TO SEE	907a	1b
		ראה	TO SEE	908c	1c
		מראה	VISION	909c	1b
		אריה	LION	1082c	
1	14	נסה	TEST	650b	1
		עשר	TEN	796d	2b
1	15	בריא	FAT	135d	
		בשר	FLESH	142c	1b
		טוב	PLEASANT	373c	1a
		ילד	CHILD	409c	D
		עשר	TEN	796d	2b
		פתבג	PORTION	834a	
		קצת	END	892d	3
		ראה	TO SEE	908c	1c
		מראה	VISION	909c	1b
1	16	היה	BE	227c	35a
		זרען	VEGETABLE	283b	
		מלצר	GUARDIAN	576d	
		פתבג	PORTION	834a	
1	17	אלהים	GOD	43d	3
		בין	DISCERN	107a	3d
		חזון	VISION	303a	1
		חכמה	WISDOM	315c	3
		חלום	DREAM	321d	2a
		ילד	CHILD	409c	D
		ספר	MISSIVE	*707c	4
		ארבע	FOUR	917a	1c4
		שכל	BE PRUDENT	968b	3
1	18	מן	FROM	583d	9 b2
		נבוכדראצר	NEBUCHADNEZZAR	613b	
		סריס	EUNUCH	710c	
		קצת	BOUNDRY	892d	4
		שר	CHIEFTAIN	978c	4a
1	19	דבר	SPEAK	181b	3d
		חנניהו	HANANIAH	337b	5
		מצא	FIND	394a	1i
		מישאל	MISHAEL	567d	2
		עזריה	ADDENDA ET COR-RIGENDA	1125d	
1	20	אשף	CONJURER	80b	
		בינה	UNDERSTANDING	108a	1
		בקש	SEEK	135a	4b
		חכמה	WISDOM	315c	3
		חרטם	ENGRAVER	355a	2
		יד	TIME	390c	4c
		מלכות	KINGDOM	575a	3
		מצא	FIND	593d	1d
		על	UPON	755a	22
1	21	היה	BE	226d	32
		כורש	CYRUS	468d	
2	1	היה	BE	227d	3
		חלם	DREAM	321c	B
		חלום	DREAM	321d	2a
		שנה	SLEEP	446a	
		מלכות	REIGN	575a	2
		נבוכדראצר	NEBUCHADNEZZAR	613b	
		על	UPON	753d	21d
		פעם	THRUST	821d	
		רוח	BREATH	925b	3e

Ch	v.	Heb	Eng	Page	Sec
2	2	על	UPON	1106b	1b
		אשף	CONJURER	80b	
		חלום	DREAM	321d	2a
		חרטם	ENGRAVER	355a	2
		כשדים	CHALDEANS	505b	1c
		כשף	PRACTICE SORCERY	506c	
		נגד	BE CONSPICUOUS	616d	2
		חרטם	ADDENDA ET COR-RIGENDA	1123c	
2	3	חלם	DREAM	321c	B
		חלום	DREAM	321d	2a
		פעם	THRUST	821d	
		רוח	BREATH	925b	3e
2	4	ארמית	ARAMAIC	74c	
		דבר	SPEAK	181b	3c
		כשדים	CHALDEANS	505b	1c
		אמר	TELL	1081b	2
		ה	AND	1091a	C
		חוה	DECLARE	1092b	
		חיא	LIVE	1092d	
		חלם	DREAM	1093a	
		ל	TO	1098b	1
		ל	AT	1098c	5
		מלך	KING	1100b	
		מלה	WORD	1100d	1
		מן	FROM	1101a	2a
		גללו	REFUSE-HEAP	1102c	
		עבד	MAKE	1105a	1
		ענה	ANSWER	1107b	1
		פשר	INTERPRETATION	1109b	
2	5	אזדא	SURE	1079b	
		אמר	SAY	1081b	1
		בית	HOUSE	1084c	1
		הדם	MEMBER	1089d	
		הן	IF	1090c	1
		ו	AND	*1090d	
		ו	AND	1091a	1
		ידע	KNOW	1095a	
		כשדי	CHALDEAN	1098a	2
		ל	TO	1098b	1
		לא	NOT	1098c	
		מלך	KING	1100b	
		מלה	WORD	1100d	1
		מן	FROM	1101a	2a
		נולו	REFUSE-HEAP	1102c	
		עבד	MAKE	1105a	1
		ענה	ANSWER	1107b	1
		פשר	INTERPRETATION	1109b	
		שום	MAKE	1113d	
		לחן	THEREFORE	*530a	
2	6	הן	IF	1090c	1
		ו	AND	*1090d	
		ה	AND	1091a	B
		חוה	DECLARE	1092b	
		חוה	DECLARE	1092b	
		יקר	HONOUR	1096a	
		לחן	THEREFORE	1099a	
		נבזבה	REWARD	1102a	
		מתנא	GIFT	1103d	
		פשר	INTERPRETATION	1109b	
		קבל	RECEIVE	1110b	
		קדם	BEFORE	1110c	2
		שגיא	GREAT	1113c	1
2	7	אמר	SAY	1081a	1
		אמר	TELL	1081b	2
		ו	AND	1090d	
		ה	AND	1091a	C
		חוה	DECLARE	1092b	
		ל	TO	1098b	1
		עבד	SLAVE	1105a	
		ענה	ANSWER	1107b	1
		פשר	INTERPRETATION	1109b	
		תנינות	THE SECOND TIME	1118b	
2	8	זבינא	ZEBINA	259c	
		מן	ON ACCOUNT OF	580c	2g
		אזדא	SURE	1079b	
		אנה	I	1081c	
		אנתון	YOU	1082a	
		די	THAT	1088a	3a
		ו	AND	1091a	
		זבן	GAIN	1091a	
		חזה	BEHOLD	1092c	3
		ידע	KNOW	1095a	
		יציב	CERTAIN	1096a	1
		מלה	WORD	1100d	1
		מן	FROM	1101a	2a
		מן	AT	1101a	2d
		עדן	TIME	1105c	1
		ענה	ANSWER	1107b	1
		קבל	BECAUSE THAT	1110b	2b
2	9	לחן	THEREFORE	*530a	
		חד	ONE	1079c	1
		אמר	TELL	1081b	2
		אמר	SAY	1081b	1
		די	THAT	1088a	3a
		די	THAT	1088a	3b
		די	THAT	1088b	4c
		דנה	THIS	1089a	B
		דת	DECREE	1089b	1
		הוא	HE	1090a	
		הן	IF	1090c	1
		ו	AND	1091a	C
		זמן	AGREE TOGETHER	1091c	
		חוה	DECLARE	1092b	
		ידע	KNOW	1095a	
		ידע	KNOW	1095a	
		כדב	FALSE	1096c	
		ל	TO	1098c	6

Ch	v.	Heb	Eng	Page	Sec
2	10	לא	NOT	1098c	
		לחן	THEREFORE	1099a	
		מלה	WORD	1100d	1
		עד	UNTIL	1105b	2a
		עדן	TIME	1105c	1
		קדם	BEFORE	1110c	1
		שחת	CORRUPT	1115a	
		שנא	CHANGE	1116c	
		איתי	THERE IS	1080b	
		אמר	SAY	1081b	1
		אנש	MAN	1081d	1
		אשף	ENCHANTER	1083b	
		דנה	THIS	1089a	C
		ו	AND	*1090d	
		ו	AND	1090d	
		חוה	DECLARE	1092b	
		חרטם	MAGICIAN	1093d	
		יבשת	EARTH	1094d	
		יכל	BE ABLE	1095d	1
		כל	ALL	1097a	2
		כשדי	CHALDEAN	1098a	2
		ל	MARK OF ACCUSATIVE	1098b	2
		לא	NOT	1098c	
		ל	TO	1098c	6
		מלך	KING	1100b	
		מלה	THING	1100d	2
		על	UPON	1106b	1a
		ענה	ANSWER	1107b	1
		קבל	BECAUSE THAT	1110b	2b
		קדם	BEFORE	1110c	1
		רב	GREAT	1112b	1
		שאל	ASK	1114a	1
		שלים	RULING	1115d	2
2	11	יקר	BE PRECIOUS	*429d	1a
		אחרן	ANOTHER	1080a	
		איתי	THERE IS	1080b	
		איתי	THERE IS	1080b	
		אלה	GOD	1080c	1
		בשר	FLESH	1085b	
		מדר	DWELLING-PLACE	1087b	
		די	WHO	1087d	1a
		חוה	DECLARE	1092b	
		יקיר	DIFFICULT	1096b	2
		לחן	EXCEPT	1099a	1a
		מלך	KING	1100b	
		מלה	THING	1100d	2
		עם	WITH	1107a	1a
		קדם	BEFORE	1110c	1
		שאל	ASK	1114a	1
2	12	אבד	PERISH	1078b	
		אמר	COMMAND	1081b	3
		בבל	BABYLON	1084a	
		בנס	BE ANGRY	1084d	
		חכים	WISE MAN	1093a	
		ל	MARK OF ACCUSATIVE	1098b	2
		ל	TO	1098c	6
		קבל	BECAUSE OF	1110b	2a
		שגיא	MUCH	1113c	3
2	13	בעא	SEEK	1085a	2
		דניאל	DANIEL	1088c	
		דת	DECREE	1089b	1
		ה	AND	1091a	D
		חבר	FELLOW	1092a	
		חכים	WISE MAN	1093a	
		ל	TO	1098c	6
		נפק	GO FORTH	1103b	
		קטל	SLAY	1111a	
		קטל	SLAY	1111a	
2	14	טבח	COOK	*371a	2
		אדין	THEN	1078d	
		אריוך	ARIOCH	1082d	
		דניאל	DANIEL	1088c	
		חכים	WISE MAN	1093a	
		טעם	JUDGMENT	1094c	2
		עטא	COUNSEL	1096a	
		ל	MARK OF ACCUSATIVE	1098b	2
		ל	TO	1098c	6
		נפק	GO FORTH	1103b	
		קטל	SLAY	1111a	
		רב	GREAT	1112b	3
		תוב	RETURN	1117d	1
2	15	פנה	FACE	818a	25a c
		אדין	THEN	1078d	
		אריוך	ARIOCH	1082d	
		די	THAT	1088a	2
		דת	DECREE	1089b	1
		ו	AND	1091a	
		חצף	SHEW INSOLENCE	1093c	
		ידע	KNOW	1095a	
		מה	WHAT	1099d	3c
		מלה	THING	1100d	2
		על	ON ACCOUNT OF	1106b	1c
		ענה	ANSWER	1107b	1
		קדם	BEFORE	1110c	2
		שלים	RULING	1115d	2
2	16	בעא	ASK	1085a	2
		די	THAT	1088a	3c
		ו	AND	*1091a	A
		זמן	TIME	1091c	
		חוה	DECLARE	1092b	
		ל	TO	1098b	1
		מן	FROM	1101a	1d
		נתן	GIVE	1103d	2

Ch	v.	Heb	Eng	Page	Sec
2	17	עלל	GO IN	1106c	
		מישאל	MISHAEL	567d	2
		אדין	THEN	1078d	
		אזל	GO	1079b	1
		בית	HOUSE	1084c	1
		ו	AND	*1090d	
		חבר	FELLOW	1092a	
		חוה	DECLARE	1092b	
		חנניה	HANANIAH	1093b	
		ידע	KNOW	1095a	
		מישאל	MISHAEL	1100a	
		מלה	THING	1100d	2
		עבדנגו	ABED-NEGO	1105a	
		עזריה	AZARIAH	1105d	
2	18	פנה	FACE	818a	2 5 a c
		שמי	HEAVENS	*1030b	2 a
		אבד	PERISH	1078b	
		אלה	GOD	1080c	2
		בעא	ASK	1085a	1
		די	THAT	1088b	3 c
		דנה	THIS	1089a	A
		ו	AND	*1091a	A
		חבר	FELLOW	1092a	
		על	ON ACCOUNT OF	1106b	1 e
		עם	WITH	1107a	1 a
		קדם	BEFORE	1110c	2
		רז	SECRET	1112d	
		רחמין	COMPASSION	1113a	
		שאר	REMAINDER	1114b	
		שמין	HEAVENS	1116b	2
2	19	אדין	THEN	1078d	
		אלה	GOD	1080c	2
		ברך	BLESS	1085c	
		גלא	REVEAL	1086c	
		די	THAT	1088a	2
		חזו	VISION	1092c	1
		ל	TO	1098b	1
		ליליא	NIGHT	1099b	
		רז	SECRET	1112d	
		שמין	HEAVENS	1116b	2
2	20	ברך	BLESS	1085c	
		גבורה	MIGHT	1086a	
		די	THAT	1088a	2
		די	THAT	1088a	3 b
		די	THAT	1088a	2
		הוא	COME TO PASS	1090a	
		הוא	HE	1090a	
		ו	AND	1091a	
		חכמה	WISDOM	1093a	
			IN REGARD TO	1098c	4 b
		מן	FROM	1101a	4
		עד	EVEN TO	1105b	1 c
		עלם	PERPETUITY	1106d	
		ענה	ANSWER	1107b	2
		שם	NAME	1116a	
2	21	יהועדה	JEHOADDAH	*221a	
		בינה	UNDERSTANDING	1084b	
		הוא	HE	1090a	
		זמן	TIME	1091c	
		חכים	WISE MAN	1093a	
		חכמה	WISDOM	1093a	
		ידע	KNOW	1095a	
		מנדע	KNOWLEDGE	1095b	
		יהב	GIVE	1095b	1
		ל	TO	1098b	1
		עדא	PASS AWAY	1105b	
		עדן	TIME	1105c	1
		קום	STAND	1110d	4
		קום	ARISE	1111a	1
		שנא	CHANGE	1116d	
2	22	גלא	REVEAL	1086c	
		הוא	HE	1090a	
		חשוך	DARKNESS	1094a	
		ידע	KNOW	1095a	
		מה	WHAT	1099d	2
		נהיר	LIGHT	1102c	
		סתר	HIDE	1104c	
		עמיק	DEEP	1107a	
		עם	WITH	1107a	1 a
		שרא	ABIDE	1117b	2
2	23	אב	FATHER	1078b	2
		אלה	GOD	1080c	2
		אנה	I	1081c	
		בעא	ASK	1085a	1
		גבורה	MIGHT	1086a	
		די	WHO	1087d	1 a
		די	THAT	1088a	3 b
		חכמה	WISDOM	1093a	
		ידע	KNOW	1095a	
		ידא	PRAISE	1095a	
		ידע	KNOW	1095a	
		יהב	GIVE	1095b	1
		מלה	THING	1100d	2
		כען	NOW	1107b	
		שבח	PRAISE	1114b	
2	24	אבד	PERISH	1078b	
		אבד	PERISH	1078b	
		אזל	GO	1079b	1
		אל	DO NOT	1080b	
		אמר	SAY	1081b	1
		אריוך	ARIOCH	1082d	
		די	WHO	1087d	1 a
		ה	AND	1091a	C
		חוה	DECLARE	1092b	
		כן	THUS	1097b	
		ל	MARK OF ACCUSA-TIVE	1098b	2
		ל	TO	1098c	6
		מנה	NUMBER	1101b	
		על	TO	1106b	4 a
		עלל	GO IN	1106c	
		עלל	GO IN	1106c	
		קבל	BECAUSE OF	1110b	2 a
		קדם	BEFORE	1110c	1
2	25	אדין	THEN	1078d	
		אמר	SAY	1081b	1
		אריוך	ARIOCH	1082d	
		בהל	ALARM	1084b	
		בר	SON	1085b	1
		גבר	MAN	1086a	
		גלו	EXILE	1086c	
		די	WHO	1087d	1 a
		די	THAT	1088a	2
		די	THAT	1088b	3 d
		ידע	KNOW	1095a	
		יהוד	JUDAH	1095c	
		כן	THUS	1097b	
		מן	FROM	1101a	3
		עלל	GO IN	1106c	
		קדם	BEFORE	1110c	1
		שכח	FIND	1115b	
2	26	איתי	THERE IS	1080b	
		בלטשאצר	BELTESHAZZAR	1084d	
		די	WHO	1087d	1 a
		ה	INTERROGATIVE PARTICLE	1089b	
		חזה	BEHOLD	1092c	3
		ידע	KNOW	1095a	
		כהל	BE ABLE	1096d	
		ענה	ANSWER	1107b	2
		שם	NAME	1116a	
2	27	אשף	ENCHANTER	1083b	
		גזר	DETERMINE	1086b	
		ו	AND	*1090d	
		חכים	WISE MAN	1093a	
		חרטם	MAGICIAN	1093d	
		יכל	BE ABLE	1095d	1
		לא	NOT	1098c	
		ענה	ANSWER	1107b	1
		קדם	BEFORE	1110c	1
		רז	SECRET	1112d	
		שאל	ASK	1114a	1
2	28	אחרית	END	31b	B
		אחרית	END	1079d	
		איתי	THERE IS	1080b	
		אלה	GOD	1080c	2
		ב	IN	1083d	1
		ברם	ONLY	1085c	
		גלא	REVEAL	1086c	
		די	WHO	1087d	1 b
		דנה	THIS	1089a	A
		הוא	COME TO PASS	1089d	1
		הוא	HE	1090a	
		חזו	VISION	1092c	1
		חלם	DREAM	1093a	
		ידע	KNOW	1095a	
		יום	DAY	1095c	
		מה	WHAT	1099d	2
		נבוכדנצר	NEBUCHADNEZ-ZAR	1102a	
		על	UPON	1106b	1 a
		ראש	HEAD	1112a	2
		רז	SECRET	1112d	
		משכב	COUCH	1115b	
		שמין	HEAVENS	1116a	2
2	29	אתר	AFTER	30b	2 b
		אחר	AFTER	1079d	
		אנתה	THOU	1082a	
		גלא	REVEAL	1086c	
		די	WHO	1087d	1 b
		דנה	THIS	1089a	A
		הוא	COME TO PASS	1089d	1
		ידע	KNOW	1095a	
		מה	WHAT	1099d	2
		סלק	COME UP	1104b	
		רז	SECRET	1112d	
		רעיון	THOUGHT	1113b	
		משכב	COUCH	1115b	
2	30	איתי	THERE IS	1080a	
		אנה	I	1081c	
		ב	WITH	1083d	3
		גלא	REVEAL	1086c	
		גברה	CAUSE	1087a	
		דנה	THIS	1089a	A
		חי	LIVING	1092d	1
		חכמה	WISDOM	1093a	
		ידע	KNOW	1095a	
		ידע	KNOW	1095a	
		לבב	HEART	1098d	
		להן	BUT	1099a	1 b
		מן	FROM	1101b	5
		רז	SECRET	1112d	
		רעיון	THOUGHT	1113b	
2	31	זו	ZIV	264c	
		חד	A	1079c	2
		אלו	LO	1080d	
		אנתה	THOU	1082a	
		דחל	FEAR	1087c	
		דכן	THIS	1088c	
		הוא	COME TO PASS	1090a	3
		זיו	SPLENDOUR	1091b	
		חזה	BEHOLD	1092c	3
		יתיר	PRE-EMINENT	1096c	
		צלם	IMAGE	1109d	
		קבל	BEFORE	1110a	1 a
		רו	APPEARANCE	1112a	
		רב	GREAT	1112b	1
		שגיא	GREAT	1113c	1
2	32	דהב	GOLD	1087a	
		די	THAT	1088a	2
		דרע	ARM	1089a	
		הוא	HE	1090a	
		חדי	BREAST	1092a	
		טב	GOOD	1094b	
		ירכה	THIGH	1096b	
		כסף	SILVER	1097c	
		מעא	BELLY	1101c	
		נחש	COPPER	1102d	
		צלם	IMAGE	1109d	
		ראש	HEAD	1112a	1
2	33	מן	FROM	580d	3 ba
		די	THAT	1088a	2
		חסף	CLAY	1093c	
		מן	FROM	1101a	3
		פרזל	IRON	1108d	
		רגל	FOOT	1112c	
		שק	LEG	1114d	
2	34	לא	NOT	*518d	1 ac
		אבן	STONE	1078b	1
		ב	WITH	1083d	1
		גזר	CUT	1086b	
		די	WHO	1087d	1 a
		די	THAT	1088b	4 c
		דקק	BE SHATTERED	1089a	
		הוא	COME TO PASS	1090a	3
		המו	THEY	1090c	B
		חזה	BEHOLD	1092c	3
		חסף	CLAY	1093c	
		יד	HAND	1094d	1
		מחא	SMITE	1099d	
		עד	UNTIL	1105b	2 a
		פרזל	IRON	1108d	
		צלם	IMAGE	1109d	
		רגל	FOOT	1112c	
2	35	אבן	STONE	1078b	1
		אדין	THEN	1078d	
		אדר	THRESHING-FLOOR	1078d	
		חד	ONE	1079c	1
		ארע	EARTH	1083a	
		דהב	GOLD	1087a	
		דקק	BE SHATTERED	1089a	
		הוא	COME TO PASS	1089d	2
		הוא	COME TO PASS	1090a	2
		המו	THEY	1090c	B
		חסף	CLAY	1093c	
		טור	MOUNTAIN	1094b	
		כל	ALL	1097a	2
		כסף	SILVER	1097c	1
		ל	TO	1098b	3
		מחא	SMITE	1099d	
		מלא	FILL	1100a	
		מן	FROM	1101a	1 c
		נחש	COPPER	1102d	
		נשא	LIFT	1103c	
		עור	CHAFF	1105c	
		צלם	IMAGE	1109d	
		קיט	SUMMER	1111b	
		רב	GREAT	1112b	1
		רוח	WIND	1112d	1
		שכח	FIND	1115b	
2	36	אמר	TELL	1081b	2
2	37	אנתה	THOU	1082a	
		די	WHO	1087d	1 a
		ו	AND	*1090d	
		חסן	POWER	1093c	
		יהב	GIVE	1095b	1
		יקר	HONOUR	1096a	
		מלך	KING	*1100b	
		מלכו	KINGDOM	1100c	2
		שמין	HEAVENS	1116b	2
		תקף	MIGHT	1118c	
2	38	אנש	MAN	1081d	2
		אנתה	THOU	1082a	
		ב	IN	1083d	2
		ב	IN	1083d	1
		ב	IN	1084a	8
		בר	SON	1085b	1
		בר	FIELD	1085c	
		דור	DWELL	1087b	
		די	WHO	1087d	1 a
		די	THAT	1088a	2
		הוא	HE	1090a	
		חוא	BEAST	1092d	
		יד	HAND	1094d	2
		יהב	GIVE	1095b	1
		כל	ALL	1097a	2
		כל	ALL	1097a	1
		עוף	FOWL	1105c	
		ראש	HEAD	1112a	1
		שלט	RULE	1115d	
		שמין	HEAVENS	1116a	1
2	39	אחרן	ANOTHER	1080a	
		ארע	EARTH	1083a	
		ארע	EARTH	1083a	
		אתר	PLACE	1083d	B
		די	THAT	1088a	2
		מלכו	KINGDOM	1100c	2

Ch	v.	Heb	Eng	Page	Sec
		מן	FROM	1101b	5
		נחש	COPPER	1102d	
		קום	ARISE	1110d	2
		שלט	HAVE POWER	1115d	
		תליתי	THIRD	1118a	
2	40	אלין	THESE	1080d	
		דקק	BE SHATTERED	1089a	
		דקק	BE SHATTERED	1089a	
		הוא	COME TO PASS	1090a	3
		חשל	SHATTER	1094a	
		ד	LIKE	1096c	
		כל	ALL	1097b	3
		מלכו	KINGDOM	1100c	2
		קבל	BECAUSE THAT	1110b	2b
		רביעי	FOURTH	1112c	
		רעע	CRUSH	1113b	
		רעע	CRUSH	1113b	
		תקף	MIGHTY	1118c	
2	41	די	THAT	1088a	3b
		חזה	BEHOLD	1092c	3
		חסף	CLAY	1093c	
		חסף	CLAY	1093c	
		טין	CLAY	1094b	
		מלכו	KINGDOM	1100c	2
		מן	FROM	1101a	3
		מן	FROM	1101a	3
		נצבה	FIRMNESS	1103b	
		ערב	MIX	1107d	
		פלג	DIVIDE	1108b	
		פחר	POTTER	1108b	
		אצבע	TOE	1109c	2
		קבל	BECAUSE THAT	1110b	2b
		רגל	FOOT	1112c	
2	42	הוא	COME TO PASS	1090a	3
		חסף	CLAY	1093c	
		מלכו	KINGDOM	1100c	2
		מן	FROM	1101a	3
		מן	FROM	1101a	3
		אצבע	TOE	1109c	2
		קצת	END	1111c	
		רגל	FOOT	1112c	
		תבר	BREAK	1117c	
		תקף	MIGHTY	1118c	
2	43	הא	LO	*210c	2
		אנש	MAN	1081d	2
		דבק	CLING	1087a	
		די	THAT	1088a	3b
		די	THAT	1088b	4aa
		הא	DEMONSTRATIVE PARTICLE	1089c	
		זרע	SEED	1091d	
		חזה	BEHOLD	1092c	3
		חסף	CLAY	1093c	
		חסף	CLAY	1093c	
		טין	CLAY	1094b	
		לא	NOT	1098c	
		עם	WITH	1107a	1a
		ערב	MIX	1107d	
		ערב	MIX	1107d	
		ערב	MIX	1107d	
2	44	אחרן	ANOTHER	1080a	
		אלין	THESE	*1080d	
		אלין	THESE	1080d	
		אנון	THEY	1081c	
		די	THAT	1088a	2
		דקק	BE SHATTERED	1089a	
		הוא	HE	1090a	
		חבל	DESTROY	1091d	
		יום	DAY	1095c	
		ל	AT	1098c	5
		מלך	KING	1100b	
		מלכו	KINGDOM	1100c	2
		מלכו	KINGDOM	1100c	2
		סוף	BE FUFILLED	1104b	
		עלם	PERPETUITY	1106d	
		עם	PEOPLE	1107a	
		קום	STAND	1110d	5
		קום	ARISE	1111a	1
		שבק	LEAVE	1114c	
		שמין	HEAVENS	1116b	2
2	45	אחר	AFTER	30b	2b
		אבן	STONE	1078d	1
		אחר	AFTER	1079d	
		אלה	GOD	1080c	2
		אמן	TRUST	1081a	
		גזר	CUT	1086b	
		די	WHO	1087d	1a
		די	WHO	1087d	1b
		די	THAT	1088a	3a
		דקק	BE SHATTERED	1089a	
		דנה	THIS	1089d	B
		הוא	COME TO PASS	1089d	1
		חזה	BEHOLD	1092c	3
		חסף	CLAY	1093c	
		טור	MOUNTAIN	1094b	
		יד	HAND	1094d	1
		ידע	KNOW	1095a	
		יציב	CERTAIN	1096a	1
		כסף	SILVER	1097c	1
		מה	WHAT	1099d	2
		מן	FROM	1101a	1c
		נחש	COPPER	1102d	
		קבל	BECAUSE THAT	1110b	2b
		רב	GREAT	1112b	2
2	46	אדין	THEN	1078d	
		אמר	COMMAND	1081b	3
		אנף	FACE	1081d	1
		מנחה	OFFERING	1101c	1
		ניחח	SOOTHING	1102d	
		נפל	FALL	1103a	1
		נסך	POUR OUT	1103a	
		סגד	DO HOMAGE	1104a	
		על	UPON	1106b	1a
2	47	אלה	GOD	1080c	2
		גלא	REVEAL	1086c	
		גלא	REVEAL	1086c	
		די	THAT	1088a	3a
		די	THAT	1088a	3b
		הוא	HE	1090a	
		יכל	BE ABLE	1095d	1
		מן	AT	1101a	2d
		מרא	LORD	1101c	
		ענה	ANSWER	1107b	2
		קשט	TRUTH	1112a	
		רז	SECRET	1112d	
		רז	SECRET	1112d	
2	48	רבה	GROW GREAT	u112b	
		אדין	THEN	1078d	
		מדינה	DISTRICT	1088c	
		יהב	GIVE	1095b	1
		מתנא	GIFT	1103d	
		סגן	PREFECT	1104a	
		על	OVER	1106b	2
		רב	GREAT	1112b	3
		רב	GREAT	1112b	3
		שגיא	MUCH	1113c	2
		שלט	RULE	1115d	
2	49	בעא	ASK	1085a	1
		די	THAT	1088a	2
		מדינה	DISTRICT	1088c	
		ה	AND	1091a	C
		מישך	MESHACH	1100a	
		מן	FROM	1101a	1d
		מנה	NUMBER	1101b	
		עבדנגו	ABED-NEGO	1105a	
		עבידה	WORK	1105a	1
		עזריה	AZARIAH	1105d	
		על	OVER	1106b	2
		שדרך	SHADRAK	1114c	
3	1	אמה	CUBIT	1081a	
		ב	IN	1083d	1
		בקעא	PLAIN	1085a	
		דורא	DURA	1087b	
		די	THAT	1088a	2
		מדינה	DISTRICT	1088c	
		עבד	MAKE	1104d	1
		פתי	BREADTH	1109b	
		צלם	IMAGE	1109d	
		קום	ARISE	1111a	1
		רום	HEIGHT	1112d	
		שת	SIX	1114d	
		שתין	SIXTY	1114d	
3	2	אדרגזר	CONSELLOR	1078d	
		אחשדרפנין	SATRAPS	1080a	
		אתה	COME	1083c	
		גדבריא	TREASURER	1086a	
		מדינה	DISTRICT	1088c	
		דתבר	JUDGE	1089b	
		ו	AND	*1090d	
		חנכה	DEDICATION	1093b	
		כל	ALL	1097a	1
		כנש	GATHER	1097b	
		ל	TO	1098c	6
		סגן	PREFECT	1104a	
		פחה	GOVERNOR	1108b	
		קום	ARISE	1111a	1
		שלח	SEND	1115c	
		תפתיא	MAGISTRATE	1118b	
		שלטון	ADDENDA ET CORRIGENDA	1127c	
3	3	אדין	THEN	1078d	
		אדרגזר	CONSELLOR	1078d	
		אחשדרפנין	SATRAPS	1080a	
		גדבריא	TREASURER	1086a	
		מדינה	DISTRICT	1088c	
		דתבר	JUDGE	1089b	
		חנכה	DEDICATION	1093b	
		כל	ALL	1097a	1
		כנש	GATHER	1097b	
		נבוכדנצר	NEBUCHADNEZZAR	1102a	
		סגן	PREFECT	1104a	
		פחה	GOVERNOR	1108b	
		קבל	BEFORE	1110a	1a
		קום	STAND	1110d	4
		קום	ARISE	1111a	1
		תפתיא	MAGISTRATE	1118b	
		שלטון	ADDENDA ET CORRIGENDA	1127c	
3	4	אמה	NATION	1081a	
		אמר	COMMAND	1081b	3
		ב	WITH	1083d	3
		ו	AND	*1090d	
		חיל	POWER	1093a	1
		כרוז	HERALD	1097d	
		לשן	TONGUE	1099b	
		עם	PEOPLE	1107a	
		קרא	CALL	1111c	1
3	5	ב	IN	1083d	1
		די	WHO	1087d	1a
		זן	KIND	1091c	
		זמר	MUSIC	1091c	
		כל	ALL	1097a	1
		נפל	FALL	1103a	1
		סגד	DO HOMAGE	1104a	
		סומפניה	BAG-PIPE	1104b	
		עדן	TIME	1105c	1
		פסנטרין	PSALTER	1108c	
		קל	VOICE	1110d	
		קום	ARISE	1111a	1
		קיתרס	LYRE	1111b	
		קרן	HORN	1111d	1
		שבכא	TRIGON	1113c	
		שמע	HEAR	1116b	
		משרוקי	PIPE	1117b	
3	6	אתון	FURNACE	1083c	
		גו	MIDST	1086b	B
		די	WHO	1087d	1b
		ה	AND	1091a	B
		יקד	BURN	1096a	
		ל	TO	1098b	1
		מן	WHO	1100d	2
		נור	FIRE	1102d	
		נפל	FALL	1103a	1
		סגד	DO HOMAGE	1104a	
		רמא	CAST	1113b	
		שעה	MOMENT	1117a	
3	7	אמה	NATION	1081d	
		די	THAT	1088b	4ab
		זמר	MUSIC	1091c	
		זמן	TIME	1091c	
		זן	KIND	1091c	
		לשן	TONGUE	1099b	
		נפל	FALL	1103a	1
		סגד	DO HOMAGE	1104a	
		עם	PEOPLE	1107a	
		פסנטרין	PSALTER	1108c	
		קבל	BECAUSE OF	1110b	2a
		קל	VOICE	1110d	
		קום	ARISE	1111a	1
		קיתרס	LYRE	1111b	
		קרן	HORN	1111d	1
		שבכא	TRIGON	1113c	
		שמע	HEAR	1116b	
		משרוקי	PIPE	1117b	
3	8	אכל	EAT	1080b	3
		גבר	MAN	1086a	
		די	THAT	1088a	2
		זמן	TIME	1091c	
		יהודי	JEW	1095c	
		כשדי	CHALDEAN	1098a	1
		קבל	BECAUSE OF	1110b	2a
		קרב	APPROACH	1111c	
		קרץ	PIECE	1111d	
3	9	ו	AND	1090d	
		חיא	LIVE	1092d	
		עלם	PERPETUITY	1106d	
		ענה	ANSWER	1107b	2
3	10	טעם	TASTE	*381b	3
		אנש	MAN	1081d	1
		די	THAT	1088a	3c
		זן	KIND	1091c	
		זמר	MUSIC	1091c	
		טעם	COMMAND	1094c	4
		כל	ALL	1097a	2
		נפל	FALL	1103a	1
		סגד	DO HOMAGE	1104a	
		סומפניה	BAG-PIPE	1104b	
		פסנטרין	PSALTER	1108c	
		קל	VOICE	1110d	
		קיתרס	LYRE	1111b	
		קרן	HORN	1111d	1
		שבכא	TRIGON	1113c	
		שום	MAKE	1113d	1
		שמע	HEAR	1116b	
		משרוקי	PIPE	1117b	
3	11	אתון	FURNACE	1083c	
		גו	MIDST	1086b	B
		די	WHO	1087d	1b
		יקד	BURN	1096a	
		ל	TO	1098b	1
		מן	WHO	1100d	2
		נפל	FALL	1103a	1
		סגד	DO HOMAGE	1104a	
		רמא	CAST	1113b	
3	12	איתי	THERE IS	1080a	
		אלך	THESE	1080d	
		גבר	MAN	1086a	
		גבר	MAN	1086a	
		מדינה	DISTRICT	1088c	
		טעם	JUDGMENT	1094c	2
		יהודי	JEW	1095c	
		ית	MARK OF ACCUSATIVE	1096b	
		מישך	MESHACH	1100a	
		מנה	NUMBER	1101b	
		סגד	DO HOMAGE	1104a	
		עבידה	WORK	1105a	1
		עבדנגו	ABED-NEGO	1105a	
		על	OVER	1106b	2
		על	TO	1106b	4a
		פלח	PAY REVERENCE TO	1108c	1
		קום	ARISE	1111a	1
		שום	SET	1113d	3
		שדרך	SHADRAK	1114c	
3	13	אדין	THEN	1078d	

Ch	v.	Heb	Eng	Page	Sec
		אלך	THESE	1080d	
		אתה	COME	1083c	
		אתה	COME	1083c	
		חמא	RAGE	1095c	
		ל	TO	1098c	6
		קדם	BEFORE	1110c	1
		רגז	RAGE	1112c	
3	14	צדה	LIE IN WAIT	*841b	
		צדה	LIE IN WAIT	841b	2 b
		אזדא	SURE	1079b	
		איתי	THERE IS	1080b	
		אמר	SAY	1081b	1
		ה	INTERROGATIVE PARTICLE	1089b	
		סגד	DO HOMAGE	1104a	
		ענה	ANSWER	1107b	2
		פלח	PAY REVERENCE TO	1108c	1
		צדא	PURPOSE	1109c	
3	15	קום	ARISE	1111a	1
		איתי	THERE IS	1080b	
		אלה	GOD	1080c	1
		אתון	FURNACE	1083c	
		גו	MIDST	1086b	B
		די	WHO	1087d	1 a
		הוא	HE	1090a	
		הן	IF	1090c	1
		הן	IF	1090c	1
		זמר	MUSIC	1091c	
		זן	KIND	1091c	
		יד	HAND	1094d	2
		יקד	BURN	1096a	
		מן	WHO	1100d	1
		מן	OUT OF	1101a	1 b
		נפל	FALL	1103a	1
		סגד	DO HOMAGE	1104a	
		סגד	DO HOMAGE	1104a	
		סומפניה	BAG-PIPE	1104d	
		עבד	MAKE	1104d	1
		כען	NOW	1107b	
		עתיד	READY	1108a	
		פסנתרין	PSALTER	1108c	
		קל	VOICE	1110d	
		קיתרס	LYRE	1111b	
		קרן	HORN	1111d	1
		רמא	CAST	1113b	
		שבכא	TRIGON	1113c	
		שיזב	DELIVER	1115c	
		שמע	HEAR	1116b	
		שעה	MOMENT	1117a	
		משרוקי	PIPE	1117b	
3	16	אנחנא	WE	1081c	
		דנה	THIS	1089a	D
		ו	AND	1090d	
		חשח	NEED	1093d	
		ל	TO	1098c	6
		לא	NOT	1098c	
		על	ON ACCOUNT OF	1106b	1 c
		ענה	ANSWER	1107b	1
		פתגם	AFFAIR	1109b	
		תוב	RETURN	1117d	2
3	17	איתי	THERE IS	1080b	
		אנחנא	WE	1081c	
		אתון	FURNACE	1083c	
		הן	IF	1090c	1
		יד	HAND	1094d	2
		יכל	BE ABLE	1095d	1
		יקד	BURN	1096a	
		פלח	PAY REVERENCE TO	1108c	1
		שיזב	DELIVER	1115a	
		שיזב	DELIVER	1115a	
3	18	איתי	THERE IS	1080b	
		די	THAT	1088a	3 a
		הוא	COME TO PASS	1090a	2
		הן	IF	1090c	1
		ה	AND	1091a	B
		ידע	KNOW	1095a	
		סגד	DO HOMAGE	1104a	
		פלח	PAY REVERENCE TO	1108c	1
		קום	ARISE	1111a	1
3	19	אדין	THEN	1078d	
		אזא	MAKE HOT	1079a	
		חד	A	1079c	2
		אנף	FACE	1081d	
		אתון	FURNACE	1083c	
		די	THAT	1088b	4 d
		חזה	SEE	1092c	4
		חמא	RAGE	1095c	
		ל	TO	1098c	6
		מלא	FILL	1100a	
		על	ABOVE	1106b	3
		על	AGAINST	1106c	4 b
		ענה	ANSWER	1107b	2
		צלם	IMAGE	1109d	
		שבע	SEVEN	1114b	
		שנא	CHANGE	1116c	
3	20	אתון	FURNACE	1083c	
		גבר	MAN	1086a	
		גבר	MIGHTY ONE	1086a	
		די	WHO	1087d	1 a
		חיל	ARMY	1093a	2
		חיל	POWER	1093a	1
		יקד	BURN	1096a	
		כפת	BIND	1097c	

Ch	v.	Heb	Eng	Page	Sec
		ל	TO	1098c	6
		רמא	CAST	1113a	1
3	21	כרבל	MANTLE	*499d	
		אדין	THEN	1078d	
		אלך	THESE	1080d	
		אתון	FURNACE	1083c	
		גו	MIDST	1086b	B
		ו	AND	*1090d	
		יקד	BURN	1096a	
		כפת	BIND	1097c	
		כרבלא	HELMUT	1097d	
		לבוש	GARMENT	1098d	
		סרבל	MANTLE	1104c	
		פטש	A GARMENT	1108b	
		רמא	CAST	1113a	1
3	22	אזא	MAKE HOT	1079a	
		אלך	THESE	1080d	
		אתון	FURNACE	1083c	
		די	THAT	1088b	4 ba
		חמו	THEY	1090c	B
		חצף	SHEW INSOLENCE	1093c	
		יתיר	PRE-EMINENT	1096c	
		מלה	WORD	1100d	1
		סלק	COME UP	1104b	
		קבל	BECAUSE OF	1110b	2 a
		קטל	SLAY	1111a	
		שביב	FLAME	1114b	
3	23	אלך	THESE	1080d	
		אתון	FURNACE	1083c	
		גו	MIDST	1086b	B
		יקד	BURN	1096a	
		כפת	BIND	1097c	
		נפל	FALL	1103a	1
		תלת	THREE	1118a	
3	24	אדין	THEN	1078d	
		בהל	ALARM	1084b	
		גדבריא	TREASURER	*1086a	
		גבר	MAN	1086a	
		גו	MIDST	1086b	B
		ה	INTERROGATIVE PARTICLE	1089b	
		הדבר	COUNSELLOR	1089d	
		ו	AND	1090d	
		יציב	CERTAIN	1096a	1
		כפת	BIND	1097c	
		לא	NOT	1098d	
		ענה	ANSWER	1107b	1
		ענה	ANSWER	1107b	2
		קום	ARISE	1110d	1
		רמא	CAST	1113a	1
		תוה	BE STARTLED	1117d	
		תלת	THREE	1118a	
3	25	איתי	THERE IS	1080b	
		אלה	GOD	1080c	1
		אנה	I	1081c	
		בר	SON	1085b	1
		גו	MIDST	1086a	A
		גבר	MAN	1086a	
		די	THAT	1088a	2
		דמה	BE LIKE	1088d	
		הא	LO	1089c	
		הלך	GO	1090b	
		חבל	HURT	1092a	
		חזה	SEE	1092c	2 a
		ענה	ANSWER	1107b	1
		רו	APPEARANCE	1112a	
		ארבע	FOUR	1112c	2
		רביעי	FOURTH	1112c	
		שרא	LOOSEN	1117b	1
3	26	אדין	THEN	1078d	
		אלה	GOD	1080c	2
		אתה	COME	1083c	
		אתון	FURNACE	1083c	
		גו	MIDST	1086b	C
		די	THAT	1088a	2
		יקד	BURN	1096a	
		מן	OUT OF	1101a	1 b
		נפק	GO FORTH	1103b	
		נפק	GO FORTH	1103b	
		עבד	SLAVE	1105a	
		עלי	HIGHEST	1106a	
		ענה	ANSWER	1107b	2
		קרב	APPROACH	1111c	
		תרע	DOOR	1118d	1
3	27	אחשדרפנין	SATRAPS	1080a	
		אלך	THESE	1080d	
		ב	IN	1083d	2
		גשם	BODY	1086d	
		די	THAT	1088a	3 a
		הדבר	COUNSELLOR	1089d	
		חזה	SEE	1092c	2 a
		חרך	SINGE	1093d	
		כנש	GATHER	1097b	
		נור	FIRE	1102c	
		סגן	PREFECT	1104a	
		סרבל	MANTLE	1104c	
		עדא	PASS ON	1105b	1
		פחה	GOVERNOR	1108b	
		ראש	HEAD	1112a	1
		שער	HAIR	1114a	
		שלט	HAVE POWER	1115d	
		שנא	CHANGE	1116c	
3	28	ברך	BLESS	1085b	2
		די	THAT	1088b	3 c
		יהב	GIVE	1095b	1
		מלאך	ANGEL	1098d	

Ch	v.	Heb	Eng	Page	Sec
		לחן	EXCEPT	1099a	1 a
		מלה	WORD	1100d	1
		סגד	DO HOMAGE	1104a	
		עבד	SLAVE	1105a	
		על	UPON	1106b	1 a
		ענה	ANSWER	1107b	2
		פלח	PAY REVERENCE TO	1108c	1
		רחץ	TRUST	1113a	
		שיזב	DELIVER	1115a	
		שלח	SEND	1115c	
		שנא	CHANGE	1116c	
3	29	אחרן	ANOTHER	1080a	
		איתי	THERE IS	1080b	
		אמה	NATION	1081a	
		אמר	SAY	1081b	1
		בית	HOUSE	1084b	1
		די	THAT	1088a	3 c
		דנה	THIS	1089a	C
		הדם	MEMBER	1089d	
		יכל	BE ABLE	1095d	1
		כל	ALL	1097a	2
		לשן	TONGUE	1099b	
		מן	FROM	1101a	2 a
		נולו	REFUSE-HEAP	1102c	
		נצל	DELIVER	1103b	
		עבד	MAKE	1105a	1
		עבדנגו	ABED-NEGO	1105a	
		על	AGAINST	1106c	4 b
		עם	PEOPLE	1107a	
		קדם	BEFORE	*1110c	2
		שום	MAKE	1113d	
		שוה	BE MADE	1114d	
		שלו	NEGLECT	1115c	
		שלה	AT EASE	1115c	
3	30	מדינה	DISTRICT	1088c	
		צלח	PROSPER	1109d	1
3	31	אמה	NATION	1081a	
		דור	DWELL	1087b	
		ל	TO	1098b	1
		לשן	TONGUE	1099b	
		עם	PEOPLE	1107a	
		שגא	GROW GREAT	1113c	
		שלם	PROSPERITY	1116a	
3	32	את	WITH	767d	1 d
		את	SIGN	1079a	
		אלה	GOD	1080c	2
		חוה	DECLARE	1092b	2
		ל	TO	1098c	6
		עבד	DO	1104d	2
		עלי	HIGHEST	1106a	
		עם	WITH	1107a	1 b
		קדם	BEFORE	1110c	1
		שפר	SEEMLY	1117a	
		תמה	WONDER	1118b	
3	33	עם	WITH	768a	1 g
		את	SIGN	1079a	
		דר	GENERATION	1087b	
		מה	WHAT	1099d	3 a
		מלכו	KINGDOM	1100c	2
		מלכו	KINGDOM	1100c	2
		עלם	PERPETUITY	1106d	
		עם	WITH	1107a	2
		רב	GREAT	1112b	1
		שלטן	DOMINION	1115d	1
		תמה	WONDER	1118b	
		תקף	MIGHTY	1118c	
4	1	אנה	I	1081c	
		היכל	PALACE	1090b	1
		רענן	FLOURISHING	1113b	
		שלה	AT EASE	1115c	
4	2	בהל	ALARM	1084b	
		דחל	FEAR	1087c	
		הרהר	FANCY	1090d	
		ו	AND	1090d	
		חזו	VISION	1092c	1
		חזה	BEHOLD	1092c	3
		חלם	DREAM	1093a	
		ראש	HEAD	1112a	2
		משכב	COUCH	1115b	
4	3	די	THAT	1088b	3 c
		חלם	DREAM	1093a	
		ידע	KNOW	1095a	
		מן	FROM	1101a	2 a
		על	GO IN	1106c	
		פשר	INTERPRETATION	1109b	
		קדם	BEFORE	1110c	1
		שום	MAKE	1113d	
4	4	אמר	TELL	1081b	
		אנה	I	1081c	
		אשף	ENCHANTER	1083b	
		בית	HOUSE	1084c	1
		גזר	DETERMINE	1086b	
		ו	AND	*1090d	
		ה	AND	1091a	B
		חרטם	MAGICIAN	1093d	
		ידע	KNOW	1095a	
		כשדי	CHALDEAN	1098a	2
		לא	NOT	1098c	
		על	GO IN	1106c	
4	5	בלטשאצר	BELTESHAZZAR	*117b	
		אחרין	AT LAST	1079d	
		אחרן	ANOTHER	1080a	
		אמר	TELL	1081b	2
		בלטשאצר	BELTESHAZZAR	1084d	
		די	WHO	1087d	1 a

Ch	v.	Heb	Eng	Page	Sec
		ד	LIKE	1096c	
		עד	EVEN TO	1105b	1 c
		קדיש	HOLY	1110d	
		רוח	SPIRIT	1112d	2 b
		שם	NAME	1116a	
		שם	NAME	1116a	
4	6	אמר	TELL	1081b	2
		אנס	OPPRESS	1081c	
		אנה	I	1081c	
		די	WHO	1087d	1 a
		חזה	BEHOLD	1092c	3
		חזו	VISION	1092d	1
		חלם	DREAM	1093a	
		חרטם	MAGICIAN	1093d	
		ידע	KNOW	1095a	
		כל	ALL	1097a	2
		לא	NOT	1098c	
		קדיש	HOLY	1110d	
		רב	GREAT	1112b	3
		רז	SECRET	1112d	
		רוח	SPIRIT	1112d	2 b
4	7	אילן	TREE	1079a	
		אלו	LO	1080d	
		גו	MIDST	1086a	A
		חזה	BEHOLD	1092c	3
		חזו	VISION	1092c	1
		ראש	HEAD	1112a	2
		רום	HEIGHT	1112d	
		שגיא	GREAT	1113c	1
		משכב	COUCH	1115b	
4	8	אילן	TREE	1079a	
		חזות	SIGHT	1092d	
		מטא	REACH	1100a	1 b
		סוף	END	1104b	
		רבה	GROW GREAT	1112b	
		רום	HEIGHT	1112d	
		שמין	HEAVENS	1116a	1
		תקף	GROW STRONG	1118c	
4	9	אב	FRUIT	1078a	
		בר	FIELD	1085c	
		בשר	FLESH	1085d	
		דור	DWELL	1087b	
		מזון	FOOD	1091b	
		זון	FEED	1091b	
		חיוא	BEAST	1092d	
		טלל	HAVE SHADE	1094b	
		כל	ALL	1097b	3
		ל	IN REGARD TO	1098c	4 d
		מן	FROM	1101a	2 a
		עפי	LEAFAGE	1107b	
		ענף	BOUGH	1107b	
		צפר	BIRD	1110a	
		שגיא	MUCH	1113c	2
		שמין	HEAVENS	1116a	1
		שפיר	FAIR	1117a	
		תחות	UNDER	1117d	
4	10	אלו	LO	1080d	
		ו	AND	1091a	A
		חזו	VISION	1092c	1
		חזה	BEHOLD	1092c	3
		מן	FROM	1101a	1 a
		נחת	DESCEND	1102d	
		עיר	WAKING	1105d	
		קדיש	HOLY	1110d	
		ראש	HEAD	1112a	2
		משכב	COUCH	1115b	
		שמין	HEAVENS	1116a	1
4	11	אב	FRUIT	1078a	
		אילן	TREE	1079a	
		אמר	SAY	1081b	1
		בדר	SCATTER	1084a	
		גדד	HEW DOWN	1086a	
		חיוא	BEAST	1092d	
		חיל	POWER	1093a	1
		כן	THUS	1097b	
		מן	FROM	1101a	1 c
		מן	FROM	1101a	1 a
		נוד	FLEE	1102c	
		נתר	STRIP OFF	1103d	
		עפי	LEAFAGE	1107b	
		ענף	BOUGH	1107b	
		צפר	BIRD	1110a	
		קרא	CALL	1111c	1
		תחות	UNDER	1117d	
		קצץ	ADDENDA ET COR- RIGENDA	1127c	
4	12	ב	IN	1083d	1
		ב	WITH	1083d	3
		ב	IN	1083d	1
		ברם	ONLY	1085c	
		בר	FIELD	1085c	
		דתא	GRASS	1089b	
		ו	AND	1091a	A
		חיוא	BEAST	1092d	
		חלק	POSSESSION	1093b	
		טל	DEW	1094b	
		מן	FROM	*1101a	2 b
		נחש	COPPER	1102d	
		עם	WITH	1107a	1 a
		עקר	ROOT	1107d	
		עשב	GRASS	1108a	
		פרזל	IRON	1108d	
		צבע	WET	1109c	
		שבק	LEAVE	1114c	
		שמין	HEAVENS	1116a	1
		שרש	ROOT	1117b	
4	13	מן	FROM	583b	7 bb
		אנש	MAN	1081d	1
		חיוא	BEAST	1092d	
		חלף	PASS	1093a	
		יהב	GIVE	1095b	1
		לבב	HEART	1098a	
		לבב	HEART	1098a	
		מן	FROM	1101b	5
		עדן	TIME	1105c	2
		על	UPON	1106b	1 a
		שבע	SEVEN	1114b	
		שנא	CHANGE	1116c	
4	14	מאמר	WORD	1081b	
		אנש	MAN	1081d	2
		אנש	MAN	1081d	2
		גזרה	DECREE	1086b	
		דברה	CAUSE	1087a	
		די	WHO	1087d	1 b
		חי	LIVING	1092d	1
		ידע	KNOW	1095a	
		מלכו	KINGDOM	1100c	2
		מן	WHO	1100d	2
		נתן	GIVE	1103d	1
		עד	EVEN TO	1105b	1 c
		עלי	HIGHEST	1106a	
		על	OVER	1106b	2
		פתגם	AFFAIR	1109b	
		צבא	BE PLEASED	1109c	2
		קדיש	HOLY	1110d	
		קום	ARISE	1111a	4
		שאלה	AFFAIR	1114b	
		שלו	NEGLECT	*1115c	
		שליט	HAVING MASTERY	1115d	1 a
		שפל	LOW	1117a	
4	15	אמר	TELL	1081b	2
		אנה	I	1081c	
		די	THAT	1088a	3 b
		חזה	BEHOLD	1092c	3
		ידע	KNOW	1095a	
		יכל	BE ABLE	1095d	1
		כהל	BE ABLE	1096d	
		לא	NOT	1098c	
		מלכו	KINGDOM	1100c	3
		פשר	INTERPRETATION	1109b	
		פשר	INTERPRETATION	1109b	
		קדיש	HOLY	1110d	
		רוח	SPIRIT	1112d	2 b
4	16	חד	A	1079c	2
		אל	DO NOT	1080b	
		בהל	ALARM	1084b	
		בהל	ALARM	1084b	
		ך	ABOUT	1096c	
		ל	TO	1098b	1
		מרא	LORD	1101c	
		ענה	ANSWER	1107b	2
		ענה	ANSWER	1107b	1
		ער	FOE	1108a	
		פשר	INTERPRETATION	1109b	
		פשר	INTERPRETATION	1109b	
		רעיון	THOUGHT	1113b	
		שנא	HATE	1114a	
		שם	NAME	1116a	
		שמם	BE APPALLED	1116b	
		שעה	MOMENT	1117a	
4	17	אילן	TREE	1079a	
		חזה	BEHOLD	1092c	3
		חזות	SIGHT	1092d	
		מטא	REACH	1100a	1 b
		רבה	GROW GREAT	1112b	
		רום	HEIGHT	1112d	
		שמין	HEAVENS	1116a	1
		תקף	GROW STRONG	1118c	
4	18	אב	FRUIT	1078a	
		בר	FIELD	1085c	
		דור	DWELL	*1087b	
		דור	DWELL	1087b	
		מזון	FOOD	1091b	
		חיוא	BEAST	1092d	
		כל	ALL	1097b	3
		ל	TO	1098b	1
		ענף	BOUGH	1107b	
		עפי	LEAFAGE	1107b	
		צפר	BIRD	1110a	
		שגיא	MUCH	1113c	2
		שכן	DWELL	1115b	
		שמין	HEAVENS	1116a	1
		שפיר	FAIR	1117a	
		תחות	UNDER	1117d	
4	19	די	WHO	1087d	1 a
		הוא	HE	1090a	
		מטא	REACH	1100a	1 b
		סוף	END	1104b	
		רבה	GROW GREAT	1112b	
		רבה	GROW GREAT	1112b	
		רבו	GREATNESS	1112c	
		שלטן	DOMINION	1115d	1
		שמין	HEAVENS	1116a	1
		תקף	GROW STRONG	1118c	
4	20	אילן	TREE	1079a	
		בר	FIELD	1085c	
		ברם	ONLY	1085c	
		בר	FIELD	1085c	
		גדד	HEW DOWN	1086a	
		די	THAT	1088a	3 b
		דתא	GRASS	1089b	
		ו	AND	1091a	A
		חבל	DESTROY	1091d	
		חזה	BEHOLD	1092c	3
		חיוא	BEAST	1092d	
		חלף	PASS	1093a	
		חלק	POSSESSION	1093b	
		טל	DEW	1094b	
		מן	FROM	*1101a	2 b
		נחש	COPPER	1102d	
		נחת	DESCEND	1102d	
		עד	UNTIL	1105b	2 a
		עדן	TIME	1105c	2
		עיר	WAKING	1105d	
		על	UPON	1106b	1 a
		עקר	ROOT	1107d	
		פרזל	IRON	1108d	
		צבע	WET	1109c	
		קדיש	HOLY	1110d	
		שבע	SEVEN	1114b	
		שבק	LEAVE	1114c	
		שמין	HEAVENS	1116a	1
		שמין	HEAVENS	1116a	1
		שרש	ROOT	1117b	
4	21	גזרה	DECREE	1086b	
		הוא	HE	1090a	
		מטא	REACH	1100a	2
		מרא	LORD	1101c	
		עלי	HIGHEST	1106a	
		על	UPON	1106b	1 a
4	22	אנש	MAN	1081d	2
		בר	FIELD	1085c	
		מדור	DWELLING-PLACE	1087b	
		די	WHO	1087d	1 b
		הוא	COME TO PASS	1090a	
		חיוא	BEAST	1092d	
		חלף	PASS	1093a	
		טעם	FEED	1094b	
		טל	DEW	1094b	
		טרד	CHASE AWAY	1094c	
		ידע	KNOW	1095a	
		מלכו	KINGDOM	1100c	2
		מן	WHO	1100d	2
		מן	FROM	1101a	2 b
		מן	FROM	1101a	1 c
		נתן	GIVE	1103d	
		עד	UNTIL	1105b	2 a
		עדן	TIME	1105c	2
		עלי	HIGHEST	1106a	
		על	UPON	1106b	1 a
		עשב	GRASS	1108a	
		צבע	WET	1109c	
		צבא	BE PLEASED	1109c	2
		שבע	SEVEN	1114b	
		שליט	HAVING MASTERY	1115d	1 a
		תור	BULLOCK	1117d	
4	23	אילן	TREE	1079a	
		אמר	COMMAND	*1081b	3
		די	THAT	1088a	3 b
		די	THAT	1088a	2
		די	THAT	1088b	4 bb
		ידע	KNOW	1095a	
		ל	TO	1098b	1
		מלכו	ROYALTY	1100c	2
		עקר	ROOT	1107d	
		קום	ENDURING	1111a	
		שבק	LEAVE	1114c	
		שליט	HAVING MASTERY	1115d	1 a
		שמין	HEAVENS	1116a	2
		שרש	ROOT	1117b	
4	24	לחן	THEREFORE	*530a	
		על	UPON	758a	2 8
		ארכה	A LENGTHENING	1082d	
		ב	WITH	1083d	3
		הוא	COME TO PASS	1089d	2
		הן	IF	1090c	1
		חטי	SIN	1092d	
		חנן	SHEW FAVOUR	1093b	
		לחן	THEREFORE	1099a	
		מלך	COUNSEL	1100c	
		עויה	INIQUITY	1105c	
		על	TO	1106c	5
		עני	POOR	1107b	
		פרק	TEAR AWAY	1108d	
		צדקה	RIGHT DOING	1109d	
		שלה	EASE	1115c	
		שפר	SEEMLY	1117a	
4	25	כל	ALL	1097b	3
		מטא	REACH	1100a	2
		על	UPON	1106b	1 a
4	26	הלך	GO	1090b	
		היכל	PALACE	1090b	1
		ירח	MONTH	1096b	
		ל	AT	1098c	5
		מלכו	ROYALTY	1100c	
		על	UPON	1106b	1 a
		עשר	TEN	1108a	
		קצת	END	1111c	
		תרין	TWO	1118b	
4	27	אנה	I	1081c	
		ב	WITH	1083d	3
		בית	HOUSE	1084c	
		בנה	BUILD	1084d	
		דא	THIS	1086d	
		ה	INTERROGATIVE PARTICLE	1089b	
		הדר	HONOUR	1089d	

Ch	v.	Heb	Eng	Page	Sec
		הוא	HE	1090a	
		חסן	POWER	1093c	
		יקר	HONOUR	1096a	
		ל	TO	1098b	3
		ל	IN REGARD TO	1098c	4 d
		ל	IN REGARD TO	1098c	4 d
		לא	NOT	1098d	
4	28	אמר	SAY	*1081b	1
		מלה	WORD	1100c	1
		מלכו	ROYALTY	1100c	1
		ענה	ANSWER	1107b	2
		רב	GREAT	1112b	1
		שמין	HEAVENS	1116a	1
		תקף	MIGHT	1118c	
4	29	אנש	MAN	1081d	2
		בר	FIELD	1085c	
		מדור	DWELLING-PLACE	1087b	
		די	WHO	1087d	1 b
		חיוא	BEAST	1092a	
		חלף	PASS	1093a	
		טען	FEED	1094b	
		טרד	CHASE AWAY	1094c	
		ידע	KNOW	1095a	
		מלכו	KINGDOM	1100c	2
		מן	WHO	1100d	2
		נתן	GIVE	1103d	1
		עד	UNTIL	1105b	2 a
		עדן	TIME	1105c	2
		עלי	HIGHEST	1106a	
		על	UPON	1106b	1 a
		עשב	GRASS	1108a	
		צבא	BE PLEASED	1109c	2
		שבע	SEVEN	1114b	
		שלט	HAVING MASTERY	1115d	1 a
		תור	BULLOCK	1117d	
4	30	אכל	EAT	1080b	
		אנש	MAN	1081d	2
		גשם	BODY	1086d	
		די	THAT	1088b	4 c
		טל	DEW	1094b	
		מפר	NAIL	1094c	
		טרד	CHASE AWAY	1094c	
		מלה	WORD	1100d	1
		מן	FROM	1101a	2 b
		נשר	EAGLE	1103c	
		סוף	BE FUFILLED	1104b	
		עד	UNTIL	1105b	2 a
		עשב	GRASS	1108a	
		צבע	WET	1109c	
		צפר	BIRD	1110a	
		רבה	GROW GREAT	1112b	
		שער	HAIR	1114a	
		שמין	HEAVENS	1116a	1
		שעה	MOMENT	1117a	
		תור	BULLOCK	1117d	
4	31	עם	WITH	768a	1 g
		אנה	I	1081c	
		ברך	BLESS	1085c	
		דר	GENERATION	1087b	
		הדר	GLORIFY	1089d	
		חי	LIVING	1092d	1
		מנדע	KNOWLEDGE	1095b	
		יום	DAY	1095c	
		ל	TO	1098b	1
		ל	AT	1098c	5
		מלכו	KINGDOM	1100c	2
		נטל	LIFT	1102d	
		עין	EYE	1105d	
		עלי	HIGHEST	1106a	
		על	TO	1106b	4 a
		עלם	PERPETUITY	1106d	
		עלם	PERPETUITY	1106d	
		עם	WITH	1107a	2
		קצת	END	1111c	
		שבח	PRAISE	1114b	
		שלטן	DOMINION	1115d	1
		שמין	HEAVENS	1116a	2
4	32	לא	NOT	*520a	3
		איתי	THERE IS	1080b	
		ב	IN	1084a	8
		דור	DWELL	1087b	
		חיל	ARMY	1093a	2
		חשב	ACCOUNT	1093d	
		יד	HAND	1094d	1
		כ	LIKE	1096c	
		כ	LIKE	1096c	
		לא	NOT	*1098c	
		לא	NOT	1098c	
		מה	WHAT	1099c	1
		מחא	SMITE	1099d	
		עבד	DO	1104d	2
		עבד	DO	1104d	2
		צבא	BE PLEASED	1109c	2
		שמין	HEAVENS	1116a	2
4	33	בעא	SEEK	1085a	
		הדבר	COUNSELLOR	1089d	
		הדר	HONOUR	1089d	

Ch	v.	Heb	Eng	Page	Sec
		זיו	SPLENDOUR	1091b	
		זמן	TIME	1091c	
		מנדע	KNOWLEDGE	1095b	
		יסף	ADD	1095d	
		יקר	HONOUR	1096a	
		יתיר	PRE-EMINENT	1096c	
		ל	IN REGARD TO	1098c	4 d
		מלכו	ROYALTY	1100c	1
		מלכו	KINGDOM	1100c	3
		על	UPON	1106b	1 a
		על	TO	1106b	4 a
		רברבן	LORD	1112b	
		רבו	GREATNESS	1112c	
		תקן	BE IN ORDER	1118c	1
4	34	גוה	PRIDE	*145b	
		אנה	I	1081c	
		אנה	I	1081c	
		ארח	WAY	1082d	
		גוה	PRIDE	1085d	
		דין	JUDGEMENT	1088b	
		הדר	GLORIFY	1089d	
		הלך	GO	1090b	
		ו	AND	*1090d	
		יכל	BE ABLE	1095d	1
		מלך	KING	1100b	
		מעבד	WORK	1105a	
		כען	NOW	1107b	
		קשט	TRUTH	1112a	
		רום	RISE	1112d	
		שבח	PRAISE	1114b	
		שמין	HEAVENS	1116a	2
		שפל	BE LOW	1117a	
5	1	בלאשצר	BELSHAZZAR	128d	
		בלאשצר	BELSHAZZAR	128d	
		אלף	ONE THOUSAND	1081a	
		בלשאצר	BELSHAZZAR	1084d	
		חמר	WINE	1093b	
		לחם	FEAST	1099b	
		עבד	MAKE	1104d	1
		קבל	BEFORE	1110a	1 a
		רב	GREAT	1112b	
		רברבן	LORD	1112b	
		שתה	DRINK	1117c	
5	2	ב	IN	89d	3 2a
		בלשאצר	BELSHAZZAR	128d	
		אב	FATHER	1078b	1
		אתה	COME	1083c	
		ב	IN	1083d	1
		ב	WITH	1083d	3
		בלשאצר	BELSHAZZAR	1084d	
		דחוה	MUSICAL INSTRUMENTS	1087c	
		די	WHO	1087d	1 a
		היכל	TEMPLE	1090b	2 a
		ה	AND	1091a	D
		חמר	WINE	1093b	
		טעם	TASTE	1094c	1
		ירושלם	JERUSALEM	1096b	
		כסף	SILVER	1097c	1
		לחנה	CONCUBINE	1099b	
		מאן	VESSEL	1099c	
		מן	OUT OF	1101a	1 b
		נפק	GO FORTH	1103b	
		רברבן	LORD	1112b	
		שגל	CONSORT	1114c	
		שתה	DRINK	1117c	
5	3	אלה	GOD	1080c	2
		אתה	COME	1083c	
		ב	WITH	1083d	3
		בית	HOUSE	1084c	2
		דחוה	MUSICAL INSTRUMENTS	1087c	
		היכל	TEMPLE	1090b	2 a
		ירושלם	JERUSALEM	1096b	
		לחנה	CONCUBINE	1099b	
		מאן	VESSEL	1099c	
		נפק	GO FORTH	1103b	
		רברבן	LORD	1112b	
		שגל	CONSORT	1114c	
		שתה	DRINK	1117c	
5	4	אבן	STONE	1078b	2
		אלה	GOD	1080c	1
		אע	WOOD	1082b	2
		חמר	WINE	1093b	
		כסף	SILVER	1097c	1
		נחש	COPPER	1102d	
		פרזל	IRON	1108d	
		שבח	PRAISE	1114b	
		שתה	DRINK	1117c	
5	5	אנש	MAN	1081d	1
		גיר	CHALK	1086b	
		די	THAT	1088a	
		היכל	PALACE	1090b	1
		חזה	SEE	1092c	2 a
		יד	HAND	1094d	1
		כתב	WRITE	1098a	
		כתב	WRITE	1098a	
		כתל	WALL	1098b	
		נברשתא	THE CANDLESTICK	1102a	
		נפק	GO FORTH	1103b	
		על	UPON	1106b	1 a
		פס	PALM	1108d	
		אצבע	FINGER	1109c	1
		קבל	BEFORE	1110a	1 a
		שעה	MOMENT	1117a	
5	6	בהל	ALARM	1084b	

Ch	v.	Heb	Eng	Page	Sec
		ארכבה	KNEE	1085c	
		דא	THIS	1086d	
		זיו	SPLENDOUR	1091b	
		חרץ	LOIN	1093d	
		נקש	KNOCK	1103c	
		קטר	KNOT	1111b	
		רעיון	THOUGHT	1113b	
		שנא	CHANGE	1116c	
5	7	ארגון	PURPLE	71a	
		אנש	MAN	1081d	1
		ארגון	PURPLE	1082c	
		אשף	ENCHANTER	1083b	
		גזר	DETERMINE	1086b	
		די	THAT	1088a	2
		די	THAT	1088b	3 d
		חמניכא	CHAIN	1090c	
		חוה	DECLARE	1092b	
		חיל	POWER	1093a	1
		כל	ALL	1097a	2
		כשדי	CHALDEAN	1098a	2
		כתב	WRITING	1098a	1
		לבש	BE CLOTHED	1098d	
		מלכו	KINGDOM	1100c	3
		על	UPON	1106b	1 a
		עלל	GO IN	1106c	
		ענה	ANSWER	1107b	2
		צואר	NECK	1109d	
		קרא	CALL	1111c	1
		קרא	READ OUT	1111c	2
		שלט	HAVE POWER	1115d	
		תלתי	THIRD	1118a	
5	8	ידע	KNOW	1095a	
		כהל	BE ABLE	1096d	
		כתב	WRITING	1098a	1
		עלל	GO IN	1106c	
		קרא	READ OUT	1111c	2
5	9	על	UPON	753d	2 1d
		בהל	ALARM	1084b	
		בלשאצר	BELSHAZZAR	1084d	
		זיו	SPLENDOUR	1091b	
		על	UPON	1106b	1 b
		רברבן	LORD	1112b	
		שגיא	MUCH	1113c	3
		שבש	BE PERPLEXED	1114c	
		שנא	CHANGE	1116c	
5	10	אל	DO NOT	1080b	
		בהל	ALARM	1084b	
		בית	HOUSE	1084c	1
		חיא	LIVE	1092d	
		מלכה	QUEEN	1100b	
		מלה	WORD	1100c	1
		עלל	GO IN	1106c	
		עלם	PERPETUITY	1106d	
		ענה	ANSWER	1107b	2
		קבל	BEFORE	1110a	1 a
		רברבן	LORD	1112b	
		רעיון	THOUGHT	1113b	
		שנא	CHANGE	1116c	
		משתי	FEAST	1117c	
5	11	בלשאצר	BELSHAZZAR	128d	
		אב	FATHER	1078b	1
		איתי	THERE IS	1080a	
		אשף	ENCHANTER	1083b	
		גבר	MAN	1086a	
		גזר	DETERMINE	1086b	
		ו	AND	*1090d	
		חכמה	WISDOM	1093a	
		חכמה	WISDOM	1093a	
		חרטם	MAGICIAN	1093d	
		יום	DAY	1095c	
		ד	LIKE	1096c	
		כשדי	CHALDEAN	1098a	2
		מלכו	KINGDOM	1100c	3
		נהירו	ILLUMINATION	1102c	
		קדיש	HOLY	1110d	
		קום	ARISE	1111a	4
		רב	GREAT	1112b	3
		רוח	SPIRIT	1112d	2 b
		שכלתנו	INSIGHT	1114a	
		שבח	FIND	1115b	
5	12	די	WHO	1087d	1 a
		אחידה	RIDDLE	1092a	
		חוה	DECLARE	1092b	
		אחויה	A DECLARING	1092b	
		חלם	DREAM	1093a	
		מנדע	KNOWLEDGE	1095b	
		יתיר	PRE-EMINENT	1096c	
		כען	NOW	1107b	
		פשר	INTERPRET	1109a	
		פשר	INTERPRETATION	1109b	
		קטר	KNOT	1111b	
		קרא	CALL	1111c	
		רוח	SPIRIT	1112d	2 a
		שום	MAKE	1113d	2
		שכלתנו	INSIGHT	1114a	
		שבח	FIND	1115b	
		שם	NAME	1116a	
		שרא	LOOSEN	1117b	1
5	13	אב	FATHER	1078b	1
		אתה	COME	1083c	
		בר	SON	1085b	1
		גלו	EXILE	1086c	
		די	WHO	1087d	1 a
		הוא	HE	1090a	
		יהוד	JUDAH	1095c	

Ch	v.	Heb	Eng	Page	Sec
		יהוד	JUDAH	1095c	
		מן	FROM	1101a	3
		עלל	GO IN	1106d	
5	14	ענה	ANSWER	1107b	2
		די	THAT	1088a	3 a
		חכמה	WISDOM	1093c	
		יתיר	PRE-EMINENT	1096c	
		נהירו	ILLUMINATION	1102c	
		על	ON ACCOUNT OF	1106b	1 e
		רוח	SPIRIT	1112d	2 b
		שכלתנו	INSIGHT	1114a	
		שכח	FIND	1115b	
		שמם	HEAR	1116b	
5	15	אשף	ENCHANTER	1083b	
		די	THAT	1088a	3 c
		חוה	DECLARE	1092b	
		חכים	WISE MAN	1093a	
		ידע	KNOW	1095a	
		כהל	BE ABLE	1096d	
		כתב	WRITING	1098a	1
		מלה	THING	1100d	2
		עלל	GO IN	1106d	
		כען	NOW	1107b	
		פשר	INTERPRETATION	1109b	
		קרא	READ OUT	1111c	2
5	16	ארגון	PURPLE	71a	
		אנה	I	1081c	
		ארגון	PURPLE	1082c	
		די	THAT	1088a	2
		המניכא	CHAIN	1090c	
		הן	IF	1090c	1
		ידע	KNOW	1095a	
		יכל	BE ABLE	1095d	1
		כתב	WRITING	1098a	1
		לבש	BE CLOTHED	1098d	
		מלכו	KINGDOM	1100c	3
		כען	NOW	1107b	
		פשר	INTERPRET	1109a	
		פשר	INTERPRETATION	1109b	
		צואר	NECK	1109d	
		קטר	KNOT	1111b	
		קרא	READ OUT	1111c	2
		שלט	HAVE POWER	1115d	
		שמם	HEAR	1116b	
		שרא	LOOSEN	1117b	1
		תלת	A THIRD PART	1118a	
5	17	אחרן	ANOTHER	1080a	
		אמר	SAY	1081b	1
		ברם	ONLY	1085c	
		ידע	KNOW	1095a	
		יהב	GIVE	1095b	1
		כתב	WRITING	1098a	1
		ל	TO	1098b	1
		נבזבה	REWARD	1102a	
		מתנא	GIFT	1103d	
		ענה	ANSWER	1107b	
5	18	אב	FATHER	1078b	1
		אלה	GOD	1080c	2
		הדר	HONOUR	1089d	
		ו	AND	*1090d	
		יהב	GIVE	1095b	1
		יקר	HONOUR	1096a	
		מלכו	KINGDOM	1100c	2
		עלי	HIGHEST	1106a	
		רבו	GREATNESS	1112c	
5	19	אמה	NATION	1081a	
		דחל	FEAR	1087c	
		הוא	COME TO PASS	1090a	3
		זוע	TREMBLE	1091b	
		חיא	LIVE	1092d	
		יהב	GIVE	1095b	1
		לשן	TONGUE	1099b	
		מחא	SMITE	1099d	
		מן	FROM	1101a	2 c
		מן	FROM	1101a	2 b
		עם	PEOPLE	1107a	
		צבא	BE PLEASED	1109c	2
		קדם	BEFORE	1110c	2
		קטל	SLAY	1111a	
		רבו	GREATNESS	1112c	
		רום	RISE	1112d	
		שפל	BE LOW	1117a	
5	20	די	THAT	1088a	4 ab
		זוד	BE PRESUMPTUOUS	1091b	
		יקר	HONOUR	1096a	
		כרסא	THRONE	1097c	
		ל	TO	1098c	6
		לבב	HEART	1098d	
		מלכו	ROYALTY	1100c	1
		נחת	DESCEND	1102d	
		עדא	PASS AWAY	1105b	
		רום	RISE	1112d	
		רוח	SPIRIT	1112d	2 a
		תקף	GROW STRONG	1118c	
5	21	אלה	GOD	1080c	2
		אנש	MAN	1081d	2
		אנש	MAN	1081d	2
		בר	SON	1085b	1
		גשם	BODY	1086d	
		מדור	DWELLING-PLACE	1087d	
		די	WHO	1087d	1 b
		חיוא	BEAST	1092d	
		טל	DEW	1094b	
		מעם	FEED	1094b	
		טרד	CHASE AWAY	1094c	
		ידע	KNOW	1095a	
		לבב	HEART	1098d	2
		מלכו	KINGDOM	1100c	2
		מן	FROM	1101a	2 b
		עד	UNTIL	1105b	2 a
		עלי	HIGHEST	1106a	
		עם	WITH	1107a	1 a
		עם	WITH	1107a	1 b
		ערד	WILD ASS	1107d	
		עשב	GRASS	1108a	
		צבע	WET	1109c	
		קום	ARISE	1111a	4
		שוה	BECOME LIKE	1114d	
		שלט	HAVING MASTERY	1115d	1 a
		שמין	HEAVENS	1116a	1
		תור	BULLOCK	1117d	
5	22	בלשאצר	BELSHAZZAR	1084d	
		בר	SON	1085b	1
		דנה	THIS	1089a	A
		ידע	KNOW	1095a	
		לבב	HEART	1098d	
		קבל	BECAUSE THAT	1110b	2 b
		שפל	BE LOW	1117a	
5	23	אבן	STONE	1078b	2
		אלה	GOD	1080c	1
		אע	WOOD	1082b	2
		ארח	WAY	1082d	
		אתה	COME	1083c	
		בית	HOUSE	1084c	2
		דחוה	MUSICAL INSTRU-MENTS	1087c	
		די	WHO	1087d	1 a
		הדר	GLORIFY	1089d	
		חזה	SEE	1092c	1
		חמר	WINE	1093b	
		יד	HAND	1094d	2
		ידע	KNOW	1095a	
		כסף	SILVER	1097c	1
		ל	IN REGARD TO	1098c	4 b
		לחנה	CONCUBINE	1099b	
		מאן	VESSEL	1099c	
		מרא	LORD	1101c	
		נחש	COPPER	1102d	
		נשמה	BREATH	1103c	
		על	AGAINST	1106c	4 b
		פרזל	IRON	1108a	
		קדם	BEFORE	1110c	1
		רברבן	LORD	1112b	
		רום	RISE	1112d	
		שבח	PRAISE	1114b	
		שגל	CONSORT	1114c	
		שמין	HEAVENS	1116b	2
		שמע	HEAR	1116b	
		שתה	DRINK	1117c	
5	24	יד	HAND	1094d	1
		כתב	WRITING	1098a	1
		פס	PALM	1108d	
		קדם	BEFORE	1110c	2
		רשם	SIGN	1113c	1
		שלח	SEND	1115c	
5	25	כתב	WRITING	1098a	1
		מנא	MANEH	1101b	
		פרס	HALF-MINA	1108d	
		רשם	SIGN	1113c	1
		תקל	SHEKEL	1118c	
5	26	מלכו	REIGN	1100c	4
		מלה	THING	1100d	2
		מנא	MANEH	1101b	
		מנה	NUMBER	1101b	
		פשר	INTERPRETATION	1109b	
		שלם	BE COMPLETE	1116a	
5	27	מאזניא	SCALE	1079b	
		חסר	WANTING	1093c	
		שכח	FIND	1115b	
		תקל	SHEKEL	1118c	
		תקל	WEIGH	1118c	
5	28	יהב	GIVE	1095b	
		מדי	MEDES	1099c	1
		מלכו	KINGDOM	1100c	2
		פרס	BREAK IN TWO	1108d	
		פרס	HALF-MINA	1108d	
		פרס	PERSIA	1108d	
5	29	ארגון	PURPLE	71a	
		אמר	COMMAND	1081b	3
		ארגון	PURPLE	1082c	
		בלשאצר	BELSHAZZAR	1084d	
		הוא	COME TO PASS	1089d	2
		המניכא	CHAIN	1090c	
		ו	AND	1090d	
		כרז	MAKE PROCLAMA-TION	1097d	
		לבש	BE CLOTHED	1098d	
		מלכו	KINGDOM	1100c	3
		על	ON ACCOUNT OF	1106b	1 e
		צואר	NECK	1109d	
		שליט	RULING	1115d	2
		תלת	A THIRD PART	1118a	
5	30	בלשאצר	BELSHAZZAR	1084d	
		כשדי	CHALDEAN	1098a	1
		ליליא	NIGHT	1099b	
		קטל	SLAY	1111a	
6	1	בר	SON	1085b	1
		דריוש	DARIUS	1089a	2
		ד	ABOUT	1096c	
		מדיא	MEDE	1099c	
		מלכו	KINGDOM	1100c	2
		קבל	RECEIVE	1110b	
		שתין	SIXTY	1114d	
		שנה	YEAR	1116d	
		תרין	TWO	1118b	
6	2	שפר	BE BEAUTIFUL	1051c	
		אחשדרפנין	SATRAPS	1080a	
		דריוש	DARIUS	1089a	2
		ה	AND	1091a	D
		ה	AND	1091a	C
		כל	ALL	1097a	1
		מאה	HUNDRED	1099b	
		מלכו	KINGDOM	1100c	3
		עשרין	TWENTY	1108a	
		קדם	BEFORE	1110c	1
		קום	ARISE	1111a	4
		שפר	SEEMLY	1117a	
6	3	חד	ONE	1079c	1
		אחשדרפנין	SATRAPS	1080a	
		אלין	THESE	1080d	
		מעם	JUDGMENT	1094c	3
		יהב	GIVE	1095b	1
		מן	FROM	1101a	3
		מן	FROM	1101b	5
		נזק	SUFFER INJURY	1102c	
		סרך	CHIEF	1104c	
		עלא	ABOVE	1106c	
		תלת	THREE	1118a	
6	4	אחשדרפנין	SATRAPS	1080a	
		יתיר	PRE-EMINENT	1096c	
		כל	ALL	1097a	1
		ל	TO	1098c	6
		מלכו	KINGDOM	1100c	3
		נצח	DISTINGUISH ONE-SELF	1103b	
		סרך	CHIEF	1104c	
		על	ABOVE	1106b	3
		עשת	PLAN	1108a	
		קום	ARISE	1111a	4
		רוח	SPIRIT	1112d	2 a
6	5	אחשדרפנין	SATRAPS	1080a	
		אמן	TRUST	1081a	
		בעא	SEEK	1085a	2
		הוא	HE	1090a	
		יכל	BE ABLE	1095d	1
		כל	ALL	1097a	2
		ל	TO	1098c	6
		מלכו	KINGDOM	1100c	3
		מן	FROM	1101a	1 a
		סרך	CHIEF	1104c	
		עלה	MATTER	1106c	
		על	AGAINST	1106c	4 b
		צד	SIDE	1109c	
		שחת	CORRUPT	1115a	
		שכח	FIND	1115b	
		שכח	FIND	1115b	
		שכח	FIND	1115b	
		שלו	NEGLECT	1115c	
6	6	אלך	THESE	1080d	
		ב	IN	1084a	7
		די	THAT	1088b	3 d
		דת	LAW	1089b	3
		להן	EXCEPT	1099a	1 a
		על	ON ACCOUNT OF	1106b	1 e
		על	AGAINST	1106c	4 b
		עלה	MATTER	1106c	
		שכח	FIND	1115b	
		שכח	FIND	1115b	
6	7	אחשדרפנין	SATRAPS	1080a	
		אלין	THESE	*1080d	
		אלין	THESE	*1080d	
		אמר	SAY	1081b	1
		דריוש	DARIUS	1089a	2
		חיא	LIVE	1092d	
		כן	THUS	1097b	
		סרך	CHIEF	1104c	
		על	TO	1106b	4 a
		עלם	PERPETUITY	1106d	
		עלם	PERPETUITY	1106d	
		רגש	BE IN TUMULT	1112d	
6	8	אחשדרפנין	SATRAPS	1080a	
		אלה	GOD	1080c	1
		אסר	INTERDICT	1082b	
		אריה	LION	1082c	
		בעו	PETITION	1085a	
		בעא	ASK	1085a	1
		גב	DEN	1085d	
		הדבר	COUNSELLOR	1089d	
		יום	DAY	1095c	
		יעט	ADVISE	1095d	
		כל	ALL	1097a	2
		כל	ALL	1097a	2
		ל	TO	1098c	6
		להן	EXCEPT	1099a	1 a
		מלכו	KINGDOM	1100c	3
		סגן	PREFECT	1104a	
		סרך	CHIEF	1104c	
		עד	EVEN TO	1105b	1 c
		פחת	GOVERNOR	1108b	
		קום	ARISE	1110d	
		קים	STATUTE	1111a	
		רמא	CAST	1113b	
		תלתין	THIRTY	1118a	
		תקף	GROW STRONG	1118c	
6	9	לא	NOT	518d	1 ab
		אסר	INTERDICT	1082b	
		די	WHO	1087d	1 a
		דת	LAW	1089b	2

Ch	v.	Heb	Eng	Page	Sec
		כתב	WRITING	1098a	2 a
		ל	TO	1098c	6
		לא	NOT	1098d	
		מדי	MEDES	1099c	1
		עדא	PASS AWAY	1105b	2
		כען	NOW	1107b	
		פרס	PERSIA	1108d	
		קום	ARISE	1111a	3
		רשם	SIGN	1113c	
		שנא	CHANGE	1116d	
6	10	בקר	MORNING	*134a	1 d
		אסר	INTERDICT	1082b	
		דריוש	DARIUS	1089a	2
		כתב	WRITING	1098a	2 a
		קבל	BECAUSE OF	1110b	2 a
		רשם	SIGN	1113c	
6	11	בית	HOUSE	1084c	1
		ברך	KNEEL	1085b	1
		ברך	KNEE	1085c	
		די	THAT	1088b	4 ab
		זמן	TIME	1091c	
		ידע	KNOW	1095a	
		ידא	PRAISE	1095a	
		יום	DAY	1095c	
		ירושלם	JERUSALEM	1096b	
		כוה	WINDOW	1096d	
		כתב	WRITING	1098a	2 a
		נגד	IN FRONT OF	1102a	
		עבד	DO	1104d	2
		עלי	ROOF-CHAMBER	1106a	
		עלל	UPON	1106b	1 a
		עלל	GO IN	1106c	
		פתח	OPEN	1109b	
		צלא	PRAY	1109d	
		קבל	BECAUSE THAT	1110b	2 b
		קדמה	FORMER TIME	1110c	
		קדם	BEFORE	1110c	1
		רשם	SIGN	1113c	2
		תלת	THREE	1118a	
6	12	אלך	THESE	1080d	
		בעא	ASK	1085a	1
		חנן	SHEW FAVOUR	1093b	
		קדם	BEFORE	1110c	1
		רגש	BE IN TUMULT	1112d	
		שכח	FIND	1115b	
6	13	בקר	MORNING	*134a	1 d
		אלה	GOD	1080c	1
		אמר	SAY	1081b	1
		אנש	MAN	1081d	1
		אסר	INTERDICT	1082b	
		אסר	INTERDICT	1082b	
		בעא	ASK	1085a	1
		גב	DEN	1085d	
		ה	INTERROGATIVE PARTICLE	1089b	
		דת	LAW	1089b	2
		יום	DAY	1095c	
		יציב	TRUE	1096a	2
		כל	ALL	1097a	2
		לא	NOT	1098d	
		להן	EXCEPT	1099a	1 a
		מדי	MEDES	1099c	1
		מלה	WORD	1100d	1
		עדא	PASS AWAY	1105b	2
		עד	EVEN TO	1105b	1 c
		על	ON ACCOUNT OF	1106b	1 e
		ענה	ANSWER	1107b	1
		פרס	PERSIA	1108d	
		קדם	BEFORE	1110c	1
		קרב	APPROACH	1111c	
		רמא	CAST	1113b	
		רשם	SIGN	1113c	
		תלתין	THIRTY	1118a	
6	14	אמר	SAY	1081b	1
		אסר	INTERDICT	1082b	
		בעא	ASK	1085a	1
		בעו	PETITION	1085a	
		בר	SON	1085b	1
		גלו	EXILE	1086c	
		די	THAT	1088b	3 d
		זמן	TIME	1091c	
		טעם	JUDGMENT	1094c	2
		יום	DAY	1095c	
		יהוד	JUDAH	1095c	
		על	TO	1106b	4 a
		ענה	ANSWER	1107b	1
		קדם	BEFORE	1110c	1
		רשם	SIGN	1113c	
		שום	SET	1113d	3
		תלת	THREE	1118a	
6	15	על	UPON	758a	2 8
		באש	BE EVIL	1084a	
		בל	MIND	1084b	
		די	THAT	1088b	4 ab
		טאב	BE GOOD	1094a	
		מלה	WORD	1100c	1
		נצל	DELIVER	1103b	
		עד	EVEN TO	1105b	1 c
		על	TO	1106b	4 a
		על	TO	1106c	5
		מעל	GOING IN	1106d	
		שגיא	MUCH	1113c	3
		שום	SET	1113d	3
		שדר	STRIVE	1114c	
		שיזב	DELIVER	1115a	
		שמע	HEAR	1116b	
		שמש	SUN	1116b	
6	16	אלך	THESE	1080d	
		אסר	INTERDICT	1082b	
		דת	LAW	1089b	2
		ידע	KNOW	1095a	
		ל	TO	1098c	6
		לא	NOT	*1098d	
		מדי	MEDES	1099c	1
		על	TO	1106b	4 a
		פרס	PERSIA	1108d	
		קום	ARISE	1111a	3
		קים	STATUTE	1111a	
		רגש	BE IN TUMULT	1112d	
		שנא	CHANGE	1116d	
6	17	אמר	COMMAND	1081b	3
		אריה	LION	1082c	
		אתה	COME	1083c	
		גב	DEN	1085d	
		תדירא	CONTINUANCE	1087b	
		הוא	HE	1090a	
		ו	AND	1090d	
		ל	TO	1098b	1
		ענה	ANSWER	1107b	1
		פלח	PAY REVERENCE TO	1108c	1
		רמא	CAST	1113a	1
		שיזב	DELIVER	1115a	
6	18	אבן	STONE	1078b	1
		חד	A	1079c	2
		אתה	COME	1083c	
		ב	IN	1084a	7
		גב	DEN	1085d	
		די	THAT	1088b	3 c
		חתם	SEAL	1094a	
		עזקה	SIGNET-RING	1105d	
		עזקה	SIGNET-RING	1105d	
		פם	MOUTH	1108c	
		צבו	THING	1109c	
		רברבן	LORD	1112b	
		שום	MAKE	1113d	
		שנא	CHANGE	1116c	
6	19	הוה	BE	*227d	3
		אזל	GO	1079b	1
		בית	PASS THE NIGHT	1084c	
		דחוה	MUSICAL INSTRUMENTS	1087c	
		היכל	PALACE	1090b	1
		טות	FASTINGLY	1094b	
		שנה	SLEEP	1096b	
		נדד	FLEE	1102b	
		על	UPON	1106b	1 b
		עלל	GO IN	1106c	
		שן	TOOTH	1116d	
6	20	אזל	GO	1079b	1
		אריה	LION	1082c	
		בהל	ALARM	1084b	
		גב	DEN	1085d	
		נגה	BRIGHTNESS	1102a	
		קום	ARISE	1110d	1
		שפרפר	DAWN	1117a	
6	21	אלה	GOD	1080c	2
		אריה	LION	1082c	
		גב	DEN	1085d	
		תדירא	CONTINUANCE	1087b	
		ה	INTERROGATIVE PARTICLE	1089b	
		זעק	CRY	1091c	
		חי	LIVING	1092d	1
		יכל	BE ABLE	1095d	1
		ך	ABOUT	1096c	
		ל	TO	1098b	1
		מן	FROM	1101a	1 d
		עבד	SLAVE	1105a	
		ענה	ANSWER	1107b	2
		עצב	PAIN	1107d	
		פלח	PAY REVERENCE TO	1108c	1
		קל	VOICE	1110d	
		קרב	APPROACH	1111c	
		שיזב	DELIVER	1115a	
6	22	חיא	LIVE	1092d	
		מלל	SPEAK	1100c	
		עלם	PERPETUITY	1106c	
		עם	WITH	1107a	1 b
6	23	אף	ALSO	1082b	
		אריה	LION	1082c	
		זכו	INNOCENCE	1091b	
		חבל	DESTROY	1091d	
		חבולא	HURTFUL ACT	1092a	
		מלאך	ANGEL	1098d	
		סגר	SHUT	1104a	
		עבד	DO	1104d	2
		פם	MOUTH	1108c	
		שכח	FIND	1115b	
		שלח	SEND	1115c	
6	24	אמן	TRUST	1081a	
		ב	IN	1084a	8
		גב	DEN	1085d	
		די	THAT	1088a	3 b
		חבל	HURT	1092a	
		טאב	BE GOOD	1094a	
		כל	ALL	1097a	2
		ל	TO	1098c	6
		סלק	COME UP	1104b	
		סלק	COME UP	1104b	
		על	TO	1106c	5
		שגיא	MUCH	1113c	3
		שכח	FIND	1115b	
6	25	אכל	EAT	1080b	3
		אלך	THESE	1080d	
		אמר	COMMAND	1081b	3
		אנון	THEY	1081d	
		נשין	WIVES	1081d	
		אריה	LION	1082c	
		ארעי	BOTTOM	1083a	
		אתה	COME	1083c	
		בר	SON	1085b	1
		גב	DEN	1085d	
		גב	DEN	1085d	
		גרם	BONE	1086d	
		די	THAT	1088b	4 c
		דקק	BE SHATTERED	1089a	
		ו	AND	1090d	
		מטא	REACH	1100a	1 a
		עד	UNTIL	1105b	2 a
		קרץ	PIECE	1111d	
		רמא	CAST	1113a	1
		שלט	HAVE POWER	1115d	
6	26	אמה	NATION	1081a	
		דור	DWELL	1087b	
		דריוש	DARIUS	1089a	2
		כתב	WRITE	1098a	
		ל	TO	1098b	1
		לשן	TONGUE	1099b	
		עם	PEOPLE	1107a	
		שגא	GROW GREAT	1113c	
		שלם	PROSPERITY	1116a	
6	27	אלה	GOD	1080c	2
		דחל	FEAR	1087c	
		די	THAT	1088a	2
		הוא	HE	1090a	
		זוע	TREMBLE	1091b	
		חבל	DESTROY	1091d	
		חי	LIVING	1092d	1
		מלכו	KINGDOM	1100c	3
		מלכו	KINGDOM	1100c	2
		מן	FROM	*1101a	2 a
		סוף	END	1104b	
		עד	EVEN TO	1105b	1 c
		עלם	PERPETUITY	1106d	
		קדם	BEFORE	1110c	2
		קדם	BEFORE	1110c	2
		קים	ENDURING	1111a	
		שום	MAKE	1113d	
		שלטן	DOMINION	1115d	1
		שלטן	DOMINION	1115d	
6	28	את	SIGN	1079a	
		אריה	LION	1082c	
		יד	HAND	1094d	2
		כורש	CYRUS	1096d	
		נצל	DELIVER	1103b	
		עבד	DO	1104d	2
		שיזב	DELIVER	1115a	
		שיזב	DELIVER	1115a	
		שיזב	DELIVER	1115a	
		שמין	HEAVENS	1116a	1
		תמה	WONDER	1118b	
6	29	דריוש	DARIUS	1089a	2
		ה	AND	1091a	A
		מלכו	REIGN	1100c	4
		פרסי	PERSIAN	1108d	
		צלח	PROSPER	1109d	2
7	1	חד	ONE	1079c	1
		אמר	TELL	1081b	2
		בלשאצר	BELSHAZZAR	1084d	
		ה	AND	1091a	A
		חזה	BEHOLD	1092c	3
		חזו	VISION	1092d	1
		חלם	DREAM	1093a	
		כתב	WRITE	1098a	
		ל	IN REGARD TO	1098c	4 c
		מלה	THING	1100d	2
		ראש	HEAD	1112a	2
		ראש	HEAD	1112a	4
		משכב	COUCH	1115b	
		שנה	YEAR	1116d	
7	2	רו	LO	1082d	
		הוא	COME TO PASS	1090a	3
		חזו	VISION	1092c	1
		חזה	BEHOLD	1092c	3
		ים	SEA	1095d	
		לילא	NIGHT	1099b	
		עם	WITH	1107a	1
		ענה	ANSWER	1107b	2
		רב	GREAT	1112b	1
		ארבע	FOUR	1112c	1
		רוח	WIND	1112d	1
		שמין	HEAVENS	1116a	1
		גוח	ADDENDA ET CORRIGENDA	1127c	
7	3	חיוא	BEAST	1092d	
		ים	SEA	1095d	
		מן	OUT OF	1101a	1 b
		מן	FROM	1101b	5
		סלק	COME UP	1104b	
		רב	GREAT	1112b	1
		ארבע	FOUR	1112c	1
		שנא	CHANGE	1116c	
7	4	אנש	MAN	1081d	1
		אריה	LION	1082c	
		גף	WING	1086d	
		די	THAT	1088a	2

Ch	v.	Heb	Eng	Page	Sec
		הוא	COME TO PASS	1090a	3
		חזה	BEHOLD	1092c	3
		יהב	GIVE	1095b	
		ל	IN REGARD TO	1098c	4 b
		לבב	HEART	1098d	
		מן	FROM	1101a	1 a
		מרט	PLUCK	1101d	
		נטל	LIFT	1102d	
		נשר	EAGLE	1103c	
		עד	UNTIL	1105b	2 a
		קדמי	FORMER	1110c	
		קום	ARISE	1111a	
		רגל	FOOT	1112c	
7	5	חד	ONE	1079c	1
		אחרן	ANOTHER	1080a	
		אכל	DEVOUR	1080b	2
		אמר	SAY	1081b	1
		רו	LO	1082d	
		בין	BETWEEN	1084b	
		בשר	FLESH	1085c	
		דב	BEAR	1087a	
		דמה	BE LIKE	1088d	
		חיוא	BEAST	1092d	
		כן	THUS	1097b	
		עלע	RIB	1106d	
		פם	MOUTH	1108c	
		קום	ARISE	1110d	3
		קום	ARISE	1111a	2
		שגיא	MUCH	1113c	2
		שטר	SIDE	1113d	
		שן	TOOTH	1116d	
		תלת	THREE	1118a	
		תנין	SECOND	1118b	
7	6	אתר	AFTER	30b	2 b
		אחרן	ANOTHER	1080a	
		רו	LO	1082d	
		אתר	PLACE	1083d	B
		אתר	PLACE	*1083d	B
		גב	BACK	1085d	
		גף	WING	1086d	
		דנה	THIS	1089a	B
		הוא	COME TO PASS	1090a	3
		חזה	BEHOLD	1092c	3
		חיוא	BEAST	1092d	
		יהב	GIVE	1095b	
		ל	IN REGARD TO	1098c	4 b
		נמר	LEOPARD	1103a	
		עוף	FOWL	1105c	
		ראש	HEAD	1112a	1
		ארבע	FOUR	1112c	1
		ארבע	FOUR	1112c	2
		שלטן	DOMINION	1115d	1
7	7	אתר	AFTER	30b	2 b
		אימתן	TERRIBLE	1080a	
		אכל	DEVOUR	1080b	2
		רו	LO	1082d	
		אתר	PLACE	1083d	B
		דחל	FEAR	1087c	
		די	WHO	1087d	1 a
		דנה	THIS	1089a	B
		דקק	BE SHATTERED	1089a	B
		הוא	HE	1090a	
		חזו	VISION	1092c	1
		חזה	BEHOLD	1092c	3
		חיוא	BEAST	1092d	
		חיוא	BEAST	1092d	
		יתיר	PRE-EMINENT	1096c	
		ל	IN REGARD TO	1098c	4 b
		ליליא	NIGHT	1099b	
		מן	FROM	1101b	5
		עשר	TEN	1108a	
		פרזל	IRON	1108d	
		קדם	BEFORE	1110c	1
		קרן	HORN	1111d	2
		רב	GREAT	1112b	1
		רגל	FOOT	1112c	
		רביעי	FOURTH	1112c	
		רפס	TREAD	1113b	
		שאר	REMAINDER	1114b	
		שנא	CHANGE	1116c	
		שן	TOOTH	1116d	
		תקף	MIGHTY	1118c	
7	8	גדול	GREAT	*153c	9
		מן	FROM	578b	1 a
		אחרן	ANOTHER	1080a	
		אלו	LO	1080d	
		אנש	MAN	1081d	1
		ב	IN	1084a	8
		בין	BETWEEN	1084b	
		דא	THIS	1086d	
		זעיר	LITTLE	1091d	
		מלל	SPEAK	1100c	
		מלה	WORD	*1100d	1
		מן	FROM	1101a	3
		סלק	COME UP	1104b	
		עין	EYE	1105d	
		עין	EYE	1105d	
		עקר	BE ROOTED UP	1107d	
		פם	MOUTH	1108c	
		קדם	BEFORE	1110c	2
		קדמי	FORMER	1110c	
		קרן	HORN	1111d	2
		רב	GREAT	1112b	1
		שכל	CONSIDER	1114a	
		תלת	THREE	1118a	
7	9	גלגל	WHEEL	1086c	
		די	THAT	1088a	2
		דלק	BURN	1088d	
		חור	WHITE	1092c	
		חזה	BEHOLD	1092c	3
		יום	DAY	1095c	
		יתב	SIT	1096c	1
		כרסא	THRONE	1097c	
		כרסא	THRONE	1097c	
		לבוש	GARMENT	1098d	
		נור	FIRE	1102c	
		נקא	PURE	1103c	
		עד	UNTIL	1105b	2 a
		עמר	WOOL	1107a	
		עתיק	ADVANCED	1108b	
		ראש	HEAD	1112a	1
		רמא	CAST	1113b	2
		שער	HAIR	1114a	
		שביב	FLAME	1114b	
		תלג	SNOW	1117d	
7	10	אלף	ONE THOUSAND	1081a	
		די	THAT	1088a	2
		דין	JUDGEMENT	1088b	
		יתב	SIT	1096c	1
		נגד	STREAM	1102a	
		נור	FIRE	1102c	
		נהר	RIVER	1102c	
		נפק	GO FORTH	1103b	
		ספר	BOOK	1104c	
		פתח	OPEN	1109b	
		קדם	BEFORE	1110c	2
		קום	STAND	1110d	4
		רבו	MYRIAD	1112b	
		שמש	MINISTER	1116b	
7	11	גדול	GREAT	*153c	9
		אבד	PERISH	1078b	
		אשא	FIRE	1083b	
		גשם	BODY	1086d	
		חזה	BEHOLD	1092c	3
		חיוא	BEAST	1092d	
		יהב	GIVE	1095b	
		יקדה	BURNING	1096a	
		מלה	WORD	1100c	1
		מלל	SPEAK	1100c	
		מלה	WORD	1100d	1
		מן	FROM	1101a	2 c
		עד	UNTIL	1105b	2 a
		קל	VOICE	1110d	
		קטל	SLAY	1111a	
		רב	GREAT	1112b	1
7	12	ארכה	A LENGTHENING	1082d	
		זמן	TIME	1091c	
		חיוא	BEAST	1092d	
		חי	LIVING	1092d	2
		יהב	GIVE	1095b	
		עד	EVEN TO	1105b	1 c
		עדא	PASS AWAY	1105b	
		עדן	TIME	1105c	1
		שאר	REMAINDER	1114b	
		שלטן	DOMINION	1115d	1
7	13	אנש	MAN	1081d	1
		רו	LO	1082d	
		אתה	COME	1083c	
		בר	SON	1085b	1
		חזה	BEHOLD	1092c	3
		חזו	VISION	1092c	1
		יום	DAY	1095c	
		ליליא	NIGHT	1099b	
		מטא	REACH	1100a	1 a
		עד	EVEN TO	1105b	1 a
		עם	WITH	1107a	1 a
		ענן	CLOUD	1107b	
		עתיק	ADVANCED	1108b	
		קרב	APPROACH	1111c	2
		שמין	HEAVENS	1116a	1
7	14	אמה	NATION	1081a	
		די	THAT	1088a	2
		חבל	DESTROY	1091d	
		יהב	GIVE	1095b	
		יקר	HONOUR	1096a	
		לשן	TONGUE	1099b	
		מלכו	KINGDOM	1100c	2
		עדא	PASS AWAY	1105b	2
		עלם	PERPETUITY	1106d	
		עם	PEOPLE	1107a	
		פלח	PAY REVERENCE TO	1108c	1
		שלטן	DOMINION	1115d	1
7	15	אנה	I	1081c	
		אנה	I	1081c	
		בהל	ALARM	1084b	
		גו	MIDST	1086a	A
		גין	ON ACCOUNT OF	1086b	
		חזו	VISION	1092d	1
		כרא	BE DISTRESSED	1097d	
		נדנה	SHEATH	1102b	
		ראש	HEAD	1112a	2
		רוח	SPIRIT	1112d	2 a
7	16	חד	ONE	1079c	1
		אמר	TELL	1081b	2
		בעא	ASK	1085a	1
		ידע	KNOW	1095a	
		יציב	TRUE	1096a	2
		מלה	THING	1100d	2
		מן	FROM	1101a	3
		פשר	INTERPRETATION	1109b	
		קום	STAND	1110d	4
		קרב	APPROACH	1111c	
7	17	אלין	THESE	1080d	
		אנון	THEY	1081c	
		אנין	THEY	1081c	
		די	WHO	1087d	1 a
		הוא	HE	*1090a	
		חיוא	BEAST	1092d	
		מלך	KING	*1100b	
		קום	ARISE	1110d	2
		רב	GREAT	1112b	1
		ארבע	FOUR	1112c	1
		ארבע	FOUR	1112c	2
7	18	חסן	TAKE POSSESSION OF	1093c	
		מלכו	KINGDOM	1100c	2
		עבד	DO	1104d	2
		עד	EVEN TO	1105b	1 c
		עליון	HIGHEST	1106a	
		עלם	PERPETUITY	1106d	
		קבל	RECEIVE	1110b	
		קדיש	HOLY	1110d	
7	19	אכל	DEVOUR	1080b	2
		דחל	FEAR	1087c	
		די	THAT	1088a	2
		דקק	BE SHATTERED	1089a	
		הוא	COME TO PASS	1090a	3
		חיוא	BEAST	1092d	
		מפר	CLAW	1094c	
		יהב	GIVE	1095b	1
		יצב	MAKE CERTAIN	1096c	
		יתיר	PRE-EMINENT	1096c	
		כל	ALL	1097a	1
		מן	FROM	1101b	5
		נחש	COPPER	1102d	
		פרזל	IRON	1108d	
		צבא	DESIRE	1109b	1
		רביעי	FOURTH	1112c	
		רגל	FOOT	1112c	
		רפס	TREAD	1113b	
		שאר	REMAINDER	1114b	
		שנא	CHANGE	1116c	
		שן	TOOTH	1116d	
7	20	גדול	GREAT	*153c	9
		אחרן	ANOTHER	1080a	
		די	WHO	1087d	1 a
		דכן	THIS	1088c	
		ה	AND	1091a	E
		חברה	FELLOW	1092a	
		חזו	APPEARANCE	1092d	2
		מלל	SPEAK	1100c	
		מלה	WORD	*1100d	1
		מן	FROM	1101b	5
		נפל	FALL	1103a	2
		סלק	COME UP	1104b	
		עין	EYE	1105d	
		עשר	TEN	1108a	
		פם	MOUTH	1108c	
		קדם	BEFORE	1110c	2
		קרן	HORN	1111d	2
		ראש	HEAD	1112a	1
		רב	GREAT	1112b	1
		רב	GREAT	1112b	1
		תלת	THREE	1118a	
7	21	דכן	THIS	1088c	
		חזה	BEHOLD	1092c	3
		יכל	BE ABLE	1095d	2
		עבד	MAKE	1104d	1
		עם	WITH	1107a	1 b
		קדיש	HOLY	1110d	
		קרן	HORN	1111d	2
		קרב	WAR	1111d	
7	22	אתה	COME	1083c	
		די	THAT	1088b	4 c
		דין	JUDGEMENT	1088b	
		זמן	TIME	1091c	
		חסן	TAKE POSSESSION OF	1093c	
		יהב	GIVE	1095b	
		יום	DAY	1095c	
		ל	IN REGARD TO	1098c	4 d
		מטא	REACH	1100a	1 a
		מלכו	KINGDOM	1100c	2
		עד	UNTIL	1105b	2 a
		עליון	HIGHEST	1106a	
		עתיק	ADVANCED	1108b	
		קדיש	HOLY	1110d	
		קדיש	HOLY	1110d	
7	23	אכל	DEVOUR	1080b	2
		אמר	SAY	1081b	1
		דוש	TREAD DOWN	1087c	
		דקק	BE SHATTERED	1089a	
		הוא	COME TO PASS	1090a	2
		חיוא	BEAST	1092d	
		כן	THUS	1097b	
		מלך	KING	*1100b	
		מלכו	KINGDOM	1100c	2
		מן	FROM	1101b	5
		רביעי	FOURTH	1112c	
		רביעי	FOURTH	1112c	
		שנא	CHANGE	1116c	
7	24	אחרן	AFTER	1079d	
		אחרן	ANOTHER	1080a	
		הוא	HE	1090a	
		מלכו	KINGDOM	1100c	2
		מן	FROM	1101b	5

Ch v.	Heb	Eng	Page	Sec
	עשר	TEN	1108a	
	עשר	TEN	1108a	
	קדמי	FORMER	1110c	
	קום	ARISE	1110d	2
	קום	ARISE	1110d	2
	קרן	HORN	1111d	2
	שנא	CHANGE	1116c	
	שפל	BE LOW	1117a	
	תלת	THREE	1118a	
7 25	בלה	BECOME OLD AND WORN OUT	115a	A
	בקר	MORNING	*134a	1 e
	ל	TO	*517a	6 b
	בלא	WEAR AWAY	1084c	
	דת	LAW	1089b	3
	זמן	TIME	1091c	
	יהב	GIVE	1095b	1
	מלה	WORD	1100c	1
	מלל	SPEAK	1100c	
	סבר	THINK	1104a	
	עד	EVEN TO	1105b	1 c
	עדן	TIME	1105c	2
	עליון	HIGHEST	1106a	
	עלי	HIGHEST	1106a	
	פלג	HALF	1108b	
	צד	SIDE	1109c	
	קדיש	HOLY	1110d	
	שנא	CHANGE	1116c	
7 26	אבד	PERISH	1078b	
	דין	JUDGEMENT	1088b	
	יתב	SIT	1096c	1
	סוף	END	1104b	
	עדא	PASS AWAY	1105b	
	עד	EVEN TO	1105b	1 c
	שלטן	DOMINION	1115d	1
	שמד	DESTROY	1116a	
7 27	יהב	GIVE	1095b	
	מלכו	KINGDOM	1100c	2
	מלכו	KINGDOM	1100c	2
	מלכו	KINGDOM	1100c	2
	מלכו	KINGDOM	1100c	2
	עליון	HIGHEST	1106a	
	עלם	PERPETUITY	1106d	
	עם	PEOPLE	1107a	
	פלח	PAY REVERENCE TO	1108c	1
	קדיש	HOLY	1110d	
	רבו	GREATNESS	1112c	
	שלטן	DOMINION	1115d	1
	שמם	HEAR	1116b	
	תחות	UNDER	1117d	
7 28	על	UPON	753d	2 1d
	אנה	I	1081c	
	בהל	ALARM	1084b	
	זיו	SPLENDOUR	1091b	
	יד	HAND	1094d	2
	כה	HERE	1096d	
	לב	HEART	1098d	
	מלה	THING	1100d	2
	נטר	KEEP	1102d	
	סוף	END	1104b	
	עד	EVEN TO	1105b	1 a
	על	UPON	1106b	1 b
	רעיון	THOUGHT	1113b	
	שגיא	MUCH	1113c	3
	שנא	CHANGE	1116c	
8 1	בלאשצר	BELSHAZZAR	128d	
	ה	THE	209c	3
	חזון	VISION	303a	1
	תחלה	BEGINNING	321b	
	מלכות	REIGN	575a	2
	ראה	TO SEE	908c	1 c
8 2	אולי	ULAI	19c	
	בירה	CASTLE	108b	2
	מדינה	PROVINCE	193d	2
	חזון	VISION	303a	1
	אובל	STREAM	385c	
	עילם	ELAM	743d	
	ראה	TO SEE	907a	1 b
	שושן	SUSA	1004d	
8 3	איל	RAM	17d	1
	אחרון	BEHIND	31a	B b
	גבה	HIGH	147b	1
	אובל	STREAM	385c	
	עלה	GO UP	748d	4
	קרן	HORN	901d	1 a
8 4	איל	RAM	17d	1
	גדל	BECOME GREAT	152c	3 b
	חיה	LIVING THING	312c	1 a
	ים	SEA	411b	9
	נגב	SOUTH-COUNTRY	616b	2
	נגח	PUSH	618c	
	ראה	TO SEE	907a	2 3
	רצון	GOODWILL	953c	3 b
8 5	אין	NOT	34c	2 e
	בין	DISCERN	107a	1
	חזות	VISION	303b	2
	נגע	TOUCH	619a	1 a
	עין	EYE	745a	5
	עז	SHE-GOAT	777c	6
	מערב	WEST	788b	
	צפיר	HE-GOAT	862b	
	קרן	HORN	901d	1 a
8 6	איל	RAM	17d	1
	בעל	LORD	127c	1 5a
	אובל	STREAM	385c	

Ch v.	Heb	Eng	Page	Sec
	חמה	RAGE	404c	2 b
	כח	STRENGTH	471a	4
	קרן	HORN	901d	1 a
	ראה	TO SEE	907a	2 3
	רוץ	RUN	930b	1
8 7	איל	RAM	17d	1
	אצל	BESIDE	69b	1
	כח	STRENGTH	471a	4
	נגע	REACH	619c	2
	נכה	SMITE	645c	1 a
	נצל	DELIVER	664d	3 a
	עת	TIME	773d	2 c
	קרן	HORN	901d	1 a
	ראה	TO SEE	907a	2 3
	רמס	TRAMPLE	942d	
	שבר	BREAK	991a	
	שלך	THROW	1021b	1 e
8 8	גדל	BECOME GREAT	152c	3 b
	חזות	VISION	303b	2
	ל	TO	511c	1 h
	מאד	EXCEEDINGLY	547c	2 b
	עלה	GO UP	748d	4
	עז	SHE-GOAT	777c	6
	עצם	BE VAST	782c	1
	צפיר	HE-GOAT	862b	
	קרן	HORN	901d	1 a
	ארבע	FOUR	917a	1 a5
	רוח	BREATH	924d	2 a
	שבר	BREAK	990d	
8 9	גדל	BECOME GREAT	152b	2 e
	מזרח	PLACE OF SUNRISE	281a	2 c4
	יצא	GO OUT	423d	1 h
	יתר	EXCESS	452a	2 b
	מן	FROM	578b	1 a
	נגב	SOUTH-COUNTRY	616b	2
	צבי	BEAUTY	840a	1 b
	צעיר	YOUNG	859a	1 a
	קרן	HORN	901d	1 a
8 10	גדל	BECOME GREAT	152b	2 e
	ו	AND	252c	1 b
	כוכב	STAR	457a	
	מן	FROM	580d	3 ba
	נפל	FALL	658a	1 g
	צבא	HOST	839a	1 b
	צבא	HOST	839a	1 b
	רמס	TRAMPLE	942d	
8 11	גדל	BECOME GREAT	152c	3 b
	מכון	FIXED PLACE	467c	1
	תמיד	CONTINUITY	556c	2
	מן	OUT OF	580a	2 ea
	צבא	HOST	839a	1 b
	צבא	ARMY	*839c	3 a
	מקדש	SACRED PLACE	874b	4
	רום	BE HIGH	927d	1
	רום	BE HIGH	927d	2
	שר	CHIEFTAIN	979a	9
	שלך	THROW	1021c	3
8 12	אמת	FIRMNESS	54b	4 d
	תמיד	CONTINUITY	556c	2 c
	נתן	GIVE	681c	1 e
	עשה	DO	794b	1 4
	פשע	TRANSGRESSION	833d	5
	צבא	WAR	839b	2
	צלח	ADVANCE	852c	2
	שלך	THROW	1021b	1 e
8 13	ו	AND	253a	1 h
	חזון	VISION	303a	1
	תמיד	CONTINUITY	556c	2 c
	פלני	A CERTAIN ONE	812a	
	פשע	TRANSGRESSION	833d	5
	צבא	ARMY	838b	3 a
	צבא	SERVICE	839b	3 a
	קדש	APARTNESS	871d	2 d
	קדוש	HOLY	872d	2 c
	רום	BE HIGH	927d	
	מרמס	TRAMPLING-PLACE	942d	2
	שמם	BE DESOLATED	1031a	2
	שמע	HEAR	1033c	1 b
8 14	בקר	MORNING	134a	1 e
	צדק	BE JUST	842d	2 b
8 15	בינה	UNDERSTANDING	108a	1
	בקש	SEEK	134d	2 b
	גבר	MAN	150a	
	חזון	VISION	303a	1
	ך	LIKE	*453d	1 b
	נגד	IN FRONT	617c	2 b
	ראה	TO SEE	906d	1 b
	מראה	VISION	909c	1 b
8 16	אולי	ULAI	19c	
	בין	DISCERN	107a	3 c
	בין	INTERVAL	107b	1
	גבריאל	GABRIEL	150c	
	הלז	THIS	229c	
	קול	VOICE	877a	1 d
	קרא	CALL	895a	1 a
	מראה	VISION	909d	1 b
8 17	אצל	BESIDE	69b	A
	בין	DISCERN	107a	1 a
	בעת	TERRIFY	130a	
	חזון	VISION	303a	1
	נפל	FALL	657c	3 b
	עמד	STANDING-PLACE	765a	
	קץ	END	893d	1
8 18	דבר	SPEAK	181c	3 e
	נגע	TOUCH	619a	1 a
	עמד	STAND	764d	3

Ch v.	Heb	Eng	Page	Sec
	עמד	STANDING-PLACE	765a	
	פנה	FACE	815d	1 1a
	רדם	BE IN HEAVY SLEEP	922b	
8 19	זעם	INDIGNATION	277a	
	ידע	KNOW	395a	
	מועד	APPOINTED TIME	417c	1 a
	קץ	END	893d	1
8 20	איל	RAM	17d	1
	בעל	LORD	127c	1 5a
	יון	GREECE	*402b	
	מדי	MEDES	552a	1
	פרס	PERSIA	828a	
	קרן	HORN	901d	1 a
8 21	חזות	VISION	303b	2
	יון	GREECE	402b	
	עין	EYE	745a	5
	צפיר	HE-GOAT	862b	
	קרן	HORN	901d	1 a
	שעיר	HE-GOAT	972c	
8 22	יון	GREECE	*402b	
	כח	STRENGTH	470d	1 c
	מלכות	KINGDOM	575a	3
	עמד	STAND	764c	6 a
	ארבע	FOUR	917a	1 a5
	שבר	BREAK	990d	
8 23	בין	DISCERN	107a	1 b
	חידה	RIDDLE	295c	4
	מלכות	KINGDOM	575a	3
	עז	STRONG	738d	
	עמד	STAND	764c	6 a
	פשע	REBEL	833b	2
	תמם	BE COMPLETE	1070c	2
8 24	כח	STRENGTH	470d	1 c
	עם	PEOPLE	767a	5 g
	עצם	BE VAST	782c	1
	עצום	MIGHTY	783a	1
	עשה	DO	794b	1 4
	פלא	BE SURPASSING	810d	3 a
	צלח	ADVANCE	852c	2
	קדוש	HOLY	872d	2 b
	שחת	GO TO RUIN	1008b	1
8 25	אפס	NON-EXISTENCE	67b	2 b
	גדל	BECOME GREAT	152c	3 b
	לבב	HEART	524a	2 c
	על	UPON	753d	2 1f
	עמד	STAND	764c	6 c
	צלח	ADVANCE	852c	2
	מרמה	DECEIT	941b	
	שכל	PRUDENCE	968d	3
	שר	CHIEFTAIN	979a	9
	שלוה	QUIETNESS	1017d	
8 26	אמר	SAY	56c	
	בקר	MORNING	*134a	1 e
	בקר	MORNING	134a	1 e
	חזון	VISION	303a	1
	יום	DAY	401a	7 i
	סתם	STOP UP	711b	2
	מראה	VISION	909d	3
8 27	בין	DISCERN	107a	3 a
	היה	BE	227d	3
	חלה	BE WEAK	317d	2
	מלאכה	WORK	522b	6 a
	מראה	VISION	909d	1
	שמם	BE DESOLATED	1031b	1
9 1	אחשורוש	AHASUERUS	31c	
	דריוש	DARIUS	201d	3
	זרע	SOWING	283a	4 f
	כשדים	CHALDEANS	505b	1 b
	מדי	MEDES	552a	1
	מלך	BE KING	574b	1
	מלכות	KINGDOM	575a	3
9 2	בין	DISCERN	106d	3 a
	דבר	WORD	182c	1 2a
	חרבה	WASTE	352a	1
	מלא	FILL	570d	3
	נביא	PROPHET	611d	1
	ספר	MISSIVE	707c	3 f
	ירמיה	JEREMIAH	941c	1
9 3	אדון	LORD	11c	3 2b
	אלהים	GOD	43d	3
	אפר	ASHES	68a	
	בקש	SEEK	134d	3 c
	תחנון	SUPPLICATION FOR FAVOR	337d	2
	נתן	PUT	680c	2 b
	פנה	FACE	816a	1 1d
	צום	FASTING	847b	
	שק	SACK	974c	2 a
9 4	אדון	LORD	11c	3 2b
	אהב	LOVE	13a	3
	אל	GOD	42c	6 a
	אנא	AH, NOW	58a	
	ברית	COVENANT	136c	2 2c
	ברית	COVENANT	137a	3 2
	ברית	COVENANT	137b	3 2
	גדול	GREAT	153b	6 c
	יהוה	YAHWEH	219a	2 1f
	חסד	GOODNESS	339a	2 1e
	ידה	CONFESS	392d	1
	ירא	BE REVERED	431d	3 a
	פלל	INTERVENE	813b	3
9 5	חטא	MISS A GOAL OR WAY	307a	2 b
	מרד	REBEL	597c	2
	עוה	COMMIT INIQUITY	731c	

Ch	v.	Heb	Eng	Page	Sec
		מצוה	COMMANDMENT	846c	2 b3
		רשע	BE WICKED	957d	3
9	6	דבר	SPEAK	181c	4 a
		נביא	PROPHET	611d	1
		עבד	SLAVE	714b	4
		שר	CHIEFTAIN	978b	2 a
9	7	אדון	LORD	11c	3 2b
		ארץ	EARTH	76c	5
		בשת	SHAME	102a	1
		ה	THE	208b	1 ha
		יום	DAY	400d	7 h
		מעל	ACT TREACHEROUSLY	591b	1 b
		נדח	THRUST	623b	2
		צדקה	RIGHTEOUSNESS	842b	2
		קרב	NEAR	898c	2 b
		רחק	DISTANT	935b	1 a
9	8	אדון	LORD	11c	3 2b
		בשת	SHAME	102a	1
		חטא	MISS A GOAL OR WAY	307a	2 b
		שר	CHIEFTAIN	978b	2 a
9	9	אדון	LORD	11c	3 2b
		ה	THE	208b	1 ha
		מרד	REBEL	597c	2
		סליחה	FORGIVENESS	669c	
		רחמים	COMPASSION	933c	1
9	10	יהוה	YAHWEH	218d	2 1c
		הלך	WALK	234c	2 3a 1d
		תורה	INSTRUCTION	435d	1 b
		נביא	PROPHET	611d	1
		נתן	PUT	680d	2 b
		עבד	SLAVE	714b	4
		פנה	FACE	817c	2 4b g
9	11	אלהים	GOD	44a	3 b
		אלה	OATH	46d	3 a
		בלת	NOT	*116d	4 a
		חטא	MISS A GOAL OR WAY	307a	2 b
		תורה	LAW	436b	2 b3
		תורה	LAW	436b	2 b3
		משה	MOSES	602c	2
		משה	MOSES	602d	
		נתך	POUR FORTH	677d	
		עבד	SLAVE	714a	3
		עבר	PASS OVER	717c	1 i
		שבועה	OATH	990a	1 b
9	12	דבר	SPEAK	181d	5
		דבר	WORD	182d	1 2b
		עשה	DO	795b	1 b
		שפט	JUDGE	1047c	1 b
		תחת	UNDERNEATH	1065b	1 c
9	13	אמת	FIRMNESS	54b	4 d
		את	MARK OF THE ACCUSATIVE	85c	3 a
		יהוה	YAHWEH	218d	2 1c
		חלה	MOLLIFY	318c	1 a
		תורה	LAW	436b	2 b3
		משה	MOSES	602c	2
		משה	MOSES	602d	
		עון	INIQUITY	731a	1 b
		שכל	BE PRUDENT	968b	2 1c
9	14	יהוה	YAHWEH	218d	2 1c
		על	UPON	754d	2 1f h
		עשה	DO	793d	1 la l
		צדיק	JUST	843a	1 d
		שקד	WATCH	1052a	1
9	15	אדון	LORD	11c	3 2b
		חזק	STRONG	305c	1 b
		חטא	MISS A GOAL OR WAY	307a	2 b
		יום	DAY	400d	7 h
		יצא	CAUSE TO GO	424c	1 a
		רשע	BE WICKED	957d	1
		שם	NAME	1028a	2 b1
9	16	אדון	LORD	11c	3 2b
		הר	MOUNTAIN	249d	1 a
		חטא	SIN	308a	1 b
		חרפה	REPROACH	358a	3
		חמה	RAGE	404d	2 c
		סביב	ROUND ABOUT	687b	2 ba b
		עון	INIQUITY	730d	1
		צדקה	RIGHTEOUSNESS	842c	7 a
		קדש	APARTNESS	871d	2 e
		שוב	TURN BACK	997d	6 f
9	17	אדון	LORD	11c	3 2b
		אור	BECOME LIGHT	21c	5
		תחנון	SUPPLICATION FOR FAVOR	337d	2
		מען	PURPOSE	775b	1 a
		תפלה	PRAYER	813c	1 e
		שמם	DEVASTATED	1031b	
9	18	אזן	EAR	24b	2 b
		תחנון	SUPPLICATION FOR FAVOR	337d	2
		נטה	INCLINE	641a	3 e
		נפל	FALL	658b	6
		עין	EYE	744b	1 j
		על	UPON	753d	2 1f
		פקח	OPEN	824d	1 a
		צדקה	RIGHTEOUSNESS	842c	7 b
		קרא	CALL	896b	6 d4
		רחמים	COMPASSION	933c	1
		שמם	BE DESOLATED	1031a	1
9	19	אדון	LORD	11c	3 2b
		אחר	DELAY	29b	1
		סלח	FORGIVE	699b	
		מען	PURPOSE	775b	1 a
		עשה	DO	794b	1 4
		קרא	CALL	896b	6 d4
9	20	יהוה	YAHWEH	219a	2 1f
		הר	MOUNTAIN	249d	1 a
		חטאת	SIN	308c	1 b
		תחנה	FAVOR	337c	2
		ידה	CONFESS	392d	1
		נפל	FALL	658b	6
		עוד	STILL	729a	1 aa
		פלל	INTERVENE	813b	3
		קדש	APARTNESS	871d	2 e
9	21	גבריאל	GABRIEL	150c	
		חזון	VISION	303a	1
		תחלה	BEGINNING	321b	
		יעף	WEARINESS	419b	
		יעף	BE WEARY	419b	4
		מנחה	OFFERING	585b	4
		נגע	TOUCH	619a	1 a
		עוד	STILL	729a	1 aa
		עת	TIME	773c	1 b
		ערב	SUNSET	788a	1 c
		תפלה	PRAYER	813c	1 b
9	22	בין	DISCERN	107a	3 a
		בינה	UNDERSTANDING	108a	1
		דבר	SPEAK	181c	3 e
		יצא	GO OUT	424a	2 c
		שכל	BE PRUDENT	968c	4
9	23	בין	DISCERN	106d	3 c
		בין	DISCERN	107a	2
		דבר	WORD	182b	1 1b
		תחלה	BEGINNING	321b	
		חמדה	DESIRABLENESS	326d	
		תחנון	SUPPLICATION FOR FAVOR	337d	2
		יצא	GO OUT	423c	1 g
		מראה	VISION	909a	3
9	24	חזון	VISION	303a	1
		חטאת	SIN	309a	1 d3
		חתך	DIVIDE	367b	
		חתם	SEAL	367d	2
		חתם	SEAL	368a	2
		כלה	FINISH	478a	1 a
		כפר	COVER OVER	497c	2 b
		משח	ANOINT	603b	3 b
		נביא	PROPHET	611d	1
		עון	INIQUITY	731a	1 c3
		עיר	CITY	746c	1 i
		עולם	LONG DURATION	762d	2 l
		פשע	TRANSGRESSION	833d	5
		צדק	RIGHTEOUSNESS	841d	5
		קדש	APARTNESS	871d	2 e
		קדש	APARTNESS	872a	3 a
		שבעים	SEVENTY	988c	1 c
		שבוע	PERIOD OF SEVEN	989a	2
		תמם	BE COMPLETE	1070c	3
9	25	בנה	BUILD	124d	1 i
		בנה	BUILD	125a	1 i
		דבר	WORD	182b	1 1b
		ו	AND	252c	1 b
		חרוץ	TRENCH	358d	1
		חרוץ	SHARP	358d	2
		מוצא	GOING FORTH	425d	1 a
		מן	SINCE	583c	7 c
		משיח	ANOINTED	603c	4
		נגיד	LEADER	618a	1
		צוק	CONSTRAINT	848a	1
		רחוב	PLAZA	932b	
		שכל	BE PRUDENT	968b	3
		שבוע	PERIOD OF SEVEN	989a	2
		שוב	TURN BACK	998b	8
		שוב	TURN BACK	999b	1 d
9	26	אין	NOT	34d	3
		חרץ	CUT	358c	
		כרת	BE CUT OFF	504a	1 b
		משיח	ANOINTED	603c	4
		נגיד	LEADER	618a	2
		צוק	CONSTRAINT	848a	
		קץ	END	893d	1
		קץ	END	893d	1
		שבוע	PERIOD OF SEVEN	989a	2
		שטף	FLOOD	1009b	
		שמם	BE DESOLATED	1031a	1
9	27	ברית	COVENANT	136b	1 2
		ברית	COVENANT	136c	1 5
		גבר	BE STRONG	149d	
		ו	AND	252c	1 b
		זבח	SACRIFICE	257c	1 1
		חצי	HALF	345c	1
		חרץ	CUT	358c	
		כלה	COMPLETE	478d	2 a
		כנף	EXTREMITY	489d	2 b
		מנחה	OFFERING	585b	4
		נתך	POUR FORTH	677d	
		צוק	CONSTRAINT	848a	1
		צוק	CONSTRAINT	848a	
		שבוע	PERIOD OF SEVEN	989a	2
		שבת	CEASE	992a	1
		שמם	BE DESOLATED	1031a	1
		שמם	BE DESOLATED	1031a	1
		שקוץ	DETESTED THING	1055a	
10	1	אמת	FIRMNESS	54b	4 a
		בין	DISCERN	106d	3 a
		בינה	UNDERSTANDING	108a	1
		בלטשאצר	BELTESHAZZAR	117b	
		כורש	CYRUS	468d	
		פרס	PERSIA	828a	3 b
		צבא	HARD SERVICE	839b	1
		קרא	CALL	896b	2 d2
		מראה	VISION	909d	3
10	2	אבל	MOURN	5c	
		יום	TIME	399d	6 b
		שבוע	PERIOD OF SEVEN	988d	1
10	3	אכל	EAT	37b	1
		בוא	COME	97d	1
		בשר	FLESH	142c	1 a
		חמדה	DESIRABLENESS	326d	
		יום	TIME	399d	6 b
		לחם	FOOD	537a	1 a
		מלא	BE FULL	570b	1 b
		סוך	ANOINT	692a	1
		שבוע	PERIOD OF SEVEN	988d	1
10	4	חדקל	TIGRIS	293c	1
		יאר	STREAM	*384c	4
		יד	HAND	391c	5 h3
		יום	DAY	398c	2 e
		נהר	STREAM	625d	1
		ראשון	FIRST	911d	2 a
		ארבע	FOUR	917b	2 b
10	5	אופז	UPHAZ	20c	
		בד	WHITE LINEN	94b	
		חגר	GIRD	291d	1
		כתם	GOLD	508d	2
		לבש	PUT ON	528a	E
		מתנים	LOINS	608a	1 c
		אופז	ADDENDA ET CORRIGENDA	1119d	
10	6	אש	FIRE	77d	6
		ברק	LIGHTNING	140c	1
		גויה	BODY	156b	1
		המון	SOUND	242c	1
		זרוע	ARM	283d	1 a
		לפיד	TORCH	542a	1
		נחשת	COPPER	639a	1
		עין	EYE	745a	4 c
		קול	VOICE	877a	1 d
		מראה	VISION	909c	1 b
		מרגלות	PLACE OF FEET	920b	
		תרשיש	YELLOW JASPAR	1076d	
10	7	אבל	HOWBEIT	6a	2
		ברח	FLEE	138a	2
		חרדה	TREMBLING	353d	1
		נפל	FALL	657c	5
		נשמה	BREATH	675d	2
		ראה	TO SEE	906d	1 b
		מראה	VISION	909b	
10	8	הוד	VIGOUR	217b	3 c
		הפך	TURN	246a	1 b
		כח	STRENGTH	470c	1 a
		כח	STRENGTH	470d	1 b
		על	UPON	753d	2 1d
		עצר	RESTRAIN	783c	2
		ראה	TO SEE	906d	1 b
		מראה	VISION	909b	
		שאר	REMAIN	984a	2
		משחית	DESTRUCTION	1008c	
10	9	פנה	FACE	815d	1 1a
		קול	VOICE	877a	1 d
		רדם	BE IN HEAVY SLEEP	922b	
10	10	ברך	KNEE	139c	
		יד	HAND	389a	1 b
		כף	HOLLOW OF THE HAND	496b	1 a
		נגע	TOUCH	619a	1 a
		נוע	TOTTER	631c	2
10	11	אנכי	I	59c	
		בין	DISCERN	107a	2
		דבר	SPEAK	180c	
		דבר	SPEAK	181c	3 e
		דבר	WORD	183b	3 2
		חמודה	DESIRABLENESS	326d	
		עמד	STAND	764b	5 b
		עמד	STANDING-PLACE	765a	
		רעד	TREMBLE	944c	
		שלח	SEND	1019b	
10	12	בין	DISCERN	107a	1 a
		ירא	FEAR	431b	1 a
		לב	HEART	525a	2 4
		נתן	GIVE	679a	1 i
		ענה	BE BOWED DOWN	776c	3
		שמע	HEAR	1034b	1
		לב	ADDENDA ET CORRIGENDA	1124c	
10	13	יתר	BE LEFT OVER	451c	
		מיכאל	MICHAEL	567c	1
		מלכות	KINGDOM	575a	3
		נגד	IN FRONT	617c	2 b
		עזר	HELP	740b	
		עמד	STAND	764c	6 c
		ראשון	FIRST	911d	2 a
		שר	CHIEFTAIN	978d	8
10	14	אחרית	END	31b	3
		בין	DISCERN	107a	3 e
		חזון	VISION	303a	1
		עוד	STILL	729a	1 ab
		קרה	ENCOUNTER	899c	2
10	15	אלם	BIND	47d	1
		דבר	SPEAK	181c	3 e
		פנה	FACE	815d	1 1a
10	16	אלם	BIND	47d	1

Ch	v.	Heb	Eng	Page	Sec
		דמות	LIKENESS	198b	1
		הפך	TURN	245d	1 a
		כח	STRENGTH	470d	1 b
		נגד	IN FRONT	617c	2 b
		נגע	TOUCH	619a	1 a
		עצר	RESTRAIN	783c	2
		פתח	OPEN	835b	
		ציר	PANG	852a	
		מראה	VISION	909b	
		שפה	SPEECH	973c	1 a1
10	17	דבר	SPEAK	181c	3 e
		היך	HOW	228a	
		זה	THIS	261a	2 ba
		כח	STRENGTH	470c	1 a
		עמד	STAND	764b	3 c
		עתה	NOW	774d	2 e
		נשמה	ADDENDA ET COR-RIGENDA	1125c	
10	18	חזק	BE FIRM	304c	1 b
		יסף	DO AGAIN	415c	2 b
		כ	LIKE	*453d	1 b
		נגע	TOUCH	619a	1 a
		מראה	VISION	909c	1 b
10	19	דבר	SPEAK	181c	3 e
		חזק	BE FIRM	304c	1 2c
		חזק	BE FIRM	304c	1 b
		חזק	BE FIRM	305b	1
		חמודה	DESIRABLENESS	326c	
		ירא	FEAR	431b	1 a
10	20	יון	GREECE	402b	
		לחם	ENGAGE IN BAT-TLE	535c	
		מה	HOW	554a	4 d
		עתה	NOW	774a	1 b
		שר	CHIEFTAIN	978a	8
10	21	אבל	HOWBEIT	6a	2
		אמת	FIRMNESS	54b	4 c
		חזק	BE FIRM	305b	4 a
		כתב	WRITING	508b	5
		מיכאל	MICHAEL	567c	1
		עם	WITH	767c	1 a
		רשם	INSCRIBE	957a	
		שר	CHIEFTAIN	978a	8
11	1	דריוש	DARIUS	201d	3
		חזק	BE FIRM	305b	6 c
		ל	TO	512b	4 a
		מדי	MEDE	552a	
		מעוז	PLACE OF SAFETY	732a	3
		עמד	STAND	764c	7 g
11	2	אמת	FIRMNESS	54b	4 a
		גדול	GREAT	153a	1
		חזקה	STRENGTH	305d	2
		יון	GREECE	402b	
		כ	LIKE	454d	3 b
		כל	ALL	482c	2 a
		כל	ALL	483a	2 bb
		מלכות	KINGDOM	575a	3
		עוד	STILL	729a	1 ab
		עור	ROUSE ONESELF	735b	1
		עמד	STAND	764c	6 a
		עשר	BE RICH	799b	2
		פרס	PERSIA	828a	
		רביעי	FOURTH	918a	1
11	3	גבור	STRONG	150a	1
		משל	RULE	605d	1
		ממשל	DOMINION	606a	1
		עמד	STAND	764c	6 a
		רצון	GOODWILL	953c	3 b
		שכל	BE PRUDENT	968c	4
11	4	אחרית	END	31b	D
		בד	SEPARATION	94d	1 e
		חצה	DIVIDE	345c	
		ל	TO	511c	1 h
		מלכות	KINGDOM	575a	3
		משל	RULE	605d	1
		משל	DOMINION	606a	
		נתש	PLUCK UP	684c	
		עמד	STAND	764c	6 a
		רוח	BREATH	924d	2 a
11	5	חזק	BE FIRM	304b	1 1c
		מן	FROM	580d	3 bb
		משל	RULE	605d	1
		ממשל	DOMINION	606a	1
		ממשלה	RULE	606a	1
		נגב	SOUTH-COUNTRY	616b	1 c
		שר	CHIEFTAIN	978c	3 a
11	6	בת	DAUGHTER	123a	1
		זרוע	ARM	284a	1 b
		חבר	UNITE	288c	
		חזק	BE FIRM	305b	6 c
		ילד	BEGET	408c	2 a
		מישר	LEVEL	449d	2
		כח	STRENGTH	*470d	1 b
		כח	STRENGTH	470d	1
		ל	TO	517a	6 a
		נגב	SOUTH-COUNTRY	616b	1 c
		נתן	GIVE	681c	1 e
		עצר	RESTRAIN	783c	2
		צפון	NORTH	861a	
		קץ	END	893d	1
		שנה	YEAR	1040b	
11	7	ב	IN	89d	3 2b
		חיל	STRENGTH	299a	4
		חזק	BE FIRM	305a	5
		כן	PLACE	487d	2
		מן	FROM	580d	3 bb
		נצר	SPROUT	666a	
		מעוז	PLACE OF SAFETY	732a	1
		עמד	STAND	764c	6 a
		עשה	DO	794b	1 2
		צפון	NORTH	861a	
11	8	שרש	ROOT	1057d	1
		זהב	GOLD	263c	1
		חמדה	DESIRE	326d	
		כלי	ARTICLE	479c	1
		נסך	MOLTEN IMAGE	651a	2
		צפון	NORTH	861a	
		שבי	CAPTIVITY	985d	1
11	9	מלכות	KINGDOM	575a	3
		נגב	SOUTH-COUNTRY	616b	1 c
11	10	גרה	ENGAGE IN STRIFE	173c	2
		גרה	ENGAGE IN STRIFE	173c	2
		המון	CROWD	242c	3 a
		חיל	STRENGTH	299a	4
		עבר	PASS OVER	717b	1 e
		מעוז	PLACE OF SAFETY	732a	1
		שכל	BE PRUDENT	968c	4
		שוב	TURN BACK	997c	3 b
11	11	שמף	OVERFLOW	1009a	1
		המון	CROWD	242c	3 a
		יצא	GO OUT	423d	2 c
		לחם	ENGAGE IN BAT-TLE	535c	
		נגב	SOUTH-COUNTRY	616b	1 c
		עמד	STAND	765a	6 g
11	12	צפון	NORTH	861a	
		המון	CROWD	242c	3 a
		לבב	HEART	524a	2 6c
		נפל	FALL	658a	2
		נשא	LIFT	671d	4
		עזז	BE STRONG	738c	
		רבו	TEN THOUSAND	914b	
		רום	BE HIGH	926d	2 b
11	13	המון	CROWD	242c	3 a
		חיל	STRENGTH	299a	4
		ל	TO	517a	6 a
		עמד	STAND	765a	6 g
		עת	TIME	773d	2 c
		צפון	NORTH	861a	
		קץ	END	893d	1
		רב	MUCH	913b	1 e
		רכוש	PROPERTY	940d	3
11	14	בן	SON	121b	1 ji
		חזון	VISION	303a	1
		כשל	STUMBLE	505d	1 b
		נגב	SOUTH-COUNTRY	616b	1 c
		נשא	LIFT	672a	
		עמד	STAND	764c	6 c
		עמד	STAND	764d	5
		עת	TIME	773b	1 a
11	15	פריץ	VIOLENT ONE	829d	
		מבצר	FORTIFICATION	*131c	
		מבצר	FORTIFICATION	131c	
		זרוע	ARM	284b	3
		כח	STRENGTH	470d	1 b
		נגב	SOUTH-COUNTRY	616b	1 c
		סללה	MOUND	700c	
		עם	PEOPLE	767a	5 i
		צפון	NORTH	861a	
		שפך	POUR OUT	1049c	1 a
11	16	כלה	COMPLETE	478d	2 b
		צבי	BEAUTY	840a	1 b
		רצון	GOODWILL	953c	3 b
11	17	בת	DAUGHTER	123c	2
		מלכות	KINGDOM	575a	3
		עמד	STAND	764b	3 c
		ישר	STRAIGHT	779b	3 c2
		שום	TO PLACE	963d	2 c
		שחת	GO TO RUIN	1008b	1
		תקף	POWER	1076a	
11	18	אי	COAST	16a	1
		בלת	EXCEPT	116d	3
		חרפה	REPROACH	358a	2 e
		לכד	CAPTURE	540a	1
		קצין	CHIEF	892d	1
		שום	TO PLACE	963d	2 c
		שוב	TURN BACK	999d	6 b
11	19	כשל	STUMBLE	505d	2 c
		מצא	FIND	594a	2
		מעוז	PLACE OF SAFETY	732a	1
		שוב	TURN BACK	999d	6 b
11	20	הדר	SPLENDOUR	214a	
		יום	DAY	399b	5 a
		כן	PLACE	487d	2
		לא	NOT	518d	1 ac
		מלכות	ROYALTY	575a	3
		מלכות	KINGDOM	575a	3
		נגש	DRIVE	620c	3
		עבר	PASS OVER	719b	4
		עמד	STAND	764c	6 a
11	21	בזה	DESPISE	102c	3
		הוד	SPLENDOUR	217a	1
		חזק	BE FIRM	305a	6 a
		חלקלקות	SMOOTHNESS	325c	2
		כן	PLACE	487d	2
		מלכות	ROYALTY	574d	1
		מלכות	ROYAL POWER	574d	1
		נתן	PUT	680c	2 b
		עמד	STAND	764c	6 a
		שלוה	QUIETNESS	1017d	
11	22	ברית	COVENANT	136b	11
		זרוע	ARM	284b	3
		נגיד	LEADER	618a	3
		שטף	FLOOD	1009b	
		שטף	OVERFLOW	1009b	
11	23	חבר	UNITE	288c	
		מן	SINCE	583c	7 c
		עצם	BE VAST	782c	1
		מרמה	DECEIT	941b	
11	24	אב	FATHER	3c	4 a
		בזה	SPOIL	103a	
		בזר	SCATTER	103b	
		מבצר	FORTIFICATION	131c	
		מדינה	PROVINCE	193d	4
		חשב	THINK	363c	2
		מחשבה	THOUGHT	364c	2
		רכוש	PROPERTY	940d	3
		שלוה	QUIETNESS	1017d	
		משמן	FATNESS	1032d	
11	25	גרה	ENGAGE IN STRIFE	173c	2
		חיל	STRENGTH	299a	4
		חשב	THINK	363c	1 2
		מחשבה	THOUGHT	364c	2
		כח	STRENGTH	470d	1 c
		לבב	HEART	524b	2 0b
		מאד	EXCEEDINGLY	547c	2 b
		נגב	SOUTH-COUNTRY	616b	1 c
		עצום	MIGHTY	783a	1
11	26	חיל	STRENGTH	299a	4
		פתבג	PORTION	834a	
		שבר	BREAK	990c	
		שטף	OVERFLOW	1009b	1
		שטף	OVERFLOW	1009b	
11	27	דבר	SPEAK	181a	2
		מועד	APPOINTED TIME	417c	1 a
		כזב	LIE	469c	
		ל	TO	510d	1 a
		לבב	HEART	523c	2 2
		עוד	STILL	729a	1 ab
		קץ	END	893d	1
		רעע	BE EVIL	949d	1
		שלחן	TABLE	1020b	1
11	28	ברית	COVENANT	136d	2 2c
		ברית	COVENANT	137b	3 2
		לבב	HEART	523c	2 2
		עשה	DO	794b	1 4
		קדש	APARTNESS	872b	4 b
		רכוש	PROPERTY	940d	3
11	29	אחרון	BEHIND	31a	B a
		מועד	APPOINTED TIME	417c	1 a
		כ	LIKE	454c	2 c
		ל	NOT	518d	1 ac
		נגב	SOUTH-COUNTRY	616b	1 c
		ראשון	FIRST	911d	3 a1
11	30	בין	DISCERN	106d	3 e
		ברית	COVENANT	136d	2 2c
		ברית	COVENANT	137b	3 2
		ברית	COVENANT	137b	3 3
		זעם	BE INDIGNANT	276d	1
		כאה	BE COWED	456c	
		כתי	KITTIM	508c	
		עשה	DO	794b	1 4
		קדש	APARTNESS	872b	4 b
11	31	זרוע	ARM	284b	3
		חלל	POLLUTE	320b	1 b
		תמיד	CONTINUITY	556c	2 c
		מן	OUT OF	579d	2 d
		מן	OUT OF	580a	2 ea
		סור	TURN ASIDE	694c	2
		מעוז	PLACE OF SAFETY	732a	1
		שמם	BE DESOLATED	1031a	2
		שקוץ	DETESTED THING	1055a	
		שקוץ	DETESTED THING	1055a	
11	32	ברית	COVENANT	136d	2 2c
		חזק	BE FIRM	305a	1 c
		חלקה	SMOOTHNESS	325c	
		חנף	BE POLLUTED	338a	2
		עשה	DO	794b	1 4
		רשע	BE WICKED	957d	3
11	33	בזה	SPOIL	103a	
		בין	DISCERN	107a	3 c
		כשל	STUMBLE	505d	1 b
		להבה	FLAME	*529b	1
		להבה	FLAME	529b	1
		שבי	CAPTIVITY	985d	1
11	34	חלקלקות	SMOOTHNESS	325c	2
		כשל	STUMBLE	505d	1 b
		לוה	BE JOINED	531a	
		מעט	A FEW	590a	1 b
		עזר	HELP	740c	1
		עזר	HELP	740c	
11	35	ברר	PURIFY	141a	
		מועד	APPOINTED TIME	417c	1 a
		כשל	STUMBLE	505d	1 b
		לבן	MAKE WHITE	526a	1
		מן	FROM	580d	3 ba
		עוד	STILL	729a	1 ab
		עת	TIME	773d	2 c
		צרף	SMELT	864b	1
		קץ	END	893d	1
11	36	אל	GOD	42b	1
		גדל	BECOME GREAT	152c	
		דבר	SPEAK	181d	5
		זעם	INDIGNATION	276d	
		חרץ	CUT	358c	
		כלה	BE FINISHED	477c	1 c
		עד	UNTIL	725a	2 1b a
		עשה	DO	795b	1 a

HOSEA

Ch v.	Heb	Eng	Page	Sec
	פלא	BE SURPASSING	810d	3 a
	צלח	ADVANCE	852c	2
	רום	BE HIGH	927d	
11 37	רצון	GOODWILL	953c	3 b
	אלה	GOD	43a	1
	אלהים	GOD	44b	4 ba
	בין	DISCERN	106d	3 e
	גדל	BECOME GREAT	152c	
	חמדה	DESIRE	326d	
	כל	ALL	482c	2 a
11 38	זהב	GOLD	263a	6
	זהב	GOLD	263c	1
	חמודה	DESIRABLENESS	326d	
	יקר	PRECIOUS	430a	1 c
	כבד	MAKE HONORABLE	457d	2 c
	כן	PLACE	487d	2
	כסף	SILVER	494b	6
	ל	TO	512c	3 b
	מעוז	PLACE OF SAFETY	732a	2 b
11 39	מבצר	FORTIFICATION	131c	
	חלק	DIVIDE	323d	1
	כבוד	HONOR	459a	3
	מחיר	HIRE	564b	2
	משל	RULE	605d	
	נכר	REGARD	648a	1
	נכר	FOREIGNNESS	648d	1
	מעוז	PLACE OF SAFETY	732a	1
	עם	WITH	767c	1 a
11 40	אניה	A SHIP	58b	
	ארץ	EARTH	76c	5
	נגב	SOUTH-COUNTRY	616b	1 c
	נגח	PUSH	618c	
	עבר	PASS OVER	717b	1
	עת	TIME	773d	2 c
	פרש	HORSEMAN	832b	
	צפון	NORTH	861a	
	קץ	END	893d	1
	שער	SWEEP	973b	
	שטף	OVERFLOW	1009a	1
11 41	כשל	STUMBLE	505d	1 b
	מלט	SLIP AWAY	572c	2
	עמון	AMMON	770a	
	צבי	BEAUTY	840a	1 b
	ראשית	BEGINNING	912b	2
	רב	MUCH	913a	1 b
	רבו	TEN THOUSAND	914b	
11 42	ארץ	EARTH	76c	5
	פליטה	ESCAPE	812d	2 b
11 43	חמודה	DESIRABLENESS	326d	
	כושי	CUSHITE	469b	D
	מכמן	STORE	485a	
	לובים	LUBIM	530c	
	משל	RULE	605d	1
	נגב	SOUTH-COUNTRY	*616b	1 c
	מצעד	STEP	857c	
11 44	בהל	DISMAY	96c	1
	מורח	PLACE OF SUNRISE	280d	2 b
	חרם	BAN	355d	1 b
	יצא	GO OUT	423d	2 c
	שמועה	REPORT	1035b	1
11 45	אהל	TENT	13d	2
	ארמון	PALACE	66a	
	הר	MOUNTAIN	249d	1 a
	ים	SEA	411b	8 d
	נטע	PLANT	642c	2
	צבי	BEAUTY	840a	1 b
	קדש	APARTNESS	871d	2 e
	קץ	END	893d	1
	ים	ADDENDA ET COR-RIGENDA	1124a	
12 1	בן	SON	121b	1 ji
	היה	COME TO PASS	227d	2
	היה	COME TO PASS	*227d	2
	כתב	WRITE	507d	3
	מיכאל	MICHAEL	567c	1
	מלט	SLIP AWAY	572c	3
	מן	SINCE	583c	7 c
	מצא	FIND	593d	1 d
	ספר	MISSIVE	*707c	3 g
	על	UPON	754c	2 lf c
	עמד	STAND	764c	6 a
	עת	TIME	773d	1 a
	צרה	DISTRESS	865b	
12 2	אדמה	EARTH	9d	3
	דראון	ABHORRENCE	201b	
	חיים	LIFE	313b	2
	חרפה	REPROACH	358a	3
	ישן	SLEEPING	445d	
	עולם	LONG DURATION	762d	2 j
	עפר	DRY EARTH	779d	1 f
	קיץ	AWAKE	884c	2
12 3	זהר	SHINING	264a	
	זהר	BE LIGHT	264a	
	כוכב	STAR	457a	
	עד	PERPETUITY	723d	2 e
	עולם	LONG DURATION	762d	2 j
	צדק	MAKE RIGHTEOUS	843a	4
	צדק	MAKE RIGHTEOUS	843a	4
	רקיע	EXTENDED SUR-FACE	956b	2
	שכל	BE PRUDENT	968c	4
12 4	דבר	WORD	183a	22
	חתם	SEAL	367d	2
	דעת	KNOWLEDGE	396a	2 d
	ספר	MISSIVE	707b	3 a
	סתם	STOP UP	711b	2

Ch v.	Heb	Eng	Page	Sec
	עת	TIME	773d	2 c
	קץ	END	893d	1
	רבה	BECOME MANY	915b	2 b2
12 5	שוט	GO ABOUT	1002a	
	הנה	HITHER	244d	A b
	יאר	STREAM	384c	4
	ל	TO	514a	5 d
12 6	בד	WHITE LINEN	94b	
	יאר	STREAM	384c	4
	כלה	BE FINISHED	*477c	1 a
	לבש	PUT ON	528b	E
	מעל	ABOVE	751c	1 b
	פלא	WONDER	810c	2
	קץ	END	893d	1
12 7	בד	WHITE LINEN	94b	
	בקר	MORNING	*134a	1 e
	חי	ALIVE	311d	1 a
	יאר	STREAM	384c	4
	ימין	RIGHT HAND	411c	1 a
	מועד	APPOINTED TIME	417c	1 b
	כלה	BE FINISHED	477c	1 a
	כלה	BE FINISHED	477c	2 c
	כלה	FINISH	478b	1 c
	ל	TO	517a	6 b
	לבש	PUT ON	528b	E
	נפץ	SHATTER	658d	
	נפץ	SHATTER	658d	
	מעל	ABOVE	751c	1 b
	עולם	LONG DURATION	762b	2 c
	עם	PEOPLE	767a	5 g
	קדש	APARTNESS	872b	A
	רום	BE HIGH	927b	1 a1
	שמאל	LEFT	969d	2
	שבע	SWEAR	989b	1
	שמים	HEAVENS	1030a	1 b
	שמע	HEAR	1033c	1 b
12 8	אחרית	END	31a	B
	בין	DISCERN	106d	2 a
12 9	דבר	WORD	183a	22
	חתם	SEAL	367d	2
	כלה	BE FINISHED	*477c	1 a
	סתם	STOP UP	711b	2
	עת	TIME	773d	2 c
	קץ	END	893d	1
12 10	בין	DISCERN	106d	2 a
	ברר	PURIFY	141a	1
	לבן	BE PURIFIED	526b	
	צרף	SMELT	864b	1
	רשע	BE WICKED	957d	3
	שכל	BE PRUDENT	968c	4
12 11	בקר	MORNING	*134a	1 e
	ל	TO	518b	7 bh
	תמיד	CONTINUITY	556c	2 c
	סור	TURN ASIDE	694c	
	שמם	BE DESOLATED	1031a	2
	שקוץ	DETESTED THING	1055a	
	תשעים	NINETY	1077d	
12 12	אלף	THOUSAND	49a	1 b
	אשר	HAPPINESS	81a	
	חכה	WAIT	314a	3
	נגע	REACH	619c	2
12 13	גורל	LOT	174d	3
	יום	DAY	399c	5 c
	נוח	REST	628b	2
	עמד	STAND	764b	5 b
	קץ	END	893d	1
	קץ	END	893d	1

HOSEA

Ch v.	Heb	Eng	Page	Sec
1 1	אחז	AHAZ	28c	1
	באֵרי	BEERI	92b	2
	דבר	WORD	182c	1 2a
	יהואש	JEHOASH	220a	2
	יותם	JOTHAM	222d	1
	היה	BECOME	226a	2 1b
	חזקיהו	HEZEKIAH	306a	1
	הושע	HOSHEA	448a	3
	עזיהו	UZZIAH	739d	1 b
	ירבעם	JEROBOAM	914d	2
1 2	אחר	BEHIND	30b	4 aa
	אשה	WOMAN	61b	1
	דבר	SPEAK	*180d	1
	הלך	WALK	234a	1 5f 1
	זנונים	FORNICATION	276a	A
	זנה	COMMIT FORNICA-TION	276a	A
	תחלה	BEGINNING	321b	
	ילד	CHILD	409b	B
	הושע	HOSHEA	448a	3
1 3	גמר	GOMER	170b	2
	דבלים	DIBLAIM	179c	
	הרה	CONCEIVE	247d	1
1 4	בית	HOUSE	110a	5 dd
	דם	BLOOD	196d	2 f
	דם	BLOOD	197b	2 k
	יהוא	JEHU	219d	1
	יזרעאל	JEZREEL	283c	2 a
	יזרעאל	JEZREEL	283c	1 b
	ממלכות	DOMINION	575c	2
	מעט	A FEW	590b	1 eb
	עוד	STILL	729a	1 ab
	פקד	ATTEND TO	823c	A 3
	קרא	CALL	896a	6 a
	שבת	CEASE	992a	2

Ch v.	Heb	Eng	Page	Sec
1 5	יזרעאל	JEZREEL	283c	1 b
	עמק	VALE	771a	
	קשת	BOW	906c	1 e
	ישראל	ISRAEL	975d	2 a2
	שבר	BREAK	990c	
1 6	בית	HOUSE	110a	5 dd
	בת	DAUGHTER	123a	1
	הרה	CONCEIVE	247d	1
	יסף	DO AGAIN	415c	2 c
	כי	THAT	473a	1 f
	לא	NOT	519d	2 d
	לארחמה	LO-RUHAMAH	520d	
	נשא	LIFT	671c	3 c
	קרא	CALL	896a	6 a
	רחם	LOVE	933c	1
1 7	ב	IN	89d	3 2c
	בית	HOUSE	110a	5 de
	יהוה	YAHWEH	218d	2 1d
	יהודה	JUDAH	397b	1 3
	ישע	DELIVER	446d	1 b
	סוס	HORSE	692c	2
	פרש	HORSEMAN	832b	
	קשת	BOW	906a	1 b
	רחם	LOVE	933c	1
1 8	הרה	CONCEIVE	247d	1
	לא	NOT	519d	2 d
	לארחמה	LO-RUHAMAH	520d	
1 9	ל	TO	515c	5 hc
	לא	NOT	519d	2 d
	לאמי	LO-AMMI	520d	
	קרא	CALL	896a	6 a
2 1	אל	GOD	42d	6 d
	אמר	SAY	56c	
	בן	SON	120b	1 c
	היה	COME TO PASS	225a	1 2b ab
	היה	BECOME	226a	2 2c
	חול	SAND	297d	C
	חול	SAND	297d	A
	חי	ALIVE	311d	1 a
	ים	SEA	411b	8 b
	לאמי	LO-AMMI	*520d	
	מדד	MEASURE	551a	
	ספר	COUNT	708a	
	מקום	STANDING PLACE	880b	4
	מקום	STANDING PLACE	880c	7 b
2 2	בן	SON	121a	1 jd
	גדל	GREAT	153a	6 a
	יזרעאל	JEZREEL	283c	1 b
	יהודה	JUDAH	397b	1 3
	יום	DAY	398d	2 g
	ל	TO	515d	5 ia
	קבץ	GATHER	867d	1
	ראש	HEAD	911a	3 a
	שום	TO PLACE	964a	3 a
2 3	אחות	SISTER	27d	1
	לארחמה	LO-RUHAMAH	520d	
	לאמי	LO-AMMI	*520d	
	רחם	LOVE	933d	
2 4	אם	MOTHER	52a	2
	בין	INTERVAL	107d	D
	הוא	HE, SHE, IT	*216a	3 a
	זנונים	FORNICATION	276a	C
	נאאפוף	ADULTERY	610d	
	ריב	STRIVE	936c	2
	שד	BREAST	994c	1
2 5	מדבר	WILDERNESS	185a	4
	יום	DAY	398c	2 f
	יום	DAY	400a	7 d1 d
	יום	DAY	400d	7 h
	ילד	BE BORN	408d	
	יצג	SET	426d	
	מות	DIE	560b	2
	ערום	NAKED	736a	
	פשט	STRIP OFF	833a	1
	ציה	DRYNESS	851a	
	ציה	DRYNESS	851a	
	צמא	THIRST	854d	
	שום	TO PLACE	964a	3 e
	שית	PUT	1011c	3
2 6	זנונים	FORNICATION	276a	C
	רחם	LOVE	933c	1
2 7	אהב	LOVE	13b	2
	אם	MOTHER	52a	2
	בוש	BE ASHAMED	102a	2
	בוש	BE ASHAMED	102a	2 b
	הרה	CONCEIVE	247d	1
	זנה	COMMIT FORNICA-TION	276a	3
	פשת	FLAX	833d	1
	צמר	WOOL	856a	
	שמן	OIL	1032b	2 b
	שקוי	DRINK	1052d	
2 8	גדר	BUILD A WALL	154d	1
	גדר	WALL	155a	
	דרך	WAY	203b	5
	זהב	GOLD	262d	2
	כן	SO	486d	3 d
	נתיבה	PATH	677b	2 a
	סיר	THORN	696c	1
	שוך	FENCE UP	962b	
2 9	אהב	LOVE	13b	2
	אז	THEN	23a	1 a
	בקש	SEEK	134c	1 b
	הלך	WALK	233d	1 5b
	טוב	PLEASANT	374c	6
	מן	THAN	582b	6 a

Ch	v.	Heb	Eng	Page	Sec
		נשג	OVERTAKE	673c	1 a
		עתה	NOW	774a	1 a
		ראשון	FIRST	911c	1 a
		רדף	PURSUE	923a	
2	10	בעל	BAAL	*127d	2 1
		בעל	BAAL	127d	2 2
		דגן	CORN	186c	
		זהב	GOLD	263c	1
		תירוש	NEW WINE	440d	
		עשה	DO	794c	2 lg
		יצהר	FRESH OIL	844a	
		רבה	BECOME MANY	915b	
		רבה	BECOME MANY	915c	1 c
2	11	דגן	CORN	186c	
		יום	DAY	398d	2 i
		מועד	APPOINTED TIME	417c	1 a
		תירוש	NEW WINE	440d	
		כסה	COVER	491c	1
		נצל	SNATCH AWAY	664d	1
		ערוה	NAKEDNESS	789a	1
		פשת	FLAX	833d	1
		צמר	WOOL	856a	
		צמר	WOOL	856a	
		רוח	BREATH	925b	3 h
		שוב	TURN BACK	998c	8
2	12	אהב	LOVE	13b	2
		נבלות	IMMODESTY	615b	
2	13	חג	FESTIVAL-GATHER-ING	291a	1 b1
		חדש	NEW MOON	294c	1
		מועד	APPOINTED TIME	417c	1 b
		משוש	EXULTATION	965c	
		שבת	CEASE	992a	1
		שבת	SABBATH	992b	1 a
2	14	אהב	LOVE	13b	2
		אכל	EAT	37c	2
		גפן	VINE	172c	
		חיה	LIVING THING	312c	1 b
		יער	WOOD	420d	E
		שדה	FIELD	961b	1 c
		שמם	BE DESOLATED	1031b	1
		אתנה	HIRE	1071d	
2	15	אהב	LOVE	13b	2
		בעל	BAAL	127d	2 3
		חליה	JEWELRY	318d	
		נאם	UTTERANCE	610b	2
		נזם	RING	633d	1
		עדה	ORNAMENT	725d	1 a
		פקד	ATTEND TO	823c	A 3
		קטר	MAKE SACRAFICES SMOKE	883a	1 b
		שכח	FORGET	1013b	1 c
2	16	דבר	SPEAK	181d	5
		הלך	WALK	236d	1 d
		כן	SO	486d	3 d
		לב	HEART	525c	2 9a
		פתה	BE SIMPLE	834c	1
2	17	יום	DAY	400a	7 d1 d
		נעורים	YOUTH	655c	
		ענה	ANSWER	772d	1 a
		ענה	SING	777b	
		פתח	OPENING	836a	
		תקוה	HOPE	876b	1
		שם	THERE	1027c	4 a
		שם	THERE	1027c	3 c
2	18	איש	MAN	35d	
		בעל	OWNER	127b	1 2
		היה	COME TO PASS	*225a	1 2b aa
		יום	DAY	400d	7 g
		נאם	UTTERANCE	610b	2
		קרא	CALL	896a	6 e1
		קרא	CALL	896a	6 c
2	19	בעל	BAAL	127d	2 3
		זכר	REMEMBER	270c	1 a
		שם	NAME	1028d	4
2	20	אדמה	GROUND	9d	4
		בטח	SECURITY	105b	
		ברית	COVENANT	137a	2 2k
		ברית	COVENANT	137a	3 1
		חיה	LIVING THING	312c	1 b
		יום	DAY	400d	7 g
		כרת	CUT	503d	4
		עוף	FLY	733d	1
		קשת	BOW	906a	1 a
		רמש	CREEPING THINGS	943a	1
		שדה	FIELD	961b	1 c
		שבר	BREAK	990c	
2	21	ארש	BETROTH	77a	
		ה	THE	*208a	1 hb
		חסד	GOODNESS	339b	2 2
		עולם	LONG DURATION	762d	2 f
		צדק	RIGHTEOUSNESS	841d	E
		רחמים	COMPASSION	933c	1
		משפט	JUDGMENT	1048d	2 a
2	22	אמונה	FIRMNESS	53c	3 b
		אמונה	FIRMNESS	53d	3 b
		ארש	BETROTH	77a	
		ידע	KNOW	394a	2
2	23	היה	COME TO PASS	*225a	1 2b aa
		יום	DAY	400d	7 g
		נאם	UTTERANCE	610b	2
		ענה	ANSWER	772d	1 b
2	24	דגן	CORN	186c	
		יזרעאל	JEZREEL	283c	1 b
		תירוש	NEW WINE	440d	
		ענה	ANSWER	772d	1 b
		יצהר	FRESH OIL	844a	
2	25	זרע	SOW	281d	3 a
		יזרעאל	JEZREEL	*283c	1 b
		ל	TO	515b	5 hb a
		לא	NOT	519d	2 d
		לא	NOT	519d	2 d
		לארחמה	LO-RUHAMAH	520d	
		לעמי	LO-AMMI	520d	
		רחם	LOVE	933c	1
		רחם	LOVE	933d	
3	1	אהב	LOVE	12d	1
		אהב	LOVE	13a	2
		אהב	LOVE	13a	5 b
		אחר	ANOTHER	29d	
		אלהים	GOD	43c	1 d
		אישישה	RAISEN-CAKE	84b	
		נאף	COMMIT ADUL-TERY	610d	1 b
		ענב	GRAPE	772a	
		פנה	TURN	815b	1 a
		רע	FRIEND	946a	1
3	2	חמר	HOMER	330d	
		חמש	FIVE	332a	2 b2
		כסף	SILVER	494b	8 b
		כרה	TRADE	500b	
		כרת	CUT	504a	
		לתך	A BARLEY-MEA-SURE	547c	
		עשר	TEN	797b	5 a
		שערה	BARLEY	972d	2
3	3	אל	TO	40a	3 c
		היה	BECOME	226a	2 2h
		זנה	COMMIT FORNICA-TION	275d	1
		ל	TO	515a	5 ha
3	4	אין	NOT	34d	4 a
		אפוד	EPHOD	65d	3 b
		זבח	SACRIFICE	257b	1 1
		מצבה	PILLAR	663b	1 c
		שר	CHIEFTAIN	978b	2 a
		תם	INTEGRITY	1070d	4
		תרפים	IDOL	1076c	
3	5	אחרית	END	31b	B
		אל	TO	39d	1
		אלה	GOD	41d	1 b
		בקש	SEEK	134d	3 c
		דוד	DAVID	188a	2
		יהוה	YAHWEH	218d	2 1d
		טוב	GOOD THINGS	375c	1
		מלך	KING	573b	2
		פחד	DREAD	808b	1
		שוב	TURN BACK	997d	6 d
4	1	אמת	FIRMNESS	54a	3 a
		חסד	GOODNESS	338d	1 2
		דעת	KNOWLEDGE	395d	2 b
		ל	TO	513b	5 ba
		עם	WITH	767c	1 c
4	2	אלה	SWEAR	46d	1
		גנב	STEAL	170c	
		דם	BLOOD	196d	2 f
		כחש	DECEIVE	471b	1
		נאף	COMMIT ADUL-TERY	610c	1 a
		נגע	TOUCH	619a	1 a
		פרץ	BREAK THROUGH	829c	7
		רצח	MURDER	953d	
4	3	אבל	MOURN	5c	
		אמל	BE WEAK	51b	
		אסף	GATHER	62d	3
		ב	IN	88c	1 2c
		דג	FISH	185c	
		חיה	LIVING THING	312c	1 b
		שדה	FIELD	961b	1 c
4	4	יכח	REPROVE	407a	5 b
		כהן	PRIEST	463b	3 b
		כמר	PRIEST	485c	
		מרה	BE REBELLIOUS	598b	2
		ריב	STRIVE	936c	2
		ריב	STRIVE	936d	
4	5	אם	MOTHER	52a	2
		בכה	WEEP	113c	6
		דמה	CAUSE TO CEASE	198c	2
		כשל	STUMBLE	505c	1
		נביא	PROPHET	611d	2
		ריב	STRIVE	*936d	
		יום	ADDENDA ET COR-RIGENDA	1124a	
4	6	בלי	WEARING OUT	115d	C a
		גם	ALSO	169d	4
		דמה	CUT OFF	198c	
		ה	THE	208b	1 ha
		ו	AND	254d	5 ca
		דעת	KNOWLEDGE	395d	2 b
		תורה	INSTRUCTION	436a	1 e
		כהן	ACT AS PRIEST	464c	1
		מאס	REJECT	549c	1 a
		מאס	REJECT	549c	1 a
		מן	FROM	583b	7 ba
		שכח	FORGET	1013b	2 a
		שכח	FORGET	1013b	1 c
4	7	ב	IN	90a	3 3b
		חטא	MISS A GOAL OR WAY	307a	2 b
		ך	LIKE	454d	2 d
		כבוד	HONOR	459a	3
		כן	SO	486b	2 ad d
		מור	CHANGE	558c	2
		קלון	DISHONOUR	885d	1
		רבב	BECOME MUCH	912d	1
		רב	MULTITUDE	914b	2
4	8	חטאת	SIN	308c	1 b
		חטאת	SIN	309b	4
		נפש	SOUL	660d	6 a
		נשא	LIFT	670d	1 b 9
4	9	עון	INIQUITY	730d	1
		דרך	WAY	203d	6 d
		היה	BECOME	226a	2 2c
		ך	LIKE	454c	2 a
		כהן	PRIEST	463b	3 b
		על	UPON	758b	4 1b
4	10	זנה	COMMIT FORNICA-TION	276a	2 a
		עזב	LEAVE	737c	2 d1
		פרץ	BREAK THROUGH	829c	8
		רצה	BE PLEASED WITH	953b	
		שבע	SATISFIED	959b	1 a
		שמר	KEEP	1037a	3 d
4	11	זנות	FORNICATION	276b	A
		יין	WINE	406c	C
		תירוש	NEW WINE	440d	
		לקח	TAKE	543a	3 c
4	12	זנה	COMMIT FORNICA-TION	276a	3
		זנונים	FORNICATION	276a	C
		מקל	STAFF	596c	3
		גד	BE CONSPICUOUS	616d	2
		עץ	TREE	782a	2 c
		רוח	BREATH	925b	3 g
		שאל	ASK	982a	2 b
		תחת	UNDERNEATH	1066b	3 2a
		תעה	ERR	1073c	3
4	13	אלה	TEREBINTH	18c	
		אלון	OAK	47c	
		גבעה	HILL	149a	3
		גבעה	HILL	149a	2
		הר	MOUNTAIN	250d	1 m
		זבח	SLAUGHTER FOR SACRIFICE	257b	2
		זנה	COMMIT FORNICA-TION	275d	1
		טוב	PLEASANT	373d	1 d
		כלה	BRIDE	483c	2 b
		לבנה	POPLAR	527b	
		נאף	COMMIT ADUL-TERY	610d	1 b
		צל	SHADOW	853b	2
		קטר	MAKE SACRAFICES SMOKE	883a	
4	14	בין	DISCERN	106d	2 a
		הם	THEY	241b	1 a
		זבח	SLAUGHTER FOR SACRIFICE	257b	2
		זבח	SLAUGHTER FOR SACRIFICE	257b	2
		זנה	COMMIT FORNICA-TION	275d	1
		זנה	COMMIT FORNICA-TION	275d	1
		כלה	BRIDE	483c	2 b
		לבט	BE THRUST DOWN	526a	b
		נאף	COMMIT ADUL-TERY	610d	1 b
		פקד	ATTEND TO	823c	A 3
		פרד	DIVIDE	825c	
		קדש	TEMPLE-PROSTI-TUTE	873d	
4	15	און	TROUBLE	20a	2
		אשם	OFFEND	79c	2
		ביתאון	BETH-AVEN	110d	
		ביתאל	BETHEL	111a	1
		זנה	COMMIT FORNICA-TION	276a	3
		חי	ALIVE	311d	1 a
		יהודה	JUDAH	397b	1 3
		ישראל	ISRAEL	975d	2 a2
		שבע	SWEAR	989b	1 a
4	16	כבש	LAMB	461a	2
		סרר	BE STUBBORN	710d	
		עתה	NOW	774a	1 b
		פרה	HEIFER	831a	
		מרחב	ROOMY PLACE	932c	
		רעה	TEND	944d	1 b
4	17	אפרים	EPHRAIM	68c	4
		חבר	UNITE	288a	1 a
		נוח	REST	629a	B 5
		עצב	IDOL	781b	
4	18	אהב	LOVE	13a	2
		מגן	SHIELD	171c	
		זנה	COMMIT FORNICA-TION	276a	2 b
		סבא	DRINK LARGELY	685a	
		סבא	LIQUOR	685a	
		סור	TURN ASIDE	694a	4
		קלון	DISHONOUR	885d	1
4	19	זבח	SACRIFICE	257c	1 2
		כנף	WING	489d	1 f
		צרר	BIND	864d	A
		רוח	BREATH	924d	2 a
5	1	אזן	HEAR	24c	1
		בית	HOUSE	110a	5 dd
		רשת	NET	440c	1 a3
		כהן	PRIEST	463b	3 b
		ל	TO	511d	2

Ch	v.	Heb	Eng	Page	Sec
		פח	BIRD-TRAP	809a	2 b
		פרש	SPREAD OUT	831b	1
		מצפה	MIZPAH	860a	2
		קשב	ATTEND	904a	
		משפט	JUDGMENT	1048c	1 e
		משפט	JUDGMENT	1048c	1 f
		תבור	TABOR	1061d	1
5	2	מוסר	DISCIPLINE	416c	2 a
		עמק	BE DEEP	770d	
		שט	SWERVER	962a	
		שחטה	THE OPPRESSION	1006b	
5	3	אפרים	EPHRAIM	68c	4
		זנה	COMMIT FORNICA-TION	276a	2 b
		טמא	BE UNCLEAN	379b	2
		ידע	KNOW	394a	2
		כחד	BE HIDDEN	470b	1
		ישראל	ISRAEL	975d	2 a2
5	4	זנונים	FORNICATION	276a	C
		ידע	KNOW	394a	2
		רוח	BREATH	925b	3 g
		שוב	TURN BACK	997b	6 c
5	5	אפרים	EPHRAIM	68c	4
		גאון	EXALTATION	145a	1 a
		כשל	STUMBLE	505c	1
		כשל	STUMBLE	505d	1 b
		עון	INIQUITY	731a	1 a
		מעלל	DEED	760b	1
		ענה	ANSWER	773a	3 a
		פנה	FACE	816d	2 3a
		ישראל	ISRAEL	975d	2 a2
5	6	בקר	CATTLE	133b	1 a
		בקש	SEEK	134b	3 c
		הלך	WALK	231c	1 1d 5g
		חלץ	DRAW OFF OR OUT	322d	2
		מצא	FIND	593a	1 a
5	7	בגד	ACT TREACHEROUSLY	93d	B
		זור	BE A STRANGER	266c	2 a
		חדש	NEW MOON	294c	1
		חלק	PORTION	324b	2 b
		ילד	BEAR	408c	1 c
		עתה	NOW	774a	1 b
5	8	און	TROUBLE	20a	2
		אחר	BEHIND	30a	2 a
		ביתאון	BETH-AVEN	*110d	
		ביתאל	BETHEL	111a	1
		בנימין	BENJAMIN	122d	1
		גבעה	GIBEAH	149b	2
		חצצרה	CLARION	348c	1
		חרד	TREMBLE	*353c	
		רמה	RAMA	928a	1
		רוע	RAISE A SHOUT	929c	2
		שפר	HORN	1051d	
		תקע	GIVE A BLOW	1075c	2
5	9	אמן	CONFIRM	52d	2
		אפרים	EPHRAIM	68c	4
		ידע	MAKE KNOWN	395b	
		תוכחה	REBUKE	407b	
		שמה	WASTE	1031c	1
5	10	גבול	BOUNDARY	148a	1 c
		סוג	DISPLACE	691a	1
		עברה	OVERFLOW	720c	3 b
		שר	CHIEFTAIN	978b	2 b
		שפך	POUR OUT	1049c	2 a
5	11	אפרים	EPHRAIM	68c	4
		הלך	WALK	235a	2 3d 4
		יאל	SHOW-WILLING-NESS	384b	3
		עשק	OPPRESS	798d	2
		צו	WORD	846c	
		רצץ	CRUSH	954c	2
		משפט	JUDGMENT	1048c	1 f
5	12	אפרים	EPHRAIM	68c	4
		בית	HOUSE	110a	5 de
		עש	MOTH	799c	
		רקב	ROTTENNESS	955a	
5	13	אשור	ASSYRIA	78d	3
		גהה	DEPART	155c	
		מזור	WOUND	267a	
		חלי	SICKNESS	318b	
		יכל	BE ABLE	407c	1 a
		ראה	TO SEE	907b	5 b
		ירב	JAREB	937a	
		רפא	HEAL	950d	2 b
		שלח	SEND	1018b	1 c
5	14	בית	HOUSE	110a	5 de
		טרף	TEAR	383a	
		כפיר	LION	498d	
		נצל	DELIVER	664d	3 a
		שחל	LION	1006c	
5	15	אשם	OFFEND	79c	3
		בקש	SEEK	134d	3 b
		הלך	WALK	233d	1 b
		עד	UNTIL	725a	2 1a b
		צר	STRAITS	865b	
		מקום	STANDING PLACE	879d	2 b2
		שוב	TURN BACK	997a	3 a
		שחר	LOOK EARLY	1007c	
6	1	הוא	HE, SHE, IT	*215b	1 a
		חבש	BIND	290a	2
		טרף	TEAR	383a	
		נכה	SMITE	645d	1 e
		רפא	HEAL	950d	1
		שוב	TURN BACK	997d	6 c
6	2	חיה	LIVE	311a	1 b

Ch	v.	Heb	Eng	Page	Sec
		חיה	LIVE	311c	3 a
		יום	DAY	401a	7 j
		מן	FROM	581c	4 b
		פנה	FACE	817a	24a b
		קום	STAND	878d	1 a
6	3	גשם	RAIN	177c	
		מוצא	GOING FORTH	425d	1 a
		ירה	THROW	435a	4
		יורה	EARLY RAIN	435c	
		כון	BE FIRM	465d	1 d
		כן	SO	486b	2 ad d
		מלקוש	SPRING-RAIN	545b	
		מצא	FIND	593a	1 a
		רדף	PURSUE	923a	2
		שחר	DAWN	1007b	
		שחר	LOOK EARLY	1007c	
6	4	הלך	WALK	232c	13
		חסד	GOODNESS	*338d	12
		חסד	GOODNESS	*338d	13
		חסד	GOODNESS	338d	13
		חסיד	KIND	339c	2
		טל	NIGHT-MIST	378d	
		ענן	CLOUD	778a	1 c
		שכם	START EARLY	1014d	
6	5	אמר	WORD	57a	1
		ב	IN	89d	3 2c
		הרג	KILL	247b	2
		חצב	HEW	345a	3
		יצא	GO OUT	423b	1 f
		נביא	PROPHET	611c	1
		משפט	JUDGMENT	1048c	1 e
6	6	זבה	SACRIFICE	257b	11
		חסד	GOODNESS	*338d	13
		חסד	GOODNESS	338d	13
		חסד	GOODNESS	*338d	12
		חסיד	KIND	339c	2
		חפץ	DELIGHT IN	342d	2 a
		דעת	KNOWLEDGE	395d	2 b
		מן	THAN	582c	6 a
6	7	אדם	MAN	9b	2
		בגד	ACT TREACHEROUSLY	93d	B
		ברית	COVENANT	136d	2 2c
		ברית	COVENANT	137b	3 3
		עבר	PASS OVER	717c	1 i
		שם	THERE	1027a	1 a
6	8	און	TROUBLE	20a	3
		דם	BLOOD	197b	21
		מן	OUT OF	580a	2 eb
		עקב	FOOT-TRACKED	784c	2
		פעל	DO	821b	1 b
		קריה	TOWN	900a	2
6	9	גדד	PENETRATE	*151a	
		גדוד	BAND	151b	1
		דרך	WAY	202d	1
		זמה	PLAN	273c	2 b
		חבר	COMPANY	288c	1
		חבר	UNITED	*288d	2 d
		חכה	WAIT	314a	2
		כהן	PRIEST	463b	3 b
		כי	THAT	472d	1 e
		רצח	MURDER	954a	
		שכם	SHECHEM	1014b	1
		שכם	SHOULDER	1014b	2
6	10	בית	HOUSE	110a	5 dd
		זנות	FORNICATION	276b	C
		טמא	BE UNCLEAN	379b	2
		ל	TO	513b	5 ba
		שערוריה	HORRIBLE THING	1045d	
6	11	מורה	FEAR	*432b	
		קציר	HARVESTING	894c	2
		שבית	CAPTIVITY	986b	2 a
		שות	PUT	1011c	3
7	1	גדוד	BAND	151b	1
		גנב	THIEF	170c	
		חוץ	THE OUTSIDE	299d	1 bb
		עון	INIQUITY	730d	1
		פעל	DO	821b	1 b
		פשט	STRIP OFF	833a	2
		רפא	HEAL	950d	2 a
		שבית	CAPTIVITY	986b	2
7	2	אמר	SAY	56b	2
		בל	NOT	115b	
		זכר	REMEMBER	270c	24
		לבב	HEART	524a	27
		נגד	IN FRONT	617b	1 aa
		סבב	SURROUND	686a	2 d
		מעלל	DEED	760b	1
		עתה	NOW	774a	1 a
7	3	הם	THEY	241b	1 a
		כחש	LYING	471c	1
		משח	ANOINT	603b	2
7	4	אפה	BAKE	66a	
		בער	BURN	129a	2
		בצק	DOUGH	130d	
		חמץ	BE SOUR	329d	
		כמו	LIKE	455d	1 a
		לוש	KNEAD	534c	
		מן	OUT OF	580a	2 ea
		מן	FROM	582a	5 c
		מן	SINCE	583c	7 c
		נאף	COMMIT ADUL-TERY	610d	1 a
		עור	ROUSE ONESELF	735c	1
		שבת	CEASE	991d	1
		תנור	FIRE-POT	1072b	

Ch	v.	Heb	Eng	Page	Sec
7	5	חלה	BE WEAK	318a	3
		יום	DAY	398d	2 i
		חמה	FEVER	404c	1 a
		ליץ	SCORN	539c	2
		מן	OUT OF	579d	2 d
		משך	DRAW	604c	7
		שכר	BE DRUNK	1016b	
7	6	אפה	BAKE	66a	
		ארב	AMBUSCADE	70c	B
		אש	FIRE	77d	6
		בער	BURN	129a	1 f
		בקר	MORNING	134b	1 f
		ישן	SLEEPING	445d	
		להבה	FLAME	529b	1
		לילה	NIGHT	539a	1
		קרב	COME NEAR	897d	2
		תנור	FIRE-POT	1072b	
7	7	אכל	EAT	37c	1
		חמם	BE OR BECOME WARM	328d	2
		קרא	CALL	895b	2 a
		שפט	JUDGE	1047c	1 b
		שקר	DECEPTION	1055c	2
		תנור	FIRE-POT	1072b	
7	8	בלי	WEARING OUT	115c	2 b
		בלל	MIX	117c	
		בלל	MIX	117c	
		הוא	HE, SHE, IT	215c	2 a
		הפך	TURN	245c	1 a
		עגה	BREAD-CAKE	728b	
7	9	אכל	EAT	37c	1
		גם	YEA	169c	3
		זור	BE A STRANGER	266c	2 c
		זרק	TO TOSS	284c	1
		כח	STRENGTH	470d	1 c
		כח	STRENGTH	*471a	5
		שיבה	OLD AGE	966d	1
7	10	בקש	SEEK	134d	2
		גאון	EXALTATION	145a	1 a
		יהוה	YAHWEH	218d	2 1d
		זה	THIS	262c	6 bg
		ענה	ANSWER	773a	3 a
		פנה	FACE	816d	2 3a
		שוב	TURN BACK	997d	6 c
7	11	אין	NOT	34d	4 a
		אשור	ASSYRIA	78d	1
		היה	BECOME	226a	2 2c
		הלך	WALK	230d	1 1d 3a
		יונה	DOVE	401d	
		לב	HEART	524d	2 3a
		פתה	BE SIMPLE	834c	1
		קרא	CALL	895d	5 c
7	12	יסר	CHASTEN	416b	
		עדה	CONGREGATION	417b	3
		ירד	BRING DOWN	434a	1 a
		רשת	NET	440b	1 a1
		כאשר	WHEN	455c	1
		ל	TO	511b	1 ga
		פרש	SPREAD OUT	831b	1
		שמע	REPORT	1034d	
7	13	אוי	WOE	17a	
		דבר	SPEAK	181d	5
		כזב	LIE	469c	
		נדד	FLEE	622b	2
		פדה	RANSOM	804a	3 c
		פשע	REBEL	833b	2
		שד	VIOLENCE	994c	1
7	14	ב	IN	89b	2 4a
		גדד	CUT	151a	1
		גור	SOJOURN	158a	
		גרר	DRAG	176a	
		דגן	CORN	186c	
		זעק	CRY	277b	2 a
		ילל	HOWL	410b	
		תירוש	NEW WINE	440d	
		סור	TURN ASIDE	694a	4
		משכב	COUCH	1012d	1
7	15	אל	TO	40b	4
		זרוע	ARM	284a	1 b
		חזק	BE FIRM	304c	1 b
		חשב	THINK	363c	2
		יסר	DISCIPLINE	416a	1
		רע	EVIL	948d	2
7	16	זו	THIS	262b	
		זעם	INDIGNATION	276d	
		לעג	MOCKING	541c	1 a
		לשון	TONGUE	546b	1 b
		נפל	FALL	657b	2 a
		על	HEIGHT	752b	1
		קשת	BOW	906a	1 b
		רמיה	DECEIT	941b	
		שוב	TURN BACK	997d	6 c
8	1	בית	HOUSE	109c	1 f
		ברית	COVENANT	136d	2 2c
		ברית	COVENANT	137b	3 3
		חך	PALATE	335a	A
		תורה	LAW	436a	2 b1
		נשר	EAGLE	676d	
		עבר	PASS OVER	717c	1 i
		יען	ON ACCOUNT OF	774d	2 c
		פשע	REBEL	833b	2
		שפר	HORN	1051d	
8	2	זעק	CRY	*277b	2
		זעק	CRY	277b	2 a
		ידע	KNOW	394a	2
8	3	זנח	REJECT	276b	

Ch v.	Heb	Eng	Page	Sec
	עבר	PASS OVER	717b	1 h
	עגלה	HEIFER	722b	2
	יעקב	JACOB	*785a	2
	צואר	NECK	848c	2
	רכב	RIDE	939a	2
	שדד	HARROW	961a	
10 12	דרש	SEEK	205b	3 a
	זרע	SOW	281d	3 c
	חסד	GOODNESS	338d	1 2
	ירה	THROW	435b	3
	ל	TO	515d	5 ia
	ל	TO	516c	5 jb
	נור	UNTILLED GROUND	644c	
	ניר	BREAK UP	644c	
	עד	UNTIL	725a	2 1b b
	עת	TIME	773d	2 b
	פה	MOUTH	805d	6 c1
	צדק	RIGHTEOUSNESS	841d	5
	קצר	HARVEST	894b	
	קצר	HARVEST	894c	
10 13	אכל	EAT	37c	1
	בטח	TRUST	105a	1 3c
	גבור	STRONG	150b	2
	דרך	WAY	203b	5
	חרש	CUT IN	360c	2
	כחש	LYING	471c	1
	עולה	INJUSTICE	732d	3
	פרי	FRUIT	826c	3
	קצר	HARVEST	894c	
	רב	MULTITUDE	914a	1
	רכב	CHARIOT	939a	1
	רשע	WICKEDNESS	957d	3
10 14	אם	MOTHER	52a	2
	בתהארבאל	BETH-ARBEL	111a	
	מבצר	FORTIFICATION	131c	
	עיר	CITY	746b	1 a
	על	UPON	755c	2 4c
	עם	PEOPLE	766c	2 b
	קום	STAND	878a	1 h
	רטש	DASH IN PIECES	936b	
	שאון	ROAR	981a	1
	שדד	DEAL VIOLENTLY WITH	994a	
	שדד	DEAL VIOLENTLY WITH	994b	
	שד	VIOLENCE	994c	2
	שלמן	SHALMAN	1025a	
10 15	ביתאל	BETHEL	110d	1
	דמה	CUT OFF	198c	
	רעה	MISERY	949b	3
	שחר	DAWN	1007c	
11 1	אב	FATHER	3b	2
	אהב	LOVE	13a	5 b
	בן	SON	120b	1 c
	ו	AND	254d	5 b
	כי	WHEN	473a	2 a
	מצרים	EGYPT	595d	1 b2
	נער	YOUTH	655a	1 d
	קרא	CALL	895c	5 a
11 2	בעל	BAAL	127d	2 3
	הלך	WALK	235a	2 4
	זבח	SLAUGHTER FOR SACRIFICE	257b	2
	כן	SO	486c	2 db
	פנה	FACE	818b	2 6
	פסיל	IDOL	820d	
	קטר	MAKE SACRAFICES SMOKE	883a	
11 3	זרוע	ARM	283d	1 a
	רגל	GO ABOUT	920b	
	רפא	HEAL	950d	2 a
11 4	אהבה	LOVE	13c	2
	אכל	EAT	37d	1
	חבל	CORD	286c	1
	ך	LIKE	*454b	1 d
	ל	TO	513a	5 ad
	לחי	JAW	534d	1
	משך	DRAW	604b	1
	נטה	INCLINE	641a	3 e
	עבת	CORD	721c	1 b
	על	YOKE	760d	
	רום	BE HIGH	927c	1 c
11 5	הוא	HE, SHE, IT	215d	2 a
	לא	NOT	519a	1 a
	מאן	REFUSE	549b	
	מצרים	EGYPT	595d	1 b1
	שוב	TURN BACK	997d	6 d
11 6	אכל	EAT	37c	4
	בד	PART	94d	3 d
	חול	WHIRL	297b	3
	מועצה	PLAN	420b	
	כלה	FINISH	478d	2 c2
11 7	יחד	ALTOGETHER	403b	2
	על	HEIGHT	752b	1
	רוח	BE WIDE	927a	
	רום	BE HIGH	927a	2 a
	משובה	TURNING BACK	1000b	
	תלא	HANG	1067d	
11 8	אדמה	ADMAH	10a	
	איך	HOW	32c	2
	מגם	DELIVER UP	171c	
	הפך	TURN	245d	1 b
	יחד	ALTOGETHER	403b	2 b
	כמר	GROW WARM	485b	1
	נחום	COMPASSION	637c	2

Ch v.	Heb	Eng	Page	Sec
	נתן	GIVE	679c	1 s
	על	UPON	753c	2 1d
	צבוים	ZEBOIIM	840b	
11 9	שום	TO PLACE	964a	3 e
	איש	MAN	35d	
	אל	GOD	42d	6 e
	חרון	BURNING OF ANGER	354c	
	עיר	AGITATION	735c	
	קדוש	HOLY	872c	1 b
	שוב	TURN BACK	998d	6 g
	שחת	GO TO RUIN	1008a	1
11 10	אריה	LION	71d	
	הוא	HE, SHE, IT	*215b	1 a
	הלך	WALK	235a	2 3d 1
	חרג	QUAKE	*353a	
	חרד	TREMBLE	353c	4
	שאג	ROAR	980d	1
11 11	אשור	ASSYRIA	78d	3
	חרג	QUAKE	*353a	
	חרד	TREMBLE	353c	4
	יונה	DOVE	401d	
	ישב	CAUSE TO SIT	443d	3 a
	מצרים	EGYPT	595c	1 a
	נאם	UTTERANCE	610b	2
	על	UPON	752d	2 1
	צפור	BIRD	862a	1
12 1	אל	GOD	42d	6 e
	אמן	CONFIRM	53a	5
	בית	HOUSE	110a	5 dd
	כחש	LYING	471c	1
	מצרים	EGYPT	595c	1 a
	סבב	SURROUND	686a	2
	עם	WITH	767d	1 d
	קדוש	HOLY	872c	1 c
	רוד	ROAM	923d	
	מרמה	DECEIT	941b	
12 2	אשור	ASSHUR	78d	2
	ברית	COVENANT	136b	1 1
	יבל	CONDUCT	385a	1
	יום	DAY	400c	7 f
	כוב	LIE	469d	
	כרת	CUT	503d	4
	קדים	EAST WIND	870b	1
	רבה	BECOME MANY	915b	
	רדף	PURSUE	922d	2
	רוח	BREATH	925a	2 a
	רעה	TEND	945b	2 b
	שד	VIOLENCE	994c	1
	שוא	EMPTINESS	996b	2
	שמן	OIL	1032b	2 b
12 3	דרך	WAY	203d	6 d
	ל	TO	513b	5 ba
	ל	TO	518b	7 bh
	יעקב	JACOB	*785a	2
	פקד	ATTEND TO	823c	A 3
	ריב	STRIFE	937a	3
	שוב	TURN BACK	999c	4 a
12 4	און	VIGOUR	20b	1
	בטן	WOMB	106a	3
	עקב	FOLLOW AT THE HEEL	784b	
	שרה	PERSIST	975b	
12 5	אל	TO	40b	4
	ביתאל	BETHEL	110d	1
	דבר	SPEAK	181c	3 e
	חנן	SHOW FAVOR	336b	2
	יכל	PREVAIL	408a	2 a
	מלאך	MESSENGER	521d	3
	מצא	FIND	593b	3 a
	שור	SAW	965a	
	שרה	PERSIST	975b	
12 6	ו	AND	253d	1 k
	זכר	REMEMBRANCE	271b	2 a
	צבא	GOD OF WAR	839b	4 a
12 7	ב	IN	88c	1 4
	חסד	GOODNESS	338d	1 2
	תמיד	CONTINUITY	556b	1
	קוה	WAIT FOR	875d	1
	שמר	KEEP	1037a	3
12 8	אהב	LOVE	13a	2
	מאזן	BALANCES	25a	
	כנען	CANAAN	488d	2 a
	כנעני	TRADER	*489b	
	ל	TO	517a	7 bc
	עשק	OPPRESS	798d	1
	מרמה	DECEIT	941b	
12 9	און	VIGOUR	20b	3
	חטא	SIN	308a	1 b
	יגיע	TOIL	388c	2
	יגיע	TOIL	388c	2
	ל	TO	515d	5 ia
	מצא	FIND	592d	1 a
	מצא	FIND	593b	2 b
	עון	INIQUITY	731a	1 a
	עשר	BE RICH	799b	
12 10	יהוה	YAHWEH	218d	2 1a
	יהוה	YAHWEH	219b	2 1d
	מועד	APPOINTED TIME	417c	1 b
	ישב	CAUSE TO SIT	443d	3 a
	עוד	STILL	729b	1 b
12 11	דבר	SPEAK	*181d	5
	דמה	BE LIKE	198a	1
	חזון	VISION	303a	3
	נביא	PROPHET	611c	1
	על	UPON	757c	2 7c b

Ch v.	Heb	Eng	Page	Sec
12 12	און	TROUBLE	20a	2
	אך	ONLY	36d	2 bb
	זבח	SLAUGHTER FOR SACRIFICE	257b	2
	זבח	SLAUGHTER FOR SACRIFICE	257b	2
	שדי	FIELD	961a	1
	שוא	EMPTINESS	996a	1
	שור	A HEAD OF CATTLE	1004b	
	תלם	FURROW	1068d	
12 13	ארם	ARAM	74c	B
	ב	IN	90a	3 3b
	ברח	FLEE	138a	1
	עבד	WORK	713a	2
	יעקב	JACOB	785a	2
	פדן	PADDAN	804c	
	ישראל	ISRAEL	975c	1
	שמר	KEEP	1036c	1 a
	שמר	KEEP	*1037b	3
12 14	ב	IN	89d	3 2c
	נביא	PROPHET	611c	1
	שמר	KEEP	1037b	3
12 15	אדון	LORD	11b	2 2
	דם	BLOOD	*197a	2 g
	חרפה	REPROACH	357d	1
	כעס	VEX	495a	2
	תמרור	BITTERNESS	601b	
	נטש	LEAVE	643d	1
	על	UPON	756c	2 7a b
13 1	אשם	OFFEND	79c	2
	בעל	BAAL	*127d	2 1
	בעל	BAAL	127d	2
	מות	DIE	560a	2 c
	נשא	LIFT	671a	1 b 1
	רתת	TREMBLING	958d	
	תבונה	UNDERSTANDING	108b	1
13 2	זבח	SLAUGHTER FOR SACRIFICE	256d	1 1 bb
	חטא	MISS A GOAL OR WAY	307a	2 b
	חרש	GRAVER	360d	1 a
	יסף	DO AGAIN	415c	2
	ל	TO	515d	5 ia
	מן	OUT OF	579b	2 ba
	מסכה	MOLTEN IMAGE	651b	2
	נשק	KISS	676c	
	עגל	CALF	722b	
	עתה	NOW	774a	1 a
	עצב	IDOL	781b	
	מעשה	DEED	796a	2 a3
13 3	ארבה	LATTICE	70c	
	גרן	THRESHING-FLOOR	175c	
	ה	THE	208a	1 f
	הלך	WALK	232c	1 3
	טל	NIGHT-MIST	378d	
	מוץ	CHAFF	558b	
	סער	STORM	704b	
	ענן	CLOUD	778a	1 c
	עשן	SMOKE	798c	1 c
	שכם	START EARLY	1014d	
13 4	אין	NOT	34c	2 c
	בלת	EXCEPT	116c	2
	יהוה	YAHWEH	218d	2 1a
	יהוה	YAHWEH	219b	2 1d
	זולה	EXCEPT	265d	1
	זולה	EXCEPT	*265d	1
	ידע	KNOW	394a	1 e
	ישע	DELIVER	446d	1 b
	מן	FROM	581c	4 a
13 5	ידע	KNOW	394b	2
	תלאבה	DROUGHT	520d	
13 6	ך	LIKE	454d	3 b
	לב	HEART	525b	2 6c
	רום	BE HIGH	926b	2 b
	מרעית	PASTURING	945c	2
	שבע	SATISFIED	959b	1 a
	שכח	FORGET	1013b	1 c
13 7	דרך	WAY	202d	3
	כמו	LIKE	455d	1 a
	נמר	LEOPARD	649d	
	שור	BEHOLD	1003d	3
	שחל	LION	1006c	
13 8	אכל	EAT	37c	2
	בקע	CLEAVE	132b	
	דב	BEAR	179a	
	ה	THE	*207d	1 f
	חיה	LIVING THING	312c	1 b
	לביא	LION	522d	
	לב	HEART	524c	2 1
	סגור	ENCLOSURE	689c	1
	פגש	MEET	803d	
	קרע	TEAR	902d	4
	שדה	FIELD	961b	1 c
	שכל	BEREAVED	1014a	
13 9	ב	IN	88d	1 7a
	עזר	HELP	740d	2
	שחת	GO TO RUIN	1008a	1
13 10	אהי	WHERE	13c	
	אפו	THEN	66b	1
	ישע	DELIVER	446c	1 a
	מלך	KING	573c	5 c
	שפט	JUDGE	1047c	1 b
13 11	לקח	TAKE	543a	1 c
	מלך	KING	573c	5 c
	עברה	OVERFLOW	720c	3 b
13 12	חטאת	SIN	308d	1 d1

Ch	v.	Heb	Eng	Page	Sec
		עון	INIQUITY	730d	1
		צפן	HIDE	860c	1
13	13	צרר	BIND	864c	A
		חבל	PAIN	287a	1 b
		חכם	WISE	314d	1
		ילד	BEAR	408c	1 b
		ל	TO	*511c	1 gb
		לא	NOT	519c	2 a
		עמד	STAND	764a	1 d
		עת	TIME	773d	2 b
		משבצר	BREACH	991b	
13	14	אתו	WHERE	13c	
		גאל	REDEEM	145c	3 a
		דבר	PESTILENCE	184a	1
		יד	HAND	391b	5 g1
		מות	DEATH	560d	3
		נחם	SORROW	637b	
		סתר	HIDE	711c	2
		עין	EYE	744c	2 a
		פדה	RANSOM	804b	3 d
		קטב	DESTRUCTION	881d	
		שאול	SHEOL	983b	4
13	15	אחו	REEDS	28a	
		אוצר	TREASURE	70a	1
		בוש	BE ASHAMED	101d	3
		בין	INTERVAL	107b	1
		הוא	HE, SHE, IT	215b	1 a
		חמדה	DESIRE	326d	1
		חרב	BE DRY	351a	2
		כי	THOUGH	473c	2 ca
		כלי	ARTICLE	479c	1
		מעין	SPRING	746a	
		פרה	BEAR FRUIT	826b	3
		קדים	EAST WIND	870b	1
		מקור	SPRING	881b	1 d
		רוח	BREATH	924b	2 a
		שסה	PLUNDER	1042c	
14	1	בקע	CLEAVE	132b	
		הריה	PREGNANT	248a	
		מרה	BE REBELLIOUS	598a	2
		נפל	FALL	657b	2 a
		עולל	CHILD	760c	
		רטש	DASH IN PIECES	936b	
		אשמנים	LUSTY	1032c	
14	2	יהוה	YAHWEH	218d	2 1a
		כשל	STUMBLE	505c	1
		כשל	STUMBLE	*505d	1 b
		עד	AS FAR AS	724a	1 1a
		עון	INIQUITY	731a	1
		שוב	TURN BACK	997d	6 c
14	3	דבר	WORD	183b	3 1
		טוב	A GOOD THING	375b	2
		כל	ALL	482b	1 f
		נשא	LIFT	671b	3 c
		עון	INIQUITY	731a	1 c2
		פר	YOUNG BULL	830d	2 e
		רצון	GOODWILL	*953c	2
		שפה	SPEECH	973d	1 a1
		שלם	BE COMPLETE	1022c	4
14	4	אשור	ASSHUR	78d	2
		אשר	PARTICLE OF RELATION	82b	1
		ב	IN	89d	3 2c
		ישע	DELIVER	446d	1 c
		יתום	ORPHAN	450c	
		סוס	HORSE	692c	2
		מעשה	DEED	796a	2 a3
		רחם	LOVE	933d	1
		רכב	RIDE	938d	2
14	5	אהב	LOVE	13a	5 b
		נדבה	VOLUNTARINESS	621d	1
		רפא	HEAL	950d	2 a
		שוב	TURN BACK	997d	6 f
		משובה	TURNING BACK	1000b	
14	6	טל	NIGHT-MIST	378d	1
		לבנון	LEBANON	527b	
		נכה	SMITE	645d	1 d
		פרח	BUD	827a	
		שרש	ROOT	1057c	1
14	7	הוד	SPLENDOUR	217b	3 a
		הלך	WALK	232d	1 3
		זית	OLIVE TREE	268c	1
		יונקת	TWIG	413c	
		לבנון	LEBANON	527b	
		ריח	SCENT	926b	1
		שושן	LILY	1004c	
14	8	גפן	VINE	172c	
		דגן	CORN	186c	
		זכר	REMEMBRANCE	271d	2 b
		חיה	LIVE	311c	3 b
		יין	WINE	406c	A
		לבנון	LEBANON	*527b	
		לבנון	LEBANON	527b	
		פרח	BUD	827a	
		צל	SHADOW	853b	2
14	9	ברוש	CYPRESS	*141c	1
		ברוש	CYPRESS	141c	1
		מצא	FIND	394a	1 h
		מה	WHAT	553b	1 dc
		ענה	ANSWER	772d	1 b
		עצב	IDOL	781b	
		רענן	LUXURIANT	947d	
		שור	BEHOLD	1003d	2
14	10	אלה	THESE	41c	A
		בין	DISCERN	106d	2 a
		בין	DISCERN	106d	

Ch	v.	Heb	Eng	Page	Sec
		דרך	WAY	204a	6 eb
		חכם	WISE	314d	5
		ישר	STRAIGHT	449a	3 a
		כשל	STUMBLE	505d	1 b
		מי	WHO	567b	G
		פשע	REBEL	833b	2
		צדיק	JUST	843b	3 b

JOEL

Ch	v.	Heb	Eng	Page	Sec
1	1	דבר	WORD	182c	1 2a
		יואל	JOEL	222b	0
		פתואל	PETHUEL	834d	
1	2	אזן	HEAR	24c	1
		אם	IF	50d	2 ab b
		זקן	OLD	278c	2 a
1	3	אחר	ANOTHER	29d	
		דור	GENERATION	190a	2 c
		ספר	COUNT	708b	1
		על	UPON	754d	2 1f g
1	4	אכל	EAT	37c	2
		גזם	LOCUSTS	160b	
		חסל	LOCUST	340c	
		ילק	LOCUST	410c	A
		יתר	REMAINDER	451d	1 a
		ארבה	LOCUST	916a	
1	5	בכה	WEEP	113b	1
		ילל	HOWL	410b	
		כרת	BE CUT OFF	504b	4
		עסיס	SWEET WINE	779b	
		קיץ	AWAKE	884c	3
		שכר	DRUNKEN	1016c	
		שתה	DRINK	1059b	1 b
1	6	אין	NOT	34d	4 b
		אריה	LION	71d	
		גוי	NATION	156a	2
		לביא	LION	522d	
		מספר	NUMBER	708d	1 a
		עלה	GO UP	748d	3
		עצום	MIGHTY	783a	1
		שן	TOOTH	1042a	1 b
		מתלעות	TEETH	1069a	
1	7	גפן	VINE	172c	
		חשף	STRIP OFF	362c	2
		לבן	MAKE WHITE	526b	2
		לבן	WHITE	*526b	
		קצפה	SNAPPING	893c	
		שריג	TENDRIL	974d	
		שלך	THROW	1021a	1 c
		שמה	WASTE	1031c	1
		תאנה	FIG-TREE	1061a	1
1	8	אלה	WAIL	46d	
		בעל	OWNER	127b	1 2
		בתולה	VIRGIN	143d	
		חגר	GIRD	291d	2
		נעורים	YOUTH	655c	
		שק	SACK	974c	2 a
1	9	אבל	MOURN	5c	
		כהן	PRIEST	464b	7
		כרת	CUT OFF	504d	
		נסך	DRINK-OFFERING	651a	1
		שרת	SERVE	1058b	2 d
1	10	אבל	MOURN	5c	
		אדמה	GROUND	9c	1
		אמל	BE WEAK	51c	
		בוש	BE ASHAMED	102a	2 c
		בוש	BE ASHAMED	102a	2 c
		דגן	CORN	186c	
		יבש	BE DRY	386d	3
		תירוש	NEW WINE	440d	
		יצהר	FRESH OIL	844a	
		שדד	DEAL VIOLENTLY WITH	994b	
1	11	אבד	PERISH	1d	1
		אכר	PLOUGHMAN	38d	
		בוש	BE ASHAMED	102a	2 d
		בוש	BE ASHAMED	102a	2
		חטה	WHEAT	334d	
		יבש	BE DRY	386d	3
		ילל	HOWL	410b	
		כרם	DRESS VINES	501d	
		קציר	HARVESTING	894c	2
		שערה	BARLEY	972d	1
1	12	אמל	BE WEAK	51c	
		בוש	BE ASHAMED	102a	2 c
		בוש	BE ASHAMED	102a	2 d
		בוש	BE ASHAMED	102a	2
		בוש	BE ASHAMED	102a	2
		גפן	VINE	172c	
		יבש	BE DRY	386d	1 d
		יבש	BE DRY	386d	3
		מן	FROM	578a	1 a
		תפוח	APPLE-TREE	656b	1
		רמון	POMEGRANATE	941d	1
		ששון	REJOICING	965b	1
		תאנה	FIG-TREE	1061a	1
		תמר	PALM-TREE	1071c	
1	13	אלהים	GOD	44d	4 c
		מזבח	ALTAR	259a	1
		חגר	GIRD	291d	2
		ילל	HOWL	410b	
		כהן	PRIEST	464b	7
		מנע	WITHHOLD	586b	
		נסך	DRINK-OFFERING	651a	1
		ספד	WAIL	704d	

Ch	v.	Heb	Eng	Page	Sec
		שק	SACK	974c	2 b
		שרת	SERVE	1058b	2 d
		שרת	SERVE	1058b	1
1	14	זעק	CRY	277b	2 a
		זקן	OLD	278d	2 b
		עצרה	ASSEMBLY	784a	1
		צום	FASTING	847b	
		קדש	BE SET APART	873b	2
1	15	אהה	ALAS	13c	
		הה	ALAS	214c	
		יום	DAY	399a	3
		יום	DAY	401a	7 i
		ך	LIKE	*454b	1 d
		קרב	NEAR	898d	3
		שד	VIOLENCE	994c	2
		שדי	ALMIGHTY	995a	1
1	16	אלהים	GOD	44d	4 c
		כרת	BE CUT OFF	504b	1 aa
		נגד	IN FRONT	617b	1 aa
		עין	EYE	745a	5
		שמחה	JOY	970d	2
1	17	אוצר	TREASURE	70a	3 b
		בוש	BE ASHAMED	102a	2 c
		בוש	BE ASHAMED	102a	2
		ממגרות	STORE-HOUSES	158c	
		מגרפה	SHOVEL	175d	
		דגן	CORN	186c	
		הרס	THROW DOWN	248d	
		יבש	BE DRY	386d	3
		עבש	SHRIVEL	721b	
		פרדה	GRAIN	825c	
		שמם	BE DESOLATED	1031a	1
1	18	אנח	SIGH	58d	3
		אשם	OFFEND	79c	
		בוך	CONFUSE	100c	
		בקר	CATTLE	133b	1 a
		בקר	CATTLE	133b	1 a
		עדר	FLOCK	727c	1 a
		עדר	FLOCK	727d	2 b
		מרעה	PASTURAGE	945c	
		אשם	ADDENDA ET CORRIGENDA	1121a	
1	19	מדבר	WILDERNESS	184d	1
		להבה	FLAME	529b	1
		להט	SET ABLAZE	529d	
		נוה	PASTURE	627d	1
1	20	אפיק	CHANNEL	67d	
		מדבר	WILDERNESS	184d	1
		יבש	BE DRY	386c	1
		נוה	PASTURE	627d	1
		ערג	LONG FOR	788b	
		שדה	FIELD	961b	1 c
2	1	בוא	COME	98c	2
		הר	MOUNTAIN	249d	1 a
		יום	DAY	399a	3
		ציון	ZION	851c	
		קדש	APARTNESS	871d	2 e
		קרב	NEAR	898d	3
		רגז	BE AGITATED	919b	
		רוע	RAISE A SHOUT	929c	2
		שפר	HORN	1051d	
		תקע	GIVE A BLOW	1075c	2
2	2	אפלה	DARKNESS	66c	1
		דור	PERIOD	189d	1 b
		היה	COME TO PASS	*227d	2
		היה	COME TO PASS	227d	2
		יום	DAY	*399a	3
		יסף	DO AGAIN	415c	2 a
		עולם	LONG DURATION	761d	1 a
		עם	PEOPLE	766c	1
		ענן	CLOUD	778a	1 e
		עצום	MIGHTY	783a	1
		ערפל	CLOUD	791d	
		פרש	SPREAD OUT	831b	2
		שחר	DAWN	1007c	
		שנה	YEAR	1040b	
2	3	גן	GARDEN	171a	
		להבה	FLAME	529b	1
		להט	SET ABLAZE	529d	
		עדן	EDEN	727a	
		פלימה	ESCAPE	812c	2 a
2	4	חשך	DARKNESS	365a	3 b
		ך	LIKE	454d	2 d
		כן	SO	486b	2 ad b
		סוס	HORSE	692d	1
		פרש	HORSE	832a	
		מראה	VISION	909c	1 b
		רוץ	RUN	930b	1
2	5	אש	FIRE	77d	6
		להב	FLAME	529a	1
		עצום	MIGHTY	783a	1
		ערך	ARRANGE	789c	1 d
		קול	VOICE	877b	2 1
		קול	VOICE	877b	2 e
		מרכבה	CHARIOT	939d	1
2	6	חול	WHIRL	297a	2 b
		כל	ALL	481b	1 a
		פארור	GLOW	802d	
		פנה	FACE	815d	1 1a
		קבץ	GATHER	868a	3
2	7	ארח	WAY	73a	1
		גבור	STRONG	150b	2
		דרך	WAY	202d	1
		דרך	WAY	203a	1
		הלך	WALK	232b	1 2
		חומה	WALL	327b	1

Ch v.	Heb	Eng	Page	Sec
	מלחמה	WAR	536b	
	עבט	TAKE A PLEDGE	716c	
	עלה	GO UP	748b	1 e
	ארבה	LOCUST	916a	
	רוץ	RUN	930b	1
2 8	את	BROTHER	26b	4
	בעד	ABOUT	126c	1 b
	בצע	CUT OFF	130b	
	גבר	MAN	150a	
	רחק	THRUST	191b	
	הלך	WALK	232b	1 2
	זכר	REMEMBER	270a	1 3 b
	נפל	FALL	656d	1
	מסלה	HIGHWAY	700c	
	ארבה	LOCUST	916a	
	שלח	MISSLE	1019c	1
2 9	בעד	AWAY FROM	126b	1 a
	גנב	THIEF	170c	
	חלון	WINDOW	319d	1
	חומה	WALL	327b	1
	עלה	GO UP	748a	3
	רוץ	RUN	930b	1
	שקק	RUN	1055b	1
2 10	אסף	GATHER	62c	4
	ירח	MOON	437a	
	כוכב	STAR	457a	
	נגה	BRIGHTNESS	618b	
	קדר	BE DARK	871a	
	קול	VOICE	876d	1 a
	רגז	BE AGITATED	919a	
	רעש	SHAKE	950b	
	שמש	SUN	1039b	1
2 11	גדול	GREAT	153a	6 a
	דבר	WORD	182d	1 2 b
	יום	DAY	399a	3
	ירא	CAUSE FEAR	431d	2
	כול	SUSTAIN	465b	2
	מי	WHO	567a	F c
	נתן	GIVE	679d	1 x
	עצום	MIGHTY	783a	1
	קול	VOICE	877a	2 b
2 12	בכי	WEEPING	113d	
	לבב	HEART	523c	2 2
	נאם	UTTERANCE	610b	2
	מספד	WAILING	704d	3
	עתה	NOW	774b	2 d
	צום	FASTING	847b	
2 13	אל	NOT	39b	A bg
	ארך	LONG	74a	
	בגד	GARMENT	94a	1
	יהוה	YAHWEH	218d	2 1 b
	חנון	GRACIOUS	337a	
	חסד	GOODNESS	339b	2 3 a
	לבב	HEART	523b	2 1
	נחם	BE SORRY	637a	2
	קרע	TEAR	902c	1 a1
	רחון	COMPASSIONATE	933d	
	רום	COMPASSIONATE	933d	
2 14	אם	IF	50d	2 ba
	ברכה	BLESSING	139d	1 b
	מי	WHO	567a	F d
	נחם	BE SORRY	637a	2
	נסך	DRINK-OFFERING	651a	1
	שאר	REMAIN	984b	4
	שוב	TURN BACK	998a	6 g
2 15	עצרה	ASSEMBLY	784a	1
	צום	FASTING	847b	
	קדש	BE SET APART	873b	2
	שפר	HORN	1051d	
	תקע	GIVE A BLOW	1075c	2
2 16	אהל	TENT	13d	1
	אסף	GATHER	62b	1 a
	זקן	OLD	278c	2 a
	חדר	CHAMBER	293c	
	חפה	CANOPY	342c	2
	חתן	DAUGHTER:S HUS-BAND	368d	2
	ינק	SUCK	413b	
	ינק	SUCK	413b	
	כלה	BRIDE	483c	2 a
	עולל	CHILD	760d	
	קבץ	GATHER	867d	2
	קדש	BE SET APART	873b	4 b
	קהל	ASSEMBLY	874d	1 d
	שד	BREAST	994c	1
2 17	אולם	PORCH	17d	1
	איה	WHERE	32c	
	אלהים	GOD	44d	4 c
	אמר	SAY	56a	1
	אנחנו	WE	59d	
	בין	INTERVAL	107c	1 c
	בכה	WEEP	113b	1
	חום	PITY	299b	B
	חרפה	REPROACH	358a	3
	כהן	PRIEST	464b	7
	מה	HOW	554b	4 d
	משל	RULE	605d	1
	נחלה	PROPERTY	635b	1 e
	שרת	SERVE	1058b	2 d
2 18	אנחנו	WE	59d	
	חמל	SPARE	328b	
	קנא	BE ZEALOUS	888c	3 b
2 19	דגן	CORN	186c	
	חרפה	REPROACH	358a	3
	תירוש	NEW WINE	440d	
	יצהר	FRESH OIL	844a	
2 20	אחרון	BEHIND	30d	A
	באש	STENCH	93b	
	גדל	BECOME GREAT	152c	3 b
	ים	SEA	410d	1
	ים	SEA	411a	3
	ים	SEA	411b	8 d
	ל	TO	517c	7 bb
	נדח	THRUST	623b	2
	סוף	END	693a	
	עלה	GO UP	748d	5
	על	UPON	758d	4 2 b
	פנה	FACE	816b	1 5
	צחנה	STENCH	850b	
	צפוני	NORTHERN	861b	
	קדמני	FORMER	870d	2
	רחק	BE DISTANT	935b	2
2 21	אדמה	LAND	10a	5
	גדל	BECOME GREAT	152c	3 a
	ירא	FEAR	431a	1 a
	שמח	REJOICE	970b	2 a
2 22	גפן	VINE	172c	
	מדבר	WILDERNESS	184d	1
	דשא	SPROUT	205d	
	חיל	STRENGTH	298c	1 a
	ירא	FEAR	431a	1 a
	נוה	PASTURE	627d	1
	נשא	LIFT	671b	2 g
	עץ	TREE	781c	1 b
	שדי	FIELD	961b	2
	תאנה	FIG-TREE	1061a	1
2 23	בן	SON	121b	1 jt
	גשם	RAIN	177c	
	ירד	BRING DOWN	434a	1 b
	מורה	RAIN	435c	
	ל	TO	516c	5 jb
	מלקוש	SPRING-RAIN	545b	
	צדקה	RIGHTEOUSNESS	842c	6 b
	ציון	ZION	851b	
	ראשון	FIRST	911d	2 a
	שמח	REJOICE	970b	2 a
2 24	בר	GRAIN	141b	
	גרן	THRESHING-FLOOR	175b	
	יקב	WINE-VAT	428c	
	תירוש	NEW WINE	440d	
	מלא	BE FULL	570a	1 a
	יצהר	FRESH OIL	844a	
	שוק	BE ABUNDANT	1003c	
2 25	אכל	EAT	37c	2
	גזם	LOCUSTS	160b	
	חסיל	LOCUST	340c	
	ילק	LOCUST	410c	A
	ארבה	LOCUST	916a	
2 26	בוש	BE ASHAMED	101d	1
	הלל	PRAISE	238b	2 b
	ל	TO	517b	7 ba
	עולם	LONG DURATION	762d	2 g
	פלא	BE SURPASSING	810d	1
	בוש	BE ASHAMED	101d	1
2 27	יהוה	YAHWEH	219b	2 2 d
	עוד	STILL	729b	1 c
	עולם	LONG DURATION	762d	2 g
3 1	בחור	YOUNG MAN	104c	
	בשר	FLESH	142d	6 c
	זקן	OLD	278c	2 a
	חזון	VISION	303b	1
	חלם	DREAM	321c	B
	חלום	DREAM	321d	2 a
	נבא	PROPHESY	612b	1 b
	ראה	TO SEE	906d	1 b
	רוח	BREATH	926a	9 b
3 2	רוח	BREATH	926a	9 b
	שפחה	MAID	1046c	1
	פך	POUR OUT	1049d	2 a
3 3	דם	BLOOD	197c	2 o
	עשן	SMOKE	798c	2 a
	תימרה	COLUMN	1071d	
	בוא	COME	98c	2
3 4	גדול	GREAT	153a	6 a
	דם	BLOOD	197c	2 o
	הפך	TURN	246a	2
	חשך	DARKNESS	365a	3 b
	יום	DAY	399a	3
	ירא	CAUSE FEAR	431d	2
	ירח	MOON	437a	
	שמש	SUN	1039b	1
3 5	היה	COME TO PASS	225a	1 2b ag
	הר	MOUNTAIN	249c	1 a
	מלט	SLIP AWAY	572b	2
	פליטה	ESCAPE	812d	2 c
	ציון	ZION	851c	
	שריד	SURVIVOR	975a	1
3 6	יון	JAVAN	402b	
4 1	שבות	CAPTIVITY	986b	2 a
	שוב	TURN BACK	999d	9
4 2	יהושפט	JEHOSHAPHAT	221d	7
	חלק	DIVIDE	323d	1
	ירד	BRING DOWN	433d	1 a
	נחלה	PROPERTY	635d	1 e
	פזר	SCATTER	808b	
	קבץ	GATHER	868a	1
	שפט	JUDGE	1048a	1
4 3	גורל	LOT	174c	2 g
	זנה	COMMIT FORNICA-TION	275d	1
	ידד	CAST A LOT	391d	
	ילד	CHILD	409b	A
	ילדה	GIRL	409c	
	מכר	SELL	*569b	
	מכר	SELL	569b	
4 4	נתן	GIVE	679c	1 o
	אם	IF	50d	2 ab b
	מהרה	HASTE	555b	
	פלשת	PHILISTIA	814b	
	צר	TYER	862d	
	קל	LIGHT	887a	
	ראש	HEAD	911b	8
	שוב	TURN BACK	999c	4 a
	שלם	BE COMPLETE	1022c	5
4 5	היכל	PALACE	228b	1
	זהב	GOLD	263c	1
	מחמד	DESIRE	327a	
	טוב	PLEASANT	374b	4 b
4 6	בן	SON	121a	1 jd
	בן	SON	121b	1 jt
	גבול	BOUNDARY	148a	2 a
	מכר	SELL	569b	
4 7	רחק	BE DISTANT	935b	2
	מכר	SELL	569b	
	עור	ROUSE ONESELF	735b	1
	ראש	HEAD	911b	8
	שוב	TURN BACK	999c	4 a
	שם	THERE	1027b	3
4 8	בן	SON	121a	1 jd
	דבר	SPEAK	180d	1
	מכר	SELL	569b	
	רחק	DISTANT	935b	1 a
	שבאי	SABEANS	985b	
4 9	גבור	STRONG	150b	2
	מלחמה	WAR	536b	
	מלחמה	WAR	536c	
	עור	ROUSE ONESELF	735b	1
	קדש	BE SET APART	8730	4 c
4 10	את	PLOUGHSHARE	88c	
	גבור	STRONG	150b	2
	מזמרה	PRUNING-KNIFE	275a	
	חלש	WEAK	325d	
	כתת	BEAT	510a	2
	רמח	SPEAR	942b	
4 11	גבור	STRONG	150b	2
	נחת	DESCEND	639c	
	סביב	ROUND ABOUT	687a	1 d
	עוש	LEND AID	736b	1
	קבץ	GATHER	867d	1
4 12	יהושפט	JEHOSHAPHAT	221d	7
	ישב	SIT	442c	1 a
	סביב	ROUND ABOUT	687a	1 d
	עור	ROUSE ONESELF	735a	
	שפט	JUDGE	1047d	3 d
4 13	בשל	GROW RIPE	143a	
	גת	WINE-PRESS	387c	
	יקב	WINE-VAT	428c	
	מלא	BE FULL	570a	1 a
	מגל	SICKLE	618c	
	קציר	HARVESTING	894c	2
	שוק	BE ABUNDANT	1003c	
	שלח	SEND	1018d	3 a
4 14	המון	CROWD	242c	3 a
	חרוץ	STRICT DECISION	358d	
	יום	DAY	399a	3
	מה	WHAT	552b	1 a
	קרב	NEAR	898d	3
4 15	אסף	GATHER	62c	4
	ירח	MOON	437a	
	כוכב	STAR	457a	
	נגה	BRIGHTNESS	618b	
	קדר	BE DARK	871a	
	שמש	SUN	1039b	1
4 16	מחסה	REFUGE	340c	B
	מעוז	PLACE OF SAFETY	732a	2 a
	ציון	ZION	851c	
	קול	VOICE	877a	2 b
	רעש	SHAKE	950b	
	ישראל	ISRAEL	975d	2 b3
	שאג	ROAR	980d	1
4 17	יהוה	YAHWEH	219a	2 2b b
	הר	MOUNTAIN	249d	1 a
	זור	BE A STRANGER	266c	2 c
	ציון	ZION	851c	
	קדש	APARTNESS	871a	2 e
	קדש	APARTNESS	871a	2 e
	שכן	SETTLE DOWN	1015b	2 c
4 18	אפיק	CHANNEL	67d	
	גבעה	HILL	149a	3
	הלך	WALK	232b	1 3
	הר	MOUNTAIN	250c	1
	חלב	MILK	316c	A 4
	יצא	GO OUT	423a	1 f
	נטף	DROP	643a	
	נטף	DRIP	*643a	1
	מעין	SPRING	746a	
	עסיס	SWEET WINE	779b	
	שטים	SHITTIM	1008d	2
	שקה	GIVE TO DRINK	1052c	1
4 19	בן	SON	121a	1 jd
	דם	BLOOD	196d	2 d
	חמס	VIOLENCE	329c	
	מצרים	EGYPTIANS	595d	2 b
	נקיא	INNOCENT	667d	
4 20	דור	PERIOD	189d	1 b
	ישב	REMAIN	442d	2 a

Ch v.	Heb	Eng	Page	Sec
	עולם	LONG DURATION	762b	2 b2
4 21	דם	BLOOD	197b	2 k
	ו	AND	253d	1 k
	נקה	BE CLEAN	667c	2
	שכן	SETTLE DOWN	1015b	2 c

AMOS

Ch v.	Heb	Eng	Page	Sec
1 1	בוקר	HERDSMAN	133c	
	דבר	WORD	183a	2 1b
	יהואש	JEHOASH	220a	2
	היה	BE	227c	3 4d e
	חזה	SEE	302c	2
	מן	OUT OF	579c	2 cb
	נקד	SHEEP-RAISER	667a	
	עזיהו	UZZIAH	739d	1 b
	עמוס	AMOS	770c	
	פנה	FACE	817c	2 4e
	ירבעם	JEROBOAM	914d	1
	רעש	SHAKING	950b	1
	ישראל	ISRAEL	975d	2 a2
	שנה	YEAR	1040b	
1 2	תקוע	TEKOA	1075d	
	אבל	MOURN	5c	
	יבש	BE DRY	386b	1 b
	כרמל	CARMEL	502a	1
	מן	OUT OF	579d	2 ab
	נוה	PASTURE	627d	1
	נתן	GIVE	679d	1 x
	ציון	ZION	851c	
	קול	VOICE	877a	2 b
	רעה	TEND	945a	1 d1
	שאג	ROAR	980d	1
1 3	ברזל	IRON	137c	1 d
	דוש	THRESH	190c	
	דמשק	DAMASCUS	199d	
	ו	AND	252c	1 c
	חרוץ	SHARP	358d	1
	חרוץ	A CUT	*359a	2
	על	UPON	754b	2 1f b
	פשע	TRANSGRESSION	833c	2
	ארבע	FOUR	917a	1 b3
	שוב	TURN BACK	999d	1
1 4	אכל	EAT	37c	3
	ארמון	CITADEL	74d	
	אש	FIRE	77c	1
	בנהדד	BEN-HADAD	122b	
	חזהאל	HAZAEL	303c	
	שלח	SEND	1019b	7
1 5	און	TROUBLE	20a	2
	ארם	ARAM	74b	A
	ביתעדן	BETH-EDEN	112b	
	בקעה	PLAIN	132c	2
	בריח	BAR	138b	1 b
	בריח	BAR	138b	2
	דמשק	DAMASCUS	199d	
	ישב	SIT	442c	1 a
	ישב	DWELL	443b	3
	כרת	CUT OFF	504c	2 c
	עם	PEOPLE	766c	1
	קיר	KIR	885b	
	שבט	ROD	987a	1 d
	שבר	BREAK	990c	
	תמך	GRASP	1069d	1
1 6	ו	AND	252c	1 c
	סגר	DELIVER UP	689c	1
	עזה	GAZA	738b	
	על	UPON	754b	2 1f b
	פשע	TRANSGRESSION	833c	2
	ארבע	FOUR	917a	1 b3
	שוב	TURN BACK	999d	1
	שלום	PEACE	1022d	1
	שלם	COMPLETE	1024a	1 a
1 7	אכל	EAT	37c	3
	ארמון	CITADEL	74d	
	אש	FIRE	77c	1
	חומה	WALL	327b	1
	חומה	WALL	327d	1
	עזה	GAZA	738b	
	שלח	SEND	1019b	7
1 8	אבד	PERISH	1c	1
	אדון	LORD	11c	4 c
	אשדוד	AHSDOD	78b	1
	אשקלון	ASHKELON	80c	
	ישב	SIT	442c	1 a
	ישב	DWELL	443b	3
	כרת	CUT OFF	504c	2 c
	עקרון	EKRON	785d	
	שארית	REST	984d	1
	שבט	ROD	987a	1 d
	שוב	TURN BACK	999a	1 a
	תמך	GRASP	1069d	1
1 9	אח	BROTHER	26b	2
	ברית	COVENANT	136b	1 1
	ו	AND	252c	1 c
	זכר	REMEMBER	269d	1 2 d
	סגר	DELIVER UP	689c	1
	על	UPON	754b	2 1f b
	פשע	TRANSGRESSION	833c	2
	צר	TYER	862d	
	ארבע	FOUR	917a	1 b3
	שוב	TURN BACK	999d	1
	שלם	COMPLETE	1024a	1 a
1 10	אכל	EAT	37c	3
	ארמון	CITADEL	74d	
	אש	FIRE	77c	1
	חומה	WALL	327b	1
	חומה	WALL	327d	1
	צר	TYER	862d	
	שלח	SEND	1019b	7
1 11	ו	AND	252c	1 c
	טרף	TEAR	383a	2
	תימן	TEMAN	*412d	
	נטר	KEEP	643c	1
	נצח	EVERLASTINGNESS	664b	4
	עברה	OVERFLOW	720c	3 a
	עד	PERPETUITY	723c	2 c
	על	UPON	754b	2 1f b
	פשע	TRANSGRESSION	833c	2
	רדף	PURSUE	922c	1 b
	רחמים	COMPASSION	933c	2
	שוב	TURN BACK	999d	1
	שחת	GO TO RUIN	1008a	1
	שמר	KEEP	1036d	2 a
1 12	אכל	EAT	37c	3
	ארמון	CITADEL	74d	
	בצרה	BOZRAH	131b	1
	תימן	TEMAN	412d	
	שלח	SEND	1019b	7
1 13	בקע	CLEAVE	131d	1
	גבול	BORDER	147d	1 a
	ו	AND	252c	1 c
	על	UPON	754b	2 1f b
	עמון	AMMON	770a	
	פשע	TRANSGRESSION	833c	2
	רחב	BE LARGE	931c	2
	שוב	TURN BACK	999d	1
1 14	אכל	EAT	37c	3
	ארמון	CITADEL	74d	
	חומה	WALL	327b	1
	חומה	WALL	327d	1
	יצת	KINDLE	428c	
	סופה	STORM-WIND	693a	
	סער	TEMPEST	704b	1
	רבה	RABBA	913d	1
	תרועה	SHOUT OF WAR	930a	1
	יחדו	TOGETHER	403c	A
1 15	מלכם	MILCOM	576a	
	שר	CHIEFTAIN	978a	1 a
2 1	ו	AND	252c	1 c
	ל	TO	512b	4 a
	מואב	MOAB	555d	2
	פשע	TRANSGRESSION	833c	2
	שיד	WHITEWASH	966d	
	שרף	BURN	976d	2 a
	משרפה	A BURNING	977c	
	שוב	TURN BACK	999d	1
2 2	אכל	EAT	37c	3
	ארמון	CITADEL	74d	
	מואב	MOAB	555d	2 a
	מות	DIE	560a	2 c
	קול	VOICE	877a	2 a
	קריות	KERIOTH-HEZRON	901a	2
	תרועה	SHOUT OF WAR	930a	1
	שאון	ROAR	981a	1
	שלח	SEND	1019b	7
	שפר	HORN	1051d	
2 3	הרג	KILL	247b	2
	כרת	CUT OFF	504c	2 c
	קרב	INWARD PART	899a	1 e
	שר	CHIEFTAIN	978a	2
	שפט	JUDGE	1047c	1 b
2 4	הלך	WALK	235a	2 3d 4
	ו	AND	252c	1 c
	חק	SOMETHING PRE-SCRIBED	349d	7 g
	חקה	SOMETHING PRE-SCRIBED	350b	2 e
	תורה	INSTRUCTION	436a	1 c
	כוב	LIE	469d	
	מאס	REJECT	549c	1 a
	פשע	TRANSGRESSION	833c	3 c
	שוב	TURN BACK	999d	1
	שמר	KEEP	1037c	3 c
	תעה	ERR	1073c	3
2 5	אכל	EAT	37c	3
	ארמון	CITADEL	74d	
	שלח	SEND	1019b	7
2 6	אביון	NEEDY	2d	1
	ו	AND	252c	1 c
	כסף	SILVER	494d	9
	מכר	SELL	*569b	
	מכר	SELL	569b	
	נעל	SANDAL	653a	
	עבור	FOR THE SAKE OF	721a	1 a
	פשע	TRANSGRESSION	833c	3 c
	צדיק	JUST	843a	2
	ישראל	ISRAEL	975d	2 a2
	שוב	TURN BACK	999d	1
2 7	דל	WEAK	195d	1
	דרך	WAY	203b	5
	הלך	WALK	231a	1 d3 ga
	חלל	POLLUTE	320b	1 c
	נטה	BEND	641d	3 g
	נערה	GIRL	655b	1
	מען	PURPOSE	775d	2 1
	ענו	POOR	776c	2
	עפר	DRY EARTH	779d	1 a
	קדש	APARTNESS	871c	1 c
	שאף	CRUSH	983d	
	שם	NAME	1028c	3
2 8	אלהים	GOD	44d	4 c
	אצל	BESIDE	69b	A
	בגד	GARMENT	94a	1
	חבל	BIND	286b	2
	נטה	INCLINE	640d	3 a
	עש	FINE	778d	
	שתה	DRINK	1059b	1 a
2 9	אלון	OAK	47c	
	אמרי	AMORITES	57c	2 d
	ארז	CEDAR	72c	1 b
	גבה	HEIGHT	147b	1
	חסן	STRONG	340d	
	מעל	ABOVE	751c	1 a
	פנה	FACE	818b	2 6a
	פרי	FRUIT	826b	1
	שמד	BE EXTERMINATED	1029b	1
	שרש	ROOT	1057c	1
	תחת	UNDENEATH	1065b	1
2 10	אמרי	AMORITES	57c	2 d
	הלך	WALK	236d	1 b
	ירש	TAKE POSSESSION	439c	1 a
	ארבעים	FORTY	917b	1 a
2 11	אף	ALSO	65a	1
	בחור	YOUNG MAN	104c	
	זה	THIS	260c	1 a
	מן	FROM	580d	3 ba
	נאם	UTTERANCE	610c	2
	נביא	PROPHET	611c	1
	נזיר	CONSECRATED	634c	2
	קום	STAND	879a	5
	ישראל	ISRAEL	975d	2 b2
2 12	יין	WINE	406c	C
	נביא	PROPHET	611c	1
	נבא	PROPHESY	612d	1 b
	נזיר	CONSECRATED	634c	2
	צוה	LAY CHARGE UPON	845c	1 a
	שקה	GIVE TO DRINK	1052c	2
2 13	ל	TO	516a	5 ic
	מלא	FULL	571a	
	עגלה	CART	722c	
	עוק	TOTTER	734b	
	עמיר	SWATH	771c	
	פוק	REEL	807c	
	תחת	UNDERNEATH	1065d	2 ia
2 14	אבד	PERISH	1d	2
	אמץ	BE STRONG	55a	1
	גבור	STRONG	150b	2
	חזק	STRONG	305d	2
	כח	STRENGTH	470d	1 d
	מלט	SLIP AWAY	572c	3
	מנום	ESCAPE	631a	1
	נפש	SOUL	660a	3 c
	קל	LIGHT	886d	
	קל	LIGHT	887a	
	תאנה	FIG-TREE	1061a	1
2 15	מלט	SLIP AWAY	572c	3
	מלט	SLIP AWAY	572c	3
	נפש	SOUL	660a	3 c
	סוס	HORSE	692c	2
	עמד	STAND	764b	4
	קל	LIGHT	886d	
	קשת	BOW	906c	1 d
	רכב	RIDE	938d	3
	חפש	LAY HOLD OF	1074d	2
2 16	אמיץ	MIGHTY	55c	
	גבור	STRONG	150b	2
	לב	HEART	525d	20
	ערום	NAKED	736a	
3 1	דבר	SPEAK	181d	5
3 2	אדמה	EARTH	10a	6
	ידע	KNOW	394b	2
	מן	OUT OF	579b	2 ac
	עון	INIQUITY	731a	1 cl
	פקד	ATTEND TO	823c	A 3
	רק	ONLY	956b	2 a
3 3	אם	IF	50c	1 ca
	בלת	EXCEPT	116d	1
	הלך	WALK	230a	1 1a
	יחדו	TOGETHER	403b	A
	יעד	MEET BY APPOINT-MENT	416d	2
3 4	אם	IF	50c	1 ca
	אריה	LION	71d	
	בלת	EXCEPT	116d	3
	טרף	PREY	383c	1
	יער	WOOD	420d	B
	כפיר	LION	498d	
	לכד	CAPTURE	540d	1
	נתן	GIVE	679d	1 x
	מעונה	DEN	733a	1
	קול	VOICE	877a	1 e
	שאג	ROAR	980c	1
3 5	אדמה	GROUND	9d	4
	מוקש	BAIT	430c	
	לכד	CAPTURE	540d	1
	נפל	FALL	656d	1
	פח	BIRD-TRAP	809a	1
	צפור	BIRD	862a	1
3 6	אם	IF	50c	2 aa
	חרד	TREMBLE	353c	1
	שפר	HORN	1051d	
	תקע	GIVE A BLOW	1075c	1
3 7	אדון	LORD	11c	4 a
	כי	THAT	472d	1 e
	כיאם	EXCEPT	474d	1

Ch	v.	Heb	Eng	Page	Sec
		נביא	PROPHET	611d	1
		סוד	COUNSEL	691c	2 b
		עבד	SLAVE	714b	4
3	8	אדון	LORD	11c	4 a
		אריה	LION	71d	
		ירא	FEAR	431a	1 a
		מי	WHO	567a	F c
		נבא	PROPHESY	612b	1 b
		שאג	ROAR	980c	1
3	9	ארמון	CITADEL	74d	
		ארמון	CITADEL	74d	
		אשדוד	AHSDOD	78b	
		מהומה	TUMULT	223a	1
		על	UPON	755d	2 5
		עשוקים	OPPRESSION	799a	
		קרב	INWARD PART	899a	1 c
		שמע	HEAR	1034c	1 c
		שמרון	SAMARIA	1038a	
3	10	אצר	STORE UP	69d	
		ארמון	CITADEL	74d	
		חמס	VIOLENCE	329c	
		ידע	KNOW	394b	4 a
		נאם	UTTERANCE	610c	2
		נכח	STRAIGHTNESS	647c	
		שד	VIOLENCE	994c	1
3	11	אדון	LORD	11c	4 c
		ארמון	CITADEL	74d	
		בזז	SPOIL	103a	
		ו	AND	252c	1 b
		ירד	BRING DOWN	434a	1 c
		ירד	BE BROUGHT DOWN	434b	1
		סביב	ROUND ABOUT	687a	1 ca
		עז	STRENGTH	739a	2 a
		צר	ADVERSARY	865d	
3	12	אזן	EAR	23d	1
		ארי	LION	71d	
		בדל	PIECE	95c	
		דמשק	DAMASCUS	*199d	
		דמשק		200a	
		טרפה	ANIMAL TORN	*383c	1
		כאשר	AS	455c	1 d
		כן	SO	486c	2 cf
		כרע	LEG	502d	
		מן	OUT OF	579a	2 aa
		משה	COUCH	641d	
		נצל	BE DELIVERED	664c	2
		נצל	SNATCH AWAY	664d	1
		עשש	COUCH	793a	
		פאה	CORNER	802a	1
		פה	MOUTH	805b	3
		רעה	TEND	945a	1 d1
3	13	אדון	LORD	11c	4 c
		בית	HOUSE	110a	5 dg
		נאם	UTTERANCE	610b	2
		עוד	BEAR WITNESS	730a	3
		צבא	GOD OF WAR	839d	4 a
3	14	ביתאל	BETHEL	110d	1
		גדע	HEW OFF	154b	
		ל	TO	511c	1 ga
		נפל	FALL	657a	1
		פקד	ATTEND TO	823c	A 3
		פשע	TRANSGRESSION	833c	3 c
		קרן	HORN	902a	3
		ישראל	ISRAEL	975d	2 a2
3	15	אבד	PERISH	1d	1
		בית	HOUSE	108d	1 ag
		בית	HOUSE	109a	1 ae 5
		בית	HOUSE	109a	1 ae 5
		חרף	HARVEST-TIME	358b	
		נכה	SMITE	646c	4 c
		סוף	CEASE	692d	
		ספה	SWEEP AWAY	705a	2
		על	UPON	752d	2 1
		קיץ	SUMMER	884d	1
		שן	IVORY	1042b	2
4	1	אביון	NEEDY	2d	
		אדון	LORD	11a	2
		בשן	BASHAN	143c	
		דל	POOR	195d	
		עשק	OPPRESS	798d	1
		פרה	HEIFER	831a	
		רצץ	CRUSH	954c	2
		שמע	HEAR	1033d	1 f
		שמרון	SAMARIA	1038a	
4	2	אדון	LORD	11d	4 c
		אחרית	END	31b	D
		דוגה	FISHING	186a	
		הנה	BEHOLD	244b	B b
		יום	DAY	400a	7 c
		נשא	LIFT	672a	4
		סור	THORN	696c	2
		צנה	HOOK	856d	
		קדש	APARTNESS	871c	1 b
		שבע	SWEAR	989b	2
4	3	אשה	WOMAN	61b	4
		הדדמון	HADADRIMMON	213a	
		הרמן	HARMON	248b	
		נאם	UTTERANCE	610c	2
		נגד	IN FRONT	617b	1 ab
		פרץ	BURSTING FORTH	829d	2
		שלך	THROW	1021a	1 b
4	4	ביתאל	BETHEL	110d	1
		בקר	MORNING	134a	1 f
		זבח	SACRIFICE	257d	2 5
		זבח	SACRIFICE	257d	2 5
		זבח	SACRIFICE	258a	2 7
		ל	TO	516b	5 ja
		ל	TO	517a	6 b
		מעשר	TENTH PART	798b	2
		פשע	REBEL	833b	2
		רבה	BECOME MANY	915b	
		רבה	BECOME MANY	915c	1 d1
		שלש	THREE	1025d	
4	5	אדון	LORD	11c	4 c
		אהב	LOVE	13a	2
		חמץ	THAT WHICH IS LEAVENED	329d	
		תודה	THANK-OFFERING	392d	4
		נאם	UTTERANCE	610b	2
		נדבה	FREEWILL-OFFER-ING	621d	2 b
		קרא	CALL	845b	3 a
		קטר	MAKE SACRAFICES SMOKE	882d	
4	6	שמע	HEAR	1034c	1 c
		גם	ALSO	169d	4
		חסר	WANT	341c	
		נקיון	INNOCENCY	667d	3
		קהיון	BLUNTNESS	874c	
		מקום	STANDING PLACE	880a	4
		רבה	BECOME MANY	915d	1 e5
		שוב	TURN BACK	997d	6 c
		שן	TOOTH	1042a	1 a
4	7	גם	ALSO	169d	4
		גשם	RAIN	177c	
		חדש	NEW MOON	294c	2 a
		חלקה	PORTION OF GROUND	324c	1 b
		יבש	BE DRY	386b	1 b
		ל	TO	517a	6 c
		מטר	RAIN	565a	
		מנע	WITHHOLD	586a	
		עוד	STILL	729c	2 ab
4	8	מי	WATER	565b	1 a
		נוע	TOTTER	631b	2
		שבע	SATISFIED	959b	1 a
		שוב	TURN BACK	997d	6 c
		שנים	TWO	1041b	1 b3
		שתה	DRINK	1059b	1 a
4	9	אכל	EAT	37c	2
		גזם	LOCUSTS	160b	
		גנה	GARDEN	171b	
		זית	OLIVE TREE	268d	1
		חרב	BE WASTE	351d	
		ירקון	RUST	439a	1
		כרם	VINEYARD	501d	
		נכה	SMITE	646c	4 a
		רבה	BECOME MANY	*915b	
		שדפון	SMUT	995b	
		שוב	TURN BACK	997d	6 c
		תאנה	FIG-TREE	1061a	1
4	10	אף	NOSE	60a	1
		ב	IN	90d	3 8
		באש	STENCH	93b	
		בחור	YOUNG MAN	104c	
		דבר	PESTILENCE	184a	1
		הרג	KILL	247b	2
		ו	AND	252c	1 b
		סוס	HORSE	692c	2
		עלה	GO UP	749c	4
		עם	WITH	767b	1 a
		שבי	CAPTIVITY	985d	2
		שבי	CAPTIVITY	985d	2
		שוב	TURN BACK	997d	6 c
		שלח	SEND	1019a	2 d
4	11	אוד	BRAND	15c	
		אלהים	GOD	44b	4 a
		את	MARK OF THE AC-CUSATIVE	85b	1 d
		ב	IN	88c	1 2b
		הפך	TURN	245c	1 b
		הפך	TURN	245c	1 b
		מהפכה	OVERTHROW	246b	
		נצל	DELIVER	665a	
		סדם	SODOM	690a	
		עמרה	GOMORRAH	771d	
		שרפה	BURNING	977b	
		שוב	TURN BACK	997d	6 c
4	12	אלהים	GOD	44b	4 c
		כון	BE READY	465d	3
		כן	SO	486d	3 da
		עקב	CONSEQUENCE	784d	1
		קרא	ENCOUNTER	897a	1
4	13	במה	HIGH PLACE	119b	2 b
		ברא	CREATE	135b	4
		דרך	TREAD	202a	2
		הר	MOUNTAIN	250a	1 c
		יצר	FORM	427d	2 a
		עיפה	DARKNESS	734a	1
		צבא	GOD OF WAR	839d	4 b
		שח	THOUGHT	967b	
		שחר	DAWN	1007b	
		שם	NAME	1028c	3
5	1	אשר	PARTICLE OF RE-LATION	82d	6 c
		בית	HOUSE	110a	5 dd
		נשא	LIFT	670d	1 b 6
		קינה	ELEGY	884d	
5	2	בתולה	VIRGIN	144a	
		יסף	DO AGAIN	415c	2 a
		נטש	FORSAKE	644a	1
		נפל	FALL	657b	2 b
		קום	STAND	877d	1 a
		קום	STAND	878d	1 a
		קינה	ELEGY	884b	1
5	3	אדון	LORD	11c	4 c
		מאה	HUNDRED	548a	1 a5
		עשר	TEN	796d	2 b
		שאר	REMAIN	984b	3
5	4	דרש	SEEK	205b	3 a
5	5	און	TROUBLE	20a	1
		בארשבע	BEERSHEBA	92a	
		ביתאל	BETHEL	110d	1
		ביתאל	BETHEL	110d	1
		דרש	RESORT TO	205a	1
		עבר	PASS OVER	717b	1 c
5	6	אכל	EAT	37c	3
		בית	HOUSE	110a	5 dz
		ביתאל	BETHEL	110d	1
		דרש	SEEK	205b	3 a
		יוסף	JOSEPH	415d	1 c
		כבה	QUENCH	459d	
		צלח	RUSH	852b	
5	7	הפך	TURN	245c	1 c4
		יצג	SET	*426d	
		ל	TO	511c	1 ga
		לענה	WORMWOOD	542a	
		נוח	REST	628d	B 1
		צדקה	RIGHTEOUSNESS	842a	1 a
5	8	בקר	MORNING	133d	1 a
		הפך	TURN	245c	1 c4
		חשך	GROW DARK	365a	1
		יום	DAY	398b	1
		כימה	PLEIADES	465b	
		כסיל	ORION	493a	
		מי	WATER	565c	1 c
		פנה	FACE	819a	2 7b
		צלמות	DEATH-SHADOW	853c	1
		שם	NAME	1028c	3
		שפך	POUR OUT	1049c	1 a
5	9	בלג	SMILE	114d	2
		מבצר	FORTIFICATION	131c	
		עז	STRONG	738c	
		שד	VIOLENCE	994c	2
5	10	דבר	SPEAK	180c	
		יכח	REPROVE	407a	5 b
		שנא	HATE	971c	1 a
		תמים	COMPLETE	1071b	5
		תעב	BE ABHORRED	1073b	1 b2
5	11	בית	HOUSE	108d	1 ag
		בנה	BUILD	124b	1 ab
		בר	GRAIN	141b	
		בשם	YOUR TRAMPLING	143c	
		גוית	HEWING	159b	
		חמד	DESIRE	326c	
		יין	WINE	406c	A
		כרם	VINEYARD	501d	
		נטע	PLANT	642c	1
		משאת	PORTION	673b	4 c
		יען	ON ACCOUNT OF	774d	1
		שתה	DRINK	1059b	1 a
5	12	אביון	NEEDY	2d	
		חטאת	SIN	308c	1 b
		כפר	RANSOM	497b	1
		לקח	TAKE	543b	4 f
		נטה	BEND	641a	3 g
		עצום	MIGHTY	783a	2
		פשע	TRANSGRESSION	833c	3 a
		צדיק	JUST	843a	2
		צרר	SHEW HOSTILITY TOWARD	865d	
		רב	MUCH	913a	1 b
		שער	GATE	1045a	2 a
5	13	דמם	BE SILENT	198d	1
		עת	TIME	773b	1 a
		רעה	MISERY	949a	1
		שכל	BE PRUDENT	968c	5
5	14	אל	NOT	39b	A bg
		דרש	SEEK	205c	6
		טוב	A GOOD THING	375b	4
		כאשר	AS	455b	1 b
		כן	SO	486c	2 da
		צבא	GOD OF WAR	839d	4 b
		רע	EVIL	948d	3
5	15	אהב	LOVE	13a	2
		חנן	SHOW FAVOR	336a	2 b
		טוב	A GOOD THING	375b	4
		יוסף	JOSEPH	415d	1 c
		יצג	SET	426d	
		צבא	GOD OF WAR	839d	4 b
		רע	EVIL	948d	3
		שארית	REST	984d	1
		שער	GATE	1045a	2a
5	16	אבל	MOURNING	5d	
		אדון	LORD	11d	6 a
		אכר	PLOUGHMAN	38d	
		הו	AH 0	214c	
		הוי	AH	*222d	
		הוי	AH	*222d	
		חוץ	THE OUTSIDE	300b	2 a
		ידע	KNOW	394b	4 b
		נהי	WAILING	624d	
		מספד	WAILING	704d	2
		צבא	GOD OF WAR	839d	4 b
		קרא	CALL	895d	5 c
		רחוב	PLAZA	932b	
5	17	מספד	WAILING	704d	2

Ch	v.	Heb	Eng	Page	Sec
5	18	עבר	PASS OVER	717c	3 a
		אוה	DESIRE	16b	
		הוי	AH	223a	
		חשך	DARKNESS	365a	3 b
		יום	DAY	399a	3
		מה	HOW	554a	4 d
5	19	ארי	LION	71d	
		דב	BEAR	179a	
		דב	BEAR	*179a	
		כאשר	AS	455c	1 d
		נחש	SERPENT	638a	1 a
		נשך	BITE	675a	
		סמך	LEAN	701d	1 a
		פגע	MEET	803b	1
		קיר	WALL	885a	1 a
5	20	אפלה	DARKNESS	66c	1
		אפל	GLOOMY	66c	
		חשך	DARKNESS	365a	3 b
		יום	DAY	399a	3
		נגה	BRIGHTNESS	618b	
5	21	חג	FESTIVAL-GATHERING	291a	1 b1
		מאס	REJECT	549c	2
		עצרה	ASSEMBLY	783d	1
		ריח	SMELL	926b	
		שנא	HATE	971c	2
5	22	כיאם	FOR IF	474d	1 b
		מנחה	OFFERING	585b	3
		מנחה	OFFERING	585b	4
		מריא	FATLING	597b	
		נבט	LOOK	613d	3
		עלה	WHOLE BURNT OFFERING	750d	
		רצה	BE PLEASED WITH	953b	2
		שלם	PEACE-OFFERING	1023c	
5	23	המון	SOUND	242c	1
		זמרה	MELODY	274b	1
		נבל	HARP	614c	
		סור	TURN ASIDE	694b	1
		על	UPON	758d	4 2b
		שיר	SONG	1010b	1
5	24	איתן	EVER-FLOWING	450d	1
		נחל	TORRENT	636a	1
5	25	ה	INTERROG PART	209d	1 b
		זבח	SACRIFICE	257c	1 1
		זבח	SACRIFICE	258a	27
		מנחה	OFFERING	585b	4
		מנחה	OFFERING	585c	6
		נגש	APPROACH	621b	
		ארבעים	FORTY	917b	1 a
5	26	כוכב	STAR	456d	
		כיון	KIYYUN	475d	
		ל	TO	515d	5 ia
		מלך	KING	573b	3
		נשא	LIFT	671a	2 a
		סכות	SIKKUTH	696d	
		צלם	IMAGE	853d	1
5	27	דמשק	DAMASCUS	199d	
		הלאה	OUT THERE	229b	A
		מן	FROM	578d	1 c
		צבא	GOD OF WAR	839c	4 b
		שם	NAME	1028c	3
6	1	אחרית	END	31b	2
		בטח	TRUST	105a	13c
		הוי	AH	223a	
		ל	TO	511c	1 gb
		נקב	PIERCE	666b	2
		ראשית	BEGINNING	912b	2
		שאנן	AT EASE	983c	3
		שמרון	SAMARIA	1038a	
6	2	גבול	BORDER	147d	1 a
		גבול	BOUNDARY	148a	2 b
		חמת	HAMATH	333a	
		טוב	PLEASANT	374c	6
		גת	GATH	387d	
		ירד	GO DOWN	433a	1 d
		כלנה	CALNEH	484c	
		ממלכה	KINGDOM	575b	1
		עבר	PASS OVER	717b	1 c
		רע	EVIL	948d	1
6	3	חמס	VIOLENCE	329c	
		שבת	SEAT	443d	
		ל	TO	512a	3 b
		נגש	APPROACH	621b	
		נדה	PUT AWAY	622d	
6	4	כר	LAMB	503a	
		מטה	COUCH	642a	
		סרח	GO FREE	710a	1
		עגל	CALF	722a	
		ערש	COUCH	793a	
		צאן	SMALL CATTLE	838b	1
		מרבק	STALL	918d	
		שן	IVORY	1042b	2
6	5	חשב	THINK	363a	15
		כלי	INSTRUMENT	479d	2 b
		ל	TO	515d	5 ia
		נבל	HARP	614c	
		פה	MOUTH	805b	2 e
		פה	MOUTH	805d	6 d1 b
		פרט	IMPROVISE	827c	
		שיר	SONG	1010c	3
6	6	ב	IN	89d	3 2a
		מזרק	BOWL	284d	1
		חלה	BE WEAK	*317d	2
		חלה	BE WEAK	317d	2
		יוסף	JOSEPH	415d	1 c
		משח	ANOINT	603a	1
		על	UPON	754b	2 1f b
		ראשית	BEGINNING	912b	2
		ריק	MAKE EMPTY	938a	
		שבר	BREAKING	991a	1
		שמן	OIL	1032b	2 c
		שתה	DRINK	1059b	1 a
		ב	WITH	*1083d	3
6	7	סור	TURN ASIDE	694a	4
		סרח	A TURNING ASIDE	*694c	3
		סרח	GO FREE	710b	1
		עתה	NOW	774a	1 b
		ציון	ZION	851b	
		ראש	HEAD	911b	4 a
		מרוח	CRY	931a	2
6	8	אדון	LORD	11d	4 c
		ארמון	CITADEL	74d	
		גאון	EXALTATION	144d	1 a
		מלא	THAT WHICH FILLS	571b	3
		נאם	UTTERANCE	610b	2
		סגר	DELIVER UP	689c	1
		צבא	GOD OF WAR	839c	4 b
		שנא	HATE	971c	2
		שבע	SWEAR	989c	2
		תאב	LOATHE	*1060b	
		תעב	BE ABHORRED	*1073b	1 b
6	9	יתר	BE LEFT OVER	451b	
6	10	אפס	NON-EXISTENCE	67b	2 b
		דוד	UNCLE	187c	2
		חם	HUSH	245a	
		זכר	REMEMBER	270d	3 a
		יצא	BRING OUT	425a	4 a
		ירכה	EXTREME PARTS	438a	2
		לא	NOT	518d	1 ab
		נשא	LIFT	670a	1 a
		עוד	STILL	729b	1 c
		עצם	BONE	782d	1 f
		שרף	BURN	977a	
6	11	בקע	FISSURE	132c	
		נכה	SMITE	646c	4 c
		צוה	CHARGE	846a	5
		קטן	SMALL	882b	1 b
		רסיס	FRAGMENT	944a	
6	12	בקר	CATTLE	*133c	2
		בקר	CATTLE	133c	2
		הפך	TURN	245c	1 c4
		חרש	CUT IN	360c	2
		ים	SEA	411a	5
		לענה	WORMWOOD	542a	
		סוס	HORSE	692d	2
		סלע	CRAG	701a	1
		פרי	FRUIT	826c	3
		צדקה	RIGHTEOUSNESS	842a	1 a
		ראש	VENOM	912c	1
		רוץ	RUN	930b	1
6	13	חזק	STRENGTH	305d	2
		ל	TO	515d	5 ia
		לא	NOT	519d	2 d
		לא	NOT	520c	4 e
		לאדבר	LO-DEBAR	520d	
		עשתרות	ASHTAROTH	800b	
		קרן	HORN	902a	5
		קרנים	KARNAIM	902b	
		שמח	JOYFUL	970d	2
6	14	בוא	COME	98d	2 e
		חמת	HAMATH	333a	
		לחץ	OPPRESS	537d	5 a
		מן	FROM	581d	5 a
		נאם	UTTERANCE	610b	2
		נחל	WADY	636c	2
		ערבה	DESERT-PLAIN	787c	1 a
		צבא	GOD OF WAR	839c	4 a
		קום	STAND	879a	4
7	1	אדון	LORD	11d	4 c
		גבי	LOCUSTS	146d	
		גז	MOWING	159c	
		הנה	BEHOLD	244b	C
		תחלה	BEGINNING	321b	
		יצר	FORM	427d	2 a
		לקש	SPRING-CROP	545b	
		מלך	KING	573c	5 d
		עלה	GO UP	748d	4
		ראה	TO SEE	908a	
7	2	ראה	TO SEE	908d	1 a2
		אדון	LORD	11c	4 a
		אם	IF	50c	1 b4 a
		היה	COME TO PASS	225a	1 2a 2
		קום	STAND	278b	7 a
		כלה	FINISH	478b	1
		מה	WHAT	*552b	1 a
		מי	WHO	566b	
		נא	PART OF ENTREATY	609a	1
		סלח	FORGIVE	699b	
		יעקב	JACOB	785a	2
		יעשב	HERB	793b	
		קטן	SMALL	882b	2
7	3	נחם	BE SORRY	637a	2
7	4	אדון	LORD	11c	4 a
		אדון	LORD	11d	4 c
		הנה	BEHOLD	244b	C
		חלק	PORTION	324b	2 e
		קרא	CALL	895d	5 d
		ראה	TO SEE	908d	1 a2
		רב	GREAT	913c	2 a
		ריב	STRIVE	936c	3
7	5	תהום	DEEP	1062d	1
		אדון	LORD	11c	4 a
		קום	STAND	278b	7 a
		חדל	CEASE	293a	2
		מי	WHO	566b	
		נא	PART OF ENTREATY	609a	1
		יעקב	JACOB	785a	2
		קטן	SMALL	882b	2
7	6	אדון	LORD	11c	4 c
		הוא	HE, SHE, IT	216d	6 a
		נחם	BE SORRY	637a	2
7	7	אבן	STONE	6d	6
		אדון	LORD	11c	3 2b
		אנך	PLUMMET	59d	
		חומה	WALL	327b	1
		חומה	WALL	327c	1
		יד	HAND	390d	5 c1
		נצב	STAND	662a	1 a
		על	UPON	756b	2 6c
		ראה	TO SEE	908d	1 a2
7	8	אבן	STONE	6d	6
		אדון	LORD	11c	3 2b
		אנך	PLUMMET	59d	
		יוסף	DO AGAIN	415c	2 a
		ל	TO	515c	5 hc
		מה	WHAT	552b	2
		עבר	PASS OVER	717c	1 j
		עמוס	AMOS	770c	
		קרב	INWARD PART	899a	1 fl
		שום	TO PLACE	963a	1 a
7	9	במה	HIGH PLACE	119b	3
		חרב	BE WASTE	351c	
		על	UPON	757d	2 7d
		עמד	STAND	764c	6 c
		יצחק	ISAAC	850c	
		מקדש	SACRED PLACE	874a	1
		קום	STAND	878a	2
		ירבעם	JEROBOAM	914d	2
		שמם	BE DESOLATED	1031a	1
7	10	אמציהו	AMAZIAH	55c	4
		ביתאל	BETHEL	110d	1
		יכל	BE ABLE	407c	1
		יכל	BE ABLE	407c	1 a
		כהן	PRIEST	463b	3 b
		כול	SUSTAIN	465b	2
		עמוס	AMOS	770c	
		קרב	INWARD PART	899b	1 fl
		קשר	BIND	905b	2
		ירבעם	JEROBOAM	914d	2
7	11	עמוס	AMOS	770c	
		ירבעם	JEROBOAM	914d	2
7	12	אכל	EAT	37b	1
		אמציהו	AMAZIAH	55c	4
		ברח	FLEE	138a	2
		חזה	SEER	302d	1 b
		ל	TO	515d	5 ib
		נבא	PROPHESY	612b	1 b
		על	UPON	752d	2 1
		עמוס	AMOS	770c	
7	13	בית	HOUSE	108d	1 a
		בית	HOUSE	109a	1 ae 1
		בית	HOUSE	109c	2
		ביתאל	BETHEL	110d	1
		יוסף	DO AGAIN	415c	2 a
		מלך	KING	573c	5 d
		ממלכה	DOMINION	575b	2
		נבא	PROPHESY	612b	1 b
7	14	אמציהו	AMAZIAH	55c	4
		בלס	GATHER FIGS	118a	
		בן	SON	121c	7 a
		בוקר	HERDSMAN	133c	
		לא	NOT	519b	1 bb
		נביא	PROPHET	611d	2
		נקד	SHEEP-RAISER	*667a	
		עמוס	AMOS	770c	
		שקמה	SYCOMORE TREE	1054b	
7	15	אחר	BEHIND	30b	4 aa
		נבא	PROPHESY	612b	1 b
7	16	בית	HOUSE	110a	5 da
		נבא	PROPHESY	612b	1 b
		נטף	DRIP	643a	2
		יצחק	ISAAC	850c	
7	17	זנה	COMMIT FORNICATION	275d	1
		חבל	CORD	286d	2
		חלק	DIVIDE	324a	
		טמא	UNCLEAN	380a	3
		נפל	FALL	657b	2 a
8	1	אדון	LORD	11d	4 c
		הנה	BEHOLD	244b	C
		כלוב	BASKET	477b	
		ראה	TO SEE	908d	1 a2
8	2	יוסף	DO AGAIN	415c	2 a
		כלוב	BASKET	477b	
		עבר	PASS OVER	717c	1 j
		עמוס	AMOS	770c	
		קץ	END	893d	1
8	3	אדון	LORD	11c	4 c
		היכל	PALACE	228b	1
		חם	HUSH	245a	
		יום	DAY	400d	7 g
		ילל	HOWL	410b	
		נאם	UTTERANCE	610b	2
		פגר	CORPSE	803d	1
		מקום	STANDING PLACE	880a	4

Ch	v	Heb	Eng	Page	Sec
		שיר	SING	1010d	
		שלך	THROW	1021a	1 a
8	4	אביון	NEEDY	2d	
		זה	THIS	260c	1 a
		ל	TO	518b	7 bh
		ענו	POOR	776c	2
		עני	POOR	776d	2
		שאף	CRUSH	983d	
		שבת	CEASE	992a	2
8	5	מאזן	BALANCES	25a	
		איפה	EPHAH	35b	2
		בר	GRAIN	141b	
		גדל	BECOME GREAT	152c	1
		חדש	NEW MOON	294c	1
		מתי	WHEN	607d	A
		עבר	PASS OVER	*717d	4 d
		עות	BE BENT	736c	1 a
		פתח	OPEN	835b	
		קטן	BE SMALL	881d	
		מרמה	DECEIT	941b	
		שבר	GRAIN	991c	
		שבר	BUY GRAIN	991d	
		שבת	SABBATH	992b	1 a
		שקל	SHEKEL	1053c	
8	6	אביון	NEEDY	2d	
		בר	GRAIN	141b	
		דל	POOR	195d	
		כסף	SILVER	494d	9
		נעל	SANDAL	653a	
		מפל	REFUSE	658c	1
		עבור	FOR THE SAKE OF	721a	1 a
		שבר	BUY GRAIN	991d	
8	7	גאון	EXALTATION	145a	1 a
		נצח	EVERLASTINGNESS	664b	4
		שבע	SWEAR	989c	2
		שכח	FORGET	1013b	2 b
8	8	אבל	MOURN	5b	
		ארץ	EARTH	76a	1 b
		גרש	DRIVE OUT	176d	
		זה	THIS	262a	6 f
		יאר	STREAM	384b	1
		יאר	STREAM	384c	1
		כל	ALL	481b	1 a
		מצרים	EGYPT	695c	1 a
		עלה	GO UP	748d	5
		רגז	BE AGITATED	919a	
		שקה	GIVE TO DRINK	1052c	
		שקע	SINK	1054b	
8	9	אדון	LORD	11c	4 c
		אור	LIGHT	21c	4
		בוא	COME	99a	1 d
		חשך	GROW DARK	365a	1
		יום	DAY	400d	7 g
		נאם	UTTERANCE	610b	2
		צהר	MIDDAY	843d	1
		שמש	SUN	*1039b	1
		שמש	SUN	1039b	1
8	10	אבל	MOURNING	5c	
		הפך	TURN	245c	1 c4
		חג	FESTIVAL-GATHERING	291a	1 b1
		יחיד	ONLY ONE	402d	1
		מר	BITTER	600d	2 b
		מתנים	LOINS	608b	1 e
		עלה	GO UP	749c	4
		על	UPON	757a	2 7b
		קינה	ELEGY	884b	
		קרחה	BALD SPOT	901b	
		שק	SACK	974c	2 a
		שיר	SONG	1010b	1
8	11	אדון	LORD	11c	4 c
		דבר	WORD	183b	3 2
		הנה	BEHOLD	244b	B b
		יום	DAY	400a	7 c
		כיאם	BUT	475a	2 b
		ל	TO	515a	5 ha
		מי	WATER	565b	1 a
		נאם	UTTERANCE	610b	2
		צמא	THIRST	854d	
		רעב	FAMINE	944b	1
		שלח	SEND	1019c	
		שמע	HEAR	1033c	1 a
8	12	בקש	SEEK	135a	3 c
		מזרח	PLACE OF SUNRISE	281a	2 c5
		ים	SEA	411b	8 d
		מצא	FIND	592d	1 a
		נוע	TOTTER	631c	2
		שוט	GO ABOUT	1002a	
8	13	בחור	YOUNG MAN	104c	
		בתולה	VIRGIN	144a	
		יפה	BEAUTIFUL	421c	
		עלף	COVER	763b	
		צמא	THIRST	854d	
8	14	אלישבע	ELISHEBA	45d	
		אשמה	WRONG-DOING	80b	2
		בארשבע	BEERSHEBA	92a	
		דן	DAN	193a	3
		דרך	JOURNEY	203a	2
		חי	ALIVE	311d	1 a
		נפל	FALL	657b	2 b
		קום	STAND	877d	1 a
		שבע	SWEAR	989b	1 a
9	1	אדון	LORD	11c	3 2b
		אחרית	END	31b	D
		בצע	CUT OFF	130b	
		הרג	KILL	247b	1

Ch	v	Heb	Eng	Page	Sec
		כפתור	CAPITAL	499b	1
		ל	TO	512b	5 aa
		מלט	SLIP AWAY	572b	2
		נוס	ESCAPE	630d	2
		נכה	SMITE	645c	1
		נצב	STAND	662a	1 a
		סף	THRESHOLD	706b	
		על	UPON	756b	2 6c
		פליט	ESCAPED ONE	812c	
		ראה	TO SEE	907a	2 3
		רעש	SHAKE	950b	
9	2	אם	IF	49d	1 a1 c
		חתר	DIG	369a	1
		ירד	BRING DOWN	434a	1
		עלה	GO UP	748b	1 c
		שאול	SHEOL	983a	1
		שם	THERE	1027c	4 a
		שמי	HEAVENS	1029d	1 a
9	3	חבא	WITHDRAW	285b	
		חפש	SEARCH	344c	2 b
		כרמל	CARMEL	502a	1
		נגד	IN FRONT	617d	2 cb a
		נחש	SERPENT	638b	3
		נשך	BITE	675a	
		סתר	HIDE	711c	2
		צוה	CHARGE	846a	4 d
		קרקע	FLOOR	903a	
9	4	שם	THERE	1027c	4 a
		אם	IF	49d	1 a1 c
		הלך	WALK	231b	1 d3 ge
		הרג	KILL	247b	2
		מובה	WELFARE	375d	1
		על	UPON	757d	2 7c d
		פנה	FACE	817c	2 4c a
		צוה	CHARGE	846a	4 d
		רעה	MISERY	949b	2
		שום	TO PLACE	963d	2 c
		שבי	CAPTIVITY	985d	1
		שם	THERE	1027c	4 a
		עין	ADDENDA ET CORRIGENDA	1125d	
9	5	אבל	MOURN	5b	
		אדון	LORD	11d	6 a
		ו	AND	253d	1 k
		יאר	STREAM	384b	1
		יאר	STREAM	384c	1
		מוג	MELT	556a	1
		נגע	TOUCH	619a	1 b
		מצרים	EGYPT	695c	1 a
		עלה	GO UP	748d	5
		צבא	GOD OF WAR	839b	4 a
		שקע	SINK	*1054b	
		שקע	SINK	1054b	
9	6	אגדה	VAULT	8b	4
		בנה	BUILD	124b	1 ab
		ו	AND	253d	1 k
		יסד	FOUND	413d	
		מי	WATER	565c	1 c
		מעלה	STEP	752b	3
		שם	NAME	1028c	3
		שמי	HEAVENS	1029d	1 a
		שפך	POUR OUT	1049c	1 a
9	7	ארם	ARAM	74b	A
		בן	SON	121b	1 jt
		כושי	CUSHITE	469d	D
		כפתור	CAPHTOR	499c	
		ל	TO	513a	5 ad
		קיר	KIR	885b	2
9	8	אדון	LORD	11c	4 a
		אפס	NON-EXISTENCE	67b	2 cb
		ב	IN	*88d	1 4
		בית	HOUSE	110a	5 dg
		חמא	SINFUL	308b	1 a
		ממלכה	KINGDOM	575b	1
		פנה	FACE	819b	2 8b
		שמד	BE EXTERMINATED	1029b	1
9	9	כברה	SIEVE	460d	
		נוע	TOTTER	631b	
		נוע	WAVE	631c	1
		נפל	FALL	657a	1
		צוה	CHARGE	846a	5
		צרור	BUNDLE	865c	
		צרור	PEBBLE	866a	
9	10	בעד	ABOUT	126c	1 b
		חמא	SINFUL	308b	2
		נגש	DRAW NEAR	620d	1
		נגש	APPROACH	621b	
		קדם	COME IN FRONT	870a	1
9	11	בנה	BUILD	124d	2 a
		גדר	BUILD A WALL	154d	
		דוד	DAVID	188a	D
		הריסה	RUIN	249a	
		נפל	LIE	657d	7
		סכה	THICKET	697c	2
		עולם	LONG DURATION	762d	1 a
		פרץ	BURSTING FORTH	829d	2
		קום	STAND	878d	1 a
9	12	ירש	TAKE POSSESSION	439c	1 b
		קרא	CALL	896b	2 d4
		שארית	REST	984d	1
9	13	גבעה	HILL	149a	3
		דרך	TREAD	202a	3
		הנה	BEHOLD	244b	B b
		הר	MOUNTAIN	250c	1 i
		זרע	SOWING	*282a	1 b
		זרע	SOWING	282b	2 b

Ch	v	Heb	Eng	Page	Sec
		זרע	SOWING	282c	2 e
		חרש	CUT IN	360c	2
		יום	DAY	400a	7 c
		מוג	MELT	556b	
		משך	DRAW	604c	6
		נגש	DRAW NEAR	621a	
		נטף	DRIP	643a	1
		ענב	GRAPE	772a	
		עסיס	SWEET WINE	779b	
		קצר	HARVEST	894c	
		מוג	ADDENDA ET CORRIGENDA	1124d	
9	14	אכל	EAT	37b	1
		בנה	BUILD	124d	1 i
		גנה	GARDEN	171b	
		יין	WINE	406c	A
		נטע	PLANT	642c	1
		פרי	FRUIT	826b	1
		שבות	CAPTIVITY	986b	2 a
		שמם	BE DESOLATED	1031a	1
9	15	יהוה	YAHWEH	218d	2 1a
		נטע	PLANT	642c	2
		נתש	PLUCK UP	684c	

OBADIAH

Ch	v	Heb	Eng	Page	Sec
1		אדון	LORD	11c	4 c
		אדון	LORD	11c	4 a
		את	WITH	86d	4 c
		קום	STAND	278b	6 b
		חזון	VISION	303a	4
		עבדיהו	OBADIAH	715d	2 1
		ציר	ENVOY	851d	
		קום	STAND	878a	2
		שמועה	REPORT	1035b	1
		קטן	SMALL	882b	2
		זדון	INSOLENCE	*268a	2
		חגוים	PLACES OF CONCEALMENT	291c	
		ירד	BRING DOWN	434a	1 a
		שבת	SEAT	444a	
		לב	HEART	525b	2 6c
		לב	HEART	525c	2 7
		מי	WHO	567a	F c
		נשא	DECEIVE	674a	
		סלע	CRAG	701a	1
		מרום	HEIGHT	928d	1
		גבה	BE HIGH	147a	
		ירד	BRING DOWN	434a	1 a
		כוכב	STAR	457a	
		נשר	EAGLE	676d	
		קן	NEST	890a	1
		איך	HOW	32c	2
		בצר	CUT OFF	131a	
		גנב	THIEF	170c	
		גנב	STEAL	170c	
		די	SUFFICIENCY	191c	1
		דמה	CUT OFF	198c	1
		לא	NOT	519a	1 ae
		לילה	NIGHT	538d	1
		מסת	SUFFICIENCY	*588b	
		עוללות	GLEANING	760a	
		שאר	REMAIN	984b	1
		שדד	DEAL VIOLENTLY WITH	994b	
		בעה	INQUIRE	126d	
		חפש	SEARCH	344b	
		עשו	ESAU	796c	
		מצפון	TREASURE	861b	
		תבונה	UNDERSTANDING	108b	1
		ברית	COVENANT	136b	1 1
		גבול	BORDER	147d	1 a
		מזור	WOUND	267a	
		יכל	PREVAIL	408a	2 b
		לחם	FOOD	537a	1 a
		מזור	NET	561c	
		נשא	DECEIVE	674a	
		שום	TO PLACE	963c	1 d
		שלח	SEND	1019a	1 d
		שלום	PEACE	1023a	5 a
		אבד	DESTROY	2b	1
		תבונה	UNDERSTANDING	*108b	2
		חכם	WISE	314d	2
		עשו	ESAU	796c	
		קטל	SLAUGHTER		
		גבור	STRONG	150b	2
		חתת	BE SHATTERED	369b	2 a
		תימן	TEMAN	412d	
		כרת	BE CUT OFF	504b	1 b
		מן	OUT OF	580a	2 eb
		עשו	ESAU	796c	
		קטל	SLAUGHTER		
		בושה	SHAME	102a	
		חמס	VIOLENCE	329c	
		כסה	COVER	492a	5
		כרת	BE CUT OFF	504b	1 b
		מן	ON ACCOUNT OF	580b	2 f
		עולם	LONG DURATION	762b	b2
		יעקב	JACOB	785a	2
		גורל	LOT	174d	2 g
		זור	BE A STRANGER	266c	2 c
		ידד	CAST A LOT	391d	
		נגד	IN FRONT	617d	2 ca
		נכרי	FOREIGN	648d	1 b
		עמד	STAND	764a	1 f

MICAH

Ch	v.	Heb	Eng	Page	Sec
		פרץ	BREAK THROUGH	829b	2
		פרץ	BREAK THROUGH	829b	1
		ראש	HEAD	911a	4 a
		שער	GATE	1044c	1 a
3	1	בית	HOUSE	110a	5 dd
		ל	TO	513b	5 ba
		ל	TO	517d	7 bd
		יעקב	JACOB	785a	2
		קצין	CHIEF	892a	3
		ראש	HEAD	911a	3 a
		משפט	JUDGEMNT	1048d	2 b
3	2	אהב	LOVE	13a	2
		גזל	TEAR AWAY	159d	
		טוב	A GOOD THING	375b	4
		עור	SKIN	736a	1
		עצם	BONE	782d	1 a
		רע	EVIL	948d	3
		רעה	MISERY	949b	3
		שנא	HATE	971c	1 b
		שנא	HATE	971c	1 b
		שנא	HATE	971d	3
		שאר	FLESH	985a	1 a
3	3	בשר	FLESH	142c	1 a
		כאשר	WHEN	455c	3
		סיר	POT	696c	1 a
		עור	SKIN	736a	1
		עצם	BONE	782d	1 a
		פצח	CAUSE TO BREAK FORTH	822d	
		פרס	BREAK IN TWO	828a	
		פשט	STRIP OFF	833a	2
		שאר	FLESH	985a	1 a
3	4	אז	THEN	23a	1
		זעק	CRY	277b	2 a
		כאשר	SINCE	455c	2
		סתר	HIDE	711d	2 c
		מעלל	DEED	760b	1
		ענה	ANSWER	772d	1 b
		רע	EVIL	949a	3
		רעע	BE EVIL	949d	2
3	5	מלחמה	WAR	536c	
		נביא	PROPHET	611d	2
		נשך	BITE	675d	
		נתן	PUT	680c	2 b
		על	UPON	756b	2 7 a a
		על	UPON	757b	2 7 c ab
		קדש	BE SET APART	873b	4 c
		שלום	PEACE	1023b	6
		שן	TOOTH	1042a	1 b
		תעה	ERR	1073c	3
3	6	בוא	COME	98a	1 i
		חזון	VISION	303a	1
		חשך	GROW DARK	364d	1
		ל	TO	511a	1 e
		לילה	NIGHT	539b	2
		מן	FROM	583b	7 ba
		מן	FROM	583c	7 bb
		נביא	PROPHET	611d	2
		על	UPON	755c	2 5
		קדר	BE DARK	871a	2
		קסם	PRACTICE OF DIVI-NATION	890d	2
		שמש	SUN	*1039b	1
3	7	אלהים	GOD	44b	4 a
		בוש	BE ASHAMED	101d	3
		חזה	SEER	302d	1 a
		חפר	BE ABASHED	344a	
		עטה	WRAP ONESELF	741d	
		מענה	ANSWER	775a	
		קסם	PRACTICE OF DIVI-NATION	890d	2
		שפה	MOUSTACHE	974a	
3	8	אולם	BUT	19d	
		את	WITH	86a	1 a
		גבורה	MIGHT	150b	2
		גבורה	MIGHT	150c	3
		חטאת	SIN	308c	1 b
		כח	STRENGTH	470d	1 e
		נגד	BE CONSPICUOUS	616d	2
		יעקב	JACOB	785a	2
		פשע	TRANSGRESSION	833c	3 a
		רוח	BREATH	925d	9 a
3	9	בית	HOUSE	110a	5 dg
		בית	HOUSE	110a	5 dd
		ישר	STRAIGHT	449b	3 c1
		עקש	TWIST	786a	
		קצין	CHIEF	892d	3
		שמע	HEAR	1033d	1 f
		משפט	JUDGEMNT	1048d	2 b
		תעב	BE ABHORRED	1073b	1 b2
3	10	בנה	BUILD	124d	1 i
		דם	BLOOD	197a	2 f
		עולה	INJUSTICE	732c	1
		ציון	ZION	851b	
3	11	ירה	DIRECT	435c	5 b
		כהן	PRIEST	463d	4
		מחיר	HIRE	564b	2
		נביא	PROPHET	611d	2
		קסם	PRACTICE OF DIVI-NATION	890d	2
		שחד	BRIBE	1005a	
		שען	LEAN	1043d	
		שפט	JUDGE	1047c	2 b
3	12	במה	HIGH PLACE	119a	1
		הר	MOUNTAIN	249c	1 a
		חרש	CUT IN	360c	

Ch	v.	Heb	Eng	Page	Sec
		יער	WOOD	420d	E
		עי	RUIN	730c	
		ציון	ZION	851b	
4	1	שדה	FIELD	961d	2 a
		אחרית	END	31b	B
		גבעה	HILL	149a	3
		גוי	NATION	156d	1 c
		היה	BE	227c	3 5a
		הר	MOUNTAIN	249c	1 a
		הר	MOUNTAIN	250d	1 m
		כון	BE FIRM	465c	1 a
		נהר	FLOW	625c	
4	2	נשא	LIFT	671d	1 a
		על	UPON	757b	2 7 c ab
		אלהים	GOD	44c	4 ba
		ארח	WAY	73b	3 b
		גוי	NATION	156c	1
		דרך	WAY	204a	6 ec
		הלך	WALK	233d	1 5b
		הלך	WALK	234a	1 5f 2
		הלך	WALK	234c	2 3a 1b
		הר	MOUNTAIN	249d	1 a
		יצא	GO OUT	423c	1 g
		ירה	DIRECT	435c	5 c
		עלה	GO UP	748b	1 c
		יעקב	JACOB	785a	2
		ציון	ZION	851c	
4	3	את	PLOUGHSHARE	88c	
		גוי	NATION	156c	1
		גוי	NATION	156d	1 c
		מזמרה	PRUNING-KNIFE	275a	
		חנית	SPEAR	333d	1
		יכח	DECIDE	407a	1
		כתת	BEAT	510a	2
		מלחמה	WAR	536b	
		למד	LEARN	540d	
		נשא	LIFT	670a	1 a
		עצום	MIGHTY	783a	1
		רחק	DISTANT	935c	2 a4
		שפט	JUDGE	1047c	2 a
4	4	גפן	VINE	172c	
		דבר	SPEAK	180d	1
		חרד	TREMBLE	353c	
		תורה	INSTRUCTION	436a	1 d
		ישב	SIT	442c	1 a
		צבא	GOD OF WAR	839c	4 c
		תאנה	FIG-TREE	1061a	1
4	5	ב	IN	90a	3 2d
		יהוה	YAHWEH	218d	2 1c
		עד	PERPETUITY	723d	2 e
		עולם	LONG DURATION	762d	2 a
		שם	NAME	1028d	4
4	6	נאם	UTTERANCE	610b	2
		נדח	BANISH	623a	2
		צלע	LIMP	854b	
		קבץ	GATHER	868a	1
4	7	גוי	NATION	156d	1 b
		הלא	REMOVED FAR OFF	229c	
		הר	MOUNTAIN	249c	1 a
		מלך	BE KING	574a	
		עולם	LONG DURATION	762c	2 c
		עולם	LONG DURATION	763a	2 m
		עתה	NOW	774a	1 c
		עצום	MIGHTY	783a	1
		צלע	LIMP	854b	
		שום	TO PLACE	964b	5 a
		שארית	REST	984d	1
		הלא	ADDENDA ET COR-RIGENDA	1122b	
4	8	אתה	COME	87c	
		בת	DAUGHTER	123c	3
		בת	DAUGHTER	123c	3
		מגדל-עדר	MIGDAL-EDER	154a	
		ממלכה	DOMINION	575b	2
		ממשלה	RULE	606a	1
		עפל	MOUND	779b	
		ציון	ZION	851b	
4	9	ראשון	FIRST	911c	1 a
		אבד	PERISH	1c	1
		חיל	A WRITHING	297d	2
		חזק	BE FIRM	305a	6 a
		ילד	BEAR	408c	1 b
		יעץ	ADVISE	419d	
		כי	THAT	472d	1 f
		עתה	NOW	774a	1 c
		רוע	RAISE A SHOUT	929d	6
		רע	ROAR	929d	
4	10	בבל	BABEL	93c	
		בת	DAUGHTER	123c	3
		גאל	REDEEM	145c	3 c
		חול	WHIRL	297a	2 a
		ילד	BEAR	408c	1 b
		יצא	GO OUT	422d	1 a
		כף	POWER	496d	2
		נצל	BE DELIVERED	664c	2
		עתה	NOW	774a	1 c
		קריה	TOWN	900b	2
		שדה	FIELD	961c	1 f
		שכן	SETTLE DOWN	1015b	2 a
		שם	THERE	1027a	1 a
4	11	חזה	SEE	302b	1 c
		חנף	BE POLLUTED	338a	1
		עתה	NOW	774a	1 c
4	12	בין	DISCERN	107a	1 b
		גרן	THRESHING-FLOOR	175b	
		מחשבה	THOUGHT	364b	1 b

Ch	v.	Heb	Eng	Page	Sec
		עצה	ADVICE	420b	
		עמיר	SWATH	771c	
		קבץ	GATHER	868a	1
4	13	אדון	LORD	11a	1 2
		בת	DAUGHTER	123c	3
		בצע	GAIN MADE BY VIOLENCE	130c	
		ברזל	IRON	137c	3
		דוש	THRESH	190c	
		דקק	PULVERISE	200d	
		חיל	STRENGTH	299a	3
		חרם	BAN	356a	2
		נחושה	COPPER	639a	2
		פרסה	HOOF	828b	1
		קרן	HORN	901d	1 a
		שום	TO PLACE	964c	5 a
4	14	בת	DAUGHTER	123d	5
		גדד	PENETRATE	151c	2
		גדוד	TROOP	151b	2
		לחי	CHEEK	534d	2
		נכה	SMITE	645b	1 a
		עתה	NOW	774d	1 c
		מצור	SIEGE	848d	1
		שום	TO PLACE	963b	1 b
		שבט	ROD	987a	1 a
		שפט	JUDGE	1047c	1 b
5	1	אלף	THOUSAND	49b	2
		אפרתה	EPHRATH	68d	2
		יום	DAY	399c	5 c
		מוצאה	ORIGIN	426a	A
		ל	TO	515b	5 hb a
		מן	OUT OF	579c	2 cb
		עולם	LONG DURATION	762d	1 a
		צעיר	YOUNG	859a	1 a
		קדם	FRONT	869d	2 c
5	2	ילד	BEAR	408b	1 a
		יתר	REMAINDER	451d	1 a
		משל	RULE	605d	1 s
		נתן	GIVE	679c	1 s
		על	UPON	755c	2 4c
		שוב	TURN BACK	997b	3 b
5	3	אפס	END	67a	1
		גאון	EXALTATION	145a	1 b
		גדל	BECOME GREAT	152b	2 e
		יהוה	YAHWEH	218d	2 1e
		ישב	REMAIN	442d	2 a
		עז	STRENGTH	739a	2 c
		עתה	NOW	774a	1 c
		רעה	TEND	945a	1 c
5	4	ארמון	CITADEL	74d	
		אשור	ASSHUR	78d	2
		דרך	TREAD	202a	2
		ו	AND	252c	1 c
		זה	THIS	260c	1 a
		כי	IF	473b	2 b
		נסיך	PRINCE	651c	
		רעה	TEND	945a	1 d2
		שלום	PEACE	1023b	6
		שמנה	EIGHT	1033a	1 b
5	5	אשור	ASSYRIA	78d	3
		אשור	ASSHUR	78d	3
		גבול	BOUNDARY	148a	2 d
		דרך	TREAD	202a	2
		נמרד	NIMROD	650a	2
		קום	STAND	879a	3
		רעה	TEND	945b	2 c
5	6	את	WITH	86d	4 c
		היה	BE	227a	3 3
		טל	NIGHT-MIST	378d	
		יחל	WAIT	404a	1
		נצל	DELIVER	665a	3 a
		עשב	HERB	793b	
		פתח	OPENING	836a	
		קוה	WAIT FOR	875d	3
		קרב	INWARD PART	899b	1 f8
		שארית	REST	984d	1
5	7	אריה	LION	71d	
		בהמה	BEAST	97a	1
		היה	BE	227a	3 3
		טרף	TEAR	382d	
		יער	WOOD	420d	B
		כפיר	LION	498d	
		נצל	DELIVER	664d	3 a
		עבר	PASS OVER	717c	3 a
		עדר	FLOCK	727c	1 a
		קרב	INWARD PART	899b	1 f8
		רמס	TRAMPLE	942d	
		שארית	REST	984d	1
5	8	כרת	BE CUT OFF	504d	1 b
		רום	BE HIGH	926d	2 b
5	9	אבד	DESTROY	2b	1
		כרת	CUT OFF	504c	2 a
		נאם	UTTERANCE	610b	2
		סוס	HORSE	692c	2
5	10	מבצר	FORTIFICATION	131c	2
		הרם	THROW DOWN	248d	1
		כרת	CUT OFF	504c	3
		מרכבה	CHARIOT	939d	
5	11	כרת	CUT OFF	504c	2 c
		כשף	SORCERY	506c	1
		ענן	PRACTISE SOOTH-SAYING	778b	
5	12	כרת	CUT OFF	504d	3
		מצבה	PILLAR	663b	1 c
		מעשה	DEED	796d	2 a3
5	13	אשרה	ASHERA	81c	B

Ch	v.	Heb	Eng	Page	Sec
		אשרה	ASHERA	81c	B
		נתש	PLUCK UP	684c	
		שמד	BE EXTERMINATED	1029c	2
5	14	חמה	RAGE	404d	2 c
		נקם	VENGEANCE	668b	1
		עשה	DO	794b	12
		שמע	HEAR	1034a	1 o
6	1	את	WITH	86a	1 c
		גבעה	HILL	149a	3
		הר	MOUNTAIN	250b	1 c
		קום	STAND	877d	1 f
		ריב	STRIVE	936d	3
6	2	הר	MOUNTAIN	250b	1 c
		יכח	ARGUE	407a	
		מוסד	FOUNDATION	414c	
		איתן	ENDURING	451a	1
		ל	TO	513b	5 ba
		ריב	STRIFE	937a	3
6	3	לאה	EXHAUST	521a	
		ענה	ANSWER	773a	3 a
6	4	אהרן	AARON	14d	
		בית	HOUSE	109a	1 ae 9
		מרים	MIRIAM	599b	1
		משה	MOSES	602c	
6	5	עבד	SLAVE	713d	1
		פדה	RANSOM	804a	3 a
		אבל	ABEL	6a	1
		בלעם	BALAAM	118d	
		בלק	BALAK	119a	
		בעור	BEOR	129d	1
		זכר	REMEMBER	270a	1 4 a
		יעץ	ADVISE	419c	
		מה	WHAT	552d	1 b
		צדקה	RIGHTEOUSNESS	842c	7 a
		שטים	SHITTIM	1008a	1
6	6	אלהים	GOD	44c	4 bb
		ב	IN	89c	3 1b
		בן	SON	122a	9 b
		כפף	BOW	496a	
		מה	HOW	553d	4 a
		עגל	CALF	722b	
		עלה	WHOLE BURNT OF-FERING	750c	
		קדם	COME IN FRONT	870a	1 b
		מרום	HEIGHT	928d	2
6	7	איל	RAM	18a	2 g
		אלף	THOUSAND	48d	1 a
		בטן	WOMB	106a	3
		חטאת	SIN	308c	1 b
		נחל	TORRENT	636b	1
		פשע	TRANSGRESSION	833d	6
		רבבה	MULTITUDE	914b	
		רצה	BE PLEASED WITH	953b	2
		שמן	OIL	1032c	2j
6	8	אהב	LOVE	13a	2
		אלהים	GOD	44d	4 c
		דרש	SEEK	205c	5
		הלך	WALK	234d	2 3b
		חסד	GOODNESS	338d	1 2
		טוב	PLEASANT	374d	0
		כיאם	EXCEPT	475a	2
		ל	TO	*517d	7 bc
		מה	WHAT	552d	1 b
		נגד	BE CONSPICUOUS	616d	1
		עם	WITH	767d	1 d
		צנע	BE MODEST	857a	
		משפט	JUDGMENT	1048d	2 b
6	9	יעד	APPOINT	416d	
		תושיה	SOUND WISDOM	444d	B
		מטה	STAFF	641c	1
		מטה	TRIBE	641d	3
		קול	VOICE	877a	1 b
		ראה	TO SEE	908b	8 c
6	10	איפה	EPHAH	35c	2
		אוצר	TREASURE	70a	2
		אש	IS	78a	
		זעם	BE INDIGNANT	276d	2
		נשה	FORGET	674c	
		עוד	STILL	728d	1 aa
		רזון	LEANNESS	931a	3
		רשע	WICKED	957b	1
		רשע	WICKEDNESS	957c	1
6	11	אבן	STONE	6d	5
		מאזן	BALANCES	25a	
		זכה	BE CLEAR	269a	2
		כיס	BAG	476a	A
		מרמה	DECEIT	941b	
		רשע	WICKEDNESS	957c	1
6	12	חמס	VIOLENCE	329c	
		לשון	TONGUE	546c	1 b
		מלא	BE FULL	570a	1 b
		עשיר	RICH	799c	
		עשיר	RICH	799c	
		פה	MOUTH	805a	2 a
		רמיה	DECEIT	941a	
		שקר	DECEPTION	1055c	3
6	13	גם	ALSO	169d	4
		חטאת	SIN	308a	1 b
		חלה	BE WEAK	318a	1
		שמם	BE DESOLATED	1031b	1
6	14	ישח	EMPTINESS	445a	
		סוג	REMOVE	691a	2
		פלט	ESCAPE	812b	1
6	15	דרך	TREAD	202a	3
		זית	OLIVE TREE	268d	2
		זרע	SOW	281c	1 a
		תירוש	NEW WINE	440d	
		סוך	ANOINT	692a	1
		קצר	HARVEST	894c	
		שמן	OIL	1032b	2 c
6	16	אחאב	AHAB	26c	1
		בית	HOUSE	110a	5 c
		חקה	SOMETHING PRE-SCRIBED	350a	2 b
		חקה	SOMETHING PRE-SCRIBED	350b	2 e
		חרפה	REPROACH	357d	1
		מועצה	PLAN	420b	
		עמרי	OMRI	771d	1
		מען	PURPOSE	775d	2 1
		מעשה	DEED	795c	1 a2
		שמה	APPALMENT	1031c	2
		שמר	KEEP	1037c	
		שרקה	HISSING	1057a	
7	1	אוה	DESIRE	16a	
		אללי	ALAS	47d	
		אסף	GATHERING	63a	
		אשכל	CLUSTER	79a	1
		בכורה	FIRST RIPE FIG	114c	
		בציר	VINTAGE	131b	
		נפש	SOUL	660d	6 a
		עוללות	GLEANING	760a	
		קיץ	SUMMER	884d	
7	2	אבד	PERISH	1c	1
		אין	NOT	34c	2 c
		איש	MAN	36b	
		ארב	LIE IN WAIT	70b	
		דם	BLOOD	197a	2 f
		חסיד	KIND	339d	2 b
		חרם	NET	357a	
		ישר	STRAIGHT	449a	3 b
		צוד	HUNT	844c	
7	3	גדול	GREAT	153b	6 b
		דבר	SPEAK	180c	
		חוה	DESIRE	217d	1
		יטב	DO WELL	405d	3
		כף	HOLLOW OF THE HAND	496d	1 d7
		עבת	WIND	721b	
		רע	EVIL	948d	3
		שר	CHIEFTAIN	978b	2 b
		שאל	ASK	981c	1 a
		שלום	REQUITAL	1024b	2
7	4	מבוכה	CONFUSION	100d	
		היה	BECOME	225c	2 1a
		חדק	BRIER	293b	
		טוב	PLEASANT	374d	0 a
		ישר	STRAIGHT	449b	3 c2
		מן	THAN	582d	6 c
		מסוכה	HEDGE	692b	
		עתה	NOW	774a	1 b
		פקדה	OVERSIGHT	824a	1 a
		צפה	KEEP WATCH	859d	
7	5	אלוף	TAME	48d	2
		אמן	CONFIRM	53b	2 c
		בטח	TRUST	105a	1 3b
		חיק	BOSOM	300d	3 a
		פה	MOUTH	805a	2 a
		פתח	OPENING	836a	
		רע	FRIEND	946a	1
		שכב	LIE DOWN	1012b	1 e
		שמר	KEEP	1036c	1 b
7	6	חמות	HUSBAND:S MOTHER	327b	
		כלה	DAUGHTER-IN-LAW	483c	1
		נבל	BE SENSELESS	614c	
		קום	STAND	878a	2
		קום	STAND	878a	2
7	7	אלהים	GOD	44c	4 bb
		אלהים	GOD	44d	4 c
		יחל	WAIT	404a	
		ישע	DELIVERANCE	447a	2
		צפה	KEEP WATCH	859c	
		שמע	HEAR	1034b	2 h
7	8	אור	LIGHT	21d	1
		איב	BE HOSTILE TO	33c	
		חשך	DARKNESS	365a	3 a
		כי	THOUGH	473c	2 cb
		נפל	FALL	657b	2 c
		שמח	REJOICE	970b	1
7	9	זעף	STORMING	277a	1
		חמא	MISS A GOAL OR WAY	307a	2 b
		יצא	BRING OUT	425b	5
		ל	TO	511b	1 ga
		צדקה	RIGHTEOUSNESS	842b	2
		ראה	TO SEE	908a	8 a5
		ריב	STRIVE	936c	3
		ריב	STRIFE	937a	3
		משפט	JUDGMENT	1048c	1 f
7	10	אי	WHERE	32b	1 a
		איב	BE HOSTILE TO	33c	
		בושה	SHAME	102a	
		יהוה	YAHWEH	219a	2 1g
		חוץ	THE OUTSIDE	300b	2 a
		טיט	MUD	376c	1
		כסה	COVER	492a	5
		עתה	NOW	774a	1 b
		ראה	TO SEE	908a	8 a6
		מרמס	TRAMPLING-PLACE	942d	2
7	11	בנה	BUILD	124d	1 i
		גדר	WALL	155a	
		ה	THE	*209b	2 b
		חק	SOMETHING PRE-SCRIBED	349c	5
		חקה	SOMETHING PRE-SCRIBED	350b	2 e
		רחק	BE DISTANT	935a	
7	12	אשור	ASSYRIA	78d	3
		ים	SEA	411b	8 d
		מן	FROM	583d	9 b
		מן	FROM	583d	9 b1
		מצור	EGYPT	596a	
		נהר	STREAM	625d	1
		עיר	CITY	746b	1 a
7	13	מן	ON ACCOUNT OF	580b	2 f
		על	UPON	753d	2 1d
		פרי	FRUIT	826c	3
7	14	בד	ISOLATION	95a	
		בשן	BASHAN	143c	
		יום	DAY	399c	5 c
		יער	WOOD	420d	D
		כרמל	CARMEL	502a	1
		כרמל	GARDEN	502a	1 e
		נחלה	PROPERTY	635b	1 e
		עולם	LONG DURATION	762d	1 a
		צאן	SMALL CATTLE	838c	3
		רעה	TEND	944d	1 b
		רעה	TEND	945b	1 c
		שבט	ROD	987a	1 c
		שכן	SETTLE DOWN	1015a	1 a
7	15	יום	DAY	400b	7 d2 g
		פלא	BE SURPASSING	810d	4
7	16	אזן	EAR	24b	3
		בוש	BE ASHAMED	101d	1
		גבורה	MIGHT	150b	1
		חרש	BE SILENT	361a	2
		יד	HAND	389c	1 d
		פה	MOUTH	804d	1 b
		שום	TO PLACE	963b	1 b
7	17	אל	TO	39d	1
		יהוה	YAHWEH	218d	2 1c
		זחל	SHRINK BACK	267b	
		חרג	QUAKE	*353a	
		ירא	FEAR	431b	1 c
		לחך	LICK UP	535b	
		מן	OUT OF	579a	2 aa
		נחש	SERPENT	638b	1 c
		מסרת	FASTNESS	689d	
		עפר	DRY EARTH	779d	1 a
		עפר	DRY EARTH	780a	2 c
		פחד	DREAD	808b	1
		רגז	BE AGITATED	919b	
7	18	אל	GOD	42d	6 d
		חזק	BE FIRM	305b	6 d
		חסד	GOODNESS	339a	2
		חפץ	DELIGHT IN	342d	2 a
		נחלה	PROPERTY	635b	1 e
		נשא	LIFT	671c	3 c
		עבר	PASS OVER	717c	1 j
		עד	PERPETUITY	723d	2 d
		עון	INIQUITY	731a	1 c2
		על	UPON	756a	2 6a
		פשע	TRANSGRESSION	833c	3 d
		שארית	REST	984d	1
7	19	חטאת	SIN	309a	1 d2
		כבש	SUBDUE	461b	3
		מצולה	DEPTH	846d	
		רחם	LOVE	933c	1
		שוב	TURN BACK	998c	8
		שלך	THROW	1021b	2 b
7	20	אמת	FIRMNESS	54a	3 b
		חסד	GOODNESS	339a	2 1e
		חסד	GOODNESS	339b	2 2
		יום	DAY	399c	5 c
		קדם	FRONT	869d	2 b
		שבע	SWEAR	989c	1
7	33	שפט	JUDGE	1047c	2 b

NAHUM

Ch	v.	Heb	Eng	Page	Sec
1	1	אלקשי	ELKOSHITE	49b	
		חזון	VISION	303a	4
		נחום	NAHUM	637b	
		נינוה	NINEVEH	644b	
		משא	UTTERANCE	672d	
		ספר	MISSIVE	707b	3 a
1	2	איב	BE HOSTILE TO	33c	
		אל	GOD	42d	6 d
		בעל	LORD	127c	1 5a
		חמה	RAGE	404d	2 c
		נצר	KEEP	643c	1
		נקם	AVENGE	668a	1 a
		צר	ADVERSARY	865d	
		קנא	JEALOUS	888d	
		שם	NAME	*1028c	3
1	3	אבק	DUST	7c	
		ארך	LONG	74a	
		גדול	GREAT	153b	8
		דרך	WAY	203a	1
		כח	STRENGTH	471a	3
		נקה	BE CLEAN	667c	2
		סופה	STORM-WIND	693a	
		ענן	CLOUD	778a	1 a
		רגל	FOOT	919d	1 b
		שערה	TEMPEST	973b	

Ch v.	Heb	Eng	Page	Sec
1 4	אמל	BE WEAK	51b	
	בשן	BASHAN	143c	
	גער	REBUKE	172a	2
	חרב	BE DRY	351b	
	יבש	BE DRY	386c	
	כרמל	CARMEL	502b	1
	לבנון	LEBANON	*527a	
	לבנון	LEBANON	527b	
	פרח	BUD	827b	
1 5	גבעה	HILL	149a	3
	הר	MOUNTAIN	250a	1 c
	תבל	WORLD	385d	
	מדד	MEASURE	*551b	2 ea
	מן	OUT OF	580a	2 ea
	נשא	LIFT	671a	1 b 1
	פנה	FACE	818c	2 6b
	רעש	SHAKE	950b	
	שאה	MAKE A DIN	980d	
1 6	אש	FIRE	77d	5
	זעם	INDIGNATION	276d	
	קום	STAND	278b	7 a
	חרון	BURNING OF ANGER	354c	
	חמה	RAGE	404d	2 c
	חמה	RAGE	*405a	2 c
	מי	WHO	567a	F c
	מן	OUT OF	580a	2 ea
	נתך	POUR FORTH	677d	
	פנה	FACE	817b	2 4b d
	צור	ROCK	849c	1 a
1 7	חסה	SEEK REFUGE	340b	
	טוב	PLEASANT	374d	9 b
	ידע	KNOW	394b	2
	ל	TO	512c	4 a
	מעוז	PLACE OF SAFETY	732a	2 a
	צרה	DISTRESS	865b	
1 8	איב	BE HOSTILE TO	33c	
	חשך	DARKNESS	365a	3 b
	כלה	COMPLETE	478d	2 a
	עבר	PASS OVER	717b	1 e
	עשה	DO	794c	2 1g
	מקום	STANDING PLACE	880c	7 b
	רדף	PURSUE	923a	
	שטף	FLOOD	1009b	
1 9	אל	TO	40b	4
	חשב	THINK	363c	2
	כלה	COMPLETE	478d	2 a
	קום	STAND	878a	4
1 10	אכל	EAT	37d	
	יבש	DRY	386d	2
	כי	THOUGH	473c	2 cb
	מלא	FULL	571a	
	סבא	DRINK LARGELY	685a	
	סבא	LIQUOR	685a	
	סבך	INTERWEAVE	687c	
	סיר	THORN	696c	1
	עד	AS FAR AS	724d	1 3
	בליעל	WORTHLESSNESS	116b	3
1 11	חשב	THINK	363a	1 2
	יעץ	ADVISE	419c	
	יצא	GO OUT	423c	1 h
	מן	OUT OF	579c	2 cb
1 12	גזז	SHEAR	159c	
	כן	SO	486d	2 db
	עבר	PASS OVER	718b	6 c
	ענה	BE BOWED DOWN	776b	3
	שלם	COMPLETE	1024a	1 a
1 13	מוסר	BAND	64c	
	מוט	BAR OF YOKE	557b	3
	נתק	TEAR APART	683d	1
1 14	אלהים	GOD	44d	4 c
	זרע	SOW	281d	1 b
	כרת	CUT OFF	504d	3
	מן	OUT OF	579c	2 cb
	מסכה	MOLTEN IMAGE	651b	2
	פסל	IDOL	820d	
	צוה	COMMAND	845d	1 e
	שום	TO PLACE	964d	5 b
	שם	NAME	1028b	2 c
2 1	בליעל	WORTHLESSNESS	116b	3
	בשר	BEAR TIDINGS	142b	3
	חגג	MAKE PILGRIMAGE	290d	1
	חגג	MAKE PILGRIMAGE	290d	1
	חג	FESTIVAL-GATHERING	291a	1 b1
	חג	FESTIVAL-GATHERING	291b	1 b
	יסף	DO AGAIN	415c	2 a
	כל	ALL	481b	1 a
	כרת	BE CUT OFF	504a	1 b
	נדר	VOW	624a	2
	שמע	HEAR	1034c	1 a
2 2	אמץ	BE STRONG	55a	1
	חזק	BE FIRM	304c	1 a
	כח	STRENGTH	470d	1 c
	מתנים	LOINS	608b	2 a
	מפיץ	SCATTERER	807b	
	פנה	FACE	819a	27a e
	מצורה	SIEGE-WORKS	849a	2
	צפה	KEEP WATCH	859c	
2 3	בקק	EMPTY	132d	
	גאון	EXALTATION	145a	1
	גאון	EXALTATION	145a	1 a
	זמורה	BRANCH	274d	
	קבב	CURSE	*866d	
	שוב	TURN BACK	998c	9
	שחת	GO TO RUIN	1008a	1
2 4	אדם	BE RED	10a	
	ברוש	CYPRESS	141c	2
	ברוש	CYPRESS	*141c	1
	גבור	STRONG	150b	2
	מגן	SHIELD	171c	
	חיל	STRENGTH	298d	1 c
	כון	ESTABLISH	466c	2 a
	פלדה	IRON	811c	
	רכב	CHARIOT	939a	1
	רעל	QUIVER	947a	
	תלע	CLAD IN SCARLET	1069a	
2 5	ברק	LIGHTNING	140c	1
	הלל	PRAISE	239b	
	לפיד	TORCH	542b	
	רחוב	PLAZA	932b	
	רכב	CHARIOT	939a	1
	שקק	RUN	1055b	
2 6	אדיר	MAJESTIC	12b	2
	הליכה	A GOING	237b	1 a
	זכר	REMEMBER	269d	12 b
	חומה	WALL	327b	1
	כון	BE ESTABLISHED	466d	1
	כשל	STUMBLE	505d	1
	מהר	HASTEN	555a	1
	סכך	PROTECTOR	697d	
2 7	היכל	PALACE	228b	1
	לבב	HEART	523b	2 1
	מוג	MELT	556a	
	נהר	STREAM	625d	1
	פתח	OPEN	835c	
2 8	אמה	MAID	51a	1
	יונה	DOVE	401d	
	נהג	MOAN	624c	
	נצב	STAND	662c	
	עלה	GO UP	750a	1
	קול	VOICE	877a	1 e
	תפף	SOUND THE TIMBREL	1074a	
2 9	ברכה	POOL	140a	
	הוא	HE, SHE, IT	216b	3 d
	מן	FROM	581b	4 a
	נינוה	NINEVEH	644b	
	עמד	STAND	764a	2 a
	פנה	TURN	815c	2
2 10	בזז	SPOIL	102d	
	חמדה	DESIRE	326d	
	כבוד	RICHES	458c	1
	תכונה	ARRANGEMENT	467d	2
	כלי	ARTICLE	479c	1
	קצה	END	892c	
2 11	מבוקה	VOID	101c	
	בוקה	EMPTINESS	101c	
	בלק	WASTE	118d	
	בלק	WASTE	118d	
	ברך	KNEE	139c	
	חלחלה	ANGUISH	298b	
	לב	HEART	525c	29 b
	מסס	MELT	587d	1
	מתנים	LOINS	608b	2 b
	פארור	GLOW	802d	
	פיק	TOTTERING	807c	
	פנה	FACE	815d	1 a
	קבץ	GATHER	868a	3
2 12	ארי	LION	71d	
	אריה	LION	71d	
	גור	WHELP	158d	1
	הלך	WALK	232a	1 2
	חרד	TREMBLE	353c	
	כפיר	LION	498d	
	לביא	LION	522d	
	מעון	REFUGE	732d	1
	מרעה	PASTURAGE	945c	
2 13	אריה	LION	71d	
	גור	WHELP	158d	
	די	SUFFICIENCY	191c	2 aa
	חנק	STRANGLE	338b	
	חר	HOLE	359d	
	טרף	TEAR	383a	
	טרפה	ANIMAL TORN	383c	1
	טרף	PREY	383c	1
	לבי	LION	522d	
	מלא	FILL	570c	1
	מענה	DEN	733a	1
2 14	אל	TO	40b	4
	בער	BURN	129c	2
	גור	WHELP	*158d	
	חרב	SWORD	352d	1 g
	טרף	PREY	383c	1
	כפיר	LION	498d	
	כרת	CUT OFF	504c	2 c
	מלאך	MESSENGER	521c	1 a
	נאם	UTTERANCE	610b	2
	עשן	SMOKE	798c	1 a
	צבא	GOD OF WAR	839c	4 c
	רכב	CHARIOT	939a	1
3 1	דם	BLOOD	197a	2 h
	טרף	PREY	383c	1
	כחש	LYING	471c	1
	כל	ALL	482c	
	מוש	REMOVE	559b	
	מלא	FULL	571a	
	עיר	CITY	746c	1 i
	פרק	PLUNDER	830a	2
3 2	אופן	WHEEL	66d	A
	דהר	RUSH	187b	
	סוס	HORSE	692c	1
	קול	VOICE	877b	2 e
	קול	VOICE	877b	2 e
	מרכבה	CHARIOT	939d	
	רעש	SHAKING	950c	1
	שוט	WHIP	1002a	2
3 3	ברק	LIGHTNING	140c	2
	גויה	CORPSE	156c	2 a
	חנית	SPEAR	333d	1
	חנית	SPEAR	334a	2 b
	חרב	SWORD	352d	1 j
	כבד	MASS	458c	2
	כשל	STUMBLE	505c	1
	להב	BLADE	529b	2
	עלה	GO UP	749c	3
	פגר	CORPSE	803d	1
	פרש	HORSEMAN	832b	
	קצה	END	892c	
3 4	בעלה	MISTRESS	128b	2
	זנה	COMMIT FORNICATION	275d	2
	זנונים	FORNICATION	276a	B
	חן	FAVOR	336b	1 a
	טוב	PLEASANT	373c	1 a
	כשף	SORCERY	506c	2
	מכר	SELL	569b	
3 5	אל	TO	40b	4
	ממלכה	KINGDOM	575b	1
	נאם	UTTERANCE	610b	2
	מערה	BARE PLACE	789b	2
	פנה	FACE	818d	27a a
	צבא	GOD OF WAR	839c	4 c
	קלון	DISHONOUR	886a	1
	ראה	TO SEE	908d	
	שול	SKIRT	1002c	
3 6	גבל	BE SENSELESS	614d	
	ראי	LOOKING	909b	3
	שום	TO PLACE	964a	3 e
	שלך	THROW	1021a	1 a
	שקוץ	DETESTED THING	1055a	
3 7	אין	WHENCE	32d	
	בקש	SEEK	134d	1 d
	גור	DREAD	*159a	1
	היה	COME TO PASS	225a	12b ag
	נדד	RETREAT	622b	1
	נוד	SHEW GRIEF	626d	2 a
	נחם	CONSOLE ONESELF	637a	
	נינוה	NINEVEH	644b	
	שדד	DEAL VIOLENTLY WITH	994b	
3 8	אמון	AMON	51b	
	חל	RAMPART	298a	1
	חומה	WALL	327b	1
	חומה	WALL	327d	3
	יאר	STREAM	384c	
	יטב	BE WELL	405c	2
	ים	SEA	411a	6
	ישב	SIT	442c	1 a
	מף	MEMPHIS	*592a	
	נא	THEBES	609d	
	סביב	ROUND ABOUT	687a	1 cb
	אמון	ADDENDA ET CORRIGENDA	*1120b	
3 9	ב	IN	89a	17 b
	כוש	CUSH	469a	2 c
	לובים	LUBIM	530c	
	עזרה	HELP	741a	2 a
	עצם	MIGHT	782c	1
	עצמה	MIGHT	782c	
	פוט	LIBYANS	806c	
	קצה	END	892c	
3 10	גדול	GREAT	153b	6 b
	גורל	LOT	174d	2 g
	הלך	WALK	231b	1 d3 ge
	זק	FETTER	279b	
	חוץ	THE OUTSIDE	300b	2 a
	ידד	CAST A LOT	391d	
	כבד	BE HONORED	457c	1 b
	עולל	CHILD	760c	
	רטש	DASH IN PIECES	936b	
	רתק	BIND	958c	
	שבי	CAPTIVITY	985d	1
3 11	איב	BE HOSTILE TO	33c	
	בקש	SEEK	134c	1 b
	מן	FROM	578b	1 a
	מעוז	PLACE OF SAFETY	732a	1 a
	עלם	CONCEAL	761a	2
	שכר	BE DRUNK	1016b	
3 12	בכורים	FIRST-FRUITS	114c	
	מבצר	FORTIFICATION	131c	
	נוע	TOTTER	631b	
	נפל	FALL	657a	
	על	UPON	756b	27a a
	עם	WITH	767b	1
	תאנה	FIG-TREE	1061a	1
3 13	אכל	EAT	37c	3
	בריח	BAR	138b	2
	בריח	BAR	138b	1 b
	פתח	OPEN	835a	
	פתח	OPEN	835c	
	שער	GATE	1045a	2 c
	מבצר	FORTIFICATION	131c	
3 14	חזק	BE FIRM	304c	1 c
	חזק	BE FIRM	305a	6 a
	חמר	CEMENT	330c	1
	טיט	MUD	376c	1

HABAKKUK

Ch v.	Heb	Eng	Page	Sec
	מלבן	BRICK-MOLD	527c	1
	מצור	SIEGE	849a	1
	רמס	TRAMPLE	942d	
	שאב	DRAW	980c	
3 15	ילק	LOCUST	410c	B
	ילק	LOCUST	410c	A
	כבד	MAKE ONESELF HEAVY	458a	1
	כרת	CUT OFF	504c	2 b
	ארבה	LOCUST	916a	
3 16	שם	THERE	1027a	1 a
	ילק	LOCUST	410c	C
	כוכב	STAR	457a	
	עוף	FLY	733c	2
	פשט	STRIP OFF	833a	1
	רכל	GO ABOUT	940b	
3 17	אי	WHERE	32b	1 a
	גוב	LOCUSTS	146d	
	גבי	LOCUSTS	146d	
	גדרה	WALL	155a	
	זרח	RISE	280b	1 a
	חנה	DECLINE	333c	2 c2
	ספר	SCRIBE	381d	
	ידע	BE MADE KNOWN	394c	1
	נדד	FLUTTER	622b	
	מנזר	CONSECRATED ONES	634d	
3 18	ארבה	LOCUST	916a	
	אדיר	MAJESTIC	12b	2
	אשור	ASSYRIA	78d	4
	הר	MOUNTAIN	250c	1 g
	נום	BE DROWSY	630b	
	פוש	BE SCATTERED	807d	
	קבץ	GATHER	868a	2
	רעה	TEND	945a	1 d2
	שכן	SETTLE DOWN	1015a	1 a
3 19	חלה	BE WEAK	*318a	1
	חלה	BE WEAK	318a	2
	כהה	DIMMING	462d	
	כף	HOLLOW OF THE HAND	496c	1 d1
	תמיד	CONTINUITY	556b	1 a
	מי	WHO	*567a	F c
	מכה	BLOW	647a	1 c
	עבר	PASS OVER	717b	1 h
	שבר	BREAKING	991a	1
	שמע	REPORT	1034d	
	תקע	CLAP	1075c	3

HABAKKUK

Ch v.	Heb	Eng	Page	Sec
1 1	חבקוק	HABAKKUK	287d	
	חזה	SEE	302c	2
	נביא	PROPHET	611d	1
	משא	UTTERANCE	672d	
1 2	אן	WHERE	33a	D
	זעק	CRY	277b	2 a
	חמס	VIOLENCE	329c	
	ישע	DELIVER	446d	1 b
	צבא	GOD OF WAR	839c	4 c
	שוע	CRY OUT	1002d	
1 3	און	TROUBLE	20a	3
	מדון	STRIFE	193b	1
	היה	BECOME	225c	2 1a
	חמס	VIOLENCE	329c	
	נבט	LOOK	613d	3
	נגד	IN FRONT	617c	2 b
	נשא	LIFT	671a	1 b 1
	עמל	TROUBLE	765d	2
	ראה	TO SEE	909a	1 b
	ריב	STRIFE	936d	1
	שד	VIOLENCE	994c	1
1 4	יצא	GO OUT	423b	1 f
	תורה	INSTRUCTION	436a	1 c
	כתר	SURROUND	509d	
	נצח	EVERLASTINGNESS	664b	4
	עקל	BEND	785c	
	פוג	GROW NUMB	806a	
	צדיק	JUST	843a	2
	רשע	WICKED	957b	2
	משפט	JUDGMENT	1048c	1 e
1 5	אמן	CONFIRM	53a	2 a
	נבט	LOOK	613d	2
	ספר	COUNT	708b	1
	פעל	DO	821b	1 a
	פעל	DOING	821c	1 a
	צבא	GOD OF WAR	839c	4 c
	תמה	BE ASTOUNDED	1069b	
	תמה	BE ASTOUNDED	1069b	
1 6	הלך	WALK	231b	1 d3 gd
	ירש	TAKE POSSESSION	439c	1 a
	כשדים	CHALDEANS	505a	1 b
	ל	TO	513d	5 cb d
	ל	TO	*516b	5 ja
	לא	NOT	519c	2 c
	מר	BITTER	600c	2 b
	קום	STAND	879a	4 b
	מרחב	ROOMY PLACE	932d	
	משכן	DWELLING-PLACE	1015d	3 a
1 7	אים	TERRIBLE	33d	
	ירא	BE FEARFUL	431d	1
	שאת	DIGNITY	673b	1
1 8	זאב	WOLF	255d	
	חדד	BE SHARP	292b	
	חוש	HASTE	301d	

Ch v.	Heb	Eng	Page	Sec
	נמר	LEOPARD	649d	
	נשר	EAGLE	676d	
	עוף	FLY	733c	1 a
	פרש	SPRING ABOUT	807d	
	פרש	HORSEMAN	832b	
1 9	קלל	BE SLIGHT	886c	2
	רחק	DISTANT	935c	2 a1
	מגמה	ASSEMBLING	169d	
	חול	SAND	297d	A
	חמס	VIOLENCE	329c	
	כל	ALL	482a	1 db
	קדים	EAST WIND	870b	1
1 10	שבי	CAPTIVITY	985d	3
	מבצר	FORTIFICATION	131c	
	עפר	DRY EARTH	779d	1 a
	צבר	HEAP UP	840d	
	קלס	MOCK	887b	
	רון	BE WEIGHTY	931b	
	שחק	LAUGH	965d	1 a
	משחק	OBJECT OF DERISION	966a	
1 11	אז	THEN	23a	1 c
	אלה	GOD	43a	1
	אשם	OFFEND	79c	2
	זה	THIS	*260d	2 a
	זו	THIS	262b	1
	חלף	PASS ON OR AWAY	322a	1 a
	כח	STRENGTH	470d	1
	ל	TO	512c	4 a
1 12	יהוה	YAHWEH	219a	2 1f
	יכח	CORRECT	407a	6
	יסד	FOUND	413d	
	מוסדה	FOUNDATION	414c	
	מן	FROM	581c	4 a
	צור	ROCK	849d	2 a
	קדם	FRONT	869d	2 c
	קדוש	HOLY	872c	1 b
	שום	TO PLACE	964a	3 d
	משפט	JUDGMENT	1048b	1 a
1 13	בגד	ACT TREACHEROUSLY	93d	D
	בלע	SWALLOW UP	118c	2 a
	חרש	BE SILENT	361b	1 b
	מהור	CLEAN	373a	3
	יכל	BE ABLE	407c	1 b
	מן	THAN	582d	6 d
	נבט	LOOK	613d	2
	עמל	TROUBLE	765d	2
	צדיק	JUST	843a	2
	ראה	TO SEE	907d	6 f
	רשע	WICKED	957b	2
1 14	דג	FISH	*185d	
	דג	FISH	185d	
	חכה	HOOK	*335d	
	לא	NOT	519b	1 bb
	משל	RULE	605d	1
	רמש	CREEPING THINGS	943a	1
1 15	אסף	GATHER	62b	1 c
	אסף	GATHER	62d	1 b
	גרר	DRAG AWAY	176a	
	חכה	HOOK	335d	
	חרם	NET	357a	
	כל	ALL	482a	1 db
	מכמרת	NET	485c	
	עלה	GO UP	749c	3
1 16	מאכל	FOOD	38b	
	ב	IN	*88a	
	בריא	FAT	135d	
	הם	THEY	241d	8 a
	זבח	SLAUGHTER FOR SACRIFICE	257b	1
	חלק	PORTION	324a	1 b
	חרם	NET	357a	
	מכמרת	NET	485c	
	קטר	MAKE SACRAFICES SMOKE	883a	
	שמן	FAT	1032a	1
1 17	הרג	KILL	247b	1 b
	חמל	SPARE	328b	
	חרם	NET	357a	
	כן	SO	487b	3 f
	ל	TO	518a	7 bg
	תמיד	CONTINUITY	556b	1 a
	ריק	MAKE EMPTY	938a	3
2 1	דבר	SPEAK	181c	4 a
	תוכחת	ARGUMENT	407b	1
	יצב	STATION ONESELF	426b	A
	מה	WHAT	552d	1 b
	מצור	SIEGE	849a	2
	צפה	KEEP WATCH	859c	
	שוב	TURN BACK	999c	3
	משמרת	GUARD	1038c	1
2 2	באר	MAKE DISTINCT	91b	
	חזון	VISION	303a	3
	לוח	TABLET	*531d	1
	לוח	TABLET	531d	1
	קרא	CALL	895c	4 b
	רוץ	RUN	930b	1
2 3	אחר	DELAY	29b	1
	חזון	VISION	303a	3
	חכה	WAIT	314a	3
	מועד	APPOINTED TIME	417c	1 a
	כזב	FAIL	469c	2
	מהה	LINGER	554c	
	עוד	STILL	729a	1 ab
	פוח	BREATHE	806b	2 d

Ch v.	Heb	Eng	Page	Sec
	קץ	END	893d	1
2 4	אמונה	FIRMNESS	53c	3 a
	חיה	LIVE	311b	1 c
	ישר	BE STRAIGHT	448a	3
	נפש	SOUL	661b	9
	עפל	SWELL	779b	
	צדיק	JUST	843a	3 a
2 5	אסף	GATHER	62b	1 a
	אף	ALSO	65a	1
	בגד	ACT TREACHEROUSLY	93d	D
	גבר	MAN	150a	
	ה	THE	207d	1 e
	חמת	WATERSKIN	*333a	
	יהיר	PROUD	397d	
	כ	LIKE	453a	1 b
	מות	DEATH	560d	3
	נוח	ABIDE	627d	
	נפש	SOUL	660c	5 c
	קבץ	GATHER	867d	2
	רחב	BE LARGE	931d	2
	שבע	SATISFIED	959b	1 a
	שאול	SHEOL	983a	1
2 6	הוי	AH	223a	
	חידה	RIDDLE	295c	1
	כבד	MAKE HEAVY	458a	1
	כל	ALL	481d	1 da
	ל	TO	513d	5 cb d
	לא	NOT	519d	2 d
	מליצה	MOCKING-POEM	539c	
	משל	PARABLE	605b	3
	מתי	WHEN	607d	C
	נשא	LIFT	670d	1 b 6
	עבמוט	WEIGHT OF PLEDGES	716b	
2 7	רבה	BECOME MANY	915c	1 c
	זוע	TREMBLE	266b	
	יקץ	AWAKE	429c	
	ל	TO	512c	4 b
	נשך	BITE	675a	
	פתע	SUDDENNESS	837b	
	קום	STAND	878a	2
	משסה	PLUNDER	1042d	
2 8	דם	BLOOD	196d	2 f
	חמס	VIOLENCE	329c	
	יתר	REMAINDER	451d	1 b
	קריה	TOWN	900b	3
	שלל	SPOIL	1021a	
	שלל	SPOIL	1021d	
2 9	בצע	GAIN BY VIOLENCE	130b	
	בצע	UNJUST GAIN	130c	
	הוי	AH	223a	
	נצל	BE DELIVERED	664c	2
	קן	NEST	890a	1
	מרום	HEIGHT	928d	1
	רע	EVIL	948c	0 d
	רע	EVIL	948d	2
2 10	בשת	SHAME	102a	1
	חטא	MISS A GOAL OR WAY	306d	1
	חטא	MISS A GOAL OR WAY	307b	3
	יעץ	ADVISE	419c	
	קצה	CUT OFF	891d	
2 11	אבן	STONE	7a	8
	זעק	CRY	277c	2 e
	כפים	RAFTER	496a	
	ענה	ANSWER	772d	1
	עץ	TREE	781d	2 b
	קיר	WALL	885a	3
2 12	בנה	BUILD	124b	1 aa
	דם	BLOOD	197a	2 f
	הוי	AH	223a	
	כון	ESTABLISH	466d	1 a
	עולה	INJUSTICE	732c	1
	קריה	TOWN	900b	4
2 13	את	WITH	86d	4 c
	די	SUFFICIENCY	191c	2 aa
	יגע	TOIL	388b	1
	יעף	BE WEARY	419b	
	לא	NOT	520c	4 bb
	לאם	PEOPLE	522c	
	צבא	GOD OF WAR	839c	4 c
	ריק	EMPTINESS	938d	
2 14	כבוד	GLORY	459a	2 c3
	כסה	COVER	492a	6
	מלא	FILL	*570b	1
	מלא	BE FULL	570c	1
2 15	אף	ALSO	65a	1
	הוי	AH	223a	
	נבט	LOOK	613d	1 a
	ספח	JOIN	705b	
	ספ	BASIN	706b	
	מעור	NAKEDNESS	735d	
	רע	FRIEND	946a	2
	שום	TO PLACE	963c	1 d
	שכר	BE DRUNK	1016b	
	שקה	GIVE TO DRINK	1052c	2
2 16	כבוד	HONOR	459a	3
	כבוד	HONOR	459a	3
	כוס	CUP	468a	
	מן	THAN	582c	6 a
	סבב	TURN ABOUT	685c	1
	על	UPON	755b	2 4a
	ערל	COUNT AS FORESKIN	790c	

Ch v.	Heb	Eng	Page	Sec
	קלון	DISHONOUR	886a	1
	קיקלון	DISGRACE	887b	
	שבע	SATISFIED	959c	3 b
2 17	שתה	DRINK	1059c	1 e
	בהמה	BEAST	97a	3
	דם	BLOOD	196d	2 f
	חמס	VIOLENCE	329c	
	חתת	BE SHATTERED	369c	2 b
	כסה	COVER	492a	5
	לבנון	LEBANON	*527a	
	לבנון	LEBANON	527b	
	מן	ON ACCOUNT OF	580b	2 f
	קריה	TOWN	900b	3
	שד	VIOLENCE	994c	2
2 18	אליל	WORTHLESSNESS	47c	B
	אלם	DUMB	48a	
	בטח	TRUST	105a	14 c
	יעל	PROFIT	418c	
	יצר	FORM	427d	1 b
	יצר	FORM	428a	2
	ירה	DIRECT	435c	5 d
	כי	THAT	472d	1 f
	מה	WHAT	552c	1 a
	מה	WHAT	553a	1 db
	מסכה	MOLTEN IMAGE	651b	2
	פסל	IDOL	820d	
	פסל	HEW	820d	
	שקר	DECEPTION	1055c	4
2 19	אבן	STONE	7a	8
	דומם	SILENCE	189b	
	הוי	AH	223a	
	זהב	GOLD	263c	1
	זהב	GOLD	263d	2 e
	ירה	DIRECT	435c	5 d
	כסף	SILVER	494b	7
	כסף	SILVER	494c	9
	עור	ROUSE ONESELF	735a	
	עץ	TREE	782a	2 c
	פסל	IDOL	*820d	
	קיץ	AWAKE	884c	4
	קרב	INWARD PART	899a	1 a
	רוח	BREATH	924c	1 a
	תפש	LAY HOLD OF	1074d	1
2 20	היכל	TEMPLE	228d	2 e
	הס	HUSH	245a	
	פנה	FACE	818c	2 6b
	קדש	APARTNESS	871c	2 a
3 1	חבקוק	HABAKKUK	287d	
	ל	TO	513c	5 bb
	נביא	PROPHET	611d	1
	תפלה	PRAYER	813c	2
	שגיון	DIRGE	993c	
3 2	זכר	REMEMBER	270b	2 3b
	חיה	LIVE	311c	1
	ידע	MAKE KNOWN	395a	
	ירא	FEAR	431b	1 b
	קרב	INWARD PART	899b	1 h
	רגז	AGITATION	919c	
	רחם	LOVE	933c	1
	שמע	REPORT	1034d	
3 3	אלה	GOD	43a	2
	הוד	SPLENDOUR	217b	2
	תהלה	PRAISE	240b	5 b
	תימן	TEMAN	412d	
	כסה	COVER	491c	1
	מלא	BE FULL	570a	1 b
	סלה	LIFT UP	*699d	
	פארן	PARAN	803a	
	קדוש	HOLY	872c	1 c
3 4	חביון	HIDING	285d	
	נגה	BRIGHTNESS	618b	
	עז	STRENGTH	739a	3 a
	קרן	HORN	902a	5
	שם	THERE	1027a	1 a
3 5	דבר	PESTILENCE	184a	1
	הלך	WALK	232c	13
	יצא	GO OUT	423b	1 g
	רגל	FOOT	919d	1
	רשף	FLAME	958b	2
3 6	גבעה	HILL	149a	3
	גבעה	HILL	149a	3
	הליכה	A GOING	237b	1 c
	הר	MOUNTAIN	250b	1 c
	מדד	MEASURE	551b	
	מוג	MELT	556b	
	נתר	START UP	684a	
	עד	PERPETUITY	723c	1
	עולם	LONG DURATION	762a	1 d
	שחה	BOW	1005d	1
	פצץ	ADDENDA ET CORRIGENDA	1126b	
3 7	אהל	TENT	14a	2
	און	TROUBLE	20a	1
	מדין	MIDIAN	193c	3
	יריעה	CURTAIN	438c	
	כושן	CUSHAN	469b	
	רגז	BE AGITATED	919a	
	תחת	UNDERNEATH	1065c	2 1cc
3 8	אם	IF	50d	2 ab a
	חרה	BURN	354a	2 a
	ישועה	VICTORY	447c	4
	עברה	OVERFLOW	720c	3 b
	רכב	RIDE	938d	2
	מרכבה	CHARIOT	939d	
3 9	אמר	WORD	57a	2
	בקע	CLEAVE	132b	

Ch v.	Heb	Eng	Page	Sec
	מטה	STAFF	641d	1
	סלה	LIFT UP	700b	
	עור	BE EXPOSED	735d	
	עריה	NAKEDNESS	789a	
	קשת	BOW	906a	1 b
	שבט	TRIBE	*987b	2 a
	שבועה	OATH	990a	2
	שבע	ADDENDA ET CORRIGENDA	1126d	
3 10	הר	MOUNTAIN	250a	1 c
	זרם	FLOOD OF RAIN	281b	
	חול	WHIRL	297a	2 b
	נשא	LIFT	670b	1 b 1
	נתן	GIVE	679d	1 x
	עבר	PASS OVER	717d	4
	קול	VOICE	877b	2 f
	רום	ON HIGH	927d	
	תהום	SEA	1063a	2
3 11	אור	LIGHT	21c	5
	ברק	LIGHTNING	140c	2
	הלך	WALK	235b	1
	זבל	ELEVATION	259c	
	חנית	SPEAR	334a	2 b
	חץ	ARROW	346c	2
	ירח	MOON	437a	
	ל	TO	516d	5 k
	נגה	BRIGHTNESS	618b	
	עמד	STAND	764a	2 a
	שמש	SUN	1039b	1
3 12	בצע	CUT OFF	*130b	
	דוש	THRESH	190c	
	זעם	INDIGNATION	276d	
	את	MARK OF THE ACCUSATIVE	85b	1 d
	יסוד	FOUNDATION	414b	1
	יצא	GO OUT	424a	2 c
	ישע	DELIVERANCE	447a	2
	מחץ	SHATTER	563c	
	משיח	ANOINTED	603c	1
	סלה	LIFT UP	700b	
	ערה	BE NAKED	788c	1
	צואר	NECK	848c	1
	רשע	WICKED	957c	2
3 14	אכל	EAT	37d	6
	כמו	LIKE	455d	1 a
	מטה	STAFF	641d	1
	נקב	PIERCE	666b	1
	סער	STORM	704a	
	מסתר	SECRET PLACE	712c	2 b
	עליצות	EXULTATION	763c	
	עני	POOR	776d	3
	פוץ	BE DISPERSED	807a	1 a
	פרו	WARRIOR	826d	
3 15	דרך	TREAD	202a	2
	חמר	FERMENT	330b	
	חמר	HEAP	330d	
	סוס	HORSE	692d	3
3 16	בטן	BELLY	105d	1 a
	גוד	ATTACK	156a	
	ל	TO	515a	5 g
	נוח	REST	628b	2
	עלה	GO UP	748c	2 c
	עצם	BONE	782d	1 c
	צלל	TINGLE	852d	2
	צרה	DISTRESS	865b	
	רגז	BE AGITATED	919b	
	רקב	ROTTENNESS	955a	
	שפה	SPEECH	973d	1 d
	תחת	UNDERNEATH	1065d	2 ia
3 17	אכל	FOOD	38a	4
	גזר	CUT	160b	5
	גפן	VINE	172c	
	זית	OLIVE TREE	268c	1
	יבול	PRODUCE	385b	
	כחש	FAIL	471b	4
	מכלה	FOLD	476c	
	עשה	DO	794d	2 2
	מעשה	DEED	796b	2 c
	פרח	BUD	827a	
	רפת	STABLE	952d	
	שדמה	FIELD	995b	
	שכח	FORGET	1013b	1 b
	תאנה	FIG-TREE	1061a	1
3 18	אלהים	GOD	44c	4 bb
	ישע	DELIVERANCE	447a	2
	עלז	EXULT	759c	
3 19	אדון	LORD	11d	5
	אילה	HIND	19b	
	במה	HIGH PLACE	119b	2 a
	דרך	TREAD	202a	3
	חיל	STRENGTH	298c	1 a
	נגינה	MUSIC	618d	1

ZEPHANIAH

Ch v.	Heb	Eng	Page	Sec
1 1	אמריהו	AMARIAH	57d	6
	יאשיהו	JOSIAH	78c	1
	גדליה	GEDALIAH	153d	2
	דבר	WORD	182c	1 2a
	חזקיהו	HEZEKIAH	306a	2
	כושי	CUSHI	469b	2
	צפניה	ZEPHANIAH	861b	2
1 2	אדמה	GROUND	9d	4
	אסף	GATHER	62c	4
	כל	ALL	482c	2 a

Ch v.	Heb	Eng	Page	Sec
	נאם	UTTERANCE	610b	2
	סוף	CEASE	692d	
1 3	אדם	MAN	9b	2
	אדמה	GROUND	9d	4
	בהמה	BEAST	97a	1
	דג	FISH	185c	
	כרת	CUT OFF	504c	2 c
	מכשלה	RUIN	506b	2
	נאם	UTTERANCE	610b	2
	סוף	CEASE	692d	
1 4	רשע	WICKED	957c	3
	בעל	BAAL	127d	2 2
	כהן	PRIEST	463a	2
	כמר	PRIEST	485c	
	כרת	CUT OFF	504d	3
	נטה	EXTEND	640a	1 a
1 5	שאר	REST	984c	
	אלישבע	ELISHEBA	45d	
	גג	ROOF	150d	1
	מלכם	MALCAM	575d	
	מלכם	MILCOM	576a	
	צבא	HOST	839b	1 c
	שבע	SWEAR	989b	1 a
	שבע	SWEAR	989b	1 a
1 6	בקש	SEEK	134d	3 2
	דרש	SEEK	205b	3 a
	סוג	MOVE AWAY	690d	1 b2
1 7	אדון	LORD	11c	4 b2
	הס	HUSH	245a	
	זבח	SACRIFICE	258a	2 6
	יום	DAY	399a	3
	כון	ESTABLISH	466b	2
	פנה	FACE	818c	2 6b
	קדש	BE SET APART	873c	3
	קרא	CALL	895d	5 c
	קרב	NEAR	898d	3
1 8	זבח	SACRIFICE	258a	2 6
	יום	DAY	*399a	3
	לבש	PUT ON	528a	A
	מלבוש	RAIMENT	528d	
	נכרי	FOREIGN	648d	1 a
	שר	CHIEFTAIN	978b	2 a
1 9	אדון	LORD	11a	2 1b
	דלג	LEAP	194c	
	חמס	VIOLENCE	329c	
	מפתן	THRESHOLD	837b	
	מרמה	DECEIT	941b	
1 10	גבעה	HILL	149a	4
	דג	FISH	185d	
	יללה	HOWLING	410c	
	נאם	UTTERANCE	610b	2
	צעקה	CRY	858d	2
	שבר	BREAKING	991b	2
	משנה	SECOND	1041d	3
	שער	GATE	1044d	1 b5
1 11	דמה	CUT OFF	198c	
	ילל	HOWL	410b	
	כנען	MERCHANT	488d	
	כרת	BE CUT OFF	504b	1 b
	מכתש	MORTAR	509d	
	נטיל	LADEN	642b	
1 12	חפש	SEARCH	344c	1
	יטב	DO GOOD TO	405d	2
	כסף	SILVER	494b	5
	לבב	HEART	524a	2 7
	לחום	BOWELS	536a	
	נר	LAMP	632d	
	רעע	BE EVIL	949c	1
	שמר	LEES	1038d	
1 13	בנה	BUILD	124b	1 ab
	היה	BECOME	226b	2 2e
	חיל	STRENGTH	299a	1
	נטע	PLANT	642c	1
	משסה	PLUNDER	1042d	
1 14	גבור	STRONG	150b	3
	גדול	GREAT	153a	6 a
	יום	DAY	399a	3
	מהר	SWIFT	555a	
	מר	BITTER	600c	2 a
	צרח	CRY	863c	
	קרב	NEAR	898d	3
	שם	THERE	1027a	1 a
1 15	אלה	DARKNESS	66c	1
	חשך	DARKNESS	365a	3 b
	יום	DAY	399a	3
	עברה	OVERFLOW	720c	3 b
	מצוקה	STRAIGNESS	748b	
	ענן	CLOUD	778a	1 e
	ערפל	CLOUD	791d	
	צרה	DISTRESS	865b	
	שואה	DEVASTATION	996c	1
	משואה	DESOLATION	996c	1
1 16	בצר	MAKE INACCESSIBLE	131a	
	גבה	HIGH	147a	1
	יום	DAY	399a	3
	פנה	CORNER	819d	1
	תרועה	SHOUT OF WAR	930a	1
	שפר	HORN	1051d	
1 17	דם	BLOOD	196c	2 b
	הלך	WALK	230a	1 1a
	חטא	MISS 0A GOAL OR WAY0	307a	2 b
	לח	FRESHNESS	*535a	
	לחום	BOWELS	536a	
	לחום	BOWELS	536a	

445

Ch	v	Heb	Eng	Page	Sec
		עור	BLIND	734c	1 a
		עפר	DRY EARTH	780a	2 a
		צור	BIND	864d	B
		שפך	POUR OUT	1049d	
1	18	אכל	EAT	37d	2
		בהל	BE DISTURBED	96c	1
		זהב	GOLD	263c	1
		יום	DAY	399a	3
		יכל	BE ABLE	407c	1 a
		כלה	COMPLETE	478d	2 a
		עברה	OVERFLOW	720c	3 b
		עשה	DO	794c	2 1g
		קנאה	ZEAL	888c	3 b
2	1	כסף	LONG	494a	1
		לא	NOT	*519c	2 b
		קשש	GATHER TOGETHER	905a	
2	2	חק	SOMETHING PRESCRIBED	349c	6 c
		חרון	BURNING OF ANGER	354c	
		טרם	NOT YET	382d	2
		טרם	NOT YET	382d	2
		יום	DAY	399a	3
		מוץ	CHAFF	558b	
2	3	בקש	SEEK	134d	3 c
		בקש	SEEK	134d	2 b
		יום	DAY	399a	3
		סתר	HIDE	711c	2
		ענו	POOR	776c	2
		ענוה	HUMILITY	776d	1
		פעל	DO	821b	1 b
		צדק	RIGHTEOUSNESS	841d	5
		משפט	JUDGMENT	1048d	1
2	4	אשדוד	AHSDOD	78b	
		אשקלון	ASHKELON	80c	
		גרש	DRIVE OUT	177a	
		עזב	LEAVE	737b	2 a1
		עזה	GAZA	738b	
		עקר	PLUCK	785c	
		עקרון	EKRON	785d	
		צהר	MIDDAY	843d	1
2	5	אבד	DESTROY	2b	1
		חבל	CORD	286d	3
		ים	SEA	411b	8 a
		ישב	DWELL	443b	1
		כנען	CANAAN	488d	2 b
		כרתי	CHERETHITE	505a	
2	6	גדרה	WALL	155a	
		חבל	CORD	286d	3
		ים	SEA	411b	8 a
		כרה	CISTERN	500b	
		כרתי	CHERETHITE	505a	
		נוה	PASTURE	627d	1
2	7	אשקלון	ASHKELON	80c	
		בית	HOUSE	110a	5 de
		יהוה	YAHWEH	218d	2 1d
		חבל	CORD	286d	3
		רבץ	LIE DOWN	918c	
		רעה	TEND	945b	2 a
		שארית	REST	984d	1
		שבית	CAPTIVITY	986b	2 a
2	8	גבול	BOUNDARY	148a	2 a
		גדל	BECOME GREAT	152c	3 b
		גדופים	REVILINGS	154d	
		חרפה	REPROACH	357d	1
		חרף	REPROACH	357d	
		עמון	AMMON	770a	
2	9	אלהים	GOD	44c	4 ba
		בזז	SPOIL	102d	
		גוי	NATION	156d	1 b
		חי	ALIVE	311d	1 a
		חרול	KIND OF WEED	355b	
		יתר	REMAINDER	451d	1 a
		כן	SO	486d	3 d
		מכרה	PIT	500b	
		מלח	SALT	571d	
		ממשק	POSSESSION	606c	
		נאם	UTTERANCE	610b	2
		נחל	TAKE AS A POSSESSION	635c	1 c
		סדם	SODOM	690a	
		עולם	LONG DURATION	762b	2 b1
		עמון	AMMON	770a	
		עמרה	GOMORRAH	771d	
		שארית	REST	984d	1
2	10	גאון	EXALTATION	145a	2
		גדל	BECOME GREAT	152c	3 b
		חרף	REPROACH	357d	
		צבא	GOD OF WAR	839c	4 c
2	11	אי	COAST	16a	
		ירא	CAUSE FEAR	431d	2
		על	UPON	755d	2 5
		רזה	GROW LEAN	930d	1
2	12	הוא	HE, SHE, IT	216a	3 b
		הם	THEY	241c	3 b
		חלל	PIERCED	319c	2
		כושי	CUSHITE	469b	D
2	13	אבד	CAUSE TO PERISH	2a	1
		אשור	ASSHUR	78d	2
		נטה	EXTEND	640a	1 a
		נינוה	NINEVEH	644b	
		צפון	NORTH	861a	
2	14	ארזה	CEDAR-PANELS	72d	
		גוי	NATION	156d	2
		חיה	LIVING THING	312c	1 b

Ch	v	Heb	Eng	Page	Sec
		חלון	WINDOW	319d	
		חרב	DESOLATION	351d	
		כפתור	CAPITAL	499c	1
		לון	LODGE	533c	1 b
		סף	THRESHOLD	706c	
		עדר	FLOCK	727d	1 a
		ערה	BE NAKED	788c	1
		קאת	PELICAN	866b	
		קול	VOICE	877a	1 e
		רבץ	LIE DOWN	918b	
		שיר	SING	1010d	
		חרב	ADDENDA ET CORRIGENDA	1123c	
2	15	אפס	NON-EXISTENCE	67b	2 b
		במח	SECURITY	105b	
		זה	THIS	261b	3
		חיה	LIVING THING	312c	1 b
		יד	HAND	389c	1 d
		לבב	HEART	524a	2 7
		נוע	TOTTER	631c	2
		עוד	STILL	729b	1 c
		עיר	CITY	746c	1 i
		עליז	EXULTANT	759c	
		מרבץ	PLACE OF WILD BEASTS	918c	
		שמה	APPALMENT	1031c	2
		שרק	HISS	1056d	
3	1	גאל	DEFILE	146a	
		ינה	OPPRESS	413a	
		מרה	BE REBELLIOUS	598a	2
		עיר	CITY	746c	1 i
3	2	אלהים	GOD	44d	4 c
		בטח	TRUST	105a	13a
		מוסר	DISCIPLINE	416c	1 a
		קרב	COME NEAR	897b	1 a
3	3	ארי	LION	71d	
		בקר	MORNING	134a	1 f
		בקר	MORNING	134a	1 e
		בקר	MORNING	134b	2
		גרם	CUT OFF, HENCE RESERVE	175a	
		זאב	WOLF	255d	
		שר	CHIEFTAIN	978b	2 b
		שאג	ROAR	980d	1
		שפט	JUDGE	1047c	1 b
3	4	בגדות	TREACHERY	93d	
		חלל	POLLUTE	320b	1 b
		חמס	TREAT VIOLENTLY	329b	2
		תורה	INSTRUCTION	436a	1 e
		כהן	PRIEST	463d	4
		נביא	PROPHET	612a	2
		פחז	BE WANTON	808d	
		קדש	APARTNESS	872a	2 g
3	5	בשת	SHAME	102a	1
		בקר	MORNING	134b	1 f
		לא	NOT	519b	1 bc
		עדר	BE LACKING	727c	
		עולה	INJUSTICE	732c	1
		עול	UNJUST ONE	732d	
		צדיק	JUST	843a	1 d
		בלי	WEARING OUT	115c	C b
3	6	חרב	BE WASTE	351d	
		ישב	DWELL	443b	3
		כרת	CUT OFF	504c	2 c
		פנה	CORNER	819d	1 b
		צדה	LAY LASTE	841b	
		שמם	BE DESOLATED	1031a	1
3	7	אך	SURELY	36c	1
		אכן	SURELY	38c	B
		מוסר	DISCIPLINE	416c	1 a
		ירא	FEAR	431c	3 b
		כרת	BE CUT OFF	504a	1 a
		מעון	REFUGE	733a	3
		עלילה	WANTONNESS	760b	2 c
		פקד	ATTEND TO	823c	B 2
		שחת	GO TO RUIN	1008b	2
		שכם	START EARLY	1014d	
3	8	אכל	EAT	37d	2
		אסף	GATHER	62b	1 a
		זעם	INDIGNATION	276d	
		זעם	INDIGNATION	277a	
		חכה	WAIT	314a	3
		חרון	BURNING OF ANGER	354c	
		יום	DAY	401a	7 i
		כי	BECAUSE	474b	3 d
		ממלכה	KINGDOM	575b	1
		נאם	UTTERANCE	610b	2
		עד	BOOTY	723d	
		קבץ	GATHER	867d	2
		קום	STAND	878a	5
		קנאה	ZEAL	888c	3 b
		משפט	JUDGMENT	1048c	1 f
3	9	ברר	PURIFY	141a	1
		הפך	TURN	245c	1 a
		שפה	SPEECH	973d	1 a1
		שכם	SHOULDER	1014b	1 a
3	10	בת	DAUGHTER	123c	3
		יבל	CONDUCT	385a	1
		כוש	CUSH	469a	2 a
		מנחה	OFFERING	585a	3
		מנחה	OFFERING	585c	6
		נהר	STREAM	625d	1
		עבר	REGION ACROSS	719b	1
		עתר	SUPPLIANT	801c	
		פוץ	BE DISPERSED	807a	

Ch	v	Heb	Eng	Page	Sec
3	11	אשר	PARTICLE OF RELATION	82d	4 c
		גאוה	PRIDE	144d	3
		גבה	BE HIGH	147a	3 b
		הר	MOUNTAIN	249d	1 a
		יסף	DO AGAIN	415c	2 a
		עליז	EXULTANT	759c	
		עלילה	WANTONNESS	760b	2 c
		פשע	REBEL	833b	3
		קדש	APARTNESS	871d	2 e
3	12	דל	POOR	195d	
		חסה	SEEK REFUGE	340b	1
		עני	POOR	777a	3
		שאר	REMAIN	984b	1
3	13	חרד	TREMBLE	353c	2
		כזב	LIE	469c	
		לשון	TONGUE	546c	1 b
		מצא	FIND	594a	2 c
		עולה	INJUSTICE	732c	1
		רבץ	LIE DOWN	918c	
		תרמות	DECEITFULNESS	941c	
		רעה	TEND	945b	2 c
		שארית	REST	984d	1
3	14	בת	DAUGHTER	123c	3
		בת	DAUGHTER	123c	3
		לב	HEART	525c	2 9a
		עלז	EXULT	759c	
		רוע	RAISE A SHOUT	929c	3
		רנן	GIVE A RINGING CRY	943b	1
		שמח	REJOICE	970b	2 a
3	15	מלך	KING	573b	3
		פנה	TURN	815c	
		ראה	TO SEE	907b	3
		רע	EVIL	948d	1
		שפט	JUDGE	1048a	
		משפט	JUDGMENT	1048c	1 f
3	16	אמר	SAY	56c	
		ירא	FEAR	431a	1 a
		ציון	ZION	851b	
		רפה	SINK	951d	2
3	17	אהבה	LOVE	13c	2
		גבור	STRONG	150b	2
		יהוה	YAHWEH	219a	2 1g
		חרש	BE SILENT	361b	1
		ישע	DELIVER	446d	1 b
		רנה	RINGING CRY	943d	3
		שוש	REJOICE	965b	
		שמחה	JOY	970d	3
3	18	חרפה	REPROACH	357d	1
		יגה	SUFFER	387b	
		מועד	APPOINTED PLACE	417d	3 a
		מן	FROM	578c	1 b
		מן	OUT OF	579c	2 cb
3	19	צלע	ZELAH	86b	1 db
		את	WITH	86b	1 db
		בשת	SHAME	102a	1
		תהלה	PRAISE	240b	5 cb
		ישע	DELIVER	446d	1 b
		נדח	BANISH	623a	2
		ענה	BE BOWED DOWN	776b	1
		עשה	DO	794b	1 2
		קבץ	GATHER	868a	1
		שם	NAME	1028a	2 b1
3	20	תהלה	PRAISE	240b	5 cb
		קבץ	GATHER	868a	1
		שבית	CAPTIVITY	986b	2 a
		שם	NAME	1028a	2 b1

HAGGAI

Ch	v	Heb	Eng	Page	Sec
1	1	דבר	WORD	182c	1 2a
		דריוש	DARIUS	201d	1
		יהוצדק	JEHOZADAK	221b	
		יהושע	JOSHUA	221c	3
		זרבבל	ZERUBBABEL	279c	
		חגי	HAGGAI	291b	
		חדש	NEW MOON	294d	2 b2
		יום	DAY	398c	2 e
		כהן	PRIEST	464b	8
		נביא	PROPHET	611d	1
		פחה	GOVERNOR	808d	
		שאלתיאל	SHEALTIEL	982d	
1	2	בנה	BUILD	125a	1 b
		לא	NOT	*519b	1 bb
		עת	TIME	773d	2 b
		עתה	NOW	774c	2 gb
1	3	דבר	WORD	182c	1 2a
		חגי	HAGGAI	291b	
		נביא	PROPHET	611d	1
1	4	בית	HOUSE	108d	1 ab
		חרב	WASTE	351d	
		ספן	COVER	706a	
		עת	TIME	773d	2 b
1	5	דרך	WAY	203c	6 a
		לבב	HEART	523b	2 3c
		שים	TO PLACE	963c	2 b
1	6	בוא	COME	99b	1 e
		זרע	SOW	281c	1 a
		חמם	BE OR BECOME WARM	328c	1
		ל	TO	517d	7 be
		לבש	PUT ON	528a	C
		מעט	A FEW	589d	1 a
		נקב	PIERCE	666b	1

Ch	v.	Heb	Eng	Page	Sec
		צרור	BUNDLE	865c	
		רבה	BECOME MANY	915a	1 e5
		שכר	HIRE	969a	
		שכר	BE DRUNK	1016b	
1	7	דרך	WAY	203c	6 a
		לב	HEART	523d	2 3c
		שום	TO PLACE	963c	2 b
1	8	כבד	BE HONORED	457c	2
		רצה	BE PLEASED WITH	953a	1 a
1	9	אשר	PARTICLE OF RELATION	82b	2 a
		הוא	HE, SHE, IT	215d	2 c
		חרב	WASTE	351d	
		ל	TO	512c	4 a
		מה	HOW	553d	4 b
		מעט	A FEW	589d	1 a
		נפח	BREATHE	656a	
		יען	ON ACCOUNT OF	774d	1
		פנה	TURN	815c	2 d
		רבה	BECOME MANY	915d	1 e5
		רוץ	RUN	930b	1
1	10	טל	NIGHT-MIST	378c	
		יבל	PRODUCE	385b	
		כלא	RESTRAIN	476b	3
		מן	FROM	583c	7 bb
1	11	אדם	MAN	9b	2
		אדמה	GROUND	9c	1
		דגן	CORN	186c	
		הר	MOUNTAIN	250c	1 i
		חרב	DRYNESS	351b	1
		יגע	TOIL	388c	2
		יצא	BRING OUT	425b	4 j
		תירוש	NEW WINE	440d	
		כף	HOLLOW OF THE HAND	496c	1 d7
1	12	יצהר	FRESH OIL	844a	
		יהוה	YAHWEH	218d	2 1d
		יהוצדק	JEHOZADAK	221b	
		יהושע	JOSHUA	221c	3
		זרבבל	ZERUBBABEL	279c	
		חגי	HAGGAI	291b	
		ירא	FEAR	431c	2
		כהן	PRIEST	464b	8
		נביא	PROPHET	611d	1
		על	UPON	757c	2 7c b
		שארית	REST	984d	1
		שלתיאל	SHEALTIEL	1027a	
1	13	חגי	HAGGAI	291b	
		מלאך	MESSENGER	521c	1 b
		מלאכות	MESSAGE	522b	
1	14	יהוצדק	JEHOZADAK	221b	
		יהושע	JOSHUA	221c	3
		זרבבל	ZERUBBABEL	279c	
		כהן	PRIEST	464b	8
		עור	ROUSE ONESELF	735b	1
		פחה	GOVERNOR	808d	
		רוח	BREATH	925b	3 g
		שארית	REST	984d	1
		שלתיאל	SHEALTIEL	1027a	
1	15	דריוש	DARIUS	201d	1
		חדש	NEW MOON	294d	2 b2
		יום	DAY	398c	2 e
		עשרים	TWENTY	798a	2 b
		ארבע	FOUR	917b	2 b
2	1	דבר	WORD	182c	1 2a
		חגי	HAGGAI	291b	
		יום	DAY	*398c	2 e
		נביא	PROPHET	611d	1
2	2	יהוצדק	JEHOZADAK	221b	
		יהושע	JOSHUA	221c	3
		זרבבל	ZERUBBABEL	279c	
		כהן	PRIEST	464b	8
		פחה	GOVERNOR	808d	
		שארית	REST	984d	1
		שלתיאל	SHEALTIEL	1027a	
2	3	אין	NOTHING	34a	1
		כ	LIKE	454b	2 a
		כבוד	HONOR	458d	2 b
		מה	WHAT	552b	1 a
		מי	WHO	566c	D
		ראה	TO SEE	907a	2 4
		ראה	TO SEE	907a	2 5
		ראשון	FIRST	911c	1 a
2	4	יהוצדק	JEHOZADAK	221b	
		יהושע	JOSHUA	221c	3
		זרבבל	ZERUBBABEL	279c	
		חזק	BE FIRM	304b	1 2c
		כהן	PRIEST	464b	8
		עם	PEOPLE	766d	5 c
2	5	את	MARK OF THE ACCUSATIVE	85c	3 a
		יצא	GO OUT	422d	1 a
		ירא	FEAR	431b	1
		כרת	CUT	504a	4
		עמד	STAND	764b	3 c
		רוח	BREATH	926a	9 f
		תוך	MIDST	1063d	
2	6	חרבה	DRY GROUND	351c	
		ים	SEA	411a	5
		מעט	A FEW	590a	1 eb
		רעש	SHAKE	950b	1
		שמי	HEAVENS	1030a	1 a
2	7	חמדה	DESIRE	326c	
		כבוד	GLORY	459a	2 c3
		מלא	FILL	570c	1
		רעש	SHAKE	950b	1

Ch	v.	Heb	Eng	Page	Sec
2	9	כבוד	HONOR	458d	2 b
		ראשון	FIRST	911c	1 a
		שלום	PEACE	1023b	5 b
2	10	דבר	WORD	182c	1 2a
		דריוש	DARIUS	201d	1
		חגי	HAGGAI	291b	
		נביא	PROPHET	611d	1
		ארבע	FOUR	917b	2 b
		תשיעי	NINTH	1077d	
2	11	תורה	INSTRUCTION	436a	1 e
		כהן	PRIEST	464b	7
2	12	מאכל	FOOD	38b	
		בגד	GARMENT	94a	1
		בשר	FLESH	142c	1 a
		ה	INTERROG PART	209d	1 b
		אם	IF	243d	B
		נזיד	THING BOILED	268a	
		כהן	PRIEST	464b	7
		כנף	EXTREMITY	489d	2 a
		לא	NOT	519a	1 ad b
		נגע	TOUCH	619a	1 a
2	13	קדש	BE SET APART	873a	2
		חגי	HAGGAI	291b	
		טמא	BE UNCLEAN	379b	3
		טמא	UNCLEAN	379d	2 a
		כהן	PRIEST	464b	7
		נפש	SOUL	660c	4 c5
2	14	גוי	NATION	156d	1 a
		חגי	HAGGAI	291b	
		טמא	UNCLEAN	379d	2 c
		מעשה	DEED	795d	1 a2
2	15	היכל	TEMPLE	228c	2 d
		טרם	NOT YET	382d	3
		יום	DAY	401a	7 j
		לבב	HEART	523d	2 3c
		מן	FROM	581b	4 a
		מעל	ABOVE	751d	2 bb g
		על	UPON	759b	4 2d
		שום	TO PLACE	963c	2 b
		מעל	ADDENDA ET CORRIGENDA	1125d	
2	16	חמשים	FIFTY	332b	1 b1
		חשף	STRIP OFF	362c	3
		יקב	WINE-VAT	428c	
		מן	SINCE	583c	7 c
		ערמה	HEAP	790d	
		עשר	TEN	797a	2 b
		פורה	WINE PRESS	807d	
2	17	אין	NOT	34b	2
		אל	TO	40a	3 c
		את	MARK OF THE ACCUSATIVE	85b	1 c
		ירקון	RUST	439a	1
		נכה	SMITE	646c	4 a
		מעשה	DEED	795d	1 b1
		שדפון	SMUT	995b	
		היכל	TEMPLE	228c	2 d
2	18	יום	DAY	398c	2 e
		יום	DAY	401a	7 j
		יום	DAY	401b	7 k
		יסד	BE FOUNDED	414a	
		לבב	HEART	523d	2 3c
		מן	FROM	581b	4 a
		מן	FROM	583d	9 b2
		מעל	ABOVE	751d	2 bb g
		על	UPON	759b	4 2d
		ארבע	FOUR	917b	2 b
		שום	TO PLACE	963c	2 b
		תשיעי	NINTH	1077d	
		מעל	ADDENDA ET CORRIGENDA	1125d	
2	19	ברך	BLESS	139a	2 a
		מגורה	STORE-HOUSE	158c	
		גפן	VINE	172c	
		זית	OLIVE TREE	268c	1
		זרע	SOWING	282b	2 d
		מן	FROM	581c	4 a
		נשא	LIFT	671b	2 g
		עד	AS FAR AS	724d	13
		עץ	TREE	781d	1 b
		רמון	POMEGRANATE	941d	1
		תאנה	FIG-TREE	1061a	1
2	20	דבר	WORD	182c	1 2a
		חגי	HAGGAI	291b	
		יום	DAY	*398c	2 e
		ארבע	FOUR	917b	2 b
2	21	זרבבל	ZERUBBABEL	279c	
		פחה	GOVERNOR	808d	
		רעש	SHAKE	950b	1
2	22	אח	BROTHER	26b	4
		הפך	TURN	245c	1 b
		חזק	STRENGTH	305d	2
		ירד	GO DOWN	433b	1 k
		כסא	THRONE	491a	3 a
		ממלכה	KINGDOM	575b	1
		ממלכה	DOMINION	575b	1
		רכב	RIDE	938d	3
		רכב	RIDE	938d	3
		מרכבה	CHARIOT	939d	
		שמד	BE EXTERMINATED	1029c	2
2	23	בחר	CHOOSE	104a	1 a
		זרבבל	ZERUBBABEL	279c	
		חתם	SEAL	368b	
		עבד	SLAVE	714a	3
		שאלתיאל	SHEALTIEL	982d	

Ch	v.	Heb	Eng	Page	Sec
1	1	יברכיהו	JEBERECHIAH	140a	4
		דבר	WORD	182c	1 2a
		דריוש	DARIUS	201d	1
		זכריהו	ZECHARIAH	272b	1 f
		חדש	NEW MOON	294d	2 b2
		נביא	PROPHET	611d	1
		עדו	IDDO	723b	2
1	2	פנה	FACE	819b	2 8b
		קצף	BE WROTH	893b	1
		קצף	WRATH	893c	1
1	3	פנה	FACE	819b	2 8b
		צבא	GOD OF WAR	839c	4 c
		שוב	TURN BACK	998a	6 g
1	4	דרך	WAY	203d	6 d
		נביא	PROPHET	611d	1
		מעליל	DEED	760b	1
		מעלל	DEED	760b	1
		צבא	GOD OF WAR	839c	4 c
		קשב	ATTEND	904a	1
		ראשון	FIRST	911c	1 a
		רע	EVIL	948c	0 d
		רע	EVIL	948c	0 d
1	5	איה	WHERE	32c	
		עולם	LONG DURATION	762d	2 i
1	6	דבר	WORD	183b	3 2
		דרך	WAY	203c	6 a
		מם	CONSIDER	273b	2 a
		חק	SOMETHING PRESCRIBED	349c	7 b
		נביא	PROPHET	611d	1
		נביא	PROPHET	611d	1
		נשג	OVERTAKE	673c	1 b
		עבד	SLAVE	714b	4
1	7	יברכיהו	JEBERECHIAH	140a	4
		דבר	WORD	182c	1 2a
		דריוש	DARIUS	201d	1
		זכריהו	ZECHARIAH	272b	1 f
		חדש	NEW MOON	294d	2 b1
		יום	DAY	398c	2 e
		נביא	PROPHET	611d	1
		עדו	IDDO	723b	2
		עשתי	ONE	799d	
		ארבע	FOUR	917b	2 b
		שבט	SHEBAT	987b	
1	8	אדם	RED	10b	
		הדס	MYRTLE	213c	
		לבן	WHITE	526b	
		לילה	NIGHT	539a	1
		לילה	NIGHT	539a	1
		סוס	HORSE	692c	2
		מעלה	SHADOW	847a	
		רכב	RIDE	938d	2
		שרק	SORREL	977c	
1	9	דבר	SPEAK	180c	
		הוא	HE, SHE, IT	*216c	4 bb
		הם	THEY	241c	4 bb
		מלאך	MESSENGER	521d	2
1	10	מה	WHAT	552b	1 a
		הדס	MYRTLE	213c	
		הלך	WALK	235d	1 a
1	11	הדס	MYRTLE	213c	
		הלך	WALK	235d	1 a
1	12	שקט	BE QUIET	1053a	1
		זעם	BE INDIGNANT	276d	1
		יהודה	JUDAH	397b	2
		מתי	WHEN	607d	C
		רחם	LOVE	933c	1
1	13	דבר	SPEAK	180c	
		טוב	PLEASANT	374d	9 b
		נחום	COMFORT	637c	1
1	14	דבר	SPEAK	180c	
		ציון	ZION	851b	
		קנאה	ZEAL	888c	2 b
		קנא	BE ZEALOUS	888c	3 b
		קרא	CALL	895c	3 d
1	15	מעט	A FEW	590a	1 d
		עזר	HELP	740c	
		קצף	BE WROTH	893b	1
		קצף	BE WROTH	893b	1
		קצף	WRATH	893c	1
		רעה	MISERY	949b	2
		שאנן	AT EASE	983c	3
1	16	בנה	BUILD	125a	1 b
		ל	TO	511b	1 ga
		נטה	STRETCH OUT	640c	
		קו	LINE	876a	
		קו	LINE	876a	
		קוה	CORNER	876a	
		רחמים	COMPASSION	933c	1
1	17	שוב	TURN BACK	997b	3 b
		בחר	CHOOSE	104a	1 a
		טוב	A GOOD THING	375a	1
		נחם	CONSOLE ONESELF	637a	
		פוץ	FLOW	807b	
		ציון	ZION	851b	
		קרא	CALL	895c	3 d
2	1	קרן	HORN	901d	1 a
2	2	דבר	SPEAK	180c	
		זרה	SCATTER	280a	1
		קרן	HORN	901d	1 a
2	3	חרש	GRAVER	360d	1
2	4	זרה	SCATTER	280a	1
		חרד	TREMBLE	353c	
		ידה	CAST	392b	

ZECHARIAH

Ch	v.	Heb	Eng	Page	Sec
		נשא	LIFT	670b	1 b 2
		פה	MOUTH	805c	6 bb
		קרן	HORN	901d	1 a
2	5	חבל	CORD	286d	2
		יד	HAND	390d	5 c1
		מדה	MEASURE	551c	1
2	6	מדד	MEASURE	551a	1
		מה	HOW	553d	4 ca
		ראה	TO SEE	907b	5 a
		רחב	WIDTH	931d	
		רחב	WIDTH	931d	
2	7	דבר	SPEAK	180c	
2	8	אדם	MAN	9b	2
		בהמה	BEAST	97a	2
		הלז	THIS	229c	
		ישב	SIT	443b	4
		פרזה	OPEN REGION	826d	
		רוץ	RUN	930b	1
2	9	חומה	WALL	327d	3
		כבוד	GLORY	459a	2 c3
2	10	גפן	VINE	172c	
		הוי	AH	223a	
		פרש	SPREAD OUT	831c	2
		צפון	NORTH	861a	
		רוח	BREATH	924d	2 a
2	11	בבל	BABEL	93c	
		בת	DAUGHTER	123c	3
		הוי	AH	223a	
		ישב	DWELL	443b	3
		מלט	SLIP AWAY	572b	2
2	12	בבה	APPLE	93b	
		כבוד	HONOR	459a	3
		נגע	TOUCH	619a	3
		שלל	SPOIL	1021d	
2	13	יד	HAND	389c	1 d
		נוף	WAVE	632a	2 b
		עבד	WORK	713a	3
		שלח	SEND	1018c	2 a
		שלל	SPOIL	1022a	2
2	14	בת	DAUGHTER	123c	3
		רנן	GIVE A RINGING CRY	943b	1
		שמח	REJOICE	970b	2 a
2	15	לוה	BE JOINED	531a	
2	16	אדמה	LAND	10a	5
		בחר	CHOOSE	104a	1 a
		חלק	PORTION	324b	2 c
		נחל	TAKE AS A POSSESSION	635c	1 d
		קרש	APARTNESS	872a	2 g
2	17	בשר	FLESH	142d	6 c
		הס	HUSH	245a	
		מעון	REFUGE	733a	2 a
		עור	ROUSE ONESELF	735a	
		קרש	APARTNESS	871c	2 a
3	1	יהושע	JOSHUA	221c	3
		ימין	RIGHT HAND	411d	2 a
		כהן	PRIEST	464b	8
		שטן	SATAN	966c	2 b
		שטן	ACT AS ADVERSARY	966c	
3	2	אוד	BRAND	15c	
		בחר	CHOOSE	104a	1 a
		גער	REBUKE	172a	2
		נצל	DELIVER	665a	
		שטן	SATAN	966c	2 b
3	3	בגד	GARMENT	94a	1
		יהושע	JOSHUA	221c	3
		לבש	PUT ON	528a	E
		צאי	FILTHY	844b	
3	4	בגד	GARMENT	94a	1
		מחלצה	ROBE OF STATE	323a	
		לבש	CLOTHE	528b	1 a
		עבר	PASS OVER	719a	4
		עון	INIQUITY	731a	1 c2
		על	UPON	758d	4 2b
		ריב	FILTHY	844b	3
3	5	בגד	GARMENT	94a	1
		מהור	CLEAN	373a	2
		לבש	CLOTHE	528b	1 a
		צניף	TURBAN	857b	
		שום	TO PLACE	963b	1 b
3	6	יהושע	JOSHUA	221c	3
		עוד	BEAR WITNESS	730a	3
3	7	דין	JUDGE	192c	2
		דין	JUDGE	192c	2
		דרך	WAY	204a	6 ec
		מהלך	GOING	237c	3
		חצר	ENCLOSURE	347a	3 b
		שמר	KEEP	1036c	1 a
		משמרת	GUARD	1038d	4 a
3	8	מופת	SIGN	69a	2
		בוא	COME	99a	2 c
		יהושע	JOSHUA	221c	3
		כהן	PRIEST	464b	8
		עבד	SLAVE	714a	3
		צמח	SPROUT	855d	3
		רע	FRIEND	946a	1
3	9	אבן	STONE	6c	2
		יהושע	JOSHUA	221c	3
		מוש	DEPART	559a	
		נתן	PUT	680b	2 a
		עון	INIQUITY	731a	1 c2
		עין	EYE	744b	1 e
		פתוח	ENGRAVING	836c	
		פתח	ENGRAVE	836c	
3	10	רע	FRIEND	946b	3
		תאנה	FIG-TREE	1061a	1
		תחת	UNDERNEATH	1066a	3 1a
4	1	דבר	SPEAK	180c	
		שנה	SLEEP	446a	
		עור	ROUSE ONESELF	735a	
		עור	ROUSE ONESELF	735a	
		עור	ROUSE ONESELF	735b	1
		שוב	TURN BACK	997c	3 b
4	2	מוצקת	PIPE	427c	1
		נר	LAMP	632d	
		מנורה	LAMPSTAND	633a	2
		ראש	HEAD	910d	2 a
		שבע	SEVEN	988a	1 b
4	3	זית	OLIVE TREE	268c	1
		שמאל	LEFT	969d	1
4	4	דבר	SPEAK	180c	
4	5	דבר	SPEAK	180c	4 bb
		הוא	HE, SHE, IT	*216c	4 bb
		הם	THEY	241c	4 bb
4	6	זרובבל	ZERUBBABEL	279c	
		כח	STRENGTH	470d	1 d
		רוח	BREATH	926a	9 f
4	7	אבן	STONE	6c	2
		גדול	GREAT	153a	1
		ה	THE	209a	2 b
		זרובבל	ZERUBBABEL	279c	
		חן	FAVOR	336b	2 b
		יצא	BRING OUT	425a	4 a
		מישור	LEVEL PLACE	449d	1
		ל	TO	512c	4 a
		ראשה	TOP	911c	2
		תשאה	NOISE	996c	
4	8	דבר	WORD	182c	1 2a
4	9	בצע	CUT OFF	130c	
		זרובבל	ZERUBBABEL	279c	
		יסד	FOUND	414a	1
4	10	אבן	STONE	6d	6
		ארץ	EARTH	76a	1 a
		בדיל	TIN	95d	3
		בוז	DESPISE	100b	
		זרובבל	ZERUBBABEL	279c	
		מי	WHO	567b	G
		קטן	SMALL	882a	2 b3
		ראה	TO SEE	907a	2 5
		שמח	REJOICE	970b	2 a
		שוט	GO ABOUT	1002a	
4	11	זית	OLIVE TREE	268c	1
		שמאל	LEFT	969d	1
4	12	זהב	GOLD	263c	0
		זית	OLIVE TREE	268c	1
		יד	HAND	391a	5 d
		צנתרות	PIPES	857c	
		שבלת	EAR OF GRAIN	987c	
		שבלת	EAR OF GRAIN	987c	
4	13	ריק	MAKE EMPTY	938a	2
4	14	אדון	LORD	11a	1 2
		ארץ	EARTH	76a	1 a
		בן	SON	121d	8 k
		על	UPON	756b	2 6c
		יצהר	FRESH OIL	844a	
5	1	עוף	FLY	733c	1 a
		שוב	TURN BACK	998b	8
5	2	אמה	CUBIT	52c	1
		עוף	FLY	733c	1 a
		רחב	WIDTH	931d	
		רחב	WIDTH	931d	
5	3	אלה	OATH	46d	3 a
		גנב	STEAL	170c	
		זה	THIS	262a	6 e
		קקה	BE CLEAN	667b	1
		על	UPON	752d	2 1
5	4	גנב	THIEF	170c	
		יצא	BRING OUT	425b	5
		כלה	FINISH	478d	2 c2
		עץ	TREE	781d	2 b
		שבע	SWEAR	989b	1 a
5	5	דבר	SPEAK	180c	
		עפרת	LEAD	780b	
5	6	איפה	EPHAH	35b	2
		מה	WHAT	552b	1 a
		איפה	EPHAH	35b	2
		כבר	ROUND	503b	3 a
		נשא	LIFT	671d	1 a
5	7	עפרת	LEAD	780b	
5	8	אבן	STONE	6d	5
		איפה	EPHAH	35b	2
		ה	THE	208b	1 ha
		פה	MOUTH	805b	4
		רשעה	WICKEDNESS	958a	2
		שלך	THROW	1021a	1 a
5	9	איפה	EPHAH	35b	2
		הם	THEY	241d	8 c
		חסידה	STORK	339d	
		כנף	WING	489c	1 e
		כנף	WING	489c	1 a
		שמי	HEAVENS	1029a	1 a
		איפה	EPHAH	35b	2
5	10	דבר	SPEAK	180c	
		הלך	WALK	237a	3 a
5	11	בנה	BUILD	124b	1 ab
		כון	BE ESTABLISHED	466d	1
		מכונה	BASE	467d	
		נוח	REST	628d	B 1
		נוח	REST	629a	A
		שנער	SHINAR	1042c	
		שנער	SHINAR	1042c	
5	12	עשרים	TWENTY	797d	1 1f
6	1	בין	INTERVAL	107d	D
		הר	MOUNTAIN	250d	1 m
		מרכבה	CHARIOT	939d	
		שוב	TURN BACK	998b	8
6	2	אדם	RED	10b	1
		אמץ	STRONG	55c	
		סוס	HORSE	692c	2
		מרכבה	CHARIOT	939d	
		שחר	BLACK	1007b	
6	3	אמץ	STRONG	55c	
		ברד	SPOTTED	136a	
		לבן	WHITE	526b	
		סוס	HORSE	692c	2
		רביעי	FOURTH	918a	2
		מרכבה	CHARIOT	939d	
6	4	דבר	SPEAK	180c	
6	5	אדון	LORD	11a	1 2
		יצב	STATION ONESELF	426c	C
		על	UPON	756b	2 6c
		רוח	BREATH	924d	2 a
6	6	אחר	BEHIND	30c	4 b
		אל	TO	40d	9
		ברד	SPOTTED	136a	
		תימן	SOUTH	412d	1 a
		יצא	GO OUT	423d	2 a
		לבן	WHITE	526b	
		סוס	HORSE	692c	2
		צפון	NORTH	861a	
		שחר	BLACK	1007b	
6	7	אמץ	STRONG	55c	
		בקש	SEEK	134d	2 d
		הלך	WALK	232a	1 2
		הלך	WALK	234a	1 5f 2
		הלך	WALK	235d	1 a
		הלך	WALK	235d	1 a
		הלך	WALK	235d	1 a
		יצא	GO OUT	423d	2 a
6	8	זעק	CRY	277c	4
		נוח	REST	628b	A 1a
		נחשת	COPPER	638d	1
		צפון	NORTH	861a	
		רוח	BREATH	925a	3 c
6	9	דבר	WORD	182c	1 2a
6	10	יאשיהו	JOSIAH	78c	2
		בבל	BABEL	93c	
		חלדי	HELDAI	317c	2
		חלם	HELEM	321b	
		טוביהו	TOBIJAH	376a	4
		ידעיה	JEDAIAH	396a	5
		צפניה	ZEPHANIAH	861b	3
6	11	יהוצדק	JEHOZADAK	221b	
		יהושע	JOSHUA	221c	3
		זהב	GOLD	263c	1
		כהן	PRIEST	464b	8
		עטרה	CROWN	742d	2
		שום	TO PLACE	963a	1 a
		בנה	BUILD	124d	1 i
6	12	היכל	TEMPLE	228c	2 d
		עבד	SLAVE	714a	3
		צמח	SPROUT	855c	1
		צמח	SPROUT	855d	3
		שם	NAME	1027d	2 a
		תחת	UNDERNEATH	1066b	3 2a
		בנה	BUILD	124d	1 i
6	13	הוד	SPLENDOUR	217a	1
		היכל	TEMPLE	228c	2 d
		עצה	ADVICE	420a	
		כהן	PRIEST-KING	463a	1
		כסא	SEAT OF HONOR	490d	1 a
		משל	RULE	605d	1
		שלום	PEACE	1023a	5 a
6	14	היכל	TEMPLE	228c	2 d
		זכרון	MEMORIAL	272a	1 c
		חלם	HELEM	321b	
		חן	HEN	336d	
		טוביהו	TOBIJAH	376a	4
		ידעיה	JEDAIAH	396a	5
		עטרה	CROWN	742d	2
		צפניה	ZEPHANIAH	861b	3
6	15	ב	IN	88c	1 2b
		בנה	BUILD	124c	1 h
		יהוה	YAHWEH	218d	2 1b
		היה	COME TO PASS	224b	1 1b
		היכל	TEMPLE	228c	2 d
		רחק	DISTANT	935b	1 a
7	1	דבר	WORD	182c	1 2a
		דריוש	DARIUS	201d	1
		זכריהו	ZECHARIAH	272b	1 f
		חדש	NEW MOON	*294d	2 b1
		חדש	NEW MOON	294d	2 b1
		חדש	NEW MOON	294d	2 b2
		יום	DAY	*398c	2 e
		כסלו	CHISLEV	493b	
		ארבע	FOUR	917a	1 a4
		ארבע	FOUR	917a	1 b3
		תשיעי	NINTH	1077d	
7	2	חלה	MOLLIFY	318c	1 b
		רגמלך	REGEM-MELECH	920d	
		שראצר	SHAREZER	974d	2
7	3	בכה	WEEP	113b	4 1
		זה	THIS	261d	4
		חדש	NEW MOON	294d	2 b2
		חמישי	FIFTH	332c	1
		כהן	PRIEST	464b	7

Ch v.	Heb	Eng	Page	Sec
	מה	HOW	553d	4 ca
	נביא	PROPHET	611d	2
	נזר	DEDICATE	634a	
7 4	דבר	WORD	182c	1 2a
7 5	כהן	PRIEST	464b	7
	כי	WHEN	473a	2 a
	ספד	WAIL	704d	
	עם	PEOPLE	766c	5 c
	צום	FAST	847a	
7 6	כי	WHEN	473a	2 a
7 7	נביא	PROPHET	611d	1
	נגב	SOUTH-COUNTRY	616b	1 a
	ראשון	FIRST	911c	1 a
	שלו	QUIET	1017c	1
	שפלה	LOWLAND	1050c	1
7 8	דבר	WORD	182c	1 2a
	זכריהו	ZECHARIAH	272b	1 f
7 9	אמת	FIRMNESS	54b	4 b
	את	WITH	86b	1 db
	ה	THE	*208b	1 ha
	חסד	GOODNESS	338d	1 2
	רחמים	COMPASSION	933c	2
	שפט	JUDGE	1047d	3 a
	משפט	JUDGMENT	1048c	1 f
7 10	אח	BROTHER	26b	4
	אלמנה	WIDOW	48b	
	גר	SOJOURNER	158b	2
	חשב	THINK	363a	1 2
	יתום	ORPHAN	450c	
	לבב	HEART	523a	2 3c
	עני	POOR	776d	2
	עשק	OPPRESS	798d	1
7 11	אזן	EAR	24a	2
	כבד	MAKE HEAVY	458a	2
	כתף	SHOULDER	509b	1 b
	מאן	REFUSE	549b	
	מן	FROM	583b	7 ba
	נתן	GIVE	680a	1 z
	סרר	BE STUBBORN	711a	
	שמע	HEAR	1033d	1 e
7 12	את	WITH	86d	4 c
	דבר	WORD	*182d	1 2a
	היה	BECOME	226a	2 1b
	תורה	INSTRUCTION	436a	1 c
	מן	FROM	583b	7 ba
	נביא	PROPHET	611d	1
	קצף	WRATH	893c	1
	ראשון	FIRST	911c	1 a
	רוח	BREATH	926a	9 b
	שלח	SEND	1018c	2
	שמור	ADAMANT	1039a	2
7 13	כן	SO	486c	2 cd
	קרא	CALL	895b	2 b
	קרא	CALL	896a	5 d
7 14	חמדה	DESIRE	326d	1
	מן	FROM	583c	7 bb
	סער	STORM	704b	
	עבר	PASS OVER	717c	3 a
	שוב	TURN BACK	997a	2
	שמם	BE DESOLATED	1031a	1
	שמה	WASTE	1031c	1
8 1	דבר	WORD	182c	1 2a
8 2	חמה	RAGE	404d	2 c
	קנא	BE ZEALOUS	888c	3 b
	קנאה	ZEAL	888c	2 b
8 3	אמת	FIRMNESS	54a	3 b
	ה	THE	208b	1 ha
	הר	MOUNTAIN	249d	1 a
	עיר	CITY	746c	1 i
	ציון	ZION	851c	
	קדש	APARTNESS	871d	2 e
	קרא	CALL	896b	2 d3
	שוב	TURN BACK	997b	3 b
8 4	זקן	OLD	278c	2 a
	יד	HAND	390d	5 c1
	רחוב	PLAZA	932b	
	משענת	STAFF	1044a	
8 5	ילד	CHILD	409b	A
	ילדה	GIRL	409c	
	מלא	FILL	570b	1
	רחוב	PLAZA	932b	
	שחק	LAUGH	966a	3
8 6	גם	ALSO	169d	4
	כי	THOUGH	473c	2 ca
	פלא	BE SURPASSING	810c	1
	שארית	REST	984d	1
8 7	מבוא	ENTERING	100a	2
	מזרח	PLACE OF SUNRISE	281a	2 e
	ישע	DELIVER	446d	1 b
8 8	אלהים	GOD	44b	4 a
	אמת	FIRMNESS	54b	3 b
	צדקה	RIGHTEOUSNESS	842b	4
8 9	בנה	BUILD	125a	1 b
	היכל	TEMPLE	228c	2 d
	חזק	BE FIRM	304a	1 1a
	יום	DAY	400b	7 d3 a
	יסד	BE FOUNDED	414a	
	נביא	PROPHET	611d	1
8 10	אדם	MAN	9b	1
	בהמה	BEAST	97a	2
	בוא	COME	97d	1 a
	היה	COME TO PASS	227d	2
	היה	COME TO PASS	227d	2
	צר	ADVERSARY	865d	1
	שכר	HIRE	969a	1
	שכר	HIRE	969a	1

Ch v.	Heb	Eng	Page	Sec
	שלום	PEACE	1023a	4
8 11	ראשון	FIRST	911c	1 a
8 12	שארית	REST	984d	1
	גפן	VINE	172c	
	זרע	SOWING	282c	2 e
	טל	NIGHT-MIST	378c	
	יבול	PRODUCE	385b	
	נחל	TAKE AS A POSSES-SION	635d	1 b
	נתן	GIVE	679c	1 t
	פרי	FRUIT	826b	1
	שארית	REST	984d	1
8 13	בית	HOUSE	110a	5 dd
	בית	HOUSE	110a	5 de
	ברכה	BLESSING	139d	2
	היה	COME TO PASS	225a	1 2b ad
	חזק	BE FIRM	304c	1 1a
	ירא	FEAR	431b	1 b
	ישע	DELIVER	446d	1 b
	קללה	CURSE	887a	
8 14	זמם	CONSIDER	273b	2 a
	נחם	BE SORRY	637a	2
	קצף	BE WROTH	893b	
	קצף	BE WROTH	893b	
8 15	בית	HOUSE	110a	5 de
	זמם	CONSIDER	273b	2 a
	יטב	DO GOOD TO	405d	2
	ירא	FEAR	431b	1 a
	שוב	TURN BACK	998c	8
8 16	אמת	FIRMNESS	54b	4 a
	אמת	FIRMNESS	54b	4 b
	דבר	SPEAK	181b	3 d
	שפט	JUDGE	1047d	3 a
	משפט	JUDGMENT	1048c	1 f
8 17	אהב	LOVE	13a	2
	את	MARK OF THE AC-CUSATIVE	85c	3 a
	חשב	THINK	363a	1 2
	לבב	HEART	523a	2 3c
	נאם	UTTERANCE	610b	2
	שבועה	OATH	990a	1 a
	שקר	DECEPTION	1055c	3
8 18	דבר	WORD	182c	1 2a
8 19	אהב	LOVE	13a	2
	אמת	FIRMNESS	54a	2
	בית	HOUSE	110a	5 de
	ה	THE	208b	1 ha
	חמישי	FIFTH	332c	1
	טוב	PLEASANT	373d	2 a
	מועד	APPOINTED TIME	417c	1 b
	צום	FASTING	847b	
	רביעי	FOURTH	918a	1
	שלום	PEACE	1023b	6
8 20	אשר	THAT	83b	8 aa
8 21	בקש	SEEK	134d	3 c
	הלך	WALK	233a	1 4b 2
	חלה	MOLLIFY	318c	1 b
8 22	בקש	SEEK	134d	3 c
	חלה	MOLLIFY	318c	1 b
	עצום	MIGHTY	783a	1
8 23	אלהים	GOD	44b	4 a
	אשר	THAT	83b	8 aa
	חזק	BE FIRM	305a	6 a
	יהודי	JEWISH	397c	
	כנף	WING	*489b	
	כנף	EXTREMITY	489d	2 a
	לשון	TONGUE	546c	2
	שמע	HEAR	1033c	1 a
9 1	דמשק	DAMASCUS	199d	2
	חדרך	HADRACH	293d	
	מנוחה	RESTING PLACE	629d	1
	משא	UTTERANCE	672d	
9 2	גבל	BOUND	148b	
	חכם	BE WISE	314c	
	חמת	HAMATH	333a	
	צידון	SIDON	851a	
	צר	TYER	862d	
9 3	בנה	BUILD	124c	1 ag
	חוץ	THE OUTSIDE	300b	2 a
	טיט	MUD	376c	1
	ירש	IMPOVERISH	440a	3
	עפר	DRY EARTH	780a	2 a
	צבר	HEAP UP	840d	
	מצור	SIEGE	849a	2
	צר	TYER	862d	
9 4	אדון	LORD	11c	3 2b
	אכל	EAT	37d	2
	חל	RAMPART	298a	1
	ירש	IMPOVERISH	440a	3
	נכה	SMITE	646c	4 c
9 5	אבד	PERISH	1c	1
	אשקלון	ASHKELON	80c	
	חול	WHIRL	297a	2 b
	ירא	FEAR	431b	1 a
	ישב	SIT	443b	4
	מבט	EXPECTATION	614a	
	עזה	GAZA	738b	
	עקרון	EKRON	785d	
9 6	אשדוד	AHSDOD	78b	
	גאון	EXALTATION	144d	1 a
	כרת	CUT OFF	504c	2 c
	ממזר	BASTARD	561c	1
	אלהים	GOD	44d	4 c
9 7	אלוף	CHIEF	49b	
	יבוסי	JEBUSITE	101a	1
	בין	INTERVAL	107d	D

Ch v.	Heb	Eng	Page	Sec
	דם	BLOOD	196d	2 f
	היה	BECOME	226a	2 2c
	עקרון	EKRON	785d	
	שאר	REMAIN	984a	1
	שן	TOOTH	1042a	1 b
	שקוץ	DETESTED THING	1055a	
9 8	בית	HOUSE	109c	1 f
	חנה	DECLINE	333c	2 c2
	מן	FROM	583c	7 bb
	נגש	DRIVE	620c	3
	מצבה	WATCH	663a	
	עבר	PASS OVER	717c	3 a
	שוב	TURN BACK	997a	2
9 9	אתון	SHE-ASS	87d	
	בן	SON	121b	4
	בת	DAUGHTER	123c	3
	בת	DAUGHTER	123c	3
	ו	AND	252c	1 b
	חמור	HE-ASS	331b	2 b
	ישע	BE DELIVERED	446b	2
	ל	TO	511c	1 gb
	מלך	KING	573b	2
	עיר	MALE ASS	747a	
	עני	POOR	777a	4
	צדיק	JUST	843a	1 a
	רוע	RAISE A SHOUT	929d	4
	רכב	RIDE	938d	2
9 10	אפס	END	67a	1
	דבר	SPEAK	181b	3 a
	ים	SEA	411b	8 d
	כרת	BE CUT OFF	504a	1 a
	כרת	CUT OFF	504c	2 a
	מלחמה	WAR	536c	
	משל	DOMINION	606a	
	נהר	STREAM	625d	1
	סוס	HORSE	692c	2
	קשת	BOW	906a	1 b
9 11	אסיר	PRISONER	64a	
	בור	PIT	92c	4
	בור	PIT	*92c	4
	ברית	COVENANT	136d	2 2c
	דם	BLOOD	197c	3 a
9 12	אסיר	PRISONER	64a	
	בצרון	STRONGHOLD	131b	
	ל	TO	511b	1 ga
	תקוה	HOPE	876b	1
	שוב	TURN BACK	999c	4 a
	משנה	DOUBLE	1041c	1
9 13	בן	SON	*121b	1 jt
	גבר	STRONG	150b	2
	דרך	TREAD	202b	4
	יון	JAVAN	402a	
	ל	TO	515b	5 hb a
	מלא	FILL	570d	2
	עור	ROUSE ONESELF	735a	
	ציון	ZION	851b	
	קשת	BOW	906a	1 b
9 14	אדון	LORD	11c	4 a
	ברק	LIGHTNING	140c	1
	הלך	WALK	231d	1 d5 ta
	חץ	ARROW	346c	2
	תימן	SOUTH	412c	1 a
	יצא	GO OUT	423b	1 f
	סערה	TEMPEST	704b	
	על	UPON	755d	2 5
	שפר	HORN	1051d	
9 15	גנן	DEFEND	171a	
	המה	ROAR	242b	5
	זוית	CORNER	265a	
	מזרק	BOWL	284d	2 a
	יין	WINE	406c	A
	יכל	PREVAIL	408a	2 c
	כמו	LIKE	455d	1 a
	כבש	SUBDUE	461b	3
	צבא	GOD OF WAR	839c	4 c
	קלע	SLING	887c	
9 16	שתה	DRINK	1059c	1 f
	אבן	STONE	7a	8
	אדמה	LAND	10a	5
	יהוה	YAHWEH	218d	2 1d
	ישע	DELIVER	446d	1 b
	נזר	CROWN	634b	1 a
	נסס	BE CONSPICUOUS	651c	
9 17	צאן	SMALL CATTLE	838b	2
	בחור	YOUNG MAN	104c	
	בתולה	VIRGIN	144a	
	דגן	CORN	186c	2
	טוב	GOOD THINGS	375c	3 a
	יפי	BEAUTY	421d	
	תירוש	NEW WINE	440d	
10 1	גשם	RAIN	177c	
	חזיז	THUNDER-BOLT	304a	
	מלקוש	SPRING-RAIN	545b	
	מטר	RAIN	564d	
	עשב	HERB	793c	
	שדה	FIELD	961c	1 d
	שאל	ASK	981c	1 a
	שקק	HISS	1056d	1
10 2	און	TROUBLE	20a	3
	הבל	VAPOUR	211a	2
	חזה	SEE	302c	2
	חלום	DREAM	321d	2 b
	כמו	LIKE	455d	1
	נחם	CONSOLE ONESELF	637a	
	נסע	JOURNEY	652b	3

Ch v.	Heb	Eng	Page	Sec
	ענה	BE BOWED DOWN	776a	3
	צאן	SMALL CATTLE	838b	2
	קסם	PRACTICE OF DIVINATION	890d	2
	רעה	TEND	945a	1 d2
	שוא	EMPTINESS	996b	2
	שקר	DECEPTION	1055c	4
	תרפים	IDOL	1076d	
10 3	בית	HOUSE	110a	5 de
	הוד	MAJESTY	217b	4
	חרה	BURN	354a	2
	סוס	HORSE	692d	3
	עדר	FLOCK	727d	1a
	על	UPON	757d	2 7d
	עתוד	HE/GOAT	800d	
	פקד	ATTEND TO	823b	A 1b
	רעה	TEND	945a	1 d2
10 4	יחדו	TOGETHER	*403c	B
	יתד	PEG	450b	A
	מלחמה	WAR	536c	
	מן	OUT OF	579d	2 cb
	נגש	DRIVE	620c	3
	פנה	CORNER	819d	2
	קשת	BOW	906a	1 b
10 5	בוס	TRAMPLE	100d	
	גבור	STRONG	150b	2
	חוץ	THE OUTSIDE	300b	2 a
	טיט	MUD	376c	1
	לחם	ENGAGE IN BATTLE	535d	
	רכב	RIDE	938d	3
10 6	בית	HOUSE	110a	5 de
	בית	HOUSE	110a	5 dz
	גבר	BE STRONG	149d	
	יהוה	YAHWEH	218d	2 1d
	יהוה	YAHWEH	219b	2 2c
	זנח	REJECT	276b	
	יוסף	JOSEPH	415d	1 c
	ישב	CAUSE TO SIT	443d	3 a
	ישע	DELIVER	446d	1 b
	כאשר	AS	455c	1 e
	רחם	LOVE	933c	1
10 7	גבור	STRONG	150b	2
	יין	WINE	406c	A
	כמו	LIKE	455c	1 a
	לב	HEART	525c	2 9a
	לב	HEART	525c	2 9a
	שמח	REJOICE	970b	2 a
10 8	כמו	LIKE	456a	1 bb
	פדה	RANSOM	804a	3 b
	קבץ	GATHER	868a	1
	רבה	BECOME MANY	915a	1 a
10 9	זכר	REMEMBER	270a	1 3 b
	זרע	SOW	281d	3 a
	מרחק	DISTANT PLACE	935d	
10 10	אשור	ASSYRIA	78d	3
	לבנון	LEBANON	*527a	
	לבנון	LEBANON	527a	
	מצא	FIND	*593c	4
	מצא	FIND	594b	3
	קבץ	GATHER	868a	1
	שוב	TURN BACK	998d	1 a
10 11	אשור	ASSHUR	78d	3
	גאון	EXALTATION	144d	1 a
	יאר	STREAM	384c	1
	יבש	BE DRY	386d	3
	ירד	BE BROUGHT DOWN	434b	1
	נכה	SMITE	646b	3
	עבר	PASS OVER	717c	3 b
	מצולה	DEPTH	847d	
	צרה	DISTRESS	865b	
	שבט	ROD	987a	1 d
10 12	ב	IN	89d	3 2c
	ב	IN	90a	3 2d
	גבר	BE STRONG	149d	
	הלך	WALK	236b	2
	נאם	UTTERANCE	610b	2
11 1	ארז	CEDAR	72c	1 a
	דלת	DOOR	195b	4
	לבנון	LEBANON	*527a	
	לבנון	LEBANON	527b	
	פתח	OPEN	835a	
11 2	אדיר	MAJESTIC	12b	2
	אלון	OAK	47c	
	ארז	CEDAR	72c	1 a
	בצר	MAKE INACCESSIBLE	131a	
	בציר	VINTAGE	131b	
	ברוש	CYPRESS	141c	2
	בשן	BASHAN	143c	
	ילל	HOWL	410b	
	יער	WOOD	420d	A
	ירד	GO DOWN	433b	1 k
	נפל	FALL	657a	1
	שדד	DEAL VIOLENTLY WITH	994d	
11 3	אדרת	GLORY	12b	1
	אדרת	MANTLE	12b	2
	גאון	EXALTATION	145a	1 c
	יללה	HOWLING	410c	
	ירדן	JORDAN	434d	
	כפיר	LION	498d	
	קול	VOICE	876d	1 a
	שאגה	ROARING	980d	1

Ch v.	Heb	Eng	Page	Sec
	שדד	DEAL VIOLENTLY WITH	994b	
11 4	יהוה	YAHWEH	219a	2 lf
	הרגה	SLAUGHTER	247c	
	צאן	SMALL CATTLE	838c	3
	רעה	TEND	945a	1 c
11 5	אשם	OFFEND	79c	3
	ברך	BLESS	138d	2 a
	הרג	KILL	247a	1 a
	חמל	SPARE	328b	
	מכר	SELL	569b	
	עשר	BE RICH	799b	2
	קנה	ACQUIRE	889a	2
	רעה	TEND	945a	1 d2
11 6	חמל	SPARE	328b	
	כתת	BEAT	510a	1
	מצא	FIND	594b	3
	נאם	UTTERANCE	610b	2
	רע	FRIEND	946b	3
11 7	הרגה	SLAUGHTER	247c	
	חבל	BIND	286b	1
	חבלים	UNION	287a	
	כן	SO	487a	3 db
	כנעני	TRADER	489b	
	לקח	TAKE	543a	4 a
	מקל	ROD	596c	
	נעם	DELIGHTFULNESS	653d	2
	צאן	SMALL CATTLE	838c	3
	צאן	SMALL CATTLE	838c	3
	רעה	TEND	945a	1 c
11 8	בחל	FEEL LOATHING	103c	1
	ירח	MONTH	437b	1
	כחד	HIDE	470c	2
	נפש	SOUL	660d	6 b
	נפש	SOUL	661a	6 g
	קצר	BE SHORT	894b	
	רעה	TEND	945a	1 d2
11 9	אשה	WOMAN	61c	4
	בשר	FLESH	142c	1 a
	כחד	BE HIDDEN	470b	2
	כחד	BE HIDDEN	470b	2
	רעה	TEND	945a	1 c
	רעות	FELLOW	946c	
11 10	ברית	COVENANT	136d	2 2c
	ברית	COVENANT	137b	3 3
	גדע	HEW	154b	
	כרת	CUT	503d	4
	מקל	ROD	596c	
	נעם	DELIGHTFULNESS	653d	2
	פרר	BREAK	830b	1 a
11 11	כן	SO	486d	2 db
	כנעני	TRADER	489b	
	פרר	BREAK	830c	2
	צאן	SMALL CATTLE	838c	3
	שמר	KEEP	1036d	1 d
11 12	חדל	CEASE	293a	1
	טוב	PLEASING	373c	5
	יהב	GIVE	396c	1
	כסף	SILVER	494d	9
	שכר	HIRE	969a	1
	שקל	WEIGH	1053c	2
11 13	אדר	GLORY	12a	1
	יצר	FORM	427d	1 a
	יקר	BE APPRAISED	429d	2
	יקר	PRICE	430b	2
	על	UPON	759b	4 2d
	מעל	ADDENDA ET CORRIGENDA	1125d	
11 14	אחוה	BROTHERHOOD	27d	
	גדע	HEW	154b	
	חבל	BIND	286b	1
	חבלים	UNION	287a	
	מקל	ROD	596c	
	פרר	BREAK	830b	1 d
11 15	אולי	FOOLISH	17c	
	כלי	INSTRUMENT	480a	2 c
	רעה	TEND	945a	1 d1
11 16	בקש	SEEK	134d	1 b
	בריא	FAT	135d	
	בשר	FLESH	142c	1 a
	כול	SUSTAIN	465a	1
	כחד	BE HIDDEN	470b	2
	נער	SCATTERING	654d	
	נער	RETAINER	655a	2 b
	נצב	STAND	662b	4
	פקד	ATTEND TO	823b	A 1b
	פרסה	HOOF	828b	1
	פרק	TEAR APART	830a	
	קום	STAND	879a	3
	רעה	TEND	945a	1 d2
	רפא	HEAL	951a	2
	שבר	BREAK	990d	
11 17	אליל	WORTHLESSNESS	47b	A
	הוי	AH	223a	
	זרוע	ARM	283d	1 a
	חרב	DRYNESS	351b	1
	יבש	BE DRY	386c	1 e
	ימין	RIGHT	412a	3
	כהה	GROW DIM	462c	
	עזב	LEAVE	737b	2 a2
	צאן	SMALL CATTLE	838c	3
	שכח	FORGET	*1013b	1 b
	יסד	FOUND	413d	
12 1	יצר	FORM	427d	2 a
	נאם	UTTERANCE	610b	2
	משא	UTTERANCE	672d	

Ch v.	Heb	Eng	Page	Sec
	קרב	INWARD PART	899b	2 a
	רוח	BREATH	925b	4 a
12 2	סף	BASIN	706b	
	על	UPON	753c	2 1c
	מצור	SIEGE	849a	1
	רעל	REELING	947a	
12 3	מעמסה	LOAD	770c	
	עמס	CARRY A LOAD	770c	
	שרט	INCISE	976b	
12 4	בית	HOUSE	110a	5 de
	ה	THE	208c	1 hb
	נאם	UTTERANCE	610b	2
	נכה	SMITE	646c	4 a
	עורון	BLINDNESS	734d	
	עין	EYE	744b	1 j
	פקח	OPEN	824d	1 a
	רכב	RIDE	938d	3
	שגעון	MADNESS	993d	
	תמהון	BEWILDERMENT	1069b	
12 5	אלהים	GOD	44d	4 c
	אלוף	CHIEF	49b	
	אמצה	STRENGTH	55b	
	לב	HEART	525c	2 7
12 6	אלוף	CHIEF	49b	
	אש	FIRE	77d	6
	אש	FIRE	77d	6
	ישב	SIT	443b	4
	כיור	POT	468c	2
	לפיד	TORCH	542a	
	עמיר	SWATH	771c	
	שמאל	LEFT	969d	1
	תחת	UNDERNEATH	1065d	2 ia
12 7	אהל	TENT	14a	1
	בית	HOUSE	110a	5 c
	גדל	BECOME GREAT	152b	3 a
	ישע	DELIVER	446d	1 b
	מען	PURPOSE	775c	2 cb
	תפארה	BEAUTY	802d	2 a
	ראשון	FIRST	912a	3 a1
12 8	אלהים	GOD	44b	4 a
	בית	HOUSE	110a	5 c
	בעד	ABOUT	126c	1 c
	גנן	DEFEND	171a	
	כשל	BE FEEBLE	505d	2
	מלאך	MESSENGER	521d	2
12 9	בקש	SEEK	134d	2 d
12 10	את	MARK OF THE ACCUSATIVE	85c	3 b
	בית	HOUSE	110a	5 c
	דקר	PIERCE	201b	
	ה	THE	208a	1 f
	חן	FAVOR	336b	2
	תחנון	SUPPLICATION FOR FAVOR	337d	2
	יחיד	ONLY ONE	402d	1
	מרר	BE BITTER	600b	2
	תמרור	BITTERNESS	601b	
	נבט	LOOK	613d	2
	ספד	WAIL	704d	
	מספד	WAILING	704d	1
	רוח	BREATH	926a	9 e
	פך	POUR OUT	1049d	2 a
12 11	בקעה	PLAIN	132c	2
	מגדו	MEGIDDO	152a	
	גדל	BECOME GREAT	152b	2 c
	הדדרמון	HADADRIMMON	213a	
	הדדרמון	HADADRIMMON	*213a	
	מספד	WAILING	704d	1
12 12	ארץ	EARTH	76b	2 f
	בד	SEPARATION	94c	1 a
	בית	HOUSE	110a	5 c
	נתן	NATHAN	682a	8
	ספד	WAIL	704d	
12 13	בד	SEPARATION	94c	1 a
	בית	HOUSE	110b	5 dk
	לוי	LEVI	532c	1 b
	שמעי	SHEMEITES	1035c	
	משפחה	CLAN	1047a	1 d
12 14	בד	SEPARATION	94c	1 a
13 1	חטאת	SIN	308d	1 b
	חטאת	SIN	309a	1 d4
	נדה	IMPURITY	622c	2
	פתח	OPEN	835c	
	מקור	SPRING	881b	1 b
13 2	זכר	REMEMBER	270c	1 b
	טמאה	UNCLEANNESS	380a	3
	כרת	CUT OFF	504d	3
	נאם	UTTERANCE	610b	2
	נביא	PROPHET	612a	2
	עבר	PASS OVER	719a	4
	עצב	IDOL	781b	
	רוח	BREATH	925b	3 h
13 3	אב	FATHER	3b	1
	אם	MOTHER	51d	1
	דבר	SPEAK	181c	4 a
	דקר	PIERCE	201b	
	ילד	BEAR	408c	3
	נבא	PROPHESY	612b	2
13 4	אדרת	MANTLE	12b	2
	חזיון	VISION	303b	1
	כחש	DECEIVE	471b	1
	לבש	PUT ON	528a	A
	נביא	PROPHET	612a	2
	נבא	PROPHESY	612b	2
	שער	HAIR	972b	1
13 5	אדמה	GROUND	9c	1

MALACHI

Ch	v.	Heb	Eng	Page	Sec
		מצא	FIND	394a	1 g1
		תורה	INSTRUCTION	436a	1 e
		מישור	UPRIGHTNESS	449d	3
		עון	INIQUITY	731a	1 b
		עולה	INJUSTICE	732c	2
		שפה	SPEECH	973c	1 a1
		שוב	TURN BACK	999d	6 a
		שלום	PEACE	1023b	5 b
2	7	בקש	SEEK	134d	2 b
		דעת	WISDOM	395d	2 a
		תורה	INSTRUCTION	436a	1 e
		כהן	PRIEST	464b	7
		מלאך	MESSENGER	521c	1 c
		שמר	KEEP	1036d	2 a
2	8	ברית	COVENANT	136d	2 2d
		דרך	WAY	203a	6 b
		ה	THE	208b	1 g
		תורה	INSTRUCTION	436a	1 e
		כשל	CAUSE TO STUMBLE	506a	1 c
		לוי	LEVITE	532d	2
		שחת	GO TO RUIN	1008a	1
2	9	בזה	DESPISE	102c	3
		גם	ALSO	169d	4
		דרך	WAY	204a	6 ec
		תורה	INSTRUCTION	436a	1 e
		ל	TO	513a	5 ad
		נשא	LIFT	670c	1 b 3
		שפל	LOW	1050c	3
2	10	אב	FATHER	3b	2
		אל	GOD	42d	6 d
		בגד	ACT TREACHEROUSLY	93d	B
		ברא	CREATE	135b	2
		ברית	COVENANT	137b	3 3
		חלל	POLLUTE	320c	3
2	11	אהב	LOVE	13b	5 c
		אל	GOD	42c	3
		בגד	ACT TREACHEROUSLY	93d	A
		בת	DAUGHTER	123d	5
		בעל	MARRY	127b	1
		חלל	POLLUTE	320c	1
		נכר	FOREIGNNESS	648c	1
		קדש	APARTNESS	872b	6
		תועבה	ABOMINATION	1072d	1 b
2	12	אהל	TENT	14a	2
		כרת	CUT OFF	504c	2 c
		מנחה	OFFERING	585b	4
		מנחה	OFFERING	585c	6
		נגש	APPROACH	621b	
		עור	ROUSE ONESELF	735a	
		ענה	ANSWER	773a	3 a
		יעקב	JACOB	785a	2
2	13	אנקה	CRYING	60c	
		בכי	WEEPING	113d	
		דמעה	TEARS	199c	
		יד	HAND	391b	5 g3
		כסה	COVER	491d	4
		מנחה	OFFERING	585b	4
		פנה	TURN	815c	2 c1
		רצון	GOODWILL	953c	2
		שני	SECOND	1041c	
2	14	אשה	WOMAN	61b	2
		בגד	ACT TREACHEROUSLY	93d	B
		ברית	COVENANT	136c	1 5
		חבר	UNITE	*288b	1 a
		חברת	CONSORT	289a	
		נעורים	YOUTH	655c	
		עוד	BEAR WITNESS	730a	1
		על	UPON	758b	3 b
2	15	אשה	WOMAN	61b	2
		בגד	ACT TREACHEROUSLY	93d	B
		בקש	SEEK	134d	1 b
		זרע	SOWING	283b	5
		לא	NOT	519a	1 a
		נעורים	YOUTH	655c	
		רוח	BREATH	925b	3 g
		שאר	REST	984c	
		שמר	KEEP	1037b	1
2	16	אלהים	GOD	44c	4 ba
		בגד	ACT TREACHEROUSLY	93d	B
		חמס	VIOLENCE	329c	
		כסה	COVER	492a	6
		לבוש	CLOTHING	528c	
		רוח	BREATH	925b	3 g
		שנא	HATE	971c	2
		שלח	SEND	1019a	1 b
		שמר	KEEP	1037b	1
2	17	או	OR	15a	1
		אלהים	GOD	44c	4 bb
		ב	IN	90a	3 2e
		חפץ	DELIGHT IN	342d	2 a
		טוב	PLEASANT	373d	2 c
		יגע	TOIL	388b	
		מה	HOW	553d	4 a
		משפט	JUDGMENT	1048b	1 a
3	1	אדון	LORD	11a	1 2
		בקש	SEEK	134d	3 c
		ברית	COVENANT	137a	2 2k
		דרך	WAY	203a	1
		היכל	TEMPLE	228c	2 d
		חפץ	DELIGHTING IN	343a	1
		מלאך	MESSENGER	521c	1 b
		מלאך	MESSENGER	521d	3
		פנה	TURN	815c	
		פתאם	SUDDENNESS	837c	
3	2	אש	FIRE	77c	3
		בוא	COME	98c	2
		ברית	LYE	141b	
		יום	DAY	*399a	3
		יום	DAY	400a	7 d1 a
		כבס	WASH	460b	1
		כול	SUPPORT	465b	3
		מי	WHO	567a	F c
		עמד	STAND	764b	1
		צרף	SMELT	864b	1
3	3	בן	SON	121a	1 je
		זהב	GOLD	262c	1
		זהב	GOLD	263c	1
		זהב	GOLD	263d	2 i
		זקק	REFINE	279b	
		מהר	BE CLEAN	372b	1 a
		טהר	BE CLEAN	372c	1 c
		ישב	SIT	442c	1 a
		כסף	SILVER	494a	1
		כסף	SILVER	494c	9
		לוי	LEVI	532c	1
		מנחה	OFFERING	585b	4
		מנחה	OFFERING	585c	6
		נגש	APPROACH	621b	
		צרף	SMELT	864b	
3	4	מנחה	OFFERING	585b	4
		עולם	LONG DURATION	762d	1 a
		ערב	BE SWEET	787a	
		קדמני	FORMER	870d	1
3	5	אלמנה	WIDOW	48b	
		גר	SOJOURNER	158b	2
		ירא	FEAR	431c	3 b
		יתום	ORPHAN	450c	
		כשף	PRACTICE SORCERY	506c	
		מהר	HASTEN	555a	1
		נאף	COMMIT ADULTERY	610d	1 a
		נטה	BEND	641a	3 g
		עד	WITNESS	729d	2 a
		עשק	OPPRESS	798d	1
		קרב	COME NEAR	897b	1 a
		שכר	HIRE	969a	1
		שכר	HIRED	969b	2
		שבע	SWEAR	989b	1 a
		משפט	JUDGMENT	1048b	1 a
3	6	בן	SON	120d	1 jb
		יהוה	YAHWEH	219b	2 c
		כלה	BE FINISHED	477d	2 c
		שנה	CHANGE	1039d	
3	7	חק	SOMETHING PRESCRIBED	349d	7 g
		יום	DAY	401b	7 k
		מה	HOW	553d	4 a
		מן	FROM	583d	9 b2
		שוב	TURN BACK	998a	6 g
3	8	אדם	MAN	9b	2
		מה	HOW	553d	4 a
		מעשר	TENTH PART	798b	2
		קבע	ROB	867b	
3	9	ארר	CURSE	76d	
		מארה	CURSE	76d	
		גוי	NATION	156d	1 b
		ה	THE	208d	1 i
		כל	ALL	481d	1 da
		קבע	ROB	867c	
3	10	אם	IF	50d	2 ba
		אוצר	TREASURE	70a	3 b
		ארבה	LATTICE	70d	
		בוא	COME	99a	1
		בחן	TRY	103c	2 c
		בית	HOUSE	109b	1 ae 0
		בלי	WEARING OUT	116a	D
		ברכה	BLESSING	139d	1 b
		די	SUFFICIENCY	191b	1
		זה	THIS	261d	6 bb
		טרף	TEAR	*383a	
		טרף	PREY	383c	2
		מעשר	TENTH PART	798b	2
		פתח	OPEN	835a	
		ריק	MAKE EMPTY	938a	2
		שמי	HEAVENS	1030a	1 b
3	11	אדמה	GROUND	9c	1
		גער	REBUKE	172a	2
		גפן	VINE	172c	
		ל	TO	515b	5 hb g
		שחת	GO TO RUIN	1008b	1
		שכל	BE BEREAVED	1013d	2 b2
		אשר	GO STRAIGHT	80d	4
3	12	חפץ	DELIGHT	343a	1
3	13	דבר	SPEAK	180d	
		זד	INSOLENT	267d	
		חזק	BE FIRM	304c	1 4a
3	14	בצע	PROFIT	130c	
		הלך	WALK	235a	2 3c
		כי	THAT	471d	1 a
		מה	WHAT	552c	1 aa
		עבד	WORK	713b	4 a
		קדרנית	AS MOURNERS	871a	
		שוא	EMPTINESS	996b	1
		משמרת	GUARD	1038c	3
3	15	אשר	GO STRAIGHT	80d	4
		בחן	TRY	103c	2 c
		בנה	BUILD	125a	2 a
		גם	YEA	169c	3
		מלט	SLIP AWAY	572b	2
		רשעה	WICKEDNESS	958a	3
3	16	דבר	SPEAK	180d	
		זכרון	MEMORIAL	272a	1 d
		חשב	THINK	363a	1 1
		ירא	FEAR	431c	3 b
		כתב	BE WRITTEN	508a	1
		ספר	MISSIVE	*707c	3
		ספר	MISSIVE	*707c	3 g
		רע	FRIEND	946b	3
3	17	בן	SON	120a	1
		חמל	SPARE	328b	
		יום	DAY	*399a	3
		ל	TO	517a	6 a
		סגלה	PROPERTY	688c	1
		עבד	WORK	713a	2
3	18	בין	INTERVAL	107c	1 d
		בין	INTERVAL	107c	1 b
		צדיק	JUST	843a	3 b
		ראה	TO SEE	907c	7 e
		רשע	WICKED	957c	3
		אשר	THAT	83c	8 b
3	19	בוא	COME	98c	2
		בער	BURN	129a	4
		זד	INSOLENT	267d	
		יום	DAY	*399a	3
		להט	SET ABLAZE	529d	
		עזב	LEAVE	737b	1 j
		ענף	BRANCH	778c	
		רשעה	WICKEDNESS	958a	3
		שרש	ROOT	1057c	1
		תנור	FIRE-POT	1072b	
3	20	זרח	RISE	280b	1 b
		ירא	FEAR	431c	3 b
		כנף	WING	489d	1 g
		עגל	CALF	722a	
		פוש	SPRING ABOUT	807d	
		צדקה	RIGHTEOUSNESS	842b	6 a
		מרבק	STALL	918d	
		מרפא	HEALING	951c	2
		שמש	SUN	1039a	1
3	21	אפר	ASHES	68a	1
		יום	DAY	*399a	3
		כף	SOLE OF FOOT	496d	3
		עסס	PRESS	779a	
		רשע	WICKED	957b	2
3	22	זכר	REMEMBER	270a	1 4 a
		חק	SOMETHING PRESCRIBED	349d	7 g
		חרב	HOREB	352a	
		תורה	LAW	436b	2 b3
		משה	MOSES	602c	
		משה	MOSES	602d	
		עבד	SLAVE	714a	3
		צוה	CHARGE	846a	4 c
3	23	אליה	ELIJAH	45b	A
		בוא	COME	98c	2
		גדול	GREAT	153a	6 a
		יום	DAY	*399a	3
		ירא	CAUSE FEAR	431d	2
		נביא	PROPHET	611d	1
3	24	חרם	DEVOTED THING	356c	3
		נכה	SMITE	646c	4 a
		על	UPON	757c	2 7 c c
		שוב	TURN BACK	999b	2 a

GENESIS

Ch v.	Heb	Eng	Page	Sec
2 13	גיחון	GIHON	161d	1
3 6	גם	ALSO	169a	1
4 4	גם	ALSO	169a	1
4 22	גם	ALSO	169a	1
4 26	גם	ALSO	169a	1
6 4	גם	ALSO	169a	1
7 3	גם	ALSO	169a	1
9 21	גלה	UNCOVER	163c	
10 18	גמדים	GAMMADIM	167d	
10 21	גם	ALSO	169a	1
12 13	גלל	ACCOUNT	164b	
12 16	גמל	CAMEL	168d	1
14 16	גם	ALSO	169a	1
15 14	גם	ALSO	169a	1
17 16	גם	ALSO	169a	1
19 21	גם	ALSO	169a	1
19 38	גם	ALSO	169a	1
20 5	גם	ALSO	169a	1
20 6	גם	ALSO	169a	1
20 12	גם	ALSO	169a	1
21 8	גמל	WEAN	168b	
22 20	גם	ALSO	169a	1
22 24	גם	ALSO	169a	1
24 10	גמל	CAMEL	168d	2
	גמל	CAMEL	168d	1
24 11	גמל	CAMEL	168d	2
24 14	גמל	CAMEL	168d	2
	גם	ALSO	169a	1
24 17	גמא	SWALLOW	167d	
24 19	גמל	CAMEL	168d	2
	גם	ALSO	169a	1
24 20	גמל	CAMEL	168d	2
24 22	גמל	CAMEL	168d	2
24 25	גם	ALSO	169a	1
24 30	גמל	CAMEL	168d	2
24 31	גמל	CAMEL	168d	2
24 32	גמל	CAMEL	168d	2
24 35	גמל	CAMEL	168d	1
24 44	גמל	CAMEL	168d	2
24 46	גמל	CAMEL	168d	2
	גם	ALSO	169a	1
24 61	גמל	CAMEL	168d	3
24 63	גמל	CAMEL	168d	3
24 64	גמל	CAMEL	168d	3
26 21	גם	ALSO	169a	1
27 31	גם	ALSO	169a	1
27 34	גם	ALSO	169a	1
29 3	גלל	ROLL	164b	
29 8	גלל	ROLL	164b	
29 10	גלל	ROLL	164c	
29 27	גם	ALSO	169a	1
30 3	גם	ALSO	169a	1
30 6	גם	ALSO	169a	1
30 15	גם	ALSO	169a	1
30 27	גלל	ACCOUNT	164b	
30 43	גמל	CAMEL	168d	1
31 17	גמל	CAMEL	168d	3
31 21	גלעד	GILEAD	167a	2a
31 23	גלעד	GILEAD	167a	2a
31 25	גלעד	GILEAD	167a	2a
31 34	גמל	CAMEL	168d	3
31 46	גל	HEAP	164d	1c
31 47	גל	GALEED	165a	
	גל	HEAP	164d	1c
31 48	גל	HEAP	164d	1c
	גל	GALEED	165a	
31 51	גל	HEAP	164d	1c
31 52	גל	HEAP	164d	1c
31 54	גלעד	GILEAD	167b	4
32 8	גמל	CAMEL	168d	3
32 21	גם	ALSO	169a	1
32 33	גיד	SINEW	161c	
35 7	גלה	UNCOVER	163a	1c
37 7	גם	ALSO	169a	1
25	גלעד	GILEAD	167b	3b
	גמל	CAMEL	168d	2
38 24	גם	ALSO	169a	1
39 5	גלל	ACCOUNT	164b	
41 14	גלח	SHAVE	164a	4
42 28	גם	ALSO	169a	1
43 18	גלל	ROLL	164c	
44 16	גם	ALSO	169a	1
47 3	גם	ALSO	169a	1
47 19	גם	ALSO	169a	1
48 11	גם	ALSO	169a	1
50 15	גמל	DEAL FULLY	168a	1a
50 17	גמל	DEAL FULLY	168a	1a

EXODUS

Ch v.	Heb	Eng	Page	Sec
2 3	גמא	REED	167d	
2 19	גם	ALSO	169a	1
3 9	גם	ALSO	169a	1
4 14	גם	ALSO	169a	1
5 2	גם	ALSO	169a	1
8 28	גם	ALSO	169a	1
9 3	גמל	CAMEL	168d	1
12 32	גם	ALSO	169a	1
16 16	גלגלת	HEAD	166b	2
20 26	גלה	UNCOVER	163a	2a
34 3	גם	ALSO	169a	1
38 26	גלגלת	HEAD	166b	2

LEVITICUS

Ch v.	Heb	Eng	Page	Sec
11 4	גמל	CAMEL	168d	4
13 33	גלח	SHAVE	164a	1
	גלח	SHAVE	164a	
14 8	גלח	SHAVE	164a	2
14 9	גלח	SHAVE	164a	2
18 6	גלה	UNCOVER	163b	1a
18 19	גלה	UNCOVER	163b	1a
20 11	גלה	UNCOVER	163b	1a
20 18	גלה	UNCOVER	163b	1a
20 21	גלה	UNCOVER	163b	1a
21 5	גלח	SHAVE	164a	2
26 30	גלל	IDOLS	165d	
	גלל	IDOLS	165d	

NUMBERS

Ch v.	Heb	Eng	Page	Sec
1 2	גלגלת	HEAD	166b	2
1 10	גמליאל	GAMALIEL	168c	
1 18	גלגלת	HEAD	166b	2
1 20	גלגלת	HEAD	166b	2
1 22	גלגלת	HEAD	166b	2
2 20	גמליאל	GAMALIEL	168c	
3 47	גלגלת	HEAD	166b	2
6 9	גלח	SHAVE	164a	1
6 18	גלח	SHAVE	164a	1
6 19	גלח	SHAVE	164a	
7 54	גמליאל	GAMALIEL	168c	
7 59	גמליאל	GAMALIEL	168c	
10 23	גמליאל	GAMALIEL	168c	
13 12	גמלי	GEMALLI	168d	
17 23	גמל	RIPEN	168b	3
18 3	גם	ALSO	169a	1
22 31	גלה	UNCOVER	163b	1b
23 25	גם	ALSO	169a	1
24 4	גלה	UNCOVER	162d	1
24 16	גלה	UNCOVER	162d	1
26 29	גלעדי	GILEADITES	167c	1
	גלעד	GILEAD	167c	6a
26 30	גלעד	GILEAD	167c	6a
27 1	גלעד	GILEAD	167c	6a
32 1	גלעד	GILEAD	166d	1a
26	גלעד	GILEAD	167a	1d
32 29	גלעד	GILEAD	166d	1a
32 39	גלעד	GILEAD	167a	2c
32 40	גלעד	GILEAD	166d	1b
34 22	יגלי	JOGLI	163d	
36 1	גלעד	GILEAD	167c	6a

DEUTERONOMY

Ch v.	Heb	Eng	Page	Sec
1 37	גלל	ACCOUNT	164b	
	גם	ALSO	169a	1
2 36	גלעד	GILEAD	167a	2b
3 10	גלעד	GILEAD	167b	3c
3 12	גלעד	GILEAD	166d	1a
3 13	גלעד	GILEAD	167a	2b
3 15	גלעד	GILEAD	167a	2b
3 16	גלעד	GILEAD	167a	2b
3 20	גם	ALSO	169a	1
4 43	גלעד	GILEAD	167a	1d
11 30	גלגל	GILGAL	166a	4
14 7	גמל	CAMEL	168d	4
15 10	גלל	ACCOUNT	164b	
18 12	גלל	ACCOUNT	164b	
21 12	גלח	SHAVE	164a	1
23 1	גלה	UNCOVER	163b	1a
27 20	גלה	UNCOVER	163b	1a
29 16	גלל	IDOLS	165d	
29 28	גלה	UNCOVER	163a	2c
32 6	גמל	DEAL FULLY	168b	1c
34 1	גלעד	GILEAD	167b	3c

JOSHUA

Ch v.	Heb	Eng	Page	Sec
4 19	גלגל	GILGAL	166a	1
4 20	גלגל	GILGAL	166a	1
5 9	גלל	ROLL	164c	
	גלגל	GILGAL	166a	1
5 10	גלגל	GILGAL	166a	1
7 11	גם	ALSO	169a	1
7 26	גל	HEAP	164d	1a
8 29	גל	HEAP	164d	1a
9 6	גלגל	GILGAL	166a	1
10 6	גלגל	GILGAL	166a	1
7	גלגל	GILGAL	166a	1
10 9	גלגל	GILGAL	166a	1
10 15	גלגל	GILGAL	166a	1
10 18	גלל	ROLL	164b	
43	גלגל	GILGAL	166a	1
12 2	גלעד	GILEAD	167a	1b
12 5	גלעד	GILEAD	167a	1b
12 23	גלגל	GALILEE	165b	2
	גלגל	GILGAL	166a	5
13 2	גלילת	TERRITORY	165c	
13 11	גלעד	GILEAD	167a	2b
13 25	גלעד	GILEAD	167a	1d
13 31	גלעד	GILEAD	167a	2b
14 6	גלגל	GILGAL	166a	1
15 7	גלגל	GILGAL	166a	2
15 8	גיא	VALLEY	161c	G
15 17	גלילות	GELILOTH	*165c	1

Ch v.	Heb	Eng	Page	Sec
15 19	גלה	BASIN	165a	1
15 51	גלה	GILOH	162b	
17 1	גלעד	GILEAD	167a	2b
	גלעד	GILEAD	167c	6a
17 3	גלעד	GILEAD	167c	6a
17 5	גלעד	GILEAD	167a	2a
17 6	גלעד	GILEAD	167a	2a
18 16	גיא	VALLEY	161c	G
18 17	גלילות	GELILOTH	165c	1
	גלגל	GILGAL	*166a	2
20 7	גלעד	GILEAD	165b	2
20 8	גלעד	GALILEE	167a	1d
21 32	גלעד	GALILEE	165b	2
21 38	גלעד	GILEAD	167a	1d
22 9	גלעד	GILEAD	167b	3a
22 10	גלילה	TERRITORY	165c	
	גלילות	GELILOTH	165c	2a
22 11	גלילות	GELILOTH	165c	2b
	גלילה	TERRITORY	165c	
22 13	גלעד	GILEAD	167b	3a
22 15	גלעד	GILEAD	167b	3a
22 32	גלעד	GILEAD	167b	3a
22 34	גל	GALEED	165a	

JUDGES

Ch v.	Heb	Eng	Page	Sec
1 15	גלה	BASIN	165a	1
2 1	גלגל	GILGAL	166a	1
3 16	גמד	SHORTCUBIT	167d	
3 19	גלגל	GILGAL	166a	1
3 31	גם	ALSO	169a	1
5 17	גלעד	GILEAD	167b	5
6 5	גמל	CAMEL	168d	1
6 35	גם	ALSO	169a	1
7 3	גלעד	GILEAD	167b	2d
7 12	גמל	CAMEL	168d	1
8 21	גמל	CAMEL	168d	3
8 22	גם	ALSO	169a	1
8 26	גמל	CAMEL	168d	3
8 31	גם	ALSO	169a	1
9 16	גמול	DEALING	168b	1
9 19	גם	ALSO	169a	1
9 53	גלגלת	SKULL	166a	1
10 3	גלעדי	GILEADITES	167c	3
10 4	גלעד	GILEAD	167a	2a
10 8	גלעד	GILEAD	167b	3c
10 17	גלעד	GILEAD	166d	1b
	גלעד	GILEAD	*167b	4
10 18	גלעד	GILEAD	167a	1c
11 1	גלעד	GILEAD	167c	6b
	גלעדי	GILEADITES	167c	2
11 2	גלעד	GILEAD	167c	6b
11 5	גלעד	GILEAD	167a	1c
11 7	גלעד	GILEAD	167a	1c
11 8	גלעד	GILEAD	167a	1c
11 9	גלעד	GILEAD	167a	1c
11 10	גלעד	GILEAD	167a	1c
11 11	גלעד	GILEAD	167a	1c
11 29	גלעד	GILEAD	166d	1b
	גלעד	GILEAD	167a	1d
11 40	גלעדי	GILEADITES	167c	2
12 4	גלעד	GILEAD	167a	1c
	גלעד	GILEAD	167b	5
12 5	גלעד	GILEAD	167a	1c
	גלעד	GILEAD	167b	5
12 7	גלעד	GILEAD	167a	1d
	גלעדי	GILEADITES	167c	2
16 17	גלח	SHAVE	164a	
16 19	גלח	SHAVE	164a	2
16 22	גלח	SHAVE	164a	
18 30	גלה	UNCOVER	163a	3
20 1	גלעד	GILEAD	167b	5
21 8	גלעד	GILEAD	167b	2d
21 9	גלעד	GILEAD	167b	2d
21 10	גלעד	GILEAD	167b	2d
21 12	גלעד	GILEAD	167b	2d
21 14	גלעד	GILEAD	167b	2d

RUTH

Ch v.	Heb	Eng	Page	Sec
3 4	גלה	UNCOVER	163b	1b
3 7	גלה	UNCOVER	163b	1b
4 4	גלה	UNCOVER	162d	1

1 SAMUEL

Ch v.	Heb	Eng	Page	Sec
1 22	גמל	WEAN	168b	
1 23	גמל	WEAN	168b	2
1 24	גמל	WEAN	168b	2
2 27	גלה	UNCOVER	163a	1c
3 7	גלה	UNCOVER	163a	2c
3 21	גלה	UNCOVER	163a	1c
4 17	גם	ALSO	169a	1
4 21	גלה	UNCOVER	163a	3
4 22	גלה	UNCOVER	163a	3
7 16	גלגל	GILGAL	166a	1
9 15	גלה	UNCOVER	162d	1
10 8	גלגל	GILGAL	166a	1
11 1	גלעד	GILEAD	167b	2d
11 9	גלעד	GILEAD	167b	2d
11 14	גלגל	GILGAL	166a	1
11 15	גלגל	GILGAL	166a	1
13 4	גלגל	GILGAL	166a	1

ADDENDA

Ch	v.	Heb	Eng	Page	Sec
13	7	גלגל	GILGAL	166a	1
		גלעד	GILEAD	166d	1a
13	8	גלגל	GILGAL	166a	1
13	12	גלגל	GILGAL	166a	1
13	15	גלגל	GILGAL	166a	1
14	8	גלה	UNCOVER	163a	1b
14	11	גלה	UNCOVER	163a	1b
14	33	גלל	ROLL	164b	
15	3	גמל	CAMEL	168d	1
15	12	גלגל	GILGAL	166a	1
15	21	גלגל	GILGAL	166a	1
15	33	גלגל	GILGAL	166a	1
17	4	גלית	GOLIATH	163d	
17	23	גלית	GOLIATH	163d	
19	20	גם	ALSO	169a	1
19	23	גם	ALSO	169a	1
19	24	גם	ALSO	169a	1
20	2	גלה	UNCOVER	162d	1
20	12	גלה	UNCOVER	162d	1
20	13	גלה	UNCOVER	162d	1
20	27	גם	ALSO	169a	1
21	10	גלית	GOLIATH	163d	
22	8	גלה	UNCOVER	162d	1
22	10	גלית	GOLIATH	163d	
22	17	גלה	UNCOVER	162d	1
24	18	גמל	DEAL FULLY	168a	1a
25	44	גל	GALLIM	164d	
27	9	גמל	CAMEL	168d	1
28	4	גלבע	GILBOA	162c	
28	20	גם	ALSO	169a	1
30	17	גמל	CAMEL	168d	3
31	1	גלבע	GILBOA	162c	
31	8	גלבע	GILBOA	162c	
31	11	גלעד	GILEAD	167b	2d

2 SAMUEL

Ch	v.	Heb	Eng	Page	Sec
1	6	גלבע	GILBOA	162c	
1	21	גלבע	GILBOA	162c	
2	4	גלעד	GILEAD	167b	2d
2	5	גלעד	GILEAD	167b	2d
2	9	גלעד	GILEAD	167b	3c
2	24	גיח	GIAH	161d	
6	20	גלה	UNCOVER	163a	1a
7	27	גלה	UNCOVER	162d	1
10	4	גלח	SHAVE	164a	2
11	12	גם	ALSO	169a	1
14	26	גלח	SHAVE	164a	2
15	12	גילני	GILONITE	162b	
		גלה	GILOH	162b	
15	19	גלה	UNCOVER	163a	3
17	5	גם	ALSO	169a	1
17	26	גלעד	GILEAD	167b	3a
17	27	גלעדי	GILEADITES	167c	3
18	17	גל	HEAP	164d	1a
19	16	גלגל	GILGAL	166a	1
19	32	גלעדי	GILEADITES	167c	3
19	37	גמל	DEAL FULLY	168b	1b
		גמלה	DEALING	168c	
19	41	גלגל	GILGAL	166a	1
21	12	גלבע	GILBOA	162c	
		גלעד	GILEAD	167b	2d
21	19	גלית	GOLIATH	163d	
22	16	גלה	UNCOVER	163a	2b
22	21	גמל	DEAL FULLY	168b	1b
23	34	גילני	GILONITE	162b	
24	6	גלעד	GILEAD	167a	2b

1 KINGS

Ch	v.	Heb	Eng	Page	Sec
1	33	גיחון	GIHON	161d	2
1	38	גיחון	GIHON	161d	2
1	45	גיחון	GIHON	161d	2
2	17	גלעדי	GILEADITES	167c	3
3	26	גם	ALSO	169a	1
4	13	גלעד	GILEAD	167a	1d
		גלעד	GILEAD	167a	2b
4	19	גלעד	GILEAD	166d	1a
6	34	גליל	TURNING	165b	
7	41	גלה	BASIN	165a	2b
7	42	גלה	BASIN	165b	2b
		גלה	BASIN	165b	2b
9	11	גליל	GALILEE	165b	2
10	2	גמל	CAMEL	168d	2
11	20	גמל	WEAN	168b	2
14	10	גלל	DUNG	165b	
14	16	גלל	ACCOUNT	164b	
15	12	גלול	IDOLS	165d	
17	1	גלעד	GILEAD	167b	2d
21	19	גם	ALSO	169a	1
21	26	גלול	IDOLS	165d	
22	3	גלעד	GILEAD	167a	1d
22	4	גלעד	GILEAD	167a	1d
22	6	גלעד	GILEAD	167a	1d
22	12	גלעד	GILEAD	167a	1d
22	15	גלעד	GILEAD	167a	1d
22	20	גלעד	GILEAD	167a	1d
22	29	גלעד	GILEAD	167a	1d

2 KINGS

Ch	v.	Heb	Eng	Page	Sec
2	1	גלגל	GILGAL	166a	3
2	8	גלם	WRAP UP	166b	
4	12	גיחזי	GEHAZI	161c	
4	14	גיחזי	GEHAZI	161c	
4	25	גיחזי	GEHAZI	161c	
4	27	גיחזי	GEHAZI	161c	
4	29	גיחזי	GEHAZI	161c	
4	31	גיחזי	GEHAZI	161c	
4	36	גיחזי	GEHAZI	161c	
4	38	גלגל	GILGAL	166a	3
5	20	גיחזי	GEHAZI	161c	
5	21	גיחזי	GEHAZI	161c	
5	25	גיחזי	GEHAZI	161c	
8	4	גיחזי	GEHAZI	161c	
8	5	גיחזי	GEHAZI	161c	
8	9	גמל	CAMEL	168d	2
8	28	גלעד	GILEAD	167a	1d
9	1	גלעד	GILEAD	167a	1d
9	4	גלעד	GILEAD	167a	1d
9	14	גלעד	GILEAD	167a	1d
9	27	גם	ALSO	169a	1
9	35	גלגלת	SKULL	166a	1
10	33	גלעד	GILEAD	167b	3a
		גלעד	GILEAD	167b	3c
15	21	גלה	UNCOVER	163a	3
15	25	גלעדי	GILEADITES	167c	3
15	29	גלה	UNCOVER	163c	
		גלילה	GALILEE	165c	
16	9	גלה	UNCOVER	163c	
17	6	גלה	UNCOVER	163c	
17	11	גלה	UNCOVER	163c	
17	12	גלול	IDOLS	165d	
17	23	גלה	UNCOVER	163a	3
17	26	גלה	UNCOVER	163c	
17	27	גלה	UNCOVER	163c	
17	28	גלה	UNCOVER	163c	
17	33	גלה	UNCOVER	163c	
18	11	גלה	UNCOVER	163c	
19	25	גל	HEAP	164d	1d
20	12	גלל	ROLL	164c	
21	11	גלול	IDOLS	165d	
21	21	גלול	IDOLS	165d	
23	10	גיא	VALLEY	161c	G
23	24	גלול	IDOLS	165d	
24	14	גלה	UNCOVER	163a	3
		גלה	UNCOVER	163c	
24	15	גלה	UNCOVER	163c	
24	16	גולה	EXILE	163c	2
25	11	גלה	UNCOVER	163c	
25	27	גולת	EXILE	163d	1

1 CHRONICLES

Ch	v.	Heb	Eng	Page	Sec
2	21	גלעד	GILEAD	167c	6a
2	22	גלעד	GILEAD	167a	2a
2	23	גלעד	GILEAD	167c	6a
2	47	גישן	GESHAN	162c	
5	6	גלה	UNCOVER	163c	
5	9	גלעד	GILEAD	166d	1a
5	10	גלעד	GILEAD	167a	1b
5	14	גלעד	GILEAD	167c	6c
5	16	גלעד	GILEAD	167a	1b
5	21	גמל	CAMEL	168d	1
5	22	גולה	EXILE	163c	2
5	26	גלה	UNCOVER	163c	
5	41	גלה	UNCOVER	163c	
6	61	גליל	GALILEE	165b	2
6	65	גלעד	GILEAD	167a	1d
7	14	גלעד	GILEAD	167c	6a
7	17	גלעד	GILEAD	167c	6a
8	6	גלה	UNCOVER	163c	
8	7	גלה	UNCOVER	163c	
9	1	גלה	UNCOVER	163c	
9	15	גלל	GALAL	165b	1
9	16	גלל	GALAL	165b	2
10	1	גלבע	GILBOA	162c	
10	8	גלבע	GILBOA	162c	
10	10	גלגלת	SKULL	166a	1
10	11	גלעד	GILEAD	167b	2d
11	36	גילני	GILONITE	162b	
12	40	גמל	CAMEL	168d	2
16	31	גיל	REJOICE	162a	1c
		גיל	REJOICE	162a	1a
17	25	גלה	UNCOVER	162d	1
19	4	גלח	SHAVE	164a	1
20	5	גלית	GOLIATH	163d	
23	3	גלגלת	HEAD	166b	2
23	24	גלגלת	HEAD	166b	2
24	17	גמול	GAMUL	168c	
26	31	גלעד	GILEAD	167a	1d
27	21	גלעד	GILEAD	167a	2c
27	30	גמל	CAMEL	168d	1

2 CHRONICLES

Ch	v.	Heb	Eng	Page	Sec
4	12	גלה	BASIN	165b	2b
4	13	גלה	BASIN	165b	2b
9	1	גמל	CAMEL	168d	2
14	9	גיא	VALLEY	161b	E
14	14	גמל	CAMEL	168d	1
18	2	גלעד	GILEAD	167a	1d
18	3	גלעד	GILEAD	167a	1d
18	5	גלעד	GILEAD	167a	1d
18	11	גלעד	GILEAD	167a	1d
18	14	גלעד	GILEAD	167a	1d
18	19	גלעד	GILEAD	167a	1d
18	28	גלעד	GILEAD	167a	1d
20	11	גמל	DEAL FULLY	168b	1c
22	5	גלעד	GILEAD	167a	1d
28	3	גיא	VALLEY	161c	G
28	18	גמזו	GIMZO	168a	
32	25	גמול	DEALING	168b	3
32	30	גיחון	GIHON	161d	2
33	6	גיא	VALLEY	161c	G
33	14	גיחון	GIHON	161d	2
36	20	גלה	UNCOVER	163c	

EZRA

Ch	v.	Heb	Eng	Page	Sec
1	11	גולה	EXILE	163c	2
2	1	גלה	UNCOVER	163c	
		גולה	EXILE	163c	2
2	61	גלעדי	GILEADITES	167c	3
2	67	גמל	CAMEL	168d	1
4	1	גולה	EXILE	163c	2
6	19	גולה	EXILE	163c	2
6	20	גולה	EXILE	163c	2
6	21	גולה	EXILE	163c	2
8	35	גולה	EXILE	163c	2
9	4	גולה	EXILE	163c	2
10	6	גולה	EXILE	163c	2
10	7	גולה	EXILE	163c	2
10	8	גולה	EXILE	163c	1
10	16	גולה	EXILE	163c	2

NEHEMIAH

Ch	v.	Heb	Eng	Page	Sec
7	6	גולה	EXILE	163c	2
		גלה	UNCOVER	163c	
7	63	גלעדי	GILEADITES	167c	3
7	68	גמל	CAMEL	168d	1
11	17	גלל	GALAL	165b	2
11	30	גיא	VALLEY	161c	G
12	29	גלגל	GILGAL	166a	1
12	36	גללי	GILALAI	165b	

ESTHER

Ch	v.	Heb	Eng	Page	Sec
1	6	גליל	CYLINDER	165b	1
2	6	גלה	UNCOVER	163c	
		גלה	UNCOVER	163c	
		גולה	EXILE	163c	1
3	14	גלה	UNCOVER	162d	1
7	9	גם	ALSO	*169a	1
8	13	גלה	UNCOVER	162d	1

JOB

Ch	v.	Heb	Eng	Page	Sec
1	3	גמל	CAMEL	168d	1
1	17	גמל	CAMEL	168d	1
3	17	גלמוד	HARD	166c	
3	22	גיל	REJOICING	162b	
8	11	גמא	REED	167d	
8	17	גל	HEAP	164d	1b
10	11	גיד	SINEW	161c	
12	22	גלה	UNCOVER	163b	2
15	28	גל	HEAP	164d	1d
15	34	גלמוד	HARD	166c	
16	15	גלד	SKIN	162d	
20	7	גל	DUNG	165a	
20	27	גלה	UNCOVER	163b	2
20	28	גלה	UNCOVER	163a	2
30	3	גלמוד	HARD	166c	
30	14	גלל	ROLL	164c	
33	16	גלה	UNCOVER	162d	1
36	14	גלה	UNCOVER	162d	1
36	15	גלה	UNCOVER	162d	1
38	8	גיח	BURST FORTH	161d	1
38	11	גל	HEAP	164d	2
38	17	גלה	UNCOVER	163a	2b
39	24	גמא	SWALLOW	167d	
40	17	גיד	SINEW	161c	
40	23	גיח	BURST FORTH	161d	1
41	5	גלה	UNCOVER	163b	1b
41	12	גיח	BURST FORTH	161d	2b
42	12	גמל	CAMEL	168d	1

PSALMS

Ch	v.	Heb	Eng	Page	Sec
2	11	גיל	REJOICE	162b	2
4	9	גלל	ACCOUNT	*164b	
7	5	גמל	DEAL FULLY	168b	1c
9	15	גיל	REJOICE	162a	1b
13	5	גיל	REJOICE	162a	1a
13	6	גיל	REJOICE	162a	1c
		גמל	DEAL FULLY	168a	1b
14	7	גיל	REJOICE	162a	1a
16	9	גיל	REJOICE	162a	1a
		גיל	REJOICE	162a	1c
18	16	גלה	UNCOVER	*163a	1b
18	21	גמל	DEAL FULLY	*168b	1b
21	2	גיל	REJOICE	162a	1b
22	9	גלל	ROLL	164c	

Ch	v.	Heb	Eng	Page	Sec
22	10	גיח	BURST FORTH	161d	2 a
27	5	גלח	BASIN	*165a	2 a
28	4	גמול	DEALING	168b	2
31	8	גיל	REJOICE	162a	1 b
32	11	גיל	REJOICE	162a	1 a
35	9	גיל	REJOICE	162a	1 c
		גיל	REJOICE	162a	1 b
37	5	גלל	ROLL	164c	
40	8	מלה	ROLL	166b	
42	8	גל	HEAP	164d	2
43	3	גיל	REJOICING	162b	
45	16	גיל	REJOICING	162b	
48	12	גיל	REJOICE	162a	1 a
49	3	גם	ALSO	169a	1
51	10	גיל	REJOICE	162a	1 a
53	7	גיל	REJOICE	162a	1 a
60	9	גלעד	GILEAD	167a	1 c
65	8	גל	HEAP	164d	2
65	13	גיל	REJOICING	162b	
71	6	גיח	BURST FORTH	161d	2 a
77	19	גלגל	WHIRL	166a	2 c
83	14	גלגל	WHIRL	166a	2 a
89	10	גל	WEAN	164d	2
89	17	גיל	REJOICE	162a	1 b
94	2	גמול	DEALING	168b	2
96	11	גיל	REJOICE	162a	1 a
		גיל	REJOICE	162a	1 c
97	1	גיל	REJOICE	162a	1 a
		גיל	REJOICE	162a	1 c
97	8	גיל	REJOICE	162a	1 a
98	2	גלה	UNCOVER	163b	3
103	2	גמול	DEALING	168b	3
	10	גמל	DEAL FULLY	168b	1 c
107	25	גל	HEAP	164d	2
107	29	גל	HEAP	164d	2
108	9	גלעד	GILEAD	167a	1 c
116	7	גמל	DEAL FULLY	168a	1 b
116	12	תגמול	BENEFIT	168c	
118	24	גיל	REJOICE	162a	1 b
119	17	גמל	DEAL FULLY	168a	1 b
119	18	גלה	UNCOVER	163b	1 b
119	22	גלל	ROLL	164c	
131	2	גמל	WEAN	168b	2
137	8	גמול	DEALING	168b	2
		גמל	DEAL FULLY	168b	1 c
139	16	גלם	EMBRYO	166b	
142	8	גמל	DEAL FULLY	168a	1 b
149	2	גיל	REJOICE	162a	1 b

PROVERBS

Ch	v.	Heb	Eng	Page	Sec
2	14	גיל	REJOICE	162a	1 b
3	30	גמל	DEAL FULLY	168a	1 a
11	13	גלה	UNCOVER	163b	2
11	17	גמל	DEAL FULLY	168a	1 a
12	14	גמול	DEALING	168b	1
16	3	גלל	ROLL	164c	
17	14	גלע	EXPOSE	166c	
18	1	גלע	EXPOSE	166c	
18	2	גלה	UNCOVER	163c	
19	17	גמול	DEALING	168b	2
20	3	גלע	EXPOSE	166c	
20	19	גלה	UNCOVER	162d	1
23	24	גיל	REJOICE	162a	1 a
		גיל	REJOICING	162b	
23	25	גיל	REJOICE	162a	1 a
24	17	גיל	REJOICE	162a	1 b
		גיל	REJOICE	162a	1 c
25	9	גלה	UNCOVER	163b	2
26	26	גלה	UNCOVER	163a	2 b
26	27	גלל	ROLL	164b	
27	5	גלה	UNCOVER	163b	
27	25	גלה	UNCOVER	163a	2
31	12	גמל	DEAL FULLY	168a	1 a

ECCLESIASTES

Ch	v.	Heb	Eng	Page	Sec
9	6	גם	ALSO	169a	1
12	6	גלה	BASIN	165a	2 a
		גלגל	WHEEL	165d	1 b

SONG OF SOLOMON

Ch	v.	Heb	Eng	Page	Sec
1	4	גיל	REJOICE	162a	1 b
4	1	גלעד	GILEAD	*167a	2 b
		גלעד	GILEAD	167a	2 a
4	12	גל	HEAP	164d	3
5	14	גליל	CYLINDER	165b	1
6	5	גלעד	GILEAD	167a	2 b
		גלעד	GILEAD	*167a	2 a

ISAIAH

Ch	v.	Heb	Eng	Page	Sec
3	9	גמל	DEAL FULLY	168a	1 a
3	11	גמול	DEALING	168b	1
3	23	גליון	TABLET	163d	
5	13	גלה	UNCOVER	163a	3
5	28	גלגל	WHEEL	165d	1 a
7	13	גם	ALSO	169a	1
7	20	גלח	SHAVE	164a	3
8	1	גליון	TABLET	163d	
8	23	גליל	DISTRICT	165b	2

Ch	v.	Heb	Eng	Page	Sec
		גלגל	GILGAL	166a	5
9	2	גיל	REJOICE	162a	1 b
		גילה	REJOICING	162b	
9	4	גלל	ROLL	164c	
10	30	גל	GALLIM	164d	
11	8	גמל	WEAN	168b	2
14	10	גם	ALSO	169a	1
16	3	גלה	UNCOVER	163b	2
16	10	גיל	REJOICING	162b	
17	13	גלגל	WHIRL	166a	2 a
18	2	גמא	REED	167d	
18	5	גמל	RIPEN	168b	3
20	4	גולת	EXILE	163d	2
21	7	גמל	CAMEL	168d	3
22	8	גלה	UNCOVER	163b	1 b
22	14	גלה	UNCOVER	163a	1 c
23	1	גלה	UNCOVER	163a	2 c
24	11	גלה	UNCOVER	163a	2
25	2	גל	HEAP	164d	1 d
25	9	גיל	REJOICE	162a	1 b
26	21	גלה	UNCOVER	163b	2
27	9	גר	CHALK	162c	
28	9	גמל	WEAN	168b	2
	28	גלגל	WHEEL	166a	
29	19	גיל	REJOICE	162a	1 b
30	6	גמל	CAMEL	168d	2
34	4	גלל	ROLL	164c	
35	1	גיל	REJOICE	162a	1 a
		גיל	REJOICE	162a	1 c
35	2	גיל	REJOICE	162a	1 c
		גילה	REJOICING	162b	
35	4	גמול	DEALING	168b	2
35	7	גמא	REED	167d	
37	26	גל	HEAP	164d	1 d
38	12	גלה	UNCOVER	163a	3
40	5	גלה	UNCOVER	163a	2 c
41	16	גיל	REJOICE	162a	1 b
45	13	גולת	EXILE	163d	2
47	2	גלה	UNCOVER	163b	1 b
47	3	גלה	UNCOVER	163a	2 a
48	4	גיד	SINEW	161c	
48	18	גל	HEAP	164d	2
49	9	גלה	UNCOVER	163a	1 b
49	13	גיל	REJOICE	162a	1 a
		גיל	REJOICE	162a	1 c
49	21	גלה	UNCOVER	163a	3
		גלמוד	HARD	166c	
51	12	גם	ALSO	169a	1
51	15	גל	HEAP	164d	2
53	1	גלה	UNCOVER	163a	2 c
56	1	גלה	UNCOVER	163a	2 c
57	8	גלה	UNCOVER	163b	1 a
59	18	גמול	DEALING	168b	2
		גמולה	DEALING	168c	
60	6	גמל	CAMEL	168d	2
61	10	גיל	REJOICE	162a	1 b
		גיל	REJOICE	162a	1 c
63	7	גמל	DEAL FULLY	168a	1 a
65	18	גיל	REJOICE	162a	1 a
		גילה	REJOICING	162b	
65	19	גיל	REJOICE	162a	1 b
66	6	גמול	DEALING	168b	2
66	10	גיל	REJOICE	162a	1 b

JEREMIAH

Ch	v.	Heb	Eng	Page	Sec
1	3	גלה	UNCOVER	163a	3
5	22	גל	HEAP	164d	2
7	31	גיא	VALLEY	161c	G
7	32	גיא	VALLEY	161c	G
8	22	גלעד	GILEAD	167a	2 c
9	10	גל	HEAP	164d	1 d
11	17	גלל	ACCOUNT	164b	
11	20	גלה	UNCOVER	163b	3
12	6	גם	ALSO	169a	1
		גם	ALSO	169a	1
13	19	גלה	UNCOVER	163c	
13	22	גלה	UNCOVER	163a	2 a
15	4	גלל	ACCOUNT	164b	
19	2	גיא	VALLEY	161c	G
19	6	גיא	VALLEY	161c	G
20	4	גלה	UNCOVER	163c	
20	12	גלה	UNCOVER	163b	3
22	6	גלעד	GILEAD	167a	2 c
22	12	גלה	UNCOVER	163c	
24	1	גלה	UNCOVER	163c	
24	5	גלות	EXILE	163d	2
25	14	גם	ALSO	169a	1
27	7	גם	ALSO	169a	1
27	20	גלה	UNCOVER	163c	
29	1	גלה	UNCOVER	163c	
		גלה	UNCOVER	163c	1
29	4	גלה	UNCOVER	163c	
		גלה	UNCOVER	163c	1
29	7	גלה	UNCOVER	163c	
29	14	גלה	UNCOVER	163c	
29	16	גלה	UNCOVER	163c	2
29	20	גלה	EXILE	163c	1
29	22	גלות	EXILE	163d	2
29	31	גלה	EXILE	163c	1
31	35	גל	HEAP	164d	2
32	5	גיא	VALLEY	161c	G
32	11	גלה	UNCOVER	162d	1

Ch	v.	Heb	Eng	Page	Sec
33	6	גלה	UNCOVER	163b	3
36	2	מלה	ROLL	166b	
36	4	מלה	ROLL	166b	
36	6	מלה	ROLL	166b	
36	14	מלה	ROLL	166b	
36	20	מלה	ROLL	166b	
36	21	מלה	ROLL	166b	
36	23	מלה	ROLL	166b	
36	25	מלה	ROLL	166b	
36	27	מלה	ROLL	166b	
36	28	מלה	ROLL	166b	
36	29	מלה	ROLL	166b	
36	32	מלה	ROLL	166b	
39	9	גלה	UNCOVER	163c	
40	1	גלה	UNCOVER	163c	
		גלות	EXILE	163d	2
40	7	גלה	UNCOVER	163c	
41	5	גלח	SHAVE	164a	
43	3	גלה	UNCOVER	163c	
46	11	גלעד	GILEAD	167a	2 c
46	19	גולה	EXILE	163c	2
47	3	גלגל	WHEEL	165d	1 a
48	7	גולה	EXILE	163c	2
48	11	גולה	EXILE	163c	2
		גם	ALSO	169a	1
48	23	גמול	GAMUL	*168c	
48	26	גם	ALSO	169a	1
48	33	גיל	REJOICING	162b	
49	3	גולה	EXILE	163c	2
49	10	גלה	UNCOVER	163b	2
49	29	גמל	CAMEL	168d	1
49	32	גמל	CAMEL	168d	1
50	2	גלול	IDOLS	165d	
50	19	גלעד	GILEAD	167b	3 b
51	6	גמול	DEALING	168b	2
51	25	גלל	ROLL	164c	
51	37	גל	HEAP	164d	1 d
51	42	גל	HEAP	164d	2
51	55	גל	HEAP	164d	2
51	56	גמולה	DEALING	168c	
52	15	גלה	UNCOVER	163c	
52	27	גלה	UNCOVER	163a	3
52	28	גלה	UNCOVER	163c	
52	30	גלה	UNCOVER	163c	
52	31	גלות	EXILE	163d	1

LAMENTATIONS

Ch	v.	Heb	Eng	Page	Sec
1	3	גלה	UNCOVER	163a	3
2	14	גלה	UNCOVER	163b	3
3	64	גמול	DEALING	168b	3
4	22	גלה	UNCOVER	163b	3
		גלה	UNCOVER	163c	

EZEKIEL

Ch	v.	Heb	Eng	Page	Sec
1	1	גולה	EXILE	163c	2
1	1	גולת	EXILE	163d	1
2	9	מלה	ROLL	166b	
3	1	מלה	ROLL	166b	
3	2	מלה	ROLL	166b	
3	3	מלה	ROLL	166b	
3	11	גולה	EXILE	163c	1
3	15	גולה	EXILE	163c	1
4	12	גל	DUNG	165a	
4	15	גל	DUNG	165a	
5	1	גלב	BARBER	162c	
6	4	גלול	IDOLS	165d	
6	5	גלול	IDOLS	165d	
6	6	גלול	IDOLS	165d	
6	9	גלול	IDOLS	165d	
6	13	גלול	IDOLS	165d	
8	10	גלול	IDOLS	165d	
10	2	גלגל	WHEEL	165d	1 a
		גלגל	WHIRL	166a	2 b
10	6	גלגל	WHEEL	165d	1 a
		גלגל	WHIRL	166a	2 b
10	13	גלגל	WHEEL	165d	1 a
		גלגל	WHIRL	166a	2 b
11	24	גולה	EXILE	163c	1
11	25	גולה	EXILE	163c	1
12	3	גלה	UNCOVER	163a	3
		גלה	EXILE	163c	2
12	4	גולה	EXILE	163c	2
		גולה	EXILE	163c	2
12	7	גולה	EXILE	163c	2
12	11	גולה	EXILE	163c	2
13	14	גלה	UNCOVER	163a	2 b
14	3	גלול	IDOLS	165d	
14	4	גלול	IDOLS	165d	
14	5	גלול	IDOLS	165d	
14	6	גלול	IDOLS	165d	
14	7	גלול	IDOLS	165d	
16	36	גלה	UNCOVER	163a	2 a
		גלול	IDOLS	165d	
16	37	גלה	UNCOVER	163b	1 a
16	52	גם	ALSO	169a	1
16	57	גלה	UNCOVER	163a	2 b
18	6	גלול	IDOLS	165d	
18	12	גלול	IDOLS	165d	
18	15	גלול	IDOLS	165d	
20	7	גלול	IDOLS	165d	

Ch	v.	Heb	Eng	Page	Sec
20	8	גלול	IDOLS	165d	
20	16	גלול	IDOLS	165d	
20	18	גלול	IDOLS	165d	
		גלול	IDOLS	165d	
20	24	גלול	IDOLS	165d	
20	31	גלול	IDOLS	165d	
20	39	גלול	IDOLS	165d	
		גלול	IDOLS	165d	
21	29	גלה	UNCOVER	163a	2 b
22	3	גלול	IDOLS	165d	
22	4	גלול	IDOLS	165d	
22	10	גלה	UNCOVER	163b	1 a
23	7	גלול	IDOLS	165d	
23	10	גלה	UNCOVER	163b	1 a
23	18	גלה	UNCOVER	163b	1 a
		גלה	UNCOVER	163b	1 a
23	24	גלגל	WHEEL	165d	1 a
23	29	גלה	UNCOVER	163a	2 a
23	30	גלול	IDOLS	165d	
23	37	גלול	IDOLS	165d	
23	39	גלול	IDOLS	165d	
23	49	גלול	IDOLS	165d	
25	3	גולה	EXILE	163c	2
25	5	גמל	CAMEL	168d	3
26	3	גל	HEAP	164d	2
26	10	גלגל	WHEEL	165d	1 a
27	9	גל	HEAP	*164d	2
27	11	גמד	SHORT CUBIT	*167d	
		גמדים	GAMMADIM	167d	
27	24	גלום	WRAPPING	166b	
30	13	גלול	IDOLS	165d	
32	2	גיח	BURST FORTH	161d	2 b
33	21	גולת	EXILE	163d	1
33	25	גלול	IDOLS	165d	
36	18	גלול	IDOLS	165d	
36	25	גלול	IDOLS	165d	
37	6	גיד	SINEW	161c	
37	8	גיד	SINEW	161c	
37	23	גלול	IDOLS	165d	
39	11	גיא	VALLEY	161c	F
		גיא	VALLEY	161c	E
		גיא	VALLEY	161c	F
39	15	גיא	VALLEY	161c	
39	23	גלה	UNCOVER	163a	3
39	28	גלה	UNCOVER	163c	
40	1	גולת	EXILE	163d	1
44	10	גלול	IDOLS	165d	
44	12	גלול	IDOLS	165d	
44	20	גלה	SHAVE	164a	1
47	8	גלילה	TERRITORY	165c	
47	18	גלעד	GILEAD	167b	3 c

DANIEL

Ch	v.	Heb	Eng	Page	Sec
1	10	גיל	AGE	162b	
10	1	גלה	UNCOVER	163a	2 c

HOSEA

Ch	v.	Heb	Eng	Page	Sec
1	8	גמל	WEAN	168b	2
2	12	גלה	UNCOVER	163b	1 a
4	15	גלגל	GILGAL	166a	1
6	8	גלעד	GILEAD	167b	4
7	1	גלה	UNCOVER	163a	2 b
9	1	גיל	REJOICING	162b	
	15	גלגל	GILGAL	166a	1
10	5	גיל	REJOICE	162b	2
		גלה	UNCOVER	163a	3
12	12	גל	HEAP	164d	1 d
		גלגל	GILGAL	166a	1
		גלעד	GILEAD	167c	5

JOEL

Ch	v.	Heb	Eng	Page	Sec
1	16	גיל	REJOICING	162b	
2	21	גיל	REJOICE	162a	1 b
2	23	גיל	REJOICE	162a	1 b
4	4	גלילה	TERRITORY	165c	
		גמול	DEALING	168b	2
		גמול	DEALING	168b	2
4	7	גמול	DEALING	168b	2

AMOS

Ch	v.	Heb	Eng	Page	Sec
1	3	גלעד	GILEAD	167b	5
1	5	גלה	UNCOVER	163a	3
1	6	גלה	UNCOVER	163c	
		גולת	EXILE	163d	2
1	9	גולת	EXILE	163d	2
1	13	גלעד	GILEAD	167b	5
1	15	גולה	EXILE	163c	2
3	7	גלה	UNCOVER	162d	1
4	4	גלגל	GILGAL	166a	1
5	5	גלה	UNCOVER	163a	1
		גלגל	GILGAL	166a	1
5	24	גלל	ROLL	164c	
5	27	גלה	UNCOVER	163c	
6	7	גלה	UNCOVER	163a	3
		גלה	UNCOVER	163a	3
7	11	גלה	UNCOVER	163a	3
7	17	גלה	UNCOVER	163a	3

OBADIAH

Ch	v.	Heb	Eng	Page	Sec
	19	גלעד	GILEAD	167b	3 c
	20	גולה	EXILE	163d	2

JONAH

Ch	v.	Heb	Eng	Page	Sec
2	3	גל	HEAP	164d	2
4	4	גמל	DEAL FULLY	168b	1 c

MICAH

Ch	v.	Heb	Eng	Page	Sec
1	6	גלה	UNCOVER	163b	2
1	16	גלה	UNCOVER	163a	3
3	12	גלל	ACCOUNT	164b	
4	10	גיח	BURST FORTH	161d	2 b
6	5	גלגל	GILGAL	166a	1
7	14	גלעד	GILEAD	167b	3 b

NAHUM

Ch	v.	Heb	Eng	Page	Sec
2	8	גלה	UNCOVER	163b	
3	5	גלה	UNCOVER	163b	1 a
3	10	גולה	EXILE	163c	1
3	11	גם	ALSO	169a	1

HABAKKUK

Ch	v.	Heb	Eng	Page	Sec
1	15	גיל	REJOICE	162a	1 a
3	18	גיל	REJOICE	162a	1 b

ZEPHANIAH

Ch	v.	Heb	Eng	Page	Sec
1	17	גלל	DUNG	165b	
3	17	גיל	REJOICE	162a	1 c

ZECHARIAH

Ch	v.	Heb	Eng	Page	Sec
4	2	גלה	BASIN	165a	2 a
4	3	גלה	BASIN	165a	2 a
5	1	מגלה	ROLL	166b	
5	2	מגלה	ROLL	166b	
6	10	גולה	EXILE	163c	2
9	9	גיל	REJOICE	162a	1 a
10	7	גיל	REJOICE	162a	1 c
		גיל	REJOICE	162a	1 b
10	10	גלעד	GILEAD	167b	3 b
10	11	גל	HEAP	164d	2
14	2	גולה	EXILE	163c	2
14	15	גמל	CAMEL	168d	1